SISTERS OF SAINT JOSEPH
PHILADELPHIA

ENCYCLOPEDIC DICTIONARY OF RELIGION

ENCYCLOPEDIC

Edited by

Paul Kevin Meagher, OP, S.T.M.

Thomas C. O'Brien

Sister Consuelo Maria Aherne, SSJ

THE SISTERS OF ST. JOSEPH OF PHILADELPHIA

Volume **F-N**

DICTIONARY OF RELIGION

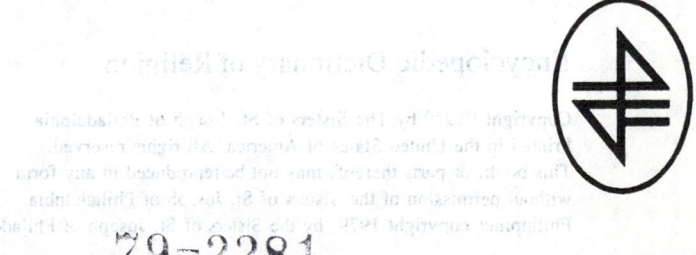

CORPUS PUBLICATIONS: WASHINGTON, D.C.

Nihil Obstat:

John P. Whalen S.T.D., J.D.
Censor Deputatus

Imprimatur:

✠ William Cardinal Baum
Archibishop of Washington D.C.
February 7, 1978

Prepared by an

Editorial Staff at Corpus Publications, Inc. (1966–1970)
Washington, District of Columbia, and at
Mt. St. Joseph (1973–1979) Chestnut Hill,
Philadelphia, Pennsylvania.

Production Manager: Gerard G. Mayer

Composition: Lexigraphics Inc.
150 Fifth Avenue
New York, N.Y. 10011

Sales Manager: Jack Heraty and Associates, Inc.
P. O. Box 875
Palatine, Illinois 60067

Encyclopedic Dictionary of Religion

Library of Congress Catalog Number: 78-62029

ISBN 0-9602572-1-7 (Volume F-N) ISBN 0-9602572-3-3 (Set)

F

FABER, FREDERICK WILLIAM (1814–63), English priest, spiritual writer. Born at Calverley, Yorkshire, he had a Calvinist background, but turned toward evangelicalism, then at Oxford, attracted by J. H. Newman, became devoted to the Oxford Movement. Ordained an Anglican priest in 1839, and rector of Elton from 1842, he followed Newman into the RC Church in 1845. He was ordained a RC priest in 1847. With most of the members of the small community called Brothers of the Will of God, which he had formed in 1846, he joined the Birmingham Oratory under Newman in 1848. The following year he founded the London Oratory at King Williams Street, and moved it to Brompton Road in 1854. His relations with Newman by reason of temperament and of interpretation of the Oratorian life were constantly strained. F.'s rather Italianate Catholicism was reflected in his preaching, his hymns, and in the devotional life he encouraged at the Brompton Oratory. He was intensely affective and emotional, widely read in the classic spiritual writers. These qualities were characteristic of his preaching and his writings. During a period of intense writing, 1853–60, he published the eight devotional works, beginning with *All for Jesus,* by which he deeply affected the spiritual life of many generations of readers, both in English and other languages. BIBLIOGRAPHY: R. Chapman, *Father Faber* (1961); L. Cognet, DSAM 5:3–13.

[T. EARLY]

FABER, JACOBUS STAPULENSIS, see LEFÉVRE D'ÉTAPLES, JACQUES.

FABER, JOHANN AUGUSTANUS (1475–1530), humanist and theologian. From 1511 he was vicar general of the Dominicans in Upper Germany, and reconstructed the priory of Augsburg. He was chosen to become an imperial councillor by Emperor Maximilian in 1515. F. believed that the classics were a necessary preparation for the study of Scripture and the Fathers, a view shared by Erasmus and many of the Reformers. He came to disagree with Luther's theology and opposed him. He had to flee Augsburg and took refuge with Card. Matthäus Lang in Salzburg. BIBLIOGRAPHY: R. Conlon, DTC 5:2046–50; N. Paulus, *Die deutschen Dominikaner im Kämpfe gegen Luther, 1518–63* (1903) 292–313.

[E. D. MCSHANE]

FABER, JOHANNES (Fabri; 1478–1541), German Catholic theologian, bp. of Vienna from 1530. Because of his friendship with *Erasmus, F. at first sympathized with *Melanchthon and *Zwingli in their efforts at reform; however, when he became aware of their doctrinal changes, he actively opposed them. As vicar-general of Constance he debated unsuccessfully with Zwingli in 1523. His sobriquet, "hammer of heretics," was suggested by the title *(Malleus in haeresim Lutheranam)* given to later editions of his tract against Luther (1524). He wrote on such doctrinal subjects as faith and good works, the Mass, and the Eucharist, and published numerous polemical treatises and sermons. He was a zealous pastor and helped prepare for the Council of Trent. BIBLIOGRAPHY: L. Helbling, RGG 2:856.

[M. J. SUELZER]

FABER, PETER, BL. (FAVRE; LEFÉVRE; 1506–46), first companion of St. Ignatius of Loyola, preacher. As a student at the Univ. of Paris he was friend and roommate of St. Francis Xavier and with him from 1528 a companion of Ignatius. Ordained in May 1534, F. celebrated the Mass in August when Ignatius and his companions made their vows together and established the nucleus of the Society of Jesus. When the Society was formally founded F. was part of it. The projected mission to the Muslims was thwarted by war with the Turks, and F. became professor of Scripture at the Sapienza in Rome. Pope Paul III sent him to attend the Diet of Worms in 1540 and the Diet of Regensburg a year later. F. recognized that these attempts of Emperor Charles V to heal the breach of the Reformation were not sufficient and began efforts to renew Catholic life in Germany. He is largely responsible for keeping the Rhineland Catholic. He established the Jesuits in Cologne and received St. *Peter Canisius. F. worked also in France, Portugal, and Spain, where he influenced St. Francis Borgia. Directed by Paul III to attend the Council of Trent, he was prevented from doing so by death. F. in his *Memoriale,* a diary of his spiritual life, reveals himself as a man of deep spirituality, charm, and strength. He was beatified in 1872. BIBLIOGRAPHY: W.V. Bangert, *To the Other Towns* (1959).

[J. R. AHERNE]

FABERT, ABRAHAM (1599–1662), French marshal who became governor of Sedan in 1642, shortly after it passed to France. He opposed the Calvinism firmly entrenched there, yet allowed freedom of conscience. His personal example and the works of charity he promoted helped much to reestablish Catholicism in the town. His outspokenness and his connection with Port-Royal did not lessen the esteem in which he was held. BIBLIOGRAPHY: R. Chalumeau, *Catholicisme* 4:1034.

[M. J. SUELZER]

FABIAN, ST. (d.250), **POPE** from *c.*236, martyr. He was elected during a lull in the persecutions; Eusebius (*Hist. eccl.* 6.29) tells that he was chosen by acclamation when a dove settled on his head as he stood by, a layman and a stranger, watching the election. The Church grew during his peaceful reign, and St. Cyprian wrote in praise of his administration. He is credited with appointing deacons to administer the seven districts of the Roman Church, and subdeacons to gather the official court records of the martyrs. Among seven bps. he consecrated and sent as missionaries to Gaul was St. *Denis of Paris. Privatus, bp. of Lambaesis in N. Africa, appealed to him without success against his condemnation for heresy by a local African synod. F. was martyred in the persecution of Decius and buried in the catacomb of Callistus where the slab that covered his tomb was discovered in 1850. The decretals ascribed to him by the Psuedo-Isidore are false. BIBLIOGRAPHY: P. G. Meier, CE 5:742–743; J. S. Brusher, *Popes through the Ages* (1959).

[P. F. MULHERN]

FABIAN SOCIETY, organization of British socialists. Founded in 1884, its early members included George Bernard Shaw, Sidney Webb, and Webb's wife, Beatrice. It was named for the Roman general Fabius Cunctator, who used tactics of delay and attrition against Hannibal. Opponents of Marxist revolution and class struggle, Fabians argued for an evolutionary development of socialism through reform of existing institutions, promoted by educational and other democratic methods. The British Labor Party is an outgrowth of the Labor Representation Committee formed by Fabians in 1900.

[T. EARLY]

FABIOLA, ST. (d.399), a Roman matron of patrician rank and great wealth who, after doing public penance because she had remarried after divorcing her husband, devoted her wealth and energies to works of charity, one of which was the foundation of a hospital for the sick, the first establishment of its kind recorded in Christian history. In 395 she visited Bethlehem, staying in the hospice of St. Paula's convent and applying herself to ascetical practices and the study of Scripture under the direction of St. Jerome, but, too restless for a contemplative life, she returned to Rome the following year. There is some reason to think she considered entering upon a second dubious marriage, but if so tempted she rejected the thought and spent the remaining years of her life caring for the sick and the poor. Her great benefactions endeared her to the people of Rome, and a vast throng attended her funeral. BIBLIOGRAPHY: Butler 4:623–624.

[R. B. ENO]

FABLIAUX, medieval French tales, usually humorous and bourgeois, varying in tone from the obscene (those of Gautier le Leu) to the burlesque ("The Peasant Doctor"). Their plots could be puns, *exempla,* folklore, satire, or legend. Often considered an origin of the modern short story, these tales influenced Boccaccio, Chaucer, and Rabelais.

[J. P. WILLIMAN]

FABORDONE, see FABURDEN.

FABRI, FILIPPO (1583–1630) Franciscan Conventual theologian. F. taught philosophy at Venice, Parma, and Cremona and was named to the faculty of the Univ. of Padua in 1603. He was preeminently the interpreter of his fellow Franciscan Duns Scotus, and was known as one who could make clear and understandable the thought of that subtle Doctor.

[J. R. AHERNE]

FABRIANO, GENTILE DA, see GENTILE DA FABRIANO.

FABRIC (Lat. *fabrica*), originally an artisan's workshop; the physical plant of a church or other ecclesiastical establishment. Canon law uses the term in reference to the funds belonging to the endowment for maintenance of church services and upkeep of the building, as distinct from income set aside for the holder of a *benefice (CIC, c. 1183–84).

[T. C. O'BRIEN]

FABRICIUS, JOHN ALBERT (1668–1736), Protestant theologian, bibliographer, and philologist. His vast philological knowledge is attested by numerous, carefully researched publications, chief of which are: *Bibliotheca graeca, Bibliotheca latina, Bibliotheca latina mediae et infimae aetatis,* and exegetical writings. He also edited some of the classic authors and the Church Fathers. BIBLIOGRAPHY: G. Marsot, *Catholicisme,* 4:1042–43.

[F. D. LAZENBY]

FABURDEN (It. *falso bordone;* Fr. *faux-bourdon;* Sp. *fabordón),* a 15th–cent. term used to designate a type of harmonization, namely a succession of first inversions or $^6/_3$ chords, and usually ending in root position. The term has also been applied to the following: any sort of monotoning; a drone bass; any metrical psalm tune harmonizing with a *cantus firmus* (already existing melody); a refrain to song verses. Like the French term faux-bourdon, this term relates to the ''false bass'' set up as a contrapuntal part and not to the *cantus firmus*. The Spanish *fabordón* was esp. highly developed. This manner of harmonization was often used, even recently, for the Passion and Lamentation in the Holy Week liturgy.

[A. M. MACK]

FACIENTI QUOD EST IN SE, the first part of a theological axiom the remainder of which is *Deus non denegat gratiam,* literally, to him who does what in him lies, God does not refuse grace. Although grace is given as an undeserved gift and not rendered as a reward for human merit or preparation, this scholastic axiom seeks to delimit the gratuity of grace and its worldwide dispensation. It has two acceptable meanings. (1) Do what you can with the help of grace offered, and you will receive further grace; i.e., fidelity to grace is a pledge of further grace. (2) Do what you can by your own natural power, and God will give you grace, not because of any merit or positive disposition of yours (this would be Semi-Pelagian) but from liberality; man's unaided good will or effort is a negative disposition for grace (it does not pose a new obstacle to grace). Taken in this sense, the axiom may be purely academic. Given the universal dispensation of grace and man's fallen state, one who does what in him lies is actually anticipated by and assisted by grace. BIBLIOGRAPHY: G.N. Buescher, NCE 5:785; J. Trütsch, LTK 3: 1336–37.

[P. DELETTER]

FACULTIES. As a canonical term a faculty (Lat. *facultas,* a capability or power) is an empowerment granted to another by a superior to whom the power belongs by office or law. There is one general usage of the term and a narrower usage, referring to ''apostolic faculties.'' (1) In the broader usage the term has two main applications. In regard to the sacrament of penance it is used to designate a confessor's competence to absolve from sin or ecclesiastical censures. In this usage it is equivalent to a delegated *jurisdiction. The power to absolve is conferred by priestly ordination; its exercise belongs to the realm of jurisdiction in the Church. That jurisdiction by reason of office is held to belong to *ordinaries; exercise of jurisdiction by others is permitted only by concession from the competent ordinary: thus from a local bp. within his diocese or from a major superior within a religious institute. A priest must receive faculties from the competent authority in order to absolve validly those who are subject to the ordinary. Such faculties are granted not only for absolving from sin, but also from censures and from reserved sins. In a second broad usage of the term and one that in practice is often linked with a confessor's faculties is the faculty to preach. The ministry of preaching belongs by office to the pope as universal pastor throughout the Church, to the bp. as first pastor throughout his diocese (CIC c. 1327§1) The ministry of preaching can be exercised lawfully by no one else except on receiving the canonical mission from the pope or from the competent ordinary (c. 1328). The license to preach (formally to proclaim the word of God, not simply to catechize) is given to priests or deacons, never to laity, even religious (c. 1342, 1 & 2). When in common parlance a priest is said to be ''silenced'' the meaning is that the license to preach is withdrawn. Allied to these broad usages of the term faculty is the permission granted to impart certain blessings reserved to a bp. or to the major superior of a religious institute (e.g., of the Vincentians in the case of the blessing of the Miraculous Medal). Vatican Council II recommended reduction of the blessings reserved to ordinaries (VatII SacLit 79); the revision of ritual blessings is still in process.

(2) Apostolic faculties are those granted by the pope with regard to powers reserved to himself. The term faculty in this narrower sense is considered in the CIC in Title V, under the heading of privileges ''beside the law'' (c. 65); faculties are habitual privileges granted either permanently or for a specified time, unrestrictedly or for a determined number of cases (*ibid.*). They are to be interpreted like all privileges, i.e., following strictly the terms of their concession.

Of long standing and history are the faculties granted by the Apostolic See to diocesan bps. esp. with regard to the power of dispensation from the universal law of the Church within their own territories. The most commonly referred to set of faculties of this type are the Quinquennial Faculties of bishops. These are apostolic faculties that have their name from the fact that they are conceded, formerly by the Consistorial Congregation now by the Congregation of Bishops, at the time the diocesan bp. makes the 5-year report on the state of his diocese. Quinquennial faculties vary according to the different regions of the Church; there are four basic sets: I, for Italy; II, for France, Belgium, Spain, Portugal; III, for the rest of Europe; IV, for North and South America and the Philippines; the roman-numeral designation is by curial convention.

Concerning bps.' faculties the CIC lays down the general principle that the bp. has power in his own diocese to dispense from diocesan law (c. 82); power to dispense from the common law of the Church belongs to the pope. Vatican Council II, however, established the principle that the bp. has the power to dispense from law for the spiritual welfare of his subjects and in particular cases, in matters the pope has reserved to himself (VatII BpPastOff 8b). To carry out the conciliar spirit and intent, Paul VI after the second session of the Council issued *motu proprio* the apostolic letter *Pastorale munus* (Nov. 30, 1963; AAS 56 [1964] 5–12), conceding under 40 headings faculties of dispensation that may be exercised by reason of office. The letter specifies that the faculties may be subdelegated only to auxuliaries or coadjutors and to vicars general. The concession is made to diocesan bps., vicars, and prefects apostolic, permanent apostolic administrators, and abbots or prelates *nullius*. The concession became effective on Dec. 8, 1963. Among the faculties granted are: the power to permit priest to binate on weekdays or trinate on Sundays and feasts for pastoral reasons (2); to permit such priests to take liquids within the hour preceding Mass (3); to permit Mass or holy communion in the evening (4); to permit infirm priests to celebrate Mass at home and seated (10); to permit chaplains in health-care facilities to administer confirmation (13); to permit confessors to absolve from some censures (14); to ordain outside the stipulated times of the year and outside of a sacred place (18); to dispense from minor matrimonial impediments (19) and from the impediments of *mixed religion and *disparity of cult (20); to make exceptions to the law of cloister (34); to give necessary permission to read and retain proscribed books (40).

In the *motu proprio, De episcoporum muneribus* of June 15, 1966 (AAS 58 [1966] 467–472), the Pope included a list of dispensations that he reserved to himself. BIBLIOGRAPHY: R. Naz, DDC 5:802–807 s.v. *''Facultés apostoliques.''*

[T. C. O'BRIEN]

FACULTIES OF THE SOUL, the operative potencies or powers of the soul. These potencies are usually designated as vegetative, sensitive, and rational or intellectual.

[J. R. RIVELLO]

FACUNDUS, ST. According to a 9th- or 10th-cent. vita that seems to derive in part from a vita of St. Felix of Gerona, he was martyred with Primitivus for not venerating idols in Galicia, Spain, where a number of churches and locales are dedicated to him. The best known is the monastery of Sahagún *(Sancti Facundi),* supposedly the site of his martyrdom, where refugee Mozarab monks from Córdoba settled *c.*870. Ties with Cluny and the pilgrimage road to Santiago spread his cult outside Spain. BIBLIOGRAPHY: J. F. Alonso, BiblSanct 5: 438–439.

[E. P. COLBERT]

FACUNDUS OF HERMIANE, (d. *c.*571), bp. in N Africa, staunch opponent of the condemnation of the *Three Chapters. From the beginning of the controversy concerning the *Three Chapters F. took a strong stand against their condemnation. In Constantinople he wrote a defense of them in 12 books, declaring that a condemnation would constitute an attack upon the authority of the Council of Chalcedon and scoring the injustice of anathematizing men long dead because they had erred occasionally and unintentionally in their work. When in 553 Pope Vigilius and the Second Council of Constantinople agreed to the condemnation, F. and most of the African episcopate broke off relations with Rome and the East and entered into a schism that lasted until 571. F. also wrote two other treatises on the same subject: *Liber contra Mocianum Scholasticum,* and *Epistola fidei catholicae in defensione trium capitulorum.* Works: PL 67:527–878. BIBLIOGRAPHY: M. Pellegrino, EncCatt 5:954–955; Altaner 589–590.

[R. B. ENO]

FAGNANO, JOSÉ (1844–1916) Italian Salesian missionary. After a brief span in the army of liberation led by Garibaldi in Italy, F. became a friend of Don Bosco, joined the Salesians, and was ordained in 1868. He became a member of his order's first missionary group in Argentina. In 1880 he went to Patagonia as a missioner, and was named apostolic delegate for southern Patagonia in 1883. F's great work was among the Indians both as peacemaker and missioner. He was also an explorer of the southmost area of S America.

[J. R. AHERNE]

FAGO, NICOLA (1677–1745), Italian composer, called ''Il Tarantino'' from his birthplace, Taranto. He studied at Naples first with A. Scarlatti, then with Provenzale. His studies completed, F. became Provenzale's assistant, and later his successor. He was also *maestro di cappella* at the Conservatorio di S. Onofrio (1704–08), and at the Tesoro di S. Gennaro (1709–31). In addition to four operas, F. composed much sacred music including two oratorios, *Faraone sommerso* and *Il monte fiorito,* and a *Te Deum.*

[A. M. MACK]

FAITH, in the classic definition of the Epistle to the Hebrews (11.1), ''the assurance of things hoped for, the conviction of things not seen.'' The brevity of this definition has often tended to obscure the complexity of faith and the difficulty of identifying its place in the total context of the Christian way of life. There is perhaps no better way to describe faith than to make clear what it is not and thus, by exclusion, to make possible some understanding of what it is or at least can be. A concordance study of how the words ''faith'' and ''to believe'' are used in the OT and the NT, combined with an examination of their occurrence in Christian theological writers, would lead to classification such as the following. Emphasis on one or another of these aspects of faith has marked the differences between various Christian traditions. Yet most Christians would agree that these are essential to the meaning of faith.

Faith is trustworthiness. Perhaps the root meaning of the word is reliability. Especially in its adjectival form, the Greek term *pistos* means deserving of faith, and this meaning is never altogether absent from the biblical use of the term. For, in the last analysis, it is God who is *pistos,* utterly dependable in his promises, reliable in what he swears. ''Every one utters lies to his neighbor'' (Ps 12.2), but God does not lie. And so ''God is faithful, by whom you were called into the fellowship of his Son, Jesus Christ our Lord'' (1 Cor 1.9). In ordinary language a person is said to have our faith when he is trustworthy and reliable in his words and deeds. Christian faith, to be sure, means more, but it never means less; and "good faith" in the Roman and legal sense of *bona fides* is never absent from even the most radically biblical discussions of faith, whether it be the faithfulness of God in his dealings with man or the faith of man in response to God.

Faith is obedience. The English word obedience does not (unless one hears in it the echoes of the word audience) show the intimate connection between obeying and hearing, as do the Greek and Latin terms for obedience. The Epistle to the Romans makes the connection clear in its use of the word faith. According to the Apostle Paul in Rom 10.17, "faith comes from what is heard, and what is heard comes by the preaching of Christ." Thus faith is a response to the proclamation of the word of God about Christ and his work of redemption. Elsewhere in the same epistle this "hearing of faith" is equated with obedience. In his opening salutation St. Paul declares that through Christ "we have received grace and apostleship to bring about the obedience of faith for the sake of his name among all the nations, including yourselves who are called to belong to Jesus Christ" (Rom 1.5–6). God has issued his call to a participation in Jesus Christ, and he has done so through the apostolic message. Those who hear the message and accept it are in "the obedience of faith." In the concluding peroration of the Epistle to the Romans the same theme recurs. There St. Paul speaks of "my gospel and the preaching of Jesus Christ, according to the revelation of the mystery which was kept secret for long ages but is now disclosed and through the prophetic writings is made known to all the nations, according to the command of the eternal God, to bring about the obedience of faith" (Rom 16.25–26). Here again the definition of faith as obedience is a way of emphasizing its close dependence on the preaching of the gospel, as this is contained in Sacred Scripture and communicated in the apostolic proclamation. At the same time, it is essential to note that when faith is called obedience, this does not refer primarily to the moral life of the believer (sometimes called "the new obedience"; see *Augsburg Confession, Art. 6), without which the faith is dead. It refers, rather, to taking God at his word when he announces his mercy in the proclamation of the gospel.

Faith is assenting knowledge. To cite the most extreme case, the NT ascribes "believing" even to the demons: "You believe that God is one; you do well. Even the demons believe—and shudder" (Jas 2.19). In such a context, presumably, to believe is to know a religious truth and to accept it as true, for the demons do not obey or trust even though they are obliged to acknowledge that monotheism is an accurate theory about the divine. Nor would it be accurate to confine to the demons this aspect of faith as assenting knowledge. Saving faith, too, attaches itself to a specific truth, which has a content. "Whoever would draw near to God," says the Epistle to the Hebrews (11.6), "must believe that he exists and that he rewards those who seek him." The object of this faith is, in the ultimate sense, nothing less than God himself. Nevertheless, it is also valid, on the basis of scriptural usage, to make a proposition of Christian doctrine the object of faith. Thus St. Paul speaks of "confess[ing] with your lips that Jesus is Lord and believ[ing] in your heart that God raised him from the dead" (Rom 10.9). To "believe that" something is so or that something has happened is to know the content of the dogmatic proposition and to assent to the truth of it. It is much more than this, to be sure, for the proposition deals with the saving will and power of God; but it is not less than this. The recurring tendency, esp. in RC theology, to define faith largely in terms of assenting knowledge has led to an excessive intellectualism, in which "the faith which one believes" *(fides quae creditur)* overshadows "the faith by which one believes" *(fides qua creditur)*, with the result that the personal dimension of faith is lost.

Faith is trust. In Luther's formula, which every major Christian theologian would affirm, "a god is that to which we look for all good and in which we find refuge in every time of need. To have a god is nothing else than to trust and believe him with our whole heart." The paradigm for this kind of faith in Scripture is Abraham, who is thus "the father of us all" because "in hope he believed against hope, that he should become the father of many nations" (Rom 4.16, 18). In this trusting faith Abraham "obeyed when he was called to go out to a place which he was to receive as an inheritance; and he went out, not knowing where he was to go" (Heb 11.8). Here the knowledge of faith is clearly subordinated to the obedience of faith and to the trust of faith. He who believes in God is one who has confidence that God can be relied upon even in times and places that are still unknown. Faith is therefore "the assurance of things hoped for, the conviction of things not seen," an assurance that may not know what awaits it but is certain who awaits it. The certainty and confidence of such a faith have been well summarized in the words of 2 Tim 1.12: "I know whom I have believed, and I am sure that he is able to guard until that Day what has been entrusted to me." Sometimes, in reaction to the sort of intellectualism described in the preceding paragraph, theologians, esp. in the Protestant and existentialist traditions, have attempted to restrict faith to trust and to regard other aspects of it, particularly the aspect of assenting knowledge, as alien or at least subordinate. Distorted though such a view is, it does make the valid point that in the Bible trust is central to faith.

Faith is courage. This meaning of the word becomes most evident not in the words that Scripture uses about faith but in the concrete examples of the men of faith whose heroic deeds Scripture recounts. The two portions of Scripture in which this dimension of faith is most visible are Heb 11 and Sir 44–50. The "famous men" praised in the latter, no less than the "men of old" whose faith is catalogued in the former, were men whose valor was not simply a heightened version of the powers that are natural to all mankind but was an affirmation of the power of God. Similar though Sampson and Prometheus are, they differ in this fundamental respect as heroes: Samson's courage came from his obedience and trust in God, while the courage of Prometheus consisted in his defiance of the gods. Early Christianity recognized the quality of faith as courage when it began to compose the lives of martyrs and saints. For example, the *Life of Antony,* which was probably written by St. Athanasius, described his many deeds of saintly heroism and quoted him as saying: "We have learned our lessons from the saints and do as they have done and imitate their courage." Bizarre though some of the exploits ascribed to some of the saints may have been, their boldness in the face of their tormentors and in the presence of death is a dominant theme of this literature. And even though fortitude was classified as one of the cardinal virtues rather than one of the theological virtues (see the next paragraph), faith as courage transcended that distinction.

Faith is a theological virtue. Its place among the virtues, together with its similarities and dissimilarities to hope and love, occupied St. Thomas Aquinas at considerable length. The greatest of the theological virtues, by apostolic authority (1 Cor 13.13), is love, and hope in turn proceeds from faith. In addition, faith pertains to the intellect, while both hope and love pertain to the will. Quoting St. Augustine's definition of faith as "a virtue whereby we believe what we do not see" and St. John Damascene's definition that "faith is an assent without inquiry," St. Thomas made its classification in the virtues dependent upon its nature as a "habit"; for "any habit that is always the principle of a good act may be called a human virtue. Such a habit is formed faith." This view of faith as a theological virtue has enabled theologians to make clear both its relation to the truth of revelation and its basis in the inner life of the believer. All the other definitions of faith listed here may thus be included in this one. BIBLIOGRAPHY: ThAq ST 1a2ae, 62–67; 2a2ae, 1–7; J. H. Newman, *Grammar of Assent* (1870, repr. 1973); P. Tillich, *Dynamics of Faith* (1957); *idem, Courage to Be* (1952).

[J. PELIKAN]

FAITH (RC THEOLOGY), the act of believing God; the gift of *grace empowering the recipient for such an act; also the truths believed, as in the phrase "Faith of our Fathers." A theological interpretation must reflect the scriptural descriptions of belief in God. The NT term for faith, already used in the LXX, is *pistis,* and it signifies a knowing, being from *peithō,* to be convinced or persuaded that some claim is true. In actual use, however, *pistis* also bears a note of affectivity—trust, commitment to God in assured confidence *(fiducia).* Faith in the OT and the NT is the fundamental and all-pervasive condition of man's relationship with God. The OT meaning is brought out in contexts that, whether in regard to Israel or to the individual, express God's faithfulness and truthfulness in his promises, and a human response that acknowledges God's fidelity. The Synoptic Gospels place faith as the condition of trust in his claims that Jesus imposes for discipleship (Mt 8.10; Mk 4.36; Lk 8.25). John's Gospel expresses the object of belief, that Jesus is from God (16.30); the Messiah (11.27); that his own words are to be believed (2.22; 5.47; 8.45). In Acts the Disciples identified themselves simply as believers (4.4; 13.12), and believers in Jesus as Lord (5.14; 9.42), having salvation through his grace (15.11). Paul proclaims above all that righteousness or salvation is by faith in Jesus Christ (Rom 1.17; 3.22, 26, 28, 30; Gal 2.16; Eph 1.15; Col 1.4); he sets justifying faith against the observances of the Old Law (Rom 4); the object of belief is the gospel he preaches (Rom 10.9,13,15); he describes it as darkness (2 Cor 5.7). The text of Heb 11.1, "Faith is the substance of things hoped for, the evidence of things not seen" (Vulg), became a definition for the medievals that stated both the cognitive and affective sides of faith. (ThAq ST 2a2ae, 4.1).

In the evolution of a theology of faith from the patristic to the medieval period the complexities of scriptural teaching received varying emphases: that belief means a share in God's own knowledge; that belief in the gospel message opens the way to understanding; that faith is a free gift of grace, contrary to *Pelagianism (D 375–377); that belief involves a complete commitment to God (a truth expressed in the formula, "to believe God; to believe in God; to believe unto God"). St. Thomas Aquinas gave the clearest medieval formulation of a doctrine on faith in his treatment of it as a theological virtue, and his analysis of belief *(credere),* the act of faith. His viewpoint and some of his teaching entered into church teaching in opposition to the Reformation position of salvation through a purely fiduciary faith. While affirming that faith and righteousness are absolutely free gifts of grace (D 1525; 1551–53), the Council of *Trent also declared that faith means assent to God's word and to what God reveals, and is not simply confidence in one's own salvation through Christ (D 1562). The medieval view on faith is also obviously contained in the fullest church document on faith, the dogmatic constitution *Dei Filius* of Vatican Council I. Its ch. 3 gives a description of faith as "the beginning of salvation, which the Catholic Church professes to be a supernatural virtue by which, under the prompting and help of God's grace, we believe what he has revealed to be true, not on the basis of the truths in themselves being perceived by the natural light of reason, but on the basis of their authentication by God himself, who can neither deceive nor be deceived" (D 3008). Vatican Council II has one particularly important remark on faith, referring to the "obedience of faith" *(obsequium fidei;* see Rom 16.26), trusting the whole self freely to God, as this means submission of mind and will (cf. D 3008) and free assent to the truth revealed (Vat II DivRev 5). Thus the fiduciary side is expressed along with the mind's cognitive assent (see also Vat II ChurchModWorld 59; MinLifePriests 4). Insistence that faith be in part interpreted as a form of knowing is a reason for criticizing the RC position as an unbiblical, intellectualist overreaction to the Reformers. A correct understanding of Aquinas's teaching, which the general RC concept of faith does reflect, shows that if the language is "intellectualist," its intent is to express both the cognitive and the affective side of faith. Two points in his teaching suffice: a description of belief as "an act of the mind assenting to the divine truth by virtue of the command of the will as this is moved by God through grace" (ST 2a2ae, 2.9); an interpretation of a parenthetical remark of Augustine (*De praedest. sanctorum* 2. PL 44: 963) taken to be a definition of belief: "to ponder with assent" *cum assensione cogitare* (ST 2a2ae, 2.1). In both cases the key word, assent, means adherence to God himself as true; it implies the point that faith is a theological virtue, its act an unmediated relationship or union with God as he is. Belief is commitment to God himself, and consequently to "content"—to what God guarantees as his truth. The interpretation of the Augustinian text is not a dialogue with Augustine at all, but the solution to previously unsuccessful attempts in medieval theology, esp. in Hugh of St. Victor's endeavor to correct Peter Abelard, to explain the sureness, the trustfulness, and firmness of belief in comparison to other kinds of mental assent. St. Thomas does a psychological analysis because that is how the problem was put; but the analysis does not isolate belief from affectivity. The meaning of the assent peculiar to belief is suggested by "to ponder"; refusing to divorce the dynamics of the grace life from man's psychological makeup, St. Thomas compares belief to other forms of knowing; agrees that it leaves unfulfilled the natural bent of the mind to see. Belief is sheer reliance on the unseen God who attests to the truths believed. The mind's pondering, its restlessness, is not unsureness, however. "Assent is an act of mind as it is brought to decision by the will" (*ibid.* ad 3). "The cognitive aspects of belief do not exist apart from the total meaning of a person's relationship to God; faith is not bestowed to provide a theoretical world view; it is the beginning of salvation. God does not address man in faith in order to provide him with information, but with the invitation to salvation . . . man is empowered by God's love to respond in love, and belief is indeed part of that response. Not only is faith not just a matter of knowledge like other knowledge, not merely a pondering; it is a pondering with assent. The God who speaks to the believer is the God who loves him and whom he loves in return. The assent is the act of the mind that does cleave to God's word, because it is the beloved Father who speaks" (O'Brien, p.215). In its integration within the whole relationship of the person to God, belief is a believing God, a believing in God, and a believing unto God; the *credere Deo, credere Deum, credere in Deum* is the medieval formula that yields an understanding of belief as both cognitive and affective, as of a piece with a total response to God's address and self-communication. A faith without love is lifeless, "unformed." BIBLIOGRAPHY: ThAq ST (Lat–Eng v.31, ed. T. C. O'Brien) App. 4 "Belief, Faith's Act."

[T. C. O'BRIEN]

FAITH, ACT OF. This note touches truth less for its biblical sense of trust and confidence in what is reliable and pledged (cf. the Hebrew root of "amen" and the Pauline *pistis,* the entire commitment to God through Christ) than for its place in the general grammar of assent, which, however, is indicated in Heb 1.1. Accordingly, to speak of its cognitive element, as an act convinced of the truth of its judgment, it differs from *doubt, a suspense of assent, and from opinion *(dōxa),* an assent mixed with some uncertainty. Yet because the object of its assent is neither evident in itself nor inferred from evident premises it differs respectively from insight *(intellectus, nous)* and from holding by scientific proof *(scientia, epistēmē).* The Greek terms above are Aristotle's. It is arrived at, as St. Paul says, from hearing (Rom 10.17), and rests on the word of another. This in effect involves an affective response in the believer to the veracity of his authority, as well as an act of will impelling the mind to assent, as it were, against its own proper inclination which is for light, not darkness. "Seeing is believing," as they say, which of course, strictly speaking, it is not, but the phrase acknowledges what the mind is made for. No great effort is called for in the case of the facts of history or geography, most of which we take on hearsay, or of the truths of more recondite sciences beyond our grasp yet vouched for by respectable experts and observed to work out in practice; the claims of religion, however, are more tasking, above all when supernatural mysteries are set forth well beyond the native scope of our mind. Yet though it is a step in the dark, Catholic theologians in general insist that such a faith is more than a feeling, or just a gamble, but a firm act of mind, based on, though not to be resolved into, thoroughly reasonable grounds for belief. Nevertheless so far does the object transcend the subject, that certitude, while remaining intact, may periodically or even constantly suffer a diminution of its assurance, as holy people, not only waverers, are well aware from experience. It is for this reason that the theological virtue of faith, human in its mode of operation, seeks some enlightenment in its obscurity; this it finds in the suprahuman operations of the *gifts of the Holy Ghost, notably understanding and knowledge. As an adhesion which does not stop at dogmas or *articles of faith, but goes through them to God himself, its beginning is not from men but from his grace. Its completion, until it disappears in vision (1 Cor 13.9-12), lies in no mere mental attitude, which may be dead faith *(fides informis),* but in the living faith *(fides formata),* which cleaves to God in charity. To cogitate with assent, the terse definition of St. Augustine, is developed by the theologians to draw the picture of human beings not yet satisfied in their minds but committing themselves to God without reserve. BIBLIOGRAPHY: ThAq ST 2a2ae, 1.2, 4 ad 5; 2.1 ad 2; 4.1 ad 4; 8 and 9; J. H. Newman, *Essay in Aid of a Grammar of Assent* (1870) many ed. since; M. C. D'Arcy, *Nature of Belief* (2d ed. 1958); H. Bars, *Assent of Faith* (1960).

[T. GILBY]

FAITH, ANALOGY OF, see ANALOGY OF FAITH.

FAITH, BEGINNING OF, the technical phrase to designate the initiative in the supernatural process that is to lead up to the life of grace. Historically the beginning of faith had been understood in two ways. St. Augustine and the Semi-Pelagians took it as including the act of belief in God's revelation and call. The Council of Trent and theologians of the time considered it to be the beginning of supernatural activity which may, but need not, be faith; it may be any salutary act. The Semi-Pelagians held that man can, without the help of interior grace, believe or assent to the word of God but that he is in need of grace to live according to this belief. This error, which includes a denial of the gratuity of grace rendered for the merit of faith, was set aside by the Council of Orange, A.D. 529 (D 375). When the Council of Trent taught that the beginning of justification comes from God's prevenient grace (D 1525, 1553), it sanctioned the Catholic doctrine about the beginning of faith understood in the sense of the beginning of the process of justification. On both these occasions the point of doctrine at stake was the gratuity of grace: the initiative in the life of grace always comes from God and not from man. BIBLIOGRAPHY: G. N. Buescher, NCE 5:804; J. Auer, LTK 5:676–677.

[P. DE. LETTER]

FAITH, CERTITUDE OF, see CERTITUDE OF FAITH.

FAITH, CONFESSION OF, see CONFESSION OF FAITH.

FAITH, LOSS OF, a term commonly but inexactly used to describe the process through which one decides to remove or annul the commitment by which he had assented to the teachings of Jesus and his church. As by the acts of faith one assents to those teachings, so by its opposite, called loss of faith, one dissents from the same teachings. The popular use of the term "loss" to describe the passage from belief to disbelief reflects an assumption that replacement of assent by dissent is an event that happens to a person rather than an event which the person brings about. Loss of faith is taken to be a privation over which one has no control, like the loss of eyesight from an injury. While, however, the power to believe is given the soul by God and each use of the power, an act of faith, is supported by God's helping grace, man's deliberative powers too are used in each commitment or act of faith he makes. He can not believe without God's help but God does not believe for him; man does the believing. So, too, if there is disbelief he does the disbelieving; it does not just happen to him. At every point in his life a man with faith has the grace to use it. But, at any point in his life the same man has the power to resist the grace offered him. Thus he who with the help of grace once began to believe can begin to disbelieve, now aided by grace because he rejects it. Usually, it is by a series of steps that one arrives at this point but to identify each step is not possible. Assenting in faith, that is, to truths not clearly seen and understood, on authority, involves a subjection of the mind. The gradual refusal to subject the mind, perhaps by playing with small, unresolved doubts can dispose one to make the final, grand refusal and to stop believing. Or, the assent of faith may be impeded by sensual objects, sinful pleasures which make one want the faith to be untrue because it forbids the sinful. Thus do pride and sensuality dispose a person to give up a faith no longer wanted, permitting him to speak of it as a valued possession "lost." BIBLIOGRAPHY: P. F. Mulhern, "Rejection and Protection of Faith," *Thomist* 3 (1941) 33–45; A. Besnard, *Faith, Its Life and Growth* (tr. J. Oligny, 1967).

[P. F. MULHERN]

FAITH, PROFESSION OF, an act of faith externalized either in word or in action and prescribed for the Christian. Christ required such an acknowledgment (Mt 10.32–33); it is, moreover, dictated by man's psychosomatic nature and his membership in the society of the Church. Common professions of faith are the Apostles Creed, the Nicene Creed, as well as the Constantinopolitan and Tridentine (D 30, 125, 150, 1862–70). The obligation to profess the faith publicly arises whenever silence, subterfuge, or a way of acting would otherwise imply a denial of faith, contempt of religion, insult to God, or scandal (CIC c. 1325.1). Yet a cryptic faith is sometimes justifiable. The Church not only wants its members to elicit acts of faith (D 2021), but obliges persons who are about to assume official positions to make a profession of faith (CIC c. 1406.1).

[J. FICHTNER]

FAITH AND MORALS, a formulary phrase referring to the full content of Church teaching, the *deposit of faith. The phrase occurs in the Council of *Trent's decrees on the sacred books of the Bible and on their interpretation (D 1501; 1507; see also 1298, 1477), and with special emphasis in Vatican Council I's dogmatic constitution, *Pastor aeternus,* ch. 4, on the infallible teaching office of the Roman Pontiff (D 3074). In theology the term belongs to the discussion of the nature and extent of the teaching office in the Church and implies that the deposit of faith received from divine revelation includes truths to be believed and to be acted upon as rules of Christian morality.

[T. C. O'BRIEN]

FAITH AND ORDER, a branch of the *ecumenical movement directed to the theological aspects of the search for unity among Christian Churches. Faith and Order took its origin from a 1910 resolution of the General Synod of the Protestant Episcopal Church in the U.S., which, conscious of the scandal of disunity as an obstacle to Christian mission work, called for a conference of Christian Churches throughout the world to work for unity, "that all may be one, so that the world may believe." After several preliminary conferences, the first World Conference on Faith and

Order met in Lausanne, Switzerland, in 1927. The conference invited the participation of all Christian Churches on the basis of a common belief in Christ and the gospel. At the second World Conference on Faith and Order (Edinburgh, 1937) it was decided to merge with the *Life and Work movement, a more socially oriented branch of the ecumenical movement. From this merger was born the World Council of Churches (WCC), within which the Faith and Order movement thereafter continued to function semiautonomously. The Constitution of the Faith and Order Commission admits to membership Churches that are not members of the WCC. As the Commission on the Faith and Orderof the World Council of Churches, it held its third world conference in Lund, Sweden, in 1952, and its fourth in Montreal in 1963. The reports prepared by these world conferences, and sometimes voted on by the delegates, are without binding power on the Churches represented, which are free to accept or reject them. After each world conference, reports are published and circulated among the Churches and their responses solicited and studied. Regional and other subgroups meet to discuss issues, and working committees undertake further theological studies, preparing preliminary reports for the next world conference and for the general assemblies of the WCC.

The initial efforts of Faith and Order were devoted largely to defining areas of doctrinal agreement and disagreement among the Churches, in the hope that a deepened understanding of their various positions might remove some of the obstacles to unity. Later studies centered about the Christological concept of the Church as the Body of Christ, united in one baptism and in the Eucharist, and associated tradition with scriptural study. At first tending to reflect doctrinal positions identified with Anglicanism, the world conferences later witnessed a growing prominence of the Lutheran and *Reformed traditions, esp. in relation to the doctrines of grace and justification. Orthodox Churches represented at the world conferences have been influential and uncompromising in their presentation of the Catholic viewpoint. Increasingly, RC theologians have taken part, as authorized observers, in recent world conferences and have contributed to the preparatory theological studies of the working committees, esp. since the creation by the Vatican of its *Secretariat for Promoting Christian Unity and the establishment, by the Secretariat on Faith and Order of the WCC, of a Joint Working Group and a Joint Theological Committee. In 1968 nine of the RC observers at the fourth General Assembly of the WCC at Uppsala, Sweden, were elected to membership on the Faith and Order Commission. Interim reports of the Commission on Faith and Order after the 1963 conference have indicated a new emphasis on a theology of man in the modern world.

In a 1971 reorganization of the WCC, Faith and Order was placed in a "faith and witness" program unit, along with the Commission on World Mission and Evangelism and the Department on Church and Society. Administratively this brought into closer relationship programs representing a continuation of the three main streams of ecumenical activity united in the WCC—Faith and Order, Life and World, and the International Missionary Council. During this period Faith and Order began shifting more definitely rom a concernd with doctrinal differences in themselves to a greater concentration on cultural, political, and other issues cutting across traditional church divisions. Such topics as relating Christian unity to the unity of all people drew greater attention. But work on traditional issues also continued. The Commission met at Louvain in 1971, and there discussed documents on the "emerging consensus" regarding baptism and Eucharist. Later a document on ministry was prepared, and all three were submitted for discussion in the Churches. A Commission meeting at Accra, Ghana, in 1974, was significant for, among other things, bringing African cultural realities to bear on the consideration of issues that previously had usually been viewed from a European-North American standpoint. In other work, the Commission has provided assistance to "bilateral" conversations between Churches. In 1977 it met at Lausanne in connection with a gathering to commemorate the 50th anniversary of the original Lausanne Conference. BIBLIOGRAPHY: J. E. Skoglund and R. J. Nelson, *Fifty Years of Faith and Order* (1963); L. Vischer, ed., *Documentary History of the Faith and Order Movement 1927–63* (1963); *New Directions in Faith and Order, Bristol 1967* (1968). *EDINBURGH CONFERENCE; *LAUSANNE CONFERENCE; *LUND CONFERENCE; *MONTREAL CONFERENCE; *UPPSALA CONFERENCE; *WORLD COUNCIL OF CHURCHES.

[T. EARLY]

FAITH AND REASON, a phrase frequently used by theologians when discussing the relationship between the act of faith and man's efforts to understand the basis and nature of this fundamental encounter with God. Three distinct although related questions are considered here.

Problems, although usually false ones, inevitably arise when knowing is thought of as acquiring knowledge on the basis of personal experience and is pitted against believing, defined by contrast as making judgments based only on another's word (see BELIEF). This view leaves out what is most essential to religious faith, i.e., the person-to-person relationship of trust and confidence involved when God reveals himself and man answers with the assent of his whole person and not merely of his intellect.

Another set of problems, much discussed in Catholic theology since 1800, revolves around the role of reason in the act of faith itself. Accepted Catholic teaching, shared by a considerable body of Protestant theologians, maintains that no one may do violence to reason even when the act of Christian faith is at stake. On the other hand, it is agreed that whatever beliefs one may entertain about God and Christ through the natural use of the intellect, they are not equivalent to faith itself. Thus the question emerges, if the act of faith is based ultimately on the authority of God revealing, then how do we know that God has in fact revealed himself at all? This much would seem to be reason's due, that we show that our act of faith is not unreasonable, an outrage against reason. How do we come to a judgment concerning the reasonableness of faith? There are signs that indicate the fact of revelation to us (e.g., miracles), but these signs are never so unambiguous as to make faith simply a rational deduction. Indeed, Jesus Christ is the definitive sign of God's self-revelation, but one can know this only insofar as one believes in him. The sign that he constitutes is not overwhelmingly convincing to the human reason apart from faith, since it does not lend itself to strict proofs of a scientific form, no more than other matters having to do with personal trust or the meaning of events. The decisive reason for believing is, therefore, the very authority of God who is revealing. But this is an element within the complex reality of the act of faith, not outside it or prior to it. Yet reason is not thereby violated, since there must be reasons or *motives of credibility for taking up the challenge of revelation at all. Such reasons will not remove the act of faith from the category of free personal decision but will justify it as such.

Third, there is a body of propositions held in the Church as true, e.g., those contained in the Creeds, which are derived from revelation. Reason's role in relation to these truths is to discover and articulate what these articles of faith mean in current concepts and language (see THEOLOGY). Here reason is clearly in service to the faith, and articulates the content of the faith decision. BIBLIOGRAPHY: R. Aubert, *Le Problème de l'acte de foi* (1958); R. Bultmann, *Faith and Understanding* (1969); H. Fries, "Faith and Knowledge," SacMund 2:329–334; J. Mouroux, *I Believe* (1959); P. Tillich, *Dynamics of Faith* (1957); B. Blanshard, *Reason and Belief* (1975).

[P. MISNER]

FAITH AND WORKS, see GOOD WORKS: JUSTIFICATION BY FAITH; SOLA GRATIA, SOLA FIDE, SOLA SCRIPTURA.

FAITH HEALING, a phrase used in two ways: (1) in its broader usage, any cure of bodily ills that relies on purely religious rather than medical means; (2) in its specific meaning, mental or metaphysical healing by the power of spiritual mind over matter, the evil cause of sin, sickness, and death. BIBLIOGRAPHY: R. J. Baker, *God Healed Me* (pa. 1974). *HEALING; *DIVINE HEALING.

FAITH, HOPE, AND CHARITY, SS. (2d. cent.), martyrs. According to an unreliable and inherently improbable legend dating from no earlier than the 6th cent., three young girls, Faith (aged 12), Hope (10), and Charity (9), were boiled in oil and beheaded under the Emperor Hadrian. Their mother, Wisdom, was killed while praying over the bodies of her children. The story spread to the East, where the children were given equivalent Greek names. BIBLIOGRAPHY: Butler 3:238–239.

[R. B. ENO]

FAITH MISSION a phrase connoting a specific type of missionary endeavor. "Faith" indicates the intention of relying completely on divine providence both for financial support and for the actual direction mission work should take. Thus the faith mission makes no provision for guaranteed sources of income, nor is it affiliated with or directed by a home mission board or organization. One of the primary aims, and accomplishments, of the faith mission is to become completely indigenous in its mission field. The faith mission often is a nondenominational project; the missionaries are bound together simply by the desire to preach the gospel; they are usually evangelicals and fundamentalists. The faith mission concept has been prominent in the growth of Pentecostalism in the US and in the remarkable Pentecostal missionary expansion throughout the world.

[T. C. O'BRIEN]

FAITH ONLY, see SOLA FIDE, SOLA GRATIA, SOLA SCRIPTURA.

FAITHFUL, those united together by reason of each one's faith in Jesus Christ as Lord and Savior, and forming the Church as the *congregatio fidelium* ("The Church is established by faith and the sacraments of faith," ThAq ST 3a, 64.2 ad 3; "Through the Spirit we are united to Christ in a union of faith and love and are made members of the Church," idem, *In Joann.*14,lect. 7). Thus the early Christians referred to themselves simply as "the believers" (Acts 2.44; 4.32). The ancient Latin *Christifideles* aptly brings out the point. The opposite of "faithful" is "infidel," one formally guilty of the sin of unbelief, i.e., of refusal to believe. Vat II Ecum recognizes that all who are baptized are "the faithful"; there are also *anonymous Christians, those who seek God according to the light of an upright conscience, and who are, therefore, not infidels. In homiletic and devotional use "the faithful" often means the laity as distinct from the clergy, but that usage is becoming obsolete since Vat II ApostLaity.

[T. C. O'BRIEN]

FAITHFUL, MASS OF THE, in the Western Church that part of the Mass which can be termed the Liturgy of the Eucharist as opposed to the antecedent Liturgy of the Word. The Liturgy of the Eucharist comprises the offering of the gifts, their consecration, and communion. It is called Mass of the Faithful because in ancient times the catechumens, those not yet baptized, were dismissed from the church before the Offertory, and only the faithful, i.e., those baptized, were permitted to remain.

FAITHFUL MAJESTY, MOST, a title bestowed upon the kings of Portugal by Pope Clement XI in 1717. It was granted to John V (1706–50) and his successors in recognition of John's aid to the Pope against the Turks.

[T. M. MCFADDEN]

FAKHR-AL-DIN II AL-MA'NI (1573–1635), father of modern Lebanon. Inheritor of a lost emirate F. expanded a small fief into the recovery of his entire lost inheritance, becoming the emir from N of Beirut to Mount Carmel and Tiberias. When he entered into a pact with the Grand Duke of Tuscany, F. was defeated in battle by Sultan Aḥmad I and fled to Florence. He returned to reconquer and was acknowledged by the Sultan Murad IV as lord of ʻArabistān. F. pursued an enlightened policy of development of his territory's natural resources, inviting in Florentine, Genoese, and French merchants. He permitted Franciscan and Jesuit missionaries to work in his country and was rumored to have been baptized a Catholic by his physician, who was a Capuchin. His Christian sympathies and contacts with the West angered the Sultan, an expedition from Constantinople was sent against him, he was captured and executed in Constantinople. BIBLIOGRAPHY: P. K. Hitti, *Lebanon in History* (1963).

[J. R. AHERNE]

FAKHR AL-DĪN AL-RĀZĪ (Fakhruddin; 1149–1209), Muslim theologian of the *Ashʻarite school. Rāzī is one of the most important theologians of the later period of the *kalâm* (see ISLAMIC THEOLOGY); a master of immense learning in the sciences and philosophy as well as theology and a polemicist of great skill. His writing shows a remarkable originality of thought at a time when Islamic theology was entering its final decline. He sets himself forth as a staunch defender of orthodox Islam and his writing contains much biting and incisive polemic against the *Shiites and the *Muʻtazilites in particular, but also against the Mâturîdîtes and some of the Ashʻarites as well, among them *Algazel (al-Ghazzâlî). Like that of most Ashʻarite thinkers of the late period, his work manifests a considerable influence of the Neoplatonized Aristotelianism of Avicenna, several of whose works he commented upon. Nonetheless, he was a relatively independent thinker who was not unwilling to reject or modify certain basic theses traditional to the Ashʻarite school (e.g., in regard to the nature of the *Koran and the *ʻiṣma* of the Prophet [see MOHAMMED]) and to make sometimes bold use of the philosophical tradition. His voluminous commentary on the Koran remains one of the most important done at any period. BIBLIOGRAPHY: G. Anawati, EncIslam²; F. Kholeif, *Study on Fakhr al-Dîn al-Râzî and his Controversies in Transoxiana* (1966) 7–25, 205–216.

[R. M. FRANK]

FAKIR (Fakeer), taken from Arab. *faqîr* (pl. *fuqarâ'*), a person who is indigent. There is some disagreement among Muslim jurists as to whether the word refers to one who is absolutely indigent and possesses nothing whatsoever or one who is simply very poor. Among the *Sûfis it is used to designate a person who has renounced all worldly possessions to live for God alone. The use of the term in English in the sense of an oriental religious ascetic or mendicant, whether Muslim or Hindu, dates from the 17th century.

[R. M. FRANK]

FALASHAS, literally "immigrants," are Ethiopians of Jewish faith, who call themselves "Kayla" or *Beta Israel* (House of Israel). Various theories exist about their origin; until the 17th century, they lived in an independent mountain province, Semyen, in northern Ethiopia. The emperor Susenyos then brought them under the control of the central government. Today, many live in the region north of Lake Tana, while many others are scattered throughout the country. The language of Falasha liturgy and literature, including the OT, is Ge'ez, or ancient Ethiopian, their spoken languages are those of their neighbors, i.e., Amharic or Tigrinya. The Falashas probably have never known Hebrew. Their religious life revolves around the synagogue *(mäs gid)*. Their high priests and priests, appointed by the community, offer animals in sacrifice, esp. at the Passover. At their synagogues, prayers are recited and the Torah read. They celebrate the principal Jewish holy days, as well as several feasts of their own; they keep Sabbath in the strictest manner. All over 7 years of age must fast every Monday, Thursday, on every new moon, and at the Passover (April 21 or 22). They also have monks who live a severe life, secluded even from fellow Falashas. Since the 19th cent., they have renewed contacts with the main body of Judaism.

[A. V. KAUFFMAN]

FALCONET, ÉTIENNE MAURICE (1716–91), French sculptor. After study with Lemoyne he carved eight statues (now destroyed) for St. Roch, Paris. As director of the National Manufactory of Sèvres he produced small allegorical groups and with his pupil Marie-Anne Collot executed the famous impressive colossal statue of Peter the Great (1766), one of the few monumental commissions for French Rococo sculptors and one which F. expressed with a baroque grandeur. In later life he published six literary volumes (1781).

[M. J. DALY]

FALCONETTO, GIOVANNI MARIA (1468–*c.*1540), Italian architect and painter of Verona. A classicist, F. relates to Pisanello, Liberale, and Mantegna and probably studied with Melozzo da Forli. F. painted frescoes (1497–99) in S. Biagio Chapel, Verona, in the Calcasoli Chapel of the cathedral, Verona (1503), and in the Maffei and Emili chapels, all works distinguished by richly ornamented architectural perspective settings. In architecture the Loggia and Casino in Verona (1524), the Porta Savonarola (1530), and Porta S. Giovanni in Padua are his works.

[M. J. DALY]

FALCONI, JUAN (1596–1638), Spanish Mercedarian from 1611. He studied at Salamanca and taught at Segovia, Valladolid, and Alcalá before devoting himself to the spiritual apostolate in Madrid (1625–38). His writings, published in Spanish, French, and Italian, advocate the imitation of Christ, daily communion, charity, prayer, and resignation. Suspicion of quietism caused his works to be put on the Index; the suspicion is no longer regarded as justified. BIBLIOGRAPHY: E. Gómez, *Fr. Juan Falconi de Bustamente, teólogo y asceta* (1956); *idem*, DHGE 16:434–435.

[E. P. COLBERT]

FALCONIERI, a noble Florentine family: (1) **St. Alexis** (1200–*c.*1310) was one of the Seven Holy Founders of the *Servites and the only one of them who lived to see the Order receive final approbation by Pope Benedict XI in 1304. (2) **St. Juliana** (1270–1341), niece of Alexis and founder of Third Order of Servite Sisters (Mantellate Sisters). J. was canonized in 1737. (3) **Lelio** (d. 1648), card. lawyer, magistrate, legate. He was greatly esteemed by Popes Paul V, Gregory XV, and Urban VIII and was effective in reconciling noblemen of differing views and in alleviating conditions for the poor. (4) **Alessandro** (1657–1734), grand-nephew of Lelio and a highly successful governor of Rome. He was made a card. by Benedict XIII in 1724. BIBLIOGRAPHY: A.-M. Dal Pino, BiblSanct 11:907–938; D. M. Montagna, *ibid.* 6:1184–88; Butler 2:581–583.

[C. CARROLL]

FALDA, a garment of white silk with a train worn over the rochet by some popes on certain solemn occasions. It may be used only by a pope.

[P. K. MEAGHER]

FALDSTOOL, a chair with arms but no back; literally, a folding stool, though many do not fold. It is used in the sanctuary by RC bps. and other prelates when not occupying the throne. Because of the absence of a back it can also be used as a prie-dieu.

[T. EARLY]

FALK, ADALBERT (1827–1900), Bismarck's minister of cult during the Kulturkampf, author of the anti-Catholic May Laws (1873–75), by which the Church's freedom was curtailed, religious orders suppressed, schools taken over by the State, Catholics deprived of the sacraments, clergy expelled. F. fell from power in 1879 and peace with the Church was gradually achieved through the initiative of Leo XIII.

[T. C. O'BRIEN]

FALKENBERG, JOHN OF, see JOHN OF FALKENBERG.

FALKNER, THOMAS (1707–84), missionary. A physician and surgeon in Manchester, England, F. served as surgeon on a slave ship of the South Sea Company on a voyage to Africa and then to S America. When he fell ill in Buenos Aires he was cared for with great kindness by the Jesuits in that city. He became a Catholic (1730) and a member of the Society (1732). He spent 38 years as a missionary, first in Paraguay, then in the region between Rio de la Plata and the Strait of Magellan. His knowledge of medicine made him an effective missioner among the natives of the area. F. had to leave S America when the Jesuits were expelled (1767) and he returned to England serving as chaplain to a number of notable Catholic families. He is known to have written several works on his experience in S America. *A Description of Patagonia* was published in a distorted version in 1774 but, in spite of that, remains a classic.

[J. R. AHERNE]

FALL OF THE ANGELS, a primordial and catastrophic sin of the angels. There is only peripheral evidence, biblical reference, to the fall of the angels; hence theological explanations are the result of reflection on this meager evidence in the light of God's total plan of salvation. There is patristic opinion that the angels sinned through envy of man, although the Fathers do not elaborate the cause of this envy other than by relating it to the fact that Christ—unlike angels—is human. Since St. Thomas Aquinas (who in this follows St. Augustine), pride has commonly been taught to be the sin by which angels fell (ThAq ST 1, 63.2); and he appropriates Is 14.12–14 (identifying Satan with Lucifer, the day star) to the fallen angels; he does, however, have difficulty in seeing how so perfect a spiritual nature as an angel's could inordinately desire likeness with God. Suárez united the lines of thought—envy of man and pride against God—in his view that the fallen angels begrudged mankind the hypostatic union: this envy of man expressed their desire to be like God in virtue of their nature rather than by God's special gift. The Scotist view that repentance was possible to angels ties in with patristic statements that repentance was possible for them prior to the Incarnation; but it contradicts the Thomistic teaching that an angel is so perfect that any angelic act of will is irrevocable. BIBLIOGRAPHY: *Satan, a Symposium* (ed. W. Farrell, 1951).

[B. FORSHAW]

FALL OF MAN. Adam's transgression, termed ''Fall'' *(paraptōma)*, is used in Wis 10.1. The story of the Fall is narrated in Gen 2.4b–3.24 which forms a literary unit, produced by a single author. The first part (2.4b–24) sets the stage: man (Adam) and woman (Eve) were created by God and placed in Eden; they were relatively free, but at God's command were obliged to abstain from the fruit of one tree. The second part (3.1–24) unfolds the drama of the temptation by the serpent; first the woman, then the man ate the forbidden fruit; by thus transgressing God's law they fell from their former friendly relationship with God.

This account belongs to the Yahwist tradition, noted for its imagery, symbolism, anthropomorphisms—a tradition more concerned with theological significance than with the historical niceties of the events. But the author wants his account to be regarded as historical. Although his style may be called primitive, folkloristic, sapiential, or mythological, he definitely wished to report certain realities of the utmost importance for religion. The account cannot be traced to any known earlier literary material. There is some evidence, however, that it incorporates Mesopotamian data. The word ''Eden'' is a Sumerian loanword; similarly the site of Eden and the motif of the tree of life betray Mesopotamian links.

Man always has been concerned with evil, death, and the possibility of immortal life. The hero in the Gilgamesh Epic, e.g., searched, although unsuccessfully, for life that would not end in death. The Yahwist who believed that God had made all things good, concluded, under divine inspiration, that man was involved in some vast aboriginal calamity. And by using the old popular stories his people knew, he not only gave the history of sin's origin, but also tried to interpret the fact of sin.

Although this story of man's fall is of the greatest importance, there are few allusions to it in the Bible: Sir 25.23 and 1 Tim 2.13–14 declare that sin began through a woman. Wisdom 2.24 and Jn 8.44 identify the serpent with the devil. Romans 5.12–21 and 1 Cor 15.21–23 stress the connection between the first man's sin and death. But the Bible always takes seriously the fact that sin is universal: ''All have sinned'' (Rom 3.23).

The Yahwist apparently did not know the precise nature of the first sin. He was content to describe it in terms applicable to any serious sin: it was a deliberate transgression of God's precept and it involved pride and defiance. The symbolism of the tree of knowledge characterizes the sin more specifically as an inordinate aspiration, as a proud claim to moral autonomy: they and not God would decide what was good and evil. There may be a sexual overtone to the account. Through the symbolism of the serpent, a power of evil, and by describing man's fall as coming through woman, the Yahwist may have lashed out against the Canaanite fertility rites which were alluring Israelites of his day to sin against God.

The status of the first man and woman, as the Yahwist indicates, has definitely deteriorated because of the Fall. They lost their wholesome relationship with all about them, with God, with one another, and with created things. Moreover, they lost these gifts not only for themselves, but also for their descendants. BIBLIOGRAPHY: L. F. Hartman, ''Sin in Paradise'' CBQ 20 (1958) 26–40; H. Renckens, *Israel's Concept of the Beginning* (tr. C. Napier, 1964) 128–304.

[F. BUCK]

FALLING ASLEEP OF MARY, see DORMITION OF THE BLESSED VIRGIN.

FALLON, MICHAEL FRANCIS (1867–1931) Canadian educator, bishop. After obtaining his doctorate in philosophy and theology in Rome, F. entered the Oblates of Mary Immaculate (1894). Ordained in 1894, he returned to his native Canada and taught English literature at the Univ. of Ottawa, and later served as vice-rector of the university. Elected provincial of the Oblates in 1904, he was appointed in 1909 bp. of London, Ontario. F. was active in discussions of public policy, a strong advocate of home rule for Ireland, and a protagonist of the Irish element in the controversy with French Canadians. He edited *Shorter Poems by Catholics* (1930).

[J. R. AHERNE]

FALLON, VALÈRE (1875–1955), Jesuit economist. He studied the social sciences at Louvain, Berlin, and Munich. He taught at Louvain and at Liège. His work on the principles of social economics was translated into several languages and widely used. He was a founder and the leader of the Belgian Family Movement, and participated from the beginning in the International Population Movement.

[H. JACK]

FALLOUX, FRÉDÉRIC ALFRED PIERRE DE (1811–86), French statesman and writer. Elected to the Chamber of Deputies in 1846 as a Legitimist, he was opposed to Louis Philippe. As a member of the Constitutional Assembly of 1848, he supported the Revolution and served as chairman of the labor committee that terminated the short-lived national workshops. He was minister of public instruction (1848–49). Author of the Falloux Law enacted after he left office, he was successful in establishing freedom of education. The new law permitted religious congregations as well as private citizens to establish schools. In 1856, he was elected to the French Academy. A liberal Catholic and a Royalist, he worked for a reconciliation of Church and State, supported the freedom of the Papal States, attempted to reconcile the Legitimists and Orleanists in 1872. His writings include: *Histoire de Louis XVI* (1840), *Histoire de Saint Pie V* (1844). BIBLIOGRAPHY: A. Joubert, *Le Comte de Falloux* (1886); E. Veuillet, *Le Comte de Falloux et ses mémoires* (1888).

[D. R. PENN]

FALSA MUSICA, see MUSICA FICTA.

FALSE DECRETALS, main work of the Psuedo-Isidorian Forgeries. Compiled *c.*850, they asserted the rights of bps. against metropolitans and secular rulers, exalting the papacy as an immediate court of appeal. Isidore Mercator, named as the compiler, came to be confused with Isidore of Seville (*c.*560–636). The Decretals comprised forged letters from pre-Nicene popes, canons of several councils (mostly authentic), and letters from various post-Nicene popes (many spurious). Influential in the Middle Ages despite occasional questioning, their falsity was proved by the 16th century. BIBLIOGRAPHY: L. Saltet, CE 5:773–780; H. Fuhrmann, NCE 5:820–824; R. Naz, DDC 4:1062–64. *CENTURIATORS OF MAGDEBURG.

[T. EARLY]

FALSE WITNESS, the sin of injustice consisting in knowingly giving untrue evidence against another. The prohibition of the Decalogue (Ex 20.16) is taken principally to refer to a court trial. The immorality of bearing false witness is threefold: it is *perjury; it is a violation of the rights of another to life, reputation, or fortune; it is *lying. Outside of a juridic procedure, the sin can also occur wherever giving evidence is obligatory, e.g., where witness to another's character or competence is required.

[T. C. O'BRIEN]

FALSE WORSHIP, a sin against the virtue of *religion, thus contrary to the honor and reverence due to God alone. Under the heading of *superstition, St. Thomas Aquinas notes that acts against religion offend by excess which either offer to a creature worship due to God alone or which offer worship to God in ways not appropriate to the right relationship intended by religion (ST 2a2ae, 92.1). The first is idolatry; the second, the many forms of superstition contrary to God's direction and lordship over man's life. *DIVINATION; *MAGIC.

[T. C. O'BRIEN]

FALSEHOOD, see LYING.

FALSILOQUIUM, literally a false statement, but historically a term taken in distinction from *mendacium,* a lie. The point of the distinction is connected with a moral theory that sought to evade the position that conscious utterance of a falsehood is intrinsically evil. (see ThAq ST 2a2ae, 11b.3). A *falsiloquium* would be the utterance of a falsehood justified by the fact that the hearer has no right to know the truth. The distinction and its use are not respected by most Catholic moralists. BIBLIOGRAPHY: D. Hughes, NCE 8:1107–10. *LYING.

[T. C. O'BRIEN]

FALSITY, the abstract form of the Lat. *falsum,* the opposite of *verum.* As *truth consists in the matching of mind and reality, so falsity is their disconformity. Some authors speak of ''ontological'' falsity, but we may dismiss the epithet here, as being altogether too grand for a sham which on analysis proves to be true for what it is in itself and as God sees it, and false only insofar as people are misled by the appearances, e.g., paste jewels, counterfeit theology, crocodile tears. Falsity, then, is not objective, but a subjective defect in the human mind; the authors speak of it as ''logical'' falsity, though the designation is scarcely adequate for a condition which is epistemological and psychological as well as logical, and may also be moral. As such it is in the mind, not simply as apprehending an object, even if that be an illusion, but as committing itself to an erroneous statement or judgment about it. Asserting that the seeming is the being, falsity is to be distinguished from mere absence of knowledge or nescience, e.g., as to which Chinese dynasty came first, the Sui or the T'ang, and from absence of knowledge which should be there, or *ignorance, e.g., that murder is always wrong (though ignorance and falsity run closely together), and from partial and incomplete judgments so long as the mind is aware of the limits in which it is working, e.g., our attribution to God of qualities we admire in this world. BIBLIOGRAPHY: ThAq ST 1a, 17 (esp. in ed. Lat-Eng, v. 4, ed. T. Gornall, 1965).

[T. GILBY]

FALSO BORDONE, It. musical term for a type of harmonization. *FABURDEN.

FAMAGUSTA CATHEDRAL, a bizarre structure of the late Middle Ages, erected by Greeks in Famagusta, Cyprus (under Frankish rulers) in the Gothic style, surmounted by a dome. The apses carry semipointed domes; the nave, quadripartite vaulting with Gothic pinnacles on the exterior. It is now in ruins.

[M. J. DALY]

FAMIAN, ST. (*c.*1090–1150), Cistercian priest, venerated esp. at Gallese, near Rome. Born of a wealthy and noble family of Cologne, baptized Gerhard (Quardus, Wardo), F. felt the call to a more perfect way of life, and as a poor pilgrim visited shrines of Italy and Spain. He entered a Cistercian monastery in Osera, Spain, where he lived a number of years as a hermit. He went on a pilgrimage —some claim that he resigned his position as abbot to do so—and died at Gallese on his return journey. He came to be called Famian because of the miracles reported at his grave. BIBLIOGRAPHY: G. Mariani, BiblSanct 5:449–450.

[G. E. CONWAY]

FAMILIAR STYLE (It., *stile familiare*), a type of polyphonic vocal music usually used in four-part harmonizations, characterized by a strict syllabic and textual progression in a ''note-against-note'' manner. Having originated around the 16th cent., this style (called also ''homorhythmic''), although employed in such types of secular music as the *frottola,* and the *villanella,* was used chiefly in harmonized hymns and chorales.

[A. M. MACK]

FAMILISTS, a religious body founded by H. *Niclaes, who called it the Family of Love (Familia Caritatis), or the House of Love. The Familists existed in Germany, Holland, and France, but principally in England, where Niclaes visited in 1552 or 1553. Their teaching was that the divine spirit of love within them raised them above Bible, creed, liturgy, or law. They were accused of *antinomianism. In spite of legal repression they survived in England until the end of the 17th cent. when most of them were absorbed into the Society of Friends. BIBLIOGRAPHY: Knox Enth 140–141, 171–172; G. Bareille, DTC 5:2070–72 s.v. ''Famille d'amour''; R. M. Jones, *Studies in Mystical Religion* (1923) 428–448.

FAMILY. Christian teaching has always sought to foster and defend the ideal of family life. Vatican Council II addressed the dignity of the family as the first of those specific issues of urgency facing the Church in the modern world (VatII ChModWorld, part II, ch.1). To implement the conciliar concern Paul VI, Jan.11, 1973, established the Pontifical Commission for the Family. The findings of the U.S. Bishops' Conference on Liberty and Justice for All (A Call to Action) during the American bicentennial year suggested the possibility and even necessity of concentrating the whole effort for justice on supporting and strengthening the family. The family ministry becomes all the more important to families themselves who are trying to follow Christian ideals because the Church is more and more becoming the sole institutional advocate of such ideals. Public policy has shown little concern for the family unit as such; both formally espoused ethical and social theories and the actual social environment increase attitudes, manners of life, cultural pressures that run absolutely counter to the existence and the dignity of the family. Christian families seeking to maintain their own values need support of the family ministry in their adherence to these values and their practice.

Simply to state that the family is the basic unit of society is a truism; the dependence of society on family is an observable fact. The Christian motivation for extolling family life is not primarily a concern for the fabric of society; statist political systems can and to a degree do attend to traditionally familial functions in order to create better servants of the State. The Christian ideal begins with and is motivated by the dignity of the family as inseparably linked with the dignity of the human person. The Genesis account of the creation of man and woman is taken as a divine message that the human being is not a solitary, but a community-directed creature. The person comes into being, grows in, and is meant to contribute to the primal community, the family. The person receives the first experience of self-worth by being one loved by others in the family; in the family as well the person experiences both the needs of others and the self-transcendence of giving in love. The dimension of the family's worth and importance is fully measured by the truth that the full dignity of the human person is in being made to God's image. That means being destined to knowing and loving and being known and loved by Father, Son, and Holy Spirit. The life of the family becomes the first setting for a realization of that destiny's meaning: not simply by parental teaching, but above all by family life as the first experience of recognition and love received from others; the family unit and communion become the first point of reference by which the child of the family can perceive what it means to be the child of God.

Because of these transcendent ideals the Church teaches that the permanence and stability of marriage must be defended as a positive objective (see GOODS OF MARRIAGE). There rests on husband and wife (even when they are not actually parents, but simply as sharers in the state of matrimony) the obligation to regard marriage not as simply a personal matter, much less a passing fancy; they must deepen their perception that growth in love and respect for each other conditions the personal growth of their own children and contributes to the wider community setting necessary to all personal development. Because the person comes into being in and through the family, the family has the first and inalienable right to educate. Because the person has the divinely given identity of being to God's image, the right to educate preeminently includes the right to inculcate Christian values. The State cannot justly interfere with the parents' rights; rather its function is limited to supporting and enhancing the resources and role of the parents themselves. The existence and dignity of the family creates a further obligation on the family itself with reference to the complex of social forces within which it exists. Only by an appreciation of its own reason for being can the family project its own values so that community standards, laws that are passed, and the whole moral climate are not a threat to the family's own meaning.

The Church's concern in facing the problems of family life in the modern world is to communicate to the family the sense of itself as a sacred institution, whose soundness directly determines the growth of children who develop a sense of personal dignity and goals and values matching that dignity. Church concern for solving economic problems follows: for these often deprive the family of the quality of life necessary as a setting in which a fully human life can be lived. The ministry of social justice is thus intimately linked with the family ministry. In order to inculcate a sense of family, there is much more attention being given to bring families together in the church community. Through sharing family liturgies together, through discussion groups, through simple parish social gatherings there is an effort being made to let families perceive their mutual sharing of values and of problems. The Church is finding, as well, that the experience of going out to other families in need is a powerful force that brings the giving family itself closer together. A further means of strengthening family life has been discovered in programs in which parents directly participate in the religious education of their children. There is a close link between the parish and the family ministry; to the effectiveness of this ministry the laity are called upon to exercise an urgently needed part.

[T. C. O'BRIEN]

FAMILY LIFE BUREAU, see UNITED STATES CATHOLIC CONFERENCE, INC.

FAMILY MOVEMENT, CHRISTIAN, see CHRISTIAN FAMILY MOVEMENT.

FAMILY PRAYER. As it is the original social unit, the family is also the first source of education to religious piety and prayer, and (with the bond of kinship and love) serves as a natural foyer of worship. Jewish liturgy is in great part realized in the home or family unit; and family prayer realizes in a fundamental way the counsel of Christ to common prayer (Mt 18.19). It is a practice encouraged recently by the Family Rosary Crusade of Patrick Peyton, CSC. BIBLIOGRAPHY: Vat II ChrEduc 3; P. Peyton, *All for Her* (1967). *PRAYER.

[W. J. READ]

FANATICISM, unreasoning devotion to a particular form of religious expression, sometimes centering around a set of doctrines, sometimes around a group (e.g., a church or sect), sometimes around an ethical code or other pattern of behavior. Devotion to the object of fanaticism is expressed without regard for rational balance or ordinary standards of prudence. Some observers interpret fanaticism as evidence of repressed doubt, which the personality subconsciously tries to deny by exaggerated devotion. Theologically, fanaticism may be interpreted as a form of idolatry. The fanatic gives to some particular object, person, or code of actions the loyalty that belongs only to God. No distinction is drawn between the being of God and the symbols and acts that relate to him. Examples that are often cited include: *snake handlers; extreme puritanical groups who attempt to make their standards obligatory for the total society; persons whose devotion to particular religious forms and their propagation becomes so consuming that they are unable to maintain normal human relationships; and those whose devotion leads them to persecute others who do not share it as enemies of God.

[T. EARLY]

FANCELLI, family of Italian sculptors of the 17th cent., several in Rome associated with the master Bernini. **Giacomo-Antonio** (1619–71) assisted Bernini (1630) and decorated St. Peter's (1640); **Cosimo** (1620?–88) decorated the buildings of Pietro da Cortona and carved the *Angel with the Sudarium* on the Ponte Sant' Angelo (1668–69).

[M. J. DALY]

FANCELLI, LUCA (1430–95), Italian sculptor and architect. It is thought that in Florence F. executed Brunelleschi's plans for the Pitti Palace. In Mantua (1450), as Alberti's envoy, F. constructed the churches of San Sebastiano and Sant' Andrea, and, for the patron Ludovico Gonzaga, the *Domus nova* of Gonzaga Castle. F.'s work for Master Alberti eclipsed his own career.

[M. J. DALY]

FANON, a term of obscure origin that has been applied in the singular or plural to a number of articles associated with liturgical worship—the *maniple, the lappets of a bishop's *miter, processional banners, the *humeral veil worn by the subdeacon while holding the paten at Mass, and, most distinctively, to the outer amice worn by the pope in addition to the ordinary amice which, like other clerics, he wears under his alb. One part of the fanon is worn over the alb and the other over the chasuble.

[P. K. MEAGHER]

FANTASTIC ART, grotesque, eccentric, irrational art in such forms as the Gorgon Medusa, gargoyles on Gothic cathedrals, the horrors of Goya, the moralities of Bosch. In the 20th cent. the *Dadaists, dethroning reason, left forms to chance; Surrealists expressed the subconscious, the dream, through exquisite optical illusions in disturbing, improbable relationships; M. Chagall produced inverted world floats, defying gravity. Intentions in fantastic art vary from the didactic and magical to those so highly personal as to defy analysis. BIBLIOGRAPHY: A. H. Barr, Jr., ed. *Fantastic Art, Dada, Surrealism* (1936), R. Callois, *Au Coeur du fantastique* (1965).

[M. J. DALY]

FANTASY, see IMAGINATION AND FANTASY.

FANTONI, ANDREA (1659–1734), Italian sculptor. F.'s most important works are a pulpit decorated with rococo reliefs from the Old and New Testament and sacristy furniture, all in the Church of S. Martino at Alzano Maggiore.

[M. J. DALY]

FANZAGO (FANZAGA) COSIMO (1591–1678), leading Italian architect and sculptor in the baroque school of Naples, with numerous exuberant works in churches, pulpits, altars, statues, palaces, and fountains. The important cloister of S. Martino in Naples, 1625, is graceful and elegant in Tuscan classical style with doors fully baroque in spiral, twisted dramatic forms. Distinctive is F.'s domination of structure by curvilinear surface designs and his inventiveness, as in trompe l'oeil cupolas of S. Lorenzo in Lucina, Rome.

[M. J. DALY]

FARA, ST. (known also as Burgundofara; d. *c.*675), foundress and abbess. Legend reports that St. Columban passed by F.'s home on his way to exile from Luxeuil. He blessed her, whereupon she vowed a religious life. After considerable parental resistance, she was able to found a house at Faremoutiers, which prospered. BIBLIOGRAPHY: H. M. Delsart, *Sainte Fare* (1911); P. Burchi, BiblSanct 3:611–612, s. v. "Burgundofara."

[B. F. SCHERER]

FĀRĀBĪ, AL-, see ALFĀRĀBĪ.

FAREL, GUILLAUME (1489–1565), French-Swiss Protestant Reformer. F., like John *Calvin, with whom his name is linked in the history of Genevan Protestantism, was born in France and studied in Paris. At first a disciple of the humanist Jacques *Lefèvre d'Étaples and a member of the reform circle of Bp. Guillaume Briçonnet of Meaux, F. was affected by Luther's writings; in 1523 he was forced to leave the country, taking refuge in Switzerland. He settled first at Basel, where his violent zeal brought him into conflict with Erasmus. During this period he came under the influence of J. *Oecolampadius and *Zwingli. Expelled from Basel in 1524, he preached reform in various localities of French-speaking Switzerland (Montbéliard, Strassburg). In this period he wrote the first Protestant treatise published in French, *Sommaire et brève déclaration* (1525), a short, not very profound work. From Berne (1526) and Aigle, he exercised an influence on many in France as well as in Switzerland. He became the Reformer of Neuchâtel in 1530; he went to Geneva in 1532 and 1533 to preach. In July 1536 he persuaded Calvin, who was passing through the city, to remain and join in the attempt to impose that strict discipline for which the city was to become famous. This first effort failed, and both he and Calvin were forced (1538) to leave the city. Calvin, of course, returned in 1541 to become the undisputed master of the godly city, while F. was content to return to Neuchâtel, where he remained pastor until his death. While he preceded Calvin in time, F. became his disciple, overshadowed by the greater man in the history of Protestantism. BIBLIOGRAPHY: Léonard HistProt 1:315–317 and *passim;* Y. Congar, *Catholicisme* 4:1095–96.

[R. B. ENO]

FAREMOUTIERS, ABBEY OF (7th cent.), foundation of nuns located E of Paris in Brie. It was guided by monks from Luxeuil and eventually became Benedictine. Its early era saw many saints and, after a 16th-cent. reform, it enjoyed another flourishing period in the 17th cent. Although it was destroyed by the French Revolution, a new foundation of Benedictine nuns was begun at the same site in 1931. BIBLIOGRAPHY: P. Sage, *Catholicisme* 4:1096–98.

[J. F. FALLON]

FAREWELL DISCOURSES OF JESUS, chapters 14–16 of the Gospel according to John. Jesus, who during the Last Supper had washed the feet of his Disciples as a proof of love and as an example and announced his betrayal by Judas, told them that he was leaving them and gave them a new commandment: "Love one another as I have loved you" (13.34). His discourses in the following chapters (14–16) are known as his "farewell discourses." They contain the testament of one who will die the following day, but one who is at the same time the "Son of Man" already "glorified" (13.31), speaking to his Disciples and through them to his persecuted Church. In the redaction of these discourses, the use of different literary patterns like dialogues, allegory, etc., may have been the cause of many repetitions and even of apparent contradictions in the chronological order of the text.

In them Jesus explains why he must die and how his Disciples will be able to follow him into his glory. Sent by his Father to bring salvation to the world, he goes back to him to prepare a place for them. In the meantime, they will have to live without him in a world which will persecute them as it had persecuted him; but they will not be left alone. Jesus is the "way" to the Father. He is one with him and they are both in one another. If his Disciples pray the Father in his name, they will always be heard. Both Father and Son will send to them the Holy Spirit who, being another Paraclete (Counselor, Advocate, Assistant), will be with them as Jesus himself was with them during his mortal life. He will reveal to them the complete truth about the world and about Jesus. He will show that the world and its prince have already been judged and condemned by God. Therefore they must not be afraid of being persecuted by it, because their sufferings will finally bring them great joy. The Paraclete will recall Jesus' teaching to them and help them to fulfill their Master's work. If they remain in his love and fulfill his commandments, the first of which is to love one another, they will no more be called his servants but his friends. He will come into them and, because he is in the Father, the Father, who loves them as he himself loves them, will come into them and both will make their home in them. Because Jesus is the true Vine, if they remain in him they will be pruned by suffering and persecution, but they will bear much fruit, the everlasting fruit of eternal life. Jesus will finally return to take them with him, and they will be with him in his Father's house forever. BIBLIOGRAPHY: C. H. Dodd, *Interpretation of the Fourth Gospel* (1960); G. M. Behler, *Last Discourses of Jesus* (tr. R. T. Francoeur, 1965).

[A. VIARD]

FARFA, ABBEY OF (6th cent.), Benedictine foundation *c.*25 miles NW of Rome in the Sabine hills. Destroyed by Lombards in the 7th cent., but soon rebuilt, it became one of the wealthiest abbeys in the Frankish Empire, extending its power over a large section of central Italy. Its luxury led to decadence, but the Cluniac reform renewed it in the 11th cent. The abbey lost much of its power and privileges with the breakdown of the empire, suffered much from absentee superiors, but flourished again in the 16th cent. under guidance from Cassino. It is now a national monument of archeological interest. BIBLIOGRAPHY: J. Roux, *Catholicisme* 4:1098–1100.

[J. F. FALLON]

FARFA BIBLE, Mozarabic illuminated manuscript of the 11th cent., now in the Vatican Library.

[M. J. DALY]

FARGES, ALBERT (1848–1926), Sulpician, leader in the revival of Thomistic studies. Ordained in 1872, he taught at several diocesan seminaries in France and at the Institut Catholique in Paris. His major work in spiritual theology is *Les Voies ordinaires de la vie spirituelle* (1925), which follows the teachings of St. Thomas Aquinas and St. Teresa of Avila. In philosophy he published a nine-volume series, *Études philosophiques pour vulgariser les théories d'Aristote et S.Thomas . . .* (1885–1907), and with his confrere, D. Barbedette, a widely used Latin-French Thomistic manual.

[T. C. O'BRIEN]

FARIBAULT PLAN, a compromise educational plan proposed in 1891 by the local RC clergy and approved by Abp. J. *Ireland, which, by agreement with the public school boards of education in Faribault and Stillwater, Minn., would make possible the use of public taxes for church-related schools. The plan involved the annual leasing of Catholic schools staffed by religious to public authorities, subject to mutual agreement. The pupils, after daily Mass, received secular instruction during school hours, and religious instruction on the premises either before or after the legal school day. The plan, although similar to the earlier Poughkeepsie Plan, became the center of a heated controversy provoked largely by T. Bouquillon's pamphlet, *Education: To Whom Does It Belong?,* to which René Holaind, SJ, responded vigorously. The ensuing vehement debate was referred to Rome and in 1893 Leo XIII declared that the plan could be tolerated. However, because of continued animus, the plan was discontinued in 1894. BIBLIOGRAPHY: J. A. Burns, *Growth and Development of the Catholic School System in the U.S.* (1912).

[M. B. MURPHY]

FARLATI, DANIELE (1690–1773), Italian Jesuit historian. The greater part of F.'s life was devoted to a work of outstanding historical scholarship, *Illyricum sacrum,* a secular and ecclesiastical history of the ancient countries Illyria and Dalmatia. It is the work of three successive authors whose labors spanned 132 years (1695–1827). F. took up the work of his Jesuit colleague Filippo Riceputi and produced five volumes rich in documentation. The contribution of this work to the history of the Balkans from the time of Justinian to the 18th cent. cannot be overestimated. BIBLIOGRAPHY: J. Lŭcić, DHGE 16:581–594.

[J. R. AHERNE]

FARLEY, JAMES ALOYSIUS (1888–1976), Catholic political leader. A native of New York state, a business man of extraordinary acumen, F. was essentially a political man. From modest beginnings in the Democratic party in New York, through years as its state chairman, as campaigner for Alfred E. Smith and Franklin D. Roosevelt, he made a unique contribution to American politics. Instrumental in securing FDR's election as governor of New York in 1930 he began making plans for his nomination as Democratic candidate for president at the 1932 convention. In the succeeding two years, F. was to establish the pattern for later campaigning as national chairman of the Democratic party. He criss-crossed the country talking to party leaders, wrote a voluminous correspondence, was on a first-name basis with an incredible number of people, and by force of charm and personality created a coalition which would dominate American politics for two decades. As postmaster-general in the Roosevelt cabinet from 1932 to 1940, F. practiced and defended the patronage system whereby appointive jobs went to party members who hewed to the line. F. broke with Roosevelt on the third-term issue and spent the remainder of his life as an internatonal business figure. He was a prominent layman in the life of the archdiocese of New York.

[J. R. AHERNE]

FARLEY, JOHN MURPHY (orig. Farrelly; 1842–1918), abp. of New York and cardinal. After study at the preparatory seminary of Clogher, Ireland, and St. Joseph's Seminary, Troy, N. Y., he was sent to the N American College, Rome, and ordained (1870) for the New York diocese. A brief parochial assignment on Staten Island was followed by successive appointments to diocesan administrative posts, culminating in his consecration (1895) as titular bp. of Zeugma and his succession (1902) to New York as fourth archbishop. In 1911 he was named cardinal priest. He was characterized by a cautious and conciliatory spirit, probably acquired, in part, from his close association with the mild *McCloskey and the conservative *Corrigan. During F.'s administration, special concern was shown for the Negroes and Italian immigrants in New York, a minor seminary was opened (1903), and support given to Catholic higher education and scholarship. His publications include *The History of St. Patrick's Cathedral* (1908) and *The Life of John Cardinal McCloskey* (1918). BIBLIOGRAPHY: M. J. Lavelle, "John Cardinal Farley, Archbishop of New York," AER 60 (1919) 113–125.

[M. CARTHY]

FARMER, FERDINAND (FERDINAND STEINMEYER, 1720–86), missionary. A German Jesuit ordained *c.*1750, he came to Pennsylvania as Ferdinand Farmer and worked out of Lancaster, traveling throughout E Pennsylvania. Moving his headquarters to St. Joseph's church in Philadelphia, he labored in Delaware, New Jersey, and New York, and established the first congregation in New York City. F. was an astronomer well known in Europe, a pioneer member of the American Philosophical Society, and a trustee of the University of Pennsylvania. BIBLIOGRAPHY: J. Kirlin, *Catholicity in Philadelphia* (1909).

[J. R. AHERNE]

FARNBOROUGH, Benedictine priory, 37 miles SW of London in Hampshire, England. Empress Eugénie resided there from 1881, and built the neo-Gothic St. Michael Church in 1886–87 as a burial place for her husband Napoleon III (d. 1873) and their son Prince Louis (slain in the Zulu War 1879). The shrine was originally under the care of French Premonstratensians, who were replaced by Benedictines of Solesmes in 1895; under them it became an abbey in 1903. Among the scholars at Farnborough were F. *Cabrol, H. Leclercq, M. Férotin, and A. *Wilmart. Since 1947, it has been a priory, staffed by Benedictines from Prinknash Abbey. BIBLIOGRAPHY: R. Gazeau, *Catholicisme* 4:1103–04.

[A. V. KAUFFMAN]

FARNE, a group of 17 islands off the NE coast of England. The largest one, bearing the same name, was so bleak that it became a favorite home of the hermit saints. Its first known inhabitant was St. Aidan (d. 651). St. Cuthbert of Lindisfarne lived there from 676 to 684, and returned to the island some time before his death in 687. His name was given to parts of the island and to the eider ducks that inhabit it. In the 13th cent. the monastery became a cell of the abbey of Durham. It ceased to be a monastic center at the time of the Reformation. BIBLIOGRAPHY: H. Farmer, DHGE 15:596–598.

[C. CARROLL]

FARO OF ST. MEAUX (known also as Burgundofaro) (d. *c.*672), bishop. One of the first known bishops of Meaux, F. was brother of St. Chainoaldus of Laon, and his sister was St. Fara (Burgundofara), first abbess of Faremoutiers. F. was raised at the court of King Theodebert of Austrasia, where he married and continued later at the court of Clotaire II. He led an edifying life, and at 35 made an agreement with his wife, Blidechild, to allow him to become a Benedictine. Later tonsured for the clergy at Meaux, he was chosen bp. in 628, and became chancellor under Dagobert I. He was noted for charity during his long episcopate, and gave St. Fiacre some of his own lands at Breuil, and founded the monastery of the Holy Cross at Meaux. BIBLIOGRAPHY: Butler 4:216–217; H. Platelle, BiblSanct 5:468.

[N. F. GAUGHAN]

FARRAR, FREDERIC WILLIAM (1831–1903), Dean of Canterbury. He studied at King's College, London, and Trinity College, Cambridge before his ordination (1857) in the C of E. He taught at Harrow and Marlborough college, served as rector of St. Margaret's, and canon of Westminster Abbey in 1876. He was also chaplain to the House of Commons from 1890 to 1895. Appointed Dean of Canterbury in 1895, F., a Broad Church evangelical, had considerable influence on the middle classes, mainly through his numerous writings, which include fiction, biography, philology, and several volumes of sermons and lectures. His *Life of Christ* (1874) went through 30 editions in as many years. This and his *Life and Works of St. Paul* (1897) had a strong impact on the religious life of his time. The doubts on eternal punishment expressed in his *Eternal Hope* (1877) aroused much debate.

[A. V. KAUFFMANN]

FARRELL, WALTER (1902–51), American Dominican theologian. A Dominican from 1920, he was ordained in 1927. The Univ. of Fribourg in Switzerland conferred on him the doctorate in theology 3 years later. His dissertation *The Natural Moral Law According to St. Thomas and Suárez* was widely hailed as a pioneer work and demonstrated that combination of clear thought and trenchant style that was to be his special mark as a theologian. F. taught at the Dominican House of Studies in Washington D.C. most of his career. He interrupted his teaching to serve as a chaplain in the U.S. Navy from 1943 to 1945. An indefatigable lecturer he gave a series of talks in New York over a period of 4 years that led to his masterly *A Companion to the Summa* (4 v., 1938–43). The work is characterized by profound grasp of the teaching of Aquinas and by its lucid and witty, if dated, English. Poor health brought F. to an untimely death. His deep spirituality as well as engaging humanity were evident in all he did and appear in the posthumous study of Christ, *Only Son* (1953). BIBLIOGRAPHY: R. Coffee, "Very Reverend Walter Farrell, O.P." AER 126 (1952) 271–278.

[J. R. AHERNE]

FASCISM, totalitarian ideology of the right which had its greatest impact upon Italy under Mussolini (1922–43) and Germany under Hitler (1933–45) but also influenced other countries of central (e.g., Austria), Eastern (e.g., Romania), and Western (Spain) Europe. Although the ideological roots of Fascism antedated World War I, it was in the period between the two world wars that Fascism enjoyed its greatest vogue. Economic distress and dissatisfaction with the Paris Peace Treaties (1919–20) facilitated the growth and triumph of Fascism. Even democratic states, such as England and France, witnessed the rise of Fascist movements.

Fascist movements and parties varied from country to country and even within a country from one period to another. Nevertheless, they exhibited certain common traits and adhered to common beliefs. Fascists were strongly nationalist and virulently anti-Marxist; they despised parliamentary forms and sought to substitute an authoritarian, corporative state. They did not tolerate the existence of any party but their own, and its machinery was interlocked with that of the State. They appealed to all social groups but esp. to the lower middle classes; conflicting interests of owners, workers, technicians and the State were resolved in the "corporation." Fascists were often anti-Semitic, with hatred and persecution of the Jews reaching its culmination in Nazi Germany. Uniforms, elaborate rituals, and myths (particularly those relating to blood and race) were characteristic of Fascist parties and movements. Although Fascism preserved the principle of private property, there was strict government control of economic affairs. Censorship of the press, as of all cultural media, was common. Both in Fascist Italy and Nazi Germany, the State clashed with the papacy.

The Italian and German Fascist movements were born in 1919. Although both brought to their respective countries some socio-economic gains, their aggressive foreign policies plunged Europe into World War II. BIBLIOGRAPHY: E. Nolte, *Three Faces of Fascism* (tr. L. Vennewitz, 1966); F. Carsten, *Rise of Fascism* (1969); *International Encyclopedia of the Social Sciences* 5:334–341; A. J. Gregor, *Fascist Persuasion in Radical Politics* (1974).

[E. A. CARRILLO]

FAST AND ABSTINENCE IN THE BIBLE. In the OT fasting is thought of as an outward expression of sorrow, affliction, and mourning, and as such is associated with the wearing of sackcloth and ashes (1 Sam 31.13; 2 Sam 1.12; 3.35). In particular it is an expression of sorrow for sin and repentance (1 Sam 7.6; Neh 9.1; Jer 14.12; Jl 1.4 etc.). It may also be an expression of supplication or entreaty. Thus David's prayer for the survival of Bathsheba's infant son is accompanied by fasting, but once the child is dead he considers it useless to prolong his fast (2 Sam 12.16). Again general fasts could be proclaimed for the whole people (Jg 20.26; 1 Sam 14.24 etc.), and the Day of Atonement was prescribed as a fast day by law (Lev 16.29). In postexilic times 4 fast days were prescribed in the course of the year to commemorate the tragedy of the fall of Jerusalem (Zech 7.3). Fasting was considered to arouse the compassion of Yahweh, and in the Psalms of lamentation the Psalmist strives to draw attention to its emaciating and enfeebling effects upon his own body (Ps 102.4-5, etc.). Through fasting and other acts of mourning he hopes to induce Yahweh to recognize him as one of the *'anawim,* the humble and afflicted, and so to accept him as his client and the object of his chivalrous protection. Fasting was much favored by the Pharisees, who were characteristically ostentatious in their practice of it. In the NT fasting as a sign of mourning is inappropriate to the time of Jesus' earthly ministry, for it would imply a failure to recognize and respond with joy to the messianic significance of this (Mt 9.14). But after Jesus' death, when his Disciples will fast, they must do so in secret and avoid the ostentation of the Pharisees (Mt 6.16). Jesus inaugurated his own ministry with a period of 40 days of fasting corresponding to that of Moses (cf. Ex 34.38).

Abstinence as prescribed in the OT applies principally to the blood of living creatures (Gen 9.4; Lev 17.10–11), which is considered the seat of life and as such sacred to Yahweh (Dt 12.23). This particular prohibition is carried down to the apostolic Church, where gentile Christians are directed to avoid consuming blood or "things strangled." For the rest the elaborate alimentary laws of the OT debarring Hebrews from various forms of unclean food were abrogated in the new dispensation so far as gentile Christians were concerned.

[D. J. BOURKE]

FASTING, the complete or partial abstinence from nourishment by way of food or drink. As part of his general obligation to care for his health, no man has the right to fast to such a degree that he endangers his health, except for a proportionately grave cause as, e.g., the good of his country. Some theologians would justify fasting even to such a degree as to endanger life, provided there was an extremely grave cause as, e.g., to obtain for one's countrymen basic freedoms not otherwise obtainable. In such a case, the obvious intent must be not to bring about one's death but to force concessions through the moral force of the publicized fast. A limited fast, in which some forms of food are given up permanently or all foods for a short time, is permitted for a good reason, e.g., to benefit health, as a form of protest against an evil or, most commonly, for a religious motive. Fasting thus inspired was common among the Jews for a variety of religious reasons. Thus, they fasted, in time of calamity, as an emphasis to their prayers for deliverance (1 Sam 7.6), and in times of mourning (1 Kg 21.9). There only one day of general fasting imposed by the Mosaic Law, the Day of Atonement (Lev 16.29–34), but four additional days were added after the Exile (Zech 8.19). Jesus was critical of the pharisaical attitude toward fasting (Mt 6.16), but he practiced fasting himself (Mt 4.1–11) and urged it as a practice to be added to prayer for the obtaining of a special favor such as the casting out of evil spirits (Mk 9.28). He left no specific regulations about times for fasting, but his followers quickly adopted fasting as a religious exercise. The Apostles, e.g., added fasting to their prayers for special guidance (Acts 13.3; 14.23) and the early Christians had regular fasting practices each week (*Didache* 8.1). Fasting, both as a regular practice of all the faithful and as a penitential observance imposed on sinners, early became a feature of Christian life, but the details of fasting practices differed from age to age and from place to place. Among the early monks of Egypt and Syria fasting—in some cases extremely rigorous—was a common feature of life and the monastic orders elaborated their own regimes of fast and abstinence which were much more stringent than the fasts of the universal Church. But throughout its history the Church has urged fasting on its members, as an accompaniment of prayer, as a way to imitate Christ in his freely accepted sufferings, and as a means of penance for sins. By the 4th cent., fast on 1 or 2 days a week had become a part of ordinary Christian observance. On such days nothing was taken outside the main meal which was served late in the day, and many foods in addition to meat were entirely excluded. During Lent and other penitential seasons, a like observance was kept for longer periods of time. A process of mitigation gradually set in, however, and in modern times such rigid fasting practices were almost unknown outside monasteries and convents. In the current discipline of the RC Church, there are few specific fasting laws which are binding on all the faithful. The Church continues to instruct its members on the universal need for penance and urges some fasting as a fitting mode of fulfilling this need, but leaves the choice of particular penances up to the individual, aside from the universal regulation of partial fasting and abstinence on Ash Wednesday and Good Friday. BIBLIOGRAPHY: P. Clancy, NCE 3:847–850; D. Faber, *Fasting: the Phenomenon of Self-Denial* (1975).

[P. F. MULHERN]

FASTING (EASTERN CHURCH). Although the ancient rules in the East that permitted on a fast day only one *(monophagia)* or two meals *(dyophagia)* consisting solely of cooked or uncooked vegetables *(xerophagia),* have been abandoned, the Christian East has preserved a certain rigor by excluding on fasting days any food deriving from a warm-blooded animal (meat or meat products, together with eggs, milk, butter, and cheese). However, it is not required that one's consumption of other kinds of food be diminished; hence the distinction between fast and abstinence has become practically obsolete. The Orthodox faithful do not regard themselves strictly obliged to observe the fast with all rigor, but according to their specific circumstances. Among Catholic Orientals the regulations of fast have been interpreted strictly, but their requirements have been so reduced that they do not differ from those of the Latin Church. In the largest Eastern Christian group, the Byzantine, the following penitential seasons exist: (1) The Great Forty Days, beginning, as in the ancient Roman rite on Monday, after Cheesefare Sunday and terminating on the Friday before Palm Sunday (although the 8 days from then until Easter are also days of strict fast). (2) St. Peter's Fast, from the Sunday of All Saints (the first after Pentecost) until June 29th. (3) The Assumption Fast, Aug. 1–14. (4) The Christmas Forty Days, Nov. 15–Dec. 24. Also observed as days of fast-abstinence are Wednesdays and Fridays, two vigils (Jan. 5 and Aug. 14), and the feasts of the Beheading of St. John the Baptist (Aug. 29), and the Exaltation of the Holy Cross (Sept. 14). Certain privileged times are free of any fast or abstinence: Christmas to Jan. 4; the week between the Sundays of the Publican and Pharisee and that of the Prodigal Son; and the weeks following Easter and Pentecost.

[V. J. POSPISHIL]

FASTRED, BL. (d.1163), Cistercian, disciple of St. Bernard, who entered Clairvaux in 1146, was made abbot of the new foundation of Cambron in his native town in 1148 and was elected abbot of Clairvaux in 1157 and of Cîteaux in 1161. BIBLIOGRAPHY: M.-A. Dimier, BiblSanct 5:470–473.

[L. J. LEKAI]

FATALISM, a religious, philosophic, or popular position that holds that all events in the universe, esp. those pertaining to human life, are predetermined by Fate, a force or power that consciously or blindly imposes a rigid necessity upon all occurrences in advance of their happening, so that these come about only when and as decreed. At times Fate has been identified with the inexorable edicts of the gods for the direction of the universe and the government of men; at times it has been conceived as an overruling force that transcends the will and power of the gods.

For the sake of clarity the notion of fatalism should be distinguished from determinism, chance, and destiny. (1) Fatalism and determinism are alike insofar as both imply that all events are necessary. Fatalism maintains that the human will cannot affect the outcome of affairs, however, whereas determinism may or may not deny the efficacy of the will as a cause. Hence, determinism may or may not be compatible with moral accountability, whereas fatalism is a resignation to events beyond human control. (2) Fatalism is opposed to chance insofar as the latter involves the activity of no cause but mere random happenings with no intrinsic necessity for the coincidence of events. According to fatalism, a cause is at work, though perhaps blind, capricious, and arbitrary. (3) Destiny is not different from Fate but rather is Fate operative in individual instances; however unlike Fate, destiny does not preclude a rational motive for that which is destined, although its rationale may not be perceived.

Non-Christian Religions. In religions in which the processes of nature are dominant, as among the Babylonians and Egyptians, fatalism is found in the recognition and dramatization of the fundamental antithesis between life and death, and in a reverence for natural necessity as personified by the Egyptian goddess, Ma'et, who stands for natural order. For the Babylonians, the order of nature was an all-controlling destiny maintained by the gods whose will was enacted in the ordinance of the State. Despite the fatalistic overtones of their naturalism, however, both peoples evidenced a high level of ethical development.

Among the ancient Greeks, the concept of *moira* or necessity prevailed, according to which each man was to receive his portion or lot in life, as meted out by the gods together or by Zeus alone. And the human could not escape the measure of misfortune contained therein, but he could surely increase it through his own folly. Prominent, too, were the *Moirai* or Fates, the three sister goddesses who determined the course of human life. Described chiefly in the poetry of Homer and Hesiod, they assigned to every man his destiny—Clotho who spins the thread of life, Lachesis who measures it, and Atropos who severs it. Moreover, the Greek tragedians such as Aeschylus and Sophocles, depicted man as pursued by the Furies or Nemesis in retribution for crime committed by himself or his ancestors, and finally overwhelmed by an inescapable destiny decreed by the Fates. At other times, to compensate for good fortune, he must be humbled by blind, arbitrary, and relentless Fate.

The Romans identified their obscure native divinities, the Parcae, with their Greek counterparts, the Fates, and named them Nona, Decuma, and Morta. While the lot of the individual or of the State was traced back to the gods, there was still the belief in Fate as an independent power. Further, the belief that an inevitable destiny awaits all men was fostered by astrology throughout the Roman and medieval periods—a destiny irreversibly determined by the stars under which each is born.

Among the Greek and Roman Stoics, there existed a conception of nature according to which everything happening is necessitated by the laws of the universe. Since the human will cannot change the course of things in this view, the wise man makes a virtue of necessity and wills and desires only what is in accord with nature and her laws. There is an omnipotent Providence, immutable and unchallenged in its rule of the universe, and Fate or Destiny is the instrument through which the will of Providence is executed.

In Oriental fatalism, esp. in China and in India, there was thought to be a cosmic causal law governing the destiny of all things. In Buddhism, the role of free will is greatly attenuated, since man acts in this life under the onus of a series of former existences. Both Buddhism and Brahmanism or Orthodox Hinduism are dominated by a doctrine of rebirth—an evil cycle from which no man can deliver himself, and in Brahmanism the caste system is evidence of the widely accepted belief in blind destiny or natural necessity, a force that grips all men from birth. For Confucianism there is some recognition of Providence, but destiny still remains the urgent necessity to which man must conform and adjust. Thus, Confucius remains primarily interested in what the order of nature prescribes.

For the Persians, Parsiism maintains the power of Fate, a blind will the force of which binds even the gods. And men are subject to a hostile necessity from which they may slowly free themselves by obeying the laws of Zarathustra, thereby siding with Ahura Mazda, the supreme power, against Angra Mainyu, the evil genius.

Orthodox Islam, so far as its philosophers and theologians were concerned, was not fatalistic, despite some passages of the Koran, which appear to inculcate fatalism, and despite the difficulty encountered by some theologians in reconciling human freedom with the will of God. Nevertheless, among the people a conviction that everyone's fate is sealed by God and that nothing can be done to change it has been widespread and has been much encouraged by poets and storytellers.

Jewish Religion. A strong consciousness of human freedom of choice left no room in Judaism for the pagan notion of Fate. In biblical literature there is no word equivalent to the Greek *moira* or the Latin *fatum*. But in rabbinical literature, in part perhaps through the influence of Stoicism, there is sometimes an emphasis upon divine foreknowledge that could have led in the direction of fatalism had it not been for Jewish conviction that man possesses freedom of will and that good or evil are the result of his own choice.

Christianity. The Christian religion has rejected fatalism on principle. Man's choice, however it is reconciled with God's foreknowledge and will, is his own. Even in the major controversies that arose concerning grace and predestination there has been no fatalism strictly socalled wherever concepts of merit or guilt or sin retain a real meaning. There is, perhaps, a benign fatalism in Origen's conception of the world process as eternally recurrent, an endless cycle in which mankind is being raised under divine protection from a sinful state to one of perfection. The Christian doctrine of the election of the good and the reprobation of the wicked could easily lead to fatalism and much subtlety of thought has been directed to the explanation of how divine foreknowledge and predestination are compatible with free choice. Some theological thought of this kind shows the tinge of fatalism. This difficulty was aggravated for the Reformers of the 16th cent., esp. for Calvin, Luther, and Zwingli, whose insistence upon the corruption of human nature by sin seemed to negate the freedom of the human will.

Modern Philosophical Fatalism. In modern thought there is a prevailing effort to make matter the sole original cause of all reality. According to this purely mechanical theory of the universe, the content and evolution of the world are the consequences of chemical and physical properties and the laws of their causation. This seems to imply that mind and will cannot affect matter, and that hence thought and volition exercise no influence in the affairs of the universe and cannot enter as efficient causes into the chain of events in physical nature. If this were true, man would labor in a complex wholly determined by fixed law, in which no assertion of freedom would be possible to him.

BIBLIOGRAPHY: A. Dorner et al., Hastings ERE 5:771–797; G. Faggin, NCE 5:850–852.

[J. T. HICKEY]

FATE, a force moving human affairs to an appointed end. Any deterministic understanding of this force is contrary to the teaching of faith in God's *providence. Thus the Fathers of the Church opposed ascribing such a power to the stars and planets (see DAIMON); modern astrology and the use of horoscopes, if pursued seriously, would seem to involve this un-Christian understanding of fate. (See DIVINATION.) Following *Boethius, St. Thomas Aquinas identifies fate with the order operating in the interrelationships of created causes in subordination to God's providence; that order involves unforeseen happenings, *chance, accidents—all of which particularly may be ascribed to fate—but these too are encompassed by providence (Th Aq ST 1a, 116). There is no such thing as a fate necessitating the human will. And the meaning of the divinely appointed order discernible to reason rests ultimately on the meaning not simply of providence and divine *government, but on God's caring love in grace.

[T. C. O'BRIEN]

FATHER (RELIGIOUS TITLE), a mode of address and appellation of honor that has had various uses in the Western Church. The title was given to all bps. from the earliest times. Somewhat later it began to be applied collectively, as in the phrase "*Fathers of the Church," to important ecclesiastical writers of the first 6 or 7 cent., most of whom were also bishops. In a similar way it has been used of the Egyptian hermits and cenobites with whom monasticism began; they are the *Desert Fathers. The head of a monastery was called father (see ABBOT). The term is applied collectively to members of Church councils, esp. ecumenical councils, e.g., Fathers of the Council of Trent. The title was given to confessors and spiritual directors, who were often called spiritual fathers. The extension of the style to priests in general in liturgical or ceremonial formulas can claim some antiquity, as in the *Confiteor*, but its use was not common in other circumstances. In Italy and commonly on the Continent the priests of the mendicant and similar orders were the first to be generally addressed as father. Secular priests, monks, and Canons Regular retained the title *domnus* or *dominus* or the vernacular equivalents such as don, signore, or monsieur. Until the latter half of the 19th cent. it was proper in England to use the ordinary mister-sir convention in addressing secular priests, although at an earlier date all priests in Ireland were commonly called father, and thence the custom spread to England and the U.S.

[S. E. DONLON]

FATHER, GOD THE, the First Person of the Blessed Trinity, considered here in terms of Christ's Trinitarian life. God's self-manifestation in the world externalizes in a sense the mystery of his inner life. What the Greek Fathers called the "economy" of salvation reproduces, beyond the "limits" of the divine life, a Trinitarian rhythm. This principle of correlation finds its deepest application in the mystery of Christ's Person. It is not a matter of indifference that he, rather than either of the other two Persons of the Trinity, was made man; he is the Son, the Word Incarnate. A Christology of the God-man cannot do justice to the mystery of Christ if it abstracts from the personal character and properties of the Son. Christ's human psychology is deeply marked by the personal character of the Son of God: his is the human psychology of the Son Incarnate. Having assumed human nature, the Word experiences on a human level, lives in human framework, the personal relations by which, within the mystery of the divine life, he is related to the Father and to the Spirit. Through the mystery of the Incarnation his humanity is in effect assumed into the orbit of the Trinitarian life. The Son originates from the Father; this is why the Son Incarnate turns toward the Father to acknowledge his dependence upon him. The sense of dependence on the Father that characterizes Jesus translates into his human psychology the consciousness of his divine origin. Thus, in his religious life Christ is not confronted with the divine Trinity but with his Father. The gospel data bear witness to the deeply filial character of Christ's human psychology. Christ prays to the Father—not to the Trinity—and acknowledges his total dependence upon him. He calls upon the heavenly Father with the familiarity of a child addressing his earthly father. The Aramaic expression *Abba* (Mk 14.36) stands for "Papa." In the entire gospel narrative, the only instance where Christ addresses the Father as God is when on the cross he quotes Ps 21 (22).1 (Mk 15.34). Christ does not only pray to the Father; he also offers his sacrifice to him, he obeys him, reveals him, and glorifies him. His entire religious life is centered on the Person of the Father, towards whom he is turned constantly in an act of self-oblation (Heb 10.5–7). As eternal Son he receives all things from the Father; so, too, as Son Incarnate. This is why in his humanity he turns back to the Father to offer all things to him. BIBLIOGRAPHY: E. Schillebeeckx, *Gott im Welt* (*Festgabe für K. Rahner* v. 2, ed. J. B. Metz and H. Vorgrimler, 1964) 43; C. Colombo, *Cor Iesu* (ed. A. Bea and H. Rahner, 1959) 1:327.

[J. DUPUIS]

FATHER DIVINE PEACE MISSION, a religious movement that began in the U.S. about 1919 and attained its peak in the decade 1935–45. It centered on the person of its leader, Father Divine, born George Baker, also known as Major Morgan J. Devine (*c.*1865–1965). He is said to have spent the first 50 years of his life in and near Savannah, Georgia. He reputedly initiated his own movement at Valdosta, Ga., *c.*1914, after a supposed earlier association with Samuel Morris. In his lifetime, Father Divine denied all of these reports, although the courts ruled that he was George Baker of Savannah. In 1919, as Major M. J. Devine, he purchased a house in Sayville, Long Island, N.Y., after gathering (1915–19) a small following in Brooklyn. At Sayville, his willingness to house and feed his followers and his habit of preaching to them at lengthy meals gained great notoriety. A determined effort to force him and his followers to leave Sayville, including judicial harassment and civil suits, gave his movement considerable publicity. After several months, he moved his headquarters to Harlem. It caught the imagination of many thousands of Negroes, as well as many whites, and within a few years missions, hostels, restaurants, stores, and other businesses conducted by Father Divine were to be found in every major city in the eastern U.S., the Midwest, on the West Coast, and to a lesser extent, in the S States.

Soon after establishing himself in Harlem, he adopted the name Father Divine and began to call his hostels heavens. Harlem in the 1920s was a "burned-over district" for both religious and social cults, dominated by Marcus Garvey and his Back-to-Africa programs. Father Divine's Peace Mission took strong root in this soil because it was primarily a social protest movement, expressed in the terminology and emotionalism of a religious revival, but completely "this-worldly." Father Divine studiously avoided giving himself the attributes of God, but his followers paid him honor as God and constantly acknowledged him as the deity in his presence. He dwelt among his followers, constantly visiting their banquets to preach to them, and provided for their daily needs. These banquets formed the worship services of the movement. A cult of his presence developed, so that his followers felt that they were blessed by seeing him and attributed cures to his presence, his touch, or even his photograph. In his daily preaching, which was published verbatim in his newspaper the *New Day,* Father Divine stressed personal morality and the ethical side of religion. Members of his sect were forbidden to drink or smoke, gamble, or own life insurance. A strict honesty, which extended to a pin found in the street, was enjoined. Members were to give an honest day's work for a day's wage. They were also encouraged to live evangelically by abstaining from sexual intercourse, even when husbands and wives continued to live together. The reward for this strict morality was immediate and tangible. Members of his sect were invited to live in one of his heavens, or hostels, where they were fed, clothed, and sheltered in considerable comfort throughout the harrowing Depression years, either at a minimal charge or by working in the heaven. The gifts of the members to their local churches made up any deficit. Nonresident members had low-cost restaurants and other services available. In New York and other states, the movement acquired rural property to move slum dwellers to farms, whose produce supplied the urban members' needs. For urban Negroes, who were often turned away by public welfare agencies at this time, Father Divine was a miracle worker.

In addition to his own role in the movement and the personal ethics of his followers, Father Divine made world peace and interracial justice the dominant theme of his movement. He greatly revered the U.S. Bill of Rights and called for its fulfillment in laws that would abolish lynching, segregation in schools and public places, prejudice in hiring for jobs or in leasing or selling houses, and every other vestige of racism. He also called for complete disarmament and interracial and international brotherhood. His movement began to decline after World War II, accelerated perhaps by his marriage to a white woman in 1946 and by judgments secured against him in the courts. Although by the time of his death in 1965 membership had diminished, the Peace Mission continued in existence. BIBLIOGRAPHY: S. Harris and H. Crittenden, *Father Divine: Holy Husband* (1953); R. A. Parker, *Incredible Messiah: The Deification of Father Divine* (1937).

[R. K. MACMASTER]

FATHER OF LIES, title given to the devil by Christ in Jn 8.44. There Christ notes that lying is the native language of the devil. This seems to be a reference to the role of the devil-serpent in Gen 3:3–4. However, the term might also be translated Father of the Liar(s), (literally, father of it or him). Then it would refer to the devil as the master of the Domain of Darkness and leader of all who are perverse and specifically of all those who deny the person and mission of Christ. BIBLIOGRAPHY: R. Brown, *Gospel according to John,* Anchor Bible (1967) 20:357–358, 364–365.

[J. A. PIERCE]

FATHERS OF ST. EDMUND, see ST. EDMUND, SOCIETY OF.

FATHERS OF SION, founded in Paris, 1852, by the brothers M. T. and M. A. Ratisbonne, a congregation of priests and brothers, approved in 1893, which under the direction of the local bp., is dedicated to strengthening Judeo-Christian relations. In an effort to overcome difficulties encountered in their apostolate, the Fathers of Sion collaborated with the sisters of the Congregation of Notre Dame de Sion, and opened centers of study and dialogue for the purpose of furthering ecumenical progress between Jews and Christians. These centers are established in Paris, Montreal and Jerusalem. The members of the Congregation number approximately 100.

[C. KEENAN]

FATHERS OF THE CHURCH, a title given to a class of early Christian writers. In the Church a bp. was frequently called "Father," either because he was looked upon as the head of the community (*Martyrdom of Polycarp* 12.2) or was looked upon as its guide and teacher (Eusebius, *Eccl. Hist.* 7.7.4), though frequently it is impossible to determine which meaning is intended. Already in the 2d cent. Christian theologians began appealing to the teaching of their predecessors, but only in the 4th cent. does an explicit appeal to individual bps. come into vogue as a proof for the traditional teaching of the Church. A fortunate extension of the title of "Father" was made by St. Augustine in citing St. Jerome, who was not a bp., as an orthodox witness on the question of original sin (*Contra Julian.* 1.7.34). A further extension of the term to include the layman Prosper of Aquitaine is made in the Gelasian decree. During the 5th-cent. controversies over the two natures in Christ, frequent appeals were made by all parties to "the Fathers," whose more important texts were set forth in *florilegia,* or anthologies. Since not all of the early Christian writers were equally sound in their teaching, Vincent of Lérins in the early 5th cent. restricted an appeal to the Fathers to "those aproved teachers who, in their respective times and places, remained in the communion and faith of the one Catholic Church" (*Commonitorium* 1.3). From such beginnings the concept of a Father of the Church was developed as an early Christian who has been approved as a witness of the faith because of the orthodoxy of his teaching and the holiness of his life. For one to be considered a Father of the Church, four conditions must therefore be fulfilled: antiquity, orthodoxy, holiness of life, and ecclesiastical approval. Writers who lack any of these criteria are called simply "ecclesiastical writers." Isidore of Seville (d. *c.*636) is considered the last of the Fathers of the West, and John Damascene (d. *c.*750) the last in the East. The orthodoxy of a Father excludes all substantial errors and implies as well a certain excellence and profundity of thought. The holiness of a Father is revealed by the harmony of his life with the faith he professed. The ecclesiastical approval required for the title of "Father" need not be a formal declaration on the part of a pope or council but a virtual consensus of the Church is sufficient. The Golden Age of the Fathers, when patristic literature reached its full development, is the period of the first four general councils, from that of Nicaea (325) to Chalcedon (451). BIBLIOGRAPHY: A. Stuiber, LTK 6:272–274; W. J. Burghardt, NCE 5:853–855; Quasten 1:9–12; Altaner 1–9.

[M. J. COSTELLOE]

FATHERS OF THE DESERT, see DESERT FATHERS.

FÁTIMA, a small town in central Portugal where the Blessed Virgin *Mary appeared to three children in 1917. The basilica and shrine built in honor of Our Lady of Fátima are a popular place of pilgrimage. The children (Lucia dos Santos and her cousins Francisco and Jacinta) were illiterate shepherds, all between the ages of 10 and 13. On May 13, 1917, they said they saw a lady brighter than the sun, standing on a cloud, who told them they should return to the spot on the 13th of each month until October. The children complied with these instructions and experienced five subsequent visions. On October 13th, the lady revealed that she was Our Lady of the Rosary, told the children to recite the rosary daily, and asked that a church be built in her honor. As she had promised, a miracle was performed on that day which many of the 50,000 people who accompanied the children also reported seeing: the sun seemed to dance in the heavens, tremble, and finally fall. An ecclesiastical commission was established to inquire into the apparitions, and after 7 years of study the local ordinary declared them worthy of credence and authorized the cult of Our Lady of Fátima. Francisco and Jacinta died within 3 years of the apparitions, but Lucia entered the convent and upon episcopal command wrote her recollections of the visions. In these she revealed that Our Lady had asked for the practice of penance, daily recitation of the rosary, and increased devotion to the *Immaculate Heart of Mary. BIBLIOGRAPHY: C. C. Martindale, *Message of Fátima* (1950); E. Dhanis, "À propos de Fátima et la critique," NRT 74(1952) 580–606; J. M. Haffert, *Meet the Witnesses* (1961).

[T. M. MCFADDEN]

FATIMIDS, a branch of the *Ismaili *Shiites that takes its name from that of Fâṭima, the daughter of *Mohammed, to whose children by ʿAlî they trace the lineage of their *Imams. The great spread of the Fatimids began with the Imam ʿUbayd Allâh (d. A.D. 934) who proclaimed himself *Mahdî and seized power in N Africa in 910. The Caliph al-Muʿizz conquered Egypt in 969 where Fatimid rule, in one of the most brilliant periods of Eygptian history, continued until 1171. From the Fatimid dynasty of Egypt is derived a large number of sects, among them the *Druses. After the death of the Caliph al-Mustanṣir (1094) there was a split between those who held that the Imamate had passed to his son al-Mustaʿlî (d. 1101) and those who held that the true Imam was his son Nizâr (d. 1095). From the former branch are derived the Boharas of India as well as several small groups found in E Africa and Yemen; from the latter derive the *Nizâris who spread extensively in the East representing today the most active Ismaili group. BIBLIOGRAPHY: M. Canard and G. Marçais, EncIslam².

FAULHABER, ANDREAS (1713–57), martyr on behalf of protecting the seal of confession. During the conflict between Prussian officials in Silesia with Catholics who supported the Habsburg dynasty, F., ordained in 1750, was a public victim. When a Prussian deserter in the Seven Years' War testified that Faulhaber in hearing his confession had condoned desertion, the priest was arrested and imprisoned. In spite of retraction by the deserter, F. was tried and by order of Frederick II was ordered to be executed. The priest refused to divulge the deserter's confession even though it might have saved him. He was hanged and his body left on the gallows for almost 3 years, miraculously preserved. Austrian troops in 1760 removed the body and buried it in the church in Glatz. His cause for canonization is pending. BIBLIOGRAPHY: E. Henseler, *P. Faulhaber der Glatzer Kaplan* (1956).

[J. R. AHERNE]

FAULHABER, MICHAEL VON (1869–1952), abp. of Munich, cardinal, foe of the Nazi movement. He was ordained in 1892, taught at the Univ. of Würzburg and the Univ. of Strasbourg. Bishop of Speyer (1911–17) and abp. of Munich and Freysing (1917–52), F. showed his humanity when World War I enveloped his diocese. He denounced the socialist philosophy of the Bavarian Soviet Republic, which had emerged from the revolution of 1918, but he was too powerful a figure to be curtailed by the authorities. In 1921 Benedict XV created him a cardinal. F.'s unswerving opposition to Hitler's Nazism began with the famous *Putsch* of 1923, which the cardinal helped to defeat. During the most fanatic years of anti-Jewish activity by the Hilter regime in the 1930s F. preached his famous Advent sermons entitled *Judaism, Christianity, and Germany* (tr. G. D. Smith, 1954) which presented the Jews as forerunners of Christianity. He spoke often and vigorously against the Teutonic myths popular with the Nazi movement. Governmental opposition and attempts on his life never deterred him. He was among the strongest and most articulate religious critics of National Socialism over a period of 22 years. His post-war years were devoted to rebuilding the archdiocese. BIBLIOGRAPHY: M. A. Gallin, *German Resistance to Hitler* (1961).

[J. R. AHERNE]

FAULKNER, WILLIAM (1897–1962), American novelist. F. belongs to that school of novelists who might be flexibly labeled "the Haunted." Like Gide, Mauriac and Camus in France and Greene, Dostoyevsky, or Melville among others, F.'s characters confront evil and sin constantly though they may not be conquered. Violence and the devastation of the old South, its decaying values and brooding sinners, mar or mark F.'s literary canvases. His Protestant background helped provide the needed tension for birth, death, and other symbolic forces that rage or meander through his novels. The conscious simplicity of F.'s style—rolling narrative including lyric restrospection—shows him as a romantic who flirted with the realities of sex and sufferings in itself beguiling. F.'s experiments with the eclipsing of time and attempts at symbolism did not make him a great stylist though he was an interesting one. He spent most of his life in his native Mississippi where his absorption of the experiences of World War I and the Civil War ultimately became traumatic. F. is remembered esp. for *The Sound and the Fury* (1929), *As I Lay Dying* (1930), *Light in August* (1932), and *Unvanquished* (1938). Yoknapatawpha County is the locale of most of F.'s best, among which such short stories as "That Evening Sun," "Dry September," "A Rose For Emily" deserve high placement. So too does the highly symbolic "The Bear" in *Go Down Moses* (1942). F. received the Nobel Prize in 1950. BIBLIOGRAPHY: I. Howe, *William Faulkner* (2d rev. ed. 1962, pa. 1975), excellent biog. and critique; *William Faulkner: Three Decades of Criticism* (ed. F. J. Hoffman and O. W. Vickery, 1960, pa. 1963).

[R. M. FUNCHION]

FAULT, a term with various shades of meaning in religious writings, from a slight offense or venial sin, whether committed knowingly and willingly or not, or even just an *imperfection, as it is called, to a graver wrong. Technically it is a synonym for the guilt of ethical, theological, or moral evil, or the lack of due good within a human act, as this implies the agent's responsibility for it, or the act's imputability to him. Accordingly, in speaking of an obligation of commutative justice to make restitution for damage or loss caused to another, traditional RC moral theologians list as one of the conditions theological fault. Some also use the term juridical fault as one of the conditions for a just court sentence for damages. This differs from theological fault in that it prescinds from formal moral guilt. It is fault as this is estimated by the law, and it may or may not be accompanied by inner moral guilt. Theological fault is removed by repentance, though some of its *sequelae* may remain. BIBLIOGRAPHY: J. J. Farraher, NCE 5:858; ThAq ST 1a2ae, 71–80 (esp. in Lat-Eng ed., v. 25, ed. J. Fearon, 1969).

[J. J. FARRAHER]

FAURÉ, ELIE (1873–1937), French essayist, art critic, and early advocate of the theory of an intrinsic relationship between artistic forms and the civilizations that engender them, the individual work of art being representative of a moment in the life of a civilization. These ideas are discussed in his 5-v. *History of Art* (tr. W. Pach; 1921–30). BIBLIOGRAPHY: P. Desange, *Élie Fauré* (1963).

[L. A. LEITE]

FAURÉ, GABRIEL URBAIN, (1845–1924), French composer and organist. Among his teachers were Niedermeyer, Dietsch, and Saint-Saens. For several years F. was church organist at Rennes, and at Paris was accompanying organist of St. Sulpice, principal organist of St. Honoré, and *maître de chapelle* of the Madeleine. His numerous compositions, written in a style of control, balance, and classical restraint, evidence as well a high-ranking melodic gift. They include songs, chamber music, piano solos, an opera, *Penelope,* short liturgical pieces, and a Requiem.

[A. M. MACK]

FAURE, GIOVANNI BATTISTA (1702–79), Italian Jesuit polemicist. A teacher all his life and a prolific writer, he published works in all the sacred sciences—the most widely used being his *Apparatus brevis ad theologiam et jus canonicum* (1751; many editions)—and esteemed works on devotion to the Sacred Heart. He also wrote bitterly against the Inquisition, and his anonymous *Commentarium in Bullam Pauli III "Licet ab initio"* (1750) attacking the Index of Forbidden Books was itself proscribed in 1757. An anti-Jansenist work was stopped from publication by the Inquisition, but issued posthumously as *In Arnauldi librum de frequenti communione* (1791), as was another anti-Jansenist tractate, *Dubitationes theologicae de judicio practico* (1840). At the time of the suppression of the Society of Jesus he was imprisoned, 1773–75, at the Castel Sant' Angelo to prevent his inciting antipapal protests.

[T. C. O'BRIEN]

FAUST, MATHÍAS (1879–1956), Franciscan administrator. Born in Germany, he migrated to the U.S. in 1896, and was ordained as a Franciscan in 1906. Most of his life he held important posts in his order. As provincial he sent missionaries to China and the American South. F. supported the St. Anthony Guild, publishers of religious works, and founded (1945) the Academy of American Franciscan History in Washington, D.C. He was procurator general for the order in Rome for 4 years. BIBLIOGRAPHY: *Franciscan Studies* 14:333–35.

[J. R. AHERNE]

FAUST LEGEND, the tales inspired by the historical figure of George (later Johann) Faust, *c.*1480-1540, which deal with the story of a man aspiring to a limitless knowledge and happiness who is goaded by his desires to the desperate step of making a pact with the powers of evil. The legend further describes Faust's ensuing torments and terrors of remorse, followed by his vain efforts to repent, and the final horror of being destroyed by demonic forces. In making a pact with superhuman figures Faust shows that he was not ignorant of its consequences; obstinacy to a conscience both hardened to crime but also prone to remorse and fear are in evidence throughout.

The Faust legend reflects the religious thinking of the Renaissance and Reformation, esp. that of 16th-cent. Germany. The life of the historical Faust coincided with the most crucial years of the Reformation. Faust capitalized upon the fears and superstitions of his contemporaries by applying pretended magical skills to all fields of human knowledge. He called himself "chief of the necromancers" and became known as a fraud and a false prophet, although his reputation seems to have improved toward the end of his life. The tales surrounding his life and deeds owe their inspiration to him, esp. in the underlying supposition that man is able to make a compact with the devil and sell his soul in exchange for spiritual power and sensual pleasure. As tales of Faust multiplied from the 16th cent. on, aspects of their plots became more complex. When the Faust of story and drama became irretrievably degraded by his search for superhuman knowledge, he turned away from spiritual questionings and various kinds of magical pranks and entered into a "swinish and epicurean" life, illustrated in his relations with Helen of Troy (e.g., Weidmann), Mathilde (Schink) and Gretchen (Goethe). Faust's fatal passion for Helen of Troy, although not a vital part of the action nor evident in every version of the legend, was present in the earliest stories. Because of the growing emphasis on sexual immorality, the greatest of sins according to medieval Western European standards, the confusion of Faust and Don Juan legends became noticeable, and culminated in the work of Christian Dietrich Grabbe (1801-36). BIBLIOGRAPHY: E. M. Butler, *Fortunes of Faust* (1952); J. W. Smeed, *Faust in Literature* (1975).

[M. SAGUÉS]

FAUSTINUS AND JOVITA, SS. (2d. cent.), martyrs of Brescia. According to the dubious stories told of them, they were brothers, natives of Brescia, who excited the wrath of the pagans by their zealous preaching of Christianity. Pagan officials had them tortured and dragged through Milan, Rome, and Naples before having them taken back to Brescia where they were beheaded at the order of the Emperor Hadrian. According to the legend, they baptized tens of thousands on their journey through Italy. Although they are considered the patrons of Brescia, they are not mentioned by the early bps. Philaster and Guadentius. BIBLIOGRAPHY: Butler 1:340–341; A. Amore, EncCatt 5:1063–64.

[R. B. ENO]

FAUSTUS, JANUARIUS, AND MARTIAL, SS. (d. 303 or 304?), martyred at Córdoba, Spain, probably in Diocletian's persecution. Since they are mentioned by Prudentius their cult evidently goes back to antiquity, but the acts of their martyrdom are legendary.

[E. P. COLBERT]

FAUSTUS THE MANICHAEAN (also called Faustus of Milevis; fl. 4th cent.), Manichaean bp., rhetor at Rome. F. was an African who won fame at Rome as a spokesman for the somewhat "Christianized" Manichaeism he had accepted. He came to Carthage in 383; Augustine eagerly consulted him, but was completely disenchanted because of F.'s resort to glibness when asked philosophical questions (see *Confessions,* 5.3.3; 6.10–11); the disappointment was a step toward Augustine's final conversion. F.'s attempt at a monumental written presentation of Manichaeism is lost, but somewhat reflected in Augustine's *Contra Faustum Manichaeum* (PL 42,207–518). The last fact known about F. is his brief banishment in 384 or 385 from Carthage by Emperor Theodosius.

[T. C. O'BRIEN]

FAUSTUS OF RIEZ (d. *c*.495), Semi-Pelagian author and bp. of Riez in Provence from 458. In 433 F. became abbot at Lérins, the center of opposition to certain extreme interpretations of St. Augustine's teaching on grace. In the years 477–485, he was exiled from his see by the Visigothic King Euric. In answering the extreme predestinarian teachings of one Lucidus, he wrote *De gratia*, urging the necessity of human cooperation with divine grace and the universal salvific will of God. His teaching was approved by the Councils of Arles and Lyons (473, 474) but was later condemned by Council of *Orange II in 529. In addition to *De gratia*, F. wrote two books on the Holy Spirit. Some of his letters and homilies also survive. Works: PL 53:681–890; 58:783–870; crit. ed. A. Engelbrecht, CSEL (v. 21, 1891). BIBLIOGRAPHY: Altaner 566–567.

[R. B. ENO]

FAUVES (meaning "wild beasts"), the name of 20th-cent. art group, derived from a phrase of derision used by a critic who, seeing a Donatello in the midst of the *avant-garde* show led by Matisse in the Paris Salon d'Automne (1905), exclaimed, "Donatello among the wild beasts!" The Fauves used a brilliant, shockingly intense palette, for subjects "freed" in color and form from visual appearance and description; the painting, an invention of unexpected shapes deriving from the feeling of the artist; the composition, a decorative arrangement; the picture emerging highly intellectualized. The Fauves, as a group, were short-lived, in 5 years each member developing a unique style. Matisse, faithful to the principles, evolved one of the strongest, most influential personal expressions in modern art. H. *MATISSE; G. *ROUAULT.

[M. J. DALY]

FAUXBOURDON, see FABURDEN.

FAVERSHAM ABBEY, former Benedictine Cluniac monastery in Kent, England, founded in 1147 by King Stephen and Queen Matilda. Prior Clarimbald and 12 monks were assigned to form the community. Independent, in deference to the rulers, it was not subject to Cluny. Despite continued and generous endowments by Stephen and Matilda and subsequent kings, the abbey was often in reduced circumstances because of the misuse of funds by some abbots. It declined also as a result of spiritual laxity. Faversham was surrendered to Henry VIII in 1538; only ruins remain. BIBLIOGRAPHY: R. Aubert, DHGE 16:755–757; G. E. Hind, CE 6:19–20.

[S. A. HEENEY]

FAVIER, ALPHONSE (1837–1905) French missionary bishop. From 1858 a member of the Vincentians, F. first served on the missions of northern China (1862). In 1897 he became auxiliary bp. of Peking and in 1899 vicar-apostolic of North Chihli (Hopeh). He was an interpreter of the missions and helped secure the decree of the Emperor that placed bps. on the level of mandarins. F's role as mediator between China and the West was a major contribution. BIBLIOGRAPHY: G. Goyan, *La France missionaire* (1948) v.2.

[J. R. AHERNE]

FAVOR OF THE FAITH, a privilege which the pope grants in dissolving a valid, but nonsacramental marriage. Sometimes it is referred to as the Petrine privilege, by parallel with the term *Pauline privilege, because the basis for granting the dissolution is taken to be the pope's apostolic power of the keys given to St. Peter (Matt 16.19). The first unmistakably clear instance was Pius XI's dissolution of a marriage in a case presented by the bp. of Helena, Mont., Nov. 8, 1924. The meaning of the phrase is that the practice has been to grant the favor to the party who became baptized after the marriage that is dissolved; because the one party was not baptized that marriage was valid, but nonsacramental. Communal life cannot have continued in that marriage after the baptism, since the marriage would then have become sacramental *(ratum)* and consummated, and as such absolutely indissoluble. The privilege has also been granted where a first marriage of an unbaptized person has been dissolved in favor of the person's Catholic partner in a second marriage.

[T. C. O'BRIEN]

FAVORITISM, see DISCRIMINATION.

FAVRE, PETER, see FABER, PETER, BL.

FAWKES, GUY (1570–1606), English conspirator. Originally a Protestant, F. became a Catholic in 1579 when his mother married a man of that faith. After serving with the Spanish army in the Netherlands (1593–1604), he joined the *Gunpowder Plot and was selected to touch off the explosion under the houses of Parliament. He was arrested on the evening before the appointed day and is said to have revealed under torture the names of his fellow conspirators. He was tried and executed. BIBLIOGRAPHY: H. Garnett, *Portrait of Guy Fawkes* (1962); E. Simons, *Devil of the Vault* (1963).

FAY, CYRIL SIGOURNEY WEBSTER (1875–1919), diplomat, an Episcopal minister, who left the Episcopal Church, entered the Catholic Church in 1907, and was ordained by Card. Gibbons in 1910. His greatest achievement was laboring to give the Vatican a voice in the peace treaty negotiations after World War I, through his friendship with Foreign Minister A. Balfour of Great Britain and members of the British Commission. Just before he was to go to London in pursuit of this mission he died of influenza. BIBLIOGRAPHY: M. Chandler, *Autumn in the Valley* (1936).

[J. R. AHERNE]

FAYOUM (FAYUM-FAIYUM) PORTRAITS, portraits, full faced or three-quarter view of head and shoulders on sycamore panels from the Fayoum oasis, Egypt, attached to the wrapped mummified body of the deceased by Hellenized Egyptians between the 1st and 3d cent. A.D., important for the study of ancient painting. Amazingly fresh in color because of an encaustic technique of great durability, in which pigments are suspended in hot wax (a few panels were done in tempera-pigment in egg) with a free, impressionistic brushwork, these vibrant personalities are caught with Roman realism and individualism. Their composure and dignity, thoughtful, soulful, almost hypnotic eyes, and tremulous expressive mouths evoke the entire philosophy of their world.

[M. J. DALY]

FAYRFAX, ROBERT (1464–1521), a composer of the Early English Tudor School and choirmaster of St. Alban's from 1502 until his death. His works include Masses, motets, Magnificats, secular songs, lute arrangements, and other instrumental pieces. F.'s style shows a trend away from a florid to a simpler chordal technique with richer sonority, distinguished for its variety in the grouping of *voices and use of imitative *counterpoint.

[P. MURPHY]

FEAR, the emotion or the will-act of dread and of drawing back in the face of a threatening evil (see ThAq ST 1a2ae, 6.7; 77.1 & 2; 2a2ae, 142.3). (1) Moral theology evaluates fear both in itself and in its effect on the fearful person's actions. Fear itself has the quality of moral rightness or wrongness by reference to the will: either as the will concurs in an emotional dread of evils threatening bodily well-being, or itself withdraws from what threatens a rightly valued human good. The fear is right when it shrinks from an evil for the sake of and in keeping with the true value of the threatened good. Thus *fear of the Lord, which is a dread of separation from the Father, is a corollary of Christian *hope, and a gift of the Holy Spirit. Thus, also, the virtue of *courage (fortitude) does not suppress fear, but sustains the experience from leading to an abandonment of a higher good to escape a lesser evil, i.e., loss of a lesser good. Fear is wrong when the scale of values among human goods is subverted: when because of a threat to physical well-being, for example, a spiritual or virtuous good is forsaken. As to its effects, fear is a factor in determining the morality of an action prompted by it. A person completely overwhelmed by terror is not morally responsible. Short of that, an action done out of fear is in principle still under the will's control, but the degree of control may be diminished, and so moral responsibility or imputability. (2) Canon law also sets down rules of law concerning fear. Grave fear, as measured by the kind and imminence of the threatening evil, and in relation to the reaction of the fearful person, excuses from violations of purely *positive law (CIC c. 2205, § 2), e.g., from attendance at Mass, from integrity of confession. Certain contractual obligations incurred out of grave fear are declared invalid, among them entrance into or profession by vow to religious life, marriage (c.1307, § 3;542,n.1; 572, § 1; 1087). Other contracts entered into out of fear may be valid, but legally rescindable (c.1684).

[T. C. O'BRIEN]

FEAR OF THE LORD, a gift of the Holy Spirit. It is a close accompaniment of the theological virtue of *hope, for, relying on God's power, promises, and mercy to reach him who is our happiness, we may yet fear to lose him. Since fear is always of some evil, and God himself is pure goodness, he cannot be an object of fear in himself. What is feared is an evil-for-us the divine may introduce into the human situation. Fearing God's justice or the pains of his service, a person may seek to avoid him as far as he can. This human and worldly fear, *timor humanus et mundanus,* is incompatible with charity. Yet a person turned to God may fear him, and in several ways: with servile fear *(timor servilis),* when the motive is the penalty (*malum poenae*) of losing him; with filial or chaste fear (*filialis* and *castus* by analogy with child-parent and sponsal relationships respectively) when the motive is fear of fault *(malum culpae),* which would offend him or cause us to be separated from him. A blend of them both is the fear proper to beginners *(timor initialis),* and may be supposed to be the condition of most of us. For servility, the opposite of liberty, is not of the essence of the fear of penalty, and the thought that we might deserve hell, if not the noblest motive for serving God, is at least a truthful and tonic response to our predicament under Providence. All the same, as we grow in the love of God so it recedes into the background, and the operation of the Spirit's gift is entirely familial. Notice, however, that the love it implies is not altruistic; in this it is like hope, and for that matter, like charity, indeed the term makes little sense in the theology of living with God, where the only self-love to be condemned is sin. A happy friend finds little need to sort out when he is loving himself and when the other. Notice, too, that scholastic theologians do not dwell on the sentiment of religious awe, of which fear is an ingredient, in face of the Holy, although they touch on it when they continue the discussion of SS. Augustine and Gregory whether the gift remains in heaven. It is traditionally related to the first Beatitude, "Blessed are the poor in spirit, for theirs is the kingdom of heaven." BIBLIOGRAPHY: ThAq ST (Lat-Eng, v. 33, ed. W. J. Hill).

[T. GILBY]

FEAST OF ASSES, see ASSES, FEAST OF.

FEAST OF FOOLS, see FOOLS, FEAST OF.

FEASTS, CONCURRENCE OF, see CONCURRENCE OF FEASTS.

FEATHERWORK. Feathers from brilliantly colored birds were tied, sewn, or woven on a sturdier foundation for elaborate ceremonial mantles and headdresses by the Indian civilizations of Mexico and South America and by the Polynesian peoples of Hawaii and New Zealand. Feathers attached to a fabric or wickerwork frame in geometric patterns are called "feather mosaic." The Japanese used featherwork in the decoration of early images and the famous 7th-cent. Tamamushi (Beetle-Wing) Shrine at Horyu-ji, ornamented with the iridescent wings of beetles, is but a variation of feather appliqué.

[M. J. DALY]

FEBRONIANISM, the radical ideas concerning *episcopacy and *Church and State proposed by N. Von *Hontheim in *On the State of the Church and the Legitimate Power of the Roman Pontiff* (pub. 1763 under pseud. "Justinus Febronius"). Von Hontheim, then auxiliary bp. of Trier, expressed both his own convictions and the grievances of the German metropolitans against the papacy and esp. the papal nuncio at Cologne. Von Hontheim claimed that the popes had usurped the rightful powers of the bps., who stood in direct succession from the Apostles. The pope was only "first among equals" and lacked jurisdiction within dioceses. A general council had legitimate authority over the pope, and his decrees could be revised by national or provincial synods. Metropolitans should have the power to confirm and depose bishops. Clement XIII put Von Hontheim's work on the Index (1764). He was protected and honored by his superiors for many years, but his abp., Klemens Wenzeslaus of Trier, finally required him to publish (1778) a qualified disavowal of his earlier views. That he actually changed his beliefs is highly doubtful, though he died (1790) in full communion with the Church. His debt to *Gallicanism was evident from his sources and his insistence that rulers should protect their churches against papal interference.

*Josephinism in Austria derived its theoretical justification from Febronianism. However, Von Hontheim and his patrons really wanted to establish a German national Church on an essentially episcopal basis, and in this the secular rulers did not aid them. On the contrary, the elector of Bavaria welcomed the establishment of a nunciature at Munich (1785), and Emperor Joseph II refused to support a program devised at the Congress of Ems (1786) to curtail papal powers in Germany. Many suffragan bps. were either unenthusiastic or were opposed to a policy that would only increase the authority of the metropolitans. The failure of the Ems program and the contemporary revolutions in France and Belgium (1789–90) led the Rhenish abps. to seek better relations with Rome. The destruction of the ecclesiastical principalities and the closing of the new Univ. of Bonn, founded to promote Febronian ideas, were serious blows to the movement. In 1815 Metternich briefly toyed with the idea of setting up a national Church in Germany, but then dropped it. The reaction against the State-Church systems prevalent in Germany after 1815 produced a new flowering of Ultramontanism in both clerical and lay circles. By mid-19th cent. Febronianism lingered at most only as an attitude of mind. BIBLIOGRAPHY: H. Holborn, *History of Modern Germany, 1648–1840* (1964) *CONCILIARISM; *PISTOIA, SYNOD OF; *CHURCH AND STATE.

[J. K. ZEENDER]

FÉCAMP, ABBEY OF (7th cent.), a cenobitic foundation of nuns in the town of that name on the NE coast of

France near Le Havre. It was destroyed by Normans in 841, but later became a monastery for Benedictine monks (11th cent.). The monastery continued to prosper, despite vicissitudes, until its suppression in the French Revolution. Its church now belongs to the local parish. BIBLIOGRAPHY: R. Gazeau, *Catholicisme* 4:1130–32.

[J. F. FALLON]

FECHNER, GUSTAV THEODOR (1801–87), German philosopher, usually associated with psychophysics and pioneering studies in experimental psychology. F. was a medical doctor who later became interested in physics, philosophy, and psychophysics. His interests were as varied as the following topics suggest: panpsychism, immortality, aesthetics, and psychological aesthetics. Basic to all these is his belief that the whole universe is spiritual in character with phenomenal representations manifesting spiritual reality. Especially in this strand of his theory F. is very close to Leibnizian monadology. F. is a forerunner of modern philosophers in the sense that he attempted to reconcile an idealist view of reality with a methodology that is scientifically modern and thus acceptable to the critical thinker.

[J. R. RIVELLO]

FEDERAL COUNCIL OF THE CHURCHES OF CHRIST IN AMERICA, a body formed in 1908 for interdenominational cooperation among Protestant Churches, predecessor of the *National Council of the Churches of Christ in the U.S.A. The idea for the Federal Council of Churches grew out of earlier cooperative ventures, e.g., the *Evangelical Alliance and the National Federation of Churches and Christian Workers, and was inspired by the *Social Gospel. Emphasis on evangelistic and social ideals rather than on theological dialogue brought together Churches of widely differing traditions. By a merger in 1950 with seven other smaller interdenominational mission boards and administrative agencies, the Federal Council became the National Council of Churches.

[T. C. O'BRIEN]

FEDERAL THEOLOGY, called also *covenant theology, a designation for the theologies in the *Reformed tradition that have used God's covenants (Lat. *foedera*) with man as a theme. In the 16th cent. the thought of *Zwingli was continued and synthesized by H. *Bullinger in *De foedere et testamento Dei unico et aeterno* (1534), presenting the biblical concept of covenant as the key to the continuity of the OT and NT history of salvation. Calvin in his *Institutes* formulated the idea of one covenant of grace manifested from Adam to Christ. The distinction between the covenant of works before the Fall and the covenant of grace afterwards, was incorporated into the *Westminster Confession (c.7) and the *Helvetic Consensus Formula (Art. 23–25). There were many variations and elaborations within orthodox Calvinism on the various covenants of God with man, but two adaptations of the covenant theme are esp. important. The biblical theologian J. *Cocceius (1603–69), whose *Summa doctrinae de foedere et testamento Dei* (1648) is regarded as a systematization of federal theology, substituted the covenant idiom for the orthodox, scholastic Calvinist terminology. He interpreted the covenant as God's expression of how to share in the divine love, and traced salvation history through the biblical manifestations of the covenant. His thought provoked resistance from the strict Calvinist theologians of the Netherlands and had influence on *Pietism as developed at Halle. Covenant theology among the Puritans of England and New England, by employing political and legal terminology to express the covenant with God, mitigated the Calvinist doctrine of absolute decrees of predestination and gave recognition to the meaning of human cooperation within the framework of a reasonable compact of salvation. Karl *Barth, in his theology of reconciliation, gave renewed prominence to God's covenant: the eternal divine covenant, God's gracious election of men in Christ, is the basis for justification and reconciliation.

[T. C. O'BRIEN]

FEDERATED CHURCHES, a term describing two or more churches of different denominations that combine for worship and work. Each congregation retains its corporate identity and denominational affiliation, but both call the same minister and carry on a common program. Such churches exist usually in rural areas where population is too sparse to make it possible for several churches to be self-sustaining. The first instances of federated churches were in Massachusetts as early as 1887. In the 1916 U.S. census they were listed as *independent churches, but in 1926 and 1936 they were called federated churches. No reliable statistics are available for this type of church; those reported in the *Yearbook of American Churches* cannot be considered accurate. BIBLIOGRAPHY: R. A. Felton, *Cooperative Churches* (1947); F. S. Mead, *Handbook of Denominations* (4th ed., 1965). *MERGER; *UNION CHURCHES.

[N. H. MARING]

FEDERATION OF PRIMARY ORTHODOX GREEK CATHOLIC JURISDICTIONS, a noncanonical inter-Orthodox organization formed in 1942 by those bishops in the U.S. who recognized patriarchal jurisdiction, viz., Greek (together with the patriarch's Carpathorussian and Ukrainian suffragans), Russian, Serbian, and Syrian, in order to obtain official standing for the Orthodox community from the civil government. It was prompted by the drafting into the armed services of Orthodox priests who did not fit into the recognized categories of Protestant, Catholic, or Jewish clergymen. The Federation had ceased to be operative by the late 1940s.

[T. BIRD]

FEDERER, HEINRICH (1866–1928), Swiss novelist and short story writer. F. was ordained in 1893 but by 1900

was forced to give up priestly work as a result of illness. He became a journalist and newspaper editor. F.'s novels and short stories are deeply influenced by his Catholicism, colored by his great admiration for St. Francis of Assisi, and by his sharp observation of the Swiss peasant and his serene life. A group of short stories also deals with Italian history.
BIBLIOGRAPHY: E. Aellen, *Heinrich Federer* (1928).

[J. R. AHERNE]

FEDERIGHI, ANTONIO (Antonio di Federigo dei Tolomei; d. 1490), Italian architect and sculptor who directed work on the Cathedral of Orvieto, was *capomastro* of Siena Cathedral, and carved statues for the Loggia della Mercanzia in the classical mode, modified by the style of Jacopo della Quercia.

[M. J. DALY]

FEDOTOV, GEORGE PETROVICH (1886–1951), historian of the Middle Ages, and of Russian Church history, hagiography, and spirituality. He taught at St. Sergius and St. Vladimir's Seminaries. From 1931 to 1940 he edited *Novy Grad* (The New City), and he is the author of *The Russian Religious Mind* (2 v., 1946–66), the 2d volume of which, published posthumously, contains a biographical sketch and a complete list of his writings.

[T. BIRD]

FEELING, a broad term that may signify either cognitive activities ranging from touch—the sense of feeling—up to more generalized and settled mental attitudes; or affective responses ranging from the experience of pleasantness and unpleasantness up to emotion, sentiment, mood, affection, sympathy, and the like. However, the term is used by some psychologists in a special sense to signify simply the experience of pleasantness-unpleasantness as distinguished from emotion or passion. In this last sense feeling exerts a polarizing influence upon human behavior and accounts ultimately, in the view of hedonists, for the distinction men draw between good and evil. On the other extreme there are those who look upon the experience of pleasure with suspicion and see it as something to be ignored or perhaps even to be repressed. This kind of thought tends to equate the good with the disagreeable and the evil with what is gratifying. In the main the classical Christian moralists have steered a middle course. Neither psychologically nor ethically is pleasure properly an object of direct pursuit; it is simply the normal accompaniment of action that is from some point of view suited to the person who performs it. The experience of pleasure is morally neutral in itself; it has ethical significance only by reason of the good or evil nature of the action with which it is associated. Pleasures arising from evil actions should be avoided; some legitimate pleasures may profitably be sacrificed with a view to future advantage; but the life of a Christian faithfully lived will by no means be barren of pleasure.

FEI, PAOLO DA GIOVANNI (fl. 1372–1410), Sienese painter working first in the Gothic lyricism of Simone Martini and later in the rigid, mannered gestures, bright palette, and decorative drapery of Bartolo di Fredi in painting *The Nativity of the Virgin* (Siena).

[M. J. DALY]

FEIJÓO Y MONTENEGRO, BENITO JERÓNIMO (1676–1764), Spanish Benedictine encyclopedist. A monk in his native Galicia in 1690, he studied at Salamanca and León before beginning in 1709 a 55-year career in Oviedo. In 1739 he withdrew from teaching at the university to concentrate on his vast *Teatro crítico* (8 v., 1726–40) and *Cartas eruditas* (5v., 1742–60), critical and moral essays to enlighten Spaniards in philosophy, philology, music, history, geography, physics, religion, agriculture, economics, medicine, and biology; these volumes saw 15 editions and were translated into five languages. In 1750 a royal decree forbade adversaries to attack him publicly. He read widely in European literature, esp. French, using and citing it in his own writings; his confrère Martin Sarmiento in Madrid helped him greatly. F.'s fame declined from some years after his death until a revival in the early 19th century
BIBLIOGRAPHY: I. L. McClelland, *Benito Jeronimo Feijoo* (1969).

[E. P. COLBERT]

FELBIGER, JOHANN IGNAZ VON (1724–88), Augustinian abbot and educational reformer in Austria and Silesia. Appointed abbot of Sagan in Silesia (1758), F. became aware of the unsatisfactory educational conditions in the nearby Catholic schools and, backed by the Silesian government, proceeded to better the situation. Returning from a visit to Berlin, where he was impressed by the Pietists' educational system, he introduced the Pietist teacher-training program into Silesia and Prussia, substituted classroom instruction for the tutoring system, integrated religious education into the curriculum, and wrote several books and a new catechism. His success attracted the attention of Empress Maria Theresa, who appointed him general minister of education (1774) in which capacity he organized both elementary and secondary schools. Joseph II, who did not approve of F.'s religious educational principles, removed him from Vienna (1782) and limited his activities to Hungary. F.'s educational influence was felt largely in methods, organization, and administration. His *Silesian Catechism* (1766) and *Method Book* were a valuable contribution to education.

[M. B. MURPHY]

FELDMANN, FRANZ (1866–1944), German RC biblical scholar. Ordained in 1891, he spent most of his career as professor of OT exegesis at the Univ. of Bonn (1903–44). He contributed to RC acceptance of critical methods in OT study, was the author of numerous studies, notably on

Isaiah, and edited *Die Hl. Schrift des Alten Testament,* a respected commentary known as the *Bonner Bibel.*

[T. C. O'BRIEN]

FELICIAN SISTERS, religious congregation (Sisters of St. Felix) founded in Warsaw, Poland, in 1855 under the leadership of Mother Mary Truszkowski. Following the rule of the Third Order of Regulars of St. Francis, the sisters engage in the education of the deaf and mentally retarded; they staff schools from kindergarten to college level, maintain hospitals, homes for the aged, and other social institutions. Their most recent endeavors have been to conduct houses of prayer and catechetical centers. Invited by Rev. J. *Dabrowski, they came to the U.S. in 1874, expanded under his guidance in Polish parishes; by 1975 the American provinces numbered over 3200 members. The motherhouse is located in Rome.

[C. KEENAN]

FELICISSIMUS AND AGAPITUS, SS. (d. 258), deacons of Rome, martyred under Valerian. On the same day that Pope *Sixtus II and four deacons were seized in the cemetery of Praetextatus, Felicissimus and Agapitus were captured elsewhere, executed, and buried in the cemetery of Praetextatus. Most of what is known of them is derived from the inscription of Pope *Damasus. BIBLIOGRAPHY: Butler 3:269–270.

[R. B. ENO]

FELICITY, ST., the name of two different women martyrs of the early Church: one from N Africa who was martyred in Carthage in A.D. 203; the other martyred near Rome probably in the 2d cent. and buried in the cemetery of Maximus on the Salarian Way. (1) **Felicity** of N Africa is commemorated along with Perpetua and her companions: Revocatus, Saturninus, Secundulus, and Saturus (see PERPETUA AND FELICITY, SS). (2) Of the Roman martyr **Felicity**, little is known other than her place of burial and the fact that her day of martyrdom (July 10) coincided with that of seven martyred men who later mistakenly came to be called brothers, and indeed her sons. BIBLIOGRAPHY: Butler 3:62–64; F. Caraffa, BiblSanct 5:605–608.

[E. J. DILLON]

FELICITY AND PERPETUA, SS., see PERPETUA AND FELICITY, SS.

FELIX I, ST. (d. 274), **POPE** from 269. Nothing certain is known of him apart from the years of his pontificate. The *Liber Pontificalis* (followed in this by the *Roman Martyrology*) declares that he was a martyr and was buried on the Via Aurelia. The *Depositio episcoporum* more reliably declares that he was buried in the cemetery of Callistus on the Via Appia and does not list him as a martyr. The Synod of Antioch had written to F.'s predecessor, Dionysius, about its action in deposing Paul of Samosata, and the letter appears to have arrived in Rome after the death of Dionysius. F. may have written to comment on the action, but scholars think the letter read at the Council of Ephesus as having emanated from him was a forgery. During F.'s reign the Emperor Aurelian settled (272) a dispute between rival Christian parties at Antioch concerning possession of the church in that city by declaring that the rightful occupant of the see was the one accepted as such by the bps. of Italy and Rome. This decision may have been politically motivated because the party of Paul of Samosata was favored by Zenobia, Aurelian's enemy in that region. BIBLIOGRAPHY: A. Amore and M. C. Celletti, BiblSanct 5:574–576.

[P. K. MEAGHER]

FELIX II (d. 365), **ANTIPOPE.** When Pope Liberius was sent into exile for his refusal to approve Arian doctrine, the Emperor Constantius invited F. to replace Liberius on the papal throne. A group of Arian bps. consecrated him and the Roman clergy accepted him, but not the Roman people. Upon the clamorous demand of the populace, Liberius was brought back to Rome (357). It was the wish of Constantius that Liberius and F. jointly occupy the papacy, but neither clergy nor people would permit such an absurdity, and F. was banished by the senate to Porto where he spent what remained of his life in retirement. The *Roman Martyrology* commemorates him as a saint. This is thought to be due to a mistaken identification of F. with a martyr of the same name who was buried on the Via Aurelia where the antipope had built a church. BIBLIOGRAPHY: J. P. Kirsch, CE 6:30.

[P. F. MULHERN]

FELIX III (II), ST. (d. 492), **POPE** from 483, of a Roman senatorial family and (acc. to the *Roman Martyrology*) an ancestor of St. Gregory the Great. His numeration as III is erroneous but persists in common usage, the antipope of 355-358 being generally called Felix II. F. is the first pope known to have officially announced his election to the Emperor. He is remembered chiefly for his courageous assertion of the right of the Church to make its doctrinal decisions without hindrance from imperial power. The **Henotikon* was published by the Emperor in 482 to circumvent the decisions of Chalcedon and thus placate the Monophysites. In 484 a synod held in Rome under Felix excommunicated *Acacius, who had drawn up or at least inspired the document, together with his supporters. This was the first grievous break between East and West. Acacius, with imperial support, ignored the excommunication and had the name of Felix stricken from the sacred diptychs. The resulting schism lasted for 35 years. A synod convened by Felix in 487 dealt with the reconciliation of those who had submitted to Arian baptism during the Vandal persecutions in N Africa. BIBLIOGRAPHY: T. G. Jalland, *Church and the Papacy* (1944); W. Ullmann, *Growth of the Papal Government in the Middle Ages* (1962).

[P. F. MULHERN]

FELIX IV (III), ST. (d. 530), **POPE** from 526, the third legitimate Roman Pontiff to bear the name Felix, but called Felix IV because of the inclusion of the antipope Felix II in many ancient listings of the popes. Upon the death of *John I, Theodoric, Ostrogoth King of Italy, favored the choice of F. as John's successor, and the Roman clergy and people yielded to his desire. F. took part in the *Semi-Pelagian controversy, sending to the bps. of S Gaul a series of "capitula" compiled from Scripture and the Fathers and drawn largely from the writings of *Prosper of Aquitaine. These capitula provided the basis for the canons of the Second Council of Orange (529). As F. faced death, his fear of the Byzantine faction at Rome led him to attempt the designation of his successor. His wishes were disregarded by the majority in the election that followed his death, although *Boniface II, whom F. had named, was ultimately accepted as pope. His portrait in mosaic, though largely reworked, is in the apse of the church of SS. Cosmas and Damian in Rome and is the earliest extant likeness of a pope. BIBLIOGRAPHY: J. Chapin, NCE 5:879–880; J. P. Kirsch, CE 6:31.

[P. F. MULHERN]

FELIX V, ANTIPOPE, see AMADEUS VIII OF SAVOY.

FELIX OF APTUNGA (Aptonga, Aptungi, Apthungi), one of the three bps. who consecrated Caecilian as bp. of Carthage in 311. The following year a council of 70 Numidian bps. meeting in Carthage declared the consecration to be invalid on the grounds that Felix was a **traditor*, that is, one who had handed over the Scriptures to pagan officials during the persecution of Diocletian. Though there was no real basis for the charge, the hostile bps. proceeded to elect Majorinus as a rival occupant to the See of Carthage, formally inaugurating the Donatist schism. In August 314 the Council of Arles declared that the ordinations of *traditores* were valid and thus destroyed the juridical basis for the Donatists' objection to Caecilian's consecration. BIBLIOGRAPHY: W. H. C. Frend, *Donatist Church* (1952) 150–151.

[M. J. COSTELLOE]

FELIX OF CANTALICE, ST. (1513–87), Italian Capuchin lay brother and first canonized Capuchin. After working as a farmhand and shepherd, in his late 20s he entered the Capuchins, made solemn vows in 1544, and was sent to Rome (1547) where for 40 years he carried on a ministry of service to his community and to the poor of the city. As the quaestor of the large community of St. Bonaventure he sought alms for his house daily. F. became a celebrated figure, walking barefoot through the city, bringing food and comfort to the poor, the sick, the dying. Among his friends and admirers were St. Philip Neri, St. Charles Borromeo and Pope Sixtus V. When Borromeo was writing a rule for his Oblates he had Felix, illiterate as he was, listen to the regulations and make recommendations for changes. F.'s personal austerity and encompassing charity for others made him a much loved influence. At his death Sixtus V urged that his process of canonization begin immediately, attesting to many miracles he had seen F. perform. It remained, however, for Clement XV to canonize the Capuchin brother in 1712. BIBLIOGRAPHY: A. Kerr, *Son of St. Francis* (1900).

[J. R. AHERNE]

FELIX OF DUNWICH, ST. (d. 648), bp. known from Bede's *Ecclesiastical History*. F., a Burgundian, was sent (631) by St. Honorius, abp. of Canterbury, at the request of Sigebert, convert king of East Anglia, to convert his people. In what are now the counties of Norfolk, Suffolk, and Cambridge, F. preached successfully for 17 years. When he died, he was buried in his see city of Dunwich (Suffolk) since submerged by the sea. His relics were transferred to Ramsey Abbey where they remained until the Reformation. F. was named in the *Roman Martyrology* as the "Apostle of the East Anglians." BIBLIOGRAPHY: Butler 1:524; J. Dolan, BiblSanct 5:542.

[C. CARROLL]

FELIX OF NICOSIA, BL. (1715–87), Capuchin lay brother. Son of a poor cobbler in Nicosia, Sicily, F. sought admission to the Capuchins but was refused for 7 years, until his persistence won out. From earliest years he displayed extraordinary sanctity and a miraculous gift of healing. His charity to the sick, the prisoner, the poor was unabated. Even at the age of 60 F. performed heroically in a time of plague ministering to the sick without concern for his own health. BIBLIOGRAPHY: Butler 2:452; M. da Alatri, BiblSanct 5:548–549.

[J. R. AHERNE]

FELIX OF NOLA, ST. (3d cent.), confessor. A native of Nola, near Naples, F. was ordained priest by Bp. Maximus. He suffered grievously during the persecution of Decius and, acc. to the life written by St. *Paulinus of Nola, was miraculously saved from death on a number of occasions. After the death of Maximus the people wanted F. as their bp., but he refused the honor, preferring a life of simple poverty and humble service to others. After his death his tomb became a celebrated pilgrims' shrine. Accounts of the wonders wrought there have been left by SS. Paulinus and Augustine. BIBLIOGRAPHY: Butler 1:80–81.

[R. B. ENO]

FELIX OF URGEL (d. 818), bp. of Ugel in Spain, with *Elipandus a leading proponent of *Adoptionism, the teaching that Jesus as born of the Father is true son of God, but as born of the Virgin Mary is only God's adopted son. The works of F. are lost; his teaching is to be seen only in the texts of his adversaries, Alcuin among them. F. was summoned before Charlemagne (792); he died in the custody of Bp. Agobard of Lyons. He is named in the condemnation of Adoptionism by the Council of Frankfurt (D

615). BIBLIOGRAPHY: L. Ueding, LTK 4:71. *ADOPTIONISM bibliog.

[E. A. WEIS]

FELIX OF VALOIS, ST. (1127–1212), hermit, asserted the cofounder (with St. *John of Matha) of the Trinitarians. Information about his life dates and indeed his very existence depends only upon late and highly dubious evidence. No biography of him exists that dates from earlier than the 17th century. According to the untrustworthy story, he was a hermit in the forest of Galeresse (Valois district) until John of Matha found him and with his help founded the new order. He has never been officially canonized, although his cult has been recognized since 1666. BIBLIOGRAPHY: Butler 4:392–393; for a presentation of the historical evidence, see I. del SS. Sacramento, BiblSanct 5:566–573.

FELIX, MARCUS ANTONIUS, freed man of Antonia, the mother of the Emperor Claudius, and the brother of Pallas, friend of Claudius. He was appointed Roman procurator of Judea by imperial decree in 52 or 53 A.D. His unprincipled behavior in office was responsible for the Jewish Revolt of 66–70 A.D. Paul stood trial before him in Caesarea after his arrest in Jerusalem (Acts 23. 22–24). Relieved of his command by Nero for maladministration, F. was spared further punishment through the intercession of his brother Pallas. BIBLIOGRAPHY: F. J. Buckley NCE 5, 881; R. Van R. Hoden, PW 1.2:2616–18; J. Schmid LTK 4:70.

[F. H. BRIGHAM]

FELIX, REGULA, AND EXSUPERANTIUS, SS., patrons of Zurich. According to legendary accounts Felix, his sister Regula, and their servant Exsuperantius brought Christianity to the region of the Limmat river in the 3d century. After many tortures they were beheaded during the persecution of Maximian. The legendary account states that the saints walked a distance of 50 cubits bearing their heads in their hands after their execution. Their relics are preserved in a chapel of the cathedral (Grossmünster) on the right bank of the Limmat. A church, the so-called Wasserkirche, is said to mark the place of the saints' martyrdom. BIBLIOGRAPHY: R. Henggeler and A. M. Raggi, BiblSanct 5:594–596.

[H. DRESSLER]

FELIX CULPA (Eng., happy fault), a phrase applied to the *original sin of Adam and Eve insofar as its redemption occasioned God's great gift of his Son through the *Incarnation.

FELIX NAMQUE, the name of several English organ works, dating from the 16th century. The words derived from the Offertory, *Felix namque es,* used for certain feasts of the Blessed Virgin Mary. Like *In nomine,* this title was frequently given to elaborate polyphonic settings.

[A. M. MACK]

FELL, MARGARET (1614–1702), "mother of Quakerism." F. was the wife of Thomas Fell, vice-chancellor of the duchy of Lancaster; they made their home, Swarthmoor (Swarthmore) Hall, a haven for itinerant preachers. When G. *Fox stopped there in 1652, she became convinced of his message. Thereafter Swarthmoor Hall became a secure base for Quakers, and F. herself advanced the movement by her counsel, preaching, correspondence, and fund-raising. She also sought mitigation of harsh anti-Quaker measures, writing frequently (1655–57) to Oliver Cromwell, and obtaining from Charles II (1661) the release of 4,000 Quakers from prison. She herself was imprisoned for 4 years, 1664–68. Her husband had died in 1658, and in 1669 she married Fox. BIBLIOGRAPHY: V. Noble, *Man in the Leather Breeches* (1953); I. Ross; *Margaret Fell, Mother of Quakerism* (1949).

FELLOWSHIP, a translation of the Greek *koinonia,* signifying varied relationships (e.g., association, partnership, community, participation). *Koinonia* and related words in the NT are used in various ways, but they refer primarily to the unique Christian communion based upon sharing new life in Christ. It sometimes indicates participation in something—e.g., God's grace (Phil 1.7), the Holy Spirit (Phil 2.1), or the body and blood of Christ (I Cor 10. 16–18). Other passages emphasize sharing with Christ (Phil 3.10) and with God (I Jn 1.3). Still others indicate the communion of Christians with one another (I Jn 1.3, 7). Recent discussions on the Church have recognized the importance of the concept of fellowship, which indicates that the Church is a divine-human community constituted and sustained by God. Emil *Brunner goes so far as to state. "The Body of Christ is nothing other than a fellowship of persons. . . . The faithful are bound to each other through their common sharing in Christ and in the Holy Ghost" (*Misunderstanding of the Church* [1953], 10–11). Although some would consider this an extreme statement, esp. since it adds that the body of Christ "has nothing to do with an organization," it illustrates the point that modern theologians consider the NT idea of fellowship essential to understanding the nature of the Church. The same viewpoint is evident in RC ecclesiology and liturgical practice esp. since Vatican Council II. In common parlance, the word has taken on more superficial meanings, ranging from a gathering for public worship to mere sociability experienced in eating or recreation. The term also has a specialized, restrictive use, namely, as applied to the place of the *local church stressing a *congregational polity in relation to centralizing organizations. This relationship is described as one of fellowship, to indicate that the local church does not surrender its autonomy; the centralizing organization does not have jurisdiction, but exists to foster mutual interests and assistance. BIBLIOGRAPHY: Kittel TD 3:789–809; J. R. Nelson, *Realm of Redemption* (1951).

[N. H. MARING]

FELO-DE-SE, a term in English law (e.g., in Blackstone), then also in literature, meaning one who does an evil to himself, and specifically, one who commits suicide or does some evil action that results directly in his own death; also the evil act itself.

[T. C. O'BRIEN]

FELTIN, MAURICE (1883–1975), French bp. and cardinal. He attended the College of St. Ignace and Saint-Sulpice, was ordained in 1909, became bp. of Troyes (1928), abp. of Sens (1932), abp. of Bordeaux (1935) and abp. of Paris (1949). In 1953 Pope Pius XII elevated him to the cardinalate. Poor health forced his resignation in 1966 as abp. of Paris. He served as chaplain of the armed forces, and was active in education and social work. He was instrumental in shaping the Debré school law of the Fifth Republic, helped found *Pax Christi* (1952), later serving as its president; he promoted the *Union Féminine Civique et Sociale,* an organization devoted to a continuing analysis of economic, civic, and social problems. He was a leading advocate of the ecumenical movement, working with leaders of other religions in promoting better relations. BIBLIOGRAPHY: W. Bosworth, *Catholicism and Crisis in Modern France* (1962).

[D. R. PENN]

FELTON, JOHN, BL. (d. 1570), English martyr who affixed Pope Pius V's excommunication of Queen Elizabeth to the gate of the palace of the bp. of London. When arrested and charged, he admitted having done so, but denied under torture that any other shared responsibility. Found guilty and hanged, he was beatified in 1886. BIBLIOGRAPHY: C. Testore, BiblSanct 5:614–615; Butler 3:284–285.

[V. SAMPSON]

FEMINISM, see WOMEN IN CHRISTIAN TRADITION.

FÉNELON, FRANÇOIS DE SALIGNAC DE LA MOTHE (1651–1715), abp., theologian, educator. Of a noble French family, F. received a classical and philosophical education, then became a priest at Saint-Sulpice in 1675. His character, though austere, was marked by delicacy and charity. He loved to preach before humble audiences; was charged for 3 years with the direction of a group of young women converts from Protestant families known as "New Catholics"; and was sent on missions to Protestants affected by the revocation of the Edict of Nantes. In 1689 he was appointed preceptor to the Duc de Bourgogne, grandson of King Louis XIV. F. had already published (1687) his *Treatise on the Education of Girls,* composed at the behest of his friends the Duc and Duchesse de Beauvilliers. He now entered with zeal upon the task of molding a royal pupil to his ideal of a cultured man and future king. To this end, the tutor prepared three pedagogical and moralistic works: *The Fables* (1690), *Dialogues of the Dead* (c.1692, published 1700–1820), and *The Adventures of Telemachus*. When the latter was published in 1699 without the author's knowledge, it brought about his final disgrace at court, since the King saw in it a satire upon his own reign. However, although F. had been honored with consecration as abp. of Cambrai in 1695, his fall into disfavor was practically complete by 1697, when he received a royal order to remain in his diocese. The cause of this punitive action dates from 1688, when he met Mme. *Guyon and was fascinated by her mystical theories. These were drawn largely from the condemned quietism of the Spaniard Molinos, although Mme. Guyon's version was ambiguous. F. defended her against Bossuet, and in 1697 he published in this connection his *Explanation of the Maxims of the Saints:* This work, largely through the persistent efforts of Bossuet, was condemned by the Holy See. F. submitted fully, and although the condemnation was based chiefly on technicalities and semantics, the quarrel was continued by others for many years. F. himself entered into an enduring silence on the matter, confining himself until the end of his life to work within his diocese, where he was esteemed as a saint. His principal importance in history is as a precursor of 18th-cent. trends. Paradoxically, he was an admirer and imitator of the ancients and yet he criticized them with modern independence. Preromantic were his love of naturalness, ease of expression, and freedom from classical rigidity. Rousseau admired him and was inspired by his educational ideals as well as by his sensitivity, quietistic tendencies, and somewhat vague aspirations toward the infinite. F., before Montesquieu, had proclaimed the sovereignty of law and opposed absolutism in monarchy. He believed in unlimited progress and the possibility of universal peace. It has been said that if his ideas for liberal reform had been followed the French Revolution might not have occurred. Works: *Oeuvres complètes* (10 v., 1852). BIBLIOGRAPHY: D. C. Cabeen, *Critical Bibliography of French Literature* (1961); M. de la Bedoyère, *Archibishop and the Lady: The Story of Fénelon and Madame Guyon* (1956); Viscount St. Cyres, *François de Fénelon* (1901, repr. 1970).

[L. TINSLEY]

FENLON, JOHN F. (1873–1943), American Sulpician professor and provincial. Ordained for the Chicago archdiocese in 1896, he joined the Society of St. Sulpice in 1898. After doctoral studies in Rome, he joined the faculty of theology, St. Joseph's Seminary, Dunwoodie, N.Y. in 1901. From 1904–24 he served at the Sulpician seminary, Washington, D.C., both as superior (1904–11), and as president of the theological school (1911–24). Provincial superior of his society from 1925, he was responsible for the opening of St. Mary's Seminary, Roland Park, Md., and St. Edward's Seminary, Seattle, Washington.

[T. C. O'BRIEN]

FENWICK, BENEDICT JOSEPH (1782–1846), second bp. of Boston. Son of a distinguished Catholic family of St. Mary's Co., Md., he became a Jesuit in 1806, was ordained in 1808. His early career included parochial work in New

York City, a time as president of Georgetown College, Washington, D.C., service in Charleston, S. C. to deal with problems of trusteeism and as vicar-general for Bp. J. *England, a second term as president of Georgetown (1822–25). He was named bp. of Boston in 1825. His tenure was marked by strong efforts to provide for the spiritual and educational needs of the greatly enlarged Catholic population; the bitterly anti-Catholic nativism, marked by the burning of the Ursuline Convent in Charlestown (1834), and anti-Irish riots in Boston (1837). He established a diocesan newspaper, afterwards called the *Boston Pilot,* sent priests throughout New England, founded and staffed parishes and schools; his greatest educational accomplishment was the founding (1843) of the College of the Holy Cross, Worcester, and staffing it with Jesuits. He dealt with the anti-Catholicism with restraint, and won the respect of many in the Protestant community. BIBLIOGRAPHY: R. H. Lord, *History of the Archdiocese of Boston* (1944).

[T. C. O'BRIEN]

FENWICK, EDWARD DOMINIC (1768–1832), missionary, first bp. of Cincinnati. Born in Maryland, he became a member of the Dominican Order and was ordained in Belgium in 1793. Imprisoned by the French Revolution he returned upon his release to America with the purpose of establishing a house of his order in the new land. He established the first foundations near Springfield, Kentucky: a parish church and the College of St. Thomas of Aquin. By his own request he was relieved of the superiorship and devoted himself to missionary work in Ohio. In 1822 he was consecrated first bp. of Cincinnati. As bishop he established the first Dominican province in the U.S. F. built St. Peter's Cathedral, established St. Francis Xavier Seminary, and founded the diocesan newspaper, *The Catholic Telegraph Register*. His efforts as a missionary and a bishop earned him the title "Apostle of Ohio." BIBLIOGRAPHY: J. H. Lamoth, *History of the Archdiocese of Cincinnati* (1921).

[J. R. AHERNE]

FERDINAND, BL. (1402–43), Infante of Portugal. A prince whose father was King John I of Portugal and whose great grandfather was King Edward III of England. F. led a life of holiness from earliest years. He refused the offer of a cardinal's hat from Pope Eugenius IV on grounds of conscience. With Henry the Navigator he headed an expedition against the Moors of Africa. The results were disastrous, and F. was given to the Moors as a hostage. There ensued years of degrading treatment in Moorish prisons which he accepted without complaint. He died as a result of ill treatment. F. was beatified in 1470. BIBLIOGRAPHY: Butler 2:483–484; I. de Villapadierna, BiblSanct 5:622–623.

[J. R. AHERNE]

FERDINAND III, ST. (1198–1252), **KING OF CASTILE** from 1217, succeeding to the throne of Castile when his mother abdicated and to that of Léon in 1230 after the death of his father Alfonso IX. Occupied at first with establishing his accession to the throne, F. from 1224 until 1248 engaged in a continuous struggle to drive the Muslims out of Andalusia, a campaign resulting in the surrender of Córdoba (1236) and of Seville (1248). Toward the Muslims who accepted his authority he showed mercy and labored to convert them to Christianity through the mendicant Orders. A patron of the Univ. of Salamanca, he consolidated the kingdoms of Castile and Léon and prepared the way for a uniform code of laws. He was declared saint by Clement X in 1671. BIBLIOGRAPHY: Butler 2:426; D. Mansilla, BiblSanct 5:624–627.

[J. R. AHERNE]

FERDINAND V, KING OF CASTILE (1452–1516), heir of Aragon (1465), King of Sicily (1468), and by marriage to Isabella (1469), King of Castile (1475); later, King of Aragon (1479). Main creator of Aragon-Castile as "Spain," he expanded it through conquest in Europe and America, his Inquisition controlling its Church. BIBLIOGRAPHY: R. I. Burns, NCE 5:887–888; F. Fernandez-Armesto, *Ferdinand and Isabella* (1975); F. Fournier-Aubry, *Don Fernando* (1974).

[R. I. BURNS]

FERDINAND I (1503–64), **HOLY ROMAN EMPEROR** from 1558. Son of the Habsburg Philip the Handsome, F. was given the Austrian territory when his older brother inherited the Habsburg and Spanish possessions. In 1526 he was elected king of Bohemia and Hungary; in 1531, king of the Romans. He succeeded his brother in 1558 as Holy Roman Emperor and accomplished important administrative reforms. He tried to stem the Reformation and was instrumental in framing the Peace of Augsburg (1555). BIBLIOGRAPHY: L. von Ranke, *Ferdinand I and Maximilian II of Austria* (1853, repr. 1975).

[M. J. FINNEGAN]

FERDINAND II (1578–1637), **HOLY ROMAN EMPEROR** from 1619. Son of the Habsburg Archduke Charles and Maria of Bavaria. F. studied at Ingolstadt, a Jesuit university, 1590-95. The combined influence of his Jesuit training and family attitudes made F. amenable to the advice of his spiritual confessors, a patron of the arts, an advocate of the "one Church, one king" doctrine, and a resolute opponent of Protestantism and restorer of Catholicism. He vowed to sacrifice his life and property before compromising his religious principles. His first official action in Styria (1598), confiscating Protestant churches for Catholic use and closing Protestant schools, forced local Protestants to choose between exile and conversion. The *Defenestration of his ministers at Prague in May, 1618, marked the beginning of Bohemian revolt against F., who had been elected king of Bohemia in 1617 and Hungary (1618). When Matthias died (1619) and F. succeeded him as Holy Roman Emperor, the Bohemians elected Protestant

Frederick V, the Elector Palatine, as their king in place of Ferdinand. With foreign support from Spain and the Catholic Maximilian I of Bavaria, F. overcame his Protestant opponents in 1620 at the battle of White Mountain, which marked the beginning of the Thirty Years' War. The enforced restoration of the Catholic Church in Bohemia after 1620 drove many Protestants into exile. F.'s military lieutenant, Albrecht von Wallenstein, raised an army which, by the end of the Danish war (1629), had essentially conquered Germany. F.'s Edict of Restitution (1629) commanded that all property of the Catholic Church alienated since the Peace of Augsburg (1555) be returned; however this act served to unite Protestant and Catholic opponents of absolute monarchy against him forcing him to remove Wallenstein (1630). Then, Gustavus Adolphus of Sweden invaded, defeating the Catholic league, utterly eroding F.'s position in non-Habsburg Germany. The Treaty of Prague (1635), which preserved the Habsburg claim to the crown while surrendering influence in Germany, was engineered by F.'s son and heir, Ferdinand III.

[R. J. LITZ]

FERENDAE SENTENTIAE (Lat., of a sentence to be passed), classification of canonical penalties. A penalty *ferendae sententiae* must be pronounced by a judge or by an ecclesiastical superior; it has no effect in canon law unless it is explicitly enjoined, even if the law mandates its imposition. Penalties *ferendae sententiae* can be contrasted with those *latae sententiae* (Lat., of a sentence already passed), which the law automatically imposes on one who commits a crime (e.g., by the fact that an individual takes part in a duel, he incurs excommunication, even if his particular fault is never discovered or condemned). A penalty *ferendae sententiae* is considered to come from the law itself *(a jure)* before the sentence is imposed, but after the sentence has been imposed, it comes from and pertains to the case of the individual *(ab homine)* while a penalty *latae sententiae* is always *a jure*. *CENSURES, ECCLESIASTICAL.

[R. A. ARONSTAM]

FERETORY, a term used to describe either a large reliquary carried in procession or a section of a church designed to enshrine the relic of a saint.

FERGUSON, FRANK W. (1861–1926), American architect and major partner in the firm with Cram and Goodhue (1899). Not as a designer but as engineer and chief of construction F. effected the firm's plans, notably the Cathedral of St. John the Divine in New York City.

[M. J. DALY]

FERIAL DAY, the "weekday" of the liturgical calendar, numbered *(feria ii)* rather than named (Monday). It received little attention until the early Middle Ages when daily Mass became customary and votive Mass formularies were developed. The term came to be used in the West of a day on which no feast or fast was kept; the original Latin meaning is "holiday" or "day of rest." Since the 1969 reform of the Roman calendar has reduced the number of saints' feasts, the weekly cycle is regaining its significance.

[J. DALLEN]

FERMENTUM (Lat., leaven), fragments of the consecrated Host which, in early Christian Rome, were sent on Sundays from Mass celebrated by the pope to other churches, to symbolize the unity of the faithful.

FERNANDES, VASCO (*c.* 1480–1543), leading Portuguese Renaissance painter of the *Lamego Altarpiece* (1506–11), a *Pietà* triptych (1520), *Pentecost* (1535), *Calvary,* and *St. Peter Enthroned* (1530). The elegant figures and detailed landscape evidence Flemish influence. The *Pentecost* is manneristic in its elongated figures but shows a monumental form extended in the *Calvary* and *St. Peter Enthroned* with their heavy figures, symmetric compositions, and deep space.

[M. J. DALY]

FERNÁNDEZ (HERNÁNDEZ), ALEJO (*c.* 1475–1543), Spanish painter evidencing a German-Flemish stylistic influence. (His brother was Jorge Fernández Alemán, "the German"). F. painted in Portuguese style related to Quentin Massys, with a *sfumato* and linear perspective in the Venetian mode, a synthesis which freed the strict 15th-cent. Hispano—Flemish manner. F. painted the *Virgen del Buen Aire* (Virgin of Favorable Winds) for the Trade House, Seville.

[M. J. DALY]

FERNÁNDEZ (HERNÁNDEZ), GREGORIO (1565/66–1636), Spanish sculptor and architect. F. created polychromed wood figures of a baroque realism; his cult and processional images (*pasos*), noted for dramatic postures and facial expressions, include *The Dead Christ* (1605) and *Veronica* (1614), harsh in color and heavy in angular drapery. F. executed the elaborate impressive high altar for the Plasencia cathedral, where reliefs, attached to a painted ground, are designed in tiered panels, the center capped by a pediment.

[M. J. DALY]

FERNÁNDEZ DE RECALDE, PEDRO (d. 1580), Spanish Dominican theologian who was sent to the Council of Trent with Juan *Gallo by Philip II of Spain. The Holy See appointed him apostolic visitator of the Carmelites in Spain, and in that capacity he was involved in the Teresan reform.

FERNÁNDEZ TRUYOLS, ANDRÉS (1870–1961), Spanish Jesuit biblical scholar. F. was vice-rector (1914–18) and rector (1918–24) of the *Pontifical Biblical Institute in Rome, helped establish its counterpart in Jerusalem where he conducted biblical study tours (1929–47), and founded the periodicals *Biblica* and *Verbum*

Domini. He published commentaries on OT books, a life of Christ, studies on the geography of the Holy Land, and was the first to propound the *sensus plenior* as a principle in hermeneutics.

[T. M. MCFADDEN]

FERNANDIS, MATEUS (fl. 1480–1515), Portuguese architect identified with the monastery of Batalha (1480) and as master of works from 1490. To him, master of the Manueline style, is attributed the portal of the Capelas Imperfeitas and the vaulting of the chapel of John II and Queen Leonor.

[M. J. DALY]

FÉROTIN, MARIUS (1855–1914), Benedictine, historian of the liturgy. A monk at Solesmes, Belgium, at Silos, Spain, and at Farnborough, England, F. is best remembered for his pioneer work on Visigothic and Mozarabic churches of Spain, together with an examination of the MS contents of the Abbey of Silos. He also collaborated on numerous bibliographies and other MS collections. BIBLIOGRAPHY: F. Cabrol and H. Leclercq, DACL 5.1:1382–98.

[B. F. SCHERER]

FERRAIOLA, an ecclesiastic cape reaching to the elbows.

FERRAIOLONE, a long black cape worn over the clerical cassock.

FERRANDUS (sometimes, wrongly, Fulgentius; d. *c.*546), deacon of Carthage. F. was a disciple and biographer of St. *Fulgentius (PL 65:378–435). He was a companion of Fulgentius's first exile at Sardinia, and there became a monk. Returning in 516 to Carthage, he cared for the Church there, which was without a bishop. His *Breviatio canonum* (PL 67:667–962) is a collection of the disciplinary decrees of contemporary Greek and African councils. BIBLIOGRAPHY: Altaner 588; *Vie de S. Fulgence de Ruspe* (ed. G. G. Lapeyre, 1929); H. Rahner, LTK 4:87 with bibliog.

[T. C. O'BRIEN]

FERRAR, NICHOLAS (1592–1637), founder of *Little Gidding community. Son of Nicholas Ferrar, an incorporator of the second Virginia Charter (1609), and Mary Wodenoth, F. was educated at Clare Hall, Cambridge. After Continental travels (1613–18), he returned to England and, like his father, became actively associated with the Virginia Company, until its charter was declared null and void in 1624. In that year he was elected to Parliament, serving only briefly. The next year his mother purchased the manor of Little Gidding in Huntingdonshire, 18 miles from Cambridge. In 1626 F. was ordained deacon by Abp. William *Laud and, referring ecclesiastical preferment as he had secular, he returned to Little Gidding, where he spent the rest of his life in prayer, study, and charitable works. F. was a friend of R. *Crashaw, literary executor of George *Herbert and probably was acquainted with John *Donne. BIBLIOGRAPHY: D. Novarr, *Making of Walton's Lives* (1958).

[M. S. CONLAN]

FERRARA-FLORENCE, COUNCIL OF, see FLORENCE, COUNCIL OF.

FERRARI (1) Giovanni Andrea de (1598–1669), Italian painter in Genoa, head of a large studio, F. studied with Bernardo Strozzi and painted the *Madonna del Carmine* (1635) at Alassio. (2) Gregorio de'Ferrari (1647–1726) established great decorative style in Genoese fresco painting. His *Death of St. Scholastica* (*c.* 1700) combines Pietro da Cortona's grand manner with the supple line and luminous color of Correggio, developing the rococo style in Italy. (3) *Lorenzo de Ferrari* (1680–1744). Son of Gregorio, he extended the decorative style of his father, executed a lavish program of *tondi,* lunettes, and ceiling frescoes in gilded stucco framework, which in strength and vivacity distinguish the Genoese School from the delicate charm of French rococo.

[M. J. DALY]

FERRARI, BARTOLOMEO, VEN. (1499–1544), cofounder of the Barnabites. A lawyer who devoted himself to charitable works he joined with Antonio Morigia and Antonio Maria *Zaccaria to establish the Clerks Regular of St. Paul, commonly known as Barnabites, for the reform of Christian morals and the defense of the faith. F. was ordained in 1532. In 1533 partly through the good offices of his brother at the papal court, the order was approved by Clement VII. Ferrari obtained the favor of Emperor Charles V and privileges from Paul III. The community enjoyed considerable expansion. F. was elected general in 1542.

[J. R. AHERNE]

FERRARI, GOUDENZIO (*c.*1480–1546), Italian painter of Lombardy who became Milan's leading artist in 1539. Influenced by Leonardo, F.'s style shows stormy dramatic action akin to late Gothic German wood sculpture. F.'s extraordinary fresco cycles in small cities near Milan and in many chapels in Varallo provided panoramic background for sculpture groups. F. also painted many agitated, vivid altarpieces and narrative pictures.

[M. J. DALY]

FERRARIENSIS (Francesco Silvestri; 1474–1528), Dominican, whose classic commentary accompanies the Leonine edition of St. Thomas Aquinas's *Summa contra gentiles* (v. 13–15, 1918, 1926, 1930). F. was master general of his order, 1525–28. His commentary and major work was completed in 1517, but only published, at the urging of *Cajetan, at Venice in 1524. F.'s interpretations differ from those of Cajetan, notably his position on the *analogy of being. BIBLIOGRAPHY: U. Degl' Innocenti, EncCatt 11:594–595 with bibliog.

[T. C. O'BRIEN]

FERRATA, DOMENICO (1847–1914), cardinal, papal diplomatist. After a period as professor of canon law at Rome, he entered the papal diplomatic service (1879). His most important single task under Leo XIII (1891) was as nuncio to Paris, with the responsibility for carrying forward that Pope's policy of *Ralliement towards the Third Republic. A cardinal from 1896, F. was successively prefect of four Roman congregations; in 1914 he was named by Benedict XV papal secretary of state, but died only a few weeks after the appointment.

[T. C. O'BRIEN]

FERRATA, ERCOLE (1610–86), Italian sculptor working in Naples and Rome. F. was an assistant of Bernini in the 1650s. *St. Agnes* (1660) and the *Stoning of St. Emerentiana* are his chief works. Through his studio F. strongly influenced the classical baroque style.

[M. J. DALY]

FERREIRA, ALEXANDRE RODRIGUES, see RODRIGUES FERREIRA, ALEXANDRE.

FERREOLUS OF UZÈS, ST. (d. 581), bishop. Fragments of a biography, uncertain as to date and historical worth, describe his zeal in clerical reform and in the conversion of Jews in his diocese of Uzès. Gregory of Tours praises him as a man of great sanctity and mentions several books of his letters written after the manner of Sidonius. The letters have not survived, but an extant monastic rule is attributed to him. BIBLIOGRAPHY: P. Viard, BiblSanct 5:650–651.

[G. M. COOK]

FERRER BIBLE, a Catalan translation of the Bible by the Carthusian Bonifacio Ferrer (1355–1417). It was one of the first vernacular Bibles printed (Valencia, 1478), but was proscribed by the Spanish Inquisition in 1490 because vernacular versions were prohibited. Copies were ordered burned; only one page of one copy is known to have survived and is now possessed by the Hispanic Society of America in New York.

FERRERI, ZACCARIA (1479–1524), Italian humanist, bp., church reformer. He became a Benedictine in 1494, abbot *c.* 1504, then transferred for a time to the Carthusians, before abandoning the monastic life. He became involved in church affairs as a participant in the *concilabulum* at Pisa in 1511 and published a defense of *conciliarism; with his colleagues at Pisa he was excommunicated by Julius II. F., however, was absolved in 1513, after addressing a heroic Latin poem in the style of Dante's *Divine Comedy* to the next pope, Leo X. F. became a member of the papal household and served as nuncio to Russia and Poland, where he contributed to church reform. On this subject he wrote *De reformatione ecclesiae suasioria* (1523), addressed to Adrian VI. To the reform of the Breviary F. contributed *Hymni novi ecclesiastici juxta veram metri et latinitatis normam* (1525); in their fulsome classical allusions the hymns lack religious style or spirit.

[J. R. AHERNE]

FERRETTI, GABRIELE (1795–1860), cardinal, papal secretary, diplomat. He pursued an important ecclesiastical career as bp. of Pieti (1827), nuncio to Naples (1833–37), abp. of Fermo (1827–42), cardinal (1839), legate to Pesaro (1846), secretary of state (July 5–Dec. 31, 1847), legate to Ravenna (1848), grand penitentiary (1852), cardinal bishop of Sabina (1853). In his political philosophy he favored Italian nationalism and closer relations with Piedmont. BIBLIOGRAPHY: R. Aubert, NCE 5:896; E. Santovito, EncCatt 5:1201–02; R. Quazza, *Pio IX e Massimo d'Azeglio nelle vicende romane del 1847* (2 v., 1954–55).

[J. J. SMITH]

FERRETTI, PAOLO (1866–1938), Benedictine abbot (1900) of San Giovanni Evangelista, Torrechiara (Parma), scholar, musicologist. When appointed (1913) to what became in 1931 the Pontificio Istituto di Musica Sacra, he studied, taught, and wrote on the nature of Gregorian chant; he became director of the institute in 1922. During the summers of 1925, 1927, and 1928, he taught at the Pius X School of Liturgical Music in New York City. Importance is attached to F.'s investigations and analyses of plainchant and to his attempts to reform sacred music in Italy. His most renowned single work is *Estetica gregoriana, ossia trattato delle forme musicali del canto gregoriana* (1938); he was a founder of *Monumenta polyphoniae italicae* and a frequent contributor to Italian and French journals on sacred music.

[A. M. MACK]

FERRI, CIRO (1634–89), Italian painter and draftsman, student and most competent follower of Pietro da Cortona F., working in Rome and Florence as a most authentic exponent of Cortona's high baroque style, often completed the work of his master.

[M. J. DALY]

FERRIÈRE-EN-GÂTINAIS, ABBEY OF (7th cent.), ancient monastic foundation near Orléans (ancient Diocese of Sens), France, over which Alcuin once served as abbot. It prospered under the Rule of St. Benedict in the 9th cent. and underwent two reforms, the Cluniac and the Maurist, until suppressed in 1790 in the French Revolution. The abbey church is now used for the local parish. BIBLIOGRAPHY: R. Gazeau, *Catholicisme* 4:1204–05.

[J. F. FALLON]

FERRINI, CONTARDO, BL., (1859–1902), Italian jurist, beatified 1947. Chaste and studious from childhood, he taught Roman law at Messina (1887), Modena (1890), and Pavia (1894), where he had received his degree (1880). His juridical works (5 v. 1929–30) deal with Roman, Byzantine, and Roman-Syriac law. His religious writings (1912, 1926, 1960) include prayers. Fame of his sanctity began at the time of his death.

[E. P. COLBERT]

FERRUCI, ANDREA (1465–1526), one of the greatest Italian sculptors of the early 16th century. F. executed the font in the cathedral of Pistoia, a bust of Marsilio Ficino (Florence), and the tomb of Antonio Strozzi (Florence).

[M. J. DALY]

FERRUCCI, FRANCESCO DI SIMONE (Francesco del Tadda; 1437–93), Italian sculptor and architect of a family of marble carvers. F. was influenced by Disiderio da Settignano and A. del Verrocchio. His fine ornament and strong three-dimensional forms are seen in his monument to Alessandro Tartagni in S. Domenico, Bologna.

[M. J. DALY]

FERRY, JULES FRANÇOIS CAMILLE (1832–93), French statesman. His strong anticlericalism was expressed in his reform of the French educational system. The Ferry Laws (1879–86) established universal free, compulsory, and secular education, and secularized all public schools by forbidding religious education in them, barring members of RC orders as teachers, and giving state facilities the exclusive right to confer degrees. Moreover, the clergy were excluded from the Higher Council of Public Education, which was granted surveillance powers over nonpublic schools. F. was also an imperialist and one of the main builders of the French colonial empire. He was assassinated by a religious fanatic in 1893. BIBLIOGRAPHY: M. Ledus, *Jules Ferry* (1947); E. M. Acomb, *French Laic Laws, 1879–89* (1941).

[J. P. REID]

FERTILITY AND VEGETATION CULTS (IN THE BIBLE), the worship of the goddess of fertility. When Israel entered Canaan, the Canaanite vegetation and fertility cults were everywhere present. They were closely associated with agriculture, and because the Israelites learned agriculture from the Canaanites, there was a danger that they might also adopt the religious festivals and practices connected with it. It is apparent from the Bible that this actually happened. The adoption of Canaanite religious practices was facilitated by the Israelite custom of speaking of Yahweh as Baal, i.e., the Lord. The use of the same name Baal for the Canaanite deity and for Yahweh caused confusion and opened the door to idolatry.

The character of the Canaanite cults has been illuminated by the Bible and, since 1929, by the discovery of the Canaanite mythological tablets of Ugarit. The nominal head of the Canaanite pantheon was the father-god El. The chief active deity was Baal and his wife Anath. In the OT almost nothing is said of Anath, but a great deal of Ashtaroth or Ashtoreth (Jg 2.13; 10.6; 1 Sam 7.3–4; 12.10; 31.10; 1 Kg 11.5 and 33; 2 Kg 23.13). Jezebel of Tyre associated Asherah with Baal (1 Kg 18.19). It is probable that among the Canaanites there was never agreement as to which of these goddesses was the wife of Baal.

Important in the Canaanite myth was the death and resurrection of Baal which corresponded to the annual death and resurrection of nature. Baal, the god of vegetation and fertility was killed each spring after a great battle with Mot (Death). Through the summer months Mot reigned supreme. Then Baal's wife vanquished Mot, and Baal came back to life. By reenacting the drama of Baal and his consort in mimetic ritual through the sexual union with a temple prostitute, it was thought that the divine pair was brought together again in a fertilizing union and that the forces of nature were reactivated and the desired fertility in soil, beast, and man thereby secured. Numerous mother-goddess figurines uncovered in Israelite archeological sites indicate how popular these Canaanite fertility superstitions must have been in Israel. The Samaria ostraca yield almost as many names composed with "Baal" as with "Yahweh." And the debasing rites of the fertility cult were practiced everywhere (cf. Hos 1–3; 4.6–14). It seems that these fertility rites continued to be in vogue, even after the fall of Jerusalem (cf. Jer 44.15–30). BIBLIOGRAPHY: G. E. Wright, *Biblical Archaeology* (1957), ch. 1.

[F. BUCK]

FERTILITY CULTS. Sets of practices, beliefs, and customs with religious or mystical significance and pertaining to the fertility of the soil, have existed in primitive cultures the world over; traces of them remain in various peasant folkways. Concerned as they were with agriculture, fertility cults—linked by ritual magic with the passage of the seasons and vegetative growth—were a means of explaining the miracle of a seed's development from planting (in the source of all life, the Earth-Mother) to harvest. Ancient rites, calculated to encourage the soil's fertility and therefore a bountiful harvest, all have, despite their diversity in various cultures, the common denominator of sacred fecundity. For example, women of the Finnish peasantry once scattered their breast-milk over furrows prior to the crops' being sown; in Germany, only women have been allowed to sow grain. The soil (identified with woman, the womb, and sexuality) was supposedly made fertile by the magic practices of the farmer. The sprinkling of water on a plough at planting time is a typical symbolic link with the fertilization of the ovum by male sperm. In Hungary, to this day, girls are sprinkled with water on Easter Monday; in exchange, they give the young men Easter eggs, cookies with nuts and flowers, all ancient fertility symbols. The Hungarian custom of planting quickly-growing grain at Christmas or Easter may go back to the Near Eastern "Harvest of Adonis." Death also played an important role in fertility cults; the burial of the dead in the soil was viewed as a completion of the cycle in which life arose from and returned to the earth. In order to effect a bountiful harvest as the culmination of the growing season, sacrifices—of grain, animals and in some cases, even of humans—were made. The preeminent harvest rituals—all involving the last sheaf of corn, wheat, etc., to be bound up—clarify the essence of the fertility cult as the worship of the natural force that controls the vegetative process of growth. (See FINNO-UGRIC RELIGION.) This force is usually feminine and venerable (like the Slavic "Baba," or Old Woman). Those who cut the sheaves are either honored (in processions and festivals) or made the objects of mockery and a kind of superstitious mistrust. The reason for this difference in attitudes is that the harvester is viewed either as part of the force that has brought the harvest, or else as a destroyer (as in Norway, where the mythical Reaper is said to eat the farmer's wheat before his final imprisonment in the last sheaf). Sacrifices, festivals, and other ceremonies celebrated the end of the harvest; these were in most respects identical to those taking place at planting time. Thus the growing season divided, at its beginning and end, the new and the old years.

Gods and divinities of fertility are common in the most diverse religions. They include a mother goddess figure and her mate—also, sometimes, her son—who are united in a sacred marriage. The Hindu Durgā is a goddess of fertility as well as of the dead. The Greek Demeter's name, changed to the Roman Ceres, was given to the grains once sacrificed to her. The consort of a fertility goddess may be Dumuzi, Tammuz, Adonis, Dionysos, etc. The Germanic Odin, usually associated with the dead, was a fertility god also. BIBLIOGRAPHY: M. Eliade, *Patterns in Comparative Religion* (tr. R. Sheed, 1963); R. Graves, *Greek Myths* (v. 1, 1955), A. Jensen, *Myth and Cult among Primitive Peoples* (1963). *ASIANIC RELIGION; *MATRIARCHY.

[D. H. BRUNAUER]

FERVOR, a metaphor for the effect of an intense love, and particularly for the desire to be united with the object of love (ThAq 1a2ae, 28.5). In theology it is used esp. of charity, and specifically with regard to its more intense acts as they are dispositions for spiritual growth, and also free the subject from the guilt and effects of *venial sin. The term is also used at times to mean *devotion, a prompt and eager readiness for God's service.

[T. C. O'BRIEN]

FESCH, JOSEPH (1763–1839), French cardinal, remembered for his role in the troubled relationship between Napoleon and Pius VII. F. was the uncle of Napoleon and Joseph Bonaparte. Archdeacon of Ajaccio, Corsica, at the outbreak of the Revolution, he took the oath of obedience to the *Civil Constitution of the Clergy. When Catholicism was reestablished in France by the Concordat of 1801, he obtained absolution and reentered the Church. He was named abp. of Lyons (1802), made ambassador to the Holy See, and was created cardinal (1803) by Pius VII. He induced the Pope to come to Paris to crown Napoleon as French emperor (1804) and, as Grand Almoner at court, F. officiated at the marriage of Napoleon and Josephine. He tried, sometimes with success, to prevent some of the harmful effects of his nephew's religious policies. In time Napoleon became dissatisfied with him and dismissed him; thereupon F. finally took residence in and reformed his own diocese, where he became a moving force in the education of the clergy. Because of Napoleon's displeasure, the last 25 years of his life were spent in Rome; he lost jurisdiction over his diocese. He lived out his days piously and died forgotten. BIBLIOGRAPHY: S. Furlani, EncCatt 5:1210–11.

[C. BUCKLEY]

FESSLER, JOSEPH (1813–72), bp. of St. Pölten, Austria, church historian. He taught church history in the seminary of Brixen (1838–52), and then spent 10 years as a professor at the Univ. of Vienna. He was consecrated as auxiliary bp. for Vorarlberg in 1862, and became the bp. of St. Pölten 2 years later. F. served as secretary of Vatican Council I. His best-known work is *Institutiones patrologiae* (2 v., 1850–51). BIBLIOGRAPHY: F. Grass, LTK 4:95; C. Testore, EncCatt 5:1211.

[R. B. ENO]

FESTA, COSTANZO (*c.*1490–1545), reputed to be the first Italian composer of madrigals. F. is represented in the first-known printed collection of madrigals, published in 1530. His most famous madrigal is familiar in English as "Down in a Flowery Vale." During the time that the Flemings were in high positions in the field of church music, F. was the musical director at the Vatican, the only Italian of the period to hold such a post in the country. In 1553 his book of litanies and in 1554 his four-part *Magnificat* were published for double choir. Two Masses are extant in the Sistine Chapel, and many of his MSS can be found in the archives of the Pontifical Chapel. Much of his music is still sung in Rome, esp. the *Te Deum* at the election of a new pope.

[H. F. REIMER]

FESTUS, PORCIUS, Judean procurator *c.*60–62 A.D. He is known only from Josephus and the Bible. According to the former he destroyed the Sicarii and supported Agrippa II in the conflict over a wall that blocked Agrippa's view of the Temple. The NT records that F. gave a hearing to Paul, whom his predecessor Felix had left in prison (Acts 24.27–26.32). After Paul's appeal to Caesar, R. also arranged for him to be heard before King Agrippa and Bernice, the King's sister.

[T. EARLY]

FÊTE-DIEU, French name for the feast of *Corpus Christi.

FETI DOMENICO (1589–1623), Italian painter in Rome (1604–13) and court painter to Duke Ferdinando in Mantua (1613–22), then transferring to Venice. F.'s *Image of the Virgin Supported by Angels* (Baltimore) and his *Six Sainted Martyrs* series (1613) show Caravaggesque light. Rubens and Tintoretto influence the rich surface and flickering lights of *Miracle of the Loaves and Fishes* and the small *Flight into Egypt*. In a late series of parables (1618–22) F. returned to Caravaggesque genre style *(Good Samaritan)*. Venetian painting led F. to accentuate painterly qualities, lighten his palette, and fuse figures in large areas of landscape, which became dominant trends in Venetian art of the 17th century.

[M. J. DALY]

FÉTIS, FRANÇOIS JOSEPH (1784–1871), Belgian musicologist, teacher, and composer. He first learned from his father how to play the violin, pianoforte, and organ. In 1800 he entered the Paris Conservatory and 3 years later won the harmony prize. In 1806 he married Adelaide Catherine Robert, a wealthy woman, and was able to continue his studies quite comfortably until she lost her fortune in 1811. In 1806 he also began a 30-year task, an edition (still unpublished) of the plainsong of the Church. In 1813 he became the organist for the collegiate church of St. Pierre in Douai. Many of his treatises and textbooks were published, but little of his church music. Among his works are seven operas, two symphonies, three piano quintets, a piano sextet, violin sonata, sonatas and other works for the piano, and a great deal of church music, including *Messes faciles pour l'orgue* and a *Messe de requiem,* which he composed for the funeral of the Queen of the Belgians.

[H. F. REIMER]

FETISHISM. (1) Anthropology and history of religions: a term, now discarded as inaccurate, once used to classify primitive religious beliefs: first, the Portuguese *feitiço,* artefact, being the origin of the term, the belief of West African tribes in magical charms; secondly, any religious belief in a spirit world (see ANIMISM). Later study showed that religious use of material figures of men or animals involved belief in human powers to imbue them with properties to protect the user and harm enemies. (2) Abnormal psychology: a sexual obsession centering on some object, physical or fantasized, as the source and means of sexual gratification, to the exclusion of interest in normal sexual intercourse. To act on such an obsession is not to act as a moral agent, but pathologically.

[T. C. O'BRIEN]

FETTI, GIOVANNI DI FRANCESCO (fl. 1355–86), Italian sculptor and architect. F. worked on the cathedral of Florence (1355–86) and was named *capomastro* there (1377) and at the Loggia dei Lanzi (1384), where he followed drawings by Agnolo Gaddi.

[M. J. DALY]

FEUCHTMAYER, JOSEPH ANTON (1696–1770), Bavarian sculptor of a family of stuccoists in Wessobrunn. F. executed in S Germany and N Switzerland ornamental religious figures of exceptional quality, expressing an ecstatic and ethereal feeling through excited surfaces and tenuous proportions.

[M. J. DALY]

FEUDALISM, a term descriptive of the political and economic system of the early Middle Ages based on land tenure. Commencing in Europe with the early Carolingian period, it differed from country to country. Its roots are found in Roman and Germanic institutions from which two basic relationships developed, the agreement between man and man and the use of land. To accept a king or a bishop or nobleman as lord was to become his vassal. To serve the lord brought the vassal the right to till his lord's land in return for military service, a benefice. It was the Carolingians' need to strengthen their defense against the Saracens that occasioned the widespread distribution of benefices. As a rule, the holder of benefices had jurisdiction over several peasants and from the time of Charlemagne was granted "immunity" from government jurisdiction, a status Charlemagne conferred upon bishops and abbots. In recognition of the benefice's new relationship to military service, it was named "fief" and included holdings of land and authority in government in return for military service and therefore became an office that could be passed on to an eldest son. These developments led to increased attention of bishops and abbots to their temporal holdings. Kings began to control appointments to ecclesiastical benefices and eventually lay investiture resulted. Then kings began "investing" abbots and bishops with the symbols not only of their temporal power but also of their sacred office and authority. The most serious effect of this control was to lessen the central authority of the church and enhance the dominance of local political as well as spiritual authority. This is best illustrated by the ebb and flow of local supremacy in Italy and a baneful influence on the selection of popes of the 9th and 10th cent. that produced men unworthy of the office and unable to give the Church the leadership needed at this time. Nevertheless Feudalism as a political and economic system was most suited to agrarian society and prepared the way for more stable and efficient government throughout Europe. BIBLIOGRAPHY: B. Lyon, NCE 5, 901–904; C. Stephenson, *Medieval Feudalism* (1942); M. Bloch, *Feudal Society* (tr. L. A. Magnon, 1960).

[F. H. BRIGHAM]

FEUERBACH, ANSELM (1829–80), German Romantic painter in Düsseldorf and Munich, in Paris (1851–53) with Couture, influenced by Delacroix and Courbet, then in Italy. During his Italian stay, influenced by antique and Renaissance painting, F. became a leader of German Romantic painters in Rome.

[M. J. DALY]

FEUERBACH, LUDWIG ANDREAS (1804–72), German philosopher, an exponent of a naturalistic humanism. The son of a famous jurist, Paul Johann Anselm (1775–1833), F. was born at Landshut, Bavaria. He studied theology at Heidelberg, and philosophy (1825) at Berlin under G. *Hegel. His career as an instructor at the Univ. of Erlangen was terminated in 1832 because of a work in which he rejected personal immortality. The rest of his life F. devoted to study and writing. His philosophy developed out of a criticism and ultimate rejection of Hegelian idealism. For F. all of reality was material nature, of which man formed a part, his consciousness being developed in dependence upon nature. By asserting human consciousness, F. was not a pure materialist; by affirming the reality of material nature he rejected idealism. Marxist *dialectical materialism was directly influenced by his thought. F.'s application of his basic ideas to religion is summed up in his aim to replace theology with "anthropology." In such major works as *The Essence of Christianity* (1841) and *The Essence of Religion* (1845) he taught that philosophy must concentrate upon man and restore to him the qualities religion had attributed to God. Religion, including its highest form, Christianity, is evidence of man's developing consciousness of his own real essence. By religion the qualities of the human essence had been projected into a deity; F. interpreted the Christian teachings on the Incarnation and the Trinity in this manner. True religion should be a study of man which would restore to himself the essence he had projected into an imaginary God. F.'s philosophy had its influence on S. *Kierkegaard, on some modern existentialists, and is currently discussed by those advocating that theology be secularized. BIBLIOGRAPHY: W. B. Chamberlain, *Heaven Wasn't His Destination: the Philosophy of Ludwig Feuerbach* (1941); Copleston, 7:293–300.

[L. DUPRÉ]

FEUILLANTS: (1) The name of an extremely austere reformed branch of Cistercians, begun in 1577 with the reform introduced by Jean de la Barrière, abbot of the monastery of Les Feuillants, near Toulouse. The reform flourished and autonomy as an order, independent from Cîteaux, was granted in 1592 by Clement VIII. The suppression by the French Revolution brought the order to an end in 1791. A separate Italian congregation, the Reformed of St. Bernard lasted until 1802. (2) The *Club des Feuillants* was a group of monarchist Revolutionaries, separating from the Jacobins in 1792, and named from the suppressed monastery, Notre Dame des Feuillants in Paris, near the Tuileries, where they met.

[T. C. O'BRIEN]

FÉVIN, ANTOINE DE (*c.*1470–1511 or 1512), at the court of Louis XII of France, composer of sacred music patterned consciously after that of Josquin Des *Prés.

[T. C. O'BRIEN]

FEY, CLARA (1815–94), foundress, in 1844 at Aachen, of the Sisters of the *Poor Child Jesus. Her cause for beatification was introduced in 1958.

[T. C. O'BRIEN]

FIACRE, ST. (d. *c.*670). Born about the beginning of the 7th cent. in Ireland, he went to France and settled as a hermit in a place on the banks of the Marne given him by the bp. of Meaux. Clearing a patch of ground for his garden, he was sought by the natives who were curious about the Christian faith. Many came to him for spiritual guidance. He is the patron saint of gardeners and cab drivers of Paris, of the latter because an early center for renting coaches was located near the hotel Saint-Fiacre in Paris. The Parisian cabs came to be known as fiacres. BIBLIOGRAPHY: Butler 3:460–461; A. Cardinali, BiblSanct 5:668–672.

[R. T. MEYER]

FIADONI, BARTOLOMEO, see PTOLEMY OF LUCCA.

FIAT OF MARY, the response of Our Lady to the angel Gabriel in the Lucan Infancy Gospel, "Be it done [*fiat* in the Vulgate] unto me according to your word" (Lk. 1.38). The words express Mary's obedience as well as the graciousness of God who would wait for her consent before commencing the work of Redemption. Augustine places great importance on Mary's consent; by it Mary conceived Christ first in faith, and only then in the flesh. Mary would have gained nothing from her physical and maternal nearness to Christ if she had not first and in a better way conceived Christ in her heart (*De virginitate* 3). Aquinas holds that the Virgin's consent stood for the consent of all mankind, and through it a kind of spiritual marriage took place between the Son of God and human nature (ThAq ST 3a, 30.1). Vat II ConstChurch (56) notes that by consenting to Gabriel's message, Mary became the mother of Jesus and manifested her complete acceptance of God's saving will for mankind. BIBLIOGRAPHY: S. Garofalo, *Mary in the Bible* (tr. T. J. Tobin, 1961); D. F. Hickey, NCE 9:906.

[T. R. HEATH]

FICHTE, JOHANN GOTTLIEB (1762–1814), German philosopher, professor at Jena and the newly founded Univ. of Berlin. F.'s philosophical system is variously described as idealistic pantheism, ethical idealism, and (his own phrase) transcendental egotism. Spinoza bulks large in F.'s early thought, but Kant is the strongest influence on him. Indeed, F.'s later work is directed to supplying a philosophy of religion to complete Kant's system. God, though infinite, is impersonal, and each man is but one of the manifold aspects of God, who is the total consciousness or the universal noumenal Ego. Thus the fundamental rule of human morality is that our life be the development and outward manifestation of God. A rigorous moralist in personal life and in theory, F. develops Kant's categorical imperative to its logical limits: Man knows and expresses himself most perfectly in freely doing his duty: "If I ought, I can." BIBLIOGRAPHY: Copleston 7:32–93; G. Von Molnar, *Novalis' Fichte Studies: the Foundation of His Aesthetics* (1970).

[W. B. MAHONEY]

FICINO, MARSILIO (1433–99), Florentine humanist philosopher. His patron Cosimo de'*Medici put him under the tutelage of Gemistos *Plethon to master Greek, and made him first director of the Platonic Academy (1459). By 1477 F. had translated all of Plato's dialogues into Latin (pr. ed., 1483–84); he also made Latin translations of Plotinus, Porphyry, and Pseudo-Dionysius. He was ordained priest in 1473. His original writings include: *Theologia platonica de immortalitate animae* (1474); *De christiana religione* (pr. ed. 1476); *De amore,* a commentary on Plato's *Symposium* (pr. ed. 1484); and from his preaching, NT commentaries. F.'s effort to overcome deficiencies in scholasticism by a return to Plato has been interpreted as an evidence of the Renaissance return to antiquity; yet scholastic thought patterns run through his writings. He did adopt a Neo-Platonic hierarchic view of the universe, and was convinced of the complete harmony between Platonic philosophy and Christian religion. The apologetic purpose of *De christiana religione* was to refute the Averroism of the Latin Aristotelians. His *De amore* inspired Renaissance literature; the grace and learning of his works gave them wide influence on Renaissance philosophers, and the *Cambridge Platonists. BIBLIOGRAPHY: P. C. Kristeller, *Philosophy of Marsilio Ficino* (tr. V. Conant, 1943); *idem,* "The Scholastic Background of Marsilio Ficino, with an Edition of Unpublished Texts," *Traditio* (1944) 257–318.

[T. C. O'BRIEN]

FICTA MUSICA, see MUSICA FICTA.

FIDEISM (Lat. *fides,* faith), the tendency to underestimate the powers of reason and overload the burden of faith in getting to philosophical, moral, and religious truths. In an extreme form, fideism is the systematic disparagement of scientific discourse and exclusive reliance on belief and affectivity. It is a perennial position in the history of Christian thought. It was advanced in the Middle Ages by holders of the "double truth theory," represented by the hardheaded thinker *William of Ockham, who taught that only by faith can we be certain about God's existence, the immortality of the soul, and the moral law, and was prominent in the reaction of *traditionalism to 18th-cent. rationalism, subjectivism, and skepticism. All the same we should proceed with caution. "Fideist, a nonce-word," the *Oxford Dictionary* declares briskly, and justly, for in truth it has been thrown about too freely, thus at such thinkers as S. Kierkegaard (d. 1855), A. Gratry (d. 1872), and A. Bonnetty (d. 1879). It is better to reserve it to controversies in the last decades of the 19th cent. and the first decade of the 20th. There it crops up in French Protestant and Catholic circles, in each case with a different emphasis. E. Ménégoz stressed the necessity of *sola fides,* faith alone, "faith" as going to God himself, not to credal statements, "alone" as being independent of the arguments of liberal Protestantism; A. Sabatier was in agreement with him (see SYMBOLOFIDEISM). Among Catholics part of the modernist controversy was about the strength of the assent that can be given to the objective grounds of rational credibility, the *preambula fidei,* on which Vatican Council I (see D 3008–09, 3026, 3033–34) had taken so firm a stand: the so-called fideists were those accused of reducing the preambles of faith to imperatives from subjective experience or inspiration. BIBLIOGRAPHY: E. Doumergue, *Le Dernier mot du fidéisme* (1907); R. Aubert, *Le Problème de l'acte de foi* (3d ed., 1958).

[T. GILBY]

FIDELIS OF SIGMARINGEN, ST. (1578–1622), German Capuchin and martyr. He was born Mark Roy of a distinguished family at Sigmaringen in Swabia. Educated at Freiburg im Breisgau, he earned doctorates in philosophy (1603) and in canon and civil law (1611). From 1604 to 1610, F. traveled through France, Spain, and Italy tutoring the children of nobility. After practicing law in Esisheim, he took holy orders and entered the Capuchins in Freiburg (1612). F. studied theology at Constance and Frauenfeld and in 1617 began preaching at Altdorf. As a member of a preaching band under the Congregation for the Propagation of the Faith, he was successful in the Rhaetian Alps in converting important leaders among the Grisons, who had turned to Protestantism and were revolting against Austria. But he went to Seewis and there was seized and slain. Canonized in 1746, F. has been named patron of lawyers and is called the protomartyr of the Congregation of the Propagation of the Faith. BIBLIOGRAPHY: Butler 2:156–157; M. da Alatri, BiblSanct 5:521–524.

[R. A. TODD]

FIDELITY, the honoring of commitments, esp. of *promises. In Roman usage one meaning of *fidelitas* was an attitude of honorableness towards outsiders as distinct from the *pietas* owed to family and country. *Fidelitas* also had the more general sense of keeping one's word. St. Thomas Aquinas classifies the *fides* or fidelity mentioned by Cicero (*De republica* 4,7) as an aspect of the virtue of truthfulness *(veritas; veracitas),* and defines it as the keeping of promises (ThAq ST 2a2ae, 80.1). As such, fidelity is concerned with honoring, not a strict contractual obligation *(debitum legale),* as commutative justice does, but a debt in honor *(debitum morale).* Such a debt is owed both to oneself out of self-respect, and to others in interactions that, while not calculable exactly, call for respect and trustworthiness as indispensable for decent, humane social living (ThAq ST 2a2ae,109.3 ad 1). Truthfulness respects the debt of speaking and acting sincerely, in keeping with one's true self and thoughts. Fidelity respects the debt assumed by one who makes a simple promise, namely, to live up to it. Thus it requires good faith in the making of a promise, and reliability in carrying it out. In a serious matter a simple promise imposes a serious obligation to faithfulness, even though neither a contract nor an oath is involved. BIBLIOGRAPHY: ThAq Lat-Eng (v. 41, ed. T. C. O'Brien) app. 1, "Legal Debt, Moral Debt."

[T. C. O'BRIEN]

FIDES DAMASI (Lat., faith of Damasus), a confession of faith at one time attributed to Pope St. Damasus I (d. 384), or to St. Jerome, his contemporary. The creed (D 71–72) originated toward the end of the 5th cent. and has two parts, the first dealing with Trinitarian theology, the second with Christology and soteriology.

[E. A. WEIS]

FIDES IMPLICITA, a belief in more specific articles of faith implied in a belief in more general truths. *Faith is essentially a holding fast to God's word, and thereby to what God proposes for belief. The two primary matters of belief are God's being and his providence (Heb 11.6). Belief in these is the implicit acceptance of all that God reveals of himself and his saving ways. As revelation gradually unfolded to disclose the mysteries of Incarnation and Redemption, the faith of the simple, uninstructed is implicit with regard to such mysteries in comparison to the more informed, explicit belief of their leaders, both in the OT and the NT. In the case of the nonbeliever, an implicit faith may be understood in the following of right conscience that puts the nonbeliever in a true relationship to God; whatever the conscious content of the relationship, it is in fact the acceptance of the actual ways of God's salvation. BIBLIOGRAPHY: ThAq ST 2a2ae, 2.5–8.

[T. C. O'BRIEN]

FIDES QUAERENS INTELLECTUM, literally, faith seeking understanding. St. Anselm of Canterbury first intended to use this expression as the title of a work for which it now often appears as the subtitle, namely, *Proslogium sive fides quaerens intellectum*. The remote inspiration for the phrase derives from St. Augustine, of whom Anselm was an ardent disciple. In Augustine's view: (1) reason has a value of its own, independently of the help it gives to faith; (2) reason can lead to faith; and (3) after the act of faith has been made, reason is of great value in helping to an understanding of what is believed by faith. In his *Sermon 43*, Augustine comments on Is 7.9 *(nisi credideritis non intelligetis*, a faulty reading of the LXX) and concludes: *Ergo intellige ut credas; crede ut intelligas* (PL 38:257–258). BIBLIOGRAPHY: G. Söhngen, LTK 4:119–120.

[E. A. MAZIARZ]

FIDES, ST., see FOY, ST.

FIELD PREACHING, a characteristic of early Methodism; preaching out-of-doors, wherever large crowds could easily gather. It was begun by George *Whitefield in 1739, when, finding many of the churches closed to him, he preached to about 200 colliers on Kingswood Hill near Bristol. John *Wesley at first opposed field preaching; but seeing the good results of Whitefield's work and finding a precedent in the life of Jesus, particularly in the Sermon on the Mount, he joined in at Kingswood. Soon he enthusiastically urged field preaching by Methodists everywhere and felt that Methodism would lose its power when it gave up preaching out-of-doors. The *camp meeting was a development in keeping with the tradition of field preaching. BIBLIOGRAPHY: J. Dawson, *John Wesley on Preaching* (1903) 149–162; R. M. Cameron, *Rise of Methodism: A Source Book* (1954).

[F. E. MASER]

FIESOLE, GIOVANNI DA, see ANGELICO, FRA.

FIFTH MONARCHY MEN (Quint Monarchy Men), a fanatical sect that, during the Puritan revolution in England, sought to establish a theocracy. They professed a form of *millenarianism, namely, that the fifth monarchy (Dt 2.44; the other four were the Assyrian, Persian, Greek, and Roman) was at hand; Christ with his saints would come to rule for 1,000 years. When Oliver *Cromwell and then the Restoration disappointed their hopes for rule by the godly (themselves), they rose in armed revolt (1657, 1661). Their leaders were beheaded and the sect was dissolved. BIBLIOGRAPHY: W. C. Braithwaite, *Beginnings of Quakerism* (2d ed., 1955) 18–19; L. F. Brown, *Political Activities of the Baptists and Fifth Monarchy Men in England during the Interregnum* (1911, repr. 1964).

[T. C. O'BRIEN]

FIGGIS, JOHN NEVILLE (1866–1919), Anglican historian and theologian. Born of a Methodist family, F. studied at Cambridge where he became an Anglican. After ordination in 1894, he lectured at Cambridge (1896–1902) and spent some years in the pastoral ministry before entering (1907) the Community of the Resurrection, an Anglican religious congregation. While he wrote books of apologetics as well, his studies of political theory have proved more durable, e.g., his *The Divine Right of Kings* (1896) and *From Gerson to Grotius* (1907).

[R. B. ENO]

FIGINI and POLLINI, 20th-cent. Italian architectural firm, among the first to work in Italy in the contemporary mode. The firm designed the main plant and complex of the *avant-garde* Olivetti Company in Ivrea (1939–42) and the Church of the Madonna of the Poor in Milan (1952).

[M. J. DALY]

FIGLIUCCI, FELIX (*c.*1525–*c.*1590), Italian humanist who joined the Dominican Order at Florence in 1551. Under his religious name, Alessio, he published by commission of Pius V, the Italian translation of the Catechism of the Council of Trent, *Catechismo cioè Istruzione secondo il decreto del Concilio di Trento* (1567). BIBLIOGRAPHY: Quétif-Échard 2.1:263–264.

[T. C. O'BRIEN]

FIGURATIVE SENSE OF SCRIPTURE, another term for the typological sense. This is the sense borne by the things, persons, events, customs or institutions signified by the actual words of Scripture. For these realities are endowed by God, the principal author of Scripture, with an intrinsic "eloquence" or meaning of their own as foreshadowing and pointing on to Christ and his Church. Thus the crossing of the Red Sea in Exodus is a type or figure of Christian baptism. The objective basis for this is the fact that these realities spoken of in the OT have a function in God's plan for the salvation of mankind, which culminated in Christ. The whole plan and all its elements are conditioned by the figure of Christ himself as the goal to which it all tends. Consequently at any given stage this intrinsic relationship between the elements involved at that stage and the final goal to which all tend and point may become clear to the reader. The fact that the figurative or typological interpretation has often been abused and pressed to extravagant lengths has brought it into discredit. Nevertheless Christian tradition from the 3d cent. attests the real and long-standing value of this method of interpretation when rightly applied. *TYPOLOGY.

[D. J. BOURKE]

FIGURED BASS, also called *basso continuo*, or thorough-bass. The bass line in the composition has figures above or below the notes to designate the chords and intervals to be played. The year 1587 shows the earliest-known use of this in a 40-part motet *Ecce beatam lucem* by Striggio; in 1594 an eight-part motet for double choir with organ accompaniment was written by Croce; in 1600 there were many motets written in this manner; and in 1610 appeared an edition of Masses by Palestrina for four and five voices with a figured bass for the organ with the soprano printed above it. This manner of composition was used in many oratorios and settings of the Passion. The church organists in England were the last to drop this type of playing.

[H. F. REIMER]

FIGURED CHORALE, a chorale embellished or ornamented in the accompaniment by using notes of faster tempo than the soprano part. There is a type of organ chorale in which a certain figure is consistently used in one or more of the inner voices or contrapuntal parts, against the plain notes of the upper voice, called the soprano. An example of this is Bach's *Orgelbuchlein,* esp. "Ich ruf zu dir."

[H. F. REIMER]

FIGURED MUSIC, a melodic line which has been embellished or ornamented with different figures, either harmonically or rhythmically, to emphasize the melody line.

FIGURISM, system of biblical interpretation invented by the Jansenist Jean-Baptiste de Sesne. Basically it asserts that a whole series of senses can be found in the words of Scripture, up to five or six or even more, over and above the immediate and obvious one (see SENSES OF SCRIPTURE). Thus all the individual figures, episodes, and actions recorded in the OT are types of corresponding figures, episodes, and actions in the New. Finally all symbols, metaphors, and images that are used in both Testaments have a figurative sense that makes them applicable to the life of the Church. In practice this means that not only the past history of the Church but its present and future situation also are found prefigured in Scripture. The system found little favor and was decisively refuted. BIBLIOGRAPHY: E. Mangenot, DTC 5:2299–2304.

[D. J. BOURKE]

FIJI ISLANDS, a British colony consisting of many hundreds of small islands (7,036 sq mi; pop. [1966] 483,247). The Fijis, which form part of *Melanesia, were discovered in 1643 by the Dutch navigator Tasman and were explored by Capt. James Cook in 1774. A native chieftain ceded them to Great Britain in 1784. Since 1970 Fiji has been an independent member of the British Commonwealth. Almost half of the inhabitants are immigrants from *India, mainly Muslims and Hindus. The Fijis were evangelized by French Marists in 1844, but the mission was temporarily abandoned in 1856. A prefecture apostolic was formed in 1863 and a vicariate in 1887. The famous leprosarium at Makogai was opened in 1911. In 1976 native Catholics numbered about 47,000. Protestant denominations in the Fijis include the London Missionary Society, Methodists, Anglicans, Presbyterians, Adventists, and Assemblies of God. BIBLIOGRAPHY: A. Burns, *Fiji* (1963); *Bilan du Monde* 2:366–368.

[M. J. SUELZER]

FILARET (Philaret; Drozdov, Vasilii Mikhailovich; 1782–1867), Metropolitan of Moscow. He took the name Filaret when he became a monk (1808). He was professor and rector at the Ecclesiastical Academy of St. Petersburg, and already renowned as a preacher when he was made a bp. in 1812. He was chosen for the Holy Synod and made abp. of Tver in 1819; of Yaroslav in 1890, and of Moscow in 1821. He was installed as metropolitan of Moscow in 1826. As metropolitan F. was devoted to preaching, the formation of the clergy, and the instruction of the faithful. During much of his tenure he was regarded as the final arbiter in theological, scriptural, and canonical questions. (See his *Comparison of the Differences in the Doctrines of Faith between the Eastern and Western Churches,* tr. R. Pinkerton, 1974.) He was also deeply involved in Church-

State relations and is said to have drafted the document of Alexander II emancipating the serfs (1861). He strove to win back the Old Believers and the Ukrainian Uniates into the Russian Church. His efforts to have the Bible translated into Russian met with eventual success, after much opposition. F. was trained in, and he himself taught, the Protestantized Russian theology that had begun under F. *Prokopovich. The *Catechism of Filaret, his principal work, however, was edited in its final form as part of the counteraction to the Prokopovian theology.

[T. C. O'BRIEN]

FILASTER, ST. (Philaster; d. *c.*397), bp. of Brescia. Probably a Spaniard, F. traveled about preaching against heretics. At Milan he became acquainted with SS. Ambrose and Augustine (*c.*384). His travels ceased when he became a bp., and he settled down to his pastoral duties in Brescia. He published a catalogue in which he listed 128 heresies (PL 12:1111–1302), but some of them were simply opinions on disputed matters at variance with his own. The work has its value for reconstructing the lost *Syntagma* of *Hippolytus from which it appears to have drawn much of its material. BIBLIOGRAPHY: Altaner 432; Butler 3:138–139.

FILIATION, the relation of the Second Person of the *Trinity to the Father as a result of the *generation of the Word. There are four Trinitarian *relations, i.e., the ordering of one person to another. Filiation expresses the relationship or order of the Son to Father because the Son is generated; *paternity expresses the relationship of the Father to the Son whom he generates. The notion is a speculative precision and is not contained in Scripture. The basis for its development is, however, clearly found in the NT where Jesus is proclaimed as the only Son of the Father (Jn 3.16); the eternal Word (Jn 1.1); the messianic *Son of Man; the *image of the invisible God (Col 1.15); and the Son of God in power (Rom 1.4). The Christological heresies of the first 5 cent. of the Christian era generally revolved around an adequate understanding of filiation (see ARIANISM; SUBORDINATIONISM; SABELLIANISM; and NESTORIANISM). The preliminary settlement at the Council of *Chalcedon (451) received a much more precise formulation during the scholastic period. According to Thomas Aquinas, this relation is best understood by analogy with the human production of a mental word or concept. The Father, contemplating the divine essence from all eternity, generates a concept which is the perfect expression of that essence. This perfect expression or Word is eternal, divine, and yet really distinct from the Father. BIBLIOGRAPHY: B. J. F. Lonergan, *De Deo Trino* (1961); L. J. McGovern, NCE 5:912–913; bibliog. for *TRINITY. *GENERATION OF THE WORD.

[T. M. MCFADDEN]

FILIOQUE, an addition to the article on the Holy Spirit in the Latin text of the *Nicene Creed. The whole phrase, *qui ex Patre Filioque procedit,* in virtue of the addition affirms the double *procession of the Holy Spirit, i.e., from both Father and Son. Historically the addition probably originates from credal formulas in 5th-cent. Spain (see D 188; also 490). Insertion of filioque into the Creed began in the liturgy, esp. in the empire of Charlemagne. At Rome the practice was first resisted, out of concern for the Greek Church, notably by Pope Leo III; in 809–810 he had the original form of the Creed, engraved in Greek and Latin on two silver tablets, placed at St. Peter's tomb. Liturgical use of the filioque did not stop, however, and *c.*1013 the addition was accepted at Rome, probably at the urging of Emperor Henry II. The accusation by *Photius in 867 that Rome had changed authoritative doctrine by use of the filioque became the fixed Eastern position in the definitive break of 1054. Eastern rejection of the filioque was based chiefly on the prohibition by the Council of Ephesus of any addition to the Nicene Creed (D 265). Theological grounds for the rejection of double precession involved its being inconsistent with the ancient Greek idea of monarchy in the Trinity, i.e., that there is but one Who is principle *(archē)* in the godhead, the Father. The preferred formula for the Greek Church was that the Holy Spirit proceeds from the Father through the Son. The Greeks attending the briefly successful reunion Councils of *Lyons (1274, D 850) and Florence (1439, D 1300) accepted the concept of double procession, but were not held to include filioque in the Creed. In the controversies between the Latin and the Eastern Churches the filioque became a symbol of the substantive issue, the meaning and seat of authority in the Church. Eastern Churches in union with Rome are not obliged to use the filioque in their versions of the Creed. BIBLIOGRAPHY: J. Gill, NCE 5:913–914.

[T. C. O'BRIEN]

FILIPPINI, LUCY, ST. (1672–1732), a foundress of the Pontifical Institute of the Religious Teachers Filippini. Even at an early age F. showed remarkable gifts which brought her to the attention of the Card. M. *Barbarigo, bp. of Montefiascone in Tuscany. He persuaded her to come to join in the work of educating young women as teachers. She was a master teacher combining great spirituality with courage and common sense. In an era when the education of women was not widespread, the center at Montefiascone was a phenomenon and it soon spread to many other areas. The Cardinal formally established the religious institute in his diocese in 1704. Clement XI in 1707 invited F. to found a similar school in Rome. Here she established the first school of *Maestre Pie* where she was a powerful educational influence on children who called her "Maestra Santa" (the holy schoolmistress). Her career was cut short by illness when she was in her middle 50s. She was canonized in 1930. BIBLIOGRAPHY: F. de Simone, *La B. Lucia Filippini* (1926).

[J. R. AHERNE]

FILIPPO DA VERONA (fl. 1509–15), Italian painter of the signed frescoes at S. Antonio, Padua, Madonnas in Bergamo, Fabriano, and Turin; and of a *St. Jerome* (London) showing influence of Bellini, Carpaccio and Raphael.

[M. J. DALY]

FILIPPUCCI, ALESSANDRO FRANCESCO SAVERIO (1632–92), Italian Jesuit missionary. He entered the Society in 1651. In 1660, F. departed for China where he became novice master and professor of literature at Macao (1663–71). He began parish work in Kwantung Province (1671), served as provincial for Japan (1680–83), and was superior in Canton (1683–88). F. wrote a work defending the Jesuits in the *Chinese Rites Controversy and also collected the letters of St. Francis Xavier. BIBLIOGRAPHY: DE 1:1118; E. Lamelle, EncCatt 5:1331.

[R. A. TODD]

FILLION, LOUIS CLAUDE (1843–1927), French Sulpician biblical scholar. F. taught at Reims (1871–74), Lyons (1874–93), and the Institut Catholique of Paris (1893–1906); was a consultor to the *Pontifical Biblical Commission and pursued a life of study in the seminary at Issy from 1906. He published nearly 40 books and numerous articles, which were generally of conservative scholarship, often attacking the conclusions of rationalist biblical studies. BIBLIOGRAPHY: A. Robert, DBSuppl 3:274–276.

[T. M. MCFADDEN]

FILLMORE, MYRTLE (1845–1931), and **CHARLES** (1854–1948), founders of the *Unity School of Christianity. They were married in 1881. While promoting real estate in Colorado and later in Kansas City, Mo., they took *New Thought courses and were influenced by Emma Curtis Hopkins. In 1889 they began *Modern Thought* magazine, which became *Unity* in 1891. The Unity School of Practical Christianity developed from the magazine, chartered as a local Kansas City association in 1903 and as a denomination in 1914. Charles Fillmore, a prolific writer on religious subjects, published *The Twelve Powers of Man* (1896), *Jesus Christ Heals* (1914), and *Prosperity* (1928), besides editing a half-dozen periodicals on Unity. Originally Methodists, the Fillmores combined traditional Christianity with belief in reincarnation, eternal life in the body, the conquest of disease by mind, and other insights drawn from New Thought sources. BIBLIOGRAPHY: H. D'Andrade, *Charles Fillmore: Herald of the New Age* (1974).

[R. K. MACMASTER]

FILM AND BROADCASTING, OFFICE FOR (OFB), a branch of the Department of Communication of the U.S. Catholic Conference. It developed from the consolidation (1972) of the National Catholic Office for Radio and Television and the National Catholic Office for Motion Pictures. The agency has two aims: through the development of the potential of the media and its utilization, to contribute to human understanding and progress, and to communicate the gospel. It supports and cooperates with diocesan communication offices throughout the U.S., and provides film and broadcasting information, evaluation of films, educational programs, and training. Its publications are *Share,* a biweekly giving religious film and broadcasting information; *Film and TV Review Service,* a weekly; *Catholic Film Newsletter,* a semimonthly; monographs issued irregularly. The organization serves as liaison between film and broadcasting industries, national media, religious organizations, and the Church. It is a member of the international Catholic organizations for film (OCIC) and broadcasting (UNDA) and has its headquarters in New York City. BIBLIOGRAPHY: *1977 Catholic Almanac* 680.

[R. A. TODD]

FIN DE SIÈCLE, "end of century" in art denotes a period at the end of the 19th cent. characterized by styles of enervation and private reverie, the decorative eroticism of Art Nouveau, the opulence of Gustave Moreau, the mysticism of the Rose Croix movement.

[M. J. DALY]

FINAL CAUSE, the *end, purpose, or goal of a being or an activity. It is described as the cause of causes, since its influence on the *efficient cause of an effect prompts the activity that brings together the *material and *formal causes that make up the effect. Paralleling the distinction of *principal causes into primary and secondary, final causes may be ultimate or penultimate. In all cases the final cause is a good, real or fancied, and its causality the attraction of the good upon appetite, whether natural or cognitive (see FINALITY, PRINCIPLE OF). In moral theology the relationship between end and moral agent is a fundamental criterion and determinant of moral good or evil.

[T. C. O'BRIEN]

FINAL PERSEVERANCE, see PERSEVERANCE, FINAL.

FINALITY, PRINCIPLE OF, the philosophical axiom that every being connaturally retains or tends towards its own completeness or full good (ThAq ST 1a, 19.1); also enunciated as "everything that acts, acts for an end." It is termed a principle because of its use in arguing to conclusions deriving from it. But it is based on the finalism or finality intrinsic to being. That is the force of the metaphysical position that goodness is a transcendental property of being; that "being" and "good" are convertible terms. Even as each being cannot contain its own contradiction, i.e., is definitely itself and not its own opposite (principle of noncontradiction), so a being "wants" to be itself and fully itself. That full being, completeness, is its good and its end. In every reality other than God there is a real distinction between the being as substance, between simply being, and the being as complete, the being as fully good. The second is thus an end to be reached (*ibid.* 1a, 5.1 ad 1; 6.3). The tendency towards end, described under the general term activity, is for the sake of an end not possessed but to be reached: the pull or attraction of the good as end is finality as causality (*ibid.* 5.4). Because the good or end is rooted in what the being is, there is a determinable proportion between the thing acting and the end for which it acts (*ibid.* 1a2ae, 109.6). The responsiveness towards end is radically identified with the very being of each thing. In nonknowing beings it is termed natural appetite; in knowing beings the natural appetite is expressed in an appetite following upon knowledge; the emotions following on sensory knowledge; the will following on intellective knowledge (*ibid.* 1a, 80. 1 & 2). As a principle for philosophic argumentation finality functions to explain a pattern to be expected in nature: not everything is a matter of *chance; and also a pattern of order in the universe wherein the particular levels of finality fit into a universal order and are related to a final, universal end proportioned to the first agent, God as governing all (*ibid.* 1a, 103.1–3). In moral philosophy and theology the principle of finality is the basis for normative judgments. To the reasoning being the end is perceivable as measuring, requiring certain acts for its attainment; an act is judged morally good or bad, so right or wrong, worthy of praise or blame accordingly as it measures up or fails to measure up to what the true good and end requires (*ibid.* 1a, 63.1; 1a2ae, 18.1).

[T. C. O'BRIEN]

FINÁN OF LINDISFARNE, ST. (d. 661), Irish monk, second bp. of Lindisfarne in Northumbria who led an austere life as a monk in the Abbey at Iona. Later he became bp. of Lindisfarne, upon the death of St. Aidan (651). During his episcopate of ten years, F. brought many souls into the faith, particularly two rulers: Sigebert I, King of the East Saxons (fl. 616–626) and Peada, King of Mercia (*c.* 656). He consecrated St. Cedd bp. of the East Saxons and Diuma bp. of the middle English. On Holy Isle off the coast of Northumbria, F. built a wooden church, after the Celtic style, with a thatched roof of sea-grass. His feast is observed in Great Britain and Ireland.

[R. A. TODD]

FINCK, HEINRICH (*c.* 1444–1527), Bavarian composer of polyphony, Cracow, Württemberg, and Vienna. He composed both secular and sacred music in contrapuntal style, gradually developing a technique of more gentle harmony. Among his sacred compositions are a Mass for six voices and a setting for five voices, "Christ ist erstanden". A collection of his works was published posthumously in 1536. BIBLIOGRAPHY: Grove DMM 3:111–112.

[T. C. O'BRIEN]

FINIGUERRA, MASO (Tommaso; 1426–64), Italian goldsmith, engraver, intarsia designer, "master of niello." He was probably assistant to Ghiberti on the E door of the baptistery, Florence and his *Creation* and *Crucifixion* show Ghiberti's influence. There are relations with Fra Filippo Lippi and a collaboration with Antonio del Pollaiuolo evidenced by a Crucifixion and Coronation of the Virgin, engraved by F. from incisive, vigorous designs of Pollaiuolo. F. designed 5 intarsia panels in the sacristy of the Florence cathedral under Giuliano da Maiano, a *Presentation of Christ* and *St. Zenobius* of Baldovinetti stiffness, and lively *Annunciation, Amos,* and *Isaiah* panels in the style of Pollaiuolo. F. produced some of the first engravings on copper and a *Florentine Picture Chronicle* or biblical history of the world which is a source of 15th-cent. motifs.

[M. J. DALY]

FINIS OPERIS AND FINIS OPERANTIS, terms used in scholastic theology and philosophy to distinguish the proposed immediate issue of an action or an operation *(finis operis)* from the ulterior purpose the agent may have in mind in causing that issue to result *(finis operantis).* Thus in the act of painting the *finis operis* is the planned disposition of paint on canvas; the *finis operantis* is (let us say) the prize the artist hopes to win by his painting, or the money he expects to gain by its sale. Sometimes, esp. by moralists, the *finis operis* is called the object or physical end of the action or operation, and the *finis operantis* the moral end, or even simply the end, of the action. The *finis operis* and the *finis operantis* in any given action may or may not coincide. In the above example they do not: the object *(finis operis)* is one thing; the end *(finis operantis)* is quite another. But if the artist paints strictly to produce a work of art, unmoved by ulterior purpose, *finis operis* and *finis operantis* are identical. BIBLIOGRAPHY: A. Chollet, DTC 2:2014–39; B. M. Ashley, NCE 5:915–919; P. J. Donnelly, "St. Thomas and the Ultimate Purpose of Creation," ThST 2 (1941) 53–83; "The Vatican Council and the End of Creation," *ibid.* 4 (1943) 3–33.

[P. K. MEAGHER]

FINK, LOUIS MARY (1834–1904), first bp. of Leavenworth, Kansas. A Bavarian, he emigrated to the U.S. entered the Benedictine Order and was ordained in 1857. He was named coadjutor bp. of Kansas and the Indian Territory in 1871. When the vicar apostolic resigned Fink succeeded and became first bp. of the newly created diocese of Leavenworth. He established mission centers into which Catholic immigrants were recruited, and for which he provided a resident priest and a parochial school. With the increasing industrialization of the cities he turned his attention to urban problems. He worked for the unionization of labor and against Sunday work.

[J. R. AHERNE]

FINLAND, predominantly Lutheran republic of Scandinavia; capital, Helsinki. By the 8th cent. Finns moving N had settled S Finland, pushing the nomadic Lapps up into Lapland. Christian missionaries began work in the area during the 11th cent. About 1160 St. Henry, an English bp. of Uppsala who became known as the apostle and patron saint of Finland, accompanied the Swedish king, St. Eric, to Finland and suffered martyrdom there. Another Englishman, Thomas (d. 1248), became the first bp. of Finland—at Turku, the capital till 1812 and still seat of Finnish archbishops. Sweden completed the conquest of Finland in the 13th cent., and retained control until it was taken by Russia. The educated classes spoke Swedish until the 19th cent. With backing from Sweden's King Gustavus I, the Reformation was extended to Finland, but gradually and without severe disruption. Lutheranism was introduced in 1523 by P. Sarkilax (d. 1530), who had studied at Wittenberg. Another prominent Reformer was M. Agricola (1512–57), who published a Finnish translation of the NT (1548) and other writings that earned him the title "Father of Finnish Literature." The Augsburg Confession was introduced in 1593, and Catholicism prohibited in 1595. The Catholic Church became legal again in 1781, but has remained small. As a result of Russian influence in its historical development, Finland also has a small Orthodox Church. Though enjoying considerable autonomy, Finland was under Russian rule from 1809 until it declared independence in 1917.

[T. EARLY]

FINN, FRANCIS JAMES (1859–1928), a native of St. Louis, Mo., who became a Jesuit (1879), was active in educational and parochial work, and between the years 1889 and 1927 wrote 25 books for boys. These stories were widely read by Catholic youth in the first quarter of the 20th century and were translated into many other languages. BIBLIOGRAPHY: D. M. O'Connor, *America* 40:132–133.

FINNEY, CHARLES GRANDISON (1792–1875), evangelist and theologian of the *Oberlin theology. F. was born in Warren, Conn., and grew up in central New York state. After his conversion in 1821, he gave up the practice of law and became a revivalist in upstate New York; later, as his reputation spread, he expanded his efforts to the larger cities of New York, New England, and England. His style of evangelism, which was referred to as "new measures" and included the use of the *anxious bench, was successful, but was criticized for its emotional effects. At first a Presbyterian, he later became a Congregationalist and assumed the pastorate of the Broadway Tabernacle, which had been built for him, in New York City. In 1835 he was called to the Oberlin Collegiate Institute as professor of theology. Although lacking and mistrusting formal theological training, he proved to be a powerful instructor. In 1837 he became pastor of the First Church in Oberlin; he was president of Oberlin College from 1851 to 1966. Influenced by the *New England theology, his views nevertheless reflected the Oberlin theology. He rejected the determination of the will and the imputation of guilt, while holding to human depravity; man (he taught) can freely respond to the claim of the divine will and embrace the aim of moral perfectionism. The will is either completely virtuous, fastening upon the good of Being in General (see EDWARDS, JONATHAN), or wholly sinful in its actions. F.'s influence as an evangelist and his sympathy for antislavery views won the support of wealthy sponsors for the struggling Oberlin institution. Mainly through his writings he influenced the establishment of the YMCA in London. BIBLIOGRAPHY: C. G. Finney, *Autobiography* (1876–1975); G. F. Wright, *Charles Grandison Finney* (1891); W. G. McLoughlin, Jr., *Modern Revivalism* (1959).

[C. A. HOLBROOK]

FINNIAN, ST. (6th cent.), bishop. Born in Leinster, F. went to Wales for his education. Returning to Ireland he founded monasteries and schools. He became bp. of Clonard and worked miracles, restoring many to health of body and soul; he is famous as "teacher of the saints of Ireland." BIBLIOGRAPHY: Butler 4:544–545; I. Cechetti, BiblSanct 5:832–833.

[R. T. MEYER]

FINNO-UGRIC RELIGION, the religion of the Finno-Ugric peoples. This family of languages, embracing Magyars, Finns, Estonians, and several smaller nations now living chiefly in the U.S.S.R., is scattered over an area as diverse as the Baltic and the Danube, the Arctic Ocean and Siberia. Some have been Christians for centuries and contributed significantly to the history and development of Roman Catholicism, Greek Orthodoxy, and Protestantism; others were baptized late or not at all. Though they speak an agglutinative language unrelated to the Indo-European family of languages, through distant kinship or cultural ties they have influenced—or been influenced by—every major ethnic group in Asia and Europe. Yet, in spite of its importance, there is no reliable and comprehensive study of Finno-Ugric religion in English. Uno Holmberg's book, volume 4 of *The Mythology of All Races* (1927), fills the need only in part, but it is valuable because of its mass of data on the Siberian tribes and its bibliography. The classical works by Castrén, Reguly, Munkácsi, Karjalainen, etc., are available chiefly in Finnish, Hungarian, German, and Russian. One important source available in English is the Finnish national epic, *The Kalevala,* a classic of world literature, introducing the culture-heroes Väinemöinen and Ilmarinen, and containing important myths of creation, redemption, the origin of poetry, agriculture, metalworking, etc. Largely untranslated are the tens of thousands of folksongs, magic songs, and children's games. These help to push back the historical perspectives by centuries, often millennia. Folk poetry reveals what historical accidents and religious persecutions obscured and destroyed. In such a reconstruction it appears that the High God (Ukko) was replaced by, and perhaps amalgamated with, the sky god (Jumala, Jumo, Ilmari) or the Thundergod, Tūrem, Tōrem, "father Tur" (Tar Tuuri). According to M. Agricola (d.

1557) he conferred victory in war; his Magyar name is Hadur or Haddur, ''lord of hosts,'' whose emblem, a lion-headed eagle, is called *turul*. He may be identical with the Near Eastern war and thunder god Haddu. *Ilma* and *Jumo* both mean ''sky'' or ''heaven''; *Tūrem* means ''sky, air, world.'' His daughter Ilmatar, ''Daughter of Heaven'' and Creatress, resembles the Sumerian Inanna, the ''Happy Lady.'' The chief Magyar holidays in her honor are called feasts of the ''boldogasszony,'' ''Happy Lady'' or ''Blessed Lady,'' now Marian feasts. There seems to have been a Mother Goddess also, the Earth Mother. In Finnish magic she was honored with a wedding (hierogamy) with Sämpsä of Pellervo, ''in the absence of whom nothing could grow,'' a vegetation god who was her own son (cf. Isis and Horus.) In addition to these chief deities, there were minor cults of lesser divinities also: sun mother or ''the Lady Clothed in the Sun;'' ''Moon King,'' astral deities such as Šub (Magyar Csaba who travels along the Highway of Hosts, The Milky Way); spirits of forest, water, fire, vegetation, and birth; family gods and heroes. In the totemistic tradition, there were two tribal ancestors, the bear and the horse, each with an elaborate cult. There is a complex belief in a double soul, one tied up with the body, the other (lél, lil) free as air. Priesthood was hereditary and during the matriarchal period held by women who divined with a magic mirror and healed with a magic drum (cf. the drum of Inanna). Later the office became predominantly but never exclusively a male prerogative; the name of Emese, legendary mother of the Magyars, means ''priestess.'' The shaman (Finnish *noita*, Magyar *táltos*) is closely analogous to the Celtic druid, his chief duty being to shepherd the souls in his care. In his drum-induced trance he could heal, conquer evil spirits by his songs, rescue souls from the powers of darkness, raise the dead, etc. Even wars were waged by pitting rival magicians against each other; the battle was decided by the magic power of song, without bloodshed. BIBLIOGRAPHY: *The Kalevala; Estonian Poetry and Language* (ed. V. Koressaar and A. Rannit 1965); N. Leader, *Hungarian Classical Ballads and their Folklore* (1967); M. Zsiray *Finnugor rokonságunk* (1937); I. Bobula *Sumerian Affiliations* (1951). *ASIANIC RELIGION; *MAGYARS; *MATRIARCHY; *MOON WORSHIP; *ANCESTOR WORSHIP; *BALTIC RELIGION.

[D. BRUNAUER]

FIORENTINO, NICCOLÒ (Niccolò de Forzone Spinelli; 1430–1514), Italian goldsmith and medalist. F. engraved seals for Charles the Bold of Burgundy (1468), repaired the silver seal of Arte de' Giudici e Notai of Florence, and made many Renaissance medals of strong portraiture: *Silvestro Daziari, Lorenzo de' Medici, Giovanna Tornabuoni,* and one of Charles VII (made in Florence rather than in France), though some attributions are questioned.

[M. J. DALY]

FIORENZO DI LORENZO (1440–1522?), Italian painter. F. introduced into Umbria the sculptural form of the Florentines, with later modifications from Perugino and Pinturicchio. F. painted the signed *Madonna with SS. Peter and Paul* and attributed works: a triptych of *The Madonna with Angels, Saints, and Donors,* an altarpiece of the *Adoration of Shepherds* (Monteluce), and a fresco of *The Mystic Marriage of St. Catherine,* all in the National Gallery of Umbria in Perugia. Eight panels of the miracles of St. Bernardino of Siena are probably from his workshop.

[M. J. DALY]

FIORETTI *(I Fioretti di San Francesco, The Little Flowers of St. Francis),* a collection of stories about St. Francis of Assisi and his early friars, which has exercised enormous influence in forming the popular conception of the saint and his order. A classic of Italian literature, the book has been translated repeatedly and is still widely read. Its unique charm and simplicity has caused it to be described as the most exquisite expression of the religious life of the Middle Ages. The *Fioretti* is the work of an unknown Tuscan friar who, sometime between 1370 and 1385, translated 53 chapters from the *Acts of St. Francis and his Companions* by Fra Ugolino Boniscambi. To this he added five chapters from another treatise entitled *Five Reflections on the Sacred Stigmata*. Many 15th-cent. MSS also include the lives of Brothers Juniper and Giles, increasing the number of chapters to 76. It is not always easy to distinguish in the *Fioretti* what is factual history, what legend, and what propaganda of the *Spirituals. BIBLIOGRAPHY: *Little Flowers of St. Francis* (ed. and tr. R. Brown, 1958), introd. 13–37; E. G. Gardner, ''The 'Little Flowers' of St. Francis,'' in *St. Francis of Assisi: Essays in Commemoration* (1926) 97–126; J. R. H. Moorman, *Source for the Life of St. Francis of Assisi* (1940) 152–169.

[C. J. LYNCH]

FIRDAUSI (Abūl Qāsim Ḥasan; *c.*932–1020), the greatest of Persian poets. His *Shah Nama* is an epic of 60,000 verses recounting the deeds of Persian royalty from mythical times to the mid-7th century. Although he was a Shiite Muslim and treated religion as one of the natural virtues of royalty, representing his characters as having faith in one God and adhering to the Muslim moral code, his orthodoxy came under some suspicion because of his enthusiastic celebration of pagan antiquity. Considering himself underpaid for his masterpiece, F. wrote a satire on the Sultan (included in many editions of the *Shah Nama*) and fled. Also attributed to F. is an 18,000-verse work known as *Yusuf and Zulaikha,* a version of the story of Joseph and the wife of Potiphar. BIBLIOGRAPHY: P. Kujoory, NCE 5:933.

FIRE, HOLY, see HOLY FIRE.

FIRE, PILLAR OF, see PILLAR OF FIRE.

FIRE, USE AND SYMBOLISM OF. The use of fire, either actual fire or the concept, has been extensive in the history of religion. The power of fire both to aid and to destroy, together with the psychological fascination of flames, has made it a natural symbol. It provides light and warmth, and serves to purify and refine. Fire also disposes of unwanted waste material, but uncontrolled can destroy homes, goods, and human life itself, while causing excruciating pain. In the Vedic Scriptures, the fire god Agni serves as a messenger between man and the gods. In Zoroastrianism, fire was worshipped as a sacred power given directly from heaven. Aztecs and Incas worshipped fire gods. In ancient Greek and Roman religion, fire symbolized power, and was borne before the Roman emperor. The fire of the hearth carried an elemental sacred quality. In the Bible, God speaks to Moses from the burning bush, and the coming of the Holy Spirit at Pentecost is marked by tongues of fire. On the negative side, Jesus describes the destiny of the wicked as a place of unquenchable fire (Mk 9.43), and 2 Pet prophesies destruction of the earth by fire (3.10–12). Related to the symbolism of fire is the widespread use of lamps and candles in religious history. The lighting of the new fire at the Easter Vigil is part of its theme of new beginning and newness of life.

[T. EARLY]

FIRE OF JUDGMENT, a phrase used to describe the eschatological testing action of God's judgment when he will decide the quality of the works of all men and declare his effective victory over evil. Fire is the usual biblical metaphor for describing the power, intensity, and thoroughness of the divine judgment. Its use in eschatological settings in the OT (e.g., Is 66.15–16; Ezek 38.22) is reflected in the NT, esp. in the Rev (8.7–8; 9.17; 11.5), but also in 2 Pet 3.7 and 1 Cor 3.13, the latter alluding to the analogy between the testing ability of fire and that of God's judgment. The fire pictured as taking place on the day of judgment seeks out the works of all men as flames search out all that is flammable. Biblical passages undoubtedly employ eschatological imagery from both apocalyptic literature and myth, but this does not preclude the reality of a final, decisive judgment by God expressed in the metaphor of fire. BIBLIOGRAPHY: K. Rahner, "The Hermeneutics of Eschatological Assertions," *Theological Investigations* 4 (1966) 323–346; *InterDB* 2:268–269.

[J. CORDOUE]

FIRMAMENT (IN THE BIBLE), the English translation of the Hebrew *raquî'a* (derived from *rqc*, to beat out as with a hammer) which properly meant a thin beaten metal plate and was thence applied to arch of the heavens. The derivation of the term in this latter sense implies the ancient conception of the heavens as a solid vault which rested on the mountains as pillars (Job 26.11). Outside of Gen 1 this Hebrew term occurs only in Gen 7.19; Ps. 19.1; 150.1; Dan 12.3, and in the description of the throne chariot in Ezek 1.22,23,25 and 10.1. Above the firmament flowed the upper waters (Gen 1.7), and above them were the "upper chambers," Yahweh's dwelling place (Ps 104.3; cf. Ps 29.10). The firmament was thought to have been provided with windows and gates which could be opened so as to allow the descent of God (Is 64.1), of angels (Gen 28.12), of blessings (cf. Ex 16.4; 2 Chr 7.1; Is 55.10; Mal 3.10), or which could be sealed shut so that no rain would fall (Dt 11.17; 1 Kg 8.35; Lk 4.25; Rev 11.6). Apocalyptic texts predicted that in the end of time the stars would fall and the sky would vanish like a scroll that is rolled up (Rev 6.12–14). BIBLIOGRAPHY: P. Van Imschoot, "World according to the OT," *Theology of the Old Testament* (1965) 1:86–89.

[F. BUCK]

FIRMAN (Turk., decree), an edict of the Ottoman sultan dealing with a wide variety of matters both ecclesiastical and civil. Many were issued to Christian Churches and monasteries under Turkish rule and are a valuable source of information for the history and life of the Church in the Ottoman Empire.

[G. T. DENNIS]

FIRMICUS MATERNUS, JULIUS, Christian author of the 4th century. Sicilian by birth, F. gave up a legal career to become a writer, producing *c*.336, when still a pagan, eight books on astrology. About 10 years later, having become a Christian, he wrote his *De errore profanarum religionum,* a violent attack upon surviving paganism, esp. the mystery religions. He advocated their forcible suppression by the imperial government. The work is an important source of information on pagan mystery cults, esp. those of Eastern origin. Critical ed. C. Halm, CSEL (v. 2, 1867).

[R. B. ENO]

FIRMILIAN OF CAESAREA (d. *c*.268), bp. in Cappadocia from *c*.230. A friend and pupil of *Origen, he supported *Cyprian in his controversy with Pope Stephen. Of F.'s writings one letter remains in the Cyprianic corpus (*c*.256?), supporting Cyprian's contention that heretical baptism is invalid. In 264 he presided over the first two Synods of Antioch against *Paul of Samosata and died on his way to the third (268 or 269).

[R. B. ENO]

FIRMIN OF AMIENS, ST. (d. *c*.284–305), first bp. of Amiens, martyr. There is much in his life that is obscure and before the 8th century no mention has been discovered of him. It is known as fact that he was a convert to the faith, a disciple of St. Saturninus of Toulouse, and a missionary in S France.

[F. G. O'BRIEN]

FIRST COMMUNION. While baptism, confirmation, and the Eucharist formed the heart of sacramental initiation in the days of the adult catechumenate of early Christian times, first communion in our times is usually taken to mean first sacramental participation in the eucharistic meal, usually on the part of a child.

Since the time of Pope Pius X the age for first communion has been about the 7th year, or when one has arrived at the age of the use of reason. The child's parents and his pastor or a priest who is well acquainted with the child are the persons to determine the child's readiness to receive communion for the first time. This may be before the 7th year in some cases. Usually, however, first communion takes place in the second grade to give the child time to adapt to the traumatic entrance into school environment.

There are two movements that have gained momentum in recent years in connection with first communion. The first concerns the involvement of the parents in the preparation of the child for first sacramental participation, a custom developing from the current realization of the centrality of the role of the parents in the child's religious formation. An abundance of materials has been produced in recent days to assist this parental function. Associated with the question of first communion is that of first confession. Many had been advocating the traditional coupling of these events in the training of children. It was argued that a child of 7 is rarely if ever in spiritual need of the sacrament of penance because he normally lacks the moral development necessary for grave sin, and because he can be better introduced to the practice of confession at a somewhat later age (e.g., at about the fifth grade). Permission was granted by Rome for a period of experiment in which, where local bishops permitted, children could be given their first communion before being trained in the practice of sacramental confession. In more than half the dioceses of the U.S. advantage was taken of this concession. However, in a joint declaration of the Congregation of the Clergy and the Congregation for the Discipline of the Sacraments, published July 9, 1973, permission for this experimentation was withdrawn. The decree was made effective at the end of the 1972–73 scholastic year. The reason for this action was stated to be a return to the "theological, spiritual, and pastoral principles" enunciated by Pope St. Pius X. Many of the clergy and others engaged actively in catechetical work, and some bishops also, have taken this revision enjoined by the Holy See in poor grace and in some cases have circumvented its enforcement.

[C. C. MCDONALD]

FIRST CONFESSION. In 1215 Lateran Coucil IV decreed that every child who has attained the use of reason or the age of discretion *(ad annos discretionis pervenerit)* was obliged along with his elders to the annual reception of the sacraments of penance and the Eucharist (D 812). So far as the annual confession is concerned, this obligation has commonly been interpreted to bind only those who are conscious of having seriously transgressed the law of God regardless of whether they are adults or children. The age at which the use of reason is attained was variously interpreted, esp. at times and places where the perfection of the dispositions required for the reception of the Eucharist was overemphasized, and quite commonly children were not admitted to either sacrament much before the age of puberty. In 1910 Pope Pius X in his decree *Quam singulari* declared that the age of reason in a child is achieved when he begins to reason, which occurs generally at about the age of 7 (D 3530). The General Catechetical Directory issued in 1971 by the Congregation for the Clergy with the approval of Pope Paul deals with the first reception of the sacraments of penance and of the Eucharist in an appendix; it declared that the legislation enacted by Lateran Council IV, as interpreted by the *Quam singulari* of Pius X was to be continued in effect, but this declaration did take note of the fact that experiments were in progress in different places in postponing the reception of the sacrament of penance until some time after the first reception of holy communion. The continuation of these experiments was sanctioned within the limits of the terms in which permission for them had been granted. But a later joint declaration of the Congregation for the Discipline of the Sacraments and the Congregation for the Clergy was issued on July 9, 1973, which stated that an end must be put to these experiments at the conclusion of the scholastic year 1972–73, and that thereafter the prescriptions of *Quam singulari* were to be obeyed by all. This declaration evoked considerable criticism among some catechists. After study and discussion this declaration was interpreted by the USCC to mean, not that children are per se obliged to make their confession before receiving their first communion (any more than an adult, not conscious of having committed serious sin is obliged to go to confession before receiving the Eucharist), but that all instruction on confession should not be systematically deferred until after the children had made their first communion. This provision in effect protects the liberty of the child and affords him the opportunity to go to confession should he be conscious of serious sin or fear that he may have gravely offended God.

BIBLIOGRAPHY: USCC, *Study Paper for First Confession* (1973).

[P. K. MEAGHER]

FIRST FRIDAY, a term used to indicate an observance based on the promises of Our Lord to St. Margaret Mary Alacoque (1647–90) that unusual graces would come to those who received communion on nine successive first Fridays of the month. The promises included the grace of final repentance, a death in the state of grace, and the assurance that the Sacred Heart would be their refuge at the hour of death.

[J. R. AHERNE]

FIRST FRUITS, the sacrificial offering from the annual crop to the deity. The custom of offering first fruits was shared by the Israelites with many other ancient nations. In the beginning these offerings were voluntary. But after the Israelite settlement in Canaan the Mosaic Law regulated the practice and requirements of these offerings. The oldest code, the Book of Covenant, required the first fruits Heb. *bikkūrîm, rē'šît* of the soil (Ex 23.19; 34.26). Other directions specifically include the first fruits of grain, wine, oil, wool (Dt 18.4), of fruit trees, but only after 3 years (Lev 19.23–25; Neh 10.35), and the first of flour (Num 15.17–21; Neh 10.36). Dt 26.1–2 indicates that only a portion of the first fruits, enough to fill a basket, was required. From the "credo" of Dt 26.1–11, which was recited at the offering of the first fruits and thanked Yahweh for the deliverance from Egypt and the gift of the land, it may be concluded that the offering of the first fruits was meant as a thank offering for the annual harvest and an acknowledgement that everything in the Holy Land belonged to Yahweh and had to be used with gratitude as a gift from him. The various first fruits were offered at the three principal Israelite feasts: Passover (Lev 23.9–14), Pentecost (Ex 34.22; Num 28.26), Tabernacles (Ex 23.16; Lev 23.33–43; Dt 16.13). After having been offered, the first fruits were left for the priests (Lev 23.20; Num 18.12–13; Dt 18.4; Neh 10.33–35; Ezek 44.30). The term "first fruits" was applied figuratively to Israel (Jer 2.3), and in the NT to Christ (1 Cor 15.20) and to Christians (Rom 8.23; 16.3; 1 Cor 16.5; Jas 1.18; Rev 14.4).

[F. BUCK]

FIRST PRESIDENCY, the supreme governing body of the Church of Jesus Christ of Latter-day Saints. It is composed of the president and two counselors, who are high priests of the priesthood of Melchizdek. "President" was a title adopted by Joseph *Smith.

[T. C. O'BRIEN]

FIRST PRINCIPLES. A principle is what is first in any order. More generic than the notion of cause, all principles are ultimately rooted in the first metaphysical principles of being and knowledge. A leading theoretical exploration of the genesis of first principles shows that direct contact with the extramental world through the senses initiates the processes which result in distinctly first concepts and from these concepts, primordial judgements. In the first intellectual apprehension, an existing essence is known; i.e., there is a prescientific notion of being as something which is. Whatever the second known reality is, it is recognized as other than the first. Thirdly, there is recognition of the division of the first two, that this being is not that being. On the basis of these first three primary concepts, i.e., being, nonbeing, division and the realization of their irreducibility, a judgment denying nonbeing of being is made. In this first inductive judgment is found the absolutely first principle. It is the best known of all principles because it is known from first human concepts; nonhypothetical, in that it cannot be dependent upon anything else; nondemonstrable, because an infinite regress in principles explains nothing and vitiates the validity of all demonstration by eliminating the certitude of other conclusions. Were first principles demonstrable, they would be simultaneously better known (as means of demonstration) and less well known (as that which is to be demonstrated).

The first principle of thought and being is phrased variously; it is impossible for the same attribute both to belong and not belong to the same subject at the same time and in the same respect; a thing cannot both be and not be; a thing either is or is not; affirmation and negation are not true at the same time and there is no intermediary between them. This principle of noncontradiction is the only first principle specified by Aristotle or Aquinas, although some others, customarily called first principles, are implicitly contained in discussions of the first.

The validity of the first principle is shown by way of negation. If the principle of noncontradiction is not true, then all predication will necessarily be accidental, which is a denial of substance; all reality would necessarily be one, for were contradiction untrue, it would be impossible to distinguish one being from another; all appearances would be true, regardless of opinion or error; all speech would be meaningless and the position itself then would be indefensible.

First concepts and the first judgment remain valid and necessary for all subsequent intellectual acts. As one's knowledge of reality is clarified and refined, it remains universally true that each concept is one of being and each judgment implicitly one of noncontradiction. This necessity is dictated by the exigencies of the extramental world and the power of the human intellect to know it realistically. Diverse opinions concerning principles vary from the skeptical, which deny principles in every sense, to those which hold innate ideas independent of experience and innate knowledge of principles, either as a birthright or grasped directly in God.

Other principles, frequently termed first principles, include identity, excluded middle, sufficient reason, and causality.

The principle of identity states that being is being; whatever is, is; whatever is not, is not; each being is what it is. Some contend that identity has the primordial role among first principles because it is stated affirmatively and is derived directly from the unity of substance. Others contest identity as a principle because principle involves judgment; judgment involves two concepts affirmed or denied one of another. In identity, the one notion "being" is treated as two. Some see a formal difference between them; others assert that it is merely an affirmation of an apprehension and hence not truly a judgment or principle. The principle of the excluded middle affirms that between being and nonbeing, there is no middle ground; a being is either this or is not this; there can be no intermediate between contradictories. Some philosophers think excluded middle a separate principle; others consider it the logical formulation of the principle of noncontradiction. The principle of sufficient reason states that every being which exists, to the extent to which it exists, has a sufficient reason for its existence; nothing happens without a good and sufficient reason to be what it is.

For Leibniz, the principle of sufficient reason makes all being intelligible. Causality requires every contingent being to have a cause; that nothing can be reduced from potency to act except by a being already in act. Hume gives this principle only psychological validity, denying man the ability to observe more than coexistence or succession of facts; Locke maintains that causality is unknowable.

One of the most serious attacks against first principles, particularly those of noncontradiction and identity is that of Hegel, e.g., "All things are in themselves contradictory"; "Movement is existing contradiction"; *(Science of Logic)*. Hegel asserts that contradiction exists in objective reality; that it is a deficiency, a mark of incompleteness and falsehood found in the lower triadic elements of the dialectic. He accuses Aristotle of absolutizing, in the principle of noncontradiction, the differences between beings: being is not nonbeing. Hegel insists that equal merit be accorded to the relatedness of being to being: being is nonbeing. Each of these formulations is partially true; absolute truth is in the synthesis: being is becoming. In the dialectical process, being is realized in going out from its immediate unity; encountering opposition, conflict, alienation; returning to itself in a reconstructed unity reflective of itself and its relationships to the whole. Hegel seems to find contradiction admissible as a necessary state of the mind in its quest for truth. BIBLIOGRAPHY: E. Trépanier, NCE 5:937–940; ThAq, ST (tr. Dominican Fathers, 3 v., 1947–48); *Basic Works of Aristotle* (ed. R. McKeon, 1941); *Syntopicon* 420–436.

[M. HALPIN]

FIRST VESPERS, that hour of the Divine Office that was said on the evening of the day before a Sunday or other major feast. Its structure was the same as that of ordinary *Vespers. First Vespers derived from the practice of beginning any liturgical celebration on the evening before the feast. On those feasts which provided for First Vespers, Second Vespers were said on the feast day itself. In the revised Liturgy of the Hours it is Evening Prayer I which, on the evening before, begins the celebration of Sunday or a solemnity.

[T. M. MCFADDEN]

FIRSTBORN, a biblical term (OT: *bekor*; NT: *prōtotōkos*) for the male offspring (human or animal) that first opened the womb. The term did not necessarily imply other offspring (cf. Zech 12.10; Lk 2.7). Firstborn sons had certain privileges and responsibilities. In the OT, the father's firstborn son had the right to succeed him as head of the family, was entitled to a special blessing (Gen 27), received a double share of the estate (DT 21.17), and held place of honor among brothers and sisters (Gen 27.29). In the patriarchal era, rights of primogeniture could pass to a younger son (Gen 48.17–20); the Mosaic Law forbade this (Dt 21.15–17). The first male born of every mother, human or animal, belonged to Yahweh (Ex 13.2, 11–15). Exodus ch. 13 explains this consecration of firstborn to Yahweh and his sanctuary as a remembrance of the 10th plague (Ex 11.4–8; 12.29), when Egyptian firstborn were slain and Israelite firstborn spared. Later, when Levites served the sanctuary, firstborn sons were redeemed from service to Yahweh by payment of five shekels (Num 3.40–51). Firstborn male domestic animals were either offered in sacrifice (Num 18.17–18) or destroyed (Ex 34.20). The OT also uses firstborn in a transferred, superlative meaning (see Job 18.13; Is 14.30), particularly of Israel as Yahweh's firstborn son (e.g., Ex 4.2). In the NT, Christ was the firstborn of Mary (Lk 2.7), and was bought back from the Lord (Lk 2.22–24). In a wider sense Christ is called "the firstborn of many brothers" (Rom 8.29), "the firstborn of all creation" (Col 1.15), and "the firstborn from the dead" (Col 1.18). BIBLIOGRAPHY: A. van den Born and E. O'Doherty, EDB 777–779; V. H. Koov, InterDB 2:270–272.

[E. MAY]

FIRSTBORN OF EVERY CREATURE, a title attributed by St. Paul to Jesus Christ (Col 1.15) in the context of a liturgical hymn exalting the God-man as the only mediator between God and men. Firstborn is applied to Christ by analogy with the OT usage. The first male child in a Hebrew family enjoyed a special dignity that entitled him to two shares in the inheritance; so Christ as man enjoys a special dignity as head of creation that entitles him to the entire universe as his inheritance (Rev 19.16). The Hebrew firstborn possessed a certain priestly character, too, which finds its fulfillment in Christ as high priest of the new convenant (Heb 4.14–15 and ch. 10). "Every creature" is better rendered by "all creation" as in the JB and RSV. It must be taken in the collective sense because Paul is comparing the ensemble of creatures to a single family. In relation to all other created beings, Christ is said to have a certain preeminence embracing both the natural order of creation and the supernatural order of grace. The title as a whole is thus a metaphorical statement of Christ's primacy, formally stated by Paul three verses later: ". . . that in all things he might have the first place." This first place belongs to Christ, as Paul also goes on to point out, because "in him dwells all the fullness of the Godhead bodily" (Col 2.9). BIBLIOGRAPHY: E. A. Cerny, *Firstborn of Every Creature (Col. 1:15)* (1938), a patristic study; D. M. Stanley, *Christ's Resurrection in Pauline Soteriology* (1961); B. R. Brinkman, "First-born of All Creation, " *Way* 2 (1962) 261–271, an exegesis of Col 1.15 that stresses the title's implications for the spiritual life.

[M. D. MEILACH]

FISCHER, JOHANN MICHAEL (1691–1766), German architect. F., coming from Bohemia to Munich (1717) was the architect of more than 50 abbeys and churches. His masterwork, the abbey church of Ottobeuren (1744–67), shows a lavish use of ornamental architectural space.

[M. J. DALY]

FISCHER, JOHANN MICHEL (1881–1956), German OT professor and scholar, who published important studies of the LXX version of the Pentateuch and of Isaiah.

[T. C. O'BRIEN]

FISCHER VON ERLACH, JOHANN BERNHARD (1656–1723), architect and sculptor of the southern German Baroque school whose magnificent works include churches, high altars, palaces, and residential chateaux. His dramatic architecture represents a blend of elements from Italian Baroque and French classical styles. Among his religious buildings are the Dreifaltigkeitskirche (1694–1702), the Kollegienkirche (1696–1707), both in Salzburg, and his masterpiece, the Karlskirche, Vienna (1715), completed by his son Joseph Emanuel in 1737. It is a combination of the antique and Borromini's Santa Agnese, Rome, even to the solution of the interpenetration of the nave and central structure, a problem with which he was concerned throughout his career. One of the most famous architects in Europe, F. by his interest in universal knowledge is related to Sir Christopher Wren and other intellectuals of the day. F.'s history of architecture embraced Oriental, Egyptian and Near Eastern elements and classical traditions of the West. BIBLIOGRAPHY: E. Hempel, *Baroque Art and Architecture in Central Europe* (1965) 88–95 and *passim;* H. Sedlmayr, EncWA 5 (1961) 396–400.

[L. A. LEITE]

FISCHER VON ERLACH, JOSEPH EMMANUEL (1693–1742), Austrian architect son of the famous Johann Bernhard Fischer von Erlach. F. completed the famous Karlskirche (1716–24) and other projects of his father. Appointed court architect after his father's death (1723), F. extended the Hofburg and the Winter Riding School in Vienna (1729–35).

[M. J. DALY]

FISCHER, THEODORE (1862–1938), German architect, building administrator in Munich, working in a simplified Romanesque revival form as seen in the Church of the Redeemer (Munich) and the Garrison Church at Ulm.

[M. J. DALY]

FISH, SYMBOLISM OF. Many religions have considered the fish sacred, including religions of India and Babylonia. Often fish has served as an offering to deities, and human consumption of fish has sometimes been prohibited, as in the *Eleusinian mystery religion. Christian art and literature from the early centuries made extensive use of fish as symbol and of the Greek word for fish, **ichthus,* as an acrostic for Jesus Christ, Son of God, Savior. Scholars remain unsure which usage came first. New Testament associations include Jesus' calling fishermen to become fishers of men, multiplying loaves and fish to feed the hungry and feeding his disciples fish after the Resurrection. Fish appear in catacomb banquet scenes, on Christian tombs, and on various church artifacts of the early centuries. In the 4th cent., fish became a eucharistic symbol.

[T. EARLY]

FISHER, GEOFFREY FRANCIS (1887–1972), abp. of Canterbury 1945–61. Born at Higham-on-the-Hill, Leicestershire, the son of the rector, F. attended Marlborough College (public school) and Oxford, and was ordained in 1913. He served from 1911 to 1914 as assistant master of Marlborough, and then until 1932 as headmaster of Repton School in Repton, Derbyshire. He was consecrated bp. of Chester in 1932, serving there until 1939. Through most of World War II, F. was bp. of London. And in 1945 Prime Minister Winston Churchill chose him to become abp. of Canterbury, succeeding William *Temple. In a 1946 sermon he called for opening discussions with the British free Churches. An outgrowth of this were the Anglican-Methodist merger talks, though F. was to oppose the actual merger scheme unsuccessfully proposed after his retirement. He was presiding at the 1948 Amsterdam Assembly when the World Council of Churches was formally constituted, and he was elected to its first presidium. In 1960 he became the first abp. of Canterbury to visit the Pope—John XXIII—since the Reformation. During the same trip he also visited Patriarch Athenagoras of Constantinople (Istanbul) and church leaders in Jerusalem. By virtue of his office he officiated at the coronation of Queen Elizabeth II and other royal events. In 1961 he resigned to be succeeded by A. M. *Ramsey. Honored with a life barony, F. subsequently served as a curate in Trent, Dorset. BIBLIOGRAPHY: W. Purcell, *Fisher of Lambeth* (1969).

[T. EARLY]

FISHER, JOHN, ST. (1469–1535), English bp., cardinal, martyr. F. was named vice-chancellor of the university at Cambridge (1501) and chancellor (1504). An outstanding scholar himself, at Cambridge he encouraged the work of *Erasmus and strove effectively to improve the standard of scholarship. Made bp. of Rochester (1504), he stood firm against the Protestant doctrines beginning to find support at the English universities, vigorously defending the Real Presence and the Eucharistic Sacrifice. F. brought royal disfavor upon himself by protesting Henry VIII's divorce and the act declaring Henry the head of the Church of England (1531). In 1534 his property as bp. of Rochester was confiscated and he was fined in lieu of imprisonment. He refused the Act of Succession and was incarcerated in the Tower of London. T. *Cromwell tried but failed to persuade him to recognize Henry as head of the English Church, and Parliament condemned him to death. By order of Henry VIII, angered at hearing the Pope had named F. a cardinal, the sentence was carried out (1535). F. was canonized by Pius XI (1936). F.'s Latin writings, many of them against Luther, exist in a Würtzburg edition of 1597. Of his treatises against the King's divorce the only known surviving one is *De causa matrimonuii serenissimi regis Angliae* (Alcalá, 1530). BIBLIOGRAPHY: T. Bailey, *Life and Death of John Fisher* (1655, ed. F. Van Ortroy, AnalBoll 10 [1891] 121–365); E. E. Reynolds, *St. John Fisher* (1955); Butler 3:45–49; E. Graf, BiblSanct 6:997–1002.

[J. P. WHALEN]

FISHERMAN'S RING, the gold ring embossed with the figure of St. Peter as a fisherman in a boat, inscribed with the name of the reigning pope, though never worn by him. At the death of each pontiff, his ring is officially broken by the cardinal camerlengo (chamberlain of the Holy Roman Church), and the succeeding pope receives his own. First mention of it dates back to 1265 when Clement IV explained its use to seal the pope's private letters, public documents being sealed with a leaden *bulla*. Since the 15th cent. the fisherman's ring seals the official documents.

[S. A. HEENEY]

FISOLE, MINO da, see MINO DA FISOLE.

FISTULA, a tube usually gold or silver, through which the laity received the sacred species from the chalice during the Middle Ages. Now it is used only in special papal Masses when the pope and his deacon receive the precious blood in this manner.

[S. A. HEENEY]

FITCH, WILLIAM, see BENEDICT OF CANFIELD.

FITERO, ABBEY OF (Santa Maria; 12th cent.), probably the first Cistercian monastery in Spain, founded first at Yerga (1140) by Alfonso VII, King of Castile, moved to Niencebas (1146) and then to Fitero (1152) in the province of Navarre. It was renowned as a spiritual and cultural center through the centuries; through the 17th and 18th cent. there flourished a series of outstanding writers who added to its luster. It was suppressed in 1834. Restored in the 20th cent., it now ministers to the surrounding countryside. BIBLIOGRAPHY: J. Goñi Gaztambide, DHGE 16:279–285.

[J. F. FALLON]

FITNESS, ARGUMENT FROM, see CONVENIENCE, ARGUMENT FROM.

FITTON, JAMES (1805–81), missionary. Instructed as a candidate for the priesthood by Bp. Fenwick of Boston, F. was ordained in 1827. In his remarkable career in missionary work for fifty years he covered every section of New England. From labors among the Passamaquoddy Indians in Maine to Vermont, Connecticut, Rhode Island and finally to Worcester and W. Massachusetts, he established churches and ministered to scattered congregations. The seminary he founded in Worcester became the College of the Holy Cross, the first Catholic college in New England. His last years were spent as a pastor in E. Boston. Among his publications is *Sketches of the Establishment of the Church in New England*. (1872). BIBLIOGRAPHY: DAB 6:432–433.

[J. R. AHERNE]

FITZALAN, HENRY (*c.* 1511–80), earl of Arundel, leader of the RC party under Elizabeth I. Godson of Henry VIII, F. served as governor of Calais (1540–43). He was appointed lord chamberlain in 1544, a post he filled until the death of Henry VIII. After the death of Edward VI, he supported Lady Jane Grey but gave his allegiance to Mary upon her accession and was employed in much diplomatic business by her. During the reign of Elizabeth, he retained his prior posts but was not trusted. F. favored lenient treatment for Mary Stuart and supported the plan to marry her to his widowed son-in-law, the duke of Norfolk. After the discovery of the Ridolfi Plot (1571), he was placed under guard until 1572 and then remained in retirement until his death. BIBLIOGRAPHY: G. Goodwin, DNB 7:88–93; Hughes RE.

[V. SAMPSON]

FITZGERALD, EDWARD (1833–1907), bishop of Little Rock, Ark. An Irish immigrant, he was ordained in 1857. After 9 years as a parish priest in Columbus, Ohio he was named bp. of Little Rock, in 1867. He inherited a bankrupt diocese with few clergy. As a bp. he worked as a missionary in a frontier diocese. At Vatican Council I he was one of the two bps. who publicly voted against the definition of papal infallibility at the final vote, July 18, 1870. He accepted the decree when it was approved by the majority. Because the diocese of Little Rock had few clergy, he brought in the Benedictines and the Holy Ghost Fathers. He was responsible for the establishment of 39 schools in his diocese. At the end of his life, Little Rock was a well-organized diocese with 20,000 Catholics.

[J. R. AHERNE]

FITZGERALD, F. SCOTT (1896–1940), American novelist and short story writer. F.'s early years until his marriage at St. Patrick's Cathedral in 1920 were sporadically touched by Catholic influences. Like most other artists and writers, F. was forever to be shadowed or guided by the tensions created in his life and his work. The body of his work is slender: five novels and some 150 short stories among others, remain. Other novelists, e.g., Jane Austen, have reached the heights despite the narrow confines and paucity of number. F. was one of the voices crying in the 1920 wilderness; it is his involvement with the expatriates, his own ill health, and the effect of wealth or the lack of it on the lives around him that make his voice unique enough to be heard. Perhaps his field and his emotions were confined to narrow limits, but they were symbols of a talent several notches above the other talents of the 20s. Hemingway and Faulkner were alive. Hemingway had been heard from (*The Sun Also Rises*, 1926), but Faulkner did not find himself before 1929 with *The Sound and the Fury*. It is perhaps that F.'s works of the 1920s (when he himself was in his 20s) stirred his readers to view more closely the disenchantment of the postwar prohibition era. Though a talented writer, one firmly entrenched in American literary history, F. was never a great writer. He lacked the broad humanity, the eternal compassion, and deeply haunted brooding over evil of Tolstoy or Dostoyevsky, but he had a feeling for form, a clear easy style, and a sense of the irony of life. BIBLIOGRAPHY: K. Eble, *F. Scott Fitzgerald* (1963); A. Mizener, *Far Side of Paradise* (1951).

[R. M. FUNCHION]

FITZGIBBON, SISTER MARY IRENE (1823–96), founder of the New York Foundling Hospital. During a cholera epidemic in Brooklyn Catherine F. was on the point of death when she vowed to enter religious life if she were spared. As Sister Irene she worked as a Sister of Charity from 1850 in elementary education. Seeing the plight of abandoned babies who were so neglected as to live only a few weeks, Abp. McCloskey proposed an asylum to be conducted by the Sisters of Charity; F. was named director. A combined effort by New York State and private donors made the Foundling Hospital a reality in 1869. F. studied similar institutions in the U.S. and Europe and brought knowledge and personal magnetism to her task. Her kindly and advanced methods for handling the problems of abandoned babies over a 25-year period saved the lives of 26,000 children. Many of her nursing methods became standard in other hospitals. In later years she founded a day nursery and a tuberculosis hospital.

[J. R. AHERNE]

FITZHUGH, ROBERT (*d.*1436), a scholar who spent many years of his life studying, first at Exeter, then at King's Hall, Cambridge where for several years he was chancellor of the University. An address on the defense of the Catholic faith delivered at the university was a model of Latin purity and style. Appointed bp. of London by the pope in 1431, he was consecrated at Foligno. He died before he could accept the see of Ely to which he was translated in 1436. BIBLIOGRAPHY: E. Venables, DNB 7:177–178.

[S. A. WARDLE]

FITZSIMON, HENRY (1556–1643), Irish missionary and controversialist. Born of a prominent Dublin family, he entered the Jesuits at Tournai and completed his theological studies at Louvain. In 1597 he volunteered for the Irish mission and his missionary success in Dublin and the Pale brought him imprisonment (1600) and exile (1604). For the next 26 years he lived on the Continent, writing, soliciting help, and acting as unofficial agent for the Irish mission. In 1630 he returned to Ireland, but thenceforth his ministry was conducted in secret. He ended his days as a fugitive during the Civil War. F. is regarded as a principal contributor to the stability and permanence of the Irish mission. BIBLIOGRAPHY: E. Hogan, *Life, Letters and Diary of Henry Fitzsimon* (1881); Sommervogel 3:766–768; P. Bernard, DTC 5:2561–62.

[V. SAMPSON]

FIVE-MILE ACT, a *Restoration measure further inhibiting activities of *Dissenters in order to safeguard the established Church of England. During a plague, many Anglican clergy fled, while Dissenters returned to former parishes, caring for the sick, burying the dead, and preaching. Fearing an increase of Dissenters, Parliament (1665) passed the Five-Mile Act. *Nonconformist ministers were to swear that "it is not lawful . . . to take arms against the king" and that they would not seek to alter "government either in Church or State." Those refusing this oath were forbidden to come within five miles of any place where they had served as ministers. They were also prohibited from teaching school. BIBLIOGRAPHY: H. Gee and W. J. Hardy, *Documents Illustrative of English Church History* (1921); G. Clark, *Later Stuarts, 1660–1714* (2d ed., 1955).

[N. H. MARING]

FIVE POINTS OF CALVINISM, designation for the basic tenets of strict Calvinism as contained in the canons of the Synod of *Dort (1618–19). The five points can be indicated by the mnemonic t-u-l-i-p: total depravity of man, unconditional predestination and reprobation, limitation of the Redemption to the elect, irresistibility of divine grace, perseverance in grace assured to the elect. BIBLIOGRAPHY: Mayer RB 225–226; bibliog. for Synod of Dort.

[T. C. O'BRIEN]

FIVE POINTS OF FUNDAMENTALISM, tenets of conservative Protestant faith, also referred to as the five fundamentals: the inerrancy of the Bible, Jesus Christ's divinity, virgin birth, substitutionary atonement, resurrection, and future second coming. They were formulated at the Niagara Bible Conference of 1895. While many denominations described as fundamentalist do adhere to such teachings, the so-called five points cannot be taken as an adequate reflection of *fundamentalism.

[T. C. O'BRIEN]

FIXED ALTAR, see ALTAR.

FLABELLUM, in Christian times a fan or disc form with handle used during the liturgy to protect the sacred species from insects. Though the earliest extant flabellum dates from the 6th cent., there are records of use as early as the 4th century. Flabella were made of feathers, leaves, precious metal encrusted with jewels and enamels, silk, linen, and parchment. The Greek flabellum termed *rhipidion* was of metal (usually silver). A 6th-cent. Syrian silver flabellum, now in the Dumbarton Oaks Collection, is engraved with winged cherubim and flaming wheels. The Hermitage duplicate of the German-Rhenish gold and jewelled flabellum (1200 A.D.) in the Metropolitan Museum Collection (The Cloisters, Fort Tryon Park, N.Y.) has led some authorities to conclude that flabella may have been used at times in pairs. BIBLIOGRAPHY: M. C. Ross, *Catalogue of Byzantine and Early Medieval Antiques in the Dumbarton Oaks Collection* (1962).

[M. J. DALY]

FLACIUS ILLYRICUS, MATTHIAS (1520–75), Lutheran theologian, polemicist, and historian. His Croatian name was Vlacic (hence Flacius); he came from the Adriatic coast of ancient Illyria (Illyricus), studied at Basel and Tübingen, and after 1541 became Luther's faithful follower. F. was one of the main editors of the *Magdeburg Centuries, in which he gave better proof of his apologetic gifts than of his objectivity as a historian. There was hardly any controversy in his lifetime in which he was not a protagonist (see ADIAPHORA; SYNERGISTIC CONTROVERSY). He held views more extreme than Luther on human sinfulness, regarding original sin as the ''essential substance'' in man's nature. This near Manichaeism required a response in the *Formula of Concord (art. 1). F. remained for life the great inquisitor of Lutheran orthodoxy. He is also known for his *Clavis scripturae sacrae* (1567), a treatise on biblical interpretation much appreciated by contemporaries, which went into several editions. He also edited the so-called **Missa Illyrica* (1557), wrongly dating it from the 8th century. BIBLIOGRAPHY: R. Seeberg, *Textbook of the History of Doctrines* (1956), 2:364ff.; C. Krauth, *Conservative Reformation and Its Theology* (1875).

[P. DAMBORIENA]

FLAGELLANTS, itinerant semiorganized bands of penitents practicing self-flagellation. This practice was an ancient form of penance, practiced in monasteries and by individual ascetics. The flagellants, however, constituted a widespread, largely lay movement, unorthodox in doctrine and subversive of social order. The first major appearance of the flagellants was in Italy at Perugia in 1260, the year when the last age of the Church was to begin according to *Joachim of Fiore (see JOACHIMISM). It was an era of devastating wars and apocalyptic foreboding. The processions of flagellants from town to town and their self-floggings had a great impact on the populace; the movement spread to Italy, and throughout and central Europe. Flagellants ignored the clergy, absolved each other, and upset the civil peace. They were repressed by ecclesiastical and civil authorities, and the first outbreak faded, although there were isolated recurrences at Strassburg (1296), Bergamo (1334), and Cremona (1346). The coming of the Black Death to Europe revived the phenomenon on a grand scale, except in England, where recruiting failed, and in France, where the flagellants were outlawed by royal decree. The confraternities of this period were more highly organized, with strict entrance requirements, a carefully detailed ritual and rule of life, and a distinctive garb. They came to claim authorization by a letter sent from heaven to Jerusalem in 1348, pardoning the sins of all who scourged themselves. The same antisacramental, antiauthoritarian, and antisocial views developed. The flagellants also engaged in anti-Jewish pogroms and massacres.

Pope Clement VI banned the flagellants in 1349. The third major appearance was in the 15th cent., esp. in Germany and the Low Countries. Conrad Schmid was one of the leaders, claiming to be a reincarnation of Elijah come to judge the world. Denials of Catholic doctrine became more detailed. Flagellation was said to be a second baptism, a baptism of blood that alone availed to salvation; other sacraments were disregarded; the doctrine of indulgences, the veneration of saints, and purgatory were rejected. The movement was violently antiecclesiastical and adopted many of John *Wycliffe's teachings. After condemnation by the Council of Constance (1414), the flagellants were gradually repressed by harsh penalties, such as imprisonment and death. From the 14th to the 16th cent. there were confraternities in Italy, the Disciplinati, under church supervision practicing flagellation. Group flagellation reappeared in some countries in Europe as late as the 19th century. In some Latin American countries and in the Archdiocese of Santa Fe, New Mexico, secret groups of *penitentes* survive in spite of ecclesiastical prohibition. BIBLIOGRAPHY: P. Bailly, DSAM 5:392–408; G. Leff, *Heresy in the Later Middle Ages* (1967) 2:485–493; N. Cohn, *Pursuit of the Millennium* (1961) 124–148.

[R. B. ENO]

FLAGELLATION, an act that may be considered as a punishment, an ascetic practice, and an aberration. This penalty was applied in episcopal courts (St. Aug., *Ep.* 133). Early councils such as Vannes in 465 and Agde in 506 legislated corporal punishment for wayward monks, as did many monastic rules. During the Middle Ages clerics were dealt with in this way. By the Council of Trent (1545–63), it seems physical punishment was already becoming obsolete for ecclesiastical offenses. As an ascetic practice of expiation and self-discipline, flagellation spread from the monastery to the general population of the Middle Ages. Peter Damian (d. 1072) helped to popularize this form of penance (PL 144:350). It has figured in many religious rules down to modern times. As an aberration, public flagellation began with penitential processions in Perugia in 1260. Papal condemnation the following year caused it to subside, but the Black Death (1348–50) induced a recrudescence. As a fanatical, anti-institutional movement, it lasted through the 15th century. Supervised by Church authorities, such processions survived until the 19th cent. in Italy. Flagellation also names a sexual deviation.

[J. E. LYNCH]

FLAGELLATION (IN THE BIBLE), punishment inflicted for two sexual offences in the OT (Lev 19.20; Dt 22.18) but possible in other cases (Dt 25.1–2). The maximum penalty was 40 lashes (Dt 25.3); later custom decreed that the last not be given. In the NT period Roman law allowed the use of rods only for beating of citizens; others could be beaten with leather whips, often weighted with pieces of bone or metal, and chains. Scourging was used as a manner of inflicting the death penalty, esp. upon slaves, a torture for obtaining information, as a preliminary to crucifixion. Jesus' scourging though not originally intended as a step toward his execution served that purpose (Lk 23.16–22; Jn 19.1–4). BIBLIOGRAPHY: C. Schneider, Kittel TD v. 4 s. v. "Mastigō, Mastizō."

[J. J. O'ROURKE]

FLAGET, BENEDICT JOSEPH (1763–1850), missionary, first bp. of Bardstown, Ky., which later became the Louisville archdiocese. A French Sulpician ordained in 1786, he became a victim of the French Revolution and left France to offer his services to Bp. J. *Carroll in the New World. Assigned to Fort Vincennes, Ind., he was conducted there by George Rogers Clarke; he restored Catholic practice among the Creoles. Recalled to Georgetown College he served for 3 years as vice-rector. For 8 years he taught at St. Mary's Seminary in Baltimore. When the See of Bardstown was established F. was named first bp., an appointment he tried unsuccessfully to decline. Consecrated at Batimore in 1810, he went to Bardstown, a diocese of 1,000 Catholic families. F.'s incredible missionary journeys took him throughout Kentucky, Tennessee, Missouri, the Northwest Territory and Canada. Always involved with work among the Indians, he represented 10,000 at a peace conference with Federal agents. During a cholera epidemic his care of the sick brought him close to death. Upon recovering he spent 2 years in Europe, during which he visited all the dioceses of France on behalf of the Society for the Propagation of the Faith. On his return to Kentucky he supervised the removal of the see to Louisville (1841). F. was an able administrator and responsible for the building of the new cathedral in Louisville, the establishment of two seminaries, numerous schools and charitable institutions. His perennial interest in the contemplative life resulted in bringing the Trappists to found the celebrated abbey of Gethsemane.

[J. R. AHERNE]

FLAMBOYANT STYLE, architectural term (from the French *flambeau,* "flame") for a late Gothic style characterized by flamelike, undulating, sinuous lines. It is seen in the "ogee" arch of double curve and extravagant decoration in elaborate elegant tracery of facades, gables, windows, and ceilings that completely denied and obscured the structural form. This style is found esp. in Normandy because of close ties with the Anglo-Norman School of "decorated" architecture. An apotheosis of the style is seen in the English Efflorescence of ribs into non-structural, purely surface ornamental network in fantastic, dazzling, virtuoso displays of "fan" and "lierne" vaulting—at its height in the overwhelming architectural elaboration of ceiling in Henry VII Chapel, Westminster Abbey, London (1503–19).

[M. J. DALY]

FLANAGAN, EDWARD JOSEPH (1886–1948), founder of Boys' Town. Ordained in 1912 F. early exhibited his compassion for the underprivileged by opening a Workingmen's Hotel in Omaha for derelicts. From there he went on to establish in 1917 a protectory for delinquent boys. This became Boys' Town when he purchased a farm near Omaha in 1922. The experiment in a self-governing community of boys, giving them a healthy environment and an education, attracted worldwide attention and support. In 1947 at the invitation of General Douglas MacArthur he assisted the governments of Japan and Korea to solve problems of juveniles. He was in Austria on the same kind of mission when he died of a heart ailment.

[J. R. AHERNE]

FLANDES, JUAN DE (fl. 1496–1519), Flemish court painter to Queen Isabella of Spain (1496), executing a predella for the Univ. of Salamanca (1505), 12 panels for the retable of the Palencia Cathedral (*c.* 1508), and some panels of a polyptych for Isabella (Prado). Influenced by Gerard David and Italian masters, F. effected spacial compositions in a manner foreign to Spanish painting of that era.

[M. J. DALY]

FLANDRIN, HIPPOLYTE (1809–64), French painter of the greatest religious murals of 19th cent. France. A student of Ingres (1829), F., in travels, was influenced by 15th cent. Italian works. *St. Clair Healing the Blind* (Nantes, 1837), frescoes in Paris in the Chapel of St. Jean at St. Severin, St. Vincent de Paul, St. Germain-des-Prés, and at St. Paul, Nîmis, earned him the title "second Fra Angelico." His style relates to that of the German Nazarenes.

[M. J. DALY]

FLATTERY, false praise given where blame is due, to curry favor or gain, or even to lead another into sin. If the evil not blamed, the gain intended, or the harm done are serious, flattery is a serious sin; if not, or if flattery is merely an undue desire to please, the sin is not serious.

[T. C. O'BRIEN]

FLAUBERT, GUSTAVE (1821–80), French novelist. For F. the one important thing was the creation of beauty in writing. He was amoral in the sense that morality was irrelevant to the aesthetic. A consuming hatred for the bourgeois mind (i.e., not only the middle-class mentality but all mediocrity) cast him often in an antireligious role.

But such an astute Catholic critic as François Mauriac regarded him as a mystic *manqué*. His most famous book *Madame Bovary* could hardly be called immoral today, though in its time it nearly sent the author to prison. *Madame Bovary* portrays evil as it truly is and it may be called rightly a morality play. A remarkable comment on the writer is contained in this statement by F.: ''The author in his work must be like God in the Universe, present everywhere and visible nowhere.'' This can hardly be construed as the affirmation of an atheist or agnostic. Other important works are *L'Éducation sentimentale* (1870), *The Temptation of St. Anthony* (1856), *Salammbo* (1862). F. was a meticulous artist, who taught his own countrymen and many writers of the English tradition the power of words. BIBLIOGRAPHY: P. Spencer, *Flaubert: a Biography* (1952).

[J. R. AHERNE]

FLAVIA DOMITILLA, ST., see DOMITILLA, FLAVIA, ST.

FLAVIAN, ST., PATRIARCH OF CONSTANTINOPLE (*d.*449), from 446 an important adversary of Monophysitism. In 448 he excommunicated Eutyches for his heretical teachings that there was but a single nature in Christ. Pope Leo I, after receiving an appeal of Eutyches, complained of F.'s failure to refer the matter to him. Later, however, after receiving the acts of the synod condemning Eutyches, he supported the patriarch with his famous *Tome to Flavin.* The following year in the ''Robber Synod'' of Ephesus, which had been convoked by the Emperor to vindicate Eutyches, F. was deposed and exiled. He died a few days later. In 451 at the Council of Chalcedon his memory was exonerated. BIBLIOGRAPHY: P. Batiffol, *Le Siège apostolique* (1924), 513–519; D. Stiernon, BiblSanct 5:889–909; O. Chadwick, ''The Exile and Death of F. of Constantinople. A Prologue to the Council of Constantinople,'' JTS 6 (1955) 17–34.

[M. J. COSTELLOE]

FLAVIAN OF ANTIOCH (fl. late 4th cent.), bp. of Antioch, succeeding *Meletius in 381. Because of the Meletian Schism, his election, protested at Rome by Epiphanius, Salamis, and St. Jerome, was recognized through Pope St. *Siricius only in 398. F. should be remembered chiefly for his appointment of *John Chrysostom as preacher in the principal churches in Antioch.

[T. C. O'BRIEN]

FLAVIGNY-SUR-MOSELLE, ABBEY OF (Flavieniacum), former Benedictine priory in the Diocese of Toul (now Nancy, Meurthe-et-Moselle, France), dedicated to St. Eustace. The body of St. Firmin, bp. of Verdun, was transferred there *c.*950. In the 17th cent., Benedictines of the Congregation of Saint-Vanne occupied the monastery, but it was abandoned at the time of the Revolution. It now houses Benedictine nuns. BIBLIOGRAPHY: Cottineau 1:1150.

[J. DAOUST]

FLAVIGNY-SUR-OZERAIN, ABBEY OF, Benedictine monastic foundation of the 8th cent. in the Côte d'Or, which participated in the Cluniac reform of the 10th cent. and the Maurist reform of the 17th cent., before it was destroyed by the French Revolution. Only a crypt of the church remains. The town fostered by the abbey became the center of a renewal of the Dominican Order under Lacordaire in the 19th cent. BIBLIOGRAPHY: J. Marilier, DHGE 17:400–405.

[J. F FALLON]

FLAXMAN, JOHN (1755–1826), English neoclassical sculptor and draftsman. A precocious child, he achieved early fame. In 1775 he produced wax models for Wedgwood's neoclassical jasper ware. F. executed classical reliefs on funeral monuments at St. Paul's, Westminster, and all over England. In 1787 he supervised the Wedgwood studio in Rome, and later attained the chair of sculpture at the Royal Academy (1810). His sketches at times sentimental are in the British Museum, University College, London, and the Royal Academy.

[M. J. DALY]

FLÉCHIER, VALENTIN ESPRIT (1632–1710), French preacher and bishop. Raised in Tarascon by his uncle, superior general of the Fathers of Christian Doctrine *(Doctrinaires),* F. entered the congregation (1648). In Paris (1659), he gained entry to the salon society of the hôtel de Rambouillet where he acquired the reputation of a man of wit and a *galant* literary style which lingers in all his works. Having become tutor in the Caumartin household (1662), he accompanied M. de Caumartin to the Clermont Assizes (1665), recording his experiences during the trip to his *Mémoires sur les grands jours d'Auvergne* (1666, pub. 1844). Chosen lector to the Dauphin (1671), for whom he wrote his *Histoire de l'empereur Théodosius le Grand* (1679), he began acquiring success as a preacher, was received with Racine into the French Academy (1673), made chaplain to the Dauphine (1681), and named bp. first of Lavaur (1685), then Nîmes (1687), where his treatment of Protestants after the Revocation of the Edict of Nantes has been the subject of both praise and criticism. He delivered funeral orations for such notables of the day as Marie Thérèse of Austria, Queen of France (1683) and the Dauphine (1690), but his oration for Turenne (1676) is considered his best and vies with the one delivered by *Mascaron (1675). Among his other works is *Histoire du card. Ximenes* (1679). BIBLIOGRAPHY: G. Grente, *Fléchier* (1934).

[R. N. NICOLICH]

FLEMING, PATRICK (1599–1631), Irish Franciscan Observant hagiographer. He studied at Louvain and Douai and was ordained in Rome (1623). He did extensive research on biographical material concerning Irish saints. He became the first president of the Irish College of the Immaculate Conception at Prague. While trying to escape from that city when it was under siege in the Thirty Years' War, he was slain by a mob of enraged Calvinist peasants. Among his writings were: *Life of St. Columba, Biography of Bishop MacCaughwell* (whose close friend he had been), and *Chronicle of St. Peter's Monastery in Ratisbon*.

FLEMING, PAUL (1609–40), German poet of the Baroque period, most gifted of the followers of Opitz. Though his poems in German and Latin belong stylistically to the Renaissance tradition, they are imbued with such vigorous and sincere feeling that he has been called the poet of life. The nature and love poems are inferior to the religious poems, of which 12 are hymns. BIBLIOGRAPHY: J. G. Robertson, *History of German Literature* (4th ed., 1962) 182–183; W. Kosch, *Deutsches Literatur-Lexikon* (1963) 90.

[M. F. MCCARTHY]

FLEMING, RICHARD (*c.*1360–1431), bp. of Lincoln, founder of Oxford's Lincoln College. At Oxford *c.*1409 he became suspect of sympathy for *Wycliffe's teachings, but if the charge was well founded, he subsequently changed his views, for he founded Lincoln College (1427) chiefly for the purpose of fostering opposition to Wycliffe's doctrine. Representing the English at the Council of Pavia, he strongly opposed its predominantly conciliarist views. BIBLIOGRAPHY: R. L. Poole, DNB 19:282–284.

FLEMING, THOMAS (1593–1655), Franciscan abp. of Dublin. He studied at the Franciscan college in Louvain where, after ordination, he taught theology and philosophy. His appointment as abp. of Dublin (1623) offended the opponents of the religious orders, but he proved an able and effective administrator, and he strove zealously to implement the decrees of Trent. He took a moderate position in the revolt of the Irish Confederation (1641) and urged peace through negotiation when Confederate defeat seemed certain. His last years were saddened by the religious persecution under Cromwell's government.

FLEMISH SCHOOL (*c.*1450–1600), often referred to as the 2d and 3d Netherland School, or the Franco-Flemish, Franco-Belgian, Franco-Netherland, or simply Belgian, the leading musical school of the Renaissance period. The titles designate either a certain geographic area or a particular musical style having certain common features that can be found in much of the music written in Europe up to about 1750. The Northerners dominated the musical scene in the 15th century. Composers of the Flemish School left their native country and held important posts in church choirs and chapels of foreign countries. One of their outstanding contributions was a new polyphonic style in which all parts were treated equally. About the middle of the 15th cent., the later works of Dufay and of Johannes Ockeghem became prominent. Ockeghem was a singer in the choir of the cathedral at Antwerp in 1443. In 1452 he entered the chapel of the King of France. From 1465 until his death in 1495, he was the *maitre de chapelle*. His known compositions include about 12 Masses, most being written in contrapuntal style, 10 motets, and chansons. His church music is close to the spirit of Gregorian chant.

Another important composer of the Flemish School was Jacob Obrecht, who held important positions at Cambrai, Bruges, Antwerp, and for 1 year at the court of Ferrara. In 1504 he joined the ducal choir but died of the plague within a year. Included among his works are about 2 dozen Masses, motets, a number of chansons, and instrumental pieces. His writings are different from Ockeghem's in that they seem to be more spontaneous and impulsive. There is a warmth of melody and, typical of the Netherlands, short, proportional phrases with periodic cadences supported by clear appropriate harmonies. The most renouned figure of the Flemish School is Josquin *Desprez.

[H. F. REIMER]

FLEMYNG, ROBERT (*c.*1417–83), an early English humanist. He matriculated at Oxford whence he went to Europe (1443) to study theology. After spending the years 1452–55 in England in service to the crown, he became king's proctor in Rome, until the accession of Edward IV (1461). At this time he returned to Oxford where he remained until 1473. F. returned to Italy, where he composed *Lucubratiunculae Tiburtinae* in honor of Sixtus IV, and other classical works. Because of his collection of Greek and Latin MSS and his introduction of humanism at Oxford, he is one of the most important of the early English humanists. BIBLIOGRAPHY: R. Weiss, *Humanism in England during the Fifteenth Century* (1957).

[A. WARDLE]

FLESH (IN THE BIBLE), a term not to be thought of as synonymous with the body, nor as the material component joined with soul and thus forming man. Flesh indicates man as a psychophysical whole and has a variety of meanings in the OT. It can mean the soft, meaty parts of animals and men and therefore what is capable of movement as contrasted with dead material, or it is sometimes applied to the entire body of man or beast, or is used to designate blood relationship. ''All flesh'' is used to include mankind and all living things collectively. It particularly signifies what is characteristically human as compared to God and what is divine. It defines a relationship of dependence and a state of transitoriness (Is 40.6; Ps 78.9). It is the relation of creature to Creator. In the NT flesh has all the connotations of the OT. Moreover, it indicates humanity without God and his spirit (Mt 16.17). Special mention must be made of St. Paul who uses the word in all the above meanings. However, in many passages he associates flesh with sin. Since flesh can mean weakness, he sees fleshly man as prone to sin. Thus flesh characterizes man in terms of his hostile attitude toward God (Rom 8.7). In Paul's writings there is a sharp contrast between flesh and spirit. To "walk according to the flesh" is opposed to "walking in the Spirit" (Rom 8.4–8) It is no longer necessary for man to be flesh since the gift of the Spirit characterizes the last times and belongs to every Christian and potentially to every man (Jl 3.1; cf. Acts 2.17–21). BIBLIOGRAPHY: J. A. T. Robinson, *Body: A Study in Pauline Theology* (1952); T. C. Vriezen, *Outline of OT Theology* (1958).

[F. GAST]

FLETCHER, GILES (*c.*1588–1623), English poet, son of Giles Fletcher, diplomat and author. Ordained for the C of E, he won fame by his sermons at St. Mary's, Cambridge. His principal literary work is his poem *Christ's Victorie and Triumph* (1610). This composition abounds in allegorical descriptions and contains some grotesque conceits, yet it displays strong devotion, great depth of melody, and exquisite imagery, particularly in the version of Paradise. Its meter shows the influence of Edmund Spenser, yet the versification is original, an eight-line stanza ending with a rhyming triplet which resumes the conceit embodied in the verse. Milton in his *Paradise Regained* borrowed from *Christ's Triumph*.

[M. J. BARRY]

FLETCHER, JOHN WILLIAM (b. de la Fléchère; 1729–85), friend of John *Wesley and the Methodist movement. Born at Nyon, Switzerland, F. studied at Geneva. He went to England in 1752, was for a time tutor in an English family, then was ordained in the Church of England. He became dedicated to Methodism, and was named by Wesley to succeed to leadership of the movement, but predeceased him. F.'s writings centered mostly upon the Arminian-Calvinist controversies of his day.

[F. E. MASER]

FLEURY, ANDRÉ HERCULE DE (1653–1743), French cardinal and minister of state under Louis XV. Born in Languedoc and educated in theology at Paris, F. began his association with the French court in 1675 as chaplain to Queen Marie Thérèse. Made bp. of Fréjus by Louis XIV in 1698, he remained in the S of France until 1715 when the dying monarch appointed him tutor to his great-grandson and successor Louis XV. It was this relationship which led to F.'s becoming both a cardinal and head of the government—in all but name—when the regency ended in 1726. F. devoted his principal energies over the next 17 years to bringing peace and prosperity to France and to regaining that initiative in foreign affairs which the diplomatic blunders of his immediate predecessor as first minister, the Duke of Bourbon, had compromised. At home, careful attention to balancing the state budget allowed F. to repair much of the damage wrought by Louis XIV's expensive wars and personal extravagances. The currency was stabilized, trade was expanded, the merchant marine enlarged, and France's road network turned into the most modern in Europe. Externally, F. maintained close ties with England and sought to avoid war on the Continent, or, when this proved impossible, at least to limit French military commitments. Popular feeling virtually forced him to enter the War of the Polish Succession (1733–35) in support of the claims of the Queen's father, Stanislas Leszczynski, to the throne; nevertheless, he initiated negotiations to end the conflict and by means of the Treaty of Vienna (1738) secured Austria's recognition of the French crown's eventual right to the duchies of Lorraine Bar. F. was also unable to prevent the war faction in the government from plunging France into the War of the Austrian Succession (1740–48). Religiously, F. opposed Jansenism and dealt harshly with both its ecclesiastical and political defenders. By and large, however, though his policies did not make him popular, his ministry brought a much-needed stability to France and can be considered one of the most successful in the 18th century.

[E. M. GATES]

FLEURY, CLAUDE (1640–1723), jurist and church historian. His first career was in law at Paris (1658–68); he published works on both civilian and canon law. He became a friend of J. B. *Bossuet, who, after F.'s ordination to the priesthood (1669), had him attached to the French court as tutor to the royal family. F.'s works on education include *Traité du choix et de la méthode des études* (1686), but he is remembered chiefly for his markedly Gallican *Histoire écclésiastique* (20 v., 1693–1720), covering the Christian era up to 1414.

[T. C. O'BRIEN]

FLEURY, see SAINT-BENOÎT-SUR-LOIRE, ABBEY OF.

FLEXA, in Gregorian chant; (1) the breath point inserted to break up an overly long first half of a psalm verse; (2) a synonym for the *clivis,* a two-tone descending *neume.

[H. F. REIMER]

FLICHE, AUGUSTIN (1884–1951), French church historian. He taught medieval history at the Univ. of Montpellier 1919–46 and produced important works on Gregory VII and on his reform. He is esp. distinguished for his editorship of 15 volumes of the monumental *Histoire de l'église depuis les origines jusqu'à nos jours* (26 v.) which he organized with the help of Victor Martin. BIBLIOGRAPHY: C. E. Perrin, *Revue historique* 208 (1952) 382–383.

[F. D. LAZENBY]

FLOATING PARISH, a name coined to describe any group of Christians who choose to form their own worship community apart from the conventional, i.e., territorial parish. The name also connotes the practice frequently followed of varying the place for each gathering of the groups. The floating parish is inspired by the desire to create a more dynamic Christian community than the participants find in the established local church or parish. The group is usually made up of whole families. Liturgical experimentation and spontaneity are prominent features, but an intense concern for social problems is also a mark of such groups. Adoption of the floating parish idea has been particularly widespread among RCs since Vatican Council II. In 6 of the 154 dioceses in the U.S. such communities operate with the approval of the bishop; elsewhere they form part of the *underground Church.

[T. C. O'BRIEN]

FLODOARD OF REIMS (Frodoard; *c*.894–966), medieval historian, author of three books of saints' lives, and two historical works that have much value as primary sources: the *Annales* (history of N France and adjacent Germany from 919 to 966) and the *Historia Remensis ecclesiae* (to 948). BIBLIOGRAPHY: PL135.

[M. F. MCCARTHY]

FLOOD, see DELUGE.

FLOREFFE, MONASTERY OF, Premonstratensian abbey near Namur, Belgium, the second foundation of the order, made in 1121 by Count Godfrey of Namur. It founded 7 daughter monasteries, served 22 parishes; 3 German convents were under its direction. It was supessed in 1797. In 1842 it became an episcopal college. BIBLIOGRAPHY: *Annales Floreffienses:* MGHS 16:618–631; N. Backmund, NCE 5:964.

[N. BACKMUND]

FLORENCE OF WORCESTER (*d*.1118), English Benedictine monk of Worcester abbey, chronicler. He supposedly began the first post-Conquest English universal chronicle, *Chronicon ex chronicis,* sometimes attributed to John of Worcester, who certainly continued it. Until the work becomes contemporary (1073), it is a laborious compilation from earlier annals but, from 1082, is an important historical source. The *Chronicon* was much used by later writers. BIBLIOGRAPHY: R. R. Darlington, *Anglo-Norman Historians* (1947); V. H. Galbraith, *Historical Research in Medieval England* (1951).

[F. D. BLACKLEY]

FLORENCE CATHEDRAL (Santa Maria del Fiore), part of a complex embracing also famous campanile and equally renowned baptistery. The cathedral, designed successively by architects Arnolfo di Cambio (1296–1301), Giotto (1334–36) and Andrea Pisano (1336–49) with "Italian Gothic" nave-vaulting (1357) and spacious side aisles (556' long-342' wide), begun by F. Talenti, has three apses (1407–21) opening from the central octagonal crossing under the epoch-making octagonal dome. The cathedral is well-named "Il Duomo" for this remarkable elliptical, first Renaissance dome, designed and engineered (1420–34) by the genius F. Brunelleschi (1377–1446) whose knowledge of ancient Roman construction, enhanced by ingenuity and skill, overcame the hitherto unsolved staggering problem of spanning the 140' wide space without traditional buttressing walls—by devising new methods, inventing necessary machinery, brilliantly reducing the weight by using 2 thin double shells (the first in history) in an ogival section (which reduced the outward thrust), the 24 ribs (8 exteriorly visible) crowned and stabilized by the lantern. On the interior, frescoes by famous Renaissance artists include *Sir John Hawkwood* (1436) by Uccello, *Niccolo da Tolentino* (1456) by A. de Castagno, a reliquary by L. Ghiberti, sculptures by Donatello and Luca della Robbia, and an unfinished Pietà by Michelangelo.

The famous detached campanile (1387) called the "Lily Tower" of Giotto by Browning, 292' high in the colored marble of the cathedral with carvings by Donatello, A. Pisano, and L. della Robbia was begun by Giotto and carried on by A. Pisano and F. Talenti.

The Romanesque Baptistery (1059) is renowned for three pairs of bronze doors—the earlier east doors (1334–36) of A. Pisano, moved to the south to make way for L. Ghiberti's first doors (1403–24) which in turn were moved to the north when replaced by the most magnificent east doors by Ghiberti with 10 Renaissance relief panels in gilded bronze (1425–52), fittingly called the "Gates of Paradise" by Michelangelo.

A disastrous flood in Nov., 1966 uncovered beneath the cathedral the ruins of the earlier church, S. Reparata, now restored with access from the upper church. BIBLIOGRAPHY: W. and E. Paatz, *Die Kirchen von Florenz* v. 3 (1952).

[M. J. DALY]

FLORENCE, COUNCIL OF, a council, regarded by the Western Church as ecumenical, convoked by Pope *Eugene IV, which first met at Ferrara (April 1438), was transferred to Florence (January 1439) and concluded in Rome (after 1445). Its principal purpose was to achieve union with the Eastern Churches, particularly the Byzantine. After an involved and bitter struggle with the conciliarists in *Basel and after long negotiations with the Byzantine Empire, the Pope succeeded in arranging for a council of Greeks and Latins to meet in *Ferrara. The Greek delegation was headed by the Emperor *John VIII Palaeologus and composed of Patriarch *Joseph II, representatives of the other Eastern patriarchs, 19 other metropolitans, as well as lay scholars and nobles. The first official session took place on April 9, but the Emperor postponed further conciliar deliberations for 4 months in the hope that he would be able to discuss military aid against the Turks with Western rulers, but his hope proved vain. During the interval discussions were held concerning the fire of *purgatory which led to no agreement. In October the council dealt with the lawfulness of the Latin addition of the *Filioque to the Nicene Creed, again coming to no agreement. Owing to the plague and the precarious state of papal finances the council was transferred to Florence, where from Feb. to June of 1439 the doctrine of the *procession of the Holy Spirit formed the subject of debate, the Greeks maintaining that the procession was from the Father alone and the Latins that it was also from the Son. The futility of the public discussions and the Latin syllogistic approach was evident. The basis for union was finally reached when both sides returned to a common tradition, the agreement of the Greek and Latin Church Fathers. Although the words might differ, the Greeks were satisfied that the Latin belief was substantially the same as their own. Other controverted points, the Eucharist, purgatory, papal primacy, were then treated with remarkable dispatch. On July 6 the decree of union, **Laetentur caeli,* was solemnly proclaimed. The sincerity of most of the Greek bps. in accepting the union can no longer be doubted, but it is also understandable that they rejected it later in the face of anti-union propaganda and popular hostility in Constantinople. The real lesson of Florence is that the way to union lies not in arguments but in a reconciliation of different legitimate views and traditions. Its teaching on the papal primacy and the authority of the patriarchs, although little heeded in the West, provides a basis for a sounder understanding of the structure of the Church. Unionistic agreements of varying firmness were also made with the Armenians (1439), the Copts (1442), the Syrians (1444), some Chaldeans and the Maronites of Cyprus (1445). BIBLIOGRAPHY: J. Gill, *Council of Florence* (1958).

[G. T. DENNIS]

FLORENSKI, PAVEL ALEXANDROVICH (1882–1940s), Russian Orthodox theologian, scientist. A native of Georgia, he studied mathematics and philosophy at Moscow Univ., then did graduate studies and became a professor at the Moscow Theological Academy. He was ordained priest in 1911. He was recognized as a man of genius, with equal distinction in philosophy, theology, the humanities, and the physical sciences. Banished by the Russian Revolution, he was recalled to Moscow in 1919 to work in research and administration, but he resolutely refused to renounce or conceal his priesthood. He was imprisoned several times in the 1930s and ultimately exiled to Siberia, where his death seems to have occurred some time in the 1940s. His chief work, influential on Sergei Bulgakov, is *Stolp i Utver Zhdeniye Istiny* (1914), *The Pillar and Ground of Truth* (An Essay on Orthodox Theodicy in Twelve Chapters). This antirationalist work takes its inspiration from themes of V. *Solovyev, pan-unity and sophiology. The idea of consubstantiality, taken from the Creed, becomes a grounding principle of F.'s synthesis. The person becomes consubstantial with all creation by the unified nonrational but intuitive experience of knowing and loving; the experience is opposed to rationalistic analysis, which only reaches the superficial otherness of things and ends in separateness and sterility. Only through the affective-cognitive realization of consubstantiality can man overcome ignorance, sin, and despair. Underlying the true consubstantiality of all creation is Sophia, in which the prototypes of all things exist; Sophia is the unified experience of the whole created universe and subsists with the eternal Trinity. F. sometimes sees it as Mary, the ideal Church, etc. On the theological level the experience of consubstantiality becomes the sole way of perceiving the truths of faith, for it means an encounter with God's reality. Concretely it is in Christ that the whole cosmos is united with the Trinity and through Christ that the experience of consubstantiality is attained by the believer. The structure of the Church, in consequence, F. interprets through A. *Khomyakov's principle of *sobornost.

[T. C. O'BRIEN]

FLORENSZ, ADRIAN, see ADRIAN VI, POPE.

FLORENTINA, ST., (fl. 600), sister of Leander of Seville, who wrote for her and her nuns a rule, *De institutione virginum et contemptu mundi,* which was known in Muslim and Christian Spain (9th–11th cent.) and in Monte Cassino (13th century). *Isidore of Seville dedicated his work against Judaism to her. Her relics, discovered with those of her brother Fulgentius near Guadalupe *c.*1330, were shared between Murcia and the Escorial in 1593. Her cult dates from the 15th century.

[E. P. COLBERT]

FLORENTINI, THEODOSIUS (1806–65), apostle of charity and social justice. A Capuchin from 1825, ordained in 1830, he became the founder of two religious congregations devoted to education and works of charity, the *Teaching Sisters of the Holy Cross (1844), and the Sisters of Mercy of the *Holy Cross (1856). His chief work, however, was the effort to establish factories where better working conditions and more equitable wages put into practice a social theology based on charity and justice.

[T. C. O'BRIEN]

FLORENTIUS RADEWIJNS (*c.*1350–1400), with Gerard Groote, founder of the Brethren of the Common Life. Born at Leerdam in Holland, he studied at Prague, became the disciple of Groote, and was ordained. With Groote he preached the **Devotio moderna* to the clerical students at Deventer. There F. established the first community house of the Brethren of the Common Life. He also established the house at Windesheim (1386). Thomas à Kempis was one of his subjects, and later his biographer. BIBLIOGRAPHY: H. Hyma, *Christian Renaissance* (2d ed., 1965); M. Van Woerkum, DSAM 5:427–434.

[T. EARLY]

FLÓREZ, ENRIQUE (1702–73), Spanish Augustinian scholar. His preparation was at Alcalá, where Ambrosio de

Morales (*d.*1591) had established a tradition of historical research. F., with the help of other Spanish scholars, edited volumes 1–29 of *España Sagrada* (1747–75), organizing Spain's ecclesiastical history by dioceses; the sources edited make the series still valuable. Dedication to Holy Spain and to historical truth characterize F.'s other works as well.

[E. P. COLBERT]

FLORIAN, ST., an officer of the Roman army who suffered martyrdom in A.D. 304, in the reign of Diocletian. F. occupied a high administrative post in the imperial bureaucracy at Noricum (now part of Austria). A reasonably authentic tradition locates his place of martyrdom at Lauriacum (Lorch), near where the Enns flows into the Danube. BIBLIOGRAPHY: Butler 2:230–231; A. Amore, BiblSanct 5:937–938. *SANKT FLORIAN, MONASTERY OF.

[E. J. DILLON]

FLORIANS (FLORIACENES), a monastic congregation of Italian origin and a branch of the Order of Cistercians that flourished between the 12th and 15th centuries. The community was founded in Calabria in 1189 by Joachim of Fire (*c.* 1130–*c.* 1202), mystic and abbot of Corazzo. He left the Cistercian abbey to organize the Florians at the abbey, S. Giovanni in Fibre, where he inaugurated Cistercian reform, which was probably the first break in the monastic orders founded by St. Bernard. In structure, the congregation was similar to the Cistercians, but in spirituality and discipline it was patterned after the Franciscans. In 1196 the Florians received papal approbation. They soon spread throughout Italy and by the 13th cent. possessed 40 foundations. During the 15th cent., however, members so decreased that those who remained were absorbed by other communities in 1505. The congregation of Florians terminated when those who had rejoined Citeaux became members of the Cistercian Congregation of Calabria. BIBLIOGRAPHY: F. Russo, *Gioacchino da Fiore e le Fondazioni Florensi in Calabria* (1959); G. Pence, *Storia del monachesimo in Italia* (1961); F. Russo, EncCatt 5:1452.

[R. A. TODD]

FLORIDA, the southeasternmost state in the Union, Florida was admitted as the 27th state (1845). Primitive Indian tribes, including the Apalachees, Timucuas, Tequestas, and Calusas, originally inhabited the area; the Seminoles did not arrive until the 18th century. The Spaniard Juan *Ponce de León discovered Florida in 1513, and it was subsequently explored by Pánfilo de Narváez and Hernando de Soto. St. Augustine, the first major settlement, was founded (1565) by Don Pedro Menéndez de Avilés. Except for a brief period of English rule, Florida remained in Spanish hands until it was acquired by the U.S. (1819). Menédez invited both Jesuits and Franciscans to St. Augustine, but Indian troubles terminated Jesuit efforts after 1572. The Franciscans, who came in 1573, were the principal missionaries in the region until 1763. Three hundred of their priests labored among the N Florida Indians and achieved 30,000 conversions. The English occupation of 1763–83 destroyed Indian morale and led to abandonment of the missions until the restoration of Spanish rule in 1784. Catholicism did not prosper under American rule and Florida Catholics had to depend on meager help from the neighboring Dioceses of Charleston, Mobile, and Savannah. Florida was a vicariate apostolic from 1857 until the creation of the Diocese of St. Augustine in 1870; its vicar, J. P. Augustin *Verot, became its first bishop. St. Augustine remained a suffragan of Baltimore until the metropolitan See of Atlanta was created in 1962. The new Diocese of Miami, founded in 1958, was a suffragan of Atlanta until 1968 when it became an archdiocese, Orlando and St. Petersburrg, dioceses.

Florida's population of 8,189,410 (over 65% urban) makes it the ninth most populous state in the Union. Catholicism has advanced rapidly in recent years, aided by the development of south and central Florida and by the growth of large urban centers. In 1976 Catholics numbered 1,146,985 or 14.0% of the total state population. The major Protestant bodies are the Southern Baptist Convention (11.9% of the total population) and the Methodist Church (5.7%). Other Protestant denominations comprised 10.8% of the population. The Jewish population (1968) was 189,280, or 2.7%.

In 1976 there were three Catholic colleges in Florida with a total enrollment of 4,189 students. Over 18,000 attended the state's 32 Catholic high schools, and 52,175 pupils were enrolled in 154 Catholic elementary schools. BIBLIOGRAPHY: H. P. Clavreul, *Notes on the Catholic Church in Florida, 1565–1876* (n.d.); K. T. Hanna, *Florida, Land of Change* (2d ed. 1948); R. W. Patrick, *Florida under Five Flags* (3d ed. 1960); T. Irving, *Conquest of Florida under Hernando De Soto* (2 v., 1869, repr. 1974).

[J. L. MORRISON; R. M. PRESTON]

FLORILEGIA, a term derived from two Latin words *flores* (flowers) and *legere* (to collect), the exact equivalent of anthologies, similarly derived from *anthe* (flowers) and *legein* (to gather, to collect), and metaphorically applied to collections of passages taken from the writings of earlier authors. Such collections with a wide variety of picturesque titles, such as *Apomnēmoneumata, Fasciculi,* and *Scintillae,* have been made from pagan and early Christian times. They consist of excerpts taken from single authors and from many authors, from profane and religious sources, or from a mixture of both. The Christian florilegia may be of a biblical or of a patristic nature. Where they consist of exegetical passages on Scripture, they are usually known as **catenae* ("chains"). The earliest Christian anthologies consisted of collections of the *logia,* or "sayings" of the Lord or the Apostles. Later were added the lists of *auctoritates* and *testimonia* used in the instruction of converts, and the *apophthegmata patrum* stating the principles of the ascetical life. Before the invention of printing and the wide diffusion of books, such florilegia were extremely useful for theologians and spiritual writers. They are still valuable in that they have preserved texts from works that have been lost and variant readings that can be used to check a MS tradition. BIBLIOGRAPHY: H. M. Rochais, NCE 5:979–980.

[M. J. COSTELLOE]

FLORINUS, ST. (7th cent.), confessor. His education was provided by the parish priest who gave up his office when Florinus was ordained. The early biographies are devotional, stressing the miracles the saint is supposed to have worked. According to the accounts, he was buried in his parish church. His relics were later brought to the collegiate church of St. Florinus in Koblenz and from there to the abbey of Schönau. He is the patron of the diocese of Chur. BIBLIOGRAPHY: W. Grundhofer, LTK 4:180–181; B. Cavanaugh, NCE 5:980; N. Del Re, BiblSanct 5:944–945.

[J. M. O'DONNELL]

FLORIS, FRANS (Frans de Vriendt; 1516–70), Flemish painter, trained by his sculptor father and later introduced to Italian works. In Rome (1542–47) F. drew from antique sculpture and the giants of Michelangelo's *Last Judgment*. Combining Michelangelo's form with rich Venetian color, he painted a *Last Judgment* (1565). Through many students F.'s northern mannerist style determined Flemish painting to the end of the 16th century.

[M. J. DALY]

FLORUS OF LYONS (*c.*800–*c.*860), Carolingian author. His life was spent in serving the Church of Lyons as deacon and teacher. Forty-four prose and poetical works are attributed to him, the most elaborate being liturgical commentaries and biblical summaries. Devoted to Bp. Agobard, he was sharply antagonistic to Amalarius and later to John Scotus Erigena. BIBLIOGRAPHY: A. Cabaniss, *Classica et Mediaevalia* 19 (1958) 212–232.

[A. CABANISS]

FLOTTE, PIERRE (also, Flote), (1260–1302), chancellor of France for Philip IV, legist, diplomat. His political policy was a defense of the sovereignty and independence of the king against papal and episcopal opposition. His activity influenced Boniface VIII to ameliorate his position against Philip's taxation of the clergy. Flotte is also named as the compiler of the accusations in the famous trial of Bp. Bernard Saisset. His more famous successor, William of Nogaret, continued his policy and spirit. BIBLIOGRAPHY: J. R. Strayer, NCE 5:980–981.

[J. J. SMITH]

FLOWERS, SYMBOLISM OF. Christian art is abundantly provided with flowers symbolically interpreted, esp. in the Middle Ages and the Renaissance. A partial list includes the following with their figurative meanings: crocus, joy; fleur-de-lys, the Virgin and possibly the conventionalized form of the Annunciation lily; daisy, the innocence of the Christ Child; hyacinth, Christian prudence, peace of mind; iris, or "sword lily," the sorrow of Mary at the Passion of Christ; lily, purity; pansy, remembrance and meditation; violet, humility; poppy, sleep, fertility, extravagance; rose, victory, pride and triumphant love; narcissus, selfishness and self-love.

[S. A. HEENEY]

FLOYD, JOHN (1572–1649), Jesuit apologist. A member of the Society from 1592, after studies at the English colleges in Reims and Rome, he labored on the English mission, and was several times imprisoned, once (1605) in connection with the *Gunpowder Plot. His later life he spent on the Continent, dying at St. Omer in France. He was a continuous contributor to the Catholic cause by his many apologetic and polemical writings.

[T. C. O'BRIEN]

FOCILLON, HENRI (1881–1943), French art historian, professor at the Collège de France and, in his last years, at Yale University. A gifted writer on a vast range of subjects, in his very influential essay on style, *La Vie des formes* (1942), he presents his method of impressive precision. His greatest contribution is a scholarly, authoritative analysis of medieval art in an impressive 2-v. work, *The Art of the West* (1963).

[P. P. FEHL]

FOCOLARE MOVEMENT (It. *focolari,* hearth, furnace, hotbed), worldwide association presently known as GEN (New Generation), begun in Trent, Italy (1943) by Chiara Lubich with several girls who had survived the destruction of the war. Members "Focolarini," joined in their gospel adherence in daily life (in accord with Jn 17.23), include youth and adult men and women of every social condition. With a core membership of 1,500, it has centers in 30 countries. Approved in 1962, though not a secular institute, it has many celibate members with vows. In its vast organization are not only laity but religious within their own orders and institutes; non-Christians are counted friends of the movement. The loose formation achieves unity by sharing the evangelical spirit, its members bound by meetings (the first in 1949 and others such as the gathering in Loppiano, the City of Youth, in Tuscany); by correspondence; by its bimonthly publications, esp. *Living City* and *Focolare News*. In Chicago, the movement was introduced (1955), and centers opened also in Boston in New York City where the women's headquarters is located and in Brooklyn, headquarters for the men's branch. In Brooklyn, is New City Press, the official publishing house; there are similarly named presses not only in Rome, but in Madrid, Clamart (France), Munich, Nijmegen (Holland), London, São Paulo, Buenos Aires, and Manila. The ecumenically minded foundress has published extensively and made translations into more than a dozen languages; she sets forth the beginnings in *That All May Be One*. (1975). Appearing next was her *It's a Whole New Scene,* brief thoughts of youth and Jesus Christ. Related to the meaning as hearth is *When Our Love is Charity,* demonstrating the presence of the Spirit in the movement; her *Meditations* is available in cassettes under title, *Contemplation in the 20th Century*. Her recent *Little ''Harmless'' Manifesto* relates to the ''hotbed'' meaning of Focolare, dynamic in its brief expression of the core of their spirituality. Contributing to the birth and vigorous development of GEN was P. Foresi, educated in the Lateran and Gregorian Universities. *Reaching for More* is his conversation with the Focolarini; he has also written *Theology of Social Man* and, for laity and religious, *Celibacy Put to the Gospel Test.*

[M. R. BROWN]

FOGGIA, FRANCESCO (1604–88), Italian polyphonist. He served in the courts of the elector of Cologne, elector of Bavaria, and the archduke of Cologne. On his return to Italy. F. held the position of *maestro di cappella* at Nemi, Montefiascone, and in several churches in Rome. His last position, held until his death, was at St. Maria Maggiore. F. was the last of the Italian church composers to write in the style of Palestrina. Much of his church music was written for two to nine voices. Among these are the oratorios *David fugiens a facie Saul* and *San Giovanni Battista* (1670). He also composed many Masses to be sung a cappella, a few with organ accompaniments, and litanies and motets.

[H. F. REIMER]

FOGGINI, GIOVANNI BATTISTA (1652–1725), Italian sculpture and architect. F. copied antique statuary in Rome (1673). His major works are reliefs (*c.* 1679) of A. Corsini and the Battle of Anghiari in the Corsini Chapel of S. Maria del Carmine (Florence). In his dry, baroque style F. restored S. Ambrogio (Florence) and further worked in Pisa and Pistoia.

[M. J. DALY]

FOGOLINO, MARCELLO (fl. 1519–48), Northern Italian painter from Vicenza. His *Adoration of the Magi* (Vicenza Museum) is reminiscent of Carpaccio in clarity, light and narrative. F. retained his anecdotal interest but changed his technical style from that of Pordenone to that of Romanino, whom he assisted in Trent.

[M. J. DALY]

FOLDED CHASUBLE, this term was formerly applied to the *dalmatic and *tunic which were worn shortened or pinned up in front *(plicata)* by the deacon and subdeacon during Solemn Mass in penitential seasons. The term was also applied to the *broad stole worn by the deacon from the Epistle to the Communion during these same seasons. These two usages no longer apply. During the Mass of Ordination to the priesthood those being ordained wear pinned up chasubles, which are progressively unfolded to signify the gradual bestowal of the various priestly powers.

FOLIOT, GILBERT (*c.*1110–87), English abbot and bp. A Cluniac monk and prior of Abbeville, he was appointed abbot of Gloucester (1139), bp. of Hereford (1148), and, with Thomas Becket's support, bp. of London (1163). Becket's chief antagonist, F. refused obedience and clashed with Becket at Clarendon and Northampton. Although twice excommunicated by Becket, F., who was royal confessor, skillfully rallied episcopal support for Henry II and defended his cause at Rome. F.'s eloquent letter, *Multiplicem,* summarizes the case against Becket. After the latter's murder, F. continued in high repute with the King.

BIBLIOGRAPHY: A. Morey and C. N. L. Brooke, *Gilbert Foliot and His Letters* (1965); M. D. Knowles, *The Episcopal Colleagues of Archbishop Thomas Becket* (1951).

[W. A. CHANEY]

FOLK CAROL (Fr. *carole*), originally meaning a round dance, then of early pagan dance songs performed in celebration of the winter solstice. The carol later became part of the Christian Christmas festivities and is known today as a traditional song of joy and devotion heard and sung at Christmas. The early Christmas festivals were celebrated by erecting the crib in churches and homes and by singing and dancing. These customs developed into mystery plays, from which the carol had its origin. At first carols were sung between the acts and later incorporated into the actual play. Eventually they were sung independently of any play.

[H. F. REIMER]

FOLK HYMN, religious song. Many Anglo-American folk hymns, essentially of English derivation, are found in the gapped modes of the pentatonic, hexatonic, and heptatonic scales. Folk hymns may be divided into four categories: (1) general hymns, which are closest to the orthodox type of hymn. Sometimes the words were put to different melodies and known by another name (''Amazing Grace'' is also known as ''Harmony Grove.'') (2) Campmeeting hymns, probably of communal origin handed down by tradition. Spirituals of both the white and Negro races are included in this group. (3) Secular songs, used as a basis for words or melody, possibly for camp-meeting use. (4) Ballad hymns, relating a story.

[H. F. REIMER]

FOLK MUSIC, the expression of communities, rather than of musically trained and self-conscious performers. In general the cultural context for folk music is one of anonymous or collective composition, and of transmission by aural rather than written means. Folk music depends on a close relationship to the less educated and less sophisticated classes of society. In content and theme folk music usually has a tangible referent in everyday life: thus cradle songs, snake charming chants, hunting calls, work chants, sea shanties, drinking songs, love songs. Because of the collective nature of folk music, its forms evince unique characteristics, ethnic and national. Thus there now exists an academic discipline called ethnomusicology. Negro spirituals are the outstanding example of folk music with a religious theme. But there has always also been the passage now of sacred music into folk melodies, now of folk melodies into hymn tunes. The contemporary use of folk tunes in liturgy, as in the folk Mass, does not have, obviously, the same spontaneity and cultural roots as the original development of folk music itself.

[D. SMUCKER]

FOLKESTONE ABBEY, originally the first convent of nuns in Anglo-Saxon England (*c.*630), later (10th cent.) a monastery of Benedictine monks. Only the church remains now and is believed to enshrine the relics of the first abbess of the original foundation, St. Eanswith.

[J. F. FALLON]

FOLKLORE, a term coined by W. J. Thoms in 1846, to signify the traditions, customs, and superstitions of the uncultured classes in civilized nations. As a category, folklore includes material as well as intellectual aspects of popular culture. Therefore, folk arts and crafts (which, under the tutelage of William Morris, became the aesthetic of a new school of 19th-cent. art) are also included. There is little difference between folklore and social anthropology, though folklore is more often a name used to label cultural expression in the peasant classes of a civilized society. Perhaps the most remarkable studies of folklore to appear just as the field had begun to attract scholarly interest were the *Kinder-und Hausmärchen* and the *Deutsche Mythologie* of the Brothers Grimm. By the mid-19th cent. folklore had become a science in its own right. Various interested personages advanced theories of its nature and origin. The most controversial of these theories was formulated by Max Müller—it stated that folk literature and mythology were remnants of religious writings related to the worship of natural phenomena. However, two other anthropologists—E. B. Taylor and later, Sir James Frazer (author of the monumental *Golden Bough*)—differed with Müller. They held that such remnants of previous cultures were not peculiar to Europe, where Müller claimed to have found traces of a form of sun and nature worship, but rather that these were common in almost every primitive culture of world civilization; and that these were not the relics of an ancient religion, but rather what had survived from phases of cultural development long since bypassed by the more advanced segments of a particular civilization. (Some other theorists disagreed in turn with the Taylor-Frazer theory and instead assumed that culture had instead been diffused from a "lost" center—like Atlantis.) Folk tales are perhaps the most elemental component of what is grouped under the category of folklore. Once passed from generation to generation (and sometimes from culture to culture) by word of mouth, they all belong to one of three subdivisions: myths, legends, and the popular, or "fairy" tales. Myths are religious stories used to explain codes of behavior, rites, taboos, and various aspects of man's environment; they have a didactic purpose. Legends, heroic, epic narratives, are frequently based on historical fact (e.g., *The Song of Roland*). Popular tales are purely and simply fictional entertainment, often with characters and settings indigenous to the cultures in which they have originated. Folklore at present is a field of study far more expansive than at its beginnings in the mid-19th century. New methods of interpretation and a general realization of folklore's relevance to modern times as well as antiquity, have helped make its study something more than rummaging through dusty, still-existing fragments of the past. BIBLIOGRAPHY: J. Frazer, *Golden Bough* (1890; 3d, enlarged edition, 12 v., 1912); W. Schmidt, *Origin and Growth of Religion* (tr. H. Rose, 1931); R. Lowie, *Primitive Society* (1920); A. Jensen, *Myth and Cult among Primitive Peoples* (tr. M. Choldin and W. Weissleder, 1951).

[D. H. BRUNAUER]

FOLLET, RENÉ (1902–56), Jesuit Orientalist. After training in Assyriology in Paris, he went on to pursue his studies in greater depth in Ankara (1938). He was appointed (1946) to the Pontifical Biblical Institute as professor of Akkadian. Later he also taught Ugaritic, the history of western Asiatic religion, and comparative Semitics. He wrote many articles on the political and religious history of the Ancient Near East, bringing to every subject upon which he touched a remarkable depth of learning. His death left a projected treatment of Babylonia in the dynasty of Hammurabi incomplete.

[C. BUCKLEY]

FOLLOWING OF CHRIST, taking Christ in his humanity as the model and exemplar of the Christian life. Our Lord's own words invited his Disciples to share in his poverty and suffering (Mt 8.19–20; Mk 8.34; 10.28–30) and in his eternal life (Mk 10.17; Jn 8.12), and pointed to himself as the Disciples' example (Jn 13.5). St. Paul instructed his converts to be imitators of Christ and to have the mind of Christ (1 Cor 11.1; Eph 5.1–2; 1 Thess 1.6). The theme in its theological interpretation means that Jesus Christ is the way of salvation, not only as the one who accomplished redemption, but as the model and exemplar of all sanctification as well. Imitation of Christ includes the truth that the grace of sonship by hypostatic union in Jesus is the exemplar of others' adoptive sonship by grace, that as the image of the Father, Jesus is the ideal according to which is fashioned the image of God in all who live by the grace of Christ. His exemplarity means that grace is Christian, giving the recipient an identity as a member of Christ; this is particularly the effect of grace received through the sacraments, so that, e.g., "the one receiving baptism shares in Christ's Passion as though he himself were the one who suffered and died "(ThAq ST 3a, 69.2). In spiritual theology the theme of the following of Christ refers to a specific emphasis on imitating the mysteries of Jesus' own human life. Devotion to these mysteries is a fundamental element in the *Rule of St. Benedict. In the Middle Ages St. *Bernard of Clairvaux, and the Cistercian tradition generally, stressed a strong affective attachment to Jesus' humanity, as did the later Franciscan spirituality. Affectivity was a particular mark of the **Devotio moderna,* out of which came the spiritual classic, *The Imitation of Christ.* *Pietism is also marked by a strongly affective devotion to Jesus. But the following of Christ is an essential element, adapted according to the distinctive spirit of each, in every form of Christian spirituality. What seems most characteristic in contemporary spirituality is a concentration on Christ's mysteries as presented in the liturgy through the Scriptures, rather than on older forms of nonliturgical, popular devotions.

[T. C. O'BRIEN]

FOLLOWING OF CHRIST (IN THE BIBLE). Jesus called his first Disciples to follow him. They came after him (Mt 4.18–22), leaving everything (Mt 19.27). Jesus' followers must suffer with him: "If anyone would come after me let him deny himself, take his cross and follow me" (Mt 16.24), even at the cost of what is dearest to men, because it is the only way to the perfection required of them (Mt 19.21): to be perfect as their heavenly Father is perfect (Mt 5.48). Jesus' Disciples are persecuted as he was persecuted (Jn 15.20). But for them, as for him, suffering and death are the way to eternal life. He went back to his Father in heaven "as a forerunner on their behalf" (Heb 6.20). By faith and baptism, his Disciples enter the same way (Acts 9.2) and are guided by him, the good Shepherd leading his sheep who follow him (Jn 10.1–8), giving them the light of life (Jn 8.12). They must remember his teaching and his example (Jn 14.26), first of all his love for them, and love one another as he loved them (Jn 13.34) even if it requires them to give their life for their brothers as he gave his own life for them (1 Jn 3.16). Christians are "sons of God through Jesus" (Eph 1.5) "the first-born among many brethren" (Rom 8.29). They must have in and between themselves "the mind which was in him" (Phil 2.5). They "walk in a newness of life" (Rom 6.4) which is, in a way, no longer their life, but Christ himself living in them (Gal 2.20). Living in him who is "the way" (Jn 14.6) they steadily run in the race they have started, looking to him who is "the pioneer and perfecter" of their faith (Heb 12.2) to be finally glorified with him (Rom 8.17), eternally united with him in a resurrection like his (Rom 6.6). BIBLIOGRAPHY: Kittel TD 1:210–216, 4:659–674; EDB 795–797.

[A. VIARD]

FONCK, LEOPOLD (1865–1930), German Jesuit biblical scholar and founder under Pius X of the Pontifical Biblical Institute. He was ordained in 1889, became a Jesuit in 1892, and continued his biblical studies from 1893 to 1899 in England, Egypt, Palestine, Berlin, and Munich. After teaching NT exegesis at Innsbruck (1901–07), he went to the Gregorian Univ. in Rome. In 1909 he became the first rector of the Pontifical Biblical Institute and served till 1919. For another 10 years he remained as professor and as editor of *Biblica*. He published numerous scholarly works, including *Parables of the Gospels* (1902; Eng. tr. G. O'Neil, 1918).

[T. EARLY]

FONOYLL, RAYNARD, 14th-cent. English architect, master builder of the South cloister of the Cistercian monastery of Santas Creus in Tarragona (1331–41) and the Church of S. Maria at Montblanch, Spain (1352).

[M. J. DALY]

FONSECA, CRISTOFORO DE (*c.*1550–1621), Augustinian from 1566. His treatise on the love of God (1592) saw 16 Spanish editions and 3 trs.; a second part had less success. His sermons on the life of Christ (1596) and for Lent (1614) were very popular. Cervantes, Lope de Vega, and St. Francis de Sales praised F.'s eloquent writings which, however, lost favor with his death, perhaps because they lack originality and form.

[E. P. COLBERT]

FONSECA, JOSÉ RIBEIRO DA (1690–1753), bp. of Oporto and diplomat. Educated at Evora and Coimbra, he joined the Franciscans and eventually became their commissary general. He had Wadding's *Annales Ordinis Minorum* annotated and completed up to 1564. In 1740 he was named to the see of Oporto.

[H. JACK]

FONSECA, PETER DA (1528–99), Jesuit professor at the Univ. of Coimbra, Portugal. A Jesuit from 1548, in addition to teaching posts in philosophy and theology, he held several administrative offices in the Society, and served Philip II of Spain, who became the ruler of Portugal in 1582. F.'s chief work is a commentary on Aristotle's *Metaphysics* (1577–89), remarkable for its preciseness and mastery of the Greek text. His teaching is marked by divergence from Aquinas on *essence and existence; and for a theory of **scientia media,* predating, some think, that of L. de *Molina.

[T. C. O'BRIEN]

FONT, see BAPTISMAL FONT.

FONT-DE-GAUME, In the Dordogne section of France, the site of impressive prehistoric cave painting (15,000–10,000 B.C.), verified in 1901 by the Abbé Breuil, dean of prehistoric archaeologists. As at other sites (Lascaux), paintings are found far within the caverns, the first images at Font-de-Gaume occurring about 70 yards behind the cave mouth. The fact that the paintings are in dark areas has confirmed deductions of archaeologists that they are ritualistic or magical and not purely decorative in intent. These subterranean ''sacred places''—engraved and painted by hunter-artists—show vital animal forms expressed in definitive gestures in body and movement and, through sculptural line and shading, evidence an amazing grasp of anatomy and 3-dimensional form. *ALTAMIRA, *LASCAUX, *CAVE PAINTING.

[M. J. DALY]

FONTANA, ANNIBALE (1540–87), Italian sculptor and gem cutter of mannerist style, first working in marble in Palermo (1570) and in crystal, bronze, and silver as well as marble at S. Maria presso S. Celso, Milan (1577).

[M. J. DALY]

FONTANA, CARLO (1634–1714), Italian architect. Apprenticed to Bernini, Rainaldi, and Pietro da Cortona, F. designed the façade of S. Marcello al Corso (1682–83)—his baroque masterpiece of concave and illusionistic surface effects—the church and college in Loyola, Spain (built by others), and numerous chapels, tombs, altars, fountains and festival settings. F. is author of *Templum Vaticanum* (1694).

[M. J. DALY]

FONTANA, DOMENICO (1543–1607), Italian architect, brother of engineer Giovanni Fontana and uncle of the renowned architect Carlo Maderno. For Pope Sixtus V F. designed the Villa Montalto and engaged in vast city-planning, designing an aqueduct (Acqua Felice), fountains, and new streets, linking basilicas, palaces, and obelisks. His masterpiece is the Sistine Chapel of S. Maria Maggiore, with its papal tombs. F.'s style is dry and unimaginative.

[M. J. DALY]

FONTANA, ORAZIO (fl. 1542–71), Italian majolica painter, son and pupil of Guido Durantino in Urbino. F.'s Renaissance *istoriato* style is established by seven signed examples (1541–44). His ornate majolica platters, richly decorated in polychrome were often enhanced by scenes and arabesques of Raphael.

[M. J. DALY]

FONTANA, PROSPERO (1512–97), Italian Bolognese mannerist painter who worked first in Florence, then in Rome with Zuccari (*c.* 1540) and with Primaticcio in France (1560). F. borrowed from Raphael in his *Beata Diana d'Andalo* (1545), while his S. Alessio (1576) evidences stylistic debt to *Parmigianino. F.'s thoroughly eclectic mannerism was strongly opposed by the Bolognese Academy of the Carracci brothers.

[M. J. DALY]

FONTANEY, JEAN DE (1643–1710), French Jesuit whom Louis XIV placed in charge of scientists conducting research in China. There he left the group to join his fellow Jesuits as missionary (1688). By 1693 he was in Nanking. The Emperor in gratitude for his gift of quinine provided the Jesuits a house within the palace area. After further missionary journeys F. became rector at La Flèche. BIBLIOGRAPHY: J. Dehergne, *Catholicisme* 4:1421.

[M. J. SUELZER]

FONTE AVELLANA, MONASTERY OF, located in central Italy, a Camaldolese monastery renouned for its ascetical, liturgical, and canonical literature, esp. under St. Peter Damian. Hermitages, priories, and monasteries were committed to the care of the Avellana congregation. In 1392, after being made a commendatory, its discipline weakened. The congregation was suppressed in 1569; the monastery was eventually suppressed until 1935, when it was restored as a hermitage.

[C. KEENAN]

FONTENAY, ABBEY CHURCH OF Cistercian monastery founded in 1119 by Raynard de Montbard as a daughter of Clairvaux and consecrated in 1147. Fontenay is an *ideal* example of the Burgundian Cistercian oratory in its simple facade, single entrance to the nave with 8 rectangular bays, 4 rectangular chapels, and a rectangular apse beyond the transept. Fenestration of the end wall supplies for the lack of a clerestory. The absence of figural decoration and the prevalence of unadorned surfaces is a witness to St. Bernard's anti-Cluniac stance against those ''monsters'' of the imagination which he denounced as barbaric and utterly distracting.

[M. J. DALY]

FONTENELLE, BERNARD LE BOVIER DE (1657–1757), French popularizer of science and man of letters. Educated by the Jesuits, he studied law but did not practice it. His *Entretiens sur la pluralité des mondes* (1686) is a witty discussion of the solar system. His *Histoire des oracles* (1686), based on a Latin treatise, exemplifies a technique exploited later by the philosophes. Criticism, apparently directed at pagan religions, indirectly applies to Christianity, for what is said about oracles can be turned against miracles. Other works revealing F.'s religious skepticism are the *Relation de l'île de Bornéo* (1686) *and De l'origine des fables* (1724). The first describes allegorically the dissensions between Catholicism and Calvinism; the second is an original approach to historiography and comparative religion. BIBLIOGRAPHY: Amédée Fayol, *Fontenelle* (1961); G. Jacquemet, *Catholicisme* 4:1424–25.

[A. S. CRISAFULLI]

FONTENELLE, ABBEY OF, Benedictine monastery in the diocese of Rouen, France, founded in 649 by St. Wandrille. During the Dark Ages it was a center of evangelization; in the early medieval period, of calligraphy and of hagiography. Out of Fontenelle were founded Fécamp, Mont-Saint-Michel, and, in the 20th cent., Saint Benoît du Lac, Quebec (1912). The abbey was joined in the Maurists in 1636, was suppressed at the time of the French Revolution, Benedictines from Limoges returned to Fontenelle in 1894. Forced to leave by the laicist laws of 1901, they returned in 1923. Monks of Fontenelle were prominent in the revival of Gregorian chant.

[C. KEENAN]

FONTEVRAULT, ABBEY OF, monastery by Robert d'Arbrissel in 1100 and dedicated in 1119 by Pope Calixtus II. The aisleless nave has four bays surmounted by domes on their original pendentives. Noteworthy are many fine capitals in the Poitevin-Angevin style. Here are the tombs of Eleanor of Aquitaine, Isabella of Angoulême; here also were the now destroyed tombs of Henry I and Richard I of England. The 12th-cent. octagonal kitchen with strange chimneys is of interest.

[M. J. DALY]

FONTEVRAULT, CONVENT OF (Fons Ebraldi), former double monastery and congregation established in the diocese of Poitiers (now Angers) France, *c.*1101 by Robert of Arbrissel, a celebrated preacher and hermit. Dedicated to the Virgin and to St. John, the convent was unique in its revival of a kind of institution that had earlier existed in Western Europe, the *double monastery. The nuns observed the Benedictine Rule and practiced strict enclosure. The monastery for men housed both clerics and laymen, who lived originally under the Rule of St. Augustine. Within a cent. the order grew to almost 5,000 members, mostly of the nobility, in many branches in France, Spain, and England. At its suppression in 1790 almost 60 monasteries were still dependent on Fontevrault. An attempt was made in 1824 to revive the congregation: three houses were opened but none of them prospered. The remains of the convent are now a public trust, accorded the care given to ancient monuments. The great Romanesque church, which dates in part from the 12th cent., is excellently preserved, as are other buildings which had been transformed into a prison in 1804. BIBLIOGRAPHY: Cottineau 1:1185–88.

[J. DAOUST]

FONTFROIDE, ABBEY OF, monastery in S France (Aude). Founded (1093) by Benedictines, it joined the Cistercians in 1145. The monks, among whom was Peter of Castelnau (martyred in 1208), were active in the struggle against the Albigenses. Abbot Jacques Fournier became Pope Benedict XII (1334–42). From the 15th cent. until its suppression in 1790 Fontfroide was under the rule of commendatory abbots. Revived in 1858, the abbey was again suppressed in 1901. BIBLIOGRAPHY: M. B. Brard, *Catholicisme* 4: 1429–30.

[L. J. LEKAI]

FONTGALLAND, GUY DE (1913–25), French child venerated in the 1930's as a model for first communicants, but whose cause of beatification was put aside by the Congregation of Rites in 1941. The same congregation issued a *monitum* on Dec. 18, 1947, firmly forbidding any further advocacy of the cause. (AAS 40 [1948] 43).

[T. C. O'BRIEN]

FOOD AND AGRICULTURE ORGANIZATION, United Nations agency established in 1945 aims to increase production from farms, forests, and fisheries, and to improve distribution and nutrition. Through intergovenmental cooperation, various studies, services, and developmental programs are conducted upon the request of a government. In November 1948, the Holy See was granted observer status in the FAO. This is to aid in continued development among Catholic workers and FAO headquarters. In this cooperative venture, then, the humanitarian purpose of FAO and the Christian concern for the hungry of the world can be solidified through the sharing of knowledge, techniques and materials.

[R. F. HEKKER]

FOOLHARDINESS, (rashness, over-confidence), a vice opposed by way of excess to courage or fortitude, the moral virtue that governs the emotions of fear and daring in the high-spirited affectivity that responds to emergencies (the "irascible appetite" of the schoolmen; *to thumikon*), not by removing them but by striking within them a reasonable balance. The foolhardy man, *thrasus* in a bad sense, is arrogantly daring, attacking an evil when withdrawal or patient endurance is called for, and sometimes with greater violence than is required. The fault is not so much an exceeding fearlessness, which, if fault it is, Aristotle leaves unnamed, though he notes it is close to madness, as in the Celts (Aquinas discussed it as *intimiditas* or insensibility to fear), but an overweening confidence, often prompted by vainglory. Aristotle refers to the rash man as an impostor, who pretends to a courage he does not possess, and is really a coward at heart. He is speaking of one who "shows off," not of one who is brave despite his fear. BIBLIOGRAPHY: Aristotle, *Nichomachean Ethics* 3.7; ThAq ST 2a2ae, 127 (esp in Lat-Eng ed., v. 42, ed. A. Ross and P. Walsh).

[T. GILBY]

FOOLS, FEAST OF, an annual celebration observed in the Middle Ages in some European countries, esp. in France, on or about Jan. 1. It had various names and is not always clearly distinguishable from other celebrations, such as the Feast of *Asses, or of the *Boy Bishop, all of which were marked by license, buffoonery, and mock liturgical observances that at times verged on blasphemy. The practice, possibly of pagan origin, bore some resemblance to the Roman Saturnalia, not only because it took place in midwinter, but also because it brought a temporary inversion of the social strata, with those of lower order being put briefly on a level with those above them, and so provided a relief from the tensions built into the rigid structure of society. The celebration was repeatedly condemned by the medieval Church and forbidden under penalties of mounting severity until it died away in the late 15th and 16th century. This celebration had no connection with All Fools' Day (April Fools' Day), which appears to be derived from a custom associated with the vernal equinox and to be completely different in character from the Feast of Fools. BIBLIOGRAPHY: H. Thurston, CE 6:132–133.

[R. B. ENO]

FOOT, SYMBOLISM OF. References to the foot abound in the Scriptures. The foot is a symbol of humility, willing service, and penitence. These are demonstrated by Christ's washing the feet of his disciples (Jn 13.4), and by the woman's bathing his feet with her tears and drying them with her hair in repentance (Lk 7.38). Because it touches the dust of the earth, the human foot is also said to symbolize humility. Victory and subjection are represented by a conqueror's placing his foot on the neck of the vanquished or using him as a footstool (Jos 10.24). The authority and power of God are described in the OT when the Lord says: "Heaven is my home and the earth my footstool" (Is 66.2–3). Naked feet symbolize mourning (Ezek 24.17); also adoration, respect, and reverence: God said to Moses "... put off the shoes from your feet, for the place on which you are standing is holy ground" (Ex 3.5).

[S. A. HEENEY]

FOOTWASHING, a practice, based on Jn 13.4–20 and 1 Tim 5.10, observed as an *ordinance by some Protestant bodies; it is also observed in some Eastern and RC Churches on Holy Thursday. Early Lutherans strongly repudiated the rite as a Roman abomination. The Anabaptists and Mennonites gave prominence to the practice to signify brotherhood and humility; it has been observed by them as equal in significance to the Lord's Supper. American Mennonites still continue the practice. The Moravians (until the 19th cent.), Particular Baptists, some Churches of God, the Evangelical United Brethren, and Seventh-Day Adventists have also observed footwashing. There are various reasons for the usage: a return to the practice of the primitive Church; the interpretation that Jesus' command at the Last Supper made it obligatory; an emphasis on brotherly love; a view of the Lord's Supper as equally and simply a symbol of fraternity.

[T. C. O'BRIEN]

FOPPA, VINCENZO (1427/30–1515/16), Italian painter from Brescia, court painter in Pavia to the Duke of Milan. F. executed a *Crucifixion* (1456), frescoes in S. Eustorgio (*c.* 1468), the *Bergamo Polyptych* (Milan), *The Martyrdom of St. Sebastian* (Brera), frescoes in S. Maria del Carmine, (Brescia), and a lost fresco, *Justice of Trajan* (Milan). Influenced by Mantegno in classical reference, modeling and perspective, F. dominated painting in the Lombard towns of his day.

[M. J. DALY]

FORAIN, JEAN LOUIS (1852–1931), French painter and illustrator. F. produced etchings (1873–86) and lithographs for journals (1886–1906) which were collected in the *Comédie Parisienne*. In their exposition of injustice, esp. in the law courts, F.'s melodramatic statements are less powerful than those of Daumier. His late work, deriving subjects from the NT, is deeply religious.

[M. J. DALY]

FORBES, ALEXANDER PENROSE, (1817–75), Anglican bp. of Brechin, Scotland. As a student at Oxford, he was much influenced by E. B. *Pusey, who secured him the Church of St. Saviour, Leeds, in 1847. The next year he was elected bp. of Brechin in the Episcopal Church of Scotland. In this position he promoted Anglo-Catholic principles and practices, and in 1860 he was censured by the college of bishops for his doctrine of the Real Presence. Among his writings is a commentary on the two-volume *Thirty-Nine Articles (1867–68) giving them a Catholic interpretation.

[R. B. ENO]

FORBES, GEORGE HAY, (1821–75), Anglican priest in the Diocese of St. Andrew, Scotland, patristic scholar. Like his brother A. P. *Forbes, he was under the influence of the *Oxford Movement, and held *high church views. He was ordained deacon in 1848, priest in 1849, and served the parish of Burntisland. From his own press he published the *Liber Ecclesiae Beati Terrenani de Arbuthnot* (1864), in advocacy of the Scottish liturgy. He also edited works of St. Gregory of Nyssa, and *Ancient Liturgies of the Gallican Church* (1855–57).

[T. C. O'BRIEN]

FORBES, JOHN, (1570–1606), Scots Capuchin. Son of the eighth Lord Forbes, a resolute opponent of Catholics, but he became a Catholic through the efforts of his older brother (a Capuchin), his Jesuit uncle, and Catholic mother, daughter of the fourth Earl of Huntly. He escaped to Flanders, entered the Capuchin novitiate in Tournai, made his studies at Lille, and was ordained. He carried on a successful apostolate in Belgium, and was stricken down by the plague on the eve of his return to Scotland. He is recognized as the *de jure* ninth Lord Forbes. BIBLIOGRAPHY: T. Cooper, DNB 7:401.

[H. JACK]

FORBIDDEN BOOKS, see INDEX OF FORBIDDEN BOOKS.

FORBIN-JANSON, CHARLES AUGUSTE DE, (1785–1844), French promoter of missions, bp. of Nancy from 1824. He was primarily a preacher. An opponent of

*Gallicanism and a monarchist, he was forced to leave France after the downfall of Charles X in 1830. His main contributions to the missions were: his founding, with Abbé Jean Bazan, of the Fathers of *Mercy, missionaries for the re-Christianization of France; his preaching mission to French-speaking Catholics in Canada and the U.S. (1839–41); his assistance in the foundation of the Society for the *Propagation of the Faith; his establishment (1842) of the *Holy Child Association, for the support of foreign missions by the children of France.

[E. P. COLBERT]

FORCE AND MORAL RESPONSIBILITY, coercion or violence inflicted with a view to making the victim act in a certain way. Any act done because of force is the direct contradictory of a voluntary action and so not imputable to the victim. Under the heading of force is included any immediate threat of death of injury; the morality of an action done under psychological or moral pressure, is to be judged under the heading of *fear. The infliction of force is a sin against *justice, and the specific kind of sin corresponds to the violated rights of the victim—to life or to property, for example. Canon law declares invalid a marriage entered into under force (CIC *c*‡1087, § 2) and forbids under pain of excommunication the use of force to deter entrance into the clerical or religious state (*c*‡.971; 2352).

[T. C. O'BRIEN]

FORCELLINI, EGIDIO, (1688–1768), lexicographer. He was educated at the seminary of Padua, which was to be his home. Together with Jacoho Facciolati, he embarked on a Latin lexicon, with Greek and Italian equivalents, to include all Latin words in literature, in inscriptions, on coins, along with extensive quotations, an undertaking that lasted 40 years. The four-volume *Totius latinitatis lexicon* was published posthumously (1771).

[H. JACK]

FORD, FRANCIS XAVIER, (1892–1952), Maryknoll missioner and bp. in China. In 1912 he became the first Maryknoll seminarian, was ordained in 1917, and in 1918 was one of the pioneer band of Maryknollers sent to China. He inaugurated the first seminary for Chinese at Yeoungkong, S China (1921). From 1925 he was prefect apostolic in Kwantung; vicar apostolic, with episcopal consecration, in 1935. During World War II he worked to aid refugees. After the Communist takeover he was arrested, and transported, in April 1951, with extreme cruelty to prison in Canton. He died there from his ordeal, Feb. 21, 1952.

[T. C. O'BRIEN]

FORDHAM UNIVERSITY, Jesuit coeducational institution of higher learning occupying three distinct campuses: Rose Hill, once the old Dutch Village of Fordham Manor, upper New York City; Shrub Oak, N.Y.; and Lincoln Center, lower New York City. Founded (1841) as St. John's College by Bp. John Hughes (later abp.), who appointed as president John *McCloskey, (later the first American cardinal), the college was chartered and empowered to grant degrees in 1846. That same year Hughes transferred the direction of it from the secular clergy to the Jesuits, who had bought the property and existing buildings (with the exception of the diocesan seminary, which remained in Rose Hill until removed first to Kingston, then to Troy, N.Y. in the 1860s). The Jesuit scholasticate was transferred to Woodstock, Md., in 1866. The development of the college kept pace with the growth of the Catholic population and in 1905 St. John's opened the school of medicine (closed in 1921) and the school of law, with the well-known international lawyer, Paul Fuller, as dean. In 1970, the charter amended, the corporate name was changed to Fordham University, with the exception of the liberal arts college for men, which remained St. John's until 1931, when it was renamed Fordham College. The College of Pharmacy was opened in 1911, followed in 1916 by the Graduate School, the School of Social Service, and Teachers College, which merged in 1938 with the graduate department of education to form the school of education. In addition, the university comprises schools of business and general studies; a college of philosophy and letters, located in Shrub Oak, for student members of the Society of Jesus, approved as an institutional branch of the university in 1955 by the Univ. of the State of New York; Thomas More College, the Institute of Contemporary Russian Studies, the John XXIII Center for Eastern Christian Studies, and a preparatory school. In 1961 the school of law was transferred to the university's new quarters in Lincoln Center where it was joined by the schools of business, education, general studies, and social service. Library holdings number approximately 750,000 vols. Enrollment averages about 11,200. BIBLIOGRAPHY: H. C. Melick, *Manor of Fordham and its Founder* (1950); A. Anastas; et al., *Validation of a Biographical Inventory as a Predictor of College Success* (1960 Pa.).

[M. B. MURPHY]

FOREIGN MISSIONS, PONTIFICAL INSTITUTE FOR, a group of secular priests engaged in missionary work under the direction of the Congregation for the Evangelization of Peoples and dedicated to establishing a native clergy in mission lands. The origins of the society go back to Pius IX and the mid-19th century. The society is the result of a 1926 merger of two groups in Italy under Pope Pius XI. Since 1948 there is an American branch with headquarters in Detroit. The society, with about 800 members, has been entrusted by the Holy See with missions in Asia, Africa, S America, and the United States.

[J. R. AHERNE]

FOREIRO, FRANCISCO, (1510–81), Portuguese Dominican theologian and scriptural commentator. F. was sent by King Sebastian of Portugal to the Council of Trent where he exerted considerable influence. He was first secretary for the *Index of Forbidden Books, contributed to the reform of the Missal and Breviary, and to the composition of the Roman Catechism. He also wrote several biblical commentaries and a Hebrew lexicon.

[T. M. MCFADDEN]

FORENSIC JUSTIFICATION, an understanding of the process of man's being made righteous usually ascribed to Martin Luther and his disciples. "Forensic" here means "by a legal act," i.e., by a declaration; accordingly, righteousness is imputed to man by God without man's being thereby inherently affected. This is doubtless the sort of theory against which the Council of Trent formulated canon 2 of the decree on justification (D 1561). It is questionable, however, whether Luther himself ever took so gross a position. According to his commentary on Galatians, for example, "righteousness *is* our possession, to be sure, since it was given to us by God out of mercy. Nevertheless, it is alien to us, because we have not merited it." Thus Luther stresses the idea of "alien righteousness," and not that sense of justification which for so long was the object of RC polemics. It does appear, however, that in the Lutheran tradition the strong emphasis on righteousness as unmerited has played down the change that takes place within man on the basis of the divine work. It also seems probable that persons formed according to this tradition might neglect the reality of the soul's union with the Lord Jesus, established by faith, and thus live as if the grace of Christ were only being imputed to them forensically. *JUSTIFICATION.

[M. B. SCHEPERS]

FORENSIC PSYCHIATRY, the application of psychiatric knowledge, techniques, and tests to matters of both civil and criminal law. The purpose is to determine legal competence or criminal liability. Thus in civil actions over wills, child custody, marriage, commitment of the mentally incompetent, psychiatric evidence may be involved. In criminal cases the main function of psychiatry concerns the issue of insanity as grounds for defense of the accused. Since, in English common law, to be criminal an act must be performed knowingly and freely, in 1843 in England a proven mental defect was recognized as grounds for acquittal (the M'Naghten Rule). Since that time in the American courts defense based on insanity has been accepted and the legal meaning of insanity expanded. Psychiatrists are called as expert witnesses for either defense or prosecution regarding the legal sanity of the accused at the time of the criminal act. The jury must decide the issue on the basis of a legal definition of insanity. There is a desire that the psychiatrist be removed from the adversary process, and be given the status of being a friend of the court. The legal issue of mental competence and responsibility is distinct from the moral issue: a person may in fact be morally responsible for a crime, yet be acquitted by the courts.

[T. C. O'BRIEN]

FORESTERS, CATHOLIC ORDER OF, a fraternal society with charitable purposes and providing insurance benefits to its members. Originating in Chicago in 1883 it has developed into a international group with "courts" in 30 states of the U.S. and 6 provinces of Canada. In its early years the Foresters provided a much needed service for many who could not obtain life insurance. It encouraged the practice of Catholicism first among men, then in later decades among boys, and in more recent years women and girls. The principles of the order are embodied in the ideals of friendship, unity, and Christian charity. In 1977 it comprised more than 170,000 members in 28 states.

[J. R. AHERNE]

FORGIVENESS OF SINS. In the OT Yahweh's readiness to forgive sins is a factor repeatedly dwelt upon (e.g., Ex 34.7; Num 14.18, etc.) and relied upon with trust (e.g., Ps 25.11; Is 33.24; 40.2). Prayers for forgiveness are frequent (Ex 32.11—; 1 Kg 8.46—; Neh 9.2; Ps 51, 130, etc.) and include reminders of Yahweh's covenant love for his people, his patience, mercy, longsuffering, etc. A frequent motive for forgiveness is the "appeal to Yahweh's honor." If Yahweh punishes his people too severely or too long, and still more if he refuses to forgive them altogether, the gentiles will say that it is because he is too weak to fulfil his promises to them (e.g., Ex 32.12). Thus the suppliant frequently appeals to Yahweh to forgive "for your *name's* sake" (Ps 25.11; 44.26; 106.8, etc.). Ultimately speaking, therefore, Yahweh's readiness to forgive is the outcome of his own attitude towards all his creatures as well as of his relationship with his covenant people in particular. Forgiveness of sin is one of the marks of the Messianic Age (Is 33.8,24; Jer 31.34 etc.). Forgiveness always presupposes sincere repentance on the part of the sinner, a radical change of heart, a turning away from sin, and an acknowledgment of the wrongness of his ways which is usually made in public (Hos 14.3; 1 Kg 8.47–48; Ps 32.5 etc.). So long as these dispositions are absent, Yahweh refuses to forgive. But when forgiveness comes it has the effect of obliterating sin completely (Ps 51.1,9), "covering" it (Ps 32.1; 85.2 etc.), and causing it to be forgotten by Yahweh. Sometimes Yahweh's forgiveness can be achieved by the intercession of one just man, as with Moses (Ex 32.11–12; Num 21.7, etc.). But even when Yahweh forgives, he does not always totally remit the chastisement he has decreed. Even when David repents of his sin in numbering the people, he still has to endure 3 days' pestilence as a punishment (2 Sam 24.1–17). The first and most obvious development which the N.T, adds to this is that forgiveness comes through Christ (Acts 13.38; Eph 1.7; Col 1.14; 1 Jn 2.12). Almost from the outset of his earthly ministry Jesus claims and exercises the power of forgiveness, vindicating his claim by healing the sick (cf. Mt 9.2; Mk 2:5). Forgiveness of sins is, in fact, an integral and primary element in the work of redemption. Jesus' forgiveness presupposes not merely the dispositions of sincere and humble repentance mentioned above, but also faith in Jesus himself and in his power to impart God's forgiveness.

[D. J. BOURKE]

FORM, in Aristotle and in scholastic philosophy, the shaping or determining element in a material being. The Latin *forma* corresponds to the Greek *morphē* that Aristotle's *hylomorphism places as the inner determining element required to explain the change in a subject from one kind of being to another. A change in substance involves primary matter's acquiring a new substantial form; a change in quantity or some quality involves a material being's acquiring a new accidental form. "Form" is transferred to an application to immaterial beings, designated as pure forms, or essences unreceived, in matter. A still further use is the designation of any distinctive element in a reality, or a resource for action—particularly for the act of knowing—as a form. In theology there is a transferred use of the term to designate the words that give use of the "matter" of a sacrament its precise signification.

[T. C. O'BRIEN]

FORM CRITICISM, BIBLICAL, the usual English version of the german *Formgeschichte*—literally "history of the forms." It is a valuable scientific method of investigating the origins, growth, and evolution of the small self-contained units of oral tradition about Jesus that lie behind the Gospels; the investigation, ostensibly based on the form of these units alone, in practice has constant recourse to questions of content and historicity. Inspired by its use in OT studies, M. Dibelius, K. Schmidt and R. Bultmann first applied the method to the NT after World War I, as a reaction to the excessively exclusive literary analysis of previous ages. While scholars differ in their form classification and terminology, V. Taylor's list is typical: *Pronouncement Stories,* which culminate in a saying of Jesus on some matter of doctrine or morals (see Mk 12.13–17); *Miracle Stories* (Mk 1.23–27); *Sayings* and *Parables* (Lk 6.27–38); *Stories about Jesus* (Mk 1.9–13); *Passion Narratives*. Each of these forms served a definite religious and sociological situation or role in the life of the primitive communities. Such a situation (a *Sitz im Leben* or "setting in life") could be preaching, teaching, liturgy and worship, controversy with Jews or Gentiles, church ministry and discipline, etc. The process of use and transmission through which the units have gone has often made it difficult or impossible to recover the exact words of Jesus (his *ipsissima verba*) or the precise chronology and topography of his ministry as shown to us in the Gospels, but the substance of his life and message is there, since the tradition has been preserved—not created, as some would have it—by communities of Christian believers led by responsible men, many of whom were eye-witnesses of Jesus' life and ministry. In short, Form Criticism has cast much new light on the vibrant life and activity of the Early Church, and though it has only limited application to the rest of the NT, it has helped to resolve many of the apparent contradictions and discrepancies found in the gospel tradition. BIBLIOGRAPHY: R. Bultmann, *History of the Synoptic Tradition* (tr. J. Marsh, 1963); V. Taylor, *Formation of the Gospel Tradition* (1933); B. Vawter, *Four Gospels: An Introduction* (1967); E. V. McKnight, *What Is Form Criticism* (1975).

[C. BERNAS]

FORM OF PRESBYTERIAL CHURCH GOVERNMENT, a statement of *polity formulated by the *Westminster Assembly (1643–49). With the arrival of the Scottish commissioners at the Assembly, the divines turned from the question of doctrine to that of church government. The Scots had already had experience of Presbyterianism, the majority of divines favored it, the English Parliament had abolished episcopacy (1642), and some provision had to be made for the ordination of ministers. The Presbyterian majority, who for the most part subscribed to the *jure divino* theory of Presbyterian polity, sought to conciliate the minority *Independents, who opposed the claim that Presbyterianism could be found in Scripture. After some delay the Presbyterian system was finally adopted by a nearly unanimous vote, and in Oct. 1645 the Form of Government was submitted for approval to Parliament. It was adopted in Scotland in the same year. The Form of Government represents a triumph for the Presbyterian view of the parity of presbyters and the regulation of the affairs of the Church by the counsel and will of the whole body; it has remained a standard for Presbyterian church government. BIBLIOGRAPHY: for Church of Scotland. *WESTMINSTER ASSEMBLY.

[J. A. R. MacKENZIE]

FORMAL CAUSE, in a material, composite being, the actuality, i.e., perfective determinant, with respect to *matter (see HYLOMORPHISM); then any constitutive, inner principle of being or activity. The *exemplar cause is sometimes called an extrinsic, formal cause. *IDEAS, DIVINE.

[T. C. O'BRIEN]

FORMAL PRINCIPLE, the source and criterion accepted by a Church for its tenets; correlative of material principle, i.e., the central doctrine or doctrines that are authenticated by this formal principle. The terminology was first used by historians and theologians to analyze what was doctrinally distinctive of the Reformation: the Bible alone was the formal principle; the material principle was the doctrine that man is saved by grace alone through faith. The headings formal principle and material principle are often used also to study or classify the doctrine of the Churches.

[T. C. O'BRIEN]

FORMER PROPHETS, also called the First or Earlier Prophets; the Books of Josue, Judges, Samuel, and Kings; modern scholars refer to them as Deuteronomic history. The distinction between Former and Latter Prophets is from the division of the *Hebrew Bible into Torah, Prophets, and Writings. The later Prophets include the Books of Isaiah, Jeremiah, Ezekiel, and the 12 *minor prophets.

[T. C. O'BRIEN]

FORMGESCHICHTE, see FORM CRITICISM, BIBLICAL.

FORMOSA, see TAIWAN.

FORMOSUS, POPE, (*d.*896), **Pope** from 891. A Roman, F. had served the Roman Curia as legate on missions to France, Germany, and Bulgaria under *Nicholas I (858–867), *Adrian II (867–872), and *John VIII (872–882). Boris, King of Bulgaria, wanted him as abp. of the Bulgarian Church, but Pope Nicholas refused because his appointment, since he was bp. of Porto, would have violated the then strong Latin tradition against the translation of a bishop from one see to another. In the Roman Council of 869 that condemned Photius, F. had a strong, perhaps even a decisive, influence. When the Frankish Emperor Louis II died in 876, the members of the imperial party in the Roman Curia took flight for fear that John VIII would take revenge for their opposition to his policies. Among these was F., whom John not only excommunicated but also degraded to the lay state. Two years later he was admitted to communion, but as a layman, and an oath was exacted of him that he would never attempt to regain his see or visit Rome. Pope Marianus, immediately on his election (882), absolved F. of his suspension and the obligation of his oath, and restored him to his See of Porto. At once F. began to be again an important influence in church affairs. He consecrated *Stephen V in 885 and was himself elected upon the Pope's death. There is no evidence to indicate that he was not an able and devoted pontiff. He continued a conciliatory policy toward Constantinople, promoted missionary activity esp. in England and N Germany, encouraged reform, and constantly fought against lay interference in the administration of the Church. But his political maneuvers evoked bitter enmity on the part of some. In an attempt to free Rome from the ''protection'' of Guy and Lambert of Spoleto (the latter crowned as coemperor by himself), F. turned to Arnulf of Germany whom he crowned emperor in 896. Within 9 months of F.'s death, when Lambert won control of Rome, he had the dead Pope tried in a formal synod known to history as the Cadaveric Synod. F.'s body was exhumed, clad in full pontificals, and arrayed in the prisoner's dock. He was found guilty in this mock trial and declared a false pope; his acts were nullified, and his remains were cast into the Tiber. The event has been attributed variously to the outraged Lambert, to a vengeful Stephen VI, and to a group in the curia with whom F. had dealt roughly. The reason alleged was F.'s translation from Porto to Rome to assume the Papacy. His successors, *Theodore (897), and John IX (898–900) reversed these infamous acts, and F.'s relics were deposited with honor in the Vatican Basilica and his name was officially cleared. But a later pope, Sergius III (904–911), renewed the calumnies against F.'s memory and even required those he had ordained to submit to reordination. Works: PL 129:837–848. BIBLIOGRAPHY: F. Dvornik, *Photian Schism* (1948); Fliche-Martin 7:20–26, 114–115.

[P. F. MULHERN]

FORMS, UNICITY AND PLURALITY OF, a controverted point in 13th-cent. scholasticism, esp. at the Universities of Paris and Oxford. The debated issue was whether there can or must be but one substantial *form in a material being, esp. in man. The problem is philosophical, but the charge was laid that the unicity position has heretical consequences. The clearest presentation for unicity, and one consistent with Aristotle's *hylomorphism and metaphysics of potentiality and act, is given in St. Thomas Aquinas, ST la, 76.1,3–8. Because the union of body and soul essentially constitutes human nature, and because the existent has a single substantial unity and actuality, there can be but one substantial *form in human nature; the rational soul in its perfection is the one source of all human vitality, vegetative, sensory, and intellective. The thesis was opposed at Paris, esp. during St. Thomas's second professorship (1269–72), by theologians in the traditional line, as being Averroistic (see LATIN AVERROISTS); but it was not condemned in the Paris anti-Averroist condemnations of 1270 or 1277. Espiscopal condemnation did come from the Oxford Dominican *Robert Kilwardby, abp. of Canterbury, in 1277, and from his Franciscan successor, *John Peckham in 1284, both alleging unicity to be incompatible with faith in human immortality, the Eucharist, and the Incarnation. The condemnations were never approved by Rome; the surrounding controversies, however, were divisive, and contributed to the decline of scholasticism.

[T. C. O'BRIEN]

FORMULA MISSAE ET COMMUNIONIS, a Latin text prepared under Luther's direction in 1523 for the celebration of the Eucharist. It was the basis for the *German Mass of 1526, which supplanted it, and so of future Lutheran liturgy. The old order of the Mass was kept as far as the Credo; there then followed a silent preparation of the elements, a preface incorporating the words of institution; the elevation took place during the Sanctus and Benedictus. The old canon was rejected; the Pater Noster and Agnus Dei were retained. The *Formula* was issued as a guide, allowing for the celebrant to improvise. Text LW 53:17–40; L. Reed, *Lutheran Liturgy* (1960).

[P. DAMBORIENA]

FORMULA OF CONCORD, the last of the Lutheran *confessions of faith, prepared in 1577 and published in the *Book of Concord (1580). The 30 years following the death of Martin Luther on Feb. 18, 1546, saw the division of his followers into theological parties. One group, the disciples of Philipp *Melanchthon, maintained his brand of irenic and humanistic doctrine; the other gave a strict construction to Luther's theology and sought to hold the line against both deviations from within and against other communions (see PHILIPPISM; GNESIOLUTHERANISM). A controversy between M. *Flacius Illyricus and Victorin *Strigel dealt with original sin; Flacius was also involved in a debate about conversion. Other doctrinal conflicts dealt with the relation between *law and gospel, esp. the "third use of the law," and with the relation between justification and sanctification.

The Formula of Concord was the climax of a series of efforts, both theological and political, to restore unity to the Lutheran party in Germany. This it did by reaffirming the validity of Luther's theology and the authority of the *Augsburg Confession. Original sin did indeed render a man incapable of taking the initiative in conversion, but it was Manichaean to call it the "substance" of fallen man, as Flacius had carelessly done (art. 1). Law and gospel were to be distinguished, and each was to be applied at the appropriate point in preaching (art. 5, 6). Good works did not cause a man's salvation, but it was wrong to say that they were inimical to it (art. 4). In addition to these intramural controversies, the differences between Lutheranism and other Protestant bodies were also specified in the Formula. In opposition to Calvinism, the Formula rejected the idea of predestination to damnation (art. 2); it also reaffirmed Luther's doctrine of the Real Presence in the Eucharist (art. 7) and the doctrine of the person of Christ that Luther had affirmed in the context of the eucharistic controversies (art. 8). Against the left wing of the Reformation (see ANABAPTISTS), art. 12 of the Formula of Concord also drew the line of Lutheran orthodoxy.

After its composition and adoption in 1577, the Formula of Concord received widespread endorsement in various Lutheran provinces of Germany. But in other provinces and in portions of Scandinavia it was not adopted, and its place within the corpus of Lutheran confessional writings has continued to be challenged from time to time. BIBLIOGRAPHY: *Book of Concord: The Confessions of the Evangelical Lutheran Church* (ed. T. G. Tappert, 1959); E. Schlink, *Theology of the Lutheran Confessions* (tr. P. F. Koehneke and H. J. A. Bowman, 1961).

[J. PELIKAN]

FORMULARIES, MEDIEVAL, collections of models for drawing up public and private documents such as decrees in civic matters, laws, administration of justice, letters, charters, wills, and such explicitly ecclesiastical matters as the consecration of churches, blessings, dispensations, excommunications, etc. They date from the 6th to the 9th or 10th cent. and are esp. useful for students of law and medieval philology, and for the preservation, in the earliest ones, of ancient Roman law and institutions, at a time when the knowledge of Latin was minimal. The existence of such formularies is attested to by extant fragmentary remains. Among the most famous and valuable are the *Formulae Marculfi* compiled in the 8th cent. by a monk, Marculf; the 9th-cent. *Liber diurnus Romanorum pontificum* of the papal chancery; and a comprehensive handbook of law, esp. of cannon law, the *Speculum iudiciale* of William Duranti (final revision 1289–91). BIBLIOGRAPHY: P. O. Kristeller, *Renaissance Thought: The Classic, Scholastic and Humanistic Strains* (1961).

[S. A. HEENEY]

FORNARI-STRATA, MARIA VICTORIA, BL., (1562–1617), religious foundress. She married and bore her husband six children. Widowed after 9 years of marriage, she devoted herself to the care of her children, one of whom died at the age of 10, but the others survived, and all in due time entered religious communities. With her children thus settled, she founded a contemplative order dedicated to honoring the Annunciation. The first house of the *Annunziate Celesti,* as the nuns were called, was established at Genoa in 1604. BIBLIOGRAPHY: C. da Langasco, BiblSanct 5:969–971; Butler 3:547–548.

FÖRNER, FRIEDRICH, (1570–1630), German bishop. For many years after his ordination (1595) he encountered much opposition in his efforts to promote Catholic renewal. His tireless activity as bp. (from 1612) contributed greatly to the preservation of Catholicism in the diocese of Bamberg. He also wrote effectively on theological subjects. BIBLIOGRAPHY: F. Dressler, LTK 4:215.

[M. J. SUELZER]

FORNICATION, sexual intercourse between a man and a woman uncommitted to one another for life, and, for that matter sexually uncommitted to anybody. A mean form of sexuality, sometimes one that cadges on a girl's generosity, and all very understandable and usually not to be blown up into an enormity, it is unequivocally condemned by God in the Scriptures and the consistent teaching of his Church. The traditional Christian view is that sexual experience is for keeps, not for an incident. That is the fundamental test which finds fornication wanting, and on the very score of sexuality. Beside it the somewhat labored arguments constructed by social moralists about the prospective wrong to possible offspring, the danger of an urgent occasion for contraception, the value of emotional reticence and non-promiscuousness for the sake of public order and stability, and the therapeutic need for discipline and control, appear supernumerary. Though valid within their just frames of reference they are not very cogent at the time.

[T. GILBY]

FORNICATION (IN THE BIBLE), Both the OT and the NT use the words for fornication (harlotry) and adultery as metaphors for the infidelity and idolatry of Israel, and for the wickedness of the pagan world (Is 1.21; Hos 2; Ezek ch. 16 and 23; Col 3.5; Rev 2.21; 14,8; 17.4–5; 18.3). The OT does not single out fornication in the literal sense of the sexual intercourse of an unmarried couple; proscriptions of sexual intercourse with or by an unmarried girl were intended to safeguard parental rights (Lev 21.9; Deut 23.18–19); or to bar intrusion of the pagan practice of sacred prostitution (Deut 23.18–19). In NT sexual morality the term *poreia* covers not only fornication, but also all forms of sexual impurity or license. Their prohibition has as its reason their incompatibility with the Christian's union with God through Christ (Mk 7.21;1 Cor 5.1; Gal 5.17; Eph 5.5; Col 3.5; 1 4.3; Heb 13.4; Rev 21.8).

[T. C. O'BRIEN]

FORSYTH, PETER TAYLOR, (1848–1921), British Congregational minister and theologian. F. was born in Aberdeen, and graduated from Aberdeen Univ. in 1869. He later studied with A. *Ritschl at Göttingen, and at New College, London. He was ordained in 1876 and held six pastorates. In 1901 he became principal of Hackney College (Congregationalist), London, a post he held until his death. Early in his career F. was militant in his *liberal theology; but, while he remained open to new currents, such as biblical criticism, he turned from the liberal doctrinal dilution of man's need for redemption. Through pastoral work and personal experience he developed a deeper appreciation for the historic doctrines of sin and redemption and new insights into the substitutionary atonement of Christ; he came to center his thinking on the cross. Among the more influential of his 25 books are *Person and Place of Jesus Christ* (1909) and *Principle of Authority* (1912). Renewed interest in F.'s theology has developed in recent years. BIBLIOGRAPHY: J. Rodgers, *Theology of Peter Taylor Forsyth* (1965), A. M. Hunter, *P. T. Forsyth (pa. 1974).*

FORT, JEAN, (1404–64), Carthusian of Scala Dei in Aragón, Spain. From the beginning of his religious life (1425) he evidenced unusual virtues and visions (mostly of Christ and the Blessed Virgin) which his confessor recorded. The 50 visions, found in an incomplete 18-cent. copy of the *Liber revelationum,* are of less interest than the remarkable humility and charity expressed.

[E. P. COLBERT]

FORT, DELHI, indian architectural complex on the Tumna River in Old Delhi, completed in 1648 during the reign of Shah Tehan. Important in the area of impressive sumptuous royal structures is the miniature Pearl Mosque (Moti Masjid) of white marble with three elegant domes erected (1657) by Aurangzeb, son of Shah Tehan.

[M. J. DALY]

FORT AUGUSTUS, ABBEY OF, Scottish Benedictine monastery and school founded by English Benedictines in 1876. Two American foundations stem from this abbey, St. Anselm's (Washington, D. C.) and Portsmouth Abbey (Rhode Island).

[J. F. FALLON]

FORTESCUE, ADRIAN, (1847–1923), English liturgist, historian, and student of Oriental Churches and liturgies. He was ordained in 1898 soon after his conversion to Roman Catholicism. He achieved his first notable success with his book *The Mass, a Study of the Roman Liturgy* (1907). His *Ceremonies of the Roman Rite Described* (1918) went through many editions and was regarded as a standard work until the changes in the liturgy in 1955. BIBLIOGRAPHY: J. G. Vance and J. W. Fortescue, *Adrian Fortescue: a Memoir* (1924).

[N. KOLLAR]

FORTESCUE, ADRIAN, BL., (*c.*1476–1539), martyr. F., a relative of Anne Boleyn, served in the campaign against France (1513) and attended Queen Catherine at the Field of Cloth of Gold (1520). He was an unusually devout man, though in outward respects very much a gentleman of his time. He was arrested in 1534 and again in 1539. Convicted of treason (he refused the oath of supremacy), he was beheaded on Tower Hill. He was beatified in 1895. BIBLIOGRAPHY: B. Camm, *Lives of the English Martyrs,* (1904) 412–461; Butler 3:72–73; C. Testore, BiblSanct 5:974–975.

[V. SAMPSON]

FORTITUDE, a gift of the Holy Spirit. It complements the cardinal virtue of courage, which may be steadfast to endure and brave to tackle the difficulties and dangers in the human scene, even including the ultimate challenge of death, but is given a superhuman strength when it reaches into the darkness beyond to the goal of eternal life, a high courage that "neither things present nor things to come, nor height nor depth, nor anything else in all creation will be able to separate us from the love of God" (Rom 8.39). Tradition attaches to this unconquerable spirit the fourth Beatitude, "Blessed are they who hunger and thirst after justice, for they shall be satisfied." BIBLIOGRAPHY: ThAq ST (Lat-Eng, v. 42, ed. A. Ross and P. G. Walsh).

[T. GILBY]

FORTITUDE, VIRTUE OF, in the wide sense, the virtue that regulates the emotions of fear and boldness so as to dispose a man to act reasonably in situations of danger. Historically it was the first of the virtues to be distinguished by ethicians, and from it the general notion of virtue itself was derived. Virtues (Lat. *virtus,* power, from *vir,* man) are powerful, manly qualities, as is most clearly evident in the case of fortitude. Most strictly, fortitude braces a man to face death bravely for a noble cause; less extreme challenges are the concern of other virtues akin to fortitude *magnanimity, *magnificence, *patience, *perseverance). From the perspective of classical philosophy, fortitude is most properly exercised in military warfare; for it is war that offers the prospect of death for the highest of human terrestrial goods, the common good of the political society. The Christian virtue of fortitude, on the other hand, finds its distinctive expression in *martyrdom, the willing acceptance of death from persecutors as the price of steadfastness in the "warfare" of Christian witness. The Gospel does not overlook the frequent necessity of resisting evils; but it does extol endurance, rather than the willingness to do battle, as the most characteristic act of Christian fortitude. BIBLIOGRAPHY: ThAq ST 2a2ae; 123–124; R. Gauthier, "Fortitude," *Virtues and States of Life* (TL 4, 1956) 483–531.

[B. A. WILLIAMS]

FORTUNA VIRILIS, TEMPLE OF, rectangular Roman Ionic temple in the Forum Boarium, also called the Temple of Mater Matuta. Prostyle in type, raised on a podium, with columnar portico and engaged columns on 3 external sides of the cella, the temple is dated as of the 1st cent. B.C. on the basis of an inscription from Caesar's time.

[M. J. DALY]

FORTUNATUS, VENANTIUS HONORIUS CLEMENTIANUS (530?–609?), bp., poet. A man of education and talent, F. became the spiritual adviser of former queen Radegunda and her nine companions in the great abbey at Poitiers, where he served for a time also as steward. After ordination to the priesthood he became chaplain to the abbey. When Radegunda received a relic of the true cross in 568, F. composed his most celebrated, poems, *Vexilla Regis* and *Pange Lingua Gloriosi,* later incorporated into the Holy Week liturgy. About 599 F. was elected bp. of Poitiers. A prolific, if not notable, poet, F. edited 10 books of verse. He is the source of much information on people and life in the Merofingian era. BIBLIOGRAPHY: Altaner 601–603; H. Leclercq, DACL 5.2:1892–97.

[J. R. AHERNE]

FORTUNE, a philosophic and popular term used in various contexts to describe the cause, character, or outcome of human events and usually identified with the word "luck." Aristotle regarded it as a species of chance, which he conceived generically as a cause of activities, whether human or simply natural, which are performed in view of an end or purpose, meaning that they are intended whether by man or by nature. Chance, generically understood, has two subclasses or species: (1) Fortune, which is involved in human actions intended by human agents to achieve definite goals or ends but which issue instead an effect or outcome neither intended nor expected by the agent, as when, in digging a well, one discovers treasure. (2) The other variety of chance is operative in the workings of nature rather than of man; the intention of these operations is only obscurely apprehended, if indeed it is apprehended at all. This type of chance has no specific name; Aristotle called it simply chance. In Greek and Roman culture, the notion of fortune was considered important because of its connection with human happiness or unhappiness. In contrast to simple chance operating in nature, fortune or luck is referred to as good or bad, as Aristotle remarked: "Fortune is called good when the result is good, evil when the result is evil. The terms good and ill fortune are used when either result is of considerable magnitude." With the Greeks, the goddess Tyche personified fortune in men's lives; she was a deity to be propitiated. The Roman counterpart was Fortuna, who was closely associated with Fate and the unpredictable will of the gods. BIBLIOGRAPHY: Hastings ERE 5:771–795; V. Cioffari, *Fortune and Fate from Democritus to St. Thomas Aquinas* (1949).

[J. T. HICKEY]

FORTUNE, CULT OF. Both the Greeks and the Romans worshiped a personification of fortune under the name of Tyche or Fortuna. Though the former is mentioned by Greek lyric and tragic poets and was represented in sculpture as early as the 6th cent. B.C., she had no mythology and no significant cult except under the form of Agathe Tyche, or "Good Luck," and as the patroness of various cities. It was only in Hellenistic and Roman times that she became prominent through an identification with the Latin Fortuna. The latter goddess was of Italic origin and was at first probably, as her name (from *ferre,* "to bring") would indicate, a bringer of fertility and increase rather than of luck. Her cult was said to have been introduced into Rome by Servius Tullius, where she was variously worshiped as *Fortuna primigenia, Fors Fortuna, Fortuna Muliebris,* and *Fortuna Virginensis*. She was particularly venerated at Antium and Praeneste. The huge remains of her oracular shrine at the latter site may still be seen. BIBLIOGRAPHY: G. Wissowa, *Religion und Kultus der Römer* (2d ed., 1912), 256–268.

[M. J. COSTELLOE]

FORTUNE, WHEEL OF. Late medieval allegorical motif showing personages (kings and hierarchy) upon the spokes of a wheel turned by Fortune—a blindfolded female figure, symoblizing the uncertainty and changeableness of life. It appeared first in the *Hortus deliciarum* of Herrade of Landsberg (*c.* 1175).

[M. J. DALY]

FORTUNETELLING, the term covering various attempts man has made to discover his future. It is a peculiarly human ability to know that there is a future. As an attempt to know impending good or bad luck, Lat. *fortuna,* Gr. *tuche,* it uncurs no more moral condemnation, and affords no more guarantee, than consulting the studbook before placing your bet on a horse: as an attempt to foretell free acts known only to God, it is a form of superstition, *superstitio divinativa*. Various objects may be employed, words and numbers are related and are suspected to contain hidden information which may be elicited by cabala and other forms of numerology. The influence of extraterrestrial bodies is predicted through astrology. Man's body is also thought to disclose his future, notably its powers of manipulation; accordingly hands are regarded as reliable predictors, hence the practice of palmistry. Among many other means of divination are special persons called mediums through whom spirits speak, entrails of "sacrificed" animals, planchettes, playing cards, dice, sticks, and tea leaves. Dreams, too, are felt to be mysterious and sometimes regarded as portents. All such predictions seem to enjoy enough success to convince some of their reliability. It seems that they fulfill a psychological need for reassurance or advance warning; and that divination is prevalent at periods of emotional instability. State laws on the subject are various, and are somewhat elastically enforced. BIBLIOGRAPHY: ThAq ST 2a2ae, 95–96, esp. in ed. Lat-Eng, v. 40, ed. T. A. O'Meara.

[C. P. SVOBODA]

FORTY HOURS DEVOTION, a period of prayer before the Blessed Sacrament marked by public services and private prayer and meditation. Originating from diverse medieval practices, the modern form began in the diocese of Milan in the early 16th cent., marked by uninterrupted exposition of the Sacrament for forty hours (the approximate time Christ's body lay in the tomb) and with one church beginning the devotion as another finished it. Recommended and regulated by several popes, esp. Clement VIII (1592), Clement XI (1711), and Clement XII (1731), the devotion began and ended with solemn Mass, procession, and the Litany of the Saints. It was characterized by penitential attitudes and prayer for peace. The second Council of Baltimore prescribed the service for the dioceses of the U.S., where St. John *Neumann had been an early advocate as bp. of Philadelphia. The practice often promoted a sense of parish community, identity, and pride, as well as of diocesan community, particularly because of the gatherings of clergy. In the 20th cent. the Forty Hours has come to be a devotion honoring the Blessed Sacrament, without the character of reparation and prayer for peace. Decline in attendance led to revision, including shortening the period of exposition (or interrupting it at night) and vernacular hymns and prayers. Regulations of the Roman Ritual (1973) now recommend exposition of the Blessed Sacrament for an extended period of time annually in each parish, if sufficient numbers would attend, but do not specify time or require continuous exposition. These regulations also state that the secondary importance of such devotions requires that exposition be interrupted during the celebration of Mass and that it be carried out in such a way that the worship of Christ present in the Sacrament is clearly related to his manifold presence in the celebration of Mass.

[J. DALLEN]

FORTY MARTYRS, see SEBASTE, MARTYRS OF.

FORTY-TWO ARTICLES, a doctrinal standard, called also the Edwardine Articles, for the C of E, completed largely by T. *Cranmer before 1552. Cranmer's original plan, overoptimistic in itself and thwarted by political events, was for a meeting of British and continental Reformers to frame a commonly accepted statement of doctrines. He was able to consult some continental Reformers resident in England, and other divines, John *Knox among them. Under authority of Edward VI the articles were published in 1553, although probably they never were approved by *Convocations. Mary Tudor's accession made them a dead letter, but under Elizabeth I they became the substantial basis of the *Thirty-Nine Articles. BIBLIOGRAPHY: J. Gardiner, *English Church in the Sixteenth Century* (1904), 308–311; Schaff Creeds I:613–615.

[F. E. MASER]

FORUM (CANON LAW), the sphere in which the power of *jurisdiction is exercised. The internal forum means *conscience, which is subject to sacramental jurisdiction in the sacrament of penance or to extrasacramental but private and spiritual jurisdiction. Matters belonging to the internal forum concern the state of a person's soul before God. The external forum means the public governmental sphere of the Church's life, which is subject to the public exercise of disciplinary jurisdiction. Matters belonging to the external forum concern the juridical status (guilt or innocence) of the members of the Church, e.g., matters dealt with by the *penal power of the Church.

[T. C. O'BRIEN]

FORUM, PRIVILEGE OF THE, a privilege that provides that a cleric who is accused of any crime must be tried by ecclesiastical rather than by civil authorities. Since clerics are leaders of the Church and are responsible for the pastoral care of the laity, and since the confidence of the laity in their pastors might be undermined by the secular trial of a cleric, the Church has actively upheld this principle from the 12th cent., when the issue of "criminous clerks" caused a breach between Henry II of England on the one hand and Thomas Becket, Archbishop of Canterbury, and Pope Alexander III on the other. Although the privilege of the forum is not often claimed today, it is still upheld in principle by the Code of Canon Law (c. 120). It was reaffirmed by Pope Pius IX in the Syllabus of Errors, and by Pope Pius X in the *motu proprio, Quantavis diligentia*.

[R. ARONSTAM]

FORUM PACIS (FORM OF VESPASIAN), in Rome on the modern Via dei Fori Imperiali the public or civic center begun by Vespasian in A.D. 71, early called the Templum Pacis. The Church of SS. Cosmos and Damian (6th cent.) was built into the one architectural remnant.

[M. J. DALY]

FOSDICK, HARRY EMERSON (1878–1969), liberal preacher and author. F. was a graduate of Union Theological Seminary, N.Y., where he later taught practical theology, 1915–46. During the same period he was pastor first at Park Ave. Baptist Church, then (1930) of the newly built

Riverside Church. F. achieved considerable celebrity as a preacher and became a spokesman for the liberal position and a target for fundamentalists. He rejected the divinity of Christ, the virgin birth, and miracles; he affirmed vital faith in God, Jesus as master, man's immortality, and the gospel power to change human life and society. BIBLIOGRAPHY: *Living of These Days: An Autobiography* (1956).

[N. H. MARING]

FOSSANOVA, ABBEY OF, Italian monastery S of Rome which was founded by the Benedictines in the 11th cent. but was taken over by the Cistercians in 1135. Patronized by Frederick I Barbarossa and Pope Innocent III, it became one of the leading Cistercian monasteries in Italy. Its monks pioneered the development and settlement of S Italy by reclaiming marsh land (*fossa nuova*) through a drainage system. Its early Gothic church built in 1208 became a model for subsequent architecture of its style throughout Italy. Also well-known as the place where St. Thomas Aquinas died (1274), it was suppressed in 1812 but revived by the Carthusians in 1826. It is now occupied by the Conventual Franciscans. BIBLIOGRAPHY: Cottineau 1:1200; A. Serafini, *L'Abbazia di Fossanova* (1924).

[L. J. LEKAI]

FOSSORS, gravediggers during the first 4 cent. A.D. regarded as minor clergy. They were also called *lecticarii* because of carrying corpses on a *lectica* or bier. Control of the catacombs came into their hands in the latter 4th and 5th cent. when they formed powerful associations. Included among them were artists who carved and painted figures for the tombs. After the fall of the city of Rome in 410, they could not function, though they are listed among the *clerici* as late as the 6th century.

[S. A. HEENEY]

FOUCAULD, CHARLES EUGÈNE DE (1858–1916), hermit. Born in Strasbourg, France, and orphaned at the age of 6, F. was reared by his maternal grandfather, a retired army officer, who directed him toward a military career. Both at the officer's academy at Saint-Cyr and the calvary school at Saumur, F. proved himself disastrously irresponsible and dissolute. In 1876 he completed his education and was given the rank of second lieutenant. His first contact with the Sahara, where he was to spend the most important years of his life, came in 1881 when he took part in stemming a local uprising. The following year he returned to study the languages and customs and to engage in exploration, publishing his findings in 1888. Meanwhile he had returned to the faith of his childhood, and his public libertinism was replaced by an equally fervid religious devotion. After several years of prayer and penance with the Trappist monks, he left the order before he was ordained to return to the Sahara. At his hermitage at Beni-Abbès he established his unique apostolate, depending not so much upon "good works" as upon bringing the "presence" of Christ to the desert tribes. His effort to win fellow workers and establish a brotherhood was doomed to failure during his lifetime. On December 1, 1916, he was murdered in his hermitage by fanatical tribesmen. In 1933, following the inspiration provided by his spiritual papers, the Little Brothers of Jesus were founded and 3 years later, the Little Sisters of Jesus. His spiritual writings, his letters, and notes for dictionaries and grammars have been variously published. BIBLIOGRAPHY: R. Bazin, *Charles de Foucauld, Hermit and Explorer* (tr. P. Keelan, 1923); M. Carrouges, *Charles de Foucauld, explorateur mystique* (1934); *Spiritual Autobiography of Charles de Foucauld* (ed. J. F. Six, 1964); P. Claudel, *Trois figures saintes pour le temps actuel* (1953).

[I. MAHONEY]

FOUCHÉ, JOSEPH (1759–1820), anti-Christian official during the French Revolution. He entered the Oratory in 1781, but was never ordained; he taught in Oratorian schools until the suppression of religious orders by the Revolutionary government. Apostatizing, he became part of that regime in 1792 as a member of the National Convention, then was put in charge of political executions at Lyons. He was minister of police, first from 1794 until 1802, then, under Napoleon I, from 1804 until 1810, when he was made governor of Rome. In all his capacities he acted against Christianity and the interests of the Church; his political treachery and scheming led finally to his downfall and banishment in 1816, under Louis XVIII, to Trieste.

[T. C. O'BRIEN]

FOUCHER DE CHARTRES, see FULCHER OF CHARTRES.

FOUNDATION MASSES, funded Masses, i.e., those to be celebrated in virtue of an obligation arising from a *pious foundation. Fulfillment must be strictly carried out and recorded; only the Holy See can, for just cause, reduce the number of Masses contracted for, or allow other alteration of the terms of the foundation.

[T. C. O'BRIEN]

FOUNDATION STONE, BLESSING OF THE, the ceremony whereby a four-square cornerstone, the altar site, and the foundation of a new church are blessed by a bp. with newly consecrated holy water. The titular saint of the church is also designated at this time. The ceremony includes the singing of Psalms 83, 126, and 86, the Litany of the Saints, and the *Veni Creator Spiritus*.

FOUNDATIONS, PIOUS see PIOUS FOUNDATIONS.

FOUNTAIN OF KNOWLEDGE (Gr. *pēgē gnōseōs*), the first attempt to put together all of theology as a connected treatise. It was written by St. John Damascene toward the end of his life. It is divided into three parts. The first section lays down the groundwork of philosophy (generally Aristotelian) on which he will base his divisions and definitions. The second gives a historical survey of more than 100 heresies from the beginning of Christianity down to Islamism. The third provides an exposition of the Niceno-Constantinopolitan Creed, treats of God and the Trinity, the creation of the angels, the world, and of mankind, the Incarnation, the Church, Scripture, the sacraments, the veneration of Our Lady, the saints, and sacred images.

[C. ENGLERT]

FOUNTAIN OF LIFE, Allegorical representation of Christ's saving power, frequently shown as a fountain of water nourishing a hart, symbol of the soul as in Psalm 42, "As the hart longs for living waters, so longs my soul for you, my God" The symbol appears in the Godescalc Gospels (*c.*761); later it is expressed as blood gushing from the side of the Lamb and flowing as rivers of salvation to the four ends of the world, as in the famous Ghent Altarpiece (completed 1432).

[M. J. DALY]

FOUNTAINS ABBEY, great Cistercian monastery in Yorkshire, England, established (1132) by the Benedictines of St. Mary's Abbey, York, who became Cistercians in 1135 at the suggestion of St. Bernard of Clairvaux. The monks founded eight other houses within 16 years. Henry Murdac, the third abbot, became abp. of York (1147). The community pioneered and prospered in sheep farming and wool trade and managed to recover from temporary hardship occasioned by King John (d. 1217) and periodic Scottish wars. The Gothic church, monumental even in its ruins, was completed in 1245, but construction continued to the eve of dissolution (1539) with the erection of the great tower which still stands. At its dissolution, Fountains had 32 monks, and possessed 60,000 acres with an annual income of about £1,000. The last legitimate abbot, William Thirsk, was executed for his part in the Pilgrimage of Grace (1537). BIBLIOGRAPHY: *Memorials of the Abbey of St. Mary of Fountains* (ed. J. Walbran, 1863); A. Gasquet, *Greater Abbeys of England* (1908) 85–98.

[L. J. LEKAI]

FOUQUET (FOUCQUET), JEAN (1415/20–1477/81), foremost painter-illuminator from Tours who achieved harmonious unification of Northern realism and Italian classical idealization. Besides the lost portrait of Pope Eugene IV, F. painted Charles VII (Louvre), the *Melun Diptych* portraying the donor Etienne Chevalier being presented by St. Stephen to the Virgin and Child, possibly a Pietà (Nouans, *c.* 1475), two medallions in the new technique painting in enamel: a *Self-Portrait* (Louvre) and *The Believing and the Unbelieving Receiving the Holy Ghost* (Berlin), with some historical and prayer books (*Antiquités judaiques,* Hours of Charles de Bourbon). His rational, sober works are exemplary of a century. BIBLIOGRAPHY: P. Wescher, *Jean Fouquet and His Time* (1947); G. Ring, *A Century of French Painting* (1949) 24–26 *passim.*

[R. BERGMANN]

FOUR ARTICLES OF PRAGUE, the reform platform (1420) of the *Utraquist party of *Hussites: (1) priests' freedom to preach; (2) *communion under both kinds; (3) public punishment for grave sins of all, even clerics; and (4) renunciation of property and civil office by clerics.

[T. C. O'BRIEN]

FOUR CROWNED MARTYRS (d. *c.*304), brothers put to death in Rome under Diocletian. Their cult is old and widespread, but the legend questioned, and is confused with the legend of five Pannonian Martyrs during the same percecution. Tradition has given them the names: Severus, Severian, Carpophorus, and Victorinus. Originally they were buried in a sand pit with other martyrs 3 miles outside of Rome on the Via Labicana. In the beginning of the 5th cent., a basilica was dedicated in their name on the Coelian hill near the supposed location of their martyrdom. Pope Leo IV placed their bodies there *c.*850. The edifice later became a titular church, which still stands after several restorations. BIBLIOGRAPHY: Butler 4:293–295; A. Amore and P. Cannata, BiblSanct 10:1276–1304.

[M. R. BROWN]

FOUR GALLICAN ARTICLES, see GALLICAN ARTICLES, FOUR.

FOUR HORSEMEN, apocalyptic image originating in Zech 1.8–12 where a rider on a red horse appears as the leader of a troop including red, sorrel or pale, and white horses. These four horsemen are sent to patrol the four corners of the earth. The number four signifies total global extension. The symbolism of the colors of the horses has been lost to us. The same image of the four horsemen is taken up and developed in Rev 6.1–7, where the four horsemen are destroying angels sent out over the earth by the four living creatures, each to wreak a separate form of destruction upon it. Here it is probable that the white horse symbolizes victory; the red horse, bloodshed and war; the black horse, famine; and the sorrel or pale horse, death. BIBLIOGRAPHY: J. Walker, *Apocalypse with Figures* (pa. 1974).

[D. J. BOURKE]

FOUR LAST THINGS, death, personal judgment, heaven, and hell, which, along with purgatory in the RC tradition, make up the personal aspects of *eschatology. These are realities that define the limit of man's personal history as an individual before God, culminating in either fulfillment in all dimensions of his existence or in final personal loss. They are distinguished from the eschatological realities connected with the cosmic fulfillment of mankind which include the parousia, resurrection of the flesh, and general judgment. Some theologians find this division artificial because events concerning mankind as a whole have meaning for the individual as well, and individual destiny has a social dimension. The tendency of contemporary theologians is to relate both the cosmic and personal eschatological realities to history in which the last things are present already in the faith, love, and hope man expresses in this life. BIBLIOGRAPHY: A. Winklhofer, *Coming of His Kingdom* (tr. A. V. Littledale, 1963); K. Rahner, SacMund 2:242–246; 3:274–276. *DEATH; *HEAVEN; *HELL; *JUDGMENT, DIVINE.

[J. CORDOUE]

FOUR MASTERS, ANNALS OF THE *Annála Rioghachta Eireann;* (*Annales quattuor magistrotum*), the most extensive compilation of the ancient annals of Ireland ''from the Deluge'' to the Flight of the Earls (1616), compiled at the Donegal Abbey (1632–1636) by Michael O'Clery (Micheál Ó Cléiright), a Franciscan brother. While attending the Irish College at Louvain, Michael was sent back to Ireland in 1620 to collect whatever important materials he could for Hugh Ward, who was preparing lives of Irish saints. During his 10 years of traveling through Ireland, Michael conceived the idea of transcribing and compiling annals from the invaluable mms, knowing that they would never be brought together again, and the preservation of the Gaelic past was foremost in his mind. On the death of Ward, the original project was partially completed by John Colgan (d. 1659). It was in the Preface of Colgan's *Acta sanctorum Hiberniae* that the title *Annals of the Four Masters* was mentioned for the first time. He claims the four antiquaires were Michael O Clérigh, Fear Feasa O Mulconry, Peregrine O Clery and Peregrine O Duignan. In the dedication of the *Annals,* Michael indicates Fergal O Gara as their patron. Copies of the MSS of the *Annals* are preserved in Brussels, Cambridge, Trinity College, and the Royal Irish Academy. BIBLIOGRAPHY: *Annala Rioghachta Eireann*; *Annals of the Kingdom of Ireland by the Four Masters from the Earliest Period to the Year 1616* (tr. and ed. J. O'Donovan, 7 v., 1854, repr. 1966); *Irish Men of Learning* (ed. C. O'Lochlainn, 1947); B. Jennings, *Michael O'Cleirigh, Chief of the Four Masters and His Associates* (1936); D. Hyde CE 6:163–164.

[R. A. TODD]

FOURIER, PETER, ST. (1565–1636), French Augustinian parish priest, reformer of his order, advocate of free education for the poor, and cofounder of a congregation of religious women dedicated to schooling indigent girls. Most of his ministry was in Mattaincourt in the Vosges Mountains of Lorraine, where he developed a lending facility for bankrupt burghers and peasants, formulated ecumenical principles for Protestants and Catholics, based on a better Christian response among the Catholics in his care, and fostered the founding and growth of his teaching sisters. In 1622 he was entrusted with the reform of the Augustinians in Lorraine, a task he performed with patient persistence. His educational aims and methods were far beyond his times in foresight and practicality.

[J. F. FALLON]

FOURNET, ANDRÉ-HUBERT, ST. (1752–1834), cofounder of the Daughters of the Holy Cross of St. Andrew. He lived most of his life near Poitiers, France. He first studied law and philosophy, but after a spiritual conversion prepared for the priesthood and was ordained in 1776. He ministered clandestinely in defiance of the *Civil Constitution of the Clergy. After a period of exile in Spain, he became spiritual director for Jeanne Elizabeth Richier des Ages; encouraged her to establish the Daughters of the Holy Cross for the care of the sick and the education of poor girls; and wrote a rule for the community. The last 14 years of his life were devoted to the sisters. He was beatified in 1926 and canonized in 1933. Emphasis in his spiritual doctrine is on the Trinity, penitence, and service to others.

[E. P. COLBERT]

FOURNIER, HENRI, see ALAIN-FOURNIER.

FOURNIER, MOTHER ST. JOHN (1814–75), founding superior of the Sisters of St. Joseph of Philadelphia. Born Julie Alexise, she entered a Conceptionist monastery at the age of 14, but transferred to the Sisters of St. Joseph, receiving the habit on June 16, 1836 as Soeur St. Jean l'Évangeliste. With Soeur Célestine *Pommerel, F. was assigned to prepare for the American mission; the two sailed for New Orleans on June 17, 1837 and arrived at the hospital of the Sisters of Charity in St. Louis, Mo., Sept. 4, 1837. From there they joined sisters of their community already established at Carondelet, S of St. Louis. With funds brought from France the community was able to build a new brick building replacing a log cabin as convent and academy. F. taught French in the academy and also taught in the school for the deaf that the sisters opened, the first W of the Mississippi. She was professed Dec. 27, 1838 and as superior with three other sisters opened a school for black girls in St. Louis in 1844; in 1846 they were forced to close and then devoted their efforts to St. Joseph's Orphanage nearby. At the invitation of Bp. Francis P. *Kenrick of Philadelphia, F. led three sisters there in 1847 to staff St. John's Asylum. In 1848 at Pottsville, Pa., she opened the first school in the East operated by her community and in 1849 undertook to provide the nursing staff for St. Joseph's Hospital, Philadelphia. From 1851 F. was superior of the first community of religious women in the Minnesota territory; she opened St. Joseph's Academy in St. Paul and in 1852 at Long Prairie a mission among the Winnebago Indians. In 1853 at the request of St. John *Neumann, bp. of Philadelphia, F. returned there and established a motherhouse for her community, first at McSherrytown, in 1854, then at Chestnut Hill, Philadelphia, in 1858, where it has remained. Under her leadership growing numbers of novices were trained and foundations made in Pennsylvania, Delaware, Maryland, West Virginia, New Jersey, New York, and Toronto, Canada; she also supervised nursing by the Sisters of St. Joseph during the Civil War. For her community instruction and devotion she herself translated many works from French. There is no definitive biography, but ample evidence of her impact on Catholic education and social ministry exists in diocesan archives, as well as in histories of her congregation (the latest, by E. de S. Dee, pa. 1975) and in its archives (notably in Chestnut Hill, Baden, Pa., Carondelet, Mo., St. Paul, Minn., Brentwood, N.Y., Buffalo, N.Y., Wheeling W. Va., and Toronto, Canada). BIBLIOGRAPHY: *History of the Archdiocese of Philadelphia (ed. J. F. Connelly, 1976)* ch. 3 and 4; M. J. Curley, *Venerable John Neumann* (1952) 369–371.

[M. R. BROWN]

FOURSQUARE GOSPEL (Fourfold Gospel), the teaching, esp. of *Holiness Churches and in *Pentecostalism, that the complete gospel message includes four themes: *justification; *entire sanctification through *baptism with the Holy Spirit; *divine healing; and *premillenarianism. Jesus is Savior, Sanctifier, Healer, and Coming Lord. BIBLIOGRAPHY: A. B. Simpson, *Fourfold Gospel* (1925).

[T. C. O'BRIEN]

FOURSQUARE GOSPEL, INTERNATIONAL CHURCH OF THE, see INTERNATIONAL CHURCH OF THE FOURSQUARE GOSPEL.

FOURTEEN HOLY HELPERS (*auxiliatores, intercessores, adiutores, coadiutores, adiuvantes, auxiliantes, quattuordecim sancti*), a group of saints whose intercession, according to popular tradition, is particularly efficacious in emergencies or afflictions, esp. in epidemics. Devotion to these saints was widespread in Switzerland, the Tyrol, Austria, Germany, Sicily, and various parts of Italy in the 14th cent., when great plagues invaded Europe. The names of the saints, as well as their particular intercessions, vary according to localities, but the usual list is as follows: Acacius (for headaches and pain); Barbara (for lightning and sudden death); Biagius (for throat ailments); Catherine (for diseases of the tongue); Christopher (for hurricanes and accidents to travelers); Ciriacus (for possession by the devil); Dionysius (for headaches and demoniac possession); Giles or Egidius (for insanity, epilepsy, and sterility); Erasmus (for intestinal diseases); Eustachius (for dangers of fire); Georgius (for skin infections); Margherita of Alexandria (invoked by pregnant women); Pantaleon (for consumption); Vitus (for hydrophobia, snake bites, and "Vitus dance"). Their cult was sponsored first by the Dominicans, then by the Cistercians, and later by the Benedictines. Hospitals, sanctuaries, chapels, and towns were dedicated to them. Pilgrimages are still made to the basilica reared in their honor at Würzburg in 1772. BIBLIOGRAPHY: B. da Arenzano, BiblSanct 2:618–623; J. Dünninger NCE 5:1045–46.

[F. D. LAZENBY]

FOURTEENTH AMENDMENT to the Constitution of the U.S. (also called the Reconstruction Amendment), ratified on July 28, 1868. Although it was first designed to protect the liberties and rights of all citizens from violations by the states, its immediate and primary concern became the newly emancipated Negroes. The amendment ultimately was interpreted as embracing all areas of human rights and civil liberties (among them education, religion, health, etc.), and not allowing any state to "abridge the privileges or immunities of citizens . . . deprive any person of life, liberty, or property without due process of law nor deny to any person within its jurisdiction the protection of the laws" (art. 14).

[S. A. HEENEY]

FOURTH CRUSADE, the name given to the Western military expedition that captured Constantinople in 1204. In 1198 Innocent III proclaimed a crusade to free Jerusalem from its Muslim captors. After many delays an army composed mostly of Northern French was gathered, and Venice agreed to transport it to Egypt. When the crusaders could not meet their financial obligations the doge, Enrico Dandolo, suggested that they aid him in taking the Dalmatian city of Zara which, despite explicit papal prohibitions, they did in Nov. 1202. In the meantime Alexius IV, the son of the deposed Byzantine Emperor Isaac II Angelus, requested their assistance in recovering his throne and in return made many impressive promises. Not only did the Pope strictly forbid an attack on Constantinople, but many of the fighting men refused to be distracted from the crusade. The Venetian doge, however, convinced the leaders, and the expedition made for the Bosporus. In July of 1203 they captured the city and placed Alexius IV on the throne. They then waited in vain for him to fulfill his lavish promises. In Jan. 1204 he was slain by the strongly anti-Latin usurper, Alexius V Murtzuphlus. In March the crusaders and the Venetians signed a treaty partitioning the Byzantine Empire and prepared again to attack the capital. In April 1204 they poured into the city and mercilessly pillaged it for 3 days. Count Baldwin of Flanders was elected emperor and Tommasso Morosini, a Venetian, was named patriarch. Although these acts were vigorously condemned by Innocent III, his role in the affair is still subject to some controversy. He does seem to have been sincere in forbidding the attack, and his shock on learning of it seems genuine. Yet he undoubtedly knew what was likely to happen and, it must be admitted, once the deed had been done he found it rather easy to live with. Constantinople never recovered from the wanton destruction and looting by the Latins. Whatever chance there might have been to restore good relations between the Eastern and the Western Churches was also destroyed by this event. The conflict was no longer one between bishops and theologians, but the average Greek was now filled with personal hatred against the Latins and against their leader the Pope, whom they believed to have ordered the assault on their sacred city. The schism between the Churches became a living reality. BIBLIOGRAPHY: E. H. McNeal and R. L. Wolff, *History of the Crusades* (ed. K. M. Setton (1962) 2:153–186.

[G. T. DENNIS]

FOX, GEORGE (1624–91), founder of the Religious Society of Friends. F. was born at Fenny Drayton, Leicestershire, and by choice received only a rudimentary education. Sensitively religious, he was early depressed by the state of the Church in Puritan England and by its Calvinist teachings. To quiet his tormented searching, there gradually dawned in him a deeply mystical conviction, a belief in the *Inner Light; and from 1647 F. was an itinerant preacher of his own individualistic brand of Christianity. In the midlands and N of England he attracted many followers, esp. from groups dissatisfied with organized Christianity: Seekers, Familists, Anabaptists, and Ranters. His preaching against the establishment also brought him eight jail sentences, totaling 6 years of periodic imprisonment. A vivid, captivating preacher, undaunted by suffering, F. gave organizational stability to the Friends, esp. with his "Rules for the Management of Meetings" (1668). He also showed himself to be rather inconsistently authoritarian (see NAYLOR, JAMES). F. undertook many journeys to spread his message, one to America in 1671–72. The last period of his life he spent in London working for the *Toleration Act (1689). In an ungrammatical but forceful style, F. set out his teachings in many books and pamphlets, esp. in his *Journals,* published posthumously in 1694 (modern eds. J. L. Nickall, 1952; H. J. Cadbury, 1963). BIBLIOGRAPHY: Knox Enth 139–175; Mayer RB 409–422, with bibliog.; V. Noble, *Man in Leather Breeches* (1953); H. Van Etten, *George Fox and the Quakers* (tr. E. Kelvin Osborn, 1959); W. C. Braithwaite, *Beginnings of Quakerism* (2d ed., H. J. Cadbury, 1955). *RELIGIOUS SOCIETY OF FRIENDS.

FOX SISTERS, the women whose "spirit rappings" at Rochester, N.Y., began the modern Spiritualist movement. They were Margaret Fox (b. 1833), Kate Fox (b. 1836), and their older sister, Leah (Fox) Fish (later Underhill). Margaret and Kate first experienced mysterious tapping and rattling sounds in 1847 at Hydesville, N.Y., and later at Leah's Rochester home. The three sisters developed an alphabet to interpret the spirit messages. In 1850 they created a sensation in New York City, with the help of Horace Greeley and the New York *Tribune*. Their lecture tours convinced thousands that the dead could send messages to the living through a Spiritualist medium. Among notable converts was Robert Dale Owen (1801–77), who became a major publicist of Spiritualism. The Fox Sisters also lectured in England, where Kate married and settled permanently. After her conversion to Catholicism in 1888, Margaret exposed the "Rochester rappings" as deliberate frauds; later she recanted and continued to lecture on Spiritualism with Leah for several years. The phenomena described by the Fox Sisters inspired the development of Spiritualist circles, which drew their ideas largely from Andrew Jackson *Davis. The three sisters contributed little to Spiritualist thought or the organization of the movement they had inspired. *SPIRITUALISTS.

[R. K. MACMASTER]

FOXE, RICHARD (*c.* 1447–1528), diplomat, bp. of Winchester, founder of corpus Christi College, Oxford. F. probably studied at Magdalen College, Oxford, received a doctorate in canon law at the Univ. of Paris, and was ordained in that city. In 1485 he was appointed principal secretary of state; for the next 30 years, under Henry VII and Henry VIII, F. did important diplomatic work for the government. During that time he was named bp. of several dioceses successively, the last being that of Winchester (1501). He gave up his secular posts as Thomas *Wolsey's powers increased and devoted himself to the care of his diocese. BIBLIOGRAPHY: T. Fowler, DNB 19:150–156.

[T. M. MCFADDEN]

FOXE'S BOOK OF MARTYRS, classical instance of a book making history, rather than history the book, first published in 1573, and reaching its seventh edition by 1684. The author, John Foxe (1516–87), had been a fellow of Magdalen and a refugee in Germany from Mary Tudor; he had already published the Latin work, begun on the suggestion of Lady Jane Grey, which was the basis of his *Actes and Monuments of these latter and perillous dayes, touching matters of the Church, wherein ar comprehended and described the great persecutions & troubles, that have bene wrought and practised by Romishe Prelates, speciallye in this Realme of England and Scotlande, from the yeare of our Lorde a thousande, unto the tyme now-present*. Its main wealth lies in materials from the 14th to the 16th centuries. It was composed in the household of the Duke of Norfolk and the printing office of John Day. Though quickly riddled by Nicholas Harpsfield, the work, with its passages of coarse ribaldry at the expense of opponents and written from a blazing hatred of Spain and the Inquisition, was a superb journalistic scoop. It met the occasion, and successive editions and abridgments, embellished with woodcuts, did more than anything to fan and maintain the flame of anti-Catholic feeling. A copy was ordered by Convocations (1570) to be placed in every collegiate church, and soon it came next only to the Bible in Protestant reading. One of the charges against W. *Laud was that he had refused to license it. Until 1837–42, when S. R. Maitland exposed the numerous errors in the narrative, a majority accepted it as authentic history. Certainly it contains falsifications and fictions, and common criminals are made into martyrs; generally it adopts the loose notions of literary ethics prevalent in the polemics of the period. But if Foxe was a man who, in the words of Anthony à Wood (1632–95), believed all he was told, the present tendency is to recognize his substantial historical learning and even to attach a socio-psychological importance to his work, though the therapeutic value of its vicarious violence may well be questioned. BIBLIOGRAPHY: W. Haller, *Elect Nation: The Meaning and Relevance of Foxe's Book of Martyrs* (1963).

[T. GILBY]

FOY, STE., see STE. FOY.

FRA ANGELICO, see ANGELICO, FRA.

FRA DOLCINO, see DOLCINO, FRA.

FRACTION, a term referring to the breaking of the Host in the Liturgy of the Eucharist. Originating at the Last Supper, the "breaking of the bread" became a name for the Eucharist in the early Church. The ritual differs in position with the Liturgy of the Eucharist according to the rite followed. In the Latin rite a small portion is broken off one half of the Host and dropped into the chalice after the Our Father (com-mixture). The prayer Lamb of God follows. In the Eastern rite the Host is broken into four parts, arranged in the form of a cross, one part icle then placed in the chalice. In the Mozarabic rite the Host is divided into nine portions, arranged in cruciform, and two particles are placed in the chalice.

[J. R. AHERNE]

FRANCA, SS., two saints of the Middle Ages. (1) Franca (fl. 11th cent.), a solitary in Fermo, who took religious vows at San Angelo in Pontano, but left there for another hermitage. A *passio* by an unknown monk, which is the main source of information about her, credits her with being a martyr in defense of her virtue. (2) Franca (d. 1218), abbess. She was of noble birth and joined the Benedictines at San Siro in Piacenza. Chosen abbess in 1198, she strengthened discipline and strict observance. In 1216 she became superior of a new Cistercian convent in Pittoli. BIBLIOGRAPHY: G. Tammi and F. Carafa, BiblSanct 5:1002–04; Butler 2:166.

[E. CONWAY]

FRANCE, predominantly Catholic country of W. Europe; however, as in other parts of Europe, much of the population is now only nominally Catholic. France has given the Church many saints, popes, theologians, and missionaries, as well as such sources of inspiration as Gothic architecture. Greeks settled at Marseilles as early as 600 B.C., but the history of the area is obscure prior to its conquest by Julius Caesar. Romans called it Gaul for the Galli (Celts) living there. Christianity was introduced in the 2d cent., perhaps from Asia Minor, and the French Church of the early centuries included such notable figures as SS. Irenaeus of Lyons, Martin of Tours, Hilary of Poitiers and Vincent of Lérins. The 5th cent. brought the breakdown of Roman authority and invasions of Arian and non-Christian tribes, including the Franks who gave the country its modern name. A new age for the Church began in 496 with conversion of the Frankish King Clovis to Catholic Christianity. In 732 near Poitiers, Charles Martel stopped the Moslem advance into W. Europe. In 751 the Carolingians took the throne from the Merovingians they had long dominated as Mayors of the Palace, and in 800 Pope Leo III crowned Charlemagne as the first Holy Roman Emperor. Alcuin of York and other educated clergy were brought in to lead a Carolingian Renaissance. Shaken by Viking attacks, Charlemagne's empire later splintered into feudal provinces. Development of the modern nation began with the crowning of Hugh Capet in 987. Ruling till 1328, the Capetians, most notably St. Louis IX (1226–70), supported the papacy—against Holy Roman Emperors, in Crusades advocated by clerics like Bernard of Clairvaux, in subduing heretics like the Albigenses. Cluny became a center of renewal for all Europe in the 10th cent., and the 13th cent. scholastic renewal of theology centered in the French capital, Paris. Under Clement V (1305–14) the papacy became virtually a French institution, with Avignon the papal residence from 1309 to 1377. An insistence on the rights of the French Church in relation to the papacy, *Gallicanism, gained support, as did conciliarism. French cardinals precipitated the Western schism in 1378 by electing Clement VII. In the Hundred Years War with England (1337–1453), France suffered severe losses, but began a resurgence under Joan of Arc. At the Reformation, the French monarchy remained Catholic. Huguenots, adherents of the Reformed faith taught by J. Calvin, gained significant strength but were decimated by the St. Bartholomew's Day Massacre of 1572. The conversion of Henry IV in 1593 secured the triumph of Catholicism, though Protestants enjoyed toleration from the 1598 Edict of Nantes till its revocation by Louis XIV in 1685. All Churches suffered in the 1789 French Revolution. But Napoleon brought freedom of worship for Protestants and Jews, and negotiated a new concordat (1801) with the Vatican that governed relations until Church-State separation was declared in 1905.

As the name of the evangelization program set up in 1941, the *Mission de France,* would suggest, France in the 20th cent. has become, as it were, a mission country; ten percent of the baptized is the estimated figure of practicing Catholics. Yet in the theological and liturgical developments, in social action, in ecumenism, in church art and architecture, the Church of France continues to play a leading role at both the theoretical and practical levels. The enlightened statements of the episcopal conference of France are models for the whole Church. The impression created by clergy and laity alike on a visitor to a French parish church is that they are making a conscious and committed choice in the face of a totally alien climate of life and opinion. In that there is promise of resources for the formidable task of evangelization.

[T. EARLY]

FRANCE, ANATOLE (pseud. of Jacques Anatole François Thibault; 1844–1924), French poet, novelist, critic. Although F. retained from his Jesuit education a classical ideal of style and culture, reminiscences of his youth show that he had lost his faith and developed an antipathy for priests. As a writer, he adopted the skepticism and pagan humanism of the 18th-cent. philosophs, Renan and the Parnassians, as evidenced in such works as *Les Noces corinthiennes* (1876), *La Vie littèraire* (1888–92), and *Le Jardin d'Epicure* (1895). The Dreyfus case changed F. from an epicurean man of letters into a political activist. After 1898 he became a militant of the Left, as reflected in *L'Histoire contemporaine* (1897–1901), and campaigned actively for social justice in *L'Affaire Crainquebille* (1901), which is a disguised treatment of the Dreyfus case. His later works reflected that F., although faithful to his convictions, was increasingly skeptical of factions. He was awarded the Nobel Prize for Literature in 1921. Because the development of his thought so accurately reflected the evolving secularistic ideals of the Third Republic and its Left wing, the government honored him with a state funeral. BIBLIOGRAPHY: C. Jefferson, *Anatole France: The Politics of Skepticism* (1965); D. Tylden-Wright, *Anatole France* (1967).

[G. E. GINGRAS]

FRANCES D' AMBOISE, BL. (1427–85), widow of Duke Peter II of Brittany (d. 1457). She founded the first cloister of Carmelite nuns in France (1463) and joined the order (1467), eventually becoming prioress of the convent at Couëts. BIBLIOGRAPHY: Butler 4:266–267; A. di Santa Teresa, EncCatt 5:1567.

[J. MULDOON]

FRANCES OF ROME, ST. (1384–1440), a Roman noble who lived a holy married life of dedication to her husband and children. With her sister-in-law, when they were still very young matrons, she practised prayerful and ascetic devotion to God, which bore fruit in many charitable services for Rome's destitute. Although she and her family eventually suffered the hardships of poverty themselves, she continued to succor the sick poor. While still living with her husband, she was the founder (1425) of a society of laywomen, Oblates of Tor de'Specchi, dedicated to religious devotion and almsgiving. Only after her husband died in 1436 did she feel free to enter the community and act as its spiritual guide. Even before her death Rome's poor considered her a saint, and her cause was immediately promoted thereafter, culminating in her canonization in 1608. She is esp. venerated in Rome, where she is considered to be a patron saint. BIBLIOGRAPHY: E. Vaccaro, BiblSanct 5:1011–1021; Butler 1:529–533.

[J. F. FALLON]

FRANCESCHI FRANCESCO DE' (fl. 1443–68?), Venetian painter known from an altarpiece (Padua) with Peter and saints signed and dated (1447) in International Gothic style. The most important work attributed to F. is the *St. Mammas Altarpiece,* sections of which are in the museums of Yale University, Verona, and Budapest.

[M. J. DALY]

FRANCESCHI, GUSTAVO JUAN (1871–1957), Argentine philosopher and sociologist. Ordained in 1902, he became a noted preacher who carried the social doctrine of the Church into the streets of Buenos Aires. He taught philosophy at the Catholic University of Buenos Aires from 1916 and Catholic social thought in the major seminary of that city from 1917 to 1941. A frequent writer of abstracts for journals, F. for some 20 years edited the journal *Criterio.* Among his books were *La democracia y la iglesia* (1918); *Tres estudios sobre la familia* (1923); *La iglesia* (1935); and *El pontificado romano* (2 v., 1945).

[J. R. AHERNE]

FRANCESCHINI, MARC ĀNTONIO (1648–1729), Italian painter from Bologna. F. was head of Bologna's Accademia Clementina and received many important commissions. Working in Modena, Piacenza, and Rome, F. drew the cartoons for the mosaics in St. Peter's and collaborated in the decorations of the Church of Corpus Domini, Bologna. F.'s highly decorative style is at times sentimental and mannered.

[M. J. DALY]

FRANCESCO d' ANTONIO DEL CHERICO (fl. 1463–85), Italian miniature painter. Working at S. Marco, F. produced antiphonaries for the Florence cathedral and in later editions of Plutarch, Petrarch, Books of Hours, and other religious works shows a vigor of style related to that of Pollaiuolo.

[M. J. DALY]

FRANCESCO BARTHOLI (fl. 1312–34), Franciscan writer. He was born in and spent most of life at Assisi. A sometime supporter of Michael of Cesena, he wrote an important source for early Franciscan history, *Tractatus de indulgentia S. Mariae de Portiuncula* (ed. P. Sabatier, *Collection d'études et de documents sur l'histoire religieuse et littéraire du moyen âge,* 7 v. 1898–1909) 2:97–100); J. L. Grassi, NCE 6:25.

[J. L. GRASSI]

FRANCESCO DI GENTILE da FABRIANO (fl. 1450), Fabrianese painter whose few signed pieces indicate at first the International Gothic Style and later the influence of Carlo Crivelli.

[M. J. DALY]

FRANCESCO DI GIORGIO (Martini; 1439–1501), Italian Sienese architect, painter and sculptor. Commissioned by the dukes of Urbino, Federigo da Montefeltro and his son Guidobaldo, F. worked on the Ducal Palace (1472), directed construction of the Church of S. Bernadino, the ducal palace in Gubbio, and many fortresses that provided the first adequate defense against cannon fire. F. advised on construction of the cathedrals of Milan and Pavia. In 1495 he successfully exploded a mine, assisting the Aragonese troops to defeat the forces of Charles VIII of France. As sculptor F. executed 4 bronze *Angels* (Siena cathedral), a *Lamentation* (Venice), and a *Flagellation* (Perugia). His most important paintings are a *Nativity* (1475) and a *Coronation of the Virgin* (1471). While his paintings and sculpture are Sienese in tradition, F.'s architectural works are important in the development of the High Renaissance. He translated Vitruvius and wrote an architectural thesis. BIBLIOGRAPHY: J. Pope-Hennessy, *Italian Renaissance Sculpture* (1958).

[M. J. DALY]

FRANCESCO MARIA OF COMPOROSSO, ST. (1804–66), a Capuchin lay brother who ministered to the poor and sick in 19th cent. Genoa. He had gifts of prophetic vision and healing, but his dedicated service to victims of a cholera epidemic in 1866 most of all manifested his holiness. He died near the end of that epidemic, after having offered his life to God that it might cease.

[J. F. FALLON]

FRANCESCO DI VANNUCCIO (fl. 1367–1403?), Italian painter whose one signed processional panel shows a *Crucifixion* on one side and *The Enthroned Virgin* on the other and in quality relates to works of the Sienese masters, Lippo Mammi and Simone Martini.

[M. J. DALY]

FRANCESCO DA VOLTERRA (fl. 1343–71/73), Italian painter. F.'s only certain work is a *Madonna with Child and Angels* (Modena), which evidences a strong influence of Taddeo Gaddi and Andrea da Firenze.

[M. J. DALY]

FRANCHI DE' CAVALIERI, PIO (1869–1960), Italian scholar and hagiographer. From 1896 F. was a scriptor of the Vatican Library, concerning himself esp. with the cataloguing of the Greek and Latin manuscripts. His principal work was done in the field of hagiography. He published nine volumes of studies and essays on the saints in the series *Studi e Testi*, as well as many articles in learned journals.

[R. B. ENO]

FRANCIA (FRANCESCO RAIBOLINI; fl. 1482–1517), Italian Bolognese master goldsmith, sculptor and painter. F.'s preserved works are paintings in the Ferrarese tradition with references to the goldsmith's technique in shining textures (St. Stephen, Rome). A mature style in blue and gray tones with sculpturesque form relating to the style of Leonardo and Perugino appears in a *Madonna* (Budapest, 1495) and distinguishes a subsequent series of altarpeices (S. Giacomo Maggioro, Bologna, 1499), the *Assumption* (Berlin, 1504), and a large number of later Madonnas. Unusual frescoes in S. Cecilia, Bologna, with graceful, elongated figures in pale landscapes unite a primitive simplicity with fully rounded forms. Remarkable is F.'s late portrait of *Federigo Gonzaga as a Child* (N.Y.; 1510).

[M. J. DALY]

FRANCIA, JOSÉ GASPAR DE (1756–1840), called "El Supremo," dictator of Paraguay. F. studied for the priesthood and obtained his Ph.D. at the seminary of Córdoba, Argentina. He practiced law in Asunción and in 1811 became one of the leaders of independence. Elected president of the republic in 1814 for a 3-year term, he remained in office for life. In his desire to make Paraguay self-supporting, he expelled foreigners and promoted domestic industris and the modernization of agriculture. His administration was both progressive and despotic. One of his victims was the Church. F. closed the seminary, suppressed religious orders, sent bps. and clergy into exile, and did his utmost to destroy Christianity among his countrymen. BIBLIOGRAPHY: C. A. Washburn, *History of Paraguay* (1871); J. R.Rengger and M. Longchamps, *Reign of Doctor Joseph Gaspard Roderick de Francia in Paraguay* (1971).

[P. DAMBORIENA]

FRANCIS, I (1494–1547), **KING OF FRANCE,** 1515–47. Often criticized for his foolish and impulsive policies, F. is best remembered as the leading French Renaissance monarch. While he encouraged Italian artists and arcitects such as da Vinci, Il Rosso and Il Primaticcio to come to his court, he did not fail in his support of French humanists, in particular Guillaume *Budé and *Lefèvre d'Etaples. The Italian Wars and the conflicts with Charles V dominated F's foreign policy. His religious policies were characterized by vacillation and inconsistency. Although there is some historical argument, he won an important victory with the Concordat of Bologna in 1516. Previously, the Pragmatic Sanction of Bourges (1438) had given significant power to the local bishops. Bologna, in effect, placed control of the French Church in F.'s hands. His attitudes toward Lutheranism varied. While he initially offered the Reformers, particularly the Meaux circle, protection because of his humanist sympathies, increased popular resentment and radical Protestant actions, such as the Day of the Placards in 1534, made him an opponent. Yet F. himself was not especially religious. Probably an answer to his confusing religious policies can be found in his political ambitions and opportunism. BIBLIOGRAPHY: D. Stone, Jr., *France in the Sixteenth Century* (1969); and R. J. Knecht, ''The Concordat of 1516: A Reassessment,'' *University of Birmingham Historical Journal, 9 (1963) 16*–32.

[C. T. EBY]

FRANCIS OF ASSISI, ST. (1182 or 1181–1226), founder of the Order of Friars Minor (*Franciscans). Born at Assisi in Umbria, the son of Peter Bernadone, a well-to-do cloth merchant, F. spent a carefree youth, more interested in revelry and romantic chivalry than in learning, business, or religion. But his life could not be characterized as licentious, and he had a deep concern for the poor. F.'s conversion began in 1202 when he was a prisoner of war for a year at Perugia. Soon after his release he was stricken with a serious illness. These experiences made him conscious of his soul's barrenness. But once recovered, he set off on a military expedition led by Duke Walter of Brienne, hoping to win fame and knighthood. At Spoleto he was overcome with fever and in a dream heard a voice asking, ''who can benefit you the most: the Lord or the servant? Why do you desert the Lord for his vassal?'' Deeply affected by this event, F. returned to Assisi, lived a more retired life, and sought to discover God's will. One day in 1205 or 1206, while at prayer in the dilapidated church of S. Damiano near Assisi, a voice from the crucifix said to him, ''Francis, repair my house.'' F. interpreted these words literally, believing his mission to be the rebuilding of the church in which he knelt. With characteristic simplicity, he took several bolts of cloth from his father's shop, sold them, and brought the money realized from the transaction to the priest in charge of the church. Indignant at his son's behavior, Peter Bernadone sumooned him to the bp. of Assisi's court, demanding that the price of the stolen cloth be returned. In a dramatic gesture of abandonment to Providence, F. gave back to his father not only the money but even the clothes he was wearing. Standing disrobed before the assembly, he said, ''Hitherto I have called Peter Bernadone father; henceforth I will say, 'Our Father, who art in Heaven.' ''

F. then went about Assisi begging materials for the repair of poor and abandoned churches. One of these, St. Mary of the Angels, he made the center of his activities. While attending Mass there in 1209, he heard read a passage from the Gospel of St. Matthew (10.4–14) that gave him a new insight into the nature of his vocation. He now saw clearly that he was called to be not only a repairer of churches and a devout hermit but likewise a joyful proclaimer of the ''good news.'' His vocation was to follow the Gospel way of poverty, simplicity, and humility. It is unlikely that F. deliberately set out to found a religious order, but his winning personality, his joyous asceticism, and his simple eloquence drew men to him. He and his earliest followers lived as itinerant preachers, possessing no permanent residence, begging their food when they could not earn it by honest labor, and refusing to accept money under any circumstances. Their sermons consisted of simple moral admonitions. The burden of their message was, ''Be converted, for the kingdom of heaven is at hand.'' Their sincerity, austerity, and joyousness deeply impressed all who saw and heard them. In 1209 or 1210, when his followers numbered 12, F. sought papal approval for the simple rule he had constructed from Gospel texts. This was granted orally by Innocent III after much hesitation. Ten years later the Lesser Brothers, as Francis wanted his followers to be known, numbered more than 5,000.

F. made three attempts to preach the gospel to the Islamic peoples; all ended in failure. In 1212 he was shipwrecked on his way to Syria. The next year he set out for Morocco but fell ill in Spain. In 1219 he succeeded in reaching Damietta in N Egypt where he preached to the Sultan who, though much impressed, did not accept Christianity. In 1221, in an attempt to provide for the needs of his expanding brotherhood, F. revised the rule. As a legal document this revision was unsatisfactory, and 2 years later another revision was undertaken. In the composition of this third and final rule F. had the aid of his close friend and adviser, Card. Hugolino (later Gregory IX). Though more legal in tone, this rule still bears the stamp of F.'s genius and breathes the spirit of the gospel which he held to be the essence of his way of life. Toward the end of his life his order attained a size and complexity F. never envisioned. His health was failing and he was almost blind. Realizing his weakness and his limitations as an executive, he resigned the direction of the order into the hands of a vicar. His last years were spent mostly in prayerful retirement in primitive hermitages among his early companions. On Sept. 17, 1224 at La Verna the marks of the five wounds of the Savior were miraculously imprinted on his body. Lying naked on the bare earth, as a final sign of his total abandonment to God, he died praying the 141st Psalm. St. Francis is best understood through a study of his own writings: *Writings of St. Francis of Assisi* (tr. B. Fahy, 1963). BIBLIOGRAPHY: J. R. H. Moorman, *Sources for the Life of S. Francis of Assisi* (1940); G. K. Chesterton, *St. Francis of Assisi* (1924, pa. 1957); O. Engelbert, *St. Francis of Assisi* (tr. E. M. Cooper, rev. I. Brady and R. Brown, 1965); J. Jörgensen, *Saint Francis of Assisi: A Biography* (tr. T. O'C. Sloane, 1949).

[C. J. LYNCH]

FRANCIS OF GERONIMO, ST. (1642–1716), the ''Apostle of Naples.'' F. was born at Grottaglie near Taranto in Italy. After receiving a dispensation because he was only 23, he was ordained in 1666. He taught at the Collegio dei Nobili and, in 1670, joined the Society of Jesus. Although he desired an assignment to the foreign missions, he was sent to Naples, where he would spend the rest of his life. Ascetical in appearance and enthralling in speech, he attracted thousands to his sermons and tens of thousands to his general communion on the third Sunday of each month. He worked tirelessly for the destitute of Naples and established several shelters for street waifs. In addition, he labored with great success among the Turkish and Moorish galley slaves. F. died after giving more than 40 years of his life to the people of S Italy, who still refer to him as the Apostle of Naples. He was canonized in 1839. BIBLIOGRAPHY: E. Papa, BiblSanct 5:1201–04; Butler 2:280–281.

[R. J. BRADY]

FRANCIS OF MARCHIA (*c.* 1290–d. after 1344), Italian Franciscan theologian who commented on the *Sentences* of Peter Lombard at Paris (1319–20) and later on Matthew. As provincial of Marca Ancona (1327–32), he supported *Michael of Cesena and Bonagratia of Bergamo against *John XXII. Expelled from the order in 1329, he was reconciled to the Church at Avignon in 1344. F. is best known as the first proponent of the theory of impetus to explain projectile motion and instrumental causality. BIBLIOGRAPHY: J. A. Weisheipl, NCE 6:32; A. Emmen, LTK 4:240–241.

[J. A. WEISHEIPL]

FRANCIS OF MEYRONNES (Mayronis; *c.* 1285–1328), Franciscan philosopher and theologian, Scotist, and Mariologist. He was probably the student of Duns Scotus at Paris (1366–67); as a professor there he became one of the originators of the Scotist school, defending in his writings the typically Scotist theses on the univocity of being and the formal distinction. His works on Mariology included an influential defense of the Immaculate Conception of Mary. He was a legate and preacher at the Court of Avignon (1324), became provincial guardian of the *Franciscans of Provence (1324), and died at Piacenza in Italy. BIBLIOGRAPHY: É. Longpré, *Catholicisme* 4:1555–58; A. Emmen, NCE 6:32–33.

[T. C. O'BRIEN]

FRANCIS OF OSUNA (*c.* 1497–*c.* 1542), Spanish Franciscan theologian and writer. He is known esp. for his *Abecedario espiritual* (Spiritual Alphabet), a series of six separate treatises on the ascetical and mystical life. It was the "Third Alphabet," a work of solid practical piety on the prayer of recollection, which more than any other book had greatest influence in the spiritual formation of St. *Theresa of Ávila and which she used as a guide throughout her life. First published at Toledo in 1527, in a short time it went through many editions and translations and established the fame of the author as one of the greatest contributors to the golden age of Spanish mysticism. BIBLIOGRAPHY: E. A. Peers, *Studies of the Spanish Mystics* (2d ed. rev. 2 v., 1951).

[D. A. MCGUCKIN]

FRANCIS OF PAOLA (PAULA), ST. (1416–1507), founder of the Order of Minims. Francis was born at Paola in Calabria to parents who dedicated him to the teachings of Francis of Assisi. At 13 he went to live in a Franciscan friary and, at 15, he began the life of a hermit in a seashore cave. In 1436, having been joined by a few other men, F. received permission from the abp. of Cozenza to erect a church and monastery. The building project signalled the beginning of a new religious order based on a strong asceticism. These Hermits of St. Francis of Assisi received official sanction from Pope Sixtus IV in 1474 and, in 1492, the name of the order was changed to Minims, "the least in the household of God." F.'s reputation as a wise and saintly man became widespread throughout the region. When he criticized the royal family of Naples, his arrest was ordered by King Ferdinand. However, when the court officers came for him, his saintly bearing intimidated them, and they returned without him. King Louis XI of France, on his deathbed, sent for F. in the hope that this legendary mystic might cure his illness. F. successfully counselled Louis on the acceptance of death and did not seek to cure the dying monarch. After the death of Louis, his son, King Charles VIII sought instruction from F., who spent the last 25 years of his life in France. F. was canonized in 1519. The order of Minims had its apex in the 16th century. Today it has approximately 40 houses. BIBLIOGRAPHY: F. Russo, BiblSanct 5:1163–75; Butler 2:10–13.

[R. J. BRADY]

FRANCIS DE SALES, ST. (1567–1622), bp. of Geneva, key figure of the Counter Reformation, Doctor of the Church. Of noble descent, F. was born at Thorens in Savoy, the eldest of 13 children. After early schooling at La Roche (1574–76) and Annecy (1576–82), he studied in the Jesuit Collège de Clermont at the Univ. of Paris (1582–88) and then went to Padua where he earned his doctorate in law (1591) and at the same time began his study of theology. Against his father's wishes he was ordained in 1593 and the next year began, with his cousin Louis, mission work in Chablais, one of the states of Savoy. After a few months he began to concentrate on the writing and distribution of leaflets defending Catholicism and attacking the doctrine of the Reformers. He engaged in frequent debates with Calvinist ministers and succeeded in winning many Protestants back to the Catholic faith. He was instrumental in establishing a group of secular priests at Thonon (1602) with the aim of combating Calvinism. He was consecrated bp. of Geneva that same year and served in that post until his death.

He was associated as spiritual director with St. Jane Frances de *Chantal who came under his influence in 1604. After 6 years he gave her and her two companions a rule for a new religious congregation (later an order) based on the virtues shown by Mary on her visit to Elizabeth (see VISITANDINES). He also took an active part in the reform of the Cistercian Abbey of *Port-Royal and was for a time director of Mère Angélique, but this was some years before she and her monastery became identified with the Jansenist cause.

F.'s greatest influence has been in the field of spirituality, in the literature of which two of his works—*Introduction to a Devout Life* (definitive revision, 1609) and *Treatise on the Love of God* (1616)—rank among the great classics. His teachings, based on Scripture, the Fathers (esp. St. Augustine), St. Thomas Aquinas, and other later writers, was put in concrete language intelligible and appealing to ordinary people. F. was the foremost exponent of what H. Bremond called Devout *Humanism, a movement that sought to steer a middle course between the pessimistic distortions of Augustinianism that overstressed the corruption of human nature by sin and the exaggerated optimism and worldliness associated with the Pelagian outlook. Characteristic of F.'s spirituality was a lessening of concentration upon prohibitions and upon negative forms of ascetical practice and an increase of attention to the positive values of virtue, esp. to that of love, upon the primacy of which he laid great stress. He emphasized the importance of a simple prayer (the mother of love) that engages the affections, the imitation of Jesus Christ, docility to the Holy Spirit, and fidelity to the duties of one's state of life. F.'s thought, method, and spirit have been incorporated in one degree or another in all the orthodox schools of spirituality in the RC Church. He was canonized in 1665 and declared a Doctor of the Church in 1877. There is an abundant literature on F. in every major language. BIBLIOGRAPHY: P. Serouet, DSAM, 5:1057–97; G. D. Gordini, BiblSanct 5:1207–26; F. Trochu, *Saint François de Sales* (2 v., 1941–42), the basic study; M. de la Bedoyere, *François de Sales* (1960); M. R. Brown, *St. Francis de Sales and Love of Neighbor* (Catholic Univ. of America, 1958); J. P. Camus, *Spirit of St. Francis de Sales* (tr. C. F. Kelley, 1953).

[T. EARLY]

FRANCIS XAVIER, ST. (Francisco de Jassu y Xavier; 1506–52), Jesuit missionary and apostle of India and Japan. F. was born in the Castle of Xavier near Sangüesa in Navarre, son of Juan de Jassu, president of the royal council of Navarre, and Maria de Azpilcueta. He received his early schooling at home, then went to Paris (1525) to study at the univ., where he obtained lodgings in the College of Sainte-Barbe. Made a master of arts in 1530, he taught as a regent at the Beauvais College (1530–34), and then studied theology (1534–36). At Sainte-Barbe he came under the spiritual influence of Ignatius Loyola. He and Ignatius, with Favre, Bobadilla, Rodríguez, Laynez, and Salmerón, who were to form the nucleus of the future Society of Jesus, bound themselves by vow to the service of God on Aug. 15, 1534. Ordained to the priesthood together with Ignatius in Venice in June 1537, F. was prevented by the war with the Turks from sailing to the Holy Land on the pilgrimage he had vowed; he spent the following autumn and winter in Bologna and went from there to Rome in April 1538. There he took part in the discussions that were to lead to the establishment and approval of the Society of Jesus. King John III of Portugal appealed to Paul III for missionaries for India, and F. and Rodríguez were sent to Portugal for training. Appointed papal nuncio for India, F. set out from Belem alone in April 1541—Rodríguez was kept by the Pope for work in Portugal. F. spent the winter in Mozambique, and arrived in Goa in May 1542. There he first began to labor among the Portuguese. In Sept. he set out for the Fishery Coast where he continued his work for 2 years among the Paravas with great success. In Aug. 1545 he left Mylapore (Madras) for Malacca on the Malay Peninsula; after a stay of 4 months he sailed on to the neglected converts in Amboyna and to the rest of the Moluccas. Returning to Malacca in July 1547, he met a Japanese named Anjiro, who inspired him with the desire to go to Japan. In April 1549, he set out from Goa, to which he had been obliged to return to supervise the activities of other missionaries who had arrived. With him were two confreres, the priest Cosmas de Torres and the laybrother Juan Fernandez, and three Japanese whom he had baptized in Goa, including Anjiro, whose name after baptism was Paul of the Holy Faith. They landed at Kagoshima in S Japan in Aug. 1549. Studying the language, writing a catechism, and instructing pagans, F. remained there a year before moving on to other cities, reaching Miyako (Kyoto), which was then the capital, in Jan. 1551. Unable to obtain an audience with the Mikado, he returned to Yamaguchi, where he put De Torres in charge of the mission that now numbered 2,000 Christians. He again sailed for Malacca, was appointed provincial of India, and returned to Goa, arriving at the end of Feb. 1552. What F. had heard in Japan about China inspired a resolve to carry the faith to that land also. Leaving Gaspar Berze in Goa as vice provincial, he sailed for Malacca and thence to Sancian (Shang Ch'uan, island nr. Canton) in the hope of finding means of entering the forbidden country. He was stricken by a fever and died on the island Dec. 3, 1552, with this last desire unfulfilled. When his body was exhumed 2 months later, it was found fresh and incorrupt. It was taken to Goa where it is still preserved. The right arm, however, which baptized so many thousands of converts, is preserved in the church of the Gesù in Rome. Of a naturally cheerful and ardent temperament, F. won the hearts of all with whom he dealt. He was beatified in 1619, canonized in 1622, and in 1927, together with Ste. Thérèse de Lisieux, was proclaimed patron of all missions by Pius XI. BIBLIOGRAPHY: G. Schurhammer, *Franz Xaver. Sein Leben und seine Zeit* (3v., 1955–73; tr. M. J. Costelloe, v. 1 and 2, 1973–77); G. Wicki, BiblSanct 5:1226–36; J. Broderick, *Saint Francis Xavier* (1952).

[M. J. COSTELLOE]

FRANCISCAN BROTHERS OF BROOKLYN In 1858, two Franciscan Brothers of Mountbellew, Ireland came to the U.S. to help Bp. John Laughlin establish a Catholic school system in his newly created diocese. Soon after their arrival, they founded St. Francis Academy, the first Catholic secondary school in Brooklyn. In 1859, the brothers became a separate congregation with the bp. of Brooklyn as superior general. They observe the Rule of the

Third Order of St. Francis under simple vows and constitute the largest autonomous congregation of Franciscan brothers in the U.S. They staff St. Francis College, which was chartered in 1884, and three high schools and seven elementary schools in the Dioceses of Brooklyn and Rockville Centre. In 1975, the congregation's professed members numbered 169.

[C. J. LYNCH]

FRANCISCAN BROTHERS OF MOUNTBELLEW (County Galway, Ireland). A community of Third Order Franciscans existed in Ireland as early as the 15th century. In 1616, this congregation had 30 houses, but because of persecution it became extinct in the 18th century. The minister provincial of the Friars Minor in Ireland reorganized the congregation in 1818 at Mountbellew where its motherhouse is still located. In 1830, the bishop of Tuam assumed jurisdiction over this group whose members profess the Rule of the Third Order of St. Francis under simple vows. The Mountbellew Brothers endeared themselves to the masses during the period of English ascendancy by conducting hedgerow schools for poor students. The educational apostolate remains the congregation's principal activity. Among its more renowned institutions is the agricultural college established at Mountbellew in 1910. More than 20 communities of Franciscan brothers in the English-speaking world trace their origins to Mountbellew. Foundations made in the second half of the 19th century in the Dioceses of Pittsburgh and Brooklyn later became autonomous congregations. The Mountbellew congregation's 111 (1975) professed members engage in educational endeavors in Ireland, Nigeria, the Republic of Cameroon, and the Archdiocese of Los Angeles. BIBLIOGRAPHY: P. McMullen, ''Franciscan Brothers' Agricultural College. Mountbellew, Co. Galway, Ireland,'' *Analecta Tertii Ordinis Regularis Sancti Francisci* (1976) 12:694–697.

[C. J. LYNCH]

FRANCISCAN FRIARS OF THE ATONEMENT, see ATONEMENT, SOCIETY OF THE.

FRANCISCAN MISSIONARY BROTHERS OF THE SACRED HEART, a nonclerical congregation founded in Poland in 1922. Professing the Franciscan Third Order Rule under simple vows, its members dedicate themselves to the care of elderly and infirm men. The first U.S. foundation was made at Eureka, Mo. in 1927. Reorganized as a diocesan congregation under the abp. of St. Louis in 1935, its membership in 1975 numbered 21 professed brothers laboring in the Dioceses of St. Louis and Joliet.

FRANCISCAN SPIRITUALITY. The originality of St. Francis consists in his lack of originality. He preached no distinctive kind of piety. The spirituality that bears his name is purely Christian, being drawn from the gospel without addition or subtraction. Thomas of Celano, his first biographer, wrote that ''Francis' highest intention, his chief desire, his uppermost purpose was to observe the holy Gospel in all things and through all things; and with perfect vigilance, with all zeal, with all the longing of his mind and all the fervor of his heart, to follow the teaching and footsteps of our Lord Jesus Christ'' (1 *Celano,* 84). It was the intensity of the love, joy, enthusiasm, and thoroughness with which Francis imitated the actions and cultivated the attitudes of Christ that made his observance of the gospel truly unique. St. Francis was deeply conscious of God's dominion and his own creaturehood. In his *Letter to a General Chapter* he admonished his friars: ''The reason he has sent you all over the world is that by word and deed you may bear witness to his message and convince everyone that there is no other almighty God besides him. . . . We must give proof in ourselves of the greatness of our Creator and of our subjection to him.'' This attitude of reverence and worship pervades all his words and deeds. But awe before God's transcendence was balanced in Francis by an intensely personal and affective appreciation of God as a Father whose every act is motivated by purest love. Francis saw creation as a communication and reflection of the goodness of a loving, caring Father. All creatures were, therefore, sisters and brothers deserving respect and reverence. But the supreme manifestation of divine love and goodness was the Incarnate Word, ''the firstborn of all creatures,'' the cause and purpose of creation. In his *Letter to All the Faithful,* Francis exclaimed: ''How glorious, holy, and great it is to have a Father in heaven. . . . How holy, beloved, pleasing, humble, peaceful, sweet, and desirable above all to have a brother who has laid down his life for his sheep.'' For Francis, the Incarnate Word was to be encountered in the Church, especially through the priesthood and the sacraments. ''In this world,'' he wrote, ''I see nothing corporally of the most high Son of God except his most holy Body and Blood which they [priests] receive and they alone minister to others'' (*The Testament*). The function he assigned to his friars within the Church was to make visible the image of the poor, humble Christ of the Gospel. ''Remember that our Lord Jesus Christ, the Son of the living and omnipotent God, was not ashamed and was poor and a stranger and lived on alms, he himself and his Blessed Mother and his disciples'' (*Rule of 1221*).

Franciscan spirituality is not a theological construct evolved by a theorist. The adjectives customarily employed to describe it include evangelical, Christocentric, apostolic, seraphic, ecclesial, Marian, and mendicant. It never occurred to Francis, who instinctively thought and spoke in concrete, personal, gospel terms, to organize the complex of elements designated by these words into a precise system. The Franciscan doctors, especially St. Bonaventure and John Duns Scotus, gave some of these elements theological explication, and the Franciscan saints gave them practical exemplification; but the efforts of those less gifted with wisdom and holiness to systematize them have not met with universal acceptance. BIBLIOGRAPHY: A. Blasucci,

DSAM 5:1315–47; *Marrow of the Gospel* (ed. I. Brady, 1958); V. Breton, *Franciscan Spirituality: Synthesis, Analysis* (tr. F. Frey, 1957); Césaire de Tours, *Franciscan Perfection* (tr. P. Barrett 1956); C. Esser, *Repair My House* (tr. M. Meilach, 1963); *id.* and E. Grau, *Love's Reply* (tr. I. Brady, 1963); A. Gemelli, *Message of St. Francis* (tr. P. Oligny, 1963); D. Lapsanski, *First Franciscans and the Gospel* (1976).

[C. J. LYNCH]

FRANCISCAN SPIRITUALS, see SPIRITUALS, FRANCISCANS.

FRANCISCANS, a religious order founded by St. Francis of Assisi. Today the order is divided into three independent and autonomous families or branches: the Order of Friars Minor, the Order of Friars Minor Conventual, the Order of Friars Minor Capuchin. The name Franciscan is also applied to members of the Second Order, popularly known as *Poor Clares, and to members of the Third Order, of whom some are bound by vows and live in religious communities, and others are lay people who try to exemplify the spirit of St. Francis in secular life. The life of the Franciscan friars of the First Order is one of prayer and apostolic service traditionally lived among and for the benefit of the poor. Franciscans are more numerous than any other religious order. Membership in the three families of the First Order totals about 40,000. Fifty-five Franciscans have been canonized, 125 beatified, and six elevated to the papacy.

St. Francis did not set out to found a religious order. His simple desire was to be a "herald of the Great King" and a "servant of the Most High God." But the authenticity of his piety and joyousness was wonderfully attractive, and soon after his conversion men began to ask to join him in his unaffected life of prayer, penance, and service. When his followers numbered 12, Francis composed a simple rule which Innocent III approved orally (1209 or 1210): This rule consisted of a collection of gospel texts interspersed with a few directives and fervent admonitions. The principal obligation imposed was "to observe the Gospel of Our Lord Jesus Christ." The early friars lived as itinerant preachers. They possessed no permanent dwellings and refused to accept money, resorting to begging when remuneration for their labor did not suffice for their needs. Periodically they retired to remote hermitages to renew their apostolic energies through prayer. The order grew with astounding rapidity. More than 3,000 friars attended the general chapter of 1221, and it is estimated that by the end of the 13th cent. the order's membership exceeded 60,000. The original rule was sufficient for a small fraternity whose activities were localized and whose members were in constant contact with the founder. But the need of a stronger legal structure became evident when the order grew into an international brotherhood most of whose members had never seen St. Francis. In 1221 Francis revised the rule, but this revision was unsatisfactory from a legal point of view and was never submitted to the Holy See for confirmation. A second revision completed by Francis in 1223 was approved by Honorius III in that same year. In preparing the final version of the rule Francis had help from his friend and adviser, Card. Hugolino (later Gregory IX). The nature and extent of "curial influence" upon the composition of the final rule has been the subject of fervent discussion since the publication of P. *Sabatier's *Vie de St. François d'Assisi* in 1894. A completely satisfactory solution to this "Franciscan Problem" has not been formulated. Many modern scholars, however, favor the view that the rule in its final form represents an amalgam of the charisma of Francis and the wisdom of the Church, rather than the surrender of an ideal to the exigencies of institutionalization. St. Francis thought instinctively in gospel terms. The medium of expression that came most natural to him was the parable and the symbol. This trait lent charm to his words, but it also created problems of interpretation. Even during his lifetime well-defined factions arose within the order, holding differing opinions on such fundamental matters as the nature of the fraternity, the apostolate of the friars, the order's organizational needs, and the manner of practicing poverty. The *Relaxati* favored a mitigated rule and a form of life similar to that of older monastic institutes. The *Zelanti,* who included some of the earliest disciples of St. Francis, insisted on the primitive form of Franciscan life and literal observance of poverty. The *Communitas,* whose spokesmen were the provincial superiors and the university-trained friars, believed that the gospel ideal could only be preserved within a more rigid legal structure, that the order's apostolate had to be given more rational organization, and that the practice of poverty had to be more responsible.

His deep humility prevented St. Francis from fully appreciating his remarkable power to inspire those with whom he came in contact, but that same humility enabled him to realize his shortcomings as an executive and a legislator. Therefore, toward the end of his life he appointed Brother Elias of Cortona to act as his vicar in the government of the order, who had great executive ability but tended to be overbearing. He earned the disfavor of the majority of the friars by undertaking the construction of a magnificent basilica to enshrine the tomb of St. Francis. In 1227 he was replaced as minister general by John Parenti, a saintly friar but an ineffective administrator, who was unable to suppress party strife. In 1230 a solution for the order's constitutional problems was sought by requesting the Holy See to issue an official interpretation of the sections of the rule on which the friars were not in agreement. The response came in the form of the bull *Quo elongati* in which Gregory IX declared among other things that the friars were bound only by the rule and not by the Testament which St. Francis had written shortly before his death; that ownership of goods given to the friars was retained by the donors; and that trustees could hold and administer money for the order. In attempting to steer a middle course the Pope succeeded only in arousing the extremists.

Elias was returned to the office of minister general this time by election, in 1232, and during his generalate the order expanded numerically and geographically. Its missionary activities were intensified and the pursuit of sacred sciences stimulated. These developments were in large part due to the minister general's energetic leadership. Nevertheless, his high-handed methods and his un-Franciscan mode of life antagonized all parties. At the chapter of 1239 he was deposed, more because he was not in agreement with the progressive opinions of the provincials than because he did not live according to the rule. For the next 20 years factional differences arising from conflicting interpretations of the rule continued to disturb the order. Another attempt was made to establish peace through papal pronouncement, but Innocent IV's bull *Ordinem vestrum* issued in 1245 accomplished nothing because it was not acceptable to all parties. By 1257 internal dissension threatened the very survival of the order. In that year St. *Bonaventure was elected general. Personifying the best principles of the moderate party, he was a man of true sanctity, deep learning, and practical political sense. It was his conviction that the order should solve its own problems. His method was the enactment of general constitutions to embody the order's own interpretation of the rule arrived at through consultation in a general chapter. The Constitutions of Narbonne, which went into effect in 1260, expressed an admirable balance between the gospel ideal and the realities of organized existence.

The *Zelanti,* who by this time were beginning to be known as Spirituals, resisted all efforts to enforce the new constitutions. The more extreme among them became fanatic in their advocacy of primitivism and aggressive in their incitement of schism. When the *Communitas* employed severe methods to secure compliance, some of the Spirituals affected an attitude of persecuted innocence and took refuge in the apocalyptic doctrines of *Joachimism. Two papal pronouncements supporting the moderate stand (1279 and 1283) were likewise rejected by the Spirituals who asserted that since the Franciscan Rule, like the Scriptures, was inspired by God, neither pope nor general chapter could change it. The history of the order during the 50 years following the death of St. Bonaventure was dominated by the struggle between the Spirituals and the *Communitas.* A separate but related controversy also disrupted the order's relations with the Holy See. The acrimonious debate over the exact nature of the poverty practiced by Christ and his Apostles ended in 1322 when John XXII renounced the Holy See's proprietorship over the goods used by the order, thus placing the Franciscans on an equal footing with other religious in the matter of poverty and forcing the friars to assume administration of their own temporalities. This turn of events met with the approval of the *Relaxati* and legalized a mitigated observance of the rule. Constant internal strife, the relaxations introduced by the decrees of John XXII, the Hundred Years' War, the Black Death, and the Western Schism were all factors that contributed to the decline of the order during the 14th and 15th centuries. Reaction to this deterioration came with the rise of the Observant movement. The proponents of this reform did not share the extreme views of the Spirituals, nor did they advocate schism. Their aim was to revive a more authentic living of the rule under the jurisdiction of legitimate superiors.

The beginnings of the Observant movement may be traced back to the second half of the 14th century. Not centrally directed in its early years, its original foundations in France, Italy, Spain, and Germany came into being and developed independently. Prominent among the leaders and organizers of the movement were Paul of Trinci, St. Bernardine of Siena, St. John Capistran, Bl. Albert of Sarteano, and St. James of the March.

As the number of Observant friars increased, several problems arose concerning their relation to the superiors of the Conventuals, as the friars who did not choose to embrace the reform now came to be known. The solution to these problems most often resorted to by the Observants was to seek from the Holy See exemptions from the jurisdiction of the Conventual superiors. By the end of the 15th cent. the Observants enjoyed a quasi-independent status in that they had the privilege to elect their own vicar provincials and vicar general. With the passage of time relations between the Observants and Conventuals became more tense. Several attempts to promote harmony, though sincere, proved unsuccessful. Finally all hope of union was abandoned, and Leo X in 1517, by the bull *Ite et vos,* separated the Observants and Conventuals into two independent orders. But once they attained autonomous existence, the Observants were not able to maintain unity among themselves. The spirit of reform felt throughout the Church in the late 16th cent. revived among the Observants the old nostalgia for small wilderness hermitages and primitive observance of the rule, esp. in matters of poverty. Eventually four new reform groups emerged within the Observants: the Discalced, the Recollects, the Reformed, and the Capuchins. These groups contributed mightily to the Counter Reformation, but in the long run they weakened the order internally by dividing its energies and resources, decreasing the effectiveness of its apostolate, weakening the vigor of its intellectual life, and rendering it vulnerable to the attacks of the anticlerical devotees of the Enlightenment. The effectiveness of those attacks is attested by the fact that the Observants decreased in number from about 77,000 in 1768 to about 14,000 in 1900.

By 1897 the tragic effects of separation and disunion were so obvious that little opposition was registered when in that year Leo XIII by the bull *Felicitate quadam* united all Observant branches with the exception of the Capuchins who retained their independent entity. In the 70 years since the Leonine Union the Friars Minor have almost doubled in number, and this in spite of the disturbances occasioned by two world wars and Communist harassment. The general chapter held at Assisi in 1967 formulated new general constitutions incorporating the principles of reform contained in the Decrees of Vatican Council II. Few Christian institutions have had as stormy a history as the Franciscan Order, yet few institutions have done more to enrich the life of the Church. The friars have made significant contributions esp. in the fields of missionary activity, preaching, theology, and welfare work. Fifty years after its founder's death the order's missionary work had attained global proportions. Franciscans were among the first to bring the gospel to large areas of Africa, America, and the Far East. Since the days of St. Francis the friars have been custodians of the shrines of the Holy Land. Popular preaching has traditionally been a specialty in which the friars excelled. The sermons of SS. Anthony of Padua, Bernardine of Siena, and Leonard of Port Maurice are examples of Franciscan preaching in which the gospel message is simply but powerfully announced in the direct language of the common people. Although St. Francis feared learning as a possible cause of pride, he did not condemn its pursuit by humble men. The order had a vigorous intellectual life almost from its first years. Alexander of Hales, St. Bonaventure, John Duns Scotus, and William of Ockham are a few of the Franciscan thinkers who contributed to the development of scholastic theology. The friars' efforts in behalf of the poor constitutes one of the order's most important apostolates. Franciscans have shown themselves particularly ingenious in devising methods to alleviate the needs of the impoverished, and in begging alms to support such activities. Projects carried on at inner-city centers is one form this apostolate has taken in more recent times. BIBLIOGRAPHY: D. Devas, *Franciscan Order* (1930); H. Goad, *Greyfriars: The Story of St. Francis and His Followers* (1947); H. Holzapfel, *History of the Franciscan Order* (tr. A. Tibesar and G. Brinkmann, 1948); K. Esser, *Order of St. Francis* (tr. I. Brady, 1959); A. Masseron, *Franciscans* (tr. W. Wells, rev. M. Habig, 1960); E. Daniel, *Franciscan Concept of Mission in the High Middle Ages* (1975); *Coming of the Friars* (ed. R. B. Brooke, *Historical Problems: Studies and Documents Series,* No. 24, 1975); C. J. Lynch, NCE 6:38–46, with bibliog.

[C. J. LYNCH]

FRANCISCANS (CAPUCHIN). The Order of Friars Minor Capuchin is one of the three autonomous branches into which the Franciscan Order has been divided since the early 16th century. In 1525, Clement VII granted Matthew of Bascio, a member of the Observant province of the Marches, permission to wear a simplified habit, reside in a hermitage, observe the Franciscan Rule in its primitive rigor, and lead the life of an itinerant preacher. While exercising this personal privilege, Matthew remained subject to his Observant superiors. His original intention appears to have been to reform the Order rather than separate from it. Three years later, another reform-minded friar named Louis of Fossombrone received the bull *Religionis zelus* from Clement VII. This document established within the Order a quasi-autonomous group known officially as the Friars Minor of the Eremetical Life, but popularly called Capuchins from the Italian word *cappuccio* designating the long, pointed hood worn by members of the reform. Besides the privilege of wearing a distinctive habit and a beard, the Capuchins were conceded the right to observe the Rule without mitigation and to live as hermit-apostles. They were also allowed to hold their own chapters and elect a vicar general subject to confirmation by the minister general of the Conventuals. In 1529, the 19 original members of the group elected Matthew of Bascio vicar general and drew up constitutions designed to safeguard primitive observance. After receiving permission in 1574 to found houses outside Italy, the reform spread rapidly throughout Europe. Despite grave internal problems and opposition from the Observants, membership grew to more than 10,000 by 1619 when Pius V granted the Capuchins complete autonomy by releasing them from the jurisdiction of the Conventuals and authorizing them to elect their own minister general.

The distinguishing marks of early Capuchin life-style were poverty and austerity. The typical friary was an unpretentious structure located in a rural setting but in the vicinity of a town or city. Ownership of the building—whose occupants were restricted to not more than 12 friars—was retained by the donor or the local government, and the community derived its support from daily alms. Common and private prayer was the principal domestic occupation and popular preaching the chief external apostolate. The Capuchins' homiletic style was simple and unadorned, and preachers accepted no remuneration. The period between 1619 and 1761 was the Capuchins' golden age. During those years, charitable services to the poor, courageous care of the plague-stricken, devoted duty as military chaplains, intrepid missionary exploits, and valiant defense of the faith against Protestantism earned the Order wide respect and popularity, especially among the uneducated masses. After the Council of Trent, theological training became a more important element in the formation of Capuchin preachers whose untiring efforts saved or recovered for the Church large areas of Switzerland and Germany. It is the opinion of Philip Hughes that "not even the Jesuits had a greater share in the victories of the Counter Reformation than these new Franciscans" (*Popular History of the Catholic Church* [1947] 179).

Primarily men of action, Capuchins have not typically been attracted to literary and scholarly pursuits, but some of their number have attained eminence in the fields of homiletic and devotional literature. The Order's theologians have shown a consistent attachment to the Bonaventurian tradition and have been particularly adept at drawing inspiration and practical directives from the Seraphic Doctor's mystical writings. St. Lawrence of Brindisi, greatest of the Capuchin preachers and theologians, was declared a Doctor of the Church in 1959. Seven of his confreres have been canonized, and 11 beatified. Capuchin membership peaked at approximately 34,000 in 1761, but was reduced to 7,722 in 1885 as a result of the French Revolution and 19th-cent.

anticlerical legislation. In spite of this drastic depletion, the Order managed to maintain its considerable commitment to the foreign missions. In 1975, Capuchins numbered 9,278, more than 1,000 of whom are missionaries. The Capuchins made their first foundation in the U.S. in 1857. In 1975, their four American provinces had a combined membership of about 1,000 friars whose principal apostolates are parochial work, preaching, and missionary activity. BIBLIOGRAPHY: Cuthbert of Brighton, *Capuchins. A Contribution to the History of the Counter-Reformation* (2 v., 1928); M. da Pobladura, "Cappuccini," *Dizionario degli Istituti di Perfezione* (1975) 2:203–252; *id.*, *Historia generalis Ordinis Fratrum Minorum Capuccinorum* (3 v., 1947–51).

[C. J. LYNCH]

FRANCISCANS (CONVENTUAL). The Order of Friars Minor Conventual is one of the three autonomous branches into which the Franciscan Order has been divided since the early 16th century. In the U.S. its members are popularly known as Black Franciscans from the color of their habit. Divergent interpretations of his Rule existed even during the lifetime of St. Francis. The observance of poverty in particular early became the focus of disagreement. Some friars insisted on an intransigent observance whatever the cost; others were willing to relax the demands of poverty to meet the needs of the Church as a whole. The internal history of the Order during its first 300 years consists in large part of a series of sincere but unsuccessful attempts to reconcile these two points of view. As early as 1250, papal documents employ the term conventual to distinguish Franciscan churches from parish churches. The meaning of the term was gradually expanded to designate friars attached to the Order's larger urban churches as opposed to those who resided at small rural hermitages. The Conventual Friars more commonly engaged in sacramental ministry, the pursuit of learning, and organized works of charity. On the grounds of apostolic necessity, they felt justified in accepting papal privileges and dispensation that allowed freer use of money and material goods. The hermitage friars, whose life-style was simpler and more austere, insisted that St. Francis had prohibited the use of money and the acceptance of papal privileges. Late in the 14th cent., groups of friars who felt called to observe the Rule in its unmitigated form received permission to live in small houses under their own superiors but still subject to the Conventual provincials. As these friars—who soon became known as Observants—sought and obtained further exemptions that allowed them a larger measure of freedom, their relations with the Conventuals became strained. The Conventuals accused the Observants of refusing to submit to legitimate authority, while the Observants charged the Conventuals with laxity, esp. in the observance of poverty. When all efforts at reconciliation failed, Leo X issued (1517) the bull *Ite vos in vineam,* which granted each group independent and autonomous existence.

In 1517 the Conventuals numbered about 25,000. Their Order was suppressed in Spain and Portugal in 1567, and its provinces in N Europe were decimated during the Protestant Reformation. The vicissitudes of the French Revolution and the repressive legislation of 19th-cent. liberal governments further depleted their ranks so that by 1893 their membership was reduced to 1,481. But the Conventuals more than doubled in number during the 20th century. In 1975 they numbered 3,967. The Conventual friars have a long tradition of scholarship, esp. in the fields of theology and history. Their theologians played an important role at the Council of Trent and have been assiduous proponents of the dogma of the Immaculate Conception and the teachings of John Duns Scotus. Conventuals are the custodians of the Basilicas of St. Francis at Assisi and St. Anthony at Padua, and since 1774 have served as penitentiaries at the Vatican Basilica in Rome. One Conventual friar, Joseph of Cupertino, has been canonized and four others beatified. Popes Sixtus V and Clement XIV both belonged to the Conventual branch of the Franciscan Order. Missionary activity has always been one of the Conventuals' principal apostolates. During the 18th cent. they labored with marked effect in E Europe. Presently they are responsible for several mission districts in Asia, Africa, Oceania, and Latin America. In the U.S., where the Conventuals began laboring in the 1850s, their principal apostolates are parochial work, popular preaching, and education. Their four American provinces have a combined membership of about 800. BIBLIOGRAPHY: L. di Fonzo, EncCatt 5:1731–38; J. Moorman, *History of the Franciscan Order* (1968); G. Odoardi, "Conventuali, Frati Minori Conventuali," *Dizionario degli Istituti di Perfezioni* (1976) 3:2–94.

[C. J. LYNCH]

FRANCISCANS (SISTERS), conventual religious women (Third Order *Franciscans) affiliated with the friars, and nuns (Second Order) with whom they share the Rule and *Constitutions* (mitigated, adapted), along with their spiritual guidance and missionary spirit (see FRANCISCAN SPIRITUALITY; FRANCISCANS, THIRD ORDER REGULAR). The term applies popularly to all women in and out of cloister who follow the way traced by SS. *Francis and *Clare of Assisi. In 1976 there was a world membership of some 103,103 in 6,639 houses; in Canada and the U.S. are 13,941 in 1,427 houses; in S. America 1,406 in 185 houses. The nuns engage wholly or partially in adoration (as *Capuchinesses, *Poor Clares) at home or in foreign missions. With the 19th cent. arose independently uncloistered communities with modified rules. Pontifical or diocesan communities, diverse in title or differing widely in form and color of habit (retaining usually the cord), share with multiple cloistered and contemplative of both second and third order, the Franciscan ideal of charity, exercised notably in teaching, care of the sick, the orphan, the aged, the handicapped. On the Continent are some 84,584 in 4,764 houses in Austria, Czechoslovakia, France, Germany, Holland, Italy, Luxembourg, Poland, Portugal,

Spain, and Yugoslavia; in Ireland are 225 in 27 houses; in England 765 in 95 houses; in Scotland 69 in 11 houses; on Malta 636 in 68 houses. Poor Clares of the Assisi protomonastery came in 1875 to the U.S. where there now are 24 autonomous monasteries. St. John N. *Neumann, by counsel of Pius IX, founded (1855) Franciscan Sisters (OSF) at Glen Riddle, Pennsylvania. These have since spread over N and S America. The Syracuse, N.Y., community stemming from that of Philadelphia has care of the lepers on Molokai. A dozen groups of Franciscan Missionaries have, moreover, bases in the U.S. (see 1977 *Catholic Almanac,* 569–572, for list of 82 Franciscan sisterhoods). In Mexico there are 1,477 in 62 houses; in the Argentine, 361 in 54 houses; in Brazil, 447 in 56 houses; Ecuador, 222 in 26 houses; Peru, 207 in 27 houses, and Venezuela, 169 in 22 houses.

[M. R. BROWN]

FRANCISCANS (THIRD ORDER REGULAR). The Third Order Regular of St. Francis of Penance is a pontifical order of men who profess solemn vows and observe the Rule of the Franciscan Third Order in accord with constitutions approved by the Holy See. In 1209 or shortly thereafter, "Many among the people, nobles and commoners, clerics and laymen, moved by the inspiration of God, came to St. Francis desiring to place themselves under his care and direction. . . . He furnished them all with a way of life (*norma vitae*) and mapped out a way of salvation for persons of every station of life" (Thomas of Celano, *Vita prima* 37).

Even during the lifetime of St. Francis, tertiaries not bound by family ties sometimes sold their possessions and retired to solitary places to live as hermits according to the rule the saint had devised for them, but without taking vows. Bl. Gerald of Villamagna (d. 1242) was one of the earliest such tertiary-hermits. It inevitably happened that disciples were drawn to these saintly recluses. The next stage of development was the formation of communities like the one that centered about Bl. Francis Cichi of Pesaro (d. 1350). In 1323, John XXII commended such congregations as "laudable and useful," and allowed their members to take vows. In 1421, Martin V merged several Third Order congregations, including those founded by Bl. Peter Gambacorti of Pisa (d. 1435) and Bl. Nicholas of Forca Palenta (d. 1440). Twenty-six years later, Nicholas V recommended that all Italian congregations assemble in chapter, compile constitutions, and elect a superior general. The present Third Order Regular is considered a continuation of this union. At the beginning of the 16th cent. there were 12 independent Third Order Regular congregations in Europe, but all of them were obliged to accept the rule promulgated by Leo X in 1521. During the 17th cent. the congregations of Sicily, Dalmatia, and Belgium united with the Italian branch of the order; but it was not until the 20th cent. that the Spanish, American, and French congregations gave up their independence. The 888 members of the Third Order Regular engage in pastoral ministry, teaching, and missionary work. The two provinces and one commissariat in the U.S. have a combined membership of 325. BIBLIOGRAPHY: J. P. Doyle, *History of the Third Order Regular of St. Francis of Penance* (1947); R. Luconi, *Il Terz'Ordine Regolare di San Francesco* (1935).

[C. J. LYNCH]

FRANCISCO DA ANUNCIAÇÃO (1669–1720), Portuguese Augustinian who fought the immorality of his time. He founded a mystical school (Jacobéa) in Coimbra which, despite rigorist and Catharist tendencies, seems to have been orthodox. Pombal in 1768 attacked his memory as a schismatic quietist, an ally of Sigilistas (those accused of violating the seal of Confession), and a public enemy. F.'s two works in print (1717, 1725–26) have not been studied.

[E. P. COLBERT]

FRANCISCO DE SANTA MARIA (Fernando del Pulgar y Sandoval; 1567–1649, Spanish Carmelite from 1586, related to St. Teresa of Ávila. A professor of theology at Alcalá and Salamanca and superior of his order, F. is best known for his history of the Carmelites; the first volume (1630) raised such controversy with Jesuits and the Inquisition that volumes 2 and 3 remained in manuscript. Volumes on St. Teresa (1644) and St. John of the Cross (1655) were translated into three languages. His spiritual writings (in MSS) show the influence of *Louis of Granada. Death interrupted his edition of the works of St. Teresa.

[E. P. COLBERT]

FRANCK, CÉSAR AUGUSTE (1822–90), French composer and organist of the romantic school. Though organist at Sainte-Clothilde, Paris, the many sacred works he composed, including a Mass for 3 voices, suffer from the romantic excesses of theatricality and discontinuity. He wrote secular works for the piano, chamber music, symphony (in D-Minor), operas, a well-known oratorio (*Les Béatitudes*), and of course his widely performed organ compositions. F. laid the foundation for the French school of organ music that still flourishes. *Six pièces* and *Trois chorales,* works for the organ, are characterized by a strong use of shifting tonalities and numerous chromatic devices. He had a passion for the excessive use of sharps and attached mystic significance to such use. F. was a deeply religious man of great faith. BIBLIOGRAPHY: L. Vallas, *César Franck* (tr. H. Foss, 1951).

[D. SMUCKER]

FRANCK, SEBASTIAN (1499–*c.*1542), German religious writer and historian. Educated at Ingolstadt and Heidelberg, where he heard Luther and met M. *Bucer, he was ordained priest in 1524, but within a year became a Lutheran. While pastor near Nuremberg he became acquainted with humanist writings, left the ministry (1529), and moved to Strassburg. There he published his *Cronica,*

Zeitbuch und Geschichtesbibel (1531), important not as a chronicle but for F.'s spiritualizing views on Christianity. In this and other works he extolled the inner word of God, the experience of Christ within, an invisible, nonsectarian Church, and the primacy of each man's conscience. He rejected creeds, sacraments, any institutional Church, and the use of force against religious adversaries, esp. the Anabaptists. He favored a personal mystical experience of Christ as the true Christian life. Some have regarded him as a forerunner of pure liberalism and subjectivism, but his writings profess belief in the divinity of Christ and in the spirit of the Scriptures. Expelled from Strassburg in 1531, he was finally able to settle at Ulm, where he published the fullest expression of his views in his *Paradoxa* (1534). He died in Basel. BIBLIOGRAPHY: W. Zeller, RGG 2:1012–13; R. M. Jones, *Spiritual Reformers of the 16th and 17th Centuries* (pa., 1959) 46–63.

[J. R. SCHULZ]

FRANCKE, AUGUST HERMANN (1633–1729), leading figure in the spread of *Pietism, educator. Born of a devout family in Lübeck, Ger., F. studied theology at Erfurt and Kiel, where he developed a special interest in biblical study and became acquainted with the work of the Pietist P. *Spener. While lecturing at Leipzig (from 1685) he met Spener and was completely converted to the Pietist position. F.'s preaching and devotional exegesis in the Collegia Philobiblica, which he helped to establish, aroused opposition from orthodox Lutherans, and he was obliged to leave Leipzig. Through Spener he eventually received (1692) a professorship in Oriental languages (later in theology) at the newly founded Univ. of Halle and a pastorate at nearby Glaucha. By lecturing, preaching, and catechizing, F. disseminated Pietist ideas: the need for a personal conversion experience; stress on sin, repentance, and grace; the practice of a godly life. To communicate his message, he drew on the witness of his own religious experience. Through him Halle became the center for the inculcation and diffusion of Pietism. He established a complex of schools, which became known as "institutes"; they became centers for training teachers, and besides contributing greatly to the spread of his religious ideas, they are important in the history of pedagogy. An orphanage he established (1697) became the first Protestant center for the formal training of foreign missionaries. He assisted his friend K. H. von Canstein (1667–1719) in the formation (1710) of a pioneer *Bible society. Although F. wrote some popular and practical works, his main influence was exercised through his personal pastoral activity and his work of organization. See bibliog. for Pietism.

[P. DAMBORIENO]

FRANCO OF COLOGNE (fl. 1250–80), pioneer musical theorist, also known as Magister Franco. In his text, *Ars cantus mensurabilis,* F. appears to be the first theorist to mention the notation of measured music. In measured notation each note has an exact time value, i.e., a precise ratio relationship to the other notes in the work. Previous to measured music, plainsong notation had fluid time values for each note. F. gathered together various notational experiments of the age, and many scholars suggest that he himself might have originated measured notation. It forms the basis for all our contemporary musical notation.

[D. SMUCKER]

FRANCO LIPPI, BL. (d. 1291), Carmelite lay-brother. He led a dissolute life, but was cured of blindness and converted at the age of 50. After pilgrimages to Compostela and Rome, he began the life of a hermit in Siena, then joined the Carmelites. He is said to have had the gifts of prophecy and visions of Our Lord and Our Lady. BIBLIOGRAPHY: L. Saggi, BiblSanct 5:1252–53; Butler 4:542.

[G. E. CONWAY]

FRANCO, FRANCISCO (1892–1975), Spanish generalissimo, head of state from 1936. Graduated from the Infantry Academy in 1910, he became a brilliant and heroic officer, head of the Spanish Foreign Legion in Morocco, and a general by 1924; he was chief of the General Staff in 1934. In that year he crushed a revolt of the Asturian miners. With the accession of the Popular Front to power (1936), F., who had identified himself with right-wing conservatism in politics, was posted to the Canaries, a *de facto* exile. In 1936 he sided with the generals' conspiracy against the Popular Front, flew to Morocco and brought back the army units garrisoned in Morocco to join the Nationalist cause. From Oct. 1936 he led the Insurgents as Generalissimo and chief of state of nationalist Spain in the Civil War, achieving victory in March 1939. During the war he had the aid of Germany and Italy; he was opposed by Russia, France, England, and the U.S. With some notable exceptions, esp. in Britain, English-speaking Catholic opinion identified F.'s cause as the Catholic cause, esp. since the Loyalists executed so many priests and religious, though the Falangists, too, were far from innocent of the same violences. F. signed an anti-Comintern pact with Germany, Italy and Japan in April, 1939, but in spite of Axis-pressure kept Spain neutral throughout World War II. From 1937 when he took the oath of office, using the title *Caudillo* (leader) of Spain, he ruled as a dictator, suspending all political parties except the Falange; but the National Movement actually included besides Falangists, Carlists, Monarchists, and Christian Democrats. The Allied countries kept up a diplomatic boycott against Spain until 1950, when the U.S. wished to open an alternate, S access to Europe. (Spain finally gained enough votes to enter the UN in 1955). Since 1950 Spain has received economic and military aid from the U.S., in exchange for military bases there. In 1947 Spain was proclaimed a monarchy with F. as head of state having the right to name the next king. In 1955 he presented Juan Carlos, grandson of Alfonso XIII, to the *Cortes* (legislature); since F.'s death Juan Carlos has become the ruling monarch. F. signed a concordat with the Vatican in 1953. During his régime the Spanish hierarchy (except the Primate, Card. Segura, the most outspoken of F.'s opponents) and most of the clergy strongly supported him, but in the later years there were among the Basques and Catalonians and throughout Spain many clerical voices speaking out for greater political liberty, and against identifying the interests of Church and State. More such opposition and other political outbreaks have followed since his death. F.'s personal life was beyond reproach; he lived in the Prado outside Madrid, and is buried in the Valley of the Fallen (for the dead of the Civil War) near the *Escorial.

[E. P. COLBERT]

FRANCO-BOLOGNESE, early 14th cent. illuminator in Bologna, the leading Italian manuscript school. Literary leadership had passed at this time to the Italians, Dante's *Divine Comedy* (1312–17) being its consummate expression. F. was praised by Dante in the *Purgatorio* section of his great work.

[M. J. DALY]

FRANCO-CANTABRIAN STYLE, term applied to the cave art of Central and Southern France and Northern Spain in the Upper Paleolithic Age from the Châtelperronian to the Magdalenian period in caverns of Altamira, Castillo, Pindal, Font-de-Gaume, Laxcaux, and others. Its best expressions are those of the famous Laxcaux caves of Aurignacio-Pêrigordian culture and the well-known paintings of Attamira from the Magdalenian period. Dominated by forms of animals vital to a hunting society, these acutely observed, intuitively grasped and sensitivity expressed images, most probably ritualistic in intent, remain unchallenged and unsurpassed by any subsequent perception of man, however enlightened by science.

[M. J. DALY]

FRANCO-FLEMISH STYLE term referring to a style of manuscript. Illumination and panel painting in the courts of the dukes of Burgundy during the late 14th and early 15th cent., combining the linear sophistication of the school of Paris and the robust realism of the Flemish style, distinctions arising from northern Flemish-German contact as opposed to southern French-Italian association. The Franco-Flemish style is exemplified by the illumination of Jan *Hennequin and the panel painting of Melchior *Broederlam. BIBLIOGRAPHY: G. Bazin, *L'Ecole franco-flamande, XIV-XV siècles* (1941).

[M. J. DALY]

FRANCO-SAXON STYLE, a manner of Carolingian manuscript illumination of the latter half of the 9th cent., with its center probably in northern France at St.-Denis or at St.-Amand near Tournai, and noted for "classical" initial letters and refinement of interlace.

[M. J. DALY]

FRANGIPANI, a noble Roman family from the 11th cent. whose power touched papacy and empire down to the 14th century. The first reference to the name is in 1014. Extensive family properties were located on the Palatine, and near the Arch of Titus and the Colosseum. The family's rise to prominence accompanied that of the reform of the papacy in the 11th cent. with Cencio favoring Hildebrand. Under his protection, Alexander II was able to enter Rome. Cencio's son, Giovanni, provided protection for Urban II against the antipope, Guibert of Ravenna. Leone Frangipani accepted the government of Beneventum from Pascal II in 1108. At the beginning of the 12th cent., the family was divided into three branches: de Cartularia, de Septizonio, and de Gradellis. With the entry of Henry V into Italy for the second time, Cencio II swung the Frangipani into the Emperor's orbit. He held Gelasius II prisoner for a short time. The family's power was strongest when Honorius II, the Frangipani's candidate, became pope in 1124. With his death, the Frangipani and their opponents, the Pierleoni, clashed in a struggle which caused a religious crisis momentarily endangering the accomplishments of Gregory VII and his successors. Support of the papacy continued during the reign of Frederick I. Then the Frangipani joined Emperor Frederick II in opposing Gregory IX and Innocent IV. They sold their properties in Rome to the Emperor and received them back as a fief. Toward the end of Frederick's reign, they abandoned him for the papacy. Frangipani power in Rome waned at the end of the 13th century; the Neapolitan branch died out in the 17th century.

Outstanding members of the Roman branch were: *Aldruda,* wife of Count Bertino, who with Guglielmo of Ferrara, led the troops that raised the seige of Ancona; *Jacoba,* wife of Graziano Frangipani, friend and follower of St. Francis of Assisi. These members of the Neapolitan branch can be noted: *Giovanni,* Lord of Astura, who captured Conradin of Swabia in 1268; *Fabio* (d. 1587), governor of the Marches and (1559) of Perugia, bp. of Cajazzo (1537), of Barletta-Nazareth (1572), carrying out the decrees of Trent in his diocese (from 1562); nuncio to Paris (1577–78 and 1586–87). BIBLIOGRAPHY: G. Opitz, LTK 4:252–254; M. G. NcNeil, NCE 6:74–75; A. Ghinato, EncCatt 5: 1696–97.

[J. M. O'DONNELL]

FRANK, JACOB (*c.* 1726–91), Jewish merchant who became the leader of a new *Shabbataiïsm. On a merchant journey to Turkey he discovered a semi-Islamic sect of Shabbataianists and brought their teaching back to his native Poland in 1755, at Polodia (Korolowska), proclaiming himself the reincarnation of Shabbatai Sevi. He secured protection of the Catholic authorities, when Jewish complaints were raised against the licentiousness of his sect, and he and his followers became public converts to Catholicism in 1759. He was soon convicted of heresy, however, and imprisoned for 13 years, until release in 1772 at the time of the Russian partition of Poland. He left that country for

Offenbach in Germany, where he lived a life of luxury until his death. His sect did not survive him.

[T. C. O'BRIEN]

FRANKENBERG, JOHANN HEINRICH (1726–1804), cardinal. Born of a noble Silesian family, F. studied philosophy under the Jesuits at Breslau, and theology at the Germanicum in Rome. In 1759 he was appointed abp. of Malines by Maria Theresa and became primate of the Low Countries. In 1778 he was created cardinal by Pius VI. He was a sturdy opponent of Josephinism. Forced to leave the country by the French Revolution, F. went first to Westphalia, and then to Holland where he died.

FRANKFURT, COUNCILS OF. The German city on the Main River was host to numerous ecclesiastical councils, of which the most enduringly important was that of 794, which condemned Adoptionism.

[E. A. WEIS]

FRANKO, IVAN (1856–1916), foremost Ukrainian novelist, poet, and dramatist in modern times. F. studied at the Univ. of Lvov, received his doctorate from the Univ. of Vienna, and gave himself to literary activity when government opposition (he was a nationalist and a proponent of Ukrainian independence) kept him from a professorship. He was at first involved with socialist and Marxist publications, but his deep faith caused him to cut his ties with these and to develop his own ideas of revolution and reform. He produced a total of 60 volumes of novels, drama, stories, poetry, translations from and into Ukrainian, and original works in Polish and German, in which he voiced his religious, philosophical, and social convictions. BIBLIOGRAPHY: W. Luciw, NCE 6:79–80.

FRANKOKRATIA (Gr., rule of the Franks), the period in which the Greeks lived under Frankish, i.e., European, domination from the Latin conquest of Constantinople in 1204 until the 15th-cent. Turkish conquests, although in some Venetian possessions it lasted into the 18th century. Even though the Byzantines recaptured their capital and other territories in 1261, Frankish lords, chiefly Italian, French, and Spanish, still ruled over much of central and S Greece and most of the Greek islands. In general, after the initial shock, Frankish rule does not seem to have been as harsh as that of the Byzantine emperors or later of the Turks. Economic and cultural life were vigorously stimulated, and there was much political and military cooperation between Latins and Greeks. Unfortunately, Latin political rule also brought the establishment of the Latin Church. Latin bps. were named for Greek dioceses (and received their revenues, often *in absentia*), while the legitimate pastors usually resided at the Byzantine capital. Greek priests were allowed to function but often under severe restrictions. It is perhaps this form of ecclesiastical imperialism which led to an understandable resentment on the part of the Greeks against anything Latin and especially against the papacy which had sanctioned these abuses. BIBLIOGRAPHY: W. Miller, *Latins in the Levant: A History of Frankish Greece, 1204–1566* (1908); K. Setton, "Latins in Greece and the Aegean", CMedH² 4.1:389–430. *LATINIZATION.

[G. T. DENNIS]

FRANKS, literally, "Freemen," The W German tribes that gave Gaul its modern name, France. The federation is first attested in A.D. 241. It included the Bructeri, Chamavi, Tenkteri, Ampsivarii, Sicambri, and others. By 258 the Franks had spread from Germany into what is now Belgium. Probus took many of them into the Roman army as auxiliaries (*c.* 280) and persuaded others to settle on abandoned farmlands in the provinces. Childeric, their king (475–481), established a Frankish kingdom in Gaul, which his son Clovis strengthened by unifying the Franks of the lower Rhine (Salians). Other Franks, who had made their homes along the Rhine near Cologne (Ripuarians, "riverbank Franks"), came into his ambit when he destroyed their dynasty and founded the Merovingian state. The conversion of Clovis and his people to Catholic Christianity (most Germanic rulers embraced the Arian creed) was of great significance for the future of the Church. BIBLIOGRAPHY: J. M. Wallace-Hadrill, *Long-Haired Kings* (1962); M. C. Pfister, CMedH 1:292–303.

[M. J. SUELZER]

FRANQUEVILLE (FRANCAVILLA: FRANCHEVILLE), PIERRE, (*c.*1548–1615), French sculptor. After studying wood sculpture in Innsbruck (1566–70), F. went to Tuscany (1574) and there became one of the best pupils and collaborators of Giovanni Bologna. He executed 6 marble saints for S. Marco, Florence (1589), a fountain with a statue of Cosimo I in Pisa (*c.*1594), and assisted Bologna in the replacement of the cathedral doors in Pisa (1595). In Paris (1604) F. did 3 reliefs for the pedestal of Bologna's equestrian statue of Henry IV, working in a style colder and drier than that of his master.

[M. J. DALY]

FRANSEN, PIET (1913–), Jesuit theologian at the Univ. of Louvain. F. studied in Louvain and Rome, became a Jesuit, and was ordained in 1943. His chief contributions to theology are well-grounded historically and concentrate on the questions of grace (*Divine Grace and Man,* 1962; *New Life of Grace,* 1969), sacramental theology, fundamental theology, and ecclesiology. He is coeditor of the theological review, *Bijdragen*.

[P. MISNER]

FRANZELIN, JOHANNES BAPTIST (1816–86), Jesuit theologian, cardinal. Born in the Austrian Tyrol, F. held the chair of dogmatic theology at the Gregorian Univ. (1857–76) where he taught most of the major theological tracts, sought a positive theological synthesis, and wrote several Latin textbooks which were widely used in seminary theology courses. F. also acted as a consultor to the Holy Office and other Roman congregations. He was designated as the papal theologian at Vatican Council I, and was instrumental in producing the dogmatic constitution *Dei Filius* dealing with faith, revelation, and reason. BIBLIOGRAPHY: H. J. Pottmeyer, *Der Glaube vor dem Anspruch der Wissenschaft* (1968); J. Courtade, *Catholicisme* 4:1564–1566; P. Bernard, DTC 6.1:765–767.

[P. MISNER]

FRASSINETTI, GIUSEPPE (1804–68), founder at Genoa of the Sons of Mary Immaculate; theological writer; brother of Bl. Paola *Frassinetti. His many published works include: *Compendio della teologia dogmatica* (1839; 26th ed., 1903); *Compendio della teologia morale di S. Alfonso* (2 v., 1865–66; 11th ed., 1948). His cause for beatification was introduced in 1939.

[T. C. O'BRIEN]

FRASSINETTI, PAOLA, BL. (1809–82), foundress of the *Dorotheans; beatified 1930; sister of G. *Frassinetti. At Quinto al Mare, near Genoa, she established (1834) her congregation for the care and education of girls, giving it a rule based on that of the Jesuits.

[T. C. O'BRIEN]

FRATER, the Latin of "brother," a form of title used in some monastic communities to distinguish a clerical or choir brother from a laybrother, the latter being designated by the vernacular "brother." *BROTHER.

FRATICELLI, a name for various factions of Franciscans who separated themselves from their order and from the RC Church in bitter disputes concerning poverty. The same (disparaging) term was also indiscriminately used in chronicles and inquisitorial reports of the 14th and 15th cent. for other groups, such as the *Apostolici and the *Beghards. The first papal use came in the bull *Sancta romana* of John XXII (1317), condemning the *Clareni, who were called contemptuously *Fraticelli de paupere vita*. The following year the same Pope excommunicated a number of Tuscan *Spirituals. The Fraticelli had their origins among the Spirituals, Franciscans who insisted on literal observance of poverty after the manner of St. Francis of Assisi and his earliest companions. So obstinate was their primitivism that they repudiated as betrayals of the Franciscan ideals the three papal interpretations of the rule issued during the 13th cent., concerning the way poverty was to be observed. Two groups of Italian Spirituals refused to heed John XXII's command to submit to the superiors of the order. They established themselves as independent bodies and declared that they alone were legitimate Friars Minor and constituted the true Church of Christ. After the condemnation mentioned above, both groups fled into S Italy and Sicily, where they were given protection by Kings Robert of Naples and Frederick of Sicily. They enjoyed a large measure of popular support, being much admired by the common people for their austere way of life. There are records of groups of Fraticelli in S France, Spain, Germany, and Bohemia; there is, however, no evidence of any historical connection between Fraticelli and the *Hussites. The eventual disappearance of the Fraticelli was brought about by the zeal of inquisitors such as SS. John Capistran and James of the March, both appointed in 1428, and by the rise of the Franciscan Observants, an order offering those zealous for primitive Franciscan poverty a life within the legitimate Franciscan family.

The Fraticelli pushed the teachings of the Spirituals to extremes. They rejected papal interpretations of Franciscan poverty and the very legitimacy of the popes beginning with Boniface VIII and consequently of all ecclesiastical power of orders or jurisdiction thereafter. They thus set themselves up as the true spiritual Church, with their own bps., priests, preachers, including women. Their ecclesiology and eschatology were markedly influenced by *Joachimism. The Michaelites are sometimes classified as *Fraticelli de opinione,* but they did not go to the same doctrinal extremes as the true Fraticelli. BIBLIOGRAPHY: D. Douie, *Nature and Effects of the Heresy of the Fraticelli* (1932); M. D. Lambert, *Franciscan Poverty: The Doctrine of the Absolute Poverty of Christ and the Apostles in the Franciscan Order, 1210–1323* (1961); C. Schmitt, DSAM 5:1167–88.

[C. J. LYNCH]

FRATRES UNITORES (Friars Unitors), a late medieval Armenian monastic order based on the Dominican rule and later assimilated with them. About 1328 the Armenian vardaped, John Kernetzi, superior of the monastery of Qrna, spent over a year studying Latin and Catholic theology with the Dominican missionary bp. of Maraghab, Bartholomew. In 1330 both went to Qrna, where groups of Armenian monks and clerics interested in union with Rome also gathered. The Dominican rule and liturgy were translated into Armenian, and the monastery reformed along Dominican lines. After receiving papal approval, *c.* 1340 John and his community took religious vows, calling themselves the Friars Unitors of St. Gregory the Illuminator, dedicating themselves to the work of reunion. They regarded the Dominicans as their spiritual fathers, wore the Dominican habit, and from 1356 were under the jurisdiction of the Dominican master general, who was represented by a vicar. In spite of initial success their Latinizing tendencies were resented by the Armenian people and lower clergy. Decline began in 1380, and in 1475 the Turkish conquest of Caffa destroyed their most flourishing convents. By 1582 they had become merely a province of the Dominican Order. BIBLIOGRAPHY: R. J. Loenertz, *La Société des Frères Pérégrinants pour le Christ* (1937) 141–50.

[G. T. DENNIS]

FRAUD, in moral theology, a sin against *commutative justice, consisting in the deceitful sale for more or the buying for less than a *just price. The sin consists in deceiving another person in a way that does harm to his right to his just possessions. Buying and selling are implicitly contracts for the mutual benefit of the parties; the balance of justice is violated if one party is injured in the transaction. In a wider sense, fraud can be taken to mean any form of *deceit, and as such has the malice and seriousness proper to *lying. (ThAq ST 2a2ae,77). In canon law, fraud, usually referred to in the phrase *fraus et dolus* (CIC cc. 52, 2049, 2361), means any deceptive activity designed to evade the law or infringe on another's rights; it generally invalidates any favor received or act performed through its use.

[T. C. O'BRIEN]

FRAUENBURG (FROMBORK) CATHEDRAL (1329–88), German Gothic cathedral of Ermland, formerly in E Prussia, since 1945 in Poland. A major example of the local school of architecture, this hall church with 8 bays is noteworthy for the huge gable of the main façade.

[M. J. DALY]

FRAVASHI, in the later Zoroastrianism, the protective spirits or genii, which were assigned individually to the followers of Ahura Mazda to aid them in the battle against the forces of Ahriman. Originally they seem to have been the spirits of the dead, the guardian spirits of ancestors and heroes. They were thought to return to earth every year, and religious feasts were held in their honor. They were invoked in battle and for fecundity. Even Ahura Mazda himself had his fravashi. Zoroaster did not include the fravashi in his own system because, despite their warlike character, they did not correspond to his moral ideal with its emphasis on the choice between good and evil. The fravashi are represented as winged figures. BIBLIOGRAPHY: J. Duchesne-Guillemin, *La Religion de l'Iran ancien* (1962) 37–38, 217–218, 327–329; *idem,* NCE 6:83.

[M. R. P. MCGUIRE]

FRAZER, JAMES GEORGE (1854–1941), author of the famous *Golden Bough: a Study in Magic and Religion.* A Scot, F. studied at the Univ. of Glasgow, was a fellow of Trinity College, Cambridge from 1879, taught classics, but was mainly interested in anthropology. The *Golden Bough* is a vast survey in comparative folklore and religion, influential on a generation of scholars and artists because of its claim to be a liberating enlightenment on the origins of religion. F.'s thesis, that a religious cult arises only after a people's failure to control natural forces through magic, and his over-reliance on the comparative method and an evolutionary scheme of human development, are no longer acceptable to anthropologists. *Golden Bough* editions: the first, 2 v., 1890; 3d rev. ed., 12 v., 1911–15; an abridgment, 1923; an abridged, annotated ed., *The New Golden Bough,* by T. H. Gaster, 1959. F. also published other anthropological works and editions of classical texts. BIBLIOGRAPHY: R. A. Downie, *Frazer and the Golden Bough* (1970); J. B. Vickery, *Literary Impact of the Golden Bough* (1973); J. Z. Smith, "When the Bough Breaks," HistRel 12 (1973) 342–371.

[E. V. GALLAGHER]

FREDEGARIUS, a compilation of six chronicles, arranged in four books with a continuation, based on *Liber generationis* of Hippolytus, works of Eusebius, Jerome, Hydatius, Gregory of Tours, and contemporary records. Earlier sections present traditional world history to the times of the compilers and continuators; the original portions cover the years 584–642; and the continuation, 642–768. The latter, done under patronage of Count Childebrand, half-brother of Charles Martel, and his son Nibelung, is valuable for Carolingian history. A work of plural authorship, it is the only important source for the period. The name Fredegarius was applied first in the 16th century. BIBLIOGRAPHY: J. M. Wallace-Hadrill, *Fourth Book of the Chronicle of Fredegar with its Continuations* (1960).

[A. CABANISS]

FREDEGUND (*c.*545–597), **FRANKISH QUEEN.** Consort of King Chilperic I of Neustria, she arranged the dismissal of his first wife Audovera and strangled his second, Galswintha. A few days later she and Chilperic were married. A feud of almost 40 years ensued between F. and Brunhilde, Galswintha's sister and wife of King Sigibert of Austrasia, resulting in the war between Neustria and Austrasia (561–613). F. was responsible for the assassination of Sigebert (575); she plotted against Audovera's three sons, who all died tragic deaths. After Chilperic's death (584) she acted as regent for her son Clotair II.

[J. R. AHERNE]

FREDERICK I, BARBAROSSA (1122–90), **ROMAN EMPEROR** from 1155. Son of Frederick II, duke of Swabia, and Judith of Bavaria, F. was crowned king of Germany at Aachen (1152); king of Lombardy at Pavia (1154); and emperor by Pope Hadrian IV at Rome a year later. A genial, uncomplicated, knightly person but with the Carolingian and Ottonian concepts of empire and imperial rule, F. struggled for twoscore years to control Italy and the papacy for his empire. He attempted to use the papal schism and the civic instability of the N Italian cities but met frequent defeat, either from the urban leagues or the papacy and the Normans or some combination of these. From the Treaty of Venice (1177) a temporary accord was reached, and F.'s son, Henry VI, married Constanza of Sicily. In 1187, when Jerusalem fell to Saladin, F. turned crusader and died in Cilicia, leaving a legend of a great emperor and a great empire. BIBLIOGRAPHY: J. M. Powell, NCE 6:84–86; LTK 4:379–380; Gebhardt-Grundmann 1:300–328; P. Munz, *Frederick Barbarossa: a Study in Medieval Politics* (1969).

[S. WILLIAMS]

FREDERICK II, (1194–1250), **ROMAN EMPEROR** from 1220. Son of Emperor Henry VI (Hohenstaufen) and Constance, daughter of Roger II of Sicily (Norman), grandson of Frederick Barbarossa. Highly intelligent, imbued with a blend of Christian, Oriental, and Islamic cultures, F. was known as "Wonder of the World." He succeeded on his father's death to the kingdom of Sicily (1198). Pope Innocent III promoted F.'s claim to the empire on condition that he relinquish Sicily in order to prevent the encirclement of the Papal States. As emperor F. continued to build a highly centralized and bureaucratic state in Sicily. After long delays he left on Crusade, and in 1229 secured the liberation of Jerusalem by negotiation, rather than by force of arms. Attempts to subdue the N Italian communes led to excommunication by Pope Gregory IX in 1239. Pope Innocent IV determined to rid Christendom of Hohenstaufen power once for all. A General Council at Lyons (1245) deposed Frederick and called for a crusade against him. Inconclusive military campaigns in Italy dragged on until his death in 1250. BIBLIOGRAPHY: J. M. Powell, "Frederick II and the Church: a Revisionist View," CHR 48(1962–63) 487–497; T. C. Van Cleve, *Emperor Frederick II of Hohenstaufen: Immutator Mundi* (1972).

[J. E. LYNCH]

FREDERICK II, THE GREAT (1712–86), **KING OF PRUSSIA** from 1740. Born in Berlin, son of Frederick William I, he turned Prussia into a great power. He took Silesia the first year of his reign, held it in a war with Austria and gained permanent possession in the Seven Years War (1756–63). Subsequent years saw reform of the Prussian judicial system and other domestic achievements. F.'s childhood tutor instilled in him a love for French culture, and through it he gained a deistic outlook that led him to practice religious toleration. A man of broad interests, F. cultivated the friendship of intellectuals, including Voltaire, played the flute, and wrote on politics. Voltaire published F.'s *Anti-Machiavel* in 1740. F. rejected the theory of the divine right of kings, but ruled according to the principles of "enlightened despotism." In relation to the Catholic Church F.'s policies were intrusive, and interfered with the Church's freedom. His kingdom, on the other hand, was one of the refuges where the Jesuits, after their 1773 suppression, were able to continue some form of corporate existence.

[T. EARLY]

FREDERICK OF MAINZ (937–954), abp., zealous preacher and reformer; enigmatic figure in the struggle between particularism and imperialism under Otto I (936–973). Though generally loyal to Otto, F. sided with the feudal dukes in the rebellions of 938 and 953, apparently because he considered Otto's antifeudalism a threat to the rights of the Church in Germany. BIBLIOGRAPHY: E. N. Johnson, *Secular Activities of the German Episcopate* (1932), 29–36 passim; F. Norden, *Erzbischof Friedrich von Mainz und Otto der Grosse* (1912).

[M. F. MCCARTHY]

FREDIANO, ST., see FRIGIDIAN, ST.

FRÉDOL, BÉRENGER (BERENGARIUS FREDOLI; *c.* 1250–1323), canonist, bp. of Béziers from 1294, cardinal in 1305, cardinal bishop of Tusculum from 1310, grand penitentiary in papal Avignon, 1311. He began his career as professor of law at Bologna. As a canonist he was one of the compilers of the *Liber sextus commissioned by Boniface VIII in 1296; author of a *De excommunicatione*. . . and a *Summa de poenitentia;* cataloguer of several decretal collections. He was also a papal diplomatist, serving both Boniface and Clement V; the latter appointed F. in 1306 to be one of the cardinals deputed to reform the Inquisition after charges of cruelty against the bp. of Albi. F. skillfully warded off Philip the Fair's demand that the planned Council of *Vienne try Boniface posthumously. In 1308 he presided at the hearings in which Jacques de Molay, Grand Master of the *Templars, made his torture-extracted confession of crimes; it is thought that F. tried in vain to save De Molay's life (he was burned at the stake in 1314). Frédol Bérenger the Younger is an undistinguished nephew of F., and successor (1310) as bp. of Béziers.

[T. C. O'BRIEN]

FREE, JOHN (Phreas; d. 1465), the first Englishman to make humanism his profession. At Guarino's studio in Ferrara, F. acquired a thorough knowledge of Greek and an excellent Latin style. His facility in translating Greek and his original Latin poems enhanced his great reputation for scholarship. He died at Rome before he could possess the see of Bath and Wells provided by Paul II. BIBLIOGRAPHY: R. J. Mitchell, *John Free* (1955).

[A. WARDLE]

FREE ASSOCIATION (MENTAL), name given to the technique originated by S. *Freud by which a patient in the psychoanalytic session relinquishes voluntary control of his thoughts and fantasies and allows them spontaneously to make connections with other thoughts and imagery. Although they are made freely, the connections are not in a casual or random way, but lead rather directly to the most sensitive areas of personal concern, even to those that are unconscious, giving the analyst clues to the patient's psychological problems. Free association also designates the technique of spontaneous word matching originated by Jung, in which a patient responds to a word presented to him by the first word that occurs to his mind. This technique also reveals sensitive problem areas in the mind.

[M. E. STOCK]

FREE CHURCHES, a description used primarily in contrast with *state Church; hence, other Churches existing alongside an *established Church. On the Continent it refers especially to Anabaptists and their descendants, but also includes other denominations. In Great Britain, this term superseded *Dissenters and *Nonconformists (*c.* 1900). During the 19th cent., Nonconformist denominations augmented their numbers and played an important role in achieving religious and political freedom, as well as social reforms. Their early loose-knit organizations (National Council of Free Churches, 1896; Federal Council of Evangelical Free Churches 1919) merged in 1941 into the Federal Council of Free Churches. In the U.S. the phrase has less significance; S. Mead, however, states that it "designates those churches under the system of separation of church and state" (*Lively Experiment,* 1963, p. 103). It is frequently used, however, to designate Churches that emphasize individual conversion, *believer's baptism, and democratic organization. BIBLIOGRAPHY: G. Westin, *Free Church through the Ages* (tr. V. A. Olson, 1958); E. A. Payne, *Free Church Tradition in the Life of England* (3d ed., 1951); P. Furneaux, *Palladium of Conscience* (1773, repr. 1974).

[N. H. MARING]

FREE WILL, considered in depth, a quality of poise inherent in the affective power of a rational being with regard to any particular good or accumulation of particular goods it may come across. The Latin term *liberum arbitrium,* free decision, the making up of your own mind, brings out, more than the English term "free will" does, the cognitive aspect of the act. However this is so closely intermingled at all its stages with the affective aspect that both Aristotle and St. Thomas Aquinas are at a loss whether to consider *choice as a decision elicited from willed *deliberation or as impulse elicited from deliberated *will. Free will marks a special function, not a faculty distinct from the will; it is like *reasoning in comparison to *understanding—indeed the analogies between mind and will processes run throughout its examination.

Before closing with this, the following outline of types of activity will help to locate the problem of free will on the map. First, freedom is a quality of a natural act, namely one that springs from within the nature of its subject and is in various degrees a fulfillment of its own proper drives; this is contrasted with the "extrinsicism" of violent, artificial, preternatural, or, in some contexts, of supernatural activity, in which a higher force intrudes so as to produce an action to which the subject scarcely contributes.

Second, this quality of being natural, which in the case of living things may be characterized as spontaneous, may issue through knowledge; then the resulting activity is called voluntary, which in technical usage is contrasted with the blind and purely natural appetites of plants and nonliving things: these last of course are also virtually present in the human organism.

Third, the knowledge in question may be conscious, at least implicitly, of purpose as such, an insight only possible to intelligence, and not to animal sensation, which may indeed relate this event to that, and even exhibit a certain balance before alternative courses of action, but which does not appreciate their meanings in the plan. Accordingly, while the voluntary in a limited scense is attributed to animals, (and in the same limited sense is found also in man), the term in its full meaning is applied only to the expression of rational appetite, namely will. We have not yet arrived at the notion of free will, for while all free activity is spontaneous and voluntary, not all spontaneous and voluntary activity is free. It is well to bear this in mind. God's free will regards the things other than himself which he creates, not his own goodness; man's will can be acting before and after the activity known as choice.

This implies a situation where the will—which has a capacity for good without restriction and can only be determined by this, its universal object—is confronted through the intelligence with an object apprehended and therefore desired as less than the all-good; some element which makes it less than compelling can always be found, even if that only be the effort entailed in achieving it. Given that the will acts for it, we do not find in such an object the necessitating cause of the action, but have to introduce a contribution from a will, a self-determinism in the human subject whereby it somehow narrows down its desires, concentrates its resources in one particular position, or from an infinite range strikes one definite posture. There is, as it were, a preceding phase of reserve where the will preserves its own equilibrium, or *indifferentia* as it is called, and this is where freedom lies.

However we have not yet done with our mapping, and three more divisions remain to be marked. First, the will may be balanced between acting and not acting at all, that is doing nothing; here the opposites are contradictory, and the ability to do either is called the freeness of contradiction or of exercise (*libertas contradictionis, libertas quoad exercitium*). Thus it may be said that nobody cannot but will to be happy in some guise, but this is on condition that he does will, which, to take an isolated abstract, he may refuse to do. It is the first step that counts, and such indeterminancy, as of Hobson's choice, is sufficient to establish the notion of free will. Nevertheless we can go further.

Second, the issue may lie between two or more alternative objects. They are contraries, and to reach for one will be to exclude the other or others. Such indeterminancy, as of the judgment of Paris, implies the freeness of contrariness or of acting thus or thus (*libertas contrarietatis, libertas quoad specificationem*).

Third, so far ethics have not entered into the question, for the alternatives may be all good, some better than others perhaps, but then, we are under no obligation always to choose the best, and we may well prefer the runt of a litter. It is only when an object is such as to induce the will to diverge from its true final end that any question of moral evil arises. Accordingly, to define freedom, as is often done in religious writing, as the ability to sin, fixes on a feature that is both provincial and incidental.

Moral theology of the classical tradition draws its theory of men's responsibility for their actions against the background of a philosophico-psychological view of the will in relation to universal and particular good. Whether men in fact are responsible, and when and how often they are healthy, nonpsychotic, and their own masters, are judgments moral theology can form only in conjunction with the witness of Scripture and the Church and by having recourse to the findings of the historical and empirical sciences. The OT teaches our responsiblity before the judgment of God, the NT exhorts us to live in the liberty of the Spirit, not under the bondage of the Law, sin, and death. We have the consciousness of being free, at least within limits, and the data are to be respected, rather than explained away. The Greek sages inculcated self-mastery, and the conviction that we are not puppets, and that rewards and punishments are deserved animates the social order and the Western tradition of law. Free will also finds some confirmation in the observations and experiments even of laboratory psychology.

It is attacked by theories generically labeled as *determinism. These may look for the determining factor of allegedly free activity either in some previous agency, or in an irresistible object, or in both. Its apparent capriciousness was a scandal to an older school of fixed-energy-and-matter scientists; a newer school is less bothered by "creativity."

Theologians themselves have had to meet the difficulty of God's omniscience of and omnipotence over all we do. Our freedom is supposed to be denied by the fact that everything is fixed for us by *fate. Psychologies of the unconscious have shown how in obsessive-compulsive reactions we are driven by forces neither of our making nor under our control. Our choices are represented as a series of counterbalancing attractions and repulsions coming to an inevitable term. Psychological determinism maintains that we always take that which most appeals to us, which of course is undeniable, for we are not like Buridan's donkey, though it rather begs the question.

In general it can be said that the philosophical elucidation of free will in terms of the universal good, though at first sight it may look somewhat remote, in reality will help to mitigate some of these difficulties by careful definition of the terms. There are philosophies that are not on the defensive about free will, but rather vaunt it as the supreme and imperative value in human life; in some cases they have in mind an *élan* such as that proposed by Bergson rather than the self-determination within limits we have outlined; in some cases they are criticizing the reduction of psychological to physiological laws; in some cases they are voicing an existential protest against the treadmill of essences according to philosophism. BIBLIOGRAPHY: ThAq ST la2ae,8–17, esp. in ed. Lat-Eng, v. 17, *The Human Act,* ed. T. Gilby (1970); A. M. Farrer, *Freedom of the Will* (1958); *DETERMINISM; *DETERMINISM, PSYCHOLOGICAL.

[T. GILBY]

FREE WILL AND GRACE, elements of a salutary act. That man's free will is not set aside by grace that invites, or precedes, and assists his salutary or meritorious actions is a doctrine of the Catholic faith. It was made explicit esp. by the Council of Trent defining that free will under the action of grace is not merely passive nor as it were, lifeless, but active (see D 1554), and the condemnation of the error of Jansen asserting that in meritorious acts there is no need for freedom from necessity but only for freedom from coercion (see D 2003). The problem of the coexistence of human freedom and grace does not concern prevenient actual grace, which God works in man without his cooperation (man cannot escape God's offer of grace); it refers to assisting actual grace, i.e., to the help of grace that is operative in man's free salutary or meritorious actions. When man accepts God's offer of grace and cooperates with grace, or when grace is efficacious, then, the doctrine of faith holds, his freedom of will remains complete (the free will, it may be added, is perfected by grace). This doctrine was stated firmly by St. Augustine, who taught the coexistence of grace and free will without attempting an explanation. Scholastic theology has made several attempts at reconciling the concepts of free will and grace. It has proposed various systems, but they are mainly of two types. Grace is said to be efficacious *ab intrinseco,* viz., of its inner nature, in such a way that the consent of the will follows infallibly, or necessarily yet freely (a paradox); or it is said to be efficacious *ab extrinseco,* viz., not of its inner nature but from God's favor granting a grace to which he foreknew man would consent freely. Some consider this explanation anthropomorphic. This much is certain: grace cannot destroy a spiritual perfection such as freedom. In actual fact, it is efficacious grace that makes the free consent actual; grace is not efficacious without this free consent. BIBLIOGRAPHY: M. J. Farrelly, *Predestination, Grace and Free Will* (1964); K. Rahner, *Grace in Freedom* (1969). *GRACE; *FREE WILL.

[P. DELETTER]

FREE WILL AND PROVIDENCE, a fundamental philosophical and theological problem which results from the dual affirmation of volitional freedom and God's *omniscience and *omnipotence. The issue is esp. significant within the Judaeo-Christian tradition which emphasizes moral responsibility and a personal God. In a more deterministic world view, e.g., in most of classical Greek philosophy, the difficulty is mitigated by a notion of *fate and the coincidence of virtue and general well-being. In Scripture, the two aspects of the problem are clearly affirmed: God is the almighty ruler of heaven and earth who knows all things (Ps 93.9), causes all things (Job 10.12), and directs the course of history (Is 2.2–9); and man is a free agent, responsible for what he does, subject to an ultimate reward or punishment (Mt 6.14–18). In characteristic Semitic fashion, however, no attempt is made to reconcile these two elements of revelation.

But the early Christian Fathers did make such an attempt. Augustine's efforts depend upon two key concepts: that evil is not something positive but negative, and that God's omniscience is not the same as advance human understanding but is based upon the eternity of God according to which earthly events are not progressively known to him but are always present. Scholastic theology deepened Augustine's insight into God's eternal "now," but also developed a further explanation based upon primary and secondary causality. God acts in all things according to their created essence; thus he acts in man as the primary cause, without whom there could be no action whatsoever, but according to the free nature of man who retains a true but secondary causality (ThAq ST 1a, 83.1 ad 3). The noted 16th-cent. controversy between Luis de *Molina and Domingo *Báñez centered on this problem, although the theological term *predestination was employed (see MOLINISM; BÁÑEZ AND BAÑEZIANISM). BIBLIOGRAPHY: M. Pontifex, *Freedom and Providence* (1960); V. J. Bourke, *Will in Western Thought* (1964); E. J. Carney, NCE 6:94–95. *FREE WILL AND GRACE; *PROVIDENCE OF GOD.

[T. M. MCFADDEN]

FREE WILL BAPTISTS, a group distinguished by belief in man's freedom to accept or reject God's saving grace, and originating in 18th-cent. American revivalism. In Perquimans Co., N.C., they were organized by Paul Palmer (1692–1763); and at New Durham, N.H., by Benjamin Randall (1749–1808), whose *Arminianism was unacceptable to the Regular Baptists. The Free Will Baptists spread through New England, the S, and the W, being reinforced by other Baptists who traced their descent from English *General Baptists. The Free Will Baptists of the N merged with the Northern Baptist Convention in 1911, but the movement in the S and W continues, with about 175,000 members. They remain Arminian, observe baptism by immersion, the Lord's Supper, and *footwashing. BIBLIOGRAPHY: N. A. Baxter, *Free Will Baptists* (1957).

[N. H. MARING]

FREE-WILL OFFERING (IN THE BIBLE), a voluntary gift offered the deity by the donor (cf. Ex. 35.27–29). The Levitical liturgy distinguishes three forms of peace offerings (Lev. 7.11–16), the thanks offering, the vow offering, and the *nedābâ* (free-will offering). This last offering, always made to God (except 2 Chr 35.8), was dictated by private devotion (Lev 7.16) and went beyond what legal demands required. At times it was offered in gratitude to God (cf. Ex 35.29; Dt 16.10), at times presented in support of prayer (Ps 54.8). The ritual of the offering is similar to that for peace offerings as set down in Lev 3.1–17. The victims suitable for offering were the same as in the case of holocausts: oxen, sheep, goats, but not pigeons. As with other peace offerings, not only male, but also female animals were allowed (Lev 3.6), and in the case of the free-will offering the principle of the unblemished character was not rigidly insisted on (Lev 22.23). In a few instances, the free-will offering referred to contributions of gold and silver for the sanctuary (Ex 35.29; Ezra 8.28; 2 Chr 31.14). It was characteristic of the peace offerings that the victim was being shared with God, priest, and offerer (Lev 7.28–34). The portion of the offerer was enjoyed at a sacrifical meal. Although in the case of the thanks offering, the whole had to be consumed the day of the sacrifice (Lev 7.15), in the free-will offering the feast might be extended to the second day (Lev 7.16). In Ps 119.108, the word "free-will offering" is used figuratively. BIBLIOGRAPHY: R. De Vaux, *Studies in Old Testament Sacrifice* (1964).

[F. BUCK]

FREEDOM, in general, the state or condition of one not subject to constraint in the exercise of his capacity to determine for himself what he shall think, believe, or do. It is not the same thing as free will, which is a natural endowment shared by all normal men, and it cannot be taken from them (although its use may be influenced or impeded in various ways, e.g., by drugs); whereas freedom is something that must be achieved. Freedom, as distinct from but implying free will, is not primarily something negative. It is not simply the absence of physical restraint (physical freedom is shared by animals not in captivity), nor is it mere spontaneity such as is found in all living things. Neither is it complete independence, for all creatures depend on God, if not also on other finite beings. Again, at least if it is to be considered as a desirable state or condition, it is not to be identified with absence of obligation, or the right to do exactly as one pleases (license), for man is the subject of duties as well as of rights. The freedom that can be reasonably claimed for man is a positive endowment, the power and right of self-mastery, consisting essentially in this, that he can rightfully be guided by his own judgment, that he can make decisions for which he alone is responsible, and that he can direct his life toward goals recognized, if not also set, by himself. This basic concept of freedom is what many modern writers call autonomy, creativity, self-transcendence, or, in existentialist terms, the power to give oneself an essence, or to pass from being to existence. The majority of philosophers today, as well as most civil constitutions, claim some such freedom for man.

Since man is not born perfect but has to reach toward perfection by his own effort, his freedom is not absolute. This is already evident from the fact that his choice is always conditioned by the situation in which it is made, a situation always dependent in large part by factors alien to the chooser. Besides, man has no alternative but to choose; or as J. P. Sartre puts it, he is "condemned to be free." The actual range of human freedom, the extent to which he can in fact realize the possibilities open to choice, cannot be settled without reference to experience; and this shows that his effective choice is limited. Freedom, as a quality of human activity, is relative to the aims of that activity. It is a means to an end, to the full development of personality. Man is meant to attain self-fulfillment by the proper use of his freedom and to attain perfect freedom through self-fulfillment. This proper use of freedom can be summed-up in the words of Vatican II: man should "direct himself toward goodness" (Vat II ChurchModWorld 17). The natural basis of such freedom is the dignity of the human person, which is now more or less universally admitted. His dignity lies in the fact that, gifted as he is with reason and free will, and created to know and embrace the truth and to seek what is good, he can mold his life by options fully his own and freely formed in the inner sanctuary of his own conscience. He is by nature open to being and to values, and ultimately to the Absolute. His nature leads him beyond himself. If freedom were used to center man on himself, it would cut him off from all other things and imprison him within the limitations of his own finite being. Such freedom would in fact deny itself. Freedom is delivered from bondage to the finite only when used to open man toward the infinite, to the God who communicates himself in love. Man is able to know God and to realize that in such knowledge, and in loving God above all things, he finds ultimate fulfillment and self-transcendence. In consequence his duties toward God are the foundation of his most sacred rights.

Man is by nature social. He can reach fulfillment only through interpersonal contacts in a social community. His duties toward the common welfare and to other members of the community give rise to further rights, while they also set limits to the exercise of his freedom. The rights resting on the individual's direct relationship to God are prior to and superior to those based on his social exigencies, and refer to the highest exercise of his freedom.

Revelation. In the words of Vatican Council II, revelation "sheds light on the dignity of the human person in its full dimensions" (RelFreed 9). Scripture clearly asserts the dignity of the human person. It "teaches that man was created 'to the image of God,' is capable of knowing and loving his Creator, and was appointed by him as master of all earthly creatures (Gen 1.26; Wis 2.23) that he might subdue them and use them to God's glory" (Sir 17.3–10; Vat II ChurchModWorld 12). "Authentic freedom is an exceptional sign of the divine image in man. For God has willed that man be left 'in the hand of his own counsel' (Sir 15.14) so that he can seek his Creator spontaneously, and come freely to utter and blissful perfection through loyalty to him. Hence man's dignity demands that he act according to a knowing and free choice" (*ibid.*, 17). The negative and positive aspects of freedom are closely linked and vividly symbolized in the OT history of the chosen people. Yahweh, having freed his people from the slavery of Egypt, offered them his alliance which would allow them to live as free men. The liberation (symbol of Easter) took place only once, but fidelity to the law promulgated on Sinai (symbol of Pentecost) remains the pledge and means of a spiritual freedom that is offered for all time to the heirs of the alliance. Similarly, Christ rose from the dead once and for all; the descent of the Holy Spirit to dwell in the Church gives man the power to live the new life offered by the risen Savior. The whole history of salvation shows God inviting man to acknowledge his sovereignty by freely loving and obeying him, and to yield assent to his revelation in faith. It portrays man as a responsible person who is able to sin or to tend to perfection by keeping God's law, as one who is able to direct his life to God through personal conviction. It reveals that God deals with man as one who is responsible and free. In the OT, God's call to union and alliance is addressed primarily to the chosen people to whom his law was given. As the new covenant draws near, the call is directed more and more to the individual also, and love begins to assume more importance than obedience. It was only when, through Christ, God's personal love for man was revealed that every individual could be seen as unique and of eternal value, as one who must fulfill himself with complete responsibility, and hence in freedom.

In the NT freedom is transformed by being founded on grace as well as on nature, by being rooted in the dignity of man as raised by grace to divine sonship. Freedom as a means to the enrichment of personality is drawn into the supernatural context of growth of the divine life in the soul toward its fullness in union with God in heaven. It is seen as most fully exercised in that charity which the Holy Spirit infuses into man. Through such love God's law ceases to be merely external; it becomes the inner law of the heart, for the lover conforms his will to that of his beloved. This "freedom of the sons of God" (Rom 8.21; Gal 4.6–7) becomes a sharing in the limitless freedom of God, a self-transcendence through union with him altogether beyond the powers of nature. The Christian's freedom flows from the conforming of man by grace to the image of the Son of God made man, and from his incorporation into the body of which Christ is the head. By thus sharing in the life of Christ, he shares also in his freedom. This aspect of the Christian life is stressed mainly by St. John (8.31–36) and St. Paul (esp. Rom 6–8; Gal 4–5). For St. John it is truth, the acceptance in faith of Christ as the Word of God, which makes man free and delivers him from the bondage of error and sin. St. Paul develops the theme of Christian freedom, first of all in its negative aspects. Through union with Christ by faith and love the Christian is set free from the obligation of obeying the Jewish Law, from the domination of death and sin, from enslavement by his passions and evil desires, from guilt and the punishment due to past sins. He is delivered from the freedom of selfishness which would center him solely on himself. Positively, it is the power to develop the life of grace in the soul, the freedom of sons who are led by love rather than by law. The will of God, made known by Christ, becomes through love the inner and personal rule of the Christian's behavior, so that he is at once both supremely free and the servant of the Lord. The meaning or purpose of freedom is revealed as love. The freedom of the children of God (Rom 8.21) is revealed as freedom for self-fulfillment through grace and love in following Christ, or, as St. Paul put it, in attaining "to the measure of the fullness of Christ" (Eph 4.13).

This moral freedom is given by the Holy Spirit, the Spirit of love, who binds those who are born again in Christ into the unity of the Church as the body of Christ and into a communion of love (2 Cor 3.17; Rom 5.5; 8.9–17). The Church is thus the home of true freedom. All, whether their natural condition is one of slavery or of freedom, are equal as sons of God by grace and love. This also means that Christian freedom is social in its exercise; it leads the baptized to place themselves through love at the service of others for God's sake since love is the fulfillment of the law (Gal 5.13–15). Grace thus draws man's natural freedom to the supernatural perfection under all its aspects.

Teaching of the Church. In the tradition and dogmatic pronouncements of the Church the scriptural teaching concerning the natural dignity of man as image of God and concerning his supernatural dignity as son of God by grace has been gradually clarified and developed in its relation to freedom. Theological disputes on original sin and its effects, on the need of grace, and on the relationship between God's sovereign or saving action and the human agent, led the Church to concentrate mainly on the affirmation of free will rather than of freedom, since this was not seriously challenged. The relation between the two is well expressed by Vatican II: "Since man's freedom has been damaged by sin, only by the help of God's grace can he emancipate himself from all captivity to passion and pursue his goal in a spontaneous choice of what is good" (Vat II ChurchModWorld 17). Until recently man's sharing in the freedom of Christ was seen mainly as freedom from error and sin. It was the modern insistence on freedom that provided the occasion for the Church to deal with its more positive aspects. The 19th-cent. rationalist claim that man is free in the sense that he has no moral obligation binding in conscience to seek out and obey objective norms of truth and proper conduct or to worship God moved Popes Pius IX and Leo III to teach that true freedom is the power to develop one's nature according to God's laws and to serve him in truth and goodness. This teaching is not new in the Church, but it does make clear what the Church understands by freedom. Pius XII could say, in an address to the college of cardinals: "Liberty . . . to reach out to what is true and good, liberty such as will be in harmony with the well-being of every people in particular and of the whole great family of peoples—such liberty the Church has ever proclaimed, guarded, and defended" (AAS [1946] 256).

The 20th cent. is characterized by its insistence on freedom as well as by man's success in winning control over nature. It has seen the emancipation of the working-class, the waning of colonialism, the recognition of the rights of women; and the reaction against totalitarian systems has led—though not universally—to the spread of democratic institutions. Owing at least partly to the influence of these movements, as well as of recent trends of thought, freedom has come to be a dominant theme in Catholic thinking. The Church's growth in awareness of its own nature has, under these conditions, led it to develop a consciousness of the implications of the freedom which it has always in principle proclaimed and which it makes possible for man. This is reflected in utterances of Pius XII, John XXIII, and Paul VI, and in the documents of Vatican II, notably in those on the Church in the modern world and on religious freedom. These texts present the full and positive notion of Christian freedom as outlined above, and they require that such freedom be effectively realized both in the Church and in civil society. Even if the Church had not made any pronouncement about freedom, by the very fact of proclaiming the gospel and of uniting man to Christ it would have made real freedom known in fact. As the community of those united in Christ by faith and love, the Church is the sign of the presence of divine freedom in the world. It is the dwelling-place of true freedom, the family in which man can through grace attain his freedom as guided and helped by those who share in the authority of Christ. The Church as a pattern of real freedom shows clearly that it is not emancipation from all authority. In the Church the kingdom of God is established on earth, and in that kingdom the rights of God are primary and absolute, and man's duty is to obey and love. Christian obedience is love-inspired as befits those who are free and who follow the "perfect law of liberty" (Jas 1.25). Christ, setting up the kingdom of God, respects man's freedom. He invites men to follow him, he does not force them. His way of seeking allegiance through love must remain that of those who represent him and share his authority in the Church.

If authority is vested in those who are set by the Holy Spirit to rule the Church of God (Acts 20.28), the manner of its exercise should not be determined by reference to the way authority is wielded in civil societies. Many of the evils complained of in the practical life of the Church have been due precisely to this foreign, and frequently baneful, influence. The ideal would be precisely the contrary, that secular rulers should learn from the example of the Church how to use their power. Christ warned his representatives quite explicitly against any abuse of authority, telling them to become the servants of all, as he had been (Mk 10.42–45; Lk 22.25–27). His first vicar on earth exhorted the elders of the Church to rule, not by force, not as lording it over others, but as guided by love and as setting an example for others (I Pet 5.3). On the other hand, the individual Christian cannot throw the burden of his most intimate and personal decisions on those who hold authority in the Church. Freedom entails responsibility; and there are many areas in which the individual, however guided by law or pastoral teaching, must decide for himself. The Christian is never just passive even in obedience, nor fully autonomous even when he is free. There will always be a certain tension, an unavoidable dialectic between authority and freedom, between obedience and inner growth, between external law and conscience. This is a healthy and essential aspect of

Christian life, and one that is receiving much attention in theology today. The Church, as founded by Christ to continue his adoring and saving mission, has to claim the freedom needed to carry out this task. Negatively, this implies that no earthly power may claim jurisdiction in the Church nor obstruct the life and work of the Church by oppressive measures. Positively, it means that the Church, as ruled by the vicarious authority of Christ, and so by its own laws, may grow and develop as the community of those who seek to imitate Christ under the guidance of the indwelling Spirit of love. Essential aspects of this growth are the development of doctrine and the activity of the prophetic element in the Church, for instance in its liturgical and religious life. Besides this inner or spiritual freedom, the Church evidently demands the civil right to religious freedom which Vatican II has claimed for individuals and communities.

Among the practical manifestations of Christian freedom are: *Freedom of conscience,* man's right and duty to follow his own conscience, to decide his destiny in accord with his conscience. *Freedom of thought,* the right to seek the truth and to adhere to it when known. This implies freedom of research and of discussion. *Freedom of action,* the right to be led not merely by obedience but by inner conviction. *Freedom of speech,* the right to make known and publish one's thoughts as well as artistic creations. *Freedom of the press,* the right to print news and comments on current events, and to have access to information about them. Such rights are relative, and they imply corresponding duties. The ideal is that men should use these rights with a sense of responsibility toward others and as guided by objectively valid moral norms, if not, as Christians, by the light of revelation. The common element running through these various kinds of freedom touched on in this article is self-determination. Free will is essentially the power to determine self by decisions formed through conscious reflection. This characteristic self-decision is retained and expressed in the different ways by which man exercises his freedom. Freedom is thus relative to the self. The value of its use depends above all on how this self is conceived, that is, on the ideal to which man freely chooses to conform. For the Christian, this self is not just human. It is self as the image of Christ who is himself the image of God as revealed in human flesh. The supreme use of freedom is to seek through love, and by God's grace, to be transformed into the living likeness of Christ. BIBLIOGRAPHY: J. Maritain, *Freedom in the Modern World* (tr. R. O'Sullivan, 1936); *idem, True Humanism* (tr. M. R. Adamson, 6th ed., 1954); D. A. O'Connell, *Christian Liberty* (1952); M. Feltin et al., *Christianity and Freedom* (1955); J. De Finance, *Existence et liberté* (1955); E. D'Arcy, *Conscience and Its Right to Freedom* (1960); J. Wild, *Existence and the World of Freedom* (1963); K. Rahner, *Theological Investigations* (v. 2, 1963) ch. 2, 8; *Freedom and Man* (ed. J. C. Murray, 1965); S. Lyonnet, "Liberté chrétienne et loi de l'Esprit selon St. Paul," in *La Vie selon l'Esprit: condition du chrétien* by I. De La Potterie (1965) ch. 6; C. Spicq, *Charity and Liberty* (tr. F. V. Manning, 1965); *Théologie morale du Nouveau Testament* (v. 2, 1965), ch. 9; B. Häring, *Liberty of the Sons of God* (tr. P. O'Shaughnessy, 1966); J. Mouroux, *La Liberté chrétienne* (1966); A. Thierry, *Liberté religieuse et liberté chrétienne* (1966); H. Küng, *La Liberté du chrétien* (1967); R. T. Osborn, *Freedom in Modern Theology* (acc. to Bultmann, Tillich, Barth, Berdyaev 1967) *FREEDOM OF SPEECH AND PRESS.

[A. MCNICHOLL]

FREEDOM, ACADEMIC, the rights of educators and students to pursue and communicate their academic investigations without interference. Such freedom is regarded as essential to effective education. Although similar rights also exist elsewhere in society, their specific institutional context in higher education makes academic freedom distinctive. Independence of inquiry has frequently been a controversial issue between scholars and either political or ecclesiastical authorities (see CENSORSHIP), but the groundwork for the contemporary formulation of academic freedom was laid in the universities of 19th-cent. Germany where freedom in teaching *(Lehfreiheit)* and in learning *(Lernfreiheit)* were defended against political interference. The situation in the U.S. is somewhat distinctive insofar as its colleges and universities are not self-constituted communities of scholars but rather religious, private, or state institutions with legal authority vested in a board of directors. Thus academic freedom has come to be protected by historical precedent, faculty professionalism and academic associations. In 1915, the American Association of University Professors was founded; it continues to formulate principles outlining the rights and responsibilities of the academic community on grounds that the faculty itself must judge the teaching and scholarship of its members. It was out of this concern that the tenure system was designed so that a faculty member, usually after 7 years of full-time service, may not be dismissed from his position except for gross neglect of his duties, moral impropriety, or the institution's extreme financial exigency. Academic freedom also entails the responsibilities to preserve scholarly objectivity, to refrain from introducing extraneous concerns into the classroom, and to distinguish the faculty member's individual positions from those of the institution.

The situation in U.S. Catholic institutions has developed considerably since a 1942 study by W. M. Mallon, S. J., indicating that only 65% of Catholic colleges recognized tenure. Since that time, the same principles of academic freedom supported by the academic community nationally have been generally adopted by Catholic institutions. The *Declaration on Religious Freedom* of Vatican Council II, noted that "truth is to be sought in a manner proper to the dignity of the human person and his social nature. The inquiry is to be free . . . ." BIBLIOGRAPHY: S. Hook, *In Defence of Academic Freedom* (1971); E. Pincoffs, *The Concept of Academic Freedom* (1975).

[T. M. MCFADDEN]

FREEDOM, RELIGIOUS, see RELIGIOUS FREEDOM.

FREEDOM, SPIRITUAL, the liberty from sin and spiritual death which Christ has won for mankind and in accordance with which the Christian acts. Spiritual freedom may be spoken of in a cosmic sense, designating the fundamental Christian vision of the world expressed in Paul's Epistle to the Romans according to which all men having sinned were under the power of death until their redemption could be secured by Christ. Within this theological perspective, characteristic also of St. Augustine and many of the 16th-cent. Reformers, man left to his own device is capable only of sin, since the possibility of attaining his unique supernatural finality is granted only through the cross. In this sense, Paul speaks of man lacking freedom while he is under the law. To this notion of the cosmic freedom granted by Christ must be added that of the personal freedom within which a Christian may make his moral decisions. This implies a liberating death to sin and an orientation of the will under grace to accomplish only what is good. Thus the person is freed from the slavery of a will constricted by selfishness and opened to the Spirit so that he may achieve the goals which he recognizes as good. BIBLIOGRAPHY: C. Spicq, *Charity and Liberty in the New Testament* (1966); S. Lyonnet, *Saint Paul: Liberty and Law* (1962) 229–251; B. Häring, NCE 6:106–107.

[T. M. MCFADDEN]

FREEDOM OF CHRIST. Christ underwent his Passion and death under the mandate of his Father. The Gr. term *entolē* (command or precept) used by St. John's Gospel with reference to Christ's death (14.31), leaves no doubt as to the binding character of the Father's will (cf. also Rom 5.19; 4.25; Phil 2.8; Heb 5.8). This mandate and the obedience due to it raise the delicate theological problem of the nature of Christ's human freedom. Did the Father's precept leave room in him for the exercise of that faculty? More precisely: how can Christ's human liberty be combined with his absolute and intrinsic impeccability on the one hand and the Father's mandate on the other? The solution of the antinomy seems to lie in a correct conception of liberty. The essence of freedom does not consist in the faculty of choice, but in the power of self-determination. Freedom is the *aseity of the will, the mastery over one's action on which responsibility is based. It is incompatible with every kind of violence suffered from without or of blind necessity intrinsic to nature; it is not, however, incompatible with a necessity that proceeds from the will itself. On the contrary, an irresistible impulse of the will resulting from full knowledge of the goodness of the object proposed to it, is the sign of a liberty fully mature. Such was in fact the human freedom of Christ. The immediate vision of the Father showed him the goodness of the Father's will. Christ embraced it in an act of perfect selfdetermination. While submitting to the Father's will (cf. Mk 14.36), he claimed to lay down his life of his own free will (Jn 10.18). BIBLIOGRAPHY: A. Durand, ''Liberté du Christ dans son rapport avec l'impeccabilité,'' NRT (1948) 811; Rahner ThInvest 1:176.

[J. DUPUIS]

FREEDOM OF SPEECH AND PRESS, the right of the individual or of the communications media to express facts and opinions without restriction from others, esp. those in authority. Freedom of speech is commonly applied to vocal communication; freedom of press is extended to films, radio, television, etc., as well as the printed word. The moral foundation of these freedoms is based upon the ontological composition of finite being itself as dynamically but not determinately inclined toward truth and goodness. The specification of the individual's movement toward actualization is the exercise of freedom, thus only as a self-determining being can a person fulfill himself. A corollary of such freedom, based upon the social nature of human existence, is the right to communicate openly. Freedom of speech and of the press is essential for the realization of human community based upon self-determination rather than an imposed homogeneity. Nevertheless, these freedoms are not absolute; they stand only in relationship to the common good which at times must be safeguarded through the regulation of the freedom of communication, e.g., the right to a fair trial precludes the press' right to print all the details of a crime. Practical and complex difficulties frequently arise when it becomes necessary to balance freedom and the common good, the latter of which is often obscure and debatable. Disagreement on specific cases is characteristic but general opinion, at least in the U.S., seems to be in favor of minimal restraints with the presumption in favor of the communicator.

The history of these freedoms is quite varied. In those social structures, either Church or State, where truth was regarded as fixed and reflected in the status quo, tolerance of independent inquiry was often nonexistent. Thus the Church, recipient of a divine revelation, often sought to limit freedom of speech and of the press when an opinion did not agree with the teachings deemed to be orthodox. Several examples of such restrictions are well known: the Index of Forbidden Books (1559), the *Nihil Obstat,* the *Imprimatur,* and the *Syllabus of Errors* (1864). But a change in attitude has been widespread in recent times. Although Vatican Council II's *Decree on the Instruments of Social Communication* was hardly innovative, Pope John XXIII's encyclical *Pacem in Terris* (1963) specifically defends ''freedom of speech and publication'' as well as the right ''to be fully informed about public events.'' In regard to the civil government's restriction of these freedoms, Christian theology has come to acknowledge more and more widely the value of Church-State separation and the concomitant freedom of religion, of speech, and of the press. A perduring problem, however, is the freedom of the Catholic press and whether such a press, as long as it remains an official organ of the Church, can escape an element of control inimical to its freedom. BIBLIOGRAPHY: J.

Deedy, *Conscience, Freedom, and Authority* (1972); J. Hohenberg, *Free Press/Free People* (1971); J. Maritain, *True Humanism* (1954); J. C. Murray, *We Hold These Truths* (1964); K. Rahner, *Free Speech in the Church* (1959).

[T. M. MCFADDEN]

FREEMASONS (Masons), members of those fraternal organizations that follow the principles, usages, and rites known as Freemasonry. Freemasons trace their origins to the medieval stonemasons, who were called free masons because they worked on free stone; these artisans, whose worksheds were called lodges and who had their own guilds, were working or operative masons. In England these fraternities of working masons, which had a religious and moral purpose, gradually admitted non-working, honorary, or "accepted" members. When the building of churches stopped after the Reformation, the lodges came to be made up mostly of nonworking Masons, and the tools and terms of the trade took on a purely symbolic meaning. The nonworking Masons, esp. after the lodges espoused deism in the 18th cent., are designated speculative Freemasons. Modern Freemasons have their origins in the Grand Lodge of England, formed from four lodges there in 1717. After 1721 the Freemasons attracted many members from the royalty and nobility, and the lodges grew in size; Grand Lodges were established also in Scotland and in Ireland (the ecclesiastical prohibitions were not promulgated there for many years). From England the organization moved to continental Europe. In France it became anticlerical and occultist; in Belgium and in the Latin countries of Europe and America it became extremely anticlerical and anti-Catholic. In Germany the Order of *Illuminati infiltrated the Masonic lodges and used them for their subversive program. The various Masonic fraternities in the world are grouped into the lodges of the Anglo-Saxon world, the Grand Orients of Europe and Latin America, Negro Masonic lodges, and splinter lodges, including some that initiate women. By far the largest representation of Freemasonry is found in the U.S., with England and the Commonwealth countries next in order of significant membership. Communist countries have banned Masonry, as has Spain, Portugal, and the United Arab Republic.

The history of the Freemasons in the U.S. begins shortly after the establishment of the Grand Lodge. Daniel Coxe was appointed Grand Master of New York, New Jersey, and Pennsylvania in 1730. Leading figures in the American Revolution, such as George Washington, Benjamin Franklin, Patrick Henry, and John Paul Jones, were Masons. Besides Washington, eleven U.S. presidents have worn the Masonic apron. The Masonic lodges not only grew enormously in membership, but they became the model for many other fraternal organizations for men of lower social rank or of beliefs incompatible with Freemasonry (see INDEPENDENT ORDER OF ODD FELLOWS). An American Mason begins his Masonic education by receiving the first, or Entered Apprentice, degree in a Blue lodge. He advances to the degrees of Fellow Craft and Master Mason. If he wishes he may elect to receive the degrees of the York rite, which culminates in the Knights Templar, or the Scottish rite, which confers the 4th to the 32d degrees and the honorary 33d degree. Masonic authorities disagree as to what are the essential features, the "landmarks," of the fraternity but are in accord that they include at least the three-degree system of initiation, the methods of recognition, acknowledgment of the Great Architect of the Universe and the immortality of the soul, acceptance of the story of Hiram Abiff, legendary stonemason for the temple of Solomon, the place of the Volume of Sacred Law on the Altar, secrecy in the lodge, and the equality of all Masons in a lodge.

Freemasonry has a religious content. In Anglo-Saxon countries the deism connoted by the designation of God as Great Architect and the general naturalism signify a neutral or nondenominational attitude rather than the hostility to religion prevalent among Freemasons of France and the Latin countries. Anglo-Saxon Freemasons are rather concerned with social and benevolent activities; the anti-Catholicism associated with Masonry was more a part of the religious antipathy between Protestants and Catholics than an essential of Freemasonry. Still, a majority of all Christians belong to denominations that condemn Masonic affiliation; not only for RCs but for Eastern Orthodox Christians, Lutherans, Quakers, Brethren, Mennonites, Jehovah's Witnesses, Mormons, Christian Reformed, and Seventh-day Adventists membership is forbidden or discouraged. The chief objections of these Christian Churches to Freemasonry have been to an avowed naturalism that ignores the essentials of the gospel, and to the imposition of an oath of secrecy with regard to something frivolous (the secrets of the lodges are not secrets at all but accessible in any public library). Roman Catholic prohibitions were chiefly prompted by the anti-Christian and anticlerical program of Freemasons in France and the Latin countries. The first condemnation was issued in a bull of Clement XII in 1738; Benedict XIV, Pius VII, Pius IX, and Leo XIII all condemned Freemasonry. In 1974 the ban was lifted against membership by the Catholic laity; active fellowship between Masons and the Knights of Columbus has been fostered. BIBLIOGRAPHY: H. S. Box, *Nature of Freemasonry* (1952); W. Hannah, *Darkness Visible* (1952); B. E. Jones, *Freemasons' Guide and Compendium* (1950); W. J. Whalen, *Christianity and American Freemasonry* (1958); *idem, Handbook of Secret Organizations* (1966); F. Bailey, *Spirit of Masonry* (2d ed. rev., 1972); W. H. Upton, *Negro Masonry* (1902, repr. 1975).

[W. J. WHALEN]

FREETHINKERS, a term brought into universal notoriety and established currency in religious controversy in England by Anthony Collins's *Discourse of Free-Thinking, Occasioned by the Rise and Growth of a Sect Called Free-Thinkers* (1713). In late 17th-cent. France, the concept of freethinking formed part of what was understood by *libertinage,* although the radical heterodoxy of the *libertin* was associated with a more or less serious moral laxity and even depravity. Freethought arose, in both countries, as a conscious reaction against some phases of conventional, traditional doctrine. It embodied a claim to pursue any question, however sacrosanct, with fearless honesty, and, in practice, the undermining of the claims of religious faith and, at times, of conventional morality as well. Both the English word libertine and the French *libertin* were reserved for the sexually vicious when Richardson created his Lovelace and Laclos his Valmont. It was from the first, however, assumed by their theological adversaries that freethinkers logically and inevitably indulged in free-living. By the beginning of the 18th cent., the English expression freethinker replaced libertine and came to stand for one who defied religious orthodoxy in an esp. outrageous and contemptuous fashion and defended the right to unbounded intellectual curiosity. Freethinkers thereafter were identified as religious skeptics, although the name concealed undoubted differences among them in point of departure, object of chief concern, and degree of unbelief. In the 19th cent., Karl Pearson stressed, paradoxically, the ''essentially religious character of freethought,'' which he identified with science and with an ethic ''superior to the Christian.'' BIBLIOGRAPHY: J. M. Robertson, *Short History of Freethought* (2 v., 1929, repr. 1969); J. S. Spink, *French Freethought from Gassendi to Voltaire* (1960).

[J. P. REID]

FREIBERG GOLDEN DOOR, main portal of the Marienkirche, the cathedral of Freiberg (now E. Germany) in what was Saxony. Originally gilded, it is the first complete statue portal in Germany (1230) with 8 jamb figures, a figural archivolt, and a tympanum carving of the *Adoration of the Magi*. The style is a German version of the French model.

[M. J DALY]

FREIBURG IM BREISGAU, CATHEDRAL, German Gothic church in red sandstone, with early 13th-cent. Romanesque transept and side towers. The nave (1235) has walls without galleries in the style of Upper Rhine Gothic. The apse was begun in 1354 by Johannes Parler and the striking net-vaulted choir by John of Gmünd in 1359 and completed 1510–13. The W tower, achieving a remarkable unity through subtle transitions from square to octagonal to pierced spire, is the first of this distinctively German type to be completed.

[M. J. DALY]

FRELINGHUYSEN, THEODORUS JACOBUS (1692–1747?), one of the principal evangelists of the *Great Awakening in America. F. was born in Westphalia, Ger., and early came under the influence of *Pietism. He was ordained by the German Reformed Church in 1717, came to New Jersey in 1720, and was made pastor of a group of Reformed Churches in the Raritan Valley. F.'s pastoral and preaching methods at first shocked his parishioners and the clergy and laymen of the Reformed Dutch Church in New York. His emphasis upon personal repentance and a more emotional expression of religion was very different from the formal kind of religion practiced in the area. Many of F.'s parishioners came to accept his revivalistic methods and experienced conversion under the pressure of the new evangelism. F. became noted, also, as a champion of self-government for the Dutch Reformed churches. Candidates for the ministry had to take the dangerous journey to the Netherlands for ordination, and two of F.'s sons died making such a journey. Victory in the fight for autonomy came only at the end of the colonial period. BIBLIOGRAPHY: P. Frelinghuysen, Jr., *Theodorus Jacobus Frelinghuysen* (1938). *REFORMED CHURCH IN AMERICA.

[E. EENIGENBURG]

FRÉMIET, EMMANUEL (1824–1910), French sculptor, who studied with his famous uncle, François Rude. F. concentrated on animal groups less violent than those of Barye. He is best known for large equestrian statues of historical figures such as *Joan of Arc* (1874), Paris) of which there is a reproduction in Fairmount Park, Philadelphia, Pennslyvania. BIBLIOGRAPHY: P. Faure-Frémiet, *Frémiet* P (1934).

[M. J. DALY]

FRÉMIN, RENÉ (1672–1744), French sculptor. Pupil of F. Girardon and A. Coysevox and court sculptor to Louis XIV, F. did decorative work in the chapel at Versailles (1705–17). In Madrid (1721–38) he was court sculptor (1727) to Philip V, executing allegorical fountains in San Ildefonso in a transitional 17th- to 18th-cent. style.

[M. J. DALY]

FREMINENT, MARTIN (1564–1619), important French painter of the second school of Fontainebleau. In Italy (1592) F. was deeply impressed by the works of Michelangelo. Journeying to Turin, he painted a *St. Martin* for the Duke of Savoy. In Paris (1603), painter to Henry IV, F. taught drawing to the young Louis XIII. His major work is the decoration of the Chapel of the Trinity (now restored, Fontainebleau). Paintings of the Fathers of the Church and the Evangelists (Orléans Museum) show agitated forms and dissonant color. An engraving of F.'s painting *Christ with the Instrument of the Passion* was made in Italy in 1615.

[M. J. DALY]

FRENCH, LEONARD (1928–), Australian painter who studied at home and in England, Ireland, Holland, and Belgium, experimenting with the cubism of Leger and Delauney. Expressing concepts of birth, death, and rebirth he painted in 1960 a series on Genesis and in 1961 a series on the life of Edmund Campion, the English Jesuit. His work in gilt and glazed enamels is magnificent in color and scale.

[M. J. DALY]

FRENCH REVOLUTION, political and cultural transformation of France, beginning in 1789 with the fall of the Bastille. French Enlightenment thinkers such as Voltaire and Rousseau had long been attacking Christian beliefs and promoting *Deism. At the beginning of the Revolution, however, leaders did not envision complete overthrow of the Church, any more than elimination of the monarchy. But privileges of the clergy were abolished in August 1789, and the Declaration of the Rights of Man, condemned by Pius VI, asserted freedom of religion. Having taken church properties in 1789, the Constituent Assembly on July 12, 1790, precipitated a decisive break between Church and Revolution by enacting the *Civil Constitution of the Clergy to make the clergy salaried, state officials. Most clergy obeyed the order of Pius VI to refuse the required oath. Supporters of the Church thereafter tended to favor restoration of the old regime, while advocates of the Revolution, *Jacobins, became more anticlerical. The French government broke relations with the papacy in 1791 and seized Avignon, then part of the States of the Church. From 1792 to 1794 the Assembly and its successor, the National Convention, carried out a dechristianization program. The monarchy was abolished in 1792 and Louis XVI executed in 1793. Many clergy were executed during the Terror, and Protestant as well as Catholic churches were closed. In Nov. 1793 the Goddess Reason was acclaimed in Notre Dame. In Dec. a revolutionary calendar replaced the Gregorian. In 1795 the Thermidorean Convention turned toward separation of Church and State, and made attempts at accommodation. Catholic opposition led the Directory to undertake a new anti-Catholic offensive from 1797 to 1799. It dispatched to Rome an army that made the Papal States a republic and brought Pius VI as a prisoner to France, where he died in 1799. *Napoleon I took power the same year, and in 1801 agreed to a concordat that reestablished the hierarchy and provided for payment of clergy salaries, but did not make Catholicism the state religion. Napoleon also legalized Protestant and Jewish worship. By its antireligious measures, the French Revolution caused a reaction in the French Church which virtually replaced *Gallicanism with *ultramontanism. The papacy and other conservative forces, both within France and elsewhere, continued the fight against the principles of the French Revolution into the 20th century.

[T. EARLY]

FREPPEL, CHARLES ÉMILE (1827–91), French bp. and polemicist. Born in Alsace, he studied at Strasbourg and was ordained there in 1849. The first years of his career were spent chiefly in Paris, where he taught homiletics at the Sorbonne; from his teaching, esp. on the Church Fathers, he published *Les origines du christianisme* (2 v., 1903). His critical response in *Le Monde* to the publication of J.*Renan's *Vie de Jésus* was widely appreciated. Called to Rome by Pius IX as a consultor for the preparation of Vatican Council I, he was named bp. of Angers in 1870, and during the council reversed his position to become an infallibilist. As bp. he spoke out against the anti-Church policies of the French government, and took his opposition into the political arena by becoming elected to the Chamber of Deputies from Brest in 1880. In the history of Catholic social policies his stand (esp. as he presided over a social conference at Angers in 1890) came to be known as the Angers School in distinction from the more radical Liège School of social thought. In politics he was a strong royalist, and instransigent against any form of Catholic liberalism. He therefore repudiated Card. Lavigerie's "toast of Algiers" and opposed the policy of *Ralliement. Leo XIII's encyclicals, *Inter innumeras sollicitudines* (officially adopting *ralliement*) and *Rerum novarum* (on the social rights of workers) contradicted F.'s views.

[T. C. O'BRIEN]

FRERE, WALTER HOWARD (1863–1938), Anglican bp. of Truro and liturgical scholar. F. was educated at Cambridge, was ordained in 1887, and joined the Anglican Community of the Resurrection in 1892. He became a bp. in 1823, resigning in 1935. He published numerous studies on the history of the liturgy, esp. a new *History of the Book of Common Prayer,* and was active in the ecumenical movement, being a participant in the *Malines Conversations.

[R. B. ENO]

FRÉRON, ELIE (1718–1776), French publicist and literary critic. In 1754, F. founded *L'Année littéraire,* a review continued by his son until the Revolution. A strong defender of religion, a man of learning and wit, he battled the philosophes and esp. Voltaire who often abused him unfairly. A controversial figure, his merits as critic have been recognized by modern scholars. Although he supported the monarchy, he advocated reforms. BIBLIOGRAPHY: François Cornou, *Trente années de luttes contre Voltaire et les philosophes au XVIIIe siècle: Elie Fréron . . .* (1922).

[A. S. CRISAFULLI]

FREUD, SIGMUND (1856–1939), founder and chief architect of *psychoanalysis. After earning his diploma in medicine from the Univ. of Vienna in 1881, F. continued study and research for a few years during which time (1886) he actually began the practice of psychiatry. Of his six children, the most famous was Anna who was also to achieve distinction as a psychoanalyst. Important intellectual influences on F. were E. Brücke who gave him the idea of rigorous science, J. Breuer who was his collaborator in the study of hysteria, and J. M. Charcot who used hypnosis in the same field at his institute in Paris. There F. realized the significance of unconscious motivation and began to concentrate on techniques for the systematic exploration of the unconscious mind. In 1900 when he was 44, he published *The Interpretation of Dreams,* which represented the real beginning of the psychoanalytic movement. The next 35 years were devoted to its development by self-analysis, therapy, and clinical research; then by dissemination of his theories to numerous disciples (the most famous, Carl *Jung and Alfred *Adler, both later 'defected' from 'orthodoxy'); finally, by the organization of psychoanalytic institutions, societies, and conventions as well as by the foundation of publications, all with international scope. The major works in which F. unfolded his developing ideas were: *The Psychopathology of Everyday Life* (1904), *Three Contributions to the Theory of Sexuality* (1905), *A General Introduction to Psychoanalysis* (1917), *Beyond the Pleasure Principle* (1920), *The Ego and the Id* (1923), *Inhibitions, Symptoms and Anxiety* (1926), and *New Introductory Lectures in Psychoanalysis* (1933). For an idea of Freud's attitudes toward religion, see *PSYCHOANALYSIS. By the time of his death, F.'s status as one of the most influential thinkers of his time was well established. Writings: ed. J. Strachey, *Standard Edition of the Complete Psychological Works of Sigmund Freud* (24 v., 1953–). BIBLIOGRAPHY: E. Jones, *Life and Works of Sigmund Freud* (3 v., 1953).

[M. STOCK]

FREY, JOHANN BAPTIST (1878–1939), German biblical scholar. After receiving his doctorate in Scripture, F. became a consultor to the *Pontifical Biblical Commission (1910) and later its secretary (1925). He contributed numerous articles to journals and reference works, specializing in Jewish theology of the time of Christ. He inaugurated a critical collection of Hebrew inscriptions from 300 B.C. to 700 A.D., two volumes of which have been published.

[T. M. MCFADDEN]

FRIAR (from Fr. *frère,* Lat. *frater,* brother), the designation adopted by the medieval mendicant orders for their members. It had the connotation both of their choice of a humble state and of their concept of a brotherhood as the source of their sanctification and apostolate. In England the four great mendicant orders were called the Austin Friars (Augustinians), the Whitefriars (Carmelites), the Blackfriars (Dominicans) and the Greyfriars (Franciscans). In the sense of community developing after Vatican II there is a frequent use of the title ''brother'' in the orders even by priest members.

[T. C. O'BRIEN]

FRIARS MINOR, see FRANCISCANS.

FRIARS OF THE ATONEMENT, see ATONEMENT, SOCIETY OF THE.

FRIARS OF THE CROSS, see CRUTCHED FRIARS.

FRIARS OF THE SACK, mendicant order (the Order of Penance of Jesus Christ) established in Provence, France. It was approved by Alexander IV in 1255 with a constitution patterned on that of the Dominicans. By 1274 it had over 100 houses with provinces in France, Spain, Italy, England, and the Holy Land. The most important of the mendicant orders forbidden by the Council of Lyons (1274) to accept any more novices or establish any new houses, it died out in the following century.

[T. EARLY]

FRIARS PREACHERS, see DOMINICANS.

FRIARY, a name commonly used to designate a monastery or convent which houses a community of men belonging to one of the earlier mendicant orders, e.g., the Franciscans, Dominicans, Carmelites, or Augustinians. It is derived from the name friar which in turn comes from OF, *frère,* and Lat. *frater,* or brother.

[M. B. PENNINGTON]

FRIBOURG, CATHEDRAL OF. The cathedral of St. Nicolas in the medieval Swiss city of Fribourg has a nave (1343–1400) preceded by an immense tower with 14th to 16th-cent. bells, an imposing sculptured S portal (1350) with statues of the Virgin, the Magi, St. Nicolas, and others, and a large *Crucifixion* (1400) on the interior. The *Loreto Chapel,* a baroque interpretation of the original Holy House of Loreto, Italy, and the Visitanerinnenkloster—a central plan covered by Gothic vaults (1653–56)—were built by H. F. Reyff.

[M. J. DALY]

FRIBOURG, UNIVERSITY OF, a state institution and center of Catholic studies financed by public subsidy and donations from Swiss Catholics. The youngest of Switzerland's seven univs., founded in 1889 with the approval of Leo XIII and the Swiss bps., it was the first Catholic institution of higher learning to exist in Switzerland since the early 1600s. With the approval of the cantonal legislature and promise of financial assistance, the univ. opened with two faculties—law and philosophy. The faculty of theology, under Dominican direction, followed in 1890; the faculty of science in 1896. In its present organization, the univ. comprises the faculties of theology (which enjoys pontifical status); law, economics, and social sciences; letters; natural sciences; and associated institutes of missiology; pastoral theology; economics and social sciences; automation and operations research; pedagogy, orthopedagogy, and practical psychology; curative pedagogy; Eastern European studies; practical French; practical English; social and political sciences; ecumenical studies, and a seminar for journalism. In theology, the language of instruction is Latin; in law, French and German; in science, French, German, and English. The remaining faculties are multilingual. The univ. confers the bachelor degree, the licentiate, and the doctorate. The highest administrative officer is the secretary; the highest authority, the senate, which is composed of the rector, deans, prorector, and prodeans. The library contains approximately 1,000,000 volumes, 1,000 MSS., and 400 incunabula. Average enrollment is 3,000. Qualified American undergraduates from Rosary College, River Forest (Ill.); Georgetown Univ., Washington, D.C.; and LaSalle College, Philadelphia (Pa.), by special arrangement, spend their junior or senior year at Fribourg. Courses are open to American graduate students in economics and social sciences; philosophy and arts; natural sciences, and premedicine.

[M. B. MURPHY]

FRIDAY, the sixth day of the week, widely observed from the early cent. of Christianity as a day of penitential observance in memory of the Passion and death of Christ. It serves a purpose in each week analogous to that of Lent in the Christian year as a whole: piety uses it to prepare, by penance, for the weekly Easter that is Sunday. Since antiquity, fasting and abstinence have been prominent among the observances thought appropriate to the day. Until Nov. 1966, abstinence from meat on Fridays was obligatory in the U.S. under ecclesiastical law. A pastoral statement of the Catholic bps. of the U.S. (Nov. 18, 1966) put an end to the obligation under pain of sin, but encouraged the faithful to continue in the penitential observance of Fridays, esp. in Lent, and declared that abstinence from meat still has first place among the acceptable practices of penance for that day, though other forms of self-denial are also commendable.

FRIDELLI, XAVER EHRENBERT (Friedel; 1673–1743), Austrian Jesuit missionary and cartographer. F. was assigned to China in 1704 and was a member of the team of *Jesuits who in 1717 mapped the Chinese Empire. Their huge chart, later reproduced from 48 engraved plates, was the only reliable map of China for more than 100 years. In 1720, F. established a school and the following year he opened St. Joseph Church in Peking. His scholarly reputation gave him the esteem of the Chinese, and his moderation helped to mitigate the persecution of Christians then in progress in the empire. BIBLIOGRAPHY: M. B. Martin, NCE 6:199.

FRIDESWIDE OF OXFORD, ST. (d. 735), patroness of the city and univ. of Oxford. According to tradition, F., daughter of an Anglo-Saxon ruler, founded a convent in Oxford and became abbess. Her foundation, suppressed under Henry VIII, is now the site of Christ Church College. BIBLIOGRAPHY: E. F. Jacob, *St. Frideswide* (1953); J. Stéphan, BiblSanct 5:1273–74; Butler 4:150–151.

[W. A. CHANEY]

FRIDOLIN OF SÄCKINGEN, ST. (fl. 6th or 7th cent.), apostle of the upper Rhine; an Irish monk who preached and founded churches throughout his native land, in France, Switzerland, and Germany. At Säckingen, an island in the Rhine, he founded a monastery and church and died there.

[J. R. AHERNE]

FRIEDLÄNDER, MAX. J. (1867–1958) German art historian and director of the Berlin Museum (Print Room, 1908; Picture Gallery, 1924). He was a noted practitioner of the methodology of connoisseurship in art history (*Die altniederländ, Malerei,* 14 v., 1924–37; *On Art and Connoisseurship,* 1942), emphasizing passionately the intuitive nature of artistic attribution and identification as opposed to coldly intellectual deductions from historic fact. BIBLIOGRAPHY: M. J. Friedländer, *Die altniederländische Malerei* (14 v., 1924–37); *idem, Early Netherlandish Painting* (v. 1 & 2, tr. H. Norden, 1967); *Neue Deutsche Biographie V* (1961) 455–456.

[L. A. LEITE]

FRIEDRICH, CASPAR DAVID (1774–1840), German Romantic painter preoccupied with landscape and who sought in his altarpiece *Cross in the Mountains* (1808) to replace traditional religious subject with landscape symbolism. With Runge, F. sought a new language for the Romantic School. *Monk at the Seashore* (1808) expresses Romantic isolation; *Ruined Cloister on the Snow* (1819) and the famous *Shipwreck of the ''Hope'' in the Ice* (1822) express a pessimism and obsession with death. F. treated natural phenomena as magical. His heroic bleak settings in a dry, smooth technique and cold, acidulous colors contrast with the emotional moods. With Runge F. is the greatest of German Romantic painters. BIBLIOGRAPHY: F. Bauer, *Caspar David Friedrich* (1961).

[M. J. DALY]

FRIEDRICH, JOHANN (1836–1917), church historian; the pseudonymous ''Quirinus,'' correspondent of J. *Döllinger from Vatican Council I. F.'s professional life was spent at the Univ. of Munich, on the theology faculty (1862–72) and on the philosophy faculty (1882 until retirement, 1905). His historical publications included a 2-volume history of German Christianity (1867–69) and a biography of J. *Möhler (1894). He is chiefly remembered for his anti-infallibilist efforts at Vatican Council I, and the material he supplied for Döllinger's *Letters from Rome* (1869–70). Excommunicated (1872) for his refusal to accept the dogmatic definition, he helped in the establishment of the *Old Catholic Church, but later abandoned it because of its rejection of clerical celibacy. He remained the friend of Döllinger, to whom he administered the last rites (1890), and whose biography he published (3 v., 1897–1901). He himself died in lonely isolation, unreconciled.

[T. C. O'BRIEN]

FRIENDS, RELIGIOUS SOCIETY OF, see RELIGIOUS SOCIETY OF FRIENDS.

FRIENDS OF GOD (Ger. *Gottesfreunde*), a term long used to denote holy persons, but applied in a specialized sense in the 14th cent. to certain pious folk of all ranks of society: laymen, diocesan priests, monks, friars, and nuns, esp. in Bavaria, Switzerland, the Rhineland, and the Low Countries. They sought to live lives of devotion, prayer, austerity, and intense union with God. They were held together in loose association by their spiritual interests, their distress at the political and social evils of the day, by the exchange of letters, visits, and spiritual writings, and the guidance of experienced leaders, esp. Henry Suso and John Tauler. Notable among them were two Dominican nuns, Margaret and Christine Ebner, and the secular priest Henry of Nördlingen, a friend of Suso and Tauler. His letters exchanged with Margaret Ebner, considered the oldest collection of letters in the German language, are a monument of German spirituality. Also prominent among the Friends was Rulman Merswin (d. 1382), a rich merchant of Strassburg, and composer of pious romances. The Friends of God were completely orthodox in their beliefs and should not be confused with the Brothers and Sisters of the Free Spirit, Waldenses, or the unorthodox Beguines, who concealed their heretical and separatist tendencies by using the same name. BIBLIOGRAPHY: DSAM 1:493–500; J. M. Clark, *Great German Mystics* (1949) 75–97; A. G. Seesholtz, *Friends of God: Practical Mystics of the Fourteenth Century* (1934, repr. 1970); R. M. Jones, *Flowering of Mysticism: The Friends of God in the Fourteenth Century* (1940, repr. 1971).

[W. A. HINNEBUSCH]

FRIENDS OF MAN, see AMIS DE L'HOMME.

FRIENDS OF THE TEMPLE (Ger. *Tempelgesellschaft*), a religious body that originated in Germany for the purpose of bringing about the kingdom of Christ on earth in their autonomous communities. The founder, Württemberg Pietist Christoph *Hoffmann (1815–85), envisaged the restoration of the Temple and a theocracy at Jerusalem. Together with George David Hardegg (d. 1879) and Christian Paulus, he set out to found other Temple communities, first in Germany and then in various places of the Holy Land. Usually good schools and hospitals were connected with each community, and the Friends thus became known for their cultural and social contributions. The Friends of the Temple spread to Russia and North America (1905), where they became closely associated with the Unitarians. The movement was suppressed in Germany during World War II; emigrants founded a Temple community in Australia in 1950. Some adherents still exist in the Württemberg area. Hardegg had separated from the group in 1876 to found the so-called Temple Union *(Reichsbruderbund)*. BIBLIOGRAPHY: C. Kolb, EncRelKnow 4:397–398; H. Hohlwein, RGG 6:688.

[J. FANG]

FRIENDS WORLD COMMITTEE FOR CONSULTATION (FWCC), an organization established to promote the purposes of the Religious Society of Friends. The FWCC was first proposed in 1920 by the London World Conference of Friends and was brought into being by the Swarthmore (Pa.) World Conference of 1927. There is an American and a European section; an African section is planned. The autonomous Friends yearly meetings freely associate themselves with the FWCC, and 29 of them in the W Hemisphere belong to the American section. The committee fosters the internal interests of Friends —communication, mutual understanding and assistance, and the establishment of new Friends meetings. The organization also seeks to bring Quaker pacifist and philanthropic concern to the world at large and is recognized at the United Nations as a nongovernmental organization with consultative status. The American section has encouraged conferences on race relations, penology, civil rights, and world peace. BIBLIOGRAPHY: E. B. Bronner, *American Quakers Today* (1966) 105–107; W. R. Williams, *Rich Heritage of Quakerism* (1962) 213–215.

FRIENDSHIP, the bond of mutual affection between persons who share common interests or values. Only such a generalized description (see Aristotle, *Ethics* VIII, ch. 1–8) can be given for an experience so treasured and diversified, and so noble that it enters into the theological meaning of *charity (see also FRIENDSHIP WITH GOD). The description given is broad enough to take in the distinctive way in which friendship is a form of love, the nuances between "loving" and "liking" a person, the analogical gradation among the kinds of friendship, even both good and base friendships. Friendship is a form of love, as love denotes a good will or a favorable responsiveness to another; but the love that makes up friendship is not one-sided, it is a bond of union, a reciprocal loving. As such it ranges from a comfortable friendliness between neighbors or associates, to a lifelong bond between intimates, even between husband and wife. The expression of this mutual bond and the measure of its intensity is companionship, a being together in which each experiences the sense of oneness with the other person. Shared interests or values are the grounds for friendship; they also differentiate its kinds and grades, for they indicate why one friend is lovable to the other. The lovable can mean something or someone good in its own right, something pleasurable, something useful or profitable. The highest form of friendship is based on the first, which may be described as "virtue," but really means every truly human good quality, including the make-up of a person's whole being and character. A friendship so based is the highest form and the ideal; each friend loves the other for his own sake. Inferior to this is a love based on the enjoyment or advantage the partners afford to each other. Friendship for pleasure or gain is not morally unworthy; in the complexity of human experience both pleasure and advantage accompany the highest form of friendship, since human love for another is not only a giving, but also a receiving: the very fact of having one's love received and returned is perfective and need-fulfilling. But purely interested friendships are less perfect forms, and are transitory, as the pleasure given or the advantage desired fades or changes. Further, such friendships can be base, evil, because the pleasure or gain sought is evil. These generalities indicate how readily the meaning of friendship is compatible with the relationship between all forms of noble human affection and charity towards others. A general "friendship" toward all, owed in charity, is based primarily on friendship with God: it is a love for others, even enemies, because they are or can be God's friends (ThAq ST 2a2ae. 23,1 ad 2). Genuine marital love is the most perfect and intimate bond of human friendship, having the most intense human otherwardness and communication, in spirit and in flesh; that love is enhanced by charity because the identity of the one loved is part of being the adoptive child of the Father. Because the highest form of friendship regards the genuinely good qualities of the friends, charity gives new reason for cherishing friends as their goodness has the special value of coming from God's love.

[T. C. O'BRIEN]

FRIENDSHIP, PARTICULAR, an association of emotional love between two persons, usually but not always of the same sex, and characterized by exclusiveness with consequent detriment to other relationships, esp. to the larger society. In one sense, every *friendship is particular, but the pejorative connotation of particular as opposed to true friendship derives from the context of some form of *community-life. While it is likely that the denunciation of particular friendship, and by unfortunate implication all friendship, proceeds from suspicions—not always altogether unfounded—of latent sexuality, the real reason for objecting is its exclusiveness. The phenomenon of the adolescent "crush," esp. when it continues beyond the boarding-school period, is reprehensible not so much because the friends are behaving like lovers, but rather because they are not accepting their adult role as true friends. Although true friendship may begin with the pleasure of the other's company, and even be useful, it should not remain so retarded that it is hardly better than disguised ego-satisfaction. Genuine friendship is based on sharing—a common life, common interests, common ideals, and for that reason it is not jealous; "Here comes another," Dante's blessed say, "who will increase our love." Thus the dangers of the erotic and even sexual element are not so pertinent to the condemnation of these friendships as the absorption of psychic and affective energies, to say nothing of the time wasted, all of which belong to a greater community. Leaders of communities whether ships' captains, colonels, or novice-mistresses, then, discourage and sometimes roundly condemn such associations. For the persons involved, there is first of all the needed conviction that this association is an obstacle to authentic maturity, which demands a wider intersubjectivity; society indulges young lovers and honeymooners in their privacy, but nature gives their love the fruitfulness of family and the exigencies of life draw them into a bigger world. Next, attention must be given to common interest rather than to friendship itself; lovers face each other and speak of their love, friends walk side by side with their gaze fixed on an ideal horizon. In situations where the friendship seems incapable of maturing, separation—physical as far as possible, mental certainly—may be the only solution for what is basically mutual emotional insecurity and instability. BIBLIOGRAPHY: C. S. Lewis, *Four Loves* (1960) 87–127; G. Kelly, *Guidance for Religious* (1956) 55–81; C. Browning, NCE 6, 205.

[J. AUMANN]

FRIENDSHIP WITH GOD, a description of the union with God that *charity means. Both the OT (e.g., Wis 7, 14, 27), and the NT (Jn 15.14–15) convey the intimacy of man's special relationship to God through the idea of friendship, and prompt Church writers and theologians to develop the same theme. For St. Thomas Aquinas the idea of friendship best fits the reality and mutuality of the bond of *charity (ST 2a2ae, 23.1). The root of his choice can be seen in the way he explains how love involves union (*ibid.*, 1a2ae, 28.1 ad 2), and in the implications of that for the life of grace. The union that causes love between persons is a likeness in being; to this corresponds the new being of grace by which the recipient becomes a *partaker in the divine nature. An affective union of wills is the essence of love; that is what charity consists in—a mutual and reciprocal loving between God and man, the dynamic expression of the relationship between Father and child. A union by companionship, life together, is what lovers seek; charity leads to the beatific vision and joyful rest in the Lord, and prompts the beginning of that through prayer. Charity is best described as friendship, then, because it is the response to God's loving man as a person, "raising him above the condition of his nature to share in the eternal good which God himself is" (*ibid.*, 1a2ae, 110.1); and because it prompts the being together that friends seek.

[T. C. O'BRIEN]

FRIENDSHIP HOUSE, a lay Catholic movement founded by Catherine *de Hueck, dedicated to social and esp. interracial justice. The first Friendship House opened in Toronto in 1931; others were established in New York City's Harlem, in Chicago, Washington, and elsewhere. The movement began as a form of welfare or settlement work carried out by associates living a common life of poverty under obedience. Baroness de Hueck withdrew from Friendship House after World War II, and emphasis shifted to such goals as equal opportunity, housing, education, and civil rights, while the staff became modestly paid employees, still dedicated to carrying out the common Christian vocation, but as lay people rather than a religious association. National headquarters is in Chicago; local houses have been discontinued. BIBLIOGRAPHY: C. de Hueck, *Friendship House* (1946); D. M. Cantwell, NCE 6:206–207. *DOHERTY, EDWARD JOSEPH.

[D. CODDINGTON]

FRIES, HANS (*c.*1465–1523), most important Swiss painter of his time; F. studied Netherlandish, Ulm, and Augsburg styles. His most important painting *The Sermon of St. Antonius* (1506) for the Franziskanerkirche relates in style to Holbein the Elder.

[M. J. DALY]

FRIGIDIAN OF LUCCA, ST., a 6th-cent. Irish priest who on pilgrimage to Italy became a hermit at Lucca. Made bishop of Lucca by papal command, he served well, rebuilding its cathedral after a Lombard invasion, but he remained dedicated to a solitary prayer life and inspired his priests to live as monks. Great miracles were ascribed to his intercession, including the rechanneling of a harmful river, a story that St. Gregory the Great credited as authentic.

[J. F. FALLON]

FRIGOLET, MONASTERY OF, a Norbertine abbey located near Tarascon in France. It was originally founded as a priory of the Benedictine abbey of Montmajour (962). Later it was taken over by Canons Regular of St. Augustine, and from 1647 to 1790 was occupied successively by Hieronimites and Discalced Augustinians. Suppressed in 1790, it was restored in 1858 by Edmund Boulbon, a former Trappist, who turned it into a house of "the primitive observance of Prémontré." In 1896 it joined the common observance. Through the years 1903–19 it existed in exile at Leffe in Belgium. It now belongs to the Circary of France. BIBLIOGRAPHY: Backmund 3:337–342.

[N. BACKMUND]

FRINS, VICTOR (1840–1912), German Jesuit theologian and spiritual director. After study at Münster and Maria Laach, F. began teaching philosophy and moral theology at Regensburg. He later taught in England and Wales. The last 20 years of his life were spent in spiritual direction. He is known esp. for his theological studies of human acts. BIBLIOGRAPHY: J. G. Bischoff, NCE 6:208.

[M. J. SUELZER]

FRISCH, MAX (1911–), Swiss novelist and dramatist. Writing in German, F. is a recorder of and commentator on the search for identity in 20th-cent. Western man. A native of Zurich, he has lived at various times in Italy, the U.S., and Mexico. He was a practicing architect who wrote plays and novels. Among the novels are *I'm Not Stiller, Homo Faber,* and *A Wilderness of Mirrors*. His plays include *Andorra, The Chinese Wall,* and *The Firebugs*. Both novels and plays, though they reflect Europe at mid-20th cent. are more concerned with men and women in their interpersonal relationships than with external events. BIBLIOGRAPHY: C. Petersen, *Max Frisch* (1972).

[J. R. AHERNE]

FRITH, JOHN (1503–33), English writer, student at Eton and King's College, Cambridge, and then a junior canon at Wolsey's college (now Christchurch), Oxford. F. wrote against the papacy, and denied that purgatory and *transubstantiation are dogmas of faith. He was eventually executed for heresy.

[E. A. WEIS]

FRÖBEL, FRIEDRICH WILHELM (1782–1852), German educator and founder of the kindergarten. F. studied at Jena, and at Frankfurt where A. Gruner, a pupil of Pestalozzi, persuaded him to become a teacher. In 1805 in Yverdun and again from 1808 to 1810 he studied Pestalozzi's methods. In 1816, with W. Mittendorf and H. Langenthal, F. opened an experimental school for children at Keilhau, where he wrote the *Education of Man* (1826). In 1829 local opposition obliged him to close the school, which he reopened in Burgdorf, Switzerland (1831–35). He later continued his work in Blankenburg, Germany, where he first called his institution the "kindergarten," a place which he conceived for young children to unfold like flowers. There he gave full rein to his educational philosophy, a fusion of idealism, realism, naturalism, and religious concepts, with a tinge of scientism acquired at Jena and Berlin. Suspecting socialistic tendencies, the Prussian government in 1851 banned all his kindergartens. BIBLIOGRAPHY: P. R. Cole, *Herbart and Fröbel* (1907).

[M. B. MURPHY]

FROBEN, JOHANNES (*c.*1460–1527), printer and publisher of Basel. He started his press in 1491 with the first Latin Bible in small type. In 1516 he issued the *editio princeps* of Erasmus's Greek NT, and followed it with Erasmus's editions of the Church Fathers.

FROBERGER, JOHANN JAKOB (1616–67), German organist and composer. Born to the conductor of a Protestant chapel in Stuttgart, F. was apparently a RC convert while a student of *Frescobaldi in Rome. As court organist in Vienna from 1641, he composed many canzones, capricios, fantasies; his suites resemble the style of French lute-playing in that era. He was one of the chief sources of Italian and French musical influence on German music.

[D. SMUCKER]

FRÖBES, JOSEPH (1866–1947), German Jesuit, who was a pioneer among Catholics in the study of experimental psychology as independent from the traditional philosophical psychology of scholasticism. Among his disciples was J. *Lindworsky.

[T. C. O'BRIEN]

FRODOARD OF REIMS, see FLODOARD OF REIMS.

FRODOBERT, ST. Cleric of Troyes, France (b. 595, d. 673), he became a monk at Luxeuil, but returned to pastoral ministry at Troyes, where he founded the monastery of Montier-la-Celle on a royal land grant. He began to be venerated as a saint in the late 8th cent., his feast being celebrated on Jan. 8.

[J. F. FALLON]

FROHSCHAMMER, JAKOB (1821–93), priest, philosopher, professor at the Univ. of Munich. F. was condemned by Pius IX in the letter *Gravissimas inter* (Dec. 11, 1862) on two points: that once supernatural truths were revealed, they could be proved by human reasoning; that philosophy is absolutely above all control from authority (see D 2850–61). F. did not submit to the prohibition of his works, was suspended, and remained unreconciled.

[T. C. O'BRIEN]

FROILÁN, ST. (832–905), bp. of León. He and his disciple Attilanus lived as hermits and preached in Galicia (Spain) until Alfonso III authorized F. to promote repopulation on the Moorish frontier under large monasteries. Unwillingly F. became bp. of León (900), where he died after a life of holiness and marvels. His vita (EspSagr 34:422–425) is a Latin literary gem. Relics were shared between León and the Cistercian monastery of Moreruela (1181–91). In 1792 he was included in the Roman martyrology. BIBLIOGRAPHY: Butler 4:18–19; J. M. Fernández Catón, BiblSanct 5:1283–85.

[E. P. COLBERT]

FROISSART, JEAN (*c.* 1337–*c.* 1410), chronicler of the beginning of the Hundred Years' War. Also the most common source for descriptions of feudalism and chivalry, his view was myopic and aristocratic, and the accounts of peasant revolt and pointless military slaughter leave a more lasting impression than the noble deeds of his patrons and heroes. Still, his long chronicle provided Montaigne, Shakespeare, Scott, and Dumas with substantial material. He also wrote a romance, *Méliador,* lyrics, *lais,* and *ballades.* Text of *Chronicles,* (Eng. tr. J. Bourchier, ed. and introd. G. and W. Anderson, 1963). French text of works, *Oeuvres de Froissart* (ed. J. Kervyn de Lettenhove, 29 v., 1867–77). BIBLIOGRAPHY: M. Wilmotte, *Froissart* (2d ed., 1948); G. G. Coulton, *Chronicler of European Chivalry* (1930).

[J. P. WILLIMAN]

FROMAGE, PIERRE (1678–1740), French Jesuit missionary, who worked in Syria where he organized catechetical instruction and provided Arabic translations of spiritual and apologetical works. F. also installed a printing press. He established a monastery of Maronite Visitandines in Antoura. In 1736 he was made preacher of the Maronite synod of Loaïsah. BIBLIOGRAPHY: P. Mech, *Catholicisme* 4:1652.

[M. J. SUELZER]

FROMENT, NICOLAS (fl. 1450–90), French painter to King René of Anjou. The triptych *Raising of Lazarus* (1461) with a realism drawn from the Netherlandish painters in Avignon, shows on the reverse Provençal portraiture at its best, combining Sculpturesque form and abstraction in the figures of the Virgin and donor. *The Legend of St. Mitre* (*c.* 1470, Aix-en-Provence) is attributed to F. His masterpiece, a documented triptych of the *Burning Bush* (Aix-en-Provence), Flemish in detail, and Provençal in simplification, shows on the wings portraits of King René and Queen Jeanne de Laval with an Annunciation on the reverse in grisaille. BIBLIOGRAPHY: M. Laclotte, *L, École d' Avignon: La Peinture en Provence aux XIV et XV siècles* (1960).

[M. J. DALY]

FRONLEICHNAMSSPIEL, the German form of the Corpus Christi play, a cycle covering biblical history from Creation to the Last Judgment.

[E. C. DUNN]

FRONTENAC, LOUIS DE BUADE (1620–98), governor of New France. After military service in Germany and Italy, F. accepted the post of governor general of New France (1672). A vigorous advocate of the fur trade, he sought peace with the Iroquois and built Fort Frontenac at Cataraqui (now Kingston, Ontario) to close the frontier. Although frequently involved in disagreements with the Jesuits and officials of the colony, he supported the explorations of Joliet, *Marquette, and La Salle. Quarrels with officials led to his recall (1682), but he managed his return to Canada (1689), harried the British along the New England frontier (1690), and defended Quebec against counterattack. He waged war on the now hostile Iroquois, destroying the Mohawk villages (1693), rebuilding Fort Frontenac (1694), and freeing Canada of the Iroquois menace (1696). BIBLIOGRAPHY: F. Parkman, *Count Frontenac and New France under Louis XIV* (24th ed., 1891); W. J. Eccles, *Frontenac: The Courtier Governor* (1959).

[R. K. MACMASTER]

FRONTO, MARCUS CORNELIUS (*c.* 100–*c.* 160 A.D.), the leading orator of his age and teacher of Marcus Aurelius. He was *consul suffectus* briefly in 143. Of his works there are extant a correspondence which contains a number of letters between himself and Marcus Aurelius, and several declamations of trivial content. The letters are filled with small talk and have little historical or even literary interest. In style Fronto went back to Early Latin for his models, and may be considered the founder of Latin archaism as a literary movement. He enjoyed a great reputation as a literary figure in his age and had a considerable influence on the Latin style of his contemporaries and the generations immediately following. He seems to have been the man from Cirta (Numidia) mentioned in Minucius Felix as having written an oration against the Christians. That he had any real influence, however, on the attitude of Marcus Aurelius toward the Christians is doubtful. BIBLIOGRAPHY: OCD 372; Loeb, text and Eng. tr. by C. R. Haines; P. De Labriolle, *La Réaction païenne* (1934) 87–94.

[M. R. P. MCGUIRE]

FROUDE, JAMES ANTHONY (1818–94), Eng. historian and biographer. F. came of a family celebrated for its religious interests—his father was an Anglican archdeacon, and his elder brother, Richard H. *Froude, was prominent in the Oxford Movement. F. was elected a fellow of Exeter College, Oxford, but the outcries that arose at the publication of two of his minor works, *Legend of St. Neots* (1844) and *The Nemesis of Faith* (1849) led to the resignation of his fellowship, though this position was restored to him (1858). His most important work was *History of England from the Fall of Wolsey to the Defeat of the Armada* (12 v., 1856–70). In this he glorified the Reformation, Henry VIII, Burghley, and the value of England's command of the sea. This work brought savage attacks upon him because of the vigor of his prejudices and the frequency of his inaccuracies. Nevertheless, his forceful and lucid style made it influential. BIBLIOGRAPHY: W. H. Dunn, *James Anthony Froude* (2 v., 1961–63); D. Wilson, *Mr. Froude and Mr. Carlyle* (1898, repr. 1970).

[C. BUCKLEY]

FROUDE, RICHARD HURRELL (1803–36), a Devonshire man, fellow of Oriel, where he and J. H. *Newman formed a close and affectionate friendship: many pages of the *Apologia* are about him. Already F. detested the Reformation, and was powerfully drawn to the medieval, but not to the primitive Church. A high Tory of the cavalier stamp, of a classical and historical temper, with no strong bent to theology as such, he became an influential figure in the early *Oxford Movement. Symptoms of consumption caused him to go to the Mediterranean to winter, where he was joined for a time by Newman; he was shocked by the degeneracy he thought he saw in the Catholics of Italy. His early death found him at the stage reached by his friend, "a catholic without popery," he professed himself, "and a Church of England man without Protestanism."

[T. GILBY]

FROUMUND OF TEGERNSEE (*c.*960–*c.*1008), Benedictine poet and educator. Educated at Füssen and Würzburg, F. learned the elements of Greek in Cologne. In the 990s he participated in the reform of the abbey of Feuchtwangen and was associated with the learned court of Otto III. His correspondence gives valuable information on the intellectual, spiritual, and economic aspects of 10th-cent. Bavarian monasticism. Of his verse, some 37 pieces survive. BIBLIOGRAPHY: O. J. Blum, NCE 6:213; H. Plechl, "Studien zur Tegernseer Briefsammlung. . . ," *Deutsches Archiv* 11:422–461.

[O. J. BLUM]

FRUCTUOSUS OF BRAGA (d. *c.*665), monk, monastic founder, abp. of Braga in what is now Portugal. Son of a Spanish general of the Visigothic kings, F. studied in Palencia. After the death of his parents, he retired to live as a hermit, but when disciples gathered around him he turned his home at Complutum into a monastery. He founded nine other monasteries in addition to a convent for women. Dissatisfied with the activities forced upon him by the dependence of his disciples, he had it in mind to go to Egypt to live as a simple hermit, but the king forbade his departure. F. was made bp. of Dumium (654) and later abp. of Braga (656). His relics are preserved at Compostela. BIBLIOGRAPHY: Butler 2:102–103; J. F. Alonso, BiblSanct 5:1295–96.

[R. B. ENO]

FRUCTUOSUS OF TARRAGONA, ST., bishop martyred in 259 in the Roman persecution of Emperors Valerian and Gallienus. The account of his death is not so legendary as most. He refused to worship Roman gods and was burned at the stake with two of his deacons. The fire burned their manacles first so that they could raise their arms to praise God before they died.

[J. F. FALLON]

FRUGALITY, the virtuous quality of being careful and sparing in the use of external goods, in particular of food. Christian teaching on the spirit of *poverty had something in common with the Neo-Platonists and Stoics. The *Summa theologiae* of St. Thomas Aquinas treats the self-sufficiency, *autarkeia,* of the Pseudo-Andronicus and the sparseness, or better, spareness *(parcitas)* of Macrobius as elements in the virtue of modesty, which is allied to the virtue of temperance or moderation (ThAq ST 2a2ae, 143). Parsimony can have a good or neutral sense, as against lavishness, but it tends to mean the skimping or being stingy or niggardly which is condemned by the same work as *parvificentia* (2a2ae, 135). Frugality is one of the virtues which, according to M. *Weber, was greatly esteemed in the *Protestant ethic.

[T. GILBY]

FRUMENTIUS, ST. (*c.*300–*c.*380), apostle of Ethiopia. A Tyrian Greek, F. was on an educational voyage with another youth, Edesius (his brother?), under the care of his uncle and tutor, Metropius, when at a port in Ethiopia all aboard the ship except the two young men were slain. They were taken as captives to Aksum and made slaves of the king (*c.*316) who, much pleased with them, advanced them in his service, and just before his death granted them their freedom. The widowed queen induced them to remain at the court to help with the education of the young prince. While so occupied they won some converts to the Christian faith. When the prince came of age, Edesius returned to Tyre, but F. went to Alexandria to beg St. Athanasius to send a bp. and priests to Ethiopia. F. was himself made bp. and returned to Axum, baptized the king, and converted many throughout Ethiopia. The Arian Emperor Constantius tried vainly to have him displaced by an Arian bishop. F. was called *Abuna (Our Father) and Aba Salama (Father of Peace), titles still borne by the primate of the dissident Ethiopian Church. BIBLIOGRAPHY: Butler 4:208–209; V. Monachino, EncCatt 5:1787; J. M. Sauguet, BiblSanct 5:1292–94.

[R. B. ENO]

FRUSTULUM (Lat., a tiny bit), breakfast on a day of fast. The term belongs to the discussion of CIC c. 1251 on the amount of food allowable on fast days, before the change in ecclesiastical laws of fast and abstinence finally formulated in Paul VI's apostolic constitution *Poenitemini,* Feb. 17, 1966. The general rule now is that on a fast day one full meal is allowed; the other two should be smaller, but this is not measured in terms of ounces, as the *frustulum* was, but in terms of local custom as to quantity and quality (*ibid.,* 3.3).

[T. C. O'BRIEN]

FRUTOLF OF MICHELSBERG (d. 1103), historian and musicologist. F. taught in the abbey school and possibly was prior. His outstanding work, the *Chronicon,* was overshadowed by the version plagiarized by Ekkehard of Aura (d. 1125). F. is also credited with several musicological works, among them a *Breviarium de musica* and *Tonarius*. BIBLIOGRAPHY: Manitius 3:350–361; J. Schmale-Ott, "Die Rezension C der Weltchronik Ekkehards," *Deutsches Archiv* 12:363–387.

[O. J. BLUM]

FRUTTUARIA, ABBEY.

FRUTTUARIA, ABBEY OF, a medieval Benedictine monastery known for its exemplary monks, founded in Volpiano, near Turin, Italy in the early 11th cent. by William of Saint-Bénigne of Dijon and his uncle, Count Arduin of Ivrea. The abbey was a center for the arts and scholarship and it was here that the notable Congregatio Fructuariensis was established. Soon the abbey became so wealthy that it fell into decline and Sixtus IV gave it into commendation in 1477. After secularization the abbey became (1617) a collegiate church. During the Napoleonic conflicts, the French destroyed Fruttuaria, and after some restoration, the abbey was suppressed in 1848 by the government of Piedmont. An unedited account of the monastery is given in *Chronicon Fructuariense*. A Salesian Institute stands on the site today. BIBLIOGRAPHY: G. Pence, *Storia del monachesimo in Italia* (1961) 206–208.

[R. A. TODD]

FRY, ELIZABETH (1780–1845), English Quaker, prison reformer, sister to J. *Gurney. She became an approved Quaker minister (1811) and an effective preacher. In 1817 F. formed an association to improve the condition of female prisoners at Newgate prison. Her efforts led to the introduction of practices now taken for granted in penology: segregation of the sexes, classification of prisoners, female supervision of women prisoners, and programs of both general and religious training. Her energies, always religiously inspired, were also devoted to other philanthropic causes. BIBLIOGRAPHY: J. P. Whitney, *Elizabeth Fry, Quaker Heroine* (new ed., 1945); D. Johnson, *Elizabeth Fry and Prison Reform* (1969).

[T. C. O'BRIEN]

FRY, FRANKLIN CLARK (1900–68), leader in the Lutheran Church in America (LCA) and in the World Council of Churches (WCC). Born in Bethlehem, Pa., F. studied theology at the Lutheran seminary in Philadelphia and was ordained in 1925. Pastor in Akron, Ohio, for 5 years, he became president of the United Lutheran Church, predecessor of the LCA, 1945–62; then of the LCA, from 1962 until a week before his death. He was also president of Lutheran World Relief (1954–60) and of the Lutheran World Federation (1957–63). He was chairman of the policy and strategy committee of the National Council of Churches, 1954–68; chairman of the Central and Executive Committees of the WCC, 1954–68. F. put his superior executive and organizing ability at the service of his highest goal, the unity of the Christian Churches; he strove to make the WCC an effective channel of ecumenical communication.

[T. C. O'BRIEN]

FRY, ROGER (1866–1934), English art critic and artist. A scientist, then a painter, F. finally achieved immense importance as an art critic. After trips to Italy (1891 and 1894) F. began to lecture, to write for the *Athenaeum,* becoming its regular art critic, published a book on Bellini, articles on Giotto, an edition of Reynolds' discourses, and established *The Burlington Magazine*. Having gained a reputation as scholar and expert, F. became a director of the Metropolitan Museum (N.Y.) 1905. In 1906 he recognized the structural quality of Cézanne's color, becoming an intense champion of modern art. Identified with the London Bloomsbury group—Virginia Woolf, Duncan Grant, Clive Bell, in 1913, F. founded the avant-garde Omega Workshops. Brilliant in his analysis of works of art and seeing that form and color have an aesthetic effect distinct from representation, he developed the idea of "pure form." His two most famous books are *Transformations* and *Vision and Design* compiled from essays and articles. Later publications from his lectures are vivid, delightful, and popular. In 1933 F. became Slade Professor at Cambridge. BIBLIOGRAPHY: V. Woolf, *Roger Fry, A Biography* (1940).

[M. J. DALY]

FUCHS, ERNEST (1930–), Austrian painter. F. was a member of the *Wiener Schule*, a contemporary group of painters, expressing a fantastic realism inspired by 19th cent. Symbolism and by Surrealism. There are obvious relations with literature and with the psychoanalytic theories of Freud; technique is based mainly on historical styles of the 16th to 19th centuries. F., influenced by Dürer, Bosch, Da Vinci, Blake and Klimt, and related to Freud in his mythical and symbolic religious themes, integrated all in a personal conception. BIBLIOGRAPHY: W. Schmied, *Malerei des phantastischen Realismus-Die Wiener Schule* (1964).

[P. H. HEFTING]

FUDO MYŌ-Ō, a favorite Japanese Buddhist deity, messenger and mighty defender of Buddha's Law, shown holding a sword to cut down the evils in the world and a rope to restrain and bind them. Fearsome with bulging eyes and 2 fangs, he is seated on a rock as the "immobile one." F. is special in the arts of Japanese Mikkyō (esoteric Buddhism). His body may be in different colors—yellow (Onjoji, 9th cent.), red (Mt. Kōya, 9th cent.), or blue (Shōren-in, 11th cent.). BIBLIOGRAPHY: E. D. Saunders, *Buddhism in Japan* (1964, D. Seckel, *Art of Buddhism* (1964).

[M. J. DALY]

FUENLLANA, MIGUEL DE (*c.* 1520–*c.* 1579), Spanish composer and lutenist. This blind musician wrote original compositions and transcriptions of contemporary music. F.'s most creative work was directed to madrigals and motets for the vihuela, a 5-stringed Spanish lute. He published *Orphenica lyra* (1554).

[D. SMUCKER]

FUENTE, MICHAEL DE LA (1573–1625 or 1626), Carmelite mystic and spiritual writer. F. spent most of his life at Toledo where he was novice master for the province of New Castile. He contributed to the development of the Carmelite *Third Order, writing a rule for the laity. He was gifted with extraordinary graces in prayer and is said to have experienced ecstasy, levitation, prophecy, and miracles. An ascetical and mystical treatise, *Libro de las tres vidas del hombre corporal, racional y espiritual* (1623) is his chief work. The cause for his beatification was introduced shortly after his death. BIBLIOGRAPHY: A. de Saint-Paul, DTC 10.2:1703–05.

[J. WILLKE]

FUGA, FERDINANDO (1699–1782), Italian architect of Baroque style and virtuoso skill. F's masterpiece is the open and lyrical façade of S. Maria Maggiore, Rome (1741–43). He rebuilt the Church of the Orazione e Morte with its unusual facade, and became (1737) leading architect in Rome, his style becoming more classical. After 1751 F. worked in Naples building among other works, the Church of the Gerolamini (1780).

[M. J. DALY]

FUGEN BOSATSU, TOKYO, 12th-cent. Japanese silk painting of Fugen, symbol of wisdom and guardian of the followers of the Lotus Sûtra shown seated on an elephant. The immaculate white bodies of Fugen and the elephant with subtly painted and gilded costume and trappings express in quiet elegance the sophisticated taste of the Fujiwara aristocrats.

[M. J. DALY]

FUGING (FUGUING) TUNE, a form of hymn or psalm-singing much employed in 18th- and 19th-cent. New England, having its origins from the late 16th cent. in England (e.g., in C. *Tye). Their extensive English and Scottish use was connected with the attempt to invigorate the moribund singing practices in 18th-cent. worship, esp. in the nonliturgical Churches. Famous American developers of the fugue tune include William Billings, Jeremiah Ingalls, Daniel Head, and Andrew Law. The structure characteristic of this form consists in a succession of voices, e.g., in four parts, coming in after an opening line and before the closing line, which are sung in unison.

[D. SMUCKER]

FUGITIVE (CANON LAW), a member of a religious order or of any clerical society who disobediently leaves his community, without permission and for a considerable period of time (at least 3 days), but with the intention of returning (CIC c. 644 §3). During his absence, he remains bound by all his religious obligations, including that of rejoining his community. The fugitive automatically incurs deprivation of office, and if a cleric, *suspension. He cannot, however, be reconciled unless he regrets his flight and undertakes to return as soon as possible to submit himself to the authority of his superior (*ibid.*, c. 645 §1). Should he die during his period of absence, his body is to be returned to the community for burial, or failing that, should receive ordinary Christian burial.

[R. ARONSTAM]

FUGUE, a form of musical composition using imitative counterpoint, developed most fully by J. S. *Bach. A fugue usually has three or four voices and is based on a short melody, the subject. At the beginning the first voice states the melody, then the other voices join in regular succession. Thus when the second voice is stating the melody, the first voice will be developing an appropriate counterpoint motif: such motifs recur in the remaining voices. A section of the fugue in which the subject is stated by each voice is called the exposition. A section where the subject is not stated is called an episode. The fugue form, of course, also is used for instrumental music, and with Bach, particularly for the organ.

[D. SMUCKER]

FULBERT OF CHARTRES, ST. (*c.*960–*c.*1028), bp. of Chartres. F. was first a master at the cathedral school; under his care as bp. (1006) the school began to achieve renown. He dedicated himself to ecclesiastical discipline, the eradication of simony, the rights of the episcopacy against interference by the nobility. Obtaining the aid of Robert, King of France, and Canute of Denmark, he undertook restoration of the cathedral after the fire of 1020; the work was not completed until 1037, after his death. Parts of this restoration, itself destroyed by fire in 1194, remain in the present 13th-cent. cathedral. He was called St. Fulbert in popular devotion, but an officially approved cult (for the dioceses of Chartres and Poitiers) was granted only in the 19th century. BIBLIOGRAPHY: Butler 2:63–64; P. Viard, BiblSanct 5:1299–60.

[T. C. O'BRIEN]

FULCHER OF CHARTRES (*c.*1059–*c.*1127), priest, chronicler of the Crusades. His *Historia Hierosolymitana* is an eyewitness account of *Urban II's proclamation of the First Crusade at Clermont (1095), and of the Crusade itself, since F. served as a chaplain. He spent the last 15 years of his life in Jerusalem, occupied with the *Historia* and duties as chaplain to the king of Jerusalem and canon of the Holy Sepulcher.

[T. C. O'BRIEN]

FULCOIUS OF BEAUVAIS (fl. 11th cent.), archdeacon and poet in Latin. He collected his voluminous writings into one work of 3 volumes: *Uter* (elegies to the dead and letters to political and church leaders), *Neuter* (lives of four French saints), *Uterque* (subtitled *De nuptiis Christi et Ecclesiae,* a recitation of the most important events in the Bible, with a theological division of the verses according to the seven gifts of the Holy Ghost). F. is important for the quantity of his work rather than for the quality, which is somewhat vague and artificial, and because he writes to some figures who would otherwise be unknown. BIBLIOGRAPHY: H. Platelle, *Catholicisme* 4:1470.

FULCRAN OF LODÈVE, ST. (d. 1006), bishop. Ordained against his wishes, he achieved a reputation for sanctity and in 949 by popular acclaim became bp. of Lodève in S France. His devotion to the poor and his building of religious houses, as well as overseeing discipline, distinguished this rather stern and uncompromising bishop.

[J. R. AHERNE]

FULDA, ABBEY OF, German Benedictine monastery in Hesse near Kassel, founded by St. Boniface's disciple St. Sturmius as a prayer and missionary center for the conversion of Germany. After Boniface's martyrdom (754), in accordance with his request, he was buried there. Its early history is glorious, productive of many saints, architects, and educators during the Dark Ages. Under Rabanus Maurus (9th cent.) it became the center of religious and cultural education in N Europe. It never was reformed, however, in any of the many Benedictine renewals and, because of its excessive wealth in land and treasures, it eventually became a pawn of ambitious nobles. After a difficult struggle to remain Catholic during the Reformation, it underwent a fruitful Counter Reformation. Napoleons's invasion of Germany ended its existence as a monastery in 1802. The 9th-cent. chapel that enshrines the relics of St. Boniface remains standing, and its 18th-cent. church has become Fulda's cathedral.

[J. F. FALLON]

FULGENTIUS, FABIUS PLANCIADES (fl. end of 5th cent.), mythographer, interpreter of Vergil. Four of F.'s productions are extant. Despite the mediocre and even bizarre character of his work, F. exercised a marked influence on the allegorical interpretation of classical writers. He was highly esteemed by Sigebert of Gembloux, Bernard of Chartres, and John of Salisbury, and enjoyed a vogue in the Renaissance. BIBLIOGRAPHY: M. R. P. McGuire, NCE 6:220–221; J. Seznec, *Survival of the Pagan Gods* (tr. B. F. Sessions, 1953); O. Friebel, *Fulgentius der Mythograph und Bischof* (1911; Eng. tr. L. G. Whitbread, *Fulgentius the Mythographer,* 1972).

[M. R. P. MCGUIRE]

FULGENTIUS OF ÉCIJA, ST. (d. *c.*619), at whose request his brother, St. *Isidore of Seville, composed *De officiis ecclesiasticis.* F. attended councils in Toledo (610) and Seville (619). The claim that he was bp. of Cartagena seems to have arisen *c.*1330 when his relics were discovered near Guadalupe; in 1593 relics were shared between Cartagena and the Escorial. His cult is immemorial. BIBLIOGRAPHY: J. F. Alonso, BiblSanct 5:1302–03.

[E. P. COLBERT]

FULGENTIUS FERRANDUS, see FERRANDUS.

FULGENTIUS OF RUSPE, ST. (Fulgenzio Claudio Gordiano; 468–533), bp. of Ruspe, near Tunis. Son of a family of senatorial rank, the Gordiani, F. received an excellent education, but renounced a civil career in order to become a monk (*c.*499). Shortly after being made bp. (507) he, with 60 other bps., was banished to Sardinia by Thrasamund, the Vandal king, who was an Arian. F. became the theological spokesman of the exiles and in this capacity returned to Ruspe in 516, but was again banished (518–523). During his exiles F. continued his pastoral and theological labors. He was not an original thinker but with thorough acquaintance and conviction applied St. *Augustine's theological principles to refute *Arianism and *Pelagianism. He is one of the authors to whom the Athanasian Creed is attributed (cf. D 75). F.'s theological treatises and sermons, not all authentic, are in PL 65:105–1018. The deacon Ferrandus of Carthage, his disciple, wrote his life (ed. G. G. Lapeyre, 1929). BIBLIOGRAPHY: Altaner 587–590; Butler 1:6–11; G. B. Proja, BiblSanct 5:1304–16.

[T. C. O'BRIEN]

FULK OF NEUILLY, BL. (Folcus; Fr., Foulques; d. 1201), preacher. After conversion from a sinful life, P., a parish priest of Neuilly near Paris, became a celebrated preacher and drew throngs throughout N France to hear his powerful denunciations of contemporary morals. Jacques de Vitry, himself a preacher of considerable stature, gives a vignette of him in *Historia orientalis et occidentalis*, telling of his triumphant success in preaching the Fourth Crusade, a work to which he was appointed by Innocent III. BIBLIOGRAPHY: Butler 1:462–463; H. Platelle, BiblSanct 5:957.

FULKE, WILLIAM (1538–89), English Puritan theologian. F. wrote ably but at times venomously in defense of extreme Protestant principles. His attack on the Reims translation of the NT had the unlooked for result of making it so well-known in England that it affected the language of the AV.

[M. J. SUELZER]

FULL GOSPEL, a phrase for the message of *Pentecostalism, used frequently in Pentecostal history and literature. The connotation of the phrase is that the complete teaching of the gospel includes: (1) justification by faith; (2) premillenarianism; (3) divine healing; (4) baptism with the Holy Spirit and its charismatic effects. *Foursquare gospel has the same meaning.

[T. C. O'BRIEN]

FULL GOSPEL BUSINESSMEN'S FELLOWSHIP INTERNATIONAL, laymen's association for mutual witness to the experience of *baptism with the Holy Spirit. The organization was Pentecostal in inspiration, and was formed in 1951 in Los Angeles by a businessman, Demos Chakarian, and the evangelist Oral *Roberts. Membership has grown greatly. The Fellowship has spread the message of spirit baptism and interest in *glossolalia throughout many denominations in the United States. BIBLIOGRAPHY: J. T. Nichol, *Pentecostalism* (1966) 241–242.

[T. C. O'BRIEN]

FULLER, THOMAS (1608–61), English divine and historian. A witty preacher, noted for calmness and moderation, F. supported the royalist cause but was criticized for lack of enthusiasm. His willingness to accommodate himself to either side brought him the reputation of being a "trimmer," yet after the death of Charles I, he lived isolated and impoverished, ejected from his prebends because of his opposition to Cromwell. He published many sermons and historical works, the best of which is *The History of the Worthies of England* (1662). Of shrewd common sense, he was one of the most popular writers and preachers of his day and one of the first to support himself by his pen. BIBLIOGRAPHY: D. B. Lyman, *Great Tom Fuller* (1935); W. E. Houghton, Jr., *Formation of Thomas Fuller's Holy and Profane State* (1938, repr. 1969).

[M. J. BARRY]

FULLER BROOCH (9th cent.), silver Anglo-Saxon disc-brooch, 4½ inches in diameter, expressing the five senses as human figures reserved in silver against niello backgrounds, within a border of roundels of human, animal, bird and plant motifs. Now in the British Museum, it is the earliest anthropomorphic depiction of the senses in European art.

[R. L. S. BRUCE-MITFORD]

FULLNESS OF TIME (Gr. *plērōma tou chronou*), a phrase that occurs only in Gal 4.4 in reference to the coming of Jesus and his redemptive action by which we became the adopted sons of God. Yet the thought which it expresses is rooted in the OT notion of history and the eschatological hopes of the later Prophets. All history was viewed as the manifestation or revelation of moments and events which God had determined from the beginning for the establishment of his kingdom on earth (cf. Eph 1.10). Thus time is considered some sort of stream whose flow carries salvation events to mankind. The earlier Prophets, because of a lack of historical perspective, looked for the immediate coming of the Day of Yahweh, the day of judgment, which would initiate God's kingdom on earth after a period of suffering which was portrayed as the birth pangs of the new age, the messianic era. But the later Prophets (see Is 2.2–4; 11.6–9; 66.22–23; Dan 7; Jer 30, 31) looked to the establishment of God's kingdom "in the days to come" (Jer 30.3; 31.1, 27, 31, 38), after the dissolution of the world as we know it and after a new creation through which the people of God, with the Son of Man at their head, will be given eternal sovereignty (Dan ch. 7). Hence the NT refers to the present time as "the end of an age" (1 Cor 10.11), the "last days" (Heb 1.2; 9.26; 1 Pet 1.20). This concept is clear in Peter's Pentecostal Sermon and the reaction of the crowds (Acts 2.15–40). Thus the "fullness of time" (the appointed time) refers not merely to the birth, life, death, Resurrection and glorification of Jesus by which our adoption as sons of God was initiated, but also to the entire Christian era in which men through conversion and commitment to Christ labor to establish the kingdom of God on earth. This is a period of suffering, likened to birth pangs, which will usher in the birth of the new age, the victorious kingdom of God (Col 1.24). BIBLIOGRAPHY: F. Prat, *Theology of St. Paul* (tr. J. L. Stoddard, 1958) 2:107–108, 352–357.

[J. A. PIERCE]

FUMO, BARTOLOMEO (d. 1545), Italian Dominican, inquisitor general at Piacenza, author. In F.'s *Summa casuum conscientiae, aurea armilla dicta* (1550), the thesis that one may follow a moral opinion that is good while knowing that another is better, is noteworthy in the evolution of *Probabilism. BIBLIOGRAPHY: T. Deman, DTC 13.456 s.v. ''Probabilisme.''

[T. C. O'BRIEN]

FUNDAMENTAL ARTICLES OF BELIEF, those basic principles of the Christian religion in which belief is necessary, according to some, for church membership and salvation. This notion caused much discussion in the 17th cent. and was the subject of a noted controversy between J. *Bossuet and P. Jurieu. Jurieu, a Protestant, maintained that Christian unity could be achieved if the various Churches recognized that certain unessential doctrines have been attached to the faith, and that those who have retained the fundamental articles of faith contained in the earliest creeds are in fact united in Christ's one Church. Roman Catholic theologians have rejected this argument insofar as they saw in it a selectivity in regard to divinely revealed truths whose veracity depends upon God's authority and not upon human judgment. Nevertheless, the deposit of faith should not be confused with its manner of presentation. In Vat II Ecum 4 it is pointed out: ''While preserving unity in essentials, let all members of the Church preserve a proper freedom . . . in the theological elaborations of revealed truth.'' BIBLIOGRAPHY: G. H. Joyce, CE 6:319–321; Vorgrimler 91.

[T. M. MCFADDEN]

FUNDAMENTAL OPTION, the primary, overall intent that directs a person's moral and spiritual life. This neologism reflects the reaction in recent moral theology against the casuistic and therefore atomistic view that assessed the moral life as though it were a series of numerically distinct, isolated choices, some good, some bad. Instead, the true moral life is seen as the life of charity, and the New Law as primarily the grace of the Holy Spirit interiorly inclining the recipient to respond personally to the Father's love. The good fundamental option is not a dramatic, single act of conversion; it is the intent of the person's whole life, responsiveness to the commandment of love of God above all; every single true act of choice is either an affirmation of the intent of charity, even where there may be no explicit reflection on that, or a failure to affirm charity's intent. The meaning allows for an appreciation of the differences in the gravity of sins that may be mortal; there can be an instance of serious infidelity for which the sinner will more quickly repent because it is a departure through weakness from the way he wishes to live his life. The evil fundamental option is the opposite: the radical refusal to accept as primary the identity given by charity, and to take other characteristics of self as the measure of one's choices. The explicit terms in which a person chooses one or the other direction in life are not always identifiable in Christian terms (see SALVATION OF THE UNBELIEVER). Whatever the terms in consciousness, however, to be a person morally means that a fundamental option underlies every truly human choice. The option, abstractly described, means in fact the choice of self as absolute or the affirmation of self as being related to God. That second always remains open in this life, and is met with God's grace that forgives and draws the respondent to himself. BIBLIOGRAPHY: G. M. Regan, *New Trends in Moral Theology* (1971) 189–208; ThAq ST (Lat-Eng., v. 18, ed. T. Gilby, 135–139, 147–150, 163–167, 174–175; *ibid.*, v. 27, ed. T. C. O'Brien, 110–117, 125–133.

[T. C. O'BRIEN]

FUNDAMENTAL THEOLOGY, the study of revelation as a possible act of God, its transmission in time and event, and man's ability to receive it. It is the foundation of theology in that it asks the basic preliminary questions: How can God's word be revealed to men? What and where is divine revelation? Although the authority of God revealing is motive and foundation of the act of faith, yet it is knowledge of the credibility of revealed truth that justifies this response intellectually. As a means of salvation, revelation must validate itself and answer men's hesitancy and doubts. Fundamental theology, therefore, weighs the credentials of revelation so that its acceptance may be seen to be reasonable, even obligatory. Moreover, since revelation cannot be substantiated by appeal to faith and revealed truth, metaphysics must provide the criteria and history must establish its actual occurrence. Thus in Christian faith, Scripture proclaims itself credible testimony confirmed by ''signs'' (Jn 20.30–31), and the preaching of Jesus and his Apostles focuses on God who reveals himself in his Word (Heb. 1.1) and on man who comes to the revealing God by faith that is reasonable. Here fundamental theology functions as bridge between philosophy and theology. Ultimately it can draw conclusions regarding the personal nature of God, man's openness to freely given revelation beyond what nature discloses, and the relation of faith to God. Other concerns include the forms of revelation, the duty to accept it, its social nature, and its transmission by the Church. In a further, missionary aspect, fundamental theology seeks to acquaint men with revelation, esp. by removing obstacles to faith such as superstition and magicism. In this way, fundamental theology is related to *apologetics. BIBLIOGRAPHY: J. V. Linden and W. T. Costello, *Fundamentals of Religion* (1956); G. Moran, *Theology of Revelation* (1966); B. Lonergan, ''Theology and Understanding,'' Greg 35 (1954) 642–644. *REVELATION.

[W. DAVISH]

FUNDAMENTALISM, a conservative theological movement in American Protestantism that arose in the 1920s in opposition to *modernism. No adequate interpretation of this movement has yet appeared. There are numerous articles and several books on the subject, some of which furnish valuable data, but most of them suffer from the tendency to explain fundamentalism in socioeconomic or psychological terms, treating the religious aspects as peripheral. While cultural factors were important, the original fundamentalist movement was rooted in genuine theological concerns. Further confusion has arisen from repeated reference to the *five points of fundamentalism, a myth that has scant foundation and provides little help in understanding the movement.

Fundamentalism should be understood primarily as an attempt to protect the essential elements (fundamentals) of the Christian faith from the eroding effects of rationalism and naturalism. It was not a monolithic movement, but had a variety of expressions. Although it emerged as a party in the fundamentalist–modernist controversy after World War I, its roots so back into the 19th cent., when evolution, biblical criticism, and other intellectual currents began to challenge old assumptions concerning the authority of biblical revelation. At the same time, new kinds of ethical problems accompanied the development of an urban-industrial society, appealing to the Christian conscience for social and economic reforms. The so-called ''higher criticism'' (historical and literary, as distinguished from textual, analysis) of the Bible was introduced into the mainstream of American Protestantism following the Civil War, and by the time of World War I, after overcoming strong resistance, came to be generally accepted in seminaries and colleges. Heated exchanges took place in scholarly journals and public forums, and Baptists dismissed a few professors (C. H. Toy, E. P. Gould), while Presbyterians held heresy trials (C. A. Briggs, A. C. McGiffert). In 1897, warning that ''the lines are being drawn, and the party spirit is gaining strength,'' a prophetic voice forecast an impending conflict between progressives and conservatives.

As more extreme liberals reduced Christianity to a sociological or psychological phenomenon, and as many seminary students and young ministers lost their faith and quit the ministry, the conservative opposition crystallized around leaders who emerged to champion the claims of the gospel. A considerable preparatory influence was the publication (1910–15), of *The Fundamentals,* distributed free to all pastors, seminary students, and many others in the United States. The emphases of these booklets were on the authority of the Scriptures, the deity of Christ, the efficacy of Christ's atoning work, etc. By 1918, the term ''fundamentals'' had become a common usage, but ''fundamentalist'' and ''fundamentalism'' were coined in 1920 by Curtis Lee Laws, Baptist editor of the *Watchman-Examiner,* who proposed that a group within his denomination adopt the name ''fundamentalists.'' Those whom he represented were moderate conservatives, who believed that the modernists in their attempt to come to terms with modern learning were surrendering the ''fundamentals'' of the gospel, namely, the sinful nature of man, his inability to save himself without divine grace, the adequacy of Jesus Christ to regenerate individuals and renew society, and the authoritative revelation in the Scriptures of God's redemptive activity. This group, which first applied the name ''fundamentalists'' to itself, was identified neither with *premillenarianism and *dispensationalism nor with a crusade against evolutionary teaching or an effort to abolish biblical criticism. They asserted repeatedly that they were concerned only about matters central to the Christian faith throughout the centuries. Before long a more militant group split off from this moderate party, calling itself the Baptist Bible Union. Gradually fundamentalism came to be used loosely for all theological conservatism, including extremists, moderates of the Laws type, and those who, like J. G. *Machen, represented a scholarly Presbyterian tradition. Eventually the fundamentalist image became stereotyped as closed-minded, ignorant, belligerent, and separatistic, and many conservatives sought a different appellation to distinguish their brand of conservatism. In the 1950s H. Ockenga renounced the fundamentalist label and proposed that ''neo-evangelical'' be the name of a conservatism that would be scholarly, balanced, and socially concerned. John Carnell, Carl F. H. Henry, Fuller Theological Seminary, the periodical *Christianity Today,* and other individuals and groups have been identified with the new evangelicalism, which considers itself the heir of the spirit and purpose of the original fundamentalists. BIBLIOGRAPHY: W. Hordern, *Layman's Guide to Protestant Theology* (1957); N. F. Furniss, *Fundamentalist Controversy, 1918–1931* (1954); S. G. Cole, *History of Fundamentalism* (1931); W. S. Hudson, *Religion in America* (1965); E. R. Sandeen, *Roots of Fundamentalism, 1830–1900* (1970); C. A. Russell, *Voices of American Fundamentalism: Seven Biographical Studies* (1976); L. Loetscher, *Broadening Church* (1954).

[N. H. MARING]

FUNDAMENTALISM, BIBLICAL, a religious movement which developed independently in different Protestant denominations in the U.S. toward the end of the 19th cent. and esp. after World War I. Its objectives were to stay what seemed to them the rising tide of modernism in theology and biblical interpretation. It attracted widespread public attention by the publication of 12 pamphlets, *The Fundamentals. A Testimony to the Truth,* issued between 1910 and 1912, subsidized by the laymen Milton and Stewart. These writings were based on an extremely literal conception of the inerrancy and infallibility of the Bible. The biblical teachings on the virgin birth, the physical Resurrection of Christ, the substitutionary atonement of his sacrifice, and his second coming were advanced as touchstones of orthodoxy. To unify their efforts, the World's Christian Fundamental Association was founded in 1919 and enlarged in 1948 to the International Council of Christian Churches and the World Evangelical Fellowship. Tensions arose between the fundamentalists and liberals in many Bible colleges and communities. H. E. Fosdick, a liberal Baptist preacher at the First Presbyterian Church in New York, was forced to withdraw from his post in 1924 when he refused to accept the Church's required doctrinal positions. Equally famous was the Scopes trial at Dayton, Tenn., in 1925, where W. J. Bryan, a fundamentalist, won the case against J. T. Scopes, a public high-school teacher accused of denying the biblical doctrine of Creation by teaching evolution. The influence of fundamentalism has diminished, but some of its extreme positions live on among a few Christian denominations. BIBLIOGRAPHY: S. G. Cole, *History of Fundamentalism* (1931, repr. 1971).

[F. BUCK]

FUNERAL RITES. The Congregation for Divine Worship by decree of Aug. 15, 1969, promulgated a revised set of funeral services that, following the mind of VatII SacLit 81–82, express more clearly the meaning of the Christian's death in the light of the Paschal Mystery of Christ. The accompanying introduction instructs those who share in the funeral rites that there is to be sensitivity both to the hope offered because of Christ's death and Resurrection and to the grief of those who mourn, as well as to legitimate regional mourning customs. The instruction points out that central place should be given to biblical readings, because of their promise of resurrection, of reunion of Christ's faithful, and the respect for the dead that the Scriptures inculcate. The prayers to be offered by the community give prominence to the Psalms, as expressions of both grief and gladness. The rites should all be marked by simplicity, with all pomp and display avoided; choice of liturgical colors should respect local custom and the wishes of the mourners; in the U.S. white, violet, or black vestments may be used. During the ceremonies it is recommended that symbols and ceremonies reflect the Christian attitude toward death. Thus the use of holy water is to be connected with the waters of baptism; a white covering may be placed over the coffin as a reminder of the white baptismal garment; the paschal candle should be carried in the funeral procession and placed at the coffin in the church. The position of the body of the deceased in the church may correspond to the person's position in the liturgical community: the faithful facing the altar, the ordained minister facing the community. The funeral rites for adults consist in three main parts called stations: a vigil service, a liturgy of the word, in the deceased's home or at a funeral parlor (the wake); the Eucharistic Liturgy in the church, the final commendation and farewell (formerly called the absolution). These three parts may be modified according to alternate forms given in the decreed ritual. According to adaptations approved for the U.S., the first service may be celebrated by the family itself (one of the elements approved for the whole Church for this service is the recitation of the Office of the Dead where that is desired). Because of the custom in the U.S. that the priest meet the body at the doors of the church, most of the elements of this first station may be included in that rite. The Eucharist should always be celebrated if possible (it is excluded on the three days of Holy Week, Sundays of Advent, Lent, and the Easter season). A homily on the Paschal Mystery is to be given, but a eulogy is forbidden. Mourners should be chosen as readers at the Mass and to carry the gifts at the Offertory; all may receive communion under both kinds. The rite of commendation and farewell should be celebrated in the church if most of the congregation does not attend the actual burial in the cemetery. All these rites are conducted also when there is a cremation, although the preference for burial is expressed by the instruction of the Congregation for Divine Worship. At the same time as the rites for the funeral of adults were issued, a new rite for the burial of children (i.e., those dying before reaching the age of reason) was also issued; it too stresses the joyful element in Christian hope, and directs that vestments should be festive and with a paschal symbolism. The rite may be celebrated for children not yet baptized whose parents intended their baptism. BIBLIOGRAPHY: *Rites of the Catholic Church* (1976).

[T. C. O'BRIEN]

FUNES, DEÁN GREGORIO (1749–1829), Argentinian priest, patriot, educator. With degrees in theology, canon law and civil law, F. was admitted to law practice before the Royal Councils in 1778. In Córdoba, Argentina, he was dean of the cathedral and vicar general. As an educator he served as rector of the Univ. of Córdoba and wrote a pioneering work called *Plan de Estudios* (1813). F., however, was primarily a political figure who played an important role in the movement for independence in Argentina. A member of the revolutionary governments and deputy to the assemblies which created the constitutions of 1819 and 1826, F. was a force for liberalism in politics. Like many of his contemporaries he believed that the **patronato real,* allowing the Spanish crown many influences on church discipline, had passed from Spain to the new Argentinian republic with the revolution. He saw that the Holy See's failure to concede to the new State similar rights could only damage the Church in Argentina. Among F.'s numerous writings is the three-volume *Ensayo de historia civil de Paraguay, Buenos Aires y Tucumán* (1816–17).

[J. R. AHERNE]

FUNK, FRANZ XAVER VON (1840–1907), church historian and patrologist. A native of Abstgmünd, Germany, F. received a doctorate in philosophy (1863), was ordained priest (1864), began his teaching career in the field of moral theology (1866), and became a contributor to the *Theologische Quartalschrift* (1867). He quickly gained a reputation for scholarship and was selected to succeed C. Hefele in church history at Tübingen in 1870. He is perhaps most widely known for his *Patres Apostolici* (first ed., 1901). Death came as he was working on an edition of the Pseudo-Clementines. BIBLIOGRAPHY: P. Godet, DTC 6.1:972–975; H. Tüchle, LTK 4:460.

[H. DRESSLER]

FURFEY, PAUL HANLEY (1896–), a leading influence in Catholic approaches to the problems of society. F. was ordained in 1922 and spent his entire professional career at The Catholic University of America. From *The Gang* published in 1926 to *The Mystery of Iniquity* in 1944 and *The Morality Gap* in 1968, F. has issued a series of sociological and pastoral studies which have had wide reading. An advocate of personalistic social action, he has been a consistent supporter of the concepts exemplified by Dorothy Day and Catherine de Hueck. *Fire on the Earth* appeared in the 1930s to galvanize American Catholics into Christian social action.

[J. R. AHERNE]

FURLONG, THOMAS (*c.*1803–75), Irish bp., religious founder. Ordained in 1826, professor at St. Patrick's Seminary, Maynooth (1827–57), he was then consecrated bp. of Ferns, Co. Wexford. F. devoted himself to deepening devotional life in his diocese; he established a diocesan seminary at Wexford, and schools for girls. In 1866 he founded a parish mission society of priests, the Missionaries of the Blessed Sacrament; in 1871 a teaching and nursing institute, the Sisters of St. John of God; in 1876, a diocesan congregation of nuns, the Institute of Perpetual Adoration.

[T. C. O'BRIEN]

FURNESS, ABBEY OF, a renowned English abbey on the peninsula of Furness, the first of the Savigny Foundations to be constructed in England. It was founded in 1123, at Tulkoth (Lancashire) by Stephen of Blois (*c.*1097–1154), later King of England, and was the most important and most prosperous of all the Cistercian abbeys of N. England. In its early days Furness had 70 monks and 120 *conversi* or lay-brothers and became known as one of the order's largest abbeys, exercising a great influence over other foundations, including some Irish houses. In time the monks decreased and their buildings became deserted, while in the late 15th cent. division and conflict prevailed between rival abbots. During the reign of Henry VIII some abbots and monks resisted the King's claim to royal supremacy, but in 1537 the abbot of Furness freely surrendered and this action led to the suppression of other abbeys in 1539. All that remains are the ruins of Furness. BIBLIOGRAPHY: Cottineau 1:1234; Knowles-Hadcock 109.

[R. A. TODD]

FURSEY, ST., (also called Furseus; d. 650), abbot of a monastery in Tuam who traveled to England and founded the monastery of Burghcastle in Suffolk. Driven out by Penda, F. went to France and settled at Lagny at the invitation of Clovis II. He was for a time vicar of the diocese of Paris. He is buried at Péronne. BIBLIOGRAPHY: R. Van Doren, BiblSanct 5:1321–22.

[R. T. MEYER]

FÜRSTENBERG, the name, distinguished by churchmen, statesmen, and soldiers, of two noble houses in Germany. The first, which originated in the Black Forest and was seated at Donaueschingen, the source of the Danube, was loyal in support of the Habsburgs, hence the saying, "The emperor fights no great battle but a Fürstenberg falls." Nevertheless, the two soldiers turned ecclesiastics noticed here were less trusty and promoted French designs on the Rhine. The first, *Franz Egon (1625–82),* instigated the policies of his friend, Maximilian Heinrich of Bavaria, abp. and elector of Cologne, and at the instance of Louis XIV was made bp. of Metz, afterwards of Strasbourg. Deprived of his emoluments by Emperor Leopold I, he was reinstated at the Treaty of Nijmegen (1679). His younger brother, *Wilhelm Egon (1629–1704),* who echoed his policies and career, succeeded him as bp. of Strasbourg, and Louis obtained for him the cardinal's hat. Disappointed in his prospects of succeeding Maximilian Heinrich, largely because of the military reverses of the French, he retired to one of his monasteries near Paris.

The second family takes its name from Fürstenberg on the Ruhr. *Franz Friedrich Wilhelm (1729–1810)* was an enlightened social reformer who eventually became vicar general of the prince bishop of Münster. *Franz Egon (1797–1859),* a member of the Prussian Upper House, was a patron of the arts and an ardent defender of Catholicism.

Maximilian von Fürstenberg (b. 1904), educated at Louvain, was apostolic delegate in Australia and Japan, and created cardinal by Pope Paul VI, 1967. He was prefect of the Sacred Congregation for the Eastern Church 1969-73 and currently serves on the Congregations for Bishops, Religious, and Secular Institutes and for the Evangelization of Peoples.

[T. GILBY]

FUTURIBLE, a neologism of scholastic theology for a conditioned, future event, one that would occur given certain conditions. The futurible is distinct from the merely, objectively, or theoretically possible, and from the future, an event, even a contingent event, that will in fact occur. The context is the discussion of God's foreknowledge. St. Thomas Aquinas describes the divine knowledge of the merely possible as purely cognitive, "the knowledge of simple understanding"; of the actual—the existent at whatever time and in whatever manner—as causative, "the knowledge of vision" (ThAq ST 1a,14.9 & 13). In dealing with the problem of the compatibility of divine foreknowledge and causality with human freedom, L. *Molina proposed a "middle knowledge," that was noncausative but infallible, and assigned the futurible as its object. The specific futurible at issue is the consent or rejection by the human will to grace offered, given various conditions or sets of circumstances. *SCIENTIA MEDIA.

[T. C. O'BRIEN]

FUTURISM, a Russian literary movement founded in 1910 as a reaction against realism and the religious and philosophical tendencies of symbolism. Its goal of repudiating tradition and creating a new "trans-sense" language found expression in the manifesto "A Slap in the Face of Public Taste" (1912). After 1917, its adherents published the journals *LEF* ("Left Front," 1923–25) and *New LEF* (1927). Their hope of controlling the art of the future by joining their literary revolution to the social and political one was thwarted by the increasing conservatism of the new regime. BIBLIOGRAPHY: C. M. Bowra, *Creative Experiment* (1949) 94–127; R. Poggioli, *Poets of Russia* (1960) 238–255.

[M. F. MCCARTHY]

FUTURISM (ART), 20th-cent. Italian art movement. Marinetti's *Manifesto* (1909) stated the attitudes of intellectuals and artists in Milan, Rome, and Florence—proclaiming the glories of movement, speed, violence, war, and the machine, and decrying Italy's fixation in her archaeological past. Leading exponents, U. Boccioni, G. Balla, G. Severini, L. Russolo, and C. Carrà expressed a universal dynamism in interesecting planes related to French analytical Cubism (M. Duchamp, *Nude Descending a Staircase,* 1912). Russolo, a muscian, invented a cacaphonous *intonarumori*. Boccioni in *La Scultura futurista* (1912) advocated the motorizing of planes (foreshadowing kinetics and mobiles) and the use of nontraditional substances (as in "collage" and "assemblage"). Marinetti's *Manifesto of Futurist Literature* introduced the free use of words. In 1915–16 C. Carrà led a metaphysical school of Futurist painters (*Pittura metafisica*). Futurism continued until *c.* 1950 (influencing American artists, J. Stella and L. Feininger) with important exhibitions in Italy, the U.S., and elsewhere. BIBLIOGRAPHY: J. C. Taylor, *Futurism* (1961).

[M. J. DALY]

FUTURIST SACRED ART, MANIFESTO OF, a declaration in 1931 stating that the Futurist timespace concept of the universal extension of objects in motion in space, and their distortion or change during movement ensured the most viable visual expression of the intangible, supernatural mysteries of the Catholic Church. A *Crucifixion* by Dottori and *Nativity-Death-Eternity* by Fillia were expositions of the movement; they met with but limited success.

[M. J. DALY]

FUX, JOHANN JOSEPH (1600–1741), Austrian composer of the baroque style. In his place as musician for the court at Vienna, he composed many sacred works, and contributed substantially to the knowledge and rules of vocal counterpoint in a theoretical work, *Gradus ad Parnassum* (1725). Translated into five languages, it became a standard reference work for that subject, and was used by Haydn and Mozart.

[D. SMUCKER]

FYLFOT, a device, esp. the *gammadion, employed to fill the foot or border of stained-glass windows.

G

GABAA, see GIBEAH.

GABAON, see GIBEON.

GABBATHA, paved court where Pilate sat in judgment on Jesus (Jn 19.13, the only occurrence of the term in the Bible). It is said to be the Aramaic name for the place called in Greek *lithostrōtos,* the pavement. It perhaps means height or elevation. The site generally favored by archeologists for its location is adjacent to Herod's Tower of Antonia, at the NW corner of the temple area. Excavators have found there beneath the Convent of Our Lady of Zion a paved area that may date from the time of Jesus. It is not certain, however, whether Pilate's palace was at Antonia or at the site of the modern Citadel, near the Jaffa Gate. BIBLIOGRAPHY: ''Game of the King,'' *Crusader's Almanac* 84 (1975) 4–5.

[T. EARLY]

GABRA, MICHAEL see GHEBRE, MICHAEL.

GABRIEL (from the Heb., *Gabrī'ēl,* usually explained as ''strong man of God''). In the OT, G. functions as the messenger of God who explains the visions concerning ''the time of the end'' (Dan 8.17), the ''time of the coming of the anointed'' (Dan 9.24). Though called the ''man Gabriel'' (Dan 8.17), his appearance strikes fear in Daniel and he comes in ''swift flight'' (9.21). In the NT, G. is clearly identified as an angel (Lk 1.11–38; the title archangel is nonbiblical). He announces the birth of John the Baptist and of Jesus, the Son of David, the Son of God (Lk 1.11–20; 1.26–38) in the fullness of time (Gal 4.4).

[J. A. PIERCE]

GABRIEL FERRETTI, BL. (1385–1456), Franciscan priest and preacher; member of the noble family of Ferretti. Having joined the Franciscan Observants at the age of 18, he preached 15 years in Le Marche near his native Ancona, becoming guardian of the Observants in that town, and attaining the status of provincial in his order. He is thought to have been responsible for promoting the Franciscan rosary in honor of the seven joys of Our Lady. He was buried in the old church of St. Francis in Ancona. His cult was approved in 1753 by Benedict XIV. BIBLIOGRAPHY: Butler 4:326–327; E. Frascadore, BiblSanct 5:654–656.

[E. J. DILLON]

GABRIEL MARY, BL. (*c.*1463–1532), Franciscan spiritual director. Gilbert Nicholas (called Gabriel Mary by Leo X because of his devotion to the Blessed Virgin) entered the Franciscans at La Rochelle after being refused entry to several other Franciscan houses because of delicate health. A philosopher and theologian, he rose in his order to the position of commissary general of Franciscan Observant houses S of the Alps. He was director of St. Joan of Valois, former wife of Louis XII, who founded the Order of the Annunciation. G. secured the approval of the order's rule (1501), and revised its constitutions. He also founded six convents of the group and served as its visitor general. BIBLIOGRAPHY: Butler 3:423–424.

[J. R. AHERNE]

GABRIEL OF ST. MARY MAGDALEN (Adrian Devos; 1893–1953), spiritual writer. A Belgian Discalced Carmelite, he was ordained after interruption of his studies by World War I and military service, during which he won the military cross of honor in 1920. From 1920–26 professor of philosophy and theology in his province, G. was appointed to the International College of the Discalced Carmelites in Rome in 1926, where he became vice-rector. In 1941 he founded the periodical *Vita carmelitana* (later the *Revista di vita spirituale*). A cofounder of the journal *Ephemerides theologicae carmeliticae* in 1947, by his contributions to these and other journals he became a recognized contemporary authority on mysticism, esp. in the Carmelite tradition.

[J. R. AHERNE]

GABRIEL SEVERUS (1541–1616), metropolitan of Philadelphia in Asia Minor, polemicist. Because his episcopal office in Philadelphia, which was under Turkish dominion, made few demands upon him, S. spent much of his career in Venice where he ministered to the Orthodox at the Church of St. George. He established a name for himself by his polemical writings, which were both anti-Latin and anti-Protestant. He wrote well on the sacraments and propounded an interesting view on purgatory. He denied that this could rightly be regarded as a place, but affirmed the existence of ''many mansions'' in hell and heaven: ''Christ, when he descended into hell, opened it and freed all his ancestors and all the just men who were there. . . . Since that time hell has not yet been closed, but up to the present it remains open.'' The difference between this and Latin theology may be more a matter of terms than of thought, since Severus, unlike some of his contemporaries, regarded the suffering of souls in hell primarily in terms of satisfaction for sin. Nevertheless, in leaving the doors open he did allow for a wider range of prayer for the dead than his Western contemporaries. BIBLIOGRAPHY: M. Jugie, DTC 6:977–983.

[G. EVERY]

GABRIEL SIONITA (1577–1648), biblical and Semitic scholar. He was a Lebanese Maronite who completed his biblical language studies at Rome and spent most of his career at the Sorbonne in Paris. His chief work was as collaborator (1614–45) in the editing of the Paris Polyglot Bible; he revised the Arabic and Syriac texts for the OT, and the Latin text for the Gospels. He also published the Arabic text with Latin translation of *Geographia Nubiensis* (1619), and *Grammatica Arabica Maronitarum* (1616).

[T. C. O'BRIEN]

GABRIEL DE TORO (d. before 1586), Spanish Franciscan. As provincial (1538–41, 1548–52) he twice sent missionaries to Guatemala. His main work (1536; 6th ed., 1599) is the first study of public care of the poor; his sources go back to antiquity. In his efforts to revive Christian poverty and social justice he condemned selfish clergy and foretold the secularization of goods. He recognized a social role for the Church, social sins, and a special sanctity of the poor. BIBLIOGRAPHY: DSAM 6:15–16.

[E. P. COLBERT]

GABRIELI, ANDREA (*c.* 1510–86), Venetian organist and composer. At his major post, first organist at St. Mark's in Venice, G. composed most creatively in the genre of madrigals. His main achievement, however, was to introduce large scale instrumentation to vocal compositions. In this way he strongly influenced his most famous pupils, a nephew G. *Gabrieli and the German Hans Leo Hassler.

[D. J. SMUCKER]

GABRIELI, GIOVANNI (*c.* 1557–1612), Venetian organist and composer. As had his uncle Andrea, Giovanni held the post of first organist at St. Mark's in Venice. He extended his uncle's compositional creativity in his own lavish and huge ecclesiastical compositions for both voices and instruments. Some works involve as many as 4 choirs singing 20 parts. Among his other lasting contributions was the first attempt at real orchestration, i.e., the assignment of individual parts to specific instruments. He influenced his pupil, the German Heinrich Schütz, and in G. even the flowering of the baroque cantata under J. S. Bach finds its origins. Most of the MSS of G.'s compositions were destroyed during the Napoleonic occupation of Venice. BIBLIOGRAPHY: E. F. Kenyon, *Giovanni Gabrieli: His Life and Works* (1966).

[D. J. SMUCKER]

GAD, in the Scriptures the name of: (a) a pagan god of fortune (cf. Gen 30.11; Is 65.11); (2) a prophet in the time of David (1 Sam 22.5; 2 Sam 24.11–14; 1 Chr 29.29); (3) the seventh son of Jacob, his first by Zilpah (Gen 30.9–11; 35.26), the ancestor of the tribe Gad. Their territory lay in Transjordan and extended from the Arnon to the Lake of Galilee (Num 32.1–36; Jos 13.24–28; 22.7–34). Harassed by Hazael (2 Kg 10.32–33), at war with the Hagrites (1 Chr 5.18–22), they were deported into captivity by Tiglath-pileser III in 734 B.C. (2 Kg 15.29; 1 Chr 5.26). BIBLIOGRAPHY: R. De Vaux, ''Notes d'histoire et de topographie transjordaniennes,'' RevBibl 1 (1941) 16–47; K. Elliger, InterDB 2:333–335.

[F. BUCK]

GADARA, city of the Decapolis about 5 miles SE of the Sea of Galilee. In the preferred reading of Mt 8.28–34, ''the country of the Gadarenes'' is given as the place where Jesus exorcised two men and sent the demons into swine. The Vulgate reading of Mt, as well as most texts of Mk 5.1–20 and Lk 8.26–39, places the incident at *Gerasa, another city. Gadara, modern Umm Qeis, was predominantly a Greek city.

[T. EARLY]

GADDI, AGNOLO (fl. 1369–96), Italian Florentine painter, son and pupil of Taddeo Gaddi and student under Giovanni da Milano. There are records that Agnolo designed reliefs and gilded and painted statues in the Cathedral of Florence (1389–95) and cartoons for stained glass windows (1394 and 1396). His only documented panel is that of *SS. Giovanni Gualberto* and *Miniato* and *Scenes from the Passion* in S. Miniato al Monte, Florence. He executed frescoes of the Virgin and the legend of the Holy Girdle and the Legend of the True Cross (Sta. Croce, Florence); with assistants, a *Madonna of Mercy, Assumption of the Virgin, Coronation of the Virgin, Pentecost, Last Supper,* and *SS. Michael, James and Julian* (Yale Univ.) Agnolo's style, sculpturesque in the manner of Giotto, though competent in technique, does not attain the monumentality of the master.

GADDI, GADDO (GADDO DI ZANOBI) (*c.*1250–*c.*1327), Italian painter and mosaicist, first of the Gaddi family and father of Taddeo G. Friend of Cimabue and contemporary of Giotto, G. is credited with the mosaics in Sta. Maria Maggiore, Rome, and the *Coronation of the Virgin* in the Cathedral of Florence. Mosaics in the Florence Baptistery are Byzantine in style—reflecting Cimabue.

[M. J. DALY]

GADDI, TADDEO (*c.* 1300–66), Italian, Florentine painter, son of Gaddo G., father of Agnolo G. and collaborator with Giotto for 24 years. In the Baroncelli Chapel of Sta. Croce Taddeo painted the *Life of the Virgin* (1332–38) showing forms in the style of Giotto but proliferations in architectural and landscape backgrounds distinctively Taddeo's, a portable triptych *Crucifixion, Nativity and Other Scenes* (1334, Berlin) with affinity to the art of Bernardo Daddi, and further commissions in Pisa and Pistoia showing sharp sculptural relief. Most remarkable are the somber *Pietá* (New Haven, Yale Univ.) and beautiful and grave *Madonna and Child* (Florence). Other works are in N.Y., Bern and elsewhere. BIBLIOGRAPHY: R. Salvini, *L'arte di Agnolo Gaddi* (1936); J. White, *Art and Architecture in Italy* (1966).

[M. J. DALY]

GAËLL, RENÉ (1871–1951), French priest, journalist. From 1909, when he published a novel about Lourdes, *Celle qui ressuscita*, he gave all his time to writing about the shrine. He founded *L'Echo de Lourdes* (1911) and was editor of *La Croix de Lourdes*, the *Revue de Lourdes*, and *Journal de la grotte*. BIBLIOGRAPHY: J. Morienval, *Catholicisme* 4:1694.

[M. J. SUELZER]

GAETANO, see also CAJETAN.

GAGARIN, IVAN SERGEEVICH (1814–82), writer on Russian Orthodoxy. A Russian diplomat he served in the embassy in Paris, where in 1842 he was converted to Catholicism. Entering the Society of Jesus (1843), he became a professor for a time before taking up at Paris his principal activity, writing polemics on Orthodox theology and history. He contributed to numerous journals and cofounded the periodical *Études* in 1856, which continues. He spent some years in Constantinople where he established the Society of St. Dionysius the Areopagite to promote the union of the Eastern and Western Churches. Among the many books and essays he wrote are: *L'Église romaine . . . .* (1865); *Les Églises orientales unies* (1867); *La Russie sera-t-elle catholique?* (1856), and *De l'enseignement de la théologie dans l'Église russe* (1856).

[J. R. AHERNE]

GAGE, THOMAS (1602–56), English Dominican missionary, then Puritan pastor, author. Member of an English recusant family, G. became a Dominican in Spain, worked in Hispanic America as a missionary (1625–37), but after returning to England abandoned his order and became a violent anti-Catholic. He was a witness in the trials of priests that led to their execution. In 1648 he published *The English-American, his Travails by Sea and Land, or a New Survey of the West Indias* (mod. ed. J. E. Thompson, 1958), a widely read travelogue marked by keen observation of the New World but marred by anti-Catholic and anti-Spanish propaganda. G. persuaded Oliver Cromwell to launch an attack on the Spanish Main and accompanied the expedition.

[J. R. AHERNE]

GAGLIANO, MARCO DA (*c.*1575–1642), Florentine composer of the early Baroque period. As canon of the Church of San Lorenzo in Florence, he inaugurated (1607) the *Academia degli Elevati*, a group of performing musicians. His opera, *Dafne* (1607), reflects a tendency found in that academy to require stronger enunciation and more vigorous emotional expression for operas. He also wrote another opera, *La Flora* (1628), secular madrigals, and sacred music.

[D. J. SMUCKER]

GAGLIARDI, ACHILLE (1537 or 1538–1607), Italian Jesuit, a fellow student of St. Robert Bellarmine at the Roman College; later friend and spiritual director of St. Charles Borromeo (at whose request he composed a catechism); spiritual writer. His treatise *De doctrina interiori*, intended as a systematic exposition of doctrine on the spiritual life, was never completed, but other writings planned as parts of this work were edited and published after his death. G.'s spiritual doctrine was strongly marked by the *Spiritual Exercises* and the Jesuit pattern of life. His teaching became known chiefly through the *Breve compendio intorno alla perfezione cristiana* (*Short Compendium of Christian Perfection*), a book that appeared anonymously in 1611. It appears to have been the work of G.'s spiritual daughter, Isabella *Bellinzaga Lomazzi, though its authorship has been attributed to G., and there is no doubt that he cooperated substantially in its composition. Translated and repeatedly republished in Italian and other languages, it must be accounted one of the most influential spiritual treatises of the 17th century. Later critics point to it as one of the influences that prepared the way for Quietism. BIBLIOGRAPHY: I. Iparraguire and A. Derville, DSAM 6:53–64, bibliog.; J. De Guibert, *Jesuits: Their Spiritual Doctrine and Practice* (tr. W. J. Young, 1964) 257–258.

[P. K. MEAGHER]

GAGUIN, ROBERT (*c.*1433–1501), humanist, priest, literary figure, diplomat. G. joined the Trinitarians (Mathurins) in his youth, and at the age of 40 was elected general of the order. He was a professor at the Sorbonne, teaching and becoming lasting friends with Erasmus and Reuchlin. G. was named dean of the faculty of canon law in 1483. He traveled a great deal both for his order and on diplomatic commissions for the king; he maintained a lively, reflective, and historically revealing correspondence with eminent leaders, including Pico della Mirandola, Bessarion, Thomas More, M. Ficino. His humanistic writings are: *De origine et gestis Francorum compendium* (1495); his *Correspondence* (1498), translations of Latin prose and verse, including Caesar's *Commentaries* (1485), and Alain Chartier's *Curial* into French. Among his religious writings are a reform of the rule of the Trinitarians, *Statuta ordinis fratrum sanctae Trinitatis et redemptionis captivorum* (1497), publications concerning the pressing theological problem of the times, the Immaculate Conception of Mary; but his poetry and prose on that subject reflect his canon law background and are appreciated more for their style than for their theological profundity. BIBLIOGRAPHY: R. J. Schoeck, NCE 6:240; A. Palmieri, DTC 6:996-998; *Catholicisme* 4:1699–1700.

[J. J. SMITH]

GAILHAC, PIERRE JEAN ANTOINE (1802–90), religious founder. Ordained for Montpellier, France, in 1826, G. taught theology in the seminary there. He refused to accept the government mandate that professors of theology teach the *Declaration of the French Clergy of 1682, though his colleagues accepted the decree. A hospital chaplain for many years, he founded a community of nuns, Religious of the *Sacred Heart of Mary, for the care of orphans and the education of young women. In 1860 G. was accused of poisoning two nuns but was acquitted. The fabricator of the story later confessed. G.'s cause of beatification was introduced in Rome in 1953. BIBLIOGRAPHY: H. Magaret, *Gailhac of Béziers* (1946).

[J. R. AHERNE]

GAIRDNER, JAMES (1828–1912), archivist and historian. An Edinburgh man, G. was at first a Presbyterian but later leaned toward Anglo-Catholicism. He was clerk in the London Public Records Office and later assistant keeper. He became an acknowledged expert on the English Reformation and edited, among other things, the letters and papers of Henry VIII and the *Paston Letters*. After his retirement he wrote several historical works, among them *The History of the English Church 1509–1558* (1902) and *Lollardy and the Reformation in England* (4 v., 1908–13). He believed that modern historians had commonly done less than justice to the RC case.

GAIRDNER, WILLIAM HENRY TEMPLE (1873–1928), Anglican missionary. G. went to Cairo in 1898, was ordained in 1901, and became a pioneer in teaching colloquial Arabic. He published a grammar of the language in 1907. He reorganized the Arabic Anglican Church and wrote many devotional, doctrinal, musical, and linguistic works in Arabic and English.

[M. J. SUELZER]

GAIUS (CAIUS), ST. (d. 296), **POPE** from 283. According to the Liber pontificalis G. was of Dalmatian origin and a relative of the Emperor Diocletian. He is reported (unreliably) to have decreed that a cleric must pass through all the lesser orders before receiving episcopal consecration and to have put deacons in charge of the administration of the seven districts into which the city was divided. With obvious anachronism, legend has involved him in the Diocletian persecution and has associated him with the martyrdom of St. Susanna. BIBLIOGRAPHY: Butler 2:144.

[R. B. ENO]

GAIUS (also Caius), presbyter of Rome. According to *Eusebius (*Hist. Eccl.* 2:25.6; 3.28.1; 6.20.3) G. wrote against the Montanist leader Proclus and against Cerinthus while *Zephyrinus was bp. of Rome (198–217). G. accepted 13 Pauline Epistles as genuine, excluding the Letter to the Hebrews. He also refers to the relics of the apostles Peter and Paul preserved in Rome.

[E. V. GALLAGHER]

GAJARD, JOSEPH (1885–1972), French Benedictine musicologist, choirmaster for 50 years at the Abbey of Solesmes, one of those responsible for the preservation of and restored interest in the Gregorian chant. G. served as director of the paleographical studio at Solesmes and succeeded Dom André *Mocquereau as director of the *Paléographie musicale,* a work first published in 1888 as compilation of sources and discussion of Gregorian chant. G. was editor for the Vatican editions of the *Officium majoris hebdomadae* (1922–). He published the *Antiphonale monasticum* (1934) and the *Agendis mortuorum* (1949). G. founded *Études grégoriennes* (1954) for scientific study of the chants and in 1957 initiated a program to publish a critical edition of the Roman Gradual.

[R. J. LITZ]

GALAAD, see GILEAD.

GALANO, CLEMENTE (d. 1666), Italian Theatine missionary. He first engaged in missionary work in Georgia and attempted to reunite the Armenians with Rome. He founded a college in Constantinople and published there an Armenian grammar and logic. Forced to leave for Rome, he was later commissioned by the Congregation for the Propagation of the Faith to work among the Armenians in Poland, but he died before their schism was finally ended.

GALANOS, DEMETRIOS (1760–1833), a Greek philologist and one of the earlier serious translators of Sanskrit literature. G. was trained to become an Orthodox priest, but left Istanbul for India, where he taught the children of Greek merchants residing in Bengal. Eventually he took up residence in Benares, the holy city of the Hindus, and devoted himself to the study, copying, and translation of Sanskrit literature. When he died there, he willed half of his considerable fortune to the founding of Athens University. His valuable MSS are kept at the National Library, Athens. G.'s Greek translations were partially published posthumously in Athens (7 v. 1845–53). BIBLIOGRAPHY: S. A. Schulz, *Journal of the American Oriental Society* 89 (1969).

[S. A. SCHULZ]

GALANTINI, HIPPOLYTUS, BL. (1565–1619), founder at Florence in 1602 of the secular Institute of Christian Doctrine. A devout layman, physically unable to enter religious life, he dedicated himself to teaching poor children at S. Lucia al Prato; the interest of Clement VIII enabled G. to establish his Institute. He was an early proponent of nocturnal adoration of the Blessed Sacrament. His beatification took place in 1825.

[J. R. AHERNE]

GALATIA (Gr. *Galatai,* earlier, *Keltoi*), the territory in Asia Minor occupied or controlled by Celtic invaders from Europe. In the strict sense the term refers to a relatively small geographical area in north central Asia Minor on both sides of the great bend of the Halys River occupied from the second half of the 3d cent. B.C. by Celtic invaders. This is sometimes called North Galatia. Its chief cities were Ancyra, Pessinus, and Tavium. After 64 B.C., the Galatians, under Roman protection, expanded southward and absorbed Lycaonia, Pisidia, a section of Pamphylia, and S. Phrygia. The last Galatian king bequeathed the entire territory to the Romans, who established it as the Province of Galatia. St. Paul, on his first missionary journey preached in the S portion of the Province of Galatia, i.e., in Pisidian Antioch, and in Iconium, Lystra, and Derbe of Lycaonia (Acts 13.14–14.22). On his second and third missionary journeys, he "passed through . . . Galatian Country" (Acts 16.6; 18.23); but there is no agreement as to the meaning of "Galatian" in these passages, nor is it certain to whom the Epistle to the *Galatians was addressed. BIBLIOGRAPHY: G. E. Wright and F. V. Filson, *Westminster Historical Atlas to the Bible* (rev. ed., 1956) 95–97.

[J. A. PIERCE]

GALATIANS, LETTER TO THE, the ninth book in the NT canon. There is no question of its Pauline authorship, but its background and date pose problems that continue to produce divergent opinions among scholars. On his first missionary journey, Paul established Christian communities in Pisidian Antioch, Iconium, Lystra, and Derbe (Acts 13.13–14.7), cities located in a territory that the Romans, shortly after 25 B.C., had made into the Province of Galatia. Galatia proper, with its key cities of Pessinus, Ancyra, and Tavium, lay to the north. In Acts, Luke does not describe Paul as having evangelized Galatia proper, although some scholars believe that Luke implies his missionary activity there in Acts 16.6 (the second missionary journey) and 18.23 (the third missionary journey). In view of these data the question arises whether the letter to the Galatians was addressed to the churches established in the Province of Galatia on the first missionary journey (the South Galatian theory), or in Galatia proper on the second journey (the North Galatian theory). Up to the late 19th cent. the scholarly assumption was that Galatians was addressed to Christian communities in Galatia proper. On this hypothesis the Epistle is to be dated between A.D. 52, the end of Paul's second missionary journey, and A.D. 57, the end of his third journey. Some scholars suggest that it was written A.D. 54 at Ephesus. The South Galatian theory has won many adherents since it was first proposed by W. Ramsay in 1895. According to him, the Epistle was written between the conclusion of Paul's first missionary journey and the Council of Jerusalem, *c.*49. Galatians would then be the first of the Pauline Epistles. This theory escapes the difficulty that the letter does not refer to the Council or to its decree formulated for gentile Christians (Acts 15.1–29). However, the South Galatian theory does not require that the letter be dated before the Council of Jerusalem. It is quite probable that the Council was actually the private meeting between Paul and Barnabas on the one hand, and James, Cephas, and John on the other, that is summarized by Paul in Gal 2.1–10. On this supposition it could have been written during the second missionary journey, about the time of the letters to the Thessalonians, *c.*52 or 53. The fact that Paul does not refer to the decree which Luke states the apostle promulgated in South Galatia (Acts 16.4) may be taken to indicate that the Judaizers adopted a position in the Galatian communities that contravened not the letter but the spirit of this decision. Basing themselves upon the actual practice of observance of the law in the Judeo-Christian communities of Palestine, they urged the same religious way of life upon the Christians of Galatia as one leading to a more secure and fuller possession of the messianic benefits promised the sons of Abraham (see Gal 3.6–9). They attacked Paul himself as a lesser light by comparison to the Twelve, alleging that he was taking the easier way out by not requiring the observance of the law from the gentiles, an objection that the Apostle reverses against them (6.12–13). This Epistle, like those to the Corinthians, addresses itself so directly to the concrete situation in the Galatian churches that interpretation of it is rendered unusually difficult by the absence of other sources of information than the Epistle itself. But the letter is well thought out and constructed, and provides a clear insight into the Pauline doctrine of justification through faith in Christ that the Apostle's continued reflection developed at greater length and with greater profundity in his Epistle to the Romans. BIBLIOGRAPHY: D. Guthrie, *New Testament Introduction* (1961); A. Wikenhauser, *New Testament Introduction* (tr. J. Cunningham, 1958); P. Feine et al., *Einleitung in das Neue Testament* (1964).

[C. P. CEROKE]

GALBERRY, THOMAS (1833–78), Augustinian friar, fourth bp. of Hartford, Connecticut. Ordained priest (1856), his 22-year career was crowded with diverse achievement. Pastor in parishes in Pennsylvania, New York, and Massachusetts, he embodied the image of 19th-cent. American building clerics wherever he went. In 1873 he was named president of Villanova College (now Univ.), Pa., where he built the main college building, still in use. The first provincial chapter of the Augustinians in the U.S. elected him first provincial superior in 1874. Named bp. of Hartford by Pius IX, an appointment he tried vainly to refuse, he was consecrated in 1876. Death came suddenly, ending a brief but vigorous term in a growing diocese. BIBLIOGRAPHY: T. Purcell, "Thomas Galberry," *Tagastan* 5 (1941) 5–14.

[J. R. AHERNE]

GALDINUS, ST. (*c.* 1100–76), a notable preacher who combated the Victorine schism and the Catharist heresy. He is still venerated in Milan for the work he did in rebuilding that city ravaged by Emperor Frederick Barbarossa. G. died while delivering a sermon and was canonized by Alexander III whose firm support he had been. BIBLIOGRAPHY: Butler 2:122–123; A. Rimoldi, Bibl Sanct 5:1359–60.

[M. A. WINKLEMAN]

GALEN (c.130–*c.*200), physician, after whom is named Galenic medicine, which relied mainly on simple vegetable drugs, and also the Galenian or fourth figure of the syllogism. G. studied at Pergamum, Smyrna, Alexandria and practiced in Rome where he was physician to Marcus Aurelius. He became the authority for East and West on medicine, anatomy, and physiology for many centuries. His observations were recorded with great clarity, and relatively few superstitions crept into his theories and conclusions. He saw God as the artificer of the human body; his philosophy, in which he followed Plato in some respects, Aristotle in most, was also his theology. He was acquainted with Judaism and Christianity but accepted neither.

[H. JACK]

GALEN, CLEMENS AUGUSTINUS VON (1878–1946), German cardinal. He was educated by Jesuits in Feldkirch and at the theological college in Innsbruck, was ordained in 1904, became bp. of Münster in 1933, and was made cardinal in 1946. He opposed Hitler's attacks on the Church as well as the euthanasia and sterilization laws of his regime. He was called the "Lion of Münster," and was frequently threatened with arrest but never taken into custody because of Hitler's fear of popular reaction. He was also critical of occupation forces after the war when he thought them guilty of injustices. BIBLIOGRAPHY: H. Portmann, *Cardinal von Galen* (tr. R. L. Sedgwick, 1957).

[M. A. GALLIN]

GALERIUS (*c.*250–311), Roman emperor of the East from 305. G., a shepherd who rose to generalship in the Roman army, was made Caesar in 293 by Diocletian and given the name Gaius Galerius Valerius Maximianus. He obtained decisive victories over the Germanic tribes on the Danube and later over the Persians. Cruel and suspicious by nature, and violent in his hatred of Christianity, he purged the army of Christian officers and, according to Lactantius and Eusebius, influenced Diocletian to inaugurate the worst 8 years of persecution in the history of the early Church. When Diocletian retired in 305 (some say G. dictated the plan), G. succeeded him as Augustus in the East. In 311 he acknowledged the failure of the persecution. In the name of the regents he promulgated an edict that admitted the right of Christians to exist, allowed them to meet for worship, and encouraged their suffrages for the empire and its rulers. In the West, this edict merely gave legitimacy to what already existed in practice; in the East, it freed prisoners, restored exiles, and brought back religious observances. BIBLIOGRAPHY: H. Mattingly, CAH 12:297–351; W. Ensslin, *ibid.*, 351–382; N. H. Baynes, *ibid.*, 646–677.

[M. J. SUELZER]

GALFRIDUS, see GEOFFREY OF VINSAUF.

GALGAL, see GILGAL.

GALGANI GEMMA, ST. (1878–1903), Italian mystic and stigmatic. Her short life and the phenomena associated with her have drawn wide attention to G. Ill-health of a serious nature accompanied her whole life. Cured by prayers to the Passionist St. Gabriel, she sought admission as a Passionist nun but was refused. G. received the stigmata, frequent visions, and briefly torment from Satan. Her cultus was immediate and widespread. In 1933 she was beatified and in 1940 canonized in spite of some opposition. BIBLIOGRAPHY: M. St. Michael, *Portrait of St. Gemma* (1950); *Letters of St. Gemma Galgani* (tr. Germano di San Stanislao, 1947).

[J. R. AHERNE]

GALIANI, FERDINANDO (1728–87), Neapolitan political economist and diplomat. A "little harlequin with the head of a Machiavelli on his shoulders," he was a priest favored by Benedict XIV, and a trusted assistant to Bernardo *Tanucci.

[H. JACK]

GALICIA, a region of E. central Europe, once an Austrian crown land, then a part of the Republic of Poland, and since World War II, a part of the Ukrainian Soviet Socialist Republic. The chief city, Lvov, is also the seat of abps. of the Latin, Armenian, and Ukrainian rites. In times past, the cities were populated mostly by Poles and Polonized Ukrainians of the Latin rite while the peasants of the countryside were Ukrainians of the Byzantine-Slavonic rite. Mentioned for the first time in the Chronicle of Nestor, Galicia or Hailach was a small kingdom with a metropolitan in the 12th century.

After the Council of Florence in 1431, movements began in the W Russian lands for resumption of communion with the Latin Church. Galicia did not participate in the Union of Brest of 1596, since both Balaban of Lvov, and Kopastinski of Przemysl, were the only Ukrainian bps. siding against their metropolitan with Constantine Ostrogsky. Within a cent., however, Galicia joined the Catholic Church of the Byzantine rite. Because they fell to Austria in the partitions of Poland, the Galicians alone remained faithful to the Union, while their Ukrainian and White Russian brethren farther N were forcibly aggregated to the Moscow patriarchate. Finally, after World War II, in 1947 Galicia was annexed to the Soviet Republic of the Ukraine. The Latin and Armenian sees have been vacant under Soviet rule, and the Ukrainian abp. has been in exile. The Church has been forced to submit to the Moscow patriarch, a jurisdiction neither the Galicians nor their forebears had ever known before.

Of the five million Galicians, only one and one-half million, living in the W hemisphere and Australia, are free to profess the faith of their fathers; the others in the Soviet Union are nominally Orthodox. The Orthodox metropolitan of Kiev now adds the name of Galicia to his title.

[A. WALKER]

GALILEE (Heb. *Galil,* circle, district or province, a shortened form of *Gelil hăggoyim,* the district or province of the nations). The full name, the Province of the nations, occurs in Is 9.1 and is noted in Mt 4.15 as Galilee of the Nations. Galilee was the northwestern-most sector of Palestine. Its N portion is mountainous, its S, hilly. As its name indicates, the inhabitants were anciently of mixed non-Israelitic origins. The territory was conquered and its population deported by Tiglath-Pileser III in 732 B.C. (cf. 2 Kg 15.29). Many Jews settled in lower Galilee after the Maccabean wars. After the Roman conquest of 63 B.C., the capital of this semi-independent sector was Sepphoris, although technically it was a part of the Province of Syria. It was placed under Hyrcanus II and later under Herod the Great. Still later (4 B.C.–39 A.D.), it was a part of the tetrarchy of Perea which was ruled by Herod Antipas. Herod Agrippa governed it from 39 to 44. It was then ruled by the Roman Procurator along with Samaria, Judea, and Idumea until the Jewish revolt of 66. Nazareth in Galilee was the town in which Jesus grew up. Galilee was the initial and principal scene of the preaching of Jesus, according to the Synoptics. Many towns of Galilee are mentioned in the Gospel: Nazareth, Cana, Bethsaida, Capharnaum, Corozain, Tiberias, Naim, and Magdala. BIBLIOGRAPHY: Orchard 55c, 57hi, 58dx, 63, 65b, 70b, 74x, 121x, 222h, 228d, 233g, 234b, etc.

[J. A. PIERCE]

GALILEE, type of porch at the entrance of English medieval curches used as a chapel for penitents and as an accessory room.

GALILEE, SEA OF, a somewhat heart-shaped fresh water lake about 13 mi long (N to S) and 7½ mi. wide (E to W). This fresh water lake is known by many names within the NT: the Sea of Galilee (Mt 4.18; Mk 1.16), the Sea of Tiberias (Jn 6.1; 21.1), and the Lake of Genesareth (Lk 5.1). Today it is known as the Bahr Ṭabarîyeh. This lake lies 700 ft. below sea level. Its depth ranges from 160 to 230 ft, and it is surrounded by hills on all sides. It is subject to sudden violent storms (cf. Mk 4.35–41; Mt 8.23–27). Its waters abound with fish today and anciently it was the scene of miraculous draughts of fish (cf. Jn 21.4–6). Capharnaum lies on its N shore, Tiberias and Magdala on its W shore. BIBLIOGRAPHY: L. H. Grollenberg, *Atlas of the Bible* (1963) 150.

[J. A. PIERCE]

GALILEI, ALESSANDRO (1691–1737), Italian architect of the Corsini Chapel in St. John Lateran, Rome. The chapel of Greek cross plan has a Baroque dome of polychromed and sculptural ornament. G. won the commission for the façade of St. John Lateran, which he designed in a severely classical style reversing the areas of mass and space of Maderno's plan for St. Peter's. In his façade for S. Giovanni dei Fiorentini (1734) G. reverts to earlier forms.

[M. J. DALY]

GALILEO (Galileo Galilei; 1564–1642), Italian mathematician, physicist, astronomer. As a lecturer at Pisa (1589–92), then at Padua (1592–1610), he became famous through his scientific discoveries, and from 1610, under the patronage of Cosimo II de' Medici, was resident at Arcetri near Florence. G. wrote on hydrostatic balance, on the laws of gravity and of dynamics; with a telescope he constructed himself, he discovered mountains on the lunar surface, the stellar structure of the Milky Way, the satellites of Jupiter, the phases of Venus, and the sunspots. G.'s importance to the methodology of modern science was his insistence on the mathematical formulation of data attained by experimental observation. His conflict with Church authority is cited as a classic instance of ecclesiastics exceeding their competence, and of religious dogmatism retarding scientific progress.

The Galileo case centered on his defense of the Copernican, heliocentric system against the then accepted geocentric systems of Aristotle and Ptolemy. His *Starry Messenger* (*Sidereus nuntius,* 1610), which claimed his astronomical discoveries as proof that the sun, not the earth, is the center of the universe, provoked opposition from the

Aristotelian academicians. With his *Letters on Sunspots* (1613), however, affirming the Copernican system not just as an hypothesis but as true, the controversy became theological: he was accused of contradicting such biblical passages as Jos 10.12–13; Ps 103.5; Ec 1.5. He went to Rome in 1615 to defend his position. In Feb. 1616 the Holy Office censured heliocentrism as heretical, and G. was forbidden to maintain or teach the truth of the Copernican system; in March the Congregation of the Index proscribed all writings attempting to harmonize the Copernican system with the Bible. After a series of conversations with his friend Pope Urban VIII in 1624, G. spent 6 years preparing his *Dialogue of the Two Chief World Systems,* published in 1632 with the approval of censors. Urban, apparently regarding the publication as a betrayal of confidence, appointed an investigatory commission. Charged with violating the 1616 ban, G. arrived in Rome in Feb. 1633; his book was put on the Index and he was condemned as suspect of heresy. On his knees he had to renounce the Copernican system; the prison sentence imposed was not carried out, but he spent the rest of his days under house arrest in his villa near Florence, working and writing. G. never achieved a conclusive demonstration of the system which his experimental observations supported. The error of the ecclesiastics who censured him as was a literalism that ascribed to the Scriptures a scientific exactness that they do not have. BIBLIOGRAPHY: J. J. Langford, *Galileo, Science and the Church* (1966, rev. 1971); G. De Santilla, *Crime of Galileo* (1953); M. Osler, "Galileo, Motion and Essence," *Isis* 64(1973) 504–509; D. Stillman, *Galileo Studies: Personality, Tradition, and Revolution* (1970).

[T. EARLY]

GALITZIN, ELIZABETH (1797–1843), figure in the history of the American religious of the Sacred Heart. She was a Russian princess, convert from the Russian Orthodox Church, who joined the Society of the Sacred Heart at Metz in 1826. Elected assistant general at a general council of the congregation in Rome, 1839, she came to the U.S. to impose sweeping changes in the religious rule approved by that council. She visited foundations in Missouri and Louisiana, exercising her authority somewhat imperiously. But in 1843 when the original rule was reconfirmed by Gregory XVI, she was given permission to return to the U.S. to rectify matters. She died while ministering to yellow fever victims in Louisiana.

[J. R. AHERNE]

GALL, ST. (*c.*560–*c.*630), Irish missionary. G. left for the Continent (*c.*590) as a missionary with St. *Columban,, under whose care he had been placed as a child in the Abbey of Bangor. He followed Columban to Bregenz on Lake Constance, where at first they worked together. After 610 G. lived as a hermit and as an apostle to the Alamanni. A century after the Abbey of *Sankt Gallen was begun at the site of G.'s hermitage. BIBLIOGRAPHY: C. Boillon, BiblSanct 6:15–19; Butler 4:126–128.

[J. R. RIVELLO]

GALL OF CLERMONT, ST. (d. 551), bishop. According to his nephew, *Gregory of Tours, he was the son of a wealthy Gallo-Roman senator and became a monk at Cournon. Later as priest, G. served first at the cathedral at Clermont, then at the court of Theodoric I of Austrasia. He succeeded Bp. Quintian to the see of Clermont (*c.*526), where his virtues and miracles won popular veneration. BIBLIOGRAPHY: Butler 3:3–4; P. Viard, BiblSanct 6:20.

[G. M. COOK]

GALLA PLACIDIA, MAUSOLEUM OF (A.D. 425–450), mausoleum of Galla Placidia, Theodosius' daughter, in Ravenna (city of the greatest 5th and 6th-cent. mosaics in Italy) and decorated with early Christian or pre-Byzantine mosaics of greatest magnificence. It is cruciform in plan with a square tower at the crossing covering the inner dome, the exterior severe walls, subtly relieved by blind arcades, the interior walls sheathed with colored marbles—every inch of the barrel vaulted ceiling (and dome) grandiose with scintillating gold and colored glass mosaics. In the deep blue dome, star-spangled in gold, glows the great gold cross and above the entrance in the glorious lunette is the Good Shepherd—a youthful Christ accompanied by six sheep in an idealized Hellenistic landscape. The other walls show martyrs, fountains, doves, chalices. A dark interior where palpitating, floating wicks flash from tiny facets of an early "imperfect," undulating wall surface creating forever moving, vital color sensations of bejewelled splendor, communicates the experience of the mysticism of intangible spiritual realitites in a pre-Byzantine glory. The Sarcophagi of Galla Placidia and Honorius are recessed in the arms of the cross plan. BIBLIOGRAPHY: F.W. Deichmann, *Frühchristliche Bauten und Mosaiken von Ravenna* (1958).

[M. J. DALY]

GALLAGHER, HUGH PATRICK (1815–82), Irish missionary who crowded two careers into his 67 years. G. was ordained in the U.S. in 1840. During his years in the diocese of Pittsburgh he is credited with bringing the Sisters of Mercy to the diocese and he edited the weekly *Pittsburgh Catholic*. At Loretto he encouraged the Sisters of Mercy to establish schools, the Franciscan Brothers to open St. Francis College. As a theologian at the First Plenary Council of Baltimore, G. met Bp. Alemany of San Francisco who persuaded him to go to the West Coast. In his new career he became a familiar figure in the mining camps and the city of San Francisco. His building of churches throughout N California and Nevada was prodigious. In 1853 he established the *Catholic Standard,* the first Catholic paper on the Pacific Coast. He brought to California Irish nuns and aided in their founding of schools, orphanages, and St. Mary's

Hospital in San Francisco. When a bank closed he took over at their request the savings of miners and laborers. In 1861 he and his brother established the first parochial school in the diocese.

[J. R. AHERNE]

GALLAGHER, SIMON FELIX (1756–1825), missionary. Ordained in Ireland, G. came to America and was sent by Bp. Carroll of Baltimore to Charleston, S.C. as pastor. He was a popular speaker and a teacher at the College of Charleston. For years he was in the center of the lay trustee controversy in Charleston, coming to a position of opposition to the new bp. of Baltimore and was suspended. His parish was placed under interdict. Bp. J. *England, appointed (1820) to the new diocese of Charleston, reinstated G., but in 1822 the maverick priest left for Florida, then Cuba, and finally New Orleans where he died. BIBLIOGRAPHY: P. K. Guilday, *Life and Times of John England* (2 v., 1927, repr. 1969).

[J. R. AHERNE]

GALLEGOS, FERNANDO (Gallego; fl. 1467–1507), Castilian painter working in the Hispano-Flemish style and injecting a subjective Spanish fervor. A very early *Crucifixion* and *Pietà* (Madrid) show primitive, distorted figures in a precise technique. Later works are mature and dignified—(*The Altarpiece of S. Ildefonso,* 1467) and an *Enthroned Virgin and Child* (Salamanca; the Madonna, Botticellian in gravity). From G.'s workshop are the *Main Altarpiece of S. Lorenzo, Via Crucis* and *Last Judgment*. A Francisco Gallegos who probably at times collaborated with G. painted the *Altarpiece of S. Catalina* (Salamanca). Francisco's works are gaudy in color and awkward in form.

[M. J. DALY]

GALLICAN ARTICLES, FOUR, a declaration of the French Clergy in 1682 asserting the freedom of the French Church. The Declaration was issued by an assembly of bps. and lower clergy, convoked by Louis IV, and representing itself as expressing the mind of the entire French clergy. The Articles stated that the king of France was independent of papal authority in temporal matters, that general councils were superior to popes, that the ancient liberties of the French Church could not be violated, and that individual popes could err (i.e., their judgments were not irreformable) though the Church was indefectible because of a reforming process helped along by the remonstrances of the assemblies of the clergy and the king. Behind this declaration was the long history of *Gallicanism, both political—that the French king had no superior within his kingdom—and ecclesiastical—that the French Church and particularly its bps. had broad freedom of action. The immediate issue was the *régale:* the claim of the French king to the income of vacant bishoprics. In line with his policy of increasing royal power and institutional uniformity Louis XIV tried to extend the *régale* to include dioceses incorporated into France since the Concordat of 1516. Pope Innocent XI chose to resist this extension. The Gallican Articles were the result. Difficulties were created on both sides by those who preferred coercion to Louis XIV's proposed negotiations. By the time of Innocent's death in 1689 the excesses on both sides had created a desire for settlement. In 1690, by the constitution *Inter multiplices,* Alexander VIII condemned the Articles. In 1693 Louis XIV had the French bps. officially withdraw those aspects of the Articles derogatory to the papacy. The Pope in return allowed some extension of the *régale.* Despite this compromise the Gallican Articles continued to be accepted by many in France. BIBLIOGRAPHY: J. B. Wolf, *Louis XIV* (1968).

[J. M. HAYDEN]

GALLICAN CHANT, plainsong used in French liturgy before the introduction of the Gregorian chant in the 8th century. Since *neume notation was not widely used, there exist no examples of pure Gallican chant. But the Roman rite incorporated some Gallican elements, e.g., the hymns *Crux fidelis* and *Pange lingua* of the old Good Friday liturgy.

[D. J. SMUCKER]

GALLICAN CONFESSION (*Confessio Gallicana, Confession de foi,* French Confession), the confessional standard adopted at Paris (1559) by the First National Synod of the *Reformed Church in France. The original draft in 35 articles was sent from Geneva by John Calvin, and revised by Antoine de la Roche Chandieu (1534–91); it was presented to Charles IX at the Conference of *Poissy (1561). A second revision in 40 articles was made by the 7th national synod of the French Reformed Church at La Rochelle in 1571 under T. *Beza; hence the document is sometimes called the Confession of La Rochelle. These original versions were all written in French. The Gallican Confession ranks as the clearest credal summary of Calvinism. Throughout its difficult history after the revocation of the Edict of Nantes in 1685, the Reformed Church in France adhered to the Confession. A new declaration of faith was adopted in 1872 and modified in 1936. BIBLIOGRAPHY: Schaff Creeds 1:490–498.

[N. H. MARING]

GALLICAN PSALTER, see PSALTER, GALLICAN.

GALLICAN RITES, the name under which the diverse liturgical forms in use in the first millennium in W Europe, excepting Rome, are grouped. Many of these rites were to be found in Gaul, but the term is not to be narrowly restricted to those rites only. Their origins are uncertain, esp. since they do not present a single form of worship but are remarkable for their diversity. The Orient, Milan, and Rome have all been suggested as places where these rites developed and from which they were translated to Gaul. Certainly a truly distinctive Gallican liturgy does not appear until after the 5th cent., when local differences in the rites began to emerge. Likewise, the sources available for a study of these rites, missals, and lectionaries, are fragmentary and date no further back than the 5th century. The disappearance of these rites from general liturgical usage, even though today one can still find a very limited and modified survival of them, occurred under the Carolingian rulers. Charlemagne's imposition of the Roman rite in Gaul to counter the growing diversity of liturgical forms was a primary factor in the sudden decline of these rites. Certainly by the end of the 8th cent., use of the Gallican liturgy, at least in France, had disappeared for the most part. The neo-Gallican rites introduced in France in the 18th and 19th cent. under the influence of Gallicanism have practically no connection with these earlier rites.

The rites grouped loosely under the designation Gallican, include certain more specific types of rite. Among these are the *Ambrosian rite, now thoroughly Romanized, which is still to be found in use in the ecclesiastical province of Milan where it was once prominent; the Celtic rite used among the Irish and Scots until the 7th cent.; the Gallican rites (in a narrower sense) found in the Frankish kingdom; and *Mozarabic liturgy which prevailed in Spain until the 15th century. In evident contrast to the starkness of Roman liturgical rites, the Gallican liturgies evidence a marked ceremonial splendor. They contain a number of oriental liturgical characteristics, e.g., the chanting of the *Trisagion and Benedictus, and the use of the *diptych for the dead during Mass. They also manifest a feature peculiarly their own, the addition of variable prayer forms to the central eucharistic proclamation. In this last respect, they are known to have influenced subsequent forms of the Roman Mass. BIBLIOGRAPHY: J. Quasten, NCE 6:258–262; N. Maurice-Denis and R. Boulet, *Catholicisme* 4:1722–28; H. Leclercq, DACL 6.1:473–593.

[B. ROSENDALL]

GALLICANISM, a 19th-cent. term for various assertions of the freedom of the French Church (*l'église gallicane*) from papal authority. Exponents of Gallicanism held that the power of the pope in France, particularly in temporal matters but also in matters of doctrine and discipline, should be limited. Though the theory was formulated in the 14th cent., it was claimed to have historical basis in ancient privileges. The most consistent advocate of the doctrine was the Paris Parlement, which after 1418, despite variations by both king and clergy, never relaxed its support. Royal power had developed from the late 10th century. At the same time the papacy asserted its claims to spiritual and temporal sovereignty over kings. Pope Boniface VIII tried to interfere with King Philip IV in the early 14th cent., and in reaction Gallicanism assumed a political aspect, contending that the king had no temporal superior within his kingdom.

In the last years of the 14th and the beginning of the 15th cent. so-called ecclesiastical Gallicanism developed. Appointments to benefices and bishoprics were declared free from papal control in an attempt to end the *Great Western Schism and bring reform to the French Church by restoring election to these positions. In practice these appointments fell into the hands of the king and, to some extent, of the nobles. This procedure was transformed into a theory by the Paris Parlement, accepted by the French clergy through the Pragmatic Sanction of Bourges (1438) and by the Pope through the Concordat of Bologna (1516).

In the late 15th and early 16th cent. the question of the legitimacy of tyrannicide added a new dimension to the problem and led to the strengthening of Gallicanism, as did attempts to introduce the decrees of the Council of Trent, since they would have interfered with the powers granted to the king by the Concordat of 1516. During the Wars of Religion in the second half of the 16th cent. the final theoretical developments took place. Popes Sixtus V and Gregory XIV were trying to prevent Henry IV from becoming a king of France because he was a Huguenot. The Popes had the suppport of the extreme Catholic League, but more and more Frenchmen, sickened by 30 years of civil war, were moving toward support of Henry IV. Though the latter's absolution by the Pope in 1595 ended the practical difficulties, the Gallican theories were greatly strengthened during the 10 years of struggle over the question, particularly through the work of Pierre *Pithou.

By the early 17th cent. the French bps. in their attempts to reform the French Church were becoming ultramontane, but the theories of the Parlement of Paris were maintained by the third estate at the Estates General of 1614. As the power of the king increased during the 17th cent. so did support for Gallicanism. Louis XIV was able to make it the accepted theory in France, and though he was forced to moderate the Four *Gallican Articles of 1682, Gallicanism remained a strong force throughout the *ancien régime*. Many of the partisans of Jansenism were Gallicans. Examples of Gallicanism in the 18th cent. include the expulsion of the Jesuits in 1764 and the reformation and suppression of a number of religious orders on royal initiative in 1768. The Synod of *Pistoia reasserted Gallican principles. After the Napoleonic era, Gallicanism lingered in France. The discussions and declarations of Vatican Council I clearly marked its incompatibility with RC teaching.

Though the ideological content of Gallicanism varied with time and group, its main points included the following: (1) The pope has no temporal power within France. He cannot prevent the legal heir from ascending the throne, release the French from obedience to the king, interfere with the rights of the crown or the exercise of duties by royal officials, or exercise absolute authority over the French clergy. (2) The king is the only head of the state. He is the protector of the Church, can convoke councils to handle discipline and temporal affairs, can ask the clergy to contribute money for the general needs of the kingdom, can reform or suppress religious communities. His courts have jurisdiction over all cases not exclusively spiritual. (3) In the spiritual realm the king has power to decide whether or not papal pronouncements are in accord with those of former councils already accepted in France. (4) Gallicans also claimed that a general council was superior to the pope, whose judgments are not irreformable; truths of faith are guaranteed by the consent of the faithful. (5) Gallican bps. claimed the right to be judges of doctrine and discipline in their own domains, independent of the Pope. BIBLIOGRAPHY: V. Martin, *Les Origines du Gallicanisme* (2 v., 1939); *idem, Le Gallicanisme politique et le clergé de France* (1929).

[J. M. HAYDEN]

GALLIENUS (*c.*218–268), Roman Emperor from 253. Publius Licinius Egnatius Gallienus was appointed coregent by his father Valerian in 253 and soon checked the Alemanni on the border of Italy and the Heruli attacking Greece. As sole emperor after 260 he put through important political, military, and religious reforms. He forbade senators to hold any military commands and created an independent mounted corps. His edict of 260, the first imperial decree of toleration, stopped persecution of the Christians and restored to them their bps., churches, and cemeteries. G. was cultured, perceptive, and energetic. Later tradition turned him into a tyrant. His end came at the hands of his own officers while he was preparing to oppose the usurper Aureolus. BIBLIOGRAPHY: A. Alföldi, CAH (1939) 12:181–231; E. Manni, *L'impero di Gallieno* (1949).

[M. J. SUELZER]

GALLIFET, JOSEPH FRANÇOIS DE (1663–1749), French Jesuit, promoter of devotion to the Sacred Heart of Jesus. G. entered the Society of Jesus in 1678; was drawn to the Sacred Heart devotion by Bl. Claude de *la Colombière. During his priestly life G. established over 700 confraternities of the Sacred Heart, and published several works on the devotion. He was charged at Rome with obtaining approval of a liturgical feast of the Sacred Heart; but the petition was only granted in 1765.

[T. C. O'BRIEN]

GALLIO, JUNIUS ANNAEUS (*c.*3 B.C.–*c.*66 A.D.), according to Acts 18.12–17, Roman proconsul at Achaea when Paul was preaching in Corinth. The dating of his tenure on the basis of a surviving letter of Emperor Tiberius to the city of Delphi permits fixing the time of Paul's work with the Corinthians from 50 to the summer of 51 A.D.

[T. C. O'BRIEN]

GALLITZIN, AMALIA (1748–1806), Catholic leader in Westphalia, Germany; mother of D. *Gallitzin. She was the Prussian Countess von Schmettau; married Prince Demetrius Gallitzin, a Russian, in 1768; bore him two children; separated from him in 1775. At Münster she became a member of a group devoted to the pursuit of learning; she gradually turned back to the Catholic faith in which she had been baptized, her final conversion coming after a serious illness in 1786. Her son, who had been reared in the Russian Orthodox Church, followed her example. The remaining years of her life were devoted to Catholic causes.

[T. C. O'BRIEN]

GALLITZIN, DEMETRIUS AUGUSTINE (1770–1840), Russian prince, convert, RC missionary. Reared in the Hague where his father was Russian ambassador and intimate friend of the French Encyclopedists, and later in Münster where his mother was of the circle of Goethe and Jacobi, he became a convert to Catholicism at the age of sixteen. His short career as aide-de-camp of the Austrian General von Lillien was ended by a decree banning foreigners from service. Travels in the West Indies and the U.S. brought him into contact with Bp. Carroll in Baltimore who had a profound influence on the young nobleman. The Prince, now using the commoner name of Augustine Smith, entered St. Mary's Seminary and was ordained in 1795, the first to receive his full theological training in the new republic.

G. volunteered for missionary work, and in 1796, using large remittances from his family to buy and build up the territory, he founded a Catholic colony named Loretto on the Pennsylvania border at the summit of the Alleghenies. From here he covered the whole countryside including Indian territory. In 1802 the Prince became an American citizen, still using his incognito, Smith. Loretto was a well-run colony despite a somewhat strong hand exercised by G., but he suffered from harsh criticism even by those he befriended. Bp. Carroll, however, continued to support him firmly. Deciding it prudent to reclaim his own name against the day of his inheritance, G. petitioned the Pennsylvania legislature to revert to his own name and title. But because of his conversion and naturalization, the Russian government disinherited G., and he was unable to pay off his debts. In 1827 he began a public appeal for donations to help pay off the land and development debts. Gregory XVI and Charles Carroll were among many who made contributions to liquidate the debt of Loretto. At the end of his life all creditors had been paid. In spite of the weight of his daily responsibility he wrote a series of letters published under the title *Defence of Catholic Principles* (1816) in answer to an attack by a local minister's sermon. The brochure was widely circulated in the U.S. and Europe and is distinguished for its polemical skill and broad tolerance. Though he showed no interest in preferment, he was considered for the Sees of Cincinnati, Philadelphia, and Detroit. The career that had begun in the glittering courts and literary centers of Europe ended in the log cabin in the heights of the Alleghenies with crowds paying tribute to the lonely shepherd of Loretto. BIBLIOGRAPHY: D. Sargent, *Mitri* (1945).

[J. R. AHERNE]

GALLO, GIOVANNI (fl. 16th cent.), Italian graphic artist (by some scholars identified with the artist Jean Salomon of Lyons). G. is known for three colored woodcuts: *Descent from the Cross, Holy Family,* and *Perseus as Slayer of Medusa,* which are signed "Johannes Gallus."

[M. J. DALY]

GALLO, ANDRÉS MARÍA (1791–1863), Colombian patriot and priest whose exploits can be gleaned from his memoirs: *Reminiscencias del Canónigo doctor Andrés M. Gallo.* He served briefly in the republican army during the war for independence, attaining the rank of military commander; was briefly under sentence of death when the royalists returned to power in 1816; served as a member of the court of justice, of the local legislature (Tunja), and of the federal congress. A student of both law and theology, he was ordained in 1818, and aided Bolívar's troops with supplies while serving as pastor of Ramiriquí; and later served as chaplain of the military staff. Throughout his life he alternated between various pastoral and political offices. Though declining the episcopacy, he was able to defend the Church against the dictator, General de Mosquera, in his capacity of vicar general of Bogotá.

[E. J. DILLON]

GALLO, MARIA FRANCESCA OF THE FIVE WOUNDS, ST. (1715–91), Italian mystic. From childhood she evinced a spirit of penance and devotion to Christ's Passion. In 1731 she joined the Third Order of St. Francis but continued to live in her parents' home. A stigmatic, she gave herself to the care of the sick and the poor and endured severe illnesses, misunderstanding, spiritual aridity, and other trials. She was canonized in 1867. BIBLIOGRAPHY: D. Ambrasi, BiblSanct 8:1065–67; M. P. Adami, *S. Maria Francesca delle Piaghedi N.S.* (1957).

[M. J. SUELZER]

GALLUS, JACOBUS, see HÄNDL, JACOB.

GALTIER, PAUL (1872–1961), Jesuit theologian. G. taught at Enghien, Belgium (1907–38) and the Gregorian Univ., Rome (1939–57). Three problems in particular received his close attention: the nature of the divine indwelling, the consciousness of Christ, and the sacrament of *penance in the early Church. G. maintained that the Trinity truly dwelt in man but, as with all operations **ad extra,* the Persons acted as from a single source of operation and no special relationship with the individual Persons was established. He also proposed a controversial and now abandoned theory on the unity of the human and divine consciousness of Christ. His work on the origins of penance demonstrated that the early Church regarded this sacrament as a "second baptism" and attributed a corresponding efficacy to it.

[T. M. MCFADDEN]

GALTON, FRANCIS (1822–1911), English scientist, explorer, and anthropometrist. A Birmingham man of Quaker ancestry and a cousin of Charles Darwin, after going down from Cambridge, he did hospital work, traveled extensively at first for hunting and pleasure, afterwards for serious African exploration. In 1857 he settled down in London to pursue his anthropological researches. He is the initiator of scientific eugenics, and the author of Galton's Law, which proposes to account for ancestral heredity and assigns to each of one's parents a contribution of one-fourth to the characters of their offspring. In his analysis he was inclined to underestimate environmental factors. He was a pioneer in the use of fingerprints for identification. His investigations into the danger of marrying an heiress, who as the sole inheritor of unprolific parents might tend to be infertile, are of interest. BIBLIOGRAPHY: D. W. Forrest, *Francis Galton: The Life and Work of a Victorian Genius* (1974).

[T. GILBY]

GALVIN, EDWARD J. (1882–1956) bp. founder of the *Columban Fathers. Born in Ireland and ordained there in 1909, he served in the U.S. before volunteering for the missions in China in 1912. Working with French Vincentians until they were recalled in World War I, G. established the St. Columban's Foreign Mission Society in 1916. It drew Irish and American candidates. G. went to Hanyang when in 1920 that area was committed to his congregation; he was successively *prefect apostolic, *vicar apostolic and bishop (1946). When the Communists overran the province in 1949 G. was put under house arrest. Tried in 1952, he was expelled from China. He died in Ireland. BIBLIOGRAPHY: R. Reilly, *Christ's Exile: Life of Bishop Edward J. Galvin* (1958).

[J. R. AHERNE]

GALVIN, WILLIAM LELAND (1886–1960), civic leader. A native of Baltimore and a lawyer, G. was prominent in civic affairs in Maryland serving on the State Department of Public Works and the Maryland Planning Commission. He served as treasurer of The Catholic Univ. of America for 22 years. G.'s main interest lay in hospitals. He served on the board of six Baltimore hospitals and was founding director of Maryland Hospital Service (Blue Cross.) Active in numerous Catholic charities, he was made a Knight Commander of St. Gregory and a Knight of the Holy Sepulcher.

[J. R. AHERNE]

GAMALIEL (Heb. Gămeliel, a name meaning God has rendered [good] to me). (1) Gamaliel, son of Pedahzur, leader-commander of the tribe of Manasseh, was a helper to Moses during Israel's wandering in the desert (Num 1.10; 2.20; 7.45–59; 10.23). (2) Gamaliel, the grandson of Rabbi Hillel, called Rabban Gamaliel the Elder to distinguish him from his grandson, Gamaliel II. He was a famous rabbi of the Pharisaic sect, a member of the Sanhedrin, who taught St. Paul the "exact observance of the Law" (Acts 22.3). He suggested the release of the Apostles by the Sanhedrin who "wanted to put them to death" on the plea that the Christian movement might be from God (Acts 5.29–39). A Christian legend (*Clementine Recognitions,* 1.65) suggests that he secretly became a Christian, but Jewish tradition insists that he was one of the most renowned rabbis before the destruction of the Temple. BIBLIOGRAPHY: J. Munck, *Acts of the Apostles,* (*Anchor Bible* 31, 1967) 48–51.

[J. A. PIERCE]

GAMBACORTA, PETER, BL., see PETER OF PISA, BL.

GAMBARA, LATTANZIO (1530–74), Italian painter of Brescia who painted among many fresco cycles those in the nave of the Parma cathedral, reflecting the mannerism of Parmigianino.

[M. J. DALY]

GAMBETTA, LÉON MICHEL (1838–82), French statesman. G. was a fiery orator, the leading republican statesman during the formative years of the Third Republic, who advocated freedom of the press, separation of Church and State, tax reform, and universal suffrage. BIBLIOGRAPHY: H. Stannard, *Gambetta and the Foundation of the Third Republic* (1921); J. P. T. Bury, *Gambetta and the National Defense* (1936, repr. 1971); *idem, Gambetta and the Making of the Third Republic (1973).*

[D. R. PENN]

GAMBLING, or betting, means risking something of value with a chance of winning more if one successfully predicts or guesses the outcome of some uncertain future event. The uncertain event can be anything from a roll of dice to a ball game or a presidential election. As distinct from "gaming" which would be betting on an event which depended on one's own skill, gambling is sometimes restricted to refer to matters of pure chance; but the term is also correctly used of both forms. Morally, gambling is indifferent and will be good and bad depending on circumstances. It is morally evil if unfair advantage is taken of the other party or if one uses money or goods belonging or due to others, esp. one's spouse or children or employer. It is taking unfair advantage if one bets on what he knows to be a certainty without warning the other party of his knowledge. Having bet on some event, it is unfair to try to bribe or persuade those involved to change the normal outcome of the event. Because gambling often leads to abuses and crime, some sects forbid it absolutely, and civil law usually controls or forbids it. BIBLIOGRAPHY: F. O'Hare, NCE, 6:276; E. Rogers, *Dictionary of Christian Ethics* (1967) 135.

[J. J. FARRAHER]

GAMMADIAE, originally the series of *Gammadion traced on the garments of Christ and the saints in early Christian iconography. By the 8th cent. the term designated the same symbols woven in purple or gold on vestments.

[T. C. O'BRIEN]

GAMMADION, a cross formed from the Greek capital letter gamma, traced four times, either intersected to form the *Swastika, or juxtaposed. This ancient symbol was adopted by Christians to signify Christ as cornerstone of the Church.

[T. C. O'BRIEN]

GAMS, PIUS (1816–92), church historian. After studies at Tübingen G. was ordained (1839) and taught history and theology at Hildesheim (1847–55) before becoming a Benedictine in Munich (1856). Besides numerous articles in journals and encyclopedias, he wrote a church history of Spain (1862–79) which is still valuable because of his understanding of patristic and early medieval events; he also compiled a lengthy *Series episcoporum* (1873) listing all known bps. of the Church.

[E. P. COLBERT]

GANDERSHEIM, CONVENT OF, former monastery of Benedictine nuns at Bad Gandersheim in Saxony. It originated in 852 in Brunshausen and was moved to Gandersheim in 856. Foundation and endowment by the Ottonian imperial family as well as other rich endowments made control over it a source of dispute until it was settled by Innocent III in 1208. In its first century the abbey developed an excellent school, represented esp. by the poet *Roswitha. At the Reformation the convent became Lutheran. It was dissolved in 1801.

[T. C. O'BRIEN]

GANDHĀRA, loosely defined region of NW India in the area now Pakistan and NE Afghanistan, famous for distinctive Graeco-Buddhist sculpture. On the trade route from India to the West, Gandhāra fell to Alexander the Great (327–26 B.C.), was successively dominated by the Mauryas of India, Bactrian Greeks, Sakos (Scythians), Parthians, and Kushāns, and was finally laid waste by the White Huns (*c.* 460). Important excavations by Sir John Marshall at Sirkap (near the ancient medical center, Taxila) discovered a royal palace, square stupa with reliefs, a Greek pediment, chaitya hall, and torana. Near Peshawar were found a Buddhist vihāra, and a great stupa built by Kaniṣhka, famous Kushan ruler, with a reliquary showing several inscriptions. Another golden reliquary from Afghanistan, round and studded with rubies, carries relief figures under arcades in the Roman manner. Buddhist sculpture at Gandhāra is of the Mahayana sect; the reliefs, an amalgam of the life of the Buddha, Jatakas, Indian deities and western iconography. The Buddha in-the-round with Western robes and halo show the head of a Greek Apollo, with wavy topknot appearing as a simple dressing of the hair, indicating a Greek artist misinterpreting the Buddhist uṣṇiṣa (swelling of the gland in intensive contemplation). Heavily bejeweled raja-like Bodhisattvas accompany the Buddha. Early forms were carved in gray schist; later ones of stucco are painted. The art of Gandhāra greatly influenced Buddhist art of Central Asia, China, and Japan, spreading by missionaries through the Khyber Pass, north over the mountains, across the Tarim Basin, finally entering China through Kansu. BIBLIOGRAPHY: B. Rowland, *Art and Architecture of India* (2d ed., 1959); *idem, Gandhāra Sculpture from Pakistan Museums* (Asia Society, 1960).

[M. J. DALY]

GANDHARVA, heavenly musician who attends the Indian gods in Hindu art. G. survived from Vedic times as servants of Indra. Apsarases are female counterparts of the male Gandharvas.

[M. J. DALY]

GANDHI, MOHANDAS KARAMCHAND (1869–1948), leader of men. G. attended Indian schools; spent 2 years at Ahmedabad University; went to London for law; was called to the bar in London in 1891. In England he came back to the Bhagavad Gita from a short-lived atheism, absorbed the Sermon on the Mount, and discovered Tolstoy, Ruskin, and Thoreau. He practiced law unsuccessfully in India, 1891–93, then went to South Africa for a business firm. Shortly after his arrival, he was put off a train on account of his color; that incident sparked a reaction that won racial equality for the Indians of South Africa and freedom for India. He was in South Africa for 21 years. The intensity of his faith enabled him to clear his life of all nonessentials, setting free the driving power that mobilized thousands of farmers, miners, and laborers into an irresistible *Satyagraha,* soul-force, that wore down the forces of injustice in the face of jails, mutilation, and death. In 1914, the Magna Charta of South African Indians achieved, he undertook the eradication of social, economic, and political injustices, and the struggle for freedom in India. In 1917, he launched his first *Satyagraha;* through the next 3 decades he used all his nonviolent resistance techniques; Satyagrahas, hartals, strikes, boycotts, noncooperation campaigns, marches, fasts, and prayer. He did not underestimate or neglect the press, conferences, personal appeal, congressional action, but used them to intensify the impact of the total "force of truth." He spent months in prison, suffered pain, contempt, derision, physical attack, and finally death for "his insatiable love of humanity." His victory was incomplete: England left India in 1947, free, but divided; religious barriers to internal peace were not leveled; but he had achieved the impossible. He provided the world with a conscience. The most important of his published works is his autobiography. BIBLIOGRAPHY: L. Fischer, *Gandhi* (1954).

GANDOLF OF BINASCO, BL. (d. *c.*1260), Franciscan hermit. He entered the order while Francis of Assisi was alive and embraced a life of solitude and rigorous penance in a hermitage in Sicily. His conspicuous sanctity won him the veneration of the Sicilians. James of Narni, 14th-cent. of Cefalù, wrote a dialogue *vita* (pub. 1632) during the process of canonization. BIBLIOGRAPHY: V. Noè, BiblSanct 6:33; Butler 2:25.

[O. J. BLUM]

GANDOLPHY, PETER (1779–1821), English Jesuit. G. became celebrated as a preacher at the Spanish Chapel in Manchester Square, London. In 1812 he published *An Exposition of Liturgy,* a work comparable to the Anglican Book of Common Prayer, in an effort to commend the Catholic faith to Anglicans. However, he was accused of heresy and suspended by Bp. W. Poynter (1762–1827). In 1817 Rome ordered him restored providing he apologize for criticisms of the bishop. His first apology was condemned by Poynter as inadequate, and he then made an unconditional apology. Disheartened, he retired the following year to his family home.

[T. EARLY]

GANESA, the elephant-headed son of Siva and Parvati, "Lord of Hosts," and remover of obstacles, with 4 arms holding his attributes—a rosary, rice bowl, goad, and tusk. He is accompanied by a mouse to deal with obstacles too small for G.'s enormous bulk.

[M. J. DALY]

GANGOLF, ST. (Gangulfus, Gengou, Gengoul; d. 760?). An illustrious native of Bourgogne, G. was left a fortune by his parents. G., raised in the military tradition, took part in the wars of Pepin the Brave. He suffered much with an unfaithful wife who refused to accept the punishment of confinement in a convent, and who succeeded in obtaining assassins to kill him in 760. He is honored as a martyr of conjugal fidelity. His cult was furthered in Germany, Italy, and England, but esp. in Varennes, France, by an account written by Roswitha in the 10th century. A tradition has him connected with the monastery of Bèze, France. The Bollandists in 1940 concluded that nothing is historically certain about G.'s death. BIBLIOGRAPHY: P. Viard, *Catholicisme,* 4:1831–32; J. Marilier, BiblSanct 6:127–128.

[N. F. GAUGHAN]

GANGRA, SYNOD OF. Held in 341, this synod issued 20 canons which described and condemned the exaggerated asceticism of Eustathius of Sebaste who had tried to impose monastic discipline on all Christians concerning dress, marriage, and abstinence. BIBLIOGRAPHY: J. Van Paassen, NCE 6:279.

[E. EL-HAYEK]

GANJIN IN TŌSHŌDAIJI, NARA, 8th-cent. Japanese lacquer sculpture, portrait of the Chinese T'ang priest

Chien-chên (Japanese, Ganjin, d. 763), who, arriving as a blind priest in Japan (753), established a proper ordination ceremony. The figure in dry lacquer technique, through poignant delineations and quiet, harmonious curves, (characteristics of Japanese realistic sculpture) conveys a deeply spiritual feeling.

[M. J. DALY]

GANO DA SIENA (fl. 14th cent.), Italian sculptor and architect who executed 2 tombs in the collegiate Church of S. Maria Assunta in Casole d'Elsa, near Siena, which show in a limited way the influence of Giovanni Pisano.

[M. J. DALY]

GÄNSBACHER, JOHANN (1778–1844), Austrian conductor and composer. As *Kapellmeister* at the Jesuit church, Innsbruck, and the cathedral of St. Stephen in Vienna (1824), G. came to know the more famous composers G. Meyerbeer and C. M. von Weber. Primarily a composer of sacred works, he wrote 35 Masses, 8 Requiems, and 2 Te Deums.

[D. J. SMUCKER]

GANSFORT, JOHANNES WESSEL (*c.* 1419–89), theologian and humanist. After early training by the Brethren of the Common Life, G. studied at Cologne, Heidelberg, Paris, and Rome. Because he attacked some teachings of the Catholic Church, some regarded him as a forerunner of the Reformation. This is, however, an oversimplification. He was deeply influenced by the *Devotio moderna* of his day, and under the protection of David, bp. of Utrecht, he spent the declining years of his life in study and the writing of ascetical works. A complete edition of his writings was published in 1614. BIBLIOGRAPHY: L. Cristiani, DTC 15.2:3531–36; Tables Générales 1772.

[H. DRESSLER]

GANSS, HENRY GEORGE (1855–1912), writer, composer. Ordained for the diocese of Pittsburgh in 1878, G. spent his life as a pastor in W Pennsylvania. He wrote on historical topics and was considered an authority on Martin Luther. Active in music, he composed the well-known hymn "Long Live the Pope" and five Masses as well as numerous hymns and songs.

[J. R. AHERNE]

GANTE, PEDRO DE (1486–1572), Flemish Franciscan and pioneer of the Mexican mission. A relative of Charles V, he arrived in Mexico in 1523 and founded one of the first elementary schools for the education of Indians. In addition to Christian doctrine the schools taught reading, writing, drawing, music, and technical skills. He was a great builder of churches and chapels. As an expert linguist and lover of the common people he exercised enormous influence among the Indians. He has been called the "first teacher of the Americas." His statue forms part of the monument to Columbus at the Paseo de la Reforma, and one of the streets of modern Mexico City bears his name. BIBLIOGRAPHY: M. Cuevas, *Historia de la Iglesia en México* (1925); Streit-Dindinger; E. A. Chavez, *El primero de los grandes educadores de las Américas, Pedro de Gante* (1941).

[P. DAMBORIENA]

GAON (pl. *geonim;* Heb. *ga'on,* glory, pride; cf. Ps 47.5, "the pride of Jacob"), title of the heads of Jewish academies at Sura and Pumbeditha in Babylonia (from 589 to 1040). The *geonim,* generally elected by the members of the academy or appointed by the exilarch (the civic leader of Babylonian Jewry), were thus honored for their contribution to the development and interpretation of the Talmud and were regarded as supreme authorities in religious matters. BIBLIOGRAPHY: E. Zolli, EncCatt 6:64; N. Ausubel, *Book of Jewish Knowledge* (1964) 175–176.

[F. BUCK]

GARAMPI, GIUSEPPE (1725–92), cardinal from 1785, scholar, prefect of the papal archives (1751), nuncio to Poland (1772) and Vienna (1782). Influenced by L. *Muratori, G. is chiefly important for his own devotion to the study of church history, for the encouragement of Catholic scholarly publications, and for the great library of valuable books and MSS. he amassed.

[T. C. O'BRIEN]

GARASSE, FRANÇOIS (1585–1631), French Jesuit polemicist. In pulpit and in print he violently and flamboyantly attacked enemies of the Society, and also the French Reformed Church. His *Somme théologique des vérités capitales de la religion chrétienne* (1625) was condemned for its intemperateness by the Sorbonne faculty of theology, and G. retired to Poitiers. There he died of the plague while ministering to its victims.

[T. C. O'BRIEN]

GARBHAGRIHA (GARBHAGRHA) Sanskrit term meaning "womb chamber" and indicating the innermost, most holy shrine room marked exteriorly by the Śikhara or tower erected over that sacred spot in Hindu temples of northern or Indo-Aryan style.

[M. J. DALY]

GARCÉS, FRANCISCO TOMÁS (1738–81), missioner, explorer. Of Spanish birth G. was ordained in 1763, proceeded to Mexico to prepare for mission work at the College of Santa Cruz de Querétaro. He was assigned to the northernmost mission, San Xavier del Bac in Arizona, Apache territory. He made several expeditions along the Gila and Colorado Rivers and became convinced that one could reach Upper California by land from Sonora. With the military commander De Anza he proceeded on a journey which led to San Gabriel Mission (near Los Angeles) and on a later expedition made important explorations to the N, finally returning to San Xavier del Bac. The Indian chief of the Gila-Colorado junction area encouraged the Spaniards to found a mission and presidio in his region. When the Spanish failed to give the chief the gifts he had expected, the Indians attacked the mission and killed G. and his companions.

[J. R. AHERNE]

GARCÉS, JULIÁN (1447–1542), missioner. Born in Spain, G. entered the Dominican Order and became preacher and confessor at the court of Emperor Charles V. In 1526 he was named to the new See of Tlaxcala (later Puebla) in Mexico. Armed with the imperial title, Protector of the Indians, he came to Mexico in 1527 where his model life enabled him to overcome the hostile Spanish officials. His record of conversions among the Indians was phenomenal. A letter G. wrote to Pope Paul III in defense of the Indians was probably the cause of the papal bull issued in their behalf in 1537.

[J. R. AHERNE]

GARCÍA VILLADA, ZACARÍAS (1879–1936), Spanish Jesuit historian executed by Leftist militia. After studies in Rome and Austria he taught history in Barcelona, wrote regularly for *Razón y Fe* (1904–33), catalogued and edited early Spanish sources (1913–35), and wrote four good popular monographs (1920–25). For 30 years he collected materials for an *Historia eclesiástica de España* (3 v. of 5; 1929–36) only to have a Leftist mob in Madrid burn his hoard (1931); parts of this work derive from introductions in the *Monumenta germaniae historica*. BIBLIOGRAPHY: E. P. Colbert, NCE 6:286.

[E. P. COLBERT]

GARDEIL, AMBROISE (1859–1931), French theologian. A Dominican of the Province of France from 1878, he became a leader in the authentic interpretation of the thought of St. Thomas Aquinas, esp. on the nature of faith, the meaning and method of theology, and the relationship of the soul in grace to the indwelling Divine Persons. On this last point he made clear that the presence of God to the soul is not simply a causal relationship, but an immediate, immanent union through knowing and loving. He was a founder of the *Revue Thomiste;* among his major works are: *Le Donnée revelée et la théologie* (1910); *La Structure de l'âme et l'expérience mystique* (1926).

[T. C. O'BRIEN]

GARDEN OF THE SOUL, a manual of prayers compiled by R. *Challoner in 1740, the name apparently borrowed from the **Hortulus animae,* a prayer book that had enjoyed great popularity in Germany and elsewhere on the Continent in the 16th century. Challoner's *Garden* contained not only prayers and spiritual exercises useful to those aspiring to devotion, but also information and instruction. His seventh and last edition, corrected and enlarged, appeared in 1755. The innumerable editions published after that time introduced so many modifications and changes that little was left of the original work. BIBLIOGRAPHY: H. Thurston, CE 12:353.

[P. K. MEAGHER]

GARDINER, HAROLD CHARLES (1904–69), editor, critic. Ordained a Jesuit in 1935, G. was literary editor of the weekly *America* from 1940 to 1962. He contributed significantly to the magazine both by his own articles and by the writers he drew to the periodical. From 1962 to 1967 he was literature editor of the *New Catholic Encyclopedia.* G. was an internationally known critic and spent much time on the lecture circuit. He was one of the founders of the publishing venture Corpus Books. Among his published works were *Fifty Years of the American Novel* (1951), *Norms for the Novel* (1953), *Catholic Viewpoint on Censorship* (1958), and *Movies, Morals and Art* (1961). Highly personable, a keen analyst of literary works, G. exerted wide influence on Catholic readers for 28 years.

[J. R. AHERNE]

GARDINER, JERMYN (GERMAN), BL. (d. 1544), English martyr. Lay secretary to the bp. of Winchester (who may have been his son), G. was condemned and executed along with John Larke and John Ireland for "attempting . . . to deprive . . . King Henry VIII of his royal dignity, title and name of 'Supreme Head of the English and Irish Church.' " He was beatified in 1886. BIBLIOGRAPHY: B. Camm, *English Martyrs* 1:543; Butler 1:564–565; M. Salsano, BiblSanct 6:38.

[M. J. SUELZER]

GARDINER, STEPHEN (*c.* 1493–1555), bp. of Winchester. He took his degree in civil and canon law, in which fields he attained eminence as secretary of Card. Wolsey and later of Henry VIII in attempting to win papal approval of the King's divorce. After some hesitation he supported Henry's claim to be head of the English Church, yet he opposed the Protestant tendencies of Thomas Cromwell and Abp. Cranmer and wrote a vigorous defense of the Real Presence and the Mass. Appointed Lord Chancellor by Mary Tudor, he supported her in restoring Catholicism. His conversion seems to have been sincere, although he was conspicuous throughout life for his skill in double dealing. His treatise *De vera obedientia* is considered the ablest vindication of Henry's claim to supremacy over the Church of England. BIBLIOGRAPHY: J. Scarisbrick, NCE 6: 287–288; J. A. Muller, *Stephen Gardiner and the Tudor Reaction* (1926).

[M. J. BARRY]

GAREMBERT, VEN. (1084–1141), abbot. A Belgian, G. founded a religious community of men, added one of women and eventually joined his community of men to the Norbertines in 1134.

[J. R. AHERNE]

GARESCHÉ, EDWARD FRANCIS (1876–1960), Jesuit writer, medical counselor. A voluminous writer of devotional and nursing-oriented works, G. was also a poet of some lyrical power. The early years were devoted to the Sodality of the Blessed Virgin Mary, for which with D. *Lord he founded the magazine *The Queen's Work*. Five books of verse appeared between 1913 and 1942. He headed the Catholic Medical Mission Board and wrote a number of books on medical ethics and other topics for nurses. In 1935 he established a congregation *Daughters of Mary, Health of the Sick, which works for medical missions; and in 1952 a community of brothers, *Sons of Mary, Health of the Sick. He conducted his varied apostolate rather apart from official Jesuit channels, and spent most of his final days with the brothers' community at Framingham, Mass., where he died.

[J. R. AHERNE]

GARET, JEAN (Garetius; d. 1571), Canon Regular of St. Augustine at Louvain; Counter Reformation preacher and writer; his *De vera praesentia corporis Christi* (1561) is a notable defense of RC Eucharistic teaching from patristic sources.

[T. C. O'BRIEN]

GARIBALDI, GIUSEPPE (1807–82), Italian military and nationalist hero. A sailor in the Sardinian navy and an early member of *Young Italy, G. was involved in a conspiracy to seize a Sardinian vessel, for which he was condemned to death. He escaped, however, and went to S America where he participated in various civil wars. After returning to Italy in 1848, he fought both Austria and the papacy. Upon the fall of the Roman Republic and the defeat of revolution in Italy, he again went into exile. He returned to Piedmont in 1854, and in 1866 led a volunteer army against Austria. His most famous exploit was his conquest of the Kingdom of the Two Sicilies (1860) with his Thousand Red Shirts. He was bitterly anticlerical, his personal religion being a synthesis of deism, pantheism, and the "religion of humanity." BIBLIOGRAPHY: D. Mack Smith, *Garibaldi* (1956, repr. 1973); G. M. Trevelyan, *Garibaldi and the Making of Italy* (1973).

[E. A. CARRILLO]

GARICOÏTS, MICHAEL, ST. (1797–1863), Basque priest, founder of the Bétharram Fathers. A Spanish shepherd boy from a household that sheltered many priests from the French Revolution, G. worked as a cook's helper in the seminary to pay his expenses. Ordained in 1823 he served in the Basque country as curate and then teacher at the seminary at Bétharram (Basses-Pyrénées). When the seminary was closed G. founded (1832) a congregation, Priests of the Sacred Heart of Bétharram, with a constitution based on that of the Jesuits. The bp. of the locality opposed and restricted the new congregation, the aim of which was to train priests for home missions. It was not until after the death of the founder that the society was approved by Rome in 1877. G. was canonized in 1947. BIBLIOGRAPHY: F. Collier, *Saint of Bétharram* (1938).

[J. R. AHERNE]

GARIN, ANDRÉ (1822–95), Oblate of Mary Immaculate, missionary and pastor. He joined his community in his native France (1842), was sent to work in Canada, where he was ordained (1845). He served the Indian missions in E Canada for 12 years. He became pastor of the first Oblate parish in the U.S., St. Joseph's, Lowell, Mass., founded to minister to Franco-Americans. His 27 years in Lowell, during which he built three other churches, made him the revered and beloved pastor of his people.

[J. R. AHERNE]

GARIZIM, MOUNT, see GERIZIM, MOUNT.

GARNET, HENRY (Garnett; 1555–1606), head of the Jesuit mission in England. A convert, he became a Jesuit in 1575, was ordained at Rome in 1586, and became superior of the Jesuits in England in 1588. He was executed for not revealing prior knowledge of the *Gunpowder Plot; it is disputed whether he had such knowledge, and if so, whether from the confessional. His work as superior was marked by a great increase in Jesuit numbers, skilled organization of the work of *seminary priests, the printing and distribution of Catholic books. He also had to intervene diplomatically in disputes among the seminary priests, and to refute accusations of Jesuit domination in England. In the years before his arrest he had been trying to secure from Rome a prohibition against the use of violence by Catholics.

[T. C. O'BRIEN]

GARNET, THOMAS, ST. (1575–1608), English martyr. G. attended grammar school at Horsham, Sussex; for a time was a page to Lord William Howard; completed his education at Saint-Omer, and entered the English seminary at Valladolid (1596). He returned to England (1599) where he labored with great success. He was admitted into the Society of Jesus by his uncle, Henry Garnet (1604). At the time of the Gunpowder Plot he was imprisoned. When he proved his innocence, he was banished (1606) and went to Louvain for his novitiate. Soon after his return to England he was betrayed by an apostate, arrested and tried at Old Bailey on the charge of treason, and was executed at Tyburn. He was canonized in 1970. BIBLIOGRAPHY: Butler 2:627; F. Baumann, BiblSanct 6:39–40.

[V. SAMPSON]

GARNIER OF ROCHEFORT, see GUARNERIUS OF ROCHEFORT.

GARNIER, CHARLES, ST. (*c.*1605–1649), Jesuit missionary, martyr. Born in Paris he became a Jesuit (1624), and was sent (1636) to the mission in Quebec with three other priests. On Dec. 7, 1649, the Indian village of Etarita where he was staying was attacked and destroyed by an Iroquois war party. Garnier perished in the massacre. *NORTH AMERICAN MARTYRS.

GARNIER, ROBERT (*c.*1544–90), French tragic dramatist. Although essentially lyrical, his plays, of Senecan or Greek inspiration, point the way to the evolution of a truly tragic action: *Porcie* (1568); *Hippolyte* (1573); *Cornélie* (1574); *Marc-Antoine* (1578); *La Troade* (1579); *Antigone* (1580); *Bradamante* (1582), one of the first important French tragi-comedies and G.'s only play without chorus; and *Les Juifves* (1583). These last two plays are considered his masterpieces. *Les Juifves,* inspired by the Bible (1–2 Kg, 1–2 Chr) and by Josephus' *Jewish Antiquities* (10.9–10), relating the vengeance of Nebuchadnezzar on King Zedekiah and his children, was intended by G. for the religious edification of his audience during the French Wars of Religion. BIBLIOGRAPHY: R. Lebègue, *La Tragédie française de la Renaissance* (1954); G. Jondorf, *Robert Garnier and the Themes of Political Tragedy* (1969).

[R. N. NICOLICH]

GARRAGHAN, GILBERT JOSEPH (1871–1942), Jesuit historian. Ordained (1904) in the Society of Jesus, G. taught at Creighton Univ. and St. Louis Univ. before becoming a research professor at Loyola Univ. in Chicago. His historical studies are all concerned with frontier history and the Midwest. *Catholic Beginnings in Kansas City, Missouri* (1920) and *The Catholic Church in Chicago, 1673–1871* (1921) are typical. In 1929 he became editor of the historical quarterly *Mid-America.* His publication (1937) of the letters of the early Jesuit Père Marquette was an event in historical research. G.'s chief work was *The Jesuits of the Middle United States* (3 v., 1938), a carefully documented account of Jesuit missionary activity in the Mississippi River area and on the Pacific coast from 1823 to 1923.

[J. R. AHERNE]

GARRIGOU-LAGRANGE, REGINALD (1877–1964), Dominican philosopher and theologian. Born in Gascony, he studied medicine at Bordeaux. As a theologian he was trained under A. *Gardeil, and taught for many years in Rome, where he wielded considerable influence, which towards the end was somewhat repressive. The list of his publications includes more than 500 titles. His work on theological apologetics, *De revelatione* (2 v., 1918) set the style for many years, and still remains a classical plan for one approach. His spiritual teaching, which stressed the universal call to holiness, was widely influential. His first outstanding work, *Le Sens commun* (1909), on the validity of a perennial philosophy of being and its relevance as the setting for the dogmas of the Christian revelation, is the one that best keeps its luster and survives its epoch.

[T. GILBY]

GARRIGUET, LOUIS (1859–1927), French Sulpician theologian and sociologist. He was professor of theology in seminaries at Nantes (1885–94) and Lyons (1894–99), and rector at Avignon (1900–09) and La Rochelle (1909–13). Among his devotional writings *Le Sacré Coeur de Jésus* (1920) is outstanding, but he was known chiefly for what he wrote on social problems in the spirit of **Rerum novarum.* Many of these writings were published in the collection *Science et religion* which he edited (1903–09). He also published a *Traité de sociologie* (3 v., 1907–08) and a *Manuel de sociologie et d'économie sociale* (1924).

GARSTANG, JOHN (1876–1956), British archeologist. G. first directed excavations in Egypt, Nubia, and various Roman sites in Britain. He is best noted for his important archeological expeditions throughout Asia Minor, the Holy Land, and Ethiopia. He was director of the British School of Archeology in Jerusalem (1920–26), and founded the British Institute of Archeology at Ankara (1947). BIBLIOGRAPHY: B. Verostko, NCE 6:294–295.

[T. M. MCFADDEN]

GARTH, an archaic term, the center garden within the surrounding cloister walk in a church or monastery.

GARUDA, mythical bird, mount of the Hindu god Vishnu, with a white, half-human face, red wings, and golden body. G. is enemy and destroyer of nagas, (snake-spirits whose cult of worship is likely rooted in an aboriginal snake ritual).

[M. J. DALY]

GARWEH (GIARWEH), family name of two Syrian-Catholic patriarchs, uncle and nephew. (1) IGNATIUS MICHAEL (1731–1800). Through the influence of Latin-rite missionaries, he secretly embraced Catholicism while a priest in the *Jacobite schism. He was consecrated bp. of Aleppo by the Jacobite patriarch George II; in 1763 with his whole flock he openly professed Catholicism, and Pius VI recognized his jurisdiction in Aleppo. In 1781 the majority of Jacobite bishops elected him patriarch, even though he was a Catholic, and Pius VI approved him in that dignity (1783). But as *persona non grata* to the Turkish government, which recognized as patriarch a Jacobite elected by the minority, he fled to Lebanon, where he died. (2) IGNATIUS PETER (d. 1851), nephew of Ignatius Michael. He was elected bp. of Jerusalem (1810), patriarch of Syrian-Catholics (1820), and confirmed in this office by Leo XII (1828). His position was recognized as independent of the Jacobite patriarchate by the Turkish government. He transferred his see to Aleppo (1830), where he labored and wrote tirelessly in the cause of union with Rome. BIBLIOGRAPHY: G. de Vries, EncCatt 5:1950.

GASBERT DE LAVAL, (d. 1347), archbishop. He was an official of the papal curia (1317–47), bp. of Marseilles (1319–23), abp. of Arles (1323–41), abp. of Narbonne (1341–47). Mentioned frequently in papal letters, G. was one of the many clerics originally from Cahors who were brought to Avignon by Jacques Duèse, Pope John XXII, and remained to serve his successors.

[J. E. WRIGLEY]

GASPARRI, PIETRO (1852–1934), cardinal secretary of state; chiefly responsible for the *Codex Iuris Canonici.* He taught canon law at the College of the Propaganda, 1877–90; then became first occupant of the canon law chair at Institut Catholique, Paris, 1890–98; he published several canonical treatises during his academic period. In the papal service from 1898, he was secretary of the committee of cardinals and head of the research work for a new codification of canon law. The new code was primarily the result of his labors; it was completed in only 12 years, submitted to Benedict XV in 1916, and promulgated in 1917. A cardinal from 1907, G. became Benedict's secretary of state in 1914, assisting that pope's efforts for peace throughout World War I. Pius XI reappointed him secretary of state in 1921, and G. carried out the negotiations that led to the signing of the *Lateran Pact with Italy, Feb. 11, 1929. During his last years he brought to a conclusion his celebrated *Fontes juris canonici.* He died of a heart attack after addressing an international congress of jurists in Rome.

[T. C. O'BRIEN]

GASQUET, FRANCIS NEIL AIDAN (1846–1929), English Benedictine cardinal and historian. A member of the Benedictine Abbey at Downside, G. was elected prior in 1878, and during his tenure the monastery and school were enlarged and improved in quality; he resigned in 1885. Because of his monumental *Edward VI and the Book of Common Prayer,* in 1896 G. went to Rome as an influential member of the Commission on Anglican Orders set up by Leo XIII. Back in England G. became abbot-president of the English Benedictine Congregation in 1900. Pius X named him president of the International Commission for the Revision of the Vulgate, and created him cardinal in 1914. G. became a permanent resident in Rome, serving on Roman congregations and holding successively the positions of prefect of the Vatican Archives and Librarian of the Holy Roman Church. His was a major contribution to the history of monasticism in the Middle Ages and during the English Reformation. Three well-known works are *Henry VIII and the English Monasteries* (1889), *Religio Religiosi* (1918), and *Monastic Life in the Middle Ages* (1922). BIBLIOGRAPHY: D. Knowles, *Cardinal Gasquet as an Historian* (1957).

[J. R. AHERNE]

GASSEL, LUCAS (HELMONT; *c.*1500–70), Flemish painter and engraver. His landscapes, generally biblical in reference, relate to those of his contemporary, Herri met de Bles (Herri Patinir, Henricus Blesius). De Bles was the nephew of the great Flemish master J. Patinir, who established the "constructed" landscape,—fantastic, epic and vast, which determined this Flemish genre of the future. The works of G. and Herri met de Bles were the bridge to landscapes of Bruegel the Elder, who finally subordinated man to the inexorable cycle of nature. BIBLIOGRAPHY: C. D. Cutler, *Northern Painting* (1968).

[M. J. DALY]

GASSENDI, PIERRE (1592–1655), French philosopher and scientist. A priest and theologian, G. taught at the Royal Bourbon College at Aix and at Digne. He saw the inadequacy of Aristotelian philosophy in physical science and devised a philosophy based on Epicurus accommodated to Christian belief. His *Disquisitio metaphysica* (1643) disputes R. *Descartes' *Meditationes de prima philosophia.* G.'s espousal of atomism prepared the way for an adequate statement of the principle of inertia. BIBLIOGRAPHY: *Pierre Gassendi: Sa vie et ses oeuvres* (ed. T. Gregory and B. Rochot, 1955).

[J. R. AHERNE]

GASSER, VINZENZ FERRER (1809–79), bishop. A Tyrolese ordained in 1833 he taught in the Brixen seminary for 19 years, being named prince bishop of Brixen in 1856. A member of the Tyrolean parliament, he defended the position of Catholicism as the sole recognized religion of the Tyrol. A leading influence in Vatican Council I, he contributed telling arguments in the question of the primacy vs. the authority of bishops. The decree on papal infallibility was G.'s work and was adopted as he composed it on July 11, 1870.

[J. R. AHERNE]

GASSNER, JOHANN JOSEPH (1727–79), an Austrian priest (from 1750) celebrated as an exorcist. While serving at Klösterle in Switzerland he became a victim of severe headaches; conceiving his affliction to be the work of the devil, he treated it successfully by invoking the name of Jesus. When he applied the same method to the infirmities of others, he obtained many remarkable cures. A work expounding his doctrine was published in 1774 and reprinted many times. G. met with strong opposition from some, who regarded his attribution of physical infirmities to diabolic action as too sweeping and without scriptural basis. However, he was protected by the bp. of Regensburg and he had many supporters, among them some physicians and the Calvinist minister, J. K. Lavater of Zurich. Imperial and university (Ingolstadt) commissions studied the case, gave their approval to G.'s methods and procedures, but recommended that he live in greater retirement to prevent the development of superstition among his followers. BIBLIOGRAPHY: F. J. Schaefer, CE 6:392.

[P. K. MEAGHER]

GASTOÚE, AMÉDÉE (1873–1943), French musicologist and composer. As professor of chant at the Schola Cantorum in Paris, he helped reform chant in various orders and served with Dom *Pothier as editor of the Vatican edition (1905–12) of the Gregorian chant books. G.'s finest text is *Les Origines du chant romain,* published in 1907; another important study is his *Musique et liturgie: Le Graduel et l'Antiphonaire romains: histoire et description* (1913).

[D. J. SMUCKER]

GATE OF HEAVEN, an explanatory term used in Gen 28.17 in relation to the sanctuary of Bethel. Such a high place—cf. ''ladder''—served, according to the ancient conception, as a point of contact between earth and heaven (Jn 1.51). BIBLIOGRAPHY: De Vaux AncIsr 291.

[C. BERNAS]

GATES OF HELL, an expression, found only once in the NT, that has claimed the attention of exegetes and theologians because it occurs in the theologically important Petrine text: ''And on this rock, I will build my church and the gates of Hell shall not prevail against it.'' (Mt. 16.18) It has been suggested that ''gates'' is merely pleonastic; that the sense is simply ''hell shall not prevail against it.'' Many exegetes, however, feel that the word gates adds something by symbolizing power and strength, since in ancient times the gates of city or citadel were specially fortified and at the gates political and social power was exercised when judgments and decisions were there handed down.

Exegetes have long disputed whether by hell (Gr. *hadēs)* is to be understood the place or region of the dead (the older biblical sense) or of the damned and of Satan (as suggested by some NT use of the word). In the first interpretation then, ''death shall not overtake the Church''; in the second, ''the power of evil shall not lay it low.'' In any case there appears to be a promise of indefectibility for the Church: in the first interpretation explicitly, in the second implicitly, for Our Lord would scarcely have made a solemn promise of abiding protection from external forces, if he foresaw that the Church was to succumb to processes of internal decay and disintegration. BIBLIOGRAPHY: J. Jeremias, Kittel TD 1:146–149; L. E. Sullivan, ''Gates of Hell,'' ThSt 10 (1949) 62–64.

[S. E. DONLON]

GATES OF PARADISE. See FLORENCE CATHEDRAL.

GATH (GETH), a Heb. word meaning ''winepress,'' one of the five Philistine cities (1 Sam 6.17), home of giants (Jos 11.22; 1 Sam 17.4; 2 Sam 21.19–22), mentioned in connection with the ark (1 Sam 5.8), Achish (1 Sam 21.11; 27.3–12; 1 Kg 2.39; Ps 56.1), David's bodyguard (2 Sam 15.18); captured by David (1 Chr 18.1), fortified by Rehoboam (2 Chr 11.8), seized by Hazael (2 Kg 12.17), by Uzziah (2 Chr 26.6). Later it disappeared from history. Possibly it is identified with Araq el-Menshiyeh, not far from Ashkelon in the Gaza strip. BIBLIOGRAPHY: B. Mazar, ''Gath and Gattaim,'' *Israel Exploration Journal* 4 (1954) 227–235; J. Simons, *Geographical and Topographical Texts of the Old Testament* (1959) 1633.

[F. BUCK]

GĀTHĀS, the hymns of Zoroaster preserved in the *Avesta* and the primary source for our knowledge of Zoroaster and his teaching. They are short metrical pieces that have clear affinities with the hymns of the *Rig-Veda* in India. They are primarily concerned with the praise of *Ahura Mazda,* and of his supporters, or moral and social attributes personified. The Evil Spirit (*Ahriman*) is attacked and likewise the cult of the ancient gods or *daēvas*. A miserable life and revolting food are emphasized as the punishment for the worshippers of the *daēvas*. On the other hand, the followers of *Ahura Mazda* who fight for justice, truth, and his other qualities are promised happiness in heaven or on a renewed earth. There will be a resurrection of the body, and man will be helped by saviors who will come in the period following Zoroaster. As the text is obscure, it is not clear whether the *haoma* (sacred liquor) sacrifice and the bull-sacrifice of the early religion are condemned or certain features of them only. BIBLIOGRAPHY: J. Duchesne-Guillemin, *Hymns of Zarathustra* (1952); *idem, La Religion de l'Iran Ancien* (1962) 33–34.

[M. R. P. MCGUIRE]

GATHERED CHURCH, the theory on the nature and polity of the Church that considers the Church to exist only in the local congregation, limited in membership to committed Christians. ''Visible churches,'' its adherents state, ''are made up of visible saints.'' A credible profession of faith and evidence of Christian character are required for admission, and members covenant together under discipline of the word of God. Such congregations believe they are led by the Holy Spirit and have authority from Christ to choose officers and determine members. The theory is in opposition to the idea of the *parish as simply a local unit of the visible, universal Church; or to the idea of the Church organized into a national or even regional entity. Beginning *c.*1580 with Robert *Browne at Norwich, the gathered church concept continued as the characteristic of the Congregationalists and the Baptists. Congregational polity was stated in England by the *Savoy Declaration (1658) and in New England by the *Cambridge Platform (1648). BIBLIOGRAPHY: P. Miller, *Orthodoxy in Massachusetts* (1933). *INVISIBLE CHURCH; *COVENANT THEOLOGY; *CHURCH (THEOLOGICAL INTERPRETATIONS); *CONGREGATIONALISM; *BAPTISTS.

[N. H. MARING]

GATHERING NOTE, a note given, usually by an organist to the congregation, to sound the correct pitch for singing.

[D. J. SMUCKER]

GATTA, BARTOLOMEO DELLA (1448–1502), Italian artist of the Arezzo school, abbot, musician, architect, and painter influenced by Piero della Francesca, Veneziano, and Antonio del Pollaiuolo. B. assisted Signorelli in the Sistine Chapel. BIBLIOGRAPHY: E. Lavagnino, EncCatt 4:1371–72.

[M. J. DALY]

GATTERER, MICHAEL (1862–1944), Jesuit professor of moral theology at Innsbruck. He entered the Society of Jesus in 1888, three years after ordination as a diocesan priest, and began his teaching career in 1892. He published several works in catechetics, and *Das Religionsbuch der Kirche* (4 v., 1928–30). His main pastoral concern in his writings is the development of charity.

GATTI, BERNARDINO (Il Sojaro; *c.*1495–1576), Italian painter in Cremona, influenced locally by Pordenone and by Correggio of Parma. G. collaborated with Pordenone on Frescoes in Piacenza (1543) and finished a project of Parmigianino in a heavy, pre-Baroque, rather than mannerist, style.

[M. J. DALY]

GATTINARA, MERCURINO ARBORIO DI (1465–1530), chancellor of Emperor Charles V, cardinal. A celebrated lawyer and teacher of law in Piedmont at the Univ. of Dôle, G. was adviser to Margaret of Austria, the guardian of the future Emperor Charles V, whom he directed in the concept of universal monarchy advocated by Dante. Named president of the Council of the Netherlands in 1513, G. was briefly accused of treason but reinstated as envoy by Emperor Maximilian. With the accession of Charles V, G. became grand chancellor and from this position exerted a powerful influence on the Emperor, esp. toward forming a general council. In 1529 he was created bp. of Ostia and cardinal by Clement VII.

[J. R. AHERNE]

GAU, FRANZ (1790–1853), architect in Paris whose iron-structured Neo-Gothic Church of Sainte-Clothilde was in advance of its time. G. also did archaeological reseach in Egypt.

[M. J. DALY]

GAUCHERIUS, ST. (d. 1140), Augustinian canon and abbot. At 18, G. retired to a forest near Limoges in order to live the contemplative life of a hermit. As others followed, he founded St. Jean of Aureil priory, in which the members followed the Rule of St. Augustine. Among his disciples were Lambert of Angoulême, Faucherius, and Stephen of Muret. BIBLIOGRAPHY: M. Salsano, BiblSanct 6:45–46; Butler 2:59–60.

[F. G. O'BRIEN]

GAUDEN, JOHN (1605–62), Anglican bishop. The son of an Essex clergyman, he studied at Cambridge and Oxford, and then became vicar of Chippenham in 1640 and dean of Bocking, Essex, in 1642. Initially a supporter of the Puritans, he came to have reservations. But though he wrote in defense of the C of E, he conformed to Presbyterianism under Cromwell. At the Restoration he became bp. of Exeter. In appealing for a more lucrative see—he sought Winchester but in 1662 got Worcester—he claimed that he deserved favor for writing *Eikon Basilike,* a book purporting to give the thoughts and prayers of Charles I in prison. Modern scholars think G. possibly wrote it from materials provided by the King. BIBLIOGRAPHY: F. F. Madan, *New Bibliography of the Eikon Basilike* (1950).

[T. EARLY]

GAUDENTIUS, ST. (d. *c.*410), bp. of Brescia. While in the East on a pilgrimage he had word of his election to the bishopric of Brescia, which he accepted with reluctance, and was consecrated by St. Ambrose (387). With two others he was sent by Pope Innocent I and Emperor Honorius to the East to defend the cause of St. John Chrysostom (404–405) and was imprisoned for a time in Thrace by Chrysostom's enemies. Twenty-one of G.'s sermons are extant (PL 20:827–1002). BIBLIOGRAPHY: AS Oct. 11: 587–604; Butler 4:199–200.

[R. B. ENO]

GAUDENTIUS OF GNIEZNO, ST. (*c.*965–*c.*1010), first metropolitan of Gniezno and brother of St. Adalbert. A member of the Benedictine Order, he was ordained in Rome in 988 and consecrated abp. of Gniezno in 999. His relics were translated to Prague in 1039. BIBLIOGRAPHY: G. Labuda, *Polski Slownik Biograficzny* (1949) 7:308–309; Z. Szostkiewicz, "Katalog Biskopów obrz. łac. Przedrozbiorowej Polski," in *Sacrum Poloniae Millennium* 1 (1954) 450; W. Meysztowicz, "Koronacje Pierwszych Piastów," *ibid.* 3(1956) 294.

[W. A. JURGENS]

GAUDERICH OF VELLETRI (9th cent.), bp., one of the chief advisors to Pope John VIII, instrumental in securing the Roman recognition of *Photius as patriarch of Constantinople in 879. He also helped to compile an account of the miracles of St. Clement, one of the principal sources for the lives of SS. Cyril and Methodius. BIBLIOGRAPHY: G. T. Dennis, NCE 6:303.

[G. T. DENNIS]

GAUDETE SUNDAY, the third Sunday of Advent in the Roman calendar, so known from the opening words in Latin of the Introit (Entrance) antiphon: "Rejoice in the Lord always. . . .'' The Epistle (Second Reading, Cycle C) supplies the reason: ''The Lord is near'' (Phil 4.4–7). The more somber period of preparation for Christmas is lightened on this day; the priest may wear rose vestments rather than the deeper violet, expressing the joy of anticipation at the approach of the Nativity celebration.

[N. R. KRAMER]

GAUDÍ Y CORNET, ANTONIO (1852–1926), Spanish innovative architect, fervid Catalonian nationalist, of extraordinary personal style. Influenced by romantic concepts of the Middle Ages, G.'s style evolved with Mudejar overtones, an *art nouveau,* monumental architecture, completely divorced from tradition, seeking to convey the dynamism and random quality of nature, with profound respect for materials, in an entirely new ''expressionistic'' architecture. He banishes the straight line, with bulky layers of rubble, rough stone, broken pottery and glass (Surrealistic Güell Park, Barcelona, 1900–14) in restless, undulating masses (Casa Milá, 1907), organic openings suggesting grottoes, iron balconies twisted as sea weed, stalagmites—leaning columns supporting bizarre roofs—suggesting unending change. G.'s masterpiece is the church of the Sagrada Familia (Barcelona, 1883–1926), the Neo-Gothic still unfinished original of Francisco de Villar which G. continued in extravagant, exotic modulations of perforated forms encrusted with native Spanish, Moorish, and African richness. The College of Santa Teresa de Jesús (1889–94) and Güell Colony chapel (1898–1914) are further examples of G.'s distinctive style. BIBLIOGRAPHY: J. L. Sert and J. J. Sweeney, *Antonio Gaudî* (1961).

[M. J. DALY]

GAUGUIN, PAUL (1848–1903), French Post-Impressionist painter, sculptor, printmaker whose search for a transcendent essence drove him beyond the industrial society and too *précieuse* Parisian culture, first to the peasants of simple faith in Brittany, and finally to the unspoiled primitive natives of Tahitia and the Marquesas. But the Parisian G. was driven to return at intervals for the confirmation of a sophisticated French society. In Paris at 23, G. collected works of Impressionists, Manet and Cézanne, and began to paint, showing in 1876. Leaving his family he became a dedicated artist in Paris (1885). In Brittany (1888) with E. Bernard he sought a ''synthetism'' and ''symbolist'' art—reducing detail and expressing a mysticism through intense, ''unnatural'' color in large, flat areas, painting Calvaries and the famous, innovative *Jacob Wrestling with the Angel* (1888). In Arles (1888) a friendship with Van Gogh failed; in Pont-Aven and Le Pouldu, G. continued his large, flat, decorative, curved shapes (*The Yellow Christ,* 1889). He moved (1891–95) between Tahiti and Paris seeking a primitive mystery and purity, painting in a brilliant tropical palette monumental figures in serene reverie as in *Ia Orana, Maria* (I Hail Thee, Mary, 1891); *Spirit of the Dead Watching* (1892); *Day of the God* (1894). Upon the death of his daughter (1897), he painted the masterful *D'où venons nous? Que sommes nous? Où allons nous?* (Where do we come from? Who are we? Whither are we going?) which is in the Boston Museum of Fine Arts. G., depressed, poor, and in bad health, went to the Marquesas (1901) where he painted until his death (1903). G. produced woodcuts in his characteristic, highly decorative, rhythmic shapes, and monotypes subtle in color, elusive in technique. BIBLIOGRAPHY: R. Goldwater, *Paul Gauguin* (1957); J. Rewald, *Gauguin Drawings* (1958); C. Gray, *Sculpture and Ceramics of Paul Gauguin* (1963); L. Skykorva, *Gauguin Woodcuts* (1963).

[M. J. DALY]

GAUHAR SHAD, MOSQUE OF, meshed Iranian mosque of the Timurid period, a noteworthy example of 15th-cent. Mohammedan architecture, built by Gauhar Shad, wife of Shah Rukh. Its dome, minarets, and portals are lavishly decorated with unusual relief designs in friezes and floral motifs of dazzling colors.

[M. J. DALY]

GAUL, EARLY CHURCH IN. At the beginning of the Christian era the term Gaul embraced the Roman administrative units of Gallia Narbonensis, Aquitania, Lugdunensis, and Belgica. The date when Christianization of this region began is unknown, and the historicity of accounts linking its evangelization with the Apostles or Disciples cannot be established. Mid-2d-century evidence attests the presence of Christians in the Rhone Valley, specifically at Lyons and Vienne. Sulpicius Severus (*Chronicles* 2.32) says that Gaul had its first martyrs during the persecution of Marcus Aurelius. At Lyons *c.*177, anti-Christian sentiment erupted into persecution. Eusebius (*Hist. eccl.* 5.1.1–61) quotes the letter of the Church of Lyons to the Churches of Asia and Phrygia describing the martyrdom of its bp. Pothinus, and the tortures endured by Sanctus, deacon of Vienne. The list of martyrs from Lyons (probably 49) includes persons from all walks of life and age groups, e.g., Blandina, a slave girl, and Ponticus, a boy of scarcely 15 years. Irenaeus, Pothinus's successor, frequently mentioned simply as ''bishop of Gaul,'' continued the evangelization of the region. If Gregory of Tours (*Historia Francorum* 1.30) is to be taken literally, seven bps. sent from Rome *c.*250 founded the sees of Tours, Arles, Narbonne, Toulouse, Paris, Auvergne, and Limoges. In any event, Cyprian, bp. of Carthage (*Letter 68*), mentions Marcian, bp. of Arles, and his severity toward the lapsed in the Decian persecution. Whatever the number of bps. from Gaul may have been at Constantine's accession (estimates vary from 20 to almost 40), 16 from the region were either present or represented at the Council of Arles in 314. Probably in 353 Hilary became bp. of Poitiers and distinguished himself as the champion of orthodoxy against the Arians at the Council of Béziers (356). His *On the Trinity* is the first extensive work in Latin on this doctrine. With Hilary's blessing, St. Martin established what may have been the first monastery in Gaul at Ligugé *c.*360 and some 10 years later became bp. of Tours. He is credited with being the first to establish rural parishes in the area. Martin's friend Victricius, bp. of Rouen, is noted for similar missionary activity; both thus extended what had been an urban-centered Church. Though the errors of Priscillianism and Semi-Pelagianism posed a threat to the progress of the Church in early Gaul, the names and work of Paulinus of Nola, Germain of Auxerre, and Sulpicius Severus indicate that Christianity had struck firm roots in many regions of the country. Even though the wars waged by Visigoths and Franks temporarily impeded the Christianization of the rural areas, the hierarchical structure of the early Church in Gaul is generally thought to have been completed by 395 or shortly thereafter. The synodal letter of the Council of Turin (398?) rendering a decision in the controversy over metropolitan rights to be exercised by the bp. of Marseilles and the bps. of Vienne and Arles seems to confirm this opinion. BIBLIOGRAPHY: É. Griffe, *La Gaule chrétienne* (2d ed., 1964) v. 1; A. Harnack, *Mission and Expansion of Christianity in the First Three Centuries* (2d ed., 1908) 2:260–269.

[H. DRESSLER]

GAULLI, GIOVANNI BATTISTA (Baciccio, Baciccia; 1639–1709), Italian painter at Rome. In 1660 he executed the *Virgin and Child with SS. Roch and Anthony* (Church of S. Rocco, Rome); the extraordinary baroque ceiling decorations in painting and stucco in the Gesù *Triumph of the Name of Jesus,* 1672–85); two major canvases, *St. Francis Xavier Baptizing an Eastern Queen* and *St. Francis Xavier Preaching in the East* in S. Andrea al Quirinale; and portraits of 7 popes.

[M. J. DALY]

GAUME, JEAN JOSEPH (1802–79), writer, controversial educationalist. Ordained in 1825, he taught dogmatic theology at the major seminary, Nevers, France, until 1828, when he became rector of the minor seminary there. He resigned in 1831, protesting against an oath imposed by the government on heads of schools run by religious, even though he himself was not affected. For his loyalty to the Church, G. was decorated by Gregory XVI with the Order of St. Sylvester. For the next 20 years he devoted himself to catechetical work; in 1843 he was named diocesan vicar general. In 1853 he resigned from that post and went to live in Paris with his brothers. His resignation was prompted by the bps.' opposition to an educational theory that became the major concern of G.'s life. Although he wrote numerous works in devotional, theological, and historical subjects, he was above all concerned with opposing the exclusive teaching of Greek and Latin classics in Catholic schools. As his *Le Ver rongeur des sociétés modernes ou le paganisme dans l'éducation* (1851) evidences, he laid to that practice the source of the paganization of France; he campaigned for the substitution of the study of ancient Christian writers and the increase of catechetical instruction. His views were welcomed by conservative, ultramontane Catholics, but opposed by the more liberal. The controversy was heated, until settled by Pius IX's encyclical *Inter multiplices* (1854), which both supported the tradition of teaching the classics and urged the addition of Christian writers to Catholic curricula. The Pope conferred on G. the title of prothonotary apostolic.

[J. R. AHERNE]

GAUNILO (d. 1083?), a monk of *Marmoutier who wrote an acute criticism of St. *Anselm's *ontological argument for the existence of God. G.'s objection to the argument is embodied in an opuscule entitled *Quid ad haec respondeat quidam pro insipiente,* but generally referred to as *Liber pro insipiente*. G. took the part of the *insipiens* (fool) mentioned in Anselm's *Proslogion*. The criticism with its two points (that the idea of God has no meaning before his existence is known; that to pass from an idea to the affirmation of real existence is unwarranted) is the first formulation of the perennial objection to the ontological argument. Anselm replied in his *Liber apologeticus adversus respondentem pro insipiente*. G.'s opuscule can be found in PL 158:241–248. BIBLIOGRAPHY: Gilson HCP 133:616–617; F. Spedalieri, "Anselmus an Gaunilo. . . ," Greg 28 (1947) 55–57.

[T. C. O'BRIEN]

GAUTAMA (Buddha), the *gotra* (clan) name of the Buddha, indicating his membership in the specific brahmanic exogamous sept (clan) descended from the primeval *ṛsi* or legendary sage, Gautama.

[M. J. DALY]

GAUTIER DE COINCY, see WALTER OF COINCY.

GAUZELIN OF TOUL, ST. (d. 962), bp. of Toul in Lorraine. He was a notary at the court of Charles the Simple when elected bp. in 923. In spite of political upheaval and Hungarian invasions he devoted himself to building up the Church and to promoting monastic reform, notably in the Abbey of St. *Asper. He also founded, near Nancy, the Abbey of Bouxières-aux-Dames, where he was buried. BIBLIOGRAPHY: P. Viard, *Catholicisme* 4:1790.

[T. C. O'BRIEN]

GAVANTI, BARTOLOMMEO (1570–1638), Milanese Barnabite, canonist and liturgist. He entered religious life in 1587. His canonical and liturgical studies became known at Rome and he was invited to collaborate in the reform of the Roman Breviary under Clement VIII and Urban VIII; he became a permanent consultor for the Congregation of Rites in 1623. Among his canonical works are a collection of the decrees of that congregation, an *Enchiridion* for the canonical guidance of bps., and a *Praxis* for episcopal visitations and diocesan synods. But his great work is the *Thesaurus* *sacrorum rituum seu commentaria in rubricas Missalis et Breviarii Romani* (1628), which went through 27 editions up to the 19th century. It presents the historical origins, symbolic interpretations, and canonical background of the rites of the breviary and missal. G. was also general of his order.

[T. C. O'BRIEN]

GAVARRI, JOSÉ (*c.*1600–89), Franciscan who by papal bull and royal decree gave popular missions through all Spain. Two of his works offer a valuable view of 17th-cent. Spanish society, one of instructions with 17 model sermons for beginning preachers (5 eds., 1673–79), and the other a dialogue examination of conscience for confessors and penitents (1676).

[E. P. COLBERT]

GAVAZZI, ALESSANDRO (1809–89), Italian apostate priest. Dismissed from the Barnabites and for a time (1848) a chaplain in the papal militia, G. went to England (1849) where he became a Protestant, and then traveled in Scotland, Ireland, Canada, and the U.S. After the Risorgimento he returned to Italy where he tried without success to unite all Italian Protestants. His anti-Catholic works include two in English, *My Recollections of the Last Popes* (1858), and *Scheme for Church Union in Italy* (1865).

GAY, CHARLES LOUIS (1815–92), French spiritual writer preacher, and bishop. He experienced a religious conversion through the preaching of H. D. *Lacordaire, entered the seminary, and was ordained in 1845. G. attended Vatican Council I as auxiliary bp. of Poiters and as theologian. He is known chiefly as a spiritual director and for his writings on the life of Christian perfection that were deeply rooted in classic Christian theology. His best-known translated works are: *Christian Life and Virtues Considered in the Religious State* (tr. A. Burder, 3 v., 1878–79; *Religious Life and the Vows* (excerpted from the preaching; tr. W. T. Gordon, 1958). G. also published *Élévations sur la vie et la doctrine de N.S. Jésus Christ* (2 v., 1897).

[T. C. O'BRIEN]

GAZA, mentioned in the *Amarna Letters, the S frontier of Canaan (Gen 10.19), inhabited by the Avvim (Dt 2.23), the Anakim (Jos 11.22), the Philistines (1 Sam 6.17). Captured, but not retained, by Judah (Jg 1.18–19), it came into the control of Assyrians (734 B.C.), Egyptians (Jer 47.1), Persians (529 B.C.), Greeks (332 B.C.), Romans (61 B.C.). Gaza, esp. associated with Samson (Jg 16.1–3; 21–30), is once mentioned in the NT (Acts 8.26). Modern Gaza is built over the ruins of the old city. BIBLIOGRAPHY: M. A. Meyer, *History of the City of Gaza from the Earliest Times to the Present Day* (1907, repr. AMS); W. Flinders Petrie, *Ancient Gaza* (5 v., 1931–52).

[F. BUCK]

GAZER, see GEZER.

GAZIER, AUGUSTIN (1844–1922), French historian of Jansenism. A professor of literature at the Sorbonne (1880–1914), G. took a keen interest in the religious history of the 17th century. His masterwork was his *Histoire générale du mouvement janséniste depuis ses origines jusqu'à nos jours* (2 v., 1922); this was entirely his work, though it appeared after his death. He was staunchly Catholic, but his works provide evidence that theologically he was somewhat imperceptive and that sympathy for *Port Royal led him to classify as Jesuit distortions the doctrines distinctive of Jansenism. Nevertheless, his works led to more precise perspectives in historical research into Jansenism. R. Knox in his *Enthusiasm* (1950) takes frequent issue with G.'s *Histoire*.

GAZZĀ (treasure), East Syrian liturgical book containing the less ancient texts of the Night Office, thus complementing the *ḥûdrā*. BIBLIOGRAPHY: J. Mateos, *Lelya-Ṣapra* (1959) 9–12. *BEIT GAZZO.

[A. CODY]

GEBENO (fl. early 13th cent.), Cistercian prior of Eberbach, Germany, whose popular *Speculum futurorum temporum* or *Pentachronon* (1220–24) attacked the Cathari and the prophecies of *Joachim of Fiore, adducing against him the visions of St. Hildegarde. BIBLIOGRAPHY: *Analecta Sacra* (ed. J. B. Pitra, 1882) 483–488; A. Borst, LTK 4:537.

[L. J. LEKAI]

GEBHARD II OF CONSTANCE, ST. (949–995), bp. of Constance (979–995). In 983, his zeal for monastic reform led him to found an abbey to which he summoned Benedictines from Einsiedeln. Though dedicated in 992 to St. Gregory the Great, the abbey, because it was modeled on St. Peter's Basilica in Rome, came to be called Petershausen. BIBLIOGRAPHY: R. Henggeler, BiblSanct 6:80.

[M. F. MCCARTHY]

GEBHARD III OF CONSTANCE (*c.*1054–1110), bp. of Constance. Having served as dean at Xanten, he became a monk at Hirsau; and *c.*1084, cardinal-legate of Ostia for Urban II. An energetic supporter of papal policy, he won over his brother Duke Berthold II, and they held complete leadership of Swabia. He was a major figure in ecclesiastical reform and a supporter of papal policy in the Empire. BIBLIOGRAPHY: H. Tüchle, LTK 4:555–56.

[S. WILLIAMS]

GEBHARD OF SALZBURG, BL. (d. 1088) archbishop. 1088. Like so many great German prelates, G. was born into a noble family; he served as royal chaplain and chancellor to Henry III. When he died at Admont, he had been abp. of Salzburg for 28 years. He strengthened eastern

German ecclesiastical organization, befriended Altmann of Passau, and was probably the strongest active supporter of Gregory VII in Germany. BIBLIOGRAPHY: J. Wodka, LTK 4:556; N. del Re, BiblSanct 6:81–82; A. Dumas, *Catholicisme* 4:1796–97.

[S. WILLIAMS]

GEBHARDT, EDUARD VON (1883–1925), German painter of religious works, following the Dutch masters and Pinturicchio in style and protesting the romanticism of the Nazarene group.

[M. J. DALY]

GEBIZO, ST. (d. betw. 1078 and 1087), monk. He was received into the Benedictine Order by Abbot Desiderius (later Pope Victor III). Noted for his self-denial, silence, and spirit of prayer, he was called a saint even in his earliest biographies. Though suffering from great pain caused by an abscess on his chest, G. begged God for even greater sufferings. He is mentioned in the monastic martyrology but not in the Roman. BIBLIOGRAPHY: A. Lentini, BiblSanct 6:82–83; G. Boing, LTK 4:557.

[F. G. O'BRIEN]

GEDDES, ALEXANDER (1737–1802), RC biblical scholar. Both as a parish priest in his native Scotland (1764–79), and in London as a scholar under the patronage of Lord Petre, he proposed critical views on the Pentateuch that shocked both Catholics and Protestants; eventually he was suspended from his priestly functions. G., however, is considered a pioneer in biblical criticism because of his questioning the Mosaic authorship of the Pentateuch and his proposal of fragmentary sources. Among his works was a translation of the Pentateuch and the historical books of the OT (2 v. 1792–97). BIBLIOGRAPHY: Gillow BDEC 2:410–415.

[T. C. O'BRIEN]

GEDELIAH (Godolia), biblical name: (1) musician of David's time (1 Chr 25.3, 9); (2) grandson of Hezekiah and grandfather of Zephaniah (Zeph 1.1); (3) one of the princes who proposed that Jeremiah be put to death (Jer 38.1–6); (4) governor of Judah under Nebuchadnezzar during the Exile (2 Kg 25.22–26; Jer 40–41) who was murdered by nationalist fanatics led by Ishmael of the exiled royal house while they were guests in his house; (5) one of the priests who put away their foreign wives (Ezra 10.18).

[T. EARLY]

GEDEON, see GIDEON.

GEERTGEN TOT SINT JANS (Gerard of Haarlem; *c.*1465–*c.*1495), Dutch painter who with other Haarlem artists (Ouwater and Bouts) studied and worked in Flanders. G. entered the monastery of the Order of St. John and produced many works. Earliest is a *Madonna* (4″ × 2¾″) on vellum, showing the influence of Bouts in an illuminated and miniature style. A *Holy Kinship* of naive charm relates to Ouwater in setting and composition. G.'s great contribution was unified distance through continutiy of space seen in *Raising of Lazarus* (Louvre), *Adoration of the Magi* (Prague), and *St. John the Baptist in the Wilderness* (Berlin). G.'s greatest work, a *Nativity*, (London) is a night scene, with the light radiating from the Child illuminating all about and a secondary warm glow suffusing the areas in half shadow. In the landscape beyond a brillant light emanates from the angel messenger touching the fields and shepherds near their bright fire. In his treatment of light G. relates to Gerard van Honthorst (1590–1650) and to other Dutch "Caravaggisti", but most precisely foreshadows the work of Georges de La Tour (1593–1652). BIBLIOGRAPHY: E. Panofsky, *Early Netherlandish Painting* (1953); M.J. Friedländer, *Early Netherlandish Painting* (tr. H. Norden, 1967).

[M. J. DALY]

GE'EZ, the liturgical language of the *Ethiopian Church. This south Semitic tongue was the official language of the Axumite kingdom when Ethiopia was converted to Christianity. Numerous Christian writings were composed in or translated into Ge'ez. When political power shifted from Axum to the SW provinces, Ge'ez gave way to Amharic as the popular language, but retained its status in literature and official documentation until the 16th century. It now survives only in liturgical usage. BIBLIOGRAPHY: W. Leslau, *Semitic Languages of Ethiopia: An Annotated Bibliography* (1964); S. A. Mercer, *Ethiopic Liturgy* (1970).

[D. W. JOHNSON]

GeHĀNTĀ (West Syrian, *gehōntō*), inclination; in Syrian rites, a prayer that the celebrant, profoundly bowed, says in a low voice.

[A. CODY]

GEHENNA, from the Hebrew *gê-hinnom*, a valley in the S of Jerusalem where children were sacrificed and burned. Jeremiah prophesied that God would punish the sins of the people there (Jer 7.30–33). Gehenna appears later as the eschatological place where the dead bodies of God's enemies are gathered (Is 66.24). The name sometimes lost its topographical meaning and was identified with *Sheol, the actual abode of the dead. In Jesus' preaching Gehenna is the place where, after the eschatological judgment (Mt. 23.33) the wicked are eternally punished (Mt 25.31–46). BIBLIOGRAPHY: I. H. Gorski, NCE 6:312–313; EDB 847–850.

[A. VIARD]

GEILER VON KAYSENBERG, JOHANNES (1445–1510), preacher of moral reform on the eve of the Reformation. The first part of his career was academic. An Alsatian he studied, then taught philosophy at the Univ. of

Freiburg in Breisgau until 1471; he obtained his doctorate in theology at Basel and returned to Freiburg to teach in 1475. He was learned in patristics; in theology, a follower of J. *Gerson, whose works he edited (4 v., 1488–1502). But preaching was his primary love, and he gave up teaching to become preacher at the cathedral of Strassburg in 1478; to that office he devoted the rest of his life, and earned the title "the Savanarola of Germany." His sermons, usually on moral topics, were carefully structured, vivid with, sometimes coarse, illustrations, and forcefully delivered. He castigated the moral decadence of rich and poor, monks and clerks; he condemned the unjust practices of lawyers and merchants, the practice of simony in filling church offices. His sermons were popular, and published from notes taken by hearers. But his crusade failed to bring about reform; Strassburg became a center of the Reformation soon after his death.

[T. C. O'BRIEN]

GEISSEL, JOHANNES VON (1796–1864), cardinal, abp. of Cologne, scholar. He was ordained in 1818, became dean of the cathedral chapter of Speyer; proposed by King Louis of Bavaria as bp. of that diocese, G. was consecrated in 1837. In 1841 he was named coadjutor with the right of succession to Cologne, then administered by a prelate who was *persona non grata* to Prussia and King Frederick William IV. G. succeeded to the see of Cologne in 1846; in 1850 he was created cardinal. In the 18 years he served as abp. of Cologne he distinguished himself as one of the outstanding German prelates of the 19th century. He greatly improved relations with Prussia, successfully ended the dominance in theological schools of the followers of *Gunther and *Hermes, called a meeting of the German hierarchy in 1858, which made decisions of great value to the Church. A zealous spiritual leader, he brought many religious communities into his diocese, fostered devotion to the Eucharist and the Blessed Virgin. For almost 20 years before his accession to the bishopric, G. did much important writing. A frequent contributor to the periodical *Katholik,* he was preeminently a historian. His principal work was *Der Kaiserdom zu Speyer* (3 v., 1828). After his death his writings were collected in a four-volume edition *Schriften und Reden von Johannes Cardinal von Geissel* . . . (ed. K. T. Dumont, 1869–76).

[J. R. AHERNE]

GEISSLERLIEDER, medieval German songs performed by the *flagellants, having melodic similarities with the later German chorales of the 16th century.

[D. J. SMUCKER]

GELASIAN DECREE, a Latin document entitled *De libris recipiendis et non recipiendis* formerly ascribed to a Roman synod of 494 A.D. held under Pope Gelasius I (492–496). Modern studies of this decree indicate that it is really a composite work. The first section (ch. 1–3) could go back to the end of the 4th cent. and be the product of the Council of Rome of 382 held under Pope Damasus I. The second (ch. 3–5) could be the product of a private individual with a great admiration for St. Jerome and the teaching of the Church of Rome. These two documents may have been put together by a cleric in N Italy or S Gaul at the beginning of the 6th cent. and circulated for some time simply as a private work. The decree is particularly important for the history of the canon of Scripture and its rejection of the legends of Roman martyrs. BIBLIOGRAPHY: G. Bardy, DBSuppl 3:579–590; A. Kleinhans, EncCatt 5:1982; T. Camelot, *Catholicisme* 4:1804.

[M. J. COSTELLOE]

GELASIAN LETTER, the letter entitled *Famuli vestrae pietatis* sent (494) by Pope *Gelasius I to the Emperor *Anastasius II (PL 59:41–47; D 347). The occasion was the *Acacian Schism, the purpose of the letter to object to imperial intervention in the realm of doctrine. The document was repeatedly cited in the medieval disputes between popes and emperors. It clearly states the autonomy of the spiritual power in deciding purely spiritual issues of teaching and discipline. The distinction between the two powers in the one, nonpluralistic society was indicated; but the letter did not attempt to delineate all possible areas of conflict between Church and State. BIBLIOGRAPHY: S. Z. Ehler and J. B. Morrall, *Church and State through the Centuries* (1954); J. C. Murray, *We Hold These Truths* (1960); W. Ullmann, *Growth of Papal Government in the Middle Ages* (1962).

[T. C. O'BRIEN]

GELASIAN SACRAMENTARY, tr. of a title given in 1748 by L. *Muratori to a Vatican MS (*Reginensis* 316), containing Mass formulas and other liturgical prayers. It is generally agreed that the title is a misnomer, that while Pope *Gelasius I did write Mass formulas, he did not write these. The correct title of the MS is *Liber sacramentorum Romanae ecclesiae anni circuli*; it is debated whether it is an 8th-cent. Frankish compilation, possibly based on a sacramentary used in the Roman churches, or a 7th-cent. Frankish compilation based on *libelli missarum* in the archives of the Lateran.

[T. C. O'BRIEN]

GELASIUS I, ST. (d. 496) **POPE** from 492. G. succeeded *Felix III (II) under whom he had strongly influenced policy as author of papal letters. G. was the most important pope of the 5th cent. after St. *Leo the Great, whom he greatly resembled in thought and style. In connection with the *Acacian Schism, G. resisted imperial interference in the realm of doctrine, and wrote the *Gelasian Letter (D 347) on the relationship of the two powers, temporal and spiritual. The acts of a synod held at Rome (495) during G.'s pontificate contain the first surviving reference to the pope as Vicar of Christ. Portions of G.'s writings were incorporated in early canonical collections and so were widely quoted during subsequent centuries. His letters and treatises (PL 59:13–190) dealt not only with the schism mentioned, but also with *Pelagianism and *Monophysitism. The *Gelasian Decree and the Gelasian Sacramentary (see SACRAMENTARIES) were not his, but of later origin. BIBLIOGRAPHY: Altaner 551–553; Bihlmeyer-Tüchle 1:318–319; W. Ullmann, *Growth of Papal Government in the Middle Ages* (2d ed., 1962).

[R. B. ENO]

GELASIUS II (John of Gaeta; d. 1119), **POPE** from 1118. Imprisoned by his enemies immediately after his election, G. was released because of an uprising. He then fled to Gaeta where he was ordained a priest and consecrated bishop. He presided at a Synod in Vienne and died at Cluny. BIBLIOGRAPHY: O. Engels LTK 4:631; A. Dumas, *Catholicisme* 4:1803–04.

[H. DRESSLER]

GELASIUS OF CAESAREA (d. *c.*395), bp., nephew of *Cyril of Jerusalem. After having ruled 5 years, G. was expelled from his see in 367 in favor of Euzoius, by the Arian Emperor Valens. Upon the accession of Theodosius in 379, G. was allowed to resume his see. He was outstanding in his loyalty to the Nicene cause and attended the First Council of Constantinople in 381. Only fragments of his works have survived. These are: an explanation of the Nicene Creed (similar to his uncle's catecheses), a treatise against the Anomoeans, and most notably a continuation of the *Ecclesiastical History* of *Eusebius, which may have served as the source for the last two books of *History* translated by *Rufinus. BIBLIOGRAPHY: Quasten 3:347–348; T. Camelot, *Catholicisme* 4:1801.

[R. B. ENO]

GELASIUS OF CYZICUS (fl. 5th cent.), historian (of NW Turkey), author of an ecclesiastical history of the Constantinian period. BIBLIOGRAPHY: T. Camelot, *Catholicisme* 4:1801.

[T. C. O'BRIEN]

GELBOE, see GILBOA.

GELIN, ALBERT (1902–60), French Sulpician, OT exegete. G. taught Scripture at the major seminary (1931–39) and at the univ. (1937–60) in Lyons. He frequently contributed scriptural articles to French periodicals and reference works, most notably the *Bible de Jérusalem*. Several of his books have been translated into English, among others: *Religion of Israel* (1959), *Key Concepts of the OT* (1963), *The Poor of Yahweh* (1964), and *The Concept of Man in the Bible* (1968).

[T. M. MCFADDEN]

GELLÉE, CLAUDE, see LORRAINE, CLAUDE.

G^e^MARAH (Aramaic, *gemara'*, completion, tradition), with the *Mishnah, on which it is a commentary, part of the Jewish *Talmud. The Palestinian Gemarah and Talmud developed between 200–400 A.D.; the more authoritative Babylonian Gemarah and Talmud, *c.*500 A.D. BIBLIOGRAPHY: *Standard Jewish Encyclopedia* (ed. C. Roth, 1966) 1783–87 s.v. "Talmud."

[T. C. O'BRIEN]

GEMBLOUX, ABBEY OF (*Gemblacense*), former Benedictine monastery founded in 940 in the Diocese of Liège (now Namur, Belgium), in honor of the Holy Savior and SS. Peter and Exuperius, by Guibert and his grandmother Gisèle. The monastery was confirmed by Otto I the Great and in 945 received a group of monks from *Gorze. It was reformed by Abbot Olbert who consecrated a new church in 1022. The abbey school was most famous in the 11th cent. under Prior Guérin, and Sigebert of Gembloux (d. 1122), author of *De viris illustribus*; a *Chronica* (MGS 6:300–374) for the period 381–1111; and *Gesta* of the abbots of Gembloux. After that, relaxation crept into the monastery and in 1505 it adopted the Statutes of Bursfeld. Shortly thereafter Abbot Papin (d. 1541) undertook important constructions, restored by Abbot Legrain in 1791. The monastery was suppressed in 1796. The 18th-cent. buildings, designed by architect Dewez, have housed the Royal Institute of Agriculture since 1860. The church, built on a Romanesque crypt, is now the parish church. BIBLIOGRAPHY: Cottineau 1:1263–65; R. Forgeur, LTK 4:643; R. Gazeau, *Catholicisme* 4:1806–07.

[J. DAOUST]

GEMEINDELIED, in general, the sacred music sung by a congregation; specifically, the Lutheran chorale sung by the *Gemeinde,* or congregation.

[D. J. SMUCKER]

GEMELLI, AGOSTINO (1878–1959), Franciscan psychologist and educator. Having received a doctorate in medicine at the Univ. of Pavia in 1902, he returned to the Catholic faith, became a Franciscan, and was ordained in 1908. He was a founder (1919) and the first rector of the Catholic Univ. of the Sacred Heart in Milan. His own intellectual efforts and most of his published works were directed to experimental psychology and its application to practical problems of human personality. His work was important to the integration of modern psychological findings into the framework of Catholic theology. From 1936 G. was president of the Pontifical Academy of Sciences. BIBLIOGRAPHY: H. Misiak and V. M. Standt, *Catholics in Psychology* (1954); G. Wagner, *Catholicisme* 4:1807–09.

[T. C. O'BRIEN]

GENEALOGIES, BIBLICAL, lists of ancestors that determined a man's rights and privileges in his clan and tribe. These were important to the Israelites for civil and religious reasons. Legal inheritance depended on one's position in the ancestral line. A priest or levite established his role in temple worship and his right to tithes and other support through them. As a literary form they have the dullness of the registry of births and deaths, but one must realize that the civil and the religious spheres were inseparable, essentially, in the Ancient Near East.

In the Priestly traditions of the Bible and in Chronicles copious genealogies served to fill in gaps between narratives pertaining to different ages. The Chronicler seems to have intended the nine chapters of genealogies at the beginning of his work to play down all the history of Israel before the glorious King David and the establishment of God's covenant with his line, just as he leaves out of his story of David anything that would tarnish the glorified image of the Davidic messianic hopes.

The most ancient lists often included topographical, ethnic, and tribal names rather than those of individuals. Frequently the affirmation of generation meant any kind of alliance between clans and families or even between groups of artisans, such as nomadic metal smiths, musicians, etc. They have afforded important evidence for biblical research on occasion, even if at times it is only negative: the investigation of the names in the lists positively dated as pre-Mosaic has failed to discover any name that has as one of its components the sacred and most revered name of God, Yahweh, which in Israel's tradition was revealed for the first time to Moses. A basic religious aim of the lists appears to have been the connecting of each era of God's progressive salvation through a linear development, which, despite its low points, continued to surge onward toward a future fulfillment. In contrast, the cyclic character of human history, familiar to the Greeks and accepted by Qoheleth, paid little attention to genealogies.

[J. F. FALLON]

GENEALOGY OF JESUS. Two genealogies of Jesus, different in theology and details, are present in the NT, Matthew's (Mt 1.1–17) and Luke's (Lk 3.23–38). The former emphasizes the messianic identity of Jesus as the heir to God's promises to David and Abraham. Three sets of 14 names symbolize Davidic fulfillment (D-V-D in Hebrew = 4+6+4 = 14); to get 14 names in set 3 one counts Mary or Christ (in glory?) as the ultimate completion of the promises. The symbolism of the four women in the list is obscure: if all four were originally gentiles, they point to the risen Christ's universal mission (Mt 28.19). David's crime of adultery and murder, evoked by "Uriah's wife" (v. 6b; cf 2 Sm 11), underlines Jesus' mission to save from sins (Mt 1.21). Luke's aim is more patently universal: he goes back from Jesus—just revealed as God's unique Son (Lk 3.22)—past Abraham all the way to Adam, "the son of God" (v. 38), thus alluding to Jesus as the new Adam, the image of God, who fathers a new humanity (Pauline themes). That Luke's names total 77 may symbolize the plenitude in Christ (seven meant fullness in Luke's mind). Various attempts to reconcile the diverse names in the two lists, which agree on only two from David to Joseph, have not received wide acceptance. Matthew's lineage of kings supports his "fulfillment" intent; Luke may have the more authentic line through Nathan. No hard evidence is extant to explain how they could differ about even Joseph's father. What is clear is that theological purposes were paramount in their treatment of whatever human evidence they had.

[J. F. FALLON]

GÉNÉBRARD, GILBERT (1537–97), Benedictine abp. and Scripture scholar. G. was a professor of Hebrew and Scripture at the Univ. of Paris. In 1593, he was named abp. of Aix-en-Provence but was forced to retire because of his opposition to Henry of Navarre, later *Henry IV of France. G. wrote many commentaries on the OT, expositions of rabbinical literature, and theological treatises, although much of his work consists in the free translation of prior studies. BIBLIOGRAPHY: B. Heurtebize, DTC 6.1:1183–85.

[T. M. MCFADDEN]

GENERAL (of an order), the name ordinarily given the head of a religious order or congregation. The term is usually combined with another noun—superior general, master general, prior general, minister general, or abbot general. The general is normally elected by the general chapter for a term of three to six years, but the general of the Jesuits and of the Dominicans for life.

[M. B. BOYLE]

GENERAL ASSEMBLY (PRESBYTERIAN), the chief *court in Presbyterianism, representative of the whole Church. It is responsible for all matters of faith and order; it institutes and supervises agencies for missions at home and overseas, for education, and for relations with other Churches. The general assembly is a conciliar, judicial, and executive body that usually meets annually, or, if necessary, as called, and consists of an equal number of ministers and elders elected by their presbyteries. Its presiding officer is termed moderator, and may be a minister or elder; his office is one of honor, not jurisdiction. The first assembly of the Reformed Church of Scotland met at Edinburgh in 1560, though the functions of the assembly were not defined until 1851, when A. *Melville's *Book of Discipline was inserted into the register of the acts of the assembly. Most Presbyterian Churches today adhere to the general definition of the powers of the assembly contained in the *Book of Discipline*. In *Reformed Churches the same court is called a general *synod.

[J. A. R. MACKENZIE]

GENERAL BAPTISTS, a designation for those Baptists who believed that Christ's atonement made salvation available to all men. Living in the Netherlands while the controversy over *Arminianism was rife, these early English Baptists rejected the Calvinistic doctrine of *predestination.

John *Smyth, the first pastor, declared that *original sin is "an idle term," and that "God doth not create or predestine any man to destruction." Thus these Arminian Baptists were distinguished from *Particular Baptists by the emphasis they placed upon the power of man's free will either to accept or to reject God's salvation in Christ. BIBLIOGRAPHY: R. G. Torbet, *History of the Baptists* (rev. ed., 1963). *BAPTISTS.

[N. H. MARING]

GENERAL CHURCH OF THE NEW JERUSALEM, a Swedenborgian body, formed in 1890 by a division of *Churches of the New Jerusalem in and around Philadelphia from the parent body, *General Convention of the New Jerusalem in the U.S.A. Denominational headquarters and educational publishing work were located at Bryn Athyn, Pa., with the generous assistance of John Pitcairn, who built a cathedral there for the General Church of the New Jerusalem in 1914. The Church has bps. who are chosen by the annual general assembly, and it asks for unanimity in the decisions of the assembly and the council of bishops. In 1968 there were 1,496 members in 10 churches.

[R. K. MACMASTER]

GENERAL CONFERENCE (METHODIST), the highest legislative body of the Methodist Church. *CONFERENCE (METHODIST).

GENERAL CONFESSION, a confession in which the penitent makes mention of the sins of his past life or of a certain period of his past life, even though in some cases these sins had been previously confessed and forgiven. A general confession is necessary when a mortal sin has been knowingly concealed in a past confession or when a past confession was invalid because the penitent lacked sorrow. In such cases, the general confession must include all mortal sins mentioned in the original bad confession and in any subsequent confessions. A general confession can be spiritually useful when made in the decisive moments of life, *e.g.*, before receiving holy orders, making religious vows, or receiving the sacrament of matrimony. On such occasions, a general confession will promote a more profound self-knowledge and thus better prepare the penitent to receive the graces of his new life situation. In this type of general confession, there is no obligation to confess all mortal sins already forgiven. If the recollection of a particular sin would be spiritually disturbing to the penitent, that sin should not be mentioned again. Penitents who are scrupulous or psychologically prone to live in retrospect, however, may be harmed by a general confession and should avoid them. BIBLIOGRAPHY: B. Häring, *Shalom: Peace, the Sacrament of Reconciliation* (1968); A. Wilson, *Pardon and Peace* (pa. 1966). *PENANCE, SACRAMENT OF.

[J. J. FLOOD]

GENERAL CONVENTION (PHILADELPHIA, 1789), the body that completed the reorganization of what had been the C of E in the colonies into the *Protestant Episcopal Church in the United States. Though established in some provinces, the C of E never had had any general organization in the colonies or any colonial bishops. As a result of the Revolution, it had lost its establishments and the aid it had formerly received from the *Society for the Propagation of the Gospel in Foreign Parts. Following the Revolution, a series of conventions (1784, 1785, and 1786), under the leadership of W. *White and representing principally the middle states, framed a constitution, obtained the consecration in England of two bps. (White of Pennsylvania and S. Provoost of New York), and through a committee recommended a radical revision of the Book of Common Prayer. This revised version came to be known as the Proposed Book, because it never received final approval. In the meantime, the clergy of Connecticut had secured the consecration of S. *Seabury by bps. of the Episcopal Church in Scotland. The General Convention at Philadelphia united these two strands of development under a revised constitution that provided for a bicameral general convention (with a house of bishops and a house of clerical and lay deputies), the body that still governs the Episcopal Church. It also adopted a more conservative revision of the BCP, which remained in force until 1890 (see AMERICAN PRAYER BOOK). Under a rule adopted by the first house of bishops, the bishop senior by consecration became presiding bishop (this office was made elective in 1919). BIBLIOGRAPHY: W. W. Manross, *History of the American Episcopal Church* (3d ed., 1959) 191–201; C. O. Loveland, *Critical Years* (1956) 236–272.

[W. W. MANROSS]

GENERAL CONVENTION (PROTESTANT EPISCOPAL), the legislative body of the Church. The deliberations of the convention, which meets every 3 years, are conducted by the *House of Bishops and the *House of Clerical and Lay Deputies. The convention also functions as the Church's judicial branch, interpreting the constitution (which it alone can amend) and the canons (which it enacts). The convention has provided courts only for the trial of bps. and for review of diocesan trials of other clergy. Historically the convention, through its officers and committees, has served also as the Church's executive branch. A gradual transfer of limited executive authority began in 1919, when the convention began electing the presiding bp.; in 1922 it created an executive council filled largely by vote of the convention. BIBLIOGRAPHY: E. A. White and J. A. Dyckman, *Annotated Constitution and Canons for the Government of the Protestant Episcopal Church in the U.S.A.* (2 v., 1954) 4–38.

[H. H. RIGHTOR]

GENERAL CONVENTION OF THE NEW JERUSALEM IN THE U.S.A., a Church founded in Philadelphia in 1817, to unite the scattered Swedenborgians into a formally organized church body (see CHURCHES OF THE NEW JERUSALEM). William Glenn first brought the works of E. *Swedenborg to America in 1784, and by 1792 the adherents of the New Jerusalem Church were sufficiently numerous to establish a church in Baltimore. Hetty Barclay of Bedford County, Pa., carried the new faith to the West. By 1817 there were congregations in W Pennsylvania, W Virginia and E Ohio, and also in Baltimore and Philadelphia. Some advances were made in New York and New England, 1820–40, but none in the South. The general convention includes 5,096 members in 62 congregations and supports a theological school and an extensive publishing program, esp. of works of Swedenborg.

[R. K. MACMASTER]

GENERAL COUNCIL, a phrase with several ecclesiastical meanings: (1) From the 6th cent., a council or *synod of all the bps. of the Church, in distinction from a particular or provincial council of a diocese or region (see D 447). The papal general councils of the Middle Ages, which evolved from the Roman synods presided over by the popes, legislated for the whole Church. Although "general" is sometimes used as a synonym for "ecumenical," only an *ecumenical council in the strict sense is authoritative for the whole Church. (2) The General Council of the Congregational and Christian Churches was the agency for cooperation formed when the local congregations of these two Churches joined together in 1931 (they became part of the *United Church of Christ in 1957). (3) In Presbyterian Churches the term General Council refers to the administrative agency of any of the church *courts.

GENERAL JUSTICE, another term for *legal justice: "general" because it is a concern for rights and duties of a person as a member of a general, collective whole, society; and because it brings into its service acts of other particular virtues, including commutative and distributive justice, to advance the collective good (ThAq ST 2a2ae, 58.6).

[T. C. O'BRIEN]

GENERAL SYNOD, in the *polity of Reformed and some Lutheran Churches, the supreme legislative and administrative agency (see SYNOD). Historically, it was the title of the union of the Lutheran bodies in Pennsylvania, New York, North Carolina, Maryland, and Virginia formed in 1820, which, because of disagreements in doctrinal points, was gradually weakened and by 1870 had disintegrated.

GENERATION (from the Latin *generatio*), a term that should have its meaning explained according to various contexts. (1) Philosophy. The passage from nonexistence to existence or from nonbeing to being (antonym: corruption), e.g., origination by some chemical or biological process. (2) Biology. Parental (sexual) act or natural process of producing a homogenous offspring (procreation, reproduction). (3) Bible. First, a contemporary group of persons (Gen 7.1; Mt 24.34), sometimes with common good or evil moral traits (Ps 13[14].5; Mt 12.39; 16.4). Second, an indefinite period of time extending either into the past (Is 61.4), or future (Gen 9.12; Ex 12.14), or both (Ex 3.15). Third, a definite period of time; a life-span (Gen 15.16). (4) Theology. First, human generation includes psychosomatic and sexual phenomena as the person of a child (body and soul) is produced both by the parents and by God, who by his transcendent dynamism acts through and in the human parents, esp. by creating and infusing the soul of a child at the moment of conception. Second, the mystery of the Incarnation of the God-man, Jesus Christ, and the divine motherhood of Mary consist in his real generation from her, i.e., in conception from the Holy Spirit, gestation in her womb, and birth of his eternal Divine Person in his human nature. Third, the inner Trinitarian generation is an analogy expressing the procession within the Godhead of the consubstantial, coeternal, coequal, and coomnipotent Son from the divine substance (in contradistinction to the spiration of the Holy Spirit). It connotes the true and natural (nonmetaphorical) sonship of the Second Person of the Trinity (divine filiation) and true and natural paternity of the First Person. It is explained as an eternal intellectual contemplation and emanation, analogous to the birth of thought, in which God the Father in contemplating the divine essence generates the concept of it (Logos, Word), or a Divine Person, differing from the Father by relation of opposition only. BIBLIOGRAPHY: P. B. T. Bilaniuk, NCE 4:428–429; A. D. Turney, *ibid.* 6:322–323; C. J. Peter, *ibid.* 6:323–324; P. C. Hoelle, *ibid.* 10:21–24; G. Sauser and M. Vodopivec, LTK 10:1362–63, s.v. "Zeugung"; M. Schmaus, *Die psychologische Trinitätslehre des Hl. Augustinus* (2d ed., 1967).

[P. B. T. BILANIUK]

GENERATION OF THE WORD, the manner according to which the Second Person of the *Trinity proceeds from the Father. It is distinguished from *spiration, the origin of the Holy Spirit within the Trinity, and from creation, the production of finite being. Although the NT does not directly consider the manner of the Son's origin, it does prepare the way for this speculative advance by referring to Jesus as the Word (John's prologue, Rev 19.13; 1 Jn 1.1) or the only-begotten (Jn 3.16), and by affirming both his equality with and distinction from the Father (e.g., Col 1.15–17; Phil 2.5–11). Several early Christian heresies centered on this issue. The Arians denied Jesus' divinity since they could not conceive of his generation as eternal and spiritual (see ARIANISM). The Subordinationists maintained that God is essentially one and unchangeable, hence he needs an agent of creation and revelation, the Word. This Word is consubstantial with the Father, but also inferior to him since he can come into contact with creatures (see SUBORDINATIONISM). *Sabellianism held that God became the Word when he assumed human nature. Against such positions the patristic writers maintained the divinity of the

Son and developed a theology of his eternal and spiritual generation by the Father from his own substance. Many, both in the East and West, contributed to such a formulation. Augustine's teaching is characteristic: just as man may conceive an idea, called a word of the heart, and thus perform a spiritual activity in time, so also God brings forth an idea, a Word which is the perfect expression of his being. This activity of the Father is also spiritual, but it is eternal and consubstantial. Scholastic theology has continued and deepened the patristic explanations, using the analogy of an intellectual emanation to describe how the Son could be consubstantial with the Father and yet distinct from him. BIBLIOGRAPHY: ThAq ST 1a, 34; M. J. Scheeben, *Mysteries of Christianity* (tr. C. Vollert, 1946); B. Piault, *What is the Trinity?* (tr. R. Houghton, 1959).

[T. M. MCFADDEN]

GENERATIONISM, see TRADUCIANISM.

GENEROSITY, a largeness or greatness of soul which prompts one to give abundantly of what one is and has to others. It can be patchy, for some easily exercise generosity in one area, for example, in money matters, and yet are niggardly with regard to other matters, for example, the gift of one's own time or sympathy. Others have an essential generosity perhaps best described as selflessness which inspires them always to see the needs of another as greater than their own. Such a quality is compounded of charity and a balanced humility which promote in a person a truly humane standard, and is a general condition of all virtue. More specifically, it is considered as an allied virtue to the cardinal virtue of courage, namely liberality which avoids the extremes of wastefulness and meanness, and exhibits the poise suggested by the etymologies: generous, i.e., high-born, and liberal, i.e., free. BIBLIOGRAPHY: Aristotle, *Nicomachean Ethics* 4.1; ThAq ST 2a2ae, 117–119 (esp. in ed. Lat-Eng, v. 42, ed. A. Ross and T. Walsh).

[T. GILBY]

GENESARETH, see GENNESARET.

GENESIS, BOOK OF, the first book of the OT, from a Greek word meaning ''origin'' or ''beginning'' and referring, by the time the name was applied to the book, to the story of creation. Described here are: the primitive history from creation to the ancestor of Abraham (1.1–11.32); the story of Abraham's call in Mesopotamia and his sojourn in Canaan (12.1–25.18); the story of Isaac and Jacob (25.19–37.1); the story of Joseph (37.2–50.26). The book closes with the sons of Jacob settled in the land of Egypt. Three principal traditions contributed to the composition of Genesis: Yahwist (J), Elohist (E), and Priestly (P). J provides the basic narrative framework, with E adding supplementary and parallel stories. P is concerned mainly with genealogies, chronological details, and legal and liturgical elements. J was probably composed in Judah toward the end of the 10th century B.C. E, a sister tradition from the North, was originally composed during the 9th century. After the fall of Samaria in 721 B.C., the two were conflated in Judah at the expense of E. P was added in the postexilic period. Although the literary analysis cannot be established with precision in every passage, the traditions are distinguished clearly enough to supply a basis for an understanding of their theologies. The J attempts a sweeping construction of the whole history of mankind seen in the light of the Exodus and of David's brilliant reign. He tells the story of man's first sin and of his gradual degradation (ch. 2–11 *passim*), and of God's choice of Abraham, Isaac, and Jacob as a preparation for his choice of his people. E has only a patriarchal history, parallel for the most part with J, but reflecting a greater concern for the holiness of God and the morality of the patriarchs. The P gives a liturgical color to the book by suggesting ritual concerns in its stories (e.g., 1.1–2.4a; 6–8 *passim*; 17). Its genealogies (ch. 5, 10, 11 *passim*) establish the link between historical Israel and the beginning of salvation history. Genesis is the book of man's rebellion and of God's saving initiative. Because of the latter, it is a book of hope and promise that would ultimately be fulfilled. BIBLIOGRAPHY: EDB 853–857; E. H. Maly, NCE 327–331.

[E. H. MALY]

GENESIUS, SS. The Genesius legends appear to be based on an account of the martyrdom of a scribe who refused to copy a decree condemning Christianity in a Roman persecution. After a church had been dedicated to him in Rome, a legend arose that identified him as a Roman actor who, while mocking Christian baptism in a play before the Emperor, actually received the gift of faith in Christ and went valiantly to torture and death. Variations of the story applied the name to many figures in the course of time.

[J. F. FALLON]

GENET, JEAN (1910–), French novelist and dramatist of the absurd, who incarnates the outsider for whom literary creation is a medium of purgation. An autobiographical novel, *Miracle of the Rose* (1943, tr. 1965) and his diary, *The Thief's Journal* (1949, tr. 1954) depict his experiences in reform school and as international outcast, pickpocket, and panderer. While in prison, G. began writing poetry and novels, asserting man's duality as criminal and saint. They attracted the attention of existentialist writers who popularized his work and won him reprieve from life imprisonment. G. found the stage's use of self-conscious artifice and its potential for ritual, magic, and myth-making an ideal medium for objectifying the absurdist theme of quest of identity. BIBLIOGRAPHY: J. P. Sartre, *Saint Genet, Actor and Martyr* (tr. B. Frechtman, 1963); J. H. McMahon, *Imagination of Jean Genet* (1963); R. N. Coe, *The Vision of Jean Genet* (1968); P. Thody, *Jean Genet. A Critical Appraisal* (1968).

[G. E. GINGRAS]

GENETICS, a biological science investigating genes as the unique messengers and interpreters of life, a study often undertaken with a view to diagnosing, preventing and treating hereditary diseases. Pioneering in the field were O.T. Avery and his associates who in 1944 discovered the properties of deoxyribonucleic acid (DNA), a substance which J. D. Watson and F. Crick in 1953 verified as the "secret of life," placing in human hands the potential to control human life and evolution. Such knowledge, according to T. Dobzhansky, poses a dilemma where a choice must be made between "the prospect of a genetic twilight" and "the certainty of a moral twilight," that is, employing medical technology to enable the weak and deformed to survive and to reproduce, thereby allowing for further degeneration of the genetic pool, or deciding to let the genetically defective suffer and die when in fact we have the means to save them.

Other alternatives are, however, also possible: the weak and defective can be assisted by various therapeutic procedures for specific genetic disorders; carriers of genetic anomalies can be confronted with the possibility or requirement either of sterilization or abstention from procreation. All of these alternatives raise ethical questions which must be faced honestly and systematically. Some facts may indeed be startling: there are more than 2,000 genetically distinct inherited defects and 15 out of every 100 newborns have hereditary disorders of lesser or greater severity. Nonetheless, worries about defective genes can be exaggerated, for humanity's well-being is threatened as much by moral and spiritual disorders as by genetic defects. Moreover, true concern for humanity's future and the integrity of the genetic pool will not look for solutions only in various kinds of genetic interventions, but will turn also to euthenics (environmental engineering) to overcome the disastrous effects of air and water pollution.

Genetically related research is developing on several fronts: eugenics, gene therapy or genetic engineering, and euphenics. (1) Eugenics may be either negative or positive. Negative eugenics attempts to curtail the transmission of defective genes by controlling or preventing procreation by genetically defective individuals. Positive eugenics seeks to enhance humanity's status, achieving a broad distribution of desirable traits by means of preferential breeding of individuals designated as superior. The danger with any large-scale use of negative or positive eugenics is that is will result in a standardization of genetic characteristics, thereby minimizing humanity's capacity to adapt to the environment and thus to maintain satisfactory evolutionary development. (2) Both gene therapy and genetic engineering involve changing the molecular structure of genes. Gene therapy or gene "surgery" refers to the attempt to alter the genes of an existing individual and is distinguished from genetic engineering, which focuses on procedures affecting the gametes (the ovum and sperm) with a view to thwarting the transmission of genetic defects and improving the status of the individual-to-be. (3) Euphenics tries to correct or prevent the expression of detrimental genes without affecting the genes themselves; thus while people with myopia or diabetes may wear corrective lenses or take insulin, they may pass on their genetically based disorders to their offspring; in a real sense, therefore, euphenics succeeds at a cost to eugenics.

It is impossible to argue with the goal of genetic progress, improvement humanity's mental and physical well-being, but discussions flourish on the ethical acceptability of the various means proposed to achieve this goal. B. Häring has observed that the real question is not whether we should or should not intervene in genetic evolutions, because, consciously and willingly or not, man "does constantly influence genetic history by how he shapes his own behaviour and his total environment" (*Ethics of Manipulation,* 183). What must be decided is whether human influence upon human evolution will continue to be haphazard or instead be systematically planned. If a sense of responsibility inspires the chosing of deliberate intervention, it must also include the caution to proceed humbly and with the utmost wisdom; hopes for future generations must be balanced by an acknowledgment of, and respect for, the personal rights of each presently existing individual, including esp. those of the weak, the defective, and defenseless. If the step is taken to modify humanity, according to what specifications will alterations be made? Who will decide upon such specifications, and who will supervise the implementation of the plan? The state of public policy-making in environmental, domestic, and foreign affairs is proof enough to that questions about genetic policy-making are not at all idle. In the effort to reshape humanity it is imperative not to undermine those very conditions of possibility for genuine human intercommunication among individuals—personal freedom, the desire for truth, the capacity to recognize goodness, and the courage to love. BIBLIOGRAPHY: The Hastings Center, *Bibliography of Society, Ethics and the Life Sciences* (pub. annually); C. E. Curran, *Politics, Medicine and Christian Ethics* (1973); J. F. Dedek, *Contemporary Medical Ethics* (1975); *New Genetics and the Future of Man* (ed. M. Hamilton, 1972); B. Häring, *Ethics of Manipulation* (1975); P. Ramsey, *Fabricated Man* (1970); "Genetic Science and Man," entire issue of *ThSt* 33 (1972).

[V. J. GENOVESI]

GENEVA BIBLE, an English version of the Bible by Protestant exiles at Geneva, Switzerland; begun during the reign of Mary Tudor (1553–58), the NT was completed in 1557; the whole Bible was published in 1560. The translation drew largely on those of W. Tyndale and M. Coverdale. The Geneva Bible was the most widely read English version until the AV, which drew from it many of its translations. The name Breeches Bible was given to the Geneva Bible because in Gen. 3.7 it speaks of Adam and Eve's making "breeches" for themselves.

[T. EARLY]

GENEVA ROBES, the garb worn usually by clergy of the *Reformed Churches. These Churches, following Calvin's directives for Geneva, discarded most of the old vestments, retaining only the outdoor dress of the clergy, which was to be used also in church services. This consisted of cassock, gown, bands (or other neckwear), black velvet cap, and scarf. The Geneva gown is somewhat fuller than the academic gown, which may be worn in its place.

[J. A. R. MACKENZIE]

GENEVAN CATECHISMS, two *confessions of faith for the *Reformed Church at Geneva; also called Calvin's Catechisms. (1) The first, entitled *Instruction and Confession of Faith according to the Use of the Church of Geneva,* was presented in its printed text to a conference at Lausanne in Feb. 1537. The document was not a *catechism at all but a doctrinal exposition in 58 sections, probably composed by Calvin and based on his **Institutes of the Christian Religion.* His conception of the Church and of the high status of the minister of the word is prominent. A short time later a confession of faith in 21 articles, obligatory for all citizens, was added. (2) The Catechism of 1541 was composed in French by Calvin to implement the section of the *Ecclesiastical Ordinances* on the education of children. It was later (1545) translated into Latin for wider circulation. Using the Apostles' Creed, the Ten Commandments, and the Lord's Prayer as a framework, this catechism, unlike its predecessor, takes the form of questions and answers, beginning with: "What is the chief end of human life?" "That men should know God by whom they are created." The work is heavily theological, and is divided into four parts: Faith, Law, Prayer, Sacraments. To facilitate summarization and memorization, the contents of the French edition were distributed to correspond to the Sundays of the year. For a long time this catechism was used as the basis for instruction in the Reformed Churches of France and Holland; it influenced the formulation of the *Heidelberg and *Westminster Catechisms. BIBLIOGRAPHY: *Calvin: Theological Treatises* (ed. J. K. S. Reid, LibCC 22; 1954); Schaff Creeds 1:467–471; Léonard HistProt 1:325–326.

[N. H. MARING]

GENEVIEVE, ST. (*c.*442–*c.*500), patron saint of Paris. Her vita, extant in three recensions, claims to have been written 18 years after her death. If authentic, the vita is an important historical document, antedating the *Historia Francorum* of Gregory of Tours (begun *c.*574, completed 594), and valuable for its details concerning the first Merovingian kings and the city of Paris before Clovis made it his capital. The authenticity of this document has been questioned by some scholars (e.g., B. Krush), but has been ably defended by G. Kurth among others (for an account of the controversy, see H. Platelle, BiblSanct 6:157–162). At the age of 15, G. was consecrated as a virgin by Bp. Vilicus, and upon the death of her parents she went to Paris to live with her godmother. St. Germain of Auxerre held her in great esteem, as did the Frankish kings Childeric and Clovis. When Paris was threatened by the Huns under Attila (451), the panic of the inhabitants was quieted by her counsel to resort to prayer rather than flight and the city would be spared. Her intercession was credited for the delivery of Paris from pestilence in 1129. Her cult has remained popular in France. Text of the *Vita Genovefae* (ed. B. Krush) MGHS rer. Mer. 3:204–238. BIBLIOGRAPHY: G. Kurth, "Étude critique sur la vie de sainte Geneviève," RHE 14 (1913) 5–80, Butler 1:28–30; H. Platelle BiblSanct 6:157–161.

[H. DRESSLER]

GENGHIS (CHINGIS) KHAN (*c.*1167–1227), Mongol ruler and one of the greatest conquerors in world history. His original name was Temuchin, the name Genghis Khan (Very Great King) being the title he received from his followers in 1206. He united the Mongol tribes and created a Mongol empire. From 1211 to 1215 his armies seized large sections of N China, and by 1221 he had conquered central Asia and destroyed Iran. In 1223 he defeated the Russian princes at the battle of Kalka. He wished to create a world empire, and showed marked ability as an administrator as well as a conqueror. He employed foreigners as advisors and adopted the Uigur script for his own language. He was a promoter of commerce and arts and crafts. He succeeded in establishing peace and order throughout most of his vast realm. The secret of his military success was his effective use of a strongly disciplined and highly mobile army. BIBLIOGRAPHY: W. Bingham et al., *History of Asia* (1964) 1:409–422; R. Grousset, *Le Conquérant du monde* (1961).

[M. R. P. MCGUIRE]

GÉNICOT, ÉDOUARD (1856–1900), Jesuit professor of moral theology at Louvain from 1899; author of a manual of moral theology used in many seminaries, *Theologiae moralis institutiones* (1896). The work was frequently reissued in editions revised by his nephew J. *Salsman. G.'s work condensed that of A. *Ballerini, leader in the 19th-cent. Jesuit defense of *Probabilism. BIBLIOGRAPHY: T. Deman, DTC 13:593–595 s.v. *"Probabilisme."*

[T. C. O'BRIEN]

GENINGS, EDMUND, ST. (alias Ironmonger; 1567–91), English martyr. G. was born in Lichfield, converted to Catholicism in his late teens, and was ordained at Reims in 1590. He returned to England but was arrested while saying Mass in 1591. Accused of treason, G. was tried and executed in that same year. Upon his death, G.'s brother, John, also became a RC and was ordained. He published a life of his brother at Saint-Omer in 1614. G. was beatified in 1929 and canonized in 1970. BIBLIOGRAPHY: Butler 4:532–534; M. Salsano, BiblSanct 6:128–129.

[T. M. MCFADDEN]

GENINGS, JOHN (1570–1660), English Franciscan. The brother of St. Edmund Genings, he resisted his brother's attempts to convert him to the old faith and in fact feared persecution so much that he was relieved when Edmund was executed. About 10 days later John experienced interior conversion, was received into the Church, studied at Douai, and was ordained in 1607. Returning to the English mission he was prompted to restore the Franciscans in England. He took the habit, joining a group of English Franciscans in Belgium (1614). From Douai he proceeded to reestablish the English Franciscan Province. G. was appointed first provincial (1629), an office he held for three terms.

[J. R. AHERNE]

GENIZA (Heb., hiding), a room attached to the synagogue where mainly worn-out copies of sacred books were deposited. Famous is the geniza of the ancient Ezra synagogue in Cairo where in the years 1896–98 S. Schechter discovered valuable MSS. BIBLIOGRAPHY: N. Gold, "Sixty Years of Geniza Research. Dedicated to the Memory of Professor Schechter," *Judaism* 6 (1957); P. Kahle, *Cairo Geniza* (1959).

[F. BUCK]

GENNADIUS I, ST. (d. 471), **PATRIARCH OF CONSTANTINOPLE** from 458. G. is known for his great sanctity and power of prayer, as well as for his theological and exegetical writing. In his position as patriarch he esp. took measures against simony and the spread of Monophysitism; he also gave staunch support to papal primacy. As a writer his commentaries on Gen, Ex, Ps, and the letters of St. Paul show his attachment to the Antiochene school of literal interpretation of Scripture. He attacked the *Twelve Anathemas* of St. Cyril of Alexandria in a work completed in 431, and in general opposed Alexandrian Christology. He established his own orthodoxy in his encomium on Pope Leo I's *Ad Flavianum* (the famous *Tome* of Leo). BIBLIOGRAPHY: G.'s works, PG 85:1613–1734; F. Dvornik, *Idea of Apostolicity and the Legend of Andrew* (1958); Quasten 3:523–526.

[L. NEMEC]

GENNADIUS II SCHOLARIUS, PATRIARCH OF CONSTANTINOPLE, see GEORGE SCHOLARIOS.

GENNADIUS OF ASTORGA, ST. (d. 936), Spanish bishop. A monk from an early age, G. was the restorer and abbot of San Pedro de Montes. He was elected bp. of Astorga *c.*899, but resigned the office a few years before his death to return to the monastic life. During his incumbency, he fostered monasticism in his diocese by founding several monasteries. BIBLIOGRAPHY: Butler 2:391–392; A. Q. Prieto, BiblSanct 6:130–132.

[R. B. ENO]

GENNADIUS OF MARSEILLES (d. *c.*500), church historian. A priest of Marseilles, G. is known chiefly as the author (*c.*480) of the continuation of the *De viris illustribus* of St. *Jerome. This work furnishes valuable information on authors of the 5th century. G. also wrote other works of an antiheretical nature: against *Pelagius, *Nestorius, *Eutyches, and eight books against all heresies, which are now lost except for fragments. Works: PL 58:1059–1120. BIBLIOGRAPHY: Altaner 567–568.

[R. B. ENO]

GENNESARET (Genesareth; Vulg, Genesar), name of a place where Jesus and his Disciples landed after a storm in the Sea of Galilee (Mt 14.34). Gennesaret may have been a settlement in the plain or the plain itself, in the NW shore of the lake, called Lake of Gennesaret in Lk 5.1, between Tiberias and Capernaum. BIBLIOGRAPHY: D. Baly, *Geography of the Bible* (1957) 189–190, 197–198.

[A. VIARD]

GENOCIDE, a hybrid word from the Gr. *genos,* tribe, race, nation, with the Lat. suffix *cida,* from *caedere,* to kill, coined at the time of the Nuremberg Trials; the grave moral wrong of extirpating a whole racial group, also extended to the destruction of a cultural, religious, or political group. Massacres of whole peoples were not uncommon in the days before tribal had been succeeded by political wars, nor were they unknown to the colonial expansion of the English-speaking people into Gaelic lands, North America, and Australia, nor in the atrocities of the Turks against the Armenians; but there had been nothing to compare with the wholesale murder of Jews, Slavs, and Romanies ruthlessly engineered with the apparatus of modern frightfulness by the Hitler regime. As a mass-killing of the innocent it infinitely multiplied and aggravated the mortal sin of murder; as done in the name of an allegedly superior Aryan race, subspecies Nordic (both of them mythical), it was a barbarianism that would have been contemptible had it not been so horrible. In addition it bore many other crimes crying to heaven for vengeance. The UN Assembly in 1946 unanimously affirmed that it was a crime under international law, and a convention was adopted in 1948 to enforce the ruling and to provide for appropriate penalties. This, however, has not yet been implemented.

[T. GILBY]

GENOVEFA, ST., see GENEVIEVE, ST.

GENTILE DA FABRIANO (Gentile di Niccolo di Giovanni di Massio; 1370–1427), leading painter of *International Gothic style in Italy, strongly influencing the art of Venice, N Italy, and Umbria. G. executed two paintings in Venice (1408) and a fresco in the Doge's Palace (1409), all destroyed; and decorated a chapel in Brescia (1414) for Pandolfo Malatesta, later working in Florence, Siena, Orvieto, and Rome (1427). His earliest works, *Madonna and Child Enthroned with St. Nicholas and a Donor,* (1390–95); the imposing altarpiece *Valle Romita Polytych* (Milan;

a *St. Francis Receiving the Stigmata;* and the badly damaged *Madonna and Child Enthroned* (Metropolitan Museum, N.Y.) are of Lombard style with Franco-Flemish and Sienese influence. G.'s major work from Florence is the large *Adoration of the Magi* (1423) with three predella panels (*The Nativity, The Flight into Egypt* and *The Presentation,* Uffizi, Florence) for the Palla Strozzi chapel in Sta. Trinità, showing a courtly procession of human and animal forms, rich in texture, of lavish color shimmering with gold leaf, the bosses on bridles in relief; the predella—in naturalism, perspective and genre details against a lyrical landscape—points to the future. A panel of the predella of G.'s great Quaratesi altarpiece (National Gallery, Washington, D.C.) and two handsome Madonnas (National Gallery, and Yale Univ.) show a later Florentine solidity, though G. at times reverted to an earlier linear style.

[M. J. DALY]

GENTILES, non-Israelite peoples; foreign nations; a term that acquired a strongly negative coloring in Jewish usage in post-Exilic times. It represents the dark side of chosen-ness and election, involving an implied aspersion on those not chosen. Before Israel's experience of life in the Diaspora, its national consciousness was apparently not vastly different from that of other peoples' of the ancient Near East, who all had their own gods and religion. It was the supranational pretensions of the world empires, which reached a peak in the cultural arrogance of the Hellenistic Seleucids who ruled Palestine in the time of the Maccabean revolt, that brought a change in attitude. Before then it had been common to accept the vision of Second Isaiah, that the gentiles were waiting for the Law; and that Israel was the Servant of Yahweh who would be the light of the Nations. But under stress of persecution it became easier to view the gods of the nations as demons to whom the foreign peoples had sold themselves, and were subsequently condemned by Yahweh to the service of these false gods. This second view had the added effect of mitigating missionary zeal. In Rabbinical writings gentiles were represented as opposed to God and to Israel; and beyond their traditional sins of uncircumcision, sabbath-breaking, and various uncleannesses, they ate food sacrificed to demons and had sold themselves to do evil. Without moral sense, they were capable of any imaginable evil. Such attitudes flourished in NT times and are reflected in words attributed to Jesus: ''Do not even gentiles do as much?'' (Mt 5:47); ''When you pray, do not go babbling on as gentiles do, who imagine the more they say the more likely they are to be heard'' (Mt 6:7). Jesus' first apostolic mandate to his Disciples expressly excluded the gentiles (Mt 10:5). Members of the community who could not accept fraternal rebuke were to be expelled as if they were gentiles (Mt 18:17). In the three Synoptic Gospels Jesus foretells his death as an event that will involve the fearful reality of being ''handed over to the gentiles.'' Other NT writings refer to gentiles as wandering in their misguided ways, separated from the Messiah, strangers to the community of God and to the covenant of promise, without hope and without God. Yet by events of history which are still the subject of much controversy, it was among the gentiles that the Christian gospel took root; and in many currents of Christian thought, it was the Jew who came to symbolize unbelief; until in the Fourth Gospel the Jewish law not only brings death to the Messiah but to the entire nation. Now one nation is to bear the kind of opprobrium that previously had been shared by all nations except one. This tradition of Jew versus gentile, close to the heart of all religious bigotry, as well as to nationalism and to cultural imperialism, is a part of biblical culture that remains problematic, and certainly affects all the traditions that claim to have their source in the biblical culture.

[E. J. DILLON]

GENTILESCHI, Italian painters. **Orazio** (1563–1639) painted in Rome, Genoa, Paris, and the court of London. ''Florentine'' manner and caravaggesque realism are seen in G.'s *Angel Gabriel* and *St. Francis Supported by an Angel* (1600), *St. Cecilia and an Angel* (1606), and *St. Peter Nolasco Carried by Angels,* with Venetian influence in an *Annunciation* (1623). He subordinated realistic detail to graceful line in his *Rest on the Flight into Egypt* (1626). In London the influence of Van Dyck was modified in his *Finding of Moses* (Madrid). An eclectic establishing a northern realism of graceful form in subtle light, G. was a forerunner of Vermeer and like painters **Artemisia** (1597–1651), studied with her father Orazio and with Tassi, traveling to Rome, Naples, and London. Her genre works, though more vigorous than her father's, are often confused with Orazio's. She executed the *Miracle of S. Carlo Borromeo,* a family scene, and a series of dramatic night scenes in the tenebroso style of Caravaggio and Honthorst: *David and Goliath, Lot and His Daughters* (both in Rome, and *Judith and the Woman Servant* (Florence). *Judith Decapitating Holofernes* (Florence) is powerful in its abrupt foreshortening and brutal violence couched in vigorous techinque. Van Dyck's painterliness characterizes the *Birth of John the Baptist* following her London visit. Her genre, subject, light effects, vigor, and painterly surfaces together with work of Ribera inspired the *Caravaggisti* in Naples.

[M. J. DALY]

GENTILI, ANTONIO (ANTONIO DA FAENZA, 1519–1607), Italian goldsmith active in Rome (1550–67). G.'s greatest masterpieces, commissioned by Card. Alessandro Farnese, were a silver and gold altar cross and silver candlesticks for the main altar of St. Peter's. G. was appointed Master of the Pope's Mint in 1585.

[M. J. DALY]

GENUFLECTION, the practice of touching the right knee to the floor, sometimes while bowing, as a gesture of homage or adoration. Originally part of imperial and feudal ceremonial, the custom entered the liturgy as a way of showing honor to persons. Its use was later extended and it became a means of showing honor to the cross, the altar, and the Blessed Sacrament. The practice of genuflecting to the Blessed Sacrament was unknown prior to the 11th cent. and was not introduced into the Mass until the 14th century. The practice is now ordinarily confined to the consecration at Mass and to honoring the reserved sacrament, particularly on entering or leaving a church, and is generally used by RCs and some Anglicans. Eastern Christians more commonly use a profound bow.

[J. DALLEN]

GENUINITY, RELIGIOUS, fidelity to God in life and worship. Man's relationship with God is true if it is determined by the divine reality revealed to him. The scriptural source for this phrase is found in the OT Hebrew term *ĕmĕt*, signifying fidelity, steadfastness, truth (Ps 31.6), and is translated in the Septuagint and NT by *alētheia* (Jn 8.44), signifying, among other things, genuineness, divine reality, revelation. God expects man, his people, to be faithful to him in response to his fidelity toward them. The Johannine writings specialize in pointing out how the Christian must conform to Jesus who incarnates, personifies, and teaches the truth (Jn 14.6), and sends the Spirit of truth to continue his work (Jn 14.17). Existentialist theologians hold that man, no matter how authentic his life of religion may be, feels the tension between who he is and who he is to be.

[J. FICHTNER]

GEOFFREY OF BRETEUIL (Godfrey; fl. latter half of 12th cent.), Victorine canon and prior. G. was much interested in the intellectual development of monks and scoffed at those who thought study incompatible with the monastic vocation. Some of his letters are extant (PL 205:827–888). In these it appears that he also wrote a spiritual treatise *De videndo Deo,* which has not survived, and a biography of St. Haimon of Savigny, which has not been satisfactorily identified. BIBLIOGRAPHY: P. Delhaye, *Catholicisme* 4:1849–50.

[M. J. SUELZER]

GEOFFREY OF CLAIRVAUX (d. 1188), author, Cistercian abbot. Originally a disciple of Abelard, G. came under St. Bernard's influence in 1140, and served as his secretary at Clairvaux. After short terms as abbot at Igny and Clairvaux, he retired to Cîteaux (1165) where he continued to support Alexander III. In 1170 he became abbot of Fossanova (Italy) and in 1176 abbot of Hautecombe (Savoy). G. collected Bernard's letters, contributed to his vita and wrote sermons, letters, and two treatises against Gilbert de la Porrée. BIBLIOGRAPHY: PL 185:301–618; J. Leclercq, "S. Bernard et ses secrétaires," RevBen 61(1951) 220–225; *idem,* "Les écrits de Geoffroy d'Auxerre," *ibid.* 62 (1952) 274–291.

[L. J. LEKAI]

GEOFFREY OF DUNSTABLE (d. 1146), abbot. Born at Maine, France, and descended from ancestors of noble rank, G. studied at the Univ. of Paris, and although a secular was invited by Richard, abbot of St. Albans, to take charge of his school. G. delayed in taking this post, but later directed a school at Dunstable, England. During this period he composed a miracle play of St. Catherine, either for the weavers of the town or his scholars; and when the choir copes that he borrowed from St. Albans abbey for his production were burned, he joined the community. He became prior and in 1119, abbot. He founded the hospital of St. Julian for lepers, and founded or enlarged and regulated a nunnery at Sopwell as a cell of St. Alban's. G. made generous gifts to St. Albans in his vigorous rule of some 26 years; his efforts saved it from demolition during the civil wars of King Stephen.

[J. D. LOUGHLIN]

GEOFFREY HARDEBY (d. 1385), English Augustinian theologian. He engaged in controversy against Abp. *Richard Fitzralph's *De pauperie salvatoris*. His most famous work is the posthumous *De vita evangelica* (1385). Twice he served as provincial of the English Augustinians and for 1 year (1376–77) he was confessor to Richard, Prince of Wales. BIBLIOGRAPHY: R. L. Poole, DNB 8:1213–14.

[J. A. WEISHEIPL]

GEOFFREY OF MONMOUTH (d. 1155), bp., historian. A cleric associated with Oxford and its archdeacon Walter, G. became bp. of St. Asaph, Wales (1152). His major work, *Historia Britonum* (completed 1136–39) is of negligible historical merit but had immense influence on later historians. Mingling British and Continental traditions with obvious fabrications, it recounts British "history" from Trojan origins to the Anglo-Saxon conquest and develops the Arthurian legend at length. G. also wrote the *Prophetiae Merlini,* incorporated into the *Historia,* and a metrical *Vita Merlini*. BIBLIOGRAPHY: J. S. P. Tatlock, *Legendary History of Britain* (1950).

[W. A. CHANEY]

GEOFFREY OF VENDÔME (*c.*1070–1132), French Benedictine abbot, cardinal. He entered the monastery at Sainte-Trinité, Vendôme, and was elected abbot before 1094. He engaged vigorously in the struggles of his time for the reofrm and independence of the Church against lay investiture and simony under all forms. In 1094 he was consecrated cardinal priest of St. Prisca on the Aventine. An intimate friend of Urban II, Paschal II, and Callistus II, he frequently served as papal legate and was present at the Councils of Clermont (1095), Saintes (1096) and Reims (1131). G. was an excellent administrator who maintained the privileges of Vendôme in a period of great unrest, and was well-versed both in Scripture and canon law; he left numerous letters (more than 185) and some short treatises, e.g., on baptism and on the Eucharist. His letters are a valuable source of 12th-cent. church politics. BIBLIOGRAPHY: PL 157:33–290; J.-C. Didier, *Catholicisme* 4:1852–53.

[J. D. LOUGHLIN]

GEOFFREY OF VILLEHARDOUIN, see VILLEHARDOUIN, GEOFFREY OF.

GEOFFREY OF VINSAUF (Galfridus; fl. *c.*1200), teacher of rhetoric and poet. His most famous work, *Poetica nova,* is a hexameter poem of 2,116 lines on the art of poetry, a work that had great influence on both Latin and vernacular poetry as well as rhetoric until the 15th century. He was educated in Oxford, taught in Hampton (and perhaps Bologna) and was associated with King Richard I. BIBLIOGRAPHY: Manitius 3:751–756.

[V. L. BULLOUGH]

GEOFFREY OF YORK (1153?–1212), English ecclesiastic and politician; elected bp. of Lincoln (1173) but resigned unconsecrated (1182); chancellor of England (1182–89); abp. of York (1191–1212). Illegitimate son and loyal supporter of Henry II, G. was forced into a church career although better fitted for secular office. He quarreled with kings and churchmen, was exiled by John (1207), and died in Normandy.

[R. W. HAYS]

GEOMANCY, a form of *divination, and as such a sin against the virtue of *religion. Geomancy is a way of expressly invoking some demonic power in order to gain a knowledge that belongs to God alone, the knowledge of contingent, future happenings. The name signifies that the alleged knowledge gained appears in some earthly element—wood, iron, stone. If the medium of communication is water, the practice is called "hydromancy"; if air, "aeromancy"; if fire, "pyromancy"; if the entrails of animals, "hepatoscopy." In the Middle Ages geomancy also had a narrower meaning: placing dots, drawings lines connecting them (*protractio punctorum*), then interpreting the configuration was called *ars· geomantiae*. BIBLIOGRAPHY: ThAq ST 2a2ae, 95.3.

[T. C. O'BRIEN]

GEOPOLITICS, a science alleged to study the effect of natural and geopolitical environment on the history of man and the destiny of nations. This "science" developed from the 19th-cent. thought that man evolved in certain relation to his environment. The word is believed to have been coined by a Swedish professor, Rudolf Kjellén (1864–1922). What began, however, as an historico-political account of man's development digresses, and in some ways, lapses into nothing more than a panegyric to nationalism and excessive national and environmental determinism.

[J. R. RIVELLO]

GEORGE, ST. (early 3d cent.?), martyr. The subject of a complicated and fantastic series of legends, including the familiar slaying of the dragon, St. George does seem to have existed, but all that can be said of him is that he was probably martyred during the persecution of Diocletian. Tradition has it that he was a soldier from Lydda in Palestine, where he was also buried. Referred to as the *Megalomartyr* (Gr. Great Martyr), his cult was immensely popular throughout the East where many frescoes and icons depict his life and martyrdom in great detail. He is usually portrayed as a young soldier, either on horseback slaying the dragon or holding the white banner with the red cross of victory. The crusaders apparently revived his cult in the West where he became the patron of knights, soldiers, and eventually of Boy Scouts. He has been chosen as the patron of many cities and nations including England, Portugal, Aragon, Catalonia, Lithuania, Georgia, and Ethiopia. BIBLIOGRAPHY: Butler 2:148–150; H. Thurston, CE 6:453–455; D. Balboni, BiblSanct 6:512–525; K. Setton, "St. George's Head," *Speculum* 48(1973) 1–12.

[G. T. DENNIS]

GEORGE CEDRENUS (late 11th and early 12th cent.), Byzantine chronicler. His *Synopsis Istoriōn* begins with creation and comes down to 1057. It is a compilation based on earlier chronicles. For the period 811–1057, it is taken almost entirely from the important chronicle of John Skylitzes. Since the latter's chronicle is not yet published, one must employ Cedrenus. BIBLIOGRAPHY: G. Moravcsik, *Byzantinoturcica* (2 v., 2d ed., 1958) 1:273–275.

[M. R. P. MCGUIRE]

GEORGE OF GHIEL (1616–52), Belgian Capuchin missionary. G. entered the Congo in 1651 and converted many hundreds within a year. The first Bantu dictionary, originally in Latin and Spanish, was begun by him. He died at the hands of natives whom he had reproved for returning to idolatrous practices forbidden even by civil law. His cause was introduced in 1936. BIBLIOGRAPHY: I. de Milano, EncCatt 6:447.

[M. J. SUELZER]

GEORGE HAMARTOLUS (George the Monk; fl. mid-9th cent.), Byzantine monk whose *Chronicle* incorporates earlier documents otherwise lost, notably writings of the 4th and 5th cent. against Manichaeism (PG 110, 883–891).

[T. C. O'BRIEN]

GEORGE OF LAODICEA (fl. 350), Arian bp. and leader of the Homoiousians along with Basil of Ancyra, Eustathius of Sebaste, and Silvanus of Tarsus. Deposed from the priesthood by Alexander, bp. of Alexandria, at the time of the outbreak of Arianism, G. failed to be received by Eustathius of Antioch but was accepted by the Arian Sophronius of Arethusa. In 331 he became bp. of Laodicea, and in 335 he took part in the Council of Tyre, which deposed Athanasius, but was himself deposed by the Catholic Council of Sardica in 343. Rejecting the radical Arianism of the Anomoean Aetius, G. took part in the Council of Ancyra, which promulgated the doctrine of *Homoiousianism. He attended the Council of Seleucia in 359 and must have died soon after it. A skilled dialectician, he wrote against heretics and the Manichaeans and composed an encomium on his friend Eusebius of Emessa. BIBLIOGRAPHY: O. Perler, LTK 4:702–703; A. Amore, EncCatt 6:447–448.

[M. J. COSTELLOE]

GEORGE METOCHITES (d. *c.* 1328), archdeacon of Hagia Sophia in Constantinople, Byzantine theologian and polemicist. He was sent by Michael VIII Palaeologus to Popes Gregory X, Innocent V, and John XXI and participated in the Council of *Lyons (1274) where he strenuously supported the union with Rome concluded there. After the union came to an end in 1282, he was imprisoned and exiled for the rest of his life, despite the fact that his son Theodore became first minister. G. wrote a large number of works favoring union with Rome, which, he felt, would assure the safety of the empire. Among his writings are a dogmatic history, five books on the procession of the Holy Spirit (still unedited), and several polemical tracts. BIBLIOGRAPHY: S. Salaville, DTC, 6.1:1238–39; Beck, 684; D. Geanakoplos, *Emperor Michael Palaeologus and the West* (1959) 287–291.

[P. FOSCOLOS]

GEORGE PACHYMERES, see PACHYMERES, GEORGE.

GEORGE OF PISIDIA (fl. 610–641), Byzantine poet, deacon of Sancta Sophia in Constantinople. He wrote three historical poems imitative of classical Greek style, on the reign of the Emperor Heraclius; a commentary on the hexaemeron; and a poem about human life.

[T. C. O'BRIEN]

GEORGE OF PODEBRAD (1420–71), leader of the *Utraquists, King of Bohemia. G. resolved the religio-political impasse between Utraquist and pro-Roman factions by seizing Prague in 1448. He then was accepted by both parties as regent during the minority of King Ladislas. In 1452 he defeated the *Taborites. At Ladislas' death (1458) G. was unanimously elected king. First conciliatory toward Rome, he took a hard Utraquist and anti-Roman line when the conflict of factions was renewed in 1462 with Pius II's annulment of the *Compactata. Paul II excommunicated him, released his subjects from allegiance, and had Bohemia invaded by *Matthias Corvinus, King of Hungary. Before G.'s death Matthias was proclaimed king of Bohemia by the pro-Romanist nobles. G.'s reign was marked by persecution of the *Bohemian Brethren. BIBLIOGRAPHY: F. G. Heymann, *George of Bohemia: King of Heretics* (1965).

GEORGE (THE BEARDED) OF SAXONY (1471–1539), German prince who resisted Luther's Reform, esp. in his own Duchy of Saxony. Intent on church reform himself, he resisted Luther only when the break with Rome became clear. G. was present at the *Disputation of Leipzig (1519), where J. *Eck debated with both *Karlstadt and Luther, and where Luther took his famous final stand. G. undertook an unsuccessful reform of monasteries in his territory, commissioned a translation of the Bible, banned Lutherans and Lutheran books. He worked for the convocation of a general council for clarification of doctrine and disciplinary reform. He died without heir, and the Duchy of Saxony did become Lutheran.

[T. C. O'BRIEN]

GEORGE SCHOLARIOS (*c.*1400–*c.*72), whose family name was Kourteses (Scholarios designated his profession), one of the most influential theologians of the late Byzantine Empire, who, after its fall in 1453, taking the name of Gennadius II, became the first patriarch of Constantinople under Turkish rule. He directed a school in Constantinople in which he stressed the philosophy of Aristotle and the theology of Thomas Aquinas, some of whose works he himself translated from the Latin. He also served as a judge, an advisor of the Emperor, and, although still a layman, preacher to the court. He participated in the debates at the Council of *Florence, and in unambiguous terms professed that council to be ecumenical and the Latin teaching on the procession of the Holy Spirit to be orthodox. But some 5 years later back in Constantinople he replied to the dying appeal of *Mark Eugenicus by taking over the leadership of the antiunionists. He spoke and wrote unceasingly and voluminously against union; his published works fill eight large tomes. BIBLIOGRAPHY: J. Gill, *Personalities of the Council of Florence* (1964); Beck 760–763.

[G. T. DENNIS]

GEORGE SYNCELLUS (d. after 810), Byzantine chronicler, who had lived in Palestine and during the patriarchate of Tarasius (784–806) served as the patriarch's secretary. He later withdrew to a monastery and there wrote his *Chronicle.* The work covers from creation to the accession of Diocletian (284). It is fullest for the period of the New Testament. He made full use, however, of the Alexandrians Panodorus and Arimanus, who established the Alexandrian era, and is second only to Eusebius as a source for the understanding of Christian chronography. BIBLIOGRAPHY: V. Grumel, *La Chronologie* (1958) 86–95.

[M. R. P. MCGUIRE]

GEORGE OF TREBIZOND (1395–1486), humanist. Born in Crete, he came to Italy about 1420 and studied and taught Greek at Mantua. By 1431 his Latin was so good that he was made a professor at the new Univ. of Rome by Pope Eugenius IV. Because of his quarrelsome character G. was despised; he sided with the Aristotelians of the day. He died in obscurity; his translations of the *Rhetoric* and the *Problems* of Aristotle are today forgotten.

[R. T. MEYER]

GEORGES-MARTIN, MARGUERITE MARIE LOUISE (1898–1944), French social worker. She became a director of the French Women's Union and labored for racial equality and the return of working mothers to their homes. In 1940 she founded a society to aid in reuniting families dispersed by war. Active in the Resistance, she was imprisoned in 1944 and killed after lengthy torture. BIBLIOGRAPHY: J. Morienval, *Catholicisme* 4:1862.

[M. J. SUELZER]

GEORGIA, a S Atlantic state, the last founded (1732) of the Thirteen Colonies, the fourth state and the first of the South to ratify the Constitution (1788). James Oglethorpe, an English philanthropist, founded the colony as a refuge for economically depressed Englishmen and persecuted religious groups. In the early years of settlement, H. Herbert organized Christ Church in Savannah. There John *Wesley, founder of Methodism, preached and founded his Sunday School (1736–37). In 1735 Presbyterianism was brought to Georgia by Scottish colonists. The Southern Baptist Convention, today the largest Protestant denomination in the state, was established in Georgia in 1845. Spanish Franciscans and Jesuits brought Catholicism to the coastal Indians in the 16th and 17th centuries. Despite this early activity, no resident priest appeared from the time the Spanish left the area until the close of the 18th century. Catholics were barred from Georgia in the early days of the colony, but in the 19th cent. their ranks were increased by immigration. The Diocese of Savannah was erected in 1850. In 1937 the name of the see was changed to Savannah-Atlanta, and in 1956 Atlanta became a separate diocese with Francis E. Hyland as its first bishop. In 1962 Atlanta was elevated to the status of an archdiocese, and Paul J. *Hallinan was named its first archbishop. Atlanta's suffragans include the Dioceses of Savannah, Ga., Charlotte and Raleigh, N.C., and Charleston, S.C. In 1976 Georgia's Catholics numbered 101,274, or 3.8 % of the total state population. The major Protestant denominations are the Southern Baptist Convention, with 27.8 of the total population in 1971, and the Methodist Church with 8.5. There are more than 12 church-related colleges in Georgia, but none are Catholic. Some 3,106 students attend the state's 6 Catholic high schools, while over 19,500 pupils are enrolled in 32 Catholic elementary schools. BIBLIOGRAPHY: W. G. Cooper, *Story of Georgia* (4 v., 1938); E. M. Coulter et al., *History of Georgia* (1954); J. T. Lanning, *Spanish Missions of Georgia* (1935); J. J. O'Connell, *Catholicity in the Carolinas and Georgia, 1820–78* (1879); D. W. Johnson et al., *Churches and Church Membership in the U.S.* (1974).

[J. L. MORRISON and R. M. PRESTON]

GEORGIA, CATHOLICOS OF, chief bp. and spiritual leader of the Georgian Orthodox Church. He is elected and consecrated by the Assembly of Bishops, who comprise the Holy Synod, and resides in Tiflis (Thlisi) with the title of "Archbishop of Mtsketa and Tiflis, Katholikos of All Iberia." Although primarily a spiritual leader, he was traditionally regarded as the king's equal, a right guaranteed by Georgian law. The catholicos (or katholikos) was recognized as head of the independent Iberian (Georgian) Church between 486 and 488, though subject to Antioch. During the golden age (11th-13th cent.), Church-State relations were formalized to guarantee the privileges of the catholicos and of the bps., who sat in the Council of State and exercised independent feudal functions. During the silver age (16th through the 18th cent.), there was a Catholic revival and ties were renewed with the West, particularly on the part of the catholicate. In 1811, however, Russia annexed Georgia, abolished the independent Georgian catholicate and banned the use of the Georgian language in liturgical functions. The catholicate was restored in 1917 when Georgia declared its independence. Although Georgia was incorporated as a Soviet Republic in 1921, the by then autocephalous catholicate was permitted to continue; and with certain notable exceptions has remained relatively free of Soviet interference.

[I. M. KASHUBA]

GEORGIA, CHURCH OF. Georgia, also known as Iberia from its principal province, is a nation S of the Caucasus Mts., between the Black and Caspian Seas. It can trace its earliest pre-Christian formation to the kingdom of Colchis in the 7th century B.C. A province of Rome since A.D. 63, Iberia came into contact with Christianity very early. According to the Roman Martyrology, Iberian legends, and archeological data, St. Nino is said to have converted King Mirian and his wife *c.*486 to 488. The earliest liturgical texts belong to the Hierosolymitan liturgy of St. James, originally celebrated in Greek, but by the 6th cent. translated into the Georgian language. Likewise in the 6th cent. monasticism began to flourish, reaching its height in the 8th and 9th centuries. The monastic tradition has been very strong in Georgia, and Georgian monks established monasteries in Palestine, on Mt. Sinai, and on Mt. Athos. Because of its geographical position, Georgia has always been subject to outside political conflicts and invasions. From the 7th to the 9th cent. it was dominated by the Arabs, who retarded its cultural development. This period however resulted in the birth of national consciousness and the adoption of the liturgy of St. Basil and St. John Chrysostom, celebrated in Georgian, with a distinctive order of prayers and melodies for chants. In 1008 the kingdom of Georgia was unified, and became a great military pan-Caucasian power. Commerce and industry developed, along with literature and the arts, esp. liturgical arts. This led to one ecclesiastical jurisdiction, under the catholicos of Mtsketa, the general acceptance of the Byzantine liturgy, and close Church-State relations. The catholicos was accepted as the king's equal and had great temporal and supreme religious power. The councils of Church and State were considered equal. During this period, known as the golden age, monasticism flourished, and schools were established at monastic centers. The Mongol invasion of 1223 brought economic and political collapse to Georgia, and the former grand culture continued to deteriorate until the 15th century. It was during this period that bonds with Rome began to weaken; without any formal break or unpleasant relations. Ties with Byzantium and the East, on the other hand, were strengthened by proximity and the use of a common liturgy. This gradual evolution led to separation from Rome. Nevertheless, during the silver age (1500–1800), centers of learning were restored and there was a rapprochement between Georgia and Rome, and both kings and catholicoi were drawn to Catholicism. In general, however, the Orthodox Church did not flourish in Georgia during this time, which was a period of corruption and worldliness of the clergy. By the end of the 18th cent., the dominant influence was Russia, which finally annexed Georgia in 1811, deported the catholicos and abolished the Georgian catholicate, and suppressed the Georgian language in liturgy and teaching. The Orthodox Church was under the domination of the Russian patriarchate until 1917, when Georgia declared its independence and reestablished the catholicate. When Georgia became a Soviet republic in 1921, the catholicate was allowed to continue, after the arrest of Catholicos Ambrose, who had protested against Soviet antireligious policies. His successors, more diplomatic, have on the whole maintained relatively peaceful relations with Moscow, despite a decline in church membership, estimated (1975) at about 750,000 practicing Orthodox Christians. BIBLIOGRAPHY: C. Toumanoff, NCE 6:361–369; M. Tarchnishvili, EncCatt 6:73–76; H. Leclercq, DACL 6.1:1029–33.

[I. M. KASHUBA]

GEORGIAN RITE. The Georgian Orthodox Church, independent since 486 though its catholicos had still to be ordained at Antioch, originally used the Hierosolymitan liturgy of St. James. Abp. John, who introduced the liturgy, used Greek, but by the 6th cent. it was celebrated in Georgian, from a translation made in the Georgian convent in Jerusalem. Manuscripts of this version are extant today in the libraries of Mt. Sinai, Gaza, the Vatican, and Tiflis (Thlisi). In the 10th or 11th cent., Georgia adopted the Byzantine liturgy of St. Basil and St. John Chrysostom, already in use in Iberia, the W province. It is celebrated in the Georgian language, and is characterized by a distinctive order of prayers and very ancient ecclesiastical chants, the oldest of which dates back to the 8th century. The liturgy is always accompanied by chants, and consists also of characteristic ''Kondaki'' or various liturgical texts, and "Kurthkhevani,'' or benedictions. Aside from the period between 1811 and 1917 when the independent catholicate was abolished, the liturgy has always been celebrated in the Georgian language. Great care is taken to preserve the integrity of the ancient liturgical chants. BIBLIOGRAPHY: A. S. Manvel, NCE 6:373–375.

[I. M. KASHUBA]

GERALD OF AURILLAC, ST. (855–909), Count of Aurillac. He lived poorly and distributed his wealth to the poor. After a pilgrimage to Rome he established the Abbey of *Aurillac but as count of the region did not become a monk. He was noted for justice as well as for the gift of healing. He died at Cézenac and was buried at the abbey he had founded. His biographer is St. *Odo of Cluny. BIBLIOGRAPHY: *St. Odo of Cluny . . . St. Gerald of Aurillac* (ed. and tr. G. Sitwell, 1958); G. Mathon BiblSanct 6:170–171.

[J. R. RIVELLO]

GERALD DE BARRI, see GIRALDUS CAMBRENSIS.

GERALD OF BRAGA, ST. (d. 1109), bishop. A Cluniac Benedictine at Moissac, G. was named bp. of reconquered Braga in N Portugal (1096) by his Cluniac colleague, Bernard of Salvetat, primate of Spain. Soon metropolitan over neighboring sees, G. introduced the Roman liturgy alongside the "rite of Braga.'' BIBLIOGRAPHY: M. Sotomayor, BiblSanct 6:172.

[R. I. BURNS]

GERALD OF MAYO, ST. (d. 732), abbot. Of Northumbrian origin, G. became a monk at Lindisfarne, later went to Ireland with St. Colman, and founded a monastery at Inishbofin because the Council of Whitby prohibited the celebration of the Celtic date of Easter in Northumbria. His monastery became a center for many Irish saints. BIBLIOGRAPHY: Butler 1:584; R. Van Doren, BiblSanct 6:174–175; R. T. Meyer, NCE 6:375.

[R. T. MEYER]

GERALDINI, ALEJANDRO (d. 1524), bp., humanist. A Renaissance man and Latin stylist, G. served at the Spanish court; he was a major force in bringing the Renaissance to Spain. Nominated by Charles V to the See of Santo Domingo in the New World, he became its second bp. in 1516. His work, *Itinerarium ad regiones sub aequinoctiali plaga constitutas* described Santo Domingo at his arrival. G. built the cathedral of Santo Domingo, the first in the New World.

[J. R. AHERNE]

GERARD OF ABBEVILLE (*c.* 1220–72), secular master of theology at Paris, friend and successor of *William of Saint-Amour in opposing the Dominicans and Franciscans. G.'s *Contra adversarium perfectionis christianae* (1256) drew replies from SS. Thomas Aquinas and Bonaventure, both defending the mendicants' rights and ways of spirituality. BIBLIOGRAPHY: P. Grand, DSAM 6:258–263, bibliog.

[T. C. O'BRIEN]

GERARD OF BOLOGNA (*c.*1250–1317), Carmelite theologian, the first of his order to receive the doctorate at the Univ. of Paris (1295). Elected general of his order (1257), he strove to promote its intellectual life. In his writings, only one of which was published, *In libros IV Sententiarum commentaria* (1622), G. follows St. *Thomas Aquinas but with variations akin to the thought of *Duns Scotus. BIBLIOGRAPHY: Glorieux L 1:128–132.

GERARD OF BORGO SAN DONNINO (d. *c.*1276), Franciscan *Spiritual. Without authorization, G. published at Paris in 1254 his *Liber introductorius in Evangelium aeternum,* also incorporating the *Concordia, Apocalypsis,* and *Psalterium* of *Joachim of Fiore. The book fostered the agitations of the Spirituals. A commission at Anagni (1255) under Alexander IV denounced 31 errors in G.'s work. The incident led to the resignation of the Franciscan minister general, John of Parma. The latter's successor, St. Bonaventure, imprisoned the obstinate G. for life. BIBLIOGRAPHY: Bihlmeyer-Tüchle 2:303–305, with bibliog. *JOACHIMISM.

GERARD OF BROGNE, ST. (*c.*880–959), abbot, monastic reformer. G. began his work of reform by rebuilding an old oratory at Brogne; he dedicated it to SS. Peter and Eugene, enriched it with relics, endowed it, and placed it in charge of monks. He was abbot in 923, having probably spent a novitiate at Saint-Denis. Various dukes, bps., counts of Flanders, Lorraine, and Ghent charged him with reforming abbeys and monasteries in their domains where he concerned himself solely with restoring regular observance of the Benedictine Rule. His ideas, however, prepared the way for the great Gregorian reform. In 1131 his body was "elevated" by the bp. of Liège: the equivalent of canonization. Since the 17th cent., the abbey at Brogne is known as St. Gérard. BIBLIOGRAPHY: Butler 4:17–18; A. D'Haenens, BiblSanct 6:178–180.

[M. E. DUFFY]

GERARD OF CAMBRAI (*c.*985–1051), bp. of Cambrai from 1012; friend and political ally of Emperor Henry II; promoter of monastic reform; patron of *Gesta episcoporum Cameracensium,* an anonymous history of the diocese and monastic foundations of Cambrai. BIBLIOGRAPHY: H. Platelle, *Catholicisme* 4:1867–68.

[T. C. O'BRIEN]

GERARD OF CLAIRVAUX, BL. (d. 1138), Cistercian monk. Second eldest brother of Bernard of Clairvaux, G. pursued a military career until 1112 when he reluctantly followed Bernard to Cîteaux. He helped to establish Clairvaux in 1115, and served there as cellarer to the end of his life. He possessed remarkable skill in manual crafts, and the direction and instruction he gave workmen was of great use to the monastery. Though unlettered, he had profound insight in spiritual matters, and Bernard depended much upon his counsel. Bernard's 26th sermon on the Song of Songs (ed. J. Leclercq in *S. Bernardi opera* 1957, 1:169–181) tells of G.'s virtues. BIBLIOGRAPHY: W. Williams, *Saint Bernard of Clairvaux* (1952) 4–29; P. Zerbi, BiblSanct 6:181–183; Butler 2:538–539.

[L. J. LEKAI]

GERARD OF CREMONA (*c.*1114–87), translator into Latin of Arabic works that decisively influenced the development of *scholasticism. G. was born in Cremona, Italy, but his literary career was spent in Toledo, Spain, the center of the spread of Arabic learning into the Latin world. His philosophical translations included Aristotle's *Posterior Analytics* and *Physics,* the *Liber de causis* of *Proclus, works of Avicenna, Alkindi, and Alfārābī. He also translated Euclid's *Elementa geometriae,* and works of astronomy and medicine.

[T. C. O'BRIEN]

GERARD OF CSNÁD, ST. (d. 1046), bishop and martyr. Born in Venice, G. became a monk and later abbot at S. Giorgio Maggiore in that city. Resigning his office to go on pilgrimage to the Holy Land, he got as far as Hungary, where the King, St. Stephen I, persuaded him to become tutor for his son, Emeric. G. was later made bp. of Csanád. He was active in the evangelization of the Hungarians; he was slain at Buda in the anti-Christian reaction that followed the death of St. Stephen. Most of his relics were taken to Venice in 1333 where he was proclaimed the city's protomartyr. BIBLIOGRAPHY: E. Pásztor, BiblSanct 6:184–186; Butler 3:629.

[P. K. MEAGHER]

GERARD OF SAUVE-MAJEURE, ST. (1025–95), abbot, monastic reformer. He entered the monastery at Corbie, in France, his birthplace, as a child oblate. As a monk *c.*1050 he was companion to the abbot on a pilgrimage to Rome where he was ordained priest by Pope Leo IV. In 1073 he was again a pilgrim, this time to the Holy Land. On his return he was elected abbot by the monastery of St-Vincent, Laon. When his efforts to reform the monastery failed, he led a group of two monks, a hermit, and five knights in establishing a new monastery near Bordeaux on land given by William VIII, Duke of Aquitaine in 1079. The abbey of Sauve-Majeure (*Silva Magna*) became a center of fervor and discipline from which daughter foundations were made. G. was venerated for his sanctity from the time of his death on and he was canonized in 1197 by Pope Celestine III. BIBLIOGRAPHY: Butler 2:35–36.

[T. C. O'BRIEN]

GERARD SEGARELLI, see SEGARELLI, GERARD.

GERARD OF STERNGASSEN (Korngin; 14th cent.), German Dominican mystic, brother of Johannes. G. was a friend, but not a follower of Meister *Eckhart. G.'s *Medela* *animae languentis,* which exists only in MS, is a complete treatise on the ascetical and contemplative life, based on the teaching of St. Thomas Aquinas. BIBLIOGRAPHY: A. Walz, EncCatt 6.90.

GERARD OF TOUL, ST. (*c.*935–994), bp. of Toul (963–994). G. solidified the temporal power of his diocese, encouraged scholarship, erected and rebuilt monasteries and churches, and is reputed to have founded the Hôtel-Dieu, the oldest hospital in Toul. He was canonized in 1050 by Pope St. Leo IX, who had been his successor in Toul. BIBLIOGRAPHY: Butler, 2:151–152; J. Choux, BiblSanct 6:190–192.

[M. F. MCCARTHY]

GERARD OF VILLAMAGNA, BL. (1174–1245?), hermit. Orphaned at an early age, he served as a page in a knightly Florentine family. With his lord he went on a crusade (1220–28), was captured by the Saracens, and after his release traveled as a pilgrim to Jerusalem. Returning to Italy, he joined the Third Order of St. Francis and lived as a hermit in his native town. BIBLIOGRAPHY: C. da Langasco, BiblSanct 9:257–258 s.v. ''Mercatti''; Butler 2:378–379.

[O. J. BLUM]

GERARD OF YORK (d. 1108), abp. of York. From a noble Norman family, he was a resolute supporter of Kings William II (Rufus) and Henry I in their quarrel with Abp. Anselm of Canterbury over lay investiture. After serving as precentor of Rouen and, from 1096, bp. of Hereford, G. was nominated by Henry I to the See of York, which he obtained, despite Anselm's opposition, in 1101. He and Anselm engaged in a bitter dispute concerning Canterbury's primacy over York, and G. was forced to acknowledge canonical obedience to Anselm. A severe rebuke by Pope Paschal II led to a change of attitude by G. and a genuine reconciliation with Anselm. His support of the King made him unpopular with the chroniclers who accused him of witchcraft and licentiousness, and with his canons, who refused him burial in his own cathedral. BIBLIOGRAPHY: J. Raine, *Fasti Eboracenses,* 158–163; R. W. Southern, *St. Anselm and His Biographer* (1963) 135–138.

[J. L. GRASSI]

GERARD OF ZÜTPHEN (b. Zerbolt; 1367–98), member of the Brothers of the Common Life and ascetical writer. At Deventer G. was a friend and confidant of *Florentius Radewijns. His writings include *De reformatione virium animae* (1539) and *De spiritualibus ascensionibus* (1539), which influenced the plans of St. Ignatius Loyola's **Spiritual Exercises*. G. defended the *Devotio moderna against the attacks of certain mendicant friars. His biography, written by Thomas à Kempis, was translated into English and published by J. P. Arthur (1905). BIBLIOGRAPHY: J. de Guibert, *Sources and Characteristic Traits of St. Ignatius' Spirituality* (tr. W. J. Young, 1964) 159.

GERARD, JOHN (1564–1637), Jesuit on the English Mission. The adventures of G. as narrated in his autobiography show him to have been one of the most colorful as well as successful outlaw priests in England during the darkest days of persecution of Catholics. He studied at Douai and the Jesuit College in Paris. Returning to England for his health, he was arrested and imprisoned (1583) for two years. Released, he went to Rome, was ordained there (1588), then entered the Jesuit novitiate. Returning to England he began his extraordinary life of hiding, escape, and ministering to the Catholic population. G. drew such trust that Catholics risked their lives for him. In an age of daily betrayal he earned unbelievable loyalty from all whom he met. He was highly successful in making converts to the old faith. G.'s capacity for physical exertion and endurance of pain was incredible. In 1594 he was again imprisoned and tortured for three years before he escaped. His apostolate continued until the Gunpowder Plot in 1605 when he was forced to flee to Spain. His last years were spent in educating young Jesuits in Flanders, then as confessor at the English College in Rome. His autobiography and his *Narration of the Gunpowder Plot* have been rich sources of Catholic history during the English Reformation.

[J. R. AHERNE]

GERARD, RICHARD (*c.*1635–80), English recusant and confessor. A descendant of the Bromley branch of the Gerard family, he was a devout and respected man of Staffordshire, known to be a friend of the Jesuits for whom he acted as trustee for certain small properties. During the Oates Plot (1679) he went to London to testify in behalf of the Catholic peers accused of conspiracy and was himself arrested on a similar charge. He was imprisoned and died while awaiting trial. BIBLIOGRAPHY: Gillow BDEC 2:432–433.

[V. SAMPSON]

GERASA, a Hellenistic city of Palestine located on the W side of the Jordan River on one of the N branches of the River Jabbok. It lies about half way between Jerusalem and Damascus. It was a settlement dating from the Early Iron Age. More likely Antiochus IV *Epiphanes (175–164 B.C.) refounded the city. Expeditions from Yale Univ., the British School of Archeology, and the American School of Oriental Research have excavated the site, where can be seen the finest ruins of a Roman city anywhere in the Near East, including an arch, theater, forum, and several temples. According to the best reading of the gospel text, Jesus with his Apostles went ashore in the vicinity of Gerasa after quieting the storm (Mk 5.1; Lk 8.26). Here Jesus exorcised Legion into a herd of swine, and the people asked him to leave the territory. BIBLIOGRAPHY: *Gerasa, City of the Decapolis* (ed. C. H. Kraeling, 1938).

[S. MUSHOLT]

GERASIMUS (d. 475), monastic founder. He was born in Lycia, SW Asia Minor. He was first a partisan of Patriarch Theodosius of Jerusalem who was said to have Monophysite tendencies, but later G. came under the influence of St. Euthymius the Great (377–473). He became the founder of the Great Laura near the River Jordan, and is reported to have lived exclusively from the Eucharist during Lent.

[J. MADEY]

GERATI, alternate name for the Concorezzenses, a group of 13th-cent. Italian *Cathari.

GERBERON, GABRIEL (1628–1711), French Benedictine (Maurist), editor of the text of St. *Anselm's works that was used in PL 158–159; author of *Histoire générale du Jansénisme* (3 v., 1700), an important source of documentation; pro-Jansenist. A monk of St-Mélaine, Rennes, he was assigned to St. Germain des Prés, Paris, in 1662. His sympathies with the Jansenist doctrine and politics forced him to flee to the Low Countries in 1682. He was convicted as a political agitator against the bps. at Brussels in 1704, remanded to France, and imprisoned until 1710. He left an autobiography, which included a bibliography of his more than 50 works.

[T. C. O'BRIEN]

GERBERT VON HORNAU, MARTIN (1720–93), German Benedictine abbot, musicologist, and liturgist. A monk of the Abbey of St. Blaise in the Black Forest from 1736, he became its abbot in 1764. His treatises and documentation on medieval chant were pioneering monuments for the study of plainchant: *De cantu et musica sacra* (2 v., 1774); *Scriptores ecclesiastici de musica sacra . . .* (3 v., 1784), His liturgical works included: *Vetus liturgia allemanica* (2 v., 1776); *Monumenta veteris liturgiae allemanicae* (2. v., 1777). G. was a strong abbot, formulated a new constitution, restored plainchant to full use, rebuilt the monastery after a fire in 1768. He was also one of the leading figures in church affairs in 18th-cent Germany.

[T. C. O'BRIEN]

GERBET, PHILIPPE OLYMPE (1798–1864), French bp., theologian. He studied at St. Sulpice and the Sorbonne, was ordained in 1822. An early collaborator with F. *Lamennais on *L'Avenir,* G. broke with him after 1836. His primary theological work was in the area of apologetics, a treatise opposing R. *Descartes on philosophical certitude in relation to theological knowledge. His *Esquisse de Rome chrétienne* (2 v., 1843, 1850) was the fruit of 10 years' research in Rome. In 1853 he was appointed bp. of Perpignan; his pastoral letter (1860) on the errors of the times was a document Pius IX considered before his own final version of the *Syllabus of Errors (''A Syllabus concerning the Principal Errors of our Times,'' 1864). The transition from liberalism to conservatism in G.'s social views paralleled that of Pius IX. Early in his career he was a forceful exponent in the movement for workers' rights, but as this cause came to be tied in with antagonism towards the Church, he reacted against both. He particularly spoke out against attacks on papal temporal power and sovereignty.

[T. C. O'BRIEN]

GERBILLON, JEAN FRANÇOIS (1654–1707), one of the first French Jesuit missionaries to China (1687). He became the tutor and confidant of the Emperor K'ag-Hsi. G. was an interpreter, through Latin, for peace negotiations between China and Russia in 1688. He published works on the sciences in Mandarin. BIBLIOGRAPHY: J. Dehergne, *Catholicisme* 4:1877–78.

[T. C. O'BRIEN]

GERDIL, HYACINTHE SIGISMOND (1718–1802), cardinal, apologete. A native of Savoy, and Barnabite from 1753, he taught philosophy and theology in houses of his order and also at the Univ. of Turin. He became tutor to the son of the king of Sardinia, the future Charles Emmanuel IV. In 1773 he was named cardinal *in petto* by Clement XIV, was brought to Rome by Pius VI in 1776; his cardinalate was proclaimed in 1777. G.'s greatest importance is in the areas of apologetics and educational theory. He brought the thought of R. *Descartes and N. *Malebranche to bear against the empiricism of J. *Locke in his *L'immatérialité de 'âme démontrée contre Mr. Locke* (1747). His own mature philosophical view he expressed in *Introduzione allo studio della religione* (1755). G. dealt with new social views of man inspired by J. *Rousseau and expressed in the revolutionary movements of the time: thus his *De l'ordre* (1770–73); *Précis d'un cours d'instructions sur l'origine, les droits, et les devoirs de l'autorité souveraine* (1799). In the field of pedagogy G. wrote a rebuttal of Rousseau's *Émile,* his *Réflexions sur la théorie et la pratique de l'éducation contre les principes de Jean Jacques Rousseau* (1763); and in many other works published the fruits of his own experience as an educator.

[T. C. O'BRIEN]

GERHARD, JOHANN (1582–1637), German theologian, important exponent of Lutheran *orthodoxy. After studying medicine at Wittenberg and theology at Marburg and Jena, G. was made superintendent at Heldburg in 1606. In 1615 he became general superintendent in Coburg and prepared a new *church order for Duke John Casimir of Saxe-Coburg-Gotha. In 1616 Elector John George of Saxony prevailed on the Duke to release G. to the Univ. of Jena, where he lectured, despite many invitations elsewhere, until his death. A prodigious worker, G. wrote numerous exegetical treatises, more than 10,000 letters, and the *Loci communes theologici* (9 v., 1609–22), which book stands as the classic exposition of Lutheran theology. In his polemical *Confessio catholica* (4 v., 1634–37) he endeavored to prove the true Catholicity of Lutheran doctrine against contemporary systematic presentations of Roman Catholicism. He also wrote patristic, exegetical, and devotional works. BIBLIOGRAPHY: A. C. Piepkorn, EncLuthCh 2:905–906, with bibliog; W. Elert, *Structure of Lutheranism* (1962).

GERHARD, NIKOLAUS, (Nicolaus von Leydon, (*c.*1420–*c.*1473), chief master of late Gothic sculpture of the Upper Rhine region. G. executed the tomb monument of Abp. von Sierck (1462, Trier), a relic of Canon van Büsang (1464, Strassburg), and the grave plaque of Friedrich IV (1473, Vienna).

[M. J. DALY]

GERHARDINGER, KAROLINA (1796–1879), foundress of the *School Sisters of Notre Dame. Of German origin, G. was chosen by the bp. of Regensburg, Michael Wittman, to found a community of sisters who would not be cloistered but could go into villages to teach. The bishop commissioned Matthias Siegert, a priest who had studied the Pestalozzi method of teaching, to serve as educational and spiritual director of the new congregation, the School Sisters of Notre Dame, headed by G., whose spirit as Sister Maria Teresia of Jesus inspired the group. Her cause was introduced in Rome in 1952. BIBLIOGRAPHY: M. Mast, *Through Caroline's Consent* (1958).

[J. R. AHERNE]

GERHARDT, PAUL (1607–76), Lutheran pastor, hymnodist. His hymns, which are intensely personal and deeply spiritual, are forerunners of Pietism. Many of them, in German and English, are still popular, esp. the profoundly reverent ''O Haupt voll Blut und Wunden'' (''O Sacred Head, surrounded/ By crown of piercing thorn'') in the beautiful setting which recurs in J. S. Bach's *Passion Music according to St. Matthew*. BIBLIOGRAPHY: *Dictionary of Hymnology* (ed. J. Julian, 1957)1: 409–412; G. Kranz, *Modern Christian Literature* (tr. J. R. Foster, 1961) 88–90.

[M. F. MCCARTHY]

GERHOH OF REICHERSBERG (1093–1169), one of the principal agents of the *Hildebrandine reforms in the Germanies. Lecturer at Augsburg, he fell foul of his simoniacal bp., Hermann, but was afterwards reconciled and accompanied him to *Lateran Council I, where he submitted plans for clerical reform. G. joined the Augustinian Canons and became provost of the house at Reichersberg. Refusing to support an imperialistic antipope, he was banished by the Emperor Barbarossa. His famous work, *On the investigation of Anti-Christ* advocates a clear delineation of the power of pope and emperor. BIBLIOGRAPHY: C. Barraclough, *Medieval Papacy* (1968).

[T. GILBY]

GERIZIM (GARIZIM), MOUNT (Heb. *Gerzzim*), a 2,900-foot mountain opposite and SW of Mt. Ebal. The ancient town of Shechem lay in the valley between these two mountains. Jotham shouted his fable to the Shechemites from the top of Mt. Gerizim (Jg 9.7). In ancient times there seems to have been a Canaanite shrine and a sacred oak there (Dt 11.30). The Samaritan Pentateuch (Dt 27.5) states that the altar for blessings and curses was built on Mt. Gerizim; this is contrary to the testimony of the MT and the LXX, but it is probably correct. A Samaritan temple existed there at the time of Christ (Jn 4.20) in spite of the fact that it had been devastated by John Hyrcanus in 128 B.C.. Today it is known as Jebel-et-Tor. A small group of Samaritans still gather there for prayer and sacrifice esp. for the Passover services. BIBLIOGRAPHY: Abel GéogrPal 1:360, 369.

[J. A. PIERCE]

GERLACH, ST. (*c.*1100–1165 or 1166), hermit. Born at Valkenburg, Holland, G. was trained in chivalry, but his wife's sudden death caused him to dispose of his wealth and make a pilgrimage to Rome and Jerusalem. He spent 7 years doing penance and caring for the sick in hospitals. He received permission from Pope Adrian IV to return to his lands at Houthem and live as a hermit, wearing the Premonstratensian habit, without formally entering a religious order. Controversies arose, however, with nearby monks (7 miles away), who refused him even the last sacraments. But his biographer relates that he miraculously received Viaticum and was anointed. He was never formally canonized although Pius IX approved his feast for Cologne, Liège and Roermond. BIBLIOGRAPHY: F. Wesselman, *Der hl. Gerlach von Houthem* (1897); G. B. Valvekens, BiblSanct 6:222–224.

[N. F. GAUGHAN]

GERLACH, PETERS (Gerlacus Petri; 1378–1411), Dutch spiritual writer. Born at Deventer, he was a disciple of Florentius Radewijns. In 1400 he entered Windesheim as a cleric. Ordained a priest, he received the religious habit in 1403 and made profession in 1404. He died at Windesheim. His works are all from the school of Gerhard Groote and the *Devotio moderna*. His writings include a *Breviloquium*, written in his youth, a lost treatise, ''Freedom of the Spirit,'' and his *Soliloquium*, his best-known work, edited after his death by a friend. It is characterized by a spirit of affective piety, some psychological insights, a Christocentric mysticism, and speculation influenced by de Ruysbroeck. G.'s central thought is ''liberty of spirit through the intuition of truth,'' and the *Soliloquium* was a favorite among the spirituals of Port-Royal. BIBLIOGRAPHY: J. Leclercq, et al., *Spirituality of the Middle Ages* (1968) 433; J. Busch, *Chronicon Windeshemense* (1887).

[N. F. GAUGHAM]

GERMAIN OF AUXERRE, ST. (*c.*378–448), bishop. Educated in rhetoric and law, G. was already successful in the practice of law and held an important administrative position in Gaul when he was elected bp. in his native city of Auxerre (418). He thereupon changed his way of life, took up the practice of poverty and austerity, and gave himself with great zeal to his pastoral duties. He was twice in England: the first time (429–430) as an emissary, along with St. Lupus of Troyes, sent by Pope Celestine to combat the Pelagianism then active among the British, and the second time (440) when he was called upon to renew his attack upon the Pelagians. On one visit to England he is said to have contributed to a victory of British over the Picts and Saxons by teaching the troops to shout loud alleluias as a battle cry. He encouraged St. Genevieve in her religious vocation and possibly had SS. Patrick and Illtud as disciples. BIBLIOGRAPHY: Butler 3:251–253; F. Cayré *Spiritual Writers of the Early Church* (tr. W. W. Wilson, 1958).

[P. K. MEAGHER]

GERMAIN OF CAPUA, ST. (d. *c.* 540), bp. of Capua from *c.* 519. He headed a mission sent by Pope Hormisdas to Emperor Justin that succeeded in persuading the Emperor to put an end to the Acacian Schism. Two details concerning G. are recorded by St. Gregory the Great: that he saw in a vision the purgatorial suffering of Paschasius, who had sinned by adhering to a schism against Pope Symmachus; and that St. Benedict, at the time of G.'s death, had seen his soul being transported to heaven by angels. G. has been esp. venerated at Monte Cassino, where there was a chapel built in his honor and adorned with works of art, among which was a precious reliquary. These were destroyed in the bombardment of 1944. BIBLIOGRAPHY: A. Lentini, BiblSanct 6:237–239; Butler 4:222.

[P. K. MEAGHER]

GERMAIN OF PARIS, ST. (*c.*496–576), bishop. An anchorite and abbot before he became bp. of Paris (*c.*556), G. worked strenuously to bring peace to the Merovingian kingdom and sought to restrain the licentiousness of the nobles, including King Childebert I whom he courageously rebuked on occasion. Nevertheless the King valued his counsel and held him in high esteem. With the King's help he founded the abbey known after his death as St-Germain-des-Prés. Two letters important for information they provide on the Gallican liturgy were formerly attributed to G., but A. Wilmart has shown that they were written at least a century after G.'s death. There is a vita of G. from the pen of his friend Venantius Fortunatus, but it abounds, unfortunately, in miracles of dubious authenticity. BIBLIOGRAPHY: Butler 2:410–411; G. Mathon, BiblSanct 5:257–259.

[P. K. MEAGHER]

GERMAINE OF PIBRAC, ST. (1579–1601), French solitary and mystic. G. from infancy was deformed and in poor health. Her father and stepmother treated her as an outcast, scarcely feeding her and forcing her to sleep in the stable, away from the other children. At an early age she was put to work tending the sheep, and it was in the quiet fields that she entered into an intimate communion with God from whom she received great gifts of wisdom. Several miraculous events were witnessed by others in her lifetime and gradually she was accepted by all as a saint. After her death at age 22 her body remained incorrupt for at least 60 years. G. was canonized (1867) by Pope Pius IX. BIBLIOGRAPHY: Butler 2:550–552.

[J. R. AHERNE]

GERMAN BAPTISTS, a name given to the Brethren who were founded in Schwarzenau, Germany, by A. *Mack. The members were not connected with the Baptists of English origin, but were called Baptists from their practice of *trine immersion. Their doctrinal origins were in German *Pietism. *DUNKERS; *BRETHREN CHURCHES.

GERMAN CATHOLICISM, see DEUTSCHKATHOLIZISMUS.

GERMAN CHRISTIANS (Deutsche Christen), Protestants under the Hitler regime who attempted to combine Christianity and Nazi ideology. While professing to complete the Reformation begun by Martin Luther, they sought to eliminate confessional differences and to engender total obedience to the *Führer*. They accepted Nazi racist ideas, rejected the OT, and attempted to de-Judaize the NT, wishing even to purge St. Paul. Germany was viewed as the true Holy Land, with Hitler the embodiment of God's law. After gaining ground, by ruse or by force, in various local areas, they demanded at the national assembly of Protestant Churches in 1933 a national Church under a national bishop. With Hitler's assistance they won a majority in the subsequent church elections, and Ludwig Müller, their most influential leader, became *Reichsbischof*. His extreme Aryanizing policies alienated many, and Müller's power was superseded with the appointment of Hans Kerrl as minister for church affairs in 1935. Strong resistance to the German-Christians was found in the *Confessing Church (Bekennende Kirche). The German-Christians declined rapidly after 1935 and in 1945 totally disappeared with the Third Reich. BIBLIOGRAPHY: A. Cochrane, *Church's Confession under Hitler* (1962).

[J. C. WILLKE]

GERMAN MASS, a formulary for divine service (*Deutsche Messe und Ordnung des Gottesdients*) composed by *Luther in 1526. While he had advocated in his writings a vernacular liturgy, Luther first issued a Latin **Formula Missae et Communionis* (1523). Alarmed by innovations introduced by T. *Münzer, and *Karlstadt, he wrote a vernacular text for the "uneducated masses." Simpler than the *Formula Missae,* the *German Mass* omitted many sections of the Roman Mass but kept the words of institution, which were to be sung. Luther also put the text to music, in order to foster *congregational singing. The formulary was not made obligatory, but was accepted by many churches. Text in LW v. 53. BIBLIOGRAPHY: L. Reed, *Lutheran Liturgy* (1960).

[P. DAMBORIENA]

GERMAN METHODISTS, the congregations established in Pennsylvania by Jacob *Albright beginning in 1796, so named because, while German-speaking, they followed Methodist doctrine, discipline, and polity. In 1816 they adopted the title Evangelical Association (Evangelische Gemeinde); in 1922, Evangelical Church. Through a merger in 1946, the Evangelical Church became part of the *Evangelical United Brethren Church, which in turn became part of the *United Methodist Church in 1968.

GERMAN REQUIEM, see DEUTSCHES REQUIEM, EINE.

GERMAN SOCIALISM, late 19th-cent. development associated with the movement to emancipate the industrial proletariat. Rival groups developed under Ferdinand Lassalle (1825–64) and Karl *Marx. The Marxian position was developed by Wilhelm Liebknecht and August Bebel, though without total consistency. The program of the German Socialists is explicated in two documents: the Gotha program (1875) and the Erfurt Program (1891). Some of their basic demands were: organization of workers; consumer cooperatives; opposition to the building of armaments; naval expansion; and an acquisitive colonial policy. The party opposed entry into World War I until the last minute. The left wing gradually became identified with the Communist party. The Social Democratic Party, which was the organizational form of German socialism, supported Brüning and fought against Hitler's rise to power, being the only group to vote against the Enabling Law of March, 1933. BIBLIOGRAPHY: K. Pinson, *Modern Germany* (rev. ed. 1966) ch. 10; W. Stark and F. Grace NCE 13:368–381; V. Lidtke, *Outlawed Party* (1966).

[G. N. SHUSTER]

GERMANIC RELIGION, religion of the Teutonic peoples (primarily in Germany and Scandinavia). Though information concerning this form of worship is scarce, the writings of some Greek, Roman, and medieval scholars provide a reasonably clear picture of polytheistic paganism in Teutonic cultures. Differences between these cultures did not obscure religious similarities, since many tribes worshiped the same gods. Germanic religion was durable; it was not replaced in Scandinavia by Christianity until the 10th century. It established, from its beginnings, a belief in various gods anthropomorphic in type. Most powerful of these was Wodan, the All-Father (Scandinavian Odin). Next came Donar (Scandinavian Thor); Tiu (Ziu, Allemanic Zîstac, Nordic Tyr) was another important deity, along with Freya (Scandinavian Frigga), Wodan's wife. From some of these gods' names have come those of some days of the week: Tuesday (Tiu); Wednesday (Wodan); Thursday (Thor); and Friday (Freya). Prayers and sacrifices—of fruit, animals and humans—were part of worship, which took place first in groves or forests, and later, under Celtic and Roman influence, in houses and temples. Because Church and State existed as one unit, priests were extremely powerful. They directed sacrifices and consulted with oracles at tribal gatherings. Teutonic religions held animistic beliefs in nature's magical powers and in the spirits of the dead. Forces of nature were personified—given human or animal form—and worshiped as divinities. Unfriendly spirits included giants, watersprites (nixes), trolls, elves, brownies, mermen and mermaids, dwarves, and numerous others. Friendly spirit-beings, esp. the Norns (Norse Fates) and Valkyries (choosers of the slain), were worshiped in a similar manner. Germanic mythology held that the world began in an abyss, from which first emerged Niflheim (frozen reaches); then Muspellsheim (arid reaches); and that the process of creation ended with the appearance of gods and man. Later, gods, giants, and man would engage in a battle like the Biblical Armageddon and perish in flames. From the ashes, a new and paradisiacal world will emerge. BIBLIOGRAPHY: G. Dumézil, *Gods of the Ancient Northmen* (ed. and tr. E. Haugen, 1974); M. Eliade, *Patterns in Comparative Religion* (tr. R. Sheed, 1958).

[D. H. BRUNAUER]

GERMANUS, see also GERMAIN.

GERMANUS, ST. (*c.*610–675), abbot and martyr. A disciple of St. Arnulf of Metz and a subject of Abbot St. Walbert at Luxeuil, G. was selected by Duke Gondo to rule his new monastery at Münster-Granfelden. He incurred the enmity of Gondo's brother Boniface by opposing the oppression of the peasants, and was murdered by him. BIBLIOGRAPHY: Butler 1:385; C. Boillon, BiblSanct 6:261–262.

[M. S. TANEY]

GERMANUS I, ST. (*c.*634–after 730), **PATRIARCH OF CONSTANTINOPLE** from 715. He was born in Constantinople of a noble family; his father was executed (668) for conspiring against the Emperor, and G. himself was castrated and forced to become a cleric at Hagia Sophia. He became an outstanding churchman and influenced Emperor Constantine IV to convoke the Council of Constantinople III (680–681) to condemn *Monothelitism. Metropolitan of Cyzicus from 706, G. was forced to give support to Emperor Philippicus's Monotheletic views. Appointed patriarch of Constantinople, however, G. repudiated Monothelitism. G.'s chief importance is his part in the history of and opposition to *iconoclasm. The most important documents on its early history are his letters. When Anastasius II, the emperor who had appointed G., was succeeded (717) by Leo III, the Isaurian, G. became faced with a fanatical imperial campaign against icons. The Emperor tried to win over both the Pope and the Patriarch to his position; G. rejected every iconoclastic proposal steadfastly. On Jan. 17, 730, Leo convened an assembly of the highest ecclesiastical and secular dignitaries, the so-called *silentium,* and demanded that all subscribe to an iconoclastic edict. When G. refused, he was immediately deposed.

Even after his death G. was attacked by the iconoclasts: in 754 his writings were condemned and his name struck from the diptychs by a synod at Hieria. He was vindicated only in 787 by the Council of Nicaea II, which cited three of his anti-iconoclastic letters in its decrees. Among G.'s works (PG 98:39–454) are his *De haeresibus et synodis*, several Mariological homilies, and dogmatic letters. He is revered for his faithful orthodoxy, his theological learning, and his piety. BIBLIOGRAPHY: Ostrogorsky 150–179; E. Kitzinger, "The Cult of Images in the Age before Iconoclasm," *Dumbarton Oaks Papers* 8 (1954) 83–150.

[L. NEMEC]

GERMANUS II (1175–1240), **PATRIARCH OF CONSTANTINOPLE** from 1222. During the Crusades, esp. following the fall of Constantinople to the Latins in 1204, G. attempted to save the Byzantine Empire, threatened with disintegration, by writing to Pope Gregory IX with a proposal for church reunion and with the hope that military aid would be sent. In this critical time Emperor John III, Ducas Vatatzes, had G. elected patriarch, since G. had distinguished himself as both patriot and negotiator. With full concurrence of the Emperor he received envoys from Rome at Nicaea in 1231 in the hope of achieving some agreement with the West; he soon realized, however, that East-West alienation was too great an obstacle. Another conciliatory attempt to win friends for Byzantium was G.'s approval of the title patriarch of the Bulgarians, assumed by the abp. of Trnovo in 1235; the one proviso was that Bulgaria would still remain under Constantinople. G. also attempted, unsuccessfully as it turned out, reunion of the Armenian Church with his patriarchate. He was a prolific writer on theological topics (opposing Latin theology on every controverted point) and his numerous homilies evince his pastoral concern. G. died in great suffering and anxiety over the sad fate of his country; he was revered as a hero of both the Byzantine Empire and the Orthodox Church. BIBLIOGRAPHY: Ostrogorsky; D. M. Nicol, *The Despotate of Empiros* (1957); *idem, The Fourth Crusade and the Greek and Latin Empires, 1204–61*, CamMedHist 4 (2d ed., 1966).

[L. NEMEC]

GERMANY. German tribes became important *c.*4th cent. B.C. as Celtic culture was weakening. From the 1st cent. B.C. they began impinging on the Roman Empire, and subsequently helped to form various European nations. The state known as Germany originated in the division of *Charlemagne's empire (843), with the E portion going to his grandson Louis the German. The region's conversion to Christianity had climaxed in the work of *Boniface (680–754), Apostle of Germany. In 744 his disciple Sturmius founded *Fulda monastery, a key center of Christian culture until dissolved under Napoleon. Norse, Slav, and Magyar attacks *c.*900 weakened the German kingdom and prepared the way for feudalism. The Holy Roman Empire, considered a renewal of Charlemagne's, began in 962 when Otto I of Germany was crowned by Pope John XII. This action forged an alliance of empire and papacy that gave the popes support, but subjected them to imperial domination. Pope Gregory VII reasserted papal authority in deposing Henry IV (see CANOSSA), and papal victory in the *investiture controversy came in 1122. After overcoming the Hohenstaufen in the next century, the papacy shifted its dependence from Germany to France. Cologne, where Thomas Aquinas studied under Albertus Magnus, gave intellectual leadership to medieval Germany.

The Reformation began in Germany in 1517 with Luther, who effectively opposed *Anabaptists seeking to make it more radical. Some German princes supported Luther, and the *Habsburg emperors were forced to conciliate them. Some regions of Germany remained loyal to Rome, and a few followed the Reformed path of Calvin. By the Peace of *Augsburg (1555), each ruler secured the right to control the religion of his area (*cuius regio, eius religio*). Protestant-Catholic strife resumed in the Thirty Years' War, concluded at *Westphalia (1648). Religious differences made Germany slower than some other countries to develop a modern unified nation state. Protestant Prussia, the former *Teutonic Knights area, began to emerge as a dominant German power, particularly under *Frederick the Great, and eventually superseded Catholic *Austria, which had led a German Confederation formed in 1815 to replace the Holy Roman Empire ended in 1806. Bismarck had the Hohenzollern William I of Prussia proclaimed German emperor (kaiser) in 1871, with Berlin as capital. Legislation against the Catholic Church in the 1870s brought a *Kulturkampf. In 18th-cent. Germany, *Febronianism paralleled French Gallicanism, and *Old Catholic resistance to Vatican I centered in Germany.

German defeat in World War I ended the empire and left problems that led to Hitler's Nazi regime (1933–45). His policies brought World War II, the Holocaust, and division of Germany into Communist East and non-Communist West (from 1945). The Churches sought to maintain unity across the political dividing line, but faced increasing E German insistence on separation.

Leibniz, Kant, Hegel, Schelling, Marx, Nietzsche, Heidegger, and other German philosophers, along with writers such as Goethe, have provided notable stimulus to modern religious thought. Germany has likewise been a world leader in theological scholarship, producing such influential men as Schleiermacher and Bonhoeffer. And the religious world has drawn heavily on such German cultural figures as Bach.

[T. EARLY]

GERMERIUS, ST. (*c.*610–*c.*660), statesman, abbot. After serving at the court of both Dagobert I and Clovis II, G. founded the monastery of Isle. He left both a secular career and the married state to enter the monastery of Pentale where he became abbot. Because of misunderstandings, he became a hermit for 5 years, but subsequently became abbot of Flay, which he also founded. BIBLIOGRAPHY: P. Rouillard, BiblSanct 6:203–204; Butler 3:628–629.

[F. G. O'BRIEN].

GERMIGNY-DES-PRÉS, ABBEY OF, an excellent example of classical Carolingian architecture near Orléans, France. The church was built in 806 by Theodulf, abbot of the nearby monastery at Fleury-sur-Loire, according to a quatrefoil design with a richly decorated interior. The church was declared a historical monument in 1839 and restored according to its original design in 1867. BIBLIOGRAPHY: DACL 6.1:1222–32.

[T. M. MCFADDEN]

GERNRODE: ST. CYRIACUS (961), Ottonian basilica church in Lower Saxony, Germany, which, though retaining the traditional 3 aisles, double apses, transept, and 2 flanking west towers, introuduces innovative subtle proportions of piers, columns, and openings in a clearly articulated interior space, marking a new direction in Romanesque building.

[M. J. DALY]

GERO OF COLOGNE, ST. (d. 976), abp. of Cologne from 969. He founded the abbeys of Thankmarsfeld and Gladbach. In 971, he headed the embassy sent to Constantinople to request the hand of a Byzantine princess for the Emperor's son, later Otto II. He is perhaps the donor of the Gero-codex of the Gospels, formerly in Cologne, but now in Darmstadt. BIBLIOGRAPHY: M. F. McCarthy, NCE 6:448; L. Berg, *Gero Erzbischof von Köln* (1913). F. Baumann, BiblSanct 6:264.

[M. F. MCCARTHY]

GEROLD, ST. (d. 978), hermit. A member of the Rhetian family of the Courts of Sax, he gave his land to the Benedictine Order in which his two sons were monks. Later he became a recluse in a hermitage built on a small plot of ground given him by Otto I. He is sometimes pictured in ducal dress with his two haloed sons, Cuno and Ulric, beside him. BIBLIOGRAPHY: R. Henggeler, BiblSanct 6:264–268.

[F. G. O'BRIEN]

GERONA CATHEDRAL, Spanish Romanesque structure (1038) retaining the original tower, cloister, altar, and throne. Master Enrique's *chevet* (1312–47) with nine radiating chapels, boasts original 14th-cent. glass. Silver-gilt retable (1309) and repoussé baldachino are famous. The Cathedral is also rich in sculptured tombs, tapestries, paintings, liturgical accessories, and noteworthy manuscripts.

[M. J. DALY]

GERONTIUS, THE DREAM OF, see DREAM OF GERONTIUS, THE.

GEROSA, VINCENZA, ST. (1784–1847) foundress of the Sisters of Charity of Lovere in Lombardy. Born Catherine and a native of N Italy, she lived the first 40 years of her life as a saintly laywoman, dedicated to works of charity. With St. Bartolomea *Capitanio she established (1824) the Sisters of Charity of Lovere in response to an appeal by the bp. of Brescia for a community to educate the young. The new congregation, following the rule of St. Vincent de Paul, taught the young and performed works of charity for the sick and the poor. Though her companion died within 9 years of the foundation, G. led the community as an admirable administrator. The congregation was approved in 1835, and by 1847 had 24 foundations. G. was canonized in 1950. BIBLIOGRAPHY: Butler 2:476–477.

[J. R. AHERNE]

GERSAM, see GERSHOM.

GERSHOM (Gersam), son of Moses and Zipporah. He was born while Moses was in Midian after fleeing from Egypt (Ex 2.22) and was circumcized by his mother (Ex 4.25). His descendants were listed among the Levites (1 Chr 23.6). According to some MSS, he was the father of Jonathan, priest to the Danites (Jg 18.30). The Bible mentions two other men of the same name (1 Chr 6.1 and Ezra 8.2).

[T. EARLY]

GERSON, JEAN (1363–1429), univ. chancellor, conciliarist, mystic, theologian. Born Jean Charlier, he studied at the Univ. of Paris and, in 1395, became its chancellor, an office that he held until his death. His career was largely devoted to seeking peace, first between conflicting factions in France and then in the Church which was divided by the Great Schism. A leading proponent of the conciliar theory and author of numerous treatises on the relation of the council to the pope, he headed the French delegation to the Council of Constance (1414–18) which ended the schism. At the same time, he also stressed in his writings the need for church reform and esp. the need to relate theology to spiritual life. His own spiritual and mystical works strongly influenced many of the leading religious figures of the later 15th and 16th centuries. BIBLIOGRAPHY: J. L. Connolly, *John Gerson: Reformer and Mystic* (1928); L. R. Loomis, et al., *Council of Constance* (1961); J. B. Schwab, *Johannes Gerson, Professeur de Theologie und Kanzler de Universitat Paris* (2 v., 1858, repr. 1967).

[J. MULDOON]

GERTRUDE OF DELFT, BL. (*c.* 1300–58), stigmatic. Born in Voorburg, Holland, G. received the stigmata on Good Friday, 1340. BIBLIOGRAPHY: G. Marsot *Catholicisme* 4:1895.

GERTRUDE THE GREAT, ST. (1256–1301/2), German nun and mystic. Educated from the age of five by the nuns of Helfta and under the special care of St. *Mechtild of Hackeborn, G. experienced a ''conversion'' at 25 years of age and from that time led a life of contemplation rich in extraordinary mystical experience. Little is known of the details of her life; the not uncommon reference to her as an abbess is probably due to an error confusing her with *Gertrude of Hackeborn. Her spirituality stressed personal union with Christ and was marked by mystical marriage. She was one of the earliest exponents of devotion to the Sacred Heart. She edited the *Liber specialis gratiae,* made up in part of notes she had taken herself and containing the revelations of St. Mechtild. Three other works are attributed to her: *Exercitia spiritualia,* comprising seven meditations; *Insinuationes,* or *Legatus divinae pietatis,* which contains an account of her own mystical experiences; and *Preces Gertrudianae,* a collection of prayers that are not the work of Gertrude herself although they may incorporate some passages that originated with her. BIBLIOGRAPHY: P. Doyère, ''St. Gertrude, Nun and Mystic,'' *Worship* 34 (1960) 536–543; G. Dolan, *St. Gertrude the Great* (1912); N. Del Re, BiblSanct 6:277–285.

[M. S. TANEY]

GERTRUDE OF HACKEBORN (1232–92), Cistercian nun; sister of Mechtild of Hackeborn.

GERTRUDE OF NIVELLES, ST. (626–659), abbess. Sister of St. Begga, daughter of Pepin of Landen and St. Iduberga, she entered the double monastery founded at Nivelles by her mother whom she (aged 20) succeeded as abbess. A defender of Irish monasticism, virtuous, mortified, and a scholar, G. resigned as abbess to study scripture. The first vita of the saint was written *c.*670. BIBLIOGRAPHY: H. Roeder, *Saints and Their Attributes* (1955); Butler, 1:620–621; *Book of Saints* (comp. by the Benedictine Monks of St. Augustine's Abbey, Ramsgate, 1966); A. D'Haenens, BiblSanct 6:288.

[M. E. DUFFY]

GERTRUDIS PORTABLE ALTAR, given *c.*1040 to Brunswick cathedral by the countess Gertrudis. It was probably made in common with her crosses by a Brunswick workshop and bears witness to the great skill of Ottonian metalworkers. Constituent elements are embossed gold, cloisonné enamel, niello, filigree, semi-precious stones, and pearls. The altar is now in the Cleveland Museum, Ohio. BIBLIOGRAPHY: O. v. Falke, et al., *Guelph Treasure* (1930). *GERTRUDIS, SECOND CROSS OF.

[R. C. MARKS]

GERTRUDIS, SECOND CROSS OF, with the portable altar of Gertrudis* formed part of the Guelph Treasure in Brunswick Cathedral. Countess Gertrudis commissioned it *c.*1040, probably from a local Brunswick workshop of highly skilled Ottonian artisans and dedicated it to her first husband's memory. It consists of gold plating with delicate reliefs and filigree work, enamel plaques, precious and semi-precious stones. BIBLIOGRAPHY: O.v. Flake, R. Schmidt, G. Swarzenski, *The Guelph Treasure* (1930). See GERTRUDIS PORTABLE ALTAR.

[R. C. MARKS]

GERULF, ST. (*c.*732–*c.*750), martyr. Legend reports that he was murdered by his godfather en route to his home after his confirmation ceremony at the monastery of St. Bavon at Gand. His body was interred in Meerendra; but after several miracles, was moved in the 9th cent. to Dronghen, Flanders, where he was venerated as a saint. BIBLIOGRAPHY: M. De Somer, BiblSanct 6:292–293.

[F. G. O'BRIEN]

GERVAISE, ARMAND-FRANÇOIS (1660–1751), Trappist, controversial author. He entered La Trappe in 1695, after having been a Discalced Carmelite. Elected (1696) to succeed A. de *Rancé as abbot, he could not rule, and resigned (1698). The rest of his life he spent in various monasteries, writing historical and biographical works, usually biased. His biography of de Rancé was published only in 1866 by Abbé Dubois, who edited G.'s manuscript. The most frequently used of G.'s works for the history of monasticism is his *Histoire générale de la réforme de l'ordre de Cîteaux* (1746). Because it calumniated the Cistericans of the Common Observance, they had G. confined at the monastery of Le Reclus near Troyes for the last 5 years of his life.

[T. C. O'BRIEN]

GERVASE OF CANTERBURY (d. 1210), English Benedictine chronicler; monk of Christ Church, Canterbury, from 1163. His writings reflect the interests of his monastery in disputes with successive abps. of Canterbury, the interests of the abps. when they coincided with those of the monks. Works: Gervase of Canterbury, *Historical Works* (ed. W. Stubbs, Rolls 73, 2 v., 1879–80). BIBLIOGRAPHY: D. Knowles, *Mappa Mundi* of Gervase of Canterbury,'' DownRev 48 (1930) 237–247.

[R. W. HAYS]

GERVASE OF MELCHELEY (d. after 1241), English Latin poet and grammarian. He probably studied at Oxford and possibly at Paris. *De arte versificatoria et modo dictandi,* his principal work, was dedicated to ''master John,'' perhaps John Blund. His verses include an epitaph (1219) for William Marshal, regent for Henry III. BIBLIOGRAPHY: Emden Ox 2:1256.

[F. D. BLACKLEY]

GERVASE OF REIMS (1008–67), the successor of his uncle as bp. of Le Mans in 1036. Named abp. of Reims in 1055, G. functioned as chancellor of the realm and as primate. He crowned Philip I king on May 23, 1059. Bibliography: H. Dressler, NCE 6:452; St. Greg 7(1960) 52; H. Glaser, LTK 4:764.

[H. DRESSLER]

GERVASE OF TILBURY (*c.*1140–*c.*1220), author. After studying and teaching law at Bologna, G. entered successively the service of Henry (d. 1183), eldest son of Henry II; of William II of Sicily (d. 1189), Henry II's son-in-law; and of Emperor Otto IV, Henry II's grandson. For Otto he wrote his famous *Otia imperialia*, a work of universal knowledge. Otto's disastrous defeat at Bouvines (1214) forced G. to return to England. The *Otia* is of special interest for the evidence it gives of what was then considered universal knowledge. Text: ed. G. W. Leibniz in *Scriptores rerum Brunsvicensium,* (3 v. 1707–11) 1:884–1004. BIBLIOGRAPHY: W. Hunt DNB 7:1120–21; M. J. Hamilton, NCE 6:453; E. Freys, LTK 4:764.

[J. L. GRASSI]

GERVASE AND PROTASE, SS. (probably d. betw. 161 and 168), reputedly the first martyrs of Milan, about whom only the fact of their martyrdom is known for certain. In 386 St. *Ambrose, having built a new basilica (later to be known as Sant'Ambrogio), but lacking relics for its solemn consecration, was shown in a dream where the needed relics could be found. Excavations made accordingly revealed the decapitated bodies of two tall young men. These were acclaimed as the bodies of Gervase and Protase about whom nothing was remembered but their names. The relics were taken to the new church and reinterred amid great demonstrations of veneration. Several miracles were reported in connection with these events, one of which is recorded by St. *Augustine who was in Milan at the time (*Confessions* 9.7). Ambrose's account of the discovery is given in a letter to his sister Marcellina, and it is mentioned also by Paulinus, his biographer. Ambrose' wish to be buried beside the bodies of the martyrs was respected. In 835 the bodies of the three were taken up and put in a porphyry sarcophagus under the high altar of Sant'Ambrogio, where they are still to be found. The acta portraying Gervase and Protase as twin sons of martyred parents, all of whom died for the faith under Nero, are purely legendary. BIBLIOGRAPHY: Butler 2:583–584; A. Amore, EncCatt 6:217–218; A. Rimoldi, BiblSanct 6:298–302; Butler 2:583–584; J. Douillet, *What is a Saint?* (tr. D. Attwater, 1958) 86.

[R. B. ENO]

GERVIN OF OUDENBURG (ALDENBURG), ST. (d. 1117), Flemish monk, hermit, abbot. After pilgrimages to Rome and to Jerusalem, G. became a Benedictine monk at Bergues-Saint-Winoc. He left the monastery to become a hermit but was recalled and made abbot at Oudenburg. About 1105 he resigned to resume his eremitic life. BIBLIOGRAPHY: E. J. Kealey, NCE 6:454; Zimmermann 2:61; F. Baumann, BiblSanct 6:304–305.

[M. J. FINNEGAN]

GÉRY, ST., see DESIDERIUS OF CAHOR, ST.

GÉRY OF CAMBRAI, ST. (*c.*550–*c.*625). G. was consecrated bp. by Giles of Reims (betw. 585–587). Zeal in uprooting paganism, and concern for the poor marked his episcopate. By the 9th. cent. G.'s name appeared in the Litany of All Saints at Cologne. BIBLIOGRAPHY: H. Platelle, *Catholicisme* 4:1901; H. Dressler, NCE 6:454; P. Viard, BiblSanct 6:71–72.

[H. DRESSLER]

GESANGBUCH, German term for church hymnbook either Protestant or Roman Catholic.

GESENIUS, HEINRICH FRIEDRICH WILHELM (1786–1842), German biblical scholar who taught at the Univ. of Halle and published grammatical and philological works, standard for the study of biblical languages: *Thesaurus philologico-criticus linguae Hebraeae et Chaldaeae Veteris Testamenti* (1829–58 posthumous); *Hebräische Grammatik* (1813). BIBLIOGRAPHY: O. Kaiser, LTK 4:814–815.

[T. C. O'BRIEN]

GESS, WOLFGANG FRIEDRICH (1819–91), German Protestant theologian. G. taught at Basel (1864), then was prof. of exegesis and systematic theology at Göttingen (1871–80) and Breslau (1880–85). In his works, such as *Die Lehre von der Person Christi* (1856) and *Christi Person und Werk* (3 v., 1870–87), G. proposed an extreme form of kenotic theory: that the abasement of Christ included the transformation of the Logos into Christ's human soul. BIBLIOGRAPHY: EncRelKnow 4:479–480.

GESSI, FRANCESCO (1588–1649), Italian Bolognese painter, at first following the style of Ludovico Carracci, then adopting the weaker style of Guido Reni. Many of G.'s works are in churches of Bologna.

[M. J. DALY]

GESTA, Lat., "deeds done," used in numerous medieval accounts of adventures, deeds of valor, or acts of a saintly person (v.g., *Gesta Romanorum*).

[J. R. AHERNE]

GESTA ROMANORUM, an anonymous compilation of *exempla,* each supplied with a moral for sermon use, ranging from the lives of saints to Eastern tales, first appearing in late 13th-cent. England. With different *exempla,* the *Gesta* was imitated on the Continent. Vernacular translations by the end of the Middle Ages, and the printing of both Latin and vernacular versions, made the *Gesta Romanorum* popular. One *exemplum* book, printed in England in the reign of Elizabeth, contained tales of Pericles, King Lear, and the Merchant of Venice. BIBLIOGRAPHY: *Early English Versions of the Gesta Romanorum* (ed. S.

Herrtage, 1879, repr. 1962); F. Douce, *Illustrations of Shakspere and of Ancient Manners* (1839, repr. 1969); E. C. Dunn, NCE 6:454–455.

[F. D. BLACKLEY]

GESTALT PSYCHOLOGY a school of psychology developed in the 20th cent. by M. Wertheimer, K. Koffka, and W. Köhler as a reaction against earlier schools of elementarism and associationism. Against the notion that perceptions and higher cognitive processes are formed from elementary "particles" of sensation associated into more complex patterns, the Gestaltists showed that perceptions are primarily of whole patterns or forms *(Gestalten),* in which the elementary parts play a relatively insignificant role, e.g., the same melody can be heard even though, if played in different keys, no single note is repeated. With many elegant and telling experiments, observations, and ingenious analyses, the Gestaltists established their basic ideas as a fundamental part of modern psychology. BIBLIOGRAPHY: R. Collin, *Evolution* (tr. J. Tester, 1959) 79–80; W. Kohler, *Task of Gestalt Psychology* (1969 pa.); J. L. Walker, *Body and Soul* (1971).

[M. E. STOCK]

GESTURES, LITURGICAL, see LITURGICAL GESTURES.

GESÙ, IL, mother-church of the Jesuit order in Rome, designed and built by Vignola (1568–84) for Card. Alessandro Farnese. The church is basilican in type, the wide, hall-like nave flanked by side chapels and the apse extending beyond a domed crossing. Its two-storied façade (1575–84) by Giacomo della Porta is united by transitional scroll forms, reminiscent of Alberti's Santa Maria Novella (1456). The Gesù is a model of the Roman Baroque that influenced ecclesiastical building for two centuries. The dramatic, magnificent interior is adorned with spiralling marble columns enhanced by gilded metal vines, and ceiling paintings by G. B. Gaulli, *Triumph of the Name of Jesus,* (1672–85) and Fra Andrea Pozzo, *The Glorification of St. Ignatius,* (1691–94) the latter an apotheosis of Baroque illusion in sculptural, architectural, and painted theatrical effects. This tumultuous, celestial terrestrial work visualizing, in addition, the four quarters of the earth to which the Jesuits carry the Gospel, gains clarity and order only when viewed from the focal point, a metal plate, at the center of the floor, which is often interpreted as symbolizing the central, authoritative Rule which governs and determines the community, ordering the diverse gifts and activities of the members in a unified plan. Pozzo who wrote an important thesis on perspective here displays his genius.

[M. J. DALY]

GETH, see GATH.

GETHSEMANE, the place on the Mount of Olives where Jesus went after the Last Supper, prayed in agony (Lk 22.39), and was arrested (Mt 26.36; Mk 14.32). It was a customary retreat of Jesus (Jn 18.2). The site now considered as the location accords with biblical data and tradition. The Aramaic name means "olive press." BIBLIOGRAPHY: J. Trinquet, *Catholicisme* 4:1904.

[J. J. O'ROURKE]

GETHSEMANI, ABBEY OF, Trappist monastery near Bardstown, Kentucky. Monks from Melleray Abbey near Nantes established Gethsemani in 1848, and in 1951 it became the first monastic community in the U.S. to achieve abbatial status. After early setbacks due to the rigor and isolation of its life, Gethsemani experienced a revival under Abbot Edmond *Obrecht (d. 1935). An extraordinary growth in community membership began in the late 1930s and reached its peak in 1952 when the community numbered 279. Various foundations have been made from Gethsemani, the first of them in Georgia in 1944. BIBLIOGRAPHY: T. Merton, *Waters of Siloe* (1949); *idem,* NCE 6:457–458; M. B. Brard, *Catholicisme* 4:1904–05.

GETINO, LUIS ALONSO (1877–1946), Spanish Dominican theologian, founder and first editor of *La Ciencia Tomista* (Madrid 1910–). His prodigious literary output included more than 3,000 books and articles. He did much to promote the revival of interest in the works of Francisco de *Vitoria through his *El Maestro fray Francisco de Vitoria y el renacimento teológico del siglo XVI en Salamanca* (1931) and his annotated edition of Vitoria's *Relecciones teológicas* (1933). When one of his works, *Del gran número de los que se salvan y la mitigación de las penas del infierno* (1934) was put on the Index, G. promptly submitted. BIBLIOGRAPHY: G. Fraile, CiT 37 (1946) 2:330–340, for a complete bibliog. of Getino; *idem,* LTK 4:847.

GEULINCX, ARNOLD (1624–69), Belgian philosopher, follower of R. *Descartes. He was first a professor at the Univ. of Louvain, where he introduced Cartesian philosophy, but became a Calvinist, and had to leave. The rest of his teaching life was spent at Leyden. His name is linked in the history of philosophy with *occasionalism, since he maintained the impossibility of any interaction between body and spirit; he also developed a personal interpretation of the Cartesian, *cogito ergo sum.* This part of his thought is contained in his *Metaphysica vera* (1695). But his main interests were in moral philosophy; his chief publication is *Disputationes ethicae* (1664–68). His ethical theory is voluntaristic: moral good and evil are explained solely by God's will; his concept of virtue contrasts his Jansenist-derived view of fallen nature with the noble ideal of goodness made possible by divine grace. BIBLIOGRAPHY: L. Baur, LTK 4:847–848.

[T. C. O'BRIEN]

GEVAERT, FRANÇOIS AUGUSTE, (1828–1908), Belgian musicologist and composer. G. held the important posts of musical director at the Paris Opera and director of the Brussels Conservatory during his life. As a scholar of early church music, he attempted to show how ancient Greek music influenced Gregorian chant.

[D. SMUCKER]

GEZER (GAZER), a Canaanite royal city (Jos 10.33; 12.12), assigned to Ephraim (Jos 16.3; 1 Chr 7.28), a Levitical city (Jos 21.21; 1 Chr 6.52), but never conquered by the Israelites (Jos 16.10; Jg 1.29). It figured in David's wars (1 Chr 14.16; 20.4). Solomon received it as a wedding gift from the Pharaoh and rebuilt it as chariot center (1 Kg 9.16–17). In Maccabean times it was a center of resistance (1 Macc 13.53; 14.7, 34; 15.28). Identified with Tell Jezer (18 miles NW of Jerusalem) where important excavations have been carried out. BIBLIOGRAPHY: R. A. S. Macalister, *Excavations of Gezer 1902–1905 and 1907–1909* (3 v., 1912); W. F. Albright, "Gezer Calendar," BASOR 92 (1943) 16–26; J. Trinquet, *Catholicisme* 4:1906.

[F. BUCK]

GFRÖRER, AUGUST FRIEDRICH (1803–61), historian. G. was unable to achieve an affirmative attitude toward Lutheran doctrine either as student or as pastor. In 1853 he entered the Catholic Church, his conversion owing, in part, to his findings when doing historical research. G. believed a reunion of Churches would effect a political unity in the German Empire. BIBLIOGRAPHY: H. Rumpler, NCE 6:459–460; R. Bäumer, LTK 4:879.

[F. G. O'BRIEN]

GHAZZĀLĪ, AL-, see ALGAZEL.

GHÉBRÉ, MICHAEL, BL. (*c.*1790–1855), an Ethiopian Coptic monk who was converted to Roman Catholicism by Bl. Justin de Jacobis in 1844. In 1851, G. was ordained and did much to convert his fellow countrymen. When Theodore II usurped the Ethiopian crown, G. began a long period of imprisonment and torture. Forced to accompany the king in chains, G. was dragged across the country, finally succumbing in 1855. He was beatified in 1926. BIBLIOGRAPHY: D. Attwater, *Book of Eastern Saints* (1938); R. Chalumeau, *Catholicisme* 4:1907.

[J. R. AHERNE]

GHELLINCK, JOSEPH DE (1872–1950), Jesuit patrologist and historian of dogma. From 1906 until his retirement in 1942, G. taught patrology and (from 1915) the history of dogma at the Jesuit scholasticate of Louvain. For one semester each year during the years 1925–32, he taught at the Gregorian Univ. in Rome. He was the author of many scholarly studies, his best known book being *Le mouvement théologique du XIIe siècle* (1914). BIBLIOGRAPHY: V. C. DeClercq, NCE 6:460–461; A. Piolanti, EncCatt 6:294.

[R. B. ENO]

GHENT, PACIFICATION OF, see PACIFICATION OF GHENT.

GHENT ALTARPIECE (Adoration of the Lamb), world-renowned masterpainting by Hubert and Jan Van Eyck in the Cathedral of St. Bavon in Ghent. *VAN EYCK, JAN.

[M. J. DALY]

GHÉON, HENRI (pseudonym of Henri Léon Vangeon; 1875–1944), French writer. G. practiced medicine, then turned to literature, and published (1897–1914) poetry (*Chanson d'aube*), criticism (*Nos directions: Réalisme et poésie*), fiction (*L'Adolescent*), and social drama (*Le Pain*). In 1915, influenced by a fellow soldier, Dominique Dupouey who was killed that year on Holy Saturday, G. returned to Catholicism, and subsequently described his spiritual development in *L'Homme né de la guerre. Témoignages d'un converti* (1919). Thereafter he became increasingly conservative, moved to the right politically, and for a time associated himself with the *Action Française* movement. His subsequent literary interests lay in founding a modern popular Christian theater by creating plays based on themes adapted from medieval mystery and miracle plays, and by establishing a company, *Les Compagnons de Notre-Dame* (1925–1930), to stage them. Representative works in this genre include *Le Pauvre sous l'escalier* (1921) (based on the medieval French hagiographical poem, *Legend of St. Alexis*), considered his best work, *Jeux et miracles pour le peuple fidèle* (2 v., 1922), *Le Noël sur la place* (1935), and *Le Jeu des merveilles de Saint-Martin* (1943). English translations include *The Comedian* (1927), *The Marvelous Story of St. Bernard* (1928), and *St. Anne and the Gouty Rector and Other Plays* (1950). His hagiographical works include lives of the Curé d'Ars and St. John Bosco. BIBLIOGRAPHY: H. Brochet, *Henri Ghéon* (1947); M. Deléglise, *Le Théâtre d'Henri Ghéon* (1947); R. Speaight, *Christian Theatre* (1960) 137–138.

[G. E. GINGRAS]

GHERARDO DI GIOVANNI DI MINIATO (1446–97), Florentine miniaturist and organist whose work is often confused with that of his brother, Monte. Known works of G. are a missal of S. Egidio (1474–76, Florence), and a Bible for Matthias Corvinus (1492, Florence), both executed with Monte. A choir book in S. Lorenzo is attributed to G. alone.

[M. J. DALY]

GHETTO, section of a city to which people of a particular ethnic group are restricted. Historically it has referred to the Jewish section, though today the term is often applied to such areas as New York's Harlem in which blacks are concentrated. In medieval Europe, Jews appear to have naturally congregated in particular areas of the cities for the sake of maintaining their community life. In the later Middle

Ages, legislation made the pattern compulsory, and in the 16th cent. ghettos became almost universal. The area was commonly walled, with Jews required to be inside by nightfall. Ghettos often contained insufficient area, and overcrowding led to epidemics and disastrous fires. Outside the ghetto the Jew had to wear an identifying symbol, often a yellow badge. The restrictions were allegedly to protect the faith of Christians. The effects on Jewish cultural life were various: the community by necessity became closely knit, but lost contact with the wider cultural world and was restricted from such basic kinds of experience as agriculture. The humiliating circumstances led to some loss of self-esteem and strengthened the anti-Semitism of the Christians who enforced the oppressive conditions. Ghettos often had a considerable degree of autonomy internally, however, particularly in such a notable ghetto as the one in Prague. Ghettos continued into the 19th cent., with the one in Rome abolished only in 1870. They were reinstituted under esp. cruel circumstances by the Nazis. BIBLIOGRAPHY: L. Wirth, *Ghetto* (2d ed., 1956).

[T. EARLY]

GHIBELLINES, see GUELFS AND GHIBELLINES.

GHIBERTI, masters at Florence, father and son. **LORENZO** (Lorenzo di Bartolo, di Bartoluccio, di Bartolo Michele; 1378–1455), sculptor, goldsmith, architect, painter and writer. G. was a member of the goldsmiths' guild (1409), painters' guild (1423), stonemasons' guild (1426), a Florentine humanist, an antiquarian and writer of *Commentarii,* an autobiography and theory of art, that is, one of the main source books of the Renaissance. G. won and executed the prestigious commissions for 2 pairs of bronze doors for the baptistery, Florence: the earlier pair (1404–24), 20 quartrefoil relief panels, relating to the Gothic first doors by A. Pisano; the second pair, 10 magnificent and famous gilded-bronze rectangular panels (1428–27; hung 1452) in G.'s masterful, innovative Renaissance style, called by Michelangelo the "Gates of Paradise." G. was involved in the early construction (1417) of the dome of the cathedral of Florence (rightfully attributed to the genius, Brunelleschi). He also executed bronze life-size statues of *St. John the Baptist, St. Matthew,* and *St. Stephen* for Or San Michele and numerous other commissions—pictorial reliefs, tabernacles, shrines, choir stalls, and bejewelled mitres and clasps for popes. G.'s workshop became a principal training ground for Florentine artists. Though avant-garde, G. was an ardent admirer of the past, combining lyrical Gothic line, Renaissance form, and spatial mastery with a scholarly adaptation of the classical. In finely graduated depths G. unites the monumentality of Renaissance design with the delicate refinements and subtle tactile qualities of the goldsmiths' art. BIBLIOGRAPHY: J. Pope-Hennessy, *Italian Gothic Sculpture* (1955); C. Seymour, *Sculpture in Italy* (1966).

VITTORIO (1416–96), goldsmith, bronze caster, and sculptor, son and pupil of Lorenzo. He assisted his father on the Gates of Paradise and after L.'s death completed the frames of all 3 baptistery doors.

[M. J. DALY]

GHIKA, VLADIMIR (1873–1954), Romanian priest. Grandson of the last king of Moldavia, G. was converted to Catholicism in 1902 and went to Rome to study theology. Later he founded numerous charitable works in Romania. Not until 1923 was he ordained, with the privilege of celebrating in both the Latin and the Oriental rites. When about to flee from communist Romania, G. gave up his place to a stranger, with the result that he was imprisoned in Bucharest until his death. BIBLIOGRAPHY: G. Wagner, *Catholicisme* 4:1909–10.

[M. J. SUELZER]

GHIRLANDAIO, Florentine painters. **Domenico** (1449–94), most accomplished frescoist of his generation in Florence and head of an extensive workshop in which Michelangelo was an apprentice. He was popular in his day for the narrative details and naturalism of his compositions in which he often included contemporary portraits (Vatican, Sistine Chapel; "Calling of the First Apostles," 1481–82). Major fresco cycles in Florence are at Santa Trinità and at Santa Maria Novella, where, in the life of the Virgin (*c.*1485–90), women of the Tornabuoni donor family in patrician elegance are prominent in the religious drama. Important for innovation in images is G.'s *Adoration of the Shepherds* (1485) in which clumsy, unprepossessing figures startle us within a panel of classical reference—evidencing the impact of Flemish naturalism in the *Portinari Altarpiece (1474–76) by Hugo van der *Goes, commissioned and brought to Florence from Bruges by T. Portinari of the Medici banking house. **David** (1452–1525), principal assistant of his brother Domenico (1475) in the library of Sixtus IV in Rome. He is credited with two mosaics: *Madonna and Child with Angels* (1496, Paris) and *Annunciation* (1510) in SS. Annunziata, Florence. The fresco *Crucifixion with Two Camaldolese Monks* (Florence) shows affinity to Castagna. **Benedetto** di Tommaso (1458–97), brother of Domenico and David. His work was probably the least refined painting of the Ghirlandaio workshop. Miniature painter until 1479, he entered the Ghirlandaio workshop, traveled to Rome, and executed frescoes on the lower walls of the Sistine Chapel (1481–82). He worked on Domenico's frescoes in S. Maria Novella in the Ghirlandaio formula of simplified form and pale color. In his *Nativity* (Aigneperse, *c.*1492), executed in France, Benedetto added Flemish conventions in the figure and head of the Virgin, with meticulously detailed ornament. **Ridolfo** (1483–1561), son of Domenico, pupil of Fra Bartolommeo, influenced by Piro di Cosimo and Granacci. He combined the literalism of the Ghirlandaio tradition with qualities of the High Renaissance (*Madonna Della Cintola,* 1514–15), which assured him commissions for works (many of which are now lost.) . see J. Lauts, *Domenico Ghirlandaio* (1943).

[M. J. DALY]

GHISI, GIORGIO (1520–82), Italian printmaker, student of Giulio Romano in Mantua, working in the style of Marcantonio Raimondi (master-engraver of Raphael's works). G. engraved Michelangelo's Last Judgment and the Prophets and Sibyls of the Sistine Chapel (1540). In Antwerp (1550) the engraved Raphael's *School of Athens* and *Disput*Insert before .ga for the publisher Hieronymus Cock who later issued G.'s *Philosopher* (1561).

[M. J. DALY]

GIACOMETTI, ALBERTO (1901–66), Swiss sculptor, painter, draftsman, poet. Beginning sculpture in 1914, G. studied Italian master-painters in Italy (1920–22), and in Paris (1922) worked with Bourdelle. G. was fascinated by the immobility of archaic forms in museums, producing idol-like cubist shapes (1926) and becoming the leader (1929–35) of surrealist sculptors. G. kept reducing the scale and volume of the human figure to express a poignant "isolation," producing after World War II distinctive hermetic figures and disembodied gestures (1947). Strongest European sculptor of his time and deeply philosophic, G. expressed the inner essence of the human subject in extremely attenuated and corrugated bronze forms. His painted figures, set in cavernous rooms, are realized in a net of brush lines in neutral palette. BIBLIOGRAPHY: A. Giacometti, *Schriften, Fotos, Zeichnungen* (ed. E. Scheidegger, 1958).

[M. J. DALY]

GIACOMO DA POIRINO (1808–85), Italian Franciscan, friend of C. *Cavour, who attended that statesman on his deathbed. Whether Cavour was absolved, either absolutely or conditionally, is not known. Defending himself on grounds of the sacramental seal, G. would give no explanation of what he had done. It is said that Pius IX, hearing that no retraction had been demanded of Cavour, suspended G.'s faculties as a confessor, and that these were restored only after 20 years. BIBLIOGRAPHY: M. Borelli, DE 2:102.

[M. J. SUELZER]

GIACOMO DELLA PORTA (1537–1602), Italian Renaissance architect in Rome. G. assisted Michelangelo at St. Peter's, completing the dome with lantern (1590) after Michelangelo's death, using Michelangelo's earlier high design, effecting probably the most beautiful dome in the world. G. designed the façade of the impressive mother church of the Jesuits, Il Gesù, Rome (*c.* 1575–84), (interior by Vignola) in a skillful synthesis of horizontal and vertical members with notes from Alberti, Michelangelo, and Palladio which, eschewing the colossal order, emphasizes the entrance in a pre-Baroque gesture, becoming a model of Roman Baroque and of Catholic churches throughout the world for 2 centuries.

[M. J. DALY]

GIAMBERTI, see SANGALLO.

GIANELLI, ANTHONY, ST. (1789–1846), bp. and religious founder. A Genoese, G. was ordained in 1812 and became a celebrated preacher and confessor. He founded two congregations: Oblates of St. Alphonsus and Daughters of Our Lady of the Garden, the latter devoted to educating poor children and nursing the sick. In 1838 G. was named bp. of Bobbio, Italy, where he proved an unusually able prelate. He was canonized in 1951. BIBLIOGRAPHY: Butler 2:500–501.

[J. R. AHERNE]

GIARWEH, see GARWEH.

GIBAULT, PIERRE (1737–1804), French Canadian missionary. Ordained in Quebec, G. was sent to the Illinois country as a missioner and in 1769 became its vicar general. When the Virginia militia captured Kaskaskia in 1778, the commander, George Rogers Clark, won over the French by his wise attitude toward the Church. G. won the acceptance of the Americans by the settlement at Fort Vincennes, Ind., and again aided the American effort to recapture it, for which he was commended by the Commonwealth of Virginia. Because of his influence on Vincennes, G. was accused of treason by the British but he asserted he was trying to bring peace. In 1790 he requested indemnification for losses in the Revolution, requesting a grant of land. Bp. Carroll objected to grants to an individual and G. withdrew to Spanish territory where he continued missionary work as pastor at New Madrid, Missouri.

[J. R. AHERNE]

GIBBON, EDWARD (1737–94), English historian. G. entered Magdalen College, Oxford, at 15, and within a year converted to Catholicism. His father at once transferred him to Lausanne, where under Calvinist influence he reverted to Protestantism. His chief work is the still authoritative *Decline and Fall of the Roman Empire* (6 v., 1776–88), the thesis of which is that Christianity caused the downfall of the Empire; the Middle Ages are "the triumph of barbarism and religion." Everything supernatural G. treated with irony and ridicule, a method more telling than direct attack, which would have alienated many readers. He assigned the rapid spread of Christianity to five causes: the intolerant zeal of Christians; their belief in a future life; the purity of their morals; the discipline enforced; and the miracles ascribed to Christianity. BIBLIOGRAPHY: *Decline and Fall* (ed. J. C. Bury, 7 v., 1904–14); S. T. McCloy, *Gibbon's Antagonism to Christianity* (1933); M. Grant, *Decline and Fall. . . A Reappraisal for Our Own Times* (1976).

[M. J. SUELZER]

GIBBONS, JAMES (1834–1921), abp. of Baltimore, cardinal, statesman of the American Church. Born in Baltimore but raised in Ireland until his 19th year, G. was ordained for Baltimore in 1861. Abp. Spalding appointed him his secretary 5 years later and within 2 years he was named vicar apostolic of North Carolina, a territory with a total of 250 Catholics and three priests. At his consecration he was the youngest bp. in the Catholic world. A quiet participant in Vatican Council I, he was made bp. of Richmond in 1872. The publication of his *Faith of Our Fathers* (1876) launched a work destined to become one of the most widely read books on religion in English. G. was named (1877) coadjutor abp. of Baltimore with the right of succession and succeeded almost immediately to the metropolitan title since his predecessor died the same year. The primary see that he now headed was the setting for a brilliant career to which he seemed predestined. A major step on the way was the convocation (1884) of the Third Plenary Council of Baltimore, presided over by G. as apostolic delegate. Its work bears his imprint, esp. in the decrees on secret societies, with G. as defender of labor unions; on the need to promote parochial schools, and in the appeal for greater efforts for the Negro missions. G. emerged from the Council as the preeminent American prelate. The conferring of the red hat on the Archbishop in 1886 and in particular the address he gave upon entering his titular church in Rome the following year made G. the undisputed spokesman for the Catholic Church in the U.S., a position recognized equally by the Holy See and by the republic. His address on the ideal relations of Church and State as exemplified in America was a new departure, incomprehensible to the European Catholic mind but a landmark for the American Church.

The original stimulus for a national Catholic university came from Abp. John Ireland and Bp. John Spalding against strong opposition from other bishops. It fell to G. as acknowledged leader of the hierarchy to carry through on the project. The idea was approved by the Council of Baltimore and ultimately, after much questioning by Rome, the papal brief of Leo XIII establishing The Catholic Univ. of America was issued in 1887. From the beginning the university was plagued with troubles rooted in the conservative nature of many members of the American hierarchy. The first rector, Bp. Keane, a liberal, was removed by Rome to the complete dismay of Gibbons. For 35 years G. would be the strong advocate of the institution, defending it against many attacks.

At a time when the cause of organized labor was in doubt because some churchmen feared the minority radical element in the movement, G. distinguished the legitimate aspects and the demands of social justice involved, and championed the Knights of Labor against the critics in the American hierarchy and in Rome. From 1887 when G. presented to the Pope his "Memorial" on the Knights of Labor with its clear statement on the Church and labor generally, to his death 34 years later, the Cardinal was a consistent leader in the new cause of social justice, acknowledged as such in Europe as well as in the United States. There is little doubt that his stand prepared the way for Leo's famous social encyclical *Rerum novarum* (1891), a document that placed the universal Church precisely where G. had declared it should be. His steadfast espousal of the rights of labor placed him in the distinguished company of Bp. von Ketteler in Germany and Card. Manning in England.

Of the manifold controversies within the American Church none was so critical as the accusation that it was infected by "Americanism," and the charge that American Catholics like G., Abp. Ireland, and the Paulist founder, Isaac Hecker, espoused doctrines that were heretical. The legitimate desire of these Catholic leaders to work out a place in American society befitting a new age was distorted by conservative bps. in the U.S., and worst of all by a reactionary element in France and in Rome. The bitter conflict was resolved, after years of storm, by Leo XIII in *Testem benevolentiae*, a letter to G. that charted a middle course and praised the American Church.

As friend and adviser to six presidents of the U.S., G. exercised tactful but enormous influence, particularly in the Spanish-American War and its aftermath, and in World War I and the uneasy peace that followed. It was to him that the government turned, just as the Vatican did in the same period for whatever related to the position of the Church in world affairs.

This gentle and, by preference, unobtrusive man almost in spite of himself became one of the most influential men in America and beyond doubt the chief voice of Catholicism in a period when it was essential to align the American Church with the burgeoning republic without in any way diminishing the perennial vigor of the ancient traditions of Catholicism. BIBLIOGRAPHY: J. T. Ellis, *Life of James Cardinal Gibbons* (1952).

[J. R. AHERNE]

GIBBONS, ORLANDO (1583–1625), English composer. As organist of the Chapel Royal and Westminster Abbey, G. performed and composed for English royalty most of his life. His sacred anthems, motets, and madrigals reflect the culmination of vocal polyphonic composition in England. Among his famous anthems are "O Lord Increase My Faith" and "Almighty and Everlasting God." His motets include "The Silver Swan" and "What Is Our Life?"

G. was considered the most skillful organist and virginalist in England during his life. While accompanying King Charles I to meet his new queen, Henrietta Maria of France, G. suffered a stroke and died.

[D. SMUCKER]

GIBBS, JAMES (1682–1754), English architect. In Rome (1707–09) G. studied with Carol Fontana. St. Mary-le-Strand (London, 1714–17), his first commission, shows mannerist rather than Baroque reference. Later G. altered his style, allying himself with Wren, showing in all work a persistent individuality. His St. Martin-in-the-Fields (1721–26) is probably the most influential of all English churches—its "Gibbs' steeple" and pedimental façade widely imitated in America. G.'s work always highly personal and characterized by technical accomplishment rather than dramatic effect, exerted profound influence. His books on architecture (1728–32) were widely used.

[M. J. DALY]

GIBEAH (GABAA), from a Heb. word meaning hill, the name of two cities in the OT: (1) a city of Judah in the hill country, mentioned only in Jos 15.57 and identified with modern El-Jeba, SW of Bethlehem; (2) a city of Benjamin (Jos 18.28), 3 miles N of Jerusalem, identified with modern el-Ful. The scene of the outrage on the Levite's concubine (Jg 19.1–20, 22–48; Hos 9.9; 10.9), it was the home and capital of Saul (1 Sam 9.1–2; 10.26; 22.6; 23.19) and hence was known as "Gibeah of Saul" (1 Sam 11.4; 15.34; Is 10.29). There occur also the names of "Gibeah of Benjamin" (Jg 20.4; 1 Sam 13.2) and "Gibeah of God" (1 Sam 10.5, 10). In 1922 and 1933 W. F. Albright excavated Tell el-Ful. BIBLIOGRAPHY: W. F. Albright, "Excavations and Results at Tell el-Ful," *Annual, American Schools of Oriental Research* 4 (1924); L. A. Sinclair, "Archaeological Study of Gibeah (Tell el-Ful)," *op. cit.* 34–35 (1954–55).

[F. BUCK]

GIBEON (GABAON), from a Heb. word meaning hill, a city inhabited by Hivites (Jos 9.7)—called Amorites in 2 Sam 21.2—allotted to Benjamin (Jos 18.25), and assigned to the priests as a Levitical city (Jos 21.17). G. is generally identified with modern El-Jib, 6 miles NW of Jerusalem. There are 45 references to Gibeon and the Gibeonites scattered through eight books of the OT (Jos, 2 Sam, 1 Kg, 1 and 2 Chr, Neh, Is, Jer). The site has been excavated by J. B. Pritchard through four seasons beginning in 1956. Among the principal discoveries may be listed the necropolis, the fortifications, the winery, inscriptions and royal stamps, water tunnels, and the great pool (2 Sam 2.13). BIBLIOGRAPHY: J. B. Pritchard, *Gibeon, Where the Sun Stood Still. The Discovery of the Biblical City* (1962); W. L. Reed, "Gibeon," *Archaeology and OT Study* (1967), 231–243.

[F. BUCK]

GIBERTI, GIAN MATTEO (1495–1543), bp., promoter of church reform. His early priestly life was spent in the service of Card. Giulio de' Medici who, as Clement VII, made him datary apostolic. Appointed bp. of Verona in 1524, G. continued active at Rome in papal political issues and did not take up residency until 1528. He immediately devoted himself to reform measures in his diocese, esp. by insistence on clerical discipline and on the improvement of sacred studies. He was a member of the reform commission set up by Paul III in 1536; and was papal legate to the Catholic-Protestant conferences at Worms in 1540.

[T. C. O'BRIEN]

GIBIEUF, GUILLAUME (*c.*1585–1650), philosopher and theologian. G. studied at the Sorbonne; entered the newly founded *French Oratory (1612); became an assistant to its founder Pierre de *Bérulle; and eventually superior of the order. G. wrote extensively in theology and spirituality, but is best known for his philosophical work *De libertate Dei et creaturae,* in which he presents free will as a faculty that participates in the infinity of God. The will is not free because it enjoys a certain active indifference before possible choices, but because it shares in the divine will's complete openness to all goodness. G.'s ideas on liberty seem to have influenced R. *Descartes, and are similar to those later defended by C. *Jansen. BIBLIOGRAPHY: É. Gilson, *Liberté chez Descartes et la théologie* (1913); A. Ingold, DTC 6.2:1347–48.

[T. M. MCFADDEN]

GIDE, ANDRÉ (1869–1951), French novelist, playwright, and poet. G. was more than a man of letters; he was a philosopher in search of truth. Truth has many faces, and G. examined many of these without committing himself irrevocably to any one. A Protestant, he studied the Scriptures ostensibly to reach truth through that cosmic channel. His lifelong interest in Christianity, his friendship with P. Claudel and perhaps with F. Mauriac mark an irregular path in the vast garden of his wanderings. His pursuits, his evasions, his convictions underscore the ambiguities of his life and work. Critics have variously praised his style and his ideas. The scintillating brilliance of his literary expression has been lavishly overpraised in compensation for the paucity of the matter. It is Sartre (*Situations,* 1965) who epitomizes what is probably most true: this play of counterbalances (Protestant law, strong sensuality, nonconformity) is at the roots of the service that G. has rendered to contemporary literature. But G. like Rousseau or Chateaubriand was more interesting than his works. It is Mauriac who ruminates over man's tendency to judge man's actions without reference to that man's particular destiny. G.'s insistence on the morality of homosexuality as he defined it is central to an understanding of his works. Likewise is an acceptance of his attempt to discredit Christianity as he knew it. His works were never banal or insincere, misguided as they sometimes were. G. founded the *Nouvelle Revue Française,* the official organ of the elite intellectual in France. He wrote *Les Nourritures terrestres* (1897), *Le Retour de l'enfant prodigue* (1907), *Dostoevsky* (1923), *Si le grain ne meurt* (1926), among other works. G. received the Nobel Prize for Literature in 1947. BIBLIOGRAPHY: *Gide: Collection of Critical Essays* (ed. D. Littlejohn, 1970); J. C. McLaren, *Theatre of André Gide: Evolution of a Moral Philosopher* (1953, repr. 1971).

[R. M. FUNCHION]

GIDEON (GEDEON), son of Joash of the tribe of Manasseh (Jg 6.11, 15), also known as Jerubbaal (Jg 6.32) and Jerubbesheth (2 Sam 11.21), was called to restore the true worship of Yahweh and to deliver Israel from the Midianites (Jg 6.11–32). A brilliant leader, he defeated and pursued the enemy (Jg 7.15–23; 8.4–21). He refused to be crowned as king (Jg 8.22). From the spoils he made an ephod, a kind of idolatrous image (Jg 8.24–28). While Yahweh made him victorious (Is. 9.4; 10.26; Ps 83. 9–10, 12), he is praised because of his faith (Heb 11.32–33). BIBLIOGRAPHY: L. Alonso Schökel, "Heros Gedeon. De genere litterario et historicitate Jdc 6–8," *Verbum Domini* 32 (1954) 3–20, 65–76; C. F. Whitley, "Sources of the Gideon Stories," VT 7 (1957) 157–164.

[F. BUCK]

GIDEONS, INTERNATIONAL (formal title, Christian Commercial Men's Association of America), a group of laymen dedicated to evangelism, chiefly through distribution of the Bible. The name is an allusion to the Book of Judges, ch. 6–8; Gideon was one of the major judges (i.e., leaders) who by his faith and obedience served God in the liberation of Israel. The account of Judges 7 also explains the emblem, a two-handled pitcher with a torch. The group was founded by two commercial travelers who met in a hotel in Janesville, Wis., in the fall of 1898; they organized the association the following July. The Gideons place Bibles in hotel rooms, hospitals, prisons, and schools. Headquarters are in Chicago, Illinois.

[T. C. O'BRIEN]

GIFFARD, BONAVENTURE (1642–1734) titular bp., vicar apostolic of the English mission. A member of an old Catholic family, G. studied at the English College in Douai, was ordained, received a doctorate from the Sorbonne in 1677, and began pastoral ministry in England. In 1687 G. was appointed one of four vicars apostolic in England, with care over the Midlands; he was consecrated bp. in April 1688. James II appointed him president of Magdelan College, Oxford, in June and G. and 11 Catholic fellows made Magdelan "a Roman Catholic establishment." They were all dismissed by the bp. of Winchester in October, 1688. With the Revolution of 1688 G. was imprisoned for 2 years. In 1703 he was named vicar apostolic of the London district. Then began a time of hiding, transfer from house to house, which continued for better than 30 years and included five arrests.

[J. R. AHERNE]

GIFFORD, WILLIAM (1554–1629), abp. of Reims and opponent of the Jesuit, Robert *Persons. Educated at Oxford, Louvain, Douai, and Rome, he was ordained (1582), taught theology at Reims, and served with Card. William Allen, his friend and benefactor (1593). After Allen's death he became dean of Lille (1595). His involvement in English church affairs brought charges from Persons that G. instigated anti-Jesuit hostility within the seminaries and connived with the English government, both charges being partially true. After G. joined the Benedictines (1608), his energies were largely directed towards order affairs until, because of his friendship with the Guise family, he was made coadjutor bp. (1617) to Card. de Guise, abp. of Reims, whom he succeeded in 1622. BIBLIOGRAPHY: *Wisbeck Stirs* (ed. P. Reynolds, 1958); T. H. Clancy, *Papist Pamphleteers* (1964).

GIFFORD LECTURES, a series given at the four Scottish universities. Founded by A. Gifford (1820–87), the first lectures were given in 1888. The lectureship was established "for promoting, advancing, teaching, and diffusing the study of natural theology, in the widest sense of that term, in other words, the knowledge of God" and "of the foundation of ethics." It is among the most highly regarded lecture series in the English-speaking world. Its holders, who are not required to hold any creed, have included numerous distinguished theologians and philosophers; many significant books are based on their authors' Gifford lectures.

[T. EARLY]

GIFT, a voluntary, spontaneous bestowal, made without intent of receiving recompense. The morality of giving and receiving gifts presupposes considerations of *justice: that the donor be capable of and truly have ownership of what is given, and that the donee be capable of receiving the gift. The act of giving also involves, obviously, the beneficence's belonging to *charity, esp. since the first gift given to another is the love that prompts the gift. The virtue of *liberality or generosity also enters gift-giving, as such a virtue means a willingness to use resources in kindness and love for others, and a respect for the right circumstances of time, place, quality of gift given. The receiving of a gift involves the decent indebtedness proper to *gratitude, which means a willingness to be indebted graciously to another's generosty and a delicacy in reciprocating both in sentiment and in kind the gift gratefully received. When gifts involve the public good order, both civil and ecclesiastical law lay down conditions. Canon law in particular determines the following: an individual religious may not give gifts out of community property, except with the superior's permission; even superiors cannot bestow gifts except officially and in keeping with the institute's resources (CIC, c. 537); those in charge of *church property are administrators and cannot give gifts except as custom or law permits (*ibid., c.* 1535); pastors or religious who receive gifts must consider them, unless otherwise stipulated, as given to the church or institute (*ibid., c.* 1536).

[T. C. O'BRIEN]

GIFT OF TONGUES, see TONGUES, GIFT OF.

GIFTS OF THE HOLY SPIRIT, see HOLY SPIRIT, GIFTS OF THE.

GIGAKU MASKS, first Japanese masks (probably the oldest extant in the world) used in farcical musical pantomime performed in court and temple ceremonies through the early Heian period. Though discontinued there are 223 such masks from the 7th and 8th cent. in the Hōryūji (now in Tokyo Museum), the Shōsō-in and the Tōdaiji. Of wood and finished in dry-lacquer technique, the large and heavy masks covering the entire head of the dancers were vividly dramatic.

[M. J. DALY]

GIGAULT, NICHOLAS (1624 or 1625–1707), French organist and composer, associated with St. Nicolas-des-Champs Church in Paris, where his son Joachim succeeded him. His work provides a comprehensive compendium of early Baroque technique. In 1685 he published *Livre de musique pour l'orgue,* which has reappeared in a modern edition, along with work by Nicholas de Grigny and others, in Guilmant and Pirro's *Archives des maîtres de l'orgue*.

[J. C. MARR]

GIGLI GIOVANNI (1434–98), canonist, English agent at the Roman Curia. G. was archdeacon of London (1482–90), of Gloucester (1489–97), and bp. of Worcester (1497–98). A naturalized Englishman of Italian parentage, with some reputation as a humanist, he served as a papal collector in England (1476–90), and was resident English proctor at Rome (1490–98). BIBLIOGRAPHY: Emden 2:764–765.

[C. D. ROSS]

GIGOT, FRANCIS ERNEST (1859–1920), Scripture scholar. Born and educated in France, G. became a Sulpician, taught at St. John's Seminary, Brighton, Mass. (1885–99), St. Mary's Seminary, Baltimore, Md. (1899–1904), and St. Joseph's Seminary, Yonkers, N.Y. (1904–20). He wrote several books and articles on biblical subjects, and translated the Apocalypse for the Westminster Bible. G. was an exemplary scholar, well-versed in the critical approach to hermeneutics which was beginning to be accepted in RC circles. In 1906, G.'s resignation from the Sulpicians to join the N.Y. diocesan clergy was interpreted by some as an effort to avoid restrictions placed on his work by reportedly ultraconservative Sulpician superiors.

[T. M. MCFADDEN]

GIHR, NIKOLAUS (1839–1924), German priest and liturgist. His professional life was spent at the Seminary of Freiburg-im-Breisgau as a faculty member and then, from 1888, as vice-rector. He published ascetical and liturgical works, but is most renowned for a major historical and theological study of the Roman Mass rite: *The Holy Sacrifice of the Mass, Dogmatically, Liturgically and Ascetically Explained* (Eng. tr. of 6th Ger. ed., 1902).

[T. C. O'BRIEN]

GIKATILLA, JOSEPH BEN ABRAHAM (1248–1305), Spanish Jew, cabalist and grammarian. As a student of Abraham Abulafia, G. acquired such deep mystical knowledge that miracles were attributed to him, and he was called "The Miracle Worker." G. worked with Hebrew numbers and letters, a mysticism which he held to be the true cabala. As a great writer, he explained his philosophy and three methods of letter combinations in the cabala: *Gematria,* numerical value of a word; *Notarikon,* interpretation of words as abbreviations; *Themurah,* permutation of letters. Some of his doctrinal works are: *Ginnoth Egoz* (Garden of Nuts; cf. S of S 6.11); *Sha'are Orah* (Gates of Light). Other works include commentaries on *Passover Haggadah,* and the *Song of Songs*. BIBLIOGRAPHY: H. H. Graetz, *History of the Jews* (ed. and tr. B. Löwy, 6 v., 1945) 4:10, 466.

[A. P. HANLON]

GIL OF ZAMORA, see JOHN GIL OF ZAMORA.

GILBERT CRISPIN (d. 1117), Benedictine abbot of Westminster. G., while a thinker and writer in his own right, was greatly influenced by St. Anselm. His commonsense argumentation is more evident in his writings than his ability in philosophical speculation. From him we get a clear insight into Anselm's influence on the times. His most important work is the *Disputatio Iudaei et Christiani*.

[F. G. O'BRIEN]

GILBERT OF HOLLAND (Hoyland; d. 1172), Cistercian abbot and biblical commentator; friend and disciple of St. *Bernard of Clairvaux. He is known to have been prior at Swineshead near Holland, Lincolnshire, England in the middle of the 12th century. He died at the Abbey of Rivour, near Troyes, France. His sermons, resuming St. Bernard's commentary on the Song of Songs (PL 184.11–252) are signal examples of 12th-cent. monastic theology and exegesis. BIBLIOGRAPHY: B. Smalley, *Study of the Bible in the Middle Ages* (1952; pa. 1964).

[T. C. O'BRIEN]

GILBERT OF MONS (*c.* 1140–1224), a priest who served Baldwin V, Count of Hainault, successively as chaplain, clerk, notary, and chancellor. After Baldwin's death (1195) he retired from public life and devoted himself to writing. His most important work, *Chronicon Hanoniense,* covers the period 1070–1195.

GILBERT OF NEUFFONTAINES, ST. (d. 1152). Born of a noble family in Auvergne at the beginning of the 12th cent., he was raised at the court of Louis the Fat. On the advice of Arnulph, first abbot of the Premonstratensians of Dilo, he set out on the Second Crusade in 1146 with King Louis VII. The failure of the enterprise affected him deeply, and, returning to Auvergne, he decided, together with his wife, Petronilla, and daughter, Pontia, to enter religious life. He restored a monastery for women at Aubeterre, Petronilla and Pontia becoming its first two abbesses. G. himself became a hermit at Neuffonts, then built there a monastery for men and a hospital where he could care for the sick. In 1151 he joined the Premonstratensians at Dilo, then returned to Neuffontaine Abbey where he was elected prior, serving only briefly before his death. Numerous miracles, esp. helping children, are attributed to him. G. was joined by his wife and daughter in sainthood. BIBLIOGRAPHY: AS June 1:749–754; G. B. Valvekens, BiblSanct 6:454–455.

[J. D. LOUGHLIN]

GILBERT DE LA PORRÉE (Gilbert of Poitiers; Gilbertus Porretanus; *c.*1075–1154), scholastic philosopher and theologian. He studied under Bernard of Chartres and Anselm of Laon. His teaching was done mainly at Chartres, where he was chancellor of the cathedral school several times, 1126–36. He became bp. of Poitiers in 1142. In 1147 he was accused of unorthodox Trinitarian doctrine by two of his archdeacons, and at the direction of Pope Eugene III the case was considered by a synod at Paris (1147) and the Council of Reims (1148). St. Bernard of Clairvaux sought to have G. condemned for errors summed up in four "chapters" (*capitula*) at Reims: (1) that God and his essence are not the same; (2) that there is a real distinction between the Divine Person and nature; (3) between the divine essence and the relations of Persons; (4) that the Divinity did not become incarnate in the person of Jesus (cf. D 745). G. was not convicted of teaching these errors. The conflict mainly centered on his commentaries on the works of Boethius; G. developed a highly technical interpretation of logic and grammar to overcome the inadequacies of language with regard to the Trinity. His other works include unedited commentaries on Psalms and St. Paul. In the Middle Ages the *Liber de sex principiis* was attributed to him, but this ascription is considered very doubtful. Through his works and many disciples G. exercised a major influence on shaping the terminology and methodology of high scholasticism. BIBLIOGRAPHY: Copleston 2:151–152; D. Luscombe, EncPhil 3:329–331; N. M. Häring, *"Case of Gilbert,"* MedSt 13 (1951) 1–40.

[T. EARLY]

GILBERT OF SAINT-AMAND (Gislebert, d. 1095), Benedictine chronicler and poet. He was a monk at Saint-Amand-les-Eaux who raised funds to restore the monastery after a fire in 1066 by leading a procession through the region with the relics of St. Amandus. G.'s *Carmen de incendio sancti Amandi* (PL 150:1435–38), chronicles in prose and verse this journey and its events. He also probably wrote scriptural commentaries and sermons.

[T. C. O'BRIEN]

GILBERT OF SEMPRINGHAM, ST. (*c.*1083–1189), founder of the Gilbertine Order. Son of a Norman knight of Sempringham in Lincolnshire, G. was presented with the benefice in his native town. He drew up a rule for a number of women who chose to live in strict enclosure in a house adjoining the parish church. The community expanded, and when G. was unable to obtain Cistercians to work the lands belonging to the sisters, he obtained religious from the Augustinian Canons for that purpose, and these came to form an integral part of the Gilbertine double *monasteries, of which there were nine by 1189. In addition there were four other monasteries for men. The Gilbertines were the only English religious order of medieval origin. At the time of its suppression by Henry VIII (1538–39) there were 24 convents. G. was blind for some years before his death at the advanced age of 106. He was canonized in 1202. BIBLIOGRAPHY: R. Graham, *St. Gilbert of Sempringham and the Gilbertines* (1901); D. Knowles, "Revolt of the Laybrothers of Sempringham," EHR 50 (1935) 465–487; N. Del Re, BiblSanct 6:453–454; Knowles MOE 204–207.

[J. L. GRASSI]

GILBERT, ROBERT (d. 1448), theologian and bishop. Fellow of Merton College, Oxford (1398), and Warden (1417–21), dean of York (1426–36), bp. of London (1436–48), he was associated with the refutation of Wycliffite doctrine at Oxford in 1411, attended the Council of Constance (1417), and was envoy to the Council of Pavia (1423). BIBLIOGRAPHY: Emden Ox 2:766–767.

[C. D. ROSS]

GILBERTINES, the only monastic order of English foundation, existing from 1131 until Henry VIII's *dissolution of the monasteries (1538–40). Named for the founder, St. *Gilbert of Sempringham, the order followed basically a Cisterican mode of life, but never became affiliated with Cîteaux. The foundations consisted of double *monasteries, since to the original community of nuns Gilbert joined lay brothers to do the farm work and Canons Regular of St. Augustine to minister spiritually to the members. The dissolution suppressed 25 monasteries with a membership of 150 canons and 120 nuns, and the Gilbertines ceased to exist.

[T. C. O'BRIEN]

GILBERTUS ANGLICUS (fl. early 13th cent.), English decretalist at Bologna; after 1220 possibly a Dominican. His collection of *decretals covering the period 1159–1202 became the basis for later compilations (see QUINQUE COMPILATIONES ANTIQUAE).

[T. C. O'BRIEN]

GILBY, THOMAS (1902–75), English Dominican, theologian, author, editor. A convert in his youth, Thomas studied at Cambridge, Emmanuel College, which stands on the site of the medieval Dominican priory, joined the order in 1919, and, after ordination in 1926, did his doctoral work in philosophy at Louvain. He taught in the Dominican studia at Hawkesyard, Staffordshire, and Blackfriars, Oxford. He ceased teaching in 1935; his assessment of the Spanish Civil War as editor of *Blackfriars,* his theology of marriage, and other positions considered to be "advanced," met with disapproval. As chaplain in the Royal Navy from 1939 he saw battle duty in the North Atlantic and the Mediterranean; he remained in service after World War II, lecturing at American universities as a good-will representative of the British government. So began a series of sojourns in America and his great affection for this country. From the end of his naval service in 1948 Blackfriars, Cambridge, was Thomas's home. There he served several terms as prior; with funds from his lectures, writing, and friends he enlarged the priory, building a library, lecture hall, and glassed-in cloister along the garden he himself laid out and cared for. He dreamt that, with its proximity to the great university, Blackfriars would become a center for Dominican scholars. Both in England and the U.S. Thomas's confreres and friends remember him for his simplicity, his wit and spirit of **eutrapelia* (life is too serious to be taken solemnly, he would say), his clear, robust grasp on principles combined with a quiet, tender care for the wayward, the anxious, the afflicted. Only God and the beneficiaries know the variety and extent of his pastoral ministering and convert apostolate. A part of Thomas lives on in his writings (see bibliog.), which culminated in his general editorship of the 60-volume Lat-Eng edition of the *Summa theologiae* of Aquinas (1965–76). In 1963 he personally placed the first volume into the hands of Paul VI; the edition occupied him literally until the eve of his death, which came in the refectory among his own a few days after he had returned the last edited proofs to the printer. He was volume editor of 11 in the series, but as general editor handled every line of every volume from MS to page proof. With characteristic fidelity to duty, work, and to friends, he carried on refusing to brood over the decline of his own health or of Catholic interest in St. Thomas. The providence of God in whom Thomas had a simple and unwavering trust arranged that the rich knowledge and serene wisdom of his mind would be expressed and remain after him in his notes and appendices to the *Summa.* Thomas would sometimes jest that he was a "theist with a tincture of Christianity"; his real insight into the theology of St. Thomas, the St. Thomas of the yogis, not of the commissars (see THOMISM) is suggested by the précis and appraisal of the *Summa* in the first volume of his edition—a paragraph unsurpassed in any era, one that says much about its author (see THOMAS AQUINAS, ST.). This first volume, on the nature of theology, volume 8, on the metaphysics of creation, and volume 18, on fundamental moral theology, are esp. to be recommended as guides to sound and discerning theological thinking and to the rediscovery of the Catholic theological heritage. BIBLIOGRAPHY: Works: *Poetic Experience* (1934); *Marriage and Morals* (pseud. T. G. Wayne, 1936, repr. 1952); *Barbara Celarent* (1949); *Phoenix and the Turtle* (1950); *Between Community and Society* (1953); *Principality and Polity* (1958; in the U.S., *Political Thought of St. Thomas Aquinas*); *St. Thomas Aquinas, Philosophical Texts* (1951); St. Thomas Aquinas, Theological Texts (1955); in ThAq ST Lat-Eng, v. 1, 5, 8, 16, 17, 18, 28, 36, 43, 44, 59; also numerous articles in the present volumes (e.g., *Alexander VI, *Barchester Towers, Maurice *Baring, *Happiness, Ronald *Knox, Hugh *Latimer, *Lepanto, *Liberalism, *Pleasure, etc.; articles in *Brittanica,* NCE, and other encyclopedias; a novel, *Up the Green River* (1955), and a military history, *Britain at Arms: a Scrapbook from Queen Anne to the Present Day* (1953).

[T. C. O'BRIEN]

GILBOA (GELBOE), MOUNT, a mountain range in Issachar, S of the plain of Esdraelon, today called Jebel Fuqu'a, rises to about 1650 feet. Its name is preserved in the modern village of Jelbun. It was the site of Saul's last battle against the Philistines (1 Sam 28.4, 31.1, 8; 2 Sam 1.6, 21, 21.12). BIBLIOGRAPHY: J. Simons, *Geographical and Topographical Texts of the OT* (1959) §§ 92.562.1604.

[F. BUCK]

GILDAS, ST. (*c.*516–*c.*570), British monk and chronicler. A native of Scotland's Strathclyde, he became an itinerant monk, visiting Wales, Ireland, and Brittany. Before 547 he wrote *De excidio Britanniae,* a highly moralizing Latin account of the British-Saxon struggle, couched in obscure verbosity in which he denounces the contemporary British kings, clergy, and laymen, and makes vague allusions to the victories of their predecessors. He was pessimistic about the moral and political future of the Britons. He may have written a penitential, a series of canons, and a hymn, and may possibly have founded the monastery of St. Gildas at Rys in Brittany. BIBLIOGRAPHY: R. W. Hanning, *Vision of History in Early Britain: from Gildas to Geoffrey of Monmouth* (1966) 44–62; Butler 1:201–202.

[J. DRUSE]

GILDUIN, BERNARD, Romanesque sculptor whose atelier established the Languedoc school, oldest of French Romanesque regional styles with monumental sculpture in carving at St. Sernin, Toulouse (*c.*1060–1120), where the altar bears the signature of B. G. This workshop executed the capitals of La Daurade Abbey (now in the Toulouse museum) and the Moissac cloister capitals and 10 large reliefs (*c.*1100). BIBLIOGRAPHY: P. Deschamps, *French Sculpture of the Romanesque period* (1930); M. Durliat, "L'Atelier de Bernard Gilduin à St. Sernin De Toulouse", *Anuario de etudios medievales* 1 (1964), 521–529; M. Schapiro, "The Romanesque sculpture of Moissac", *Art Bulletin* 13 (1931), 249–350, 464–531; P. Deschamps, NCE 12:625–627.

[R. C. MARKS]

GILEAD (GALAAD). a biblical name (1) used of persons only twice (Num 26.29; 36.1), and (2) designating originally a small area S of the Jabbok (e.g., Gen 31.25; Jos 13.25; Jg 10.27; 2 Sam 17.26), then also the part N of the Jabbok (cf. Dt 3.10; 1 Sam 13.7; 1 Chr 5.9, 10, 16), and finally including all Transjordan from the Arnon to the Yarmuk (cf. Dt 34.1; Jos 22.9.13; Jg 10.8; 20.1). A mountainous region, famous for its woods, its balm (Gen 37.25; Jer 8.22; 22.6–7; 46.11), and its pastures (S of S 4.1), Gilead is mentioned in the story of Jacob (Gen 31.21–23), of the tribes Gad and Manasseh (Jos 13.24–31), and of Saul and David (1 Sam 13.7; 2 Sam 17.24–26). It was the home of Jephthah (Jg 11.7) and of Elijah (1 Kg 17.1). BIBLIOGRAPHY: J. J. Mauchline, "Gilead and Gilgal" VT 6 (1956) 19–33; J. Simons, *Geographical and Topographical Texts of the OT* (1959) §§93, 284, 299–300, *passim*.

[F. BUCK]

GILES, ST. (*c.*720), venerated as an abbot and hermit at the abbey of St.-Gilles near Marseilles. His shrine there was a famous pilgrimage spot in the Middle Ages, and he was particularly venerated in England. But the *Vita S. Aegidii*, the legend of his life, dates from the 9th cent. at the earliest and has no historical value. He was dropped from the calendar of saints in the reform of 1961 by the Congregation of Rites. BIBLIOGRAPHY: Butler 3:457–458; G. Jacquemet, *Catholicisme* 5:19–20.

[T. C. O'BRIEN]

GILES OF ASSISI, BL. (d. 1262), early companion of Francis of Assisi. A simple, dedicated follower of the Franciscan ideal, G. was noted for his tendency to give away all he had to any stranger in need. He resolutely refused alms unless he could earn the gift by menial work. Most of his life was spent in Italy, but he made a pilgrimage to the Holy Land and embarked on an unsuccessful attempt to convert the Saracens at Tunis. G. was a lover of silence whose prayer life was crowned by a vision of Christ. The sayings of G. have been often published and are remarkable for their shrewd insight.

[J. R. AHERNE]

GILES OF CORBEIL (Pierre; Aegidius Corboliensis; *c.*1165–*c.*1220), canon of Notre Dame of Paris, physician to Philip II Augustus of France. Graduate of Salerno Univ., the first medical school in W Europe, G. studied both Greek and Arabic medical literature, in the tradition handed down the preceding cent. by Constantine of Carthage (Constantinus Africanus), and taught at the Univ. of Paris and Montpelliér. He wrote in Latin verse *De pulsibus*, an analysis of 15 kinds of pulse-beats, and a satire on ranking members of the clergy, *Hierapigra ad purgandos prelatos*.

GILES OF FOSCARARI (*c.*1230–1304), first lay canonist at the Univ. of Bologna, author of *De ordine iudiciario* (*c.*1260), important to the history of canon law. BIBLIOGRAPHY: C. M. Rosen, NCE 6:484.

[T. C. O'BRIEN]

GILES OF LESSINES (*c.*1240–*c.*1305), Dominican philosopher who strongly defended St. Thomas Aquinas's teaching on the unity of substantial form against *Robert Kilwardby. A native of what is now Hainant, Belgium, he probably was a student of St. Thomas at Paris (1269–72), and certainly was a disciple of St. Albert the Great, as is reflected in his interest in the natural sciences. Some of his physical theories have been the subject of modern research. BIBLIOGRAPHY: J. C. Vansteenkiste, NCE 6:484.

[T. C. O'BRIEN]

GILES OF ROME (*c.*1243–1316), founder of Augustinian school, abp. of Bourges, known as *Doctor Fundatissimus*. G. was among the first students sent to Paris for studies 4 years after the canonical foundation of his order in 1256. During the course of his theological studies there, he probably attended the lectures of Aquinas between the years 1269 and 1272. Following the famous condemnation by Abp. Tempier in 1277, which also included doctrines of Aquinas, he left Paris, but returned in 1285, when, at the insistence of Honorius IV, he resumed his status and became the first master of theology in his order. His doctrines and writings were made mandatory for all teachers of the order at the general chapter of Florence in 1287, which marks the beginning of the Augustinian school as a new and distinctive entity. He was elected general of the order in 1292, and 3 years later was named abp. of Bourges. Controversies arising from the abdication of Celestine V, and the subsequent conflict between Boniface VIII and King Philip of France, were the occasion for Giles' treatises, *De renuntiatione papae* and *De ecclesiastica potestate*. In the latter, G. propounds a theory of papal theocracy characteristic of his school; this was to be presented in its most extreme form by Augustine of Ancona in the next century. Although G. follows the Thomistic teaching on individuation, as well as the hylomorphic doctrine and the unity of the substantial form, he rejects the intellectualism of Aquinas in favor of an Augustinian voluntarism. In the *Theoremata de ente et essentia,* he appears to defend an ultrarealistic interpretation of the real distinction between essence and existence. A more pronounced *Augustinianism obtains in his theology, which he characterizes as neither speculative nor practical, but affective. Other doctrines inspired by Augustine, developed more fully in the later Augustinian school, include, among others, man's quasi-natural capacity for beatific vision, the primacy of grace for salutary works and its necessity even for acts possessed of a natural morality, and the role of the *delectatio victrix* to explain the nature of efficacious grace. BIBLIOGRAPHY: Gilson HCP; G. Bruni, *Le opere di Egidio Romano* (1936).

[R. P. RUSSELL]

GILES OF SANTAREM, BL. (Giles of Portugal; *c.*1184–1265), Dominican preacher. Third son of Coimbra's governor, he was in early life a dissolute necromancer at Toledo and Paris, but was converted by dreams and became a Dominican (1220) at Palencia, Spain, and later lived at Santarem, Portugal. After studies at Paris, where he knew Jordan of Saxony and Humbert of Romans, he distinguished himself as preacher, theologian, and provincial. BIBLIOGRAPHY: A. Silli, BiblSanct 4:964–965; Butler 2:308–309.

[R. I. BURNS]

GILES OF VITERBO (1469–1532), humanist, reformer, prior general of the Augustinian Order. The considerable achievement of G. has been obscured if not distorted by his contemporary admirers and even more by historians. He was a Renaissance scholar, a pioneer in biblical studies, and a staunch defender of the faith. A celebrated scholar of the Renaissance, Pontano, made him the central figure of his work *Aegidius*. He was not the polished cleric of the period but a man of letters whose erudition was matched by his piety. One of the great orators of his age, he was for 12 years prior general of the Augustinians, in which position he labored for reform of his order. He was selected to deliver the opening sermon of Lateran Council V in 1512. In that address he declared: "It is right to change men through religion, not religion through men." G. was a scholar who mastered Oriental languages in his pursuit of biblical studies, a poet of some eminence, and a classicist. Though praised by the witty and immoral Card. Bembo, often a kiss of death to the reformers, G. as a fellow cardinal made a deep impression on his age as a man who sought to renew his order and the Church. BIBLIOGRAPHY: F. X. Martin, *Augustiniana* 9 (1959) 357–379.

[J. R. AHERNE]

GILGAL (GALGAL), (Heb. *gilgal,* circle of stones), where the Israelites encamped (Jos 4.19; 5.9) and set up 12 commemorative stones (Jos 4.20). It became a political (cf. Jos 10.6–11; 14.6; 1 Sam 13.4; 15.12) and religious center (1 Sam 7.16; 10.8; 13.12; Am 4.4; 5.5; Hos 4.15; 9.15; 12.12) and figures in the stories of Elijah and Elisha (2 Kg 2.1; 4.38). Its identification with Khirbet el-Etheleh (or en-Nitleh), between Jericho and the Jordan seems probable. BIBLIOGRAPHY: L. H. Grollenberg, *Atlas of the Bible* (1956) 150; J. Simons, *Geographical and Topographical Texts of the OT* (1959) 87–88 *passim.*

[F. BUCK]

GILGAMESH EPIC. The most ancient epic known to man, the story of Gilgamesh dates in composition back to the 3d millennium B.C. in some form. The account, written on cuneiform tablets in Sumerian, the language of Mesopotamia, dates back to the 1st centuries of the 2d millennium B.C. The epic is therefore at least 1,500 years older than Homer's *Iliad.* Knowledge of the story of Gilgamesh derives from archeological excavations dating from the middle of the 19th cent. and continuing into the 1930s. Early discoveries of parts of the epic received wide attention because they contained a Sumerian parallel to the Deluge account in Genesis. The long narrative of Gilgamesh centers on the hero-king of Uruk, an adventurer, a brooding man whose preoccupation with mortality and search for immortality run through the various episodes of the story as a dominant theme. Though it reflects a society long buried in forgotten history, the epic is a human document and carries perennial fascination for readers. BIBLIOGRAPHY: *Epic of Gilgamesh* (ed. and tr. N. K. Sandars, 1960); A. Heidel, *Gilgamesh Epic and Old Testament Parallels* (2d ed., 1949).

[J. R. AHERNE]

GILL, ERIC (Arthur Eric Rowton; 1882–1940), English artist and author. A Catholic convert and Dominican tertiary, G. worked for the integrity of both art and artist in face of the proliferating "art-nonsense" he saw in the secular industrial culture. His range of activity included engraving, type and book design (*Four Gospels,* 1931), sculpture ("Stations" in Westminster Cathedral), and writings on art and life *Art-Nonsense* (1929), *Necessity of Belief* (1936), and *Sacred and Secular* (1940). BIBLIOGRAPHY: Eric Gill, *Autobiography* 1941; R. Speaight, *Eric Gill* (1966).

[R. J. VEROSTKO]

GILLESPIE, ANGELA, MOTHER (1824–87), foundress in the U.S. of the Sisters of the Holy Cross. A native of Pennsylvania, Elisa Gillespie attended Visitation convent school, Washington, D.C., and became active in religious teaching and care of the sick. A meeting with Father E. F. *Sorin, founder of the Univ. of Notre Dame, caused her to join (1853) the Sisters of the Holy Cross. For nearly 30 years Mother Angela was superior of her congregation in the United States. Her administrative and personal qualities gave the community extraordinary growth: she established 45 foundations throughout the nation. St. Mary's Academy at Notre Dame she designed to give superior education to young women; it became eventually St. Mary's College. Mother Angela founded a number of other academies and established several hospitals. During the Civil War she and her sisters labored in military hospitals.

[J. R. AHERNE]

GILLET, MARTIN STANISLAS (1875–1951), French Dominican master general (1929–46), titular abp. of Nicaea from 1946. His earlier life was spent in teaching: at Louvain (1905–16); Le Saulchoir (1916–22); the Institut Catholique, Paris (1923–27). His chief interests were in moral philosophy, esp. in the education and moral formation of youth, themes on which he published several works, notably *L'Éducation du caractère* (1908). In 1925 G. inaugurated the *Somme Théologique* (edition of the *Revue des Jeunes*), a French-Latin, annotated edition of St. Thomas Aquinas's *Summa theologiae,* and edited the volume on human acts. He was provincial of the province of France from 1927 until his election as master general. His generalate was marked by great Dominican growth, esp. in the

U.S.; by his major letters to the order on study and preaching; by the establishment of what later became the pontifical Universitas S. Thomas Aquinatis, at Rome; but his tenure also coincided with the difficult years of World War II. He suffered recrimination over his attitude towards the Vichy government.

[T. C. O'BRIEN]

GILLIS, JAMES MARTIN (1876–1957), preacher and editor. A native of Boston and an early member of the Paulist Fathers, G. was ordained in 1901. He taught theology until 1910, then as a member of the Paulist mission band became a renowned preacher. In 1922 he was named editor of the *Catholic World* and from that position exercised great influence on Catholic thought in the United States. For many years his syndicated column "Sursum Corda" was read in most Catholic weeklies of the country. From 1925 to 1937 his "Timely Topics" on radio station WLWL, operated by the Paulists, was popular. He wrote *False Prophets* (1925), *The Catholic Church and the Home* (1928), *Christianity and Civilization* (1932), and *This Our Day* (1933). G. was a conservative in politics in an era of liberalism. From retirement as editor in 1948 until death he served as a contributing editor for the *Catholic World*.

[J. R. AHERNE]

GILM ZU ROSENEGG, HERMANN VON (1812–64), Austrian poet whose life and literary style parallel, at a lower level of excellence, those of Switzerland's G. *Keller. Born in Innsbruck as the son of a magistrate, he was educated by the Jesuits, whose influence is clear in some of his poems. He became and remained a professional civil servant, but his poetic nature could not be restrained and writing became a lifetime preoccupation. Known primarily for love and nature poems, his main contribution in the religious field was a work concerned with All Souls, "Stell auf den Tisch die düftenden Reseden."

[B. F. STEINBRUCKNER]

GILMOUR, RICHARD (1824–91), bishop. A Scottish-born Covenanter, G. came to Pennsylvania where he entered the RC Church in 1842, and was ordained in 1852. Pastoral duties in Ohio proved him to be adept at reconciling fractious elements among Irish, German, and French Catholics, and he was named bp. of Cleveland in 1872. G. was a vigorous promoter of Catholic education and the parochial school. A strong-willed administrator, he incurred hostility from his own clergy as well as religious orders. On the positive side he was an able champion of the rights of Catholics in an era of prejudice. His role at the Third Plenary Council of Baltimore and later in seeing its decrees sanctioned by Rome were important contributions to the American Church.

[J. R. AHERNE]

GILPIN, BERNARD (1517–83), priest during the Reformation period in England who favored a reform of abuses in the Church but found it difficult to accept doctrinal change. He was an admirer of Erasmus, spoke out boldly against sacrilege before Edward VI, loathed the persecution under Mary, and vigorously denounced clerical scandals. Under Elizabeth he was offered the bishopric of Carlisle (1559) and the provostship of Queen's College (1560), but refused both. He was widely respected, even in some Puritan circles, for his successful missionary labors in the N of England. BIBLIOGRAPHY: G. G. Perry, DNB 21:378–380.

[M. J. SUELZER]

GILSON, ÉTIENNE (1884–), French historian of philosophy; a leading 20th-cent. Thomist. After having taught at the Univ. of Lille and Strasbourg, he became professor of medieval philosophy at the Sorbonne in 1921. Since 1929 he has been director of the Pontifical Institute of Medieval Studies at Toronto, and during the same period until 1959, was professor of the Collège de France. He was elected to the French Academy in 1946. G. found his way to medieval philosophy through his studies of scholastic influence on Descartes. His approach to medieval thought has been historical, and on that basis he developed both his distinctive thesis on Christian philosophy and his personal interpretation of Thomism. While discrediting a widespread impression that scholastic philosophy was one system, he maintained that the diverse philosophical interpretation of the scholastics did have in common an intrinsic dependence on the content of revelation. His predilection for Thomism, understood as the philosophy of St. Thomas Aquinas as distinguished from that of the Thomist school, was based on his conviction that St. Thomas's understanding of *esse,* the act of existing, provided the most fruitful and intellectually justifiable metaphysics and epistemology. While some critics regard his "Thomistic existentialism" as an in-reading, rather than a doctrinal exegesis of Aquinas's texts, he has had an extensive influence among Thomists. His historic-philosophical studies are numerous; of primary importance are *Spirit of Medieval Philosophy* (1936), *Unity of Philosophical Experience* (1937); *Being and Some Philosophers* (2d ed., 1952); and *Christian Philosophy of St. Thomas Aquinas* (1956). BIBLIOGRAPHY: A. Maurer, NCE 14:137–138 bibliog.; T. C. O'Brien, *Metaphysics and the Existence of God* (1960); *Étienne Gilson Tribute* (ed. C. J. O'Neill, 1959).

[T. C. O'BRIEN]

GINAKUJI, Japanese Buddhist temple in Kyoto, originally the mountain-retreat of the Shogun Yoshimasa (between 1'69 and 86). After Yoshimasa's death, it was converted into a Buddhist temple popularly known as Ginkakuji (Temple of the Silver Pavilion). On the opposite side of a reflecting pond is the Tōgudō-Yoshimasa's study. Both buildings are fine examples of Muromachi architecture. The garden also is renowned.

[M. J. DALY]

GINOULHIAC, JACQUES MARIE ACHILLE (1806–75), abp. of Lyons from 1870, anti-infallibilist at Vatican Council I. After being a seminary professor from 1830, he was named vicar general of Aix in 1839, bp. of Grenoble in 1852. His theological reputation rests on a sound study of the development of dogma, his *Histoire du dogme catholique pendant les trois premièrs siècles* (2v., 1852; 3v. rev ed., 1865). In the period preceding Vatican I, G. sought, like J. H. *Newman in England, to avert a precipitate definition of papal infallibility, against extreme ultramontanists like L. Veuillot; he was accused of ''liberalism'' for doing so. At the council with F. *Dupanloup, he was a leader of the opposition, voted against the definition in the closed session of July 13, 1870, and in a letter of regret with other opposed bps., excused himself to Pius IX and left Rome before the solemn public reading of the dogma on July 18.

[T. C. O'BRIEN]

GINZKEY, FRANZ KARL (1871–1963), Austrian lyricist, novelist, whose spiritual home was the old multinational Austrian Danube–monarchy. He once called himself a cross between a poet and a soldier. Born in Pola at the Adriatic Sea, be became an army officer and later an archivist in Vienna. During World War I he was a war correspondent at the Italian front. After the war he lived in Vienna, Salzburg, and after 1944 Seewalchen, Upper Austria. His neoromantic novel *Prinz Tunors* (1934) deals with the Biedermeier era (1804). A collection of short stories was published as *Meistererzählungen* (1940).

[B. F. STEINBRUCKNER]

GIOBERTI, GIAN MATTEO (1495–1543), card. As a young man G. became a member of the household of Card. Giulio de Medici and rapidly emerged as a scholar and member of the *Academia Romana*. Sent on diplomatic missions by Pope Leo X, a deeply religious as well as scholarly man, G. was ordained and continued his diplomatic missions especially to Emperor Charles V. Named bp. of Verona he was involved in the attempt to make peace between Charles V and Francis I. His advocacy of the latter made him a target when Charles sacked Rome in 1527 and G. was imprisoned. He then devoted himself entirely to reform of his own diocese. He was sent to Trent to prepare for the great Council. In Verona he had remarkable success in raising the standards of clerical knowledge and was regarded by St. Charles Borromeo as a model bp. L. Bopp, LexThK 4:885.

[J. R. AHERNE]

GIOBERTI, VINCENZO (1801–52), Italian priest, political figure, and philosopher. He was sent into political exile in 1834 for his activities in the cause of a united, independent Italy. His banishment, spent mainly in Brussels, was the period of most of his philosophical writing. He returned triumphantly to Turin in 1847, became president of the chamber of deputies, then a cabinet minister of Victor Emmanuel II; but in a dispute over policy he quit public life in 1848 and spent the rest of his days in Paris. G.'s basic philosophical position was *ontologism (although he wrote against *Rosmini), which he interpreted in a pantheistic sense; he also held for a continuous divine revelation manifested in human history. All his works were placed on the Index in 1852. BIBLIOGRAPHY: L. Stefanini, EncCatt 6:414–422.

[T. C. O'BRIEN]

GIOCONDO, FRA GIOVANNI (*c.*1433–1515). Dominican friar, architect, engineer, and humanist. He was probably responsible for a system of canals to divert the course of the Brenta in order to prevent flooding in Venice (1506) and for the construction of fortifications at Padua and Treviso. G. was in the court of Naples (1489–93) and was called (1495) to Amboise by Charles VIII of France, where he was associated with the Château at Blois. Among his humanistic activities was the discovery and publication of the *Letters* of Pliny the Elder. A leading scholar of the Roman architect Vitruvius G. published in Venice (1511) his first edition of Vetruvius's work, *De architectura*. BIBLIOGRAPHY: B. Biadego, *Fra Giocondo* (1917).

[L. A. LEITE]

GIORDANO, LUCA (1632–1705). After study in Naples, G. traveled to Rome (*c.*1650), Florence, Venice, Bergamo, and was finally called to Spain by Charles II (1692–1702). In his vast output G. evidenced the styles of Ribera, the *Caravaggisti*, and esp. the Venetians (*Marriage at Cana*, 1689), of Lucas van Leyden and Dürer (*Ecc Homo*, Baltimore), creating a personal style of Venetian color in the grand concepts of Pietro da Cortona (*St. Anne and the Virgin*, 1657). G.'s *Christ Driving the Money Changers from the Temple* (1684) is intense, whereas frescoes in the Medici-Riccardi Palace (Florence) and a *Triumph of Judith* are characterized by a Tiepolo rococo lightness which greatly influenced 18th-cent. fresco decoration.

[M. J. DALY]

GIORGIO, FRANCESCO DI (1439–1502), Sienese architect and military engineer for Federigo da Montefeltro, painter and sculptor. He is reported by Vasari to have built the Ducal Palace at Urbino a fact now debated. His masterpieces are four bronze angels (1489–97) on the high altar of the cathedral of Siena. He advised on Renaissance architectural forms in other cities when traveling, and wrote *Trattato di architettura* (1841) a humanistic basis for architectural designs and city-planning. BIBLIOGRAPHY: A. S. Weller, *Francesco di Giorgio* (1943); A. S. Weller, NCE 6:493.

[P. P. FEHL]

GIORGIONE (GIORGIO DA CASTELFRANCO, 1478–1510), one of the greatest Venetian painters; with Titian, a student of the master Giovanni Bellini. Upon an early death G. bequeathed his ''Giorgionesque'' qualities of poetic, romantic landscape to 16th-cent. Venetians. Many of G.'s works are lost or extensively ''restored.'' Renowned is *The Tempest* (1505), a sensuous, enchanted idyl of controversial ''non-subject,'' in which a soft pervasive light is the very theme, establishing, not form, but a lyrical mood. G. painted the more conventional *Castelfranco Altarpiece* and probably the debated *Adoration of the Shepherds* (also called the *Allendale Nativity*, Washington, D.C.). In the magnificent *Fête Champêtre* G. again induces his pastoral reverie with sensuous figures rich in the warm, golden tones that distinguish Venetian art from cool, intellectual Florentine works. A *Sleeping Venus* set in landscape is the first in a long series of like subject through subsequent centuries. The *Three Philosophers* and some portraits further express the sensitive, poetic intimacy and melancholy of G.'s style. BIBLIOGRAPHY: G. B. Giorgione, *All the Paintings of Giorgione* (1962); G. M. Richter, *Giorgio da Castelfranco* (1937).

[M. J. DALY]

GIOTTINO (Giotto di Maestro Stefano, Tommaso di Stefano; fl. 1325–75). G. is mentioned in compilations of 15th-cent. Florentine artists and identified (controversially) under the names above, Vasari's attributions having been refuted. G.'s identity rests on a brilliant *Deposition* (Uffizi) in which decorative refinement and high-keyed color point to north Italian painting, though the figure composition is Florentine and monumental in the tradition of Giotto.

[M. J. DALY]

GIOTTO DI BONDONE (1266–1337). Italian painter and architect, trained by Cimabue and influenced by P. Cavallini in Rome. B. Berenson recognizes G. as ''Father of Western Painting'' in his contribution of ''sculptural form''—solid and weighty, the drapery determined by articulation of the form beneath; tactile value—illusionistic textural realization; and significant form—figures eloquent in posture and gesture carrying the message fully, in monumental, classic grandeur, rhythmically composed within a controlled space. In stylized backgrounds of trees, crags and architectural notes against a flat blue ground, G. did not break with the Byzantine modes. His essays in foreshortening and perspective foreshadow Renaissance investigations. G. does more than observe; he seeks the secrets of nature, divining and revealing her order. Establishing *outward* vision vs. medieval *inward* vision, G. set western painting on its course for centuries to come. Famous are the series of frescoes: *Life of the Virgin and Christ* and *Last Judgment* in the Arena (Scrovegni) Chapel, Padua; frescoes and altarpieces in four chapels, Sta. Croce, Florence, (Bardi and Peruzzi chapel frescoes alone survive); panels of the *Dormition of the Virgin* (Berlin); and *Madonna and Child Enthroned with Angels and Saints* (both for the church of the Ognissanti, Florence); altarpieces from G.'s workshop: *Coronation of the Virgin* (Sta. Croce); *Madonna and Saints* (Bologna); and St. Francis Receiving the Stigmata (Louvre); *Christ with the Virgin and Other Saints* (National Gallery, Washington, D.C.); a mosaic—*Navicella* in the narthex, St. Peter's, Rome; and frescoes of the *Legend of St. Francis* in the Upper Church, Assisi. G. has been identified with the Isaac Master of frescoes above the St. Francis paintings. BIBLIOGRAPHY: B. Berenson, *Italian Pictures of the Renaissance: Florentine School* (2 v., 1968); L. Tintori and M. Meiss, *Painting of the Life of St. Francis in Assisi* (1962); *Giotto in Perspective* (ed. L. Schneider, 1974).

[M. J. DALY]

GIOVANNA MARIA OF THE CROSS, VEN. (1603–73). Bernadine Floriani was born in Rovereto, Italy. At the age of 13 she came under the tutelage of Thomas of Bergamo. Affter the death of Thomas, she continued her instruction with the Franciscans. In 1650, with the approval of Pope Innocent X, she opened a convent of Poor Clares at Rovereto. Taking the name Giovanna Maria of the Cross, she dedicated this convent to the care of the poor and the sick. In 1672, Giovanna Maria established another convent of Poor Clares at Borgo Valsugana. G. was an author and poet who was forced to endure the scrutiny of the Inquisition in 1643; the Inquisition exonerated her. Her major works included a commentary on the Canticle of Canticles and a treatise entitled *Evangelici spirituali sentimenti*. BIBLIOGRAPHY: C. Callovini, BiblSanct 6:588–589; *Studi francescani* 25 (1928) 306–346.

[R. J. BRADY]

GIOVANNI BATTISTA DI SAN MICHELE (1695–1765), the younger brother of St. *Paul of the Cross, whom G. aided as confidant, confessor, and collaborator in the foundation of the Passionists. His cause of beatification was introduced in 1930, and the decree affirming his heroic virtue was published in 1940. BIBLIOGRAPHY: AAS (1940) 563–567.

[P. K. MEAGHER]

GIOVANNI DA FIESOLE, See ANGELICO, FRA.

GIOVANNI DI PAOLO (Giovanni del Poggio; 1403–83), Italian painter of the Sienese school, pupil of Taddeo di Bartolo. G. was influenced by Gentile da Fabriano, who was in Siena 1424–25, and by the art of Sassetta. G. painted a *Madonna and Child with Angels* (1426), *Madonna and Child* (1427 and 1428), *Crucifixion* (1440), *bcoronation of the Virgin* (1445), and a *Presentation in the Temple* (1447) based on that of A. Lorenzetti and showing stereotyped figures in monotonous colors. His genius is evident in small, narrative pictures combining Sienese medieval poetic fantasy with Renaissance perspective and composition; the most beautiful of them are scenes from the *Life of St. John the Baptist* (1450, Chicago). Later narrative works are four predella panels (1426, Baltimore), a *Paradise* and *Creation* *of the World* (New York). Sienese mysticism and religious fervor made possible and acceptable G.'s delicate and often grotesque inventions. BIBLIOGRAPHY: J. Pope-Hennessy, *Giovanni di Paolo* (1937).

[M. J. DALY]

GIOVANNI DA VERONA, FRA (1457–1525), Italian sculptor and architect, a monk at Monte Oliveto Maggiore. G. executed the paschal candlestick for the cloister of S. Maria in Organo, Verona (before 1506), intarsia decorated panels and benches for the Camera della Segnatura in the Vatican (1511–12), and choir stalls at S. Maria in Organo, considered his major work.

[M. J. DALY]

GIOVANNI, ANTONIO DE SACCHI, See PORDENONE.

GIOVANNI, STEFANO DI, See SASSETTA.

GIOVANNINO DE'GRASSI (*c.*1340–98), Italian sculptor, painter, and miniaturist of the Lombard school, extensively active as "architect-in-charge" at the cathedral of Milan. G. executed the relief *Christ and the Samaritan Woman* (1396), probably painted the illuminations in the Codex Berolo and in the prayerbook of Gian Galeazzo Visconti, Milan, and produced a notable sketchbook of animals (Bergamo Library). Showing relationship to the art of the Burgundian court, G. was the leading International Style artist of his time.

[M. J. DALY]

GIOVINE ITALIA, see YOUNG ITALY.

GIRALDUS CAMBRENSIS (Gerald de Barri, Gerald of Wales; *c.*1147–1223), Welsh historian. Educated in his native Pembrokeshire, G. also studied in Paris under *Peter Comestor. While serving as archdeacon of Brecknoch (1175–1203) he was twice elected bp. of St. David's (1176 and 1198) but was denied consecration because of the fear that as a Welshman he would attempt to separate his church from Canterbury. Of his writings, the *Topographia hibernica, Expugnatio hibernica, Vita S. Remigii, Itinerarium Cambriae,* and *De iure Menevensis Ecclesiae* are important as historical sources, but allowance must be made for some exaggeration and distortion due to party feeling. Works: ed. J. S. Brewer and J. F. Dimock (8v., 1861–91); in Eng tr., historical works, tr. T. Forester and R. C. Hoare, rev. and ed. T. Wright (1863); autobiography, (tr. H. E. Butler, 1937). BIBLIOGRAPHY: H. R. Luard, DNB 7:1268–72; J. A. Corbett, NCE 6:496–497.

[M. S. TANEY]

GIRALDUS OF SALLES, BL. (1070–1120), monastic founder. G. entered the Canons Regular of St. Avit-le-Senieur when quite young and later studied under *Robert of Arbrissel. He became a hermit and then an itinerant preacher. He founded numerous monasteries (for both sexes), which later adopted the Cistercian Rule. Included among these was Notre Dame des Châtelliers. BIBLIOGRAPHY: C. Dupont, BiblSanct 6:1078; M. B. Brard, *Catholicisme* 4:1874.

[F. D. LAZENBY]

GIRARD OF ANGERS, ST. (d. 1123), monk. He was a secular cleric before becoming a Benedictine. In 1097 he founded the priory of Ste.-Madeline in Brossay. He reportedly had visions after prolonged fasts and predicted the time of death for both Pope Gelasius II and William, son of King Henry I. Numerous miracles were attributed to him and in 1468 he was canonized. BIBLIOGRAPHY: P. Rouillard, BiblSanct 6:1105–06.

[F. G. O'BRIEN]

GIRARD D'ORLÉANS (d. 1361), court painter at Paris to King Jean II ("Jean le Bon", who reigned 1350–64). Bouchot attributes to G. the portrait of *Jehan Roy de France* (Louvre). Painted *c.*1360 it is probably the earliest royal portrait in Europe.

[M. J. DALY]

GIRARD, JEAN BAPTISTE (1765–1850), Franciscan scholar, known as Père Girard. Ordained in 1788, G. was the first Catholic priest after the Reformation to be named chaplain to the Swiss government. Pastor at Bern (1800–04) and later superior at Fribourg where he directed an experimental primary school for indigents, he served as commissioner of French schools until 1823. Remarkable for his tolerance and understanding of youth, he developed a monitorial system of "mutual education," and advocated a triple school system—for the working class, businessmen, and professionals—with no bars between categories when such transition was a practical possibility for a student. An admirer of Pestalozzi, whom he had visited at Yverdun (1809), G. accepted his theory of harmonious development, but lamented his emphasis on the intellectual to the neglect of moral and religious values. His *De l'enseignement régulier de la langue maternelle* received the French Academy award (1844). BIBLIOGRAPHY: A. Maas, *Père Girard, Swiss Educational Reformer* (1931).

[M. B. MURPHY]

GIRARDON, FRANÇOIS (1628–1715), French sculptor who studied in Rome and Paris, becoming a member of the Royal Academy (1657). G. worked under Le Brun in the Louvre (1664–71), fulfilled commissions at the Tuileries and Versailles, carved a *Christ* (1690) for Saint-Rémi, and the high altar for Saint-Jean (1692). His masterpiece is the tomb of Card. Richelieu (1694) in the chapel of the Sorbonne, Paris. G.'s colossal statue of Louis XIV probably inspired Falconet's *Peter the Great.* A second equestrian statue of Louis XIV (destroyed 1792) was an innovative casting by B. Keller (1692), having been poured as a single unit rather than composed of assembled parts. G.'s work is the embodiment of 17th-cent. French classic sculpture.

[M. J. DALY]

GIRAUD, SYLVAIN MARIE (1830–85), an early member of the Missionaries of Our Lady of La Salette, spiritual writer. He joined the La Salette community in 1858, 5 years after his ordination, and 6 years from its foundation. But his *La Pratique de la dévotion à Notre Dame de la Salette* (1863), and *De la vie d'union avec Marie* (1864) gave expression to the spirit of the community and shaped its spirituality. His many other spiritual writings reflected his activity as spiritual director and retreat master, esp. for cloistered nuns and for seminarians.

[T. C. O'BRIEN]

GIRAUDET, RENÉ (1907–45), French worker priest. After ordination (1931) G. served in rural parishes for 11 years and then became a laborer among young Frenchmen sent to Germany as forced laborers. His secret ministry led to his arrest by the Nazis. The army of liberation freed him from the concentration camp at Bergen-Belsen, but he died of exhaustion directly upon his return to France. His tomb at Chantonnay is an object of veneration. BIBLIOGRAPHY: L. Guéry, *Catholicisme* 5:35.

[M. J. SUELZER]

GIRGENTI CATACOMBS, AGRIGENTO, early Christian catacombs in Agrigento, southern Sicily, possibly of the 2d cent. but probably of the 4th. One is circular with vaulted tombs.

[M. J. DALY]

GIRLANI, ARCANGELA, BL. (Arcangela of Trino; *c.*1460–95), Italian Carmelite nun (from 1477) who in 1492 founded a new convent at Mantua at the invitation of the Gonzaga family. She reputedly had mystical experiences. BIBLIOGRAPHY: L. Saggi, BiblSanct 6:1107–08.

GIROLAMO DA CREMONA (fl. 1467–75), Italian miniaturist and painter. G. executed many miniatures in antiphonals in the Piccolomini Library, Siena; a signed miniature in London; and painted a large altarpiece of *The Risen Christ* (1472, Viterbo). G.'s works relate with modifications to Mantegna's style and that of Liberale da Verona.

[M. J. DALY]

GIRY, FRANÇOIS (1635–88), French Minim. He entered his order in 1652 and was trained by Nicolas Barré, founder of the Schools of Charity of the Infant Jesus. When the latter died, G. succeeded him. He wrote many ascetic, hagiographic, and historical treatises. BIBLIOGRAPHY: J. Daoust, NCE 6:498; G. Jacquemet, *Catholicisme,* 5:35–36.

[F. D. LAZENBY]

GISELA, BL. (*c.*973–*c.*1060), **QUEEN OF HUNGARY,** sister of Emperor Henry II, wife of St. Stephen I, King of Hungary, and mother of St. Emeric. She cooperated in her husband's effort to Christianize the Hungarians. Expelled from Hungary by Stephen's successor, she took refuge in a Benedictine monastery near Passau. There is no evidence that she ever enjoyed an official cult, but her name is included in the Benedictine martyrology. BIBLIOGRAPHY: Zimmermann 2:159, 161; E. Pásztor, BiblSanct 6:1149.

[P. K. MEAGHER]

GISLEBERT, see also GILBERT.

GISLEBERTUS, 12th-cent. Burgundian sculptor responsible at Autun Cathedral for 50 nave capitals and the Last Judgment tympanum, remarkably vital and fantastic. The tympanum is one of the finest and most awe-inspiring works of Romanesque sculpture with its majestic figure of Christ and terrifying portrayal of the fate of the damned; it illustrates perfectly G.'s sense of drama and tension. Previously employed, probably as chief assistant working on the great W doorway at Cluny and at Vézelay, G. was active at Autun, 1125–35. BIBLIOGRAPHY: D. Grivot and G. Zarnecki, *Gislebertus, Sculptor of Autun* (1961). *AUTUN.

[M. J. DALY]

GISLENUS, ST. (Ghislain; *c.*650–*c.*680), abbot. Although no satisfactory account exists about his life, G. was a hermit in the forest of Hainault. He founded the (Frankish) Monastery of SS. Peter and Paul at a place called *Ursidongus* (the "Bear's Den"), which is now the Abbey of Saint-Ghislain near Mons. He seems to have influenced St. Vincent Madelgarius and his wife, St. Waldetrud, to establish a convent at Castrilocus near Mons; and Waldetrud's sister St. Aldegundis to establish one at Maubeuge. The Roman martyrology account says G., born in Greece, resigned a bishopric at Athens to become a hermit, but this is apocryphal. He is invoked against epilepsy and in difficult childbirth. BIBLIOGRAPHY: Rainerus, AnalBoll (1887) 5:209–294. For a different view, see G. D. Gordini, BiblSanct 6:1149–50.

[N. F. GAUGHAN]

GIULIANI, GIOVANNI (1663–1744), Italian sculptor in Vienna in 1690. G.'s greatest works in St. Maria in Heiligenkreuz were the pulpit (1719), organ (1720), column of the Trinity (1730), and Stations of the cross (1732) in an 18th-cent. eclectic Italian and Alpine High Baroque style.

[M. J. DALY]

GIULANI, VERONICA, ST. (1660–1727), mystic. Ursula Giulani was born at Mercatello in Urbino, Italy. Her parents, of noble lineage, sought to arrange a suitable marriage for her, but she pleaded for permission to enter the religious life. When a serious illness befell her, her father gave his approval to her vocational decision. In 1677, she entered a convent of the Poor Clares and chose the name Veronica. From the time of her profession in 1678, she evidenced a total absorption in the Passion of Christ. In 1693, the physical phenomena of Christ's sufferings appeared in Veronica. The bp. of Città di Castello affirmed the signs of the stigmata in G., who endured great spiritual and physical pain until her death. Pope Gregory XVI canonized her in 1839. BIBLIOGRAPHY: F. da Mareto, BiblSanct 12:1050–55; Butler 3:57–58.

[R. J. BRADY]

GIUSTI, Italian sculptors. **Antonio** (1479–1519) and **Giovanni** (1485–1549) carved 12 Apostles for the chapel of Cardinal d'Amboise at Gaillon. Working together after 1504, they produced their masterpiece—the tomb of Louis XII and Anne de Bretagne (1516–31, St.-Denis). Akin in style to that of Michel Colombe, they represented the Italianate proto-Renaissance mode in France.

[M. J. DALY]

GIUSTINIANI, prominent family of statesmen and churchmen. **Lawrence, St.** (1381–1455), the most illustrious member of the family, became general of the Canons Regular of St. Augustine 1413, in 1433 was appointed bp. of Castello, and in 1451 patriarch of Venice. Renowed for his concern for the poor and his ascetical writings, he was canonized by Alexander VIII in 1690. **Bernardo** (1408–89), nephew of Lawrence, humanist and historian. Venetian ambassador to France and to Popes Paul II and Sixtus IV, he wrote the life of his uncle and a history of Venice. **Agostino** (1470–1536), a Dominican in 1488, he was appointed bp. of Nebbio in Corsica in 1514 and in 1517 became the first professor of Hebrew at the Univ. of Paris. **Paolo, Bl.** (1476–1528). About 1505 he began to live in solitude and eventually established the Camaldolese Hermits of Monte Corona. Most of his spiritual writings are unedited. **Benedetto** (1551–1622), Jesuit exegete. For 12 years he taught theology at Toulouse, Messina, and Rome, and for more than 20 years he was rector of the Sacred Penitentiary. He accompanied Card. Cajetan as his theologian to Poland. He is best known for his commentaries on St. Paul and the Catholic epistles. **Orazio** (1580–1649), Oratorian and scholar. He was the choice of Card. Francis Barberini to be custodian of the Vatican Library. This enables him to find and publish the acts of the Council of Florence. In 1640, he was made bp. of Montalto; in 1645, he became bp. of Nocera and was elevated to the cardinalate. BIBLIOGRAPHY: A. De Mazis, DHGE 11:523–526; P. Bernard, DTC 6.2:1381–1382; J. Kraus, LTK 4:904–905; M. G. McNeil, NCE 6:500–502.

[J. M. O'DONNELL]

GIVALIOR, SITE OF, an Indian fortress complex embracing 6 temples and a mosque (A.D. 525), taken by the Muslims (1232). The fortress wall, with windows receding 6 times within frames in Hindu style, is covered with carvings of Hindu and Jain scriptural writings. Givalior is further the site of the *Bāgh caves, famous for fine Indian classical painting.

[M. J. DALY]

GIZZI, PASQUALE TOMMASO (1787–1849), diplomat in the papal service, cardinal from 1844, secretary of state to Pius IX (1846–47). At the period when Pius IX was still trying to make liberal concessions within the Papal States, G. took a much more conservative stand, and strongly advocated forceful repression of those opposing the Pope's temporal power. The disagreement on policy led to G.'s resignation.

[J. R. AHERNE]

GLABER, RAUL (Rudolf the Bald; *c.*985–*c.*1046), Cluniac monk–chronicler, whose life spanned the "dreaded" end of the first millennium, famed particularly for his authoritative reference (1002–03) to the surge of church building following the year 1000: "there occurred all over the world, esp. in Italy and Gaul, a rebuilding of churches . . . each people vying with the others . . . as if the whole world, casting off its rags, were clothing itself in a white robe of churches," The marvelous, the curious, and the calamitous fill his writing. BIBLIOGRAPHY: E. G. Holt, *Literary Sources of Art History* (1947).

[M. J. DALY]

GLADSTONE, WILLIAM EWART (1809–98), four-time prime minister of England (1868–74; 1880–85; 1886; 1892–94). Religion and moral principle were essential elements in G.'s thought, interests, and political stands throughout his life. As a student at Oxford he was prevented from taking orders in the C of E only by his father's strong objections. While reared rather in the evangelical tradition within the Church, he early became attached to High Church principles as advocated in the *Oxford Movement. He remained throughout his life a strong adherent to the doctrine of the *Real Presence, and to *apostolic succession; when the question of Anglican orders was being debated in Rome, G. wrote a letter urging recognition of their validity. His relationship with the RC Church was in part a sympathetic attitude in the area of doctrine, but in part an intense opposition in regard to its mode of government. He denounced Vatican Council I's definition of papal infallibility, and in an open letter after the Council, answered by both J. H. *Newman and H. E. *Manning, questioned the civil allegiance of Catholics. In his political offices G. assisted in the spread of the C of E throughout the expanding British Empire; he defended the integrity of the Church as it operated under the headship of the sovereign; yet he also was responsible for a law exempting nonconformists from supporting the established Church. His moral convictions were strongly at issue when in his first tenure as prime minister he effected disestablishment of the Church of Ireland (1869) so that Catholics were no longer obliged to support an alien Church. In 1886 his continued concern for the Irish Catholics led to his advocacy of home rule, an issue that led to defeat of his government; his bill for the same cause was defeated again in 1893. He secured passage of improved land acts for the Irish in 1861 and 1881. He was a forthright champion of social welfare and manhood suffrage, and the opponent of imperialist exploitation of Africa. G's writings on theological and religious subjects include: *The State in its Relations with the Church* (1838); *Church Principles Considered in Their Results* (1840); *Studies Subsidiary to the Works of Bishop Butler* (1896). D. C. Lathbury edited G's *Correspondence on Church and Religion* (2 v., 1910). BIBLIOGRAPHY: A. R. Vidler, *Orb and the Cross* (1945).

[T. C. O'BRIEN]

GLAGOLITIC, a Slavic alphabet of 38 letters, based on Greek minuscules or cursives. This, not the *Cyrillic, was the alphabet designed by St. *Cyril. It was supplanted for the most part by the Cyrillic, except in the liturgical books of some *Uniates of Dalmatia and Istria. BIBLIOGRAPHY: F. Milović, "La Langue liturgique chez les Yugoslaves," ÉO (1905) 294–298; R. Rogošić, LTK 4:906–908, for history of the use of Glagolitic in liturgical books.

GLAIRE, JEAN BAPTISTE (1798–1879), French biblical scholar. After ordination in 1822 he taught Hebrew, first at Saint-Sulpice in Paris, then at the Sorbonne, where in 1841 he became dean of the theology faculty. His published works include lexicons and manuals for the study of biblical languages; *La Sainte Bible en latin et en français* (3 v., 1834); *Introduction historique et critique aux livres de l'Ancien et du Nouveau Testament* (6 v., 1836). He also edited a widely used *Encyclopédie catholique* (18 v., 1839–48) and *Dictionnaire universel des sciences écclésiastiques* (2 v., 1868).

[T. C. O'BRIEN]

GLANTZ, LEIB (1898–1964), Russian-born Jewish cantor and composer. He led congregational prayers at age 8 in Kiev, where his father was cantor. He held positions in Kishinev and Romania, and came to the U.S. in 1926, serving as cantor in Brooklyn and Los Angeles. In 1954 Tel Aviv became his home; there he was chief cantor at a synagogue until his death. He researched and arranged Jewish liturgical music, and founded Tel Aviv Institute of Religious Jewish Music.

[J. C. MARR]

GLAREANUS, HENRICUS (1488–1563), Swiss musical theorist. In addition to his contribution to musical theory, through his poetry G. earned him the crown of poet laureate from Maximilian I. Like François Gavaert, he claimed that plainsong chant was heavily formed by ancient Greek music. His chief work was *Dodecachordon* (1547).

[D. SMUCKER]

GLAS, JOHN, see GLASITES.

GLASITES (Sandemanians), a small body that separated from the *Church of Scotland under the leadership of John Glas (1695–1773). He was a Presbyterian minister who repudiated the idea of a *state Church in his treatise *The Testimony of the King of Martyrs* (1729). He was deprived of his ministry by the national presbytery in 1734 for his dissent from the *Westminster Confession. In polity, the Glasites observed *independency; elders were in charge of each congregation, and personal property was at the disposal of the community. They strived to live in strict imitation of the early Christians, esp. after Glas's son-in-law Robert Sandeman (1718–71), took over the leadership (1739). They adopted the practice of footwashing and celebrated the agape (with broth). The designation Sandemanians was used esp. in England and the U.S. The body has not existed since the beginning of the 20th century. BIBLIOGRAPHY: J. Ross, *History of Congregational Independency in Scotland* (1900).

[T. C. O'BRIEN]

GLASTONBURY, ABBEY OF, located in Somerset, considered the oldest and among the most important English monasteries. Glastonbury was built on a Celtic foundation, but its early development is somewhat obscure and mixed with legend. It became a noted pilgrimage site and its history is mingled with references to Joseph of Arimathea, King Arthur, and the Holy Grail. Following the Benedictine rule, Glastonbury was extremely influential in the great monastic revival of the 10th century. Its missionaries were sent throughout England and Scandinavia. It was known in the 13th cent. for its vital intellectual life and outstanding library. Its last abbot, Richard Whiting (1524–39), was executed during the reign of Henry VIII. The abbey was then suppressed and its riches pillaged by the English crown. Very little remains, but archeological digs conducted on the site have made possible ground tracings of the outlines of the church and monastic buildings. The site has become again a place of pilgrimage, esp. of an annual, ecumenical sutdents' pilgrimage.

[M. A. MCFADDEN]

GLASTONBURY THORN, originally a hawthorn tree at Glastonbury Abbey that, according to the legend of the abbey's foundation by Joseph of Arimathea, sprouted from his staff. Thorn trees in England that bear the name are from slips taken from the tree at Glastonbury, which was uprooted as part of Cromwell's destruction of the abbey because it was a place of pilgrimage. The Glastonbury thorn is unique in that it flowers twice a year, in spring and in fall, often at Christmas time. Botanists call it a "sport," or random development, because it does not reproduce naturally but must be budded and grafted.

[T. C. O'BRIEN]

GLEBE, land, used particularly of land set apart by public authority to support the minister of a parish under an established church system. It could be cultivated by either a tenant or the minister himself. The parsonage was sometimes called the glebe house. Glebes became a point of controversy during the disestablishment debates of 18th-cent. Virginia.

[T. EARLY]

GLENCOE, MASSACRE OF, an atrocity that occurred on Feb. 13, 1692 and stained the Glorious Protestant Revolution of 1689. It was partly due to clan enmities. Glencoe is a dark and beautiful glen in the W Highlands. There the MacDonalds, traditionally devoted to the Stuarts and the old religion, hospitably entertained for 12 days a company of "Black Campbells," who supported William of Orange, and who, with the connivance of authority, were planning their destruction. Early in the morning, during a winter storm, 38 persons, including a woman and child, were murdered before the survivors could escape, many to perish in the wild hills. BIBLIOGRAPHY: J. Prebble, *Massacre at Glencoe* (1973).

[T. GILBY]

GLENDALOUGH, MONASTERY OF, founded in Co. Wicklow, Ireland, by St. Kevin *c.*570, an influential ecclesiastical center for 800 years. The impressive round tower where the monks took refuge from Norse raiders still stands. The walls which remain show that a remarkable series of buildings existed. A famous abbot was St. *Lawrence O'Toole. In the 12th cent. Glendalough was the seat of a large diocese, but in 1214 was merged with Dublin. In the 18th cent. officials and local Protestant settlers destroyed most of the buildings. BIBLIOGRAPHY: L. Price, "Glendalough . . .," *Essays and Studies Presented to Professor Eain McNeill* (ed. J. Ryan, 1940).

[J. R. AHERNE]

GLENLUCE ABBEY, a Cistercian monastery founded by Roland, Lord of Galloway in Wigtownshire, Scotland, in 1192, and colonized from Dundrennan Abbey. Its monks were expelled at the Reformation in 1560 and it is now a ruin. BIBLIOGRAPHY: D. E. Easson, *Medieval Religious Houses: Scotland* (1957) 64; M. Barrett, *Scottish Monasteries of Old* (1913) 167–169.

[L. J. MACFARLANE]

GLENMARY HOME MISSION SISTERS, also known as the Glenmary Sisters. This community was founded in Glendale, Ohio (1941) by Fr. W. H. *Bishop when two women joined him drawn by the plan he had published earlier for orders of men and women to serve in the predominantly non-Catholic rural areas and small towns of the U.S. In 1946 the first sisters began to receive instruction on the fundamentals of religious life from the Dominican Sisters of Adrian, Mich., whose constitutions they adapted, while choosing to follow the Rule of St. Augustine. The community was canonically established on July 16, 1952 by Abp. Alter of Cincinnati. The sisters maintain nine social and catechetical centers, one house of study, one promotional center, and one nursing service. In 1976 the community numbered 19 professed sisters and were represented in two archdioceses and seven dioceses.

[M. B. BOYLE]

GLENMARY HOME MISSIONERS, common name for the Home Missioners of America, established in 1939 by Fr. W. H. Bishop for the pastoral ministry in rural areas of the U.S. where there are no resident priests. The society consists of secular priests and brothers who assist the priests as catechists, recreational leaders, sacristans, youth directors, etc. As of 1976 the 73 priests and 23 professed brothers conducted 41 mission bases, and 2 houses of study, 1 novitiate, and 3 vocational centers, and were represented in 5 archdioceses and 13 dioceses.

[M. B. BOYLE]

GLENNON, JOHN JOSEPH (1862–1946), archbishop, cardinal. Born in Ireland and completing there his seminary training, he came to Kansas City, Mo., and was ordained in 1884. At age 34 he was named coadjutor bp. and 7 years later was transferred as coadjutor bp. to St. Louis. The same year (1903) he began his tenure as abp., which was to last for 43 years. An able administrator and preacher, notably at several Eucharistic Congresses, G. built a number of schools, a major and minor seminary, erected a new cathedral in 1926, and was the patron and friend of two famous hostels: Fr. Dempsey's Hotel for the Homeless and Fr. Dunne's Newsboys' Home. In 1946 he was named cardinal by Pope Pius XII, and died in Dublin en route from the consistory. BIBLIOGRAPHY: Catholic World (1946) 83–84.

[J. R. AHERNE]

GLICENSTEIN, ENRICO (1870–1942), Polish sculptor studying in Munich, who, awarded the Prix de Rome, settled in that city until his coming to the U.S. in 1928. Rodin admired G.'s work and confirmed him in a double showing at the Grand Palais. G. showed in the Venice Biennale (1926), at the Chicago Art Institute (1929), in Brussels, and Paris. His figures retain the form of the block expressing a tension between the energy of forms and the restraint of the medium as seen in his *St. Francis* exhibited at the Venice Biennale, 1926.

[M. J. DALY]

GLODESINDIS (GLODESINDA, GLOSSINDIS), ST. (578–608), abbess. Shunning marriage, she took refuge in the church of St. Stephan at Metz. Thereafter her parents allowed her to enter a convent at Trier under the direction of her aunt Rotilde. G. founded a convent at Metz, gave it the Rule of St. Benedict, and directed it for 6 years. BIBLIOGRAPHY: C. Dupont, BiblSanct 7:60–62; PL 137:211–218.

[F. D. LAZENBY]

GLORIA DEI (1698–1700), oldest surviving church in Philadelphia, Pa., erected by its Swedish congregation. Originally a simple rectangular shape, a porch and vestry were added (1703) as buttress against the spread of the vaulted ceiling. Though Swedish in origin, the cornice and window trim are English; the interior, with gallery on slender posts, simple and pure of line. John Smart and John Brett possibly designed the church.

[M. J. DALY]

GLORIA IN EXCELSIS DEO (Eng., Glory to God in the Highest), an ancient Greek hymn of praise to the Triune God, sung or recited in the vernacular following the Penitential Rite in the new order of the Mass on most Sundays, solemnities, and feastdays. It is known as the greater doxology because of its length, and also as the angelic hymn, since its opening phrases are those proclaimed by the angels in the biblical account of Christ's birth. The hymn is of anonymous origin, an unconnected compilation of acclamations extolling the majesty of God the Father and his Son, "with the Holy Spirit." It reflects scriptural doxologies and early liturgical prayers and prefaces. BIBLIOGRAPHY: J. A. Jungmann, *Mass of the Roman Rite* (rev. ed., tr. F. A. Brunner, 2 v., 1950–55); P. Parsch, *Liturgy of the Mass* (3d ed., tr. H. E. Winstone, 1957); F. Amiot, *History of the Mass* (tr. L. Sheppard, 1959) 39–41.

[N. R. KRAMER]

GLORIA PATRI (Eng., Glory be to the Father . . .), a short acclamation of praise to the Triune God, known as the lesser doxology. It is used principally as a conclusion to the Psalms in the Roman Breviary, but also in many other devotions, e.g., after each decade of the rosary. In a variable form it is also used frequently in the Eastern Liturgies (see TRISAGION). Besides proclaiming the glory of God throughout and beyond the ages, it has served from early times as a brief profession of faith in the equality of the Divine Persons. It seems to be a development from the baptismal formula of Mt 28.19. BIBLIOGRAPHY: J. A. Jungmann, *Mass of the Roman Rite* (rev. ed., tr. F. A. Brunner, 2 v. 1950–55); *Place of Christ in Liturgical Prayer* (2d rev. ed., tr. A. Peeler, 1965).

[N. R. KRAMER]

GLORIFIED BODY, the human body of the just endowed with the preternatural qualities it will have after the general resurrection. These qualities are given in 1 Cor 15.42–44. It will enjoy a splendor or glory (*doxa*), which is primarily the glory of God in the face of Christ (2 Cor 4.6) but which passes through him to the blessed (2 Cor 3.18; Phil 3.21), who will shine like the sun in the kingdom of their Father (Mt 13.43). It will have the gift of incorruption or imperishable life. Corruption was the result of sin (Rom 5.12). When sin is entirely conquered, the just lives only for God, like Christ (Rom 6.10). Death is absorbed into life, and as a consequence all concomitant needs like nutrition (1 Cor 6.13) and procreation (Mt 22.30) will cease. It will have power for it is the immense power of God, so strikingly manifested in Christ's Resurrection (Eph 1.19), that will transform the human body, and, according to the constant law of Pauline soteriology, that which is characteristic of the cause passes into the effect. It will be spiritual. This is the deepest root–cause of all the other qualities. The body is now fully seized by the Spirit who renders it spiritual as opposed, not to material, but to weak and infirm. The human body, once temple of the Spirit (1 Cor 6.19) dwells now in God as in a temple (Rev 21.22). The glorification of the body is nothing but the final outcome of the Indwelling of the Spirit (Rom 8.9–11). The body's numerical identity should be explained not by a mere permanence of the informing principle (Origen, Basil, Gregory of Nyssa) but rather by the vivification of the same body: "The flesh will surely rise, all flesh, the same flesh, the whole flesh" (Tertullian, *De resurr. carnis* 63; similarly Epiphanius and Augustine). This constant tradition becomes the official teaching of the magisterium: "Not in an ethereal or any other flesh . . . but in this, in which we now live, exist, and move" (D 540; cf. 684, 797). Once the body is raised to life, the soul itself, already in possesion of the Vision, will probably experience an intrinsic increase in glory, for only then will man be really glorified and given his full reward. BIBLIOGRAPHY: S. B. Marrow and H. M. McElwain, NCE 12:419–427; A. Chollet, DTC 3.2:1879–1906.

[A. M. BERMEJO]

GLORY, biblical term with varying meanings. **Old Testament.** In its primary significance the Hebrew word *kabod,* usually translated by "glory," signifies weight or worth. From this it comes to mean the outward expression of a man's importance, his standing among his fellows, and the respect in which he is held. By a further derivation it is used to signify that which causes him to be so esteemed, the wealth or substance he has gained. It is with this sense in mind that the pious Israelite confesses that Yahweh is his glory.

A more important aspect of glory comes to the fore when it is the glory of Yahweh himself that is in question. In the *Priestly tradition the visible expression of Yahweh's presence to his people is the cloud of radiant fire, and this, too, is called the glory, the *kabod*. The *kabod* advances before the people at the Exodus and comes down to rest upon the "mercy-seat," the ark-throne in the tabernacle in their midst, creating a radiant sphere of holiness about itself in which the people constantly dwell.

From this basic conception a whole theology of the Divine Presence known as "*kabod* theology," grows up and associated chiefly with the Priestly tradition of the Pentateuch and with Ezekiel. Isaiah's vision, too, as described in ch. 6, is basically a vision in which he is privileged to see right into the radiant fiery cloud where the heavenly beings attend upon Yahweh himself enthroned at its center. Thus in *kabod* theology, brilliant light, fire, and smoke become visible expressions of the numinous presence of Yahweh to his people. In later traditions the concept of the divine glory appears vaguer, and becomes identified with his mighty feats of salvation, etc. (Is 35.2; 40.5; 59.19; 66.18–19; Ps 63.3).

To glorify Yahweh or give him glory is to give him the praise due his divine holiness (Ps 29.1, 9; 96.7; 30.13; 66.2, etc.), and also to confess one's own sinfulness and unworthiness in his sight (Jos 7.19; Jer 13.16). Not only man but the heavens and the cosmos declare the glory of Yahweh (Ps 19.2; 96.3).

New Testament. In three episodes in the Gospels Jesus appears as the focal point of the divine glory or *kabod:* at his birth, when the brilliant light illumines the heavens above Bethlehem (Lk 2.9), at his Transfiguration, when the light appears to shine out of his own countenance and person (Lk 9.31–36), and in the predictions of the Parousia, when he will come "in the glory of his Father with his angels" (Mt 16.27), "on the clouds of heaven with great power and glory" (Mt 24.30), and "take his seat upon the throne of glory" (Mt 25.31; cf. Mk 8.38; 13.26; Lk 21–27). The Johannine writings offer a new and almost unprecedented insight, in which the Passion, death, and Resurrection of Jesus are taken as a single event and said to be his "glorification" (Jn 12.23; 13.31; 17.1–5). The glory he thereby achieves is imparted to his Disciples also (Jn 17.22) when the Spirit is given to them and they are enabled to understand the significance of his words (Jn 7.39; 12.16). In the Pauline writings Christians are offered the hope of sharing in the glory of God (Rom 5.2) and being glorified with Christ by identifying themselves with him in his Passion (Rom 8.17) so that the glory of God is manifested in and through them (Rom 8.18), for "it is the same God that said 'Let there be light shining out of darkness' who has shone in our minds to radiate the light of the knowledge of God's glory, the glory on the face of Christ" (2 Cor 4.6).

BIBLIOGRAPHY: Kittel TD 2:236–255; E. Pax, "Ex Parmenide ad Septuaginta. De notione vocabuli doxa," *Verbum Domini* 38 (1960) 92–102.

[D. J. BOURKE]

GLOSSES, collections of explanatory notes on the biblical text. For the purpose of explaining obscurities in the Bible text the practice arose of inserting brief marginal or interlinear notes. In the course of time these grew longer and more elaborate, and appeared in separate collections, either in the order of their occurrence or in alphabetical order. This is the origin of the 5th-cent. lexicon of Hesychius of Alexandria, the 10th-cent. lexicon of Suidas, and of several others. Eventually glosses were elaborated to the point where they became running commentaries upon all or most of the contents of the Bible. The best-known example, the so-called *Glossa ordinaria* is from the 12th or 13th century. It appears to have been compiled under the direction of Anselm of Laon from Latin translations of Origen and Hesychius, certain of the Latin Fathers, and the works of earlier medieval glossators. This work exercised an immense influence on theology throughout the Middle Ages.

BIBLIOGRAPHY: B. Smalley, *Study of the Bible in the Middle Ages* (2d ed., 1952, repr. 1964) 46–66.

[D. J. BOURKE]

GLOSSOLALIA (Gr. *glossa,* tongue; *lalia,* talking), ecstatic speaking in tongues. In *Pentecostalism tongues-speaking is regarded as the manifestation of *baptism with the Holy Spirit. "Over and against all objections the Pentecostal Movement affirms a baptism in the Holy Spirit accompanied, as at the beginning, with scriptural evidences of speaking with tongues as the Spirit gives utterance. . . ." (statement of the World Pentecostal Conference, 1952). The occurrence of this charismatic gift in the early Church is attested by Acts 2.4–21, 23–32; 8.9–24; 10.46; I Cor 12–14. Pentecostal authors point to the recurrence of the phenomenon in the case of some medieval groups and the *Camisards, the Jansenists, American revivalists, and the *Catholic Apostolic Church. In no form of Christianity since apostolic times, however, has glossolalia been stressed to such a degree, or so claimed to be part of the ordinary Christian life, as in Pentecostalism. Tongues-speaking is for Pentecostals "the reason for their separate existence even to the point of divergence with other evangelical churches" (Brumback). It is the landmark of the beginnings of Pentecostalism, and separated it from the *Holiness Churches. Some distinguish between glossolalia as a sign, initial evidence of Spirit baptism, and glossolalia as a more permanent gift of grace to be exercised as witness to the Spirit-filled character of the Pentecostal message. Glossolalia is usually in the form of unintelligible sounds or utterances, although cases of xenoglossy (or xenolalia, ecstatic speaking of a language by a person who had no previous knowledge of that language) have been cited. Consequently, for glossolalia to be profitable to others the gift of interpretation (I Cor 14.10) is required; often the interpreter restricts himself to conveying a comprehensive meaning of what the tongues-speaker has said. Abuse of glossolalia has caused many Pentecostals to point to the need for control over its use. Some Pentecostal bodies seem to have deemphasized its importance.

*Neo-Pentecostalism is the term for the growing interest in tongues-speaking within other Churches. In 1968 the General Assembly of the United Presbyterian Church instituted an inquiry into the spread of glossolalia. There has been a manifestation of interest among members of the Protestant Episcopal Church, the American Lutheran Church, the American Baptist Convention, the Reformed Church in America, the Methodist Church, and the Evangelical United Brethren. Interest has been in part attributed to the *Full Gospel Businessmen's Fellowship International (Nichol, 240–244). The growing charismatic movement in the RC Church gives prominence to tongues-speaking in prayer (see NEO-PENTECOSTALISM, ROMAN CATHOLIC). Neo-Pentecostalism, however, seems to look upon charismatic occurrences as a sign not of Spirit baptism but of the active presence of the Holy Spirit in the Christian community. BIBLIOGRAPHY: C. Brumback, *What Meaneth This?* (1947); M. Kelsey, *Tongue Speaking* (1964); J. P. Nichol, *Pentecostalism* (1966); N. Bloch-Hoell, *Pentecostal Movement* (1964); J. L. Sherrill, *They Speak with Other Tongues* (1964); *New Testament*, M. F. Unger, *Teaching on Tongues* (1971); G. T. Montague, *Spirit and His Gifts* (1974 pa.).

[P. DAMBORIENA]

GLOUCESTER, ABBEY OF, monastery in the Diocese of Worcester, England. The site was first occupied in the 7th cent. by a nunnery and later by Benedictine monks. William the Conqueror named his chaplain Serle abbot in 1072. Edward II (d. 1327) was buried at the abbey. Known for its interesting building (a forerunner of the Perpendicular style), the church became a cathedral under Henry VIII in 1541 after the monastery had been dissolved.

[M. A. MCFADDEN]

GLOUCESTER CATHEDRAL, English cathedral with Romanesque nave, gallery, and clerestory (1089–1160), the south transept in 14th-cent. English Perpendicular Gothic (''decorated'') style, relating to St. Stephen's Chapel, Westminster. The remarkable choir (1332–57) is of English Late Gothic, the piers in unbroken verticals rising from floor to vault where nonstructural ribs are multiplied in a dense, ornamental network—a dazzling display of the distinctively English lierne vaulting. The style, harmonious with the delicate, affected conventions of the dying Middle Ages had its culmination in the Chapel of Henry VII, Westminster.

[M. J. DALY]

GLUBOKOVSKY, NIKOLAI NIKANOROVICH (1863–1937), lay theologian, professor, and lecturer. G. left Russia in 1921 and lived in Sofia, Bulgaria, from 1923 until his death. His theology is traditional in tendency; he did not recognize *Khomyakov, but did accept the Slavophiles as authorities. He was also active in Russian church affairs and in the ecumenical movement. His major literary contribution was as editor of the Russian Theological Encyclopedia. He also published scriptural commentaries, exegetical essays, and tracts on the reunion of Christians.

[I. M. KASHUBA]

GLUTTONY, a sin and *vice against *temperance, consisting in immoderate eating or drinking, and numbered among the *capital sins. Its rather coarse Latin name, *gula* (gullet or palate), indicates that the immoderation is in the pleasures of tasting and swallowing, pleasures of touch that temperance is meant to moderate. The excess may mean swilling food or drink; or may mean craving extreme sumptuousness and delicacy. Ordinarily gluttony is a kind of excess that is seriously sinful only if the pleasures of the table become the dominant concern in life. It is numbered among the capital sins because of the attraction of the pleasures it seeks. BIBLIOGRAPHY: ThAq ST 2a2ae, 148.

[T. C. O'BRIEN]

GLYCAS, MICHAEL (Sicidites; *c.* 1118–*c.* 1200), Byzantine monk, noted for teaching that Christ's body in the Eucharist is present as mortal before communion, then becomes the resurrected body. His writings on the point were proscribed by the Holy Synod of Constantinople. G. as secretary to Emperor Manuel I Comnenus fell into disfavor, was imprisoned and partially blinded. Upon release he became a monk and devoted himself to study and to writing, notably a chronicle from creation to the year 1118 and his *Kephalaia*, a work of biblical exegesis in which he also dealt with the main theological themes of Christian belief.

[T. C. O'BRIEN]

GNANA PRAKASAR, SWAMINADAR (1875–1947), Ceylonese Oblate of Mary Immaculate, missionary. Ordained in 1901, G. labored in the vicariate apostolic of Jaffna for more than 40 years and was responsible for many conversions. He left a number of writings, among them a history of the Church in Ceylon 1502–1602 (1925) and a Tamil dictionary. BIBLIOGRAPHY: J. Rommerskirchen, EncCatt 6:875.

[M. J. SUELZER]

GNECCHI SOLDO, ORGANTINO (1532–1609), Italian Jesuit missionary to Goa (1567), Macao (1568), and Japan (1570). In Kyoto he built a church (1576) and at Azuchi a seminary (1582).

[D. J. SMUCKER]

GNESEN CATHEDRAL, cathedral in western Poland. It was the earliest Romanesque building (1040–64) in Poland; rebuilt in 1097, in the 12th cent. it was finally replaced by the present Gothic structure (1342–1415). The magnificent early Romanesque bronze doors, executed (1135–38) in the reign of Boleslaw III, depict the life of St. Wojciech (St. Adalbert, Apostle of the Slavs). The nine panels in low relief on each door, framed by a vine rinceau enmeshing the forms, are related to the Hildeshein or Mosan (Liège) workshop, probably the latter, since the *Rétable of St. Remaclius* in Stavelot is from Liège. BIBLIOGRAPHY: A. Goldschmidt, *Die Bronzetüren von Nowgorod und Gnesen* (1932).

[M. J. DALY]

GNESIO-LUTHERANISM (Gr. *gnesios*, true, genuine), name given *c.* 1700 to the conservative segment of second-generation Lutheranism led by M. *Flacius Illyricus (1520–75), which claimed to be the defender of genuine Lutheranism against anyone who would compromise the Reformation, even among those who called themselves disciples of Luther. The controversies belonged to two principal categories. First, the doctrine of justification had to be defended against the synergists, who tended to compromise with the doctrine of the Church of Rome concerning the necessity of good works for salvation (see SYNERGISTIC CONTROVERSY). Second, the Gnesio-Lutherans were concerned with the doctrine called *Crypto-Calvinism, concerning the person of Christ and the Lord's Supper.

[M. B. SCHEPERS]

GNOME, the virtue of coming to a sound practical decision in exceptional cases which escape the ordinary working rules of conduct according to *synesis*. A virtual part (*pars potentialis*) of the virtue of prudence, it provides close intelligent backing to the justice of **epikeia*, and should be distinguished from a declaration of exemption, an interpretation of law, and a profiting from dispensation. In moral theology *gnome* keeps the original Greek meaning of being pithy and pointed, but, since its occasions are unique, sheds that of being sententious or of delivering a maxim, apothegm, or aphorism.

[T. GILBY]

GNOSIS, CHRISTIAN, a special knowledge (Gr. *gnosis*) of divine things, concerning which a doctrine was developed by early Christian writers. Indeed there is some probability (but no certainty) that some passages in the NT are directed against one or another form of Gnosticism. There is, however, also a doctrine of Christian Gnosis (although some Catholic scholars do not like the term), to be distinguished from heretical Gnosticism as well as from Jewish Gnosticism, that is undoubtedly found in St. Paul and St. John. To the former, as to the latter, knowledge of God, not knowledge of self, is most important. This knowledge of God is primarily knowledge of Christ. In dignity it is less than the love of God. Among early Christian writers Clement of Alexandria and Origen significantly developed the doctrine of Gnosis BIBLIOGRAPHY: R. Schnackenburg, LTK 3:996–1000.

[E. A. WEIS]

GNOSTICISM, from the Gr. *gnosis,* knowledge, a term first applied by orthodox Christians in the 2d cent. to various syncretistic systems that exalted arcane knowledge. The devotees mixed some fundamental Christian ideas and traditions with their basically non-Christian, pagan speculations and theories. This early limited application of the term persisted until the 18th cent., when historians began to extend it to include Gnostic types of religion that had no immediate connection with early Christianity, e.g., Hermetic sects, Mandaeism, Manichaeism, Catharism, etc. The narrower notion is treated here. Gnosticism was reported by Irenaeus as a Christian aberration, a heresy. It certainly threatened Christianity by its allurement to esoteric, salvational knowledge and the cult and desire for the higher spiritual life; but it was not, in its multifarious forms, an offshoot of Christian traditional thought. Rather it used Christian tradition and writings by forcing their themes into, and subordinating them to, notions that were essentially incompatible with Judaeo-Christian thought. These basic anti-Christian themes may be described as: God is so transcendent, aloof, and unconcerned with the universe and humanity as to be utterly unknowable by any means. Men and matter are evil in themselves, not the work of a loving, concerned, and provident God, but the product of deficient and corruptive emanations from God, over which he has no immediate control. God and creation are as opposite as being and nothing, light and dark, good and evil. The hidden powers that govern the world, e.g., angels, princes of darkness, etc., are essentially evil and in no way under God's control. Men are all evil, except those few elect in whom the original divine spark has been rekindled, the spiritual Gnostics, who are destined to return to the divine world from which the divine spark descended. Redemption, liberation, and salvation are not offered to all by God through Christ but only to a limited number. These receive and assimilate the mysterious, esoteric knowledge that comes from a Christ who is only a semidivine agent of God and who never was a real man who suffered an atoning death for mankind's sin. Further to describe the Gnostic claims, they alone have true knowledge revealed to them and alone can accept it. This revelation is not subject to any scrutiny or criticism: it is pure, unassailable, divine knowledge, no matter how it may clash with human intellect, logic, common sense (all of which are essentially evil), or with Sacred Scripture (esp. the OT, which is the work of the evil God of the Jews), or with apostolic traditions. Since Gnostics are basically pure through their knowledge, whenever they do what others call sin or evil, they really do no wrong. The ideal is the divine life of the spirit within (which some strove to live through severe asceticism, condemning marriage and the right uses of sex, and disdaining the rest of mankind), but sexual licence and every other kind of immorality are allowable. They even are a way to show contempt for ordinary human behavior. Such teachings are obviously in extreme opposition to the basic doctrinal traditions of biblical and institutional Christianity.

The most famous Gnostics of the 2d cent. were Basilides, Carpocrates, Valentinus, Marcion, and Bardesanes. Marcion is most noteworthy for his emphasis on the evil character of the OT and its God, his attempt to repress the heritage that Christianity received from Judaism, and his excessive, self-glorifying asceticism. The commingling of ideas and trends in Gnosticism indicates no single, continuous source or even group of sources, but an assemblage of many disparate elements: Iranian myths, Greek philosophies, mystery religions, Egyptian cults of Isis and Osiris, Babylonian astrologies, Judaism and Christianity, esp. for the idea of a Savior who leads the saved to deeper knowledge.

Knowledge of Gnosticism has been increasing since the 18th cent. through various discoveries of original Gnostic writings that add to what was recorded by anti-Gnostic Christians of the 2d and 3d centuries. The greatest discovery took place in Egypt in 1946 when a library of Gnostic works in Coptic translation (see *Chenoboskion Gnostic Texts*) was discovered. These texts discredit the theory once advanced that Gnostic "gospels" influenced the Gospel of John. BIBLIOGRAPHY: G. W. MacRae, NCE 6:523–528; R. M. Grant, *Gnosticism* (1961); F. B. Vawter, JBC 63.13–16.

[J. F. FALLON]

GOA, civil and ecclesiastical capital of Portuguese India and the Portuguese empire of the East; now part of the Indian territory of Goa, Daman, and Diu. Located on India's W coast, 250 miles below Bombay, it was captured by Muslims in 1312, incorporated in a Hindu kingdom in 1370, and recaptured by Muslims a century later. In 1510 it was taken by the Portuguese Alfonso de Albuquerque. It was the first territorial possession of Portugal in Asia and remained under Portugal until seized by India in 1961. Ecclesiastically, Goa was under the *Order of Christ until 1514, when it was transferred to Funchal, Madeira Islands. In 1533 Goa became a diocese, suffragan to Funchal and exercising authority from the Cape of Good Hope to the Moluccas. In 1558 it became an archdiocese and in 1606 the abp. of Goa was named primate of the East. Since 1886 he has been patriarch of the East Indies, and since 1928 also abp. of Cranganore. In 1542 St. Francis Xavier took over the Franciscan College of Santa Fé in Goa and renamed it the College of St. Paul, which became the headquarters of Jesuit missions in the East. Relics of Xavier remain in the Bom Jesus Church of Goa. Like other Spanish and Portuguese possessions, Goa was under the royal patronage (Port., *padroado*) system that allowed state selection of church officials. But the Congregation for the Propagation of the Faith, established in 1622, appointed vicars apostolic for non-Portuguese regions of India, leading to conflict between *padroado* missionaries directed from Goa and those sent by the Congregation. Dual claims in British-ruled Bombay led to the Goa schism, deal with in concordats of 1857 and 1886 but extending its effects into the 20th century. The *padroado* in India was not finally abolished until 1953. BIBLIOGRAPHY: R. N. Saksema, *Goa into the Main Stream* (1973).

[T. EARLY]

GOAR OF TRIER, ST. (fl. 6th cent.), priest and hermit. Probably from Aquitane, G. built a chapel and hermitage along the Rhine near Oberwesel in the diocese of Trier. Though mentioned by Gregory of Tours, the earliest definite information about him dates from *c.*765, when the chapel and hermitage were given by King Pepin to the monastery of Prüm, a donation later confirmed by Charlemagne. It became a famous center of pilgrimage. Because of the courtesy and hospitality G. had shown to those who came to see and consult him, he is venerated as patron of innkeepers. BIBLIOGRAPHY: A. Amore, BiblSanct 7:64–65; Butler 3:24–25.

[P. K. MEAGHER]

GOAR, JACQUES (1601–54), Dominican historian of Eastern liturgies. He is esp. known for his *Euchologium seu Rituale Graecorum* (1647), which is still an indispensable source of information for the study of the Greek liturgy. The work provides, in addition to G.'s valuable notes, the original text and a Latin translation. BIBLIOGRAPHY: Quétif-Échard 2:574–575; A. Duval, *Catholicisme* 5:75; A. Strittmatter, "Barberinum S. Marci of J. Goar," EphemLiturg 47 (1933) 329–367.

[N. KOLLAR]

GOBAT, GEORGE (1600–79), Swiss Jesuit, moralist. A Jesuit from 1618, he first taught philosophy at the Univ. of Fribourg, 1631–40, then for the rest of his life moral theology in several Jesuit houses, notably at Constance, 1641–66, where he was also cathedral penitentiary. At the command of his superiors he gathered into one work the many separate treatises he had written; this was his *Opera moralia* (v. 1, 1679; v. 2–3, posthumous, 1681). His defense of *probabilism against B. *Pascal's *Provincial Letters*, published first in 1659 as *Clypeus clementium judicum*, defends a position regarded as leaning towards *laxism. BIBLIOGRAPHY: J. Salsmans, CE 6:607; R. Hofman, LTK 4:1032–33.

[T. C. O'BRIEN]

GOBEL, JEAN BAPTISTE JOSEPH (1727–94), bp. of Paris under the Civil Constitution of the Clergy. Ordained a priest, he was made a canon in Basel and vicar general of the diocese. In 1722 he was named coadjutor of Basel and vicar for Alsace. He plotted to create a new diocese with himself at the head. A deputy of the Estates General in 1789, he supported the Civil Constitution of the Clergy, under which he was elected metropolitan bp. of the Seine, with his center at Paris. Conspiring to overthrow the prince bishop of Basel, he was sent to the area as commissioner of the republic. His weakness led to his formal abdication of the priesthood in 1793 during the Terror. A year later Robespierre saw to his condemnation and execution. In prison G. was reconciled to the Church. BIBLIOGRAPHY: G. Gautherot, *Gobel, évêque métropolitain constitutionnel de Paris* (1911).

[J. R. AHERNE]

GOD (IN ISLAM). According to the Koran, Allah is the name God gave himself when he revealed himself to Moses through the burning bush (Sura 20.14; Ex 3.4–6). The name, Allah, is found scores of times in the Koran (hereafter, K), and with it begins the great Koranic leit-motiv: *bismillâh al-rahmân al-rahîm,* "in the name of God, Most Gracious, Most Merciful," which opens each sura. The Arabic word *Allâh* is a shortened form of *al-ilâh,* "the god." In pre-Islamic times, Allah certainly was a creator god, and possibly the supreme deity of the Meccan pantheon. In the Koran Mohammed preached an absolute monotheism. No systematic exposition on the nature and the attributes of God is found in the Koran, but there emerge from it many ideas which constitute the ground of such a treatise. The first and foremost idea the Koran insists upon, is the Oneness (*tawhîd*) of the Godhead. Sura 112, one of the early Meccan suras, is known as the *tawhîd*'s sura. It reads, "Say: he is Allah, the one and only; Allah the eternal, he begetteth not, nor is he begotten; and there is none like unto him." The *shahâda* professes, "There is no god but Allah. . . ." The Koran gives to Allah a good number of attributes out of which the Muslims have put together the 99 "most beautiful names" of God. They express either God's immanent qualities, like Immortal, Supreme, The Living, or his activities *ad extra,* like Creator, Omnipotent, Supreme Judge, Avenger, Guide, The Merciful, The Protector. When the Muslim divines began to rationalize their faith in *'ilm al-kalâm* (theology), they came upon some particularly difficult passages in the Koran that described God in anthropomorphic terms ascribing to him eyes, hands, a face, and portraying him as speaking and sitting on a throne (Sura 2.254–7.54). The two rival views about the nature of God were *tashbîh* or comparing God to man and *ta'tîl* or divesting God of all attributes. The *ta'wîl* or the allegorical interpretation of the anthropomorphic expressions was invented and applied to explain away what was offensive in *tashbîh*. The *ta'wîl* method was particularly used by the Mu'tazilites for whom God is more similar to the Greek Absolute than to the Allah of the K. They affirm his unity and the identification of his essence with his attributes. Close to the Mu'tazilistic theology is the "negative theology" of the Isma'iliya sect: because the mystery of God is inscrutable, "no name or attribute can be attached to God's essence." The *falâsifa* (philosophers) developed a rationalistic theology whereby the existence of God is proved by the contingency of the world. God is being, necessary and perfect, supreme intelligence and supreme love. In *Sufism the essence of God is love. The Sufi seeks an intuitive mystic experience at the moment of *Kashf*. For the Sufi, God is not the object of knowledge but of love. Orthodox kalâm clings to the Koranic texts. The intricate passages must be believed without questioning (*bilâ-kaifa*), as objects of faith. BIBLIOGRAPHY: *Hour Qur'ân*. Text, translation and commentary by Abdullah Yusuf Ali (3d ed. 1946); M. S. Seale, *Muslim Theology* (1964); A. J. Wensinck, *Muslim Creed* (1932).

[J. R. GHANEM]

GOD (IN THE BIBLE). The biblical revelation of God describes him, not abstractly, but through concrete, personal relationships to his people in the history of salvation.

The God of Israel. For the people of the OT the existence of God is axiomatic and unquestioned. He is known not in his intrinsic nature, but by his actions and in his dynamic impact upon nature and history, whether to destroy or to create. For the people of the OT the vital question is whether there is one God or many, and, so far as their earlier traditions are concerned, they achieve not a theoretical but a practical *monotheism by refusing (though often only after prolonged struggles and failures) to attribute activities conceived to be divine to any other being apart from him. Thus for instance they learn very early to ascribe the characteristic activities of the war gods and destroyer gods of the various mythologies of the ancient Near East to the God of Israel alone, thereby giving that impression of ferocity and even cruelty which Christian readers from the time of *Marcion onward have found so repellent. Only by ascribing opposite activities, such as those of the fertility gods and raingivers of the Semitic pantheons, to one and the same God of Israel do the OT people gradually and progressively learn to think of him as a God who can both destroy and create, and who does both according to the just decrees of his will. Through their strivings to ascribe all activities conceived as divine to their God alone they progressively develop an idea of his transcendence; his power is confined to no one characteristic activity. Perhaps it was not until the age of David and Solomon, when Israel came into direct, sustained and peaceful contact with Egypt, Phoenicia, etc., and so became familiar with the great cosmogonic myths of these countries, and esp. with Egyptian ideas of Creation, that her own ideas of her convenant God as creator of the cosmos as well as controller and manipulator of all its nations, were fully developed. It has been suggested that hitherto the Israelites had thought of their God as intervening at isolated moments in the world's history, interrupting its normal course for a time, until that particular divine "visitation" had ended. But from the time of David and Solomon onwards (so the theory goes) Israel learned to think of him as continuously presiding over, controlling, and determining the course of nature and history from his place in heaven. Adapting Egyptian ideas of creation, Israel even conceives of all created life depending constantly on the exhalations of the divine breath. "You stop your breath; they die and revert to dust. You breathe out and fresh life begins . . ." (Ps 104.29–30). These theories can be accepted only with the vital reservation that Israel's idea of God is originally and basically the outcome of a direct and indigenous revelation; it was not made up of an amalgam of ideas borrowed from foreign peoples. Nevertheless it was developed and deepened under the stimulus of challenges from without. And perhaps it is not until Deutero-Isaiah and the Exilic Age that a completely developed idea of the divine transcendence is achieved. Here it is expressed spatially and vertically by representing the God of Israel as above the created order and so fashioning and controlling its course that the fates of all creatures are determined by his mysterious decrees, which no mere creature can expect to anticipate or understand (Is 40.12–30; cf. 55.8–9). It is also expressed in temporal and horizontal terms by representing God as the first and the last, the one who was already there before any other god or creature existed, and who will be there after the last god or creature has perished (e.g., Is 43.10; 44.6). Side by side with this developing sense of Yahweh's transcendence and absolute power over all creation goes a deepening sense of his intimacy with, and tenderness toward his covenant people. This too comes to its climax in Deutero-Isaiah, where the expression of Yahweh's covenant love as that of husband for wife (cf. Hos ch. 1–2) or parent for child (cf. Dt 1.31; 14.1), finds its most intense expression (cf. Is 40.1–11; 43.6; 49.15), though never at the expense of that awareness of Yahweh as *numen,* as *mysterium tremendum et fascinans,* which so clearly characterizes Israel's encounters with him from first to last.

The God of Jesus Christ. The fact that God as presented in the NT is identical with God in the OT is a first principle of orthodox Christian belief. The basic difference is that in and through God's relationship with Jesus Christ we are taught to recognize him and to accept him as Father, without for one moment losing sight of his numinous transcendence or his absolute power (SEE e.g., Rom 15.6; 2 Cor 11.31; Eph 1.3). The action of God through which he is known in the OT converges upon, and becomes one with, his action in and through the ministry, death, and Resurrection of his incarnate Son, Jesus Christ. In Jesus the plan and purpose underlying God's activity achieve their initial fulfillment. The deeds and words of Christ are identical now with the deed and word of his Father (Jn 4.34; 5.17; 9.4; 14.10–11). More than this, Jesus himself in his own person is one with the Father (Jn 6.57; 10.30, 38), the Word which the Father utters into the world (Jn 1.1–18), so that he who sees Christ in the flesh and recognizes him for what he is sees the Father also in and through him (Jn 14.9–11). He knows God now as one term of a relationship in which the Father is the sender and Christ the one sent, and both are one in their divinity. The effect of the grace and truth which Christ brings (Jn. 1.14) is to allow men, who in the OT have been admitted to a knowledge of God *ab externo,* to enter into his intrinsic nature and to know this in a "Father-Son" relationship which is actually extended to themselves also (Jn 17.21–23). This is achieved through the sending of the Spirit from the risen and glorified Christ (Jn 14.23–29; 15.26) into men so that for believers the Spirit is, as Paul tells us, a Spirit of adoption enabling them to call God "Father," too (Rom. 8.15), in virtue of their union with Christ through faith and baptism (Acts 1.5, 41; 10.48; 11.15–17; 18.8; 19.5–7; 1 Cor 12.13). BIBLIOGRAPHY: W. Eichrodt, *Theology of the Old Testament* (2 v., Eng. tr., 1961, 1967); D. Barthélemy, *Dieu et son image. Ébauche d'une théologie biblique* (1963); J. Blenkinsopp, *Sketchbook of Biblical Theology* (1968); G. von Rad, *Theology of Old Testament* I-II (2 v., Eng. tr., 1965, 1968); P. van Imschoot, *God (Theology of the Old Testament,* Eng. tr. 1965); H. Conzelmann, *Outline of the Theology of the New Testament* (Eng. tr. 1969); O. Cullmann, *Salvation in History* (Eng. tr. 1967); E. Stauffer, *New Testament Theology* (1963); G. Lindstrom, *Kingdom of God in the Teaching of Jesus* (1963); N. Perrin, *Kingdom of God in the Teaching of Jesus* (1963); R. Schnackenburg, *God's Rule and Kingdom* (Eng. tr. 1963).

[D. J. BOURKE]

GOD, EXEMPLARITY OF, see EXEMPLARITY OF GOD.

GOD, INTUITION OF, the created mind's unmediated vision of God as he is. "Intuition" here means, not a swiftly felt, unreasoned conviction, but, like the Latin *intuitus,* a gazing or looking upon. Because the bodily sense of sight apprehends objects immediately present to the beholder, words referring to vision become metaphors for the cognitive union of mind with God as he is immediately present to it. The knowing is termed an intuition because it involves no mental image, concept, or idea as medium; only the eternal Word, no created representation, expresses the divine being as it is, and the cognitive union intended is directly with God himself. The *beatific vision is the only certain instance of the intuition of God (see ONTOLOGISM); theology speculates about biblical references to Moses (Ex 33.11; Num 12.8; Deut 34.10–11) and St. Paul (2 Cor 12.2) seeing God "face to face" (ThAq ST 2a3ae, 175.3); and about the theoretical possibility of the created mind's being elevated to the intuition of the divine being. *DESIRE FOR GOD, NATURAL; *LIGHT OF GLORY.

[T. C. O'BRIEN]

"GOD," THE NAME. As a proper name it translates the biblical words *Yahweh, *Elohim, *Theos*. The OED traces in detail the possible etymology of "god"; the term, however, is impregnated with its Judaeo-Christian meaning. The labor of etymologists to trace precisely the origin and meaning of either the Greek *theos* or the Latin *deus* has yielded little. Thus it would be difficult to substantiate on etymological grounds that "God" means for all who use it a being who has universal providence over things (ThAq ST 1a, 13.8 and ad 2.10 ad 5). St. Thomas does make the valuable distinction between the basis for applying a name and the referent intended in its use. The basis in human experience for applying any name to the divine can only be effects of divine activity; then the referent becomes the being to whom the action belongs. Thus in the case of "God" in its theoretically possible origin it signifies action, particularly providence; in its reference it signifies the divine nature: "it is used to mean something that is above all that is and that is the source of all things and distinct from them all" (*ibid.* 13.8 ad 2). Antecedent, however, to such speculative determinations is the NT meaning of the proper name *Theos,* which "God" translates. No conception in pagan poetry or philosophy corresponds to the meaning of this name in the NT. For the whole Christian view of life and of the world it is a momentous fact that in almost its every NT use *Theos,* or better *ho Theos* (the God) means the Father of Jesus. The abstract and pedagogic order of theology in which "God" is discussed first in the unity of his nature, then in the Trinity of persons, should not be projected into reality. God as proper name should be taken first according to its NT sense, and the revelation of the Father of Jesus Christ through the Holy Spirit be seen as the preeminent revelation of the meaning of "God." The causal identification of God lies open to the human mind and should therefore be pursued; but reasoned discoveries and findings are to be measured and evaluated in subordination to the revelation of Father, Son, and Holy Spirit. BIBLIOGRAPHY: Kittel TD 3:79 s. v. "Theos."

[T. C. O'BRIEN]

GOD, NAMES OF. The names by which God is known are supremely important for OT theology. According to the *Elohist source of the Pentateuch, his exclusive covenant name Yahweh was revealed only from the time of Moses onwards. The *Priestly source, with its intrinsic sense of climax, goes still further. Up to the time of Abraham, God is known as Elohim. To the patriarchs he is El Shaddai, a title which, for all its obscurity, does imply a closer and more positive relationship between the patriarchs and their God than that which had previously existed. Finally, with the age of Moses, the new name Yahweh is revealed, indicating a progressive deepening in the Israelites' knowledge of their covenant God. Of the various names by which Yahweh is known the most significant are the following: (1) *El, Elohim* or, far less frequently, the poetic form *Eloah*. *El,* the generic Hebrew word for God, is applied to the covenant God of Israel as a proper name—a fact that expresses a practical monotheism that consisted in excluding all other gods, and left the more speculative question of their existence or nonexistence largely unexplored, at any rate, in the earlier traditions. The central concept here appears to be that God is wholly other to and utterly above all other creatures. The prohibition of images is a further expression of this. (2) *El Shaddai*. The most plausible explanation of this mysterious appellation is that it means "God of the mountain." The "mountain" here is the mountain in the N (sometimes identified with *Hermon) which was roughly the equivalent in Semitic mythology of the Greek Olympus. It implies that the God of Israel has all the attributes, powers, and privileges elsewhere ascribed to the supreme god of Semitic pantheons, and is therefore known by an honorific title expressive of this. (3) *Adonai, "Lord."* The primary note here is one of royal power over nature and history alike. With the same concept in mind (perhaps with the added idea of a dynamic assumption of power at specific moments in history or in cultic reenactments of history on the supreme festival day), he is also called "king" or, less frequently, "baal." Both epithets signify supreme authority, but the latter title is rarely used because of its associations with Baal the Canaanite deity.

(4)*Yahweh*. This is God's covenant name, revealed to the Israelites alone, and so sacred that many traditions have found it necessary to devise ways of avoiding either writing it in full or pronouncing it. The interpretation given to this name in Ex 3.14, namely "I am who I am," is as mysterious as the name itself. The discussions that have arisen concerning both the real meaning of this phrase and the more primitive meaning which the name itself may once have borne, are interminable. Most scholars would derive it from some form of the Hebrew word *hāyāh,* meaning "to be," perhaps from the causative form of this verb, implying that Yahweh causes all things to be. With regard to the actual etymology of the name Yahweh, Goitein has put forward a particularly attractive suggestion. He would relate it, not to the Heb. word *hāyāh,* but to the Arabic root *hawa,* meaning passionately to devote oneself to some person or thing. From this he deduces that ". . .the name implies two things: that its bearer passionately demands exclusive devotion, and that he is himself passionately devoted to those that worship him. . . YHWH is the passionate, a disposition which can work in two different ways: 'I am the one who is passionately extreme both in punishing and rewarding'." Even those who are not convinced by Goitein's philological argument must surely recognize that it is precisely this idea of the covenant God that does in fact lie at the heart and center of Israel's religion. If this is correct (and the point is an extremely controversial one), then it follows that the interpretation "I am who I am" attached to the name in the Elohist source is an artificial one. This too, however, has an inspired meaning to convey. We should notice that elsewhere in the OT exactly the same construction is used with many other verbs as is used here with the verb "to be." Thus for instance: "I will be gracious to whom I will be gracious and I will show mercy to whom I will show mercy" (Ex 33.19b); "Send by the hand of him who you will send" (Ex 4.13); "Sojourn where you will sojourn" (2 Kg 8.1), etc. Now the common factor in each of these instances is that the speaker either claims for himself or ascribes to his hearer complete freedom of choice. It seems no more than logical to suppose that a similar meaning lies behind the phrase: "I am who I am" in the passage under consideration. By revealing himself in this manner Yahweh seems to make himself available and accessible as a person to his elect while at the same time leaving his nature still wholly mysterious and undefined. But what is of primary importance here is the idea that this God, so holy and transcendent, allows himself to be known by name at all. For to a Semitic mind the name establishes a mystic union between knower and known. To know the name of another is in some sense to have him in one's own soul. To pronounce his name is to make him present there. Now Yahweh allows Israel to know him by name, to have him present as person in the community and in the individual's heart while the mystery of his nature still remains impenetrable.

(5) *Yahweh Sebaoth*. The epithet Sebaoth appears originally and primarily to belong to the context of the holy war, and to be associated with the ark as the shrine of Yahweh's presence to the armies of Israel as the source of their warrior strength. Whether it signifies the hosts of heaven, as has sometimes been suggested, is less certain. But it does seem to designate Yahweh primarily as all-powerful Lord, who has the forces of heaven and earth at his command. (6) Finally, a number of titles by which the God of Israel is known indicate his intimate attachment to persons. He is the God of Israel or the God of Abraham, or Isaac, or Jacob, or frequently of all three. This way of referring to him expresses above all that deep and unshakable bond of his covenant

union with his elect which lies at the center of Israel's faith.

BIBLIOGRAPHY: A. M. Besnard, *Le Mystère du Nom* (1962); J. D. Goitein, ''YHWH the Passionate, the Monotheistic Meaning and Origin of the Name YHWH,'' VT 6 (1956) 1–9; M. Reisel, ''Mysterious Name of YHWH'' (1957); P. van Imschoot, *Theology of the Old Testament,* (v. 1, *God;* Eng. tr. 1965); W. F. Albright, *From the Stone Age to Christianity* (2d ed., 1957) 15–17; J. L. McKenzie, JBC 2:737–740.

[D. J. BOURKE]

GOD, PROOFS FOR THE EXISTENCE OF, arguments that verify with certainty the proposition ''God exists'' (ThAq ST 1a.3, 4 ad 2). In the Christian, theological context of the topic, ''God'' means the one God of the Creed. Theologians who have developed such arguments have acknowledged that while God is pure, unreceived existence, the fact that he exists is not self-evident to the human mind (see ONTOLOGISM; ILLUMINATIONISM), but that by reasoning the mind can infer it as a certain truth (see Rom 1.20). Such reasoning is intended to advance strictly probative evidence, not simply allege such persuasive probability as a general human consensus or aspirations toward the transcendent. Historically the two approaches to the argumentation have been either strictly reasoned and intellectual, or experiential and affective. The two classic forms of the first type are the arguments developed by St. *Anselm of Canterbury and by St. *Thomas Aquinas. Anselm (*Proslogion* 2; see ONTOLOGICAL ARGUMENT) argues that God's real existence is a fact necessarily involved in the idea or meaning of God, ''a being than which nothing greater can be conceived.'' The validity of the proof has been both accepted and rejected; and whether Anselm intended it strictly as a proof is a controverted point. Aquinas's celebrated *quinque viae* (the five ways, ThAq ST 1a.2, 3), as well as similar arguments by both Catholic and Protestant authors, proceed rather from observation of the created world and argue to a first cause (other causal arguments have been developed on the basis of the existence of moral obligation or of the human desire for transcendent fulfilment, happiness).

The *quinque viae* begin from three kinds of actuality or given data observed ''here and now'': the first way from movement, as this is a process towards a not yet attained term; the third and the fourth ways begin from actual existence (the third from material existence acquired by a coming-to-be, and the fourth from gradated existence, measurably more or less perfect); the second and the fifth ways begin from exercised activity (the second from an activity exercised in subordination and the fifth from an activity exercised purposively). Each way leads to a first, or intermediary, conclusion: that its observed starting point has actual reality, by reason of an agent cause, i.e., a cause other than the subject or possessor observed to be in movement, existence, or activity. Thus the first conclusion of the first way is ''whatever is in movement is being moved by some other.'' Each way then proceeds to a second conclusion: the observed starting point (the movement, existence, or activity) is an actual fact not because of just any cause, but because there actually is a first cause. The argument toward this second conclusion consists in the rejection of a false hypothesis: that the given fact can be explained by an infinite regress or antecedent series of causes, e.g., whatever is in movement is moved by an infinite series of movers. The rejection does not mean that a temporally or numerically infinite series is impossible (see ThAq ST 1a.46, 1 & 2). An infinite series is rejected because it would not explain the present actuality, the observed, given starting point. This requires a first which is not itself part of the dependent series; the possibility of an infinite series is ruled out by the necessity that there be a first cause. Unless dependence had in fact been transcended, i.e., unless there is a first, not dependent as the original starting point of the argument is, there would be no present actuality here and now. If indeed there is a proximate cause of the present observed fact which is of the same level or dependence as that fact, such a cause would itself not be actually functioning except there be a first cause. Since the here and now starting point of each argument is a given, experienced fact, it is impossible that there not be a first cause; e.g., the fact of movement here and now requires a first absolutely unmoved mover.

The general conclusion of the *quinque viae* is that the proposition ''God exists'' is necessarily true, on the grounds that the first cause denominated by the originating point of each of the five ways (first mover unmoved; first necessary being; limitless first being; first uncaused cause; first purposive agent), coincides with what is intended by the term ''God.'' No claim is made to a knowledge of God's proper and unique being, since that is communicated only through grace (see FAITH; GRACE, HABITUAL). Neither is there the expectation that even one who follows the reasoning in the arguments must inevitably and decisively give religious assent to God's reality. Seeking ways to evoke such a religious response, other thinkers have turned towards experience and affectivity to prove God's existence; thus B. *Pascal, to reasons of the heart; F. *Schleiermacher, to the experience of absolute dependence; R. *Otto, to the sense of the numinous or holy; E. LeRoy, to the method of *immanence; M. Scheler, to the experience of God as existential value.

As to proofs in a purely philosophical context, Christian apologists from earliest times have pointed to the philosophies of Plato, Aristotle, Plotinus, the Stoics, and others as evidence of reason's discovery of God. In modern philosophy, e.g., in R. *Descartes, B. *Spinoza, G. *Hegel, the Judaeo-Christian idea of a transcendent God has been simply assumed as an element in a philosophical system. Contemporary positivistic and analytic philosophies that regard any statement about God as meaningless, assume that I. *Kant has destroyed the possibility of any objectively valid knowledge of the transphenomenal or metempirical. Proponents of a *natural theology patterned after Aquinas have often ignored his own position (*In Boethii De Trin.* 5.4) that no philosophic discipline can have God as its subject of inquiry. BIBLIOGRAPHY: T. C. O'Brien, *Metaphysics and the Existence of God* (repr., 1970).

[T. C. O'BRIEN]

GOD, RIGHTEOUSNESS OF, see RIGHTEOUSNESS OF GOD.

GOD THE FATHER. In Jesus Christ, his only begotten Son made man, God is the Father of men. This fundamental truth of the faith has been revealed progressively in and by Christ himself. In order to make the mystery of men's divine sonship understood, Christ made use of and completed the OT revelation. To his disciples he spoke of Yahweh, the God of the covenant, who throughout the history of his people had proved himself a loving Father. Christ exhorts his disciples to cultivate, as Israel did—and better than Israel did—an attitude of sons toward God. The foundation for the old and for the new people's filial attitude toward God is, however, vastly different. In the OT this was based on Yahweh's fatherly kindness and unfailing faithfulness to a saving promise made to the people of his choice; his name itself, which he revealed to Moses (Ex 3.14), was on the part of God a protestation of fidelity calling for faith and confidence in return. In Christ, however, something entirely new is manifested and revealed: not only is Yahweh like a Father to his own people; he is truly their Father, for he has sent his own Son, Jesus Christ, into the world to adopt them in him as sons.

The intimate relationship that binds Christ to his Father is a theme everywhere present in the Gospel narrative. Christ addressed his Father in prayer with the familiarity of a child calling upon his earthly father: "Abba" (Mk 14.36). He instructed his disciples to follow his own example: they too were to call upon Yahweh as "Our Father who art in heaven" (Mt 6.9). St. Paul witnesses to the fact that the first Christians did address God with the familiarity used by Christ himself (Gal 4.6). This fact demonstrates the novelty brought about by Christ and the originality of the Christian message. In a sense every man is entitled to call upon God as Father, for the universal Creator has toward all men a fatherly attitude. Yet, the full meaning of men's divine sonship is revealed only in Christ. All men are called to be sons of the heavenly Father; many are so unknowingly. Every sincere Christian, however, is so explicitly and knowingly. This is why it is the Christian's unassailable privilege to call upon God after Christ's own example: "Abba, Father." BIBLIOGRAPHY: DBT 144, 179; K. Rahner, *Theological Investigations* 1 (1961) 79.

[J. DUPUIS]

GOD-MAN, a term expressing the basic Christian mystery and belief that Jesus Christ is both God and man. He is man, in the fullness of human nature—conceived and born of Mary of the lineage of David through the power of the Holy Spirit—and God, born before all time of the Father. The God–man is proclaimed as Lord and Savior of men in the NT Scriptures, in the apostolic preaching, and in the abiding faith of the Church. Though the term itself is not biblical, the doctrine that Jesus is both God and man is clearly stated in the Epistles (e.g., Gal 4.4) and in the Gospel according to John (1.14). It was first used by Origen. Only with Augustine, however, is the title accepted as a succinct term for Christ in Latin theology, with a clear implication of the hypostatic union of the two natures in the one Person. In the field of comparative religion the title must indicate the unique claim for the founder of the Christian religion. Jesus is not mere man favored by God, nor a god in human guise, but true God and man in the closest of unions. Clearly excluded are a God-man person or nature in the Monophysitic sense, as well as any dual personality with a moral bond between the persons—a Nestorian understanding. The Divine Person is the bearer of both natures, each perfect in itself, inseparably united without confusion or commingling. Thus the Chalcedon formula is faithfully reflected. Theologically the term God–man suggests the common possession of the attributes of both natures by the one Person-subject and therewith the true basis for the communication of idioms. It also suggests the theandric work of Christ (two wills, two operations) in which the sanctified and exalted humanity is the instrument of the Divine Person, and the Christ presence and action in the Church and in the world. BIBLIOGRAPHY: B. J. F. Lonergan, *De Verbo Incarnato: Pars prima* (3d ed., 1964); *De constitutione Christi ontologica et psychologica* (4th ed., 1964).

[E. G. KAISER]

GODARD OF HILDESHEIM, ST. (960–1038), Benedictine abbot and bishop. G. became abbot of Niederaltaich in 996. An advocate of the Cluniac reform, he reformed a number of abbeys. In 1022 at imperial request, G. assumed the bishopric of Hildesheim. Saint Gotthard Pass bears his name. BIBLIOGRAPHY: O. J. Blecher, *Das Leben des heiligen Godehards* (1957); O. Schmucki, BiblSanct 7:134–140; Butler 2:231–232.

[B. F. SCHERER]

GODDEN, THOMAS (Tylden; 1624–88), controversialist. He was converted to Catholicism at Cambridge and attended the English College, Lisbon, where, after ordination, he joined the faculty and eventually became president. In 1661, he was appointed chaplain to Catherine of Braganza, consort of Charles II. He was falsely accused at the time of the Oates Plot, escaped to Paris, but returned under James II and again served as chaplain to the Queen Dowager. He was famous for his controversy with Edward Stillingfleet, chaplain to Charles II. BIBLIOGRAPHY: Gillow BDEC 2:503–506; J. Lane, *Titus Oates* (1949); S. J. Quinn, CE 6:621–622.

[V. SAMPSON]

GODEAU, ANTOINE (1605–72), French bp., writer, and one of the first members of the Académie Française. After early years of worldliness as a favorite at the Hôtel de Rambouillet, where he was known as "the dwarf of Julie (d'Angennes)" because of his unimposing stature, G. was named, with Richelieu's patronage, bp. of Grasse (1636). Although the apparent haste of his ordination and consecration (both 1636) caused unfavorable comment, he devoted himself in an exemplary fashion to his pastoral duties, eventually renouncing his earlier salon poetry for serious religious verse of Counter Reformation inspiration in accord with his theological outlook. Among his poetic works, some of which entitle him to front rank among the 17th-cent. writers of religious verse in France, are: *Saint Paul,* an epic (1654); *Poésies chrétiennes* (1660); *Hymnest,* his famous *Paraphrase des Psaumes* frequently set to music (by Louis XIII, Du Mont, Gobert); and his *Les Fastes de l'Église* (1674). Among his many publications meant as religious edification for his flock are his *Histoire de l'Église,* lives of saints, moral treatises, letters, funeral orations, and his *Nouveau Testament.* Named bp. of Vence (1639) for the additional revenue he would derive from that see, he was eventually forced to relinquish Grasse (1653). He played an important part in the assemblies of the French clergy (1645, 1646, 1653), and is said to have had Jansenistic sympathies. BIBLIOGRAPHY: A. Cognet *Antoine Godeau* (1900); G. Doublet, *Godeau, évêque de Grasse et de Vence* (1911).

[R. N. NICOLICH]

GODEFROY DE CLAIRE (Godefroid; fl. 1130–50), famed Romanesque goldsmith from Huy on the Meuse, probably from the workshop of the great master, Renier de Huy. In the service of Wibald of Stavelot, G. executed the engraved silvergilt reliquary *Triptych of the Holy Cross;* a reliquary head of St. Alexander in Stavelot abbey (1146); and the bronze aquamanile in Brussels (*c.*1130–40). The Crucifix of St. Bertin (1160–75) in the St. Omer Museum reflects G.'s style.

[M. J. DALY]

GODESCALC GOSPELS, two important Carolingian illuminated Gospel MSS produced by the scribe Godescalc, one *c.*781 for Charlemagne, now in the Bibliothéque Nationale, Paris, its vellum leaves dyed purple for royal use, a Byzantine mode adopted in the West in the early Middle Ages.

Also by Godescalc are the Ada Gospels (*c.*800), now in the Trier cathedral. Both MSS are in the style of the Ada School, characterized by monumental figures, solid color and gold, as opposed to the Palace style of linear impressionism and color-washed pen drawings.

[M. J. DALY]

GODFREY OF AMIENS, ST. (*c.*1050–1115). G. entered the Benedictine abbey at Mont-Saint Quentin at 5 years of age and was later ordained and professed there. He was elected abbot of Nogent-sous-Coucy in Champagne despite the opposition of the previous superior; in 1104 he became bp. of Amiens. Guibert, his successor at Nogent, praised his career as abbot, but felt that as bp. he disappointed expectations. Unpopular because of his severity, he retired to La Grande Chartreuse. He was recalled to Amiens by his abp. but died within the year. His zeal in combating simony during the Gregorian reform was noteworthy. BIBLIOGRAPHY: PL 162:683, 735–748; P. Villette, BiblSanct 7:83–84.

[J. D. LOUGHLIN]

GODFREY OF BOUILLON (*c.*1060–1100), Crusader, King of Jerusalem. Descendant of Charlemagne, second son of the count of Bouillon, lord of its castle N of Verdun (1076), and duke of Lower Lorraine, G. was the only major prince of the Empire on the First Crusade; he led overland a Walloon-Flemish army of 8,000. G. was pious, reasonably capable, and generally respected—characteristics soon exaggerated by legend. Reluctantly, he accepted the crown of the Crusaders' Kingdom of Jerusalem (refused by Raymond of Toulouse), but only as a subordinate "Advocate of the Holy Sepulcher" for the Church. His reign of 1 year stabilized and founded the secular kingdom. BIBLIOGRAPHY: J. C. Andressohn, *Life and Ancestry of Godfrey of Bouillon* (1947); S. Runciman, *History of the Crusades,* 3 v. (1951–54) v. 1.

[R. I. BURNS]

GODFREY OF BRETEUIL, see GEOFFREY OF BRETEUIL.

GODFREY OF FONTAINES (*c.*1250–betw. 1306 and 1309), scholastic, known as *Doctor venerandus.* He was a secular master at Paris from 1285. In his teaching he opposed the Augustinian school, adhered closely to Aristotle, but did not agree with St. Thomas Aquinas on all points, esp. on the real distinction between essence and existence and on cognition. G.'s 15 *Quodlibeta* were edited and published in modern times at Louvain (1904–37). BIBLIOGRAPHY: J. T. Wippel, NCE 6:577–578; J. C. Didier, *Catholicisme* 5:79–80.

[T. C. O'BRIEN]

GODFREY GIFFARD (*c.*1235–1302), bp. of Worcester from 1268, and chancellor of England (1267–68) under Edward I. He cleared himself of some 36 counts charged against him for illegal actions in support of his see. BIBLIOGRAPHY: A. R. Houge, NCE 6:578; Emden Ox 2:761–762.

[J. A. WEISHEIPL]

GODFREY OF SAINT-VICTOR (*c.*1125–*c.*1195), canon regular at the Abbey of Saint-Victor in Paris, theologian, and poet. His poetry includes a panegyric on St. Augustine, and verses of Marian devotion. His doctrinal sermons and writings on the Eucharist and the body of Christ are rich in biblical and patristic metaphors concerning Christ's humanity. G.'s major work, the *Microcosmus,* was written *c.* 1185 during a period when he had been exiled by a prior (Walter of Saint-Victor) hostile to his ideas. The work, which contains moral and spiritual interpretations of man's Creation and God's natural and supernatural gifts to man, reflects G.'s positive evaluation of nature in contrast to Augustinian pessimism. BIBLIOGRAPHY: P. Delhaye, DSAM 6:552–556.

[T. C. O'BRIEN]

GODFREY OF TRANI (d. 1245), Italian canonist and jurist at Naples and Bologna; glossator of the *Decretals of *Gregory IX* (*c.* 1241) and author of a *Summa* on the law of the *decretals (1241–43); created a cardinal deacon in 1244.

[T. C. O'BRIEN]

GODFREY OF VITERBO (*c.* 1129–after 1191), German chronicler and poet. He studied at the cathedral school of Bamberg (from 1133) and eventually became a court chaplain to Conrad III, Frederick Barbarossa, and Henry VI. Frederick took him along on many campaigns and assigned him diplomatic missions. In 1181, G. wrote the *Gesta Friderici* (MGHS 22) which has some historical merit. The *Memoria saeculorum* of 1183 is a universal chronicle. The *Pantheon* (PL 198), another world history, enjoyed wide popularity during the Middle Ages.

[J. E. LYNCH]

GODFREY, WILLIAM (1889–1963), cardinal abp. of Westminster. After ordination in Rome (1916) and his doctorate in theology there (1917), he taught at the seminary of Ushaw, England (1918–30), was rector of the English College in Rome from 1930. He was appointed apostolic delegate to England in 1938, abp. of Liverpool in 1953, and of Westminster in 1956. He was created a cardinal in 1958.

[T. C. O'BRIEN]

GODHEAD, the Supreme Being or Deity. The term is almost used with the definite article, often as a title for *God with connotations of divine majesty and power.

[T. M. MCFADDEN]

GODIN, HENRI (1906–45), French worker priest. After ordination (1933) G. was named vicar at Clichy. He was assistant chaplain to the Jocists there and in 1935 was given complete charge of the Jocists of Paris-Nord and Vincennes. His *France, Pays de mission?* made a great impact and led to his collaboration with a number of other priests in founding the Mission de France. Accidental death by asphyxiation cut short his work. BIBLIOGRAPHY: P. Glorieux, *L'Abbé Godin* (1946); J. Cronin and H. Flannery, *Church and the Workingman* (1965) 136–137.

[M. J. SUELZER]

GODO, ST. (d. 690) abbot, patron of glove makers. G. was the nephew of St. Wandrille who founded the monastery of Fontenelle, where G. lived until 661. He left to found another monastic house at Oyes, later known as Saint Gond. His relics were taken to the cathedral at Langres. BIBLIOGRAPHY: O. L. Kapsner, NCE 6:580; C. Boillon, BiblSanct 7:79–80.

[F. G. O'BRIEN]

GODOLIA, see GEDALIAH.

GODPARENTS, see SPONSORS.

GODWIN, WILLIAM (1756–1836), English political philosopher, author. Son of a dissenting minister, G. was raised in the liberal intellectual world of the Enlightenment. After a brief career as a minister, he took up free-lance writing. His *Enquiry Concerning the Principles of Political Justice* (2 v., 1793) expressed his belief in the perfectability of man, in the effect of environment in shaping character, and in the necessity of abolishing all restrictive institutions such as the family, marriage, State, Church, etc. The effect of his anarchistic thought is evident in the work and lives of Coleridge, Byron, and Shelley. BIBLIOGRAPHY: F. K. Brown, *Life of William Godwin* (1926, repr. 1974); H. N. Brailsford, *Shelley, Godwin and Their Circle* (1913, repr. 1973).

[T. C. O'BRIEN]

GOES, HUGO VAN DER (*c.* 1435–1482), painter of Ghent who depicted with great originality the psychological drama of religious scenes. After serving as dean of the painters' guild at Ghent, he entered the Roode Kloster near Brussels, where, as a lay brother, he continued to receive commissions. G. went to Louvain (1479–80) to evaluate the unfinished *Justice Panels* of Dirk Bouts. In 1481 he suffered severe mental illness and died the following year. His most notable work is the large triptych of the *Adoration of the Shepherds* or *Portinari Altarpiece (*c.* 1474–76; Uffizi, Florence). G. was commissioned by Tommaso Portinari, representative of the Medici banking firm in Bruges, for the Portinari Chapel in S. Egidio, Florence. The famous central panel of the *Adoration of the Shepherds,* showing emotional intensity hitherto foreign to the Flemish School, is remarkable for the three ordinary shepherds, simple, clumsy, dazed, who affected the history of Florentine painting, appearing in *Ghirlandaio's *Adoration of the Shepherds* (1485) in strange company with the Italian classical motif of a Roman sarcophagus as manger. BIBLIOGRAPHY: E. Panofsky, *Early Netherlandish Painting, Its Origins and Character* (1953); M. J. Friedländer, *Early Netherlandish Painting* (tr. H. Norden, 1967); C. D. Cuttler, *Northern Painting* (1968).

[M. J. DALY]

GOESBRIAND, LOUIS DE (1816–99), bp. of Burlington, Vermont. After studies at Saint-Sulpice in Paris, G.

was ordained in 1840. He came to the U.S. as a missioner and labored in Cincinnati and Cleveland, Ohio. Named first bp. of Burlington, Vermont (1853), he came to a diocese with few parishes and no institutions. His tenure saw the growth of parishes and schools to a phenomenal degree. He is the author of *Catholic Memoirs of Vermont and New Hampshire* (1886) and *History of Confession* (1889).

[J. R. AHERNE]

GOETHE, JOHANN WOLFGANG VON (1749–1832), German poet, dramatist, scientist, statesman. Nothing need be said of the details of his life or the singularly broad range and immense fertility of his genius; information about these is readily available in many sources. He was profoundly concerned with creativity, human aspiration, the beauty of nature, and morality. He was also a man of deep religious convictions, but is uninterpretable in terms of ordinary denominational or theological labels. He recognized the omnipotent God as force, intelligence, and order in nature and at times appears to verge upon pantheism, yet without clearly identifying God and nature. He shunned the usual images of God proposed by conventional religion and religious thinkers because they seemed to him to narrow and humanize divinity. His dramatic poem *Faust* was the work of a lifetime, the completion of *Faust II* coming shortly before his death. In the full acceptance of earthly limitations of human existence Faust attained perfection. It was a poetic expression of G.'s vision of human salvation, shrouded in the symbols of Christianity. BIBLIOGRAPHY: R. Friedenthal: *Goethe: His Life and Times* (1965); A. Schweitzer, *Goethe: Four Studies* (Eng. tr., 1949).

[I. MERKEL]

GOETTSBERGER, JOHANN BAPTIST (1868–1958), pioneer Catholic biblical scholar in Germany. Ordained in 1894, G. spent the major part of his career as professor of biblical studies at the Univ. of Munich. He was cofounder, with Joseph Sickenberger, of the *Biblische Zeitschrift* (1903). His main publications were *Einleitung in das Alte Testament* (1928); commentaries on Daniel (1928), and on Chronicles for the *Bonner Bibel*. BIBLIOGRAPHY: V. Hamp, LTK 4:1143.

[T. C. O'BRIEN]

GOG AND MAGOG, a code phrase in later Jewish eschatology referring to the leaders of a final abortive assault of the powers of this world upon the kingdom of God. According to Rev 20.7–9, after the saints rule with Christ for 1,000 years, Satan will be let loose from his dungeon and will muster the countless hosts of Gog and Magog from the ends of the earth to lay siege to the camp of God's people and the city he loves. The essential idea in an earlier stage of expression is contained in Ps 2, with its allusions to the nations in turmoil, the peoples plotting, the kings of the earth and the rulers conpiring against the Lord and his anointed king. The basic notion of the final battle occurs in the apocrypha, in rabbinic literature, and in Arabic legend. The code phrase "Gog and Magog" derives eventually from Ezek 39, 39, where the actual repeated reference is to Gog, the chief prince of Meshech and Tubal of the "land of the Magog." This Gog is envisioned leading a great host of nations from the N against humbled, purified, and restored Israel, only to be awesomely shattered anc crushed by Yahweh's intervention on the mountains of Canaan. There may have been an actual land of the Magog somewhere in Asia Minor, since Assyrian records place Meshech and Tubal NE of Cilicia. Biblical genealogies list Magog among the sons of Japheth and locate the people of that name between the Cimmerians (Gomer) and the Medes (Madai). The name Gog may derive from a famous king of Lydia mentioned by Herodotus, called by the Greeks Gyges, and in Akkadian Gugu. The Assyrian King Ashurbanipal (7th cent.) credits his help in repelling the invading Cimmerians. Or the name may be a corruption of the place name Gasga, a wild district in the region of Armenia and Cappadocia, and apparently mentioned in the *Amarna Letters. When the memory of the people of this area faded, the name survived as a synonym for barbarian.

[E. J. DILLON]

GOGARTEN, FRIEDRICH (1887–1967), existentialist theologian, important proponent of theological personalism. He was a Lutheran pastor, then became professor of theology at Jena (1927) and later at Göttingen (1933). With Karl *Barth, he rejected the optimistic, man-centered theology of the 19th cent. in favor of *dialectical theology. Fundamental Lutheran positions on the sovereignty of God, the gratuity of grace, and the crisis in which God's word places man were central to his early thought. He maintained that Christianity is not found in a realm of ideals or universal truths but in the continuing interaction between persons, a Thou-I relationship in which man is always dependent upon God's initiative. In 1933, G. broke with Barth and moved toward a more existential theology in which traditional doctrine could be rethought in historical rather than metaphysical categories. He strongly supported the biblical demythologizing of R. Bultmann and often confronted the speculative problems raised by liberal NT exegesis. Acceptance of the gospel message should be viewed not as the subjective assent to objective truths but as the affirmation that God's saving action, revealed in the historical Jesus, continues in the present.

After World War II, he recognized secularism as the major issue facing Christianity and tried to indicate man's radical responsibility for the world. Since man is saved by faith alone, he is free to work in the world with true objectivity and is able to avoid any divinization of the historical process. Grace renders man free from the world as a source of justification, yet man remains responsible for the world as his possession. These notions strongly influenced D. *Bonhoeffer, Harvey Cox, and the *death of God theologians. Works in English: *Demythologizing and His-*

tory (tr. N. H. Smith, 1955), *Reality of Faith* (tr. C. Michalson, 1959). BIBLIOGRAPHY: L. Shiner, *Secularization of History* (1966); Y. Congar, *Catholicisme* 5:90.

GOGOL, NIKOLAY VASILYEVICH (1809–52), leading Russian humorist and writer. His most important works are two collections of *novelle* about the Ukraine, *Evenings on a Farm near Dikanka* (1831–32) and *Mirgorod* (1835); the three *novelle* in *Arabesques* (1835), which, together with the short stories *The Nose* (1835) and *The Overcoat* (1842), comprise the "Petersburg novelle"; the comedy *Revizor* (*The Inspector General* [1836]); and the famous "epic in prose," *Dead Souls* (Part I, 1842), which he had intended as a trilogy on the model of Dante's *Divine Comedy*. In 1845, discouraged by his failure to portray the moral rehabilitation of its hero, Chichikov, G. burned the nearly completed second part of *Dead Souls*. In 1848, after a pilgrimage to Palestine in search of spiritual strength and peace, he resumed work, but, in 1852, shortly before his death, again destroyed the manuscript. G.'s reputation among his contemporaries as the founder of Russian Naturalism (Realism) rested on a misunderstanding of his literary purpose, which the radical and liberal intelligentsia regarded as socio-political, but which G. himself regarded as moral. Thus he was able, in *Selected Passages from a Correspondence with Friends* (1847), to champion without inconsistency, the very autocracy and serfdom which he had seemed to condemn in other works. His most characteristic achievements are his portrayal of man's universal weaknesses as manifested in the lives of St. Petersburg's "little people" and his inimitable combination of romanticism and realism, satire and idealism, grotesquerie and humor, rich imagery and homely idiom. BIBLIOGRAPHY: V. Setchkarev, *Gogol: his life and works,* (tr. R. Kramer 1965); J. Lavrin, *Nikolai Gogol* (1962); H. Troyat, *Divided Soul* (tr. N. Amphoux, 1973).

[M. F. MCCARTHY]

GOGUEL, MAURICE (1880–1955), French NT scholar and historian of early Christianity. From 1905, G. belonged to the Protestant theological faculty at Paris where he taught NT studies. He applied the established critical methods in his exegesis, but was esp. significant in maintaining the historical basis for the life of Jesus and the growth of the early Church. His trilogy, *Jésus et les origines du Christianisme* (1933–47), is an important study of primitive Christianity. BIBLIOGRAPHY: T. W. Buckley, NCE 6:587; Y. Congar, *Catholicisme* 5:90–91.

[T. M. MCFADDEN]

GÓIS, DAMIÃO DE (1502–74), Portuguese humanist. He was in the royal service, beginning as a page in the court of King Manuel I. G. lived a good part of his earlier life in Flanders, both as a royal servant and as a student at Louvain, where he also married. During this part of his life he twice visited Erasmus of Rotterdam at Freiburg-im-Breisgau. His more famous work of this period is *Fides, religo, moresque Aethiopum* (1540), proscribed by the Inquisition (1541) for its tolerant spirit toward Coptic Christians. G.'s most significant contribution is considered to be his *Crónica do felicissimo rei Dom Emanuel* (4 v., 1566–67) and *Crónica do Principe Dom João* (1567). Uncomplimentary statements about Portuguese royalty in these works along with his remembered friendliness with Protestants in Flanders led to G.'s arrest and imprisonment by the Inquisition in 1571; he was released as a penitent only in time to die.

[T. C. O'BRIEN]

GOLD AND SILVER WORK. The intrinsic value of the material involved generally brought a correspondingly high degree of technical expertise to the production of gold and silver work, but has doomed most of it to the melting pot. All great civilizations have produced such work, which is often preserved in such burial hoards as the fabulous treasure of Tutankhamen, and Etruscan and Scythian finds. The Church ensured continuity of possession in medieval times, later broken by such cataclysms as the English Reformation and the French Revolution. Germany provides a large proportion of surviving magnificent medieval gold and silver works, such as the portable altar at Bamberg commissioned by Henry II (1014–24). Whereas medieval gold and silver work was predominantly in the form of liturgical and other sacred objects, exquisite in workmanship, fabulous in inlay of precious stones and enamel, the Renaissance brought a renewal of secular patronage and a preference for worldly display (Rospigliosi Cup, Saltcellar of Francis I). A revival of interest in this art has taken place in the late 19th & 20th cent. in *Art Nouveau* and contemporary jewelry. BIBLIOGRAPHY: EncWA 6:399–459, esp. bibliog. from 454.

[S. D. MURRAY]

GOLD GLASS, an effect achieved by covering a sheet of glass with gold leaf, upon which a design is then drawn, finally covering all with a thinner layer of glass. Developed first at Alexandria in the 3d cent. B.C. the technique became extremely popular in 3d- and 4th-cent. Rome; many disks with figural decoration have been found in the catacombs. For making gold mosaic tesserae the same technique is used, but the design omitted.

[S. D. MURRAY]

GOLDAST, MELCHIOR (1578–1635), Protestant polemicist and historian. He studied at Ingolstadt, Altdorf, Geneva, and Sankt Gallen, and served as chancellor of the Univ. of Giessen. He was one of the first in Germany to research ancient and medieval sources for his numerous writings on law and history. Most important of his works are *Monarchia Sancti Romani Imperii sive tractus de jurisdictione imperiale et pontificali* (3 v., 1610–14) and *Collectio constitutionum imperialium* (4 v., 1615). BIBLIOGRAPHY: O. Vasella, LTK 4:1039.

GOLDEN AGE, symbolic designation of a time of general well-being. Many religious traditions attempt some periodization of history, but the association of each period with one in a series of metals of declining value is less frequent. The Iranian *Bundahish,* for example, divides time into four periods of trimillennia, but relates them to stages in the struggle between light and darkness. Among the Greeks, Hesiod (*Works and Days,* 109 ff.) presents a succession of five ages (golden, silver, bronze, heroic, and iron); similar traditions are alluded to in the *Odyssey* (15.403) and discussed by Plato (*Laws,* bk. 3). Interest in a golden age is a specific instance of the widespread nostalgia for the preeminently sacred time of the beginnings. Whether in a cyclic or linear time framework, the progressive decline in the value of the metals is intended as a negative comment on the contemporary situation. The present has been surveyed and found wanting, particularly in comparison with the distant past. In linear systems, that remains a rueful meditation, but in cyclic systems the culmination of the final stage signals the return to the blissful state of the golden age. *Apocalyptic appropriated the concept of the golden age to express the imminent renewal of this world. That sentiment is clearly portrayed by Virgil: "Now the last age by Cumae's Sibyl sung / Has come and gone, and the majestic roll / Of circling centuries begins anew: / Justice returns, returns old Saturn's reign / With a new breed of men sent down from heaven. / . . . / The iron shall cease, the golden age arise" (*Eclogue 4,* 5–11). Nebuchadnezzar's dream in Dan 2:31–35 echoes a similar conception.

[E. V. GALLAGHER]

GOLDEN BULL, a seal impressed on gold to authenticate exceptional papal, imperial, or royal acts. The finest collection of bulls of this type is that of the Vatican Archives. The best-known example is that attached to the celebrated constitution ("Golden Bull") of 1356 that regulated the election of kingsof Germany until the dissolution of the Holy Roman Empire in 1806. BIBLIOGRAPHY: G. Tessier, *Diplomatique royale française* (1962) 197–198.

[L. E. BOYLE]

GOLDEN CALF, the image made, according to Ex 32, in connection with the worship of Yahweh. The term refers to the young bull or cow. Calves were slaughtered for sacrifice (Lev 9.2–3) and for food (1 Sam 28.24). A golden calf, probably a wooden core overlaid with gold, was made by Aaron at the request of the people (Ex 32.4–8; Dt 9.16, 21; Neh 9.18). The calf, a figure of strength and usefulness, was meant to be a visible representation of their God. Jeroboam later erected two golden calves in Bethel and Dan to affirm the unity of the northen kingdom (1 Kg 12.26–33). Such practices, being superstitious and idolatrous, were severely condemned by Moses (Ex 32.19–30) and the Prophets (e.g., Hos 8.5). BIBLIOGRAPHY: L. Lewy, "Story of the Golden Calf Reanalysed" VT 9 (1959) 318–322.

[F. BUCK]

GOLDEN FLEECE, ORDER OF THE, a chivalric order of nobles that surived until the fall of the monarchies in Austria (1919) and Spain (1931). The origin of the name in unknown. The order was first established by Philip the Good, Duke of Burgundy in 1429; the dukes of Burgundy were grand masters until the title passed by marriage to the Habsburgs in 1477. From the time of Charles V, the heads of the Spanish Habsburgs were grand masters until the extinction of the Spanish line in 1700; then Charles VI of Austria claimed the title and established a separate Austrian order. The Spanish order continued under the Bourbons. In its flourishing period, the Order of the Golden Fleece exercised power, gave its members prestige and privilege. BIBLIOGRAPHY: J. F. O'Callaghan, NCE 6:599.

[T. C. O'BRIEN]

GOLDEN LEGEND, THE (LEGENDA AUREA), the compilation by Bl. *James of Voragine, 13th-cent. Dominican bp., of readings on the lives and miracles of the saints, arranged to follow the church calendar. The work was derived from other sources, and itself became the source of many familiar anecdotes in Catholic folklore about the saints. The *Golden Legend* has a simple charm and style, but little historical accuracy. Modern tr., G. Ryan and H. Ripperger, 1941. It was an inspiration for mystery plays and particularly a chief source book for themes and symbolic details (iconography) of Flemish religious painting of the 15th cent. and of certain Italian works: *Temptations of St. Anthony* (Bosch, Grünewald); Memling's *Reliquary of St. Ursula* with its hyperbole of 11,000 virgins; and 10 legendary episodes of the *Finding and Proving of the True Cross* of the fresco cycle of Piero della Francesca in Arezzo (*c.* 1455).

[T. C. O'BRIEN]

GOLDEN MADONNA (*c.* 1000), German work also known as the Essen Madonna. The 29-inch gold, enameled, and jeweled wooden figure, one of the oldest imbued with monumental Romanesque grandeur, likely produced by the remarkable school of goldsmiths in the abbey at Essen, is now in the Essen cathedral treasury with two similarly magnificent gold, enameled, and jeweled crosses bearing the name of the Abbess Matilda (971–1011), sister of Duke Otto.

[M. J. DALY]

GOLDEN MASS, a votive Mass in honor of the Blessed Virgin, also known as the Rorate. It was formerly celebrated with great pageantry on Ember Wednesday in Advent. It was also the custom to celebrate it in the early morning hours through Dec. 17–24. The Blessed Sacrament was usually exposed during the whole Mass. With the revision of the liturgical calendar this custom is obsolete.

[N. KOLLAR]

GOLDEN NUMBER, the number belonging to a particular year in the 19-year lunar cycle once used to determine the date of Easter. It may have been called golden for this reason or because it was so colored in Roman and Alexandrian Calendars. Anatolius, bp. of Laodicea *c.*258 reckoned the date of Easter with it in his computus. Dionysius Exiguus transmitted it through *Liber de paschate* in 526 until it was succeeded by the epact (the age of the moon on January 1) in the Gregorian Calendar of 1582. BIBLIOGRAPHY: A. E. Boyle, NCE 4:99; V. Grumel, NCE 3:674b; M. Noirot, *Catholicisme* 2:1430–31.

[F. H. BRIGHAM]

GOLDEN ROSE, an award made by the papacy since *c.*1049 to those who have performed some extraordinary service for the Church. Originally a single rose, by the mid-15th cent. it consisted of a gem-encrusted golden branch with leaves and several flowers. BIBLIOGRAPHY: A. Shield, *Month* 95 (1900) 294–304.

[J. M. MULDOON]

GOLDEN RULE, modern name for a precept of Jesus in the Sermon on the Mount: "Whatever you wish that men would do to you, do so to them" (Matt 7.12; cf. Luke 6.31). In popular discourse it is often rendered, "Do unto others as you would have them do unto you." The rule is given in negative form in Tob 4.15 and in various nonbiblical sources. Though sometimes regarded as the central teaching of Christianity, the golden rule is found in one form or another in many religious and ethical systems, and is not distinctively Christian. The origin of the name is obscure.

[T. EARLY]

GOLDEN SEQUENCE, a name given to the 12th-cent. Veni Sancte Spiritus, the Sequence for the Mass of Pentecost. The appellation refers to the purity of its simple, poetic style, the clarity of its theological expression, and the richness of its devotional inspiration. Like gold, as well, it has become a lost treasure since the sequence can only be perceived when read in Latin.

GOLDSTEIN, DAVID (1870–1958), RC apologist, convert from Judaism. In Boston (1888) he joined the Socialist Labor Party, and came under the influence of one of its leaders, Mrs. Martha Moore Avery. She became a Catholic in 1903, and G. resigned from the Socialist party and in 1905 was himself received into the Church. The two began an apostolate of apologetic preaching on street corners and in parks, and formed what became the Catholic Campaigners for Christ. G. spent his entire life traveling and lecturing to carry on this apostolate. Among his writings were an exposé of Socialist doctrine, in collaboration with Mrs. Avery, titled *Socialism, the Nation of Fatherless Children* (1905), the well-known *Campaigners for Christ Handbook* (1932), and his autobiography (1935). From 1945 until the end of his life he wrote a weekly column for the *Boston Pilot.*

[J. R. AHERNE]

GOLDWELL, JAMES (d. 1499), canonist, fellow of All Souls, Oxford (1441–52), king's secretary (1460–62), king's orator at Rome (1468–69, 1471–72), bp. of Norwich (1472–99). He was responsible for building work at Norwich. G. bequeathed MSS and printed books including Aquinas, Scotus, and classical authors to All Souls. BIBLIOGRAPHY: Emden Ox 2:783–786.

[C. D. ROSS]

GOLGOTHA, the site of Jesus' Crucifixion. The Greek equivalent *kraniou topos* (Mt 27.33; Mk 15.22; Jn 19.17), "place of the skull," translated into Latin as *Calvariae locus* gives origin to the English "calvary." Traditionally it is located within the present basilica of the Holy Sepulcher. BIBLIOGRAPHY: R. H. Smith, "Tomb of Jesus," *Biblical Archaeologist* 30 (1967) 74–89.

[J. J. O'ROURKE]

GOLIARDIC POETRY, a type of secular poetry written in Latin, by wandering scholars of France and Germany in the 12th and 13th centuries. The name may be derived from that of a fictional bp. "Golias." Many of the poets were students. There were also some others who were fairly important in the Church. Some of the poems are marked by ribaldry, some are satirical attacks on clerical loose living and greed; some are stylistically well done and, at least one poet, known simply as *Archpoet is well known. Most of the poetry, however, was anonymous. It shows strong influences of Ovid, which probably account for its satirical character. One of the principal collections *Carmina Burana,* has been put into orchestral and choral arrangements by the contemporary German composer, Carl Orff. BIBLIOGRAPHY: H. J. Waddell *Wandering Scholars;* P. Pascal NCE 6:602.

[J. R. RIVELLO]

GOLIATH, Philistine hero (1 Sam 17.1–10), type of the pagan who defies the Lord (1 Sam 17.45), slain by David (1 Sam 17.48–51). The conflicting tradition of 2 Sam 21.19 (Elhanan the slayer of Goliath) is best referred to 1 Chr 20.5.

[F. BUCK]

GOLTZIUS, HENDRICK (1558–1617). Son of the glass painter Jan Goltz, G. studied engraving under D. V. Coornhert and P. Galle and became famed for skill in control of shaded strokes in a brilliant mannerist style showing influences of Dürer and Italian painters. G.'s *Story of Ruth and Boaz* is intricate in detail and dramatic in chiaroscuro effects. A series of large plates on the life of Christ and a large *St. Jerome* are superbly rendered in an amazing eclecticism of Italian and German masters.

[M. J. DALY]

GOLUBINSKIJ, EVGENIJ EVSTIGNEEVIČ (1834–1912), Russian church historian. Professor of history at Moscow Academy from 1860, G. wrote a history of the

Russian Church (4 v., 1880–1916) that occasioned both civil and ecclesiastical censure because his critical treatment of sources led him to conclusion at variance with tradition. The onset of blindness prevented his continuing his history beyond 1398. BIBLIOGRAPHY: L. Müller, RGG 2:1691.

[M. J. SUELZER]

GOMARUS, FRANCISCUS (Gomar; 1563–1641), Dutch Calvinist theologian. After studies at several universities, including Oxford, Cambridge, and Heidelberg, G. became (1587) pastor for the Dutch residents of Frankfurt-am-Main. From 1594 to 1611 he was professor of theology at the Univ. of Leiden. Theologically he was a rigid supralapsarian, and vigorously opposed J. *Arminius; because of his leadership the strict Calvinists, anti-Arminians, were called Gomarites. He was one of the five official theologians at the Synod of *Dort (1618–19). From 1618 he was professor at Groningen, and in this period collaborated in the revision of the Dutch version of the OT books. Works: *Opera theologica omnia* (1644 and 1664). BIBLIOGRAPHY: Bihlmeyer-Tüchle 3:202; W. F. Dankbaar, RGG 2:1691–92; D. Nauta, EncRelKnowlSuppl 1:467.

[T. C. O'BRIEN]

GOMBERT, NICHOLAS (*c.*1500–*c.*1556), Franco-Flemish singer and composer; follower and possibly a pupil of Josquin Després. He held positions in Courtrai, Brussels, Madrid, and Tournai. Some consider him founder of strict "classical Netherlands style." Two elements of his innovative method were the parody Mass and motets containing variations on a theme. Published between 1529 and 1613, his many sacred works include 11 Masses and numerous motets, contained in various collections.

[J. C. MARR]

GOMIDAS KEUMURGIAN, BL. (1653–1707), a priest declared blessed by Pius XI in 1929 and venerated as a martyr for Christian unity. Born in Istanbul, he was first a priest of the Orthodox jurisdiction; but from 1694 became a *Uniate, continuing in the Armenian Rite, but acknowledging the primacy and jurisdiction of Rome. He was beheaded by the Turks in Istanbul, presumably at the instigation of his fellow countrymen and former coreligionists.

[E. J. DILLON]

GOMMATEŚVARA OF ŚRAVANA BELGOLĀ (947–984), colossal rock-cut image, fifty-seven feet high, at Śravana Belgolā, center of the Jain religion in Mysore State, India, representing the holy ascetic Gommateśvara (son of the first of the 24 Jinas), so long a time in the erect meditation posture (*kayotsarga*) that vines have twined round him to his shoulders.

[M. J. DALY]

GONÇALVES, NUNO (fl. 1450–72), Portuguese court painter (1450) to Alfonso V. He is famed for two large altarpieces of St. Vincent, patron saint of Lisbon and of the royal house. One altarpiece was destroyed in an earthquake (1755); the other (1460–70), intended for the convent of St. Vincent-beyond-the-Walls and discovered in 1882, is a polyptych of six panels. The left central *Panel of the Infante* shows the saint reverenced by the king, nobles, and the artist himself; to the right the *Panel of the Archbishop* carries figures of the clergy and knights. The saint's skull and coffin appearing in the panel were relics held by the convent. Though the three-quarter view of heads suggests Flemish influence, G., painting without landscape or architectural detail, was an innovator and true founder of the Portuguese school of the 16th century.

[M. J. DALY]

GONCHAROV, IVAN ALEXANDROVICH (1812–91), Russian novelist; leading representative of the psychological novel of pragmatic realism. Contemporaries (cf. e.g., Dobrolyubov's criticism of G.'s masterpiece in the essay "What is Oblomovism?" [1859]) regarded G.'s three novels, *A Common Story* (1847), *Oblomov* (1859), and *The Precipice* (1869), as attacks on the existing social orders, esp. on the institution of serfdom and the ineffectiveness and spiritual lethargy which it engendered among the liberal nobility. In reality, however, G. seems to have intended nothing more than a psychological study of two contrasting types: the impractical, vegetative "superfluous man" and the efficient, energetic "practical man." BIBLIOGRAPHY: D. S. Mirsky, *A History of Russian Literature* (1927) 231–236; J. Lavrin, *Goncharov* (1954); M. Eyre, *Oblomov and his Creator: Life and Art of . . . Goncharov* (1974).

[M. F. MCCARTHY]

GONCOURT, EDMOND AND JULES HUOT DE (Edmund, 1822–96; Jules, 1830–70), French writers, popularly known as "les frères Goncourt," whose novels, art criticism, and social histories offer a remarkable example of literary collaboration. Independent means permitted them to study 18th-cent. life and art, and contribute to emerging naturalism with their documentary novels and realistic theater. From adolescence their religious outlook was characterized by skepticism bordering on atheism; they were materialists in philosophy and regarded life as a matter of chemistry. Yet as politically conservative aristocrats with antirepublican and anti-Semitic biases, who personally rejected the Christian ethic and denied divine providence, they considered themselves by "racial and family sympathies" within the social and cultural orbit of Catholic tradition. Edmond's will provided funds for establishing the Académie Goncourt, which annually awards a prize to a novelist. BIBLIOGRAPHY: R. Baldick, *Goncourts* (1960); A. Billy, *Goncourt Brothers,* (tr. M. Shaw, 1960).

[G. E. GINGRAS]

GONDRIN, LOUIS HENRI DE PARDAILLAN DE (1620–71), French bishop. An uncle by marriage of Mme. de Montespan, G. became bp. of Sens through a cousin's influence. After a time he replaced his princely style of life with one of austerity. When Louis XIV and Mme. de Montespan came to Fontainebleau (in the diocese of Sens), G. was present and spoke out fearlessly against concubinage. He was relegated to his see city in punishment but disregarded Louis' order, threatening excommunication if the King proceeded against him. BIBLIOGRAPHY: M. Rigal, *Catholicisme* 5:98.

[M. J. SUELZER]

GONDULPHUS OF METZ, ST. (d. 823), bp. of Metz from *c.*816, venerated as a saint from the time of his death and still at Gorze Abbey where he was buried and where his shrine is. BIBLIOGRAPHY: J. Choux, BiblSanct 7:96; G. J. Donnelly, NCE 6:606.

[T. C. O'BRIEN]

GONET, JEAN BAPTISTE (1616–81), Dominican theologian, professor at the Univ. of Bordeaux. A man of the Midi, clear-edged in his ideas and language, he fell into royal disfavor for his refusal to condemn Pascal's *Lettres provinciales* on the charge of Jansenism; he himself was no friend of the *probabilists. His main work, for which he acknowledges his debt to the writings of his Spanish confrere, Peter Godoy, was entitled "a shield for Thomist theology against its new assailants." There were those who charged it with Calvinism.

[T. GILBY]

GONFALONIERI, an archconfraternity which began in 1264 at Rome when 12 noblemen who were *gonfalonieri* (standard-bearers) joined together at the Church of St. Mary Major to form the Compagnia de' Raccomandati di Madonna Sta. Maria. Among their many activities during the late medieval period were those of ransoming Christians captured and held by the Saracens, and an annual presentation of a Passion Play in the Roman Colosseum each Holy Week. In 1549, however, Paul III banned the presentation. Sixtus V made them a sort of third order in 1588. The most important modern confraternity is the Arciconfraternità del Gonfalone, centered at Sta. Lucia del Gonfalone with affiliates throughout the Christian world.

[R. J. LITZ]

GONIN, MARIUS (1873–1937), French Catholic journalist. G. founded several sociological journals and became director of three daily newspapers. He also established a youth group, Christian unions, and schools for workers. He is best known, however, as the organizer of the Semaines Sociales de France (1904). His cause was introduced in 1952. BIBLIOGRAPHY: J. Folliet, *Catholicisme* 5:99–100.

[M. J. SUELZER]

GONSALVUS HISPANUS (d. 1313), Spanish scholastic, minister general of the Franciscan order (1304–13). He was bachelor of theology at Paris in 1288 and regent-master of the Franciscan studium (1302–03) when Duns Scotus lectured there. His generalship largely was concerned with maintaining stability amid the upheavals of the *Poverty Controversy. His philosophical and theological writings were mainly anti-Thomist defenses of Augustinianism. BIBLIOGRAPHY: G. Gál, NCE 6:608–609.

[T. C. O'BRIEN]

GONZAGA, ALOYSIUS, ST., see ALOYSIUS GONZAGA, ST.

GONZALÉZ, BARTOLOMÉ (1564–1627), Spanish painter to the royal family. G. worked in the detailed miniaturist style of S. Coello, by 1621 having painted 91 royal portraits in a dull and labored technique. G.'s religious works, e.g., *St. John the Baptist* (1621), are stronger in dramatic realism and tenebrist chiaroscuro.

[M. J. DALY]

GONZÁLEZ, ROQUE, BL. (1576–1628), Paraguayan Jesuit missionary and martyr, whose life was dedicated to the evangelization of the Indians. Born in Asunción, Paraguay, he had attained the rank of vicar general of his diocese (1609) when he decided to enter the Society of Jesus. In 1615 he began his missionary work, founding settlements (reductions). In 1620 he was assigned to give instruction the inhabitants of the area that is now the Brazilian state of Rio Grande do Sul. He was martyred there in the last reduction that he founded: Todos los Santos (All Saints). He was beatified in 1934. BIBLIOGRAPHY: F. Baumann, BiblSanct 7:109–111; Butler 4:376–377.

[E. J. DILLON]

GONZÁLEZ DÁVILA, GIL (1570–1658), Spanish clergyman and historian, born in Ávila. After his ordination and long residence in Rome, G. became archivist of the cathedral of Salamanca and subsequently official chronicler of the kingdom of Castile. In the latter capacity he wrote, under the curious title *Teatro eclesiástico,* the history of the Church in Spain. The first parts appeared in 1643 and the last posthumously in 1700. Two of the volumes are devoted to the Church in the Western Hemisphere: *Teatro eclesiástico de la primitiva iglesia de las Indias Occidentales*. His information regarding the Church in the Iberian Peninsula is more detailed and trustworthy than the material on the West Indies. BIBLIOGRAPHY: A. Millares Carlo, *Tres estudios biobibliográficos* (1961); F. Esteve Barba, *Historiografía Indiana* (1964).

[P. DAMBORIENA]

GONZÁLEZ DE SANTALLA, TIRSO (1624–1705), Spanish moral theologian, 13th general of the Society of Jesus. He taught at Salamanca (1655–87) before being elected general. His election was connected with *Innocent

XI's efforts to turn the Jesuits away from advocacy of *probabilism in moral theology, a position that G. declared to be as official as the theory of **scientia media*. The latter he defended vigorously in his *Selectae disputationes ex universa theologia* (4 v., 1680–86); probabilism he assailed as the cause of moral *laxism, even of sin. In 1674 G. submitted a work against probabilism, intending to oppose its being taken as the official position of the Society; permission to publish was denied by the general, P. Oliva. Innocent XI, after his condemnation (1679) of a series of laxist propositions (D 2101–67) was made aware of the refusal of an imprimatur to G.'s work that was in fact against the 3d of the condemned propositions (D 1203). The Pope sent for the book, then had issued (1680) through the Holy Office an approval of G.'s teaching as acceptable to the Holy See and enjoining Oliva to inform the Jesuits of His Holiness's own preference for it (D 2175–76). Historians dispute whether the decree prescribed *probabiliorism; whether and how Oliva obeyed (see D 2177); in any case probabilism prevailed in the Society until modern reaction away from the *moral systems towards a more solidly based and interiorized interpretation of morality. At Innocent's urging G. was elected general (by a vote of 48–46), and expressly because of the Pope's conviction that probabilism lay at the source of the condemned laxist propositions. As general G., to further his cause, first published a brief work on the issue, *Tractatus de recto usu opinionum probabilium* (1691), which led to conflict with his own assistants. The revised edition of his 1674 book was published as *Fundamentum theologiae moralis,* in spite of Jesuit resistance, with an imprimatur from the Dominican master of the sacred palace, after approval by the appointed censors, a Discalced Carmelite and a Carthusian. The subtitle was the same as that of the *Tractatus;* G. was identified as *Praepositus generalis Societatis Jesu*. In the Society the work provoked both attacks and support; G. was engaged in controversy until his physical decline in his last years. In his thorough account of the ''Gonzalez case,'' T. Deman intends to show that G.'s ''probabiliorism'' marked a return to the classical moral teaching that the immediate basis for right moral action is a person's interior decision that an action is good. The quality of such a judgment at most can be moral *certitude; at times only probability is possible. But probabilism's position that a person can follow the less probable opinion of one author when he knows the more probable, opposite opinion of another, completely exteriorizes morality, and implies that a person can act on an opinion he is certain may be false. A sign of the times was the accusation of a pseudonymous opponent that G.'s insistence on a responsible moral judgment of truth was an advocacy of pure subjectivism. BIBLIOGRAPHY: T. Deman, DTC 13:534–546 s.v. ''Probabilisme.''

[T. C. O'BRIEN]

GONZÁLEZ PRADA, MANUEL (1848–1918), poet, political figure. A Peruvian aristocrat and onetime seminarian, G. became the leading anticlerical of Peru and defender of the Indians. He labored to integrate the Indian into the national life, to suppress the clergy, and reform education. The literary circle he established became in 1888 the National Union Party. G. became ultimately head of the National Library of Peru. His poetry is noted more for its innovation and form than for its conveyance of his social ideals. Among his works are *Minúsculas* (1901), *Exóticas* (1911), *Baladas* (1935), and *Grafitos* (1937).

[J. R. AHERNE]

GONZÁLEZ SUÁREZ, FEDERICO (1844–1917), bp., historian. He was an Ecuadorian who first joined the Jesuits but then became a secular priest. His great work, *Historia general de la república* (8 v., 1890–1903), is based on an intensive study of sources. G. corrected the history of the 17th-cent. Jesuit Juan de Velasco, which was full of errors, and established a new standard in Ecuadorian historiography. He was a member of the Assembly of 1878 and served as mediator between the Liberal and Conservative parties. As bp. of Ibarra in 1895 he enjoined neutrality on his diocese when Conservative forces attempted to destroy the Liberal reforms. In 1906 G. was appointed abp. of Quito. He remained a Liberal even though the Conservatives professed to be guardians of the Church. BIBLIOGRAPHY: L. J. Barrera, NCE 6:613–614.

[J. R. AHERNE]

GONZÁLEZ Y DÍAZ TUÑON, CEFERINO (1831–94), Dominican philosopher and prime restorer of Thomism in Spain. An Asturian, he was a professor at Manila, and afterwards abp. of Seville, cardinal, abp. of Toledo and primate of Spain, which office he resigned after a year and returned to Seville. He did not slip into the mold; his mind was open to contemporary philosophical problems; he was deeply interested in the sciences; and his principles for scriptural exegesis were acknowledged by M. J. Lagrange in the first number of the *Revue Biblique*.

[T. GILBY]

GOOD (Lat. *bonum,* Gr. *agathon*), that which fills a want. The term looms large in philosophy, from Plato to our own days, when it has been subject to much analysis. As being true is the object of mind, so being good is the object of appetite (*orexis*), and in its fulness of rational appetite or will. As a quality of being as such, it has as many meanings, transcends the categories, and the concept is arrived at by the same sort of abstraction. Nobody thinks that it is open to proper definition. What follows is a map drawn from the standpoint of Aristotelial and Thomist philosophy.

Goodness sets up a relation of final causality. An end is called a value (*bonum honestum*), and a delight (*bonum delectabile*); the first indicates its objective worth, the good in itself; the second, the terminal quality of giving fulfillment, the good as enjoyed. A means to an end is called a useful good (*bonum utile*). The division, which is sometimes called that between an intrinsic and an extrinsic or instrumental good, has been customary since St. Ambrose. Notice that a true end is not necessarily the ultimate end or supreme good (*summum bonum*), for it may be an intermediate or penultimate end, which, though subordinate to a further end, is not thereby purely a means. The point, which is based on a pluralist metaphysics that reality is composed of God and his creatures, not the One alone, is of importance in spiritual guidance: it implies a doctrine of a hierarchy of true values. God is our ultimate end, yet we are not to treat his creatures, esp. when they are persons, as utilities; they are to be respected and appreciated for the worth they hold and the pleasure they give. As real things, not symbols or shadows, they are good in themselves, though not of or for themselves, for their being flows out from God and returns toward him. A means as such is never desirable for its own sake, nor is it ever enjoyable: the stock example in the *Summa* is unpleasant medicine.

Good, like *evil, can be in being and in acting. The first is sometimes, not altogether happily, dignified as ontological good; the second in its reference to human beings is called moral good, and is variously identified according to differing ethical theories. Since moral good, according to theologians of the central Catholic tradition, lies in *human acts, and there is a goodness beyond them and even in our acting beyond them, e.g., the *beatific vision, it follows that moral good is not the highest good, though it may be called such by an ethical theory of another tradition, which has a more exalted view of morality and puts duty by itself on a peak.

The term, which is analogical not univocal, may be used substantively, adjectivally, and adverbially, thus, respectively, "the good of the State," "a good bet," "fixed for good." Thorough-paced nominalists will urge that it is purely equivocal, and serves as a blanket for utterly different meanings, or rather incidents. Linguistics philosophers, too, will be chary about investing it with any metaphysical value—unless they are not able to help themselves. Others will find it useful to distinguish between the Good, a good, and good as an epithet. With respect to moral good, the controversy set off by G. E. Moore's (*Principia Ethica,* 1903) exposure of the so-called Naturalistic Fallacy has not yet been settled: he powerfully argued that it was a unique and irreducible good-making property. *Deontologists, too, have entered the fray, and argued that no "ought" can be elicited from a descriptive proposition. Few contemporary philosophers are found to reduce the concept of moral goodness to an expression of the speaker's approval, though here it may be well to recall that in philosophy, not least moral philosophy, neither objectivism nor *subjectivism bear single, exactly defined senses.

For RC theology, moral good is a teleological notion to start with, but the treatment soon becomes transmoral as the discourse moves into the dimensions of grace and the theological virtues and living in Christ, and the final effect is eschatological rather than ethical.

[T. GILBY]

GOOD, THE SUPREME (Lat. *summum bonum*), the superlative in respect to all created goods and to human desire. As the first and universal object of appetite, it is signified in the abstract as "pure goodness" (*ipsa bonitas*), by contrast with any particular kind of goodness, and in the concrete as "the subsisting good" (*bonum subsistens*), by contrast with a derivative good (*bonum participatum*). Theological language attributes both terms to God, who embraces in himself the whole range of *good though infinitely transcending his creation. The supreme good belongs to the being who is his own whole, not to the whole of created things. The Manichaean dualism, which treats a supreme evil as a counterpoise, is rejected by Christian thought and can be shown by analysis to be a contradiction in any but rhetorical terms.

Usage in speaking of God as the supreme good can be twofold. It is sometimes metaphorical, as often in the Scriptures, when an essentially creaturely perfection is projected into God on the principle that every effect somehow reflects its cause: it is his supremely, yet virtually (*virtualiter*), that is, it is in his power. Thus the sheen of skin and the ripple of muscle, indeed every good proper to created things, are God's, down to the least flicker, even, says St. Thomas Aquinas, when it is a vanity (*bonum tantum apparens*). Sometimes, however, the usage is according to philosophical *analogy: when we are dealing with terms, such as living, knowing, and loving, which imply no imperfection in their meaning, but only in our mode of meaning them, then the perfection is his formally (*formaliter*) and, in the order of reality, though not in the order of our discovery, is foremostly his (*per prius*). Thus the supreme good is good in the most proper sense of the term.

So then when we speak of God as being the sovereign good we mean more than the *negative theology, e.g., of Maimonides, according to which all that can be said literally of God is that he is not-evil, or at most that he is an unknown *x* who somehow is the cause of what we call good. Nevertheless we have to be guarded in our attribution lest we carry along with it the limitations inherent in our present mode of signifying meanings. The connection is made in a double way, by elimination (*via remotionis*), i.e., by canceling any suggestion of imperfection, and by enhancing (*via excellentiae*), i.e., by affirming that the truth is beyond human categorization. Thus, respectively, that the supreme good is a justice not at all antithetical to mercy, and that it is not a "quality" of being good.

The term also centers with special force into moral philosophy and theology as the ultimate end of the human will. It charges every *intention and *choice of intermediate objects with the value and delight of what is final and paramount for human beings, namely *happiness (*beatitudo*). For deontologism this lies in doing what is right; for Christian eudemonism in rejoicing with God. BIBLIOGRAPHY: K. E. Kirk, *The Vision of God. The Christian Doctrine of the Summum Bonum* (1931); ThAq St 1a, 4–6; 1a, 13; 1a2ae, 1–5, (esp. in ed. Lat-Eng, v. 2, ed. T. McDermott; v. 3, ed. H. McCabe; v. 16, ed. T. Gilby).

[T. GILBY]

GOOD FAITH, a term generally used to indicate honesty and integrity of intention in entering into a contract or agreement, or in the making of a statement.

[P. K. MEAGHER]

GOOD FRIDAY, the Friday before Easter. It has always been an *aliturgical day in the West, i.e., a day on which the Eucharist is not celebrated, and the liturgy of the day is the solemn commemoration of the grim aspect of the Easter mystery, Christ's Passion and death, and of the meaning this has for all mankind. The Holy Week Ordinal of 1955 changed the official liturgical name of the day from *Parasceve (*feria sexta in parasceve*) to the ''Friday of the Passion and Death of Our Lord.'' Before 1955 the liturgical observances proper to the day centered about the Mass of the *Presanctified, and they were celebrated in the morning of Good Friday. Since 1955 the simplified rite has been celebrated in the evening hours between 3 and 8 o'clock. It consists of three parts: a reading (now the Liturgy of the Word) and a prayer service (now the General Intercessions), the *adoration of the cross, and a Communion service. (1) The theme of the readings is the Passion of Christ. There are three readings, the most important of which is St. John's narrative of the Passion. The prayers that follow the readings are an ancient example of the *bidding prayer. They ask that Christ's Passion be effective for the Church and all mankind. (2) The adoration of the cross, which originated probably with a popular devotional practice in Jerusalem in the 4th cent. and spread (with relics of the Cross) to the West, has been commonly observed in the Roman Good Friday ritual from the 10th cent. (3) The Communion rite first appeared in the West in Italy in the 7th cent. at the earliest. As the reception of Communion by the faithful declined in frequency, it became customary for the celebrant alone to communicate on this day, and his communion was elaborated during the Middle Ages into the Mass of the Presanctified. The Holy Week Ordinal now encourages all to receive communion at this solemn service. BIBLIOGRAPHY: J. G. Davies, *Holy Week, a Short History* (1963); A. Lohr, *Great Week* (tr. D. H. Bridgehouse, 1958); L. Bouyer, *Paschal Mystery* (1950); W. J. O'Shea, *Meaning of Holy Week* (1958).

[P. K. MEAGHER]

GOOD NEWS (Lat. *evangelium*; Gr. *euangelion*), a term used in the Septuagint and NT for the announcement of God's action to save his people. The literal ''evangel'' was archaic by the 17th cent. in England, later in Scotland; in any case the Middle English ''gospel'' from the Old English ''god spel'' (glad tidings), which passed into the languages of the Teutonic peoples evangelized from England, was an exact rendering. For the sake of freshness this is sometimes replaced in modern translations as, e.g., when Mk 1.1 is rendered: ''This is the good news of Jesus Christ, the Son of God.''

GOOD SAMARITAN, THE, a parable in Lk 10.29–37 in which Jesus teaches the meaning of the love of neighbor. The story is told in answer to a lawyer's test question concerning eternal life and his subsequent question, ''And who is my neighbor?'' Refusing to give a technical definition, Jesus instead tells a story in which he shows that what is important is not knowing who is a neighbor, but acting with charity to all men whoever they may be. One of the Gospel's richest teachings on the love of charity, which is seen to be spontaneous, prompt, and disinterested, as well as personal, active, and effective, the story also conveys the contrast between the letter of the Old Covenant and the spirit of the New.

[M. A. MCNAMARA]

GOOD SHEPHERD, SISTERS OF OUR LADY OF CHARITY OF THE, commonly known as the Sisters of the Good Shepherd (RGS), commit themselves to rehabilitation of delinquent girls and young women. The institute was founded by St. John Eudes in 1641 to care for the penitent fallen women for whom he established a shelter. The community, known as Religious of Our Lady of Charity of the Refuge, held its first profession on Jan. 2, 1666. The congregation had seven houses when the Revolution overpowered France. In the reestablishment that followed, the refuge, which had been situated at Tours, was restored. On Oct. 20, 1814, Rose Pelletier, receiving the name Mary of St. Euphrasia, was received as a novice. At the age of 29 she became superior and worked vigorously to unify the then independent houses of the institute by forming a generalate and central motherhouse at Angers, France. In 1835 a pontifical decree sanctioned the establishment, which took the distinctive name of the Congregation of Our Lady of Charity of the Good Shepherd. Living under the rule of St. Augustine, the sisters take the four vows of poverty, chastity, obedience, and zeal for souls. Bp. B. J. *Flaget of Louisville, Ky., requested them to work in his diocese. On Sept. 8, 1843 five sisters, each of a different nationality, began their labors in America. For their professional work in guiding girls of varied emotional needs, the sisters are trained as social workers, psychologists, guidance counselors, teachers, nurses, and home economists. In 1976 there were 9,894 members in 580 houses throughout the world.

[M. B. BOYLE]

GOOD THIEF, traditional designation of the one crucified with Jesus who in Lk 23.29–44 did not rail against the Savior. But Mt 27.44 and Mk 15.32 speak of the robbers who upbraided Jesus. Various explanations of the differing accounts have been attempted, but none is completely satisfactory. In some later traditions the Good Thief is called *Dismas and his companion Gestas. BIBLIOGRAPHY: F. Prat, *Jésus Christ,* (tr. J. Heenan, v. 2, 1950).

[J. J. O'ROURKE]

GOOD WORKS, or simply works, the upright deeds or actions of man. The Christian Churches in their official teaching reject *Pelagianism, the doctrine that works prompted by man's natural good will win salvation or God's grace. Reliance on good works in this sense is rejected as opposed to the gratuitousness of grace. In Christian practice, however, this opposition has not always been respected; in liberal or rationalist theological trends, man's capacity for good has been exalted to the point of obliterating the specific meaning of grace (see LIBERAL THEOLOGY). In the framework of a recognition of the divine initiative in grace, there are still diverse understandings of good works. According to one understanding they are deeds through which one attempts to fulfill the law and so please God, or appear innocent in his sight (see Rom 3.20). In another understanding good works are synonymous with "fruits of the Spirit" (Gal 5.22), against which "there is no law"; they are the effect of coming under the dominion of the indwelling Spirit. In the Renaissance Church, the two understandings appear not to have been adequately distinguished (see NOMINALISM), and the Reformation may be viewed as an attempt to reestablish the distinction. Even where there is agreement that only the good works which are the fruit of the Spirit have any relation to salvation, there is difference as to what the relation is. On the basis of the Lutheran position that man's righteousness comes from faith alone through grace, Protestants, rejecting the idea of works being meritorious, regard them as necessary only in the sense that they are an inevitable evidence of the presence of the Spirit. According to the Council of Trent good works are at once gifts of the Spirit and meritorious of salvation (D 1582). Contemporary theologians view the opposition between authentic RC and Lutheran teaching as more verbal than real. *JUSTIFICATION; *JUSTIFICATION BY FAITH; *LAW AND GOSPEL; *ARMINIANISM; *MAJORISTIC CONTROVERSY; *LUTHER, MARTIN.

[M. B. SCHEPERS]

GOODHUE, BERTRAM GROSVENOR (1869–1924), American architect trained under J. Renwick. He joined the firm of Cram, Goodhue, and Ferguson, designing his finest ecclesiastical interior in St. Thomas' Church in New York (1906). Earlier an ardent Gothicist, G. initiated the Spanish revival in California (1914), and completed designs for the San Diego Exposition (1915) and the Nebraska State Capitol (1922). In later work G. eschewed Gothic ornament, conceiving in smooth surfaces a restrained modernism.

[M. J. DALY]

GOODIER, ALBAN (1869–1939), abp. of Bombay, spiritual writer. Born of an old English Catholic family, G. entered the Society of Jesus and was ordained in 1903. Sent to the Jesuit college in Bombay in 1914, he was named abp. in 1919. A scholarly man he was not happy in the administration of his diocese, which was beset by many problems, and in 1926 he resigned his see to return to England and the life of writing that was his true gift, and to preaching retreats. His experience in India and tours of the Holy Land gave him a background that made the two-volume *Public Life of Our Lord Jesus Christ* (1931) unusual; the distinctive style also made the work memorable. He wrote with insight and considerable learning, but made no claims to biblical scholarship. *The Passion and Death of Our Lord Jesus Christ* (1933) used the same method: geographical emphasis, strong support from OT quotations, and a liveliness quite rare in works of its kind. It was as a writer on spirituality, however, that G. made the strongest impression. The small treatise *A More Excellent Way* was a pioneering effort in spiritual writing. His more ambitious *Introduction to Mystical and Ascetical Theology* (1939) reveals the deep spirituality that characterized his own life. BIBLIOGRAPHY: E. Graf, "Archbishop of Hierapolis," DublinRev 205 (1939).

[J. R. AHERNE]

GOODMAN, GODFREY (1583–1656), Anglican bp. of Gloucester. Educated at Cambridge, G. held various pastoral posts in England until 1616, when the publication of his most noted work, *The Fall of Man,* brought him to the attention of the court. Thereafter, he was rapidly promoted until he was named bp. of Gloucester in 1625. His sympathy with and tendencies toward Rome frequently caused him difficulties, not only with the Puritan faction in Parliament, but also with the High Church abp. of Canterbury, William *Laud. During the Civil War (1642–46), he was imprisoned and deprived of his see. After his release, he remained in London, where he died in communion with Rome. BIBLIOGRAPHY: G. Soden, *Bishop of Gloucester, 1583–1656* (1953); J. Hanlon, NCE 6:629.

[R. B. ENO]

GOODS OF MARRIAGE, a formula from Augustine (*De bono conjugali* 6. PL 40.377) expressing the values matrimony serves; *proles, fides, sacramentum,* children, matrimonial fidelity, sacramental indissolubility. In traditional Catholic theology the first two were taken to belong to marriage as it is a natural, human institution and contract. Without the intention of the connatural purpose of begetting and caring for children and of mutual conjugal fidelity, there is no genuine marital consent or contract. Further, the primary value and intent of marriage, according to the tradition, is the begetting and rearing of children; that is the essential reason and need for mutual fidelity. The personal elements, mutual love, conjugal pleasure, supportive corelationship between husband and wife, are secondary. The "good of the sacrament" is a further enhancement, as the natural contract is transformed into a sacrament: both as it is a sign of the perpetual loving union between Christ and the Church, his spouse (Col 3.18; Eph 5.25–33), and as it is a source of grace for the marital state. The *sacramentum* surpasses the other goods of marriage—even though these are essential to the being of matrimony—because it belongs to the order of grace, and it gives indissolubility a special, permanent reenforcement. Besides being standard in theology from the Middle Ages on, this teaching was taken up into church documents, as is reflected by CIC c. 1012–13, and by its prominence in Pius XI's *Casti connubii,* and in Paul VI's *Humanae vitae* (1968). As to contemporary theological discussions on marriage, it is noteworthy that historically the term good was applied to marriage to express benefits and ends that offset the liabilities it included: the lustful loss of reason in the act of intercourse, the besetting familial concern for temporalities (see ThAq Suppl. 41.3 ad 4; 49.1; but also *ibid.* ad 2 & ad 3). A more positive contemporary assessment of personal conjugal values, including marital sexuality, views the priorities between the *bonum prolis* and the *bonum fidei* differently. As to the *bonum sacramenti,* indissolubility is more and more seen as the essential and distinctive characteristic of the sacramental bond; the sacrament does not simply add an accessory value to a natural indissolubility: indissolubility is the sacramental signification of matrimony, i.e., the reflection of Christ's permanent, loving union with the Church. Such reevaluations have bearing on the problems concerning both contraception and remarriage of the divorced Catholic.

[T. C. O'BRIEN]

GOODSPEED, EDGAR JOHNSON (1871–1962), American biblical scholar. Professor at Univ. of Chicago (1902–37), he was a powerful advocate of biblical translation into idiomatic English. He published the NT in 1923, and with J. M. P. Smith the whole Bible in 1939 as *The Complete Bible: an American Translation,* popularly named Chicago Bible, which at the time was regarded by many as the best English version available. BIBLIOGRAPHY: autobiography, *As I Remember* (1953); J. H. Cobb and L. B. Jennings, *Biography and Bibliography of Edgar Johnson Goodspeed* (1948).

[T. EARLY]

GOOSSENS, PIERRE LAMBERT (1827–1906), cardinal abp. of Mechelen (Mechlin), Belgium. He was vicar general there before his consecration in 1883 as coadjutor bp. of Namur, where he succeeded as bp. in 1884. That same year he was named abp. of Mechlin and in 1889 cardinal. G. became a primary force in establishing the Catholic party in Belgium. He labored to keep working classes faithful to the Church. In his tenure, he established 86 new parishes, created 840 primary schools and numerous academies for boys and girls, founded 10 colleges and was a principal benefactor of the Univ. of Louvain, although he slowed the revival of Thomism there. Devoted to the economic betterment of workers and following Leo XIII's *Rerum Novarum,* he organized two general congresses and five district congresses to discuss the social question. A diplomat, he was able to avoid conflicts with the State. He published *Charges and Pastoral Letters* (5 v., 1889–1906), *Occasional Addresses* (1906) and *Talks on the Social Question* (1894).

[J. R. AHERNE]

GOOSSENS, WERNER (1899–1949), theologian. G. taught at the seminary in Ghent, and published numerous books and articles on positive theology. In Mariology, G. denied Mary's cooperation in the objective Redemption, limiting Mary's role to the application of Christ's merits. Among his more important works are: *Les Origines de l'eucharistie sacrement et sacrifice* (1931); *L'Église corps mystique du Christ d'après St. Paul* (1949); and *De cooperatione immediata matris Redemptoris ad redemptionem objectivam . . .* (1939). BIBLIOGRAPHY: J. Coppens, NCE 6:630.

[T. M. MCFADDEN]

GÖPFERT, FRANZ ADAM (1849–1913), priest and professor of moral theology at the Univ. of Würzburg from 1879, author of the first moral text written in German, *Moraltheologie* (3 v., 1879–98).

GOPURA, South Indian Hindu temple tower over the gateway entrance on each of the four sides of the walled temple area, pyramidal in structure, encrusted with a florid exuberance of sculptured tiers. Earlier gates surmounted by watchtowers developed into the soaring gopuras of the 12th century. The largest Vaishnavite temple of Srirangam (13th-18th cent. A.D.) shows 7 concentric walls, all with gopuras.

[M. J. DALY]

GORDIAN AND EPIMACHUS, SS. (fl. probably *c.* 362 and 250 respectively), martyrs whose names have been linked by all the Western martyrologies since the 6th century. Their cult is ancient, and the fact of their existence and martyrdom seems well established, but the legends surrounding their names are without basis. For example, legend has made G. a Roman official charged with conducting the trials of Christians, who was himself converted to Christianity and beheaded; but Pope Damasus I in his epitaph describes him as a youth. The identity of E. is altogether uncertain. He may have been martyred in Alexandria, or more probably in Rome. BIBLIOGRAPHY: J. Brückmann, NCE 6:630; A. Amore, BiblSanct 7:117–120; Butler 2:265.

[R. B. ENO]

GORDON RIOTS (also called No Popery Riots), anti-Catholic uprising in London, June 2–7, 1780. Lord George Gordon (1751–93), heading the Protestant Association against the Catholic Relief Act of 1778, led several thousand supporters to present a petition to Parliament. Violence broke out and the mob burned Catholic churches, prisons, and the houses of some public figures. When officials of the City of London showed themselves unwilling to take effective countermeasures, George III sent troops to restore order. Probably the number of those who lost their lives in the riots, or in consequence of injuries sustained in them, was greater than the official count of 285. Twenty-one of the rioters were later hanged. Gordon was tried for treason but was acquitted. Excommunicated from the C of E in 1786, he was later converted to Judaism. He died while in prison for libel. BIBLIOGRAPHY: P. Colson, *Strange History of Lord George Gordon* (1937); C. Hibbert, *King Mob* (1958); J. Kazantzis, *Gordon Riots* (1967).

GORDON'S CALVARY, proposed alternative to the traditional Crucifixion site. Otto Thenius of Dresden suggested the spot, a hill NE of the Damascus Gate, in 1842. Gen. Charles D. (Chinese) Gordon visited Jerusalem in 1883, he took up the theory and published it in 1885. The Crucifixion site had the Hebrew name Golgotha (Jn 19.17), which means skull (Lat. *calvaria*), and some people see the outline of a skull in the hill proposed by Thenius. In 1889 the discovery of a tomb nearby, completed the picture, and for decades there was great enthusiasm about Gordon's Calvary and Garden Tomb. The "discoveries" and theories, however, have been completely rejected by scholars, notably L. H. *Vincent of the École Biblique. BIBLIOGRAPHY: ThAq (Lat-Eng, v. 54, ed. R. Murphy) 202–207.

[T. EARLY]

GORE, CHARLES (1853–1932), Anglican bp., educated at Harrow and Balliol. B. became fellow of Trinity, Oxford; librarian at Pusey House (1884); canon of Westminster; and bp. successively, of Worcester (1894–1902), Birmingham (1902), a see he was largely responsible for founding (1905), and Oxford (1911). He resigned in 1919. He was a man of academic distinction, pastoral zeal, radical tastes, and devotion to the cause of social justice. He was a founder of the Community of the Resurrection (the Mirfield Fathers). His was perhaps the chief formative influence in modern *Anglicanism. He fought *modernism, defended *episcopacy, and resisted the Romanizers with much learning and cogency in speech and writing. His mind was open to the conclusions of biblical criticism, and his **lux Mundi* article "The Holy Spirit and Inspiration" (1889) grieved conservative contemporaries, yet his candor ultimately emphasized his completely committed *Anglo-Catholicism. Among his writings, *The Ministry of the Christian Church* (1888) defended the apostolic origins of *episcopacy in the Church; the *Body of Christ* (1901) was an exposition of an Anglican eucharistic theology of the *Real Presence. His trilogy, the *Reconstruction of Belief* (1926), is a monument to his liberal orthodoxy. BIBLIOGRAPHY: life by G. L. Prestige (1935).

[T. GILBY]

GORETTI, MARIA, ST. (1890–1902), martyr. One of the six childen of a farm worker, after her father's death in 1900, she cared for the other children while her mother worked in the fields. A neighbor, Alessandro Serenelli, tried to induce her to submit to his advances; when she resisted he struck her and wounded her fatally with a knife. After serving a prison term, Serenelli worked for the beatification of the girl he had killed. She was canonized June 24, 1950, during the pontificate of Pius XII. BIBLIOGRAPHY: M. C. Buehrle, *Saint Maria Goretti* (1950); C. F. Nerone, BiblSanct 8:1072–76.

[E. A. CARRILLO]

GORGIAS OF LEONTINI (*c.*483–376), one of the leading Sophists and the founder of rhetorical prose style. Under the influence of *Empedocles and *Zeno of Elea he wrote a philosophical work (not extant), *On Nature or on Not Being,* in which he maintained: nothing exists; if anything exists, it is unknowable; if anything can be known, the knowledge cannot be communicated in language. Whether he intended these propositions to be taken seriously from a philosophical point of view is disputed. At any rate he devoted his talents chiefly to rhetoric as the art of persuasion and to the elaboration of prose style that could approach poetry in its effects. He stressed the importance of the emotional appeal, "the tragic element," to achieve persuasion, and he seems to have been the founder of epideictic oratory. The rhetorical devices known as the Gorgianic figures bear testimony to his contributions in rhetoric. BIBLIOGRAPHY: OCD 391; LexAW 1110–11; Copleston 1:93–94; M. Untersteiner, *Sophists* (tr. K. Freeman, 1954) 176–202.

[M. R. P. MCGUIRE]

GORGON, Greek mythical female guardian monster with wings, snaky locks, and grimacing hideous face. Homer speaks of one, Hesiod of three Gorgones—Stheno, Euryale, and Medusa. An early example on the pediment of the Temple of Artemis on the island of Corfu, *c.*600–580 B.C., is famous.

[M. J. DALY]

GORGONIA, ST. (d. *c.*375), elder sister of St. Gregory of Nazianzus. Nothing significant is known of her except what can be gathered from her funeral oration which her brother delivered in praise of her virtues. G. was married and the mother of three children. Baptized only in middle age, she was twice cured of serious illness through her strong faith. BIBLIOGRAPHY: Butler 4:524–525; J. Brückmann, NCE 6:632; R. Janin, BiblSanct 7:121–122.

[R. B. ENO]

GORGONIUS, ST. (d. *c.*303), martyr. G. was an official of the imperial residence in Nicomedia in Asia Minor, who, together with two other Christians of life status, Peter and Dorotheus, was cruelly tortured and put to death at the beginning of the persecution of Diocletian (see Eusebius, *Eccl. hist.* 8.6). Another Gorgonius was commemorated by the Roman Martyrology which erroneously identifies him with the martyr of Nicomedia and declared that he was buried on the Via Labicana. Scholarly opinion holds that they were distinct martyrs of the same name. BIBLIOGRAPHY: Butler 1:573–574; 3:512; A. Frutaz, LTK 4:1057; J.-M. Sauget, BiblSanct 7:125–130.

[R. B. ENO]

GORIBAR, NICOLAS JAVIER DE, (fl. *c.*1688–1736), Spanish colonial painter in Ecuador, pupil of Miguel de Santiago. G.'s best paintings are the 2 series—*Prophets* and *Kings of Judah* in Quito and a rare signed work, *The Assumption* in the sanctuary of the Virgin of Guápulo near Quito.

[M. J. DALY]

GORINI, JEAN-MARIE-SAUVEUR (1803–59), French church historian. Ordained in 1827, G. was for some unkown fault relegated to a remote parish for 18 years. There he devoted himself to research and traveled long distances on foot to obtain books. In 1847 he was named curé at Bourg. He wrote *Défense de L'église contre les erreurs historiques de MM. Guizot, Thierry, Thiers, Michelet, Ampère, Quinet, Fauriel, Henri Martin* (2 v., 1853). So courteous was his criticism that he won the friendship of some of the scholars he opposed. In his honor the Société Gorini was founded on the centenary of his birth. BIBLIOGRAPHY: J. Morienval, *Catholicisme* 5:106–107.

[M. J. SUELZER]

GORKI, MAXIM (Alexey Maximovich Peshkov; 1868–1936), Russian proletarian writer. Though he became a Marxist in 1898 and a Bolshevist shortly afterwards, he was and remained a romantic revolutionary who soon became disillusioned with the stark reality of 1917. In 1921, he emigrated to Capri. Returning to Russia in 1928 at the invitation of the Soviet government, he was influential in formulating the doctrine of Socialist Realism and became the first president of the Union of Soviet Writers (1932). His sudden death in 1936 has never been fully explained. The success of G.'s writings is due more to the timeliness of their proletarian themes than to their literary merit. In his earlier works (e.g., *Chelkash,* 1895), he tends to see in the self-reliance and asocial independence of the derclicts and outcasts whom he depicts the qualities necessary for future leaders of the revolution. After 1895, his stories employ objective realism and naturalistic detail to convey the hopelessness engendere by this same proletarian milieu (e.g., *Former People,* 1897,). His masterpiece, *Twenty-Six Men and a Girl* (1899), reflects both his romantic idealism and his objective realism. Between 1899 and 1910, G. wrote novels and plays of no great significance. Among the novels mention should be made of *The Mother* (2 v., 1906), sometimes hailed by Soviet critics as the first novel of the revolution, and *Confession* (1908), which reflects the then current religious concept that the masses "construct" their own God (*bogostroitelstvo,* i.e., "God-construction"). Best known of the plays is *The Lower Depths* (1902). G.'s greatest works, the autobiographical trilogy *Childhood* (1913–14), *In the World* (1915–16), and *My Universities* (1923), span the period of the Revolution. His *Reminiscences* (1924–31) of Russian writers, esp. of Lev Tolstoy, are also worthy of note. BIBLIOGRAPHY: F. M. Borras, *Maxim Gorky, the Writer* (1967); D. Levin, *Stormy Petrel; the Life and Work of Maxim Gorky* (1965).

[M. F. MCCARTHY]

GORKUM, MARTYRS OF, eleven Franciscans of the Observance, members of the friary at Gorkum, Holland, and eight other religious and secular priests, hanged at Briel near Dordrecht July 9, 1572, by Calvinist extremists. The martyrs could have gained their freedom by denying the Real Presence and papal primacy. The episode occurred in connection with the Dutch struggle to overthrow Spanish rule in the Low Countries. The martyrs were beatified in 1675, canonized in 1867. BIBLIOGRAPHY: G. Jansen, BiblSanct 7:111–112.

[T. C. O'BRIEN]

GÖRRES, JOHANN JOSEPH VON (1776–1848), Catholic scholar, political philosopher, writer; leading figure of Heidelberg romanticism. Except for the editing of some medieval German texts (e.g., *Die teutschen Volksbücher,* 1807), his writings are largely religious in content (e.g., *Die christliche Mystik,* 4 v., 1836–42) or political. In 1814, he founded the liberal journal *Der rheinische Merkur* (which Napoleon labeled "the fifth great power"); it was suppressed in 1816 for attacking the reactionary policies of Germany after the Congress of Vienna. Called to the Univ. of Munich as professor of history in 1826, G. made it the center of German Catholic intellectual life in the 19th century. BIBLIOGRAPHY: A. Dru, *Contribution of German Catholicism,* (1963) 65–77; W. Kosch, *Deutsches Literatur-Lexikon* (1963) 108–110, bibliog.

[M. F. MCCARTHY]

GÖRRES-GESELLSCHAFT, the German Catholic learned society named after Joseph *Görres (1776–1848), the noted publicist and patriot. Its foundation took place on the centenary of his brith, Jan. 1876, during the *Kulturkampf. The basic aims of the society were to promote the development of Catholic scholarship along scientific lines and to provide assistance to young Catholic scholars, who had to contend with anti-Catholic discrimination in German universities. Its main founder, Georg von Hertling, later German chancellor (1917–18), was the society's first president (1876–1919) and in this position became the leading German spokesman for the aspirations, needs and problems of German Catholic education and scholarship. The Görres-Gesellschaft established an Institute at Rome (1886), an Oriental Institute at Jerusalem (1908), a Spanish Institute at Madrid (1926), and an International Institute for Relations between Natural Science and Faith at Munich (1957). Its journals include the *Historisches Jahrbuch* (1880), the *Römische Quartalschrift* (1887), the *Philosophiches Jahrbuch* (1888), the *Oriens Christianus* (1911), as well as several others begun after World War I. Its *Staatslexikon,* a multi-volumed work, went through six editions between 1896 and 1957. The society has also published the Acts of the Council of Trent in 12 volumes (1901–65) BIBLIOGRAPHY: W. Spael, *Die Görres-Gesellschaft, 1876–1941* (1957); *idem,* LTK 4:1060; N. Backmund, NCE 6:634.

[J. K. ZEENDER]

GORTON, SAMUEL (*c.1592*–1677), founder of the Gortonites. A native of Lancashire in England, G. emigrated to Massachusetts in 1637 in search of religious freedom. He established a sect at Plymouth, but his views turned the Puritan authorities against him. Together with some of his followers he went to Rhode Island and there at Shawomet purchased land from the Indians. When harassment from the Massachusetts government continued, he went to England (1643); after 5 years he finally was able to return to the settlement in R. I. with a letter of protection from the Earl of Warwick. In the settlement, renamed Warwick, he composed several religious treatises during the remainder of his life. Among the doctrinal points that involved him in difficulties was his denial of the Trinity and of the reality of heaven and hell. Gortonites survived as a small sect into the 18th century. BIBLIOGRAPHY: A. Gorton, *Life and Times of Samuel Gorton* (1907); E. Winslow, *Hypacrosie Unmasked by the True Relation of the Proceedings . . . against Samuel Gorton* (1916, repr. 1969).

[T. C. O'BRIEN]

GORZE, ABBEY OF (Gorziense), former Benedictine monastery established *c.*745 in honor of SS. Peter, Stephen, and Gorgonius by St. Chrodegang, bp. of Metz. The founder transferred the relics of the martyr Gorgonius to the abbey in 765 and was buried there himself. The monastery became prosperous, but its discipline deteriorated after its destruction by the Hungarians. St. John of Gorze (Jean de Vendrières) saved it in 932 by his reform and placed it under the Benedictine rule. In the Rhineland and Lorraine 29 monasteries quickly adopted the reform of Gorze. The abbey flourished in the 12th cent.; it was sacked and set on fire in 1542 and 1543 and served as a fortress for the Lutherans. It was secularized in 1572; in 1580 a college of 12 canons succeeded the monks. The land of the abbey was given to the King of France in 1661, and in 1790 the chapter was dissolved. The abbey church (choir dating from the 12th cent., nave from the 14th and 16th), the main portion of the abbey (1696), and ruins of the fortifications are still standing. BIBLIOGRAPHY: Cottineau, 1:1303–04; A. A. Shacher, NCE 6:634–635.

[J. DAOUST]

GOSCELIN (Gotselin, d. *c.*1099),, English hagiographer. Originally a Benedictine in France, G. went to England with Hermann of Salisbury in 1053. He based his biographies of English saints upon older sources, but his personal elaborations lessen their historical value. BIBLIOGRAPHY: G. C. Alston, CE 6:655.

[M. J. SUELZER]

GOSLING, SAMUEL (1883–1950), English priest remembered for his active promotion of the use of the vernacular in the liturgy. He began to advocate this before the cause was yet popular. He founded the English Liturgy Society (1943) to win support for his views, and through this exerted an influence in The U.S. where a similar association, the American Vernacular Society, was established in 1946. BIBLIOGRAPHY: C. W. Howell, NCE 6:635.

[N. KOLLAR]

GOSPEL, from the Anglo-Saxon *godspel,* ''good news,'' an accurate rendering of the Greek *evangelion.* The major background for its usage derives from the LXX where the cognate verb *evangelizesthai* (to announce good news) translates the Hebrew *bisser* found in the Deutero-Isaiahan texts announcing God's eschatological salvation to Zion (Is 40.9; 41.27; 52.7), which brings comfort to the afflicted and release to the captive (Is 61.1). The NT nowhere uses the word to designate a written document. For the NT authors, the gospel is the divine proclamation of the realization of God's plan for man's salvation in Jesus the Christ. The basis of this proclamation is the life and activity of Jesus, who presented himself as God's agent, announcing the presence of the definitive divine act of salvation in his person, his preaching and healings. Jesus preached that through him God's kingly rule was being established, asked commitment to his person and message, and taught that the reality of this rule would be both completed and manifested to all through a coming eschatological event. For the early Church, the gospel content focused on the fact that the salvation preached by Jesus had been realized in the eschatological event of his death and Resurrection, inaugurating the final era of salvation, which all may share in through faith, repentance, baptism, and which was hopefully to be soon consummated in the return of Jesus as Son of Man (Acts 2.22–42; 4.8–12; 13.26–39).

This same stress on the eschatological effects of the death and Resurrection realized within the believer is the content of the gospel preached by Paul. The essence of ''the gospel of God'' (Rom 1.1, 9,15–16) or ''the gospel of Christ'' (1 Cor 9.12; 2 Cor 2.12; 9.13; Rom 15.19) concerns the Son whom God ''has raised from the dead, Jesus, who delivers us from the coming wrath'' (1 Thess 1.10). Paul stresses the "now" character of the gospel in conceiving it to be a salvific force that God has directed toward the world of man. It is "the power of God for the salvation of every man who believes" (Rom 1.16). As the power of God, the gospel is neither preached apart from the presence of God's Spirit (1 Thess 1.5; 1 Cor 4.20) nor without ethical demands made upon the hearer (Gal 5.16–26; 1 Cor 6.14–20; Rom 8.5–11). Since in the gospel has been revealed the divine economy of salvation in Christ Jesus, it has the character of *mysterion* (1 Cor 4.1; Rom 11.25; Col 4.3; Eph 3.4–10). So taken was Paul by his mission to preach the gospel that he speaks of "my gospel" or "our gospel" (Rom 2.16; 1 Cor 15.1; 2 Cor 4.3).

While the focus of the earliest gospel was the redemptive effects of the death and Resurrection, the earthly ministry of Jesus formed part of the community's interest and preaching (Acts 10.34–43). Yet it is with Mark that the meaning of gospel assumes that form which makes it the "one unique literary product of NT Christianity" (Perrin). In Mark, there is to be found a dimension missing in Paul: Jesus is viewed as the eschatological agent of salvation in the context of his historical public ministry. Pre-Gospel traditions, written and oral, topically ordered yet considerably developed beyond the *ipsissima verba et acta* stage, Mark first systematized along both chronological and theological lines. The author fit his selected material into a simplified narrative of the public ministry (baptism, ministry in Galilee, outside Galilee, journey to Jerusalem, Passion, death, Resurrection), inserting incidents where, according to his purpose, they seemed to fit either theologically or chronologically. Of utmost importance in determining Mark's selection and ordering of material were his theological perspectives and the needs of the particular community for which he was writing. The reason for this is evident: Jesus is significant to Mark's community because of what he has done in the past, of what he does now within the community, and of what he is to do in his future coming as Son of Man. The later synoptic Gospels, Matthew and Luke, while addressing different problems in their communities and employing expanded traditions, still basically follow the Markan sequence. The survival and eventual canonization of the four accounts of the Gospel were due in part to the names connected with them, the prominence of the communities from which they originated, and the extent of their dissemination and use in the expanding Christian Churches. BIBLIOGRAPHY: X. Léon-Dufour, *Les évangiles et l'histoire de Jesus* (1965); N. Perrin, *What is Redaction Criticism?* (1969); C. H. Dodd, *Apostolic Preaching and Its Developments* (1939); R. H. Mounce, *Essential Nature of New Testament Preaching* (1960); M. Burrows, "Origin of the Term Gospel." JBL 44(1925) 21–33. *GOSPELS, THE HOLY.

[T. J. RYAN]

GOSPEL (LITURGY), a section from the four Gospels customarily read or sung as the most prominent part of the Liturgy of the Word in Roman and other Christian worship services. Lectionaries containing such sections, determined for daily Mass, feasts, and Sundays, are borne in solemn procession to a prominent place in the church, are venerated by an incensation before being read by no one of lower rank than a deacon, while the congregation stands out of respect for God's Word being proclaimed. At the reading's conclusion praise of thanksgiving is offered to God in acclamation or song by the whole assembly for the gift of his revealing word. The term Last Gospel refers to the prologue of St. John's Gospel which in the RC Church was read at the end of Mass. In the revised order of the Mass this custom has been discontinued.

[J. F. FALLON]

GOSPEL OF NICODEMUS, see NICODEMUS, GOSPEL OF.

GOSPEL OF THE EBIONITES, see APOCRYPHA (NT) 18.

GOSPEL HYMN, a term coined by Ira D. *Sankey in the decade of the 1870s. The source was the practice of printing a biblical quotation under the title of the hymn that usually mentioned the subject or major phrase in the hymn. These quotations often came from the first four books of the NT, the Gospels. Sankey and evangelist D. *Moody combined talents in years of widespread revival services, publishing a series of gospel hymnals and developing specific techniques for using these hymns to shape the emotional climate of their mass revival meetings. Sankey, the first paid musician in the revival tradition, sang these hymns at the mass meetings and composed many including "There Were Ninety and Nine," "Hold the Fort," and "Pull for the Shore, Sailor." Although such other composers as George Stebbins, Fanny Crosby, George Washington Doane, and P. P. Bliss were more prolific, the techniques of the Moody-Sankey team have left an indelible stamp of the character of American religion. Gospel hymns have a pervasive appeal in many Christian denominations for both musical and theological reasons. First, the gospel tradition is in the mode of popular music, with readily assimilated and straightforward melodies. Rather than the complicated harmonies of a Bach chorale or the sophisticated verses of a Charles Wesley, they are musically direct and often repetitive. Various strains of American popular music are evident throughout the development of gospel hymns. These strains include quick-step marches, a syncopated ragtime beat, minstrel songs, Tin Pan Alley chord progressions, and college fight songs. In general the texts of gospel hymns are also a simple appeal to the heart using sentimental language and urging the hearer to accept Jesus as savior and friend. Without complex theological demands, the saved Christian is urged to lead a pure and cheerful life, show God's love to others, and rest in assurance of heaven's tangible rewards. Wherever the influence of American revivalism exists in any part of the globe, there is also present a variation on the theme of gospel hymns.

[D. SMUCKER]

GOSPELS (ART), among celebrated extant examples of the art of manuscript illumination are the following:
Gospels of the Abbess Hitda of Meschede (*c.*1030), MS produced at Cologne in modified Reichenau style during the Ottonian Renaissance and now in the Darmstadt Library, Cologne.
Gospels of the Abbess Uta (Uota; 1002–25), illuminated MS of the Abbess Uta of Niedermünster, produced at Regensburg during the Ottonian Renaissance in a modified Reichenau style, showing the abbess presenting the MS to the Virgin. It is now in the Bayerische Staatsbibliotek, Munich.
Gospels of Charlemagne (Schatzkammer Gospels), early 9th–cent. The Carolingian illuminated MS of the Palace School style, showing linear expressionism and color-washed drawings, is now in the Schatzkammer, Vienna. See ADA, SCHOOL OF; GODESCALC.
Gospels of Henry II (1002–14), Ottonian illuminated MS from Bamberg, now in the Bayerische Staatsbibliotek, Munich.
Gospels of Mount Athos (10th cent.), Byzantine illuminated MS from the Stavronikita Monastery on Mt. Athos, one of the finest examples of the miniaturists of the Macedonian Renaissance, deriving from early Christian models with architectural background.
Gospels of Otto III (*c.*1000), illuminated MS in the Bayerische Staatsbibliotek, Munich, combining both Byzantine and Roman styles in a manner characteristic of the age of Otto III (980–1002).
Gospels of St. Chad, Hiberno-Saxon illuminated MS in the cathedral library, Lichfield, England.
Gospels of St. Médard of Soissons (early 9th cent.), MS of the Palace School of Charlemagne from the notable scriptorium at Metz, now in the Bibliothèque Nationale, Paris.

[M. J. DALY]

GOSPELS, APOCRYPHAL, see APOCRYPHA (NT).

GOSPELS, HARMONY OF THE, see HARMONY OF THE GOSPELS.

GOSPELS, THE HOLY, the four books of the NT in which the story of Jesus' preaching the good news of redemption is set forth. They constitute a literary genre that is *sui generis.* Although they have the same general theme, they often differ in the chronological setting of the narratives and even in the wording of important sayings of Jesus. Their authors used not only oral but also written sources in which parts of apostolic teaching were already gathered according to different patterns. This teaching was founded on what Jesus has said and done. It often reproduces his actual words; but it has also adapted and completed them to answer the theological, practical, and liturgical needs of the Christian communities. In the Gospels, these sources were used to fulfill a theological purpose which was fundamentally the same: "that you may believe that Jesus is the Christ, the Son of God, and that believing in him you may have life in his name" (Jn 20.31). The differences between the personalities of the authors and the communities for which they wrote explain the differences in the pictures they give of him. The four Gospels supplement one another to help us discover who he was and what he remains for his disciples. BIBLIOGRAPHY: D. M. Stanley, "New Understanding of the Gospels," *Bible in Current Catholic Thought* (ed. J. M. MacKenzie, 1962); "Instruction on the Historical Truth of the Gospel." CBQ 26 (1964).

[A. VIARD]

GOSSAERT (MABUSE), JAN (*c.*1478–1533), Flemish painter (called Mabuse from his birthplace Maubeuge). Working for Prince Philip of Burgundy, with whom he traveled to Rome (1508), he was deeply impressed by Italian art. Moving with the Habsburg-Burgundian rulers to residences in Utrecht, Bruges, and Brussels, G. achieved his mature style (1516–17), painting the diptych of his patron *Jean Carondelet Adoring the Virgin and Child* (1517, Louvre). Major panels dated on stylistic grounds are the *Adoration of the Kings* (London) and the *Malvagna Triptych* (Palermo) with *Agony in the Garden* (Berlin), all *c.*1512; *St. Luke Painting the Virgin* (*c.*1515, Prague) with another version in 1520, and an *Ecce Homo* (1527), often copied. G.'s classicism, showing from the influence of Dürer's engravings, fulsome figures denying ideal proportions and characterized by a meticulous Flemish technique and realism, resulted in an artificial Mannerist style, decorative and often bizarre. BIBLIOGRAPHY: M. J. Friedländer, *Die altniederländische Malerei* (1930).

[M. J. DALY]

GOSSIP, conversation or other exchange of information about the private affairs of others, usually acquaintances or neighbors. It centers commonly on matters less than creditable to the persons who are discussed and is often based upon unsubstantiated rumor. The attraction of conversation of this sort to some people seems to lie in its utility as an ego-building device; in a competitive world it is easier to think well of oneself if it is possible to think poorly of others. Although the ducking stool has passed out of fashion and the offender is now subject to no worldly penalties, except perhaps some loss of esteem and the risk of a possible (but highly improbable) suit for slander, the reprehensible nature of the popular diversion is still generally recognized. Its morality is judged according to the *rash judgment or suspicion, the unjust invasion of another's privacy, the *detraction or *calumny that may be involved, and the gravity of the harm done to the victim. BIBLIOGRAPHY: J. D. Fearon, NCE 6:640.

[P. K. MEAGHER]

GOSSNER, JOHANNES EVANGELISTA (1773–1858), influential German pastor and preacher, famous for his zeal for social welfare and the foreign missions. Born at Hausen near Günzburg, he was ordained in 1796. As a priest he was strongly influenced by J. M. Sailer and M. Boos. In 1819 he withdrew from the Catholic ministry and in 1826 converted to the Evangelical faith; became a preacher in 1829, serving in the Bethlehem Church in Berlin from 1829–1846. He founded schools for children, a hospital, and in 1838 a mission society. His numerous writings, much read in his day, reflect his concern for a humane system of social welfare and his zeal for foreign missions.

[E. J. DILLON]

GOSWIN, ST. (d. 1165 or 1166), abbot of Anchin, near Douai, scholar. As a student at Paris he engaged in controversy with Peter Abelard, then teaching at Mont Ste.-Geneviève. G. was a canon and also a teacher at Douai before becoming a Benedictine at Anchin *c.* 1112. He was devoted to monastic discipline. As prior at St. Médard, Soissons, he gave Abelard hospitality after the condemnation by the Council of Soissons in 1121. G. was elected abbot of Anchin in 1131 and under his direction the monks produced many superbly illuminated manuscripts. From the time of his death he was venerated as a saint. BIBLIOGRAPHY: R. Van Doren, BiblSanct 7:132–133; M. G. Blayo, DHGE 2:1516–24, s.v. "Anchin."

[T. C. O'BRIEN]

GOTHER, JOHN (d. 1704), English Catholic priest. In 1668 G. entered the English College in Lisbon. After ordination he became prefect and supervisor of studies there. His most famous work, *A Papist Misrepresented and Represented* (1685, 1687), gave rise to much controversy. He later became chaplain at Warkworth Castle, where he received R. Challoner into the Church. Gillow, BDEC 2:540–546.

[M. J. SUELZER]

GOTHIC ART, an artistic phase originating in 12th-cent. Northern France and spreading throughout Western Europe from the 13th through the 15th century. First developed in ecclesiastical architecture, the Gothic structure an ogival construction (raising of all ribs to equal height) of ribbed vaults, clustered piers and flying buttresses. This skeletal system carried the heavy masonry load, thus opening the walls for large areas of stained glass and raising vast other-worldly interiors in the great cathedrals of Chartres (1194), Amiens (1220) and Reims (1211). Along with this, new religious themes and devotional images emerged in sculptural ornamentation, manuscript illumination, tapestries, textiles, embroideries, and virtually all the arts and produced a rich variety of regional and national styles ranging from Early to Late "Gothic" art. BIBLIOGRAPHY: A. Martindale, *Gothic Art From the Twelfth to Fifteenth Centuries* (1967). *CATHEDRALS; *CHARTRES, *AMIENS.

[R. J. VEROSTKO]

GOTHIC BIBLE, the translation (perhaps of only the NT) by *Ulfilas (*c.*311–382 or 383) for which he invented a Gothic alphabet based on Greek, Latin, and runic characters. The best MS is the 6th-cent. *Codex Argenteus* in Upsala. BIBLIOGRAPHY: *Die gotische Bibel* (ed. W. Streitberg, 2 v. in 1, 3d ed., 1950); G. W. S. Friedrichsen, *Gothic Studies* (1961).

[M. F. MCCARTHY]

GOTHIC REVIVAL, 18th-cent. romantic revival of Gothic architectural and decorative forms introduced in English domestic buildings of exotic charm and playfulness (Strawberry Hill, 1755, of Horace Walpole), witty anomalies of "artful wildness" and "built ruins" in parks (Hagley Park) and the apotheosis in the exotic Royal Pavilion (1815–18) at Brighton by Sir John Nash. The 19th-cent. Gothic Revival extended to civic and ecclesiastical buildings (1830–75) with pseudo-Gothic Houses of Parliament (1836) by C. Barry and A. Welby Pugin, work by Viollet-le-Duc (France), an alternate Gothic plan by B. Latrobe for his final neoclassical cathedral of Baltimore, designs by R. A. Cram and Goodhue in the U.S., and others.

[M. J. DALY]

GOTHIC RITE, see MOZARABIC RITE.

GOTHIC VESTMENTS. "Gothic" has reference to the artistic style of the 13th, 14th, and 15th centuries. In recent usage it has referred to chasubles of full and flowing cut, as distinguished from the clipped, abbreviated, and stiffened Roman or "fiddleback" chasuble. The Roman vestments of ancient and medieval times were of Gothic style.

[J. DALLEN]

GOTTFRIED VON STRASSBURG (fl. 1210), medieval stylist and author of the Middle High German courtly epic *Tristan* (*c.* 1210); probably a burgher, though well-educated and thoroughly familiar with courtly manners. His *Tristan,* often referred to as the "Canticle of Canticles of Courtly Love," presents an aesthetic and humanistic idealization of illicit love, emancipating it from the *Gott und der Welt gefallen* (to please God and the world) of the courtly code and giving it—whether with blasphemous intent or not is still a moot question—its own theology and its own transcendent code of morality. For a good discussion in English, see the Introduction to Gottfried von Strassburg's *Tristan,* (in the edition tr. A. T. Hatto, 1960); for bibliography, see W. Kosch, *Deutsches Literatur-Lexikon* (1963) 122.

[M. F. MCCARTHY]

GOTTHARD, ST., see GODARD OF HILDESHEIM, ST.

GOTTHELF, JEREMIAS (pen name of Albert Bitzius; 1797–1854), Swiss novelist. A Protestant pastor in Switzerland, G. was from 1835 to 1845 commissioner of primary and secondary education for the Canton of Bern. As an educator he was a follower of Pestalozzi. A sharp observer of peasant life, a foe of materialism and secularism, G. devoted many years to the writing of novels. They are notable for faithfulness to village life, their Christian themes and moral purpose, and their psychological insight. Of his 24 volumes of fiction the most memorable are *Ulric the Farmhand* (1841), *Ulric the Tenant-Farmer* (1847) and the novellas *Elsie die seltsame Magd* (1842) and *Die schwartze Spinner* (1842).

[J. R. AHERNE]

GOTTI, VINCENZO LUDOVICO (1664–1742), Dominican theologian, cardinal-priest, and titular patriarch of Jerusalem from 1728. A native of Bologna, he became professor of theology at the university there in 1695, after having taught in studia of his order. He became known for his many apologetical and polemical writings in defense of the RC Church, esp. against Calvinist authors. His *Theologia scholastico-dogmatica iuxta mentem D. Thomae* (16 v., 1727–35), also emphasizes defense of Catholic teaching against heresy. He strongly opposed Jansenism. BIBLIOGRAPHY: Quétif-Échard 2.2:814.

[T. C. O'BRIEN]

GOTTSCHALK, ST. (d. 1066), martyr. G. was a prince, educated in Lüneburg which he left to avenge the murder of his father, Uto; then, forced into exile in England, he served King Canute whose daughter he married. In 1043, G. returned as ruler and apostle of his people with Adalbert of Bremen; they founded the dioceses of Mecklenburg and Ratzeburg. In the reaction to Adalbert's fall in 1066, G. was martyred. BIBLIOGRAPHY: F. Dvornik, *Slavs: Their Early History and Civilization* (1956) 297–300; Butler 2:496; N. Del Re, BiblSanct 7:77–78.

[M. E. DUFFY]

GOTTSCHALK OF LIMBURG (*c.*1015–1098), a monk of the monastery of Limburg, court chaplain to Henry IV, and provost of the church of the Bl. Virgin in Aachen. G.'s chief distinction is his authorship of more than 20 Sequences which have been preserved with their melodies. These compositions were written for use at Mass on various feast days esp. those of Our Lord and the Bl. Virgin. The sequences are surprisingly rich in biblical allusions and show deep poetical feeling. G. wrote in the great tradition of *Notker Balbulus. BIBLIOGRAPHY: Raby CLP 224–225; H. Dressler, NCE 6:647–648.

[H. DRESSLER]

GOTTSCHALK OF ORBAIS (*c.*803–*c.*868), monk, theologian, poet. Committed as a child by his parents to the Abbey of Fulda, G. left the monastery before receiving major orders and was absolved of his monastic obligations by the Synod of Mainz (829). This dispensation was rescinded upon the objection of Rabanus Maurus; and he was obliged to return to the monastic life and take an assignment to the monastery of Orbais, where he devoted himself to theology. He developed a doctrine of extreme predestinationism, holding for a double predestination, one to life, and the other a positive reprobation to death. Hincmar of Reims, charged by the Synod of Mainz (848) with the responsibility of dealing with him, had him imprisoned by the judgment of another synod held at Quiercy-sur-Oise (849). Hincmar also wrote against his doctrine on predestination as well as against his trinitarian theology. G. was mentally deranged toward the end of his life, possibly in consequence of the harsh treatment he had received, and refused to the end to abjure his errors. His few extant poems show him to have been among the leading poets of the Carolingian era. Works: *Oeuvres théologiques et grammaticales de Godescalc d'Orbais,* SSL, 20 (1945); poetry, MGH Poetae 3:707–738; 4:934; 6:86–106. BIBLIOGRAPHY: Szövérffy 1:235–244; P. Delhaye, *Medieval Christian Philosophy* (tr. S. J. Tester, 1960) 47–48.

[M. S. TANEY]

GÖTTWEIG, ABBEY OF, founded in the Diocese of St. Pölten, Austria, *c.*1070 by Bp. Altmann of Passau for Augustinian Canons, it was in 1090 committed to Benedictines from St. Blasien. Still today the abbey is an important center of culture and cares for many parishes. The magnificent baroque buildings situated on the top of a mountain were almost totally destroyed by fire in 1718, and the splendid reconstruction planned and begun the same year by L. v. Hildebrand was never completed. BIBLIOGRAPHY: L. Koller, *Abtei Göttweig* (1953); *Festschrift,* ''Der hl. Altmann'' (1965).

[F. H. RÖHRIG]

GOUDIN, ANTOINE (1639–95), Dominican philosopher and theologian, a native of Limoges, professor at Avignon and Paris, where he was prior of the convent of St.-Jacques. He was not the last French Thomist to run athwart the narrower and more rigorous Thomism professed by his order in Rome, represented in G.'s case by A. Massoulié. G.'s four-volume *Philosophy according to the unshaken and secure teachings of St. Thomas* remains a compendium esteemed for its accuracy and rare elegance (12th ed., 1859). His posthumous *Theological treatises according to the unshaken, etc.* (2d ed. A. M. Dummermuth, 1874) have been suspected by some of having been touched up by the Roman authorities. In fact, however, it seems he would not have resented the corrections, which were made by a German Dominican sympathetic to his views. The evidence for his position afforded by the correspondence of his close friend, Richard Simon, is to be treated with caution; if not a Molinist, Simon was irked by an exclusively Augustinian doctrine of grace and appealed to a sunnier humanism in

Chrysostom, Damascene, and even Jerome. What seems certain is that G.'s exact Thomism found nothing in common with the hatchetmen in the controversies on grace, not least when they were clumsy. His effort was to disengage his master from Jansenism, and in doing so, why should one not speak with a smile? He pleasantly compared those Dominicans who shunned the Jesuits to the Jews forbidden to have commerce with the Samaritans. BIBLIOGRAPHY: R. Coulon, DTC 6.2:1508–16.

[T. GILBY]

GOUGAUD, LOUIS (1877–1941), historian. Ordained as a Benedictine in 1909, he served in the French army in World War I. The rest of his life of scholarship was spent at St. Michael Abbey in England. His work became well known in the fields of Celtic and monastic history. Among his published works are *Les Chrétientés celtiques* (1911), *Gaelic Pioneers of Christianity* (1932), and *Les saints irlandais* (1936).

[J. R. AHERNE]

GOUJON, JEAN (1510–betw. 64–68), finest French sculptor of the 16th century, G. executed in Rouen columnar supports of the organ in the church of St. Maclou and the tomb of Louis de Brézé in the cathedral. With architect P. Lescot, G. carved the rood screen in the church of St. Germain l'Auxerrois (Louvre) and in 1547 did woodcuts for a French publication of Vitruvius. For the Louvre Pavilion of Henry II, which P. Lescot designed, G. carved (1546) the famous Gallery of the Caryatids, quite destroyed by 19th-cent. "restoration." His most famous *Fontaine des Innocents* (1548–49; Louvre), with elongated figures in the style of Primaticcio, evidences the blend of classical purity with French delicacy, which was the unique distinction of 16th-cent. French art.

[M. J. DALY]

GOULD, SABINE BARING-, see BARING-GOULD, SABINE.

GOUNOD, CHARLES FRANÇOIS (1818–93), French romantic composer. As a youth G. studied organ and composition in Rome. Upon return to his birthplace, Paris, he studied theology for 2 years, but decided against taking orders. Instead he spent most of his life composing operas, among them the familiar *Faust* and *Romeo and Juliet*. He turned to writing religious music in the last decade of his life, esp. in the oratorio form. Dating from an influential 5-year stay in London, these oratorios include *Redemption, Death and Life,* and *Mass in the Memory of Joan of Arc*. Both Gounod's sacred and secular compositions favor lyrical, sensual, and often mystical elements. His main influence on church music today can be found in numerous Anglican anthems.

[D. SMUCKER]

GOUPIL, RENÉ, ST. (1606–42), surgeon, martyr. Born at Anjou, he entered the Jesuits but was forced by ill health to leave. He became a surgeon and in 1638 went to Quebec to work with the Jesuits on the Huron missions. While traveling in 1642 with Isaac *Jogues, he and his companion were captured by Iroquois. After 2 months of torture, he died under the tomahawk Sept. 29 in the presence of Jogues, near Albany, New York. *NORTH AMERICAN MARTYRS.

[P. K. MEAGHER]

GOUSSET, THOMAS MARIE JOSEPH (1792–1866), French theologian, bp., and cardinal. He was ordained in 1817 and taught theology at the Grand Séminaire, Besançon. He gained renown by his theological publications: *Conférences ecclésiastiques d'Angers* (26 v., 1823); *Dictionnaire théologique* (1826); *Théologie morale* (2 v., 1844); *Théologie dogmatique* (2 v., 1848, 1856); *Exposition des principes du droit canonique* (1859); and *Du droit de l'Église touchant . . . la souveraineté temporelle du pape* (1862). In 1836 G. was appointed, because of his anti-Gallican leadership, bp. of Périgueux; there he wrote his *Observations sur la liberté d'enseignement,* a defense of freedom in university teaching. He was created cardinal in 1858 and was named commander of the French Legion of Honor.

[J. R. AHERNE]

GOVERNMENT, DIVINE, the execution of the plan of divine *providence for the universe through the causal workings toward their ends of all things set in being by divine *creation and maintained in being by divine *conservation. "It is thy providence, O Father, that steers the course" (Wis 14.3). That God is the first cause, efficient, final, and exemplar, of all activity is the key notion; that creatures themselves are true causes has to be made compatible with this. Special difficulties arise when they are also free and possibly rebellious causes: cf. *predestination, *premotion, *Bañezianism, and *Molinism. The following remarks are meant to clear the ground.

A Dionysian tradition takes biblical references to God's being jealous in the sense less of his tolerating no unfaithfulness than of his zealous cherishing of the natures he has created so that his governing respects and fosters their own proper activities. The thought that divine Wisdom "reaches mightily from one end of the earth to the other and orders all things sweetly and well" (Wis 8.1) runs throughout the classical treatises on divine government, which do not agree with *Malebranche that the first cause is the unique cause and that creatures are only occasions for its productive action. The motivation of his *occasionalism was mainly religious, as it had been with the Muslim Mutakallims in upholding the exclusive causality of God against the Aristotelian teaching that natures were principles and centers of activity.

True causality might still be credited to creatures by allowing that they were *instrumental causes, acting in virtue of a transient activation communicated to them from above. Hallowed usage refers to us as instruments in the hands of God. Nevertheless, the word has not its special and technical sense when applied to activities within our own proper field, which embraces grace as well as nature, for charity is *our* loving (cf. ST 2a2ae, 23.2), but only when applied to activities which are lifted out of this field, *praeter ordinem,* as with the working of miracles. St. Thomas speaks for the majority of Catholic theologians when he holds that the world is composed of real things, and in particular of human beings who are real substances, which are true efficient causes in virtue of their own stable active forms. In other words dividing efficient causes into the first cause and instrumental causes becomes a bit like dividing humanity into men and unmarried women. Rather the initial division should be between the first cause and secondary causes (always remembering of course that the former does not really fall within the division but transcends it), followed by a subdivision of secondary causes into principal and instrumental causes.

Since government implies purpose, this division should be transposed from efficient into final causality, so that the initial division should not be between the ultimate end and the means, but between the ultimate and the intermediate, this last being subdivided into objects of value in themselves, and therefore ends, and objects of value only for the sake of something else, and therefore purely means. All this has an important bearing on the spiritual teaching on "attachment to creatures" and on a teleological theology which maintains that while the objective end of things is God who is "outside" the world, the fulfillment of processes is in their subjects: thus that God made men for himself also means that he made them to be happy. "The Lord hath made everything for its purpose" (Pr 16.4).

The universe as governed by God, which should be pictured as a polity rather than a despotism, is a hierarchy of true values in subordination. The notion of a cause which is at once both secondary and subordinate will become easier than it looks at first sight if we treat "principal" less in the superlative than in the comparative sense, of being the chief in a particular order which is secondary to a wider order, or even in its sense according to law, namely of being the responsible agent.

So much for the grammar. Now for some headings. The whole universe is governed by divine wisdom down to every particular, even the least, down to every nuance, even the slightest. It all converges to a unity, for the one Lord is its sole ruler; his purpose is not to gain anything thereby, but to bring all things to perfection by somehow reflecting some of his perfection, his power, his justice, above all his happiness in theirs. Each and every effect is immediately present in his vision, yet some effects are produced through intermediate agents, though divine causality continues into all that is positive in their actions. None, even though he set up a faction against some secondary order or system, can escape from God's universal rule. BIBLIOGRAPHY: ThAq ST 1a, 103 (esp. in ed. Lat-Eng, v. 14, ed. T. C. O'Brien).

[T. GILBY]

GOWER, JOHN (*c.*1325–1408), English poet, friend of Chaucer. His three major works, written in three different languages (French, Latin, and English) are concerned with the ills of contemporary society in England due in G.'s opinion to man's deviation from virtue, good order, and reason. The English poem, *Confessio Amantis,* praises the moral order which can be preserved only by wisdom and virtue, and displays G.'s gift as a storyteller. The tales are drawn from classical or medieval sources to illustrate the seven deadly sins, and the poems show G. as a poet of reform, not of revolt. G. did much to help establish a standard English literary language and for this reason is often linked with Chaucer, but he does not possess Chaucer's genius. BIBLIOGRAPHY: P. J. Lennox, CE 6:685–686.

[M. J. BARRY]

GOYA Y LUCIENTES, FRANCISCO JOSÉ DE (1746–1828), Spanish painter, graphic artist, master tapestry designer. He is acclaimed for his "presumed" satirical portraits of the Spanish royal family (*Family of Charles IV,* 1800), certain macabre and familiarly known paintings (*Saturn Devouring His Son, c.*1820–22; *Maja desnuda,* 1800–02; *Third of May, 1808, c.*1814); and cycles of etchings dealing with human folly, abuse in the Church, war, and bullfights (*Los caprichos,* 1796–98; *Los desastres de la guerra,* 1808–14; *Los proverbios,* 1813–18; and *Tauromachia,* 1815). Considered a revolutionary G. was a passionate observer and critic of his time seeking despairingly for reason in man's actions. He executed some exceptional and sincere religious paintings, among them the famous *Fiesta of S. Isidoro* (1787, Prado), a masterpiece of 18th-cent. *peinture claire,* and the technically advanced frescoes of the life of St. Anthony at S. Antonio de la Florida, Madrid (1798–99), *The Last Communion of St. Joseph of Calasanz* (1819), and *The Agony in the Garden* (1819). G.'s genius in decoration, portraiture and graphics, prefiguring the Romanticism of Delacroix, Manet, and Daumier in urgency and expressionistic style, made Spain a dominant influence in 19th cent. French painting. BIBLIOGRAPHY: F. Sánchez-Cantón, *Goya* (tr. H. Mins, 1964); A. Malraux, *Saturn, an Essay on Goya* (1957).

[L. A. LEITE]

GOYAU, GEORGES (1869–1939), layman, church historian. A close student of history, G. taught at the Institut Catholique of Paris and was a consultor in history for the Sacred Congregation of Rites. G. wrote nearly 100 works on ecclesiastical history; well-known among them were *Allemagne religieuse* (9 v., 1898–1913), on the Church in modern Germany, and *Histoire religieuse de la nation* *française* (1922). BIBLIOGRAPHY: F. Veuillot, *G. Goyau* (1942).

[J. R. AHERNE]

GOYENECHE Y BARREDA, JOSÉ SEBASTIÁN DE (1784–1872), Peruvian prelate during the crisis of emancipation, during the period of transition between the viceroyalty and the republic. Having studied law and theology at the Univ. of San Marcos, he was ordained in 1807 and became bishop of Arequipa in 1817. Although he fought for the integrity of the Church, he was loyal to the republic and helped consolidate republican institutions. He was one of the few bishops who had the wisdom to maintain his see during tumultuous times, so that he had to look after other dioceses as well. G. was made apostolic delegate in Peru (1832) by Gregory XVI, and later became abp. of Lima (1859).

[E. J. DILLON]

GOZZOLI, BENOZZO (1420–97), Italian painter, student of Fra Angelico, famous for the fresco, *Journey of the Magi* (1459), in the Medici-Riccardi Palace, Florence, showing, in Renaissance convention, members of the Medici family as the wise men and a self-portrait. The fresco, though relating in decorative quality to Gentile da Fabriano's work, is quite distinct, evidencing G.'s impressive command of foreshortening and perspective in figures posed in challenging anatomic juxtapositions. The figures move around the chapel toward Fra Filippo Lippi's *Madonna Adoring the Child* over the altar. G. painted a *Madonna and Saints* (1461) and worked in Viterbo, Perugia, and San Gimignano (1463). In 1467–84 he painted important frescoes in the Camposanto, Pisa (destroyed in World War II). His banners and other commissions in variety of form and fantasy relate to the International Style while including his distinctive genere details.

DM. J. DALY]

GRABMANN, MARTIN (1875–1949), theologian, historian. He was professor of dogma at Eichstätt Seminary (1906–13), of Christian philosophy at the Univ. of Vienna (1913–18), and of dogma at the Univ. of Munich (1918–39; 1945–48). His special fields of activity were the history of scholasticism and Aristotelianism, Thomism, and German mysticism. He was particularly assiduous in reproducing lost MSS of Siger of Brabant, Albert the Great, Boethius, Meister Eckhart, and other medieval scholars. There is a Grabmann Institute at the Univ. of Munich to promote the study of medieval philosophy and theology. BIBLIOGRAPHY: J. Van der Meersch, DTC 16.1:1843–44.

[J. J. SMITH]

GRACE (*gratia*, Vulg tr. of Gr. NT word *charis*), understood to mean God's favor, either in the sense of divine gratuitous love for man or as a gift received in virtue of that love.

Gratuitousness of Grace. In the West, *Pelagianism viewed man's own nature as ''grace,'' with the capacity to achieve eternal life without any special divine assistance. The essential reaction of St. Augustine became a position to which almost all Christian Churches have given common assent, at least in principle. Grace comes from the special divine favor of *predestination; it is absolutely gratuitous; no disposition native to man, nor anything that he can do on his own as a *good work does in fact call down or merit God's favor; the gratuitousness of grace is the greater because of the sinfulness of man's fallen state. In the foremost medieval theological synthesis on grace, St. Thomas Aquinas largely incorporated Augustine's teaching but took a more restrained view of the Fall, precisely distinguished man's natural from his grace-given capacities, and affirmed that grace is inwardly received in man, enabling, transforming, and empowering him for a new life.

*Luther's intuitive reassertion of the gratuitousness of grace was a reaction to what seemed a new Pelagianism, the optimistic exaltation of good works by *nominalism. The Lutheran doctrine is characterized first of all by close association between grace and faith. By faith alone, which is itself a gift of God and not a good work, the believer is made receptive to the graciousness of the merciful God. Grace is utterly beyond merit in any sense, even after justification through faith. The graciousness of God's gift is in contrast with man's utter sinfulness; if not Luther himself, his followers understood the justified man to remain inherently sinful, with righteousness not inherent in, but imputed to, him (see FORENSIC JUSTIFICATION). *Calvinism and the *Reformed Churches use the term grace almost exclusively in reference to the divine good pleasure. God's graciousness is emphasized by the characteristic doctrine of *double predestination, according to which God chooses some men to be saved from sin, while reprobating others. The mystical doctrines of some Anabaptists, and the Quakers' *Inner Light teaching, regarded man more optimistically and God's grace as within the believer. But the predominant emphasis in Protestant teaching remained the free grace of God saving ever-sinful man. *Liberal theology made most of this emphasis irrelevant by effacing in effect the distinction between grace and nature and by diluting the meaning of sin and of God's saving interventions in human history.

The Council of *Trent enunciated RC teaching by reaffirming the gratuitousness of grace and its saving, transforming effect on man. The transformation consists in a share in God's own righteousness imparted to the recipient, so that he inwardly has the power to live the life of grace. Man by the free grace of God is given the power to consent in the process of his justification and to work out the progress of his salvation. The good works that proceed from the grace-given life in him are at once a gift, since God is their first source, and are meritorious, since these acts are a real exercise of freedom by man living under grace. RC theology seeks to express this teaching by elaborating the distinction between actual grace (enlightenment, inspiration, influence upon the human will) given in sufficiency to all men according to the foreknowledge of God; and sanctifying grace, an inner, abiding share in God's own righteousness, a source of new life.

Dynamics of Living in Grace. The relationship of grace to human responsibility and freedom has led to controversies, even to the formations of new Churches or new emphases in the Christian life. Against Pelagian exaltation of free will, St. Augustine insisted that fallen human nature is so corrupt that no act of free choice (*liberum arbitrium*) has any effectiveness for salvation. *Irresistible grace alone, the effect of God's predestination, gives the freedom (*libertas*) of the sons of God. Man needs this grace to keep his power of free choice from leading him into personal sin, for which he is responsible. *Semi-Pelagianism gave to human freedom the power to initiate the process of salvation, which grace would perfect. Council of *Orange II (529) taught that the whole process of salvation, which includes man's own willing, is a gift of grace. St. Thomas Aquinas sought to explain human freedom under grace through God's transcendent causality, acting effectively but without coercing the will to bring about man's free choices. The Council of Trent stressed man's free, active cooperation in receiving grace and living in grace. the *Congregatio de auxiliis (1597–1607) centered on the question whether grace became fruitful, either in conversion or subsequently, from its inherent efficacy or from the response of the human will. *Quietism was an extreme interpretation of the passivity of man under grace. *Jansenism, which claimed the authority of St. Augustine, stressed the total sinfulness of human nature and man's need of the irresistible, necessitating power of grace.

To Luther free will and its native activities belonged to the level at which man was a sinner, and from which he was saved by grace; human freedom was irrelevant to the order of grace. The *Synergistic Controversy, however, arose within Lutheranism because of P. *Melanchthon's theories of human cooperation in conversion. Freedom and responsibility were simply not entertained as problems in the Calvinist system, with its roots in the absolute sovereignty of God's predestination of the elect. Historic *Arminianism, however, rejected absolute predestination and irresistible grace, defending the role of human freedom; it gave its name, as well, to an interpretation of salvation and the Christian life stressing human effort. This attitude has been a particularly pronounced feature in American Protestantism, esp. through *revivalism. While many of the Churches retained their adherence to classic Lutheran or Calvinist doctrines, the widespread effect of revivalist preaching put an emphasis upon the believer's power to choose to be saved and to live righteously. In liberal theology human capacity to prepare oneself for grace was simply an irrelevancy. In recent years both RC and Protestant theologians have sought to free their explanations of the mystery of grace from overtones of polemics and controversy; to interpret the essential meaning of historic confessional formulations; and esp. to give a richer, more biblical expression to the nature of grace.

[M. B. SCHEPERS]

GRACE (IN THE BIBLE), a translation of the Gr. *charis,* which in profane Gr. meant that which causes joy, and in its scriptural use signified the gratuitous supernatural gift of God, God's favor, resulting in the new economy and favors of external providence. In Hebrew it was usually *ḥēn* (first, God's favor; then later, effects of that favor). A few times it was *raḥămîm* (tender mercy), or *rāṣôn* (benevolent love), or *ḥesed* (dutiful love, which should cause kinsmen to help one another). The OT first stresses the favor of being God's chosen people, living in a kinship bond (*ḥesed*) with him, since by the covenant he bound himself to act as father and *gō'ēl* (kinsman-rescuer). The OT mentions other effects, esp. *b^e^rākâ* (blessing), which gives joy, strength, fullness of life, special relationship to God, and wisdom, making one spiritually perfect. The Synoptic Gospels give a similar picture: Grace brings man under a new covenant (Mt 26.28) into the kingdom of the Father (Mt 22.1–14) as his children (Mt 6.9–10) who must imitate him (Mt 5.48). John stresses grace as light and truth, passage from death to life (Jn 5.24), a share in divine life (Jn 10.10) through rebirth (Jn 3.3). Paul pictures progressive transformation making man a new creation (Gal 6.15), a temple of the Spirit (1 Cor 3.16–17), a member of Christ (1 Cor 6.15), son of the Father (Rom 8.14–17), no longer coerced by external law (Rom 7.4–6), but moved inwardly by the Spirit (Rom 8.14), who effects both exterior performance of good and the inner act of will (Phil 2.13) and even the thought of good (2 Cor 3.5). Paul distinguishes greater gifts (1 Cor 12.13) open to all, conferring the above effects, and charismatic gifts, giving roles as apostles, prophets, teachers, or gifts of tongues, interpretation, healing, etc. (1 Cor 12.30).

There is a theme of restriction and another of universality in the OT's treatment of the receiver of grace. Restriction appears in the fact that Israel is a special people—a favor not given to all, nor from merit (Ex 33.19). Universality appears in Gen 12.3 and Is 49.6 and in other passages that foretell the call of all nations. The NT seldom expresses restriction (e.g., Mt 10.5–6; Rom 9; 1 Cor 1.26–31), but often universality: the Father gave the Son for all (Jn 3.16), even sinners (Mt 5.45; 18.23–25; Lk 15.3–9) and has even bound himself in a new, eternal covenant (Mt 26.28; 1 Cor 11.25) in which the infinite price (1 Cor 6.20) for each individual (Gal 2.20) testifies to infinite love, so that he wills to give all graces (Rom 8.32), even perseverance to the end (1 Cor 1.5–8; 1 Th 5.23–24). The two themes are compatible: restrictive statements refer to internal grace aimed immediately at eternal eschatological salvation; universal statements, to his will that all be saved (1 Tim 2.4), and the fact that one can be saved without the external favor (Rom 2.14–16). Not only the external favor, but even justification, the first step to eschatological salvation, is gratuitous (Rom 11.6; 4.4), not depending on works of the Law (Rom 3.20, 28). Yet reception of justification depends on faith (Rom 1.17; 3.28), which is not only intellectual assent but also confidence, obedience of will adhering to God (Rom 10.16), and active love (Gal 5.6). This condition is in our power: Paul urges that the grace be not received in vain (2 Cor 6.1). Although we cannot earn justification, it is offered to all; since God wills all saved and bound himself in covenant to offer all graces to each man (Rom 8.32; Gal 2.20). Though we cannot even accept grace by our own power (Phil 2.13), we can reject or not reject. Gratuity does not preclude merit. ''Merit'' does not occur in Scripture, but its basis does (2 Tim 4.8; 2 Cor 5.10). But we earn only on a secondary level, in that the Father has bound himself by covenant and promises to reward. Yet, the basic reason he gives is still because he is our Father. We can reject grace even in a basic sense (cf. Rom 6.23). BIBLIOGRAPHY: J. Bonsirven, *Theology of the New Testament* (tr. S. F. Tye, 1963) 34–127; 130–139; 251; 270–351.

[W. G. MOST]

GRACE, ACTUAL, the divine help given to a person, prompting those acts of mind and will that belong to salvation. The term actual serves to distinguish it from sanctifying grace, which later scholastics referred to as *habitual grace; it denotes the help as given at the moment of the exercise of a concrete action of mind or of will. Against *Pelagianism St. *Augustine emphasized continual dependence upon this divine help, both for the beginning and completion of *justification, and for the subsequent process of salvation; the strongest church declaration on this dependence was given by the Council of Trent, Decree on Justification (D 1520–83). *GRACE, CONTROVERSIES ON; GRACE AND FREEDOM.

[T. C. O'BRIEN]

GRACE, BAPTISMAL, the sanctifying newness effected through the sacrament (see GRACE, SACRAMENTAL): rebirth into adopted sonship and liberation from all sin, original and, in the case of adults, personal; incorporation into Christ and thereby into the Church, Christ's body. The baptismal liturgy and theology both seek to express the Pauline teaching of a complete death to sin and a resurrection to new life in Christ (Rom 6.3 ff). ''The one baptized shares in the Passion of Christ as though he himself had undergone that Passion'' is the reason Aquinas gives for the unique completeness of sanctification effected by baptism (ThAq ST 3a, 69.2). Baptismal grace, though not the *sacramental character, is received extrasacramentally by *Baptism of desire or of blood.

[T. C. O'BRIEN]

GRACE, CONSCIOUSNESS OF, an experienced awareness of the presence and working of grace in oneself. Grace empowers a person to live a life of knowing and loving God; self-awareness, a concomitant reflexiveness, is characteristic of such vital actions. Even as in the case of purely natural knowing and willing (ThAq *De ver.* 10.8), the concomitant consciousness is first of all of the acts themselves; then and thereby of their objects, i.e., uncreated grace, the Divine Persons present, and of their inner source, i.e., created grace, the gifts of God abiding in the soul (see GRACE, HABITUAL). The cognitive quality of this consciousness, however, is limited by faith, the objects of which always remain believed, not evident; thus awareness of grace is not equivalent to *assurance of salvation (ThAq *De ver.* 6.5 ad 3). The awareness, however, is more intense and more interior than simply a moral certitude about one's state of soul derived, e.g., from an examination of conscience. On the basis of affectivity, esp. of charity's union with God, there can be a quasi-experiential sense both of the affections themselves and of their divine object (ThAq ST 1a, 43.3 ad 1; 5 ad 2). Such experience is particularly associated with the gifts of the *Holy Spirit; since these are necessary for salvation (*ibid.* 1a2ae, 68.2) the experience need not be regarded as exclusive to mystics, nor as a suspect idea.

[T. C. O'BRIEN]

GRACE, CONTROVERSIES ON. The more noteworthy are: (1) The conflict with *Pelagianism, and then with *Semi-Pelagianism. The anti-Pelagian writings of St. *Augustine largely shaped Western theology of grace; he esp. defended the completely unmerited quality and the absolute sovereignty of grace for the beginning, continuance, and completion of the process of salvation (see ORANGE, COUNCILS OF). (2) Hincmar of Reims opposed the absolute predestinationism of *Gottschalk of Orbais in the 9th century (see QUIERCY, COUNCIL OF). (3) Their opponents in the 14th and 15th cent. branded the Nominalists' teaching on God's foreknowledge and predestination and on the natural power of free will to merit first grace a new Pelagianism (see DURANDUS OF ST. POURÇAIN; WILLIAM OF OCKHAM; GREGORY OF RIMINI; BIEL, GABRIEL, THOMAS BRADWARDINE). (4) The Reformation and Counter Reformation doctrinally centered chiefly on the meaning and workings of grace. The protest *sola fide, sola gratia* against the exaltation of good works, was an accusation that Rome had denied the absolute gratuitousness of grace and the sinful bondage of man; the Council of Trent both affirmed the primacy of grace and denied its irresistibility, man's total depravity and merely imputed grace. (5) The *Congregatio (divinae gratiae) de auxiliis (1597–1607) was an attempt at Rome to adjudicate a dispute, originating between Spanish Dominicans and Jesuits, on the infallible efficacy of grace. From this era on, two basic Catholic positions emerged as orthodox: grace is effective because of its inner influence on man's will, prompting consent either directly (Dominican position) or by persuasive attraction (Augustinian position); grace is effective because of circumstances or other factors favorable to its acceptance and infallibly foreseen by the divine *scientia media* (see MOLINISM). In the tortuous doctrinal and political history of *Jansenism, the critical issue was Rome's proscription (D 2001–06) of five propositions extracted from the *Augustinus* of Cornelius *Jansen, because they limited God's saving will and efficacious grace to the few elect, and denied a truly sufficient grace given to all. (6) Modern theological debate has been marked by attempts to give a more Trinitarian emphasis to the treatment of grace and to recover the neglected riches of the early Eastern Fathers on sanctifying grace as a deification; and to achieve a more objective Catholic-Protestant interchange on each other's tradition in this matter. BIBLIOGRAPHY: E. M. Burke, NCE 6:666–668.

[T. C. O'BRIEN]

GRACE, CREATED, a gratuitous gift of God to a created intellectual being. This grace may be external, i.e., something outside the one to whom it is given; e.g., the Church or the sacraments in relation to man. It may also be internal, i.e., a special effect produced by God in the substance or the powers of a rational creature. To be a grace this effect must be supernatural, that is, beyond the power of nature to produce or attain and not due to nature as such. Instances of created internal graces are sanctifying grace, a habit produced in the soul by God, and actual grace. Illuminations of the mind concerning things that pertain to salvation are actual graces, so also impulses of the will toward some supernatural good. The habit that will be infused into the soul of the just man after death, called the light of glory and also the act of seeing God face to face, called the beatific vision, are created graces. The word created does not mean, according to the more common opinion of theologians, that the grace is created in the strict sense of that word, that is, produced by God out of nothing. The word is used rather to express the fact that the supernatural effects of God's action are distinct from God himself and caused by him in the rational creature. BIBLIOGRAPHY: I. Willig, *Geschaffene und Ungeschaffene Gnade* (1964).

[T. J. MOTHERWAY]

GRACE, EFFICACIOUS, a term used primarily to signify a grace that infallibly moves a man to perform an act leading to salvation while leaving him perfectly free to consent or resist. It is an actual grace, i.e., a help conceived of as an impulse or a movement bestowed on the recipient. An efficacious grace not only gives a man the power to act but unfailingly secures the free use of that power. It is efficacious, therefore, not merely in the event of man's cooperation but from the moment it is given by God, before man's consent is given.

The difficult problem of grace that efficaciously brings about the will's consent and still leaves the freedom of the will intact has vexed theologians for many centuries. Among the various solutions, two that were defended by the 16th-cent. Spaniards Domingo Báñez, O. P., and Luis de Molina, S. J., are historically famous. Báñez ascribed the efficaciousness to the grace itself, to the divine movement that directly affects the will itself, and called this movement physical predetermination. Man is unfailingly prompted to perform salutary acts but with freedom; God predetermines him to determine himself freely. Molina conceived of the efficaciousness as something extrinsic to the grace itself. The grace is efficacious, he said, because imparted by God in the light of man's foreknown consent; i.e., by the foreknowledge called *scientia media* God has foreseen that a particular grace, a moral persuasion offered, would be accepted if it were given. Because God has foreseen the effect it will have, the grace is said to be efficacious before it is actually conferred; once given, it cooperates with the act of the will consenting, and the salutary act is performed. The RC Church grants full freedom for the teaching of these and other theories provided two truths are safeguarded: the dominion of God over man's actions and the freedom of the will. BIBLIOGRAPHY: H. Lange, *De gratia* (1929). *CONGREGATIO DE AUXILIIS.

[T. J. MOTHERWAY]

GRACE, EXTERNAL, in a broad sense, any objective divine gift external to man, not demanded by his nature or constitution. Riches, power, and such things fall under this definition. In the strict theological sense this gift must be a supernatural one, ultimately directed to salvation. F. Suárez and other theologians consider external also those interior graces that are not strictly spiritual, such as those that affect the senses. External grace may be something supernatural in itself or at least supernatural in the manner in which it is produced. Again this grace may consist of a created gift or it may be God's self-donation objectively considered. From the viewpoint of man's perfection, external grace has relevance only inasmuch as it is conducive to the production and increase of internal sanctifying grace. More in particular, external graces are objective realities, initially perceived by the senses, that make their way under the influence of internal grace to the mind and the will to stir up supernatural life. The proclamation of the gospel, which according to the Scripture, is the beginning of salvation (Rom 10.14), is the classic example. Other external created graces are works of supernatural providence ordained for man's salvation, such as the Church and the sacraments. Christ, the Word Incarnate, is the visible symbol of God's irrevocable self-gift to man. His work of Redemption constitutes objectively in itself the exclusive source of human salvation. The divine acts of benevolent love in themselves, such as God's predestination of the elect, are to be considered uncreated gifts external to man. The Scriptures, particularly St. Paul, speak of these realities in terms of grace (Eph 1.3–14). BIBLIOGRAPHY: P. Fransen, *Divine Grace and Man* (tr. G. Dupont, rev. ed., 1965); R. Garrigou-Lagrange, *Grace* (tr. Dominican Nuns, 1952, repr. 1957).

[R. J. TAPIA]

GRACE, HABITUAL, the gifts of God's love abiding in the recipient as the source of a new, supernatural being, knowledge, love, and action. The wide currency of the term dates from the Counter Reformation, with its emphasis on the interiority of grace in opposition to the teaching ascribed to the Reformers of *justification by extrinsic imputation. The medievals distinguished between grace as an ''habitual gift'' and grace as ''the help of God moving the soul'', i.e., *actual grace (ThAq ST 1a2ae, 109.6; 110.2). Habitual grace is also called sanctifying grace and in their broader sense both terms include grace as a new being given to the soul as well as the theological and infused moral *virtues, the gifts of the Holy Spirit. In their restricted sense the terms mean only that grace present in the soul itself as a kind of share in the divine nature. Besides distinguishing grace as a settled status from grace as passing or actual, the designation ''habitual,'' deriving from the Lat. translation of Aristotle's category *hexis* (having), intends that God's grace-love truly regenerates the soul to a new state of being and confers resources enhancing man's powers so that he may live a life in keeping with that new being. Scholastic theology further nuanced the terminology by categorizing grace in the soul as ''entitative habit,'' the virtues as ''operative habits.'' The accuracy of terminology needs to be measured by St. Thomas Aquinas's remark: ''There is nothing like grace among the accidents of the soul known by philosophers; they knew only of those categories that have reference to acts proportioned to human nature.'' (*De ver*. 27.2 ad 7). The central meaning of ''habitual grace'' is that the grace-life is truly lived from within, and that God's love gives the recipient a positive, inner source of response to him (see: ThAq ST 1a2ae, 110.2).

[T. C. O'BRIEN]

GRACE, ILLUMINATING, a description of grace from its enlightening effect on the recipient. Light has been a constant metaphor to describe grace in general; thus, ''once you were darkness, but now you are light in the Lord; walk like sons of light'' (Eph 5.8; cf. Jn 1.9). Particularly because of the writings of Pseudo-Dionysius and St. Augustine medieval theology used ''the light of grace'' as a stock phrase, contrasting it with ''the natural light of reason,'' i.e., human nature and all its intellectual powers as sharings in ''the divine light'' (see ThAq ST 1a2ae, 91.2; 110.3; cf. Pseudo-Dionysius *On the Divine Names* ch. 4; Augustine, *On the Trinity* XIV, ch. 12, 14). The light metaphor remains in liturgical language, e.g., in the rite of baptism. As theology sought to describe the functioning of grace as the source of every salutary act, illumination, or enlightenment came to describe a specific effect of grace as human powers were raised to a vital communion with God; illuminating grace is the effect of grace on the mind and knowing as distinct from the effect directly on the will. Habitual grace is illuminating particularly as it gives the abiding gift of faith as a power bestowed on the mind enabling it to assent to God's word and so to accept truths surpassing the power of the natural light of reason (ThAq ST 1a2ae, 109.1). All the *gifts of the Holy Spirit that imply a form of knowledge of God are included as habitual illuminating graces. Actual grace is described as illuminating both with regard to the initial acts in the process of *justification or conversion, and in the subsequent use of the habitual gifts of grace. In justification enlightenment by the Holy Spirit is, according to the Council of Trent (D 1525), part of the process; illuminating grace enables the sinner to perceive and to believe that God is the true good and to evaluate sin as evil. This enlightenment is a step towards bringing the will's response to God to fulfillment. The life of grace after conversion requires the constant assistance of actual grace on the mind so that its judgments will remain in conformity with the orientation of charity towards loving God above all.

[T. C. O'BRIEN]

GRACE, IMPUTED, the righteousness (justice) and merits of Christ accredited to the justified sinner because of his faith; contrasted with interior *grace, bringing *justification as an inner transformation, given in virtue of Christ's Passion. In the Reformation controversies a merely imputed grace was taken to be the teaching of both Luther and Calvin. During its deliberations the Council of *Trent considered, but rejected, G. *Seripando's proposal of a *double justice, consisting in both an interior and an imputed grace; the Decree on Justification condemned the doctrine of a merely imputed grace (D 1561,–62). Modern Reformation studies, together with ecumenical discussions, have clarified Protestant-Catholic positions, both historical and actual, on the point. BIBLIOGRAPHY: S. Pfurtner, *Luther and Aquinas on Salvation* (tr. E. Quinn, 1964).

[T. C. O'BRIEN]

GRACE, INTERIOR: (1) grace as received inwardly to transform the recipient, in contrast to merely *imputed grace (see also GRACE, HABITUAL); (2) grace as directly affecting the soul and its powers, in distinction from helps of God for salvation that remain external: preaching, the salutary events of life, or even the mysteries and sacraments of faith.

[T. C. O'BRIEN]

GRACE, NATURAL, any endowment of nature, esp. of human nature, so designated because it is an effect of God's causal goodness, and as such a gift freely given; distinguished against grace in its proper sense, the gift of God's love drawing man above the natural to share in the divine life. Natural endowments or experiences can also be called graces in that all of God's causality over man relates to his saving love.

[T. C. O'BRIEN]

GRACE, PREVENIENT, a designation, chiefly of actual *grace, from St. *Augustine (*De natura et gratia,* 31) and based on its diverse effects in the recipient; in general it is grace preceding all the actions dependent on it (D 1553); in particular it is grace given for effects that are prior in the process of salvation; for justification in comparison to sanctification; for sanctification in comparison to glorification; for an act of belief in comparison to an act of hope. Grace given for the second member in such comparisons is termed "subsequent." BIBLIOGRAPHY: ThAq ST 1a2ae, 111.3.

[T. C. O'BRIEN]

GRACE, SACRAMENTAL. In theology *grace can mean only one concrete reality, the divine gift given through Jesus Christ the Savior. To speak of sacramental grace in RC theology involves the presuppositions that grace is a created gift interiorly affecting the being and the acting of the recipient and that his gift is conferred through the sacraments, both teachings of the Council of Trent (1545–63). There is also, by contrast, a further implication, "extra-sacramental grace," i.e., that grace is given in ways other than through the sacraments. (A recent and to-be-treasured church statement on this point is that catechumens—not yet baptized—are already in many cases living the life of faith, hope, and charity; Vat II MissAct, #14.) Classical theology has inquired, consequently, into the precise meaning of grace as it is received in virtue of the sacraments. There is a first, general response that applies to all of the sacraments. The sacraments are signs witnessing the union in faith with Jesus Christ in his Passion, death and Resurrection; their effectiveness consists in and is derived from Christ as the universal and first saving Mediator. In serving as signs of faith the sacraments bring about what they signify. They are signs of the past, the paschal mystery of Christ, of the actual effectiveness of that mystery here and now, and of the future, final sharing in the fruits and purpose of that mystery. All sacramental grace, then, is a gift conforming the recipient to Christ in his paschal mystery and giving a participation in its effectiveness, and promising future glory. (St. Thomas Aquinas expresses this by saying, for example, that the recipient of baptism is before God as though he himself were the Christ who suffered, died, and rose again; ST 3a, 69.2 ad 1).

Each sacrament is a distinctive form of witnessing and of being conjoined with the paschal mystery. The further theological issue, then, is the nature of the grace given by each of the seven sacraments. Centuries of theological discussion have developed a variety of categories, usually scholastic in origin, to classify the quality of the grace proper to each sacrament (e.g., that each confers a right to the actual graces needed to carry out the essential meaning of the sacrament). A more contemporarily fruitful evaluation may be seen in the documents of Vatican II and in their subsequent implementation, esp. in the general instructions issued concomitantly with the revised liturgical rites. The teaching of *Lumen gentium* is that the baptized are consecrated into a "spiritual house and a holy priesthood" (Vat II ConstChurch, #10). The document adds that through the sacraments and the exercise of the virtues the sacred nature and organic structure of the priestly community are brought into operation. (ibid, #11). Each of the sacraments brings about, and in a way appropriate to each person, the ways of living as the priestly people of God (ibid.). In *Sacrosanctum concilium* the point is summarized thus: "Rightly, then, the liturgy is considered as an exercise of the priestly office of Jesus Christ. In the liturgy the sanctification of man is manifested by signs perceptible to the senses and is effected in a way which is proper to each of these signs; in the liturgy full public worship is performed by the Mystical Body of Jesus Christ, that is by the Head and His members (VatII SacLit, #7; tr, Abbott, p. 141). The general instructions for the new liturgical rites contain a rich theology that directs the rites to be carried out in such a way as to manifest more clearly how each sacrament brings about a special mode in which the recipient is enabled to live as a sharer in Christ's priestly, paschal mystery. Sacramental grace so understood is not taken as static and objectified. The sacraments and their graces point to an abiding manner of living, the life of the faithful as such. Even the graces given that were traditionally referred to as "actual graces," as well as the *charisms, are to be seen as related to sacramental grace, in the sense that they are gifts to those who are constituted as a priestly community by the grace of the sacraments.

[T. C. O'BRIEN]

GRACE, SANCTIFYING, in general, any grace given directly for the salvation of the recipient—*gratia gratum faciens* (grace that makes holy) as against **gratiae gratis datae*, the charisms. But the term is generally used restrictively to mean *habitual grace.

[T. C. O'BRIEN]

GRACE, STATE OF, the abiding disposition of one who possesses sanctifying or habitual grace. It is opposed to the state of sin, or the situation of one who is without sanctifying grace. Although the phrase is not expressly used in the NT, the idea it represents is clearly implied in biblical terms. The description of salvation as a new birth (Jn 3.3–7) and of the status of believers as children of God (1 Jn 3.1), or as partakers of the divine nature (2 Pet 1.4), indicates an abiding condition. Through baptism one is incorporated into the mystical body of Christ and enters into the state of grace. He may fall from this state, but only through mortal sin. If grace is lost, it may be recovered by perfect contrition or by the sacrament of penance received with *attrition. The state of grace is nourished and strengthened through the Eucharist. The state of grace is a necessary predisposition to the fruitful reception of the sacraments of the living. Apart from a special revelation from God, according to RC theology, one cannot know with the certainty either of faith or of scientific knowledge that he is in the state of grace; he may, however, have conjectural or moral certainty of it based on indications cumulatively more or less incompatible with a state of sin. Even this limited degree of certainty, however, may be beyond the reach of an individual, either because of the ambiguity of the indications he discerns in his own case, or because anxiety and scruple may cause his judgment to be clouded. His doubtful state of mind need not keep him from the sacraments of the living; what the Church requires of him in the proper reception of such a sacrament is not certainty that he is in the state of grace, but a conscience unburdened by the certain consciousness of sin. BIBLIOGRAPHY: Davis, MorPastTh 4:207–208; J. P. Browne, NCE 6:682–683.

[P. K. MEAGHER]

GRACE, SUBSTANTIAL, God as communicating himself, not simply his created gift, to man: as the loving source of created grace (ThAq ST 1a2ae, 110.1); as the Word made flesh in the *hypostatic union; as object of knowing and loving in the divine *indwelling. The term substantial comes from scholastic theology, applying Aristotelian categories to the classification of supernatural realities: "substance" refers to a complete, distinct being in itself, as against "accident," not a separate being, but a quality belonging to one. Grace being understood as God's self-communication, the idea of a substantial grace received into another being would have pantheistic or even polytheistic implications. Thus in scholastic terminology the created gifts of grace are necessarily classified as accidents. Substantial grace taken as God's beneficent love does not involve his becoming part of the recipient; the hypostatic union does not involve a commingling of natures; in the divine indwelling, Father, Son, and Holy Spirit are present as known and loved, not as compositively part of the soul or its powers (see: ThAq CG 3.51).

[T. C. O'BRIEN]

GRACE, SUFFICIENT, a grace that confers on man the capability of a salutary act (that is, one leading to salvation) and moves him to it, but that man refuses to use. The Jansenists denied the existence of such graces. For them all grace is efficacious and cannot be resisted. The Church condemned their error and defined the truth that God sometimes gives a grace that remains without salutary effect because man chooses not to cooperate. Absolutely speaking, the term sufficient grace taken in itself means a sufficiency of power for a supernaturally good action; it prescinds from use or nonuse of the power. Therefore, in strict theological terminology the modifying adverb "merely," or the adverb "purely" is added to bring out the notion of rejection of the grace. So it is that theologically and historically considered, with reference to Jansenism, sufficient grace is purely, or merely, sufficient. This expression always signifies a grace that God bestows with the intention that it be accepted but at the same time foreseeing and permitting its nonacceptance. The existence of purely sufficient graces is a corollary of some of the words and actions of Jesus himself. For instance he condemned the people of Chorazin and Bethsaida for not believing in him (Mt 11.21). But they could not have believed without grace. Their sin, therefore, was a refusal to accept the grace of faith, and this grace was what one calls purely sufficient. BIBLIOGRAPHY: H. Lange, *De gratia* (1929).

[T. J. MOTHERWAY]

GRACE, UNCREATED, God himself considered as a gift to man. The words grace of God are sometimes used in Holy Scripture to signify God himself under the aspect of his supernatural favor and benevolence toward men. Thus in the Incarnation "the grace of God our Savior has appeared" (Tit 2.11). This is the uncreated grace showing itself to men for the purpose of redeeming and saving them (2 Tim 1.9–10). Jesus called himself the "gift of God" (Jn 4.10), and the Holy Spirit is a gift "which has been given to us" (Rom 5.5). But the gift in both instances is grace, uncreated grace, Persons of the Blessed Trinity. With the gift of created habitual grace is given the indwelling of the Father, Son, and Holy Spirit in the soul of the sanctified man. This indwelling is uncreated grace, God in the redeemed soul. Of all the gifts of grace received in the present life, this is the most precious, the dynamic presence of the three Divine Persons imprinting on the soul their own image and moving it to those acts by which it will gain eternal life. But the uncreated grace par excellence is granted in the afterlife, when the Blessed Trinity unites itself with the beatified soul as the object of immediate intellectual vision and beatific joy. BIBLIOGRAPHY: I. Willig, *Geschaffene und Ungeschaffene Gnade* (1964).

[T. J. MOTHERWAY]

GRACE AND FREE WILL, see FREE WILL AND GRACE.

GRACE AND FREEDOM, the theological problem of the way man depends on God's help for salvation. Apart from some Nominalists of the 14th and 15th cent., orthodox theologians have followed Augustine's affirmation, against *Pelagianism, of the absolute primacy of divine grace; no such unanimity, however, has existed with respect to the condition of the will under the justifying and sanctifying power of God's help. The irresistibility of grace and the total enslavement of the will to sin for some have meant that the power of free choice has no place in the grace life. Augustine's writings have been cited both in support and in denial of such a position. The Council of Trent, Decree on Justification (D. 1544–55), directed its condemnation of this position against the Reformers; and it was part of the doctrinal case against *Jansenism (D. 2002–03). Roman Catholic theologians have sought to maintain an understanding that the gospel of grace as primary and as pure gift is still addressed to man to invite his free response. Variations in explaining the relationship between grace and this response are reducible to two: the one views freedom as existing in the actual exercise of choice, and because grace is the first source of any saving act, in empowering man to act, it gives him his free act. The other position views freedom as a state of suspension, open to various possible alternatives; the exercise of choice is explained, not by the inner influence of grace itself, but by God's arrangement of circumstances or other elements favorable to overcoming the suspension so that the person consents to the grace offered. The theological problem involves the mystery of God's unique love and inner action on the heart of man; theology may see the separate lines of the problem, but not their convergence. Contemporary theologians are wary about straitening the gospel message of God's call through Christ into categories of causality. *GRACE, CONTROVERSIES ON.

[T. C. O'BRIEN]

GRACE AND NATURE, the natural and supernatural life in man. They have between them a complex relation that can be viewed either essentially or existentially. In the first aspect, grace is distinct from nature; it is of a higher order; it perfects and does not destroy or warp nature. Man's spiritual nature is of its essence open to grace, though he cannot of himself acquire or merit it. When he receives grace, man is raised to a divine level, to a filial relationship with God the Father in Christ and the Spirit; he is made capable of divine faith, hope, and love—attaining God in Himself; this is his sharing in the divine nature. In thus perfecting nature grace does no violence to it; it respects the pattern of human nature and adapts itself to it. It does not intensify man's powers with regard to their connatural activities and objectives. Remaining man and creature, man is made the adoptive son of God.

Existentially or historically speaking, this formal distinction between what in a man living in grace corresponds to grace and what to nature, does not mean that the two are only extrinsically connected, or placed side by side. Rather grace permeates and transforms nature; there are not, as it were, two layers in man. The whole of man is supernaturalized or divinized by grace. Nor is grace merely superadded to nature as though by a divine afterthought. In fallen man, moreover, grace has a medicinal effect; it remedies the consequences of the Fall and to that extent perfects nature on its own level.

A similar relation exists between the order of grace and the order of nature, or of creation. The natural order is not suppressed or modified by the order of grace. In the divine plan that governs the existential order, nature exists for the sake of grace. Yet grace respects the natural and temporal values, which keep their own consistency and activity. The order of grace subsumes and crowns the order of nature.

BIBLIOGRAPHY: M. J. Scheeben, *Nature and Grace* (tr. C. Vollert, 1954); K. Rahner, *Nature and Grace* (1963); C. Regan, NCE 6:683–685.

[P. DELETTER]

GRACE AT MEALS. One of the meanings of the Lat. *gratia* is thankfulness. Grace before meals is an ancient Christian custom, recommended by many Church Fathers, and following the example of Christ (Mk 8.6, 7). The prayer may include thanksgiving to God, a petition for his blessing on the food and those gathered at the table. The grace after meals, less common, is also a prayer of thanks. These prayers, as in monastic or religious houses, may follow a formula. They also are frequently improvised and spoken by the head of the family, or by a member of the gathering invited to "say grace." Whatever form grace may take, it is a practice that makes the common meal both an act of worship and a symbol of the love of charity that binds those gathered at the table.

[T. C. O'BRIEN]

GRACES, THE, three beautiful goddesses personifying beauty, grace, and joy, who attend Aphrodite, Apollo, and Dionysius (usually as dancers). The Three Graces in a circle may be seen in Roman wall painting, works of Botticelli, and other Renaissance painters reviving the classical.

[M. J. DALY]

GRACIAN DE LA MADRE DE DIOS, see GRATIAN, JEROME.

GRADINE, a shelf at the back of the altar, slightly above the level of the mensa or altar table, introduced near the end of the 16th cent. to provide a place for cross, candlesticks, and reliquaries. The gradine is found only on altars placed against the wall ("eastward position").

[J. DALLEN]

GRADO-AQUILEIA, PATRIARCHATE OF. The Church of Aquileia in the province of Udine in NE Italy was probably founded in the mid-3d century. Nevertheless, a legend traceable as far back as the mid-3d cent. attributed the foundation to St. Mark the Evangelist and provided a basis for the claim made by the bps. of Aquileia to a right to patriarchal status. This right was generally recognized by the 8th century. In 568, when the Lombards overran Italy, the patriarch moved to the island of Grado, which still belonged to the Byzantine exarchate of Ravenna. In consequence of the conflict between Byzantium and the Lombards, two patriarchs were elected in 607: one in Aquileia, John, who was sponsored by the Lombard duke, and the other in Grado, Candianus, who was supported by the Byzantine exarch. Candianus styled himself patriarch of Nova Aquileia. The competition between the two patriarchates continued even after 716, when Rome formally recognized the patriarchate of Aquileia and divided the diocese between Grado and Aquileia. After the Byzantines left N Italy, the doge of Venice became the protector of the patriarch of Grado, whereas the Franks favored the Aquileian patriarch. After 1156 the patriarch of Grado made Venice his place of permanent residence, and in 1451 the patriarchate of Grado officially became the patriarchate of Venice. The patriarchate of Aquileia lasted until 1751 or 1752, when Pope Benedict XIV under Austrian pressure divided the diocese into two archbishoprics, one (Udine) Italian, and the other (Görz) Austrian. BIBLIOGRAPHY: O. Demus, *Church of San Marco in Venice* (1960); M. M. Roberti, EncCatt 6:982–983; *ibid.* C. Cecchelli, 1:1722–27.

[V. VON FALKENHAUSEN]

GRADUAL, a term that describes the interposing of a Psalm or parts thereof between the First Reading and the Gospel Reading in the Liturgy of the Eucharist. In the revised order of the Mass it is called the Responsorial Psalm and occurs between the OT and NT readings. One of the most ancient parts of the liturgy, the Gradual was always responsorial, between lector and people. The ancient practice was to use a Psalm after each of three readings. The term Gradual derives from the Latin word *gradus* or step, because originally it was delivered from a higher position in the sanctuary. Before Vatican Council II the Gradual was immediately followed by the Alleluia (or in penitential seasons, the Tract) but in today's liturgy the Alleluia is separated from the Responsory by a reading. The *Graduale* is a liturgical book, containing the Latin Mass chants of the Roman rite.

[J. R. AHERNE]

GRADUAL PSALMS, a name given to the group of Psalms 120–134, each of which contains a title generally translated as "Song of Ascents," referring most likely to the trek of pilgrims up to Jerusalem at festival time. BIBLIOGRAPHY: W. Oesterley, *Psalms* (1939).

[C. BERNAS]

GRADUALE ROMANUM, liturgical book containing the chants of the Roman Mass, both proper and ordinary, whether done by choir or soloist. The latest edition of the *Graduale Romanum Simplex* is 1966.

[J. DALLEN]

GRAECO-BUDDHIST ART. See GANDHARA.

GRAF, GEORG (1875–1955), German historian of Christian Arabic literature. A priest of the diocese of Augsburg, G. was active in pastoral work until 1930 but managed to continue his studies in Christian Arabic literature at the same time. In 1930 he became an honorary member of the theological faculty of Munich. From 1926 G. was coeditor of *Oriens Christianus* and he was director of the Arabic section of *Corpus scriptorum Christianorum orientalium*. His greatest work is his *Geschichte der christlichen arabischen Literatur* (5 v., 1944–53). BIBLIOGRAPHY: P. Skehan, NCE 6:687.

[R. B. ENO]

GRAF, URS (1485–1527 or 28), Swiss graphic artist, goldsmith, and glass painter. G. executed woodcuts for the *Passion of Christ* (1506), *Decretales diu papae Gregorii* (1511), *Decretum Gratiani* (1510), and shows the influence of Dürer in *Ritter vom Turn* and *Das Narrenshyff* (1490). G. executed numerous signed energetic drawings, whiteline woodcuts, and ornamental engravings for jewelers and armorers.

[M. J. DALY]

GRAFFIN, RENÉ (1858–1941), French priest and Orientalist. In 1886 G. organized the school of Semitic and Egyptian languages at the Institut Catholique of Paris. He published first a *Patrologia Syriaca* (3 v., 1894–1926), followed by the more ambitious *Patrologia orientalis* (25 v., 1907–42). He also founded and edited the *Revue de l'Orient chrétien* (1896–1938). His efforts made available to contemporary scholars a great deal of valuable material that would otherwise have been difficult to find. BIBLIOGRAPHY: P. Skehan, NCE 6:687–688; S. Lyonnet, EncCatt 6:988.

[R. B. ENO]

GRAFT, the sin against justice of a public official who receives money or other advantage by dishonest use of his office (see EXTORTION). By making appointments for pay, awarding contracts in view of a pay-off, by promoting private interests that conflict with political responsibilities, a public official offends against various forms of justice: legal justice requiring any governing officer to promote the common good; commutative justice that bars *fraud or extortion; distributive justice that restrains any member of society from gaining unjust, i.e., disproportionate, advantages. Since graft usually involves the community's being cheated and overcharged by those who participate in it, it calls for restitution. The beneficiary of graft always remains an unjust possessor; the prevalence of the practice can never change that moral fact. Political patronage as such need not be the equivalent of graft; it is not wrong to appoint political supporters to positions that need to be filled and for which the appointees are qualified; it is an obvious advantage to have personnel supportive of legitimate policies of government. But if patronage is equivalent to buying votes, e.g., the creation of sinecures to reward supporters, it is a form of graft, and the appointees themselves are culpable participants in the injustice.

[T. C. O'BRIEN]

GRAHAM, WILLIAM FRANKLIN (BILLY) (1918–), foremost contemporary evangelist. G. was born in Charlotte, N.C., was graduated from Wheaton (Ill.) College in 1943, became a lay preacher while still a student at Bob Jones Univ. and Florida Bible Seminary, and was ordained a minister in the Southern Baptist Convention in 1939. His evangelistic work began in 1946 with Youth for Christ International. The first of the many campaigns for which he has become famous was in Los Angeles, Cal., in 1949; since that time he has conducted them in all parts of the world. Through his broadcasts, the *Weekly Hour of Decision,* he has reached millions. His preaching is eloquent, impassioned; he stresses fundamental biblical themes, above all grace, sin, salvation, the need for repentance, and the Second Coming. The objective of his campaigns is to bring about a "decision for Christ," and the return of those converted to their own Churches.

[T. C. O'BRIEN]

GRAIL, THE HOLY, name of the cup or chalice that became the subject of a cycle of medieval romances, most of which concern its loss and the search for it by knights of King Arthur's court. The hero of the search is in turn Perceval, Lancelot, and finally Galahad, Lancelot's son and Perceval's kinsman. The Grail romances developed fully between 1180 (*Perceval* by *Chrétien de Troyes) and 1230 (the Vulgate Cycle of prose Arthurian romances). Most of these tales are in French. They fall into two classes: those concerned with the history of the Grail, called early history versions, and those concerned with the knights searching for it, called quest versions. The earliest history version is a verse romance by Robert de Boron (1170–1212), known as *Joseph d'Arimathie*. To the incident of Joseph's asking Pilate for the body of Christ, mentioned in the Gospels it adds legendary material of Joseph's imprisonment by the Jews (from apocryphal *Gospel of Nicodemus,* late 4th cent.), of his possession of the cup used by Christ at the Last Supper, of his exile, and of the appointment of a Grail keeper, Bron the Fisher King, a relative of Joseph. Later history versions (the *Grand Saint Graal*) make Joseph's son the keeper of the Grail and trace his descendants down to King Pelles, grandfather of Galahad, thus connecting the period of early Christianity with King Arthur's court. The earliest extant quest version (12th cent.) is Chrétien de Troyes' *Perceval*. The Grail here is pagan in origin, and R. S. Loomis (*The Development of the Arthurian Romances* [1963], 63) says that early Celtic literature offers "prototypes of the Fisher King, the Grail Bearer, Perceval, and Galahad." Chrétien died before he finished his romance. Malory's version in the *Morte d'Arthur* (1485), the best-known account, uses the Christian signification given in the Vulgate Cycle. Some versions say that the Grail disappeared when an impure person approached it. The relationship of the Grail stories and their chronology is uncertain. The medieval accounts are already fully developed legends coming from sources that are partly heathen and partly apocryphal Scripture. Famous modern versions are Tennyson's "Holy Grail" in the *Idylls of the King* (1869) and Wagner's *Parsifal* (1882). BIBLIOGRAPHY: *Arthurian Literature in the Middle Ages* (ed. R. S. Loomis, 1959); *Grail: From Celtic Myth to Christian Symbol* (1963).

[M. M. BARRY]

GRAIL MOVEMENT, an international apostolic movement organized in Holland (1921) by Jacques van Ginneken, SJ, which aims through a training period of about 2 years to prepare married or single Catholic young women of all ethnic backgrounds to be leaders in the lay apostolate and to bring spiritual values to all areas of modern society. These women, whose spirituality stresses personal commitment to Christ, personal prayer, community worship, and concern for the dignity of the individual, devote their lives to the service of their fellowmen in both Christian and non-Christian lands. By 1977 the movement had spread to 20 countries. It was established in the U.S. (1940) with headquarters in Loveland, Ohio.

[M. B. BOYLE]

GRANACCI, FRANCESCO (1477–1543), Italian painter trained by Domenico Ghirlandajo, using the compact dynamic contours of Michelangelo, his friend whom he assisted (1508) on the Sistine ceiling (later dismissed). Fra Bartolomeo's shadows within personal, broader silhouettes characterize G.'s *Madonna in Glory with Four Saints* and *Madonna with SS. Zenobius and Francis* (both 1514–16). G., prolonging late 15th-cent. mannerisms in emotional, elongated figures, was a transitional master of dignity and restraint.

[M. J. DALY]

GRANCOLAS, JEAN (1660?–1732), theologian, liturgist. Chaplain to the brother of King Louis XIV, he earned the displeasure of the Duke of Orléans, later Regent of France, who dismissed him. G. turned first to writing on the liturgy. Among these studies were: *Traité de l'antiquité des cérémonies des sacraments* (1692); *Les Anciennes liturgies . . . dans les Églises d'Orient et dans celles d'Occident* (1697); *Traité de la Messe et de l'office divin* (1713). G., however, really preferred theological controversy. His *Le Quiétisme contraire à la doctrine des sacraments* (1693) is a refutation of the Spanish mystic M. *Molinos and his doctrine. A keen theologian and a writer who used ancient sources well, G. was a careless stylist and poor organizer of his valuable material. BIBLIOGRAPHY: H. Leclercq, CE 6:724–725.

[J. R. AHERNE]

GRAND PENITENTIARY, the cardinal presiding over the Sacred Penitentiary, the Vatican tribunal dealing with all important matters affecting the sacrament of penance, as regards the internal forum, and with the granting of indulgences. The post seems to have originated from the appointment of a personal confessor for the pope. The title seems to have come into use in the 13th century; from the 14th it has been attached to a cardinal living in Rome. The tribunal itself was organized in the 14th century.

[J. DALLEN]

GRANDE-CHARTREUSE, LA, motherhouse of the Carthusian Order, situated in the Dauphine Alps, 15 miles N of Grenoble. When St. *Bruno and six companions desired a more contemplative life, at the advice of Benedictine Abbot Seguin of Chaise-Dieu, they sought help from a former novice, Hugh de Châteauneuf, bp. of Grenoble. St.

Hugh led them to a plateau in the Alps where they built wooden huts (one hut for two men) and a chapel of solid masonry. This was the beginning of the Grande Chartreuse *c.*feast of the Nativity of St. John, 1084). A charter was issued in December 1084. In 1090, Bruno was summoned by Pope Urban II as counselor, but when his followers did not want to stay without him, he ceded the land back to Seguin. After an unsuccessful attempt at eremetic life at Rome, some of Bruno's disciples returned to Grande Chartreuse. Again, Abbot Seguin ceded the land to Landuin, the new prior, who was not successful as superior. He was dispatched to Rome to confer with Bruno; neither ever returned to Grenoble. A lay brother did return with a letter from Bruno, called the "Testament of St. Bruno." It was not a formal rule, but rather notes for the experiment in religious living. The fifth prior, Guigues du Pin (surnamed also du Chastel), Guigo I, was elected in 1110. He established six colonies from the Grande Chartreuse and compiled the "Customs of La Grande Chartreuse," the first formal rule. In it, he declared that the Carthusians drew inspiration for the eremitic side of their life from St. Jerome and the cenobitic from St. Benedict. In 80 chapters, Guigo devotes himself to the subjects of the Divine Office, the solitary life (the upper house—i.e., from its position on the mountain), and the lay brothers (in the lower house). In 1131, St. Hugh of Grenoble died. In 1132 an avalanche destroyed the Chartreuse killing six monks and one novice. Among the new novices who came to the Chartreuse was Anthelme, who became prior in 1139. He supervised new building and had the foundation of the great cloister laid. He convoked the first Carthusian chapter at La Chartreuse (1142) with its prior to serve as perpetual president of the chapter, but having only primacy of honor. The chapter established a unity of ritual practices and stabilized the rule. It was Basil (prior 1151–53) who obtained from Alexander II in 1162, confirmation of papal privileges for the Grande Chartreuse, taking it and all Carthusian houses under papal protection and freeing them from episcopal control, while enlarging the spiritual powers of the prior. La Grande Chartreuse was destroyed a number of times by fire and rebuilt. The present monastery was begun in 1676. In 1904, the monks were forcibly ejected from their home under the Association Laws of 1901; the Grande Chartreuse was secularized. In 1940, the Carthusians were permitted to return to the venerable site. BIBLIOGRAPHY: C. M. Boutrais, *La Grande–Chartreuse* (1881; English tr. 1891).

[N. F. GAUGHAN]

GRANDERATH, THEODOR (1839–1902), church historian. A Jesuit of the Rhine province, he taught in England and the Netherlands, succeeding *Schneemann as editor of Vatican Council I's *Acta et decreta*. In 1893 Leo XIII opened the Vatican Archives to him. His master work was the history of the Vatican Council, *Geschichte des Vatikanischen Konzils*. Two volumes were published in 1903, a year after his death, and the work was completed in 1906 by Konrad Kirch. The first history of the Council did not objectively present the minority view on papal infallibility.

[J. R. AHERNE]

GRANDI, ALESSANDRO (d. 1630), Italian choirmaster and composer. He held several church positions in Venice and Bergamo, and was the first to use the term *cantata,* or *cantada*. His sacred works include Masses, psalms, and motets. Of the few of his many compositions known to have survived there are MSS in libraries in England, Vienna, and Berlin. BIBLIOGRAPHY: K. H. Worner, *History of Music* (tr. W. Wager, 5th ed., 1973) 282.

[J. C. MARR]

GRANDIDIER, PHILIPPE ANDRÉ (1752–87), historian. Born in Strasbourg, he completed his classical studies at the age of 13. With encouragement from the Card. Louis de Rohan, G. entered the priesthood and soon became archivist of the Strasbourg Cathedral. When he was 25, he published the first volumes of the *Ecclesiastical History of Alsace*. The work was praised by some but attacked vehemently by many of G.'s peers because it deflated many myths. When his critics questioned the sincerity of his religious principles, G. for a time abandoned the study of history. However, he soon resumed and his work was recognized with his acceptance into 21 French and German academies. In addition to the unfinished history of Alsace, his major works included: the *History of the Diocese and the Bishops of Strasbourg* (1777–78); a review of the 9th-cent. German poet, Ottfrid; the *History of the Valley of Lièvre;* a Strasbourg Breviary; and contributions to a new edition of *Vies des Saints*. BIBLIOGRAPHY: *Revue Catholique d'Alsace* (1926) 28–40.

[R. J. BRADY]

GRANDIER, URBAIN (1590–1634), French priest whose scandalous conduct, open hatred of religious orders, and sympathy for the Reformation led to his suspension, but after a time he was restored to his pastorate at Loudon by the abp. of Bordeaux. He was later charged with casting a spell on the sisters of a local Ursuline convent. He confessed, was condemned to death for sorcery, and burned at the stake. The story with much fictional accretion was long exploited in prurient antireligious books. BIBLIOGRAPHY: A. M. Bozzone, DE 2:243–244.

[M. J. SUELZER]

GRANDIN, VITAL, VEN. (1829–1902), French-born Canadian missionary of the Oblates of Mary Immaculate. After his ordination (1854) he was sent to Saskatchewan as an Indian missionary, and much of his long career was devoted to pioneer mission efforts among Indians, métis, and white settlers. He was consecrated as auxiliary bp. of the vast St. Boniface diocese (1859); he assisted Bp. Taché in the development of frontier parishes, but primarily as an Indian missionary. BIBLIOGRAPHY: P. E. Breton, *Vital*

Grandin (1960); C. A. Liederbach, *Canada's Bishops from 1120 to 1975 . . . from Allen to Yelle* (pa. 1975).

[R. K. MACMASTER]

GRANDMAISON, LÉONCE DE (1868–1927), French Jesuit theologian and apologist. After teaching in France and England, G. served as editor of *Études* (1908–10) and founded the scholarly periodical *Recherches de science religieuse* to help combat *Modernism. He published numerous articles, generally apologetic in nature. Most notable is his 2-volume life of Christ, *Jésus Christ: sa personne, son message, ses épreuves*. BIBLIOGRAPHY: J. Geuser, "Mélanges Grandmaison," RechSR 18 (1928) 281–295.

[T. M. MCFADDEN]

GRANDMONT, ABBEY AND ORDER OF (Grammont, *Grandimontensis*), chief monastery of the Order of Grandimont, founded in honor of St. Michael in 1067 by St. Stephen of Muret near Limoges (Haute-Vienne, France) on the mountain of Muret. He established a society of hermits there, who after his death (1124) settled in the desert of Grandmont, 3 miles from Muret. Stephen of Liciac (d. 1163) gave them a rule inspired by the teachings of their founder and very rigorous in the matter of poverty. The austerity of the monks and the support of the Plantagenets during the second half of the 12th cent. favored the extension of the order, but it was soon halted by the revolts of the lay monks. The monastery was raised to an abbey in 1317, but in that year Pope John XXII concentrated its total strength in an abbey of 60 members and in 30 conventual priories of 16 to 18 members. Grandmont became a commendatory abbey and was the victim of the 16th-cent. disorders. It was reformed in 1634 by Prior Charles Fremon, who instituted strict observance, grouping together 7 or 8 houses out of the 30 or more that remained among the Grandmontains. The order was suppressed in 1768. The church of Grandmont, now destroyed, had a single nave that served as a model for the houses of the order in France and England. BIBLIOGRAPHY: Cottineau 1:1326–28; J. C. Dickinson, NCE 6:694–695.

[J. DAOUST]

GRANT, FREDERICK CLIFTON (1891–), biblical scholar. Born in Wisconsin, educated at the General Theological Seminary (New York) and Western Theological Seminary (Chicago), he was ordained to the priesthood in the Protestant Episcopal Church (1912). After serving as assistant and rector in several parishes (1912–24), he was dean of Bexley Hall at Kenyon College (1924–26), professor at Berkeley Divinity School (1926–27), president and dean of Seabury-Western Theological Seminary (1927–38), and professor of biblical theology at Union Theological Seminary in New York (1938–59). His scholarly work in various areas, esp. NT studies, is represented by some 30 books and scores of articles. The following are representative: *The Economic Background of the Gospels* (1926), *The Gospels: Their Origin and Their Growth* (1953), *The Earliest Gospel* (1943), *Ancient Judaism and the New Testament* (1959), *Roman Hellenism and the New Testament* (1962), *Introduction to New Testament Thought* (1958), *Nelson's Bible Commentary, New Testament* (1962), and his work as joint editor of *Hastings Dictionary of the Bible, Revised Edition* (1963). He was editor-in-chief of the *Anglican Theological Review* (1924–55). He was a member of the committee on revision of the American Standard Revised Version and also a member of the versions committee of the American Bible Society (1944–54). He was one of the three Anglican observers at Vatican Council II.

[H. H. GRAHAM]

GRANT, THOMAS (1816–70), first bp. of Southwark, England. Born in France of Irish parents, G. was educated at Ushaw College in England, then in Rome at the English College, where he was ordained in 1841. Secretary to Card. *Acton and agent for the English bps, he translated into Italian the documents which prepared the way for the reestablishment of the English hierarchy. G. was also rector of the English College from 1844. Appointed bp. of Southwark in 1851, he was frequently consulted by the government on points of civil vs. canon law. Though gravely ill, he attended Vatican Council I but had to withdraw in Feb. 1870.

[J. R. AHERNE]

GRANTH SĀHIB, see ĀDI-GRANTH.

GRANVELLE, ANTOINE PERRENOT DE (1517–86), French cardinal and diplomat in the service of the Habsburgs. Son of Charles V's minister, G. frequently accompanied the Emperor on his journeys and represented him at the opening of the Council of Trent. He was made abp. of Malines in 1560 and cardinal in 1561. Meanwhile he became chief counselor to Margaret of Parma, regent of the Netherlands. He was opposed by the Dutch nobility because of his adherence to the principles of absolute monarchy, and Philip was forced to remove him in 1564. G. assisted in drawing up the Holy League (1570) and served as viceroy of Naples (1571–75). In 1579 he was recalled to Madrid to become secretary of state. He was a better diplomat than churchman and showed more interest in politics than in religion. BIBLIOGRAPHY: R. Palmarocchi, EncCatt 6:1002; W. Keller, NCE 6:695–696; P. Geyl, *Revolt of the Netherlands against Spain 1555–1609* (1932).

[D. NUGENT]

GRASSEL, LORENZ (1753–93), missionary. A native of Germany, he was forced to leave the Jesuit seminary by the suppression of the Society and became a diocesan priest. In response to an appeal for priests to work in America, he came to Philadelphia in 1787. His ministry took him to the missions of New Jersey and Pennsylvania. During the plague of yellow fever in 1793 in Philadelphia, he contracted the disease. The same year he had been selected as coadjutor bishop to Bp. Carroll. Death, however, from yellow fever came to G. before he could be consecrated. BIBLIOGRAPHY: P. Guilday, *Life and Times of John Carroll* (1922).

[J. R. AHERNE]

GRASSI, ANTHONY, BL. (1592–1671), Oratorian. Born to a noble family in Fermo, Italy, at the age of 17, he joined the Oratory at Fermo, where he soon gained a reputation for gentleness and sincerity. At the age of 29, he survived being struck by lightning. In 1635, he was elected superior of the Fermo Oratory, a position to which he was reelected twelve times. G. was said to have prescience, and Popes Clement X and Innocent X relied on his counsel. He was beatified by Leo XIII in 1900. BIBLIOGRAPHY: C. Gasbarri, BiblSanct 7:150; Butler 4:554–556.

[R. J. BRADY]

GRASSI, GREGORIO, BL. (1833–1900), missionary, bishop, martyr. An Italian Franciscan ordained in 1856, he spent his life in China from 1861. He was titular bp. of Ortosia from 1876 and later vicar apostolic of northern Shansi Province from 1891. During the Boxer Rebellion he was put to death. He was included in the beatification of martyrs in China in 1946.

[J. R. AHERNE]

GRASSMAN, MARCELO (1925–), Brazilian draftsman and printmaker from São Paulo. Self-taught, G. has won many prizes; first graphic award São Paulo Bienal (1955) and the prize for sacred art, Venice Biennale (1958). His images show monstrous human-animal fusions (*Taming of the Beast* 1958).

[M. J. DALY]

GRATIAN (Flavius Gratianus; 359–383 A.D.), **ROMAN EMPEROR** from 367. The son of Valentinian I, G. received a good education under the rhetorician Ausonius. He became consul in 366, Augustus in 367, and Emperor of the West after the death of his father in 375 but had to share his rule with his half-brother Valentinian II, who had been proclaimed emperor by the troops in Pannonia. In 378 G. went to the East to assist Valens against the Goths, and when Valens was slain that same year he became ruler of the East as well. In 379 he handed this portion of the empire over to the Spanish general Theodosius. In 383 G. was assassinated near Lyons by followers of the rebellious Magnus Maximus, governor of Britain. Generous, cultured, and a convinced Christian, G. began *c.* 378 to take an active interest in religious questions under the influence of St. Ambrose. He proscribed pagan sacrifices, deprived the priestly colleges and Vestals of state support, removed the statue of Victory from the senate, and renounced the title of *pontifex maximus*. He was also a staunch upholder of Nicene orthodoxy against the Arians. BIBLIOGRAPHY: O. Seeck, RAC 7:1831–39.

[M. J. COSTELLOE]

GRATIAN, JEROME (1545–1614), Carmelite theologian, writer, coworker of St. Teresa of Avila. After his ordination to the priesthood G. became acquainted with the Teresian reform and entered the Carmelite monastery at Pastrana (1572), taking the name, Jerome of the Mother of God. Shortly after his profession (1573) he was made apostolic visitator to the Carmelites of Andalusia, in which position he sponsored and/or approved the establishment of new reform houses. From his first meeting with St. Teresa (1575) until her death (1582), G. remained her close confidant and collaborator. He was elected first provincial of the Discalced Carmelites when they became a separate order in 1581. After Teresa's death and the expiration of his provincialate, G.'s opposition to the policies of his successor caused him to be charged with rebellion, and he was expelled from the order in 1592. His appeal to the Holy See and his attempts to find refuge in other orders were unsuccessful. Captured by Turkish pirates, he endured 2 years of imprisonment. After his liberation he was permitted by the Pope to live among the Calced Carmelites. BIBLIOGRAPHY: O. Rodriguez, NCE 6:706; A. Peers, *Studies on the Spanish Mystics* (3 v., 1927–60) 2:149–189; 421–427.

[J. C. WILLKE]

GRATIAN, DECRETUM OF, a canonical collection of *c.* 1150, entitled in early MSS *Concordantia discordantium canonum,* to reflect its dialectical purpose of resolving conflicts among its authorities (*auctoritates*). The author, Gratian, is known only as a Camaldolese monk who taught in the monastery school of SS. Felix and Nabor in Bologna. Although not the first such collection, the *Decretum* rather quickly won universal acceptance as the canonical text par excellence; was surrounded by glosses and commentaries (see DECRETISTS); and was used in the schools of law. A version corrected to delete spurious decretals was published at Rome in 1582 in the official *Corpus Juris Canonici. In composition the *Decretum* consists of its *auctoritates*—a vast array of papal and conciliar as well as patristic texts, deriving in the main from *Ivo of Chartres—and of Gratian's commentary, and resolution of conflicts. The collection covers the sources of law, ecclesiastical discipline, monastic life, matrimony, and the sacraments. Work on a corrected, critical text has been in progress since the eighth centenary of the *Decretum* was observed.

[T. C. O'BRIEN]

GRATIEUX, ALBERT 1874–1951), student of Russian religious thought, ecumenist. G. traveled to Russia repeatedly between 1907 and 1910 for the purpose of study and research, but in the Modernist reaction he was changed from the Institut Catholique to a country parish. While serving as chaplain in World War I, he was able to return to

Russia as a member of several delegations, and in 1923 he resumed his researches. He published several important volumes on the Slavophile movement. BIBLIOGRAPHY: Y. Congar, *Catholicisme* 5:206–207.

[M. J. SUELZER]

GRATITUDE, a virtue, allied to justice, acknowledging and honoring indebtedness for kindnesses received. The connection with justice is tenuous to the extent that gratitude does not concern a quid pro quo; yet it does respect a real indebtedness, in responding to the spontaneous beneficence of another person, and so requires a sense of honorableness, a sensitivity to the proper way and opportunity to show thanks. St. Thomas Aquinas ranks it with other virtues of reverence and honor towards those who are sources of benefits received, and in that sense are like God in his fatherliness (ThAq ST 2a2ae, 106.1). Since the first gift that a giver bestows is the goodwill or love that prompts the gift, the delicacy and nobleness of true gratitude is obvious—and so the despicableness of ingratitude; it is obvious, as well, that the first measure of gratitude is the heart and goodwill entering thankfulness. The sentiments should be immediate and unforced; goodheartedness and grace should also measure the external expression of thanks. The intent should be to try to return something better to the benefactor in order to remove any suggestion of merely exactly acquitting a debt. Yet the favor returned should match the circumstances and a sense of proportion; extravagance would seem also like not wanting to be obligated. Gratitude is very close to *charity towards God and neighbor; part of loving them is to be happy to be indebted in thankfulness, and to keep green the memory of every kindness.

[T. C. O'BRIEN]

GRATIUS, ORTWIN (van Graes; *c.*1480–1542), German humanist and theologian. G. studied under the celebrated humanist Alexander Hegius (*c.*1433–98) at Deventer in Holland (so he was also called *Deventianus*); became a member of the arts faculty at Cologne (1507), and at the Quentell publishing house supervised the publication of many Latin classics. In 1514 he became a priest. G.'s academic and personal reputation were tarnished by the **Epistolae obscurorum virorum*, addressed to him for joining the opponents of J. *Reuchlin. His belated replies, *Epistola apologetica* (1518) and *Lamentationes obscurorum virorum* (1518), were rather weak. His principal work, *Fasciculus rerum expetendarum ac fugiendarum* (1535), a collection of historical and legal documents pointing to the need for church reform, was judged to be anticlerical and placed on the Index by Pope Benedict XIV after G.'s death. BIBLIOGRAPHY: G. Krodel, RGG 2:1831; D. Reichling, *Ortwin Gratius* (1885); F. G. Stokes, *Epistolae obscurorum virorum: The Latin Text with an English Rendering, Notes and an Historical Introduction* (1909).

[T. C. O'BRIEN]

GRATRY, AUGUSTE JOSEPH ALPHONSE (1805–72), French Oratorian, whose main interest was apologetics. He was ordained in 1833, after emerging from a period of religious indifference. He taught at Strasbourg and at Paris, becoming professor of theology at the Sorbonne in 1863. He joined the revived French Oratory in 1853, but his relationship to the community was a troubled one. He also experienced difficulties because of his opposition to the dogma of papal infallibility prior to Vatican Council I (after the Council he publicly accepted the teaching). G.'s main apologetic concern was to show the harmony between faith and science. Through his numerous writings, esp. *Les Sources* (1862), he was for several generations of readers an influence counteracting rationalism and indifferentism, mainly by the warmth and affectivity that animated his writings. BIBLIOGRAPHY: M. Join-Lambert, *Catholicisme* 5:267–309.

[T. C. O'BRIEN]

GRATZ, PETER (1769–1849), NT exegete. G. taught Scripture at the Univ. of Ellwangen and Bonn, and helped found the *Theologische Quartalschrift*. While at Bonn, he was initially sympathetic to the rationalistic theories of G. *Hermes but soon rejected them. Among his important publications are a Greek-Latin NT and an extensive commentary on Matthew's Gospel. BIBLIOGRAPHY: J. Schmid, LTK 4:1172–73.

[T. M. MCFADDEN]

GRAU, FRIEDRIC, see NAUSEA, FRIEDRICH.

GRAVAMINA, complaints made formally to a superior authority, generally about encroachments of that or of some other authority on the rights of the plaintiffs. A well-documented set of *gravamina* is that occasioned by the Council of Vienne (1311), where many bps., at the invitation of Clement V, listed incursions of secular authorities into purely ecclesiastical realms, claiming, for example, that these authorities continually frustrated the decisions of church courts. BIBLIOGRAPHY: F. M. Powicke and C. R. Cheney, *Councils and Synods* (1964) 2:1350–56.

[L. E. BOYLE]

GRAVES, MORRIS COLE (1910–), American painter. Born in Fox Valley, Ore., after study with Mark Tobey and travel in Europe and the Orient, G. expressed an eastern mysticism in haunting, lyrical paintings of birds and flowers. He worked with the Federal Arts Program in the 1930s and in the 1960s was engaged in paintings for the space program. BIBLIOGRAPHY: F. S. Wright, *Morris Graves,* 1956; G. M. Cohen, "Bird Paintings of Morris Graves," *College Art Journal* 18 (1958).

[M. J. DALY]

GRAVISSIMAS INTER, a letter of Pius IX to the abp. of Munich (Dec. 11, 1862; publicized later) strongly condemning the doctrinal errors of Jakob *Frohschammer (1821–93), who, exaggerating the powers of human reason, taught that reason of itself can perceive and understand the mysteries of faith. The Pope delineates the proper function of philosophy in investigating revealed truths and points out that human reason has its limitations and must not set aside divine revelation and the teaching authority of the Church (D 2850–61).

[J. H. ROHLING]

GRAY, WILLIAM (d. 1478), humanist and patron of scholars; chancellor of Oxford Univ. (1441–42). He studied in Cologne, Padua, and Ferrara (1442–46); was king's proctor at the Roman Curia (1445–54); bp. of Ely (1454–78). G. bequeathed a considerable library to Balliol College, Oxford. BIBLIOGRAPHY: R. Weiss, *Humanism in England* (1957) 86–96; Emden Ox 2:809–814.

[C. D. ROSS]

GRAYMOOR FRIARS, see ATONEMENT, SOCIETY OF THE.

GRAZIANI, BONIFAZIO (Gratiani; 1605–64), Italian composer, *maestro di cappella* at the Jesuit church in Rome and at the Roman Seminary from 1649. His works, including oratorios, Masses, and motets, were first published in 1652 and then in 1678. BIBLIOGRAPHY: Wörner, K. H., *History of Music* (tr. W. Wager, 5th ed., 1973) 282.

[J. C. MARR]

GREAT AWAKENING, a series of religious revivals that spread throughout the American colonies from approximately 1725 to the early 1760s in reaction to religious indifference and secularism. The opening phases of the movement occurred in New Jersey with the vigorous preaching of T. J. *Frelinghuysen of the Dutch Reformed Church. G. *Tennent carried on a similar ministry among the Presbyterians, becoming the most prominent revivalist in the middle colonies. Jonathan *Edwards, Congregationalist of Northampton, Mass., began the New England phase of the Awakening by his forceful and logical sermons emphasizing the dangers of punishment in hell for the unrepentant and the hope of heaven for the converted. Into this scene came G. *Whitfield about 1740 with his own itinerant preaching, which was to extend the fervor of the movement throughout all the colonies. His work provided a measure of geographical unity and a uniformity of pattern to the revival. Samuel Davies proved to be the leading figure in introducing the Awakening to the Presbyterians of Virginia in its later phases. Less balanced preachers, such as James Davenport, by their extravagant charges against clergy who would not support the revival, and by their histrionics in the pulpit, brought the movement into disrepute. Charles *Chauncy of Boston led the attack upon the movement, sharply criticizing it as encouraging eccentric behavior and irrationality while yielding few, if any, moral effects. Edwards, a careful observer, as well as an agent of the revival, defended it as a work of the spirit of God. In *Some Thoughts Concerning the Present Revival* and later in his treatise on the *Religious Affections,* he discriminated between its beneficial and detrimental effects and described in detail the nature and function of the emotions. In New England those who followed Edwards and other defenders of the Great Awakening were known as New Lights and became proponents of the *New England theology; those who opposed it were known as Old Lights. The Presbyterians also split into New Side and Old Side groups.

The Awakening tended to weaken the authority of the clergy, as laymen claimed to be able to judge for themselves the validity of their spiritual condition. Some Churches were invigorated; many were divided, giving rise to sectarian differences in the same denominations or to shifting memberships from Congregational to Baptist Churches. Antagonism toward the Calvinism of the Churches participating in the revival arose among the more liberal-minded members, and many of them later moved into the ranks of the Unitarians and Universalists. Dissenting groups growing from the revival in Virginia helped to overthrow the established Anglican Church in that colony. Increased missionary activity among the Indians is also traceable to the movement, as represented by the work of David Brainerd, Eleazar Wheelock, and Samuel Kirkland. Early antislavery sentiment was fostered, as well as increased interest in education, evidenced by the founding of many academies and of Dartmouth, Princeton, Brown, and Rutgers. BIBLIOGRAPHY: M. Gewehr, *Great Awakening in Virginia, 1740–1760* (1936); E. S. Gaustad, *Great Awakening in New England* (1957). *REVIVALISM.

[C. A. HOLBROOK]

GREAT BIBLE, so called from its size, the English Bible ordered by T. *Cromwell in 1538, to be placed in all churches. Based on *Coverdale's Bible, *Matthew's Bible, W. *Tyndale's notes, it was a revision prepared by M. *Coverdale and was issued in 1539. As an official version, it influenced the *Geneva Bible and the *Bishops' Bible, which replaced it in 1568. The Psalter in the BCP is from the Great Bible. It is called also "Whitchurch's Bible," from the name of one of its English printers, E. Whitchurch (the other was R. Grafton); a 1540 edition had a preface by T. *Cranmer and is known as Cranmer's Bible; the translation of Jer 8.22 gave the Great Bible the popular title "Treacle Bible."

[T. C. O'BRIEN]

GREAT CHURCH, THE, in the Byzantine tradition, the church Hagia Sophia; then also the patriarchate itself of *Constantinople, because of its pride of place in the history of Eastern Christendom. Historical forces have greatly curtailed the power and influence of the patriarchate, but it retains its dignity, as the exchanges in 1963 and 1965 between Paul VI and Athenagoras I, Patriarch of Constantinople symbolized; Hagia Sophia, after the fall of Constantinople to the Turks (1453), became first a mosque and in modern times (1934) a museum.

[T. C. O'BRIEN]

GREAT DEPARTURE, theme in Buddhist art, showing Prince Siddhārtha's secret leave-taking from his father's palace to seek enlightenment. The Buddha-to-be, accompanied by his faithful groom, Channa, rides his horse Kaṇṭhaka, while genii hold up its hooves that no sound betray his escape.

[M. J. DALY]

GREAT LAURA, the oldest and most prominent monastery on Mount Athos; it was founded in 963 by the monk Athanasius, who became its first abbot and organized its life according to the cenobitic rule of St. Theodore of Studius. He had the encouragement and support of Emperor Nicephorus II Phokas, who gave the monastery an annual grant, a particle of the Holy Cross, and other relics. Conflicts between the Great Laura, the only cenobium on the Holy Mountain, and the hermits who had settled there previously caused Emperor John I to regulate their relations in a **typikon* for Mount Athos in 972. Thereafter the monastic system of the laura type became popular on the Holy Mountain. By favor of Byzantine emperors, the Great Laura prospered and was able to increase the size of its community. In the beginning there were 80 monks; by 1045 there were 700. In the 14th cent. *idiorrhythmic monasticism was introduced on Mount Athos. This permitted individual monks greater freedom and the possession of private property. It is not known when this system was adopted at the Great Laura, but it must have been well before 1573, when Patriarch Sylvester of Alexandria reestablished the cenobitic system. But during the 17th cent. idiorrhythmic practices were again introduced at the Great Laura, and they have continued down to the present time. The monastery church, dedicated to the Annunciation, became the architectural model for other monastic churches on Mount Athos. The wall paintings date from the 16th century. BIBLIOGRAPHY: F. W. Hasluck, *Athos and Its Monasteries* (1924).

[V. VON FALKENHAUSEN]

GREAT SAINT BERNARD, HOSPICE OF, refuge for travelers run by Canons Regular of St. Augustine at the Great St. Bernard Pass in the Pennine Alps (Switzerland). The once treacherous pass, which crosses from Martigny, Valais, Switzerland to Aosta, Italy, has been used from Celtic days. Founded *c.* 1050 by St. Bernard of Aosta, it has housed popes and emperors. With the aid of the famous St. Bernard dogs the canons have rescued many travelers and in modern times extend their hospitality to tourists and skiers.

[M. A. MCFADDEN]

GREAT SILENCE, the period of solemn quiet in religious houses, formerly extending from after *Compline until *Prime, now from after night prayer until some suitable time the next morning. Almost all the monastic codes have made some provision for this, e.g., Rule of St. Benedict 42. Its purpose is to produce an atmosphere of deeper recollection, inviting one to enter into the rhythm of nature and to watch for the coming of the Lord. BIBLIOGRAPHY: B. Steidle, *Rule of Saint Benedict: A Commentary* (tr. U. Schnitzhofer, 1967).

[M. B. PENNINGTON]

GREAT WESTERN SCHISM, the period of divided allegiance (1378–1417) when Western Christendom was torn between two, and at times three, rival claimants to the papacy. The roots of the schism can be traced to the period when the papal curia, under French influence, preferred Avignon to Rome. The actual beginning, however, is dated in 1378, shortly after Pope Gregory XI (1370–78) restored the papacy to the Eternal City. Not until the Council of Constance (1414–17) was the schism healed.

The death of Gregory XI in Rome set the stage for the first papal election in that city in 75 years. The 16 cardinal electors, aware of the popular desire for a Roman or at least an Italian pope, went outside their own numbers for a candidate. They selected Bartholomew Prignani, Abp. of Bari. Taking the name Urban VI (1378–89), and crowned on April 18, he began almost immediately to alienate the cardinals who had elected him. Either Urban's extreme tactlessness or, as modern authors suspect, evidence of his dementia led the cardinals to flee the Papal States. Regrouping at Anagni, they repudiated Urban VI and held a new election. This time their choice was Card. Robert of Geneva who took possession of the papal palace in Avignon as Clement VII (1378–94).

The support given the rival claimants reflected national interests; most of Italy, the Holy Roman Empire, Hungary, England, and Scandinavia supported Urban VI; Naples, Sicily, France, Spain, and Scotland were loyal to Clement. Division, confusion, and scandal were caused by the schism, yet there was no recognized canonical machinery for healing the breach. Each obedience, convinced of its own position, continued the rivalry. Urban's successors in the Roman line were Boniface IX (1389–1404), Innocent VII (1404–06), and Gregory XII (1406; d. 1417). The proposals to end the schism generally fell under one of three headings: (1) the *via cessionis* called for the resignation of both claimants; (2) the *via compromissi* proposed that a tribunal be appointed to judge the rival claims; and (3) the *via concilii* looked to a general council to decide the issues.

When the procrastination of Gregory XII and the intransigence of Benedict XIII further worsened the situation, cardinals from both obediences agreed to solve the crisis *via concilii*. Although both Popes opposed it, a council met at Pisa in 1409 for the express purpose of ending the schism. The end result, however, was further division, since Pisa elected a third claimant to the papacy, Alexander V (1409–10); and upon his death, John XXIII (1410; d. 1419).

Finally in 1414 the *via concilii* was tried again at the Council of Constance. More careful planning, better leadership from the "conciliarists," and a prominent role for the Emperor Sigismond, contributed to its success. The Roman Pope Gregory XII gracefully resigned, July 4, 1415. John XXIII had been formally deposed March 29, 1415, and when Benedict XIII was declared deposed on July 26, 1417, the way was open to elect a pope who would be accepted by the entire Western Church. On Nov. 11, 1417, the council ended the schism by electing Martin V (1417–31).

Much of the confusion about the legitimacy of the rival claims of Rome, Avignon, and Pisa still remains. Those who elected Urban VI and Clement VII argued that the Roman mob during the first balloting inspired so much fear that a free election was impossible. Just as the canonical means for resolving the impasse were inadequate in the 14th cent., so today historical and ecclesiological criteria for judging the conflict remain unclear. Certainly, however, the doubt and disputes about the real pope and the real Church deeply affected all levels of Christian life; the schism directly prepared for the destruction of Christian unity a century later in the Reformation. BIBLIOGRAPHY: W. Ullmann, *Origins of the Great Schism* (1948); O. Prerovsky, *L'elezione di Urbano VI e l'insorgere dello scisma d'Occidente* (1960); Hughes HC 3:299–305.

[B. L. MARTHALER]

GREATER LITANIES, a day of prayers and originally also of fasting, traditionally observed in the Roman Church on April 25th, the feast of St. Mark, to invoke God's blessing and protection upon the crops. Its full observance calls for a procession through the fields while the Litany of the Saints and other prayers are chanted or recited alternately by the priest and the people. The word litanies thus came to designate the procession itself, called greater or major because of its earlier origin than the Lesser Litanies in Gaul. The observance in Rome began at least in the 4th cent. to Christianize a similar pagan practice on the same day. Most recently such days for public prayer are to be designated by the various national episcopal conferences. BIBLIOGRAPHY: F. X. Weiser, *Handbook of Christian Feasts and Customs* (1958); J. H. Miller, *Fundamentals of the Liturgy* (1959).

[N. R. KRAMER]

GREBEL, CONRAD (*c.* 1498–1526), leader of the Swiss Anabaptists. The son of a prominent Zurich family, G., as a student and scholar at Basel, Vienna, and Paris, was a humanist with little religious interest. Returning to Zurich (1520) he was converted by H. *Zwingli, but by 1524 broke with him, advocating a religion of inner experience, the rejection of *infant baptism, and the complete separation of Church from State. G.'s followers were known as the Swiss Brethren. In Jan. 1525 he put into practice *believer's baptism by rebaptizing G. *Blaurock. He suffered persecution until his early death from the plague. BIBLIOGRAPHY: H. S. Bender, *Conrad Grebel ca. 1498–1536, the Founder of the Swiss Brethren, Sometimes Called Anabaptists* (1950).

[T. C. O'BRIEN]

GRECO, EL (Domenikos Theotokopoulos; Theotocopuli, Greco, Griego; 1541–1614), Greek-Spanish painter, perhaps greatest of the Mannerists. Born in Crete, so known as "El Greco" (the Greek), G.'s Byzantine background set him in the mystical tradition. In Venice (1558), G. absorbed Titian's architectonic composition and rich palette, Tintoretto's dynamic movement, and Veronese's opulence, *The Marriage at Cana* (1568–70). In Rome (1570), G. infused Michelangelo's late mannerism with his Cretan mysticism, *The Healing of the Blind Man* (1571–73). In *Purification of the Temple* (1574–75), G. attests to the masters, Titian, Michelangelo, Guilio Clovio in portraits. Settling in Toledo, Spain (1575), G. fitted ideally into the fervid atmosphere of the Inquisition and was akin to A. Berruguete, Toledo's mannerist sculptor, but fell from the favor of Philip II because of non-Italianate, intangible, spiritual interpretations in the *Martyrdom of St. Maurice and the Theban Legion* (1580–82). G. painted his most resplendent work, *The Burial of Count Orgaz* (1586), evidencing both earthly and heavenly spheres—the former sumptuous, serene; the latter ecstatic in dynamic, swirling, attenuated, flamboyant shapes, bathed in light spirits immaterial in their weightless, unearthy shapes. Distinctively G.'s are the sharply torn, knife-edged shapes, true to the torn skies of Spain's plateaus *(View of Toledo)* and a framing of forms in embryonic, womblike patterns *(Agony in the Garden)* that confirm the basic rhythms, in the pink and sharp greens of his incandescent palette *(Adoration of the Shepherds, Pentecost, Resurrection)* within long, vertical panels that extend the aspirational, ecstatic feeling. Venetian is G.'s portrait mastery in *Fray Felix Hortensio Paravicino* (1605, Boston), the mystic and intellectual who praised the painter in sonnets, and *The Inquisitor*. G. gained fresh fame in 20th-cent. expressionism. BIBLIOGRAPHY: J. Camón Aznar, *Doménico Greco* (1950).

[M. J. DALY]

GREDT, JOSEPH AUGUST (1863–1940), Benedictine, Thomist philosopher. Born in Luxembourg, he became a diocesan priest (1886) and studied at Rome under some of the leading figures in the 19th-cent. Thomistic revival. He joined the Benedictines at Seckau, Austria, in 1891, and from 1896 until his death was professor of philosophy at San Anselmo in Rome. His principal work, *Elementa philosophiae aristotelico-thomisticae,* was first published in 1899–1901 and went through 13 editions (13th ed. rev. 1961). This textbook, in formal scholastic style, attempted to present authentic Thomistic teaching by relying on the texts of St. Thomas Aquinas, but as interpreted by the principal commentators in the Thomistic tradition. G.'s consideration of human cognition was of particular merit.

[T. C. O'BRIEN]

GREECE, CHURCH IN. At the time Christianity emerged, Rome ruled the entire Mediterranean world, including Greece, but culturally that world was ruled by Hellenism. There were people in many places who by ancestry or education were Greeks, and Greek became the language of the NT and of the universal Church in its first centuries. As to the country of Greece, during Paul's second missionary journey he crossed from Asia Minor to Greece in response to a vision in which a Macedonian appealed for help (Acts 16–17). He preached at Philippi, Thessalonica, Berea, and Athens, where he spoke in a synagogue and on the Areopagus to Stoics and Epicureans. He then spent 18 months in Corinth, headquarters for the Roman proconsul. He again visited Greece on his third missionary tour, and wrote letters to Greek Churches (Phil, Cor, Thess). The history of the Church in Greece during the postapostolic period is obscure, but a number of martyrdoms are recorded. Some of the Apologists worked in Athens, a pagan center until Theodosius II turned the temples into churches (426) and Justinian closed the philosophical schools (529). The Parthenon, temple of Athenae, became a church, and later a mosque after the Turks took Athens in 1458. Slavs moved into Macedonia in the 6th-7th cents., and the Greek Church gradually won them to Christianity. Their dialect became Church Slavonic for all Slavs through the work of *Cyril and Methodius, natives of Thessalonica. After Constantine's death, Rome and Constantinople competed for ecclesiastical supremacy in Greece. Constantinople prevailed, and the schism of 1054 left Greece allied with Eastern Orthodoxy. Greece today remains over 95 per cent Orthodox. In the iconoclastic controversy (8th-9th cents.) Greece upheld icons. Following the conquest of Constantinople by Venetians and Frankish crusaders in 1204, much of Greece came under Western rule. A Catholic abp. took over the Parthenon, but the Greek Church generally was little affected. After 1482 no Latin bps. were appointed till 1875. Through the centuries Greek Orthodoxy became identified with Greek nationalism as the Church represented the national viewpoint in times of conflict with emperors, patriarchs, and occupying forces. In 1821 Abp. Germanos of the Lavra monastery at Patras initiated the fight for Greek freedom. Since Constantinople (Istanbul) remained part of Turkey, in 1833 the Greek Church declared *autocephaly to prevent the exercise of Turkish influence through the patriarchate, which however retained jurisdiction over certain Greek areas, including Mt. *Athos. In 1850 Greece acknowledged Constantinople's primacy of honor and it recognized Greek autocephaly. But the Church had not in fact become free but state-controlled. Today it is governed by a synod of bishops, with the abp. of Athens as primate. Under the constitution of 1975, the Orthodox Church remained the established religion. The primate is appointed by the government from a list of three nominees chosen by the synod.

[T. EARLY]

GREED, a synonym for avarice, the vice and *capital sin of inordinate attachment to the getting and keeping of material possessions, esp. money.

[T. C. O'BRIEN]

GREEK CATHOLICS, a term given often to a variety of meanings. Strictly speaking, it should apply to both the Roman as well as the Byzantine rite Catholics who live in Greece. The Roman rite was introduced into Greece as a result of the Crusades, esp. that of 1204, and many Greek dioceses were placed under Latin bishops. Today there remain three abps. (Athens, Naxos-Tinos and Corfu) and one bp. (Syros) who administer to 45,605 faithful. The term is more specifically applied to the small group of Byzantine rite Greek Catholics who owe their origin to a movement started in 1856 by Rev. John Marango in Constantinople. In 1911 Isaias Papadopoulos became the first Byzantine Greek Catholic bp. and was succeeded in 1920 by George Calavassy, who moved his small group to Greece in 1922. There is one bp. who resides in Athens, 18 native Greek priests and 25 nuns ministering to 2,000 faithful who reside mostly in Athens and in the N town of Ioannitza. They operate a minor seminary, a hospital, an orphanage, a home for the aged, hostels for students and young workers and also engage in the publication of Catholic books and pamphlets in Greek. The term is also used, although improperly, to designate Slavic and other Eastern rite Catholics.

[G. A. MALONEY]

GREEK CHANT, see BYZANTINE CHANT.

GREEK COLLEGE (ROME), a college in Rome for seminarians of Greek descent erected by Pope Gregory XIII in 1576. The second national college of pontifical right to be founded, it is connected with the Church of St. Athanasius. The student body has included principally Greeks and Italo-Greeks, some Melkites, and until 1896, the Ruthenian seminarians. Since 1950 Greek clerics of the Latin rite have also enrolled. The Greek College has been administered by secular priests and various religious orders. In 1773 it came under the direct jurisdiction of the Sacred Congregation for the Propagation of the Faith. In 1896 Pope Leo XIII established a separate college for the Ruthenians, and the Greek College was entrusted to the Confederated Benedictines, in 1919 to the Belgian congregation, and in 1956 to the Monastery of Chevetogne. In 1586 the students of the Greek College received from Pope Sixtus V the privilege of singing the Epistle and Gospel in Greek at solemn pontifical Masses. The students' distinctive apparel includes a blue cassock and red sash.

[T. BIRD]

GREEK FATHERS. In a narrow sense the great Fathers of the Eastern Church are those prominent in the golden age of establishing Christian orthodoxy in the Trinitarian and

Christological controversies; thus SS. *Athanasius the Great, *Basil the Great, *Cyril of Alexandria, *Gregory of Nazianzus, *John Chrysostom (see DOCTORS OF THE CHURCH). St. *John Damascene is often referred to as the last of the Greek Fathers, who synthesized orthodox teaching in his *De fide orthodoxa*. In a wider sense the term means all the great writers of the Eastern Church, including SS. *Cyril of Jerusalem, *Peter Chrysologus, and *Ephrem of Syria. Until the inauthenticity of his name and title was established, *Pseudo-Dionysius the Areopagite had a quasi-apostolic authority and an immense influence on theology, esp. in the West. *APOSTOLIC FATHERS; *FATHERS OF THE CHURCH.

[T. C. O'BRIEN]

GREEK LANGUAGE, BIBLICAL AND EARLY CHRISTIAN, Hellenistic Greek, the dominant language of the Roman Empire. It was derived from classical Greek, from both the Ionic and Attic dialects. Beginning from approximately 300 B.C. it gradually became the language of the cultural elite throughout the lands bordering the Mediterranean, and retained this dominance until approximately 550 A.D. It was the language of commerce as well. This common (*koinē*) Hellenistic Greek was shorn of the subtleties and complexities of classical Greek. In the written documents that have come down to us it comes across as close to spoken language, because it is vivid, emphatic, with a preference for direct discourse and the present tense. The abundant usage of prepositions, adverbs, and the coordinate conjunction "and" also distinguish it from classical Greek. The subject peoples of various cultures had to assimilate as well as they could the Greek language and culture. The Jews living in diaspora found it essential to translate their Scriptures into Greek. The most famous example of this came to be called the *Septuagint (believed to be the work of 70 or 72 translators), a work undertaken for the hundreds of thousands of Jewish inhabitants of Egypt. The Pentateuch translation probably dates from the middle of the third cent. B.C., and most of the other books were probably completed by the beginning of the Christian era. There were later attempts to do the same thing. Theodotion's version dates from the end of the 2d cent. A.D.; Aquila, a Jewish proselyte, made a slavishly literal translation *c.* 130 A.D.; Symmachus, an Ebionite Christian, completed *c.* 170 A.D. a version that tried to be at once good Greek and faithful to Hebrew meaning. That was indeed the problem. Can one translate into fluent Greek without putting on the Greek culture and developing Greek sensibilities? The Jewish leaders who decided at Jamnia (end of 1st cent. A.D.) to restrict the canon of Jewish Scriptures to those works written in Hebrew on Palestinian soil were responding to the danger of syncretism. Their decision helped chart the way for Judaism to become a minority subculture in an alien world-culture. Similarly, the fact that the Christian sacred writings were all written in *koinē* Greek paved the way for the Christian faith to become the religion of the empire. The Septuagint and the NT writings are the most important documents of Hellenistic (*koinē*) Greek, because of their impact on subsequent history. Yet there are other impressive examples of Hellenistic Greek, originating in all corners of the empire: Polybius, Josephus, Philo; the various Christian *apocrypha; Apollodorus the mythographer; Strabo the geographer; Plutarch the biographer; Nicolaus of Damascus and Diodorus the historians. The diatribes of the Stoic philosopher Epictetus bear a remarkable resemblance to the writings of his contemporary, St. Paul. Within the Christian canon there are various levels of success in converting Semitic culture and idiom to good Greek expression. The apocryphal Wisdom of Solomon, which bridges the gap between the Testaments, is at once the most Greek and the best Greek. Among the NT writers, the author of Hebrews and the author of Luke-Acts are the most fluent. Paul and James have the style of Stoic preachers. John, Matthew, and Mark use indifferent Greek, not much removed from the vernacular. The author of Revelations has the distinction of writing the most barbarous Greek.

[E. J. DILLON]

GREEK LANGUAGE IN THE WEST, DECLINE OF. Greek ceased to be commonly spoken in the West (except in some Sicilian cities, e.g., modern Girgenti), at the end of the 2d century. Fairly common usage of Greek began after the Roman conquest of Greece (Pydna, 167 B.C.) and went on crescendo with the influx of prisoners of war and slaves from the Levant and Eastern Mediterranean. It is not easy to determine the peak of Oriental immigration; yet, though the remarks of the satirist Juvenal (d. *c.* 135 A.D.) cannot be taken at face value ("I cannot abide a Rome of Greeks," Sat. 3, 60–61), the *Corpus inscriptionum latinarum* (6) in page after page of Greek names on funerary inscriptions shows that a Greek-speaking population was numerous in the 1st and 2d centuries. The last massive influx occurred at the end of Trajan's reign (117 A.D.) and after the Jewish War of Hadrian (134–136).

Such large numbers of Greek-speaking immigrants to Rome makes understandable St. Paul's use of the language. Hence also Greek was the liturgical language until the second half of the 3d century. It was completely replaced by Latin, probably under Pope St. Damasus (366–384), while St. Jerome was his secretary for Greek affairs. However, Greek expressions persisted, e.g., *Kyrie eleison*, and others were even added as late as the pontificate of Pope Gelasius (end of the 5th century). Significantly, the exclusive series of Greek-speaking popes ceased from Miltiades (311) to Zosimus (418).

Among the educated classes Greek reached its apogee in the age of Cicero, and all cultured Romans strove to speak it. Both Cicero and Caesar composed works in that language. However, with a literature of their own, mastery of Greek by Romans was markedly on the decline. For instance, Quintilian (last quarter of 1st cent., A.D.) in his *Institutio Oratoria,* though obviously familiar with Greek literature, is far more lavish with Latin references. Yet, until the reign of Marcus Aurelius, who composed his *Meditations* in Greek, a whole series of Roman writers also published works (no longer extant) in that language: Pliny the Younger, Tacitus, Juvenal, Suetonius, Fronto of Cirta (*c.*100 to 170), tutor of Marcus Aurelius, and Apuleius of Madaura in Africa are thoroughly conversant with it. "In the 3d cent., the stranger who did not understand Latin would still be able to make his way in the larger cities of the West." (Harnack, *Die Mission und Ausbreitung des Christentums,* 1:17 n. 2). In the 4th cent. a traveler could not get by without Latin. However, even in the 2d cent. it is now established that the gospel was propagated in Latin (as early as 150 A.D.), and the need arose for a Latin version of the Bible. In the completely new vocabulary for liturgical needs, the resultant terminology is heavily influenced by Hebrew, as were the Septuagint and the NT. The rest of the vocabulary and the syntax were not drawn from "classical" Latin but from the every-day language of the common folk.

In the 4th cent. only those who had the means could achieve linguistic facility. St. Ambrose was able to read, in contrast to St. Augustine, the works of the Greek Fathers and thus enrich Latin patristic literature. Only in the Eastern half of the Balkans did Greek persist as a spoken idiom when Emperor Theodosius the Great (379–395 A.D.) achieved for the last time the union of the two halves of the empire. From then on attempts to recapture a knowledge of Greek became, in the West, an arduous task, taken up by such men as *Boethius (480–524) and Cassiodorus (480–575), a task reserved to scholars. BIBLIOGRAPHY: P. Langlois, NCE 6:731–732.

[J. M. F. MARIQUE]

GREEK ORTHODOX CHURCH, see EASTERN ORTHODOX CHURCH.

GREEK ORTHODOX ARCHDIOCESE OF NORTH AND SOUTH AMERICA, the official Greek Orthodox jurisdiction for the Americas. The first parish was founded in New Orleans in 1864, but the Orthodox Church in America did not develop until the turn of the century with the acceleration of immigration from Greece, which continued into the 1920s. Originally the American parishes were under the jurisdiction of the Patriarchate of *Constantinople, but in 1908 that jurisdiction was transferred to the Orthodox Church of *Greece. This arrangement lasted until 1918 and was unfortunate since it deferred the organization of Greek-American Orthodoxy. One step in solving this difficulty was the appointment of Metropolitan Meletios as delegate of the ecumenical patriarch. The latter established a Synodical Council that prepared the way for centralization, and when he was elected patriarch of Constantinople in 1922, one of his first acts was to restore ecclesiastical jurisdiction to Constantinople. On May 11, 1922, the archdiocese was officially created and Abp. Alexander was appointed patriarchal exarch. Political events in the homeland also brought division in the Greek-American community during the 1920s. When *Athenagoras became abp. in 1930, he inaugurated a brilliant program of organization that brought about the union of most Greek parishes. Athenagoras became ecumenical patriarch in 1948 and his successor, Abp. Michael Constantinides, continued to strengthen Greek Orthodoxy in America. Abp. Iakavos contributed greatly to the ecumenical movement and was responsible for establishing the *Standing Conference of Canonical Orthodox Bishops of America in 1960. The archdiocese maintains numerous schools, philanthropic associations, and Holy Cross Theological School. The faithful number about 2,000,000 in 380 parishes.

[F. T. RYAN]

GREEK PHILOSOPHY. The purpose of this article is to outline and characterize very briefly the development of Greek philosophy period by period in its long history from *c.*600 B.C. to the closing of the philosophical schools at Athens by the Emperor Justinian in 529 A.D. Details on the more significant individual philosophers, movements, and schools are given in separate articles as indicated.

Early Greek Philosophy (*c.*600–*c.*450 B.C.). This may also be called, more specifically, Pre-Attic or Pre-Socratic philosophy. Five subdivisions will help to indicate the stages of progress and also the growing recognition of problems. However, during the whole period the chief concern of the early Greek thinkers, who should be called philosopher-scientists rather than simply philosophers, was to find the origin of things, to discover the nature of the universe.

The Milesian or Ionian Schools. *Thales, *Anaximander, and *Anaximines of Miletus were the founders of science and philosophy proper. Thales sought the *archē* or the beginning of things in water; Anaximander, in the Infinite or Indeterminate in Nature; Anaximines, in air. No distinction was yet made between the material and the immaterial or spiritual, and from the beginning of Greek philosophy and science, the eternity of matter was taken for granted.

Pythagoras and the Pythagorean Brotherhood. *Pythagoras, who migrated from Ionia to Italy, founded a religious society or brotherhood. The Pythagoreans, however, were likewise concerned with the search for the *archē* which they sought in numbers. Unlike the rest of the Pre-Socratics, they were equally preoccupied with asceticism and ethics.

**Heraclitus of Ephesus* sought the *archē* in fire and identified fire with the logos, or reason, or ordering principle of all things. He maintained that all things are in a state of flux, and that there is a harmony in opposites. He is the deepest thinker of the Pre-Socratics.

*The *Eleatics.* This school takes its name from the town of Elea in S Italy. They are represented chiefly by

*Xenophanes of Colophon, *Parmenides, and *Zeno of Elea. Xenophanes attacked the traditional polytheism and regarded God as the motionless One. His concept of God, however, is monistic, not monotheistic. *Parmenides taught that Being, the One, is, and that becoming, change, is an illusion. He is regarded as the first to enunciate the principle of contradiction. He also made a sharp distinction between reason and sense. Zeno of Elea, the inventor of dialectic, formulated elaborate proofs against the possibility of motion. Thus, Heraclitus and Parmenides represent directly opposite positions, one maintaining a doctrine of flux and the other a doctrine of changelessness.

The Eclectic, Pluralist Systems. Under this heading come **Empedocles, *Anaxagoras, *Leucippus, and Democritus,* the younger group of philosopher-scientists; all are older or younger contemporaries of Socrates. Empedocles attempted to reconcile Ionian cosmology and Pythagoreanism, to deal with the problem of the one and the many. He taught a doctrine of the all as a spherical *plenum,* recognized four basic roots or elements—fire, air, water, and earth, and maintained that in nature there was an eternal process of mingling of these elements under the contrary impulses of love and strife. The major contribution of Anaxagoras was the introduction of mind (*nous*) as the initial source of cosmic motion and as the life-principle of plants and animals. His *nous,* however, would seem to be thought of in material terms, and not as yet a teleological principle. Leucippus and Democritus were the founders of the atomic theory, which in many respects was the logical development of the philosophy of Empedocles. Soul and mind are considered identical and made up of small fiery atoms. The motion of the atoms and the vortex bringing them together are postulates. The system has been made widely familiar by the *De rerum natura* of the great Latin poet Lucretius.

Attic Philosophy. (The Age of the Sophists, Socrates, Plato, and Aristotle; *c.*450–*c.*300 B.C.). The investigations of the philosopher-scientists did not cease in the age of Socrates, or even later, as is evident from the career of Democritus, who did not die before *c.*370 B.C. However, with the destruction of Miletus by the Persians (494 B.C.), Athens became the chief intellectual center of the Greek world, and, with the rapid growth and prosperity of Athens as well as of other Greek states in the 5th cent., it became increasingly necessary for men to turn their attention to man himself as a citizen, as a magistrate, and as a person. Political, social, and economic life were becoming more complex, and trained leadership was needed.

*The *Sophists*. They appeared on the scene as educators who claimed that they could teach *aretē*, i.e., efficiency or skill in any subject, provided the learner had a normal endowment of native talent. They catered to the well-to-do and charged fees for their instruction. They elaborated a systematic program of education which culminated in the curriculum of the liberal arts. Their philosophical outlook varied, reflecting the various philosophical currents with which they made contact. They tended, on the whole, to be superficial in their philosophical views and to disseminate doctrines, the full implications of which they did not perceive. Individual Sophists adopted a relativistic attitude toward the validity of knowledge, an agnostic attitude toward the traditional divinities, and challenged the divine origin of the state and its laws. Furthermore they ignored or rather neglected the moral side of education. The conservative Aristophanes is severe in his condemnation of the Sophists as destroyers of traditional values and morality. Men like Alcibiades were regarded as the products of Sophistic education. A serious intellectual and internal political crisis was only too manifest, esp. at Athens in the last quarter of the 5th cent.

**Socrates*. He marks an epoch in the history of philosophy. He believed that the soul, as the most important part of man, should receive his major attention. He was the first to recognize the soul as the intellectual and moral personality. He held that if man had right knowledge, he would necessarily act rightly. For him such knowledge is identical with virtue. His method of questioning was intended to reveal a man's ignorance of right knowledge to which he could then be led. He exercised a unique influence not only by his thought but also by his own personality and by his willingness to die for his principles. He was the chief inspiration of Plato.

*The *Minor Socratics*. The term is employed to designate several schools or movements, in part of extreme tendencies, that claimed Socrates or Socratic teaching as their source. Their connection with Socrates was really very tenuous. The groups in question were the *Megarians, the *Elean-Eretreans, the *Cynics, and the *Cyrenaics. Of these the most important and the longest to endure were the Cynics.

**Plato and *Aristotle*. It is unnecessary here—and practically impossible in a short space—to outline the contributions of Plato and Aristotle, the greatest of Greek philosophers whose thought continues to have an active influence in the modern world. Both, if in somewhat different ways, worked out comprehensive philosophies—although Plato did this in less systematic form. Aristotle was the first philosopher to attempt a general classification of knowledge. Both had this in common, namely, that they lived in the 4th cent., and that they were familiar at first hand with the political decline of Athens and with the internal disintegration of the Greek city-state, and, in particular, that of Athens. Plato's hostility to democracy and Aristotle's preoccupation with a mixed constitution are based on personal experience or observation. Both were concerned with ways and means of restoring the city-state as the best of all polities and the only one in which man as a person and as a citizen could realize his full potentialities.

The Alexandrian and Early Roman Periods (*c.*300–*c.*50 B.C.). Alexander changed the whole character of the Greek world. The sovereign city-state was replaced as the norm of political and social life by the Hellenistic monarchy and the rise of a cosmopolitan society. There was a need to find new standards of values and of making radical adjustments under new conditions of life. The new philosophies, and to some extent the old, were preoccupied, accordingly, in meeting the needs of the individual in an international, cosmopolitan society, and with setting before him a goal of peace, security, and happiness—an ideal of self-sufficiency and the means of attaining it. Stoicism met the need most successfully and was the most influential of ancient systems of philosophy from *c.*300 B.C. to the early 3d cent. A.D. Epicureanism was also important, but far less so than Stoicism. Philosophy must be regarded, furthermore, as a way of life, a religion, and the adoption of a given philosophy was increasingly regarded as a form of conversion. Athens was the home of the philosophies, old and new, although the chief representatives of the various schools were usually not Athenians.

Stoicism. This is a comprehensive philosophical system founded by *Zeno of Citium, with emphasis on ethics and the ideal of the wise man, the individual who is master of himself. The individual, however, is a citizen of the world and has definite responsibilities to his fellowmen. For an account of the system in some detail and its development see STOICISM.

Epicureanism. Founded by Epicurus of Athens, this is likewise a comprehensive philosophical system. It is based in its cosmology on the atomic theory, but is primarily concerned with ethics and with its own ideal of the wise man—the individual of abstemious life who withdraws from all activities that could disturb his tranquillity and devotes himself to the cultivation of friendship. For an outline of the system in some detail see EPICUREANISM.

The Peripatetic School (or the Lyceum, or the School of Aristotle). This was organized and developed to a marked degree by *Theophrastus of Lesbos (372–288), the founder of botany, and active in a number of other fields. The school was chiefly concerned with scientific and historical research. Among other representatives may be mentioned, Aristoxenus of Tarentum (fl. last half of 4th cent. B.C.), most important ancient writer on musical theory; Straton of Lampsacus (d. *c.*270), physicist and important for his theory of space; and *Andronicus of Rhodes (fl. middle of 1st cent. B.C.), who arranged, classified, and edited Aristotle's works. The Peripatetics made important contributions in biography and to the development of the genre.

The Academy (or School of Plato). The Old Academy, under Plato's first successors, continued to maintain the teachings of Plato but gave greater emphasis to mathematics, astronomy, and ethical questions. However, the two first scholarchs, *Speusippus (d. 339 B.C.) and *Xenocrates, already went beyond Plato on certain points, and their views were to have an influence later on Middle Platonism and on Neoplatonism. The Platonist Crantor of Soli (*c.*335–*c.*275) wrote the first commentary on Plato's *Timaeus* and a treatise *On Grief*, the most influential of the ancient *Consolations*. The Middle Academy, founded by *Arcesilaus of Pitane (scholarch, 268–240), taught an extreme form of logical skepticism which was modified by the theory of probabilism held by *Carneades of Cyrene (244–129), founder of the New Academy. *Philo of Larissa (160–80) broke largely with the skepticism of the Middle and New Academies, and his pupil *Antiochus of Ascalon (*c.*130–120–*c.*68) returned to the epistemology of the Old Academy. Philo and Antiochus are regarded as the founders of the so-called ''Fourth'' and ''Fifth Academies'' respectively. Cicero attended the lectures of Antiochus in Athens in 78. Strictly, Antiochus was an eclectic rather than an Academic or Stoic, esp. in his ethics.

The Older Skeptics. The founder of skepticism proper was Pyrrho of Elis (*c.*360–270), who was followed by his pupil Timon of Phlius (*c.*320–230). Like the Stoics and Epicureans, they were primarily concerned with ethics. Their doctrine of uncertainty was intended to give philosophical support to their ethical objective of imperturbability of mind.

The Cynics and Other Minor Socratics. The Cynics show no marked changes in the teachings and attitudes of their founder. Their tenets are faithfully reflected in the wandering preacher and writer *Crates of Thebes (*c.*365–285) and his wife Hipparchia. Bion of Borysthenes (*c.*325–255) developed the satirical style of ''saying the truth with a laugh,'' which was to have its influence on Horace. The Cynic diatribe was now given literary form and a whole series of Cynic or Cynico-Stoic *topoi* was developed. The *Cyrenaics were represented by *Theodorus the Atheist (*c.*330–270), who repudiated all moral restraints and the existence of divinity, and by *Hegesias of Cyrene (*c.*330–270), who advocated suicide as a release from pain and grief. Under *Stilpon (*c.*380–300) the Megarian School was the most popular in Greece. He wrote a number of dialogues and adopted the ethical doctrine of *apatheia* from the Cynics (see CYNICISM).

Through the first half of this period (*c.*300–*c.*50 B.C.), the Stoics and the Platonists in particular carried on a sharp polemic esp. on epistemology, and it was only gradually that the Platonists recognized rhetoric, so cultivated by the Stoics, as a subject worthy of philosophical attention. In the second half of the period, however, all the schools or movements, with the exception of Epicureanism, exhibit more or less marked eclectic tendencies. Philo of Larissa and Antiochus of Ascalon, for example, are definitely eclectic, and the same is true of *Panaetius and *Posidonius, the founders of Middle Stoicism. The eclecticism of the Romans like *Cicero and *Varro reflects the eclecticism of their Greek teacher of philosophy.

Hellenistic-Roman Philosophy (from *c.*50 B.C.–*c.*250 A.D.). This period is characterized by a return to the founders, to the renewed study, editing of, and commenting upon, their works, by a widespread eclecticism and syncretism and by a preoccupation with theology and mysticism, including Egyptian and Oriental treatises and revelations.

*Late *Stoicism.* The Stoicism of *Seneca, *Musonius,

*Epictetus, and *Marcus Aurelius marks a return to the Early Stoics. However, it is almost exclusively ethical in content and profoundly religious. Yet it not only exhibits a softening or modification of Early Stoic dogmatism, but also the acceptance of Platonic dualism, at least in part, in respect to the *nous*.

**Neopythagoreanism*. There was a revival of Pythagoreanism in the 1st cent. B.C. and most probably at Alexandria. The Neopythagoreans stressed devotion to Pythagoras and his ascetical ideal, and emphasized numbers and their mystical qualities. However, in keeping with the contemporary eclecticism, they borrowed elements from Platonism, Aristotelianism, and Stoicism, and showed a marked bent for the occult and for theurgy, embracing the *Hermetic Literature and the *Chaldean Oracles with enthusiasm. However, one can hardly speak of a Neopythagorean School. There is a wide range in the actual tenets held by those who called themselves Pythagoreans. At the higher philosophical level, some Neopythagoreans maintained that all things are derived from the monad or point; others, while admitting the monad as the ultimate origin, stressed the opposition between the *monas* and the indefinite dyad (*aoristos dyas*). Among the representatives of Neopythagoreanism, it will suffice to mention P. *Nigidius Figulus (*c.*98–45 B.C.); *Apollonius of Tyana (1st cent. A.D.), a wonderworker and prophet; *Moderatus of Gades (2d half of 1st cent. A.D.), who regarded numbers as the symbols of metaphysical concepts; *Nicomachus of Gerasa (1st half of 2d cent A.D.), who dealt with mathematics in the spirit of Pythagoras; and esp. *Numenius of Apamea (2d half of 2d cent. A.D.), in whom the syncretism of Neopythagoreanism reached its high point and helped to prepare the way for *Neoplatonism.

Middle Platonism. This term is employed to designate a body of doctrines that in part derive from Plato himself and his disciples, Speusippus (scholarch of the Academy, 347–339) and Xenocrates of Chalcedon (scholarch 339–314 B.C.), and in part from Aristotelian logic and metaphysics, Stoicism, and Neopythagoreanism. Despite wide divergences on many points, all Middle Platonists were primarily concerned with theology and a religious way of life. Middle Platonism can hardly be called a system, but it is of greatest importance in the history of philosophy, because the doctrines falling under this title constitute, along with Neoplatonism, the chief Platonic influence on early Christian philosophy and theology. It will suffice here to mention some of the principal Middle Platonists and to refer to the individual articles for details on their doctrines. The following are especially important: *Eudorus of Alexandria (1st cent A.D.), *Plutarch of Chaeronea (*c.*45–125 A.D.), *Albinus (2d cent. A.D.), *Apuleius of Madaura (*c.*125–d. after 163), *Atticus (*c.*150–200), *Celsus (2d half cent. A.D.), and *Maximus of Tyre (fl. 180 A.D.).

The Peripatetics, Later Skeptics, and Cynics. The Peripatetics in this period were mainly concerned with commenting on the works of Aristotle and they tended to be dogmatic and relatively conservative. The greatest of the commentators was *Alexander of Aphrodisias (2d–3d cent. A.D.). Stoic influence, however, is evident as in the pseudo-Aristotelian *peri kosmou (De mundo)*. The geographer Claudius Ptolemaeus (fl. 121–151 A.D.) and the physician Galen (129–199 A.D.) were eclectic Aristotelians. The Later Skeptics are represented by Aenisodemus of Cnossus (2d half of 1st cent. B.C.) and *Sextus Empiricus (fl. *c.*250 A.D.) (see also SKEPTICISM). The most illustrious representative of Cynicism in this period was Dion Chrysostom of Prusa (*c.*40–d. after 112), who, however, became progressively Stoic in his teachings and outlook. Mention may be made here, too, of the fantastic Christian Cynic, *Maximus of Alexandria, the intrusive bp. of Constantinople in A.D. 380. Throughout this period, the Cynics were often charged with theatrical display and insincerity, for example, by *Lucian of Samosata, but some of the criticism at least seems to have been exaggerated.

Neoplatonism (*c.*250–529 A.D.). The term has been employed since the early 19th cent. to designate the comprehensive system of philosophy elaborated by *Plotinus, the last of the great original Greek thinkers, and its further development or modification by his successors. Plotinus himself regarded his philosophy as authentic Platonism, but a critical examination of the system indicates that he contributed something new, and, reflecting the eclecticism of Middle Platonism, it contains Neopythagorean, Aristotelian, and Stoic elements—and also Egyptian and Oriental features, esp. in *Iamblichus and Plotinus. Neoplatonism was so important that they are given separate articles, and likewise the other more significant Neoplatonists. See NEOPLATONISM, ANCIENT CHRISTIAN. For Hellenistic-Jewish philosophy see the article PHILO JUDAEUS. It will suffice here to list the founders, the chief schools, and their representatives: Ammonius Saccas (teacher of Plotinus), Plotinus (205–270), and *Porphyry of Tyre (232–d. after 301); the Syrian and Pergamene Schools—*Iamblichus (*c.*250–330), *Aedesius (d. *c.*355), Secundus *Sallustius (before 377), *Eunapius of Sardes (*c.*345–414), and *Julian the Apostate (332–363); the Athenian School—*Plutarch of Athens (*c.*350–433), *Syrianus (scholarch, *c.*431), *Proclus (*c.*411–485), Marinus (scholarch, 484), *Damascius (*c.*458–d. after 533); and *Simplicius (1st half 6th cent, A.D.); the Alexandrian School—*Hypatia (*c.*370–415), *Synesius of Cyrene (370–375–413). *Hierocles of Alexandria (5th cent., a pupil of Plutarch of Athens), *Ammonius Hermion (*c.*445–517–526), Joannes Philoponus (d. *c.*570), *Olympiodorus (early 6th cent.); the Latin Neoplatonists—*Calcidius (fl. *c.*400 A.D.), *Macrobius (fl. 400 A.D.), *Martianus Capella (2d half 4th cent. A.D.), and *Boethius (*c.*480–524). BIBLIOGRAPHY: A. H. Armstrong, *Introduction to Ancient Philosophy* (1959); Copleston v. 1; Guthrie 1 and 2; CHGMP; Ueberweg v. 1.

[M. R. P. MCGUIRE]

GREEK RELIGION, the complex beliefs and religious practices of the ancient Greeks in numerous communities throughout Greece proper and the Mediterranean and Pontic world from pre-Homeric times down to the disappearance of paganism in the 5th and 6th cent. A.D. Knowledge of this religion is derived from both literary and archeological sources. The writings of Homer, Hesiod, the elegiac, lyric, and tragic poets, and the historians and philosophers contain numerous references to, and descriptions of, various rites and a great many myths. Excavations at Athens, Eleusis, Olympia, Delphi, Epidauros, and elsewhere have turned up numerous temples, statues, treasuries, altars, and inscriptions containing calendars, lists of priests, oracles, and sacred decrees. The assessment of this material is frequently difficult, not simply because of the differences of time and place, but also because of the character of Greek religion itself. It had no specifically sacred books such as the Bible or the Koran, no dogmas or creed, that is, a prescribed body of doctrine, no powerful priestly castes, no code of ethics, and no theology in the sense of a rational investigation of the data of religious experience or revelation. Nevertheless, the Greeks were an essentially religious people (cf. Acts 17.22), and their interpretation of life and of the world about them was definitely religious. This may be seen in their faith in the power and omniscience of the gods, their trust in them, their gratitude for favors received, their friendly regard for their divine protectors, and their joy and enthusiasm in honoring them, particularly during the public festivals.

Though Greek religion retained traces of more primitive practices, a worship of rocks, trees, and animals, a belief in taboos (*miasmata*) and magic, and the conducting of fertility rites, in its developed form it was essentially an anthropomorphic polytheism. This was brought about through a fusion of a belief in sky gods and the use of bloody sacrifices that belonged to the Indo-European invaders of Greece with earlier belief in chthonic deities and the offering of unbloody sacrifices on the part of the peoples already living there. To these were later added other gods borrowed, particularly from the East, and other rites such as the ecstatic dances in honor of Dionysius and the temple-harlotry of Aphrodite at Corinth.

By the time of Homer, the Greek deities had already been associated into a kind of clan with Zeus, "the father of gods and men," exercising a kind of patriarchal authority over the rest of the Olympians. Among these latter were his wife Hera, his daughters Artemis and Athena, and his sons Ares and Apollo. Associated with these gods were the heroes, men such as Heracles who had been divinized for their noble deeds. In contrast with these celestial deities were those of the Lower World, particularly Hades and his wife Persephone. As gods of the dead rather than the living, they received little worship. When an animal was offered to them in sacrifice, it was always an appropriate black. Over all these gods and their mortal clients there reigned, however, in some mysterious fashion Destiny (*moira, moros,* or *aisa*), at times in conflict with the gods but far more frequently expressive of their will.

Greek literature, particularly in Homer and in the tragedians, portrays the role of individual men such as Calchas and Tiresias who, as seers or prophets, proclaimed the will of the gods. Much more important than these diviners, however, were the oracular shrines at Dodana, Delos, Didyma, and above all at Delphi. There through the medium of a priest or priestess, the will of the gods could be discovered with respect to the advisability of proposed courses of action. The oracle at Delphi could be consulted by individuals, as it was by Socrates, or by cities with regard to the founding of colonies and the waging of war. It could even be consulted by foreigners such as Croesus, king of Lydia, and the Roman Senate. Its answers were frequently ambiguous and occasionally partial; but because of the respect in which it was held, it was probably the most important single unifying element among the Greeks in religion as it was in politics.

Prayers and sacrifices were offered to the gods by individuals, families, the members of a clan or phratry, and esp. by the city-states, for Greek religion was essentially of a communal nature. Prayers addressed to the gods usually consisted of an invocation, the reasons why it should be heard, and the actual petition. In the official festivals these prayers would be accompanied by hymns, processions, and sacrifices. One of the most famous of these festivals was the Great Panathenaea held every 4 years at Athens, a vivid representation of which is given in the lengthy frieze that surrounded the cella wall of the Parthenon. Religious in character also were the Panhellenic games held at Olympia, Delphi, and Corinth.

In contrast with the Judaeo-Christian tradition, Greek religion was to a large extent amoral and in its mythology even in the minds of some Greeks themselves at times, quite immoral. This deficiency was to an extent remedied by the reflections and ethical teachings of Pindar and the tragedians, particularly Aeschylus and Sophocles, and by the philosophizings of the Greek sages, of Socrates, Plato, Aristotle, and the Stoics, all of whom subscribed to the religion of the state but taught at the same time a more or less perfect kind of monotheism.

The separation in the cities of the public worship of the gods from its agrarian foundations, the decline of the city-states in the 4th cent. B.C., the rationalizations of the philosophers, and the disappointment of personal hopes as the result of the constant civil and foreign wars that plagued the Greeks, weakened the influence of traditional religion and turned the minds of men to more personal types of worship that would at the same time give promise of a happy immortality. Already in the classical period the Eleusinian mysteries and those connected with Orpheus and Dionysus promised purification and survival after death to their initiates. The feeling for the importance of the individual is also reflected from the 5th cent. on in the popularity of Aesclepius, the god of healing, the worship of Tyche, the goddess Fortune, during the Hellenistic Age, and the widespread cult of such foreign deities as the Egyptian Isis and the Persian Mithras under Roman rule.

Probably the most lasting achievement of Greek religion was the profound influence it had on the whole of Hellenic art—the painting of vases, the engraving of gems and coins, the carving and casting of exquisite statues, the erection of altars such as that of Zeus at Pergamum and of hundreds of temples throughout the Mediterranean world. The same inspiration is to be seen in the poetry of Homer, of Pindar, and the Greek tragedians, and in the philosophy, at least by reaction, of Plato. In its highest philosophical reaches, its influence can also be seen in the borrowings made under divine inspiration by the authors of the Sapiential Books of the Old Testament. BIBLIOGRAPHY: M. P. Nilsson, *Geschichte der griechischen Religion,* 2 v. (1955–1961); M. Camozzini, EncCatt 6:1040; A. J. Festugière, *Personal Religion among the Greeks* (1960); E. R. Dodds, *Greeks and the Irrational* (1951).

[M. J. COSTELLOE]

GREEN, JULIEN (1900–), French born novelist and dramatist who expressed the tensions between grace and a world marked by the disorders of sin. Born of American parents living in Paris, educated in France and in the U.S., G., though writing in French, reflects aspects of both cultures in his work. Reared a Presbyterian, after his mother's death G. read Cardinal Gibbons's *Faith of Our Fathers*; he then sought instruction from a Jesuit priest through the influence of his father, an earlier convert who never discussed religion with his children. Soon after, G. received Catholic baptism (1916) and contemplated entering the religious life. The tepid and pharisaical attitude of his French coreligionists led him to write *Pamphlet contre les catholiques de France* (1924). There followed a period of unbelief, lasting until 1934, when he sought spiritual insight in Buddhism. In 1939 a reading of George Herbert's poetry and St. Catherine of Siena's *Treatise on Purgatory* led to his return to Catholicism. His *Journal,* 6 v. (1928–54), with additional pages of *Le Bel aujourd'hui* (1955–57), is a significant contemporary religious document, recording his spiritual evolution. His early novels, though not directly concerned with religious questions, nevertheless reflect supernatural anguish. A spiritualistic orientated fiction was inaugurated with *Varouna* (1940) and with *Si j'étais vous* (1947), criticism of false piety. Religious themes have come to occupy a larger role in his later novels and dramas. BIBLIOGRAPHY: S. E. Stokes, *Julien Green and the Thorn of Puritanism* (1955); J. L. Prevost, *Julien Green ou l'âme engagée* (1960); J. Sémolue, *Julien Green ou l'obsession du mal* (1964).

[G. E. GINGRAS]

GREEN, THOMAS HILL (1836–82), English philosopher. Educated at Oxford, he was elected Whyte's Professor of moral philosophy in 1878. His two most important published works are *Prolegomena to Ethics* (1883) and *Lectures on the Principles of Political Obligation* (1895). G. reacted against Hume's empiricism and Spencer's theory of biological evolution, which represented man as a "being who is simply the result of natural forces." G. held that self-reflection reveals man's acting for an end, a good, and that this self-determination is not determined but rational and free. In political philosophy he taught that the purpose of the State is to work for the common good of its citizens. G. exercised a powerful philosophical influence on 19th-cent. England, yet his vagueness makes his true principles often difficult to grasp. BIBLIOGRAPHY: M. Richter, *Politics of Conscience: T. H. Green and His Times* (1964); W. H. Walsh, EncPhil 3:387–389.

[M. J. BARRY]

GREENE, GRAHAM (1904–), English novelist, born at Berkhamsted, Herfordshire. Before publishing his major novels, G. led a varied active life that gave grist and impetus to his novels of the tortured and potentially damned. G. attended Balliol College, Oxford (1922–25). The next year he spent as a reporter on the *Nottingham Journal.* In 1926, he was received into the RC Church. From then on his literary career was sprinkled with journeys providing him with literary and personal background and framework. He visited West Africa, Mexico, Sierra Leone, Kenya, Malaya, and the Congo. G. might be considered an experimenter with the psychological in his concern for the sinner and his final penitence or impenitence. His critics are not all beneficent. Orwell labels his characters "the sanctified sinner" and regrets that concentration on such persons as Scobie can lead easily to a cult. G.'s novels and his plays, e.g., *The Potting Shed,* reveal his preoccupation with the moral dilemma of humanity, with the dark places in the human heart, and with man's final confrontation and reconciliation with Christ. His style has been praised and equally defamed as "nervous," "vivid," "astringent," or "grim" and "functional." He invites comparison with Dostoevsky, Camus, or Mauriac. A paeon by Mauriac states that G. counteracts the absurdity of the worlds of Sartre or Camus.

G. wrote thrillers (which he calls entertainments) such as *Confidential Agent* and *The Ministry of Fear* (1943). His reputation, however, rests on the major novels: *Brighton Rock* (1938), *The Power and The Glory* (1940), *The Heart of the Matter* (1948), *The End of the Affair* (1951), and *The Quiet American* (1955). He gained some fame in the dramatic world with *The Living Room* (1953), *The Potting Shed* (1957), and *The Complaisant Lover* (1959). G. has written journals, essays, and an autobiography, *A Sort of Life* (1971). More recently he returned to the novel in *The Honorary Consul* (1973). BIBLIOGRAPHY: P. Stratford, *Faith and Fiction: Creative Process in Greene and Mauriac* (1964); D. Pryce-Jones, *Graham Greene* (1963).

[R. M. FUNCHION]

GREENE, ROBERT (*c.*1560–92), English dramatist, prose writer, and poet, a "university wit," who attacked the young Shakespeare because he came from the country, had no university degree and thus was an "upstart crow." He lived a dissolute life but repented, probably sincerely, in *Greene's Groatsworth of Wit Bought with a Million of Repentance,* licensed, 1592. His narrative writing is declamatory and static; his "cony catching" pamphlets realistic in scenes from the London underworld, in their humor and slang; his best poems are songs and eclogues interspersed throughout his prose works; his plays are partly conventional retorts to Marlowe's "atheism." He was one of the first Elizabethans to make his profession the entertainment of a broad reading public. BIBLIOGRAPHY: G. Jones, *Garland of Bays* (1938), a fictionized biography.

[M. M. BARRY]

GREENLAND, world's largest island (Australia regarded as a continent). Formerly a Danish possession, since the revision of the constitution (1953), it has been an integral part of Denmark. Greenland is predominantly Lutheran and ecclesiastically under the bp. of Copenhagen. It lies NE of Canada and almost entirely within the Arctic Circle, more than 80% of its area covered by ice. Settlement began *c.*985 by Eric the Red, a Norwegian-born resident of Iceland. He had sailed to the island earlier and on his return to Iceland, he named the new discovery Greenland to encourage settlement. The sagas record that Leif, Eric's son, brought the Christian faith on his return from a trip to Norway *c.*1000, and that Leif's mother, Thjohild, built a church, the first in the Western hemisphere. Like Iceland, Greenland was ecclesiastically under Bremen at first, transferred to Lund in 1104, and to Nidaros (Trondheim) in 1152. A diocese was established in 1124, and the first bp., Arnald, arrived 2 years later. In 1261 Greenland came under the jurisdiction of Norway. In the 14th and 15th cents., the Greenland colonies died out or became assimilated with the Eskimos. Recolonization began in 1721, led by the Lutheran minister H. P. Egede of Norway. In 1380, Norway, and therefore Greenland also, came under the Danish crown. When Norway became independent in 1815 (in union with Sweden), Greenland was left under Danish control.

[T. EARLY]

GRÉGOIRE, HENRI (1881–1964), Belgian Orientalist and historian. After taking his doctorate at Liège, G. made further studies in Germany, France, Palestine, and Greece, and then returned to teach Greek philology in Brussels. In 1923 he helped to found the journal *Byzantion.* A productive worker with a broad range of interests, he published numerous monographs and studies, the best known of which is his *Les Persécutions dans l'Empire Romain* (2d ed., 1964). BIBLIOGRAPHY: F. X. Murphy, NCE 6:754–755.

[R. B. ENO]

GREGORIAN CHANT, music of the texts of early Western RC Latin liturgies. Synonyms are: plainchant, plainsong (distinguished from figured or measured song, the polyphonic music of the Middle Ages and Renaissance), sometimes simply chant, in German *choral.* It is the oldest musical art form still in use in the West. It is music that uses a single-line melody, derived from Greek, Hebrew, and Syrian influences; it is vocal, diatonic, modal. The range is not large; often all is contained within an octave. It is monophonous, without the third dimension of harmony. The melodic intervals are small, and conjunct (stepwise) motion is primary. The rhythm is that of prose or free verse, coming from the natural accents of the spoken words. There is rarely any repetition of text. Syllables that are accented may be emphasized by high notes, or sometimes by more notes on a particular syllable. Every Gregorian melody is divided into periods or phrases, and these are often arch-shaped, beginning on low pitched notes, ascending, then descending. The part of Pope St. Gregory I for whom this chant is named, in its development and organization is difficult to define. He could hardly have accomplished all that some medieval traditions ascribe to him in the space of 14 years, but he probably ordered and supervised at least the beginnings of a codification of many areas of church life, including the liturgy. One result of his work is that chants were assigned for different parts of services and for particular feasts of the year. The standards for liturgical ceremonies dating from this era were virtually unchanged until the 16th century. Use of the term Gregorian Chant dates from as early as the 9th cent., and this is also the era from which we derive the first traces of the music in its present forms. Originally, these chants were handed from one generation to the next orally; in about the 7th cent., a form of notation was devised; it gave the singers only an outline of the contour of each melody. This was done by means of ascending and descending lines indicated above the words. These lines were called neumes ("nods" or "signs"), and this term still persists for the note or notes to be sung on any one syllable. Later neumes became more complicated, showing how many tones were to be sung on a given syllable, and finally a form of notation was devised that uses a staff of four lines with clefs indicating relative pitches. Today many chants are also transcribed and printed in modern notation. It is not known for certain whether the chant was always sung unaccompanied in the early Church. Before the 12th cent., information regarding musical instruments comes from scattered visual and literary sources, including sculptures, reliefs, and miniatures and similar pictorial decorations in Psalters and other books. There are many references to instruments in French poetry of the 12th and 13th centuries. Manuscripts of chant are extant from the 9th cent. and later. Many of these come from vastly differing times and places, and the similarities between them are surprisingly close, often amounting almost to identity, an indication that in earlier times they were transmitted very faithfully by oral tradition or by some form of notation of which no specimens survive. The missionaries of the Church took the chants over the ancient Roman roads to all parts of Western Europe, and with Western and Northern influences came several notable developments. Chief among these are: the range was enlarged; the melodic line acquired more skips, gradually gravitating toward a harmonic center, and ultimately leading to major and minor modes; new forms were added, chiefly tropes (additions of music and/or words; this became overdone, and all were abolished by the Council of Trent in 1560), sequences (a special kind of trope, most of which were abolished by Trent; four were retained, and one more was added in 1757), and liturgical drama (one of the earliest, 10th cent., came from the trope to the Introit of the Easter Mass). One of the more obvious ways in which Western music has been influenced by the chant is in the Hexachord System. Guido d'Arezzo, an 11th-cent. monk, devised a method of teaching sight-reading by memorizing the pattern of the six tones c,d,e,f,g,a. In the hymn to St. John the Baptist *Ut queant laxis,* the first note of each succeeding line was one of these tones in ascending order. By using the initial syllable of the first word on each line, he devised the pattern *ut, re, mi, fa, sol, la*. The first syllable has been changed to *do,* except in France, and the syllable *si* or *ti* (from "*S*ante *I*oannes"?) added above *la,* the result, the major scale.

The Gregorian melodies may be classified in numerous ways. According to the nature of the texts, there are: biblical or nonbiblical and prose or poetic chants; examples of these are: biblical prose, Gospel of the Mass, biblical poetry, psalms; nonbiblical prose, *Te Deum,* and nonbiblical poetry, hymns and sequences. As to manner of performing, chants are: responsorial, alternating from solo to choral singing; antiphonal, alternating from chorus to chorus (less flexible and less elaborate than responsorial). By relation of notes to syllables: chants are syllabic, most syllables having one note; neumatic, the syllable having two, three, or four notes (a neume); or melismatic, an extended series of notes on each syllable. According to form or structure chants are: two balanced phrases, as in psalm tones; strophic, same melody used for several stanzas of text, as in hymns; free forms, including all other types, which do not allow concise description. One more method of categorizing chants is according to the portions of liturgical services (Mass and Office) for which they are used. Parts with changing texts include: reciting tones (for prayers, reading from the Bible), one note, with occasional inflecting notes inserted; psalm tones, one for each mode, and one extra, the *tonus peregrinus* or "pilgrim tone" and slightly more complex than the reciting tone; antiphons (most numerous chants, 1,250 in the modern Antiphonale). Evidence of the Eastern origins of the early Church, antiphons are mainly sung on the same melody with slight variations; the older ones are simpler, because intended for singing by a chorus, while moderately ornate ones have developed for the Introit and Communion of Mass,. The most highly developed musically are the chants for these parts of the Mass: Gradual, Alleluia and Offertory; often several melismatic formulas are joined in them in the manner of Jewish synagogue chants. Parts for the Ordinary (unchanging portions) of the Mass were originally syllabic, for congregational singing, and this form is retained in the Gloria and the Credo. The other parts lend themselves naturally to three part arrangements, and are commonly heard thus: Kyrie, ABA or ABC, Sanctus, ABB', and Agnus Dei, ABA or all three the same.

In order to understand the present form of various books containing the Gregorian chants used in connection with the liturgy (as it existed prior to introduction of the vernacular after Vatican Council II) it is necessary to review the printing history the various collections have had since the 17th-century. An edition published by the Medici Press in Rome (1614–15) represented an arbitrary treatment of traditional Gregorian by editors with little sense of the development of the chant. In 1869 F. X. Haberl published the Ratisbon edition, repeating the errors of the Medician. Published by Pustet, this edition had Vatican approval. At the Benedictine abbey of Solesmes, France, a program of liturgical reform initiated by Dom Prosper Guéranger (1805–75) included the restoration of Gregorian chant by diligent investigation of the varying MSS in the abbey library. Guéranger also introduced a free-flowing, rather than mechanical singing of the chant. Under the direction of Guéranger, a new edition of chants was produced, based on a study of the diverse MSS from earlier times. In 1880 Dom Joseph Pothier published *Les Melodies grégorienne d'après la tradition,* a radically new interpretation of traditional chant, restoring its pre-Medicean character. In 1883 Pothier's *Liber Gradualis* appeared and was savagely attacked by adherents of the Ratisbon truncated version. To support Pothier, Dom André *Mocquereau published a number of MSS, sources of Gregorian, in his monumental *Paléographie musicale* (1888), a painstaking study of chants in MSS from the 9th to the 17th cent., demonstrating a rediscovery of the essentially common attributes in Gregorian chant history. Mocquereau in this and other writings proved that editions popular at his time contained serious distortions. Mocquereau published later *Le Nombre musical grégorien* defining the rhythm of chant as musical but free. It is the work of Solesmes which underlies the Vatican edition of Gregorian chants (1905 to 1912). Although some disputes concerning rhythmic signs on the notation continued, the Solesmes method prevailed.

In the 20th cent., Pope St. Pius X initiated a reform of church music, and in 1911 founded the Pontifical Institute of Sacred Music, one of the principal functions of which is to further the study of Gregorian Chant. In the U.S., the Pius X School of Liturgical Music at Manhattanville College of the Sacred Heart in Purchase, N.Y., was affiliated with the Institute in Rome. The monks of *Solesmes have developed critical chant texts. Vatican Council II, in its Decree on Sacred Liturgy, urges that the typical editions of the books of the Gregorian Chant be completed, and that a more critical edition be prepared of those books already published since the restoration by St. Pius X. It also calls for an edition containing simpler melodies for use in smaller churches, and urges musicians to find practical means of preserving and using this rich heritage in liturgical services.

[J. C. MARR]

GREGORIAN MASSES, 30 Masses said on consecutive days, to which a plenary indulgence applicable to a soul in purgatory is attached. The name is derived from a story in the *Dialogues* of *Gregory the Great (d. 604) about a monk who was released from purgatory after such a series of Masses. The Sacred Congregation of Indulgences last declared the practice to be a reasonable one in 1888.

[T. M. MCFADDEN]

GREGORIAN REFORM, that reform movement of the Church which began in the middle of the 11th cent. and was extended through the first decade of the 12th. Although it began before and continued after his pontificate, it received its name from Pope Gregory VII, because of his significant leadership, his reform decision, and the strength he brought to the papacy. Recent studies have clarified the influence of Cluny throughout this reform movement. It centered on these areas; the strengthening of the primacy of the pope and the centralization of authority, reform of the clergy, and the elimination of lay investiture. BIBLIOGRAPHY: J. Gaudemet, NCE 6:761–765; A. Fliche, *La Réforme grégorienne* (3 v., 1924–37); J. J. Ryan, *St. Peter Damiani and his Canonical Sources* (1956). *CHURCH, HISTORY OF.

[F. H. BRIGHAM]

GREGORIAN SACRAMENTARY, a "family" of Mass books whose origin is attributed to Pope St. Gregory I (d. 604) and which exists in various forms: a 9th-cent. pre-Hadrian Paduan MS; the descendants of the *Hadrianum,* the papal service book sent to Charlemagne by Pope Hadrian I *c.*784; and a mixed type originating in Gaul. Charlemagne obtained and mandated the Roman Sacramentary in an effort to unify his empire. But the papal service book (already outdated in Rome) had to be supplemented and adapted to parish use. A supplement of Gallican and Mozarabic materials (introduced by the *Hucusque* preface attributed to Alcuin) was added. These materials were gradually intermixed with the Roman texts. After being added to during the 9th and 10th cent., this fusion of texts found its way back to Rome, where it was subsequently adopted and became the basis of the Missal of Pius V. The text for the Roman Mass dominant in the West was thus a hybrid of the original Roman liturgy and the Gallican-Mozarabic liturgies. BIBLIOGRAPHY: *Le sacramentaire grégorien,* (ed. J. Deshusses, 1971).

[J. DALLEN]

GREGORIAN UNIVERSITY, THE PONTIFICAL (Pontificia Università Gregoriana), institution of higher learning for ecclesiastical studies in Rome staffed by the Jesuits. As the *Collegio Romano* it was founded by Ignatius of Loyola in 1551, raised to university status by Pope Paul IV in 1556; Gregory XIII, after whom it was subsequently named, put it (1583–85) on a secure basis with its own building. In 1930 it moved into new quarters on the Piazza della Pilotta. Until the pontificate of John XXIII it was the only institution of ecclesiastical studies having the title of university. Its alumni are active as diocesan bishops and cardinals, seminary professors and canon lawyers throughout the Catholic world. Especially since its new start in 1824, it has played an important role in fostering closer contact between the Roman center of church operations and the dioceses or regional groupings of the RC communion. Its theology, represented by influential Jesuits such as G. Perrone, J. B. Franzelin and L. Billot, emphasized the leading position of the hierarchy and its head, the pope (cf. T. H. Sanks, *Authority in the Church,* 1974). Since Vatican Council II many adaptations have been introduced, including the admission of nonclerical students. It publishes several international reviews and scholarly series, including *Gregorianum* (since 1920). To it are conjoined the Pontifical Biblical Institute and the Pontifical Institute of Oriental Studies.

[P. MISNER]

GREGORIAN WATER, the water, named for St. Gregory I the Great, who first prescribed its blessing and use in the dedication of a church (see CHURCHES, DEDICATION OF) for the *lustrations, i.e., the sprinkling of the walls and altars by the officiating bp. as a symbol of the expulsion of evil powers. The water is mixed with salt, wine, and ashes and is blessed before the lustrations.

[T. C. O'BRIEN]

GREGOROVIUS, FERDINAND (1821–91), German historian of medieval Rome. He studied Lutheran theology before beginning his historical researches in Rome (1852). His monumental study, *Geschichte der Stadt Rom im Mittelalter* (8 v., 1859–72; A. Hamilton, tr., *History of the City of Rome in the Middle Ages,* 1894–1902) covers the period from 410, Alaric's sack of the city, to 1527, its sack by Charles V's soldiers. Because of its antipapal interpretation of medieval politics the work was put on the Index in 1877. G. also wrote on medieval Athens and a journal of his Italian travels.

[T. C. O'BRIEN]

GREGORY I THE GREAT, ST. (540–604), **POPE** from 590, last of the "four great doctors of the West" and founder of the medieval papacy. He was born of a patrician family that had already given two popes to the Church. After receiving an excellent education and entering the civil service, he was made prefect of the city in 572–573. Following the death of his father Gordianus, G. erected six monasteries on his family's estates in Sicily and converted his ancestral home on the Clivus Scauri into a monastery dedicated to St. Andrew. There he subjected himself to the Benedictine Rule under the abbot Valentio. Ordained by one of the regionary deacons, G. was later sent in 579 by Pope Pelagius II as *apocrisiarios, or papal legate, to the imperial court at Constantinople. There he made numerous acquaintances and came to know the political and ecclesiastical problems of the age and the indifference of the Byzantine court to the situation in the West. Recalled to Rome in 585, he continued in his monastic life but at the same time acted as counselor and secretary to the Pope. When Pelagius died in the pestilence of 590, G., despite his genuine reluctance to accept the honor, was elected his successor by popular acclamation. After this choice had been ratified by the Emperor, he was consecrated and began to attack ills that afflicted both Church and State in a manner that was to be decisive for the future of the West. He reorganized the administration of the large land holdings of the Church (the *Patrimonium Petri*), using the increased revenues to alleviate the sufferings of the poor and destitute. Aware of the weakness of Byzantine authorities in Ravenna, G. appointed governors to Italian cities and supplied them with means of self-defense. He saved Rome from the Lombards by negotiating the equivalent of a separate peace treaty (552–553). The Franks and Visigoths responded favorably to his diplomacy. His most successful missionary endeavor brought St. Augustine and his monks to England. Adopting the title of ''Servant of the Servants of God,'' G. steadfastly upheld the prerogatives of the Holy See against the claims of the Patriarch of Constantinople, who had adopted the title of Ecumenical Patriarch.

G.'s numerous writings emphasize the practical. His 854 extant letters are of great historical interest and reflect his administrative genius. His *Liber regulae pastoralis,* written shortly after his elevation to the papacy, became the vade mecum of the hierarchy during the Middle Ages. In four books he describes the character of one who is to be a spiritual guide, the virtues he must possess, his manner of preaching, and his need of daily recollection and examination of conscience. G.'s *Moralia* is a lengthy commentary on the Book of Job dealing with problems of moral and ascetical theology. He also wrote other commentaries on the Gospels and on Ezechiel. His *Dialogi,* in four books, narrate the lives and miracles of St. Benedict and other early Latin saints and discuss the immortality of the soul. The popularity of this work was enhanced by the medieval fascination for the wonderful.

Besides these strictly literary activities, Gregory has been traditionally credited with composing a sacramentary. No copy of this has survived, and what portion of the sacramentary that bears his name was written by himself is debated among scholars. His role in the creation of Gregorian chant is disputed. An ardent promoter of monasticism, G. laid the foundation for the exemption of religious orders by granting monasteries certain privileges that partially exempted them from episcopal jurisdiction. Though more of a follower of tradition than innovator in theology, he developed the doctrine of purgatory, enriched Christology by his refutation of the Agnoetae, and promoted the veneration of the relics and images of the saints. G.'s personal leadership and administration preserved the positive elements of a declining political structure and established the bp. of Rome as the undisputed political and moral power for the new emerging nations of medieval Europe. BIBLIOGRAPHY: B. Pesci, EncCatt 6:1112–24; Altaner 556–565; Daniélou-Marrou, 437–440; V. Monachino, BiblSanct 7:222–278; R. Gillet, DSAM 6:872–910, esp. for G.'s theological, ascetical, and mystical doctrine.

[M. J. COSTELLOE]

GREGORY II, ST. (d. 731), **POPE** from 715. He is sometimes called the Younger in the West, and Dialogus by the Greeks, who confused him with Gregory I. After serving several popes in various capacities, G. accompanied his immediate predecessor in the papacy, *Constantine I, on a journey to Constantinople to deal with the Emperor Justinian II, who was attempting to wrest from the Pope an approval of the decrees of the *Quinisext Synod long since disavowed by Pope *Sergius I. His distinguished service on the occasion was followed on the death of Constantine by his own election to the papacy. As Pope, G. was firm in dealing with the Emperor Leo III (717–741); he resisted the imposition of imperial taxes and later reacted to Leo's iconoclastic decrees with definitive condemnation and a vigorous protest against the Emperor's interference in doctrinal matters. G.'s reign marks a turning point in the history of the Church; the papacy began to ally itself to the emerging Germanic peoples of the West, as the politically decadent but still autocratic Byzantines attempted to retain their arbitrary control of Rome. When Leo III tried to have G. kidnapped in an attempt to impose his iconoclasm by force, a treaty with the King of the Lombards and military aid thwarted the design. Never again was the Holy See altogether dependent on Constantinople. G. encouraged St. Boniface and his missionary work in Germany, blessing the enterprise and consecrating Boniface in 722, and continuing to follow developments by correspondence. This active interest left an imprint of the Roman spirit on the organization of the nascent German Church. In addition, G. renewed much church property in Rome and contributed to the liturgy especially by the addition of Lenten Masses. BIBLIOGRAPHY: C. Dawson, *Making of Europe* (1932); Hughes HC 2:122–123; Butler 1:308.

[P. F. MULHERN]

GREGORY III, ST. (d. 741), **POPE** from 731. Born of a Syrian family, G. was the last pope for whose election imperial confirmation was sought through the exarch of Ravenna. He continued the struggle against *iconoclasm, first attempting to dissuade the Emperor Leo III from his policy, and then condemning iconoclasm in a Roman synod and excommunicating image breakers. The Emperor took revenge by taking jurisdiction over the province of Illyricum from Rome and giving it to Constantinople. He also dispatched a fleet to humble Rome and make G. a prisoner. The fleet was scattered by storms, but imperial forces appropriated papal territories in S Italy and in Sicily. When the Lombards, whose growing power had been useful to the Holy See in resisting imperial pressure, themselves became a menace, G. appealed, not to the Emperor, but to *Charles Martel for protection. Although the appeal went unheeded, the step marked a new weakening of ties between East and West and foreshadowed important developments soon to come. G. continued his predecessor's encouragement of St. *Boniface, whom he made an abp. in 732 with a commission to set up dioceses in the newly evangelized lands of Germany. He also bestowed the pallium on *Egbert of York and conferred upon him the authority of a metropolitan in the North of England. BIBLIOGRAPHY: Butler 4:531; Mann 1.1; H. K. Mann, CE 487–489.

[P. F. MULHERN]

GREGORY IV (d. 844), **POPE** from 827. In accordance with the Roman Constitution approved by *Eugene I in 824, the consecration of G. (a Roman, cardinal priest of St. Mark's at the time of his election) was delayed until imperial commissioners had reviewed and certified the circumstances of the election. During his long reign, G.'s energies were largely absorbed in efforts to preserve intact the unity of Charlemagne's vast empire, which the Pope conceived as necessary to the peace of the Church. He dispatched a succession of legates to the warring descendants of Charles and even went in person to Alsace in the hope of blocking the dismemberment of the empire, which, despite his efforts, was accomplished, shortly before his death, at the Treaty of Verdun (843). On another front, G. saw the Church menaced by the ever-extending influence of the Muslims as they took Sicily and threatened the entire Italian coast. In the North, however, G. was able to advance the cause of Christianity. He bestowed the pallium on St. *Ansgar, naming him legate to Scandinavia and encouraging him in the establishment of a hierarchy there. BIBLIOGRAPHY: Mann 2.1:187–231; H. K. Mann, CE 6:789–790.

[P. F. MULHERN]

GREGORY V (Bruno of Carinthia; 972–999), **POPE** from 996, the first German to occupy the papacy. A great-grandson of Emperor Otto I (963–973), he was prepared for the clerical life from his youth and served as chaplain to his cousin Otto III (982–1002). On the death of John XV, who had been restored to his see in 995 through Otto's influence, the German king presented G., then only 24 years old, as pope and the Romans accepted him without opposition. One of G.'s first acts was to crown Otto as emperor (996). The two ruled in a harmony that was not unmarked by some tension. G., a man of virtuous life, was sincerely intent upon reform and maintained independence of the Emperor in achieving his purpose. He sustained the policy of his predecessor by refusing to permit Hugh Capet to install in the See of Reims, Gerbert, a personal friend of Otto, destined to succeed G. in the papacy. Yet he sent Gerbert the pallium when he was named abp. of Ravenna. G. withstood the Emperor also in his plan to recreate the See of Merseburg, which had been absorbed into Magdeburg at the will of the German hierarchy. When Hugh Capet's son and heir, Robert the Pious, entered into an unlawful marriage, G. excommunicated him and imposed on him 7 years of penance. Through G.'s influence at the beginning of his reign, the Emperor had pardoned Crescentius II who had expelled John XV from his see. But Crescentius once more involved himself in a struggle to gain control of the papal office, this time by promoting the cause of Abp. John Philagathos of Piacenza in a claim to the papal throne. Crescentius forced G. out of Rome, but the Emperor invaded the city, beheaded Crescentius, blinded and imprisoned the antipope (who had taken the name John XVI), and restored G. to power. BIBLIOGRAPHY: F. Dressler, NCE 6:771; Hughes HC 2:197; Mann 4:389–446.

[P. F. MULHERN]

GREGORY VI (John de Gratiano; d. 1047), **POPE** 1045–46. A man of unblemished character and, perhaps, a leader of the reforming element in Rome, he arranged to provide Benedict IX with a sum of money sufficient to induce his resignation. Reformers hailed his accession, but soon changed their opinion of G. upon learning of his supposed simoniacal advancement. Emperor Henry III investigated his title to the papacy and at the Synod of Sutri deposed him, opening the way for the election of the German pope, Clement II. G. went into exile in Germany, accompanied by his chaplain, Hildebrand. BIBLIOGRAPHY: R. L. Poole, "Benedict IX and Gregory VI," *Proceedings of the British Academy* 8 (1917–18) 199–235; G. B. Borino, "Invitus ultra montes. . . ," StGreg 1 (1947) 3–46; O. J. Blum, NCE 6:772.

[O. J. BLUM]

GREGORY VII, ST. (Hildebrand; *c.*1020–1085), **POPE** from 1073. Educated at Rome, he was one of the chaplains of Gregory VI when that pope was deposed at the Synod of Sutri in 1046. Hildebrand went with him into exile in Germany (1047) and on Gregory VI's death late that year became a monk of Cluny. He journeyed with Leo IX, the new pope, to Rome in early 1049. Soon after his arrival in Rome, Hildebrand was made a cardinal by Leo, and in 1050, abbot of St. Paul's. In 1054 he went as legate to France, where he presided at a synod at Tours to discuss the Eucharistic teaching of Berengarius; later he went on other missions to France (1056), Tuscany, and Germany (1057). Shortly after the election of Nicholas II, he made a spirited appeal at the Lateran Synod of 1059 for the renewal of regular life among canons; he maintained that clerics who embraced the common life should relinquish all their goods. In 1059 he was made archdeacon of the Roman Church. From then on his activities were largely those of any curial cardinal, until the day of the funeral of Alexander II when Hildebrand was elected pope by popular acclamation.

From the outset, at Lenten synods in Rome, G. promoted clerical reforms, particularly with respect to simony and incontinence. If his decrees on simony and celibacy were resisted with some show of strength in France and Germany, his efforts toward the abolition of secular appointments of bps. resulted in a complete break with the Emperor Henry IV. Repeated warnings to Henry had no effect; a Diet convoked at Worms in Jan. 1076 labeled G. ''no true monk'' and actually declared him deposed from the papacy. Gregory retaliated at the Lenten synod of 1076 with the excommunication of Henry and his suspension from royal office. Although the Emperor sought and obtained absolution from Gregory at Canossa in Jan. 1077, the alienation of Emperor and Pope continued; it was further complicated when Rudolf of Swabia was elected in place of Henry by dissident German princes later in 1077. When G. recognized Wilbert as Emperor in 1080 and excommunicated Henry again because of his failure to fulfill the promises made at Canossa, Henry set up Wibert, the excommunicated abp. of Ravenna, as antipope and then marched on Rome. When Henry captured Rome some 2 years later, G. who had called on Robert Guiscard and his Norman troops for help, fled from Rome in the protection of the Normans; he found refuge in Salerno, where he died. BIBLIOGRAPHY: G. Miccoli, BiblSanct 7:294–379; *Gregorian Epoch: Reformation, Revolution, Reaction* (ed. S. Williams, 1964).

[L. E. BOYLE]

GREGORY VIII (Alberto de Mora; d. 1187), **POPE** for 57 days in 1187. He was an Augustinian Canon who had filled many offices, including chancellor of the Roman Church. With the Church in a time of crisis, the cardinals elected him on the death of his predecessor. The election took place Oct. 21; he was consecrated on the 25th and died after a pontificate of less than 2 months. He planned a general peace and a crusade, but died before any action could be taken on these projects. BIBLIOGRAPHY: S. McKenna, NCE 6:775; A. Ghinoto, EncCatt 6:1134; Mann 10:312–340.

[S. WILLIAMS]

GREGORY IX (Ugolino; *c.*1170–1241), **POPE** from 1227. A nephew of Innocent III, he became cardinal in 1198 and bp. of Ostia in 1206. When elected pope he was already an old man. Most of his 14 years as pope were taken up with Frederick II, who at his coronation as emperor in 1220 had vowed to go on a Crusade; and Gregory now insisted that he should fulfill his promise. In 1227 he declared Frederick excommunicate, and although Frederick went on a Crusade and entered Jerusalem in 1229, G. did not release him from excommunication until 1230. In fact while Frederick was in the Holy Land, G. had freed his subjects from their oath of fidelity to him, and had actually preached a Crusade against him. A relatively quiet period followed from 1230 to 1237, but in 1237 Frederick became a distinct threat to Rome after his victory over the Lombard League. In 1239 G. excommunicated him, and when Frederick invaded the Papal States in 1240, G. called a council for Rome in 1241. Frederick showed his disdain of the council by seizing 100 bps. and 3 legates, who were on their way by sea to Rome, and then he marched on Rome. Shortly after Frederick had captured Tivoli and was within sight of Rome, G. died. A great friend and admirer of St. Francis and St. Dominic, G. canonized Francis in 1228 and Dominic in 1234; and he enlisted the Dominicans and Franciscans as agents of reform. His concern for the Univ. of Paris caused him to institute a commission for the reform of the curriculum and for the examination of the writings of Aristotle. His bull *Parens scientiarum Parisius* (Paris, the mother of sciences) is a landmark in the history of the university. The act of his pontificate that had the most lasting effect was his promulgation in 1234 of a volume of papal constitutions which had been put together at his request by Raymond of Peñafort ''for the use of schools and tribunals.'' Into this volume, *Decretales Gregorii IX* or *Decretales Extravagantes,* Raymond placed in classified form the main constitutions of G.'s predecessors for a century or more, many decretals of G. himself, as well as any decretals ''circulating apart from the usual collections.'' The result was the first authentic general collection of papal decretals and constitutions. It formed the core of the official *Corpus iuris canonici* of 1582. BIBLIOGRAPHY: *Registres de Grégoire IX* (4 v., ed. L. Auvray, 1890–1955); G. Mollat, NCE 6:775–777; O. Bonmann, EncCatt 6:1134–40.

[L. E. BOYLE]

GREGORY X, BL. (Teobaldo or Tedaldo Visconti; 1210–76), **POPE** from 1271. He held minor offices and gained vast experience in ecclesiastical matters; he was widely known and highly respected. While in the Holy Land on Crusade with Edward I, the cardinals, after a 3-year conclave, elected him. Invested at Rome G. planned a general council to strengthen the constitution of the Church, unite Greek and Latin Churches, save the Holy Land, end the interregnum, and bring peace to Italy. The Second General Council of *Lyons was only partially successful; the interregnum ended, but neither the general peace nor a Crusade was achieved. Bl. Gregory was acclaimed by contemporaries as a humane, wise administrator anxious for peace and Christian brotherhood. BIBLIOGRAPHY: M. François, NCE 6:777; Mann 15:347–501; F. Molinari, BiblSanct 7:379–387.

[S. WILLIAMS]

GREGORY XI (Pierre Roger de Beaufort; 1329–78), **POPE** from 1370, the last French pope. He determined to reestablish the seat of the papacy at Rome. Leaving Avignon on Sept. 13, 1376, he reached Rome on Jan. 17, 1377. G. succeeded in ending the quarrel between Naples and Aragon; thus he gained for the Church large yearly amounts of gold from Sicily. Though troubled by temporal matters, G. reformed abuses in religious orders and did not neglect pastoral duties. The rigorous Italian climate and political upheavals hastened his death. BIBLIOGRAPHY: J. B. Villiger, LTK 4:1188; G. Mollat, *Catholicisme* 5:242–244; A. Clerval, DTC 6.2:1807.

[F. D. LAZENBY]

GREGORY XII (Angelo Correr; *c.*1325–1417), **POPE,** 1406–15. The major thrust of G.'s pontificate was the effort to end the Great Schism. His failure to reach an agreement with the antipope Benedict XIII at Avignon led to the calling of a council at Pisa; there the two popes were declared deposed and a third elected. When this maneuver failed to resolve the issue, the Council of Constance was convoked (1414) at which Gregory XII was recognized by all as the lawful pope. Later G. resigned (1415) and paved the way for the end of the schism and the election of Martin V. BIBLIOGRAPHY: Pastor 1:166–202; L. R. Loomis et al., *Council of Constance* (1961).

[J. MULDOON]

GREGORY XIII (Ugo Buoncompagni; 1502–85), **POPE** from 1572. He had already been a famous professor of law at Bologna, and from 1539 an official in the papal service at Trent and Rome before entering the clerical state *c.*1542. He had also fathered a natural son. He was made bp. of Viesti in 1558 and was the canonist for the papal legate, L. *Simonetta, at the Council of Trent (1561–63). Created cardinal priest of San Sisto in 1565, he filled several posts under Pius IV and Pius V, whom he was elected to succeed at the conclave of 1572. As pope he strove to offset the losses of the Reformation by aiding Catholics in England, Scotland, Sweden, Germany, and the Low Countries; Poland's allegiance was firmly established. G. zealously promoted the decrees and aims of Trent. Among his contributions to church reform were: his approval of the Oratory of *Divine Love of St. *Philip Neri and of the Carmelite reform of St. Teresa of Ávila; the favor he showed the Jesuits; establishment of the English and German Colleges in Rome for the training of clergy; rebuilding of the Collegium Romanum, afterwards named for him the Gregorian University; the completion and promulgation of the *Corpus juris canonici*. Because of his reform of the calendar, the result, published in 1582, is known as the Gregorian Calendar.

[J. R. AHERNE]

GREGORY XIV (Niccolò Sfondrato, 1535–91), **POPE** from Dec. 5, 1590 to Oct. 16, 1591. A jurist and bp. of Cremona at the age of 25, he participated in the Council of Trent (1561–63), and sought to implement its decrees in his diocese. He was created a cardinal in 1583. Unexpectedly, after the death of Urban VII he was elected pope. He shared the friendship and spirit of St. *Philip Neri and enforced several Tridentine reform measures on episcopal residence and other disciplinary matters. He also commissioned the correction and revision of the Sistine Vulgate. His inexperience led him to unwise political interventions on the side of Spain in opposition to Henry IV of France. BIBLIOGRAPHY: Pastor 22:351–408 and *passim*.

[J. R. AHERNE]

GREGORY XV (Alessandro Ludovisi; 1554–1623), **POPE** from 1621. After receiving a degree in canon law, he became a priest and entered papal service as a canonist and member of diplomatic missions under Gregory XIII, Clement VIII, and Paul V. He became abp. of Bologna in 1612 and strove to implement the Tridentine disciplinary decrees there. His pontificate accomplished a reform in papal elections, replacing acclamation by strictly regulated, secret balloting that required a two-thirds majority for election; the legislation remained in effect until the reign of Pius X. He also established the Congregation for the Propagation of the Faith (see CURIA ROMANA), which added to the effectiveness of the Church's missionary work, and condemned Indian slavery in the New World. His political interventions helped the Catholic cause in Bohemia.

[J. R. AHERNE]

GREGORY XVI (Mauro Cappellari; 1765–1846), **POPE** from 1831. An ascetic Camaldolese monk and theologian, champion of reactionary policies within the Roman Curia, who reigned at a time of new challenges from the ideological forces of the 19th cent., G. viewed problems from a base of theoretical principles rather than pragmatic experience. Liberalism he condemned completely in *Mirari vos* (1832). Respecting legitimate authority, he opposed revolutionary change even at the expense of persecuted Catholics in Poland. Acute problems in the government of the Papal States affected his political thinking generally. Everywhere he strove to protect traditional ecclesiastical rights from State encroachment. His reign coincided with the flowering of Catholic Romanticism. BIBLIOGRAPHY: E. E. Y. Hales, *Church and the Modern World* (1960).

[R. H. SCHMANDT]

GREGORY, PATRIARCH OF ANTIOCH from 570 to 593. A monk, he was appointed by Emperor Justin II to succeed the deposed Athanasius I. G. is said to have been a friend of Pope St. Gregory I, the Great, an influential preacher and writer. The texts of but a few of his sermons have survived.

GREGORY II, CYPRIUS (1241–90), **PATRIARCH OF CONSTANTINOPLE** 1283–89. In the era of the Council of Lyons (1275), as a cleric under Emperor *Michael VIII Palaeologus, G. supported reunion with Rome. But as patriarch he became anti-reunion. His refutation of the *Filioque doctrine in his *Tomos pisteos* and a later apologia for it antagonized all sides in the controversy and he was forced to resign. G. also wrote hagiographical works and an autobiography, *Diēgēsis merikē* (PG 142, 233–300).

[T. C. O'BRIEN]

GREGORY III MELISSENES (Mamme; 1400–59), **PATRIARCH OF CONSTANTINOPLE** from 1433. A monk and superior of the Pantocrator monastery in Constantinople, he was sent to the reunion Council of Florence (1439–41) and there became a principal force in the success of the union; he wrote apologies in its defense as well as a treatise on papal primacy. Elected patriarch he was forced to flee by antiunionists, esp. the monks; he spent the last years of his life in Rome, ruling the Greek Church in the territories controlled by Venice, holding fast to his claim to the patriarchate, and living a life of great holiness.

[T. C. O'BRIEN]

GREGORY ACINDYNUS, see ACINDYNUS, GREGORY.

GREGORY OF AGRIGENTUM, ST. (*c.*559–after 603), Greek bp. of Agrigento, Sicily from *c.*590, friend of St. Gregory the Great, probable author of a 10-book commentary on Ecclesiastes that influenced Byzantine ecclesio-literary style.

[T. C. O'BRIEN]

GREGORY BARBARIGO, ST., see BARBARIGO.

GREGORY OF BERGAMO (late 11th cent.–1146), monk of Vallambrosa, bp. of Bergamo (1133). As a friend of Bernard of Clairvaux, G. attended the Council of Pisa of 1134 and introduced the Cistercian Order and reform into his diocese. He defended the Real Presence of Christ in the Eucharist (*Tractatus de veritate corporis et sanguinis Christi*) against Berengarius. It is said that G. died a martyr. BIBLIOGRAPHY: M. M. McLaughlin, NCE 6:789.

[M. E. DUFFY]

GREGORY OF CATINA (*c.*1060–*c.*1132), Benedictine historian. As archivist of the Benedictine monastery at Farfa, he transcribed many of the documents into a single *Regestum,* and later added several corrective and amplifying books. His collections give valuable insights into the history of the Church and of Italy from the time of the Lombards to the 11th cent. and give evidence of critical and scholarly examination of documents. M. J. Kishpaugh, NCE 6:789.

[M. S. TANEY]

GREGORY OF CERCHIARA, ST. (*c.*930–1002), abbot. Driven from his monastery of San Andrea at Cerchiara by Saracen invasions, G. founded the monastery of San Salvatore in Rome (*c.*990). At the request of Empress Theophano, he founded a Basilian monastery at Burtscheid, Germany, which became a center of Byzantine culture in the North. BIBLIOGRAPHY: Zimmermann 3:258–260; R. Van Doren, BiblSanct 7:174–175.

[M. A. WINKLEMAN]

GREGORY DEKAPOLITES, ST. (*c.*762–862), Byzantine monk in Isauria, but forced into exile by the iconoclasts; he died at Constantinople. BIBLIOGRAPHY: R. Janin, BiblSanct 7:176.

[J. R. RIVELLO]

GREGORY OF EINSIEDELN, BL. (d. 996), abbot. G. entered the Benedictine monastery of Einsiedeln in 949. As its third abbot (964–996), he introduced the *Regularis concordia*. Under his guidance the monastery acquired a reputation for sanctity and enjoyed the patronage of the Saxon emperors. BIBLIOGRAPHY: O. Ringholz, *Geschichte des fürstlichen Benediktinerstiftes U.L.F. von Einsiedeln* (1904) 43–53.

[M. F. MCCARTHY]

GREGORY OF ELVIRA, ST. (*c.*320–392), first recorded bp. of Elvira, Spain, strong defender of Nicene teaching against Arianism, esp. in his *De fide orthodoxa*. Historians have cleared him of the charge that he joined in the schism led by *Lucifer of Cagliari. G.'s sermons and commentaries on the Bible are important evidence of the development of Christology and a theology of the Church in the West. G. is known to have persecuted Jews in Spain.

[T. C. O'BRIEN]

GREGORY THE ILLUMINATOR (ENLIGHTENER), **ST.** (*c.*240–*c.*332), Apostle of Armenia, called the Illuminator because he brought the light of faith to his native land. According to the Armenian legend, G., born of noble family, was brought up as a Christian in Cappadocia where he was taken as an infant when the others of his family were murdered. Grown to manhood, he returned to Armenia and won King Tiridates and many of the nobles to Christianity. This was followed by mass conversions of the people, the turning of the pagan temples into Christian churches, and the establishment of Christianity as the official religion of the country, which thus became the first Christian state. G. was consecrated bp. (*catholicos) of Armenia by Leontius of Caesarea *c.*315 and made Ashtishat his see. He consecrated many bps. (among others his two sons, Aristakes and Vhartanes) and ordained innumerable priests. The office of catholicos was hereditary in his family for more than 100 years. He is venerated in the Armenian Church as its chief patron, is commemorated in the canon of the Armenian Mass, and a number of the wonderful events of his life, as recorded in the legend-filled vita written by Agathangelos (traceable to the 5th cent.), are celebrated with distinct feasts in the Armenian liturgy. BIBLIOGRAPHY: Butler 3:693–695; P. Ananian, BiblSanct 7:180–190.

[R. B. ENO]

GREGORY MAGISTROS (*c.*990–1058), Armenian scholar at Constantinople. He gave up his title and dominion as prince in Armenia and devoted his life to teaching and writing. He left a paraphrase of the Bible in verse, letters on theology and philosophy, Armenian translations of classic Greek works.

[T. C. O'BRIEN]

GREGORY NAREK (951–1003), monk in the East Armenian monastery of Narek. The Armenian Church venerates him as a saint. He belongs to the great mystic theologians and religious authors of the Eastern Churches. He composed religious poems, prayers, and hymns. His is also a commentary on the Song of Solomon. His prayer book, "The Narek," is highly esteemed by Catholic and Orthodox Armenians alike. BIBLIOGRAPHY: P. Ananian, BiblSanct 7:192–194.

[J. MADEY]

GREGORY OF NAZIANZUS, ST. (330–390), *Father of the Church, one of the "three great Cappadocians" (the others being his friends St. *Basil the Great and the latter's younger brother St. *Gregory of Nyssa), surnamed the Theologian because of the eloquence of his doctrinal discourses. Delicate and restless, perhaps not perfectly stable psychologically, he was able to cope only briefly with the monastic life under Basil, and then was helpless to keep his hold on the turbulent, Arian-controlled See of Constantinople longer than a few days. But he was a master of the Greek tongue and literature, a powerful preacher of orthodoxy, and a leader in the anti-*Apollinarian polemic. He joined the other great Cappadocians in master-minding the gradual drift of the *Semi-Arians towards orthodoxy. BIBLIOGRAPHY: Quasten 3:236–254; J. M. Sauget, BiblSanct 7:194–204.

[R. R. BARR]

GREGORY OF NYSSA, ST. (332–394), *Father of the Church, one of the "three great Cappadocians" (the others being his elder brother St. *Basil the Great and their friend St. *Gregory of Nazianzus), the one genuinely original and speculative philosopher among the golden age (350–400) Fathers in the East. G. had married but later retired to a monastery of St. Basil in Pontus. Then he held the See of Nyssa in Cappadocia in Asia Minor, then that of Sebaste, each briefly and with little success, as G. was a poor politician and administrator. G. was a major adversary of *Apollinarianism and *Arianism; he was instrumental in the gradual drift of *Semi-Arianism towards orthodoxy. Mystic, heir of the thought of *Origen, G. is perhaps the deepest and tenderest spirit of the patristic Church. BIBLIOGRAPHY: Quasten 3:254–296; J. M. Sauget, BiblSanct 7:205–210; Butler 1:533–536.

[R. R. BARR]

GREGORY OF OSTIA, ST. (d. 1048), abbot of SS. Cosmas and Damian in Rome (998–1004), whom Pope Benedict IX named bp. of Ostia (1033) and later papal legate to the kingdom of Navarre. BIBLIOGRAPHY: G. D. Gordini, BiblSanct 7:210–212.

[G. E. CONWAY]

GREGORY III PAHLAV (*c.*1093–1166), Armenian catholicos for 54 years, from 1113, notable for his reunion contacts with contemporary popes and his acceptance at Latin councils at Antioch (1139) and Jerusalem (1142) of Chalcedonian Christology.

[T. C. O'BRIEN]

GREGORY PALAMAS, see PALAMAS, GREGORY.

GREGORY OF RIMINI (d. 1358), Augustinian theologian and philosopher, known as *Doctor Authenticus* and *Doctor Acutus*. Following earlier studies at houses of his order in Italy, France, and England, G. became a master of theology at Paris in 1345, where he occupied the Augustinian chair of theology at the university for nearly 10 years. He was elected prior general in 1357 but died a year later in Vienna. His most important work is a commentary on the *Books of the Sentences*; only the parts on the first two books are extant. Except for nominalistic tendencies in his theory of knowledge, G. remains faithful to the basic tradition of his school, as he is careful to point out in the prologue to his commentary. Because of new directions introduced within the school by G., he forms a link between the early school of Giles and the later so-called school of H. *Noris. These include a greater reliance on the authority of Augustine, a vigorous polemic against alleged Pelagian tendencies of the period, and the development of a more positive theology based upon Augustine and the Fathers of the Church. Concerning the end of theology, G. teaches that it is preeminently affective; but he denies, in opposition to the traditional view of his school, that theology is a strict science, since this would seem to render faith superfluous. Though he rejected the Scotistic teaching on the Immaculate Conception, G. did not, as sometimes alleged, hold that Mary had been guilty of venial sin. BIBLIOGRAPHY: G. Leff, *Gregory of Rimini* (1961).

[R. P. RUSSELL]

GREGORY SINAITES, ST. (d. 1346), canonized in the Greek Orthodox Church, monk and ascetical writer. He was a monk in Crete, on Mt. Sinai and Mt. Athos before founding a new monastery at Mt. Paroria in Bulgaria. G. was a proponent of *Hesychasm; his most widely read work on prayer is entitled *137 Chapters or Spiritual Meditations;* he also wrote on liturgical and doctrinal subjects.

[T. C. O'BRIEN]

GREGORY OF TAT'EW (1340–1411). He is the most esteemed theologian of the medieval Armenian Church. Born at Vayo Jor, he became a disciple of John Kachick. He studied occidental scholasticism, and taught philosophy and theology in the monastery schools of Aprakouniq, Mecop, and Tat'ew. He opposed the Catholic Fratres Unitores as well as the schismatic catholicate of Aghtamar. He wrote commentaries on many OT and NT books, discussed various philosophers, and is the author of polemical works, the Great and Small Books of Questions, Oksep'orik and Paramanc Girq. He died at Tat'ew in 1411.

[J. MADEY]

GREGORY IV TEGHA (1133–87), paternal nephew of Armenian Catholicos Nerses IV Shnorhali, who became catholicos himself upon the latter's death in 1173. He continued his predecessor's negotiation for a union with Byzantine Emperor Manuel Comnemnus, which was broken off at the Emperor's death (1180). For this attempt at union he was attacked by the clergy and the monks of East Armenia. He corresponded also with Pope Lucius III. He wrote an elegy (1187) or lamentation on the conquest of Jerusalem by the Muslims.

[J. MADEY]

GREGORY THAUMATURGUS, ST. (213–*c.*270 or 275). first bp. of Neocaesarea. Born of an aristocratic pagan family at Neocaesarea in Pontus, he received his early training in literature and rhetoric in his birthplace. While visiting at Caesarea in Palestine, he chanced to hear Origen, and remained there for 5 years as his pupil. During this time, he and his brother became Christians. Upon his departure for Pontus (238), he delivered a panegyric for Origen, which is valuable as a description of Origen's teaching method. A short time after G.'s return to Pontus, he was consecrated bp. of Neocaesarea. He survived the persecution of *Decius, was active at the Council of Antioch (265), and died sometime during the reign of Aurelian. The many miracles assigned to him by early tradition reflect the salutary influence of his dedicated life on his people, most of whom became Christian through his zeal.

Of his writings five authentic works have survived. The so-called *Canonical Epistle to the Bishops of Pontus,* dealing with problems of conscience resulting from cooperation of Christians with invading Goths and Boradi, is a significant source for the history of penitential discipline. The *Panegyric in Honor of Origen* mentioned above; the *Exposition of Faith,* important for its statement of trinitarian teaching; the *Metaphase of Ecclesiastes,* a free version of the Septuagint; and a work on the *Impassibility and Passibility of God* describing the way in which Jesus suffered, but willingly in his triumph over death. BIBLIOGRAPHY: Quasten 2:123–128; R. Janin, BiblSanct 7:214–217.

[F. H. BRIGHAM]

GREGORY OF TOURS, ST. (*c.*538–*c.*594), bp. of Tours from 573, historian, and hagiographer. Born at Averni (now Clermont-Ferrand, France) of a distinguished family, G. was a great grandson of St. Gregory of Langres and a nephew of St. Gallus. Tours, the see of St. *Martin (d. 397), enjoyed great prestige in Gaul, and this was heightened by G.'s able and zealous administration. In a time of turbulence, when Roman order was breaking down under the Frankish invaders, G. had to contend esp. in the early years of his episcopate, with obstreperous royalty and aristocracy, but after 584, under King Guntram and later King Childeric II, he enjoyed royal favor and was permitted to rule his diocese and to proceed unhampered with the writing upon which his fame chiefly rests. His *Historia Francorum* in 10 books is a universal history and a source of primary importance for events in France during the period near his own time. His *Miraculorum libri* is a hagiographical work dealing with the lives of, and wondrous events associated with, the martyrs and confessors, esp. those of Gaul. Judged by modern hagiographical standards, this work shows excessive credulity, but it contains much information of historical value concerning contemporary customs and manners. Works: PL 71; crit. ed. W. Arndt and B. Krusch, MGHS rer. Mer. 1 (2 parts, 1884–85); revision of the *Historia Francorum,* B. Krusch and W. Levison (1951); incomplete Eng. tr. of the *Historia,* O. M. Dalton (2 v., 1927). BIBLIOGRAPHY: H. Leclercq, DACL 6.1:1711–53; CE 7:18–21; Butler 4:367–369.

[R. B. ENO]

GREGORY OF UTRECHT, ST. (*c.*707–*c.*775), disciple of St. Boniface (722–754), abbot of St. Martin's in Utrecht (754–776). After the martyrdom of St. Eoban in 754, he was administrator of the diocese of Utrecht. Under G. the school at Utrecht became a thriving center of missionary activity. BIBLIOGRAPHY: Butler 3:402–403.

[M. F. MCCARTHY]

GREGORY OF VALENCIA (*c.*1549–1603), Spanish Jesuit theologian. He was born in Spain and educated as a Jesuit at Salamanca and Valladolid, but spent the major part of his life as professor of theology at Ingolstadt in Germany. Works published there were his *De rebus fidei hoc tempore controversis* (1591), a collection of his acerbic, anti-Calvinist and anti-Lutheran writings; and *Commentariorum theologicorum tomi quatuor* (1591–97), a work following the order of St. Thomas Aquinas's *Summa theologiae,* in which G. is credited with anticipating the teaching of L. *Molina on free will and grace. The last years of G.'s life were spent at Rome in active defense of Molinism at the **Congregatio de auxiliis;* during the 1602 sitting he collapsed in the midst of a debate and died a few months afterwards in Naples.

[T. C. O'BRIEN]

GREGORY II VKAJASER (Martyrophile, Lover of Martyrs; d. 1105), Armenian catholicos from 1065, venerated as a saint in the Armenian Church. The name "Lover of Martyrs" rests on his Armenian compilation of the acta of the martyrs; he also translated Proclus's life of St. John Chrysostom. From 1074 G. was in correspondence on reunion with Pope Gregory VII.

[T. C. O'BRIEN]

GREGORY THE WONDERWORKER, ST., see GREGORY THAUMATURGUS, ST.

GREGORY, ISABELLA AUGUSTA (1852–1932), Irish playwright, cofounder of the Abbey Theatre. G.'s literary career began after the death of her husband in 1892. She wrote or translated more than 40 plays, the most popular of which are *The Rising of the Moon* and *Spreading the News*. Despite her Protestantism, her knowledge of Catholicism at the folk level was deep; she entered into the minds of Catholic peasant characters and transposed Irish saintly legends into religious plays acceptable to both Catholics and Protestants. *The Story Brought by Brigit,* an Irish passion play (1924), and *Dave,* a modern miracle play (1927), reveal the healing power of love, the main theme of her religious plays. BIBLIOGRAPHY: L. Robinson, *Lady Gregory's Journals* (1947); E. Coxhead, *Lady Gregory: A Literary Portrait* (1966).

[V. SAMPSON]

GREGORY IX, DECRETALS OF, the collection of papal legislation promulgated in the bull *Rex pacificus* by Gregory IX, Sept. 5, 1234, and abrogating any *decretals not contained in it. In 1230 Gregory commissioned the Dominican jurist *Raymond of Peñafort to systematize the various decretals and other legislation compiled in *Gratian's *Decretum* and in many subsequent collections (see DECRETISTS, DECRETALISTS). Raymond used as the primary basis the *Quinque compilationes antiquae* to produce his single volume of *Decretals*. The collection came to be known as the *Liber extravagantium* or *Liber extra* (see EXTRAVAGANTES); it was the principal component of the official *Corpus Iuris Canonici* (Rome 1582).

[T. C. O'BRIEN]

GREGORY DIALOGOS, LITURGY OF, see PRESANCTIFIED, LITURGY OF THE.

GRELLET, STEPHEN (Étienne de Grellet du Mabillier; 1773–1855), evangelical Quaker preacher. Fleeing Revolutionary France, where he had been reared a Catholic, G. came to Newtown (Queens), N.Y., where he became a Quaker in 1795 and an approved minister in 1798. In his lifetime he traveled 100,000 miles in missionary journeys in North America and Europe. His preaching expressed the evangelical Protestant strain introduced into American Quakerism. The conflict of this point of view with the *Inner Light teaching as interpreted by E. *Hicks, whom G. opposed, led to the orthodox-liberal split of 1827 in Quaker ranks. G.'s memoirs were edited by B. Seebohm (2 v., 1860). BIBLIOGRAPHY: W. W. Comfort, *Stephen Grellet* (1942); B. Forbush, *Elias Hicks, Quaker Liberal* (1956).

[T. C. O'BRIEN]

GREMIAL VEIL (Lat. *gremium,* lap), the originally functional but later purely ceremonial apron or lapcloth put over the knees of the ministers at a pontifical Mass or other rite when they are seated at the sedilia. The gremial veil at Mass is of the same texture and color as the vestments; when used in other liturgical rites, it is of white linen.

[T. C. O'BRIEN]

GRESSMANN, HUGO (1877–1927), German Protestant OT scholar, specializing in comparative religion. G. taught in Kiel and in Berlin (1902–1927). His interest was *Traditionsgeschichte* (transmission of oral accounts). Unorthodox in his thinking, he was a follower of H. Gunkel in the use of literary genre and applied his modern methods to his studies of ancient mythologies and religions. His work vindicated that of others in the field and was of value to both Protestant and Catholic Scripture scholars. His religious relativism led him to deny a special revelation or a divine election of any one people. Among his works are *Der Ursprung der israelitisch-jüdischen Eschatologie* (1905), and *Der Messias,* opus posthumous, ed. H. Schmidt (1929), and *Altorientalische Texte und Bilder zum AT* (2 v., 1909).

[A. P. HANLON]

GRETSER, JAKOB (1562–1625), Jesuit theologian and scholar, fierce Counter Reformation polemicist, playwright. His 23 dramas in Latin (of which the best is the *Dialogus de Udone archiepiscopo*) are an important landmark in Jesuit drama, marking the transition from Renaissance to Baroque. BIBLIOGRAPHY: *Opera omnia,* (ed. P. G. Kolb, 17 v., not including the dramas, 1734–41); A. Dürrwächter, *Jakob Gretser und seine Dramen* (1912).

[M. F. MCCARTHY]

GREY NUNS, the Sisters of Charity commonly called Grey Nuns (SGM), founded by Marie Marguerite d'*Youville, a widow, in 1738 in Montreal, Canada. In 1975 they numbered 5,755 members in 6 autonomous congregations, staffing educational and charitable institutions in Canada, the U.S., Africa, Latin America, and the Far East.

Grey Nuns of Montreal. In 1737 Madame d'Youville and companions privately professed their dedication to the poor and sick, without any intention, however, of forming a religious community. In 1738 they began to live together in a rented house to better carry out their work. This beginning of their community life enraged many citizens, who could not believe that the widow of François d'Youville, confidential agent of the government in illegal trade with the Indians, would honestly help the poor. In the face of violence, insulting and abusive language, including their title, *les soeurs* *grises* (the drunken sisters), the women persisted in their dedication and work. Anticipating their Rule, they made the first formal promises in 1745, living together in charity, wearing plain black dresses, uniform only in simplicity. In 1747 the General Hospital of Montreal was entrusted to their care and was to become their first motherhouse. In 1755, it was decided to design a habit. Having been called *les soeurs grises* for 18 years, they chose grey—also *gris* in French—for the color of their habit, thus giving a new meaning to an old title. The first papal approval was granted in 1865. In 1855 a foundation was made in the U.S. In 1975 total membership was 1,465 sisters in 128 houses.

Grey Nuns of St. Hyacinthe (SGSH). The first independent foundation was made in 1840 at St. Hyacinthe, near Montreal. From this foundation another was made at Nicolet in 1886, but in 1940 it became a province of the original institute in Montreal. The first U.S. foundation was made in 1878. In addition to care for the sick, aged, poor, orphans special attention is given to mentally retarded children. In 1975 total membership was 604 sisters in 32 houses.

Grey Nuns of Quebec (SCQ), an independent foundation established in 1849 in Quebec City, with the first U.S. foundation being made in 1890 in Massachusetts. Staffing educational and charitable institutions, these sisters give their greatest service in immense hospitals for the mentally ill. In 1975 total membership was 1544 sisters in 84 houses.

Grey Nuns of the Cross (SGC). In 1845, the Grey Nuns of Montreal founded this autonomous congregation in Ottawa, Ontario. Papal approval was given in 1889. In 1857 a foundation was made in the U.S. Their work includes teaching, nursing, social work, and foreign and home missions. In 1975 total membership was 1,478 sisters in 109 houses.

Grey Nuns of the Sacred Heart (GNSH). This autonomous congregation was founded in 1857 from the Grey Nuns of the Cross. At the invitation of Card. Dennis Dougherty of Philadelphia, Pa., they established their motherhouse there in 1921; its present site is at Yardley, Pennsylvania. The sisters are active in the administration of hospitals, a home for the aged, and teaching in parochial and private schools on the primary, secondary, nursing, and collegiate levels. In 1975 total membership was 349 sisters in 33 houses.

Grey Sisters of the Immaculate Conception (GSIC), English speaking sisters of the Grey Nuns of the Cross who established a separate motherhouse in 1926 in Pembroke, Ontario. Besides educational and charitable work the congregation maintains Chinese missions in Canada and schools in Santo Domingo. In 1975 total membership was 315 sisters in 29 houses.

[C. J. NOONE]

GREYFRIARS, written as one or two words, a name given to Franciscans or Friars Minor in medieval England and sometimes, in the plural, to a friary in which they lived. They were called Grey Friars because of the grey or indeterminate color of the habits they were accustomed to wear in England at that time.

[J. C. WILLKE]

GRIEN, HANS. See BALDUNG-GRIEN, HANS.

GRIESBACH, JOHANN JAKOB (1745–1812), NT scholar at the Univ. of Jena from 1775. His name is associated with the thesis that Mark is the last of the Synoptic Gospels. Of particular importance in his published criticotextual studies is his principle of favoring a textual reading supported by two MSS families in order to establish the best biblical text from Alexandrian, Constantinopolitan, and Western manuscripts.

[T. C. O'BRIEN]

GRIFFIN, MARTIN IGNATIUS JOSEPH (1842–1911), American journalist, historian. He was a native and lifelong resident of Philadelphia, Pa. His journalistic career began on the *Catholic Herald* (later *Standard*) of Philadelphia, but he was a correspondent for many diocesan papers. An amazing organizer of societies, he founded the National Catholic Beneficial Society in 1871, edited the *Journal* of the Irish Catholic Benevolent Union of which he was secretary, worked with the archdiocesan Temperance Union, and was one of the founders of the Catholic Total Abstinence Union of America. G.'s contribution to historical documentation about Catholicism in the Middle Atlantic States was of inestimable value to later historians of the Church in America. A careful recorder of events and on balance an objective appraiser of controversial matters, he labored hard to offset the narrowly conceived non-Catholic views of the Catholic Church. Though strongly partisan he was never a bigot. Ever a figure who drew criticism, he boldly took part in the affairs of the Irish Land League which many bps. feared. As a result of his forthright stands, he was not a popular man and in fact received too little credit from his contemporaries. He was a founder of the American Catholic Historical Society of Philadelphia and contributed frequently to the *Records* of that society. From 1886 to 1911 he edited *American Catholic Historical Researches*. G. was the author of *History of Rt. Rev. Michael Egan, D.D., First Bishop of Philadelphia* (1893), *Commodore John Barry* (1903), *General Count Casimir Pulaski* (1909), and *Catholics and the American Revolution* (3 v., 1907–11).

[J. R. AHERNE]

GRIFFITH, MICHAEL, see ALFORD, MICHAEL.

GRIFFITHS, THOMAS (1791–1847), titular bp., vicar apostolic in England. A convert to Catholicism as a boy, G. was ordained in 1814. Made president of St. Edmund's

College in Ware in 1817, he governed it with great care for 15 years. In 1833 he was named coadjutor bp. with the right of succession to the vicar apostolic of the London district, where he succeeded in 1836. In London he represented before the government the interests of the Catholic Church in the colonies. G.'s concern was to maintain the relative freedom Catholics had achieved, nor did he regard with warmth converts from the *Oxford Movement.

[J. R. AHERNE]

GRIGNION DE MONTFORT, LOUIS MARIE, ST. (1673–1717), religious founder. After studies at St. Sulpice and the Sorbonne, he was ordained in Paris in 1700. The center of his preaching and spirituality was devotion to Mary; he called himself simply Louis Marie de Montfort. His life, lived in dedicated poverty, was a mission of preaching to the simple people of the towns and villages of France. He founded the Daughters of Wisdom in 1702 as a teaching and nursing order; the Missionaries of the Company of Mary (Montfort Fathers) in 1705. The work most associated with his name, *True Devotion to the Blessed Virgin Mary,* is the title given to one of his MSS found and published in 1842; his own basic work, *The Love of Eternal Wisdom,* gives the full doctrinal context to this Marian devotion, slaveship to Mary as the way to Christ. He was canonized in 1947.

[J. R. AHERNE]

GRIGNY, NICOLAS DE (1671–1703), French organist, choirmaster, and composer. He succeeded his father Louis as organist of Notre-Dame at Rheims in 1695. G.'s most famous work, *Livre d'orgue contenant une messe et quatre hymnes pour les principales fêtes de l'année,* was published in 1711. It is outstanding among the products of the classical French school, and Bach copied it out for entertainment and instruction. Guilmant's *Archives des maîtres de l'orgue* includes it, with an introduction, along with work of G. and others, in a modern reprint.

[J. C. MARR]

GRIJALVA, JUAN DE (d. 1638), historian of the missions. A Mexican Augustinian, G. served as superior in several houses of his order in Mexico. His great contribution was to the history of Augustinian missionaries. In 1624 G. published a major historical work in four books, *Crónica de la Orden de N.P.S. Augustín en las provincias de la Nueva España*. . . . The book draws on original sources and is precise in its treatment. It covers the early years of Augustinian work among the Indians of New Spain, and their adventure into the Far East, esp. China and the Philippines. One section deals at length with mission methods, and another with the lives of Augustinian missionaries.

[J. R. AHERNE]

GRILLE, screen impeding contact and sight, used by certain cloistered orders to separate sisters from the outside world even when meeting visitors and, more commonly, since the late 16th cent. used in the confessional to separate priest and penitent. While now generally seen as ensuring anonymity, it was introduced to prevent possible scandal in hearing women's confessions, the only time it was legally required. Since 1973 its use is at the penitent's option.

[J. DALLEN]

GRILLPARZER, FRANZ (1791–1872), one of Austria's greatest dramatists, whose plays combined German classicism and Romanticism; he brought the Viennese form of the baroque theater to dramatic perfection, and his work marked the beginning of the psychological drama. Born in Vienna, G. was the son of a lawyer of peasant descent; his mother came of an old Viennese family. He studied law at the university, but after the death of his father (1809) he became tutor in the house of Count Seilern. G. entered civil service in 1813 in order to support his brothers and rose to the position of director of the imperial archives (1832–56). A victim of melancholy and hypochondria, G. shrank from decisions and never married his early love, though he was devoted to her until his death. Some of his plays involved him in trouble with the official censors. In 1817 his fate tragedy, *Die Ahnfrau,* gained him an international reputation. *Sappho,* which followed in 1818, won him a place next to Goethe as the Austrian classicist. The dramatic trilogy, *Das goldene Vliess* (1821), is based on the plot of Euripides and gives a powerful characterization of its heroine Medea. Two tragedies deal with Austrian history, *König Ottokars Glück und Ende* (1825) and *Ein treuer Diener seines Herrn* (1828), the first containing G.'s famous "praise of Austria"; it is a tragedy of the fall of a man caused by his pride; the second's thesis is loyalty for the sake of law and order manifested through the Christian humanism of the hero. *Des Meeres und der Liebe Wellen* (1831) is a dramatic masterpiece with Hero and Leander plot. Calderon's influence shows in *Der Traum ein Leben* (1834) with its dual action of reality and dream and its Biedermeier emphasis on the inner contentment of an honest life rather than upon external glory. When G.'s only comedy, *Weh dem der lügt* (1838) met with small success, he gave up playwriting. Three of his greatest dramas were not discovered until after his death: *Libussa,* dealing with the founding of Prague; *Ein Bruderzwist in Habsburg,* in which Rudolf II's inaction results in the Thirty Years' War; and *Die Jüdin von Toledo,* wherein the king sacrifices his personal love for the good of the state. BIBLIOGRAPHY: A. Burkhard, *Franz Grillparzer in England and America* (pa. 1961).

[B. F. STEINBRUCKNER]

GRIMALD, NICHOLAS (*c.*1519–*c.*1559), English *recusant poet. In his youth he was a moderate adherent of the Reformation in England. His *Christus Redivivus* is a forerunner of the passion play of Oberammergau. The tragedy *Archipropheta* has been counted among the finest verse of the period. Imprisoned in 1555, G. returned to Catholicism. As a Catholic and protégé of the Catholic bp. of Ely, he wrote his most notable work, *Marcus Tullius Cicero;* he edited and contributed to *Tottel's Miscellany* (1557), the first anthology of English poetry. His death may have occurred in prison or in exile, but there is no record. BIBLIOGRAPHY: L. I. Guiney, *Recusant Poets* (1939).

[J. R. AHERNE]

GRIMALDI, FRANCESCO (1545–*c.*1630), Italian architect and Theatine priest, designing churches in classical style in Rome and Naples: S. Andrea della Dame (1585–90) and S. Paolo Maggiore (1591–1603).

[M. J. DALY]

GRIMANI, DOMENICO (1461–1523), humanist cardinal; in the papal service from 1471, created cardinal in 1493; patriarch of Aquileia in 1497; bp. of Porto in 1511. At his villa in Rome he collected a rich library, left to the monastery of San Antonio di Castello, Venice, and many art treasures.

[T. C. O'BRIEN]

GRIMBALD, ST. (d. 901), monk and teacher. He was prior of Saint-Bertin (Flanders) before going to England *c.*887. He participated in the Alfredian revival as royal tutor, adviser, and musician. He also encouraged Edward the Elder to build the Newminster, Winchester. BIBLIOGRAPHY: P. Grierson, ''Grimbald of St. Bertins,'' EHR 55 (1940) 529–561; R. Van Doren, BiblSanct 7:406–407.

[W. A. CHANEY]

GRIMFRIDUS, CHALICE OF, 9th-cent. Carolingian chalice, of gilded copper with silver inlay. Formerly known as the chalice of St. Chrodegand, 8th-cent. bp. of Séz in Normandy, it belonged successively in the treasure of the priory of Saint-Martin des Champs, the Basilewsky collection (Paris), and the Hermitage (Petrograd). The chalice was acquired in 1933 by Mildred and Robert Woods Bliss for their discriminating and scholarly collection at Dumbarton Oaks, Harvard's Byzantine and medieval-studies center in Washington, D.C.

[M. J. DALY]

GRIMMELSHAUSEN, HANS JAKOB CHRISTOFFEL VON (1625?–76), German novelist. The details of his life are unknown. He seems to have served on both sides in the Thirty Years' War and was made mayor of Renchen under the bp. of Strasbourg in 1667. His many satirical works and novels of gallantry (published from 1659 on, under a number of pseudonyms) are less important than the picaresque novel *Der abenteuerliche Simplicissimus* (1668–69), which, beneath its baroque exterior, is one of the most valuable historical documents of the age. BIBLIOGRAPHY: M. F. McCarthy, NCE 6:807.

[M. F. MCCARTHY]

GRISAR, HARTMANN (1845–1932), German Jesuit church historian and Luther scholar. In the year of his ordination (1868) he joined the Jesuits, and after a novitiate at Rome was appointed professor of church history at the Univ. of Innsbruck (1871). He was a founder (1877) of the *Zeitschrift für Theologie*. Relieved of teaching in 1889 for the sake of his research and writing, he worked in Rome until 1901, and produced a number of authoritative studies on the history of the ancient and medieval Church and papacy. But his major life's work was a series of historical studies on Luther, developed and published after his return to Innsbruck: *Luther* (3 v., 1911–12); *Lutherstudien* (6 v., 1920–23); *Martin Luthers Leben und sein Werk* (1926); all were translated into English. Among RC Luther scholars, G. stands as a transition between the extreme, polemical negativism of H. *Denifle and the revolutionary, more positive appraisal begun by J. Lortz's *Die Reformation in Deutschland* (2 v., 4th ed., 1962). Many of G.'s positive insights remain fundamentals in the study of the Reformation.

[J. R. AHERNE]

GRISWOLD, ALEXANDER VIETS (1766–1842), bp. of the Protestant Episcopal Church in the Eastern Diocese. Born in Simsbury, Conn., he was ordained priest in 1795. After serving three parishes in Litchfield County, Conn., he became rector of the Episcopal church in Bristol, R.I., in 1804. The Episcopal churches in all of the New England states except Conn. combined in 1811 to form the Eastern Diocese, and Griswold was chosen bishop. During his long episcopate, he built the Church up to such strength that each of the member states was able to support its own bishop. He was a leader in the formation of the Domestic and Foreign Missionary Society in 1820. After the death of Bp. W. *White (1836), G. became presiding bishop of the Episcopal Church. BIBLIOGRAPHY: J. S. Stone, *Memoir of the Life of the Rt. Rev. Alexander Viets Griswold* (1854).

[W. W. MANROSS]

GROCYN, WILLIAM (*c.*1446–1519), great English humanist, educated at Oxford. While residing at New College, he was tutor to William Warham who later, as abp. of Canterbury, provided many preferments for him. G. left his position as divinity reader at Magdalen in 1488 to study in Italy for 2 years. When he returned, he was the first to give public lectures in Greek at Oxford. Both More and Erasmus praised his learning and his teaching; Erasmus, his excellent Latin style. Apparently none of his works are extant. Warham made Grocyn master of the collegiate church of All Hallows, Maidstone (1506), where he died. Linacre, his executor and a principal beneficiary of his will, made an inventory of his library, and this is preserved in the Oxford Historical Society's *Collectanea*. BIBLIOGRAPHY: Emden OX 2:827–830; S. Lee, DNB 8:709–712; R. Weiss, *Humanism in England during the Fifteenth Century* (1957).

[A. WARDLE]

GROENENDAEL, ABBEY OF (*Viridis Vallis*), former priory founded in honor of Our Lady in 1304, nine miles from Brussels (diocese of Cambrai, now Malines-Brussels, Belgium). The famous mystic Jan van Ruysbroeck (1294–1381) returned there in 1343. He formed a community, which in 1350 joined the Canons Regular of St. Augustine, and became their first prior. The monastery became a renowned center of intense mysticism, where the doctrine of Ruysbroeck formed the basis of the spiritual movement known as the *Devotio moderna*. The monastery was suppressed during the Revolution and the few remaining ruins have been made into a restaurant. BIBLIOGRAPHY: Cottineau, 1:1347.

[J. DAOUST]

GROOT, JOSÉ MANUEL (1800–78), Colombian historian and apologete. His father, of Dutch extraction, had been very influential in the last years of the colony. G., an avid reader of French anticlerical literature, early lost his faith; but a deeper contact with the sources restored it and converted him into an ardent defender of the Church. He wrote many polemical treatises. His main work, however, was historical: *Historia eclesiástica y civil de Nueva Granada,* a systematic attempt to recount the evangelization of the Colombian territory. G. also tried to prevent the admission of Protestants to Colombia with writings like *Réplica al ministro presbiteriano, H. B. Pratt* and *Los misioneros de la herejía*. BIBLIOGRAPHY: M. A. Caro, *Don José Manuel Groot, 1800–*78 (1950).

[P. DAMBORIENA]

GROOTE, GERARD (1340–84), spiritual leader in the Lowlands whose ideas inspired the founding of the *Brethren of the Common Life, the **Devotio moderna,* and its spiritual classic, the **Imitation of Christ.* Well educated and the holder of ecclesiastical benefices, he gave up all to become a preacher of church reform. He was not a priest, but was ordained a deacon in 1374. His attacks against abuses of discipline and morals led to his suspension from preaching. He founded the Sisters of the Common Life, but died before his plan for a community of canons regular could be realized. G.'s preaching and writing concentrated on the apostolic ideals of poverty and community and on following the example of Christ's human life. Ascription of the *Imitation* to him, however, has been proved unwarranted. His sermons and letters have been published in a modern edition. BIBLIOGRAPHY: T. P. Van Zijl, NCE 6:809, with bibliography.

[T. C. O'BRIEN]

GROSJEAN, PAUL (1900–64), Belgian Jesuit Bollandist and Celtic scholar. One of the outstanding contemporary Bollandists, G. was chosen for the task by H. Delehaye. He studied at Oxford and Dublin in preparation for his special work and in fulfillment of it published many previously unedited lives of the Celtic saints as well as studies on various unsolved problems in this area of hagiography.

[R. B. ENO]

GROSS, WILLIAM HICKLEY (1837–1898), bishop. A native of Baltimore, he was ordained as a Redemptorist in 1863. He was engaged in preaching for 8 years throughout the East. He was named bp. of Savannah in 1873. A supporter of Card. *Gibbons, he was a member of the progressives in the hierarchy. In 1885 G. was made abp. of Portland, Ore. and in his 13 years there did much to expand parishes and schools in his vast territory and to strengthen the Indian missions.

[J. R. AHERNE]

GROSSETESTE, ROBERT, see ROBERT GROSSETESTE.

GROSSETESTE, PSEUDO, the unknown author(s) of more than 65 works falsely attributed to the Oxford master *Robert Grosseteste (1175–1253). Among these works, the *Summa philosophiae,* written after 1270, has received special study as representing the more common theological and philosophical doctrines of the 13th cent. that were the basis for opposition to the innovations of St. Thomas Aquinas. BIBLIOGRAPHY: Gilson HCP 265–274.

[T. C. O'BRIEN]

GROTE, FEDERICO (1853–1940), German Catholic social leader in Argentina. A Redemptorist seminarian, he was exiled at the height of the Kulturkampf in 1873, continued his studies in Luxembourg, and was ordained in 1877. Sent first to the missions in Ecuador he went to Argentina in 1884 and was soon identified with Catholic social action efforts in Buenos Aires. He traveled the country preaching Catholic Action. In 1900 he founded the daily *El Pueblo,* and in 1907 the weekly *Justicia Social.* In addition G. established the Christian Democratic League and a nationwide credit union for Catholic workers.

[J. R. AHERNE]

GROTIUS, HUGO (1583–1645), Dutch jurist and humanist. Born at Delft, Holland, G. completed studies at the Univ of Leyden at the age of 15. He began legal practice in 1599 at The Hague and became attorney general of Holland in 1607 and first magistrate of Rotterdam in 1615. In the religious conflict of the day he supported the *Remonstrants against the strict Calvinists, and after the Synod of *Dort (1618), was condemned to life imprisonment. With the assistance of his wife, he escaped in 1621 and went to Paris. In 1631 he returned to Holland but left again the following year. He served as Sweden's representative in Paris 1635–45. G.'s main religious work was *Concerning the Truth of the Christian Religion* (1622), a handbook for missionaries. It sought to show how natural theology supported Christianity over other religions. The liberal theories of the atonement he proposed were to be developed in the 19th and 20th centuries. In other writings he pioneered in scientific biblical exegesis. He is chiefly noted for his work *De iure belli ac pacis libri tres* (*On the Law of War and Peace,* definitive ed., 1631), which won him the title "father of international law." He knew and cited the writings on law of F. de Vitoria and F. Suárez. According to G., natural law is a body of self-evident commands and prohibitions, known by reason or by the fact of consensus. Human law is developed by the positive will of lawgivers in the nation or community. With regard to the just war, he acknowledged the possibility of justifying a war on the basis of human, public law that would be unjust according to natural law. The positivistic approach to war and to other actions of nations came to be G.'s chief influence on later developments of international law. BIBLIOGRAPHY: E. Dumbauld, *Life and Legal Writings of Hugo Grotius* (1969).

[T. EARLY]

GROTTAFERRATA, MONASTERY OF, a Basilian monastery of the Catholic *Italo-Albanian rite located in the Alban hills near Rome. Founded by the Greek St. *Nilus of Rossano *c.* 1004, it became a center of Greek learning for several centuries but gradually came under Latinizing influences. During the Renaissance its *commendatory abbots included Cardinals Bessarion, Guilio della Rovere (afterwards Pope Julius II), and Consalvi. In 1881 Pope Leo XIII reestablished the observance of the Byzantine rite, freed from Latinization. In 1939 Pope Pius XI elevated the monastery to the equivalent status of an *abbey nullius. An excellent collection of Greek MSS is preserved there, and the monastery publishes many liturgical books for the Catholic Eastern rites. BIBLIOGRAPHY: A. A. King, *Rites of Eastern Christendom* (1948) 2:10–12; P. Battifol, *L'Abbaye de Rossano* (1891).

[F. T. RYAN]

GROTTO OF THE NATIVITY, a cave at Bethlehem where, according to a tradition that goes back to the 2d cent., Jesus was born. A basilica was built over it in 325.

[M. F. MCNAMARA]

GROU, JEAN NICOLAS (1731–1803), Jesuit spiritual director. A Jesuit from 1746, he worked first in the classics and published several translations of Plato. After 1766, however, he devoted himself exclusively to spiritual direction. The French Revolution led to his exile in England, where he lived out his life in the household of Thomas Weld at Lullworth Castle. His works include: *Morale tirée des Confessions de St. Augustin* (1786); *Caractère de la vraie dévotion* (1789); *Méditations en forme de retraits sur l'amour de Dieu* (1796); *Manuel des âmes intérieures* (1833). He was widely read in the several English translations made in the 19th cent.; still available is *How to Pray* (tr. J. Dalby, pa. 1972).

[T. C. O'BRIEN]

GRUDEN, JOHN CAPISTRAN (1884–1962), theologian. G. was born in present-day Yugoslavia but completed his theological studies in the United States. He taught for 27 years at the St. Paul, Minn., diocesan seminary; published *The Mystical Christ* (1937), an influential study of the Church as the mystical body of Christ that anticipated later theological developments.

[T. M. MCFADDEN]

GRUEBER, JOHANNES (1623–65), Jesuit missionary and explorer. Joining the Society of Jesus in 1641 he was ordained and sent to China in 1656 as a missioner. In Peking he served at the court as professor of mathematics. Recalled to Rome in 1661 he undertook an overland journey because of the Dutch blockade of the China coast. With another priest (who died on the way) G. crossed China, Thibet, and through passes of the Himalayas to India. The journey, carefully recorded, made G. one of the great explorers of his century. The great achievement of indicating an overland route from China to India and the possibilities of the Himalayan passes was acknowledged immediately. G. attempted to return by the overland route to China but died on the way. BIBLIOGRAPHY: A. Hounder, CE 7:41–42.

[J. R. AHERNE]

GRUENTHANER, MICHAEL (1887–1962), Jesuit exegete. A Jesuit from 1905 and ordained at St. Louis in 1920, he taught for 3 years, then obtained his doctorate from the Pontifical Biblical Institute in Rome. His doctoral dissertation theme, *The Authorship and Date of Daniel,* was of such a controversial nature in those days as to be called daring; nevertheless he defended it in 1927 with persistence and conviction. He was a noted teacher, interested in the languages and history of Mesopotamia. With zeal he strove for the advancement of biblical scholarship in America, contributing to collective works and journals, esp. on the Book of Daniel, and was one of the founders of the Catholic Biblical Association. In 1939 he was appointed to translate the book of Ezekiel for the revision of the Challoner Douay Old Testament. G. was second editor-in-chief of the *Catholic Biblical Quarterly* (1941–61) and elevated its standard. He taught at St. Mary's, Kansas (1936–61), The Catholic Univ. of America (1941–56), and St. Mary's College, South Bend, Indiana (1943–56) where he was chancellor of the Graduate School of Sacred Theology for lay women. In addition to being a scholar himself, G. was a fine inspiration to his students to carry on his work. After his death, a commemorative volume, *The Bible in Current Catholic Thought* was dedicated to him. BIBLIOGRAPHY: J. L. McKenzie, *Bible in Current Catholic Thought* (1962) ix-xiii, 1–2; R. North, "A Frontier Jerome: Gruenthaner, Part 1," AER 148 (1963) 289–302.

[A. P. HANLON]

GRÜN, ANASTASIUS (pseud. of Count Anton Alexander Auersperg; 1806–76), Austrian poet, influential representative of the liberal aristocracy, who belonged to the Young Germany group. Born in Laibach (now in Yugoslavia), he studied in Vienna and Graz and lived on his estates from 1831. He traveled extensively through Italy, Germany, France, and England. Because of his political ideas he was temporarily placed under police surveillance. He became a member of the German parliament in Frankfurt (1848) and of the Austrian parliament (1860). His patriotic, lyrical poetry defended human freedom in the political as well as religious area. Best known are his poems collected as *Spaziergänge eines Wiener Poeten* (1831).

[B. F. STEINBRUCKNER]

GRUNDTVIG, NICOLAI FREDERIK SEVERIN (1783–1872), Danish theologian, church reformer, historian, and hymn writer. His powerful attacks upon the rationalism of his time and the Church as he found it in Denmark provoked reprisals from the churchmen he had criticized so outspokenly, and he was at different times forbidden to preach or to publish anything without the approval of the royal censor. However, he survived these troubles, as well as several periods of mental disturbance, and won the support of many who came to be called Grundtvigians. Before his death his influence had already done much to revitalize the Danish Church. He was made a bishop in 1861. BIBLIOGRAPHY: A. Jansen, *European Authors* (1967).

GRÜNEWALD, MATTHIAS (Mathis Gothart Nithart, *c.*1470–1528), German painter, chiefly active at Mainz (court painter to the Elector, Card, Albrecht) and Frankfurt. His work combines a sophisticated use of Renaissance techniques with Late Gothic imagery and is distinguished by its emotional power. His greatest accomplishment is the Isenheim altarpiece (Colmar, Musée), painted (1509/10–1515) for the monastery church of the Order of St. Anthony—a polyptych of eight panels enclosing and surrounding a sculptured shrine. In the closed portion the central panel, a *Crucifixion* (probably the most impressive ever painted) shows a terrifying view of Christ, covered with a multitude of wounds, as a dead body on the cross. When the panels are opened they reveal, in staggering contrast, the joys of the Annunciation, the Nativity, and the Resurrection, a triumph in the painting of brilliant supernatural light as symbol of heavenly glory. On the reverse of the innermost panels, a singularly grotesque and yet deeply moving *Temptations of St. Anthony,* a gesture to the monks of St. Anthony is esp. remarkable. BIBLIOGRAPHY: N. Pevsner, *Grünewald* (1958).

[P. P. FEHL]

GRYPHIUS, ANDREAS (1616–64), Silesian dramatist, scholar, poet. Using the Alexandrine verse recommended by Opitz, Gryphius composed five original German tragedies in the baroque style, among them *Leo Arminius* (1646), a German classicistic tragedy; *Cardenio und Celinde* (1648), the first German *bürgerliches Trauerspiel* (middle-class tragedy); and *Carolus Stuardus* (1649), a drama on a contemporary theme. He was, however, more successful as a writer of fresh and original comedies, e.g., *Die geliebte Dornrose* (1660) and *Horribilicribrifax* (1663), a variation on the *Miles gloriosus*-theme of Plautus. The transitoriness of human life is a frequent theme of his sonnets (published in 1639 and 1663) and his religious lyrics. BIBLIOGRAPHY: J. G. Robertson, *History of German Literature* (1962) 183–185; W. Kosch, *Deutsches Literatur-Lexikon* (1963) 135–136.

[M. F. MCCARTHY]

GUADAGNI, BERNARDO GAETANO (1674–1759), Discalced Carmelite, bp. and the first cardinal from his order. A civil and canon lawyer and canon at the cathedral of Florence, he became a Carmelite in 1700. After serving as provincial in Tuscany, he was named bp. of Arezzo, 1724. Created cardinal in 1731, he received several curial appointments and also served as vicar of Rome (1732–59). Because of his own devout life and his zeal for reform, his cause for beatification was twice proposed.

[J. R. AHERNE]

GUADALUPE, FRIARY OF, shrine of royal foundation (*c.*1300) near Cáceres, Spain, entrusted to the Franciscans since 1909, after having been suppressed in 1835. It was founded to enshrine a miraculous picture of the Virgin Mary, became a center of pilgrimage, celebrated for its art and the architecture of its church. The Hieronymites who staffed it from 1389 were renowned for their learning and for fostering the spiritual and mystical life.

GUADALUPE, OUR LADY OF. According to tradition, the Virgin *Mary twice appeared to a Mexican Indian, Juan Diego, at Tepeyac near Mexico City in December 1531 and instructed him to tell the local bp. that a church should be built in her honor on that spot. When Diego appeared before Bp. Zumárraga, roses fell from his mantle and it bore a painting of Mary as she had looked in the apparitions. Accordingly, a small church was erected in 1533, and a larger edifice was begun in 1556, and was dedicated in 1709, with additions in 1893 and 1930. Devotion to Our Lady of Guadalupe is widespread, esp. throughout Mexico and Latin America, and many miracles are attributed to her intercession. In 1754 Benedict XIV authorized a Mass and Office on December 12 in honor of this devotion, and in 1910 Pius X declared Mary, under this title, the Virgin Patroness of Latin America. Pius XI extended this patronage to the Philippines (1935) and Pius XII named her patroness of the Americas (1945).

Documentation for the apparitions is slight, and much of it considerably later than 1531. A summary of the report written by the interpreter at the interview between Diego and Bp. Zumárraga is extant, but it is not a detailed account. Another account, called the *Valeriano Relation,* was written between 1560 and 1570 under the direction of Bernardino de *Sahagún. Its account of the events coincides with the interpreter's report. BIBLIOGRAPHY: D. Demarest and C. Taylor, *Dark Virgin: The Book of Our Lady of Guadalupe: A Documentary Anthology* (1956).

[T. M. MCFADDEN]

GUAL, PEDRO (1813–90), Spanish-born Franciscan whose apostolate in South America, beginning in 1845 at Lima, included establishment of colleges under the Congregation for the Propagation of the Faith, and apologetical preaching and writing.

[T. C. O'BRIEN]

GUALA OF BERGAMO, BL. (*c.*1180–1244), Dominican bishop. Guala Roni (Walter Romanoni) entered the order in 1217 and became prior at Brescia and Bologna. He was also founder of the convent at Bergamo. Honorius III and Gregory IX employed him on diplomatic missions. He became bp. of Brescia *c.*1229. When exiled from his see in 1239 he went to live with the Benedictines of Astino. He was beatified in 1868. His cult is observed among the Dominicans and in the dioceses of Bergamo and Brescia. BIBLIOGRAPHY: Butler 3:482–483; M. J. Finnegan, NCE 6:823; A. Brontesi, BiblSanct 7:412–419.

[M. J. FINNEGAN]

GUALTIERI DI GIOVANNI DA PISA (*c.*1389–1445), Pisan artist who painted (1409–1411) ceilings of the sacristy of the cathedral of Siena and the vaults of three chapels with Niccolò di Naldo. Berenson attributed to G. frescoes in the Chapel of the Virgin, cathedral of Siena (*c.*1410) and panels now in the Opera del Duomo.

[M. J. DALY]

GUANELLA, LUIGI, BL. (1842–1915), founder, champion of social justice. A native of Italy, Guanella was ordained in 1866. He was a zealous worker for orphans and neglected children, for whom he established institutions in a number of Italian cities. He founded the clerical congregation, Servants of Charity and the Daughters of St. Mary of Providence to continue his work. Part of the apostolate of both groups became the care of Italian immigrants in North America. He became the associate in working for social justice of D. *Albertario and G. *Toniolo. G. was beatified in 1964.

[J. R. AHERNE]

GUARANTEES, LAW OF, unilateral concessions, enacted May 13, 1871, by the newly formed Italian parliament, to the person, office, and property of the pope. The Law was repudiated immediately by Pius IX, in the encyclical, *Ubi nos,* May 15, 1871. Acceptance would have jeopardized papal sovereignty and submitted the pope to the jurisdiction of the Kingdom of Italy, even to the whim of politicians. The popes preferred to remain "prisoners of the Vatican" until the Law was repudiated as part of the *Lateran Pact (1929). BIBLIOGRAPHY: E. E. Y. Hayles, *Pio Nono* (1954; pa.1962) 332–337; Eng. tr. of the Law, J. Carrère, *The Pope* (n.d.) 264–268.

[T. C. O'BRIEN]

GUARDIAN, superior of a Franciscan friary, a term used in keeping with the angelic nomenclature customary with the Franciscans. St. Francis of Assisi did not want a local superior to be called "prior," since he was to be the servant of the friars. The term guardian appears in the *Testament of St. Francis* (1220). The guardian is appointed for a term of 3 years by the provincial chapter and has a vote in the election of provincial superiors. In his office he bears the responsibility for the regular observance in the friary and for the spiritual welfare of the friars.

[T. C. O'BRIEN]

GUARDIAN ANGEL, an angel believed to be entrusted with the care of an individual or group. The biblical teaching concerning angels includes reference to the "angels of the nations," Michael being the guardian angel of the people of God, promised in Ex 23.20, who apparently strives with the guardian angel of the Persians (Dan 10.13–14,21). This function is carried out also in favor of individuals, as the Book of Tobit shows in recounting Raphael's constant help to Tobias; and Christ attributes to all children a guardian angel (Mt 18.10). Hebrews 1.14 calls angels "spirits whose work is service, sent to help those who will be the heirs of salvation." Acts 12.15 reflects a popular belief that guardian angels were a kind of spiritual double of their charges. The Church accepts belief in guardian angels; since 1670 it has observed the feast of Guardian Angels (Oct. 2), but it has made no definition concerning them. Their functions are to protect the Church, nation, group, or individual both spiritually and bodily and to present their prayers to God (Rev 8.3–4). Theologians agree that in virtue of their ontological perfection they are able directly to influence human imagination; but the view of SS. Jerome and Basil that sin drives them away seems gratuitous. BIBLIOGRAPHY: J. Duhr, DSAM 1:580–625; P. R. Régamey, *What Is an Angel?* (tr. M. Pontifex, 1960).

[B. FORSHAW]

GUARDINI, ROMANO (1885–1968), theologian. G. was Italian by birth, but was educated in Mainz where his father was Italian consul. He remained in Germany as an adult, was ordained a priest, and taught at the Univ. of Berlin (1923–39), Tübingen, and Munich (1948–63). His emphasis on a distinctly Christian interpretation of life and culture, combined with an openness to change, a world-affirming spirituality, and an awareness of contemporary currents of thought, made G. a preeminent leader in European Catholic renewal. His life of Christ, *The Lord* (1937), became immensely popular. BIBLIOGRAPHY: J.

Laubach, ''Romano Guardini'' in *Theologians of Our Time* (ed. L. Reinisch, 1964) 109–126.

[T. M. MCFADDEN]

GUARINI, GUARINO (1624–83), Italian Piedmontese architect in the Theatine order (1639). G. studied in Rome, was ordained and became lecturer in philosophy in Modena (1647) and teacher in mathematics. G. designed (1660) the church of the Annunciation in Messina (destroyed in the earthquake of 1908) and in Paris (1662) designed Ste.-Anne-la Royale (destroyed 1823) with a Baroque Borromini façade. In Turin (1660) for Carlo Emanuele II of Savoy with other works G. designed 2 centralized churches—Cappella della Sta. Sindone (1667–90) and S. Lorenzo (1668–87), both with his highly original extravagantly complex domes, achieving a dizzying effect of height, suggestive of infinity, by light filtering through the grid of ribs. G.'s domes, suspended and diaphanous, were copied by European Baroque architects, his undulating façades in abstract geometric poetry (a natural development from *Borromini) having significant influence beyond Italy. G. was town architect of Turin, capital of Savoy, which became the creative center of Baroque toward the end of the 17th cent. through his architectural genius. He extended Borromini's synthesis, achieving through his mathematical theories structural ''miracles'' which reached their climax N of the Alps in Austria and Southern Germany.

G. is author of *Architettura civile* and a mathematical treatise, *Placita philosophica* (1665). BIBLIOGRAPHY: M. Anderegg-Tille, *Die Schule Guarinis* (1962).

[M. J. DALY]

GUARINUS OF PALESTRINA, ST. (*c.*1080–1159), cardinal bishop. Already a cleric when he joined the Augustinians (*c.*1104), G. was elected by popular acclaim to the See of Pavia (*c.*1139). He was imprisoned for refusing the honor. In 1144, however, he was required by Pope Lucius II to accept a cardinal's hat and the See of Palestrina. BIBLIOGRAPHY: AS Feb. 1:923–925; G. D. Gordini, BiblSanct 7:435; Butler 1:264–265.

[W. A. JURGENS]

GUARINUS OF SION, ST. (GUÉRIN: *c.*1065–1150), abbot and bishop. A monk at the Abbey of Molesme from *c.*1085, he led a group from there in 1094 to live a more austere life; they formed an abbey at Aulps, Savoy and in 1110 G. became second abbot. After a visit of St. Bernard of Clairvaux, G. put the abbey under the rule of Cîteaux in 1136. He became bp. of Sion, Switzerland in 1138. He died while on a visit to Aulps and was buried there. He has always been venerated as a saint in Savoy and in the Valais.

[T. C. O'BRIEN]

GUARNERIUS (GARNIER) OF ROCHEFORT (*c.*1140–after 1225), Cistercian monk, bp., and author. Abbot of Clairvaux and the preacher of the Third Crusade, he later served as bp. of Langres but was forced to retire (1199) by Pope Innocent III. Several letters and sermons of his are extant. (PL 217:283–286; 205:555–828). BIBLIOGRAPHY: J.-C. Didier, *Catholicisme,* 4:1759–60; *idem,* ''G. de R., sa vie et son oeuvre,'' CollOCR (July 1955).

[V. BULLOUGH]

GUAS, JUAN (*c.*1450–97), Breton–Spanish architect. G. worked on the Lion Gate of the cathedral (1459–69), built S. Juan de los Reyes, Toledo (1479–80), the Infantado Palace, Guadalajära (1480–83), and the chapel of S. Gregorio, Valladolid (1488), reconciling in his work medieval, Mudejar, and Italian styles.

[M. J. DALY]

GUASTALLA, COUNCIL OF. In 1106 Pope Paschal II summoned a council to treat problems arising out of the Investiture Controversy. It was held in N Italy at Guastalla, between Verona and Mantua. BIBLIOGRAPHY: A. Condit, NCE 6:828.

[B. L. MARTHALER]

GUASTO, ANDREA DEL (1534–1627), founder of an order of hermits at Centorbi, Sicily, the *Congregatio centum urbium,* which he had affiliated to the first-order Augustinians. The congregation was suppressed in 1873.

[J. R. AHERNE]

GUATEMALA, a Central American country situated to the S and E of Mexico (42,042 sq mi; pop. [est. 1976] 5.4 m., Catholics 4,854,233; ethnic distribution: 45% Indian, 30% mestizo [Ladino], Europeans and N Americans 14%). The Spanish conquest of Guatemala was undertaken (1523–24) under Pedro de Alvarado, who became captain-general of Guatemala under the vice-royalty of New Spain (Mexico). Its early capital, Antigua, founded in 1542 after the destruction of Ciudad Vieja, came to rival Mexico City in splendor; the capital was moved to its present site, Guatemala City, after earthquakes destroyed Antigua in 1773. Guatemala became independent from Spain in 1821, and after the collapse of Iturbide's Mexican Empire (1823), of which it formed a part, it joined the Confederation of Central America. Following the dissolution of the Confederation (1838), Guatemala suffered a succession of dictators, some of conservative, some of liberal persuasion; and, as elsewhere in Central America, the opposition between right and left has been bitter and violent. In 1945 a liberal constitution was adopted under the presidency of Juan José Arevala, and progress was made toward social reform; but the Agrarian Reform Law of 1952 and reaction to the charge of Communist influence led to the overthrow of the liberal regime and a return to conservatism in 1954. Ferment has continued and the persistence of guerrilla warfare makes it clear that an effective political unity has not yet been achieved.

The necessity of social reform is admitted by all. Despite the potential wealth of the country, the great mass of the people live in poverty; the illiteracy rate is 70%; in 1950 no less than 75% of the land was owned by 2% of the people. Guatemala was evangelized by Dominicans, Franciscans, Augustinians, Jesuits, and Mercedarians. The Dominican apostolate esp. was marked by an effective use of the Indian language. The See of Guatemala was established in 1534, the University of San Carlos in the years 1579–89. Native vocations gradually increased the self-sufficiency of the Guatemalan Church; scholarship and art flourished, and Catholicism became a dominant influence in the social and family life of the people. In the 18th cent. decadence set in. After independence from Spain had been achieved, anticlericalism was rampant, esp. under liberal regimes, and the Church was an object of systematic persecution—bishops, priests, and religious were exiled; orders were suppressed; education was secularized, and property was confiscated. Dictator Justo Rufino Barrios sought Protestant missionaries from the U.S. The situation improved in the late 1930s, and a concordat was signed with the Vatican. The 1945 Constitution contains some restrictive clauses but allows ample freedom of action to the Church. After World War II much help has come from the U.S. and European countries; priests and sisters are active in the educational field and much attention is being given to social works. In 1961 the Rafael Landívar University was founded and now has faculties of economics, juridical and social sciences, and humanities. Guatemala forms an ecclesiastical province. The archiepiscopal see is located in Guatemala City. The six suffragan dioceses are Quezaltenango, Vera Paz, San Marcos, Zacapa, Jalapa, and Sololà. There is an apostolic administration in El Petén and prelatures *nullius* in Esquipulas and Huehuetenango. In 1976 Guatemala had 668 priests, of whom 478 were religious, and 1,037 nuns. Among the problems faced by the Church in this country are: the great scarcity of vocations among the native-born population and the prevalence of religious ignorance and superstition. The Catholic laity has been slow to involve itself in religious activity, although some progress in this matter is being made. The principal Protestant denominations engaged in missionary effort in Guatemala have been the Presbyterians, Methodists, Lutherans (Missouri Synod), and Baptists, although many other groups have lately joined in the work.

[P. DAMBORIENA]

GUBERNATIS, DOMENICO DE (d.1690), Italian Franciscan historian. His *Ordo Seraphicus*, one of the main source works for the study of Franciscan history, he planned as a 30-volume work. He himself published (1682–85) volumes one to four on the order's own history; volume five on its missions (1689). Two other volumes were added in 1741 and in 1886.

[J. R. AHERNE]

GUDULA, ST. (d. *c.*712), patroness of Brussels. A grand-niece of Pepin, she led a life of extraordinary asceticism and charity toward the poor while living at home. After her death she was buried at Hamme, near Brussels. Charlemagne venerated her relics and built a monastery nearby. In 978 Duke Charles of Lorraine conveyed her relics to Brussels. She holds a lantern in art, representing the wax taper miraculously relighted after being extinguished by a demon during her prayers. BIBLIOGRAPHY: Butler, 1:54; AS Jan. 1:513–530.

[J. E. LYNCH]

GUDWAL, ST. (d. *c.*640), early apostle of Brittany, probably from Cornwall, founder of the monastery of Plec, Island of Locoal-Mendon. Little else is known of G.'s life, his relics were brought to Ghent, the Abbey of SS. Peter and Paul in the 10th century. BIBLIOGRAPHY: J. Evenou, BiblSanct 7:444–445.

[T. C. O'BRIEN]

GUELF TREASURE (Welfenschatz), **COLLECTION OF,** 11th–through 14–cent. medieval metal, enamel, and jewelry work first belonging to the German house of Brunswick and sold (1929) by Duke Ernest Augustus of that family through art dealers to museums throughout the world. Among 44 works—Byzantine Italian, Rhenish, and North German in the Museum of Arts and Crafts, Berlin—is the famous Guelph cross given (1038) by the widow Gertrude in memory of the first duke; it is unparalleled in Romanesque metalwork of enameled gold, gems, silver, and filigree, with enameled gold plaques of the Evangelists on each arm. Of like richness are the reliquary arm of St. Blasius, and the *Gertrudis Altar* in niello, cloisonné—enamel and gems (Cleveland, Ohio). Henry the Lion in 1173 gave bejeweled metal reliquaries of the Apostles and a 12th–cent. portable altar inscribed ''Eilbert of Cologne made me,'' glorious in enameled copper with six figures in a colonnade and an unusual top with miniatures of the life of Christ on vellum—the entire surface covered by solid rock-crystal. A 12th-cent. Rhenish reliquary in the shape of a Byzantine dome covered with cloisonné plaques and ivory figurines, all raised on griffin supports, is equally important.

Duke Otto the Mild (d. 1344) added an illuminated gospel book (1339) with silver cover, vellum miniatures and rock-crystal cross holding portions of the True Cross. Engraved on the reverse of the cover is St. Blasius enthroned between Duke Otto and the Duchess Agnes.

[M. J. DALY]

GUELFS AND GHIBELLINES, names of German origin given in the 13th cent. to papal partisans (Guelfs) and the imperial partisans (Ghibellines) in internecine warfare that wreaked havoc in what is now Italy. Eventually, with the death of Emperor Frederick II (1250) and the defeat of his grandson Conradin (1268) by Charles of Anjou, King of Sicily, over possession of which the dispute had begun, the fighting ceased, but residual animosity between local factions that had followed one or the other side continued into the next century.

[J. F. FALLON]

GUÉNON, RENÉ MARIE JOSEPH (1866–1951), French religious theorist. After taking an early interest in the occult, G. became a Muslim. He also studied other oriental religions, wrote extensively on symbolism and religious esoterica, and constructed somewhat vague and confusing theories to account for Christian belief.

[M. J. SUELZER]

GUÉRANGER, PROSPER (1805–75), French Benedictine liturgist and scholar whose writings did much to put in motion the liturgical revival in France. As a secular priest, G. became profoundly convinced that the spiritual life of Christians had to be integrated with the Church's liturgy to achieve its best development. With the financial assistance of friends he bought the deserted priory of Solesmes. There he settled to live according to the Benedictine Rule in company with five other priests. The community was juridically incorporated into the Benedictine Order in 1837, and Solesmes was accorded the status of an abbey. G. was appointed its abbot. Under his guidance the abbey became the center of the liturgical movement in France in its early years and the center also of a rejuvenated monasticism. Two of G.'s best-known works are: *Institutions liturgiques* (3 v., 1840–52) in which he attacked local liturgical practices in France; and *L'année liturgique* (15 v., 1841–66), which was translated into English by L. Sheppard under the title *The Liturgical Year* (15 v., 1895–1903). BIBLIOGRAPHY: L. C. Sheppard, ''Dom Guéranger and the Liturgical Revival in France,'' *Thought* 6 (1932) 624–649; H. Leclercq, CE 7:58–59.

[N. KOLLAR]

GUERCINO (GIOVANNI FRANCESCO BARBIERI; 1591–1666), Bolognese baroque painter. Influenced by Lodovico Carracci he later became an emulator (in the presentation of sacred subjects) and competitor of Guido Reni. His greatest work is probably the *Aurora* fresco on the ceiling of the *casino* in the Villa Ludovisi in Rome, a painting at once innovative and surprising in his form-dissolving *sfumato* style of illusionism, yet full of dignity. Unfortunately he later changed to a linear clarity ''correct'' but uninspired. BIBLIOGRAPHY: M. Marangoni, *Guercino* (1959); A. K., Moir, NCE 6:832.

[P. P. FEHL]

GUÉRIN, PIERRE (1596–1654), French priest, founder of a religious congregation. As a curé in Roye, G. brought together a number of young women to establish a school, and out of this developed the Daughters of the Cross (Filles de la Croix, sometimes called Guérinettes). From 1629 G. came under suspicion of illuminism, and twice formal charges were brought against him; but the accusations were not substantiated. Nothing heterodox was found in his writings. The attacks may have stemmed in part from exaggerations and misinterpretations of his teachings by some who professed to be his followers, but they were also a manifestation of the then current suspicion of even orthodox mystical doctrine. BIBLIOGRAPHY: A. Dodin, DSAM 6:1106–10.

[M. J. SUELZER]

GUÉRIN, THÉODORE, MOTHER (1808–56), educator, foundress. Born in France, she entered the Sisters of Providence at age 25. After 17 years of teaching in France, where she studied medicine and pharmacy for 4 years, she volunteered for the work in the diocese of Vincennes, Indiana. At St. Mary-of-the Woods she established the first academy for girls in the state, and was foundress of the community of Sisters of Providence of St.-Mary-of-the-Woods. An educator of great ability, she was a woman of deep spirituality and influence on her community.

[J. R. AHERNE]

GUÉRINETS, name given to a group of illuminists in Picardy in the late 17th cent. by many historians because of their supposed connection with Pierre Guérin (*c.*1596–1654), a parish priest at Roye. He did found a congregation of nuns, Filles de la Croix, who were popularly called Guérinettes; he was also twice investigated for alleged novelties in doctrine, but was acquitted. Any association with the suspect *Illuminés is questionable.

[T. C. O'BRIEN]

GUERRA, ELENA, BL. (1835–1914), religious foundress. A native of Lucca, she established there in 1872 a community of sisters, popularly known as Sisters of St. Zita (approved in 1911 as Oblate Sisters of the Holy Spirit) whose purpose was to promote devotion to the Holy Spirit. Her influence is evident in the encyclical **Divinum illud munus* of Leo XIII, issued in 1897. Her community spread from Italy to Iran, Lebanon, Brazil, Canada, and the Philippines. She was beatified in 1959.

[J. R. AHERNE]

GUERRERO, FRANCISCO (1527 or 1528–99), Spanish composer, cantor, director of church music esp. in Seville. He was a diligent student of the work of Morales, and, like him, particularly devoted to sacred music. G. composed 18 Masses, with some words from the Mozarabic liturgy, more than 100 motets and other works, many of which were printed during his lifetime in Rome, Venice, Paris, and Louvain. Some MSS may be found in Spanish cathedrals, notably Ávila and Madrid. *Opera Omnia* (1955 *et seq.*) prepared by the Instituto Español de Musicología, includes his *Canciones y Villanescas espirituales* (1589).

[J. C. MARR]

GUERRIC OF IGNY, BL. (betw. 1070 and 1080–1157), French Cistercian theologian. G. became a canon at Tournai (1101?) but attracted to the contemplative life, he entered Clairvaux before 1125. In 1138 he was elected abbot at Igny. His writings, elegant in style, reveal him as a classical scholar and master of spirituality. Noteworthy is his emphasis on Mary as mediatrix. G.'s cult was approved by Leo XIII (1889). BIBLIOGRAPHY: M. B. Brard, *Catholicisme* 5:363–364; C. Waddell, NCE 6:833–834.

[S. A. HEENEY]

GUERRILLA WARFARE. From Spanish *guerrilla,* diminutive of *guerra,* war, the word came into English in Napoleonic times when the Spaniards, though their field armies were defeated, yet maintained their war of independence against the invader and prepared the way for Wellington's successful campaign. The Spanish guerrillas called themselves *partidos,* and the word has come back in recent years as "partisans." It is important to distinguish between guerrilla warfare and guerrilla-type warfare, which is most successfully conducted by highly trained regulars acting as commandos or as special service groups. Both operate in difficult country and adopt the same tactics of ambush, sudden surprise, and rapid disengagement; both have the strategy, not of taking terrain but of denying its exploitation by the enemy, of threatening him in the flank or rear, and of interfering with his lines of communication; both need the support of a regular army for final victory and reoccupation of the country—thus the withdrawal of Cornwallis from the Carolinas was dictated by the mountain men, but his capitulation at Yorktown was dictated by the French and American army. The essence of guerrilla warfare is that it is conducted by irregulars, and on the degree or kind of the "irregularity" displayed will depend its status according to international law and morality. For people to fight against occupation by an alien power was not considered wrong, and they were accorded the rights of belligerents from the tribal wars fought by the Romans until those fought by the British. The tradition was crystallized in The Hague Conventions (1899, 1907) where it was required that the command of groups should be exercised by a responsible authority, that fixed signs or uniforms recognizable at a distance should be worn, that weapons should be carried openly, and that operations should be conducted in accordance with the law and customs of war. Otherwise punishment could be severe and final. On the whole the Germans in World War II were effective against the *Banditen,* as they called them, who were active against them, and whom they repressed, though without discrimination. But with the decline of war as a legalized and limited kind of art into undisciplined violence, many distinctions have gone by the board.

[T. GILBY]

GUEST-MASTER, in monastic tradition, a monk or lay brother charged with the reception and care of guests. He is the subject of specific legislation in almost all monastic codes (e.g., Rule of St. Pachomius 30–32; Rule of St. Benedict 53) since great emphasis was placed on the reception of Christ in guests. "I was a stranger and you received me" (Mt 25.35; RB 53,1). The duties outlined for him are usually concerned with the guest's physical well being, but his reverence, joy, and peace are to give witness and convey a deeply spiritual message. BIBLIOGRAPHY: B. Steidle, *Rule of Saint Benedict: A Commentary* (tr. U. Schnitzhofer, 1967).

[M. B. PENNINGTON]

GUEUX (Beggars), a name taken by the party in the Netherlands who opposed the policies of Philip II. In 1566 a group of noblemen organized to petition Margaret of Parma, the Spanish regent, for a redress of grievances and for the suspension of the Inquisition and the laws against heretics. When, under the leadership of Louis of Nassau and Henry of Brederode, some 250 signers presented the "Request," a Spanish counselor used the term in derision. The title was then proudly claimed by the noblemen and those from all levels of society who joined them in defense of political, economic, and religious rights. Mob violence and the desecration of churches brought swift Spanish reprisals and an end to the Gueux movement. The name was revived in 1569 when the *gueux de mer* (sea beggars), under William (the Silent) of Orange, began raiding Spanish ships. In 1572 they seized the seaport of Brielle, inspiring a general revolt in the N provinces.

[J. C. WILLKE]

GUEVARA, ANTONIO DE (*c.*1480–1545), Franciscan humanist, bp. of Guadix (1528) and of Mondonedo (1537). He was preacher and chronicler at the court of Charles V of Spain; author of *Libro llamado Relox de Príncipes o Libro áureo del emperador Marco Aurelio* (1529), a pretended translation from a Florentine MS and a treatise in novel form on moral instruction. His 85 *Epístolas familiares* and *Menosprecio de corte y alabanza de aldea* (1539) were widely read, translated, and by their ornateness strongly influenced the baroque style of literature, even what is known as euphuism in the history of English literature.

[T. C. O'BRIEN]

GUEVARA Y LIRA, SILVESTRE (1814–82), abp. of Caracas, Venezuela (1853–76), defender of the Church against the secularization policies of the dictator A. *Guzmán Blanco.

[T. C. O'BRIEN]

GUFFÂRAH, outer garment, made like a Western cope, worn by Maronite episcopal celebrants before and after the anaphoric part of the Mass (during which they wear the *badlah*). The *guffârah* is also worn by certain nonepiscopal

Maronite celebrants, for the entire Mass, like the West Syrian *phainō*.

[A. CODY]

GUGLIELMO DA MODENA (fl. 12th cent.). An Italian sculptor, G. worked on the cathedral at Modena (1099–1106), executing reliefs of the Creation on the S façade of the main portal and ornamental friezes. The "Enoch-Elias" tablet gives his name as Wiligelmus, indicating of Germanic origin. G. executed the bishop's throne at Bari (1098) and the archivolt of angel heads at Monopoli (1107). He is master of narrative monumental figural reliefs.

[M. J. DALY]

GUIBERT OF GEMBLOUX (also Guibert-Martin *c.*1125–1213), Benedictine abbot, historian. G. studied at the Abbey of Gembloux under Abbot Arnold (1136–55). Because of his correspondence with St. *Hildegard of Bingen, he became her literary assistant for a time. He was abbot at Florennes in 1188, and Gembloux in 1193, but returned to Florennes as a simple monk in 1202, remaining there until his death. He had a great devotion to St. Martin of Tours, visited his tomb and wrote much about him. Sixty-four of his letters (some to St. Hildegard) remain, as do a work on her life and various treatises on monasticism. BIBLIOGRAPHY: R. Gazeau, *Catholicisme* 5:370–371.

[N. F. GAUGHAN]

GUIBERT OF NOGENT (1053–1124), historian and ecclesiastical controversialist. Abbot of the monastery of Nogent-sous-Cousy in the diocese of Laon, G. is best remembered for his autobiography, *De vita sua*, an invaluable account of the time. He also wrote a history of the First Crusade, *Gesta Dei per Francos*, which, though based on the anonymous *Gesta Francorum*, still managed to achieve some originality. His most controversial work was *De pignoribus sanctorum*, a critical treatise on the use of relics. Guibert also wrote against Berengarius' rejection of transubstantiation. BIBLIOGRAPHY: V. L. Bullough, NCE 6:836 (bibliog.)

[V. BULLOUGH]

GUIBERT OF RAVENNA (*c.*1025–1100), imperial official, antipope. A man of obscure birth, he entered imperial service (*c.*1054–55) and rose to the post of imperial chancellor for Italy (1058). He was interested in church reform and became a supporter of Hildebrand until the latter's election to the papacy (1073). G. was excommunicated (1078) and later (1080) elected as an antipope by the imperial party in opposition to Gregory VII. As Clement III, Guibert aroused support for the imperial cause. He remained in favor of reform but objected to the methods used by the Gregorian party to secure it. BIBLIOGRAPHY: W. Ullmann, *Growth of Papal Government in the Middle Ages* (2d ed., 1962).

[J. MULDOON]

GUIBERT OF TOURNAI (Gilbert, Wibert; *c.*1200–84), Franciscan theologian and preacher. He was a master at Paris *c.*1235 when he joined the Franciscans. Possibly he succeeded to St. Bonaventure's chair of theology, but he was more famous as a preacher than as a theologian. BIBLIOGRAPHY: *Antonianum* 32 (1957) 431; G. Fussenegger, LTK 4:1266 gives a list of recent editions of some of G.'s works.

GUIBERT, JOSEPH DE (1877–1942), French Jesuit theologian, author of studies of first rank in ascetical and mystical theology. A Jesuit from 1895, after graduate studies at the Sorbonne, he was ordained in 1906, taught at houses of the Society, and was a chaplain in World War I. But his major life's work was as professor of ascetical and mystical theology at the Gregorian Univ. in Rome from 1920 until his death. He was also a founder of *Revue d'ascétique et de mystique* in 1919. His published works include: *Theologia spiritualis, ascetica et mystica* (1937; Eng. tr. P. Barrett, 1953); *La Spiritualité de la Compagnie de Jésus* (1953; Eng. tr. W. J. Young, *The Jesuits; Their Doctrine and Practice*, 1964).

[T. C. O'BRIEN]

GUICCIARDINI, FRANCESCO (1483–1540), Italian historian and statesman. Born in Florence, G. inherited from his parents strong Medicean sentiments. He studied law at Ferrara and Pisa, married (1508), and established a respectable law practice. During this period, he wrote his first work, *Florentine History from 1378 to 1509*. In 1512, he began his political career as ambassador to the court of Ferdinand V of Castille, in 1514 entered the service of the Medici and became governor of Modena and Reggio, and, later, commissioner general of the papal army. After the brief Republican rule (1527–30), the Medici returned to Florence and G. along with them. He became advisor to Duke Alessandro and was instrumental in the election of Cosimo de' Medici (1537). But his inability to control Cosimo's absolutism led to the decline of G.'s political importance. He retired to his villa to write the *History of Italy*. This work, his most important, is the principal piece of historical writing of the 16th century. He breaks away from the standard local type of chronicle characteristic of the period and presents an overall view of Italy from 1494 to 1534. A historian's historian, he departed from the rhetorical conventions of the humanist historians. BIBLIOGRAPHY: R. Ridolfi, *Vita di Francesco Guicciardini* (1960); F. Gilbert, *Machiavelli and Guicciardini: Politics and History in the 16th Century Florence* (1964).

[D. G. NUGENT]

GUICHARD OF TROYES (d. 1317), French bishop. G. was brought to trial and deposed on charges of having killed, with the help of magic, the wife of Philip IV and her mother. The Pope was unable to prevail on the secular court to turn the trial of the bishop over to the ecclesiastical court. BIBLIOGRAPHY: G. Mollat, *Catholicisme* 5:371–372.

[M. J. SUELZER]

GUIDI, FILIPPO (d. *c.* 1874), Dominican theologian and cardinal archbishop of Florence. Although a respected figure among the ultramontane majority at Vatican Council I, he worked against a definition of an oracular and personal papal infallibility. He was applying the principles of his Dominican predecessor, St. *Antoninus. For this he was severely rebuked by Pius IX. Nevertheless, with other moderates he was instrumental in securing the present definition, which guards against claiming infallibility in any abstractist or autocephalous sense or as a positive and habitual charismatic endowment.

[T. GILBY]

GUIDI, IGNAZIO (1844–1935), Italian Orientalist. A master of Semitic languages, G. was professor of Hebrew and comparative Semitic languages at the Univ. of Rome (1876–1919). In this capacity he helped to train an outstanding group of Semitic scholars, among them his son, Michelangelo (1886–1946). G. contributed numerous editions of texts to the *Corpus scriptorum christianorum orientalium* and the *Patrologia orientalis*. In addition he furthered Islamic studies by his scholarly efforts. His special field was Ethiopic studies in which he published a dictionary of Amharic. He spoke this language fluently though he never visited Ethiopia. In general, his work was characterized by minute and rigorous research. BIBLIOGRAPHY: P. Skehan, NCE 6:839–840; G. Levi della Vida, EncCatt 6:1284–86.

[R. B. ENO]

GUIDO (GUY) OF SPOLETO, GERMAN EMPEROR (891–894), Duke of Spoleto and Camerino (882). After failing to obtain the West Frankish crown, Guido defeated Berengar, Margrave of Friuli, thus becoming King of Italy (889). In 891, when the Carolingian king (later emperor) Arnulf failed to aid Pope Stephen V against the Saracens, the Pope bestowed the imperial crown on Guido. BIBLIOGRAPHY: CMedH 3:63–64 and *passim;* L. Duchesne, *Beginnings of the Temporal Sovereignty of the Popes, A.D. 754–1073* (tr. A. H. Mathew, 1908) 190–196.

[M. F. MCCARTHY]

GUIDO (GUY) OF ANDERLECHT, ST. (d. 1012), Flemish confessor, also called St. Wye. G. was a sexton at Laeken near Brussels. Later, for having turned merchant to gather money for alms, he went on a 7-year expiatory pilgrimage to Rome and Jerusalem and died soon after his return. BIBLIOGRAPHY: K. van den Bergh, BiblSanct 7:496–501; Butler 3:546–547.

[M. J. FINNEGAN]

GUIDO OF AREZZO (b. *c.* 990), monk and musical theorist, reformer of musical notation and instruction. His fame rests chiefly on his system of solmization, by which he established the nomenclature of the steps of the scale (*ut, re, mi, fa, sol, la*) from the initial syllable of each line of the hymn **Ut queant laxis* for the feast of St. John the Baptist. He also popularized the music staff of four lines which made possible the precise notation of pitch. Another invention, the Guidonian hand, related each scale degree to a different place on the hand, to which a teacher or choir director could point to indicate pitch. A diagram of the Guidonian hand became a feature of every music treatise through the Renaissance. G.'s most important work, the *Micrologus*, is also an early source of information about *organum. BIBLIOGRAPHY: J. Smits van Waesberghe, MGG 5:1071–78; Reese MusMA.

[P. MURPHY]

GUIDO OF BAYSIO (d. 1313), Italian canonist. He compiled a classic source for the history of canon law, his *Apparatus ad Decretum* (1300), also called the *Rosarium Decreti;* the work contains material on Gratian's **Decretum* not otherwise available. He also wrote *Apparatus ad Sextum* (1306–11), a commentary and supplement for the study of the **Liber sextus*. In connection with the proposed posthumous trial of Boniface VIII and the suppression of the Templars at the Council of *Vienne (1311), he wrote *Tractatus super haeresi et aliis criminibus in causa Templariorum et D. Bonifacii D. P. Papae VIII*. During his career G. held a canonry at Chartres (1295), was archdeacon of Bologna (1296), and from 1301, professor of canon law there; from 1304 he served in the papal curia at Avignon.

[T. C. O'BRIEN]

GUIDO OF CORTONA, BL. (1187–1214), Franciscan, priest. As one of the early followers of St. Francis (1210) he is esp. prominent in the *Fioretti*. He founded the hermitage of Le Celle near Cortona where he was revered by the people for his ascetical life and the miracles ascribed to him, among which were the healing of a priest's paralyzed arm and the bringing back to life of a girl who had drowned in a well. His cult was approved in 1583. BIBLIOGRAPHY: N. Bruni, *Le reliquie del beato Guido da Cortona* (1947); Butler 2:556–557.

[J. J. SMITH]

GUIDO THE LOMBARD, BL. (b. *c.* 1100), a venerable person about whom not much is known except that he had some connection of preeminence with the Order of Humiliati. The male branch of the order was suppressed in 1571; but there are still some few communities of women in Italy who revere Guido as their founder. BIBLIOGRAPHY: F. Russo, EncCatt 6:1291–92.

[W. A. JURGENS]

GUIDO PAPA (Guipape; *c.*1405–77), French jurisconsult. After legal studies at Montpellier, Pavia, and Turin, he practiced law in Lyons but soon thereafter went to Grenoble where he held a variety of posts in civil administration. In 1444 he became legal counsel for the regional council which became the parliament of the Dauphiné during his tenure, until 1461. His most famous work is the *Decisiones parlamenti dalphinalis,* a collection of *quaestiones,* a term he used to include legislative decrees, curial practice, autobiographical and historical material. BIBLIOGRAPHY: G. Letonnelier, DDC 5:1009–11.

[J. E. BIECHLER]

GUIDO OF POMPOSA, ST. (d. 1046), Benedictine abbot. After living for 3 years as a hermit, he went to the abbey of Pomposa where he was soon elected abbot. Under his leadership Pomposa became one of the outstanding abbeys of N Italy. At his invitation Peter Damian came to Pomposa and lectured on Sacred Scripture for 2 years (1039–41). In 1046 G. joined the retinue of Emperor Henry III when he entered Italy, but took sick and died at Parma. The next year his body was taken for burial to Speyer, Germany. BIBLIOGRAPHY: Butler 1:709–710; Zimmermann, 1:394–396; D. Balboni, BiblSanct 7:510–512.

[O. J. BLUM]

GUIDO DA SIENA (fl. 13th cent.), Italian painter. The *Madonna Hodetria* of 1221, repainted in the 14th cent., is disputed. *Christ with Angels* is in a modified Byzantine style; a *St. Dominic* (Cambridge), *Madonna and Four Saints,* and *St. Peter Enthroned* (both in Siena), though humanized in figures, retain a Romanesque hieratic majesty.

[M. J. DALY]

GUIGO I (1084–1136), fifth prior of La Grande Chartreuse, 1109, its rebuilder in 1132, author (basing himself on St. *Bruno's oral teaching) of the Carthusian rule, *Consuetudines Cartusiae* (1121–27), codifier of the order's liturgy. G.'s *Meditationes* express the primitive ideals of Carthusian prayer life.

[T. C. O'BRIEN]

GUIGO II (d. *c.*1188), ninth prior of La Grande Chartreuse, from 1173 until resigning in 1180, spiritual writer. He is known primarily for his *Scala Paradisi seu Tractatus de modo orandi* (*c.*1150; ME tr., *A Ladder of Four Rungs by Guy II,* 1953). The four rungs, reading, meditation, prayer, contemplation became an accepted grouping of the elements of the spiritual life, one adopted by St. John of the Cross in his writings. G. also wrote *Meditationes,* edited by M. M. Day, *La Vie spirituelle, Suppl,* 1932–34.

[T. C. O'BRIEN]

GUIGO DE PONTE (Guigue du Pont; d. 1297), Carthusian mystical writer whose description in *De contemplatione* of a natural, a scholastic or acquired, and a mystical contemplation was adopted by *Denis the Carthusian. G. described mystical contemplation as an overshadowing by a darkness in the innermost heart; his stress was on the noncognitive, affective experience as the essence of mystical contemplation.

[T. C. O'BRIEN]

GUILDAY, PETER (1884–1947), church historian. A native of Pennsylvania, G. was ordained in 1909. After spending two years of postdoctoral study and research in several European countries, he published *The English Colleges and Convents in The Catholic Low Countries 1558–1795* (1914). He was appointed to The Catholic Univ. of America in 1914 and remained on its faculty for the rest of his life. In 1915 he founded the *Catholic Historical Review,* of which he remained editor until his death; it was a great catalyst for the study of American church history. In 1919 under his leadership, the American Catholic Historical Association was founded, and from that year until 1941 he was the moving force of its annual meetings. Among his many works, *The Life and Times of John Carroll* (1922) and *The Life and Times of John England* (1927) are landmarks in the field of church history. G. also wrote extensively for periodicals. Through the American Church History Seminar at Catholic Univ., he exerted great influence on a generation of writers on church history, and was responsible for a renewed development of this discipline in Catholic circles. BIBLIOGRAPHY: J. T. Ellis, "Peter Guilday," CHR 33(1947) 257–268.

[J. R. AHERNE]

GUILDS, associations for economic, social, and religious purposes. The medieval craft guilds, which often achieved political as well as economic power, constitute the most significant examples. Guilds, known as *collegia,* were prominent in the Roman Empire, where children were often required to enter the profession and guild of their parents. In Byzantium guilds survived until the fall of Constantinople (1453). In the West, most of these *collegia* disappeared after 476, though some may have continued until the medieval revival. As clan ties weakened among the peoples of N Europe in the Carolingian era, they formed peace (frith) guilds, devoted largely to mutual protection. Merchant guilds began in N Europe *c.*1000, and craft guilds a century later, the latter gaining dominance in the 13th and 14th centuries. Guild statutes such as those of Abbotsbury, Exeter, and Cambridge date as early as the 11th century. Craft guilds served social as well as economic purposes. They met extraordinary needs that arose in cases of sickness and disaster and after a member's death helped his widow and orphans. All medieval guilds had a religious dimension, normally adopting a patron saint and keeping the saint's feast day. In some, the religious purpose was dominant, but these generally had less wealth and power than the craft guilds. The latter served many functions of a modern labor union in protecting the economic interests of their members, including regulation of hours and prices. They usually maintained an apprenticeship system and set the requirements for certification as a qualified craftsman. When masters, seeking to hold down competition, became too restrictive in admitting new members to their ranks, journeymen sometimes formed their own guilds.

Universities arose from guilds of scholars, who regulated their profession and set requirements for entry into their ranks. Practitioners of the various arts also formed guilds. A significant role in Western political development was played by guilds as intermediate powers between the individual or family and the State. Recognition of the guild as a corporate person with certain rights contributed toward the growth of a pluralistic social structure in which there were checks against state absolutism or individuals of great power and wealth. Guilds sometimes came under criticism from church authorities for reasons as various as drinking brawls, unorthodox beliefs, and price fixing. The Reformation was generally hostile to guilds, and Adam Smith condemned them as selfish monopolies. They gradually declined in the late 18th and 19th cent., but at their height they formed a dominant part of the society, particularly in areas where central governmental authority was weak. Evidence of their importance remains in the splendid guild halls surviving in many European cities.

[T. EARLY]

GUILELMUS MONACHUS (fl. 15th cent.), Italian music theorist whose treatise *De praeceptis artis musicae et practicae* contains information concerning the practice of *faux-bourdon. BIBLIOGRAPHY: H. Hüschen, MGG 5:1084–87; Reese MusMA.

[P. MURPHY]

GUILLAUME DE LORRIS (fl. 1225–37). Orléans poet, beginner of the **Roman de la Rose,* otherwise unknown. His possibly autobiographical allegory, influenced by Ovid, Chrétien de Troyes and *courtly love is graceful, idealistic, and youthful. Its abrupt ending may be due to Guillaume's marrying the "Rose."

[J. P. WILLIMAN]

GUILLAUME DE MACHAUT, see MACHAUT, GUILLAUME DE.

GUILMANT, (FÉLIX) ALEXANDRE (1837–1911), French organist and composer at the Trinité church, Paris (1871–1901). With Bordes and d'Indy, he founded the Parisian *Schola cantorum*. Dupré, Bonnet, Jacob, and Cellier were his pupils. He successfully toured England, America, and the Continent. He did valuable editorial work, publishing *École classique de l'orgue,* and, with André Pirro, *Archives des maîtres de l'orgue*. He resurrected long-forgotten music, adapting it to the modern organ, notably that of Nicolas de Grigny and Nicholas Gigault.

[J. C. MARR]

GUILT, a word derived from the Anglo-Saxon *gylt*. There are no equivalents in other Teutonic languages, and the alleged connection of the word with the roots of owing a debt is, says the *Oxford Dictionary,* "phonologically inadmissible," although there is, as shall be seen, an attraction between the ideas. The term has rather different meanings in psychology, in jurisprudence, and in theology. Its theological meaning varies according to the stress on philosophical or on juridical morals.

In its common and fundamental notion, guilt involves two closely associated elements: first, misdirected human action, i.e., a failure or a sin in general terms and a moral fault (*malum culpae*) more specifically; and second, a condition of being deficient or of lacking some integrity in oneself, or of being displaced with respect to one's environment. Under this latter aspect it approaches the notion of being penalized (*malum poenae*). The first of these elements is presupposed to, rather than constitutive of, guilt as it is generally understood. Guilt is thus less the wrongdoing than the resulting condition of dislocation. In this condition we may distinguish between the dislocation itself and the being held responsible and having the fault imputed for blame. Though guiltiness is commonly blurred with culpability, both in popular speech and in theological rhetoric, it seems that the two should at least be separately discerned.

Phenomenologically considered, guilt seems to spread beyond the field of morals. There is an experience of uneasiness, to put it no more poignantly, and of anxiety rising from one's recognition that he is a "stray," one who does not belong, that he is not what and where he should be. Four theological levels in this experience may be discerned, and in attempting this in so summary a treatment, the use of labels is unavoidable.

To begin with, man is a creature, and that very fact may produce an *Angst,* even a sort of resentment of the split in himself between essence and existence, when, like Nietzsche, he would be as a god. He may even regard God as an antagonist against whom he cannot possibly win. This ruefulness may be changed into love and gratitude and acceptance of oneself for what one really is, but until that transformation is brought about, one may live in a state of what can, for want of a better term, be called ontological guilt.

Second, one sees oneself not merely as a creature, but as a mixed-up creature to boot, i.e., as a combination, at once monstrous and benign, of intelligence and sense and avoirdupois. That alone, but for the grace of original justice, which we lack, is bound to produce a sort of grievance of one part against another. This we may speak of as psychosomatic guilt. Notice that neither this nor ontological guilt are the result of a lapse, as the Gnostics thought; both are God's doing, not man's own, and both are conditions of his health and salvation.

Third, to introduce a morbid note, mankind has somehow spoiled the mixture, and all men are born prone to disorder and subject to decay. This is the guilt of original sin. But the fault by which this came about had its happy side. It was a *felix culpa* because it brought to men their Savior, and it communicates to an authentic Christianity the smell of a race both cursed and blessed beyond the comprehension of a eupeptic humanism. Furthermore, it is something a man may be sorry about, yet not exactly repentant for.

Fourth, the matter grows worse, for an individual adds to this mass guilt the results of his own wickedness by turning in on himself apart from God and so getting thoroughly "lost"; this, the condition of being a cheat, a coward, a whoremonger, or whatever, is his personal guilt before God. Yet wretched as may be the state of a man under the weight of it, he is not without hope. He may cry out: "God be merciful to me, a sinner." This is the true beat of the life of Christian devotion, namely man's contrition and God's forgiveness.

So far theology; now for other settings to the notion of guilt. Man is a social animal and must adjust himself to his community which will not tolerate the breaking of its customs and laws. A human being is not at home where he is without honor; he becomes an outcast by ostracism or by being put out of circulation by imprisonment or by banishment; he suffers a deprivation by being fined. All these are instances of the guilt of punishment (*reatus poenae*), which comes into theology largely from Roman law conceptions, and is adopted by St. Thomas Aquinas (ThAq 1a2ae, 87.1), though he explains the "depression" it involves along the meta-legal lines already indicated. This, which may be called social or juridical guilt, answers more to what the community considers a crime than to what the conscience considers a sin. The plea of diminished responsibility tends to muffle the notion of moral guilt, and though a satisfactory substitute for the McNaghten rule has not been found, few modern penologists are content with it.

Under the heading of social guilt we may touch on the problem of collective guilt, as when a whole national group is indicted at the bar of international law. Unless this implies a consensus in *natural law, and not just an agreement on private law among the nations, and particularly among victorious nations, and unless an active conspiracy can be proved, the notion does not commend itself to canonists and moralists who, since the days of Innocent IV and St. Thomas Aquinas, have adopted the principle that human authority may directly punish only because of personal crime.

So far we have spoken of "objective" guilt, which may strike at the root of a man's existence, or cause him no more than a momentary discomfort, but in its intervening stages is a potent cause of guilt in its most prominent contemporary form, namely "subjective" guilt, or guilt-feelings. On this both Freud and Jung have given theologians much food for thought, although their theories cannot be recapitulated here. It is enough to remark that a mature realization of a failure in personal responsibility can only with strain be explained by the operation of superego mechanics; all the same it is to be admitted that feelings of shame and remorse or crypto-remorse and of being condemned by a taboo amount to a disease when we are so hag-ridden by them that essential non-self–regarding activities are spoiled or prevented. As a form of self-punishment, a payment of forfeits demanded only by illusion, it might be called a clinical entity were its manifestations not so diverse. A person completely shameless would be a pathological case, a dangerous criminal at worst, a little Jack Horner at best, and so a psychotherapist should train a patient out of healthy feelings of shame only to the extent that a physician should anaesthetize against healthy feelings of pain. In this matter a moralist may be permitted to have the last word. Our fears keep us from God more than our pleasures do: overindulgence in either is wrong, and a form of intemperance, but to luxuriate in the first, or in guilt-feelings, lacks even the shadow of recommendation.

Here Christian theology has much to offer for strength and comfort. It discerns between the wrongdoing and its effects, and in the latter it refuses to identify estrangement with total depravity. The fault is obliterated by God's free mercy and forgiveness, the "cost" is more than paid and amendment made when we are joined with Christ in his atonement; we who used to be "far off have been brought near in the blood of Christ. For he is our peace. . ." (Eph 2:13–14). Only when all things are restored in him shall we be beyond guilt. BIBLIOGRAPHY: J. C. Falcone, *Guilt and the Sense of Guilt* (1961); J. G. McKenzie, *Guilt: Its Meaning and Significance* (1962); V. White, "Guilt, Theological and Psychological," in *Christian Essays in Psychiatry* (ed. P. Mairet, 1956).

[T. GILBY]

GUILT OFFERING, a type of OT sacrifice which was offered in reparation for all voluntary and involuntary sins against justice. It is mentioned in Ezek 40.39; 42.13, and prescribed in the Priestly Code (Lev 5.6–25; 7.1–10) where an additional reparatory penalty is also imposed. The guilt offering is distinguished from the sin offering, which concerned ritual holiness, although the distinction is often obscure.

[T. M. MCFADDEN]

GUINEY, LOUISE IMOGENE (1861–1920), poet, literary critic. She inherited the militant Catholicism and devotion to country of her father, Major General Robert Guiney, a distinguished officer in the Union Army during the Civil War. Postmistress in Auburndale, Mass., she was victim of anti-Catholic feeling that caused a boycott of the postoffice, but she was reappointed by President McKinley. Publication of *The Roadside Harp* (1893) made her a favorite of Oliver Wendell Holmes and others of the magic circle in Boston. G. was too vigorous, unconventional, and down-to-earth to stomach the respectability of Boston for long. Her last 20 years were lived in England, chiefly at Oxford, where her love of the 17th-cent. poets created an extraordinary work, *Recusant Poets,* part of which was published long after her death (1938). It is a critical work of very high order. In both her poetry and her criticism G. displayed a vigor and lucidity unusual for the turn of the century. BIBLIOGRAPHY: C. Alexander, *Catholic Literary Revival* (1935).

[J. R. AHERNE]

GUIRAUD, JEAN (1866–1953), historian, editor. Born and educated in France, G. studied medieval religious history at the École Française in Rome. For that institution's publication of 13th-cent. papal registers, G. edited the *Régistres d' Urbain IV* and the *Registres de Grégoire X*. In 1896 he published *L'État pontifical après le Grand Schisme,* his main thesis. In 1907 he published *Cartulaire de Notre Dame de Prouille,* noted for its essay on the Albigensian heresy. In 1898 he was named professor of medieval history at Besançon. The law of 1905 separating Church and State in France led to a vigorous career in opposition to the legislation and encroaching secularism in his country. From 1917 to 1940 he directed the powerful Catholic daily *La Croix*. His *Histoire de L'Inquisition au Moyen Age* (2 v., 1935–38) is but a part of the uncompleted plan for the study of the Inquisition. He published as well popular historical studies.

[J. R. AHERNE]

GUISE, the name taken from the town on the Oise in N France, of a cadet branch of the house of Lorraine descended from the house of Anjou, of a noble family with royal pretentions of capable soldiers, churchmen, and statesmen. Their energy, solidarity, and popularity with the people of Paris formidably contributed to the political maintenance of Catholicism in the French 16th-cent. Wars of Religion. The second duke, Francis, the grand Guise (d.1563) was a splendid figure, the idol of his soldiers, and conspicuous for his humanity after battle. His uncle was John, first Card. of Lorraine (d.1550), dissolute but well-liked, a patron of learning and the arts, the friend and protector of Erasmus and Rabelais; his brothers included Charles, second Card. of Lorraine (d.1574), and Louis, first Card. of Guise (d.1578); a sister was Marie de Guise, regent for her daughter Mary Queen of Scots. His son Henry, the third duke, continued his father's work and was treacherously assassinated with royal contrivance, and his brother, Louis, second Card. of Guise, murdered in prison (1588). His 14 children, who included Louis, third Card. of Guise (d.1621), remembered for his liaison with the king's mistress, maintained the cause of the Catholic League, the policies of which without the alliance with Spain, were established with the succession of the Bourbon.

[T. GILBY]

GUITMOND OF AVERSA (d. *c.*1095), monk, bp., writer on the Eucharist. He was, with St. *Anselm of Canterbury, a student of Lanfranc; he became a monk at the monastery of La Croix-Saint-Leufroy, Évreux; declined a bishopric in England after the Norman Conquest. Dissension at his election as bp. of Rouen led him to depart for Italy; there Gregory VII befriended him and made him bp. of Aversa (NE of Naples). There has been recent historico-theological interest in his *De corporis et sanguinis Domini veritate libri tres*. Written in dialogue form as a refutation of *Berengar of Tours, this defense of the Real Presence is largely dependent on *Paschasius Radbertus. But G. is thought to be the first to use the term "accidents" of the species in discussing the Eucharistic change; and, without employing the term, to have explained this change in a way equivalent to *transubstantiation. The early scholastic dialectic of the work is also noteworthy. BIBLIOGRAPHY: P. Shaughnessy, *Eucharistic Doctrine of Guitmond of Aversa* (1939); S. Furlani, EncCatt 6:1302–04.

[T. C. O'BRIEN]

GUITTARD, LOUIS (1903–55), French Christian Brother, educator. He taught philosophy for some years, and was made director of several schools of his congregation. His doctoral thesis and its sequel, *Pédagogie religieuse des adolescents* (1952), urged the application of the findings of characteriology to the religious training of the young. BIBLIOGRAPHY: J. Jacquemet, *Catholicisme* 5:423.

[M. J. SUELZER]

GUIZOT, FRANÇOIS PIERRE GUILLAUME (1787–1874), French statesman and historian, main intellectual prop of the July Monarchy of Louis Philippe. He adopted a liberal attitude toward the Church and sponsored an education law giving the Church control of French primary education. Under his premiership France achieved a stable government. G.'s political creed stressed the middle course between absolutism and democracy. His *General History of the Civilization of Modern Europe* and *History of the Revolution in England* put him among the leading French historians of his time BIBLIOGRAPHY: D. Johnston, *Guizot* (1963).

GUJARAT TEMPLES. In Gujarat, an 11th– to 13th–cent. trading center in W India are numerous richly designed Hindu and Jain temples of Northern "Indo-Aryan" style, elaborate in décor with clustered śikharas, extensively damaged by the Muslims (1298) and an earthquake in the 19th century. Important is the Sūrya temple at Modhera, and temples of exquisite marble detail at Mt. Abu in Rajasthan.

[M. J. DALY]

GUMBERT OF ANSBACH, ST. (fl. 8th cent.), founder (before 748) and abbot of St. Mary's Abbey at Ansbach, which he donated to Charlemagne in 786 in exchange for the privileges of immunity and free election of abbots. His legendary vita (see AS 4:61) is unreliable. BIBLIOGRAPHY: P. Cousin, NCE 6:860–861; A. Bayer, *S. Gumberts Kloster und Stift in Ansbach* (1948); F. Baumann, BiblSanct 7:519. [M. F. MCCARTHY]

GUMILYOV, NIKOLAY STEPANOVICH (1886–1921), Russian poet; he was shot in 1921 on charges of anti-Soviet activities. In 1912, with Gorodetski, he founded the Guild of Poets (better known as the Acmeists). The best collections of his poems are *Pearls* (1910), *The Pyre* (1918), and *Pillar of Fire* (1921). BIBLIOGRAPHY: L. I. Strakhovsky, *Craftsmen of the Word: Three Poets of Modern Russia* (1949) 5–52; R. Poggioli, *Poets of Russia: 1890–1930* (1960) 223–229. [M. F. MCCARTHY]

GUMMAR, ST. (d. *c.*775), a hermit of noble birth. A life of him, dating from the 11th cent. but claiming to be drawn from an otherwise unknown earlier account, is the source of what information we have of him. At the urging of Pepin III he married a woman whose perverse ways caused him much grief and shame. Ultimately he gave up his efforts to salvage her and retired to a life of solitary prayer at Lier. In the Low Countries he is reputed to have been a great wonder worker. BIBLIOGRAPHY: Butler 4:88; AS Oct. 5: 674–697; A. D'Haenens, BiblSanct 7:521–522. [J. E. LYNCH]

GUNDECAR, BL. (GUNZO; 1019–75), bp. of Eichstätt, author of a source work for the study of the history of the diocese and the liturgy of the period, now referred to as the *Gundecarianum*. BIBLIOGRAPHY: F. Baumann, BiblSanct 7:526. [T. C. O'BRIEN]

GUNDISALVI, DOMINIC, see DOMINIC GUNDISALVI.

GUNKEL, HERMANN (1862–1932), German biblical scholar, pioneer in the study of biblical *literary genres and *form criticism. He insisted on the need to discover, for biblical interpretation, the oral tradition that anteceded the actual literary composition of the books; and on the *Sitz im Leben* (life situation) as determinative of the development of these preliterary traditions. His own application of his theories is esp. important in *Die Psalmen* (1926). G. was founding editor of the first edition of *Religion in Geschichte und Gegenwart* (RGG). BIBLIOGRAPHY: A. Suelzer, JBC 2:598–601. [T. C. O'BRIEN]

GUNPOWDER PLOT, in England the conspiracy discovered in 1605 to blow up the Houses of Parliament. The conspirators were all Roman Catholics; their leader was R. *Catesby. The plan was designed to better the condition of Catholics under James I; it was hoped that in the confusion following the explosion Catholics could gain control over the government; a rising in the Midlands was also part of the plot. Initial steps were taken in 1604, but the actual laying of gunpowder kegs under the House of Lords took place in the fall of 1605. The plot was discovered at the last moment, and almost by accident. Guy *Fawkes, appointed to set off the powder, was caught, and soon afterwards the other principal plotters. Most of them were executed. The plot became the occasion for further repressive measures against Catholics, and was used esp. to curtail the efforts of the Jesuits. Historians agree that the plot was not a general conspiracy of English Catholics. Controversy as to the true motives of the conspirators, the reliability of official versions of the plot, and the propaganda made of it by the government remain unresolved. BIBLIOGRAPHY: P. Renold, NCE 6:862–864 with bibliog. [T. C. O'BRIEN]

GÜNTER, HEINRICH (1870–1951), historian. G. began his career with a Württemberg commission for local history, and after several professional chairs, went to Munich in 1923. He is best known for his series of works on the role of legend as it affects the intellectual history of peoples and institutions. BIBLIOGRAPHY: J. Spörl, *Historisches Jahrbuch* (1951) 70. [B. F. SCHERER]

GÜNTHER OF NIEDERALTAICH, ST. (*c.*955–1045), Benedictine monk. After an irreligious youth in Thuringia, G. made a journey to Rome. On his return he joined the Benedictines at Hersfeld as a lay brother but later received tonsure at Niederaltaich. He lived as a hermit with several companions in the Bavarian forest and thereby helped open a trade route to Bohemia. Adviser to three emperors and missionary to the Lusatians, G. founded several monasteries, including Rinchnach, an affiliate of Niederaltaich. BIBLIOGRAPHY: G. Spahr, NCE 6:864–865; E. Pásztor, BiblSanct 7:528–531. [M. J. FINNEGAN]

GUNTHER OF PAIRIS (d. *c.*1220), Cistercian author. He was tutor to Frederick Barbarossa's sons; then he joined the Cistercian abbey of Pairis (Alsace) and wrote three historical works of limited originality: *Solimarius* (1180–86), a verse narrative of the First Crusade; *Historia Constantinopolitana;* and *Ligurinus* (1186–87), an epic of Barbarossa's Italian campaigns. BIBLIOGRAPHY: F. Brunhözl, LTK 4:1276; H. MacKinnon, NCE 6:865. [L. J. LEKAI]

GÜNTHER, ANTON (1783–1863), Austrian priest-theologian whose teaching was proscribed as rationalistic by Pius IX in letters to the abp. of Cologne in 1857 (D 2828–31) and to the bp. of Breslau in 1860 (D 2833), as well as in the Syllabus of Errors (D 2914). The Vatican Council I's dogmatic constitution on faith directed its c.5

on God the Creator against his thought (D 3025). When nine of G.'s works were put on the Index in 1857, he submitted sincerely and completely and wrote no more; Pius IX's strictures were prompted by the continued dissemination of G.'s teachings by former students, many of whom were professors in Germany. G. before studying theology had become thoroughly read in modern philosophy, being esp. attracted to the thought of Hegel. He was ordained in 1837, spent 2 years in a Jesuit novitiate, then took up residence in Vienna, teaching privately and doing parochial work; he never accepted a university post.

[T. C. O'BRIEN]

GÜNTHER, IGNAZ (1725–75), German sculptor, who worked at Mannheim (1751–52) and finally settled in Munich. G.'s work shows elongated proportions, ecstatic expressions, and angular movement of bodies in a radial rhythm more complex than that of E.Q. Asam, his inspiration. At Rottam Inn (1760–62) he carved the high and side altars, executed the polychrome *Guardian Angel* (Munich, 1763), a *Pietà* and *Annunciation* of elegant, dynamic forms at Weyarn (1763–65). G.'s soft colors unite the intangible and the real. Late works (*Pietà*, Nenningen, 1774), and reliefs of St. Joseph and St. Theresa are tragic—the complexities no longer a visual idiom but rather expositions of tensions of body and spirit. BIBLIOGRAPHY: H. Gundersheimer, *Matthäus Günther* (1930).

[M. J. DALY]

GUNTHILDIS SS. There are reputedly three saints of this name who are probably separate manifestations of one individual. Gunthildis I, an Anglo-Saxon nun and abbess in Thuringia, is mentioned in Othlo's *Life of St. Boniface*. Gunthildis II was honored in the diocese of Eichstätt by 1075; and Gunthildis III, honored in the same diocese, probably had no historic existence. BIBLIOGRAPHY: Zimmermann 3:405–407; L. Meagher, NCE 6:865–866; V. Boublík and J. Baur, BiblSanct 7:532–533.

[J. L. GRASSI]

GURIAN, WALDEMAR (1902–54), editor, political scientist at the Univ. of Notre Dame, founder of the *Review of Politics* in 1939. He was born in Russia, taken to Germany in childhood, there became a Catholic, and earned a doctorate in journalism at Cologne (1923). Before being invited to Notre Dame in 1937 he had escaped Nazi rule in Germany and from Switzerland edited a weekly, *Die deutschen Briefe*, attacking Naziism. In the U.S. he came to be known as a foremost authority on Soviet political theory and practice, and established a center for Soviet studies at Notre Dame.

GURNEY, JOSEPH JOHN (1788–1846), English Quaker, philanthropist, and writer. G. worked with his sister, E. *Fry, for penal reform and the abolition of slavery; he visited Canada and the U.S., 1837–40. His name was given to those orthodox Quakers who in the 1840s stressed evangelical Protestant belief more than the *Inner Light. They were called Gurneyites as distinct from the Wilburites (see WILBUR, J.). Among G.'s works were *Observations on the Distinguishing Views and Practices of the Society of Friends* (1824) and *Essays on the Habitual Exercise of Love to God* (1834). BIBLIOGRAPHY: *American Quakers Today* (ed. E. Bronner, 1966) 20–21. *RELIGIOUS SOCIETY OF FRIENDS.

[T. C. O'BRIEN]

GURNEYITES, those 19th-cent. Quakers who followed the evangelical emphasis of J. *Gurney; also the Quaker bodies that trace their origins to that movement. *RELIGIOUS SOCIETY OF FRIENDS.

[T. C. O'BRIEN]

GURY, JEAN PIERRE (1801–66), French Jesuit professor of moral theology at Vals, near Le Puy, from 1847; author of *Compendium theologiae moralis*. The work following the moral system called *probabilism, had immense influence. The first edition was published in 1850; the definitve edition, revised on the basis of criticisms from readers, appeared in 1865. The work was a seminary text both in Latin and vernacular editions; it was the basis for the *Sabetti-Barrett text, a stand-by in American seminaries for several generations. G.'s *Casus conscientiae in praecipuas quaestiones theologiae moralis* (1862) was the casuistic companion volume to the *Compendium;* Deman credits it with clearly bringing out the probabilism of the *Compendium* and giving this moral system its widespread acceptance into the 20th century in RC moral theology. BIBLIOGRAPHY: Th. Deman, DTC 13:592–593, s.v. "Probabilisme."

[T. C. O'BRIEN]

GUSTAVUS II ADOLPHUS (1594–1632), **KING OF SWEDEN** from 1611. G. came to the throne (1611) in an era of internal unrest and foreign wars. Aided by the skill of his chancellor, Axel Oxenstierna (1585–1654), he overcame these problems. One of the great captains of history, he has been called the "Protestant Hero" because of his decisive intervention on the Protestant side during the Thirty Years' War. The *Edict of Restitution (1629) issued by the Habsburg Emperor, Ferdinand II, outlawed all Protestant bodies except Lutherans of the Augsburg Confession. G. entered the war (1630) for motives that were at least in part genuinely religious. He was aided by the support of Cardinal Richelieu, given at first secretly, but later publicly through the treaty of Bärwalde (1631). G. led the army of small, highly mobile units on a march through Germany, defeated the Catholic imperial army under Count Tilly at Breitenfeld (1631), on the Lech (1632), and at Lützen, near Leipzig (1632). In the last battle G. fell in a cavalry charge, mortally wounded. He was not only an innovative military tactician but also a great king, raising

Sweden to the status of a great power and enhancing its economic and cultural life. BIBLIOGRAPHY: M. Roberts, *Gustavus Adolphus: A History of Sweden 1611–32* (2 v., 1953–58).

[E. D. MCSHANE]

GUTENBERG, JOHANN (*c.*1396–1468), printer, traditionally regarded as the first European to print with movable type. Details of his life are uncertain, but he is generally thought to have been born at Mainz and later to have gone to Strasbourg, where possibly he developed his printing methods *c.*1436–39. He returned to Mainz, and the printing attributed to him was done there, minor works *c.*1445–50, and preparation for the first Bible 1450–55. In 1456 the first Bible, known as the *Mazarin (also called the Gutenberg) Bible appeared on the market. Its text (the Vulgate) was printed in double columns of 42 lines. G. later produced other works, including the *Catholicon* (dictionary) in 1460. He received a pension from Adolph, abp. of Mainz. BIBLIOGRAPHY: V. Scholderer, *Johann Gutenberg* (1963).

[T. EARLY]

GUTHLAC, ST. (d. 714), Anglo-Saxon hermit of Mercian royal stock. In G.'s early life he served in the army of Ethelred of Mercia until he was 24, when he gave up his arms and entered the monastery at Repton. After 2 years he took up the life of a hermit at Crowland, then an island in the Fens. In the abbey built later at Crowland, the shrine containing his relics became a popular center of pilgrimage. BIBLIOGRAPHY: Mabillon AS 3.1:264–284; *Felix's Life of St. Guthlac* (ed. and tr. B. Colgrave, 1956).

[J. DRUSE]

GUTIÉRREZ, RODRIGUEZ BARTOLOMÉ (1580–1632), Augustinian missionary and martyr. A native of Mexico City, he was professed in the Order of St. Augustine in 1597. After his ordination he volunteered for the missions in Japan. He spent 6 years in the missions of the Philippines and was sent to Japan in 1612. In 1614 the imperial edict banished all missionaries, and G. returned to Manila. In 1618 he and others returned secretly to Japan and from hiding ministered to the Christians throughout the country. Finally at Nagasaki G. and his companions were arrested. From 1629 until his martyrdom in 1632, life became a series of prisons and torture chambers. He and six companions were burned alive; he thus became the first American-born martyr. Beatification was in 1867. BIBLIOGRAPHY: A. Hartmann, *Tagastan* 22(1961) 39–49.

[J. R. AHERNE]

GUTOLF (d. *c.*1300), a Cistercian of the Holy Cross monastery in Baden who became abbot of Marienberg in Hungary. He is best known for his poetry and other writings which were almost encyclopedic in scope. His description of 13th-cent. Vienna in his *Translatio S. Delicianae* is particularly important. BIBLIOGRAPHY: V. L. Bullough, NCE 6:869.

[V. BULLOUGH]

GUY OF BAZOCHES (1146–1203), French chronicler, whose family name was derived from Basilicae, a holding in the area of Soissons. His works include those found in the 19th century by Count Paul Riant in the Bibliothèque Nationale de Paris (B. N. lat. 4998, fol. 35–64v). *Liber apologia contra maledicos* contains 11 books which deal with apologetics, regions of the world, and the history of the world up to 1199. BIBLIOGRAPHY: J. Daoust, NCE 6:869; F.–J. Schmale, LTK 4:1267–68.

[J. R. RIVELLO]

GUY DE MONTPELLIER (d. 1208), founder of the Order of the Holy Spirit, a lay community dedicated to the care of the sick, and the author of its rule (1198). G. opened hospitals in Montpellier and, at the invitation of Pope Innocent III, also in Rome, whence his theories and practice concerning the care of the sick spread throughout Europe. BIBLIOGRAPHY: J. Daoust, NCE 6:869.

[M. A. WINKLEMAN]

GUYON, JEANNE MARIE BOUVIER DE LA MOTTE (1648–1717), French controversial spiritual writer. Born at Montargis, at 15 she married Jacques Guyon de Chesnoy, 20 years her senior. He died in 1676, leaving her with three children and a large fortune. In 1681 she left her family to help found a community of Nouvelles Catholiques, converted Huguenots, near Geneva. The Barnabite priest François La Combe, who was imbued with certain quietist tendencies, became her director, and the two traveled through Italy and southern France expounding ideas on prayer contained in G.'s *Moyen court et très facile de faire oraison* (1685). At Paris in 1687 by order of G.'s half-brother, then Barnabite provincial superior, La Combe was imprisoned in the Bastille, then moved to Lourdes, where, having become insane, he died in 1715. De Harlai, Abp. of Paris, had been encouraged by Louis XIV to quell quietist tendencies in France, and the arrest of La Combe paralleled that of M. *Molinos in Rome in 1685. Mme. Guyon was restrained in a Visitation Convent in Paris from January to August of 1688, when release was secured by Mme. de Maintenon, who initiated Mme. Guyon into the "Court Cenacle" and into St. Cyr, where her *Moyen Court* became influential. In October 1688 she met F. Fénelon, then superior of a Paris community of Nouvelles Catholiques, and the two met occasionally and corresponded until 1693, when a proceeding against possible quietist ideas in Mme. Guyon's writings was begun by J. B. Bossuet; this was later expanded into the famous Issy Conferences of 1694–95, attended by Bossuet, L. de Noailles, Abbé Tronson, and Fénelon. The resultant 34 articles condemning aspects of the *Moyen Court* and *L'Explication du Cantique* *des Cantiques* were signed by Fénelon and Mme. Guyon, but Bossuet, dissatisfied with the temperateness of the Issy condemnation, angered by G.'s sudden departure from his diocese of Meaux, and aided by a now jealous Mme. de Maintenon, had the State arrest G. on Christmas Eve, 1695. She was imprisoned in Vincennes, then in Vaugirard, and finally in the Bastille until her release in 1703 into the custody of her daughter, who brought her to Blois, where she died. During part of her imprisonment Bossuet and Fénelon carried on the great controversy over mystical prayer and *l'amour pur,* pure or disinterested love of God, in which Fénelon never denied G.'s good faith and intentions, despite the obvious excesses in her writings. Contemporary scholarship, which radically challenges the condemnation of Fénelon by Rome in 1699, would also disagree with those who have too readily labeled G. as a quietist. BIBLIOGRAPHY: M. De La Bedoyère, *Archbishop and the Lady* (1956); H. Bremond, *Apologie pour Fénelon* (1910); L. Tinsley, NCE 6:869–871. *SEMI-QUIETISM.

[W. J. MUELLER]

GUZMÁN Y LECAROS, JOSÉ JAVIER (1759–1840), Chilean Franciscan, preacher in the cause of his country's independence from Spain, and author of a popularized portrayal of Chilean cultural and political history, *El chileno instruido en la historia topográfica, civil y política* (1834).

[T. C. O'BRIEN]

GWYN, RICHARD, ST. (*c.*1537–84), martyr. He was educated at Oxford and Cambridge, became a schoolmaster at Overton, and was converted to the Catholic faith. As an influential person, his absence from Anglican services was noted, and he was arrested in 1579. He escaped to Erbistock, but in 1580 was arrested again, imprisoned, fined, and tortured. After eight indictments, he was found guilty of treason and executed. He was canonized in 1970. BIBLIOGRAPHY: N. Del Re, BiblSanct 7:565–566; Butler 4:202–204; T. P. Ellis, *Catholic Martyrs of Wales* (1933).

[V. SAMPSON]

GYNECAEUM, in the Eastern Churches a part of the church building set apart for women (Gr. *gunē*, woman). The separation of the sexes at liturgical functions is still observed in the Eastern Churches.

[T. C. O'BRIEN]

GYROVAGUE (gyrovagus), as the name indicates, wanderer or tramp. They are the fourth kind of bad monk mentioned by the *Rule* of St. Benedict: ". . . who spend all of their lives wandering about diverse provinces, staying in different cells for three or four days at a time, ever roaming with no stability, given up to their own pleasures and to the snares of gluttony." BIBLIOGRAPHY: F. A. Gasquet, *English Monastic Life* (1905).

[U. VOLL]

H

HAAS, FRANCIS JOSEPH (1889–1953), bp., sociologist. Ordained for the Archdiocese of Milwaukee in 1913, he taught at Marquette Univ. and The Catholic Univ. of America, where he became dean of the School of Social Science. President F. D. Roosevelt named him to several posts: the conciliation service of the U.S. Department of Labor, the National Recovery Administration, the National Labor Relations Board, and the Fair Employment Practices Commission. H. founded the Catholic Conference on Industrial Problems. His book *Man and Society,* was a widely used sociology text. He served as bp. of Grand Rapids, Michigan from 1943 until his death.

[J. R. AHERNE]

HABAKKUK (HABACUC), BOOK OF, the book containing the prophecy of Habakkuk, the eighth among the minor prophets in the OT canon. Scripture has preserved no biographical details concerning this prophet. The book's composition displays a variety of literary forms in its three chapters. Two complaints against God, each answered by an oracle, constitute the substance of the first two chapters. The second oracle is further developed by five imprecations against oppressors in chapter 2. Chapter three is a liturgical psalm with mythological overtones; this is often referred to as the prayer of Habakkuk. Most exegetes favor a date of composition *c.*600 B.C. The prophet expresses to God his impatience with the injustice perpetrated against the righteous by the oppressors, probably the Chaldeans. God gives the only solution to the prophet's problem: ". . . but the upright man will live by his faithfulness" (2.4). BIBLIOGRAPHY: E. A. Leslie, InterDB 2:503–505; H. Freeman, *Nahum, Zephaniah, Habbakuk* (pa. 1973).

[N. L. VAILLANCOURT]

HABERL, FRANZ XAVAR (1840–1910), German music editor and scholar. H. was educated at Passau, where after ordination in 1862, he became Kapellmeister of the cathedral and music director of the seminary. He subsequently held posts in Rome and Regensburg where, in 1874, he founded the School of Ecclesiastical Music. In 1879, H. founded the Palestrina Society for the publication of the complete works of that master, completed in 1894. He contributed much valuable material to musical journals and was editor of many valuable collections such as the *Musica divina,* begun by Joseph Schrems, *Bertalotti's Solfeggien, Wilhelm Dufay*. His *Magister choralis* had 12 editions and several translations. He was editor of the periodical *Musica Sacra* and *Caecilienkalender*. In 1899 he was chosen president of the Allgemeiner Caecilienverband (see CAECILIAN MOVEMENT). H. received the honorary degree of doctor of theology from Würzburg Univ. and held several posts under Pius IX. Most notable among these were the supervision of a revision of the liturgical chant (the Ratisbon edition) which, however, was later suppressed and supplanted by the Vatican edition in 1904. As a result of this, H.'s works on plainchant, among which were the *Magister choralis,* became practically worthless. The value of his other writings, however, remains undiminished.

[M. T. LEGGE]

HABERT, ISAAC (*c.*1600–68), French anti-Jansenist writer, and bp. of Vabres from 1645. He wrote against Richelieu's reputed Gallicanist plan to make France a patriarchate independent of Rome. As canon and theologian at Notre Dame de Paris (from 1641), he was commissioned to preach against Jansen's *Augustinus;* he published *La defense de la foy de l'Église* (1644) in reply to A. *Arnauld's attack on these sermons. His main polemic was *Theologia graecorum patrum vindicatae circa universam materiam gratiae libri tres* (1646), a response to Arnauld's *Apologie pour les Pères de de l'Église, defenseurs de la grace de Jésus Christ*. As bp. of Vabres he delated (1850) to the Holy See in a letter signed by 85 bps. the five propositions censured but without ascription by the Louvain faculty in 1649; the letter explicitly ascribed them to the *Augustinus*. Thus began the long and acrid dispute about the authorship of the propositions, condemned by Innocent X in 1653.

[T. C. O'BRIEN]

HABERT, JOHANNES EVANGELISTA (1833–96), Bohemian organist, composer, and writer. H. studied at Linz, was organist at Gonunden from 1861, composed church music and organ pieces, and founded and edited the *Zeitschrift für katolische Kirkenmusik.*

[M. T. LEGGE]

HABIRU (HABIRI), bands of seminomadic peoples, widespread in the Fertile Crescent from lower Mesopotamia to Egypt in the 2nd millenium B.C., to whom the ancient Hebrews may have been related. The word Habiru comes from the Akkadian and has cognates in Egyptian and Ugaritic. The Hebrew word for Hebrew (Hibri) seems obviously related. The Habiru are first mentioned in texts from the Third Dynasty of Ur (2050 B.C.), and from then on are mentioned in documents from all the important archives of the Near East: Babylonia, Mesopotamia, Mari, Syria, and Phoenicia. Anything said about them is subject to dispute by scholars. The earliest references to Habiru seem to refer to a social class or function. Perhaps the word connotes hired mercenary troops recruited from seminomadic bands who moved along the fringes of the settled cultures of the Near East. They may have served as client soldiers for one king or another, and their rank in the social order was assigned to a level between the free citizens and the slaves. Gradually the term apparently acquired an ethnic meaning, so that by the time of the Amarna Letters the Habiru all have West Semitic names. The ancient text found in the narrative of Gen 14, in which Abraham is depicted drawn into the battles between different confederations of kings, refers to Abraham "the Hebrew." The text may date from a period in which the word Hebrew retained its class meaning of mercenary fighter recruited from the bands of seminomads. Elsewhere in the OT "Hebrew" has a gentilic, ethnic force primarily. The words Habiru and Hebrew would then have evolved in a way similar to that of the word Canaanite, which originally meant merchant before it acquired its ethnic meaning. The word Amorite may have a similar history.

[E. J. DILLON]

HABIT, in scholastic philosophy is, according to its most important meaning, a permanent quality that disposes a subject well or badly in itself or in its faculties. Traditional theology defines habit in a positive sense as a supernatural permanent quality that conditions the soul or its faculties in relation to supernatural life. In Catholic thought God's gracious ordination of man to personal communion with him already in this life suggests the actualization of a new quality of being and the furnishing of capacity and disposition to act accordingly (ThAq ST 1a2ae, 110.2–4). The Council of Trent, while asserting the existence of these realities in man, abstained from referring to them under the precise scholastic term of habit. There are two kinds of supernatural habits according to the subject they inhere in or perfect: entitative and operative. Sanctifying grace is considered to be the only entitative habit. It perfects the very soul or being of man. It is the stable principle of supernatural life that renders man "a new creature" (2 Cor 5.17). Operative supernatural habits are the infused theological and moral virtues as well as the gifts of the Holy Spirit. They inhere in and perfect man's powers or faculties, enabling them to act in a supernatural manner. All these habits differ from natural habits not only in their quality of being, but also in their causes and effects. They are produced and infused entirely by God at the time of justification. They develop exclusively under the action of God. Natural operative habits condition human faculties, rendering their activity easy and pleasurable. Supernatural habits provide these faculties with the capacity for supernatural operation, and in doing so they perform the role of quasi-faculties themselves, but it is questionable whether or not they add external facility of operation. Modern theology avoids thinking in terms of duality of natural and supernatural habits in the same individual. It prefers to view the supernatural as merely uplifting and conditioning the natural. Supernatural habits, save faith and hope, are believed to be lost with the loss of sanctifying grace. Faith and hope are lost by the performance of their contrary acts. BIBLIOGRAPHY: C. M. Lachance, "La Grace est en nous par mode d'habitus entitatif; ou l'ontologie de la grace," *Revue de l'Université d'Ottawa* 26 (1956) 23–51, 75–89; M. J. Scheeben, *Nature and Grace* (tr. C. Vollert, 1954). SANCTIFYING *GRACE, *VIRTUE.

[R. J. TAPIA]

HABIT, RELIGIOUS, the distinctive garb worn by members of religious communities that commonly serves as a means of identifying the religious organization to which an individual belongs. The custom of a special mode of dress for religious was begun by St. Pachomius (d. 346) and adopted by St. Basil (d. 397) and promoted by his Rules, which were widely influential in both East and West. He saw the religious habit as a reminder of the wearer's monastic obligations and as a protection against worldly conduct. Gradually the use of a habit for religious extended itself through the Church and by the 13th cent. all religious were bound under grave penalty not to throw it off. In modern times, the Holy See has frequently claimed its right to regulate religious costumery, particularly for women. BIBLIOGRAPHY: Vat II RenRelLife 17.

[P. F. MULHERN]

HABIT FORMATION. The word habit is used in psychology in several senses, which have in common the central idea of a repetitive pattern of behavior along with the underlying psychological structure that accounts for the pattern. In one sense, *addictions are said to be habits, e.g., alcoholic drinks and some drugs are sometimes called habit-forming. In these cases, the substances used at first to relieve pain, tension, or anxiety, or to produce euphoria eventually create a physiological need, which makes itself felt as a craving, often for progressively greater amounts.

Somewhat similarly, activities like eating, fidgeting, knuckle-cracking, etc., can become habitual because they are mildly tension relieving, although the aspect of addiction is absent. Smoking however may be slightly addictive. Other habit patterns are formed for convenience, e.g., patterns of dressing in the morning, driving to work, etc. Still other habit patterns are the object of direct and deliberate formation; much of the educative process is concerned with these. Thus speaking, reading, and writing language, learning how to organize and classify data, arithmetic calculations as well as the development of manual skills, use of tools, and physical prowess in general are all exercises in habit formation. The general principle of habit formation is repetition of action with the gradual elimination of useless or erroneous movements and the strengthening and refinement of effective movements. In the beginning, the simpler actions or thought processes are fixed, then elaborations are worked in, until finally the mental or physical skill is sufficient for the purposes intended. If appropriate rewards are given at each successful step of the development and proportionate punishments for mistakes, the process of habit formation takes place more quickly. Likewise, habits of character can be formed, e.g., honesty, industry, cleanliness, etc. Like skill habits, the successive steps should be graded from simpler to more complex to engender a feeling of success from the beginning; additional rewards along the way hasten the process. Other psychological phenomena having the characteristics of habits are called habits in some schools, e.g., attitudes, prejudices, opinions, beliefs, and interests are formed through the interaction of complex factors, of which probably the most significant is social influence and pressure, particularly the influence of the immediate family. The other factors include personal experiences, esp. key experiences, and individual temperament, which determines how a person will react both to experience and social influence. Goals and purposes in life are similar to attitudes and beliefs in their mode of formation. The effect of habit formation is to make action quick, easy, and pleasant. In the case of skills, manual or mental, this increases efficiency. In the case of tension-relieving habits, this primary effect is also easily attained, but if there are injurious after-effects, these also occur easily. Whenever habits are formed, including attitudes, interests, and goals, there is a tendency for parts of the operations connected with the use of the habit to begin to operate unconsciously, e.g., a typist does not think of individual finger movements when typing a letter, a politician does not think of the reasons he belongs to his party when he is organizing a rally. This tendency for habitual operations to recede to an unconscious level contributes to the efficiency of the habit, but can also allow a person to fall into stereotyped behavior which may be inappropriate on many occasions.

[M. E. STOCK]

HABITUAL SINNER. (1) A person who sins because of an acquired *vice, i.e., a morally evil, settled disposition, Lat. *habitus*. Sinful acts that are expressions of the vice are willful, and even more so than isolated lapses from virtue, since any moral disposition, good or bad, increases the willingness and pleasure of its exercise. A habitual sinner in this sense of the term sins out of clear *malice (ThAq ST 1a2ae, 78.2). (2) In pastoral theology, a penitent who does have a habit of sin, and has committed sins consistent with it. The penitent, however, may have a resolve against such lapses; the influence of habit may mean a surge of passion or an instance of heedlessness that diminishes culpability. The penitent's condition thus differs from *recidivism. The penitent who is a habitual sinner and the confessor have to judge both the effectiveness of the penitent's past resolve and his proposal of means of amendment.

[T. C. O'BRIEN]

HABSBURG, the family name, from the castle of Habichtsburg, "hawk's castle," near the confluence of the Aar with the Rhine (Switzerland), of the great family which provided a series of kings of the Germans from 1273, Holy Roman Emperors continuously from 1438 until 1806, Austrian emperors, 1804–1918, kings of Bohemia and Hungary after 1526, kings of Spain, 1516–1700. On the marriage of the sole heiress, the great Maria Theresa, 1736, the name of the house became Habsburg-Lorraine. Staunchly conservative, often ill-starred, throwing up more than their quota of eccentrics towards the end, they were a major force in the history of Europe, and not least as affecting religion. Their accession to power after the extinction of the Hohenstaufens marked the end of the great conflicts between the Empire and the Papacy; they were the main bulwark for the forces of the Counter Reformation and for the defense of the West against the Turks in the Danubian lands and for their recovery. Their power was extended by family alliances rather than by conquest, hence the adage, *Bella gerant alii, tu, felix Austria, nube*—Let others make war, do you, happy Austria, marry.

[T. GILBY]

HACELDAMA, name of a potter's field near Jerusalem whose purchase is connected in the NT with Jesus' betrayal by Judas (Acts 1.18; Mt 27.6–9). According to a 4th-cent. tradition it was located on the S side of Hennom Valley but this is suspect (Jer 19.11).

[J. J. O'ROURKE]

HADALINUS, ST. (d. *c.*690), known also as Adelinus and Haulin, a Benedictine abbot who left his native Aquitaine to live first as a recluse in Cougnon and later in the Abbey of Stavelot, which was founded by his teacher, St. Remalcus. At Celles in Belgium he founded an abbey which was later reestablished at Visé and of which he is the patron. BIBLIOGRAPHY: H. Roeder, *Saints and Their Attributes* (1955); Benedictine Monks of St. Augustine's Abbey, *Book of Saints* (1966).

[M. E. DUFFY]

HADELOGA, ST. (d. *c.*750), monastic foundress. Protégée and friend of St. Boniface, H. is reputed to have been daughter of Charles Martel. In protest against a marriage arrangement, she fled from court to Kitzingen where, under Boniface's tutelage, she founded a double monastery. Her father, eventually reconciled, became its patron. BIBLIOGRAPHY: A. M. Zimmermann, BiblSanct 1:246–247.

[A. CABANISS]

HADES, one of the three sons of Kronos and lord of the Lower World. A grim and pitiless deity, he had practically no cult and only a slight mythology. The sole place where he was worshiped was in his precinct at Elis. Becoming identified with Pluto, the god of wealth (esp. that of grain), he enters into the great myth associated with Eleusis as husband of Persephone and son-in-law of Demeter, the goddess of vegetation. In classical Greek, Hades is always the name of the deity, and never of the place over which he rules, as it came to be employed in later times. BIBLIOGRAPHY: M. P. Nilsson, *Geschichte der griechischen Religion,* (2d ed., 1955) 1:452–456.

[M. J. COSTELLOE]

HADEWIJCH, BL. (fl. first half of 13th cent.), a Flemish woman who achieved distinction as a poet and mystical writer. Nothing is known of her life but the little that can be inferred from her writings. Probably of noble birth, H. seems to have held a position of leadership in a group of pious women whose type of life foreshadowed that of the beguinages. Her extant writings consist of *Visions* in which she described her own religious experiences for the benefit of her companions, *Letters,* and *Poems* (17 in rhyming couplets and 45 in stanzas). She was much preoccupied with God's love for man and man's for God, and with man's return to God. She was a pioneer in the adaptation of lyric poetry to the theme of mystical love; her imagery and technique show the influence of the troubadors. H. is not to be confused with another Flemish Beguine of the same name and adversary of Bl. Jan van *Ruysbroeck (see P. Doyère, *Catholicisme* 5:469–470). For crit. ed. of text and commentary, see J. Van Mierlo, ed.: *Hadewijch, Visioenen* (2 v., 1924); *Hadewijch, Strophische Gedichten* (2 v., 1942); *Hadewijch, Brieven* (2 v., 1947). Translations can be found in T. Weevers, *Poetry of the Netherlands in Its European Context, 1170–1930* (1960). BIBLIOGRAPHY: J. Van Mierlo, "Hadewijch, une mystique flamande au treizième siècle," RAM 5 (1924) 269–289.

[M. J. BARRY]

HADITH (Arab. *al-ḥadîth*), a term that originally meant a report or account of an event, but specialized in *Islam to designate the body of traditions recounted of the actions and sayings of the Prophet *Mohammed; in this sense it is most commonly rendered in English as tradition. The Hadith is universally recognized in Islam as the canonical source of religious doctrine, second to the *Koran. As manifesting the words and deeds of the Prophet, which are held to constitute the normative custom of the Muslim community (see ISLAMIC LAW and SUNNITES), esp. in matters of ritual and law, it is often referred to as the *sunna* (i.e., *sunnat al-nabî,* the "custom of the Prophet" as normative and binding upon the believer). Many traditions were early passed down from the "companions" (*ṣaḥâba*) of the Prophet and their successors" (*tâbi 'ûn*) on various matters concerning law and the life of the Prophet. Collections of such material were compiled from the early 8th century. Progressively, however, and esp. through the influence of al-Shâfi (d. 820; see ISLAMIC LAW) there came to be a consensus that only traditions from the Prophet were valid and binding. The major canonical collections of hadith are found in the Six Books, i.e., those of Bukhârî (d. 870) and Muslim (d. 875), which are universally considered the most authoritative, and those of Ibn Dâwûd (d. 888), al-Tirmidhî (d. 892), al-Nasâ'î (d. 915), and Ibn Mâja (d. 886), though the *Muwatta'* of Mâlik ibn Anas (d. 795; see ISLAMIC LAW) and the *Musnad* of Ibn Ḥanbal (d. 855; see HANBALITES) are also of great authority. Numerous other collections and compendia have also been compiled but do not enjoy such prestige. The *Sûfîs frequently cite traditions not found in the canonical collections and the *Shiites, who accept only traditions from Ali, have their own sectarian body of canonical traditions.

A tradition or hadith is divided into two parts, the text (*matn*) and the chain of authorities (*isnâd*) who have reported it. The specialists in matters of tradition (*al-muḥadditûn*) commonly classify traditions into four main categories (valid, good, weak, sick) with many distinctions and divisions according to their plausibility. To avoid passing a subjective judgment on its content, however, the traditional Muslim critique of the validity of a given hadith is based almost exclusively on the study of the personages mentioned in the *isnâd,* and consequently one finds in some cases, even in the canonical collections, contradictory traditions listed side by side. Because of the authority of the Prophet, there was from the beginning a notable tendency to forge traditions, sometimes to support a custom or a legal decision, sometimes simply to embellish preaching. In some cases, the *isnâd* of a tradition from one of the companions or some other person of noted piety was simply extended back to the Prophet by adding names. Many traditions considered valid by all the best authorities clearly reflect legal and dogmatic problems of a period later than that of the Prophet, and there is even a tradition to accommodate these. Unquestionably many reported traditions do go back to the Prophet and his immediate companions, but it is almost impossible in most cases to distinguish them from those which are fictitious. The Traditionists or "People of the hadith" (*ahl al-ḥadîth*), i.e., those devoted to the study of traditions, have from the beginning represented the most conservative and fundamentalist group in Islam.

BIBLIOGRAPHY: I. Goldziher, *Muslim Studies* (v. 2, tr. R. Barber, 1967); F. Robsen, EncIslam².

[R. M. FRANK]

HADOINDUS, ST. (d. *c.*653), bp. of Le Mans. Little is known of him before he succeeded Bertram in the See of Le Mans (*c.*623). He founded the abbey of Evron and attended the Councils of Clichy and Reims. His veneration as a saint dates from the 9th century. BIBLIOGRAPHY: C. DuChesnay, DHGE 16:214–219; H. Dressler, NCE 6:886.

[H. DRESSLER]

HADRA VASES, inscribed sepulchral Alexandrian vases found (1883–84) in the ancient cemetery of Hadra, Egypt. The hydria-shaped vessels with brown glaze on clay ground, or polychrome on white ground, carry floral friezes on the neck, shoulder, and handle, with names and dates inked or incised on the front. There are several in the Metropolitan Museum, New York.

[M. J. DALY]

HADRIAN (Publius Aelius Hadrianus; 76–138 A.D.), **ROMAN EMPEROR** from 117. H. became the ward of his cousin Trajan in 85 and his adopted son in 117. He promoted peace in the Empire through a renovation of civil and military administration. Conscientious, enlightened, romantic, a devotee of Greco-Oriental cults, H. followed Trajan's policy in his treatment of the Christians: punishing those who refused to abandon their faith, but freeing those who yielded. He placed a statue of Venus on Calvary and one of Jupiter at Jesus' tomb. His insulting treatment of the Jews, particularly his erection of a shrine to Jupiter on the Temple site, aroused them to the ill-fated revolt of Bar-Kokhba (132–135). H.'s mausoleum on the Tiber is now a national museum, the Castel Sant'Angelo. BIBLIOGRAPHY: B. W. Henderson, *Life and Principate of the Emperor Hadrian* (1923).

[M. J. SUELZER]

HADRIAN'S TOMB, see CASTEL SANT'ANGELO.

HADRIAN OF CANTERBURY, ST. (d. 710), abbot and scholar. African-born and an abbot near Naples, H. declined papal appointment as abp. of Canterbury in favor of Theodore of Tarsus, whom he accompanied to Canterbury (669). Here H. became abbot of St. Augustine's monastery, organized schools of Latin and Greek learning, and emphasized Roman usage and authority. BIBLIOGRAPHY: P. Burchi, BiblSanct 1:268–269; Butler 1:58–59.

[W. A. CHANEY]

HADRIANA COLLECTIO, a compilation, deriving from the **Dionysiana collectio,* of creeds, conciliar canons, and decretals given by Adrian I to Charlemagne in 774 and adopted formally as a code for the Frankish Church in 802. It is important not only to the history of canon law, because of its use, but also because it was the vehicle of transmission for such documents as the Nicene and Constantinopolitan Creeds, and the profession of faith of Chalcedon. It was coupled later with the *Hispana collectio* into the *Hadriana-Hispanica collectio,* a basic text for the *decretists. BIBLIOGRAPHY: J. Rambaud-Bukot, NCE 6:887.

[T. C. O'BRIEN]

HADRUMETUM, wealthy Roman colony (Sallust, *Jugurtha* 19) on the E coast of modern Tunisia. It has an excellent harbor. Designated a free city by the Romans after the Punic Wars, it became a Latin colony under Trajan and the capital of Provincia Valeria by order of Diocletian *c.*300 A.D. Its defenses weakened by the Vandals and vulnerable to attack by nomadic tribes in the 5th cent. it was renewed and renamed Justinianopolis by Justinian I in 533. It was destroyed by the Arab invasion of the 7th cent. and rebuilt by the French in the 19th as modern Sousse (Susa). It has an early tradition and was the center of several church councils up to the 7th century. Significant remains of its five catacombs have survived, the earliest dating back to the 3d century. BIBLIOGRAPHY: H. Dressler, NCE 6:887–888; A. Audollent, DHGE 10:1460–1500; H. Leclercq, DACL 6.2:1981–2010.

[F. H. BRIGHAM]

HAECKEL, ERNST HEINRICH (1834–1919), German zoologist, propagandist of Darwinism. He was a professor of zoology at the Univ. of Jena from 1862 till his death. In his many, often hurried writings, of which *Riddle of the Universe* (1899) was most widely read, he sought to extend evolutionary theory to philosophy, theology, and religion. His position became one of pantheistic materialism that rejected a personal God, human free will, and immortality. The zeal for his cause made him neglect or distort scientific methods. All of his scientific theories were discredited.

[T. EARLY]

HAECKER, THEODOR (1879–1945), German Catholic writer and polemicist. Reared a Protestant and with little formal education, as an adult H. developed his own mind by reading the classics and philosophy. He became interested in *Kierkegaard, then in *Newman, through whose writings he was led to Catholicism (1921). H. was convinced that man could find the key to existence only in the revelation of the Word of God. His political vision was of a Europe united on the basis of a true Christian humanism. A relentless opponent of Nazism, he was forbidden to speak publicly (1935) or to publish (1939), and barely escaped execution (1943). His works include *Christentum und Kultur* (1927), *Vergil, Vater des Abendlandes* (1931), and *Der*

Begriff der Wahrheit bei Søren Kierkegaard (1932). BIBLIOGRAPHY: W. Hug, LTK 4:1303, with bibliog.

[T. C. O'BRIEN]

HAFIZ (Khājeh Shams al-Dīn Mohammed ibn Bahā al-Dīn; *c.*1325–89), Persia's most celebrated lyric poet. His major work, *Divān,* a collection of about 500 lyric poems or *Ghazals,* sometimes referred to as odes or sonnets of 5 to 16 rhymed couplets apiece, has been used in conjunction with the Koran as an allegorical religious guide and text for divination. H. ("Rememberer of Koran"), a name he adopted because he had memorized the Koran, was a Shi'a who studied the mystical philosophy of Sufism and entered a Sufi confraternity. His knowledge of Arabic and Persian literature, the Koran, and theology qualified him as an expert commentator on literature and as a lecturer on exegesis of the Koran. His poems, often compared by Westerners to the sensuous and amatory verse of Anachreon, are considered symbolic and allegorical by Islamic commentators; this religious aspect of the poetry has gained him the names "interpreter of mysteries" (Tarjumān al-Asrār) and "tongue of the Unseen" (Lisān al-Ghayb). Prose and poetic translations of H.'s *Divān* have appeared in many Western languages, G. Bell, A. J. Arberry, and H. B. Lister being notable English translators.

[R. J. LITZ]

HAGAR (AGAR), the slave of Sarah, given by her to Abraham as a concubine lest he remain childless. H. then became the mother of Ishmael. The two traditions concerning her (Gen 16.1–16; 21.9–21) are generally regarded as parallel accounts joined artificially by Gen 16.9 Their antiquity is confirmed by related legal material dating from the patriarchal period (Code of Hammurabi, Nuzu tablets). These sources also contain ancient explanations for the remote habitat of Israel's Bedouin kinsmen and for the origin of the cult at a sacred well. At some early period, H. was perhaps regarded as the ancestor of the Hagrites (1 Chr 5.10; Ps 83.6; cf. Gen 25.15 and 1 Chr 5.19). In final form, the Genesis traditions illustrate the election of Israel and contribute to the story of Abraham's faith. In the NT (Gal 4.21–31), Paul allegorically reinterprets the Sarah-Hagar relationship, making H. the symbol of the Jews who did not accept Christ. The identification of H. and Sinai (Gal 4.24) is probably occasioned by Ishmaelite inhabitation of the Sinai area. BIBLIOGRAPHY: G. von Rad, *Genesis* (tr. J. H. Marks, 1962) 186–196, 225–230.

[P. J. KEARNEY]

HAGEN, the name of two brothers, both Austrian Jesuits. (1) **Johannes Georg** (1847–1930), renowned astronomer. A Jesuit from 1863, he studied philosophy and theology in England. He was director of the astronomical observatory at Georgetown Univ. (1880–1905); from 1906 onward, of the Vatican Observatory. Two of his astronomical works on the variable stars are classics, *Veränderliche Sterne* (2 v., 1913–24) and *Atlas stellarum variabilium* (6 v., 1899–1908). See J. Stein, *Atti della Pontificia Accademia delle Scienze dei Nuovi Lincei* (1930–31) 60–81, which contains complete list of his works. (2) **Martin** (1855–1923), exegete. He composed *Lexicon biblicum* (3 v., 1905–11) and *Atlas biblicum* (1907), both in the *Cursus Sacrae Scripturae* of R. *Cornely. He also completed and revised Cornely's *Compendium introductionis historicae et criticae in utriusque testamenti sacros libros* and J. *Knabenbauer's *Commentarium in prophetos minores.*

[P. K. MEAGHER]

HAGENAU, CONFERENCE OF, an unsuccessful reunion meeting in June 1540 between Catholics and Protestants of Germany, convened by the Emperor Charles V. The conference was poorly attended, became bogged down in procedural matters, and postponed its business until the Disputation of *Worms.

[T. C. O'BRIEN]

HAGERTY, JAMES EDWARD (1869–1946), educator, sociologist. A native of Indiana, H. spent his mature years as a professor and administrator at Ohio State University. Active in Catholic sociological circles he was president of the Catholic Conference on Industrial Problems from 1928 to 1937. H. was the author of many studies in sociology and penology.

[J. R. AHERNE]

HAGERTY, JAMES LEO (1899–1957), educator. In his 38 years as professor and administrator at St. Mary's College, Moraga, Calif., H. was a pioneer in building a liberal arts curriculum around World Classics (1942). He served as associate editor of *New Scholasticism* and was a member of the executive commission of the Great Books Foundation. A vigorous proponent of Catholic Action, he helped to establish the program in San Francisco.

[J. R. AHERNE]

HAGGADAH, a type of midrash. The Haggadah assumes the form of a narration that freely develops a biblical text regardless of its literal sense. The association of ideas is ground enough to warrant such reflections whose primary aim is edification. Consequently it most frequently contains fictional or legendary material contributing much to the formation of later Jewish tradition. It also designates the order of the Passover ritual. BIBLIOGRAPHY: P. Ellis, *Men and the Message of the Old Testament* (1963) 445–456.

[N. L. VAILLANCOURT]

HAGGAI (AGGAI), BOOK OF, the discourses of Haggai, the first of the post-Exilic prophets, in which he was concerned with the rebuilding of the temple of Jerusalem. His exhortations, dated in the year 520, seek to bolster the religious ardor of the people, stirring them to reconstruct the temple which was still in ruins. Prosperity will then ensue;

the new temple will outstrip the old in glory; Zerubbabel will be exalted. The book reflects messianic hope, an outstanding feature of the Restoration period. BIBLIOGRAPHY: C. Stuhlmueller, NCE 1:201–202; EDB 42–43.

[N. L. VAILLANCOURT]

HAGIA (Gr. for holy things; Sl., *svatea*), a term used in Greek liturgical books to designate the eucharistic bread and wine both before and after their consecration.

[A. J. JACOPIN]

HAGIA IRENE, Constantinople, originally a Byzantine double church with the Hagia Sophia, begun by Constantine. Rebuilt after destruction (532) Hagia Irene is one of the major early-Justinian domed basilicas. The present church from the 8th cent. following the earthquake (740) with 14th-cent. and Turkish modifications, has most interesting vaulting of the two nave bays: the eastern, square, with a high dome on a drum upon four large piers with an arcade of columns; the western bay, a rectangle vaulted by a low elliptical dome. The masonry alternates hewn stone and brick bands in typical Constantinopolitan style. Iconoclastic and Turkish destructions have left little decoration.

[M. J. DALY]

HAGIA SOPHIA (Gr., holy wisdom), the principal church in Constantinople where the most solemn patriarchal and imperial ceremonies took place. Most probably built by the Emperor Constans *c.*350 and consecrated in 360, it was known simply as the Great Church because of its vast dimensions. In the 5th cent. it was called the church of the Divine Wisdom (Gr. *Theia Sophia*) in honor of the Word, the Second Person of the Trinity, and its patronal feast was the Nativity of the Word Incarnate. Later it was referred to as Hagia Sophia as it still is (*Aya Sofya* in Turkish), but in English it is misleading to call it St. Sophia as though it were a saint's name. The center of religious life in Constantinople, the church was damaged and restored several times. The most famous restoration, actually a new construction, was that of Justinian begun in 532 and completed 5 years later. The result was a magnificent and immense cathedral still one of the world's architectural and artistic marvels. Resplendent with marble, mosaics, and an altar of gold, the nave was surmounted by a cupola 33 meters in diameter and 60 meters above the pavement supported by arches on enormous pillars. In the 7th cent. it was served by 80 priests and 150 deacons, many of whom were members of the patriarchal curia. In 1453 it was made into a mosque by the Turks and since 1934 has been a museum. American archeologists have been engaged in examining it and in restoring the mosaics plastered over by the Turks. BIBLIOGRAPHY: R. Janin, *La géographie ecclésiastique de l'empire byzantin* (1953) 471–485; J. Mateos, *Le Typicon de la grande église* (2 v., 1962–63); R. L. Van Nice, *St. Sophia in Istanbul: An Architectural Survey,* Installment I (1966).

[G. T. DENNIS]

HAGIASMA (Gr., a consecrated thing), in the singular water that has been blessed in the manner prescribed by the Church. In the plural (*hagiasmata*) it is used of anything consecrated or blessed by the Church as bread, holy water, and even the consecrated Eucharist.

[A. J. JACOPIN]

HAGIASMATARION (Gr. for instrument for blessing), the name given to the liturgical book containing the Offices, prayers, and blessings excerpted from the *Euchologion that are most often used by the priest. It is similar to the pocket rituals in use in the Roman rite. The term is also applied to a vessel used to contain holy water.

[A. J. JACOPIN]

HAGIASMOS (Gr. for sanctification, consecration), the liturgical rites that by the power and prayer of the Church sanctify water to be used in the sacraments and sacramentals. The minor blessing for water may be used at any time, while the solemn major blessing occurs once a year at the *Theophany (Epiphany) after the Liturgy. Baptismal water is blessed by the priest each time he baptizes. *HOLY WATER.

[A. J. JACOPIN]

HAGIASTERA (Sl., *kropelo*), an instrument used to sprinkle holy water on persons or things during blessings. It may be simply a branch of a tree, a shaft with a brush-like device attached, or a metal sprinkler.

[A. J. JACOPIN]

HAGIOGRAPHY, the literature on the saints and their cults. The term embraces an extensive variety of writings that may be classified as popular hagiography and that reflect the written memorials of an active cult of the saints of a given period. Included are narratives of martyrdom such as the *Passion of the Scillitan Martyrs, The Passion of SS. Perpetua and Felicitas,* and the *Acts of St. Cecilia;* hagiographic collections such as the lost Acts of the Ancient Martyrs of Eusebius of Caesarea, the *In gloria martyrum* and *In gloria confessorum* of Gregory of Tours, and the *Dialogues* of Gregory the Great; legendaries or local, long stylized accounts of saints of a particular area; *Legenda aurea* or smaller versions which first appeared in the 13th cent.; the Collectives of the Middle Ages esp. those of Lippomano and Surius and the best known collection, Alban Butler's *Lives of the Fathers, Martyrs and other Principal Saints* of the 18th century. Most of these collections were written to inspire the faithful, with no primary concern for historical accuracy. The science of hagiography had its beginnings in the 17th cent. with the Jesuit Heribert Roswegde and Jean Bolland. The publication by the latter of the *Acta sanctorum* in 1643 gathered all extant authentic texts of the lives of the saints. His collaborators were known as the Bollandists. Since that time, advances in epigraphy, philology, paleography, and archeology have enabled

20th-cent. hagiographers to develop significant critical texts and interpretations of material pertaining to individual saints. The twelve-volume *Bibliotheca sanctorum* (1961–69) published by John XXIII Institute of the Lateran Univ. is an outstanding example of contemporary hagiography. BIBLIOGRAPHY: C. F. Halkin, NCE 6, 895–897; R. Algrain, *L'Hagiographie, ses sources, ses méthodes, son histoire* (1953); H. Delehaye, *The Legends of the Saints* (tr. D. Attwater, 1962).

[F. H. BRIGHAM]

HAGIOLOGY, the study of the lives and cult of the saints. *HAGIOGRAPHY.

[F. H. BRIGHAM]

HAGIOS DIMITRIOS (St. Demetrius), Thessalonika, 5th-cent. Greek church rebuilt in 629, 643, and 1917. The five-aisled basilica with spacious transept and galleries around the entire building boasts capitals in antique, Early Christian and Byzantine styles. Seventh-cent. mosaics preserved on the piers, showing St. Demetrius with ecclesiastical and civil personages in frontal poses (coming from the age of the iconoclastic controversy) are historically significant.

[M. J. DALY]

HAGIOS PANTOCRATOR, name applied to Byzantine and Greek churches in honor of Christ as World Ruler (Pantocrator), the central cupola carrying a mosaic or fresco of Christ, Pantocrator, one hand raised in a teaching gesture, the other holding a book.

[M. J. DALY]

HAGIOSCOPE (Gr. *hagios,* holy; *skopein,* to view), an architectural term coined in 19th-cent. England for a small aperture in the interior wall of a church that allowed a view of the altar from a side chapel, aisle, or transept. Squint is an earlier name.

[T. C. O'BRIEN]

HAHN, JOHANN MICHAEL (1758–1819), German founder of the Michelians. Born at Altdorf, a peasant's son, he traveled and spoke extensively to reveal his interpretation of the Bible, based on Pietism and the mysticism of J. Boehme. H. viewed Creation as the development of divine attributes and believed that man's fall was the result of his awakened sexual desires and that consequently he was redeemed by Christ's blood, which enables man to shed his carnal nature. Some Michelians in Würzburg and Baden still follow H.'s teachings.

[P. J. HENNESSEY]

HAI (AI), a Canaanite town near Bethel. The account of its conquest by the Israelites (Jos 7.2–5; 8.1–29) presents a problem. Archeological evidence shows that Hai (The Ruin) was unoccupied at that time. Many scholars believe that the account of its destruction is unhistorical. They argue that the scene of the battle was transferred from Bethel to Hai to explain the ruins of the latter. BIBLIOGRAPHY: W. F. Albright, "Israelite Conquest of Canaan," BASOR 74 (1939) 11–23.

[N. L. VAILLANCOURT]

HAID, LEO MICHAEL (1849–1924), Benedictine abbot and titular bishop. He was professed as a monk at St. Vincent's Abbey, Latrobe, Pa. (1869), ordained in 1873, and became an esteemed professor in St. Vincent's College there until 1885. He then became first abbot of Belmont Abbey, Belmont, N.C.; he built a college there, as well as a seminary. In 1887 he was named vicar apostolic of North Carolina and was consecrated bp. with the titular See of Messene. He devoted himself to building up the Church in the vicariate, to the expansion of Belmont Abbey and its college, and to new Benedictine foundations in Florida. He was also (1890–1902) president of the American Cassinese Congregation of Benedictines. When Belmont Abbey was made an abbey nullius, detached from the North Carolina vicariate, H. became the *abbot nullius.

[T. C. O'BRIEN]

HAIL MARY, a prayer addressed to *Mary. It has three parts: the salutation of the Archangel Gabriel, "Hail (Mary) full of grace, the Lord is with you" (Lk 1.28); the words of Elizabeth, "Blessed is the fruit of thy womb" (Lk 1.42); and a later petition, "Holy Mary, Mother of God, pray for us sinners now and at the hour of our death. Amen." The combination of Gabriel's and Elizabeth's words appears in the liturgy and Divine Office in the 6th cent., mainly as an Offertory Prayer. These two verses became a popular prayer in the 11th cent., and various forms of the concluding petition began to be added in the 15th century. BIBLIOGRAPHY: H. Thurston, DSAM 1:1161–65; A. A. De Marco, NCE 6:898.

[T. M. MCFADDEN]

HAIMO OF AUXERRE (d. *c.*855), monk and exegete. H. taught at his Abbey of Saint-Germain in Auxerre. His largest work is an explanation of the Epistles of St. Paul. Commentaries on the Canticle of Canticles, Revelation, the Minor Prophets, and two groups of homilies are now also recognized as his work. BIBLIOGRAPHY: J. Gross, LTK 4:1325; H. Dressler, NCE 6:898–899.

[H. DRESSLER]

HAIMO OF LANDECOP, BL. (d. 1173), Cistercian mystic. Born in Landecop (Brittany) he joined the Abbey of Savigny and became widely reputed for his holy life, visions, and miracles. He was confessor of Henry II of England and advisor of Louis VII of France. BIBLIOGRAPHY: R. Klopfer, "Der selige Haimo von Savigny," *Cistercienser-Chronik* 50 (1938) 102–104; G. Venuta, BiblSanct 1:640–641.

[L. J. LEKAI]

HAINMAR OF AUXERRE, ST. (*fl.* 717–31), Frankish magnate, bishop. Although possibly never consecrated, he served as bp. *c.*717–*c.*731. A military rather than a spiritual leader, he twice led troops against Aquitaine under Charles Martel's direction. Later he quarreled with his chief. Imprisoned at Bastogne, he made his escape to Toul where he was arrested and executed. BIBLIOGRAPHY: A. Codaghengo, BiblSanct 1:639.

[A. CABANISS]

HAIRSHIRT, a garment of rough cloth made of goat's hair or other prickly material and used as a penitential robe from early Christian times. This was understood to have been the sackcloth of which Jesus spoke as a penitential garb (Mt 11.21), its appropriateness to that purpose stemming from its irritating effect when worn next to the skin. It was adopted for clothing and bedding by public penitents and by ascetics as a work of supererogation. Its use by cenobites began in the East, as St. Jerome attests, and thence spread to the West where it became the distinctive livery of the monk. Cassian denounced it for making a parade of virtue, but saints like Thomas Becket and Louis of France were reputed to have worn such a garment under their silk. In a modern version it is sometimes used in the form of a strip of haircloth worn about the waist or as a scapular. BIBLIOGRAPHY: G. Alston, CE 7:113–114; P. F. Mulhern, NCE 6:899.

[P. F. MULHERN]

HAITI, a Carribean republic occupying the W third of the island of Hispaniola (10,700 square miles; pop. [est. 1976] 4,681,004; ethnic distribution: 95% Negro and 5% mulatto, with a few thousand whites and Indians). The land was discovered by Columbus (1492). The W portion of Hispaniola was neglected by Spain and from 1625 was a base for French and English pirates. The French drove out the English, and Spain recognized the territory as a French possession in 1697. Under the French it was called Saint Domingue. The first missionary was B. Buyl (Boyl), who was later followed by Franciscans, Mercedarians, Hieronymites, Dominicans, Discalced Carmelites, and Jesuits. The Indian population, fairly large at the time of the island's discovery, was all but exterminated by disease and harsh treatment. To provide labor, Negroes were brought in as slaves and their number grew until they made up the great bulk of the population. The evangelization of the slaves was superficial, and they retained many of the religious practices brought from Africa. Insurrections compelled the French to abolish slavery in 1793. After a period of revolt (1801–03) Haiti became an independent nation in 1804. Ecclesiastically the country was separated from Rome by schism from that time until 1860, when a concordat with the Holy See was signed and provision was made for the establishment of an archdiocese and four dioceses. During the separation from Rome the Church in Haiti was served by a clergy made up in large part of cast-offs from other countries. After union with Rome was reestablished, the Montfort Fathers in France recruited and trained missionaries to work in Haiti, and gradually, esp. in the 20th cent., other orders became active in that field. Missionary work was hampered by the fact that it was customary to use French, the official language in instructing the people, although 75% of them do not understand that tongue. Efforts to replace French with Créole in instruction and worship have achieved some success in the last 20 years.

In 1922 a seminary was established at Port-au-Prince. This was put under the care of Canadian Jesuits in 1953 in an effort to improve the quality of the training given to the seminarians. The government expelled the Jesuits in 1964 and the seminary was closed, but it reopened later that same year under the Viatorians. The relations of the Church with the Duvalier regime were untroubled at first, but tension began in 1960. The abp. was expelled in 1960, Bp. R. Augustin in 1961, and Bp. P. Robert in 1962. The government and the Vatican agreed upon a *modus vivendi* in 1966, and five native bps. were consecrated. Haiti has one ecclesiastical province with an abp. (Port-au-Prince) and four suffragan sees: Les Cayes, Port-de-Paix, Cap-Haitien, and Les Gonaives. There are 191 diocesan priests of whom 88 are Haitians, and 191 religious priests of whom only 25 are Haitians. In 1976 Catholics numbered 4,110,628 or 85% of the population, Protestants about 10%, and the remaining composed chiefly of followers of the voodoo cult. Protestant missionary effort, which began during the period of the U.S. protectorate (1915–34), has been remarkably effective. In 1965 the total Protestant community was approaching the half million mark. Prominent among the groups engaged in it are the American Baptists, Episcopalians, West Indies Missions, the Pentecostals.

Haiti is in need of a gigantic apostolic effort. Vocations among the native Haitians must be fostered. An enormous amount of catechetical work should be done, esp. in the Créole language. Educational effort must be extended and intensified (Haiti's illiteracy rate is 80%). The quality of family life must be improved (almost 85% of the children are of illegitimate birth). The relief of misery through hospitals and dispensaries, and the relief of poverty through education and the establishment of cooperatives and credit unions cannot be neglected, not only because the evils of disease and want cry for remedy (Haiti's per capita income is less than $100 per year), but because it is the helplessness against them that accounts for much of the appeal of voodoo. BIBLIOGRAPHY: J. M. Salgado, NCE 6:899–901.

[P. DAMBORIENA]

HAJJ (HADJ; Arab., *ḥajj*), the ritual pilgrimage to Mecca, one of the five cardinal duties prescribed by *Islam. To make the hajj at least once in his lifetime is incumbent upon every free, adult Muslim who has the means to do so. The ritual, fixed according to precedent set by *Mohammed on his "farewell pilgrimage" 3 months before his death (June, 632), embraces two ancient rites, the *'umra* and the hajj. Upon his arrival at *Mecca the pilgrim, in a state of ritual purity (*iḥrâm*), seven times makes the ritual circumambulation of the Kaaba (Great Mosque). The hajj proper begins on the 8th of *dhû l-Hijja* (the 12th month of the Muslim calendar) when the pilgrims leave the Holy City to make the ritual "halt" (*wuqûf*) at Arafat from noon until sunset on the 9th. Another "halt" is made on the 10th at the Great Mosque after which the pilgrims go to Mina where they cast seven stones at a pillar (symbolically at Satan). This is followed by the Great Feast (*al-'îd al-kabîr*), on which animals (mostly sheep and goats) are sacrificed, whereupon the hajj is ended. The sacrifice of the Great Feast is celebrated as an obligation throughout Islam. A person who has made the pilgrimage is called a hajji (hadji). BIBLIOGRAPHY: A. J. Wensinck et al., EncIslam².

[R. M. FRANK]

HALAKAH, a type of midrash used by the rabbis to interpret and explain the Mosaic Law. It sought to enact precepts based on the Torah but adapted to new situations. These commentaries were granted authoritative value and account for the formation of the Jewish legal tradition. Rabbi Judah ha-Nasi compiled them in the Mishnah which became the object of the deliberations for the next 3 centuries. The Gemarah, the record of these deliberations, and the Mishnah form the Talmud, the sum of Jewish jurisprudence. BIBLIOGRAPHY: J. Z. Lauterbac, JE 8:569–572.

[N. L. VAILLANCOURT]

HALBERSTADT CATHEDRAL (1239–1491), German Gothic structure retaining Ottonian westwork in its twin-tower W façade. Later additions were a 14th-cent. Lady Chapel, choir (1402), transept and nave (after 1450). Noteworthy are a *Crucifixion* sculpture group (1220), many pier statues, an *Entombment* (*c.*1360). *Twelve Apostles* (1427), *St. George* (1487), an unusually dynamic *St. Jerome* with lion (*c.*1500), and *St. Sebastian* (1510).

[M. J. DALY]

HALF HOLY DAYS, feast days in the RC Church that required attendance at Mass but not abstention from work. Such feasts as the Virgin's Presentation, Birth, and Immaculate Conception were once observed in this way.

[R. J. LITZ]

HALF-WAY COVENANT, in 17th-cent. New England Congregationalism, a compromise measure on church membership. Only members of the Church enjoyed citizenship, and in 1643 only 11% of the population enjoyed this privilege. In pure Congregational doctrine there were two ways of joining the Church: (1) by joining through a covenant, living a godly life, submitting to church discipline, and partaking of the Lord's Supper, after testifying to an experience of regeneration; and (2) by being born of parents in covenant relation to the Church and being baptized. Persons joining by the second method, however, were never admitted to the Lord's Supper until they personally claimed regeneration and joined in the covenant relationship. The question then arose as to whether those who were members only because of their birth and baptism and remained "unregenerate" might have their own children baptized.

A ministerial body was appointed by the General Court of Massachusetts in 1657 to study the question and present a decision. Its findings were accepted by the Court in 1662, and became known as the Half-Way Covenant. Its decision was that members by birth who "owned the covenant," lived respectable lives, and promised to support and obey the Church might have their children baptized though they themselves had no conversion experience and could not partake of the communion or participate in ecclesiastical affairs. Many persons of standing and position in New England took advantage of these provisions. By 1665, under pressure from the Crown, the right of franchise had ceased to be restricted to members of the Congregational Churches. In church life itself the principle of the Half-Way Covenant was extended, esp. by Samuel Stoddard, pastor at Northampton, Mass., to admit all baptized of upright lives to communion even though they had not experienced conversion. His son-in-law Jonathan *Edwards, in the *Great Awakening, restored the requirement of the conversion experience. BIBLIOGRAPHY: Olmstead 84; W. Walker, *History of the Congregationalists* (1894) 170–182.

[F. E. MASER]

HALIFAX, CHARLES LINDLEY WOOD (1839–1934), Second Viscount Halifax; ecumenist. Pusey, Liddon, and Wilberforce shaped his *high church piety and devotion at Oxford. Closely attached to the Cowley Fathers, he was also a great benefactor of the first Benedictine communities in the C of E. As president of the *English Church Union (1864–1919; 1927–34), he was in the thick of the fights of the period, e.g., the *Public Worship Regulation Act and the *Revised Prayer Book. Together with his friend Abbé Portal, he opened an ecumenical approach to Rome that ended unhappily with the bull **Apostolicae curae* (cf. H.'s *Leo XIII and Anglican Orders,* 1912; J. J. Hughes, *Absolutely Null and Utterly Void,* 1968); but with true Yorkshire doggedness he reopened it in the famous *Malines Conversations with Card. Mercier. In England the authorities on the Anglican side fought a delaying action and on the RC side opened a counteroffensive; both were looking backward rather than forward. The Conversations themselves, which were conducted in an admirable spirit, set in motion a series of talks that for 2 decades were private and informal, but that now are official and recognized. BIBLIOGRAPHY: life by J. G. Lockhart (2 v. 1935, 1936).

[T. GILBY]

HĀLĪL, a biblical musical instrument similar to the Greek *aulos* and having a sharp, penetrating tone like that of the oboe. BIBLIOGRAPHY: C. Sachs, *History of Musical Instruments* (1940) 118–121.

[M. T. LEGGE]

HALINARD OF LYONS (d. 1052), Benedictine abbot, abp. of Lyons. He was a cathedral canon at Langres before becoming a Benedictine at the Abbey of St. Benigne, Dijon; he was elected abbot there in 1031. He was consecrated abp. of Lyons in 1046. He became a prominent ecclesiastical figure and was even proposed for the papacy. He was of considerable assistance to Leo IX in that Pope's visits to Germany, France, and Italy. H. was also important to the spread and success of the Cluniac monastic reform movement. Some of his letters are to be found in PL 141:1157 and 142:1345–48 and a vita in PL 162:839–848.

[T. C. O'BRIEN]

HALL, FRANCIS JOSEPH (1857–1932), Episcopalian priest and theologian. He studied at Racine College as well as at General Theological Seminary in New York City and at Seabury-Western Theological Seminary, Evanston, Illinois. Ordained in 1886, he was professor of dogmatics at Western Theological Seminary and later at General. His *Theological Outlines* (3 v., 1892–95; rev. ed., 1933) and his *Dogmatic Theology* (1907) are classics of Anglo-Catholic theology and have had a widespread influence upon many priests of the Protestant Episcopal Church. A foe of *modernism, he wrote *Christianity and Modernism* (1924). He served as a member of the world Conference on *Faith and Order in Lausanne (1927) and wrote *Christian Reunion in Ecumenical Light* (1930).

[M. A. GARDNER]

HALL, JOSEPH (1574–1656), English writer and bp. of Exeter and Norwich. His devotional writing attracted Henry, Prince of Wales, who made him one of his chaplains in 1608. He became bp. in 1627. In the controversy between the Arminians and the Calvinists within the English Church, he sought a middle way with the result that Bp. Laud investigated his Calvinistic tendencies. He defended the English Church in *Episcopacy by Divine Right* (1640). Tried for high treason in 1641, condemned by Parliament, imprisoned for some months, he retired after his release to a place near Norwich, where he wrote and preached. Thomas Fuller says: "He was commonly called our English Seneca, for the purenesse, plainesse and fulnesse of his style. Not unhappy at *Comments,* very good in his *Characters,* better in his sermons, best of all in his *Meditations.*" BIBLIOGRAPHY: G. G. Perry, DNB 24:75–80.

[M. M. BARRY]

HALL CHURCH, distinctively German type of medieval *dreischiffe* (three-aisled) church, so called because the nave and side aisles are of the same height. Lacking a triforium and clerestory, they receive light from the aisle windows. St. Stephen and St. Quentin, Mainz, the Frauenkirche, Nürnberg, and St. Elizabeth, Marburg are examples.

[M. J. DALY]

HALLAHAN, MARGARET MARY, MOTHER (1803–68), foundress of the English Congregation of St. Catherine of Siena, a third order Dominican community. Until 1842 she was in domestic service and while maid to a Catholic family in Bruges became a Dominican tertiary. In that same year she began her formal service to the Church, teaching school at Conventry. Two years later she established her congregation there; in 1853 the motherhouse and novitiate were transferred to Stone, Staffordshire (the novitiate is now at Stroud, Gloucestershire). She included in the community observance the choral recitation of the Divine Office. Under H.'s leadership the congregation established five convents, schools, an orphanage, and hospitals. The Congregation of St. Catherine joined with other English Dominican communities in 1929 and in the 1970s had some 200 sisters. H. was a friend of Card. Newman, who often wrote to her for prayers in his times of trial. Her cause for beatification has been in process since 1936. BIBLIOGRAPHY: Sr. Mary Catherine, *Steward of Souls* (1952).

[T. C. O'BRIEN]

HALLÂJ, AL- (al-Ḥusain ibn Manṣûr; 857–922), Muslim mystic and saint. Al-Ḥallâj, the Carder (of souls), is commonly recognized as one of the greatest of Muslim mystics (see SUFISM). Devoted to the ascetic life from an early age, he followed first the teaching of Sahl al-Tustarî and later, at Basra, became a disciple of 'Amr al-Makkî and al-Junaid. At his first (year-long) pilgrimage to *Mecca he gave up the usual sufi custom of secrecy and later the wool tunic also, in order to be able to reach more people in his preaching. Basically his doctrine was one of the bond of love that unites God and the believer, and of the value of faith for the interior life of the soul. He was accused by both *Sunnites and *Mutazilites of performing false miracles, for *Shiite tendencies, and also of being a *Karmatian agent. Because of these accusations he was forced to flee Iraq and traveled widely in Persia and India. Subsequently he was denounced, particularly by the Ẓâhirite (see ISLAMIC LAW) Ibn Dâwûd, for claiming mystical union with God and imprisoned for 9 years, during which period some of his most important works were written. Finally, after considerable court intrigue, he was crucified, decapitated, and cremated at Baghdad. Though condemned by many, he had a large following and many—even some *Hanbalites—have considered him a saint. BIBLIOGRAPHY: L. Massignon, *La Passion d'al Ḥallâj, martyr mystique de l'Islam* (2 v., 1922); L. Massignon and L. Gardet, EncIslam².

[R. M. FRANK]

HALLE, UNIVERSITY OF (Martin-Luther-Universität Halle-Wittenberg), a coeducational institution of higher learning in E Germany, whose theological faculty played an important role in the history of Protestant theology. Based on an earlier papal *privilegium* of 1531, the Elector Frederick III of Brandenburg (later Frederick I, King of Prussia) established the university in 1694 as an expansion of an existing academy for noblemen (*Ritterakademie*). Intended as a center for Lutheranism, and incorporating the new educational ideas of a state institution, the university was under the influence of Pietism (esp. through Philipp Jakob *Spener and A. H. *Francke) and the Enlightenment (C. *Thomasius). Thomasius, a jurist, was the first to use German as language of instruction instead of Latin—a procedure soon imitated by other German universities. In the 18th cent. it became obligatory for Prussian theology students to study 2 years of philosophy at Halle under C. *Wolff (1679–1754), a leading exponent of the German Enlightenment. Pietistic opposition caused Wolff to be dismissed and banished from Prussia, only later to be recalled by Frederick the Great and made chancellor (1743). With J. S. *Semler, historian and pioneer in biblical criticism, and other scholars, Halle became a center of Protestant theology during the 18th cent., a place it later shared with the Univ. of Göttingen. Intermittently closed during Napoleonic times, the university was reestablished in 1817 when it merged with the Univ. of Wittenberg, which had been founded by Elector Frederick III the Wise (1502) and under Luther and Melanchthon as professors had become the starting point of the German Reformation. In 1933, on the occasion of the 450th anniversary of Luther's birth, the name of the university was changed to Martin-Luther-Universität Halle-Wittenberg. Since 1946 it has been under Communist administration, with expanded programs in agriculture and economics. The library (founded in 1696) contains 2,608,000 volumes. BIBLIOGRAPHY: E. Wolf, RGG 3:34–38.

[M. B. MURPHY]

HALLEL, ritual psalms (113–118), sung as an expression of thanks and joy on all the major Jewish festivals except Rosh Hashanah and the Day of Atonement.

[M. T. LEGGE]

HALLELUJAH (Lat. *Alleluia*), a biblical word meaning "praise ye the Lord." It occurs frequently in Gregorian chant and has been the subject of treatment in many choral compositions, esp. of the 17th and 18th centuries.

[M. T. LEGGE]

HALLER, JOHANNES (1865–1947), historian. A graduate of Heidelberg, H. served in several posts in Rome and in Tübingen. His researches led him to publish work on the Council of Basel and the papacy itself. The latter is one of the most exhaustive works dealing with institutional history. BIBLIOGRAPHY: R. Bäumer, LTK 4:1334–35.

[B. F. SCHERER]

HALLER, LEONHARD (d. 1570), German theologian, representative (1562–63) of the bp. of Eichstätt during the final phases of the Council of Trent; spoke out against concession of the chalice to the laity in the Eucharist (see D 1725–34).

[T. C. O'BRIEN]

HALLERSTEIN, AUGUSTIN VON (1703–74), Jesuit missionary to China from 1736. In his official position at the imperial Chinese court his reputation as a mathematician and astronomer secured good favor for Christian missionaries. The Royal Society of London granted him membership as a foreign associate on the basis of his excellent astronomical observations.

[D. J. SMUCKER]

HALLOIX, PIERRE (1571–1656), Belgian Jesuit, patrologist. A Jesuit from 1592, H. was renowned for his austerity of life and unrelenting scholarly labors. These he devoted to studies in patristics, classical languages, and hagiography. His *Vita et documenta D. Justini philosophi et martyris* (1622) was one of his chief works. H.'s *Origines defensus* (1648), part of a larger collection of works of the Fathers, begun in 1636, was placed on the Index (1655), pending its correction, for its zeal in vindicating some of *Origen's less acceptable positions. BIBLIOGRAPHY: P. Bernard, DTC 6:2039; Hurter 3:1099; Sommervogel 4:52–55.

[T. C. O'BRIEN]

HALLOWEEN, see ALL SAINTS, FEAST OF.

HALLUCINATION, a psychic disturbance in the order of gross sensory deception. Objects are perceived which are either altogether nonexistent or only remotely suggested by the existing sensory cues. Hallucinations are often visual (seeing things) or auditory (hearing voices) although hallucinatory pains and sensations of touch are not uncommon. Hallucinations are characteristic of toxic psychoses, i.e., psychotic states induced by excessive use of alcohol or narcotics, or by sudden withdrawal of intoxicants. The delirium tremens of the alcoholic offers prime examples of terrifying hallucinatory visions. Hallucinations are also symptomatic of more severe mental and emotional disorders, e.g., schizophrenia. Sometimes those who suffer from hallucinations will "explain" them in terms of *delusions. If religious feelings and ideas are bound up with such psychological disturbances, hallucinatory phenomena may be interpreted as supernatural visions or voices, a point for spiritual directors to take into account.

[M. E. STOCK]

HALLUM, ROBERT (*c.* 1365–1417), bishop. A doctor of canon law at Oxford by 1403, he was chancellor of the university (1403–07), becoming bp. of Salisbury in 1407. He was present at the Council of Pisa (1409); and at the Council of Constance (1415–19), where he was the president of the English "nation"; H. preached before the Council on at least five occasions. BIBLIOGRAPHY: Emden Ox 2:854–855; E. F. Jacob, *Essays in the Conciliar Epoch* (3d ed. 1963).

[L. E. BOYLE]

HALLVARD VEBJÖRNSSEN, ST. (Alvardo or Halward; d. 1043), patron of Oslo. According to legend he was related to King Olaf II and was murdered while defending a woman unjustly accused of theft. His cult (from the 15th cent.) was primarily within Norway, Iceland, and in Skara, a diocese of Sweden. In both Norwegian and Swedish iconography, H. is usually pictured bearing a millstone. BIBLIOGRAPHY: Butler 2:322; N. Rasmussen, BiblSanct 1:894.

[F. G. O'BRIEN]

HALO, the luminous crown encircling as a sign of glory the head, first of Christ (4th cent.), then of Mary, the Apostles, and saints (5th cent.) as they were represented in Christian art. At present only images of saints, not of the blessed, may have a clearly defined halo. Scripture speaks of golden crowns in connection with the glory of the blessed (Rev 14.14). St. Thomas Aquinas understands this as being the special reward of spiritual joy granted to virgins, martyrs, and doctors in the Church for their triumph over the flesh, death, and the devil. In a related way a halo sometimes also surrounds the name of Jesus or its monogram.

[A. M. BERMEJO]

HAMAN (Aman), in the Book of *Esther, the highest official in the court of King Ahasuerus (Xerxes). Out of enmity towards Mordecai, he sought to exterminate all of the Jews of Persia, but was thwarted through Esther's influence and was himself hanged by the king on the gallows he had prepared for Mordecai.

[T. C. O'BRIEN]

HAMANN, JOHANN GEORG (1720–88), German Lutheran religious writer. H. studied various disciplines at Königsberg. While in London on business (1756–58) he experienced a sudden conversion and devoted the rest of his life to opposing the *Enlightenment with Christian ideas based on lived experience and intuition. He considered the only reality to be God's giving himself humbly to the world. With deep conviction he championed the views of Luther on sin and redemption. Some of his ideas were taken over by S. *Kierkegaard; others were reflected in the theology of the irrational proposed by F. E. *Schleiermacher and A. *Ritschl. BIBLIOGRAPHY: I. Ludolphy, EncLuthCh 2:975–976; R. G. Smith, *J. G. Hamann: A Study in Christian Existence, with Selections from His Writings* (1960).

[T. C. O'BRIEN]

HAMARTIOLOGY, a rare term for the theological study of sin; *hamartia* in the Greek NT means sin (Mt 7,2,5,9; Acts 7,60; Rom 5,12; 2 Cor 5,21).

[T. C. O'BRIEN]

HAMATH (Emath), town on the Orontes River in Syria, at the site of the modern Hama, *c.* 130 miles N of Damascus. It marked the northernmost extension of the Israelite kingdom (1 Kg 8.65; Num 34.8). It was the center of an independent kingdom from *c.* 900 B.C. until destroyed by Sargon in 720 B.C. and is frequently mentioned in the Bible (2 Kg 17.24; 2 Chr 8.4; Is 11.11; Amos 6.2; Zech 9.2).

[T. EARLY]

HAMERLING, ROBERT (Ruppert Hammerling; 1830–89), Austrian poet, novelist. His poetry, rather academic in character, tends in its polished form toward a historicism of vivid colors, involving historic-philosophical thoughts. From 1852 he was a teacher in Vienna, Graz, and Triest. Later he settled in Graz. He brought about a revival of new aesthetic culture. Works: *Sangesgruss von der Adria* (1857), poems; *Aspasia* (1876), a novel.

[B. F. STEINBRUCKNER]

HAMILTON, JOHN (1511–71), abp. of St. Andrews and primate of Scotland from 1546. He had previously been keeper of the privy seal (1542), then bp. of Dunkeld (1544). As abp. he was the unyielding foe of John *Knox's Reform movement; H.'s *Catechism* (1552) was part of the attempt to keep the people true to the old faith. But he failed to stop the progress of Calvinism and its parliamentary approval, and was himself imprisoned in 1563 for continuing to celebrate Mass and hear confessions. He was released through the influence of *Mary Queen of Scots. Less noble was his unscrupulous annulment (1567) of Bothwell's marriage to Lady Jane Gordon so that Bothwell could marry Mary. In spite of H.'s efforts the Queen fled Scotland in 1568; he was finally arrested for treason and 3 days after his arrest was hanged at Stirling. Involvement in the murders of Lord Darnley and the Earl of Moray was a trumped-up charge against him.

[D. J. SMUCKER]

HAMILTON, PATRICK (1504–28), a Scot of noble birth who was burned at the stake for preaching Reformed doctrine at St. Andrews. While studying on the Continent, he was influenced by Lutheran doctrines; he returned to Scotland to preach his faith, and was summoned on a charge of heresy. He was offered life if he would recant. His courage and steadfastness at his execution (it took 6 hours to burn him) had a far-reaching effect, and his short book *Loci communes (Patrick's Places* or *Patrick's Pleas)* became a cornerstone of Protestant theology. The text is in J. Knox, *History of the Reformation in Scotland* (W. C. Dickinson, ed., 2 v., 1949). BIBLIOGRAPHY: P. Lorimer, *Scottish Reformation* (1860); *idem, Patrick Hamilton* (1857); A. R. Macewan, *History of the Church in Scotland* (1913); J. McKinnon, *Luther and the Reformation* (1925).

[L. P. O'CONNOR]

HAMITES, descendants of Ham, the second of Noah's three sons (Gen 5.32). A curse pronounced by Noah upon Ham's son Canaan for the offense of Ham, who looked upon his father's nakedness, has been the subject of considerable discussion (Gen 9.20–27). In the table of nations Ham is also the father of Cush, Egypt, and Put (Gen 10.6). The identification of Put is uncertain, but some scholars suggest it is Cyrene. Cush is identified as the father of Nimrod, whose kingdom was in the Tigris-Euphrates area (Gen 10.8–10). Cush originally was used as the name for both the area of Ethiopia and that of Babylonia. The principle of classification was apparently not ethnographic or linguistic but geographic, with the Hamites extending from Phoenicia through W Palestine into Africa. In the poetic parallelism of the Psalms, Ham is used as a synonym of Egypt (78.51; 105.23,27; 106.22).

[T. EARLY]

HAMMURABI, KING OF BABYLON from *c.*1792–50 B.C. He expanded his hegemony far beyond any of the five kings of his first dynasty, but had to battle constantly against invasions during his last 12 years. He is most famous for the law code named after him.

[J. F. FALLON]

HAMON, ANDRÉ JEAN MARIE (1795–1874), Sulpician biographer and spiritual writer. After 31 years as professor and religious superior, H. was appointed curé of St. Sulpice (1851) and began a pastoral ministry that lasted 23 years. He wrote a treatise on preaching (1846) that was much used in seminaries; a series of meditations (1872) whose English title is *Meditations for All the Days of the Year* (tr. A. T. Bennett, 5 v., 1894); a life of St. Francis de Sales (1854; Eng. tr. H. Burton, 2 v., 1926, 1929), and the first biography of J. *Cheverus (Eng. tr. E. Stewart, 1839). BIBLIOGRAPHY: L. Branchereau, *Vie de M. Hamon* (1877).

[P. K. MEAGHER]

HAMPTON COURT CONFERENCE, a meeting in Jan. 1604, presided over by James I, between Anglican bps. and Puritan leaders. The latter presented grievances against the liturgy of the *BCP (see MILLENARY PETITION) and the Anglican notion of episcopacy; they received little satisfaction. The conference did, however, lead to the publication of the Authorized Version of the Bible.

[T. C. O'BRIEN]

HAṀSA. Hindu and Buddhist motif, the *haṁsa* (goose or swan) is the mount of Brahmā.

[M. J. DALY]

HANBALITES (Arab *Ḥanâbila,* from sing. *ḥanbalî*), the followers of the school of Aḥmad ibn Ḥanbal (d. A.D. 855), one of the four orthodox schools of *Islamic law. Ibn Ḥanbal, a brilliant jurist and theologian who held that the only sources of religious knowledge, dogmatic as well as legal, are the *Koran and the Sunna (see SUNNITES), was imprisoned and flogged during the reigns of the two *Mutazilite caliphs, al-Ma'mûn and al-Mu'tasim because of his refusal to acknowledge the doctrine that the Koran is created. For this he became and remains the great hero of conservative orthodoxy and the model of antitheological traditionism (see HADITH). Although from the beginning the Ḥanbalite school has stood opposed to all forms of speculative theology, whether orthodox or Mutazilite, and above all to philosophy, it has nonetheless produced some of Islam's most remarkable theologians. Outstanding among these is Ibn Taymîya (d. 1328) whose work had a profound influence on the doctrine of Mohammed ibn 'Abd al-Wahhâb (d. 1792), the founder of the ultraconservative Wahhabite movement that is now dominant in Saudi Arabia. BIBLIOGRAPHY: H. Laoust, "Aḥmad ibn Ḥanbal" and "Ḥanâbila" in EncIslam².

[R. M. FRANK]

HANC IGITUR, the fourth prayer of the Roman Canon, (Eucharistic Prayer I), which is a prayer for the acceptance of the offering of bread and wine, and in the English text begins with the words, "Father, accept this offering." There are two special forms: (1) that of Holy Thursday, in which Christ's institution of the Eucharist is specified; and (2) one used from the Easter Vigil to the Second Sunday of Easter inclusively, in which the newly baptized are mentioned. Before the year 600 this prayer was mobile and variable; originally it was used only on special occasions. As the prayer is recited the celebrant extends his hands over the offering, a gesture that entered the Mass rite after the Middle Ages.

[C. J. NOONE]

HANDEL, GEORGE FREDERIC (1685–1759), German-born, naturalized English composer of the Baroque period. Though of nonmusical parents, H.'s talent was early discovered, and he was allowed to study with Zachau, the organist at Halle. H. became organist himself there (1697–1703), during which time he finished the study of law to which his father had set him. He then went to Hamburg where he secured employment, mainly as a harpsichordist, and went on to complete his musical training. In 1706 he went to Italy, performing and composing in Florence, Rome, Venice, and Naples. In 1710 he left Italy to become *Kapellmeister* to the Elector of Hanover. While holding that post, he visited England twice, the second time remaining there since his master, at that time, ascended the English throne as George I. H. held various appointments in England, including that of director of the new Royal Academy of Music. He produced numerous operas and oratorios in London. The *Messiah,* however, saw its first production (1742) in Dublin. His works number 46 operas, 32 oratorios, 71 cantatas, 20 chamber duets, plus other sacred and secular music. Of H.'s music it may be said that his operas represent an important phase in the development of that form; that the body of instrumental music was enhanced by his *concerti grossi,* his organ concertos and his sonatas; but that it was the oratorio that reached its climax with him. In this form he effectively combined his own, basically Italian, style with the English tradition of choral music. Though his *Messiah,* gave H. the reputation of being a great church musician, it must be noted that this work was a unique composition. H. must be regarded essentially as a composer for the theater rather than for the church. He wrote German, Italian, and English church music of value and himself possessed a profound religious spirit, but his music is not ecclesiastic. He chose biblical themes because of their universal validity, not their dogmatic significance. H. dealt with his subjects as a moral humanist, not as a member of a specific sect.

[M. T. LEGGE]

HÄNDL (HÄHNEL), JACOB (Gallus; 1550–91), German Cistercian composer of polyphonic music. He held important court and church positions in Vienna, Olomouc, and Prague. His works include 16 Masses, motets, and other church music. H. ranked among the best composers of his time. He published *Opus musicum,* motets for the liturgical year. Other works were published in Prague, during and after his lifetime and have appeared in old and later musical collections. They are contained in various volumes of the *Denkmäler der Tonkunst in Österreich.*

[M. T. LEGGE]

HANDMAIDS OF THE BLESSED SACRAMENT AND OF CHARITY, SISTERS ADORERS (AASC), a pontifical congregation founded by St. María Desmaisières *c.*1850 in Madrid. The institute was established to meet the needs of wayward girls with whom the foundress had come in contact during her labors in San Juan de Dios hospital. She and her sisters established trade schools where the rehabilitated girls might live. For them she also founded a religious society in which they took private vows; they were called Mínimas de Santa María Miguela del Santísimo Sacramento. The apostolate of the congregation now also embraces the education of children and domestic work. The sisters are devoted to adoration of the Blessed Sacrament. Houses are located in Spain, Portugal, Italy, Argentina, Chile, Bolivia, Colombia, Venezuela, and Japan. Established in the U.S. in 1961, they have served in the Diocese of San Diego. With their general motherhouse in Madrid, they have 2,315 members in 111 houses (1976).

[M. B. MONAGHAN]

HANDMAIDS OF CHARITY, a religious congregation founded in Brescia, Italy, in 1840 by the wealthy Paula DiRosa (Maria Crocifissa DiRosa) with the assistance of Msgr. Faustino Pinzoni and Gabriella Echenos Bornati. Papal approbation was granted in 1921. The original object of the new congregation was the care of the sick in hospitals, not only nursing but giving the whole of their time and interest unreservedly to the sick and suffering. The early years of the institute found the members serving in military hospitals, esp. during the Revolution of 1848, and succoring the needs of plague-ridden Italian towns. The congregation expanded to 3,058 members (1975) serving Italy, Switzerland, Yugoslavia, and Brazil. The foundress was canonized in 1954. The motherhouse is in Brescia.

[M. B. MONAGHAN]

HANDMAIDS OF THE SACRED HEART OF JESUS (ACJ; ANCILLAE SACRI CORDIS JESU), a religious congregation founded in Madrid, Spain (1877) by Dolores and Raphaela Mary Porras y Ayllón, which received papal approval in 1887. Raphaela became the first superior general of this institute which follows an adaptation of the Rule of St. Ignatius Loyola. The Handmaids who take simple, perpetual vows combine contemplation with active works. Characteristic of the former is the daily adoration of reparation before the exposed Blessed Sacrament. Their apostolic works include education, catechetics, retreats, and foreign mission activities. The congregation numbered (1975) 2,273 in 112 houses in 14 countries. In the U.S. they are in the Archdioceses of Baltimore, Philadelphia, and Miami. The foundress Raphaela Mary Porras was canonized by Paul VI in 1977.

[M. B. BOYLE]

HANDS, IMPOSITION OF, see IMPOSITION OF HANDS.

HANEBERG, DANIEL BONIFATIUS (1816–76), German biblical and Oriental scholar; Benedictine abbot; bp. of Speyer. Ordained in 1839, he was a professor at the Univ. of Munich from 1841 until 1872, and published works of meticulous scholarship on biblical themes as well as an edition, with Latin translation of *Canones S. Hippolyti arabice* (1870). He became a Benedictine in 1850 at the Abbey of St. Boniface, Munich; he was elected abbot in 1854. After Vatican Council I, he was appointed bp. of Speyer. In part because of the influence of J. *Dollinger, he was in opposition to the definition of papal infallibility, but bowed to the decision of the Council; he also repudiated his own view of biblical inspiration, namely that it consisted in church acceptance of the biblical books, once the Council had rejected it.

[T. C. O'BRIEN]

HANIWA FIGURES, 3d-cent. clay images *(haniwa)* around early Japanese mounded tombs, representing men, women, animals, and buildings, and considered both ritualistic and practical (stabilizing the earthen pile). The hollow, expressive forms, grave and serene, inserted by pin-extensions at the base rise three and four feet high. In an amazing degree distinctively Japanese, they are authentic evidence of costume, gesture, and various aspects of the life of the period.

[M. J. DALY]

HANNA, EDWARD JOSEPH (1861–1944), abp. of San Francisco. A native of Rochester, N.Y., he was ordained in Rome in 1885, remained there until 1887, then returned to Rochester and from 1893 taught at St. Bernard's Seminary.

When first proposed as coadjutor of San Francisco in 1907, he was attacked by some theologians as a Modernist because of his writings on Christology. Five years later, however, he went to San Francisco as auxiliary bp., succeeding to the see in 1915. His work among migrant workers and in settling labor disputes won him national recognition. He was chairman of the administrative board of the National Catholic Welfare Conference from its inception in 1919 until 1935. President F. D. Roosevelt in 1934 appointed H. chairman of the National Longshoreman's Board which settled a crucial dock strike. In 1935 he retired to Rome, where he lived until his death.

[J. R. AHERNE]

HANNO OF COLOGNE, ST., see ANNO II OF COLOGNE, ST.

HANS OF COLOGNE (JUAN DE COLONIA; 1410–*c.* 1481), Spanish architect in Burgos (1454), designing its cathedral towers with tracery as at Cologne. H. built the Carthusian church of Miraflores and the chapel of Concepción in the Burgos cathedral (1477).

[M. J. DALY]

HANSIZ, MARKUS (1683–1766), Austrian Jesuit historian. He spent his entire life on one work, entitled *Germania sacra,* which dealt with the medieval ecclesiastical history of the bishoprics of Passau, Salzburg, and Regensburg; he did not complete the work. He taught in the cities of Vienna and Graz.

[D. J. SMUCKER]

HANTHALER, CHRYSOSTOMUS (Johannes Adam; 1690–1754), Cistercian monk from 1716 at the Abbey of Lilienfeld, Lower Austria, compiler of the valuable *Fasti Campililienses* (3 v., 1747–54), a documented history of Austria until 1550; but also author of *Notulae anecdotae* (1742), alleged early chronicles that he in fact forged.

[T. C. O'BRIEN]

HANUKKAH, see DEDICATION OF THE TEMPLE, FEAST OF.

HANXLEDEN, JOHANN ERNST (1681–1732), German Jesuit missionary to India, author of the first European Sanskrit grammar and compiler of a Portuguese-Sanskrit dictionary.

[T. C. O'BRIEN]

HAOMA, in Persian religion the sacrificial liquor made from the juice of a plant in a mortar. It was also regarded as a god as well as a sacred liquor. Sacrifice was offered to this divinity, and, although he was a god, he was killed as he was crushed in the mortar. The Hindu *Soma* corresponds closely. The *Haoma* sacrifice is that of a dying god offered to a god. In the *Haoma* ritual, portions of the victims sacrificed were reserved for the god. The participants in the ritual drank the *Haoma* and were thus thought to participate in the god's immortality. There is a superficial resemblance between this ritual and the Catholic Mass, but on closer analysis there are basic differences. BIBLIOGRAPHY: J. Duchesne-Guillemin, *La Religion de l'Iran ancien* (1962) 95–99.

[M. R. P. MCGUIRE]

HAPPINESS, as understood here, man's final end and the fulfillment of his every potentiality. It is taken, outside ethical formalism, as the purpose of moral activity; different accents are laid on its nature as theories range up, in accordance with underlying philosophical and theological presuppositions, from the various stages of humanist utilitarianism, through more or less explicit recognitions of value beyond human life on earth and a supreme good *(summum bonum)* apart from the universe, to the uncompromisingly nonpantheist affirmations by Judaism, Christianity, and Islam, of the transcending and subsisting goodness of God. Happiness is defined comprehensively by Boethius as the state made perfect by the accumulation of every good, and more pointedly by Aristotle, as the culminating activity of the human mind; their terms are filled out by the Christian theology of the face-to-face vision of God. Two sides are to be considered in happiness, as in any end *(finis),* namely, the real object that is the cause of happiness, sometimes called objective happiness, and the possessing of it by the subject, sometimes called subjective or formal happiness or beatitude, since this is the how *(finis quo)* man is happy, whereas the first is the why *(finis cuius gratia)* he is happy. As to the first, the theologians build on the foundation of the *Nicomachean Ethics* but rise much higher than did Aristotle. They list the blessings in which happiness might lie; and decide that it is not in riches, either natural or artificial, for they are for something else, whereas happiness is desirable for its own sake; nor in honors or fame, for these derive from being blessed or happy; nor in power, for that as such can work for good and ill; nor in health of body, for that is subordinate to health of soul; nor in pleasure, for that is the resonance of being happy; nor in virtue, for that is a quality of soul, and soul is not its own end; nor in any created good, not even the good of the whole world, for that is finite, and man has a heart for the good without reserve, eternal and incommutable. The stage is set for the doctrine that in nothing less than God is happiness found.

But how? The theologians turn then to consider subjective happiness. Perhaps it is quite noncreaturely? Awed by the mystery of intimacy with God, and not seeing any real sense in which it could be said that God was shared in himself, not merely in his effects, some great theologians and mystics left it at this, that God's own joy is somehow shed on us, *per illapsum,* just as his life becomes grace for us and the Holy Spirit becomes charity for us. St. Thomas Aquinas, however, characteristically tough and tender about creatures, firmly insisted that it was for men to be happy without being absorbed into the divinity and while remaining themselves, just as it is for men to be in God's favor and to be in love with him with a friendship which is their own. And so Aquinas and others, many of whom did not agree with his later findings, set themselves to define the formal note or decisive moment in our holding of happiness, and this without losing sense of the whole: they were helped by a theory of knowledge and love more developed than that of earlier theologians. Subjective beatitude, they agreed, was an activity, for creatures find their achievement in this *actus secundus;* only with God is being his acting. Furthermore, it must be a spiritual activity, not a sensation or emotion. The debate arose as to whether it was an act of mind, or of will, or of both. Into its intricacies we cannot now enter: here it is enough to note that Scotus opted for the second, St. Bonaventure and Suárez for the third, while St. Thomas and the Dominican school after him, recognizing the tragic inability of love alone to bring about the real presence of the beloved, taught that the happiness-making form can be held only by an act of mind. This, however, was not a form as the Arab-Hellenists understood the term, a bodiless meaning such as a spectator might contemplate in a philosopher's heaven, but the embrace of the living God in the *beatific vision promised by revelation.

And so it is significant that St. Thomas turns to man's natural desire in order to show the consonance of this mystery with human experience, not, of course, to demonstrate what lies beyond man's rights and claims and thoughts. Then also, before the vision there has been the cleaving to God himself in the darkness of faith by charity. Charity never falls away and now that God is seen, rejoices in his presence; here the theologians dwell on 1 Cor 9.24 and the 'comprehending' of God, not a special act, but a relation in the will to what is held in the mind, without fear of any relapse from perfect bliss, such as was entertained by some Gnostically-tinged Alexandrian theologians. The glory of soul brims over into the body, and charges it with its own immortality, invulnerability, clarity, and lissomeness—the dowry brought by spirit to sense was much meditated on by medieval theologians. Then, too, there is the companionship of friends, in an *agape* going beyond the bounds of the somewhat prim associations of the ethical authors. Though the aim of moral action, happiness itself is a post-moral condition, not to be discovered by a moral sense nor evaluated by science about the moral virtues. It is not a question of the incomplete felicity of living according to reason, nor even of the natural beatitude which is a useful methodological fiction in theology, though even these, it might be argued, pass out of purely ethical situations, but of the complete happiness which can be achieved, not from man's own native resources, but only by God's free mercy and loving kindness. How men can be caught up into the inner life of God is inexplicable in terms of any ontological category. It can be suggested, however, by the theme as stated by St. Augustine in the *De Trinitate* and half-developed by St. Thomas; that the relations of knowing and loving to their objects are not strictly causal, and so open an entrance into the "processions" of the three Blessed Persons. BIBLIOGRAPHY: ThAq St (Lat-Eng, v. 16, ed. T. Gilby, 1969); K. E. Kirk, *Vision of God: Christian Doctrine of the Summum Bonum* (2d ed. 1932); A. Gardeil, *La Structure de l'âme et l'expérience mystique* (1927).

[T. GILBY]

HAPSBURG, see HABSBURG.

HARBAVILLE TRIPTYCH, 10th-cent. Byzantine ivory relief panels of a consular triptych. The central panel is distinctively Persian in the cross motif decorated with rosettes and in the elliptical Persian trees on either side of the cross—the Christian Tree of Life—entwined with vines and grapes eastern in style—though iconographically Christian. In contrast, the side wings are austerely classical, the frontal parallel figures separated by heads in Roman medallions.

[M. J. DALY]

HARD SHELL BAPTISTS, derogatory name for *Primitive Baptists, applied to the group because of its ultraconservatism and literalism.

[T. C. O'BRIEN]

HARDENBERG, ALBERT RIZÄUS (*c.*1510–74), German Lutheran theologian. Educated at Groningen, H. entered Aduard Monastery *c.*1527; but after study at Louvain and Mainz he embraced the Reformation in 1539. In 1542 he became a disciple of Philipp *Melanchthon at Wittenberg and in 1544 helped the abp. of Cologne introduce reforms. He held a pastorate in Kempen and then became cathedral preacher in Bremen; but because of his Crypto-Calvinist doctrine of the Lord's Supper he was forced to leave the city in 1561. He spent 5 years in a monastery near Oldenburg and then accepted invitations to Sengwarden (1565) and Emden (1567). H. is regarded as the founder of the Reformation in Bremen. BIBLIOGRAPHY: C. Bertheau, EncRelKnow 5:145–147; J. Moltmann, RGG 3:74.

[M. J. SUELZER]

HARDENING OF HEART, a biblical metaphor (see Is 6.10; Mt 19.8; Rom 9.18) taken in theology to mean both a sin and a punishment for sin. As a sin it is equivalent in meaning to *malice, understood as both the obdurately sinful intent in a given act or as fixity of will in a habit of sin, in a *vice. Such a hardening of heart is particularly associated with *sins against the Holy Spirit, such as despair, presumption, spurning the known truth, obstinacy in evil; these all harden the heart against the very principle of forgiveness and of living the spiritual life (ThAq ST 2a2ae, 14.2). In a lesser sense hardening of heart may simply refer to failure to respond to inspirations towards the good, as in Ps 94 (95).8. As punishment hardness of heart means the deprival of grace and charity that makes a person amenable and responsive to the things of God. The obdurate sinner places an obstacle to the communication of grace; the punishment of deprival corresponds to what an unrepentant attitude deserves (ThAq ST 1a2ae, 78.3–4; 2a2ae,15). St. Paul, Rom 1.24–32 seems to be describing this kind of divine punishment.

[T. C. O'BRIEN]

HARDOUIN, JEAN (1646–1729), historian and polemicist, theologian, and librarian at the Jesuit College of Louis-le-Grand in Paris (1683–1718). His major contribution is a critical collection of the texts of church councils (12 v., 1714–15), generally regarded as the most reliable edition of conciliar texts. H. did scholarly work in a variety of fields: numismatics, history, theology, and Scripture, although his conclusions were often extreme and the subject of controversy. BIBLIOGRAPHY: P. Bernard, DTC 6.2:2042–46.

[T. M. MCFADDEN]

HARDT, HERMANN VON DER (1660–1746), Lutheran church historian. Born in Melle, Westphalia (Germany), he studied at Leipzig, showing proficiency in Greek, Latin, and Hebrew. He was chosen curator of the library of the Duke of Brunswick and later, in 1690, was appointed professor of languages at Helmstedt University. From 1690 to 1693 he published three volumes of his *Autographa Lutheri aliorumque celebrium virorum ab anno 1517 ad annum 1546, reformationis aetatem et historiam egregie illustrantia*. In 1709, he was named rector of an academy in Marienburg, spending the remainder of his life there, teaching and writing. Among his other important works are: *Historia litteraria reformationis* (1717); *Aenigmata prisci orbis: Jonas in luce in historia Manassis et Josiae ex eleganti veterum Hebraeorum stylo solutum aenigma* (1723), a collection of novel interpretations of the OT which resulted in his being censured; *Tomus primus in Jobum, Historiam populi Israelis in assyriaco exilio* (1728), which also dealt with a biblical topic (i.e., the Book of Job) and which was also banned; *Histoire de la réformation* (6 v.,), which was not published during his lifetime. BIBLIOGRAPHY: H. Bardthe, NDB 7:668–669; *Realencyklopädie für protestantische Theologie und Kirche* 7:417–420; M. Schmidt, RGG 3:75.

[R. J. BRADY]

HARDWICK, THOMAS (1752–1829), English architect, pupil of Sir William Chambers, and clerk of works at Hampton Court and Windsor Castle. H. built the famous St. Marylebone New Church, London (1813–17).

[M. J. DALY]

HARDY, EDMUND (1852–1904), German priest, historian, esp. of the religions of India. Born in Mainz, he was professor at Freiburg, Fribourg, Würzburg, and Bonn, and was cofounder of the *Archiv für Religionswissenschaft*, as well as the author of many works, among them *Die vedisch-brahmanische Period der Religion des alten Indien* (1893); *König Asoka* (1902); and *Buddha* (1905). BIBLIOGRAPHY: J. Haekel, LTK 5:6.

[P. K. MEAGHER]

HARE, JULIUS CHARLES (1795–1855), English theologian. Ordained for the C of E, he succeeded to a rich family living in Sussex and, in 1840, became archdeacon of Lewes. His writings are mainly theological and controversial, and though full of thought, have a heavy German style and sentence structure, and show strongly the influence of German speculation in which H. throughout his life took great interest. Among his chief works are: *Vindication of Niebuhr's History of Rome* (1829) and *Recent English Assailants* (1854). H. belonged to the so-called *Broad Church Party, and while some of his opinions approach closely the evangelical Arminian school, others are very vague and indecisive.

[M. J. BARRY]

HARENT, ÉTIENNE (1845–1927), French Jesuit theologian. He entered the society in 1864, taught dogmatic theology in its houses in France and in England. Besides publishing several dogmatic treatises, he made substantive contributions to the DTC, esp. articles on theological faith and hope.

[T. C. O'BRIEN]

HÄRING, BERNARD (1912–), German Redemptorist moral theologian. His *Das Gesetz Christi* (3 v., 1954; Eng. tr. E. G. Kaiser, *The Law of Christ,* 1961–66) was the major transitional work in moving Catholic moral theology to a more biblical and personalist orientation. Some 15 other books in English have followed. H. has been a retreat master to Pope Paul VI and was a *peritus* (theological expert) at Vatican Council II, where he contributed significantly to the *Constitution on the Church in the Modern World*. He teaches at the Alphonsianum, his order's graduate school of theology in Rome, and has been a visiting lecturer at several universities and divinity schools in the U.S. BIBLIOGRAPHY: C. E. Curran, *New Look at Christian Morality* (1968) 145–158.

[R. VAN ALLEN]

HARLAY, French family whose members were prominent in the 16th and 17th centuries. **Achille de** (1536–1619), jurist and leading proponent of *Gallicanism during the French wars of religion. He was an ardent supporter of Henry III in his struggles with the Catholic League and the Guise family and after Henry's assassination in 1589, he backed the Protestant pretender to the throne, Henry of Navarre, becoming a close adviser to the now nominally Catholic King *Henry IV. As such, he supported the principle of absolute monarchy versus the claims of papal supremacy, in opposition to the Jesuits and such ultramontanist political theorists as Juan de Mariana and Card. Bellarmine. **Achille de (Baron de Sancy)** (1581–1646), bp., scholar. Bp. of Lavour from an early age, he acted as France's ambassador to the Sublime Porte (1610–19), in which capacity he protected the Jesuits against the Turks, and later formed part of Louis XIII's retinue under the guidance of Card. Richelieu. As bp. of Saint-Malo from 1631, he tried and persecuted those bps. of Brittany who had participated in the Duke of Montmorency's rebellion against the King. He was also an expert in Oriental languages, with a valuable collection of ancient Hebrew Bibles (now in the Bibliothèque Nationale), and served as the editor of Richelieu's *Memoirs*. **François de** (1586–1653), abp. of Rouen from the age of 30. He was known for his papal sympathies in an age of Gallicanism, for the social reforms he instituted, for the school of theology he founded, and for the ill-advised pamphlet satirizing the papal court he wrote (and soon retracted) when his ambitions were foiled. **François de Harlay de Champvallon** (1625–96), nephew of François I, whom he succeeded as abp. of Rouen in 1651 when only 26, despite his scandalous private life and worldly ambitions. As abp. of Paris after 1671, he supported Card. Mazarin, whose position as prime minister he hoped to inherit, and advised Louis XIV in ecclesiastical affairs. His support of the Gallican claims advanced by the Assembly of the Clergy in 1682 won him the King's favor, as did his acceptance of Louis' secret marriage to Mme. de Maintenon. A harsh opponent of both Jansenism and Protestantism, he personally persecuted the Huguenots at Dieppe and was instrumental in securing the revocation of the Edict of Nantes (1685).

[E. M. GATES]

HARLESS, ADOLPH GOTTLIEB CHRISTOPH VON (1806–79), Lutheran theologian. A devoted exponent of the thought of Martin Luther on justification, H. taught Scripture and theology at Erlangen from 1830 to 1845. In 1837 he founded the journal *Zeitschrift für Protestantismus und Kirche*. He was removed from Erlangen for his defense of the Lutheran stand on genuflection and taught at Leipzig (1845–50) when he became court preacher at Dresden. In 1852 he was named president of the Lutheran supreme consistory where he was able to accomplish many reforms esp. in liturgy. Two notable works are *Theologische Enzyklopädie und Methodologie vom Standpunkte der protestantischen Kirche* (1837), and *Christliche Ethik* (1842; Eng. tr. *System of Christian Ethics*, 1865). BIBLIOGRAPHY: M. Schmidt, RGG 3:75–76.

[J. R. AHERNE]

HARLEZ, CHARLES JOSEPH DE (1832–89), student of Eastern religions. Ordained priest in 1858, H. did most of his scholarly work at the Univ. of Louvain, where he was professor of Oriental languages, developed an important school of Oriental studies, and began the periodical *Le Muséon*. Among his scholarly achievements are a translation of the **Avesta*, the sacred book of the Zoroastrian religion; a Sanskrit manual; a lexicon for the Manchu language; and a study of the relationship between Vedic religion, Brahmanism, and Christianity.

[T. M. MCFADDEN]

HARMANDSZOON, JACOB, see ARMINIUS, JACOBUS.

HARMEL, LÉON (1829–1915), French industrialist, Catholic social activist. A man of intense faith and broad concern for workers, H. established a Catholic-centered factory where the religious betterment of the employees was paramount and labor participated in the management of the factory. H. lived with his family among the workers. He was well known to Pius IX, Leo XIII, and Pius X, all of whom approved his stance. He led a number of pilgrimages to Rome in which management and labor joined. The influence of this Christian industrialist, through congresses of workers and encouragement of study groups to ponder the social question, contributed to the development of the fruitful *Semaines Sociales de France which began in 1904. An early advocate of the Christian Democratic movement, H. placed more reliance on social than on political action.

[J. R. AHERNE]

HARMENOPOULOS, CONSTANTINE (1320–83), the chief Byzantine judicial official in Thessalonica, who compiled in 1345 a handbook of civil and canon law in six parts, called the *Hexabiblos*. He also composed a highly regarded epitome of canon law. BIBLIOGRAPHY: Beck 788.

[E. EL-HAYEK]

HARMONIUM, a keyboard instrument of the reed-organ family, the tone of which is produced by thin metal tongues, "free reeds," set in vibration by a steady current of air. The harmonium was long considered a popular substitute for the organ, but when used properly it is an instrument in its own right. It resembles the organ in features such as wind supply, keyboard, sustained tones, and stops producing various timbres. Since its development from, among other instruments, *Grenie's orgue expressif*, it has had many improvements: the *percussion, prolongement, melody attachment*. Vatican Council II retains the preeminence traditionally given to the pipe organ, but accepts other instruments suitable for liturgical use (Vat II SacLit 120).

[M. T. LEGGE]

HARMONY OF THE GOSPELS, an arrangement of the individual Gospels woven into a single continuous narrative by the elimination of repetitions. Tatian's *Diatessaron* is the most famous example. Harmony is also sometimes used, less properly, for a synopsis—an arrangement of the complete Gospels in individual parallel columns for the purpose of investigation. BIBLIOGRAPHY: B. Metzger, *Text of the New Testament* (1964); K. Aland, *Synopsis Quattuor Evangeliorum* (1964).

[C. BERNAS]

HARMONY SOCIETY, a group of separatists and Pietists, also known as Harmonists or Rappites after their founder, the Württemberg farmer Johann Georg Rapp (1757–1847). Rapp immigrated to the U.S. with some followers in 1803 for a freer exercise of belief. After founding the Harmony settlement in Butler County, Pa., the members moved to establish New Harmony, Ind., in 1814. They sold this property in 1824 to Robert Owen, the socialist reformer and agnostic, who continued his own community there, and Rapp and his followers moved back to Pennsylvania and set up a third colony, named Economy, now the town of Ambridge, NW of Pittsburgh. They recognized no authority save the Bible, denied the Eucharist, advocated celibacy, rejected school attendance of children, led a communal life without individual possessions, and believed that in an imminent regeneration of the world the "harmony" of male and female elements in man would be reestablished. By their simple and strict life they developed prosperous agricultural communities. The Harmonists adopted children and also sought new emigrants from Germany; but neither these measures nor a temporary merger with a similar group, the Bernhardusbrüder, prevented extinction by the end of the 19th century. BIBLIOGRAPHY: J. S. Duss, *Harmonists* (1943); T. Horgan and R. Brown, "Communal Movements," NCE 4:29–32, esp. 30 and bibliog; W. H. Larrabee, EncRelKnow 3:187.

HARNACK, ADOLF VON (1851–1930), German church historian and liberal theologian. Next to F. *Schleiermacher, H. was probably the most influential Protestant thinker of the 19th and the early 20th cent. because of his immense historical scholarship and his contributions to *liberal theology. H. studied at the Univ. of Leipzig and taught there for 5 years. He then became professor of church history at Giessen and at Marburg. In 1889 he was called to Berlin despite the strenuous opposition of the Lutheran Church Senate because of his liberal views. He was also the director of the state library in Berlin. With T. Mommsen he founded the series *Griechische christliche Schriftsteller,* to provide definitive texts of the Fathers of the first 3 centuries. In 1899 he gave a course of lectures stressing the moral side of Christianity, esp. the message of universal brotherhood. These appeared the following year as the epoch-making *Das Wesen des Christentums.* H. traced the infiltration of Greek metaphysics into early Christianity until the emancipation effected through Luther's reform and his ethical approach to the God of goodness. H.'s capacity for work (his bibliography numbers about 1,700 items), clearness of vision, powers of organization, brilliance of style, and ability as a lecturer were matched by his gift both for planning and for scholarly detail. BIBLIOGRAPHY: W. Schneemelcher, RGG 3:77–79; Y. Congar, *Catholicisme* 5:516–519; F. X. Murphy, NCE 6:929–930.

HAROLD, WILLIAM VINCENT (*c.*1785–1856), Irish Dominican who was vicar general of the Diocese of Philadelphia under Bp. H. *Conwell. H. is known for his opposition to *trusteeism, but also for his appeal, after a dispute with Conwell, to the U.S. civil courts to defend his rights against transfer by ecclesiastical authority. The American government would have nothing to do with interfering in a purely religious matter. H. returned to Ireland, became a renowned preacher, and was provincial of Ireland, 1840–44. BIBLIOGRAPHY: H. J. Nolan, *Most Reverend Francis Joseph Kenrick* (1948).

HARPSFIELD, NICHOLAS (*c.*1519–75), English theologian. Preferring to leave England rather than adopt the religious changes imposed under Edward VI, he returned in Mary Tudor's reign, was appointed archdeacon of Canterbury, and led the bps. in protest against the changes proposed by Elizabeth. Imprisoned in the Tower for refusing to accept the BCP (1559), he remained there until his death. His writings include a history of the English Church, six dialogues defending papal supremacy, the invocation of saints, monasticism, and a treatise on the divorce between Henry VIII and Catherine of Aragon, this latter written in opposition to the universities' favorable reply to Henry's famous question and containing a strong defense of Fisher and More. Extant also in MS are lives of Cranmer and of Thomas More, the latter based mainly on Roper's account. BIBLIOGRAPHY: Gillow BDEC 3:154–157.

[M. J. BARRY]

HARRIS, HOWELL (1714–73), founder of the *Calvinist Methodists. H. was born at Trevacca, Wales, in 1714 and had a conversion experience in 1735. A student at Oxford in the same year, he became disturbed by the immorality there and returned to Wales, and though not ordained, he began to preach. He became an itinerant evangelist, and separated from the Church of England. In 1743 with George *Whitefield, whom he had met in 1739, and some others, he formed the Welsh Calvinistic Methodist Church. He was also a friend and admirer of John *Wesley. He was persecuted by mobs, and when his health broke, founded a community for needy persons at Trevacca. He was befriended and assisted by Selina, Countess of *Huntingdon. BIBLIOGRAPHY: H. E. Lewis, *Howell Harris* (1912); W. Williams, *Welsh Calvinistic Methodism* (1872).

HARRIS, JOEL CHANDLER (1848–1908), humorist, writer on blacks in the Old South. A native of rural Georgia, a state that produced a number of writers of humor in the 19th cent., H. as a boy went to work on Turnwold Plantation where he had ample direction in the two chief interests of his life: journalism and observing plantation life, esp. the ways of the Negro. The owner was a colorful figure who published a weekly newspaper on which H. worked. Journalism brought him finally to the Atlanta *Constitution,* which was to be his base for 24 years. It was here that his first stories of Negro folklore and his *persona* Uncle Remus appeared. A shy man who dreaded publicity, H. through the influence of his Catholic wife and reading Newman and other Catholic writers, was long convinced of the truth of Catholicism but deferred entrance to the Church until a few weeks before his death—a delay he said was his only real regret. The witty, compassionate, and warmly human observer of Southern life enriched the lives and broadened the understanding of millions all over America. BIBLIOGRAPHY: P. M. Cousins, *Joel Chandler Harris* (1968).

[J. R. AHERNE]

HARRISON, PETER (1716–75), American architect born in England, H. was the first thoroughly Palladian architect in the colonies, though absorbing influences in a unique style. His King's Chapel (Boston, 1749–58) with slender Corinthian columns is in James Gibbs' style. His Touro Synagogue (1759–63) and Brick Market (1761–72), both in Newport, R. I. derive from Inigo Jones.

[M. J. DALY]

HARRISSE, HENRY (1829–1910), historian. A native of France, H. came to the U.S. before 1847, remaining in America until 1869. He taught at the Univ. of North Carolina and at Georgetown Univ. where he studied law. Interest in the records of the discovery of the New World led him to publish *Notes on Columbus* (1866), and as a bibliographer he brought out his great work *Bibliotheca Americana Vetustissima* (1866), which described books on America published between 1492 and 1551. A man who delighted in controversy, he published *The Discovery of North America* (1892) and *John Cabot, Discoverer of North America* (1896). Most of his extensive library at his death he left to the Library of Congress and the Bibliothèque Nationale in Paris.

[J. R. AHERNE]

HARROWING OF HELL, the medieval English term for the descent of Christ into hell to release the OT saints. It was a favorite theme for medieval plays and featured the dramatic confrontation between Satan and the majestic, risen Christ.

[T. M. MCFADDEN]

HART, CHARLES ALOYSIUS (1893–1959), philosopher, professor at The Catholic Univ. of America from 1921 until his death. H. was prominent in the neoscholastic movement in the U.S., and was particularly effective as a teacher. His main interest was in metaphysics; the influence of É. Gilson's interpretation of Thomism as an existential metaphysics is apparent in H.'s *Thomistic Metaphysics* (1959).

[T. C. O'BRIEN]

HARTMAN, LOUIS FRANCIS (1901–70), biblical scholar. A Redemptorist ordained in 1927, H. spent 3 years of study at the Pontifical Biblical Institute in Rome. Two years later he earned the licentiate in Oriental languages in Rome. He was conversant with 14 languages, including 6 of the ancient Near East. From 1948 to 1970 he was prominent for his work on the *New American Bible*. From 1950 to 1970 he taught Semitic languages at The Catholic Univ. of America, Washington, D.C. Executive Secretary of the Catholic Biblical Association for over 20 years, H. was the author of countless journal articles, scripture editor of the NCE, and editor of the EDB. BIBLIOGRAPHY: *Catholic Biblical Quarterly* 32 (1970) 497–500.

[J. R. AHERNE]

HARTMANN VON AUE (*c.*1160–*c.*1210), medieval German minnesinger and author of courtly epics and legends, credited with having introduced the Arthurian romance into Germany. His two extant epics, based on Chrétien de Troyes, illustrate the role of *mâze* (moderation) in knightly conduct: in *Erec* (after 1190), the hero places marital love above knightly duty; in *Iwein* (*c.*1202), knightly duty outranks marital love. Both heroes repent and are rehabilitated. The legend *Gregorius* (*c.*1195) contains a medieval version of the Oedipus motif. Gregorius, child of an incestuous marriage and married to his own mother, is purified by penance and called, by God's grace, to be pope. H.'s masterpiece, *Der arme Heinrich* (*c.*1196), recounts how Heinrich is cured of leprosy through a young girl's readiness for sacrifice. H. also wrote love lyrics, crusading songs, and a rhymed disputation on love: *Das Büchlein*. His technical mastery reveals itself in his graceful narrative style and vivid imagery, but his works are chiefly noted for their awareness of the duality of life and their moral and didactic purpose. BIBLIOGRAPHY: M. O'C. Walshe *Medieval German Literature* (1962) 142–156; *Gregorius* (tr. E. H. Zeydel and B. Q. Morgan, 1955); *Der arme Heinrich* (tr. C. H. Bell, in *Peasant Life in Old German Epics*, 1931).

[M. F. MCCARTHY]

HARTMANN OF BRIXEN, BL. (*c.*1090–1164), bishop. Educated by the Augustinians in Passau, Germany, H. spent 20 years organizing religious houses and groups at Salzburg, Herren-Chiemsee, and Klosterneuberg. After he became bp. of Brixen in 1140, he established another Augustinian house near Brixen. He had the respect of both Alexander III and of Frederick I during their struggles. BIBLIOGRAPHY: Butler 4:601–602.

[S. WILLIAMS]

HARTMANN, ANASTASIUS (1803–66), Swiss Capuchin, missionary to India, vicar apostolic of Patna. Ordained in 1825, he was a novice master, then professor of theology in Rome before going to India in 1844. He was appointed first vicar apostolic of Patna in 1845 and built churches, schools, infirmaries, and mission stations. He returned to Rome to serve in the Congregation for the Propagation of the Faith and as procurator for Capuchin missions (1856–60); during this period he assisted in arranging the first permanent Capuchin foundation in the U.S. (Milwaukee, 1857). H. again became vicar apostolic for Patna in 1860. Among his writings were a Hindustani NT and catechism.

[T. C. O'BRIEN]

HARTMANN, EDUARD VON (1842–1906), German pessimist philosopher. Barred by an injury from an army career, he turned to philosophy. Schopenhauer, Schelling, and Hegel are perhaps most influential on his thought. H.'s epistemology is (his phrase) "transcendental realism." He rejects the irrational intuitionism of Schopenhauer's "World as Will," but does not fully accept Hegel's "World as Idea." H. would build his philosophy on data from the historical and positive sciences. He opposes the mechanistic materialism and the myth of progress accepted by many of the 19th cent., and rejects Christianity, at least as he saw it in contemporary Protestantism, for it, too, had fallen prey to "progress." The world must be seen as teleological. Thus, while he uses many evolutionary concepts, he is not Darwinian. His pessimism was not such that he held this to be the worst of all possible worlds. Rather, it is a world which, on balance, will bring happiness neither here nor hereafter. Man finds and fulfills himself by accepting the partial teleologies of the world as he finds it. Paradoxically, H. insists that only on this pessimism can one found a valid ethical system. His attitude to the divine is monistic and pantheistic. His insights on man mark him as the "philosopher of the unconscious," and anticipate the vitalism of some 20th-cent. existentialists. BIBLIOGRAPHY: R. Tsanoff, *Problem of Evil* (1931) ch. 12; L. E. Loemker, EncPhil 3:419–421.

[W. B. MAHONEY]

HARTMANN, NICOLAI (1882–1950), German philosopher born at Riga, Latvia, who, though originally a member of the Marburg school, rejected Neo-Kantian idealism in favor of developing a new ontology. He did not advocate the building of a system but adopted a method combining a phenomenological description of the facts and treatment of their implicit antinomies that arise from the problematic (aporetic) side of reality. In conceiving his realist philosophy, H. was influenced by E. *Husserl, but instead of emphasizing the internal constitution of mental acts he focused his research on concrete reality. He maintained that although Being is not totally explainable, there is an intelligible side and the very acts of knowing, willing, and feeling prove that there is an "in-itself" because of their objective (noematic) content. In his earlier works, H. proposed a division of Being into various spheres, modalities, and categories but after Heidegger's *Sein und Zeit* (1927) he did not principally concern himself with the problem of the unity of beings and Being. In ethics H. adopted Scheler's theory of value, but expanded it by rejecting the notion of the collective person and emphasized the absolute freedom and autonomy of the individual. The will is not limited by the determinations of nature nor by an extrinsic teleological principle. Nature does present determined situations but the freedom of the will is the highest determining force and introduces all values into the world. There is no need for God as the unifying principle of reality since man brings Being and value together, thereby giving history its course. Further, the world is accidental and contingent. Thus, though he recognized that the problem of religion could not be ignored, he thought it one that would eventually disappear. H. had a strong but brief influence on German philosophy, esp. his ethics, but existentialism quickly dominated European philosophy. BIBLIOGRAPHY: W. Cerf, EncPhil 3:421–426; I. M. Bochenski, *Contemporary European Philosophy* (1961) 212–226.

[F. T. RYAN]

HARTWICH OF SALZBURG, BL. (Hartwig, Herwig, *c.*955–1023), abp. of Salzburg from 991. He enjoyed the respect and favor of Emperors Otto III and Henry II; the former awarded him the rights of market and coinage (996), and the latter, large grants of property. He yielded part of his diocesan territory to be helpful to St. Stephen of Hungary who was then organizing the Hungarian hierarchy. Heedless of personal danger he labored tirelessly to relieve the material and spiritual necessities of his people when they were suffering from famine and plague in 994. He is credited with the reform of the Salzburg cathedral school and the restoration of the cathedral itself and numerous monasteries. In the Middle Ages he was venerated as a saint; he is now more commonly titled "blessed." BIBLIOGRAPHY: G. M. Fusconi, BiblSanct 2:492–493.

HARTY, JEREMIAH JAMES (1853–1927), bishop. Ordained for St. Louis, Mo., H. spent 25 years in parish work there. In 1902 he was appointed temporary administrator of the archdiocese. Named abp. of Manila, Philippines in 1903, he faced a Church in disarray after the defeat of Spain. Church property had been confiscated, the religious orders of men were under attack, the *Aglipayan schism was threatening the islands, and financial support by the Spanish crown was gone. H. was no diplomat and knew little Spanish and no Philippine dialect. In spite of limitations, he made progress for the Church. Transferred to Omaha, Neb. in 1916, H. worked vigorously to build up a diocese with few institutions, promoted charities and Catholic Action, and built parishes and schools. Ill health forced him to resign in 1925.

[J. R. AHERNE]

HARVARD, JOHN (1607–38), Puritan minister for whom Harvard Univ. is named. Born at Southwark, England, H. received his M.A. in 1635 from Emmanuel College, Cambridge, a Puritan stronghold. He came to Charlestown, Mass., in 1637 and became assistant to the pastor and teaching elder of First Church. He willed the college (founded in 1636 by a grant from the Massachusetts Bay Colony), his library of over 400 volumes (mostly theological works in Latin) and half his estate. In gratitutde for the gift, the college was named for him in 1639. BIBLIOGRAPHY: S. E. Morison, *Founding of Harvard College* (1935).

[T. EARLY]

HARVEY NEDELLEC, see HERVAEUS NATALIS.

HASE, KARL AUGUST VON (1800–90), German Lutheran church historian and theologian, professor at Jena from 1830 until retirement in 1883, five times vice-rector. He was respected for his literary style, though it became more and more cryptic in his later years. H. must be described as a liberal theologian, bent on presenting Christianity as an instantiation of the eternal, inner laws of the spirit. He had a polemicist's interest in Catholicism, journeyed many times to Rome, wrote on Italian subjects (on Catherine of Siena, 1850, Francis of Assisi, 1856), and his *Handbuch der protestantischen Polemik gegen die römisch-katholische Kirche* (1862, *Handbook of the Controversy with Rome,* 2 v., 1906) was occasioned in part by J. A. Möhler's *Symbolik.* His most highly regarded work is the *Kirchengeschichte* (2 v., 1834; tr. *History of the Christian Church,* 1859). An edition of H.'s collected works was published in 12 volumes, 1890–93.

[T. C. O'BRIEN]

HASIDAEANS, a Jewish religious group among the stalwart men who participated in the Maccabean revolt against Antiochus IV Epiphanes in 167 B.C. They were strong supporters of the legitimate priesthood and undoubtedly joined in the revolt for religious motives. They remained seditious at least until 161 B.C., during the reign of Demetrius I, but faded out of history after the time of Judas Maccabeus. The Essenes and Pharisees are probably offshoots of this group. BIBLIOGRAPHY: D. B. Eerdmans "Chasidim," *Oudtestamentische Studien* 1 (1942) 176–257; W. R. Farmer, InterDB 2:528.

[N. L. VAILLANCOURT]

HASIDISM, a movement founded in the 18th cent. as an organ of religious renewal for the oppressed Jews of E and SE Poland. These Jews turned to magic healers hoping to obtain deliverance from their oppression. The most outstanding healer was Rabbi Israel ben Eliezer, the founder of Hasidism, who was called Baal Shem Tov (Master of the Good Name), abbreviated into Besht. He was greatly influenced by the Lurianic Cabala which substituted ritual practices for Talmudic studies. He emphasized joy as characteristic of those who turn to God. Each group of *hasidim* gathered around a *tzaddik* who, through a singular communion with God, was a mediator between God and the masses. Song and dance often accompanied their religious celebrations. The *Hasidim* remain quite influential. BIBLIOGRAPHY: M. Buber, *Origin and Meaning of Hasidism* (ed. and tr. M. Friedman, 1960).

[N. L. VAILLANCOURT]

HASKALAH (Heb., enlightenment), movement among Jews of Eastern Europe *c.* 1750–1880 to combine traditional Jewish studies with modern European science and philosophy. Leaders of the movement, *Maskilim* (those who bring understanding), wished to absorb Western culture without losing Jewish identity. The movement originated in Berlin, where M. *Mendelssohn (1729–86) published a Hebrew-language periodical expressing modern ideas. It became esp. important in 19th-cent. Russia, despite vigorous opposition from orthodox Jews. As it led to a resurgence of Jewish nationalism, the Haskalah was a forerunner of *Zionism. BIBLIOGRAPHY: M. J. Stiassny, NCE 6:942–943.

[T. EARLY]

HASKINS, CHARLES HOMER (1870–1937), historian. Educated at Johns Hopkins, H. taught at Wisconsin and Harvard Universities. He pioneered in the study of the 12th-cent. transmission of Greco-Arabic learning to the West and was a member of the American delegation to the Versailles Peace Conference. BIBLIOGRAPHY: J. R. Strayer, DAB 22:289–291.

[B. F. SCHERER]

HASMONAEANS, dynasty of Jewish priestly family that ruled Jerusalem and parts of Palestine from *c.* 135 B.C. until the Roman conquest of Judea in 63 B.C. (see MACCABEES). From being guerrilla leaders against Greek oppression they became petty kings, John Hyrcanus being the first to assume royal power (135–105 B.C.).

[J. F. FALLON]

HASOR (HAZOR), the name of several fortified Canaanite cities in OT times. The most important stood on the site of Tell el-Qedah in N Galillee. Mentioned in Egyptian texts and the Mari tablets, its destruction is attributed to Joshua (Jos 11.4–15), although the same King Jabin is mentioned in Jg 4. Fortified by Solomon, it was finally destroyed by Tiglath-Pileser III in 733 B.C. BIBLIOGRAPHY: EDB 940–941.

[N. L. VAILLANCOURT]

ḤĂṢÔSᵉRÂ (hatzotzrah), a biblical silver trumpet used for religious functions, to beg God's help upon going into battle and on solemn days.

[M. T. LEGGE]

HASSE, JOHANN ADOLPH (1699–1783), German composer, director (1731) of the Dresden Opera House. H. wrote over 100 operas in the Italian style, oratorios, cantatas, Masses, a *Te Deum,* and a well-known *Salve Regina.*

His church music is operatic in style, manifesting his gift as a melodist, but is somewhat superficial.

[M. T. LEGGE]

HASSLER, HANS LEO VON (1564–1612), German organist and composer. H. was the son and pupil of Isaac H., organist at Nuremberg. After an Italian training under Gabrieli, he held positions in Augsburg, Nuremberg, Dresden, and in other places, and became one of the most celebrated composers of his time. His works include madrigals, motets, Masses, organ pieces, hymns, and other works for the Lutheran church. Most of his compositions are reprinted in *Denkmäler Deutscher Tonkunst*.

[M. T. LEGGE]

HASTENING OF DEATH, see DEATH, HASTENING OF.

HASTINGS, JAMES (1852–1922), Scottish minister and editor. Educated in Aberdeen at the university and Free Church Divinity College and ordained a Presbyterian minister (1884), H. was active in the ministry until his retirement in 1911. He founded (1889) and edited the monthly *Expository Times* until his death. But he is best known for several widely used reference works which he also edited. These include: *Dictionary of the Bible* (5 v., 1898–1904; 1-v. ed., 1909; rev. 1-v. ed., 1963); *Dictionary of Christ and the Gospels* (2 v., 1906–08); *Encyclopedia of Religion and Ethics* (12 v., 1908–21; index v., 1926); and *Dictionary of the Apostolic Church* (2 v., 1915–18).

HASTINGS, SELINA, see HUNTINGDON, COUNTESS OF.

HATHORIC CAPITAL, Egyptian column capital, shaped as the head of Hathor, the cow goddess, seen in Temples of Hathor, Dendera, and Philae. Hathoric columns at times imitate the handle of a sistrum rattle. Early cubic capitals carry the face on two sides; in the New Kingdom four faces top a square pillar, and later a cylindrical shaft. In the Saitic period the capital was one-third the total height.

[M. J. DALY]

HATIKVAH (Hatikva, Hatikwah), Zionist hymn that became the Zionist national anthem in 1907 and was adopted by Israel in 1948. The original poem was written by Naftali Herz Imber (1856–1911), and the English version by Nina Salaman. The tune is based on a much-used Hebrew melody.

[M. T. LEGGE]

HATRED. (1) Psychologically, aversion from what is perceived as repulsive or harmful. As an emotion it is the opposite of sensory love, i.e., the positive response to the agreeable. Perhaps hatred as a term has too many moral overtones to express simply an emotion, and dislike would be a better term. Paralleling the emotional aversion, there is also one of will, its turning away from what is contrary to the good connatural to the will's love for the human good. (2) Morally, as an emotional or volitional response, hatred is a matter to be controlled by virtue. The emotional shirking from what goes against the sensory side of nature must be kept from hindering the pursuit of the higher goals of human life, by virtues allied to *courage. (3) The full theological and most specific meaning of hatred is aversion directed against other persons, and is the direct opposite of the virtue of *charity, and accordingly among the worst of sins. Hatred of God is possible in that through effects that go counter to the human will he is regarded as the evil hinderer of will and the punisher; such hatred is particularly possible for the obdurate sinner. Hatred of God takes on and, as it were, ratifies the turning away from God that in lesser sins is simply the consequence of choosing a good incompatible with the union of charity with God. Hatred directly rejects and impugns the loving communion with God that is the life of the soul; as such it is the worst of sins, and numbered among the *sins against the Holy Spirit, i.e., those that undermine the very basis of reconciliation. Hatred of neighbor—which is more than simply an emotional dislike or distaste for another's uncongenial qualities—is also a serious offense against charity (see 1 Jn 2.11; 3.15). Instead of willing to another the divine good and all that is related to it, which God himself wills, hatred wills the opposite: wills the other to be deprived of such benefits. Such hatred may not of itself inflict actual injury in the way outward acts do, but it has a worse perversity, since it is the radical willing of evil, and the will is the seat of all sins. Sins of hatred are enmity towards God and neighbor. But there is a form of detestation that may be good. It is good and in right order to hate the divine punishments due to sin, not as they reflect God's justice, but as avoidable evils against self, and so as reasons for fidelity to the demands of charity. ''Hatred for what is bad for someone and loving what is good for him amount to the same thing'' (ThAq ST 2a2ae, 25. 6 ad 1). Detestation of what is sinful, or also hostile and harmful to self, on the part of another person is charity's displeasure for what is contrary to God's love: but the detestation is for the evil, not for the person. Hatred of sin is also part of charity's love for self: part of conversion and *contrition, and the negative side of loving God with one's whole heart.

[T. C. O'BRIEN]

HATSHEPSUT, TEMPLE OF, see DIER EL BAHRI.

HATTO OF REICHENAU, BL. (763–836), confidant of Charlemagne, bp. of Basel (802), abbot of Reichenau (806), and envoy to Constantinople (811). Resigning in 823, he founded the school at Reichenau, contributed to theology and canon law, and was the author of a prose version of the famous vision of his pupil Wettin. BIBLIOGRAPHY: PL 105:770–780; 115:11–16; A. M. Zimmermann, BiblSanct 2:572.

[A. CABANISS]

HATZFELD, JOHANNES (1882–1953), German priest, church musician and composer. H. was a founder (1929) of the International Society for New Catholic Church Music and of the periodical *Musik im Leben*. His interest in the revival of German folk song as enriching family life led him to produce several collections of folk music.

[M. T. LEGGE]

HAUCK, ALBERT (1845–1918), German Lutheran church historian, professor at Erlangen and Leipzig, and also director of the Ecclesiastical Archeological Institute. His notable (unfinished) work, *Kirchengeschichte Deutschlands* (6v., 1887–1920), is scrupulously documented but occasionally prejudiced. He collaborated with other scholars on the 3d edition of *Realencyklopädie für protestantische Theologie und Kirche* (24 v., 1896–1913). BIBLIOGRAPHY: M. Borelli, DE 2:326; B. Stasiewski, LTK 5:30.

[F. D. LAZENBY]

HAUPT, PAUL (1858–1926), biblical scholar. Born and educated in Germany, early in his career he accepted the post of professor of Semitics at Johns Hopkins Univ., Baltimore, Maryland. He was a pioneer in Sumerology and Assyriology; his most illustrious student was W. F. *Albright. H. published two series of OT books, printed in various colors so as to illustrate the source theories of J. *Wellhausen; they are thus known as the Rainbow Bibles (1896–1904; 1899–1904).

[T. C. O'BRIEN]

HAUPTMANN, GERHART (1862–1946), German dramatist and novelist, influenced by Ibsen, Zola, and Tolstoy. H. became the foremost representative of naturalism; his basic themes were the misery of the hopeless proletariat, social compassion or the lack of it, quest for God, and the decay of the bourgeoisie. BIBLIOGRAPHY: H. Sinders, *Gerhart Hauptmann, The Prose Plays* (1957).

[S. A. SCHULZ]

HAURÉAU, JEAN BARTHÉLEMY (1812–96), French historian and scholar. At an early age H. entered politics and journalism. After the Revolution of 1848, he became *conservateur* of French MSS at the Bibliothèque Nationale; when he refused to swear allegiance to Napoleon III, he was discharged. He is chiefly remembered for his continuation of *Gallia christiana* (v. 14–16), for his collaboration on *Histoire littéraire de la France* (v. 25–32), and esp. for *Notices et extraits des manuscrits de la Bibliothèque Nationale et autres bibliothèques* (v. 21–35). His independent work, six volumes of *Notices et extraits de quelques manuscrits latins de la Bibliothèque Nationale,* is still highly regarded. BIBLIOGRAPHY: P. Delhaye, *Catholicisme* 5:529–530; E. Borghese, DE 2:326.

[F. D. LAZENBY]

HAURIETIS AQUAS, Pius XII's encyclical on the nature and theological basis of devotion to the *Sacred Heart. It marked the centenary celebration (1956) of Pius IX's extension of the Feast of the Sacred Heart to the universal Church. The encyclical refutes several criticisms of devotion to the Sacred Heart and shows that the devotion is solidly grounded in Scripture as well as in the theological traditions of the Church. It teaches that the Church has not based devotion to the Sacred Heart merely on the strength of the private revelations made to St. Margaret *Alacoque but on the Word of God, and stresses that the Church had already given official approval to this devotion long before the writings of the saint had been known. When viewed in the light of divine revelation and practiced according to the directions of the Church, this devotion can lead men to a deeper and fuller understanding of the divine plan of salvation. BIBLIOGRAPHY: A. Bea *et al., Cor Jesu* (2 v., 1959); M. J. Donnelly, ''Haurietis Aquas and Devotion to the Sacred Heart,'' ThSt 18 (1957) 17–40.

[M. GRIFFIN]

HAUSKNECHT, JOHANN PETER (1799–1870), founder of the Hausknechtians. After studying theology in Strasbourg, H. went as a tutor to Paris, where he came under Mormon and Adventist influence. He founded a sect characterized by separatism, chiliasm, and an ascetic way of life. He was honored as a martyr because of an imprisonment; but the failure of his prophecies caused some of his adherents to return to the state Church and others to join related sects or emigrate to America. BIBLIOGRAPHY: P. Rohmer, RGG 3:97–98.

[M. J. SUELZER]

HAUTECOMBE, ABBEY OF, Benedictine abbey on Lake Bourget, Savoie, France. Founded by Benedictines of Aulps in 1121, it became Cistercian in 1135. Commendatory abbots in the 15th cent. caused it to decline. In the 18th cent. the abbey was rebuilt in Baroque style, but was suppressed in the French Revolution. Restored by King Charles Felix of Savoy (1824), it was repopulated first by Italian, then by French Cistercians. In 1922 the Benedictines of Marseilles acquired Hautecombe. BIBLIOGRAPHY: B. Laure, *Hautecombe* (1955).

[L. J. LEKAI]

HAUTERIVE, ABBEY OF, Cistercian abbey near Fribourg, Switzerland. Founded in 1138 by William of Glâne, pillaged by mercenaries (1387) and eventually impoverished, the abbey was suppressed (1848) and became an agricultural school and teachers college. The church was restored in the 18th cent.; the Cistercians reestablished Hauterive as a priory in 1939.

[M. A. MCFADDEN]

HAVEY, FRANCIS PATRICK (1864–1945), educator. Ordained for the Diocese of Hartford, Conn., (1889), he became a Sulpician in 1896. His teaching career brought him to St. Joseph Seminary in Dunwoodie, N.Y.; St. John's Seminary in Brighton, Mass.; and St. Mary's Seminary in Baltimore, Maryland. From 1917 to 1935 he taught in Washington, D.C., mostly at the Sulpician Seminary where he was rector from 1919 to 1925. He is author of many works on spirituality for priests and seminarians, among them *Meditations on the Passion and Eastertide* (1928) and *Retreat Companion for Priests* (1946). BIBLIOGRAPHY: C. J. Noonan, NCE 6:951–952.

[J. R. AHERNE]

HAWAII, a state in the central Pacific Ocean; admitted to the Union as the 50th state (1959). An archipelago consisting of eight major islands and a series of islets, atolls, and shoals, it was first explored by Polynesians who settled there in the 5th century. When the English explorer, James Cook, visited the islands in 1778, they were being united by the Hawaiian chief, Kamehameha. The popular religion was animistic until the arrival of Congregationalist missionaries in 1820. Most Protestant sects subsequently sent missionaries who contributed greatly to cultural and economic life, helping to devise a written language, and to draft the first Hawaiian constitution (1839). Prior to annexation by the U.S. (1898), a number of Chinese, Korean, and Japanese laborers came to Hawaii. Their presence resulted in the introduction of the Confucian, Taoist, Shinto, and Buddhist faiths. The first Catholic missionaries, members of the French Congregation of the Sacred Heart, arrived in 1827. They experienced little success until the Church was granted legal freedom by the Constitution of 1839. Among later missionaries the most famous was Father Damien (Joseph de Veuster), who worked among the lepers of Molokai from 1873 until his death in 1889. Hawaii became a prefect apostolic in 1826 and a vicariate in 1844. With James J. Sweeney as its first bp., the diocese of Honolulu was created in 1941 as a suffragan of the metropolitan See of San Francisco, California. The Church has grown enormously during Sweeney's episcopacy, and a number of religious orders have responded to the bp.'s pleas for aid. These include the Marianists, the Sisters of St. Joseph from St. Louis, Mo., and from Orange County, California.

Hawaii's population of 832,000 is over 75% urban and makes it the 40th most populous state in the Union. In 1976 Catholics numbered 205,000 or 24.11% of the total state population. Most Protestant denominations, including the Mormons, are represented among the population, which is more heterogeneous and racially mixed than that of any other state; the Jewish population is less than 1%.

Chaminade College, a coeducational institution founded (1955) by the Marianists, has an enrollment of some 800 and is the only Catholic college in Hawaii. There are 8 Catholic high schools with a total enrollment of 4,106 students, and 31 Catholic elementary schools with over 11,403 pupils. BIBLIOGRAPHY: R. S. Kuykendall and A. G. Day, *Hawaii: From Polynesian Kingdom to American State* (rev. ed. 1961); N. Webb and J. F. Webb, *Hawaiian Islands: From Monarchy to Democracy* (1956); R. Yzendoorn, *History of the Catholic Missions in the Hawaiian Islands* (1927); D. W. Johnson et al., *Churches and Church Membership in U.S.* (1974); *Jewish Yearbook* (1972).

[J. L. MORRISON AND R. M. PRESTON]

HAWARDEN, EDWARD (1662–1735), English theologian and controversialist. A member of a Lancashire recusant family, H. was ordained at Douai (1686) where he then taught philosophy. He was briefly a tutor in theology at Magdalen College, Oxford, but with the revolution of 1688 he returned to Douai to teach at the English College. Factionalism kept him from the royal chair of theology and led to his denunciation at Rome for Jansenism, but he was subsequently cleared of the charge. He was back in England in 1707 and established a reputation as a polemicist. In 1717 he engaged in a dispute with the anti-Trinitarian S. *Clarke in the presence of Queen Caroline. His collected works were published in Dublin (1808). BIBLIOGRAPHY: Gillow BDEC 3:167–182.

[T. C. O'BRIEN]

HAWKINS, DENIS JOHN BERNARD (1906–64), English Thomist philosopher. He completed undergraduate and doctoral studies at the Gregorian Univ., Rome, and was ordained in 1930. H. devoted his life to both the pastoral ministry and philosophical study and writing. His works were marked by concern to vindicate Aquinas's metaphysics against the critique of I. *Kant, and by a style and tone attuned to the English intellectual temper. Most influential were his *Sketch of Medieval Philosophy* (1946) and *Essentials of Theism* (1949).

[T. C. O'BRIEN]

HAWKS, EDWARD (1878–1955), priest, convert from Anglicanism. He was of Welsh origin, worked in Canadian mining camps as a lay missionary before studying for the Episcopal ministry at Nashotah House in Wisconsin, where he was ordained priest and became a faculty member. He also joined an Anglican religious community, the Companions of the Holy Savior. In 1907 he with most of his confreres left the Episcopal Church because it opened its pulpits to Protestant ministers. H. was received into the RC Church in 1908 and was ordained for the Archdiocese of Philadelphia. He served as a chaplain in World War I. In 1919 he established the parish of St. Joan of Arc in Philadelphia. Throughout his life as pastor there he was a contributor to the *Catholic Standard and Times,* the diocesan newspaper.

[T. C. O'BRIEN]

HAY, GEORGE (1729–1811), titular bp., vicar apostolic in Scotland. A Scot, son of a father exiled for his Stuart sympathies, H. interrupted his study of medicine, served with the army of Prince Charles as an apprentice surgeon, spent 15 months under arrest for his participation in Edinburgh and London, Returning to Edinburgh he became a convert to Catholicism in 1748. Barred from medical practice by the penal laws, he was persuaded by Bp. R. *Challoner, vicar apostolic of London, to study for the priesthood at the Scots College in Rome, and was ordained there in 1758. Returning to Scotland H. labored as a missionary. In 1769 he was named coadjutor to the vicar apostolic of the Lowlands and succeeded to the vicariate in 1778. Hay is chiefly responsible for preserving Catholicism in Scotland in a time of persecution. His devotional and theological writings achieved celebrity in the 18th and 19th centuries. A 5-volume edition of his *Works* was published in 1871, but individual books had by then run through many editions. In abbreviated form, his principal writings are listed as *The Pious Christian, The Sincere Christian,* and *The Devout Christian*. DNB 9:261–263.

[J. R. AHERNE]

HAYDN, FRANZ JOSEPH (1732–1809), Austrian composer of the Classic period. Son of a small farmer, H. early showed unusual musical ability and left his home at the age of five in order to receive musical instruction and later to become a choir boy for the Viennese cathedral. At 17, when his voice broke, H. was set adrift in Vienna. He taught for a while, then found employment, first as an accompanist and later as music director to Count Morzin. Then, at 27, he wrote his first symphony. H. married, not too happily, in 1760 and in 1761 was engaged as *Vize-Kappellmeister*. Later he was Kapellmeister at the court of the Esterházy at Eisenstadt, a post he held for thirty years. His activities were extremely diverse, yet the post offered an ideal place in which to develop and perfect his style in composition. Many of his greatest works were composed during this period. At the age of 58, H. left the court, following the death of Prince Nikolaus, and went to Vienna. Upon the invitation of J. P. Salomon of London, H. embarked in Dec. 1796 upon a two-year stay in the British Isles. Concerts, social activities, honors, and many great new compositions filled his days there. He returned to Vienna in 1792 and there Beethoven became his pupil. In 1794 he was again in England, staying for about 18 months; his successes there made him financially secure for life. Inspired by the great oratorios he had heard in England, he turned from symphonic to vocal music and produced his two immortal oratorios, *The Creation* (1797–98) and *The Seasons* (1799–1801), the latter almost completely exhausting his creative powers. He died a man much revered by the artistic world. The bulk of H.'s musical compositions was secular: 104 symphonies, 85 string quartets, 16 overtures, 52 piano sonatas, numerous concertos, stage works, songs, and other instrumental and vocal music. To the body of religious music H. contributed, in addition to the oratorios already mentioned, several Masses, two *Te Deum* and two *Salve Regina* settings and other shorter works. Though he composed religious music throughout his career, the time from his return to Esterházy was the most fruitful in number and quality of compositions. The *Te Deum* and the last Masses display the mastery of his final period. H.'s church music is characteristically cheerful, a quality which, many felt, made it inappropriate for liturgical use. BIBLIOGRAPHY: K. Geiringer, *Haydn, A Creative Life in Music* (rev. Ed., 1963).

[M. T. LEGGE]

HAYDN, (JOHANN) MICHAEL (1737–1806), Austrian organist and composer. Brother of Franz Joseph, H. was (1762) music director and *Konzertmeister* to the abp. of Salzburg at the time of the Mozarts. Although he wrote symphonies and other secular music, he is best known for his church music: Masses, Introits, Offertories, etc., and for his oratorios and cantatas. One of the few composers of his time who gave his energies first and foremost to writing for the Church, H. became the most respected church music composer in Austria.

[M. T. LEGGE]

HAYDON, BENJAMIN ROBERT (1786–1846), English painter. H. planned grand compositions in the manner of Raphael and Michelangelo—often beyond his capacity. Among his main works are *The Entry into Jerusalem* (1820, St. Mary's Seminary, Norwood, Ohio) and the *Raising of Lazarus* (1823, Tate, London). H. spoke eloquently for acquisition of the Elgin marbles. His *Lectures on Painitng and Design* were published in 1846.

[M. J. DALY]

HAYDT, JOHANN VALENTIN (John Valentine Haidt; 1700–80), colonial artist and Moravian preacher. Born in Europe, he arrived in Pennsylvania in 1754. H. painted religious subjects and portraits, combining his European training with a personal manner of composition and color. BIBLIOGRAPHY: W. L. Peters, "Religious Paintings of J. V. Haidt," *Moravian* 109.1 (1964) 10–15.

[F. S. GRUBAR]

HAYES, CARLTON JOSEPH HUNTLEY (1882–1964), historian, diplomat. A convert to Catholicism while a student at Columbia Univ., H. had a long career at that institution as teacher and writer in the field of history. He began his teaching career in 1907 and retired from Columbia in 1950; the only two interruptions were during World War I and during 1942–45 when he served as ambassador to Spain. His fresh approach to European history made his *Political and Social History of Modern Europe* (1916) the most widely used college text of its kind; second version completely revised, *Political and Cultural History of Modern Europe* (1932), was equally popular. His *Modern History* written in collaboration with Parker Moon was attacked for its Catholic orientation. As ambassador to Spain H. succeeded in minimizing Spanish collaboration with Germany. Out of the experience came *Wartime Mission in Spain, 1942–1945* (1946). H. was an astute historian of nationalism and studied the phenomenon in *Essays on Nationalism* (1926) and *The Historical Evolution of Modern Nationalism* (1931). He was a founder and co-chairman (1938–46) of the National Conference of Christians and Jews. BIBLIOGRAPHY: J. L. Morrison, NCE 6:957–958.

[J. R. AHERNE]

HAYES, PATRICK JOSEPH (1867–1938), abp. and cardinal. Of Irish immigrant parents, he was born in New York City, studied at Manhattan College there and at St. Joseph's Seminary, Troy, N.Y., and was ordained (1892). In 1894 he received the S.T.L. degree from The Catholic Univ. of America, Washington, D.C. He served successively as parish assistant (1894–1903); chancellor and president of Cathedral College (1903–14); was titular bp. of Tagaste (1914) and pastor of St. Stephen's in New York City (1915–17), first ordinary (1917) of the U.S. military ordinariate, and fifth abp. of New York (1919). In 1924 he was made a cardinal priest. His major achievement was the founding (1920) of the model organization, Catholic Charities, to unify and expand private welfare activities. BIBLIOGRAPHY: J. B. Kelly, *Cardinal Hayes* (1940).

[M. CARTHY]

HAYMARUS MONACHUS (fl. *c.*1171–1202), a native of Florence who became chancellor of Jerusalem (1171), abp. of Caesarea (1181–92), and patriarch of Jerusalem (1192–1202). As patriarch he resided in Acre because Jerusalem was under Muslim control. He was noted for his poem *De expugnatione civitatis Acconensis*. BIBLIOGRAPHY: V. L. Bullough, NCE 6:959.

HAYMO OF FAVERSHAM (d. 1244), English minister general of the Franciscans. H. entered the Franciscans at the Univ. of Paris (*c.*1226), where he was already an established professor. Against the unfortunate regime of *Elias of Cortona, he was a leader in the movement that resulted in Elias' being deposed by the General Chapter of 1239. H. was himself elected minister general (1240) after the death of Albert of Pisa, Elias' successor. H. strengthened Franciscan legislation, promoted studies in the order, and unified its liturgical practices. The Breviary revised and adapted by him for the friars from the Breviary of the Roman Curia spread throughout Europe and was the basis of the *Roman Breviary of St. *Pius V.

HAYMO OF HALBERSTADT (d. 853), monk of Fulda, bp., theologian. He studied at Tours *c.*802 with Rabanus Maurus under Alcuin, became bp. of Halberstadt in 840, and took part in the synods of Mainz in 847 and 852. Not all the writings credited to him in PL 116–118 are authentic; some are the work of Haymo of Hirschau, and some of other writers. He gives interesting witness to contemporary doctrine on the subject of the transubstantiation, purgatory, and the Last Judgment. His *De vanitate librorum, sive de amore coelestis patriae libri tres* is a not very original gathering of patristic thought; its chief interest lies in its evidence of 9th-cent. piety. The Benedictine martyrology lists H., but there is no evidence that his cult received official recognition. BIBLIOGRAPHY: Zimmermann 1:383; A. M. Zimmermann, BiblSanct 1:640; M. Mähler, DSAM 1:261–262.

[T. C. O'BRIEN]

HAYNALD, LUDWIG (1816–91), abp. of Kalocza, Hungary, from 1867, cardinal from 1879. He had been a seminary professor, then secretary to the abp. of Esztergom (1845–49) when named (1851) coadjutor bp. of Alba Julia in Transylvania, bp. in 1852. From 1861 he was a political exile in Rome, then became abp. of Kalocza. He was an anti-infallibilist at Vatican Council I, proclaimed that he would publicly vote against the definition, but submitted at the actual solemn session of definition.

[T. C. O'BRIEN]

HAZAEL, KING OF DAMASCUS (the last half of the 9th cent. B.C.). From a vision of Elisha that he would inflict much evil on Israel H. was provoked to murder his lord Ben-Hadad II, to usurp his kingdom (2 Kgs 8.7–15). He wrested Transjordan completely from Israel's king, Jehu (10.32,33) and even succeeded in a campaign against the Philistine coastland in exacting a heavy tribute from King Joash of Judah (12.18,19).

[J. F. FALLON]

HE WHO COMES, a messianic title used of Jesus in the NT. Its use by the Baptist underlines its eschatological emphasis (Mk 1.7; Mt 11.3; Jn 1.15,27. See also Mk 11.9; Lk 13.35; Jn 11.27; Acts 19.4; Heb 10.37). The background for the name is found in the OT hope that God will come in the last days (Ps 96.13; cf. Rev 1.4,8; 4.8) It soon lost currency as a name of Christ since the richer title Lord expressed more forcefully all its eschatological meaning.

[J. J. CUNNINGHAM]

HEAD OF BODY, a metaphor used in late Pauline Epistles to signify the superiority and authority that the resurrected Jesus Christ maintains over the community that God has called together under his lordship (Col 1.18; Eph 1.22,23). Christ's headship is unique and extends beyond the Church to hold sway over every superhuman power (Col 2.10,15). The analogical basis for the figure comes from Hebraic precedents of religious and political leadership (Jg 10.18; 11.8,9,11; 2 Chr 13.12; Hos 2.2), and not from the head's neurological centrality. Christ's headship, according to this pattern or model, is that of a mysterious, human and divine reality, governing from God's right hand his faithful and all creation through his Spirit.

[J. F. FALLON]

HEADCOVERING, on the basis of 1 Cor 11.2–16, the practice of men's being bareheaded, women's wearing hats or veils in church. Paul speaks of the practice as of long standing in a context on the hierarchic order in Christian life: the subjection of the man to Christ and of the woman to man. But the headcovering usage was a custom (see *ibid.*, 16), and its importance was as a symbol; the text need not be taken as prescriptive. The long-observed custom of women's wearing hats or veils in church is becoming obsolete in most places.

HEADLAM, ARTHUR CAYLEY (1862–1947), Anglican exegete and ecumenist. After professorships in theology at London and Oxford he served as bp. of Gloucester from 1923 until his retirement in 1945; he exercised a strong, moderating influence in the Church of England. The commentary on the Epistle to the Romans (1895) on which he collaborated with W. Sanday (1843–1920) was a work of merit. His ecumenical efforts included the 1920 Bampton Lectures, *Doctrine of the Church and Christian Reunion.* BIBLIOGRAPHY: life by R. Jasper (1960).

[T. EARLY]

HEALING, the cure of bodily ills by religious means, a teaching and practice that appear in various forms among Christian bodies. Beside Jesus' own ministry of healing, the NT attests to the charisma of healing given to the Apostles and to the early Church (Mt 10.1; Acts 3.1–16; 8.7; 9.32–42; 1 Cor 12.9, 28, 30) and to the connection between bodily ills and sin (Jn 9.2–3). The instruction in Jas 5.14–16 was followed in the early Church in both liturgical anointings and prayers for the sick. The RC Church came to regard the anointing of the sick as one of the seven sacraments (D 1696), and its meaning as a sacrament for the sick has been reaffirmed in recent times (Vat II SacLit 73). Besides this sacramental healing, private blessings and prayers for the sick, sometimes involving the use of relics, have continued in RC practice. Other Christian bodies, while not recognizing a sacrament for the sick, still have retained the use of prayers, blessings, laying on of hands, and anointing as profitable for bodily health. The continuance of charismatic healing has been recognized by the RC Church in the miracles performed by saints or attached to places of pilgrimage such as Lourdes as authentication of the Christian message. Through the centuries other groups, e.g., the Waldenses, Moravians, and the Irvingites, have claimed the presence of this charism among them. Particular importance has been attached to it in *revivalism, the *Holiness Churches, and as part of the *foursquare gospel message that healing is an essential part of the Christian message; that as Jesus saves from sin, so also he heals the body from the consequences of sin. In Pentecostalism charismatic, *divine healing is regarded as an essential part of the Christian life, connected with *baptism with the Holy Spirit. *Faith healing has come to mean not just the power of belief to obtain an answer to prayer for health but a specific teaching: mental or metaphysical healing, the power of spiritual mind over matter, which is considered to be evil, the source of sin, sickness, and death. In this sense faith healing is associated with New Thought, Spiritualism, and esp. Christian Science.

[T. C. O'BRIEN]

HEALTH, CARE OF. The moral obligation to take the measures necessary for the life of the body has several bases. The fifth commandment of the Decalogue rests on the truth that God alone is the author of life; a person thus cannot take or jeopardize his own life. The positive direction of the virtue of *temperance means the maintenance of physical well-being as a condition for a fully human existence (ThAq ST 2a2ae, 141.6); by implication that includes preventive and curative measures as needed. The virtue of *courage requires restraint from recklessness in the face of threats to life (*ibid.* 123.3 & 4). *Charity as it applies to self includes a regard for one's own body, the temple of the Holy Spirit as 1 Cor 6.19 puts it, and for physical life as part of God's loving gift and the medium in which the process of salvation and serving God is worked out (*ibid.* 25.5). Even the virtue of *penance as an imitation of Christ's suffering that calls for mortification of the flesh includes avoidance of damage to health. All of these virtues mean that care of health is the object of virtuous choice. How that choice is worked out in particular requires the judgment of prudence. Common guidance is given by the norm that no unnecessary risk of bodily injury or death is morally permissible. But the meaning of "unnecessary" varies with circumstances: sometimes a person's obligations as a parent, for example, requires work that is dangerous; to rescue another person from peril is not an unnecessary risk (see LIFE, RISKS TO). A further general norm is that ordinary means must be taken to preserve health and life; but the meaning of ordinary and extraordinary is broadly flexible. (see LIFE, PROLONGATION OF).

[T. C. O'BRIEN]

HEALY, GEORGE PETER ALEXANDER (1813–1894), American portrait and historical painter. He was encouraged by Thomas Sully. In 1834 he was a student of Gros in Paris. H. achieved an extraordinary reputation in Europe before settling in Chicago. He was probably America's most successful and prolific 19th-cent. portrait artist. His distinguished clientele included Longfellow, Emerson, Pope Pius IX, Cardinal John McClosky, Liszt, Bismarck and several U.S. presidents. Although the aesthetic merits of his more than 700 portraits are considered uneven, there is no denying their historical significance. A younger brother, Thomas Cantwell Healy (1820–1873), was also a portrait painter. BIBLIOGRAPHY: M. de Mare. *G.P.A. Healy, American Artist* (1954).

[F. S. GRUBAR]

HEALY, JAMES AUGUSTINE (1830–1900), bishop. Son of an Irish immigrant plantation owner of Georgia and of a Negro slave, H. was educated in New England,

Canada, and Paris, where he was ordained in 1854. Chancellor and vicar general of Boston as a young priest, he was named bp. of Portland, Maine, in 1875. As bp. he expanded churches and missions and took special pains to help the French Canadians in his diocese. BIBLIOGRAPHY: A. Foley, *Bishop Healy, Beloved Outcast* (1954).

[J. R. AHERNE]

HEALY, JOHN (1841–1918), abp. of Tuam, Ireland, historian. He was ordained in 1867, did parochial work, then taught at Maynooth from 1879 to 1884. There he was editor of *The Irish Ecclesiastical Record*. Named coadjutor bp. of Clonfort in 1884, he succeeded to that see in 1896; he built a new cathedral there as well as a seminary. In 1903 he was appointed abp. of Tuam. H. opposed home rule and efforts against landlords, both of which made him unpopular. His books are uneven but had considerable popularity: *Ireland's Ancient Saints and Scholars* (1890); *Life and Writings of St. Patrick* (1905), and his most scholarly work, *Centenary History of Maynooth College* (1895). H.'s work in education was important, and he contributed much to the strengthening of The National Univ. of Ireland. He was the first president (1889–1914) of the Catholic Truth Society of Ireland. BIBLIOGRAPHY: P. Joyce, *John Healy, Archbishop of Tuam* (1931).

[J. R. AHERNE]

HEALY, PATRICK JOSEPH (1871–1937), church historian, educator. Of Irish birth, H. was ordained for New York in 1897. Most of his career was in the School of Theology at The Catholic Univ. of America, where he taught church history and served a number of terms as dean of the faculty of theology. He edited the *Catholic University Bulletin* when it was a scholarly journal. A frequent contributor to historical journals, he was author of *The Valerian Persecution: a Study of the Relations between Church and State in the Third Century* (1905.) H. was a contributor of articles for the *Catholic Encyclopedia* (1907) and was Catholic editor of *Webster's New International Dictionary* (2d edition). BIBLIOGRAPHY: A. Ziegler, NCE 6:964–965.

[J. R. AHERNE]

HEART (IN THE BIBLE), the center of man's inner life and the source of his spiritual activities. The English word translates the Hebrew *lēb* or *lēbāb* and the Greek *kardía*. Only rarely in the Bible does "heart" refer to the physical organ in a literal sense, whereas its use in a figurative sense is frequent and varied. Contrary to the usual English connotation of the heart as the source only of man's affective life, biblical usage emphasizes the unity of spiritual functions, both intellectual and volitional, proceeding from the inner man. This OT usage of the heart as the seat of inner life in contrast to external appearance may be seen from 1 Sam 16.7, "Man looks upon the outward appearance, but the Lord looks upon the heart." Similarly, to exchange a heart of stone for a heart of flesh (Ezek 18.31; 36.26) is to undergo an interior regeneration or transformation of character. The OT also uses heart to refer to the source of rational life: the common idiom, to say "in the heart," means simply to think; wisdom and knowledge reside in the heart (Ezek 28.3; Dt 8.5); Solomon's breadth of heart (1 Kg 5.12) is prudent judgment, not magnanimity; and someone lacking in heart is not cowardly but unintelligent (Pr 6.32). The heart is also the basis for man's emotional life: sorrow proceeds from the heart (Dt 15.10), as does joy (Ps 45.1), fear (Gen 42.28), and every other passion. Planning and volition come from the heart (Jer 23.20), which is also the source of religious and moral conduct (1 Sam 12.20).

The LXX uses *kardîa* to translate the Hebrew, and it is this word which is also used in the New Testament. However, the NT also uses the word *nous* to denote a purely intellectual function. Thus, in the NT as in the OT, feelings and emotions dwell in the heart (Acts 2.26; Jn 16.22); the heart is the source of understanding and of reflection (Mk 7.21; Ap 18.7); and is used even to stand for the person himself (Col 2.2; 1 Jn 3.19). If there is any variation in usage between the OT and the NT, it is in the NT emphasis on the heart as the receptive center of the divine operations which transform a man: the Spirit is sent into the heart (Gal 4.6), and through the Spirit love is poured into the heart (Rom 5.5). Finally, it is in the heart that Christ dwells (Eph 3.17). BIBLIOGRAPHY: F. Baumgärtel and J. Behm, Kittel TD 3:605–614; EDB 947–948. *SPIRIT; *FLESH; *SOUL.

[T. M. MCFADDEN]

HEART OF JESUS, see SACRED HEART.

HEART OF JESUS, INSTITUTE OF THE, a secular institute of diocesan priests, founded to develop fully the grace of the priesthood and dedication to priestly work in its members. The society was established in Paris (1791), by Pierre Joseph Picot de Clorivière, SJ; it was revived in 1918 by Rev. Daniel Fontaine, then became a secular institute in 1951. The institute received papal approbation (1952) affirming this way of life, which includes the taking of the three vows, observing a flexible rule of life, receiving spiritual direction regularly, observing an hour of meditation daily, and sharing fraternal community. The priest members, however, retain their assignments and are subject to the authority of their bishops. Only in spiritual matters are they subject to their superiors, who do not govern their apostolates. The society was introduced in the U.S. in 1957 by Rev. Yves M. Guenver. Headquarters is located in Putnam, Connecticut; in 1975 the institute had 1,900 members worldwide.

[M. B. MONAGHAN]

HEART OF MARY, see IMMACULATE HEART OF MARY.

HEART OF MARY, DAUGHTERS OF THE (DHM), a religious congregation founded in (1790) in France for the preservation of the religious life against the threat of the French Revolution, Pierre Joseph Picot de Clorivière, SJ; together with Marie Adelaide de Cicé, placed the congregation under the Rule of St. Ignatius of Loyola and required the taking of public vows but no habit or cloister. Pope Pius VII (1801) granted initial approval to the institute; Pope Leo XIII gave final approval in 1890.

The scope of the apostolate varies with the needs of the times. Teaching, retreat work, catechetics, social service, home and foreign missions comprise the many endeavors of the congregation. The U.S. foundation was made in Cleveland, Ohio, in 1851. The American members are sometimes referred to as Nardins. The American province, headquarters in New York City, numbered 258 members (1976). Worldwide membership totaled 3,482 (1975); the general motherhouse is in Paris.

[M. B. MONAGHAN]

HEATH, NICHOLAS (*c.* 1501–78), last Catholic abp. of York. Well-educated and talented, he gained court favor by his witty exposure of Elizabeth Barton, nun of Kent. During Henry VIII's reign he received a series of royal and ecclesiastical appointments including the Sees of Rochester (1539) and Worcester (1543). During the period of Edward VI, he broke with the Reformers and was imprisoned (1550) for opposing their policies. With the accession of Mary, his episcopal consecration was confirmed by Rome and he became abp. of York and then lord chancellor (1556). Under Elizabeth he refused the oath of supremacy, was deprived of his see, and was imprisoned until 1571.

[V. SAMPSON]

HEATHEN, one who is not a believer in the God of the Bible, or one who is neither Jewish, Christian, nor (in some usages) Muslim. The term probably derives from "heath" and is related to the fact that the first Christians lived in the towns, while the country people continued to worship pagan deities. The word came to have the derogatory implication of not living by Christian moral standards, and sometimes meant more broadly one uncultured or unenlightened.

[T. EARLY]

HEAVEN, the traditional term for the state and "place" of happiness for those who are finally and fully saved. In the OT, "heaven" is the figure of speech used to describe the highest segment of the tripartite universe which was understood to be the dwelling place of God. In the NT the same cosmological imagery is employed with God's abode conceived as a place high above the earth from which Christ came, to which he raised his eyes in prayer, and toward which he is described as ascending. Heaven is the ultimate destiny of those who share in the death and Resurrection of the Lord who has returned to the Father in heaven (Jn 6.62; 13.1), who is the first fruits of the Resurrection (1 Cor 15.20), the first-born among many brethren (Rom 8.29), the one who has gone to prepare a place for his followers (Jn 14.3). From this evidence of the NT, it follows that heaven is essentially Christological in structure. It is based upon Christ's victory over death and his glory which are recognized as necessary so that creatures may enter into the eternal life of God. Those who share in the death and Resurrection of Christ are to be gathered into his body in order to be united with him in his glorified humanity and with one another. Theology has expressed the nature of this definitive sharing in the eternal life of God as primarily an experience of the heart and mind of man. The beatifying union with God is described as a personal love relationship between God and the creature as well as being the *beatific vision of God. According to Catholic tradition this union with God may be experienced immediately after death or after whatever purification is necessary in *purgatory (D 1000–02). In this view these holy souls await reunion with their bodies at the resurrection of the flesh after which the soul and the glorified body together will enjoy the happiness of heaven eternally (see BODY, GLORIFIED). The concept of heaven as a place grows out of the understanding that glorified bodies, since they are bodies, imply space. However, tradition reflects the reserve of Sacred Scripture about spatiality in heaven and gives greater stress to it as a state or condition of salvation than as a place. At the same time it affirms the actuality of the glorified body of Christ in the mystery of the Ascension and, in Catholic tradition, that of Mary in her Assumption. While heaven is the finality and fullness of salvation, tradition (D 693, 1305) has spoken of the unequal glory of those who share it. The person who is finally saved is conditioned by the life he has lived, and it is in conformity with that history that God fully saves him, i.e., God fills him and loves him fully in a measure preconditioned by the merit of his historical experience. Here, no less than in the case of hell, the stress is on the continuity between life after death and life on earth. Finally, heaven, though it is rightly described as the consummation of salvation for those who presently share it, is not yet complete. It awaits that consummation of all things to be accomplished in the parousia and the resurrection of the dead. BIBLIOGRAPHY: J. Plastaras and B. Forshaw, NCE 6:968–975; A. Winklhofer, *Coming of His Kingdom* (tr. A. V. Littledale, 1963); R. Guardini, *Last Things* (tr. C. E. Forsyth and G. B. Branham, 1954).

[J. CORDOUE]

HEBDOMADARY, HEBDOMADARIAN (Gr. *hebdomas,* week), in a monastery, cathedral chapter, or other place where the choral chanting of the Liturgy of the Hours is observed, the person charged all during a week with beginning the canonical hours, chanting the prayer of the day, and, where appropriate, being principal celebrant of the day's Mass.

[T. C. O'BRIEN]

HÉBERT, JACQUES (1757–1794), journalist, French revolutionary. Among exponents of violence and scurrilous attack in the era of the French Revolution, none outdid Hébert. Known as Père Duchesne from the name of his journal, he was a crude writer whose chief targets were the Catholic clergy, people and institutions. His writings were popular and his mob influence great. Merciless in urging the guillotine for others, he was finally condemned to death himself as an insurgent opposing Robespierre.

[J. R. AHERNE]

HÉBERT, JEAN FRANÇOIS (1739–97), bp. missionary. Born in Quebec, H. was ordained in 1766. He volunteered for the Huron missions near Detroit in 1781. Named coadjutor bp. of Quebec in 1785, he succeeded to that diocese in 1788. His opposition to the plan for an interdenominational university doomed the project, though H. showed great interest in education generally. He was a wise and able administrator of his diocese.

[J. R. AHERNE]

HÉBERT, MARCEL (1851–1916), French priest-philosopher, Modernist. He came gradually to the position that God is simply a symbol or category for expressing the objective Absolute and Ideal, not, so to speak, a concrete reality. He argued his thesis in *Souvenirs d'Assise* (1899), was suspended from the ministry for refusing to retract. From 1903, living as a layman in Brussels, he devoted himself to efforts in behalf of the workers and to the promotion of a humanistic religion of conscience.

[T. C. O'BRIEN]

HEBREW BIBLE, the 24 books accepted by modern Jews as Sacred Scripture (some reckon the books as numbering 22, like the letters of the Hebrew alphabet, by counting Jg-Ru and Jer-Lam as single books). The modern Hebrew acronym TNK (*T^e^nāk*) is based on the conventional division into the Law (*Tôrâ*), the Prophets (*N^e^bî'îm)*, and the Writings (*K^e^tûbîm*). The acceptance of them as *the books* (Gr. *biblia*) in an absolute sense was a gradual process. The Law, the five books of the Pentateuch, was the first to receive this status. Much later the same sacredness was attributed to the Prophets, divided in to the Former Prophets (Jos, Jg, 1–2 Sam, 1–2 Kg), and the Later Prophets (Major—Is, Jer, Ezek, and the twelve, the minor prophets, taken as a single book, Hos, Jl, Am, Ob, Mic, Jon, Nah, Hab, Zeph, Hag, Zech, Mal). The Writings, comprising Ps, Pr, Job, the five Megilloth or scrolls—S of S, Ru, Lam, Ec, Est—Dan, Ezra-Neh, and 1–2 Chr were almost cerainly the last to receive acceptance.

There is no conclusive record of the fixing of this canon of the Hebrew Bible (see BIBLICAL CANON). In Sir ch. 44-50 (written *c.* 180 B.C.), all the books listed above are included, except Dan, Ezra, and Est, a fact that suggests that these were not recognized as fully "sacred" at this time. The implication that the canon was recognized as including Law, Prophets, and Writings may be present in Lk 24.44; the same division is found in *Josephus, with a list of 22 books, and *Philo Judaeus. It was long held that a rabbinical synod held at *Jamnia *c.* 100 A.D. representing Palestinian Jews fixed the actual Hebrew canon, excluding the deuterocanonical books (Tob, 1–2 Macc, Jdt, Sir, Wis, Bar, parts of Dan and Est) that were in the LXX translation and allegedly accepted in an Alexandrian canon. The existence of an Alexandrian canon differing from the Palestinian, and the occurrence of any synod at Jamnia are now seriously questioned. The fixing of the Hebrew canon is dated from the late 2d or early 3d cent.; the *Qumram MSS have not clarified the issue.

The present Hebrew Bible is written in the "square" or "Assyrian" script initially used for inscriptions and ornamental writing, which replaced the earlier "Samaritan" script about the 4th-3rd cent. B.C. The best critical edition of the Hebrew Bible is the *Biblia Hebraica* edited by R. *Kittel and P. *Kahle, which, from the 3d ed. onwards, has been based on the *ben Asher Masoretic text as preserved in the Leningrad Codex B 19a [L] of 1008 A.D. This antedates all other Hebrew MSS by some 600 years. More recent editions record variants from the Qumram biblical MSS, which again antedate L by at least 900 years. BIBLIOGRAPHY: P. Kahle, *Cairo Genizah* (2d ed., 1959); *idem,* "Vorwort," *Biblia Hebraica Kittel* (3d ed., 1937) and all subsequent eds.; B. J. Roberts, *Old Testament Text and Versions* (1951).

[D. J. BOURKE]

HEBREW PSALTER, see PSALTERIUM JUXTA HEBRAEOS.

HEBREW STUDIES (IN THE CHRISTIAN CHURCH), the reverent and scholarly study of the Hebrew language and literature, esp. of the Hebrew texts of the Jewish canon of Scripture. It is striking how quickly and how thoroughly the Christian Church lost contact with the Hebrew language and with the tradition of Jewish scholarship. The fact attests to the tragedy of the early Church's traumatic break with Judaism. The great Alexandrine scholar, Origen, laboring in Caesarea (230–240 A.D.), produced the Hexapla to bridge the gap somewhat. It survived until the 6th cent. and was written in six columns, two of which contained the Hebrew text of Scripture: one in Hebrew script, the other transliterated into Greek. The fifth column was a version of the Septuagint with emendations based on the Hebrew text. The Hexapla was used as a guide by those who were responsible for ancient versions of the Bible, esp. the Armenian version. More important even than the Hexapla for the Western Church was the immensely influential Vulgate of St. Jerome, a Latin translation from the Hebrew, commissioned by Pope Damasus *c.* 382 and completed in 405. The opposition it faced attests to the fear of Hebrew and of Judaism at that time and the almost universal attitude that embraced the Septuagint as the Bible par excellence. The Septuagint, after all, had been the version used even by the authors of the New Testament. It was not until the humanists of the Renaissance had convinced the powerful of the need to go back to the sources that it became at all safe to pursue the serious study of Hebrew. The Christian scholar ran the risk of being considered a convert to Judaism; the Jewish scholar who consented to teach a Christian ran the deadlier risk of being accused of perverting the faith of a Christian. Johann *Reuchlin (1455–1522), German layman, doctor of law, and professor of Greek and Hebrew, had to pay learned Jews for instruction. His *De rudimentis Hebraicis* (1506) consisted of a Latin-Hebrew dictionary and a grammar adequate to provide the basis for serious Hebrew studies in Christian Europe. He had to face condemnation in 1517, the same year as Luther, by the great humanist pope, Leo X. Another Catholic scholar, Sebastian Münster of Basel (1488–1552), produced the first Aramaic grammar written by a Christian (1527). He also made available the works of Elias Levita (*c.*1468–1549), the greatest Jewish grammarian of the age. The Protestant scholar, Paul Fagius of Strassburg (1504–1549), one-time Regius professor of Hebrew at Cambridge, translated into Latin the Pirke Avoth and the Targum of Onkelos. The Catholic spirit of reaction became dominant at the Council of Trent (1546), which gave the Vulgate "authentic" status, probably because scholastic theology was felt to be threatened by any threat to the integrity of the Latin Bible. Since then the main thrust of papal initiative in biblical studies has been to restore the Vulgate in a corrected edition. First came the Sixtine edition (Sixtus V, 1590), then the Clementine (Clement VIII 1592); and in renewed reaction to modern studies, Pius X in 1907 commissioned the Benedictine Order to prepare a comprehensive new edition of the Vulgate. By 1969 only the Prophets awaited publication. In 1970 a papal commission under Cardinal Augustinus Bea was charged with still a new revision of the Vulgate taking the Benedictine edition as its working base. Meanwhile in Hebrew studies a new revolution occurred when scholars broke with the rabbinic tradition that treated Hebrew as the incomparable *lingua sacra.* Albert Schultens of Leiden (1686–1750) in his *Institutiones ad fundamenta linquae Hebraicae* (1737) was the first to treat Hebrew as a branch of the Semitic family of languages. Archeological findings of the last century have brought much new light to show that Hebrew is indeed one of the NW Semitic language group, which comprises Aramaic and Canaanite; that Hebrew is a dialect of Canaanite, along with Ugaritic, Hamathite, Phoenician (which has several dialects of its own), and Moabite. Now it is more precise to speak of Semitic studies, and to acknowledge the immense debt of Israel to the Canaanites, in language, culture, and religion; not only to Canaan, but to many other peoples and languages of the ancient Near East.

[E. J. DILLON]

HEBREWS, GOSPEL ACCORDING TO THE, see APOCRYPHA (NT), 21.

HEBREWS, LETTER TO THE, one of the NT Epistles, accepted as part of the canon from the 2d century. Early tradition included it among the Pauline Epistles, but there were also early doubts about this, e.g., by Origen and Tertullian. Though it was traditionally included among the Epistles of Paul, serious doubts have existed from earliest times as to whether this Epistle was in fact composed by him. Most modern critics agree that the difference in language, style, interpretative method, general approach, and subject matter are so great that it must certainly be the work of another author, familiar indeed with Pauline ideas, yet possessing an independent genius of his own. The style of the Epistle is polished and cultivated, and the method of interpretation shows the influence of rabbinical exegesis and perhaps more particularly of the typological approach of *Philo Judaeus and his school. The Epistle must have been written not earlier than 60 and not later than 90 A.D. Most modern scholars suggest a date between 80 and 90, though some have used the absence of any reference to the destruction of Jerusalem in A.D. 70 as an *argumentum ex silentio* to suggest that it must have been written before that date. The reference to Italy in 13.24 suggests that this must have been its place of origin. The title, found from the 2d cent., was possibly derived from the many references to OT practice; but it is not at all certain that the destinaries were Jewish and not gentile Christians.

The Epistle is addressed to a group that has suffered persecution and that is in danger of becoming disillusioned in its faith. Its basic message is fidelity to Christ, the eternal and preexistent Son of God. As High Priest tried and proved perfect by his obedience in suffering and the last and supreme messenger of God's word, Christ has now ushered in the new dispensation of grace as the final consummation of the Law and the Prophets, achieving what they could never achieve, a sacrifice that *effects* the Redemption it signifies, and a truth that comes directly and immediately from God. By the final, supreme, and unrepeatable sacrifice of himself, this High Priest has made void all the transient and figurative sacrifices of the Old Law, and brought into being the new and heavenly covenant, effective and definitive.

Unlike the Prophets he is not merely the spokesman of God but his own Son, "the effulgence of his glory" (1.3), higher than the angels both by his nature and in the glory that he has achieved in his Resurrection (1.5–2.9), yet nevertheless for a time making himself lower than the angels in order wholly to identify himself with our humanity (2.10–18). Moreover, as Son rather than steward in God's house, he is higher than Moses (3.1–6), higher too than Aaron and the Levitical priesthood, since his priesthood, like that of Melchizedek, is not based on human descent and is eternal (4:14–6:20). Finally, he is higher than Abraham who paid tithes to Melchizedek (7.1–12) at a time when his descendant Levi was yet unconceived (7.9–10). Hence the fact of Christ's identity with God on the one hand, and with our suffering humanity on the other, makes him the perfect mediator between God and man and the inaugurator of the new and eternal covenant foretold by Jeremiah (Jer 31.31–4), which supersedes the old and, unlike it, is effective to redeem, to save, and to make perfect (12.18–29). In his death and Resurrection he has, as High Priest, celebrated the final and supreme Day of Atonement, and carried once and for all the blood of his own sacrifice into the holy of holies which is the kingdom of heaven on behalf of all mankind.

In view of these facts the readers are exhorted to steadfast perseverance in their faith (12.14–17) etc.), despite all persecutions and sufferings. They must strive to deepen and intensify their faith, watching for the coming of Christ. They are reminded of a long and glorious series of OT figures who have practiced these virtues to a heroic degree (11.1–12:13). They are a people on pilgrimage, even now advancing toward the heavenly city (13.8–14), and in order to arrive there safely they must practice love, purity, gratitude to God, and detachment from this world (13.1–7). BIBLIOGRAPHY: F. F. Bruce, *Epistle to the Hebrews. (New International Commentary on the New Testament,* 1964); A. B. Davidson, *Epistle to the Hebrews* (1950); J. Héring, *L'Épître aux Hébreux* (*Commentaire du Nouveau Testament,* 12, 1954); O. Michel, *Der Brief an die Hebräer* (11th ed., 1960); J. H. Davies, *Letter to the Hebrews* (*Cambridge New English Bible,* 1967).

[D. J. BOURKE]

HEBRON, biblical city near Mamre; the modern city, in Arabic El Kahlil, probably on the site of ancient Hebron, is 18 miles SSW of Jerusalem. Abraham was camped in the area, then known as Kirjath-arba, when his wife Sarah died, and he bought the field of Machpelah with its cave for a burying place (Gen ch. 23). It was a Canaanite royal city, built, according to Num 13.22, 7 years before Zoan in Egypt. During the 14th cent. B.C. the area was ruled for a time by Shuwardata, a prince mentioned in the *Amarna Letters. At the Conquest Joshua destroyed Hebron (Jos 10.36–37), later giving it to Caleb (Jos 14.13). It was made a city of refuge (Jos 20.7) and was given to the Levites (Jos 21.10–13). David was anointed king of Judah at Hebron and reigned there more than 7 years (2 Sam 2–3), while Ish-bosheth, Saul's son, ruled the rest of Israel from Mahanaim. Six of David's sons were born at Hebron. Two of Ish-bosheth's own men cut off his head and brought it to David at Hebron, but David had them killed (2 Sam 4). David then became ruler of the whole nation and moved to Jerusalem. Absalom used Hebron, where he was born, as the headquarters for his revolt (2 Sam 15.7–10). Rehoboam strengthened Hebron, along with several other cities (2 Chr 11.5–12). The Idumeans (Edomites) occupied Hebron from the Exile until 164 B.C., when Judas Maccabeus destroyed it. It was rebuilt, however, and elaborate buildings were constructed over the Cave of Machpelah during the time of Herod the Great. It is not mentioned in the NT. It was again destroyed by the Romans in 68 A.D.

[T. EARLY]

HECKER, ISAAC THOMAS (1819–88), founder of the *Paulists. A friend of O. *Brownson and the Transcendentalists of *Brook Farm, H. was a convert (1844) to Catholicism. He joined the *Redemptorists (1845), studied in England, and was ordained there (1849). Back in the U.S. (1851), he undertook missions to Catholics and interested himself in the conversion of non-Catholics, publishing two books: *Questions of the Soul* (1855) and *Aspirations of Nature* (1857). When Pius IX released him and several companions from their vows as Redemptorists (1858), H. founded the Paulists, the first American community to work for the conversion of non-Catholics in America. A successful preacher and lecturer, he also established (1865) the monthly *Catholic World,* organized (1866) the Catholic Publication Society for the national distribution of inexpensive literature, and began the *Young Catholic* as an illustrated monthly for youth. His last publication was *The Church and the Age* (1887). BIBLIOGRAPHY: V. F. Holden, *Yankee Paul: Isaac Thomas Hecker* (1958) bibliog., 415–422.

[M. CARTHY]

HEDDA (HEDDI), ST. (d. 705), bp. of Wessex. Consecrated by Abp. Theodore, he moved both the see and St. Birinus' relics from Dorchester to Winchester. Advisor to King Ine, H. was noted for his sanctity. After his death, Wessex was divided into two dioceses, Winchester and Sherborne. BIBLIOGRAPHY: G. M. Fusconi, BiblSanct 4:903–905; Butler 3:34–35.

[W. A. CHANEY]

HEDGE PRIEST, in Ireland a priest who had studied at Douai and Salamanca and taught in secret schools during the days of the Penal Code which forbade Catholic schools.

[F. H. BRIGHAM]

HEDGE SCHOOL, in Ireland a secret school set up in the 1730s to circumvent the Penal Code, which forbade Catholic schools, refused Catholics admission to Trinity College, Dublin, and did not permit any person to teach members of a Catholic family privately. The hedge schools emphasized elementary subjects in the beginning, but eventually priests educated at Douai and Salamanca taught the humanities.

[F. H. BRIGHAM]

HEDLEY, JOHN CUTHBERT (1837–1915), bp., author. An English Benedictine of Ampleforth Abbey, H. was ordained in 1862. He taught philosophy and directed candidates for the order at Belmont Abbey, Hereford, for 11 years, when he was named auxiliary bp. of Newport and Menevia, Wales. In 1880 H. succeeded to the see. Spokesman for the English bps, H. is best known for his writings on spirituality, distinguished for their felicitous style. Best known are *Lex Levitarum* (1906), *A Retreat* (1894), and *The Holy Eucharist* (1906). From 1879 to 1894 he was editor of the *Dublin Review.* BIBLIOGRAPHY: J. Wilson, *Life of Bishop Hedley* (1930).

[J. R. AHERNE]

HEDONISM, (Gr. *hēdonē,* meaning pleasure), the ethical doctrine that *pleasure is the sovereign good and the main object of human action. It appears with *Aristippus of

Cyrene hence his followers were called Cyrenaics—they were too loosely knit and eclectic to form a school—who, influenced by the empiricism of *Protagoras of Abdera, fastened on the manifest pleasures of the moment, and held that the art of living lay in cultivating them in abundance; he is misrepresented as inculcating the coarser forms of self-gratification and voluptuousness. However, *Epicurus of Samos (b. 342 B.C.) hence Epicureans, is more elevated; he emphasized the delights of wisdom and friendship, comprehended all pleasure in serenity of soul, *ataraksia,* which he described almost negatively, as absence of disorder, and taught a way of life as disciplined and austere as that according to the Cynics or Stoics. Hedonism reappeared in ethical thought with the English Utilitarians of the Enlightenment; a representative exponent was Jeremy Bentham (1748–1832), who was certainly no softener of social morals; a representative critic was Bp. J. Butler (1692–1752), still worth study. No serious hedonist has advocated debauchery or the indiscriminate pursuit of pleasure, yet relatively few moralists have been hedonists. There is little fault to be found with their lessons of moral practice; indeed St. Thomas Aquinas regards pleasure charged with intelligence as a fair index of the rightness of an action. The failure lies elsewhere, in psychology and epistemology, by confusing pleasure-in-idea with idea-of-pleasure, and by not discerning in *happiness the distinction between the essential form and essential consequence, that is, a good object, present and possessed in cognition, and the delight-response of appetition. BIBLIOGRAPHY: H. Sidgwick, *Methods of Ethics* (repr. 1962); R. B. Brandt, EncPhil 3:432–435.

[T. GILBY]

HEDWIG, ST. (*c.* 1174–1243), duchess of Silesia, widow. H. married Henry I, duke of Silesia, and proved an able consort. Her personal piety and prudence are said to have exerted great influence on the factious nobility. H. is credited with the introduction of Franciscans and Dominicans into Silesia. She also instituted a house for religious women, the Cistercians at Trzebnica, to which she retired upon her husband's death. Regarded as a saint in her lifetime, she was canonized by Clement IV in 1267. BIBLIOGRAPHY: Butler 4:124–125; E. Markowa, *Glowing Lily* (1946); P. Naruszewicz, BiblSanct 4:933–934.

[B. F. SCHERER]

HEENAN, JOHN CARMEL (1905–75), abp. of Westminster, church leader in England. Ordained in 1930 and having earned two doctorates in Rome, H. made an extended visit to the Soviet Union in the turbulent 1930s, posing as an engineering student, an experience that gave him a firsthand picture of communism at work. During World War II he was pastor of a parish in London's East End. Through the war years he was a regular speaker on BBC programs directed to America and Europe. It was in these years also that he produced his best-known book *Priest and Penitent*. Commissioned by the English hierarchy to revive the dormant Catholic Missionary Society, which aimed at the conversion of England, he undertook a long visit to America to study the apostolate there. Four years of intense activity in every part of England and a revitalization of the society followed. Named bp. of Leeds (1951), he showed himself an able administrator and a bridge between Catholics and non-Catholics. In 1956 H. was made abp. of Liverpool where his skill and interest in civic affairs continued to show. Here he built a new cathedral of ultramodern design which he selected from a competition of 300 entries. He was appointed abp. of Westminister by Pope Paul VI in 1963 and named cardinal in 1965. He played a prominent role at the Vatican Council II, speaking in defense of religious freedom and for a decree on the Jews (see Vat II NonChrRel 4). A strong ecumenist, he became vice president of the Secretariat for Christian Unity under Card. Bea. In England, H. was Catholic spokesman for the new spirit of friendliness with the C of E and a close friend of Abp. Michael Ramsey of Canterbury. The publication in England of the encyclical *Humane vitae* caused a considerable uproar among Catholics, and H. showed his remarkable skill in preserving unity without repudiating the document. A man who spoke frequently on television and the lecture platform, he had his share of controversy but won most Englishmen's admiration for his courtesy and understanding. In the difficult postconciliar era he was a firm administrator but a flexible one, though regarded by some as conservative. His chief aim and achievement was to preserve the unity of the Catholic Church in England.

[J. R. AHERNE]

HEERBRAND, JAKOB (1521–1600), German Lutheran theologian and professor. After study at Wittenberg (1538–43) H. served at Tübingen until his opposition to the Augsburg Interim (1548) resulted in his removal. He was one of the Württemburg theologians sent to the Council of Trent (1552). Entrusted by Archduke Christoph with many commissions, he helped introduce the Reformation into Baden (1556) while pastor at Pforzheim. In 1557 he began 42 years of teaching at Tübingen, where he was second in influence and honors only to J. *Andreä. H. was outstanding as a preacher and as an exegete of the Pentateuch. His *Compendium theologiae* (1573), which in its 2d edition followed the *Formula of Concord, enjoyed wide distribution.

[M. J. SUELZER]

HEERINCKX, JAMES (1877–1937), Flemish theologian. A Franciscan from 1894 and ordained in 1901, he was a professor of theology in Belgium until 1921, then in Rome at the Pontifical Anthenaeum Antonianum for the rest of his career. A specialist in ascetical and mystical theology, he published *Introductio in theologiam asceticam et mysticam* on Franciscan spirituality (1931), and other works in the field.

[T. C. O'BRIEN]

HEESWIJK, MONASTERY OF, Premonstratensian house near 's Hertogenbosch, Netherlands. Founded in the early 12th cent. at Bern near Heusden, it was destroyed in 1579, leaving the monks without a permanent cloister for some 300 years until the monastery was reestablished in 1857 at Heeswijk. St. Norbert Abbey in De Pere, Wis., was founded by Heeswijk; it also directs a missionary diocese in India (Jubbulpore).

[M. A. MCFADDEN]

HEFELE, CARL JOSEPH VON (1809–93), church historian, patrologist, bp. of Rottenberg, Germany from 1869. He succeeded J. A. *Möhler at the Univ. of Tübingen in 1836, and was rector there from 1852 to 1853. He was a consultor (1868) in the preparations for Vatican Council I. As a bp. at the Council itself, he strongly opposed both the doctrine of papal infallibility and the opportuneness of its definition, and was one of those bps. who left Rome before solemn promulgation. He did finally publish the decree of the Council in his diocese on April 10, 1871, the last German bp. to do so. H.'s great work of scholarship was his monumental *Conciliengeschichte* (1855–74); he brought the work up to 1449 (v. 1–7), and J. *Hergenröther, up to the Council of Trent (v. 8–9). The work remains a solid source for the study of church history, as it treats conciliar and synodal documents in their historical setting. It is used mainly in the revised and updated French edition of H. *Leclercq (11 v., 1907–52). H. also published an edition of the Apostolic Fathers in 1839. BIBLIOGRAPHY: S. Furlani, EncCatt 6:1385–86.

[T. C. O'BRIEN]

HEGEL, GEORG WILHELM FRIEDRICH (1770–1831), German philosopher. Educated at Tübingen, H. began his career as a tutor, first in Basel, then at Frankfurt (1793–1800), a period called his mystic-pantheistic phase. In 1801 he became a lecturer at Jena, where with F. *Schelling he edited the *Critical Journal of Philosophy*. After a period in Nuremberg H. obtained a professorship at Heidelberg (1816), then at Berlin (1818), where he enjoyed tremendous popularity and exerted great influence. During his younger years H. was primarily interested in theological questions and wrote a number of theological tracts important to his subsequent intellectual development. These early writings have been collected and edited by H. Nohl in *Hegels Theologische Jugendschriften* (1907). H.'s philosophy of religion follows the dictates of his absolute idealism. In its highest expression, religion is the ultimate determination of the Absolute Idea itself; hence philosophy can embrace and surpass religion. Proofs for the existence of God are possible and religion can be taught but it differs from philosophy. Philosophy grasps the Absolute notionally; religion, only through representations. The dialectical stages of historical development enter into the constitution and evaluation of religion, i.e., mankind progresses from God as the substance of nature, through God as a divine subject, to the final and absolute religion, Christianity. H.'s is a pantheistic religion of pure intellectuality, sublimated into philosophy. BIBLIOGRAPHY: G. W. F. Hegel, *On Christianity: Early Theological Writings* (tr. T. M. Knox, 1961); G. P. Adams, *Mystical Element in Hegel's Early Theological Writings* (1910); K. Lowith, *From Hegel to Nietzsche* (1964); E. L. Fackenheim, *Religious Element in Hegel's Thought* (1968).

[J. P. REID]

HEGELIANISM, the dialectical method of G. *Hegel and his notion of Absolute Spirit as these were incorporated into a wide range of disciplines, including theology, philosophy, historiography, law, aesthetics, the scientific study of nature, economics, and religion. A group of personal disciples surrounding Hegel in the early 19th cent., particularly during the 1820s while he was associated with the Univ. of Berlin, formed a movement, "The Society for Scientific Criticism," which was explicitly Hegelian and whose members worked in the fields of systematic philosophy (G. Gabler, L. von Henning, J. Schaller), theology (K. Daub, P. K. Marheineke), jurisprudence (E. Gans), ethics (K. Michelet), aesthetics (H. Rotscher, H. Hotho, K. Rosenkranz, H. Hinrichs), and physiology (K. H. Schultz). This group edited and published Hegel's *Collected Works* (1832 ff.). Around the time of Hegel's death (1831), tension between Hegelian theologians erupted in a divisive debate over theism. L. Feuerbach, in his *Thoughts Regarding Death and Immortality* (1830), and F. Richter, in both *The Doctrine of Last Things* (2 v., 1833–44) and *The New Doctrine of Immortality* (1833), arguing for strict pantheism based on Hegel's religious thinking, insisted that personal, individual immortality was a mistaken notion that ought to be replaced by a concept of Infinite Spirit, immortal, pantheistic, and having no taint of private egoism. A Christological controversy followed when D. F. Strauss argued, following the historical criticism of Vatke and Baur, that the miracles and supernatural acts ascribed to Jesus by the NT authors could not be supported historically. The thesis of Strauss' *Life of Jesus* (1835–36) was that the divine spirit was incarnate in the human race as a whole, not in the individual person of Jesus of Nazareth. This radical position was countered by more conservative Hegelians (Goschel, Gabler, Bauer) and by moderates like Rosenkranz. But Bauer eventually went further than Strauss, denying any divinity, asserting that the Gospels were a myth created by a single author, stating that "true" Hegelianism led to atheism, not to pantheism, and certainly not to theism. Feuerbach's *The Essence of Christianity* (1841) presented humanism as the primary shape and content of religion. God, he argued, is the creation of man, an Idea like other ideas, reflecting human striving for ideals. Feuerbach saw his approach as an affirmation and restoration of human nature, and his subsequent *Lectures on the Essence of Religion* (1848) presented a religion of nature and individual self-preservation. The leftist side of political and economic Hegelianism, associated with Arnold Ruge, Karl

Marx and F. Engels, evolved from that side of Hegel's thought which envisioned higher, more rational forms of reality emerging from the imperfectly real present world and which justified dissatisfaction with present conditions and revolutionary reaction to those conditions. The Hegelian Journals, which Ruge edited, reflect the shift of liberal Hegelians toward the left during the 1830s and 40s. Marx went beyond Feuerbach and Bauer when he argued that religion was only a symptom of humans alientated from their humanity; religion was not the cause of that alienation; it was socio-economic and political institutions that tyrannized humans, Marx's historical dialectical materialism was an heir to Hegel's philosophy of history. Right-wing Hegelians, liberal by contemporary political standards, favored minor reforms of German government and society; they antagonized the more revolutionary left. The disappointing failure of the 1848 social revolutions, however, discouraged both right and left. During the latter half of the 19th cent. studies of history reflecting the Hegelian notion of an unfolding Absolute Spirit widely influenced secular and religious historiography and philosophy. Among the more important of these works are F. K. A. Schwegler's *Outlines of the History of Philosophy in Epitome* (1848; tr. Seelye, 1856), Fischer's *History of Modern Philosophy* (8 v., 1852–93), Michelet's *The History of Mankind in its Course of Development from 1775 to the Most Recent Time* (2 v., 1859–60), and Erdmann's *Outline of the History of Philosophy* (2 v., 1866). S. Kierkegaard's criticism of Hegel and his Danish disciples focused on the impossibility of upholding complete ''systems'' of reality, a criticism found particularly in Kierkegaard's *Concept of Dread* (1844) and *Concluding Unscientific Postscript* (1846). Nonetheless, this critique developed into an existential dialectic which shares certain Hegelian categories and methods with the systematic philosophy Kierkegaard was criticizing. A. Ott and L. Prevost wrote and promoted Hegelian philosophy in France during the 1840s; A. Vero's studies and translation were instrumental in making Naples a center of Hegelian thought; and Polish A. Cieszkowski, while objecting to the typical Hegelian celebration of German ascendancy, incorporated Hegel's methods at the same time that Russian and Polish academics and political activists were importing Hegelian thought to Eastern Europe. George Eliot, the English novelist, translated Strauss' *Life of Jesus* (1846) and Feuerbach's *Essence of Christianity* (1854) but not until J. H. Stirling published *The Secret of Hegel* (1865) did Hegelianism become evident in traditionally empirical and utilitarian England. E. Caird and T. H. Green joined Stirling in his advocacy of Hegelianism. A St. Louis school of Hegelian thought centering on H. C. Brokmeyer, W. T. Harris, and *The Journal of Speculative Philosophy* during the latter part of the 19th cent., indulged many interests but particularly emphasized the Western expansion of America and its regional tensions as elements of a Hegelian dialectic. Associated with St. Louis was a Cincinnati group including A. Willich, J. B. Stallo, and M. D. Conway, who were usually further left on political and religious issues than the St. Louis circle. Hegel's effect on 20th-cent. thought has been subtle and broad but not as direct and explicit as it had been during the 19th. The two sides of Hegel—the rational is the real, which fostered new idealism; and the real is rational, which fostered a new history-based thinking —made it possible to put Hegel's technical and visionary powers as well as his multitude of themes to diverse and often contradictory uses.

[R. J. LITZ]

HEGEMONIUS (4th cent.), author of the *Acta Archelai,* an anti-Manichaean treatise. Composed in the form of a dispute between Mānī, his disciple Turbo, and Archelaus, bp. of Kashkar, Mesopotamia, the work gives valuable information on the beginnings of Manichaeism, although the dialogue recorded is merely a literary device. The work, written probably *c.*350 in Greek, exists now in relatively complete form only in a poor Latin translation, but some Greek fragments have survived.

[R. B. ENO]

HEGESIAS OF CYRENE (*c.*330–270 B.C.), Cyrenaic philosopher. He taught that pleasure was the end of life, but that pleasure was really unattainable to such a degree that one should strive rather for absence of pain and sorrow. This pessimism led him not only to permit suicide but to advocate it. It is said that some of his hearers committed suicide and that Ptolemy I forbade him to continue his teaching at Alexandria. BIBLIOGRAPHY: LexAW 1223; Copleston 1:122–123.

[M. R. P. MCGUIRE]

HEGESIPPUS, ST. (2d cent.), a Judaeo-Christian writer against the *Gnostics. H.'s *Memoirs,* composed *c.* 180, are known only through *Eusebius. They are not properly a chronological history, but a collection to show that doctrinal purity had survived in the succession of bps. in the Churches of the Apostles. To compile information H. traveled by way of Corinth to Rome, and a list of popes down to *Anicetus (155–166) is attributed to him. His *Memoirs* are of interest, but not of historical value, for the study of Judaeo-Christianity. BIBLIOGRAPHY: W. Telfer, ''Was Hegessippus a Jew?'' HTR 53 (1960) 143–153.

[R. B. ENO]

HEGIRA (Arab. *hijra*), Mohammed's ''flight'' from *Mecca to *Medina. The term is taken from the verb *hajara* meaning to depart from one's clan, severing all bonds of kinship obligations. As a proper name, it designates Mohammed's emigration from Mecca to Medina in Sept. 622, with a number of his followers. It was in Medina that the Muslims first came to constitute an autonomous political community, and consequently, during the reign of the *Caliph 'Umar I (d. 644), the year of the Hegira was fixed as the first year of the Islamic era. Hegira dates are usually designated by the abbreviation A.H. (*Anno Hegirae*).

[R. M. FRANK]

HEGUMENOS, in the Eastern Church, the elected head of a monastery, esp. of *Basilian monks; counterpart of an abbot in the West. His term is for life; he rules subject to the patriarch or bishop.

HEHN, JOHANNES (1873–1932), Catholic biblical scholar. Professor of OT literature and Oriental languages at the Univ. of Würzburg (1903–32), by his research in Assyriology he increased knowledge of the Bible's historical background.

HEIDEGGER, MARTIN (1889–1976), German philosopher, noted esp. for his phenomenological and existential analysis of the meaning of Being (*der Sinn von Sein*). He was born into a Catholic family at Messkirch, Baden, (now West) Germany. After public school there, he attended the gymnasium in Constance (1903–06), and then transferred to the Bertholds-Gymnasium in Freiburg-im-Breisgau, receiving his diploma in 1909. Religious in outlook, he then joined the Jesuits as a novice.

At the Univ. of Freiburg, where he studied first philosophy and theology and then, having decided against the priesthood, philosophy, mathematics, and the natural sciences, the atmosphere was dominated by neo-scholasticism and neo-Kantianism, The challenge of responding to the latter's claim that Immanuel Kant (1724–1804) had forever destroyed the metaphysics so important to the former never ceased to preoccupy H. But the basic elements of his response were already evident. Thus, while still only 18 yrs. old, he had read the *Von der mannigfachen Bedeutung des Seinden nach Aristoteles* (1862) of Franz *Brentano (1838–1917), reflections on which lie at the origin of H.'s crucial distinction between the Being of beings (*das Sein des Seinden*) and the beings of which it is the Being. Then, while still in theology, he discovered, in the *Logische Untersuchungen* (1900–01) of Edmund *Husserl (1859–1938), the phenomenological method of bracketing and suspending all judgments about real existence and causality and directing the attention uniquely to the pure and uncontaminated data of consciousness; as H. adapted it, this came to be the method by which he approached the question of Being. Finally, in his *Habilitationschrift, Die Kategorien und Bedeutungslehre des Duns Scotus* (1916), largely a study of the *Grammatica speculativa* of pseudo-Scotus, Thomas of Ehrfurt, H.'s inquiry into the ultimate theoretical foundations of language began, destined to lead him to see language as the "house of Being" (*das Haus des Seins*).

Now a recognized disciple of Husserl, H. taught philosophy in Freiburg as *Privatdozent,* 1915–23, except for a brief period of military service. In 1923 Nicolai *Hartman (1882–1950) was instrumental in obtaining for him appointment as *professor ordinarius* at Marburg. H. here came under the influences that led him in the direction of existentialism. Rudolf *Bultman introduced him to the theology of Karl *Barth, and the two led him to the study of Martin Luther (1483–1546) and Søren Kierkegaard (1813–55), the "father" of existentialism. H. also read Pascal and Dostoyevsky, came to value the work of the phenomenologist Max *Scheler, and befriended Karl *Jaspers, the second greatest German existentialist.

In 1927 H. published the first two divisions, of three, of the first part of his *magnum opus, Sein und Zeit,* the essentials of the approach of which are as follows. First, to H.'s distinction between Being and beings corresponds one between his ontological inquiry into Being and the traditional ontology of beings, the tradition having quite forgotten the problem of Being. Second, Heidegger attempted to base his *general ontology* of Being on a preliminary *fundamental ontology*. Here Being would be found through an analysis of the one being whose way of being is none other than the asking of the question of Being and who has, therefore, an implicit comprehension of Being. This, the human being as oriented to Being, Heidegger calls Dasein (there-being). Third, the analysis must be a phenomenological and existential analysis; it is not made in terms of such sophisticated theoretical conceptions as the "substance" and "cause" of classical philosophy, but in terms of the pretheoretical modes of orientation to Being that are the *existentials,* the elements constitutive of the very being of Dasein.

The fundamental *existential* discovered in Heidegger's fundamental ontology is that of "being-in-the-world" (in-der-Welt-sein). Dasein is self-transcendent *(über sich hinaus),* its existence transcending itself to the world, the world being indeed Dasein's relational structure as transcendent. But Dasein's existence is also one of dereliction (*Geworfenheit*, "thrown-ness") and facticity; Dasein finds himself to be what he is already in, and having been "flung" into, a given world. Further, phenomenological analysis shows everyday existence to be inauthentic (*uneigentlich*) existence, where one surrenders to the many objects and people and stands in alienation from one's true self; it is dread (*Angst*), the sense of nothingness that arises when the whole structure of being-in-the-world, the ground, boundary, and end of which is death, is faced and that induces Dasein to lose himself in inauthentic existence. Consciousness (*das Gewissen*), i.e., awareness, self-awareness, and conscience, call man back to authentic existence, to the knowledge of self as being-to-death (*Sein zum Tode*). Finally, H.'s analysis, in which Dasein's existence, as transcendence and projection, is constitutively oriented to the future and in which the future is originative of the past and present, reveals the constitutive temporality of Dasein's existence; indeed, authentic time is existence and temporality is the answer to the question of the meaning of being.

Sein und Zeit's massive analysis proved to be a failure. At one level, the virtual impossibility of its interpretation and the nature of its influence provide one measure of failure. That both the atheistic existentialism of J.P. Sartre (1905–) and the biblical exegisis of Rudolf Bultman are largely derived from Heidegger's project indicates clearly its indeterminacy. Again, Heidegger himself came to abandon the attempt to base the quest after Being upon a phenomenological analysis of Dasein that revealed but the nothingness of his being, and to believe that the meaning of Being can only be revealed through the initiative of Being. But ultimately the very basis of the quest after Being rests in confusion. Heidegger's Being, as that by which beings exist, can be neither a principle intrinsic to them, as it is not reducible to them, nor a principle extrinsic to them, as it is not itself a being.

Despite its incompleteness and its obscurity, *Sein und Zeit* made Heidegger famous. He was offered the chair of philosophy at Freiburg in 1928, succeeding Husserl, who had requested that the appointment be made. And in 1933, when the anti-Nazi *rector magnificus* of the university resigned in protest against the pressure to support the "national revolution", H. was unanimously elected to the post. Even his participation in National Socialism, ambiguous but including early pro-Hitler speeches and membership in the Party, did little to permanently diminish his standing in philosophy. Thus, although the occupying powers forbade him in 1945 to resume the official teaching position from which he had just resigned in 1944, having held it since stepping down as rector in 1934, H. was permitted to continue his influential lectures until his retirement in 1959. Further, his numerous post-*Sein und Zeit* publications, marked by his assigning to poetry the role of ultimate witness to Being, have continued to find an enthusiastic audience. And, even after his retirement, numerous pilgrimages were made to his *Heimat* in the Black Forest. There is a German edition of his voluminous unpublished writings and lectures in progress by Klostermann. BIBLIOGRAPHY: *Being and Time* (tr. J. Macquarrie and E. Robinson, 1962); W. J. Richardson, *Heidegger: Through Phenomenology to Thought* (1963) with a letter from H.; *Philosophy Today* 20 no. 3/4 (1976) H. on his rectorship.

[R. E. HENNESSEY]

HEIDELBERG CATECHISM, the *Reformed *confession of faith published in 1563. While officially approving Calvinism, the elector of the Rhine Palatinate, Frederick III, desired a formula of belief, catechetical in form and temperate in content, to quiet the violence of theological conflict between Lutherans and Calvinists. The exact authors are not certain, but Z. *Ursinus and C. *Olevianus had a principal part in its preparation. The Catechism incorporates Lutheran ideas on man's sinful condition, tones down rigid Calvinist teaching by not mentioning double predestination or limited atonement, and is more concerned with Christian living than theological preciseness. Simple and warm in language, it was translated into Latin at the time of publication. Gradually the Catechism was accepted by the Reformed Churches, not only in Germany but throughout Europe; one of the main concerns of the Synod of *Dort was approval (1619) of this document as a confessional standard. The first English translation appeared in 1572; in English-speaking Reformed Churches the Catechism ranks second in importance after the *Westminster Confession. The three parts of the Catechism, on man's misery in sin, redemption, and the new life, were designed to correspond to the Epistle to the Romans. There are 129 questions divided into 52 lessons for the weeks of the year. The answer to Question 80 (inserted into the 2d and 3d eds., according to some, by Frederick himself; according to others, by Olevianus) is an embarrassingly bitter attack on the Mass, probably as a rejoinder to the Council of Trent. BIBLIOGRAPHY: K. Barth, *Heidelberg Catechism for Today* (tr. S. C. Guthrie, pa., 1964); H. Hoeksema, *Heidelberg Catechism, an Eposition* (1944); W. Hollweg, *Neue Untersuchungen zur Geschichte des Heidelberger Katechismus* (1961); A. Péry, *Heidelberg Catechism* (tr. A. O. Miller, M. B. Koons, 1963); Schaff Creeds 1:535–550.

[T. C. O'BRIEN]

HEILIGENKREUZ, ABBEY OF, Austrian Cistercian abbey, archdiocese of Vienna. Founded in 1133 by Margrave Leopold III at the request of his son Otto of Freising, it was settled from Morimond. The foundation of many other monasteries (Zwettl, Lilienfeld, Neuberg, etc.) testified to the great generative spirit of this abbey. Its monks still carry on important theological studies. Nearly all medieval buildings of the abbey are conserved: church (12th and 13th cent.), cloister (1220–50) with famous lavabo, chapterhouse, dormitory (*c.* 1240), etc.

HEILSBRONN, ABBEY OF, German Cistercian monastery near Ansbach which was established by monks from Ebrach with the help of Bp. Otto of Bamberg (1132). Its Romanesque church served as the burial place for the Franconian Hohenzollern family until 1625. Damaged during the 16th cent., the abbey was subsequently converted into an outstanding school by the Lutherans (1581).

[L. J. LEKAI]

HEIM, KARL (1874–1958), Protestant systematic theologian of pietist bent, at the Univ. of Halle (1907–14), Münster (1914–20), and Tübingen (1920–58). His translated works include: *God Transcendent* (1935), *Jesus the World's Perfector* (1959); *The World: its Creation and Consummation* (1962). He presented in terms of contemporary knowledge the crisis between skepticism and Christian commitment and its resolution by a decisive faith in Jesus Christ with acceptance of the biblical view of history as the working out of God's saving will; the Satanic threat is opposition of will to God.

HEIMBUCHER, MAXIMILIAN JOSEPH (1856–1946), German theologian and author, professor of apologetics at Munich and Bamberg. His principal work, *Die Orden und Kongregationen der Katholischen Kirche* (2v., 1896–97; 4th ed. 1965), is regarded as a fundamental source for the study of the origins and history of religious orders and congregations. BIBLIOGRAPHY: G. Marasà, DE 2:332; M. Csáky, NCE 6:997.

[F. D. LAZENBY]

HEIMERAD, ST. (Heimo; d. 1019), wandering priest, eccentric, hermit. He was popularly regarded as a "holy fool." Many had no patience with him, but some, even among the prelates and nobles of his time, visited him and appear to have held him in esteem. Miracles followed his death, and after some 50 years a monastery was built over the place where he was buried. However, his cult remained no more than a popular one, for it never received official sanction. BIBLIOGRAPHY: Butler 2:660–661.

[S. WILLIAMS]

HEIMO OF MICHELSBERG (d. 1138). Nothing is known of the origins of this ecclesiastical chronicler. Originally an Augustinian Canon of St. James in Bamberg from 1108, he was educated at and later taught at Michelsberg Abbey in Bamberg until his death. In 1135 he completed his *De decursu temporum ab origine mundi,* which with his work on the Paschal Cycle established his fame. BIBLIOGRAPHY: E. Santovito, EncCatt 1:602; PL 173:1363–68.

[S. WILLIAMS]

HEINE, HEINRICH (1797–1856), German poet; intellectual leader and most gifted writer of the group known as Young Germany (1830–48); originator of the German *feuilleton.* H. is most famous as a lyric poet (*Gedichte,* 1821; *Lyrisches Intermezzo,* 1822–23; *Buch der Lieder,* 1827; *Neue Gedichte,* 1847; *Romanzero,* 1851; *Letzte Gedichte,* 1853–54). He also wrote ballads (e.g., *Die Grenadiere),* prose works (e.g., the witty and informative *Reisebilder,* 1826–31), and satire (e.g., *Atta Troll,* 1843). BIBLIOGRAPHY: S. S. Prawer, *Heine, the Tragic Satirist* (1961); *Poetry and Prose of Heinrich Heine* (ed. F. Ewen, 1948).

[M. F. MCCARTHY]

HEINICHEN, JOHANN DAVID (1683–1729), German composer and theorist. H. studied at the Thomasschule, Leipzig, and held posts in Rome and Dresden. He composed numerous operas, concertos, Masses, oratorios, *Te Deums,* and other church music. He is best known, however, for his treatise, *Neu erfundene und gründliche Answeisung,* and esp. for its explanation of thorough bass.

[M. T. LEGGE]

HEINISCH, PAUL (1878–1956), OT biblical scholar. H. taught at Breslau (1908–11), Strassburg (1911–18), and Nijmegen (1928–45). He was a scholarly and rather conservative exegete, best noted for his contributions to the *Bonner Bibel* series, his *Theology of the OT* (1951), and *History of the OT* (both tr. W. G. Heidt, 1952). BIBLIOGRAPHY: J. Trinquet, *Catholicisme* 5:571; W. G. Heidt, NCE 6:997–998.

[T. M. MCFADDEN]

HEINKE, FRANZ JOSEF (1726–1803), organizer of the *Josephinism in the Austro-Hungarian Empire. After being dean of the law school at the Univ. of Prague, H. went to Vienna in 1767 where he remained in the high regard of both Maria Theresa and her successor *Joseph II. H.'s Church-State theory elevated the sovereignty of the State, and ecclesiastical reforms became guided by reasons of State. Naturally, Rome and the Austrian bps. struggled against the whole system and fought the suppression of the contemplative orders.

[D. J. SMUCKER]

HEINRICH VON LAUFENBERG (*c.*1390–1460), German lyric and religious poet, notably of an epic poem on salvation and of a popular German version of the *Salve Regina, Bist grüsst maget reine.*

[T. C. O'BRIEN]

HEINRICH, JOHANN BAPTIST (1816–91), German theologian and apologete. He began his career as professor of law at the Univ. of Giessen; he took up studies for the priesthood in 1842 and was ordained in 1845 for the Diocese of Mainz. He was professor of theology at the diocesan seminary from 1851. His main dogmatic work, the last four volumes of which were completed by his friend K. Gutberlet, was *Dogmatische Theologie* (10 v., 1873–1904); it incorporates Thomistic theological principles. In other writings and activities he worked for the cause of religious freedom in Germany. He also published apologetic works against J. *Döllinger, D. F. *Strauss, and E. *Renan.

[T. C. O'BRIEN]

HEIRIC OF AUXERRE (*c.*841–*c.*876), Benedictine, teacher at Auxerre, known mainly for his hagiographical and historical works: *Vita S. Germani Antissiorodensis; Miracula;* part of the *Gesta. episcoporum Antissiodorensium.* His knowledge of classical literature also made his teaching an important channel for the recovery of ancient learning.

[T. C. O'BRIEN]

HEISS, MICHAEL (1818–90), missionary, scholar, archbishop. A native of Germany, he was influenced as a student in Munich by J. A. Möhler. After ordination in 1840 he was drawn to the American missions and went to the U.S. in 1842. In Milwaukee he became secretary to Bp. John Henni. After serving as first rector of St. Francis Seminary in Milwaukee, where he was a much revered teacher, H. was named first bp. of La Crosse, Wis., in 1868. In 1881 he became abp. of Milwaukee, which he administered with humility and skill. He called the First Provincial Council of Milwaukee, participated in the Second and Third Plenary Councils of Baltimore, and was an infallibilist at Vatican Council I. A strong advocate of the parochial school, he opposed the idea of establishing The Catholic Univ. of America in Washington, D.C. H.'s name is prominent in the bitter controversy over German interests that split the American hierarchy in the 19th century. His very appointment to Miluwakee was opposed by the "Americanizers." He strongly defended the need for Rome to appoint more German-speaking bps. in the Midwest and the right to have parochial school courses taught in the German language. His appointment of P. *Abbelen to represent the cause for Germany to the Holy See in 1886 caused bitterness. The controversy was not settled till after H.'s death.

[J. R. AHERNE]

HEISTERBACH, ABBEY OF, German Cistercian monastery near Bonn, established by monks of Himmerod (1189). Its most notable period of achievement was reached under Abbot Henry (1208–42), a mystic who erected the great church and sponsored the literary activity of Caesarius of Heisterbach. Secularized in 1803, the abbey was razed except for the apse and choir of the original church. BIBLIOGRAPHY: H. Pauen, *Die Klostergrundherrschaft Heisterbach* (1913); L. J. Lekai, NCE 6:999.

[L. J. LEKAI]

HEJAZ (Arab., al-Hijaz), NW region of Saudi Arabia in which the Islamic holy cities of Mecca (the capital) and Medina are located. It is esp. known for the pilgrimages made to the holy cities, many of the pilgrims coming through the seaport Jiddah. Previously controlled by the Baghdad caliphate and later by Egypt, Hejaz was under Turkish control most of the time from 1517 until 1916 when T. E. Lawrence assisted Husein ibn jali, sherif of Mecca, in gaining independence. Husein was defeated in 1924 by Ibn Saud, who formally incorporated Hejaz in Saudi Arabia in 1932. Hejaz has an area of *c.* 150,000 square miles, with a predominantly Muslim population of some 2 million.

[T. EARLY]

HELEN OF SKÖVDE, ST. (fl. 12th cent.). Given the title patron saint of Västergötland and of all Sweden by Brynolf Algotsson, bp. of Skara, in the Offfice of her feast. Few facts are known concerning her life other than that she was a young widow, who, according to legend, was murdered after a family quarrel. Her cult was popular in Denmark as well as in Sweden. BIBLIOGRAPHY: Butler 3:228; A. L. Sibilia, BiblSanct 4:996–997.

[F. G. O'BRIEN]

HELEN OF UDINE, BL. (*c.* 1396–1458), Augustinian tertiary. Of the Valentini family and married to the nobleman Antonio dei Cavalcanti, she was widowed when she was 40. While continuing to maintain her household, she became a tertiary and practiced prayer, penance, and charitable works. Miracles were attributed to her intercession and she was beatified in 1848. BIBLIOGRAPHY: Butler 2:155.

[M. J. FINNEGAN]

HELENA, ST. (*c.* 255–*c.* 330), mother of Constantine, who honored her with the title *Augusta* after he became Emperor (306) and, according to Eusebius (*Vita Const.* 3.41), was responsible for her conversion to Christianity (*c.* 312). Eusebius also describes her pilgrimage to Palestine (324) and her founding basilicas on the Mount of Olives and at Bethlehem (*ibid.* 3.41–43). Apart from later references of St. Ambrose (*De obitu Theod.* 43) and Rufinus (*Hist. Eccles.* 10.7–8) and the basilica built at Rome by Constantine in honor of her devotion to the cross, there is no historical evidence to support her legendary role in the finding of the True Cross. Her burial at Rome and Constantinople is disputed, and the alleged 9th-cent. translation of her remains to the abbey of Hautvilliers near Reims is questionable. Nor is there any historical foundation for the medieval legend that H. was a native of England, the daughter of Coel (Old King Cole) of Colchester. BIBLIOGRAPHY: Butler 3:346–347; P. T. Camelot, *Catholicisme* 5:574; A. Amore, BiblSanct. 4:988–992.

[T. EARLY]

HELENTRUDIS, ST. (Helmtrud, Hiltrud; d. *c.* 950), an anchoress of Neuenheerse (Westphalia) to whom, (according to the *passio* of St. Ursula) St. Cordula, one of the legendary 10,000 virgins, appeared to tell the story of her martyrdom.

HELFMAN, MAX (1901–63), Polish-born conductor and composer. H. studied in the U.S. and became a choral conductor of Jewish groups. He wrote and edited Jewish liturgical and choral music.

[M. T. LEGGE]

HELFTA, CONVENT OF medieval monastery of nuns near Eisleben, Germany. Founded in 1228, it was originally established in Mansfeld and eventually Helfta in 1258. The convent followed the Cistercian constitutions but the nuns were not of that order. It became the most famous center of German mysticism in the 13th century. Mystics such as Gertrude the Great and Mechtild of Magdeburg belonged to this convent whose liturgical devotions to Christ the Bridegroom were filled with rhapsodic emotion. The convent was dissolved in 1545. BIBLIOGRAPHY: Cottineau 1:1398.

[M. A. MCFADDEN]

HELGA, see ILGA; OLGA.

HELGESEN, POVL (Paulus Heliae; *c.* 1485–after 1534), Swedish Carmelite, opponent of the spread of Lutheranism in Scandinavia. Only some periods of his life are known: 1519–22, professor of theology at Copenhagen; 1522–34, provinical of the Carmelites of Scandinavia; 1533–34, professor at the cathedral school of Roskilde, Denmark; thereafter nothing is known. His writings include translations of Erasmus' works and an edition of Erasmus' translation of St. Paul; polemical works in Danish and Latin against Lutheran theology. In the history of Lutheranism he is regarded as a forerunner of the Reformation by his humanism and biblical orientation, but as resisting the break with Rome.

[T. C. O'BRIEN]

HELI, see ELI.

HELIAND ("Savior"), an Old Saxon religious poem of 5,983 lines modeled on OE epics in the Latin style. According to the Latin preface, the poem was written at the command of Louis the Pious (814–840) by a *non ignobilis vates,* who was almost certainly a monk, perhaps at Fulda. In alliterative verse characterized by variation (*Hakenstil*), and overlong lines (*Schwellenverse*), the poet adapted the NT to the Germanic heroic background of his hearers without sacrificing Christian orthodoxy. BIBLIOGRAPHY: J. K. Bostock, *Handbook on Old High German Literature* (1955) 141–156.

[M. F. MCCARTHY]

HÉLINAND OF FROIDMONT, BL. (*c.*1170–*c.*1230), Cistercian monk, writer. A nobleman who was a skilled musician and poet, he entered the monastery at Froidmont, near Beauvais, *c.* 1194. His writings include sermons, ascetical essays, scriptural commentaries, chronicles. He belongs to the history of French literature because of his Old French poem *Vers de la mort* (modern ed. J. Coppin, 1930). He preached in the mission against the *Albigensians under Bp. Foulques of Toulouse.

[T. C. O'BRIEN]

HELIODORUS Syrian statesman of the 2d cent. B.C. Seleucus IV (Philopator) sent him to Jerusalem to take the treasure from the Temple. Forcing his way past the protesting high priest Onias, he was stopped by an apparition of horsemen charging him. He was carried out at the point of death but restored when Onias offered a sacrifice for him (2 Macc ch. 3). A Heliodorus, who may not have been the same person, murdered Seleucus IV in 175 B.C. and tried unsuccessfully to take the throne. He was driven out by Antiochus IV (Epiphanes), who became king.

[T. EARLY]

HELIODORUS OF EMESA Greek author, perhaps of the 3d cent. A.D. Born in Emesa, Syria, he wrote *Aethiopica,* a prose romance celebrating the love of Theagones of Thessaly for the dark-skinned Princess Chariclea of Ethiopia, daughter of the king. H. influenced numerous European writers, including Racine and Cervantes. The church historian Socrates said he was a bp. of Tricca in Thessaly, but scholars today generally reject that assertion.

[T. EARLY]

HELIOPOLIS, one of the most important cities of ancient Egypt, situated at the S vertex of the Nile Delta, just NE of modern Cairo. In ancient Egypt it had no major political role, although it was the capital of the Thirteenth Lower Egyptian Nome and an outstanding cult center. The Greek name Heliopolis, "City of the Sun," was sometimes rendered in Hebrew as Beth Shemesh, "House of the Sun." It was the home of the prestigious Heliopolitan theology, which attained its basic form in the Third Dynasty (the beginning of the 3d Millennium B.C.). The chief deity Atum was syncretized with Re into Atum-Re, the sun god. The other deities of the pantheon—the Great Ennead—included gods whose names meant Atmosphere, Moisture, Earth, and Sky; as well as the gods of birth, death, the underworld and rebirth: Isis, Osiris, Seth, and Nephthys. This ennead was adopted by Memphite theologians, who made Ptah the central figure, the emanation and manifestation of the ennead itself. The ruins of this ancient city, which, according to Strabo (17.805–6), was laid waste during the Persian invasion under Cambyses, include many cult objects; the most famous is perhaps the prototype of the obelisk, which may have symbolized the primordial hillock on which Atum stood when he first emerged from the waters of chaos. The name of the sun-god came into Hebrew as "On" or "Aven." The wife that Pharoah gave Joseph in Egypt was Asenath, daughter of Potiphera, priest of On. She became the mother of Ephraim and Manasses (Gen 41.45,50; 46.20). When Jeremiah foretells the smashing of the sacred pillars of Beth-Shemesh (Jer 43.13), it is the humiliation of Egypt's religion that he foresees. Also when Isaiah foresees the day when the City of the Sun will speak the language of Canaan and swear allegiance to Yahweh of Hosts, it is Egypt's conversion to the faith of Israel that he sees. (Is 19.18).

[E. J. DILLON]

HELIOPOLIS, LEBANON, see BAALBEK.

HELL, traditional term for the state and "place" of final loss and eternal punishment for those who die unrepentant. The NT imagery used to describe hell reflects contemporary Jewish thought, which had developed out of a concept of *sheol or the underworld, as simply a place and state of the dead. This abode of the dead eventually came to be understood as shared differently by the good and the wicked, the latter consigned to a place of punishment called *Gehenna. In extrabiblical literature it was a place of punishment after death, a place of darkness and burning flame. Each of the Synoptics mentions Gehenna, and it is described there as a place of unquenchable fire (Mt 5.22; Mk 9.43) of torture (Mt 5.25–26), of darkness, weeping, and gnashing of teeth (Mt 8.12; 13.42,50; Lk 13.28), and of never-ending corruption (Mk 9.48). This imagery reflecting contemporary Jewish thought is to be understood as a persuasive rhetoric about the truth that there is judgment and punishment, and not as a statement of descriptive detail. Images about Gehenna are all directed toward expressing the truth about the possibility of man's losing himself with finality. Hence questions concerning the real or metaphysical nature of hell's fires, or the location of hell, are pointless and misinterpret the nature of the eschatological discourses used by Christ in the NT.

Tradition affirms the existence of hell (D 72, 76, 801,

etc.) and its eternity (D 411), but there is no definitive declaration about the nature of the pains of hell. Scholastic theology taught a dual punishment of hell: that is, the unrepentant suffer both a *pain of loss, or privation of union with God, and a *pain of sense, or affliction coming from an external agent. The concept of the eternity of hell was forged against the background of the doctrine of *apocatastasis, or universal salvation, defended by Origen. Although this expression of universalism has had defenders into modern times, there is no firm scriptural or traditional support for the doctrine, nor, on the other hand, for the position that anyone has actually been judged as lost finally.

It should be stressed that hell is the result of one's own choice and therefore a judgment upon oneself. Rather than a punishment inflicted by God, it should be conceived as the working out of sin itself, the logical consequence of free actions that reject God and others in order to serve the interest of the self. In this sense hell begins within the present situation where man freely disposed of himself and can turn away to such a degree that he irrevocably estranges himself from God.

The teaching about hell emphasizes the freedom of man and the possibility of loss; it heightens the importance of the history of each man and calls man to reverse himself from a movement toward death to that of life. The eternity of life and death expressed in the traditional terms of heaven and hell form a continuity with the freely chosen direction of life in this world. BIBLIOGRAPHY: A. Winklhofer, *Coming of His Kingdom* (tr. A. V. Littledale, 1963); R. Schnackenburg, *God's Rule and Kingdom* (tr. J. Murray, 1963); K. Rahner, SacMund 3:7–9; *idem,* "The Hermeneutics of Eschatological Assertions," *Theological Investigations* 4 (1966) 323–346; E. G. Hardwick, NCE 6:1004–07.

[J. CORDOUE]

HELL SCROLL (Jigoku Sōshi), 12th-cent. Japanese *emaki* showing the eight Buddhist hells, each with 16 minor hells attached, illustrating the Six Roads of Reincarnation. The small paintings depict vividly the torments and terrors of the damned. The dynamic lines of the flames have been compared with the calligraphic curves of Botticelli. Portions of the scroll are preserved in the National Museum, Tokyo, the remainder in the National Commission for the Protection of Cultural Properties.

[M. J. DALY]

HELLENISM, a term that may signify (1) a complex of religious and social ties and cultural achievements that united the ancient Greeks (Hellenes) into a distinctive and recognizable group; or (2) the adoption of salient features of this Hellenic civilization by other ethnic groups in the East and West to constitute a richly varied and widely diffused Hellenistic culture; and (3) a contemporary enthusiasm for the art, literature, and philosophy of the ancient Greeks. The conquests of Alexander in the East (334–323 B.C.) and the contacts of Rome with the Greeks of S Italy, Sicily, and Greece had the effect of spreading Greek, at least as a second language, and Greek culture throughout the whole of the Mediterranean world. But since this culture was to a large extent polytheistic in religion, rationalistic in philosophy, and lax in its standards of morality, it was bound to be at odds with the monotheism and strict ethical codes of Judaism and Christianity.

The artistic and intellectual achievements of the Hellenistic world undoubtedly had a strong appeal for a considerable number of Jews both in Palestine and the diaspora. During the 2d cent. B.C., when Palestine was ruled by the Seleucids, Hellenizing Jews in Jerusalem even adopted the practice of exercising in the nude, an excess which, along with others, led to the Jewish revolt under the Maccabees. The internal tensions created in Judaism by the problem of Hellenism were eventually resolved by the rejection of all foreign influences and the adoption of a superior, "pharisaical" attitude, which was ultimately canonized in the rabbinical writings of the Talmud.

Since the first Christians were drawn from both Aramaic- and Greek-speaking Jews, it was only natural that occasional disputes over certain practices should have arisen between the Christian Hebrews and Hellenists (Acts 6.1). The difficulty was compounded when Christianity was preached to the gentiles. Since the latter did not think like the Jews (cf. 1 Cor 1.22), some adaptations obviously had to be made to make the teachings of Christ more acceptable to the pagan mind.

The Christian apologists of the 2d and 3d cent. were frequently ambivalent in their attitude toward the pagan, Hellenistic culture. Tatian, an extremist, rejected it outright as a work of the devil. Tertullian rhetorically asked, "What has Athens to do with Jerusalem?" (*De praescr.* 7), but he was nonetheless heavily indebted to his former legal training in his theology and to Stoicism in his ethical teachings. Justin Martyr was strangely persuaded that the truths found in pagan authors were ultimately derived from the Old Testament. Clement of Alexandria, on the other hand, who was well versed in Greek poetry and philosophy, could see the role of Greek culture in preparing the world for the acceptance of Christianity: "Before the advent of the Lord, philosophy was necessary to the Greeks for righteousness, but now it is conducive to piety, being a kind of preparatory training for those who attain faith through demonstration" (*Stromata* 1.5). Origen, Clement's successor as the head of the catechetical school at Alexandria, continued the tradition of interpreting Christianity in terms of Greek culture, making admirable use of Hellenistic philological principles in his exegesis of Scripture and of Greek philosophy in elaborating his theology. With Arius in the 4th cent., however, Greek rationalism was used to explain away the real mystery of the Trinity, an aberration that had to be combated by Athanasius through an insistence upon the traditional teachings of the Church.

The Christian writers in the West of the 3d, 4th, and 5th cent., even though many of them were deficient in their knowledge of Greek, were all strongly imbued with the Greco-Roman, Hellenistic culture. St. Jerome even narrates an experience in the desert during which he was called "a Ciceronian and not a Christian" by the devil (*Ep.* 22.30). Though Augustine, particularly in *De civitate Dei*, has vividly described the errors of the ancient pagan world, he was convinced that "every good and true Christian should know that truth, wherever it is found, is his Lord's" (*De doctr. christ.* 1.18) and thus felt free to make use of the learning of the Greeks. In this he and other Christian humanists such as Basil of Caesarea, who in his little essay "To Young Men on How They May Profit by the Writings of the Hellenes," simply restated a principle that had already been enunciated by St. Paul: "Whatever things are true, whatever honorable, whatever just, whatever holy, whatever lovable, whatever of good repute, if there be any virtue, if anything worthy of praise, think upon these things" (Phil 4.8). BIBLIOGRAPHY: C. N. Cochrane, *Christianity and Classical Culture* (1944); W. Jaeger, *Early Christianity and Greek Paideia* (1961); J. Shiel, *Greek Thought and the Rise of Christianity* (1968).

[M. J. COSTELLOE]

HELLENIST, (Gr. *Ellenistes*), a Greek-speaking Jew (Acts 9.29) or a Greek-speaking convert from Judaism (Acts 6.1) and thus distinct from and frequently at odds with the Hebrews (*Ebraioi*), Hebrew or Aramaic speaking converts in the primitive Church (cf. Acts 6-7). C. S. Mann considers Hellenists to be Hellenized Jews and Hebrews to be Samaritan Christians. Since the Greek-speaking Jews were often more earnest in their religion than the Hebrews, they offered strong resistance to the spread of Christianity in Jerusalem and elsewhere (cf. Acts 6.9; 9.29; 13.50), but once converted they became earnest proselytes of the new faith, as at Antioch (Acts 11.20). Among the first to be converted by Peter's preaching were many Hellenists (Acts 2.5–11). The most famous of the Hellenists are the first seven deacons, all of whom bore Greek names, and St. Paul, the Apostle to the Gentiles, who was both a Hebrew and a Hellenist (Phil 3.5; Acts 22.3). BIBLIOGRAPHY: F. C. Grant, InterDB 2:580; H. Windisch, Kittel TD 2:508–509; M. Simon, *St. Stephen and the Hellenists* (1958) 1–19; J. A. Fitzmeyer, JBC 2:181; W. F. Albright and C. S. Mann, "Stephen's Samaritan Background; Hellenists and Hebrews in Acts 6:1," *Acts, Anchor Bible* (tr. J. Munck, rev. W. F. Albright and C. S. Mann, 1967) 31:285–304.

[M. J. COSTELLOE]

HELL-FIRE, the principal physical punishment or *pain of sense suffered by the damned. Along with *pain of loss it describes the dual aspects of eternal punishment as elaborated by scholastic theology. The NT description of punishment by fire was influenced by Jewish writing concerning *Gehenna and reflects contemporary apocalyptic language. The Synoptics, for example, speak of a place of punishment for sinners where fire is eternal and unquenchable (Mt 5.22; 18.8–9; Mk 9.43). In the same vein the final state of the wicked in Rev is the pool of fire which is a second death (19.20; 20.1–5; 21.8). Christian tradition has no definitive statement on the kind and quality of the pains of hell. From the patristic era, theologians have questioned whether hell-fire is real or metaphorical. Until relatively recent times, the majority opinion was that the fire was material and real, but it seems to be commonly held today that it is a metaphor which, along with other apocalyptic expressions, helps describe the final state of loss which is possible for man, a condition of alienation not only from God but from creation as well. Theology growing out of the scholastic tradition has speculated that material creation, principally under the image of fire, somehow subjects and restricts the damned, thereby causing them pain. BIBLIOGRAPHY: K. Rahner, SacMund 3:7–9; A. Michel, DTC 5.2:2196–2239; A. Winklhofer, *Coming of His Kingdom* (tr. A. V. Littledale, 1963).

[J. CORDOUE]

HELLO, ERNEST (1828–85), French publicist and religious philosopher. A critic of positivism and of Prussian rationalism—a characteristic feature of patriotic French Catholicism of the time—he was as intransigent as his close friend. *Veuillot, and his vigorous, if uneven, polemics challenged bourgeois mediocrity with the mystical, apocalyptic, and miraculous elements in Christianity.

[T. GILBY]

HELMARSHAUSEN, ABBEY OF, German abbey on the Weser River famous for Romanesque goldwork of high quality by Roger von Helmarshausen and his followers. Roger's silver altar (*c.*1100, Paderborn cathedral treasury) and a silver-plated and niello crucifix (12th cent.) in Minden are examples.

[M. J. DALY]

HELMOLD, (*c.*1120–77), German chronicler. After some schooling and early experience, H. came under the influence of St. Vicelinus. Between 1167 and 1172 his *Cronica Slavorum* told the history of the German settlement in the lower Elbe Basin; the part covering the period 1075–1170 is the best source for Germano-Slavic history. BIBLIOGRAPHY: *Helmoldi presbyteri Bozoviensis cronica Slavorum,* (ed. B. Schmeidler, 2d ed., 1909); *Chronicle of the Slavs* (tr. F. J. Tschan, 1935).

[S. WILLIAMS]

HÉLOÏSE (*c.*1098–1164), abbess. She is best known for her learning, her love for Peter *Abelard, and later devotion to the religious life. After her liaison with Abelard she entered the convent, later becoming prioress of the Abbey of Argenteuil, and finally abbess of the Paraclete, a Benedictine abbey in the Diocese of Troyes, built by Abelard. BIBLIOGRAPHY: É. Gilson, *Héloïse and Abelard* (tr. L. K. Shook, 1951); J. T. Muckle, Med St 12 (1950) 163–213; 15

(1953) 47–94; 17 (1955) 240–281. For a more romantic version of her troubles, see H. Waddell, *Peter Abelard* (1933). [J. D. LOUGHLIN]

HELP OF CHRISTIANS, a title for the Blessed Virgin *Mary which was added to the Litany of *Loretto by Pius V after the battle of *Lepanto (1571). The Christian fleet had sailed under a blue, Marian banner at this battle, and the Pope attributed the victory to her intercession. Pius VII approved a feast under this title to commemorate his release from captivity under Napoleon I.

[T. M. MCFADDEN]

HELPERS OF THE HOLY SOULS (HHS), missionary congregation of sisters founded in Paris in 1856 by Bl. Eugénie de Smet. Encouraged by the Curé of Ars and assisted by two Jesuits, Hippolyte Basiau and Pierre Olivaint, De Smet dedicated the group to charitable works and to the assistance of the souls in purgatory by prayers, sufferings, and labors. From the beginning, lay collaborators were encouraged to extend the Helpers' mission; affiliation of secular members to the society was approved by Rome in the revised constitutions of 1961. The congregation established its first U.S. foundation in New York City (1892). Foreign missions in Asia and Africa are also staffed by the society, which numbered 1,235 members in 1975. The general motherhouse is in Paris; the sisters nurse the sick poor, give religious instruction, and are engaged in social work.

[M. B. MONAGHAN]

HELPIDIUS THE PRISCILLIANIST (4th cent.), Spanish rhetor who, with the noblewoman Agape, was led astray by Mark, an Egyptian Manichean magician. H. and Agape won over Priscillian to their sect.

[E. P. COLBERT]

HELVETIC CONFESSIONS, two Swiss *confessions of faith. (1) The *Confessio helvetica prior,* sometimes called the Second Confession of Basel, was composed there in 1536. The document was prepared by a group of Swiss theologians, headed by H. *Bullinger, for the purpose of a conference with M. *Bucer and W. *Capito. The original was written in German, and a Latin version was immediately made. The 27 articles embodied Zwinglianism, esp. concerning the Holy Eucharist, but also sought for concord with Luther's teaching. (2) The *Confessio helvetica posterior* was written by Bullinger alone in 1562 as a kind of last testimony of his own belief. The desire of the Calvinist elector of the Rhine Palatinate, Frederick III, to defend himself against Lutheran charges of heresy and the need felt by the Swiss *Reformed Churches to have a new confession of faith led to the public adoption of Bullinger's confession at Zurich in 1566. The author himself made the German translation; it was also translated into French. One of the lengthiest of the Reformed confessions (more than 20,000 words), its 30 chapters discourse upon all the main Christian teachings. Continuity of the Reformed Church with the early creeds and patristic witness is emphasized, but the primacy of authority is given to the Scriptures. The influence of both Zwingli and Calvin upon Bullinger is plain in the discussions of the Lord's Supper and predestination; with regard to the latter, the Confession is softer than is Calvin's later thought (see CALVINISM). Dissent from both Lutheran and RC doctrine is expressed. This Confession was accepted or highly regarded in all the Reformed Churches. As a theological document it was unsurpassed; in influence and practical use, it ranked only below the *Heidelberg Catechism and the *Westminster Confession. BIBLIOGRAPHY: E. Routley, *Creeds and Confessions* (1962) 73–86; Schaff Creeds 1:390–420; 3:237–306 (Lat. text).

[N. H. MARING]

HELVETIC CONSENSUS FORMULA, last of the *confessions of faith officially adopted by the *Reformed Church in Switzerland. Composed in 1675 by J. H. Heidegger (1633–98), prof. of Zurich, the Formula, in its preface and 26 canons, was a reaction to the mitigations of Calvinism by the theologians of Saumur, esp. L. Cappell, M. Amyraut, and J. de la Place. The Formula asserted the literal inspiration of Scriptures (even the integrity of the Masoretic Hebrew text); the particular predestination of the elect alone, excluding any hypothetical will of God to save all men; and the imputation of original sin to every man because of a share not simply in the depraved nature but in the sinful act of Adam. The Formula was imposed upon all teachers and preachers; within a generation, however, because its conservatism was divisive, it became a dead letter. BIBLIOGRAPHY: Schaff Creeds 1:477–489.

[T. C. O'BRIEN]

HELVIDIANS, the followers of *Helvidius. St. Augustine (*Haer.* 83) identifies them with the Antidicomarianites of Arabia. BIBLIOGRAPHY: H. Quillet, DTC 1:1378–82.

HELVIDIUS (4th cent.), an adversary of St. Jerome. He may have been a disciple of Auxentius, the Arian bp. of Milan and predecessor of St. Ambrose. About 380, H. wrote a treatise denying the perpetual virginity of Mary and asserting that she had other children by Joseph (the "brothers of the Lord" in the NT). His principal purpose was to attack the prevailing exaltation of virginity above marriage. Jerome, in reply, wrote *De perpetua Mariae virginitate adversus Helvidium* (PL 23:183–206), stating that these "brothers" were Jesus' cousins.

[R. B. ENO]

HELWYS, THOMAS (*c.* 1550–*c.* 1616), pastor of the first Baptist Church in England and author of the first plea in English for full religious liberty. By 1607 he had become a *Separatist and fled to Holland. In Amsterdam, he was a member of John *Smyth's congregation, which was organized on the basis of *believer's baptism and is regarded as the first Baptist Church. When Smyth made overtures to join the Dutch Mennonites, the Church divided, and H. became pastor of the objecting minority. In 1612, he returned to England, and his Church settled at Spitalfields, near London. Rejecting *limited atonement, his followers were known as *General Baptists. In his *Short Declaration of the Mystery of Iniquity* (1612) he asserted that the king ''hath no authority as a king, but in earthly causes'' and that since religion is a matter between man and God, the civil government had no right to punish ''heretics, Turks, or Jews.'' Because of this work it is probable that H. died in prison. BIBLIOGRAPHY: W. H. Burgess, *John Smyth the Se-Baptist, Thomas Helwys and the First Baptist Church in England* (1911); A. C. Underwood, *History of the English Baptists* (1947).

[N. H. MARING]

HÉLYOT, HIPPOLYTE (1660–1716). In 1683 H. took the habit of the Third Order Regular of St. Francis. As secretary of his much-traveled provincial, he collected information on many religious institutions. After 25 years he published his monumental *Histoire des ordres monastiques, religieux et militaires, et des congrégations séculières de l'un et l'autre sexe* (5 v., extended to 8 v. by P. M. Bullot, 1714–21). BIBLIOGRAPHY: DE 2:334–335; R. Gazeau, *Catholicisme* 5:594–595; J. Daoust, NCE 6:1014.

[F. D. LAZENBY]

HEMEROBAPTISTS, a Jewish sect, so named because of their practice of daily washing, known from the scattered mention made of them by Christian writers. According to *Epiphanius, their religious tenets were similar to those of the Scribes and Pharisees. The second Pseudo-Clementine homily states that John the Bapist was a hemerobaptist. The sect is also mentioned by Hegesippus (cited by Eusebius *Hist. Eccl.* 4.22) and by Justin Martyr (*Dial.* 80). BIBLIOGRAPHY: E. Peterson, EncCatt 5:283; ODCC 620.

[R. B. ENO]

HEMMA, BL. (*c.*808–876), Carolingian queen, abbess. A sister of Judith, second wife of Louis I the Pious, H. married his son, Louis the German. Among her children were Charles III the Fat and Bl. Irmengard. She was patroness of the abbey of Obermünster where in later years she was professed and chosen abbess. BIBLIOGRAPHY: A. Cabaniss, NCE 6:1015.

[A. CABANISS]

HEMMER, MARIE HIPPOLYTE (1864–1945), French church historian. Ordained in 1887, he worked in the parochial ministry in Paris most of his life. But he also dedicated himself to the study and teaching of church history, giving courses at the Sorbonne, establishing the series, *Textes et documents pour l'étude historique du christianisme* (1904); translated P. Funk's church history, *Histoire de l'Église* (2 v., 1892, 1911). He was called on as consultant historian for the *Malines Conversations of 1923.

[T. C. O'BRIEN]

HEMMING, BL. (d. 1366), bp. of Åbo, Finland. In 1340 he instituted the office of provost at his cathedral; he was responsible for much of its construction and to it willed his library of theological and canonical works. Highly thought of by St. Bridget of Sweden, he acted as her messenger to several kings and to the Pope. BIBLIOGRAPHY: T. Schmid, NCE 6:1015–16; A. L. Sibilia, BiblSanct 7:584–586.

[T. C. O'BRIEN]

HENANA (d. *c.*610), director of the theological school at Nisibis (Nusaybin, Turkey) from 572 until his death. He took a position singular in the Church of Persia, the rejection of *Nestorianism and the acceptance of the Christology of the Council of *Chalcedon. He was charged by his opponents with subscribing to Origen's doctrine of universalism (*apocatastasis) and of being a fatalist. His writings, surviving only in fragments, include commentaries on OT books, on Mark's Gospel, and on St. Paul, as well as theological treatises.

[T. C. O'BRIEN]

HENDRICK, THOMAS AUGUSTINE (1849–1909), bishop. Ordained for Rochester, N.Y., in 1873, he was named first American bp. of Cebu, Philippine Islands, in 1903. His episcopate was taken up entirely with reorganizing his diocese following the American occupation after the Spanish-American War.

[J. R. AHERNE]

HENNEPIN, LOUIS (1640–1701?), explorer, missionary. A French Franciscan Récollet, H. early manifested a keen interest in exploration and discovery. Sent to Quebec in 1675, he spent several years there, making excursions into the surrounding Indian country and learning much of both the wilderness and its natives. H. was assigned to a mission which was to be Fort Frontenac (now Kingston, Ontario). In 1678 he joined the expedition of La Salle to explore the Great Lakes. The expedition followed the lakes and rivers of Michigan, Illinois, and Minnesota. When La Salle left to return to Quebec, H. was directed to follow the Illinois River and then go N on the Mississippi. Twice a prisoner of the Indians and forced to accompany them on their nomadic journeys, H. was finally released and joined the explorer Du Lhut on a voyage down the Mississippi and northward on the Wisconsin River. H. returned to France in 1681 where he published the first of three accounts of his explorations. The title may be abbreviated to *Description de la Louisiane* (1683), a work of accurate observation and factual strength. Two later works *Nouvelle découverte* (1697) and *Nouveau voyage* (1698) made claims disputed by historians. BIBLIOGRAPHY: J. W. Willis, CE 7:215–218.

[J. R. AHERNE]

HENNEQUIN, JAN (Jean Bandol or Bondol; Jean de Bruges; fl. *c.*1368–81), Franco-Flemish miniaturist. H. restored to French miniature painting the vitality lost after the death of Jean Pucelle. He completed the *Heures de Savoie,* begun by Pucelle for Blanche of Burgundy, and painted for Charles V the famous *Bible historiale* (1371), which in treatment of space, volume, and distance relates to panel painting. *The Apocalypse* tapestry was woven *c.*1381 by Nicolas Bataille from cartoons of Jean de Bruges (Jan Hennequin). *APOCALYPSE TAPESTRY; *NICHOLAS BATAILLE.

[M. J. DALY]

HENNI, JOHN MARTIN (1805–81), first bp. of Milwaukee, missionary. Swiss by birth, H. came to the U.S. and was ordained for Cincinnati in 1832, and in 1834 became vicar general of the diocese. Founder and editor of the first German Catholic weekly in the U.S., *Warheitsfreund,* he wrote on political, moral, and social questions with tact and courage. His espousal of American democracy was clear and unqualified. In 1844 H. became the first bp. of Milwaukee. Immediately after installation he set out on a voyage of exploration of Wisconsin. Founder of St. Francis Seminary, which was to become a powerful center of Catholicism in the West, he also assisted the founding of Marquette University.

He strongly promoted the establishment of parochial schools, which included the teaching of courses in the language of the people, German. He succeeded in building up the Catholic community by the homesteading system, defended immigrants against Know-Nothingism, and refuted charges of priests' having political control over the people. He brought religious congregations of men and women to supply clergy and teachers for the diocese and established a series of newspapers in his apostolate of the press. At Vatican Council I, H. was an anti-infallibilist, but acceded to the majority decision. While espousing and implementing the German cause in his diocese for sound reasons, he saw that cause lead to a split in the American hierarchy (see HEISS, M.). H. was raised to the rank of abp. in 1875 when Milwaukee became a metropolitan see.

[J. R. AHERNE]

HENOCH, see ENOCH.

HENOTHEISM (Gr. *henos,* one; *theos,* god), a term invented by M. Müller (1823–1900) to describe the stage between polytheism and monotheism in the evolution of primitive religion. He concluded that in the Vedic and other religions there was a process in which worship and all divine attributes were centered successively in a single one one of the gods. He called this kathenotheism (Gr. *kat hena,* one after another) or simply henotheism. His thesis gained little support. Henotheism is also used to signify the exclusive worship given to the god of a nation or people; the religion of Israel during the Mosaic period has been so described by some scholars. The term may also connote concentration, within a monotheistic system, on some particular divine attribute.

[T. C. O'BRIEN]

HENOTICON, document of compromise, issued in 482 by the Emperor Zeno in order to win back the Monophysites. Largely the work of Acacius, patriarch of Constantinople, it neutralized the teaching of the Council of *Chalecedon by dropping its precise terminology, esp. on the person and natures of Christ. Circulated for acceptance throughout the East, it was repudiated at Rome for conceding too much to the Monophysites; it thus occasioned the *Acacian schism.

[T. C. O'BRIEN]

HENRARD, ROBERT ARNOLD (1617–76), Belgian sculptor in the Carthusian Cloister, Liège, who executed statues of the saints, a *Madonna* in the tympanum, and a relief of the *Martyrdom of St. Lambert* (*c.*1659) in heavy baroque style.

[M. J. DALY]

HENRICIANS, followers of *Henry of Lausanne.

HENRICUS ARISTIPPUS (d. after 1162), translator and scientist. He was ambassador to Constantinople for King William I of Sicily (1158) and was chief minister at the Sicilian court (1160–62) until he lost favor. He died in prison. H. brought Greek MSS to Sicily, including a copy of Ptolemy's *Almagest,* and wrote the first Latin translation of Plato's *Meno* and *Phaedo.* He also translated Aristotle's *Meteorologica,* Book IV. BIBLIOGRAPHY: C. H. Haskins, *Studies in the History of Medieval Science* (2d ed., 1927).

[G. E. CONWAY]

HENRIETTA MARIA (1609–69), Queen of England and wife of Charles I. In May 1625 H., the youngest daughter of Henry IV and Marie de Médicis, married Charles I. Their early years together were not happy. The young French princess was spirited and accustomed to the gay life of the French court. On the other hand, Charles's character was more restrained and scholarly. In addition, she was infuriated by the King's devotion to his favorite, George Villiers, the Duke of Buckingham. After Buckingham's assassination in 1628, earlier personal discord disappeared and she and Charles became extremely devoted and faithful. Throughout the Civil War, for example, H. was tireless in her efforts to support her husband's cause. After Charles's execution she retired to a life of religious contemplation. Although she died at Colombes in France, she lived to see her son Charles II return to the English throne. H.'s Catholicism is a highly debatable topic. It is fairly clear that Card. Richelieu intended that her marriage should alleviate anti-Catholic laws and improve relations between England and France. Other historians argue that she directly influenced Charles' later leniency towards Catholicism. Yet the most recent research maintains that her impact was indirect and personal. Charles was responsible for his own religious policies. BIBLIOGRAPHY: Q. Bone, *Henrietta Maria, Queen of the Cavaliers* (1972); C. V. Wedgwood, *Great Rebellion* (2v., 1955, 1959).

[C. T. EBY]

HENRION, MATHIEU RICHARD AUGUSTE (1805–62), French lawyer, church historian. His best work is considered to be *Histoire générale des missions depuis le XIIIe siècle jusqu'à nos jours* (2 v., 1846–47); he also wrote a history of the papacy, a church history down to Gregory XVI, and several biographies of churchmen.

[T. C. O'BRIEN]

HENRIQUES, HENRIQUE (1520–1600), Portuguese Jesuit, coworker of St. *Francis Xavier in the missions of India from 1564 until his death. He wrote catechisms, a grammar, and devotional works in the native language (Tamil).

[T. C. O'BRIEN]

HENRIQUEZ, ENRIQUE (1536–1608), Jesuit moral theologian. Born in Portugal, he was brought up at the Spanish court. He taught theology and philosophy at Córdoba and Salamanca. Two of his students were Suárez and Gregory of Valencia. He used his considerable influence with the Inquisition to denounce Suárez, Molina, and Bellarmine. At one point he obtained papal permission to transfer to the Dominicans, whose position against Molina he favored; his own three volume *summa* of moral theology brought him difficulties with his order. His work on the authority of the Roman pontiff was placed on the Index and ordered burned by the papal nuncio. It survives as a book rarity at El Escorial. St. Alphonsus Liguori held him in high esteem as a moralist.

[E. J. DILLON]

HENRY I (1068–1135), **KING OF ENGLAND** from 1100. William the Conqueror's youngest son, H. solidified support after Rufus' reign by confirmation of baronial rights, by marriage with the Anglo-Scottish Princess Edith, and by reconciliation with Abp. Anselm of Canterbury. H. settled the investiture controversy (1107) by ceding investiture with ring and staff but preserving royal control by having bps. perform homage and receive temporalities before consecration. His use of royal writs, shire and hundred courts, itinerant justices, and the exchequer made for peaceful, efficient administration. These ecclesiastical and governmental policies were vital for future development. His reign was marked by the arrival of Cistercians and Premonstratensians in England and the abp. of York's independence of Canterbury. He supported church reform, founded Ely and Carlisle Dioceses and Reading Abbey. BIBLIOGRAPHY: A. L. Poole, *From Domesday Book to Magna Carta* (1955); N. Cantor, *Church, Kingship and Lay Investiture in England* (1958).

[W. A. CHANEY]

HENRY II (1133–89), **KING OF ENGLAND** from 1154. Already duke of Normandy (1150) and count of Anjou (1151), he gained much of France by marrying Eleanor of Aquitaine (1152). H. strengthened royal authority and common law with the use of writs, itinerant justices, and juries, but his centralization of administration caused conflict with Abp. Thomas Becket concerning criminous clerics. Becket's murder (1170) necessitated granting ecclesiastical immunity from secular courts, but this was limited in practice by royal jurisdiction. H. suppressed rebellion, gained overlordship of Scotland (1174), and annexed Ireland (1177). BIBLIOGRAPHY: A. L. Poole, *From Domesday Book to Magna Carta* (1955).

[W. A. CHANEY]

HENRY III (1207–72), **KING OF ENGLAND** from 1216. Son of John, he married (1236) Eleanor of Provence. Various officials, including papal legates, controlled Henry's realm (1216–34). In his middle years, he suffered military defeats in France and Wales, and alienated English barons and clergy by favors to the Poitevins and acceding to papal demands, esp. requests for benefices for Romans. By the Provisions of Oxford (1258), a step toward parliamentary government, Simon de Montfort forced him to rule in conjunction with a baronial council. After regaining power (1265), he ruled through his son Edward. Personally virtuous, H. patronized hospitals and rebuilt Westminster Abbey. BIBLIOGRAPHY: W. Hunt, DNB 9:463–482; F. M. Powicke, *King Henry III and the Lord Edward* (2 v., 1947).

[R. W. HAYS]

HENRY VI (1421–71) **KING OF ENGLAND** from 1422. By terms of the Treaty of Troyes (1420), H. also became King of France at the death of Charles VI. The two kingdoms were ruled by his uncle John, Duke of Bedford, who was appointed protector. At Bedford's death H. assumed an active role in government. He met with opposition that culminated in open rebellion—the Wars of the Roses. Between bouts of mental illness H. was imprisoned, restored to his throne, but finally murdered. Despite his recurrent illness, he was a great scholar. He founded Eton College and King's College, Cambridge, and assisted in establishing Queens' College. Interest in his canonization, first proposed by Henry VII, has recently revived. BIBLIOGRAPHY: C. M. Aherne, NCE 6:1023.

[F. G. O'BRIEN]

HENRY VII (1457–1509), **KING OF ENGLAND** from 1485. The first Tudor king, H. spent many years in exile in Brittany before invading England in 1485, defeating Richard III at Bosworth, and securing the throne. Despite several rebellions against him, including those of Lambert Simnel and Perkin Warbeck, H. consolidated his position. Avoiding foreign entanglements, he strengthened the government, esp. financially, and repressed lawlessness. A pious man, he completed Edward IV's building of St. George's Chapel, Windsor, and he himself built a great chapel in Westminster Abbey and palaces at Richmond and Greenwich. Described by Francis Bacon as "a wonder for wise men," H. lacked popular appeal and proved a hard taskmaster; but he was an able, industrious, and realistic ruler who left the English monarchy far stronger than he found it. BIBLIOGRAPHY: R. L. Storey, *Henry VII* (1968).

[C. D. ROSS]

HENRY VIII (1491–1547), **KING OF ENGLAND** from 1509. This article is confined to the steps whereby H. separated the Church of England from Rome. He was influenced to some degree by the example of Protestant princes and the writings of men like William Tyndale; yet he might never have caused England to separate from Rome had it not been for his dynastic interests. Since only a girl survived of his children by Catherine of Aragon and since he feared the Tudor succession would be disputed, he wanted to marry again to obtain further issue. Besides, he was in love with Anne Boleyn, lady-in-waiting to the Queen. Accordingly, in 1527 he asked Pope Clement VII to revoke the dispensation given him 18 years before to marry Catherine, his brother's widow. He reasoned that his failure to have a male heir was proof of the divine displeasure that is threatened in Lev 20.21. When it was rejoined that his illicit relations with Anne's older sister Mary made him related to Anne in the same degree as to Catherine, he shifted his argument: not all such dispensations were invalid, but his was, for a number of reasons. A flood of polemical literature followed. To gain his end, H. asked Card. Wolsey to try the case in his legatine court and only then to proceed to obtain the Pope's approval. When Wolsey learned that Catherine might appeal his decision, he attempted to gain the Pope's approval beforehand. Clement temporized by ordering Wolsey and Card. Campeggio to hear the case in France but gave the latter secret instructions to persuade H. to drop the suit or Catherine to enter a convent. By threatening to join the Lutherans, H. forced Wolsey to open proceedings in May 1529. After lengthy hearings the court was recessed in July, to resume in Rome in October. H. feared a decision given in Rome would be unfavorable and therefore resolved to try the case in his own courts. Thomas Cranmer now advised H. to submit the question of annulment to university scholars with the proviso that if their verdict proved unsatisfactory, he declare himself head of the Church in England and settle the case in his own courts. H. thereupon called Parliament and laid the issue before it. By attacking clerical abuses, he and Parliament intimidated *Convocations, which acknowledged him as supreme head of the English Church "as far as the law of Christ allows."

The next year H. extracted from Convocations the Submission of the Clergy, whereby it was agreed that ecclesiastical laws be revised by a committee consisting of laymen and clerics chosen by the King and that no new laws be enacted by Convocations without the King's consent. H. also obtained from Parliament an act depriving the Pope of his customary annates whenever the King saw fit. When Clement remained unintimidated, H. decided to end all papal authority in England. He proceeded, Jan. 1533, to marry Anne. Parliament then passed the retroactive Act for the Restraint of Appeals, which made invalid both Catherine's recourse to Rome and H.'s original suit. Anne was crowned in June and on July 11 the Pope excommunicated Henry. At that point Parliament proceeded to legalize the break with Rome. It stopped all payments to the papacy and by the Act of Supremacy (1534) made H. the only supreme head on earth of the Church of England (*Anglicana Ecclesia*). It also passed an Act of Succession in favor of Anne's heirs. The *dissolution of the monasteries took place in 1536 and 1539. While the views of the continental Reformation were reflected in the *Ten Articles of 1536, and in liturgical reforms favoring the vernacular, doctrinally H. sought to conserve the substance of Catholic belief (see SIX ARTICLES; KING'S BOOK) during his reign. BIBLIOGRAPHY: H. J. Grimm, *Reformation Era* (1965) 289–300; E. Doernberg, *Henry VIII and Luther* (1961).

HENRY I (c. 1008–60), **KING OF FRANCE** from 1031, notorious as the weakest of the Capetians, instigator of a perennial conflict between the French kings and the dukes of Normandy by his opposition to William the Conqueror, and for his venality.

[T. C. O'BRIEN]

HENRY IV (1553–1610), **KING OF FRANCE** from 1589, ruler whose accession marked the end of the French Religious Wars. A flamboyant, vigorous man, Henry of Navarre was far from a religious dogmatist. His early religious life was dominated by his Protestant mother, Jeanne d'Albret. He made a forced conversion to Catholicism during the St. Bartholomew's Day Massacre (August 22–23, 1572), but shortly after abandoned it. His abjuration on July 25, 1593, marked his final return to Catholicism and ended most resistance to his succession. Religiously, H. can be best characterized as a *politique*. He firmly believed that the unity of France was more important than religious uniformity. The *Edict of Nantes (April 13, 1598) was an example of his *politique* attitudes. This famous decree was not an act of toleration, but rather a recognition that the Huguenots could not be defeated, without further bloodshed and harm to France. H.'s efforts were largely successful in bringing France order and prosperity after nearly forty years of religious and political strife. BIBLIOGRAPHY: D. Seward, *First Bourbon King, Henri IV, King of France and Navarre* (1971); R. S. Dunn, *Age of Religious Wars, 1559–1689* (1970).

[C. T. EBY]

HENRY II, ST. (*c.*972–1024), **HOLY ROMAN EMPEROR.** Born near Hildesheim, he was educated for the Church but crowned king of Germany at Mainz (1002), king of Italy at Pavia (1004), and emperor at Rome by Benedict VIII (1014). The early part of his reign was devoted to internal peace and to establishing acceptable borders with his neighbors. This entailed long wars with Poland, Lorraine, and Flanders, and with his brothers-in-law in Luxembourg. He made three trips to Italy. The first was to suppress Count Ardoin of Ivrea; the second, at papal request, to bring order to Rome; the last, in 1021–22, into S Italy to overcome the Byzantines. H. supported monastic reform stemming from Gorze, was an active church builder and the founder of Bamberg. No small debt is owed him for the artists, gathered at Bamberg, who contributed to the Romanesque style. To rule, he employed the higher clergy, thus establishing a custom which led to the investiture struggle. BIBLIOGRAPHY: Gebhardt-Grundmann 1:210–225; H. Holtzmann, *Geschichte der sächsischen Kaiserzeit*[3] (1955), 381–487; Butler 3:105–106; G. and C. Spahr, BiblSanct 4:1240–46.

[S. WILLIAMS]

HENRY III (1017–56), **HOLY ROMAN EMPEROR,** Born at Osterbeck, H. was well educated and was crowned coruler with his father, Conrad II, at Aachen in 1028. In 1039 he succeeded his father and in 1046 he and his queen, Agnes of Poitou, were crowned emperor and empress at Rome by Clement II. To strengthen the empire he had used a great number of ecclesiastics for administration. After the Council of Sutri (1046), the naming of Roman popes devolved entirely on him. He died at Bodfeld—near Goslar—in 1056 and was buried at Speyer. His son, Henry IV, was only a young child, to the detriment of the empire his father had tried to build. BIBLIOGRAPHY: J. M. Powell, NCE 6:1031–32.

[S. WILLIAMS]

HENRY IV (1050–1106) **HOLY ROMAN EMPEROR** from 1056, of the Franconian or Salian line, son of Emperor Henry III whom he succeeded as king. Under the regency the power of the monarchy declined alarmingly. In 1069 H. began to exercise effective leadership. He first had to assert his authority in Germany over the nobles and esp. over the independent-minded Saxons. The crown's traditional policy of control over the German episcopate brought H. into conflict with the reform movement of Pope Gregory VII (Hildebrand) over lay investiture. To escape the political isolation resulting from his excommunication, H. sought papal absolution at Canossa in Jan. 1077. After defeating a movement to set Rudolf of Swabia up as king, H. had himself crowned emperor (1084) by an antipope of his own creation. The arrival of the Normans, coming to the aid of Pope Gregory, caused him to return to Germany. The revolts of his sons Conrad (1093) and Henry V marred the last years of his reign. It was during battle with the latter that H.'s death occurred. BIBLIOGRAPHY: J. M. Powell, NCE 6:1032.

[J. E. LYNCH]

HENRY V (1081–1125), **HOLY ROMAN EMPEROR** from 1106, son of Henry IV, elected king of the Germans in 1098, crowned emperor by Paschal II in 1111. A person of great ability, admired on all sides, but loved by none. H. pressed the Church relentlessly and, even more than his father, pursued a policy of total control of the empire by using ecclesiastics and nobles. In 1106, he deposed his own father, but after being defeated by the German rebels in 1116, he made the Concordat of Worms in 1122 with Callistus II. In 1125, he was defeated by the Saxons, and the electors rejected his candidate for Duke Lothar of Saxony, thus ending both the Salian line and an hereditary monarchy. BIBLIOGRAPHY: S. Williams, NCE 6:1032–34; A. Amore, EncCatt 5:379–381; Gebhardt–Grundmann 1:273–281.

[S. WILLIAMS]

HENRY VI (1165–97), **HOLY ROMAN EMPEROR,** The second son of *Frederick Barbarossa, H. was crowned king of the Germans (1169), of Italy (1189), of Sicily (1194), and emperor (1191). In spite of papal opposition this brilliant man succeeded in having his son, Frederick II, elected king both of the Germans and of Sicily. He died suddenly at Messina and with his death both the Third Crusade and an attempted hereditary monarchy collapsed. BIBLIOGRAPHY: S. Williams, NCE 6:1034; H. Schaller, LTK 5:182; A. Poole, CMedH 5:454–480; *History of the Crusades* (ed. K. M. Setton, 1962) 2:116–122.

[S. WILLIAMS]

HENRY VII (*c.*1275–1313), **HOLY ROMAN EMPEROR** from 1308. Born Henry IV of Luxembourg, he was elected emperor, and crowned king of the Romans at Aachen in 1309 and emperor of Rome (1312), after entering the city by force; he then laid siege unsuccessfully to Florence. He died of malaria while on the way to invade Naples. He is the ''alto Arrigo'' of Dante's *Divine Comedy.* BIBLIOGRAPHY: W. M. Bowsky, *Henry VII in Italy* (1960); R. Davidsohn, *Geschichte von Florenz* (4 v., 1896–1927) 3:345–552.

[W. A. JURGENS]

HENRY (BATE) OF MICHELN (d. after 1310), Flemish medieval philosopher, mathematician, astronomer, linguist, canon of Liège. His major work, *Speculum divinorum et quorundam naturalium,* is important for the history of medieval Platonism and as a source for contemporary philosophical controversy at the Univ. of Paris. He was a friend of William of Moerbeke and translator of several Hebrew treatises of Abraham ben Ezra. BIBLIOGRAPHY: J. R. O'Donnell, NCE 6:1041; Lynn Thorndike, *History of*

Magic and Experimental Science (8 v., 1923–34) 2: 926–30.

[J. E. WRIGLEY]

HENRY OF BLOIS (d. 1171), monk, bishop, statesman, brother of King Stephen of England, and a leading figure of his reign. Educated at Cluny, he was a lifelong friend of Peter the Venerable. He became abbot of Glastonbury (1126), bp. of Winchester (1129) with a dispensation to hold the two offices in plurality, and papal legate (1136–43). Respected as abbot and bp., he was an outstanding administrator and a firm but moderate supporter of Thomas Becket. BIBLIOGRAPHY: L. Voss, *Heinrich von Blois, Bischof von Winchester, 1129–71* (*Historische Studien* 210, 1932); Knowles MOE 282–298; W. Hunt, DNB 8:563–568; M. M. Chibnall, NCE 6:1034.

[J. L. GRASSI]

HENRY OF BOLZANO, BL. (of Treviso; *c.*1250–1315), Italian ascetic. Born of poor parents in Bolzano, he moved to Treviso where he worked as a menial laborer. After the death of his wife and his son, his devotion to poverty, prayer, and penance increased. He gained a reputation for great sanctity, and many miracles were reported after his death. BIBLIOGRAPHY: I. Rogger, BiblSanct 4:1226–27; Butler 2:520–521.

[G. E. CONWAY]

HENRY OF BONN, BL. (*c.*1100–47), a knight from Cologne on the Second Crusade. On the way, when the fleet stopped to conquer Muslim Lisbon, H. was killed in the siege. There he was buried near St. Vincent's Church, and was soon venerated as a result of miracles at his grave. BIBLIOGRAPHY: AS Oct. 8:281.

[R. I. BURNS]

HENRY OF BRACTON (*c.*1210–68), English cleric and jurist. He possibly did his legal studies at Oxford, became a king's clerk by 1240, and a justice by 1244. In his unfinished *De legibus et consuetudinibus Angliae* and his *Notebook* of cases, he sought to systematize English common law. These works had a marked influence on English constitutional law. BIBLIOGRAPHY: Emden Ox 1:240–241; B. Tierney, "Bracton on Government," *Speculum* 38 (1963) 295–317.

HENRY OF CLAIRVAUX, BL. (Henry of Marcy; d. 1189), Cistercian cardinal-bishop of Albano and papal diplomat. Burgundian by birth, H. joined the Cistercians in 1155, became abbot of Hautecombe (Savoy) in 1160, of Clairvaux in 1176, and cardinal in 1179. He served the Holy See in French and English affairs, in negotiations concerning the Albigensians, and in the matter of the Third Crusade. He was considered as successor to Pope Urban III (1187) but refused the office. Writings: PL 204:215–402. BIBLIOGRAPHY: S. Steffen, "Heinrich, Kardinal-bischof von Albano," serial in *Cistercienser-Chronik 31* (1909); M. A. Dimier, BiblSanct 4:1230–31.

[L. J. LEKAI]

HENRY OF DIESSENHOFEN (*c.*1302–76), canon of Constance; at the papal court in Avignon, author of *Historia Ecclesiae*, a continuation to the year 1361 of *Bartholomew of Lucca's *Historia ecclesiastica* which covered Christian history up to 1314.

[T. C. O'BRIEN]

HENRY OF FRIEMAR (the Elder; *c.*1245–1340), theologian and preacher. A member of the Order of Augustinian Hermits, H. wrote numerous influential works on ascetical and mystical subjects. Among his writings are a treatise on the origin of his order and its development to 1256, an explanation of the Mass, and a description of the Passion of Christ. BIBLIOGRAPHY: R. Arbesmann, NCE 6:1035.

[M. J. FINNEGAN]

HENRY OF GHENT (*c.*1217–1293), scholastic philosopher and theologian, *Doctor solemnis,* who lectured at the Univ. of Paris from 1276 to 1292. A secular master in theology, he was the most renowned teacher of his era, a leading figure in university affairs, and an active opponent of the mendicant friars. His *Summa theologica* (modern ed. 1953) and his 15 *Quodlibeta* represent the disputations, ordinary and solemn, that he conducted during his teaching career. He also wrote on Aristotle's *Metaphysics* and *Physics*. His doctrinal synthesis was a type of Augustinianism distinct from that of the Franciscan school; it combined elements from Plato, Augustine, and Avicenna, and for four centuries was cultivated by Christian Platonists not attracted by Thomism. His thought, particularly in metaphysics, had a direct effect upon individual scholastics, most notably on Duns Scotus; in many ways as well, he inspired the critical spirit characteristic of 14–cent. scholasticism. BIBLIOGRAPHY: Gilson HCP 447–454.

[T. C. O'BRIEN]

HENRY OF GORKUM (*c.*1386–1431), theologian at Cologne; early exponent of the teaching of St. *Thomas Aquinas; author of *Compendium summae theologiae S. Thomae,* edited posthumously (1473).

[T. C. O'BRIEN]

HENRY OF HARCLAY (1270–1317), English scholastic. He was a secular master at Oxford when elected chancellor of the university in 1312. In this capacity he was involved in a dispute with the Dominicans over academic procedures and died at Avignon while seeking papal solution. His philosophical position was Augustinian and anti-Thomist; Gilson also regards his opposition to Duns Scotus' realism as a step towards the nominalism of *William of Ockham. BIBLIOGRAPHY: Gilson HCP 480–483.

[T. C. O'BRIEN]

HENRY HEINBUCHE OF LANGENSTEIN (*c.* 1330–97), conciliarist, theologian, academician. No adequate biography of this many-sided man exists in any language. Entering the Univ. of Paris in 1358, H. became a master of arts (1363), taught and wrote on astronomy, but later turned to theology and became a doctor (1375), then professor of Scripture and vice chancellor in 1378, the year of the Western Schism. In his letter *Epistola pacis* (May 1379) he was the first to advocate a general council. Exiled from Paris, he was called to Vienna to refound the univ. in 1380. He served one term as rector and taught there until his death. Though some works have been printed, large numbers remain in MS such as his exegesis on Genesis, his ascetical theology, his work on the Immaculate Conception, translations into German of hymns and psalms and his Hebrew grammar. BIBLIOGRAPHY: S. Williams, NCE 6:1037–38; J. Zemb, DTC 8.2:2574–76; Pastor v. 1 *passim.*

[S. WILLIAMS]

HENRY OF HEISTERBACH, BL. (d. 1242), Cistercian abbot, mystic. Noble by birth, H. studied in Paris, became a canon in Bonn, but *c.* 1200 joined the Cistercians in Heisterbach, where he became prior and in 1208, abbot. His abbey flourished materially and spiritually. He encouraged Caesarius of Heisterbach's literary activity. BIBLIOGRAPHY: G. Wellstein, *Die Cistercienserabtel Marienstatt,* (1955) 19; C. Spahr, BiblSanct 4:1228–29.

[L. J. LEKAI]

HENRY OF HERFORD (d. 1370), German Dominican philosopher, theologian, and historian. His chief work was *Liber de rebus memorabilioribus,* a rather pedestrian chronicle of the world from creation to 1355. This was edited by A. Potthast in 1859.

[L. E. BOYLE]

HENRY OF HERP (Harphius van Erp; *c.* 1405–77), mystical writer. He was first a member of the Brethren of the Common Life at Delft, Holland; at Rome in 1450 he became a Franciscan of the Observance; he lived and died at Mechlin as a member of the Cologne province. H.'s chief work is *Spieghel der Volcomenheit,* composed in middle Dutch between 1455 and 1460 (modern ed., J. L. Verscheuren, ed., 2 v., 1931). The work lays out the process of the interior life from the interior-active through the interior-contemplative to the interior-''superessential''; in the last stage the soul reaches a direct vision of the divine essence. H. marks out the grades of ascent within each of the three stages; his particular emphasis, dependent on *Hugh of Balma, is on the prayer of aspiration, i.e., a repeated desire of will for union with God. In overall content the *Spieghel* strongly reflects the influence of Jan van *Ruysbroek.

[T. C. O'BRIEN]

HENRY OF HUNTINGDON (*c.* 1080–85–1155), English churchman and chronicler. He was ordained a priest before 1110 and a year later was made archdeacon of Huntington. He made Bede's work the foundation for his *Historia Anglorum,* which he divided into four periods: Roman, Saxon, Danish, and Norman. Between 1130 and 1154 he brought out five editions of his history, eventually adding three books which are cast in epistolary form. As a chronicler, H. is a valuable independent source for his own age, but as an historian and stylist he is inferior to William of Malmesbury and Robert of Torigny. BIBLIOGRAPHY: M. R. McGuire, NCE 6:1039, H. R. Luard, DNB 9:569–570; Manitius 3:481–485; Ghellinck Essor 2:153–155.

[M. R. P. MCGUIRE]

HENRY OF KALKAR (1328–1408), Carthusian, spiritual writer. He was a master at Paris, then canon at Cologne before entering the Cologne Charterhouse in 1365. As prior of Arnheim (1368) he was the spiritual guide of Gerard de Groote, and through his writings and preaching played a strong part in the development of the *Devotio moderna. Some have even attributed authorship of the *Imitation of Christ* to him, but the ascription has little probability.

[T. C. O'BRIEN]

HENRY OF LAUSANNE (Henry the Heretic; d. *c.* 1145), an apostate monk who began to preach at Le Mans early in the 12th century. His eloquence and commanding appearance won him many followers, called Henricians. H. bitterly attacked the worldliness of the clergy and urged all to practice poverty. He rejected *infant baptism and veneration of the saints, and was finally expelled from Le Mans by Bp. Hildebert of Lavardin. He then moved through S France castigating the official Church and arousing mobs to desecrate churches, assault clerics, and pull down crosses. He was condemned at the Council of Toulouse in 1119, recanted at the Synod of Pisa in 1135, and was again condemned at Lateran Council II in 1139. St. Bernard was sent to preach against him in 1145. The same year H. was imprisoned and died shortly afterward. BIBLIOGRAPHY: H. Daniel-Rops, *Cathedral and Crusade* (1957) 523; E. Delaruelle, *Catholicisme* 5:622–624; J. Guiraud, *Histoire de l'Inquisition au Moyen-Age* 1:3–13 (1935).

[C. J. LYNCH]

HENRY THE LION (1129–95), Duke of Bavaria, son of Henry the Proud. He received title to Saxony in 1142 but had to wait until 1154 for Bavaria, which was bestowed on him by his cousin Frederick Barbarossa in return for military aid. By 1162 he had subjected the Wendish territory beyond the Elbe to German rule. As the most powerful prince in the empire, he married Matilda, daughter of Henry II of England, in 1168. A breach between the Emperor Frederick Barbarossa and H. over certain German lands led to the Diet of Gelnhausen in 1180, where H. was stripped of most of his possessions. In 1182 he was banished for three years. He returned to Brunswick where he devoted himself to intellectual and artistic interests. His son Otto IV was Innocent III's candidate for the imperial crown in 1209. BIBLIOGRAPHY: A. L. Poole, *Henry the Lion* (1912).

[J. E. LYNCH]

HENRY OF LIVONIA (Henricus de Lettis; d. after 1259), chronicler of the Baltic Church. H. was educated in Saxony and went to Livonia *c.* 1205. After ordination in 1208 he settled among the Letts. His *Chronicle,* begun *c.* 1225, records the Saxon conquest of the Baltic. He served (1225–27) as interpreter for the papal legate of the Baltic, Bp. William of Modena. BIBLIOGRAPHY: J. A. Brundage, NCE 6:1040–41.

[M. J. FINNEGAN]

HENRY MURDAC (d. 1153), Cistercian abp. of York. A noble of Yorkshire, H. joined the secular clergy, then transferred to the Cistercians at Clairvaux. Commissioned by St. Bernard himself, he became in 1135 founder and first abbot of Vauclair (France), and in 1143 was elected abbot of Fountains in Yorkshire. He rebuilt Fountains magnificently and founded five new monasteries. Supported by St. Bernard and the Cistercian Pope Eugene III, he was created abp. of York in 1147, but his position was hotly contested and he was unable to take possession of his see until 1151. A strict ascetic, a zealous reformer, he was unyielding in his defense of principles. BIBLIOGRAPHY: T. F. Tout, DNB 13:1218–20; J. H. Baxter, NCE 6:1041.

[L. J. LEKAI]

HENRY THE NAVIGATOR (1394–1460), prince, crusader, explorer. Fourth surviving son of John I of Portugal, H. conquered Ceuta in N Africa (1415). As grand master of the Military Order of Christ, he presided over a campaign of discovery down the African coast, gathering experience and information and initiating the Age of Discovery. BIBLIOGRAPHY: J. B. Heffernan, NCE 6:1042.

[R. I. BURNS]

HENRY OF NEWARK (d. 1299), archbishop of York, diplomat. He began his career about 1270 from clerk to Edward I, to abp. of York, to which office he was elected in 1296 but not consecrated until 1298 because the wars prevented him from appearing before Boniface VIII, who confirmed the election in 1297. H. served the king in several important capacities. He represented Edward at the Roman court (1276–77); in 1281 he arbitrated a dispute with subjects of the Count of Holland; in 1283 he was appointed to arrange the services due to the king from knights and others N of the Trent and to collect subsidies in the Diocese of Durham for the Welsh wars; in 1296 he was one of those appointed to treat with the counts of Gelderland and Holland. He was also a member of the council of the Prince of Wales. He was buried in the cathedral church at York. BIBLIOGRAPHY: W. H. Dixon, *Fasti Eboracenses: Lives of the Archbishops of York* (ed. J. Raine, 1863) 349–353; W. Hunt, DNB 14:310–311.

[J. J. SMITH]

HENRY OF ST. IGNATIUS (*c.* 1630–1719), Belgian Carmelite theologian. His major work, inspired by his vehement opposition to casuistry and *probabilism in moral theology, was *Ethica amoris sive theologia sanctorum* (1st ed., 1709). It had the merit of stressing the primacy of *charity in the moral life, but its extreme polemic against enemies of the Jansenists for *laxism caused Bp. *Fénelon to denounce the work at Rome in 1711. In 1714, Book I was proscribed by the Inquisition and in 1722 the whole opus. Earlier, H. had published an anti-Jesuit work (*Artes jesuiticae in sustinendis pertinaciter novitatibus damnabilibusque Sociorum laxitatibus*); the first ed. (1703) was put on the Index in 1709; a second, rev. ed., in 1711, but a third escaped condemnation.

[T. C. O'BRIEN]

HENRY OF SETTIMELLO (d. perhaps 1194), priest and poet, author of a narrative poem, *De diversitate fortunae et philosophiae consolatione,* popular in the Middle Ages. Written in the elegiac meter, the poem shows the influence of Martianus Capella and treats of the many woes of life for which philosophy provides the only basis of endurance. BIBLIOGRAPHY: H. MacKinnon, NCE 6:1043.

[M. A. WINKELMAN]

HENRY SUSO, BL. (1295–1366), preacher and mystical writer. H. entered the Dominican Order at the age of 13 at Constance. Meister Eckhart was his teacher at Cologne (1322/24–25). After a brief professorship at Constance (1326–27/30), he developed a lively ministry as preacher and spiritual director, esp. among nuns and the *Friends of God in Switzerland and the Rhineland. He was prior of the Constance Dominicans (in exile at Diessenhoven) during 1343–44. His life as a mystic began with a spiritual conversion when he was 18 and was matured by physical hardships, hostility, persecution, and calumny. When slander caused even friends to desert him, H. was transferred to Ulm (*c.* 1347) where he died. His *Little Book of Truth* (*c.* 1327) is an exposition of profound mystical questions and is also a defense of Meister Eckhart. His *Little Book of Eternal Wisdom* (*c.* 1328), a mystical dialogue with Christ and occasionally Mary, was the most popular spiritual book of the 14th and 15th centuries. It has been called "the finest fruit of German mysticism" (Denifle). H. published *c.* 1334 a reworked Latin version of this, called the *Horologium sapientiae*. H.'s *Life of the Servant* is his spiritual biography. Two sermons and 28 spiritual letters (also in an abridged form) are extant. The brief *Soul's Love Book* is doubtfully authentic. H. collected his Middle High German works in an *Exemplar c.* 1362. Some scholars deny his connection with this collection and his authorship of the *Life,* which they claim is largely fictional. The authenticity of both is upheld by reliable authors. His spiritual teaching, illustrated by constant reference to his own experiences and dominated by a tender love of Christ, is psychological, practical, and largely ascetical but touches at times on profound mystical, speculative points. Venerated immediately after his death and continuously, H. was beatified on April 16, 1831. English tr. of works: Sr. M. Ann Edward, *Exemplar. Life and Writings of Bl. Henry Suso, O.P.*, (2 v., 1962). BIBLIOGRAPHY: J. Ancelet-Hustache, *Master Eckhart and the Rhineland Mystics* (tr. H. Graef, pa. 1958); J. M. Clark, *Great German Mystics* (1949).

[W. A. HINNEBUSCH]

HENRY OF UPPSALA, ST. (d. *c.*1156), bp., martyr, patron saint of Finland. H. is believed to have accompanied King Eric IX of Sweden on his crusade to Finland where they converted many pagans. H. remained in Finland to meet martyrdom at the hands of a convert. Many legends grew concerning him and a cult spread rapidly. In 1300 his relics were translated from Nousis, Finland, to Åbo (Turku), Sweden. BIBLIOGRAPHY: T. Schmid, NCE, 6:1045; Butler 1:123; A. L. Sibilia, BiblSanct 4:1232–34.

[F. G. O'BRIEN]

HENRY OF VITSKÓL, BL. (d. late 12th cent.), Cistercian monk at Clairvaux where he spent his noviceship under the abbot, Bernard of Clairvaux. Henry himself was later founder and abbot of the abbey of Varnhem in Sweden (1150). He is connected with two other foundations—one at Vitskól in Denmark, which he directed (1158) and the other at Clara-Insula which he founded (1166). BIBLIOGRAPHY: A. M. Zimmerman, BiblSanct 4:1238.

[J. R. RIVELLO]

HENRY OF ZWIEFALTEN, BL. (*c.*1200–62), German Benedictine monk. From a family which resided in Zwiefalten, H., after a youth spent as a knight, became a Benedictine and in 1238 was named prior of Ochsenhausen, a dependency of the abbey of Sankt Blasien. H. expanded the monastic library, obtained generous gifts for the adornment of the church, and earned renown for miraculous powers. BIBLIOGRAPHY: G. Spahr, NCE 6:1045; J. F. Alonso, BiblSanct 4:1238–40.

[M. J. FINNEGAN]

HENRY, CARL F. H. (1913–), theologian, professor, editor, writer, and outstanding leader of *Evangelicalism. Born in New York City, he was educated at Wheaton College (B.A., M.A.), Northern Baptist Seminary (B.D., Th.D.), and Boston University (Ph.D.). His career includes teaching at Northern Baptist Seminary (1942–47), Fuller Theological Seminary (1947–56), Eastern Baptist Theological Seminary (1969–74), and visiting lectureships at numerous institutions. From 1956 to 1968 he was editor of *Christianity Today,* a fortnightly founded to foster Evangelicalism. He became Lecturer-at-Large for World Vision, Inc. in 1974. His career has been devoted to recalling Protestanism to renewed evangelistic endeavor, recovery of theological orthodoxy, and a deepening of ethical concern. In 1948 he challenged conservatives with *The Uneasy Conscience of Modern Fundamentalism,* and subsequently he has written and edited more than two-score books, as well as countless articles in support of his understanding of evangelical Christianity. He has also furthered the cause by establishing The Institute for Advanced Christian Studies, promoting the World Congress on Evangelism (Berlin, 1966), and speaking at conferences around the world. In 1976, the first two volumes of *God, Revelation, and Authority* appeared, and the rest is to be published by 1980. This work represents the culmination of a lifetime of study on what he considers the most critical issue in theology today, viz., an authoritative basis for Christian belief. Assuming that in the Bible God has given his revelation in propositional form, H. places heavy emphasis upon the law of noncontradiction in support of a doctrine of the inerrancy of Holy Scriptures. His presuppositions lead him to minimize subjective, nonrational, and mythopoetic elements in human experience, and to stress the role of reason and logic in arriving at ultimate truths of revelation.

[N. H. MARING]

HENRY, HUGH THOMAS (1862–1946), scholar, hymnodist, educator. Born in Philadelphia, he was ordained in 1889. He served as professor at St. Charles Seminary, 1887–1919, and was director of the choir. He edited *Church Music* (1905–12), and wrote for the *Catholic Encyclopedia.* When in 1902 his *Poems, Charades, and Inscriptions of Pope Leo XIII,* appeared the Univ. of Pennsylvania conferred on him an honorary doctorate. In 1912 he was made rector of Roman Catholic High School. From 1919 at The Catholic Univ. of America, he taught homiletics. He published on the art of preaching (1924, 1925, 1941). His historical acumen found outlet in the *American Catholic Historical Society of Phila.*, of which he was president (1897–98) and corresponding secretary (1910–13). His popular hymn *Long Live the Pope,* for which H. G. Ganss wrote the music, was translated into 15 tongues including American Indian. In Jessup, Pa., H. died on the feast of St. Gregory the Great, the correct rendition of whose chant he had ably fostered. His impact on the *liturgical movement, as in his CE article, "Congregational Singing," was notable. BIBLIOGRAPHY: "Report of E. F. Halsey to Library Committee for 1970," RACHS 82 (1971) 48–49; R. H. Schmandt, *History of the Archdiocese of Philadelphia* (ed. J. F. Connelly, 1976) 605–613.

[M. R. BROWN]

HENRY BRADSHAW SOCIETY, a society founded in England in 1890 for editing and publishing liturgical MSS, rare editions of service books, and related documents of historical interest bearing on the Anglican liturgy, esp. the BCP; named in honor of Henry Bradshaw (1831–86), librarian of the Univ. of Cambridge. Among its important publications are the *Gregorian Sacramentary* and the *Bobbio Missal*.

[E. J. DILLON]

HENSCHEN (HENSKENS), GOTTFRIED (1601–81), Flemish Jesuit and Bollandist. He was chosen (1653) to assist his former teacher, J. van *Bolland, in the preparation and publication of the **Acta Sanctorum* and spent the remaining 46 years of his life in that hagiographical work. He contributed importantly to the development and improvement of the critical methods for which the *Bollandists became famous. BIBLIOGRAPHY: C. De Smedt, CE 2:632–634; H. Delehaye, *A travers trois siècles, L'oeuvre des Bollandistes de 1615–1915* (1920).

[R. B. ENO]

HENSON, HERBERT HENSLEY (1863–1947), Anglican bp. of Hereford (1918) and Durham (1920–39). A graduate of Oxford, H. was ordained in 1888. He gave up an early sympathy for the High Church cause and aligned himself with the Broad Church party. His liberal theology caused some to protest when he was nominated for the See of Hereford. He favored a comprehensive and tolerant national Church, but later turned against the Establishment in his disappointment at the rejection by Parliament of the revision of the *Book of Common Prayer (1927–28). His writings include *Ad clerum* (1937) and *Retrospect of an Unimportant Life* (3 v., 1942–50).

[R. B. ENO]

HEPBURN, JAMES (rel. name Bonaventure; 1573–1621), *Minim Orientalist. A native of Scotland, H. was converted to Catholicism while a student at the Univ. of St. Andrew, Edinburgh. He entered the Minims at Avignon. His labors on oriental manuscripts in the Vatican Library and at Venice resulted in more than 30 works.

[T. C. O'BRIEN]

HERACLEON (*c.*145–180), leading representative of the Italian school of the Gnosticism of *Valentinus. The works of H. survive only in fragments. H. is one of the earliest commentators on the NT; Origen frequently cites his commentary on the Fourth Gospel. His highly allegorized commentaries set forth the teachings of Valentinus. Epiphanius gave the name Heracleonites to a group of Gnostics (*Penar.* 36). BIBLIOGRAPHY: G. Bareille, DTC 6:2198–2205.

[L. G. MÜLLER]

HERACLES, Greek hero, who, as Hercules, was worshipped as a god in Rome. Though he appears originally to have been a prince in Tiryns *c.*1100, a complex mythological tradition accords H. heroic (and sometimes divine) status by virtue of his exploits, particularly his twelve labors. In late Antiquity, H. frequently served in literature and in art as a model for athletes, philosophers, and rulers. BIBLIOGRAPHY: L. R. Farnell, *Greek Hero Cults and Ideas of Immortality* (1921); J. Bayet, *Les Origines de l'Hercule romain* (1926); M. Simon, *Hercule et le Christianisme* (1955).

[E. V. GALLAGHER]

HERACLIAN OF CHALCEDON, an early bp. of Chalcedon, of whom little is known beyond Photius' reference to him as a vigorous opponent of the Manichaeans and the author of a 20-volume work *Adversus Manichaeos,* presumably a compendium of the opinions of opponents of the Manichaeans. There is also a fragment of H.'s letter to a certain Achillius that is cited by Maximus the Confessor and may be found in PG. The fragment deals with an attempt to harmonize the humanity of Christ with the divinity. BIBLIOGRAPHY: C. Hole, DCB 2:901; PG xci:125–126.

[E. J. DILLON]

HERACLITUS OF EPHESUS (fl. *c.*500 B.C.), the deepest thinker of all the pre-Socratics, and the most obscure because of the oracular form of the utterances attributed to him. He taught that all things are in a state of flux, but esp. that Reality is One and Many at the same time, unity in difference. There is harmony in opposites; the world is an ever-living fire and hence is in an eternal state of process. His most important contribution, however, is that he turned inwards for an explanation of knowledge and the soul: "I searched myself," thus becoming the first philosopher of mind. He stressed the concept of Logos or the Word as eternal truth, the divine "thought by which all things are steered through all things." He opposed the moral dualism of the Pythagoreans and based his own ethics on the harmony of opposite tensions. Reason and consciousness in man is the fiery, and therefore, the valuable element. There is one immanent Law and Reason in the universe. The God of Heraclitus is the immanent ordering principle of all things and not a personal God. He identifies his Eternal Fire with Thought, Reason, God, and Eternal Justice. He exercised a great influence on the Stoics, although their belief in periodic world conflagrations is not found in him. BIBLIOGRAPHY: A. H. Coxon, OCD 415; LexAW s.v.; Copleston 1:38–46; Guthrie 1:403–492.

[M. R. P. MCGUIRE]

HERACLIUS (*c.*575–641), **BYZANTINE EMPEROR** from 610. He seized power by a revolt against the Emperor Phocas, whom he executed. Most of H.'s reign was spent in military campaigns to hold his territory against the Persians, Slavs, and Arabs. In ecclesiastical affairs he tried to satisfy his Monophysite subjects by enforcing *Monothelitism in the edict *Ecthesis* (638). Pope Severinus repudiated the edict and Pope John IV condemned Monothelitism.

HERBART, JOHANN FRIEDRICH (1776–1841), German philosopher and educator. Although influenced by Kant, Leibniz, and Fichte at Jena, H. did not subscribe wholly to an idealistic philosophy. As tutor (1796) he began to develop ideas on method, which were later influenced by contact with Pestalozzi in Burgdorf (1799). At Bremen, where he resumed his philosophical studies, he made a scientific formulation of Pestalozzi's educational ideas. He lectured at Göttingen in 1805 and in 1809 accepted the chair of philosophy left vacant by Kant at Königsberg, where he also lectured on education and in 1810 instituted a teacher's seminary and model school. He returned to Göttingen in 1833. His contribution to education consists mainly in his psychological principles applied to method. His theory of interest and apperception helped unify educational process and promote the correlation and coordination of studies. His *Outlines of Educational Doctrine* (1841) describes his system. BIBLIOGRAPHY: J. S. Brubacher, *History of the Problems of Education* (1947).

[M. B. MURPHY]

HERBERT, EDWARD (1583–1648), English poet, philosopher, historian, and diplomat; brother of George Herbert, the poet. In politics he steered a middle course between Charles I and Parliament but in 1645 submitted to the Parliamentarians. His *Autobiography*, discovered and printed by Horace Walpole in 1764, is a very readable account of the period to 1624. He is a metaphysical poet of the style of Donne and Carew. In philosophy he has been called the father of Deism, whose principles he formulated at the end of *De veritate* (1624), developed fully in *De religione laici* (1645), and in *De religione gentilium* (1663). He sought a set of universal truths established by reason, which would stand between traditional religion and its excesses (as he saw them) and irreligious skepticism. He subjected scriptural revelation to critical scrutiny. BIBLIOGRAPHY: S. L. Lee, DNB 26:173–181.

[M. M. BARRY]

HERBERT, GEORGE (1593–1633), Anglican priest and religious poet, distinguished scholar, musician, university orator at Cambridge. Giving up civil preferments, he was ordained (1630) and served at Bemerton. Just before his death he sent his English poems to his friend, Nicholas *Ferrar, founder of the religious house, *Little Gidding, to be published or burned. His poetry is intensely personal and human, often revealing a sense of doubt as how best to serve God. He and Donne (his mother's friend) are the most important of the metaphysical group. His language is simple, his meter flexible, his imagery largely dependent upon the Bible, liturgy, nature, and everyday activities. His best poems are in *The Temple; Sacred Poems and Private Ejaculations* (1633); *A Priest to the Temple, or the Country Parson* (1652), which reveals his happy sense of fulfilled vocation. Works: *The Works of George Herbert* (ed. F. E. Hutchinson, 1941); BIBLIOGRAPHY: M. Bottrall, *George Herbert* (1954); J. H. Summers, *George Herbert, His Religion and Art* (1954).

[M. M. BARRY]

HERBIGNY, MICHEL D' (1880–1957), Jesuit Orientalist. Made president of the *Pontifical Institute for Oriental Studies in 1922, H. became editor of *Orientalia Christiana* in 1923 and a consultor for the Sacred Congregation for the Oriental Churches in 1924. In 1925 the *Commissio pro Russia* was created within that congregation, and H. served as its president (1931–34). In 1926, having obtained a visa to enter Russia, he was consecrated bp. by Abp. Pacelli in Berlin and traveled in the USSR from April until September to replace bps. who had been executed or deported . Shortly after Beauduin's exile in 1932, H. appears to have fallen into disfavor with the Holy See; his resignation from the *commissio* on grounds of health was accepted in 1934. From 1938 he lived in complete retirement in a novitiate house. His *De ecclesia* (2 v., 1920–21) was a work of considerable importance in the field of apologetics. It struck a new note in works on that subject with its wealth of scriptural and patristic documentation, its breadth of view, its ecumenical orientation. BIBLIOGRAPHY: Y. M. J. Congar, *Catholicisme* 5:633; H. Beylard, DTC, *Tables Générales* 2049–50.

HERDER, JOHANN GOTTFRIED VON (1774–1803), German critic, philosopher of history. Under the influence of Rousseau and Hamann, H. developed his organic interpretations of literature (e.g., in *Fragmente über die neue deutsche Literatur,* 1766), of language (e.g., in *Über den Ursprung der Sprache,* 1772), and of history (e.g., in *Ideen zur Philosophie der Geschichte der Menschheit,* pt. 1, 1784; pt. 2, 1785). In *Auch eine Philosophie der Geschichte zur Bildung der Menschheit* (1774), he describes history as God's action on nations. His concept of *Urpoesie* and his collection of folksongs (*Stimmen der Völker in Liedern,* 1778), as well as his contention that each language has its own genius (*Genie*), make him the harbinger of Romanticism. BIBLIOGRAPHY: E. A. Blackall, *Emergence of German as a Literary Language, 1700–1775* (1959) 451–481, *passim;* F. McEachran, *Life and Philosophy of Johann Gottfried Herder* (1939).

[M. F. MCCARTHY]

HERDTRICH, CHRISTIAN WOLFGANG (1625–84), Jesuit missionary, mathematician, and translator. A native of Graz, Austria, he spent 28 years of his life in the Far East, mostly in China, where in 1671 he joined the intellectual entourage of the Emperor K'ang-Hsi in Peking. There he compiled the first Chinese-Latin dictionary and, along with two other members of the Society of Jesus, produced a Latin translation of the teachings of Confucius, *Confucius, Sinarum Philosophus, sive Scientia Sinensis exposita.* This work (1678) introduced the West to Confucian thought. H. was superior of the mission at Hangchow at the time of his death.

[E. M. GATES]

HEREFORD, NICHOLAS, see NICHOLAS OF HEREFORD.

HERESIARCH, founder of a heresy or leader of a heretical movement; an arch heretic. The term is commonly applied to such historical figures as Arius, Marcion, and Pelagius. It has been sometimes applied polemically to influential writers or leaders whose teaching has been considered unorthodox.

[T. EARLY]

HERESY (Gr. *hairesis,* what is chosen), originally a particular school or tenet of philosophy, e.g., the Stoics, or a party within Judaism, e.g., the Pharisees or Sadducees. Thus St. Paul refers to himself as having lived "according to the strictest sect of our religion" (Acts 26.5; cf. 5.17 and 15.5). He alse denies that the Christian "way" is that of a Nazarene sect (Acts 24.5). When applied by the NT to the Christian body it loses its neutral meaning, and is condemned as a division or faction that threatens or destroys unity (1. Cor 2.19; Gal 5.20; Tit 3.10; 2 Pet 2.1). In these passages on the danger to Christian unity, the term heresy is not differentiated from *schism. From the 2d cent. the Fathers begin to draw that distinction; thus Augustine, "heretics violate the faith by thinking falsely about God, while schismatics break away from fraternal love by their wicked separation, though they believe as we do" (*Fid. et symbol.* 8.21). The Fathers also allowed that not all error was heresy, for it might be based on misapprehension and misunderstanding without intention of setting itself up against church teaching when this had been made clear. The grave wrong lay in obdurate persistence in setting up a sectarian body against the Church. Bad faith was readily suspected, yet Augustine was not alone in holding that "those who have not fathered it but have received it from others, yet who still seek the truth are by no means to be reckoned among the heretics" (*Epist.* 43.1). Catalogues of heresies were drawn up by Justin Martyr, Irenaeus, Hippolytus, Epiphanius, Augustine, and John Chrysostom. The growth of systematic theology in the Middle Ages with its more specific classifications led to a closer and juridically stiffer notion. In practice, however, the term continued to be elastic, and stood comprehensively for all willful separation from the living body of the Church, whether by the rejection of revealed doctrines or opposition to the principles of disciplined life inculcated by authority (see D 902, 906, 1800). Given the strong community sense of Christians, even those of some eccentric and anarchic groups it was a wickedness too dangerous to be tolerated, and the persecutions and barbarities by orthodox and heterodox alike, which have marked history, reflect and caricature the horror in which heresy was held.

Since the Reformation not only did the RC Church continue in its rejection of heresy, but confessional Churches of the Reformation shared in the same zeal for orthodoxy. The Lutheran and *Reformed *confessions of faith reject as heresy teachings that are contrary to the gospel. In modern times the notion of heresy is often ridiculed. This is in part explained by the minimizing of dogma, rooted in rationalism and in theological liberalism, and in part by the widespread acceptance of the adage "deeds not creeds." Yet many of the Churches continue to recognize the possibility of heresy, the need to resist it, and have juridic processes for those accused of heresy. There is also, however, a healthy contemporary restraint from use of the word "heresy" both by Catholics and Protestants. The term is less frequently used to impugn the genuineness of the belief of fellow Christians. This involves a recognition of past polemical exaggeration, and a hesitancy to accuse others of consciously preferring their own opinions over what is known to be the authentic word of God. Heresy in its strict meaning would be such a choice. BIBLIOGRAPHY: K, Rahner, *On Heresy* (tr. W. O' Hara, 1964;) H. E. W. Turner, *Pattern of Christian Truth* (1954).

[T. GILBY]

HERESY, CATHOLIC MORAL THEOLOGY OF, As might be expected, the notion of heresy is more precise in scholastic theology and canon law than in the Scriptures and patristic writings. It is classed under a heading of disbelief, *infidelitas,* a vice directly contrary to the theological virtue of faith. This refusal to assent is differentiated from schism, the refusal to remain in communion, which is directly contrary to the theological virtue of charity. Clearly the condition of just not believing, or of unbelief with respect to Christian truth, implies no moral fault, since many have not had the Gospel preached to them, or if so then not acceptably; sin enters only when grace is refused and God's revelation denied or positively doubted. Hence the distinction, here as in other fields, between material sin, which is objectively deficient, mistaken, or even wrongful but no personal sin at all, except in a Pickwickian sense, and formal sin, a moral fault for which we are responsible and to blame, and which may also be a juridical crime. We are concerned only with formal or culpable infidelity.

This may go so deep as to strike at the roots of Christian belief in the revelation of God in the Incarnation. The effect is confessedly non-Christian, except in a purely ethical sense, and too total to be called heresy. It may be called pagan infidelity; in early medieval Augustinianism it used to be called the infidelity of the Gentiles or Jews. But there can be a more partial rejection of revealed truth, a more domestic affair within Christianity, or at least, as sticklers would once have put it, within Christendom, when for instance the following of Christ is professed but truths taught by his Church are rejected at various stages of their development. The rule of the Church for deciding what is of faith is set aside and some other norm is substituted at an individual's own choice, *hairesis.* Since all the truths of faith hang together in the assent to God's authority manifested through his Church, the denial of one involves them all, and so in theory at least the loss of Christian faith. However, we cannot draw the conclusion in practice, for God alone knows for certain when formal heresy is present.

The 1918 Code of Canon Law (c. 1325) requires conscious and intentional resistance to the will of God, and defines a heretic as one who after baptism, while remaining nominally a Christian, pertinaciously denies or doubts any one of the truths which must be believed by divine and Catholic faith; the statement dates from the pre-ecumenical period, yet it does not impugn the genuineness of Christian faith among non-Catholic bodies. "Heresy" is also a juridical term of censure for teaching which in various degrees—heresy, near to heresy, smacking of heresy—is contrary to truths of faith. It should be distinguished from theological "error," about which is conclusions inferred from the premises of faith, and of course from "rashness," "offensiveness," and sheer bad manners in dealing with religious doctrine. BIBLIOGRAPHY: St. Thomas Aquinas, *Summa theologiae,* 2a2ae, 11; K. Rahner, *On Heresy* (1964).

[T. GILBY]

HERETIC (Lat. *haereticus,* Gr. *hairetikos*), one who professes a *heresy. The history of heretics is a long record of how men may hate one another for the love of God; often savagely persecuted and usually in vain, heretics retorted in kind when they gained the ascendancy. With the decline of dogmatic certainty among Christian bodies, the term is less frequently used in English-speaking countries, and the milder "dissenter," "nonconformist," or "dissident" are preferred. It survives to the extent that fundamentalism survives, and in the RC Church, where it is given a technical and juridical sense. Popularly it has acquired, like a naval swear word, a jocular and even endearing ring. Official practice, too, has been more generous since Vatican Council II in acknowledging a unity of faith among Christian denominations. Only one who is pertinacious, i.e., who knowingly, willingly, and culpably sets himself up against the Church's divine teaching authority is a "formal" heretic, whereas one who does not recognize this authority, and consequently denies its ruling, is merely a "material" heretic.

[T. GILBY]

HERETICS, BAPTISM OF, see BAPTISM OF HERETICS.

HERGENRÖTHER, JOSEPH (1824–90), German church historian. Born at Würzburg, he studied in Rome where he was ordained (1848), and in Munich. He taught at the Univ. of Würzburg from 1855 and was a consultor for the preparation of Vatican Council I. In 1879 Leo XIII brought him to Rome as Vatican archivist and created him cardinal. A convinced ultramontane and infallibilist, from 1860 H. engaged in polemics against I. *Döllinger, his former teacher and published *Anti-Janus* (Döllinger's pseudonym) in 1870. H.'s more detached and scholarly works are his *Photius Patriarch von Constantinopel* (3 v., 1867–69); his additions, v. 8 and 9, to K. J. von *Hefele's *Conciliengeschichte* (1887–90), and his ed. of Photius' works for PG 101–104. His somewhat apologetically slanted *Handbuch der allgemeinen Kirchengeschichte* (3 v., 1876–80) became a long-lived standard work. BIBLIOGRAPHY: H. C. Fischer, "Hergenröther," *Church Historians* (ed. P. Guilday, 1926) 289–319.

[R. H. SCHMANDT]

HERIBERT OF COLOGNE, ST. (*c.*970–1021), abp. of Cologne (999–1021). Under Otto III, H. was appointed chancellor of Italy in 994 and of Germans in 998; but in 1002, after Otto's death, he lost both chancellorships because of a misunderstanding with Duke Henry of Bavaria (later Emperor Henry II). BIBLIOGRAPHY: Lambert of Deutz, *Vita* and *Miracula,* MGHS 4:740–753; 15.2: 1245–60; *Geschichte des Erzbistums Köln* (ed. W. Neuss, 1965) 1:174–180; G. and C. Spahr, BiblSanct 4:1317–19.

[M. F. MCCARTHY]

HERIGER OF LOBBES (d. 1007), writer. Although the date and place of his birth are not certain, H. entered the Abbey of Lobbes under Abbot Folquin (965–990). His later writing reveals that Heriger was well trained as a scholar. Wazo, future bishop of Liège, was his pupil and he was also a friend and co-worker of Notker, the bp. of Liège (972–1008). After Folquin's death, Heriger became abbot (990). He rebuilt the abbey and added a chapel in honor of St. Benedict. Although he wrote some hagiographical works (life of Saint Landoald, Saint Usmer), some theology, a treatise on the Eucharist against Ratramnus of Corbie, and a mathematical work, he is principally known for his historical writing. Because of his *Gesta episcoporum,* recording the history of Liège from the 4th to the 7th cent., and other historical writings, H. has been called the first Belgian historiographer. BIBLIOGRAPHY: G. Kurth, *Biographie nationale de Belgique,* v. 9.

[N. F. GAUGHAN]

HERINCX, WILHELM (1621–78), Flemish Franciscan Recollect; from 1677 bp. of Ypres. He taught theology at Louvain and is remembered for his *Summa theologica scholastica et moralis* (1660–63). He was a staunch defender of *probabilism, and had to revise elements in the moral part of his work after Alexander VII's condemnations of laxist propositions in 1665 and 1666 (see D 2021–65).

[T. C. O'BRIEN]

HERKENNE, HEINRICH (1871–1948), German priest, biblical scholar. Professor of OT literature in the Catholic faculty of the Univ. of Bonn (1903–32) and in Aachen's seminary (1932–48). His most important work was on the Book of Psalms.

[J. F. FALLON]

HERKUMBERT, ST. (d. *c.*813), bp., who has been identified with Ercambert, first bp. of Minden; he was also probably the monk of Fulda who led the mission sent from Fulda to Minden. He is not, however, mentioned in the early chronicles of the Minden diocese. Possibly he is the Herenbert said to have been installed as bp. in a church erected in Minden by Charlemagne (780). BIBLIOGRAPHY: L. Falkenstein, BiblSanct 4:1298.

[M. S. TANEY]

HERLIN, FRIEDRICH (*c.*1435–*c.*1500), German painter from Nördlingen. In Rothenburg (1467) H. painted the high altar of St. Jakob showing the strong Netherlandish influence of Rogier van der Weyden. Two major works are the high altars in St. Blasius-Kirche, Bopfingen, blending the Flemish with a personal style of fierce, intense facial expression, and the altar of St. Georgskirche, Nördlingen (1477–78), a more subtle expression of emotion.

[M. J. DALY]

HERLUIN OF BEC, BL. (*c.*995–1078), founder in 1035 and first abbot of Bec, the monastery joined by both *Lanfranc and St. *Anselm of Canterbury. H. had been a knight at the court of Count Gilbert of Britonne before embracing a life of asceticism at the age of 38; the companions he attracted formed the first community of Bec. Lanfranc as abp. of Canterbury consecrated the abbey church in 1077, before H.'s death. BIBLIOGRAPHY: P. Knowles, "Bec and its Great Men, *Downside Review* 52 (1934): 567–585.

[T. C. O'BRIEN]

HERLUKA OF BERNRIED, BL (*c.*1060–1127), a religious woman about whom little accurate information has survived. Her entire life was spent in Swabia, Germany, at the convents of Epfach am Lech and at Bernried (1122). An ardent supporter of reformation, her important correspondence with the nun Diemoth has unfortunately perished. BIBLIOGRAPHY: AS April 2:549–554; H. Mackinnon, NCE 6:1072; A. M. Zimmerman, LTK 5:249; N. Del Re, BiblSanct 5:7–9.

[S. WILLIAMS]

HERMAN THE GERMAN, BL., (*fl.* early 13th cent.), Dominican missionary. H. received the habit from St. Dominic himself with Bl. Ceslaus of Silesia and St. Hyacinth. In 1219 he helped to found Friesach, the first Dominican house in Germany. Later in his career he preached in Silesia. BIBLIOGRAPHY: B. Altaner, *Die Dominikanermissionen des 13 Jahrhundert* (1924); W. Lampen, Bibl Sanct 5:25.

[O. J. BLUM]

HERMAN JOSEPH, ST. (1150–1241), Premonstratensian mystic and author noted for his treatise on the "Canticle of Canticles," which is now lost. One of the Church's most noteworthy mystics, he earned the title Joseph because of his blameless life. The earliest hymn to the Sacred Heart, *Summi regis cor aveto* is accredited to him, though this is open to question. His cult was approved in 1958 in an action equivalent to canonization. BIBLIOGRAPHY: M. J. Hamilton, NCE 6:1072; J. B. Valvekens, BiblSanct 5:25–28; Butler 2:48–49.

[F. G. O'BRIEN]

HERMAN THE LAME (Hermannus Contractus, Herman of Reichenau; 1013–54), monk, chronicler, poet, musician, mathematician, astronomer. From early childhood he was educated at the monastery of Reichenau where he eventually made his religious profession and spent the rest of his life. Although crippled from birth, he possessed a remarkably gifted mind and an attractive personality. He set to music a number of Offices and sequences and has been credited on unsatisfactory evidence, with the composition of the *Salve Regina* and the *Alma Redemptoris Mater*. His *Chronicon augiense* is a world history from the Incarnation to 1054; in its composition he used the best sources available, and it is valuable, esp. for its record of contemporary events. His *De musica* was used as a textbook by monks for their study of the chant. H. has been the object of local veneration, which was confirmed by the Holy See (1863). Works: PL 143:9–458; crit. ed. of his *Chronicon*, G. H. Pertz, MGHS (1844) 67–133. BIBLIOGRAPHY: Raby CLP 225–229; W. C. Korfmacher, NCE 6:1073.

[M. S. TANEY]

HERMAN OF LEHNIN (fl. 1300), Cistercian monk. He composed a prophetic poem in leonine hexameters about a family which would rule for 11 generations and then go into eclipse because of a notorious scandal. Thereupon the pope would regain his flock; Germany, its true ruler; and the Abbey of Lehnin, a glorious renaissance. The MS is lost, but a forgery (1690) based on the tradition was used against Prussia and the Hohenzollern. BIBLIOGRAPHY: J. Allendorff, LTK 6:884.

[M. J. SUELZER]

HERMAN OF METZ, bishop *c.*1072–1090. He was one of *Gregory VII's few staunch episcopal supporters against Henry IV in the German *investiture struggle. At Worms in January 1076, H. tried vainly to forestall royal and episcopal denunciation of the Pope. Although he signed the episcopal statement, he quickly returned to allegiance to Gregory and for years thereafter experienced intense royalist pressure. He fled into exile briefly in 1078 and was deposed by a royalist synod in 1085, but returned in 1088 and died in possession of his see. Two letters of Gregory VII to him (25 August 1076 and 15 March 1081) contain important statements of the Pope's political theory. BIBLIOGRAPHY: Gregory VII, *Correspondence of Pope Gregory VII*, (tr. E. Emerton, 1932); A. Hauck, *Kirchengeschichte Deutschlands* (repr. 1954) v. 3.

[R. H. SCHMANDT]

HERMAN OF SALZA (d. 1239), grand master of the Teutonic Knights. H. was elected grand master at Acre, Syria, in 1209. In 1216 he became counselor of Frederick II. As mediator with Pope Honorius III, H. was instrumental in having Frederick crowned emperor and in promoting the interests of the Teutonic Knights. His order was charged with protecting and Christianizing areas in Hungary and

Prussia; but four years later Gregory IX took control of the new mission territory, thereby excluding the order from further political action. In 1237 H. consented to the incorporation of the Livonian Knights of the Sword into the Teutonic Order. BIBLIOGRAPHY: M. Hellmann, NCE 6:1072.

[M. F. FINNEGAN]

HERMAN OF SCHEDA (*c.*1109–70), also known as Herman the Jew. H. was converted to Christianity in 1128 at Mainz where he entered the Premonstratensian Order, and became abbot of Scheda in 1143. He wrote an autobiography, *Opusculum de vita sua,* in which he appealed to his fellow Jews to accept Christ. BIBLIOGRAPHY: J. C. Didier, *Catholicisme* 5:656–657.

[B. F. SCHERER]

HERMAN OF SCHILDESCHE (d. 1357), Augustinian priest, theology professor, provinicial in Saxony and Thuringia. He wrote some 30 treatises, 11 of which are extant. Two manuals, *Speculum manuale sacerdotum* and *Introductorium juris,* were widely used. In 1338 he was a member of a Bavarian embassy which attempted to reconcile Emperor Louis IV with Pope *Benedict XII. BIBLIOGRAPHY: J. E. Bresnahan, NCE 6:1073; A. Zumkeller, LTK 5:253.

[J. E. WRIGLEY]

HERMAN OF WIED (1477–1552), abp. and elector of Cologne (1515–46). By his own admission H. was more successful as a secular than as an ecclesiastical ruler. Though at first opposed to Martin *Luther, he became friendly to the Reformation and through meetings with Lutheran princes and with P. *Melanchthon, *Erasmus, and M. *Bucer. The last worked at Bonn (1542–43) at H.'s invitation; but the cathedral chapter, the university, and civil authorities at Cologne opposed H.'s attempts at reform. When he caused communion to be celebrated according to the evangelical rite, his clergy petitioned the Emperor Charles V to intervene. H. was excommunicated in 1546. He retired to his estates at Wied and died a Lutheran. His removal helped keep northwest Germany Catholic. BIBLIOGRAPHY: J. F. G. Goeters, RGG 3:240–241; A. Franzen, LTK 10:1097–98.

[M. J. SUELZER]

HERMANDSZOON, JAKOB, see ARMINIUS, JACOBUS.

HERMANN OF NIEDERALTAICH (*c.*1200–75), Benedictine abbot and historian. Educated in the monastery school of Niederaltaich, where he became a monk, H. was entrusted by Abbot Dietmar with the office of *custos* and with missions to the emperor at Verona and to the Holy See. During his own abbacy (1242–73) the monastery's economic situation and discipline were improved. H. wrote the *Annales Hermanni,* covering the years 1137–73, as well as other chronicles and historical works. His complete works are published in MGHS 17:351–427 (ed. P. Jaffé).

[S. A. SCHULZ]

HERMANOS MINIMOS, see OBREGONIANS.

HERMANT, GODEFROY (1617–91), pro-Jansenist member of the Sorbonne (1642–56), rector (1646–48), and doctor (1650). He wrote against Jesuit attacks on the university, *Apologie pour l'université* (1643) and *Vérités académiques* (1643). In defense of A. *Arnauld he published *Apologie pour M. Arnauld* (1644). From the time of Arnauld's condemnation H. abandoned controversy in favor of research and writing in patristics; among his works were lives of St. John Chrysostom (1664) , St. Athanasius (1671) and St. Ambrose (1678). His *Mémoires,* published by the modern pro-Jansenist historian A. Gazier (1905–10), added to modern research on the Jansenist movement. H. is one of the most frequently cited sources, after Sainte-Beuve, of Gazier's own *Histoire du mouvement Janséniste* (2 v., 1923–24).

[D. J. SMUCKER]

HERMAS, SHEPHERD OF, see SHEPHERD OF HERMAS.

HERMENEGILD, ST. (d. 585), son of the Visigothic King Leovigild of Spain, and brother of *Reccared. He was brought up with his brother in the Arian heresy, and from 573 Leovigild associated the two young men with him in the ruling of the kingdom. Under the influence of his Catholic wife and of Leander, Abp. of Seville, H. became a Catholic. Enraged by this, his father demanded that he resign his civil office and dignities, but H. took arms in the vain expectation that the Romans would come to his assistance. The revolt was crushed and H. was imprisoned and later executed. His claim to the title of martyr accorded him by Gregory the Great and Gregory of Tours has been warmly disputed. Some have held that he was put to death simply as a rebel. BIBLIOGRAPHY: Butler 2:82–83; Bihlmeyer-Tüchle 1:225.

[P. K. MEAGHER]

HERMENEUTICS, BIBLICAL, the part of theological science that treats of the of the principles of biblical interpretation (Gr. *hermeneuein,* ''to interpret'') applied in actual practice by exegesis. Hence it deals with the meaning of the Scriptures. Hermeneutics presupposes that the Bible has been written by men in human fashion, but under the inspiration of the Spirit of God (2 Tim 3.16); as a result it contains the Word of God in the words of men. The literal sense of Scripture is the meaning God intended to be conveyed by the sacred writers to their contemporaries, and ultimately, to men of all time. To ascertain this meaning, the text and the oral and written traditions that lie behind it must be studied with the help of philology, archeology, history, textual and literary criticism. Attention must also be paid to the unity of the Bible, for each word, sentence, section, or book possesses its complete meaning only as part of a larger whole—namely, the progressive revelation of God in the history of salvation culminating in the NT. When the persons, objects, or events of the OT are explained as types or figures of the mystery of Christ, they are said to possess a typical sense; when the very words of the OT foreshadow the Christian dispensation, they are said to contain a fuller sense. The value of the above distinctions is disputed, however, and in any case, neither of them is really independent of the literal meaning. The so-called accommodated sense—an application of a text to a new situation based on mere verbal similarity—cannot be considered a genuine sense of Scripture; much the same can be said of the consequent sense, understood as a theological conclusion, not implicitly contained in, but only deduced from, a sacred text. Catholics, moreover, believe that the Church in the light of its living tradition and by the power of the Holy Spirit authoritatively interprets the Bible, hands it on, and explains it to the faithful. Scientific studies aid in this service of the Word of God; they help the judgment of the Church to mature and serve to show more clearly how the Bible teaches ''without error that truth which God wanted put into the sacred writings for the sake of our salvation'' (*Dei Verbum,* 11). BIBLIOGRAPHY: L. A. Schökel, *Inspired Word* (1965); Vat II DivRev; Robert–Tricot 1:678–780; J. Levie, *Bible, Word of God in Words of Men* (tr. S. Treman, 1961); L. Bouyer, *Meaning of Sacred Scripture* (tr. M. Ryan, 1958).

[C. BERNAS]

HERMES TRISMEGISTUS (Hermes the Thrice Greatest), Gk. name for Thoth, Egyptian god of wisdom and the alleged author of the *Hermetica* (Hermetic literature), Gk. writings dating from *c.*50–300, and combining elements of philosophy, Eastern religions, and astrology. BIBLIOGRAPHY: G. Van Moorsel, *Mysteries of Hermes Trismegistus* (1955); H. J. Rose, OCD 418.

[T. EARLY]

HERMES, GEORG (1775–1831), German RC theologian whose *rationalism was the occasion of condemnations in Vatican Council I, the dogmatic constitution *Dei Filius,* on faith and reason (D 3035–36). Gregory XVI in the brief *Dum acerbissimas* (D 2738–40) had already proscribed H.'s works *Philosophische Einleitung* (1819) and *Positive Einleitung in die christkatholische Theologie* (1829); in 1836 the first part of the posthumous *Christkatholische Dogmatik* was also proscribed and by 1836 all H.'s works were put on the Index. He was a priest-professor at Münster from 1807 and at Bonn from 1819. As Gregory XVI's brief indicates, there was a great alarm because many of the theological chairs in Germany were being filled by ''Hermesians''; H. was also a highly respected personage to the government of Prussia, and publication of *Dum acerbissimas* was prevented there. The fundamental direction of H.'s work was to reconcile Catholic apologetics and dogma with *Enlightenment rationalism. His theology reduced the act of faith to an assent reached by reasoning alone, and neutralized the meaning of grace and the supernatural order.

[T. C. O'BRIEN]

HERMETIC LITERATURE, a body of texts of a theological, philosophical, and magical character, produced in Egypt, but in a Greek milieu, chiefly in the 2d cent. A.D. The texts were presented as the revelations of Hermes Trismegistus, an approximate Greek translation of the Egyptian name ''Thoth the Very Great.'' The *Corpus hermeticum* proper is a collection of 18 treatises, extant in a mutilated form. In addition we have the *Asclepius* that has come down under the name of Apuleius, the eight chapters in Iamblichus' *De mysteriis* concerned with Hermetic literature, and a number of fragments in the Church Fathers, but esp. in Stobaeus. There are also several Hermetic works found in Coptic translation in Codex VI of the Chenoboskion (Nag Hamâdi) MSS discovered *c.*1945. The material deals throughout with God, the cosmos, man, and salvation. Astrology and other forms of magic play a major role. While the Hermetic literature shows some Oriental influence, it may be characterized as being based essentially on a popularized and distorted application of Platonic doctrine, esp. as found in the *Timaeus* and *Phaedo,* with an admixture of Aristotelian and Stoic elements. The *Corpus hermeticum* does not constitute in any sense a unified system. It exhibits close affinities with certain aspects of *Gnosticism and exercised considerable influence in antiquity. As Egyptian ''wisdom,'' it had an amazing vogue in the Renaissance. Modern scholarship, however, has established its true character. BIBLIOGRAPHY: W. G. MacRae, NCE 6:1076–77; LexAW s.v. ''Corpus hermeticum,'' 669–670; Nilsson 2:582–612. Cr. ed. of the texts by A. D. Nock and A. J. Festugière, *Hermès Trismégiste* (4 v., 1945–54). Fundamental authoritative study on the texts by A. J. Festugière, *Révélation d'Hermès Trismégiste* (4 v., 1944–54; v. 1, 2d ed., 1962).

[M. R. P. MCGUIRE]

HERMIAS, a Christian writer of uncertain date; the author of a ten-chapter treatise entitled *Mockery of the Pagan Philosophers.* In this work H. satirizes conflicting opinions of pagan philosophers culled from popular compendia concerning the nature of God, the soul, and the universe. The date of composition is assigned to various times between 200 and 600 A.D. Internal evidence suggests the 3d cent. as the likely date. BIBLIOGRAPHY: Altaner 136–137; C. Andresen, RGG 3:265–266.

[H. DRESSLER]

HERMIT, a religious ascetic who lives alone in order to attain complete openness to God through solitude, silence, penance, and prayer. Although the first monks were hermits, the great monastic legislators differed in their evaluations of the eremitical life. *Basil thought it inferior to life in community, while *Benedict seemed to present it as an extraordinary crowning of a cenobitic life. Hermits have most often associated in loosely formed colonies, coming together for the celebration of the Eucharist at set intervals. Closer union led to the establishment of the laura and, in the 11th cent., semi-eremitical orders (e.g., *Carthusians, Camaldolese). Eremitical life has always flourished more abundantly in the East, but is experiencing a present-day renaissance in the West. BIBLIOGRAPHY: T. Merton, *The Silent Life* (1957). *ANCHORITE.

[M. B. PENNINGTON]

HERMITS OF ST. AUGUSTINE, see, AUGUSTINIANS.

HERMITS OF ST. PAUL (OSPPE), popularly named Paulites or Paulines, a religious order of priests and brothers founded in the Middle Ages, now concentrated in Poland at Czestochowa and Cracow. The order, named for St. Paul, 3d-cent. Egyptian and first Christian hermit, originated from the merger of two monasteries in Hungary and received papal approval in 1308 to live, according to the Rule of St. Augustine, a contemplative life; in the 16th cent. the Holy See directed it into works of the apostolate as well. Before the Reformation the Paulites existed in central and eastern Europe, in Sweden, and in Italy; in Poland the order established the sanctuary of Our Lady of Czestochowa in 1382. After a decline, a 17th-cent. revival saw the Paulites established in France and Portugal. Suppression under *Josephinism in Habsburg lands and then the French Revolution led to there being only the two Polish monasteries to continue the order's existence. In 1975 the Paulines numbered 229 in 20 monasteries. In the U.S. there are 26 members and headquarters are at their Monastery Shrine of Our Lady of Czestochowa, Doylestown, Pa.

[T. C. O'BRIEN]

HERMOGENEANS, followers of the Gnostic Hermogenes. He began his career in Antioch in the 2d cent., but moved to Carthage after his teachings had been refuted by St. Theophilus. H. taught that God had formed the world out of externally existing, uncreated matter; that the soul of man is derived from matter; that after the Ascension Jesus deposited His body in the sun. The chief source of information is Tertullian's *Adv. Hermogenem*. Augustine (*Haer.* 41 and 59) inherited the confusion of Filaster (*Haer.* 54 and 55) about the identity of the Hermogeneans. BIBLIOGRAPHY: G. Bareille, DTC 6:2306–11.

[L. G. MÜLLER]

HERMON, mountain forming the S spur of the Anti-Leban Range, the modern Jebel el-Sheikh. It has three peaks and is 9232 ft. high, the tallest mountain in the Syria-Palestine area, and marked the N limit of the Hebrew Conquest E of the Jordan (Jos 12.1). Hermon is called Baal-hermon in Jg 3.3, indicating Baal worship was carried out there (for other names see Dt 3.8). Its features provide figures for the poetry of the Bible (Ps 89.13; 133.3; S of S 4.8). Its proximity to Caesarea Philippi has led some writers to suggest it as the Transfiguration site (Mt 16.13; 17.1).

[T. EARLY]

HERNANDEZ, FRANCISCO (1514–87), physician, explorer. A physician in Spain, Hernandez was sent to Mexico by King Philip II to investigate medicine there. He compiled a vast amount of scientific data in Mexico. Poor health forced his return to Spain. His writings were not published until 1651 in Rome. In the 18th cent., first drafts H. had made were found in Madrid and published. Though the complete writings were not available until recently, his observations on medicine and natural science in Mexico were the only source of information on that area for three centuries.

[J. R. AHERNE]

HERO-CULT, the worship of deceased men and women, either real or imaginary, who have been raised to a superhuman level because of their singular benefits to mankind. Though such worship is not found in Homer, it was very common in classical and Hellenistic Greece. Among the objects of such worship could be figures who had originally been divine, such as Hyacinthus and, possibly, Asclepius, but who had "faded" into the status of mortal men. Others, like Theseus and Orestes, were legendary heroes. Still others, like the Spartan Brasidas, who was worshiped after his death at Amphipolis, were prominent historical figures. The cult of heroes differed from that offered to the Olympian deities, resembling that given to the gods of the nether world and the expiatory rites offered for the dead. Thus it was usually performed in the evening or at night, when a black animal was slain in sacrifice, or blood or other liquids were poured into a trench or over a hearth or low altar. Under the guise of a worship of the deceased emperors, hero-cult became one of the unifying elements of Roman rule, though it was strongly opposed by such men as Cicero, Asinius Pollio, Thrasea Paetus, Seneca, and Tacitus.

[M. J. COSTELLOE]

HEROD AGRIPPA, see AGRIPPA.

HEROD ANTIPAS, the son of Herod the Great and Malthace, brother of Archelaus; he ruled Galilee as tetrarch from 4 B.C. to 39 A.D. In the NT and on his coins he is called Herod. In 22 A.D. he made Tiberias his capital. His adultery with Herodias, wife of his half-brother Philip, and his execution of John the Baptist blacken his name. He was deposed by Caligula and exiled to Lyons. BIBLIOGRAPHY: H. Holzmeister, *Historia aetatis Novi Testamenti* (2d ed., 1938); A. H. N. Jones, *Herods of Judaea* (1938).

[J. J. O'ROURKE]

HEROD THE GREAT, son of Antipater and Cyprus. born *c.*73 B.C., appointed governor of Galilee in 47 B.C. through the influence of his father with Julius Caesar. While at first siding with Pompey, he went over to Anthony and Octavian in 42 and was named tetrarch of Galilee in 41. Named king of Judea in 40, he captured Jerusalem in 37. After Anthony's defeat at Actium he gained the favor of Octavian. He exterminated the remnants of the Hasmonean dynasty and deposed high priests at will. His reign was marked with magnificent construction including the rebuilding of the Temple, though this was not completed in his lifetime. He married 10 times. He killed many members of his own family, including his favorite wife Mariamne, for fear of treason. In the NT in Lk 1.5 and in the story of the Magi and killing of children in Bethlehem (Mt 2.1–12, 15–18), he is mentioned. BIBLIOGRAPHY: S. Sandmel, *Herod: Profile of a Tyrant* (1967).

[J. J. O'ROURKE]

HERODIANS, a group mentioned occasionally in the Gospels (Mk 3.6; 12.13; Mt 22.16). Their identity is the object of dispute: those opposed to Roman rule in Palestine, or the troops of Herod Antipas, his courtiers. The last seems most likely. They certainly were opposed to Jesus. BIBLIOGRAPHY: H. H. Rowley, "Herodians in the Gospel" JTS 41 (1940) 14–72.

[J. J. O'ROURKE]

HERODIAS, daughter of Aristobulus, wife of Herod Philip, who entered an adulterous relationship with Herod Antipas and caused the death of John the Baptist. Salome was her daughter by Philip. She went into exile with Herod Antipas. BIBLIOGRAPHY: A. H. N. Jones, *Herods of Judea* (1938).

[J. J. O'ROURKE]

HÉROËT, ANTOINE (surnamed La Maisonneuve; 1492–1568), French bp. of Digne, poet of the Lyonnaise school and forerunner of the *Pléiade, who participated in the "feminist quarrel" of the period. His chief work, *La Parfaicte amye* (1542), was a reply to Bertrand de la Borderie's antifeminist *L'Amye de court*. In it H. developed the Neoplatonic theories of virtuous love inspired by Marsilio *Ficino's commentary on Plato's *Symposium,* which he had imitated in his *L'Androgyne*. He also wrote *Autre invention extraite de Platon* and *La Complainte d'une dame surprise nouvellement d'amour*. BIBLIOGRAPHY: A. Héroët, *Oeuvres poétiques* (ed. F. Gohin, 1943) introd.

[R. N. NICOLICH]

HEROIC ACT OF CHARITY, a name given to a particular practice of piety whereby a person offers to God for the soul in purgatory any and all *indulgences he might gain, expiatory works he might perform, or prayers offered for him after his own death. The practice was promoted by the Theatines. The "heroism" consists in the complete selflessness of the offering. The practice, however, should not be confused with the offering made by the so-called victim soul. This is a self-donation to God that wills to accept suffering without reservation in atonement for sin and in union with the self-offering of Christ. Such heroism presupposes an advanced degree of spiritual growth and cannot be lightly assumed nor readily permitted by a spiritual director. The fundamental validity of either form of heroism, however, is the same: the communion of saints, i.e., the union of members in Christ's mystical body with him and therefore with one another. BIBLIOGRAPHY: J. Wilhelm, CE 7:292.

[T. C. O'BRIEN]

HEROIC VIRTUE, human virtue, whether moral or theological, in a superlative degree, even to an extreme that may somewhat baffle a sober and rational moral theologian. The notion, though not the term, appears in the *Summa theologiae* of St. Thomas Aquinas; he was well aware that although the moral virtues of living according to right and Christian reason observe a measure between the two extremes of excess, or too much, and of defect, or too little, no such middle course is prescribed for faith, hope, and charity which go out unreservedly to God himself. The backwash of this extravagance, or *magnificence as he calls it, appears in his treatment of the moral virtues; thus *fortitude or courage is expressed to the utmost in *martyrdom and so is *chastity in virginity, which is lauded as a loving for what it does do, not for what it does not do. But the heart of the matter is the depth of the being in love with God and the range of the being in love with the friends of God.

Now the heroic will be variously exemplified in different cultures; styles and mannerisms vastly admired by one may strike another as affected or eccentric. The hagiographical models which appealed to the taste from the Renaissance to the Post-Baroque were caught up in the miraculous and ecstatic when they were not presented as practitioners according to a very specialized routine. Some saints were too toughly themselves, too racy, and too implicated in human history to conform to the convention, which was admirable when expressed with the zest of Bernini or the imagery of Crashawe, but less so in the more pedestrian exercises of religious repository art. One effect was that the saints came to be considered as experts in a special and professional style of living that was not for the ordinary people of God, who on the whole were prepared to admire and even to humor what sometimes was felt to be really either all rather odd or all rather prim.

It was the providential role of Prospero Lambertini's classic, *On the Beatification and Canonization of the Servants of God* (1734–38), to help toward correcting this. He became Pope Benedict XIV, and his work became authoritative and canonical for the Congregation of Rites. In its careful siftings of the evidences of heroic sanctity and of its counterfeits, it emphasized first of all the faithful and constant discharge of the duties of a person's state of life, manifested in a steady glow of goodness, by which others were helped and for which they were grateful, rather than in exceptional occurrences. Though we may still distinguish between heroic virtue as a juridical category used in the process of putting a venerated individual in the calendar and as a theological meaning for his being utterly a friend of God, its argument was a restatement of old and hallowed doctrine: the *perfection of charity lies in the precepts, not the counsels, and preternatural phenomena are quite marginal. Indeed there is nothing bizarre or even optional about heroic sanctity; one may not achieve it now as a steady condition, but a crisis can come when one is asked to touch its height, by refusing at dire cost to betray a friend or deny the faith.

[T. GILBY]

HEROIN, a white powdery substance derived from morphine, but more potent. It is the favorite of narcotic addicts in the U.S. where, because of its addictive powers, it is illegal even for medical purposes. Obtainable on the black market, it is sniffed or injected into a vein or at least under the skin. Severe infections may result from unsterile needles or impure heroin, and an overdose can be fatal. Under its influence the user has a brief feeling of euphoria and may even fall asleep. The body eventually develops a tolerance that will cause the addict to increase the dosage; he becomes physically dependent so that withdrawal of the drug will result in severe physical discomfort. The need for and the difficulty of obtaining heroin prevent the user from fulfilling his obligations to his family and society and often turn him into a criminal. Since heroin weakens or destroys the user's freedom, endangers his health and life, and even injures society, moralists are unanimous in condemning its use. BIBLIOGRAPHY: I. Chien, et al., *Road to Heroin* (1963). *ADDICTION.

[P. SMITH]

HEROISM, through the Lat. from the Gr. *hērōs,* a human person, godlike in his deeds, who renders exceptional service and is honored by posterity. The notion appears in a more defined sense in Aristotle's *Nicomachean Ethics* and, more importantly, in the *Eudemian Ethics;* it applies to acts that are motions of a divine instinct rather than of deliberation according to right reason, superhuman in their virtue, unearthly touches quite unlike Dr. Johnson's description of genius as the infinite capacity for taking pains. So it is enlarged on by St. Thomas Aquinas, who analyzes it more precisely, takes it into Christian theology, and relates it to the gifts of the *Holy Spirit, which dominate his teaching on the mystical life. They are not considered as operating according to the modes of the virtues, either moral or theological, whereby a man acting through his intelligence and will as a principal, though secondary, cause comes to his own choices, but as operating according to a superhuman mode whereby his virtues, his charity above all, are so lifted up by the Spirit that as an instrument he reaches to knowledge, love, and deeds surpassing the "meaningful," the "rightful," and the "exemplary." He flies, says John of St. Thomas, not walks. The gifts, however, are so closely connected with the virtues, of which they are the complement, that the special meaning here indicated is not very evident in the notions of *heroic virtue in the lives of the saints and of heroism as attributed to superb exhibitions of courage. There a maximum in virtuous acting is signified rather than a transcendence of the mode proper to virtuous acting.

[T. GILBY]

HERP, HENRY OF, see HENRY OF HERP.

HERRAD OF LANDSBERG (*c.*1130–95), abbess and writer. Under her direction the convent at Hohenberg attained reknown for its culture and for the preparation of a famous MS, *Hortus deliciarum* (Garden of Delights), which contained some 350 miniatures and a vast compendium of medieval knowledge. This, unfortunately, was destroyed in the Strasbourg bombardment and fire of 1870. BIBLIOGRAPHY: PL 194:1537–42; F.M. Beach, NCE 6:1082; G. Webb, "Herrad and Her Garden of Delights," *Life of the Spirit* 16 (1961–62) 475–481.

[S. WILLIAMS]

HERRERA, BARTOLOMÉ (1808–65), bp. of Arequipa, Peru, from 1859; twice deputy to the Peruvian congress, 1849–53 and 1858–60. He was ordained in 1832, after having completed studies in law, became rector of the Convictorio de San Carlos in 1842. In politics he was a conservative, favoring an aristocratic form of government. In both terms in the legislature he was elected president of congress; in his first term he also served as a cabinet minister. But his conservatism and his attachment to the Holy See caused conflict with Peruvian liberals. As bp. he was esp. concerned with clerical education and discipline.

HERRERA, JUAN DE (*c.*1530–97), Spanish architect, accompanying Philip II to Italy and Brussels (1547–51), assisted (1563) Juan Bautista de Toledo at the Escorial, completed roofs and additions to the W façade of the palace-monastery; reorganized workshops, designed the church (1574–82), and built the infirmary. Working at the cathedral of Valladolid (1585) H., by his refined proportions, influenced Spanish church and palace plans for generations.

[M. J. DALY]

HERRERA Y TORDESILLAS, ANTONIO DE (1559?–1625), Spanish historian, best known for his authoritative treatment of the Spaniards in the New World. Popular in his day and generally reliable in presenting factual content, H. was an exhaustive investigator into 16th-cent. European developments. He thus wrote on

Portugal's conquest of the Azores, on Scotland and England in the time of Mary Stuart, on the religious wars in France, on Church-State conflict in Milan, on the difficulties in Aragon, on the last three centuries of Italian history (1281–1599), and on the reign of his patron, Philip II, 1556–98. In all his work he showed an interest not only in chronicling events but in geographical, social, and ethnic material as well. His greatest work, the *General History of the Spanish in the Indies* (4 v., 1601–15), was written after his appointment in 1596 to the position of royal chronicler. Based on both MS sources from the state archives and previously published accounts, the history comprehensively and eulogistically describes Spain's discovery and conquest of and rule in the New World from 1492 up to 1554.

[E. M. GATES]

HERRERO, ANDRÉS (1782–1838), Spanish Franciscan missionary, restorer of the missions after the wars of independence. From 1810–33 he labored in the missions among the Indians of N Bolivia. In 1833 he returned to Europe, was named apostolic prefect of South American missions; through this and a subsequent visit to Europe he was able to recruit over 100 missionaries for Bolivia and Peru. The result was the renewal of the missions as well as of the colleges sponsored by the Congregation for the Propagation of the Faith in Bolivia, Peru, and Chile.

[T. C. O'BRIEN]

HERRGOTT, MARQUART (1694–1762), German ecclesiastical historian and antiquarian. Born in Freiburg and ordained as a Benedictine in 1718, H. studied *Maurist historical methodology at the Abbey of Saint-Germain-des-Près in Paris and there gathered together the writings of Italian, French, and German Benedictines on monastic life for inclusion in his major work, the *Vetus disciplina monastica* (1726). Attached to the court of Emperor Charles VI in Vienna from 1728 to 1748, H. thereafter returned to the Abbey of St. Blasien in the Black Forest and devoted himself principally to the study of German and local church history.

[E. M. GATES]

HERRICK, ROBERT (1591–1674), English poet and clergyman, friend of Ben Jonson and of the wits of the court of Charles I. He was appointed rector of Dean Prior and grieved for a time that he was out of London life but he grew contented and wrote lyrics about flowers, trees, country beliefs and customs. His collection of *c.* 1200 short lyrics is entitled *Hesperides: the Works both Human and Divine of Robert Herrick* (1648). He is fanciful, polished but without complexity of ideas or of poetic discipline. Dismissed from the rectorship by the Puritan government in 1647, he was restored under James II in 1662. BIBLIOGRAPHY: E. S. White, NCE 5:400.

[M. M. BARRY]

HERRISVAD, ABBEY OF, the oldest Cistercian abbey in Denmark, located near Helsingborg, in what is now Sweden; founded 1144 by Eskil, abp. of Lund; settled by monks from Cîteaux; and founding in its turn daughterhouses in Tvis 1163, Holme 1172, and Logum *c.* 1173. All the abbeys in Denmark suffered serious decline in the 14th cent., and all were dissolved in the Reformation, after 1536. Although Herrisvad Abbey was demolished, recent excavations have brought to light its architectural plan. BIBLIOGRAPHY: Cottineau I:1409–10.

[E. J. DILLON]

HERRMANN, WILHELM (1846–1922), Lutheran liberal theologian. He studied at Halle in 1866, was university lecturer there in 1875, and finally was professor at Marburg from 1879 until his death. To I. Kant he owed his notion that God is an object of practical knowledge, not theoretical knowledge, and that faith can neither be supported nor rejected by science or philosophy. His personalism may derive from F. Scleiermacher, including the notion that faith is a matter of personal experience, not of doctrines; a living personal relationship with God. He was a student of A. Ritschl, from whom he derived his emphasis on ethics and his rejection of metaphysics. He was a teacher of both K. Barth and R. Bultmann, both of whom carried forward the problematic of faith as presented to them by him. His best-known work was the *The Communion of the Christian with God* (1886, Eng. tr. 1895); his *Faith and Morals* and *Essays on the Social Gospel* (with A. Harnack) were also translated. BIBLIOGRAPHY: P. Fischer-Appelt, *Metaphysik im Horizont der Theologie Wilhelm Herrmans* (1955); R. T. Voelkel, *Shape of the Theological Task* (1968).

[E. J. DILLON; P. MISNER]

HERRNHUT, a town in Saxony, Germany, established in 1722 as the mother community of the Renewed *Moravian Church. It was founded on the estate of Count *Zinzendorf as an asylum for refugees from Habsburg lands who sought to keep alive the *Unitas Fratrum of their ancestors. Growing into a flourishing center of *Pietism with worldwide missionary outreach, Herrnhut became a prototype for Moravian communities throughout the world. Its archives contain valuable source material on the Moravian movement. His stay influenced J. *Wesley. BIBLIOGRAPHY: K. G. Hamilton, *History of the Moravian Church* (1967).

[J. R. WEINLICK]

HERSFELD, ABBEY OF, former Benedictine abbey near Mainz, Germany. The abbey was founded in 769–770 by Lullus, a monk of Malmesburg and companion of St. *Boniface. It became an imperial abbey under Charlemagne, controlled large tracts of land and during the 10th and 11th cent. became an important spiritual and intellectual center. Its prestige waned in the later Middle Ages, and Protestantism was introduced in the 16th century. Important ruins of the abbey remain. BIBLIOGRAPHY: P. Beckman, NCE 6:1086.

[T. M. MCFADDEN]

HERTFORD, COUNCIL OF, the first general assembly of the English church. It was convoked by the abp. of Canterbury, Theodore of Tarsus in 673, to establish diocesan government; it also laid down guidelines for uniform practice regarding divorce and the date for keeping Easter. BIBLIOGRAPHY: R. S. Hoyt, NCE 6:1086–87.

[B. L. MARTHALER]

HERTLING, GEORG VON (1843–1919), German statesman, Catholic philosopher, first president of the Görres Society, university professor in Bonn and Munich; member of the Reichstag (1875–90 and 1896–1912); German chancellor (1917–18). He wrote on the Aristotelian concept of the soul, Albert the Great, John Locke and the Cambridge School, natural law, social justice, St. Augustine, scholasticism, and Catholicism vis-à-vis art and science. Despite the breadth of his interests, he cannot be described as a philosopher of eminence; his chief contribution to religious and philosophical thought lay in the encouragement he gave to Catholic thinkers to emerge from their ghetto-like retreat.

[S. A. SHULZ]

HERVAEUS NATALIS (HARVEY NEDELLEC; d. 1323), French Dominican theologian who taught at Paris (1302–09), was provincial of the French Dominicans (1309) and master general of the order (1318–23). During his generalate he promoted the cause of canonization of St. Thomas Aquinas and rebuked *Durandus of St. Pourçain for departing from the teachings of St. Thomas. In his own works he rejected a real composition between essence and existence in created being. His explanations of the sacramental theology of Aquinas are remarkable for their lucidity. BIBLIOGRAPHY: Gilson HCP, extensive bibliog.; Glorieux R 1:64; E. B. Allen, NCE 6:939.

[P. K. MEAGHER]

HERVÉ OF BOURG DIEU (end of 11th cent.–1150), French Benedictine biblical commentator, best known for his commentaries on Isaiah and the Pauline Epistles. The second were for a long time ascribed to St. Anselm of Canterbury, among whose homilies (PL 158:585–674) are printed some that have also been shown to be H.'s work. His exposition of the *Celestial Hierarchies,* using Erigena's translation, helped to promote interest in the thought of Pseudo-Dionysius.

[P. J. HENNESSEY]

HERVET, GENTIEN (1499–1584), French theologian and translator. Originally Greek tutor to Cardinal Pole's brother, H. supplied him and the future Pope Marcellus II with translations of the Greek fathers and accompanied his patrons to the Council of Trent. He was ordained in 1556. He wrote a treatise recommending the enforcement of episcopal residence as the best means of reforming the Church. He also wrote numerous pamphlets against the Protestants and published a French translation of the Tridentine decrees and of St. Augustine's *City of God.* BIBLIOGRAPHY: A. Duval, *Catholicisme* 5:693–697.

[M. J. SUELZER]

HERWEGEN, ILDEFONS (1874–1946), German Benedictine liturgist, abbot of Maria Laach from 1913. Under his leadership his abbey became a leading center of the liturgical movement. H. did much personally by his preaching and writing to stimulate interest in the liturgy. He founded the popular *Ecclesia Orans* series in 1918, edited scholarly works, and also wrote himself on monastic history, art, and the liturgy. In 1931 he founded the Benedictine Academy for Liturgical and Monastic Research known since 1948 as the Abt-Herwegen-Institut. BIBLIOGRAPHY: T. A. Michels, "Abbot Ildefons Herwegen," OrFrat 21 (1946) 2–7; H. A. Reinhold, NCE 6:1087.

[N. KOLLAR]

HERWIG, FRANZ (1880–1931), German novelist, journalist, a figure in the Catholic literary revival in Germany. His early interest centered on the world of history (*Wunder der Welt,* 1910). Later he turned to social themes (as in *Sankt Sebastian vom Wedding,* 1921; *Hoffnung auf Licht,* 1931). His best-known novel, *Der grosse Bischof* (1930), is built upon the life of Ketteler.

[I. MERKEL]

HERZEN, ALEXANDER IVANOVICH (1812–70), radical Russian thinker and journalist; leader of *Westerners and Populists; liberal socialist. In 1847 he left Russia and, in 1852, settled in England, where he published the influential Russian émigré newspaper *Kolokol* (*The Bell*; 1857–67). Though he disagreed with the *Slavophiles in their concepts of orthodoxy and autocracy, he shared to a large extent their idealization of the Russian peasant commune (hence his influence on the Populists). BIBLIOGRAPHY: M. Malia, *Alexander Herzen and the Birth of Russian Socialism, 1812–1855* (1961).

[M. F. MCCARTHY]

HERZL, THEODOR (1860–1904), the leader of modern World *Zionism. A native of Budapest, H. was sent (1894) to Paris as correspondent for the *Neue Freie Presse* of Vienna to cover the *Dreyfus affair. From that time the idea of a sovereign Jewish state as an answer to anti-Semitism occupied all his energies. H. published his thoughts in the pamphlet *Der Judenstaat* (1896; often reprinted). His political and diplomatic efforts included an unsuccessful meeting with the Sultan (1896) and the assembling of the first World Congress of Zionism at Basel (1897). In 1949 the remains of H. were transferred with great honor to Israel.

His diaries were edited by R. Patai (1960). BIBLIOGRAPHY: Biog. by A. Bein (1939); I. Cohen (1959); J. Adler (1960).

[T. C. O'BRIEN]

HERZOG, JOHANN JAKOB (1805–82), German Reformed theologian, prolific author. He taught historical theology at Lausanne until he resigned in 1846 because of his convictions. He later taught at University of Halle where he developed a strong interest in the Waldenses. Among his contributions are *Das Leben Oecolampadius und die Reformation der Kirche zu Basel,* and the editing of the *Realencyklopädie* for which he also wrote 529 articles.

[P. J. HENNESSEY]

HERZOGENBURG, Austrian monastery of Augustinian Canons in the Diocese of St. Pölten. It was founded in 1112 by Bp. Ulrich of Passau in St. Georgen on the Danube. As a consequence of frequent inundations, the monastery was transferred to Herzogenburg (1244). In this place it prospered, and during the Baroque period its buildings were monumentally renovated by the famous architects J. Prandtauer, J. B. Fischer, V. Erlach, and F. Mungenast (1714–85). The monastery is rich in art collections. BIBLIOGRAPHY: *Bibl. Herzogenburg, das Stift und seine Kunstschätze* (1964).

[F. H. RÖHRIG]

HESCHEL, ABRAHAM JOSHUA (1907–72), Jewish theologian. Born in Warsaw, H. succeeded M. *Buber at Frankfort and later taught in Warsaw and London. In 1940 he joined the faculty of Hebrew Union College in Cincinnati. From 1945 he was professor of Jewish ethics and mysticism at the Jewish Theological Seminary in New York. A noted interpreter of *Hasidism and prophetism, he was also active in the civil rights and anti-Vietnam War movements, and in Jewish-Christian dialogue. BIBLIOGRAPHY: F. Sherman, *Promise of Heschel* (1970).

[T. EARLY]

HESDIN, JACQUEMART DE (fl. *c.*1384–1410 or 11). Franco-Flemish MS illuminator from Artois, H. worked for Jean Duc de Berry producing the magnificent *Petites heures du Duc de Berry* (Paris), *Très belles heures de Notre-Dame* (Turin-Milan Hours), *Très belles heures de Jehan de Franco* (Brussels), and *Grandes heures du Duc de Berry.* Influenced by Jean Pucelle and the Italianate style, J.'s work, distinguished by a delicate; idyllic quality, is prelude to Flemish panel painting.

[M. J. DALY]

HESKYNS, THOMAS (fl. 1566), English RC priest. Educated at Oxford and Cambridge, he became vicar of Briworth and chancellor of the Church of Sarum. In 1559, having refused to swear to the supremacy of Queen Elizabeth over the C of E, he was deprived of his positions and income, and he retired to Flanders where he entered the Dominican Order. Later he returned secretly to England where he ministered to Catholics and was highly esteemed by them. He wrote *Parliament of Christe* in defense of the Real Presence of Christ in the Holy Eucharist, against which treatise William Fulke in 1579 wrote *Heskins' Parliament Repealed.* Nothing is known of the cause or time of H.'s death. BIBLIOGRAPHY: Gillow BDEC 3:292–294.

[M. J. BARRY]

HESPERINOS (Gr., evening), the vespers or evening prayer of the Byzantine rite. It has always been the custom of the Church to begin the liturgical day with evening prayer. At this beginning of the new day, Evening Prayer is said in memory of the beginning of the day on which God started the creation of the visible world. The theme is carried out during the week with Psalm 103, dealing with the six days of creation from the creation of light to the creation of man. Evening Prayer consists solely of beseechings and supplications, with the repetition of the peace petition, the offering of incense, and the chanting of Psalm 140. On certain days of great solemnity, the Vespers are more solemn in their tone and composition.

[P. A. MORLINO]

HESS, BEDE FREDERICK (1885–1953), minister general of the Order of Friars Minor Conventual from 1936. A Franciscan from 1900, he was ordained in 1908 and worked in teaching, parish missions, and parochial assignments before becoming provincial of the Province of the Immaculate Conception in 1932, until his election as minister general. He was the first American-born general of a major religious order; his tenure was the longest since the generalate of St. Bonaventure. During World War II H. was able to save Assisi from Nazi destruction and after the war protected the provinces of his order in the Iron Curtain countries. He is highly regarded by his brethren for his reform work and his writing on the internal life of the order.

[T. C. O'BRIEN]

HESSELIUS, American painters. **Gustavus** (1682–1755), portrait, religious, and mythological artist, arrived from Sweden (1712) and was a major painter in Pennsylvania, Maryland and Delaware (1750). He did the first religious paintings known to have been commissioned in the Protestant colonies. *The Last Supper* (1721, now lost), and his two Indian portraits are early masterpieces of characterization. The most important collection of his works is owned by the Historical Society of Pennsylvania, in Philadelphia. **John** (1728–1778), colonial portrait painter in Maryland, Virginia, Delaware, and Pennsylvania trained by his father, Gustavus, was later (1750's) influenced by the fashionable itinerant English artist, John Wollaston (*Charles Calvert and His Slave,* 1761). BIBLIOGRAPHY: J. H. Pleasants, DAB (1932) 598–599; R. E. Fleischer, *Gustavus Hesselius* (The Johns Hopkins University, 1964); *idem,* NCE 6:1089.

[F. S. GRUBAR]

HESSLER, GEORG, (*c.*1427–1482) cardinal and statesman. Born of a bourgeois family from Würzburg, he completed canonical studies in Cologne, Heidelberg and Pavia, and then entered the service of Cardinal Giovanni Castiglione in 1457, and that of Duke Albrecht of Austria in 1459. He was canon and provost before becoming chancellor for Emperor Frederick III in 1474. He handled the marriage of Maximilian with Marie of Burgundy. He was made a cardinal in 1477, consecrated a bishop by Sixtus IV in 1479, and died three years later near Melk on the Danube. BIBLIOGRAPHY: J. Wodka LTK 5:307.

[E. J. DILLON]

HESYCHASM, a method of prayer of the heart, then an Orthodox doctrine on prayer. Essentially it is a contemplative interpretation of the Pauline phrase of "life hidden in Christ" which passes through Origen and the Alexandrians, Gregory of Nyssa, Evagrius of Ponticus, the Desert Fathers, the Sinaites (John of Climacus etc.), Simeon the New Theologian, and the great Hesychasts of the 13th and 14th centuries. When Orthodox writers use the term "prayer of the heart," they usually have in mind one particular prayer, the *Jesus Prayer. Among Greek spiritual writers, Diadochus of Photice in the 5th cent. and later John Climacus of Mt. Sinai, in his *Ladder of Perfection,* recommended as an esp. valuable form of prayer for certain chosen monks (who were warned against the vice of *acedia) the constant repetition or remembrance of the name of Jesus. In the course of time, the invocation became crystalized into a short sentence known as the Jesus Prayer: "Lord Jesus Christ, Son of God, have mercy on me." By the 12th cent. the recitation of the Jesus Prayer had become linked to certain physical exercises designed to assist concentration. Breathing was carefully regulated in time with the prayer, and a particular body posture was recommended: bowed head, chin on chest, eyes fixed on the place of the heart. This is often called the Hesychast method of prayer, but it should not be thought that for the Hesychasts these exercises constituted the essence of prayer. They were regarded not as an end in themselves, but as a help to concentration, as useful to some but not obligatory on all. The Hesychasts knew that there can be no mechanical means of acquiring God's grace, and no techniques leading automatically to purity of heart (an Eastern Orthodox concept that corresponds to the Western Christian concept of contemplation).

For the Hesychasts of Byzantium, the culmination of religious experience was the vision of Divine and Uncreated Light. The works of Simeon the New Theologian (940–1022), the greatest of the Byzantine mystics, are full of this light-mysticism. When he writes of his own experiences or those of others, he speaks again and again of the "Divine Light," like a fire uncreated and invisible, without beginning, and immaterial. The Hesychasts believed that this light they experienced was identical with the Uncreated Light seen by the three Disciples surrounding Jesus at his Transfiguration. But to reconcile this vision of the Divine Light with the apophatic doctrine of God, the transcendent, unapproachable, ineffable became a controverted issue in the 14th cent., as did the role of the body in prayer and the Divine Light. The Hesychasts were violently attacked by a learned Greek from Italy, Barlaam the Calabrian, who stated the doctrine of God's otherness and unknowability in an extreme form. Barlaam's views have some resemblance to the Nominalist philosophy current in the West at this date; but he was also learned in the Greek Fathers, particularly *Dionysius the Areopagite (see PSEUDO-DIONYSIUS).

Emphasizing the negative theology in Dionysius' writings, he argued that God can be known only indirectly; he felt Hesychasm was wrong to speak of an immediate experience of God, for any such experience is impossible. Because of the bodily exercises the Hesychasts employed, Barlaam accused them of holding a grossly materialistic concept of prayer. He was also scandalized by their claim to a vision of the Divine and Uncreated Light and again he charged them with materialism, that a man can see God's essence with his bodily eyes. The light that the Hesychasts beheld, in his view, was not the eternal light of the divinity, but a temporary and created light. The defense of the Hesychasts was taken up by Gregory Palamas (1290–1359), Abp. of Thessalonica. He upheld a doctrine of man that allowed for the use of bodily exercises in prayer, and he argued against Barlaam that the Hesychasts did indeed experience the Divine and Uncreated Light of Thabor. To explain how this was possible, Gregory developed the distinction between essence and energies of God, also a Dionysius theme. It was Gregory's achievement to set Hesychasm on a firm dogmatic basis, by integrating it into Orthodox theology as a whole, and by showing how the Hesychast vision of Divine Light in no way undermined the apophatic doctrine of God. His teaching was confirmed by two synods held at Constantinople in 1341 and 1351. BIBLIOGRAPHY: Diadoque de Photice, *Oeuvres spirituelles* (ed and tr. É. des Places, *Sources chrétiennes* 5, 1955); V. Lossky, *Mystical Theology of the Orthodox Church* (1973); J. Meyendorff, *Byzantine Theology* (1974); *Writings from the Philocalia on the Prayer of the Heart* (ed. E. Kadloubovsky and G.E.H. Palmer, 1957).

[M. T. HANSBURY]

HESYCHIUS OF ALEXANDRIA (fl. 5th cent.), otherwise unknown author of a Greek lexicon, an important resource on ecclesiastical Greek, esp. that of St. Cyril of Alexandria and other Fathers. There was a 19th-cent. edition by M. Schmidt (5 v., 1858–68). BIBLIOGRAPHY: V. Laurent, *Catholicisme* 5:706.

[T. C. O'BRIEN]

HESYCHIUS OF JERUSALEM (d. after 451), monk and exegete. Ordained *c.*412, sometime after having embraced the monastic life, H. became widely known as a preacher. He was still alive at the time of the Council of

*Chalcedon (451). In the Greek Church he is commemorated as a saint. Of his extensive biblical commentaries, which reflect Alexandrian, allegorical exegesis, only some survive, e.g., on Lev (PG 93:787–1180); on Job (in an Armenian tr., 1913); two on Ps (PG 93:1179–1340 and among the works of *Athanasius, PG 27:649–1344). He also wrote against *Arianism and *Apollinarianism. BIBLIOGRAPHY: Altaner 389–390; Quasten 3:488–496; A. Vaccari, EncCatt 5:581–582.

[R. B. ENO]

HESYCHIUS OF MILETUS (fl. 5th cent.), Greek chronicler and also biographer. He lived during the reign of Justinian I and was also known as Hesychius Illustris. He was the author of *A Compendium of Universal History,* work in six books; a portion of the sixth, which deals with the history of Byzantium, still exists. Another work, *A Biographical Dictionary of Learned Men* was a source used by later Greek writers. BIBLIOGRAPHY: F. Dolger LTK 5:309–310.

[J. R. RIVELLO]

HETHITES. The biblical Hethites (Hittites) are probably connected with the Hittites who lived in the 2d millennium B.C. in W Asia Minor. Although the Bible sometimes links the Hethites with the Canaanites, it usually considers them to be distinct and as settlers in Canaan, esp. around Jerusalem and Hebron, before the Israelite conquest. The Hethites of David's time are probably from the surviving Hittite city states with whom Solomon later engaged in horse trade. BIBLIOGRAPHY: L. F. Hartman, NCE 6:1090–91; E.O. Forrer, "Hittites in Palestine," *Palestine Exploration Fund Quarterly Statement* 68 (1936) 190–203; 69 (1937) 100–115. *HITTITES.

[E. J. CROWLEY]

HETTINGER, FRANZ (1819–90), German theologian, author. He spent most of his career at the Univ. of Würzburg, where he was the associate of H. *Denzinger. He served as a consultor (1868) in the preparations for Vatican Council I; was the German translator of Leo XIII's encyclicals; and the author of many works on priestly spirituality. His major achievement was *Apologie des Christentums* (5 v., 1863–67), a work of theological apologetics reprinted many times and translated into other languages; he also published *Lehrbuch des Fundamentaltheologie* (1879). H. was a renowned preacher and a recognized Dante scholar, publishing several works of theological interpretation on the *Divine Comedy.*

[T. C. O'BRIEN]

HETZENAUER, MICHAEL (1860–1928), Austrian Capuchin biblical scholar whose most lasting work is his *Biblia sacra Vulgatae editionis,* a critical ed. of the Clementine Vulgate; he also published a 2-volume edition of the Greek New Testament. H. taught at Innsbruck and in Rome, where he became a consultor of the Pontifical Biblical Commission. Much of his work was directed against the spread of Modernism.

HEUSER, HERMAN JOSEPH (1852–1933), writer, editor. Born in Germany, he came to the U.S. and was ordained in 1876. During his entire career H. taught at St. Charles Seminary in Philadelphia, largely in the field of Scripture. In 1899 he founded *The American Ecclesiastical Review,* which he edited for 23 years, a magazine that exercised great influence in the U.S. and in Europe. H. was the publisher in the U.S. of the novels of Canon Patrick Sheehan of Ireland, whose most popular work *My New Curate* was written for the *Review* and published there serially. H. established the Dolphin Press and edited the quarterly *The Dolphin,* a Catholic literary journal. He wrote the constitutions for the Sisters of Mercy of Merion, Pa., and the Sisters of the Blessed Sacrament. In 1907, during the Modernist controversy, he was named censor of all Catholic publications in the U.S. BIBLIOGRAPHY: E. Galbally, AER (1933) 337–360.

[J. R. AHERNE]

HEVIA BOLAÑOS, JUAN DE (*c.*1570–1623), Spanish-born jurist and author of influential legal treatises. He had already been an office boy and clerk in a law office in Spain before leaving for Spanish America at age 14. He worked first at Quito and then in Lima. It is not certain that he was an attorney, but there is much practical legal advice contained in his *Curia Philipica* (1603): a guide to civil and criminal cases of both Church and State courts; and his *Labyrintho* (1617): a favorite guide for judges, lawyers, merchants, and seamen in unraveling legal problems of land and sea commerce.

[E. J. DILLON]

HEVITES (or Hivites), a term that appears in the OT mostly in the stereotyped lists of peoples expelled from Canaan by the Israelites; however, it is not found in any extrabiblical source. Many scholars think the name is a synonym of "Horrites" (Hurrians), probably to distinguish them from the Horrite pre-Edomite population of Seir. BIBLIOGRAPHY: E. A. Speiser, *Genesis* (Anchor Bible 1 1964) 276–283. *HURRIANS.

[E. J. CROWLEY]

HEWIT, AUGUSTINE FRANCIS (1820–97), Paulist editor, educator. After study at Amherst College, Mass., and the Congregationalist seminary at East Windsor, Conn., he joined the Episcopal Church, trained for the ministry, and was ordained a deacon (1843). He converted to Roman Catholicism (1846), was ordained (1847), and made his vows as a Redemptorist (1850). In 1858 he was released from his vows and assisted Isaac *Hecker in founding the *Paulists, succeeding him as superior general (1889). H. founded a house of studies (St. Paul's College) at The Catholic Univ. of America, Washington, D.C., the first religious house affiliated with the university. Under his direction, the Catholic Missionary Union was established (1896) and the Columbus Press (later the Paulist Press) was begun (1891). BIBLIOGRAPHY: J. P. Flynn, *Early Years of Augustine F. Hewit, C.S.P.* (1945); J. McSorley, *Father Hecker and His Friends* (2d ed., 1953).

[M. CARTHY]

HEXACHORD, an antecedent of the do-re-mi scale, a succession of six notes at semitone intervals, comparable to the first six tones of the major scale. Guido d'Arezzo (d. *c.* 1050) designated these tones by the names: *ut, re, mi, fa, sol, la,* from the first syllable of the first word in the first six lines of a hymn for the feast of St. John the Baptist: *Ut* queant laxis, *Re*sonare fibris, *Mi*ra gestorum, *Fa*muli tuorum, *So*lve polluti, *La*bureatum, Sancte Johannes. Each line began one note higher than the last. Under Guido's influence the hexachord system superseded the Greek tetrachord system. These six tones have been used repeatedly as the theme in both vocal and instrumental compositions.

[M. T. LEGGE]

HEXAEMERON, a term derived from the Greek adjective "six-day" to designate the work of creation in Genesis, ch. 1, or the narrative of this work. It was probably first used by Philo and adopted by the Greek and later by the Latin Church Fathers. The name is also used of the patristic commentaries on ch. 1 of Genesis, notably St. Basil's and St. Ambrose's. The term leaves out of consideration the seventh day when "God finished his work" (Gen 2.2). BIBLIOGRAPHY: J. Tringuet, *Catholicisme* 5:711–712.

[E. J. CROWLEY]

HEXAPLA, Origen's parallel edition of the OT, completed at Caesarea in 245, showing the relationship between the original Hebrew of the OT and the Greek translations. It comprised six columns (Hexapla): the Hebrew text, a Greek transliteration, Aquila's version, Symmachus' version, the Septuagint, and Theodotian's version. The fifth column was Origen's critical edition of the Septuagint, and signs employed at Alexandria in editing secular authors were used to show the divergences from the Hebrew. BIBLIOGRAPHY: D. N. Freedman, InterDB 2:597–598.

[E. J. CROWLEY]

HEXAPTERYGON, (Gr. for six-winged) in Eastern Churches a disk fashioned in the form of an angel's head surrounded by six wings. Mounted on a pole, it is borne in liturgical processions; it is one of the instruments passed to the deacon at ordination as a sign of office. In its functional origin it was a fan to brush away flies from the gifts during the Eucharistic canon (anaphora). Another name is the *ripidion.*

[T. C. O'BRIEN]

HEXATEUCH (Gr. for "six books"), a modern desgnation for the first six biblical books, first used by J. Wellhausen in 1876. The emphasis on the Promised Land theme in the Pentateuch seemed to link the conquest in Joshua to the Pentateuch. However, most scholars now consider Joshua to be more integrally a part of the Deuteronomic history. BIBLIOGRAPHY: H. Cazelles, DBSuppl 7:735–858, esp. 749–750. DEUTERONOMIC HISTORY, PENTATEUCH.

[E. J. CROWLEY]

HEXENFOOS, magical decorative designs (hexagonal stars in circles, whirls, rosettes) painted on Pennsylvania German barns to protect from evil spirits and lightning and to keep animals from being bewitched or *ferhexed.*

[M. J. DALY]

HEXHAM, MONASTERY OF, former Benedictine monastery, then priory of Canons Regular of St. Augustine, Hexham, England. Founded *c.*673 by Wilfrid, abp. of York, as a Benedictine abbey, it was destroyed during the 10th–cent. Danish invasions. Rebuilt in the 12th cent. it was a priory for Canons Regular of St. Augustine until it was dissolved (1536) under Henry VIII. This monastery church is now the parish church of St. Andrew.

[M. A. MCFADDEN]

HEYWOOD, JASPER (1535–98), classicist, English Jesuit of penal days. Son of John *Heywood, the epigrammatist, he became a fellow of All Souls, Oxford. In early years noted for wildness of spirit, he undoubtedly suffered all his life from some form of psychological illness. He is known in literature for his translation of three plays by Seneca. Ordained a priest and admitted to the Society of Jesus, in 1581 he became superior of the English Mission where he enjoyed extraordinary success. In 1583 H. was imprisoned and later tried at Westminster, then committed to the Tower. Deported to France, he experienced again the mental illness of former days. He died at Naples, in the words of the famous Jesuit Father Persons, "like a good religious man." BIBLIOGRAPHY: L. I. Guiney, *Recusant Poets* (1939).

[J. R. AHERNE]

HEYWOOD, JOHN (1497–1578), playwright, poet. A friend and possible collaborator of St. Thomas More, H. married the granddaughter of More's sister and was close to a number of More's friends and relatives. During the reigns of Edward VI and Mary Tudor he was a royal pensioner. When Abp. Cranmer was attacked by the Catholic party in 1540, H. was condemned to death but was pardoned. In 1544 appeared his best-known play *The Four P's,* which played a major role in the development of pre-Shakespearean drama. He was most famous for his epigrams collected in 1546. Exiled in 1564, he emigrated to Flanders with his family. Two sons became Jesuits, his daughter Elizabeth became the mother of the celebrated poet John Donne. H. to the last endured persecution for his faith, narrowly escaping death several times. BIBLIOGRAPHY: L. I. Guiney, *Recusant Poets* (1939).

[J. R. AHERNE]

HEZEKIAH (Ezechias), king of Judah *c.*715–687 B.C. (2 Kg ch. 18–20; 2 Chr ch. 29–32). He was the son and successor of Ahaz, but under the influence of Isaiah and Micah he reversed his father's policy and promoted the exclusive worship of Yahweh. He also sought to end Ahaz's policy of subordination to Assyria by an alliance with Egypt, a move condemned by Isaiah (Ch. 20; 30.1–7; 31.1–3). Sennacherib retaliated by forcing heavy tribute from H. (2 Kg 18.14). Sennacherib gave up his siege of Jerusalem, however, when his army was decimated by "the angel of Yahweh" (2 Kg 19.35). H. dug the Siloam Tunnel to secure a water supply during sieges. He was succeeded by his son Manasseh.

[T. EARLY]

HIBERNENSIS COLLECTIO, compilation of the canon law of the Church in Ireland, made *c.*700. It is an important source on the life of the Irish Church from its beginnings, reflects the predominance of the monks and zeal for discipline. The collection had its influence on the canon law of the Continent through the Irish monk-missionaries.

HIBERNO-SAXON ART, a synthesis of Celtic (Irish) nonclassical, linear style, and the Northumbrian humanistic, classical narrative tradition, effecting a culture spread on the Continent by Irish and Northumbrian monks who founded (from Iona and Lindisfarne) major monasteries at St. Gall, Bobbio, and Echternach. Exquisite metalwork in the Tara Brooch (*c.*800) and cover of the Lindau Gospels (8th-9th cent.) from St. Gall show a complex, dynamic zoomorphic interlace evidencing marvelous skill. Early Irish work contrasts with the delicate quality of Northumbrian design. The Celtic *Book of Durrow* (7th cent.) is heavy in detail with large open spaces, whereas the Hiberno-Saxon *Book of Kells* (8th cent.) displays an elaboration of spirals, interlaces, and ornament of most refined delicacy. The cursive script, which finally flowered in Carolingian miniscule, was the greatest contribution. The Gospels of Echternach (*c.*690), St. Gall (8th cent.), Cuthbert (760–770) show the influence of Hiberno-Saxon culture.

[M. J. DALY]

HICKEY, ANTONY (1586–1641), Irish Franciscan theologian. After teaching theology at Louvain and Cologne, he went to Rome in 1619 where he collaborated with Luke Wadding in editing the works of Duns Scotus, and also wrote a commentary on Book IV of the *Sentences*. He also served as definitor general of his order (1639). BIBLIOGRAPHY: É. d'Alençon, DTC 6.2:2358–59; A. J. Gondras, *Catholicisme* 5:712–713.

[V. SAMPSON]

HICKEY, JOSEPH ALOYSIUS (1883–1955), Augustinian prior general. Reared by Maurice Dorney, the pastor of St. Gabriel's Church in Chicago, H. entered the Augustinian Order and was ordained in 1906. After serving in many offices of his order in the U.S., H. was elected assistant general in 1925, prior general in 1947, the first American so honored. His chief accomplishment as general was the reorganizing of Augustinians in the wake of World War II. H. served for many years in Rome as consultor and commissary of the Congregation for the Sacraments.

[J. R. AHERNE]

HICKS, EDWARD (1780–1849), American painter and leading Quaker preacher, head of a workshop for painting signs and furniture, carriages, and other items. His art reflects his practical nature and religious convictions. H. is famous for more than 50 versions of *The Peaceable Kingdom* (Isaiah 11), depicting the animal kingdom in the foreground and William Penn's treaty with the Indians in the background—as Quaker fulfilling the Biblical prophecy. BIBLIOGRAPHY: A. Ford, *Edward Hicks, Painter of the Peaceable Kingdom* (1952).

[M. J. DALY]

HICKS, ELIAS (1748–1830), American liberal Quaker. H. was a Long Island farmer who was active in Friends meetings from *c.*1765 and became an approved minister in 1778. For 50 years he gave himself to arduous preaching journeys, and in his sermons and correspondence he became a foremost exponent of Quaker liberal mysticism, developing G. *Fox's *Inner Light teaching to the fullest, but advocating a rationalist attitude toward traditional Christian beliefs. He opposed the imposition of evangelical Protestant tenets upon American Quakerism (see GRELLET, S.). When the Quaker separation of 1827 occurred, the evangelical group labeled the liberals "Hicksites," although H. did not have a direct part in the actual process of schism. The schism began in the Philadelphia Yearly Meeting, spread elsewhere, and is still reflected in Quaker divisions. H. wrote a powerful pamphlet against slavery, *Observations on the Slavery of the Africans and Their Descendants* (1811), and his *Journal* was published posthumously (1832). See *American Quakers Today* (ed. E. B. Bonner, 1966); R. B. Doherty, *Hicksite Separation* (1967); B. Forbush, *Elias Hicks, Quaker Liberal* (1956); R. M. Jones, *Later Period of Quakerism* (2 v., 1921.)

[T. C. O'BRIEN]

HICKSITES, a label attached to those Quakers who accepted the interpretation of Quakerism given by Elias *Hicks, and beginning in 1827, separated from the "orthodox" or evangelical Quakers. The name still connotes the lineage of Quaker bodies that originated in that separation. *RELIGIOUS SOCIETY OF FRIENDS.

[T. C. O'BRIEN]

HILDALGO Y COSTILLA, MIGUEL (1753–1811), Mexican patriot, "Father of Mexican Independence." A priest under surveillance of the Inquisition because of doctrinal and moral changes, as pastor of Dolores he called for revolt against Spain on Sept. 16, 1810 with his "Grito de Dolores" (Cry of Dolores). He led a motley army, mostly of Indians, to the edge of Mexico City, but was defeated near Guadalajara in 1811, taken prisoner, defrocked by the Inquisition, and executed.

[J. R. AHERNE]

HIDULF, SS., name of two saints, contemporaries. (1) Hidulf (d. *c.*707), founder of the abbey of *Moyenmoutier, in the Vosges Mountains. He was a hermit there and founded the abbey when others came to share in his ascetical life. (2) Hidulf of Lobbes (d. 707), a Frankish noble who assisted in the founding of the abbey of Lobbes in Belgium, where he became a monk after his wife's death. BIBLIOGRAPHY: R. Gazeau, *Catholicisme* 6:713–714; R. Van Doren, BiblSanct 7:645–646; Butler 3:72.

[T. C. O'BRIEN]

HIERACITES, Egyptian ascetics and followers of Hieracas (Hierax; fl. 3d cent.), a native of Leontopolis and a man learned in the Scriptures as well as in the science and literature of his day. Epiphanius, the principal source of information about him (*Panar.*, 67), said that he interpreted the Scriptures in an allegorical fashion, denied the reality of the terrestrial paradise, and maintained that there would be no resurrection of the body. He held that the body was nothing more than a prison from which the soul would be liberated, and a resurrection would only mean a new imprisonment for the soul. He regarded marriage as absolutely forbidden. BIBLIOGRAPHY: G. Bareille, DTC 6:2359–61.

[L. G. MÜLLER]

HIERARCH, a member of the hierarchy (Gr. sacred rule), esp. a patriarch or a bishop. In Oriental Churches in union with Rome, a major religious superior (e.g., a *provincial) is classified as a hierarch.

[T. C. O'BRIEN]

HIERARCHICAL RANK, see RANK, HIERARCHICAL.

HIERARCHY (from the Gr. *hierarchēs,* one who presides at sacred rites; hence *hierarchia,* the power and office of one who so presides), a collective term used in the Christian Church for the body of men empowered to administer sacred things, a body organized in ranks and orders with a subordination of the lower to the higher ministries. In the disputes that have arisen concerning the hierarchial structure of the Church, opinion has differed not so much about its existence, or about the legitimacy of a gradation of those who exercise sacred functions, as it has about the origin of such offices. Those who hold what is called the hierarchical theory (Catholics, Eastern Dissidents, Episcopalians, Anglicans) maintain that these functions—or at least the principal ones—were permanently instituted by Christ himself in his establishment of the apostolic college, and that there is no power in the Christian community to change or abrogate them. Those who defend the Protestant or democratic concept hold that the functions in the Church result from arrangements made by the Christian community itself and that consequently there remains a radical right in the community to modify them or to dispense with them.

In the Catholic view the existence of the apostolic college made up of men mandated by Christ to stand in his place and act in his name, and the consciousness of apostolic rights in the first Christian communities, along with the witness in early postapostolic times for the succession to apostolic functions warrant the assertion of hierarchical structure. Nor does it seem surprising to those who hold this position that the corporate powers and visible external functions in the society that is His mystical body should be fixed by Christ, from whom as head the internal life and vigor flow into the members. Such a provision would appear almost connatural in a body altogether unique in its continuing dependence on its founder and permanent invisible head. The traditional distinction (cf. CIC *c.*108.3) into a hierarchy of orders (bishops, priests, ministers) and a hierarchy of jurisdiction (supreme pontificate and episcopate) need not lead to the denial of a basic unity in hierarchical structure. While discussions on this point will probably not end until it is more clearly established exactly how the priestly power of Orders and the pastoral powers of jurisdiction are interrelated, Vatican II has brought some clarification to the matter by teaching (Vat II ConstChurch 21) that episcopal consecration confers along with the function of sanctifying (the priestly function) the functions of teaching and ruling (the pastoral function). Perhaps it may be suggested that in the hierarchy the sacramental power of Orders precedes and demands the pastoral power, much as the physical procreative powers of man and woman precede and demand the moral parental power over those whom they have begotten. BIBLIOGRAPHY: B. Dolhagaray, DTC 6:2362–82; *L'Épiscopat et l'Église universelle* (ed. Y. M. J. Congar and B. D. Dupuy, 1962).

[S. E. DONLON]

HIERARCHY, CELESTIAL, the orders or ranks of *angels. St. Paul gives two enumerations of angels (Eph 1.21; Col 1.16) which mention five different classes: thrones, dominations, virtues, powers, and principalities. To this group are added the seraphim (Is. 6.2) and cherubim (Ezek 1.5), and finally angels and archangels considered as a separate species of being. This series of nine choirs or classes of angels has been common since the 4th century. *Pseudo-Dionysius further grouped these nine choirs into a hierarchical structure of three triads.

[T. M. MCFADDEN]

HIERATIC (ART), term (Gr. *hieratikos,* meaning sacerdotal) used in art to denote a style subject to the rules of religion. Generally it implies monumentality, formalism, or rigidity, and may refer to Egyptian sculpture, Byzantine iconastasis, or African woodcarving.

[M. J. DALY]

HIERATIC SCRIPT (Gr. *hieratikos,* devoted to the sacred, priestly), stage between the hieroglyphic and the demotic in writing. Developed during the Middle Kingdom (*c.*2100–1800 B.C.), it continued in regular use until the end of the New Kingdom (*c.*1100 B.C.). Originally used for administrative, literary, and other writings, after the rise of the demotic script, hieratic was reserved for religious writings.

[T. EARLY]

HIERIA, SYNOD OF, in the history of *iconoclasm, the synod (754) of 338 bps, under Emperor Constantine V (741–775) that condemned use of icons or veneration of the saints as idolatrous. The synod proclaimed itself the seventh *ecumenical council, and iconoclasm the official, orthodox teaching. Only the monks of the Byzantine Empire remained faithful to ancient traditions, and Constantine used the synodal decrees as a justification for persecuting them.

[T. C. O'BRIEN]

HIEROCLES (fl. end of 3d cent.), governor of Bithynia under Diocletian, later prefect of Egypt, author of an anti-Christian treatise in two books. This work, no longer extant, was entitled *Lover of Truth.* H. was the first to present Apollonius of Tyana as a rival and equal of Christ as a religious leader, wonder-worker, and exorcist. Eusebius of Caesarea refuted the work in his *Against Hierocles.* Lactantius in his *The Deaths of the Persecutors* charged H. with having played a part in preparing the Diocletian persecution. BIBLIOGRAPHY: Quasten 3:333–334; A. Amore, EncCatt 6:181–182.

[H. DRESSLER]

HIEROCLES OF ALEXANDRIA (5th cent. A.D.), Neoplatonic philosopher. H. was a pupil of *Plutarch of Athens. Closer to Middle Platonism than to his Neoplatonic predecessors, he admitted only one superterrestrial being, the Demiurge. He seems to have come under Christian influence in maintaining free creation *ex nihilo* for the Demiurge and in his interpretation of Fate not as mechanical determinism, but as the allotment of certain effects to man's free actions. He thus reconciled the doctrine of Necessity or Fate with the Christian concept of human freedom and Divine Providence. He composed a commentary on the Pythagorean *Golden Verses* which is extant. BIBLIOGRAPHY: P. Merlan, LexAW 1296; H. Langerbeck, RGG 3:314–315; Copleston 1:483; CHGMP 314–315.

[M. R. P. MCGUIRE]

HIERODULES, men or more often women temple prostitutes in Mesopotamia and esp. in Canaan, whose earnings went to the temples. Despite the Law (Dt. 23.17ff.), this practice became part of Israelite cult (1 Kg 14.24), even in the Temple of Jerusalem (2 Kg 23.7), a defilement reintroduced by Antiochus Epiphanes (2 Macc 6.4). BIBLIOGRAPHY: H. Cazelles, *Catholicisme* 5:723–724.

[E. J. CROWLEY]

HIEROGLYPHICS, an ancient Egyptian style of writing with signs or pictures, socalled from the Greek for "sacred carvings." A myth of origin attributes their invention to the god Thoth. Strictly, hieroglyphics are limited to picture writings on Egyptian temples and monuments, but the term is commonly extended to picture writing in other cultures. Egyptian hieroglyphic writing is to be distinguished from hieratic (religious) and demotic (ordinary) cursive scripts. Traces of hieroglyphics are preserved from the end of the fourth millennium, and the most recent example dates to A.D. 394. Knowledge of hieroglyphics decreased as Christianity promoted the use of Greek in Egypt in the 2d and 3d centuries. Throughout Egyptian history there were limited literacy and knowledge of hieroglyphics, and the expansion of the common domain of signs from about 700 in the classical period to several thousand *c.*500 B.C. coincides with the progressive restriction of their use to an esoteric circle of priests. Greeks typically viewed hieroglyphics not as writing but as symbols or allegories. Not until the discovery of the Rosetta Stone in 1799 could informed attempts at translation be made. By comparing the Greek, demotic, and hieroglyphic versions of a single inscription preserved on the stone, François Champollion deciphered the writing in 1822. BIBLIOGRAPHY: N. M. Davies, *Picture Writing in Ancient Egypt* (1958); I. Gelb, *A Study of Writing* (1963); A. H. Gardiner, *Egyptian Grammar* (3d ed., rev. 1957).

[E. V. GALLAGHER]

HIEROGNOSIS (Gr., knowledge of the holy), a form of spiritual clairvoyance enabling the recipient to recognize the holiness (or its opposite) of another person, a place, or thing. It is a gift in the same class as the reading of hearts and was manifested in the lives of many saints. Authors differ, however, on whether it invariably is a gift given only to those who are in God's grace.

HIEROMONK, (Gr., sacred monk), in the Eastern Church a monk who has been ordained to the priesthood. According to Eastern practice the majority of monks do not receive holy orders.

[F. T. RYAN]

HIERON (TEMENOS), sacred place or temple, or the enclosure containing the temple. A wall surrounding the sacred precinct, entered by gateway or propylaeum, often embraced further auxiliary shrines, groves, and treasures, as at Olympia and Delphi.

[M. J. DALY]

HIERONYMITES (LOS JERONIMOS), name, meaning Hermits of St. Jerome, applied to several religious orders founded in the 14th and 15th cent. in the Iberian peninsula and Italy. At their height in the late 15th and 16th cent. when they enjoyed the favor of the Spanish and Portuguese monarchies, they wielded considerable power and influence, playing a prominent role in the Americas as well as in Europe. The first Heironymite congregation, organized in Toledo *c.*1370 by Pedro Fernando Pecha, court chamberlain to Peter the Cruel, was recognized by Pope Gregory XI in 1374. The next year, María Gracías of Toledo founded a Hieronymite order of nuns in the convent of San Pablo. Many houses sprang up thereafter, the most important Spanish monasteries being Santa Maria de Guadalupe in Cáceres; San Jerónimo el Real in Madrid; San Yuste in the province of Guadalajara, to which the Habsburg Emperor Charles V retired in 1556, 2 years before his death; San Isidor in Seville; and the imposing fortress-like palace-monastery of Escorial built by Philip II between 1563 and 1584 not far from the capital. In Portugal, the Hieronymite monastery facing the sea at Belém, built by Manuel I near Lisbon in 1499, probably constitutes the most impressive and beautiful example of the distinctive Manueline style of architecture to be found in that country.

The order followed the strict Augustinian Rule, with individual monasteries exercising considerable autonomy until they were placed under a single head by Philip II. Their habit consisted of a white tunic covered by a black scapular and a black hood. The order was put down during the Carlist wars of 1835, but reemerged in 1957 in Segovia. In Italy, Hieronymite establishments included the Poor Hermits of San Geronimo, founded near Montebello by Pietro Gambacorti of Pisa in 1377; a congregation in Fiesole established by Carlo de Montegranelli in 1406, which was dispersed in 1668; and the Observantines of Lombardy, founded by the third general of the Spanish order—Lope de Olmedo—and recognized by Martin V in 1426.

[E. M. GATES]

HIEROPHANY, from Gr., literally a manifestation or appearance of the holy. In the comparative study of religions such phenomena as religious symbols or sanctuaries are classified as hierophanies; they exist for the sake of an experience of the sacred, the divine presence or power. The term hierophany is intended to convey the idea that the religious symbols or holy places are not themselves the object of cult or devotion, but the divine realities that they are meant to make manifest.

[T. C. O'BRIEN]

HIGH ALTAR, see ALTAR, HIGH.

HIGH CHURCH, a term first used in 17th-cent. England as a descriptive phrase for persons or movements that emphasized the continuity and authority of the C of E and its sacramental life. As with *low church, the phrase has had different connotations during its 2 or 3 cent. of use, sometimes referring to political matters, such as the divine right of kings, and sometimes identifying, very often pejoratively, mere ceremonial usages. Also as with low church, it refers to a school of thought within the Church, not to a separate Church. The terms high church and low church are tending to disappear from common usage.

[S. F. BAYNE]

HIGH HOLIDAYS, the first ten days of the Jewish year, a season of penitence and prayer opening with Rosh Hashanah and ending with Yom Kippur. BIBLIOGRAPHY: H. Harper, *Days and Customs of All Faiths* (1957) 244–245.

[M. T. LEGGE]

HIGH MASS, a term to indicate a form of the former Tridentine *Mass in the Roman rite celebrated and sung by one priest accompanied by a chanter, choir, and/or the entire congregation. It is designated in Latin as the *Missa cantata* or chanted Mass. In a previously fixed form it became regarded as the more elaborate (hence high) Mass usually celebrated in the local churches on Sundays, holy days, and on occasion weekdays. It was thus distinguished from the ordinary *low or recited Mass and the *solemn Mass offered with the assistance of a deacon and a subdeacon on festive occasions. It developed as the nearly unique form of the Mass for the ordinary priest in the early local Roman churches, derived from the *pontifical Mass the bp. celebrated with his lower clergy and people. Its own ritual became more fixed, however, through parochial and monastic celebrations. With the revision of the Liturgy of the Mass by Vatican Council II such distinctions as solemn, low, or high Mass are no longer applicable. See J. A. Jungmann, *Mass of the Roman Rite* (rev. ed., tr. F. A. Brunner, 2 v. 1950–55). J. H. Miller, *Fundamentals of the Liturgy* (1959). *MASS, ROMAN.

[N. R. KRAMER]

HIGH PLACE, biblical term referring mainly to a cultic center. Originally Canaanite, high places were frequently adopted by Israelites (1 Sam 9.11–14), and Yahweh was sometimes worshiped there (2 Chr 33.17). Dating from as early as the 3d millennium B.C., the high places were generally situated on hills, though the ''high'' may also refer to the elevated platform on which cultic objects were placed. The high places could be either open-air or covered, and they were equipped with altars, facilities for ablutions, stone pillars, poles, and trees. Because of their associations with pagan worship, they were frequently condemned by biblical writers. Yahweh's hostility to them was stressed (Num 33.52; Ps 78.58), and Deuteronomy demanded centralization of all worship in Jerusalem (12). Solomon, who had his vision at a high place (1 Kg 3.4), built high places for pagan gods (1 Kg 11.7). Hezekiah (2 Kg 18.4) and Josiah (2 Kg 23.8) were noted for their action against them.

[T. EARLY]

HIGH PRIEST, chief official of the Jewish priesthood. Of special importance was the fact that he alone was allowed to enter the holy of holies in the Temple, and he went in only once a year, on the Day of Atonement (Lev ch. 16). A part of his dress was a breastplate with the names of the 12 tribes of Israel, indicating that he represented the whole people. His function was to make atonement for the sins of the people, and the regulations concerning his office showed a marked feeling for the holiness of God and God's demand that his people be holy. The high priesthood was normally hereditary and conferred for life (Num 25.10–13). Ordination, which took 7 days, involved an elaborate ritual (Lev ch. 8). Though sprinkling the mercy seat with the blood of the sin offerings on the Day of Atonement was by far the most important of his duties, he apparently also carried out other priestly functions (Lev 6.19–23).

Scholars generally think the conception of the office expressed in the Pentateuch reflects developments some centuries later than Moses, some contending it arose only after the Exile. The office undoubtedly increased in importance after the end of the Davidic monarchy. The high priest Joshua and the Davidic governor Zerubbabel were considered the "two anointed" (Zech ch. 4). With the end of the Davidic line, the high priest became the chief Jewish official, presiding over the Sanhedrin. The author of Hebrews used the office in his interpretation of the work of Christ (2.17; 9.11–12). *PRIESTHOOD OF CHRIST.

[T. EARLY]

HIGH-PRIESTLY PRAYER OF JESUS, the name given to Jn ch.17 by David Chytraeus in 1600 A.D., although the thought had been earlier expressed by St. Cyril of Alexandria *c.*444. It is the last of the three farewell discourses given by Jesus at the Last Supper, the other two being Jn ch. 13–14 and Jn ch. 15–16. The position in the book of the last of the three discourses and solemnity of tone make of it a fitting preface to John's Passion account, which begins in the following chapter (18). On the eve of heavenly glory (the words at times suggest that the speaker has already entered into glory), Jesus looked first backward, upon the task he had just accomplished (1–8), and then forward to what the future held for those who believed in him (9–19). He had bestowed eternal life upon those who had believed in him (2), by making known to them the person (i.e., the name) and love of the Father (6–8). Next, offering himself as a sacrifice for the protection (9–16) and consecration (17–19) of those who were to pass his revelation on to the world, Jesus prayed for disciples and believers yet to come. His prayer attains its climax in 20–23: ". . . that they may be one, even as we are one." He had in mind both his immediate Disciples and all the people of God, and his prayer envisaged in these a joyful unity of mind and heart which would faithfully reflect the oneness existing between himself and the Father; such unity also establishes in believers a genuine mystical union with God (24–26).

BIBLIOGRAPHY: G. Behler, *Last Discourse of Jesus* (1965); C. H. Dodd, *Interpretation of the Fourth Gospel* (1953).

[R. T. A. MURPHY]

HIGHER CRITICISM, literary and historical analysis of the Bible with concentration on provenance, formation, vocabulary and style, authorship and redaction of its various books and sections of books, for the purpose of better understanding their content, meaning, and aim. It is distinguished from lower, or textual, criticism, which attempts to determine the exact original texts of the Bible as they were published by their various authors and editors.

[J. F. FALLON]

HIGHER EDUCATION FACILITIES ACT OF 1963, passed by Congress on Dec. 16, 1963 as Public Law 88–204, an act that provides public and private (secular and church-related) non-profit colleges and universities with financial assistance in grants and loans solely for academic facilities such as the construction or renovation of libraries and classrooms. The latter are to be used solely for foreign languages, engineering, mathematics and the natural and physical sciences. The program, which is administered by the Bureau of Higher Education through the interested parties, is the most extensive federal aid authorized for higher education. Loans and grants are made on a matching basis and may not exceed one-third the construction cost. The act provides matching grants on the same conditions to graduate schools, with the approval of the Commissioner of Education on recommendation of his advisory committee. They are to help provide much-needed expert professional personnel in the various fields of activity: research, teaching, government, industry, and community.

[M. B. MURPHY]

HILARION, ST. (291–371), Eastern monk, credited by St. Jerome with the introduction of monasticism into Palestine. Born near Gaza of pagan parents, H. became a Christian in his teens as a student in Alexandria and for a few months he joined the desert father St. Anthony. Returning home in 306 H. began first to lead the life of a solitary anchorite, but in 329 he established the first monastery in Palestine. Because the fame of his miracles and his austere life attracted many pilgrims, he left, *c.*360, for Egypt to visit the places connected with St. Anthony. With the persecution under Julian the Apostate, which he had predicted, H. was forced to flee to Libya and then to Sicily, where his hermitage was again soon overrun by pilgrims. This forced him to continue his journey, leading him finally to Cyprus where he died. H.'s life written *c.*391 by St. Jerome (PL 23:30–54) in order to spread the fame of Palestinian monasticism is more rhetorically embellished hagiography than historical biography.

[V. J. POSPISHIL]

HILARIUS OF SEXTEN (1839–99), Tyrolean Capuchin, moral theologian. Born Christian Catterer, he became a Capuchin in 1858; for most of his life he taught at the Capuchin friary of Merano. He published *Compendium theologiae moralis* (1889), and was also well known for his solutions to moral problems in the pastoral review *Linzer Quastalschrift*.

[T. C. O'BRIEN]

HILARUS OF MENDE, ST. (d. *c.*540), hermit, bishop. A dubiously accurate biography written some 4 or 5 cent. after his death describes how he lived as a hermit on the banks of the Tarn, where a group of disciples for whom he built a monastery gathered about him. That he became bp. of Mende some time before the synod of Clermont (535) is attested to by the signatures of that snyod. BIBLIOGRAPHY: G. M. Cook, NCE, 6:1113, P. T. Camelot, *Catholicisme* 5:731.

[G. M. COOK]

HILARY, ST. (d. 468), **POPE,** from 461. H. had been a legate of Leo at the *Robber Synod of Ephesus in 449. In a letter to the Empress Pulcheria before his election, he told of making his escape from the clutches of Dioscurus after insisting, as legate, on the policy of Leo. During much of his reign H. was involved in disciplinary matters in Spain and Gaul. His Roman Synod of 465 is the earliest of which the original records have survived. He was a vigorous ruler, once firmly taking the Emperor Anthemius to task for the heretical tendencies of one of his court. H. erected several buildings, among them an oratory dedicated to St. John the Evangelist. Over its door H. had inscribed the account of his escape from Dioscurus by hiding in a church of St. John. BIBLIOGRAPHY: J. Chapin, NCE 6:1113; J. P. Kirsch, CE 7:348–349.

[P. F. MULHERN]

HILARY OF ARLES, ST. (401–449), monk, bishop. Encouraged by St. Honoratus, H. became a monk at Lérins and upon the death of Honoratus succeeded to the See of Arles *c.*429. As bp. of this important see he presided at a number of councils, among them that of Orange in 441. With the support of a council he deposed Chelidonius, bp. of Besançon (accused of ineligibility for episcopal office because he had married a widow before receiving orders, and because as a civil magistrate he had passed sentence of death) and later he appointed a successor to Projectus, an ailing bp., before his see was vacant. Projectus recovered and there were thus two claimants to the see. Both Chelidonius and Projectus appealed to Pope Leo I. After an exchange of views, marked by some asperity on both sides, between the Pope and H., Arles lost its metropolitan status and H. was no longer permitted to appoint bishops. The authentic works of H. include a sermon on St. Honoratus, a letter to Eucherius, and some verses. BIBLIOGRAPHY: M. Jourjon, DSAM 7:463–464; É. Griffe, *La Gaule chrétienne* (2d ed., 1966) 200–206, 242–246; Butler 2:236–238; V. Boublík, BiblSanct 7:713–715.

[H. DRESSLER]

HILARY OF CHICHESTER (d. 1169), canonist, bishop. He was an influential political figure during the reign of Stephen (1135–54) and was appointed bp. of Chichester by Eugene III in 1147. During Henry II's controversy with Thomas Becket (1163-64), H. took the King's side. BIBLIOGRAPHY: D. Knowles, *Episcopal Colleagues of Archbishop Thomas Becket* (1951).

[L. E. BOYLE]

HILARY OF POITIERS, ST. (*c.*315–*c.*367), bp., Doctor of the Church, called the Athanasius of the West because of his works on the Trinity. He was a convert from paganism through his reading of the Bible; was named bp. of Poitiers *c.*353. Because of Arian domination in the Roman Empire at the time and his refusal to comply in a condemnation of St. *Athanasius, he was exiled to Phrygia. During his exile he completed his own *De Trinitate* (Eng. tr., S. J. McKenna, *Fathers of the Church* 25, 1954) and compiled the *De synodis,* a translation with his own annotations of Greek church pronouncements on the Trinity (e.g., from the Synods of Ancyra and of Sirmium). Through H.'s works the Church in the West received the Latinized Nicene terminology that was to become part of medieval theology's vocabulary on the Trinity. H. himself was not always precise nor felicitous in his pioneering effort to render the Greek terms into Latin. He also wrote scriptural commentaries, is credited with encouraging St. *Martin of Tours' introduction of monasticism into Gaul, and with promoting hymn-singing as a way of teaching and of defense against Arianism. BIBLIOGRAPHY: J. Pelikan, *Emergence of the Catholic Tradition* (Christian Tradition 1, 1971) 199–200; 203–207.

[T. C. O'BRIEN]

HILDA OF WHITBY, ST. (614–680). Grandniece of King Edwin of Northumbria, she was baptized by Paulinus of York in 627. In 647 she became a nun, founding in 657 the double monastery of Whitby in Yorkshire. There are many scholars and at least five bps. were educated; and there the famous synod was held in 664. The sole source is Bede, *Hist. eccl.* 4.23. BIBLIOGRAPHY: Butler 4:369–370.

[L. E. BOYLE]

HILDEBERT OF LAVARDIN (d. 1133), abp. of Tours. His ecclesiastical career was marked by a series of confrontations with political leaders. H. emerged from these undaunted in his determination to serve the Church. Both William II of England and Louis VI of France gave H. trouble; William once removed him from his diocese for a time and had him confined to England as a prisoner (of sorts). Besides presiding at the Synod of Nantes in 1127 he attended Lateran Council I in 1123. His literary works are both religious and secular in content. BIBLIOGRAPHY: V. Besse, DTC 6.2:2466–68; A. M. Zimmerman, BiblSanct 4:1238.

[J. R. RIVELLO]

HILDEBRAND, see GREGORY VII, ST., POPE.

HILDEBRAND, DIETRICH VON (1889–1977), Catholic moral philosopher. V. obtained his doctorate in philosophy from Göttingen University (1912), and taught at the Univ. of Munich (1919–33) and Vienna (1933–38) until his opposition to the Nazis forced him to flee. He began his long association with Fordham Univ. in New York City in 1941, where he became a professor emeritus in 1960. His writings, several of which were done in collaboration with his second wife, Alice Jourdain V., were characterized by a deep Christian spirituality, a personalist approach, and a rejection of modern secularism. BIBLIOGRAPHY: *Liturgy and Personality* (1943; rev. ed. 1960); *Fundamental Moral Attitudes* (1950); *Transformation in Christ* (1948); Schwarz, ed., *Human Person and the World of Values: A Tribute to Dietrich von Hildebrand by his Friends in Philosophy* (1960).

[T. M. MCFADDEN]

HILDEGARD, ST. (1098–1179), Benedictine abbess of Rupertsberg, at Bingen, Germany, writer, churchwoman, mystic. She lived in a monastery from early childhood, received the habit in 1113 and was elected abbess in 1136. She was a phenomenon in her own age, traveling extensively throughout Germany, the correspondent of popes, cardinals, bishops, and princes, the counsellor to the troubled, the reformer of the wayward. She wrote homilies, saints' lives, hymns, studies of medicine and natural history, countless letters. H. experienced mystical visions from childhood; when in later life she sought the counsel of her confessor, Godfrey, he advised her to write them down. They were submitted to the examination of theologians for the abp. of Mainz and for Pope Eugene III. Both found nothing objectionable in H.'s descriptions. The visions continued throughout her life and brought her revelations on the mysteries of faith. Her biographer after her death was the monk Theodore. His account as well as the report of miracles contributed to her cult. No canonization process was ever completed, but H. is listed as a saint in the Roman Martyrology and the object of devotion in parts of Germany. Extant MSS of her writings are preserved in the state library at Wiesbaden. BIBLIOGRAPHY: Butler 3:580–585; R. Van Doren, BiblSanct 7:762–765.

[T. C. O'BRIEN]

HILDEGARD OF KEMPTEN, BL. (738–783), queen. Of noble Alamannian origin, second (or third) wife of Charlemagne, she was the mother of 9 of his 18 children, among them his successor, Louis I. Foundress of many churches, close friend of Lioba (kinswoman of St. Boniface), she rebuilt and endowed Kempten (773). She was buried in the church of St. Arnulf at Metz. BIBLIOGRAPHY: AS Apr 3:797–811; P. Viard, BiblSanct 7:760.

[A. CABANISS]

HILDEGUNDE OF MEER, BL. (d. 1183), foundress of the convent of Meer of which she was first prioress. Born of a countess, H. married Count Lothair of Are and Meer. Of their sons, Herman became abbot of the Premonstratensians at Cappenberg while another son, Theodoric, abetted the sack of Rome in 1167. In expiation for Theodoric's deed, H. caused a replica of the destroyed church of St. Lawrence to be built at Meer. BIBLIOGRAPHY: Butler 1:265–266; J. B. Valvekens, BiblSanct 7:766.

[B. F. SCHERER]

HILDEGUNDE OF SCHÖNAU (d. 1188), Cistercian. A twin daughter of a burgher of Neuss am Rhein, she accompanied her father to the Holy Land disguised as a boy. On her return she joined the Cistercian monks of Schönau near Heidelberg, but died as a novice. Only then was her true sex discovered. Among Cistercians she was venerated as a saint, but the cult was never approved by Rome. Her curious vita was preserved in at least five versions, one life being written by a Cistercian monk who was a fellow novice with her, and the basic fact seems well established. BIBLIOGRAPHY: H. Thurston, "Story of St. Hildegunde, Maiden and Monk," *Month* 127 (1916); M. A. Dimier, BiblSanct 7:767–768; E. Pfeiffer, *Cistercienser-Chronik* 47 (1935) 198–200.

[L. J. LEKAI]

HILDELIDE, ST. (d. *c.*717), Benedictine abbess. Of Anglo-Saxon royalty, she became a nun at Chelles or Faremoutiers. Summoned back to England to prepare St. Ethelburga for religious life, she followed her pupil as abbess of Barking *c.*678. To her *Aldhelm dedicated his treatise *De laudibus virginitatis;* both *Bede and *Boniface expressed admiration for her. BIBLIOGRAPHY: Bede, *Hist. eccl.* 4.6–10; E. I. Watkin, BiblSanct 7:769; Butler 3:481.

[A. CABANISS]

HILDESHEIM, ART OF. This city in Lower Saxony was a leading center of early medieval art. It reached its apogee with Bps. Bernward (993–1022) and Godhard (1022–38), under whose patronage great churches were built (e.g., St. Michael's Abbey) and illuminated MSS and metalwork were produced (e.g., Bernward's column and bronze doors). In 1061 the new cathedral, a major Ottonian building, was consecrated. Although Hildesheim's preeminence gradually waned, fine work was still produced in the early 13th cent. (e.g., St. Michael's stucco screen and ceiling paintings). A sumptuous silver treasure of the Roman Augustan period was discovered in 1868. BIBLIOGRAPHY: H. Jantzen, *Ottonische Kunst* (2nd ed., 1959); R. Wesenberg, *Bernwardinische Plastik* (1955), *BERNWARD OF HILDESHEIM, ST.

[R. C. MARKS]

HILDIGRIM, ST. (d. 827), bp. and missionary; brother of St. Ludger. H. was bp. of Châlons-sur-Marne (802–827) and, after Ludger's death in 809, abbot of the monastery of Werden. He was active in missionary work among the East Saxons, and may have been the first bp. of Halberstadt. BIBLIOGRAPHY: P. Rouillard, BiblSanct 7:768–769.

[M. F. MCCARTHY]

HILDUIN OF SAINT-DENIS (*c.*775–*c.*855), abbot of St. Denis near Paris. He was the nephew of Emperor Louis I the Pious, and so was involved in many of the ecclesiastical and political affairs of the imperial court. But he is primarily remembered for making the first Latin translation of the writings of *Pseudo-Dionysius and for his vita of "St. Denis." A Greek MSS copy of the works of Dionysius was presented as a gift to Louis from the Byzantine emperor, Michael II, in 827. At Louis' request H. made his rather rudimentary translation, which in turn became the basis for the revised translation made by *John Scotus Erigena. The vita reenforced the false identity Dionysius had given himself as the Areopagite of Acts 17.16–34, and further identified him with St. Denis, first bp. of Paris. H. thus began the introduction of the major influence Dionysius's works had in the West. BIBLIOGRAPHY: ThAq ST (Lat-Eng, v. 14, ed T. C. O'Brien) app. 3; *Denys l'Aréopagite, La Hiérarchie céleste* (SC 58, ed. R. Roques, 1958) i–xix.

[T. C. O'BRIEN]

HILLEL AND SHAMMAI, the leaders of two opposed rabbinical schools of the time of Christ. The followers of Hillel maintained a relatively benign and lenient interpretation of the Law, and showed themselves tolerant and conciliatory to Jew and gentile alike in matters of political or religious controversy. The Shammaites, on the other hand, were uncompromising rigorists, the allies of the Zealots, whose attitude brought them into frequent conflict with the Roman authorities. After A.D. 70 the power of the Shammaites declined in favor of that of the Hillelites. BIBLIOGRAPHY: I. Sonne, "Schools of Shammai and Hillel Seen from Within," *Louis Ginsburg Jubilee Volume* (1945) 275–291.

HILLEL FOUNDATIONS, campus organization founded and supported by B'nai B'rith for Jewish students attending non-Jewish schools. Comparable to Methodist Wesley Foundations and Newman Clubs for Catholic students, Hillel provides a variety of religious, cultural, and social services. Named for the Jewish scholar Rabbi Hillel (*c.*70 B.C.–10 A.D.), the chapters are normally directed by rabbis. They have been established in Israel and other countries, as well as in the U.S. and Canada.

[T. EARLY]

HILTON, WALTER (d. 1395 or 96), mystical theologian, spiritual director and Canon Regular of St. Augustine; one of the chief contemplatives of the 14th-cent. English mystical school. His known works show a wide field of interest, including a defense of the veneration of images, practical advice concerning a religious vocation, and purest mystical speculation, but his fame rests mainly on his *Scale of Perfection,* the clearest, most balanced treatise on the spiritual life that the late Middle Ages produced. This work shows H. as a close follower of Augustine, Gregory, Bernard, Bonaventure, and the Victorines in regard to doctrine, but the author's originality appears in his homely practical analysis of the progress of a soul, his insistence on the necessity of ascetical preparation for true contemplation, and his striking metaphors drawn from ordinary life. H. agrees with his contemporaries that the contemplative life is best, but he breaks with medieval tradition in teaching that perfection is not confined to the cloister or the solitary, but results from the fuller development of sanctifying grace common to all baptized Christians, and can be attained in any walk of life through close imitations of Christ in his love and service of men. *The Scale* is more sober and academic than most of the 14th-cent. English mystical writings. Its enduring popularity is due primarily to the author's quiet tone, his sane and methodical presentation of ascetical and mystical doctrine, his humility which makes him treat the reader as his peer, and his understanding of the needs and sincere desires of simple folk. The early date of its printing, 1494, evidences the esteem in which *The Scale* was held.

[M. J. BARRY]

HIMMEROD, ABBEY OF, German Cistercian monastery near Wittlich (Eifel). Founded by monks of Clairvaux in 1134, the abbey cleared the marshy land, cultivated famous and profitable vineyards and by 1453 had a library of 2000 volumes. Although badly damaged in the wars of religion, the monastery was totally rebuilt in Baroque style. It was suppressed in 1802, but was successfully revived in 1922. BIBLIOGRAPHY: A. Schneider, *Die Cistercienserabtei Himmerod im Spätmittelalter* (1954).

[L. J. LEKAI]

HIMYARITES, people of ancient SW Arabia. They are thought to have ruled from *c.*115 B.C. until the 4th cent. A.D., when they were defeated by Christian Abyssinians. Persia dominated the area from 575 until Muslim forces gained control in 628. Classical authors picture the Himyarites as successors to the Sabeans (of biblical Sheba), but modern scholars think they probably inhabited one province of the Sabean area. Prior to the time of Christ they were split into two groups—an Eastern and a Western. Their original home is unknown.

[T. EARLY]

HINAYANA, Buddhist, Sanskrit sectarian term, meaning literally the "lesser (*hina*) vehicle (*yana*)" of salvation. It was originally used by those Buddhists who called themselves the *Mahayana* ("greater vehicle") as a derogatory reference to their Buddhist opponents because of an alleged self-centeredness, elitism, and impoverished conception of salvation or enlightenment. The term has come to be used, popularly but inappropriately, in two ways: to refer to the Buddhism of SE Asia, more properly called Theravada Buddhism; to refer to the whole early series of sects or schools which arose between the 4th and 1st cent. B.C. (including Sthaviras, Sarvastivadins, Theravadins, etc.).

The second usage was fairly common among earlier scholars, but the term "archaic" Buddhism is preferable.

[D. P. EFROYMSON]

HINCMAR OF LAON (d. 879), nephew of Hincmar of Reims, who had H. made bp. of Laon in 858. H. came into conflict with *Charles the Bald on the issue of church property. An interdict leveled by H. to affront the king was lifted by Hincmar of Reims as metropolitan and brought the bps. into conflict in 870. Part of the interest in the controversy is Hincmar of Reims' demonstration of forgeries in the *False Decretals, on which H. was basing his case. H. was deposed in 871, exiled, and blinded. He was released only in 878, shortly before his death, by Pope John VIII. BIBLIOGRAPHY: Fliche-Martin 6:403–411.

HINCMAR OF REIMS (*c.*806–882), abp. of Reims from 845, canonist and theologian. Under his presidency in 853 the Council of Quiercy (Carisiacum) condemned the double predestination teaching of *Gottschalk of Orbais (D 621–624). This condemnation climaxed a long controversy that began with an earlier condemnation at Mainz (848). H. imprisoned Gottschalk for failing to recant after Mainz and composed *Ad reclusos et simplices,* a treatise defending predestination to glory alone. After Quiercy prompted attacks against H. by other theologians, he wrote two other treatises on the matter. He was also author of canonical opuscula, a life of St. Remigius, a treatise on the Trinity, and a philosophical study of the soul. Politically as abp. he was in frequent conflict both with the papacy over his refusal to admit the legitimacy of bps. appointed to suffragan sees of Reims and with Lothar II, King of Lorraine, composing *De divortio Lotharii* disputing the right granted to the King to put away his first wife and remarry.

HINDEMITH, PAUL (1895–1963), German-born composer. H. studied at Frankfurt where he later became concertmaster of the opera house and a member of the Amar String Quartet. He was soon a leading figure in German and European musical composition, but when he came into conflict with the Nazi regime, he left the country. In 1940 he settled in the U.S. and became a citizen. Among other positions he held a professorship at Yale (1940–53). A prolific composer, H. wrote works in literally all genres and published books on harmony and composition. Best known among his compositions are *Ludus Tonalis,* a set of fugues and *Mathis der Maler,* an opera. H. was an ardent champion of both "Gebrauchsmusik" (music for use) and "Hausmusik" (music for amateurs). His religious music include a Mass, a setting of Psalm 100, and *Das Marienleben,* a collection of songs based on poems of Rilke.

[M. T. LEGGE]

HINDERER, ROMAN (1669–1744), Alsatian Jesuit, missionary to China from 1707, attached to the imperial court because of his knowledge of cartography and mathematics. He was permitted to preach throughout China, was visitor (1722 and 1730) to all missions in China, Japan, and Tonkin.

HINDUISM, the predominant religion of India and, as such, the foundation on which Indian culture is primarily based. Though other religions exist in India—including Christianity and Judaism—only Islam is a rival religious force to be reckoned with. It must be remembered, moreover, that in the past Hinduism has not been limited to India; there are traces of it, due to missionary influence, in Cambodia, Ceylon, Nepal, and other SE Asian countries. The complexity of Hinduism—different sects, varied mythology, manifold modes of worship—is the result of a combination of influences which have existed, side by side, as equally important components of a religion not subject to sweeping, radical change. One set of influences has never supplanted the others in Hinduism. It absorbed, at its beginnings, the religion of the fair-skinned Aryan tribes which invaded India in ancient times, as well as the pre-Zoroastrian religion of Iran. (Resulting from this integration of classical Hinduism and Aryan religion was a split between Aryan and Iran-influenced forms of Hinduism, and the later formation of the Vedic religion.) Subsequent influences included the appearance of sects, of *bhakti, and of *Tantrism.

In its essence, Hinduism is a variety of approaches of the individual toward his spiritual self-discovery. The Hindu may participate in religious ritual or seek moksha (Sanskrit *moksa*, liberation) through renunciation and meditation. The Hindu thinks of his religion as a philosophy that integrates, organizes, and formalizes the mythic-symbolic aspects of Indian culture. This understanding is the hallmark of the Hindu's faith: all life is sacred. Therefore, all that occurs in life, good or bad, is sacred also. The Hindu, who believes that he lives countless lives, also believes in dharma—the maintenance of the "right path" that will lead him to a higher plane of existence in his next incarnation.

Religious rituals in Hinduism have increased in importance since Vedic times. Their variety signifies the diverse ways in which a Hindu may worship his chosen god. The Hindu word for worship is *pūjā;* it is the most important part of religious ritual. Puja often consists of the worship of a god in the form of an idol (which is considered by some Hindus to be the god himself). The idol will be treated as an honored guest in his temple; anointings, dances, and offerings are used to celebrate his presence. The temples themselves, each dedicated to a particular god, range from village sanctuaries to large religious communities. These sustain a clergy. Among members of the clergy there are spiritual advisors (gurus), teachers and astrologers who serve one family and are supported by it; there is also the *samnyāsin* or "renouncing individual"—a priest who lives in self-imposed detachment from secular life. Temple ceremonies are not obligatory for the individual Hindu, but some religious practices are considered essential in the home. Prayer at morning, at noon, and at night is accompanied by sacrifice to gods and ancestors. Sacraments, or samskara, in connection with birth, religious initiation, marriage, and death, are conducted with the ritual worship of fire. Vows, or *vrata,* using self-denial or prayer to obtain a desirable end, are very common.

Most Hindus consider Hinduism a polytheistic religion or rather culture. Some philosophers maintain that the supreme divine influence is that of a Lord (Ishvara) or an impersonal Absolute (Brahman); common worshipers, however, accept the many gods and their attendant cults as part of the order of things. Each Hindu selects a god from the Hindu pantheon and joins his cult. Chief deities are: Brahma, creator of the universe; Vishnu, god of preservation in the universe and his other manifestation, Krishna, chief hero of the Hindu pantheon; and Siva, god of destruction. The Mother Goddess, in several personifications, is both a benevolent force (as Uma) and a destructive force (as Durga or Kali). The widely worshiped god Ganesa is a remover of obstacles. Great men, heroes, and saints of the past have also been integrated into the pantheon of various sects. Neither absolute evil nor absolute good is personified by any of these deities. While Siva and his attendant demons are recognized as destructive forces, destruction itself is considered part of the order of nature. The Mother Goddess, too, is in this respect similar to other female deities, the Egyptian cow-goddess Hathorr, for instance, who is credited with having punished mankind with the Flood. Another parallel would be the Great Goddess of Crete, giver of life and death. Conversely, ''good'' as such is not specifically worshiped; Brahma, as High Gods in general, lacks any noticeable following.

Even though the earliest literary monuments lack references to class division, in historical times Hindus have been divided into four castes. The top three of these four castes are ''free'' castes, dominated by the highest, the brahmans, wielders of spiritual influence. Second in rank are the kshatriyas, powerful in secular life; third are the vaisyas; artisans, farmers, and others who maintain the Indian economy. These three castes are comprised of ''twice-born'' Hindus, those initiated into Brahmanic life. Separate from them are the sudra, who function more or less as serfs, and the untouchables, descendants of the dark-skinned Dravidian peoples who lived in India at the time of the Aryan invasion.

According to Hinduism, the individual's birth in a caste is the standard by which his relationship with the divine is determined. Members of a particular caste are prohibited from marriage with those of another caste; they are also prohibited from eating meals outside the caste or inviting a nonmember of the caste to eat with them. Thus the fragmentation of Hindu society is maintained.

On a spiritual plane, the Hindu belongs to one of three phases of earthly activity: from *kama* (pleasureful activity), to *artha* (interested activity), to *dharma* (moral activity). In their proper order, these phases lead to liberation.

The extent to which Hinduism has benefited India has been widely questioned. It is seen by some as a millstone around the neck of progress; cow-worship, child marriage, and the social stagnation caused by the caste system are some features commonly criticized. It may be true that Hinduism has hindered progress, but it has also earned worldwide respect for its search for spiritual truth and its practice of nonviolence. Contrasted with the materialism inherent in almost every other major culture, Hinduism shines in an admirable light. It is possible, in light of recent developments of Indian political life, that the caste system, with its attendant rejection of millions of untouchables, will undergo considerable change. Should Hinduism find a solution to this and other problems, it will be able to meet the needs of its followers more satisfactorily, and attract greater world-wide admiration. BIBLIOGRAPHY: *Hinduism* (ed. L. Renou, 1962). *INDIAN PHILOSOPHY

[D. H. BRUNAUER]

HIPPIUS (GIPPIUS), ZINAIDA NIKOLAYEVNA (1867–1945), symbolist author of poems, novels, and dramas. As cofounder with her husband, D. S. Merezhkovski, and Minski (pseud. of N. M. Valenkin) of the Religious and Philosophical Society and its journal, *The New Road* (1903–04), she contributed to the religious and philosophical awakening of the young Russian intelligentsia at the turn of the century. Her brilliantly intellectual and genuinely lyrical poems are often statements of mystic and metaphysical problems, e.g., the ego as refuge from a banal and futile world. The volume *Living Faces* (1925) contains valuable reminiscences about contemporary literary figures. BIBLIOGRAPHY: R. Poggioli, *Poets of Russia: 1890–1930* (1960) 105–111; G. Donchin, *Influence of French Symbolism on Russian Poetry* (1958).

[M. F. MCCARTHY]

HIPPO REGIUS, a seaport city of Numidia where St. Augustine was bp. 393–430, now a titular see, the ancient city having been abandoned in favor of the present Algerian city of Bône, a mile and a half to the NE. ''Hippo'' meant ''port'' in Punic, and the Romans called it ''Regius'' (royal) because it was a place of residence for Numidian kings, a coincidence of names that the friends of *Port-Royal later pointed to with delight. Originally a Phoenician colony, the city early came under Roman rule and became a place of splendor and importance second only to Carthage in Proconsular Africa. Even in the time of Augustine, Punic was still the tongue of a substantial portion of its population. Christianity was introduced in the mid-3d cent., but in the late 4th and early 5th cent. there were many Manichaeans and Donatists among its inhabitants. BIBLIOGRAPHY: For an account of the city, esp. its social structure and mode of life in Augustine's day, see F. Van Der Meer, *Augustine the Bishop* (1961) 16–198; E. Josi, EncCatt 7:180–181; E. Marec, *Monuments chrétiens d'Hippone ville épiscopale de saint Augustin* (1958).

[R. B. ENO]

HIPPOCRATES OF COS (a contemporary of Socrates), the founder of scientific medicine. The most famous of all Greek physicians, he is the least known personally. On the testimony of Plato, H. considered the body an organism, that its parts must be considered in relation to the whole, and that natural causes must be sought for diseases through careful observation. The voluminous Hippocratean Corpus, which comprises works spread over many centuries, does not contain a single treatise that can be ascribed to H. with certainty. He became a legendary figure at an early date and even contradictory medical doctrines and practices were ascribed to him by later medical writers. The famous "Oath of Hippocrates" sheds valuable light on Greek medical practice, education, and ethics, but whether it goes back to H. himself cannot be determined. BIBLIOGRAPHY: OCD 430 and 549; LexAW 1304 and 1305–06; PW Suppl. 6 (1935) 1290–1345. For the "Oath of Hippocrates," see W. H. S. Jones, *Hippocrates,* Loeb (1923) 1:298–301.

[M. R. P. MCGUIRE]

HIPPOCRATIC OATH, an oath traditionally ascribed to Hippocrates of Cos (460–377 or 354 B.C.) or to his school; concerns the ethical relationships of physician and patient. It is among the earliest documents of Greek medical thought and practice built on a secure philosophic basis. The oath is a covenant to "guard my life and my art in purity and holiness" (Gk. text 11 15/16), to work "for the benefit of the sick" (11, 12 and 19), and to respect confidentiality. The proscription against drugs and abortion, sound a strongly contemporary message. Consistent with Christian and also non-Christian principles, the oath continues to be the basis of national and international medical codes. BIBLIOGRAPHY: L. Edelstein, *Hippocratic Oath: Text, Translation, and Interpretation* (1943).

[M. G. SCHUMACHER]

HIPPOLYTUS OF ROME, ST. (*c.*170–235), important Christian author in Rome during the times of persecution, first antipope, martyr. Little is known of his origin or early life, but in the early 3d cent. he was an influential presbyter in the Roman Church, zealous for orthodoxy and penitential discipline. His concern for these brought him into conflict with successive popes, *Zephyrinus (198–217) and esp. *Callistus (217–222). His followers elected him antipope in opposition to Callistus, whom H. accused of heresy and laxity. He continued in his schism during the reigns of the two successors of Callistus, *Urban (222 or 223–230) and Pontius (230–235). During the persecution under Maximinus Thrax both H. and Pontius were exiled to Sardinia where they died. Apparently they had become reconciled, for the bodies of both were brought back to Rome, and H. was soon accorded honor as a martyr. His works, or at least those known to us, were written in Greek, and that at a time when Greek was no longer generally understood in the Christian community at Rome. This may explain in part why so much of H.'s writing has been lost. His *Philosophumena (Refutation of all Heresies)* was recovered and published in 1851 and is one of the most important sources of history for the early heresies. He wrote a shorter treatise against heresy called *Syntagma,* which has been partially reconstructed from later adaptations. According to H., all heresies were derived from one or another of the ancient philosophies. He also wrote the earliest known exegetical treatises, commentaries on Daniel and the Song of Solomon. Of great importance for the history of the liturgy is his *Apostolic Tradition*. His doctrine on the Trinity was inadequate and his attitude toward penance and sinners rigoristic. Works: PG 10:261–292; *Commentary on Daniel,* SC 14 (ed. G. Bardy, 1947); *Apostolic Tradition* (SC 11, tr. only ed. B. Botte, 1964; text and tr. ed. B. Botte, 1963). BIBLIOGRAPHY: Quasten 2:163–207.

[P. K. MEAGHER]

HIRAM, KING OF TYRE, ruler over what is now Lebanon in the time of Solomon. He entered into a commercial agreement with Solomon to supply trees and skilled workers for the construction of Jerusalem's Temple. H. was paid with farm products and granted rule over 20 towns in N Israel (1 Kgs 5.15–26).

[J. F. FALLON]

HIRMOLOGION, a collection of *hirmoi*. *HIRMOS.

HIRMOS (Heirmos), in early Byzantine music a melody composed for the first stanza of a hymn and then used, somewhat in the manner of a psalm tone, for subsequent stanzas.

[M. T. LEGGE]

HIRSAU, ABBEY OF, former Benedictine abbey of SS. Peter and Paul in the Black Forest, Diocese of Speyer, Germany. Founded in 830, it was not permanently established until 1065. In the 11th cent., the Hirsau reform spread throughout many of the German and Austrian monasteries. The spiritual force behind this reform came from Hirsau's Abbot William, who had inaugurated substantial reforms at Hirsau itself, adapted the Cluniac usages to the German manner, severed attachments to the State and revitalized monastic life. Prototype of German Romanesque in architectural style, Hirsau was known for its library, its style of MS illumination, and its music. It joined the Bursfeld Union in 1458; was secularized in the 16th cent. and became a school. The monks were banished in 1648. It is now a ruin. BIBLIOGRAPHY: P. Beckman, NCE 6:1141–42.

[M. A. MCFADDEN]

HIRSCH, SAMSON RAPHAEL (1808–88), rabbi, defender of traditional Judaism. He was rabbi of the separatist *Israelitische Religionsgesellschaft*.

[P. J. HENNESSEY]

HIRSCHER, JOHANN (1788–1865), controversial German author of homiletic and catechetical works. He taught moral and pastoral theology at Tübingen from 1817, and from 1837 at the Univ. of Freiburg until retirement in 1863. Liberal views on the vernacular in liturgy, abolition of private Masses, communion under both kinds caused his *De genuina missae notione* (1821) to be put on the Index in 1823. A collection of his writings on Church and State was also prohibited in 1849. He published many volumes of sermon guides; a very successful catechism, *Katechismus der christkatholischen Religion* (1842), as well as a course for moral theology, *Die christliche Moral* (3 v., 1835–36), a work that reflects his aversion for scholasticism and casuistry; a dominant theme is the presence of the new kingdom of God. Decried in his own time as extreme, many of his views are now commonplaces in the Church.

[T. C. O'BRIEN]

HISPANA VERSIO, an *Old Latin (pre-Vulgate) version of the Bible. A number of Spanish MSS, the usages in the Mozarabic liturgy, and other sources have led scholars to accept the *Hispana versio* as a third Old Latin textual tradition, at least partially independent of the long-recognized African and European Old Latin texts. BIBLIOGRAPHY: T. Ayoso Marazuela, *Vetus Latina Hispana I–II* (1967).

[D. J. BOURKE]

HISPERICA FAMINA, fragments of a composition written in Ireland in the 5th or 6th century. The term means "Italian, i.e., urbane utterances." The language is an obscure amalgam of Latin, Greek, and Hebrew with curious suffixes added to known Latin words. Forms and meanings of the words are far-fetched and may have been from Old Latin glossaries, themselves collections of hard and strange words. Gildas and Aldhelm wrote Latin poetry using the same technique. A short example must suffice: *caerimonicant vates Missam unitum,* "priests ceremoniously transact the assembled Mass." It is thought to be the invention of Gaulish rhetoricians.

[R. T. MEYER]

HISTORIA AUGUSTA, a collection of biographies of Roman emperors from Hadrian to Numerian (A.D. 117–284) allegedly developed from the writings of six authors in the reigns of Diocletian and Constantine. Its anonymous author or authors attempt to portray the lives of pagan emperors as models of Roman virtue equal, if not superior, to that of Christian ideals. Recent scholarship leaves the question of authorship open, allowing a date as late as 410 A.D. BIBLIOGRAPHY: *Scriptores Historiae Augustae* (tr. D. Magie, 3 v., Loeb 1.6, 1953); A. Momigliano, *Secondo contributo alla storia degli studi classici* (1960); N. H. Baynes, *Historia Augusta* (1926).

[F. H. BRIGHAM]

HISTORIA MONACHORUM, translation by *Rufinus of Aquileia (d. 410) of a Greek text dealing with Egyptian monastic life. It was probably written (*c.*400) by Timothy, an archdeacon of Alexandria, and describes a visit of seven pilgrims to the Egyptian ascetics in 394–395. It was confused with Palladius' *Lausiac History,* but C. Butler established its autonomy to the satisfaction of most scholars in 1904. BIBLIOGRAPHY: PL 21:387–462; C. Butler, *Lausiac History of Palladius* (2 v., 1904); Quasten 3:177–178.

[M. B. PENNINGTON]

HISTORIC EPISCOPATE, phrase used in two senses. (1) Understood strictly, it describes the office of bp. as derived from the Apostles through an unbroken series of ordinations. The idea of the historic episcopate has always been central in the Anglican and Episcopal Churches; the specific phrase has been prominent, esp. in ecumenical discussions, since the *Lambeth Quadrilateral (1888). The fourth point of the Quadrilateral declared as essential to Christian unity: "The Historic Episcopate, locally adapted in the methods of its administration to the varying needs of the nations and peoples called of God into the unity of His Church." The *Lambeth Conference of 1930 explained historic episcopate in the sense of historical continuity in ordination. (2) Taken in a wider sense, the historic episcopate means episcopacy as a historically accepted institution or function in the Church. This broader sense of the historic episcopate leaves aside the question of a valid succession of ordinations, and whether the office of bp. is a human or divine institution. In the first sense, the historic episcopate is one aspect of *apostolic succession, as understood by the RC, Eastern, and Old Catholic Churches and by those in the Anglican Communion. In the broader sense, the Constitution of the *Church of South India (1941) accepted the historic episcopate, but without declaring any theory of its meaning. The success of the *Consultation on Church Union may partially depend on the acceptance of historic episcopate in its broader sense, to accommodate those Churches that do not have an episcopal tradition. Yet such an understanding creates an obstacle in the search for church unity for those Churches that regard the historic episcopate in its strict meaning as an essential in the structure of the Church.

[T. C. O'BRIEN]

HISTORICAL BOOKS (OT). In the modern, as opposed to the traditional, Jewish method of classifying the books of the Bible, the following are grouped under this head: Gen, Ex, Lev, Num, Dt, Jos, Jg, 1–2 Sam, 1–2 Kg, 1–2 Chr, Ezra-Neh, Ru, Est and, for Catholics, Tob, Jdt, and 1–2 Macc. Of these Ru, Est, Tob and Jdt have only the most vestigial contact with history, and are far closer to the modern conception of the "novel" designed to edify. Large areas of the Pentateuch, though ultimately rooted in historical fact, are historical only in a highly specialized sense peculiar to the world of the ancient Near East. Of the rest perhaps the approach of 1–2 Kg approximates most closely (though still not very closely) the modern conception of history. BIBLIOGRAPHY: J. Bright, *History of Israel* (1960), *idem, Early Israel in Recent History Writing* (1956); De Vaux AncIsr; M. Noth, *History of Israel* (2d ed., Eng. tr. 1960); W. Beyerlin, *Origins and History of the Oldest Sinaitic Traditions* (1965).

[D. J. BOURKE]

HISTORICAL SOCIETIES, AMERICAN CATHOLIC, a phenomenon of the growing awareness of the importance of documentary and critical American Catholic historiography, originating in the last quarter of the 19th century. John Gilmary *Shea (1824–92), rightly called the father of American Catholic church history, had published in both periodical and book form numerous studies before the advent of journals devoted to historical studies on Catholicism in the U.S. In 1884 he joined with Charles George Herbermann to found the U.S. Catholic Historical Society and its publication, *United States Catholic Historical Magazine,* which after the death of Shea was replaced by the annual *Historical Records and Studies,* edited by Herbermann. In 1884 also, Fr. Andrew Arnold Lambing of the Diocese of Pittsburgh, Pa. established the Ohio Valley Catholic Historical Society and began publication of *Historical Researches in Western Pennsylvania, Principally Catholic*. This quarterly (renamed *American Catholic Historical Researches* in 1886) was ultimately merged with the publication of the Philadelphia American Catholic Historical Society, *Records*. The last-named society was founded in 1884 by Martin I. J. *Griffin and Thomas Cooke Middleton, OSA. In the 20th cent. the pioneer among Catholic historians was Fr. Peter *Guilday, professor at The Catholic Univ. of America. In 1915 he established the *Catholic Historical Review,* of which he was editor until 1941. In 1919 he founded the American Catholic Historical Association. The Academy of American Franciscan History, established in 1944, is made up of Franciscan scholars devoted to research and publication of early documents in Latin American history. The Academy publishes the quarterly *Americas*. A more specialized society is the Academy of California Church History, founded in 1946.

[J. R. AHERNE]

HISTORICAL THEOLOGY, see POSITIVE THEOLOGY.

HISTORICISM, a theory emphasizing the importance of events as determinants of a given human situation and its standards of value. As a method it serves to keep the historian to ''the shape of Cleopatra's nose'' without straying into ideological and meta-historical dialectics. Nevertheless as a philosophy of history it can lapse into a *nominalism, denying reality and significance to the recurrences and progressions of certain common forms of structures. From these are composed the economic, cultural, social, political, and theological explanations and interpretations, all of which are allowed to be valid disciplines so long as they are not forced. Though an exclusive historicism can scarcely be practiced, for it would leave out all but the incidental—and facts of themselves provide no clue to the laws of their development—nevertheless a moderate historicism is a corrective to the opposite extreme, for which the correspondingly academic barbarism of ''mysticism'' may be coined. The opposition between fact and value, which runs through contemporary moralism, has encouraged the views of certain authors that some Christian truths, such as the Crucifixion and the Resurrection, can be historically significant without having a basis of fact, like the Magna Carta of the Whigs, which started as a myth and ended as a powerful force in politics, and unlike Queen Victoria, who started as a fact and ended as a no less powerful myth. BIBLIOGRAPHY: M. C. D'Arcy, *Meaning and Matter of History* (1959).

[T. GILBY]

HISTORICITY, in its common use by exegetes, the historical validity of the words and events narrated in the NT, esp. regarding the person of Jesus Christ. The NT itself verifies Christianity as a historical religion. Luke began his Gospel by explaining that, ''after carefully going over the whole story from the beginning,'' he would ''write an ordered account,'' in order to show ''how well founded the teaching is that you have received'' (Lk 1.3–4). John said he was writing of events ''that we have heard, that we have seen with our own eyes; that we have watched and touched with our hands'' (1 Jn 1.1). And Paul appealed to the objective facts of Christ's life, death, and Resurrection as proof that faith in Christ was not a vain fancy. Beginning with Ignatius of Antioch (d. 107) and during the Gnostic controversy, the Church defended the historicity of the gospel narrative: ''Jesus Christ . . . was really (*alēthōs)* born and ate and drank, really persecuted by Pontius Pilate, really crucified and . . . really rose from the dead'' (*Trallianos* 9–10). Following the lead of Peter, ''It was not any cleverly invented myths that we were repeating'' (2 Pet 1.16), apologists like Justin and Irenaeus argued that Christianity had a historical center, unlike the vagaries of Greek and Roman mythology. With the rise of radical *Form Criticism in modern times, the historical validity of the Gospels has again been challenged and a whole literature has developed on the subject. The issue centered on the claim made by men like Bultmann and Dibelius that the Gospels cannot be authentic history because they are not objective narrative but *Heilsgeschichte,* or the story of man's salvation. Since the Evangelists embellished and reinterpreted the data, Christians now have only a distillation of these reflective thoughts. They cannot come into contact with the facts themselves.

Roman Catholicism recognizes the unique character of NT history, yet one that squares with empirical observation. The sacred authors selected some things in preference to others from the many words and events which were handed on by word of mouth or in writing; they reduced certain facts to a synthesis, ''explicating some things in view of the situation of their Churches, and preserving the form of proclamation, but always in such a fashion that they told us the honest truth about Jesus" (Vat II DivRev 19). Their intention was to share with others the evidence of what eye-and-ear-witnesses had actually experienced. The historicity of Christian origins is closely identified with the Church's *apostolicity. If the doctrine and ministry are apostolic only as somehow reflecting the spirit of the Apostles, then what Christ said and did may be considered historical (*geschichtlich*) even though much of what the Gospels say is only mythical, i.e., describing general truths in factually undemonstrable terms. But if the doctrine and ministry are literally apostolic, and what the Church now believes and does is essentially what the Apostles witnessed Christ teaching and doing, then the Evangelists must have written historic (*historisch*) narratives. Although shaped to meet religious needs, their accounts give the substance of what really took place. This makes Christianity not only spiritually or psychologically but historically apostolic. BIBLIOGRAPHY: D. Geels, NCE 6:636–640; L. Alonso Schökel, NCE 5:1017–23.

[J. A. HARDON]

HISTORY, PHILOSOPHY OF, the branch of knowledge that studies the events of history in order to determine an identifiable purpose, or plan, or pattern. This process is usually the product of a historian's own theory of knowing together with those presuppositions which establish and interpret causes of what has happened, *res gestae*. The cyclic interpretation of history had its beginnings in Chaldean astronomy, an explanation of events and their repetition through predictable seasonal changes. Later exposition of this can be found in the writings of Herodotus, Empedocles, in a number of the myths of Plato, the astronomical teaching of Aristotle, Seneca's *Epistula 24,* Justin's *Dialogue with Trypho,* and Origen's *Contra Celsum* 4, 67 and *De principiis* 2, 3. Rejected by Augustine in his *De civitate Dei,* it appears again in the Aristotelianism of Siger of Brabant and Dante. The most recent exponent of eternal recurrence is F. W. Nietzsche.

With St. Augustine, Western European thought developed what in effect was a theology of history. According to Augustine's view as stated throughout the *De civitate Dei,* the source of history is God's creative act which brought the world into being and which continues to shape its subsequent development. Divine wisdom in so creating the world is manifested by succeeding human generations, which advance according to a plan toward a divinely appointed goal through the exercise of free will. This approach dominated Western thinking for over 1,000 years and was restated in 1621 in the *Discours sur l'histoire universelle* of J. B. Bossuet, for whom the rise and fall of governments and peoples are the result of God's providence and are to be so understood. This interpretation of the philosophy of history was succeeded in the 18th and 19th cent. by one that turned away from theology and providence to natural science. Voltaire was the first to use the term philosophy of history in insisting that the historian establish his independent interpretation of events. Hegel and his followers saw it as world history, and the 19th-cent. positivists looked to uniform laws to explain human happenings. R. Collingwood is of the opinion that the objects of philosophy of history are those problems that have been presented by scientific historical research, problems that cannot be adequately explained by theology, mathematics, or natural science exclusively. It is this trend which began with Vico in his *Scienza nuova* (1744), in which he emphasizes the uniqueness of the philosophy of history and its differences in methodology from that of the natural sciences. Herder continued the same thinking in his *Ideen zür Philosophie der Geschichte der Menchheit* (1784–91), in which he claims that historical research requires examining the actions of men in their particular society in order to determine patterns of life and their causes apart from a preconceived universal plan or unchanging human consciousness. These interpretations have been advanced and expanded in the 20th cent. by Croce and Collingwood. A. *Toynbee's *Study of History* (1934–1961) is the most celebrated English-language 20th-cent. interpretation of history and the most religiously oriented. His work reviews the pattern of rise and fall of 21 civilizations; it concludes to the ultimate emergence of the great world religions as the hope of humanity's future. That hope does not, however, refer to theological content, esp. not Christian theological content, but on the expression in the great religions of the psychological aspirations of men. BIBLIOGRAPHY: R. G. Collingwood, *Idea of History* (1946); K. Lowits, *Meaning in History* (1949); M. C. D'Arcy, *Meaning and Matter of History* (1959); P. L. Hug, NCE 7:26–30; B. Croce, *History, a Story of Liberty* (tr. S. Sprigge, 1941); C. Dawson, *The Judgement of the Nations* (1942).

[F. H. BRIGHAM]

HISTORY, THEOLOGY OF, the interpretation of history which relates all events to the wisdom of God and his providence. *HISTORY, PHILOSOPHY OF.

[F. H. BRIGHAM]

HISTORY OF RELIGIONS SCHOOL (Ger. *Religionsgeschichtliche Schule*), a 20th-cent. method of biblical criticism according to which the NT is to be understood on the basis of the principles of comparative religion. The ideas of early Christianity are interpreted as syncretistic derivations from other religious phenomena of the period. The foremost exponent was W. Bousset (1865–1920), esp. in his *Kyrios Christos* (1913). The History of Religions School was an influence on the thought of R. Bultmann. BIBLIOGRAPHY: J. S. Kselman, JBC 2:13.

[T. C. O'BRIEN]

HITLER, ADOLF (1889–1945), Chancellor of Germany, 1933–45. His career perhaps posed more problems of conscience for more people than any other individual in history. Although raised in a Catholic family in Upper Austria, H. rejected Christian beliefs in favor of a vulgar creed that praised war instead of peace, racism instead of brotherhood, ruthlessness instead of compassion, and force over right. His political activities began in Munich after World War I, where he became an extraordinarily successful public speaker by attacking the Versailles Treaty and the government of the Weimar Republic which had accepted it. H. conspired to seize power in Munich as a base for the overthrow of the German Republic, but his radicalism offended the traditional Bavarian separatists whose support he expected. The failure of this *Putsch* convinced him to seek political power through legal means. In the effort to win as many votes as possible, H. dealt on religious issues mostly with generalities in his speeches and avoided any specific discussion. Many sincere Christians, both Catholic and Protestant, saw in him a forceful opponent of communism, a nationalist who might restore Germany to a position of strength in the world, and a force for order who might heal the divisions within German society. Almost immediately after H. became Chancellor in 1933, however, the Nazis introduced legislation discriminating against Jews and Marxists and began to undermine the Churches by attempting to gain administrative control, by ideological indoctrination of the populace, and by terror and intimidation. As a result of the Concordat with the Vatican in July 1933, the Catholic Center Party was dissolved in return for a formal regulation of Church-State relations. Frequent Nazi violation of the Concordat prompted many protests from Pope Pius XI, including the condemnatory encyclical *Mit Brennender Sorge* in 1937. As the Hitler regime strengthened its hold on the German people, it also began preparations for war. The first violations of the Versailles Treaty and the annexations of Austria and the Sudetenland occurred peacefully under the guise of self-determination. The attack on Poland in September 1939 started World War II, which brought several military successes in the early stages, but the downfall and ruin of Germany in the end. During the war H. increasingly demanded destructive war crimes, the liquidation of the Jews of occupied Europe, medical experiments and euthanasia, and other unspeakable atrocities. For Germans these events raised the question of the legitimacy of disobedience to the State and even of assassination of a tyrant. For other nations the question of a just war was placed in a wholly new perspective, rendering pacificism in the face of such untold evil virtually indefensible. Finally the Hitlerian nightmare contributed to an intense revival of theological studies in Germany. BIBLIOGRAPHY: A. Bullock, *Hitler: A Study in Tyranny* (1964). *BARMEN DECLARATION.

[R. J. GIBBONS]

HITTITES, ancient people of Asia Minor, in the OT referred to as Hethites. The original Hittites, who spoke a non-Indo–European language called Hattic or Proto-Hittite, lived in central Anatolia. Invasion by Indo-Europeans resulted in the development of the Hittite state into an empire that spread southward for a time (*c.* 1600 B.C.), even overcoming Babylon. The empire lasted until *c.* 1200 B.C., when it was broken into small kingdoms under the impact of invaders from across the Aegean. The last of those states, Carchemish, was conquered by the Assyrian King Sargon II *c.* 717 B.C.

The official language of the Hittite Empire was cuneiform Hittite, an Indo–European language. Its use, attested from *c.* 1600 to *c.* 1200 B.C., was centered at Hattusas (modern Boghazkoy), capital of the empire. a second important language was hieroglyphic Hittite, an Indo-European language spoken throughout the empire down to *c.* 700 B.C. Both languages have been deciphered in the 20th century. In religion the Hittites were syncretistic, borrowing gods from Sumer, Nineveh, Babylon, Egypt, and Syria.

Hittites are mentioned frequently in the OT, where the term is used for all inhabitants of the Hittite Empire, regardless of language or ethnic identification. Neither the empire before 1200 B.C. nor the Hittite kingdoms afterward extended into Palestine, however, and the references to them are a problem for OT interpretation. Hittites were identified as "the people of the land" in the time of Abraham (Gen ch. 23; see also Gen. 26.34; Ex 3.8; 2 Sam 11.3). Some scholars suggest the reference may have been to Horites, a people important in Palestine during the 2d millennium B.C. but rarely mentioned in the OT. BIBLIOGRAPHY: O. R. Gurney, *Hittites* (2d ed., rev. 1961).

[T. EARLY]

HITTORP, MELCHIOR (1525–84), German liturgist best known for his *De divinis catholicae ecclesiae officiis ac ministeriis* (1565), a collection of medieval liturgical writings and an important Roman Ordinal that dated from ancient times. It is still regarded as the most complete collection of its kind.

[N. KOLLAR]

HIVITES, see HEVITES.

HLOND, AUGUSTYN (1881–1948), Polish cardinal. Ordained in Cracow in 1905 after first receiving his education in Italy, he served as apostolic administrator from 1922. Thereafter his rise in the ecclesiastical hierarchy was rapid: in 1925 he became the first bp. of Katowice and the same year helped to negotiate the concordat between Poland and the Vatican. The year 1926 saw his elevation to the archbishopric of Gniezno-Poznań; the following year he was raised to the cardinalate. As primate of Poland, he promoted the development of Catholic Action and the press's role in propagating the faith. Forced to flee his native land early in World War II, he lived in exile in Vichy France from 1940 to 1944, when the Gestapo arrested and transported him to a prison in Germany. Liberated by the Americans in 1945, he returned that summer to Poland, where in the remaining years of his life he strove to repair the damages visited upon the Church during the years of Nazi occupation as well as to defend it against the attempted inroads of the new Communist regime. In both efforts he was successful. From 1946, he was abp. of Warsaw as well as of Gniezno.

[E. M. GATES]

HOBART, JOHN HENRY (1775–1830), bp. of the Protestant Episcopal Church in New York. Born in Philadelphia, he graduated from the College of New Jersey (now Princeton Univ.) in 1793. From the time of his ordination in 1801, he spent his life at Trinity Parish, New York City. In 1812 he was elected and consecrated as assistant bp. of New York; in 1816 he became the bp. as well as rector of Trinity Parish. He established a society for ministerial studies that developed into the present General Theological Seminary in New York City. In his preaching and writing he emphasized *high-church themes on *apostolic succession and the sacramental-liturgical life of his Church, and was largely responsible for the dominance of a high-church tradition in the Episcopal Church in his era. BIBLIOGRAPHY: M. T. Gardner, *Conquerors of the Continent for Christ and His Church* (1911); *Correspondence of John Henry Hobart,* (6 v., 1911–12).

[M. A. GARDNER]

HOBBES, THOMAS (1588–1672), English political philosopher. Educated at Magdalen College, Oxford, in an era of decadent scholasticism, H. acquired a firm grasp of Aristotelian method and a lifelong aversion to Aristotle. A royalist, H. fled to France during the Long Parliament, where he served as a tutor to the exiled Charles II. He met Mersenne, the friend of Descartes, and Galileo. Banished from France for his violent anti-Catholicism, H. returned to the England of the Commonwealth. After the Restoration, H. was granted a pension by his former pupil. H.'s long years were marked by heated and acerb polemics over his denial of free will, his views on geometry, and his advocacy of the superiority of statute to common law. Much of H.'s philosophical method anticipates that of the modern analytical philosophers, as his philosophy of law does that of modern analytical jurisprudence. H. is a thoroughgoing materialist (even God is corporeal), seeking to explain all change and all thought in terms of matter and local motion. He was fascinated by contemporary physics and saw the world as mechanically determined. Classically educated (his first publication was a translation of Thucydides), H. was nevertheless very much a man of his times. The emerging individualism becomes egoism in his view of men and morals. His gloomy view that man is motivated solely by fear affects his whole political philosophy. Life is a race, men the runners, and all men run in fear. To achieve peace and to reduce fear, men form the commonwealth (Leviathan is H.'s word) by a unity of wills. By the social contract which begets the State, men cede certain of their rights, mutually and to the whole. The social contract is the only moral imperative. Under this view and the position that natural law is based on the principle that man's one inalienable natural right is the wish to protect life and limb as long as possible, H. concludes logically to state absolutism as the only rational form of government. The executive power of the state must increase, whether it be vested in representative government or, preferably, in a monarch. Law is the command of the ruler and it is authority, not conformity to usage or reason, that makes law. H. carefully sets philosophical and moral questions apart from faith. As to religion, the ruler must be head of Church as well as State, and his decision is supreme. Since there is a diversity of nations, there cannot be one religion for all. We can know that God exists, can affirm only negative attributes of him, and can know nothing of his nature. H.'s influence was less in his own day than among the economists and philosophers of the next century. BIBLIOGRAPHY: L. Strauss, *Political Philosophy of Thomas Hobbes* (1963); R. S. Peters. *Hobbes* (1956).

[W. B. MAHONEY]

HOBERG, GOTTFRIED, RC biblical scholar, professor at Paderborn (1887–94) and Freiburg (Breisgau) in Germany. His research and publications were devoted esp. to the Pentateuch and the Latin Psalter. He was a defender of biblical conservatism against *Modernism.

[T. C. O'BRIEN]

HOCEDEZ, EDGAR (1877–1948), Jesuit historian of theology. H. taught theology at several Jesuit houses, mainly at Louvain and the Gregorian Univ. in Rome, and was editor of the *Nouvelle revue théologique* (1920–26). He is esp. noted for his *Histoire de la théologie au XIXe siècle* (3 v., 1949–52), a classic history of 19th-cent. Christian theology. BIBLIOGRAPHY: J. Levie, NRT 70 (1948) 786–793; *idem,* NCE 7:43–44.

[T. M. MCFADDEN]

HOCHHUTH, ROLF (1931–), controversial German author whose first drama *Der Stellvertreter* (*The Deputy,* 1962) deals with the role of Pope Pius XII during World War II and raises the question of whether he did enough to prevent mass slaughter of Jews. In *Soldaten* (1967) Winston Churchill's total airwar, the bombing of civilians, and his part in Marshall Sikorski's tragic death are examined. The problems involved rather than great dramatic qualities have made his dramas successful.

[S. A. SCHULZ]

HOCKET (hoketus, hocquet, ochetto), a medieval technique of composition in which two (sometimes three) notes of a section were distributed among the various parts so that each voice alternately sang and then rested. This device was used only in sections, for contrast.

[M. T. LEGGE]

HODAJOTH (Thanksgiving Psalms), a group of 30 to 40 psalms (or hymns) found among the writings of Qumran, so called because they often begin with the words: "I give thanks to you, O Lord." They are contained in the so-called Thanksgiving Scroll (1QH) found in the original Cave I; fragments of the same poems were later discovered in Cave IV. Their style is similar to the individual lamentations and thanksgivings of the biblical Psalter and, as in the latter, the individual suppliant often serves as a mouthpiece for the whole community. The language itself is modeled on biblical Hebrew, influenced by Palestinian Aramaic. The doctrinal content of these psalms follows the general tenor of the Qumran writings: a strong moral dualism; eschatological expectation; the majesty of God contrasted with the frailty of man; a developed angelology. All in all, their deeply religious tone shines through the literary conventions in which they are framed. BIBLIOGRAPHY: T. Gaster, *Dead Sea Scriptures* (2d ed., 1964) 121–222; M. Mansoor, *Thanksgiving Hymns* (1961).

[C. BERNAS]

HODEGETRIA VIRGIN, an icon venerated at Constantinople until destroyed by the Turks when the city fell in 1453. It was regarded as an authentic portrait of Mary drawn by St. Luke and was the pattern of many icons of Mary, as exemplified by the well-known "Our Lady of Perpetual Help."

HODEGETRIA MADONNA. This Byzantine Madonna holding the Christ Child on her left arm, is hieratic in contrast to the humanistic *Eleousa Madonna. The Child in frontal position blesses with his right hand, while holding a scroll in his left hand.

[M. J. DALY]

HODGE, CHARLES (1797–1878), American Presbyterian theologian. H. graduated from the College of New Jersey (now Princeton Univ.) in 1817 and studied at Princeton Theological Seminary under Archibald *Alexander. H. was licensed to preach by the Philadelphia Presbytery in 1819, and in 1822 accepted a call to Princeton Seminary as professor of OT and NT literature. During 1826–28 he studied at Halle and Berlin, where he was influenced by Tholuck, Neander, and the Pietist circle of Ludwig von Gerlach. In 1829 he established the *Biblical Repertory and Princeton Review,* serving as editor until 1868. In 1840 he became professor of systematic theology. H. was the chief theologian of the Old School Presbyterians, and his theological system was a conservative exposition of the *Westminster Confession and other *Reformed doctrinal standards. His *Systematic Theology* (3 v., 1871–73) was explicitly intended as a bulwark against doctrinal aberration. He personally trained more than 3,000 clergymen, and his influence contributed greatly to the intellectual and doctrinally conservative tradition of *Princeton theology and to the conservative forces both in Presbyterianism and in other Protestant traditions. BIBLIOGRAPHY: Smith-Jamison 1:260–266; A. A. Hodge, *Charles Hodge,* (1889); H. T. Kerr, *Sons of the Prophets* (1963).

[R. K. MACMASTER]

HODUR, FRANCIS (1866–1953), founder of the *Polish National Catholic Church in America. Born of peasant stock near Cracow, he studied at Cracow Univ. and was ordained a RC priest (1893). He became assistant pastor in Scranton, Pa. (1893), and then (1894) pastor at nearby Nanticoke. Partly inspired by a nationalistic messianism, H. heeded a call (1897) to lead a Scranton Polish parish in a dispute with its bp. over church administration. He vainly brought his cause to Rome, and the bp. excommunicated him (1898). In 1904 H.'s congregation and others formed the Polish National Catholic Church in America; the Synod elected him bishop. Old Catholic bps. consecrated H. in Utrecht (1907). Organizer, theologian, liturgist, and humanitarian, H. was the most influential person in the Church, which he headed until his death. In 1914 he helped establish the Lithuanian National Catholic Church. BIBLIOGRAPHY: T. Andrews, *Polish National Catholic Church* (1953).

[E. E. BEAUREGARD]

HOEBEN, HEINZ (d. 1942), Dutch Catholic journalist. In 1928 H. founded the *Katholische Weldpost,* which was important in developing an international organization of Catholic journalists. When the Nazis suppressed it, he devoted himself to aiding German journalists in many countries. He returned to Holland in 1942 to turn himself over to the Nazis, who were holding his brother as hostage. He died in prison after prolonged interrogation.

[M. J. SUELZER]

HOEHN, MATTHEW (1898–1959), librarian, biographer. A Benedictine ordained in 1925, he taught at St. Benedict's Preparatory School, Newark, N.J., for a number of years before studying for a degree in library science; he was prior of St. Mary's Abbey from 1946–56. H. performed a needed task for Catholic letters in his two biographical works *Catholic Authors: Contemporary Biographical Sketches 1930–1947*. The first appeared in 1948, and the second (1952) added several hundred new writers.

[J. R. AHERNE]

HOENSBROECH, PAUL VON (1852–1923), German count, Jesuit from 1878, ordained in 1886, who abandoned the Society in 1892 and the Church in 1895, then devoted his life to anti-Jesuit and antipapal diatribes: *14 Jahre Jesuit* (2 v., 1909–10; Eng. tr., *Fourteen Years a Jesuit,* 2 v., 1911); *Das Papsttum in seiner sozialkulturellen Wirksamkeit* (2 v., 1900–02); *Der Jesuitenorden* (2 v., 1926–27). The Nazis are said to have used his works for anti-Catholic propaganda.

[T. C. O'BRIEN]

HOFBAUER, CLEMENT MARY, ST. (1751–1820), pioneer Redemptorist. Born in Moravia, H. overcame unbelievable obstacles in his lifetime to become the "second founder of the Redemptorists," with whom he was ordained in 1785 in Rome. Returning to Vienna with the object of establishing Redemptorist houses N of the Alps, he encountered the antireligious decrees of *Josephinism. In Warsaw he and two companions were given charge of a church where they ministered to the Poles as well as to the many Germans in that city. His preaching and work in the confessional attracted thousands. H. was keenly sensitive to the plight of the poor and founded an orphanage and a school for boys. With the growth of the Warsaw community, H. established houses in Poland, Germany, and Switzerland. The decree of Napoleon suppressing religious orders brought imprisonment to the Redemptorists. Eventually each returned to his own area but H. chose to go to Vienna. His fame in pastoral work grew to a point where his influence thwarted the effort at the Congress of Vienna (1814–15) to separate the Austrian Church from Rome. Called the "apostle of Vienna," he was protected by Emperor Francis I. Shortly after H.'s death the Redemptorists were legally established in Austria. He was canonized in 1909. BIBLIOGRAPHY: Butler 1:601–604.

[J. R. AHERNE]

HOFFMANN, CHRISTOPH (1815–85), German founder of the *Friends of the Temple. At an early age H. began to write against the conventional Christianity of his time. In 1848 he established the Evangelischer Verein, consisting of about 450 local branches and a school for lay preachers, to revive *Pietism. He sought to regenerate society by centering God's people on one point, the Temple, thought of partly in a spiritual and partly in a physical sense. He tried to restore a theocracy in Jerusalem, even pressuring the Frankfurt Assembly to prevail on the Sultan to sanction a settlement in Palestine. When his overtures failed, H. undertook to found the new Jerusalem in Germany, near Marbach. He had meanwhile left his Evangelischer Verein and was formally expelled from the national Church in 1859. BIBLIOGRAPHY: C. Kolb, EncRelKnow 4:397–398; G. Lang, RGG 3:413.

[M. J. SUELZER]

HOFHAIMER, PAULUS VON (Hoffheimer, Hoffhaymer; Paulus von 1459–1537), Austrian organist and composer. Hailed by his contemporaries as an organist without peer, he held posts in the court of Maximilian I, at Innsbruck, and at Salzburg. Though only a few of his organ compositions remain, several of his songs are extant. His settings of Horace's *Odes* helped to forward the movement for homophonic music and to develop the note-for-note setting of the Protestant chorale.

[M. T. LEGGE]

HOFMANN, GEORG (1885–1956), German Jesuit priest and ecclesiastical historian specializing in Byzantine and modern Greek history. His forte was archival investigation that would result in critical editions of documents, and so provide the groundwork for future works of historical synthesis. Born in Friesen near Bamberg, Bavaria, he studied philosophy and theology at the Gregorian Univ. in Rome; was ordained in 1912; and after serving as chaplain in World War I, entered the Jesuits in 1918. He studied ecclesiastical history under Grabmann and Döberl at the Univ. of Munich, where he received his doctorate. From 1922–56, he was professor of Oriental church history at the Pontifical Oriental Institute in Rome. Between 1928–34, he produced a series of monographs on the Holy See and the Eastern patriarchs. From 1934–41, he produced five volumes on the modern Catholic apostolate on some of the Greek islands. His chief work was his contribution to the critical edition of the documents concerning the Council of Florence. Besides being the founder and director of that work, he contributed seven fascicles of papal letters and other documents, and the *Acta Latina* of the council. In addition. he was an expert in Greek and Latin paleography.

[E. J. DILLON]

HOFMANN, MELCHIOR (Hoffmann; *c.*1500–*c.*1543), Anabaptist preacher. H. was first a Lutheran lay preacher in northern Germany and the Scandinavian countries. Between 1523 and 1533 he wrote more than 35 religious treatises. H. visited Luther in 1525, but by 1527 had lost his initial approval. In 1530 at Strassburg he became an Anabaptist and from 1530 to 1533 propagated his message in Friesland and Holland. Returning to Strassburg he was imprisoned until his death. Along with the usual Anabaptist message of a religion of inner experience, H. strongly accented *millenarianism (1533 was to be the dawn of the new age, and he was to be one of the prophets of Rev 11.3) and held Docetist views on Christ's humanity, i.e., that Christ was seemingly, not really, human. B. *Rothmann of Münster was among those strongly influenced by H.'s teachings (see JOHN OF LEIDEN). The followers of H. were called Hoffmanites or Melchiorites; many of them, because of persecution in Holland, fled to England in the 16th century. BIBLIOGRAPHY: MennEnc 2:778–785; bibliog. for Anabaptists.

[T. C. O'BRIEN]

HOGAN, WILLIAM (1788–1848), schismatic priest, leader of "Hoganism." Ordained for the diocese of Limerick, Ireland, where he seems to have been suspended from ministry, H. came to the U.S. and the diocese of New York. He left New York in 1820 without consulting his bp. and went to St. Mary's Cathedral in Philadelphia. Winning over the lay trustees of St. Mary's, he publicly denounced Bp. Conwell and proposed an American Catholic Church in charge of lay trustees. "Hoganism" was repudiated by the Supreme Court of Pennsylvania in 1832. Obliged to resign because of charges against his moral life, H. became an anti-Catholic lecturer and writer of such pamphlets as *Popery as It Was and Is*. In 1843 H. became U.S. consul in Nuevitas, Cuba. BIBLIOGRAPHY: F. E. Tourscher, *Hogan Schism* (1930).

[J. R. AHERNE]

HOGER OF BREMEN-HAMBURG, ST. (d. *c.*916) abp., monk at the Abbey of Corvey. H. succeeded Adalgar (d. 909) as abp. of Bremen. Details of his life are unknown, but tradition relates his sanctity and his strictness in upholding ecclesiastical and monastic discipline even during the invasion of his diocese by the Slavs and Magyars. BIBLIOGRAPHY: Adam of Bremen, *History of the Archbishops of Hamburg-Bremen,* (tr. F. J. Tschan, 1959).

[M. F. MCCARTHY]

HOHENBAUM VAN DER MEER, MORITZ (1718–95), Benedictine of the abbey of Rheinau in Schaffhausen, Switzerland. From 1776 he was secretary of the Swiss Benedictine Congregation; but his greatest renown rests on his archival studies of Benedictine history and of his own monastery's history.

[D. J. SMUCKER]

HOHENSTAUFEN, a great Suabian family that rose to eminence at the end of the 11th cent. and produced two great Holy Roman emperors, Frederick I, or Barbarossa (d. 1190), and his grandson, Frederick II, *Stupor mundi* (d. 1250), of whom St. Thomas Aquinas was kinsman. Legend, afterwards transferred to Barbarossa, tells of him still alive in the mountains, sitting at a stone table through which his beard grows, waiting for the call to restore the golden age of peace to the Empire. Their claims in Sicily were a weakness, and the male line became extinct when Conradin, defying the Pope and Charles of Anjou, asserted them and was beheaded after the defeat of Tagliacozzo, 1268.

[T. GILBY]

HOHENZOLLERN, a noble family, named from Zollern between the Neckau and Danube, which began its rise toward the end of the 12th century. The older or Franconian branch was transplanted to Brandenburg and, through the grand mastership of the *Teutonic Knights, became possessed of Prussia (king, 1701) and Protestant: German emperors 1871–1918. The younger or Suabian branch remained close to its ancestral lands, and continued to be Catholic, with the exception of the occupants of the throne of Romania (1866–1947).

[T. GILBY]

HOKKEDO (733 or 746), Japanese Buddhist temple in the compound of the Todaiji, Nara, where the Lotus Sutra ceremony is held each March. Enlarged in 1196, it boasts impressive clay statues of the Nara period.

[M. J. DALY]

HOLAIND, RENÉ (1836–1906), Jesuit educator, writer. After entering (1851) the Jesuits in his native France, H. came to the U.S. in 1861. His teaching career brought him to several colleges in the South, to Woodstock, Md., and to Georgetown University. He was active in defense of parochial schools, opposing the view of Abp. Ireland and others who defended public education for Catholics. H. wrote on private property, *Ownership and Natural Right* (1887); on jurisprudence, *Natural Law and Legal Practice* (1889); on education, *The Parents First* (1891). BIBLIOGRAPHY: P. Dooley, *Woodstock and Its Makers* (1927).

[J. R. AHERNE]

HOLBEIN, HANS, THE YOUNGER (1497–1543), German painter. After initial training by his father Hans, in Augsburg, H. became a member of the painters' guild at Basle, executing murals (Town Hall), woodcut designs *(Dance of Death),* altarpieces (Solothurn), Madonnas with donor portraits (Meyer). He enriched his prodigious gifts by journeys to Italy and France. Introduced by Erasmus to Thomas More, he settled permanently in London (1532), becoming court painter to Henry VIII. Although H. treated religious themes (Madonna, Passion, OT), his keen sense of observation, great draftsmanship, and cool objectivity found ultimate realization in a predominant portrait *oeuvre* of humanists (ambassadors), German merchants (Gisze), and royalty (Jane Seymour). He was the first cosmopolitan German Renaissance artist. BIBLIOGRAPHY: P. Ganz, *Paintings of Hans Holbein* (1956); K. T. Parker, *Drawings of Hans Holbein in the Collection of His Majesty the King at Windsor Castle* (1945).

[R. BERGMANN]

HOLCOT, ROBERT, see ROBERT HOLCOT.

HOLDEN, HENRY (1596–1662), theologian and controversialist. Of an English recusant family, he studied at Douai and the Sorbonne, where he later taught theology. Though vicar general of Paris, H. was a leader in English church affairs and supported the seculars against the regulars in the controversy over the appointment of a bp. for England. BIBLIOGRAPHY: Gillow, BDEC 3:332–338; A. Gatard, DTC 7:31–32.

[V. SAMPSON]

HÖLDERLIN, JOHANN FRIEDRICH CHRISTIAN (1770–1843), famous German poet, friend of Hegel, Schelling, and Fichte, whose works on themes of transcendence and mortality have influenced both philosophers and theologians of the 20th century. Most of his works were published by his friends, since after 1802 he became more and more mentally unbalanced.

HOLES, ANDREW (d. 1470), canonist, trained in Padua; archdeacon of Wells (1449–70); king's proctor at Rome; papal chamberlain; Keeper of the Privy Seal (1450–52).

Notable for his very large library, probably second only to that of his patron, Humphrey, duke of Gloucester, he maintained contacts with humanists in Rome, Padua, and Ferrara. BIBLIOGRAPHY: Emden Ox 2:949–950.

[C. D. ROSS]

HOLINESS. The early biblical concept of the holy embraced two elements: negatively, a removal from the common and ordinary; positively, a reservation for the Lord (furniture, vestments, persons). The uniquely holy One was Yahweh, utterly other, transcendent, removed from the tangible world. Men and other created realities were holy because of their relationship with him, for he was the source of all sanctity: "Be holy, for I, the Lord, your God, am holy" (Lev 19.2). The high priest was "sacred to Yahweh" (Ex 28.36), and the Nazarite was holy while under his vow because "he remains consecrated to the Lord" (Num 6.5–8). This perspective continues into the NT, where Christ is proclaimed as holy because of his divine sonship and the presence of the Holy Spirit in him. Thus Christian holiness is to be like Christ: one dies and rises with the Lord, lives in him, reflects his image, puts him on, and shares in his sonship. Christian holiness retains the positive and the negative in the constant gospel theme of exchange; a man must always give up something in order to have Christ: "none of you can be my disciple unless he gives up all his possession" (Lk 14.33).

The key to Christian holiness is love. Since this is the characteristic of God's relationship with the world, it is also the essential element in Christian life. Since it is love that most effectively unites persons, holiness consists simply in love, and relatively in the other virtues (ThAq ST 2a2ae, 184.1). Love is formally present in every virtuous act and is the fulfillment of all the precepts (Gal 5.14). Nevertheless, since human life is diverse, the concrete acts of love which characterize Christian holiness take different forms. Thus holiness expresses itself in justice, mercy, humility, prudence, etc. Christian love is also worldly insofar as it participates in the redeeming love of Christ for all creation. Holiness manifests itself in a reverence for the total created order. Moreover, genuine love of the world will strive to express itself in action so that the goodness of creation may grow to fullness.

Holiness is also one of the *marks of the Church, since the Church is sustained by Christ precisely as a fellowship of love and service. As Vat II ConstChurch (64) points out, the whole Church must ". . . preserve with virginal purity an integral faith, a firm hope, and a sincere charity." This is not to deny the great holiness found outside of the Church, since God gives "life and breath and every other gift" to all men, and effectively wills their salvation. (*ibid.* 16). BIBLIOGRAPHY: G. Thils, *Christian Holiness* (1961).

[T. DUBAY]

HOLINESS (IN THE BIBLE). The Heb. root *qds* from which the words *quodes* and *quados* are derived, has the general Semitic meaning of "separateness" from all that is *profane. A related but not identical term is *purity. (1) In its actual biblical use holiness is said properly of God alone in his absolute transcendence (e.g., 1 Sam 2.2; Ex 15.11); the trisagion of Isaiah (Is 6.3; Rev. 4.8) in whom the reference to the Holy One of Israel is most frequent. The meaning of this holiness is generally taken to be that of Rudolph Otto's "numinous," that mysterious quality associated with the entirely other which is both attractive and frightening (*mysterium fascinans ac tremendum*). (See *The Idea of the Holy,* tr. J. W. Harvey, 1958.) Nevertheless God's holiness is revealed in the Bible esp. as the antonym of sinfulness (Gen 18.16; Ex. 3.5). (2) As a religious, moral quality the divine holiness is the reason and norm for human imitation (Lev 19.2; Mt. 5.48). Human holiness manifests itself as moral irreproachability and stainlessness; both LXX and NT prefer *hagios* and *agnos* (clean) as closer to the Hebrew usage than the more common *hieros*. But while Yahweh demands that Israel be holy (Ex 19.6; 1 Pet 3.9), his covenant is not merely punitive but loving, forgiving, and redeeming (Is 41.14; Hos 11.9). The NT emphasis on the personal, moral character of holiness is even stronger. The holy Father (Jn 17.11) who sent his holy servant Jesus (Acts 4.27) also sends his Spirit who is called holy par excellence because he has a special function in making the people of God holy (Rom 15.16; 2 Th 2.13). (3) This moral holiness has a close connection with cultic holiness. Sometimes the cultic notion became so important, not only in primitive religions but in Israel, that the Prophets and esp. Jesus had to intervene to reassert the spiritual, moral meaning of holiness. Still the union with Christ which is the NT way of holiness is not simply by faith and righteousness but by the liturgical actions of baptism and the Eucharist (Eph 5.26). BIBLIOGRAPHY: J. de Fraine, EDB 1012–18; J. Lachowski, NCE 7:51–52.

[U. VOLL]

HOLINESS, HIS, a title applicable to all bps. in the early Church, but used by patriarchs of the Eastern Church since the early 6th cent. and exclusively by the pope in the West since the 14th century.

HOLINESS, LAW OF (*Heiligkeitsgesetz*), name given by Klostermann to ch. 17–26 of Lev, which are characterized by the frequent exhortation, "Be holy, for I, Yahweh your God, am holy." Purportedly "the laws, customs and rules the Lord laid down between himself and the sons of Israel on Mt. Sinai through the mediation of Moses" (26.46), these chapters probably attained their present form during the Exile. The age of the units which now make them up is uncertain, but much of the material is of great antiquity (references to Moloch [18.21; 20.1–5] point to *c.*750 B.C., and some authors find traces of far earlier dates). No satisfactory logical order governs the chapters; they contain laws about animal sacrifice and blood (17), sexual purity (18–20), the priesthood and food (21–22), a liturgical cycle both annual and periodic (23–25); they conclude with blessings and threats (26). They have much in common with the spirit of Dt and the preaching of the prophets, esp. Ezekiel. In general, they aimed at building up a national community which would be holy in a land of Exile, in preparation for a life of holiness back home after the Exile was over (18.3; 19.23). BIBLIOGRAPHY: E. Robertson, *Old Testament Problem* (1950).

[R. T. A. MURPHY]

HOLINESS CHURCHES, those Christian Churches that emerged from the 19th-cent. *Holiness movement and its emphasis on *entire sanctification. The Church of God (Anderson, Ind.) is one of the oldest; the Church of the Nazarene is the largest. The Holiness Churches are strongly evangelical and fundamentalist; neither the Church nor sacraments are needed for man's sanctification, which is the direct work of the Spirit. They insist on the *foursquare gospel—Jesus as Savior, sanctifier, healer and coming Lord (see PREMILLENARIANISM)—and on the reality of a supernatural, experienced sanctification (see BAPTISM WITH THE HOLY SPIRIT). While they have joined other denominations to promote fundamentalism, Holiness bodies have not generally been enthusiastic about the ecumenical movement. In a practical way, however, there are signs of possible rapport with other Christian Churches in fraternal ties and cooperative contacts established in some mission fields. As a classification, Holiness Churches are distinguished from Pentecostal Churches by a conservative interpretation of entire sanctification. Many of the bodies, e.g., the Christian and Missionary Alliance, refuse to accept the connection, essential for Pentecostals, between sanctification and charismatic gifts, esp. *glossolalia. Many of the Holiness groups still endorse *divine healing, but not as a necessary sequel to conversion and sanctification; they also reject the exuberant emotionalism often found among Pentecostals as a concomitant of Spirit baptism. BIBLIOGRAPHY: Mayer RB 305–323; H. S. Smith et al., *American Christianity* (1963); E. T. Clark, EncRelKnowSuppl 11:520–521.

[P. DAMBORIENA]

HOLINESS METHODISTS, Methodist bodies or denominations that were originally formed or that broke away from other Methodist bodies because of their belief that the denominations in general, and the Methodist denominations in particular, were not placing sufficient stress in their doctrinal emphasis on personal holiness. Most Holiness Methodists make special claim to fidelity to the true doctrine of *Christian perfection as taught by John *Wesley and as found in the Bible. *HOLINESS MOVEMENT.

[F. E. MASER]

HOLINESS MOVEMENT, a post-Civil War emphasis on *entire sanctification that led to the emergence of the Holiness Churches. John *Wesley's doctrine of *Christian perfection was the immediate inspiration of the teaching elaborated during the course of the Holiness movement. Early signs of the movement appeared in Thomas Merritt's *Guide to Christian Perfection* (1839) and in Phoebe Palmer's *Guide to Holiness* (1860). But the Holiness movement proper began, esp. among Methodists, after the Civil War with revivals in which the need of a return to holiness was preached. In 1867 a group of Methodists at Vineland, N.J., formed the National Camp Meeting Association for the Promotion of Holiness; soon similar associations were formed (esp. in Indiana), and the movement became interdenominational; it also spread to England. Some Holiness Churches came into being informally as outgrowths of the Holiness associations; others were separations from the organized Churches, which, as in the case of Methodism, viewed the interpretation of Holiness doctrine as unorthodox. Pentecostalism was a further development of the Holiness movement. BIBLIOGRAPHY: HistAmMeth 2:608–627; H. S. Smith et al., *American Christianity* (1963); J. T. Nichol, *Pentecostalism* (1966) 5–7.

[P. DAMBORIENA]

HOLINESS OF GOD, the transcendent loving perfection of the divine life and being, the mysterious, unique quality of God that sets him apart from all creation, making him (in R. Otto's terms) simultaneously attractive or "fascinating," and fearful or "tremendous." This concept appears frequently in the OT: Isaiah consistently uses the title "The Holy One of Israel" to designate Yahweh (also Jer 50.29). God cannot sin (1 Sam 2.2; Job 4.17; 25.5), but exercises judgment upon sin (Num 20.13; Ps 5.5; 44.8; Ezek 28.22; 38.16). The angels who stand before him cry out, "Holy, holy, holy is Yahweh Sabaoth" (Is 6.3). Indeed, man's call to holiness is established upon his relationship with God, and frequently in the OT man is described as holy in a liturgical context. God manifests his holiness by establishing a reign of holiness upon earth: the salvation of Israel is the prime revelation of Yahweh's righteousness. Thus Ezekiel records, "I will show my greatness and my holiness, and make myself known in the eyes of nations. Then they will know that I am the Lord" (Ezek 38.23). The notion continues into the NT but with much less frequency: Christ speaks of God's holiness (Jn 17.11; 1 Jn 3.3; Mt 6.9) and designates it as the norm for man's perfection (Mt 5.48). God's will is the holiness of man (Eph 1.3–6).

For speculative theology the foundation for God's holiness is the love which he has for his own absolute perfection. Since he is totally good, he must respond to that goodness by an outpouring of love. This is of the very nature of God and hence he is holiness itself, substantial holiness without the possibility of sin. It is only insofar as man and all creation participate in this divine goodness that they also participate in God's holiness. BIBLIOGRAPHY: R. Otto, *Idea of the Holy* (tr. J. W. Harvey, 2d ed., pa. 1950).

[T. M. MCFADDEN]

HOLINESS OF THE CHURCH, one of the attributes of the Church professed in the Apostles' and Nicene Creeds. The close attachment of the title "holy" to the Church in both RC conciliar documents and Protestant and Anglican confessions of faith indicates belief that holiness is of the essence or nature of the Church. There is a common belief in the reason for this holiness: the whole Church is not just a body of believers, but Christ the head and those who believe in him. From Christ, the chosen Son of the Father, the body of believers is made holy, set apart as the *People of God. The vital communion of Christ with his members and of the members with one another through Christ is the Church, called for this reason even a communion of saints. Protestants and Roman Catholics differ in their understanding of the implications of this holiness, however, because they differ in their understanding of the Church itself. There are two principal points of divergence. RC theology asserts that the holiness of the Church includes power communicated by Christ to the Church itself to sanctify its members. The essentials of the visible structure and life of the Church, its sacraments, its special priesthood, its hierarchical agencies, are understood as part of the holiness of the Church. Such a mediating role of the Church in the sanctification of its members is denied in principle by Reformation teaching on the *priesthood of all believers and the sacraments. The essential holiness of the Church is the holiness of Christ in himself and as given to the believer. None of the forms or institutions of the Church truly mediate in the sanctification of the believer; in this sense the *visible Church is not holy.

Protestants and RCs also understand the holiness of the members of the Church differently, although both seek to reconcile the sinfulness in the Church with its essential holiness. Roman Catholic teaching has refused to accept the notion of the Church as the congregation of the predestined or elect. The Church is holy in its members first because all have the same calling to holiness, to become sanctified. At the same time the Church is a pilgrim Church, never to be completely holy on this earth. The different states of life lived in the Church are meant to reflect the call to holiness and to bring about its fulfillment. The Holy Spirit, the Spirit of Christ, sanctifies the members of the Church individually and corporately (see Vat II ConstChurch 5–7). In the Reformation the earlier idea of John *Wycliffe and Jan *Hus that the true Church is the congregation of the predestined was repeated in the Lutheran and *Reformed traditions. The contrast between the true, *invisible Church and the external, imperfect visible Church runs through Protestant history. The endeavor to make the visible Church conform to the invisible Church inspired emphasis on church discipline, as well as the *gathered church idea of the Puritans and Congregationalists. While less concerned with the corporate structure of the Church, the spiritualizers, Anabaptists, Mennonites, and Quakers still enforced discipline to keep the brotherhood free of those who were unworthy. Wesleyan and Holiness *perfectionism concentrated on the individual; yet their traditions also imposed strict moral codes in order that the outward conduct of believers might reflect their inward conversion and freedom from sin. BIBLIOGRAPHY: J. Pelikan, *Riddle of Roman Catholicism* (1959).

[T. C. O'BRIEN]

HOLISM, theory originated by Jan Smuts (1870–1950) emphasizing the importance of wholes in contrast to scientific dissection and analysis. Stressing the inner structure and outward function of inorganic units, plants, animals, and men, Smuts contended that wholes were more than the sum of their parts. The theory has some kinship with *Gestalt theories in psychology, and in politics was illustrated by Smuts' preference for larger, inclusive units—the Union of South Africa; the British Commonwealth; the United Nations. He saw the concept as a way of overcoming the dichotomy between matter and spirit. BIBLIOGRAPHY: J. Smuts, *Holism and Evolution* (3d ed., 1936).

[T. EARLY]

HOLL, KARL (1866–1926), eminent Protestant church historian and patrologist, collaborator with A. von *Harnack. H. taught at the Univ. of Tübingen from 1901, then from 1906, at the Univ. of Berlin. His patristic studies include: *Die Sacra Parallela des Johannes Damascenus* (1896); *Enthusiasmus und Bussgewalt beim griechen Mönchtums* (1898, a study of Simeon the New Theologian); *Amphilochius von Ikonium* (1904), and an edition of the works of Epiphanius of Constantius (3 v., 1915–33). With Von Harnack he took part in the renowned edition of the Greek Fathers of the first 3 cent., *Griechischen Christliche Schriftsteller,* the so-called Berlin Corpus. He also produced studies on Martin Luther.

[T. C. O'BRIEN]

HOLLAZ, DAVID (*c.* 1648–1713), Lutheran pastor, preacher and theologian. In his *Examen theologicum acroamaticum* (posthumous 1717) he produced the last comprehensive, dogmatic systematic text of the period of Lutheran orthodoxy. Written when *Pietism had just surfaced in German-speaking Europe, the treatise represents the zenith of Lutheran "Scholasticism."

[D. J. SMUCKER]

HOLLWECK, JOSEF (1854–1926), German canonist. Professor of canon law at Eichstätt from 1892, he was the author of numerous works in his field, and an important consultor for the revision of canon law promulgated in CIC, 1917.

[T. C. O'BRIEN]

HOLOCAUST, the most solemn of Israelite sacrifices in which the offering, preferably an unblemished male animal, was completely burned. The word is derived from the LXX translation (*holokauston*) of the Hebrew 'ōlâ. The verb form of Hebrew 'ōlâ means "to go up"; the holocaust thus was a sacrifice whose smoke "went up" to God. This sacrifice is also referred to as kālîl, "complete" (1 Sam 7.9; Dt 33.10; Ps 51.21). The holocaust had a long history in Israel. Gideon's sacrifice (Jg 6.26, 28) was an 'ōlâ. When the ark returned safely from the land of the Philistines, a holocaust was offered (1 Sam 6.14). Samuel (7.9;10.8), Saul (13.9ff), David (2 Sam 6.17ff), Solomon (1 Kg 3.4; 9.25), and Elijah (1 Kg 18.38) all offered holocausts. Though the historical books give no description of the ritual followed, the characteristic feature of the holocaust remains constant, i.e., that the victim was completely burned. Because of the belief in post-Exile theology that this sacrifice had propitiatory value, laws concerning holocausts dominated the cultic legislation of the Priestly tradition. According to the prescriptions of Lev 1.3–17, the victim of a holocaust had to be an unblemished male from the herd of flock. The offerer laid his hand on the victim's head to signify that the sacrifice was to be offered in his name and for his benefit. After the laying on of hands, the victim was slaughtered, cut up, laid on the altar, and its blood poured around the altar. After the animal had been skinned and quartered, the pieces were washed and placed on the altar to be consumed "as a sweet smelling oblation to the Lord" (Lev 1.13, 17). If the victim was a bird, the priest performed the ritual directly on the altar. Such offerings were usually made by the poor (Lev 5.8; 12.8; 14.22). The Levitical liturgy made extensive use of holocausts, prescribing its offerings every morning or evening in the Jerusalem Temple (Num 28.3), with additional holocausts on the Sabbath (Num 28.9–10), the Feast of Booths (Lev 23.36) and New Year's Day (Num 29.2) as well as such occasions as purification after childbirth (Lev 12.6–8), cure of leprosy (Lev 14.10–13), and the consecration of the high priest (Lev 8.18). In the latest development of the holocaust ritual, the law called for an accompanying gift (minhâ) of flour mixed with oil and a libation of wine (Lev 23.18). The only NT reference to holocaust one quotes from the LXX (Mk 12:33; Heb 10:6, 8). BIBLIOGRAPHY: De Vaux AncIsr 415–417.

[T. J. RYAN]

HOLST, GUSTAV (THEODORE; 1874–1934), English composer. H. studied at the Royal College of Music in London and subsequently held various positions playing in orchestras and teaching. In 1919 he returned to the Royal College as a teacher of composition. H. composed about 50 works, mainly in the larger choral and instrumental forms. Some of his best known compositions are *The Planets* (1915), a suite of seven tone-poems; and *The Hymn of Jesus* (1917), a large choral work.

[M. T. LEGGE]

HOLT, JOHN (d. 1504), English schoolmaster; educated at Magdalen College, Oxford; usher of Magdalen College School. While master of Abp. Morton's boys at Lambeth Palace, *c.* 1496, he wrote *Lac puerorum,* "the English first gate to grammar." In 1502 he was appointed schoolmaster to Prince Henry, later Henry VIII. BIBLIOGRAPHY: F. Watson, *English Grammar Schools to 1660* (1908).

[C. D. ROSS]

HOLTZMANN, HEINRICH JULIUS (1832–1910), Protestant theologian and biblical scholar of the liberal school. After studies at Berlin and a pastorate at Baden (1854–57), he taught at Heidelberg (1858–74) and Strassburg (1874–1904). In *Die synoptischen Evangelien* (1863) he published the results of his painstaking study to verify the Two-Source Theory. A major contributor was his conclusion that Mark was the first Gospel, and that Matthew and Luke had used a common sayings source in their Gospels, but had relied on Mark for the basic framework and major narrative content. However, H. mistakenly assumed that the establishing the priority of Mark, he could logically conclude that the order of events in the life of Jesus as reported in Mark was historically trustworthy. In his later works, he argued for a psychological development in Jesus' self-consciousness, holding that there were two principal periods in his earthly life; that of "success" which reached its climax at Caesarea Philippi and a subsequent period of "failure" when the concept of a suffering messiah supervened. This idea in various forms still appears in some contemporary Christological studies. The most important of his works are: *Kanon und Tradition* (1859); *Lehrbuch der historisch-kritischen Einleitung in das NT* (1885); *Lehrbuch der neutestament Theologie* (1896–97). He was one of the founders of, and contributors to, the *HandCommentar zum NT,* for which series he wrote *Die synoptischen Evangelien* (1889); *Die Apostelgeschichte* (1891); *Die johanneischen Schriften* (1891). BIBLIOGRAPHY: W. Bauer, *Heinrich Julius Holtzmann* (1932); H. C. Kee, *Jesus in History* (1969) 1–27.

[T. J. RYAN]

HOLTZMANN, WALTHER (1891–1963), historian of the papacy, medievalist. He was ordinary professor of medieval history at Halle (1931–36); at Univ. of Bonn (1936–55). From 1953 to 1961 he was director of the Historical Institute in Rome. His research was primarily oriented to English history in the Middle Ages and to the papacy of the High Middle Ages. Closely associated with Paul Kehr, H. continued Kehr's *Regesta Pontificum Romanorum: Italia pontificia.* BIBLIOGRAPHY: K. H. Schwarte, NCE 7:59–60, for a complete bibliography.

[J. J. SMITH]

HOLY, the mysterious and encompassing reality experienced by man and yet beyond human experience, attractive but awesome, subsuming everything yet totally other. An awareness of the holy has always been a part of human experience, and has been reflected upon as such in man's earliest philosophical efforts. But it is only recently, esp. through the writings of É. *Durkheim, R. *Otto, and M. *Eliade, that the concept of the holy has become a central issue in comparative religion (see RELIGION, COMPARATIVE STUDY OF).

The interpretative value of the holy became obvious as soon as attempts were made to come to grips with religious phenomena on a comparative basis. When Durkheim analyzed the religion of the Australian aborigines on the premise that as human beings they were no less religious than the so-called civilized peoples, he concluded that all religions have one common characteristic—the dichotomy between the sacred and the profane. As ideal and transcendental the holy is radically opposed to the profane. But Durkheim thought that since the world of the sacred is real only in and through human community, its basis is nothing but society itself. The experience of the community's life and power induces man to develop his sense of God and of the holy. Otto came to a similar conclusion, though on different grounds and with a different interpretation of the relationship between the individual and society. Religion is not an epiphenomenon of morality (Kant), nor a mere matter of feeling (Schleiermacher), but has its independent roots in the depth of the mind and heart as well. The mind discovers the holy as an irreducible category of experience, the wholly other as being different from the profane. The heart reacts upon this discovery by attraction (the holy as *fascinans*) and repulsion (the holy as *tremendum*), which in turn gives rise to the variety of religious phenomena. Consequently religion is defined as the spontaneously experienced encounter with the holy and man's responsive action as determined by that encounter.

Presupposing that religion is indeed a reality of its own, M. Eliade has shown that the idea of the holy is highly significant for the description and classification of religious phenomena. The concept of the holy permits us to comprise both the human response within the process of religious expressions and the instances that mark these expressions as religious. In this sense the holy is neither a totally different world nor, epistemologically speaking, an a priori category, but the hypostatized significance of religious manifestations. These manifestations indicate that something other than the profane really exists, and that there are absolute values which give orientation and meaning to human existence. Therefore, to talk about the sacred is tantamount to speaking about *hierophanies, i.e., manifestations of the sacred.

But as the empirical study of religious phenomena shows, the discovery of the universal character of the holy is not in itself a total answer to the question about the meaning of religion. The sequence of hierophanies is bound up with the constitution of consciousness in particular, the emergence of mankind in the world, and history in general. Man not only finds his orientation in the world by growing up in and with hierophanies, but he also interferes with them through a variety of attitudes. For instance, the tension between ideology and society or magic and religion is mirrored in the dialectics of the sacred and the profane, and points back to actual events of history as the necessary medium of hierophanies. Some contemporary philosophers of religion maintain that the idea of the holy is not sufficiently explained by hypostatizing the sacred and regarding it as an a priori category, as R. Otto did. An adequate theory of the sacred has to clarify its relationship to the person, in particular to the divine person as the highest value, and its relationship to mythology, i.e., the meta-rational framework that qualifies the character and the significance of hierophanies. The holy has to be seen as an integral feature of the mythological process by which the world is qualified and modified as a place for man to live in. The holy would no longer be identical with the wholly other, but becomes understandable as a myth-related and multi-structured medium and value, in which man as person originates and continues to grow. BIBLIOGRAPHY: É. Durkheim, *Elementary Forms of the Religious Life* (pa., 1965); R. Otto, *Idea of the Holy* (tr. J. Harvey, pa., 1958); M. Eliade, *Patterns in Comparative Religion* (tr. R. Sheed, pa., 1963); M. Scheler, *On the Eternal in Man* (tr. B. Noble, 1960); G. van der Leeuw, *Religion in Essence and Manifestation* (tr. J. Turner, 1963); W. Dupré, *Religion in Primitive Cultures* (1970). *SACRED AND THE PROFANE.

[W. DUPRÉ]

HOLY ALLIANCE, an international compact, created for the purpose of preserving European peace after the downfall of Napoleon. It was signed by the Tsar of Russia, the Emperor of Austria, and the King of Prussia, Sept. 26, 1815. Alexander I of Russia had drafted the document and then asked all Christian princes of Europe to sign, pledging themselves to follow an international system based on the principles of Christian justice, charity, and peace. To many of the statesmen of Europe, the Alliance was the product of intellectual Romanticism, unrealistic and impractical. Eventually, however, the invited princes, except George III and the Pope, joined the Alliance out of deference to Alexander who had first started Napoleon on the road to defeat. The Tsar was probably sincere in his efforts to establish a peace based on Christian principles, but the liberals placed a different interpretation on his action. To them, it represented a common policy of reaction among the rulers of Europe. Some historians think that the Alliance did possess some moral force, but many others agree that there is slight evidence that it ever affected the conduct of a single European ruler. When Alexander died in 1825, the document was conveniently shelved. BIBLIOGRAPHY: *France and the European Alliance 1816–21* (ed. Guillaume de Bertier de Sauvigny, 1958).

[M. A. WATHEN]

HOLY CHILD JESUS, SOCIETY OF THE, a congregation of religious women devoted to educational work; founded at Derby, England, in 1846 by an American convert, Cornelia Connolly. The rule, adapted mostly from St. Ignatius, won papal approval in 1893 (after her death). The congregation expanded into 5 European countries, the U.S., and Africa; and engages in the full spectrum of education, from elementary schools to sophisticated teachers colleges. In 1963 there were 950 members. In 1976 this congregation claimed 814 members living in 83 houses. In 1937 the sisters established an African sisterhood, which was given independent status in 1960.

[E. J. DILLON]

HOLY CHILDHOOD, PONTIFICAL ASSOCIATION OF THE (also known as Missionary Childhood), a work of children's support of the missions. The organization was established in 1843 by Charles Forbin-Janson, bp. of Nancy and Torel, in France. The founder wished to draw all Catholic children from infancy to their 12th year to share in the mission apostolate, particularly to assist establishment of a native clergy and Church in mission lands. The children's help consists in their prayers, practice of virtues, their offerings saved by small sacrifices, all to assist missionaries in their care and ministry to mission children. The intention is that the children's efforts will lead to the fostering of Christian family life and native vocations. Headquarters are in Paris but there are national branches in many countries. In the U.S. the Missionary Childhood is under the care of the Holy Ghost Fathers, with headquarters in Pittsburgh, Pa. There is also a council for this association attached to the Congregation for the Evangelization of Peoples.

[T. C. O'BRIEN]

HOLY COAT, the coat of Jesus without a seam described in Jn 19.23 and since the 12th cent. identified as the property of the parish churches of Argenteuil and Trier, with each holding their own to be the authentic garment mentioned by John. BIBLIOGRAPHY: F. Lauchert, CE 7:400–402.

[F. H. BRIGHAM]

HOLY COMMUNION, a term used by many Churches for the celebration of the *Eucharist, or *Lord's Supper. It is often called simply communion or the communion service. Although disagreements about the meaning of the rite have been numerous and deep among Christians, they generally agree that one of its meanings is the unity that people of diverse backgrounds have through Christ; they therefore regard the existence of separate Churches not in *intercommunion as an anomaly to be overcome.

[T. EARLY]

HOLY COMMUNION, REFUSAL OF. As in the case of all the sacraments, the Eucharist cannot be denied to any one of the faithful who is capable of receiving it and requests it in reasonable circumstances. The minister of the Eucharist also has the obligation of protecting the sacrament from any misuse and of protecting the community from scandal. Thus communion is not given to one who is too young or otherwise mentally incapable of recognizing the meaning of the sacrament. (The discipline of some Eastern Churches includes, however, giving communion to newly baptized infants.) The minister also has the obligation of refusing the sacrament, even publicly, e.g., at a public Mass, to those who are commonly known to be unworthy because of a public excommunication or infamy or because they are openly living a sinful life, inpenitently and with no regard for scandal. The minister cannot deny communion to one publicly approaching the sacrament even when the minister knows the person to be unworthy as long as that unworthiness is not publicly known; the person retains the right to a good name. (Confessional knowledge has no bearing on the case, since a confessor can never act outwardly on the basis of such knowledge.) In certain specific cases of public scandal to the community, the local bp. may publicly exclude a person from communion until repentance and repair of the scandal are clear. A religious superior may forbid a subject who has gravely injured the community from receiving communion until the subject has received the sacrament of penance. Even though *intercommunion has not yet been sanctioned by the Church, in practice some ministers give communion to other Christians who approach the sacrament at a Catholic Eucharistic Liturgy.

[T. C. O'BRIEN]

HOLY CROSS, ABBEY OF, Irish Cistercian monastery near Thurles, Co. Tipperary, which was founded by monks from Nenay with the help of Domnall Mór O'Brien, king of Thomond, who entrusted the monks with the guardianship of a relic of the True Cross. Although the abbey was suppressed by Henry VIII, the people continued to regard it as a shrine because of the presence of the relic, and the Butler family who received the property from Queen Elizabeth allowed the monks to use the buildings into the 17th century. The relic is now kept in the Ursuline convent of Cork. Only the ruins of the abbey remain. BIBLIOGRAPHY: M. Hatry, *Triumphalia chronologica monasterii Sanctae Crucis in Hibernia* (ed. and tr. D. Murphy, 1891).

[L. J. LEKAI]

HOLY CROSS, CONGREGATION OF THE, an order of priests and brothers dedicated to education, home and foreign mission work. It was founded at Le Mans, Sarthe, France by B. A. *Moreau in 1837, who united into one religious institute the Congregation of the Brothers of St. Joseph and the Auxiliary Priests of Le Mans. The former had been founded to provide primary education for children where the system had been destroyed by the French Revolution; the latter, to assist parish clergy. Thus the congregation became a clerical institute composed of two societies which, while canonically united, remain nevertheless distinct. Their union is maintained by the same general administration and the same constitutions and religious practices. The members are bound by the usual vows of poverty, chastity, and obedience. The vow of obedience, however, binds them only to any house or activity dependent on the province. A religious must have made a fourth vow known as the mission vow to be sent into any territory under the Congregation for the Prapagation of Faith. The salvation of souls for the glory of God through preaching, education, and social work is the means through which each member perfects himself and contributes to the expansion of the kingdom of Christ. The congregation has had its greatest number of members and works in the U.S., where it expanded very quickly. In 1976 it numbered throughout the world 291 houses, 1,020 priests and 1,312 brothers.

[R. C. CLIGGETT]

HOLY CROSS (LIÈGE), DAUGHTERS OF THE (FC), a papal congregation founded at Liège, Belgium (1833), by Maria Theresia Haze and Canon Jean Habets for educational work and the care of the sick and aged. The congregation has expanded to Germany, India, England, the Netherlands, Italy, Brazil, and the United States. It is governed from Liège by the superior general and her council. The members numbered 1,518 in 1975.

[M. B. MONAGHAN]

HOLY CROSS SEMINARY, a seminary under the jurisdiction of the Greek Orthodox Archdiocese of North and South America. It is located in Brookline, Mass., a suburb of Boston. Founded at Pomfret Center, Conn., in 1937, it was authorized by the State of Massachusetts to grant the B.A. in theology in 1956 and in 1965 to confer the B.D. and S.T.M. degrees. A college of liberal arts was opened in 1961. The seminary publishes the *Greek Orthodox Theological Review.*

[T. BIRD]

HOLY CROSS SISTERS. Two congregations of the Holy Cross Sisters emerged as counterparts of the Congregation of the *Holy Cross, a community of priests and brothers founded in Le Mans, France, by B. A. Moreau. From the original congregation founded by Moreau in 1841, the Marianites of the Holy Cross, there were established from the missions in the U.S. and Canada, the Congregation of the Sisters of the Holy Cross (CSC) and the Sisters of the Holy Cross and Seven Dolors (CSC). (1) The Congregation of the Sisters of the Holy Cross, with its general motherhouse in Notre Dame, Ind., since 1855, developed when the first four sisters arrived in South Bend, Ind., in 1843, to join Rev. Edward Sorin, CSC, founder of the Univ. of Notre Dame. By the 1860s this group became autonomous. Their apostolates including nursing, education on elementary, secondary, and college levels in seven U.S. regions, and foreign missions in, among others, Bengal, India (1927), São Paolo, Brazil (1947), and Pakistan (1934), where Sr. Rose Bernard Gehring founded a native community, the Associates of Mary, Queen of the Apostles. Significant contributions to the higher education of women are St. Mary's College, Notre Dame, Ind. (1844), St. Catherine's, Baltimore (1847), a teacher-training school, and a graduate school of sacred theology at St. Mary's, Notre Dame (1944). Membership in 1976 numbered 1,130 professed sisters. (2) Sisters of the Holy Cross and Seven Dolors, a congregation formed when Sisters of the Holy Cross came to Montreal, Canada, in 1847 to take charge of the Catholic schools. From this group sisters were sent to the Diocese of Hartford, Conn., in 1887 at the request of the bishop. The sisters are engaged in teaching from preschool to college level in the New England states. In 1975 the congregation had 1,883 sisters and 207 houses; the motherhouse is in Montreal. The provincial house for the U.S. province of 388 sisters is in Pittsfield, N.H.

[M. B. MONAGHAN]

HOLY DAY, a solemn feast of the Church, other than a Sunday, on which the faithful are obliged to attend Mass and abstain from servile work. In the 4th cent. attendance at Sunday Mass was enjoined, and it was not long before other feasts were celebrated with special solemnity, and their observance in the same manner as Sundays began to be required. The list of these feasts gradually increased until, in the 13th cent., there were more than 50 such days in the year. In 1642, to diminish the ever-growing number, Urban VIII reduced them to 36 and limited the right of bps. to institute new ones.

The current calendar of the RC Church lists 10 holy days of obligation: Christmas, the Nativity of Jesus, Dec. 25; Solemnity of Mary the Mother of God, Jan. 1; Ascension of the Lord, 40 days after Easter; Assumption of the Blessed Virgin Mary, Aug. 15; All Saints' Day, Nov. 1; Immaculate Conception of the Blessed Virgin Mary, Dec. 8; Epiphany, Jan. 6 or (in the U.S.) a Sunday between Jan. 2 and 8; St. Joseph, March 19; Corpus Christi, a movable observance held in the U.S. on the Sunday following Trinity Sunday; and SS. Peter and Paul, June 29. By enactment of the Third Plenary Council of Baltimore, and with the approval of the Holy See the first 6 of the above 10 are observed as holy days of obligation in the United States.

[P. F. MULHERN]

HOLY DOORS, see DOORS, HOLY.

HOLY FACE, the image of Christ which, according to various medieval legends, was impressed on a linen cloth or veil belonging to St. *Veronica. Such a cloth received great devotion in the Middle Ages; in Rome from as early as the 10th cent.; where one such cloth, now almost completely faded, is preserved as a relic at St. Peter's Basilica. Stories as to the origin of the image vary, but most popular is the legend that when Veronica wiped the face of Jesus on the way to Calvary, he caused his features to appear on it. There is also a famous portrait known as the Holy Face of Edessa, supposedly painted by Christ himself or by his secretary, Hannan, which is preserved at the Bartholomite church in Genoa. An Archconfraternity of the Holy Face was established (1851) in Tours in reparation for offenses against Christ.

[T. M. MCFADDEN]

HOLY FAMILY, THE, Jesus, Mary, and Joseph as the object of a special devotion which attained widespread popularity in post-Tridentine Catholic piety. The persons of Jesus, Mary, and Joseph as a domestic unit are viewed as embodying the ideal of family life. This subject matter for iconography and meditation was derived from the Infancy narratives of Luke and Matthew where the gospel account presents the objects of this special devotion acting as a unit. The devotion first appeared in 17th-cent. Europe and then spread to French Canada through the special initiative of the first bp. of Quebec. In 1921 Benedict XV made the feast of the Holy Family a feast of the universal Church, to be celebrated on the Sunday within the octave of the Epiphany. In the liturgical reforms following Vatican Council II, the feast still has a place within the Christmas-Epiphany celebrations. BIBLIOGRAPHY: B. Fischer et al., LTK 5:93–95; G. Löw EncCatt 10:1551–52)

[E. J. DILLON]

HOLY FAMILY, CONGREGATION OF SISTERS OF THE (SSF), a community of black sisters who work among the poor, established in 1842 in New Orleans, Louisiana. Motivated by zeal and compassion, the founders Henriette DeLisle and Juliette Gaudin, two freeborn black women, were directed by Étienne Rousselon, vicar general of the diocese, and assisted by Marie Jeanne Aliquot, a French immigrant. The congregation is of pontifical status; its members take simple vows and follow the Rule of St. Augustine. Their apostolate is directed toward the needs of the poor, particularly in Southern U.S. and Central America. Numbering 281 members (1976) the community staffs elementary schools, high schools, a college, nurseries, orphanages, a nursing home for the aged; it conducts catachetical schools and provides domestic services for seminaries.

[M. B. MONAGHAN]

HOLY FAMILY, SISTERS OF THE (SHF), a papal congregation founded specifically to instruct and train in the practice of the Catholic faith children otherwise deprived of religious education. In 1872 Elizabeth Armer (Mother M. Dolores) under the direction of Abp. J. S. Alemany of San Francisco, Calif., founded this institute to undertake this task. The sisters engage in various aspects of religious education. They conduct vacation schools, retreats for public high school students, day-care centers for children of working mothers; engage in relief work, mission work in Hawaii, education of the mentally retarded, and religious education of the blind. The 254 members (1976) are active in California, Nevada, Texas, Utah, and Hawaii. The motherhouse is situated in Mission San José, California.

[M. B. MONAGHAN]

HOLY FAMILY, SONS OF THE (SF), a congregation of priests and brothers founded in 1864 in Tremp, Lerida, Spain, by Rev. Jose Manyanet. This papal congregation (approved 1901) has for its purpose the promotion of devotion to the Holy Family and the fostering of true Christian family life by means of education of youth and organization of a family movement. In spite of the difficulties brought about by political upheaval and persecution in Spain, the Sons of the Holy Family began to prosper after the Spanish Civil War. They are well established as educators in Spain, Italy, and Argentina. At the request of Pope Pius XI, they maintained the general secretariat for the International Association of the Holy Family. Pius XII commissioned them to build an international shrine to the Holy Family in Rome. In 1920 the congregation came as missionaries to the Diocese of Sante Fe, N. Mex. to work among the Spanish-speaking people of the Southwest. The American headquarters and seminary are located in Silver Spring, Maryland. Worldwide membership in 1976 was 170 of which 132 were priests; their generalate is in Barcelona, Spain.

[M. B. MONAGHAN]

HOLY FAMILY MISSIONAIRIES, also known as the Congregation of Missionaries of the Holy Family (MSF); a missionary society founded by Jean Baptiste Berthier (1840–1908), a La Salette Missionary, for fostering priestly vocations among the poor and those advanced in years. It was approved by Leo XIII in 1894, then founded in 1895 at Grave, Netherlands, with the approval of the bishop of s'Hertogenbosch. Forty of its members were killed in World War I; 150 in World War II, including 50 Polish members killed by the Nazis. By 1964 there were 733 priests, 233 scholastics, 181 lay brothers, and 58 novices in 17 countries, 9 provinces, and 4 regions. There were 45 priests and 12 parishes in the U.S. with headquarters in St. Louis. The generalate is in Rome. In 1976 the congregation included 1,072 religious members (of whom 865 were priests) living in 289 religious houses.

[E. J. DILLON]

HOLY FAMILY OF NAZARETH, SISTERS OF THE (CSFN), a religious community following the Rule of St. Augustine, originally contemplative, whose apostolic works include teaching, caring for the sick and working girls, retreat and missionary work. The community was founded (1875) in Rome by a Polish noblewoman, Frances Siedliska (declared venerable in 1935). The constitutions were given final approval in 1923. International in scope, the congregation has convents in Poland, Italy, England, France, the U.S., Puerto Rico, Australia, and Peru. The American foundation was made in 1885 in Chicago by the foundress and 11 sisters. Today the congregation has expanded and been divided into five provinces. In 1975 membership was 2,050. The generalate is in Rome.

[M. B. MONAGHAN]

HOLY FAMILY OF VILLEFRANCHE, SISTERS OF THE, a religious congregation of women founded in 1816 by St. Émile de Rodat with the assistance of Abbé Anton Marty for the education of girls, the care of the sick, and other works of mercy. Its motherhouse is in Villefranche, France. It is organized with papel approval into two branches: cloistered and noncloistered. The congregation has spread to nine countries in addition to France. In 1976 the congregation numbered 1,047 members living in 152 houses.

[E. J. DILLON]

HOLY FATHER, a title of the Pope, first used in England *c.*1380.

HOLY FIRE, a legend associated with the blessing of the new fire during the Easter Vigil as conducted according to the Orthodox rite in the Church of the Holy Sepulcher in Jerusalem. Early versions of the legend date from the late 11th and early 12th cent. (the *Gesta Francorum,* Abbot Daniel Palomnik's account of his pilgrimage to the Holy Land, etc.). The legend varies in content, but the following may be regarded as the most widespread elements: (1) The fire is of miraculous origin, descending as the tongues of fire at Pentecost. Some commentators hold that this "spontaneous flame" is caused by a chemically treated torch that ignites after a certain period of time or upon contact with water. This procedure may have been intended as a symbolic dramatization, but because of the widespread belief that it is a miracle some have viewed it as a deliberate deception. (2) The fire neither gives heat nor consumes. (Some Greek accounts describe it as *phōs,* (light), not *pur*, (fire). In some descriptions it resembles St. Elmo's fire. (3) The fire is selective, bypassing the candles of all those who are not of the Orthodox faith. This aspect of the legend seems to have originated shortly after the schism of 1054.

BIBLIOGRAPHY: G. Klameth, *Das Karsamstagsfeuerwunder der Heiligen Grabeskirche* (1913); P. Dörfler, "Das heilige Osterfeuer in Jerusalem," *Hochland* 24 (1927) 1–11.

[R. H. MARSHALL]

HOLY GHOST, see HOLY SPIRIT.

HOLY GHOST, SISTERS OF THE (CHG), a diocesan institute founded in 1913 by Bp. F. R. Canevin. The first motherhouse was located in Donora, Pa.; in 1926 it was moved to its present location, Westview, Pittsburgh. The sisters live a life dedicated to the Holy Spirit, observe the Rule of St. Augustine, and make simple vows. Their principal works are education of youth in parochial and private schools, care of the aged, and nursing of the sick in their hospital. The congregation labors in the Dioceses of Pittsburgh, Greensburg, Charleston, and Wheeling. In 1976 they numbered 111 professed sisters.

[M. B. MONAGHAN]

HOLY GHOST AND MARY IMMACULATE, SISTERS OF THE (SHG), an American congregation founded (1893) in San Antonio, Texas, by a widow, Margaret Healy Murphy. Its purpose, to bring Catholic truth the blacks of the South, inspired a degree of opposition in the early stages of the congregation's development. Its 223 members (1976) conduct schools, a home for the aged poor, and catechetical centers in Texas, Louisiana, and Mississippi. The sisters take simple vows. Final papal approval was granted the institute in 1938. In 1964, they established a training house for candidates in Galway, Ireland. The general motherhouse is in San Antonio, Texas.

[M. B. MONAGHAN]

HOLY GHOST FATHERS, official title, Congregation of the Holy Ghost under the Protection of the Immaculate Heart of Mary (CCSp), founded in Paris in 1703 by Claude François Poullart des Places. The group became known as the Seminary and the Congregation of the Holy Ghost. In 1734 the congregation received papal approbation. Interested in the missions, the institute sent missioners to China, India, and the French colonies. The community flourished until the French Revolution (1789) when it all but disappeared. However, it was restored in 1805. At the suggestion of Pius VII, Francois *Libermann, a converted Jew and the founder of the Society of the Immaculate Heart of Mary, combined his institute (1848) with that of the Congregation of the Holy Ghost. The approved rule of the latter was retained and the constitutions of Libermann's society were incorporated into it; he also became the superior general. The members make simple vows, temporary for 3 years, then perpetual. The congregation undertakes the direction of home and foreign missions, seminaries, and colleges. Its numerous foreign missions are located principally in Africa. Its worldwide membership in 1976 was 4,344. The permanent establishment of the Holy Ghost Fathers in the U.S. dates from 1873. The congregation operates Duquesne Univ., Pittsburgh, Pennsylvania.

[M. B. BOYLE]

HOLY GRAIL, THE, see GRAIL, THE HOLY.

HOLY HEART OF MARY, SERVANTS OF THE (SSCM), a papal congregation founded (1932) in Paris at the Shrine of Our Lady of Victory, by François Delaplace, CSSp in 1860. An orphanage established by Father Delaplace and directed by Jeanne Marie Moysan was the first work undertaken by the women who were to form the nucleus of the new congregation. At the request of J. Marsile, CSV, the sisters emigrated to the U.S. (1889) where they undertook domestic work at St. Viator College, Bourbonnais, Illinois. Later foundations were established in the archdioceses of Chicago, St. Paul, and Washington, D.C., and in the dioceses of Joliet, Little Rock, Peoria, and Rockford. The congregation is also found in Canada where the general motherhouse is located, and in Africa. The sisters engage in many apostolates: education, hospital work, catechetics, black missions, administration, secretarial and domestic duties. The congregation totaled 1,033 members (1975), of whom 125 were American. The American provincialate is located in Kankakee, Illinois.

[M. B. MONAGHAN]

HOLY HEARTS OF JESUS AND MARY, SISTERS OF THE, a congregation of Syrian and Lebanese religious founded in 1874 by the merger of two groups dedicated to assist the missionary work of the Jesuits. The first group, the Mariamettes, was founded (1853) in Lebanon, by J. Gemayel, a Maronite priest, with the aid of Raymond Esteve, SJ; the second, the Poor Sisters of the Sacred Heart, had its origins in Lebanon (1857), under the direction of Paolo Riccadonna, SJ. The combined group was a pious union of persons with private vows when first organized. In 1875 Remi Normand, superior of the Jesuits in Syria, disbanded the congregation because he felt that the direction of this group was not in accord with the Jesuit constitutions. The apostolate was resumed, however, 9 years later because of the persistence of 60 sisters and the realization of the harmful effects of the withdrawal of the Jesuit ministry to them. They numbered (1974) 537 members staffing 69 institutions. Papal approbation was granted to the institute in 1931 and to its constitution in 1957. The congregation is at once Latin and interritual. All members are permitted to retain their original rite, e.g., Maronite, Greek Melchite, Syrian, Armenian, but follow the Latin rite calendar feasts of obligation and fasting. The Divine Office and sacraments were observed according to the rite prevailing in the place of residence. The scope of the apostolate until 1930 was limited to educational institutions and dispensaries. Subsequently, it has expanded to government hospitals, social work, and missions in Morocco and Chad. From this congregation a separate community, the Coptic rite Congregation of Egyptian Sisters of the Sacred Heart, was formed in 1912. The Sisters of the Holy Hearts of Jesus and Mary staff high schools, grade schools, Syrian and Lebanese hospitals, orphanages, dispensaries, and mission stations. The superior general and council reside in Beirut, Lebanon.

[M. B. MONAGHAN]

HOLY HOUR, a nonliturgical, devotional service of reparation and adoration of the Blessed Sacrament, usually exposed, and consisting of appropriate prayers, hymns, a sermon, and *Benediction. With the greater emphasis on the Eucharistic Liturgy itself, in recent times the Holy Hour is less frequently held. The origin of the practice is traced to St. *Margaret Mary Alacoque who kept a holy hour in response to a message from Christ that promised her a share in his agony in Gethsemani; thus Thursday and Friday were esp. the days set aside for the devotion. An Archconfraternity of the Holy Hour was established at *Paray-le-Monial in 1829.

[T. C. O'BRIEN]

HOLY HUMILITY OF MARY, SISTERS OF THE (HHM), or Blue Nuns, a pontifical institute with two different motherhouses, which was established (1854) by the parish priest John Joseph Begel and Mother Magdalen Poitiers, in the Diocese of Nancy, France, to teach poor rural children. In 1864, because of the anticlericalism prevalent in France, the entire community of 10 sisters emigrated to Cleveland, Ohio, at the invitation of Bp. Amadeus Rappe. Shortly after their arrival, the sisters moved to New Bedford, Pa., then a part of the Cleveland diocese. There they opened parochial schools and established their motherhouse at Villa Maria, Pennsylvania. In 1870 four sisters were sent to St. Joseph, Mo., where 11 years later a separate congregation, the Congregation of the Humility of Mary, was formed. Their motherhouse is at Ottumwa, Iowa. The two congregations are working in 5 archdioceses and 19 dioceses, as well as in Guam and Mexico, in which they staff schools, colleges, hospitals, and other institutions. They also conduct a social service mission in Chile. As of 1975 the Iowa branch numbered 290 members, and the Villa Maria community had 448.

[M. B. MONAGHAN]

HOLY INDIFFERENCE, a quality in a person's love for God above all that excludes preference for any person, object, or condition of life. The possibility of such an attitude is implicit in the totality that measures charity and so the determination at the commandment of charity must be fulfilled by loving nothing to the exclusion of God, but may be more fully fulfilled by loving nothing except in direct relation to the love of God (ThAq ST 2a2ae, 44.4 and 2 & ad 3; 184,2). The choice to strive so to love God totally in the second way is freely embraceable and open to endless progress, since God is boundlessly lovable. The attitude of holy indifference, however, is not one to be taken, so to speak, simply for a pious practice. Rather it is first of all a description of what has in fact been given to souls at a certain stage of spiritual development. It may be related as a culmination, for example, to the purification of sense and spirit described by St. John of the Cross in the *Dark Night of the Soul*. It may also be associate with the intense operation of the Gifts of the Holy Spirit, esp. the Gift called Knowledge (*scientia*) and its experience as typified by the beatitude of "those that mourn." The gift and the beatitude describe the perception that with all the beauty and value in God's creation and in his creatures, there is as well the threat that they can by their very goodness distract from the intensity of union in love with God (ThAq St 2a2ae, 9). What holy indifference describes is not an undervaluing of the creation, and esp. of the children of God; the intensity of charity which is its basis rather will make the recipient of the gift more loving, more tenderly reverent. The indifference means, however, the purification from self-interest and the intensification of the universality of love, but with the increasingly more explicit motivation in loving solely because of love for God and what is of God in all. That is not to value things and persons less, but more.

[T. C. O'BRIEN]

HOLY INFANT JESUS, SISTERS OF THE (Ladies of St. Maur), a papal institute founded near Rouen, France *c.* 1662 by Nicolas Barré, OMinim, for the education of poor girls. The motherhouse is situated in Paris, on the former Rue Saint-Maur, hence their popular name, Les Dames de Saint-Maur. Their apostolate comprises staffing primary, secondary, and technical institutions; serving in the foreign missions; and undertaking parish and social work. Foundations have also been established in Ireland, England, Italy, Spain, Malaysia, Japan, Siam, Thailand, and the United States. In 1974 the congregation had grown to 1,617 members.

[M. B. MONAGHAN]

HOLY INNOCENTS, see INNOCENTS, HOLY.

HOLY KISS, see KISS, HOLY.

HOLY LANCE, see LANCE, HOLY.

HOLY LAND, see HOLY PLACES.

HOLY LEAGUE, anti-Protestant French Catholic organization in the 16th century. The weakness and indecision of the French monarchy towards the threat of Protestantism caused the formation of the Holy League, *c.* 1560. Initially local unions headed by nobility and townsmen, the League combined to form a national organization of Catholic sentiment and political action. The League rose to prominence in 1576 during the Estates General at Blois. Henry III, declaring himself its head, hoped that he could use the League to offset his opponents. After it proved uncontrollable, Henry disbanded it in Sept. 1577. The death of Francis, Duke of Alençon, on June 10, 1584 prompted a dramatic resurgence of this union. Henry of Navarre (see HENRY IV), a Protestant, became heir to the French throne. Under the leadership of Henry, Duke of Guise, the League denounced the Protestant succession and supported a Catholic, Charles of Bourbon. From its Paris headquarters the Leaguers were a danger to the Huguenots and the French monarchy. Yet the League lacked unity, esp. after the murder of Guise in Dec. 1588. Many Catholic nobles disliked the radical acts in Paris. League factions grew, particularly over Spanish interference: the Maheustre faction argued that Spain should only intervene until the Catholic succession was assured, while the Manant faction was unconcerned about Spanish intrusion. Henry of Navarre's abjuration on July 25, 1593 was the final turning point. A Catholic king was now certain and the League gradually disappeared. BIBLIOGRAPHY: H. G. Koenigsberger, "The Organization of Revolutionary Parties in France and the Netherlands during the Sixteenth Century," *Journal of Modern History,* 27 (1955) 335–351; De L. Jensen, *Diplomacy and Dogmatism* (1964).

[C. T. EBY]

HOLY MAID OF KENT, see BARTON, ELIZABETH.

HOLY MAN OF LILLE, see VRAU, PHILIBERT.

HOLY MAN OF TOURS, see DUPONT, LÉON.

HOLY MOUNTAIN, in the Greek Orthodox Church Mount *Athos, so called because it is the seat of 20 monasteries.

[T. C. O'BRIEN]

HOLY NAME, DEVOTION TO THE. Evidence that devotion to the holy name began among the early Christians is found in MSS, monuments, and the works of the Fathers. During the Middle Ages, reverence for the holy name was the chief aspect of devotion to the sacred humanity. The wide use of the Prayer to the Name of Jesus of Anselm of Canterbury, of the hymn Jesu Dulcis Memoria, and the preaching of Bernard of Clairvaux testify to the diffusion of the devotion. In 1274 Gregory X, in pursuance of canon 25 of the Council of Lyons II, commanded the Dominican master general to engage his order in preaching greater reverence for the holy name. During the 14th cent., Richard *Rolle of Hampole in England, Henry Suso in Germany, and John Columbini of Siena in Italy esp. fostered the devotion. In the 15th cent. *Bernardine of Siena revitalized devotion to the name of Jesus. Martin V's endorsement in 1427 of his displaying a tablet bearing the monogram of the holy name at the end of his sermons added to the growing devotion. The victory over the Turks at Belgrade, July 14, 1456, is attributed to the preaching of the holy name by John Capistran, who stressed the devotion in many sermons in Italy, France, and Germany. During this cent. the people inscribed the holy name over doorways and at the head of letters and documents. Many local liturgies incorporated votive Masses, feasts, and litanies of the holy name. Innocent XIII universalized the feast in 1721, and Leo XIII the present litany, which enjoyed limited approval, in 1886. The popes repeatedly approved the Holy Name Confraternity, which was founded in the 15th century. Charles H. McKenna, OP, by his preaching, made the society a feature in the life of Catholic men in the United States. The society also spread to other English-speaking countries and to Malta. Public veneration of the holy name was fostered by rallies, parades, conventions, and the taking of the holy name pledge. BIBLIOGRAPHY: A. Cabassut, "La Dévotion au nom de Jésus dans l'Église d'occident," VieS 86 (1952) 46–69; P. R. Biosiotto, *History of the Development of Devotion to the Holy Name* (1943).

[W. A. HINNEBUSCH]

HOLY NAME SOCIETY, officially the Confraternity of the Most Holy Name of Jesus, a confraternity (since 1564) dedicated to reverence for the name of Jesus and reparation for blasphemy and profanation of the divine name. The society is established in a parish ordinarily by receiving a charter from the master general of the Dominican Order, since the Dominican master general, Bl. *John of Vercelli was commissioned (1274) by Gregory X to foster reverence for the holy name. But many other saints and orders have preached the same devotion. Legally the society is for all Christians, but in practice has been largely a society of men, and exclusively so in the United States. Besides its primary objective, the society seeks to aid its members to live a genuinely Christian life and to receive the sacraments at least monthly. In English-speaking countries meetings and devotions include recitation of the Holy Name Pledge, 12 promises expressing dedication to the ideals of the society. In the U.S. the spread to so many parishes stems from the pioneering preaching of the Dominican C. H. *McKenna in the 19th century. The reform of the liturgy and the pattern of parish life in recent decades have diminished the prominence of the Holy Name Society.

[T. C. O'BRIEN]

HOLY NAMES OF JESUS AND MARY, SISTERS OF THE (SNJM), a native Canadian religious congregation dedicated to Christian education and the mission apostolate. Their foundation by Bp. Ignatius Bourget was modeled on the spirit and rule of the Sisters of the Holy Name of Jesus of Marseilles, where he had tried unsuccessfully to gain recruits for the Canadian apostolate. Under the direction of the Oblates of Mary Immaculate at Beloeil, Quebec, Éulalie Durocher and two companions made a kind of novitiate and the congregation was formally established by Bp. Bourget in 1844, with Éulalie, as Mother Marie Rose, the first superior. From the beginning the community generously responded to appeals throughout Canada and the U.S. by sending its sisters to staff schools for children and young women. The first foreign mission, in Basutoland, South Africa, was accepted in 1931. A school in Japan is staffed by native sisters. Since 1961 the community has worked in Peru. There are 10 provinces in Canada, 5 in the United States. The motherhouse is in Montreal, Canada. In 1976 there were 3,504 sisters in 252 houses of the congregation.

[T. C. O'BRIEN]

HOLY OF HOLIES, the most sacred shrine of the religion of the Hebrews of ancient time. It was the most secluded room of the Temple of Solomon (1 Kg 6.16; cf Ex 26.33), a perfect cube, about 30 feet on all sides, which contained in its middle the Ark of the Covenant with its contents, guarded by hovering cherubim, on which Yahweh, the invisible Hebrew God, was believed to dwell in all his glory, apart from his real existence in his own sanctuary, heaven (Ex 26.34; 1 Chr 28.2). In later Judaism this inner sanctum was entered only once a year by the high priest on the Day of Atonement (Lev 16.15–16), on which occasion alone, of all Jews, he was allowed to pronounce the sacred name of Yahweh in his prayer for forgiveness of sins. In the Letter to the Hebrews this ritual became a symbol of Jesus' entering once for all time into heaven with the atoning value of his own sacrifice for the sins of all men (Heb 9.11–28; 10.19–25).

[J. F. FALLON]

HOLY OFFICE, CONGREGATION OF THE, see DOCTRINE OF FAITH, CONGREGATION FOR THE.

HOLY OILS, oils used for sacramental anointings and other consecratory purposes, specially blessed by the bp. in the Mass of the Chrism on Holy Thursday morning. The new oils are then distributed to the diocesan parishes and institutions to replace the oils of the previous year. They are of three types: *oil of the catechumens, mainly used at baptism and priestly ordinations; holy *chrism, used at baptism, confirmation, and episcopal consecrations, etc.; and *oil of the sick used for the anointing of the sick. Oil has always been regarded as an agent of healing, strengthening, and beautifying. Its Christian usage symbolizes spiritual strengthening and sacralizing, and the imparting of the special grace of the Holy Spirit. The holy oils are kept in silver or pewter vessels, usually under lock and key in the church (see AMBRY), though priests may keep smaller "stocks" more immediately available. BIBLIOGRAPHY: J. H. Miller, *Fundamentals of the Liturgy* (1959), E. J. Gratsch, NCE 7:81–83.

[N. R. KRAMER]

HOLY ORDERS, in the RC, Old Catholic, and Eastern Churches, a sacrament of the New Law that confers the spiritual power and grace to perform the sacred acts proper to the different grades of the ministry. The word order comes from the Latin *ordo* in the sense of a rank, class, or degree of status. From relatively early times the term was used to distinguish the position of the cleric from that of the layman. The term takes the plural form in reference to the sacrament in its totality, because clerical rank embraces several distinct grades. RC belief with regard to the graded ministry was put in these words by Vatican Council II: "Christ, whom the Father sanctified and sent into the world (Jn 10.36) has, through his Apostles, made their successors, the bishops, partakers of his consecration and his mission. These in their turn have legitimately handed on to different individuals in the Church various degrees of participation in this ministry. Thus the divinely established ecclesiastical ministry is exercised on different levels by those who from antiquity have been called bishops, priests, and deacons" (Vat II ConstChurch 28). Thus the episcopacy, priesthood, and diaconate are held to be of divine origin, but it is now commonly agreed that the former subdiaconate and minor orders were of ecclesiastical institution. Scripture mentions only bps., priests (presbyters), and deacons. That there was a clear distinction between bps. and priests cannot be gathered simply from the words used in Scripture, but this may be inferred from the contexts in which the terms are used, or from what appears to have been signified in particular instances. Precision of terminology began to appear only in the 2d century. In the 3d cent. Eusebius in his *Ecclesiastical History* mentions other particular offices: subdeacons, acolytes, exorcists, readers, and doorkeepers. It was not until the Middle Ages, however, that there was any settled determination of the number of orders, or of the distinction between major orders (as then recognized, priest, deacon, subdeacon) and minor orders (acolyte, exorcist, lector, doorkeeper). Until Vatican Council II, RC theologians did not agree as to whether the episcopate was an order distinct from the priesthood. The Council's statement that ". . . it devolves on the bishops to admit newly elected members into the episcopal body by means of the sacrament of orders" (*ibid.* 21) appears to have settled that controverted point.

Because holy orders is numbered as one of the seven sacraments held by Catholics to have been instituted by Christ, holy orders is but one sacrament. The manner in which the different orders form only one sacrament is a matter of theological opinion. The view most commonly accepted is the essence, power, and character of this sacrament reside fully in one who has received the highest order, and less fully in those who have received only the lower orders. It was once held by some that the same essence, power, and character, in lesser degree, resided in those who had recieved the subdiaconate and the minor orders. More recent opinion, however, denied true sacramentality to these now obsolete orders. The conferral of the sacrament of holy orders is through a sacred sign. That Christ instituted a specific sign is the more common theological teaching. However, some maintain either that he established only the signification of the sacrament and left it to the Church to determine the material element that would, under a form or formula of words, convey this signification, or that he instituted an indeterminate material element or merely an imposition of hands and left the rest to the determination of the Church. It is most probable that the imposition of hands was always the matter of this sacrament, even by divine institution. Until the 10th cent. the sacrament was conferred only in this manner, but subsequently in the Latin Church the handing over of the instruments of the particular order was considered an essential rite. In 1947 Pius XII declared in the Apostolic Constiution *Sacri ordinis* that thenceforth the episcopacy, priesthood, and diaconate would be conferred in each instance by the one and only essential and valid rite, namely, the designated imposition of hands, the designated form, the consecratory preface. The Apostolic Constitution of Paul VI, *Pontificalis Romani* (June 21, 1968) added to the bishops ordination the consecratory prayer from the *Traditio S. Hippolyti* (3d cent.) and clarified further the meaning of the essential of the three sacred orders. The same document made additions to the ordination of deacons (AAS 60 [1968]: 369–373). Scripture indicates (Acts 6.6, 13.3; 1 Tim 4.14, 5.22; 2 Tim 1.6) bps. alone as minister of sacred orders, and Catholic doctrine holds that the bp. is the ordinary minister by divine right. Common theological opinion today rejects the claim that a simple priest may act as extraordinary minister in the conferring of the priesthood and diaconate. The practice and legislation of the Church permitted in some circumstances, a priest lacking episcopal character to confer minor orders. In view of the ancient practice of the Greek Church it seems probable that a priest could also have been permitted to confer the subdiaconate.

Holy orders is held to imprint an indelible and inadmissible character on those who receive it ". . . shaping sacred ministers to the likeness of Christ the Priest, and enabling them to perform the lawful acts of religion by which men are sanctified and God duly glorified according to the divine ordinance" (Pius XII, *Mediator Dei* 42). It confers the power over the real body of Christ to consecrate, offer, and administer his body and blood, and over his mystical body to prepare the faithful by the sacraments and the preaching of the Word to be fit and worthy for the sacrament of the Eucharist. It is an active power whereby the recipient, according to his order, can accomplish in the name and person of Christ the sacramental rites destined for Christian worship and for the sanctification of the people of God, and by which he is also established a leader of the Christian community in liturgical functions. The grace bestowed by this sacrament is noted by St. Paul (1 Tim 4.14; 2 Tim 1.6–7). This sacramental effect is specified by the purpose of the sacrament. The Council of Florence (*Decree for the Armenians*) speaks of an increase of grace so that one may be a suitable minister, that is, receive the virtues and helps attendant upon the proper and worthy exercise of the order. The form of the ordination of a deacon prays that the Holy Spirit might strengthen the candidate "with the sevenfold gift of grace to carry out faithfully the work of the ministry"; the form for the priesthood asks the Father to "renew within him [the ordinand] the spirit of holiness so that he may hold the office of second rank which he has received from thee, O God, and by the example of his life give a pattern of upright conduct"; the form for episcopal consecration beseeches: "give to thy priest the fullness of thy ministry, and sanctify with the dew of heavenly anointing him who is adorned with the vesture of the highest dignity." In 1967, Pope Paul VI, in the document *Sacrum diaconatus ordinem,* authorized the restoration of the permanent diaconate in the Roman rite, whereby it became possible for men to become deacons permanently without going on to the priesthood. This restoration was approved for the U.S. by the Holy See in 1968. A revision of the orders was begun by the Holy See in 1971. An indult of Oct. 5, 1971, permitted bps. of the U.S. to omit ordaining porters and exorcists, and an indult of Oct. 8, 1971, permitted the use of revised rites for ordaining acolytes and lectors and inaugurated the use of a service celebrating one's dedication to God and the Church in place of the ceremony of tonsure. In 1972 the revision was completed when Paul VI abolished the orders of porter, exorcist, and subdeacon, and decreed that laymen, as well as candidates for the diaconate and priesthood, can be installed (rather than ordained) in the ministries (rather than orders) of acolyte and lector. He reconfirmed the suppression of tonsure and its replacement with the service of dedication to God and the Church and stated that entrance into the clerical state comes with ordination to the diaconate. It is to be noted that there were no obstacles to the Pope's action because the abolished orders had been instituted by the Church for functional purposes and were not considered to be parts of the sacrament of holy orders. In most rites of the Eastern Churches, the subdiaconate is not recognized as a major order, nor is there uniformity among the Eastern Churches in the number and names of the minor orders that are conferred. (For other communions see *ORDERS) BIBLIOGRAPHY: D 1326, 1740, 1764–68, 1774, 1777; CIC c. 949, 951; Leo XIII, *Apostolicae curae,* D 3317; Pius XII, *Sacramentum ordinis,* D 3857–3861; Vat II ConstChurch 18–21, 28–29; E. Doronzo, *De ordine* (3 v. 1957–62); A. Michel, DTC 11.2:1193–1405; A. d'Alès, DAFC 3:1143–62. *ORDERS

In Old Catholic, Eastern, and Anglican teaching there is agreement that diaconate, priesthood, and episcopate are essential orders of ministry in the Church. There are designations of diverse ministries in Acts and in the Epistles of St. Paul (e.g., Acts 11.30, 14.14; 1 Cor 12.28; Eph 4.11; 1 Tim 3.2, 5.17), with mention of bishop, (overseers), presbyters (elders), and deacons. Since the 1550 revision of the Anglican Ordinal made no mention of minor orders, the Anglican Communion does not observe them; in other Churches of a Catholic tradition, there is no uniform practice with regard to minor orders. The term "orders" is not prominent in the purely Protestant traditions. But a distinction and gradation of offices in the ministry of word and sacraments were developed in the Lutheran, *Reformed, and *free church traditions on the basis of their varying concepts of the Church and *ministry.

In the Old Catholic, and Eastern Churches, orders, or holy orders, is numbered among the seven sacraments. The Protestant Churches do not regard orders or the offices of ministry as a sacrament. The Anglican *Thirty-Nine Articles regard orders as one of the five commonly called sacraments but not to be counted a sacrament of the gospel (Art. 25). The sacrament is administered only by a bishop; the essentials of the administration are the *laying on of hands, together with the authorized form of words. Through episcopal administration of orders the line of apostolic succession is maintained by these Churches.

[N. HALLIGAN]

HOLY ORDERS, IMPEDIMENTS TO, see IRREGULARITY.

HOLY PLACES, the sites in Palestine and its environs connected with the life of Christ. Several are associated with Christ's Passion and Resurrection: the Upper Room, the Garden of Gethsemane, the Way of the Cross, Calvary, the Holy Sepulcher, and the site of the Ascension. Others are linked with the public life of Christ: the Jordan River, Sea of Galilee, the site of the Transfiguration, and the Temple at Jerusalem. The places mentioned in the infancy narratives also receive special veneration: the Church of the Annunciation at Nazareth, the Grotto of the Nativity at Bethlehem, and the Church of the Visitation. The place of Mary's Assumption is also venerated, as are many of the lesser known places popularly connected with events described in the Gospels. There can be no general claim concerning the authenticity of these places. The judgment of historians and archeologists must be evaluated for each particular site. The care and custody of most of the holy places has been exercised by the Friars Minor since the 13th cent., although the Eastern Orthodox care for some. Unfortunately, dissent among these two groups, the Greek Armenians, and the Mohammedans, who similarly venerate many sites in Jerusalem, has caused an attitude of mistrust and rancor at many of the holy places. Pope Paul VI has endeavored to secure from the State of Israel guaranteed free access to Jerusalem and the holy places. BIBLIOGRAPHY: D. Baldi, NCE 7:875–889; B. Bagatte, NCE 10:920–921; C. Kapp, *Holy Places of the Gospels* (tr. R. Walls, 1963). *PALESTINE; *JERUSALEM.

[T. M. MCFADDEN]

HOLY REDEEMER, SISTERS OF THE (previously known as Daughters of the Most Holy Redeemer), a religious congregation founded as the Daughters of the Divine Savior in Alsace by Elizabeth Eppinger in 1849 and established as an independent branch in 1866 in Würzburg, Bavaria. Originally committed to nursing the sick poor in their own homes, the sisters later expanded their apostolate to include hospital nursing, teaching, care of the aged, and domestic work in seminaries. The community came to the U.S. in 1924, opening a house in Baltimore, Md. and in 1926 began to serve in Philadelphia where their Dreuding Infirmary and Home for the Aged, and Holy Redeemer Visiting Nurse Agency (organized and placed under certification in 1973) are located. Near Philadelphia in Meadowbrook, Pa., they conduct St. Joseph's Manor for the Aged and Holy Redeemer Hospital. In 1975 the congregation numbered worldwide 1,922 in 201 houses; the general motherhouse is in Würzburg.

[P. NEAL]

HOLY ROLLERS, a derogatory nickname for religious groups whose meetings are characterized by high emotionalism, manifested by physical agitation. In particular, the name has been attached to Pentecostal groups. The name Holy Jumpers has been similarly used. Pentecostals regard the names as offensive, even libelous.

[T. C. O'BRIEN]

HOLY ROMAN EMPIRE, the state founded in A.D. 800 by Charlemagne and Pope Leo III. Theoretically universal, like the old Roman Empire, after 962 when the German kings acquired the title it embraced only German and Italian lands, with occasional feudal suzerainty over other areas. From Frederick I's reign the word "Holy" was added, as were later the words "of the German Nation." It endured until Francis II's resignation in 1806. Because the Empire was considered the secular counterpart of the Holy Roman Church, and because the pope alone could bestow the imperial title, the Empire's history saw frequent conflicts with the papacy over theoretical questions of supremacy or over Italian territory. BIBLIOGRAPHY: G. Barraclough, *Origins of Modern Germany* (1947).

[R. H. SCHMANDT]

HOLY ROOD, ABBEY OF, a former royal monastery of the Canons Regular of St. Augustine, next to Holyrood Palace in Edinburgh, Scotland. The monastery was founded *c.* 1128 by David I of Scotland and was frequently used by the Scottish kings, esp. during the reign of the Stuarts. The monastery fell into ruins in the 16th cent. at the hands of the English and Reformers; was restored by Charles I and James II; sacked again in 1688, and now remains in ruins.

[T. M. MCFADDEN]

HOLY SATURDAY, the day before Easter on which the Church commemorates the stay of Christ's body in the tomb. From the 12th to the mid-20th cent. the *Easter Vigil was celebrated in the Latin Church on the morning of Holy Saturday. The reform of 1951 restored the Vigil to the night intervening between Saturday and Sunday. Although the ceremonies preceding the Mass of the Easter Vigil take place before midnight on the night of Holy Saturday, and sometimes the Mass itself (when the ordinary judges the advancement of the hour of its celebration to be necessary), the Easter Vigil is an Easter Sunday Mass of the Resurrection and does not belong to the day of Holy Saturday.

[N. KOLLAR]

HOLY SEE, term used to designate the residence and the authority of the pope. Originally the word see (Lat. *sedes,* chair) was applied to the five great centers of Antioch, Alexandria, Jerusalem, Constantinople, and Rome. The last named was regarded as the primary see of Christendom. Though in theory and in fact, with several notable exceptions, the pope and curia reside in Rome, it is not necessary that they do so. Wherever the pope and his officials are, technically is the Holy See. Used in reference to the governance of the Church, the term refers to the supreme pontiff, the Sacred College, and the Curia Romana.

[J. R. AHERNE]

HOLY SEPULCHER, BROTHERHOOD OF THE, association of monks in the Orthodox Patriarchate of Jerusalem, influential in its affairs and in charge of Orthodox interests in the Christian shrines of the Holy Land.

[T. C. O'BRIEN]

HOLY SEPULCHER, CHURCH OF THE, basilica in Jerusalem, built according to early Christian tradition, on the site of Christ's Crucifixion, burial, and Resurrection. Though the present church dates only to the 19th cent., it incorporates features from several of the earlier structures, the first and most famous of which was dedicated in 335. Here on Golgotha (or the hill of Calvary), according to the historian Eusebius of Caesarea, the Emperor Constantine constructed his church after first razing the temple to Venus that had stood on the site since 135 A.D. and excavating the rubbish that had accumulated in layers above the tomb. (A variant tradition attributes the discovery of the tomb to Constantine's mother St. Helena, who at the same time was supposed also to have found the true cross.) Whether Christ's Passion took place here or, as some modern scholars believe, elsewhere, the rocky place did contain both a cave tomb and the large stone used to cover its mouth, and it was around these that Constantine placed a pillared rotunda, beyond which stretched the three-aisled basilica in whose S aisle stood the place of Crucifixion. The rock surrounding both sacred spots was hewn away so as to allow them to dominate the building. This structure was burned by the Sassanian Persians in 614, but a new building was completed in 626 under Modestus, abbot of the monastery of Theodosius. In the 10th cent. the Arabs erected a mosque where Constantine's atrium had been, but early in the 11th ordered the destruction of the church. A third foundation, similar in conception to Modestus' plan, was in place by 1050; this the Crusaders, after their conquest of Jerusalem in 1099, replaced by a Romanesque edifice, built on a much larger scale and consecrated in 1149. Once more destroyed (1244) and again rebuilt (1310), the church remained substantially the same until 1808 when, apart from the bell tower, much of the building succumbed to fire. It was last rebuilt in 1810, the dome covering the Holy Sepulcher being added in 1868.

Superficially, there is little about the present site to recall to the pilgrim or tourist its antique associations; the church today is hemmed in by the streets of the city, while the hill on which it was founded is obscured beneath the massive structure, visible only occasionally in its rocky lower depths. Something even of an atmosphere of clutter and busyness is imparted to the church proper by the many chapels and special areas pertaining to each of the Christian sects sharing the shrine and esp. by the simultaneous conduct of their varying rites on Sundays. The religious bodies permitted to hold services in the church include the Greek Orthodox, RC, Armenian, Syrian, Coptic, and Anglican Churches; Protestants are barred from this privilege. Yet for all the sectarian quarrels it has inspired and despite the prodigious damage and alterations it has sustained over the centuries, the church remains the holiest site in Christendom, the final goal of Holy Week celebrations enacted annually in commemoration of the suffering and miracle which lie at the heart of the Christian faith. Here can be seen, in two chapels within the rotunda, the Holy Sepulcher together with the stone rolled away by the angel; and to the E, in the church proper, the site of Calvary, the tomb of Joseph of Arimathea, the tombs of the Crusader kings Baldwin and Godfrey, and the Chapel of St. Helena.

[E. M. GATES]

HOLY SEPULCHER, GUARDIANS OF THE, see COMMISSARIAT OF THE HOLY LAND.

HOLY SEPULCHRE, ORDER OF THE, see ORDER OF THE HOLY SEPULCHRE.

HOLY SHROUD, see SHROUD, HOLY.

HOLY SOULS, according to RC teaching, those who depart this life in the grace of God but who are not yet free from all imperfection. In a state called purgatory, they make expiation for the temporal punishment due to venial and mortal sins that have already been forgiven and, probably, for unforgiven venial sins. In this they can be helped by the intercession of the faithful. The condition of purification they experience is to be considered not only as a purging but also as a recompense for a life faithfully lived. It is a preparation for the completion in heaven of the salvation which they have already substantially achieved. Recent theological speculation about the effects of sin upon the personality has stressed the need for the person to undergo a purifying process by which he is gradually freed from the consequences of sin in order that the richness of the personality can emerge. The emergence of the true self is necessary as a preparation for beatifying union with God which, as a personal love relationship, requires the openness of the whole person to him. BIBLIOGRAPHY: H. J. Cargas and A. White, *Death and Hope* (1970).

[J. CORDOUE]

HOLY SPIRIT, in the mystery of God's inner life, the last of the three Persons in the order of origin; he is also last in the order of revelation. His public manifestation took place at Pentecost, when the glorified Christ, by pouring his Spirit over the Church, ushered in a new era in the history of salvation, the era of the Spirit, or the Church era. The Spirit of God (Heb., *ruah;* Gr. *pneuma*) is well known to the Old Testament. Originally wind, breath of life, the term when applied to Yahweh refers to a divine energy, or power. God gives life through his Spirit (Gen 1.2; Ps 104.29–30); the Spirit of God, at work within men, quickens them and gives them strength and enthusiasm by which they become the powerful instruments of God's saving deeds. Thus the Spirit fell upon Saul (1 Sam 11.6); he took possession of King David (1 Sam 16.13); he opened the minds of the Prophets. Above all, the dawn of the messianic age was to be marked by an outpouring of God's Spirit (Jl 3.1); the Spirit would be for all men the principle of an inward renewal (Ezek 36.26–27). Not unlike the Word, the Spirit of God is spoken of as a Person (Is 40.13). He is not however distinct from Yahweh. Rather, he represents God himself, acting upon men, enlivening them and transforming them from within. When Christ spoke of the Spirit of his Father, the OT presuppositions made the divine character of the Spirit unmistakable. Not so with his personal character. However, Christ explained to his Apostles that the Spirit, sent by him after his glorification, was to continue his own personal action among them. He would be with them and would teach them all truth. Above all, after Christ Himself, he would be for them "another Advocate" (Jn. 14.16). In the light of the Pentecostal experience, the apostolic Church understood that the Spirit too belongs to the sphere of divine personal relationships. The proper character of the Spirit is mysterious, his action hidden and secret. Nevertheless, of the three Divine Persons he it is whose presence directly enlivens the Church. This presence is most intimately experienced by every man living by the divine life. As the common bond of Father and Son, the Spirit is in the order of God's personal relations with men the intimate link, whose indwelling within men guarantees God's personal presence to them. BIBLIOGRAPHY: *Dictionary of Biblical Theology* (ed. X. Leon-Dufour, 1967) 1:500; J. Guillet, *Themes of the Bible* (1960) 225.

[J. DUPUIS]

HOLY SPIRIT, DAUGHTERS OF THE (DHS), a pontifical institute founded in Plerin, Brittany, France in 1706. Renée Burel and Marie Balavenne, under the direction of Jean Ledeuger, founder, sought to provide care for the sick and to educate the youth of the area. The community prospered until the French Revolution, during which its members survived only by living in secrecy. By 1810, the reconstituted community was granted official government recognition; the sisters, because of rapid expansion, moved the motherhouse from Plérin to Saint-Brieuc in 1834. In 1902 and 1903 when the repressive French *Law of Associations led to the expulsion of teaching communities, the sisters made new foundations in Belgium, Holland, England, Canada, and the United States. They also served in Manchuria from 1936 until they were expelled in 1951. They have missions in Canada and S America; the U.S. congregation, with its motherhouse in Putnam, Conn., serves the New England area, Alabama, California, and New York where the 360 members engage in teaching and catechetical work, conduct hospitals, nursing centers, and day nurseries. The general motherhouse remains at Saint-Brieuc, with a worldwide membership of 3,007 sisters (1975).

[M. B. MONAGHAN]

HOLY SPIRIT, FRUITS OF THE. "The fruit of the Spirit is love, joy, peace, patience, kindness, goodness, faithfulness, gentleness, self-control" (Gal 5.22–23). The text contrasts these 12 with the "works of the flesh" (*ibid.* 19) and points to them as the effects of the grace that sanctifies, whereas the law condemned but did not sanctify.

They represent the ways in which grace is manifested in the life of the recipient. St. Thomas Aquinas takes the term fruit as a metaphor, not for the virtues, but for the actions, whether of the virtues or of the *Gifts of the Holy Spirit (see also BEATITUDES) which, by the grace of the Holy Spirit, the just man produces and in which he finds spiritual delight. The enumeration is not exhaustive of all the ways in which the sanctifying presence of the Holy Spirit is manifested, but the fruits as given point to certain salient movements of charity toward the good and away from evil. BIBLIOGRAPHY: ThAq ST 1a2ae, 70 (Lat-Eng, v. 24, ed. E. O'Connor, *Gifts of the Holy Spirit*) 148–150.

[T. C. O'BRIEN]

HOLY SPIRIT, GIFTS OF THE. These endowments are known only through revelation; the classical scriptural reference is Is 11.1–3. The text itself refers to Christ, but in view of Rom 8.29, that all are to be conformed to the image of Christ, it can be concluded that the gifts of the Holy Spirit are also conferred on the just. Although other biblical texts have been cited as a basis for their existence (e.g., Gen 41.38; Ex 31.3; Num 24.2; Dt 34.9; Ps 31.8; 32.9; 118.120; 142.10; Lk 12.12; 24.25; Jn 3.8; 14.17; Acts 2.2; Rom 8.14; Cor 2.10; 12.8), theological and liturgical tradition, taken into the magisterium of the Church, has rested primarily on the text from Isaiah.

Their nature is explained in various ways; St. Thomas Aquinas considers them to be special habits given together with grace and the infused virtues; St. Gregory the Great regards them as perfections of the virtues, Hugh of St. Victor, as seeds of virtue or certain predispositions to virtue; G. Vázquez holds that they are acts or operations but not habits; L. Billot, that they are types of actual grace. However the common view is that they are distinctive habits that accompany sanctifying grace and operate under a particular movement of the Holy Spirit. Unlike the infused virtues, which are supernatural powers whereby we act as principal causes, the gifts are supernatural powers by which we act as instrumental causes in a divine mode; they are therefore not under our total control although their readiness to divine influence renders them meritorious. They are conferred in baptism. For the majority of theologians, their constant operation constitutes the mystical state. They are sevenfold: wisdom, understanding, knowledge, fear, counsel, piety, and fortitude. They produce certain acts that are called the fruits of the *Holy Spirit as well as eminently perfect works that are called *beatitudes. BIBLIOGRAPHY: ThAq ST 1a2ae, 68; John of St. Thomas, *Gifts of the Holy Spirit* (tr. D. Hughes, 1951); A. Gardeil, DTC, 1728–81; L. Lallemant, *Spiritual Doctrine* (1955).

[J. AUMANN]

HOLY SPIRIT MISSIONARY SISTERS (SSPS), a pontifical congregation, officially called the Missionary Sisters Servants of the Holy Spirit; founded in 1889 at Steyl, Holland by Fr. Arnold Janssen, SVD (1837–1909) for the purpose of propagating the faith in less privileged countries of the world. The community is characterized by its zeal for souls and devotion to the Holy Spirit and its members engage primarily in social, educational, and medical work. The sisters made rapid progress and soon their apostolate, under the guidance of the Sacred Congregation for the Evangelization of Peoples, extended into countries of Africa, Asia, and North and South America. In 1901, the first American foundation was established at Techny, Illinois, and later they founded other houses in Arkansas and Mississippi, where the sisters attended to the education of southern blacks, conducted retreat houses, and trained subjects for the foreign missions. The generalate is located in Rome, Italy. In 1975 the community maintained 269 houses and had a total membership of 4,303 sisters. BIBLIOGRAPHY: Heimbucher 2:409–411.

[R. A. TODD]

HOLY SYNOD OF RUSSIA. When Patriarch Adrian of Moscow died in 1700, Czar Peter I would not permit appointment of a successor. In 1721 the patriarchate was abolished and a collegial council or Holy Synod patterned on German Protestant synods was introduced. It was composed of 11 members from various ranks of the clergy, but bps. were in the minority. The Czar appointed the members of the Synod which was presided over by a layman with the title over-procurator (*oberprocuror*). The Revolution of 1917 allowed a new rapport between Church and State and a national council of church leaders met which elected Metropolitan *Tikhon as patriarch of Moscow. Since the restoration of the patriarchate, such synods, under the leadership of the patriarch, are composed of three permanent members: the metropolitans of Leningrad, Kiev, and Moscow; three elected members along with the president of foreign affairs and the bp. in charge of patriarchal affairs. The Synod controls the appointment and removal of bishops. BIBLIOGRAPHY: N. Zernov, *Russians and their Church* (1945).

[T. BIRD]

HOLY THINGS TO THE HOLY, the formula in the Eastern Eucharistic Liturgies *(ta hagia tois hagiais)* and in the Mozarabic *(sancta sanctis)* accompanying the holding of the chalice and host aloft, reminding the faithful of the reverence and freedom from serious sin required of the communicant.

[T. C. O'BRIEN]

HOLY THURSDAY (also called Maundy Thursday, and in Latin*feria quinta in coena domini*), the day on which the Church celebrates the institution of the Eucharist, which it sees inseparably connected with the entire paschal mystery. The Proper texts speak of Christ's redeeming passion, the institution of the Eucharist, obedience on the cross, the washing of the feet, and the paschal mystery. Only one Mass may be celebrated in noncathedral churches on this day; in cathedrals, in addition to the Mass of Holy Thursday, the Mass of the Chrism is celebrated. The Mass of Holy Thursday (now called the Mass of the Lord's Supper) is now normally celebrated in the evening. After the Gospel there is provision for a washing of feet, and after the Mass there is a procession with the Blessed Sacrament to the altar of repose, and the liturgy ends with the stripping of the altars. Holy Thursday was originally a day of preparation for the Easter Vigil. A reconciliation of penitents was held so everyone could participate in the sacred triduum, which then consisted of Friday, Saturday, and Easter Sunday. The chrism was consecrated at the Easter Vigil. The practice of celebrating Mass at the approximate hour of the Last Supper originated in Jerusalem in the 4th century. The washing of feet became a part of the Mass only in the 7th cent; the procession after Mass developed from the custom of putting hosts aside for communion on aliturgical days. Pius XII's reform (1955) restored the simplicity of the early Middle Ages by eliminating many ceremonial accretions and creating a special Mass for the blessing of the chrism. BIBLIOGRAPHY: W. J. O'Shea, *Meaning of Holy Week* (1958); J. G. Davies, *Holy Week: A Short History* (1963); L. Bouyer, *Paschal Mystery: Meditations on the Last Three Days of Holy Week* (1950); A. Lohr, *Great Week* (tr. D. H. Bridgehouse, 1958).

[N. KOLLAR]

HOLY WAR: (1) the second allegory of John Bunyan, the author of **Pilgrim's Progress* in which the City of Mansoul is conquered by the devil and freed by Emanuel; (2) in Islam the *jihad is war fought in the name of God and was important in the early centuries of Muslim conquest.

[F. H. BRIGHAM]

HOLY WATER, water which has been blessed for religious purposes, esp. for use as a sacramental. In Western, although not Eastern, usage the bp. or the priest who blesses and exorcises the water also adds a small quantity of blessed salt to it. The use of holy water, esp. for the frequent blessing of persons and objects, is an ancient custom in the Church. It is attested to as early as the 2d cent. (*Apocryphal Acts of Peter*) and may even be of apostolic origin. The natural symbolism of water as a purifying agent and as necessary to life and abundance led to its liturgical use in blessings, dedications, and exorcisms. Today the use of holy water is seen primarily as a renewal of the baptismal spirit and as an aid to devotion. The custom of taking holy water upon entering a church needs to be seen in the context of this symbolism. BIBLIOGRAPHY: E. J. Gratsch, NCE 14:825–827.

[B. ROSENDALL]

HOLY WEEK, the week immediately prior to Easter, and the central period in the Church's liturgical cycle. The central mystery of Christianity, God's saving action through Christ's Passion and Resurrection, is celebrated in a special way during this week, and its effects are made present to the believing community.

The heart of Holy Week, as well as its original 3d-cent. structure, is found in the 3-day celebration of the Paschal Feast (*Good Friday, *Holy Saturday, *Easter Sunday). Expansion of this observance into the present structure, which spreads the commemoration over a whole week, was begun in the 4th cent. with the addition of *Holy Thursday. The development probably began with the frequent Christian pilgrimages to Jerusalem where the natural desire to reenact the last events of Christ's life in liturgical drama could be carried out. The liturgical ceremonies of Holy Week evidence a number of interesting peculiarities. Since they represent in many cases the preservation of earlier liturgical rites, they manifest a simplicity unknown to later liturgical forms. The intent of these rites is to provide commemoration of and participation in the events of the last days of the life of Christ, or an opportunity to relive the paschal mystery by which Christ reconciled the world to his Father. Each of the events commemorated contributes to the overall liturgical representation of the mystery of Redemption, while at the same time providing a special coloring to the prayers, praise, and adoration of the individual days. Pope Pius XII sought to restore the prominence of Holy Week in the liturgical cycle of the Church by introducing a new *Order for Holy Week* (1956). His immediate concern was to provide for a more active participation of the people in the celebration of the paschal mysteries. The hours of the services were rearranged and many irrelevant features of the rites were eliminated. The English version of revised Holy Week rites went into effect in 1971. They introduced concelebration of Mass, place new emphasis on commemorating the institution of the priesthood on Holy Thursday, and modified Good Friday prayers for other Christians, Jews, and other non-Christians.

[B. ROSENDALL]

HOLY YEAR, a year during which the Holy See grants a solemn plenary indulgence, under the usual conditions, to all those who visit Rome and venerate the tombs of the Apostles Peter and Paul. The practice recalls the pre-Exilic Jewish custom of designating every 50th year as a Jubilee in which debts were remitted and slaves freed (Lev 25.25–54). Pope Boniface VIII sought to transform this ancient practice into a spiritual year of remission, and proclaimed the first Holy Year in 1300. Succeeding popes have continued the practice, and have reduced the interval between Holy Years to 25. Extraordinary circumstances may also occasion the proclamation of a Holy Year outside of this regular interval. The latest Holy Year began on Christmas Day, 1974, and its object as proclaimed by Paul VI was prayer for reconciliation and peace. BIBLIOGRAPHY: J. J. Gavigan, NCE 7:108–109.

[T. M. MCFADDEN]

HOLYHEAD (Welsh, Caer Gybi) **MONASTERY,** founded by St. Cybi in the 6th cent., had a monastic parish with houses in Cornwall, Monmouthshire in Wales, and possibly in Ireland; which eventually took over those of SS. Gwndaf, Cyngar, Peulan, and Caffo. By 1291 Holyhead had become a secular college; and was dissolved *c.*1547. BIBLIOGRAPHY: A. W. Wade-Evans, *Welsh Christian Origins* (1934); J. E. Lloyd, *History of Wales* (2 v., 1948).

[C. MCGRATH]

HOLYWOOD, CHRISTOPHER (1562–1626), superior of the Jesuit mission in Ireland. H. was born in Dublin, studied at Padua, and became a Jesuit in 1579. After teaching theology in France and Italy, he was arrested, imprisoned, and deported. When Elizabeth I died, he returned to Ireland (1604) and was appointed Jesuit superior there. Under his leadership, the mission made substantial progress even during the period of persecution following the imposition of the Oath of Allegiance. He established five active missionary centers, founded a school at Kilkenny, and encouraged the Sodality of the Blessed Virgin to offset the Protestantizing influence of the government. BIBLIOGRAPHY: Sommervogel 4:446–447.

[T. M. MCFADDEN]

HOLZBAUER, IGNAZ (1711–83), Austrian composer. H. became court conductor at Stuttgart in 1750 and in 1753 music director at Mannheim, where he remained for most of his life. A composer mainly of operas and symphonies, he also wrote Masses, motets, and other church music, highly praised by Mozart.

[M. T. LEGGE]

HOLZHAUSER, BARTHOLOMEW (1613–58), Bavarian priest, founder of the Institute of Secular Clergy of Community Life, known as the Bartholomites or the United Brothers. His purpose was to restore and reform church life through the teaching and example of diocesan priests living in small groups at seminaries or in parishes. The members did not take religious vows. The Institute was refused papal approval during H.'s own life but in 1680 received it. It flourished for a century, but then died out; there was a restoration in France in the 19th century. H. also wrote works on the spiritual life for diocesan clergy and for the laity: *Constitutiones et exercitia spiritualia clericorum saecularium in communi viventium; De diversis orandi modis et de modo meditandi; De humilitate; Epistola fundamentalis.*

[T. C. O'BRIEN]

HOME, DANIEL DOUGLAS (1833–86), Scottish born spiritualist and medium, reared in Connecticut. From 1850 he gave many séances in the U.S. and in Europe, often before persons of prominence. He took no money for his demonstrations, though he did accept gifts; he was never detected in fraud. He became a RC in Italy, but this did not prevent his expulsion from the city of Rome as a sorcerer. BIBLIOGRAPHY: J. Burton, *Heyday of a Wizard* (1944).

[M. J. SUELZER]

HOMER, epic poet of the *Iliad* and *Odyssey*. Though both works bear distinct marks of oral composition over a period of time, the guiding hand of a creative poet is equally in evidence. Committed to writing *c.*700 B.C., the poems preserve several layers of early traditions which provide indispensable information about pre-Homeric Greek culture. Throughout late Antiquity, the myths and characters of the Homeric poems dominated Greek thought. Stoics, Pythagoreans, and other philosophical schools developed distinctive styles of interpreting H. according to their own tenets. Both Christian writers and their opponents noticed the similarities between certain biblical narratives and Homeric myths; and Christians typically dealt with the resemblance by asserting H.'s dependence upon the Bible. Christian apologists also frequently assailed the immorality of the anthropomorphic Homeric deities. BIBLIOGRAPHY: G. S. Kirk, *Homer and the Epic* (1965); A. Lord, *Singer of Tales* (1960); F. Buffière, *Les mythes d'Homère et la pensée grecque* (1956); J. Daniélou, *Gospel Message and Hellenistic Culture* (tr. and ed. J. A. Baker, 1973) 75–105.

[E. V. GALLAGHER]

HOMICIDE, the unjust and intended killing of another human being. This gravest of sins against *justice is the act proscribed by the fifth commandment of the Decalogue. To qualify the act as "unjust killing" is to set homicide apart from the taking of life by one resisting an unjust aggressor (see SELF-DEFENSE), or by a combatant in a just *war (whether modern warfare and nuclear bombing can ever be justified is a moot point in current theology), or by one exercising public authority in inflicting *capital punishment. As "intended," homicide must be a morally complete exercise of choice. Civil law on this point makes distinctions between first and second degree murder, as well as between the crimes of murder and of manslaughter, voluntary or involuntary. The moral norms affecting the issue of intent are as follows. When the death of another results from a morally good action as a complete accident there is no homicide. Where the death of another is foreseeable, but is an unintended side effect of a good act there is no homicide; the principle of *double effect is applicable (e.g., a refusal in the name of the common good to accede to the demands of terrorists when that leads to their executing their hostages). Where the death of another is the result of *negligence, even where a person is performing a good action, the negligence means the incurrence of a proportionate degree of guilt. Where the death of another ensues upon his act, a malefactor or criminal is guilty of that death. In all cases, however, where the intent is not direct, culpability is lessened. BIBLIOGRAPHY: ThAq ST 2a2ae, 64.2,3, 6,8.

[T. C. O'BRIEN]

HOMILETICS, the general title in common use since the 17th cent. to denote the theory of preaching. According to Vat II SacLit (35), the homily is part of the liturgical service and "should draw its contents mainly from scriptural and liturgical sources, and its character should be that of a proclamation of God's wonderful works in the history of salvation, the mystery of Christ, ever made present and active within us, esp. in the celebration of the liturgy." The post-conciliar *Instructions on the Liturgy* (1964) adds "by a homily from the sacred text is understood an explanation either of some aspect of the readings from Holy Scripture or of another text from the Ordinary or Proper of the Mass of the day, taking into account the mystery which is being celebrated and the particular needs of the hearers" (54). The homily serves as a bridge between the mystery proclaimed in the sacred readings and the mystery celebrated in the liturgical action of ritual and word. It expounds the mysteries of the faith and the guiding principles of the Christian life during the course of the liturgical year (Vat II SacLit 52).

Generally speaking, a homily should involve the proclamation of one of the themes of God's redemptive love found in the readings. It should attempt to arouse a faith response on the part of the liturgical assembly, and establish a relationship with their everyday world. Finally, as a link with the subsequent liturgical action, the unity between word and sacrament should be highlighted. A more fruitful liturgical participation is thereby encouraged through the prolongation, amplification, and adaptation of the liturgy of the word.

Early Christian homilies were more exhortative than exegetical and were part of the liturgical service. By the beginning of thr 3d cent., homilies were no longer reserved to bps., priests, or even laymen in some places, engaged in preaching. It appears that Origen was the first to distinguish a homily from a *sermon, the latter involving the classical style of oration; but the great patristic homilies in the East and West were more than mere commentaries on Scripture. They usually involved both an explanation and application of a sacred text, but sometimes centered on the great feasts of the church year. A period of spiritually oriented homilies emerged with the growth of medieval monasticism. By the 9th cent. there were collections of homilies and sermons in use, and preachers began to translate their message into the vernacular.

The *mendicant orders introduced a new style of preaching into the life of the Church. Pious discourses developed independently of the liturgical action and talks outside the church in the public square became common. Scholastic preachers tended, on the other hand, to introduce the style and logic of the classroom into the homily or liturgical discourse.

The Reformation insistence on the genesis of faith through the preached word placed great emphasis on the preaching office. For many Protestants, the sermon was of divine command and, if it in fact served the gospel, became the principal means whereby salvation was made possible for the individual.

The Council of Trent reemphasized the necessity for the Sunday sermon in which bps. and priests were to instruct the people in the things necessary for salvation. Penalties were established for those who neglected this duty. In the 19th cent., the Third Council of Baltimore prescribed that the essential themes of faith and morals be explained over a period of a year or two, with the Roman Catechism as a guide. Five minute sermons on Sundays and feastdays were legislated. In the Code of Canon Law (1917) a number of canons stress the necessity for sermons on Sundays and feastdays (CIC cc. 1344, 1345, 1347). Homilies were emphasized also by the *Instruction on the Liturgy* of the post-conciliar liturgical Consilium. Homilies are to be delivered on Sundays and major feasts, and at other weekday and seasonal times whenever fitting. Generally speaking, they are both exegetical and thematic. Involved in the whole liturgical renewal is an emphasis on the homily during the administration of sacraments and during paraliturgies or Bible services. Dialogue homilies have also enjoyed increasing popularity. BIBLIOGRAPHY: *Sunday Homily* (ed., J. Burke, 1966); R. Fuller, *What is Liturgical Preaching* (1957); D. Grasso, *Proclaiming God's Message: A Study in the Theology of Preaching* (1965); *Recent Homiletic Thought: A Bibliography 1935–65* (ed. W. Toohey and W. Thompson, 1967). *PREACHING, *SERMON.

[W. J. TOBIN]

HOMILY from a Greek word meaning familiar conversation, applied in early Christianity to the explanation of Sacred Scripture preached at liturgical services. Jews had observed a similar practice in the synagogue, after reading the sacred writings. Jesus himself is reported as having done this in the synagogue at Nazareth (Lk 4.16–20), and the Apostles adopted the custom at the gatherings for the "breaking of the bread" (Acts 2.42). First directly referred to by St. Justin Martyr (d. *c.*165), the homily became the accepted type of preaching in the Church by the end of the 2d century. It was a deliberately artless form of discourse which explained one or more of the texts used in the Mass with some application of their lessons to the daily life of the hearers. The homilist was ordinarily the celebrant of the liturgy, in most cases the local bishop. Slowly, against the resistance of those who felt it desecration to mix the gospel with purely human rhetoric, the principles of the art of persuasion began to enter in. With Origen (d. 153), a decided development took place through the widespread influence of his teaching on the spiritual interpretation of Sacred Scripture. His numerous homilies, which illustrated the Alexandrian view that there were multiple meanings under the literal sense, made his interpretations well known. Following him, the use of allegory in commenting on the Scriptures grew common in the 3d century. Then in the 4th and 5th cent. the great preachers began to depart from the verse-by-verse explanation to use the thematic sermon which centered on the explanation of a doctrine or an event, rather than on a passage from the Bible. St. Augustine (d. 430) gave the homily new vogue but added to the simple explanation used by earlier homilists all his art of persuasion. His numerous homilies and those of other Fathers served the preachers of the Middle Ages, when most preaching consisted of either paraphrase or outright repetition of patristic homilies. The later Middle Ages saw a wide development of literature on preaching which has continued to the present day, and the term homily became practically synonymous with any kind of preaching esp. preaching within the Mass. Vatican Council II gave a new focus to the concept of the homily by insisting on its importance as a integral part of the liturgy and by returning to the ancient emphasis on its scriptural foundation: "It is from Scripture that lessons are read and explained in the homily" (Vat II SacLit 24). "The sermon is part of the liturgical service" and "should draw its content mainly from scriptural and liturgical sources . . . its character should be that of a proclamation of God's wonderful works in the history of salvation, that is the mystery of Chirst (35). BIBLIOGRAPHY: O. Semmelroth, *Preaching Word: On the Theology of Proclamation* (tr. J. J. Hughes, 1965); D. Grasso, *Proclaiming God's Message* (1965).

[P. F. MULHERN]

HOMINES INTELLIGENTIAE, (Williamites), a mystic sect that flourished in Brussels *c.* 1411. When the bp. of Cambria set out to investigate the Brethren of the Free Spirit, and particularly that facet called "Bloemmardine's heresy," the examiners discovered a man named William of Hildernissen, of noble birth, a successful lecturer in theology, and twice prior of a friary. Upon questioning him, they turned up a secret community calling itself the *homines intelligentiae;* they chose the word *intelligentia* because in the popular medieval mysticism that was the highest faculty of the soul which made mystical ecstasy possible. The community had its origin in the revelation experienced by Aegidius de Leeuive or Sanghers (Latin, Cantor), a layman from a prominent Flemish family, who was already dead at the time of the mentioned investigation. This group also included a number of women, probably of the Beguines sect. The extent and nature of William's complicity was never clear, so he was sentenced only to some years of penance and seclusion. BIBLIOGRAPHY: "Errores sectae hominum intelligentiae," in E. Baluze, *Miscellanea,* (4 v., 1678–83) 2:277–297; J. J. Altmeyer, *Les précurseurs de la Réforme aux Pays-Bas* (1886) 82–83.

[N. F. GAUGHAN]

HOMINIZATION , Teilhard de Chardin's description of the process within evolution by which primitive world stuff gradually became a species capable of self-reflective consciousness. The human being as an organized center of consciousness knows that he knows. This capability sets him apart from all other elements of organized matter. Man can turn back upon his consciousness and in so doing leap to new levels of conscious organization. Presently man represents the most intensely organized conscious element of living matter. The total species of man has become hominized and with hominization of matter the personalization of the individual begins. BIBLIOGRAPHY: Teilhard de Chardin, *Phenomenon of Man* (1959); *idem, Future of Man* (1964).

[W. J. DUGGAN]

HŌMNÎKŌ (*hemnîkō*), a Syriac word used (1) by Syrian Catholics for the sacerdotal *ûrōrō*; (2) by Jacobites for the episcopal *ûrōrō rabbō*.

[A. CODY]

HOMOBONUS, ST. (d. 1197), Italian merchant. H. was noted for his deep spirituality and his charity to the poor. The letter in which Innocent III declared him a saint (1199) is of great historical interest because of the details it furnishes about the process (see PL 214:483–485). H. is patron of the merchants and tailors of N Italy. BIBLIOGRAPHY: G. D. Gordini, BiblSanct 9:1173–75; Butler 4:334–335.

[M. J. SUELZER]

HOMOEANS, post-Nicene Arians, their leader, *Acacius of Caesarea, who proposed the term *homoios* as a catch-all term, meaning vaguely that the Son is like the Father, but suppressing the force of the Nicene or the anti-Nicene *homoousios.* *ARIANISM; *NICAEA I, COUNCIL OF.

[T. C. O'BRIEN]

HOMOIOUSIOS, the term adopted by one Arian faction in the 4th cent. to designate the Trinitarian relationship between Father and Son. The word is a Greek compound adjective derived from *homoios* (like or similar to) and *ousia* (essence or substance). Despite the fact that the Council of Nicaea (325) had declared that the Son was *homoousios,* i.e., consubstantial or of one nature with the Father, there were many bps. in the East who were not satisfied with that term. The difficulty was one of interpretation. Since many Eastern bps. would have understood *ousia* to mean person, the Nicene definition would have been for them a denial of the distinct personality of Father and Son. At the synods of Ancyra and Sirmium (358), the true Semi-Arians, who denied the equality of the Son with the Father, were able to prevail upon the scruples of the more orthodox bps. who were mindful of the interpretative difficulties connected with *homoousios.* These synods taught, therefore, that "the Son is of like substance (*homoiousios*) with the Father." Though the majority of these Homoiousians were probably orthodox in their belief in the divinity of the Son, many of them later became Macedonians and denied the divinity of the Holy Spirit. *ARIANISM.

[T. M. MCFADDEN]

HOMOOUSIOS, a compound Greek adjective derived from *homos* (one, joint, common) and *ousia* (essence or substance). It was used by the Gnostics in the sense "of the same kind of material as" in expounding their theory of emanations, and by the Christians of Alexandria in the sense "of one substance with" in their explanation of the generation of the Son from the Father. Its use by *Paul of Samosata was, however, condemned by a synod of Antioch in 267, probably because he understood it in a Modalistic sense that would have denied a real distinction of persons in the Trinity. The Council of Nicaea used the term in 325 to define the consubstantiality, and hence equality, of the Son with the Father, a doctrine that had been denied by Arius. Despite some scruples about the use of the term on the part of many Eastern bps., who preferred **homoiousios*, the former became "the rampart and wall of orthodoxy" (Marius Victorinus) and "the bond of faith" (St. Epiphanius). BIBLIOGRAPHY: A. Grillmeier, LTK 5:467–468.

[M. J. COSTELLOE]

HOMOSEXUALITY. The term *homosexuality* is used in so many different senses by different authors that it is necessary to describe how the term is used here. The more recent employment of the term "gay" has tended to confuse the public concerning the meaning of homosexuality. As Barnhouses notes, literally, "homosexual" means having sexual proclivities toward those of the same sex as oneself, while *homosexuality* refers to an *adult* adaptation characterized by *preferential* sexual behavior between members of the same sex. The emphasis on *adult* is extremely important. "Much of today's rhetoric does not allow for the fact that adolescence is often accompanied by a period of transitional anxiety or confusion about sexual identity. . . . To lump discussion of homosexual phenomena in teenagers with those occurring in adults is such an inappropriate confusion of disparate categories as to render meaningful discourse virtually impossible." (Barnhouse, 21–22).

Homosexuality is said to be either an "obligatory" or a temporary (facultative, situational) condition. It is doubtful that one can be classified as an obligatory homosexual until the mid-20s. Often a person inclined during adolescence and early adulthood to homosexuality, at least in phantasy if not in overt activity, experiences a change in his sexual orientation in the mid-20s. Likewise many individuals of both sexes indulge in homosexual activity because they have no opportunity for social contact with persons of the opposite sex (as in prisons, military life, and boarding schools). Even with the help of therapy, however, many find they cannot change their basic drive to psychological and physical intimacy with persons of their own sex. No scientific information yet available holds out the hope that the condition of persons of this latter type is not permanent and irreversible. Although many can and do control their inclinations, which are in themselves no more vehement than those of the heterosexual, they have to face the fact that they cannot alter the direction of their drive.

Homosexuality is still regarded by many psychiatrists as a neurosis originating in very early childhood and involving a variety of psychogenic factors. The most important of these is the lack of the right kind of relationships with the parents or their surrogates, in consequence of which the homosexual is unable to identify with members of his own sex. While the hostility of society, experienced perhaps by the homosexual before he recognizes the fact that he is an invert, aggravates the neurotic condition, the principal source of disturbance remains the individual's inability to accept himself.

The bulk of scientific knowledge of the etiology and dynamics of homosexuality derives from the study of the male homosexual. Attempts to apply this research to a female homosexual (lesbian) are questionable because she differs from the male in many respects. She can keep her anomaly secret more easily because she can live with a female partner with little fear of detection; her manifestations of affection are less likely to be recognized as deviant; she is less prone than man to stress the physical and unambiguous extreme in her expression of love. She can establish a more lasting relationship with another woman because she is given more opportunity and security than the male homosexual has with another man. She is less alienated from heterosexual society than the male, whose degree of neurosis often seems deeper.

Like male inverts, female homosexuals differ so widely in appearance and character that it is not possible to identify them. There are no consistent anatomical or hormonal differences between the homosexual and heterosexual members of either sex. Homosexuals differ from one another in personality traits as much as heterosexuals.

Some homosexuals claim that it is as natural to be homosexual as it is to be left-handed. But when questioned whether they would want their children to be homosexual, inverts usually reply in the negative. A person does not choose to be homosexual; he discovers that he is during a period in life when it is often too late to do more than to learn to control the impulses.

Like heterosexuals, homosexuals vary greatly in their degree of freedom to control sexual impulses. Some achieve a high degree of mastery; others appear as compulsive as alcoholics. Compulsive impulses are found more often in the male than in the female, to judge by the squalid circumstances, often coupled with great risk, in which some male homosexuals meet. Unless he has professional guidance to help him toward self-knowledge and self-control, the plight of the compulsive homosexual is almost hopeless.

At the present psychiatric opinion remains pessimistic about the probability of redirecting a homosexual's sexual orientation. Group therapy, however, has enjoyed some success in helping homosexuals progress to an exclusively heterosexual pattern of adjustment. Through group dynamics the invert often comes to see that his preschool inability to form effective peer relationships was a contributing factor in his deviation. Significantly, in group therapy homosexuals often drop their defenses and abandon the arguments proposed by homophile associations in favor of overt homosexuality.

In determining the morality of homosexuality, one must distinguish between the condition itself and the overt acts in which the homosexual may engage. The condition itself is not properly an object of moral judgment, since one cannot help being a homosexual.

It is the teaching of the Church, rooted in Holy Scripture and in human reason, that homosexual actions are immoral. The argument from Holy Scripture is based upon two related considerations. (1) Genital sexual expression between a man and a woman should take place only in marriage, as marriage is a permanent, exclusive, procreative, and loving union. (2) Besides the argument from biblical teaching on marriage there are at least five clear references to male homosexual actions, and one to female which have been understood throughout the tradition of the Church as condemnatory of homosexual activity (male homosexuality: Lev 18.22; 20.13; Rom 1.27; 1 Cor 6.9–10; 1 Tim 1.9–10; female: Rom 1.26–27). The question, however, is not one of isolated interpretations of specific biblical passages, but a massive unified understanding of the Scriptures in the Church as disapproving of homosexual actions.

The first argument is reaffirmed by Vatican Council II, which draws upon the Scriptures of both Testaments to show that the man-woman relationship in marriage is the norm of genital sexual expression (Vat II ChModWorld 48–52). The Genesis accounts (1.27–28; 2.23–24) are both an ideal and norm of sexual behavior and the sexual behavior is heterosexual. Matthew's reference to this norm (Mt 19.1–9) strengthens the argument that Genesis teaches a heterosexual norm of morality in permanent marriage. This man-woman relationship is stressed from Genesis to Ephesians (5.21–33). Significantly, nowhere in Holy Scripture is the homosexual *person* condemned, but always the action is condemned. Nowhere is there any approval of homosexual unions, but the heterosexual union of man and wife is confirmed as a perennial principle. Efforts to reinterpret biblical references to homosexuality in such a way as to infer that the contexts are not treating the immorality of homosexual action are really forms of special pleading. They lack scholarly documentation.

In addition to the argument from Holy Scripture and tradition there are cogent considerations on the level of human reason. Just as masturbation is a failure of proper self-integration of genital activity into the good of the whole person, so, likewise, in their physical manifestations, homosexual acts share in precisely the same privation as masturbation. There is the same dualistic separation of enjoying subject and body-object, albeit the body of another. Yet homosexual activity involves something beyond mutual masturbation. One person attempts to communicate with another. The difficulty in this endeavor, however, is that the two individuals do not have a common substantive good to serve, as do two married persons who have a common transcendent purpose (union and procreation) fostered by the very act of intercourse. In homosexual relations, moreover, there is a lack of real unity. The lack of bodily coadaptation mirrors the lack of a truly unifying good for the action. In short, homosexual actions have built-in frustration. It is not only the inability to have a physical union, but also a lack of psychological complementarity. Homosexuals are denied so many of the spiritual and emotional rewards available to the man and woman who enter into a long term relationship. The enriching otherness of the other sex is tragically absent, and so the relationship fails to be totally human.

Finally, there are arguments of a more traditional kind against homosexual activity which have a limited persuasive value. Insofar as homosexual acts by their very nature do exclude all possibility of the procreation of life, they do not fulfill an essential purpose of human sexuality. *The Declaration on Certain Questions Concerning Sexual Ethics* says that "according to the objective moral order homosexual relations are acts which lack an essential and indispensable finality" (8).

Frequently, the attempt is made to justify homosexual acts between persons who insist they have no other outlet through which to express their love. Unions between such persons, if they are faithful to one another, are even claimed to be a kind of marriage, legitimate for those who have no other means of fulfillment. This view of homosexual "marriage," however, can appeal only to those whose minds are closed to the arguments of reason and faith mentioned above, and who choose, moreover, to ignore the psychiatric evidence that the homosexual is the victim of a deep-seated neurotic disorder, and his counterfeit "marriage" with another of his kind tends to truncate whatever potential each person has for authentic growth. It should be stressed, however, that the homosexual person is not responsible for his condition, but for the control of his tendencies. His responsibility to control his desires is in proportion to the *degree* of freedom he possesses. Where the homosexual tendency has become a compulsion, very special guidance is necessary to help the person regain the freedom necessary for true responsibility.

Many personal and fulfilling relationships of a legitimate kind remain open to the homosexual. A teenager or a young adult who is troubled by homosexual tendencies should seek some form of therapy. The probability of a successful redirection of the sexual drive is greater if this is attempted at an early age. An older person who can afford therapy may also find it helpful; at least he stands to gain insights into other aspects of his personality and this may help him to understand his deviant tendencies better and to cope with them more successfully. If he accepts the probability that it is too late to change the established direction of his sexual inclination, he will come to see the importance of looking for other ways of becoming a more complete person. He is capable of opening himself to deep communion with God. He is capable of dedicated service to the poor or to the other works of Christian charity. The suffering and frustration he has endured as the result of his condition will make him more empathetic with other suffering individuals and particularly with other homosexuals who remain in alienation from society. Undeniably, his way of life is lonely, but he can give it Christian meaning as many have done. He needs spiritual guidance from experienced Christian psychologists and theologians; he needs an ascetic plan of life; he needs inspiration that will help him give himself to others in actual works of charity. Through openness to God, who communicates to him through revelation, he can come to see that he is loved by God and so must love himself and others in response to God. In this way many homosexuals have found fulfillment in a profound sublimation of their deviant inclinations. Space does not permit a summary of theological opinions on the morality of homosexuality, but the bibliography will bring the reader up to date on the controversies concerning both the morality and psychology of homosexuality. Through all the current confusion the Church continues to hold that homosexual actions are immoral, but the homosexual person must be shown respect and affection. His civil rights to housing and employment must be supported, except in the area of teaching the young, where the rights of parents not to have an *overt* homosexual as a model for their children take precedence. BIBLIOGRAPHY: D. S. Bailey, *Homosexuality and the Western Christian Tradition* (1955); R. T. Barnhouse, *Homosexuality: A Symbolic Confusion* (1977); J. R. Cavanagh, *Counseling the Homosexual* (1977), updating of author's *Counseling the Invert* (1966); Congregation for the Doctrine of the Faith, *Declaration on Certain Questions Concerning Sexual Ethics* (USCC Publ., Washington, D.C., 1977); C. E. Curran, "Dialogue with the Homophile Community: the Morality of Homosexuality," *Catholic Theology in Dialogue* (1972) 184–219; A. Guidon, *Sexual Language* (1976) 299–377; J. F. Harvey, "Homosexuality and Marriage," HPR 5 (1961) 227–234; *idem,* "Morality and Pastoral Treatment of Homosexuality," *Continuum* (Summer 1967) 279–297; *idem,* "The Controversy Concerning the Psychology and Morality of Homosexuality," AER 167 (1973) 602–629; *idem,* "Female Homosexuality," *Linacre Quarterly* 36 (1969) 100–106; *idem,* "Homosexual Marriages," *Marriage and Family Living* (Jan 1974) 18–23; *idem,* "Changes in Nomenclature and Their Probable Effect," *Counseling the Homosexual* (by J. R. Cavanagh, 1977) 30–36; *idem,* "Contemporary Theological Views," in *ibid.* 222–238; *idem,* "Chastity and the Homosexual," *The Priest* (July-Aug. 1977) 10–16; A. Karlen, *Sexuality and Homosexuality: A New View* (1971); J. J. McNeill, *The Church and the Homosexual* (1976); National Conference of Catholic Bishops, "Principles to Guide Confessors in Questions of Homosexuality" (NCCB, Washington, D.C., 1973); R. Shinn, "Homosexuality: Christian Conviction and Inquiry," *The Same Sex* (ed. R. W. Weltge, 1969) 43–54.

[J. F. HARVEY]

HOMUNCIONITAE (Melitonii), those teaching that it is the body, not the soul, that makes man the image of God. In his attempt to match a list of heresies to a list of heresiarchs, Filaster probably invented a sect professing such a teaching (*Haer.* 97); Augustine (*Haer.* 76) repeats him. The name Homuncionitae (Lat., *homunculus,* diminutive of *homo,* man) comes from **Praedestinatus* (76); Danaeus, in his edition (1576) of Augustine's *De haeresibus* (PL 12:1209) calls them Melitonii. BIBLIOGRAPHY: G. Bardy, "Le *De haeresibus* et ses sources," *Miscellanea Agostiniana* (1931) 397–416.

[L. G. MÜLLER]

HONDURAS, a Central American republic, situated E of Guatemala and NW of Nicaragua (43,227 sq mi; pop [est. 1971] 2,839,000, ethnic distribution, 91% mestizo, 6% Indian, 2% Negro, 1% white; illiteracy rate, 55%). Columbus on his fourth voyage (1502) reached the coast of Honduras. Settlement began (1524) under Cristóbal de Olid but proceeded slowly because of resistance by the Indians. In 1539 the territory was put under the captaincy general of Guatemala. In 1821 it declared its independence of Spain and became part of Iturbide's brief Mexican Empire (1821–23). From 1823 it was associated with its neighbors in the Central American Federation until that union collapsed in 1838 and Honduras declared itself an independent republic. It joined with El Salvador and Nicaragua in a loose confederation that lasted from 1848 until 1863. The history of the republic has been marked by a bitter conflict between conservatives and liberals. The country was evangelized by Franciscan missionaries. In 1531 Trujillo became its first episcopal see. In 1631 several priests were martyred by the Indians. At the beginning of the 19th cent. there were 145 churches and Christian life was relatively flourishing, but the Church suffered greatly until the country was separated from Spain. From 1819 until 1840 the episcopal see was without an incumbent. There began in 1880 a systematic curtailment of the rights and privileges of the Church, which was disestablished and its properties were expropriated. Religious instruction in schools was prohibited, and subsidies for the support of the clergy were withdrawn. Not until the Constitution of 1957 was there a notable improvement in this situation. The prohibition of religious instruction was rescinded, and private educational institutions were granted subsidies by the government. Divorce is permitted, and only civil marriage is recognized by the State. The general disorganization of family life is evident in the high illegitimacy rate (55%). The metropolitan see has been located in Tegucigalpa since 1916. It has four suffragans: Santa Rosa de Copán (1916), San Pedro Sula (1963), Comayagua (1963), and a prelature *nullius,* Immaculada Concepción de la B.V.M. en Olancha (1949). There is a great shortage of priests who number only 249. Of those no more than 66 are diocesan and only half of them are native Hondurans. In recent times the activity of clergy, brothers, and sisters of various orders and missionary societies has helped much with the first difficult steps toward a revitalization of Catholic life. Protestant denominations have been active in the country, esp. in San Pedro de

Sula. The total Protestant community numbers about 36,000, with more than 200 ministers and pastors.

[P. DAMBORIENA]

HONEGGER, ARTHUR (1892–1955), composer, born in France of Swiss parentage. H. studied at the Conservatories of Zurich and Paris. In Paris he began to become known as a composer and was one of the group called "Les Six." He was a prolific composer in many genres: operas, ballets, incidental radio and film music, choral, orchestral, chamber, and solo music, songs. Of his religious music, the more important compositions are *Le Roi David,* a sort of concert opera or dramatic oratorio based on the play of René Morax; *Judith,* a biblical opera; and *Jeanne d'Arc au bûcher,* another dramatic oratorio, based on a text of Paul Claudel.

[M. T. LEGGE]

HONESTY, a term now popularly identified with the uprightness of character of one disinclined to lie, steal, cheat, defraud, or deceive another. It had a wider meaning in the ethics of Aristotle, the Stoics, and the schoolmen. With them it stands for the general comeliness, the beauty, or decorum of virtue, and is connected with the division between goods that are valuable in themselves (*honesta*) and those that are merely means to something else (*utilia*), and developed from the rather prim and civic conceptions of esteem in the classical world into the more gallant notions of chivalry. Since then it has rather dulled again into respectability. Moral theologians in the scholastic tradition connect it particularly with the cardinal virtue of temperance, esp. in sexuality, because of its characteristic qualities of candor, delicacy, and fineness of temper. Hence the now archaic use of "honesty" for "chastity." BIBLIOGRAPHY: ThAq ST 2a2ae, 145 (esp. in ed. Lat-Eng, v. 43, ed. T. Gilby).

[T. GILBY]

HONG KONG, British crown colony in SE Asia (398 sq mi; pop. [1970 est.] 4.1 million). A free port and trade center, it is made up of an island ceded to Great Britain by China in 1842 and of land leased in 1898. The inhabitants are mainly Chinese. Cantonese and English are the official languages. Hong Kong became a prefecture apostolic in 1841. In 1846 it was entrusted to the Paris Foreign Mission Society but was taken over in 1867 by the Pontifical Institute for Foreign Missions. The diocese of Hong Kong was created in 1946, suffragan to Canton. Because of the influx of refugees from Communist China in 1949, the Catholic population has almost doubled. Conversions are also numerous. Catholics in 1976 numbered 265,806. Hong Kong became an Anglican diocese in 1848. More than 50 Protestant mission groups are stationed there at present. The most prominent are Anglicans, Methodists, Lutherans, the Church of Christ in China, Elim Church, the Oriental Missionary Society, the Southern Baptist Convention, Evangelicals, and the United Presbyterian Church. BIBLIOGRAPHY: A. Lazzarotto, *Catholic Hong Kong* (1958); *Bilan du Monde* 2:448–452.

[P. DAMBORIENA]

HONNECOURT, VILLARD DE, see VILLARD DE HONNECOURT.

HONOR, a somewhat ambiguous term in moral theology, blended from three sources, the ethical teachings of Aristotle and the Latin Stoics, and the customs of knighthood. Aristotle's essentially social morality treats honor as the proper tribute to be accorded to virtue, and an element that rightly enters into the calculations of the good life, so long as it is not made an end in itself. Properly speaking honor is in the one who shows it, not in him who receives it; but in both respects it is to be controlled by virtue. In the first, by the just distribution of rewards (distributive justice) and by respect for merit (observance, Lat. *observantia*); in the second, by a loftiness of spirit (*magnanimitas*), which is part of courage. The Stoics, no less civic-minded but with an ideal of passionless virtue, saw it as being uplifted above all animal and therefore shameful motions. Cicero identifies being virtuous and being honorable (*honestum*), and this again with being beautiful (*decorum*) because of the light of reason which shines clearly in what is virtuous but shows only murkily where fears and lusts prevail. Though not subscribing to their premises, St. Thomas Aquinas embodies much of their conclusions, though he relegates feelings of honor, like sensitiveness to shame (*verecundia*) to the condition of components (*partes integrales*) of the virtue of temperance. Finally, the early Middle Ages went to school with the Stoics, and their influence continued into the tradition of chivalry and courtesy, particularly in the field of Mars and the court of Venus, and still persisted in later codes of conduct prescribed for members of a caste, sometimes deviously, as in the case of dueling, and in defiance of common morality. BIBLIOGRAPHY: ThAq ST (Lat-Eng v. 23, ed. A. Ross and P. G. Walsh; v. 43, ed. T. Gilby).

[T. GILBY]

HONORATUS OF AMIENS, ST. (d. *c.*600), bishop. All that can be taken as historically valid from an 11th-cent. biography is that he was born and died (6th cent.) in the diocese of Amiens. Miraculous cures that occasioned the elevation of his body (1060) gave momentum to his cult. In 1204 a Paris church was put under his patronage and the following year, the charterhouse at Abbeville. Today the *faubourg* and Rue Saint-Honoré in Paris perpetuate his name. BIBLIOGRAPHY: H. Platelle, BiblSanct 9:1201–02; Butler 2:330.

[G. M. COOK]

HONORATUS OF ARLES, ST. (*c.*350–*c.*430), monk and bishop. Born of a consular family, H. became a Christian and received baptism in early manhood. With his brother Venantius he embraced monasticism and *c.*410 founded the famous monastery of Lérins. Reluctantly ordained to the priesthood, he became bp. of Arles probably late in 427 or early in 428. None of his writings are extant. Under the influence of H., *Hilary of Arles, became a monk at Lérins, delivered the sermon at the saint's burial, and succeeded him as bishop. BIBLIOGRAPHY: G. Mathon, BiblSanct 9:1202–03; É. Griffe, *La Gaule chrétienne* (2d ed., 1966) 2:241–245.

[H. DRESSLER]

HONORATUS OF MARSEILLES (d. after 496), bishop. Little is known of him, but that he associated with the group of theologians who made SE Gaul a vital center of Catholic thought and asceticism in the 5th and 6th centuries. *Hilary or Arles esp. influenced H., who composed a biography of his mentor as an expression of his esteem. It is not known when H. became bp., but he held the See of Marseilles during the pontificate of Pope Gelasius I (492–496), who is known to have entertained reservations about H.'s orthodoxy. These were removed when he sent Gelasius a personal profession of faith.

[R. H. SCHMANDT]

HONORIUS I (d. 638), **POPE** from 625. Of his early life nothing is known except that he was of noble birth and from the Campagna. As pope he was active in many matters. He took an interest in the Church in Britain, conferring the pallium on Honorius of Canterbury and Paulinus of York and sending St. *Birinus to preach in Wessex. He also sought to induce the Irish bps. to conform to Roman usage in the matter of the date of Easter. His legate took an active part at the Council of Toledo VI in Spain, urging stronger action to curb the infidels. In Italy he dealt successfully with the Exarch Isaac, enforced discipline, and brought to an end the schism of the patriarchs of Aquileia-Grado that stemmed from resentment over the approval given to the condemnation of the *Three Chapters by Pope *Vigilius. The Italians hailed him for his wise use of the Patrimony of St. Peter, despite the heavy expenses occasioned by his extensive building program. But H. is chiefly remembered in history for the questionable statements he made with regard to the points at issue in the Monothelite controversy. Perhaps in sympathy with the Emperor's desire for religious unity, he responded to a letter of Patriarch *Sergius of Constantinople, with whose proposal that there should be no further discussion of one or two operations in Christ he agreed, and appeared to conclude that there was but one will in Christ. The expressions he used could, at least in other contexts, be understood in an orthodox sense, but they were taken by Monothelites as an endorsement of their position, and the *Ecthesis,* published the year of H.'s death, made much of his statement. This initiated a debate about H.'s personal orthodoxy and its connotations in the matter of papal infallibility, that continued down to Vatican Council I. That H.'s language savored of the Monothelite denial of two wills in Christ is clear, but it seems equally clear that he was not personally a Monothelite, despite his condemnation by the Roman Synod of 649 and the Council of Constantinople III (680–681). Pope Leo II in passing judgment upon the acts of Constantinople III blamed H. not for heresy but for permitting the unsullied standard of apostolic tradition to be soiled. Pope *John IV, who condemned Monothelitism and the *Ecthesis,* defended the orthodoxy of H. in a letter to Emperor Constantine III and declared that H. in affirming the unity of will in Christ had meant no more that to underline the perfect harmony in him, because of his sinless humanity, between the law of his members and the law of his mind (cf. Rom 7.23). This explanation has been used by many apologists (see P. Galtier, ''La Première lettre du Pape Honorius,'' (Greg 1948 29:42–61). Others have preferred to point out that H.'s statement was not an ex-cathedra utterance; that his fault lay in his negligence and failure to take clear issue with the Monothelites (see J. Chapman, CE 7:452–459). The evasion to which some scholars once resorted of questioning the authenticity of the letter of H. and of the acts of Constantinople III as well has long since been abandoned by all. Letter: PL 80: 470–474, or better in the Gr., Mansi 11:537–544. BIBLIOGRAPHY: in addition to the references given in the text, J. Chapman, ''Condemnation of Pope Honorius,'' DublinRev 139 (1906) 129–154; 140 (1907) 42–72; É. Amann, DTC 7:93–132; H. G. J. Beck, NCE 7:123–125.

[P. F. MULHERN]

HONORIUS II (Lambert Scannabecchi; d. 1130), **POPE** from 1124. A significant figure at the papal court from the time of his entry into papal service under Urban II, H. represented Callistus II in the negotiations with Emperor Henry V which culminated in the Concordat of Worms (1122) and ended the investiture conflict in the Empire. As pope, he strove to consolidate the gains secured by the Concordat. He also devoted much of his time to pacifying the rebellious nobles of the papal states. BIBLIOGRAPHY: Mann 8: 228–305.

[J. MULDOON]

HONORIUS III (Cencio Savell; d. 1227), **POPE** from 1216. H. was born at Rome at an unknown date, spent his entire life in the service of the Roman Church, first as a canon of St. Mary Major, later as chamberlain, at which time (1192) he drew up the *Liber Censuum*. He succeeded the great Innocent III, and though aged and of a gentler disposition, sought to emulate Innocent by carrying out the legislation of the Lateran Council IV (1215). Faced with heresy in the Church and Jerusalem in infidel hands, H. first fostered the Dominicans to deal with heresy but was curbed by the French spirit of political expansion. Next he tried to settle the Hohenstaufen problem by recognizing Henry, Frederick's son, and by crowning Frederick emperor at Rome but binding him with an oath to go on crusade.

Honorius's Fifth Crusade came to nought, but he succeeded in having heresy suppressed in imperial territory and Aragon and laid the ground for the papal Inquisition. To the Franciscans he granted a rule (Nov. 23, 1223), and his legislation was collected in the *Compilatio quinta* formally promulgated by the constitution *Novae causarum* (May 2, 1226), the first official book of canon law. BIBLIOGRAPHY: S. Williams, NCE 7:126–27; Mann 13:1–164; *History of the Crusades* (ed. K. M. Setton, 1955–) 2:377–428.

[S. WILLIAMS]

HONORIUS IV (Giacomo Savelli; 1210–87), **POPE** from 1285. From his appointment as cardinal (1261), his career was devoted largely to papal negotiations concerning Sicily, and his pontificate was devoted to an unsuccessful attempt to restore Sicily to papal control. BIBLIOGRAPHY: Mann 16:357–450; S. Runciman, *Sicilian Vespers* (1958).

[J. MULDOON]

HONORIUS (Flavius Honorius; 384–423), **ROMAN EMPEROR** from 395. Upon the death of his father, Theodosius the Great, H. became emperor of the West, and in 398 he married the daughter of his great general Stilicho. In 403 or 404 he moved his capital to Ravenna and in 408 had his father-in-law executed on the suspicion of treason. From then on his rule was plagued by revolts and invasions, the most notable being the sack of Rome by Alaric in 410. Honorius was not an able ruler, but he did much to hasten the demise of paganism by a series of laws depriving pagan priests of their privileges and immunities, closing temples, and forbidding public sacrifices. He also took strong measures against the Manichaeans, Donatists, and Pelagians. In his concern for orthodoxy he betrays the early influence of St. Ambrose upon him at Milan. BIBLIOGRAPHY: A. Amore, *EncCatt* 9:139–140; O. Seeck, PW 8:2277–91.

[M. J. COSTELLOE]

HONORIUS OF AUTUN (d. *c.* 1156), early scholastic, who wrote under the name Augustodunensis, but it is more likely that this refers to Regensburg where he was perhaps a recluse who joined the Irish Benedictines there than to Autun in Burgundy. His encyclopedic writings on history, natural science, and theology in the Platonist tradition, partly deriving from *John Scotus Erigena, were widely circulated and are good witnesses to the state of contemporary learning. Works: PL 172.

[T. GILBY]

HONORIUS OF CANTERBURY, ST. (d. 653), abp. of Canterbury. Probably one of the companions of Augustine in 597, he was consecrated abp. in 627. He sent Felix as missionary to East Anglia and received the pallium in 634. His jurisdiction seems to have been exercised only in Kent, Essex, and East Anglia. BIBLIOGRAPHY: Bede, *Eccl. Hist.* bks 2 and 3; E. John, NCE 7:129–130; Butler 3:695.

[J. DRUSE]

HONORIUS MAGISTER (d. *c.* 1213), English *decretist who taught both at Paris, *c.* 1185, and at Oxford, *c.* 1192. His *Summa decretalium quaestionum* influenced the systematization and methodology of canonical studies. His academic career ended in 1195 when he became a member of the curia of the abp. of York.

[T. C. O'BRIEN]

HONTHEIM, JOHANN NIKOLAUS VON (1701–90), auxiliary bp. of Trier, 1748–90, chiefly known for his major work: *On the State of the Church and the Legitimate Power of the Roman Pontiff* published in 1763 under the pen name Justinus Febronius. H. affirmed an essentially episcopal concept of church government, charging that the popes had usurped powers initially held by the bishops (see FEBRONIANISM). His ideas reflected his early exposure to Gallican and Jansenist doctrines and an apparent hope to promote Christian reunion in Germany, but also his involvement in the jurisdictional differences of the German metropolitans with Rome. H. formally disavowed his teachings in large measure in 1778, but only under pressure. He died at peace with the authorities. BIBLIOGRAPHY: F. Maass, NCE 7:130–131; M. O'Callaghan, NCE 5:868–869; Y. Congar, *Catholicisme* 5:933.

[J. K. ZEENDER]

HONTHORST, GERRITT VAN (1590–1656), Dutch painter in Rome (*c.* 1611). Influenced by Caravaggio, H. was called Gerardo delle Notti for his use of artificial light sources *(Christ as a Child with St. Joseph)*. A *Madonna and Child with SS. Francis and Bonaventura and Princess Colonna-Gonzaga* (1618) reflects the classical Baroque of the Caracci. In *Christ Crowned with Thorns,* H. continued to blend Dutch and Italianate styles. Following a visit from Rubens (1627) and royal commissions in England and Denmark, H. cofounded a school introducing Italian Baroque into the Netherlands.

[M. J. DALY]

HOOD, see COWL.

HŌŌDŌ OF BYŌDŌIN, the Amida Hall (Phoenix Hall) of the Byōdōin originally a palace for Yorimichi (Fujiwara) near Kyoto, converted to a Buddhist temple in 1052. The Hōōdō derives its name from layout in the form of a winged phoenix bird and phoenix acroteria on the roof. A painting of the descent of the Amida (Buddha), a carved Amida by Jōchō with ornate aureole and pierced canopy, bodhisattvas in wall reliefs, and the gardens seek to express the Amida Paradise.

[M. J. DALY]

HOOGSTRAETEN, JACOB VAN (Hochstraten; 1460–1527), Dominican theologian and polemicist. A native of the Brabant, H. became successively regent of studies at the Dominican house in Cologne (1505) and prior (1508). As prior he was ex officio inquisitor general for

Cologne, Mainz, and Trier. He engaged in vigorous controversy, first in defense of the mendicant orders, then against J. *Reuchlin, and finally against Luther. Against Reuchlin, who sought to preserve Hebrew, esp. Talmudic, literature from burning, H. sided with the Jewish convert J. *Pfefferkorn and had Reuchlin's *Augenspiegel* burned (1514). This caused H. to be labeled an enemy of the New Learning, and he was made a target of the biting shafts of the **Epistolae obscurorum virorum* (1515, 1517). H. was himself condemned by the abp. of Speyer (1514) and removed from his office by the Dominican provincial chapter (1517). Leo X, alarmed by events in Germany, reversed both these actions (1520), reinstating H. and silencing Reuchlin. There is no doubt that H. was intemperate in his zeal and wanting in good judgment, but his writings, though lacking conspicuous theological merit, reveal him as something less than the complete fool the *Epistolae* made him out to be. His three anti-Lutheran works were edited by F. Pipjer, *Bibliotheca reformatoria Neerlandica* (3 v., 1905).
BIBLIOGRAPHY: R. Coulon, DTC 7:11–17; F. C. Stokes, *Epistolae obscurorum virorum: The Latin Text with an English Rendering, Notes and an Historical Introduction* (1909).

[T. C. O'BRIEN]

HOOK, SIDNEY (1902–), American philosopher and student of John Dewey, professor of philosophy at New York Univ., author of innumerable books and articles on matters of philosophical and social concern. The general tendency of his philosophy is naturalistic, and represents a development of the mature position of John Dewey. His most important work is generally considered to be *The Quest for Being* (1961). The title essay of this book establishes the grounds upon which H.'s philosophical position must rest. He here takes the position that the term Being, as it has traditionally been used in ontological discussions, is meaningless and that therefore it is senseless to talk about ontology as the study of Being-as-such. His argument about Being is based on the linguistic principle that in order for a term to have a meaning, it must specify that which it does not include within its scope. The only thing that Being-as-such does not include within its scope is Nothing, which, as H. points out, is not a term designating an entity. Thus, Being "as an all-inclusive category does not seem to possess an intelligible opposite." Being is therefore an empty term, and if ontology is to be anything at all it cannot be the study of Being. H. therefore proposes another task for ontology. It should be restricted to a study of "those statements or propositions which we believe to be cognitively valid, or which assert something that is true or false, and yet which are not found in any particular science . . . but which are taken for granted by the sciences."

[F. J. CUNNINGHAM]

HOOK, WALTER FARQUHAR (1798–1875), Anglican vicar, dean of Chichester, writer. Son of an Anglican vicar, H. attended Oxford. In 1821 he was ordained deacon and served for 5 years as his father's curate on the Isle of Wight. An early sermon, "The peculiar character of the Church of England independently of its connection with the State" preached in 1822 gives clear indication of views later made famous by the *Oxford Movement. In 1828 H. was appointed to Holy Trinity parish, Coventry, where his zeal and vigorous promotion of church attendance revived the parish. His sermons were notable (2 v., 1841–42), and his solicitude for the betterment of his flock prompted him to set up a savings bank, a dispensary, and a library. Named vicar of Leeds in 1837, he began the most effective period of his ministry. The population was growing, the state of religion declining when H. took charge. In his tenure at Leeds, churches increased from 15 to 36, schools from 3 to 30. In 1846 he proposed a concept of education that made the State responsible but provided for facilities and time in each school for ministers to give instruction to children of their faith. A sermon preached in 1838 before Queen Victoria, entitled "Hear the Church" created a stir when it was published, and over 100,000 copies were printed. It proposed the thesis that the English Church was not founded but reformed in the 16th century; that Roman Catholics left it; that the Anglican bps. enjoyed apostolic succession. In spite of sympathies with the Oxford Movement, H. was never one of them. He fell out with E. B. *Pusey over the issues. In 1859 H. was appointed dean of Chichester where he worked on his masterly *Lives of the Archbishops of Canterbury* (12 v., 1860–76). Though offered more attractive deaneries, H. declined and lived the rest of his life at Chichester. He was a man of extraordinary pastoral zeal, compassion for the disadvantaged, and keen powers of theological reasoning.

[J. R. AHERNE]

HOOK NEUMES, medieval musical notational signs such as the epiphonus, ancus, salicus, etc., so-called because they were drawn with a rounded hook.

[M. T. LEGGE]

HOOKER, RICHARD (1553–1600), Anglican theologian and political philosopher. H. studied at Corpus Christi College, Oxford, where he obtained a fellowship (1577). In 1585 he was presented with the mastership of the Temple Church in London. There he came into conflict with Walter Travers, a representative of the Puritan faction, pressing for the polity of Calvin's Geneva as alone suited to the reformation of the Church. In the ensuing controversy H. saw the need of a systematic defense of the Elizabethan ecclesiastical polity; to prepare such a work he had himself appointed to a country rectory (1591), where he wrote his classic of Anglican theology, *Of the Laws of Ecclesiastical Polity*. The first five books of this appeared 1594–97; posthumously, Books 6 and 7 were published in 1648; Book 8, in 1662. Against the Puritan reliance upon the Scriptures alone, he established the necessity of reason and patristic tradition and presented a view of natural law very much like that elaborated by Aristotle and adapted to the context of Christian thought by Thomas Aquinas. Although Aquinas is not cited, H.'s dependence upon his thought is unmistakable. However, where neither reason nor tradition could adequately justify the particular arrangements of the Elizabethan settlement, H., turning from Aquinas, had recourse to the thought of *Marsilius of Padua who had completely subjected Church to State. H.'s work, in its vindication of episcopacy and the Book of Common Prayer, was the classic apologia for Anglicanism as a middle course, *via media*, between Roman Catholicism and Calvinistic Protestantism. Works: ed. J. Keble (3 v., 1836; rev. ed., R. W. Church and E. Paget, 1888); *Of the Laws of Ecclesiastical Polity* (2 v., 1954). BIBLIOGRAPHY: P. Munz, *Place of Hooker in the History of Thought* (1952); J. Marshall, *Hooker and the Anglican Tradition* (1964).

[R. B. ENO]

HOOKER, THOMAS (1586–1647), English Puritan leader and a founder of the Colony of Connecticut. H. studied at Emmanuel College (then a Puritan center), Cambridge (B.A., 1608; M.A., 1611). For some years he was a fellow of Emmanuel; he received a conversion experience that became a constant theme of his preaching. From 1620 to 1629 he held various parochial positions in Surrey and Essex, but his Puritan preaching was brought to an end by Abp. W. *Laud. In 1630 he fled to Holland and 3 years later, to Massachusetts, where he became pastor of a congregation at Newtown, now Cambridge. Finding the government too autocratic, he led a group of his followers to the Connecticut Valley, where they founded the city of Hartford in 1636. He has been called the father of American democracy because of his insistence that the power to choose public officials lies with the people. He advocated, however, a very limited sort of democracy at most, for the people vested with the power of choice included only those of established social status; the number of these probably did not exceed one-third of the colony's adult males. He did rule out religious tests for citizenship. H. was above all a Puritan preacher; his topics, the experience of conversion and moral duty; his style, the plain and orderly exposition of Scripture. BIBLIOGRAPHY: S. E. Ahlstrom, *Theology in America* (1967) 98–99 (bibliog.), 111–114.

[R. B. ENO]

HOONACKER, ALBIN VAN (1857–1933), biblical scholar. Professor of OT literature at Louvain (1889–1927), he concentrated his higher critical research on the evolution of the Pentateuch or Torah, e.g., in his *De compositione litteraria et de origine Mosaica Hexateuchi* (1949). He was a leader of the revival of serious biblical studies among Catholics.

[J. F. FALLON]

HOOPER, JOHN (d. 1555), English Reformer; bp. of Gloucester and later of Worcester; martyred under Mary Tudor. A Cistercian monk, H., upon the *dissolution of the monasteries, went to London and became attached to the ideas of *Zwingli and J. H. *Bullinger. Exiled for his views on the Eucharist, H. lived in Strassburg and Basel until the death of Henry VIII. On his return he received promotion to the episcopacy. He was a powerful preacher, liberal to the poor, but combative and of irksome severity. He stood for the full Protestantizing of the Reformation in England and was highly regarded by the Puritans of the 17th century. Under Mary he was degraded and sent to the stake at Gloucester, enduring his passion with unshaken constancy.

[T. GILBY]

HOORNAERT, GEORGES (1876–1950), Belgian Jesuit retreat master and spiritual writer. H. entered the Society of Jesus in 1894, taught humanities 1901–20, and then engaged in the active ministry for the rest of his life. His retreats for priests were esp. influential. BIBLIOGRAPHY: C. Martin, *Catholicisme* 5:938.

[M. J. SUELZER]

HOPE, the theological virtue according to which the Christian tends toward God as the fulfillment of his confident expectation for the fully realized reign of God. It is man's openness to the future, and issues from the reality of faith and the occurrences of God's saving acts in history. In the OT, the term hope has several nuances but one basic meaning: the expectation of a future good in view of the promises which the Lord made to his people. Hope is necessarily linked with faith; it proceeds from that faith as the assurance that God will provide his continual protection. Its object, therefore, is not the future as such but God who controls the future. False hope would be to transfer this confidence from the Lord to merely human security, e.g., through foreign alliances at the time of the Israelite kings (Is 7.10–16). Gradually, this expectation extended to an ultimate deliverance which will be accomplished in the final day of the Lord. Thus the NT confession of faith attests that Jesus is this "consolation of Israel" and "redemption of Jerusalem" (Lk 2.25,38). His Resurrection is the new source of Israel's hope for the future (Acts 23.6), which hope is inseparable from faith and love (1 Th 1.3). Scholastic theology applied the same careful analysis to hope as it did to the other virtues. According to this system, the primary material object of hope is God himself. What hope ultimately seeks is the *beatific vision, the full knowledge and love of God as he is in himself (Rom 8.24–25). Secondarily, hope extends to all those means which serve man in his journey toward God: natural endowments, grace, the sacraments. They are the object of hope insofar as the primary object, God, could not be attained without them. The motive of hope is also God; his love, power, and mercy constitute the reason why we hope. The radical monotheism of the Judaeo-Christian tradition insists that man trust only in him before whom there can be no strange gods. Thus Christ is the foundation of our hope (1 Cor 15.19) because he is the Divine Son. The secondary motives of hope, derivative from the principal motive, are the presence of sanctifying grace which orders the Christian to the beatific vision, the good works upon which merit is based, the humanity of Christ, the Church, and the sacraments. Finally, it is man the wayfarer who hopes precisely insofar as he is still marking his pilgrim way; he hopes both for himself and for the community of men.

The theology of hope has recently undergone a major resurgence, shaped by those theologians (J. Moltmann, W. Pannenberg, J. *Metz) who saw with R. *Bultmann that an eschatological perspective is central to Jesus' message but who were unwilling to interpret this eschatology solely in terms of its existential, moral repercussions. In accord with the Marxist philosopher E. *Bloch who maintains that the key to human existence is the hope which man holds for the future state of the world, these theologians are attempting to reactivate Christian hope by pointing to the eschatological significance of Christianity. The Christian is able to negate the present empirical fact of suffering and sin in the light of his hope, thus establishing the "condition for the possibility of new experiences." The basis for this hope, as in scholastic theology, is God; but it is God as revealed in Jesus and specifically in his Resurrection. Jesus' Resurrection and man's share in it enables us to understand the world as it really is—with meaning, order, and a future thrust which is entrusted to man's revolutionary energies. BIBLIOGRAPHY: R. Bultmann, Kittel TD 2:517–523; Thomas Aquinas, *De spe; idem,* ST 2a2ae, 17–23; J. Moltmann, *Theology of Hope* (1967); W. Pannenberg et al., *History and Hermeneutics* (1964); F. Kerstiens, SacMund 3.61–65.

[T. M. MCFADDEN]

HOPE (IN THE BIBLE). The Hebrew OT vocabulary of hope displays a surprising richness of variety and nuance lacking in the Greek of the LXX and the NT: *bth,* to be confident, to feel secure (Ps 25.2; Is 30.15); *qwh,* to wait for, be tense (Pr 23.18; 24.14); *yhl,* to expect (Ps 33.18; 42.5, 11). In both the LXX and the NT, *elpis* and *elpizein* express the virtue of hope. Hope in the Bible means confidence in the person of God, whose very name in the Hebrew implies hope, and in his fidelity to his promises, for the future, whether formally expressed through convenants, esp. the Mosaic, or through the Son, Jesus the Christ, in the New Testament. Thus, this virtue is rooted in faith in the reality of God's existence and in his continuing activity in the history of the world, the history of a people, and the history of the individual believer. Accompanying hope is the responsibility of expressing hope through confident communal and individual prayer, and through the exercise of mutual justice and love.

In the Old Testament. Hope in the OT bears witness to an historical reality; the frequent and varied event of the people of Israel clinging to God as the hope upon whom the realization of its future good depends (Jer 14.8). Israel understood its history as the fulfillment of God's promises: the rise of the nation, the gift of the Promised Land (Gen 12.1–3,7; Dt 5–6); the kingdom and continuance of the house of David (2 Sam 7.11–16; Ps 89.20–37); the catastrophes of the period of judges (Jgs 2.1–3) and of kings (1 Sam 8.7–18); the Babylonian Exile (Jer 27.12–15, Ezek 21.18–23); the return from the Exile (Is 40.9–11); the new beginning in Jerusalem, and the fulfillment of the promises in Israel's new covenant (Ezek 36.24–32). The expectation of these transformations had their basis solely on the word of God, which became known to Israel as promise to the patriarchs, as covenant to Moses, and as the proclamation of judgment and pledge of salvation through the later prophets. Not only was the function of Israel's prophets to purify Israel's hopes, but also to open the people's horizons of hope. The nation often forgot that its future was God's gift (Hos 2.10; Ezek 16.15–30) and attempted to guarantee its future as did the nations, by idolatry, by self-sufficiency, and international treaty. The prophets denounced these misplaced hopes (Jer 8.15; 13.16), insisting that without fidelity to God there is no salvation (Hos 12.7; Is 26.8–11), and that the penalty for infidelity would be a wrathful Day of the Lord (Amos 5.20). Yet paradoxically in the actual moments of judgment, the prophets had the insight to perceive a future for the people. A remnant would be spared (Is 10.19–20); for the scattered and exiled a homecoming is promised (Jer 32.42–44; Ezek 37; Is 40–55) with full pardon for past sins (Hos 11; Is 54.4–10). To pardon and return the prophets coupled their vision of a future, expanded horizon of hope, diversely expressed as involving a new creation (Ezek 34; 13–16; 36.26–27; Is 43.16–21), a new exodus (Is 40.3–5); a new covenant (Jer 31.31–34); an age of prosperity and blessing (Is 61) under a new David (Jer 23.5–6). The new age would be a time when the people would truly know God (Is 11.9), when their hearts would be renewed (Ezek 36.25–29), when perfect worship would be offered (Ezek 40–48), when the nations would acknowledge the God of Israel. The biblical expression of hope finds no more eloquent testimony than that of the Psalms which nourished the pious in the critical stages of Israel's history. God is the refuge and the fortress of security to the poor and the righteous in their afflictions (Ps 14.6; 61.3; 73.28). The pious commit their cause to the Lord, hold fast to him, and live in serenity under his protection (Ps 9.10; 22.8–9; 40.4). Confidence and patient expectation of salvation and happiness are also voiced in the prayer of Israel (Ps 13.15; 31.24; 33.18–22; 71.12–14; 119.114–16). These same sentiments are found in the wisdom literature (Pr 22.19; 10.28), and yet wisdom itself casts new light upon the hope of the people. Toward the end of the Exile a prophet had taught that Israel's suffering should foster rather than impede hope, because pain had a redemptive character (Is 52.13–53.12), while on the other hand Job had tested the limits of hope in the face of God's seemingly arbitrary omnipotence (Job 42.1–6). Apocalyptic somewhat resolved the tension of suffering by teaching the hope of future resurrection and glory for the just and the martyr (Dan 12.1–15), and triumph for the people (Dan 7). Later wisdom continues this thrust by locating peace and salvation in immortality (Wis 3.1–3). Thus, hope in the OT is indissolubly linked with the God of the patriarchs and promises, the God of promises and threats, the God of all who pray and the God of the wise.

In the New Testament. Besides *elpizein,* the vocabulary for hope in the NT includes *hypomenein,* to endure patiently, and *gregorein,* to be watchful. In John and to some extent in the Synoptics, hope coincides with faith; in Rev, hope with patient endurance and in 1 Pet faith with hope. Hope takes on a variety of forms, determined largely by differing eschatological concepts. But basic to the concept is the reign of God which has come in Jesus and the Messiah, in his life and teachings, death and Resurrection. The power of death, sin, the elements of the world have been essentially conquered by Christ. The believer in Jesus has been liberated to live a new life in anticipation of glory (Rom 8.29–30). The Christian, because of God's love manifested in Jesus and because of the indwelling Holy Spirit, is to live in the hopeful tension of present faith and awaited fulfillment with the return of Jesus. The focus of hope for earliest Christianity was the imminent return of Jesus as Son of Man, bringing completion to the reign of God initiated during his public ministry. Though the Church came to understand that it must live in history until God chooses to reveal the moment of the eschaton, hope in Jesus' soon return persisted in the prayer of the Church, esp. during times of persecution, and to a large extent determined the imagery employed in connection with the last day both in the NT and later theology. Thus, though there may be surprise at its delay (2 Pet 3.8), the day will arrive "as a thief in the night" (1 Th 5.1–4). The time of waiting calls for vigilance (1 Th 5.6; 1 Pet 5.8) and patient endurance in trial (Jas 5.7–9; 1 Th 1.4; 1 Pet 1.5). Hope of glory engenders present seriousness (1 Th 5.8; 1 Pet 4.7) and detachment (1 Cor 7.29–32; 1 Pet 1.13; Tit 2.13). For St. Paul, God is the source of hope (Rom 15.13), who gratuitously has willed the salvation of all mankind (1 Th 5.9; Rom 1.16; 10.10) and brought salvation to realization through the death and Resurrection of his Son, Christ Jesus (1 Cor 15.17; 2 Cor 1.3; Rom 4.25). The death and Resurrection of Jesus have restored sinful mankind to union with the Father (2 Cor 5.18–20; Rom 5.10–11), made expiation for sin (Rom 3.23–25), and freed mankind from the power of the law, sin, and death (Rom 5–8). Sinful man becomes hopeful man only through justifying faith gratuitously offered by God through the preaching of the gospel (Rom 10.9, 17), and through baptism, which incorporates a person into the death and Resurrection of Christ (Rom 6.4–5; 1 Cor 6.17) and into a salvific community (1 Cor 12.13; Gal 6.16). Hope as faith's expectancy is virtually synonymous with the inheritance to which God's people are called (Rom 5.2; 12.12). The power to hope is found in the indwelling of Christ's Spirit, the Holy Spirit (Rom 5.5; 15.13; Gal 5.5) who gives assurance of the full harvest (Rom 8.23–30). In Paul's thought hope's object is the continuation and completion of the work of the Father, Son, and Holy Spirit. The undeniable elements of his future hope are the parousia (1 Th 4.15), the resurrection of the dead (1 Th 4.16; 1 Cor 15.13), the judgment (2 Cor 5.10), and the glory of the justified believer (Rom 8.18,21). Yet for the believer the eschaton in a real sense has begun and man is saved (2 Cor 6.2). For the Christian who has become a "new creature" (Gal 6.15), hope is associated with unshakeable confidence (Rom 4.18), steadfast endurance (Rom 5.4; 8.25), responsible freedom (Rom 8.21; Gal 5.5), rejoicing (Rom 5.2), boldness (2 Cor 3.12) and above all with love (1 Cor 13.7). While the hope of the individual believer is important, the growth of the hoping Church is decisive, for man is baptized "in one Spirit to form one body" (1 Cor 12.13; Eph 4.4). The captivity letters present the basis as well as the object of the Church's hope: hope in cosmic terms, a hope based upon the role of the Son in creation and in the reconciliation of the universe through his death and Resurrection (Col 1.13–20). While the creation of one new man composed of Jew and gentile is an accomplished fact (Eph 2.11–19), the Church must continue to mature in hope in order to become a holy temple with Christ himself as the keystone (Eph 2.20–21) and source of hope (Col 1.27) in that special representation of his body, the Eucharist (1 Cor 11.26–32). According to Hebrews, the substance of the future was attested to in the OT by Moses and the patriarchs (Heb 11.1–28), while now Jesus is both the pioneer and perfecter of faith (Heb 12.2). By his obedience unto death, he has become mediator of the new covenant and supreme example of a better hope. Christian hope is the anchor of the soul for Christians because it rests with Christ, the high priest (Heb 6.19–20) who makes intercession with the Father (Heb 9.23–24). Johannine hope stresses the possession of eternal life already granted the believer (Jn 3.15; 6.54; 1 Jn 5.11–13), who in a sense has been raised (Jn 11.25–27; Jn 3.14) and judged (Jn 3.19; 5.24). The Christian's passage to eternity will be the manifestation of a reality already existing (1 Jn 3.2). However, in the Book of Revelation, apparent triumphs of the satanic power threaten hope. Yet the Word fights and reigns at the side of his people (Rev 19.11–16; 20.1–6) and decisive victory is near (Rev 2.5; 3.11; 22.6, 12). The ultimate expression of the Christian hope for the consummation of God's total plan of salvation is found in the prayer of the Church: "Come, Lord Jesus" (Rev 22.20). BIBLIOGRAPHY: H. W. Wolff, *Anthropology of the Old Testament* (1974); W. Zimmerli, *Man's Hope in the Old Testament* (1970).

[T. J. RYAN]

HOPE OF SALVATION, the theological virtue of *hope insofar as it is ordered to man's trusting expectation of final deliverance from the powers of evil. In the OT, this notion underwent a gradual development. At the time of the

Judges, Israel's hope was rooted in Yahweh as the one who would continue to give his people military victories over their enemies (Jg 15.18). The perfect expression of the Lord's delivering presence was the Exodus, delivering his covenanted people from their slavery in Egypt (Ex 14.30). Among the pre-Exilic Prophets, however, a longing for a salvation greater than political security emerged. These Prophets condemned the nation's confidence in their temporal kings, and warned that a day of wrath was approaching when only a remnant, the poor and humble servants of the Lord, would be saved from destruction (Am 5.18–20; Is 2.6–21; 4.2–3; Zeph 1.14–18). The post-Exilic Prophets expanded this vision even further: the fact that some exiles did return to Jerusalem is clear evidence that Yahweh is still the savior of his people. Through this pious remnant, the Lord's dominion will be exercised over all the world (Is 45.22)—a time of justice and joy will dawn upon the earth. Moreover, a sense of salvation beyond this life comes to be experienced at this time (Is 25.6–9; 26.17–19).

The NT draws this hoped for salvation to its ultimate conclusion in Jesus. The kingdom of God that Jesus proclaimed is in the future, but it is a future that breaks into the present because of Jesus' actions. He comes to bring deliverance from sin and death (Mt 8.17; Lk 7.11–17), and his Resurrection is the pledge that this salvation is granted to all who believe in him (Acts 2.37–41; Rom 10.9–13). Christ is the sole mediator between God and man, and his life with the Father is the assurance of our hope and type of our salvation (Rom 5.9–10; Col 3.1–4). BIBLIOGRAPHY: EDB 2101–07; J. E. Fallon, NCE 7:142–144.

[T. M. MCFADDEN]

HOPEDALE COMMUNITY, an American communal society founded in 1842 in Worcester, Mass., by Adin Ballou. His intent was to form a Christian utopia whose members would agree to avoid violence, the taking of oaths, and strong drink. No common beliefs were to be required. In 1857 one of the members, Draper by name, bought up the community stock and forced Ballou out. Thereupon the experiment lost momentum. The group was sometimes called the Miniature Christian Republic. BIBLIOGRAPHY: T. Horgan, NCE 4:80.

HÖPFL, HILDEBRAND (1872–1934), Benedictine biblical scholar who taught in Rome (1903–16, 1920–34) and Jerusalem (1916–20). A consultor of the Pontifical Biblical Commission and other congregations, he is most widely known for a conservative introduction to the whole Bible (reprinted as late as 1950 as *Introductio generalis in Sacram Scripturam,* ed B. Gut). He also published *Introductio specialis in Novum Testamentum* (5th ed., 1949).

[J. F. FALLON]

HOPKINS, GERARD MANLEY (1844–89), English poet. He was the eldest son in a family staunchly Anglican. He attended school in Highgate, then studied at Balliol College, Oxford, where he had Walter Pater as tutor, distinguished himself in Greek, and won prizes for essays and poetry. His deeply religious spirit led him after severe struggles into the Catholic Church. Baptized by Card. Newman, he taught for a year in the Birmingham Oratory School, and then entered the Society of Jesus. After this he followed the pattern of Jesuit life—scholastic, teacher, parish priest, and college professor. When he entered the Society, he destroyed his early poems thinking that poetry and the Jesuit life were incompatible. On December 7, 1875, a ship carrying Catholic exiles from Germany was wrecked, and H.'s rector suggested that someone should commemorate the tragedy. H., taking this as an indication that he should return to poetry, wrote his longest and most sustained poem, "The Wreck of the Deutschland." From this time on he wrote when he had time, but he was not successful in publishing. H.'s early poems are largely meditations on the relationship of nature, man, and God, often showing that nature reveals God while man fails to do so. The themes of God's mercy and justice and of the Incarnation of Christ run through his poems. His last sonnets show severe interior struggles and discouragement borne with patience and trust. H.'s poems remained in MS in the care of his friend Robert Bridges until 1918. The first edition drew attention slowly, but H. became influential in the 1930s. His position as a poet now seems secure. His thought is not unusual, and his interest in God, man, and nature relate him to his age, but his method of expression, his "sprung rhythm," odd placement of words, and unusual diction give his poems a sound structure interesting and stimulating to the reader. Works: *Poems* (ed. W. H. Gardner, 3d ed. 1948); *Journals and Papers* (ed. H. House and G. Storey, 1959); for a complete list of editions of other writings, see R. Boyle, NCE 7:147. BIBLIOGRAPHY: *Gerard Manley Hopkins,* essays by Kenyon critics (1945); *Hopkins: A Collection of Critical Essays* (ed. G. H. Hartman, 1966).

[M. M. BARRY]

HOPKINS, SAMUEL (1721–1803), American Congregationalist theologian. H. was born in Waterbury, Conn., graduated from Yale (1741), and studied theology under Jonathan *Edwards. H.'s theological system, inspired by Edwards and known as Hopkinsianism, the *New England theology or (in England) American Theology, is presented in many closely reasoned works, esp. in *A System of Doctrines Contained in Divine Revelation* (1793). He mitigated rigid Calvinist predestinationism and emphasized God's goodness: God wills what is advantageous for the greater number, for this end even permitting sin; and man's duty is to be completely submissive to God's benevolent purposes, even to the extent of a willingness to be damned. From 1770 H. spoke out against the slave trade and urged Negro emancipation. His works, with a biography, were edited by E. A. Park (3 v., 1852). BIBLIOGRAPHY: T. H.

Foster, *Genetic History of the New England Theology* (1907).

[T. C. O'BRIEN]

HORAE DIURNAE, (Day Hours; also called Little Hours) before recent liturgical changes comprised Prime, Tierce, Sext, and None, the hours of the Roman day. The term also refers to a book (diurnal) containing these, but not the major Hours of the Breviary, Matins, Lauds, Vespers. The medieval Book of Hours, of which so many artistic examples survive, was usually a lay person's prayerbook, containing the Little Office of the Blessed Virgin Mary.

[T. C. O'BRIEN]

HOREB, MOUNT, presumed to be another name for Sinai and is referred to as the "mountain of God." It has been noted by Pentateuchal scholars that Horeb is used in the Elohist and Deuteronomic traditions. Sinai is used by the Yahwist and Priestly traditions. Horeb's location is more commonly thought to be in the S part of the Sinai peninsula. It was the scene of the burning bush (Ex 3.2) and of the worship of the golden calf (Ex 33.6). It was here that the covenant was made and promulgated (Dt 4.10, 15) and Yahweh encountered Elijah (1 Kg 19.8). Lagrange suggested that Horeb was the name of the entire mountain range and Sinai a particular peak; W. F. Albright suggests just the opposite. It is possiible that the same mountain or range had more than one name. BIBLIOGRAPHY: D. Baly, *Geography of the Bible* (1957), L. H. Grollenberg, *Atlas of the Bible* (1956).

[F. GAST]

HORMISDAS, ST. (d. 523), **POPE** from 514. He was a deacon of the Roman Church under Pope Symmachus, whom he succeeded in the papacy. Earlier in life he had been married, and his son Silverius, later became pope (536–537). H. received back into the Church the last adherents of the antipope *Laurentius. He is best known for healing the schism of Acacius with the acceptance by Constantinople of the "Formula of Hormisdas," a great victory of orthodoxy and Chalcedon, and an assertion of papal authority at that time without precedent in its scope as well as a unique example of Byzantine submission. He was buried in the portico of St. Peter's. More than 100 of his letters are extant (CSEL 35). BIBLIOGRAPHY: Butler 3:271; I. F. Corti, BiblSanct 9:1237–40.

[P. F. MULHERN]

HORMISDAS, FORMULA OF POPE. For 30 years the Eastern Church was troubled by a controversy known as the Acacian Schism. Some Eastern bps. wrote to Rome for help to bring about a solution. In 519 Pope Hormisdas issued his famous Formula. With it he obtained the signature of 2,500 Eastern bps. and brought about peace and reunion. This document is very important because of the uniquivocal assertion of papal authority: " . . . it is in the Apostolic See that the Catholic religion has been preserved undefiled."

[A. MORHBACHER]

HORNS OF THE ALTAR, the most sacred parts of the altars of holocaust (Ex 27.2; 38.2) and of incense (Ex 30.2; 37.25). They extend the four top corners. The blood of victims was rubbed on them in rites of expiation (Lev 4), and a fugitive could gain asylum by grasping the horn of the altar (1 Kg 2.28). The altar itself was a symbol of Yahweh's presence; the horn a symbol of power and strength. Perhaps therefore, the horn of the altar signified Yahweh's power and strength. If the horn were knocked off, the altar was considered profaned (Am 3.14). Horned altars have been found in excavations of Shechem and Megiddo. BIBLIOGRAPHY: J. Pedersen, *Israel: Its Life and Culture* (4 v., 1940); De Vaux AncIsr.

[F. GAST]

HOROLOGION (Gr., book of hours), a liturgical term used in the Orthodox Church to signify a Byzantine liturgical book that contains the ordinaries for the canonical Hours, together with a supplement that includes votive canons and hymns and various prayers, and an appendix with rules for the computation of the liturgical calendar and a paschal table. Among Eastern Catholics it signifies a drastically abbreviated, portable collection of liturgical texts meant to be used as a kind of Breviary by some Eastern Catholic rites, which accept the principle of private, daily recitation of the Office.

[A. CODY]

HOROSCOPE, the astrological sighting of the stars and planets; then a schema showing their position on a given date, e.g., of a person's birth, used to forecast the future. The most sophisticated work in antiquity on astrology and horoscopy was the *Tetrabiblos* of Claudius Ptolomaeus; The Romans relied heavily on astrological forecasts; in spite of patristic condemnations and official Church rejection, even Renaissance popes consulted them. Astrology itself was treated as an exact science until the 18th cent., when the full development of astronomy totally discredited its systems and calculations. The contemporary, resurgent reliance on horoscopes is probably a sign of a search to replace lost faith. The theological repudiation of astrology and horoscopy rests on two points. First, they presuppose a direct influence of astral bodies on human action that is incompatible with the nature and freedom of the will, as well as with the primacy and particularity of God's *providence (ThAq ST 1a, 22.1–3; 115.4; 116.1 & 4). Secondly, horoscopic predictions and a reliance on them amount to *divination, a sin of superstition against the virtue of *religion; they amount to seeking in an untoward way knowledge belonging to God alone. The casting of horoscopes on the basis of birth signs is the particular type of divination called "genethlialogy" (*ibid.* 2a2ae, 95.3).

[T. C. O'BRIEN]

HORRITES, see HURRIANS.

HORSIESI, ST., see ORSISIUS, ST.

HORT, FENTON JOHN ANTHONY (1828–92), Anglican NT scholar. Born in Dublin, Ireland, he studied at Trinity College, Cambridge; and after ordination in 1856 was appointed to the parish of St. Ippolyts, near Hitchin, Hertfordshire. In 1872 he returned to Cambridge, where he taught until his death. Though he also wrote on historical and philosophical theology, he is chiefly known for the critical Greek NT that he published (1881–82) with B. F. *Westcott. This work became the basis for all modern textual criticism, esp. by its classification of NT MSS traditions. BIBLIOGRAPHY: A. F. Hort, *Life and Letters of Fenton John Anthony Hort* (2 v., 1896).

[T. EARLY]

HORTON, DOUGLAS (1891–1968), Congregationalist theologian and ecumenist. H. was born in Brooklyn, N.Y.; graduated from Princeton (1912); studied at Edinburgh, Oxford, and Tübingen; prepared for the ministry at Hartford Theological Seminary; and was ordained in 1915. H. was pastor in Brookline, Mass. (1925–31), and in Hyde Park, Ill. (1931–38). He taught *practical theology at Newton Theological Institute (1930–31) and the Chicago Theological Seminary (1933–38), and Congregational polity at Union Theological Seminary, New York City (1943–55). He was also dean of Harvard Divinity School (1955–59). H. made an impact on theology in the U.S. by his 1928 translation of Karl *Barth's *The Word of God and the Word of Man*. But his chief contribution was to ecumenism. Among other works, he edited an important guideline for the ecumenical movement, *Basic Formula for Church Unity* (1937), and wrote *Toward an Undivided Church* (1967). As minister of the General Council of Congregational Christian Churches (1938–55) he led the discussions that resulted in union (1957) with the Evangelical and Reformed Church, forming the *United Church of Christ. He was prominent in the formation of the National and World Councils of Churches, and for the latter served as chairman of the committee on *Faith and Order (1957–63). As an official observer for the International Congregational Council, he attended Vatican Council II, on which he commented in *Vatican Diary* (4 v., 1962–65).

[T. C. O'BRIEN]

HORTULANUS SCENE, the third and climactic section of the *visitatio sepulchri* in its more elaborate forms. In it the risen Christ appears to Mary Magdalene and is at first mistaken for a gardener (*hortulanus*). In terms of dramatic structure this scene contains the recognition that causes a reversal (*peripeteia*) of the plot movement. It thus satisfactorily concludes the aesthetic pattern, balancing the lamentation with rejoicing.

[E. C. DUNN]

HORTULUS ANIMAE (Little Garden of the Soul), a manual of prayers published first in Germany in 1498, and republished there and elsewhere in innumerable Latin and vernacular editions, different publishers appropriating, changing, rearranging according to their pleasure. The basic contents were similar to those of the *Primer or *Book of Hours. *GARDEN OF THE SOUL.

[P. K. MEAGHER]

HORYUJI, Japanese Buddhist temple near Nara, dedicated to the Healing Buddha (Yakushi) in 607 by the Emperor Yomei. Though rebuilt after destruction (670), the pagoda, Golden Hall or Kondō, gate and corridors are the world's oldest wooden structures. Other parts date from the Nara, Heian and Kamakura periods. The strange E-W orientation of the Golden Hall permits two Buddha shrines. Magnificent paintings from the Asuka period—the oldest wall paintings in Japan (*c.*670–711) were destroyed by fire (1949). Important were the Paradise of the four Buddhas (Historic, Healing, Future, Amida), bodhisattvas in Paradise and flying angels (apsaras). These last alone survived the destruction. The Amida Buddha preaching the Law, surrounded by the good souls on lotus flowers, evidences serenity and languid grace in a Sino-Indian synthesis. Their grandeur of conception makes their loss a tragedy.

[M. J. DALY]

HOSANNA, a Hebrew term *hoshi'ah-na* "do save" used in Ps 118.25 as a prayer for success after victory. Because it was part of the great prayer of praise *Hallel* the cry was aptly used to greet Jesus on his triumphant arrival in Jerusalem on Palm Sunday (Mt 21.9, 15; Mk 11.10; Jn 12.13). Thus it passed into Christian liturgy.

[J. J. O'ROURKE]

HOSEA (OSEE), variant of the same name that Jesus had, and the name of a great prophet of the mid-8th cent. B.C. whose oracles were gathered in the Book of Hosea, the first of the 12 prophetic smaller books of the Old Testament. H. lived at a time of crisis after the prosperous reign of Jeroboam II and predicted dire punishment from God because of Israel's infidelity. He was a great poet with a brilliant aesthetic sense who thought of symbols that penetratingly described God and man's relationship. He pictured his own relationship with his unfaithful wife, real or imagined, as the pattern of God's loving marriage with an unfaithful people; God would eventually allure them back to their first loving response. Thus H. became the author, under God, of the mystical marriage theme of the Bible. He influenced many Prophets who came after him, esp. Jeremiah.

[J. F. FALLON]

HOSEA, BOOK OF. Hosea was a Prophet of the Northern Kingdom, and his message is addressed exclusively to his fellow Israelites there. He began prophesying in the closing years of the prosperous reign of Jeroboam II, almost certainly lived through the terrible period of menaces and defeat by Assyria and the dynastic murders ensuing upon this, and probably died shortly before the final ruin and deportation in 721. The first three chapters of the book consist of what appears to be two distinct biographical accounts of his unhappy marriage to an unfaithful wife, Gomer, whom he divorces yet still loves and seeks to win back in spite of her betrayal. This is taken as an image of Yahweh's relationship with Israel, who persistently and flagrantly betrays him by "going a-whoring after the baalim," looking to the fertility gods of Canaan for her sustenance instead of showing loving loyalty to a convenant God who has proved himself so relentlessly faithful and devoted to her. Hosea evinces a profound sense of sacred history, constantly relating the sins of his own time to the terrible prototype sins of the past. As he sees it, Israel must be so crushed and broken that she returns in spirit to the time of the desert wanderings, and revives that spirit of steadfast love and devotion which she has since lost through the corrupting influence of Canaan, the guilt and treachery of her priests and prophets, the perverted forms of her worship (the "calves of Bethel and Dan"), and the folly of her political intrigues. BIBLIOGRAPHY: W. R. Harper, *Amos and Hosea* (1905); L. W. Batten, "Hosea's Message and Marriage," JBL 48 (1929) 257–273; N. H. Snaith, *Mercy and Sacrifice. A Study of the Book of Hosea* (1953).

HOSIOS ELEUTHERIOS (11th cent. A.D.), a Byzantine domed church in Athens also known as the "Small Metropole." Amongst the marble slabs with which the church is faced are some ancient sculptured fragments built haphazardly into the walls. BIBLIOGRAPHY: R. Krautheimer, *Early Christian and Byzantine Architecture* (1965); T. F. Matthews, NCE 3:783.

[S. MURRAY]

HOSIOS LOUKAS (*c.* A.D. 1040), a Byzantine double church monastery in Stiris, Phocis, Greece, having a dome supported on squinches, and a Greek-cross plan. Its famous mosaics follow the severe Byzantine iconic program of hierarchy showing the Pantocrator in the dome, the enthroned Virgin and Child in the apse, and a cycle of nine scenes of the life of Christ. The work of a provincial school rooted in the Eastern Christian monastic tradition of Syria and Palestine, the mosaics express emotional intensity heightened by an abstract use of color and line. Figures at Hosios Loukas appear stiff and rigid when compared with the 11th cent. mosaics at Daphni. BIBLIOGRAPHY: R. Krautheimer, *Early Christian and Byzantine Architecture* (1965); E. Diez and O. Demus, *Byzantine Mosaics in Greece* (1931); W. C. Loerke, NCE 2:928ff.

[S. MURRAY]

HOSIUS OF CÓRDOBA (OSSIUS; *c.*256–*c.*358), bp. of Córdoba *c.*295, confessor of the faith in the persecution of the Emperor Maximian, 303–305, anti-Arian counselor of Constantine I. H. left Spain *c.*312, where he had taken part in formulating the decrees of the Council of Elvira, including the requirement of clerical celibacy, and joined the court of Constantine. It was on H.'s advice that the emperor convened the Council of Nicaea I, and under H.'s presidency that the Council incorporated the **homoousios* into its creed. He also formulated the canons of the Council of Sardica (lower Dacia) in 343 on the primacy of the Roman pontiff in settling episcopal disputes (D 133, 135). Because of his defense of St. Athanasius and of the Church's liberty against Constantine II he was placed in confinement at Sirmium (in modern Bosnia) and forced by torture to subscribe to the extreme Arian (Anomoean) Second Formulary of Sirmium (that the Son is inferior and subject to the Father, the Holy Spirit has existence through the Son). H. returned to Córdoba and repudiated that submission before he died.

[T. C. O'BRIEN]

HOSIUS, STANISLAUS (1504–79), cardinal, leader of the Counter Reformation in Poland. He studied at Cracow, Padua, and Bologna, there concentrating on law. He was ordained in 1543, made bp. of Culm in 1549 and of Ermland (E Prussia) in 1551. He contributed to the Catholic cause by his writings, esp. *Confessio catholicae fidei christiana* (1532; over 30 subsequent editions). His episcopal administration helped keep Poland Catholic; he took particular care over both the supervision of the clergy and clerical education, introducing the services of the Jesuits; he successfully offset Lutheran influences upon Polish princes. In 1561 he was brought to Rome to serve the papacy, and was created cardinal. Pius IV named him one of the five papal legates for the final period of the Council of Trent. After the Council he succeeded in having its decrees officially recognized in Poland; Pius V charged him with seeing to the Polish translation of the *Catechism of the Council of Trent.* From 1869 he served as ambassador of the Polish king, and continued to work for church reform and for the Catholic cause in the Nordic countries.

[T. C. O'BRIEN]

HOSPITAL OF THE INNOCENTS, Florence. Planned 1419, built 1421–24, this first Florentine Renaissance building designed by Filippo Brunelleschi, shows a portico of nine arches on Corinthian columns, with glazed terracotta medallions by Andrea della Robbia in the spandrels. Housed here is the important *Adoration of the Magi* by Domenico Ghirlandaio.

[M. J. DALY]

HOSPITALITY, from Lat. *hospes,* which refers either to host or to guest, so that it covers both in a mutual relationship, a gracious virtue, all the better for being so often unselfconscious and uncanonized by the run of spiritual writers. Hospitable folk are unaware of their quality: of such is the kingdom of God. It is rooted deeply in the customs of primitive and pagan peoples; only faint correspondences with it appear in the animal kingdom.

Abraham's entertainment of the three heavenly visitors (Gen 18.1–15) sets the note for biblical teaching. The Jews were taught to cherish wayfarers, for they had been wayfarers themselves in the land of Egypt (Dt 10.19). Many stories point the moral; Elijah begs from the widow a share of her last handful of meal (1 Kg 17.11). Their overtones are not always conventionally edifying; it is Rahab the harlot who harbors the two spies (Jos 2) and becomes a heroine for the Christian Church (Heb 11.31; Jas 2.25), though Jael who drove the tent peg into Sisera's skull (Jdt 5. 157) is not condemned as a bad hostess in the Song of Deborah.

In the NT our Lord sets the supreme example by himself washing the feet of his guests (Jn 13) and breaking the bread for them to eat; before that he had told them of the Lord coming "hungry, and you gave me to eat, thirsty, and you gave me to drink, a stranger and you welcomed me" (Mt 25.35). "Practice hospitality ungrudgingly to one another (1 Pet 4.9)." This apostolic theme was insisted on and repeated in the early Church; bps. were charged with the special duty of hospitality, and numerous *xenodochia* and *nosocomia* were the forerunners of modern hotels and hospitals, not so clean and antiseptic, though perhaps more genial. Particular mention should be made of the important place held by hospitality in the monastic life (*Rule of St. Benedict* ch. 53); the tradition still flourishes in religious houses.

We are the losers when, with the advance of civilization, a growth in security, now somewhat dubious, and of urban conditions, hospitality is not now so readily claimed and so readily offered. Even so relics remain, and their merits are by no means to be despised, such as giving a party or offering a drink to a stranger from a genuine warmth of friendliness. It is hard to pigeonhole hospitality in an Aristotelian scheme of the Christian virtues. Theologically it flows from charity, as *mercy, (*misericordia*), *beneficence (*beneficentia*), and giving relief (*eleemosyna*) (cf. ThAq ST 2a2ae, 30–33), but it is most important that any suggestion of patronage should be drained from all these, which are appropriately expressed on both sides through the virtues of *gratitude, *friendliness or kindly manners, *liberality, *magnificence, and **eutrapelia* or good fun (cf. respectively ThAq ST 2a2ae, 106, 114, 117, 134, 168).

[T. GILBY]

HOSPITALLERS, THE KNIGHTS, see HOSPITALLERS AND HOSPITAL SISTERS.

HOSPITALLERS AND HOSPITAL SISTERS, name given to a variety of orders, lay or religious, secular or monastic, which, beginning in the Middle Ages, consecrated themselves primarily to nursing the sick in institutions specifically designed for their medical treatment and care. Members of such orders, whether or not they had taken solemn vows, generally lived in organized communities according to Augustinian, Benedictine, or Franciscan Rule. Those attached to monastic orders or to canonries came under episcopal jurisdiction or the direct control of the pope. The first hospitals in Western Europe probably grew out of the simple hospices that were maintained for the poor, the incurably ill, and the insane. As these were often administered by monastic orders, many monasteries in effect turned into hospitals once they became oriented to healing. Early medieval Europe was of course far behind the Islamic world in the provision of medical services in an institutional setting, individual charity having sufficed during the 1st millennium, but after 2 cent. of frenzied hospital growth beginning in the 11th cent., the Continent had caught up by the early 13th. So numerous in fact were the foundations during this period that by the 14th cent. such leading Italian cities as Florence and Rome could boast 30 hospitals apiece, while England at the same time could claim nearly 1,000. The nursing orders were directly responsible for much of this expansion, and their rise in turn could be attributed in part to the Crusades.

The most celebrated of all Hospital orders, for instance, was that of the Knights of St. John of Jerusalem, established early in the 12th cent. to cater to the needs and infirmities of pilgrims in the Holy Land. In spite of becoming a military order shortly after their foundation, medical work remained a top priority with them, and hospitals founded and administered by the order flourished throughout Europe and the Near East. The main hospital in Jerusalem, which the Knights hung onto until 1187, provided for 2,000 patients, while their infirmary on the Island of Rhodes, which, after its capture from the Turks, became their headquarters from 1309 to 1523, was professionally staffed by lay doctors, surgeons, chemists, and nurses. The 300-bed hospital established by the Knights on Malta (headquarters of the order, 1530–1798) was one of the largest and most modern of its day, though by the early 16th cent. nearly every country could claim possession of architecturally impressive hospital facilities. Other important nursing orders included the Antonines, who, starting in 1100 with the founding of the hospital of Saint-Antoine-de-Viennois attached to the monastery of the same name, set up hospitals all over France, Spain, Italy, and Germany, as well as at Constantinople and Acre in Palestine; the Order of the Holy Spirit, which within a century of its establishment at Montpellier in 1145 had daughter houses throughout Western Europe; the Order of St. William of the Desert; the Bethlehemites; and the hospital sisters of the Order of St. Catherine. The mendicant orders—Franciscans and Poor Clares—were also influential in the development of the hospital movement, as were the Beguines in the Belgian Netherlands, and the later Alexian Brothers, who first emerged in the 15th cent. to minister to victims of the plague and ultimately spread throughout Flanders and Germany.

The principles of nursing practiced by the medieval Hospital orders—isolation of the gravely ill, constant attendance on the sick, and emphasis on the needs of new mothers—were in a sense more advanced than the rudimentary medical knowledge of the university-trained physicians under whose supervision they worked. Hospitallers were responsible for administering drugs and anesthetics (made from combining the fumes of opium and mandragora), for taking temperatures before the invention of the thermometer, for the treatment of fractures by traction, for urine analysis, and for assisting at operations, which, in addition to blood letting, cupping, and trephining, included procedures for treating cataracts, ruptures, fistulas, hemorrhoids, and strictures.

The chief contributions of the hospital movement lay in regulating the character of care to be given patients in hospitals, in establishing and staffing the institutions to provide this care, and, by their existence, in enabling municipal hospitals to function independently of the monasteries which formerly controlled them. But perhaps the greatest single service rendered by the Hospitallers was in helping to rid Europe of the scourge of leprosy. By their service in leper houses, by orders such as the Hospitallers of St. Lazarus, founded in the 12th cent. especially to deal with leprosy in Jerusalem, and later active throughout the West, and through their massive attack on the disease waged by means of confining the infected, leprosy, prevalent on the Continent for nearly 1000 years, was effectively conquered by 1500. This success in turn influenced the approach to other infectious diseases and consequently the health of the whole Western world. *ST. LAZARUS OF JERUSALEM, ORDER OF.

[E. M. GATES]

HOSPITALLERS OF ST. JOHN OF GOD, a nursing order of brothers in Spain who were dedicated to the sick and needy. They were founded by a Portuguese shepherd boy, St. John of God, in 1537 and were recognized by Pius V as the Hospitaller Order of St. John of God in 1571. Following the Rule of St. Augustine, they added a fourth vow of hospitality and summed up their spirit in the word *Caritas*.

As the order spread through Europe some of its hospitals were renowned for the medical and surgical skill of its brothers. The rural areas had hospitals from which the brothers made daily home visits to the sick; the brother-pharmacist grew herbs to heal diseases, and the chaplain cared for the spiritual needs of all. The brothers played a great part in the conversion of the Indians since 70 of their hospitals were opened in S. America in the 17th century.

During the French Revolution the brothers were expelled from 40 hospitals but they opened new ones when the Revolution was over. The brothers, who worked in 34 countries by 1975, numbered 2,039 serving in 116 hospitals. In 1941 they arrived in the U.S. and are currently located in the Archdioceses of Los Angeles and St. Louis and the Diocese of Ojai.

[R. C. CLIGGETT]

HOSPITALLERS OF ST. LAZARUS OF JERUSALEM, see HOSPITALLERS AND HOSPITAL SISTERS.

HOSPITALS, CATHOLIC. Institutions for the care of the sick and injured have always been closely allied with the practice of religion. In Greece and Rome temples in honor of Asclepius Hygeia or Saturn were primarily built to treat the sick. In early Christian times there were hospices for the infirm, for travelers, or victims of war or natural disasters. Religious orders of men and women stressed ministry to the sick and built hospitals attached to religious houses; throughout the Middle Ages nursing of the sick was largely in the hands of the Church. The modern Catholic hospital is in continuity with the ancient practice of the care of the sick as a corporal work of mercy. But medical advances of the modern era have changed the work of the hospital from being, as it generally was prior to the 18th cent., a place for care of the terminally ill, to a place of healing. The complexities faced by the modern hospital press on the Catholic hospital in many distinctive ways. In the U.S. there were in 1975 over 660 hospitals operated under RC auspices and caring for more than 5 million patients annually. As private institutions these hospitals are hard pressed by the rising costs of medical care; the ancient charitable characteristic and motivation of the care of the sick has often to be tempered in practice by the rigors of economic necessity. The private status of Catholic hospitals before the law has assumed major importance because of legal and medico-moral controversies. Legislative and judiciary bodies, both state and federal, have incorporated into laws and court decisions so-called conscience clauses that grant immunity to private health care facilities from the legal obligation public hospitals have to provide patients with elective abortions or sterilization procedures. It has been established legally that the fact of private hospitals' receiving federal grants for some of their programs does not deprive them of the right to take a moral stance on certain medical issues. In order to stress the pro-life commitment of the Catholic hospital as such the National Conference of Catholic Bishops (NCCB) at its annual meeting in Nov. 1971 approved and issued *Ethical and Religious Directives for Catholic Health Facilities* (text in *Origins* 1:408, 410–413). The document was a strong affirmation of moral absolutes in the area of medical ethics; it covered the issues of abortion, sterilization, determination of the moment of death, postmortem examinations, organic transplants, and other medical issues. The National Federation of Catholic Physicians Guilds registered the formal dissent of some members with respect to the NCCB statement (*Origins* 1:425). The Catholic Theological Society of America in 1973 at its annual meeting received the report of a study commission on the NCCB statement. The report was a strong dissent from the NCCB document. It called into question the assertion of moral absolutes in areas where there was no agreement among theologians or ethicians about the moral quality of certain medical procedures; it also called into question the right to impose absolute directives on the consciences of hospital personnel. The report also argued against the right of hospitals to claim to be Catholic and private institutions in the face of the pluralistic society in which they exist and which to some extent shapes their identity and status (text of the report, *Origins* 2:469–472; 477–484). The issues on which the dissent was registered continue to be controverted. NCCB Committee on Pro-life Activities in 1973 issued another statement, *Pastoral Guidelines for the Catholic Hospital and Catholic Health Care Personnel* (*Origins* 2:696–698). This was in reaction to the Supreme Court decision of Jan. 22, 1973 that made elective abortion an absolute part of the woman's right to privacy. The NCCB statement forbade direct abortion and contraceptive sterilization in Catholic hospitals and forbade Catholic medical personnel working in hospitals where these procedures are carried out from participating. The teaching of the American bps. on Catholic hospitals is clear; dissent, however, continues.

HÖSS, CRESCENTIA, BL. (1682–1744), Franciscan. Anna Höss was born to parents of modest means at Kaufbeuren in Bavaria. During her teenage years she desired to join the Franciscan community of Mayerhoff but was denied because her father could not provide a dowry. At the age of 21, she was able to enter the community because the burgomaster of Kaufbeuren purchased a tavern adjoining the convent, turned the deed over to the nuns, and stipulated that she must receive admittance in return for his favor. In 1704, H. received the habit and took the name Maria Crescentia. During the first years of her religious life, she suffered harsh treatment by the superior, Theresa Schmidt. With the appointment of Maria Altwoegerin as superior in 1707, H. was given her rightful place in community life, and the sisters finally began to recognize her saintliness. In 1726, she was appointed mistress of novices and in 1741, superior. She had several mystical experiences including a sharing in Christ's Passion, and her reputation as a woman of wisdom brought her visitors from throughout Germany. She was beatified by Pope Leo XIII in 1900. BIBLIOGRAPHY: R. Lioi, BiblSanct 8:601–603; Butler 2:38–39.

[R. J. BRADY]

HOST, the Eucharistic bread, so called because it is Christ's body ''given up for us'' as victim (Lat. *hostia*) in the sacrifice of the Cross. Sometimes the unconsecrated communion wafers are called ''hosts'' in distinction from the consecrated Eucharistic bread.

[T. C. O'BRIEN]

HOSTIENSIS SEGUSIO (Henry of Segusio, Susa; *c.*1200–71), canonist, cardinal. One of the most renowned and influential *decretalists of the medieval church, H. studied at Bologna under Jacobus de Albenga (canon law) and under Jacobus Balduinus and Homobonus of Cremona (civil law). His mastery of the law earned him the title ''iuris utriusque monarcha.'' Whether he taught at Bologna is not certain, but in 1239 he was archdeacon of Paris where he lectured on the decretals. He spent much of the time between 1235 and 1244 in England in the service of Henry III and his wife Eleanor of Provence. From late 1243 until about 1250 H. was bp. of Sisteron and then became abp. of Embrun. He enjoyed the favor of both Innocent IV and Urban IV and served both in various canonical and diplomatic capacities. In 1261 Urban IV named him cardinal bishop of Ostia (whence the name ''Hostiensis''). The illness that led to his death forced him to resign (June 1270) from the papal conclave that followed upon the death of Clement IV. H.'s reputation as canonist rests chiefly upon his *Summa super titulis decretalium (Summa aurea, Summa archiepiscopi, Summa ''copiosa'')* begun in 1239 and completed in 1253. Despite its dependence on the work of such predecessors as Godfrey of Trani, the *Summa* is no mere assemblage of opinions, distinctions, and questions relating to the decretals but an original and comprehensive synthesis of canon and civil law. His *Lectura in quinque libros decretalium,* allegedly begun while he taught in Paris, was completed only shortly before he died. This work shows a more religious or theological concern than does the *Summa* and this may in some way explain its lesser influence on the subsequent tradition. H. also composed a commentary on the decretals of Innocent IV and several other minor works. He is mentioned by Dante in the *Paradiso,* 12, 82. BIBLIOGRAPHY: J. F. von Schulte, *Die Geschichte der Quellen und der Literatur des kanonischen Rechts* (1875–80) 2:123–129; A. Van Hove, *Commentarium Lovaniense in Codicem iuris canonici* 1:476, 478.

[J. E. BIECHLER]

HOSTS, LORD OF, an ancient designation for Yahweh. It stands for the fuller title, Yahweh, the God of the Hosts of Israel (1 Sam 17.45). Israel is considered an army with Yahweh as its leader. The designation is later used most frequently by the Prophets, esp., Is, Jer, and Zechariah. Another opinion holds that Hosts refers to the angels or stars. This is certainly not its original meaning. Perhaps the universalism introduced by the classical prophets widened its meaning. If so, the title would later express Yahweh's supremacy over earthly and heavenly agencies as instruments of his purpose. BIBLIOGRAPHY: W. Eichrodt, *Theology of the OT* (tr. J. A. Baker, 2 v., 1961); R. W. Gleason, *Yahweh: the God of the OT* (1964).

[F. GAST]

HÔTEL (MAISON DIEU), see HÔTEL DIEU DE PARIS.

HÔTEL-DIEU DE PARIS, oldest hospital in Paris, now located on the N side of Place Notre Dame, though the original hospital complex was on the S side. According to legend, it was founded (651) by St. Landri, bp. of Paris. More certainly, an establishment for the poor was endowed by Bp. Inchade in the 9th cent., and this was dependent on the cathedral chapter by the early 11th century. It was under Bp. Sully that the important medieval institution known as the Maison-Dieu began to take shape, started *c.* 1160 simultaneously with the cathedral of Notre Dame and the episcopal palace; from this date on, emphasis shifted to care of the sick rather than of the poor. Extended along the Seine in the 13th cent., the hospital thereafter was many times added to, reinforced, remodeled, and even reconstructed, eventually expanding across the river onto the Left Bank during the 17th century. Nevertheless, until the 15th cent., the Hôtel-Dieu accommodated no more than 300 beds, these often seeing triple service—a standard practice of the time—esp. during epidemics when up to 1500 patients were treated. The hospital was originally staffed by laity, but these were replaced by religious personnel in the late 13th century. During the reign of Louis XI (1461–83), however, the administration of the hospital was plagued by scandals, discipline among the religious collapsing completely into an abusive regime. In an attempt to stamp out this anarchy, Francis I (1515–47) confided the hospital's administration to the abbey of St. Victor, placed the nursing brothers and sisters under Augustinian Rule, and drew up a new constitution for the Hôtel-Dieu. Even so, discipline was not fully restored until the 17th cent. when St. Vincent de Paul installed the zealous Ladies of Charity (1634) to bolster the institution's religious staff and to set higher standards. At the same time, the treatment of foundlings was revolutionized. On December 30, 1772, most of the Hôtel-Dieu, which had long since proved inadequate, was destroyed by fire. The new hospital established by Louis XVI according to modern precepts, though intended for 3,000 patients, could still not accommodate Parisian needs, and so was rebuilt early in the 19th cent. as a place for serious illnesses only. Under Napoleon III, this too was torn down in accordance with Baron Hausmann's ambitious planning schemes, but rearose, 1868–78, larger than ever, in a slightly different spot, now facing the square that is the heart of Paris as well as of France.

[E. M. GATES]

HOUBIGANT, CHARLES FRANÇOIS (1686–1783), French Oratorian biblical scholar. H. established a printing plant at Avilly where he published his major works: a vocabulary of Hebrew roots; an introduction to Scripture (2 v.); and, most significantly, a Hebrew Bible with critical notes (4 v., 1753–54), followed by a Latin translation of the OT based upon his Hebrew text. Although well received at the time, H.'s Hebrew Bible is marred by a lack of vocal signs and too many unwarranted changes from the Masoretic text. BIBLIOGRAPHY: H. Lesêtre, DB 3.1:765–766; C. Souvay, CE 7:498–499.

[T. M. MCFADDEN]

HOUCK, GEORGE FRANCIS (1847–1916), diocesan chancellor, writer. Ordained in 1875 he became the first chancellor of the Diocese of Cleveland, a capacity in which he served from 1877 to 1909. His influence on a fast growing jurisdiction was considerable. As a writer he refuted the frequent anti-Catholic statements appearing in the *Cleveland Leader* and published the extensive work *History of the Catholic Church in Northern Ohio and the Diocese of Cleveland* (1903).

[J. R. AHERNE]

HOUGHTON, JOHN, ST. (*c.* 1487–1535). English Carthusian martyr. After ordination he entered the London charterhouse (1514) and became prior there (1531). In 1534 he was briefly imprisoned for refusing to swear to the Act of Succession, but eventually took the oath with reservations. The following year the Act of Supremacy was more encompassing and the required oath more stringent. H. and two other Carthusian priors appeared before Cromwell in hopes of obtaining a version of the oath satisfactory to conscience. They were immediately imprisoned, tried and found guilty of treason, and executed at Tyburn in brutal fashion. H. was canonized in 1970. BIBLIOGRAPHY: S. Mottironi, BiblSanct 3:1140–42; Butler 2:277–280; L. E. Whatmore, *Blessed Carthusian Martyrs* (1962) 224–232.

[V. SAMPSON]

HOUR OF JESUS, in the Synoptic Gospels, "the hour" is used significantly but not quite thematically to designate the appearance of the Son of Man (Mt 24.44; 25.13), the testing of the Disciples by persecution (Mk 13.11), and above all, the Passion of Jesus (Mk 14.35, 41; Mt 26.45). John employs "the hour" or "my hour" thematically to denote a particular and significant period in Jesus' life, the hour of his return to the Father, the hour of the cross, which in the fourth Gospel is one phase of Jesus' glorification. The hour of Jesus is opposed to the hour of darkness (12.35) and yet paradoxically it is in the hour of darkness that Jesus' hour arrives (12.21–32). Despite outward appearances, it is the hour of triumph because the world is being judged, and the power of evil broken definitively. John's usage of "the hour" encompasses passages in two categories: those affirming that it has not yet come or is still coming (2.4; 7.30; 8.20); those affirming that "the hour" has come (12.23, 27; 13.1; 17.1). The fourth Evangelist also refers to "an hour" in passages that apply by anticipation the effects of Jesus' own hour to those believing in him during his public ministry. Such references include: passages referring to a coming hour (4.21; 5.28–29; 16.2, 25) involving, e.g., clear understanding of Jesus' words or persecution of believers; passages stating that "an hour" is both coming and has already come (4.23; 5.25; 16.32). In 4.23 a coming yet present hour has to do with the worship of the Father in spirit and in truth. Although the Spirit was not given until after the Resurrection (7.39; 20.22), the experience of Jesus during his earthly ministry offered to those who believed in him an anticipation of the divine gifts. The fourth Evangelist views the events of Jesus' earthly ministry as prophetic signs in which past and future coalesce in the present. The moment when all prophetic signs of Jesus' life are fulfilled and come to reality in the new born community is "the hour" of the Cross which begins the glorification of Jesus. BIBLIOGRAPHY: R. Brown, *Gospel According to John* (1966) 1:517–518; B. Vawter, JBC 80:33–34 (834–835).

[T. J. RYAN]

HOUSE OF BISHOPS, one house of the *General Convention of the Protestant Episcopal Church. The original draft of the Church's constitution, following the civil polity of the U.S. under the then-effective Articles of Confederation, provided a unicameral governing body, the House of Clerical and Lay Deputies. The House of Bishops was added to win approval of the Constitution from Bp. Samuel S. *Seabury of Connecticut and his followers. Voice and vote in this House are given to all active bps. and to those retired for specified reasons. The House of Bishops acts independently in issuing pastoral letters and in organizing and electing bps. for missionary districts. BIBLIOGRAPHY: E. A. White and J. A. Dyckman, *Annotated Constitution and Canons for the Government of the Protestant Episcopal Church in the U.S.A.* (2 v., 1954) 4–38.

[H. H. RIGHTOR]

HOUSE OF CLERICAL AND LAY DEPUTIES, together with the House of Bishops, the constitutive houses of the *General Convention of the Protestant Episcopal Church. Each diocese is represented in the House of Deputies by four clergymen and four laymen; each missionary district, by one member of each order. The constitution is being amended to permit women to serve as lay deputies, and there is a growing movement to make representation from dioceses more proportionate to diocesan church membership. A "vote by orders" on any measure must be granted when requested. Passage of a measure on such a vote requires both a majority of clerical representatives and a majority of lay representatives from a majority of dioceses. BIBLIOGRAPHY: E. A. White and J. A. Dyckman, *Annotated Constitution and Canons for the Government of the Protestant Episcopal Church in the U.S.A.* (2 v., 1954) 4–38.

[H. H. RIGHTOR]

HOUSE OF DAVID, communal body established by Benjamin Purnell at Benton Harbor, Mich., in 1903. He proclaimed himself to be the last of the seven messengers referred to in Rev 8.6 and 11.15, with the mission of gathering the 144,000 true Israelites to establish the kingdom of God on earth. He was crowned King Benjamin of the House of David. The group is sometimes called the Israelite House of David, since Benton proclaimed the members to be the "ingathering" of the descendants of the 12 lost tribes of Israel. Belief includes acceptance of the doctrine of Jesus Christ, *millenarianism, and *universalism. Members turn over all their property to the community; they are vegetarians; the men must not cut their hair or shave. In the 1920s and 1930s the traveling House of David baseball team and band gave national publicity to the movement. The House of David survived the scandal of Purnell's trials on charges of immorality. A board of directors maintains control over spiritual and temporal affairs; the community supports itself by agriculture and small shops. Membership in 1964 was 350; in 1969 there were 77 members. BIBLIOGRAPHY: W. J. Whalen, *Faiths for the Few* (1963).

[T. C. O'BRIEN]

HOUSE OF PRAYER. The term in a generic use refers to a center with a core community intended to provide an experience of prayer within an interpersonal setting. It refers to a center, then, where Christians, whether laity, clergy, or religious, may pass a period of retreat or retirement to share in this experience. The permanent (relatively speaking) community provides a setting, a continuity, and the resources developed through its life so that others may profit by participating for a time. In this sense houses of prayer are maintained by religious communities or other interested groups. There are some general characteristics: prayer is communal and based on Scripture; there are discussions and exchanges of experience; there may be guided retreats, which seek to match the spiritual needs and conditions of the participants; there is a commonly recognized goal, a deepening of prayer life that manifests itself in and permeates the whole life of the individual. There is also a common reliance: that the Holy Spirit will be present to those who are so gathered together. But the house of prayer as such is not necessarily focused on *charismatic prayer or part of the charismatic movement. In a specific and historical meaning the House of Prayer Experience (HOPE) is a movement that began among women religious in the U.S. in 1968, with the Immaculate Heart of Mary Sisters, Monroe, Mich., providing the initial organization. The HOPE 6 weeks experiment of 1969 has been followed by similar programs since, whether within religious communities or with members of many communities coming together.

[T. C. O'BRIEN]

HOUSEHOLD OF THE POPE, see PAPAL HOUSEHOLD.

HOUSEL, a word, now obsolete, used in England from ancient times down to the Reformation. As a noun it signified the consecrated eucharistic elements, or sometimes the Mass itself, or the distribution of communion. As a verb it meant to administer communion, or, in the passive, to be given communion.

[P. K. MEAGHER]

HOUSELANDER, CARYLL (1901–54), Catholic writer. In 1941, while working in a London first-aid post, H. published *This War is the Passion* and in 1944 *The Reed of God,* spiritual books of great originality speaking directly to the hearts of modern men. Both became best sellers and brought a stream of men and women to her door seeking direction. A psychiatrist brought her his patients for therapy and in 1951 she published *Guilt.* Intensely Bohemian, she earned her living in advertising, wood-carving, teaching, illustrating, and finally in writing as her books and poems and "rhythms" poured out, all written at white heat and on every page a flash of wisdom. All express her passionate conviction of the presence of Christ in all men. She drove herself hard, got up early to pray, and in whatever she did, according to her friends, was both "endlessly amusing" and "continually aware of the divine." A complete list of her writings can be found in E. Falloux, NCE 7:175. BIBLIOGRAPHY: M. Ward, *Caryll Houselander: That Divine Eccentric* (1962).

[M. O'CONNOR]

HOUSELING CLOTH, a white linen cloth spread before communicants to prevent the host or crumbs from falling to the floor. The cloth is held by altar boys, or is attached to the altar rail, or is clipped along the top of the pews, possibly to give the impression of a prepared table. Its use originated in the Middle Ages and in some places continues at the present time.

[N. KOLLAR]

HOUTIN, ALBERT (1867–1926), French priest who apostatized during the period of *Modernism. His main works were *La Question biblique chez les catholiques de France au XIXe siècle* (1902) and *Histoire du modernisme catholique* (1913). He left the priesthood in 1912 and by degrees came to reject all revealed truth and to regard all organized religion as fraudulent and hypocritical.

[T. C. O'BRIEN]

HOWARD, EDWARD D. (1877–), abp. of Portland, Oregon. Ordained for the archdiocese of Dubuque in 1906, H. was a professor and later president of Columbia (now Loras) College. In 1924 he was named auxiliary bp. of Davenport, Iowa. Appointed bp. of Oregon City, later the archdiocese of Portland, Oregon, he was a vigorous administrator of his see, establishing 23 parishes, centralizing the Catholic school system, and building new schools. H. inaugurated the Catholic Charities organization and promoted the Confraternity of Christian Doctrine. He resigned in 1960.

[J. R. AHERNE]

HOWARD, FRANCIS WILLIAM (1867–1944), bp., educator. A native of Ohio, H. was ordained in 1891. After 4 years of study at Columbia Univ. and in Rome, he was assigned to educational and parish work in Columbus, Ohio. In 1923 he was named bp. of Covington, Ky., where he enhanced his reputation as an innovative educator, esp. with his "Bishop's Schools" for the gifted. He was secretary-general of the National Catholic Educational Association (1904–28) and president (1929–35). BIBLIOGRAPHY: P. Ryan, *History of the Diocese of Covington, Kentucky* (1954).

[J. R. AHERNE]

HOWARD, HENRY (1517–47), Earl of Surrey by courtesy, English poet, son of Thomas Howard, Duke of Norfolk. Accused of treason by the Seymours after the death of Henry VIII, he was beheaded. H. was well known in his own day for his translations of the Psalms and for his *Songs and Sonnets,* of which numerous editions in the 16th cent. attest his popularity. His chief importance in the field of English literature, however, lies in his attempts to adapt new meters to English poetry: he and Thomas Wyatt were the first to employ the sonnet and the "octave rima" in English; he first tried English blank verse in his translation of the *Aeneid,* and first imitated Italian poetry in English, using Petrarch and Dante as his favorite models.

[M. J. BARRY]

HOWARD, PHILIP, ST. (1557–95), Earl of Arundel and martyr. H. was eldest son of the 4th Duke of Norfolk. When young he lived a worldly life as a courtier and favorite of Elizabeth I, neglecting his wife, Anne Dacre, whose fortune and his own he squandered. His conscience was troubled, however, and after hearing Edmund *Campion dispute with Protestant divines, he was reconciled to the Church of Rome and to his wife, already a Catholic. He fell from royal favor, and when discovered in an attempt to fly the country, he was sent to the Tower where he lived a holy life for more than 10½ years. Though he greatly desired to see his wife and the son born after his imprisonment, he was never allowed that comfort. Tried for treason, he was condemned on fabricated evidence but was never executed, and indeed his freedom was offered him on condition he take part in a Protestant service. He died in the Tower. He was canonized in 1970. BIBLIOGRAPHY: H. G. F. Howard, *Lives of Philip Howard and Anne Dacre* (1857); G. E. Cokayne, *Peerage of England* 11; M. Waugh, *Bl. Philip Howard* (CTS 1961); Butler 4:152–154.

[M. O'CONNOR]

HOWARD, PHILIP THOMAS (1629–94), cardinal. H. was born at Arundel House, London, and his education was controlled by his grandfather Thomas Howard, Earl of Arundel, who in 1615 had conformed to the new religion. While traveling with his grandfather, H. met an Irish Dominican who was teaching theology in Milan and in spite of strong opposition from his family became a Dominican friar. He returned to England, rallied the spirits of the few remaining Dominicans and from his own resources, and those of friends, raised £1600 for the founding of a priory at Bornhem in Flanders. Here the sons of English, Irish, and

Scots were received into the Dominican Order and trained for the home mission. This foundation is credited with saving the English Dominicans from extinction. After the Restoration, he became chaplain to Queen Catherine (1662) but resigned 10 years later and returned to Bornhem. He later became a card. (1675) and served in the papal curia. BIBLIOGRAPHY: C. F. R. Palmer, *Life of Philip Thomas Howard O.P.* (1867); W. Lescher, *Cardinal Howard* (1905); B. Jarret, *Letters of Philip Cardinal Howard* (1925).

[M. O'CONNOR]

HOWLETT, WILLIAM JOSEPH (1847–1936), missionary, writer. Ordained for Denver, Colo. in 1876, H. labored there as a missionary and pastor. From 1903 until his death, he was chaplain to the Sisters of Loretto in Loretto, Ky. where he did considerable historical and biographical writing on mission figures.

[J. R. AHERNE]

HOYSALESVARA TEMPLE, Halebīd, S Indian double Temple of Şiva in Mysore State, begun in 1235. It is unfinished due perhaps to the Muslim invasion (1310). Oriented E on a platform, the exterior is profusely carved in narrow friezes with scenes from mythology and legend.

[M. J. DALY]

HRABANUS MAURUS, see RABANUS MAURUS, BL.

HROZNATA, BL. (*c.*1170–1217), Bohemian Premonstratensian canon and monastic founder. When the Crusade of Henry VI, which H. had vowed to join, disintegrated, the Pope commuted the vow to that of founding a religious institute. He established the Premonstratensian nuns in his family castle at Choteschau. In 1201 he himself took the habit of a Premonstratensian in Rome and later settled down to the life of a lay brother in the Premonstratensian monastery at Tepl, which he had founded before his departure for the Crusade. On a journey undertaken in defense of the community's property he was captured by brigands and died of the maltreatment he received at their hands. Leo XIII approved his cult as a martyr. BIBLIOGRAPHY: J. Polc, BiblSanct 7:606–608.

HSIANG-T'ANG-SHAN CAVES, in N Honan and W Hopei, China, two series of cave temples called the Northern and Southern Hsiang-t'ang-shan from the Northern Ch'i period (550–577), explored by Japanese scholars in the 20th century. The sculpture, of great simplicity, has a three-dimensional quality indicating Indian influence. Several fine examples are in the University Museum, Philadelphia, Pennsylvania.

[M. J. DALY]

HUBER, SAMUEL (1547–1624), Swiss Protestant controversialist, advocate of Lutheranism, critic of Swiss Reformed Calvinism. His opposition to A. Muslin and others in Berne over the novel use of broken bread instead of the communion wafer restored the traditional practice until the 17th century. After sharply criticizing the Reformed doctrine of predestination at the Mümpelgart Colloquy (1586) and publicly disputing his position at Bern (1588), he was silenced, and refusing to obey, was exiled (June, 1588). At Tübingen, he formulated his doctrine of the Atonement which stressed the universality of Christ's sacrificial death for all men, a doctrine to which the Württemberg theologians objected. In 1592 he went to Wittenberg, but after controversy was dismissed from his professorship and banished (1595).

[R. J. LITZ]

HUBER, WOLF (1490–1553), Austrian painter, designer of woodcuts and with A. Altdorfer (to whom he was apprenticed), a chief representative of the Danubian school, which he enriched by his spontaneity. H. painted a *St. Anne Altar,* one of the greatest of Danubian works, and *Christ Taking Leave of His Mother* (1519), showing Altdorfer's influence. His later work is expressive and mysterious in light (*Raising of the Cross, Crucifixion, Crowning of Thorns*). Early woodcuts, *St. George* and *St. Christopher* are remarkable for landscapes.

[M. J. DALY]

HUBERT OF MAASTRICHT, ST. (*c.*655–727), bp. of Tongerer-Maastricht and Liège. Legend enters his life-history: he is one of those reportedly converted upon seeing a cross in the antlers of a stag when hunting. After his conversion, he worked with St. Lambert of Maastricht whom he succeeded as bp.; he later transferred the see to Liège. He was buried in the abbey, later called "of St. Hubert," in the Ardennes, center of his cult. BIBLIOGRAPHY: J. Barnow, *Pageant of Netherlands History* (1952); Butler 4:247–248; *Book of Saints* (comp. Benedictine Monks of St. Augustine's Abbey, 1966).

[M. E. DUFFY]

HUBERT WALTER (d. 1205), abp of Canterbury chancellor of England. H. was a nephew of Ranulf de Glanville, the famous legist, who influenced him in his taste for law and civil service. He became dean of York (1186); bp. of Salisbury (1189); abp. of York (1193). On the Third Crusade, he accompanied King Richard, whose chief agent he became in negotiations with Saladin. In 1194, Richard designated him justiciar of England, and in this capacity he successfully governed the country in the King's absence. He resigned the office in 1198 when Innocent III reinvigorated the law against priests' holding secular office. In 1199 until his death he held the office of chancellor under King John. His service was characterized by efficiency, dedication, and prolonged litigation with Bp. Hugh of Lincoln, Giraldus Cambrensis, his cathedral chapter at York, and others. His tomb is said to be at Canterbury cathedral. BIB-

LIOGRAPHY: K. Norgate, DNB 10:137–140; C. R. Cheney, *From Becket to Langton* (1956).

[J. J. SMITH]

HUBERT, JEAN-FRANÇOIS (1739–99), ninth bp. of Quebec. A native of Quebec, he was ordained in 1766. He taught at the seminary, labored in the Huron Mission at Detroit for 4 years, was named coadjutor of Quebec in 1786 and became bp. in 1788. When American Tories from the U.S. attempted to establish a university for Catholics and Protestants he saw it as a threat to French Canadians and effectively opposed the scheme. H. administered a fast-growing diocese, in territory larger than Europe. He resigned shortly before his death.

[J. R. AHERNE]

HUBMAIER, BALTHASAR (*c.*1485–1528), Anabaptist leader and writer. H. was born at Friedberg near Augsburg, was a student of J. *Eck, became a priest and a celebrated preacher at Regensburg (1516–21). Having become pastor at Waldshut near the Swiss border, he soon embraced Reformation teaching. He formed a bond with *Zwingli, but through C. *Grebel turned to Anabaptist ideas—a religion of inner experience, the rejection of *infant baptism, and the complete freedom of the Church from secular power. H. broke with Zwingli after disagreements on infant baptism at Zurich in 1525. He took part in the *Peasants' War (some attribute the Twelve Articles to him) but opposed the violence preached by T. *Münzer. Early in 1526, H. was imprisoned at Zurich for his Anabaptist views and temporarily renounced them. He found refuge in Nikolsburg in Moravia, where he engaged in controversy with H. *Hut and wrote a number of Anabaptist tracts. In 1527 he was arrested, brought to Vienna, and burned as a heretic. His works, esp. *Von dem Tauf der Glaübigen* (1525), are a clear exposition of the essential Anabaptist teaching on individual and mystical experience in religion. Works: *Balthasar Hubmaier Schriften* (ed. G. Westin and T. Bergsten, 1962). BIBLIOGRAPHY: T. Bergsten, *Balthasar Hubmaier* (1961); R. Döllinger, RGG 3:464–465; R. M. Jones, *Studies in Mystical Religion* (1923) 379–383.

[T. C. O'BRIEN]

HUBY, JOSEPH (1878–1948), French NT scholar, apologist, and spiritual writer. He entered the Society of Jesus at Laval in 1897 and was ordained in England in 1910. He taught in England until 1927, then was professor of New Testament at Lyon-Fourvière until 1936. He was founder (1924) of the *Verbum Salutis* NT commentary series, to which he contributed commentaries on Mark, Luke, John, and the Pauline Epistles. In 1940 he was appointed a consultor to the Pontifical Biblical Commission. In addition to his books, he contributed numerous articles to *Études, Recherches de Science religieuse, Dictionnaire apologétique de la foi catholique,* and *Construire*. His books include *L'Évangile et les Évangiles (Church and the Gospels*, tr. F. Moran, 1931) and *Mystique paulinienne et johannique* (1947).

[T. J. RYAN]

HUC, EVARISTE RÉGIS (1813–1860), French Vincentian missionary explorer. A member of the Congregation of the Missions from 1836, he went to China in 1839, residing in the Vicariate of Tartary-Mongolia for 5 years, when he and a confrere, Joseph Gabet (1808–53), were asked by the bp. to explore the vicariate and observe Mongol customs. For 18 months they journeyed across China, arriving at Lhasa, capital of Tibet, in 1846. Expelled from Lhasa soon after through the machinations of the Chinese commissioner, they made a difficult journey of 7 months to Canton. H. returned to France in 1852 and left the Vincentians the next year. He wrote two notable books, *Souvenirs d'un voyage dans la Tartarie et le Tibet* (1850) and *Le Christianisme en Chine, en Tartarie et au Tibet* (1858).

[J. R. AHERNE]

HUCBALD OF SAINT-ARMAND (*c.*840–930), Benedictine teacher, hagiographer, and poet; but remembered esp. for his *De institutione harmonica,* one of the earliest theoretical treatises on Gregorian chant.

[T. C. O'BRIEN]

HUCH, RICARDA (1864–1947), German novelist, lyricist, essayist, historian, and literary critic. Originally a neoromanticist, H. became increasingly conscious of the great European traditions and undertook works on Italian and German history. Her imaginative narration is combined with solid historical research. She is pro-Protestant, sometimes to the point of being conspicuously anti-Catholic in her sympathies. Among her works are: *Golden Age of Romanticism* (1899); *Luther's Faith* (1916); *Roman Empire of the German Nation* (1934).

[S. A. SCHULZ]

HUDDLESTON, JOHN (1608–98), English Benedictine. Born in Lancashire and educated at St. Omer's College, he entered the English College in Rome and was ordained there in 1637. He returned to England and served at Moseley, Staffordshire, where, for a few days in 1651, he secretly harbored Charles II after Cromwell's victory at Worcester. Sometime thereafter, H. joined the Benedictines of the Spanish Congregation and was professed on the mission. When Charles II was restored, he appointed H. chaplain to Queen Mother Henrietta Marie and later to Queen Catherine of Braganza. When Charles II was dying, H. received him into the Roman Church and administered the last sacraments. BIBLIOGRAPHY: G. R. Hudleston, CE 7:511–512; Gillow, BDEC 3:463–465.

[V. SAMPSON]

ḤÛDRĀ (cycle), East Syrian liturgical book containing the older propers of the Mass and Office; complemented for the

Night Office by the *gazzā, and filled out by the *kashkull. BIBLIOGRAPHY: J. Mateos, *Lelya-Ṣapra* (1959) 5–12.

[A. CODY]

HUDSON, DANIEL ELDRED (1849–1934), Holy Cross priest, editor of *Ave Maria*. As a young man working for Lee and Shepherd, book publishers in Boston, he enjoyed the acquaintance of Hawthorne, Emerson, Whittier, and Longfellow. H. wished to be a Trappist but was persuaded by a visit to Notre Dame, Ind., to join the Congregation of the Holy Cross, in which he was ordained in 1875. His entire life was spent at Notre Dame as editor of the magazine *Ave Maria*. Ascetic, hard working, and keen in his critical writing, he made the periodical a notable one, both by his own editorial contribution and by the writers he attracted to its pages.

[J. R. AHERNE]

HUEBER, FORTUNATUS (d. 1706), reformed Franciscan of the province of Bavaria, cathedral preacher at Freising. He was the author of many volumes of sermons and theological essays, but most importantly of *Menologium Franciscanum* (1698), on the Franciscan saints and blesseds, a rich source work for Franciscan history.

[T. C. O'BRIEN]

HUECK, CATHERINE DE, see DE HUECK, CATHERINE.

HUELGAS DE BURGOS, ABBEY OF, the Cistercian convent of Sta. Maria la Real, established near Burgos, Spain, in 1187 by Alfonso VIII of Castile. This royal convent soon became the head of all Cistercian convents in Castile and Leon. Although a daughterhouse of Tulebras, it affiliated in 1199 with Cîteaux. Its abbesses were of royal lineage, its nuns were drawn from the nobility, kings were crowned there, 64 villages were under its civil jurisdiction, it was exempt from episcopal jurisdiction, and exercised a virtual episcopal jurisdiction of its own for centuries. This immemorial custom was confirmed by Urban VIII in the 17th cent., despite the protests of the bp. of Burgos and the abbot of Cîteaux; but the exempt status was finally suspended in 1873 by Pius IX. Looted by Napoleonic troops in 1808, it was the site of the swearing in (1938) of the Franco government after the Spanish Civil War. The abbey possesses many medieval art treasures and manuscripts. BIBLIOGRAPHY: Cottineau 1:1435.

[E. J. DILLON]

HUERTA, JUAN MARÍA (1854–1916), Mexican statesman. Born at Cotoblan (Jalisco), he attended the military academy through Benito *Juárez's good offices. He sided with Porfirio *Díaz and in 1893 executed those who had taken part in the revolt of Guerrero. His relations with Madero, whose downfall he prepared, were always tense. Elected president of Mexico in 1913, he governed the country in the midst of many difficulties: Carranza's revolt, civil war, and the American landing at Veracruz. Having failed in his efforts to take the Mexican case to the International Court of The Hague, H. went into exile in Europe. On his return to America, he was arrested and imprisoned at Fort Bliss, Tex., where he died. BIBLIOGRAPHY: L. Pérez, *La cuestión religiosa en México* (1935); P. González-Blanco, *De Porfirio Díaz a Carranza* (1916).

[P. DAMBORIENA]

HUFNAGELSCHRIFT, see NAGELSCHRIFT.

HUG, JOHANN LEONARD (1765–1846), biblical scholar. H. taught exegesis at the Univ. of Freiburg from 1791. He was highly critical of the rationalistic trends in hermeneutics advanced by J. Semler, insisted upon a truly historical study of the NT, and was the most influential Catholic exegete of his day. His widely translated *Introduction to the Writings of the NT* is his most important work. BIBLIOGRAPHY: M. C. McGarraghy, NCE 6:187.

[T. M. MCFADDEN]

HÜGEL, FRIEDRICH VON (1852–1925), RC scholar and writer. His father, from whom he derived the title baron by which he was commonly known, was German; his mother was of Scottish family and a convert to Roman Catholicism. Privately educated, he married in 1873 and from 1876 until his death lived in England, though he traveled much on the Continent. His concern for religion began with a spiritual crisis (1870) in which he was much helped by a Dutch Dominican, R. Hocking; some years later the Abbé H. Huvelin's spiritual counsels exerted a strong influence upon him. He was greatly interested in reconciling religious thought with contemporary developments in the fields of science, philosophy, and critical scholarship. Cismontane rather than ultramontane in his sympathies and distrustful of the prevalent scholastic methods of theological investigation, he visited and corresponded with many leaders in Catholic liberal thought, some of whom, such as A. *Loisy and G. *Tyrrel, were to be leaders of the Modernist movement. The breadth of H.'s interests and esp. his concern with adoration and mystical prayer kept him from exclusive involvement in the issues of Modernism; he accepted the condemnation of the movement when it came. In 1905 he founded the London Society for the Study of Religion, which put him into close association with many prominent scholars of his time. As an author, his best work was in the field of mystical theology. In his *The Mystical Element of Religion as Studied in St. Catherine of Genoa and Her Friends* (1908) and in his letters he reveals a profound insight into the spiritual life. BIBLIOGRAPHY: M. De La Bedoyère, *Life of Baron von Hügel* (1952); J. Steinmann, *Friedrich von Hügel* (1963).

[M. A. WATHEN]

HUGH OF AMIENS (*c.* 1080–1164), abp. of Rouen. Entering the monastic life at Cluny, he became prior of Lewes

(1123) and abbot of the foundation at Reading (1125). He actively supported the claims of Pope Innocent III against those of Anacletus II. He was elevated to the see of Rouen (1130) and often served as an arbiter in secular and ecclesiastical matters, with the support of Henry I, Stephen, and Henry II. The author of exegetical and polemical writings, including *Dialogi* and *Contra haereticos,* he was a redoubtable champion of the 12th-cent. Church.

[J. D. LOUGHLIN]

HUGH OF BALMA (fl. 13th cent.), Carthusian of Meyriat (Burgundy), known only for his *De theologia mystica,* which has been dated between 1246 and 1297; also called *De triplici via,* and *Viae Sion lugent,* its opening words. It is one of the first works to develop the doctrine of Christian *perfection according to the three ways, *purgative, illuminative, and unitive. Influential on subsequent mystical theology, the treatise reflects many themes from *Pseudo Dionysius. It has sometimes been falsely attributed to St. Bonaventure.

[T. C. O'BRIEN]

HUGH OF BOLOGNA, early 12th-cent. priest, canon, and writer. His extant writings, among them a treatise on epistolography dating from *c.*1120, the *Rationes dictandi prosaice,* show him to have been a skilled rhetorician, versed in the classics as well as in the best authors of his own time. BIBLIOGRAPHY: *Briefsteller und Formelbücher des 11. bis 14. Jahrhunderts 1* (ed. L. von Rockinger, 2 v., 1863) 47–94.

[W. A. JURGENS]

HUGH OF BONNEVAUX, ST. (d. 1194), Cistercian abbot. Nephew of St. Hugh of Grenoble, H. entered the Cistercian abbey of Miroir, then changed to Léoncel, where he became abbot in 1162. Elected abbot of Bonnevaux (1166), he established three new foundations from there. He supported Pope Alexander III. BIBLIOGRAPHY: M. A. Dimier, *Saint Hugues de Bonnevaux* (1942); G. Müller, "Der hl. Hugo, Abt von Bonnevaux," *Cistercienser-Chronik,* 11 (1899); M. A. Dimier, BiblSanct 12:749–751.

[L. J. LEKAI]

HUGH OF CLUNY, ST. (1024–1109), abbot of Cluny. Educated by Bp. Hugh of Auxerre, H. became a novice at Cluny (1038), was ordained (1044), became prior (1048). He was arbiter in a controversy between Emperor Henry III and the abbey of Payerne. He was elected (1049) abbot of Cluny. He participated in numerous synods and councils (e.g., Lateran in 1050, 1059, and 1080, Vienne in 1060, Clermont in 1095), and spent 60 fruitful years as abbot, bringing Cluny to its apogee. He performed important diplomatic duties in Hungary (1051) and in Germany (1072); established new monasteries, aggregated older ones, and founded the first convent of Cluniac nuns at Marcigny in 1056. He was canonized by Callistus II (1120). BIBLIOGRAPHY: Butler 2:188–189; J. Leclercq, BiblSanct 12:752–755.

[J. D. LOUGHLIN]

HUGH OF DIE (*c.*1040–1106), Gregorian reformer, bp. of Die, then abp. of Lyons. He was ordained and served as precentor of the cathedral of Lyons. Elected bp. of Die (1073), he was consecrated at Rome (1074) by Gregory VII in the course of a council that condemned simony. The Pope named him his legate in Gaul to enforce the council's decrees there. H. labored vigorously to this effect, visiting the dioceses and convoking councils. He performed his task with excessive severity, suspending and even deposing bps. and became unpopular with the French clergy. He was raised to the archbishopric of Lyons (1082–83). After Gregory VII's death, H. criticized his successor Pope Victor III for compromising the principles of the Gregorian Reform. He was excommunicated at the Council of Benevento (1087). In 1094 Pope Urban II restored him to the post of papal legate. H. was a patron and supporter of the Cistercians.

[J. D. LOUGHLIN]

HUGH OF DIGNE, (d. *c.*1254), venerated in some localities as blessed. H. became a Franciscan and is well known for his commentary on the Rule of St. Francis and for two treatises on poverty. He was affected by the teachings of Joachim of Fiore and is regarded as a leader of the Spirituals. BIBLIOGRAPHY: J. Poulence, *Catholicisme* 5:1020–22.

[H. DRESSLER]

HUGH ETHERIAN (*c.*1110–82), Italian lay theologian, attached for a time to the court of Emperor Manuel I at Constantinople; author of a work on Greek patristic teaching about the procession of the Holy Spirit from the Son; translator into Latin of Greek patristic texts on person and nature in the godhead. Just before his death he was made a deacon and cardinal by Pope Lucius III.

[T. C. O'BRIEN]

HUGH OF FLAVIGNY (1065–1115), Benedictine abbot, chronicler. He came of illustrious parentage (his mother was related to Emperor Otto III) and at an early age entered the abbey of St. Vanne, Verdun. When the monks there were expelled by Bp. Thierry of Verdun (a member of the imperial party, whereas the monks supported the Pope against the Emperor), they took refuge at St. Bénigne in Dijon. He was elected (1096) abbot of Flavigny, but soon was involved in disputes with his bp. and with his own monks, who were defenders of the papacy. Bp. Norgaud dismissed him in 1099; H. returned to St. Bénigne, but brought his case before the synods of Valence and Poitiers during 1100. Ultimately Norgaud was deposed for simony, but H. did not recover his office at Flavigny, as prior Gérard had succeeded him. In 1111 he was made abbot of Verdun, when the lawful abbot, Laurentius, was removed, by a bp.

in revolt against the Pope: from a staunch supporter of papal claims H. had become a determined adversary. He wrote the *Chronicon Virdunense seu Flaviniacense*, a valuable source for events from 1002 to 1102. BIBLIOGRAPHY: F. J. Schmale, LTK 5:513–514; P. Schlager, CE 7:519.

[J. D. LOUGHLIN]

HUGH OF FLEURY (d. after 1118), historian, biographer. As Benedictine priest of St.-Benoît-sur-Loire, also known as Hugh of Sainte-Marie, he completed a *Historia ecclesiastica* to the death of Charlemagne in 1109, divided into four books and dedicated to Adela, Countess of Blois. About 2 years later he wrote a chronicle of the kings of France, *Modernorum regum Francorum liber* (842–1108). Sometime after 1102 he addressed a *Tractatus de regia potestate et sacerdotali dignitate* to Henry I of England, which presented his position in the investiture struggle, restating the divine rights of both royal and ecclesiastical authority and condemning those who held that the temporal power came from man and not God. In addition to a biography of Bp. Sacerdos of Limoges, several other works have been attributed to him, including the *De miraculis s. Benedicti*. BIBLIOGRAPHY: B. Heurtebize, DTC 7:239–240.

[J. D. LOUGHLIN]

HUGH OF FOSSE, BL. (1093–1164), early follower of the founder of the Premonstratensians, St. Norbert, whom H. succeeded as abbot. He set up the constitutions of the order, and became its first general. Among his writings are the first *Vita Norberti* and directories for the order. His cult was not approved until 1927. BIBLIOGRAPHY: P. F. LeFèvre, *L'Ordinaire de Prémontré* (1941); *Book of Saints* (comp. Benedictine Monks of St. Augustine's Abbey, 1966).

[M. E. DUFFY]

HUGH OF FOUILLOY (*c.*1110–*c.*1173), Canon Regular of St. Augustine, prior of St. Laurent-au-Bois, near Amiens; author of *De claustro animae, De medicina animae, De nuptiis,* treatises on the spiritual life wrongly included among the works of *Hugh of St. Victor in PL 176:1183–1218.

[T. C. O'BRIEN]

HUGH OF GRENOBLE, ST. (1052–1132), bp. and reformer. His first ecclesiastical office was a canonry at the cathedral of Valence, which he filled as a layman. Impressed by his learning and other qualities, Bp. Hugh of Die took him into his service at the age of 27, and although not yet ordained, he was elected bp. of Grenoble, a see much in need of reform. Ordained at once, he was consecrated at Rome by Pope Gregory VII. For 52 years he labored strenuously and successfully, despite the fact that he repeatedly asked to be replaced when discouraged. He was greatly comforted by his friendship with Bruno the Carthusian and the monks of La Grande Chartreuse. Guigo I, prior of La Grande Chartreuse and his contemporary, left his biography. H. was canonized by Innocent II in 1134. BIBLIOGRAPHY: M. O. Garrigues, BiblSanct 12:759–763; Butler 2:3–5.

[J. D. LOUGHLIN]

HUGH OF HONAU (2d half 12th cent.), theologian and canon regular. He was a scholar and ''deacon of the Sacred Palace'' at the court of Frederick Barbarossa. The emperor sent him as legate to Constantinople, where he consulted Hugh Etherian on the teachings of the Greek Fathers. H. of Honau wrote two works on the clarification of Trinitarian terms.

[M. J. FINNEGAN]

HUGH OF LINCOLN, ST. (1140–1200), Carthusian bishop. H. received his education from the Augustinian Canons at Villarbenoît, then entered the Grande Chartreuse where he became procurator some years later. In 1179 Henry II of England employed H. to resuscitate the charterhouse at Witham. Again Henry II urged him to accept the see at Lincoln. Here, H. demonstrated his zeal, devotion, and resourcefulness. He remained on friendly terms with Henry's sons as well, even when he opposed them. At his funeral his remains were borne by three kings and three bishops. He was the first Carthusian to be canonized. BIBLIOGRAPHY: Adam of Eynsham, *Life of St. Hugh of Lincoln* (ed. D. L. Douie, and H. Farmer, 2 v., 1961–62); Butler 4:370–374; H. Farmer, BiblSanct 12:765–767.

[B. F. SCHERER]

HUGH OF LINCOLN, ST. (d. 1255), 9-year-old boy, supposed victim of ritual murder by Jews of Lincoln. The charge, to which some Jews confessed under duress, has been refuted but was widely believed in medieval times. His body was credited with miracles and buried in Lincoln Cathedral. Many literary sources mention him. BIBLIOGRAPHY: W. Hunt, DNB 10:169–72; H. Fenning, BiblSanct 12:764–765.

[R. W. HAYS]

HUGH OF NEWCASTLE (NOVOCASTRO; *c.*1280–*c.*1322), Franciscan theologian. His birthplace is usually given as Newcastle in England, though it may possibly have been Neufchâtel in France. He studied and taught at Paris; earned the honorific, *Doctor scholasticus*. He was highly regarded as a teacher by Franciscans; was an earlier defender of the Immaculate Conception doctrine, using arguments from Duns Scotus, whom he followed generally.

[T. C. O'BRIEN]

HUGH OF ORLÉANS (*c.*1093–*c.*1160), also called Hugh Primas; wandering scholar, author of some 50 secular lyrical poems and satires (see CARMINA BURANA); composer of one of the melodies to which the *Pange lingua gloriosi,* in honor of the Blessed Sacrament, was sung.

[T. C. O'BRIEN]

HUGH OF PISA, see HUGUCCIO.

HUGH OF REMIREMONT (Candidus; 1020–after 1098), cardinal, sometime promoter, sometime adversary of Gregorian Reform. A Benedictine at Remiremont, he was named, by Leo IX, cardinal priest of S. Clemente (1049). He opposed the reform party in 1061 and supported Cadalus of Parma, the antipope Honorius II. Disillusioned, he submitted to the lawful pope, Alexander II, who appointed him legate to Spain (1063), where he enforced clerical celibacy. He played a leading role in the election of Gregory VII, but from 1075 joined the anti-Gregorian party, incurred excommunication (1076), deposition in 1078. He supported Guibert of Ravenna as the antipope Clement III, was excommunicated (1085), and in 1098 signed the proclamation against Pope Urban II as bp. of Palestrina.

HUGH OF SAINT-CHER (*c.*1200–63), French Dominican biblical scholar. He was a doctor in law at Paris when he joined the Dominicans (1225). Twice he was provincial of France (1226–30; 1236–44) and served as vicar general of the Dominicans 1240–41. He was the trusted adviser and envoy of Popes Gregory IX, Innocent IV (who made him the first Dominican cardinal, 1244), Alexander IV, and Urban IV. At Innocent's request he adapted the Carmelite Rule to permit an apostolate in the manner of the mendicant friars (1247). He was influential in bringing about the institution of the feast of Corpus Christi (1264), produced the first verbal concordance of the Bible, left a set of exegetical notes (*Postillae*) that continued in use up to the 17th cent., and attempted a correctory of the Vulgate text. BIBLIOGRAPHY: Quétif-Échard 1:194–209.

HUGH OF ST. VICTOR (*c.*1096–1141), philosopher and theologian. H. was probably born in Saxony, descended from the family of the counts of Blankenburg. He joined the Canons Regular of St. Augustine and entered the monastery of St. Victor in Paris (1115). From 1120 until his death, H. was the leading theologian of the Victorine school and an important influence on subsequent medieval theology. He contributed significantly to the development of Scholastic theology since he was the first to systematize biblical and esp. patristic thought into a complete body of doctrine. Philosophically, he argued for man's natural ability to know the existence and major properties of God. As a theologian, he was much concerned with accurate biblical exegesis based on the literal sense of the passage. His speculative synthesis, strongly dependent upon St. *Augustine, is contained in his *Summa sententiarum* and the *De sacramentis christianae fidei*. H. developed an accurate theory of the sacraments; stressed the role of absolution in penance; denied *Abelard's tendencies toward *adoptionism; but erred in attributing divine attributes to Christ's human nature. H.'s mystical writings are also significant. In them, he outlines the soul's gradual ascent to God and the reacquisition of man's intimate sense of God, which was lost through original sin. BIBLIOGRAPHY: D. Van Den Eynde, NCE 7:194–195 with bibliog.

[T. M. MCFADDEN]

HUGH OF TRIMBERG (*c.*1235–*c.*1313), lay educator and poet. He taught in Bamberg for more than 40 years as schoolmaster of St. Gangolf. His best known work is a German didactic epic *Der Renner* (courier) written between 1280 and 1313, an ethical instruction based on the seven capital sins. Other works are: *Registrum multorum auctorum*, a textbook in verse on Latin writers; *Solsequium*, a prose collection of short narratives and legends; and *Laurea sanctorum*, a list of saints in verse.

[J. E. LYNCH]

HUGHES, ANGELA, MOTHER (Ellen; *c.*1806–66), foundress, social worker, sister of Abp. J. Hughes of New York. Born in Ireland but educated in the U.S., H. entered the Sisters of Charity of Emmitsburg, Md. in 1825. She was elected assistant general of the Sisters of Charity upon their separation from Emmitsburg (1846). Founder of St. Vincent's Hospital, the first Catholic hospital in New York City (1849), she became superior general in 1855. From New York two new groups of Sisters of Charity were founded: Halifax, Nova Scotia, and Newark, New Jersey. H. was responsible for the rapid growth of the New York community.

[J. R. AHERNE]

HUGHES, ANSELM (1889–1974), English Benedictine prior of Nashdom Abbey (1936–45), musicologist. In addition to numerous publications of his own such as *Early English Harmony* (1912), *Latin Hymnody* (1923), *Medieval Polyphony in the Bodleian Library* (1951), H. contributed to *Grove's Dictionary of Music and Musicians*, the *Oxford History of Music*, and was an editor of the *New Oxford History of Music*.

[M. T. LEGGE]

HUGHES, HUGH PRICE (1847–1902), Wesleyan Methodist preacher and supporter of social reform and Methodist union. He was born at Carmarthen, Wales, and entered the ministry in 1867, establishing West London Mission in 1887. He emphasized its philanthropic work and conducted a popular preaching service; he founded the *Methodist Times* in 1885, passionately supporting social reform. He worked indefatigably for Methodist union, founding the National Council of the Evangelical Free Churches (1896). He was president of the Wesleyan Methodist Conference in 1898. BIBLIOGRAPHY: D. P. Hughes, *Life of Hugh Price Hughes* (1904); M. Edwards, *Methodism and England* (1943) 147–164.

[F. E. MASER]

HUGHES, JOHN JOSEPH (1797–1864), abp. of New York. As a youth he emigrated from Ireland and settled with his family in Chambersburg, Pennsylvania. In 1820 he entered Mt. St. Mary's Seminary at Emmitsburg, Md., and was ordained in 1826 for the Diocese of Philadelphia. Successful in various parochial assignments, H. also acquired a reputation for his forceful defense of Catholicism in public debate and in the press. He founded (1833) the *Catholic Herald,* a weekly newspaper. In 1838 he was consecrated titular bp. of Basileopolis and coadjutor, with right of succession, of New York. When Bp. John *Dubois suffered a stroke, H. was named (1839) apostolic administrator and succeeded to the see (1842). In 1850 New York was made an archdiocese and H. its first archbishop. He was tireless in his efforts to improve the status of Catholic immigrants, providing aid societies, leading the fight against the unfair treatment of Catholic children in the allegedly nonsectarian public schools and trying to get public support for Catholic schools, and protecting Catholic property against the attacks of nativist rioters. His firm handling of lay *trusteeism helped to prevent its spread in New York. H. established a seminary and a college at Fordham in New York City, introduced many religious communities into the archdiocese, and laid the cornerstone (1858) for the nobly conceived and superbly located St. Patrick's cathedral. The most influential American prelate of his time, H. promoted the establishment (1859) of the North American College in Rome, staunchly defended the rights of Pius IX, opposed plans for Irish colonization of Western lands, and publicly supported the American separation of Church and State. In 1861, at the request of President Lincoln and Secretary of State Seward, H. visited Europe and successfully represented the Union cause to the French government and to the Holy See. Ill at the time, H. made his last public appearance, at the request of New York's Governor H. Seymour, to urge the draft rioters of New York City to end the disorders and obey the laws of their country. BIBLIOGRAPHY: *Complete Works* (comp. and ed. L. Kehoe, 2 v., 1865). J. R. Hassard, *Life of the Most Reverend John Hughes, D.D., First Archbishop of New York* (1866); H. J. Browne, ''Archbishop Hughes and Western Colonization,'' CHR 36 (Oct. 1950) 257–285.

[M. CARTHY]

HUGHES, PHILIP (1895–1967), English church historian. He studied history at Louvain and at Rome under F. *Gasquet. After ordination in 1920 he did parochial work until being appointed archivist for the Archdiocese of Westminster in 1931. He was able to accept the post of professor of church history at the Univ. of Notre Dame in 1955, and there he spent his remaining days, enjoying high academic and personal esteem. H.'s best-known work is the three-volume *History of the Church* (1933–47), which covered only the period up to the Reformation. His most thorough study is his *History of the Reformation in England* (1951–54). Other works include: *Popular History of the Church* (1938); *Popular History of the Reformation* (1957), and, in the era of Vatican Council II, *Church in Crisis: A History of the General Councils 325–1870* (1961). H.'s historical writing is marked by objectivity and candor about the Church and churchmen, grace of expression, and the most perceptive theological and historical interpretation. He esp. admired, and thoroughly knew, the thought of St. Thomas Aquinas, and among H.'s devotional works is *Meditations for Lent from St. Thomas Aquinas* (1938).

[T. C. O'BRIEN]

HUGHES, THOMAS (1849–1939), English Jesuit and historian of work of the Society in the United States. After becoming a Jesuit in England (1866), he came to the U.S. as a volunteer for the missions and was ordained at Woodstock, Md., in 1878. His great work, *History of the Society of Jesus in North America, Colonial and Federal* (4 v., 1907–17), was composed mainly in Rome and reflects the author's careful archival research.

HUGO, see HUGH.

HUGO, VICTOR MARIE (1802–85), French novelist and poet. Like many French writers of his time, H. was a victim of the controversies, political and religious, that raged throughout the 19th century. His father was one of Napoleon's officers. It was his mother who exerted a subtle influence on him with her Voltairian bias and religious indifference. His attachment to her was strong, as were his attachments to Juliette Drouet and to his daughter Leopoldine. He revered Chauteaubriand and was interested in the theology of Swedenborg, though his own religious views of the period after 1830 became cloudy infiltrations into his submerged anticlericalism. His works in any case were often influenced by personal disaster. So his daughter's death (1843) evoked some of his finest poetry. The turmoil created by Napoleon III's rise and fall (1851–71) drove him to a dramatic conviction and exile for 20 years. His return to France (1870) brought him additional glory and admiration. He was elected to the national assembly and to the senate. As a final testimony to this great romantic, his burial in the Pantheon reinforced his already brilliant reputation. In his own century H. was a towering figure of romanticism; the 20th cent. views him more rationally from an imposed aesthetic distance. Some of his works are: the novel *Les Misérables* (1862); *Les Rayons et les ombres* (1840), a book of poems; *Ruy Blas* (1838), a play. BIBLIOGRAPHY: E. M. Grant, *Career of Victor Hugo* (1945).

[R. M. FUNCHION]

HUGOLINO OF GUALDO CATTANEO, ST. (d. 1260), the first Augustinian prior of Gualdo in the Diocese of Spoleto. This monastery had earlier belonged to the Benedictine monks. Long before his cult was officially approved, he was venerated by a penitential society devoted to charitable works. BIBLIOGRAPHY: Butler 1:14–15; M. Sensi, BiblSanct 12:784–787.

[M. A. WINKLEMANN]

HUGON, ÉDOUARD (1867–1929), French Dominican theologian. A Dominican from 1885 and ordained in 1892, he taught in various houses of the Dominican Lyons province before becoming a member of the first faculty of the pontifical institute Angelicum in Rome (now the Universitas S. Thomae Aquinatis). His teaching was marked by orderly and succinct clarity, and by its emphasis on key themes from St. Thomas Aquinas; the same qualities characterize his published works, among them: *Cursus philosophicus* (1903–07; many repr.); *Tractatus theologici* (5 v., 1920–27); *Les Ving-quatre thèses thomistes* (8th ed., 1938). His draft contributed to the preparation of Pius XI's *Quas primas*, an encyclical on Christ the King. H. also wrote popular works on the Eucharist and on Mary; he was a consistent contributor to the review *La Vie spirituelle*.

[T. C. O'BRIEN]

HUGUCCIO (HUGH OF PISA; d. 1210), philologist, *decretist at Bologna; from 1190 bp. of Ferrara. He figures in the history of language studies because of his early works on grammar, and esp. for the *Liber derivationum*, on word origins. He also wrote commentaries on the Creed and the Lord's Prayer. But his *Summa super Decreta* is his greatest achievement, first in excellence among all the commentaries on *Gratian's work. This *Summa* became the primary source work for all subsequent medieval canonical studies; its excellence consisted in both its rich presentation of sources, its orderly, critical exposition, and the author's resolution of opinions. The work remains an important resource for the history of canon law and even for historical theology.

[T. C. O'BRIEN]

HUGUENOTS, the nickname of French Calvinists—in common use after the Conspiracy of Amboise (1560)—which may derive from the German *Eidgenossen* (confederates, conspirators) or from a legendary King Hugon. The French who favored the Reformation received doctrinal inspiration from Jacques *Lefèvre d'Étaples and Martin Luther, but above all from John Calvin's **Institutes of the Christian Religion*. In organization, both ecclesiastical and political, the Huguenots were influenced by the theocratic state of Geneva—an international center for Protestant missionaries and a model of authoritarian republicanism and collective parochial living.

The movement grew in France, and with it the opposition of the crown; Francis I (1515–47) initiated persecution and Henry II (1547–59) systematized it by appointing a special commission of the Paris Parlement to try heretics and by codifying the enactments against them. By 1555, however, Paris had its first *Reformed Church and for 70 years the Reformed Church in France played an important political life. The organization of the Church developed gradually; the final structure emerged at the Assembly of Saumur, 1611.

Although the Dukes of Guise intensified persecution of the Huguenots during the short reign of Francis II (1559–60), many of the nobility, such as Admiral de Coligny and the Dukes of Bourbon and Condé, became leaders of the party, which remained mainly aristocratic until the end of the 16th century. By the edict of January 1562, Chancellor M. de l'Hôpital and Catherine de Médicis attempted to ward off war between the religious factions by granting the Huguenots civic status and the right to worship outside the towns; the powerful Guises, however, opposed a policy of conciliation: in the two decades following the massacre of Vassy (March 1, 1562)—which began the *Wars of Religion—there were seven wars and the *St. Bartholomew's Day Massacre (1572).

Soon the Huguenot organization was so strengthened and unified that it resembled a state within a state. Two organizational structures emerged, each with a system of representation: the religious, which included consistories, colloquies, and provincial and national synods; and the political—with its provincial councils, circle assemblies, and general assemblies. Academies were established at Montauban, Montpelier, Nîmes, Sedan, and Saumur—the last being particularly important in the history of Reformed theology (see HELVETIC CONSENSUS FORMULA).

A decline in the power of the Guises, the rise of the Huguenot Henry de Navarre, and the influence of the *politiques*, who were anxious to end hostilities, led to the *Edict of Nantes (1598), a compendium of previous edicts granting some toleration, which remained nominally in effect for 87 years, though it was never applied in its entirety because France was not ready to adopt its principles. The assassination of Henry IV in 1610 removed the sense of comparative security enjoyed by the Huguenots, and the reign of Louis XIII (1610–43) ended their political hopes. Cardinal Richelieu, although he earned a reputation for tolerance, saw a threat to the state in the Huguenot party with its strongholds ("places of surety"). He launched a campaign against the Huguenots, took La Rochelle and Privas, and dictated the terms of the Peace of Alais (June 1629). The Huguenots were made subservient to the state and their party was doomed, but there was no overt persecution. However, Louis XIV (1661–1715), by gradually depriving the Huguenots of their rights, authorizing dragonnades (persecution by troops, 1683–86), and finally by revoking the Edict of Nantes in 1685, probably carried out the Cardinal's real intentions. The revocation caused a massive exodus of from 200,000 to 300,000 Huguenots. French Protestants were granted partial equality of rights by the Edict of Toleration (1787) and full equality by the Napoleonic code. The Reformed Church of France remains the largest French Protestant body; it forms, with other Protestant groups, the Fédération Protestante de France, established in 1907. BIBLIOGRAPHY: W. J. Stankiewicz, NCE 7:201–204 with bibliog.

[W. J. STANKIEWICZ]

HŬGUET, JAIME (1415?–1492), Spanish painter, central figure in Catalan art at Barcelona, directing a studio with assistants (Vergós family) doing wood and goldwork. In many retables at Vallmoll and in Barcelona in, *S. Miguel, Consecration of St. Augustine, and St. Bernardine and the Guardian Angel,* H. in linear, elongated figures united decorative patterns with a 15th-cent. naturalism.

[M. J. DALY]

HUIZINGA, JOHAN (1872–1945), historian of culture, born in the Netherlands, and trained as a linguist and Sanskritist at Groningen and Leipzig. Beginning as a high school teacher, he obtained a doctorate in 1897, later occupying the history chair at the Univ. of Groningen, and in 1915 at the Univ. of Leiden. First imprisoned by the Germans as a hostage, he was released in 1942, but forced to live in retirement. Although he first achieved fame as an expert on the culture of the 12th cent. with his study "The Waning of the Middle Ages," he afterwards ventured into studies of the pathology of modern culture. He was deeply influenced by a conviction of inescapable antinomies in human thinking, which made him uncommonly sensitive to the complexities of historical matter. He is best known for his 1938 "Homo Ludens," a study of the role of play in culture. See *Verzamelde Werken,* (9 v., ed. L. Brummel et al, 1948–53); for his major writings on theoretical historical problems, see *Verzamelde Werken,* VII, 1–258; his lesser writings are listed in *Verzamelde Werken,* I, 203–411; on the European crisis, *Verzamelde Werken,* VII, *passim.*

[N. F. GAUGHAN]

HÛLLĀLĀ (East Syrian), a large division of the Psalter, which is divided into 20 *hûllālę̄* plus a 21st containing OT canticles. Each *hûllālā* is subdivided into two, three, or four *marmyātā* (sing., **marmîtā*). *Hûllōlō* among the West Syrians signifies an alleluiatic versicle to be sung before a Gospel reading. Compare the Byzantine division into **kathismata* and *staseis.*

[A. CODY]

HULST, MAURICE D' (1841–96), French churchman, a founder and sometime rector of the Institut Catholique at Paris. Before ordination (1865) he completed doctoral studies in Rome both in theology and canon law. After a period of parish ministry, he was assigned to planning and inaugurating a Catholic university; when the Institut Catholique opened in 1875 he was its vice-rector, became rector in 1881, and held that post until death. He is credited with firmly establishing the Institut in spite of the anti-Catholic political climate at the time; with recruiting an eminent faculty; with leading the Institut through the crisis that led to the dismissal of A. *Loisy from the faculty (1893). In ecclesiastical affairs H. strongly opposed *Ralliement, but acquiesced when Leo XIII made Catholic allegiance to the French political regime a matter of church policy. Leo XIII's encyclical *Providentissimus Deus* (1893) rejected a theory of biblical inspiration H. had proposed. H's activities also included writing (he published a series on the foundations of morality, and on family, civil, and social morality), spiritual direction, and preaching (he was successor to J. M. Monsabré as preacher at Notre Dame in 1891). Near the end of his life he became a member of the Chamber of Deputies.

[T. C. O'BRIEN]

HUMAN ACT, in scholastic moral theology, an act deliberately willed. It is called human because the source of such an act is the powers of mind and will that set the human being apart from lesser creatures. The distinctive name also implies that in a person's activity some actions are not human in the full sense. Every action belongs to the one who acts, but some are purely physical phenomena, biological or sentient, some are reflexes, some are unthinking. The greater number of human acts are choices. To be fully human these must be acts of will that correspond to a sufficient mental evaluation of the good chosen. The same basis for distinguishing a human act from other sorts of human activity ("acts of man") is also a basis for recognizing acts that are only partially human, i.e., that lack sufficient mental awareness and evaluation, and complete willingness. The possibility of morality, i.e., of any moral good or evil requires the capability for making deliberate choices. To deny such possibility is not only to deny the possibility of sin, but also of moral good.

[T. C. O'BRIEN]

HUMAN DEVELOPMENT, CAMPAIGN FOR, a national education and action program of the U.S. Catholic Conference (USCC), initiated in 1968 by the National Conference of Catholic Bishops. The national organization has its center in Washington, D.C.; there are diocesan offices to function at the local level. The aim of the campaign is to fund innovative projects that reach the root causes of poverty and to work year-round in educating the American people concerning the dimensions and reality of poverty and powerlessness. In 1970 there was the first annual collection for this purpose taken up in all 18,000 Catholic parishes in the U.S. on the Sunday before Thanksgiving. During the next 2 years guidelines were gradually established by a national committee of 40 (including 25 laymen), all of whom were involved as active leaders among the poor. Accordingly each diocese was to keep one-quarter of the amount raised for local self-help projects. The remaining portion was to be distributed through the national committee. All groups seeking funds were to be given equal consideration, including those religiously unaligned. The poor were to be involved in the planning and the operation of any self-help project funded by the campaign. From the beginning the campaign has averaged $8 million in the annual collection; and has funded an average of 150 projects a year, in such areas as housing, jobs, health care, legal aid, education, and communications. Refunding can extend to 3 years pending financial and progress reports.

[E. J. DILLON]

HUMAN RESPECT, as a weakness, excessive concern for the good opinion of others. To be honored is a true blessing, and to seek for it is right and natural (ThAq ST 2a2ae, 145), besides being a compliment to one's neighbor. Yet to be preoccupied with praise is to set a false store on it. If Aristotle noticed that it was a flaw in the true pride of a lofty character (*megalopsuchos*), still more is it a strain inimical to the true sturdiness and humility of a Christian. The classical moralists do not use the term human respect but treat of it under the headings of faults against magnanimity, which is part of the cardinal virtue of courage. BIBLIOGRAPHY: Aristotle, *Nichomachean Ethics* 4.3–4; ThAq ST 2a2ae, 130–134 (esp. in ed. Lat-Eng v. 42, ed. A. Ross and P. Walsh).

HUMAN RIGHTS, the claims that are to be respected in *justice on the grounds simply of human dignity. In a narrow sense they are the rights traditionally recognized in moral theology as arising from the basic direction in human nature to self-preservation, the rearing of children, amicable living in the society of men. But as human every person has a life that is individual, familial, political, economic, cultural; "human rights" has come to embrace a complexus of guarantees to a way of living out all these aspects of human existence that is decent and enhancing. The United Nations Declaration of Human Rights (1948) is an instance of the attempt to universalize a recognition and fostering of such rights. In part a result of the barbaric crimes of World War II, the document is also a culmination in the process of historical enlightenment that began with the Declaration of the Rights of Man in the French Revolution and in the Bill of Rights of the U.S. Constitution. But the UN declaration was meant to be a basis for internationally accepted laws that would guarantee the rights of self-determination, freedom of conscience, worship, property, and adequate standards of living for all peoples. One significance of this appeal to international laws is that for centuries there has been no consensus on the foundations of human rights. Thus their attainment and enforcement is largely left to the operation of political forces and the enactment of laws. As law is a work of reason it is perfectly "natural" that with the increasing intricacies of human existence laws should reflect a more reasoned determination of how men can live together for the best interests of all. Greater sophistication is required to assure a life in keeping with human dignity. But there is an obvious need for a referent to determine what is genuinely in keeping with that dignity. Politically no such referent is agreed upon by all nations; there are no truly international laws guaranteeing human rights. For Christian theology the referent is God's creation of man to his image; the guarantees are the ideals of justice and charity.

[T. C. O'BRIEN]

HUMAN SACRIFICE, the offering of a human being's life as part of a cultic ceremony. It is found primarily among agricultural societies and in archaic high cultures. The Aztecs, for instance, offered thousands of prisoners of war to the sun, which was thought to be strengthened by human blood, symbolized in the still beating heart torn out of the breast of the victim. These rituals symbolized man's fight with the earth, the fertilization of the earth, and its continuous renewal. The Mayas sacrificed young girls by drowning them in a deep well, and the Incas celebrated the initiation of a new ruler with a human sacrifice. In some of the African kingdoms a king sacrificed himself or was slaughtered when his term was ended, when his health declined, or when land and people were endangered by a catastrophe. A very common form of human sacrifice is the mortuary sacrifice upon the death of a king, chieftain, or feudal husband. Human beings were offered, occasionally voluntarily, to provide a guide, servant, or messenger for the king, or just to honor and strengthen the deceased by the life of the living. Sometimes a widow was burned on the pyre to accompany her deceased husband. Other occasions for human sacrifice were crisis situations (famine, war, etc.), when the best possession was offered, e.g., a child to Moloch, to please the godhead; or when the fertility of man, cattle, and crops had to be secured, e.g., by offering slaves on occasion of the first fruit; or when, as in Greece, a crime had to be expiated. The ideology of human sacrifice revolves around two poles: that of the demi-godhead, who by death provides life through plants, food supply, etc., and that of the ruler godhead, whose lordship cannot be pleased except by man's most precious possession, life.

Although human sacrifice was practiced among ancient people of the Middle East, and appeared even in Israel in times of religious degeneration (see, e.g., Ps 106.37–39; Ezek 16.20), there is no evidence to support the contention that it ever formed a part of Israelite ritual. If Hiel's laying of the foundation of Jericho at the cost of Abiram, his firstborn, and its gates at the cost of Segub, his youngest son (1 Kg 16.34) refers (as is by no means clear) to a foundation-sacrifice, the incidents can be regarded as exceptions meant to be viewed with abomination. The same can be said of *Jephthah's sacrifice of his daughter (Jg 11.30–40). The proper Jewish view is clearly stated in Lev 18.21; 20.2–5; Ezek 20.31; and Jer 7.31. BIBLIOGRAPHY: A. A. Crawley *et al,* Hastings, ERE 6:840–867; J. G. Frazer, *Golden Bough* (12 v., 3d ed., 1907–12); G. Hogg, *Cannibalism and Human Sacrifice* (1958); M. Eliade, *Patterns in Comparative Religion* (tr. R. Sheed, 1963); JBC 2:723.

[W. DUPRÉ]

HUMAN SOUL, see SOUL, HUMAN.

HUMANAE VITAE, papal encyclical "on the right ordering of the procreation of children" published by Paul VI, July 29, 1968. The letter opens with the statement that the transmittal of human life (*humanae vitae*) is a most serious duty; the letter's positive purpose was to teach the sanctity of human life, the sacredness of marital responsibility, and the Church's concern for true human values. The decade passing since the encyclical has only increased the need that one constant voice proclaim its positive message, since any other institutional defense of marital and family life grows fainter and fainter. But *Humanae vitae* is remembered almost exclusively for its exclusion, as morally unjustifiable, of "any action which either before, at the moment of, or after sexual intercourse, is specifically intended to prevent procreation . . ." (n. 14). This includes the use of anovulants ("the pill") for a purely contraceptive (not therapeutic, cf. n. 15) reason. This ban has led to two levels of dissent in the Church. One amounts to a denial of the cogency of the Pope's arguing from the inherent and inseparable connection between the unitive and the procreative significance of the marriage act (n. 12). Those who repudiate this line of thought recall that the 1966 majority report of the commission appointed during Vatican Council II to study the issue was repudiated by the Pope in issuing *Humanae vitae*. They maintain further that the central theme of inseparability between the procreative and the unitive takes the marital act in isolation from the full personal values of married love and rests on an antiquated, "biological" view of natural law. The second form of dissent is more concrete and probably more serious. Surveys of American Catholics indicate that the papal ban is simply being ignored; that Catholics of good will are deciding on their own what responsible parenthood is and whether it requires artificial methods of contraception. In this decision such Catholics have received the public support of theologians and, presumably, private pastoral concurrence. A concrete authority crisis has thus emerged and this has raised the theological question of how close *Humanae vitae* is to being an act of the ordinary teaching authority (*magisterium*) of the Church. Ten years after the encyclical neither crisis can be said to have been settled. It seems an exaggeration, or a misinterpretation of what the personally responsible decision of faith means, to say that *Humanae vitae* has driven people from the Church. At the same time, the Catholic mind has never been comfortable with leaving inconsistencies unresolved. The good that the crises have served is an emphasis on all moral choices being decisions of conscience that are genuine, i.e., personal evaluations and responses to every determinant of moral good, including the guidance of ecclesiastical authority. BIBLIOGRAPHY: *Contraception: Authority and Dissent* (ed. C. Curran, 1969); R. McCormick, "Notes on Moral Theology," ThSt 29 (1968) 707–741.

[T. C. O'BRIEN]

HUMANI GENERIS, an encyclical letter of Pope Pius XII (Aug. 12, 1950) that examines and passes judgment on various contemporary theological trends. It curbs certain novel and extreme views in philosophy and theology. As opposed to these views the encyclical states the traditional Catholic teaching. Nevertheless, it encourages Catholic philosophers and theologians to study such philosophies as evolutionism, existentialism, and historicism in order to combat them and to garner whatever of truth they might contain. It condemns merely relativistic conceptions of dogmas and reaffirms the teaching authority of the Church. BIBLIOGRAPHY: AAS 42 (1950) 561–578; Eng. tr. NCWC (1950); J. M. Connolly, NCE 7:215.

[J. H. ROHLING]

HUMANISM, in the specific historical sense, the program of learning prevailing during the *Renaissance. Thus the principal humanists were the great Renaissance literary figures. While interpretations of historical humanism are many, its techniques of learning and attitudes toward man's life were significant for religion. Humanism above all consisted in the *studia humanitatis,* the cultivation of the humanities through classical texts. Consequent interest in philology and textual criticism opened a new era in biblical and patristic studies. The humanist program of learning consciously rejected the medieval *scholasticism of the immediate past. Humanist presentation of theological truths sought to be more personal, warm, and direct, in contrast to the scholastic use of logic and philosophy for theological discourse. The celebrated **Epistolae obscurorum virorum* discredited the scholastics before the intellectual world and diminished confidence in traditional theology. Humanism developed in a Christian context; humanists did not assail essential Christian truths; many were eager for the reform of the Church. There was a distinctive interpretation of Christian life, however, in the world view of many humanists. Human values were stressed and the capacity of man to transform self, society, and the Church. The virtues extolled by the ancients were looked upon as a rediscovery of a nobler view of life that the medievals had lost. The humanist interpretation of the Christian life was a highly moralistic one, in which pagan and Christian virtues seemed as one, and the significance of Christ, the Church, and the sacraments were diminished. The humanist program for reform was one of re-education; the ignorance of the clergy came under bitter attack. Optimism and the idealization of the good life made many humanists severe critics of monastic asceticism and institutions. Tolerance in matters of belief, a recurrent theme, suggested a conviction that all religious belief is the expression of the lofty aspirations shared by all men. Extreme exaltation of man contributed to the corruption of the Renaissance papacy; criticism of established institutions created an atmosphere conducive to the breakup of Christianity in the Reformation. The humanist spirit was not compatible with the pessimism of the Reformers toward human nature. But simply as a cultural transition and a concentration upon man, humanism affected the forms and emphasis in both RC and Protestant life. BIBLIOGRAPHY: H. Baker, *Image of Man* (1947); R. R. Bolgan, *Classical Heritage and Its Beneficiaries* (1954); E. Cassirer, *Individual and Cosmos in Renaissance Philosophy* (tr. M. Domandi, 1963).

[D. NUGENT]

HUMANISM, CHRISTIAN, a description applied to theories that see a positive relationship between purely human values and the life and destiny of man under grace. One such modern form of Christian humanism was given prominence by Jacques Maritain. He saw an integration between nature and grace, so that the capacities for the true and the good inherent in man's nature were fully realizable, not negated or irrelevant, under grace. Teilhard de Chardin's world view, in which the gradual perfection of the universe and its subjection to man will be culminated in Christ the Omega Point, has also been called Christian humanism. The contemporary theory that the living and the pursuit of the Christian message consist precisely in concern for the secular and authentically human is also referred to as Christian humanism. In any of its forms this world view opposes a humanism that would make man absolute to the exclusion of God and his grace and opposes any purely superterrestrial interpretation of the Christian message that would negate human culture, traditions, and values. Thus incarnationalism in theology can be called a form of Christian humanism. BIBLIOGRAPHY: L. Bouyer, *Christian Humanism* (tr. A. V. Littledale, 1959); J. Maritain, *Integral Humanism* (tr. J. W. Evans, 1968). *SECULARITY.

[T. C. O'BRIEN]

HUMANISM, CLASSICAL, that style of life and view of man from the 14th cent. (the "quattrocento"), mainly in Italy, continuing to the Reformation. Jacob Burckhardt in *Civilization of the Renaissance in Italy* (1860) said it ushered in the modern world, but a century of scholarship has produced varying opinions.

Whereas general humanism embraces all that men have done in every era to explore the infinite variety of man's nature and relationships, classical humanism includes the professional class of scholars who saw in the classical languages and literatures (mostly Latin, later Greek) a world of knowledge and well-defined moral virtue which they strove to comprehend and transmit. It was re-statement of the Platonic ideal of virtue through knowledge. When Giovanni Pico della Mirandola delivered his "Oration on the Dignity of Man", he conceived of a dignity bestowed on Adam as the power to control his own destiny, which could allow the new movement to take a strictly secular bent (as it did in later centuries), or to remain within the Christian tradition, as classical humanism mainly did.

The word *umanista* was student slang in the mid-15th century. A teacher of the *studia humanitatis* was a grammarian, the arts professor, involved in the scholarly disciplines, grammar, rhetoric, history, poetry, and moral philosophy. This involved the rediscovery of classical antiquity in a different way from the humanism of the Middle Ages. First, the literary form became important for study and imitation (not merely the facts, allegories or sentiments to be drawn from them). Second, the ancient texts were to disclose a new concept of life, freer, more joyous than heretofore, which could give unfettered scope to the play of human feelings, to the sense of beauty, to the activities of the intellect. These studies were *litterae humaniores,* and the comparative implied, not more secular (as opposed to theological), but distinctively humane, more than any other kind of literature.

This new world view found its prophet in Francesco Petrarca (1304–74), who as the poet Petrarch, proclaimed this vision and became the champion of classical learning. Crowned at 37, with the laurel at the Capitol at Rome in 1341, he was the foremost man of letters in Europe. He cultivated the Latin style assiduously, and his cry "back to the ancients" was eagerly embraced. The success of the new learning was not, as with Scholasticism, due to the universities; it was supported by powerful and wealthy individuals, and grew as each teacher developed his own inner circle of disciples. Thus Lorenzo de Medici (d. 1492) supported the Platonic academy at Florence, attended by Pico, Marisilio Ficino, Michelangelo, and others. The Roman Academy founded about 1460 by Julius Pomponius Laetus had three eminent scholars who later became cardinals: Bembo, Sadoleto, and Egidio Canisio. The movement was further aided by the discovery of lost manuscripts. Giovanni Francesco Bracciolini Poggio, apostolic secretary, found treasured works at the abbey of St. Gall and elsewhere. Others collected and housed MSS in private libraries as did Cosmo de Medici, who established one at Venice in 1433, and the Medicean Library at Florence in 1441. The Vatican Library (begun under Pope Zacharias, 741–752) received definite formation under Pope Nicholas V (1447–55) who added to it several thousands of manuscripts.

From Italy, classical humanism spread throughout Europe, producing Erasmus in the North, Johann Müller or Regiomontanus (1436–76), Rudolph Agricola (Roelof Huysmann; 1443–85), and Melanchton (1497–1560) in Germany, Cardinal Ximenes in Spain, Budaeus (Guillaume Budé; 1467–1540), and Turnebus (Adrien Turnèbe; 1512–65) in France.

Classical humanism replaced the medieval elements of society with others drawn from the Graeco-Roman heritage. Because it was philological in much of its emphasis, it emphasized analysis, with memorization of linguistic and illustrative detail. It did prepare the way for some of the intellectual aspects of the Reformation, the rationalism of the 18th cent., and the thrust towards cultural anthropology that is man's current humanistic accent. BIBLIOGRAPHY: M. Gilmore, *World of Humanism (1453–1517)* (1952); P. O. Kristeller, *Classics and Renaissance Thought* (1955).

[N. F. GAUGHAN]

HUMANISM, SECULAR, a more or less systematic body of thought or action concerned with merely human interests, as opposed to divine, with the implication that it offers a substitute for the service of a being who is altogether out of this world. It tends to be a protest against religion, which it regards as profoundly inhuman. Nevertheless humanism does not itself compose a well-defined creed, code, or cult, nor does it as such either deny or affirm the existence of God. But it insists that humankind must rely on its own resources without looking for outside help or without passive resignation to God's providence to attack misery and bring it to goodness and happiness; all the means at its disposal must be used—science, technology, the communications media, political programs, and the fine arts. The attitude is sober and courageous, and contemporary humanism accordingly exhibits an activist character in contrast to the more contemplative graciousness of historic humanism. It is argued that humanism avoids the great and constant questions of human life and reaches an impasse: man is man's only hope, and human life is the supreme value; life, however, is disclosed as reaching out to beyond. Yet humanism casts out some of the cant that is associated with religion and that has served to impede the progress of the humane decencies. Its challenge is that if only Christianity were eliminated then the ideals of unity and love, originally Christian in inspiration, would no longer be a sort of pie in the sky, but could be realized completely in this world. Humanism argues not from the failure of Christians in history but from the intrinsic and irremediable powerlessness of the Christian faith to make real its promises, and from the fact that belief in an ''other'' world exhausts the believer's energies from doing what is required in this world. BIBLIOGRAPHY: C. Lamont, *Philosophy of Humanism* (5th ed., 1965); *Humanist Frame* (ed. J. Huxley, 1962); *idem, Essays of a Humanist* (1964); N. Rotenstreich, *Humanism in the Contemporary Era* (1963); R. E. Osborn, *Humanism and Moral Theory* (1959). *SECULARISM.

[T. GILBY]

HUMANITARIANISM, the advocacy and action of promoting the welfare of mankind at large, often associated with schemes of organized philanthropy, and sometimes professed as a ''religion of humanity,'' as though this chiefly or wholly comprised human duty. Yet its positive aspiration should be effectively integrated in Christianity. In fact, for many centuries it was under the aegis of the Church that hospitals for the sick and homes for orphans, the aged, the friendless, and strangers were founded; the history of European medicine takes it back to medieval religious sources. However, with the widening separation between the sacred and the secular from the time of the Renaissance and Reformation, and in the climate first of the Enlightenment, then of Positivism, then of moral indignation with the inhuman after-effects of industrial capitalism, the cause of humanitarianism has been presented in nonconfessional terms, and widespread and effective campaigns of social reform, extending even to the humane treatment of animals, have been conducted without appeal to religion. It has reflected the nobler side of Utilitarian social philosophy, ameliorated Manchester School economics, communicated a kindly and sometimes sentimental glow to socialism. Nevertheless, all has not been secular, far from it. The Evangelical Movement was a prime agent in the abolition of slavery and the improvement of factory conditions; the Anglo-Catholic Movement has a noble history in the social apostolate; the Social Gospel has been actively and effectively preached from the 19th cent.; and even when RC were most absent-minded about the values of secular humanism, they were often leading the way in the effort to alleviate human suffering. Even today the Christian Church remains the public conscience on many points. BIBLIOGRAPHY: R. T. McNally, NCE 7:229–230.

[T. GILBY]

HUMANITY OF CHRIST: (1) As a dogmatic theme, the genuineness and completeness of Christ's human nature as well as its *hypostatic union with the Word are matters of faith (see CHRISTOLOGICAL CONTROVERSIES). The denial of the reality of his humanity is the heresy of *Docetism; the denial of its perduring distinctness from Christ's divinity is the heresy of *Monophysitism; the position that Christ is also a human person, united only by excellence or holiness to divinity, is the heresy of *Nestorianism. (2) As a theme in spiritual theology, the humanity of Christ, i.e., the events and example of his life, death, and Resurrection, is a central emphasis in the *following of Christ as the model for Christian life.

[T. C. O'BRIEN]

HUMANN, LOUISE (d. 1836), a lay leader of the Catholic renaissance in France. Brilliant and well educated, she was especially versed in German philosophy and biblical exegesis and was instrumental in the conversion of L. Bautain and a number of Jews. These she assembled along with other intellectuals in a Strasbourg circle from which the Society of St. Louis developed. The inflexibility of Bautain brought on censure in 1834, but only after her death was the group dispersed. BIBLIOGRAPHY: M. Join-Lambert, *Catholicisme* 5:1085.

[M. J. SUELZER]

HUMBELINE, BL. (1092–1135), sister of Bernard of Clairvaux. H. lived a worldly life as the wife of a wealthy nobleman until a visit to her brother at Clairvaux, which shaped her future. When Bernard refused to see her because of her extravagant dress and retinue, as a sinner she begged his forgiveness and sought his direction. Thereafter she dedicated herself to a life of prayer and fasting, and later, with her husband's consent, entered the Benedictine priory at Jully, where she spent her remaining years. BIBLIOGRAPHY: Butler 3:376–377.

[J. D. LOUGHLIN]

HUMBERT OF MAROILLES, ST. (b. early 7th cent., d. *c.*680), abbot. According to legend H. was either first abbot or first bp. of Maroilles, or both. His cult was already widespread in the Frankish kingdom in the 8th century. H.

is thought to have visited Rome twice. BIBLIOGRAPHY: P. Rouillard, BiblSanct 12:808.

[B. F. SCHERER]

HUMBERT OF ROMANS (de Romanis; *c.*1200–77), fifth master general of the order of Preachers. Already a master of arts, he entered the order in 1224. He was professor of theology (1226) and prior (1237) at Lyons, provincial of the Roman (1238–40 or 1243–44) and French (1244–54) Dominican provinces, and master general (1254–63, resigned). During his generalate, the order's liturgy was perfected (1256), its scholastic regime coordinated and completed, its position at the Univ. of Paris vindicated, and the office of procurator general created (1254 during the university crisis). H. wrote several homiletic, ascetical, and pastoral works. His *Expositio Regulae B. Augustini, Expositio in constitutiones De officiis ordinis,* and encyclical letters exercised a wide and continuing influence on the Dominican spirit and administration. BIBLIOGRAPHY: F. Heintke, *Humbert von Romans* (1933).

[W. A. HINNEBUSCH]

HUMBERT OF SILVA CANDIDA (*c.*1000–61), cardinal, canonist, and reformer. H. was born in Lorraine and at the age of 15 entered the monastery of Moyenmoutier. In 1049 he was named cardinal bishop of Silva Candida and became an influential advisor to four popes. One of the great reform churchmen of the 11th cent., he is unfortunately remembered chiefly for his narrow and intransigent attitude toward the Byzantine Church which he regarded as subject to the same canonical regulations as the Western Church. As legate of Pope Leo IX to Constantinople in 1054 he pronounced the controversial excommunication of Patriarch Michael Cerularius. Pope Stephen IX named him chancellor and librarian, and under Nicholas II he formulated regulations for papal elections. Attention was focused on him as a reformer and theologian by his *Libri tres adversus simoniacos,* in which he denied the validity of sacraments administered by simoniacs and heretics. His writings supported the distinction between spiritual and temporal jurisdictions and the limitation of lay ownership of church property. BIBLIOGRAPHY: J. Gilchrist, ''Cardinal Humbert of Silva Candida,'' *Annuale mediaevale 3* (1962) 29–42; A. Michel, *Humbert und Kerullarios,* (2 v., 1929–30).

[L. NEMEC]

HUME, DAVID (1711–76), Scottish philosopher, perhaps the most powerful of the empiricists. Of moderate means, he was educated at Edinburgh but declined to follow the legal career for which he was destined. He spent some 3 years in France writing his *Treatise of Human Nature,* a work that died aborning. Serving as secretary to several diplomats, he continued to revise the work in a more literary style. *An Enquiry Concerning the Human Understanding* and *An Enquiry Concerning the Principles of Morals* brought him the fame that he had sought. A man of note and great personal charm in life, he remains today a vital influence in philosophy. H.'s basic philosophical position is skepticism, variously qualified as ''radical'' or ''mitigated.'' In its background lies the Cartesian notion of the clear and distinct idea, though H. was to battle continually against the Cartesian tenet that the ultimately real is rational. The natural science of the day, the physics of Galileo and esp. of Newton bulk large. (The title of the *Treatise* goes on: '' . . . being an attempt to introduce the experimental method of reasoning into moral subjects.'') The immediate starting point is Locke's approach to the problem of knowledge. H. is distinguished by a more systematic and rigorous development of the empiricist premises than Locke exhibits. As with Locke, the object of knowledge is the fact of consciousness, the perception. Perceptions of sense data are ''lively'' (impressions) or ''less lively'' (ideas). H. forthrightly abandons Locke's representational theory: we know ideas, not things through them. He atomizes experience: each impression or idea is unique. The mind associates ideas (a key point in H.'s thought) in terms of resemblance, contiguity, and causality. These are empirically observed laws of thought, not intrinsically necessary ones. There are no universal ideas, for universals cannot be empirically verified, but only universal terms. This nominalism goes far beyond that of the 12th cent., or even that of Ockham.

From such premises, no notion of substance can be drawn, and H. adheres to the logic. Substance is an ''idea . . . of a particular collection of qualities.'' Even spiritual substances: myself, other selves, are ''nothing but a bundle or collection of different perceptions.'' We imagine the continuity of personal identity as we imagine the external world. (H. did not deny the external world, merely the certitude of our knowledge of it.) So, too, with causality. We cannot know that A causes B, only that B follows A. From repeated experience we associate the ideas of A and B as causally connected. H., of course, must reject any ontological or causal argument for the existence of God. He admits order in the world and some slight evidence, therefore, for a designer, but none for the omnipotent God of religion. H. denies the possibility of constructing a moral philosophy in rationalistic terms, or even those of Locke and Berkeley. He bases his ethics on empirical grounds, rejecting pleasure and even enlightened self-interest (utilitarianism) as the criterion of moral goodness. Moral goodness for him is the pleasure arising from the consideration of character expressed in disinterested approbation. Goodness is in the mind of the judge. H. escapes subjectivism here by observing that men, for the most part, agree in judgment about vice and virtue, good and evil acts. He denies, of course, the existence of any moral absolutes. The skepticism of H.'s position is a philosophical, not a practical one. We must live as though the world is out there, as though inductive reasoning were valid. His attitude is still seen in the empiricism and pragmatism of today. The force and rigor of its presentation awoke Kant from his ''dogmatic [*rationalistic*] slumber.'' BIBLIOGRAPHY: A. Flew, *Hume's Philosophy of Belief* (1961); C. W. Hendel, *Studies in the Philosophy of David Hume,* (rev. ed. 1963).

[W. B. MAHONEY]

HUME, NELSON (1881–1948), educator. A teacher and founder of two preparatory schools, H. is known esp. for establishing and acting as headmaster of the Canterbury School, New Milford, Conn., conducted by Catholic laymen under the patronage of the bp. of Hartford. He served as headmaster there from 1915 to 1948.

[J. R. AHERNE]

HUMERAL VEIL, a rectangular piece of cloth covering the back of the shoulders and used to hold liturgical vessels. It is used for Benediction of the Blessed Sacrament and in some countries for taking Viaticum to the sick. It originated from the custom of avoiding, out of reverence, the touching of holy things.

[N. KOLLAR]

HUMFREY (HUMPHRY, HUMPHRYS), PELHAM (1647–74), English composer in the Chapel Royal. H. wrote several fine anthems, services, religious and secular songs, and composed the music for Shakespeare's *The Tempest*.

[M. T. LEGGE]

HUMILIANA DE CIRCULIS, BL. (d. 1246), Franciscan tertiary. Married at 16, she suffered for 5 years in a difficult marriage until her husband's death. Her obligations toward her two children prevented her joining the Poor Clares, but she became a Franciscan tertiary, living a life of prayer and austerity in a tower of her father's house in Florence and receiving notable graces. Her cult was confirmed in 1694. L. de Clary, *Lives of the Saints and Blessed of the Three Orders of St. Francis,* (4 v., 1885–87) 2:275–279. AS May 4:384–418.

[O. J. BLUM]

HUMILIATI, first a lay fraternity, then a religious order for men and women, inspired by the ideal of apostolic poverty and simplicity. Members were also called Berettini from their attire of undyed, grayish wool (It., *beretto*). Their origins are unknown but they existed in Lombardy as early as the mid-12th cent.; they were another manifestation of the desire of laymen of the time to restore the Church to simplicity and to remove the abuses of the clergy (see PATARINES; WALDENSES). The Humiliati sought to live in poverty not by begging but by manual labor; they abhorred lying, refused oaths, practiced fasts, and cared for the poor. Some lived at home, others in community, in double monasteries. The Humiliati began to preach in public for reform in the Church; in 1179 Pope Alexander III ordered them to cease; when they continued, they were excommunicated, together with the Waldenses, by Lucius III in 1184. Many rejoined the Church in 1202, and they became effective counter-agents against groups of similar inspiration who were attacking the Church, especially the *Cathari. Innocent III organized the Humiliati into one order with three parts: regulars, living the religious vows in double monasteries; lay members, living a community life, also in double monasteries; and tertiaries, living at home (these Humiliati were the first to be called tertiaries). The order spread through N Italy and S France and by 1216 had 150 houses. The communities prospered through their interest in the wool industry; by their wealth they were able to become moneylenders. They also began to grow lax, and their numbers decreased sharply; St. Charles Borromeo tried to reform them, and one of them in 1569 attempted to assassinate him. The male houses of the order were suppressed in 1571 by Pius V. In Italy monasteries of nuns, Berettine, still survive. BIBLIOGRAPHY: E. S. Davison, *Forerunners of St. Francis* (1928) 168–200; M. F. Laughlin, NCE 7:234; M. H. Vicaire, *Catholicisme* 5:1097–98.

[C. J. LYNCH]

HUMILITY, generically a candid attitude towards what we really are, an avoidance of humbug at two extremes, namely of inordinate self-esteem which claims too much and of unwarranted and sometimes hypocritical self-abasement that claims too little. St. Thomas notes its closeness to *magnanimity. Consequently, it is not at all wormlike, but sturdily truthful about one's human and creaturely condition. It has been caricatured by hagiographers writing in one genre as also by Charles Dickens in the character of Uriah Heep: the word now tends to have a pejorative sense. Specifically it means the part of the *moral virtue of *temperance that controls the pleasures connected with the assertion of the self and its acknowledgment by others; more specifically it is that part of such *modesty as relates to one's inward feelings rather than to outward show.

Enjoined by Our Lord (Mt 11.29, 18.4, Lk 14.11), the spiritual writers treat it as a *sine qua non* of Christian living, indeed as the most potent of the moral virtues after justice. St. Benedict's *Rule* sets forth its 12 degrees, St. Ignatius Loyola's *Exercises* proposes its systematic development. It is specifically opposed by the sin of pride: this, however, should be regarded less as the self-seeking implicit in all sin or as Luciferian pride than as a more emotional and often more petty conceit and vanity. BIBLIOGRAPHY: ThAq ST 2a2ae, 161–162.

[T. GILBY]

HUMMEL, JOHANN NEPOMUK (1778–1837), pianist and composer of the Viennese school. H. early displayed a remarkable facility on the piano and for 2 years studied and lived with Mozart. H. continued his studies (with Clementi, Salieri, Albrechtsberger), served Prince Esterhazy for 7 years, taught for a while, then held the posts of Kapellmeister at Stuttgart and later at Weimar. H. will best be remembered for his work the *Pianoforte School* and for his contributions to the art of piano playing; but he also composed operas, piano, chamber, and other forms of secular music as well as Masses and other choral church works.

[M. T. LEGGE]

HUMMELAUER, FRANZ VON (1842–1914), Jesuit biblical scholar. H. studied and taught at Jesuit houses in Germany, England, and Holland where he devoted himself to anthropology and Oriental studies, and later to Scripture. He cofounded the *Cursus Scripturae Sacrae* with R. Cornely and J. Knabenbauer, and contributed commentaries on several OT books to this series. He developed a theory on a pre-Mosaic priesthood, and sought to establish a principle to solve any apparent difficulties between OT exegesis and scientific knowledge. H. was a liberal scholar whose insights have been vindicated by subsequent studies. BIBLIOGRAPHY: A. Bea, DBSuppl 4:144–146; F. X. Weiser, NCE 7:236–237.

[T. M. MCFADDEN]

HUMPHREY OF GLOUCESTER (1390–1447), patron of English humanism. H. ranked with his father, King Henry IV, and his brothers, Henry V and John, Duke of Bedford as a bibliophile. But Duke Humphrey was the first to invite Italian humanists to England and in 1440 he donated an impressive number of MSS (nearly 300) to Oxford Univ., which named the central part of the library after him. BIBLIOGRAPHY: R. J. Schoeck, NCE 7:237; Emden Ox 2:983–985.

[J. A. WEISHEIPL]

HUNEGUNDIS, ST. (d. *c.*690), monastic foundress. Compelled to marry against her will, she persuaded her husband to go on pilgrimage to Rome. She received the veil from Pope Vitalian, in whose presence she took her vows. Returning to Frankland, she founded the monastery of Homblières where she lived. Her husband served as chaplain. BIBLIOGRAPHY: R. Van Doren, BiblSanct 12:823–825.

[A. CABANISS]

HUNFRIED, ST. (Hunfrid, Humphrey; d. 870), Benedictine abbot and bp. of Therouanne, France. He was abbot of Prum when elected bp. in 836. Therouanne was ravaged by the Normans in 861, but Pope Nicholas I refused to allow H. to return to the monastery, and Therouanne was restored. He was elected abbot of St. Bertin near St. Omer and continued to rule his diocese. He was present at the Third Council of Soissons in 866. H's relics are venerated at St. Omer. BIBLIOGRAPHY: Butler 1:525–526.

[T. C. O'BRIEN]

HUNGARIAN BYZANTINE RITE, a body of Hungarian Byzantine Catholics. Conditioned and influenced by a strong Hungarian nationalism, the liturgical rite replaced an Old Slavonic vernacular with Hungarian. The conclusion of the *Union of Brest-Litovsk* (1596) and the *Union of Užhorod* (1696) consolidated the position of Uniates and exercised pressure on the Orthodox toward the reunion. The Uniates were protected against further abuses from the Latins by the decree of the Empress Maria Theresa issued under the title ''Apostolic Kings'' on Sept. 16, 1756. However, the plan of the bishop of Eger to bring about the Magyarization of the Ruthenian Church in Hungary greatly hindered the cause of union. In 1870 the Greek Catholic Bp. Bachnynsky transferred the episcopal see from Mukachevo or Užhorod for a more central location. The success of this event prompted the Hungarians to form in 1818 the new Eparchy of Prešov by taking ninety parishes from the Eparchy of Mukachevo. The Uniate bishop of Prešov was subjected to the metropolitan jurisdiction of the Latin abp. of Esterdom *pro tempore* for the purpose of supervision.

It is hardly to be wondered that Ruthenians were weakened in regard to national feeling, and that soon there appeared the strange anomaly of Hungarians-Ruthenians, who succeeded so well that on June 8, 1912 Pius X created for them the Magyar Eparchy of Hajdudorogh out of eighty former Ukrainian parishes taken from the Carpathian Ruthenian eparchies. Pressure for this action was exerted by the Hungarian government for the benefit of ''Hungarian Greek Catholics'' with Magyar as the official language. The National Committee ventured further in trying to eliminate Old Slavonic as liturgical vernacular and tried to safeguard ecclesiastical traditions by prescribing Greek as the liturgical language for the Hajdu-Dorogh Eparchy. That the Old Greek language was more foreign to the Hungarians than the Old Slavonic gives some indication of the dislike that the Hungarians held for Ruthenians. The endless struggle to maintain the Old Slavonic liturgy against encroachment by the Hungarians caused a great division among the faithful, some of whom defended Magyarization and some of whom became Russophiles because of it. This situation was, of course, exploited by the Orthodox.

This led to emigration to the U.S.A. and elsewhere. Fragmentation into ethnic groups of those emigrating from Galicia and those of Subcarpathian Russia caused Pope Pius XI to give to each group their bp. by decree of the Congregation for the Oriental Church, May 8, 1924, namely Kyr Constantine Bohatchevsky for the Galicians and Kyr Basil Takacs for those from Subcarpathian Russia. Eparchies were accordingly established for Galicians—under the metropolitan in Philadelphia and suffragan bps. in Stamford, Conn. and in Chicago. Jurisdiction for the Subcarpathian Ruthenians was established in Pittsburgh (1924), Passaic, N.J., and Parma. Among the Ruthenians considered to be from Subcarpathian Russia there actually are represented such diverse ethnic groups as the Rusini, Hungarians, and Slovaks.

It must be said that Greek, Hungarian, Slovak, and English are the liturgical vernaculars for Catholics of Byzantine rite, settled in Hungary and other parts of Europe and in the Americas. The number of Catholics of the Hungarian Byzantine rite (1976) is about 323,112. BIBLIOGRAPHY: L.

Nemec, "The Ruthenian Uniate Church in Its Historical Perspective," *Church History* 38 (1968) 1–24; B. Boysak, *Fate of the Holy Union in Carpatho-Ukraine* (1963); B. J. Kidd, *Churches of Eastern Christendom from A.D. 451 to the Present Time* (1927, repr. 1973).

[L. NEMEC]

HUNGARIAN CONFESSION (Confession of Czenger), a principal *confession of faith of the *Reformed Church in Hungary adopted in 1557 or 1558 at a synod in Czenger (Csenger, NE border of Hungary); it was supplanted (1567) by the Second *Helvetic Confession and the *Heidelberg Catechism. In eleven chapters the Confession expresses Calvinist teaching on salvation (without mention of *double predestination) and the sacraments; it is also a polemic against Unitarianism and Anabaptist teaching on baptism.

BIBLIOGRAPHY: Schaff Creeds 1:591–592.

[T. C. O'BRIEN]

HUNGARY (*Magyarország*), a country in E central Europe (area 35,911 square miles; pop. 10,460,000, nearly all Hungarian-speaking Hungarians [Magyars]). The population is 60% Catholic, 27% Protestant, and the rest are chiefly Greek Orthodox and Jewish. For 1050 years (896–1946), Hungary was a monarchy; since 1945 it has been a republic. The historical territory of Hungary had an area of 125,402 square miles. Its boundaries were the Carpathian Mountains, and the country had a seaport on the Adriatic. Prior to the arrival of the *Magyars, the area was sparsely populated by a variety of peoples, including Celts and Thracians, various Slavic and Teutonic tribes, Huns and Avars. For a period, two Roman provinces, Pannonia and Dacia, were also established in the Danubian valley. In 896, the Magyars, a Finno-Ugric people, migrated across the Carpathians under its elected leader Árpád, and for the first time in history, the whole area was under one ruler. The House of Árpád ruled Hungary until 1301, when the crown passed in the female line. With the exception of the freely elected Mátyás Hunyadi in the 15th cent., all Hungarian kings and ruling queens traced their descent from Árpád. At first, the rulers were called dukes (a custom revived later by the princes of Transylvania, the SW section of Hungary with a strong tradition of its own). Stephen, the son of the great Duke Géza, asked for and received a royal crown from Pope Sylvester II and in 1000 had himself crowned king. In the history of the Christian Church, the House of Árpád is unique; starting with Stephen and his son Imre, and continuing through László who reigned 1077–1095, it numbers 18 canonized saints among its descendants. These include such distinguished daughters and granddaughters as SS. Elizabeth of Hungary; Margaret, a Dominican nun; Margaret of Scotland, a granddaughter of St. Stephen; Elizabeth of Portugal; and Hedwig, the great "Queen Jadwiga" of the Poles and Lithuanians.

As V. Juhász maintains, "the transcendental and spiritual content of the shamanist view of the world facilitated the nation's inner acceptance of Christianity and inspired a live, original folk religiosity which—side by side, but never at odds with the Church—permeates the peasantry to this day." Historians consider the Hungarian nation exceptionally religious, with an almost mystical faith in its God-given mission to be "the bastion of the West and the defender of Christianity." Traditionally "the land of Mary," it has a unique record of religious tolerance. Already King Koloman the Wise (1095–1116) decreed, "Of witches, which do not exist, no more mention shall be made." Later, the 1552 Transylvanian Parliament of Torda was the first in Europe to guarantee complete freedom of religion, providing a haven for nonconformists of all creeds.

Being a "bastion of the West" proved to be a costly privilege. Throughout their history, Hungarians fought to defend the West, which was indifferent, even ignorant of Hungary's existence, against Easterners, who often wished no quarrel with their distant kinsmen, the Magyars. The West, when it noticed Hungary at all, did so with an eye to colonization and exploitation.

The Hungarian nation, originally as populous as and far more wealthy than England or France, was often decimated. Twice—during the Tatar invasion (1241–42) and the Turkish occupation (1526–1686) it was nearly exterminated. The predicament of being caught between the millstones of Vienna and Istanbul for 400 years is best expressed by the rebel song, "Does it matter who shall eat us/Whether the wolf eats us or the bear eats us/We shall be eaten surely." The song was sung with great conviction prior to, during, and following World War II also; this time the wolf and the bear had changed to Berlin and Moscow. Among such trials, the Hungarian nation regarded even the fact of its continued existence as a miracle of God and Hungary was grateful for such leaders as the Árpád kings, of whom Béla III (1173–96), and Béla IV (1235–70) deserve special mention, and even for a weak one, Andrew II (1209–35), who, just 7 years after the Magna Charta, gave Hungary its Golden Bull (1222). After the male line of the Árpáds died out, the female line brought in the Anjou kings, Charles Robert (1308–42) and Louis the Great (1342–82) King of Hungary and Poland. When King Sigismund (1395–1437) became Holy Roman Emperor, Hungary grew in prestige but the honor proved to be a mixed blessing. The rise of the Hunyadis, János (d. 1456) and Mátyás (Matthias Corvinus, who ruled 1458–90) marks one of the proudest periods in Hungarian history, with the father exemplifying the virtues of Christian warrior and statesman, and the son, known as the Just, shining as Renaissance humanist and the people's own elected king. Even those blessings, however, cost the blood of László Hunyadi, victim of foreign intrigue.

After Hunyadis, the Austrians liberated Hungary to try to annex it; Buda, freed from the Turks in 1686, was effectively destroyed in the process. The Zrinyis, Rákóczys, Imre Thököly, fought Habsburg absolutism in the 17th and 18th cent. in vain. They died by violence, treachery, or in exile. Refuge for the exiles, ironically, was provided by the enemy—the Turkish Empire. In the long line of Habsburg rulers, only two stand out as not intent upon the destruction of Hungary: Maria Theresa (1740–80) and Joseph II (1780–90); but they contributed to making the country economically and politically dependent on Austria.

Economical and cultural exploitation was responsible for the rise of the peaceful reformer Count István Széchenyi, and with him Hungary's "Augustan Age" of poetry and music (Petőfi, Arany, Vörösmarty, Erkel, Liszt). Political oppression brought about the War of Independence (1848–49), sparked by the charismatic Lajos Kossuth and brutally put down by the Austrians after their ally the Czar of Russia conquered the victorious Hungarian armies. The hanging of the 13 Hungarian generals as war criminals and the execution of the moderate Prime Minister Count Lajos Batthányi embittered the nation as much as the 18 years of terror that followed. A wise statesman, Ferenc Deák, with the help of Queen Elizabeth, effected the nation's reconciliation with King Francis Joseph in 1867, and Hungary found its place in the community of nations once more. After the millennial celebrations of 1896, Hungary rose to new heights in culture. Starting with 1905, a generation of poets, writers, composers equal to or even surpassing the galaxy ruling the early 1800s flourished (Ady, Babits, Kosztolányi, Móricz, Bartók, Kodaly).

World War I, into which Hungary was pressured over the protest of its prime minister, Count István Tisza, put an end to the only interlude of peace and relative prosperity Hungary had in nearly 500 years. Crippled by the Treaty of Trianon (1919), 71.4% of its territory and 61% of its population having been given to the succession states (Austria among them), Hungary seemed destined to permanent decline as an impoverished, dependent nation. Temporary occupation by Romanian troops, 5 months of terror under Béla Kun's Communist regime, the influx of refugees from the territories which were taken away, and the harsh terms of the treaty all but crushed the country completely. Yet under the leadership of the governor, Miklós Horthy, the country embarked on another period of relative prosperity. New writers and poets, many of peasant origin, continued to search for a new spiritual identity in the mutilated country. (A Eucharistic Congress was held in Budapest in 1938 to commemorate the millennium of the death of St. Stephen).

The clash of ideologies sharpened as Hitler's rise to power, on the one hand, threatened Hungary, which had been stripped of its military defenses, and on the other, tantalized it with a hope that, under a revision of the Treaty of Trianon, at least those parts of the country could be returned that were inhabited solidly by Hungarians. After holding out against Hitler longer than any of its neighbors, Hungary was occupied by German troops in March 1944. Occupation by the Soviet Union followed in 1945. Free elections that year brought to power a democratic, non-Communist government, but its power was broken by Communist pressure. The Revolution of 1956 was put down; for the second time in a little over a century, Russian troops crushed Hungary's fight for independence. The head of the Hungarian Church, Joseph Cardinal *Mindszenty, imprisoned in 1948, freed in 1956, found refuge in the American Legation in Budapest. Under these circumstances, relations between Church and State improved slowly, and while the political lot of Hungary has eased considerably under János Kádár and Gyorgy Lázár, its economic situation continues to be difficult. In 1964–69, under the terms of two agreements between Hungary and the Vatican, an apostolic administrator was appointed, two new abps. and four new bps. were invested; in 1972 the government accepted the appointment of five new bps; the appointment (1976) of a new bp. and an auxiliary bp. marked the first time since the Communists came to power that all 11 dioceses of Hungary had bishops. BIBLIOGRAPHY: I. Lukinich, *History of Hungary* (tr. C. Dallas, 1937); J. Montgomery, *Hungary the Unwilling Satellite* (1947); *Facts About Hungary* (ed. I. Kovács, 1958); X. Szunyogh, *Magyar szentek, szent magyarok* (1938). *HUNYADI, JÁNOS; *PÁZMÁNI, PÉTER; *FINNO-UGRIC RELIGION.

[D. H. BRUNAUER]

HUNGARY, ORTHODOX CHURCH IN. The small number of Orthodox believers in Hungary (about .02% of the population) is divided jurisdictionally among the patriarchates of Bulgaria, Romania, Russia, and Serbia, and include, in addition to people of those nationalities, some Greeks and Magyars.

[T. BIRD]

HUNGER, WORLD, problems of human starvation and malnutrition as viewed from an international perspective. To some extent, world hunger has afflicted the human family throughout history, as illustrated in the Joseph story of Genesis. And the need for alleviating the hunger of people in other parts of the world has long been emphasized as a moral duty. In the modern missionary movement, the Churches have customarily made hunger relief a part of their work, both through donation of food to the hungry and through aiding agricultural development. Christian theology, with its use of bread as a sign for the body of Christ, has found it natural to make the giving of physical food a concomitant part of the Christian ministry. In taking this approach, the Churches were also responding to Christ's identification of himself with the hungry (Matt 25.35, 42). But though this emphasis has been perennial, world hunger assumed a new degree of urgency for the Churches in the 1970s. A number of factors converged to bring this concern to a focus in 1973–74–75. A drastic rise in oil prices had made production and distribution of food much more expensive. Years of drought had brought disaster to several African countries in the Sahel. Bad harvests in the Soviet Union had resulted in its decision to make large purchases of wheat, particularly in the U.S., and world grain prices rose sharply. Political disturbances in such chronically poor areas as Bangladesh made their food needs more acute.

World population continued to soar in most of the countries suffering food shortages.

In late 1974, a United Nations-sponsored World Food Conference in Rome brought increased attention to the need for action. Many church representatives attended the conference, and Churches of various denominations subsequently gave world hunger a higher priority in their programs. When the Catholic International Eucharistic Congress was held at Philadelphia in 1976, its theme was world hungers, and the need of the hungry for physical food was emphasized along with the hungers for justice, freedom, and spiritual fulfillment. Churches responded to the world hunger crisis through gifts of food as in the past. But they gave more attention than had been usual to the need for dealing with "root causes." They discussed the need for people in affluent areas of the world to adopt simpler patterns of living, with less consumption, so that the world's resources might be more equitably distributed. And they talked of the need for political changes in both poor and affluent countries to facilitate more adequate production and distribution of food. While church members of diverse viewpoints could find agreement on the importance of combating starvation, the religious community remained divided over the question of population control, its importance in relation to dealing with world hunger, and what methods were acceptable for limiting population growth.

[T. EARLY]

HUNGER STRIKE. Total refusal of any nourishment whatsoever as a means to dramatize or promote a cause is an intended suicide as surely as is the act of burning oneself to death; it is the use of an immoral *means and cannot be justified by any end, however noble. Refusal of nourishment as a calculated risk, however, is morally a different kind of act. Risks to life for a proportionately serious and right cause are permissible on the grounds of the hierarchy of values among human goods and objectives (see LIFE, RISKS TO). A hunger strike that involves a definite period of total fast, or one undertaken with a fair probability of success within a sustainable time of fasting, may be permissible. Intended suicide is not involved; the fast as a calculated risk is not immoral in itself; a proportionately serious purpose is involved. The principle of *double effect may thus apply. Even if death should occur, then, it is morally speaking incidental to the faster's intent and mode of action. A further consideration has arisen in recent hunger strikes, the right and/or obligation of authorities, e.g., jailers, to force-feed the striker. Civil law has sometimes required forced feeding. The moral obligation towards prisoners, however, seems to stop at providing nourishment in the ordinary manner, and does not include forcing nourishment intravenously.

[T. C. O'BRIEN]

HUNNAEUS, AUGUSTIN (1521–78), Thomist scholar. He served as president of the College of St. Anne. His major works were a discussion of the doctrine of St. Thomas as it concerns the sacraments (1570), and two editions of Commentaries on the *Summa* of St. Thomas (1569), (1575).

[P. J. HENNESSEY]

HUNS, a Turanian people, the Hiungnu, who lived originally in central Asia. United into an empire, they long threatened the Chinese, who in 214 B.C. built the Great Wall against them. In the 2d-cent. A.D. some of the Huns began a slow spread westward. They made Persia tributary in 448; and in India the so-called White Huns destroyed the Gupta empire *c.*480. A third horde pushed out the Alans and the Goths, settling in the middle basin of the Danube. In 448 their king Attila exacted a huge tribute from the Eastern Roman Empire. He was, however, defeated 3 years later by a coalition of Roman and Germanic forces. He was later turned aside from plundering Italy by an embassy headed by Pope Leo I. Soon after Attila's death in 453, most of his followers retired E of the Carpathians; but other Turkish peoples and some Slavic tribes that had taken over their name and fierce reputation remained a threat to central Europe. BIBLIOGRAPHY: W. M. McGovern, *Early Empires of Central Asia* (1939); E. A. Thompson, *History of Attila and the Huns* (1948).

[M. J. SUELZER]

HUNT, DUANE GARRISON (1884–1960), fifth bp. of Salt Lake City. A convert to Catholicism in 1913 from Methodism. H. studied for the priesthood and was ordained for the Diocese of Salt Lake City in 1920. He served as vicar general there and was named bp. in 1937. A celebrated preacher, H. conducted a popular radio program in the Mormon capital which brought many into the Church. He was author of *The People, the Clergy and the Church* (1936).

[J. R. AHERNE]

HUNT, WALTER (d. 1478), Carmelite friar, canon of Hereford (1465–78). English representative at the council of Ferrara-Florence (1438–39), he attended the General Chapter at Rome for the reformation of his order (1446). He wrote extensively on the theological and historical aspects of relations with the Greek Church. BIBLIOGRAPHY: Emden Ox 2:986–987.

[C. D. ROSS]

HUNT, WILLIAM HOLMAN (1827–1910), English painter and writer. Trained in the Royal Academy school, H. founded—with Rossetti and Millais—the Pre-Raphaelite Brotherhood (1848). He was the most moralistic and literal member of the movement. To be certain of the accuracy of his biblical pictures, he made three trips to the Near East between 1854 and 1873. Unlike the rest of the Brotherhood, Hunt remained loyal to the tenets of Pre-Raphaelitism throughout his career. Representative paintings are *The*

Light of the World, Hireling Shepherd, The Scapegoat, and *The Awakening Conscience*. BIBLIOGRAPHY: W. H. Hunt, *Pre-Raphaelitism and the Pre-Raphaelite Brotherhood* (1913); A. C. Gissing, *William Holman Hunt* (1936); J. Maas, *Victorian Painters* (1969).

[F. S. GRUBAR]

HUNTING. From a moral point of view the killing of animals is not an act of injustice, since justice is a person-to-person relationship; if there is injustice it would be in killing animals that are the possession of another person. Hunting as a means to obtain food is obviously morally right, since, according to Genesis and the understanding of theology, the *order of the universe includes the service and usefulness of lesser creatures to man (see ThAq ST 2a2ae, 64.1 & 2). Hunting as sport is justifiable as part of man's regulation of his environment, i.e., where animals are predators or their number upsets environmental balance; it is also justifiable on the grounds of man's legitimate need for recreation (see LEISURE, THEOLOGY OF). But whether for need or for sport hunting must be a morally reasonable action. Simply because it is base, *cruelty is contrary to right reason and is immoral on that account; because man must respect his environment (see POLLUTION, ENVIRONMENTAL) wantonness must be avoided, whether that means indiscriminate slaughter or the impoverishment of future natural resources or the upsetting of the ecological pattern.

[T. C. O'BRIEN]

HUNTINGDON, COUNTESS OF (Selina Hastings; 1707–91), foundress of the *Countess of Huntingdon's Connexion. She and her husband, the ninth Earl of Huntingdon, joined the Fetter Lane Methodist *Society in London, 1739. After the Earl's death, she became an active leader in Methodism, the close associate of G. *Whitefield and of John and Charles *Wesley. She built many chapels, with the Methodist-trained chaplains, and established a college for preachers at Trevecca, Wales. A strong Calvinist, she broke with J. Wesley over his *Arminianism. Invoking the protection of the *Toleration Act, she established the Connexion as an association of dissenting chapels; there were 64 chapels at the time of her death. BIBLIOGRAPHY: S. Tytler, *Countess of Huntingdon and Her Circle* (1907).

[F. E. MASER]

HUNTINGTON, ANNA V. HYATT (1876–1973), American sculptor from Cambridge, Mass., who lived in France, and is best known for animal forms of intense energy. H. executed the equestrian *Joan of Arc* (1915) on Riverside Drive and the *El Cid* (1927–37) at the Hispanic Society of America, both in New York City.

[M. J. DALY]

HUNTINGTON, WILLIAM REED (1838–1909), liturgical scholar, author of the Chicago-*Lambeth Quadrilateral. H. was a liberal Episcopalian leader of the House of Deputies of the *General Convention of the Protestant Episcopal Church for 30 years, until his death. As rector, first of All Saints Church, Worcester, Mass. (1862–83), and then of Grace Church, New York City (1883–1909), he led significant movements for the reform of the *BCP and for the organic reunion of the Churches in the United States. Influenced by William White, S. T. Coleridge, and Horace Bushnell, among others, H. continued the search for church unity begun by W. A. *Muhlenberg and in turn contributed to the later ecumenical movement through his influence upon C. H. *Brent and E. L. Parsons. H. sought a national Church for the U.S., based on unity by contribution, and at the same time realized the necessity of making the Episcopal Church more "American" in outlook. His major publications were *Church-Idea, An Essay toward Unity* (1870), *Peace of the Church* (1891), *A National Church* (1898), *Theology's Eminent Domain* (1902), *Tract 91* (1907), and *Four Theories of Visible Church Unity* (1909). BIBLIOGRAPHY: W. R. Huntington, *Church-Idea, An Essay toward Unity* (5th ed., 1928); J. F. Woolverton, "William Reed Huntington: Liturgical Renewal and Church Unity in the 1880s," *Anglican Theological Review* (April 1966).

[J. F. WOOLVERTON]

HUNYADI, JÁNOS (JOHN; 1387?–1456), regent of Hungary, Christian warrior. The origins of this deeply religious, popular leader have never been definitely established. While still in his teens, he attracted the attention of the King—soon Holy Roman Emperor— Sigismund. Under successive rulers, H. attained their greatest trust in matters both military and administrative. His native genius and sterling character inspired confidence and admiration in kings, lords, and peasants alike. His life's goal was to drive the Turks out of Europe, and he succeeded in forcing them into a 10-year truce. Unfortunately, King Wladislaw I, persuaded by Card. Cesarini, papal legate, over H's protests, broke the truce and lost his own life in the Battle of Varna (1444). H. barely escaped with his life. During László V.'s minority, H. ruled Hungary as the nation's elected regent. With the ascension of Mohammed II and the fall of Constantinople (1453), H. redoubled his efforts to avert the Mohammedan conquest of Europe. In July 1456, with his sole ally a Franciscan, John Capistrano, H. raised a volunteer army and won a decisive victory at Nándorfehérvár (now Belgrade). In commemoration of the victory, and in accordance with a bull by Pope Callixtus III, to this day, the *angelus* bell tolls every noon in many Christian countries. H. averted the Turkish conquest for another 70 years, saving Western Christianity; he himself died of the plague, in his camp, the following month. Though his elder son László was treacherously slain by the jealous king, his younger son Mátyás became a splendid Renaissance king (Matthias Corvinus, 1458–90). BIBLIOGRAPHY: D. G. Kosáry, *History of Hungary,* (1941); L. Elekes, *Hunyadi* (1952). *HUNGARY.

[D. H. BRUNAUER]

HUONDER, ANTON (1858–1926), Swiss-born Jesuit ascetical writer and a pioneer in the search for a deeper and more critical understanding of the missionary impulse; famous for his polemic against Europeanism in the missions. He entered the Jesuits in 1875; studied theology in Holland and England; was ordained in 1889; became famous for his retreats for priests; was for many years editor of *Die Katholischen Missionen;* was the author of a series of meditations entitled *Zu Füssen des Meisters* (At the Feet of the Master, 4 v.); a character study of Ignatius Loyola; and esp. important, his three-volume work entitled *Die Mission auf der Kanzel und im Verein,* which refers to mission in and out of the pulpit, in which one learns in fraternal dialogue as much as one teaches. He worked efficaciously for the development of native clergies.

[E. J. DILLON]

HÛPPŌYŌ, a small square of cloth used in West Syrian churches to cover the chalice or the paten; also called *kûppōrō*. It is sometimes replaced by a metal cover.

[A. CODY]

HUREZI (HOREZI), ABBEY OF, a Greek Orthodox monastery in the forest of Hurezi in Moldavia, Romania, in the district of Vîlcea, built by John Constantin Brâncoveanu, Prince of Walachia, in 1690, the year of his victory over the Austrians. The most important Romanian monastery of its time, it was subject directly to the patriarch of Constantinople. There is Venetian influence in its decor. In the 20th cent. it has been settled by nuns.

[E. J. DILLON]

HURLEY, MICHAEL (*c.*1780–1837), missionary. The first American candidate for the Augustinian Order, H. was ordained in 1803. In New York he became the spiritual adviser of St. Elizabeth Seton. In 1826 he was made superior of the Augustinians in the U.S. and was influential in bringing the Sisters of Charity of Emmitsburg to Philadelphia to work with orphans. During the cholera epidemic of 1832, H. won wide recognition for his aid to the stricken.

[J. R. AHERNE]

HURRIANS, ancient Near Eastern people, known in the Bible as Horites and Hivites (Gen 14.6; 36.2, 20; 1 Kg 9.20). Probably originating in Armenia, they spread widely in the Near East, achieving their greatest influence from *c.*2500 to 1000 B.C. The peak of their political strength came *c.*1500 B.C. when their Mitanni Empire, centered in the Middle Euphrates Valley, dominated Assyria, Their culture known from writings found at Boghazkoy, Ugarit, Nuzi, and Mari, greatly influenced their neighbors, including perhaps the Israelite patriarchs. Hurrians were also a part of the pre-Conquest population of Palestine.

[T. EARLY]

HURTADO, CASPAR (1576–1646), Jesuit professor of theology at Alcalá. He wa already a professor there when he became a Jesuit in 1607; he returned to the university in 1616 and taught there for the rest of his life. His writings, which make no pretense of conforming to the contemporary fashion of following St. Thomas Aquinas, include treatises on principal themes in Christology, on the general principles of moral theology, and on the theological virtues.

[T. C. O'BRIEN]

HURTER, HUGO VON (1832–1914), Austrian Jesuit historian and theologian. With his father, Frederick, a Protestant clergyman and historian, H. was received into the Catholic Church in 1844. After studies in Rome, he became professor of dogmatic theology at the Univ. of Innsbruck in 1858 and remained in that position until shortly before his death. He was the author of a three-volume manual of dogmatic theology but is remembered more for his three-volume *Nomenclator literarius theologiae catholicae* (1871–86), an annotated catalogue of Catholic theologians from the Council of Trent on. Later editions of this work carried the list back to the Patristic period.

[R. B. ENO]

HUS, JAN (John Huss; *c.*1369–1415), a Bohemian reformer, executed as a heretic. At the Univ. of Prague, H. began his studies *c.*1386 and lectured from 1396 onward. As preacher at Bethlehem Chapel from 1402, he decried clerical abuses, urging reform in the Church and in Christian life. He was guided by the ecclesiology of John *Wycliffe. H. ignored the condemnation of 45 Wycliffite statements in 1403 by the predominantly German faculty of the university. When the King revised university voting powers in favor of Bohemians in 1409, the Germans departed and H. was made rector. His troubles with ecclesiastical authorities began the same year, when the abp. decreed that Wycliffe's writings be burned and H. excommunicated. He continued to preach; other measures against him followed, climaxed by a major excommunication in 1412 for leading resistance to an indulgence proclaimed by John XXIII (antipope). H. left Prague and in seclusion wrote his *De ecclesia,* drawing freely from Wycliffe's work of the same title. In 1414, through the urging of Emperor Sigismund, who promised him safe conduct, H. was persuaded to appear before the Council of *Constance. Arriving there in Nov., he was imprisoned until his trial the following June. H. refused to recant the errors extracted from his works, and, in the presence of Sigismund, was condemned as a heretic on July 6 and on the same day was burned at the stake by the town officials. He died bravely and in prayer. At Prague he was proclaimed a martyr and saint.

H. has renown as a Czech patriot; but that he himself conceived his role at Prague as a nationalistic crusade against foreign (German) domination is open to doubt. The Hussites were named for him, but he never taught the practice that became their battle cry *communion under both kinds (see *UTRAQUISTS). He did resist the ecclesiastical authorities, but he could not be called a precursor of the Reformation doctrine of "faith alone" and "Scripture alone." Martin V. confirmed (1418) the decree of Constance condemning H.'s errors (D 1201–30; 1250–51). These include a denial of the primacy of Peter, a description of the true Church as the assembly of the predestined, and the judgment that personal holiness alone gives legitimate jurisdiction to pope, bishop, or priest. H. himself disavowed not only Wycliffe's eucharistic teaching, but any share in the heretical sense of Wycliffe's ecclesiology. While condemnatory qualifications are attached to them (D 1251), these propositions are not so startling when viewed in historical context, the age of the *Great Western Schism, and with allowance for H.'s zealous rhetoric. His own intransigence and the doctrinal and political predispositions of his judges did much to bring about his tragic end. BIBLIOGRAPHY: Bihlmeyer-Tüchle 2:438–441; J. Boulier, *Jan Hus* (1958); M. Spinka, *Jan Hus and the Czech Reform* (1941); *idem, Jan Hus's Concept of the Church* (1966); *Tractatus de Ecclesia* (ed. S. H. Thomson, 1956); P. de Vooght, *L'Hérésie de Jean Hus* (1960).

[T. C. O'BRIEN]

HUSSERL, EDMUND (1859–1938), German philosopher and mathematician, founder of phenomenology as a philosophic movement. Born of Jewish parentage at Prossnitz or Prostejov in Moravia, then part of Austria, he was educated in mathematics at the Univ. of Leipzig and Berlin, then attended the philosophy lectures of F. Brentano at Vienna (1884–86), which influenced him to follow philosophy as a career. He taught at Halle (1887–1901), at Göttingen (1901–1916), and at Freiburg (1916–1929), where he spent the balance of his life following retirement. He joined the Lutheran Church in 1887.

In 1900–01 his best-known and most influential work appeared—*Logische Untersuchungen (Logical Investigations)*—outlining his phenomenonological method as a philosophic avenue for describing the basic nature of conscious data. Conceived as a new foundation for both science and philosophy, phenomenology was to have for its purpose the investigation and description of all consciously experienced phenomena but free of all theories as to their cause. With the motto "Back to things themselves," H. advocated the abandonment of all prior speculations and preconceptions as a means of delineating the content of consciousness. His writings were considerably influenced by William James, the British Empiricists, Leibnitz, and Kant, and they exerted distinct effects in thinkers such as Max Scheler and Martin Heidegger in Germany and Jean Paul Sartre and Maurice Merleau-Ponty in France. The descriptive method and his theories of intentionality and intuition have universal acclaim. BIBLIOGRAPHY: W. R. Boyce Gibson, *General Introduction to Pure Phenomenology* (1931).

[J. T. HICKEY]

HUSSITES, adherents of the religious and political movement inspired by Jan *Hus. Antipapal and nationalistic agitation in Bohemia became violent after Hus's execution, and a national Church emerged. The Hussite program far exceeded Hus's teachings; e.g., *communion under both kinds, forbidden by the Council of *Constance (D 1198–99; 1257–58), was not the teaching of Hus but of *Jacobellus. On religious and political grounds the Hussites were divided. The *Utraquists—university people, nobles, and merchants—were moderates. Their religious goals were contained in the Four Articles of Prague (1420): (1) that priests be unhampered in fulfilling Christ's mandate to preach;(2) that communion under both kinds be obligatory; (3) that mortal sins, even of clerics, be punished publicly; (4) that the clergy renounce temporal ownership or office. The *Taborites, mostly artisans and peasants, were far more extreme in doctrine and were violently antipapal; they advocated a communistic society, and the Hussite Wars (1420–33) were marked by the confiscation of ecclesiastical and patrician properties. These wars were a successful resistance, led by the Taborites J. *Žižka and Prokop the Great (d. 1434), against the crusades promoted by Martin V (1420, 1426, 1427) and Eugene IV (1431), and carried out by Emperor Sigismund. The final crushing defeat of the imperial-papal forces came at Taus (Domazlice; 1431). Between the wars there was bloody internal strife among the Hussites. At the invitation of Eugene IV negotiations with Utraquist and Taborite representatives began at the Council of *Basel in 1433, continued at Prague, and resulted eventually in the *Compactata. The only concession to the Four Articles, and that in a limited sense, was on the point of communion under both kinds. The Taborites rejected the Compactata, and were crushed by the combined Catholic and Utraquist forces at Lipany in 1434. The Compactata were accepted at Iglau (Jihlava) by the Hussites, and Sigismund was proclaimed king of Bohemia (1436). The agreement was approved by Basel (1434) but never received papal approval. In the subsequent religious and political history of Bohemia the Hussites are referred to as Utraquists, and the *Subunists as Catholics, but both considered themselves to be orthodox. The Utraquists, however, were continually in conflict with Rome (see *GEORGE OF PODĚBRAD). Internal conflict brought about a split in Utraquist ranks, which eventually led to the establishment of the *Bohemian Brethren (c.1458). At the time of the Reformation, many of the remaining Utraquists went over to Lutheranism, a union expressed in the *Bohemian Confessions of 1535 and 1575; later, however, the *Reformed tradition became dominant. The practice of communion under both kinds was suppressed by the *Edict of Restitution (1629). The Hussite era had important consequences for the evolution of the Reformation and for the rise of nationalism in Europe. BIBLIOGRAPHY: Bihlmeyer-Tüchle, 2:438–444; P. de Vooght, *Catholicisme* 5:IIII–13; F. H. Heymann, *John Žižka and the Hussite Revolution*

(1955); J. Macek, *Die Hussite revolutionäre Bewegung* (1958).

[T. C. O'BRIEN]

HUSSLEIN, JOSEPH CASPAR (1873–1952), American Jesuit educator, editor. Ordained in 1905, he early became interested in social problems and wrote extensively on the subject for *America* magazine, of which he was associate editor for 16 years. He was one of the founders of Fordham Univ.'s School of Social Work and was also a prominent force in the Catholic Conference on Industrial Problems. In 1936, H. founded the School of Social Service at St. Louis University. In 1931 he began to edit a successful series of books in the Science and Culture Series and in 1934 continued with the Religion and Culture Series. Of the 212 books he edited, none was more popular than his own *The Christian Social Manifesto* (1931) on the social encyclicals and *Social Wellsprings* (1940–42), a two-volume work made up of statements by the popes on the social question. BIBLIOGRAPHY: G. Higgins *Social Order* (1953), 3:51–54.

[J. R. AHERNE]

HUT, HANS (*c.*1491–1527), an Anabaptist preacher. H. was a Franconian bookbinder and accountant, who first became a fanatical preacher of revolution under the influence of T. *Münzer. After the *Peasants' War, H. was converted to the Swiss Anabaptist idea of passive nonresistance by H. *Denk, who rebaptized him at Augsburg in 1527. After a controversy with B. *Hubmaier, H. had to escape from Nikolsburg in Moravia and spent his last years in apocalyptic preaching throughout Austria. He died in prison. BIBLIOGRAPHY: R. M. Jones, *Studies in Mystical Religion* (1923) 390; MennEnc 2:846.

[T. C. O'BRIEN]

HUTCHESON, FRANCIS (1694–1747), British philosopher. A native of Ireland, H. studied at the Univ. of Glasgow (1710–16) where from 1729 he was professor of moral philosophy. He was among the first to make aesthetics a philosophical discipline, and his ethical theory, for which he is better known, closely parallels his aesthetics. Under the influence of Shaftesbury he emphasized benevolence against the crude individualism of Hobbes; his formulation of the criterion of moral goodness, "the greatest happiness for the greatest numbers," anticipated that of the *utilitarians. He also took from Shaftesbury—and further developed—the idea of a moral sense, divinely implanted, that, like the other senses, is passive and intuitional in regard to its object. H. had a marked influence on D. Hume, Adam Smith, and Immanuel Kant. BIBLIOGRAPHY: Copleston 5:178–184; D. D. Raphael, *Moral Sense* (1947); L. Vignone, *L'Etica del senso morale in Francis Hutcheson* (1954).

[T. C. O'BRIEN]

HUTCHINS, ROBERT MAYNARD (1899–1977), American educator. He was born in Brooklyn, N.Y.; his higher education, begun in 1915 at Oberlin College, was interrupted by service as an ambulance driver in World War I; he completed college at Yale. There he also took a law degree (1925) and became a professor and acting dean of the law school (1927). From 1929–51 he was president of the Univ. of Chicago. The "Chicago Plan" he inaugurated there organized higher education into four broad areas—the humanities, the physical, social, and life sciences—to be pursued through the program of the Great Ideas (reflected in the Great Books series and the Syntopticon). H.'s own publications evidence his interest in Greek thought and the philosophical ideas of St. Thomas Aquinas; among them are: *Higher Learning in America* (1936) *Education for Freedom* (1943) *St. Thomas and the World State* (1949) *Morals, Religion, and Education* (1950), *University of Utopia* (1953), *The Learning Society* (1968). The second great phase of his career was devoted to fostering research into the science of politics as he headed the Center for the Study of Democratic Institutions at Santa Barbara, Cal; one of H.'s concentrations during these years was the ideas set forth by John XXIII's *Pacem in terris*. H.s' theories on education were followed by some, disputed and scorned by many; their value and need may yet be more recognized in this or a later generation as the bankruptcy of positivistic education, without links to tradition, becomes increasingly apparent.

[T. C. O'BRIEN]

HUTCHINSON, ANNE (*c.*1590–1643), the leader in the Antinomian Controversy in colonial Massachusetts. She migrated from England to Boston in 1634. There her neighborliness and intellectual insights brought her a large following of both laymen and ministers, among them John *Cotton, who later repudiated her teaching. The strife that ensued between her supporters and those who accused her of heresy and sedition affected even the gubernatorial election of 1637. She branded the legalistic discipline of the Massachusetts Puritans as a covenant of works, in contrast with her own conviction, the covenant of grace. Her opponents attached the reproach "antinomian" to her teaching because of her rejection of works of the law, rather than the interior assurance of faith and grace, as the essence of righteousness. She was tried by the civil court and sentenced to banishment; the Boston Church excommunicated her. She then joined with others to make the first settlement in R.I., at Portsmouth. BIBLIOGRAPHY: A. H. Newman, EncRelKnow 1:200–201; R. P. Bolton, *Woman Misunderstood* (1931). *ANTINOMIANISM.

[M. J. SUELZER]

HUTER, JAKOB (Hutter; d. 1536), founder of the *Hutterian Brethren. After the death of G. *Blaurock, H. was the leader of the Tyrolean Anabaptists. Because of persecution he brought a group of his followers to Austerlitz, Moravia. There, for the practice of their belief, he organized them (1533–35) in an agricultural settlement with a communal form of life (see BRUDERHOF). On a journey to Austria, H. was captured, condemned, and burned at the stake in Innsbruck. BIBLIOGRAPHY: H. Fischer, *Jakob Huter* (1956); MennEnc 2:851ff., 854ff.

[T. C. O'BRIEN]

HUTTEN, ULRICH VON (1488–1523), German humanist and polemicist. H. was sent to the monastery at Fulda when he was 11, but fled 6 years later and became an itinerant poet and mercenary. After study at Cologne, Erfurt, and Frankfurt he lived for a time in Leipzig, Greifswald, and Rostock. His first meeting with Erasmus occurred before he went to Rome to study law (1515–17). On his return to Germany H. criticized the Roman Curia in a number of violent tracts. With Crotus Rubeanus he wrote **Epistolae obscurorum virorum*, satire directed against the Cologne scholastics. In 1517 he edited Lorenzo *Valla's *De donatione Constantini*. He published a series of anti-Roman pamphlets in defense of Martin Luther, though the latter disapproved of his threats of force. When H. vainly sought asylum with Erasmus in Basel, *Zwingli gave him refuge and sent him for medical help to the Island of Ufenau in Lake Zurich, where he died. BIBLIOGRAPHY: H. Holborn, *Ulrich von Hutten and the German Reformation* (tr. R. H. Bainton, 1937).

[M. J. SUELZER]

HUTTERIAN BRETHREN, a religious body founded by the Anabaptist J. *Huter. The first of the *Bruderhofs, agricultural settlements following a strictly communal form of life (see Acts 2.44–45), was organized by Huter in Moravia (1533–35). Because of persecution the Brethren migrated first to Russia in 1622 and then to Bon Homme Co., S. Dak., in 1874. There were about 7,600 American members, in 24 groups in S. Dak. and one in Minn. in 1967. Other communities exist in Manitoba and Alberta Provinces, Canada, in England, and in Paraguay. In the substance of their belief and practice the Hutterian Brethren are Mennonites, but their communal form of life is distinctive. BIBLIOGRAPHY: G. Horsch, *Hutterian Brethren, 1528–1931; Story of Martyrdom and Loyalty* (1931); J. W. Bennett, *Hutterian Brethren* (1967), MennEnc 2:851–865.

[T. C. O'BRIEN]

ḤÛTTŌMŌ (East Syrian, *ḥûttāmā,* seal), prayer of dismissal in Syrian churches.

HUVELIN, HENRI (1838–1910), spiritual director at the Church of St. Augustin in Paris. He was the counselor of Charles de *Foucauld, and F. von *Hügel. His spiritual conferences, directed particularly to young people, became famous. Many were published posthumously, some quite recently: *Bossuet, Fénelon et le quiétisme* (2 v., 1911–12); *Écrits spirituels et paroles de l'Abbé Huvelin* (1959); *Le Regard du Christ* (1960); *Venez et voyez* (1961).

[T. C. O'BRIEN]

HUXLEY, ALDOUS LEONARD (1894–1963), English novelist and essayist; grandson of T. H. Huxley, grandnephew of Matthew Arnold, and brother of the biologist Julian Huxley. His center of interest was contrapuntal to that of his brother who looked to science for the realization of the best in human values; H., on the contrary, thought poorly of the transformations already brought about in contemporary life by scientific progress and took an even dimmer view of future possibilities. He was profoundly convinced that man must somehow transcend himself. The idea that this can best be achieved by mystical experience came to dominate much of his later thought, but it was a mysticism divorced from any form of religious orthodoxy. He took a deep interest in the Catholic mystical tradition, but was also concerned to study and explore other avenues to mystical experience, even the pharmacological. From 1939 he resided in the U.S. Among his works are: *Proper Studies* (1927); *Point Counter Point* (1928); *Brave New World* (1932); *Eyeless in Gaza* (1936); *Perennial Philosophy* (1945); *Doors of Perception* (1954); *Heaven and Hell* (1956); and *Literature and Science* (1963). BIBLIOGRAPHY: P. H. Thody, *Biographical Introduction* (pa., 1973); P. Bowering, *Aldous Huxley: A Study of the Major Novels* (1969).

[M. J. BARRY]

HUXLEY, THOMAS HENRY (1825–95), English biologist. One of the best known biologists and literary figures of his age, he spent most of his life studying, lecturing, and writing in the fields of science, education, sociology, and religion. Although an ardent advocate of human evolution, he never quite agreed with Darwin's theory of natural selection as he shows in *Man's Place in the Universe* (1863). He rejected Christianity since "the exact nature of the teachings and convictions of Jesus is extremely uncertain," yet he insisted on the teaching of the Bible in the schools as a great literary heritage and an essential basis of conduct. His 25 books, over 100 articles, almost countless lectures, and the number of scientific and royal commissions on which he served are an indication of his importance in the 19th-cent. scientific world. BIBLIOGRAPHY: biographies by E. Clodd (1902) and C. Bibby (1960).

[M. J. BARRY]

HUYSMAN ROELOF, see AGRICOLA, RODOLPHUS FRISIUS.

HUYSMANS, J.-K.(1848–1907), French novelist of the Catholic Revival. Of Dutch-French parentage, H. changed his given names Charles-Marie-Georges to Joris-Karl on publishing his first work (1874). Early novels like *Les Soeurs Vatard* (1879) and *En Ménage* (1881) reflect the epoch's dominant naturalistic style, but with *À vau-l'éau* (1882; Eng. tr. *Down Stream*), embodying a Schopenhauer-like pessimism, a reaction set in and his spiritual evolution began. In 1884, H. published *À rebours* (Eng. tr. *Against the Grain*), with the decadent symbolist Des Esseintes as hero, prompting Barbey d'Aurevilly to remark, "After such a book the author is left with choosing between the barrel of a revolver and the foot of the Cross." *Là-Bas* (1891), the style of which H. called spiritual naturalism, marked a further alienation from materialism, this time via the occult and an examination of satanism by the autobiographical hero Durtal, who is researching the career of Bluebeard, Gilles de Rais. In contrast to this "black novel," H. began writing a "white novel" of Catholic mysticism, which he left unfinished to go in 1892 on retreat to the Trappist community at Igny. He later transposed the conversion that followed into the novel *En route* (1895). Thereafter, H. focused his refined aesthetic sensibility on predominantly religious motifs, developing in the novels *La cathédrale* (1898) and *L'Oblat* (1903) the symbolism of the medieval cathedral and of the liturgy, and in *Trois primitifs* (1905) the sturdy spirituality of Grunewald's paintings which he found lacking in 19th-cent. Catholic art. While idealizing medieval spirituality as a whole, H. preferred that era's waning centuries, the modalities of its mysticism, and its emphasis on physical suffering. This accounts for his study on the 15th-cent. Dutch ascetic Bl. Lydwine (*Sainte Lydwine de Schiedam,* 1901), his interest in more recent examples of vicarious and expiatory suffering (e.g., the Augustinian nun Anna Catherine *Emmerich) and his work *Les Foules de Lourdes* (1905), in which H. proposed to depict "a realistic Lourdes, to bring out its vulgar and its beautiful aspects and to do justice to the authenticity of its miracles." H. viewed a personal experience connected with Lourdes in a supernatural light; he had lost his sight during his second visit, but recovered in time to write his study. He had hoped to join a religious community. Discouraged from entering the novitiate, he became a Benedictine oblate at Ligugé (1901). Although aestheticism and heterodox religious notions did influence his spiritual development, H. was committed to an orthodox albeit rigorous concept of Catholicism. BIBLIOGRAPHY: J. Daoust, *Les Debuts bénédictins de J.-K. Huysmans* (1950); R. Baldick, *Life of J.-K. Huysmans* (1955); H. R. T. Brandreth, *Huysmans* (1963).

[G. E. GINGRAS]

HY, ABBEY OF, see IONA, ABBEY OF.

HYACINTH, ST. (d. 1257), Dominican apostle to Poland. He became a Dominican along with his brother (or cousin), Bl. *Ceslaus at Rome while there on a visit; legend has it that they were drawn to the order after witnessing St. Dominic perform a miracle. H. is known to have preached throughout Poland, the Baltic countries, Scandinavia, Russia, and perhaps in Tibet. He established many Dominican priories in his native land. His miracles include walking across the waters of a river, bearing the Blessed Sacrament and a statue of Mary, to escape invading Mongols. He died on the feast of the Assumption; he was canonized in 1595. BIBLIOGRAPHY: Butler 3:338–339; B. Stasiewski, LTK 5:553–554; V. Koudelka, BiblSanct 6:326–331.

[T. C. O'BRIEN]

HYACINTH AND PROTUS, SS., see PROTUS AND HYACINTH, SS.

HYDATIUS (*c.*395–after 468), historian and bp. of Chaves(?) in Portugal. As priest (416), bp. (427), and legate to the Roman general Aetius (431), he had to deal with the ravages of the barbarian Suevi and with Manichaeism and Priscillianism. Besides maintaining a list of Roman consuls, he continued Jerome's chronicle through what were for him portentous years (379–468). Isidore's chronicle superseded that of Hydatius.

[E. P. COLBERT]

HYDATIUS AND HYTHACIUS (Idatius and Ithacius), bps. of Mérida and Ossonoba in Lusitania who led the attack on Priscillian at the Council of Saragossa I (380), which charged Hythacius to carry out its general decisions against Manichaeans. So zealous were the two that a reaction in favor of Priscillianists occurred. Hydatius withdrew from the attack and resigned his see; later he tried to regain it, probably without success. Hythacius, described by Sulpicius Severus as a loquacious gourmet, fled to Trier and continued the attack, though he was not the prosecutor in the final trial when Priscillian was condemned to death (385). Bishops at Trier communicated with him, but Martin of Tours later regretted it. After the fall of Maximus (388), Hythacius was excommunicated (389), deposed, and exiled to Naples (by 392); none of his works are extant.

[E. P. COLBERT]

HYDE, ABBEY OF, former Benedictine monastery in the Diocese of Winchester, England. It was founded by King Edward the Elder in 901, was originally named New Minster, and was built near Winchester cathedral. It was turned over to Benedictine monks in 965. New buildings were constructed at Hyde in 1111, and the monastery became famous for its liturgical and biblical manuscripts. The monastery was dissolved in 1538 and its buildings destroyed.

[T. M. MCFADDEN]

HYDRAULIS (Hydraulos, Hydraulus), ancient Greek organ invented by Ctesibius (Ktesibios) of Alexandria *c.*250 B.C. Its wind supply was provided by water rather than by bellows. From a description of Hero of Alexandria, from a clay model found in the ruins of Carthage, and from portions of an actual instrument found near Budapest, details were discovered of its construction and appearance. It was very much like any small organ of today. Its remarkable playing mechanism was rediscovered in the 10th cent. and used in the construction of modern organs. The hydraulis was probably a very loud-sounding instrument since it seems to have been used at festivals and in outdoor arenas. However, Cicero described it as being used indoors and as being "delectable to the ears." It is interesting to note that its use was forbidden in early Christian worship, possibly because of its associations with the gladiatorial contests.

[M. T. LEGGE]

HYDROMANCY, a form of divination using water. In some cases springs or fountains are observed for signs, particularly after casting in offerings. If the water refuses to accept the offering, that is, if the offering floats, the outlook is unfavorable. Hydromancy has also been practiced with water in a basin, sometimes watching globules of oil in the water or the ripples caused by dropping in a pebble. In that form it is known as lecanomancy. BIBLIOGRAPHY: W. R. Halliday, *Greek Divination* (1913) 145–162. *DIVINATION.

[T. EARLY]

HYDROPARASTATAE (i.e., advocates of water), a name given to Christians who used water instead of wine in the Eucharist. Filaster (*Haer.*, 77) calls them *aquarii* (from the Lat. *aqua,* water). The same custom was observed by the Ebionites, Tatianites, Marcionites, and Manichaeans. The practice of substituting water appears also to have been resorted to in certain circumstances without heretical intent. Thus St. Cyprian (*Ep.*, 63) relates that some Christians celebrated a Eucharistic Service in the morning without wine, and again in the evening with wine. The custom evidently arose in the time of persecution, for Christians were daily communicants and could be detected by the smell of wine, which pagans would not have used in the early morning. BIBLIOGRAPHY: A. Lehaut, DHGE 3:1102.

[L. G. MÜLLER]

HYGINUS, ST. (d. 142), **POPE** from 138. Little is known for certain about the pontificate of Hyginus. According to the *Liber pontificalis* he was an Athenian philosopher, who as pope organized the lower orders of the clergy. The value of these statements is doubtful. The Gnostics Valentinus and Cerdo came to Rome during his pontificate. Although H. has been honored as a martyr, there is no record in ancient writings of his martyrdom. BIBLIOGRAPHY: Butler 1:67.

[R. B. ENO]

HYGINUS OF CÓRDOBA, successor to Osius (*c.*358). He was probably the first bp. to oppose Priscillian (*c.*375), and he seems to have opposed Luciferians. But he accepted communion with Priscillianists and was deposed by Hythacius of Ossonoba after the Council of Saragossa I (380). Emperor Maximus exiled him; Ambrose relieved his physical distress in Gaul (387).

[E. P. COLBERT]

HYLICS (Gr., *hylē*, matter), in Valentinian Gnostic speculation, for which matter results from the passion of Sophia, people enmeshed in matter and the passions, and thought to be less enlightened than the *psychics or pneumatics.

[E. V. GALLAGHER]

HYLOMORPHISM (also hylemorphism; from the Gr. *hulē,* matter, and *morphē,* form), the Aristotelian theory, adopted by the scholastics, that corporeal or physical substances are composed of two constitutive principles, primary *matter and form (substantial form). Hylomorphism is a dualistic explanation of the process of change, or coming to be, observed in nature; its correlation with the contemporary science of physics continues to be explored by some scholastic philosophers. An analogous use of the terminology of hylomorphic theory was made in the RC theology of grace, the sacraments, the human soul.

[T. C. O'BRIEN]

HYLOSYSTEMISM, a philosophic theory as to the essential composition of inorganic natural bodies, thought by its proponents to be more attuned to the findings of modern science than the view of hylomorphism—the traditional Aristotelian-Scholastic position on the same subject. According to the latter, the essences of all natural bodies—organic and inorganic—are composed of two complementary substantial principles, primary matter and substantial form, each incomplete without the other, neither perceptible by the senses, but both intelligible to the intellect. In contrast, hylosystemism centers its attention upon inorganic natural bodies only—the elements and compounds of chemistry and physics—describing their ultimate constitution in terms of "hylons," heterogeneous subelemental and subatomic particles of matter usually referred to as electrons, protons, neutrons, and positrons. These form an energy system of functioning units designated as "hylomeric"—signifying the material particles stressed by the theory, each being in itself a complete substance, varying in number in the respective elements. Further, there is a heterogeneity in the coordination and subordination of the hylons, each particle remaining distinct from the others, permitting space between them. BIBLIOGRAPHY: A. Mitterer, *Wandel des Weldbildes von Thomas auf Heute,* (2 v., 1935–36); C. Bittle, *From Aether to Cosmos* (1941).

[J. T. HICKEY]

HYLOZOISM, a term derived from the Gr. *hulē* (matter) and *zōē* (life) to designate the philosophic doctrine that all matter is animated or alive, and sometimes extended to the doctrine that all life and spiritual processes are to be conceived as properties of, or as deriving from, matter. As a philosophical position it is closely associated with, though not the same as, animism and panpsychism, the former holding that all nature is filled with innumerable spirits and thus possesses life somewhat akin to human life, the latter that not only man and brute but also plants and inanimate objects enjoy a form of sensation or other psychic life.

Hylozoism has its known origins among the early Greek cosmologists. Their concern to reduce all reality to a single primordial substance inevitably issued in a form of hylozoism, which was more or less explicit in *Xenophanes, whose eternal principle was God in whom all things are, and even more clearly in *Empedocles who ascribed psychic life to all beings. Greek Stoicism followed in this hylozoic tradition by seeing the cosmos as animated by reason or world soul, which stood in much the same relation to the world as the human soul does to the body.

Similar tendencies of thought appeared in modified form in the Middle Ages and to a greater degree in the Renaissance philosophy of nature as expounded by men such as P. *Gassendi, B. *Telesio, and G. *Bruno. The theme also recurred in the thought of some of the Cambridge Platonists, e.g., R. Cudworth (who coined the term) and H. More. In more recent times hylozoistic views have been drawn from the findings of physical and esp. organic science. In materialistic form hylozoism was revived by the German biologist, E. H. Haeckel. F. Paulsen conceived the earth as a unitary organism having an inner life as well as a body, and G. Fechner, pioneer in psychophysics, conceived of a highly animistic universe in which plants and stars are alive and endowed with consciousness.

[J. T. HICKEY]

HYMN, see HYMNS AND HYMNALS.

HYMNODY, see HYMNS AND HYMNALS.

HYMNOLOGY, the science that treats of Christian sacred poetry set to music. Only in the 19th cent. did scholars begin the systematic study of texts, settings, authorship, liturgical use, MS tradition, translations, etc. Investigators of Latin hymnody include: H. A. Daniel, F. J. Mone, G. M. Dreves, C. Blume, J. M. Neale, R. C. Trench, J. U. C. Chevalier, W. Bulst, and J. Szövérffy; of Greek-Byzantine: W. Christ, M. Paranikas, J. B. Pitra, E. H. Wellesz, and H. Follieri; of the hymns of the Protestant church: J. Julian, L. Schäberlein, W. Buszin, E. E. Koch, A. F. W. Fischer, and W. Tümpel. BIBLIOGRAPHY: *Historical Companion to Hymns Ancient and Modern* (ed. M. Frost, 1960); J. Szövérffy, *Die Annalen der lateinischen Hymnendichtung* (2 v., 1964).

[M. J. SUELZER]

HYMNS, ANCIENT AND MODERN, title of a hymnal important to the doctrinal and liturgical life of the Church of England. It was first produced because of the *Oxford Movement's emphasis on the ancient and medieval heritage of the English Church. The first text was edited by H. W. Baker, the music by H. Monk. The first edition appeared in 1861; supplements were issued periodically; the Standard Edition incorporating these was published in 1922. The Revised Edition of 1950 pared down the number of hymns to 636. BIBLIOGRAPHY: W. K. L. Clarke, *Hundred Years of Hymns, Ancient and Modern* (1962).

[M. T. LEGGE]

HYMNS AND HYMNALS. The word hymn, at one point in time, came to be defined as a newly written, i.e., nonscriptural, sung poem in praise of God, usually metrical and strophic in form. However, the term, in its broader sense means also simply a religious song for use in Christian worship. The first Christians, in their gatherings for worship, continued the Hebraic tradition of the singing of the Psalms, but gradually distinctively Christian hymns came to be composed, traces of which we find in Luke, Ephesians, 1 Timothy, Revelations, and other books of the New Testament. Evidence of continued use and composition of hymns during these early cent. exists, but most of these hymns have been lost. Around the 4th cent. two distinct types began to emerge, hymns used to express devotion and those intended to teach doctrine. To this period belong some of the first significant composers of hymns: St. Ephrem the Syrian in the Eastern tradition; St. Gregory Nazianzen, writer of early Greek hymns; and, for early Latin hymns, St. Hilary of Poitiers. With St. Ambrose of Milan (*c.*339–397) the singing of hymns began to become an integral part of public worship. Written, it is believed, to offset the errors of Arianism, his hymns were the first of a large body of Latin metric compositions that grew up during the next half cent. in the works of such men as Prudentius, Sedulius, Fortunatus, Gregory the Great, Bede, and Notker of St. Gall. Side by side with the Latin hymns grew the largely dogmatic Eastern troparia, stichera, and contaria of such writers as Romanos, Sergios, and St. John of Damascus. The Middle Ages witnessed the appearance of some of the best of all Latin lyrics, the great *sequences. St. Thomas Aquinas composed his great doctrinal Eucharistic hymns (1264) and devotional Latin hymnody arose in works such as Jesu Dulcis Memoria (anon).

To the Reformation belongs the period of development of hymns for church use written in the vernacular. Martin Luther, himself a musician, was responsible for the beginning of a great and important body of German hymns that would continue to be written into the 18th cent. and to be sung up to the present day (Now Thank We All Our God and O Sacred Head Surrounded belong to this time). The Calvinists, who used only scriptural texts, sang metrical versions of the Psalms, collected in the *Genevan Psalter* (1563). In England and Scotland this same restriction held and psalm-singing remained the staple of the C of E up until the 19th century. In the RC Church, the Council of Trent ordered a reform of the chant, but the result was anything but felicitous and Latin hymnody began to decline. At the same time, however, sacred polyphony reached its highest peak with the works of Palestrina. In Germany the demand for congregational singing in the vernacular during the Liturgy led to permission for *Singmessen* (portions of the ordinary sung in German) and the publication of Catholic hymnbooks with German text, the first of which, Michael Vehe's *Ein neues Gesangbuch geystlicher Leider*, appeared in 1537. The *Singmessen*, whose popularity caused an ever-widening separation from the action of the Liturgy, was one of the objects of the reforms of the Caecilian movement (19th century).

In contrast to the largely doctrinal hymns of the previous cent., Isaac Watts, a Congregationalist, began early in the 18th cent. to use the hymn to express the spiritual experiences of the singers. In 1737 John Wesley's *Collection of Psalms and Hymns,* the first hymn book of modern type, was published and 2 years later *Hymns and Sacred Poems* by John and Charles Wesley appeared. The singing of these Methodists soon spread to the Evangelical party of the Church of England and, in 1779, J. Newton and W. Cowper put out *Olney Hymns,* a collection of the subjective type characteristic of the Evangelical school.

Prejudice against hymn singing in the C of E had almost completely broken down by the 19th cent. through the efforts of R. Heber and the influence of the Oxford Movement. Translations, notably those of John Mason Neale, were made of ancient and medieval hymns and some original compositions appeared so that by the middle of the 19th cent. collections of both began to be published, among them *Hymns Ancient and Modern* (1861). This collection, which contained hymns both for the liturgical calendar and of the type to express personal emotion, has had several editions and continues in use up to this day.

In America, meanwhile, a desire for better versions of psalm-settings prompted a committee to compil the **Bay Psalm Book* (1640), the first actual book produced in the North American colonies. It had several editions and soon included hymns. American hymn composers include William Billings (18th cent.), Thomas Hastings, and Lowell Mason (19th century). Mention must indeed be made also of the flowering, in America, of negro spirituals and of the development of the "white spirituals," folk hymns and gospel songs which grew in popularity during the 19th-cent. revival meetings and appeared in such volumes as *The Sacred Harp* (1844).

Catholic vernacular hymnody in America reflected the religious heritage of all the cultures represented there. Efforts were made in Spanish and Indian missions to adapt hymnody to the culture, but there is not much other documentation on American Catholic church music until almost the 19th century. By that time several hymnals were being published, but many were in poor taste and often included adaptations of secular music and of themes of instrumental and operatic works of composers such as Haydn, Mozart, and Beethoven. In the late 19th and early 20th cent., hymnals reflected the results of the instructions of the *motu proprio* (1903) of Pope Pius X and the reform efforts of the American Caecilian Society: incorporation of chant melodies, elimination of improprieties in text and melody, but also production of hymns characterized by the use of stock devices and by an absence of creativity. However, the interest in improving hymnody did bear fruit in many fine hymnals which incorporated the best European traditions plus some American compositions.

In the second half of this cent., the liturgical reform initiated by Pope Pius XII (*Musicae sacrae disciplina,* 1955) and reinforced by the *Constitution on the Sacred Liturgy* (1963) of Vatican Council II has emphasized the importance of the use of religious songs of the people and the need skillfully to foster that singing. The paragraphs on sacred music of the Council documents, as well as subsequent teachings, are marked by a great freedom of spirit and were intended to call forth the creative efforts of talented and inspired musicians. The results have been mixed. The incorporation of folk, pop, and rock elements has not always been aesthetically or religiously successful; texts have often been trite and otherwise badly written; quality of performance is often poor; choirs have been needlessly disbanded and the heritage of almost 2 cent. of art music is all but totally ignored in many churches. However, the scene is not totally bad. Much that is good is happening in the parish liturgies and much good music is being written to meet the needs of 20th-cent. worshippers. There are many fine collections of psalm-settings: *The Gelineau Psalms* (Grailville, Ohio); *Biblical Hymns and Songs* (2 v.) of Lucien Deiss (World Library Publications); and *Psalms for Singing* by Stephen Somerville (also World Library). New hymn books continue to appear bearing evidence of a scholarly, discriminating, broad-visioned, and pastoral approach to the task of assembling hymns for the faithful: *The People's Mass Book* (World Library); *New Hymns for All Seasons* (Geoffrey Chapman, London); *The New Catholic Hymnal* (Faber, London); *Morning Praise and Evensong* (Fides); *The Catholic Liturgy Book* (Helicon Press, Baltimore); *Praise the Lord,* rev. (Geoffrey Chapman); *The Westminster Hymnal* (Search Press, London); *The English Hymnal* and its supplement *English Praise* (Oxford Univ. Press); and *Worship II* (G. I. A. Publications).

In the hymnal of today, attempts are being made to incorporate the finest of the various traditions and styles of the past with the music of such contemporary composers as V. Williams, A. Peloquin, J. Langlais, and others. Numerous groups and individuals are trying to fulfill liturgical needs in collections of religious songs. Many of these may last but for a specific need and time but others may endure. Among such efforts are the works of the Jesuits of St. Louis (North American Liturgy Resources); the monks of the Weston Priory (The Benedictine Foundation of the State of Vermont), the Damians and Sr. Suzanne Toolan. BIBLIOGRAPHY: J. Szoverffy, NCE 7:287–295, with extensive bibliography; J. V. Higginson, *Handbook for American Catholic Hymnals* (The Hymn Society of America, 1976).

[M. T. LEGGE]

HYPAPANTE (Gr., for encounter), in the Byzantine liturgy the name given to the feast of the Presentation (February 2). It commemorates the first public appearance of Christ in the Temple and thus his first formal encounter with the chosen people. It is one of the 12 major feasts of the Byzantine calendar. The Western Church formerly used a similar name (*occursus Domini*) for this feast. Among other Eastern Churches it is celebrated with great solemnity and called variously, "Presentation," "Purification," or "The

Entry of the Lord into the Temple." *PRESENTATION OF JESUS.

[A. J. JACOPIN]

HYPATIA (*c.*370–415 A.D.), mathematician and Neoplatonic philosopher at Alexandria. She was the daughter of Theon, a mathematician and astronomer, and held the chair of Platonic philosophy. She perished as a victim of Christian mob violence. Her chief pupil was *Synesius of Cyrene, who in 411 became bp. of Ptolemais. He held Hypatia in high esteem both as a philosopher and as a person. BIBLIOGRAPHY: Ueberweg 1:640; P. Merlan, LexAW 1346.

[M. R. P. MCGUIRE]

HYPATIUS (properly Hypatios; d. 446), hegumen (406–446) of the famous Monastery of the Twelve Apostles (Rufinianae, from the name of its initial benefactor, Rufinus). From the principal primary source, the *Life* (between 447 and 450) by Callinicus, a monk of the Rufinianae, we know he was born in Phrygia about June 366 (*Life* 136.3) and fled his father's house at the age of 18 after a whipping (*Life* 59.16). His initiation to asceticism was under the guidance of Jonas, a former Armenian soldier in the Imperial Guard (*Life* 61.7). A maximum of penances, a minimum of intellectual activity characterized the first steps and the whole of his monastic life (the latest translation and commentary by A. J. Festugière, OP, in *Les Moines d'Orient,* I and II, 1961) as was also the case with too many monks in Egypt, the Syrian desert, and the area in and around Constantinople. At every turn rock-bound orthodoxy vitiated by antiintellectualism becomes manifest. His relations with Nestorius, the patriarch of Constantinople whose fall he "predicts," bring this out. Bp. Eulalios of Chalcedon, his immediate superior, also experienced his arbitrary independence (*Life* 107.3ff). From 406 until his death at the age of 80 he governed the Rufinianae. Like many contemporary monks his motto was: "Either sanctity *or* learning"—a masterly answer to the "dilemma" in the work of Festugière (I, esp. ch. 4).

[J. M.-F. MARIQUE]

HYPATIUS OF EPHESUS (d. after 537), principal ecclesiastical adviser of the Emperor Justinian during the years 531–536. At a colloquy with the *Monophysite followers of *Severus *c.*532, H. was the spokesman for the Catholic bishops. At this meeting Justinian was convinced (and he was supported in this by *Leontius) that the *Theopaschite formula "One of the Trinity suffered," would provide a bridge to bring Catholics and Monophysites together. H. was despatched to Rome where he persuaded a reluctant Pope John II to recognize the orthodoxy of the formula. In 536 at the Synod of Constantinople, H. again stood forth as the spokesman for the bishops. Of his writings only fragments have survived. BIBLIOGRAPHY: Altaner 617–618; J. Reuss, LTK 5:574.

[R. B. ENO]

HYPERBOLIC PARABOLOID, a warped surface generated by a straight line moving to touch two other straight lines not in the same plane, and parallel to a plane director. The hyperbolic paraboloid is a recent lyrical structural determinant in 20th-cent. architectural designs by E. Saarinen, F. Candel, Le Corbusier and others.

[M. J. DALY]

HYPERDULIA (Gk. *uper,* more than, *douleia,* veneration), the special homage paid to Mary because of her eminent dignity as Mother of God. It is distinguished from **latria,* the worship due only to God, and **dulia,* the veneration given to the saints and angels. This distinction reflects the difference between the Almighty God and Mary, a creature, but also emphasizes her unique holiness which surpasses that of all other creatures.

[T. M. MCFADDEN]

HYPNOSIS, from the Gr. *hupnos* (sleep), a condition similar to sleep induced by concentration and suggestion. The term hypnotism was coined by J. Braid in 1842. It refers both to the temporary condition of general relaxation and selective concentration of attention and to the artificial process of producing it. It is marked by an alteration of consciousness, a decrease of inhibition, an increase of susceptibility to suggestion, attention to a single stimulus, and disregard of distraction; it is accompanied by physiological changes in the muscular, circulatory, and respiratory systems. As an occult practice, a reputation that still lingers in the popular mind, it goes back to the mists of time. The Jesuit, A. Kircher (d. 1680), was the first to make it the subject of scientific report, F. Mesmer (d. 1815) made it famous, but "mesmerism" was committed to his theory of animal magnetism, soon discarded, and the real originator of it as a branch of clinical psychology was D. Faria, an Indo-Portuguese priest, who began work in 1814, and held that its effects were contributed by the subject. His conclusions were clarified by Braid (d. 1860). Its scientific control has been developed, and proper training for its professional practice is now promoted by the American Society of Clinical Hypnosis. As a therapeutic instrument its value is undoubted. Yet it is not without medical and moral dangers. As for the first it may remove symptoms so as to obscure and prolong addictive delusions; as for the second, though the subject will not act against his will, or, it seems, commit acts directly harmful to others, yet he may respond to unconscious impulses or perform acts under posthypnotic suggestion that he has come to be persuaded are quite acceptable. Certainly treatment should be properly qualified and responsible, but the general principle is that hypnosis is right when employed for a good purpose and applied by skilled art observant of good morals. It depends on the cooperation of the patient, and so is not a form of violence. BIBLIOGRAPHY: J. M. Bramwell, *Hypnotism: its History, Practice and Theory* (1903, 1930, 1956); L. W. Wolberg,

Medical Hypnosis (2 v., 1948); B. Wolfe and R. Rosenthal, *Hypnotism Comes of Age* (1949).

[C. P. SVOBODA]

HYPOCRISY, a form of *simulation directly against the virtue of truthfulness, an acted lie whereby a person uses the appearance of good deeds to cloak unworthy designs of self-glorification or some sort of fraudulent credit. Our Lord's rebuke to the Pharisees was on account of their hypocrisy (Mt 22.23). Though in itself a mean and ugly sin, in fact it is often more of a pathetic weakness, a vanity, as Aristotle remarks, more than a malignity, and is rarely exemplified as in Uriah Heep. In the individual it is the "tribute vice pays to virtue," and commonly comes from some appreciation of goodness unaccompanied by the exertions required to achieve it, and is sometimes less a contrived pose of virtue than a complacency about unmerited esteem. Peoples not rarely preen themselves on the very qualities they lack, and conspicuously so in the eyes of other people, but this, which is not confined to English-speaking countries, is really more a form of mass-delusion than of rational hypocrisy. No man is a hypocrite for concealing his faults; he is not bound to advertise them, but rather the reverse, though a decent reticence will prevent his parading his virtues. Nor is he a hypocrite if, while failing with one commandment, he strives to observe another. For instance, persons who are wedded to a sexual irregularity should be encouraged to keep in touch with the Church: there is a faithfulness, modesty, and truthfulness in this sometimes desperate hanging on. The pretence to a vice one does not practice is a mock humility which is a sort of inverted hypocrisy. BIBLIOGRAPHY: ThAq ST 2a2ae, 111.

[T. GILBY]

HYPORRHOE (HYPORRE), in Byzantine music a character of descent.

HYPOSTASIS, literally *substantia,* or substance, a term that has played an important part in the development of the Trinitarian and Christological dogmas. Originally it referred somewhat ambiguously to concrete reality and was open to various developments. The Greek and the Latin traditions evolved it in opposite directions. The Greek tradition understood hypostasis in the sense of person and preferred it to *prosōpon* because it expressed more clearly the ontological reality of the subject. The Latin tradition took *substantia* to mean nature. Not before the ambiguity of terminology was clarified could the Trinitarian and Christological faith of both traditions appear clearly identical. The Council of Constantinople II (553) is a clear witness to the understanding arrived at between the two traditions (D 421). The term hypostasis is linked to the history of the Trinitarian dogma, even before the Christological. Origen seems to have been the first to enunciate the mystery of God's inner life as one of three hypostases and one essence (*ousia*) at a time when Tertullian spoke of God as "one substance [substantia] in three who coinhere" (*Adversus Praxaeam* 12). The dogmatic meaning of hypostasis, or person, implies a concrete subsisting subject: God is three persons; Christ, the God-man, is one. BIBLIOGRAPHY: G. L. Prestige, *God in Patristic Thought* (1936) 157. *HYPOSTATIC UNION.

[J. DUPUIS]

HYPOSTATIC UNION, the unity of the divine and human natures of Christ in the Person of the Word. The mystery of Christ's Person is at the center of the Christian faith, for the Christian message of salvation is entirely dependent upon Christ's ontological makeup. Jesus Christ is the God-man; more precisely, he is the eternal Son of God become a member of the human race. The Son of God has assumed a human nature into the unity of his Person (hypostasis); thus, both natures, the divine and the human, are hypostatically united in him. The dogma of the hypostatic union is based on the NT revelation of the twofold condition of Jesus Christ, at once truly human and truly divine. The early centuries witness to a twofold approach, upward and downward, to the mystery. The Antiochene school, starting from the man Jesus, explains how his humanity is personally united to the divine Word; the Alexandrian, how the Word of God becomes man by assuming a human condition. The development of the Christological dogma consists to a great extent in the progressive elaboration of a well-balanced synthesis of these two distinct and complementary viewpoints. It culminates in the dogma of Chalcedon (301–302): in Christ both natures, the divine and the human, are united in the Person of the divine Word; yet, they remain "unconfused, unchangeable, undivided and inseparable." Theologically the mystery of the hypostatic union can be formulated as follows: though whole and entire, the individual concrete nature of the man Jesus is not hypostatized so as to constitute a human person; it is not ontologically self-possessed. The absence of a human personhood leaves Christ's human nature open for integration into the divine personhood of the Word of God. How this integration takes place is subject to different interpretations according to the different views on the ontological constitution of the Person. To posit two acts of being in Christ, a divine and a human, may seem to rule out the oneness of his Person. The theory of the "ecstasy of being" however, which postulates the divine act of being only, may seem to belittle the reality of Christ's human existence. It must be shown that, while communicating with the human nature, the divine act of being of the Son of God provides it with human existence. The Son of God exists as man through the creative assumption of a true humanhood. BIBLIOGRAPHY: Rahner ThInvest 4:105; B. Lonergan, *De constitutione Christi ontologica et psychologica* (1964) 57; F. Malmberg, *Über den Gottmenschen* (Quaestiones disputatae 9, 1960).

[J. DUPUIS]

HYPOSTATIC UNION, GRACE OF. The "grace of union" is a technical term in scholastic Christology. Its origin is ultimately to be traced to the Vulgate usage of the word *gratia* in passages concerning the Incarnation (Jn 1.14–17; Tit 2.11). Then St. Augustine developed the idea of the personal union of man and God in Christ as the ideal analogy for the union of man and God in grace. With these elements on hand it was a simple step to speak of the "grace of union," as Peter Lombard did in the 12th century. The term was taken up and used in somewhat different senses in the 13th cent.: (1) the Holy Spirit producing the hypostatic union; (2) a created disposition in Jesus for that union; or (3) the hypostatic union itself. In favoring for the third meaning, St. Thomas Aquinas explains: "the union is called grace inasmuch as it is not from merit." (ThAq ST 3a, 2.12 ad 2).

This gift, the "grace of union," is the greatest of God's gifts to men and the foundation of all others. It is defined as "the personal being that is given gratis from above to the human nature in the person of the Word, and is the term of the assumption" (*ibid.* 3a, 6.6). In Christ's human soul and powers, sanctifying them, there is also the habitual grace and by its fullness Christ as man is Head of his members, the mystical body. BIBLIOGRAPHY: A. Michel, DTC 7.1:437–568.

[J. J. MEGIVERN]

HYPSELE (HYPSILE), in Byzantine music a marking or character to indicate ascent.

HYPSISTARIANS, a 4th-cent. sect that worshiped God as all high ruler (Gr. *hypsistos*), but not as Father, and that is known only from the writings of St. Gregory Nazianzus (*Orat.* 18.5).

[T. C. O'BRIEN]

HYSSOP, a small shrub growing out of crevices (1 Kg 4.33); not the southern European *Hyssopus officinalis,* but *Origanum Maru L.,* marjoram of the mint family. Its stiff branches and the absorptive qualities of its hair-like leaves made it ideal for ceremonial sprinkling (Ex 12.22; Lev 14; Num 19.6, 18; Heb 9.19). Hyssop in Ps 51.7 is metaphorical and perhaps should be translated "gushing water." The hyssop of Jn 19.29 seems less suitable than the reed of Mt 27.48; Mk 15.36; possibly it is symbolic, since hyssop is linked with OT sacrifices. BIBLIOGRAPHY: J.C. Trever, Inter DB 2:669–670; H. N. and A. L. Moldenke, *Plants of the Bible* (1952) 160–162.

[E. J. CROWLEY]

HYSTERECTOMY, surgical removal of the womb. Since this represents a major *mutilation of the woman's body, its moral justification requires a proportionately grave cause. Danger to the patient, however, need not be immediate: a condition, such as may arise from repeated Caesarean sections, in which the womb could here and now be repaired, but will eventually require hysterectomy, suffices as a reason for the surgery. Because of the nature of this operation medical science itself indicates that the surgery in all cases be only as radical as is necessary.

[T. C. O'BRIEN]

HYTHACIUS, see HYDATIUS AND HYTHACIUS.

HYTREK, THEOPHANE, SISTER (1915–), Franciscan, church musician, educator, organist, and composer. H., who is professor of music at Alverno College, Milwaukee, Wis., holds master's degrees in organ and composition, has a doctorate in composition from the Univ. of Rochester and is a Fellow of the American Guild of Organists, a member of its National Council and of several other national and local organizations and committees. She is a recognized leader in the field of liturgical music. Her published works include Masses, motets, psalms, hymns, and organ compositions. One of her recent works, the *Pilgrim Mass,* was commissioned for the 41st International Eucharistic Congress in Philadelphia, 1976.

[M. T. LEGGE]

HYVERNAT, HENRI (1858–1941), Orientalist. After studies in his native France, H. taught Assyriology and Egyptology at the Roman Seminary and in 1889 came to The Catholic Univ. of America where he remained until his death. He contributed articles on Coptic studies to periodicals and reference works, cofounded the *Corpus scriptorum Christianorum Orientalium,* catalogued the Coptic MSS found at Hamuli, and began a catalogue of Coptic learning.

[T. M. MCFADDEN]

I

I AM MOVEMENT, an American religious cult that gained a considerable following in the 1930s and rapidly declined thereafter. Guy W. Ballard and his wife Edna organized and promoted the movement; its ideas were drawn exclusively from *Unveiled Mysteries, The Magic Presence,* and other books written by Ballard, under the pen name Godfrey Ray King. In 1934 he published *Unveiled Mysteries,* describing interviews with the Ascended Master St. Germain that began on Mt. Shasta, Calif., in 1930. He and his wife launched the I Am Movement with lecture series in Chicago, Philadelphia, New York, Washington, and other American cities; in 1936 they established their headquarters in Los Angeles. The thought of the I Am Movement was a maze of borrowings from occult and *New Thought sources. An original veneer of Christianity was dropped, and the Ascended Master St. Germain, who in one of many incarnations had been the 18th-cent. Comte de St. Germain, took the chief place in the pantheon of Ascended Masters. Through successive reincarnations, every member of the movement could become an Ascended Master. Death was impossible because of the immanence of the Great I Am Presence in every man. By using certain affirmations and incantations, each member could harness the I Am power for health, prosperity, and happiness. The I Am Presence is impersonal, while St. Germain is at once a benevolent demiurge and one of the myriad Ascended Masters. The Ballards were reincarnations of George Washington and Joan of Arc, respectively. I Am study groups were required to purchase Ballard's many publications and to tithe their wealth. They were also obliged to abstain from sexual intercourse, astrology, drugs, garlic and onions, and playing cards. The I Am movement borrowed ideas and members from the Silver Shirt Movement and was characterized by superpatriotism and condemnations of the New Deal, labor unions, and liberals. Ballard's death in 1939 and a series of trials, 1939–47, that culminated in Edna Ballard's imprisonment for mail fraud, made considerable inroads on the I Am membership, and it disappeared altogether in the 1950s.

[R. K. MACMASTER]

IACOPINO (IACOPO) DA TRADATE (fl. 1401–40), Italian sculptor. I. worked on the cathedral of Milan (1401–25), served the Duke Giovanni Francesco Gonzaga at Mantua (1440), and carved the statue of Pope Martin V (1421) in detail and rhythmic drapery, an apotheosis of Lombard Gothic sculpture.

[M. J. DALY]

IAMBLICHUS OF CHALCIS IN SYRIA (*c.* A.D. 250–330), Neoplatonist philosopher and founder of the Syrian School. He was the leading representative of theurgy among the Neoplatonists, combining Neopythagorean and Oriental elements in his system. He made full use of the *Chaldaean Oracles* and is now recognized as the author of the *De mysteriis Aegypti*. He was reputed to be a practitioner of magic as well as an advocate of its efficacy, and of the necessity of theurgy for the salvation of the soul. However, the scholarship of the last decades has demonstrated that he also made important contributions on the metaphysical side and undoubtedly deserved in many respects the prestige that he enjoyed among later Neoplatonists. He went much beyond Porphyry in working out a kind of systematic theology of the most diverse forms of pagan beliefs and practices. He developed further the metaphysical speculation of Plotinus and Porphyry by his division and multiplication of the stages of being. He introduced a second One, divided the sphere of the *nous* into the Intelligible and the Intellectual, and taught that there was a triad of souls. He recognized numerous classes of divinities within and above the world, which constituted stages in the ladder of being. In similar fashion he assigned an appropriate order to angels, heroes, and demons. In his interpretation of Plato's *Dialogues,* he adopted a definite method. He abandoned the prevailing arbitrary use of allegory and established Neoplatonic metaphysics in methodological fashion on Plato. BIBLIOGRAPHY: P. Merlan, LexAW 1354; Copleston 1:476–477; CHGMP 283–301; Ueberweg 1:612–617; É. des Places, *Iamblique: Les Mystères d'Égypte* (1966).

[M. R. P. MCGUIRE]

IARF, see INTERNATIONAL ASSOCIATION FOR LIBERAL CHRISTIANITY AND RELIGIOUS FREEDOM.

IBARRA, JOSÉ DE (1688–1756), 18th-cent. Mexican painter whose prolific work adorns the cathedrals of Mexico City and Puebla and many other churches.

[M. J. DALY]

IBARRA Y GONZALEZ, RAMON (1853–1917), Mexican abp. of Puebla—the first and last to hold that title. He was a zealous and energetic man, much interested in education, who worked tirelessly to found new schools and bring religious to work in his diocese to promote the establishment of workers' circles. He founded two Mexican missionary congregations. He was subject to grievous religious persecution from which he was in hiding at the time of his death.

[P. K. MEAGHER]

IBAS OF EDESSA (d. 457), bp. who attempted a difficult middle course between the teaching of Nestorius and that of St. Cyril of Alexandria. During the episcopate of Rabbula, his predecessor in the see of Edessa, I. was the leader of the theological school of that city. At the Council of Ephesus (431) he sided with the representatives of Antioch, and when peace was established by the agreement of 433 between Cyril of Alexandria and John of Antioch, Rabbula expelled him from Edessa for refusing to condemn the works of *Theodore of Mopsuestia. About this time he summarized his views in a letter to Bp. Mari of Ardascir in Persia. After his election to the bishopric of Edessa (435), Alexandrian theologians repeatedly denounced him for heresy throughout his episcopate. He was deposed by the Robber Synod of Ephesus in 449 because of his letter to Mari, but the Council of Chalcedon restored him 2 years later after he had condemned Nestorius. After the lapse of a cent., however, his celebrated letter was one of the *Three Chapters condemned by the Second Council of Constantinople. BIBLIOGRAPHY: Altaner 406; PSO 91–93.

[R. B. ENO]

IBLÍS, in the Koran of Islam a personal name for the devil. Iblís plays a role similar to that of the serpent in Gen in the Koran account of the creation of man. Iblís became a source of evil when he refused to bow down in reverence before Adam as God's creation. His final punishment is postponed until the end of the world, and he possesses a power conceded by God to tempt those who are not God's true servants. Elements of the account derive from the apocryphal, *Life of Moses*. In Islamic tradition it is disputed whether Iblís is truly an angel or one of the "genies" (jinn).

[T. C. O'BRIEN]

IBN 'ARABĪ (Muhyī al-Dīn ibn 'Arabī; 1165–1240), Spanish-born Islamic philosopher and writer. While he was studying the Koran and Islamic law in Lisbon and Seville, his association with two elderly Sufi women reinforced his familial ties with Sufism. Following a vision in 1200, he wandered throughout the Near East and Asia Minor, finally settling in Damascus (1223). His complex doctrine was never presented in systematic form, though at the core of his thought is a vision of multiple and sequential theophanies or manifestations of the primordially undifferentiated Divine Essence. As these manifestations of the Divine Essence incorporate more of the names of the Divine, each theophany (*tajalliyāt*) becomes increasingly complex and brighter, a more intense effusion of Light. Perfect Man is an epiphany of all the Divine Names; all other individual beings manifest one or more Names, each of which is a particular manifestation of the primordially undifferentiated Divine Essence. These Names are the Lords over their respective individual creatures, thus total God in all his manifestations is the Lord of Man. Good is described by I. as a growing realization of God's being manifest in himself and in all beings; evil is the illusion that creatures, beings, and God are independent and autonomous. Among his numerous works, his *Tarjumān alashwāq* (Interpreter of Eager Desires, 1215) is a famous collection of poems written for a young Meccan woman whose role parallels Dante's Beatrice; his own esoteric commentary on the poems is appended. His major doctrinal work is *Futuḥāt al-makkiyah* (Revelations at Mecca on the knowledge of the secrets of the King and Kingdom, 1230 ff.). His *Fuṣus al-Ḥikam* (Gems of the Wisdoms of the Prophets, 1230) is a summary of his teachings.

[R. J. LITZ]

IBN EZRA, ABRAHAM (1092–1167), Jewish poet and biblical commentator. He was born and died in Spain, but during his last 30 years took on the mission of traveling teacher to the Jewish communities throughout Europe. All of his written works are from this period. The most important is his commentary on all the books of the Hebrew Bible except Chronicles; this was one of the standard commentaries incorporated into the *Rabbinical Bibles. His commentary sought out the literal sense; it is noteworthy for its anticipation of later biblical criticism, esp. as to the sources of the *Pentateuch. He was a man of broad learning in grammar, philology, mathematics, astrology, and astronomy; some of his sacred poetry became part of Jewish liturgy. BIBLIOGRAPHY: A. Brunot, NCE 7:313–314, bibliog.

[T. C. O'BRIEN]

IBN EZRA, MOSES (*c.* 1070–*c.* 1138), Jewish poet who lived and died in Spain. His religious, penitential poetry, much of which became part of Jewish liturgy, reflected on the vanity of the world and the need of resignation. His poems as well as a treatise on the subject manifested his mastery of the poetic techniques of the Hebrew language. He also left an undistinguished philosophical treatise.

[T. C. O'BRIEN]

IBN GABIROL, SOLOMON, see AVICEBRON.

IBN KHALDŪN (1332–1406), Arab historian and social theorist. His original approach to history noted in the rise and fall of civilizations a similarity of cause and effect from which conclusions could be deduced and sociological laws determined. Many of his conclusions are applicable to modern problems. The *Muqaddimah,* one of four volumes of *Kitāb al-'Ibar,* his Islamic history, is important for its philosophy of history. His writings are backed by his experiences in positions of official capacity in Tunis and Granada.

[A. P. HANLON]

IBN PAQŪDA (Baḥya ben Joseph ibn Pakūda; fl. late 11th cent.), Jewish moralist, who lived in Moorish Spain. His great treatise became a classic of Jewish piety and spirituality. Written in Arabic, it was translated into Hebrew in the 12th cent. and became known as *Ḥovot ha-levavot* (Duties of the Heart). The work reflects a Neoplatonic view of the relationship of the soul and body, and of the world to God. Its teaching on the ascetical and mystical ascent to God is phrased in beautiful language and has been recognized as reflecting not only Jewish, but also Islamic and Christian influences. BIBLIOGRAPHY: M. R. Nôtre, NCE 7:316, bibliog.

[T. C. O'BRIEN]

IBN RUSHED, see AVERROËS.

IBN SHAPRUT, HASDAI (*c.*915–*c.*970), Spanish Jewish diplomatist at the court of the caliphs in Córdoba and patron of Jewish letters. His statesmanship was remarkably successful in fostering amicable relations with Christian kingdoms of Spain and of Europe. His interest and financial support made Córdoba the center of Talmudic scholarship and the study of the Hebrew language, a fact that had effects on both Jewish and Christian cultural and intellectual history.

[T. C. O'BRIEN]

IBN SĪNĀ, see AVICENNA.

IBN TIBBON, Jewish family, originally from Granada in Spain, famous for Hebrew translations from Arabic, which contributed to learning by their spread of ideas and development of precise technical vocabulary. (1) **Judah ben Saul** (*c.*1120–*c.*1190) left Granada because of persecution, settled the family in S France. Among his translations were works of *Avicebron and *Juda Ha-Levi. His *A Father's Admonition* is a famous testament on the care of books and the scholar's life. (2) **Samuel ben Judah** (*c.*1150–1230), son of the preceding, translated, under the author's own supervision, *Maimonides's *Guide of the Perplexed,* an introduction to the *Mishnah and *Pirke Avoth,* as well as works of Averroës and the Arabic of Aristotle's *Meteora.* (3) **Moses ben Samuel** (*c.*1240–*c.*1283), son of the preceding, translated Arabic versions of Euclid's *Elements* and works of Alfārābī and Avicenna. (3) **Jacob ben Makhir** (Don Profiat; Profatius Judaeus, *c.*1230–*c.*1312), grandson of Samuel, translated Averroës's *Compendium of Logic* and commentaries on Aristotle. He was also a brilliant astronomer, whose astronomical tables were used by Dante in the *Divine Comedy,* and whose writings on a new quadrant he himself invented were known to Kepler and Copernicus. BIBLIOGRAPHY: B. Krinsky, NCE 7:316–317, bibliog.

[T. C. O'BRIEN]

IBN-ṬUFAIL (Abū Bakr Muhammad; *c.*1110–85), Spanish Muslim philosopher, physician, and court official. He is author of *Ḥayy ibn 'Yaqzān,* a philosophical novel that describes the educational and philosophical development of a man who lived in isolation for 50 years on an uninhabited island. The author was secretary to the governors of Granada, Ceuta, and Tangiers in N Africa. As court physician to the Almohad sovereign, he aided the career of *Averroës by his influence with the Sultan. He also wrote Arabic works on medicine and astrology. BIBLIOGRAPHY: H. Corbin, EncPhil 4:109–110.

[A. P. HANLON]

IBURG, ABBEY OF, Benedictine abbey located on the most important mountain pass in the district of Osnabrück, Germany. It was founded in 1080 by Benno II, bp. of Osnabrück. The abbey made its greatest cultural and intellectual contributions under Abbot Maurus Rost (1676–1706). Secularized in 1803, the buildings were restored in 1956 and are now used as a boarding school.

[T. M. MCFADDEN]

IC XC NIKA, a Greek acclamation appearing in several different forms on Christian monuments, particularly of the Byzantine period. The "C" in inscriptions of this type is an old but rather rare form of the Greek "Σ," technically known as a "sigmate *s*." The first two words by a common mode of contraction stand for the Holy Name: the first four letters are Iota (I), Sigma (C), Chi (X), Sigma (C), thus I(esou)S X(risto)S-Iesus Christos. The NIKA may be taken as a survival of a pagan invocation to the goddess Victory. It later came to be used at Greek and Roman race tracks as an exclamation of encouragement to the contestants. It may also be taken as a verb, more properly spelled NIKAI, and would then mean "he conquers." It may also appear as NIKAIS, or "you conquer." Probably the best sense would be that of the Latin *Iesus Christus vincit,* "Jesus Christ conquers." BIBLIOGRAPHY: H. Leclercq, DACL 12.1:1269–72.

[M. J. COSTELLOE]

ICELAND, predominantly Lutheran island republic 500 miles NW of Scotland, just under the Arctic Circle. Perhaps the Thule of the ancient Greeks, it was the home of Irish monks for a century or more prior to the first Viking settlement of Ingolfur Arnarson, traditionally dated 874. The monks felt compelled to leave, though some of the Norse had been in Scotland and Ireland and their number included Christians. However, Christianity virtually died out, to be revived by missionaries sent by Olaf I of Norway (995–1000). When a Christian-pagan war threatened, the Althing (established 930) decided in 1000 that the country as a whole would become Christian. Much of N Europe was then under the abp. of Bremen, and the first bp. of Iceland, Isleifur Gissurarson, was consecrated there in 1056. He established his see on his family lands at Skalholt. In 1106 the N Diocese of Holar was established. For a time under the Archdiocese of Lund, Iceland was assigned in 1152 to Nidaros (Trondheim). Churches were originally built by laymen on their farms, and clergy later undertook a struggle for independence. The climax began *c.* 1230 when the abp. of Nidaros appointed Norwegian bps. to both Icelandic sees. The Norwegian King supported the bps. and brought Iceland under Norwegian rule (1262–64). By a concordat of 1297, the bps. gained control of church properties. In the 12th and 13th cent. were written the noted sagas that brought the old Scandinavian culture to its peak. In 1380 Iceland, along with Norway, passed to the Danish crown. In 1540 Gissur Einarsson of Skalholt became the first Lutheran bp. of Iceland. In 1550 Bp. John Arason of Holar and his two sons were beheaded for resisting Lutheranism. Since the new order was imposed by the Danish crown, Arason became a symbol of national resistance, and the Reformation gained popular acceptance only with the work of Gundbrandur Thorlaksson (1541–1627), bp. of Holar for 56 years and translator of the Bible into Icelandic (1584). The two dioceses were merged in 1801 and the bp.'s seat located at Reykjavik. Iceland gained limited home rule undcr a constitution in 1874 and in 1918 received sovereign status, though remaining in union with the Danish crown. In 1944 it declared independence, with Lutheranism remaining the established religion. BIBLIOGRAPHY: J. Hood, *Icelandic Church Saga* (1946); *Iceland 874–1974* (ed. J. Nordal and V. Kristinsson, 1975).

[T. EARLY]

ICHTHUS (ICHTHYS), transliteration of the Greek ixous, meaning fish. The fish has been a symbol of Christ from early 2d century. Together with loaves of bread (the multiplication of the loaves and fishes in the Gospels), it was taken as a symbol of the *Eucharist. The Greek word was used as a confession of faith in the form of an *acrostic: I(ēsous) X(ristos) TH(eou) U(ios) S(ōtēr): Jesus Christ, Son of God, Savior. BIBLIOGRAPHY: H. Leclercq, DACL 7.2:1990–2086.

[R. B. ENO]

ICHYI KINRIN IN CHUSONJI, HIRAIZUMI, 13th-cent. Japanese wood icon worshiped in the True Word sect (Shingon) in connection with solar and lunar eclipses.

[M. J. DALY]

ICON, (Gr. *eikon,* image), a term in Christian art referring to images of the Savior, the Trinity, the Mother of God, angels, saints, as well as sacred events and theological mysteries. Icons, usually portable, are to be distinguished from statues and also from idols that had cultic purposes in pre-Christian Hellenism and other Near Eastern religions. Generally they are made on slabs of wood, but at times the Romanians use glass, and there have been small portable icons of mosaic. On these surfaces the iconographer, following rules ecclesiastically established, sketches the outlines of the figures he wishes to depict. He then lays down the background in paint or goldleaf. When this is completed, the figures are filled in with paints generally prepared from vegetable colors mixed with egg whites. The finished product is coated thoroughly with linseed oil which makes the colors appear brilliant for a time, but they soon darken. In the 17th cent. metal covering (in Russian, a *riza*), began to be used to cover the entire icon except the face and hands of the figures. This was done partly to preserve the icon and partly to express veneration. These coverings were often of silver or gold and further enhanced by having precious stones inserted into them in decorative patterns such as crowns and necklaces.

Icons ideally are painted by monks or nuns who live contemplating the persons and mysteries they depict for the veneration and instruction of their fellow Christians. The iconographer is an evangelist in paints; in his work he hopes to be moved by a kind of inspiration analogous to that enjoyed by the writers of Scripture. He begins his work with fasting and prayer, and by his painting he seeks to concretize his own vision of the transfigured cosmos through Christ, the Trinity, the Mother of God, the angels, and saints. For this reason the genuine iconic style is never naturalistic or sentimental, but always strives to make the glorified state of its subject shine through its earthly portrayal, so that the worshiper may behold the presence of the world to come. A special liturgy consecrating the icons for church use is prescribed and the wording of the prayers shows traces of the controversies over *iconoclasm.

Icons are venerated by bows, or prostrations, during which the worshiper continually makes the sign of the cross. They are also kissed and the forehead is pressed against them as gestures of respect and honor. Lamps and candles burn before them both during liturgical services and in private devotion. During the Liturgy the holy icons are incensed by the celebrant or deacon three times in veneration of the Church, both earthly and heavenly. They are borne in procession on certain feast days, and blessings are given with them at the end of some services. On certain occasions the faithful are anointed with oil from the lamp burning before an icon. The icon is venerated as an extension of the Incarnation of the Savior; the image is believed to participate in Christ as the Image of God, and is an expression of man as the Image of God, who is renewed and deified by the redemptive Incarnation. Icons mediate to man the presence of those whom they depict in much the same way that the words of the Gospels mediate the message of salvation. BIBLIOGRAPHY: L. Ouspensky and V. Lossky, *Meaning of Icons* (tr. G. Palmer and E. Kadloubovsky, 1956); E. Benz, *The Eastern Orthodox Church* (tr. E. and C. Winston, 1963) 1–19.

[A. WALKER]

ICONIUM, a city in Asia Minor pertaining to the region of Lycaonia in NT times. Today it is Konya in Turkey with a population of *c.*65,000. Paul and Barnabas preached the gospel there on their first missionary journey (Acts 13.51–14.6), and Paul visited the community he had founded on his second and third missionary journeys (Acts 16.2, 18.23). It was dominated by the Turks in the 9th cent., the Crusaders in the 13th, then the Muslims and the Ottoman Empire in 1472.

[S. MUSHOLT]

ICONOCLASM (Gr., *eikonoklasmos,* image breaking), the heresy denouncing the veneration of sacred images as idolatry. Combined Jewish and Islamic influence resulted in some Christian opposition to such veneration, and Paulician heretics in Constantinople claimed the support of certain Catholic bishops. In 730 Emperor Leo III the Isaurian ordered the destruction of all holy icons. The Patriarch Germanus, who was opposed to this policy, was deposed, and Leo's attempts to force the Pope to accept iconoclasm led to a serious rupture in relations between Rome and Byzantium. Emperor Constantine V Copronymos, seeking ecclesiastical condemnation of images, summoned 340 bps. to a synod in Hieria (754). Here they decreed that the Eucharist alone could be held to be a lawful representation of Christ. Publicly denounced were Patriarch Germanus, St. John Damascene, and George of Cyprus, staunch iconodules (Mansi 13:205 ff.). Constantine, the new patriarch, and all the bps. were required to sign the synodal Acts. The Emperor then embarked on a savage persecution of the iconodules, particularly the monks. Leo IV, Constantine's son (775–780), sanctioned the return of exiled monks and attempted reconciliation, but the Patriarch Paul IV (780–784) failed to revoke the imperial decrees. Upon Leo's death Empress Irene, regent for her son, attempted to repair the damage inflicted by the iconoclastic emperors. Patriarch Tarasius (784–806) with imperial approbation sent a delegation to confer with Pope Adrian I (772–795). At the Seventh General Council, convoked at Nicaea (787), the bishops repudiated the synodal decrees of Hieria (754). The doctrinal decree defining the veneration of images included the theological distinction between the terms **latria* and **dulia.* On abjuration of their error Pariarch Tarasius admitted former iconoclastic bps. to their original status. Soon, however, Emperor Leo V (813–820) dismissed the orthodox Patriarch Nicephorus, and had a synod (815) annul the decrees of the Council of 787 and recognize the ecumenical status of Hieria. Renewed persecution continued under the Emperors Michael II (820–829) and Theophilus (829–842). Theodora, imperial regent (842–856), named Methodius (842–846) to replace the iconoclastic patriarch and at a synod in March 843, the decrees of the Council of Nicaea were reinstated and unrepentant iconoclasts excommunicated. The first Sunday of Lent is still kept by the Eastern Churches as the Sunday of Orthodoxy in commemoration of the triumph over heresy. The *Photian Synod of 879–880 conferred on the Council of Nicaea (787) the title of Seventh Ecumenical Council to emphasize the decline of iconoclasm. The famous *Libri Carolini* and the Frankfurt Synod of 794 rejected both the Synod of 754 and the Council of 787, pressuring Pope Adrian I to defend the cult of images. BIBLIOGRAPHY: A. Grabar, *L'Iconoclasme byzantin: Dossier archéologique* (1957); P. J. Alexander, *Patriarch Nicephorus of Constantinople: Ecclesiastical Policy and Image Worship in the Byzantine Empire* (1958); Ostrogorsky.

[L. NEMEC]

ICONOGRAPHY From Gr. *eikōn,* image, and *graphein,* to write, a term referring generally to the representation of objects and persons, as well as to the description or study of images and symbols found in artistic works. The study of Christian subject matter and its meaning in the visual arts dates from such 16th-cent. iconographers as J. Molanus, *De picturis et imaginibus sacris* (Louvain 1570). The lack of sufficient graphic material and photo documentation created a need for minute descriptions of art works for classifications based on subject matter. By the 18th cent. the methods of iconography were used to document and classify art works by subject matter as in Ph. de Caylus, *Recueil d'antiquités* (Paris 1752–67). Up to and even into the 20th cent. the term has often been used more broadly to include the interpretation and contextual meanings of images. For some modern scholars (E. Panofsky) this latter stage of image study is more properly termed *iconology BIBLIOGRAPHY: EncWA 7:769–785.

[R. J. VEROSTKO]

ICONOLOGY, from Gr. *eikōn,* image, and *logos,* word, the study of images. The term refers generally to the historical analysis and interpretive study of symbolic representations and artistic images. Iconology considers the cultural context of symbols and images as a means of interpreting their content. Thus a 15th-cent. Italian Virgin Mary though in subject the same as a 12th-cent. Byzantine representation reflects from a different time and place significant cultural differences. Iconology investigates the complex stylistic and cultural relationships that converge to shape the symbolism and imagery of a given artist or artistic period. Although the term was used as early as the late 16th cent. for a manual of symbols, allegories and personifications (Cesare Ripa, *Iconologia,* Rome, 1593), it was not used in reference to the interpretive study of images until modern times. Addressing a need for greater depth in research into images, iconological studies were pioneered in the 20th cent. by

German and Austrian scholars (M. Dvorak, A. Warburg, E. Panofsky). Following psychoanalytical studies of artists by Freud and Jung, iconology has also come to include exploration of subconscious elements in composition and symbolism. BIBLIOGRAPHY: E. Panofsky, *Studies in Iconology* (1939).

[R. J. VEROSTKO]

ICONOSTASIS. After the resolution of the Iconoclast controversy (726–843 A.D.), the way was open in the East for the proliferation of iconographic art. This activity was eventually focused on and reached its zenith in the embellishment of the iconostasis. Basically, the iconostasis is a screen, usually of wood, that separates the sanctuary from the main body of the church. The oldest known form of chancel screen was a simple affair which did not restrict the worshipers' view of the altar or the frescoes and mosaics in the sanctuary. (In certain Orthodox churches today there is a return to this less elaborate type of screen.) Such early screens, approximately 3 to 4 feet in height, on which was placed a single row of small icons, were first introduced in Byzantium. Although in Kievan Rus (11th–13th cent.) the iconostasis was of comparable size to its Byzantine models, it was ultimately among the Russians that the most lavish and ornamental screens were produced. Opinions vary as to the date of the first solid iconostasis, reaching from floor to ceiling and serving to display three to five tiers of icons. (Ware, 276; Rice, 68; Billington, 641, footnote 69). However, such screens, which date from the 14th cent., have survived to the present. G. P. Fedotov explains the Russian prediliction for such ornamental screens in the light of certain special qualities of Russian piety, which, he says, regarded the sanctuary as a shrine within a shrine and the sacred mysteries performed therein as suitable only to be witnessed by the clergy. Whatever the case, the fact remains that in medieval Russia the Eucharist was surrounded by a very ascetic theology, and the liturgy witnessed a growth in the number of secret prayers. It was logical to expect that in such conditions the sanctuary would be progressively closed to the congregation. As a direct result of this, the importance of icons grew, both as objects for veneration and as worthy of great artistic effort.

The iconostasis of the tradition described above is pierced by three doors. In the center is the double-gated Royal Door, behind which stands the altar, which is visible when the gates are open and the curtain is drawn aside, as is the case at certain moments during the liturgy. (Today liturgical usage varies widely in this regard. See Ware, 277.) The left door, as one faces the apse, leads to a side altar at which the rite of preparation or *prothesis* is accomplished. The right door leads to the *diakonikon* where the Book of Gospels and the vestments are kept. These doors are used for various purposes, such as the procession of the gifts (Offertory), the proclamation of the Gospel, and the distribution of communion. Laymen are not permitted behind the iconostasis, except as acolytes, and only an officiating priest may stand between the altar and the Royal Door.

The arrangement of icons on the iconostasis is according to a precise pattern. Those on the lowest tier are the largest and most important. They are called the "local icons." To the right side of the Royal Door is an icon of Christ, holding the Gospels in one hand and giving his blessing with the other. To the left is an icon of the Mother of God holding the infant Jesus. (For both of these icons there are several stylized poses, each of which has a name.) On the Royal Door itself are six small icons: the two in the center depict the Annunciation, and the four others, the Evangelists. The Archangels Michael and Gabriel are shown on the two side doors. The remaining icons of the first tier include the patron saint or feast of the church and other popular and national saints. The second row of icons, just above the doors, commemorates the 12 principal feasts or holy days of the Church. A third row contains the icons of the prophets, facing the Virgin, seated in the center. Above this are the Apostles, headed by Peter and Paul, all facing a central group or Deisis (Christ seated as judge, with the Virgin and John the Baptist at his sides). As noted, there is some variation of the foregoing, based on national usage. BIBLIOGRAPHY: J. H. Billington, *Icon and the Axe* (1967); G. P. Fedotov, *Russian Religious Mind,* (v. 2, 1966); T. T. Rice, *Concise History of Russian Art* (1963); T. Ware, *Orthodox Church* (1963).

[R. H. MARSHALL]

ICTINUS (fl. 450 B.C.), Greek architect of the Parthenon (with Callicrates). I. brought the Doric order to highest perfection, made innovative changes at the Temple of Apollo, Epikourios, Bassae, and codesigned the Periclean Telestrion, Eleusis. One of the first masters of interior space, I. wrote on architecture (Vitruvius 7, 12).

[M. J. DALY]

ICTUS, a term applied by the monks of Solesmes in the explanation of their interpretation of Gregorian chant. It is not a notational marking, nor does it describe the prolongation of one note in a neume. In their conception of the rhythm, in which notes have equal value, the ictus is said to fall, e.g., on the first note in a neume. It may thus designate a pulsation in the rhythm.

[T. C. O'BRIEN]

ID, a Freudian term with *ego and *superego applied to a basic mental structure of the human psyche. It contains instinctual drives, and the fantasies, thoughts, attitudes, etc., related to them. Since an infant at birth has no capacity for meaningful relationship to reality and morality, Freud concluded the whole psyche at birth consists of the id. The instinctual drives of the id arise spontaneously from underlying biological processes as modified in each individual by hereditary dispositions. These fundamental drives (libido or sex-pleasure and aggressive motivating hostile and destructive activities) always work together in a mixed way. The continual generation of instinctual drives causes a constant rise in internal tensions or pressures which are discharged by the activity gratifying the drive, e.g., by the infant's oral activity of sucking. The principle used to explain the id process is the constant striving to reduce rising tensions by means of appropriate activities, i.e., those discharging drive-energy. Since the release of tension is conceived as pleasure, it is called the pleasure principle. In infancy these instinctual drives are discharged by activities such as biting, defecating, or withholding feces; and masturbation. To the degree that these can be carried out without delay, interruption, or interference, the psyche fixes on them as modes of drive discharge. If prevented, however, by circumstances or parental prohibitions, they must be abandoned and the impulse repressed. In the course of development, the child normally abandons one activity and proceeds to the next in a determinable order, but if at any point he represses into the unconscious, the fantasies connected with a mode of gratification, he remains unconsciously attached or "fixated" and in the future will strive unconsciously to obtain satisfaction according to this mode. In the course of development, esp. *oedipal, the child almost inevitably represses many fantasies, and later by processes of association, other fantasies are repressed so that eventually the id becomes filled with repressed fantasies. These develop according to the laws of the unconscious mind to form complexes and constellations which in later life characterize the contents of the id. Although Freud's concept of the id has perhaps offended and frightened many, it is not altogether strange to traditional Christian thinking. Church Fathers used the notion of *fomes peccati,* the tinderbox of sin, by which they meant the eruptive propensity of passion. St. Thomas Aquinas's consideration of the scholastic term *sensualitas* also bears relation to the meaning of sensual or sexual tendencies (ThAq *In 2 Sent.* 24, 2, 1 and ad 3; ST 1a2ae, 74.3; 85.3; 91.6).

[M. E. STOCK]

IDA, BL., name borne by three Belgian Cistercian nuns of the 13th century. (1) **Ida of Leeuw** (d. *c.*1260). Born at Leeuw, Belgium, she entered the convent of La Ramée in Brabant and is said to have experienced mystical visions. (2) **Ida of Louvain** (d. *c.*1300), who entered the Cistercian abbey of Roosendael (Val-des-Roses) near Malines and also had a reputation for mystical experiences and for working miracles. (3) **Ida of Nivelles** (1199 or 1200–31), who entered Kerkhem abbey near Louvain and later moved with her community to La Ramée in 1215. She was esp. known for her devotion to the Passion and to the Eucharist. BIBLIOGRAPHY: K. Spahr, LTK 5:600; S. Roisin, BiblSanct 7:638–642.

[N. F. GAUGHAN]

IDA OF BOULOGNE, BL. (*c.*1040–1113). I., whose parents descended from Charlemagne, was the child of Godfrey IV, duke of Lorraine, and his first wife Doda. At 17 she was married to Eustace II, Count of Boulogne, and was the mother of Eustace III, Godfrey of Bouillon, and King Baldwin of Jerusalem. Her spiritual advisor was St. Anselm, then Abbot of Bec, in Normandy. In her widowhood, she spent her wealth and time in caring for the needy, and the construction of monasteries. She founded St. Wulmer at Boulogne and Vasconvilliers, and even though she never took the veil, she favored the Cluny reform. She is buried in the monastic church at St. Vaast. BIBLIOGRAPHY: F. Ducatel, *Vie de Sainte Ide de Lorraine* (1900).

[N. F. GAUGHAN]

IDA OF HERZFELD, ST. (d. 825[813?]), widow. Born in Alsace, a descendant of Charles Martel, she married the Saxon duke Egbert. After the death of her husband, she devoted her life to doing penance and to serving others and became noted for her patient suffering in illness. She is buried in the cemetery of the convent at Herzfeld which she and her husband had founded. Two of her children were Bl. *Warin and Bl. Hedwig, abbess of Herford. BIBLIOGRAPHY: G. Marsot, *Catholicisme* 5:1172; Butler 3:486.

[J. R. RIVELLO]

IDA (IDDA) OF TOGGENBURG, ST. (*c.*1138–*c.*1410). Nothing is known of I. save that she has been honored at Fischingen, near Lake Constance in Switzerland, since 1410. A spurious legend concerning her has existed since the late 15th century. There is some reason to believe that she was a recluse. Her cult was confirmed in 1724. BIBLIOGRAPHY: L. Kern, *Die Ida von Toggenburg-Legende* (1928); J. Duft, BiblSanct 7:637.

[B. F. SCHERER]

IDAHO, a Rocky Mountain state, admitted to the Union (1890) as the 43rd state. Among the early pioneers in Idaho were Christian missionaries, who followed the Oregon Trail seeking access to the Indians of the Northwest. Jason Lee of the Methodist Episcopal Church, the Presbyterians Marcus Whitman and Henry H. Spalding, and the Jesuit Pierre Jean *De Smet, all did missionary work in the region during the 1830s and 1840s. Mormon homesteaders made their first permanent settlement at Franklin in 1860. Today the Mormons have the largest church membership in the state. The Jesuits first worked among the Coeur d'Alene Indians, establishing the Sacred Heart Mission on the St. Joseph River (1842). The area was made a vicariate apostolic (1868), and in 1893 the Diocese of Boise was established. A suffragan of the Archdiocese of Oregon City (now Portland) Boise's first bp. was Alphonse Glorieux. His successors were Daniel M. Gorman (1918–27), Edward J. Kelly (1928–56), and James J. Byrne (1956–62). The present bp., Sylvester W. Treinen, has served since 1962.

Idaho's population of 820,000 (over 50% urban) makes it the 42nd most populous state in the Union. In 1976 Catholics numbered 64,499, or 7.9% of the total state population. The major Protestant sects are the Mormons, with 27.1% of the total population in 1971, and the Methodist Church, with 3.4%. Other Protestant denominations comprised 18.5%. The Jewish population is less than 1%.

Among the three church-related colleges in Idaho, one is

a Catholic college. There is one Catholic high school with an enrollment of 444 students, and 12 Catholic elementary schools with 2,049 pupils. BIBLIOGRAPHY: C. Brosnan, *History of the State of Idaho* (4th ed., 1948); C. Bradley and E. Kelly, *History of the Diocese of Boise* (1953).

[J. L. MORRISON; R. M. PRESTON]

IDATIUS AND ITHACIUS, see HYDATIUS AND HYTHACIUS.

IDEALISM, any of a variety of philosophic positions that stress the mental or spiritual at the expense, or to the complete exclusion, of the material in accounting for the nature of human knowledge and of reality. In Western thought, the concept is extremely complex because of its application to a wide variety of theories, some of which approach a pure form of idealism, while others are admixtures of idealism and other elements. In a broad sense, scholars use the term to include all philosophies, maintaining that the immaterial or spiritual is the basic reality in the universe and its processes, in opposition to the naturalistic view of emergent forces in nature. But in a narrower sese, idealism usually identifies those philosophic outlooks that pose a critical dependence of the universe upon the mental or mind. While idealistic movements exist also in the Hindu and Buddhist thought of the East, present treatment is confined to the principal subdivisions of Western idealism—the subjective and the objective.

Subjective Idealism. Emphasizing the knowing subject as the true reality, and either minimizing or denying the existence of matter, this type of idealism is often called phenomenalism or mentalism. Only minds or spirits and their products—perceptions or ideas—exist, and these together constitute the totality of all that is. The so-called objects of ordinary human experience are not material realities but rather personal experiences of the knower; they exist only in the mind that knows them. In the final analysis, only minds and ideas exist.

The doctrine of the Irish epistemologist, George *Berkeley (1685–1753), sometimes termed ''immaterialism,'' typifies the attitudes of the subjective idealist. Presenting a logical extension of the reasoning of John Locke (1632–1704), Berkeley proclaims the basic tenet of his system, *esse est percipi* or ''to be is to be perceived.'' What man customarily refers to as the known object, (e.g., a tree or a dog) is ultimately but a collection of ideas in the human mind. The only existents, then, are the perceiver (the mind) and the perceived (the idea). These—the mind and the ideas it knows—constitute the whole of reality in man's experience, for he has truly experienced nothing apart from them. To explain the apparently independent, given world, God is introduced, the Supreme Mind, who determines the order and succession of our ideas and who in fact causes them to exist by constantly perceiving them. Hence, matter does not cause our ideas but rather do they come to us from God as an Infinite Spirit. In this view, the whole order of nature exists when not being perceived by man because God perceives it, since only as perceived can it exist. But man knows neither nature nor exterior reality, but only ideas concerning it which come to him from God.

Objective Idealism. Here, there is stress also upon the mental aspects of reality and of knowledge, but it is also affirmed that reality in its very nature is essentially mental or ideal, apart from any consideration of the knower. The universe is seen as an orderly and intelligible realm, the ultimate nature of which is mental or mind, and recognized as such by the human intellect.

Prominent among proponents of this view was *Plato in his theory of separated forms or ideas. According to this account, the truly real or the fundamental existents are the separated forms, otherwise termed ideas or essences, existing in a state apart from the ordinary phenomenal world of flux and change experienced by the senses. These are the exemplars or prototypes after which individual material objects are but copies. Hence, for Plato, there exist two realms. The first is that of the immaterial, immutable, and eternal ideas which serve as the models after which the things of creation are fashioned; only these are real in an ultimate sense. Secondarily, there is the sphere of the lowly material—the seen, the heard, the touched—the dwelling place of the copies; these are real, too, but only in an inferior and secondary sense. When the mind of man recognizes the identity of the classes of things it confronts, then, it does so because of a ''reminiscence'' or ''recollection'' of the forms or ideas with which the intellect is connatural and akin in its own immateriality.

Apart from the classic instances of subjective and objective idealism cited above, there exist many refinements of both, each with its own unique approach, and depending upon context and interpretation for classification. These would include the thought of René Descartes (1596–1650), Immanuel Kant (1724–1804), Georg Hegel (1770–1831), Friedrich Schelling (1775–1854), Josiah Royce (1855–1916), F. H. Bradley (1846–1924), T. H. Green (1836–82), Johann Fichte (1762–1814), Hermann Lotze (1817–81), and Hans Vaihinger (1852–1933). BIBLIOGRAPHY: A. C. Ewing, *Idealism: A Critical Survey* (3d ed., 1961); W. E. Hocking, *Types of Philosophy* (3d ed., 1958); *Idealist Tradition from Berkeley to Blanshard* (ed. A. C. Ewing, 1957).

[J. T. HICKEY]

IDEAS, DIVINE, the exemplars in God's mind of all actual and possible beings in their kind and perfection. For Christian theology the first expression of the divine being is the *Word of the Father; in the Word are uttered the divine being itself and all its created reflections, actual or possible (ThAq ST 1a, 34.3); the term idea is not, however, properly used of the Word, since it has the connotation of causality (*ibid.* ad 4; 15.1 ad 2). Adapting Platonic philosophy, esp. as read through *Plotinus, Augustine gave prominence to the divine ideas as patterns and sources both of angelic and human knowledge of truth, and of the gradated perfections in the universe; in this he was followed closely by St. *Bonaventure (see EXEMPLARISM). St. Thomas Aquinas considers the divine knowledge as causative, i.e., that all creation preexists cognitively in God as he is an intelligent being (1a, 14.3.5.8). The divine essence itself as intelligible "contains" the objective meanings and patterns of all things created or creatable; the multiplicity is one of objective meaning, not of ontological addition (*ibid* 15.1 & 2). As the intelligent cause of all, God does not act haphazardly; He is the exemplar cause of all reality (see EXEMPLARITY OF GOD). Trinitarian theology transforms these considerations through the doctrine of the Word, and of the pattern of communication among the divine persons being the model of the coming forth of creation (*ibid*. 45.6 & 7).

[T. C. O'BRIEN]

IDELSOHN, ABRAHAM ZEVI (1882–1938), Latvian musicologist. He founded in Jerusalem the Institute for Hebrew Music and taught at the Hebrew Union College in Cincinnati. Among his many lectures and writings, his best known work is the *Thesaurus of Hebrew Oriental Melodies* in 10 volumes.

[P. J. HENNESSEY]

IDENTIFICATION, a psychological reaction by which an individual, esp. in childhood, unconsciously imitates the attitudes, words, gestures, etc., of others, particularly parents, and incorporates them into his own self-image and his own ways of thinking and behaving. The main motivations behind identification with others are love and awe. Thorough self-knowledge, which is important in making moral and vocational decisions, must include conscious reflection on the people a person was identified with, and how the identification took place. The successful rearing of children demands the presence of adults who are religious, moral, and personal models, with whom the children can profitably identify.

[M. E. STOCK]

IDESBALD VAN DER GRACHT, (*c.*1100–67), a monk born in Flanders and brought up at court. In 1135 he was made canon of the church of St. Walburga at Furnes, but at midpoint of his life, he resigned. He then joined the abbey of Our Lady of the Dunes (on the sandhills between Dunkirk and Nieuwpoort), which followed the Savigny reform. He held the post of cantor, and later abbot. Pope Alexander III granted many privileges to the abbey under I., who died with a reputation of sanctity. His body was discovered (1623) incorrupt 450 years after his death, and since 1831 is in the church of the Augustinian nuns at Bruges. His cult was confirmed in 1894. He is patron of sailors and is invoked against rheumatism, gout, and fever. BIBLIOGRAPHY: J. De Cuyper, *Idesbald van der Gracht* (1946).

[N. F. GAUGHAN]

IDIOMELON, any Byzantine hymn with its own original melody (Gr. *idios*). It is distinguished from the *prosomoion,* which borrowed its melody.

[P. J. HENNESSEY]

IDIORRHYTHMIC MONASTICISM, a type of monastic life in which the monks, though subject to a superior whom they must obey in his regulation of external matters, nevertheless enjoy a considerable freedom in their private lives and may even retain possession of private property. This mode of life, adopted in imitation of early colonies of ascetics in the desert, was gradually introduced in certain Eastern monasteries and has persisted down to the present time.

[P. K. MEAGHER]

IDLENESS, as a moral defect, avoidance of activity because of its difficulty. In this sense it is a tendency that has to be controlled by the virtue of *courage and its connected virtues. Idleness also connotes *sloth and *negligence, because it implies a failure in matters of obligation. The term also describes a moral danger; there is a necessary and virtuous *leisure, but idleness as a failure to pursue positively any worthwhile activity is warned against in the sense that the vacuum will be filled by sinful activity. The term idle also has another connotation, as in the expression idle (baseless) gossip, and describes a word or act that is trivolous, pointless, or even irresponsible. In the sense that a morally defective act is one that fails to attend to the genuine moral good, idleness, the lack of right purpose and order in thought, word or action, is a characteristic of every sin.

[T. C. O'BRIEN]

IDUBERGA (IDA: ITTA), ST.(*c.*592–652), widow. Daughter of a count of Aquitaine and wife of Pepin of Landen, and thus, with him ancestor of the Carolingian line, I. was also the mother of SS. Begga and Gertrude, both of the abbey of Nivelles (Belgium), which she founded and where she is buried. Her cult and the cults of her husband, her daughters, and others are kept and renewed yearly at Nivelles. BIBLIOGRAPHY: J. J. Hoebanx, *L'Abbaye de Nivelles* (1952) 22–55; A. D'Haenens, BiblSanct 7:988.

[M. E. DUFFY]

IDUMEA, term used in LXX and Josephus for Edom. Idumea extended farther N than Edom, its N boundary being N of Hebron. Invading Nabateans had taken over Edom and forced the Idumeans north. Idumea was conquered by John Hircanus (125 B.C.) and Judaized. The family of Herod the Great was Idumean. BIBLIOGRAPHY: A. Robert, DB Suppl 4:195–199.

[E. J. CROWLEY]

IFE, see PHILIPPINE INDEPENDENT CHURCH.

IFFLEY, CHURCH OF, beautiful, small English Romanesque building (1170) in Iffley, Oxfordshire, England. The elaborate English decoration is in zigzag and other geometric designs upon the W front, extending into the elaborate interior, with west vaulting from the 13th century. The English Romanesque sculpture, though strongly influenced by France, shows at Iffley a revival of Anglo-Saxon "beak-head" ornament characteristic of the Herefordshire school, further seen at Kilpeck (*c.*1140) and Leominster priory (after 1141).

[M. J. DALY]

IGNATIAN SPIRITUALITY, see JESUIT SPIRITUALITY.

IGNATIUS, ST. (*c.*798–877), **PATRIARCH OF CONSTANTINOPLE** (847–858; 867–877). Son of Emperor Michael I, Ignatius became a monk under compulsion. His appointment as patriarch in 847 was irregular, but he consented to submit his case to Pope Leo IV. Amid growing political turmoil, however, he abdicated (858). *Photius succeeded him, but soon enemies of the government questioned the validity of Photius's accession, and another appeal was taken to Rome. Papal legates in Constantinople confirmed Photius, but Pope Nicholas I excommunicated him and supported Ignatius. Emperor Basil I reinstated I. in 867. Soon I. clashed with Pope John VIII about jurisdiction over the nascent Christian Church in Bulgaria. I. and Photius were reconciled and Photius, restored after I.'s death, canonized him. BIBLIOGRAPHY: F. Dvornik, *Photian Schism* (1948).

[R. H. SCHMANDT]

IGNATIUS OF ANTIOCH, ST., (d. shortly after 110 A.D.), bp. of Antioch, Apostolic Father, martyr. During a brief persecution at Antioch in the reign of Trajan, I. was condemned to be thrown to wild beasts and brought under guard to Rome. En route he wrote seven letters, four from Smyrna to the Churches at Ephesus, Magnesia, Tralles, and Rome; three from Troas to the Churches at Philadelphia and Smyrna and to Polycarp. In general, the letters warning their addressees against Judaizers and Docetist errors reveal a man totally devoted to Christ and yearning for martyrdom. Specifically, they refer to the aggregate of Christian communities as the Catholic Church (*Smyrnaeans* 8.2), bear early witness to the monarchic episcopate (*Magnesians* 3.1; 6.1; *Smyrnaeans* 8.1; *To Polycarp* 4.1, 6.1), and show special reverence for the Church at Rome (*Romans,* salutation). BIBLIOGRAPHY: Altaner 106–109; O. Penler, LTK 5:611–612; G. Bosio, BiblSanct 7:653–664.

[H. DRESSLER]

IGNATIUS OF JESUS (Carlo Leonelli; 1596–1667), Italian Carmelite Missionary who labored in Persia (1629–56) and Syria (1656–64). As superior in Basra he strove to convert the Mandaeans, a valuable account of whose cult he sent to Rome. He also compiled a Persian-Latin Dictionary and translated Robert Bellarmine's *Doctrina christiana* into Persian. BIBLIOGRAPHY: Ambrogio di S. Teresa, EncCatt 6:1601.

[M. J. SUELZER]

IGNATIUS OF LACONI, ST. (1701–81), Capuchin lay brother. From 1721 he led a humble life in various houses of his order in Italy. For years his mission was to beg alms for his monastery; he was celebrated for his kindness to children, the sick, the destitute, and for his power of healing, both natural and supernatural. He was canonized in 1951.

[J. R. AHERNE]

IGNATIUS OF LOYOLA, ST. (1491–1556), founder of the Society of Jesus and author of the renowned **Spiritual Exercises*. Little is known about his early life; his education was that of the young Spanish gentleman destined for military service and was characterized by an outmoded belief in chivalric virtues. When recovering from wounds received in Pamplona in 1521, I. partially rediscovered true fulfillment of these ideals in the books he read about the heroism of the saints and the perfection of Christ. In March 1522 he renounced the evils of his former life and at Manresa underwent a mystical experience that inspired the beginning of his *Exercises*. A pilgrimage to Jerusalem proved disillusioning, and he returned to Spain unsure of his future. In the next few years of study, ending at Paris (1528–35), he laid the foundations for the society. Francis Xavier and D. *Lainez were among the first companions who made vows with him in Paris, Aug. 15, 1534. After years of hardship and diligent work, I. witnessed the creation of what became the leading religious institute in the Counter Reformation, when Pope Paul III signed the bull of approval, *Regimini militantis Ecclesiae,* Sept. 27, 1540. The heart and spirit of the Jesuits can be found in the *Spiritual Exercises;* while essentially the record of their author's own religious conversion, they are also flexible enough to serve as a spiritual directory for others. They became a symbol of the spirit of Counter Reformation Catholicism. Significant as well among I.'s foundational contributions were the educational direction given the Society by his establishment in 1551 of the Collegio Romano and his fashioning and revisions, after experimentation, of the Jesuit *Constitutions*. BIBLIOGRAPHY: M. Foss, *Founding of the Jesuits* (1969); H. Outram Evennett, *Spirit of the Counter Reformation* (ed. J. Bossy, 1970).

[C. T. EBY]

IGNORANCE, the want of knowledge in a subject capable of it. In a subject incapable of it, a want of knowledge is a negation rather than a privation, and moralists usually call it nescience rather than ignorance. The capacity to know, however, is commonly estimated morally rather than physically, and a person is not called ignorant unless he lacks knowledge he could reasonably be expected to possess. Ignorance, being a lack of cognitive activity, differs from error, which is a mistaken judgment, though the two may be closely connected.

With respect to its influence on the morality of human action, Catholic moralists commonly distinguish between vincible and invincible ignorance, depending on whether or not it is capable of being dispelled by the application of reasonable diligence. Because it can be dispelled and is not, vincible ignorance is in one degree or another voluntary, and tends therefore to be identified with culpable ignorance when it is likely to lead or does in fact lead to wrongdoing. Invincible ignorance, being involuntary, is inculpable.

A distinction is drawn between ignorance of law (as when a person does not know it is illegal to possess heroin) and ignorance of fact (as when he is unaware of the fact that he is in possession of heroin).

Moralists in the Thomistic tradition distinguish between antecedent, concomitant, and consequent ignorance, a distinction based on a double consideration: the causal relationship of the will with respect to the ignorance itself and the causal relationship of the ignorance with respect to what is done. Antecedent ignorance precedes any act of the will accounting for the ignorance itself. But it is the cause (in a negative sense) of an agent's willing or doing something. He would not do what he does if he were not ignorant. Therefore the effect of such ignorance is to make the action involuntary and inculpable, and the agent is said to act out of ignorance.

Concomitant ignorance, like the antecedent, is not the result of the will's act, but unlike antecedent ignorance it has no causal relationship to what is done. One does not know what he is doing, yet would be quite prepared to do it, even if he did know, as when a man administers an unconscious snub to somebody he would gladly snub given an opportunity. One acting in concomitant ignorance acts not out of but with ignorance. What he does is not actually voluntary, but neither is it altogether involuntary, for it is not contrary to the agent's disposition. Therefore St. Thomas called such an act nonvoluntary rather than involuntary.

Consequent ignorance is the lack of knowledge which is voluntary because it is willed either directly or indirectly. In the former case it is called studied or affected ignorance, as when one deliberately closes his eyes to the truth in order not to be diverted from his evil ways. This worsens rather than lessens the wrong that is done.

Ignorance is indirectly voluntary when it is the result of no direct desire to be ignorant but rather of an unwillingness to take the trouble to dispel the ignorance. It could and should be dispelled by the use of reasonable diligence, and one fails to make the effort. The extent of the diligence that ought to be employed depends upon the circumstances such as the nature of the act and the extent of one's opportunities. In some situations, with something of importance at stake, great pains should be taken to be rid of the ignorance; in others, a considerably lesser effort would suffice. Reasonable diligence would be that which a good and prudent man would exercise in like circumstances. When little or no effort is made to dispel the ignorance, it is called crass or supine; when some, but still an inadequate, effort is made, it is called the ignorance of simple carelessness or negligence. In either case what is done under the influence of such ignorance is, simply speaking, voluntary, but it also contains an element of involuntariness that may attenuate in one degree or another the extent of one's culpability. BIBLIOGRAPHY: ThAq ST 1a2a, 6. 8 (Lat-Eng v. 17, ed. T. Gilby; v. 18, ed. T. Gilby; v. 25, ed. J. Fearon).

[T. GILBY]

IHS, a monogram for Jesus taken from the first three letters of his name in Greek (iota, ēta, sigma). It is often found in liturgical art and serves as an emblem for the Jesuits.

[T. M. MCFADDEN]

ILDEFONSUS, ST. (*c.*607–677), nephew and successor of St. Eugene as abp. of Toledo from 657. After becoming a monk of Agalia (near Toledo) against the will of his parents, I. soon rose to the office of abbot. In that capacity he attended the Councils of Toledo in 653 and 655. Of his many writings only four survive, the most famous of which is his *De viris illustribus,* a work important for the history of the Spanish Church of the 7th century. In his treatise on the Blessed Virgin, he defends the perpetual virginity of Mary and otherwise fosters devotion to her. His works on baptism and on the postbaptismal life journey of the Christian are also notable. Works: PL 96:9–330. BIBLIOGRAPHY: Butler 1:155–156; A. Braegelmann, *Life and Writings of St. Ildephonsus of Toledo* (1942).

[R. B. ENO]

ILGA, BL. (Hilga, Helga; d.*c.*1115), recluse. She reportedly lived in Schwarzenberg in the forest of Breganz. Tradition makes her the sister of Bl. Merbod and Bl. Diedo. Persons suffering from diseases of the eye visited a spring named for her. I. has never been canonized. BIBLIOGRAPHY: M. J. Finnegan, NCE 7:358.

[M. J. FINNEGAN]

ILLATIVE SENSE, in Scholastic philosophy, an inner sense relating to, or denoting inference from, premises to conclusions. It is another name for the *estimative power in man, also called the "particular reason." Such a sense is postulated on the theory that the sensory knowledge of man serves his mind; the illative sense perceives sense images in their order to intellectual assimilation and reasoned discourse.

[T. C. O'BRIEN]

ILLEGITIMACY, in canon law an *irregularity that bars reception of holy orders; also called an irregularity "from defect of birth." The irregularity is removed by religious profession in solemn vows or by *legitimation. Illegitimacy ceases automatically if the parents marry after the child is born.

[T. C. O'BRIEN]

ILLICIT, a term that qualifies an action as one that the law does not allow (Lat. *licet*). Particularly in canon law it is taken in distinction from "invalid," which categorizes an action as null and void. Thus some ecclesiastical laws invalidate contrary acts; others are merely prohibiting laws (CIC, c. 11). Matrimonial *impediments, for example, that are classified simply as "impediment," make marriages contracted without dispensation from them illicit; diriment impediments, even the concealed or unknown, make a marriage invalid.

[T. C. O'BRIEN]

ILLINOIS, a midwestern state, admitted to the Union as the 21st state in 1818. Fur traders, soon followed by missionaries, were the first white men to enter the area. In 1673 Louis Jolliet and Jacques *Marquette explored the river basins of Illinois, and in 1680 Robert Cavelier, de *la Salle, established Fort Crèvecoeur. The first white community was established (1700) near the mouth of the Kaskaskia River. When the area was ceded to Great Britain (1763), many French Catholic settlers moved to St. Louis or New Orleans. Protestant gains accompanied British control and increased with rapid American settlement after 1812. In 1839 Mormons entered Illinois, settling at Nauvoo. The murder of their leader, Joseph *Smith, by a mob at Carthage led to their departure for Utah in 1846. The first Catholic jurisdiction was established when the Illinois Country became part of the Diocese of Quebec in 1674. After the French lost control of the area, jurisdiction was transferred to the Diocese of Baltimore until 1808, when it became part of the Diocese of Bardstown, Kentucky.

The Diocese of Chicago was created by Gregory XVI in 1843. The first bp., William Quarter, finding only eight priests in the entire state, opened the College of St. Mary's as a seminary. During the next 4 years he ordained 29 priests, built 30 churches, and established national parishes for the Irish and Germans. Quarter's successors from 1849 until 1879 were James Oliver van de Velde, Anthony O'Regan, James Duggan, and Thomas Foley. In 1879 Chicago became an archdiocese. Its suffragans now include Belleville, Joliet, Peoria, Springfield, and Rockford. The first abp. Patrick A. Feehan, was an able administrator. During his episcopacy the number of churches increased to 298, priests to 538, elementary school students to 62,000, and the Catholic population to 800,000. Feehan died in 1902, and the following year Bp. James Edward Quigley was transferred from Buffalo to Chicago. He opened Cathedral College of the Sacred Heart as a preparatory seminary and supported the Catholic Church *Extension Society, founded (1905) by Francis C. *Kelley. After Quigley's death (1915), George William *Mundelein was appointed as Chicago's third archbishop. Mundelein expanded facilities at the new Quigley Preparatory Seminary and the old University of St. Mary of the Lake. A strong supporter of social reform, he founded Catholic Charities (1918) to conduct the welfare work of the archdiocese. Some 82 new parishes had been established and over 1,000 priests ordained by the time Samuel Alphonsus *Stritch succeeded Mundelein in 1940. Stritch's accomplishments included wider circulation of the *New World,* the archdiocesan newspaper; establishment of the the Confraternity of Christian Doctrine; expansion of Catholic Charities to include aid to the deaf and blind and to alcoholics; recognition of the Christian Family Movement and the Cana Movement; creation of special commissions on sacred music, radio, and television; and formation in 1945 of the Catholic Interracial Council to deal with the increase in Chicago's black population. In 1958 Albert Gregory Meyer succeeded Stritch, who had died in May. Although devoting himself largely to institutional problems, Meyer also supported the integration of Chicago's parishes, schools, and hospitals. A major figure in the American delegation to *Vatican Council II, he died in April 1965, and was succeeded by John P. Cody, Chicago's sixth archbishop. Cody has supported liberal, social, and ecclesiastical reforms, including civil rights and a more democratically structured church government.

Illinois' population of 11,231,439 is over 80% urban and makes it the 5th most populous state in the Union. In 1976 Catholics numbered 3,545,629, or 32.1% of the total state population. The major Protestant sects are the Methodist Church, with 5.3% of the population in 1971, and the Lutheran Church (Missouri Synod), with 3.2%. Other Protestant denominations comprised 13.3% of the population. The Jewish population, as of 1968, was 283,180, or 2.5%.

Twelve of the church-related colleges in Illinois are Catholic colleges. Six of these are in the Archdiocese of Chicago, which also contains 76 of the state's 114 Catholic high schools. Catholic high school enrollment in the state exceeds 85,000. There are 694 Catholic elementary schools in Illinois, with a total enrollment of 225,464 pupils. BIBLIOGRAPHY: *Centennial History of Illinois* (ed. C. W. Alvord, 6 v., 1917–20); T. C. Pease, *Story of Illinois* (rev. ed., 1949); G. J. Garraghan, *Catholic Church in Chicago, 1673–1871* (1921).

[J. L. MORRISON; R. M. PRESTON]

ILLITERACY, the inability to read or write any language, a defect that puts a person at a disadvantage in a society in which the culture is transmitted, and people communicate with one another, by means of script. The disadvantage becomes notable at an age when the child becomes less dependent on his parents and begins to fend for himself. Hence the illiteracy rate in a society is generally expressed in terms of the percentage of the population beyond 10 years of age who cannot read or write. In Christian lands and cent. the use of written language has always been important for religious as well as other cultural purposes. At some times and in some places other means of communication have been used with varying success. After the decline of Roman civilization, the Church took the lead, often under unfavorable circumstances, in promoting education, establishing cathedral, monastic, guild, chantry, and grammar schools, as well as colleges and universities. In modern society civil government generally recognizes the need of an enlightened citizenry and is concerned to provide educational opportunity and to enforce school attendance. Despite these efforts, UNESCO reported in 1975 that the number of illiterate adults had risen to 800,000,000 from 735,000,000 in 1965. The effort to overcome this deficiency goes on, and the Churches, esp. in their missionary programs, devote a large part of their manpower and other resources to that end.

[P. K. MEAGHER]

ILLTUD, ST. (5th–6th cent.), one of the founders of Welsh monasticism, in whose story fact and legend are inextricably intertwined. Probably of Breton origin, he is believed to have founded a monastery and school at Llantwit Major (Llanilltud Fawr), Glamorgan, where many Welsh monastic leaders were among his pupils. BIBLIOGRAPHY: I. Evans, NCE 7:366; Butler 4:274–276; G. H. Doble, *St. Iltut* (1944).

[R. W. HAYS]

ILLUMINATED MANUSCRIPTS. Illumination is the use of color (including gold and silver) for decoration, text, or illustrations in books. Colored illustrations in papyrus rolls can be dated at least to the 20th cent. B.C. in Egypt where the *Book of the Dead* provides numerous examples. In Hellenistic times the book trade was significantly stimulated by the Alexandrian Library (3d cent.), and it is probable that de luxe, illustrated editions of Homer were regularly for sale. The 4th-cent. *Milan Iliad* (Ambrosiana Cod. F. 205) and the *Vatican Vergil* (Lat. 3225) with their profusion of illustrations are probably replicas of ancient, de luxe book production, but in the later codex form. In spite of the OT attitude towards graven images, illuminated Bibles appeared in the West at least by the 6th cent., for Cassiodorus mentions illustrations of the tabernacle and temple appearing in one of his Bibles. In the East, Byzantine portraiture became stylized, but illumination was lavish, including purple parchment with gold and silver inks for text and decoration (e.g., *Cotton Genesis,* British Museum; *Rossano Gospels,* Rossano Cathedral; *Codex Anicia Juliana,* Vienna Cod. Graec. Med. I). In the West, Irish and Northumbrian illumination begins about the 7th cent. and owes much to Eastern influence, although the *Book of Kells* (Trinity College, Dublin) and *Lindisfarne Gospels* (British Museum) exhibit a startling amount of native artistic creation. Manuscripts of Fulda, Luxeuil, and St. Gall (abbeys founded by English and Irish monks) as well as Byzantine styles influenced the artists of the Caroline Renaissance (e.g., *Ada Gospels,* Trèves, Cod. 22).

From Alfred's time (d. 899) English illumination was strongly influenced by Continental styles (e.g., that of the *Utrecht Psalter*), but the *Winchester Bible* (*c.*1160, Winchester, Old Minster) and the *Queen Mary's Psalter* (*c.*1330, British Museum) are magnificent examples of an independent artistic creativity that persisted through the centuries. On the Continent the Caroline tradition was carried on under the Ottos, particularly at Reichenau (e.g., *Heidelberg Sacramentary,* Heidelberg Univ.). Later, under Renaissance influence which emphasized realistic portrayal of nature, MS illumination became more elaborate with full borders and pictures; here *Books of Hours* (*Horae*) are the most outstanding examples (e.g., those of the Duc de Berry), although Psalters, Missals, Breviaries as well as secular works were lavishly illuminated (including gold leaf) throughout Western Europe in these last years before MS illumination was relegated to an esoteric art by the invention of Gutenberg. BIBLIOGRAPHY: D. Bland, *History of Book Illustration* (1958); J. Herbert, *Illuminated Manuscripts* (1911); K. Weitzmann, *Ancient Book Illumination* (1959).

[F. J. WITTY]

ILLUMINATI, ORDER OF, established (1776) in Bavaria, a secret organization first called the Perfectibilists. The founder was Johann Adam Weishaupt (1748–1830), prof. of law at the Univ. of Ingolstadt. A system of gradually more elaborate degrees initiated the members into the arcana of the society; they were to achieve progressive illumination through the study of rationalistic philosophy and the humanities. Initiation included an exhaustive life confession and oaths of absolute secrecy and blind obedience to the leaders, whose identity was known only to the highest initiates. The spread of the society throughout Germany and Austria and into France was achieved by infiltration of the lodges of Freemasons. Through revelations by disaffected members, the secrets of the society became known to the civil authorities, and it was outlawed by the elector of Bavaria in 1785. Some historians classify the Illuminati simply as a rationalistic movement, embodying the spirit of the *Enlightenment and mingling itself with the Freemasons. G. Bareille, however, offers evidence that the secrecy and recruitment of the order were aimed by its founder at destroying all authority—domestic, civil, and ecclesiastical. The aim was to retrieve the liberty and equality supposed as a natural primitive human condition suppressed by law and private property. In 1896 a form of the Illuminati was restored in Germany; it went through a reorganization in 1925, but apparently was disbanded under the Nazi proscription of secret societies. BIBLIOGRAPHY: G. Bareille, DTC 7:756–766; R. Le Forestier, *Les Illuminés de Bavière et la Franc-Maçonnerie Allemande* (1950). *ROSICRUCIANS; *ALUMBRADOS.

[T. C. O'BRIEN]

ILLUMINATION OF THE DYING, a special grace at the moment of death which, according to a recent theological conjecture, enables each man (and according to some theologians, the unbaptized infant) to perceive himself and his past life in relationship to the infinite perfection of God. Enlightened by this illumination, each individual makes an ultimate decision for God or against him. The proponents of this theory argue that it is only with such a clear vision of God's goodness and the separation from him that sin entails, that eternal salvation or damnation should depend. Although there is no specific basis for this theory in Scripture or tradition, it does not seem to be contrary to Christian doctrine, for nothing in revelation compels us to believe it lies beyond the power of God to grant such a grace. BIBLIOGRAPHY: A. Winklehofer, *Coming of His Kingdom* (tr. A. Littledale, 1963).

[T. M. MCFADDEN]

ILLUMINATIVE WAY, the second general stage in the spiritual growth of a person who is striving after *Christian perfection according to the three spiritual ways (see WAYS, THREE SPIRITUAL). It is marked with a progressive movement toward total generosity in God's service. Deliberate sin has generally been left behind, and there is a concentrated effort to overcome imperfections. The *night of the senses has been experienced and the *night of the soul is approaching. Religious practices are less numerous, more simple and fervent, prayer attains a certain simplicity, and mystical illumination leading to infused contemplation is an increasingly frequent experience. While there is a genuine increase in love for God and one's fellow man, there is a growing attraction for silence and solitude, and a yearning for complete union with God in heaven. This stage is equivalent to the Fourth and Fifth Mansions in Teresa of Avila's *Interior Castle*. BIBLIOGRAPHY: A. Royo, *Theology of Christian Perfection* (tr. J. Aumann, 1962); R. Garrigou-Lagrange, *Three Ages of the Interior Life* (2 v., tr. M. T. Doyle, 1947–1948).

[M. B. PENNINGTON]

ILLUMINÉS, also called, with doubtful accuracy, *Guérinets; a group in Picardy in the late 17th cent. affected by religious *illuminism and accused of heresy. They were suppressed by ecclesiastical and civil powers.

[T. C. O'BRIEN]

ILLUMINISM, RELIGIOUS, a classification for teachings that rely upon a mystical or intuitive divine enlightenment. In this sense it has been applied most regularly to the doctrines of the Gnostics, the *Alumbrados, the *Illuminés of P. Guérin. It has also been used as an equivalent to *enthusiasm, and has been so applied to individuals and movements throughout church history that have deviated from authority or official teaching on the basis of appeal to a higher light. Illuminism has also been used to refer to the exaltation of the clear light of reason characteristic of the *Enlightenment.

[P. DELETTER]

ILLUSION, either a perceptual error by which one object or event is wrongly taken for another or a judgmental deception based on a faulty premise or misleading data. Everyone is subject to illusions; the magician's trade depends on producing illusions for the entertainment of an audience. Some objects or events are structured so ambiguously that they cannot be definitely perceived in one way, e.g., the familiar optical illusions. Since emotions affect perception and judgment, people are frequently under illusions concerning things that touch them deeply, e.g., parents about their children, lovers about their beloved. When illusions are the effect of deep, unconscious attitudes and prejudices they become psychologically harmful. Morally, a constant and serious effort to rid oneself of illusions in order to arrive at truth, esp. about God, self, and neighbor, is part of the progress toward Christian maturity.

[M. E. STOCK]

ILLYRICUM, the ancient name given the Balkan peninsula region, encompassing Dalmatia, Rhaetia, Noricum, Pannonia, Moesia, and Macedonia. It remained within the Western half of the Roman Empire at its division in 324 with Sirmium the praetorian residence of this prefecture. A further division in 379 left W Illyricum subject to the Italian prefect, while the rest became absorbed into the Eastern Empire (395). Ecclesiastically under papal jurisdiction, it belonged politically to Byzantium, a situation that precipitated and prolonged East-West tension. During the Acacian schism, the bps. of Thessalonica, the leading see, withdrew from communion with Rome, but in 515 reaffirmed their loyalty to Pope Hormisdas. The *Notitiae episcoporum* shows that at the close of the 9th cent. E Illyricum was under the patriarchate of Constantinople. Western Illyricum was subjugated by the Avars in the 6th cent. and by the Serbs and Croats a century later. The E coast and the islands of the Adriatic remained under Byzantine control until they came under Venetian dominion in the 11th century. Eastern Illyricum was divided among the Byzantines, Bulgarians, and Serbs and in the early Middle Ages disappeared as a cohesive entity. BIBLIOGRAPHY: E. Dvornik, *Making of Central and Eastern Europe* (1949).

[L. NEMEC]

ILLYRICUS, MATTHIAS FLACIUS, see FLACIUS ILLYRICUS, MATTHIAS.

ILLYRICUS, THOMAS (*c.*1485–1528), Slavic Franciscan of the Observance, anti-Lutheran preacher in Italy, Germany, and France. He also published polemical writings; in his *Libellus de potestate summi pontificis* (1523) he favored the superiority of a general council over the pope.

[T. C. O'BRIEN]

IMAGE, see IMAGES, VENERATION OF.

IMAGE AND LIKENESS, phrase used in Gen 1.26 to describe man's creation according to the divine *ṣelem* (image) and *demût* (likeness). By using both terms, the author softens the usual meaning of *ṣelem,* exact reproduction, to resemblance or similarity. The phrase does not mean that God has a body of which man is the physical image. For the Jew, image would not necessarily imply any identity of corporeal form between the image and its object. Rather man is in the divine image and likeness insofar as he is God's representative on earth. Man acts upon and has dominion over the world of creation, thereby reflecting the reality of the living, creating God of Genesis. Although the OT must not be interpreted in the light of theological systems foreign to the authors' minds, the phrase is open to the interpretation that man represents God insofar as he enjoys an intellect and will. The creation narratives present God as choosing and ordering all things by his wisdom: these attributes constitute him as an active agent exercising his sovereignty over the universe. By application, man can exercise this same domination only by his faculties of knowing and willing. BIBLIOGRAPHY: P. Van Imschoot, *Theology of the Old Testament* (1965). *IMAGE OF GOD.

[T. M. MCFADDEN]

IMAGE NOT MADE BY HANDS (Gr., *acheiropoiētos*), term applied to images reputed to be of divine, or at least supernatural, origin. The best-known icon of this sort, often called simply the *acheiropoiētos,* is that which Byzantine tradition claims to be the face of Christ miraculously imprinted by the Savior himself on a piece of linen and sent to King Abgar V of Edessa. The East has always regarded this image as a material testimony of the Incarnation and of the possibility of representing the divine. In many places this icon is carried in procession and venerated on the Sunday of Orthodoxy which recalls the defeat of iconoclasm. The icon depicts only the face of Christ with neither neck nor shoulders visible and with long hair falling in locks on either side. As is customary, the halo is inscribed with a cross, whose top three segments contain the Greek letters, OWH, referring to Ex 3.14: "I am who am." Then, the letters, IC XC (abbreviation of Jesus Christ), are written on either side of the head. The two inscriptions, traditionally found on all icons of Christ, visually recall the divine and the human natures of the Savior. The term has also been applied to the image of Christ preserved in the Lateran basilica in Rome. It is also used metaphorically of the body of the Virgin Mary as a tabernacle for the Incarnate Word. BIBLIOGRAPHY: H. Leclercq, DACL 7:225–226; 8:1611; L. P. Siger and L. A. Leite, NCE 7:961–962.

[A. J. JACOPIN]

IMAGE OF GOD, the theological description of man based on Gen 1.26 (see IMAGE AND LIKENESS). Theology has taken this description both as the key to the makeup of man's being and as the revelation of the fulfillment towards which God's loving care is moving him. Latin theology's understanding of the imaging of the divine was strongly dependent on *Pseudo-Dionysius's theme, the dynamic likening to the divine that constitutes the hierarchic governance of angels and men in their going forth from and return to God (*proodos-epistrophē*). St. *John Damascene was also a notable authority used. But St. Augustine's development of the image within the spiritual being (*mens*) of man as an analogue of the Trinity was the primary inspiration of later theological anthropology. The preeminent image of the Trinity is the *mens,* its self-knowledge and its self-love: the *mens* (the soul as it includes the spiritual powers of knowing and loving) is the source that begets a "word" in knowing itself and breathes forth a love for what is known in the word. The completion of the image consists in being united to the divine Persons in knowing and loving them. St. Thomas Aquinas, adapting Augustine's language to his own conception of knowing and loving, speaks of the "image of creation," the "image of recreation," and the "image of completed likeness," a triplet taken from a gloss on Ps 4.7 (ThAq ST 1a, 93.4). Under the image theme he organizes the essentials of RC belief about the economy of grace. The "image of creation" present in everyone is the openness of the human being to being drawn into God's own life; the power to know all being intellectually and to love the good appreciatively are a receptivity to a kind of likening to God that surpasses that of any other being in the material creation. That likening is a share in the divine good that God is (*ibid.,* 1a2ae, 110.1; see DIVINE NATURE, PARTAKER OF); it is "having to do with" God as the immediate object of knowing and loving (see *ibid.* 1a, 8.3). Any other likening to the divine consists in the creature's relationship to its own created perfection, which de facto reflects God as cause of every created good. But the unmediated relationship to the divine that is proper to the divine life itself is the kind of relationship that being in God's image means. For this reason the "image of creation" is described as "aptitudinal," and in the scholastics' terminology, an *obediential potency to be the recipient of God's grace. Only this gift can form man into being a sharer in the divine life itself; the truth of that gift being believed, however, theology has the key to an evaluation of man's highest dignity that by creation itself God has made the reception of his grace possible. The "image of recreation" is actually present where grace is fully received; but this image is neither an ethical goodness nor a static possession. The Christian life of grace consists primarily in the operation, the activity of the theological virtues; everything else is subordinated to the actual working of faith, hope, and charity. For God's own Trinitarian life is the knowing that begets the Word and the love that breathes forth the Holy Spirit. To be in God's image means sharing in a life of knowing and loving Father, Son, and Holy Spirit. That concretely is an "image of recreation" because it is the redemptive Incarnation that fashions it. Christ is the exemplar and the truest image of God (see Rom 8.29; Col 1.15), for he is the Son of God; being in God's image means being in the likeness of Christ; it is adoptive filiation conformed to Christ's natural filiation (see Eph 1.5; ThAq ST 3a, 23). That comes about, of course, in virtue of Christ's Passion and Resurrection; the recreation of man is reconciliation and restoration after the disfigurement of sin. The Christian life of the virtues and of the sacraments is a redemptive process in its negative, purgative, and expiatory side; but the objective is always the intensification of the imitation of Christ, in uttering with him ''Abba, Father'' through the Holy Spirit (see Rom 8.15; Gal 4.5–7). The ''image of completed likeness'' is the term of the process of salvation. It is the sharing in the inheritance of sons of God; the completed being with and likeness to the Trinity is the contemplative and loving rest in the Word proceeding from the Father and the Holy Spirit coming forth as the expression of their love. That is why the immediate anticipation of that fulfillment consists in the indwelling of the divine Persons in the soul through the more intense spiritual experiences of the gift of *wisdom and the quickening of charity (see ThAq ST 1a, 43.3 & 6).

BIBLIOGRAPHY: J. E. Sullivan, *Image of God: the Doctrine of St. Augustine and Its Influence* (1963); ThAq ST (Lat-Eng. v. 13, ed. E. Hill) xxi–xxxi; 209–212; *ibid.* (v. 7, ed. T. C. O'Brien) 259–265; *ibid.* (v. 50, ed. C. E. O'Neill) 250–257.

[T. C. O'BRIEN]

IMAGE OF GOD (IN THE BIBLE). In the theology of the Priestly creation narrative (Gen 1.1–2.4a) God's final act was the creation of mankind in his image: ''Let us make man in our image, after our likeness, and let him have dominion over . . . all creatures. . . . So God created man in his own image; in the image of God he created him; male and female he created them.'' (Gen 1.26, 27.) Given the monotheistic intent of the priestly account to exalt God as the one and only Creator of the ordered universe, which was ''very good'' (Gen 1.31), the use of the word image (*ṣelem*) is surprising, for it is used in other texts for idols (Am 5.26; Ezek 7.20). The inference is that in all creation only mankind is a true image and graphic representation of God. Men, then, are more akin to God, and the unseen beings of his court in heaven, than they are to animals over whom, like God, they enjoy rule and dominion. The later Greek elaboration of this concept, which makes man's higher intelligence and will the specification of the imaging of God, is more dependent on Greek than on Hebrew anthropology and actually shifts the imaging from man's closeness to God (the obvious intent of the passage) to his superiority over animals. But for the Hebrew theologian man's superiority over animals at creation is the result of his closeness to God, not of his observed difference from other living beings. The conclusion from this doctrine is that there is nothing in the created order before which man must bow down: he must worship and serve God alone, not simply as creature before his Creator, but as a divine servant in God's intimate family, who is to act as God's regent and to share in the creative and governing power over all other beings. Such an exalted revelation of man's worth and identity, one of the highest points of Hebrew theology, finds its ultimate culmination in the NT's theology of the Incarnation and the identity of Jesus as the unique Son of God and the new Adam: through his service offered to his Father for man's Redemption from sin and death, he reconciles man to God and recreates him to be a participant in the divine nature itself. Those who accept Jesus as the ultimate regent for God in God's final act of creation and governance will share with Christ, the first-born of many brothers, eternal, intimate presence with the Father.

[J. F. FALLON]

IMAGES, BIBLICAL PROHIBITION OF. It is not absolutely clear from the texts exactly what is forbidden: images of foreign gods, of Yahweh, or of both. Images of foreign gods seem to be forbidden by the first commandment (Ex 20.3; Dt 5.7). These images would have been familiar to the Israelites from surrounding peoples. The polemic of both the preaching and writing prophets against idols makes it evident that this was forbidden. There are scholars who argue that the second part of the commandment (Ex 20.4; Dt 5.8) refers to a prohibition of images of Yahweh since the preceding verse clearly has reference to images of other gods and would not have to be repeated. This is not absolutely clear. It seems to have been taken for granted, however, that Yahweh could not be imaged. Perhaps it was only explicitated in later times. Deuteronomy 4.15 mentions the reason why no image is to be made of Yahweh: at Horeb in the great theophany there was no form seen and therefore nothing to imitate. The golden calves mentioned in connection with the N kingdom (1 Kg 12.26–30) and in Ex 32 seem to have been understood rather as pedestals for the invisible Yahweh than as an image of him. The bronze serpent and the seraphim mentioned in the OT were apparently not images of Yahweh and therefore not forbidden in early times. It was only later when a more rigid interpretation was given to the prohibition (perhaps because of popular confusion of the cult object and the deity) that these things were totally outlawed. To date archeology has discovered nothing that appears to be an image of Yahweh. The ark was only to be a symbol of Yahweh's presence. The cherubim adorning it are more difficult to understand. They seem to be copies of images of a type that represented guardians of important places—the palace, throne, or temple—in contemporary cultures. The purpose underlying the prohibition of images is to preserve the transcendence of Yahweh and to emphasize his total otherness (Is 40.12–19). Some of the later rabbis understood the prohibition to include all images of anything at all. This was neither universally taught nor accepted. BIBLIOGRAPHY: W. Eichrodt, *Theology of the Old Testament* (tr. J. A. Baker, 2 v., 1961); A. S. Herbert, *Worship in Ancient Israel* (1959); and G. von Rad, *Old Testament* (tr. D. M. G. Stalker, 2 v., 1962).

[F. GAST]

IMAGES, VENERATION OF, a practice declared at the Council of Nicaea II in 787 (D 600–603) to be sacred and sanctioned by the most ancient traditions of the Church. This solemn declaration against *iconoclasm applied to representations, in whatever form, of the Crucifixion; figures on sacred vessels or vestments; icons of Christ, Mary, the angels, and saints. The veneration, distinct from the *latria offered to God alone, is right because it is directed towards the person imaged. Expressions of veneration include the kissing and incensation of images, placing lights and candles before them. St. Thomas Aquinas indicates that images of Christ are venerated with the latria due to the Divine Person; the true cross is venerated in the same way that Christ crucified is, because it represents him suspended on it, and because of its contact with his body; other crucifixes are venerated purely as images. The relics of saints are included in the meaning of images and are venerated accordingly (ThAq ST 3a, 25). Abuses in the Church led to the Reformers' condemnation of the whole practice, as contrary to the OT proscriptions against graven images. Superstition does occur, but that is not the intent of the teaching on venerating images; and the antiquity as well as the purpose of it are well attested by Christian archeology.

[T. C. O'BRIEN]

IMAGINATION AND FANTASY, the mental capacity to reproduce in imagery sense apprehensions and perceptions (not only visual but also auditory, tactile, etc.) in the absence of the original objects. When related directly to past experiences as actually experienced, this capacity is called memory; when related to future possibilities of action, to problem-solving and the expression of thoughts and feelings, it is creative. In imagination, images tend to associate with each other on the basis of similarities, contrasts, and contiguity in past experience. In actual perceptions, therefore, the results of past experiences are associated with the objects presently perceived, and this contributes to the depth and richness of the present encounter. Fantasy or imagination elicits drives and *emotions which may motivate practical action or be merely experienced in daydreaming. Human intelligence depends on imagination for its source materials from which to draw rational meaning and order. Imagination is generally weaker and vaguer than sense perception except for so-called eidetic images and hallucinations.

[M. E. STOCK]

IMAGINES, painted waxen Roman portrait masks of ancestors, worn in funeral processions by the nobility, displayed on ceremonial occasions, and kept in family shrines with a record of the life of the person.

[M. J. DALY]

IMAGINISTS, members of a literary group in Moscow (1919–24), distinguished by their use of free verse forms and by the excessive, often crude, imagery of their poetry. The ''hooliganism'' by which they expressed their disenchantment with the Revolution and its aftermath is described by Sergey Alexandrovich Yesenin (1895–1925), the only great poet whom the movement produced, in *Tavern Moscow* (1924) and *Confession of a Hooligan* (1924). BIBLIOGRAPHY: R. Poggioli, *Poets of Russia: 1890–1930* (1960) 238–240, 252–253; D. S. Mirsky, *Contemporary Russian Literature* (1926) 265–266.

[M. F. MCCARTHY]

IMAM, an Arabic term (pl. *a'imma*) commonly used in *Islam in three senses, all derived from a basic notion of ''leader.'' It is used to designate (1) the person who leads the congregational prayer (whether a professional, formally attached to a religious institution, or any layman). By the *Sunnites it is used (2) to indicate the *caliph as leader of the Muslim community and also as an honorific title given to a number of renowned religious figures. The *Shiites, who hold that the only true caliphs are descendants of Ali, use the term (3) as a strict equivalent of caliph, referring exclusively to those whom they recognize as divinely ordained successors of the Prophet, wherefore they are frequently called the Imamites or, in Arabic, Imâmîya. For all Shiite sects other than the *Zaidis, the term takes on a special significance in that they hold that the Imam is endowed with supernatural knowledge and powers, passed down through the descendants of Ali and Fatima, from father to son in specially designated individuals. The divinely ordained Imam, they hold, is the unique guardian of Islam and the sole authoritative teacher of the true faith. It is their belief that the Imam (different with each sect) is presently ''hidden'' and they await his glorious return as **Mahdi*, when he will usher in a new era. BIBLIOGRAPHY: W. Ivanov, EncIslam[1].

[R. M. FRANK]

IMELDA, BL. (1321–33), declared in 1910 child patroness of first communicants. Before the age of 12 she entered the Dominican cloister at Valdipietra near Bologna, Italy. She died after receiving her first communion, given to her because of the appearance of a Host over her head as the nuns were receiving and she was waiting, not yet of sufficient age. She was beatified in 1826; more recently some have questioned details of her vita.

[T. C. O'BRIEN]

IMHOTEP, architect of the famed Stepped Pyramid at Saqqara (in stone rather than brick), built for King Djeser of the Third Dynasty. I., later worshipped by Egyptians as god of healing, was called Imouthes by the Greeks, who identified him with Asclepios.

[M. J. DALY]

IMITATION OF CHRIST, a popular devotional book. Since its anonymous appearance about 1418, this has become after the Bible the most widely circulated book in Christian literature, translated into more than 50 languages, and many times into English, by John Wesley among others. Its authorship by *Thomas à Kempis has been questioned yet now seems more established than ever (cf. summary of recent scholarship by W. Jappe Aberts, NCE 7:375–377). It is a juxtaposition without logical connection of four treatises or sets of soliloquies probably composed independently. They consist of "admonitions," first, about freeing oneself from worldly cares and preparing for conversation with God; second, for promoting the interior life; third, concerning the consolations that follow; and fourth, on the devout reception of holy communion. It was a classical expression of the **devotio moderna*, which not only reacted against an arid scholasticism in theology, but also sought a style simpler, more artless, and more popular than that of the Dominican Rhineland mystics (though it lingered over *Henry Suso's *Eternal Wisdom*), and went back to evangelical and early monastic sources and notably to St. *Bernard. Its emphasis was on loving rather than knowing: "better to feel compunction than to know what it is." This, almost amounting to an exclusion, combined with a lack of exactness in its contempt for creatures, makes it noncompulsory and even embarrassing reading for those whom our Lord calls to follow him without violence to their intellectual passion for the truth and their humanist sympathies. There are many more, however, who are warmed by the practical persuasions of this famous manual and by the "positivist" communication of the author's own experience. BIBLIOGRAPHY: S. Axters, *Spirituality of the Old Low Countries* (tr. D. Attwater, 1954).

[T. GILBY]

IMMACULATE CONCEPTION, the conception by her mother of the Blessed Virgin Mary. "In the first instant of her conception, by a singular grace and privilege of almighty God in consideration of the merits of Jesus Christ, savior of the human race, the Blessed Virgin Mary was preserved from all stain of original sin. This doctrine has been revealed by God and must, therefore, firmly and constantly be believed by all the faithful" (Pius IX, *Ineffabilis Deus,* Dec. 8, 1854; D 2803). This belief, infallibly defined as above, is a derivative of the nearly universal acceptance, among Eastern Churches as well as among Western Protestants, of the unique holiness of Mary; but only the RC Church has so carefully defined it as to include this Immaculate Conception.

The scriptural basis for believing Mary's complete holiness, including her exemption from the inherited sin of all men, is said to begin with as ancient a text as Gen 3.15: "I will make you enemies of each other, you and the woman, your offspring and her offspring. It [in Hebrew; "he" in Greek; "she" in Vulgate] will crush your head and you will strike its heel." The text "Rejoice, so highly favored!" for Lk 1.28 is less a tribute to Mary's perfect holiness, but is more faithful to the Greek, than the "Hail, full of grace!" which is the translation of the Vulgate. More relevant to the present question is Lk 1.30–32: "You have won God's favor. You are to conceive and bear a son . . . Jesus . . . Son of the Most High"—a unique, God-directed role that calls for a preeminent resemblance of Mary to what Paul (Rom 8.2) calls "the spirit of life in Christ Jesus . . . free from sin and death." What he says of Christians would be perfectly true of Mary: " . . . the Spirit of God has made his home in you. . . . If Christ is in you . . . then your spirit is life itself because you have been justified" (Rom 8.9–10).

The history of the development of this dogma is the longest and most philosophically debated of all the Church's beliefs about Mary. Her holiness and virginity were accepted during the first centuries as corollaries of the divinity of her Son; her Assumption would be declared a dogma later (1950), but it never was the controversial issue among theologians that the Immaculate Conception had been. St. Justin (d. *c.*165) in his *Dialogus cum Tryphone Judaeo* (100; Pl 6:710), St. Irenaeus (d. *c.*202) in *Contra haereses* (5.1.2; PG 7:1122), and Tertullian (d. after 220) in *De carne Christi* (17; PL 2:781–782) apply to Mary and Eve Paul's parallel of Christ and Adam (Rom 5.12–21; 1 Cor 15.45–49) and attribute sinlessness to Mary in contrast to the sinfulness of Eve. St. Hippolytus (d. 235 or 236) compares, in much detail and complexity, Jesus and Mary, calling the Messiah an ark of incorruptible wood formed of material that had never known corruption (*Apud Theodoretum, Eranistes;* PG 10:610). St. Ephrem of Syria (d. 373) writes, "There is in thee, Lord, no stain, nor any spot in thy mother" (*Carmina Nisibena,* ed. J. Bickell, 1866), an accommodation of S of S 6.7. St. Ambrose (d. 397) wrote of Mary as "virgin incorrupt, a virgin by grace, entirely free from every stain of sin" (*In Ps. 118 exp.;* PL 15:782) who "alone obtained a grace none other can claim: to be filled with the very Author of grace" (*In exp. Luc.* 1.29.9; PL 15:1556). St. Augustine (d. 430) is the most explicit of the Fathers: "From him we know what abundance of grace . . . was conferred upon her who undoubtedly had no sin" (*Nat. et grat.* 36.42; PL 44:267).

The official theology of the RC Church concerning this mystery began with the Ecumenical Council of Ephesus (431), which insisted on the true divinity of Christ and specified the corollary that Mary is Mother of God (Gr. *theotokos,* Lat. *Dei genitrix*). Christ's divinity required, for St. Proclus (d. 446), patriarch of Constantinople, that God "make her for himself without any stain" (*Or. laud. BVM;* PG 65:683). Pope St. Anastasius I (d. 401) and St. Sophronius (d. 638), patriarch of Jerusalem, added their tributes to Mary's sinlessness.

It was opposition to the notion of the Immaculate Conception that clarified its subtleties and established its theological basis. In England arguments for and against a feast of the conception of Mary led to the composition of *De conceptione BVM* by the Benedictine monk Eadmer *c.*1130

(PL 159:301–318) in its favor, and to its condemnation by St. Bernard of Clairvaux in a letter to the canons at Lyons *c.*1140 (Letter 174; PL 182:332–336)—because God could not be associated miraculously with an evil like conception! St. Thomas Aquinas (d. 1274), because of his concepts of the universality of both original sin and Christ's Redemption, could exempt Mary from neither the contagion of, nor salvation from, sin (ST 3a, 27.2 ad 2). St. Thomas distinguished between Mary's ordinary conception and an extraordinary purification from sin before birth, but it was Duns Scotus (d. 1308) who distinguished between Mary's deserving original sin like all human creatures and her being purified by preservation at the moment of conception—a prevenient grace that would include her among those saved by Christ—a unique gift (*In 3 sent.* 3.1; Vivès 14:171). This distinction dominated the Dominican-Franciscan disputes, which continued into the 16th cent., and became the basis of Church declarations like Sixtus IV's *Cum praeexcelsa* of 1477 and *Grave nimis* of 1483. The Council of Trent (1545–63) in its statement on original sin specifically denied any intention to deal with the case of Mary, while including her among those redeemed by Christ (D 1516). St. Pius V's condemnation of Baius in 1567 included a defense of Mary's preservation from sin; in 1568 he established the feast of the Immaculate Conception. Alexander VII's *Sollicitudo omnium ecclesiarum* of 1661 described Mary's exemption in words similar to those which were to be used by Pius IX in 1854.

In the 20th cent. Pope Pius XII proclaimed (1950) the *Assumption of Mary as the crowning event of a life of unique sinlessness, holiness, proximity to and cooperation with Christ's divinity and Redemption. In 1964 Vatican Council II (ConstChurch 59) reiterated Mary's perfect holiness and described it as a model for the Church. Paul VI's *Credo of the People of God* (1968) repeated the traditional belief in her special sinless conception. BIBLIOGRAPHY: E. D. O'Connor, NCE 7:378–382; A. Carr and G. Williams, Carol Mariol 1:328–394; C. Vollert, *Theology of Mary* (1965) ch. 6.

[J. W. LANGLINAIS]

IMMACULATE CONCEPTION, DAUGHTERS OF MARY OF THE, religious community founded in 1904 in New Britain, Conn., raised to the status of a pontifical institution in 1939. Rev. Lucian Bojnowski, in the year of the golden jubilee of the proclamation of the dogma of the Immaculate Conception, with sodalists from his parish formed the nucleus of a community for the care of orphans. Numbering 141 members (1975), they engage in teaching, nursing, and other social services in more than 20 institutions in New England, New York, and New Jersey.

[C. KEENAN]

IMMACULATE CONCEPTION BROTHERS, religious community founded at Maastricht, Netherlands, by Louis Rutten, a secular priest and Jacob Hoecken, a layman, receiving papal approval in 1848 and 1870. Members take simple, perpetual vows and are governed by a superior general and four assistants—all elected for 6-year terms. Their apostolate is teaching boys between the ages of 6 and 15, including the mentally retarded and deaf, and directing training schools for teachers. They have missions in Java, Chile, Sierra Leone, Nyasaland, W Pakistan, and Borneo. In 1975 they had 63 institutions and a membership of 735.

[C. KEENAN]

IMMACULATE HEART OF MARY, a Marian devotion propagated in the 17th cent. by St. John Eudes (1601–80) and approved by Pope Clement X during his papacy (1670–76). Eudes, a follower of the French school of spirituality founded by Card. de *Bérulle, advocated this school's central tenet that Christ could never be considered without his mother, since the two are one in will and purpose. Though he preached that in herself Mary was nothing, but owed her entire merit to her Son, he did understand Mary as a secondary source of grace, and defended the cult of the Heart of Mary as distinct from that of the Heart of Jesus. Centering on Pr 3.30 and Lk 2.19, he tried to root his reflections in Scripture. Mary's heart was seen as the perfect reproduction and living image of the divine attributes of mercy and wisdom. The popularity of this devotion, once it was acknowledged by the Church, greatly enhanced the role of Mary in the interior life of Catholics, and Pius XII consecrated the world to the Immaculate Heart of Mary in 1942. Contemporary Mariology tends to view Mary's role not as perfectly parallel to that of her Son, but as the archetype of a profound theology of grace, which, based on the need for human cooperation with God's Spirit in salvation history, properly belongs to pneumatology and ecclesiology. Mary's heart can be venerated, since her blessed and grace-filled existence reflects what God has done for all mankind. BIBLIOGRAPHY: J. Eudes, *Admirable Heart of Mary* (1681; tr. 1948); P. Hérambourg, *St. John Eudes: A Spiritual Portrait* (1960); K. Rahner, *Mary, Mother of the Lord* (1963).

[P. J. ROSATO]

IMMACULATE HEART OF MARY, CONGREGATION OF, religious community, the Scheut Fathers, founded in 1862 by Theophile *Verbist at Scheut (Brussels, Belgium), to enlist missionaries for China, both priests and brothers. Although originally limited to Belgian and Dutch membership, the congregation became international in 1947. After the death of Verbist in 1868, his followers continued their efforts to improve the social conditions of the Catholic converts in Inner Mongolia; they purchased farm lands, introduced irrigation, formed small Catholic towns, and discovered a vaccine against spotted typhoid that saved hundreds of Catholic missioners in China. A number of Scheut missionaries suffered violent deaths at the hands of bandits, Communists, and Japanese troops. At the present time, the beatification of 10 Scheut missionaries, who were victims in the Boxer uprising in 1900 is in process. Between 1885 and 1961 their work spread to the former Belgian Congo, Philippines, Chile, and South America. In 1975 their membership numbered 1,702. In the U.S. they are devoted to work in black and Spanish-speaking parishes. The congregation, directly subject to the Congregation for the Evangelization of Peoples, also staffs seminaries for native clergy.

[C. KEENAN]

IMMACULATE HEART OF MARY, SISTERS, SERVANTS OF THE (IHM), a teaching congregation founded by Rev. Louis Florent Gillet, CSSR (1813–92) at Monroe, Mich. in 1845, for the purpose of giving religious instruction in the mission schools of French settlers. The members use the Rule of St. Alphonsus, which was adapted by the founder to the teaching apostolate and which received final approval of the Holy See in 1920. The sisters conduct schools at all levels and also engage in hospital and social work. Since the original foundation, the congregation has become three independent communities, each having papal approval and its own general motherhouse. These houses are located at Monroe, Mich. (1845), which serves in 7 archdioceses and 11 dioceses in U.S., Puerto Rico, S America, Africa, and the West Indies; Scranton, Pa. (1871) serving in 4 archdioceses and 14 dioceses in the U.S. and Peru; and Immaculata, Pa. (1872), working in 5 archdioceses and 8 dioceses in the U.S., Peru, and Chile. In 1975 the Monroe Congregation had 270 houses and 1,229 sisters; the Immaculata motherhouse maintained 173 houses and had 2,168 members; the Scranton community supported 87 houses and a total membership of 1,082. BIBLIOGRAPHY: M. R. Kelly, *No Greater Service* (1948).

[R. A. TODD]

IMMANENCE, GOD'S, see TRANSCENDENCE AND IMMANENCE, GOD'S.

IMMANENCE APOLOGETICS, a method of vindicating the truth of Christianity on the basis of inner experience; specifically, the method developed by M. *Blondel. He proposed that the experience of the insufficiency of human action to satisfy the needs of the inner will leads the nonbeliever to postulate as necessary a transcendent supernatural source of fulfillment. That in turn leads to the discovery in the teachings of Christianity that there is a hypothetical specific response to his aspirations. That is a disposition for the gift of faith, through which he can accept the hypotheses as realities. Because of the campaign against Modernism, any form of immanence apologetics was for a long time suspect; more recently the recognition of the need for both subjective and objective dimensions in an effective apologetics has led to a better assessment of Blondel's thought. BIBLIOGRAPHY: J. M. Sommerville, *Blondel's L'Action* (1968).

[T. C. O'BRIEN]

IMMANENTISM, in a theological context, a classification censuring any explanation of the universe based exclusively on its inner components and/or processes. The label thus applies to any form of *atheism, including secular *humanism, evolutionism, *materialism, *panentheism, *pantheism. Christian orthodoxy asserts the distinct reality of both God and his creatures; God's absolute, entitative transcendence and his causal immanence in the reality and processes of creation. To some a philosophy of process (see WHITEHEAD, ALFRED NORTH) seems adaptable to this orthodoxy and more effective than a metaphysics of being to express it; some forms of process theology, however, are immanentistic by intent. In moral theology ''immanentism'' is sometimes a label for any moral theory rejecting objective moral norms.

[T. C. O'BRIEN]

IMMANUEL, see EMMANUEL.

IMMATERIALITY, in Aristotelian and Thomistic philosophy distinction and independence from matter. According to the Aristotelian theory of actuality and potentiality, the existent-subject-to-change is both material and determined by form. Matter, or the material cause, is that intrinsic principle of potentiality by which an existent can be changed. The correlative intrinsic principle of actuality is form, or the formal cause; both the actuality or determination lost in change and that gained are forms. The existent-subject-to-change further stands in privation to, or lacks, the form to which it is to be changed. Thus lacking the actuality to be received, the material existent is necessarily passive, being changed only through the activity of an agent, or efficient cause. This agent is in turn activated by a further factor, the goal, or final cause. All of the above-named principles distinct from matter are, of course, immaterial. But, more importantly, only the existent-not-subject-to-change enjoys the immateriality that is independence from matter. In that aspect in which it is immaterial, such an existent must be by nature simply formal, standing in privation and in potency to no determining actuality.

True change is either substantial or accidental. Substantial change is change with respect to existence itself, while accidental change is change with respect to mode or manner of existence. The principles of form, matter, and privation, and the efficient and final causes as well, are analogously operative in both substantial and accidental change. Likewise, immateriality is verified in both existence itself and mode of existence. Thus the existent which is material with respect to substantial existence is subject to both generation, change from nonexistence to existence, and corruption, change from existence to nonexistence. The same is true of the accident, considered as an existent and in precision from the subject in which it exists. But the existent which is immaterial with respect to existence itself is not subject to such changes. Being by nature simply formal, it has no intrinsic capacity or potentiality for nonexistence.

The human soul, but not the body, the angel, and God are said to be such immaterial existents.

But it must be understood that immateriality is not the same as pure actuality. As St. Thomas Aquinas saw clearly, the Aristotelian theory of act and potency requires that the immaterial creature possess potency other than the potency for change. While it is not a composite of form and matter, it is, as much as the material existent, a composite of the two distinct intrinsic principles of being, *essence and existence. Its essence is its nature or that intrinsic principle of potency by which it is capable of existence; the essence is yet a principle of passive potency in that it always actualized by existence; its existence is the intrinsic principle of act by which essence as potency for existence is actualized. But this actualization can only be achieved through the agency of that existent which alone is purely actual existence itself, without a distinct principle of potency, and for the sake of that agent. Thus the immaterial creature, even though immutably perfect by its very nature, is immutably dependent in its very being upon its purely actual creator. Only the creator, God, is absolutely independent.

But while no creature is absolutely independent as to its existence, immateriality as to mode of existence does give a certain autonomy lacking in the merely material existent. Simply formal and standing in potency and privation to no actuality, the immaterial existent is by nature perfect and complete, being, in a certain way, both its own efficient and final causes: while it is capable of genuine activity from within by which it contributes to its own enrichment, i.e. to its own purpose in being.

Knowledge is such an immaterial activity. It is true that human intelligence and the power of sensation shared with the lower animals are subject to a becoming, i.e. the process from ignorance to knowledge. However, actual knowing is not, strictly speaking, change, but an analogue of change. Change is the actualization of the material and not actual, of the potential as potential. It is therefore the act of a strictly passive recipient. But the activity of knowledge is rather the act of the formal and the perfect, of the already actual; the capacity for such an act is said to be an active, not a passive, potency. The knower is already actual, in that it is, again, but formal and in potency and privation to no act. The actualized potency is the potency for knowing the knowable, for being the knowable, not just for being what it, the knower, is by nature. The becoming of the knower is indeed a becoming the knowable. According to Aristotle, "Mind is what it is by virtue of becoming all things." The power of sense is potentially any sensible existent, and the power of understanding is potentially all intelligible existents. The knower, then, is distinguished from the non-knower in that while the latter is just what it is ontologically, i.e., substantially and accidentally, the former is not restricted to simple ontological being. It also enjoys the being of the reality known; thus it is, not merely ontologically, but intentionally, that which the known is. In sum, the knower's knowledge, rooted in immateriality, is actually the known itself as existing in the knower. Prior to actual knowing some knowledge presupposes a becoming that is the acquisition of the means and act of knowing. But not all knowledge is the term of a becoming. Only that knower which is but one of many existents of the same ontological level must proceed from ignorance to knowledge. For such an existent the direct and proper object of knowledge is another existent, separate and distinct, of the same ontological level. Knowledge here depends on the knowable being made present to the knower; both the knower and the knowable must be capable of change so that the presence of the knowable to the knower may be accomplished. This is the case for man, for whom then the proper object of knowledge is the changing existent. The divine and angelic knowers, for whom the direct and proper object of knowledge is identical with the subject knowing, enjoy a knowledge that is free from dependence upon change and from becoming. Thus an angel, being the only one of its kind or member of its species, and being thus its own proper object of knowledge, is unchangingly present to itself, and its knowledge is a being without becoming. But the angel's act of knowing is still the actuality of the potency to know, and distinct from the angelic essence and existence; the angel's being itself intentionally in knowledge is distinct from its being itself substantially. Only God, as pure act, with no distinct potency, enjoys a substantial being so elevated as to be identical with his intentional being. It is for this reason that Aristotle called God "Thought Thinking Itself."

St. Thomas, building upon the indications of Aristotle and Boethius, based his classification and division of the sciences upon the relation of the knowable object to matter and motion. He saw an existent to be the object of intellectual speculation insofar as it is immaterial, for the intellect is an immaterial power, and to be an object of scientific knowledge insofar as it is immobile, for science is of the necessary. The different objects of the different sciences have different relations to matter and motion. The object of physics depends upon matter for both its being and its being known, that of mathematics depends upon matter for its being but not for its being known, and that of metaphysics is so dependent for neither its being nor its being known.

[R. E. HENNESSEY]

IMMERSION, the most ancient manner of baptizing, i.e., by submerging the candidate, still the practice of the Eastern Churches. Baptism so received is the allusion of St. Paul (Rom 6.3–4) to being buried together with Christ. The other forms of baptizing are by sprinkling (aspersion) and by pouring (effusion) the water. Baptism by sprinkling is not allowed, although to baptize in this way would not invalidate the sacrament.

[T. C. O'BRIEN]

IMMERSION, ALIEN, see ALIEN IMMERSION.

IMMERSION, TRINE, see TRINE IMMERSION.

IMMERSION BAPTISTS, a name connoting baptismal practice. Concerned primarily with *believer's baptism, the earliest Baptists baptized by affusion. They adopted immersion *c.* 1640 as the proper mode and have almost universally used it since then. Their main arguments are: (1) the Greek word *baptizein* signifies total submersion; (2) NT examples indicate that candidates were taken into a body of water; (3) the symbolism of baptism as identification with Christ in his death and resurrection requires immersion; and (4) this mode was useful for centuries, as attested by written records and remains of baptistries in ancient churches. BIBLIOGRAPHY: *Christian Baptism* (ed. A. Gilmore, 1959); W. L. Lumpkin, *History of Immersion* (1962).

[N. H. MARING]

IMMODESTY, the lack of modesty, that virtue being understood in the technical sense it has in systematic moral theology, i.e., a virtue attendant on *temperance, moderating our pleasures about being esteemed, *humility, about acquiring knowledge, devotion to learning (*studiositas*), about sport and games (*eutrapelia* or playfulness), and about outward habit such as decency in dress. All these are opposed respectively by the following forms of immodesty—vainglory and pushfulness, prurience and curiosity, boorishness and frivolity, sloppiness, and underdressed or overdressed ostentation. Common usage, however, refers modesty to temperate sexuality (*pudicitia*), which is purity in thought, word, and deed not amounting to a directly willed climax. Immodesty is its opposite, and is a kind of sinful *lust. It may be thin, but a line is to be drawn between such immodesty and immodesty in the wider sense referred to above, though they may be closely connected; also between such immodesty and sentimentality; also between the vain sentimentality that tends to be psychologically and morally dissolving and the healthy play of fancy and sensuousness. BIBLIOGRAPHY: ThAq ST 2a2ae, 150–159.

[T. GILBY]

IMMOLATION, in its primary theological usage the distinctive element in *sacrifice. The Christian theology of sacrifice, its vocabulary deriving from the language of the OT ceremonial precepts, was developed in relation to Christ's Passion and Death and to Eucharistic teaching. Sacrifice, an act of the virtue of *religion, is one form of offering (obligation) by which the spiritual sacrifice of interior submission to God, is expressed, the offering distinctive of sacrifice, however, is one in which there is a living victim or a burning or pouring forth of the fruits of the earth. Immolation particularly refers to the victim-offering; Christ's sacrifice is his immolation on the Cross. Of the Eucharist the Council of Trent teaches that in the sacrifice of the Mass the same Christ contained and is immolated bloodlessly who once for all offered himself bloodily on the altar of the cross (D1743; cf. VatII ConstChurch 6; MinLifePriests 2). RC teaching on the Eucharist as sacrificial has been accused—and the accusation has often been warranted by shabby theology and *verismo* preaching—of making the Mass a distinct sacrificial act, thereby a derogation from the value of Calvary and a contradiction of Heb 10,14. St. Thomas Aquinas states simply that the essence of the Eucharist consists in the consecration of the matter (ST 3a,73.1 ad 3); such a position avoids attributing to any act of ecclesial initiative anything constitutive of the sacrifice in the Mass. The oblation and immolation are essentially the Eucharistic consecration. (Happily the reform of the liturgy avoids even the terms "offertory" in favor of "preparation of the gifts.") Like all the sacraments the total reality of the Eucharist consists in its signifying function: the Eucharistic consecration by that signification (i.e., by the act of consecrating bread and wine) brings about what it signifies; it makes present in the twofold consecration the unique,' unrepeatable sacrificial act of Christ. The immolation is Christ's immolation present as signified. The "reality and the sacrament" (*res et sacramentum*) is the reality of Christ's act made present and itself further pointing to the fruits of his sacrifice in those conjoined to him. The Mass is not the repetition of Calvary; it is the being present of Calvary. It is the memorial of Christ's paschal mystery, but—this is the genius of the sacrament as effective sign—the memorial that means the actuality of the mystery itself.

A second use of "immolation" occurs in spiritual theology and refers to the act of the *victim soul, a heroic act of self-offering in union with Christ for the salvation of others. BIBLIOGRAPHY: A. Vonier, *Key to the Doctrine of Eucharist* (1925); J. M. Powers, *Eucharistic Theology* (1967).

IMMORTALE DEI (1885), an encyclical letter of Pope Leo XIII on Church and State, that in 1885 opened the discussion which eventually prepared the way for European Catholics to assume conscious and comfortable citizenship in the fully secular, liberally democratic State. The doctrine contained in *Immortale Dei,* however, is difficult to reconcile with the American political experience. Moreover, from any national viewpoint, the gap between the contents of *Immortale Dei* and the Vatican Council II's *Declaration on Religious Freedom* is wide and illustrates the fact that the Council intended to and did "develop" Catholic doctrine.

The encyclical assumes that the State derives its authority from God. Consequently, temporal power has a sacred character and the State should therefore make public profession of religion, indeed of the one true religion. However, Church and State are two distinct powers and no conflict is seen between them.

Today's reader might easily misunderstand the Pope's insistence that all men are not by nature equal (no.24). To argue the opposite, at least in practice, would be to say that no man has the right to rule over other men. Even if people choose their ruler in an egalitarian state, they hand over "not the right so much as the business of governing," and this, in Pope Leo's view, is dangerous: "The authority of

God is passed over in silence, just as if there were no God; or as if he cared nothing for human society; or as if men, whether in their individual capacity or bound together in social relations, owed nothing to God; or as if there could be a government of which the whole origin and power and authority did not reside in God himself''(no.25).

The wellbeing of every State greatly depends, the pontiff says, on the instruction of youth in religion and morality. Accordingly, Catholics should work for laws that would provide for such instruction. The goal to be pursued by all Christians is "to bring back all civil society to the pattern and form of Christianity." Pope Leo lays down no fixed way to achieve this because the means "must suit places and times widely differing from one another." BIBLIOGRAPHY: E. T. Gargan, *Leo XIII and the Modern World* (1961); for text of the encyclical, see *Church Speaks to the Modern World* (ed. É. Gilson, 1954) 157–187.

[W. J. BYRON]

IMMORTALITY. Although God is conceived of as the only being who essentially *has to be* or to exist without end (see 1 Tim 6.16), the human creature has long pondered the possibility of life exempt from death. Responding to the Gilgamesh epic, which understood death as fate, Gen (2–3) viewed the possibility of life without death as a lost opportunity because of humanity's own sinfulness. In that context an early death and lack of descendants were long considered punishments (Jer 18.21; cf. Wis 4.7–19). Nevertheless, burial practices and evidence of attempts at communication with ancestors (necromancy) reveal that even the early Hebrews did not simply consider the dead as totally nonexistent. They were *refāʾīm* or shadowy bodies having an unreal existence in the underworld pit of Sheol (Gen 37.35; Ps 39.13, 88.3–10; Is 14.9, 26.14; Job 3.13, 7.9,21; Pr 2.18, 9.18, 21.16). Death was originally thought to break all relationships with God. One who entered Sheol was without hope (Ps 6.5, 30.9, 88.3–5, 115.17, 118.17; Is 38.18; Sir 17.27–28; Bar 2.17). As Jewish hopes for national autonomy, nurtured by the past glories of David's kingdom, were smashed by the Assyrian invasion, the Babylonian Exile, and the subsequent Persian and Hellenistic domination, there gradually emerged a new concern for divine justice toward righteous individuals whose earthly lives were filled with absurd suffering (Jer 12; Job). When such concern took its place alongside the earlier preoccupation with national or societal fortunes, God's power was extended over Sheol, which thus became a place of ethical retribution. The unjust were pursued even into Sheol (Amos 9.2). The Book of Daniel 12.2 (cf. Is 25.8, 26.19; Jdt 16.17) contains the first indisputable reference to a resurrection for both good and wicked, either to everlasting life or to shame and everlasting disgrace. Intertestamental literature such as 1 Enoch, 2 Baruch, Apoc. of Moses, and Secrets of Enoch vividly portrayed the situations of heaven and hell. Because Judaism envisioned a human being as equally or inseparably body and spirit, it followed that full retribution for earthly suffering or injustice would require bodily resurrection. Later Judaism also adapted Greek philosophical notions of an immortal soul. In the perspectives of Plato the soul was deathless (*athanasia*) because its immateriality rendered it incorruptible or imperishable (*aphtharsia*). When Judaism integrated such Platonic perspectives, it placed them into the ethical context of righteousness (Wis 1.15; 6.18–20). God created human beings for incorruption (*aphtharsia*); sin brought death (Wis 2.23–24). For Wisdom only the just live forever. The death of a just person is only an apparent destruction since righteous living brings immortality (Wis 3.1–9, 5.15; see 2 Macc 7.9–14, 12.39–45). Paul likewise interprets the death of the righteous as only a seeming death (Rom 5.10–17). By the victory of Jesus the mortal puts on immortality (1 Cor 15.21–23, 53–57). The death of Jesus becomes an event which Christians seek to share in order to gain eternal life (Rom 6.5; Gal 2.20). Eternal life is a free gift from God whereby the dead in Christ will rise (1 Thess 4.16; Rom 6.23). The Gospels repeatedly present Jesus as sharing the expectation of a general bodily resurrection that is related to God's kingdom. In this he agreed with the Pharisees against the Sadducees (Mk 12.18–27; Acts 23.6–8). Two conditions, heaven and hell, are attributed to the afterlife, which emphasizes the reality of our present potential to create the ultimate meaning of our life (Mt 5.12,29, 10.28, 25; Mk 9.42–48; see D 1000–02).

Tatian (*Address to the Greeks* 7 and 13) and Theophilus (*To Autolycus* 2, 26–27) stress immortality as a gift from God over against the natural immortality lost through sin. For Irenaeus immortality is a quality acquired after a period of growth and development (*Against the Heresies* III, 20, 2; IV, 38, 2–3; V, 8, 1, and 12, 1–3 vs. *Proof of Apost. Preaching* 15). Tertullian maintains that human beings were not created for death; it is an unnatural event, the result of sin (*De Anima* 52, 2). The younger Origen believed that the body was created only to express the diversity required by the present state of fallen spirits consequent on their sin in an unembodied *preexistence. By death the flesh is transformed into a "spiritual body" (*De Principiis* 1, 6, 1–4; 2, 10, 3; 3, 6, 4–9). Methodius of Olympus countered Origen by insisting that human beings have a body previous to sinning and that it is not simply its "form" which will resurrect (*De resurrectione* 1, 32, 7; cf. D 403). Augustine follows Athanasius and Ambrose in saying that man was created immortal (able not to die vs. unable to die) but was separated from the Tree of Life because of sin (*De Gen. ad litt.* 6.36; cf. *De immort. animae*). The notion of bodily immortality as a preternatural gift thus emerged (see D 222, 372, 1511, 1978, 3514). Thomas Aquinas later refers to individual, incorporeal, subsistent souls as incorruptible (ThAq ST 1a, 75.2 & 6; CG 2.79 & 84; cf. D 1440–41). Although he recognizes bodily death to be natural for material beings, he considers it a punishment for human beings because it involves the loss of a divine gift of bodily immortality, which God miraculously restores at the final resurrection (ThAq ST 1a2ae, 85.5–6; 2a2ae, 164.1–2; 3a, 46.6; Suppl. 75.3; cf. CG 4.79). Contemporary theologians such as Karl Rahner (*On the Theology of Death*) relate immortality to the human potential for freely transcending the necessities and inertia of nature. A life of free decisions seeking not to have or possess but to love within time and space thus culminates in a death that is not merely a fated, biological, passive event, but that can be a free, human action, a trusting decision to break through emptiness, futility, and loneliness into an open, unrestricted relationship with the entire cosmos, the innermost part of the world. In this sense eternity is either the fulfillment or the void of meaning created by an incarnate spirit living in time. Christian immortality is radically distinguished from the natural immortality of the human soul. Christian immortality is not simply a freeing of the soul from the body but a communion of the human spirit in God's own life (see D 3771). Since God communicated with us in an "embodied" Jesus and since our own transcendence in this life is "embodied," a resurrected person and not an unembodied human spirit is the focus of Christian teleology. *SOUL-BODY RELATIONSHIP.

[B. P. PRUSAK]

IMMURATION (Lat. *murus,* wall), the walling up of a person as punishment. The immuring of nuns in order to smother them is a myth sometimes found in literature or anti-Catholic diatribes. There was a monastic punishment, a kind of solitary confinement in a cell with only a narrow slit for light, air, and receiving food; St. John of the Cross suffered it. There was also a penitential practice of voluntary self-enclosure in a cell with the exit blocked in.

[T. C. O'BRIEN]

IMMUTABILITY OF GOD, a negative divine attribute, the impossibility of God's changing, "in whom there is no change or shadow of alteration" (Jas 1.17). Theology explains this attribute, a constant of biblical belief in God (but see PROCESS THEOLOGY), on the basis that change (see MOTION) connotes perfectibility. Change in its first sense is proper only to material beings, subject to coming-to-be and to passing away, or subject to material alteration; by an analysis of change Aristotle concluded to the necessity of there being an absolutely unmoved (unchangeable) mover (Acts 17.27-28). Change in a wider sense is the process towards achieving an unrealized potentiality. Since God can neither be material nor lack any actuality (see PURE ACT), there can be no change of any kind in the divine being. The consideration of the *eternity of God, as he is absolutely and all at once, as it were, all that he is, is an attempt to give positive expression to the divine changelessness.

[T. C. O'BRIEN]

IMOLA, INNOCENZO DA (*c.*1490–*c.*1550), Italian painter settling in Bologna (1517). He painted *The Madonna with SS. Sebastian, Roch, Cosmas, and Damian* (signed 1515); frescoes of the life of the Virgin (1517–22); and the main altarpiece for the Monastery of S. Michele, Bologna. Influenced by Raphael, I. taught P. Fontana and Primaticcio.

[M. J. DALY]

IMPANATION (Lat. *panis,* bread), a term devised to express or describe certain theories of the *Real Presence. In the 12th cent. this parallel was advanced: as by the Incarnation the Word is personally and substantially united to human nature, so in the Eucharist by impanation Christ is personally and substantially united to bread and wine. The idea was admitted as a tenable alternative to *transubstantiation by John of Paris (*c.*1306) and was espoused by the Lutheran A. *Osiander (d. 1552). In affirming the Real Presence Luther himself rejected any such idea. Nevertheless, when C. *Schwenkfeld and others called his sacramental realism impanation (*Einbrödtung*), Luther conceded the designation, for the sake of argument, in his *Confession concerning the Lord's Supper* (1528). RC theologians sometimes described Lutheran eucharistic theory as impanation, but the designation is not apt. *CONSUBSTANTIATION.

[T. C. O'BRIEN]

IMPASSIBILITY, one of the four qualities traditionally attributed to glorified bodies in heaven whereby they are placed beyond pain or any physical inconvenience. The scriptural foundation for it is traced to 1 Cor. 15.42: "So it is with the resurrection of the dead. What is sown in the earth as a perishable thing is raised imperishable." Theologians reasoned that the cessation of any physical suffering is implied in the conquest of death upon the *resurrection of the dead. Thomas Aquinas links this gift with the glorified soul's complete dominion over the body (ST Suppl, 82.1). The Catechism of the Council of Trent lists impassibility among the endowments of the resurrected body. BIBLIOGRAPHY: C. J. Corcoran, NCE 7:394–395.

[T. M. MCFADDEN]

IMPECCABILITY, not merely the absence of sins committed by a free agent but also the impossibility of sinning. In RC theology this quality is said to extend to three categories of existent free agents: the triune God, the humanity of Jesus and his mother, and the blessed in heaven. The question of sin (basically a missing of the mark, a disorientation from life's purpose) obviously cannot apply to the Triune God. In regard to the humanity of Jesus, Scripture (Jn 8.46, 14.30; Heb 7.26) and church teaching (Council of Constantinople III, D 291) maintain that Jesus was sinless in fact and impeccable in theory.

A common objection is that the inability to sin destroys the concept of human freedom. Yet human freedom is a faculty (power or ability) designed to enable man to orient himself properly toward life's purpose (in general, a state of perfect love of God and neighbor). Man sins when he chooses, not evil as such, but an "apparent" good in preference to a ''real'' good, because his limited, finite intelligence does not inform him with unquestionable certitude of life's purpose as it lies dormant within the context of specific issues. The human ability to choose a sinful rather than a virtuous course is really a sign of imperfection to be remedied as far as possible. Human freedom is more of a means to an end rather than the end itself.

Jesus, by virtue of the special aid (grace) concomitant with the hypostatic union, always kept his intellect and will perfectly in tune with the purpose of his life. Mary his mother, according to the dogma of the Immaculate Conception, was also given special aid (grace) by God in virtue of her foreseen intimate relationship to Jesus, to enable her to freely choose not to sin. The blessed in heaven are also impeccable since they are eternally realizing the purpose of their lives. The eternity of this state is guaranteed either by the clarity of the beatific vision which renders sin impossible (Aquinas), or by a special prevenient grace which guides the will so that as long as this grace remains, sin is rendered impossible (Bonaventure). BIBLIOGRAPHY: P. J. Kelly, NCE 7:395; E. A. Weis, NCE 7:395–396; J. R. Gillis, NCE 9:146; *idem, op. cit.* 7:948.

[C. NEELY]

IMPECCABILITY OF CHRIST, his inability to sin. This stems from his supreme holiness, which is in turn rooted in the grace of union. Because his human nature belongs to the Divine Person, its acts are acts of an infinitely holy Person who cannot sin. Excluded are all mortal and venial sin, and all possibility of sinning and of any inclination to sin; excluded is all interior temptation to sin. The Christian sense has always viewed with horror the thought that Christ did or could sin. He is the high priest ''tried as we are in all things except sin'' (Heb. 4.15). He is ''holy, innocent, undefiled, set apart from sinners''(Heb 7.26). He ''knew nothing of sin'' (2 Cor 5.21), ''did no sin, neither was deceit found in his mouth'' (1 Pet 2.22). Christ himself could challenge the Jews: ''Which of you can convict me of sin'' (Jn 8.46; cf. 8.29). ''. . . Sin is not in him'' (1 Jn 3.5). The Fathers of the Church and theologians unanimously teach the impeccability of Christ. Chalcedon (D 301) restates the doctrine of Heb 4.15 and of one of the creeds found in the *Ancoratus* of St. Epiphanius (D 44): He is like his fellow men in every respect except sin. See also the Council of Florence's Decree for the Jacobites (D 1347). If the impeccability of Christ rests on the hypostatic union and the intuitive vision that the human nature possessed from the beginning (theologians offer various explanations), it is also demanded by the perfection and holiness required for his life of merit, his sacrifice (1 Pet 1.19), and the supreme example of holiness he gives as a pattern for men's lives. BIBLIOGRAPHY: E. A. Weis, NCE 7:395–396.

[E. G. KAISER]

IMPEDIMENT, in a strict sense, an obstacle to marriage (see IMPEDIMENTS TO MARRIAGE). Impediments to the reception or exercise of holy orders are properly called *irregularities. Canonists also at times speak of obstacles to admittance to, or profession in, a religious institute as impediments.

[T. C. O'BRIEN]

IMPEDIMENTS TO MARRIAGE, see MARRIAGE, IMPEDIMENTS TO.

IMPEDIMENTS TO ORDINATION, see IRREGULARITY.

IMPENITENCE, the condition of the person who has neither sorrow for his sinful actions as an offense against God nor intention to avoid future sins and make amends for past ones. Impenitence is distinguished into simple and willful. The former is simply the fact of nonrepentance or repentance negligently postponed for a period beyond the commission of sin; the latter is voluntary impenitence in which one wills not to do penance and resolves not to be converted to God. Willful impenitence is an attitude blatantly antithetical to the gospel message of **metanoia* expressed through John the Baptist (Mt 3.8; Lk 3.7) and adopted by Jesus (Mk 1.15). According to St. Thomas, this voluntary and malicious impenitence is a sin by itself, even a sin against the Holy Spirit (ThAq ST 2a2ae, 14.2), whereas simple impenitence is not. Both kinds of impenitence have serious consequences. It is generally held that a person in a state of alienation from God is prone to further sinful actions; and when this alienation is voluntary, it is a serious predisposition to final impenitence (see IMPENITENCE, FINAL). BIBLIOGRAPHY: P. Richard, DTC 7:1280–85.

[J. CORDOUE]

IMPENITENCE, FINAL, the state of the unrepentant person at the moment of death. It may be the result of simple impenitence in which repentance has been postponed for a period beyond the commission of sin, or it may be the result of a willful, final resolve not to be converted, an ultimate rejection of grace that may be described as a sin against the Holy Spirit (see IMPENITENCE). What may be observed as final impenitence at the moment of death is generally considered to destine a person to a condition of final loss in *hell, but there is no absolute support in Scripture or tradition for the position that anyone has been judged as actually lost finally. Although Christian theology has generally supposed that there are those who die in a state of final impenitence, some contemporary writers have conjectured that at the moment of death an individual's freedom and clarity of mind may be heightened in such a way as to give him an opportunity to choose God by affirming the fundamentally right orientation that may have marked his life, or of rejecting a wrong orientation. BIBLIOGRAPHY: ThAq ST 2a2ae, 14; P. Richard, DTC 7:1280–85.

[J. CORDOUE]

IMPERFECTION, etymologically a lack of completion or perfection, commonly in Catholic moral theology, an action that could be better. Negative imperfection usually means that a good action was done with less perfect dispositions and motivation than the agent was capable of. Positive imperfection usually means the deliberate choice to do something less perfect than a real alternative, and yet not in violation of any command of God. Smoking is sometimes cited as an example. It is often impossible to know what is best for one in a given real situation. The most common application of any doctrine on the matter concerns the violation by a member of a religious order of rules which the constitutions of the order say do not bind under pain of sin. Theologians hold that as long as what is done is not a sin for some other reason, for instance, contempt, it is not a sin; it may be less pleasing to God—according to the trite phrase—but not displeasing; less good but not evil. This seems to agree with the teaching of St. Paul in 1 Cor 7.38 where the Apostle says that for a man to give his daughter in marriage is good, but not to give her in marriage is better. Some theologians have held the stricter view, although even the rigorists are usually liberal in applying their doctrine to actual situations, and some respectable moral theologians hold that, like Mrs. Harris, there is no such thing. BIBLIOGRAPHY: J. J. Farraher, NCE 7:396–398; "Is Religious Disobedience Always a Sin?" *Review for Religious* 19 (1960) 215–224.

[J. J. FARRAHER]

IMPERIALISM, like *colonialism, a term around which various emotional suggestions have clustered in recent decades, mostly to its disrepute; thus of aggression, exploitation, and arbitrary despotism. In fact it can stand for something highly honorable; to be an imperialist in the 17th cent. often meant you were defending Christendom with your life, and in the afterglow of the British and French Empires, many missionaries have had occasion to recall their benefits. St. Augustine was an imperialist, and so was Dante. However, in our present world of fragmented and discordant nationalism, the image of empire has rather gone out, together with its glitter and panoply, though the reality may survive under other names. In early political history an empire was not distinguished from a kingdom or even a state: in principle it came to mean the rule of a sovereign state over dependencies or even an aggregation of independent states under one head: in essence it does not require subject peoples, nor even an emperor. In a phase of American history imperialism was a movement that advocated extending the rule of the American people to foreign countries and gaining and holding distant dependencies. The mood has passed, but a critic would be callow in the extreme, and indeed very ungrateful, who dismissed its driving force as just aggrandizement and its effects as just a blot.

[T. GILBY]

IMPETRATION, a term in Latin theology expressing several aspects of *prayer. In essence prayer is impetration, an asking that what it petitions be accomplished by God; the impetration functions dispositively in regard to its fulfillment, as God's commanding prayer means that it is a condition for the working out of certain effects of his providence (ThAq ST 2a2ae, 83.2). Impetration also brings out the source of prayer's effectiveness, namely its reliance in faith and hope on God's gracious love and willingness to answer prayer, even the prayer of sinners (*ibid.* 13;15 & ad 3;16 & ad 2). In a narrower sense impetration designates the kind of prayer addressed to the saints: only God is petitioned as the one who answers prayer; the prayer to the saints intends to ask their share in the petition, their *intercession (*ibid.* 83.4). Because the Eucharistic Sacrifice is the supreme form of prayer, impetration is given as one of the purposes for its celebration.

[T. C. O'BRIEN]

IMPLUVIUM, in the atrium of a Roman house, the sunken area receiving the rain water, adopted by the early Christian Church as the area for baptism.

[M. J. DALY]

IMPOSITION OF HANDS, in the sacrament of *holy orders the ordaining bp.'s placing his hands on the head of the ordinand: deacon, priest, or bp., which alone is the essential *matter of the sacrament, exclusive of the handing over of the instruments of office, (*traditio instrumentorum*). This determination was made by Pius XII (1947) in the apostolic constitution, *Sacramentum ordinis* (D 3857). (For the history and usage of the practice, see LAYING ON OF HANDS.)

[T. C. O'BRIEN]

IMPOTENCE, lack of the capability to have sexual intercourse. Canon law lists the perpetual impotence of either party that is antecedent to an intended or ostensible marriage as a diriment *impediment, i.e., as nullifying; such impotence may be absolute or relative, known to the other party or not. The reason for the nullifying character of the impediment is that impotence negates the meaning of true matrimonial consent; no matrimonial contract is possible (CIC, c. 1068, § 1); doubtful impotence does not constitute the impediment (*ibid.* § 2). Absolute impotence means that the man or the woman is altogether incapable; relative impotence is the incapacity of one partner with respect to the other. An impotence occurring subsequent to the marriage does not invalidate. Nor does temporary impotence, whether functional or caused by remediable organic or psychological causes (even if in fact they are never remedied). The law also indicates (*ibid.* § 3) that *sterility does not constitute any sort of impediment. The determination of the existence of impotence in the canonical sense is not a generalized procedure; each case has to be considered in its precise circumstances.

[T. C. O'BRIEN]

IMPRECATION, the utterance of a curse, and particularly in a solemn way. To call down evil on anyone by wish or command with an evil intent is a sin contrary to both justice (ThAq ST 2a2ae, 76.1) and charity (*ibid.* 25.6). The condemnations in Scripture pronounced by the Prophets are imprecations made with good intent, the correction of sin or the affirmation of God's justice (*ibid.* 25.6 ad 3; 83.9 ad 1). The anathema in solemn church documents is a pronouncement of *excommunication, i.e., of the separation of those denying a declared teaching from the body of the faithful.

[T. C. O'BRIEN]

IMPRIMATUR (Lat., let it be printed), term for the permission of the competent ecclesiastical authority that a book touching on religion or morality may be published. Not an endorsement, it indicates negatively that the work contains nothing detrimental to faith or morals. For most works the competent authority is the bp. of the diocese where the work has been written or will be printed or published. Granting of the imprimatur presupposes the **nihil obstat* by appointed censors. According to current canon law the imprimatur, dated, and with the name and place of the bp., must appear at the beginning or end of the work approved (CIC c. 1393.4). This prescription is frequently not observed in practice, esp. since the whole issue of *precensorship has come under discussion in the Church.

[T. C. O'BRIEN]

IMPRIMI POTEST (Lat., it can be printed), formula indicating the permission of a major religious superior for the publication of a work written by one of his subjects. Such permission must be obtained before the work can be submitted for an *imprimatur (CIC c. 1385.3). The *imprimi potest* is usually printed in the work in question, although this is not canonically required. *PRECENSORSHIP.

[T. C. O'BRIEN]

IMPROPERIA (Lat., reproaches), a set of verses deriving from Scripture, formerly chanted or sung as part of the Good Friday veneration of the cross before the reform of the liturgy after Vatican Council II. The words convey the divine reproaches that Jesus' death became necessary. The *Improperia* were given polyphonic musical settings by Palestrina and Luis de Victoria. One possible reason for this suppression in the liturgy is the ridding of the Good Friday service of any suggestion of anti-Semitism.

[J. DALLEN]

IMPROVISATION (LITURGY), see LITURGICAL EXPERIMENTATION.

IMPULSE, the sudden, unthinking stirring of the emotions towards some real or seeming good or away from some harm. In general an impulse cannot have a fully virtuous or fully sinful quality, in that it is not marked by deliberateness. To be virtuous an emotive act must be intentionally directed towards moral good; to be sinful the lack of such intent must have been deliberate. Yet impulses to good or away from evil are not altogether without any moral quality. They exist not in instinctual isolation, but within the human, moral agent, and that gives them a natural amenability to contribute to the fully human good. They admit of subordination to reasonable direction. An impulse towards a good offers the possibility of a fully virtuous, intended good. An impulse with regard to something morally evil itself lacks the subordination possible for the moral agent to achieve; that is its inordinateness. On these grounds St. Thomas Aquinas recognizes the possibility of such disordered emotional impulses being venial sins. The position represents at once a high idealism with respect to the capacity for virtuous control and a realism with respect to the continuousness of salvation as a process. Any single, indeliberate venial sin could have been forestalled; that is the meaning of the potential for virtue. Actual virtuous control over the whole range of impulses is not possible, both because of their sudden spontaneity, as contrasted with the relatively slower capacity for deliberation, and because of the fallen state of human nature. The implication is the constant need of grace and of its growing domination until the final redemptive reintegration. BIBLIOGRAPHY: ThAq ST 1a2ae, 74.3 & 4;109.8 *CONCUPISCENCE.

[T. C. O'BRIEN]

IMPURITY, in general, the state or act of sinfulness, often with sexual connotation. (1) The origin is probably primitive disgust with the loathsome. The OT term *tāmē* meant the mysteriously dangerous; in magical thinking, it was closely related to what cultural anthropologists call "taboo," a Polynesian term signifying the prohibition against unleashing powerful and perilous forces. (2) In OT, particularly Lev, the notion of legal impurity is applied to a great series of things: certain foods, sex (notwithstanding legitimacy or even involuntariness), contact with death and diseases such as leprosy. It is difficult to bring all these under a single concept, since apparently the only common element is life itself, esp. in its beginnings and conclusion. Still all of these are considered the areas of divinity. The idea is closely related to that of the *holy; the Semitic root *hrm* (banned, anathema) has a polarity of meaning, signifying both the *sacred and the abominable. (See W. Albright, *Stone Age to Christianity* [1948] 176). (3) The NT along with its moral idea of purity uses the notion of impurity in both its substantive (*akarthasîa*) and adjectival (*akártaros*) forms, adapting their original meaning of physical filth or ritual uncleanness to that of moral dirtiness. Because of the sexual decadence of the Hellenistic world, impurity was increasingly used with a sexual connotation, with overtones of unnatural sexuality (Rom 1.24; 6.19; 2 Cor 12.21; Gal 5.19; Eph 4.19, 5.3; Col 3.5). Its synonyms were *sensuality (*aselgeîa*) and *fornication (*porneîa*). BIBLIOGRAPHY: EDB 1055. For unchastity, *lust, see Davis, Mor-Past Th.

[U. VOLL]

IMPUTABILITY, the praiseworthiness or blameworthiness of a voluntary action. Praise or blame implies that the one acting is judged by another. But the imputation of an act to its doer reflects the inner meaning of an action, namely that it is under the power or control of the one acting (see RESPONSIBILITY). He is one intending and accomplishing the true human good chosen, or in choosing fails to attend to the relationship of a good chosen to the full value of the human good. The "good-as-meant" constitutes the good moral action; the "lack-of-good-as-meant" vitiates the bad moral action (see Gilby). Imputability presupposes the voluntarily good or bad character of an action; it also presupposes that the human action has a relationship to other human beings and to God. To be laudable or blamable is a sign and a consequence of the inner goodness or malice of a human action, and of its interpersonal or social ramifications. BIBLIOGRAPHY: ThAq ST 1a2ae, 21.2 (Lat-Eng v. 18, ed. T. Gilby) app. 10, 13.

[T. C. O'BRIEN]

IMPUTATION OF JUSTICE AND MERIT, a doctrinal position rejected by the Council of Trent. What the council repudiated was the conception of justification as a mere imputation of the justice of Christ, who satisfied for men's sins on the cross, to the sinner in whom no objective change was effected. He remains the sinner that he was, with his sins covered over by, or not imputed to him because of, the justice of Christ, which is reckoned to his credit for his trustful faith. Such a view of justification leaves no room for merit. A sinner does not merit. Hence, just as trustful faith was the only condition (not cause, whether effective or meritorious) of his justification, so also the good works following on justification as its fruit and sign do not bring about (or merit) a growth in justice. The trustful faith that inspires them is the only condition of this development. It may be doubted whether the Protestant doctrine restricted justification to a mere imputation of Christ's justice; it did, rather, allow for a real change in man. The imputation of justice included in *double justice need not preclude merit. BIBLIOGRAPHY: T. J. Motherway, NCE 7:408–409.

[P. DELETTER]

IMRE, ST., see EMERIC OF HUNGARY, ST.

IN ARTICULO MORTIS (Lat., at the moment of death), a term used in RC manuals of theology and canon law to indicate that moment when death is imminent and when, therefore, certain sacramental and canonical norms become operative. In traditional dogmatic theology this moment marks both the separation of the soul from the body and the end of the time of merit and demerit. In recent writing the moment of death is described as a most free one in which a person, reflecting what he has become by his free choices, can affirm his life or, according to some theories, reject it. In either case death is understood as a personal act in which man brings himself to completion and definitively becomes himself. BIBLIOGRAPHY: K. Rahner, *On the Theology of Death* (tr. C. H. Henkey, 1961); L. Boros, *Mystery of Death* (tr. G. Bainbridge, 1965). *DEATH, THEOLOGY OF.

[J. CORDOUE]

IN CAMPO APERTO (Lat., in an open field), refers to musical notation, particularly in early *Gregorian chant MSS, written without a staff, the graphlike system of one or more parallel horizontal lines indicating fixed pitches. Such notation indicates at least the approximate melodic contour of the music; in later MSS the neumes are often diastematic, indicating precise musical intervals by their height and vertical spacing.

[A. DOHERTY]

IN COMMENDAM, (Lat. in trust), a way of holding a legally vacant ecclesiastical benefice. Historically, the phrase connotes the abuses connected with *commendation.

[T. C. O'BRIEN]

IN HOC SIGNO VINCES, "In this sign you will conquer," a motto originating from the stories of Constantine's conversion after the battle of the Milvian Bridge (312) near Rome. In Lactantius's version the sign in question was the Christian monogram *Chi Rho* (*De morte* 44); in Eusebius of Caesarea's (*Vita Constantini* 1.17–32), it was the *labarum, a staff with globe surmounted by the *Chi Rho*. Both authors speak of a vision before the battle in which Constantine was instructed to paint the sign on his soldiers' shields. Eusebius narrates that Constantine heard the words, "in this sign conquer." Lactantius's version is accepted as authentic, and the events of the emperor's vision and victory are connected with the consequent peace of the Church. EDICT OF *MILAN.

[T. C. O'BRIEN]

IN NOMINE, a class of instrumental compositions having a *cantus firmus* foundation. The designation of these English works derives from the melody forming the *cantus firmus* for the words *In nomine Domini* in the *Sanctus* of John Taverner's Mass, *Gloria tibi Trinitas*.

[P. J. HENNESSEY]

IN PARTIBUS INFIDELIUM (Lat. for in the regions of unbelievers), a designation used for those sees held by bps. who were not residential or diocesan. Canon law requires that every bp. have a see, hence auxiliary bps. are granted a formerly residential see which has been abandoned because of disuse or the absence of Christians. These sees were said to be held *in partibus infidelium*. Pope Leo XIII substituted the term titular bp. or see in 1882.

[T. M. MCFADDEN]

IN PETTO (It., in the breast), a manner of designating a cardinal. The pope, at his discretion, may inform the *College of Cardinals in consistory that he has appointed a new cardinal, but has decided that the appointee's name shall be kept secret until some future date. Until that time, the cardinal *in petto* does not have the rights or duties of his office, although his seniority is determined from the time of his appointment. The practice generally occurs when undesired political repercussions would follow upon a public announcement.

[T. M. MCFADDEN]

INADVERTENCE, a lack of awareness with respect to an act that in itself belongs to the realm of morals; and regarding either the act itself or some moral *circumstance (see also IGNORANCE). Since a human, therefore moral act is a deliberate choice, a total lack of awareness, i.e., complete inadvertence, makes an action nonmoral, neither good nor bad. But an action may be partially advertent and partially inadvertent, and so have an incomplete moral quality e.g., in the case of indeliberate venial sins. Further, an actual inadvertence does not rule out a virtual advertence, i.e., an action is done in virtue of an abiding, deliberate *intention, but without that being made explicit in the given instance.

[T. C. O'BRIEN]

INCA RELIGION, a Peruvian system deeply concerned with ritual and the organization of life and society during the Imperial Inca Period which began around 1440 A.D. with the Inca conquests and declined with the coming of the Spanish. Reflecting a subdued interest in mysticism and spirituality, ritual worship of the supreme deity, Viracocha, the creator, was less important than prayer to the lesser, more accessible deities, the *huaccas*. These were associated with the food supply, significant places, physical cures, and the agricultural lunar calendar. Viracocha, though represented in human form, was considered too distant and withdrawn from the world to be approached by any but members of a royal cult. Of major importance, however, was the sun, protector of crops and the personal ancestral god of the ruling family. Represented by a golden disk with rays around a face, the Sun shared his temple in Cuzco with other astral deities—stars, Moon, and the Weather-god. In contrast to most Mesoamerican religion, the concept of the four directions of the universe had little significance for the Inca. During the Inca conquests, idols of conquered peoples were sent to Cuzco along with priests to attend them, making Cuzco an important religious site. Many special places, passes, summits, springs, bridges, as well as outstanding rock formations were considered dwelling places for natural powers. Evil spirits were feared but not worshipped, since they could do no good. The temples served to store images and ritual objects and to house priests and chosen women. They were maintained by produce of land assigned as the Sun's portion, official religious land as distinct from land reserved for government rulers and for the people. The major public ceremonies were linked to the agricultural lunar year and were held in the open air. Ritual cleanliness was required of all participants in the services, thus making confessions of transgressions to a confessor, penance, and purification in running water, ideally at the confluence of rivers, an important feature of religious practice. Magical and religious methods were used to cure injuries and disease, since maladies were considered to be of supernatural origin. A broken bone for example might have been caused by the anger of the spirit at the place where the bone was broken; thus sacrifice to the spirit was considered an essential part of the cure. Most of what is known about Inca religion relies heavily upon Spanish sources of the 16th century. BIBLIOGRAPHY: J. A. Mason, *Ancient Civilizations of Peru* (pa., 1963).

[R. J. LITZ]

INCANTATION, a superstition numbered among *vain observances and consisting in the utterance of esoteric words, or even in wearing inscriptions of them, for the purpose of bringing about magical effects. The power is ascribed to the words or their inscription; thus incantation is a sin against the virtue of *religion.

[T. C. O'BRIEN]

INCARDINATION AND EXCARDINATION, the juridic terms (CIC, c. 111–117) for a cleric's formal affiliation into and disaffiliation from a diocese. No secular cleric is admitted to the clerical state or to any sacred order without incardination; nor can a cleric be excardinated from one diocese without and until being incardinated into another. The power to incardinate or excardinate belongs to the ruling bp. of the diocese in question; exercise of the power requires a clear and just cause, formal evidence given to the incardinating bp. of the cleric's good character; the cleric's sworn intent to remain permanently in the diocese of incardination. Since the *motu proprio* of Paul VI *Ad pascendum,* admission to the clerical state and incardination come at ordination to the diaconate. A cleric who is a religious becomes excardinated from his diocese of origin by reason of final profession in simple or solemn vows; his affiliation is to his own religious institute; but this is not termed incardination. No religious who is a priest can become a secular priest unless and until he is incardinated by a diocesan bishop. The legislation in force, deriving from the Council of Trent, rests on the early, unhappy experience in the Church of wandering clerics, the *acephali,* having no authority to which they were subject. The *motu proprio, Ecclesiae sanctae* (Aug. 1, 1966) simplified incardination in order to provide for needs of dioceses short of priests (see Vat II MinLifePriests 10).

[T. C. O'BRIEN]

INCARNATE WORD, SISTERS OF CHARITY OF THE (CCVI), a congregation of women religious originating in Lyons, France, in 1866, when the founder, Bp. Claude Marie Dubuis (1817–95) visited his native France and requested sisters for his diocese in Galveston, Texas. In immediate response, Mother Angélique, superior of the congregation of Sisters of the Incarnate Word and Blessed Sacrament, recruited three new subjects, giving them religious training in preparation for their new mission in America. Upon their arrival at Galveston the sisters were immediately engaged in the care of those who were plague-stricken with yellow fever. The new community was founded for the purpose of attending the sick and honoring in a special way the sacred humanity of Christ. Today their apostolate involves educational, hospital, and social work. Foundations were established throughout Texas and in Arkansas, Louisiana, Utah, and California. The congregation, with a general motherhouse at Houston, has a membership of 412 and maintains 27 houses; an independent branch of the same community with a generalate at San Antonio, has 917 sisters and 129 houses.

[R. A. TODD]

INCARNATE WORD AND BLESSED SACRAMENT, CONGREGATION OF THE (IWBS), an originally cloistered congregation of women religious founded at Roanne (later at Lyons), France in 1625 by Mother Jeanne Marie Chézard de Matel. The members follow the rule of St. Augustine.The congregation was approved by Innocent X in 1644 and it was not until 1913 that the cloister was lifted. Suppressed during the French Revolution, the community was reorganized in 1832. The sisters engage in an apostolate of educational and hospital work. Besides the motherhouse in France, the community extended its work to Mexico and U.S. (1853), where it established three autonomous foundations in Texas, with a total membership of 480 sisters, maintaining 30 houses; the congregation in Guadalajara, Mexico has 48 sisters and 4 houses.

[R. A. TODD]

INCARNATION (Lat. *caro,* flesh), the Christian dogma that the Second Person of the Trinity became a human being in the historical person, Jesus of Nazareth. The doctrine asserts that Jesus is fully and completely God as well as fully and completely a human being. As such it is the pivotal affirmation of Christian faith, giving direction and specific content to all other Christian mysteries. The Incarnation is the ultimate self-communication of God and his redeeming acceptance of the world and sinful humankind. The normative scriptural text for the Incarnation is John 1.14: "The Word became flesh," i.e., the divine agent of creation, governance, and redemption assumed the complete physical reality of a particular man. This perspective is characteristic of the fourth Gospel which presents the Word's actual "becoming flesh" as decisive for human salvation rather than, for instance, the cross and Resurrection. The other Gospels also assert the complete humanity of Jesus, proclaiming his birth from a woman, his physical activities of eating, drinking, sleeping, etc., his death, and the corporal nature of his risen body. At the same time, the Gospels present the unique relationship between Yahweh and Jesus who, esp. in the Son of Man title, is regarded as the preexistent agent of God's definitive act of salvation. In Paul, the preexistence of Jesus is explicitly acknowledged as well as his complete human nature: Jesus was in the form (mode of existence) of God but was subsequently "born in the likeness of men" (Phil 2.6 ff.); he is "the image of the invisible God" and in his incarnate state the one in whom "the fullness of God was pleased to dwell" (Col 1.15–18).

In the first 5 cent., the early Church—esp. in the East—labored extensively to formulate the true manner of union between God and man in Jesus. The issue was not an easy one to resolve; conceptual variations, terminological shifts, and political machinations all contributed to the difficulties encountered. It is important to note, however, that no matter how varied the explanations and acrimonious the debates, the Church was never content to accept a formulation that denied either Christ's humanity (such as the several forms of Docetism), or Christ's divinity (the various forms of Adoptionism; Arianism). Two principal conceptual models emerged. The Word-man or Antiochene formulation was consistent with an Aristotelian anthropology which stressed the essential union of soul and body in man. This approach argued that in order to preserve the complete humanity of Jesus, it was necessary to assert that he had a human or rational soul. The eternal Word came to dwell in this complete human being. While this approach clearly safeguarded Jesus' true humanity, its deficiency was its tendency to regard the unity of the Incarnate Christ in a rather superficial way. The Antiochene school also questioned whether an attribute which pertained to only one nature in Christ could be applied to the single Incarnate Person, e.g., whether it was legitimate to say that God died on the cross or that Mary was the mother of God. The second conceptual model was the Word-flesh or Alexandrian model, consistent with a Platonic anthropology which regarded the soul as fundamentally separable from the body. This approach maintained that the eternal Word assumed flesh but not a human soul. The Word was the one governing principle in Jesus even after it had become united with human flesh. Thus the Alexandrian model easily explained the complete and total unity of the Incarnate Word as well as the interchange of communication of attributes, but tended to deny Jesus' full humanity. The controversy reached its culmination at the Council of Chalcedon (451), where the two natures/one person explanation was agreed upon and became the nearly universal solution to the prior Christological controversies. Chalcedon defined that Christ had two complete natures or principles of activity: a divine soul and a human soul. Yet there is only one person in Christ, the Second Person of the Trinity. The union between the human and divine nature is hypostatic, i.e., there is only one complete individual being, or person, the eternal Word, who unites himself with a human body and soul.

Subsequent reflections on the Incarnation have, until relatively recent times, remained within the two natures/one person framework. The speculative synthesis attained in the 13th cent. employed this perspective exclusively. Thus

Thomas Aquinas defines the Incarnation as "the communication of the divine personal Being on a created nature through the goodness of God." The Incarnation is a free act of God, not one that is necessarily implied by the relationships within the Divine Trinity itself. Through the Incarnation, a Divine Person without any modification in his being communicates himself to a complete human nature. According to the Thomistic analysis, the Incarnation is also contingent, i.e., it would not have taken place if man had not sinned. In Christ there is only one Person, one complete and final individual being, realizing full existence in the ontological order and complete responsibility in the moral order. Christ's human nature has no subsistence (hypostasis) aside from its realization in the Word.

Some contemporary theologians question whether this classical explanation of the union between God and man in Jesus remains adequate at a time when the categories of person and nature are no longer used within an Aristotelian/Scholastic frame of reference. Some affirm Jesus as the unique mediator between God and man but refuse to postulate his divinity (Bultmann); others classify this emphasis on Jesus' uniqueness just as mythological as his divinity (Ogden). Some prefer an entirely new terminology, e.g., Jesus is the New Being who manifests the essential "Godmanhood" of all human beings (Tillich). Process theologians also reject the classical explanation, preferring to base their explanation on the uniquely effective relationship between God and Jesus whereby God completely realizes his living presence to human beings, and Jesus comes to the fullness of his humanity through his relationship with the Father (Pittenger). Some contemporary RC theologians have also probed some new speculative interpretations: Piet Schoonenberg holds that there is only one person in Christ—the human person—who operates through both a human and a divine nature. In spite of these variations, as eminent and contemporary a theologian as Karl Rahner maintains that the key concepts for understanding the Incarnation are person, nature, and hypostatic union —Chalcedonian terms which he insists have never been improved upon. BIBLIOGRAPHY: R. Brown, "Who Do Men Say That I Am? Modern Scholarship on Gospel Christology," *Horizons* 1 (1974) 35–50; D. Griffin, *Process Christology* (1973); A. Grillmeier, *Christ in Christian Tradition* (rev. ed., 1975); S. Ogden, *Christ Without Myth* (1961); K. Rahner, *SacMund.* 3:110–118; P. Schoonenberg, *Christ* (1971).

[T. M. MCFADDEN]

INCARNATIONAL THEOLOGY, a type of theology that in major questions draws explanation from the mystery of the God-man. A contemporary RC resurgence of this emphasis reached its apex approximately during the years 1933–55. It stemmed from a rethinking of faith in the Incarnation of the Son of God and extended to the Christian involvement in all phases of human activity—economic, political, social, and cultural. M. I. Montuclard, P. Teilhard de Chardin, Y. Congar, H. de Lubac, and G. Thils endeavored to show how the Christian, to be fully human, must assume earthly realities and human values for whatever they are worth so that he can help to build up the mystical body of Christ. The need of a theological explanation of the Christian's involvement in the world has given an incarnational direction to both Protestant and RC theology, and explains the appeal of existentialist and phenomenological philosophies to contemporary theologians. There is no total agreement among theologians about the values of the world. The Christian cannot escape in his life the practical question of the continuity and discontinuity between the material and spiritual, sacred and profane, natural and supernatural, worldly achievement and the kingdom of God. Incarnational theology has to be balanced by an eschatological point of view. BIBLIOGRAPHY: N. Sharkey, NCE 7:415–416; B. Besret, *Incarnation ou Eschatologie?* (1964); J. M. Connolly, *Human History and the Word of God: The Christian Meaning in Contemporary Thought* (1965), esp. ch. 6, "The Catholic Theologies of History." *ESCHATOLOGICAL THEOLOGY.

[J. FICHTNER]

INCENSE (Gr., *thumiama;* Sl., *ladan),* perfumed resinous gum substances which are burned in church services or in the home and give off an aromatic odor. Pure frankincense (gum olibanum) is predominantly used, but other fragrances and mixtures are also found. The use of incense in the Christian Church probably derives from its use in the Jewish temple services and, although its early history is not clear, it would seem that St. John (Rev. 8.3–5) implies that its use was known in the Apostolic Church. At the end of the 2d cent. Tertullian mentions the use of incense at funeral processions, and by the 5th cent. it is often mentioned, esp. in regard to the placing of fixed censers before the shrines of martyrs and saints. Incense in the early Church was probably associated with the idea of a sin offering and the purifying sweet-smelling smoke was considered a sign of forgiveness and cleansing. By the 6th cent. it was definitely used in the entry procession of the bp. at the Liturgy, and by the 9th cent. the custom of incensing the altar, Gospels, and holy things was common.

Incense is used today as a symbolic representation of the prayer of the Church rising before the Divine Majesty and also of the pouring out of the individual Christian as grains of incense to be consumed in the service of the Lord. The actual incensing of the altar, the Gospels, the icons, the clergy, and the congregation relate to the presence of Christ in each of these things. It is Christ himself who is reverenced in his holy altar, in his revealed word, in his actual image, or in the images of those who share most perfectly in the Christ-life (saints), in his ordained ministers who are dispensers of the mysteries of God, and in his people who by their baptismal consecration stand as images of God by the indwelling of the Trinity and as sharers in the royal priesthood of Christ.

In the newly revised Liturgy, the RC Church has made the use of incense optional in any form of Mass, but the times and manner of its use are prescribed in "General Instructions of the Roman Missal," in the *Sacramentary* of 1974, 235–236.

[A. J. JACOPIN]

INCEST, sexual intercourse between a male and a female closely related by blood (consanguinity) or marital kinship (affinity); the term is also given a broader application to sexual acts short of intercourse. Incest in its fullest and most reprehensible sense is between parent and child; the degree of relationship that categorizes sexual intercourse as incestuous varies according to varying determinations of law, and the remoter the relationship the less incestuous the union. The degrees of relationship that in canon law constitute the matrimonial *impediments of consanguinity (CIC c.96;1042;1076;1990) or affinity (CIC c.97; 1041;1077;1990) are a practical norm for moral theology in regard to incest. The OT evidences both incidents of incestuous union and their proscription in various forms (Lev 18.3–18;Dt 27.20–23; 3 Kgs 2.13–21; Am 2.7). In the NT John the Baptist condemned the incest of Herod with Herodias (Mk 6.17–18) and St. Paul, the union of a man with his father's wife (1 Cor 5.1–12). The special moral disorder of incest is that it introduces libidinousness into a family's intimate life, and that is a threat to the higher bond of affection among the members; it also could prevent the widening of the family's contacts with others and threaten the benefits derived from mutual assistance in society (see ThAq ST 2a2ae, 154.9). Psychologists, anthropologists, and sociologists discuss and variously interpret the incest taboo, but generally agree that it is almost universally observed. The risk that incest may bring together dangerously recessive genes and so cause congenital defects is not thought to be the reason for the taboo. Not all geneticists agree that there is such a risk.

[T. C. O'BRIEN]

INCEST (IN THE BIBLE). Leviticus 18.6–18 sets forth the different kinds and degrees of relationship between a man and woman, whether of affinity or consanguinity, that constitute a special legal and moral bar to their engaging in sexual intercourse (cf. Dt 27.20, 22–23). Leviticus 20.11–21 lists the penalties to be inflicted on those who violate the prohibition. The law is explicitly imposed on the man, because he was regarded as the active party in sexual relationship. Inferentially, however, the woman also was bound by it, for she as well as the man was subject to the penalty. There is no mention of a prohibition of intercourse between a father and his daughter. Such a prohibition may possibly have dropped out of the text. The list is late in the history of Israel, for in patriarchal times there was marriage between brother and sister. In the NT Paul's observation about the conduct of the man who was living with his stepmother, that such a thing was not found even among pagans (I Cor 5.1), suggests that the Jews and early Christians were stricter in their views of incest than were the pagans. BIBLIOGRAPHY: De Vaux AncIsr; M. Noth, *Leviticus: A Commentary* (tr. J. E. Anderson, 1965).

[F. GAST]

INCHCOLM ABBEY a monastery situated on an island in the Firth of Forth, Scotland, founded by King Alexander I for Augustinian Canons *c.* 1123 on an earlier Celtic site. Its vulnerable position made it a frequent target for English raiders in the Middle Ages, who occupied it in 1547. It was suppressed in 1560; its substantial ruins are still impressive BIBLIOGRAPHY: D. E. Easson, *Medieval Religious Houses: Scotland* (1957) 76; S. Cruden, *Scottish Abbeys* (1960) 75–76.

[L. J. MACFARLANE]

INCHMAHOME PRIORY, an Augustinian house founded on an island in Loch Menteith, Perthshire, Scotland (1238), and now a well-preserved ruin. It was here, after the Battle of Pinkie in 1543, that the child Mary Queen of Scots was sheltered before leaving for France. BIBLIOGRAPHY: D. E. Easson, *Medieval Religious Houses: Scotland* (1957) 76.

[L. J. MACFARLANE]

INCIPIT, the opening letters or words of medieval MSS (later of early printed books), usually highly ornate; similarly the *explicit* at the end of the manuscripts. The two Latin terms mean "begins" and "ends."

[T. C. O'BRIEN]

INCOMBUSTIBILITY (*mystical phenomenon*), a person's capacity to withstand the physical effects of fire. As an authentic mystical occurrence, this phenomenon can testify to an individual's holiness or truthfulness. BIBLIOGRAPHY: H. Thurston, *Physical Phenomena of Mysticism* (1952).

[T. M. MCFADDEN]

INCOMMUNICABILITY, a theological term signifying the self-containedness of the ontological subject. Paradoxically, the possibility of interpersonal communication supposes the absolute incommunicability of personhood. Personhood is formally constituted by the completeness of an individual subject subsisting in a spiritual nature. The integration of being that constitutes a subject as an ontological center, makes it at once self-possessed and absolutely incommunicable. It gives it the ontological consistency that is at the root of every personal relationship. Short of the incommunicability of the ontological subject, exchange and relationships would result in disintegration of being.

The coincidence of incommunicability and communication is verified at its deepest level in the mystery of the Trinity. There, communication is complete within the numerical identity of one nature; at the same time, the incommunicability of the Persons is ensured by the opposition of their mutual relationship. The mystery of the Trinity throws light on the mystery of the human person. It shows that distinction between subjects is in direct proportion to the intimacy of their relatedness. As a center of being, the person is self-possessed, but it is turned to other persons. BIBLIOGRAPHY: B. Lonergan, *De constitutione Christi ontologica et psychologica* (1964) 9; *idem., De Deo Trino v.2: Pars systematica* (1964) 152.

[J. DUPUIS]

INCOMPREHENSIBILITY OF GOD, the excess of the divine being over the power of any created mind's knowing power. Because the intelligibility of being corresponds to its actual perfection (see PURE ACT), the only mind commensurate with the divine intelligibility is the divine mind itself; the only adequate intellectual expression of the divine reality is the Divine Word, the Son. The vision of God given to the blessed, their mind being strengthened by the *light of glory, is an unmediated but not exhaustive intuition of God. BIBLIOGRAPHY: ThAq St 1a, 12.1.2.5–7;14.3.

[T. C. O'BRIEN]

INCORPORATION IN CHRIST, the action by which, or the state into which, one is united with Christ, and, consequently, with all already united with him. The expression derives from Pauline comments on unity in diversity in the dynamic, Spirit-given, Christ-centered, and God-operated communal life of the Church at Corinth (1 Cor 12.12,27; cf. 6.15; 10.17; Rom 12.4,5; etc.). The analogous concept tries to delve into the mysterious union of the resurrected Lord Jesus with his believers on earth. Incorporation begins when an adult believes the gospel about Jesus' saving death, Resurrection, and lordship—an invisible act governed by God's grace; it becomes apparent when he professes his faith before men by receiving the initiating sacraments, so that his hidden faith takes visible form; it is completed when, after complete growth in Christ, the person is united with him forever in God. In infant baptism, since the baby cannot make an act of faith, the parents and the sacred community are said to supply this lack so that there is an ontological incorporation of the child into Christ. In any case, the cradle-Christian must eventually by an act of faith accept Christ as his Savior when he is able.

The union of Christians in the Body of Christ is correlative to their union with him. The spiritual gifts and powers flowing from participation in the Spirit's ordered government must lead not to personal exaltation but to the building up of the common fellowship through Christ's love as Lord of his servants. Paul constantly returns to this principle when he has to solve problems of personal relationships of Christians living in community (1 Cor 12–14 and parallels). The biblical analogues, although stemming from organic types, are figures of spiritual, supernatural realities that govern the living, visible community of the Church of Christ. They thus are societal in intent rather than organic, a fact that harmoniously connects them with other important biblical analogues derived from the Church's description as the People of God. Modern ecclesiologists are in the process of applying both sets of figures to the problems of the nature of the Church in the modern world. BIBLIOGRAPHY: H. Küng, *Church* (1967) 203–241; A. Dulles, *Models of the Church* (1974) 43–57.

[J. F. FALLON]

INCORRUPTIBILITY, (1) in Aristotelian philosophy an immunity from substantial change characteristic of beings not composed of matter and form, and also of heavenly bodies; (2) in theology a property of Christ's glorified body and the bodies of those who share in his Resurrection (1 Cor 15.42). Before the Resurrection Christ freely accepted the natural subjection of the body to death, and so merited for himself and his faithful the glory of the Resurrection. As a manifestation of the power of Christ's grace, the bodies of some of the saints have remained free of corruption after death, even as Christ's own body was not subject to the process of decay during its entombment.

[T. C. O'BRIEN]

INCUBATION, the practice observed among Greeks and Romans of sleeping within the precincts of certain temples in order to experience visions, revelations, and, more esp. in order to secure relief from disease or pain. Some deities were thought more amenable than others to this kind of approach; the incubation, usually accompanied by the observance of some specific ritual, was considered an effective means of inducing them to do as the suppliant wished. The observance was esp. associated with temples of *Aesculapius. BIBLIOGRAPHY: A. J. Festugière, *Personal Religion among the Greeks* (1954).

[P. K. MEAGHER]

INDEFECTIBILITY, a gift, a charism, given the earthly Church through the presence of the Spirit whereby it exists in Christian dynamism from Pentecost to the Parousia. As charismatic reality, the gift of indefectibility is given to the Church not as a title of boasting but for others. It is for the good of the human family that the new family of God in Christ is indefectible.

The Son of God became incarnate at a given moment of human history. He entered man's universe, man's humanity, at a certain moment of time and in a certain location. His saving deeds, however, were for all men of all ages and every location. The Church, therefore, which prolongs the presence of Christ and makes present concretely in human availability his saving mystery, is for all ages. It possesses the charism of indefectibility. Through the Church the gospel is announced to every creature, the paschal mystery is liturgically celebrated in every age, all men are invited to communion with Christ and with one another in God's family. The Church as sacrament of Christ's presence among men exists among men until the end of human life on earth.

Otherwise the grace and love of Christ would no longer be actual in present humanness for all men.

While the Church possesses the charism of perpetuity in dynamic presentation of the gospel, the Church is not changeless. Rather, in its indefectibility, the Church experiences the growth of living organism. The permanent message of Christ is announced down the ages in terms meaningful to each age. The paschal mystery is celebrated in signs relevant to each age. The ministry is exercised according to the needs of each age. Loving service to others finds diversity of concrete expression. The Church must maintain its essential mission and permanent structure, while at the same time resisting the temptation to rigidity in accidental forms throughout its indefectible earthly life. BIBLIOGRAPHY: E. Dublanchy, DTC 4.2:2145–50; M. E. Williams, NCE 7:429; Vat II ConstChurch 48; C. Journet, *Church of the Word Incarnate* (tr. A. Downes, 1955) 1:530–554; R. Latourelle, *Theology of Revelation* (1966) 417–424.

[J. F. GALLAGHER]

INDEPENDENCY, that *polity which recognizes local congregations of believers as autonomous under Christ and denies any but ministerial and persuasive authority to any wider fellowship of churches or to any priestly order. In the 17th cent. the word was gradually replaced by the more positive term *Congregationalism. The word and the concept, however, still persist in Wales in the Union of Welsh Independents. In certain parts of England also the term ''Independent Chapel'' continues to be preferred to Congregational Church. *BROWNE, ROBERT; *INDEPENDENTS.

[R. F. G. CALDER]

INDEPENDENT CHURCHES, in England a synonym for Congregational churches, or those churches that have a congregational polity (see INDEPENDENCY), but in the U.S. a designation for churches having no denominational affiliation. Such churches have proliferated since the fundamentalist-modernist controversy after World War I. This movement had diverse origins, but underlying it was an erosion of the doctrine of the universal Church, to which several influences contributed. *Rationalism, *individualism, and *revivalism fostered a concept of the Church as simply a voluntary association of believers (see VOLUNTARYISM). Plymouth Brethren ideas of the Church, disseminated through the *Scofield Bible, used in many Bible schools, reinforced this tendency. As doctrinal disputes aroused suspicions of major denominations, many churches severed ties with such bodies and existed without relationship to other churches. Independent churches often furnish generous support to missionary and evangelistic causes through numerous independent missionary organizations. There are also *community churches that are independent but that emphasize cooperation on the basis of a comprehensive Christian unity. *INTERDENOMINATIONAL CHURCHES.

[N. H. MARING]

INDEPENDENTS, an early designation for Congregationalists. The term was in use in England until the 18th cent.; in Wales the Welsh-speaking Congregationalists continue to be called Welsh Independents. The origin of the name is R. *Browne's idea that the local church is itself a full expression of the kingdom of God and thus free of superior authority, civil or ecclesiastical. The Independents were the strongest of the Puritan parties and had a notable influence upon the evolution of the rights of *Nonconformists. There is a second usage of the name among the Disciples of Christ, who call members of their churches engaged in autonomous foreign mission work Independents. BIBLIOGRAPHY: bibliog. for Congregationalism. *GATHERED CHURCH.

[R. B. ENO]

INDETERMINISM, a point of view which maintains the real possibility of undetermined, uncaused, unnecessary, or chance events occurring and which questions the logic and significance of arguments in support of divine providence or of fate, utter necessity, determinism, or of any other purposiveness. Indeterminism, historically, has been a reaction to deterministic philosophies, particularly those arising from 17th-cent. natural sciences. The Newtonian universe is, by definition, utterly determined in all of its subsequent events by its state at any single time, since the laws of its operation are uniformly fixed. Descartes' ontological determinism posited the fundamental quantitative, mechanical nature of the material (not spiritual) universe. With Laplace's *Celestial Mechanics* and Kant's *Critique of Pure Reason,* determinism with the distinctive stamps of Newton's mechanics and Descartes' subjectivism became firmly established in 19th-cent. physics and philosophy. C.S. Pierce's objection to determinist arguments that the real was exactly as it is and could not have been otherwise, was that such arguments are trivial and specious; he himself presented a doctrine of real chance and utter indeterminism in certain cases. A. Cournot criticized the extension of Newtonian theoretical physics to the real world of physical bodies as being logically unsound. The revolution in physics following the appearance of relativity and quantum and wave mechanics, which occurred during the early 20th cent., fundamentally subverted the classical mechanics of the Newtonian world view. Werner Heisenberg offered an ''indeterminacy principle,'' which stated that either the position or momentum of a subatomic particle could be assigned a value, but not both, and for Newtonian physics to apply, both must be possible. The question of indeterminism has been debated since ancient times when Lucretius and Epicurus maintained that novel, uncaused, chance events can and do occur, and that these spontaneous actions are the physical basis upon which a philosophy of human freedom can be defended. More typically the debate between determinists and indeterminists has centered on the key issue of human freedom: can and do humans rationally and/or willfully decide to act in ways that alter the shape of events? William

James posed the problem in pragmatic fashion: walking home, one can choose between a number of different routes all of which end at the same destination; all choices are thus real possibilities and the route chosen reflects a real choice by the traveler. The determinist response is that one and only one route was taken and could have been taken; the other possible routes have the semblance of real possibilities but in actuality are not—the real is exactly what it is and cannot be otherwise; "might have beens" do not really exist in the real world. The ancient form of this question appears in Aristotle's *De Interpretatione:* given a naval battle, were correct predictions about its outcome "true" before the battle itself was finished; in other words, were victory and defeat equal possibilities? The Christian form of the question raised the difficult problem of consistently maintaining God's absolute foreknowledge and will as well as freedom of the human will: if God is omniscient, omnipotent, and good, how can there be evil in the world; how can God permit the willful choice of evil, human sin? Augustine and Aquinas both resolved this issue by stressing God's eternity as being independent of temporal, transient events, insisting that God's eternal thoughts do not necessitate temporary events. Predestination, a concept central to the Protestantism of Calvin and Luther, is a related issue; the Reformers maintained that humans cannot be saved by their will alone but must be saved by divine grace of faith and that God saves those whom he has predetermined shall be saved. The perennial problem that indeterminists must face is whether or not it is merely the limitation of human intelligence, reason, or knowledge and thus the human incapacity to explain the full content and context of events which makes these seem indeterminate. Yet indeterminists, given their belief in spontaneity and chance, must also explain the apparent order and regularity of the cosmos; and religious indeterminists must deal with the omnipotence of God in a universe that seems to be freely altered in its lesser aspects by human will. The core issue is the future: indeterminists claim that there are many equally possible futures, each as likely and real as the next; determinists, that there is and can be only one. *GOVERNMENT, DIVINE.

[R. J. LITZ]

INDEX OF FORBIDDEN BOOKS (*Index librorum prohibitorum*), an alphabetical listing of books banned by the RC Church. The ban extended to the publication, sale, reading, translation, or possession of these books. Violators of the prohibition incurred excommunication (CIC c. 2318.1). This penalty and the binding force of the Index itself were abrogated in 1966.

The Council of Nicaea I (325) condemned a work of Arius; the so-called Gelasian Decree (496) condemned certain apocryphal writings; the practice of banning works regarded as heretical continued through the Middle Ages. With the Reformation and the invention of printing, the first general Roman Index of proscribed books was published in 1559. Since this catalogue was considered too severe, the Council of Trent took up the work of revision at its 24th session (1563), but turned the task over to Paul IV for completion. He promulgated the Tridentine Index in 1564, together with 10 norms on censorship and reading. Pius V instituted a special Congregation of the Index in 1571. The Tridentine Index, periodically revised, and with norms added by Benedict XIV (*Sollicita ac provida,* 1753), remained in force down to the 19th century. Carrying out a proposal made during Vatican Council I, Leo XIII issued new norms (*Officiorum ac munerum,* 1897) and a new Index (1900). The Leonine rules were substantially incorporated into the revised CIC in 1917; in the same year the Congregation of the Index was absorbed into the Congregation of the Holy Office. The Leonine Index was periodically amended, the last edition appearing in 1948. Discussions on censorship at Vatican Council II led to the 1966 decision to discontinue the Index.

The Index was never meant as an exhaustive list; the 1948 edition contained 4,126 books condemned since 1600, 255 of them in the 20th century. Works banned were those that the Roman Congregations, or in some cases the pope personally, ruled to be particularly dangerous. Most prohibitions were directed against theological or philosophical works, not against the obscene. The prohibition always admitted of exceptions in favor of educational or professional requirements. While the Index has ceased to exist, the Church retains the right to condemn books, but only after the author has been heard. Members of the Church remain bound by general canonical legislation, and by the requirements of Christian prudence in regard to literature that may endanger faith or morals. BIBLIOGRAPHY: R. A. Burke, *What Is the Index?* (1952); G. H. Putnam, *Censorship and the Church of Rome* (2 v., 1967). *BOOKS, PROHIBITION OF; *PRECENSORSHIP.

[T. EARLY]

INDIA, republic of SE Asia (1,261,597 sq mi; pop [est. 1974] 586,270,000). Northern India was the seat of a great civilization which was swept away by Aryan invasions around 1500 B.C. The land has been overrun from ancient times by foreign armies. From the 16th cent. A.D. onward it became the prey of European nations: of Portugal and Holland, which controlled its shores; and of Great Britain, which annexed it in 1877. Independence was achieved in 1947 on the following terms: India and Pakistan are independent states; Kashmir is a disputed territory; and the N boundaries remain as an occasion of conflict with Communist China. There are more than 800 languages and dialects, 14 of them official. The country continues to be predominantly rural, although steps are being taken to create industries as well as to modernize farming. Most Indians profess Hinduism, believe in reincarnation, and are not yet ready to give up the caste system. Mohammedans, in spite of their exodus to Pakistan in 1947, form the largest minority group, perhaps 61,417,934. There are also several million aborigines attached to animistic beliefs and practices. The Indian Christians of the Malabar coast claim their conversion can be traced to the preaching of the Apostle Thomas. In 1329 Rome created the Diocese of Quilon. At the beginning of the 16th cent., Portugal brought missionaries to preach the Gospel. Goa was made an episcopal see in 1534, as were Cochin and Malacca in 1557. India became a center of St. Francis Xavier's activities. By 1600 Catholics numbered 250,000; synods were organized; schools, colleges, and seminaries were opened. In 1606 Robert de Nobili began his efforts to adapt Christianity to Indian culture and customs, taking up residence as a *sanyasi* and devoting his time to the sacred books of Hinduism; but his method, which had already become controversial among missionaries, was condemned by the Pope in 1774. The 18th cent. was a period of decadence for the Indian Church, with growing conflicts between Propaganda and Padroado, suppression of the Jesuit order, and a lessening in number of missioners and their activities; but the next 50 years, in spite of the Goan "schism," were a time of great progress. Missionary societies came from many European countries and, profiting from the religious freedom granted by the British, carried on systematic evangelization. There has been a steady increase of foreign missionaries, but more esp. of native clergy. In 1976 the total Catholic community numbered 8,992,384. The Church is divided into 16 ecclesiastical provinces, 55 suffragan sees, and 4 prefectures. India has 10,012 priests, 3,828 brothers, and 40,302 sisters (almost three-fourths of them native). The clergy are prepared in 14 major and 49 minor seminaries. There are 32 colleges for men and 30 for women, 140 industrial schools; and over 450 high schools. The Catholic press is well developed but needs to adapt itself to non-Christian readers. Much social work remains to be done. Viewed as a whole, the Church in India holds great promise. Vocations to the priesthood and religious life abound. The laity is being organized, often despite material poverty.

Protestantism has made great progress in India. Work was begun by Zingenbald and Plutschau in 1706 and continued by Schwartz (1750–89). American and European societies have shared in the task. Men like Bp. Azariah have pioneered in the ecumenical movement. Nationalization is well advanced. The Union of the Church of South India might well serve as a pattern for similar mergers. Protestants have contributed greatly to education and medicine. Currently, Pentecostals and Adventists are working hard to attract followers. The total Protestant membership in 1976 numbered 5,230,888 served by many thousands of native and foreign ministers. BIBLIOGRAPHY: C. B. Finth, *Introduction to Indian Church History* (1961); G. M. Moraes, *History of Christianity in India* (1965); *Bilan du Monde* 2:461–476.

[P. DAMBORIENA]

INDIA, CHRISTIANITY IN. The history of Christianity in India is quite ancient, though Christians in India are not numerous. The Thomas Christians of SW India claim that their Church was established by the Apostle Thomas himself; there are not enough historical proofs to justify the claim. However, there is historical evidence (writings of the Greek, Cosmos Indicoplustes) of the presence of Christianity in India as early as the 6th century. The Portuguese excavation near Madras in 1547 suggests the presence of Christianity in India in the 9th century. In the 11th cent. the Pope sent a few representatives to India, and they baptized a few people. However, the first major impact of Christianity was felt in India after Vasco da Gama's discovery of the sea route from Europe to India. The Portuguese settled in Goa (SW India) and brought Roman Catholicism along with them. They did not try to convert the local people. However, they converted a whole community of fishers in return for protecting them from the pirates. In the middle of the 16th cent. when St. *Francis Xavier came to Goa, he took measures that were decisive for the whole future of the Indian Church. He translated the Lord's Prayer, the Apostle's Creed, and the Ten Commandments into local language, and so paved the way for evangelization. He established St. Paul's College in Goa to prepare the local students for Christian ministry. In the 17th cent. the Italian Jesuit, Robert de *Nobili, achieved considerable success in converting some high caste Hindus by his Indianization of Christianity and observance of some Hindu customs. But soon his measures were abandoned in favor of Roman practices. From the end of the 18th cent., the Roman Church declined in India for political and ecclesiastical reasons, e.g., suppression (1773) of the Jesuits by the Pope. Protestantism came to India along with the British, Dutch, and Danish traders. The Danish Lutheran Ziegenbalg translated and printed the NT in Tamil. Later, a German translated the Old Testament. However, in the 18th cent. because of the lack of missionary zeal in Europe, there was a dearth of Western missionaries; a native Indian ministry did not develop, and the Protestant Churches declined. After the establishment of British rule in India in the 18th cent. the British were against missionary activity among the local people for political reasons. However, in the end, they had to yield to the pressure of the evangelists at home and granted freedom to missionaries of all denominations to settle in India. A Baptist from England, W. *Carey, together with two others, translated and printed the Bible in many Indian languages as well as in Chinese. They established a college in Serampore to instruct Asiatic Christians. They endeavored to study Hinduism and translated some of its classics. Churches and missionary societies of different denominations from the U.S. and also from continental Europe took a great part in missionary activities in India. During the colonial time the gospel was spread in many ways; there were medical, industrial, and agricultural missions. Many centers for the study of medicine, technology, different arts and sciences as well as theological studies were established. Women missionaries started to take part in evangelization and education of the Indian women. One woman convert, Panditae Ramabai, had a marked impact on the community. With all their zeal, however, the missionaries were not very successful as far as the number of actual converts was concerned. They were somewhat successful among lower caste Hindus and aboriginal communities in India, but could convert only a few high caste Hindus and Muslims. The causes seem to lie in the nature and character of the Indian community as well as the nature and character of the missions. Hinduism, the religion of the majority of Indians, has great flexibility and variety as far as faith structure is concerned. The Hindus could incorporate what they understood about Christianity within their own faith. Many of the Hindu elite of the 19th and the 20th cent. admired and wrote highly about Jesus Christ without giving up their own religion. Acceptance of conversion seemed to many the giving up of their own customs in favor of foreign ones. The missions also did not try to dissociate Christianity from Western culture. Very few and futile attempts were made to Indianize Christianity. The Western superiority complex of the missionaries, as well as the lack of education among converts and their underprivileged background, hindered the development of India's ministry and India's Church. In modern times most of the Churches are trying to adjust Christianity to the local cultures. This, together with the suspicion towards foreigners of the government of the present independent India, calls for the development of a native ministry. A number of Indian Christians are trying to adapt Christian theology to Indian terms.

[K. MITRA]

INDIA, CHURCH OF SOUTH, see CHURCH OF SOUTH INDIA.

INDIAN MISSIONS (U.S.). The apostolate to the Indian tribes in what is now the U.S. has a long, continuous, and creditable history, antedating the earliest white settlements. Its fundamental objective has been to bring Christ's message to men and second, to promote the Indians' temporal welfare. Two main thrusts of continued and systematic activities are observable. The first of these occurred during the colonial period (1565–1825) mainly in the Spanish borderlands from Florida to California and was manned by Franciscan friars. Jesuits also established scattered missions on the fringes of New France (1613–1768). Considerable success was attained in these regions, but the effort on the whole was hindered, and results were all but obliterated by attacks of wild tribes, hostility of neighboring whites, or secularization of the missions. This first effort's legacy to the young American Church was a few scattered and abandoned groups of Catholic Indians. The second and renewed advance of the apostolate was initiated by Bp. John *Carroll in the 1790s by the appointment of four priests to the remnants of the mission in his jurisdiction. The work advanced slowly, but the appearance of the mission school, first elementary, then manual-training, was an importance advance. Strong impetus was given to the apostolate by the *Bureau of Catholic Indian Missions after its establishment in 1874, and by the kindling of interest in the work among Jesuits, Franciscans, Benedictines, and numerous sisterhoods. The apostolic effort spread rapidly from tribe to tribe. Missions were established and are now functioning on all the large Indian reservations and on many of the smaller ones in 23 states. Obvious results have been a steadily increasing number of Catholic Indians, reported to be approximately 125,000 at present, or 40% of the Indians living on or near reservations. This increase has been due largely to births, but converts in recent years have numbered about 1,000 annually. An undetermined number of other Catholic Indians from the missions, many thousands in the aggregate, are living in white communities. Work on the missions is now principally pastoral and educational in character. In 1976, Catholic Indians on the reservations were served by 271 priests, mainly at 397 churches; 5,947 Indian children attended 37 Catholic schools. BIBLIOGRAPHY: J. B. Tennelly, NCE 1:402–408; P. de Smet, *Western Missions and Missionaries* (1863, repr. 1972); J. G. Shea, *History of the Catholic Missions among the Indian Tribes of the U.S. 1529–1854* (1855, repr. AMS).

[J. B. TENNELLY]

INDIAN MISSIONS, BUREAU OF CATHOLIC, see BUREAU OF CATHOLIC INDIAN MISSIONS.

INDIAN PHILOSOPHY. The aim of philosophical thought in India is medicinal; philosophy is not simply an intellectual enterprise, it is also a practiced device for curing the existential ailments. Emphasis on the problems of life tends to give a pessimistic tone to Indian philosophy, for which it is often criticised; however, pessimism is only initial and not final. With the exception of Cārvāka, no other school thinks that the problems of life cannot be dealt with and have simply to be tolerated. Each school offers some resolutions of the problems of life. Use of reason in philosophical endeavor is emphasized by all. Each school deals with the epistemological question of how and how far one can know, and bases its ontological investigation on its epistemological position. Axiological issues or values systems are settled by ontological answers. Each philosopher has to state the view of his opponent (Pūrvapakṣa), refute it (Khandana), and then state and prove his own view (Uttarapakṣa). However, the majority of the schools believe that the ultimate truth is transrational and can be grasped only by direct apprehension. The Sanskrit name for philosophy is *darshana* (seeing), and philosophy and religion are intimately related to each other. Out of the nine classical schools of thought, six (Sankhya-Yoga; Nyaya-Vaiseshika; Mimamsa-Vedanta) try to trace their views to the Veda, the Hindu Scripture. The other three, Cārvāka, Buddha, and Jaina are anti-Hindu; however, Buddhism and *Jainism are both important religions of India. Cārvāka is a realistic and materialistic school of thought; it depends only on perceptual knowledge, regarding inference and authority as unreliable and misleading. Perception reveals only the material world, but neither soul nor God. The aim of life, therefore, is enjoyment, as much as and as far as possible. The Jaina school is based on the teaching of its saints. Jainism points out that besides perception, valid inference and authority are reliable. These sources of knowledge prove the existence of soul as above the material world, though there is no necessity to accept the existence of God. Human soul has infinite potentiality and by proper cultivation can reach perfection, the goal of life. The Buddhist system, based on the teachings of Buddha, in the course of history became divided into many schools, and their philosophical conclusions are quite different from one another. However, all accept the four noble truths taught by Buddha, viz, there is suffering; there is cause of suffering; if the cause is removed, so is the suffering; and the cause can be removed. Thus, by proper development one can stop suffering. The Nyaya is a school of realism based on logical thinking. It deals with the epistemological questions in minute detail, and epistemology in India is named after the school, viz, Nyaya-Vidya. By skillful argument it tries to prove the existence of God, whose guidance helps man to be free from suffering. The Vaiseshika system is allied to Nyaya and accepts the epistemological conclusions of Nyaya. It makes a detailed investigation of the different ontological categories; its treatment of the category of relation and nonexistence is quite unique. Its view of the goal of life and how it can be reached is similar to that of Nyaya. The Sankhya is a school of dualistic realism. Two ultimate realities, purusha (consciousness) and prakriti (unconscious force), are distinct from each other. In ordinary life one gets confused about this distinction and suffers; a grasp of the distinction ends the suffering. The Yoga system is allied to Sankhya. It deals with the practical techniques that help the realization of truth. Yoga discusses the different layers of mind and indicates the importance of the unconscious on conscious motives and actions. The Mimamsa system attempts to justify Vedic ritualism on philosophical grounds. It tries to prove that valid knowledge is always self-evident and on this ground indicates that Veda is infallible. The *Vedanta is allied to Mimamsa. It is supposed to be the culmination of Vedic philosophy and thus named as Vedanta or end of the Veda. It has many schools that disagree about philosophical issues; however, all agree about the basic unity of the ultimate reality, which they name Brahman. Whereas one of the well-known advocates of Vedanta, Shankara tries to disprove any duality between Brahman on the one hand and world and man on the other, another well-known Vedantist, Ramanuja, admits distinctions within the unity of Brahman. The Vedantists indicate that ignorance about the true nature of reality causes man's suffering, and possession of Truth, which is the birthright of every man, is bliss.

[K. MITRA]

INDIANA, a Midwestern state admitted to the Union (1816) as the 19th state. Originally inhabited by Indians, including the so-called Mound Builders and the Miami. Indiana was first discovered in the 17th cent. by a party of French explorers under Sieur de *la Salle. In the 18th cent., the French established three forts and trading posts in the area, the most notable of which was Vincennes (1732). After 1787 Ind. became part of the Old Northwest Territory of the U.S. Following statehood it became the site of Robert Owen's experimental socialist community at New Harmony (see HARMONY SOCIETY). Missionary activity in the area began at Vincennes in the 18th century. The first church built in Ind., St. Francis Xavier's, also served as cathedral for Simon *Bruté when he became the first bp. of the Diocese of Vincennes. Before his death (1839) Bruté had established a college and seminary and founded an academy staffed by the Sisters of Charity from Emmitsburg, Maryland. His successor, Celestine de la Hailandière, helped the Sisters of Providence to establish the convent of St. Mary-of-the-Woods (1840), and contributed to the founding (1842) of the University of Notre Dame by the Congregation of Holy Cross. The fourth bp. of Vincennes, Maurice de St. Palais, built numerous churches and orphanages, and encouraged the Franciscans and Dominicans to open schools, convents, and a seminary. He also helped the Sisters of Charity to begin St. Mary's Hospital in Evansville (1872). During St. Palais' episcopacy, the Diocese of Fort Wayne was created (1857), leaving only the southern portion of Ind. under the control of Vincennes.

Francis Silas *Chatard succeeded St. Palais (1878) and took up residence in Indianapolis. Twenty years later the title of the diocese was changed from Vincennes to Indianapolis. Chatard died in 1918 and was succeeded by Joseph Chartrand. During Chartrand's active administration the *Knights of Columbus founded Gibault Home for delinquent boys; orphanages were enlarged; Margaret Mary Hospital was opened in Batesville; and several high schools were founded, including Reitz Memorial High School in Evansville and Cathedral High School in Indianapolis. Joseph E. *Ritter, who succeeded Chartrand (1934), was responsible for rapid institutional growth, the founding of the Confraternity of Christian Doctrine, and the creation of the Catholic Information Bureau. The Archdiocese of Indianapolis was erected (1944), with Fort Wayne, Lafayette, and Evansville as suffragan sees. When Ritter was transferred to St. Louis (1946), Paul C. Schulte succeeded him as archbishop. Schulte commenced a huge building program that resulted in the creation of 27 new parishes, more than half of which were in Indianapolis.

Of Indiana's population of 5,193,172 (1975) Catholics numbered 717,712, or 13.8% of the total state population. The major Protestant sects are the Methodist Church (8.0% of the total population, 1971) and the Christian Churches and Church of Christ (3.0%). Other Protestant denominations comprised 18.7% of the population. The Jewish population is less than 1% . There are more than 20 church-related colleges in Indiana. Of these, nine are Catholic and have a total enrollment of 16,431. Some 16,453 students attend 27 diocesan and parochial Catholic high schools in the state, while 282 Catholic elementary schools have over 66,484 pupils. BIBLIOGRAPHY: J. D. Barnhart and D. F. Carmony, *Indiana from Frontier to Industrial Commonwealth* (4 v., 1954); T. T. McAvoy, *Catholic Church in Indiana, 1780–1834* (1940); M. C. Schroeder, *Catholic Church in the Diocese of Vincennes, 1847–77* (1946); G. B. Lockwood, *New Harmony Movement* (1905).

[J. L. MORRISON; R. M. PRESTON]

INDIANS AND COLORED PEOPLE, BLESSED SACRAMENT SISTERS FOR, see BLESSED SACRAMENT SISTERS FOR INDIANS AND COLORED PEOPLE.

INDICTION, ancient Roman term for fiscal year. The term originally meant compulsory purchase, and referred to the imperial government's manner of requisitioning food and clothing for its court and army employees during the devastating inflation of the 3d cent. A.D. People were forced to sell at prices determined by the government, in what amounted to an arbitrary and inequitable system of taxation. The reforms of Diocletian (284–305) instituted an annual levy, or land tax, based on land and population censuses which involved an assessment that was valid for a 15-year cycle. The word indiction then referred to the complete cycle, but could apply to the individual years of the cycle as well (as in indiction 2, indiction 7, indiction 15 etc.). The cycle as a whole would not have a number by which it could be related to previous cycles. The indictional year began with the autumnal equinox (September 23), but was soon altered to begin September 1. The Byzantine Church adopted a feast of the indiction to mark the beginning of the liturgical year and to bring it in harmony with the civil year. At first this coincided with the commemoration of the Conception of John the Baptist (September 23); but later came to commemorate the first preaching of Christ in the synagogue, as narrated in Lk 4.16ff (September 1). The popes used the imperial indictional year until 1087, after which papal indiction began December 25. Finally, in the 16th cent., Gregory XIII established January 1 as New Year's Day.

[E. J. DILLON]

INDIFFERENT ACTS, a Latinism, which does not mean "not up to much," or apathetic, or uncaring, but not yet determined about one of two alternatives; thus it is applied to the poise of balance of free will before opposite courses. Its usage in ethics, which echoes Cicero and Seneca, refers to human acts that are morally neutral of their kind; that is, looked at in the abstract, not in the concrete. In the concrete, according to the commoner opinion, acts are invested with personal intentions and individual circumstances and will be either reasonable or unreasonable; that is, right or wrong. The morality of what one does was regarded by Abelard as depending on what one intends, and by the Nominalists generally as depending on what God wills more or less arbitrarily, in the matter. St. Thomas Aquinas, however, while quite aware of the truth in situation ethics and of the limits to be set to moralizing about the Good, held that some types of activity are to be judged rightful, and others wrongful, quite impersonally and irrespective of their case histories, where what was good might be enhanced, lowered, or even spoiled, and what was evil might be aggravated, lessened, or even excused. He has been followed by most Catholic moral theologians in such setting of objective moral standards. There are kinds of acts that are always to be approved whatever their surroundings, e.g., cherishing the baby, others that as flatly are to be condemned, e.g., neglecting the baby. Yet there are many which in themselves carry no implication of right or wrong. It is difficult to think of a case with regard to one's treatment of a baby, but let us say, having a baby. Is it right or wrong? In answer to this one might say "it all depends" even in wedlock. One hesitates over intentions, prospects, circumstances, and so forth, in a manner that is not called for in the judgment of the other two examples. By morality the classical moral theologians do not mean good morality; it was a frame of reference according to which human acts could be considered in relation to human happiness with God, and insofar as they were classified into kinds or species they divided into the morally good, bad, and neutral (indifferent). How far "indifference" represented a species of morality, though keenly debated, was a luxury-point. (See ThAq ST 1a2ae, 18.8–9, esp. Lat-Eng v. 18, ed. T. Gilby).

This view, however, presupposes the acceptance of intrinsic morality regarding certain actions. Proponents of situation ethics regard all human actions objectively considered as indifferent, with the motivation of love as the only factor capable of giving them moral qualification.

Protestant theologians were little concerned with the speculative problems that centered about the idea of indifference; they were rather concerned with the propriety of classifying certain specific forms of human activity as indifferent: the following of certain Catholic rites and observances, as in the first *adiaphorist controversy; or indulgence in worldly amusement, as in the second. BIBLIOGRAPHY: O. Lottin, *Psychologie et morale aux XIIe et XIIIe siècles* (6 v., 1942–60) 2:469–489.

[T. GILBY]

INDIFFERENTISM, RELIGIOUS, a term often used in reference to the view and attitude of those who hold that the differences of belief that separate Christians of different denominations, or even adherents of any religion, are of no significance. The term is also applied to the position of those who attach no importance to religious belief of any kind. This article is chiefly concerned with indifferentism in the latter sense.

So understood, indifferentism is the least conspicuous form of irreligion; it is rarely militant and aggressive and rarely given doctrinal expression, because God is totally disregarded. It is often accompanied by indifference to any serious purpose in life and to spiritual values or ideals. As such it is all but closed to religious dialogue or to any exposition of sacred doctrine. Such indifference seems connected, in ways not precisely determined, with certain major characteristics of modern civilization and thinking. Some philosophical and theological conception of religion is undoubtedly involved in the attitude of indifference, but it is hardly worked out in detail by those for whom the things of religion are of little concern. There are degrees of indifference and, in more or less marked forms, it can penetrate the attitude even of believers. The religious problem does not even arise for a person or milieu in the grip of indifference. Whether or not God exists makes no impact on the way things are seen and interpreted or on the way life is lived; everything happens and is understood as if the question of God were totally meaningless. Even for a believer God can be accepted as the ultimate ''explanation'' of reality but make no significant impression in real life. The line between religious indifference and a kind of lived atheism is much less clear in practice than in theory.

The man of technological civilization is ''diverted'' (in Pascal's sense) by many immediate attractions. He is, further, distressed by an acute awareness of evil in its individual, cosmic, economic, social, political, and moral dimensions. Religious values must compete with a hypercritical spirit, the pluralist atmosphere, the view taken by exponents of different ideologies that their own values are autonomous, and the alleged existential inefficacy of religion. Religious indifference emerges as a sign of the time and not simply as a personal attitude. Whatever one thinks of God, it is claimed, everything in fact happens as if he did not exist. On the personal level believers seem to be men like others, or at least they are not so different as to make one think that faith has a power to renew and transform. On the social level the great religions, including Christianity, do not seem to have grasped the world's leading problems or contributed to their solution. The most dramatic aspect of the contemporary situation is not so much the rejection of old solutions as the decline of interest in the problems themselves. Indifferentism raises the problem of the authenticity of the image of religion and stresses the need for a profound rethinking of Christianity. BIBLIOGRAPHY: P. H. Simon, ''Athéisme, incroyance, indifférence,'' *Dieu aujourd'hui* (1964); E. Borne, *Atheism* (1959); J. Girardi, ''Reflections on Religious Indifference,'' *Concilium* (v. 23) 60–69. *SECULARISM.

[J. P. REID]

INDISSOLUBILITY OF MARRIAGE, see MARRIAGE, INDISSOLUBILITY OF.

INDIVIDUAL PSYCHOLOGY, the creation of Alfred Adler, an early disciple of Freud who soon separated from the master. The name derives from the postulate that an individual is more than the sum of his parts; he is not comprehensible in terms of isolated functions even taken all together, but only in terms of his overall purpose or aim. Adler's most famous contribution to contemporary psychology is the notion of the inferiority complex, i.e., the defensive reaction of the individual to real or imagined personal defects, which makes him respond by overcompensation, i.e., some form of futile and inappropriate striving, which becomes patterned as a self-defeating style of life. Therapy consists in helping the individual to accept himself and relinquish ineffective styles of life. It has had most success with adolescent problems. BIBLIOGRAPHY: A. Adler, *Individual Psychology of Alfred Adler* (ed. H. L. and R. R. Ansbacher, 1956); *Understanding Human Nature* (tr. W. B. Wolfe, 1962).

[M. E. STOCK]

INDIVIDUALISM, as a religious term, a tendency to reduce Christianity to the vertical relation between God and the individual person. Beginning with the Renaissance, many influences have contributed to a one-sided emphasis upon individual freedom, competence, and self-reliance, which have affected Christianity. Nowhere has this trend been more apparent than in the United States. The frontier experience fostered self-confidence, the *Enlightenment stressed the competence of the individual's reason and conscience, and *revivalism made individual *conversion the primary focus of concern. The New England circle of *transcendentalists asserted the immediacy of divine guidance, making intuition authoritative in morals and religion, and *liberal theology made ''the infinite worth of the individual'' a major plank in its platform. Although the Scriptures teach the value of individuals (e.g., Lk 15.7), they also reveal a corresponding acknowledgment of human solidarity, esp. within the Christian community. The Great Commandment(Mk 12.30–31) enjoins both love of God and love of neighbor. Religious individualism has had as consequences: the *subjectivism that makes individual reason and conscience the sole arbiter in faith and morals; the proliferation of sectarian divisions; reduction of the Church to a convenient means by which the individual receives occasional help, but which he may easily ignore; and loss of awareness that the Church of Jesus Christ exists for service and that this ministry is shared by all members.

[N. H. MARING]

INDIVIDUALISM, ECONOMIC, see ECONOMICS.

INDIVIDUALITY, according to scholastic analysis, that constitutive factor by which an existent is individual, both undivided in itself and distinct from others. There are three kinds of individuality. In the first, individuality is the same as unity. As such it is a transcendental property of being, for every existent is one. In the second, individuality is incommunicability. The individual or singular existent has incommunicability in that it is not common, as is the universal, to many similar existents. The third kind of individuality is that of the person, the individual endowed with rationality, that by which the person's intellectual nature is unitary in itself and distinct from that of others. On the other hand, individuality and personality can also be distinguished. Individuality then is that aspect by which the person is distinct from and related to society, while personality is the perfection, or total of actualities and potentialities, of his own person.

[R. E. HENNESSEY]

INDIVIDUATION, that by which an existent of a specific kind has an individual or singular existence, distinct from others of the same kind and from that nature which is common to them. That there are such individuals and that there are such common natures might seem equally evident. But just how an individual could be differentiated from others and from a common nature has not proven to be evident at all. Indeed, antirealism has been led to deny that there is individuation. Nominalism, believing only words to be universal, and conceptualism, for whom universal terms signify universal concepts which correspond to nothing in reality, posit only the existence of bare singulars. Such need no individuation. Both nominalistic and conceptualist antirealisms, however, then face the equally difficult task of explaining the apparent similarities found in reality. Philosophers in this vein have included William of Ockham, John Locke and David Hume, and innumerable theorists of the 20th century. But philosophical realism, granting the common nature a real basis in the individual existent or even, in the case of extreme realism, an independent existence, cannot avoid confronting the problem of individuation. Many types of solution to this problem have been offered. Thus *Boethius, an extreme realist and a major source for the medieval discussions, thought the essence or common nature to be individualized by its accidents, such as being in this or that time and place. But, as the substantial existent is that upon which the accident depends for its existence, most thinkers recognized that the individual accident presupposes the individual substance. Hence the most penetrating analyses have attempted to find the principle of individuation in a substantial principle. The moderate realism of Aristotle, denying to the common nature an independent existence, thought individuation, like change, to result from indeterminacy and potency. Thus Aristotle affirmed the principle of individuation to be matter. Form, as the principle of act and determination, could not on this basis be the basis of multiplicity, but was universal in itself, individuated by union with matter.

The Aristotelian position was generally followed by the major Arabian philosophers and was adopted by St. Thomas Aquinas. But Thomas, seeing too that matter itself, capable of determination by many forms, is common, proposed matter as related to quantity, which in this context he called signate matter, to be the principle of individuation. His Dominican commentators tried to clarify the exact relation between matter and quantity. Cajetan taught that matter itself, as the basis of quantity, was capable of numerical distinction. And John of St. Thomas believed matter to have an intrinsic ordination to quantity, quantity causing both the extension and the division of the material subject. But Francesco Silvestri Ferrariensis, while retaining signate matter as the principle of individuation, in effect abandoned the Aristotelian position that individuation is a result of indeterminacy. Ferrariensis proposed that signate matter must be matter already actuated by some act distinct from that matter before it can individuate a form.

Outside the immediately Thomist tradition, John Duns Scotus and Francisco Suárez have provided the most profound analyses. Finding individuation to be a positive determination, Scotus believed that the real distinction between individuals had to be based upon different intrinsic realities. Within the individual, an analogue of the specific difference distinguishing one species from the rest of the genus, the *haecceitas,* was added to the common nature. The *haecceitas,* then, differentiated the individual from the species. Suárez, on the other hand, thought the principle of individuation could be nothing other than the individual entity itself. That which the individual unity added to the common nature, he explained, was only mentally, not really, distinct from the nature.

[R. E. HENNESSEY]

INDONESIA, republic of SE Asia (formerly called Netherland Indies or Dutch East Indies), an archipelago whose most important islands are Sumatra, Java, Madura, the Sunda and Tenggara groups, the Moluccas, Celebes, part of Borneo, and W New Guinea (735,268 sq mi; pop. [est. 1975] 126,513,015. Indonesia is potentially very rich in natural resources. The official language is Bahasa Indonesian. The territory, strongly influenced by Hindu and Buddhist tradition, was overrun after the 12th cent. by Moslems from India and Persia. Then Islam became the leading religion. The Portuguese, who early held important outposts, were expelled in 1596 by the Dutch East India Company. Indonesia's formal annexation to Holland took place in 1848. Independence in 1949 was followed by serious trouble, some provoked by members of the Chinese Communist Party, which was later suppressed (1966–67). Indonesia has the largest Moslem population (87%) in the world. Hinduism flourishes in Bali; and Buddhism and Confucianism are practiced by Chinese residents. Christianity was introduced in the 16th cent. by the Portuguese, who established mission stations in the Moluccas and Ternate, some of which St. Francis Xavier visited. In 1562 Dominicans began work at Solor, Adonare, and Ternate, while Carmelites evangelized N Sumatra. The Christian community grew to 50,000; but the arrival of the anti-Catholic Dutch meant the end of the Church. Chapels were taken over by Protestants or turned to commercial use. Missionary work was forbidden, and many Catholics were forced to give up their faith. The Dutch conquerors established the Church of the Indies, not a missionary agency but rather an extension by the Company of the Dutch State Church for the convenience of its employees. Napoleon's occupation of Holland brought religious freedom to the islands. In 1828 Batavia became a vicariate apostolic. Jesuits 20 years later began methodic evangelization, training teachers and helping to raise the status of women. Missionaries were fewer than 50, however, at the end of the 19th cent., and the government barred many regions to them.

Until World War II the territory was entrusted to Jesuits, Picpus, and Capuchins. Divine Word missionaries, mainly from Holland, also evangelized and conducted primary schools. In 1940 there were 570 Jesuits, 550 brothers, and 1,768 sisters serving 543,000 Indonesian and 93,045 white Catholics. Independence in 1949 brought difficulties: withdrawal of many Dutch missionaries; problems of replacement; and the natural suspicion of some government authorities. Nevertheless, the Church made notable progress: the total Catholic community stands at 2,717,099; there is complete freedom of religion; and often the authorities welcome the collaboration of Christians. Many foreign missionaries have become Indonesian citizens. Indonesia is divided into 7 metropolitan sees, 25 suffragan dioceses, and 2 prefectures apostolic. Efforts are being made in education (3 universities, 520 high schools, 49 normal schools, and 134 professional centers) and in the training of clergy in 20 minor seminaries and 11 major seminaries. Catholics are active in schools and in politics; but missionaries have yet to spread the faith from the isl. of Flores, where it is now concentrated, to other parts of the republic. Protestantism was identified with the Dutch Reformed Church and a few German groups during the colonial period. At present many American denominations are represented, most of which belong to the World Council of Churches. Missionaries have greatly increased in number, as have native ministers. The total Protestant membership in 1968 was estimated at 5,000,000. BIBLIOGRAPHY: Latourette CRA 3, 5; *Bilan du Monde* 2:476–484.

[P. DAMBORIENA]

INDRA, storm- and warrior-god of early India whose importance and popularity are attested in the 250 hymns honoring him of the Rig-Veda (*c.* 1000 B.C.?). He seems to personify the exuberant and warlike ideals of the Aryans, who pushed into India in the 2d millennium B.C. I.'s most significant achievement was probably the slaying of Vritra, the demon-serpent who held back the waters or rains. In striking contrast to the Mesopotamian Marduk (and many other creator gods) who slew Tiamat and "contained" or "restrained" the waters of chaos (thus imposing order on creation), I.'s slaying of Vritra with a heavenly thunderbolt "releases" the waters. Thus both violence and fertility are associated with him. Like other Vedic gods, his cult eventually declined, and he is no longer worshiped. BIBLIOGRAPHY: W. D. O'Flaherty, *Hindu Myths* (1975) 56–96; G. Dumezil, *Destiny of the Warrior* (1970).

[D. P. EFROYMSON]

INDRECHTACH, ST. (Indractus; d.854), martyr, Irish abbot of Iona. From all the accounts of his life only two or three facts are certain. He was the son of a king or prince, and he was murdered by a Danish highwayman either at Glastonbury on a return from Rome or on his way to Rome. It is also certain that his body and those of his murdered companions were claimed by the abbey of Glastonbury. At the time of his murder he was carrying the relics of St. Colomba. BIBLIOGRAPHY: L. Boyle, BiblSanct 7:796–797; Butler 1:258.

[J. R. RIVELLO]

INDUCTION, in the technical terminology of Aristotelian logic, the mental operation of inferring from one or more given propositions about some members of a class to a proposition about all members. There are two types of induction. One is formal or complete induction. Such induction, basically nothing more than predicating of every member of a class that which has been predicated of each member separately, is completely apodictic or demonstrative, and is in fact but one form of deduction. Amplifying induction, or induction in the ordinary sense, is the other type. Here what is affirmed of some members of a class is inferred to belong to all. Necessary as it is to the empirical sciences and the practice of living, amplifying induction is never absolutely apodictic.

[R. E. HENNESSEY]

INDULGENCE, DECLARATIONS OF, see DECLARATIONS OF INDULGENCE.

INDULGENCE CONTROVERSY, the dispute between Martin Luther and J. J. Tetzel, regarded as the immediate starting point of the Reformation. Whether the posting of the *Ninety-Five Theses, Oct. 31, 1517, be fact or legend, Luther did challenge the Dominican Tetzel's doctrine on indulgences. Tetzel had been licensed by Albert of Brandenburg, Abp. of Mainz and Magdeburg, to solicit alms for the building of a new St. Peter's in Rome. The indulgence campaign was tied in with sordid and simoniacal financial arrangements. The abp.'s instruction made no mention of sorrow for sin or confession, but only of the contributions as the condition for gaining an indulgence. Luther protested against Tetzel's doctrine on four points; that an indulgence guarantees salvation; that money given immediately frees a soul from purgatory; that through an indulgence the worst sins were forgiven; and that Tetzel's indulgence freed from all guilt and punishment. Luther mainly protested against the misunderstanding caused in people's minds by the indulgence preaching. But in the storm provoked by his protest, his alienation from Rome, in doctrine and in practical measures of reform, became manifest. In Rome Tetzel's order promoted the canonical process that led to Luther's excommunication. BIBLIOGRAPHY: E. Iserloh, *Theses Were Not Posted* (tr. J. Wicks, 1968); J. P. Dolan, *History of the Reformation* (pa., 1965) 233–238.

[P. DeLETTER]

INDULGENCES, according to CIC c. 911, "the remission before God of the temporal punishment due to sins which have been effaced with respect to guilt, which ecclesiastical authority grants from the Church's treasury, for the living by way of absolution, for the dead by way of suffrage." This definition reflects several magisterial statements, esp. the Council of Trent which defined that the Church has the authority to grant indulgences and that they are of benefit to the faithful (D 989; 1471). Although there is no scriptural testimony to indulgences, their usage is based upon two fundamental Christian principles that came to be variously elaborated in the history of the Church: that there is a process of reconciliation whereby the punishment due to sin is gradually eliminated after the guilt itself is forgiven, and that the Church, through the intercession of Christ and the members of his mystical body, participates in this process. Thus, the solidarity of all Christians in the life of Christ was extended to the corporate character of penance. From the 2d cent., the Church exercised supervision over a sinner's penitential acts, even to the degree of assigning a certain scale of penance based upon the gravity of the sin committed. Severe penances were the general rule in the early Church, but this severity was mitigated by the early Middle Ages when the practice of frequent confession began. Hence confessors came to diminish the usual scale of penances, substituting other less vigorous prayers and pious practices. These commutations were, in a broad sense, the beginnings of indulgences. Another early form of indulgence was the solemn assurance, given by popes and bps. in apostolic letters or sermons, of the Church's intercession with God for the forgiveness of sins. An act of jurisdiction accompanied these declarations which remitted part or all of the person's canonical penance. These redemptions or absolution grants were juridical acts, but they were not connected with the sacrament of penance and were too general to regard as indulgences in the strict sense. The true indulgence appeared only in the 11th cent. when the fulfillment of specified conditions (a pilgrimage, almsgiving, prayers) caused the relaxation of a sacramental penance. Enlistment in a *Crusade was one of the most important of these conditions, and was "reckoned in place of all penance" at the Council of Clermont (1095), provided that the Crusader had already confessed his sins.

The theology of indulgences developed slowly and did not always keep pace with actual practice in the Church. It need not be held that even now theological theory of indulgences in all its details has been definitively settled. But one point is beyond dispute: any interpretation of indulgences must be built upon the distinction drawn by Catholics between the eternal and the temporal punishment due to sin. Repentance and absolution restore the sinner to a state of friendship with God and remit the eternal punishment to which the sinner exposed himself by turning away from God. Nevertheless repentance and hence absolution are rarely so perfectly effective that they wipe away, along with the substantial guilt, all the damage sin has caused in the person of the sinner. Generally speaking, this damage can be overcome only by prolonged penitential effort. In the early Church this effort commonly preceded absolution; after confession became frequent, the absolution was given first, and the reparatory penance followed later.

In early practice indulgences were closely associated in popular consciousness with the canonical penances imposed by bps. and confessors on those to whom absolution (i.e., from the substantial guilt of sin) was given. Indulgences represented the relaxation or commutation of such penances, and the granting of an indulgence was looked upon as an act of jurisdiction on the part of a person whose office it was to impose canonical punishment, i.e., the pope, bps., or confessors.

This accounted for the commutation of the penalty required by the Church. But the judgment of an ecclesiastical official, based necessarily on external considerations or upon the penitent's inadequate perception and confession of his own guilt, is not necessarily identical with God's judgment of what penalty is due. The elaboration in the 13th cent. of the notion of the "treasury of the Church" provided a basis for the remission of the penalty due in the sight of God. What substitutes for the actual payment of this penalty is the superabundance of good works of Christ and the saints whose merit is more than enough to make satisfaction for the temporal punishment due to the sins of those to whom indulgence is accorded. This also provided a basis for restricting the right to grant indulgences to the pope, who alone is entitled to dispense authoritatively the treasures that belong to the Church as a whole. Others may lawfully grant indulgences only to the extent to which they are delegated to do so.

The application of indulgences to the dead cannot be understood in any strict sense as a jurisdictional act, for the dead have passed beyond the Church's jurisdiction. It must therefore be considered to have its effect through the intercessory prayer of the Church. The offering of such an indulgence is in effect the Church's certification that the indulgenced work on behalf of the dead will have the support of the Church's prayer.

Thus theologians have distinguished two ways in which an indulgence may operate: by way of absolution (*per modum absolutionis*), as when a penalty is authoritatively remitted, and by way of suffrage (*per modum suffragii*), as when the Church pledges the support of its intercession.

Although the Council of Trent taught that the Church has the right to grant indulgences and that these are spiritually beneficial to the faithful, it acknowledged that the concession of indulgences had not been free from abuse (D 1835). The most conspicuous examples of abuse were connected with indulgences granted to those who contributed to collections for certain good causes. The need of material support for pious causes is so constant and multifarious that the danger of multiplying indulgences of this kind beyond reasonable measure can hardly be avoided without prohibiting them entirely. Trent called for the reform needed to correct abuses (see Shroeder T, 142, 253–254) and Pius V in his bull *Etsi dominici* (1567) completely abrogated indulgences associated with the taking of collections. Ecclesiastical legislation and practice have attempted to keep other forms of abuse under control. Most recently Paul VI in an apostolic constitution *Indulgentiarum doctrina* established several new norms in the discipline of indulgences, e.g., that sacramental confession, communion, and prayer for the pope's intentions are necessary for each plenary indulgence; that indulgences are always attached to a particular good work, even though they may be linked to some object or place (see INDULGENCE, APOSTOLIC); and that no specification of days or years will be attached to partial indulgences.

There is a disposition on the part of some contemporary RC theologians to look with disfavor upon the distinction between partial and plenary indulgences and also to question the basic validity of the distinction between indulgences that operate by way of absolution and those that operate by way of suffrage. The explanation of all indulgences, even those gained by the living, in terms of suffrage seems to these theologians to make it easier to defend the soundness of the idea of indulgences without prejudice to the need of personal penance. BIBLIOGRAPHY: K. Rahner, SacMund 3:123–129; *idem,* "Remarks on the Theology of Indulgences," Rahner ThInvest 2 (1963) 175–202; P. F. Palmer, *Sacraments and Forgiveness: History and Doctrinal Development of Penance, Extreme Unction and Indulgences* (1960).

[T. M. MCFADDEN]

INDULGENCES, APOSTOLIC, those *indulgences, either plenary or partial, that are attached to rosaries, crosses, crucifixes, statues, or medals blessed by the pope or by a priest having the necessary faculties. Originally they were attached by the popes to objects sent by them to kings or other important personages, but later they were extended for the benefit of all the faithful. The first list of such indulgences was that of Benedict XIII (d. 1730). Now every new pope issues a similar list shortly after his election. Each indulgence can be gained only on certain feast days which, since Pope Paul VI added the Feast of Our Lady of the Rosary, now number 32. The 1967 apostolic constitution on indulgences emphasized that indulgences are dependent upon actions of the faithful even though at times they may be linked with some object. To acquire a plenary indulgence one must perform the work to which the indulgence is attached and fulfill three conditions: sacramental confession, communion, and prayers for the pope. BIBLIOGRAPHY: W. Herbst, *Indulgences* (1955).

[A. M. BERMEJO]

INDULT, a term signifying a concession. But the term has no precise and determined juridical meaning. In general it signifies a grant or benefit unprovided for by the common law, bestowed by the Apostolic See or by the ordinary, for a time or to meet a particular situation. It may be identical with a dispensation, which is a relaxation from a law, or a privilege granting immunity from a general obligation, or by rescript if the grant or faculty is given in answer to a request submitted to the Apostolic See or the ordinary. Sometimes the indult has the force of a general law, e.g., the faculty granted to parish priests to administer the sacrament of confirmation in certain circumstances, as provided for in the decree *Spiritus Sancti* (Sept. 14, 1946). Privileges may be granted to bps. and others by indult, e.g., to say Mass at sea. Dispensations similarly are given by indults, as for instance permission for a religious to be secularized, or for a priest to be reduced to the lay state or to marry.

[A. FARRELL]

INDUSTRIAL CHRISTIAN FELLOWSHIP, (ICF) Anglican organization formed in 1918 for the Christianization of man's life in an industrial society. At the Malvern Conference of 1941 the ICF advocated, in the name of Christian teaching on human existence, an end to the private ownership of major industrial resources. Headquarters are in London.

[T. EARLY]

INDUSTRIALISM, a 19th-cent. word that has outstripped the sense of its etymological root, the Lat. *industria* (intelligent diligence), and now stands for an economic system, and, somewhat ominously as well, for a social and political system, in which consumer goods, and other things too, neither consumable nor good, are produced, processed, and distributed by machinery exploiting the thermal resources of matter and concentrated in increasingly large units. It began with the English Industrial Revolution of the 18th cent.; it is impossible to say when it will end, or whether it ever will. By its historical association with individualistic capitalism, the competitive society, and the profit motive, it has been the subject alike of lively attack and dogged defense by Christians. But neither attack nor defense need concern us in glancing at some of the problems for human decency, morality, and religion it raises, whether it be run by conservatism, liberalism, socialism, or communism. One is noted by Aristotle; it may lie at the root of the matter. A regulator seems to be built into natural lusts, more noticeably perhaps in animals than in men, whereas artificial greeds set themselves no limit; one can always add zeros to the checks he would like to draw from life, and the machines will always run to multiply their quantities, often to the detriment of quality. Other points call for second thoughts and effective action. The earth itself needs to be protected against rape and conversion into a refuse dump, for industrialism is prodigal in its waste. The air and the waters have to be saved from pollution, not just for the sake of flora and fauna, though they are reason enough, but in order to keep the world habitable by human beings.

The industrialization of farming increases the threat. Its effect can be to denature things—food, drink, and even sex—and to cut us off from the rhythms expressed in the liturgy. This goes deeper than the destruction of a peasant society, which itself has its own occupational diseases. A Christian need not cry woe, nor seek to get back to the land and lead the simple life so long as he uses his wits, exercises his proper responsibilities, and does not allow himself to be mesmerized by the slogan of "progress." While grateful for and profiting from the gains of scientific technology, he should be well aware of the mutations industrialism has brought about in family structures, the diminution of parental care of children and of the domestic position of women; he should be critical of social relations when machine-menders and paper-workers are herded into conurbations that are choking themselves; of the decline of craftsmanship, of ceremonies, and of play springing from work; of the power of a professional managerial class and of commercial parasites, some less benign than others, to stimulate consumption for an ever–increasing production, often not of necessities for which millions starve, but of amenities and sometimes of luxuries we could do without. Whether this vicious spiral could be remedied by complete state control of the economy is open to doubt. What is certain is the need for an energetic Christian humanism, critical, compassionate, and courageous, lest industrialism come to spell, not the triumph of man over nature, but the triumph of the machine over man. BIBLIOGRAPHY: J. L. and B. Hammond, *Rise of Modern Industry* (9th ed. 1966); G. Friedmann, *Industrial Society* (1955).

[T. GILBY]

INDWELLING, DIVINE, a special presence of the three Divine Persons in the soul of the baptized just man, really different from the natural immensity by which God is in all things sustaining and activating them. This indwelling, or inhabitation, as it is called, a matter of ordinary Catholic teaching, is coexistent with sanctifying grace. It is terminated by mortal sin.

Faith in the divine indwelling is based on the teaching of Holy Scripture, esp. St. John and St. Paul. But the particularities of the doctrine are not set forth in these sources. St. John (ch. 14) quotes Our Lord as saying that he and his Father will take up their abode in the man who loves Christ. St. Paul (in, e.g., Romans, 1 Corinthians, and 2 Corinthians) speaks almost always of the indwelling of the Holy Spirit without explicit mention of the Father and the Son. Hence there is no clear and certain teaching of the Church concerning the exact nature of the indwelling and its relation to the infused habits of grace and virtues and to the gifts of the Holy Spirit.

One usually speaks of the inhabitation of the Holy Spirit rather than of the Blessed Trinity. Hence the question arises, is the indwelling so special and proper to the Third Person that the Father and the Son are present only because of their inseparability from him? To this question St. Thomas Aquinas and other great theologians have replied that the inhabitation is not proper to any one Divine Person but common to all three. In the expression inhabitation of the Holy Spirit the common indwelling is spoken of as though it were proper to the Third Person because he proceeds by the love of the Father and Son, and the indwelling is likewise the work of God's love. Other theologians however prefer a proper presence of the Holy Spirit. They speak of a special union with him through sanctifying grace. Some have even proposed a proper presence and union with each of the three Divine Persons.

There is a general consensus that the ensemble of sanctifying grace and the other infused gifts differentiates the supernatural from the natural presence of God in the soul. But what is there in this supernatural endowment that makes the difference? Two replies to this question may be indicated.

The first solution is that the Blessed Trinity is present as a friend to a friend. This presence, as among men, is characterized by a special bond of knowledge and love. His presence as creator presupposed, God becomes for the justified soul the object of a new and supernatural knowledge and love. This knowledge and love need not be actual. It suffices that a man have the power, given in his justification, to know and love God supernaturally. In this way the Trinity, his supreme friend, is always present to him.

The other opinion suggests that the Blessed Trinity is supernaturally present because the Divine Persons are in the soul imprinting on it their own very image: of the Holy Spirit in the virtue of charity, of the Son in the gift of wisdom, of the Father in sanctifying grace itself, the source from which the virtues and gifts emanate. This assimilative action is of its very essence supernatural because it imparts to man proper personal likenesses of the three Divine Persons. Such likenesses could not be natural to a creature. BIBLIOGRAPHY: P. De Letter, NCE 7:492–494; P. Galtier, *L'Inhabitation en nous des trois personnes divines* (rev. ed., 1949); J. Trütsch, *SS. Trinitatis inhabitatio apud theologos recentiores* (1949).

[T. J. MOTHERWAY]

INE, KING OF WESSEX. (d. 726). Of West Saxon royal blood and kinsman to Aldhelm, he succeeded Caedwalla, his half brother, in 688. I. extended his rule over all Britain S of the Thames and enacted laws (690–693). He abdicated in 725 and went on pilgrimage to Rome where he died. BIBLIOGRAPHY: F. M. Stenton, *Anglo-Saxon England* (2d ed., 1947).

[J. DRUSE]

INEDIA, one of the principal charismatic phenomena, it is complete abstinence from all forms of nourishment, the requirements of nature notwithstanding. BIBLIOGRAPHY: F. C. Happold, *Mysticism: A Study and an Anthology* (1963).

[F. H. BRIGHAM]

INEFFABILIS DEUS, the encyclical letter of Pius IX explaining his definition of *Mary's *Immaculate Conception (1854). Pius had promulgated the definition earlier that year after consultation with theologians and all the bps. of the Church. The encyclical published the official text and added a considerable exposition of the dogma's significance and presence in Christian tradition.

[T. M. MCFADDEN]

INEFFABILITY OF GOD (Lat., *effari,* to utter), usually in the sense of defining or settling, the transcendence of the divine over the signifying power or any word or statement (see NEGATIVE THEOLOGY). Since human beings can only name things accordingly as they can know them, all language about God is deficient. The mind's own, rational level of knowledge about God is limited to the degree that the created sources and objects of such knowledge reflect the divine perfection as their source; that reflection is necessarily inadequate (see UNICITY OF GOD). Further, the words in their structure and signifying power reflect the reasoned experience of reality: e.g., the concrete word good denotes a subject's having some good quality; God is not a subject having attributes distinct from the divine being itself. Faith as a form of knowing is expressed in propositions, particularly the articles of the Creed. The mind needs the mediation of concepts that the words of the Creed express. But the assent of faith is not based on the intelligible content of the concept signified by the articles of the Creed, but solely on the authority of God's word guaranteeing the truth of what is believed (see CERTITUDE OF FAITH). The dogmatic declarations by the Church of the authentic meaning of what is believed remain limited in their power to signify; they do not, as it were, capture the divine mystery. The positive function of all true statements about God, however, is that they intend or point to the divine reality; they are neither pure equivocations nor irrelevancies (see ANALOGY). Where the genuinely intelligible is expressed, the fact that faith is an assent to the truth is a guarantee that a true statement about God is a positive reference to the ineffable and incomprehensible divine reality itself.

[T. C. O'BRIEN]

INERRANCY, the quality of truthfulness or, negatively, of freedom from error, attributed to the Bible because it is inspired (see INSPIRATION). The assertion of inerrancy in the absolute sense that every line of the Bible is free of factual, historical, scientific, or ethical error is characterized as fundamentalism and is regarded as extreme and contrary to evidence internal to the Bible itself. The rationalistic or liberalist opposite extreme is an outright denial of inerrancy, or at least of the relevance of objective truth or falsity, the Bible being taken as mere devotional literature. There is, however, a constant tradition in Judaism and Christianity affirming the objective truthfulness of the Bible; rabbinical and patristic allegorizing were attempts to get around the obvious difficulties. In RC teaching the truthfulness of the Bible is regarded as an article of faith even though not formally defined. Biblical inerrancy understood as truthfulness is, however, given a moderate interpretation.

Such an interpretation is reflected in Vatican Council II's decree on revelation. The words of the inspired author must be held to be asserted by the Holy Spirit, but as teaching "that truth which God wanted to put into the sacred writings for the sake of our salvation" (Vat II DivRev 11). The truthfulness of the Bible is related to teaching the meaning and history of salvation; that is the criterion. Since this truth is communicated by a human author through his words, what he wrote and what he intended (see LITERAL SENSE) must be discerned and evaluated (Vat II DivRev 12). Judgment about the truth of the biblical text, therefore, is closely dependent upon the tasks of *textual criticism to determine what was actually written and of biblical *exegesis and *hermeneutics to determine what the author intended. In this connection the study of any text in its context and above all within the unity of the Bible as a whole, the findings of form criticism (see LITERARY GENRES), and *redaction criticism are essential. BIBLIOGRAPHY: K. Rahner, *Inspiration in the Bible* (tr. C. R. Henkey, 2d ed. 1964); P. Synave and P. Benoît, *Prophecy and Inspiration* (tr. A. Dulles and T. Sheridan, 1961); R. F. Smith, JBC 2:512–514.

[D. J. BOURKE]

INFALLIBILITY, insusceptibility or immunity to error in matters pertaining to divine revelation. It is a corollary of Christian faith that the believer is certain of the object of his faith: "I know whom I have believed and I am sure that he is able to guard until that Day what has been entrusted to me" (2 Tim 1.12). The NT promises that the Holy Spirit "will guide you into all the truth" (Jn 16.13) apply, at least in some sense, to every Christian and not only to the corporate experience of the Church as a whole. From the history of the Church, as well as from the personal experience of every Christian, it is clear that such promises do not exempt the individual from susceptibility to error at every moment in his Christian life, but they do promise the guidance of the Holy Spirit to protect him from a fundamental error in his faith (see ThAq ST 2a2ae, 1.3; 8.4 ad 1 and ad 2). This subjective infallibility must, however, be seen in relation to the infallibility that, as a concomitant of divine inspiration, is predicated of the Bible. Not only is divine revelation itself infallible, but its bearer and medium, Sacred Scripture, is also protected from error by the Holy Spirit. This quality of Scripture is evident from the way the OT is handled in the New, as when Jesus is represented in the Gospel of John as arguing on the basis of the assumption that "scripture cannot be broken" (Jn 10.35). The promise to the Apostles that they will be guided into all the truth would seem to apply with special force to their exercise of their apostolic office, a major component of which was the writing of the NT. Yet it does not necessarily follow that this infallibility of Sacred Scripture implies an absolute scientific accuracy concerning the universe and the laws of nature. Nor does it imply that the writers of the Old and the

NT did not make use of literary forms and ideas that were current in the world around them. The chronological data or biological information of the Bible are not on the same level with its message of salvation (see BIBLE, AUTHORITY OF).

The apostolic office is, however, by no means restricted to the composition of the NT. It is an office for the Church and in the Church, and it is to the Church that the promise of divine guidance—and therefore the right to infallibility—is granted. "The church of the living God" is "the pillar and bulwark of the truth" (1 Tim 3.15). In the exercise of this prerogative, the earliest "church council" felt qualified to invoke the formula. "It has seemed good to the Holy Spirit and to us" (Acts 15.28). In one way or another, the post-apostolic Church has continued to claim this right to speak infallibly as the custodian of divine revelation. Here again it is necessary to note that, from the evidence of history, this right did not prevent the councils and officials of the Church from mistakes of fact and errors of judgment that have been corrected by later generations. Ethical judgments —including, e.g., the prohibition of "what is strangled" in the decree of the apostolic council in Acts 15.29—and dogmatic formulas have been changed, clarified, and even revoked, as the development of the Church and of her teaching office has brought new insights into divine revelation (see Vat II Ecum 6).

It is in the context of the infallibility of the Scriptures and of the Church that the doctrine of the infallibility of the pope is to be understood. *Pastor aeternus* of Vatican Council I (see D 3074) was careful to specify that the pope exercises "that infallibility with which the divine Redeemer willed that His Church be instructed in defining doctrine on faith and morals"; papal infallibility is not separated from the infallibility of the Church. It also identified the infallibility as applying to the pope "when he speaks *ex cathedra,* i.e., in the exercise of his office as pastor and teacher of all Christians"; it is part of this office to be the authoritative interpreter of Sacred Scripture. At the same time Vatican I stated that this infallibility pertained to the pope without "the consent of the Church." The clarification of this combination of statements has continued to engage the attention of theologians. The calling of Vatican Council II would seem to refute any idea that Vatican Council I had vested all authority and all infallibility in the papal office as such (see Vat II ConstCh 25); nevertheless, the decisions of Vatican II were also proclaimed and promulgated by the pope.

In recent RC theology, Hans Küng (*Infallible? An Inquiry,* 1971) has challenged the very possibility of infallibility with regard to dogmatic propositions. Others, whether agreeing or disagreeing, have searched for explanations more consonant with contemporary theological epistemology and hermeneutics. BIBLIOGRAPHY: B. C. Butler, *Church and Infallibility* (1954); J. H. Newman, *On the Inspiration of Scripture* (ed. J. D. Holmes and R. Murray, 1967); J. J. Hennesey, *First Council of the Vatican* (1963); P. Chirico, *Infallibility: The Crossroads of Doctrine* (1977).

[J. PELIKAN]

INFAMY (CANON LAW), an ecclesiastical, vindicative penalty, meaning that the person punished has lost both good name and rights in the Christian community. Infamy of law is a penalty attached to certain grave offenses and is incurred automatically or imposed by a competent authority on an offender (CIC c. 2293, §2). A *de facto* infamy (*infamia facti*) arises from an action or way of life that discredits a person in the eyes of the faithful; its existence is determined by the local bp.; those of such ill-repute are to be excluded from holy orders, from any ecclesiastical dignity, or from exercise of the ministry (*ibid.,* c. 2294, §2). Infamy of law (*infamia juris*) according to current legislation may be incurred by such crimes as formally joining another Church, violating corpses or graves, profaning the eucharistic species, doing violence to the person or liberty of the pope. Incurrence of such a penalty deprives a person of any share in ecclesiastical benefice, privilege, office and from the legal exercise of any function in the Church; it also gives rise to an *irregularity, barring reception of holy orders. Since infamy is a vindicative, not a medicinal penalty, (see PENALTY, REMEDIAL) it is a punishment over and above *censure. The 1973 draft revision of the penal law of the Church proposes that the penalty of infamy be dropped. *PENAL POWER OF THE CHURCH.

[T. C. O'BRIEN]

INFANCY, canonically (CIC, c. 88 §3) the condition before the law of a person who has not yet completed the 7th year of age, who is, therefore, presumed not to have reached the use of reason, even if in fact use of reason has begun. The condition of a person who habitually lacks the use of reason is equivalent to infancy. The determination of the law is made in view of the exercise of certain rights or the liability to certain obligations that presuppose the use of reason and are stipulated by law, e.g., the law of fasting.

[T. C. O'BRIEN]

INFANCY GOSPELS. Two quite different compositions come under this head: the canonical narratives of the birth and early childhood of Jesus in Mt 1.18–2.23; Lk 1.5–2.52; and the various apocryphal stories about Christ's birth and childhood, which were in circulation in the early Church.

(1) The infancy narratives of Mt and Lk, two widely divergent accounts, have in common only the basic assertions that Jesus was conceived while his mother was still a virgin, that he was born at Bethlehem, and that the circumstances of his birth show him to be the Davidic *Messiah foretold in OT prophecy. Both accounts are now held to contain a strong element of Christian *midrash; i.e., in accordance with the traditional canons of Jewish interpretation, they elaborate upon the basic facts in such a way as to show that in the events of Jesus' infancy the designs of God as revealed in the OT find their fulfillment. This means that the narratives are presenting a level of significance in the earthly Jesus deeper than the merely factual and historical, and that many elements in them belong to the dimension

rather of theological reflection than of literal historical fact. Thus for instance in Mt the episode of the Magi is designed to show that the wisdom of the gentiles discerns the truth of Jesus' kingship, to which the Jews are blind. The star in the East is the star of Jacob (Num 24.17). The coming of the ruler of Judah was foretold in the blessing of Jacob (Gen 49.10); and the birth of the Messiah at Bethlehem was foretold in Mic 5.1–3; the coming of the gentile kings with gifts echoes Ps 72.10, Is 49.23. The inspired truth which these details are intended to convey is the Messiahship of Jesus. Again it has been argued that Luke's account is a tissue of implicit references to the OT, the prophecies of Dan ch 7–9 and Zeph 3:14–17 being particularly strong influences on Luke's interpretation. In their infancy narratives both Mt and Lk also convey, in quite different ways, an anticipation of Christ's Passion and death.

(2) Speculations about the birth and childhood of Jesus proliferated in the early Church, and many are preserved in pseudepigraphical works which abound in apocryphal miracle stories of the grossest kind (see APOCRYPHA NT). The two most notable of these are the "book" or *Protoevangelium of James* and the *Gospel of Thomas*. BIBLIOGRAPHY: K. Bornhäuser, *Die Geburt- und Kindheitsgeschichte Jesu* (1930); E. Burrows, *Gospel of the Infancy and Other Biblical Essays* (1945); H. Pernot, *Les Deux premiers chapitres de Matthieu et de Luc* (1948); J. P. Audet, "L'Annonce à Marie," RevBibl 63 (1956) 346–374.

[D. J. BOURKE]

INFANT BAPTISM, the administration of the sacrament of baptism to those who have not yet attained the use of reason, a topic controverted among Christians.

The Case for Infant Baptism. There is no direct evidence in the NT that infants received Christian baptism. However, since male children were initiated into the Jewish religion by the rite of circumcision and since the children of adult converts to Judaism were baptized along with their parents in Jewish proselyte baptism, it is not unlikely that the children of Christian parents were initiated into the Christian religion by baptism. In the earliest detailed rite of baptism, that of Hippolytus (*c.*215), the following rubric occurs: "And they shall baptize the little children first. And if they can answer for themselves, let them answer. But if they cannot, let their parents answer or someone from the family" (*Trad. apost.* 21.3). According to Augustine, the faith of the child is supplied by the faith of the Church, expressed in the baptismal formula. The Council of Trent anathematized anyone who "denies that infants newly issued from their mother's womb are to be baptized, though born of baptized parents" (D 1514), and in its Decree on Justification it taught that justification "cannot take place without the laver of regeneration or its desire (*votum*), as has been written: 'Unless a man be born again of water and the Holy Spirit, he cannot enter into the kingdom of God' [Jn 3.5]" (D 1524). RC theologians are generally agreed that infants are incapable of the *votum,* or desire, for baptism. There is, however, a growing number of theologians who suggest that the *votum* need not be the child's, but that as part of the parents and the community into which he is born, the child may participate in their Christian desire that he be baptized.

The Case against Infant Baptism. Those who reject infant baptism do so both on biblical grounds and for theological reasons. Since the NT accounts of baptism make no mention of the baptism of infants, but always indicate that the rite is being administered to persons who have repented and made a profession of faith, the lack of such a precedent furnishes one basis for refusing to adopt the practice. Moreover, many understand baptism to be a human response to God's grace, signifying submission to God's judgment and mercy, identification with Christ in his death and Resurrection, and a testimony to others that one has become a Christian; they therefore see no reason for baptizing infants. Furthermore, in the belief that the visible Church should include only those who consciously manifest their faith in Jesus Christ and submit themselves to the disciplines of the Christian community, they contend that baptism should be reserved for those old enough to make a responsible decision. An examination of extrabiblical literature reveals no clear, explicit reference to infant baptism earlier than Origen and Tertullian in the 3d century. Such documents as the *Didache* or the *First Apology* of Justin Martyr imply that the subjects were adults; the former requires the candidate to fast prior to receiving baptism, and the latter says that the recipients are those who "are persuaded and believe" and have been instructed.

Infant baptism appears to have become the usual practice; although some medieval sects, such as the Waldenses, may have renounced it, there was not a strong renewal of emphasis upon *believer's baptism until the Reformation of the 16th century. At that time, Lutherans, Anglicans, and *Reformed retained the practice of infant baptism, but the *Anabaptists, esp. the *Swiss Brethren of Zurich (and their descendants, *Mennonites, Hutterites, and others), insisted that baptism was only for those old enough to repent and seek a personal profession of faith. Seeking to restore the faith and practice of the primitive Church, they restricted church membership to persons baptized upon a profession of faith. In the 17th cent. English Baptists emerged from congregational Puritanism and became a distinct denomination because of their emphasis upon believer's baptism and a concept of the *visible Church composed only of committed and disciplined Christians. Whether there was any but an indirect connection between the earlier Anabaptist groups and the Baptists is not entirely clear. In 1708 the Church of the Brethren arose in Germany under the leadership of Alexander *Mack, and a few years later moved to America. Several other Brethren Churches in the U.S. also derived from German *Pietism in the 18th century. The Disciples of Christ originated under the leadership of Alexander *Campbell in the U.S. around 1830. All of these groups come within the category of "believers' Churches," admitting to membership only persons baptized after reaching a mature age and having professed their faith in Jesus Christ as Lord and Savior.

Some European theologians have had qualms about infant baptism in recent years. Emil *Brunner was an early critic of infant baptism, declaring in 1937 that the contemporary practice of infant baptism is nothing short of scandalous (*The Divine-Human Encounter* [1937], 132). In 1943 Karl *Barth launched an attack on infant baptism, asserting that such a practice has no biblical basis and that in the NT baptism is in every case the "indispensable answer to an unavoidable question by a man who has come to faith" (*The Teaching of the Church Regarding Baptism* [tr. E. A. Payne, 1948], 41–44). Barth's son, Markus, has written a more thorough book on baptism, in which he rejects the rite of infant baptism (*Die Taufe–Ein Sakrament?*, 1951). Likewise considerable discussion has taken place within the C of E and among some Lutherans concerning the propriety of infant baptism. Catholic theologians are also discussing the issue esp. since the restoration of the catechumenate for adults and the implications of the revised rites. BIBLIOGRAPHY: D. F. Durnbaugh, *Believers' Church: the History and Character of Radical Protestantism* (1968); A. Gilmore, *Christian Baptism: A Fresh Attempt to Understand the Rite in Terms of Scripture, History, and Theology* (1959); P. Palmer, *Sacraments and Worship* (Sources of Christian Theology I, 1955).

[N. H. MARING]

INFANT COMMUNION, the practice in Eastern Churches of including the Eucharist in the Christian initiation of infants. The possibility of taking up the practice in the Latin Church is being discussed since revision of the rites of Christian initiation.

INFANT JESUS OF PRAGUE, a statue of the Christ Child, preserved since 1628 in Our Lady of Victory Church in Prague. The carved wooden statue depicts the Infant dressed in regal robes, holding a globe in his left hand, and extending his right hand in blessing. Thus the kingship of Christ is united with his holy childhood. Many legends surround the statue's origin. The Christ Child, under this title, is the object of much popular devotion which has received ecclesiastical approbation through the granting of many indulgences. BIBLIOGRAPHY: L. Nemec, NCE 7:500–501.

[T. M. MCFADDEN]

INFANTICIDE, child murder, or the crime of taking the life of a newly born or very young child. Morally, if not legally, the term includes not only the direct killing of a child but also such gross maltreatment that a child's death could or should be foreseen as a probable consequence. Indirectly it includes also the culpable withholding from the child of the care necessary to preserve its life, or the abandonment of the child in circumstances in which it probably cannot survive. In some primitive societies infanticide has been practiced—sometimes for economic reasons, sometimes in cases of deformity, or when the child was believed to be of tainted origin. In early Greek and Roman societies a right was variously accorded, generally to the father, but in some cases to the mother or to some public official, to determine whether a child should be allowed to live. Among some peoples infanticide has been practiced as a form of human sacrifice, as in the worship of Moloch. This was regarded as an abomination under Mosaic law (Lev 18.21; Dt 12.31). Judaism, and later Christianity and Islam, have considered infanticide as gravely sinful. Civil law in the U.S. treats infanticide as homicide. The occasional lenience of courts in dealing with mothers charged with taking the lives of their own children reflects not so much a condonation of the crime itself as an unwillingness of juries to believe that a mother could be capable of so abhorrent an act except under circumstances of extreme mental and emotional stress, which would diminish her subjective responsibility for the deed. In the current debate among moralists on the subject of abortion, some have suggested that the infant *in utero* is not yet a person in the sense in which they want the term understood, and hence the taking of its life cannot be considered homicide. A few isolated writers have gone so far as to extend the argument to infants after birth, whose status as persons they hold to be equally doubtful, and hence they question the propriety of classifying the taking of the life of a newborn infant as homicide. This position is commonly rejected.

[C. NEELY]

INFANTILE SEXUALITY, a postulate of Freudian psychoanalysis which has aroused greatest criticism, namely, the assumption that children up to the age of 6 or 7 experience sexual desires substantially the same as those of adults. The evidence comes from observing and talking to children between the ages of 3 and 5 when there is a tendency to masturbate, and the similarity between their sexual wishes and those of adults seems to be striking. Further evidence comes from psychoanalysis of adults, from which it appears that many infantile wishes persevere into adult sexual fantasies, esp. in cases of abnormal sexual development. The stages of infantile sexuality are the oral, anal, phallic, and Oedipal, in which erotic desire centers successively on mouth, anus, genitals, and parents. In criticism of this theory, it is noted that, while many aspects of adult sexuality become intelligible in terms of infantile yearnings, the maturing of the sex organs and the formation of adult interpersonal relations undoubtedly change the sex drive profoundly.

[M. E. STOCK]

INFANTS, BAPTISM OF, see INFANT BAPTISM.

INFANTS, UNBAPTIZED. Several aspects of Christian belief make the eternal fate of infants dying without baptism problematic: the unlimited extension of original sin, God's universal salvific will, and the necessity of baptism for salvation. Original sin is present in human beings by the very fact of their human existence, and baptism is the sacramental rite through which sin is forgiven and entrance into the redemptive life of Christ accomplished. Thus Jn 3.5: "No one can enter into God's kingdom without being begotten of water and Spirit." Even when baptism by desire or baptism by blood (martyrdom) is acknowledged, it does not appear how an infant dying without the sacramental rite could attain the participation in Christ's life which is necessary for salvation. Yet the eternal condemnation of such an infant would seem to contradict God's will to bring every person to salvation (1 Tim 2.4). The issue is not raised in the NT and infant baptism became the usual practice in the Church only by the 4th or 5th century. The controversy first emerged at the time of Augustine (d. 430), when he began to argue against the teachings of Pelagius. Pelagius maintained that human beings are by nature good, that the sin of Adam is bad example only, and God does not restrict unbaptized infants from heaven.

Contrarily, Augustine insisted upon the absolute necessity of Christ's Redemption, the reality of original sin, and hence the unconditioned requirement of baptism. Augustine defended the position that unbaptized infants suffer both the pain of loss (absence of the beatific vision), and pain of sense (the physical suffering characteristic of hell, although in a mitigated way). During the emergence of the Scholastic Age, however, Augustine's strict interpretation was rejected. Thomas Aquinas taught that infants dying without baptism experienced the pain of loss but not of sense, and he reasoned to the probability of a place called Limbo (from the Latin *limbus,* border or edge) where unbaptized infants would enjoy a state of natural happiness even though they would be denied the total fulfillment available only through the beatific vision. According to Thomas, original sin was a sin of nature and not of the person and as a result the punishment for both would have to be different.

Some sects at the time of the Protestant Reformation, esp. the Anabaptists, rejected infant baptism because of their emphasis on personal faith in the reception of the sacraments, and returned to the position that infants dying without baptism were condemned. The Jansenist movement also reverted to the Augustinian doctrine, against which Pius VI issued (1794) the bull *Auctorem fidei* which taught that Scripture does not exclude the theological conclusion of Limbo. Several contemporary attempts to deal with the problem have rejected the notion even of Limbo in favor of a more liberal interpretation. The grounds for this interpretation vary: that the faith of the parents or of the Church supplies for the actual baptismal rite, that a special moment of illumination is granted the infant at the moment of death through which the infant is made capable of a supernatural act of love for God, or that the cosmic unity of all creation in Christ's Redemption renders improbable the condemnation of anyone except those who have resolutely turned against God. In 1958, however, the Holy Office declared that these interpretations lacked solid foundation in either Scripture or tradition. The question therefore remains an open one in Christian theology. BIBLIOGRAPHY: G. J. Dyer, *Limbo, Unsettled Question* (1964); V. Wilken, *From Limbo to Heaven* (1961); W. A. Van Roo, "Infants Dying without Baptism: A Survey of Recent Literature and Determination of the State of the Question," *Gregorianum* 35 (1954) 406–473.

[T. M. MCFADDEN]

INFESSURA, STEFANO (*c.*1430–*c.*1500), historian. I. was professor of Roman law at the Univ. of Rome and sided with the Roman commune against Pope Nicholas V. Sixtus IV's economies curtailing salaries and funds of the university and the Pope's friendship with the Orsini faction deepened his antipapal hostility. His *Diario della città di Roma,* a history of Rome from 1303 to 1494, is important for its account of the Renaissance papacy. The author's antipapalism makes this a biased and distorted work that is to be used with discretion. BIBLIOGRAPHY: P. Wasner, LTK 5:668; C. L. Hohl, Jr., NCE 7:502; P. Paschini, *Roma nel Rinascimento* (1940).

[J. M. O'DONNELL]

INFIDEL, SALVATION OF, a question that concerns not those who deliberately and sinfully refuse the faith but those nonbelievers in God and Christ who through no fault of their own are ignorant of God and his revelation. Many attempts at solving the question have been made in theology throughout its development, particularly in these last decades. (See L. Capéran, *Le Problème du salut des infidèles* [1934]; R. Lombardi, *Salvation of the Unbeliever,* [tr. D. M. White, 1956]; M. Eminyan, *Theology of Salvation* [1960]. This theologizing is reflected in Vat II ConstChurch 16: "Those who through no fault of their own are still ignorant of the gospel of Christ and his Church yet sincerely seek God and with the help of grace strive to do his will as known to them through the voice of conscience, can attain salvation." A similar answer is given about those who do not know God explicitly but endeavor to live a good life "not without divine grace." Accordingly, non-Christian believers in God and even nonbelievers can with the help of grace (which the Council supposes is given to those in good faith) attain salvation.

Contemporary theology seeks to show how this is possible. Until recently it endeavored to make out how they can, without revelation, come to the minimal material object of faith (existence and providence of God) and its formal object. Recently one school has rather sought the solution on the side of the subjects. They can be saved as "anonymous Christians" (K. Rahner) by a fundamental option that determines their entire way of life. In the context of the universal salvific will, which offers to every individual person a real chance of salvation by ways unknown and untraceable to men, the basic life attitude of a man gradually building up and deciding for or against God is in fact an acceptance or a refusal of God's grace. Acceptance includes faith, hope, and charity (or baptism of desire). It is a yes to God revealing himself in the offer of grace while remaining anonymous. Thus all nonbelievers who live dedicated lives, submitting to the Absolute (but only these), are anonymous Christians. This possibly widespread anonymous Christianity does not make the Church's missionary activity superfluous. See Vat II ConstChurch 16: "Consequently the Church anxious to promote . . . the salvation of these men . . . fosters the missions with great solicitude." (Cf. *ibid.* 17). BIBLIOGRAPHY: J. A. Hardon, NCE 7:502–504.

[P. DELETTER]

INFIDELITY, faithlessness. (1) As a sin against theological *faith, infidelity means more than nonbelief, the simple absence of faith; it is a lack of belief, a privation, i.e., the unbelief or disbelief of one who can and ought to believe. Culpable infidelity describes both the unbelief of one who refuses ever to believe, and the disbelief of one who by rejection ceases to believe. The culpability is to be understood by the oppositeness of infidelity to faith: it is essentially an obstinate resistance against assenting to God's word, the motive of belief. That dissent is instigated by the will's attachment to personal judgment or to some other objective incompatible with the commitment to God in faith. These are the essential and the motive constituents of infidelity, rather than any particular, rejected teaching of faith. That precise meaning of infidelity allows, first of all, for the recognition that both unbelief and disbelief do exist; but, secondly, the recognition that lack of explicit faith in the Christian creed by non-Christians, or differences among Christians as to the contents of explicit faith, do not necessarily establish either infidelity or lack of the essential element in faith, trusting commitment to God. Vatican Council II clearly and positively recognized the reality of faith and the elements of holiness in others not outwardly united with Catholics (Vat II ConstChur 13–17; Ecum 2–4; NonChrRel 2–4). (2) Taken as an equivalent of *adultery, infidelity offends against one of the *goods of marriage, the *bonum fidei*. It violates the mutual commitment owed by the spouses in both justice and conjugal charity; it disfigures, as well, what the sacrament of matrimony signifies, namely, Christ's constant love for his Spouse, the Church.

[T. C. O'BRIEN]

INFINITY OF GOD, the boundless character of divine perfection, conceived as an attribute of God inasmuch as he is subsistent and pure being without limitation of any sort. In accordance with the biblical emphasis upon God's presence and power rather than upon philosophical qualities, references to divine infinity are few and indirect. Generally they are connected with affirmations of other attributes: his power (Gen 17.1; Ps 32.9; 134.6; 144.3; Bar 3.25; Jn 1.3), eternity (Gen 21.33; Dt 32.40), perfection, and incomprehensibility (Mt 5.48; Rom 11.33–36). Latin and Greek Fathers speak of God's infinity in this way: he is infinite because he is omnipotent, eternal, incomprehensible, and the sum of all perfections. Later scholastic theology treats extensively of infinity: by his very nature God is pure act without any limiting potentiality, and therefore infinite (see ThAq ST 1a, 7). In the Thomistic view, matter causes the determination of form in this or that existing reality even though matter is in itself indeterminate. God, without material principle, is subsisting form and hence infinite. Contemporary philosophy confronts the question quite differently: *Spinoza and *Hegel, insofar as they can be interpreted as monists, consider God as the unique reality and hence perfect. The so-called process philosophers, esp. A. N. *Whitehead, do not recognize divine infinity but see God and all reality in a continual movement toward the creative production of new and more perfect structures of being. BIBLIOGRAPHY: L. Sweeney, NCE 7:504–509; G. Haeffner, SacMund 3:138–139.

[T. M. MCFADDEN]

INFRALAPSARIANISM, equivalent alternative for sublapsarianism or postlapsarianism, the interpretation in Calvinist doctrine that God predestined men to heaven or hell only after the Fall. *SUPRALAPSARIANISM.

[T. C. O'BRIEN]

INFULAE, in classical Lat., a headband of red cloth worn as a sign of religious consecration; then any insignia of office; in Christian use, the hanging bands or tabs at the back of a bishop's miter.

[T. C. O'BRIEN]

INGE, WILLIAM RALPH (1860–1954), English philosopher and religious thinker. Educated at Eton and King's College, Cambridge, he taught at both Oxford and Cambridge before his appointment to the deanship of St. Paul's Cathedral, London (1911); he held that office until his retirement in 1934; the remaining 20 years of his life he spent in scholarly retirement. He was a keen critic of modern civilization and from the pessimistic tone of his epigrammatic comments upon it he was known as the Gloomy Dean. He saw the rationalism of the modern mind as too narrow to reach beyond the world of sense to the world of values and to the supreme value that is God, and hence insisted upon intuition of the mystic as necessary to supplement the defective vision of contemporary rationalism. He was greatly attracted to Plotinus, in whose Neoplatonism he saw a blend of true rationalism and mystical insight. Among his works are *Christian Mysticism* (Bampton Lectures, 1899), *Philosophy of Plotinus* (Gifford Lectures, 2 v., 1918), *Platonic Tradition in English Religious Thought* (1926), and *Mysticism in Religion* (1947). BIBLIOGRAPHY: A. Fox, *Dean Inge* (1960); R. M. Helm, *Gloomy Dean* (1962).

[R. B. ENO]

INGEGNERI, MARC ANTONIO (1545–92), Italian composer. The choirmaster of Cremona cathedral, he composed 27 Responsoria for Holy Week which were for some time thought to be the work of Palestrina.

[P. J. HENNESSEY]

INGENUIN, ST. (Genuinus, Geminus; d. *c.*605), bishop. He seems to have been one of those bps. who refused for some time to assent to the condemnation of the Three Chapters. His See of Säben was transferred to Brixen in the 10th cent., his relics following the same route at a later time. BIBLIOGRAPHY: AS Feb. 1:675–681; R. Heuberger, *Festschrift Albert Brackmann* (1931) 17–39.

[W. A. JURGENS]

INGLESANT, JOHN, a hero of fiction in a novel of that name, a minor masterpiece, by J. E. Shorthouse (1834–1903), a Birmingham businessman, the son of Quaker parents, who became a Pre-Raphaelite and a devout member of the Church of England. At first privately printed, it was published by Macmillan in 1881 and was widely welcomed for its sympathetic understanding of religious history in England and Italy in the 17th cent., not least for its picture of the community of Nicholas *Ferrar at *Little Gidding. The story of a gallant and sensitive cavalier with papist connections but high church convictions, it is still admired.

[T. GILBY]

INGRES, JEAN-AUGUSTE-DOMINIQUE (1780–1867), famous French painter and great master of line in the classical school. I. studied (1797) with J. L. David, painting Greek and Roman mythological and historical panels, and impressive portraits. In Rome (1806) and in Florence (1818) I. painted the masterworks *Oedipus and the Sphinx* (1808) and *Jupiter and Thetis* (1811). Though not a religious painter, I. executed *Christ Giving the Keys to St. Peter* (1820), *The Vow of Louis XIII* for the cathedral of Montauban (1821), and the *Martyrdom of St. Symphorian* for the cathedral of Autun (1834). In 1827 he painted the *Apotheosis of Homer* on the ceiling of the Louvre. Renowned for innumerable, distinguished portraits (Rivière family) and the famous *Turkish Bath* (1859–63), I. included a self-portrait in *Jeanne d'Arc* (1854) and completed *Jesus among the Doctors* in 1862. Degas, Renoir, Matisse, and Picasso were influenced by I.'s genius and his masterpieces are treasured throughout the world. BIBLIOGRAPHY: J. Alazard, *Ingres et l'Ingrisme* (1950).

[M. J. DALY]

INGRESSA, an entrance chant in the Milanese rite, corresponding to the Introit of the Roman rite.

INGRID ELOVSDOTTER, VEN. (d. 1282), the first Dominican nun in Sweden. She became a nun after being widowed. Besides founding a cloister in Skänninge, she also served as prioress of a convent in Germany where her niece (daughter of her brother Valdemar) had entered. The canonization process for her was begun in the early 15th cent. but it was never formally completed because of the Reformation. BIBLIOGRAPHY: A. L. Sibilia, BiblSanct 7:816–817; A. Duval, *Catholicisme* 5:1632–33; J. F. Hinnebusch, NCE 7:515.

[J. R. RIVELLO]

INHERITANCE (SCRIPTURAL USE). The basic religious meaning of inheritance derives from the Israelite concept that God saved the Hebrew tribes from Egyptian servitude to bring them to the possession of Canaan as their land in view of their acceptance of him as their one, only God and Lord. Because of their covenant with him they became his particular possession as a sacred nation dedicated to loving him; correlatively, he became their Lord, provider and Savior as long as they acknowledged him as their only God. Having led them to conquer and possess the land promised to their father Abraham in Israel's religious lore, God became the donor of Israel's inheritance by promise and fulfillment.

In the judgment of their prophets, God's people were unfaithful to his convenant with them and he was good to his word: he first took away the northern part of the inheritance, the land and people of Ephraim, by the Assyrian invasion of the 8th cent. B.C. and, finally, the land and people of Judah in the early 6th cent. by the Babylonian conquest. The covenant that promised the land had been broken; a new covenant, however, promised to establish for the faithful, and henceforth adamantly monotheistic, remnant of Judah's exiles a more exalted inheritance than merely having a territory as their own. The Judean remnant returned to what was once their land as subjects of the Persian empire that in its religious tolerance under God granted a partial religious and ethnic freedom that never again became a national political and religious independence under the royal dynasty of David. The covenant with David's house, and God's promise for a permanent inheritance through it, seemed to have been abrogated because of his people's unfaithfulness. Their religious aims began to center on a new inheritance, a much closer relationship with God beyond the hopes of ordinary human existence. In oppressive destitution they longed for a messianic inheritance, the final kingdom of the faithful remnant who went on serving the Lord in trial and poverty.

Jesus of Nazareth proclaimed the good news of such an inheritance, the kingdom of God. He symbolized it by his control of demons, and by healings and other mighty works. He inaugurated it by his death to purge mankind from sin and by his Resurrection and exaltation to give eternal life to men who confessed him to be the Messiah, Lord, and Son of God. Henceforth, he was the inheritor of the universe (Heb 1.2). He established his reign on earth by sending the promised Holy Spirit, who emboldened his disciples to proclaim Jesus to be the archleader who brings men to immortal life with God.

Christians became, through Jesus, God's sons and heirs of the life of glory with the Father, if they suffer with Christ (Rom 8.17; Gal 3.26–4.7). The secure bond and down payment of this inheritance was the Holy Spirit; he leads the faithful to the fullness of Redemption, God's possession of them as his special heritage set aside for the eternal praise of his glory (Eph 1.14). Christians have not merited this inheritance by their own upright actions; God, rather, mercifully saved them by the cleansing bath that regenerated and renewed them through the Holy Spirit poured out on them so richly by their Savior, Jesus, the Messiah. Once made upright by that gracious favor, they were heirs, through constant hope, of eternal life (Tit 3.5–7). This inheritance is God's final creative act accomplished through his Son; it is incorruptible life in the presence of God and the victory over sin and death (1 Cor 15.50–55).

[J. F. FALLON]

INHIBITION (literally a holding in), a restraint or a holding back of an otherwise natural and spontaneous thought or action; the blocking of one psychological process by another. Some distinguish inhibition from self-control, pointing out that the latter is essentially a conscious restraint, whereas the former is largely automatically functioning. Psychoanalysis and other psychotherapies aim, not at removing inhibitions indiscriminately, but at rechanneling or relieving those that represent psychically destructive forms of control.

[R. VAN ALLEN]

INITIARII (Lat. *initium,* beginning), those who believed that the Second Person of the Blessed Trinity was coeternal with the Father but became the Son only by being born at a point in time. Filaster (*Haer.* 127) reports such a belief, and Augustine repeats him (*Haer.* 80); it is mentioned in Tertullian (*Adv. Hermonegenem* 3). Adherents are called Initiarii (or Nativitarii; Lat. *nativitas,* birth) by Danaeus in his edition (1576) of Augustine's *De haeresibus* (PL 12:1254).

[L. G. MÜLLER]

INITIATION, SACRAMENTS OF, baptism, confirmation, and the Holy Eucharist. The model that sets these three as sacraments of initiation is the Christian initiation of adults, particularly as it is solemnly celebrated at the Paschal Vigil. The rite includes reception of these three sacraments. In its introduction to the Rites of Christian Initiation the revised Roman Ritual explains the reason for the designation. Baptism incorporates the recipients into Christ; forms them into God's people; forgives sin; raises them to the condition of adopted children of the Father. Confirmation signs the recipients with the gift of the Spirit; makes them more perfectly the image of the Lord; fills them with the Holy Spirit; empowers them to give witness of their faith. The Eucharist draws them to the table of the Lord so that they show forth the unity of God's people; makes them share in Christ's sacrifice; makes them an offering made by Christ the high priest. The three sacraments, together then, bring the recipients to the full stature of Christ and enable the people of God to carry out their mission in the Church and in the world. BIBLIOGRAPHY: *Rites of the Catholic Church* (1976) 3–4.

[T. C. O'BRIEN]

INITIUM, in Gregorian Chant the first few notes of a psalm tone.

INJURY, in moral theology, a general term for the object of sins against justice; the unjust thing done (see HOMICIDE; ADULTERY; DETRACTION; THEFT). The general moral evaluation of an injury done is that it is sinful because it deprives another of what is rightfully his; the sinfulness may be worsened where, because of the injury, the victim suffers further loss, e.g., where theft of an auto causes a person to lose work and wages (see DAMAGE). To be truly unjust, the injury must be intended and be against the victim's will. Thus to harm another by sheer accident and without culpable *negligence is morally speaking not an unjust injury, even though there is a *de facto* injury. Or a person may steal, but the victim willingly accept the loss; the thief is guilty of the sinful intent, but the outward act itself is not objectively a theft. There are, however, certain matters which a person cannot rightly surrender. Thus, a suicide commits an injury; he cannot rightly give up his own life because he is subject both to God's authorship of life and to obligations to the community of which he is a member.

[T. C. O'BRIEN]

INNATISM, the epistemological thesis that genuine knowledge is inborn or innate. Innatism has two bases. The first, shared by nominalism, is the denial that true knowledge, as opposed to mere opinion, is achieved through direct experience or intuition of the real. This denial in turn rests upon one of two beliefs. The one is that the real experienced does not in itself possess an intelligibility commensurate with genuine knowledge; this was the case for Plato. The other belief, that of Descartes, holds that our means of experience, the senses, yield obscurity and confusion of knowledge, rather than clarity and distinctness. The second basis of innatism, this time shared with realism, is the belief that we do indeed enjoy a supraopinionative knowledge. Mathematical laws, the first principles or laws of thought, and the existence of God are the commonly cited examples. As innatism holds that such knowledge cannot be derived from experience, it must conclude that such knowledge is a priori, prior to and independent of experience. Thus Plato held that innate ideas are actually memories, the representations of the direct intuitions of higher reality enjoyed before the soul entered the body. And Descartes went so far as to identify thought and the nature of the soul.

Occidental philosophy has not been sparing in its criticism of innatism. Locke, among others, argued that if innatism were true, such ideas as that of God and the principle of identity would be possessed by all and used in all reasonings. But this is manifestly not the case. And long before, Aristotle had pointed out that innatism runs counter to our experience of development in knowledge, from merely potential to actual knowledge. Yet innatism continues to attract adherents well into the second half of the 20th cent.; the Cartesianism of the linguist Noam Chomsky is but the most notable example.

[R. E. HENNESSEY]

INNER CITY, popular expression for that part of a metropolitan area which includes the central business district and the nearby densely populated residential sections. The residents are generally poorer than those who live in the suburbs, and the black population of the metropolitan area is usually concentrated there because of a *de facto* segregation pattern in the housing opportunities of the city. In most of the large cities of the U.S. there is a continuing exodus of white middle-class families from the downtown areas in large urban centers, and their places are taken by poorer, rural families coming to the city to seek employment. There is a trend also for industries to move into less densely populated areas, and the revenue loss from the diminishing industrial and personal income taxes makes it increasingly difficult for the city authorities to supply the necessary public services to those who live in the inner city. Thus, there is a widening gap between the needs of the area's residents and the ability of the city to supply for those needs. The inner city is the focal point of the problems of race, poverty, and human misery in the often otherwise affluent American society. It has been the locale of the civil disturbances, the rioting, looting, and racial disorders of the 1960s. It has therefore become the object of increasing social concern on the part of Churches and other organizations interested in human welfare.

[G. A. VANDERHAAR]

INNER LIGHT, the basic and distinctive belief of the *Religious Society of Friends. While others earlier, e.g., among the Anabaptists, had similar ideas, the doctrine of the Inner Light most probably came to G. *Fox, founder of the Quakers, from his own personal religious experience. Neither in Fox's enthusiastic writings nor in R. *Barclay's more formal *Apology of the True Christian Divinity* (1678) was the Inner Light precisely categorized. God is its source and dwells within it; Fox called it the Light of Christ; Barclay at times seemed to identify it with Christ himself. While evangelical emphases within Quakerism on the Bible and the historical Christ have sometimes subtly altered its role, the Inner Light has remained for Quakers the essential rule of faith; Scripture or anything else outside the soul is simply confirmatory. Although some moderns, e.g., Edward Grubb (1854–1939), have given it a naturalistic interpretation, for most Quakers the Inner Light is neither conscience nor reason, but a unique religious sense; an immediate revelation, a personally experienced contact with God, it is unerring, self-authenticating and saving. Barclay stressed its being a corporate experience. All men, even those predating or not knowing the historical Christ, have received it; for those who use it rightly it means consciousness of Christ's inner saving presence. The American Quaker Rufus M. Jones (1863–1948) stressed the affinity between the Inner Light and mysticism. Belief in the Inner Light underlies the Quaker deemphasis of dogma, their understanding of sin and redemption, their benevolence toward all men as sharers in the light, and their proper mode of worship. BIBLIOGRAPHY: Knox, Enth 152–171; L. Eeg-Olofsson, *Conception of the Inner Light in Robert Barclay's Theology* (1954); Mayer RB 409–422, with bibliog.

[T. C. O'BRIEN]

INNER MISSION (Ger. *Innere Mission*), a term first used by J. H. Wichern in 1848 to designate mission work within Christendom as opposed to mission work outside it. It included all charitable, social, and religious endeavors of German Lutherans except parish work. By means of a central committee it endeavored to coordinate such efforts. The movements grew out of *Pietism, the Awakening (a return to the historical and confessional roots of Lutheranism), and industrialization. The chief aims were to reclaim lapsed Christians and to assist the needy of all social classes. The organization soon spread to other European countries. In the U.S., Lutherans promoted it; changing its name after a time to Christian Social Welfare. In Germany, the Inner Mission merged in 1957 with Hilfswerk, a society that had been set up in 1945 by the *Evangelical Church in Germany (EKD). Even in its early years Inner Mission was criticized for obscuring the importance of doctrine, ignoring church authority, and overstressing social action. BIBLIOGRAPHY: W. Schütz, RGG 3:756–763.

[M. J. SUELZER]

INNITZER, THEODOR (1875–1955), abp. of Vienna, cardinal. Born in Bohemia, I. was educated in Vienna and ordained in 1902. He was professor of Scripture at the Univ. of Vienna (1913–32). Noted for his interest in social reform, he served as minister of social welfare (1929–30), was made abp. of Vienna in 1932, and cardinal in 1933. Though a loyal supporter of the Austrian government under Dollfuss and Schuschnigg, he offered, with the Anschluss, to collaborate with the Nazi regime in the hope of keeping peace between Church and State. This brought upon him the rebuke of Pius XI, whose disapproval proved justified shortly after, when the liberties of the Church were severely curtailed. After the war, he dedicated himself to the rebuilding of the Church in Austria. BIBLIOGRAPHY: J. Kosnetter, *Theodor Kardinal Innitzer zum Gedächtnis* (1957); J. Wodka, *Kirche in Österreich* (1959); W. B. Slottman, NCE 7:518–519.

[A. WATHEN]

INNOCENCE, BAPTISMAL, the state of complete freedom from sin consequent upon the reception of *baptism.

One of the effects of this sacrament is the total remission not only of original sin but also, in the case of the adult recipient, of actual sin. A person who has never committed any actual sin is said to remain in a state of baptismal innocence.

[T. M. MCFADDEN]

INNOCENCE, ORIGINAL, a term used by St. Thomas Aquinas as a synonym for *original justice, INTEGRITY, STATE OF.

[T. C. O'BRIEN]

INNOCENT, ST. (4th cent.), bp. of Tortona, of whom nothing is known except that he was a zealous bishop. According to legend, however, I., an orphan boy, was condemned to death at Tortona for his faith but was miraculously rescued from prison. Thence he made his way to Rome where he came under the protection of the Pope, who eventually sent him back to his native city as bishop. BIBLIOGRAPHY: Butler 2:113; A. Frutaz, LTK 5:696.

[R. B. ENO]

INNOCENT I, ST. (d. 417), **POPE** from 402, during whose reign Rome fell to Alaric (410). He is remembered for his vigorous assertion of the powers of the papal office. In letters to Victricius of Rouen, Exuperius of Toulouse, and Decentius of Gubbio, he insisted upon a uniform discipline in the Western Church based on Roman usage and custom. He demanded as well that more important cases be referred to the Holy See for judgment. He extended the powers of the metropolitan of Thessalonica as papal vicar and thus helped to bring E Illyricum (part of the Eastern Empire) under the authority of the Western Patriarchate. He prevailed upon the civil power to take steps against the *Donatists and he confirmed the anti-*Pelagian decisions of the African councils of Carthage and Milevis. During his pontificate his friend St. *John Chrysostom, whom he had tried to defend against Theophilus of Alexandria, died in exile (407). Works: PL 20:463–636; CSEL 35:92–98. BIBLIOGRAPHY: Altaner 416; E. Weltin, *Ancient Popes* (1964) 259–280.

[R. B. ENO]

INNOCENT II (Gregorio Parareschi; d. 1143), **POPE** from 1130. I. was a cardinal deacon and papal mediator for the Concordat of Worms. After the death of Honorius II, a double election occurred. A committee of eight cardinals had been designated to elect a new pontiff. Though two members were absent Gregorio was chosen and hastily enthroned at the Lateran as Innocent II. Thereupon the majority of the cardinals elected Peter Pierloni who was enthroned at St. Peter's as Anacletus II. Through the efforts of St. Bernard of Clairvaux and St. Norbert of Xanten, I. was ultimately acknowledged as pope. BIBLIOGRAPHY: H. Wolter, LTK 1:467–468 s.v. "Anaklet II"; Jedin-Baus (1968) 3:2.

[H. DRESSLER]

INNOCENT III (Lotario de Segni; *c.*1160–1216), **POPE** from 1198. After studies at Paris in theology and at Bologna in law, he was made a cardinal by his uncle Clement III (1191). While still a deacon, he was elected pope. Possessed of a keen intelligence, he was also a man of prodigious activity. The chief record of his pontificate is his *registers of letters, now in the Vatican Archives. From the outset he saw himself as the vicar, not simply of Peter, but of Christ (*Vicarius Christi*). As vicegerent of God he concerned himself ceaselessly with the affairs of all of Christendom. He used every opportunity to strengthen his political power in those cities and lordships which formed the patrimony of St. Peter; and he obtained recognition of feudal lordship over the kingdoms of Sicily, Aragon, Portugal, Hungary, England, and Ireland. In the matter of the Empire, he asserted the right to examine the credentials of the emperor-elect before consecrating him (see *Regestum super negotio Romani imperii,* ed. F. Kempf, 1947). In general his concern was to secure peace between states and to reconcile monarchs with subjects, but where exhortation failed he often resorted to threats: he excommunicated the Emperor Otto IV and released his subjects from their allegiance; he placed England under interdict for years on end, as a result of a dispute with King John about the election of the archbishop of Canterbury. His concern for the poor is all too often lost sight of, as is his promotion of hospitals in Rome and elsewhere. His many sermons (see PL v. 217) are remarkably rich from this point of view; some of his treatises, particularly *De miseria conditionis humanae,* were very influential. His greatest achievement, perhaps, was Lateran Council IV, which in a few weeks in late 1215 promulgated a series of pastoral constitutions that not only had a profound effect on the day-to-day life of the Church for the next 3 cent., but also gave rise to a wealth of treatises of practical theology and to higher standards of clerical education than hitherto. BIBLIOGRAPHY: A. Luchaire, *Le concile de Latran et la réforme de l'Église* (1908); C. Cheney and W. H. Semple, *Selected Letters of Innocent III concerning England (1198–1216)* (1953); C. R. and M. Cheney, *Letters of Innocent III, 1198–1216, concerning England and Wales* (1967).

[L. E. BOYLE]

INNOCENT IV, (Sinibaldo Fieschi; *c.*1200–54), **POPE** from 1243. Trained in civil and canon law at Bologna where he also taught briefly, he entered papal service in 1226. His pontificate spanned the climactic years of the papal-imperial struggle. At the Council of Lyons I, he declared the previously excommunicated Emperor Frederick II deposed and ordered a Crusade against him. At Frederick's death (1250) the Hohenstaufen dream of a strong, centralized kingdom uniting Germany, Italy, and Sicily was destroyed and the papacy's freedom from imperial control assured. I.'s last years were devoted to securing the fruits of victory by preventing Frederick's son from taking the throne by permanently severing Sicily from Hohenstaufen control, and by granting it to a family loyal to the papacy. The struggle with the Empire had overshadowed I.'s interest in missionary expansion, the Crusade, and in ending the schism with Constantinople. He was one of the foremost canon lawyers of his day, and his *Commentaria* on the *Decretales* included a major treatment of the role of the secular power in Christian society. BIBLIOGRAPHY: Mann 14; E. Kantorowicz, *Frederick II, 1194–1250* (tr. E. O. Lorimer 1931, repr. 1957); J. M. Muldoon, NCE 7:524–525.

[J. MULDOON]

INNOCENT V, BL. (Peter of Tarentaise; *c.*1224–76), **POPE** for 5 months in 1276. A Burgundian by birth, he was trained as a theologian. He was himself a Dominican and a friend of St. Thomas Aquinas. He served his order and the French Church before his election to the papacy in 1276. Though he was a theologian of note, his modest skill as a diplomat failed to implement union with the Greeks or a Crusade. BIBLIOGRAPHY: W. H. Principe, NCE 7:525; A. P. Frutaz, EncCatt 7:14–17.

[S. WILLIAMS]

INNOCENT VI (Étienne Aubert), **POPE** (1352–62). Intent upon reform, he did not hesitate to resort to prisons and the stake to insure obedience in religious orders. To reconquer States of the Church, he engaged the shrewd Card. Albornoz who, though successful, required much money for military operations which I. raised by selling silver, *objets d'art,* and jewels. Feeling that Avignon was threatened, he barricaded it with wooden walls. He died soon after. BIBLIOGRAPHY: G. Mollat, DTC 7.2:1997–2001; G. Mollat, Catholicisme 5:1664–65.

[F. D. LAZENBY]

INNOCENT VII (Cosimo de' Migliorati; *c.*1336–1406), **POPE** from 1404. When elected he was cardinal archbishop of Bologna (from 1389); he had previously been abp. of Ravenna (1387), and papal collector of taxes in England for 10 years. He was the third pope of the Roman line during the Great Western Schism, eager to end it, and directed most of his efforts to detaching King Charles VI of France and the Univ. of Paris from the cause of the antipope, *Benedict XIII. I.'s relations with King Ladislaus of Naples occasioned many problems. A scholar by inclination, I. tried to revive the decrepit Univ. of Rome, and he introduced humanist influences into the Roman Curia. But his pontificate was too short to be effective in these projects or in putting an end to the Schism.

[R. H. SCHMANDT]

INNOCENT VIII (Giovanni Battista Cibo; 1432–92), **POPE** from 1484. Giving up the dissipation of his early youth, he became a priest, was made bp. of Savona (1467) and later was transferred to Molfetta (1472). By the influence of Card. Della Rovere (later Julius II), he was made cardinal (1473). At the death of Sixtus IV, Della Rovere, seeing that his own candidacy was not likely to prosper, managed by bribery to secure Cibo's election to the papacy. I. was a weak and ineffective pope. He involved the Holy See in wars and quarrels that depleted the papal treasury. In an effort to cope with his financial troubles, he sold offices. Although he saw the need of reform, his efforts to bring it about were pitifully inadequate; unsuccessful also was his attempt to organize a crusade to ward off the threat of Turkish attack. BIBLIOGRAPHY: Pastor 5:229–357; 375–378.

[P. K. MEAGHER]

INNOCENT IX (Giovanni Antonio Facchinetti; 1519–91), **POPE** from Oct. 29 to Dec. 30, 1591. Educated in law at Bologna, he participated as bp. of Nicastro in the Council of Trent and became papal nuncio at Venice in 1566; there he facilitated the formation of the grand alliance that defeated the Turks at Lepanto. In 1576 he became titular patriarch of Jerusalem and cardinal in 1583. At the Roman Curia he was principally responsible for many of the actions and decisions of Gregory XIV, his ailing predecessor. During his own brief reign he labored to improve the organization of the Curia and of the Papal State. BIBLIOGRAPHY: Pastor 22:409–427.

[R. H. SCHMANDT]

INNOCENT X (Giambattista Pamphili; 1572–1655), **POPE** from 1644. A canon lawyer, he served as auditor of the Roman Rota for 25 years, before becoming nuncio to Spain. As pope he carried on an active diplomacy but without signal success. He vainly condemned the Treaties of Münster and Osnabrück ending the Thirty Years' War in 1648, since these treaties deprived German Catholics of the rights guaranteed in 1555. The Jansenist controversy in France demanded papal intervention; after a 2-year study by a commission he appointed, I. issued the bull *Cum occasione* (1653) condemning the five Jansenist propositions (D 2001–07). In subsequent pronouncements he banned Jansenist publications, yet he failed to stifle the dispute (see JANSENISM). Personally pious, he was responsible for a scandalous nepotism in Rome. BIBLIOGRAPHY: Pastor v. 30.

[R. H. SCHMANDT]

INNOCENT XI, BL. (Benedetto Odelscalchi; 1611–89), **POPE** from 1676. He was a canon lawyer who entered the clerical state when he was 28 years old, and not until he was 39 was he ordained a priest. As a cleric he entered the papal service, was created cardinal in 1645, legate to Ferrara in 1648, and from 1650 until 1656 was bp. of Novara. He resigned to return to the papal curia; his election to the papacy was blocked in the conclave of 1670 by *Louis XIV of France. Elected in the following conclave, I. took firm action against Louis' encroachments on the liberty of the Church: his claim to revenues from vacant episcopal benefices (the *régale*) and his reaction to I.'s resistance by having enacted the Four Gallican Articles (1682; see GAL-

LICANISM). The Pope immediately condemned them and the bps. who enacted them. Doctrinal problems also arose. His correction (1679) of the position making frequent communion obligatory, commended both frequent communion and reverent restraint according to conscience (see D 2090–95). I.'s condemnation of *laxism (1679; D 2101–67) and his directive by a decree of the Holy Office (1680; D 2175–77) that the Society of Jesus not oppose the *probabiliorism of Tirso*Gonzalez de Santalla, belong to the decline of *probabilism in the history of moral theology. I. also condemned the *quietism of M. *Molinos (1687; D 2201–69; cf. 2181–92) and propositions from the work of the Oratorian, by then cardinal, Pier Matteo Petrucci (1687). I. was beatified in 1956.

[R. H. SCHMANDT]

INNOCENT XII (Antonio Pignatelli; 1615–1700) **POPE** from 1691. He served in papal curial and diplomatic posts, became a cardinal under Innocent XI in 1681, and abp. of Naples in 1687. At his election he took his name as a sign of his intent to follow the policies of Innocent XI. As pope, I. was devoted to the poor; took firm actions to suppress nepotism and to reform religious life. He brought about Louis XIV's reconciliation with Rome and the withdrawal of the Declaration of the French Clergy (see GALLICANISM). He put an end to the haggling over the five Jansenist propositions (see JANSENISM), and in 1699 condemned Mme. *Guyon's quietist teaching as found in the *Maximes* of F. *Fénelon (see D 2351–74).

[R. H. SCHMANDT]

INNOCENT XIII (Michelangelo dei Conti; 1655–1724), **POPE** from 1721. I. suffered from poor health and physical disabilities that limited his activity as pope. In doctrinal matters he endorsed Clement XI's **Unigenitus* against Jansenism. From his diplomatic service as nuncio in Lisbon I. had acquired a distrust of the Jesuits' position of missionary adaptation in the *Chinese rites controversy and insisted on their obedience. His international relations focused on a vain reaffirmation of papal rights over various Italian lands formerly possessed by the pope, yet Charles VI of Spain recognized his sovereignty over Naples. I. supported James Stuart, "the Old Pretender," to the English throne and brought Card. G. *Alberoni to trial for treason, but exonerated him. BIBLIOGRAPHY: J. S. Brusher, NCE 7:531; Pastor 34.

[R. H. SCHMANDT]

INNOCENT OF LE MANS, ST. (d. 542), bp. of LeMans from 496. Under his rule the first cathedral of Le Mans was finished; he strove to establish monasteries of the Benedictine rule in his diocese. He died on a visit to Monte Cassino to secure monks. His relics were returned to his cathedral, where his cult grew rapidly. BIBLIOGRAPHY: E. Griffe, *Catholicisme* 5:1673; G. Mathon, BiblSanct 7:838.

[T. C. O'BRIEN]

INNOCENTS, HOLY, male infants killed by Herod in Bethlehem (Mt 2.16). When the Magi returned home without telling Herod where the newly born "king of the Jews" was, he had all males under 2 years of age in the town killed. The event has been called the slaughter of the Innocents; the Feast of the Holy Innocents has been celebrated since as early as the 5th cent. On the basis of Bethlehem's population at the time, scholars have estimated the number killed could have been perhaps between 10 and 30. Ancient legends sometimes gave much higher figures. Matthew's account is the only known reference to the event.

[T. EARLY]

INNOCENZO OF BERZO, BL. (1844–90). An Italian ordained a diocesan priest in 1867, Giovanni Sclavinoni was vice rector of the seminary in Brescia, joined the Capuchins in 1874, and took the name Innocenzo. He devoted his life in the order to preaching and hearing confessions. BIBLIOGRAPHY: C. da Langasca, BiblSanct 7:834–836.

INNSBRUCK, UNIVERSITY OF (Leopold-Franzens-Universität), an autonomous institution of higher learning in the Tyrolean capital under the jurisdiction of the Austrian Ministry of Education. The university, established in 1669 and confirmed by papal brief of Innocent XI and imperial decree of Leopold I in 1677, opened with the four faculties of philosophy, theology, law, and medicine. The Jesuits were entrusted with theological and philosophical chairs, but with the suppression of their order (1773) anticlerical Josephinism brought increased state supervision until Emperor Joseph II reduced the university to the status of a lyceum (1873) with greatly restricted faculties. In 1791 Emperor Leopold II restored the university to its original rank, but in 1810 under Bavarian rule the school was again lowered to a lyceum. After Tyrol was returned to Austria, Emperor Francis I restored university rank (1826) with faculties of law and philosophy, although it was not until 1857 that the faculty of theology was reinstalled under Jesuit direction, and the faculty of medicine in 1869. The faculty of theology was closed by the Nazi regime from 1938 to 1945. Theological studies have won international recognition through distinguished teachers such as H. Grisar, H. Hurter, H. Noldin, J. A. Jungmann, K. Prümm, and H. and K. Rahner, and through publications such as the *Zeitschrift für Katholische Theologie* (1877–). Other outstanding professors were Julius von Ficker (1826–1902), founder of the Innsbruck Historical School, and Ludwig von *Pastor, papal historian. The library, founded in 1746, contains some 620,000 volumes, 1,650 incunabula, and 1,150 manuscripts. BIBLIOGRAPHY: E. Wolf, RGG 3:769.

[M. B. MURPHY]

INORDINATENESS: (1) in its wider and stronger sense, the quality of a sinful action as such, sin being taken as a human act lacking the order it should have; *actus debito* *ordine privatus* is St. Thomas Aquinas's most characteristic definition of sin (ThAq ST 1a2ae, 72. 2 ad 2); (2) in a narrower and weaker sense a slight excess or defect in an otherwise good act that may introduce venial sin into an act or pattern of acts. In the second sense inordinateness has frequently entered into the literature on the spiritual life to mean a retardant to spiritual growth.

[T. C. O'BRIEN]

INQUISITION. The harshness of the old Judaic death penalty for heresy (Dt 13.5–19; 16.21–17.13; 18.20) was opposed by early Christians, who saw religion as a matter of conscience and free will and regarded excommunication as a sufficient punishment.

History. The caesaropapist emperors viewed the protection of religion as their first concern and would have made heresy tantamount to high treason. St. Optatus of Milevis (d. *c.*400), citing the OT, defended the imperial position; but the execution of Priscillian (386) brought strong objections from Siricius, Ambrose, and Martin of Tours, besides the reaction in Spain. By the 11th cent., with the revival of Roman law, the idea of a perfect and sovereign Christian society based upon objective revelation was current enough in Europe for heretics to be hanged by Henry III (1051–52), burned by Robert I (1122), and lynched by several mobs. Why the papacy in 1231 moved to establish a special Inquisition in the hands of the newly founded mendicant orders, the Franciscans and Dominicans, is not clear. It appears that the decision, long in developing, was prompted as a defense against the caesaropapism of Frederick II Hohenstaufen. Neo-Manicheans entered Western Europe from the Balkans *c.*1000 (see BOGOMILS) and by the late 12th cent. gave alarm to the authorities of Church and State, esp. in N Italy, S France, and Germany. England had little heresy, although some 30 heretics were branded under Henry II and turned out to die in the winter of 1166. Peter II expelled heretics from Aragon (1197), but they came back during the Albigensian War; Aragon feared heresy less than the loss of her lands in S France. In Flanders and N France a fair number of heretics died at the stake.

Ecclesiastical measures began with Lateran Council II (1139), which required civil rulers to prosecute heretics; Alexander III called for prison and confiscation (1163); Lateran Council III (1179), soon after a council of *Cathari met near Toulouse, ordered the use of force. In 1184 Lucius III in *Ad abolendam* initiated the episcopal inquisition, which required aid from secular rulers, denunciations of heretics by the faithful, semiannual diocesan visitations, and strong measures against supporters of heresy. Neither episcopal nor secular aid was forthcoming, and Innocent III put his hopes in the holy life and holy thought of Cistercians working with local parish commissions of inquiry. In 1206 St. Dominic began to work with the Cistercians in S France. When the papal legate was slain in 1208, Innocent excommunicated the Count of Toulouse and gave all Catholics freedom to persecute his person and occupy his lands. The Albigensian War followed, and dynastic and regional rivalries prevailed over religious interests.

While Paris was extending its sway into S France, Frederick II was issuing decrees against heresy (1220, 1224, 1227). Innocent III and Lateran Council IV (1215) had acted to safeguard episcopal authority and to defend heretics against secular judgment, and Innocent disapproved of the death penalty; but Gregory IX in 1227 gave support to the 1224 law of Frederick II, all those convicted by bishops be burned. When Frederick was excommunicated in late 1227, the papacy had to assume direct control. The Council of Toulouse (1229) only confirmed regulations already in use; but the Statutes of the Holy See (1231), sent to all bishops, initiated the Inquisition. The Statutes consisted first of Gregory's constitution, which offered life imprisonment as a penance for abjurers of heresy and restricted secular punishment to those condemned by the Church, and secondly of the statutes of the Roman Senator Annibald, which confiscated heretics' goods, demolished their dwellings, fined or exiled sympathizers, and required future senators to prosecute them. Episcopal zeal was still lacking, and Gregory in 1232 advanced the Dominicans as agents of the new Inquisition. What was peculiar to the new institution was that the jurisdiction over heretics was reserved to a legal system controlled by the papacy. The hunting of heretics, the judicial procedure, and the punishments had existed for years; torture would not be accepted until later.

The first Inquisitors went to the Rhineland, Burgundy, Aragon, and Lombardy. Local bishops and nobles in France and Italy opposed them; Lombard cities, except Bologna, resisted the intrusion of a new judicial authority. Kings supported the Inquisition as long as it was in their interest. By 1255 the new system was established. Areas of jurisdiction varied according to the intensity of heresy but respected ecclesiastical and political boundaries. Only the pope could reverse the judgments of the Inquisitors, who were practically irremovable from office. At first, Inquisitors rode the circuit in pairs, but they soon took up residence in centers where their persons and records were safe; several were slain. In 1254 Innocent IV required episcopal consent in sentences of life imprisonment and death, and this order was confirmed in 1262, 1265, and 1273. Boniface VIII required episcopal approval for all judgments. Everywhere the Inquisition depended on the support of the local force.

Some early Inquisitors were quite harsh. Robert le Bougre, a former member of the Cathari, burned 137 people in Champagne (1239); 200 more were burned in Moissac; 200 Perfecti (members of the elite group of the Cathari), at Montségur (1244); and 50 heretics and 18 cadavers at Castelbon in Aragon. From 1227 Conrad of Marburg, a diocesan priest at Mainz, and two associates burned "countless" peasants and then turned against the nobility in a reform of the German Church, and were assassinated.

Inquisition Procedures. The conduct of an Inquisition began with a sermon exhorting aid from the faithful and repentance of heretics within a month's period of grace.

Penitents were treated leniently but had to name their associates; the Inquisitors had to prove the guilt of those remaining suspect after a month. Roman and OT law required at least two witnesses for trial, but the Inquisitor could be accuser as well as judge. False witnesses were liable, as in OT, to the same penalty as was the accused; the testimony of heretics and other infamous persons was not accepted until 1261. To prevent retaliation, the accused did not know the witnesses against him until Boniface VIII ruled otherwise; but he could name his enemies, whose testimony would be stricken from the record. Rarely did witnesses appear for the accused and risk incriminating themselves. Eventually, the accused was allowed legal aid, mostly exhortations to confess by lawyers whose orthodoxy was above suspicion. The accused could reject a judge because of prejudice and at any time before sentence could appeal to Rome, which would then render the verdict. Such appeals were not rare, and Inquisitors strove to make their trials irreproachable. A permanent council of judges assisted them, and a jury of *boni viri* reviewed the cases without knowing the names of the accused; they had to decide on the reliability of the witnesses, the nature of the guilt, and the penalty. While advisory, their judgment was usually followed; any modification of their opinion was toward leniency.

Papal bulls based on the acts of provincial councils determined procedure. Inquisitors also composed manuals, the most famous being that of Bernard Gui, Inquisitor of Toulouse (1307–24). Charges were read twice to the accused, who was then asked to swear on the Bible. The list of questions varied according to the heresy. Promises of indulgence and planted informants were used to elicit confessions, which were the goal of the Inquisitor. When a person strongly suspect would not confess, constraint could be employed: prison, chains, fasting, sleeplessness, and (after 1252) torture so long as it did not mutilate or cause danger of death. It could be applied only once for one half-hour, unless new evidence appeared. The grand solemnity of torture sessions was calculated to produce confessions through terror rather than through pain. Confessions obtained through torture had to be repeated voluntarily. Most Inquisitors put little faith in torture, but some abused it. When there was no confession, the testimony of two witnesses in agreement was enough to convict, although more witnesses were usually required. Punishments for repentant heretics, imposed by the Inquisitor, were viewed as salutary penances. Those unconfessed and convicted by the testimony of witnesses were handed over to civil authorities as obstinate heretics for punishment, death at the stake. Penitents beforehand agreed to accept the sentences, from which there was no appeal. Death and life imprisonment entailed confiscation of goods, and so many posthumous trials were held. Sentences were pronounced at a solemn assembly of notables and populace (*sermo generalis*). Lesser penalties were public or private and included scourging, visits to churches, pilgrimages, wearing the cross of infamy, fines, and alms. Commutations and suspensions of penalties were frequent, as were escapes from prisons, which were the unwelcome responsibility of bishops. Ordinary imprisonment was tolerable, but solitary confinement had no regard for health. Relapsed heretics, even though repentant, were liable to death but were often spared. The death penalty was not frequent. Confiscations accrued to the king and great nobles; but unless these personages met the expenses of the Inquisition, which were heavy, a part of the confiscations went for expenses. Houses frequented by heretics were subject to demolition; but because of conflict with other interests, such as confiscation, this penalty was rarely applied.

After 1300 the power of the Inquisition was restricted, mainly because it became dependent upon episcopal approval. It lost importance as the Cathari disappeared, although Waldenses, Franciscan Spirituals, Fraticelli, Beguines, Lollards, crypto-Jews, and witches attracted its attention. Philip IV used it to destroy the Templars (1312). The 15th-cent. decline in papal prestige caused by the Great Western Schism also hurt the Inquisition, which fell into the hands of the secular rulers. By the 16th cent. the Inquisition was generally inoperative, except in Spain and Portugal; in France it gave way to the king's authority and parliament. The Inquisition did develop objective rules that not rarely operated as protections against popular prejudice. As an institution it cannot be defended but merely explained by that social intolerance of deviations that was general in all communities and continued even long after the Reformation. BIBLIOGRAPHY: Y. Dossat, NCE 7:535–541, bibliog. *INQUISITION, SPANISH.

[E. P. COLBERT]

INQUISITION, SPANISH, the institution in Spain that followed the same procedure as the papal *Inquisition but differed in two respects from the Inquisition elsewhere: (1) royal control played a much more prominent part in it; and (2) it acted mainly against secret adherents to established religions, i.e., to Judaism (the Marranos) and to Islam (the Moriscos), who overtly professed Christianity, rather than against heresies. The medieval Inquisition was of little note in Spain. Several Inquisitors were killed; Nicholas Eymerich, an Inquisitor known for moderation, wrote a manual (1346) based on 44 years of experience. In 1478 Sixtus IV, in the interest of peace, agreed to revive the Inquisition in Spain against crypto-Jews. So strong did crypto-Judaism prove to be in Seville (1481) that the Inquisition quickly extended to Córdoba, Ciudad Real, Segovia, and Aragon. In 1483 Isabella established a tribunal of appeal under the abp. of Seville, without prejudice to Rome, and Tomás de Torquemada (d. 1498) began a 15-year career in which as Inquisitor General he established the machinery of the Spanish Inquisition. His *Instructions* (1485, 1488, 1498) were completed by Cisneros (1516) and issued in definitive text by Valdés (Toledo 1561). The Inquisitor General, an expert in theology or canon law, presided over a supreme council of seven Inquisitors that held nine sessions a week; eight other officials, several theologians, and clerks assisted them in Madrid. Staffs also assisted particular Inquisitors in 15 Spanish, 3 Portuguese, 2 Italian, and 3 American tribunals. There was also an Inquisition of the Fleet. Until 1647 the supreme council dealt only with appeals from lower tribunals; after 1647 it had to confirm all judgments. There seems to be no way to estimate the number of sentences pronounced at Spanish *autos-da-fé but they were fewer, it appears, than condemnations for witchcraft in the rest of Europe.

Moriscos, baptized en masse in 1499 and forced to choose between Christianity and exile in 1502, rose against the Inquisition and allied with enemies of Spain in 1568. Expelled by Philip III in 1609, they disappeared. In the era of the *Alumbrados (16th–17th cent.) there were few harsh punishments administered to those guilty of immorality. Some Protestants suffered, but the Inquisition was mainly concerned with preventing circulation of unauthorized Bibles and the works of Luther and Calvin. The Spanish Church consistently opposed ties with Protestant countries. Witchcraft was practically ignored. Under the Inquisition, Spanish authors were quite free in their choice and treatment of topics, and Spanish readers had access to almost all European philosophical and scientific literature. The era was probably the greatest in Spanish literary history.

In 1579 Philip II used the Inquisition against Antonio Pérez, but Aragonese patriots protected him in a defense of their political rights. In 1644 Philip IV prevailed over the Inquisition in the case of a seduced nun. There were few trials in the 18th century. Suppressed by Napoleon (1808) and the Cortés of Cadiz (1813), the Inquisition was restored in theory by Ferdinand VII (1814) and finally suppressed by Maria Cristina (1834).

The Inquisition came to the New World on Columbus's second voyage (1493). From Hispaniola it went to Mexico (1532) and Lima (1539). In 1569 Philip II put the New World Inquisition directly under the supreme council; permanent tribunals were established at Mexico and Lima in 1571 and at Cartagena (Colombia) in 1610. The New World Inquisition sought to control undisciplined clergy and to keep out Protestantism, Judaism, and Islam. It dealt with a few captive English and Dutch pirates but did not concern itself with the Indians. By 1650 there was not much for it to do. BIBLIOGRAPHY: Y. Dossat, NCE 7:540–541; E. Hibbert, *Spanish Inquisition* . . . (3 v. in 1, 1967); D. W. Lomax, NCE 14:205, s.v. "Torquemada, Tomás de."

[E. P. COLBERT]

INRI, an abbreviation formed of the initial letters of the title Pilate had affixed to the cross on which Jesus was crucified—*Iesus Nazarenus Rex Iudaeorum,* according to the Vulg version of Jn 19.19. This abbreviation is often used in Western art in representations of the crucifixion. *TITLE OF THE CROSS.

[P. K. MEAGHER]

INSANITY, with reference to morality, any pathological mental state that precludes moral *responsibility. As rendering truly human action impossible, any form of derangement, as well as mental or behavioral disorders, can be understood under the term insanity. Criminal law recognizes a temporary insanity as excusing from guilt (see FORENSIC PSYCHIATRY); moral evaluation would, however, not always concur with the legal criteria.

[T. C. O'BRIEN]

INSCRIPTIONS, see EPIGRAPHY.

INSIGHT, etymologically a word that refers to internal sight, a way of seeing with the eye of the mind. Used in this sense in Old and Middle English, its meaning later included mental vision, internal sight, and in this sense it was used as early as 1297. Its definition as inner penetration with the eyes of understanding into the character or hidden notion of things is traceable to the works of Sidney, Coleridge, and Wordsworth. In the Bible the word, or its analogue, was used to mean inner vision and discernment of the just man and it was used in both the Old and New Testaments (1 Kg 3.9, 12; Pr 4.7; Ec 8.5; Acts 26.19; 1 Cor 2.14; Heb 11.27; 2 Pet 1.9, among others). The word is of special interest in theology and philosophy where it is generally accepted to mean an understanding into the intelligibility of X (ThAq ST 1, 84.7; 1, 85.1 ad 8; 3, 11.2). In its common-sense meaning the word is closer to the meaning ascribed to it by B. J. F. Lonergan: "an understanding of X." Since the word is subject to arbitrary and selective use, esp. in the prolix of current philosophical analysis, it is perhaps best to use Lonergan's definition. BIBLIOGRAPHY: B. J. F. Lonergan, *Insight: A Study of Human Understanding* (1957) *passim.*

[J. R. RIVELLO]

INSPIRATION, BIBLICAL, "unique divine influence in virtue of which the men responsible for the OT and NT were so moved and enlightened by God that their work may truly be called the Word of God." (Forestell, see below). Some such basic notion is common to Jewish writings, to such intertestamental books as Sirach and 1 and 2 Maccabees, to the NT itself, and to the entire history of the Christian Church. Inspiration is linked to the notion of prophecy, the word of God mediated through the prophets; and to *torah,* the commandment of God mediated through the priests. It is reflected in such NT phrases as "it is written" or "to fulfil what was spoken by the prophets." Nevertheless determining which books were in fact inspired was a complicated matter, involving the long process fixing on the *canon of the Bible. The canon of the Council of Trent is the most "catholic," including as it does the Jewish canon as well as intertestamental books of the Septuagint and accepting as deuterocanonical what Protestants and other call the apocrypha. Referring to the books of the OT and the NT, Vatican Council I declared that "The Church holds them as sacred and canonical, not because, having been composed by human industry alone, they were afterwards approved by her authority, nor only because they contain revelation without error, but because, having been written under the inspiration of the Holy Spirit, they have God as their author and, as such, have been handed over to the Church." (EnchBibl[4] 77). Regarding the human writers who were instruments of the Holy Spirit in this achievement, Leo XIII (1893) taught: ". . . by supernatural power, he so moved and impelled them to write—he was so present to them—that the things that he ordered, and those only, they, first, rightly understood, then willed faithfully to write down, and finally expressed in apt words and with infallible truth" (*Providentissimus Deus*: EnchBibl[4] 125). The notion of inerrancy has been problematic, leading some to treat every part of every biblical book as a collection of timeless definitions of truth, rather than the record of the divine pedagogy and human response, as the Fathers of the Church did. They viewed the core of Scripture to be Christ's revelation, which gave coherence to the entire biblical record. The problem of hermeneutics was addressed by Pius XII in *Divino afflante Spiritu* (1943), in which he pointed out the importance of appreciating the various literary genres and cultural forms of the various ancient authors in order to grasp the true literal meaning of their words. The new hermeneutic goes beyond this and questions how words spoken and written long ago can have relevance and speak to men today. This has called into play the traditional Catholic and Orthodox view of the role of the Church (in the sense of the People of God) in producing the Scriptures and that only in the life and liturgy of the Church can the written word attain its full dimension. BIBLIOGRAPHY: J. T. Forestell, NCE 2:381–386; K. Rahner, *Inspiration in the Bible* (tr. C. H. Henkey, 1961).

[E. J. DILLON]

INSPIRATIONISTS, an early name for members of the *Amana Church Society, which was called also the Community of True Inspiration.

[T. C. O'BRIEN]

INSPIRATIONS OF THE HOLY SPIRIT, in its primary and active sense the special assistance of the Holy Spirit prompting the exercise of one of the gifts of the *Holy Spirit. The doctrine of the gifts is maintained in keeping with the constant NT affirmation of the Holy Spirit's active presence in those who live under grace. The intervention primarily denoted by the term inspiration is the activation of the gifts, because that activation is necessary for salvation (ThAq ST 1a2ae, 68.2). The immediate, unitive relationship with God given by grace and the theological virtues, charity above all, occasions crises in the Christian's life in which the ordinary way of acting is insufficient to maintain the life of grace. The inspiration of the Holy Spirit, an intervention coming, as it were, swiftly and from outside, effects a higher manner of acting consistent with the demands of charity. That does not mean the performance of an objectively heroic or extraordinary deed or, in the order of knowledge, a special revelation. The inspiration of the Holy Spirit is an assistance that raises the mind and affections over their own insufficiency in order that the recipient may remain constant in faith, hope, and charity. The term St. Thomas prefers for this special assistance is *instinctus* (*ibid.* 1–2; see O'Connor). In a secondary sense inspiration, whether attributed simply to God or specifically to the Holy Spirit, also refers to such *charismatic gifts as prophecy, or to the actual grace prompting any holy thought or affection. Both the active divine inspiring and the effect inspired are included in the term inspiration. The term has special development in the theology of biblical *inspiration, prophecy, and the charismatic gifts for the teaching office in the Church. Prayer for inspiration is part of Christian practice when difficult decisions are to be made. Claims are also advanced, at times presumptively, that an idea or course of action is an inspiration of the Holy Spirit. There are such inspirations, but because they are supernatural realities there can be no human assurance infallibly certifying the claim; only a docility, humility, and sincere intent of charity can safeguard against presumptive claims. BIBLIOGRAPHY: ThAq (Lat-Eng v. 24, ed. E. D. O'Connor) 131–141.

[T. C. O'BRIEN]

INSTALLATION, in its precise sense, the formal seating of a canon in his cathedral stall, symbolizing conferral of his office. The term also is used more broadly for inauguration into any ecclesiastical office: for taking "canonical possession" of a diocese by a RC bp. or of a parish by a pastor; as an Anglican term, enthronement of a bp. or induction of a rector. Lutherans, Presbyterians, Baptists, and others in the U.S. frequently call the public recognition of a new minister or church officer an installation.

[T. C. O'BRIEN]

INSTANTIUS AND SALVIAN, Spanish bps. of unknown sees who joined Priscillian (*c*.375) and probably consecrated him bp. of Ávila (382). They accompanied Priscillian to Italy on his vain appeal to Damasus I and Ambrose against the bps. of Spain and Aquitaine. Salvian died in Rome. While Priscillian appealed to Emperor Maximus, Instantius defended their group before the Council of Bordeaux (384–385), which deposed him and exiled him to the Scilly Isles. Instantius may be the author of 11 anonymous Priscillianist treatises in an uncial MS discovered in 1889, as well as three apologies, seven sermons, and a prayer (CSEL 18:1–106).

[E. P. COLBERT]

INSTITUTE OF CHARITY, see ROSMINIANS.

INSTITUTE OF JUDAEO-CHRISTIAN STUDIES, a scholarly program inaugurated on March 25, 1953 at Seton Hall University, South Orange, New Jersey by Monsignor John M. Oesterreicher for the purpose of increasing knowledge of the Church's roots in Judaism and furthering a better mutual understanding and relationship between Jewish and Christian communities. The idea for such an institute had its origin in Vienna when a similar effort entitled *Opus Sancti Pauli* was conducted by Monsignor Oesterreicher and given the support of a number of European bps. as well as the praise and approval of the then Card. Pacelli in 1938. In his booklet, *The Rediscovery of Judaism,* Oesterreicher writes: "for all their differences, the Church and Judaism need not be antagonists, rather does the Covenant bind them to a common task, to a partnership before God." The program of studies in Jewish and Christian traditions provides a rich background for all phases of ecumenical discussion and encounter. A vital part of the Institute is the program in graduate studies which offers a master's degree. Among its many courses are: foundations of Judaeo-Christian studies; biblical thought in the Hebrew Scriptures and the NT; Jewish mysticism; Jewish texture of the Gospels; the Holocaust; history and theology and the Middle East. Besides a variety of studies, the Institute engages in lectures, seminars, workshops, and publications, particularly, *The Bridge: Essays in Judaeo-Christian Studies*.

[R. A. TODD]

INSTITUTE OF MARY, see LORETTO, LADIES OF.

INSTITUTES, RELIGIOUS, see RELIGIOUS INSTITUTES.

INSTITUTES, SECULAR, see SECULAR INSTITUTES.

INSTITUTES OF THE CHRISTIAN RELIGION, English title of the treatise by John *Calvin, the most important theological exposition of early Protestantism. It was first published in Basel in 1536; the final and definitive edition was published in Geneva in 1559. Calvin called the work "a summary of the principal truths of the Christian religion." He originally composed the treatise shortly after his own conversion to Protestantism as a statement and defense of the beliefs of the French Protestants, and he revised and enlarged it several times during the course of his life. The original version was in Latin (*Christianae religionis institutio*); revised Latin texts appeared in 1539, 1543, 1550, and *1559*. Calvin's French translations of these revisions were published in 1541, 1545, 1551, and 1560. The first draft of the *Institutes* was printed by Thomas Platter in Basel, where Calvin had taken refuge after his flight from France. He was then but 26 and on the threshold of his great career. The *Institutes* introduced him to the world as a Reformer and was an immediate success. The first edition consists of six chapters that observe the order of Martin Luther's *Larger Catechism:* (1) the Ten Commandments, (2) the Creed, (3) the Lord's Prayer, (4) the sacraments of baptism and the Eucharist, (5) the other sacraments (rejected by Calvin), and (6) the theme of Christian liberty. The doctrine is largely Lutheran. The second edition was published in Strassburg in 1539, during the time Calvin lived there in temporary exile from Geneva. It is three times larger than the original text and contains, among other new material, an extended statement of the doctrine of *election or *predestination. The formulation of this tenet, so closely associated with Calvin, was greatly influenced by the Strassburg Reformer Martin *Bucer, whose tutelage during these years shaped the development of Calvin's thought. This edition, translated by Calvin into French and published in Geneva in 1541, was an important event in French literature and religious history. The final edition of the *Institutes* appeared in 1559, followed by a French translation in 1560. This definitive edition is five times the length of the 1536 edition and consists of 80 chapters divided into four books, which follow generally the topics: Father, Son, Holy Spirit, and the Church. The organization and additions render it practically a new book, the fullest statement of Calvin's biblical theology and the *Summa* of *Reformed Protestantism. The famous statement on "Eternal Election" is found in Book 3, Chapter 21; Calvin's distinctive exposition of the role of civil government, in Book 4, Chapter 20, concludes the work. The 1559 *Institutes* was soon translated into most of the languages of Europe. A Dutch version appeared in 1560, an English translation in 1561, and a German edition in 1572. The best English edition is in the *Library of Christian Classics* (v. 20–21, ed. J. T. McNeill, tr. F. L. Battles, 1960). BIBLIOGRAPHY: F. Wendel, *Calvin* (tr. P. Mairet, 1963).

[J. C. OLIN]

INSTITUTION, admission into one of the lay ministries, e.g., as reader or acolyte. According to the *motu proprio* of Aug. 15, 1972, conferral of these ministries is not to called "ordination" but "institution" since there are no longer minor orders in the Latin Church, according to the same apostolic letter.

INSTITUTIONAL CHURCH, a term used in two senses. (1) A description of any Church as organized with some structural form of authority, pursuing a special mission and accepting set means of sanctification and modes of worship. The Church as institutional for any or all of these reasons is often contrasted unfavorably with the "charismatic Church," i.e., the spiritual assembly or community of those living under the direct guidance and gifts of the Holy Spirit, or is regarded as an impediment to the "desacralization" or secularization required of the Church in the modern world. Disparagement or dismissal of the institutional Church is not acceptable to many of the Protestant Churches that recognize certain objective elements as constitutive of the Church established by Christ. In RC teaching, Vatican Council II taught that the visible and invisible elements are not opposed but are necessarily two aspects of one reality, the Church (Vat II ConstCh 8). (2) An instrument of the *Social Gospel movement. The term was applied to churches that also sought to be agencies for social service on behalf of the urban poor. St. George's Episcopal Church in New York City and Grace Baptist Church in Philadelphia were famous examples.

[T. C. O'BRIEN]

INSTRUCTION, CLEMENTINE, see CLEMENTINE INSTRUCTION.

INSTRUMENTAL CAUSE, an *efficient cause that in its use by a *principal cause, produces an effect greater than itself. The qualities and function proportionate to the instrument enter into the makeup of the final effect, but that effect matches the genius or power of the user of the instrument. Theology uses the meaning of instrumental causality in assigning the function of Christ's human powers with regard to divine effects, e.g., miracles; or the function of the sacramental signs (see SACRAMENTS) with regard to grace.

[T. C. O'BRIEN]

INSTRUMENTS IN CHURCH, see MUSICAL INSTRUMENTS IN CHURCH.

INSTRUMENTS OF THE PASSION, the cross, the nails, hammer, scourge, crown of thorns, and lance used in the crucifixion of Jesus.

[F. H. BRIGHAM]

INSTRUMENTUM PACIS (instrument of peace), a small disc or tablet bearing a sacred image, presented to be kissed by those assisting at Mass, as a way of conveying the celebrant's kiss of peace to them; also called simply the *pax* or the *osculatorium* (Lat. *osculum,* kiss). The usage, dating from the Middle Ages, was continued in modern times into some liturgies, e.g., the Dominican and the Carthusian, and at some pontifical Masses.

[T. C. O'BRIEN]

INSUFFLATION, a blowing or breathing upon a person or thing to symbolize the giving of the Holy Spirit and the expulsion of an evil spirit (Jn 20.22). This ritual action is used in exorcism, the stages of the catechumenate, and in the blessing of chrism. As this action signifies the expulsion of an evil spirit, it is sometimes referred to as exsufflation.

[P. K. MEAGHER]

INSULT, the English term used for the offense against the honor and dignity of another that RC moral theologians called *convicium.* It is a sin against commutative justice and charity, and theologians are not agreed as to whether it is essentially distinct from upbraiding or taunting speech (*improperium*). Like contumely, insult dishonors another, but contumely does so by calling attention to his moral lapses, while insult may fault him even for his natural defects, as when scorn is heaped upon him for racial or ethnic reasons. That such offenses are not to be viewed lightly is evident from the serious disorders to which they can lead. The gravity of the sin of insult depends upon the seriousness of the offense given by what is said or done, upon the intention of the one who gives the insult, and upon other circumstances of time and place. Often insult is a symptom of some other moral fault, e.g., anger, hatred, envy, etc. BIBLIOGRAPHY: ThAq ST 2a2ae, 72.1, esp. ad 3.

[J. HENNESSEY]

INSURRECTION, see REVOLUTION.

INTEGRALISM (Fr. *intégrisme*), a campaign by conservatives in the Church that carried to extremes the condemnation of *Modernism by Pius X's **Pascendi dominici gregis* (1907). The purport of the title is that the campaign intended to preserve integrally the teachings of faith in resistance to the "Modernist" reductionism of those who favored critical scholarship in the sacred sciences. The chief agency of the campaign was the *Sodalitium Pianum, French name *Sapinière,* the secret society founded (1909) by U. *Benigni; its organ, *Correspondenza di Roma.* Benigni and most of the leading integralists were shallow obscurantists in theological learning but skilled in casting suspicion by anonymous or pseudonymous accusation or by innuendo. The most intense activities were in France, then the chief center of Catholic scholarship; but the integralists found victims in Italy, Belgium, Germany, Austria, and Switzerland as well. Prominent among them were those who led the hue and cry against *Americanism; many also became associated with *Action française. The names of but a few of the scholars on whom they cast a cloud and whose work they suspended, in some cases permanently, is an indication of their virulent effectiveness: L. *Duchesne; L. De *Grandmaison; J. M. *Lagrange; P. *Battifol; D. *Mercier; A. D. *Sertillanges. Gradually the danger came to be recognized; *Correspondenza* was suppressed; Benedict XV in his encyclical *Ad beatissimi Apostolorum* (1914) noted that the term integral is tautological as a qualifier of "Catholic faith," since the body of belief is adhered to in its entirety or not at all; matters of theological inquiry, however, are open to research and debate (D 3625–26). When the Sodalitium, disbanded after Pius X's death (1914), attempted to resume its activities, it was suppressed by Rome (1921). As a concrete movement, Integralism died; in less definable or extreme forms, similar attitudes remained the aftermath of the alarm over Modernism until almost mid-20th cent.; their almost complete disappearance since Vatican Council II is perhaps symbolized by the abrogation of the *Oath against Modernism (1967).

[T. C. O'BRIEN]

INTEGRATION, the result of a process whereby people previously not accepted or discriminated against because of their race become full members of a community with the same rights and opportunities as others. The term is applied to the movement for equality of Negroes with whites in all areas of social, economic, and political life. It calls for a change of attitude on both sides. In the process of integration the three basic areas of social reform are employment, education, and housing. Many more jobs must be made available to blacks so that all who want to do so will have the opportunity to work. This will involve a massive training program for those who by lack of previous education or discrimination do not have the ability to perform as skilled workers. In education there must be mixing of white and black children in the classrooms, as well as efforts to improve the quality of schools already functioning in predominantly black neighborhoods. In housing, all sections of the cities must be opened to blacks, and help in financing low and moderate rental must be made available to those who temporarily cannot afford it.

[G. A. VANDERHAAR]

INTEGRITY, STATE OF: (1) in its use by St. Thomas Aquinas, the stable condition of rightness proper to human nature before the Fall; thus synonymous with the state of *original justice (ThAq ST 1a2ae, 109.2,3,4,8,10 ad 3; 114.2): (2) in later theology, a hypothetical condition, like that of ''pure nature,'' the condition human nature would be in without grace, but with the harmonious rightness of natural moral faculties and immunity from physical evils that were the secondary elements in the state of original justice. The hypotheses, states of pure and integral nature, were entertained in theology with a view to categorizing more precisely the essence and necessity of grace and the damage to nature done by original sin. These hypotheses were particularly prominent in connection with the rejection of the teachings of *Baius (see D 1921, 1923–24, 1926, 1978), *Quesnel (D 2434–35), and the Jansenist Synod of *Pistoia (D 2616–17).

[T. C. O'BRIEN]

INTEGRITY OF CONFESSION, an obligation imposed upon the penitent to insure that the confession of sins, a necessary part of the sign of the sacrament of penance, is entire and complete. It requires the penitent to confess all serious sins not yet remitted by the power of the keys, thereby submitting them to the judgment of the Church. This means that the penitent must avow all serious sins committed since baptism which have either never been confessed, or which were confessed but were not forgiven because of some obstacle such as ill-disposition on the part of the penitent, which prevented the sacrament from being effective. The moral nature of the sin must be indicated as clearly as possible; this is done by providing the confessor with the necessary facts relative to number, species, and circumstances so as to enable him to make a correct judgment concerning the sin (c. 901). Integrity of confession, however, as here described is not always possible, and a wide variety of extenuating circumstances can lessen the obligation. Thus, the psychology of the individual (emotional disturbances, loss of memory, etc.) or physical and material circumstances (deafness, dumbness, danger of death) can be legitimate impediments to the making of an integral confession. In normal circumstances, integrity of confession can best be insured by a serious examination of conscience before reception of the sacrament. Attention should be directed toward sins of omission as well as those of commission. Of greatest importance, however, is the need to see these requirements for an integral confession as part of a sacrament intended for man, and therefore adaptable to a degree to various situations and circumstances.

BIBLIOGRAPHY: A. G. Martimort, *Signs of the New Covenant* (2d and rev. ed. 1963) 256–257; P. E. McKeever, NCE 11:78–83.

[B. ROSENDALL]

INTELLECTUAL LIFE, that part or dimension of life belonging to the mind's pursuits. The ideal of an intellectual life seems to derive from the early Greek philosophers, among whom the attainment of wisdom was seen as the goal or perfection of human existence, bringing with it a participation in the divine life. Thus, to reach for wisdom was no incidental affair but a way of life. The intellectual life, and respect for knowledge and intellectual achievement, have, at times, been lacking in Christianity when an exaggerated stress has been placed on the salvific aspect of revealed truth to the point of holding in disdain all knowledge thought not to bear immediately on salvation. Such a viewpoint failed in its understanding of the completeness of the Incarnation. But if there have been anti-intellectual movements in the history of the Church, there have also been countermovements promoting an integral Christian intellectual life, and a better understanding of the relationship between nature and grace. Within the past 100 years such figures as Card. D. *Mercier, Card. J. H. *Newman, A. G. *Sertillanges, J. *Maritain, and P. *Teilhard de Chardin have been associated with this. Within the U.S. there have been periodic examinations of conscience concerning the adequacy and vigor of Catholic intellectual life and achievement. G. Shuster (1925) and J. T. Ellis (1955) wrote to challenge American Catholics to greater intellectual activity and participation in American life. In the 1960s and 1970s, A. Greeley has pointed to continuing religious and ethnic bigotrys, partially preventing this broader participation by Catholics. He has also maintained that sociological analysis indicates that Catholics are about equal to other Americans as regards their inclination to the intellectual life. Some feel, however, that this simply means that Catholics like many other Americans are basically anti-intellectual, not because of any excessive zeal for revealed truth, but because of an excessive attachment to a pragmatic and utilitarian perspective.

BIBLIOGRAPHY: P. T. de Chardin, *Divine Milieu* (1960); J. T. Ellis, *American Catholics and the Intellectual Life* (1956); A. Greeley, *Religion and Career* (1963); H. R. Reith, NCE 7:560–561; A. G. Sertillanges, *Intellectual Life* (tr. M. Ryan, 1956).

[R. van ALLEN]

INTELLECTUALISM is here taken, not in a frequent modern sense, that is as according a primacy to thought, conceptualization, or abstract reasoning over loving, doing, or being existentially committed, or as an impersonal rationalism, scientism, and perhaps determinism as against a dynamism more pulsing, capricious, and moving, but as the Dominican and Thomist contrast with and pendant to Franciscan and Bonaventuran voluntarism in the high theology of the Middle Ages and afterwards, above all with respect to the doctrine of union with God. The fundamental point was whether the decisive moment of the activity of *happiness lay in the mind or in the will: there was no question of an either-or exclusion as to its integral nature. From a comparative analysis of the functions of knowing, which brings its objects "in," and loving, which sends its subject "out," St. Thomas Aquinas concluded that only the first was a possessing or holding activity, whereas the second was powerless of itself to ensure the difference between desiring its object when absent and enjoying it when present: this was at once its noble and tragic burden. The nobility was that we could love God beyond our knowing him; the tragedy was the inevitable ache until we could see him face to face. He agreed that affective knowledge through the gifts of the Holy Spirit brought some glow into the darkness of faith. His characteristic intellectualism scales down to lesser positions, thus his emphasis on reason in the reign of law, in moral command, in freedom, and in the response to beauty. BIBLIOGRAPHY: ThAq ST 1a2ae, 3, 4 (esp. in ed. Lat-Eng v. 16, ed. T. Gilby); P. Rousselot, *Intellectualism of St. Thomas* (tr. J. E. O'Mahony, 1935).

[T. GILBY]

INTENTION. (1) In theology, an objective sought by a purposeful act of the will; the purposeful act itself. As signifying some intended object, intention refers esp. to matters petitioned of God in prayer and in the offering of Mass. As an act of will, according to the theology of the sacraments, the minister's intention, required for validity, means his proposal to do what the sacramental sign expresses, e.g., to administer baptism as a sign of cleansing from sin; the recipient's intention, required for fruitful reception, means the proposal to receive the sacrament as such, not simply to go through the externals. In the case of matrimony, the spouses' intention makes up the essence of the sacrament itself; in penance, the penitent's intention is in fact his contrition and is the matter of the sacrament. Moral theology takes into account the psychological structure of the *human act, the effective development of which begins with the resolve to achieve some goal or end. On that basis intention may refer to the fundamental purposiveness that a person gives to his moral life. Concretely in the life of grace that is either the bent of charity upon loving God above all, or is attachment to a created good incompatible with charity. Under such general moral orientations, there are immediate and proximate ends; intention is the resolve to attain them by effective means. In both its senses, intention has the effect of coloring subsequent moral judgments; these are affective evaluations, seeing as good or evil what is consonant with the will's intention. In a further, notable moral usage, intention refers to a person's subjective motivation. The underlying thought here is the almost endless range of possibilities for perceiving true or seeming good in any given moral situation. The intention of good does not negate or justify the moral values intrinsic in a situation, however; no end can justify bad means. An intention that is an ulterior motive can give even the decisive moral goodness or evil to an action, since the ulterior motive is predominant in the one who acts (see also INTENTION, PURITY OF). As far as its influence in any of these senses on acts following from it, intention is described as implicit or virtual, where the one acting does not explicitly renew it; or actual and explicit, where he does. (2) In scholastic psychology both cognitive and affective experiences are described as intentional in that each in its own way is otherward. The vocabulary is particularly developed with respect to knowledge. The mental concept (idea) is called an intention because it functions totally to signify; its primary signification is the reality known, and the concept is described as a first intention; but what is known also has a logical classification (genus, species) by reason of its presence in the mind; signification of the concept is called a second intention.

[T. C. O'BRIEN]

INTERCESSION, prayer offered on behalf of others. The term bears on one meaning of *impetration: that prayer is addressed to the saints, not as though they have power to answer it—that kind of prayer is offered to God alone—but to obtain their supportive petitioning, their intercession. The most important meaning of intercession, however, is that it is an inherent element in the *communion of saints, i.e., the vital communication existing in the mystical body of Christ. That vitality means that all can share in the benefits and graces of the whole; first of all, in those of Christ the Head; then, of each other. Thus Christ himself "always lives to make intercession for those who draw near to God through him" (Heb 7.25; cf. Jn 17). Those who are joined to Christ in faith and charity are joined to one another. Intercession, then, becomes a primary expression of charity, which above all wishes the divine good to neighbor; and it is because of the union in charity that there are grounds for prayers offered for another being heard. Because intercession belongs to the vitality of charity, nearness and intensity of union with God make intercessory prayer more effective. Thus the communion of saints includes the special power of Mary and the blessed as an aid for those who are still striving toward eternal life.

[T. C. O'BRIEN]

INTERCOMMUNION, a relationship between Churches in which each accepts members of the others for holy communion and authorizes its own members to receive communion from another. It is allowed by the RC Church only with regard to Eastern Churches (cf. Vat II EastCath 26–29; Ecum 8); these Churches do not ordinarily practice it. The Anglican Communion has maintained intercommunion with Old Catholic Churches since 1932 (see BONN AGREEMENT); the *Lambeth Conference of 1968 permitted Anglicans to receive communion even in Churches not recognizing the *historic episcopate, admitted non-Anglicans to communion and encouraged full intercommunion with Churches with which merger discussions are in progress. In Protestant Churches generally there is a wide diversity of practice, depending on the view of what constitutes a valid ministry (see OPEN COMMUNION). In the *ecumenical movement intercommunion receives two interpretations: one, that it is a means of expressing unity despite diversity; the other, that it should be practiced only when the goal of unity has been achieved.

[T. EARLY]

INTERCONFESSIONALISM, movements of thought and action relating Churches that have different *confessions of faith. With the rise of the *ecumenical movement the importance of Christian unity has made it seem necessary for Christians to seek some way of securing a united witness despite their differences of doctrinal expression. This is done not by ignoring differences between the confessions but by searching for greater mutual understanding. It is seen in certain cases of *intercommunion, in ecumenical agencies, e.g., the World Council of Churches, and in interfaith dialogue. BIBLIOGRAPHY: *Intercommunion* (ed. D. Baillie and J. Marsh, 1952).

[T. EARLY]

INTERDENOMINATIONAL CHURCHES, a term that may designate two types of churches. (1) The *community church, which may be either federated (two or more congregations, retaining identities but sharing one minister, service, and community program) or union (people of diverse denominational backgrounds united in one congregation upon a broad Christian platform). These are sometimes loosely affiliated through the International Council of Community Churches. (2) This type is exclusive rather than inclusive. Rejecting denominational differences, this group stresses agreement in doctrinal orthodoxy (usually understood as *fundamentalism) and evangelistic interest. While adhering to *independency, some of these churches have fellowship in the *Independent Fundamentalist Churches of America. BIBLIOGRAPHY: J. R. Howe, "Community Churches," EncRelKnowSuppl 1:278–279; Mayer, RB 376–378. ANTIDENOMINATIONALISM.

[N. H. MARING]

INTERDICT, an ecclesiastical penalty barring those punished from certain sacred rites. An interdict may be imposed by the pope or a local bp. within his jurisdiction. It is a personal interdict if imposed upon an individual or a group of people; local, if it is imposed on a whole place—parish, diocese, nation, for example. No interdict prevents reception of the sacraments in danger of death. Local interdicts are suspended on Christmas, Easter, Pentecost, and the feast of the Assumption of Mary. Also where there is a local interdict the cathedral church, or the church in a one-church-town, liturgical celebrations on Sundays or holy days are permitted, but in a subdued manner. Personal interdict prohibits those penalized from administering or receiving the sacraments, from participation in liturgical rites, and from Christian burial. The legislation on interdict is far more detailed; while the canons remain in force, their application is obsolescent and canons generally urge that interdict has no place in a revised draft of the penal code. *PENAL POWER OF THE CHURCH.

INTEREST, an amount charged or paid for the use of money and ordinarily consisting in a percentage of the money used. The moral issue of charging interest touches on the wider issue of *usury. Usury, condemned in Scripture, in theology, and in canon law, always has been and remains morally wrong: it is the unjust extortion of payment for the use of money. But an extreme view equated any charging of interest with usury. Various theological attempts have been made to give an exact moral justification for interest; basically the justification seems to amount to the right of the one charging interest to compensation for the loss of the money's power to bring profit. The possibility of usury always remains and esp. where the amount of interest charged includes administrative costs, protection against risk, monetary speculation (as in the case of mortgage lending). Where interest is usurious it creates the obligation to restitution.

[T. C. O'BRIEN]

INTEREST, CONFLICT OF, see CONFLICT OF INTEREST.

INTERFAITH DIALOGUE, conversation between representatives of different communions with the aim of developing greater understanding and finding a basis for greater cooperation. It is distinguished from debate in which representatives try to prove that the position of their communion is right and the others wrong. It proceeds from the conviction that one may learn from his partner in dialogue, particularly that one will be enriched by mutual sharing with fellow Christians of different background and outlook. Dialogue requires a willingness to listen to representatives of other communions with the intent of gaining greater understanding, and to explain one's own point of view with candor and courtesy. It emphasizes respect for other communions, but insists that participants speak honestly about points of disagreement. Through the process of dialogue it is hoped that misunderstandings may be overcome, that the extent of basic disagreement may be clarified, and that the sense of what is held in common may be deepened. In interfaith dialogue participants speak responsibly as representatives of their communions; therefore they should have thorough knowledge of what their communions teach, and should refuse to sacrifice convictions in the interest of a superficial unity. In the *ecumenical movement various agencies, notably the *World Council of Churches, have been established to further interfaith dialogue. It was commended in the Decree on Ecumenism (9) of Vatican Council II.

A development of special importance in recent years has been the establishment of numerous formal dialogues involving two communions. Known as bilaterals, these customarily consist of meetings by officially appointed representatives and of publication of reports on areas of agreement reached and on remaining disagreement. These reports do not constitute official action by the communions, but are nonetheless regarded as highly significant since the dialogue participants have been officially appointed and are generally theologians and church officials of high standing. The bilateral dialogues involving the largest numbers of Christians are those conducted internationally by the Vatican Secretariat for Promoting Christian Unity and various world confessional families. Following a 1966 visit of Anglican Abp. M. Ramsey to Pope Paul, an Anglican-RC International Consultation was set up and began meeting in 1970. It reported substantial agreement on the Eucharist in 1971 and on the ministry in 1973. A 1977 report expressed agreement on Roman primacy in any future union, but not on papal infallibility. International *Lutheran-Catholic dialogue began in 1967, and a joint statement issued in 1972 (Malta Report) provided the basis for later discussions. Dialogue by representatives of the Vatican and the World Methodist Council also began in 1967. Roman Catholics began dialogue with the World Alliance of Reformed Churches in 1970 and with Pentecostals in 1972. In the U.S. the following bilateral consultations are active: Anglican–RC; Southern Baptist–RC; Disciple of Christ—RC; Lutheran–RC; Presbyterian–RC; United Methodist–RC; Orthodox–Roman Catholic. In 1964 the Third Pan-Orthodox Conference at Rhodes agree to set up an Inter-Orthodox Theological Commission for the dialogue with the Anglicans, and meetings began in 1966. The Rhodes Conference also established a commission for dialogue with Old Catholics, and conversations began in 1966 at Belgrade. After unofficial consultations since 1964, The Fourth Pan-Orthodox Conference in 1968 formed an Inter-Orthodox Theological Commission for Dialogue with the Oriental Orthodox Churches. Establishing inter-Orthodox-Catholic dialogue proved more difficult, but in 1967 Catholic conversations began with the Russian Orthodox Church. The latter has also entered into dialogue with other Churches. Other formal dialogues between world confessional families include the Anglican-Lutheran, Anglican-Old Catholic, Baptist-Reformed, and Lutheran-Reformed. A dialogue between representatives of Lutheran and Reformed Churches of Europe resulted in a 1973 Leuenberg (Switzerland) statement that expressed theological agreement moving beyond the historic differences of these two Reformation traditions. In addition to world and regional activity, communions within particular countries have conducted dialogues. These have served both to improve relationships within the country concerned and through publication of reports to aid dialogue elsewhere. Interfaith dialogue in recent years has also involved Christian conversations with Jews and other non-Christians, though in these cases the goal of unity has not been in view.

BIBLIOGRAPHY: N. Ehrenstrom and G. Grassman, *Confessions in Dialogue* (1972; rev. ed. 1975).

[T. EARLY]

INTERFAITH MOVEMENTS, cooperative efforts by members of different religious communions to work for common goals. In the development of the *ecumenical movement many Christians came to desire cooperation with Christians of other Churches. In some cases this cooperation was in regard to a particular project, as in the case of Bible societies organized to promote distribution and use of the Scriptures. In other cases this cooperation was more general. Christian youth work, as in the YMCA and the World Student Christian Federation, developed largely on an interfaith basis. The ecumenical movement itself, with the development of the World Council of Churches and regional ecumenical bodies, may be considered the most important interfaith movement. Interfaith movements are based on the conviction that men who are divided on some things may nonetheless profitably cooperate on matters upon which they agree, and particularly that Christians despite their divisions share a significant body of common conviction and common concern for the welfare of the general society. Critics warn against the dangers of *indifferentism, with participants ignoring the basic distinctive elements of their Churches. *DENOMINATIONALISM, *VOLUNTARYISM.

[T. EARLY]

INTERIMS, three Reformation edicts designed to achieve for the time being (*ad interim*) a religious truce in Germany. (1) Regensburg Interim (1541). Charles V terminated the fruitless reunion Conference of *Regensburg on July 29, 1541. In the document of recess, over the objection of Card. Contarini, papal legate, the Emperor Charles V deferred doctrinal settlement to a national council in Germany. To win the Protestant princes to help him in his war against the Turks, Charles also granted them freedom in the interpretation of disputed doctrines, the right to receive Protestants into their territories from others, and guaranteed to the princes the church property they had secularized.

(2) Augsburg Interim (1548). The formula of this truce, approved by the Diet of Augsburg, was a crucial issue in the Reformation. The document was prepared by Protestant and Catholic theologians. On the main points of justification, the nature of the Church, and the sacraments, it imposed

Catholic interpretations. To the Protestants it conceded the points of a married clergy and communion under both kinds. It also guaranteed secularized church property to the Protestant princes. Most of the Protestant princes refused to sign. In Rome, Paul III gave reluctant approval only in Aug. 1549. Since the Interim was to be imposed, many of the Reformation leaders had to flee from their pastorates; the South German cities resisted vigorously; M. *Bucer departed from Strassburg for England. Among the Lutherans, there was strong reaction to the doctrinal implications, esp. by N. *Amsdorf and M. *Flacius Illyricus. P. Melanchthon was blamed for compromising Luther's teaching (see GNESIOLUTHERANISM).

(3) Leipzig Interim (1549). This was an effort to ease the resumption of some RC rites by Protestants. It was drawn up by Maurice of Saxony, Melanchthon, and George II of Anhalt-Dessau. Some RC ceremonies were classified as *adiaphora, neither good nor bad in themselves, and thus permissible. The document led to further bitter controversy (see ADIAPHORISTS). Only in the Duchy of Saxony was there any acceptance. BIBLIOGRAPHY: *Documents Illustrative of the Continental Reformation* (ed. B. J. Kidd, 1911) 340–346, 359–362; H. Holborn, *History of Modern Germany* (2 v., 1959) v. 1, *Reformation;* Léonard HistProt 1:260–262.

[E. D. MCSHANE]

INTERIOR CASTLE, a literary device used by St. *Teresa of Avila (1515–82) to describe the advance of a soul in the love of God. Her work of that name likens the Christian soul to a crystal castle constructed of seven chambers, or mansions, through which a person passes on the way to complete union with God. In the innermost mansion dwells the King, God, and from him as from the center a light of diminishing intensity spreads through the mansions lighting the way to him. Outside the castle there is only the darkness of sin; one enters through prayer, and all of the journey to the King at the center is by prayer. The first, or outer, mansions, to which the light penetrates least, are devoted to meditation on the eternal truths and the removal from the soul of attractions for sin. As one goes on, prayer develops, the attraction for God increases, sin grows ever less influential, until God possesses the soul completely at the very center. Simple meditation is practiced in the first mansions, leading to the beginning of contemplation in the third and its completion in the fourth. This leads to the initiation of the spiritual betrothals and the fifth mansion; they are fulfilled in the sixth and crowned by the spiritual marriage and the resulting transforming union of the seventh mansion. BIBLIOGRAPHY: "Interior Castle," *Complete Works of St. Teresa* (ed. and tr. E. Allison Peers, 3 v. 1946, pa. 1973); Marie Eugène de L'Enfant-Jésus, *I Want to See God* and *I Am a Daughter of the Church* (tr. M. V. Clare, 1953–1955).

[P. F. MULHERN]

INTERIOR LIFE, the life given by sanctifying grace and expressed above all in the exercise of the theological virtues. This vital communion with God is primary in the Christian life and the preeminent meaning of the life of prayer. It is equivalent to the contemplative life in the broadest sense that includes all stages of union with God. To speak of the interior life is not simply a question of contrasting it with outward and apostolic activity, but of indicating that it consists in the immanent acts of faith, hope, and charity, along with the assistance of the gifts of the Holy Spirit. The connotation also includes a more intense effort to live the life of grace and charity. This interior life is distinguishable from what theological tradition terms the active life. But while there can be an exclusive concentration on the life of prayer, as in the case of contemplative religious, there can be no active life separable from the interior life. The active life, whether it means fulfillment of the duties of the lay state or explicit dedication to an apostolate of spiritual or corporal works of mercy, has its base, its resources, and its motivation in the life of prayer, in the vitality of the theological virtues. *APOSTOLATE AND SPIRITUAL LIFE.

[T. C. O'BRIEN]

INTERIORIZATION, a cosmic process described by Teilhard de Chardin in which the expanding universe as a whole places great pressure on its constitutive parts, causing the less complex forms of matter to become more complex and closely knitted structures. In this shift from the less complex to the more complex forms of matter there is also a shift in the interior psychism of matter causing a move from the less intensely conscious to the more intensely conscious. This process includes not only the exterior complexity of matter but also the interiorization of matter in which consciousness intensifies to the extent that matter complexifies. BIBLIOGRAPHY: Teilhard de Chardin, *Phenomenon of Man* (1959), *Future of Man* (1964). *COMPLEXIFICATION.

[W. J. DUGGAN]

INTERLUDES, a general term usually applied to all types of early Tudor drama in England, from the late 15th to the mid-16th cent. Interludes were short plays, though often of several scenes, and may have been performed between courses of a banquet. They continue late medieval dramatic traditions of biblical and morality plays, often with a Protestant rather than Catholic viewpoint. Some of them are political allegories on problems of government and public life, and still others are of a comic nature related to the French farces called *sotties*.

[E. C. DUNN]

INTERNATIONAL ASSOCIATION FOR LIBERAL CHRISTIANITY AND RELIGIOUS FREEDOM (IARF), an organization founded at Sankt Gallen, Switzerland, in 1932 for the purpose of promoting communication and fellowship among liberals of all religious beliefs. The organization in its present form developed from an earlier international council founded by Unitarians in Boston in 1900, which held congresses with delegates from as many as 30 nations, including liberal Muslims and Hindus as well as Jews, Catholics, and Protestants. The movement declined as the liberalism of the early years of the century passed its peak, but was revitalized by the revival of humanism in the decade preceding World War II. The IARF permanent secretariat, established in The Hague in the 1930s, suspended activity when the Netherlands was overrun by Germany early in the war, but resumed afterward, and the first postwar international congress was held in Amsterdam in 1949. The IARF, while maintaining its distinctively humanist approach, reflects the tendencies of European Christian theology, with emphasis on Scripture and on the one Church. The influence of its American heritage is seen in its stress on ethics, brotherhood, and "practical Christianity" as its basic principles. BIBLIOGRAPHY: W. Gaade, *IARF and Its Vision* (1955).

[D. CODDINGTON]

INTERNATIONAL CATHOLIC AUXILIARIES, a laywomen's volunteer organization founded in Belgium in 1937 by V. Lebbe to supply workers for the missions. After 3 years' training, members take an oath to devote themselves to the missions. Working as part of a team, they give technical and professional help in collaboration with local groups and have labored in many countries including Belgium, Brazil, Canada, the Congo, Formosa, India, Rwanda, Syria, Vietnam, and the Volta Republic. In the U.S. there is a training center in Evanston, Illinois. Headquarters are in Geneva.

[J. R. AHERNE]

INTERNATIONAL CATHOLIC CHILD BUREAU (Le Bureau International Catholique de l'Enfance), an organization, founded in Paris (1948) with members in 75 countries throughout the world. It undertakes studies and projects for the welfare of children everywhere. Regional meetings and international meetings are held. The bureau serves Catholic and other organizations in child welfare work and is consultant to the United Nations Economic and Social Council and the United Nations Children's Fund.

[J. R. AHERNE]

INTERNATIONAL CATHOLIC DEAF ASSOCIATION, an organization founded in 1949 to bring instruction to the Catholic deaf and, in general, to assist in promoting social, educational, and recreational opportunities. A lay society, its members are deaf adults and deaf children, the religious and clergy who work with them. There are diocesan chapters in the U.S., Canada, and other areas. Organized in committees for research, athletics, and missions to the deaf, the association conducts missions and retreats, provides catechetical materials, maintains a survey of the Catholic deaf, promotes a specialized liturgy, and supports priests and religious who work with the deaf. Among its programs are institutes to train persons for work with the deaf, cooperation with national and United Nations agencies, distribution of books on religious education for the deaf.

[J. R. AHERNE]

INTERNATIONAL CATHOLIC MIGRATION COMMISSION, society established in 1951 at the request of Pius XII to aid refugees and migrants and to work for international recognition of their rights. It publishes the bimonthly *Migration News*. Headquarters are in Geneva.

[T. EARLY]

INTERNATIONAL CATHOLIC ORGANIZATIONS, CONFERENCE OF. The present conference was established in 1953 as successor to a council of presidents of Catholic organizations of international scope, founded in 1927. The conference is made up of a number of organizations with interest in international problems. A permanent secretariat is maintained in Fribourg, Switzerland; information centers are located in Paris, New York, and Buenos Aires. A general assembly governs the conference which holds annual meeting in different countries. A representative of the Holy See attends. The conference cooperates with UNESCO and the International Information Center in Geneva, as well as the World Consultation on the Laity.

[J. R. AHERNE]

INTERNATIONAL CATHOLIC YOUTH FEDERATION, see WORLD FEDERATION OF CATHOLIC YOUTH.

INTERNATIONAL CHURCH OF THE FOURSQUARE GOSPEL, Pentecostal denomination growing out of the evangelistic work of Aimee Semple *McPherson and incorporated in Los Angeles in 1927. The Canadian-born evangelist served as a missionary in Hong Kong and as a tent revivalist before arriving in Los Angeles in 1918. There she built Angelus Temple and founded a Bible college and a radio station. Once widowed and twice divorced, Mrs. McPherson received widespread notoriety in the 1920s and 1930s, most of which she was able to turn to the promotion of her cause. When she died in 1944 her son Rolf assumed leadership of the Church. *Divine healing has been emphasized by the International Church of the Four-square Gospel, as has the *baptism of the Holy Spirit, Christ's second coming, and speaking in tongues (see GLOSSOLALIA). All members of the Church must subscribe to the fundamentalist Declaration of Faith composed by Mrs. McPherson. Each congregation makes a monthly offering for home and foreign missions. The Church supports 961 missionaries and native pastors in 1,300 mission stations in 27 countries. It also operates 18 day schools, 20 Bible schools, and 3 orphanages. In the U.S. there were in 1968 about 89,000 members in 741 congregations; worldwide membership was about 218,000. Rolf McPherson holds the lifetime position of president of the Church, but other officers are elected by delegates to the annual convention. An eight-member board of directors governs the Church and appoints field supervisors in charge of 10 districts. Ministers are trained at the Lighthouse of International Foursquare Evangelism (LIFE) Bible College in Los Angeles, which has graduated more than 5,000 men and women.

[W. J. WHALEN]

INTERNATIONAL CONFERENCE ON THE SOCIOLOGY OF RELIGION (Conférence internationale de sociologie religieuse), society founded in 1946 by Canon Jacques Leclercq of the Univ. of Louvain, its first president, for research in sociological theory. It holds triennial conventions. Most members are European Catholics.

[T. EARLY]

INTERNATIONAL COUNCIL OF CHRISTIAN CHURCHES (ICCC), an organization founded at Amsterdam, The Netherlands, in August 1948, as a conservative counterpoise to the *World Council of Churches. Carl McIntire, former minister of the Presbyterian Church in the U.S. who was deposed in 1936 after being found guilty of ''violation of his ordination vows'' and other charges, has been president from the beginning, and was reelected at the Seventh Plenary Congress in 1968. The ICCC reported 61 Protestant evangelical Churches of 29 countries at its founding, and 116 constituent and 60 affiliated members in 1968. The number of persons represented by these Churches is unknown, but none of the larger Churches is included in the Council. The ICCC headquarters are in Amsterdam, and an American office is maintained at Collingswood, N.J.; the official publication is the *Reformation Review,* a quarterly. Major emphasis of the ICCC has been opposition to the World Council of Churches, which it has charged with theological error in failing to uphold biblical infallibility and other emphases of *fundamentalism, with Communist influence on the part of churchmen from Communist countries and some church leaders in the West, and with betrayal of Protestantism through acceptance of Orthodox Churches and cooperation with the RC Church.

[R. K. MACMASTER]

INTERNATIONAL EDUCATIONAL AND CULTURAL EXCHANGE, a blanket term including the various forms of organized intercommunication among widely divergent nations through various scholarly pursuits—arts, sciences, education, technology, and their related fields—to preserve, develop, expand, and disseminate what is best in intellectual, cultural, and artistic achievements. It is an expression of narrowing geographical distances, a desire to contribute to the ''universal common good'' as expressed in John XXIII's *Pacem in terris,* and the awakening of nations to the existence of rich cultures and traditions different from their own. International exchange overseas projects and programs for teachers, students, scholars, and leaders are sponsored privately, or by Church or government. Some predate World War I: the establishment of national theological centers in Rome (North American College, 1859); the French and German government exchange programs (1900); the Rhodes Scholarships for Oxford University (1902); the Carnegie Corporation (1911). Others predated World War II, among them, the Commonwealth Fund (1918); the Institute of International Education (1919); the Belgian-American Foundation (1920); the China Foundation for the Promotion of Education and Culture (1925), and those established in Switzerland, with the assistance of the Laura Spelman Rockefeller Memorial (1925); by the U.S.S.R.(1934); and the British Commonwealth (1938). After World War II there was an increase in the number of foreign students at American univ., and a world-wide increase in international scholarships. Private organizations expanded their services and new ones appeared: the National Catholic Educational Association, the Ford Foundation, Pax Romana, and the Papal Volunteers. Outstanding among governmental projects are the Fulbright-Hays program; the Agency for International Development (AID), and the Peace Corps. BIBLIOGRAPHY: *Cultural Affairs and Foreign Relations* (ed. R. Blum, 1963).

[M. B. MURPHY]

INTERNATIONAL FEDERATION OF CATHOLIC ALUMNAE federation of alumnae associations of Catholic universities, colleges, schools of nursing, and high schools. The IFCA was founded in 1914 by two alumnae of St. Joseph's College, Emmitsburg, Md., to promote Catholic education and ideals for women. Headquarters are at The Catholic Univ. of America, and the vice-rector of that institution acts as director. The IFCA is organized in state groups, 4,000 members in the United States. The programs of the federation are many, mostly concerned with education for women in Catholic institutions. An important program is the granting of scholarships annually to religious women.

[J. R. AHERNE]

INTERNATIONAL GOTHIC, a style, primarily in painting, which flourished throughout W and Central Europe (*c.* 1390–1400), characterized in general by a realism of content rather than form, and employing the latest developments in space, light, and modeling, while retaining a late Gothic predilection for elegant curvilinear patterns and gilded surfaces. In architecture it is represented by flamboyant Gothic and in sculpture by the *Weicher Stil.* International Gothic originated on French soil (Avignon, Dijon, Paris) from a confluence of two currents of art, a Franco-Flemish and a north Italian, showing a preference, aside from religious themes, for motifs taken from courtly life. BIBLIOGRAPHY: E. Panofsky, *Early Netherlandish Painting I* (1958) 51–74.

[L. A. LEITE]

INTERNATIONAL LAW, see LAW, INTERNATIONAL.

INTERNATIONAL MISSIONARY COUNCIL (IMC; 1921–61), an organization of Protestant national missionary organizations and Christian councils designed to facilitate the presentation of the gospel to non-Christian peoples through the development of coordinated activities, common study and consultation, and united action. The historical background of the IMC was the rise of Protestant missions in the 19th cent. with the consequent increase in problems of duplicated and splintered efforts on the part of disunited denominations. Six Anglo-American Conferences (1854–1900) called to deal with the situation preceded the 1910 World Missionary Conference held in Edinburgh, which in turn led directly to the formation of the IMC at Mohonk Lake, N.Y., in 1921 (see EDINBURGH CONFERENCES). The IMC, through its creation of a global network of national Christian councils, its stimulation to cooperative activities in the mission field, and its meetings (Jerusalem 1928; Madras 1938; Whitby, Ontario, 1947; Willigen, Germany 1952; Ghana 1958), substantially prepared the way for the establishment of the World Council of Churches. In 1961 at New Delhi, the IMC formally joined the World Council, becoming the Division of World Mission and Evangelism. BIBLIOGRAPHY: W. R. Hogg, *Ecumenical Foundations* (1952).

[R. MATZERATH]

INTERNATIONAL SOCIETY OF CHRISTIAN ENDEAVOR, see CHRISTIAN ENDEAVOR, INTERNATIONAL SOCIETY OF.

INTERNATIONAL STYLE, in the 1920's and 1930's a major European architectural style emphasizing space, not mass, showing rectilinear volumes, undecorated planes, and symmetrically balanced voids and solids. Gropius, Dudok, and Mendelsohn had introduced a quasi-International style in geometric masses (1910–20). Mies van der Rohe's glazed, steel-framed skyscrapers (1920) anticipated his Barcelona Pavilion (1929) and his Chicago "curtain walls" (1950). Strongly determinant were: Le Corbusier's Citrohan houses (1922), with *pilotis* elevations and usable roofs (1927). The brilliant essay of Hitchcock and Johnson on the occasion of the International Exhibition of Modern Architecture in New York, 1932, defined and christened the movement. Though resisted in Russia and Fascist Germany, the International Style spread throughout the world, establishing a basis of new forms and determining the orientation of 20th-cent. architecture. BIBLIOGRAPHY: H. R. Hitchcock, *Architecture, Nineteenth and Twentieth Centuries* (1958). *BAUHAUS; *LE CORBUSIER.

[M. J. DALY]

INTERNATIONAL UNIONS OF SUPERIORS GENERAL (UISG), worldwide organizations in liaison with the Sacred Congregation for Religious and Secular Institutes, one of men general superiors, the other of women general superiors. The men's organization was established in 1957, the women's in 1965; the statues of both were approved in 1967 as implementations of VatII RenRelLife. The purpose of the unions is to share in and to support the endeavor to safeguard and to renew religious life. Headquarters are at the Vatican, where there is a permanent secretariat. The unions function as a body in general assembly; also has a general council and an executive committee. The Congregation for Religious and Secular Institutes maintains a council for liaison with each international union.

[R. A. TODD]

INTERPELLATIONS, in canon law (CIC, c. 1121), the questions put to the nonbelieving spouse in an existing marriage before the other baptized (or about to be baptized) spouse can contract a new marriage on the basis of the *Pauline Privilege. The questions, which must be put under episcopal auspices and which must receive a negative answer (or no answer at all) in order for the privilege to be operative, are: whether the nonbelieving spouse is willing to be converted and receive baptism; if not, whether the spouse will live peacefully, without prejudice to the baptized spouse's new faith and spiritual welfare ("without offense to the Creator"). The interpellations are required in order to establish the fact of the "departure," in fact or in spirit, of the nonbelieving partner (see 1 Cor 7.15). Interpretation by skilled canonists of the conditions surrounding the interpellations and their intent is part of the complexity of verifying the applicability of the Pauline Privilege.

[T. C. O'BRIEN]

INTERPRETATION OF LAW, see LAW, INTERPRETATION OF.

INTERRACIAL COUNCILS, CATHOLIC, see NATIONAL CATHOLIC CONFERENCE FOR INTERRACIAL JUSTICE.

INTERSTICES, in canon law regulating holy orders, the time interval that must elapse between reception of one order and the next, e.g., 3 months between major orders (CIC, c. 978 §1). According to the *motu proprio, Ministeria quaedam* (Aug. 15, 1972) some interval should be set when a person receives institution in more than one lay ministry (reader, acolyte). The same is true of the interval between institution as reader and acolyte and ordination to diaconate (*motu proprio, Ad pascendum,* Jan. 1, 1973). The interstices are intended for preparation, training, and observation of the candidate. The term also may refer to the interval required between successive tenures in the same office that has a juridically set term. The purpose is to prevent perpetuation in office.

[T. C. O'BRIEN]

INTERVENTION, DIVINE, that function of divine *providence which, according to human understanding, causes an effect different from the usual order of events. The term is acceptable insofar as it indicates the total openness of the world to God's saving action; it is erroneous when it implies a self-sufficient universe whose natural order is disturbed by an agent extrinsic to its operations. The concept is important for a proper understanding of *miracle.

[T. M. MCFADDEN]

INTINCTION (Lat. *intingere,* dip in), method of administering holy *communion under both kinds simultaneously. Either the consecrated hosts are simply dipped into the chalice, or they are dropped in and a spoon is used to give them to the communicants. The practice is known to have existed in the East from the 7th cent. and became widespread by the 9th; it continues there esp. with the use of the spoon. In the West intinction was practiced from the 7th to the 12th century. There was objection to it, e.g., by the Council of Braga in Spain (689) and by Pope Paschal II (1099–1188), on the grounds that it did not conform to Christ's action at the Last Supper. It seems to have been practiced chiefly in giving communion to the sick. As communion under both kinds ceased in the West, so did intinction. In the modern RC restoration of communion under both kinds, the two are received either separately or by intinction.

[T. C. O'BRIEN]

INTOLERANCE. (1) As a moral attitude, the unwillingness to honor the rights of other persons, as such is an attitude contrary to *justice. Usage has drawn the meaning of ''tolerance'' from its original, etymological sense (Lat. *tolle,* to bear), the enduring of some evil, real or apparent, for the sake of a higher good, so that it now suggests a kind of benign impartiality. The connotation of intolerance, then, is that of a refusal to bear with what is objectively a good, the rights, civil, social, or religious, of other people. In effect it is understood as either a euphemism for bigotry, or as a less virulent form of it. Civil or social intolerance is based on grounds extrinsic to the *equality that derives from natural or from positive law, and that justice respects as an objective standard; intolerance is based on considerations of race, color, creed, and social position. Religious intolerance refuses to recognize the freedom and dignity that every person invests in committing himself to a religious belief or decision. Vatican Council II gave a particularly positive RC statement on the right to religious freedom (Vat II RelFreed 1–3). Intolerance also sins against charity, since love of neighbor rests on the regard for every person as actually or potentially the child loved by the Father. (2) Intolerance as a physical disability to sustain certain influences has bearing on *sobriety: a person experiencing his intolerance for alcohol must abstain in order to avoid the sin of drunkenness.

[T. C. O'BRIEN]

INTONATION, (1) the agreement of tone among the members of a musical group; (2) also the initial section of a Psalm tone in Gregorian chant or of any musical setting of a liturgical text sung by the cantor.

[P. J. HENNESSEY]

INTONAZIONE, a liturgical prelude of 16th-cent. Italy. Andrea Gabrieli was the most famous exponent of this form.

[P. J. HENNESSEY]

INTORCETTA, PROSPERO (1625–96), Italian Jesuit spokesman at Rome, 1672–74, in the *Chinese Rites Controversy. He had been a missionary in China since 1657, and suffered imprisonment. From Rome he returned to China in 1674 for the remainder of his life. He translated St. Ignatius Loyola's *Spiritual Exercises* into Chinese, and collaborated on a Latin edition of Confucian studies.

[T. C. O'BRIEN]

INTRAUTERINE DEVICES, see CONTRACEPTION.

INTROIT, the opening (Lat. *introitus*) or entrance chant of the Roman Mass sung during the entrance procession of the ministers. Introduced into the rite by Pope Celestine I (d. 432) as a psalm with refrain, it became reduced to a refrain with one or two psalm verses. In the present order of the Mass either the psalm or a hymn may be sung. If there is no singing, either the congregation or the priest is to recite the entrance antiphon (refrain) without the psalm. The opening words of the Latin Introit generally gave the name to the Mass formulary (*Requiem*) or even to the Sunday (*Laetare, Gaudete*), a usage retained by some Reformation Churches. The Introit frequently sets the tone or theme for the celebration, as should the hymn which may replace it. It functions also as a means of establishing a sense of community at the beginning of the celebration. In sacred music the *introitus* referred to an introduction to a polyphonic motet or to an instrumental processional piece.

[J. DALLEN]

INTROJECTION (IDENTIFICATION), a mental process by which a person, esp. in early childhood, unconsciously incorporates into his own self-image the qualities, attitudes, modes of behavior, and even appearances of those persons he loves and fears. Introjection is a mode of mastering the yearning one has for people whose love cannot be possessed absolutely or the fear one has of threatening persons. From the point of view of personal moral and spiritual development, it is important to recognize that major aspects of any individual's personality are in effect replications of the personalities of others, esp. parents.

[M. E. STOCK]

INTUITION, an immediate, nonconceptual termination of the mind in what it knows; as such it has several theological applications. St. Thomas Aquinas describes the divine eternal knowledge as an intuition, God's gazing (*intuitus*) on all things as eternally present to himself (ThAq ST 1a,14.13). In the divine knowledge there is no conceptual medium acquired from the objects known; the expression of the divine knowledge is the eternal Word, the Person proceeding in the single divine nature. Intuition has another instance in the explanation of the *beatific vision; in this vision, while the mind of the blessed is strengthened and elevated by the *light of glory, the term of its vision is immediately the divine being itself. The self-intuition in regard to its own acts, implicit or explicit, characteristic of human thought (*ibid.* 1a, 16.5 ad 2) is a basis for understanding the prayer of contemplation as a kind of intuition of the divine, a quasi-experimental knowledge.This self-consciousness is applied to the vitality of the grace life, particularly to acts of the theological virtues and the gifts of the Holy Spirit, whose object is the Divine Persons indwelling in the soul. This grace experience is not literally an intuition like the beatific vision, since the darkness of faith remains. It is, however, in a sense a termination in the divine itself beyond the conceptual. Whatever thought or verbal formulation may be present, it is surpassed by the intimacy, penetrativeness, and quasi-experimental perception of the divine. The basis of that quasi-intuitive contact is affective, the connaturality of love with the persons experienced. The instance of this par excellence is the activation of the gift of *wisdom; as in the Trinitarian life itself this knowledge experience is said to be a *verbum spirans amorem,* a word breathing forth love; the contact with the divine is penetrative and intuitive because it is vivified by love's union with the Divine Persons. (*ibid.* 1a, 43.3, 5 & ad 2). *INSPIRATION OF THE HOLY SPIRIT.

[T. C. O'BRIEN]

INVALID, (1) in matters of canon law, any act in violation of an invalidating, not merely prohibiting, law (CIC, c. 11). The effect of such a law is to render an act in violation null and void (see ILLICIT). (2) In theology a sacrament is classified as invalid, i.e., not a true sacrament, when an element essential to its makeup and signification is missing (see MATTER OF A SACRAMENT). Thus the use of any liquid in the sacrament of baptism other than that which is water (according to the common estimation of man) would mean that there was no true sacrament.

[T. C. O'BRIEN]

INVALIDES, LES, PARIS home for disabled French soldiers, built 1671–76 to designs by Libéral Bruant. The institute of several wings and courtyards boasts impressive sculptured reliefs and statues by G. Coustou. The monumental church (Dôme), added to the S side, designed by Jules-Hardouin-Mansart, and built 1680–1706, blends classical and baroque elements. The triple dome, lighted between shells and painted by C. de Lafosse (*St. Louis Returning his Sword to Christ*), rises high externally, its gilded ornament seen from afar. Napoleon's tomb designed by Visconti (1843) and set in a well beneath the dome has weakened the interior organization.

[M. J. DALY]

INVARIATA (*Confessio Augustana invariata*), the version of the *Augsburg Confession (1530) prepared for the *Book of Concord (1580). It is designated as "Unaltered" in relation to the *Variata, the revision of the Confession prepared by Melanchthon in 1540. This revision included expressions on the *Real Presence conciliatory to the Swiss *Reformed Churches but unacceptable to most Lutherans. The Invariata is the text accepted as the chief Lutheran *confession of faith. This version differs in minor points from the 1530 text of the Confession. BIBLIOGRAPHY: F. Bente, *Historical Introduction to the Book of Concord* (1959) 15–28.

[R. BEESE]

INVASATI, a sect, probably related to the Turlupians, that arose in Germany and spread into France during the 14th century. Adherents engaged in obscene dances while invoking the demons. For these practices and for their *antinomianism they were condemned by Gregory XI in 1373.

[C. J. LYNCH]

INVESTITURE STRUGGLE, controversy (1075–1122) between the popes and medieval monarchs over the right to install bishops. Feudal practice allowed this, but *Gregory VII challenged the authority of the German King Henry IV. Henry's resistance provoked strong countermeasures from the pope; the King submitted at Canossa in Jan. 1077, but civil war erupted in Germany 3 months later when the princes became involved. Not until 1122 did the Concordat of Worms effect a workable compromise. In England St. *Anselm of Canterbury quarreled with William II and Henry I until the Concordat of London in 1107. Other lands witnessed lesser controversies. From the investiture struggle grew the great political influence of the medieval papacy. BIBLIOGRAPHY: G. Tellenbach, *Church, State, and Christian Society at the Time of the Investiture Contest* (1959).

[R. H. SCHMANDT]

INVISIBLE CHURCH, a description intended to designate the true Church, a spiritual, eschatological community, as a reality distinct from the visible Church, an empirical, imperfect, organized institution. Modern RC rejection of this distinction appears in the theme, repeated in documents from Pius IX's *Syllabus of Errors* to Pius XII's *Mystici corporis,* that the Church is essentially a visible society. The *Constitution on the Church* of Vatican Council II holds that the visible and invisible are two aspects of the one reality, that there is a necessary and objective, not merely a psychological, relationship between spiritual discipleship and visible communion. Accordingly, in the visible structure of the RC Church the true mystical body of Christ achieves its fullest realization on earth; through these structures the body is drawn into closer union with the risen Savior. The Church also insists that visible communion without interior adherence is of no avail; that many elements, interior as well as visible, of its own reality are found in persons and Churches not in communion with it. The Council speaks of a dynamic tendency of all Christians toward a visible unity, the achievement of which, however, may be eschatological (Vat II ConstChurch 8, 9, 14, 18, 23; Ecum 3). John *Wycliffe and Jan *Hus, in their dissatisfaction with the conditions of the contemporary Church, proposed the idea of an invisible Church, known only to God, and rejected the Church as a hierarchical institution. The Reformers believed in the ''holy, catholic church'' of the creeds but did not equate it with a particular organization. Martin Luther held that the true Church is invisible, known only by faith; not wishing to reduce the Church to a Platonic idea, however, he taught that the invisible aspects of the one Church are hidden in its visible aspects. In keeping with his doctrine on predestination, John Calvin defined the invisible Church as ''the true members of Christ sanctified by the Holy Spirit''; this Church of the elect was an indiscernible object of faith. The visible Church was a society of those who accepted the Scriptures, partook of the sacraments, and led godly lives; Calvin's system of discipline was meant to detect some of the more obvious nonelect. The *Thirty-Nine Articles of the C of E made no mention of the invisible Church, but the definition of the visible Church as a ''congregation of faithful men'' implied the idea of an invisible Church. The miscellaneous Anabaptist groups did not all use the actual terms visible and invisible, but most of them did insist that true Churches must restore the faith and practice of the primitive Church and must restrict membership to professing Christians. Many stressed individual experience and attached little importance to organization.

The Puritans, with rigid logic, sought to make the visible Church correspond in membership to the true, invisible Church. The terms visible and invisible appeared in the Presbyterians' *Westminster Confession, the Congregationalists' *Savoy Declaration, the General Baptists' *Orthodox Creed, and the Particular Baptists' *Second London Confession. For Congregationalists and Baptists the distinction was basic to the *gathered church principle. Affirming belief in the ''holy, catholic church,'' they held that it was invisible; the visible Church was a congregation of visible saints.

In the 18th cent. the emphasis of the evangelical revivals upon subjective experience further weakened objective institutional authority. The Church was thought to be the total number of saved people, mingled in many denominations. Since religion was personal, individual, and spiritual, the Churches were simply of instrumental value for winning people to Christ and nurturing them. In the 19th and 20th cent. the tradition of *liberal theology in the U.S. spread the idea of a universal Church, which was made up of those who lived practical Christian lives, but was invisible, not an organization. A consequence of this viewpoint, which was quite general among evangelical Christians in the U.S., has been a certain reluctance, e.g., among Baptists and others related to this tradition, to be interested in any organized ecumenical movement; since spiritual unity is all that is necessary or desirable, they see no point in seeking organic union of Churches. Contemporary theologians generally avoid the terms visible and invisible, but some of them have views that seem similar. For Karl *Barth, e.g., the true Church cannot be seen, but the word of God quickens men in the visible Church, where the word of Scriptures is read and preached. Although Barth emphasized the oneness of the Church, he did not urge all Christians to unite in a single institution. Emil *Brunner did not find the terms visible and invisible useful, but his sharp distinction between the *ecclesia as a fellowship of persons in Christ and the Church as an institution seems an echo of these ideas; the ecclesia, the true Church, can never be identified with any specific Church. Paul *Tillich referred to a ''latent'' and a ''manifest'' Church and judged that one can belong to the former without ever being connected with any outward organized Church. BIBLIOGRAPHY: P. Althaus, *Theology of M. Luther* (1966); K. Barth, *Church Dogmatics* (1958); E. Brunner, *Misunderstanding of the Church* (1953); J. Calvin, *Institutes of the Christian Religion* (ed. J. T. McNeill, tr. F. L. Battles, 1960); *Nature of the Church* (ed. R. N. Flew, 1952); F. Littell, *Anabaptist Concept of the Church* (2d ed., 1958); A. H. Strong, *Systematic Theology* (v. 3, 1909); P. Tillich, *Systematic Theology* (v. 3, 1963); C. W. Williams, *John Wesley's Theology Today* (1960); H. F. Woodhouse, *Doctrine of the Church in the Anglican Reformers* (1954). *UNITY OF THE CHURCH.

[N. H. MARING]

INVITATORY, in the Western liturgical tradition, the introduction to the daily office or Liturgy of the Hours, esp. morning prayer, generally consisting primarily of Psalm 94 (95). It is an invitation to join in the praises of God. *LAUDS; *MATINS.

[J. DALLEN]

INVOCATION OF SAINTS, praying to those who have reached eternal life, because of their nearness to God and so their special powers of *impetration and *intercession. The antiquity and constant sanctioning of the practice was declared by the Council of Trent against the Reformers' charge that it was a form of idolatry (D 1821). Invocation of the saints is prompted by reverence for God whose friends they are; by the regard of *charity for those who are more perfectly united to God; and relies on the vital communion in love that joins all the members of Christ's mystical body. The fact of official canonization gives a firmer confidence in calling on the saints so honored; in their lives they have shown forth in a singular way the graces won by Christ for the building up of his body, the Church (see EDIFICATION); and their continuous share in the intercessory power of Christ is assured by their blessed union of vision and charity in heaven. BIBLIOGRAPHY: Vat II ConstChurch 7.

[T. C. O'BRIEN]

INVOLUNTARINESS, in an action or its effect, the lack of origin in inner, deliberate willing. Such an action or effect is contrary to the moral agent's will or intention. Antecedent *ignorance causes its consequences to be involuntary. The influence of *fear, passion, or moral pressure can bring about a degree of involuntariness; *force by definition can only cause an involuntary act. As to the involuntariness of an effect, the distinction is made between what is involuntary in itself and what is voluntary in its cause. The moral agent may act or even refrain from acting (see OMISSION, SIN OF) without averting to or intending some result. That outcome is not voluntary in itself, not the direct concern of his action. If, however, it could and should have been foreseen, it is voluntary in its cause, and as such, imputable. The voluntary action chosen contains its foreseeable result.

[T. C. O'BRIEN]

INVOLUTION, a process described by Teilhard de Chardin in which the universe is in a state of expanding outward from the infinitesimal to the immense but at the same time turning back in upon itself, causing the simple structures of matter to move to the more complex. According to Teilhard, cosmic layers of matter not only expand explosively as a wave but also condense into corpuscular units. The explosive force of expanding matter places great pressure on atoms and molecules to form more complex exterior structures. As the exterior structures become more complex, the interior psychism becomes more intensely conscious. Man originates in the layers of cosmic dust which in the process of involution not only expanded outwardly but contracted inwardly, causing particles of matter to move up the evolution scale from the less complex to the more complex, from primitive psychism to self-reflective consciousness. Man represents a high point of matter within the process of involution. BIBLIOGRAPHY: Teilhard de Chardin, *Phenomenon of Man* (1959); *idem.*, *Future of Man* (1964).

[W. J. DUGGAN]

INWOOD, WILLIAM (fl. 1800–43), English architect, with his eldest son Henry best known for a Greek revival style (St. Pancras, New Church, London, 1819–22). Henry published two books on Greek art.

[M. J. DALY]

IOANNES PHILOPONUS of Alexandria (d. *c.*570), Neoplatonic philosopher; a pupil of Ammonius Hermiou before going to Alexandria. He lectured on Aristotle esp., but abandoned the Aristotelianism of his master for Stoic theory. On his conversion to Christianity, he eliminated from his teaching all that was incompatible with the Christian faith. He wrote a work against Proclus' concept of the eternity of the world and attempted to support his own position by interpreting Plato's *Timaeus* as teaching creation in time. He maintained that Plato was heavily indebted to the Pentateuch for his wisdom, and that our resurrected body will be a different one from our present body. As many Platonists before him, he explained the Platonic ideas as the creative thoughts of God. BIBLIOGRAPHY: Armstrong, CHGMP 477–482 (excellent); Ueberweg 1:643.

[M. R. P. MCGUIRE]

IONA ABBEY, a monastic house founded by *Columba in 563 and ruled by priest-abbots. It was regarded as the head of the Irish Church and of the Christian Scots in North Britain. From it were converted the Picts and the English of Northumbria. Although it declined after 664, Iona remained the primatial church of an extensive monastic parish in Ireland and Scotland until the Scandinavian raids of the 9th cent. when the primacy passed to abbots in Ireland. Iona had a brief period of resurgence *c.*844; had Culdees there in the 12th cent. but was taken over by Benedictines *c.*1204. It was dissolved and dismantled during the Reformation in Scotland. BIBLIOGRAPHY: C. McGrath, NCE 7:605; A. Bellesheim, *History of the Catholic Church of Scotland* (tr. D. O. H. Blair, 4 v., 1887–90); J. F. Kenney, *Sources for the Early History of Ireland* (1966).

[C. MCGRATH]

IONA COMMUNITY, a community of clergy and laymen, married and unmarried, established in 1938 by G. MacLeod, a minister of the Church of Scotland, with which the community is associated. It has restored the monastic buildings at Iona, an island famous for its association with St. Columba, and sponsors programs there for visitors. It also maintains a Community House in Glasgow and its headquarters in Edinburgh. Members commit themselves to an economic and devotional discipline and meet periodically at Iona and elsewhere to further their community life. Concerns of the community include world peace, the healing ministry of the Church, and the renewal of church life in industrial areas. It had (1970) about 150 members and 600 associates. BIBLIOGRAPHY: T. Morton, *Iona Community Story* (1957).

IONIAN (also *undecimus tonus,* 11th mode), the mode or scale equivalent to a white-key scale beginning on C. Its existence was not recognized in theory until the 16th cent., and modern chant books classify pieces whose final is C as Lydian. It is identical in form to the modern major scale. Its plagal form is termed hypoionian (*duodecimus tonus,* twelth mode).

[A. DOHERTY]

IOWA, Midwestern state admitted to the Union (1846) as the 29th state. Jacques *Marquette and Louis Jolliet traveled through the area (1673). The first major settlement was made (1788) by French-Canadian Julien Dubuque in the E portion of the territory. As part of the Louisiana Purchase acquired (1803) by the U.S., Iowa was explored by the Lewis and Clark expedition the following year. C. F. *Van Quickenborne, SJ, and S. *Mazzuchelli, OP, inaugurated Catholic missionary activity in Iowa during the 1830s. In 1837 the Diocese of Dubuque was created and Mathias Loras named as its first bishop. With six French priests and numerous French donations, Loras firmly established Catholicism in Iowa. He organized (1839) St. Raphael's College and Seminary, which was relocated (1850) at Table Mound and renamed St. Bernard. Under Loras, too, the first Irish national parish was founded (1840), and the first German parish (1846). When he died (1857), his diocese had 46 priests, 60 churches, and 54,000 Catholics. Loras was succeeded by Clement Smyth, prior of the Trappist Monastery of New Melleray. Numerous troubles plagued Smyth's episcopacy, among them financial problems and a nationalistic conflict between French and Irish clerics. Irish-born John Hennessy became the third bp. (1866) and was named Dubuque's first abp. (1893). Its suffragans are now the Dioceses of Davenport, Des Moines, and Sioux City.

Under Hennessy's successor, John Joseph *Keane, the rapid growth of the archdiocese, already stimulated by immigration and railroads, caused the number of priests to increase to 232 and parishes to 171. Keane was followed (1911) by James John Keane (no relative), who expanded the archdiocesan Columbia College and founded the archdiocesan newspaper, the *Witness*. The fourth bp., Francis J. L. Beckman, used the *Witness* as a vehicle for political conservatism during the 1930s. Recent bps. have included Leo Binz, consecrated in 1954, who greatly expanded educational facilities before his transfer to St. Paul, and James J. Byrne, the present incumbent.

Iowa's population of 2,780,669 (over 50% urban) makes it the 25th most populous state in the Union. In 1976 Catholics numbered 538,599, or 19.4% of the total state population. The major Protestant sects are the Methodist Church (13.1% of the total pop., 1971) and the American Lutheran Church, (7.3%). Other Protestant denominations comprised 23.3% of the population. The Jewish population (1968) was 7,500 or 0.27%.

There are more than 20 church-related colleges in Iowa, 8 of which are Catholic and enroll a total of 7,244 students. About 14,739 students attend the state's 33 Catholic high schools, while 37,989 pupils are enrolled in 173 Catholic elementary schools. BIBLIOGRAPHY: W. J. Peterson, *Story of Iowa* (4 v., 1952); J. F. Kempker, *History of the Catholic Church in Iowa* (1887); D. W. Johnson, et al., *Churches and Church Membership in U.S.* (1974).

[J. L. MORRISON; R. M. PRESTON]

IPPEN SCROLLS, set of twelve Japanese silk *emaki* (1299) in Kankikōji, Kyoto, made by En-i, depicting the life of the priest Ippen (1239–89) who traveled through the country to spread the Jishū teachings of Buddhism. Charming, lyrical scenes of small figures of all types in towns and villages capture the rich coloring of different seasons in beautiful landscape paintings.

[M. J. DALY]

IPSISSIMA VERBA OF JESUS. To what extent do we have the exact words (*ipsissima verba*) spoken by Jesus? A comparison of the Synoptic Gospels reveals surprising variants in his words on one and the same occasion, in one and the same parable. The Lord's Prayer itself is recorded differently by Matthew (6.9–15) and Luke (11.2–4); the same is true of the Beatitudes (Mt 5.3 ff; Lk 6.20 ff) and of the words of the institution of the Eucharist (Mt 26.26–29; Mk 14.22–25; Lk 22.15–20; 1 Cor 11.23–25). These are just a few outstanding examples of what is a rather general phenomenon.

Apparently the primitive Christian communities, within which the gospel tradition was formed for 3 or more decades before being consigned to writing, were concerned with getting the mind of Christ on matters of importance to them without too much concern about the exactness of the words in which that mind was expressed. It was what he had said that was important to them, rather than how he had said it. As his words were remembered and applied to various situations, they underwent a transformation of varying extent. Each community had its own problems, its own preoccupations. They sought answers in the teaching of Jesus as remembered by those who had heard him. That teaching was then applied to the actual situation and, in the process, transformed, but not deformed. Compare, for instance, his remarks on the indissolubility of marriage as recorded in Mt 5.32; 19.9 and in Mk 10.11–12. By the time the Evangelists set about their work, they had at their disposal large blocks of prefabricated material, material formed by the living tradition of the Christian communities. This is not to say that these communities created this material out of whole cloth. It had been given them by authentic witnesses who were quite jealous of its integrity. But adaptation had occurred, with apostolic sanction, and this adaptation is reflected in the actual Gospels. It has been suggested, for example, that the variants in the words of the institution of the Eucharist mirror differences in the celebration of the Eucharist in several communities. *FORM CRITICISM; *SYNOPTIC PROBLEM.

[J. J. CASTELOT]

IPSO FACTO, in canon law on censures, a qualification indicating that a penalty (e.g., *excommunication) is incurred by the very commission of a censured act and does not await imposition by judicial sentence.

[T. C. O'BRIEN]

IPSO IURE, a Latin phrase meaning "by the law itself" or "by operation of law" and having special relevance in the penal code of the canon law of the Latin Church. Such phrases as "ipso iure," "ipso facto," or "eo ipso" are used to express the automatic nature of a penalty, incurred upon commission of a canonical crime. Without such phrases it is presumed that the penalty attached to the violation of a law or precept is not incurred without a separate judicial action imposing the penalty.

[E. J. DILLON]

IRAN, SW Asian monarchy, known as Persia before 1935 (636,367 sq mi; pop. [1974 UN est.] 31,960,000). Location of a great empire of the ancient world, the region was conquered by Arabs in 636 and by Mongols in the 13th and 14th centuries. The present Kadjar dynasty was established in 1796, the present constitution proclaimed in 1906. The official religion is Islam (*c.*98%). The constitution grants religious freedom but forbids proselytization. There were Christians in the land in apostolic times; in the 4th and 5th cent. the church there suffered severe persecution. Early modern missions under Dominicans, Franciscans, Carmelites, Capuchins, and Jesuits were not successful. Religious liberty was granted in 1834, but religious massacres occurred even as late as 1918. French missionary efforts began in 1840 with the creation of a perfecture apostolic and the reestablishment in 1847 of the episcopal see for the Chaldean and Armenian-rite adherents. In 1872 an apostolic delegate was assigned to Ispahan. In 1900 many Orthodox groups entered into union with Rome, but the persecution of 1918 brought ruin to the Church. Missionaries had returned, however, and diplomatic relations were established with the Vatican. In 1976 Catholics numbered 28,395 (.08%). At present there are two patriarchates in communion with Rome (Chaldean and Armenian) as well as an apostolic visitor for the Latins. The Evangelical Church of Iran (Presbyterian) conducts schools and hospitals. Pentecostals are also active. BIBLIOGRAPHY: R. Etteldorf, *Catholic Church in the Middle East* (1959); *Bilan du Monde* 2:490–495.

[P. DAMBORIENA]

IRAQ, Asian republic (252,116 sq mi; pop. [1974 est.] 10,770,000). In A.D. 630 the Arabs gave the name Iraq to Mesopotamia, the land between the Tigris and Euphrates Rivers, and made it a great center of Muslim culture. It fell to the Ottoman Turks in the 15th cent; after World War I it was mandated to Great Britain and governed as a monarchy from 1921 to 1958, when it became a republic upon the assassination of King Faisal. Islam is the official religion. Children are forbidden to attend primary schools operated by foreigners. According to an old tradition, the Apostle Thomas brought the gospel to the region. At any rate, Christianity was established there by the 2d cent. and was persecuted by King Sapor and his successors. The Muslim invasion (640) did not altogether destroy the Church in Iraq; Christian scholars took an active part in the theological and philosophical revival that preceded scholasticism. Baghdad, an important center of Christian learning, is the see of the Chaldean patriarch. There are suffragans in Akra, Alquoc, Amadiya, Zakho, Bassra, and Kirkuk. Syrian Christians acknowledge the patriarchate of Antioch, which has suffragan sees in Baghdad and Mossul. Armenian and Latin bps. reside at Baghdad. Iraq has a Catholic community of 290,508 (1976), the majority of whom follow the Chaldean rite. There are 152 priests and 224 sisters. A Catholic univ. (Al-Hikma) and several high schools are greatly appreciated by the Muslims. Nestorians, Jacobites, and Armenians not in communion with Rome total 100,000. Protestant missions are comparatively few. The United Mission to Iraq, the Assemblies of God, Anglicans, Lutherans, and Adventists are at work. Their combined membership reported in 1968 was 4,648. BIBLIOGRAPHY: *Bilan du Monde* 2:486–490.

[P. DAMBORIENA]

IRASCIBILITY, a disposition towards *anger (Lat. *ira*). One of the sensory *appetites, it was termed the "irascible" by the medievals, naming it from the strongest of the contending emotions, the concern of which is gaining a difficult good, or repulsing an afflictive evil. Irascibility may also denote a naturally choleric temperament (ThAq ST 1a2ae, 46.5). In neither sense does a disposition to wrath have a moral quality. But as all human emotions and even temperament are to be controlled by virtue, failure at such control with regard to anger can come under the name irascibility (Lat. *iracundia*), a vice bent upon an uncontrolled lashing out against any sort of opposition to one's comfort or self-will (*ibid.*, 2a2ae, 158); it is the vice contrary to *meekness.

[T. C. O'BRIEN]

IRELAND, JOHN (1838–1918), archbishop. As a youth I. emigrated (1848) from famine-stricken Ireland with his parents, who settled in St. Paul, Minn., after temporary residence in New England and Chicago, Illinois. He was sent in 1853 to study in France and after completing his minor and major seminary training he returned to the U.S., was ordained (1861). Serving as an army chaplain, (1862–63) he began a long career of active involvement in public causes. He was consecrated (1875) as coadjutor bishop of the Diocese of St. Paul, and succeeded to that see (1884), becoming its first abp. (1888). I.'s eloquence won him fame in the U.S. and Europe, and he was the featured speaker at many important events. He was a leading champion of the cause of temperance, a foremost promoter of Americanizing the immigrants, a strong supporter of Card. *Gibbons in his defense of labor's right to organize, a vigorous opponent of racial prejudice and discrimination, and an aggressive defender of American separation of Church and State. In education, he supported the establishment of The Catholic Univ. of America and its location in the nation's capital; favored the growth of religious schools, colleges, and seminaries; defended the public schools and was the sponsor of the controversial *Faribault-Stillwater

Plan—a forerunner of the later "shared-time" arrangement. In an effort to give needy immigrants in the crowded cities of the East a fresh start in the open lands of the West, he provided, on easy terms, huge tracts of land in Minnesota to colonizers and helped to found the *Irish Catholic Colonization Association of the United States. He represented his diocese at Vatican Council I (1870) and played an active part in the Third Plenary Council of Baltimore (1884). I. was a controversial figure; some of his fellow Catholics in the U.S. and France accused him of holding the doctrine condemned under the name *Americanism, but he vigorously denied the charge. At the request of the Holy See, he interceded with President William McKinley in an effort to prevent the Spanish American War; after the war he aided in settling the friars' land problem in the Philippine Islands.

BIBLIOGRAPHY: J. H. Moynihan, *Life of Archbishop John Ireland* (1953); J. Ireland, *Church and Modern Society* (1896).

[M. CARTHY]

IRELAND, SERAPHINE, MOTHER (1842–1930), educator. Sister of Abp. John Ireland, Ellen Ireland became a Sister of St. Joseph of St. Paul, Minnesota. In 1882 she became provincial of her community. Under her administration the community grew in numbers and apostolates, including the establishment of the College of St. Catherine in St. Paul.

[J. R. AHERNE]

IRELAND, CHRISTIANITY AND. The religious importance of Irish people who have migrated has been beyond all proportion to that of those who stayed at home. There were many flights of wild geese before and after 1691 when the Protestant ascendancy was finally established for nearly 2 centuries; in the Dark Ages the monks under St. Columba did much to Christianize Scotland; those under St. Columban spread over all Europe except the Iberian Peninsula to restore religion and learning, while in recent centuries they played a large part in the U.S. and the major part in Australia and New Zealand in building up the Church. Most Catholics in the United Kingdom are of Irish stock, and even now in India and Pakistan many churches remain as memorials to the Irish regiments who served the British Raj.

Christian history begins with the coming of missionaries from Roman Britain and Gaul; the decisive achievement was that of St. *Patrick in the mid-5th cent., though evangelization was less rapid than was thought at one time, and paganism lingered in pockets until the 7th century. This was the golden age of a specifically Gaelic religious culture when the rest of Europe was still overrun by the barbarians; it excelled in metal work, illumination, and the characteristic treatment of letters in MSS; it wrote in Latin and was familiar with the classics; but its temper and discipline contrasted with the Roman order. In effect the centers of ecclesiastical power were monastic, not episcopal, and were associated with the great families who ruled minor kingdoms. Bishops were kept for their sacramental functions; but for the rest were subordinate to the monks, among whom were many remarkable characters, who spread learning and from whom derived the earlier *Penitentials. The export of this system, or if that is too tight a word for a style of Christian living at once free and easy and austere—notes which are still discernible in the Irish religious character —and the claim to immunity from the more formal and episcopal system set up strains when the Celtic monks from the West met the returning tide of Rome and the waves of Benedictinism from the south. The results of the Synod of *Whitby (664) were to extend to Ireland. The great Irish monasteries were ravaged by the piratical raids of the Norsemen, who settled in the seaports and became Christian, yet looked to Anglo-Saxon rather than to Celtic models. Already before the Anglo-Norman invasion in 12th cent., the ecclesiastical polity of Ireland was substantially, if somewhat raggedly, that of the rest of Europe, with properly constituted territorial archbishoprics and bishoprics and a growing force of Cistercians.

The coming of the Anglo-Normans, then, produced no abrupt religious change; they were backed by a reforming group within the Church, supported by the papacy, and not resented by the people at large. Nationalism had not the emotive force or political meaning it later came to possess, and Strongbow might as well be called a Cambro-Norman as an Anglo-Norman. England no more ruled Ireland than New England ruled the U.S. under President Kennedy. Henry II of England was recognized as Lord of Ireland, but exercised direct control only over Dublin and other seaports, while the Norman lords established themselves in the lands they had won, by arms or arrangement, married Irish wives, spoke Gaelic, kept their sense of English law, and became a kind of "middle-nation," Irish to the English, English to the original Irish.

So far the history of Ireland had not been more distressful than that of other European countries. The troubles were to come from the Protestant Reformation and the regalism of the English state under the Tudors, two causes which coalesced to produce a shameful oppression for three centuries. The first, which was to prove the more outrageous, was slow in beginning. Henry VIII's breach with Rome had relatively little effect: he proclaimed himself King of Ireland, but his and succeeding Tudor viceroys moved gently in face of the unanimous attachment of the people to the Mass and the Holy See. There was spoliation of the monasteries, intrusion of Protestant bps., but no effective persecution and few martyrs: outside the Pale the Anglo-Irish families proved as staunch to the old religion as the old Irish. Yet with the conversion of elective chieftainships to hereditary peerages, some loose attachment to the royal supremacy was secured, and this, combined with a policy of informal toleration, enabled the vice-regal government to ride out various rebellions so that the kingdom was sufficiently firm in support of the Stuarts against the English Parliament.

That was to lead to the disaster of the Cromwellian Settlement, achieved after many barbarities in 1653 and made permanent 40 years later by the victory of William of Orange over James II. The only plantation of English colonists of lasting importance had been made in Ulster at the beginning of the century; this was now reinforced by Scottish Presbyterians, and the effects remain with us in the partition of Ireland, a still unresolved political problem.

Catholicism was not proscribed during the 18th cent., but rather more bleeding was the subordination of Ireland to English mercantile interests, and even more odious was the condescension with which the Irish were sometimes treated as likeable and licensed barbarians. Though not bad at insults themselves, they have in fact heaped coals of fire on the British head, and not only for reasons suggested in the opening paragraph. The tragedy for their country in the 19th cent. was "the Great Hunger," the catastrophic potato famine (1845–50), which scattered them and Catholicism all over the English-speaking world. The political union of Ireland with Great Britain operated to the benefit of Catholics, largely through the efforts of Daniel O'Connell to achieve Emancipation: it was supported by many, particularly among the higher clergy, and some, not very generous, support for the Catholic Church in Ireland was forthcoming from Westminster.

The Protestant Church of Ireland was disestablished (1869–71). But the union was weakened by the movement for Home Rule, which for a variety of reasons, including the revival of a feeling for the Gaelic culture, led to the establishment of an independent Irish Free State in 1922. There the special position of the Catholic Church is recognized, yet complete toleration for other religions is both acknowledged and practiced, a contrast to the regime in the six counties, the legacy of the Cromwellian settlement, where Catholics, though a good third of the population, are not free from disabilities. The whole country remains very church-going, and both Catholics and Protestants provide more than their quota of missionaries in distant lands. The proud clericalism of the Catholic Irish, which in many cases served as a blanket over their native genius, is now being drawn aside, and true piety and theology have not suffered. The true problem seems to be that this gifted and fruitful Christian people can neither find a living in their own country nor exert a respectable influence in world affairs, civil and ecclesiastical, proportionate to their virtues. There are signs that this is lessening.

[T. GILBY]

IRELAND, CHURCH OF, see CHURCH OF IRELAND.

IRELAND, NATIONAL UNIVERSITY OF, a coeducational, nonsectarian institution of higher learning in the Irish Republic, established by the British Parliament under the Irish Universities' Act of 1908. The university has three constituent colleges, each established under separate charter: University College, Dublin (1909); University College, Cork (founded 1845 as Queen's College, Cork); and University College, Galway (founded 1845 as Queen's College, Galway). In addition the university also includes St. Patrick's College, Maynooth, a major seminary for all the dioceses of Ireland and a pontifical univ., founded in 1795, and since 1908 recognized as pertaining to the National University. Until the founding of the Queen's Colleges by Sir Robert Peel (1845), there was only one university in Ireland, Trinity College, Dublin, which was founded in 1592 by Queen Elizabeth I. Established to reinforce Protestantism in Catholic Ireland, Trinity was closed to Catholics until 1793, and until 1873 did not admit them to fellowships or scholarships. The National Univ. on the contrary, together with its constituent colleges, is secular in nature, open to all, and enjoys considerable academic latitude, although, with the exception of St. Patrick's, Maynooth, it is not permitted to teach theology. Each college has its own governing body and academic council composed of professors appointed by the university. All the university colleges comprise the faculties of arts; Celtic studies, which in Dublin and Cork is combined with arts; science; law; medicine; commerce; and engineering, which in Dublin includes architecture. University College, Dublin, also has faculties of philosophy; general agriculture; and veterinary medicine; and Cork, dairy science. St. Patrick's, Maynooth, besides the faculties of arts, science, and philosophy, has faculties of theology and canon law. Enrollment in Dublin averages about 8,500; in Cork, 2,400; in Galway, 2,020; and in St. Patrick's, Maynooth, 570. The Univ. College Library in Dublin houses 207,200 volumes; in Galway, 90,000; in Cork, 487,800; and St. Patrick's, Maynooth, has about 125,000, besides rare works on Irish history, incunabula, pamphlets on Irish history, a number of special collections, and the archives from the Irish College, Salamanca, Spain.

BIBLIOGRAPHY: *National University of Ireland Handbook 1908–32* (1932); D. Meehan, *Window on Maynooth* (1949).

[M. B. MURPHY]

IRENAEUS OF LYONS, ST. (betw. 130 and 140–202), influential early church Father and bp. of Lyons; an effective 2d-cent. defender of apostolic tradition against the rising tide of Gnosticism. Little is known for certain of his life except that he was born in Asia Minor; that he was a disciple of St. Polycarp of Smyrna; that he migrated to Gaul, was a presbyter of the Church of Lyons during the reign of Marcus Aurelius, was sent as an envoy to Rome during the Montanist controversy, and succeeded the martyr Pothinus as bp. of Lyons. Gregory of Tours speaks of I.'s being a martyr. As bishop he opposed Gnosticism and advised Pope Victor I to be conciliatory in the Easter controversy between Rome and the Churches of Asia Minor. He wrote in Greek and two complete works are now extant, but only in translation: a five-volume work usually cited by its Latin title *Adversus haereses* and an Armenian version of his *Demonstration of the Apostolic Teaching*. Numerous Greek citations of these works are found in other church Fathers, in Eusebius, who cites various other of his writings as well. I. defended the importance of history in revelation of the OT as well as the NT; of the tradition that reveals history and is handed down in history by a historical process involving concrete persons and communities. He opposed the timeless systems of any form of ahistorical Gnosticism. BIBLIOGRAPHY: F. Vernet, DTC 7.2:2394–2533; G. Bosio, BiblSanct 7:891–899; Butler 2:656–658.

[E. J. DILLON]

IRENAEUS (d. 450), bp. **OF TYRUS,** defender of *Nestorius. As an imperial count, I. went to the Council of Ephesus and there attempted to use the influence of his position in defense of his friend Nestorius. For his pains he was deprived of his imperial rank and banished to Petra. He was consecrated bp. of Tyrus *c.*445 but through the machinations of *Eutyches and other enemies of the Antiochene theology, he was deposed and banished to his native city. He was condemned by the *Robber Council of Ephesus and seems to have died before the convening of *Chalcedon. He wrote a history of the Nestorian controversy, rich in documentary materials, called the ''Tragedy.'' Some of this work survives in the 6th-cent. *Synodicon* of Rusticus the Deacon (PG 84:548–814). BIBLIOGRAPHY: G. Bareille, DTC 7.2:2533–36; K. Junack, RGG 3:892.

[R. B. ENO]

IRENE, BYZANTINE EMPRESS, (*c.*752–803), wife of the iconoclast Emperor Leo IV. Upon the latter's death in 780, I. became regent and, later, coruler with her son Constantine VI. She reversed the policies of her predecessors by appointing Tarasius, a less iconoclastic patriarch. During her rule the Council of Nicaea II (787) met and condemned *iconoclasm. After failing to depose her son in 790, she lost her imperial power for 2 years but finally succeeded in overthrowing Constantine in 797. The aims of the Byzantine Empire were greatly jeopardized in 800 when *Charlemagne was crowned Emperor by Pope Leo III, a title that Byzantium did not accept until 814. Some historians maintain that the coronation could take place since there was no male ruler in Byzantium. In the Byzantine Empire, however, I. was considered the legitimate ruler although her reign was the first instance of a woman's possessing full imperial power. Official documents refer to her not as empress but as emperor (*basileus*), but she is not considered a political success. She was herself overthrown in 802. BIBLIOGRAPHY: Ostrogorsky 156–165; A. A. Vasiliev, *History of the Byzantine Empire* (1964) 1:234–269.

[F. T. RYAN]

IRENE OF PORTUGAL, ST. Several vitae of Braga and Évora after 1100 describe her as a virgin martyr victimized by a magic potion in 653; equally magical is the course of her body downstream to the Tagus and her entombing in a pool at Scallabis, which then became Santarém. Called *virgo in Scallabi Castro* in a 10th-cent. Mozarabic antiphonary, she was added to the Roman martyrology in 1586.

[E. P. COLBERT]

IRENICISM (Irenics; Gr. *eirēnē,* peace), an attitude or approach seeking peaceful or conciliatory resolution of theological differences for the sake of Christian unity; the opposite of polemics or *polemical theology. A false irenicism is tantamount to indifferentism and is generally rejected as ultimately harmful to the ecumenical movement. Genuine irenicism includes more than an emphasis on points of agreement, or on separation of essentials from nonessentials of belief; it also seeks in mutual understanding and charity to discover beyond controversial associations or connotations the true meaning intended in points of doctrine. *ECUMENISM.

[T. MANTEUFEL]

IRISH ART (2000 B.C.–1200 A.D.). A brilliant phase of megalithic art and goldsmith's work in the 2d millennium B.C. was followed by decline; there was a revival in the 3d and 2d cent. B.C.; and during the next 4 or 5 cent. primitive human figures and stones covered with swelling curvilinear ornament were matched by brilliant achievements in metalwork (Broighter collar, Armagh trumpet, Lisnacroghera scabbards, etc.). The scrolls and curvilinear designs of Celtic tradition were rendered in *repoussé* technique and in engravings (Lisnacroghera scabbard, Lough Crew bone trial pieces). Figural scenes were sometimes attempted (Lough Crew stag hunt on bone). Although it escaped Roman occupation, Ireland to the end of the 2d cent. A.D. reflected the changes in Celtic style in Roman Britain. Individual works of art cannot be dated except by such analogies for chronology is uncertain. From the end of the 2d cent. A.D. to *c.*600 A.D. there are no evidences. Then began a brilliant revival of old Celtic elements and impulses in a new phase of Irish Christian art which produced masterpieces such as the Ardagh Chalice, the Tara Brooch, and the Book of Kells, as well as a prolific decorative sculpture chiefly associated with high crosses. The 9th cent. saw foreign modifications in Hiberno-Viking and Anglo-Saxon styles. Distinctively Irish are the stone round towers with conical tops (11th and 12th centuries). Norman incursions (1169) ended the separate tradition of Irish art. BIBLIOGRAPHY: R. L. S. Bruce-Mitford, NCE 7:633–636.

[R. L. S. BRUCE-MITFORD]

IRISH ARTICLES, a ''rule of public doctrine'' formulated by the first convocation of Protestant clergy in Ireland (Dublin, 1615). The principal author is thought to have been James Ussher (1581–1656), later (1625) abp. of Armagh. The 104 articles under 19 titles express rigid *Calvinism, and Puritan Sabbatarianism; they do not mention the need for ordination by a bishop. The Articles were supplanted as a *confession of faith when in 1635 the

*Thirty-Nine Articles were adopted. The chief interest of the Irish Articles is that they served as a model for the *Westminster Confession. BIBLIOGRAPHY: Schaff Creeds 1:662–665; 3:526–544.

[T. C. O'BRIEN]

IRISH CATHOLIC COLONIZATION ASSOCIATION OF THE U.S., an organization proposed in 1879 by William J. Onahan, representing the leading organizations promoting Irish immigrant settlements, and formally set up the same year under the chairmanship of Bp. John Lancaster Spalding of Peoria, Illinois. Set up as a stock company with capital of $100,000 and shares sold at $100, the project gained support with difficulty in spite of the strenuous appeals of Abp. John Ireland and Bp. Spalding. Railroad land, 10,000 acres in Minnesota and 25,000 acres in Nebraska, was purchased. Immigrants who had saved some money were sold acreage at a low cost. Included in the cost was a percentage to support the building of a church, rectory, school, and immigrant depot in each colony. The association also leased land in Arkansas already owned by Bp. Fitzgerald of Little Rock, but few Irish came to this area. When the colonies were flourishing, the Association redeemed its stock and in 1891 dissolved. BIBLIOGRAPHY: M. Henthorne, *Irish Catholic Colonization Association of the United States* (1932).

[J. R. AHERNE]

IRISH CHRISTIAN BROTHERS, men religious formerly known as Brothers of the Christian Schools of Ireland, are members of the Congregation of Christian Brothers (CFC) founded at Waterford, Ireland, in 1802 by Edmund Ignatius Rice (1762–1844). The brothers take simple perpetual vows of poverty, chastity, and obedience, perseverance in the congregation, and voluntary teaching of the poor. In their apostolate of the instruction and Christian formation of youth, the members conduct elementary and secondary schools, technical schools, colleges, orphanages, and institutions for the deaf and blind in countries throughout the world. Papal approval was granted the institute in 1820. The two American provinces of Eastern and Western U.S. have headquarters in New Rochelle, N.Y. and Vallejo, California. In 1975, the congregation maintained 344 houses and had a total membership of 3,322 brothers governed by a superior general residing in Rome. BIBLIOGRAPHY: Heimbucher 2:433–453.

[R. A. TODD]

IRISH CONFESSORS AND MARTYRS, those members of the Irish clergy, religious and laity who suffered and/or died during the period of the penal laws in Ireland (1535–1714) for whom the most reliable documentation on the Catholic side includes several martyrologies assembled between 1590–1629; 1659–1669 notably those of John Howling (1539–1599), continued by Bishop Cornelius O'Devaney (1611), Bishop David Rothe (1619) and two priests from Cork who worked on the Continent, John Coppinger (1620) and John McLean (1629). Later, two Franciscans, Maurice Morison (*Threnodia-Hiberno Catholica*) and Antony Bruodin (*Propugnaculum*) together with the records of several religious orders supplemented these accounts. The most recent complete work documenting extant sources is *Our Martyrs* by Father Denis Murphy (Dublin 1896).

Fear of reprisal and extension of the penal laws was responsible for restraint in advancing the causes of these witnesses to the faith. It was not until 1861 that preliminary efforts began culminating in the research of Father Murphy. In the 20th cent., Oliver Plunkett was beatified by Benedict XV and canonized by Paul VI. BIBLIOGRAPHY: F. Finigan, NCE 7, 641–644.

[F. H. BRIGHAM]

IRISH CROSSES, an important body of sculptural and monumental art, some 50 examples of which date from 800 A.D. The series continues into the Romanesque age. Starting with pillars and roughly hewn stones, the series includes upright cross-bearing slabs, closely analogous in form and ornament to the monuments of the Christian Picts, and culminates in high wheel-headed crosses such as those of Moone (Kildare, 16 feet) and Muiredach (at Monasterboice, Louth, 18 feet). Such crosses were probably set up as preaching-stations in the countryside, and were also regularly erected in and around monasteries and churches. Elaborate iconography of biblical and lay scenes and rich Celtic ornament were developed. BIBLIOGRAPHY: R. L. S. Bruce-Mitford, NCE 7:644–645; F. Henry, *La Sculpture Irlandaise* (1930).

[R. L. S. BRUCE-MITFORD]

IRMENGARD, BL. (*c.*832–866), Carolingian princess. The daughter of Louis the German and Bl. Hemma, hence great-granddaughter of Charlemagne and sister of Charles the Fat, she was professed as a Benedictine nun at an early age, and became abbess of Bachau and later of the royal monastery at Chiemsee in Upper Bavaria. BIBLIOGRAPHY: Butler 3:119; A. Cabaniss, NCE 7:657; F. Baumann, BiblSanct 7:904–905.

[A. CABANISS]

IRMGARDIS OF COLOGNE, ST. (d. betw. 1075 and 1100), countess of Aspel. It is said that I. disposed of her inheritance in the foundation of churches and charitable institutions. According to some accounts she lived as an anchorite at Süchteln, where she is honored with a 15th-cent. chapel. I. is buried in Cologne Cathedral. BIBLIOGRAPHY: A. M. Burg, LTK 5:758.

[B. F. SCHERER]

IRMHART, ÖSER (d. betw. 1350 and 1400), theologian, translator. Having studied law in Bologna and served in two Austrian pastorates, he was promoted to a canonry at the Augsburg cathedral. I. made Latin translations of the works of the Spanish Dominican Alfonsus Bonihominis and a German translation of an Arabic treatise on the Messiah. BIBLIOGRAPHY: M. Csáky, NCE 7:657.

[M. J. FINNEGAN]

IRMINA, ST. (d. *c.*708), abbess. Unreliable evidence has identified I. as putative daughter of Dagobert II and his Anglo-Saxon wife Mechtild; all that is known of her is that she was abbess of the monastery of Öhren, that she befriended Anglo-Saxon and Irish missionaries, and was in particular a generous benefactress of St. *Willibrord. BIBLIOGRAPHY: F. Caraffa, BiblSanct 7:906; Butler 4:605–606.

[A. CABANISS]

IRRATIONALISM, a position or attitude toward the nature and role of reason in human experience and philosophical inquiry that questions the existence (ontological presence), ability (epistemological limits), or relevance (moral efficacy) of reason in the world and in human existence. Philosophical irrationalism usually indicates a recognition of the fundamental and impenetrable mystery of the essence of all things, and as such reflects a desire to transcend logic and reason and to reach truth and wisdom by mystical, transcendental, or spiritual paths. A philosophy of irrationalism tends to subordinate mind to heart, reason to emotion, explanation to experience. Irrationalism in philosophy frequently emerged as a religious reaction to the scientific and mathematical rationalism of 17th- and 18th-cent. thinkers (Descartes, Locke, Leibniz, and their heirs). An early critic of rationalism, harshly derided by Voltaire, was the French mathematician-philosopher Blaise Pascal (1623–62) who experienced (1654) what he described as a discovery of "the God of Abraham, Isaac, and Jacob, not of philosophers and men of science." Pascal held that reason can never prove first principles, but is merely the power to build and improve systems of axioms; awareness of first principles derives not from reason but from revelation, instinct, and submission to God. By the end of the Enlightenment, Kant had developed a critical philosophy that questioned the natural limits of human reason and explored transcendental awareness. Hamann, Herder, and Jacobi sought to reaffirm the place of faith and emotion in human life, which they felt Kant had displaced by his overriding epistemological concerns. The reaction to Hegel's Idealism took a decided irrationalist turn. Schopenhauer in particular questioned smug presumptions on the part of philosophers that the universe is rationally ordered, that it is readily available to rational human investigation, and that reason is a common bond between man and world. Kierkegaard, too, felt the utter discrepancy between attempts to order experience by human intellect and the deep resistance of the world and of experience to intelligibility. The tension between the order expected and the chaos too often found, coupled with a metaphysical questioning of the very existence of reason as a first principle, carefully elaborated in the existentialist philosophies of Sartre, Camus, and others, yielded a doctrine of absurdity. Nietszche, in an extreme reaction to what he considered the delusions ("lies and frauds") of accepted rational thoughts, arguments, and conclusions about the world, denied them a real foundation in the real world but celebrated them as human creations. In psychology, a belief in subconscious irrational motivations for human behavior found consistent expression in the works of Freud, Jung, and others. Irrationalism has always provided an alternative perspective on the achievements of science and scientific philosophies; it serves as a reminder that rational explanation, while logically sufficient, does not fully describe human experience of self and of the world.

[R. J. LITZ]

IRREGULARITY, an impediment designated by canon law as a bar to the reception of holy orders or the exercise of an order already received (CIC, c. 968). An irregularity makes the reception or exercise *illicit but not *invalid. Irregularity can be removed by dispensation. Current legislation classifies irregularities as arising from a defect (e.g., *illegitimacy), or as arising from an act classified by the law as a crime (*ex delicto; ibid.* cc. 984–985). Similar to irregularities are "simple impediments" (*ibid.* c. 987); however, unlike irregularities, these are of such a nature as to be temporary.

[T. C. O'BRIEN]

IRRESISTIBLE GRACE, a formula to express the power of divine grace to bring about man's conversion. The idea is found in St. *Augustine, who speaks of grace acting *indeclinabiliter et insuperabiliter,* i.e., as excluding the possibility of man's refusal impeding its effect; such effectiveness is attributed to grace because of fallen man's need to be protected against the defectiveness of his own free choices (*liberum arbitrium*). The actual phrase "irresistible grace" is historically associated with *Calvinism and the teaching that grace has its source in the absolutely sovereign will of God. The Synod of *Dort reaffirmed the irresistibility of grace against *Arminianism. Appealing to St. Augustine, *Jansenism included the view that grace interiorly necessitates man's consent.

[T. C. O'BRIEN]

IRVING, EDWARD (1792–1834), Scottish Presbyterian minister, whose ideas strongly influenced the beginnings of the *Catholic Apostolic Church. First a student at the Univ. of Edinburgh and then a schoolmaster, I. became a preacher in the Church of Scotland in 1815 and worked among the poor. He received an appointment to a small Presbyterian chapel in London in 1822, became interested in *millenarianism, and published *The Coming of the Messiah in Glory and Majesty* (1827), a translation of a Spanish work. He also was an advocate of *glossolalia, *divine healing, and *baptism with the Holy Spirit, and is regarded by some to have been a forerunner of Pentecostalism. Because of the revivalistic outbursts in his chapel and a book in which he claimed Christ had a sinful nature, I. lost his place in the Presbyterian Church (1832). He had, however, received a welcome in the prayer circle at the home of Henry Drummond (1786–1860), where interest in recapturing the spirit of the primitive Church made the members responsive to I.'s preaching. His ideas on Christ's second coming, the restoration of a college of Twelve Apostles, and a new outpouring of charismatic gifts, led to the formation of the Catholic Apostolic Church. Members were often called Irvingites by outsiders. I. himself, however, never received high rank in the Catholic Apostolic Church. BIBLIOGRAPHY: A. L. Drummond, *Edward Irving and His Circle* (1937).

[W. J. WHALEN]

ISAAC II ANGELUS, BYZANTINE EMPEROR, from 1185–95. He ruled at a time of turmoil and was unable to check the decadence of the Empire. I. dominated the Church, deposing the patriarch and appointing three others in rapid succession, enforcing discipline on the clergy, and seizing property. The prevailing anti-Latin sentiment in Constantinople induced him to ally with Saladin to acquire for the Greeks ecclesiastical rights and properties in the lands the Muslims had recently captured from the Latin Kingdom of Jerusalem. I. harrassed and impeded the army of Barbarossa crossing Byzantium on the Third Crusade; this action inflamed Western hostility and contributed to the Latin attack on Constantinople in 1204. BIBLIOGRAPHY: C. Brand, *Byzantium Confronts the West, 1180–1204* (1968).

[R. H. SCHMANDT]

ISAAC, PATRIARCH, a rather obscure person in the OT, overshadowed by his father Abraham and his son Jacob. In Gen 26 there are some narratives concerning I., but even these seem to be imitations of like stories concerning his father. I.'s name is popularly explained as meaning "he laughs" and is connected with the laughter of Abraham (Gen 17.17–18) and Sarah (18.11–15) at the promise of a child in advanced old age. I. came close to being sacrificed by his father, as happened among surrounding peoples (Gen 22). Yahweh intervened, however, to stay the act. The story was told as a polemic against child sacrifice and later interpreted as an example of sublime obedience. I. married Rebekah, the sister of Laban (Gen 24) and she gave him twin sons, Esau and Jacob (Gen 25.19–26). In the NT Paul pictures I. as a type of the gentile Christian Church (Rom 9.7; Gal 4.28–31). This is based on the fact that I. was a son by promise as well as by flesh. Thus all who accept the promises through faith are true sons of Abraham and therefore heirs; those who refuse the promises even though descended carnally from Abraham are cast out like Ishmael. In Rom 9.10, I. is called "our father" and in Heb 11.20 he is presented as a hero of faith. BIBLIOGRAPHY: J. Daniélou, *From Shadows to Reality: Studies in Biblical Typology of the Fathers* (tr. W. Hibberd, 1960); N. Glueck, *Rivers in the Desert* (1959); E. A. Speiser, *Genesis: Introduction, Translation and Notes* (1964).

[F. GAST]

ISAAC BEN ABRAHAM (Troki; 1533[25?]–1594[86?]), Lithuanian Karaite controvertist and opponent of Christianity. His apologetic defense of Judaism, *Hizzuk Emunah* (Strengthening of the Faith), reflects his intimate knowledge of both Testaments and Christian doctrine; half of it examines Christian arguments against Judaism, the other half reviews and critiques the NT for its textual inconsistencies. The MS was unfinished at his death and, though his disciple Joseph ben Mordecai Malinovski was to have supplied both an index and preface for publication, the unpublished work was altered and corrupted by self-interested copyists. A Talmudic rabbinite rendering of the work, accompanied by a Latin translation and extensive refutation, was published by Johann Christoph Wagenseil in 1681 as *Tela Ignea Satanae* (Fiery Darts of Satan). A Judaeo-German translation appeared in 1717; other translations include: English, by Moses Mocatta in 1851 (1970); German, by David Deutsch, in 1865 and 1873. Anticlerical writers of the 18th cent., Voltaire in particular, found the *Hizzuk Emunah* an arsenal of criticism in their attack on Christian dogma.

[R. J. LITZ]

ISAAC THE GOOD OF LANGRES, ST. (d. 880), bp. of Langres from 859; author of *Canones seu selecta capitula,* a set of diocesan statutes, participant in church councils at Soissons and Troyes.

[T. C. O'BRIEN]

ISAAC THE GREAT, ST. (Sahak; *c.*347–438), the son of St. Nerses and a leading bp. of the early Armenian Church. His role in the beginnings of Armenian literature was a very important one. His opposition to Nestorianism and his contacts with the Byzantine Empire led the Persians to drive him from his see, so that his last years were troubled ones. BIBLIOGRAPHY: P. Ananian, BiblSanct 7:916–918.

[G. T. DENNIS]

ISAAC ISRAELI (Isaac Judaeus; d. *c.*932), Jewish physician and philosopher. Born in Egypt, he imigrated to Tunisia and became a physician to the Fatimid Caliph 'Ubayd Allah al-Mahdi. His medical treatises, the *Book of Fevers,* and the *Book of Foodstuffs and Drugs,* among others, were written in Arabic. Regarded as classics, they were translated into Hebrew and Latin and thus became accessible to Jews and Christians as well as to Muslims. In philosophy, I. was largely Neoplatonic. Among his philosophical works are: the *Book of Definitions,* the *Book on Spirit and Soul,* and the *Book of Elements.* He had no influence on Muslim philosophers, but he was read by the Jewish Neoplatonists in Spain. In Latin translation he was used, among others, by Dominic Gundisalvi, Albert the Great, and Thomas Aquinas. BIBLIOGRAPHY: A. Altmann and S. M. Stern, *Isaac Israeli: A Neoplatonic Philosopher of the Early Tenth Century* (1958).

[M. R. P. MCGUIRE]

ISAAC MASTER (fl. *c.*1300), anonymous Italian painter of the Florentine school to whom are attributed frescoes (*Pentecost, Ascension, Lamentation,* with two scenes from the life of Isaac—which give the painter his name), in bays nearest the entrance of the upper church of S. Francesco at Assisi. Recent scholars attribute the Isaac scenes to Giotto, and the other works to his assistants.

[M. J. DALY]

ISAAC OF MONTE LUCO, ST. (Isaac of Spoleto; d. after 550), hermit. A native of Syria, I. fled the Monophysite persecution and became a recluse on Monte Luco near Spoleto, where he directed a kind of laura or colony of hermits. BIBLIOGRAPHY: *Dialogues* of St. Gregory the Great, PL 77:244–248; AS April 2:27–30; V. Monachino, EncCatt 7:232.

[W. A. JURGENS]

ISAAC OF NINEVEH, 7th-cent. Syrian ascetic, monk, and writer; one of the earliest theoreticians of Christian mysticism. His works have had a great influence in both East and West. He himself was dependent on *Evagrius. Born in Beit' Quatrajē on the Persian Gulf, I. was Nestorian bp. of Nineveh but soon resigned that office as being inimical to the spiritual life. He was first an anchorite, then an abbot, and lived to an old age; but became blind from much study and abstemiousness. His writings teach self-mastery through watching, fasting, silence, and solitude. His main themes are the life of prayer, the mystery of God, judgment, and temptation. He delineates the three grades of solitaries: the novices, the proficients, and the perfect. He believed the worth of human actions was to be gauged by the degree of the love of God that inspired them.

[E. J. DILLON]

ISAAC OF STELLA (*c.*1100–*c.*1169), Cistercian abbot at Étoile in France, theologian. He was an English cleric, studied theology at Paris, became a Cistercian *c.*1145 and 2 years later was elected abbot. His works, mainly sermons (PL 194:1689–1893) reveal his profound knowledge of St. Augustine and Pseudo-Dionysius, esp. in a series of sermons for monks that amounts to a theological course. His treatise on the soul, written to *Alcher of Clairvaux, while philosophical, was written as a psychological background for the process of prayer. I.'s ideas were incorporated in Alcher's *De spiritu et anima*. One other known treatise by I. is his *De officio missae* (PL 194:1889–93). BIBLIOGRAPHY: L. Bouyer, *Cistercian Heritage* (tr. E. A. Livingstone, 1958).

[T. C. O'BRIEN]

ISAAK, HEINRICH (*c.*1450–1517), composer. He was born in Brabant and is thus described as a great German composer, but he spent most of his career in Italy, for a long period in the service of Lorenzo de'Medici in a variety of musical capacities. After Lorenzo's death I. served Maximilian of Germany as court composer at Innsbruck from 1497 until his own death, though most of his time was still spent in different parts of Italy. One of the great composers of the time, he was a master of the contrapuntal style. Among his many compositions are the harmonization of the German folk song, "Innsbruck ich muss dich lassen," the "Choralis Constantinus" and numerous Masses, motets, and songs.

[P. J. HENNESSEY]

ISABELLA I (1451–1504), **QUEEN OF CASTILE** from 1474, succeeding her brother Henry IV. By marriage (1469) to Ferdinand II of Aragon and V of Castile I. succeeded also to the throne of Aragon (1479), thus uniting Aragon and Castile under the *Reyes Católicos,* or Catholic Kings. Under Isabella and Ferdinand, Spain was reformed socially and ecclesiastically; civil war and banditry were suppressed; a regular army established; trading and agriculture improved. The monarchy became dominant in affairs of the nobility, the cities, and the Church, obtaining a papal right to appoint all bps. in Spain. A papal bull of 1478 established the Spanish Inquisition under royal control and the monarchs appointed Tomás de *Torquemada to administer it. Under the Inquisition's influence, Isabella expelled the Jews from Spain (1492). She commissioned Columbus' voyages and sought colonization and evangelization of the New World. After the successful conquest of Granada and failure of the Moorish rebellion (1502), all unconverted Moors were expelled.

[R. J. LITZ]

ISABELLE OF FRANCE, BL. (1225–70), sister of Louis IX (St. Louis). She founded and drew up the regulations for the convent of Poor Clares in Longchamp (Paris), and though she lived a penitential life there she refused to take vows or become abbess. Her cult was approved by Pope Leo X in 1521. Her life was written shortly after her death by Agnes of Harcourt (AS Aug. 6:798–808). BIBLIOGRAPHY: A. Garreau, *Bienheureuse Isabelle de France, soeur de saint Louis* (1955); R. T. d'Arenzano, BiblSanct 7:908–909; Butler 1:427–428.

[V. L. BULLOUGH]

ISAIA DA PISA (fl. 15th cent.), sculptor in Rome who carved the monument of Card. Antonio Martinez Chaves in St. John Lateran, and of Pope Eugenius IV in S. Salvatore in Lauro (1450–55).

[M. J. DALY]

ISAIAH, ASCENSION OF. Three distinct compositions appear to have been assembled under this heading: (1) "The

Martyrdom of Isaiah'' (most of ch. 1–5); (2) ''The Vision of Isaiah'' (ch. 3.13–4.18), probably an originally independent composition subsequently inserted into (1); (3) ''The Ascension of Isaiah'' (ch. 6–11). Fragments of the complete work have been preserved in Greek, Latin, Coptic, and Old Slavonic, but the only complete version extant is Ethiopic.

Martyrdom of Isaiah. This certainly goes back to a Hebrew original. The author seems to have taken as his basis the passage in 2 Kg 21.1–18 in which we are told that the apostate king Manasseh actively supported idolatrous practices of every kind and ''flooded Jerusalem from end to end'' with innocent blood. Isaiah had previously foretold to Hezekiah the apostasy of Manasseh as well as his own martyrdom. At Manasseh's accession Isaiah had fled to the wilderness with a small band of his disciples and there taken refuge on a lonely mountain. But he was falsely denounced by a lying Samaritan prophet named Balchira, at whose instigation Manasseh had him sawed in half while he prayed. It has been suggested that behind this legend lies a motif borrowed from Iranian saga, or more probably from the myth of Adonis, and now transferred to Isaiah. The allusion to prophets being ''sawn in half'' in Heb 11.37 must surely refer to this legend, and it was certainly known to Justin, Tertullian, and Origen. In fact, however, it must be considerably earlier and may ultimately have its roots in the religious persecution of Antiochus IV (167–164 B.C.). At this time and after it stories of martyrs were freely being circulated. The story of Isaiah's martyrdom also has numerous points of contact with the sectarian writings of Qumran, and it has even been suggested that Isaiah has here been taken as a type of the Teacher of Righteousness who figures in those writings.

Vision of Isaiah. This describes how Isaiah is inspired to foresee the coming of Christ, the establishment of his Church, the advent of Belial or Antichrist, and the end of the world. This is manifestly of Christian provenance and stems from *c.* 100 A.D.

Ascension of Isaiah. This relates how Isaiah is taken up into the seventh heaven where he receives a vision of God himself. He also witnesses the command of God to Christ that he shall descend to earth, and sees in a vision the circumstances of his birth, earthly mission, Passion and death, Resurrection and Ascension. This composition too is manifestly of Christian provenance and should probably be assigned to the 2d cent. A.D.

Finally, at a much later date, possibly in the 3d or 4th cent., these three originally independent pieces seem to have been roughly united into a single composite story. At this time, too, a number of Christian additions were made.

BIBLIOGRAPHY: R. H. Charles, *Ascension of Isaiah Translated From the Ethiopic Version* (1900); R. H. Charles et al., eds., *Apocrypha and Pseudepigrapha of the Old Testament* (1913) 2:155–162; H. H. Rowley, *Relevance of Apocalyptic* (2d ed., 1947) 108–111, 144–145.

[D. J. BOURKE]

ISAIAH, BOOK OF. This book is divided into three main parts known respectively as Isaiah (ch. 1–35), Deutero-Isaiah (ch. 40–55) and Trito-Isaiah (ch. 56–66). Chapters 36–39 have really been excerpted from 2 Kg 18. 13–20.19.

(1) *Isaiah,* or First Isaiah, as it is sometimes called, is itself made up of a number of minor collections not all of which can be ascribed even substantially to the prophet himself, whose career extended from c.742–701 B.C. The principal themes here are these: the faithlessness, ingratitude, pride, luxury, and obstinacy of Judah and Jerusalem, and their superstitious reliance on the cult instead of on righteousness to ensure Yahweh's favor. These amount to such deep guilt and betrayal that in spite of all Yahweh's love and longsuffering these crimes will bring about the downfall of his people. Obstinately relying on their own counsel and the powers of this world for support, instead of accepting and staunchly relying upon Yahweh's counsel as conveyed by his Prophet, and keeping themselves holy to him alone, they will find that from his temple in their midst he will inspire those very foreign powers to whom they have turned to purge his land of all faithless elements until only a remnant of those still faithful remains to inherit the predestined glories of his chosen people. This remnant will be led by Emmanuel, a figure supremely equipped with Yahweh's divine counsel and strength, who will replace the present faithless representatives of the house of David.

(2) Deutero-Isaiah is a more unified collection written much later by a different author in the utterly altered circumstances of the years shortly before the return from the Babylonian captivity in 538. The basic message here is of consolation. Israel's sufferings have only been the parental chastisement of her covenant God, who has never ceased to love her deeply and who, faithful to all his promises, is now about to bring her back to her land in a new exodus more glorious than the first, and to initiate a new stage of unprecedented glory in her covenant life with him. To do this he will engage his powers as sole creator God of heaven and earth, and will employ Cyrus as his consecrated servant, thereby demonstrating the worthlessness of all idols and the stupidity of worshipping them. Thus the Gentiles will come to recognize him as the sole God and Lord of all that is in heaven and earth, the controller and guider of history. They will learn to reverence the people, who have never ceased to be his own, as the mediators of his truth and blessing to them.

Into this section four poems, possibly, though by no means certainly, by a different hand, have subsequently been inserted. These are the Servant Songs of Is 42.1–9; 49.1–7; 50.4–9; 52.13–53.12. The Servant is a figure consecrated by Yahweh from birth, to bring light and salvation to the Gentiles and to remain staunch in his deputed task in spite of unjust persecution and ultimate death in ignominy. His sufferings have an atoning force for the sins of his persecutors, and he is ultimately vindicated by glories received after death.

(3) Trito-Isaiah (ch. 56–66) appears to be the work of a later disciple of Deutero-Isaiah, resuming many of his themes and reapplying them in a situation in which the temple has already been rebuilt, and a considerable measure of repopulation has already been achieved. The failure to bring to realization the highly idealized picture of the new age in Deutero-Isaiah is ascribed to the sins of the people and their leaders, such as deficiencies in Sabbath observance, excessive reliance on the cult and temple instead of on personal ''righteousness'', and even on idolatrous practices. Nevertheless, the ideal of a new heaven and a new earth with a new and more glorious Jerusalem as its center is still maintained, and humble acknowledgments of sin are interspersed with entreaties that Yahweh may soon accomplish this on his Day of Judgment, crushing the unrighteous and the people's enemies, and delivering them from their present tribulations. BIBLIOGRAPHY: P. Auvray, J. Steinmann, *Isaïe* (2d ed. 1957); G. Fohrer, *Jesaja I–III* (1961–64); G. B. Gray, *Isaiah I (1–27)* (1912); E. J. Kissane, *Book of Isaiah: Translated from a Critically Revised Hebrew Text with Commentary I* (1941), *II* (1943); E. J. Young, *Studies in Isaiah* (1954); S. H. Blank, *Prophetic Faith in Isaiah* (1958); J. Lindblom, *Study on the Immanuel Section in Isaiah* (1958); P. A. H. de Boer, *Second Isaiah's Message* (1956); C. R. North, *Second Isaiah* (1964); J. Lindblom, *Servant Songs in Deutero-Isaiah* (1951); C. R. North, *Suffering Servant in Deutero-Isaiah* (2d ed. 1956); G. Rignell, *Study of Isaiah 40–55* (1956).

[D. J. BOURKE]

ISAIAS BONER OF CRACOW, BL. (*c.*1400–71), friar. After entering the Order of Augustinians in Poland, he studied and later taught at the Univ. of Padua. He served as visitor of his order in Poland, as vicar general at a chapter (1452) in Bavaria, as well as master of theology at the Univ. of Cracow. Though recognized for his sincere virtue during his life and honored with the title Blessed in Augustinian martyrologies, he has never been beatified by Rome. BIBLIOGRAPHY: Butler 1:282–283; *Book of Saints* (comp. by the Benedictine Monks of St. Augustine's Abbey, 1966).

[M. E. DUFFY]

ISAPOSTOLOS (Gr. equal of the Apostles), a term used in the Byzantine Church to denote certain saints who greatly propagated the Christian faith, such as SS. Constantine and Helena, SS. Vladimir and Cyril and Methodius.

[A. J. JACOPIN]

ISÉ SHRINE, ancient Japanese Shinto shrine duplicated or ''restored'' from the 7th cent., as is the custom, until 1953 (date of the present building); carries the heavy thatched roof (*chigi*) and *katsuogi* (billets over the roof ridge), featured in the prehistoric architecture of Japan. An inner shrine is dedicated to the goddess Amaterasu, ''ancestor'' of the Japanese, and an outer shrine to the god Toyuke.

[M. J. DALY]

ISENBRANDT ADRIAEN (Ysenbrandt, d. 1551), 16th-cent. Netherlandish artist combining Italianate and German conventions with a Northern style. Active in the Bruges workshop of G. David, I. used a warm palette and strong contrasts of light and dark. He painted *The Seven Sorrows of the Virgin,* a diptych (Bruges), and a triptych *The Adoration of the Kings* (1518, Lübeck), having on the wings an Adam and Eve derived from the *Ghent Altarpiece*.

[M. J. DALY]

ISENHEIM ALTARPIECE, see GRÜNEWALD, MATTHIAS.

ISFRIED, ST. (d. 1204), Premonstratensian bishop. Canon of Cappenberg and provost of Jerichow, he became bp. of Ratzeburg in 1180. As spiritual leader of the Premonstratensians in N Germany, he exerted a wide influence as colonizer and Christianizer. He was confessor to Henry the Lion. His cult has been approved for the Premonstratensian Order.

[M. J. FINNEGAN]

ISH-BOSHETH (Is-Baal), king of Israel (2 Sam ch. 2–4). He succeeded his father Saul, but the tribe of Judah followed David. He ruled only 2 years, with his capital at Mahanaim, the main town of Gilead. Abner, commander of his army, deserted him. Then two of his men cut off his head and took it to David, hoping to be rewarded. David, however, had them executed. His name, which means man of shame, is also given as Esh-baal, man of Baal (1 Chr 8.33).

[T. EARLY]

ISHMAEL (ISMAEL), son of Abraham and Hagar. After the birth of Isaac, he was expelled from the household with his mother (Gen. 21.8, 25) and became a nomad and archer. In Gen 25.9 it is stated that he was present at the burial of Abraham. I. is considered to be the ancestor of a number of Arabian tribes and is claimed by the Mohammedans as their ancestor.

[A. P. HANLON]

ISHMAELITES, a group of wandering tribes dwelling in the Negev, the Sinai peninsula and N Arabia (Gen 25.12–18) and tracing their descent from an eponymous ancestor Ishmael (Gen 25.18–19). Considered partially Egyptian in origin (Gen 16.2) but kinsmen of the Israelites (Gen 16.15), they were also linked with the Midianites (Gen 37; Jg 8). BIBLIOGRAPHY: G. M. Landes, InterDB 2:748–749.

[E. J. CROWLEY]

ISHO 'DAD OF MERV (mid 9th cent.), Persian exegete and Nestorian bp. of Hedhatha on the Tigris. Little is known of his life, though his works have been preserved. He combined the historical-grammatical method of exegesis developed by Theodore of Mopsuestia utilized by Nestorian exegetes and the allegorical methods of the Jacobite or Monophysite school.

[R. J. LITZ]

ISHTAR, the Mesopotamian equivalent of the Canaanite Astarte. The Sumerian goddess Inanna (''Lady of Heaven'') was, like *Astarte, manifest in, or identified with, the planet Venus; and the arrival of the Semitic element in Mesopotamia led to the application of Astarte's name, in its Akkadian form Ishtar, to her Sumerian counterpart, Inanna. Her nature was complex. Endowed with the role of goddess of warfare and of love and fertility, her position became so great that her name could be used for ''goddess'' in general. Her cult may well have figured among the astral cults introduced into Palestine when the Assyrian Empire was at its zenith (cf. Am 5.26; 2 Kg 21.5), but it is not certain whether references to the ''Queen of Heaven'' in the Bible are to Ishtar or to Canaanite Astarte. BIBLIOGRAPHY: E. Dhorme, *Les Religions de Babylonie et d'Assyrie* (1945) 67–78. *TAMMUZ.

[A. CODY]

ISHTAR GATE, Babylon, double arched gateway dating from Nebuchadnezzar II (604–561) B.C.), dedicated to Ishtar, goddess of love and war. Spanning the sacred way and the starting point of processions to the temple of the god Marduk (at the summit of a seven-story ziggurat), it is decorated with symbolic glazed polychrome animal reliefs on a lapis lazuli ground, with a narrow frieze of white and yellow rosettes at bottom and top. The 575 yellow-clawed white dragons, sacred to Marduk, the brown bulls with green horns and blue tail tips, and the 120 white and yellow lions, move with grace and dignity. A ''ceramic architecture'' of impressive splendor, these clay forms, cut-up for firing and reassembled, flashed and dazzled the populace.

[M. J. DALY]

ISHVARA, Sanskrit divine title (''Supreme Lord'') used in two separate contexts. (1) In the *Yoga system, I. becomes an object of the student's concentration and thereby facilitates the eventual achievement of *samadhi or liberation. (2) In one version of the *Vedanta system, Ishvara is the title given by *Shankara to *Brahman (God) as personified, as involved in the universe and knowable by humans (as opposed to Brahman which transcends personality and which is beyond knowledge). In another version, that of *Ramanuja, the Ishvara whom humans can know and esp. love is the transcendent Lord himself. BIBLIOGRAPHY: M. Eliade, *Yoga* (1970); S. Prabhavananda, *Spiritual Heritage of India* (1963).

[D. P. EFROYMSON]

ISIDORE, THE FARMER, ST. (1070–1130), patron saint of Madrid and of farmers. He lived a life of holiness and fidelity to his employer; I.'s wife also was renowned for her sanctity. He was regarded as a miracle worker during his lifetime and prayers to him after his death brought a cure from a severe fever to King Philip III of Spain. I. was canonized in 1622 by Gregory XV. The National Catholic Rural Life Conference also took him as patron. BIBLIOGRAPHY: J. F. Alonso, BiblSanct 7:953–956.

[T. C. O'BRIEN]

ISIDORE OF KIEV (*c.* 1385–1463), metropolitan, humanist, theologian, diplomat, cardinal. A well-educated native of the Peloponnesus, I. was highly regarded in Constantinople and Mistra. After being named an abbot he became intimately involved in the negotiations between Byzantium and Western rulers. In 1436 he was consecrated metropolitan of Kiev and All Russia and, despite some difficulties in Moscow, represented the Russian Church at the Council of *Florence (1438–39). Articulate and influential, particularly in the private debates, he was instrumental in effecting agreement on the *Procession of the Holy Spirit by showing that the Greek formula, ''through the Son,'' meant the same as the Latin ''from the Son.'' On returning to Russia he was confronted with strong antipapal and antiunionistic feelings and was forced to flee. With a contingent of archers he was present at the fall of Constantinople in 1453, barely escaping alive. The rest of his days were passed quietly in Rome (he had been named a cardinal) in curial and scholarly pursuits. Many of his MSS are now in the Vatican Library. BIBLIOGRAPHY: J. Gill, *Personalities of the Council of Florence* (1964).

[G. T. DENNIS]

ISIDORE OF MILETUS, born in Asia, codesigner with Anthemius of Tralles of the Hagia Sophia, Constantinople (532–538)—a commission imaginative, daring, resulting in a Byzantine building never again equalled in scale or concept. In common with Anthemius, with whom he had probably previously completed the dome of nearby SS. Sergius and Bacchus, I. was not an architect by training although he had written a commentary on a treatise on vaulting and had taught geometry and physics at the Univ. of Alexandria and Constantinople. BIBLIOGRAPHY: R. Krautheimer, *Early Christian and Byzantine Architecture* (1965); *ANTHEMIUS OF TRALLES.

[R. C. MARKS]

ISIDORE OF PELUSIUM, ST. (*c.*360–*c.*435), monk and theologian. Born in *Alexandria, I. lived most of his life in Pelusium, a town to the E of the Nile delta. Contrary to common opinion, he probably was not an abbot. Famous for his sanctity and learning, he was a friend of *Cyril but also honored the memory of *John Chrysostom by imitating him. More than 2000 of his letters are extant, though a critical edition is lacking. These writings reveal him as an astute and orthodox theologian. Works: PG 78:9–1674. BIBLIOGRAPHY: Quasten 3:180–185; Butler 1:249; J. M. Sauguet, BiblSanct 7:967–971.

[R. B. ENO]

ISIDORE OF SEVILLE, ST. (*c.*560–636), abp., Doctor of the Church. After his parents' death, I. was educated under the care of his older brother *Leander, then a monk and later I.'s predecessor in the See of Seville. As abp. I. sought to strengthen Catholicism against the Arians and to this purpose encouraged and commanded the founding of schools, esp. for the education of the clergy. During his tenure of office several noteworthy synods were held, the most important of which was the Fourth Council of Toledo (633) which established liturgical uniformity in Spain, brought Church and State into closer union, and did much to weld the various peoples of the Hispano-Gothic kingdom into a homogeneous nation. I. was one of the most learned men of his time. His numerous works have all been preserved. They are important less for what they contain than for their great influence in the Middle Ages. His *Etymologiae* in 20 books is a general encyclopedia and summary of all the learning of the time, valuable on that account rather than for the etymologies proper, which are often defective and fanciful. Smaller works of the same kind are *Synonyma, De differentiis rerum,* and *De differentiis verborum.* In the field of history, I., drawing upon Julius Africanus, Eusebius, Jerome, and Victor of Tunnuna, produced his *Chronicon,* a world history up to the year 615. His *History of the Kings of the Goths, Vandals and Swabians* is valuable for the early history of Spain. Like Jerome and Gennadius, I. also wrote a *De viris illustribus.* His several excursions into biblical exegesis show a propensity for allegorical and mystical interpretations. The doctrinal writings of I. include three books of *Sentences,* a general doctrinal work, the forerunner of many of its kind in the Middle Ages. He also wrote a history of heresies and a work on the liturgy of Spain, *De ecclesiasticis officiis.* Although there is little originality in I., his accomplishment by way of summary and conservation was a distinguished one and most necessary for his time. He was named a Doctor of the Church in 1722. Works: PL 81–84. BIBLIOGRAPHY: A. Humbert, NCE 7.674–676; Altaner 594–598; K. Baus, LTK 5:786–787; LexAW 410–411; J. Fontaine, *Isidore de Séville et la culture classique dans l'Espagne wisigothique* (2 v., 1959); Butler 2.26–27.

[R. B. ENO]

ISIDORIANA, see HISPANA COLLECTIO.

ISIS AND OSIRIS, Egyptian divinities. By the early 3d millennium B.C. Osiris was a royal god of waxing and waning in nature, with Isis as his sister-wife. By the 2d millennium Osiris had become an important figure in popular religion, with ideas of afterlife centering around assimilation to him. Isis, already the faithful wife and mother, came to be concerned for all the dead as she was for Osiris. In the earliest form of the Osirian myth, Osiris was drowned in the Nile; his body was recovered by Isis and he became the king of the underworld, while his son Horus (with whom the pharaohs were identified) assumed the rule of Egypt. Secondary additions to the mythological cycle were the role of Seth in Osiris' death and bodily dismemberment, Isis' quest for the body, the conflict between Seth and Horus. The cult of Isis, transformed into a mystery-cult, became esp. popular throughout the Greco-Roman world, where Osiris was identified with Serapis. BIBLIOGRAPHY: H. Bonnet, *Reallexikon der ägyptischen Religionsgeschichte* (1952) 326–332, 568–576.

[A. CODY]

ISLA (Y ROJO), JOSÉ FRANCISCO DE (1703–81), Spanish Jesuit, novelist, satirist. Entering the Society in 1719, he was ordained and taught at Segovia, Santiago, and Pamplona. When the Jesuits were expelled from Spain he went to Bologna, Italy, where he was befriended for the remainder of his life by Count Tedeschi. I. was a famous preacher himself, and in 1758 he wrote a celebrated satire on pulpit oratory, *Historia del famoso predicator Fray Gerundio,* immediately popular but condemned by the Inquisition in 1760. The second volume appeared 18 years later. In Italy I. did his admirable translation of *Gil Blas* by Le Sage, for some unaccountable reason claiming that he was restoring the original, a claim not true. The book was issued after his death. His *Cartas Familiares* (6 v.) is a collection of lively letters.

[J. R. AHERNE]

ISLAM, the religion, counting presently well over 300 million adherents, founded upon the *Koran as the scripture revealed to the Prophet *Mohammed. The term Islam (Arab. *'islâm*) is the infinitive of the verb *'aslama,* "to submit totally [to God]." Already in the Koran the word is used formally to designate the religion taught therein; e.g., "Today I have perfected for you your religion and have completed my blessing upon you; I have approved Islam as your religion" (5.3; cf. also 3.19). The participle of this verb is *muslim* (i.e., the one who submits completely to God) by which term the followers of Islam are called. The practice, common in European languages, of referring to Islam as Mohammedanism and to its followers as Mohammedans is in some respects offensive to Islamic doctrine.

Within a century of the death of the Prophet the power of Islam had spread far beyond the Arabian peninsula, extending from the Atlantic coasts of Spain and North Africa eastward as far as Ferghana in Transoxiana (now in the Uzbek S.S.R.) and across the Indus River into Sind (present-day West Pakistan). Islam is currently the predominant religion throughout North Africa, the Near and Middle East, the Sudan, Iran, the Kazakh, Uzbek, Turkmen, Tadzhik, and Kirgiz Republics of the U.S.S.R., in Afghanistan, Pakistan, Kashmir, in Sinkiang province of China, and southeastwards into the Malay Peninsula and Archipelago: in Malaysia, Sumatra, Java, and Borneo. There are strong Muslim minorities in Albania, India, the southern Philippines, in Somalia, Mozambique, Madagascar, and Nigeria, and its influence is expanding rapidly in both East and West Africa.

Ever since the election of *Ali, the fourth caliph, Islam has been torn by theological and political dissension. The principal division in Islam remains that between the *Shiites, who hold that the caliphate belongs only to the descendants of the Prophet, and the orthodox or *Sunnites, who affirm that the caliphate belongs to Quraysh, Mohammed's tribe. There is no centrally organized religious authority or magisterium in Islam and for this reason its character varies sometimes widely from traditional norms, esp. in areas of Africa and the Far East where it has only recently taken root and mixtures of pagan and Islamic practice still mingle.

The primary religious obligations, called the "pillars (*arkân*) of Islam," incumbent upon every Muslim are five: (1) to pronounce the *shahâda* or testimony, "There is no God but God and Mohammed is the Apostle of God"; to utter this formula before a witness is sufficient to make one legally a Muslim. (2) The ritual prayer (*ṣalât*), which is performed five times a day (at dawn, noon, afternoon, sundown, and evening) facing *Mecca. In larger towns the times for prayer are announced by a *muezzin. The prayer is an individual obligation and may be performed in any place, save at noon on Fridays when the faithful are obligated to attend, if possible, the public service in the mosque. (3) Almsgiving: the alms known as *zakât* or *ṣadaqa* (both terms occur in the Koran) are given in a fixed percentage, varying according to the goods on which they are levied, in different proportions according to the several law schools. The *zakât* is given to the community for the use of the community and, from the earliest times, has constituted, in effect, a tax levied by the government upon the faithful; it is, in fact, the only tax which has official sanction of the religious law, though many other taxes and duties (*mukûs*) have inevitably been collected by Muslim states. (4) The fast during the month of *Ramadan. (5) To make the pilgrimage (*hajj,) to Mecca at least once in his lifetime is incumbent upon every Muslim who is capable of it. To contribute to the spread of Islam (*jihad) has been considered by some as a sixth "pillar." Faith *(îmân),* which is sometimes distinguished from *'islâm,* is generally held to consist in belief "in God, his angels, his Scriptures, his prophets, and the resurrection after death" together with at least a minimal fulfillment of the cultic and moral prescriptions of the law, though the community was sorely divided over this matter in the early centuries (see MURJI'ITES and KHARIJITES). Islam recognizes the basic validity of Judaism and Christianity and conceives, in conformity with the teaching of the Koran, that Mohammed, "The Seal of the Prophets," was sent with essentially the same message as that of Abraham, Moses, John the Baptist, and Jesus (who is held to be simply a prophet), as well as of the other prophets, to reaffirm this message against the distortions *(taḥrîf)* and innovations that had crept into them and to bring the essential message to its final and perfect form. The distinctive focus of Islam is on the Koran and the Prophet. The Koran holds a relatively more important place in Islam than do the Scriptures either in Judaism or in Christianity. It is considered by orthodox Muslims to be the verbatim, uncreated "speech of God" *(kalâm Allâh)* and, because of the power of its language has from the very beginning been held to be the unique miracle that confirms the divine origin of Mohammed's mission and teaching. Orthodox doctrine adheres remarkably to the text of the Koran and its recitation is one of the most common forms of popular devotion. For all essential matters of religion not explicitly set forth in the Koran the Prophet is considered the source and the model. His actions and words as the norm and model for the believers, individually and as a community, are called Sunna and these are embodied in the written form of reports or traditions (*Hadith), which though not strictly considered revealed have canonical authority. The formal religious law of Islam (see ISLAMIC LAW) is based on the Koran and the Sunna; some authorities give precedence to the latter, considering it to be the sole criterion for the interpretation of the revelation.

All men, the Koran says, before their creation were made to testify to God's lordship and, according to orthodox belief, each person is examined in his tomb by two angels, Munkar and Nakîr, concerning the basic articles of faith. Subsequently, on a day known to God alone, after the coming of the *Mahdi, there will be a general resurrection (*ba'ṯ, qiyâma, ma'âd*) when the deeds of all men will be judged and weighed in the balance (*mîzân*), whereupon they will be divided into two main groups, "those of the right" and "those of the left," the former going into eternal fire and the latter into "the Garden" *(al-janna)*. Most orthodox authorities affirm that through the intercession *(shafâ'a)* of the Prophet for his followers, all Muslims not guilty of outright apostasy or idolatry will enter paradise. Some schools hold that the pains of hell are eternal for all men who once enter there, but others assert that after an appropriate period of chastisement most believers, if not all, will be released from the fire into blessedness. There is also disagreement as to whether the pleasures of paradise, depicted in the Koran and Hadith are to be interpreted in a literal or purely spiritual sense.

Islamic law touches, in theory, every aspect of the believer's life, but since, in practice, most matters of public law were from an early period brought under the jurisdiction of various civil authorities, Sharia, the religious law, primarily affects matters of ritual, family, and inheritance. The Koran forbids gambling and the drinking of wine (*ḫamr*) and three of the four schools of law have extended the latter prohibition to include all intoxicants. Though there is much variation of detail among the schools of law, the dietary laws are basically these: unless constrained by necessity a Muslim may not eat anything sacrificed to an idol, pork, or the flesh of carnivorous animals (whether mammals or birds), nor may he eat blood or carrion (*mayta*: basically any animal not slaughtered or taken in hunting). A Muslim may not eat the food of pagans and it is preferred that he not eat that prepared by Christians or Jews. The basic Koranic legislation in these matters resembles somewhat the Jewish regulations but in origin most probably derives from common Semitic practice current among the pagan Arabs. A Muslim is allowed to marry four wives and may keep as many slave women (see ISLAMIC SLAVERY) as he can afford. Children born to him by a slave woman, if recognized, have equal status with children born of his legitimate wife and inherit equally with them. Marriage, which requires the consent of both parties, is legitimated through a formal contract negotiated generally by the bride's "agent" (*walî*), most often a male relative, and a member of the husband's family and through the husband's giving a stipulated bride-price (*mahr*); it may be terminated at any time simply by the husband's pronouncing the formula of talak or divorce (Arab. *ṭalâq*), following which the woman, after a specified period (*'idda*), generally 3 months, is free to remarry. The Shiites allow temporary marriage, called *mut'a,* the length of which is specified in the contract.

The Prophet was the political chief of the Muslim community and following his death, they elected a successor (or *caliph) for him. With the rise of the Abbasid caliphate (750), however, the process already begun under the Umayyad caliphs of Damascus (661–750) of turning the caliphate into an oriental monarchy was completed. Nonetheless, the caliph remained, in theory at least, the temporal and spiritual leader of Islam. Islam constitutes a people or community (*umma*) and all Muslims are supposed, if possible, to live under the rule of a Muslim government that will facilitate the fulfillment of the religious duties of the individual and the community. Since it is the obligation of the community to spread Islam by all means available and theoretically, therefore, the Muslim state may not be at peace with the governments of the nonbelievers, the world is canonically divided into the "region of Islam" (*dâr al-Islâm*) and the "region of war" *(dâr al-ḥarb*), though, again according to classical legal theory, a truce may be negotiated with a state ruled by "people of the Scripture" *(ahl al-kitâb),* i.e., Christians or Jews. Christians or Jews living under Muslim rule are classed as "protected people" (*ahl al-dhimma*) or *dhimmîs* and have, as such, somewhat the status of permanent subject aliens. Through the *dhimma* they are entitled to the protection of the State and to the regulation of their internal affairs through their own religious courts. They are, however, subject to a special poll tax (the *jizya*) and a special tax (the *ḥarâj*) on the produce of their lands. In actual practice, there has been considerable variation in the tolerance shown to religious minorities.

Already in the 9th cent. the Islamic empire was breaking up and the real authority of the caliph diminishing, as he became progressively dominated by his officers, most often Turkish mercenaries, and was forced to recognize the *de facto* power of numerous independent princes and *sultans. Constitutional theory accommodated itself to this state of affairs. Genuine religious authority ever remained with the *ulema, for Islamic religious tradition had, from the earliest times, looked upon government as something evil and corruptive of religion. Consequently the termination of the caliphate with the Mongol invasions in the 13th cent. did not per se produce any radical change in the real structure of religious authority in Islam. Sunnite Islam had from early times produced a diversity of theological schools (see ISLAMIC THEOLOGY); of these, the four main trends were represented by the conservative or fundamentalist traditionists (see HADITH), most notably the *Hanbalites, by the "orthodox" Ash'arites, the *Mutazilites, and the Sufis (see SUFISM). Though the Mutazilites enjoyed the favor of the government briefly in the 9th cent., traditionism which had always held the greatest popular support, gained almost complete predominance over the Mutazilites and Ash'arites in the 11th century. From this time too, Sufism, in both orthodox and nonorthodox forms, grew in importance and influence and from the 13th cent. on—in part in reaction to the ever more oppressive government of foreign rulers—the anti-intellectual trends of traditionism and Sufi mysticism held almost total dominance of the religious consciousness of Islam.

The expansion of European influence and colonialism in the East began, from the 19th cent., to have a profound impact on Islam as Muslims came more and more to reflect on their economic and political subordination to the great Western powers and their universal scientific and technological backwardness. The reform movement, originating first in India, combined a program of anticolonialism and a major effort to effect social and educational reform within the context of Islam. The primary impediment to social reform and religious renewal, responsible for the general stagnation of Islamic culture, was seen to be the ulema's insistence on *taqlîd* (obligatory doctrinal submission to established school tradition) and the wide influence of the Sufi congregations, while the influence of Western "materialism," present in the institutions of the colonial governments, was conceived as a threat to the very principles of Islam. The true founder of both the modernist movement and of Islamic nationalism was *Jamâl al-Dîn al-Afghânî (d. 1897), who initiated the movement known as the *Salafiya* (from Arab. *salaf,* the ancestors). This movement, continued by *Mohammed 'Abduh (d. 1905) and Rashîd Riḍâ (d. 1935) published an influential journal, *al-Manâr,* in which they sought to establish their interpretation of the Koran and to reopen "the gate of free interpretation" (*bâb al-ijtihâd*) of the Koran and Sunna. Despite a rather bold beginning, in the end the theology of the Salafîya tended towards a Hanbalite conservatism, though it remained far more liberal than the reactionary doctrine of the *Muslim Brethren. Reform movements, many of them similar to the *Salafiya,* such as the Mohammediya in Indonesia, have spread throughout most of Islam in the 20th century. One of the most influential of all reformers was Mohammed Iqbal (d. 1938), whom Pakistanis consider the father of their country.

In general, because of a common hesitancy to make a genuine critique of the content and value of the traditional sources of orthodox dogma or to review the question of the nature of the Koranic revelation, the modernization of Muslim theological thought has made little progress. The most significant effort has been in terms of political and social doctrine but here the actual changes in society, law, and economics go forward independently of the religious theorists and the new constitutions tend to be purely secular, based on Western models. The Turkish constitution of 1928 is completely secular, giving to Islam no official recognition at all. The majority of reformers claim ijma, or consensus (Arab. *ijmâ'*) as the ground and justification for their ideas but it is difficult to say for how much of the community they speak. With the rapid spread of Islam in Africa and the Far East, diversity increases and a religious center in a reconstituted caliphate, having exclusively religious authority, suggested by Rashîd Riḍâ, has found no acceptance. BIBLIOGRAPHY: H. A. R. Gibb, *Mohammedanism* (1949); *idem, Modern Trends in Islam* (1947, repr. 1971); G. E. von Grünebaum, *Medieval Islam* (1946); *idem, Modern Islam* (1962); Fazlur Rahman, *Islam* (1966); *Islam* (*Religion in the Middle East* 2, ed. A. J. Arberry, 1969); P. M. Holt, et al., *Cambridge History of Islam* (2 v., 1970); F. E. Peters, *Allah's Commonwealth* (1973); bibliog. in EncCatt 7:293.

[R. M. FRANK]

ISLAMIC ART. The principal achievement of Islamic religious art is the mosque (*masjid*), and its most exclusive accomplishment is the development of calligraphy as a decorative style. The mosque reflects the integral relationship between the social organization and the religious faith of Islam. It is marked by great congregational space, orientation toward Mecca, the tall minaret (*minar*) for summoning to prayer, and a pulpit-like place within for the *imam* who leads prayers. Later were added an interior niche to accentuate the direction toward Mecca and a screen to indicate the prince's place. Types of mosques include the Romano-Byzantine, as in Syria (Damascus); the great hall with columns, as in Egypt and Spain (Córdoba); the courtyard with vaults and arcades, as in Iran (Isfahan); and the central plan, derived from Christian churches after 1453. The basic design of a court surrounded by halls derives from the house of the Prophet in Medina. The huge outer gates of some mosques show the direct influence of palace architecture.

Islamic art has expressed itself also in small mosques, educational institutions, and memorials, among the earliest of which is the Dome of the Rock in Jerusalem. The most spectacularly lovely architectural form of impressive grandeur is the *Taj Mahal in India. Decoration of architecture and religious articles with words and phrases from the Koran, beautifully and intricately inlaid, evidence the preeminence of calligraphy as a decorative art deriving principally from Moslem reverence for the text of the holy Koran. BIBLIOGRAPHY: K. A. C. Creswell, *Bibliography of the Architecture, Arts and crafts of Islam to 1st Jan., 1960* (1961), O. Grabar, NCE 7:684–689.

[L. P. SIGER]

ISLAMIC LAW, the basic law of *Islam, considered by Muslims to be divinely ordained, called the Sharia (Arab., *Sharî'a* sometimes also *Shar'*). The science that studies its sources and applications is called *fiqh* and the specialist in its study is called *faqîh* (pl. *fuqahâ'*).

Since the *Koran contains few specific legal prescriptions, the judges or Cadis (*Qâḍî*, pl. *quḍâ*) appointed by the earliest caliphs acted on the basis of local customs, using their own prudential judgment (*ra'y*), so that, from the outset, Islamic law took on many diverse elements of Arabian custom, Byzantine and Roman provincial law, and also some Talmudic and Sassanian elements. By the beginning of the 8th cent. A.D., Islamic law began to take on its distinctive character, as local practice was examined in the light of Islamic religious principles. The development of law in each area reflected the social and cultural background of the region and specific doctrines were generally attributed to the Prophet (especially in Medina) or to important "companions" (*ṣaḥâba, aṣḥâb*) of the Prophet or their "successors" (*tâbi 'ûn*) who had settled in the locality. Most early legal material, consequently, comes to us in the form of traditions (see HADITH). In the latter part of the 8th cent. we find the beginnings of the major schools, those of abû Hanîfa (d. 767) in Iraq and Mâlik ibn Anas (d. 795) in Medina. Subsequently, a disciple of the Medina tradition, al-Shâfi 'î (d. 820), the true founder of Islamic jurisprudence, succeeded in imposing almost universally the traditionist thesis that *sunna* (i.e., established custom as morally and legally binding) could be determined only on the basis of traditions from the Prophet. Rejecting the use of *ra'y* altogether, he insisted on a systematic use of kiyas, or analogy (*qiyâs*), in studying the data of the *Koran* and *sunna*. Later, one of his students, Aḥmad ibn Ḥanbal (d. 855; see HANBALITES) went further to restrict even the use of analogy and thereafter another school, that of the Zâhirites, went so far as to reject the use of analogy altogether, insisting on adherence to the literal sense (*al-ẓâhir*) of the canonical sources completely. By the end of the 9th cent., the four orthodox or *Sunnite schools or rites (*maḏhab, pl. maḏâhib*) of jurisprudence (Hanafite, Malikite, Shafi'ite, and Hanbalite) were commonly recognized, and within a short time it became generally accepted opinion that the elaboration of the law through the exercise of independent judgment (*ijtihâd*) was no longer permissible, but that the followers of each school had to give unquestioning adherence (*taqlîd*) to the principles of the founder. Some development continued nonetheless as the decisions of individual *muftis were incorporated into the tradition of particular schools. Despite their significant differences, the four schools are agreed on al-Shâfi'î's definition of the four "principles" *(uṣûl)* of *fiqh*, viz, the Koran, the Sunna (as established in the canonical Hadith), consensus *(ijma),* and analogy, ijma being the principle by which one knows what is juridically binding in the Koran, and Sunna and kiyas the method of its application to particular cases.

The Sharia is considered by the Muslims to consist of a set of divine ordinances (*aḥkâm Allâh*) which as such cannot (save in the thinking of the *Mutazilites) be rationally explained or justified. Since the mind of the lawgiver cannot be known, one is free to employ any casuistic device *(ḥîla)* to avoid its prescriptions. The *fiqh* divides all acts into two basic classes, religious acts (*'ibâdât*) and nonreligious acts *(mu'âmalât)*. All acts are juridically divided into five categories: (1) the obligatory (*farḍ*), including what is obligatory on every believer (*farḍ al-'ayn*) and what is obligatory on the community as a whole (*farḍ al-kifâya*); (2) what is praiseworthy but not obligatory (*sunna*), as recommended, preferable, or supererogatory; (3) what is indifferent (*mubâḥ*); (4) what is blameworthy (*makrûh*); and (5) what is absolutely forbidden (*ḥarâm*).

In practice, as the *fiqh* became more and more strictly elaborated as a religious law, it tended to lose touch with many practical problems and, from the beginning of Abbasid times, although cadis were appointed in each city, their actual jurisdiction became restricted. Criminal law and most matters of commerce and finance were taken under the jurisdiction of the police and other administrative officials operating under non-Sharia laws (*qânûn*, pl. *qawânîn)* enacted by the government, so that in the end the Sharia courts came to deal almost exclusively with religious obligations and matters of family, marriage, and inheritance. The prestige of the Sharia, however, as the divinely revealed law of Islam remained undiminished and as non-Sharia laws and regulations were looked upon by pious men as indications of the corruption of the religious purity of the community, many religious persons, even from a quite early period, refused to accept appointment to public office.

The law of the *Kharijites and of the *Shiites does not differ radically from that of the orthodox Sunnites, save in matters concerning the head of the community (see IMAM). In the case of the Shiites, however, this involves a profound difference of attitude, since whereas the Sunnites hold that the community is the guardian of the law and the guarantor of its authoritative interpretation through ijma, they hold that only the divinely designated imam could hold this position.

From the 19th cent. a tendency has arisen to promulgate codes based on European models and in recent years the Sharia courts have been abandoned altogether in a number of Muslim countries. BIBLIOGRAPHY: J. Schacht, *Introduction to Islamic Law* (2d ed., 1966); N. J. Coulson, *History of Islamic Law (Islamic Surveys* 2, 1964).

[R. M. FRANK]

ISLAMIC PHILOSOPHY, in Arabic termed *falsafa* (a loan word based ultimately on the Gr. *philosophia*), the philosopher being called *failasûf* (pl. *falâsifa*), though frequently the terms *ḥikma* (wisdom) and hakim (Arab. *hakîm* pl. *ḥukamâ'*) are used in the same sense. In *Islam *falsafa* is distinct and separate from speculative theology (*kalâm*; see ISLAMIC THEOLOGY) as the two rest upon quite different sources and are developed in comparative independence, representing quite divergent attitudes in almost all fundamental matters. The *falsafa* is rooted in Greek philosophy which was transmitted and, for the most part, translated by Christians, most significantly those of the school of the Nestorian Ḥunain ibn Isḥâq (d. after 870). The process of translation and study of the Greek heritage began early in the Abbasid age; a number of works of the Aristotelian corpus and other works, including the pseudo-*Theology of Aristotle* (a work based on the *Enneades* of Plotinus) were put into Arabic before 850 and within a century not only the works of Aristotle but those also of Alexander of Aphrodisias, Themistius, Simplicius, John Philoponus, Galen, and many others had been rendered in excellent translations. Filtered as it was through the end of the Hellenistic age, the Greek philosophical tradition was presented to Islam as a single, basically unified system, Aristotelian in its form but containing a heavy admixture of Neoplatonism and already adapted to theological perspectives. The Muslims, thus, viewed "philosophy" as a single system elaborated by Plato, perfected by Aristotle (under whose name they had some of Plotinus), and further elaborated in matters of detail by successive generations of commentators. Because of its apparent unity as presented in the contemporary tradition, they saw philosophy as giving the rational, analytic structure of the universe; i.e., as the one (and so necessary and true) description of the nature of the universe discovered by reason or mind (*'aql*) without the aid of divine revelation. The Muslim *falâsifa* then began to study and carry on this tradition with an Islamic context to which certain of its elements and vocabulary had inevitably to be adapted; the system was in some respects, however, inseparable from a basically Greek view of the universe; and a thoroughgoing commitment to the system in its unity demanded a proportionate commitment to a universe, some of whose essential structures and underlying principles were altogether alien to the native Arab and Islamic intuition of the nature of being and the universe, which was elaborated in the classical *kalâm*. Among these elements are the doctrines of the nature of "form" (Arab. *ṣûra,* Gr. *eidos*) and "matter" (Arab. *hayûlâ, mâdda*), that of the nature of the "soul" (*nafs*) and intellect (*'aql*), their interrelations and cosmological functions, etc., as also of great importance for the Muslim philosophers was the Aristotelian logic which too was rejected by the classical kalâm and the traditionists (see HADITH). The system which had the widest and most profound influence within Islam is that elaborated by al-Fârâbî (d. 950) and Ibn Sînâ (Avicenna; d. 1037). Following Neoplatonic conceptions of the nature of the intellect and of God's unity, Avicenna conceives God's action as absolutely simple, necessitated by his nature from which there flows eternally first one and then a growing multitude of ever more complex beings in a descending ontological hierarchy. The being of all beings is, he holds, either "necessary in itself" (God) or "necessary through another" (everything else). In order to escape an unqualified monism, Avicenna holds a doctrine of the distinctness of a thing's "essence" (*ḏât*) from its "existence" (*wuǧûd*), a theory taken from the *kalâm*. Of perhaps even greater influence in later Islam is his psychology according to which the "agent intellect" (*al-'aql al-fa''âl*), the last in a series of separated celestial intelligences, illuminates, in varying degrees, according to their "aptness," the minds of all men and of the prophets in a special and immediate way. This doctrine was particularly significant in the development of later *Sufism. Somewhat parallel systems of *falsafa* were elaborated in the Islamic West by Ibn Bâjja (Avempace; d. 1138) and Ibn Ṭufail (d. 1185), while Ibn Rushd (Averroës; d. 1198), reacting against the heavy Neoplatonization of Avicenna's system, sought to return to a more strictly Aristotelian philosophy. The *falsafa* was condemned as heretical by most orthodox authorities, and as manifested in its foremost proponents, seems to die out after the 12th cent., but its influence becomes ever more widespread in the later periods as, in one direction, it is transformed and integrated into the doctrines of various Sufis and, in another, is taken up by later orthodox theologians such as al-Ghazzâlî (*Algazel), a violent opponent of the Avicennan system, *Fakhr al-Dîn al-Râzî and others, including the great historian, Ibn Khaldûn. BIBLIOGRAPHY: T. J. de Boer, *History of Philosophy in Islam* (1903); *History of Islamic Philosophy* (ed. M. M. Sharif, 1963–66); R. Arnaldez, EncIslam², s.v. "Falâsifa" and "Falsafa"; M. Fakhry, *History of Islamic Philosophy* (1970).

[R. M. FRANK]

ISLAMIC THEOLOGY, the speculative theology that is native to *Islam and is referred to in Arabic by the term *kalâm* (discourse), a word taken, in this technical sense, from Greek *dialexis*, as it was used by the Stoa. The earliest theological debates in Islam centered around the questions of faith (which involves the notion of belonging to the Muslim community) and of the imamate (see IMAM), which was the focus of the contentions of the *Shiites and the *Kharijites. Though according to tradition a speculative system of theology, seemingly founded on a Neoplatonist model, was propounded by Jahm ibn Ṣafwân (d. 746) and although the *Mutazilite school was in some sense founded before 750, we have no clear view of Islamic theological speculation before the year 800, about which time a number of diverse systems appear, already well elaborated. The most important masters of this period were abû l-Hudhayl (d. *c.*840 at the age of nearly 100), al-Naẓẓâm (d. before 845), both of whom were Mutazilites, Ḍirâr ibn 'Amr (d. *c.*815), and the more orthodox Ibn Kullâb (d. *c.*854).

From the beginnings, the various systems that were attempted show a building of diverse elements, eclectically chosen from past traditions, Greek and Christian, tending in the main to follow a fundamentally Stoic pattern in their conception of created (i.e., material) reality and a more Aristotelian or Neoplatonic conception of the being of God and his attributes. The most important traditions were those of the school of al-Jubbâ'î (d. 815) and his son abû Hâshim (d. 833) in the Mutazila and that founded by abû l-Hasan al-Ash'arî (d. 935) which in significant elements of its essential dogmatic theses seems to follow the thought of Ibn Kullâb. While the *Ash'arites, who came progressively to be associated with the Shafi'ite school of jurisprudence (see ISLAMIC LAW) constituted the predominant orthodox school of *kalâm*, that of al-Mâturîdî (d. 944), associated almost exclusively with the Hanafite tradition and, in most essential elements, closely akin to the Ash'arite theology, flourished for many centuries in the easternmost provinces where the Hanafite school was strong. The religious teaching of the traditionist jurists and, esp. in the later cent., of the *sufis was far more influential in Islam than was the *kalâm*, so that rational theology never held as important a place in Islamic culture as it did in the Christian tradition. Despite their open hostility to rational theology, the *Hanbalites nevertheless counted among them some of the greatest theologians of Islam, most notably perhaps the great polemicist Ibn Taymîya (d. 1328), as did also the Ẓâhirites (see ISLAMIC LAW) in the great poet theologian Ibn Ḥazm of Córdoba (d. 1064).

The history of the *kalâm* can be divided into three periods, that of its formation up to the end of the 9th cent., the classical period, embracing the 10th and 11th cent., and the period of its Hellenization from the 12th cent. until the demise of the *kalâm*. The main schools of *kalâm* of the classical period, opposing the Aristotelian and Neoplatonic character of late Hellenistic philosophy (*falsafa*), considered all being other than God to be material, composed of an atomistic substrate with its inherent qualities or accidents. Considerable attention was devoted to the problem of reasoning by analogy from the (material) "phenomenal" to the (immaterial) "nonphenomenal."

Although the Ash'arites and the Mutazilites were in fundamental agreement on the conception of the metaphysical structure of the material world, the way in which they handled the central theological problems diverged widely. Where the Ash'arites held that God's attributes are subsistent perfections in his essence, the Mutazilites taught that God's essential attributes are modalities of his being as it exists in itself and that his attributes of action are contingent perfections. God's names, according to the Ash'arites, are perfections or attributes of his being that are made known through revelation, but according to the Mutazilites, they are simply names applied to him because of their appropriateness, as established by convention and reason.

Similarly the Ash'arites held that speech, strictly defined, is the unarticulated understanding of the speaker that underlies the verbalization, and accordingly they held that God's speech (i.e., the Koran) is an essential attribute of his being. The Mutazilites, on the contrary, defined speech as phonemes that are articulated according to human convention and so taught that God's speech is created. Finally, whereas the Ash'arites, like the traditionists (see HADITH), held that the good and the just consist simply in what God commands and evil in what he forbids, the Mutazilites insisted that moral right and wrong are known universally by intuition and reason and that God, too, is bound to do what is just and good.

At the end of the 11th cent. the Mutazila began to pass out of existence as a living tradition while the orthodox theology of the Ash'arites and the Mâturîdites, moved by apologetic needs and the increasing popularity of Sufism, began to turn for inspiration towards the philosophical tradition that had been rejected by the earlier *kalâm* and so took on a more Aristotelian appearance. For a brief period the *kalâm* seems to have a new life with a number of great theologians, among them the Ash'arites, abû Ḥâmid al-Ghazzâlî, known in the West as *Algazel (d. 1111), al-Shahrastânî (d. 1053) and Fakhr al-Dîn al-Râzî (d. 1206), and the Mâturîdite, al-Nasafî (d. 1142), but the *kalâm* had passed into senescence and declined into a long series of pedantic handbooks and commentaries such as those of the Ash'arite al-Jurjânî (d. 1413) and the Mâturîdite, al-Taftâzânî (d. 1390).

Except in the doctrine of the imamate the theology of the moderate Shiites tends to follow that of the Mutazilites very closely. There have been, since the 19th cent., a number of attempts by various authors, all of whom have been much influenced by modern Western thought, to revive theological thought in Islam, but it is not yet possible to speak of a coherent trend in modern Muslim religious thought. The most important of the modern reformers are Jamâl al-Dîn al-Afghânî (d. 1897), his follower, the Egyptian Mohammed 'Abduh (d. 1905), and Mohammed Iqbal, (d. 1938), the great poet, statesman, and religious thinker, who was, in a sense, the founder of Pakistan. BIBLIOGRAPHY: L. Gardet and G. Anawati, *Introduction à la théologie musulmane* (1948); A. S. Tritton, *Muslim Theology* (1947); W. M. Watt, *Islamic Philosophy and Theology* (Islamic Surveys 1, 1962); *idem, Formative Period of Islamic Thought* (1973); J. R. T. M. Peters, *God's Created Speech* (1976).

[R. M. FRANK]

ISLAMIC TRADITION, see HADITH.

ISMAILIS (Arab., *al-Ismâ'îlîya*), one of the main branches of the *Shiites, commonly referred to as The "extremists of the Shî'a" by *Sunnites. The Ismailis takes its name from that of Mohammed ibn Ismâ'îl (d. 765) whom they consider as the seventh *Imam after *Ali. While professing a doctrine rather similar to that of orthodox Islam, they teach, according to various stages of initiation, an esoteric doctrine heavily influenced by Neoplatonism, Neopythagoreanism, and Hermetic Gnosticism. They have been the chief exponents of alchemy in Islam and have played a great role in the development of the exact sciences. Their basic religious doctrine seems to originate in the propaganda of abû l-Khaṭṭâb (d. 755), who taught that God was somehow immanent in the Imam. After the death of Mohammed ibn Ismâ'îl, his adherents split into two main branches one (called the "seveners" and later the *Karmatians) who held that he was the last and hidden Imam and the other, the *Fatimids, who held that the imamate passed on to one of the sons of Mohammed ibn Ismâ'îl. Both branches spread extensively from the end of the 9th century. Later, the Imam 'Ubaid Allâh (d. 934) proclaimed himself the *Mahdi and established a dynasty that came to rule Egypt and N Africa for many years. From this dynasty there arose a number of subsects, including the *Druses and the *Nizâris among whose subdivisions are the Assassins of Syria and a number of groups still active in Persia, the Indian subcontinent, and East Africa. BIBLIOGRAPHY: H. Laoust, *Les Schismes dans L'Islam* (1965); B. Lewis, *Origins of Ismailism* (1940); S. M. Stern, "Ismā'īlīs and Qarmatians," *L'Elaboration de l'Islam* (Colloque de Strasbourg, 12–14 juin 1959, pub. 1961) 99–114.

[R. M. FRANK]

ISNARD OF CHIAMPO, BL. (d. 1244), Dominican preacher and director of souls. A native of Chiampo in Vicenza, Italy, he received the Dominican habit from St. Dominic himself *c.*1219. In 1231 he founded and became prior of the Dominican foundation at Pavia. His life was one of prayer, study, preaching, and spiritual direction. He was regarded as a saint while he lived, and his cultus began immediately after his death and continued. The formal beatification decree was published in 1919. BIBLIOGRAPHY: L. Boyle, BiblSanct 7:986.

[T. C. O'BRIEN]

ISOCEPHALY, a convention in composition by which in figures of diverse positions all heads are placed in the same zone, effecting an impressive harmony and serenity. Isocephaly was used significantly in classical Greek art in the Panathenaic frieze of the Parthenon where enthroned deities, mounted youths, and watercarriers on foot present heads in one zone, with no violent distortion of form nor agitation to the spectator, realizing the noble Greek ideal of grandeur and serenity, aesthetic qualities inherent in isocephaly, no matter the period.

[M. J. DALY]

ISOCRATES (436–338 B.C.), Greek educator and publicist. Highly trained in rhetoric in the tradition of *Prodicus, *Gorgias, and *Protagoras, he worked for some time as a speech writer, but *c.*393 opened his own school as a professor of rhetoric at Athens and taught there for the rest of his life. He planned his school as a training center for political leaders. Unlike the less admirable sophists, he regarded rhetorical education as a kind of philosophy, and he insisted on the importance of ethics for both the teacher and pupil. His curriculum, with rhetoric as its capstone, was the fully developed *enkuklios paideia,* and he may be considered, if not the founder, at least the most influential promoter of the rhetorical or literary education that became the dominant form of education in antiquity. In fact, it was destined to remain the dominant form of modern education as well until the later part of the 19th century. In the field of education, his *To Demonicus* (374), and *To Nicocles* (372), were esp. important in Renaissance education, as is evidenced by their translation into Latin and into the chief vernacular languages of Europe. I. developed a rich periodic style, with emphasis on the use of figures and rhythm, and he exercised a marked influence on subsequent Greek prose and on Latin oratorical prose as well—in particular on that of Cicero. As a publicist, he attempted in his oratorical treatises to promote peace among the Greek states and friendly relations with Macedonia. He was the founder of encomiastic or epideictic oratory, of which his *Panathenaicus,* on the greatness of Athens, is an example. BIBLIOGRAPHY: J. F. Dobson, OCD 460–461; Marrou, *History of Education in Antiquity* (1956) 79–91; W. Jaeger, *Paedeia* 3 (1944) 46–155; R. R. Bolgar, *Classical Heritage and Its Beneficiaries* (1954), esp. 516–518.

[M. R. P. MCGUIRE]

ISOLATION, a term applied to two different *defense mechanisms first described by psychoanalysts. The more common phenomenon is the *repression of the affect or emotion connected with a wish or memory, e.g., the repression of the grief connected with the memory of the death of a loved person, or the affect connected with a sexual fantasy. Some people extend such repressions so far that their mental life becomes apparently almost emotionless. A less common form of isolation involves the separation of a thought from any preceding or following thoughts, by brief periods of mental blankness, a process that decreases the thought's chances of affecting consciousness.

[M. E. STOCK]

ISON, in *Byzantine chant notation, the sign indicating a repeated note.

ISORHYTHMIC, term applied to the repetition of the rhythmic pattern, but not necessarily the melody, of the tenor in 14th- and 15th-cent. French motets. The technique was developed by Philippe de Vitry.

[P. J. HENNESSEY]

ISRAEL, HISTORY OF. Modern scholars differ as to when the history of Israel as a nation truly begins but it seems a sound procedure, even on purely natural grounds, to regard it as commencing with the patriarchs and ending with the Roman period. The total span thus defined may be divided into 12 stages as follows:

1. The Patriarchs (*c.* 1800–1600). Texts discovered at Nuzi and Mari attest the fact that many of the social customs and institutions ascribed to the patriarchs Abraham, Isaac, and Jacob in Genesis 12–50 were indeed practiced by semi-nomadic peoples of precisely their type during the Middle Bronze age (*c.*2000–1550) and *not at any later stage.* Even on natural grounds, therefore, it seems reasonable to infer that the biblical accounts are substantially accurate. The message of these, reduced to its barest essentials, is that Israel's forebearers originated in Mesopotamia and thence journeyed to Palestine where they established themselves to some limited extent. Later some of them went to Egypt where, after an initial period of prosperity, their descendants were reduced to forced labor by the Egyptians.

2. Moses and the Exodus (*c.*1280–1260). Though the exact historical details are difficult to recapture, it is clear that as a result of events subsequently interpreted as divine portents Moses was enabled to lead a specific ethnic group of the semi-nomadic Semites, known to the Egyptians as the *hapiru,* out of Egypt to Mount Sinai. Here, in a striking experience the precise nature of which cannot be reconstructed from the biblical text, the God of their fathers manifested himself to them, bound them to himself in covenant and revealed his will to them. Subsequently, during a period of sojourning centered upon Kadesh-barnea, the implications of this central experience seem to have been drawn out to a point where Israel came to realize more fully her destiny as a chosen people consecrated in a unique sense to the God of the Patriarchs. They pledged themselves to the task of achieving his glory and their own happiness by faithfully fulfilling his will for them as revealed at Sinai and as expressed in his laws. Thus Israel as a people in the true sense was born.

3. Joshua and the Judges (*c.*1260–1040). Canaan, the land promised by Yahweh to his people, seems to have been weakened by internal conflicts and by invasions from the West by elements of the "sea peoples" shortly before the Israelites themselves made their incursion from the East. Thus extraneous factors contributed to the limited degree of success the Israelites achieved under Joshua in acquiring a firm foothold in the land. Groups of tribes within Israel at this time seem to have formed amphictyonies, loosely knit confederations of tribes bound together by a common religion and a central shrine, and pledged to assist one another against attacks by outsiders. The judges were charismatic leaders raised up from the individual tribes to deal with particular moments of crisis in the form of onslaughts from external foes. Their authority seems to have been limited to particular tribes or groups of tribes, and they never seem to have achieved a power that was either permanent or extending over all the tribes at once. Finally a particularly persistent and menacing enemy arose, the Philistines, and a new and more permanent form of leader came forward to meet a menace that had become endemic.

4. Saul (*c.*1040–1000). The introduction of kingship, regarded as un-Israelite and offensive to Yahweh by one important current of Israelite thought, entailed special difficulties for a people whose previous formation and development left so little room for this institutional type of leader. In attempting to maintain and ameliorate his position as king, Saul transgressed the covenant customs and laws and so, in spite of initial successes, failed to establish a lasting dynasty to survive him when he fell victim to the Philistines.

5. The Reign of David (*c.*1000–961). Where Saul had failed David succeeded. He established a lasting dynasty and made kingship a permanent institution in Israel. Among the factors contributing to his success were his establishment of a quasi-professional standing army independent of the tribal factions of N and S and owing allegiance only to himself. With this army he succeeded not merely in conquering the Philistines but in founding a sort of miniature empire, in which the small nations surrounding Judah were forced to pay tribute to him and accept some degree of subordination to him. Above all he conquered the Canaanite stronghold of Jerusalem which Joshua had failed to overcome, and which had been a key point of Canaanite resistance to Israel ever since. Now he not merely conquered this city, hitherto a sacred city of the Jebusites, but succeeded in making it the shrine of the ark, the symbol and focal point of Yahweh's covenant with the tribes. At the same time David himself became the divinely appointed guardian of the shrine and upholder of the traditions of the amphictyony. Situated as it was on neutral territory between the rival factions of the northern and southern tribes, Jerusalem was ideally suited to become the capital of the newly united kingdom. David's kingship, accepted and ratified by the men of Judah (2 Sam 2.4) and then by the elders of Israel (2 Sam 5.3), had long before been charismatically bestowed upon him by Samuel (cf. 1 Sam 16.12–13). Now it was further ratified by the oracle of Nathan (2 Sam 7.8–16) promising divine protection and guidance to himself and his "house" for ever. These are the main factors which enabled David to survive rebellions and intrigues on the part of his own sons, and his dynasty to survive as kings of Judah for more than 400 years.

6. The Reign of Solomon (961–922). The enormous prosperity which accrued to Solomon and his kingdom was owing in no small measure to the position of his kingdom on the route between Egypt and Phoenicia. This position enabled him to profit from the trade between these two powers, esp. in horses and chariotry; to build a fleet and enter into world commerce; and to develop a metal industry in the extreme S of his kingdom at Ezion-Geber. It also meant that his kingdom was open as never before to cultural influences from abroad, and above all from Egypt and Phoenicia. Indeed there are grounds for believing that at this period Israel was to some extent politically subject to Egypt. However it was precisely this increase in prosperity which enabled Solomon to consolidate the position of David's dynasty in their new role as guardians of the ark, and to build a temple for it in which the resources of Phoenician craftsmanship were so largely laid under contribution. At the same time the political and social structure of Israel was radically modified. Apart from the professional soldiers of the king's personal army, and the new class of merchants and capitalists which emerged, a new class of civil servants and professional administrators grew up, educated largely on Egyptian lines, to cater for the new centralized administration of the kingdom. Inevitably these innovations brought in their train numerous corruptions in the religious sphere, and also oppressions and exactions in the social sphere. Many were dispossessed from their land and forced into slavery, conscripted with the army, or taxed beyond endurance to pay for the king's grandiose schemes.

7. The Divided Kingdom to the Fall of Samaria (922–721). The attempts of Solomon's son Rehoboam to maintain, and even to intensify these exactions led to the 10 northern tribes, which had long constituted a distinct faction, breaking away from Judah and Benjamin in the south, choosing their own king Jeroboam, and eventually setting up their own independent capital at Samaria. This northern kingdom, which endured for about 200 years, was cut off from Jerusalem, the center of the orthodox religion of Yahweh, and thrown open to the corrupting influences of Phoenicia and Syria. The notorious bull or calf images set up by Jeroboam may have been due to Canaanite influence. Although the northern kingdom seems to have prospered (cf. Amos and Hosea), its political security was constantly disturbed by dynastic disputes and assassinations. Finally the entire kingdom was virtually obliterated by the Assyrians in 721.

8. The Survival of Judah Alone until Her Fall (720–587). Judah did not escape the savagery of the Assyrian attacks, but Jerusalem itself was spared by what appeared to be a miraculous dispensation. However, under the two worst of her kings, Manasseh and Amon, she seems very largely to have succumbed to Assyrian influence in the religious sphere. The successor to Amon, Josiah, undertook a far-reaching religious reform, and this seemed at first to bring a blessing on the nation. For with the waning of the Assyrian power he was able to reconquer a considerable extent of the old Davidic kingdom. But his religious and military successes were brought to an abrupt end with his death in battle at Megiddo in 609. The remaining history of Judah is a story of petty and disastrous intrigues against the new Babylonian power, culminating in the final defeat and sacking of Jerusalem in 587 and the deportation of the king and many of the people to Babylon.

9. The Exile and Restoration (587–538). Though this disaster evoked reactions of despair and disbelief on the part of some, others realized that in it the warnings of the Prophets had been fulfilled to the letter. Thus a new and even higher premium was set upon the revealed Word of God (this being taken to include both the Law and the Prophets). Inspired by this the Jewish exiles survived as a relatively united people still clinging to faith and hope in Yahweh who, through the mouth of the Prophets had promised them a future restoration. In 538 Cyrus, the conqueror of the short-lived Babylonian Empire, authorized and even actively encouraged the return of the Jews to Jerusalem, and this was naturally hailed as the fulfillment of the Prophets' promises and the inauguration of a new and more glorious epoch in Jewish history.

10. The Persian Period (538–333). Under the tolerant rule of the Persians the state of Judah was reconstituted and the temple and walls of Jerusalem itself were rebuilt. At this time a new danger to Israel arose, that of allowing the purity of its religion to be contaminated by intermarriage with inhabitants of mixed race who had occupied its territories during the Exile. Further religious and social reforms were carried out by Ezra and Nehemiah. At the same time a number of the Babylonian Jews who had not returned home began to join others in developing further communities in other parts of the Middle East, esp. Babylonia and Egypt. Thus the Diaspora was born, with its special emphasis on the synagogue form of worship developed during the Exile, and on the written word of God (as distinct from the temple cult) as the center of Jewish religious practice.

11. The Hellenistic Period (333–167). By 331 the Persian empire had suffered a crushing defeat at the hands of Alexander, but it was not until *c.*300, when Alexander's empire was divided up among his successors, the Diadochi, that Palestine was allotted to the Ptolemies of Alexandria, and so became directly involved in these world-shattering events. Another branch of the Diadochi, the Seleucids ruling from Antioch, claimed to be the lawful rulers of Palestine, which thus became disputed territory between the two dynasties. Even during the Persian era Greek cultural influences had made their impact, and under Alexander and the Diadochi the process was intensified. The Jewish community in particular was split into two groups, the progressives who wished to adapt the old faith to the new culture, and the conservatives who were anxious to preserve the purity of their Jewish religion and culture unalloyed. In 198 Palestine finally fell to the Seleucids and the reigning representative of these, *Antiochus IV Epiphanes, began to seek by every means in his power to force Greek cultural practices and Greek religious beliefs upon his Jewish subjects.

12. The Maccabeans and Hasmoneans (167–63). The attempt of Antiochus to erect a statue of Zeus Olympus in the Temple, to abolish circumcision, and to force the Jews to eat unclean food instigated the Maccabean revolt under the three brothers Judas (166–160), Jonathan (160–142) and Simon (142–134). This movement, brilliantly daring and successful as it was, was initially purely religious in inspiration but came progressively to be dominated by political motivations. In their struggle against the Seleucids the Maccabean leaders turned to Rome for help, thereby, though unwittingly, taking the first step towards subsequent domination by Rome. The descendants of Simon, the Hasmoneans as they are called, ruled Judah until Pompey's conquest of Judah and Jerusalem in 63 B.C. Largely secular in outlook and ambitions, the greatest of them, Alexander Jannaeus, succeeded in regaining the lost territories and extending his domain almost to the boundaries of the ancient kingdom of David. The reign of the Hasmoneans was ended by a dynastic dispute between two brothers, Hyrcanus II and Aristobulus, each of whom appealed to Pompey for arbitration. When Aristobulus refused to accept Pompey's decision, the latter attacked and took Jerusalem in 63 B.C. and made Judea part of the Roman province of Syria. BIBLIOGRAPHY: G. W. Anderson, *History and Religion of Israel, New Clarendon Bible,* (1966); J. Bright, *History of Israel* (1960).

[D. J. BOURKE]

ISRAELITE HOUSE OF DAVID, see HOUSE OF DAVID.

ISRAELITES (ABRAHAMITES), see ABRAHAMITES.

ISSACHAR, son of Jacob and Leah and father of one of the twelve tribes. It is said in Gen 30.18 that the name means: "God has paid me my wages."

[J. J. CASTELOT]

ISSOUDON FATHERS, see SACRED HEART MISSIONARIES.

ISSY, ARTICLES OF, the series of articles drawn up at Issy (1695) by J. B. *Bossuet, L. de *Noailles, and M. *Tronson acting as a commission to pass judgment on the doctrine of Mme. de *Guyon. These articles were directed against quietist errors contained explicitly or by implication in Mme. Guyon's writings, e.g., the uselessness of the prayer of petition; the idea that perfection should be sought through passive prayer rather than through positive acts of faith, good works, and the practice of virtue; the desirability of indifference to one's own salvation. Mme. de Guyon signed these articles, as did Bossuet and Fénelon, but their publication led to further trouble. Their ambiguity opened the door to the epic controversy between Bossuet and Fénelon. BIBLIOGRAPHY: R. Knox, *Enthusiasm* (1950) 337–352.

[P. K. MEAGHER]

IŠTAR, see ASTARTE.

ITA OF KILLEEDY, ST. (d. 569), also known as Ida, Ite, Ide, one of the most famous of the Irish women saints. She was born of the royal tribe of Daisi. With the consent of her father, she dedicated her virginity to God and went to Cluaincrudhail where she founded a religious community and kept a school for small boys, the most famous of her pupils being the great St. Brendan. The name Killeedy (Cill Ite) indicates today the site of her foundation. I. traveled much, participating in the affairs of the clan. The Ua Conaill who had given "land and protection" attributed a great military victory to her prayers. BIBLIOGRAPHY: AS, Jan. 1:1062–68; L. E. Boyle, BiblSanct 7:988; Butler 1:96–97.

[A. WARDLE]

ITALA (Vetus Itala), a name given to Latin versions of the Bible, but with a confusing variety of uses. The term comes from St. Augustine, who, in writing of Latin interpretations (i.e., versions), says *Itala caeteris praeferatur (De doctrina christiana,* 2.15). Critics have not succeeded in determining the text to which he refers. Some authors have used Itala to refer to all pre-Vulgate or *Old Latin versions, or at least for the European as distinct from the African family of texts. Others have sought to identify the *versio itala* as a text in use in N Italy. Others have identified it with the translation of the Gospels, Job, and Psalms made by St. Jerome (see VULGATE). Because of its ambiguity the term has lost acceptance. BIBLIOGRAPHY: F. C. Burkitt, *Old Latin and the Itala* (1896; repr. 1967); B. Botte, DBSuppl 4:777–782.

[D. J. BOURKE]

ITALO-ALBANIANS, a designation applied to the greater portion of the Italo-Greeks, Byzantine-rite Catholics scattered through S Italy and the neighboring islands of Sicily, Malta, and Corsica. The Italo-Albanians are chronologically the last great wave of Byzantine-rite immigrants from the Balkans. There had always been a large number of Greeks in S Italy (called *Magna Graecia* in ancient times) and Sicily, and at different times they came under the jurisdiction of the patriarch of Constantinople (as in 731). Beginning in the 11th cent., Roman jurisdiction was gradually restored throughout the region with the substantial help of the Norman invaders. However, after the Turkish conquest of the Balkans and the fall of Constantinople (1453), several thousand Eastern Christians took refuge in Italy. Albania, the nearest Balkan country across the Adriatic, provided most of the refugees. For several centuries these Byzantine-rite Christians, largely of Albanian origin, were subject to the local bishops and were encouraged, sometimes forced, to become Latins. A special congregation was established in Rome by Gregory XIII (1573) to take care of the "reform" of the Greeks. Several papal documents, now quoted for the Catholic Uniates in general, were actually issued for the Byzantine-rite Christians of S Italy (the *Etsi pastoralis* of Benedict XIV in 1742, the *Inter multiplices* of Clement XII in 1732, the *Commissa nobis* of Pius VI in 1784). The Italo-Albanians have been organized ecclesiastically only in the 20th century. First came the eparchy of Lungro in Calabria in 1919, which now comprises 24 parishes. In 1937 the eparchy of Piana dei Greci (now Piana degli Albanesi) was established in Sicily with 15 parishes. In the same year the Greek monastery of Grottaferrata at the gates of Rome was made an exarchic monastery (abbey nullius) with ordinary jurisdiction over the residents of the monastery itself. The seminarians study at Grottaferrata and the Greek College in Rome. The Italo-Albanians now number about 80,000. They follow the Byzantine liturgy, using both Greek and Albanian, but many Latin elements were introduced into the rite, although the monks of Grottaferrata have been effective in restoring original Byzantine forms. BIBLIOGRAPHY: A. Fortescue, *Uniate Eastern Churches* (1923); OrientCatt, 225–234.

[G. ELDAROV]

ITALUS, JOHN, see JOHN ITALUS.

ITHACIUS (d. before 392), bp. of Ossónoba (in modern Portugal) by 379. He prosecuted Priscillian after the Council of Saragossa, thereby incurring the disfavor of Pope Damasus, Ambrose, and Martin of Tours. He regained favor after being excommunicated at Bordeaux (384), but was condemned anew after the fall of Emperor Maximus (387) and died in exile. Sulpicius Severus criticizes him for worldliness; Isidore calls him noble in birth and eloquence. BIBLIOGRAPHY: DTC 8:242–243.

[E. P. COLBERT]

ITINERANCY, the system characteristic of early Methodism whereby preachers were frequently transferred from one station to another and never allowed to remain in one *charge for more than a year. The term referred secondarily to the custom of appointing a preacher to serve a group of *societies or *circuit over which he presided by "itinerating," i.e., traveling among them. Itinerancy was in sharp contrast to the system practiced in the C of E, where a priest often served only one parish throughout his lifetime. John *Wesley began the system when he and his colleagues, as missionaries in Georgia, established their headquarters both at Frederica and Savannah, exchanging places with one another at frequent intervals. He continued the practice in England, and he defended it in a letter to Samuel Walker, Vicar of Truro (1756). He stated that should his preachers remain for too great a time in one place, "they will 'ere long grow dead themselves, and so will most of those that hear them. I know, were I myself to preach one whole year in one place, I should preach both myself and most of my congregation asleep. . . . We have found . . . that a frequent change of teachers is best. . . . No one whom I ever yet knew has all the talents which are needful for beginning, continuing and perfecting the work of grace in a whole congregation." The system was also used in early American Methodism. While it is no longer mandatory that a minister transfer from one church to another after a stated time, Methodists still tend to "move" more often than preachers in other denominations. Furthermore, in most Methodist bodies every preacher's assignment is for one year only, although he may be reassigned to the same place year after year. Other Protestants also speak of traveling preachers or evangelists as "itinerating."

[F. E. MASER]

ITINERARIA, ancient accounts of travel routes. The extant *itineraria* indicate the relay posts (*mutationes*), hostelries (*mansiones* or *stationes*), and distances between cities along a given route. They are valuable for our knowledge of ancient geography. Some include descriptions of noteworthy sights. The *Iter Antoninianum, c.*300 gives in 17 sections the travel routes of the entire Roman Empire. In the *Iter Hierosolymitanum sive Burdigalense* the so-called Pilgrim of Bordeaux gives data for the path he followed from his home city to Jerusalem. Valuable for the study of topography and linguistics is the partially preserved *Peregrinatio sanctae Egeriae ad loca sancta,* the travel account of a nun who journeyed *c.*385 to Palestine. Pilgrimages to Rome are also the subject of *itineraria*. The *Notitia Regionum Urbis XIV*, drawn up in the 4th cent., indicates the chief points of interest in that city. Details of a route from Cadiz to Rome are engraved on four ancient silver vases discovered in Italy. A 13th-cent.-copy of a portable road map, the *Tabula Peutingeriana,* is judged by scholars to be a revision at sixth hand of the lost *Orbis pictus* mentioned by Pliny the Elder. The *Iter Alexandri,* prepared by a courtier for the Emperor Constantius, purports to be a consecutive narrative of the stages taken by Alexander the Great in his conquests 6 cent. earlier. Some other *itineraria* are also extant. BIBLIOGRAPHY: H. Leclercq, DACL 7.2:1841–1922; K. Miller, *Itineraria romana* (1916).

[M. J. SUELZER]

ITSUKUSHIMA SHRINE, Japanese Shinto shrine near Hiroshima, extensively restored in 1169. The buildings at high tide—inundated by the sea—seem to float. Hideyoshi built here a famous Noh stage projecting into the sea. Thirty-three sutras and other excellent decorative arts of the Fujiwara period are housed in the shrine.

[M. J. DALY]

ITURBIDE, AUGUSTÍN DE (1783–1824), Mexican soldier, politician, and "emperor." Born in Morelia, I. was an officer in the royalist forces and became head of the army in 1816. When in 1820 the anticlerical laws of the Spanish Cortes of Cadiz angered the Mexicans and forced them to declare independence, I. and Guerrero devised the Plan of Iguala, which preserved the Catholic religion, political independence, and equality of Creoles and Europeans. Upon Ferdinand VII's refusal to accept the Mexican throne in 1822, I. was proclaimed emperor as Augustín I. His reign was short-lived. In 1823 he went into exile in Europe. Upon his return he was captured and shot by order of the state of Tamaulipas; but in 1833 he was honored with the title "Liberator." BIBLIOGRAPHY: V. Riva Palacio, *México a través de los siglos* (1888–89); C. Bustamente, *Historia del emperador Augustín de Iturbide* (1846); E. W. Shield, "Church and State in the First Decade of Mexican Independence," CHR (1942) 206–228; A. Iturbide, RACHS 26 (1915) 287–310; 27(1916) 16–44.

[P. DAMBORIENA]

IUS CIRCA SACRA, in the terminology of natural-right jurists in Germany (e.g., H. Grotius), the sovereign power of the State over religious organizations. What had previously been regarded as the duty of the Christian prince became a right inherent in the power of the State. Included were church legislation, appointment to ecclesiastical offices, discipline, and administration of church finances. The *ius circa sacra* tended to make civil functionaries of church officers and to subordinate religion to politics. The **ius in sacra* was a contrasting concept. BIBLIOGRAPHY: J. Hachel, "Cura religionis, Ius circa sacra, Ius in sacra," *Festschrift Ulrich Stutz* (1938); A. L. Drummond, *German Protestantism since Luther* (1951).

[T. C. O'BRIEN]

IUS DEVOLUTUM, a law in the Church of Scotland according to which the *presbytery must take steps to appoint a minister to a vacant charge when the time limit for the congregation to elect its minister (6 months, with extension to 9 at most in exceptional circumstances) has expired.

[J. A. R. MACKENZIE]

IUS GENTIUM, division introduced by Roman jurists to explain the diversity of laws. Ulpian proposed a three-fold division: *ius naturale* (what nature teaches all animals), *ius gentium* (what is common to all men), *ius civile* (what is proper to one city). Gaius maintained a two-fold division: *ius civile* and *ius gentium* (what natural reason constitutes among all men). These divisions were influenced by Aristotle's division of political justice into natural and legal (*Ethics* 1134b18–1135a13) and law into universal and particular (*Rhetoric* 1373b1–18) and by Stoic emphasis on universal reason. During the patristic era various writers introduced a chronological distinction based on the Fall. The *ius naturale* became an ideal state, existing before sin, while the *ius gentium,* including property, war, and slavery, became the human condition after sin. Albert the Great wrote of the *ius naturale* without separating human activity into rational and animal. Thomas Aquinas relied upon both Gaius and Ulpian, whom he reconciled in teaching that it is natural for man to act reasonably. According to Thomas Aquinas, if one begins with man's ontological structure, then one finds certain activities generically common to men and animals. Thus the *ius gentium,* since it depends upon man's reason for its existence, would pertain to positive rather than to natural law (ST 1a2ae, 95.4). If one more properly considers law's relationship to man's specific, rational nature, then the *ius gentium* pertains to natural rather than positive law, for it includes activities close to man's most basic inclinations (ST 2a2ae, 57.3). *Ius gentium* and *ius naturale* may be related as conclusion and principle if one remembers that this is only an analogy. The one is derived from the other by rational reflection upon experience, not by *a priori* deduction. The *ius gentium* of the Romans and the early scholastics is not the *ius inter gentes* of the later scholastics. BIBLIOGRAPHY: J. M. Aubert, *Le Droit Romain dans l'oeuvre de Saint Thomas* (*Bibliothèque Thomiste* 30, 1955); O. Lottin, *Psychologie et morale aux xii*e *et xiii*e *siècles,* v. 2 (1948).

[P. STENGER]

IUS IN SACRA, the right of the Church over its own affairs. It was first called *ius in ecclesiastica* by 17th-cent. Protestant theologians in Germany (J. Gerhard, D. Pareus) who sought to defend the spiritual autonomy of the Church. The contrasting concept was the **ius circa sacra*.

[T. C. O'BRIEN]

IVANIOS, MAR (Givergis Panikervirtis; 1882–1953), leader in the union movement under the Jacobite Christians in Kerala that resulted in 1930 in the union of the Malankar Church with Rome (see MALANKAR RITE). As rector of the Jacobite seminary in Betania, he founded the Order of the Imitation of Christ. He was consecrated bp. of Betania in 1928 and became metropolitan of his Church in 1928. With the support of many of the bps. he began negotiations for reunion with Rome in 1926. With a confrere, Mar Theophilos, and a few others he made profession of the Catholic faith in 1930; and in 1932 Rome appointed him metropolitan of the newly erected Catholic Malankar Church province. BIBLIOGRAPHY: "Reunion Movement in Malabar 1930–1955," a special number of ECQ 9 (1955).

[J. MEIJER]

IVANOV, ALEXANDER (1806–58), Russian painter, son and pupil of A. I. Ivanov at St. Petersburg Academy. Living in Rome after 1831, I., deeply religious and influenced by the Nazarene Overbeck, subordinated his interest in luminous landscape to an engagement in monumental religious works. He labored 25 years on *Christ's First Appearance to the People* (Leningrad). Later work is marked by a Russian-Byzantine style.

[M. J. DALY]

IVANOV, VYACHESLAV IVANOVICH (1866–1949), symbolist theoretician and poet. Under the influence of Nietzsche and Solovyov, he sought to create a new spiritual reality by the use of poetic symbols. His poetry, which is erudite and stately, has a mosaic-like quality that is reminiscent of Byzantine iconography (cf. *Cor Ardens* [2 v., 1909–11]). In his correspondence with the literary historian Gershenzon, published as *Correspondence Between Two Corners* (1921), I. defends humanistic traditions and culture. He was converted to Roman Catholicism in 1926. BIBLIOGRAPHY: O. Deschartes, "Vyacheslav Ivanov," in *Oxford Slavonic Papers*, 5 (1954); R. Poggioli, *Poets of Russia: 1890–1930* (1960) 161–170.

[M. F. MCCARTHY]

IVERNY, JACQUES (fl. 1411–38), French painter in Avignon after withdrawal of the papal court, I. shows the influence of the Sienese school in his decorative, aristocratic style, painting the signed triptych *Virgin Suckling the Child* (Turin).

[M. J. DALY]

IVES, ST., the English name of three persons venerated as saints; the Latin form of the name is Ivo, the French, Yves. (1) The Ives associated with the English town in Huntingdonshire was reputed to have been a Persian bp. and itinerant preacher who visited England and died in Huntingdonshire in the early 7th century. His relics were discovered in 1001 and were transferred to the abbey of Ramsey. See ODCC 707; Butler 2:157–158; (2) St. Yves-des-Bretons (Hélory de Kermartin; 1235–1303), a priest of humble and charitable life greatly honored among Bretons and regarded as the secondary patron of Brittany. Devotion to him was spread far and wide by Breton sailors and emigrants. See J. Evenou, BiblSanct 7:997–1002. (3) Yves (Ivo) de Chartres (*c.*1040–1110), reformer, bp. of Chartres. He was the most celebrated canonist of his day. In the investiture struggle then raging, he took a moderate position. For extensive bibliography see M. Noirot, BiblSanct 7:994–997, and ODCC 707. The St. Ive, near Liskear in Cornwall, is not properly associated with any of the above. The name appears to be a corruption of a name of a female saint, Ia, Hia, or Iva, about whom nothing beyond legend is known.

[P. K. MEAGHER]

IVES, LEVI SILLIMAN (1797–1867), Episcopalian bp., convert to Catholicism. Ordained in the Episcopalian Church in 1823, he was named bp. of North Carolina in 1831. I. published several works including *The Apostle's Doctrine and Fellowship* (1844) and *The Obedience of Faith* (1849). Though he labored to improve the education of blacks and wrote a catechism for slaves, he was accused of favoring slavery, an institution he abhorred. Coming under the influence of the *Oxford Movement, he introduced high church practices and founded the Brotherhood of the Holy Cross. He was rebuked by the Convention of Episcopalian bps. and dissolved the Brotherhood, but on a journey to Rome, resigned his see and entered the Catholic Church in 1852. His years as a Catholic were financially difficult though a number of bps. and communities gave support. His great work was in the field of charity, with the St. Vincent de Paul Society and as founder (1863) and first president of the New York Catholic Protectory. Staffed by the Brothers of the Christian Schools, it cared for deprived Catholic youth. As a Catholic he wrote *Trials of a Mind in Its Progress to Catholicism: A Letter to his Old Friends* (1853).

[J. R. AHERNE]

IVO, ST., see IVES, ST.

IVO OF CHARTRES, ST., see IVES, ST.

IVO OF CHARTRES, COLLECTION OF, a group of canonical compilations originating most likely during the last decade of the 11th cent. and consisting of three separate collections of canonical material, the *Tripartita,* the *Decretum,* and the *Pannormum (Pannormia)*. Part I of the *Tripartita* contains decretal material; Part II, canons of councils and texts from the Fathers; and Part III, compiled perhaps a year or two later, is an abridged version of Ivo's *Decretum*. The latter work (Migne, PL 161:59–1022) is an unwieldy assemblage of legal and theological material composed with some intention of system and comprehensiveness—it ranges from faith and baptism (Part I) to the four last things (Part 17)—but far short of this in achievement. Much more successful was the *Pannormum* (PL 161:1037–1344), which takes nearly all its material from the former work but far excels it, not only in conciseness and arrangement, but also in originality. Evidence of its marked contribution to the development of canonical science may be found especially in the carefully worded summaries that precede each text, enhancing the general usefulness of the work and accounting for its attested popularity. Ivo's *Pannormum* offers an excellent example of the state of the art at the close of the 11th century. BIBLIOGRAPHY: É. Amann and L. Guizard, DTC 15.2:3625–40; P. Fournier and G. LeBras, *Histoire des collections canoniques en Occident depus les fausses décrétales jusqu'au Décret de Gratien* (1931–32) 2:55–114; A. Van Hove, *Commentarium Lovaniense in codicem iuris canonici,* 1:331–332.

[J. E. BIECHLER]

IVO HELORY, ST. see IVES, ST.

IVORY. In the biblical world, ivory was considered to be a decorative luxury. It was among the desirable goods that Solomon's ships brought, and his throne was made of it (1 Kg ch. 10). It was generally thought of in connection with palaces and other places of great luxury (Ps 45.8). Amos denounced those who "lie upon beds of ivory" and do not concern themselves with the problems of the nation (6.4–6). Since elephants roamed northern Syria in the 2d millennium B.C., some ivory presumably came from there. Some may have come also from Egypt. A great quantity of carved ivories have been found by excavators, providing evidence of the great skill of ivory craftsmen in OT times and giving insight into aspects of ancient Near Eastern culture. The most important collections of ivories have been found at Megiddo (*c.* 1350–1150 B.C.) and Samaria (*c.* 850 B.C.).

[T. EARLY]

IZUMO SHRINE, one of the oldest Japanese Shinto shrines. Rebuilt in the Kamakura period in reduced size, and in its present form in 1744, it retains a primitive off-center entrance.

[M. J. DALY]

J

JABBOK (JABOC), VALLEY, the valley of the Jabbok River of the Transjordan side in ancient Gilead, for much of its distance a deep gorge. The river is a tributary of the Jordan, and its modern name is Nahr ez-Zerqa. Its route to the Jordan forms a kind of half circle. Its first direction is E for several miles, then N for several more miles. It begins to flow NW and finally directly W toward the Jordan Valley where it moves S by SE until it empties into the Jordan at Tell ed-Damiyeh (ancient Adama). Its course is about 50 miles long and during the journey it drops from 2,500 feet above sea level to 1,150 below sea level. Along this river the scene of Jacob's wrestling with the angel was staged (Gen 32.22–26). The only other mention of Jabbok in the Bible is for establishing boundaries between the kingdoms of Sihon and Ammon (Num 21.24) and Israel and Ammon (Jg 11.13, 22). BIBLIOGRAPHY: D. Baly, *Geography of the Bible* (1957); N. Glueck, *Other Side of the Jordan* (1940).

[F. GAST]

JACA CATHEDRAL, one of the most important Spanish Romanesque churches, dedicated in 1063. With three apses, a barrel-vaulted transept, and a dome on squinches, the cathedral was further constructed in the 11th and 12th cent., the nave and aisles star-vaulted in the 16th century. Excellence of sculptured capitals and corbels, and beauty of architecture made Jaca a most important Spanish Romanesque church on the pilgrimage route to Santiago de Compostela—with influence far beyond its province.

[M. J. DALY]

JACKSON, MAHALIA (1911–72), famed contralto gospel singer. Born in New Orleans, the daughter of a preacher, she began her musical career after moving to Chicago at age 16. Among her albums are *Move on Up a Little Higher, Bless This House,* and *Sweet Little Jesus Boy*.

[P. J. HENNESSEY]

JACOB, PATRIARCH, the son of Isaac and Rebekah, younger twin of Esau, and the ostensible progenitor of the 12 tribes of Israel. By popular etymology his name is linked with "heel" (Gen 25.26) and with the verb "to deceive" (Gen 27.36). It probably means "may God protect." He won Esau's birthright for a good meal (Gen 25.27, 34) and with the help of his mother deceived his father Isaac into granting it to him (Gen 27.1–42). J. left the family circle after this event—either in fear of his brother's wrath (Gen 27.42–45) or to find a woman relative to marry (Gen 27.46–28.5). He could have been motivated by both considerations. The covenantal promise passed to J. and was confirmed at Bethel in a vision (Gen 28.10–22). In Paddan-Aram he met Rachel and was invited by her father Laban to stay on as a helper. He worked 7 years for the hand of Rachel and in the end was outwitted by Laban who gave him the elder sister Leah. He worked another seven years for Rachel (Gen 29). Leah was fertile; Rachel was not. This caused dissension in the household. Bilhah, Rachel's maid, was substituted for her. Zilpah, Leah's maid, added children to the family also. J. had the following offspring: from Leah—Reuben, Simeon, Levi, Judah, Issachar, Zebulun; from Rachel—Joseph, Benjamin; from Zilpah (Leah's maid)—Gad, Asher; from Bilhah (Rachel's maid)—Dan, Naphtali. From these offspring, along with Joseph's sons Ephraim and Manasseh, the eponymous names of the 12 tribes (Gen 29.31–30.24; ch. 48) are taken. J. finally took his family and returned to Canaan. On his way he wrestled with an angel at Penuel in the Jabbok Valley (Gen 32). He appeased Esau with gifts and was permitted to settle in Shechem. J. later moved to Bethel and there Rachel died in childbirth (Gen 35). J.'s partiality for Joseph caused the latter to be sold into slavery. Joseph became vizier of Egypt and during a famine in Canaan, J. sent his sons to get grain in Egypt. Joseph recognized his brothers and identified himself. The rest of the family was brought to live in Egypt (Gen 42.1–45.28). J. died in Egypt after having blessed Joseph's two sons, Ephraim and Manasseh (Gen 48), and was buried at Machpelah (Gen 49.29–50.13). It is possible that this material seemingly told of one individual could be narrated of Israel as a people. In fact the name J. and its equivalent, Israel, is often attached to the whole people. In the NT, J. is frequently associated with Abraham and Isaac. He is mentioned in a sermon by Stephen (Acts 7.8–16); Jesus uses the vision of the ladder to show himself mediator between heaven and earth (Jn 1.51); St. Paul uses the transfer of the birthright from Esau to J. as an example of election on the part of God (Rom 9.10–13). BIBLIOGRAPHY: N. Glueck, *Rivers in the Desert* (1959); G. von Rad, *Genesis: A Commentary* (tr. J. H. Marks, 1961); E. A. Speiser, *Genesis: Introduction, Translation and Notes* (1964).

[F. GAST]

JACOB BARADAI (Ya'-qôb Burde'-āyā; Baradaios; *c.*500–578), organizer of the Monophysite *West Syrian Church and its derivative branches. Trained in the monastery of Phesilta, J. became a disciple of the Monophysite leader *Severus and eventually went to Constantinople to defend *Monophysitism before Empress *Theodora I who had him consecrated bp. of Edessa (543). He returned to Syria and for almost 40 years went about ordaining priests and consecrating bps., thus creating a new hierarchy that was organized by Sergius the Monophysite patriarch of Antioch (see ANTIOCH, PATRIARCHATE OF). His persistence guaranteed the existence of Monophysite Churches, and for this reason those Christian groups who derive from him are also called Jacobites. BIBLIOGRAPHY: E. Hammerschmidt, LTK 5:836; J. P. N. Land, *Anecdota syriaca* (1862–75) 2:364–383.

[F. T. RYAN]

JACOB OF SERUGH (451–521), Syriac bp. and writer. J. studied at Edessa, served for a time as chorbishop in Haura in the district of Serugh, and in 519 was made bp. of Batnae, chief city of the province of Serugh in Osrhoene. He wrote both prose and poetry, including letters, sermons, some liturgical texts, and at least one biography. He left a large number of metrical homilies, mostly on biblical themes. He appears to have been a Monophysite, although the authenticity of a letter upon which this opinion is based is open to question and he certainly took no significant part in the Christological controversy of his time. Many of his works remain unedited and even unpublished. Works: *Homiliae selectae Mar Jacobi Sarugensis* (ed. P. Bedjan, 5 v., 1905–10). BIBLIOGRAPHY: A. Baumstark, *Geschichte der Syrischen Literatur* (1922) 148–158; I. Ortiz de Urbina, PS (1958) 97–101; Altaner 407–408.

[R. B. ENO]

JACOB, MAX (1876–1944), convert from Judaism to Catholicism. J. led a Bohemian existence as painter, astrologer, and poet until he was converted through the experience of three apparitions of Christ (1909–15). He lived 1921–28 in the practice of penance near a Benedictine priory at St. Benoît-sur-Loire, then reverted to his former mode of life, but in 1936 returned permanently to his penitential observances. Arrested as a Jew in 1944, he survived the rigors of Nazi imprisonment for only a few days. BIBLIOGRAPHY: J. Morienval, *Catholicisme* 6:244–245.

[M. J. SUELZER]

JACOBAZZI, DOMENICO (*c.*1458–1528), cardinal and canonist. His career as a lawyer progressed rapidly in Rome, and he was made auditor of the Roman Rota in 1493 and in 1511, bp. of Nocera dei Pagani as well as vicar of Rome. In 1517, he was raised to the cardinalate. His virtue, piety, and learning were widely known. His main work, *De concilio*, long recognized as a classic, was written during Lateran Council V. He treated all aspects of a council and in general opposed the viewpoint of the Gallican cardinals. He firmly adhered to the position that a council and its decrees were not above the pope. He was a loyal defender of pontifical power with Vallambrosa and Cajetan. He clearly stated, however, that a council could be held without papal consent in a state of emergency or if the pope refused to heed the summons to convoke a council. BIBLIOGRAPHY: R. Gillet, DDC 6:75–77; R. Bäumer, LTK 5:831; H. Jedin Trent 1:97–100, 109–116.

[J. M. O'DONNELL]

JACOBELLUS (James of Mies; 1372–1429), colleague of Jan *Hus, who from 1414 onward, in teaching and practice, advanced the theory that communion under both kinds is necessary for salvation (see UTRAQUISTS).

[T. C. O'BRIEN]

JACOBI, FRIEDRICH HEINRICH (1743–1819), German romantic philosopher, major critic of both Spinoza's dogmatic rationalism and Kant's critical philosophy. Along with his friend J. G. Hamann, he was a leading proponent of a philosophy based on the belief that what is felt, the immediately and sensually given, is in fact the real world of things and that these perceptions must precede all and any discursive thought. Faith, for J., is a mode of knowledge; he extended faith to the realm of objects and objective knowledge, whereas Kant restricted the function of faith to validating principles of religion and morality. Faith, an assured sense or feeling of the immediate reality of things, cannot be explained rationally or proved, yet it is absolutely essential to our human consciousness of the world. The world of things-in-themselves is revealed through external perceptions, and God is revealed internally through intellectual intuition, yet both revelations assuredly yield the objective reality of their content. Thus science and religion are both grounded on faith, feeling, and immediacy. Though J. appreciated the significance of Spinoza's rationalist metaphysics (he considered it the most important since Plato), he criticized the pantheistic tendency of Spinoza's thought, arguing that Spinoza's rigorous mathematical-logical system required that God, like world, be bound by laws of causality and thus that God be neither free nor independent. J. considered Kant's critical philosophy pure subjective idealism. Kant's system, he maintained, could not support the existence of objective reality independent of human mind and thus the concept of thing-in-itself (*Ding an Sich*) was incompatible with the rest of Kant's system. J.'s works were published in 6 volumes (ed. F. Roth, 1812–25). His system must ultimately be classified as an extreme reaction to rationalism: it is a form of irrationalism, accepting an unbridgeable gap between his concept of faith and reasoned knowledge, while affirming the objective validity of each.

[R. J. LITZ]

JACOBINA OF PISA (*c.*1280–*c.*1370) the wife of Peter Cascina of Pisa, who became a Dominican Tertiary after his death (1361), and was prioress of the Tertiary Sisters in Pisa from 1366. After her death she had a local cult.

[L. E. BOYLE]

JACOBINI, LUDOVICO (1832–87), cardinal, papal diplomat. As a member of the Roman Curia, he became secretary for Oriental Affairs in the Congregation of the Propagation of the Faith. At Vatican Council I he was undersecretary. Named titular abp. in 1874 he was appointed nuncio to Vienna, where his finesse helped to improve relations with the Empire, still clinging to the principles of *Josephinism. J. met with Chancellor Bismarck of Germany in 1879 to ease the problems of *Kulturkampf. Created cardinal in 1879, J. was appointed secretary of state to Leo XIII in 1880, in which position he brought an end to the conflict with Germany. BIBLIOGRAPHY: F. Engel-Janosi, *Österreich und der Vatikan, 1846–1918* (v. 1, 1958–1960).

[J. R. AHERNE]

JACOBINS, CHURCH OF THE (1260 or 65–1304), medieval fortress-church in Toulouse, France, established by the Dominicans. The lengthy nave and choir are divided into two parts—for the clergy and for the public—by lofty round columns, the easternmost supporting 22 ribs of the "palm-tree" vault. The severe brick exterior supports an octagonal tower. Portions of the cloisters, the chapter house, and 14th-cent. chapel of St. Antonin, decorated with impressive 14th- and 15th-cent. frescoes, survive.

[M. J. DALY]

JACOBIS, JUSTIN DE, ST. (1800–60), Vincentian missionary bishop. The Ethiopian Church has since the Monophysite heresy of the 5th cent. harbored a violent dislike of Rome. In 1839, J. was sent as prefect apostolic to Ethiopia, which he found an almost impossible mission field because of the local clergy and monks. His humility and friendliness, however, won over some dissidents. In early years there he was chosen to accompany a deputation going to Egypt to request the Coptic patriarch of Alexandria to appoint a bp. for the Ethiopian Church. He went to Cairo on condition that he could request the Patriarch to be reconciled with Rome. The Patriarch refused and appointed a young monk as bp., one who was to oppose J. so long as he remained in Ethiopia. J. founded in 1845 a college to train clergy for the mission. A new and savage persecution was set in motion by the Ethiopian bishop. The college was closed and J. was proscribed. In 1848 he was secretly consecrated vicar apostolic. The college reopened and for a while Catholicism made good progress. Once again persecution brought imprisonment and exile to him. He died from the continued harrassment suffered in his last year. He was beatified in 1939, canonized in 1975. BIBLIOGRAPHY: Butler 3:230–235.

[J. R. AHERNE]

JACOBITES (SYRIAN) Christians of the Monophysite heresy, they dissented from the Council of Chalcedon that defined Jesus to be both fully divine and fully human in nature, because they believed that whatever humanity he had had was somehow and variously absorbed into his divinity. This outlook originated with Apollonarius and Eutyches who were reacting to Arianism that denied the divinity of Jesus. The name Jacobite comes from a Syrian monk and bishop, *Jacob Baradai who preached Monophysitism amid much persecution from the entrenched orthodoxy. Many Jacobites were wiped out by the Muslim invasions of the 7th cent., but a few still exist today, although some have reunited with Rome. The tendency toward this doctrine seemed to result from an excessive emphasis on Jesus' Godhead to the detriment of his human reality and, consequently, to the weakening of the salvational process by which Jesus recreates mankind from within itself by his resurrected eternal humanity that continues to be united to the divine Son of God forever. *WEST SYRIAN CHURCH.

[J. F. FALLON]

JACOB'S ORACLES, the blessings of Jacob on the 12 tribal patriarchs contained in Gen 49. 1–33. In reality they are prophetic summaries of the subsequent histories of the tribes concerned. They were probably composed in the period of the judges (1200–1050 B.C.) and appear to be based on Canaanite models. The blessing of Judah, however, far the most prominent and adulatory in tone, represents an exception to this, and was probably added during the Davidic period (1000–962 B.C.). BIBLIOGRAPHY: J. Coppens, "La Bénédiction de Jacob, son cadre historique à la lumière des parallèles ougaritiques," VT Suppl 4:97–115.

[D. J. BOURKE]

JACOB'S WELL, part of the property which Jacob purchased outside the town of Shechem (modern Balata, about 2 miles E of Nablus; Gen 33.18–20). The patriarch Joseph was buried nearby. It was here that Jesus had the conversation with the Samaritan woman (Jn 4).

[J. J. CASTELOT]

JACOBUS OF LIÈGE (fl. *c.*1270), obscure musical theorist. He is thought by some to have written the

Speculum musicae, which has been attributed to Johannes de Muris.

[P. J. HENNESSEY]

JACOPO DA VERONA (fl. 1370), Italian painter of impressive frescoes of the life of Christ and of the Virgin in the Oratory of S. Michele, Padua, Giottesque in three-dimensional figures and resembling Altichiero in his treatment of space. J. did illuminations for the *Bibbia istoriata padovana* (British Museum and Library of the Concordi, Rovigo).

[M. J. DALY]

JACOPONE DA TODI (*c.*1230–*c.*1306), Franciscan poet. J. is said to have been an Italian nobleman and lawyer before the tragic death of his wife, *c.*1268, turned him away from the world and to a life of prayer and piety. In 1278 he became a Franciscan and showed tendencies toward extremes of asceticism. Some of his *laudi,* or poems, reveal this extremism. He often employed the *laudi* for polemics, as in the bitter controversy between the Franciscan *Spirituals, with whom he sided, and Conventuals. He insulted Pope Boniface VIII for condemning the Spirituals, and was censured and imprisoned for 5 years. His *Donna del paradiso,* still performed to music in Italy, is a beautiful portrayal of Our Lady at the foot of the Cross; but it is doubtful that he is the author of the sequence, *Stabat Mater,* which has a similar theme. While the object of a popular cultus, he has not been officially beatified. BIBLIOGRAPHY: E. Underhill, *Jacopone da Todi, Poet and Mystic* (1919).

[R. H. SCHMANDT]

JACQUEMART DE HESDIN was a Flemish miniaturist-painter commissioned (c.1384–1413) by the Duc de Berry for some of his finest manuscripts (e.g., ''*Les Très riches heures*'' (1404–09) which became a model of so-called International Gothic pictorial art, the last phase of the Gothic era.). J. here introduced (Lombard-Sienese) *trecento* influences into French painting—the play of light, new color-relationships, and elegant gesture, in an atmosphere of restraint and composure. BIBLIOGRAPHY: M. Miess, *French Painting in the Time of Jean de Berry* (3 v. 1968); L. P. Leite, NCE 7:576;A. Emiliani, NCE 6:644.

[R. C. MARKS]

JACQUES DE BESANÇON (fl. *c.*1450), French illuminator. Follower of the Master Francis with whom he worked and emulator of Fouquet, J. also executed woodcuts for printed books.

[M. J. DALY]

JACQUES DE MOLAY, (betw. 1243 and 1254–1314), last Grand Master of the Knights Templar. Little is known of his life prior to his entrance into the Templars (*c.*1265). After becoming Grand Master (1298), he faced Philip the Fair's drive to seize control of the Templars' wealth. Arrested by Philip (Oct. 13, 1307), he underwent a series of trials on the charges of heresy and immorality, charges which were never proven. He was finally put to death as a relapsed heretic and the order's wealth confiscated by Philip. BIBLIOGRAPHY: G. Mollat, *Popes at Avignon, 1305–78* (tr. J. Love, 1963).

[J. MULDOON]

JACQUES DE VITRY (*c.*1170–1240), cardinal, historian, bp. of Acre (1216–28), and cardinal bishop of Tusculum (1228). A series of his letters (1216–21) provide a history of the Fifth Crusade and his *Historia orientalis et occidentalis* presents the history of the Church in his own day. He was also very interested in contemporary reform movements and esp. with the new Orders for women which later became known as *Beguines. BIBLIOGRAPHY: E. W. McDonnell, *Beguines and Beghards in Medieval Culture* (1954).

[J. MULDOON]

JAEGEN, JEROME (1841–1919), German banker, member of the Prussian *Landtag* (1899–1906), writer on the spiritual life. He was himself a mystic and sought to convince fellow Christian laymen that contemplative union with God was open to them and was the normal fruit of a prayerful Christian life. His works stressed the theme of the intensification of charity, not extraordinary phenomenon, as the essence of perfection. His publications include: *Der Kampf um die Krone* (1883); *Das mystische Gnadenleben* (1911).

[T. C. O'BRIEN]

JAEGER, WERNER WILHELM (1888–1961), German classical philologist. After receiving the Ph.D. from Berlin in 1911, he taught at Basel (1914), Kiel (1915–21), and Berlin (1921–36). Because of Nazi restrictions on university freedom, he emigrated to the U.S. and taught at Chicago (1936–39) and Harvard (1939–59). At Harvard he founded the Institute for Classical Studies, largely to aid the production of his critical edition of St. *Gregory of Nyssa. His scholarship reflected deep interest in classical, patristic, and humanistic thought. Among his writings he is noted particularly for *Aristotle* (2d ed., 1955), *Paideia: The Ideals of Greek Culture* (tr. C. Hishet, 3 v., 2d ed., 1955), and *Early Christianity and Greek Paideia* (1961).

[T. EARLY]

JAEGGI, OSWALD (1913–), Swiss Benedictine monk and composer. His large output includes numerous liturgical compositions and other sacred works both instrumental and vocal, as well as many secular pieces. Choral compositions are prominent among the latter, and J.'s reputation is chiefly in choral music, both as composer and conductor. He is noted also as director of music at the abbey of Einsiedeln and of the ''Leonhard Lechner'' Chorus and Chamber Chorus in Bozen-Gries. His training included study at the Pontifical Institute of Sacred Music, Rome, where he wrote a dissertation under H. *Anglès. BIBLIOGRAPHY: A. Hiebner, MGG 6:1655–56.

[A. DOHERTY]

JAFFA, see JOPPA.

JAFFE, PHILIPP (1819–70), German historian. Of Jewish parentage he became a Protestant 2 years before his death. He is remembered for his *Regesta pontificum Romanorum* (1851), a collection of papal documents to the year 1198, and for his contribution *Scriptores* to the *Monumenta Germaniae historica* (v. 12, 17–20; 1856–68). Both he did as the associate of G. Pertz; after their estrangement in 1868 J. began his own *Bibliotheca rerum Germanicarum* (6 v., 1864–73), a work of less merit.

[T. C. O'BRIEN]

JAGIEŁŁO (WŁADISŁOW II) (*c.* 1350–1434), king of Poland, grand duke of Lithuania. Son of the grand duke of Lithuania, Olgierd, J. consented to accept Catholicism together with all of Lithuania in order to marry Jadwiga of Anjou. Through her, he became king of Poland; his power then included Ruthenia as well as his native Lithuania. Encouraged by his wife and by the true fervor of his conversion, J. renewed the Univ. of Cracow, established Poland as a great Catholic power, destroyed the power of the Teutonic Knights (Battle of Grünwald, 1410), and reached international Catholic as well as political status at the Council of Constance. In 1413, the Poles and Lithuanians signed the Union of Horodlo, a document uniting the regal and noble families of the two countries as a single family in the "Mystery of Charity." BIBLIOGRAPHY: O. Halecki, *History of Poland* (1961); *Cambridge History of Poland* (1941–50) 1:161.

[M. E. DUFFY]

JAHVEH, see YAHWEH.

JAINISM, a religion originating in India in the 6th cent. B.C. Its founder Vardhamāna was a contemporary of the Buddha. Called the Great Hero (Mahāvīra), he was born *c.* 540, and like the Buddha he was of a princely family in the region of the Ganges Valley. At the age of 30 he renounced his wife and family to lead an ascetical life. He attained enlightenment and became a conqueror (*jina:* hence the name jainism, the religion of the conquerors). He died *c.* 468 B.C. at age 72, of self-starvation. His extreme asceticism led him to go naked at the end; as did many of his followers for centuries. This was part of the original cause of schism between the Dîgambaras (white-clad) and the Shvetāmbara (space-clad). Like Buddhism, Jainism represents a protest against the ritualistic emphasis of early Hinduism. There has been very little doctrinal development. Jainism seeks the perfection of man's nature through the ascetical life; a return to an original state of pure knowledge and bliss; purification from *karma: the adherence of matter. Only monks can attain this perfection through their five vows: abjuring killing, stealing, lying, sexual intercourse, and property. A distinguishing mark of the religion is the practice of noninjury to all living creatures, including insects and plant life. Gandhi's practice of nonviolence is dependent on this tradition. Finally, early Jainist monks took an interest in secular literature and knowledge, and preserved and copied ancient texts. Followers of Jainism in India number about 1½ million.

[E. J. DILLON]

JALABERT, LOUIS (1877–1943), French Jesuit epigraphist. Teaching in Beirut, Lebanon, before World War I, J. conceived the project of publishing a new collection of the Greek and Latin inscriptions of Syria. Unable to complete the project, he turned over the preliminary work he had done to René Mouterde, SJ, who published the first volume in 1929. From 1916 on, J. was closely associated with the Jesuit monthly review *Études* to which he regularly contributed articles on the Near East and related subjects until his death. BIBLIOGRAPHY: J. Lecler, *Catholicisme* 6:296–297.

[R. B. ENO]

JALAL-UD-DIN MOHAMMED, see AKBAR.

JALÂL-UD-DÎN RÛMÎ (1207–73), *Sufi teacher and writer. He was born in Persia but spent most of his life in Konya, Asia Minor; Rûmî in his name refers to Rûm, the region where he lived. Succeeding his father in 1230, he established his reputation as a teacher in the Konya school. After 1244 he came completely under the influence of a wandering Sufi mystic, Shams Tabrîzî. After the mystic's death J. composed poems as if in Sham's person, *The Dîwân-i Shams-i Tabrîz*. His most famous work, a classic of the Persian language, *Mathnâwî*, is a vast collection of mystical couplets. After his death his son succeeded him and founded the Sufi order of the Mawlawîya in his honor. This is the origin of the still extant Whirling Dervishes of the Near East, who venerate him as master (*Mawlânâ*).

[J. F. FALLON]

JAMÂL AL-DÎN AL-AFGHÂNÎ (1838–97), a Muslim reformer, the first to launch an effective campaign in favor of the modernization of *Islam and the elimination of European colonialism. Jamâl al-Dîn insisted that the backwardness of Islamic countries in relation to the West was due to their having lost touch with the true Islamic tradition which he held to be completely compatible with true modern science. He saw the materialistic atheism of the West (esp. Darwinism) as the greatest present threat to a true social, cultural, and religious revival in Islam. These ideas were set forth in many writings, esp. in his *Refutation of the*

Materialists, written originally in Persian *c.*1880 (French tr. A. M. Goichon, 1942). He preached a reform of Muslim education and the value of science within an Islamic framework and the necessity of the expulsion of all colonial and Western influence from Islamic lands. He considered the elimination of colonialism of first importance and toward that goal he directed his greatest efforts. He traveled widely in both the East and Europe but was constantly in difficulty with both Muslim officials and the colonial powers because of his vehement political agitation. His influence was most felt in Egypt where his disciple, Muhammad 'Abduh managed to reform the University of al-Azhar. BIBLIOGRAPHY: I. Mélikoff, EncIslam^2, s.v. "Djamāl al-Dīn al-Afghānī."

[R. M. FRANK]

JAMES, in the NT the name of two Apostles, and of one of the "brothers of the Lord." (1) James, son of Alphaeus, one of the Twelve (Mt 10.3; Mk 3.18; Lk 6.15; Acts 1.13). (2) James, "brother of the Lord," (Mt 13.55; Mk 6.3; Gal 1.19), head of the early Church at Jerusalem. He defended retention of some Jewish traditions, but also the freedom of gentile converts to the gospel(Acts 15.13–23; cf. Gal 2.12). He was martyred *c.*62 A.D., either by stoning or by being cast from the pinnacle of the Temple. Tradition holds him to be the author of the letter of James in the NT canon; modern scholarship has largely rejected his authorship. (See JAMES, LETTER OF). Tradition also identified this James with James son of Alphaeus and refers to the one person as James the Less, i.e., the younger, or perhaps smaller. Because the NT separates the Apostles from the brethren of the Lord, who at first did not believe in him (Mk 3.21; Jn 7.3), modern biblicists deny the identification. (3) James, Son of Zebedee, one of the Twelve (Mt 10.3; Mk 3.18; Lk 6.15; Acts 1.13; 12.2). He and his brother John were working with their father Zebedee mending nets by the sea of Galilee when Jesus called them (Mt 4.18, 21–22; Mk 1.19–20). With Peter and John he formed an inner circle within the Twelve (Mk 5.37; 9.2; 14.33). James and John were rebuked, however, for seeking preferment (Mk 10.35–45). Executed by Herod Agrippa I, James is the only one of the Twelve whose death was recorded in the NT (Acts 12.1). The tradition of a journey to Spain that is the basis for the cult at the shrine of *Santiago de Compostela lacks historical basis.

[T. C. O'BRIEN]

JAMES I (1208–76), **KING OF ARAGON** from 1213. He transformed feudal Aragon-Catalonia into a protokingdom, reorienting its energies S from Languedoc-Provence and conquering the Muslim Valencia and Balearics. He cofounded the Mercedarians, participated at the Council of Lyons II, and composed an autobiography, *The Chronicle of James I* (tr. J. Foster, 2 v., 1883), which is a classic. BIBLIOGRAPHY: R. I. Burns, NCE 7:806.

[R. I. BURNS]

JAMES II (1267–1327), **KING OF ARAGON** from 1291 and Sicily from 1286. Named Captain-General of the Church by the Pope, J. continued his predecessors' expansionist policies, annexing Castile's Murcia, crusading to Gibraltar, conquering Sardinia, conniving at the Catalan Company's Byzantine adventures, and replacing the fallen Templars with his Montesa Knights. BIBLIOGRAPHY: R. I. Burns, NCE 7:808.

[R. I. BURNS]

JAMES I, KING OF ENGLAND (1566–1625), King of Scotland from 1567 and of England from 1603. Son of Mary Queen of Scots and Henry Stuart, Lord Darnley, he was proclaimed James VI of Scotland after his father's murder and his mother's enforced abdication. The child was controlled by a succession of regents, but slowly shook himself free, and by his teens was deviously and in his characteristically shambling fashion pursuing policies of his own, in the main in alliance with England. He was reared as a Protestant and, tutored by the humanist G. Buchanan (1506–82), became a man of considerable learning, if somewhat of a pedant. His best-known literary work is the *Counterblast to Tobacco.* In 1589 he married Anne of Denmark (1574–1619), who later became a Catholic. Upon the death of Elizabeth in 1603, he became King of England and Ireland. Following a religious policy offensive to both Puritans and Catholics, and an economic policy aptly represented by the "Addled Parliament" of 1614, he left his son and successor Charles I a situation of great difficulty. Notable events of his reign include the translation of the Bible (King James Version) and the settlement of the first American colonies. BIBLIOGRAPHY: W. McElwee, *Wisest Fool in Christendom* (1958).

[T. EARLY]

JAMES II (1633–1701), **KING OF ENGLAND** from 1685–88. Second son of Charles I and Henrietta Maria, he was created Duke of York, and succeeded his brother Charles II. During the Protectorate he had served in the French and Spanish armies and won the praise of the great Turenne. He returned to England at the Restoration and married Anne Hyde, daughter of Clarendon, the chancellor; she later became a Catholic, though their two daughters, Mary and Anne, both future queens, were reared as Anglicans. Before 1671 he became a Catholic and, following the death of his first wife he married a Catholic, the devout and gracious Mary of Modena. As Lord High Admiral he was a resolute fleet-commander in the great actions of the Dutch Wars, and loyally served by Samuel Pepys, was the true begetter of the Royal Navy. As king, however, he lacked his brother's political judgment. His efforts for religious toleration were looked upon as attempts to push Catholicism; his lack of tact inflamed the Protestants, alienated the great patricians and the city, and when his queen bore him a son, which would have meant a Catholic successor, William of Orange, who had married Mary, until then his heir presumptive, was invited to supplant him. William's invasion was favored by the "Protestant wind," which prevented interception by the King's ships. Deserted by his friends, even by his daughter, Anne, James escaped to France, and "the Glorious Revolution" of 1688 was over. The final defeat of his cause came in Ireland, at the Battle of the Boyne, 1690. Already he had lost his energy for politics, and progressively withdrew into a life of religious devotion. BIBLIOGRAPHY: F. C. Turner, *James II* (1948).

[T. EARLY]

JAMES DE BENEFACTIS, BL. (Giacomo Benfatti; mid-13th cent.–1332), Dominican preacher and bishop. Born in Mantua, he entered the Dominicans at a young age, gained a degree in theology, and became an esteemed preacher with a concern for correct doctrine. His position as advisor and secretary to the Dominican Pope Benedict XI led to his appointment as bp. of Mantua in 1304. His pastoral care earned for him the title Father of the Poor. His cult was approved by Pius IX in 1859. BIBLIOGRAPHY: N. Del Re, BiblSanct 2:1220–21; L. Jadin, DHGE 7:1293–94.

[E. J. DILLON]

JAMES BIANCONI, BL. (De Blanconibus; James of Bevagna; 1220–1301), Italian Dominican preacher who led the way to a revival of civil and religious life in his native city of Bevagna (then known as Mevania), which had been sacked by Ghibellines and was suffering from an outbreak of heresy in the form of an attack upon clerical celibacy. No early life of J. exists; the later documents appear to draw much from legend. BIBLIOGRAPHY: Butler 3:390–391; L. A. Redigonda, BiblSanct 3:175–176.

[J. A. WEISHEIPL]

JAMES OF CERTALDO, BL. (d. 1292), abbot and parish priest. Son of a knight of Volterra, J. became a Camaldolese monk at the Abbey of San Giusto in 1230. He was abbot there for a short time, but resigned the office to labor for 40 years as parish priest at the monastery church. He was renowned as a pastor of souls. BIBLIOGRAPHY: C. Somigli, BiblSanct 6:352–353; Butler 2:85–86.

[G. E. CONWAY]

JAMES CINTI DE CERQUETO, BL. (d. 1367), Augustinian ascetic. From Cerqueto in Umbria, J. became an Augustinian at Perugia and spent most of his life there in obedience, patience, and austerity. He was famed for his preaching and miracles. He was formally beatified by Leo XIII in 1895, but had been venerated and prayed to throughout the intervening centuries.

[T. C. O'BRIEN]

JAMES GAETANI STEFANESCHI (*c.*1270–1343), cardinal, historian. After studying and teaching at Paris, he entered papal service, eventually becoming a cardinal (1295). His loyalty to Boniface VIII in the conflict with Philip the Fair brought him into disfavor with Boniface's successors so that his later years were spent in literary endeavors. His works include the *Monumenta Coelestiniana* (a life of Celestine V), a history of the jubilee of 1300, and notes for a projected study of the early Avignon popes. BIBLIOGRAPHY: G. Mollat, *Popes at Avignon, 1305–1378* (tr. J. Love, 1963).

[J. MULDOON]

JAMES GRIESINGER OF ULM, BL. (1407–91), Dominican lay brother. He left home in Germany for Italy, served in army of Alphonse of Aragon (Naples), and later entered the employ of a prominent jurist at Capua. At the age of 34, he became a Dominican lay brother at Bologna. He excelled in the art of painting on glass; according to tradition he discovered silver stain by accident. He has been honored as the patron of glaziers and of painters on glass and was beatified in 1825.

[J. E. LYNCH]

JAMES OF THE MARCHES, ST. (1393–1476), Italian Franciscan Observant, canon and civil lawyer, papal nuncio. Born into a humble family, educated at the Univ. of Perugia, he entered the Friars Minor (1416) at Assisi. Besides his missionary work in Bohemia, Poland, and Hungary, he was inquisitor against the *Fraticelli (1441) along with *John Capistrano; both were closely associated with St. Bernardine of Siena. J. was largely instrumental in Bernardine's canonization in 1450. His work to unite Franciscan Conventuals and Observants was less successful. Part of J.'s mission in Italy was the establishment of **montes pietatis*. He died in Naples and was canonized in 1736. BIBLIOGRAPHY: Butler 4:440–441; R. Lioi, BiblSanct 6:388–396.

[T. C. O'BRIEN]

JAMES OF METZ, Dominican theologian; it is uncertain whether he was a student or a teacher of Durandus of Saint-Pourçain. He is known to have commented on the *Sentences* of Peter Lombard at Paris; to have advanced a position on the distinction between nature and person in the Trinity that his order condemned (1314) as heresy; and to have departed from St. Thomas Aquinas on major philosophical points.

[T. C. O'BRIEN]

JAMES OF MIES, see JACOBELLUS.

JAMES OF MILAN (fl. 13th cent.), Franciscan known only as the author of *Stimulus amoris*, a late 13th-cent. mystical treatise on spiritual progress, influenced by the thought of St. Bonaventure.

[T. C. O'BRIEN]

JAMES OF NISIBIS, ST. (d. 338?), very popular saint of the Eastern Church, venerated throughout the world from ancient times. His real history has long been submerged in legends of all kinds, but he seems to have been a renowned ascetic and a teacher of St. Ephraem; as well as the first bp. of Nisibis in Mesopotamia (*c.*308), and an effective opponent of Arianists at the Council of Nicaea (325). He may have died while defending his city against the Persian siege under Sapor II. He was revered as the savior of that city by the townsfolk. His body was buried within the town walls, and his grave became a shrine. He is commemorated by the Greeks, Copts, Maronites, Armenians, and Syrians. In the Syrian and Maronite liturgy his name occurs in the canon. BIBLIOGRAPHY: E. Tisserant, DTC 292–295; E. Beck, LTK 5:844.

[E. J. DILLON]

JAMES OF SALAMONIUS, BL. (James of Venice; 1231–1314), Dominican. After divesting himself of a rich inheritance, he became a Dominican in 1248 in Venice, but spent most of his life at Forli. He was renowned as a man of prayer, a charismatic preacher, a worker of miracles, and a father to the poor. He was formally beatified in 1526 by Clement VII.

[T. C. O'BRIEN]

JAMES STREPA, BL. (*c.*1340–*c.*1410), missionary, archbishop. He became a Franciscan and worked as a missionary among the Lithuanians, Wallachians, and schismatic Russians for some 15 years. He was named abp. of Halicz in 1391. BIBLIOGRAPHY: J. J. Sarneta, BiblSanct 6:419–421; *Acta Ordinis Fratrum Minorum* (1909) 28:211.

[H. DRESSLER]

JAMES OF VITERBO, BL. (*c.*1225–1308), Augustinian scholastic, abp. of Naples. He taught at Paris as bachelor in 1288 and succeeded *Giles of Rome as regent master, 1293–1300. From 1300 he was in charge of the Augustinian *studium generale* in Naples, until he was made bp. of Benevento in 1302. A year later he was promoted to the See of Naples. Besides scholastic disputations on theological and philosophical points prepared at Paris, J. wrote commentaries on Matthew, Luke, and Paul; these are now lost. His *De regimine Christiano* (1302) is the earliest extant ecclesiological treatise. As abp. he was a theological defender of Boniface VIII against the attacks on the papacy by Philip IV of France. BIBLIOGRAPHY: P. Glorieux, NCE 7:813; U. Mariani, EncCatt 6:333–334.

[T. C. O'BRIEN]

JAMES OF VORAGINE, BL. (*c.*1230–1298), Italian Dominican, author of the *Golden Legend,* abp. of Genoa. He is known for his personal piety, his scholarly writings, his endeavors as abp. to quell the feud between the Guelphs and Ghibellines, and for his goodness to the poor. As a Dominican he taught theology and Scripture for the order. His *Legenda Aurea,* a popular collection of stories about the saints was published first in Latin (1470), then later translated into Italian, French, and even English (by Caxton at Westminster, 1483). J. was prior provincial of the Dominican Lombard province in 1267–77 and 1281–86. After refusal a first time, he accepted the See of Genoa in 1292. His cult began immediately after his death and was confirmed in 1816 by Pius VII. BIBLIOGRAPHY: A. M. Zimmermann, LTK 5:849–850; M. J. A. McCormick, NCE 7:813.

[J. R. RIVELLO]

JAMES, HENRY (1845–1916), essayist, critic, novelist. A New Englander, he made his home in England from the age of 31. He had no religious upbringing, but developed into a deist with some interest in the surface aspects of the Church. His characterizations were founded on Christian moral standards. He studied his narrow, though cosmopolitan, world from the sidelines, fascinated, yet unattached and uninvolved.

[H. JACK]

JAMES, MONTAGUE RHODES (1862–1936), English biblical scholar and paleographer. After graduating, at Cambridge J. became an assistant at, later (1893) director of the Fitzwilliam Museum where he catalogued and described thousands of the medieval MSS in the libraries of England. In the field of biblical studies, he published a valuable collection of NT Apocrypha—the *Apocryphal New Testament* (1924). A scholar of encyclopedic knowledge, J. served as vice-chancellor of Cambridge during World War I. From 1918 until his death he served as provost at Eton. BIBLIOGRAPHY: R. Schork, NCE 7:815.

[R. B. ENO]

JAMES, WILLIAM (1842–1910), American psychologist and philosopher. Son of a Swedenborgian philosopher and theologian, J. was educated at home, then in Germany and at Harvard, where he was to teach from 1872 on. His early interests were in natural science and in art, then in psychology, and finally in philosophy. These should be regarded as continuing strands rather than as different segments of his thought.

''Radical empiricism'' (his own phrase) perhaps best describes J.'s turn of mind. The pragmatism with which he is identified (although C. S. Peirce is its father and the Metaphysical Club of Cambridge its cradle) is an attitude and methodology rather than a philosophy. In approaching the problem of knowledge, J. stands against rationalism and with, to some extent, positivism, in admitting only sensibly verifiable knowledge, and utilitarianism, in insisting on practical consequences as a criterion of truth. An idea is true only if verifiable in experience and if it produces practical or ''pragmatic'' (not merely expedient) consequences. These are social as well as individual.

For J., the knower is active in the process of cognition. Against the English empiricists, he sees knowledge as related to the "stream of consciousness" of the knower, not merely as a series of isolated experiences. Ideas framed from the stream of consciousness are checked against experience. If they are verifiably true or false they are to be accepted or rejected. If the evidence is insufficient, the "will to believe" comes into play. Through the will to believe, the individual makes it true. The will to believe is a factor not only in religious thought, but in all thought, including the construction of scientific theories. Truth is a process, not an absolute.

In his *Varieties of Religious Experience* (1902) he analyzed such experiences and sought to give a psychological account of their origin. But in his evaluation of religious experiences he would have them subjected to the same pragmatic test by which other judgments are to be verified. His philosophy left him open-minded so far as religious truth is concerned, for he did hold that some religious hypotheses were capable of empirical confirmation. He was personally disposed to believe that some higher power (or higher powers), indefinable in the present state of human knowledge, was operative in the universe and working toward good, but he preferred to conceive this power as limited.

J.'s moral philosophy stems from his position on the value of the individual and the pluralism of individual wills rather than from supernatural or confessional conviction.

J.'s influence on American philosophy is a sturdy and continuing one. He left no complete system, but his insights are valuable. His is a lecturer's style and the phrases ring: "tough and tender-minded philosophies," "the moral equivalent of war," "the stream of consciousness," and "the will to believe." BIBLIOGRAPHY: R. B. Perry, *Thought and Character of William James* (2 v., 1935); W. J. Earle, EncPhil 4:240–249.

[W. B. MAHONEY]

JAMES, APOCALYPSE OF, see APOCRYPHA (NEW TESTAMENT), 22.

JAMES, ASCENTS OF, see APOCRYPHA (NEW TESTAMENT), 23.

JAMES, LETTER OF, the first of the so-called *Catholic Epistles, addressed to "the twelve tribes in the Dispersion (1.1), a description that must surely refer to Jewish converts scattered throughout the Roman-Hellenistic world. With its constant echoes of OT *wisdom, its frequent Semitic idioms and thought-forms, and its typically Jewish turns of phrase, this Epistle is certainly itself the work of a Jewish Christian. It is not, as had been pretended by F. Spitte and J. Meyer, an originally Jewish work subsequently "Christianized" by an editor. Its affinities with the Gospels and other NT Epistles are too strong, too numerous, and too radical for this. It is written in polished Greek, and shows a mastery of the methods of argument developed in Greek literary and philosophical circles. All of this makes its traditional ascription to *James the brother of the Lord problematical but not impossible. It is unlikely to be earlier than A.D. 60 or later than A.D. 150, but it is difficult to assign it a more precise date within these two extremes.

A striking feature of this Epistle is the absence of references to the person of Christ and of doctrinal instruction. It consists almost entirely of moral exhortations, and its form is that of the synagogue homily rather than of the Epistle. Its basic message is that for faith and religion to be true they must be made fruitful in good works (1.22 ff.; 2.14–25). These good works are not only the duties of practical charity (1.27 etc.), but also the joyful enduring of temptations for the sake of future glory (1.2–12), the rejecting of the false values entailed in honoring the rich and powerful and despising the poor (2.1–13; 5.1–6), the bridling of the tongue with its capacity for evil (3.1–12), the avoidance of the sins of lust, arrogance, and presumption (4.1–17), and the cultivation of the virtues of peaceableness (3.13–18), patience (5.7–11), and a charitable and uncensorious attitude toward others. *Anointing of the sick by the Church (5.13–18) and mutual confession of sins (5.16) are also recommended.

The canonicity of this Epistle was recognized in the East from the time of Origen onwards, and in the West from the mid-4th cent. onwards. The Epistle has found little favor in orthodox Protestant circles since the Reformation and Luther desired to exclude it from the canon, because of its theme of good works. BIBLIOGRAPHY: C. L. Mitton, *Epistle of James* (1966); J. Chaine, *L'Épître de Saint Jacques: Études Bibliques* (1927); B. Reicke, *Epistles of James, Peter and Jude,* (Anchor Bible 37, 1964) 1–66; T. W. Leahy, JBC 2:369–377.

[D. J. BOURKE]

JAMES, LITURGY OF ST., a liturgy whose *anaphora, attributed without foundation to James, the "brother of the Lord" and first bp. of Jerusalem, was the principal anaphora, if not the only one, used in Jerusalem in the late 4th century. The same anaphora came to the patriarchate of *Antioch, where it was eventually translated into Syriac. The division of the Antiochene patriarchate into an orthodox church adhering to Constantinople and an independent Syrian Monophysite Church is responsible for a double history of this anaphora. Only the anaphora itself is shared by both the Greek liturgy of St. James, developed in the Orthodox Church, and the Syriac liturgy of St. James developed in the *West Syrian Church. The Greek liturgy of St. James must have remained the principal anaphora of the orthodox patriarchates of Jerusalem and Antioch until at least the 8th century. It is known that the Orthodox of the patriarchate of Antioch and Jerusalem still used it on a few feasts in the 12th cent. despite its general replacement by Byzantine liturgies. The liturgy was also in use in Thessalonica, Bulgaria, Georgia, and the Byzantine communities of S Italy in the 11th or 12th century. Use of the Greek liturgy on the feast of St. James has been retained officially in modern times by the Orthodox Church on the

Greek isle of Zante. In the early 20th cent. it was revived for a while on Dec. 30 in the church of the Orthodox Monastery of the Cross near Jerusalem. BIBLIOGRAPHY: F. E. Brightman, *Liturgies Eastern and Western* (1896) 1:31–110; A. Rücker, *Die syrische Jacobosanaphora* (1923); B. Mercier, PO 26 (1946), 119–256.

[A. CODY]

JAMES, PROTOEVANGELIUM OF, see APOCRYPHA NEW TESTAMENT, 24.

JAMES THE GREAT, ACTS OF, see APOCRYPHA (NEW TESTAMENT), 25.

JAMMES, FRANCIS (1868–1938), French writer who utilized the mores and landscape of his native Pyrenees to create a spiritual bucolic poetry characterized by genuine belief, yet free of pious sentimentality. While working as a lawyer's clerk, J. won fame after 1890 for his naturist verse and regional novels in which religious motifs found a natural setting. Between 1898 and 1905, under the influence of Barrès and Claudel, J. experienced a reawakening of his youthful religious convictions, culminating in a formal return to Catholicism. Thereafter, he fused so intimately his traditional nature themes with a conscious religious outlook as to be called "a child of Virgil, but of a Virgil who might have belonged to the Third Order of St. Francis." BIBLIOGRAPHY: A. Moreau, *Le Patriarche d'Hasparren. Francis Jammes,* in *Convertis du XXe siècle* (v. 5, 1952); R. Mallet, *Francis Jammes* (1961); R. and L. Van der Burght, *Francis Jammes. Le faune chrétién* (1961).

[G. E. GINGRAS]

JAMNIA, Gr. name of the biblical city Jabneel or Jabneh, on the border of Judah, *c.*12 miles S of Joppa; the modern Yebna. The city is mentioned in Jos 15.11, 2 Chr 26.6, and in 1 and 2 Maccabees. After the fall of Jerusalem in 70 A.D. it became a center of learning for the Palestinian Jews. It has been maintained that the council of rabbis at Jamnia *c.*90–100 A.D. definitively fixed the *canon of the Hebrew Bible. Modern studies, however, can find no sure support for any authoritative list determined at Jamnia. BIBLIOGRAPHY: J. C. Turro and R. E. Brown, JBC 2:521–522.

[T. C. O'BRIEN]

JANDEL, VINCENT ALEXANDRE (1810–72), French Dominican, master general and reformer of his order. Ordained in 1834, he became rector of the seminary at Pont-à-Mousson. He joined the Dominicans in 1841 and with H. D. *Lacordaire reestablished the Friars Preachers in France. In 1862 J. was elected master general and promoted reform of the order throughout Europe. The reform was marked esp. by strong emphasis on the primitive, monastic observances, as is evident from J.'s edition of the Dominician *Constitutiones.* Lacordaire did not share in J.'s views, holding rather to an accommodation of the monastic to the apostolic life. The two strains of emphasis characterized the Dominican Order's history well into the 20th century. BIBLIOGRAPHY: R. Devas, *Dominican Revival in the 19th Century* (1913); *idem, Ex umbris* (n.d.); M. H. Vicaire, *Catholicisme* 6:310.

[T. C. O'BRIEN]

JANISSARY (from Turkish *yeni çeri,* "the new troop"), an elite corps of infantry belonging to the Ottoman sultan. The Janissary organization was created by the Sultan Orkhan in the first half of the 14th cent. as a special body of infantry subject directly and exclusively to the Sultan. The manner of their recruitment was unique; it was accomplished by a periodic levy or draft (called *devshirme*) of non-Muslim children of ages generally 14 to 20, carried out chiefly among the rural peasantry of the Balkan provinces of the empire. These recruits, most of them Christian by birth, were screened in Istanbul and those thought morally and physically the best were sent directly to the palace for training. After the 16th cent. the *devshirme* became less frequent as there were many aspirants to membership in the elite corps. Promotion within the corps was based strictly on seniority and members were subject to discipline exclusively by the organization. Because of the privileges attached to the Janissaries, membership came ultimately to be purchased and in the 18th cent. the organization, having completely lost its military virtue, became altogether corrupt and embroiled in palace politics. It was finally disbanded in 1826 by Sultan Mahmud II in favor of an army based on European models. The Janissary corps had also a special relationship to the *Bektashi order of *dervishes who had exclusive spiritual direction of the organization. BIBLIOGRAPHY: J. A. B. Palmer, "Origin of the Janissaries," *Bulletin of the John Rylands Library* 35 (1953) 448–481; H. A. R. Gibb and H. Bowen, *Islamic Society and the West,* v. 1, part 1 (1950), index.

[R. M. FRANK]

JANNEQUIN, CLÉMENT (*c.*1475–*c.*1560), French composer. Very little is known of this composer's life. He wrote two Masses and an abundance of four-part descriptive chansons, which latter made him famous. Many of his works, such as "La Bataille" and "Le Chant des Oiseaux", are included in *Les Maîtres-Musiciens de la Renaissance Française,* edited by Henri Expert.

[P. J. HENNESSEY]

JANNES AND JAMBRES, names given by popular Jewish tradition to the two Egyptian magicians who matched wits with Moses (Ex 7.11–12). This tradition is reflected in 2 Tim 3.8, where the Latin version gives the variant spelling, Mambres. There is also evidence that an apocryphal book was once attributed to them.

[J. J. CASTELOT]

JANSEN, CORNELIUS (THE ELDER) (1510–76), bp. and Bible scholar. J. studied at the Univ. of Louvain and, after serving as pastor at Courtrai (1542–62), became a professor of theology there. He attended the Council of Trent, and reluctantly accepted the Diocese of Ghent in 1568. He implemented the Tridentine decrees with great zeal, established a seminary, and published a diocesan ritual. He is also known for his exegetical works, notably a *Concordia evangelica* (1549) which emphasized the literal interpretation of the text and the importance of working from the original biblical languages.

[T. M. MCFADDEN]

JANSEN, CORNELIUS OTTO (Jansenius; 1585–1638), Dutch theologian and bishop, from whom *Jansenism received its name and doctrine. Born at Accoi in Holland, he was aided by benefactors to study at the Univ. of Louvain, winning first honors in 1604. From Jacques Jansson he imbibed the "positivism" of Baius (see BAIANISM), as well as a contempt for scholasticism and for the Jesuits. In France he studied the early Fathers and councils with Jean Duvergier de Hauranne, later the Abbé de *Saint-Cyran. J. was ordained in 1614. He became bachelor of theology in 1609 and doctor in 1619. As professor of exegesis at Louvain and director of Ste. Pulchérie Seminary (1619–21), he studied St. Augustine's teachings on grace and found Baianist allies in Saint-Cyran and Florent Conry, an Irish Franciscan. J. corresponded with Saint-Cyran in elaborate codes about "Pilmot," their ambitious and mysterious project of radically reforming the Church from laxity and rationalism. At the court and universities of Spain in 1624 and 1626, J. thwarted expansion of Jesuit education in Louvain. As Regius Professor of Scripture after 1630, he stressed literal exegesis and patristic teaching; he also undertook anti-Protestant polemics. Named rector of Louvain in 1635, he developed its library and archives. His pamphlet *Mars gallicus* attacked the policies of the French king and Richelieu, and Protestant alliances. Rewarded as a loyal scribe of his Spanish sovereign, J. was consecrated bp. of Ypres in 1636. Meanwhile his work *Augustinus, begun in 1627, proceeded with interruptions. Viewing Augustine's doctrine as the last word on nature and grace, J. adopted Baius's interpretations, already condemned by Pius V and Gregory XIII. He completed his revisions in April 1638 and died peacefully on May 6, apparently of plague. His will entrusted publication to friends, who achieved it secretly on July 19, 1640; the papal internuncio Stravius obtained a prohibition from Urban VIII just too late. Louvain's faculty declined to condemn *Augustinus,* and the three ponderous Latin folios sold widely among Catholic and Calvinist clergy. They were reprinted in Paris and Rouen (with Conry's treatise consigning unbaptized infants to hell appended). A long controversy between Jansenists and Jesuits ensued. Dying after 18 months as bp., J. had said, "If the Holy See wishes any change, I am an obedient son of the Church." He was remembered as pious, austere, learned, and eloquent, a tireless worker devoted to the Church, rather cold and inflexible but with a lofty sense of duty.

BIBLIOGRAPHY: F. Mourret, *History of the Catholic Church* (tr. N. Thompson, 8 v., 1931–57) 6:362–389; H. Daniel-Rops, *Church in the Seventeenth Century* (tr. J. J. Buckingham, 1963) 327–346; *Theology of Man and Grace* (ed. E. J. Fortman, 1966) 271–284; J. Orcibal, *Origines du Jansénisme* (1947); J. Carreyre, DTC 8.1:319–330.

[W. DAVISH]

JANSENISM, a religious movement chiefly among 17th- and 18th-cent. French intellectuals, originating with a distinctive doctrine on grace, but developing also into an adherence to *Gallicanism and moral rigorism. It lasted beyond 1800 and is survived by a small schismatic Jansenist Church founded in Holland in 1723 (see LITTLE CHURCH OF UTRECHT). Its name and doctrine derive from Cornelius *Jansen; its organization, from Jean Duvergier de Hauranne, Abbé de *Saint-Cyran. These friends, after studying the church Fathers, developed an ambitious project to reform the Church from rationalism and laxity. Jansen, as professor of Scripture at Louvain, produced **Augustinus,* a study of St. Augustine's doctrine on grace, posthumously published in 1640. He taught that: (1) divine grace is man's by right; (2) its loss through original sin has mutilated man's very nature; (3) fallen man's will no longer controls his decisions but necessarily obeys the stronger attraction, either of *concupiscence or of grace; (4) all acts of sinners are sins; (5) salvation and damnation depend on God's eternal predestination alone; and (6) Christ died not for all but for the predestined few. Jansen thus systematized *Baianism, which had already been censured in 1567 and 1579 (see D 1901–80); consequently, Urban VIII formally condemned *Augustinus* in the bull *In eminenti,* 1643. Meanwhile Saint-Cyran organized support for Jansen's doctrine, aided by the influential *Arnauld family. Mère Angélique Arnauld was the reforming abbess of *Port-Royal convent near Paris, where Saint-Cyran became director in 1635 and established the center of Jansenism. Suspicious of Port-Royal and resentful of Saint-Cyran's refusal to rebut the anti-Richelieu pamphlet *Mars gallicus* (actually Jansen's work), Richelieu imprisoned Saint-Cyran, 1638–42. Freed at the cardinal's death, Saint-Cyran died in 1643.

Jansenism might have died with him, but Antoine Arnauld became a second founder, defending *Augustinus* and counterattacking with *De la fréquente communion* (1642), in which he teaches that, since no one is worthy to receive Christ, respectful abstention honors him more than frequent communion does. Furthermore, absolution requires perfect contrition and should be withheld pending severe penances. Arnauld's attack on Jesuit casuistry shifted the controversy from grace to morality. But Innocent X convoked a commission of cardinals to study a résumé of doctrine in five questionable propositions attributed to *Augustinus* and condemned all five in **Cum occasione,* 1653. Arnauld devised his famous distinction between *droit* and *fait,* admitting the condemnation of the propositions as heretical but denying that they in fact reflected Jansen's thought. Alexander VII, however, with *Ad sanctam beati Petri sedem,* 1656, explicitly reaffirmed this fact. Required to accept this censure, the nuns of Port-Royal quibbled and protested, and finally 12 were dispersed to other convents. Blaise *Pascal, brother of one of the nuns, produced in 1656 his classic epistolary series, the *Provincial Letters, which deride Jesuit probabilism. Read everywhere, they were condemned by the Holy Office and ordered burned by Louis XIV, but they popularized Jansenist ideas. The sensational cure of Pascal's niece furthered the movement, and Jesuit rebuttals fell on deaf ears. After the *Peace of the Church under Clement IX in 1669, Jansenist influence grew in the Sorbonne and in the seminaries and spread abroad. The party published Pascal's *Pensées,* a French Bible, numerous impressive textbooks, and a voluminous assault on Jesuit moral doctrine. But as Port-Royal continued loudly recalcitrant, in 1679 a new abp. forbade receiving novices, and thus the community declined. In 1709 Louis XIV dispersed the score of nuns remaining and 2 years later razed the convent. Louis saw the Jansenists as heretics and rebels, hence Arnauld's persistent polemic led to his exile in the Netherlands, where he died in 1694.

Arnauld's companion and successor, Pasquier *Quesnel, reorganized Jansenism, emphasizing Gallicanism and moral austerity. His *Réflexions morales* expounded a Protestant view of the Church, and in 1713 Clement XI in **Unigenitus* proscribed 101 propositions verbatim (see D 2400–2502), whereupon nine Jansenist bps. held that the Pope had erred in faith. Rigorist, Gallican Jansenism thrived on the subsequent pamphlet war and won temporary favor from the regent Philip of Orléans after Louis's death. In 1717 four bps. appealed from *Unigenitus* to an ecumenical council; though these *Appellants enlisted a dozen bps. and 3,000 of the 100,000 French clergy, they were excommunicated. Compromise failed and a decade of exiles and imprisonments ensued.

In Paris Abp. Vintimille, successor to the vacillating Noailles, had *Unigenitus* made law and exacted acceptance by the Sorbonne, Parlement, dioceses, and religious communities. As convinced Appellants died out and no new leaders appeared, moribund Jansenism lapsed further into bigotry and gloom. The journal *Nouvelles ecclésiastiques* sustained its martyr mentality, 1728–1803, recounting marvels such as those claimed by the *convulsionaries of Saint-Médard. Jansenism was dogmatic under Saint-Cyran, moralistic with Arnauld, political after Quesnel, and anti-Jesuit first to last. A moral Puritanism and the infrequent reception of holy communion were effects on RC life that lingered into the 20th century. BIBLIOGRAPHY: N. Abercrombie, *Origins of Jansenism* (1936); J. Orcibal, *Origines du Jansénisme* (1947); A. Gazier, *Histoire générale du mouvement janséniste* (1922); Knox Enth; DTC *Tables générales* 2:2387–2415; L. J. Cognet, NCE 7:820–824. *PISTOIA, SYNOD OF.

[W. DAVISH]

JANSENIST CHURCH OF HOLLAND, a commonly used name for the *Little Church of Utrecht (OBC), also called the Old Catholic Church of the Netherlands. In 1889 it became an Old Catholic body, but its beginnings date from the 18th-cent. Schism of Utrecht, a separation from Rome partly over *Jansenism.

JANSENISTIC PIETY, the religious piety (attitude, spirit, devotion) that had its doctrinal roots in the *Augustinus* of Cornelius Jansen (the soil was prepared by Baianism), furthered principally by Jansen's friend and close associate, Jean Duvergier de Hauranne, Abbot of Saint-Cyran, who became in 1633 director of Port-Royal, the "geographical and spiritual heart of jansenistic piety" (NCE 7:824). Reacting against humanism in all forms, it was a piety insistent upon the need for personal austerity and for ecclesiastical reform. It regarded God with an unwholesome fear and preached of the severity of Christ. Based on a narrowly interpreted Augustinian teaching on grace, it found little good in human nature, was preoccupied by a sense of sin and of the sinfulness of man, and was imbued by a spirit that demanded rigorous moral discipline and a severe penitential practice (advocating long preparation for confession, with absolution deferred until the penance had been fulfilled). It discouraged frequent communion.

Jansenism allowed little or no place in the spiritual life for devotional feeling, for familiarity with God, for joy or warmth in attachment to Christ. The resultant piety was cold and harsh; the prayer abstract (going directly to God without concern for intermediaries). And the disregard for emotions and other human factors in the spiritual life led to a tension in many, and to a lack of religious balance that encouraged the excesses of Port-Royal.

Saint-Cyran and his disciples encouraged a profound spirit of adoration, a simple realism in the spiritual life, and reverence for the liturgy. Yet at the same time they distrusted theological reasoning, the casuistry of moral theology, and, regarding themselves as an elite, even questioned church pronouncements (doctrinal and disciplinary) as favoring laxity and undue liberty. With the antimysticism that followed the quietist controversies, Jansenistic spirituality revived and (largely under the influence of Quesnel) spread widely through the 18th and into the 19th century. It vigorously opposed the devotion to the Heart of Jesus. More recently any spirit that appears to reflect the harsh aspects of the piety of Saint-Cyran and his followers is, not always accurately, termed "Jansenistic." BIBLIOGRAPHY: L. Cognet, *Catholicisme* 6:313–331; B. Matteucci, NCE 7:824–826; P. Pourrat, *Christian Spirituality* (tr. D. Attwater, 4 v., 1955) 4.

[W. J. READ]

JANSSENS, ALOYSIUS (1887–1941), theologian. J. was professor of dogmatic theology for the missionary Congregation of the Immaculate Heart of Mary (Scheut Fathers), and dedicated himself to producing in Flemish a series in contemporary dogmatic and biblical theology for missionaries. He edited 17 of the 28 volumes in that series. He also wrote on Card. Newman and was a founder (1931) of the first Belgian Mariological society. BIBLIOGRAPHY: G. Philips, NCE 7:827.

[T. M. MCFADDEN]

JANSSENS, HENRI (1855–1925), Benedictine theologian. J. studied at the Gregorian Univ., was ordained in 1877, then entered the Benedictines in Belgium at the abbey of Maredsous. He was appointed rector and professor of dogmatics at the Collegio San Anselmo in Rome (1893), and subsequently held a variety of positions in the Roman Curia. His principal work is a theological *Summa* (9 v., 1899–1921). He was appointed a titular abbot (1909), and titular bp. of Tiberias (1921).

[T. M. MCFADDEN]

JANUARIUS, ST., see FAUSTUS, JANUARIUS, AND MARTIAL, SS.

JANUARIUS OF BENEVENTO, ST. Patron saint of Naples, bp. of Benevento, martyred during the persecution decreed by the Emperor Diocletian in 303 A.D. The accounts of his life are late and of doubtful validity. The most noteworthy fact about him is that a vial containing a solid, brownish matter, said to be his blood, is publicly venerated by great crowds to this day in the Naples cathedral, because 18 times a year it softens and is seen to flow when the vial is tipped. The wonder attracts the curious, the devout, and the skeptical. On occasions when the substance does not liquefy on schedule dire consequences seem to occur, such as the great earthquake in NE Italy in May 1976. Attempts to explain the liquefaction scientifically have failed.

[J. F. FALLON]

JANUS, Roman god having one head with two faces in opposite directions, guarding public and private entrances and exits from evil. The Janus head appears on Roman coins as patron of business, promising fresh beginnings.

[M. J. DALY]

JANUS (PSEUD.), see DÖLLINGER, JOHANNES JOSEPH IGNAZ VON.

JAPAN, isl. country located in the Pacific to the East of the Asiatic mainland (142,726 sq mi; pop. [1971] 104,660,000). It comprises four major islands and many hundreds of small ones. Its present form of government is democratic; the hereditary emperor being regarded less as actual ruler than as a symbol of the states and the unity of the people. The racial origins of its people are not clearly known. In the 5th cent. B.C. Buddhism and the civilization of China became known to the islands. Japan was opened to commerce in modern times by Commodore M. Perry in 1854. Its modern constitution dates from 1889. By defeating Russia and China and by occupying Formosa, Korea, and Manchuria, Japan became a major world power, but its defeat in World War II marked the end of territorial expansion and the beginning of a more modern and industrialized economy. The religion of the masses is Shintoism, with elements of Confucianism, Buddhism, and ancestor worship (see JAPANESE RELIGION). However, the modern, educated citizen of Japan tends to be a religious skeptic.

Christianity came to Japan with St. *Francis Xavier and his companions in 1549. By 1582 the Church had 150,000 members. The chief organizer of the mission was A. *Valignano, whose program of evangelization included seminaries for the training of priests. The death of the Shogun Nobunaga, the mission protector, brought conflict among religious orders over procedures, suspicion of the motives of Europeans, and the pressure of Shintoists led to persecution in which many lost their lives. Despite the heroic steadfastness of the Christian community, the number of the faithful diminished and few remained by the end of the 18th cent., and those were centered in pockets (Nagasaki and Kyushu) in which the Christian faith persisted with remarkable hardihood through 2 cent. of persecution. Missionary work was resumed in 1847 by the Paris Foreign Mission Society. Religious freedom was established by law in 1889, but from 1930 till 1945 mission activities were curtailed because the Church was obliged to sever many of its ties with the West in consequence of political developments. The first Japanese bp. was consecrated during this period.

After World War II there was a great influx of missioners. Forty religious orders of men and 86 of women were established in Japan. At first there were many conversions, but during the 1960s their number has declined. The Catholic Church in Japan is at present working to lay solid foundations for the future. There are archbishoprics at Nagasaki, Tokyo, and Osaka with suffragan sees at Fukuoka, Hiroshima, Kagoshima, Kyoto, Sapporo, Sendai, Urawa, Yokohama, Nagoya, Niigata, and Takamatsu, all under Japanese bishops. The clergy are trained at seminaries in Nagasaki, Tokyo, and Kyushu. Catholics publish a number of periodicals and are active in the other media of communication. In 1976 the total Catholic community was estimated to number about 377,637. The increasing agnosticism of the younger generation, however, and the materialism resulting from the new prosperity are poor preparation for the acceptance of the gospel. On the other hand, the steadfast attachment of Japanese Catholics to the faith as well as the openness of the Church to new ideas inspires hope for the future.

Protestant denominations (Episcopalian, Baptist, Methodist, Presbyterian, Lutheran, and Congregational) began work in 1859. They were followed by Adventists, Pentecostals, and other denominations. After World War II there was a notable increase in the number of missionary societies—almost 200 of them. A unifying agency, the United Church of Christ in Japan (*Kyodan*), includes half of the 818,476 Protestants in the country. There is also a no-church Christian Movement (*Mukyokai*), which shuns ecclesiastical organization. BIBLIOGRAPHY: A. Ebizawa, *Christianity in Japan* (1960); J. Laures, *Catholic Church in Japan: A Short History* (1954); *Bilan du Monde* 2:531–540.

[P. DAMBORIENA]

JAPAN, MARTYRS OF. European missionaries brought Christianity to Japan in the 16th cent. and made many converts. In 1587 an edict of prescription against Catholics was published, and the first bloody persecution took place in 1597. Early that year, a Castilian ship was captured and guns were found on board; this led to the belief that the missionaries were attempting to annex Japan to either Portugal or Castile. A list of all Christians in Miyado and Osaka was drawn up; reprisals began in Nagasaki with the crucifixion of 26 missionaries and converts on Feb. 5, 1597. This group was beatified by Urban VIII on Sept. 14, 1627, and canonized by Pius IX, June 8, 1862. Persecution continued sporadically through the 17th, 18th, and 19th cent. until the granting of religious freedom in 1873. A group of 205 martyrs who died 1617–32 (see Butler 2:445–451) were beatified by Pius IX. BIBLIOGRAPHY: Butler 3:533–535; L. C. Profillet, *Le Martyrologie de l'église du Japon* (3 v., 1897); L. Delplace, *Le Catholicisme au Japon* (2 v., 1869); C. R. Boxer, *Christian Century in Japan* (1951); for lists of martyrs see J. F. Schütte, NCE 7:835–845.

[P. K. MEAGHER]

JAPAN, ORTHODOX CHURCH IN. A mission of the Russian Orthodox Church was initiated in the 1860s and its clergy were mostly Japanese by the turn of the century. The first Japanese bp., Nicholas Ono, was consecrated in 1941 and died in 1944. A majority of Japanese Orthodox are subject to a bp. associated with the Russian Metropolia in the U.S. in consequence of manipulation by the American military occupation authorities in 1946. There is a seminary in Tokyo. A minority of Japanese Orthodox are subject to a Japanese bp., Nicholas Sayama, consecrated in 1967 with canonical ties to the Patriarchate of Moscow. BIBLIOGRAPHY: R. Stephanopoulos, *Encyclopedia of Modern Christian Missions* (1967) 237.

[T. BIRD]

JAPANESE RELIGION. The concept of religion as a distinct category in social and psychological life is not native to Japan. The Japanese language contained no word corresponding to the Western "religion" until contact with the West in the 19th cent. led to the adaptation of many words, including *shukyo* for religion, to meet the sort of categories in which foreign investigators thought. One can still encounter arguments that Shinto or Buddhism are not religions, meaning religions in some Western sense. The argument, being highly semantic, is usually sterile. The modern phenomenological approach to comparative studies detects, contrariwise, an almost embarrassing richness of forms in traditional Japan which play the role of religion as generally defined cross-culturally. Acts of awareness of the numinous or sacred, techniques of spiritual rebirth, and human commerce with superhuman forces provide fundamental contexts for family, community, or sect activities of coinherence.

Influences. The complexity of Japanese religion is due to the great diversity of cultural influences which have flowed into the island empire. It is as though all of Asia and the South Seas emptied themselves into this land beyond the E rim of the continent. The flood could go no further; at least until very recently, remarkably little of Japanese influence touched the culture of any other land. But what had been there received was held tenaciously, and was subtly modified while being preserved. The Japanese race itself, although now highly homogeneous, is ultimately a mixture of several strands. Comparably, it is as difficult to find a purely indigenous religious phenomenon in Japan as to find one that does not bear the mark of distinctive Japanese adaptation.

Seven discernible threads are worked into the fabric of contemporary Japanese religion. These are folk religion, Shinto, Buddhism, Taoism, Confucianism, Christianity, and the recent New Religions. Of these, the first five were already in Japan by the time of the emergence of literary civilization in the 7th cent. A.D. Folk religion in Japan possesses certain definable patterns that have survived to the present and have exercised a subtle but incalculable impact on the Japanese modification of the great religions. But almost by definition folk religion has no more than local and nonliterary institutional life. The great institutional religious form has been Buddhism. The *samgha* entered Japan as a distinct and at first alien structure actively shaping and being shaped by the life around it. Shinto acquired institutional form largely in response to the Buddhist challenge to preserve certain values of the pre-Buddhist milieu. The great Chinese traditions of Taoism and Confucianism achieved minimal institutional form in Japan, but have had a pervasive intellectual influence, particularly on folk religion, Shinto thought, and political ideology. Christianity, first entering Japan with St. Francis Xavier and his missionaries in 1549, revived by a new influx of missionaries in the 19th and 20th cent., has remained institutionally aloof. Yet characteristically Japanese modifications of Christianity have appeared. Moreover, the last entity to arrive, the New Religions, sectarian movements of the last century and a half, have represented syncretisms of all that had gone before, including motifs borrowed from Christianity. The highly organized institutional forms the New Religions have taken derive from a specific response to modernity.

It is important to preserve, in the face of this complexity, what has been called a "unified interpretation of Japanese religion." It would be going too far to hold that there is really only one religion of Japan, of which all these forms are only epiphenomenal faces. Yet with a few exceptions the greater error would be to see them as separate, monolithic, and exclusive faiths or denominations. Traditionally, Japanese are married in Shinto rites and buried in Buddhist obsequies, associating Shinto with family and this-worldly affairs, Buddhism with the concerns of private spirituality and the afterlife. For 1,000 years before the Meiji Restoration of 1868, Shinto shirines and Buddhist temples commonly existed side by side in a kind of symbiosis. The interaction of Confucianism, Taoism, and folk religion with these two visible faiths can be compared to the role of Greek philosophy, hermeticism, and European folk-faith respectively on the development of medieval Christendom. (Taoism came to Japan largely in the guise of "spiritual technologies" involving directional and calendric magic, esoteric deities, and the like.) Without becoming major institutions, these three helped mold the specific shapes of religious and cultural structures.

The Phenomena of Japanese Folk Religion, Shinto, and Buddhism. It is difficult to isolate a distinct group of practices that can unambiguously be termed folk religion, for the nature of its continuity has been such that most of its contents—i.e., the names of the gods and the like—are one with those of Shinto, Buddhism, and Taoism. But its structures have permeated the greatest of the shrines and monasteries, and have provided the dynamic of the newest religious movements. Archaic and popular Japanese religion has been said to focus around two polar experiences of divinity: the *ujigami,* or deity of place and clan, and the *hitogami,* the divine being who breaks in from outside the circle of the familiar. The celebration of the *ujigami,* in archaic times before the emergence of architectural shrines, typically centered upon the sacred mountain above the rice fields. In the spring, the populace would make their way up the mountain to greet the deity and escort him (or her) into the fields to fructify the crop and guard it until the harvest. In the fall the god would be conveyed with the harvest into the granary or home and celebrated with first-fruit offerings and festival, then be returned to the mountain. The leader of the clan would be priest. Between the mountain and the village the worshipers would purify themselves in water, preferably in a stream. These basic motifs—the sacred mountain, spring and fall festivals, the deity as patron of a clan, purification—underlie village practice today, even if associated in part with Shinto shrine or Buddhist temple.

The divine is not experienced only as the familiar god of the clan, however. It may also come as the *hitogami,* the "manlike god," at once more human and more alien than the village patron. He is the heavenly deity who descends to mate with the local god, and is the god or ancestral spirit who visits at uncanny, pivotal times like harvest and New Year's. He possesses shamans in ecstasy. The importance of New Year's should be emphasized. In it themes of harvest and spring, of *ujigami* and *hitogami* merge. It has become the central festival of Japanese religion. Shamanism is also typologically important. While shamanistic phenomena have seemingly been repressed in the major traditions, local shamans—mostly female and blind—still pursue their mediumistic craft in a few places. More important, the shamanistic structure—the pattern of ecstatic journeys and new revelations that give charismatic authentication to elect persons—has never disappeared from the dynamics of Japanese religion, as the stories of the origins of many of the New Religions show. Shinto can be understood only as a religion whose major mode of expression is rite, and whose foundation is sociological. Its essential locus is the shrine. The Shinto shrine, jinja, beautifully illustrates the dichotomy of sacred and profane space. It is usually a simple, rustic edifice containing no anthropomorphic image, but built around some relic of the divine presence—a mirror or sword, perhaps—kept behind closed doors. The shrine precincts are demarcated by the distinctive torii, or Shinto gate. At the time of service, offerings of rice, wine, food, salt, and water are presented by robed priests in a liturgy of simple dignity, followed (on the occasion of a matsuri, or public festival) by sacred dance, perhaps a rapid bearing of the *mikoshi* or divine palanquin through the streets, and carnival.

The Buddhist temple is easily distinguishable from the Shinto shrine. Whereas the shrine has no image or incense, the temple lacks the torii; but within, the visitor is greeted with a solemn likeness of a Buddha, or Bodhisattva, with offerings of incense, fruit, and flowers, and perhaps the chanting of sutras. It is in the family or private spirituality of believers, though, that the impact of traditional Buddhism is seen. Funeral and memorial services occupy a large part of the time of Buddhist clergy. Before many household Buddhist altars are tablets with the names of ancestors. In the great historic Buddhist temples and monasteries, such as those of Mt. Koya, Mt. Hiei, or various Zen centers, one can participate in the aesthetic and atmosphere of the Mahayana interior path. The major temples of the Pure Land schools, such as the two Honganji in Kyoto, are pilgrimage centers for devotees of these large sects. On the other hand, numerous humble roadside shrines, such as those of Jizo, the bodhisattva protector of travelers and children, testify to the pervasive influence of Buddhism on popular piety.

History. The introduction of Buddhism into Japan from China via Korea is traditionally set at 532 or 552 A.D. This period coincides with the beginning of Japan's exact history. After several vicissitudes Buddhism secured a strong position as the dominant religion of the imperial court in the regency of Prince Shotoku (573–621). It is worth noting, however, that in the famous constitution attributed to him, Confucian virtues are enjoined upon civil servants in language as positive as that in which they are exhorted to reverence the Three Treasures of Buddhism. Toward the end of the 8th cent., during the reigns of the Emperor Temmu (672–686) and his widow and successor, Jito (686–697), a certain Shinto reaction set in. Decrees attributed to them established the main pillars of that official Shinto which determined the faith's institutional shape: the preeminence of the Grand Shrine of Ise dedicated to the imperial patron deities, the control of shrines by the throne, the cycle of court Shinto rites, and the compiling of the official mythological-historical chronicles, the *Kojiki* (issued 712) and the *Nihonshoki* (or *Nihongi,* issued 720). When the ancient theocratic regime was reorganized on the model of Chinese ministerial government by the Taiho Code of 701, the Jingi-kan, or ministry, was given a place of honor above all other bureaus.

However, the subsequent Nara period (710–784) saw a great flourishing of Buddhism. The establishment of a permanent capital in the city of Nara allowed the production of those great works of art and architecture inseparable from Buddhist culture. Its triumph was symbolized in the dedication of the Great Buddha in the Todaiji, a sort of national cathedral, in Nara in 752. The Buddhism of the capital was consolidated around officially recognized schools (the so-called six sects) gathered by prominent priests in endowed temples. Their Buddhist learning and credentials, together with other desiderata of culture, had been brought from China. This aristocratic Buddhism suffered competition from rural evangelists who combined a patina of Buddhism with a display of magic and shamanic powers. Often operating out of traditionally sacred mountains, they made Buddhism speak the language of Shintoistic indigenous spirituality tinged with Taoist magic. The reconciliation of this wing with official Buddhism was a major problem of the Nara period. It was partly achieved when Gyogi Bosatsu (Gyogi the Bodhisattva, 670–749), a leader in this charismatic popular Buddhist tradition, was made high priest of all Japanese Buddhism by the Emperor Shomu.

In 794 the capital was moved from Nara to Heian (modern Kyoto), in large part because of the reaction against the excessive influence of monks on the court. Abandoned by the center of national culture, the Nara schools withered. They were replaced in the mainstream of Buddhism during the Heian period (794–1185) by two new schools. These were Tendai, headquartered on Mt. Hiei NE of Kyoto and founded by Dengyo Daishi (766–822), and Shingon, headquartered on Mt. Koya some distance from the capital and founded by Kobo Daishi (773–835). Both of these masters had studied in China, and both were vigorous and active men of the stamp of Gyogi as well. Their sects asserted a Japanese Buddhism rich in the charismatic, mountain-centered, quasi-magical indigenous tradition, yet authenticated by transmission of important mainland teachings. Tendai was the Chinese T'ien T'ai, a broad and syncretistic Mahayana culminating in belief that the Lotus Sutra is the supreme statement of Buddhist faith. Shingon represents the tradition of esoteric Buddhism, with its emphasis on achievement of the eternal Buddha-nature now in this life through intense meditation, mystic gestures (mudra), and words of power (mantra). One advanced to Buddhahood through 10 stages of consciousness. Shingon was esp. lavish in the use of art and ceremonial. Tendai soon emulated Shingon in both its color and esotericism. Both sects also sought, and in large measure achieved, a reconciliation of Shinto with Buddhism through doctrines that first made the *kami* guardians of the Buddhist faith, and later manifestations of the Buddha-nature. This was practically expressed through the attachment of shrines and temples to each other. Both sects also had orders of *yamabushi* (mountain priests) attached to them, at least nominally. These were Buddhist ascetics, magicians, and diviners who perpetuated the old charismatic tradition. Wandering about, guiding pilgrims, evangelizing the countryside, they were popular among villagers for their healings and strange feats, and had a great influence on provincial religion.

Yet the splendid ceremonies of Tendai and Shingon did not exhaust the spiritual life of the Heian court. The dignified and austere official Shinto rites prescribed by the Taiho Code were continued. Under the supervision of the ministry of Yin-yang divination (*ommyo-ryo*), concepts concerning lucky and unlucky days, directions, times of life, and purification were widely observed. Many such practices have persisted into modern times on the folk level. At the same time, Confucian ideas such as the supreme moral value of filial piety were widely regarded in aristocratic circles. The life of the court centered upon a garish and eclectic cycle of ceremonial observances.

The Heian regime was overthrown in the middle of the 12th cent. by rough-hewn warrior chieftains from outlying provinces. The religious life of the following periods (Kamakura, 1192–1333, and Muromachi, 1338–1573) was dominated by the soldier mentality. But the revolution was popular as well as military and represented a reaction against the monastic, aesthetic, and complex Buddhist systems of the Tendai and Shingon priesthoods. The new demand was for simple, powerful styles of religion as effective for salvation on the battlefield or in the peasant village as in court or cloister. Once again strong charismatic leaders rose up, men who spoke alike of the particular degeneracy of the age and of the radically simple means by which salvation must be achieved in such an age. Three major types of Buddhism, which now embrace the great majority of Japanese Buddhists, emerged: Pure Land, Nichiren, and Zen.

Pure Land Buddhism in Japan was promulgated by Honen (1133–1212), founder of the Jodo sect, and his even more radical disciple, Shinran (1173–1262), founder of the Jodo Shinshu sect. They taught that dependence solely on the help of an outside spiritual power, specifically Amida Buddha who was believed to have vowed that any who called upon his name would be brought into his Western Paradise (the Pure Land), was a greater way to Buddhist peace and liberation than the former techniques based on individual effort. Followers of Pure Land, forsaking other practices, chant "*Namu Amida Butsu*" (Hail to Amida Buddha).

Nichiren (1222–82), founder of the sect that bears his name, believed with a passion typical of the charismatic tradition that the only answer to the spiritual crisis of the age was a return to devotion to the Lotus Sutra exclusively. For his followers, the chanting of *Namu Myoho Renge Kyo*

(Hail to the Marvelous Teaching of the Lotus Sutra) indicated implicit faith in all its doctrines and Buddhas and was a formula of great power. The movement was characterized by fervor, nationalism, and a polemical spirit. Much of its tone is found today in a modern offshoot, Soka Gakkai.

The third movement, Zen (see ZEN BUDDHISM), was a very different sort of answer, but in its own way suited the new attitude. Brought from China by Eisai (1141–1215) and Dogen (1200–53), it taught that enlightenment is achieved quietly and unexpectedly in the course of meditation and self-control. Its simplicity of atmosphere and approach contrasted with the techniques of the older esotericism. Zen was popular with the new military aristocracy for its compatibility with their stoical code, yet also with artists and poets for its patronage of a new aesthetic of allusive understatement.

The next important era, the Tokugawa (1600–1868), began with persecution of Christians and the requirement that all families be registered as members of a Buddhist temple. *Yamabushi,* however, remained important in popular religious life. But the intellectual foundation of the Tokugawa regime was Confucian. Against all of this a scholarly movement, called Kokugaku, in favor of what was thought to be pure Shinto, emerged under the leadership of Azumamaro Kada (1669–1756), Norinaga Motoori (1730–1801), and Atsutane Hirata (1776–1843).

The Meiji Restoration of 1868 brought a triumph of the kind of Shinto represented by Kokugaku scholarship. A violent separation of Shinto and Buddhism, and "purification" of the former, was ordered. The ancient cycle of imperial Shinto practices was made central to the official spiritual life of the nation. However, religious Shinto proved inadequate as the basis of a modern state. The increasingly nationalistic official ideology came to emphasize a Confucian concept of filial loyalty to sovereign and State (as stated, e.g., in the important Imperial Rescript on Education of 1890), undergirded by Shinto myths of the imperial ancestors and symbolic acts of loyalty in Shinto shrines, which were declared to be "nonreligious."

At the same time Christianity won acceptance from a certain number of Japanese, esp. during waves of Western prestige. Its influence has usually outweighed its numbers. The New Religions, which have grown at phenomenal rates in the last 100 years, have similarly helped shape the modern religious picture. Examples are Tenrikyo, Konkokyo, Omoto, Odori Shukyo, and Soka Gakkai. They have typically grown up around strong charismatic leaders, frequently women, and have emphasized tight organization, healing, optimism, modern publicity techniques, fervent loyalty, and evangelism.

[R. S. ELLWOOD]

JARICOT, PAULINE MARIE (1799–1862), foundress of the Society for the Propagation of the Faith. At the age of 17 she vowed perpetual virginity, and her whole life was lived in great self-denial. She established in Lyons a group among servant girls that dedicated itself to reparation to the Sacred Heart (Réparatrices du Sacré-Coeur de Jésus-Christ). Beginning among her associates, she began to solicit funds for the missions. Each promoter was to find 10 contributors who would give a minimal weekly sum. J. also established other pious associations and a home for working girls. The Society for the Propagation of the Faith was formally founded at Lyons in 1822 when her original group merged with a similar one started by Angelo Inglesi, vicar general of New Orleans; the first name was Missionary Society of Lyons, or St. Francis Xavier Society. The society prospered in spite of formidable opposition and became a mainstay for the missions all over the world. J.'s cause for beatification was introduced in 1930 and advanced in 1963 to a declaration of her practice of *heroic virtue.

[J. R. AHERNE]

JARRATT, DEVEREAUX (1733–1801), first C of E, then Protestant Episcopal, rector of Bath, Va., from 1763 until his death. His parents belonged to the class of small landowners, sometimes called yeomen, who were held to rank socially between the great planters and the landless populace. Though his opportunities for education were limited, J. succeeded in acquiring enough learning to become a schoolmaster and, eventually, to obtain ordination in the Established Church. As the C of E had no bps. in the colonies, he had to go to England for orders. He was ordained deacon and priest by the bp. of London in 1762 and on his return to Virginia was chosen rector of Bath. His religious awakening had occurred under the influence of Presbyterians who had been converted in the *Great Awakening, and his preaching retained a revivalistic flavor. When Methodist preachers appeared in the colony on the eve of the Revolution, he encouraged them but opposed their separation from the Anglican Church. He supported the Revolution, but with well-controlled enthusiasm, for, while he favored separation from the mother country, he disliked the "leveling" tendencies that accompanied it. In addition to his autobiography, *Life of the Reverend Devereaux Jarratt* (1806), he published *Sermons on Various and Important Subjects in Practical Divinity* (3 v., 1795).

[W. W. MANROSS]

JARRETT, BEDE (1881–1934), English Dominican historian, spiritual writer, and preacher. Born of a military family, educated at Stonyhurst, Oxford, and Louvain, J. became provincial of the English Dominicans in 1916 and remained in office for 16 years. In 1921 he reopened the Oxford house of the Dominicans on the 700th anniversary of its first founding. Despite his many charges, J. kept up his literary and scholarly activities. He founded the review *Blackfriars* and found time for careful and imaginative historical writing. He had a genius for friendship, and was never too busy for patient and protracted counsel to those who sought it. He was a very effective preacher; his voice rang like a bell and he spoke without clichés, turgidity, or false heroics. Among his writings were *Medieval Socialism* (1913), *St. Antonino and Medieval Economics* (1914), *Social Theories of the Middle Ages* (1926), *Meditations for Layfolk* (1915), and *Emperor Charles IV* (1935). BIBLIOGRAPHY: K. Wykeham-George and G. Mathew, *Bede Jarrett* (1952).

[T. GILBY]

JARROW, ABBEY OF, Benedictine monastery in Northumbria, England, founded in 681. It functioned as a joint foundation with Wearmouth, both usually ruled by the same abbot. The Venerable Bede spent his life at Jarrow; and from its scriptorium came the *Codex Amiatinus*. Both monasteries were dissolved in 1536. BIBLIOGRAPHY: H. Leclercq, DACL 7:2163–64; Knowles-Hadcock (1953).

[C. MCGRATH]

JASHAR, BOOK OF, a prebiblical, Israelite work containing some material now recorded in the OT, including Joshua's poetic words to the sun and moon (Jos 10.12–13) and David's lament over Saul and Jonathan (2 Sam 1.17–27). The significance of the title is unknown. Jashar means straight or upright, so it may have been Book of the Upright. Since the known quotations from it are poetry, however, some scholars suggest the title was originally Book of Song, a work cited in the Greek (LXX) version of 1 1 Kg 8.12–13, with the change made by the accidental transposition of two Hebrew letters. Others suggest that Book of Song was the original title, with the transposition forming the name Jashar. Nothing is known of the book other than what may be inferred from the OT citations. Some scholars identify it with the Book of the Wars of the Lord(Num 21.14). Modern forgeries claiming to be the long-lost book are sometimes published.

[T. EARLY]

JASOV, ABBEY OF, Premonstratensian monastery near Košice in Slovakia. Founded in *c.* 1220, it was under Turkish attack in the 15th and 16th centuries. Restored in the 18th cent. by the Premonstratensians, it was briefly suppressed by Joseph II. The Institute Norbertinum in Budapest was controlled by Jasov (schools were organized in several cities). Jasov was named an abbey *nullius* in 1922. With the suppression of the clergy after World War II, Jasov was turned into a concentration camp for religious.

[M. A. MCFADDEN]

JASPERS, KARL (1883–1969), German psychologist and philospher. J. studied law at Heidelberg and Munich, and medicine at Berlin, Göttingen, and Heidelberg. His M.D. was awarded with the completion of a dissertation, *Heimweh und Verbrechen (Nostalgia and Crime)* in 1909. He served as assistant in psychiatry at Heidelberg and was professor of psychology there (1916). W. *Dilthey's writings were a significant influence in the shaping of J.'s existential philosophy. In 1919 J. published a work based on Dilthey's theories of world views, thereby moving into the field of philosphy. He was greatly influenced by his friendship with Ernst Meyer and Max *Weber his teacher, J. was professor of philosophy at Heidelberg from 1921 until forced out of that position by the Nazis (1937). He returned there in 1945 and also taught at the Univ. of Basel. Concern with the events of World War II led him to write *Die Schuldfrage, ein Beitrag zur deutschen Frage* (1945); he had personal knowledge of the atrocities against the Jews since he was married to Meyer's sister, a Jewess. The first volume of the major work, *Philosophische Logik* was published in 1947. In his philosophy J. is best described as a Kantian existentialist; in fact, he is viewed by some to be the foremost philosopher of contemporary existentialism. J. adapts Kierkegaard's theory of crisis and limiting situations, making the central point of it the foundering, the *Scheitern*. Those situations which provide man with the crisis are the limiting situations, the *Grenzsituationen*. Within the quest for truth that each man makes, he negotiates the limiting situations that bind him; yet he does so within the same circumscription that provides the knowledge for him to make that quest in the first place. J. parts company with Kierkegaard at this point for he believes that the whole of reality (*das Umgreifende*) eludes man. Notwithstanding this, he believes one is able to transcend these limitations through contact with the "Encompassing" that is never fully grasped. It is this ascent through transcendence that he describes as *Aufschwung in die Transzendenz*. Thus one is able to replicate knowledge through decodification of the rationally intelligible signs (*Chiffren*) in life. Kant's dualism, phenomenon and noumenon, is traced in J.'s description of the limits of knowledge and the "Encompassing." His philosophy covers the range from epistemology to metaphysics and theology. He holds that one depends solely on intuitions and decisions of the ego for knowledge. But if such a view is, as he wishes, counter to scientific theory, it disavows as well the possibility of gaining certainty in religion, politics, and philosophy. But then the very principle that is meant to underpin J.'s philosophy undercuts it by dooming man to a futile quest. The clearest insights are those found in his philosophy of psychology. The real, the authentic in man is *Existenz*—always open to newsness and new possibilities—in opposition to *Dasein*. The attainment of *Existenz* is not possible but the tension (*Spannung*) between it and *Dasein* provides man with the best mode of existence. While J. subscribes to the theory of free will he does so within a frame that seems only to rob man of freedom—one identifiable with choice and selfhood. The implication for ethics is that man provides the norms by which he lives as he himself explores the possibilities and probabilities inherent in the tension. He collaborated with R. Bultmann in the writing of *Myth and Christianty* (1954). Although there are marked differences between J.'s philosophy and traditional Christianity, he does not deny that man is perfectible; however, the perfectibility that he affirms is one without the redemptive support of faith and grace. Some of his major works include: *Psychologie der Weltanschauungen* (1919); *Philosophie* (3 v., 1932); *Existenzphilosophie* (1938); *Philosophie und Welt* (1958); *Wahrheit und Wissenschaft* (1960). BIBLIOGRAPHY: P. Koestenbaum, EncPhil 4:254–258; L. H. Ehrlich, *Karl Jaspers: Philosophy as Faith* (1975); S. Samay, *Reason Revisited: The Philosophy of Karl Jaspers* (1971); C. Fabro, EncCatt 5:586–591; *EXISTENTIALISM.

[J. R. RIVELLO]

JASSY, SYNOD OF (1642), a synod of the Orthodox Church called to root out Protestant influence, particularly after Patriarch Cyril Lucaris of Constantinople had signed a profession of faith submitted to him by Dutch Calvinists. After synods held by the Greeks in 1638 and 1642, this meeting was convoked to obtain the support of the non-Greek Orthodox Churches against Calvinism. It was held in the Romanian city of Jassy in the autumn of 1642, with the participation of the Metropolitans Barlaam of Moldavia and Peter Moghila of Kiev and of the special delegate of the patriarch of Constantinople, the theologian Meletios Syrigos. Two documents were approved, both of a definitely anti-Calvinistic character: the synodical letter of Patriarch Parthenios, and a catechism written by Peter Moghila, with its Catholic terminology toned down by Syrigos. This catechism was later submitted to the four Greek patriarchs (1643) and was widely accepted as a genuine expression of Orthodox faith. BIBLIOGRAPHY: Jugie v. 1.

[G. ELDAROV]

JASUB, see SHEAR-JASHUB.

JĀTAKAS, a collection of folk tales and other stories (jātakas) incorporated in the Pāli canon which were the source and inspiration for carvings and paintings of the life of the Buddha and, further, important vehicles of Buddhist ethics, teaching virtues of prudence, generosity, self-abnegation—through birds and animals as in Aesop's fables.

[M. J. DALY]

JAZZ MASS, refers either to a celebration of the Mass in which jazz is performed or to a musical work of that type in the style of jazz. Both forms of Mass arose in the 1960s with the movement to render the liturgy more meaningful to the worshipers. The use of jazz in a liturgical setting is consistent with the history of jazz as inseparable from the history of Negro gospel music. The two most profound differences made by the presence of jazz in the Mass are: its rhythmic nature as primarily dance music, thus providing a new dimension to the Mass; its sponteneity, the music is often largely composed as it is being performed.

[P. J. HENNESSEY]

JEALOUSY, as a sin against *charity, a form of *envy (ThAq ST 2a2ae,36.3); displeasure at another's having or threatening to have what is regarded as exclusively one's own. Purely emotional twinges are not seriously sinful; jealousy in its full sense requires full displeasure of will. The object of jealous resentment may be some person loved or good possessed, and seen to be threatened by another's rivalry. Or it may mean regret over another's having or sharing in some possession. Envy is a more general term; jealousy stressed a sense of exclusiveness and a particular kind of distorted perception based upon an inordinate self-esteem. Because of the meaning of charity toward neighbor, which should rejoice in others' sharing in divine blessings and in a sense of communion in God's love, St. Paul lists being jealous (*zēloi*) among attitudes ill-befitting the Christian (2 Cor 12.20–21). In its common usage jealousy also connotes unfounded suspicion, and as such may be a sin of false or rash judgment contrary to justice. There is also a sense, close to the meaning of *zeal, in which jealousy simply means an intense vigilance about one's rights, which may be both warranted and morally good (ThAq ST 2a2ae, 36.3).

[T. C. O'BRIEN]

JEALOUSY OF GOD, a figure of speech used in the Scriptures (see Ex 20.5, and esp. 34.14: ". . . for the Lord, whose name is Jealous, is a jealous God") to guard from every manner of attenuation the absolute unity and uniqueness of the one true God. He cannot be conceived capable of sharing with another what is proper to himself without debasing the notion of divinity. As in all figures of speech, something in the unfigurative sense of the words is not transferable to that to which they are figuratively applied. God is without passion and the spiteful vengeance that characterizes human jealousy. Nevertheless, one who makes him share with others what in truth is uniquely his will not escape hurt, which will come, if not from the punishing hand of God, from the damage he does himself by counterfeiting divinity. God's jealousy in this sense is provoked most obviously by idolatry, but also, inferentially, by the infidelity of his creatures through disobedience and sin.

[R. J. BUSCHMILLER]

JEAN BODEL (Jehan; *c.* 1167–1210), versatile and gifted author in several genres, familiar with ecclesiastical institutions. In his epic *Chanson des Saisnes* (Song of the Saxons) he described three categories of vernacular literature: *matières de Rome* (pagan), *de Bretagne* (Arthurian), and *de Charlemagne* (national). Author of the **Jeu de Saint Nicolas*, a miracle play, and probably several **fabliaux;* he composed the lyric *Congés* (leave-taking) in 1202 upon entering a leper colony. BIBLIOGRAPHY: C. Foulon, *L'Oeuvre de Jehan Bodel* (1958).

[J. P. WILLIMAN]

JEAN DE BRUGES, see HENNEQUIN, JAN.

JEAN DE CAMBRAI (d. 1438), French sculptor, who succeeded André Beauneveu in 1397 as first Sculptor to the Duc de Berry, creating statues for the palace-chapel at Bourges and working (1405–16) on the tomb of the duke (Bourges Cathedral). J.'s style is hard and realistic, lacking the grace of Beauneveu.

[M. J. DALY]

JEAN DE LIÉGE (fl. 1361–82), Flemish sculptor. J. studied with and assisted Jean de Huy, becoming a favorite of Charles V of France, executing many commissions including a sepulchral monument (destroyed) to hold the heart of the king in Rouen Cathedral. The monument for Charles IV and Jeanne d'Evreux (Louvre) is of heavy proportions quite unlike the graceful statues of Charles V and Beatrix de Bourbon (Louvre) at times attributed to Jean.

[M. J. DALY]

JEAN DE MEUN (*c.*1240–*c.*1300), nicknamed Jean Chopinel (Clopinel), a prolific versifier and translator. A master of arts, familiar with classical and medieval authors, J. lived in Paris, the intellectual center of his age. Famed for his cynical continuation of the **Roman de la Rose,* he also translated Boethius, Abelard, and Vegetius into French, and composed a *Testament* and perhaps a *Codicille* which anticipate Villon in tone and format. His work is vigorous, tough minded, and naturalistic.

[J. P. WILLIMAN]

JEAN, CHARLES FRANÇOIS (1874–1955), Semitic and biblical scholar. J. taught Hebrew and Semitic epigraphy at L'École du Louvre. In addition to his scholarly publications in Assyriology, he wrote a Hebrew grammar, a catalogue of Semitic inscriptions, and *Le Milieu biblique avant Jésus-Christ* (3 v., 1922–26).

[T. M. MCFADDEN]

JEANNE MARIE DE MAILLÉ, BL. (d. 1414), Franciscan tertiary and mystic. She was of noble birth and at 16 was married to Robert de Sillé, with whom she lived in continence for 16 years. Dispossessed by the Sillé family after his death, she returned to Tours where she devoted herself to prayer and good works, living in seclusion near the church of St. Martin. She prayed incessantly for the end of the Western Schism and pleaded for the reform of the court of Charles VI. BIBLIOGRAPHY: M. de Crisenoy, *Bienheureuse Jeanne-Marie de Maillé* (1948); G. Mathon, BiblSanct 6: 589–590; Butler 4:279–281.

[O. J. BLUM]

JEANNERET, PIERRE, see LE CORBUSIER.

JEANNERET-GRIS, CHARLES ÉDOUARD, see LE CORBUSIER.

JEBUSITES, a pre-Israelite people of Palestine oftentimes enumerated in the conventional list of six or seven Palestinian peoples (Gen 15.21; Ex 3.8,17). The Jebusites are important in Israelite history because they were a major obstacle to the Israelite conquest of Palestine. They inhabited the strongly fortified city of Jerusalem, which remained independent of Israelite rule until David captured it and made it his citadel (2 Sam 5.6–10). Even then the Jebusites must have continued to live there, for David later bought the threshing floor of the Jebusite Araunah to build an altar to Yahweh (2 Sam 24.18–25). BIBLIOGRAPHY: G. A. Barrois, InterDB 2:807–808.

[E. CABEY]

JEDBURGH, MONASTERY OF, former abbey of the Canons Regular of St. Augustine, situated on the Jed River (Roxburghshire, Scotland). The monastery was founded in *c.*1138, has an architecturally significant church, but was damaged in the Anglo-Scottish wars (1297–1300). Suppressed and nearly destroyed in the 16th cent., it was later used as a Reformed church but is now in ruins.

[T. M. MCFADDEN]

JEDNOTA BRATRSKA, Czech name for the *Unitas Fratrum, also known as the *Bohemian Brethren, later to become the Moravian Church.

JEGHER, CHRISTOFEL (1596–1652 or 53), Flemish wood engraver, renowned for nine expressive works after Rubens, including *Coronation of the Virgin, Temptation of Christ,* and *Rest on the Flight into Egypt.* Rubens supervised and often retouched the proofs (1632–35 or 36). J.'s monogram "C. I.," with a knife beneath, is distinct from that of his son Jan Christofel which reads "I. C. I."

[M. J. DALY]

JEHOIACHIN, ("Yahweh establishes"; it also occurs in the variant forms Jeconiah and Coniah), king of Judah 598–597 B.C., son and successor of Jehoiakim. J. became king at the age of 18 and reigned 3 months. His father Jehoiakim had rebelled against Nebuchadnezzar, but died soon afterwards, leaving his son at the mercy of the Babylonians. J. quickly surrendered to Nebuchadnezzar and was deported to Babylon with some of his people. Evil-Merodach, Nebuchadnezzar's successor, released him from prison and had him dine royally at his table as long as he lived. This gave a ray of hope to the exiles that the Davidic dynasty had not been snuffed out. (2 Kg24.10–17; 25.27–30). BIBLIOGRAPHY: H. G. May, InterDB 2:811–813.

[E. CABEY]

JEHOSAPHAT, VALLEY OF (Josaphat), the scene where, according to Jl 3.2, Yahweh will judge the nations that have dared to attack Jerusalem; called in 3.14 the "valley of decision.'' Apocalyptic traditions that have sought to identify it as a place, e.g., Kidron, as the scene of the Last Judgment, are unfounded. In the text the name simply means the place where Yahweh judges.

[D. J. BOURKE]

JEHOVAH, a hybrid name for God resulting from the arbitrary combination of the consonants of the sacred name, *YaHWeH* and the vowels of *AdOnAi* (Lord). In late Judaism there developed a somewhat exaggerated reverence for the sacred name; it was not even to be pronounced. The reader was alerted to this when he saw the form, YaHoWah, indicating that he was to substitute the word Adonai for the revealed name of God. Hence the translation, Lord, for Yahweh.

[J. J. CASTELOT]

JEHOVAH'S WITNESSES, religious body that traces its beginning to the *millenarianism of Charles Taze *Russell. Russell was succeeded by Joseph F. *Rutherford, who devised new missionary techniques that have helped this movement to grow from 50,000 in 1938 to worldwide membership of more than 1 million in 1971. Until 1931 adherents of the movement were known as Watch Tower People, Millennial Dawnists, Earnest Bible Students, and Russellites, but Rutherford gave them the name Jehovah's Witnesses. Present head of the legal corporation, the Watch Tower Bible and Tract Society, is Frederick Franz. As their central doctrine the Witnesses have their own form of millenarianism. The present world is the reign of Satan and his tools—government, business, and organized religion—in conflict against the theocratic rule of Jehovah. All men have mortal souls, but they will be recreated and given a second chance at salvation during the millennium. Those who reject it by wickedness will be annihilated; the just will reign everlastingly in this renewed world. Christ and the 144,000 elect alone have immortal souls, as a reward for their obedience to Jehovah, and reign as spiritual creatures in heaven, not on this earth. The task of the Jehovah's Witnesses is to announce the second coming of Christ, which will be marked by the Battle of Armageddon, in which Satan and his allies will be defeated. Witnesses declare that the doctrine of the Trinity is a pagan addition to Christianity. Their Christology is vague but resembles a crude Arianism. They teach that Jesus did not rise from the dead in his physical body but as a spirit creature subordinate to Jehovah.

All baptized members, including children and women, are considered ordained ministers. An active witness will attend three of four meetings a week at which the Bible and Watch Tower materials are studied. The sect schedules only one communion service a year, on Nisan 14; only those who consider themselves to be among the 144,000 elect may partake of the bread and wine. In 1966, 1,971,107 people attended this memorial service, but only 11,179 actually received communion. Witnesses consider themselves to be citizens of a theocracy and therefore refuse to serve in the armed forces of any nation, salute the flag, vote, or hold political office. They are willing, however, to pay taxes. Their refusal to allow blood transfusions, because they are believed to be forbidden by the Bible, have brought them into conflict with the law. Avoidance of the secular world characterizes the committed Witness. He is encouraged to find fellowship in the congregations that meet in Kingdom Halls. Witnesses may not celebrate feasts such as Christmas and Easter. They abstain from active participation in labor unions, lodges, or secular organizations. Smoking, drinking, dancing, and card playing are discouraged but not flatly forbidden. After providing a decent living for themselves and their families, Witnesses are asked to turn over the excess of their income to the Watch Tower Society.

Each member is expected to devote at least 10 hours a month to door-to-door missionary work; some sell copies of the Society's publications on street corners. About 35,000 ''pioneers'' devote their full time to missionary efforts around the world. There are 1,500 men and women who work at Bethel headquarters in Brooklyn, N.Y., and at other centers. They set type, print, and bind the books and magazines, write, and handle correspondence. The Watch Tower Society has always relied heavily on the printed word. *The Watch Tower* magazine reports a circulation of 4,950,000; and its companion, *Awake!*, 4,550,000. Thus they have the widest circulation among all religious periodicals published in the U.S. The Witnesses also publish books, tracts, and copies of their own New World translation of the Bible. This edition is edited and annotated according to their beliefs.

During the 1930s and 1940s the sect grew as much as 25% A year, but this has leveled off to about ⅜% a year. About 450,000 Witnesses live in the United States. Large concentrations are also found in West Germany, Canada, Nigeria, the Philippines, Mexico, Zambir, the British Isles, and Brazil. They are banned in Iron Curtain countries. Many thousands attend meetings in Kingdom Halls, read the Society's literature, and attend Bible classes, but have not been baptized and are not recorded on membership rolls. Members have usually come from the lower socioeconomic class, but as the movement has evolved more members have risen to a higher social and educational level. In the U.S. the Witnesses have made a special effort to attract blacks, Spanish-Americans, and members of other minority groups. Their proselytizing techniques have become noticeably less aggressive in recent years. BIBLIOGRAPHY: R. Pyke, *Jehovah's Witnesses* (1954); W. J. Whalen, *Armageddon around the Corner* (1962); W. C. Stevenson, *Inside Story of Jehovah's Witnesses* (1968).

[W. J. WHALEN]

JEHU, KING OF ISRAEL, founder of a new dynasty. J. reigned from 842 to 815 B.C.. With the backing of the prophets, he wiped out the last rulers of the dynasty of Omri. After his royal anointing at Ramoth-gilead (2 Kg 9.1–10), he carried out a bloody coup. At Jezreel he killed the incumbent king, Joram, and had the queen mother, Jezebel, thrown from a palace window. He then drove his chariot over her body and went into dinner while dogs consumed her flesh. The blood bath continued until the whole royal family had been exterminated, together with the adherents of Baal, both priests and laity. The prophet Hosea later condemned his excessive cruelty (Hos 1.4). Jehu is mentioned on the Black Obelisk of Shalmaneser III as paying tribute to Assyria. BIBLIOGRAPHY: J. Bright, *History of Israel* (1959) 231–236.

[J. J. CASTELOT]

JELLETT, MAINIE (1897–1944), English painter who studied (1920–21) with Andre Lhote and with Albert Gleizes (1923). J. frequently painted religious themes, for example, *Let There Be Light* (1941), *Ninth Hour* (1943), and a cubist *Crucifixion.*

[M. J. DALY]

JENATSCH, GEORG (1596–1639), Swiss statesman. J. opposed the Spanish Habsburg party during the Thirty Years' War and succeeded in freeing his country. He became a Catholic in 1635. The discovery of his letters to the Protestant theologian St. Gabriel containing detailed defense of controverted dogmas has now erased all doubt as to the genuineness of his conversion. BIBLIOGRAPHY: O. Vasella, LTK 5.889.

[M. J. SUELZER]

JENINGEN, PHILIPP, VEN. (1642–1704), Bavarian Jesuit mystic, preacher of parish missions and of devotion to Mary. He had an admired Marian shrine, in Baroque style, built on Schönberg, a mountain overlooking the town of Ellwangen, center of his work. His popular preaching carried out the message given to him during his mystical prayer.

[T. C. O'BRIEN]

JEPHTHAH (Jephte; Hebr. *yiptah,* ''God frees captives''), military leader and judge of Israel. J. was a valiant warrior who became an outlaw chieftain after he was expelled from his clan (Gilead) by his brothers because he was the son of a harlot (Jg 11.1–3). Oppressed by the Ammonites, the elders of Gilead begged J. to return as their commander. He accepted on condition that he become the ruler of Gilead (Jg 10.6–18; 11.1–11). To deliver his people he had to sacrifice his only child in fulfillment of a vow he had made (Jg 11.29–40). He also had to deliver Gilead from the jealousy of the Ephraimites (Jg 12.1–6). BIBLIOGRAPHY: DeVaux AncIsr 150–154.

[E. CABEY]

JEREMIAH, one of the major prophets who most resembles Christ in his life and preaching. Born of a priestly family in Anathoth, J. received his call as a young man (Jer 1.6) in 626 B.C., the 13th year of the reign of King Josias (Jer 1.2; 25.3). He preached in the tragic years preceding and following the destruction of the Kingdom of Judah. He warned and admonished kings, priests, and people that they were bringing disaster on the nation because they would not live according to the covenant they had made with Yahweh. The very institutions of Judah, the Temple and sacrifices, had become corrupt because they were now being used as an excuse for breaking the covenant: for not treating each other fairly, for exploiting the stranger, the orphan, and the widow, for shedding innocent blood, for following alien gods. Therefore Yahweh would destroy the Temple as he destroyed Shiloh; he does not want their holocausts, but adherence to the way of life he had marked out for them. Such preaching earned for Jeremiah the hatred of the people, priests, and kings, who persecuted him. Like Christ, he preached against the established order, stood up for justice for the poor, the widow, the orphan, and was persecuted by those to whom he came to preach. In the end he was carried off to Egypt (*c.*680), where, according to Hebrew legend, he was stoned to death. BIBLIOGRAPHY: J. Bright, *Jeremiah* (1965); P. Ellis, *Men and the Message of the Old Testament* (1963) 295–311.

[E. CABEY]

JEREMIAH, BOOK OF. Jeremiah's prophetic career extended from his youth in 626 B.C. to a date considerably later than the ruin of Jerusalem in 587. Thus he witnessed the brief renewal of the covenant people under Josiah; the latter's death in 609 at Megiddo; the obstinate, weak, and futile resistance of Josiah's successors to Babylon, and the continued intrigues by those left in the land after the mass deportations of 598 and 587, these intrigues culminating in the murder of Gedaliah, Babylon's representative. After this episode the assassins forced Jeremiah to accompany them on their flight into Egypt.

More than any other prophet, Jeremiah not merely preached his inspired message but lived it, too. incurring the hatred and persecution of the anti-Babylonian party throughout his life, and suffering intense personal anguish and conflicts from the part he was forced by Yahweh to play in these events. This is recorded in the autobiographical material of his ''confessions'' (11.18–12.6; 15.10–21; 17.12–18; 18.18–23; 20.7–18) and the biographical material (some of it composed by Baruch, Jeremiah's disciple and scribe) of prose narrative in the third person, which together constitute a major element in his book.

The existing text of Jeremiah is in a state of some disorder, and a comparison between the Hebrew and Greek versions reveals many discrepancies both in the order of the chapters and in the total length of the book. Furthermore a number of oracles are reduplicated at different points. Broadly speaking, however, the contents fall into three main parts: (1) 1–25.14 comprises three groups of oracles mainly belonging to the reigns of Josiah (ch. 1–6), Jehoiakim (ch. 7–20), and Zedekiah (much of ch. 21–25). (2) Ch. 26–45 consists mainly of biographical material, but includes the famous temple discourse (ch. 26), and the prophecy of the new covenant (31.31–34). (3) Comprises oracles against the nations, notably Egypt (46.2–28) and Babylon (ch. 50–51.), the two chief protagonists in the contemporary international scene.

Jeremiah's message as a whole is dominated by a fourfold opposition: first between Yahweh as true God and the false gods; second between Jeremiah as the true prophet and the false prophets; third between the ineffective externalism of the official cult and the transforming power of the true religion of mind and heart; fourth between Babylon, designated by Yahweh to be his "servant" and Egypt, the beguiler and deceiver. Yahweh is consistently thought of as dwelling not in the temple at Zion (as in Isaiah) but transcendently in heaven, looking down upon the world and presiding over all that it contains from the vast cosmic forces to the most interior thoughts and dispositions of its inhabitants. The prophetic word of Jeremiah himself is not merely a message but an irresistible weapon that forces itself from his lips and has immense destructive power. Israel is not merely to be purged to a righteous remnant, but is to be like a pot crushed back into the original clay and radically reshaped anew (Ch. 18). BIBLIOGRAPHY: J. Skinner, *Prophecy and Religion* (1922); W. Rudolph, *Jeremia* (2d ed., 1958); S. Mowinckel, *Zur Komposition des Buches Jeremia* (1914); H. Cunliffe Jones, *Jeremiah* (1960); A. Gelin, *Jérémie, Les Lamentations, Le Livre de Baruch*, (2d ed. 1959); A. C. Welch, *Jeremiah, His Time and His Work* (1928).

[D. J. BOURKE]

JEREMIAH LETTER OF, for Catholics, a *deuterocanonical book; for others, one of the *apocrypha. Although in the LXX the work appears as a separate treatise, in the Vulg and derived versions it has been made the sixth and final chapter of the book of *Baruch. The surviving Greek version of it derives from a lost Hebrew original by an unknown author, probably of the 2d cent. B.C. It consists of a prolonged satire on the Greek idols, plainly inspired by the anti-idolatry polemic as exemplified in Jer 10.1–16 and Is 44.9–20. It is important as reflecting the interests and outlook of the Judaism of the Diaspora and its contacts with Palestinian Judaism. BIBLIOGRAPHY: A. Robert, "Jérémie (lettre de)", DBSuppl (1949) 4:849–857; W. Baars. "Two Palestinian Syrian Texts Identified as Parts of the Epistle of Jeremy", VT 11 (1961) 77–81; A. Fitzgerald, JBC 1:618–619.

[D. J. BOURKE]

JEREMIAH, PARALIPOMENA OF. This compilation, otherwise known as "The Rest of the Words of Baruch," is an apocalyptic work, originally Jewish, but heavily worked over by a Judaeo-Christian adapter probably of the 2d cent. A.D. It draws extensively upon earlier apocalyptic works such as the Apocalypse of Baruch, 2 Esdras, the Ascension of Isaiah. It itself has been described, not without justice, as "the degenerate offspring of an illustrious line, perhaps the very last scion of a noble house," i.e., of Jewish apocalyptic (cf. J. R. Harris, *Rest of the Words of Baruch,* p. 2).

The three chief protagonists of the story are Jeremiah, Baruch, and their virtuous servant, Abimelech. It opens with God's decree, which Jeremiah is unable to avert, that Jerusalem is to be destroyed by the Chaldaeans. Jeremiah is to accompany the exiles to Babylon, Baruch is to remain at Jerusalem, while Abimelech is sent to fetch figs from the "gardens of Agrippa" as a pretext for saving him from the distressing spectacle of the city's being destroyed. On his way back he is miraculously sent to sleep for 66 years. Baruch sends a message by a miraculous talking eagle to Jeremiah at Babylon, whereupon Jeremiah joyfully leads back from exile all those who are prepared wholeheartedly to reject Babylon and its customs. A number of those who accompany him, however, are unwilling to do this, and in particular refuse to put away their Babylonian wives. These return to Babylon, only to find that they are denied entry into that city as well. Thus they are forced to form a degenerate sect neither wholly Jewish nor wholly Babylonian.

This is the origin of the Samaritans. After once being miraculously raised from death Jeremiah is finally martyred by his fellow countrymen for saying that he has seen God and the Son of God, and foretelling the coming of Jesus, still 365 years distant. He is buried by Baruch and Abimelech.

J. R. Harris argues ingeniously that this work reflects the conditions under Hadrian in A.D. 136 when Jews were prohibited by imperial decree from entering their holy city, now rebuilt as Aelia Capitolina. "Our document is the Church's Eirenikon to the Synagogue . . ." appealing to Jews wholeheartedly to embrace Christianity on the grounds that as Christians they will be allowed into the city. Thus the destruction of 587 is taken as a type of that under Hadrian and a Christian message is drawn from it. BIBLIOGRAPHY: J. R. Harris, *Rest of the Words of Baruch: A Christian Apocalypse of the Year 136* A.D. (1899).

[D. J. BOURKE]

JEREMIAS II, PATRIARCH OF CONSTANTINOPLE (1530–95), *ecumenical patriarch three times, 1572–79, 1580–84, 1589–95. He established the patriarchate of *Moscow during a visit to Russia in 1588–89. He refused to accept the Gregorian calendar since it was regarded as heretical by the Greeks. J. is also known for his correspondence with the Lutheran theologians of Tübingen, and gave the first official Orthodox verdict on Lutheranism, specifying six basic points of disagreement: procession of the Holy Spirit, free will, justification and good works, invocation of the saints, and the monastic life. BIBLIOGRAPHY: L. Petit DTC 8:886–894; E. Schelstrate, *Acta Orientalis Ecclesiae contra Lutheri haeresim* (1739) 69–252.

[P. FOSCOLOS]

JEREMIAS, JOACHIM (1900–), Lutheran theologian and NT scholar. In 1927–28 he was *Dozent* at the Herder

Institute in Riga; 1928–29 professor of NT at the Univ. of Berlin; 1929–35 professor at Greifswald; from 1935 until his retirement professor at Göttingen. Many of his voluminous works have been translated into English including *Jerusalem zur Zeit Jesu* (1962), *Die Gleichnisse Jesu* (1947), *Unbekannte Jesusworte* (1948), *Die Abendsmahlworte Jesu* (1967), and his *Studien zur neutestamentliche Theologie und Zeitgeschichte* (1966). BIBLIOGRAPHY: *Judentum, Urchristentum, Kirche* (ed. W. Eltester, 1974).

[T. J. RYAN]

JERICHO, a city in Palestine located about seventy miles NW of the Dead Sea. The ancient site down to Canaanite and OT times was at Tell-es-Sultan, beginning with a walled city about 7000 B.C. After a gap in occupation before 3100 B.C., it was occupied from 3100 to 2100 B.C., although its walls were destroyed (frequently by earthquakes) and rebuilt 17 times in this period. After being an open town for 200 years, Jericho was refortified 1900–1580 B.C. and again *c.*1400–1325 B.C., after which it seems to have been unoccupied for some 400 years. If there was a town there in the time of Joshua (Jos 2.6), all traces of it, including pottery, have been eroded. The town was later destroyed by the Babylonians (587 B.C.) and by the Persians (353–351 B.C.). In Hellenistic-Roman times the town was built 1¾ miles to the SW, and it was this town, with many public buildings built by Herod, that Jesus visited. The Jericho of Byzantine-Arab times stood at a third site, more than a mile SE of Tell-es-Sultan. BIBLIOGRAPHY: J. and J. B. E. Garstang, *Story of Jericho* (1948); K. Kenyon, *Digging Up Jericho* (1957).

[E. J. CROWLEY]

JEROBOAM I, KING OF ISRAEL, first ruler of the northern kingdom, who reigned from 922 to 901 B.C. During the reign of Solomon he was put in charge of a forced labor battalion. The northern tribes resented being pressed into this degrading type of work and found in him a champion of their cause. A prophetic tradition mentions his being appointed king by Ahijah the prophet (1 Kg 11.29–39). Whether news of this leaked out or whether he actually led an abortive revolution, he had to seek asylum in Egypt until Solomon's death (1 Kg 11.40). He came back to play a leading role in the resistance of the northern tribes to the demands of Solomon's son and successor, Rehoboam (1 Kg 12.2–3). These demands led to the secession of the 10 northern tribes and the establishment of the Kingdom of Israel. One of his first acts was the setting up of shrines at Bethel and Dan. The worship at these shrines soon became infected with Baalism; hence the frequent references in the Books of Kings to "the sin of Jeroboam and the sins into which he led Israel." BIBLIOGRAPHY: J. Bright, *History of Israel* (1959) 210–219.

[J. J. CASTELOT]

JEROBOAM II, KING OF ISRAEL a member of the dynasty of Jehu; he enjoyed a long and prosperous reign from 786–746 B.C. (2 Kg 14.23–29). Economically, Israel reached the heights; politically, it enjoyed peace at home and success against foreign enemies. Its armies were victorious over the Aramaeans, who had hitherto been a constant thorn in their side (2 Kg 14.28), and extended the borders of the kingdom northward to Hamath (2 Kg 14.25). However, immorality and social injustice came in the train of peace and prosperity, and the prophets Amos and Hosea preached against these abuses. Amos was particularly vehement; his prediction of the fall of the royal house was relayed to the king by Amaziah, the high priest at Bethel (Am 7.9–11). BIBLIOGRAPHY: J. Bright, *History of Israel* (1959) 238–241.

[J. J. CASTELOT]

JEROME, ST. (Eusebius Hieronymous; *c.*347–419/20, Scripture scholar, Doctor of the Church. Born of wealthy parents at Stridon in Dalmatia, he studied grammar, rhetoric, and philosophy in Rome, where he had Aelius Donatus, the most famous grammarian of the 4th cent., as one of his teachers. Baptized by Pope Liberius *c.*365, he went for a short time to Trier to study theology. Moving to Aquileia, he lived for a number of years (368–374) with a group of ascetical friends. Setting out on a pilgrimage to Jerusalem, he fell ill at Antioch but took advantage of his stay there to attend the lectures of Apollinaris of Laodicea and to perfect his knowledge of Greek. For 3 years (375–378) he lived as a hermit in the desert E of Antioch, taking up the study of Hebrew to combat the temptations that assailed him there. Ordained in 379, he left Antioch for Constantinople, where he followed the lectures of Gregory of Nazianzus. In 382 he accompanied Paulinus of Antioch and St. Epiphanius to Rome to attend a synod being held to remedy the Antiochene schism. He there became the friend and secretary of Pope Damasus, who asked him to revise the Latin versions of Scripture then in use. His sharp criticism of ecclesiastical abuses created so much hostility among the clergy that in 385, the year after Damasus' death, he again left Rome. While there he had been the spiritual director of a number of devout women, and at Antioch he was joined by two of them, the wealthy widow Paula and her daughter Eustochium. Together they continued on to Jerusalem, but first visited Egypt. They eventually settled at Bethlehem, where they founded a monastery for men and another for women, and where J. continued his ceaseless writing until his death.

A keen and indefatigable, if at times somewhat careless worker, J. was without doubt the most learned, if not the most profound, of the Latin Fathers. More of a philologist than a philosopher, he mastered Greek and Hebrew in addition to his own native Latin. Interested in problems of history, geography, and archeology, he had neither the temperament nor the talent to become a great speculative theologian like St. Augustine. His undoubted literary talents are manifest in his many works, which include the following: (1) Letters. Carefully written on a wide variety of subjects, his 117 still-extant letters are an admirable mirror of his mind and of the times.(2) Historical works. These include the biographies of Paul, Malchus, and Hilarion, and the *De viris illustribus*, hastily written but invaluable for details on the lives of prominent Christians. (3) Homiletic and exegetical writings on both the Old and New Testament. These are important because of his great knowledge of Scripture and tradition. (4) Polemical writings. Jerome's own ardent temperament caused him to become involved in practically all the religious controversies of his day, particularly those centered about Arius, Origen, and Pelagius. (5) Translations. These may be divided into two types: those of ecclesiastical writers and Scripture. Among the former are works of Origen, Epiphanius, Theophilus of Alexandria, Eusebius, Pachomius, and Didymus the Blind. The latter comprise the whole of the Old and New Testament (see VULGATE). As scholar, exegete, and spiritual guide, J. had a profound influence throughout the Middle Ages, combining within himself as he did the best in the classical, Hebrew, and early Christian cultures. Works: PL 22–30. BIBLIOGRAPHY: B. Altaner 462–476; A. Penna, BiblSanct 6:1109–32; Butler 3:686–693.

[M. J. COSTELLOE]

JEROME EMILIANI, ST., see EMILIANI, JEROME, ST.

JEROME OF PRAGUE (1380–1416), friend and lay collaborator of Jan *Hus. At Prague, while a student of Hus, and later at Oxford, J. pursued an interest in the philosophical and theological teachings of John *Wycliffe. He brought Wycliffe's writings back to Prague (*c.*1401) and became a violent proponent of Hus's reform ideas in Prague, Hungary, and Austria. He went to the Council of *Constance to defend Hus, was himself arrested in 1415, and after an initial abjuration of errors, again became suspect. He thereupon renounced his first recantation and was burned at the stake as a relapsed heretic. BIBLIOGRAPHY: Bihlmeyer-Tüchle 2:440.

[T. C. O'BRIEN]

JERON, ST. (Hieron; d. *c.*856), priest, martyr, born probably in Noordwijk, N Holland (Frisia), although claimed also by the Scots. Little is known of his life, save that he was missionary to the Frisians and died under the Danish (Northmen) invasions as a martyr to the faith. His relics are at Noordwijk and at St. Adalbert's Monastery in Egmond. He was invoked in the Middle Ages for lost causes, and his cult has been recently revived. BIBLIOGRAPHY: W. Böhne, LTK 5:325.

[N. F. GAUGHAN]

JERUSALEM, the pivotal city of the Bible and the holy city of Christians, Jews, and Muslims. The name is of Semitic origin, and through the centuries such meanings as "city of peace," "vision of peace," "possession of peace," are more popular than exact. Most probably, the name means "City of Shalem," Shalem being a well-known Semitic god who appears in the texts of Ugarit. Today the Arabs call the city el-Quds (The Holy City), while in the State of Israel it is called Yerushalayim.

Jerusalem is situated on Palestine's central limestone plateau, at an elevation of 2493 feet above sea level, 32 mi W of the Mediterranean Sea, and 14 miles E of the N tip of the Dead Sea. The N part of the city is a continuation of the central plateau, but the city itself generally slopes downward toward the south. The city is skirted on three sides by protecting valleys, the Kidron to the E and the Hennon (whence Gehenna) on the W and south. These two valleys meet at En-Rogel whence they work their way southeastward to the Dead Sea as one valley. The city is divided into two hills by another, smaller valley, called the Tyropoeon Valley (Cheesemakers' Valley) by Josephus, which has accumulated from 40 to 70 feet of filling in the course of centuries. The two hills are cut through with other depressions so that the terrain of the city is quite uneven. The S narrow extremity of the E hill is the Ophel (City of David) and to the N is the site of several temples in the general area of the present Mosque of Omar. The Basilica of the Holy Sepulcher containing Calvary, and the Cenacle are located on the larger, W hill.

No doubt, the water sources determined the location of the city originally. The most interesting is the spring located low on the E slope of the Ophel which the Bible calls Gihon (1 Kg 1.33) (today: "Spring of the Mother of the Steps" or "Spring of Lady Mary"). Even before David captured the city, this spring was artificially blocked up so that the water could be reached through a shaft from within the city above. Joab entered the city through this shaft and captured it for David (2 Sam 5.8). Water flowed through canals from this spring into two pools at the lower end of the Ophel until King Hezekiah's engineers cut a tunnel through the rock so that the flow of water would not be exposed to enemies. The reservoir at the end of the tunnel is called the Pool of Siloe. Further to the S where the Kidron and Hennon Valleys join is another, but poorer spring, En-Rogel. In the N part of the city, a large pool near the Sheepgate served the city in later times. This is Bethzatha with five porticoes (Jn 5.2) which has been located near the church of St. Ann. Today Jerusalem's main water supply comes from Wadi el-Fara, 10 miles to the northeast.

Primitive peoples inhabited the area around the Gihon Spring from earliest times. By 3000 B.C. Early Bronze Age people (Canaanites) settled there. By 2000 B.C. the Amorites were invading Canaan and one of their clans, the Jebusites, made the Ophel above the Gihon Spring their stronghold. The shaft for reaching the spring's water from within the walled stronghold dates from this period. The biblical reference (Gen 14.18) to Melchizedek, King of Salem and priest of "God Most High" refers to this city. Jerusalem returned to the domination of Egypt under Thutmose III (1490–36 B.C.). Even though Joshua defeated and killed Adonizedek King of Jerusalem (Jos 10.26), the city remained independent of the Israelites until David. David's general, Joab, caught the Jebusites off guard by gaining entrance to the city through the shaft leading up from the Gihon Spring. David repaired the city's walls, built his palace and royal buildings, and had the ark of the covenant carried within the city, thus centralizing the political and religious life of the Twelve Tribes in his own city. After the death of David his son Solomon ushered in the city's most glorious period by erecting a protective wall and many buildings including his palace and his famous Temple.

Upon the death of Solomon the kingdom split in two, and Jerusalem became the capital of only the two S tribes of Judah and Benjamin. Under King Rehoboam (917 B.C.) the Egyptian King Shishak (Shoshonk) attacked and carried off treasures from the King's palace and from the Temple (1 Kg 14.25–26). Around 783 B.C. King Jehoash of the N kingdom defeated the Judean King Amaziah and tore down a 600-foot section of the wall and carried off treasures and prisoners from the king's palace and the Temple (2 Kg 14.13–14). However, his successors, King Uzziah and Jotham seem to have repaired this damage. Under pressure of Sennacherib's invasion King Hezekiah strengthened the city's walls, and tunneled the water passage from the Gihon Spring to the Pool of Siloe. The next king, Manasseh, also strengthened the defenses of the city. Antiochus IV Epiphanes, in forcing the process of Hellenization, sacked the city, desecrated the Temple, and built a Syrian stronghold known as the Acra to enable them to maintain control of the city. The reaction against the Syrians resulted in the Wars of the Maccabees in which Judas Maccabee captured the Temple and purified it, and later under Simon Maccabee the city was strengthened and the Syrians were driven from the Acra (1 Macc 13.50). After a period of peace and prosperity, war broke out in 69 B.C. between the two Hasmonaean brothers, Hyrcanus II and Aristobulus II. In 63 B.C. the Romans came in to settle the conflict, made Hyrcanus high priest and appointed the Idumean, Antipater as procurator. Herod the Great, son of Antipater, had the Romans declare him king of Palestine in 40 B.C. His building accomplishments include an agora, theater, gymnasium, hippodrome, palace, the fortress Antonia, and esp. the Temple which was completed only in 63 A.D. During this period Jerusalem was ruled by the Romans through their procurators. In 66 A.D. the Jews revolted against Rome which led to the destruction of the city and Temple by Titus in 70 A.D. Another revolt in 135 A.D. led by Bar Kokhba was suppressed by Hadrian and resulted in a complete Romanizing of the city even to the extent of imposing a new name: Aelia Capitolina.

Jerusalem regained its importance after 312 when Constantine the Great restored peace to the Empire and his mother, St. Helena, visited Palestine and erected the Basilica of the Holy Sepulcher. The city played an increasing role as a pilgrim place and as a power in the Church during the period of heresy. In 614 Jerusalem was taken by the Persians; churches and monasteries were destroyed (including the Constantine Basilica); citizens were slaughtered; and the relic of the holy cross was carried off. The relic was returned and buildings reconstructed, the monk Modestus rebuilt the Basilica of the Holy Sepulcher, only to have the city fall into the hands of the Arabs under Caliph Omar in 636. Under Caliph 'Abd al-Malik (684–705) the renowned Dome of the Rock (also called Mosque of Omar) was erected on the site of Solomon's Temple. In 1010 the Fatimid Caliph al-Hakim completely leveled the basilica and even the Holy Sepulcher itself. The structure was redone by 1048, and more or less it has remained to the present day. In 1072 the Muslims prohibited the Christians access to the city, a step that provoked the Crusaders to occupy the city by force. In 1099 Godfrey of Bouillon became the first Christian ruler of Jerusalem and by 1187 the impetus of the Crusades was gone, and Jerusalem was again under the control of the Muslims in the person of Saladin, head of the Seljukian Turks.

After the Crusades, control of Jerusalem passed from the Seljukian Turks to the Mamelukes of Egypt and by 1516 Palestine became part of the Ottoman Empire. Turkish rule ended in 1917 when Jerusalem fell to General Allenby and by the Treaty of Versailles Palestine was placed under the British Mandate. In 1948, with the creation of the two states of Jordan and Israel, Jerusalem became a divided city, the Old City belonging to Jordan and Israel occupying the newer sections of the city to the West. In June 1967 war broke out between the two states. Israel occupied all of Palestine W of the Jordan, acquiring complete control of Jerusalem. BIBLIOGRAPHY: J. Simons, *Jerusalem in the O.T.* (1952); L. H. Vincent and A. M. Stève, *Jérusalem de l'Ancien Testament* (3 v., 1954–56).

[S. MUSHOLT]

JERUSALEM, ARMENIAN PATRIARCHATE OF, one of the four principal jurisdictions of the Armenian Church. As Christianity expanded in Armenia during its first millennium, ecclesiastical organization remained unsettled. A patriarch for the Gregorian Armenians resided in Jerusalem since 1311, but this was purely a nominal title for several centuries. Finally, a synod held in Jerusalem in 1625 determined the ecclesiastical primacy of the catholicate of *Echmiodzin, over the catholicate of *Sis and the Armenian patriarchates of Jerusalem and *Constantinople. Although the patriarchate increased its numbers during the early 20th cent., the patriarch now rules approximately 6,400 faithful in Jordan and Israel. *ARMENIAN CHURCH.

[F. T. RYAN]

JERUSALEM, CATHOLIC-MELKITE PATRIARCHATE OF, a patriarchate subsumed under the Greek-Melkite Catholic patriarchate of *Antioch. In 1772, the Melkite patriarch of Antioch was given jurisdiction over

Melkites in Jerusalem and Alexandria, but in 1838 Patriarch Maximos III Mazlūm(1833–55) was given the personal title of patriarch of Antioch, Alexandria, Jerusalem and the whole East. This title has been handed down to his successors and a patriarchal vicar of Jerusalem actually governs in his place. At present there are about 6,500 Melkite Catholic faithful in 13 parishes. *MELKITE RITE

[F. T. RYAN]

JERUSALEM, COUNCIL OF, the apostolic meeting of Acts 15.1–29 (cf 16.4; 21.25) called to settle problems about gentile converts to Christ. Two distinct problems were combined in the Lucan account: whether gentiles were saved by faith and Christ's grace and were brothers having the same spiritual status as Christian Jews—this doctrinal question was settled by Peter's decree in a semiprivate assembly of Apostles and elders (Acts 15.6–11) and was substantially the same as the conclusion reached in the Cornelius story (10.1–11.18); and, how much gentile Christians, once saved, were bound by Jewish customs—this practical question was settled before the whole Church by a compromise proposed by James and accepted by all (15.4, 12–29). The proposal bound the gentiles to avoid practices linked with idolatry and cultural customs obnoxious to Jewish Christians (consumption of blood, a sacred symbol of God's life in animals). This James was very likely the leading elder of the mother Church, the Lord's brother, author of the Gospel of James, and not one of the 12 Apostles (Gal 1.19; Gr. text may readily mean, ". . . . but [I did see] James, the brother of the Lord.", rather than, "except James. . . ."). Chronologically, the compromise, which did not insist on circumcision, probably happened later than Luke's logical placing of it. Paul made no reference to it in Galatians, in which he argued forcefully against circumcision's being obligatory for gentile converts. (But, perhaps this Epistle preceded the date usually ascribed to the Jerusalem decree [*c.*49–51 A.D.], as many scholars argue, Galatians would then be the very earliest writing of the NT). Such logical combinations of two events, similar but not identical in content, are observable Lucan constructions (e.g., Lk 4.16–30; Jesus' visit to Nazareth, which combines at least two distinct visits). When Luke wrote Acts 15 (*c.*80 A.D.), his main purpose was didactic: to exemplify how gentile and Jewish Christians should live together as brothers in the peace of Christ, while respecting each other's drastically different cultural heritages.

[J. F. FALLON]

JERUSALEM, KINGDOM OF, the chief unit among the four Crusader States established in the Near East. Founded on feudal concepts of government, the kingdom was structurally weak, with power divided between the king and the High Court, and revenues shared with merchant groups. Sultan Saladin captured the city and much territory in 1187–88; Acre became the capital of the small remnant state until 1291, when the Mameluke sultans of Egypt ended the kingdom's existence. It represented a brief restoration of Christianity in the land of its birth. The Latin patriarchs of Jerusalem ruled the Church, with a full panoply of bishoprics, monasteries, and ecclesiastical institutions. Its inhabitants took little interest in the conversion of the Muslims. BIBLIOGRAPHY: *Feudal Monarchy in the Latin Kingdom of Jerusalem* (1932); S. Runciman, *History of the Crusades* (3 v., 1951–54).

[R. H. SCHMANDT]

JERUSALEM, LATIN PATRIARCHATE OF, RC see in Jerusalem. When the Crusaders seized the holy city in 1099, the church structure of Palestine was adapted to a Western model with Latin-rite clergy. Because the Greek patriarch had taken refuge in Constantinople during Moslem invasion, a Latin-rite patriarchate of Jerusalem was established. During the time of Crusader rule, many churches were built and the Basilica of the Holy Sepulcher restored. When the Muslims regained Jerusalem (1187), the patriarch fled to Accho where his eight immediate successors remained until that city fell in 1291. Afterwards, there were only titular patriarchs who resided in Rome until Pius IX restored the patriarchate in Jerusalem in 1847. All of these Latin patriarchs have been Italian. At the present time, the patriarch resides in Jerusalem and governs 53,450 Latin-rite faithful in Jordan, Israel, Cyprus, and the Gaza Strip.

[F. T. RYAN]

JERUSALEM, LITURGY OF, the liturgical order proper to the Holy City and its environs, partially known through 4th-cent. allusions in the catecheses of Cyril of Jerusalem and in the *Peregrinatio Aetheriae,* the latter work being esp. valuable for its description of the actual ritual and of the special celebrations, e.g., Lent and Holy Week. The Jerusalem lectionaries from the 5th to the 8th cent. are preserved in Armenian and Georgian with schematic indications of the ritual's structure for the liturgical year. The anaphora to which Cyril's catecheses refer is essentially that which came to be known as the anaphora of St. James. By the 4th cent. Jerusalem had developed a cycle of feasts, the practice of stational liturgies, and a system of scriptural readings for the year. The liturgy of *Antioch was quite similar, for the two Christian centers were mutually influential, their liturgies being of the same Syrian or Antiochene type, and it is difficult to distinguish their specific traits. In the ecclesiastical separations following the Council of *Chalcedon (451) the patriarchate of Jerusalem remained overwhelmingly in the orthodox camp, and the liturgical creativity of orthodox Syrian monks of Antiochene origin but who lived in Palestinian monasteries, deeply marked liturgical development in Palestine. This developed Palestinian usage had some influence on the sung parts of the Byzantine liturgies, less influence, however, on the formation of the Byzantine Divine Office. Between the 9th and 12th cent. the local liturgy of Jerusalem and Palestine was gradually replaced by that of Constantinople itself. BIB-

LIOGRAPHY: F.E. Brightman, *Liturgies Eastern and Western* (1896) 1:464–470; M. Tarchnischvili, CSCO (1959–60) 188–189 (text Georgian) and 204–205 (translation).

[A. CODY]

JERUSALEM, NEW, see HEAVEN.

JERUSALEM, PATRIARCHATE OF, one of the four eminent patriarchates of the Eastern Church. Ecclesiastically speaking, the patriarchate can be traced to the Apostle, St. James the Less, first bp. of Jerusalem. In spite of its religious importance, the city did not receive the recognition it deserved and was merely a suffragan see to *Caesarea in Palestine, itself under the patriarchate of *Antioch. After Constantine the Great gave freedom to the Church (313), many shrines and monasteries were erected in and around Jerusalem, thus making it a pilgrimage center. The Council of *Nicaea I (325) conferred honorary precedence upon Jerusalem after Rome, Alexandria, and Antioch, although, jurisdictionally, it was still subordinate to the metropolitan See of Caesarea in Palestine. Ultimately the Council of *Chalcedon (451) elevated the Holy City to the status of a genuine patriarchate, independent of Antioch which ceded 58 dioceses. This elevation was achieved mainly through the presistence of Juvenal, bp. of Jerusalem (422–458). During the Monophysite conflict, the patriarchate remained orthodox, but there were sufficient Monophysites in Palestine for the Jacobite patriarch of Antioch to appoint Severus as bp. of Jerusalem in 597, thus creating a line of Jacobite bps. for Jerusalem. The prosperity that had grown from the 4th to the 7th cent. ended with the Persian and Arab invasions in 614 and 637, respectively. The Latin Kingdom established through the Crusades (1099–1187) brought with it a Latin hierarchy that displaced the Melkite patriarchate. The Melkite patriarch took up residence in Constantinople and the ecumenical patriarch of the imperial city actually ruled the Jerusalem patriarchate until the dissolution of the Latin kingdom. During this difficult era, the patriarch of Jerusalem followed Michael Cerularius in his break from Rome (1054). Temporary reunion was achieved by the patriarchs of Jerusalem, Antioch, and Alexandria, after the Council of *Florence (1439). But before the end of the 15th cent., relations between Rome and the Orthodox patriarch of Jerusalem were completely severed. In 1838 the Catholic Melkite patriarch of Antioch, Maximos III Mazlūm, received the title of patriarch of Jerusalem and Alexandria with authority over Catholic Melkites in these jurisdictions. In 1847, the Latin patriarchate was restored. Jerusalem is also claimed as an Armenian patriarchate. From the beginning of the 20th cent., cooperation between Greek and Arab members of the Orthodox Church has been greatly strained. The Orthodox patriarch resides in Jerusalem itself and governs 60,000 faithful in three eparchies. BIBLIOGRAPHY: G. A. Maloney NCE 7:891; E. Amann, DTC 8.2:998–1010.

[F. T. RYAN]

JERUSALEM BIBLE, the 1966 English edition of the Bible derived from *La Sainte Bible* of the Dominicans at the École Biblique in Jerusalem. *La Sainte Bible de Jérusalem*, a multi-volume translation with critical introductions and notes, was first published in France, 1948–54; a one-volume abridgement appeared in 1956. The English *Jerusalem Bible* corresponds to this one-volume edition. The English of the biblical text is presented as a translation from the original biblical languages, guided by the interpretations of the French edition. The introductions and notes are translations, with some revisions, of the French edition; the index of biblical themes has been considerably expanded. The *Jerusalem Bible* has proved eminently helpful to students; some use of its text has been made for liturgical readings. The translators' endeavor to achieve a straightforward modern English prose, devoid of archaisms, has been regarded by critics as reasonably successful, and the text is considered clear and reliable.

[D. J. BOURKE]

JERVAULX, ABBEY OF, Cistercian monastery in Yorkshire, England. Founded by Byland abbey in 1150, it prospered for a century but by the dissolution (1537) had only 26 monks. One of them, George Lazenby, refused to take the Oath of Supremacy and was executed. The last abbot, Adam Sedbergh, suffered the same fate with two other monks for taking part in the Pilgrimage of Grace; several others were imprisoned; none received a pension. BIBLIOGRAPHY: F. Gasquet, *Greater Abbeys of England* (1908) 120–130; J. O'Dea, NCE 7:891–892.

[L. J. LEKAI]

JESSE WINDOW, church window showing the descent of Jesus from Jesse (Ru 4.22). It normally shows a tree growing from a reclining figure of Jesse (see Is 11.1) with the intermediary descendants on the foliage and ending with Jesus or the Virgin and Child. Notable examples are at Wells and Chartres cathedrals.

[T. EARLY]

JESUATI, popular name of a religious order suppressed by Clement IX in 1668. The name is based on their practice of frequently using the name of Jesus as an ejaculation. They were originally a lay group in Italy founded by Bl. *John Colombini, and given papal approval by Urban V in 1367; they were dedicated to works of mercy and to a penitential life. They first followed a Benedictine rule of life, but after 1426, the Rule of St. Augustine. In the 17th cent. some members received priestly ordination. There was also a women's congregation, the Poor Jesuatesses of the Visitation of the Blessed Virgin Mary, contemplatives whose order survived until 1872 in Italy.

[T. C. O'BRIEN]

JESUIT CENTER FOR SOCIAL STUDIES, a scholarly organization of members of the Society of Jesus established in 1939 under the direction of John P. Delaney, SJ. Besides his activities in the institute, Delaney also supported the Cana movement and the labor school movement. Originally, the Center was founded for the purpose of engaging in research and publication of works on social issues written in view of Christian values. Its members also plan and promote social action programs through Jesuit schools, universities, retreat houses, and other affiliated organizations. When it was first established, it was called the Institute of Social Order of the Society of Jesus and under this name it published a monthly, entitled the *Social Order* (1948–63). In 1971, it was known as the Cambridge Center for Social Studies. Presently named the Jesuit Center for Social Studies, its headquarters are located at Georgetown Univ., Washington, D.C.

[R. A. TODD]

JESUIT DRAMA, the drama performed in Jesuit schools and colleges throughout Europe from the 16th to the 18th century. It was uniformly didactic and moral in purpose, though its form and style differed at different times and in different places. Its development is easily traced in the various revisions of the *Ratio studiorum* (the program of studies in Jesuit institutions) and in the annals of the older Jesuit foundations. Initially a scholastic disputation in Latin delivered in dialogue form before a small audience, the genre soon developed (under such varied influences as the school drama of the humanists, Spanish secular drama, the *tableaux vivants* of the Low Countries, and Italian opera) into a grandiose spectacle which anticipated the Wagnerian *Gesamtkunstwerk* in its employment of large casts, light, music, color, and pageantry. Latin was replaced by the vernacular, the school platform by the sophisticated baroque stage; women's roles were introduced; audiences grew larger. The first recorded performance—at the Mamertine College in Messina in 1551—was quickly imitated. By 1770, more than 100,000 performances had been presented at more than 500 institutions. Most of the plays were written by Jesuits: Jakob Gretser (1562–1625), Jakob Bidermann (1578–1637), Nicolaus Avancinus (1612–86) in German-speaking countries; Stefano Tuccio (1540–97) in Italy; Nicolas Caussin (1580–1651) in France; Joseph Simeon (1594–1671), an Englishman writing in Rome; Pedro de Acevado (fl. 1560) in Spain. Jesuit drama reached its peak in the 17th cent., esp. in Bavaria and Austria, where it enjoyed the patronage of the courts. Several factors contributed to its eventual decline: the Thirty Years' War (1618–48); the growing spirit of rationalism from France; the increasing demand for plays on political, rather than spiritual, themes; and, finally, the suppression of the Jesuits in 1773. BIBLIOGRAPHY: E. Purdie, *Oxford Companion to the Theatre,* (1957) 415–422; W. Grenzmann, NCE 7:893–897.

[M. F. MCCARTHY]

JESUIT RELATIONS. From the beginnings of the Society of Jesus the founder, St. Ignatius Loyola, insisted on getting reports from missionaries in Protestant and non-Christian lands. Francis Xavier's letters from the East encouraged numerous vocations and support for his work of evangelization. In French Canada these reports took the form of *Relations des Jésuites*. It was the duty of the Jesuit superior at Quebec to draw upon the letters of the individual missionaries and draft an annual report to the Jesuit provincial at Paris. There they were edited and published in yearly volumes. The *Relations* touched not only on the progress of the Church in Canada, but on the geography, ethnography, and history of the St. Lawrence Basin and the Mississippi Valley. The original *Jesuit Relations* constitute 41 small volumes, a number for every year from 1632 to 1672. In 1673, at the insistence of the Congregation for the Propagation of the Faith, Clement X issued a brief forbidding the publication of any literature on the missions without the Congregation's approval. Because of the strain then existing between France and the Holy See, that directive meant the end of the *Jesuit Relations*. In their own day these reports succeeded in winning recruits and support for the Canadian missions. They are still regarded as a precious source for the history and ethnography of North America. The Wisconsin historian Reuben Gold Thwaites, published the original text of the *Jesuit Relations* together with an English translation and many supporting documents in 73 volumes entitled *The Jesuit Relations and Allied Documents* (1896–1901).

[T. H. CLANCY]

JESUIT SPIRITUALITY. The basic foundation of Jesuit or Ignatian spirituality is the book of the **Spiritual Exercises* of St. Ignatius Loyola, which is the result of his experience in trying to find God after his conversion in 1521. The text of this little masterpiece is brief and jejune, almost forbidding. It is not meant to be read, but to be a manual to guide the director who is leading a person through the experience of the *Spiritual Exercises*. The best commentary is to be found in Ignatius' *Autobiography* and letters. The first note of Jesuit spirituality is its emphasis on method. It is founded on the belief that any soul can be taught to pray and to find the will of God by the use of one of the many methods found in the *Spiritual Exercises*, and this not at the end of years of spiritual apprenticeship but in the course of an intense month spent under the guidance of a capable director. There is a strong ascetical note in Jesuit spirituality. The purpose of the *Spiritual Exercises* is "the conquest of self and the regulation of one's life in such a way that no decision is made under the influence of any inordinate attachment" (n. 21). The first goal of the Exercises is Ignatian "indifference," which is a readiness to follow whatever one perceives to be more for the glory and praise of God. In achieving this goal bodily penance has a place, but more important is that abnegation of will and intellect which leads to the Ignatian emphasis on obedience. The chief spur to virtue and abnegation is the imitation of Christ. A smaller place is given in Jesuit spirituality to the nature, classification, and abstract considerations of virtue. The motive to ask for poverty and humiliations is that these things characterized Christ's life. The chief devotion of Jesuit spirituality is to the Heart of Christ. Ignatius gives a large part to reflection and discernment. He believes that a person who has achieved indifference can find out the will of God by noting the motions of the Spirit in his soul. His rules for discernment are included in the *Spiritual Exercises* and have been developed through the years by spiritual writers of all schools. Following their founder, Jesuits have always insisted on the examination of conscience as a prayerful reflection on God's dealing with the soul. Finally, Jesuit spirituality is apostolic. All prayer is meant to impel towards enthusiastic and energetic service of God for his greater glory. The summit of this spirituality is that a person be able to find God in all things, to become a contemplative in action, joined to God not only in prayer but in work for Christ's kingdom. Perhaps the best summary of Jesuit spirituality is the terse lines jotted down by Ignatius' faithful collaborator, Jerónimo Nadal, in 1561: "Do all for the greater glory of God. Love the Institute. Love the end (of the Society). Love and desire to work for that end. Perfect obedience. Prayer which is practical and carried into execution (*practica y extendida a la obra*). Simplicity. Love of mortification. Love of suffering. Modesty in speech coupled with edification. Love to be despised. Dilgence in daily observances. Walk before God and always in his presence. Practice the acts of the theological virtues, esp. of charity. Develop the habit of an ever-activated love of God, in such a manner that this love may always be the motivating force in all one's actions, and that it may be the form of all the virtues and give them the superior value of charity."

[T. H. CLANCY]

JESUITS, the Society of Jesus, a religious order of clerks regular that grew out of an association of friends who formed around St. *Ignatius Loyola at Paris. They were all students at the university there, and on 15 August 1534 they vowed poverty, chastity, and the apostolic life at Montmartre in Paris. Their first plan was to work in the Holy Land, but when it proved impossible to find passage there they put themselves at the disposition of Pope Paul III and eventually formed a religious order, which he confirmed in 1540. Special features of the rule include: the name, the lifetime term for the superior general, a two-year novitiate, the absence of any obligation to the choral Divine Office, to an official habit or daily horarium, and a strong emphasis on obedience. Their early works included preaching, the corporal works of mercy, hearing confessions and conducting the *Spiritual Exercises of St. Ignatius, which later came to be known as retreats. They had a special vow to undertake missions for the Holy Father in any part of the world and in 1540 Francis Xavier departed for India. In their first decade Jesuits were sent to Ireland, to Germany, to Ethiopia and to the Council of Trent at the command of the Pope. In 1548 the first real Jesuit school for the instruction of youth was begun in Messina in Sicily. From that point the two major efforts of the Society were the foreign missions in the New World and the East and colleges and seminaries in Europe, esp. in Germany. By the death of St. Ignatius in 1556 there were 1,000 members; by the death of the fifth general, Claudio Aquaviva in 1615, the number had risen to 13,000. For the next 350 years Jesuit growth was steady, although from 1773 to 1814 they were suppressed worldwide by papal order (see CLEMENT XIV, POPE). In 1965 there were 36,038 Jesuits. Since then the number has declined to about 29,000, but the order still ranks as the largest religious order of men. Of this number, about one in four is an American. Their main works are still education and the foreign missions. In the U.S. the Jesuits conduct 26 colleges and universities and 47 high schools. There are Jesuit retreat houses in almost every country, and the Society is notable too for the number of learned and popular books and periodicals it produces. Among the 38 Jesuit saints the best known after St. Ignatius Loyola and St. Francis Xavier are John Francis Regis, Robert Bellarmine, Isaac Jogues, and Edmund Campion.

[T. H. CLANCY]

JESUS (THE NAME). In Mt 1.21, 25b; Lk 1.31; 2.11, it was divinely ordained for the Messiah before his conception. Matthew's Gospel explains it as symbolic of his mission, "For he will save his people from their sins." This agrees with its popular meaning as "Yahweh saves," although the original unshortened form meant "Yahweh helps." In Luke its bestowal is related to Jesus' eternal reign as the Davidic Messiah and the great Son of the Most High God. Both outlooks may well derive from Peter's primitive, apostolic proclamation of Acts 4.10–12, in which the name of Jesus is the only one given by God to men for their salvation, a text that underlies the biblical notion that one's name expresses one's very person and essential function. The "name above every other name" awarded to Jesus by God in the exaltation text of Phil 2.10–11 is not Jesus but Lord.

[J. F. FALLON]

JESUS, GENEALOGY OF, see GENEALOGY OF JESUS.

JESUS, WISDOM OF, see APOCRYPHA (NEW TESTAMENT), 26.

JESUS CHRIST (IN THE BIBLE), a Jewish itinerant preacher from Nazareth in Galilee, Palestine, who attempted a reformation of the Judaism of his day, acquired a reputation as a religious teacher and wonder-worker, and who was executed by crucifixion at Jerusalem under the Roman governor, Pontius Pilate, on a charge of sedition, with the cooperation of Jewish religious authorities, *c.*30 A.D. but whose memory and teaching were kept alive by certain of his followers, led by Simon Peter of Galilee, who proclaimed him raised from the dead by an act of God on the 3d day after his burial, and who succeeded in establishing in Jerusalem a strong community of believers in him as the expected Messiah of Israel and religious savior of the world, whence similar communities were reduplicated in Palestine and in major cities of the Roman world, inspired by the hope of his coming (parousia), his presence in history (the Eucharistic Liturgy), and his activity and teaching (the gospel tradition), that by A.D. 100 left permanent records in a body of writings known as the NT and in the emergence of Christianity as a vital religious force in world history.

The origin and 1st-cent. history of the Christian movement is not documented by ancient historians. Tacitus and Suetonius, reflecting the early adoption of Christ as the proper name of Jesus, merely mention him under this name in connection with their observations on the Christian presence in Rome. New Testament literature is religious in character, written from the standpoint of faith in Jesus as messiah and savior, and must be assessed critically for an accurate understanding of Jesus in the historical context of the religious milieu of his time. Accordingly, this article discusses Jesus Christ (1) in terms of the understanding of him developed by the faith of the Christians of NT times (*Christology*); (2) in the context of the historical milieu of his life as his history can be assessed from the data of the gospel tradition (''*the Jesus of history*''); and (3) as the person accepted in NT faith as the God-man and the same person who taught and died in the brief span of scarcely more than several years' duration (''*the Christ of faith'' and ''the Jesus of history*'').

NT Christology, the prophetic assessment of the religious significance of Jesus' person. There is no question that Christian faith arose historically out of the conviction that Jesus of Nazareth, crucified, dead, and buried, was raised from the dead by God to live a transcendent life related to the history of this world, but no longer a part of it in his physically present person (cf. Acts 2.14–36; 3.11–26; 10.34–43; 13.16–41). The earliest presentation of Jesus' person in the Jewish milieu of Jerusalem understandably stressed his messianic dignity: he was ''the Christ,'' i.e., he summed up in his person all the religious characteristics that God had destined the Messiah to possess as the savior of Israel and which were already mysteriously stamped upon the prophetic teaching of the OT (cf. Acts 4.11, citing Ps 118.22). This concept of Jesus as messiah embraced some elements of Jewish messianic expectation such as his Davidic lineage and his glorious reign, but diverged significantly from contemporary views in the acceptance of a single, crucified Messiah, in attributing to him the power to forgive sin and dispense the gifts of the Spirit (Acts 2.38), and in consigning his physical presence as ruler of Israel to an order outside history (Acts 2.33; 3.21; cf. 1.9–11). The earliest conception of the risen Jesus transcendentalized his person by making him the direct source of forgiveness and righteousness, divine prerogatives ascribed in the OT to Yahweh alone (Ps 130.3–4; 37.39–40). This early Christology is reflected in Acts 2.36–38: the risen Jesus possesses in his own person qualities and powers that reflect the lordship of Yahweh. At the same time his perfect humanity is recognized in the description of him in terms of the suffering servant of Is 53.12 (cf. Acts 3.13, 26). Thus early NT Christology displays the two key strands of thought about the person of Jesus that dominate practically the whole of the NT: truly and perfectly human, Jesus is also capable of identification with the divine.

The NT view of Jesus as in some way divine as well as admittedly human does not represent two different approaches toward the understanding of his person. It is a single view that attempted to express the fullness of the Christian understanding of him. But with the exception of Jn 1.1–14 no systemized formulation was worked out in NT times to unify these two ideas about his person under a single conceptualization. Throughout the NT the divine and human aspects of his person are reflected upon separately. This tradition is illustrated in Phil 2.5–11, though by many scholars to be an early Palestinian liturgical hymn retouched by Paul. This composition is a reflection upon the person of Jesus: throughout his ministry he was the hidden God, whose divinity was concealed by his evident humanity (2.6–8), until with his Resurrection his true identity was made known in his lordship that demands divine worship from all creatures as due to his very person (2.9–11).

Between the earliest Christology that presented Jesus as a divinized messiah and the later Christology appearing in Phil (*c.* A.D. 57–61) that places him on a level with God there was a period of developing understanding of his person. Although the data of the NT are incomplete and overlapping, it may be judged that the key factors in the acceptance of his person as fully divine were the use of Ps 2.7 to explain the significance of his person and the transference to him, esp. in liturgical worship, of the OT concept of Yahweh as savior. According to Acts, Jesus as messianic Son of God in the sense of Ps 2.7 was a title early conceded him and was esp. emphasized by Paul (cf. Acts 9.20). It was found applicable to Jesus, however, not in consideration of his birth but of his Resurrection (cf. Acts 13.33). The latter event revealed him as Son of God in a messianic, i.e., a salvific sense (cf. Rom 1.4) and opened the way to ascribing to him the salvific function traditionally conceded in the OT to Yahweh. Particularly significant for the perception of this line of development is the Pauline expression in 2 Cor 5.19, ''God was in Christ reconciling the world to himself,'' where the Apostle does not hesitate to identify the OT conception of the saving presence of Yahweh in history with the presence of Jesus in history; i.e., it is in the very person of Jesus that God manifests himself to men as their savior. This high Christology of the Pauline Epistles is given a cosmic significance in Col 1.15–20, wherein the risen Jesus is declared to be the omega-point of all creation, in whom all creatures are ultimately to find their *raison d'être* in view of his divinity and of his reconciling death upon the cross. The final touch to the NT conception of Jesus as God and man is supplied by the fourth Gospel.

Here the concept of Jesus as God in person is presented most clearly in the affirmation of the *Logos* become flesh (Jn. 1.14). The *Logos*, "Word," is the Evangelist's term for the pre-existent Son of God, creator (Jn 1.3) and source of all religious life and knowledge among men (Jn 1.4). The risen Jesus is revealed to be both Lord and God (cf. Jn 20.18,28). This entire Christological development is neatly resumed in Heb 1.1–6, and alluded to in Jn 14.9: Jesus is the culmination of God's revelation of himself as savior, begun in the prophetic tradition of the OT, not simply because of the unique authority of his word, but because of the divinity of his person; to understand God as the loving Father who effects the salvation of men, it is sufficient to understand Jesus.

The "Jesus of History." All four Evangelists present the same broad conception of Jesus' ministry: his work began in the setting of the preaching of John the Baptist announcing a coming divine judgment, and ended with his crucifixion under Pontius Pilate. The central theme of his ministry was the reign (kingdom) of God. The reign is present in a new way (Mk 1.14–15), but is preparatory to a reign of God still to come (Mt 18.23–35; 20.1–16). In his teaching Jesus drew out the implications of the arrival of God's new reign. It demanded radical conversion, i.e., a total surrender of the individual person to God and his demands. The practice of love of God and of neighbor as fundamental to the acceptance of the reign was declared by Jesus to be key to its understanding (Mk 12.28–34). Many of his individual sayings, teaching the meaning of love of God and neighbor, are incorporated in the Sermon on the Mount (Mt 5–7) and the Sermon on the Plain (Lk 6.20–49). Jesus also made use of the parable to express his ideas about God's reign (cf. the collections of parables of the kingdom in Mk 4.1–34 and Mt. 13.1–52). According to these parables, the reign of God is not imposed upon men by divine force. Its presence is announced to them in the ministry of Jesus, and they are invited to accept it on these terms and to persevere in their adherence to its reality despite the difficulties posed by faith in it (the parable of the Sower; cf. Mk 4.3–9). The reign is the presence of God in history, which has its own inevitable climax (the parable of the self-growing seed; cf. Mk 4.26–29). It has an intrinsic power that exerts a beneficent effect within history (the parable of the leaven; cf. Mt 13.33). Although the reign of God as announced by Jesus may seem a triviality compared to other forces, its ultimate effect will surpass human expectations (the parable of the mustard seed; cf. Mk 4.30–32). Matthew includes other parables emphasizing the necessity of making every sacrifice for the sake of God's reign (the parables of the treasure and the pearl; Mt. 13.44–46), and declares that its temporal reality within history includes the just and the unjust (Mt 13.24–30), a view of the reign that differed from the Baptist's, who expected that the unrepentant would be summarily excluded from it by the one to come (Mt 3.11–12).

In addition to the parables as memorable lessons on the varied aspects of God's reign, Jesus employed the highly dramatic means of the miracle to make visible to the eyes of faith the actuality of the sovereign presence of God announced in the new reign. His healing miracles, usually effected by simple command, made it clear that his prophetic word on the reign of God was itself the vehicle that introduced this new dominion of God into history. To accept his word was to accept his miracles as acts of God making evident his royal presence; to accept Jesus' miracles as acts of God was to accept his word about God's reign (cf. Mk 10.46–52; Jn 4.46–53). Efforts to explain Jesus' miracles as natural phenomena, however unique, or as legends created by the Christian communities of NT times to enlarge the significance of his person, misconstrue the religious dimension of the miracles: historically, they were intended primarily to underscore the significance of Jesus' message, not of his person, and were invitations to faith in him as the bearer of God's new message, and not as its creator and lord (cf. Mt 12.28; Jn 10.38). As Jesus' preaching and teaching can be appreciated only in the context of faith, so also his miracles can be appreciated only in the same context.

The eloquent testimony of the four Gospels that Jesus "went about doing good" (Acts 10.38) makes all the more tragic his condemnation to death by crucifixion. This manner of execution, which was the capital punishment meted out at the time to the worst criminals, is sufficient indication that his activity created considerable public stir and became a concern to the authorities. The possibility of his messianic role was a topic of popular discussion (Jn 7.40–42; 10.22–24) and was the conviction of his Disciples (Mk 8.29; Lk 24.21). Jesus was reticent on the subject (Mk 8.30), and before the Sanhedrin refused to be drawn into an admission of a messianic function at variance with his own views (Mt 26.64; Lk 22.67).

In the account of Jesus' execution the gospel tradition assigns key roles to Caiaphas, Annas, the Sanhedrin as a whole, and Pontius Pilate. According to the fourth Gospel, Caiaphas, the reigning high preist, persuaded the Sanhedrin that Jesus' death was in the best interests of the Jewish people (Jn 11.49). He had the support of his father-in-law, Annas, whom the Romans had deposed as high priest in A.D. 15. After the arrest of Jesus, probably on Thursday night of Passion Week, he was first brought to Annas, who interrogated him on the orthodoxy of his teaching (Jn 18.19–24). The following morning the Sanhedrin was convoked under the leadership of Caiaphas (Mk 15.1; 14.55–64); the Synoptic tradition places the content of the morning session before the Sanhedrin at a night session to conserve the tradition of Jesus' appearance before Annas recorded in Jn 18.19–24. Gospel scholars are not in agreement about whether this convocation followed juridical procedure and whether or not the Sanhedrin actually condemned Jesus to death. It is clear, however, that his responses to the questions put to him were not satisfactory to the court, and that at the least the Sanhedrin judged him to be subject to the death penalty for blasphemy (Mk

14.63–64; Lk 22.70–71; Mt 26.65–66; Jn 19.7). For reasons that are obscure the Sanhedrin did not carry out the death penalty in accordance with Jewish law, but turned Jesus over to Pilate on a charge of sedition against the Roman authority (cf. Lk 22.2). Pilate was already aware of the action taken against Jesus, as is clear from the fact that a detachment of Roman soldiers accompanied the temple police who made the arrest (Jn 18.3). As Roman governor, Pilate was not bound by the decision of the Sanhedrin, but was required to make his own independent determination of guilt. The Gospels depict him as dissatisfied with the evidence offered for Jesus' seditious activity and as inclined to release him, but he succumbed to the pressure of the Jewish religious authorities backed by a mob, perhaps bribed for this purpose (cf. Lk 22.13–25).

It can scarcely be questioned that the execution of Jesus of Nazareth was judicial murder for which both the Jewish religious authorities in Jerusalem and Pilate bore the responsibility. Although the gospel tradition does not analyze the motives of the religious authorities, its data as a whole indicate that they hoped to stamp out a religious movement they could not comprehend but which they feared as a threat to their own authority. It is possible that some among them were sincerely convinced that Jesus' activity could only lead to an attempted popular revolt against Roman authority, for which the time was not ripe. The material of the gospel tradition reflects both Jesus' popularity among the masses of the people (cf. Mk 1.28, 37; 6.53–56; 14.2) and also a hostility between him and the religious authorities (cf. Mk 2.1–3.6; 11.27–12.17) with whose application of the OT religious tradition to the lives of the people he was frequently in disaccord.

The "Christ of Faith" and the "Jesus of History." Critical study of the four Gospels in the 20th cent. has resulted in the conclusion that these documents contain more material and thought than can be accounted for by the historical ministry of Jesus itself. The conviction of his Resurrection as an act of God that vindicated his mission against the judgment of religious authority (cf. Acts 2.23) not only created the early Christian communities, but also furnished an entirely new perspective from which to view his person and work (cf. Heb 1.1–2). Actually, we possess no data from documentary sources of the time concerning the origin of the material of the Gospels. Careful study of the material itself, however, has compelled gospel scholarship to conclude that each of the four Evangelists was the heir of 40 to 60 years of tradition during which accounts of Jesus' suffering and death were formulated, and collections made of his parables, miracles, and sayings. Luke ascribes such activity to the Twelve (Acts 6.4; Lk 1.2) and also acknowledges the work of others (Lk 1.1) in the production of these materials. The prevailing standpoints from which materials from and about Jesus were developed were his Resurrection, the life of the Christian communities (e.g., the Eucharistic Liturgy), and their relationship to their environments. In the light of the Resurrection Jesus' death was no longer viewed as an historical disaster (cf. Mk 14.49; Lk 23.48) but as the salvation of mankind; so also his parables, sayings, and miracles were recounted afresh in the same light. "Everything that Jesus had done and taught" (Acts 1.1) was taken up as his legacy to the Christian community, to be reworked for the illumination and deepening of its faith, and for its encouragement and guidance in discovering and maintaining its place in the cultural environment of its time. The material of the gospel tradition so interwove the religious experience of the Christian communities with the life and mission of Jesus that the majority of gospel scholars believe it to be impossible to cut through the gospel narratives to distinguish the historical Jesus as he appeared to his contemporaries from the figure of Jesus presented in the light of the faith of NT Christianity. For the creators of the gospel material such a distinction was meaningless (cf. Heb 13.8), for the risen Jesus was one and the same person with the Jesus of the ministry. The personal limitations of his mortal life were but the evidence of the reality of his human condition (cf. Phil 2.5–8), which concealed his actual divine identity as well as the religious significance finally manifested in his Resurrection (cf. Rom 1.1–4). Thus the material of the gospel tradition coalesced into a unified portrait the Christian understanding of Jesus as messiah, Son of God, and savior of the world (cf. Lk 2.11) with the memory of the events of the ministry. But the authors of the tradition were also concerned to instruct the Christian community in the varied circumstances of its history. In the formulation of the gospel material they addressed themselves to contemporary questions and needs among Christians, such as the reality of persecution (Mk 8.34–38), the authenticity of the relationship of Christian teaching to the OT (Mt 5–7), and the primary attitudes and values in Christian teaching (Lk 15.1–32; 16.19–31; 19.1–10). There is little doubt that the person and teaching of Jesus are faithfully reflected and interpreted in these gospel formulations. The gospel tradition is a remarkable combination of historical fidelity and living interpretation that constantly kept Jesus and his teaching freshly before the faith of the Church. BIBLIOGRAPHY: for NT Christology: L. Cerfaux, *Christ in the Theology of St. Paul,* (tr. G. Webb and A. Walker, (1959); O. Cullmann, *Christology of the New Testament,* (tr S. C. Guthrie and C. A. M. Hall, (1959) R. H. Fuller, *Foundations of New Testament Christology* (1965). For "the Jesus of history": G. Bornkamm, *Jesus of Nazareth,* (tr. I and F. McLuskey (1960); X. Léon-Dufour, *Gospels and the Jesus of History* (tr. J. McHugh, 1967); J. Blinzler, *Trial of Jesus* (tr I. and F. McHugh, 1959). For "the Jesus of history" and "the Christ of faith": C. E. Braaten and R. A. Harrisville, *Historical Jesus and the Kerygmatic Christ* (1964); H. K. McArthur, ed., *In Search of the Historical Jesus* (1969).

[C. P. CEROKE]

JESUS CHRIST, EXALTATION OF, see EXALTATION OF JESUS.

JESUS CHRIST, HUMAN KNOWLEDGE OF. Classical Christian theology has maintained that Jesus had both a divine nature and a human nature as well as the operations (acts) proper to those natures without any mixture or confusion. (cf., for instance, the Creed of the Council of Chalcedon). Thus Jesus had a human intellect and human knowledge. Scholastic theology tended to maximize Jesus' human knowledge: Thomas Aquinas attributed acquired (experiential) and infused knowledge to Jesus' human intellect as well as the knowledge that would follow from the beatific vision (ST 3, 8–12). Some contemporary theologians (especially P. Galtier, K. Rahner and B. Lonergan), while fully acknowledging the humanity and divinity of Jesus, have denied that Jesus' human intellect during his earthly life enjoyed the beatific vision and have questioned the psychological aspects of the divine-human union in Jesus. Their opinion is that there was a psychologically independent I-center in Jesus whereby Jesus came to know the relationship between his humanity and the eternal Word, not as one would come to know an object but rather through the awareness of the self that is present in and through all conscious activity. Thus Christ's created mind became aware of itself in its lifelong acts of knowledge, pointing beyond itself to that with which it was united, the eternal Word. BIBLIOGRAPHY: K. Rahner, *Theological Investigations* I (1961) 149–200; B. Lonergan, *Collections* (1967) 164–197.

[T. M. MCFADDEN]

JESUS CHRIST, THE CORNERSTONE, a title coming from a saying of Jesus (Mt 21.42) that applies Ps 118.22,23 to himself. The passage predicts his rejection by the religious leaders who had him crucified ("the builders") and his subsequent power as the support and foundation of "the kingdom of God" that "will be given to a people producing fruits for it." In the Lucan parallel (Lk 20.17,18) immediate reference is made to the destructive force of this stone for any who attack it or who are attacked by it. Therefore, it was a gospel figure of Christ's powerful and supportive rule after his victory over sin and death. In Acts 4.11 Peter uses the same symbol, with emphasis on God's raising of Jesus from the dead to make him the only source of salvation. In 1 Pet 2.4–8 the symbolism is extended from a rejected stone to the foundation stone of the new Zion of Is 28.16 for those who put their trust in it and to the obstacle stone of stumbling for disbelievers (Is 8.14). The same texts are combined in Rom 9.33 to explain the Jews' failure to gain uprightness because of disbelief in the redemptive death of their Messiah. Ephesians 2:20–22 uses the symbol for Christ as the foundation that binds and supports the whole household of the Church (cf. Col 2.7). Modern theories that the cornerstone means an ornamental copestone or a keystone of an arch hardly fit the architecture of ancient Israel. Further, the stone must not be conceived as a final dedicatory stone of a building.

[J. F. FALLON]

JESUS MOVEMENT, youth movement distinguished particularly for drawing youth of "hippie" or "counterculture" communities to conservative evangelical Christianity. Though adherents gave up drugs and promiscuous sex, they commonly retained many other aspects of their former way of life, including dress, hair styles, and communal living patterns. Their enthusiastic advocacy of Jesus as the "one way" in a time when many Churches found difficulty in reaching youth created widespread public interest, intensified by the unfamiliar juxtaposition of conservative theology with cultural patterns alien to most church members. The movement emerged *c.*1967 on the West Coast of the U.S., and then spread to other parts of the country and to some foreign lands. For the most part, the movement developed outside existing church structures, with adult leadership coming mostly from smaller denominations and independent para-church groups. Critics accused the movement of theological shallowness and insufficient commitment to the total life and ministry of the Church. But it was praised for an ability to reach a segment of the younger generation estranged from mainstream Churches. Boundaries of the movement remained somewhat vague. In a broad sense the term was used to designate almost any expression of evangelical faith among youth. But in its original, specific form it began subsiding in the early 1970s. BIBLIOGRAPHY: E. E. Ericson et al., *Jesus People* (1972); E. E. Plowman, "Whatever happened to the Jesus movement?" *Christianity Today* v. 20, no. 2 (1975) 102–104.

[T. EARLY]

JESUS PRAYER, see HESYCHASM.

JESU'S PSALTER, often called the Jesus Psalter, a favorite devotion of English Catholics of the 16th and 17th cent., which appears never to have spread beyond English-speaking countries. Written by Richard *Whitford, it consisted of 150 invocations of the name of Jesus, separated by verses composed in imitation of the Psalms. It was many times reprinted both separately and as part of the *Primer and other devotional works.

JETHRO, a Midianite priest, father-in-law of Moses (Ex 3.1; 4.18), who married his daughter Zipporah while sojourning in Midian. She and her two sons remained with him when Moses went to Egypt to effect the liberation of the Israelites. They were all reunited after Moses had led the people into the desert of Sinai. J. offered sacrifice to Yahweh on this occasion (Ex 18.1–12) and suggested to Moses a reorganization of the people, delegating to minor officials the handling of less important legal disputes. There is considerable confusion about his name; he is called Reuel in Ex 2.18 and Hobab in Num 10.29, but here Reuel is the father of Hobab.

[J. J. CASTELOT]

JEU DE SAINT NICOLAS, a play composed by Jean Bodel before 1202; its pungent vernacular and sense of staging are remarkable. The plot is a legend in which St. Nicolas overpowers criminals and pagans with a miraculous apparition.

[J. P. WILLIMAN]

JEUNESSEE OUVRIÈRE CHRÉTIENNE (JOC), see JOCISM.

JEWEL, JOHN (1522–71), Anglican apologist and bp. of Salisbury. At Oxford J. achieved some prominence as an intellectual leader in the reforming party. Under Queen Mary he went into exile and became closely associated with *Peter Martyr Vermigli in Strassburg and Zurich. In 1560 Elizabeth appointed him to the See of Salisbury. He was active in the defense of the C of E against Catholics and Puritans. In 1562 he published his *Apologia Ecclesiae Anglicanae,* which led to a long and acrimonious controversy on the papacy with Thomas Harding of Louvain, important for its influence upon the course of subsequent polemics. Works: ed. J. Jelf (8 v., 1848) Eng. tr. of his *Apologia: Apology of the Church of England* (ed. J. Booty, 1963). BIBLIOGRAPHY: W. Southgate, *John Jewel and the Problem of Doctrinal Authority* (1962); J. Booty, *John Jewel as Apologist of the Church of England* (1963).

[R. B. ENO]

JEWISH EMANCIPATION, see EMANCIPATION, JEWISH.

JEWISH LITURGY. The ruin of the temple in 587 B.C. put a temporary end to the sacrificial forms of Israelite worship by which the covenant people had responded to the quasi-physical presence of their God in the Holy of Holies. Cut off from their holy temple, city, and land, the Jewish exiles in Babylon had to devise a new form of worship which no longer depended on this presence of the divine to them in a particular, holy place, but rather on his presence through his revealed word. According to many scholars, therefore, it was during the exile that the synagogue was born. It was essentially a meetinghouse for Jewish laymen, in which the role of the priest was minimal, and its focal point was, and still is, the place where the written scrolls of the law were kept. The term ark had acquired this new signififance: from being the throne on which Yahweh's *kabod* or glory rested it had become the shrine of his written word, and this word alone still effectively guaranteed his abiding presence to and union with his people. From being a people of the presence they had become a people of the book. The synagogue, therefore, was presided over not by priests but by the elders of the community, and its management was in the hands of the *archisynagogos* or ruler of the synagogue (cf. Lk 8:41; Acts 18:8 etc.). Here services were held on the sabbath and festivals, though a minimum of 10 male members had to be present for public worship. The morning service originally opened with a recitation of the Decalogue, but from the Christian era onwards this was suppressed and the first act consisted of the Jewish profession of faith known as *shema*. This was set in a framework of three blessings or prayers of thanksgiving, the first thanking God for his creation, the second for his election of and revelation to Israel, and the third for his redemption and protection of his people. In the evening service an additional blessing was added to these, invoking divine aid for the approaching night. This first act was followed by the official prayer or *tephillah,* which was originally extempore, but gradually acquired fixed and traditional form as the *shemone esre* or 18 benedictions. Additional psalms and prayers were also added. The third stage consisted of a reading or readings from the Law in Hebrew (the prophets were soon added as prescribed reading at this stage), followed by a loose translation or paraphrase in Aramaic (cf. Targum). A member of the congregation then delivered a homily on the reading, and both Jesus and his followers seem to have taken this as an opportunity for proclaiming the Christian gospel within the framework of the synagogal liturgy. The deliverer of the homily concluded with a supplication known as the *gaddish,* and later this came to be repeated at several points in the course of the liturgy. Finally the blessing was given, the only part in which a priest exercised his specifically sacerdotal function. The pentateuchal readings were arranged in a cycle designed to last over a period of 3 years. BIBLIOGRAPHY: I. F. Elbogen, *Der jüdische Gottesdienst in seiner geschichtlichen Entwicklung* (1913).

[D. J. BOURKE]

JEWISH MUSIC. In spite of the diversity of language and culture to which the Jews have been introduced, their music, particularly the sacred, has maintained a distinctive identity throughout a long, largely oral tradition. The most abrupt change in the sacred music occurred in the transition from Temple worship to the service of the synagogues after 70 A.D. Before that time the complex musical organization of the Temple was directed by the powerful Levites and included choral groups accompanied by large numbers of ancient instruments, many of which are cited in the Bible. From numerous marginal notes it is clear that the musical rendition of the Psalms, psalmody, occupied much of the effort of early Jewish musicians. With the destruction of the Second Temple, instrumental music was abolished and the professional Levites replaced by individual precentors chosen from the congregations. It is believed that the traditional melodies may themselves have undergone certain changes at this time, but the general practice of cantillation, the singing of the parts of the Bible and the oldest form of Jewish chant, continued in the new system. Cantillation consisted of the singing of certain melodies or chants, each represented by a sign, *ta'amin,* the presence of which, in conjunction with a text, indicated how that text was to be sung and even how it was to be interpreted, because the signs also indicated stress values. That fact alone provides an insight into the traditional importance of the cantor, particularly in view of the fact that the significances of those signs were transmitted orally for over 1000 years.

The chanting of prayers was a somewhat later type, in which the goal was development on a basic theme and consequently revealed the need for a return to the professional musician in that it allowed for more melodic freedom and thus demanded greater skill. The 9th-cent. development of fixed chants reconstructed from ancient modes was achieved because of this new role of *hazzanim* or cantors. With these later forms, the basic theme occupied a meager portion of the chant—the major part being improvised. When the necessarily vulnerable nature of improvisation was combined with the already widespread and ever-increasing dispersion of the Jews in the medieval period and the somewhat later influence of the artistic climate of the Renaissance, not surprisingly the original modes became all but unrecognizable, as almost did the Jewish character of the music. Beginning in the 18th cent. a concerted effort was made to reconcile modern trends with tradition. The controversy still rages today, although with the growth of Jewish nationalism the tendency to restore the old styles gains headway.

In the secular realm, attempts have also been made to extract the strictly Jewish folksong from the multitude of versions in which each is found—clearly a monumental undertaking. In addition, the remarkable contributions of Jewish composers to occidental music has also led Jewish leaders to try to channel the efforts of these artists into the production of music that reflects more of their own heritage.

[P. J. HENNESSEY]

JEWISH PHILOSOPHY. Jewish biblical and rabbinical literature is essentially theological and religious, being based on divine revelation and the prophetic interpretation of sacred history. But from Hellenistic times Greek philosophies influenced Jewish thought, as is evident in **Qoheleth* and **wisdom*. Not until Philo (20 B.C. –*c.*50 A.D.) may any Jewish author be identified strictly as a philosopher, i.e., one who, while remaining basically Jewish in thought and interest, attempted to relate purely philosophical thought to Jewish themes. Jewish philosophy may be divided historically into the Philonic, the medieval (9th–15th cent.), and the modern (18th–20th cent.). *Philo Judaeus accommodated Jewish sacred writings to various Greek philosophies, *Neoplatonism, *Stoicism, etc., by means of forced allegorical interpretations. Some salient concepts were: the linking of Greek metaphysics with the unique, spiritual identity of the God of Israel, his infiniteness in dynamic force and beneficence, and his creation of the cosmos from preexistent matter through Platonic-like ideas that existed in the logos, the word, an intermediate created force above the seen world but outside the uncreated divinity. Philo's anthropology, while not neglecting the body's sensing faculties, emphasized the soul's striving for a spiritual happiness. That resulted from self-control of evil desires and the contemplation of God and his creation, and led to a mystical grasp of the ultimate truth. Philo never created a school among Jews but influenced later Christian writers of the Alexandrian tradition.

The medieval period began when Muslim philosophers of the *kalām* schools influenced Jewish thought in the E Islam of the 10th cent. Saadyah ben Joseph adopted Platonic, Aristotelian, and Stoic concepts and used them in rational explanations of biblical and rabbinical tradition: knowledge of God could be defended and confirmed by human reasoning; creation was wrought in time from no previous matter; God was one, while having many attributes; no evil escaped his ultimate control; a Trinity in God is inconceivable. Neoplatonic influence became prominent in the work of *Isaac Israeli (d. *c.*955): the world emanates from God through his power and will, primary matter and first form antecede intellectual realities, souls and the world. For man's perfect union with divine wisdom a drastic purgation and illumination must occur.

In the Islamic West, Solomon ibn Gabirol, known in the Latin world as *Avicebron (d. *c.*1060), approached the definition of a pure philosopher, since in his widely acclaimed *Source of Life,* a Neoplatonic metaphysical treatise, he evinced no explicit dependence on the Bible and the Rabbis. He extended the composition of matter and form even to intelligences and evoked debate about his doctrine among Latin philosophers down to the 14th cent. (they mistakenly took him to be a purely rational Arab philosopher). Other Neoplatonists, though much more Judaic in outlook, were Baḥya (late 11th cent.), a moralist mainly, and the famous *Judah Halevi. His greatest work *Kuzari* is a classic and forceful apology for Judaism that makes use of philosophy to promote a more conservative view of the value of Jewish revelation and prophetism. The Neoplatonic trend continued into the 12th cent. in the works of Abraham bar Ḥiyya, Joseph ibn Zaddik, and Moses and Abraham ibn Ezra.

Aristotelianism, stemming from the great Arab thinkers, *Alfarabi, *Avicenna and *Avempace, dominated Jewish philosophy of the later Middle Ages. Abraham Halevi (Ibn Daud, *c.*1110–80) compared the physics and metaphysics of Aristotle to revealed religion and reacted forcefully to the poetic Neoplatonism of Avicebron with a lengthy critique. Moses *Maimonides, however, became the most famous of all Jewish Aristotelians, and indeed the most renowned Jewish philosopher of the Middle Ages. His *Guide of the Perplexed* was a masterpiece of the use of Aristotelian concepts to bolster and clarify biblical themes. His clear insights on how to interpret the human actions and emotions attributed to God in the Bible opened up a more realistic hermeneutic of Sacred Scripture. Maimonides' work was soon translated into Latin and had a great impact on Christian theologians of the 13th cent., esp. on Albert the Great and *Thomas Aquinas. Henceforth, most medieval Jewish philosophers either commented upon or disputed Maimonides' work. Among the more famous were Falquera, Kaspi, Moses of Narbonne, Levi ben Gerson (Gersonides) and Ḥasdai Crescas.

In the modern period Moses *Mendelssohn, a proponent

of Jewish "enlightenment," was followed by philosophers who viewed Judaism through German idealistic concepts: S. Formstecher, S. Hirsch, N. Krochmal, M. Lazarus, and Hermann Cohen. Existentialism influenced the philosophy of F. Rosenzweig, L. Baeck and M. Buber. Other philosophers, who happened to be Jews, such as B. *Spinoza, E. *Husserl and H. *Bergson, are important for their contributions to philosophy in general, but were not proponents of an identifiable Jewish philosophy.

[J. R. RIVELLO]

JEZABEL (JEZEBEL), the daughter of King Ethbaal of Sidon and the wife of King Ahab of Israel (1 Kg 16.31). With Ahab's toleration, she persecuted the prophets of Yahweh and fostered the worship of the Canaanite Baal in Israel, even supporting 450 prophets of Baal (1 Kg 18). Her chief opponent was Elijah who stirred up a popular movement that led to the killing of the prophets of Baal (1 Kg 18.19–19.2). The pernicious influence of this strong-willed woman on Ahab is seen in the murder of Naboth (1 Kg 21.1–24). Her death at Jehu's command is described in 2 Kg 9. Her daughter, Queen Athalia of Juda (2 Kg 8.18), continued her evil ways. In Rev 2.20 the name Jezabel is used symbolically of some individual or group leading the Christians of Thyatira into idolatry. BIBLIOGRAPHY: Kittel TD 3:218.

[E. J. CROWLEY]

JEZREEL, VALLEY OF, see ESDRAELON, PLAIN OF.

JIHAD (Arabic *jihâd,* exertion), in the specialized Muslim sense, exertion in the way of God. The word is specifically applied to military activity carried on to expand or preserve the rule of *Islam. The jihad is to be carried out against all nonbelievers, against pagans until they become Muslims or against Christians and Jews, as the People of the Scripture until they either convert to Islam or agree to pay the prescribed taxes. The jihad is counted as one of the five obligations incumbent on every fit Muslim. It is the only legitimate form of war recognized by fundamental Islamic doctrine. According to *Sunnite doctrine the term is not applicable to warfare carried on against other Muslims, even schismatics, while for the *Shiites, who consider other Muslims as nonbelievers, it is allowed. BIBLIOGRAPHY: EncIslam², s.v. "Djihād."

[R. M. FRANK]

JIMÉNEZ DE ENCISO, SALVADOR (1765–1841), Spanish-born bp. of Popayán, Colombia from 1818 who first resisted then became a supporter of the war for Colombian independence and was esteemed by Simón Bolívar.

[T. C. O'BRIEN]

JINA (Sanskrit, conqueror), the founder of *Jainism, Vardhamāna, who in the 13th year of his asceticism, attained spiritual perfection as Tirthankara—"Ford-maker" (bridge-builder).

[M. J. DALY]

JINN (Arab. *jinn*; sing., *jinnî*; fem., *jinnîya*), spirits or demons among the Muslims. Among the pagan Arabs of the time of *Mohammed, the jinn were considered quasi-divine beings and sacrifices were offered and petitions addressed to them. The **Koran* describes them as created of fire and called upon to worship God under the same conditions of reward and punishment as men. In popular tradition and stories they are conceived as normally invisible to humans, but capable of taking on various forms, human and animal, endowed with magical powers which they may employ maliciously or beneficently. The jinn have always held an important place in Islamic magic and a great number of works have been written on how to compel them to service. The term *'ifrît* is often used to denote a jinni, generally a powerful and evil one. BIBLIOGRAPHY: D. B. MacDonald, et al, EncIslam², s.v. "Djinn."

[R. M. FRANK]

JOAB, biblical name. (1) David's nephew (1 Chr 2.16) and commander of David's army (1 Chr 11.6). He successfully fought the Ammonites and Syrians (2 Sam 10.6–14), carried out David's plot against Uriah (2 Sam 11), gave David the honor of personally taking Rabbah (2 Sam 12.27–28), reconciled David with Absalom (2 Sam 14), killed Absalom when he later rebelled (2 Sam 18.14), was replaced temporarily by Amasa (2 Sam 19.13), but regained his position by killing Amasa and defeating Sheba (2 Sam 20). J. favored Adonijah as successor to David (1 Kg 1.7) and was killed at Solomon's command (1 Kg 2.28–35); (2) father of Ge-harashim (1 Chr 4.14); (3) eponym of a Judean family (Ezra 2.6; 8.9; Neh 7.11).

[T. EARLY]

JOACHIM, ST., see ANNE AND JOACHIM, SS.

JOACHIM OF BRANDENBURG, two imperial electors, father and son. **Joachim I** (1484–1535), elector from 1499. He was one of the few German princes—another being Duke George of Saxony—who remained firmly loyal to the Church during the early Reformation. In fact his convictions were so deep that his wife, Elizabeth, fled to Saxony because he could not tolerate her Protestant leanings. Throughout his rule he was also a staunch supporter of the Emperor. He was a member of the Catholic Dessau League, created in the aftermath of the *Peasants' Revolt in July 1525. In May 1527 he became active in the Breslau League, whose aim, like that of Dessau, was the crushing of the Lutheran heresy. Each of these Catholic alliances was countered by Protestant unions. When the powerful *Schmalkaldic League appeared in May 1533, the Catholic union at Halle, which he joined, proved no match. At his death J. divided Brandenburg between his two sons, Joachim II and John, but he made them swear to uphold the Catholic faith in their territories. This promise was soon broken. **Joachim II** (1505–71), elector from 1535. Although he had earlier contacts with Lutheranism, J. initially kept his promise to his father to maintain the Catholic faith.

In 1539, however, he permitted Lutheran preaching in the electorate and by 1542 Protestantism was largely introduced. Yet his own religious convictions are unclear. In fact he tried to steer a middle course in order to gain advantage from both sides. Catholic irenicists, in particular George Witzel, served in his court and he even won the approval of Charles V for his church ordinances. He was careful not to antagonize the papacy until he was able to secure the bishopric of Halberstadt for his son, Frederick, in 1551. J.'s politics followed the same pattern. He often acted as a mediator between the Emperor and other Protestants. In 1548, for instance, he urged that the *Interim* be used as a basis for compromise. His church reforms can be compared with Henry VIII's Reformation. He wanted sole control of the Church; the closing of monasteries and convents offered him economic gain while his reform of the bishops increased his political power; finally, like Henry VIII, he retained much of Catholic ritual. J.'s conversion to Protestantism was significant in upsetting the balance of religious forces in Reformation Germany. BIBLIOGRAPHY: F. Lau and E. Bizer, *History of the Reformation in Germany to 1555* (tr. B. A. Hardy, 1969); H. Holborn, *History of Modern Germany,* v. 1, *The Reformation* (1964); *New Cambridge Modern History* (ed. G. R. Elton, v. 2, *The Reformation,* 1958).

[C. T. EBY]

JOACHIM OF FIORE (Flora; 1132?–1202), Cistercian abbot and visionary. Born at Celico, Italy, son of a notary to the Norman Kings of Sicily, J. spent his youth at court. His experiences during a pilgrimage to the Holy Land occasioned his decision to retire from the world. About 1159 he took up the life of a lay preacher, but later chose to enter the Cistercian Order at Sambucina, Sicily. He was ordained in 1168 and elected abbot of Corazzo in 1177. Five years later he resigned this office to devote himself to biblical study and contemplation. In 1191 he obtained permission to found a community of hermits at Fiore (Flora) in Calabria for the more austere observance of the Cistercian Rule. The foundation was given autonomy as the Order of Fiore by Pope Celestine III in 1196.

A fervent monk and dedicated scholar, J. was held in high esteem by popes and nobles. Soon after his death the title of blessed was attached to his name by popular acclaim. The religious ideas of J. centered on biblical prophecy as applied to the future reform of the Church and his speculation displayed a clear tendency toward *illuminism. His three major works, *Liber concordiae novi et veteris testamenti, Expositio in Apocalipsim,* and *Psalterium decem chordarum,* are strongly marked by *apocalypticism (see JOACHIMISM). Toward the end of his life J. submitted his writings to the judgment of the Holy See, instructing his followers to accept whatever decision might be forthcoming. In 1215 Lateran Council IV condemned his teaching on the Trinity but did not censure J. personally as a heretic (D 803–807). Joachim's allegorical interpretation of history created a contagious excitement during the 13th century. Commentators and popularizers produced a host of pseudo-Joachimite treatises containing extreme and heretical interpretations of the abbot's thought (see GERARD OF BORGO SAN DONNINO). This literature was the source of the Joachimism that served as a rationale for such discontented groups in medieval society as the Franciscan *Spirituals. BIBLIOGRAPHY: H. Bett, "*Joachim of Fiore* (1931); M. W. Boomfield, "Joachim of Flora: A Critical Study," *Traditio* 13 (1957) 249–311; B. D. Dupuy, *Catholicisme* 6:878–887; E. Jordan, DTC 8:1426–58; M. F. Laughlin, NCE 7:990–991.

[C. J. LYNCH]

JOACHIMISM, a name given to an apocalyptic theology of history and a reform spirit derived from writings of *Joachim of Fiore, or from Joachimite apocrypha. During his lifetime Joachim's orthodoxy was hardly questioned, but after his death zealous enthusiasts gave his eschatological theories interpretations that inspired a whole spectrum of reformers, ranging from fervid idealists to crass opportunists. Joachim claimed to have acquired through mystical experience a supernatural insight into the true spiritual meaning of history and the inner relationship between the Old and New Testaments. His writings consisted principally of allegorical interpretations of the Scriptures interspersed with prophecies concerning the future of the Church. He was a lyrical rather than a systematic thinker, and the meaning of his highly figurative language is often far from clear. As conceived by Joachim the historical process is dominated by a double pattern of two's and three's corresponding to the OT and the NT and the persons of the Trinity. Time is divided into Three Ages, each lasting about 40 generations and influenced by pairs of historical personages. The First and Second Ages were merely preparatory to, and images of, the Third—the apotheosis of history —which will evolve by a double procession from the First and Second. The First Age, the epoch of the Father (Law), began with creation and terminated with the advent of Christ; the Second, the epoch of the Son (Grace), was to end in the year 1260, when the Final Age of the Holy Spirit (Love) would begin. With the passing of the Ages the human race would progressively grow to a fuller realization of the meaning of the historical process and would gradually become perfect. Each Age would be announced by a prophet and be brought to fulfillment by a fructifier. In the Third Age Spirit and Love will prevail; *viri spirituales,* members of a new religious order will win all mankind to true faith; liberty, peace, and equality will unite the world in mystic fellowship; structured disciplinary institutions will become obsolete; and a spiritualized Johannine Church will take the place of the carnal Petrine Church of the Second Age.

Both Dominicans and Franciscans saw in themselves the *viri spirituales* of Joachim, and in their foundation his Age of the Spirit. But Joachim's writings and the many spurious works attributed to him provided a rationale esp. for the numerous radical reform groups of the 13th century. One such group was composed of dissident Franciscans known as *Spirituals. This uncompromising minority refused to tolerate the slightest mitigation of poverty, insisting that all friars live after the manner of St. Francis and his earliest companions. When this extreme position was rejected by the Franciscan Order, the Spirituals appealed from man to God, invoked the higher law of heaven, and took refuge in apocalyptic fantasy. Their conviction of persecuted innocence, their feeling of impotent fidelity, and their weak theological background all combined to predispose the Spirituals to find prophetic justification for their cause in Joachimist writings.

In 1254 a sensational book entitled *Liber introductorius in evangelium aeternum* was published in Paris by *Gerard of Borgo San Donnino, an ardent young Spiritual. He applied the prophecies of Joachim in a garbled but provocative manner to the Franciscan Order. Joachim was identified as the prophet of the Third Age, St. Francis as its fructifier, and the Friars Minor as the *viri spirituales*. The Masters of the Univ. of Paris found 31 errors in the *Liber introductorius*. A year after its publication it was censured by Pope Alexander IV. William of Saint-Amour singled it out as a typical example of mendicant perfidy; John of Parma had to resign as Franciscan Minister General because of his penchant for Joachimite prophecy. The preaching of Gerard *Segarelli, *Fra Dolcino, and the *flagellants of Italy were inspired by Joachimism.

About the beginning of the 14th cent. the hardcore Spirituals in France and Italy became known as *Fraticelli. The writings of their spokesmen, such as *Angelus Clarenus, *Ubertino of Casale, and *Peter John Olivi, were heavily tinged with Joachimism. The effectiveness of such groups was virtually destroyed by the energetic measures taken against them by Boniface VIII and John XXII. Nevertheless, Joachimism did not lose its fascination for the medieval mind, and vestiges of it can be detected in many apocalyptic groups even up to the 16th century. BIBLIOGRAPHY: E. Algerton, *L'Évangile éternel* (1928); E. Antichkof, *Joachim de Flore et les milieux courtois* (1931); M. W. Bloomfield and M. E. Reeves, "Penetration of Joachimism into Northern Europe," *Speculum* 29 (1954) 772–793; B. D. Dupuy, *Catholicisme* 6:887–895; F. Russo, *Bibliografia Gioachimita* (1954); D. L. Douie, *Nature and Effect of the Heresy of the Fraticelli* (1932) 22–48; A. S. Turberville, *Medieval Heresy and the Inquisition* (1920, repr. 1964) 34–54.

[C. J. LYNCH]

JOAN, POPE, a woman supposed to have reigned as pope in 855, between Leo IV and Benedict III. The story goes that she was an English girl educated at Cologne who fell in love with a Benedictine and fled with him to Athens, disguised as a man. On his death she went to Rome, was ordained priest, created cardinal, and elected pope under the title of John VIII. During a papal procession between the Colosseum and San Clemente she gave birth to a child and died. The tale is found in the writings of popular authors in the second half of the 13th cent.—e.g., the Polish Dominican Martin of Troppau and the French Dominicans Étienne de Bourbon and Jean de Mailly—and was widely believed and relished in the Middle Ages, even at Rome, though John Hus made it a cause of complaint at the Council of Constance. An ancient statue of a pagan priest and serving boy near San Clemente and an inscription were thought to refer to Joan: according to a 1575 guidebook to Rome, Pius V had them destroyed. The invention was finally exploded in the 17th cent., largely through the work of David Blondel, a French Calvinist.

[T. EARLY]

JOAN OF ARC, ST. (1412–31), French heroine of the 100 Years War. Born in Domremy in Lorraine, J. is also known as La Pucelle and the Maid of Orléans. She was the daughter of a farmer and began to hear her "voices" about the age of 13 but kept them secret for nearly 5 years. They told her that her mission was to deliver France, much of which was then under the rule of the English crown in alliance with the Burgundians. In 1429 J. left home and made her way to the dauphin, later Charles VII, who after some hesitation consented to follow her counsel. Directed and inspired by her, his troops raised the siege of Orléans, and the victory of Paray threw open the road to Reims. There in the cathedral he was crowned, with Joan standing at his side. It had been a brilliant campaign, but Charles was to prove a listless and unreliable master. In the next campaigning season she was captured by Burgundians and sold to the English in 1430. The English determined to get her out of the way, rigged her trial for heresy, presided over by Pierre Cauchon, bp. of Beauvais. Her visions were condemned as "false and diabolical," and she was tricked into a recantation she later disavowed. She was excommunicated, turned over to the secular arm, and burned in the marketplace, May 30. Four years later the Duke of Burgundy abandoned the alliance with the English, their power crumbled, and by 1453 they held only Calais. Joan had done more than any other person to bring that about. She was solemnly rehabilitated in 1456 and was canonized in 1920. BIBLIOGRAPHY: V. Sackville-West, *Saint Joan of Arc* (1936); W. P. Barrett, *Trial of Joan of Arc* (translation of the documents, 1931); R. Pernoud, *Joan of Arc by Herself and Her Witnesses* (tr. E. Hyams, 1964); *idem*, BiblSanct 6:568–577.

[T. EARLY]

JOAN OF AZA, BL. (*c.*1140–*c.*1190), mother of St. Dominic, founder of the Dominicans, and of Bl. Mannes. Her dream before Dominic's birth that she would bear a dog with a torch in its mouth to set the world afire with faith is the reason for that symbol in Dominican iconography. Her cult was approved in 1828.

[T. C. O'BRIEN]

JOAN OF FRANCE (VALOIS), ST. (1464–1505), religious foundress. Daughter of Louis XI of France, J. was espoused before she was a month old to her 2-year-old cousin, Louis of Orleáns, who was later to become Louis XII of France. The marriage was celebrated when J. was 12. In 1498, upon the death of her brother, Charles VIII, her husband succeeded to the throne and within a few months sought an annulment of the marriage, which he declared under oath had not been consummated, despite J.'s claim to the contrary. The annulment was granted and J., no longer queen of France, became duchess of Berry (1498). She occupied herself with the duties of this office and with good works. With the encouragement and help of her confessor, Gilbert Nicolas (later known as Gabriel Marie), she undertook the foundation of a contemplative order, which came to be known as the *Annonciades of Bourges, dedicated to the imitation of the virtues of the Blessed Virgin. Approval of the rule she had drawn up was granted by the Pope in 1502. Her cause was introduced in 1632; she was beatified in 1742, but though she was widely venerated as St. Joan (Jeanne), formal canonization did not come until 1950. BIBLIOGRAPHY: Butler 1:252–253; A. M. C. Forster, *St. Joan of France* (1950); A. Combes, BiblSanct 6:560–565, bibliog.

[P. K. MEAGHER]

JOAN OF ORVIETO, BL. (1264–1306), Dominican tertiary, stigmatic, and mystic. Refusing marriage, she entered the Third Order of St. Dominic. Her special devotions were to the holy angels and the Passion of Christ. Devoted to the poor and venerated by the townspeople, she was distinguished by her forgiveness of persons who injured her. BIBLIOGRAPHY: Butler 3:171–172; A. Silli, BiblSanct 6:556–557.

[M. J. FINNEGAN]

JOAN OF PORTUGAL, BL. (1452–90), Dominican. First child of King Alphonsus V, she was heiress to the throne of Portugal. Despite regal environment in her youth she manifested an interest in the religious life and at the age of 16 asked her father to allow her to enter the convent. Alphonsus denied the request, directing her to choose a husband from such suitors as Maximilian of the Holy Roman Empire, Richard III of England, and Charles, brother of Louis XI of France. In 1471, while Alphonsus waged war against the Moors in N Africa, J. became regent of Portugal and ruled the nation with charity and wisdom. Upon the King's return she again sought to join the convent and received his consent. She entered the Dominican convent at Aveiro in 1472 but in the interest of keeping open the royal line of succession was forbidden to take vows. Despite continuous pressure from her family, she led the life of an ordinary Dominican nun. She died at the age of 38, after drinking water possibly poisoned by women of Aveiro who were angry over her admonitions regarding their conduct. She was beatified in 1693. BIBLIOGRAPHY: A. Silli, BiblSanct 6:557–558; Butler 2:291–292.

[R. J. BRADY]

JOAN OF SANTA LUCIA, BL. (d. *c.*1105), Camaldolese nun of the convent of Santa Lucia at Bagno in the Romagna. Her remains were transferred to the parish church in 1287. The cessation of a plague was ascribed to her intercession, and Bagno made her its patron saint in 1506. Her cult was confirmed in 1823. BIBLIOGRAPHY: Zimmermann 3:13–14; M. R. P. McGuire, NCE 7:994.

[M. R. P. MCGUIRE]

JOAN OF SIGNA, BL. (*c.*1245–1307), Italian hermitess at Signa near Florence, renowned for her sanctity and miracles. She was formally beatified in 1798. There is no certainty to the claims of several orders that she was a tertiary. BIBLIOGRAPHY: F. Baumann, BiblSanct 6:559.

[J. R. RIVELLO]

JOANA ANGÉLICA DE JESÚS, SISTER (1761–1822), Brazilian abbess from 1817 of the Conceptionist Franciscan cloister of Lapa in Salvador, Bahía, slain at the monastery door for refusing admittance to Portuguese soldiers to search for Brazilian patriots in the war of independence.

[T. C. O'BRIEN]

JOANNA MARIA OF THE CROSS, VEN., see GIOVANNA MARIA OF THE CROSS, VEN.

JOANNES ANDREAE (*c.*1270–1348), lay canonist. He spent most of his life at the Univ. of Bologna, where he studied both theology and canon law, and where, from *c.*1300 he became its most renowned teacher of canon law. His compilations, prepared for his students, were marked by such care for the chronology and authorship of legislation that he may be considered the first historian of canon law. His commentaries on the **Liber Sextus* and the **Clementinae* became standard texts. His masterworks were the *Novella* on the Decretals of *Gregory IX, the *Quaestiones Mercuriales,* and the *Novella* on the Liber Sextus.

[T. C. O'BRIEN]

JOANNES PARVUS (Jean Petit; *c.*1360–1411), theologian. A graduate of and later teacher at the Univ. of Paris, J. achieved some recognition in his own lifetime because of his views on the Great Schism, but he is most famous for his *Justification,* a defense of tyrannicide. The *Justification* was written specifically to justify the assassination of Louis, Duke of Orléans and brother of King Charles VI of France. The crime was committed at the instigation of John the Fearless, Duke of Burgundy, whose family had served as a patron of J.'s career. Although John the Fearless eventually obtained a royal pardon for the crime, attempts led by Jean Gerson, chancellor of the Univ. of Paris, were made to have J.'s ideas condemned as heretical. The struggle ended when a condemnation issued by the bp. of Paris (1414) was annulled at the Council of Constance (1416). BIBLIOGRAPHY: E. Perroy, *Hundred Years War* (tr. W. B. Wells, 1951).

[J. MULDOON]

JOANNES TELLENSIS, see BAR-CURSUS.

JOANNICIUS, ST. (754–846), a monk celebrated for miracles and prophecy. A native of Bithynia, he was first a swineherd, then a soldier. He was converted from a licentious life and the promotion of Iconoclasm by a monk. Leaving the army, he entered a monastery on Mt. Olympus and thereafter preached zealously on behalf of the veneration of icons. He was a close friend of SS. Theodore of Studius and Methodius of Constantinople. BIBLIOGRAPHY: J.-M. Sauget, BiblSanct 6:1065–66.

[P. FOSCOLOS]

JOASAPH AND BARLAAM, see BARLAAM AND JOASAPH.

JOB, BOOK OF. On the basis of language and ideas this book is generally assigned to a period some time between the 5th and 3d centuries B.C. Though parallels to it do exist in the literature of the Near East, it far exceeds any of them in profundity and originality of thought. Two sections, which probably should be regarded as late interpolations, are the praise of wisdom in ch. 28 and the speeches of Elihu (ch. 32–38). It falls clearly into three main parts, two narrative sections at the beginning and end (ch. 1–2 and 42.7–17) framing a long and complex intervening section of dialogue. In the opening section Job's steadfast piety is made the subject of a contest between God and Satan, and is put to the test by a series of afflictions that reduce him from a state of supreme prosperity amid a large and happy family to one of childlessness, destitution, and disease. This introduces the long section of dialogue in which we see Job living through this experience and striving to reconcile it with the truth, which he never ceases to cling to, of God's justice, love, and care. Three other figures take turns in proposing interpretations of his misfortunes, all of which ascribe them in some sense to his own sinfulness. Job's speeches in rejoinder represent a radical criticism of this orthodox attitude to suffering. He protests passionately against his lot, and against the injustice and hypocrisy of trying to induce him to confess to sins of which he knows he is innocent. In particular his protest takes the form of longing to "take God to court," to confront him in a situation in which he can argue his case and demonstrate the injustice of his fate (e.g., 13.3; 16.18–19; 19.23–27). The climax comes when God responds not by solving the problem of evil as Job himself experiences it, but by confronting him with a direct manifestation of his own holiness and power as seen in the created order (ch. 38–41). Faced with this, Job no longer expects, or feels that he has a right, to understand God's ways. Once this lesson is learned his prosperity is restored and his comforters are sternly rebuked for their hypocrisy. BIBLIOGRAPHY: C. Larcher, *Le Livre de Job,* (2d ed., 1957); H. L. Ellison, *From Tragedy to Triumph* (1958); G. Fohrer, *Hiob* (1963); E. D. Eerdmans, *Studies in Job* (1939); E. J. Kissane, *Book of Job* (2d ed., 1946); M. B. Crook, *Cruel God, Job's Search for the Meaning of Suffering* (1959); H. W. Robinson, *Cross in the Old Testament* (1954); T. H. Robinson, *Job and His Friends* (1954); W. B. Stevenson, *Poem of Job* (2d ed., 1948).

[D. J. BOURKE]

JOB, TESTAMENT OF, a work, written in Greek the 2d cent. A.D., essentially *midrash in character. Though ultimately based on the biblical story of Job it elaborates upon it in a more or less extravagant manner so as to bring out moral aspects which are of special interest to its author. The original work may well have been Essene in tendency in view of its particular interest in Satan and its highly developed angelology (ch. 48) together with the value it attaches to ascetical practices, patience, almsgiving, and virginity. The Jewish prototype has, however, been heavily worked over by later Christian hands.

Job, here identified with Jobab, king of Edom (see Gen 36.32–33), bequeathes a last message to the children of his second wife, Dinah, an Israelite, his former wife Sitidos, together with her ten children, having died in the course of Job's own afflictions. He relates how he incurred the wrath of Satan by destroying an idolatrous temple. Satan thereupon attempts to exact vengeance upon him (ch. 1–8) by reducing him to such extremities of want and distress that Job's wife is forced to barter her hair for three loaves of bread from Satan. At this point, however, Satan has to acknowledge himself defeated in his futile struggle to overthrow Job's heroic steadfastness in virtue (ch. 16–27). Job's three friends, kings like himself, incur sin and are liable to death by reason of their rash judgments upon him, but they are forgiven and pardoned. Only Elihu, wholly given over to Satan, has "no memorial among the living" (43.17). Each of Job's three daughters in turn receives the gift of prophecy as her portion of his inheritance, and is inspired to utter a canticle of praise (ch. 46–50). Finally Job's brother Nereus describes how he saw Job's soul carried off by a heavenly chariot which carried him eastwards to Paradise. For critical Greek text see *Testamentum Jobi* (*Pseudepigrapha Veteris Testamenti Graeci* 2, ed. S. P. Brock, 1967). BIBLIOGRAPHY: M. R. James, *Apocrypha Anecdota* (v. 2, repr. 1967); C. C. Torrey, *Apocryphal Literature* (repr. 1963).

[T. C. O'BRIEN]

JOC, see JOCISM.

JOCELIN OF BRAKELOND (d. *c.*1215), Benedictine of Bury St. Edmonds whose Latin chronicle (tr. H. C. Butler, 1949) of the abbey's life from 1173–1202 ranks as the most faithful of all pictures of medieval monastic observances and spirit. The chronicle was the inspiration for Thomas Carlyle's *Past and Present.*

[T. C. O'BRIEN]

JOCELIN OF GLASGOW (d. 1199), Scottish Cistercian; abbot of Melrose (1170); bp. of Glasgow (1175). Prominent in attempts to assert independence of Scottish bps. from the abp. of York, J. conducted negotiations between William the Lion and Lucius III, and is also famous for rebuilding and enlarging Glasgow Cathedral. BIBLIOGRAPHY: D. Nicholl, NCE 7:1001.

[R. W. HAYS]

JOCELIN OF WELLS (d. 1242), English ecclesiastic and royal administrator; bp. of Bath and Glastonbury (1206). His title was changed, by agreement with Glastonbury monks, to bp. of Bath and Wells (1217). Papal interdict caused his absence from England (1208–13). He reorganized the clergy of Wells Cathedral and contributed to its construction. BIBLIOGRAPHY: D. Nicholl, NCE 7:1001–02.

[R. W. HAYS]

JŌCHŌ (d. 1057), Japanese sculptor. Given high priestly rank in recognition of his work, J. carved the Amida Buddha of the Western Paradise in the Phoenix Hall of Byōdōin (1053). A model for later such images, it alone of his work survives.

[M. J. DALY]

JOCISM, from the acronym JOC, *Jeunesse Ouvrière Chrétienne,* a social action apostolate for youth that includes specialized groups like the *Jeunesse Agricole Chrétienne, Jeunesse Étudiante Chrétienne* and others. *YOUNG CHRISTIAN WORKERS.

[J. R. RIVELLO]

JŌDO, Japanese term for the Buddist Paradise, associated with the teaching of the Amitābha (Japanese, Amida) and rebirth in his Western Paradise. The Jōdo (Pure Land) sect had a strong following in China (3rd cent.) and Japan (10th century). The Raigō concept (joyous descent of the Amida and bodhisattvas) inspired magnificent sculpture and paintings. The entire temple of the Phoenix Hall (Hōōdo) in Byōdōin, Uji (1053) and a 12th-cent. painting at Mt. Kōya are impressive examples of Raigō art. *JŌCHŌ, HŌŌDŌ OF BYŌDŌIN.

[M. J. DALY]

JOEL, BOOK OF. This work dates from the period of the second temple, that is, well after 515 B.C. and possibly as late as the 4th century. It is apparent that the author is an anthologizer, borrowing words and phrases from many earlier prophets. The book as it now stands is divided into two parts. The first part (ch. 1–2) concerns a plague of locusts that threatens to ravage the land. They are depicted in the apocalyptic imagery of the "foe of the north," and their advent is interpreted as the "day of Yahweh," on which he comes with his army to punish wrongdoers. But the prayer of the priests at the temple succeeds in securing Yahweh's forgiveness, and prosperity and fertility are restored and intensified. The theme of the second part (ch. 3; in the Hebrew, 3–4), is the eschatological march of the Gentiles against Jerusalem. Their army corresponds to the locust army as eschatological macrocosm to historical microcosm. This is the day of Yahweh on a macrocosmic scale. Yahweh destroys them from the temple, and thereby ushers in the new age of paradisal prosperity and peace. BIBLIOGRAPHY: L. Dennefeld, *Les Problèmes du livre de Joël* (1926); A Kapelrud, *Joel Studies* (1948); J. M. Myers, "Some Considerations Bearing on the Date of Joel," ZATW 74 (1962) 177–195; R. Pautrel, "Joel, le livre de," DB Suppl 4 (1948) 1098–1104.

[D. J. BOURKE]

JOGUES, ISAAC, ST. (1607–46), Jesuit missionary, martyr. He became a Jesuit in 1624, and when ordained, was sent to the Quebec mission at his own request. He was seized with René *Goupil in 1642 by Iroquois and was tortured, mutilated, and humiliated during a year's captivity. Escaping with Dutch help, he returned to France in 1644, but was back in Canada that same year. He and John *Lalande set out for Iroquois country in 1646 and were captured by a band of Mohawks. On Oct. 18, Jogues was tomahawked and beheaded. For bibliog. see NORTH AMERICAN MARTYRS.

[P. K. MEAGHER]

JOHANAN (YOHANAN) BEN ZAKKAI (d. *c.*80 A.D.) Jewish teacher and leader, founder of the pharisaic/rabbinic academy at Javneh (*Jamnia). What is known of him comes from later rabbinic traditions. He was a disciple of *Hillel and seems to have continued and developed his teacher's approach to the interpretation of Scripture. Early in the Jewish revolt against Rome (66–70 A.D.) J. appears to have opposed the war, or at least the military policies, of the *Zealot party. His attitude toward Rome was probably a kind of realistic accommodation to a far superior military power; he thus fled Jerusalem before its destruction (70 A.D.) and was apparently allowed by the Romans to establish the academy at Javneh, from which came the mainstream Judaism that has survived and flourished until today. His political and theological stance might be described as a middle way between prophetic charisma and priestly routine, or as an alternative to the revolutionary excitement of messianic movements and to the loyal conservatism of the Jerusalem priesthood. He contributed heavily to the ability of Judaism to survive the war, without political autonomy and without temple and sacrifice. God, he firmly believed, had not rejected Israel; what was necessary was an implementation of the prophetic concern for a Judaism which found its center in atonement through "loving-kindness" (see *HESED: cf Hos 6.6) in daily life. BIBLIOGRAPHY: J. Neusner, *A Life of Yohanan ben Zakkai, Ca.1–80 C.E.* (2d ed., 1970).

[D. P. EFROYMSON]

JOHANNES CORNUBIENSIS (also John of Cornwall, John of St. Germans; d. 1199 or 1200), theologian. He studied under Thierry of Chartres and Peter Lombard and taught, probably at Oxford. His main works were a translation and commentary on the Welsh *Prophetia Merlini* and *Eulogium ad Alexandrum papam tertium*. Texts: *Prophetia Merlini*, (ed. C. Greith in *Spicilegium Vaticanum* (1838) 82–106; *Eulogium* in PL 199:1043–86. BIBLIOGRAPHY: J. N. Garvin, NCE 7:1003.

[J. L. GRASSI]

JOHANNINE COMMA (also known as the "Three Witnesses"), the gloss in 1 Jn 5:7–8 ("comma" in the sense of the Gr. *Komma*, clause). The words are not found in any early Greek MSS or any early translations (except a few witnesses of the Old Latin) or in the best MSS of the Vulgate. The 1897 decree of the Holy Office, clarified in 1927, was a practical directive before the non-authenticity of the gloss was settled. BIBLIOGRAPHY: T. Ayuso Marazuela, *Biblica* 28 (1947) 83–112, 216–235; *idem*, 29 (1948) 52–76; Robert-Feuillet, v. 2 (Eng. tr.) 683–685.

[E. J. CROWLEY]

JOHANNITIUS (Hunain ibn Ishak; d. *c.*873), Christian translator of Greek medical (Galen) and philosophical works into Syriac and Arabic. He spent most of his life as a physician at the court of the caliph in Baghdad. Through his and his pupils' translations, the Arabic world became acquainted with Greek thought that enlightened their own culture, while many important works, lost in the Dark Ages in the West, were preserved in Arabic and eventually enriched the Western Middle Ages. Translations of some of his medical works, e.g., *Introduction to Medicine* and, his *Sayings of the Ancient Sages* carried his fame and erudition to the West.

[J. F. FALLON]

JOHN, see also JUAN.

JOHN, APOSTLE, ST., son of Zebedee and James's brother, one of Jesus' first disciples. Both, with Peter, were chosen by him as witnesses to the raising of Jairus's daughter, to his Transfiguration, and to his agony. He was one of the pillars of the Church of Jerusalem (Gal 2.9). According to tradition he later went to Ephesus where he died at a very old age, having written the Book of Revelation, the fourth Gospel, and three of the catholic epistles. BIBLIOGRAPHY: EDB 1177–79; P. C. Landucci, BiblSanct 6:757–785; *JOHN, EPISTLES OF ST.; *JOHN, GOSPEL ACCORDING TO ST.

[A. VIARD]

JOHN I, ST. (d. 526), **POPE** from 523. J. was a Tuscan and an archdeacon at Rome. He succeeded *Hormisdas, under whom the *Acacian Schism was brought to an end. With the restoration of unity the Emperor Justinian I began taking harsh measures against the Arians, closing their churches in Constantinople. The Ostrogoth king of Italy, *Theodoric, forced J. to head an embassy to Constantinople on behalf of the Arian cause. J. was the first pope to set foot in Constantinople, and on his arrival, Oct. 525, he was received with great acclaim, the Emperor himself prostrating before him "as if he were Peter in person." He stayed in Constantinople 5 months and there received from the Eastern clergy honors befitting his primacy, but his mission, from the point of view of Theodoric, was a failure. On his return to the West, J. was thrown into prison in Ravenna, where he died from mistreatment. His body was brought back to Rome in 534, and he was revered as a martyr. During J.'s pontificate the system of dating years from Christ's birth was adopted, and the paschal cycle was drawn up by Dionysius Exiguus in accordance with the practice at Alexandria. BIBLIOGRAPHY: L. Clugnet, CE 8:421; C. Callovini, BiblSanct 6:926–927; Butler 2:406.

[P. F. MULHERN]

JOHN II (Mercurius; d. 535), **POPE** from 532. He took the name John because he thought his pagan name unsuitable for a Roman pontiff. He was the first pope to take a new name, a custom that did not become common until the 10th century. J.'s election followed a stormy vacancy of more than 2 months, marked by riots and attempted bribery. After his election, the Roman senate passed a severe decree against simony, and J. secured its confirmation by King Athalaric. *Justinian asked J.'s approval of the Theopaschite formula which the *Acoemetae monks in Constantinople were refusing to accept. *Hormisdas had been dubious about it, thinking it orthodox but superfluous. J. tried to persuade the Acoemetae to accept it, and when they would not, he excommunicated them and gave his own approval to the formula. In the deferential interchange of letters between the Emperor and pope, later incorporated in the Justinian Code, the Emperor acknowledged the Apostolic See as head of all the churches. J. exercised his authority in Gaul, ordering the imprisonment of the unruly bishop of Riez in a monastery. J. was buried in the portico of St. Peter. Extant letters: PL 66:17–32. BIBLIOGRAPHY: J. Chapin, NCE 7:1007–08; J. G. Jalland, *Church and the Papacy* (1944).

[P. F. MULHERN]

JOHN III (Catelinus; d. 574), **POPE** from 561. A Roman of distinguished family, J. was elected on the death of Pelagius I, but his consecration did not take place till 5 months later, probably because of a delay in obtaining imperial confirmation. The Lombard invasion, encouraged by the recall of *Narses by the Emperor, made his pontificate a time of great trial. Even the return of Narses, at the Pope's entreaty, could not restore order at Rome, and J. was obliged to take refuge in the catacomb of Praetextatus to avoid involvement in the strife. When he was able to emerge, toward the end of his reign, he ordered the catacombs repaired and arranged for Mass to be offered in them regularly. Little else is known of him because records of the time were lost. He was buried in St. Peter's. BIBLIOGRAPHY: J. Chapin, NCE 7:1008; Mann 1.1:351.

[P. F. MULHERN]

JOHN IV (d. 649), **POPE** from 640. J. was a Dalmatian, son of an official in the court of the exarch of Ravenna. Like other popes of the era, he was much involved in Monothelitism, presiding over a synod that reasserted the condemnation of the heresy. Later, he rejected the **Ecthesis* attributed to the Emperor Heraclius (610–641) because the work maintained a single will in Jesus Christ; the Emperor, perhaps influenced by this condemnation, disavowed the *Ecthesis*. J. defended the orthodoxy of Pope *Honorius I, insisting that his apparent denial of two wills in Christ was in reality only an insistence on the harmony between his divine and human wills. A chapel built by J. to house the relics of St Venantius contains a contemporary mosaic picturing the Pope. Letters: PL 80:601–608. BIBLIOGRAPHY: Mann 1.1:351–368; H. G. J. Beck, NCE 7:1008; Hughes, HC 2:292–296.

[P. F. MULHERN]

JOHN V (d. 686), **POPE** from 685. A native of Syria, J. as a deacon had been legate of Pope *Agatho (678–681) to the Third Council of Constantinople (the Sixth Ecumenical Council). He was the first pope to make use of the concession granted by Emperor Constantine IV to his predecessor, *Benedict II (683–685), permitting a pope to be consecrated without awaiting the imperial confirmation of his election. Of J.'s pontificate of 13 months little is known beyond the fact that he presided over a Roman synod in which he declared irregular the consecration of a bp. in Sardinia by the abp. of Cagliari because it invaded the pope's traditional patriarchal rights in that area. BIBLIOGRAPHY: Mann 1.2:64–67; H. G. J. Beck, NCE 7:1009.

[P. F. MULHERN]

JOHN VI (d. 705), **POPE** from 701. J. was of Greek descent. By the circumstances of his pontificate he was cast in the role of a peacemaker. When the Roman militia threatened Theophylact, Exarch of Ravenna, as he was passing through Rome, J. secured his freedom and safety. J. won a respite from war for the people of the Campania, by convincing—with the inevitable tribute—the invading Lombard Duke Gisulf, that he should withdraw his troops and free his prisoners. In a Roman synod (704) the Pope sought to compose a continuing disagreement between Wilfrid of York and a group of British bishops. The quarrel was referred for settlement to the abp. of Canterbury, with the understanding, however, that his decision could be appealed to Rome. BIBLIOGRAPHY: Mann 1.2:105–108; H. G. J. Beck, NCE 7:1009.

[P. F. MULHERN]

JOHN VII (d. 707), **POPE** from 705. J.'s father, Plato, of a prominent Byzantine family, won renown for his restoration of the imperial palace on the Palatine. As Pope, J. himself restored parts of several Roman churches, including St. Peter's. The fierce, half-mad Emperor Justinian II, during his second occupancy of the throne, tried to extort from J. a reevaluation of the decrees of the *Quinisext Synod, all of which had been condemned by Pope *Sergius I (687–701). J. is sometimes accused of showing human frailty in allowing himself to be intimidated by the emperor, but he sent the decrees back without comment or signature, and the significance of this did not escape the emperor. BIBLIOGRAPHY: Mann 1.2:109–123; Hughes HC 2:304; H. G. J. Beck, NCE 7:1009.

[P. F. MULHERN]

JOHN VIII (d. 882), **POPE** from 872. J. was an archdeacon of the Roman Church for 20 years before he was elected to succeed Adrian II. Throughout his reign he faced constant harassment from Saracen pirates who with the help of petty Italian princes preyed on the States of the Church. Looking to the Frankish Emperor for help, he became involved in Frankish politics, but his efforts brought no practical assistance. In the end J. had to be his own military organizer. He fortified Rome, defended the coasts, even at one point made an alliance with the Saracens, but was involved in fending off attackers until his death. In an attempt to mend the widening breach between East and West he recognized Photius as patriarch of Constantinople and there was much to commend the decision, since Photius seemed the only one capable of restoring peace to the Church of the East which was still divided in the aftermath of Iconoclasm. J. supported the missionary work of St. Methodius among the Slavs and after an investigation approved the use of the Slavic tongue in the liturgy, despite the opposition of the German bishops. J. was an able and strong pope in a period of great disorder. A story, based on less than satisfactory evidence, is told of his being clubbed to death by enemies within the papal curia after an attempt to poison him had failed. BIBLIOGRAPHY: Mann 3:231–252; F. Engreen, "Pope John VIII and the Arabs," *Speculum* 20 (1948) 318–330; F. Dvornik, *Photian Schism* (1948).

[P. F. MULHERN]

JOHN IX (d. 900), **POPE** from 898, a Roman, ordained by *Formosus, and at the time of his election abbot of a monastery in Tivoli. Despite strong opposition from Sergius, leader of the anti-Formosan party, who tried with the aid of *Theophylactus to seize the papacy, J. was consecrated. Despite its violent beginning, J.'s reign was a time of conciliation, influenced by the circumstance that in 898 he presided over the Roman synod that accepted as Emperor the same Lambert of Spoleto, who had been behind the "Cadaveric Synod" which had desecrated the memory of Formosus. In a series of synods, J. was able to reinstate Formosus and to reverse *Stephen VI's annulment of his acts. Those who had lost positions because they had been ordained by Formosus were restored, but members of the opposition party were treated with a moderation unusual in that time. J. also was able to establish peace between the contending Photians and Ignatians in Constantinople, and between Rome and Constantinople he brought amicable relations that lasted 8 years. In an attempt to assure order in future elections, the Constitution of Lothair of 824 was reenacted. It was further decreed that bishops and priests alone were to choose the pope on the request of senate and people and that the consecration was to take place in the presence of imperial legates. But, with J.'s death, all he planned came to nought and an era of chaos descended on the papal see. BIBLIOGRAPHY: L. Duchesne, *Beginnings of the Temporal Sovereignty of the Popes, A.D. 754–1073* (tr. A. Mathew, 1908); Mann 4:91–102.

[P. F. MULHERN]

JOHN X (d. 928), **POPE** from 914. From *c.*905 J. was abp. of Ravenna; he was chosen to succeed Pope Lando through the patronage of the family of *Theophylactus whose influence was then dominant in Rome. He was nevertheless a vigorous and able pope. In alliance with the Eastern Emperor, *Constantine VII, *Berengar I, and several Italian princes, he succeeded in breaking the grip of the Saracens upon S Italy. He strengthened the recently established (910) monastery of *Cluny with many privileges, especially that of *exemption. His legates made his influence felt at national synods in France, Germany, and Spain, and he promoted peace throughout the West by encouraging the loyalty of the lesser nobility to the kings. In 915 he bestowed the imperial crown on Berengar I, and after Berengar's murder (924) he entered into an alliance with Hugh of Italy. This gave offense to the infamous *Marozia, daughter of Theophylactus, who stirred up a rebellion that ended with J.'s deposition and imprisonment. Eventually he was murdered, apparently by order of Marozia. BIBLIOGRAPHY: Mann 4:149–187; S. McKenna, NCE 7:1011.

[P. F. MULHERN]

JOHN XI (d. 935 or early 936), **POPE** from 930, son of the infamous *Marozia. The story that he was the natural son of Pope *Sergius III has often been repeated as definite fact, but its sources are questionable. Through his mother's influence J.'s rise to ecclesiastical prominence was rapid. He was cardinal priest of S. Maria in Trastevere and still in his early 20's when he became pope. He was completely dominated by his mother, who sought to increase her power by entering into marriage (her third) with her brother-in-law, Hugh of Provence, King of Italy. J. compliantly witnessed the ceremony, but his brother, Alberic II, seeing the defeat of his own ambitions in his mother's new marriage, stirred up a rebellion, drove Hugh from Rome, and made prisoners of Marozia and the Pope. Thereafter J. was permitted to concern himself with ceremonial functions only. In matters of ecclesiastical government his decisions appear to have been dictated by Alberic—for example, his bestowal of the pallium on Artold, abp. of Reims, and his approval of the consecration of the teenaged Theophylactus, son of the Eastern Emperor Romanus I Lecapenus, as patriarch of Constantinople. During his reign important privileges were granted to the monastery of Cluny and its filial houses. BIBLIOGRAPHY: L. Duchesne, *Beginnings of the Temporal Sovereignty of the Popes,* A.D. *754–1073* (tr, A. Mathew, 1908); Mann 4:191–204; M. Mulholland, NCE 7:1011.

[P. F. MULHERN]

JOHN XII (Octavian; *c.*936–964), **POPE** from 955. J. was the only son of Alberic II, the Theophylact dictator of Rome from 932. J. at the age of 19 was elected pope in compliance with an oath exacted from the nobles by the dying Alberic. J. was the first pope after *Sergius III (904–911) to be at the head of civil as well as religious affairs in Rome; he was at once Pope and Prince of Rome. Authors have been generally content to repeat uncritically a history bad enough in truth but rendered even blacker by the chronicler Liutprand of Cremona, who strongly favored the German party. The Pope is pictured as a simoniacal profligate in whom no redeeming feature can be found. J. overreached himself in aspiring to recover from Berengarius, King of Italy, certain sequestered papal lands, and he appealed for help to Otto I, then King of Germany. Otto accepted the invitation, occupied Rome, and received the imperial crown from the Pope (962). An agreement between J. and Otto granted the Church extensive lands in Italy, but with the stipulation that the emperor would be suzerain of the States of the Church, and was to receive an oath of fealty from the pope before his consecration. This, the *Privilegium Ottonianum,* was accepted by J., but only grudgingly and because of his immediate need, and as soon as Otto left Rome, J. began to conspire against him. The Emperor returned and summoned a synod at which John was accused of grievous crimes, deposed, and replaced by Leo VIII. But when Otto again left Rome, J. returned and easily regained his position. He nullified the acts of Leo VIII and returned to his licentious ways, but only for a short time. Within a few months he died, stricken with paralysis under shameful circumstances. BIBLIOGRAPHY: Mann 4:341–372; W. Ullmann, "Origins of the Ottonianum," *Cambridge Historical Journal* 11 (1953) 114–128; *Antapodosis: Liber de rebus gestis Ottonis* (tr. F. A. Wright, 1930).

[P. F. MULHERN]

JOHN XIII (d. 972), **POPE** from 965, a Theophylact, son of Marozia's younger sister Theodora, brother of Crescentius I, and so cousin to John XII (955–964). Unlike his cousin, J. had a strict upbringing in a school for clerics at the Lateran. He was then employed in the papal chancery; he was bp. of Narni when he became pope by choice of Emperor Otto I (963–973). Two months after his consecration, a group of anti-imperial Roman nobles kidnapped J. and held him prisoner until he escaped and was returned to his see by Otto's army (966). The Emperor's residence in Rome for the rest of J.'s reign insured the peace necessary for some accomplishment. In a synod at Ravenna (967) laws on clerical reform, including insistence on the law of celibacy, were passed. The Diocese of Posen in Poland was set up (966) as a missionary center and despite some opposition from the German hierarchy J. succeeded in completing the establishment (968) of the Archdiocese of Magdeburg, begun in the time of John XII: this was to become the center for the conversion of the Slavs. J. crowned Otto II, a boy of 12, coemperor with his father (967) and, in his last year, he presided at the marriage of the young Otto to Theophano, the Byzantine princess, daughter of the Eastern Emperor Romanus II (959–963). The promise offered by the progress effected during J.'s reign was marred by the gradual rise to power as leaders of the Roman aristocracy, of J.'s own family, the Crescentii. BIBLIOGRAPHY: Mann 4:282–304.

[P. F. MULHERN]

JOHN XIV (Pietro Canepanova; d. 984), **POPE** from 983, a native of Pavia. J. became bp. of his home city and chancellor of the kingdom of Italy. On the death of Benedict VII (983) he became pope on the nomination of Emperor Otto II (974–983). A good churchman, J. was interested in reform and he might have accomplished much under the patronage of the earnest young Emperor. But, on the latter's early death (983), the Crescentii reestablished the antipope Boniface VII, reputed murderer of Pope Benedict VI (973–974). J. was imprisoned in the Castel Sant'Angelo where he starved to death or was poisoned. BIBLIOGRAPHY: Mann 4:330–338; Hughes HC 2:196.

[P. F. MULHERN]

JOHN XV (d. 996), **POPE** from 995. J. was a Roman and cardinal priest of St. Vitalis, when elected to the papacy after the death of the antipope whom Crescentius II had put on the papal throne to replace the imprisoned *John XIV. Although the details of his election are not known, it is generally conceded that J. was created and managed by Crescentius II. Yet he achieved some independence of action and restored a measure of papal authority. Through a legate he established peace between King Ethelred of England and Duke Richard of Normandy. Further, again through a legate, J. overruled the decision of Hugh, King of France, replacing Arnulf, rightful abp. of Reims, with Gerbert, the future Pope Sylvester II (999–1003). J. also introduced the solemn act which has come to be known as *canonization when, at the Roman Synod of 993, he proclaimed Bp. Ulric of Augsburg a saint. J.'s dictatorial manner and nepotism caused opposition among the Romans and, as a result, he was driven from Rome by Crescentius. J. had enjoyed peaceful relations with the regents of Otto III, and when J. appealed to the German king, Crescentius was forced to reinstate him. But he died shortly thereafter, while Otto was en route to Rome to be crowned. BIBLIOGRAPHY: Hughes HC 2:196; Mann 4:343–388.

[P. F. MULHERN]

JOHN XVII (John Sicco; d. 1003), **POPE** for about 6 months. A Roman, J. became a pope through the influence of Crescentius III, on the death of Sylvester II (999–1003). Before becoming a priest, J. was married, and he had three sons who also entered the clerical life. J.'s name has more significance than his pontificate. John XVI was a puppet whom Crescentius II, father of Crescentius III, had used in an attempt to displace the rightful pope, Gregory V (998). J.'s title as the 17th of that name is thought a device used by Crescentius III to justify his father's memory by making John XVI seem to have been a true pope. Nothing is known of J.'s reign. BIBLIOGRAPHY: Mann 5:126–141.

[P. F. MULHERN]

JOHN XVIII (Joannes Fasanus; d. 1009), **POPE** from 1003. A Roman, J. was chosen through the influence of Crescentius III, who controlled the city. Crescentius seems to have kept J. from cooperating with the attempts of Henry II of Germany to influence affairs in Italy, although J. did deal with the King in matters affecting the German Church. Merseburg was strengthened as a missionary base for central Europe, and Bamberg was made a diocese that became a center for missionary activity among the Slavs. J. also continued the papal policy of drawing monastic foundations close to the Holy See by exempting them from the authority of local bishops. He also bestowed the pallium on the abps. of Trier and Canterbury. At the end of his life he retired to the monastery of St. Paul-Outside-the-Walls. He lived there as a monk for his last months; there he died and was buried. BIBLIOGRAPHY: Mann 5:126–141.

[P. F. MULHERN]

JOHN XIX (Romanus; d. 1032 or 1033), **POPE** from 1024. During the pontificate of his brother, Benedict VIII, he assumed the title "Consul of the Romans." At Benedict's death, though still a layman, he took possession of the papacy and received all the orders on one day. Dominated by Emperor Conrad II, whom he crowned at Easter, 1027, John was an inconsistent and simoniacal administrator. The account of his recognition of the patriarch of Constantinople as "ecumenical," may be seriously doubted. His interest in the liturgy, the Cluniac reform, and in the *Truce of God are positive achievements to his credit. BIBLIOGRAPHY: L. Santifaller, "Chronologisches Verzeichnis der Urkunden Papist Johanns XIX," *Römische historische Mitteilungen* (1956–57) 1:35–76.

[O. J. BLUM]

JOHN XX, POPE. This is the curious case of the pope that did not exist. The one who for a time went under that number is now referred to as John XIX (1024–1032). The confusion arose from a list of popes that inserted a fictive interloper between Boniface VII and John XV (985), thus numbering the latter erroneously as XVI. By the time the error was caught, John XXI and esp. XXII had fixed their place in history. However, the numbering of the less illustrious popes of the 10th and 11th cent. could be and was corrected.

[P. MISNER]

JOHN XXI (Peter of Spain; *c.*1215–1277), **POPE** from 1276. Born in Lisbon, Portugal, J. was pope for less than a year. Trained at the Univ. of Paris in dialectics and medicine, he taught medicine at Siena before serving as dean and later, abp. of Braga. His book, *Summulae logicales,* was for centuries widely used.

[S. WILLIAMS]

JOHN XXII (Jacques Duèse; 1249–1334), **POPE** from 1316. Son of a shoemaker, J. was born at Cahors, France. He studied law at Paris and Orléans before being appointed chancellor of Charles II of Naples. He was elevated to the See of Fréjus in 1300, transferred to Avignon in 1310, and created cardinal in 1312. After his election to the papacy, he chose to reside at Avignon. Although frail and elderly, he was the most energetic of the Avignon popes. Over 60,000 official documents were issued during his pontificate. He enlarged the curia, advanced centralization of church administration, reorganized papal finances, made important contributions to the development of canon law, and zealously promoted missionary activity. His manner of life was austere and his tastes simple, but he was much given to nepotism.

Early in his pontificate John became involved in the struggle between the Spirituals and the *Communitas,* two factions within the Franciscan Order. He issued three bulls (1317–18) sharply condemning the former group, four of whom he had burned for heresy. He also played a major role in the poverty controversy. When the Franciscan general chapter unanimously declared to be sound Catholic doctrine the proposition that Christ and his Apostles owned nothing either individually or in common, the Pope countered with the Bulls *Ad conditorem* (Dec. 8, 1322), by which the Holy See renounced ownership of the goods used by the Franciscans, and *Cum inter ionnullos* (Nov. 12, 1323), which declared the doctrine of absolute poverty heretical. Michael of Cesena, the minister general, together with William of Occam and a few other prominent Franciscans, refused to submit and sought the protection of Emperor Louis of Bavaria.

Louis had denied the Pope's right to settle the disputed imperial election of 1314 and had eliminated his rival, Frederick of Austria (Habsburg), by an appeal to arms. To protect his position Louis aided the Pope's enemies in Italy, declared him a heretic because of his condemnation of absolute poverty, and appealed to a general council on the basis of the theories of Marsiglio of Padua and John of Jandun. In 1324 J. excommunicated Louis and declared his imperial rights forfeited. In 1328 Louis had himself crowned at Rome, declared John deposed, and set Peter Rainalducci of Corbara, a Franciscan Michaelist, on the papal throne. Soon after Louis' departure from Italy in 1330, this antipope (Nicholas V) made his submission to John at Avignon. But the empire and the papacy were not reconciled during John's lifetime.

In sermons delivered in 1331 and 1332 John advanced the theory that the blessed are denied enjoyment of the beatific vision until after the last judgment. Theologians, especially those of the Univ. of Paris, raised such a storm of protest that the Pope found it necessary before his death to retract the statements containing this theological opinion. BIBLIOGRAPHY: G. Mollat, *Popes at Avignon 1305–78* (tr. J. Love, 1963); J. P. Kirsch, CE 8:431–434; Pastor 1:58–84.

[C. J. LYNCH]

JOHN XXIII, ANTIPOPE (d. 1419), rival to Popes *Benedict XIII and Gregory XII from 1410 to 1415. After a military career, J. studied law at Bologna and entered the clergy. He had great administrative abilities and was papal legate in Romandiola and Bologna. The cardinals who accepted the validity of the Council of *Pisa elected him pope, and of the three claimants to the papacy John had the largest number of supporters. At the insistence of King Sigismund, he convoked a general council in Constance to end the *Western Schism but later fled Constance to deprive the council of its authority. He was imprisoned by Sigismund, subscribed to the election of Martin V, and died as bp. of Frascati. BIBLIOGRAPHY: G. Mollat, NCE 7:1020–21.

[T. M. MCFADDEN]

JOHN XXIII (Angelo Giuseppe Roncalli; 1881–1963), **POPE** from 1958. Son of peasant farmers from Bergamo in N Italy and ordained in 1904, he was formed in his early career as a priest by his appointment as secretary to the bp. of Bergamo, Radini-Tadeschi, a man with strong interests in the social mission of the Church. Although suspected of *Modernism, J. also taught in a seminary, wrote church history, did social work, and served during World War I in the medical corps and as a chaplain. Pope Benedict XV called him to Rome in 1921 to direct the Society for the Propagation of the Faith in Italy, and in 1925 J. was made an abp. and began a diplomatic career as apostolic visitor to Bulgaria. During 10 years there and 9 years as apostolic delegate to Turkey and Greece, he showed diplomatic ability in dealing with various hostile nationalities, governments, and religious factions as well as concern for ecumenism, for an indigenous clergy, and for the social needs of various groups. As nuncio in Paris at the end of World War II, J. sought to heal the divisions between the followers of De Gaulle and the discredited members of the Vichy regime. He displayed caution and a characteristic tolerance of the theological, biblical, and pastoral experiments that flourished in postwar France. Pius XII made J. in 1953, at the age of 71, cardinal, then patriarch of Venice, a position in which he initiated peace-making contacts with socialists and resumed direct pastoral work. His major accomplishments as 262d pope were Vatican Council II and two encyclicals, *Mater et magisra* on social questions and *Pacem in terris* on the basis for world peace. The Council sought, in his words, "to restore the simple and pure lines which the face of Jesus's Church wore at its birth." Although J. opened the Council to observers from non-Catholic churches, international organizations, and governments, its primary mission was to reform the teachings and practices of the Catholic Church itself. J.'s purposes encountered resistance from certain curial factions, and, although he did not attend the Council deliberations, his guidance and occasional intervention supported the majority favoring change. He died between the first and second sessions of the Council. His life was marked by a deep but simple spirituality, an open, friendly personality, and broad experience in which charitable and gracious diplomacy sought to conciliate seemingly insuperable differences. BIBLIOGRAPHY: M. Trevor, *Pope John* (1967); E. E. Y. Hales, *Pope John and His Revolution* (1965); P. Johnson, *Pope John XXIII* (1974).

[J. R. ZUREK]

JOHN PAUL I (Albino Luciani; 1912–78), **POPE** Aug. 26–Sept. 28, 1978. A native of Forno di Canale in N Italy, he was ordained to the priesthood in 1934. For 10 years he taught in the seminary of Belluno, became vicar general of that see in 1954. Named bp. of Vittorio Veneto in 1958, he was distinguished for his concern for the poor and illiterate. In 1969 he became patriarch of Venice, a larger scene for his solicitude for the poor. Elevated to the cardinalate in 1973, he adhered firmly to the decrees of Vatican Council II. Elected the first day of the conclave following the death of Paul VI, he chose the name John Paul I, marking the first time in history a pope had chosen a double name, and the first time since the 10th cent. that a new name had been selected. The extraordinary choice of the names of his two immediate predecessors indicates an intention to continue the work begun by John XXIII and Paul VI.

[J. R. AHERNE]

JOHN PAUL II, POPE, elected October 16, 1978. Born Karol Wojtiła, May 18, 1920, in Wadowice, near Krakow, Poland, he came from a working-class background and during the Nazi occupation of Poland himself worked in a quarry and in a chemical plant, and was involved in the anti-Nazi resistance movement. As priest and bishop he has always remained devoted to the betterment of workers. In 1939 he began his university studies at Krakow as a student of literature, particularly poetry and drama, but in 1942 decided to study for the priesthood. He was ordained in 1946, then was sent to the Angelicum in Rome where he earned a doctorate in philosophy. As a young priest he did pastoral work in Krakow, then began his career (1953) as a professor of Christian ethics at Krakow and at the Catholic University of Lublin. He published many articles in scholarly journals, especially on ethics. Pius XII on July 4, 1958 named him a titular bishop and auxiliary to the Administrator Apostolic of Krakow; on January 13, 1964 Bp. Wojtiła was named archbishop of that see, vacant because of government obstruction since 1951. Pope Paul VI created him cardinal, June 26, 1964. The Archbishop became the staunch ally of Cardinal Stefan Wyszinski in defense of the rights of the Polish Church. Cardinal Wojtiła participated in all the sessions of Vatican II and in all the assemblies of the Synod of Bishops, where his role was particularly important in the work of the 1974 Synod on evangelization. His election as pope to succeed John Paul I came on the second day of the papal conclave and was greeted by surprise, since he is the first non-Italian pope since Adrian VI (1522–23). The new Pope has shown himself to be a strong and magnetic personality, dedicated to the ideas and implementation of Vatican II. He has expressed particular interest to further the functioning of episcopal collegiality and to provide human rights, especially religious freedom. His election was warmly welcomed in the U.S., where he has visited often, most recently for the 1976 Eucharistic Congress in Philadelphia.

[T. C. O'BRIEN]

JOHN I TZIMISCES (925–976), **BYZANTINE EMPEROR** from 969–976. A member of the Macedonian dynasty of soldier emperors, J. campaigned successfully in the Balkans and the Near East where he warred against the Fatimids of Egypt. Syria and much of the Holy Land, but not Jerusalem, fell to him in 974–975. Toward the Church J. showed himself completely submissive to Patriarch Polyeuctes, who induced him to do penance and reform his life. J. also revoked his predecessor's law restricting monastic and ecclesiastical property-holding. He is credited with a statement about Church-State relations that reads much like the Western Gelasian principle.

[R. H. SCHMANDT]

JOHN II COMNENUS (1088–1143), **BYZANTINE EMPEROR** from 1118–1143. The second of the Comneni dynasty, J. strove to reassert Byzantine authority against Armenians, Danishmen, Turks, and the Latins at Antioch. As guaranteed by the crusaders' oaths and the Treaty of Devol, Antioch was to be a Byzantine possession under a Greek patriarch. The Latins refused to honor their obligations, and mutual hostility long impeded the Crusade effort. In 1137–38 J. forced Raymond of Antioch to acknowledge his supremacy, but he could not enforce it because of Latin opposition within the city. Again in 1142 J. prepared to assert his rights but he died before carrying out his plan.

[R. H. SCHMANDT]

JOHN III DUCAS VATATZES (fl. 13th cent.), **BYZANTINE EMPEROR.** In Nicaea during the Latin occupation of Constantinople (1204–1261), he married the daughter of the German emperor *Frederick II and carried on unionistic negotiations with Rome, chiefly with the purpose of recovering Constantinople. He is considered one of the greatest of the Byzantine emperors; his charitable measures made him so popular that soon after his death he was honored as St. John the Merciful.

JOHN V PALAEOLOGUS (1331–91), **BYZANTINE EMPEROR** from 1341. At the age of 10 John succeeded to the throne, but from 1346 to 1354 he was forced to share it with *John VI Cantacuzenus, whose daughter, Helen, he married. In 1352 John V broke with his father-in-law, and with Genoese aid assumed sole authority in 1354. He inherited an empire torn by civil warfare and critically endangered by the advancing Ottoman Turks. In the hope of obtaining military aid he journeyed to Hungary and in 1369 to Rome, where he accepted papal primacy as an individual. Still, he received no aid, and on his return was held in Venice until his debts were paid. The rest of his reign was marked by constant strife among his sons and by continual Turkish conquests, which led him to follow a policy of collaboration with the Turks, and in effect to reign as a puppet emperor. BIBLIOGRAPHY: O. Halecki, *Un Empereur de Byzance à Rome* (1930); Ostrogorsky 415–487.

[G. T. DENNIS]

JOHN VI CANTACUZENUS (*c.*1290–1383), **BYZANTINE EMPEROR** from 1347 to 1354. As leader of the powerful landed aristocracy John claimed the regency for the young John V Palaeologus in 1341, but was opposed by the Empress Anne of Savoy and the Patriarch John XIV Calecas. The association of Cantacuzenus with the Hesychast party assured both his success in the civil conflict and theirs in the ecclesiastical. In 1341 he had himself proclaimed emperor and, with Turkish aid, was crowned in 1346. He strove to consolidate Byzantine territory, esp. in the Morea. His enemies supported John V Palaeologus, and Cantacuzenus was forced to share the throne with him, but soon abdicated and became a monk, taking the name Joasaph. He is best known for a history of his era and theological works, chiefly in defense of Hesychasm.

[G. T. DENNIS]

JOHN VIII PALAEOLOGUS (1390–1448), **BYZANTINE EMPEROR** from 1425. A well-educated and competent ruler, J. concentrated on seeking aid against the Turks. To this end he entered into negotiations with Pope *Eugene IV, which culminated in the Council of *Florence (1438–39). He actively moderated the Greek delegation at the Council, earning the respect of all, and after signing the decree of union returned to his capital in 1440.

[G. T. DENNIS]

JOHN (1167–1216), **KING OF ENGLAND** from 1199. Henry II's youngest son, J. plotted against his brother, King Richard. As King, John murdered his nephew Arthur, Richard's recognized heir in Maine and Anjou, and lost Normandy and his continental Angevin possessions to King Philip II. J. refused to recognize Stephen Langton as abp. of Canterbury, but when faced with papal interdict against England (1208), his own excommunication (1209), and threatened French invasion, he submitted to Pope Innocent III (1213). Becoming a papal vassal for England, he aimed to destroy justification for foreign invasion or domestic rebellion. After Bouvines (1214) the English barons, roused by financial exactions and foreign defeat, forced his agreement to the Magna Charta (June, 1215), which asserted feudal prerogatives and the liberties of the English Church against royal authority. Innocent III annulled the charter at J.'s request, and J. died during the ensuing baronial revolt. BIBLIOGRAPHY: S. Painter, *Reign of King John* (1949); W. L. Warren, *King John* (1961).

[W. A. CHANEY]

JOHN III SOBIESKI (1624–96), **KING OF POLAND** from 1674. His election brought some hope of a revived Polish state. A wealthy landowner, J. had already established a reputation as a successful general. The first decade of his reign witnessed some significant achievements. Poland's foreign policy moved forward with a French alliance in 1675 and later a treaty with Sweden. Both alliances were aimed at stopping Prussian expansion. His moderate religious policies temporarily improved relations with the Cossacks. The high point of his career was his victory against the Turks at the relief of Vienna on September 12, 1683. He believed that his kingship obligated him to defend Christendom. While the international crusade he envisioned failed, his efforts and leadership proved decisive at Vienna. The years of his later rule were marked by foreign and domestic disasters. Some critics maintain that J.'s military adventures so weakened Poland that it could not recover. It cannot be denied, however, that he was instrumental in halting the final Turkish threat to Western Europe.

[C. T. EBY]

JOHN III SCHOLASTICUS (d. 577), **PATRIARCH OF CONSTANTINOPLE,** 565–577. He was born in Antioch, either *c.*505 or as late as 530. At Constantinople he was *apocrisiarius of the patriarch of Antioch when Justinian I appointed him patriarch, to succeed the exiled Eutychius. His office was marked by his share in Justin II's persecution of the Monophysites. J's primary accomplishments, however, were as a canonist: his *Synagoga L titulorum* is the first Byzantine canonical compilation; he also composed a *Collection of 87 Chapters,* from ecclesiastical matters in Justinian's *Novellae.*

JOHN IV THE FASTER, PATRIARCH OF CONSTANTINOPLE (d. 595). Famous for his asceticism, he was the first abp. of Constantinople to call himself "The Oecumenical (universal) Patriarch," a title his successors keep to the present day. The title caused friction with Rome, because it seemed to indicate that J.'s office had primacy over all Christendom, whereas Rome, Antioch, Alexandria, and many other sees were much more ancient and had greater claim to apostolic succession. Since Constantinople was also the capital of the Roman Empire, its prime importance, which he promoted at the imperial court, prevailed in the Eastern Churches despite Rome's displeasure. His only extant, authentic work is a sermon on penance and asceticism, which is much dependent on St. John Chrysostom.

JOHN VII GRAMMATICUS (fl. 9th cent.), **PATRIARCH OF CONSTANTINOPLE** (837–842) and prominent Iconoclast theologian. J. composed treatises against the veneration of images, and as patriarch violently persecuted those opposed to *Iconoclasm. With the restoration of orthodoxy in 843, he was excommunicated and died in prison sometime before 863.

[G. T. DENNIS]

JOHN VIII XIPHILINUS (*c.*1005–75), **PATRIARCH OF CONSTANTINOPLE** from 1063, canonist. In his earlier career he had been, from 1045, a member of the law school, then its head, at the Univ. of Constantinople, before becoming a monk with his friend M. *Psellus. J. was head of a monastery when elected patriarch. Some of his works on Byzantine canon law survive.

JOHN X COMATEROS (d. 1206), **PATRIARCH OF CONSTANTINOPLE,** 1198 until retirement in Feb. 1206, five months before his death. He was against reunion with Rome, fleeing when the Fourth Crusade occupied Constantinople in 1204, refusing to receive the pallium from Innocent III, rejecting papal primacy, and writing against the *Filioque. In his own jurisdiction he convened a synod (1199–1200) to deal with the odd Eucharistic teaching of Michael *Glycas. J. is known also as the author of a treatise on the Holy Spirit's indwelling in the soul.

JOHN XI BECCOS (*c.*1235–97) **PATRIARCH OF CONSTANTINOPLE** (1275–82), theologian, and proponent of union with Rome. A learned patriarchal official, J. was sent on several embassies by Emperor *Michael VIII. After an exhaustive study of the origins of the schism between East and West, he turned from opposition to strong support of union. As patriarch he worked and wrote tirelessly in favor of the union concluded at the Council of *Lyons (1274), and his writings formed the major part of the argumentation employed by subsequent Byzantine advocates of union. With the death of Michael VIII (1282) the union, such as it was, ended and J. was deposed, eventually excommunicated, and died in prison.

[G. T. DENNIS]

JOHN XIII GLYKYS (d. *c.*1319), **PATRIARCH OF CONSTANTINOPLE** from 1315. He was a prominent intellectual and literary figure and also held a number of responsible positions in the Byzantine government. He was named patriarch in the hope that he would end the factional strife within the Church, but he resigned in 1319 because of illness. He is the author of a grammatical work, and some essays and letters.

[G. T. DENNIS]

JOHN XIV CALECAS (1283–1347), **PATRIARCH OF CONSTANTINOPLE** from 1334. A married priest in Constantinople, he was selected by *John VI Cantacuzenus for the patriarchate. In 1341 he brought about the condemnation of *Barlaam of Calabria and prohibited any further discussion of the Hesychast controversy. He then broke with Cantacuzenus and had Gregory Palamas condemned and imprisoned. But in 1347 he found himself deposed by a synod. He compiled polemical works and is noted for his disciplinary, dogmatic, and canonical decisions.

[G. T. DENNIS]

JOHN OF ACTON (d. 1349), English canonist. He was a doctor of civil law from Oxford and of canon law from Cambridge. He left an important canonical work, the *Constitutiones legatinae* (*c.*1333–35), a gloss on the constitutions of the legates Otto and Ottobuono. The work contains many of J.'s critical views of church abuses. He also left a work of moral theology, *Septuplum* (1346). In his career he was rector of Willingham-by-Stow and served as an official of the court of York.

JOHN THE ALMSGIVER, ST. (d. 619 or 620), patriarch of Alexandria from 610. Born of a noble and wealthy family of Cyprus, J. married in early life. All his children died in infancy or early childhood, and upon the death of his wife he gave away his possessions and devoted himself completely to the service of God and to works of charity. In 610 he was acclaimed patriarch of Alexandria; in that office he distinguished himself by his effort to reform his church. He built monasteries and churches; and his charities on behalf of refugees from regions overrun by the Persians as well as of the poor of his own city account for the title by which he is known. After Egypt fell to the Persians, J. returned to Cyprus, where he died. BIBLIOGRAPHY: J.-M. Sauget, BiblSanct 750–756, esp. for bibliog.

[P. FOSCOLOS]

JOHN OF THE ANNUNCIATION, see JUAN DE LA ANUNCIACIÓN.

JOHN OF ANTIOCH (d. *c.*441), controversialist at the Council of Ephesus, bp. of Antioch from 429. He was a friend of Nestorius, but did not share Nestorius's rejection of the *theotokos title of Mary, writing in 430 to urge Nestorius to drop his teaching. Angered because at Ephesus

Cyril of Alexandria did not wait for the arrival of the Antiochenes before anathematizing Nestorius on June 22, J., arriving on June 26, convened a rival synod that condemned Cyril. The two were only reconciled in 433, but their reconciliation angered the bps. of J.'s jurisdiction and led to the Church of Edessa's becoming separated as the East Syrian Nestorian Church, to protest J.'s concessions. Some of his correspondence is extant.

JOHN OF APPLEBY (d. 1389), ecclesiastical lawyer, dean of St. Paul's, London (1365–89). His services as a lawyer were much in demand and he served on diplomatic missions for King Edward III. He was present at the condemnation of Wycliffe's doctrines (London, 1382).

[F. D. BLACKLEY]

JOHN ASSER, see ASSER, JOHN.

JOHN OF AUSTRIA, DON (1547–78), victor of the naval battle of Lepanto. The natural son of Emperor Charles V and half-brother of King Philip II of Spain, he was reared as a prince. After the death of Charles V, Philip gave Don John his title and a substantial household. Handsome and dashing J. desired a military career and began such at the age of twenty-one. He was in command when the Spanish subdued the Moriscos of Granada. In 1571 Philip made him commander of the naval forces of the Holy League against the Turks. His personality and commanding presence pulled the dissident admirals together, and at Lepanto in 1571 the Christian fleet won one of the great decisive battles of history, putting an end to the myth of Turkish invincibility in the Mediterranean. J. saw himself as a crusader against Islam but was held back by Philip. Named governor general of the Netherlands, he planned to invade England and marry the imprisoned Mary Queen of Scots. He attempted to bring a peace to the Netherlands and restore Catholicism there but was frustrated by the refusal of some provinces to accept the treaty. Again in war J. conquered the rebels. His work in the Netherlands was hampered by Philip's intrigues and lack of support. J. was, in his short lifetime, one of the most fascinating personalities of the age and an extraordinary military commander.

[J. R. AHERNE]

JOHN OF ÁVILA, ST. (1500?–69), Spanish mystical writer, preacher, spiritual counselor, reformer. After studying law at Salamanca and theology under D. de *Soto at Alcalá, J. prepared to leave from Seville in 1527 to do missionary work in the Americas, but was persuaded to join in the Andalusia preaching mission (1527–36). There his sermons drew great crowds and his condemnations of high officials brought charges by the Inquisition in 1533 of rigorism and distortion of the dangers of wealth. J. was, however, quickly exonerated. After 1537 he began organizing colleges in Spain, among them the beginning of the Univ. of Baeza; the Jesuits took his foundations as a model for their own schools. His friendship and support promoted the Society's rapid spread in Spain. J. was also spiritual director to St. Teresa of Ávila. He spent the last years of his life, from 1552, in constant pain patiently borne. His major spiritual work, *Audi filia* (*c.*1530), is a guide to Christian perfection; a modern Spanish ed. of his writings, L. Sala Balust, ed., was published in two volumes in 1952. J. was canonized by Paul VI in 1971. BIBLIOGRAPHY: X. de Silió, BiblSanct 2:649–656; Butler 2:268–269.

[R. J. LITZ]

JOHN BACONTHORP (*c.*1290–*c.*1348), English Carmelite philosopher and theologian, *Doctor resolutus*, who lectured at Paris (1323–30) and at Cambridge *c.*1330. He was for a long time known as the prince of Averroists, but in fact he strongly rejected Averroism. His philosophical theories on cognition were opposed to those of St. Thomas Aquinas. In theology he defended the doctrine of the Immaculate Conception.

JOHN THE BAPTIST, ST., preacher of a conversion baptism for the forgiveness of sins in view of the imminent and final coming of the Lord (Mk 1.2–4). In Luke he is identified as the miraculously predicted and begotten son of the elderly Zechariah and Elizabeth, a cousin of Jesus through Mary (Lk 1.36), a Nazarite and prophet (1.13–25). He leaped for joy in his mother's womb at Mary's salutation (1.41–44), was divinely named (1.13, 59–64), and, when old enough, lived in uninhabited regions until his commission as God's herald began (1.80). Wearing the garb of an ascetic prophet like Elijah (Mk 1.6; 2 Kgs 1.8), he preached that reception of baptism must lead to works worthy of conversion to prepare for the final judgment (Mt 3.7–10; Lk 3.7–9); that beneficence and almsgiving must be practised, greed and extortion shunned (3.10–14); that he was not the Christ, but baptized with water, and one much greater would follow who would baptize with the Holy Spirit and fire and would accomplish the final judgment (3.15–17; Mt 3.11, 12). The fourth Gospel insists that he was not the Messiah but his herald and witness (Jn 1.6, 7, 15, 19–21, 26, 27, 29–34; 3.24–30). Soon after Jesus accepted John's baptism to fulfill "every kind of uprightness" (Mt 3.15), the Baptist was imprisoned for accusing Herod Antipas of incest and other evil deeds (Lk 3.19). When he heard of Jesus' healing ministry, he sent his disciples to ask Jesus if he really was the final "coming one." Jesus answered that one should not be dismayed by his merciful works. He then called John the greatest prophet, the final messenger of the Lord (Mal 3.1), greater than any man, yet less than the least in God's kingdom (Mt 11.2–11). This startling contrast showed how different their functions were: John preached conversion in view of imminent wrath; Jesus preached conversion in view of present mercy. Jesus then indicated how John was his precursor in a deeper sense: God's reign was being violently attacked in the person of John and by his death he would foreshadow Jesus' (Mt 11.12–15; cf.

17.10–13). When Herod and others heard of Jesus' fame they thought that John, raised from the dead, was performing these wonders—so John's presumed resurrection was another type of Jesus' (Mk 6.14–16; Mt. 14.2). Jesus used John's rejection by religious leaders as the reason why he would not defend his own authority (Mt 21.23–28). The resurrected Jesus' final word about John contrasted his own baptism in the Holy Spirit and John's water baptism (Acts 1.5; cf 18.24, 25): John's was an external act of penance; Jesus' was the immersion in the promised gift, divine power from the Father. Two decades after the Resurrection people still honored the Baptist (Acts 18.24–28; 19.27) and his downgrading in the fourth Gospel indicates that even later his followers gave him honor, equal or superior to that due Jesus, and needed to be corrected (Jn 10.40, 41).

The *Qumran discoveries have increased our knowledge about John's ambience: he must have had a clear awareness of the *Essenes, whose monastery he could easily see from where he was baptizing. That John was an Essene or was directly influenced by them cannot be established with certainty, since we know so little of John's own way of life and teaching. Yet a purgative return to the desert, asceticism, ritual washings, and end-time imminence are all themes common to John, the Qumranites, and the Old Testament. Perhaps other Qumran themes, such as light and darkness, opposition to Pharisees and Sadducees, etc., came into NT literature through the Baptist's disciples of whom at least three became Jesus' disciples (Jn 1.35–42).

Josephus reported that John's imprisonment and death happened at Herod's fortress, Machaerus, on the cliffs east of the Dead Sea (Antiq. 18, v. 2). Christian veneration of John as a saint is ancient (there is evidence that his relics were venerated at Sebaste, Samaria, in the 4th century). His original feast celebrated his witnessing at Jesus' baptism (Epiphany octave, 4th cent.), but was later fixed on June 25 (East) or 24 (West), i.e., six months before Christmas, to celebrate the theological belief of many Fathers that he was born without original sin, having been cleansed from it in the womb (Lk 1.41, 44). Another feast commemorated his death (5th cent., Aug 29). Early veneration is further indicated by his place in the Canon of the Mass, the Confiteor, and the Litany of the Saints. It is now generally accepted that the Gnostic Mandaeans inherited their cultus of John from Christianity rather than from 1st-cent. non-Christian Baptist circles. Early Christian iconography generally portrayed John as the ascetic herald of Christ, the Lamb of God (Jn 1.29, 36), and as his baptizer.

[J. F. FALLON]

JOHN THE BAPTIST OF THE CONCEPTION, ST. (1561–1613), Trinitarian reformer, mystic. J. was born at Almodóvar del Campo in Spain and was educated first by the Jesuits, then by the Discalced Carmelites at Baeza and Toledo. During his youth he was greatly impressed by the teachings of St. Teresa of Ávila. J. received the Trinitarian habit in Toledo and learned the strict Trinitarian rule under Father Alonso de Rieros. He was ordained in 1585. In 1594 the Trinitarians, meeting in general chapter, pledged a renewal of the strict rule, but many apparently disregarded the reform effort. J., now superior at Valdepeñas, began his own reform movement in 1597, stressing the apostolic nature of the priesthood and the necessity of union with Christ through meditation. In 1599, he received approval from Rome for his Discalced (Barefooted) Trinitarians and in the following years he opened houses in Salamanca, Pamplona, Baeza, Córdoba, and thirty other locations. He died in Córdoba, and was beatified by Pius VII in 1819. BIBLIOGRAPHY: J. del Carmen, BiblSanct 6:940–943; Butler 1:339–340.

[R. J. BRADY]

JOHN BASSANDUS, BL. (1360–1445), Celestine. Born in Besançon, at eighteen he joined the Canons Regular of St. Augustine at the Abbey of St. Paul. In 1390, he transferred to the Celestines in Paris and was given the task of opening a monastery in Amiens, where he befriended St. Colette. From 1411 to 1441, he was named provincial of France five times. Charles VII sent J. on an unsuccessful mission to antipope Felix V, urging that papal usurper to renounce. In 1443, Pope Eugene IV asked him to reform the monastery of Collemaggio, near Naples. He died shortly after succeeding in this task. BIBLIOGRAPHY: P. Gini, BiblSanct 2:961–963.

[R. J. BRADY]

JOHN OF BASTONE, BL. (d. 1290), friend of St. *Silvester Guzzolini and from 1231 monk at the first Sylvestrine Benedictine monastery at Montefano. J.'s cult was officially approved in 1772 by Clement XIV.

JOHN OF BELETH (d. 1182), master, probably English, at Paris, whose *Rationale divinorum officiorum* provides rare documentation on 12th-cent. liturgy. He was one of those referred to in medieval theological literature as the *Porretani*, followers of *Gilbert de la Porrée.

JOHN BENINCASA, BL. (1376–1426), Servite hermit. In his early youth he entered the Servite Order and in 1401 was permitted to begin a life of solitude near Siena. People were attracted to his isolated retreat by the reports of his austere life of prayer. They received spiritual counsel and at times bodily cures. John considered this attention a temptation to pride and retired to a more remote cave near Monticelli. The news of his death was supposed to have been announced by the spontaneous ringing of the local church bells. His cult was approved Dec. 19, 1829.

[J. M. O'DONNELL]

JOHN BERCHMANS, ST. (1599–1621), Belgian-born Jesuit scholastic. After his mother's death, J.'s father became a priest. A Jesuit from 1616, J. was sent, following his father's death, to Rome for his studies in 1618. In his short years as a scholastic at the Collegio Romano, he achieved sanctity by his fidelity in the everyday duties of religious and student life, and received the gift of unitive prayer. He was canonized in 1888.

JOHN OF BEVERLEY, ST. (d. 721), bp. of York. A student of Hilda of Whitby and Theodore of Canterbury, J. became bp. of Hexham (687). He ordained Bede. Translated to York (705), he founded the monastery of Beverley and died there in retirement. Greatly venerated in N England, he was canonized 1037. BIBLIOGRAPHY: Bede, *Ecclesiastical History;* N. Del Re, BiblSanct 6:627–628.

[W. A. CHANEY]

JOHN OF BICLARO (*c.*540–after 621), historian and bp. of Gerona. A Catholic Visigothic noble from Lusitania, he studied in Constantinople for 16 years and on his return to Spain *c.*576 was exiled to Barcelona by Arian King Leovigild (569–586). He continued the chronicle of Victor of Tunnuna, giving a valuable account of critical years of Spanish history (567–590). Isidore's chronicle superseded John's. A rule that John wrote for a monastery (of Biclaro?) which he founded before he became bp. is not extant.

[E. P. COLBERT]

JOHN BLUND (d. 1248), English scholastic at Oxford and Paris, master there in 1220, again at Oxford in 1229, canon of Chichester, 1233, chancellor of York, 1234. His *Tractatus de anima* is significant in the process that combined traditional Augustinian teaching with the newly discovered philosophical works of Aristotle through Arab sources. The work also influenced later 13th-cent. masters, Albert the Great among them, and touched on points of later controversy, including the unicity and plurality of forms and the spirituality of the soul.

JOHN BONUS OF MILAN, ST. (d. 660), bishop. John Camillus the Good was bp. of Milan from 649 until his death. The cognomen Bonus was attached to him in his own lifetime because of his many endearing virtues; but his cult grew only after the discovery of his relics in the 11th cent., which are at present enshrined in the cathedral at Milan. BIBLIOGRAPHY: AS Jan. 1:622–623; AnalBoll (1896) 15:356–358; A. Tamborini, *I santi milanesi* (1927) 46–51.

[W. A. JURGENS]

JOHN BOSCO, ST., see BOSCO, JOHN, ST.

JOHN OF BRIDLINGTON (JOHN TWENGE), ST. (*c.*1320–79), Augustinian Canon. He studied at Oxford 1335–38 before entering the Austin Canons of St. Mary's, Bridlington, near Thwing. He led a quiet, prayerful life. He reluctantly accepted the office of prior of his monastery and served in that capacity for 17 years. His shrine became a center of pilgrimage after the translation of his relics in 1404. He was canonized in 1401, the last native of England to be so honored until 1935 (*Osmund, d. 1099 and canonized in 1457, was born in Normandy). BIBLIOGRAPHY: AS Oct. 5:135–144; J. S. Purvis, *St. John of Bridlington* (1924); Butler 4:171–172.

JOHN DE BRITTO, ST. (1647–93), martyr. He was born of a noble family in Lisbon and educated with the future King Pedro II. After recovering from tuberculosis J. entered the Society of Jesus in 1662. While studying, he directly petitioned the superior general, Oliva, for an assignment to the missions in India. Soon after ordination in 1673, J. was sent to Goa and then to India proper, where he became superior of the Madura mission. By observing the secular customs and by following the example of Robert de Nobili and Baldassare de Costa in leading an ascetic life, he had access to all castes in India. In 1686 he was arrested by officials in Marava. After being tortured he was given his freedom and returned to Portugal in 1687. In 1690 he went back to Madura. In 1693 he converted a nobleman named Teriadevem and instructed him to relinquish four of his five brides. The father of one of the four women was a powerful rajah who ordered J.'s arrest and execution. He was beheaded in Oriur on February 3, 1693. Pius XII canonized him in 1947. BIBLIOGRAPHY: A. Bessières, *Le Nouveau François-Xavier* (1946); F. Baumann, BiblSanct 6:989–993.

[R. J. BRADY]

JOHN BURIDAN (fl. 1357–68), secular master at the Univ. of Paris for over 50 years, who was influential in the spread of nominalism in philosophy, and whose theory of impetus in the explanation of motion was important to the development of modern physical science. BIBLIOGRAPHY: Gilson HCP 511–516.

JOHN CANONICUS (Juan Marbres; fl. early 14th cent.), Catalan Scotist, canon of the Tortosa cathedral, and master in arts of Toulouse, whose *Questiones super physicorum Aristotelis* (written *c.*1321–23) so expertly defended the fundamental principles of John Duns Scotus that legend falsely considered Marbres an English Franciscan disciple of Duns Scotus. His *Questiones* was in great demand during the late medieval period and went through multiple printings.

[R. J. LITZ]

JOHN CANTIUS (JOHN WACENGA), ST. (1390–1473), theologian. John's early promise persuaded his parents to send him to Cracow where he earned degrees in liberal arts and theology, and where he taught, after an interval of 8 years, at the school of the Templars at Miechów. Conscientious as a professor, he was also devout, mortified, a servant of the poor. Fearing the responsibilities of a pastor (he served at Olkusz for a time), he returned to teaching. Buried at St. Anne's in Cracow, he was canonized and declared a patron of Poland and Lithuania in 1767. BIBLIOGRAPHY: Butler 4:154–155; C. Skowron, BiblSanct 6:644–645.

[M. E. DUFFY]

JOHN CAPISTRAN, ST. (1386–1456), Franciscan preacher, reformer. After studying law at Perugia, he entered the Franciscans (1415) where he became a leader of the Observants in their struggle with the Conventuals. He was also a famous preacher, eventually being sent to E Europe (1451) to preach against the Hussites and then (1454) being requested to preach a new Crusade against the Muslims. BIBLIOGRAPHY: J. Hofer, *St. John Capistran, Reformer* (tr. P. Cummins, 1943); P. O. Bonmann *Catholicisme* 6:420–421; A. Chiappini, BiblSanct 6:645–654.

[J. MULDOON]

JOHN OF CARAMOLA, BL. (d. 1339), Cistercian lay brother, mystic. Born in Toulouse, he spent most of his life in S Italy, first as a hermit on Mt. Caramola (Lucania), later as a brother in the Cistercian monastery of S. Maria de Sagittario near Chiaramonte. He lived on bread and water and had the gifts of prophecy and miracles. BIBLIOGRAPHY: F. Ughelli, *Italia sacra* (2d ed.), 7:91–93; Zimmermann 2:625–627; M.-A. Dimier, BiblSanct 6:654–655.

[L. J. LEKAI]

JOHN CASSIAN, see CASSIAN, JOHN.

JOHN OF CHÂTILLON, ST. (sometimes called J. of Craticula, or in French, Jean de la Grille, because of the grating around his tomb; *c.*1098–1163), Canon Regular of St. Augustine (not a Cistercian, as has been claimed), abbot, bishop. He was sent to the diocese of Tréguier with a group of canons to found the monastery of Sainte-Croix de Guingamp, of which he became abbot. Elected bp. of Aleth, he later transferred his episcopal see to the more populous Saint-Malo. There he installed Canons Regular in his cathedral, a move that involved him in years of litigation, eventually successful, with the Benedictines of Marmoutiers. BIBLIOGRAPHY: Butler 1:229–230; G. Ollivier, *Catholicisme* 6:462.

[P. K. MEAGHER]

JOHN CHRYSOSTOM, ST. (betw. 344 and 354–407), patriarch of Constantinople, Father of the Church, most prolific early Eastern Christian author, classic Christian orator of all time. Typical of the Golden Age (*c.*350–*c.*400) of the Fathers, J. was born a Christian in Antioch to parents of high social standing, was deeply influenced by his mother (who was widowed at the age of 20), received the education of a gentleman of leisure, fled the world to become a monk in the mountains near Antioch, was elected to the episcopate, and was much more a guardian of Nicaea than a theologian of originality. J. was ordained deacon in 381 and priest in 386 in Antioch. During the decade that followed, he won his reputation as a preacher with some of his best homilies. He was transferred to Constantinople and consecrated bp. of that see, over his protestations, in 398. His fearless denunciations of all that seemed morally out of order in church or civil life, along with the political intrigues of many a high-ranking official, and the pique of an offended empress, brought upon him persecution, attempted assassination, and repeated banishment from his see. He died en route to his last exile. Of all ancient Christian writers only Augustine matches J. for sheer quantity of extant material. By far the most significant of his writings are his exegetical homilies. Typically Antiochian in its literal approach to the interpretation of Scripture, as opposed to Alexandrian allegorism, J.'s exegesis remains captivating and persuasive even in our own day. BIBLIOGRAPHY: Quasten 3:424–481; C. Baur, *John Chrysostom and His Time* (tr. M. Gonzaga, 2 v., 1960–61); D. Stiernon, BiblSanct 6:669–699.

[R. R. BARR]

JOHN CHRYSOSTOM, LITURGY OF ST., the Eucharistic rite used most frequently in the Churches of the Byzantine tradition. Its origin lies in Antioch from where it was taken to Constantinople and there found its final development. St. John Chrysostom who was bp. of Constantinople (387–407) did much in shaping this liturgy and some of the prayers are from his hand. It differs from the Liturgy of St. *Basil principally in its *anaphora. One easily recognizes in the Liturgy of St. John Chrysostom the general pattern of Christian worship: a service of the Word of God, or Liturgy of the Catechumens, and the Eucharistic celebration. Ceremonies of the imperial court were adopted that give this Liturgy its present beauty and splendor, the form of which became fixed in the 11th–12th century.

This Liturgy assumes the presence of a bishop. When he is absent it keeps the same order but is less solemn. After the **proskomide* the congregation and the clergy wait for the entrance of the bishop. Originally this was accompanied by the singing of some prayers and antiphons which now form the first part of the Liturgy. Preceded by the book of the Gospels the bp. makes his entrance into the sanctuary (see LITTLE ENTRANCE). The congregation expresses its adoration in the singing of the **trisagion*. The reading of the Epistle and Gospel is concluded by the *ektenia*. While the congregation then prepares itself for the Holy Sacrifice, singing the **cherubikon,* the altar is prepared and incensed. Solemnly the gifts are brought through the church to the altar (see GREAT ENTRANCE). After another *ektenia* for the sanctification of the gifts, the congregation professes its faith reciting the Nicene Creed. Then the deacon invites the faithful to "stand aright, to be attentive to offer the holy oblation in peace." The anaphora is, as it were, "covered" by the devout singing of the people; only the central words of the consecration are sung aloud by the bishop. The **epiclesis* then follows and the congregation joins again in prayer singing the Our Father. The deacon declares: "the holy things are for the holy," and the bp., clergy and people receive holy communion "approaching with faith and the fear of God." On finishing the communion the remaining gifts are brought to the side table where they are consumed by the deacon. A prayer of thanksgiving and the blessing by the bp. conclude the Liturgy. BIBLIOGRAPHY: S. M. Sophocles, *Liturgy of the Orthodox Church* (1960); A. A. King, *Rites of Eastern Christendom* (1950) 1:151–234.

[J. MEIJER]

JOHN CLIMACUS ST. (579–649), abbot of the Greek monastery at Mt. Sinai. He was the author of a celebrated spiritual manual, *The Stairway to Paradise,* which describes in 30 stages the ascetical and mystical discipline that leads to the control of self and to Christian perfection through the practice of monastic virtue and withdrawal from everything profane and mundane. This work, widely used by Greek ascetical writers and in Latin translation during the Middle Ages, became the first book to be printed in America (1532, in Spanish tr. in Mexico). The name Climacus derives from *klimas*, a Greek word for ladder or staircase. BIBLIOGRAPHY: AS March 3:834–837; G. Zannoni, BiblSanct 6:664–666.

[J. F. FALLON]

JOHN COLUMBINI, BL. (1304–67), founder of the Jesuati. The chance reading of the life of the penitent, St. Mary of Egypt, changed his life-style. He gave himself to prayer, penitential exercises, and the practice of charity toward the poor and needy. With his wife's agreement and after providing for her, he distributed his possessions to be free to care for the sick poor. When others joined him, a society of lay-brothers known as the Jesuati was organized to do penance and the corporal works of mercy. Urban V approved this community in 1367. J. was buried in Siena and was beatified by Gregory XIII. BIBLIOGRAPHY: Butler 3:228–230; J. Baur, LTK 5:1022.

[J. M. O'DONNELL]

JOHN OF CORNWALL (Joannes de Sancto Germano; fl. 1170). The facts of his life are uncertain, but it is generally agreed that he was born in Cornwall. A student of Peter Lombard and of Robert of Melun at Paris, J. also studied in Italy. He wrote *Eulogium ad Alexandrum Papam III* opposing the teaching that Christ had only a divine nature. Several other works are ascribed to him, but none with certainty.

[A. WARDLE]

JOHN COTTON (11th–12th cent.), musical theorist. He is known for his treatise on harmonics, of which six copies are extant.

[P. J. HENNESSEY]

JOHN OF THE CROSS ST. (1542–91), Discalced Carmelite founder, Doctor of the Church, because of his spiritual theology. A Carmelite from 1563, he received his theological education at the Univ. of Salamanca during the golden era of Thomistic studies there. The influence of Aquinas's *Summa* is most apparent in J.'s making the theological virtues central to his own spiritual teaching. Soon after ordination (1567) he began his collaboration with St. Teresa of Ávila in a reform effort—he concentrating on the friars—based on primitive Carmelite observance and giving priority to the contemplative life. He took the name Juan de la Cruz when he vowed observance of the Primitive Carmelite Rule in Nov. 1568. His reform efforts brought persecution from the Carmelite "establishment"—including a 9-month monastic imprisonment at Toledo—and ostracism even by some of the Discalced who disagreed with his views. He nevertheless, during a relatively short life, contributed to the nurturing of the reform by his spiritual direction and service as superior. But J.'s greatest contribution both to the Discalced Carmelites and the Church is through his writings. He is renowned for his mystical poetry, some of which was written during his imprisonment, and the three great treatises that are accorded eminence in the corpus of RC ascetico-mystical theology and literature. The three are: *Ascent of Mt. Carmel—the Dark Night of the Soul; Spiritual Canticle; Living Flame of Love*. They are recognized for their solid theological grounding, but also for as clearly the expression of the author's own intense inner experience, spirit of prayer, and high mysticism. Much of J.'s terminology, analysis, and descriptions of the phenomena of the interior life in the process of Christian perfection and its culmination in mystical union have become standard in spiritual theology. The *Ascent of Mt. Carmel* is an account of the way, followed in the darkness of faith, in which the person is purged through the ascetical purification of sense and spirit and through the passive subjection to God's refining action. The *Spiritual Canticle* describes the enlightenment given by the beginnings of mystical union with the affective knowledge it brings. The *Living Flame* is a poem with commentary on the transforming union at the apex of mystical experience. J. was canonized in 1726; in declaring him a Doctor of the Church in 1926 Pius XI gave specific endorsement to the three great treatises as a guide in the pursuit of Christian perfection, BIBLIOGRAPHY: *Works* tr. K. Kavanaugh and O. Rodriguez (1964); *Complete Works* tr. and ed. E. A. Peers (repr. 3v. in 1,1963); Bruno de Jésus Marie, *St. John of the Cross* (1957). *CARMELITE SPIRITUALITY; *DISCALCED CARMELITES.

[T. C. O'BRIEN]

JOHN DAMASCENE, ST. (*c.*650–*c.*750), last *Father of the Church. Born in Damascus of Arab-Christian parents, J. worked for a time with his father, the caliph's minister of finances, but as the government became more and more inimical to Christianity J. entered a monastery near Jerusalem. There his talents as scholar, hymnologist, and preacher were commandeered by the bp. who had him ordained a priest. Like most of the later Fathers, J. was not an original theologian, and he stated explicitly that he did not wish to be. He was an eclectic and compiler, but with an extraordinary gift for synthesis. He gathered the texts and teachings of the Fathers before him into a self-consistent theological system constituting the final patristic synthesis of the doctrines of God, creation, and salvation. Only in the area of image-worship did he make significant original contributions; hence his condemnation by the iconoclasts in 754 and his rehabilitation by the seventh ecumenical council (Nicaea II, 787). J.'s most important work is *The Exposition of the Orthodox Faith,* a synthesis of his compilations from the Fathers on the central dogmas of Christianity; it is usually regarded as the third part of his *Fount of Knowledge.* BIBLIOGRAPHY: B. Kotter, NCE 7:1047–49; J.-M. Sauget and C. Colafranceschi, BiblSanct 6:732–740.

[R. R. BARR]

JOHN THE DEACON OF NAPLES (*c.*900), hagiographer, who wrote lives of several saints and a chronicle of the bps. of Naples from 762–872.

[G. T. DENNIS]

JOHN THE DEACON OF ROME (fl. *c.*1250), canon of the Lateran Basilica, who wrote a somewhat tendentious work, incorporating much legendary material, to prove the precedence of the Lateran canons over those of the Vatican.

[G. T. DENNIS]

JOHN THE DEACON OF VENICE (d. after 1008), chronicler. His account of Venice, *Chronicon Venetum* (MGS 7:4–38), traces the history of the city from its origins until 1008, the year before the death of Peter II Orseola, doge of Venice (991–1009), his friend and patron. J. also served the doge as envoy to the court of Emperor Otto III. BIBLIOGRAPHY: PL 139:871–940; P. L. Hug, NCE 7:1050.

[M. A. WINKLEMANN]

JOHN DISCALCEATUS, BL. (1280–1349). After serving as parish priest in the Diocese of Rennes he entered the Franciscan Order. He is called *Discalceatus* because of his custom of going barefooted. He died of the plague contracted while serving the sick. BIBLIOGRAPHY: W. Lampen, CollFran (1956) 29:421–424. G. Odoardi, BiblSanct 6:748–749.

[H. DRESSLER]

JOHN DOMINICI, BL. (*c.*1356–1419), Dominican writer, reformer, cardinal. J. entered the Dominican Order where he became a theologian and preacher after studies at the Univ. of Paris. Later he served as prior of several monasteries, among them Santa Maria Novella; he also founded new houses and a convent for Dominican nuns in Venice. Reformer of his order, he extended his influence in the Church, urging Gregory XII (who had made him abp. of Ragusa and cardinal of San Sisto) to resign and facilitate the end of the Great Schism.

Pope Martin V sent him to Bohemia where he arrived after the execution of John Hus and where he urged repressive measures which were not accepted. Continuing on to Hungary, he died there of a fever. Among his works are *Lucula noctis* and *Regola del governo di cura familiare* (on education); *Il libro d'amore di carità* (on asceticism). His life was written by one disciple, St. Antoninus; his portrait was made in San Marco by another, Fra Angelico. BIBLIOGRAPHY: Butler 2:521–522; *Book of Saints* (comp. Benedictine Monks of St. Augustine's Abbey, 1966); A. Duval, *Catholicisme* 3:993–994.

[M. E. DUFFY]

JOHN OF DUKLA, BL. (*c.*1414–84). Joining the Franciscans as a Conventual he transferred to the Observants and was known for his love of contemplation. In spite of blindness in his last years J. was a zealous preacher and confessor. He was proclaimed Patron of Poland and Lithuania by Clement XII in 1739. His cause for canonization was introduced June 25, 1948. BIBLIOGRAPHY: K. Kantak, AFH (1929) 22:434–437; K. Grudzinski, BiblSanct 6:749.

[H. DRESSLER]

JOHN OF DUMBLETON (fl. 1338–49), philosopher at Merton College, Oxford, Okhamist (see WILLIAM OF OCKHAM), and mathematical theoretician; known through the MSS of his *Summa logicae et philosophiae naturalis.*

[T. C. O'BRIEN]

JOHN DUNS SCOTUS, see DUNS SCOTUS, JOHN.

JOHN OF EGYPT, ST. (*c.*300–394), monk and hermit. He lived in a cave on Mt. Lykos for about 40 years and was highly regarded for his spiritual advice, and as a prophet. BIBLIOGRAPHY: A. J. Festugière, *Historia monachorum in Aegypto* (1961); Butler 1:691–692.

[G. T. DENNIS]

JOHN OF EPHESUS (*c.*507–586), Monophysite monk and bp. of Ephesus (*c.*542), the most important Syriac historian of the Church. His Syriac *Ecclesiastical History,* covering down to 585, survives only in its third and final part (571–585). He also wrote a hagiography, important for the history of monasticism. As Monophysite bp. of Ephesus, through the favor of the Emperor Justin I, he converted many thousands from paganism and built churches and monasteries. Under Justin II, however, he was imprisoned for his teaching, and on release lived a nomadic life for his remaining years.

[T. C. O'BRIEN]

JOHN OF FALKENBERG (*c.*1365–1435), Dominican polemicist. Professor of theology in the Vienna studium of the Dominicans in 1385, he was an inquisitor at Magdeburg in 1411. His chief claim to fame is that as a result of his defense of the Teutonic Knights against the king of Poland (*De monarchia mundi,* 1410), he went so far as to maintain at the Council of Constance that it was quite licit to assassinate the Polish king and to exterminate the Polish people because of their attitude toward the Knights. (*Tres tractati,*

1417). Although the Lithuanians and the Poles at the Council urged his condemnation for preaching the doctrine of tyrannicide, J. escaped with a short period of confinement in Rome. BIBLIOGRAPHY: *Council of Constance,* (tr. L. R. Loomis, 1961).

[L. E. BOYLE]

JOHN OF FÉCAMP (*c.*990–1078), Benedictine abbot, spiritual writer. He reformed the Abbey of the Trinity at Fécamp, in France on the English Channel. His mystical and ascetical writings, many long attributed to others, rank him close to St. Bernard of Clairvaux. He derived much of his teaching from St. Augustine and St. Gregory the Great. BIBLIOGRAPHY: F. Dressler, NCE 7:1051, bibliog.

[T. C. O'BRIEN]

JOHN OF FECKENHAM (*c.*1512–*c.*1584), Marian abbot of Westminster. He was professed at the Benedictine abbey of Evesham and graduated from Oxford (1539). After his monastery was dissolved by Henry VIII (1540), he became successively chaplain to Bp. Bell of Worcester and Bp. Bonner of London. As an orator and controversialist, he accepted royal supremacy, but rejected Protestantism. Cranmer ordered him imprisoned (1551–53), but he was released by Queen Mary and made dean of St. Paul's, London (1554). With hopes of reestablishing the Benedictine Order in England, Westminster abbey was restored in 1556 with J. elected as abbot. Under Elizabeth the community was dispersed, and in 1560 J. was again sent to prison where he remained for the rest of his life. BIBLIOGRAPHY: Knowles ROE 3:421–443; B. Heurtebize, DTC 5:2124–25; Gillow BDEC 2:233–238.

[V. SAMPSON]

JOHN OF FREIBURG (d. 1314), Dominican moral theologian who lectured at Freiburg im Breisgau, Germany. His *Summa confessorum* (1280–98; Ger. tr. 1300) became the prototype of many similar pastoral guides for confessors.

[T. C. O'BRIEN]

JOHN OF GAETA, see GELASIUS II, POPE.

JOHN OF GARLAND (*c.*1195–1272), grammarian, poet, humanist. At Oxford J. became interested in language, literature, science, music, and medicine. He taught Latin literature at the Univ. of Paris, and for a short period at the newly founded Univ. of Toulouse. His works though inferior in style are valuable for the study of medieval Latin. They include *De mysteriis ecclesiae* (*c.*1245); *Stella Maris* (1249), important in the study of medieval hymnology; *Morale scolarium* (1241), a student guidebook, and nearly 40 other works. BIBLIOGRAPHY: *J. de Garlandia, Morale scolarium,* (ed. L. J. Paetow, 1927); *Stella Maris of John of Garland* (ed. E. F. Wilson, 1946); G. E. Conway, NCE 7:1051–52.

[G. E. CONWAY]

JOHN GIL OF ZAMORA (*c.*1250–after 1318), Franciscan encyclopedist, secretary to Alfonso X the Wise of Castile and tutor to Sancho IV. Despite the loss of the original MSS of his works and of a copy made in 1797, his writings can be rather well restored. The *Liber de Jesu* (vita), and *Liber de Maria* (vita, miracles, and poems) are long excerpts from his *Book of Famous People* (mostly popular saints). His other writings include sermons, lives of kings of Spain, and works on natural history, rhetoric, grammar, and music. BIBLIOGRAPHY: M. de Castro, *Catholicisme* 6:645–647; Hurter 2:414.

[E. P. COLBERT]

JOHN GILBERT (d.1397), Dominican theologian. Chancellor of Oxford (1378), confessor to the Black Prince, Treasurer of England (1386–91), he was employed by Richard II on embassies abroad (1373–81). He became bp. of Bangor in 1372, of Hereford (1375), and of St. David's (1389). BIBLIOGRAPHY: Emden Ox 2:765–766.

[L. E. BOYLE]

JOHN OF GOD, ST. (1495–1550), founder of Hospitallers of John of God. John Ciudad was born in Portugal to parents of modest means. In 1522, he became a soldier of the Count of Oroprusa (Castile) in the war between the Spanish and the French. He was captured (1523) by the French and barely escaped a sentence of hanging. In 1532 he fought under Charles V in the defense of Vienna, which was under Muslim siege. In 1535, having repented of his immoral life, J. undertook an ill-prepared venture among the Christian slaves in North Africa. Returning to Spain, he was so impressed with the words of John of Ávila, whom he heard in Elvira (1538), that he ran through the streets crying for repentance—with a fervor that resulted in his confinement to a lunatic asylum until 1539. In that year, he opened his first house to care for the sick and the poor. In the next few years, he took in the sick from every part of Granada and in 1646 was joined by his first disciple. Ramírez Fuenleal, of the Royal Chancellery gave him the name John of God. In 1548, he opened a hospital in Toledo and received aid from Philip II. When J. died in 1550, his work among the destitute had already become legend throughout Spain. Codification of the rules of the Order of Hospitallers of John of God was completed in 1584, although the congregation was divided into two entities until 1867. J. was canonized in 1690 by Alexander VIII and declared patron of the sick in 1886 by Leo XIII. BIBLIOGRAPHY: G. Russotto, BiblSanct 6:740–745; Butler 1:517–520.

[R. J. BRADY]

JOHN OF GORZE, BL. (d. 976). Carrying out a long-cherished desire for monastic life, John entered the abbey of Gorze in 933. He became abbot and played a significant role in the reform movement that began at Gorze. BIBLIOGRAPHY: S. Hilpisch, LTK 5:1038; R. Van Doren, BiblSanct 6:813–814.

[H. DRESSLER]

JOHN OF GOTO (John Magnus; 1488–1544), Swedish archbishop. J. wrote *Metropolis ecclesiae upsalensis* (1557), a work of considerable historical value.

[M. J. SUELZER]

JOHN THE GRAMMARIAN (fl. early 6th cent.), theologian of Caesarea, Palestine, who clearly expressed the Council of Chalcedon's Christology: that the *hypostatic union consists in the union of Christ's two natures in the one hypostasis. His *Apologia* for Chalcedon, dating from 514–518, is known only through quotations given by its attacker, Severus of Antioch in *Contra impium Grammaticum*. J. was the first theologian to state that the humanity of Christ cannot be conceived of as existing without a hypostasis, since the first moment of its existence was in its union with the Word.

[T. C. O'BRIEN]

JOHN DE GRANDISSON (1292–1369), bp. of Exeter. He studied civil law at Oxford where he returned when he was created bp. (1326–27). J. was devoted to his obligations while bp. and opposed the numerous papal provisions in England. He composed a *Legenda de sanctis* and a life of Thomas *Becket. BIBLIOGRAPHY: V. Murdoch, NCE 7:1053; Emden Ox 2:800–801.

[J. A. WEISHEIPL]

JOHN DE GREY (Gray; d. 1214). Under King John, in whose service he had been for some years, J. became archdeacon of Cleveland and then bp. of Norwich in 1200. Apart from judicial duties in England, he also functioned as justiciar in Ireland (1209–13). An able administrator, he reformed Irish coinage, brought Irish law and administration into line with that of England, and raised money and troops for John. Elected unsuccessfully to Canterbury in 1205, his steadfast adherence to John during the Interdict earned him a lengthy excommunication from Innocent III. On his way back from a reconciliation with Innocent, who appointed him bp. of Durham, he died in France. BIBLIOGRAPHY: S. Painter, *Reign of King John* (1949), L. Warren, *King John* (1961), *passim*.

[L. E. BOYLE]

JOHN GUALBERT, ST. (*c.*995–1073), abbot, founder of Vallombrosans. Born in Florence, member of the Visdomini family, J. was a knight, until the murderer of one of his kinsmen came on Good Friday to beg his forgiveness. He forgave the man, and was soon professed as a Benedictine monk. In order to live a more austere and eremitic life he founded (1058) a monastery at Vollombrosa, a mountainous, wooded site 16 miles from Florence. The rule was Benedictine but with eremitical adaptations. His reforming spirit put him in conflict with corrupt ecclesiastics. He was canonized in 1193 by Pope Celestine III. BIBLIOGRAPHY: AS July 3:297–433; E. Lucchesi, *S. Giovanni Gualberto: Dai boschi d'Italia alle foreste del Brasile* (1959).

[W. A. JURGENS]

JOHN OF HAUTEVILLE (fl. late 12th cent.), poet of Norman origin, best known for his Latin satirical epic *Architrenius*, composed near the end of the 12th century. The poem, of 4,296 unrhymed hexameters, is divided into nine books; it is an allegory about a disillusioned young man in search of Lady Nature. After various symbolic adventures he reaches his goal and a remedy for his trouble, marriage to a beautiful maiden known as Moderation. BIBLIOGRAPHY: T. Wright, *The Anglo-Saxon Satirical Poets and Epigrammatists of the Twelfth Century* (RollsS 59; 1872) 1:240–392.

[V. BULLOUGH]

JOHN OF HOVEDEN (d. after 1275), English mystical poet. J., who seems to have had Oxford training, by 1268 was a clerk of Queen Eleanor of Provence, mother of King Edward I. His poetry, which reflected Franciscan spirituality, was of uncommonly high order, esp. *Philomena*, a poem of 4,000 lines on the birth, Passion, and Resurrection of Christ. J. had great influence on 14th-cent. mystics, particularly on Richard Rolle of Hampole. Works: *Poems of John of Hoveden*, ed. F. J. E. Raby (1939). BIBLIOGRAPHY: Emden Ox 2:974–975; M. J. Hamilton, NCE 7:1055.

[J. A. WEISHEIPL]

JOHN THE IBERIAN, ST. (d.*c.*1002). After many years in the service of the Iberian (Georgian) rulers, John became a monk in Asia Minor and then on Mt. Athos together with his son Euthymius. There they established a monastery for Iberian monks known as Iviron (Gr., of the Iberians), which still exists. John was succeeded as abbot by his son (d. 1028), who translated patristic, hagiographical, and liturgical works into Georgian.

[G. T. DENNIS]

JOHN ITALUS (b.*c.*1025), Byzantine philosopher and humanist. He wrote a number of commentaries on works of Aristotle, Plato, and the Neoplatonists. In 1077 certain doctrines attributed to J. were condemned by a synod, and in 1082 he himself was solemnly condemned and banished to a monastery. Although he very probably was not guilty of any erroneous doctrine, his use of Platonic philosophy and his attempt to employ reason in explaining dogma brought the wrath of the Church upon him. BIBLIOGRAPHY: P. Stephanou, *Jean Italos, philosophe et humaniste* (1949); LTK 5:1043.

[G. T. DENNIS]

JOHN JENŠTEJNA (1348–1400), archibishop. J. became bp. of Meissen (1375) and 3 years later succeeded his uncle as abp. of Prague. He was for a time chancellor of King Wenceslaus. Serious illness and the influence of certain devout canons deepened his interest in the spiritual life and led him to initiate reforms in the spirit of the Devotio moderna. Estranged from Wenceslaus, he resigned his see in favor of his nephew and devoted himself to writing hymns and ascetical treatises. BIBLIOGRAPHY: F. Seibt, LTK 5:1043–44.

[M. J. SUELZER]

JOHN OF JERUSALEM (*c.*356–417), nephew and successor to St. *Cyril as bp. J., is chiefly remembered for his part in the first *Origenist controversy in which he joined with *Rufinus in defending *Origen against *Epiphanius of Constantia and St. *Jerome. J. denied the charge of Origenism in an apology addressed to *Theophilus of Alexandria, of which only the fragments cited by Jerome have survived. Some inconclusive evidence exists suggesting that J. wrote or completed the *Mystagogical Catecheses* ascribed to St. Cyril. Toward the end of his life J. befriended *Pelagius, receiving him hospitably at Jerusalem, acquitting him of the charge of heresy at a diocesan synod at Jerusalem (415), and using his influence to secure an equally favorable verdict at the Metropolitan Synod of Diospolis the following year. In this matter he opposed the efforts of *Orosius, whom St. Augustine had sent to Palestine to obtain the support of St. Jerome in the struggle against Pelagianism. BIBLIOGRAPHY: A. A. Stephenson, NCE 7:1056; G. Garitte. LTK 5:1043.

[R. B. ENO]

JOHN OF JESUS MARY (1564–1615), Discalced Carmelite, general of his order (1611–14), and writer on the religious life. He became a Carmelite in 1583, held positions as professor and master of novices in Spain and in Italy, where he helped establish the Italian Congregation of the Discalced. His writings on Carmelite religious formation were published in 3 volumes in 1622.

[T. C. O'BRIEN]

JOHN JOSEPH OF THE CROSS, ST. (1654–1734), Franciscan religious reformer and ascetic. Carlo Gaetano Calosioto, a Neapolitan, became in 1670 a Franciscan of the reform of St. Peter Alcántara. J. wished to remain a deacon, but his community insisted on his ordination to the priesthood in 1677. Though he preferred solitude and the penitential practices begun in early youth, he was for years novice master and three times superior of the house in Piemonte. His reputation as a wonder-worker was widespread. When the continued existence of the Franciscan reform in Italy was threatened by differences with the Spanish, J. led the way to separation and became first provincial superior of the independent group. It was he who saw the small province through years of privation. A number of miracles are ascribed to him. He was canonized in 1839.

[J. R. AHERNE]

JOHN OF KASTL (fl. *c.*1400), Benedictine representative of late medieval mysticism. Little is known of his life. J. probably received the baccalaureate from Prague University in 1388. The work *De adhaerendo Deo,* formerly ascribed to either Albert the Great or Bonaventure, was shown by Grabmann and Huyben to be J.'s. He was well versed in the Church Fathers, St. Thomas Aquinas, and German mystical writings. These sources provided him with material for prayers, contemplative expositions on religious life, the Bible, Christ's life and passion; he also wrote lives of famous Benedictines. BIBLIOGRAPHY: M. Grabmann, *Mittelalterliches Geistesleben* (1926) 487–524; J. Huyben, VieS (1922) Suppl. 32–37 (1923); 1 Suppl. 80–101.

[J. R. SCHULZ]

JOHN KLENKOK (d. 1374), German theologian and polemicist. Trained in both civil and canon law, J. became an Augustinian at Herford. He received a doctoral degree in divinity at Oxford in 1359 and in the next decade was made provincial of his order in Saxony. His opposition to some articles of the civil law of E Germany (the Sachsenspiegel) caused his confrontation with both civil and ecclesiastical authorities, who gave judgment against him. In 1370 he was teaching at Prague. The next year he submitted a revision of his treatise *Decadicon* to Gregory XI, who agreed that 14 of the 21 Sachsenspiegel articles, which J. had denounced, were indeed condemnable. As papal penitentiary J. opposed Milíč, Bohemian nationalist and enemy of the mendicant orders. BIBLIOGRAPHY: F. Roth, NCE 7:1057.

[M. J. FINNEGAN]

JOHN OF KRONSTADT, ST. (John Sergiev; 1829–1908), a married priest, the dean of St. Andrew's Cathedral at Kronstadt, chief naval base of the Russian Empire. He was renowned as an eloquent preacher and an influential spiritual director, catechizer, and healer. Pastorally he reduced the iconostasis and encouraged public communal confession and frequent reception of holy communion. Author of a spiritual autobiography, *My Life in Christ* (tr., 1897), he was canonized by the Russian Orthodox Church Outside of Russia on Nov. 1, 1964.

[T. BIRD]

JOHN KYNYNGHAM (CUNNINGHAM), (d. 1399), Carmelite theologian. J. studied at Oxford and early opposed John *Wycliffe. At the Council of Blackfriars, London (1382), he signed the condemnation of 24 propositions against Wycliffe and preached the concluding sermon. He was one of a number of Carmelite confessors to John of Gaunt. BIBLIOGRAPHY: *Fasciculi Zizaniorum* (RollsS 5; 1858) 4–104; K. J. Egan, NCE 7:1057; Emden Ox 2:1077.

[J. A. WEISHEIPL]

JOHN OF LANGTON (d. 1337), chancellor of England, 1292–1302, 1307–10; bp. of Chichester, 1305–37. He had a long but undistinguished career in the royal chancery. A political moderate, he helped negotiate the treaty of Leake (1318). After 1327 he devoted himself to his diocese. BIBLIOGRAPHY: Emden Ox 2:1099–1100.

[F. D. BLACKLEY]

JOHN OF LA ROCHELLE (De Rupella; *c.*1195–1245), Franciscan theologian and preacher. Parts of the *Summa universae theologiae* of Alexander of Hales are the work of J., who was the friend and colleague of Alexander. He also wrote the first scholastic text in philosophical psychology, *Summa de anima* (ed. T. Domenichelli, 1882), was a renowned preacher, and wrote a celebrated treatise *De arte praedicandi.* BIBLIOGRAPHY: *Eleven Marian Sermons* (ed. K. Lynch, 1961); J. C. Brady, NCE 7:1057–58.

[T. C. O'BRIEN]

JOHN LATHBURY (d. 1362), English Franciscan theologian and Oxford teacher with an interest in the classics. His commentary on Lamentations *(Liber moralium in threnos Hieremiae),* popular for sermons, was one of the first books printed by Oxford Press (1482). BIBLIOGRAPHY: B. Smalley, *English Friars and Antiquity in the Early Fourteenth Century* (1960).

[F. D. BLACKLEY]

JOHN OF LA VERNA, BL. (1259–1322), Franciscan priest. At first an Augustinian canon (1269), he became a Franciscan (1272), residing in various hermitages of the order and finally at La Verna. He was devoted to penance and solitude, received many mystical graces, and was a preacher of renown. Opposed to the Franciscan Spirituals, he nevertheless gave the last rites to their partisan poet, Jacapone da Todi. His testimony in favor of the *Portiuncula* indulgence in 1311 is of significance for its historicity. BIBLIOGRAPHY: *Fioretti di San Francesco,* ch. 49–53 (Eng. ed. R. Brown, 1958); Butler 3:324–325; G. Pagnani, BiblSanct 6:919–921.

[O. J. BLUM]

JOHN OF LEIDEN (Jan Beuckelszoon, Bockelson, Beuckels, Johann Buckholdt; 1505–36), Anabaptist fanatic. A native of Leiden in Holland and a tailor by trade, he became an Anabaptist through M. *Hofmann. With Jan *Matthys and other refugees from persecution in Holland, he was able with the aid of B. *Rothmann to take over Münster in 1534. After Matthys's death, J. claimed new revelations and proclaimed himself king of a new Zion. His theocratic reign was marked by religious extravagance, extreme cruelty, and moral excess, including the practice of polygamy. With the fall of Münster in 1535 to the forces of the bp., F. von Waldeck, J. was captured and, after months of torture, executed. BIBLIOGRAPHY: Van der Aa, *Biographisch Woordenboek der Nederlanden* (1853). C. Krahn, *Dutch Anabaptism* (1968); see ANABAPTISTS (bibliog.).

[T. C. O'BRIEN]

JOHN OF LICHTENBERG (Joannes Picardi de Lucidomonte; d. after 1313), early Thomist at Cologne, defender of St. Thomas Aquinas on the real distinction between *essence and *esse* in every created being. He was named bp. of Regensburg in 1313, but never took possession of his see.

[T. C. O'BRIEN]

JOHN OF LOBEDAU, BL. (*c.*1231–64), Franciscan. Outstanding for his learning and piety, John was endowed with the gift of contemplation. He was zealous in hearing confessions and served as spiritual director for Jutta of Sangerhausen. BIBLIOGRAPHY: Wadding Ann 4:266–267, 375–376 (1931); H. Westphal, LTK 5:1057.

[H. DRESSLER]

JOHN OF LODI, ST. (*c.*1025–1105), bishop. Educated in the liberal arts, he forsook the world for a hermitage. Later, as a priest, he became the companion of St. Peter Damian, writing a biography of him following the latter's death. After 1080 he was made prior of the hermitage at Fonte Avellana; and about a year before his death he was consecrated bp. of Gubbio, in which cathedral his relics now repose. BIBLIOGRAPHY: A. Potthast, *Bibliotheca historica medii aevi* 2:1400; AS Sept. 3:146–175.

[W. A. JURGENS]

JOHN LYDUS (John of Philadelphia; 490–*c.*565), a Byzantine writer at the time of Justinian. Among his works were *De ostentis,* which dealt with the origin and development of divination, and *De mensibus,* a valuable source for the festivals of the year, but he is esp. remembered for his *De magistratibus,* a long confused account of the Eastern praetorian prefecture, in which he described the overripe bureaucracy in detail and included many personal reminiscences. Though proud of his office of *cornicularius,* he complained of the degradation of the civil service under John of Cappadocia. He was appointed by Justinian to one of the ten chairs of Latin grammar in the university at Constantinople. BIBLIOGRAPHY: E. Gibbon, *Decline and Fall of the Roman Empire* (ed. J. B. Bury, 7 v., 1909–13); A. H. M. Jones, *The Later Roman Empire* (3 v., 1964).

[M. F. MCNAMARA]

JOHN MAGNUS, see JOHN OF GOTO.

JOHN MALALAS (fl. mid-6th cent.), Byzantine historian of Syrian origin (*Malel* in Syriac is "rhetorician"). His *Chronicle* begins with creation and closes with the death of Justinian (565). Malalas, although an uncritical compiler, had available first class sources now lost, and from these he supplies valuable information not found elsewhere in extant remains of Byzantine literature. He wrote a simple nonclassical Greek. His Greek text is extant in a somewhat abbreviated form, but an Old Slavonic translation of the 10th or 11th cent. reflects a fuller Greek original. The *Chronicle* of Malalas is utilized by all subsequent Byzantine compilers of world-chronicles. BIBLIOGRAPHY: R. Browning, NCE 7:1060; G. Moravcsik, *Byzantinoturcica* (2d ed., 1958) 1:329–334.

[M. R. P. MCGUIRE]

JOHN DE MASSIAS, BL. (1585–1645), Dominican lay brother. He was a shepherd in his native Spain before going to America in 1619. He became a lay brother and served as porter in St. Mary Magdalen's Cloister in Lima, Peru. His porter's lodge became a meeting place for the poor, the sick, and the outcasts of the city. He begged and even taught the priory donkey to make the rounds collecting food and clothing without him. At his death the whole city went into mourning. He was declared blessed in 1837. BIBLIOGRAPHY: Butler 3:593–594.

[E. J. DILLON]

JOHN OF MATERA, ST. (John of Pulsano; 1070–1139), Benedictine abbot. Much of his life was spent in journeying from one religious house to another in search of a more ascetical way of life. He finally settled at Pulsano where he governed a small group of followers in accord with a strict interpretation of the Benedictine rule. BIBLIOGRAPHY: AS June 5:33–50; A. F. Pecci, *Vita S. Iohannis a Mathera abbatis, Pulsanensis Congregationis fundatoris* (1938).

[W. A. JURGENS]

ST. JOHN OF MATHA (1160–1213), founder of the Order of the Most Holy Trinity for the Redemption of Captives (O.S.S.T.). He founded the Trinitarians (*c.*1197) for ransoming Christian captives of the Moslems. The order received papal approbation from Innocent III (1198). BIBLIOGRAPHY: Butler 1:276–278.

[J. MULDOON]

JOHN OF MECKLENBURG, ST. (d. 1066), bp. of Mecklenburg *c.* 1055, martyr. Recognized in Iceland as one of the apostles of the faith there, John returned to Europe where, late in life, he became the first bp. of Mecklenburg. Probably of Anglo-Saxon origin, he was sent to the Slavic tribes and to the Wends in Saxony (Viendland: land of the Wends). During an attack upon the Christians there, he died a martyr to his faith, beheaded in 1066. BIBLIOGRAPHY: K. Schmaltz, *Kirchengeschichte Mecklenburgs* (3 v., 1935–52).

[M. E. DUFFY]

JOHN MILÍČ (*c.*1305–74), ascetic, Bohemian reform preacher. First a layman active in the court of Emperor Charles IV (1358–60) , and an official (1360–62) in the chancery, John then became a priest. His zeal and ascetic life (cf. *Devotio moderna*) combined to make him an ardent reformer; his example in giving up all dignities was intended as a rebuke to current corruption among the clergy. He preached ardently, urging the people to communicate daily; he pleaded for a vernacular translation of the Bible; he went to Rome and proclaimed the coming of the antichrist. Imprisoned there by the Inquisition, he wrote *Libellus de Anti-Christo* (1368). Pope Urban V listened to him and sent him back to Prague. Even though considered a heretic, or at least of heretical tendencies, he sought only reform within the Church. He was allowed to defend himself before the Pope and cardinals at Avignon where he died. BIBLIOGRAPHY: F. Dvornik, *Slavs in European History and Civilization* (1962).

[M. E. DUFFY]

JOHN OF MIRECOURT (1345–47) Cistercian, hence referred to as *monachus albus*, who is known chiefly for the condemnations at Paris in 1346 and 1347 of propositions from his commentary of the *Sentences*. The condemnations were based on the theological consequences he drew from his skepticism about human certitude and his insistence on the arbitrary freedom of God's absolute power *(potentia absoluta)*. BIBLIOGRAPHY: J. R. O'Donnell, NCE 7:1661.

[T. C. O'BRIEN]

JOHN OF MONTE CORVINO (d.*c.*1330), Franciscan, first Western missionary to China. Already an experienced missionary, John was sent out by Pope Nicolas IV in 1289 as bearer of letters to the Great Khan at Peking. After making numerous converts in India, he and his companion, Peter Lucalongo, were received with courtesy in 1294 by the Khan, Ch'en Tsung. Another companion, Nicolas of Pistoia, a Dominican, had died in India before the party reached China. In 1307, John was named abp. by Clement V. He built three churches in Peking, made more than 6000 converts, and translated the NT and Psalter into the native speech. Dying at the age of 82, he was mourned by Christians and non-Christians alike. BIBLIOGRAPHY: *Sinica franciscana* (ed. A. van den Wyngaert, 1929) v.1; K. S. Latourette, *History of Christian Missions in China* (1929).

[W. A. JURGENS]

JOHN OF MONTE MARANO, ST. (fl. late 11th cent.) Benedictine monk, bp., of whom there is no reliable information except that Gregory VII, at the earnest entreaty of the clergy, people, and nobles of Monte Marano, ordered that he be consecrated bp. of that city. According to tradition, he was revered for his great charity to the poor. He is patron of the city, and he is buried in its cathedral. BIBLIOGRAPHY: P. Burchi, BiblSanct 6:844.

[G. E. CONWAY]

JOHN OF MONTFORT, BL. (d. 1200 or 1248), a Knight Templar and crusader. He was wounded in battle against the Saracens at Jerusalem and was taken to Cyprus, where he died at Famagusta. His body was transported to the abbey church of Beaulieu in Nicosia. He was venerated there by the Cypriots until the Turkish conquest in 1571. BIBLIOGRAPHY: M. A. Habig, NCE 7:1062; L. Welti, LTK 5:1063; Zimmermann 2:220–221.

[M. R. P. MCGUIRE]

JOHN OF MONTMIRAIL, BL. (d. 1217), Cistercian monk. A knight under Philip II Augustus, he fought the Albigenses; then he established a hostel and cared for the sick in his own castle. Finally, in 1210, he entered the Longpont Abbey where he was noted for his obedience and humility. BIBLIOGRAPHY: M. A. Dimier, ''Le Bienheureux Jean de Montmirail moine de Longpont,'' *Mémoires de la fédération des sociétés savantes de l'Aisne* 7 (1960–61) 182–191; *idem,* BiblSanct 6:846–847.

[L. J. LEKAI]

JOHN MOSCHUS (*c.*550–619), monk and spiritual writer. He entered the monastery of Theodosius near Jerusalem, but in the course of his monastic life also lived among the hermits in the valley of the Jordan and in the monastery of St. Sabas near Bethlehem. He traveled with *Sophronius, visiting the monks of Egypt and Sinai. The last five years of his life were in Rome, where he wrote the *Spiritual Meadow*, his chief work. This collection of stories and anecdotes about the lives of the monks was read widely during the Middle Ages. Works: PG 87:2851–3112; Latin tr. PL 74:119–240; French tr. ed. M. Rouët de Journel, SC 12 (1946). BIBLIOGRAPHY: P. Sherwood, NCE 10:7; C. Testore, EncCatt 8:1468–69.

[R. B. ENO]

JOHN OF NAPLES (fl. 1310–36), Dominican, early defender of Thomism. He entered the Order of Preachers at the Univ. of Naples, studied at Paris, and was a master there in 1317 when he was assigned to the Dominican studium in Naples. He was one of the Dominican censors against the anti-Thomism of Durandus of St. Pourçain, and a witness (1319) and promoter (1323) in the process of canonization of St. Thomas Aquinas. J. also defended the right to teach St. Thomas's doctrine in spite of the 1277 condemnations by the abp. of Paris. BIBLIOGRAPHY: P. Glorieux, NCE 7:1062.

[T. C. O'BRIEN]

JOHN OF NEPOMUC, ST. (*c.*1350–93), canon of St. Augustine, patron of the Czechs, alleged martyr. As canon of the cathedral of Prague and vicar general (1389) of the archdiocese, John often opposed King Wenceslaus IV. One story, for which there is no contemporary documentation, would have him refuse to reveal to her husband the confession of Queen Sophie. In a conflict over the appointment of the abbot of the Benedictines at Kladruby, John's swift action prevented the king's confiscating the property. At another confrontation with the king, John and counselors of the abp. were seized and tortured. John was so critically injured that he was thrown into the river Vltava by his torturers. The people honored him as a martyr and national hero. Legend and history continued to be mingled in the story of his life, and he was canonized in 1729. BIBLIOGRAPHY: H. Roeder, *Saints and Their Attributes* (1955); Butler 2:332–333; *Hussiana* (1960) 400–441.

[M. E. DUFFY]

JOHN DE OFFORD (d. 1349), chancellor of England and archbishop-elect (1348) of Canterbury. A doctor of civil law by 1334, probably of Cambridge, J. entered royal service before 1328 and for the next 20 years was engaged therein. As the cathedral chapter's choice to succeed *Thomas Bradwardine in the see of Canterbury, he was nominated to that position by Edward III but died before he could be consecrated. BIBLIOGRAPHY: V. H. Baxter, NCE 7:1063; Emden Camb 431–433.

[J. A. WEISHEIPL]

JOHN OF OTZUN (650–729), Armenian catholicos, theologian, and canonist. J. worked at reforming the liturgy and discipline of the Armenian Church and, although his terminology was suspect, seems to have been orthodox in his Christology.

[G. T. DENNIS]

JOHN OF OXFORD (d. 1200), English ecclesiastic, statesman, jurist, and diplomat; bp. of Norwich (1175). After minor ecclesiastical appointments in Oxford, he became deeply involved in royal affairs, sided with *Henry II against Thomas *Becket, presided at the Council of Clarendon (1164), and through Henry's influence but against Becket's and Alexander III's wishes, was elected dean of Salisbury (1165). The antiroyal party denounced J. for allegedly submitting to *Paschal II, antipope, and Becket excommunicated him, but he was reconciled with Alexander (1166). John acted for Henry as emissary to Rome, the Emperor, and France, and in judicial, administrative, and family matters. BIBLIOGRAPHY: Emden Ox 2:1414.

[R. W. HAYS]

JOHN (GIOVANNI) PARENTI, Franciscan minister general (1226–32). A Roman citizen and doctor of law, J. joined the order soon after its establishment. He was made provincial minister to Spain (1219) and was elected minister general of the order and the first successor to St. Francis (1227). He held fast to Francis' ideas, but was not a strong leader. At the chapter of 1230 controversy arose over the binding force of the Testament of St. Francis and portions of the Rule. The questions were submitted to Pope Gregory IX, who issued the bull *Quo elongati* (1230), the first papal explanation of the Rule. Although J. had been elected to the office of minister general for life, at the chapter of 1232 he succumbed to the pressure of the majority, who were supporters of *Elias of Cortona, and resigned. BIBLIOGRAPHY: R. B. Brooke, NCE 7:1064.

[F. G. O'BRIEN]

JOHN (QUIDORT) OF PARIS (d. 1306), Dominican theologian. At Paris *c.* 1284 he wrote a rebuttal, *Correctorium circa* (ed. 1941, J. P. Müller) to the attack on St. Thomas Aquinas's doctrine in *William de la Mare's *Correctorium fratris Thomae*. J.'s treatise of 1302, *De potestate regia et papali* (ed. 1942, J. Leclercq) is an important work on the relations of the papacy to civil power. His Eucharistic views became suspect when in a *Determinatio* of 1304 he maintained that transubstantiation, while acceptable, was neither defined by the Church nor the only explanation of the Real Presence, but that another orthodox explanation was the theory later called *consubstantiation. For this he was silenced and suspended from teaching. BIBLIOGRAPHY: A. J. Heiman, NCE 7:1064.

[T. C. O'BRIEN]

JOHN OF PARMA, BL. (1208?–1289), Franciscan minister general (1247–57). Handsome, charming, learned, and energetic, he was a master of logic, taught theology and became an eloquent preacher. As general he enhanced the order's repute by his example, visitations, and by legislation. He was esteemed by all Franciscans despite his academic adherence to Joachim of Fiore's teachings. When Joachim became a major issue, Alexander IV insisted on John's resignation (1257). Acquitted at his trial, he lived in retirement till his death. BIBLIOGRAPHY: R. B. Brooke, *Early Franciscan Government* (1959); Butler 1:646–647.

[O. J. BLUM]

JOHN PECKHAM (Pecham; *c.* 1225–1292), English theologian and philosopher. Born in Sussex and educated at the monastery at Lewes, he joined the Franciscans in 1250, continuing studies at Oxford and Paris. After serving as provincial of the English Franciscans and as the first lecturer in theology at the papal court, he became abp. of Canterbury in 1279, and as such was notable for a vigorous program of ecclesiastical reform and support of papal policies over those of temporal authority. In philosophy, he was a strong upholder of the Franciscan tradition grounded in St. Augustine; his entire career was an effort to perpetuate and revitalize the Augustinian corpus against the tide of allegiance to Aristotle among the Dominicans, particularly in the person of St. Thomas Aquinas. Among other doctrines, he maintained particularly those of divine illumination in knowledge, the seminal reasons, and the real unity of the powers and essence of the soul. BIBLIOGRAPHY: *Registrum epistolarum Fratris Johannis Peckham* (ed. C. T. Martin for RollsS, 3 v., 1882–86); D. L. Douie, *Archbishop Pecham* (1952).

[J. T. HICKEY]

JOHN PELINGOTTO, BL. (d. 1304), Franciscan tertiary. Born into a prosperous family in Urbino, he led an exemplary life. He joined the Third Order of St. Francis at 15, devoting himself completely to prayer and to service of God. His remarkable asceticism was noticed at Rome during his pilgrimage there in 1330. BIBLIOGRAPHY: Wadding Ann 4:38–42; Butler 2:443–444.

[O. J. BLUM]

JOHN PHILOPONUS, see IOANNES PHILOPONUS.

JOHN DA PIAN DEL CARPINE (Plano Carpini; *c.* 1180–1252), early recruit of St. Francis of Assisi, emissary of Innocent IV to the Great Khan of the Mongols, 1245–47, author of a descriptive account, *Istoria Mongalorum quos nos Tartaros appellamus,* a valued source on 13th-cent. Mongolia and its people.

[T. C. O'BRIEN]

JOHN DE PONTEYS (d.1304), English bp. and diplomat. He was born in the diocese of York, probably studied in Oxford, and was invited *c.* 1270 to lecture in civil law at Modena, Italy. John was chosen by the clergy of Canterbury to protest against the manner of laying tithes for deliverance of the Holy Land. He became papal chaplain and legal advisor of *John Peckham at the curia. In 1282 he became bp. of Winchester and was entrusted with many diplomatic missions. BIBLIOGRAPHY: J. Daoust, NCE 7:1067; Emden Ox 3:1498–99.

[J. A. WEISHEIPL]

JOHN PRANDOTA OF CRACOW, BL. (early 13th cent.–1266), bp. of Cracow from 1242. In his work as bp. John was a reformer and a politically wise leader. He expelled the Flagellants (heretics) from Cracow, excommunicated Duke Conrad of Moravia for seizing church property, and led the Polish lords and King Charles V the Chaste and his wife Kinga in advancing the political and moral welfare of the country. BIBLIOGRAPHY: *Monumenta Poloniae historica* (1864–1893); L. Siekdniec, NCE 7:1067.

[M. E. DUFFY]

JOHN OF PUEBLA (1453–95), Spanish Franciscan. J. entered the monastery of the Hermits of St. Jerome in Guadalupe in 1471. After ordination he went to Rome (1480), where he asked permission of the pope to join the Franciscan Observants. In 1480 he returned to Spain as tutor to his nephew and founded there a number of convents of his order. BIBLIOGRAPHY: M. de Castro, *Catholicisme* 6:558–559.

[M. J. SUELZER]

JOHN OF RAVENNA (*c.* 812–after 863) abp. whose episcopate at Ravenna (850–861) was marked by conflict with Pope *Nicholas I. Seeking to enlarge his own see at the expense of surrounding dioceses, he did injury to people living within the papal territory. When he failed to heed warnings sent by the Pope, Nicholas commanded him to come to Rome and explain his actions; J., refusing to obey, was excommunicated by the Pope. Nicholas himself went to Ravenna and secured the restoration of stolen property. After a period of reconciliation with the papacy, J. again opposed the Pope, this time over the divorce of Emperor Lothair II. He was again deposed. The strong stand taken by Nicholas contributed to the strengthening of the papacy in the West. BIBLIOGRAPHY: J. P. Halton, NCE 7:1067; F. Dvornik, *The Slavs: Their Early History and Civilization* (1956).

[G. E. CONWAY]

JOHN OF READING (*c.*1285–1346), English Franciscan theologian. One of the staunchest followers of*Duns Scotus, whom he knew personally, J. lectured on the *Sentences* at Oxford before 1320 and became 45th regent master of the Franciscans, *c.*1320 or 1321. During his Avignon sojourn (1322) he strongly opposed the nominalism of *William of Ockham. BIBLIOGRAPHY: E. Longpré, ''Jean de Reading et . . . Duns Scot,'' *La France Franciscaine* 7 (1924) 99–109; Emden Ox 3:1554; J. A. Weisheipl, NCE 7:1067–68.

[J. A. WEISHEIPL]

JOHN OF RÉÔME, ST. (*c.*450–*c.*544), early monastic founder in Burgundy. At Réôme he introduced an Egyptian form of the monastic life, which he himself had embraced at Lérins. The monastery, near what is now Ménétreux, was later named St.-Jean-de-Réôme. He was renowned for his holiness and miracles.

[T. C. O'BRIEN]

JOHN DE RIDEVALL (John of Musca; fl. 1331–1340), Franciscan writer and lector of Franciscans at the Oxford convent. A number of theological and philosophical works are attributed to him. He wrote the following: *Commentarius super Fulgencium;* a commentary on St. Augustine's *De civitate Dei,* (books 1, 2, 3, 6, and 7 are still extant); a commentary on the Apocalypse, *Lectura super Apocalypsi*. A commentary on Ovid formerly ascribed to him has been shown to be that of Peter Bersuire. BIBLIOGRAPHY: B. Smalley, ''J. Ridewall's Commentary on *De Civitate Dei,*'' *Medium Aevum* 25 (1956) 140–153; J. J. Smith, NCE 8:1068.

[J. J. SMITH]

JOHN OF RILA, ST. (Rilsky; d. 946). One of the first native Bulgarian monks, J. spent some 60 years in the mountains south of Sofia where he established the influential monastery of Rila.

[G. T. DENNIS]

JOHN OF RIPA (fl. 1357–68), Italian Franciscan theologian at the Univ. of Paris. The distinctive feature of his work was his organization of theology around the doctrine of beatitude or happiness; through a personal metaphysics of forms, he sought to show how God's own beatitude was present in creatures. BIBLIOGRAPHY: J. R. O'Donnell, NCE 7:1068.

[T. C. O'BRIEN]

JOHN OF RODINGTON (*c.*1290–1348?), Franciscan scholastic at Oxford, 19th provincial minister of the English Franciscans, author of a work on moral theology, *De conscientia* and of a commentary on Lombard's *Sentences*. He is notable for an Augustinian *illuminationism, holding that those thinkers alone attain the truth free of doubt who are enlightened by the divine Ideas. BIBLIOGRAPHY: Gilson HCP 453.

[T. C. O'BRIEN]

JOHN LE ROMEYN (*c.*1230–1296), abp. of York from 1285. A dispensation from illegitimacy enabled him to be ordained after studying at Oxford and Paris, where he took his doctorate in theology (1276). His episcopate was a stormy one involving quarrels over jurisdiction with Bp. Anthony Bek of Durham and King Edward I. BIBLIOGRAPHY: B. F. Byerly, NCE 7:1069; Emden Ox 2:1134–35.

[J. A. WEISHEIPL]

JOHN OF ROQUETAILLADE (d. *c.*1365), Franciscan preacher and alchemist. At various times he has been thought to have been Catalan and even English, but he was probably a Gascon, born at Marcoles near Aurillac in the province of Aquitane. He studied philosophy for 5 years at Toulouse and entered the Franciscan monastery at Orléans. His work as an alchemist was recorded in *De consideratione quintae essentiae* (1561). J. became a bitter critic of the papacy; his denunciation of ecclesiastical abuses brought him into conflict with his superiors and led to his imprisonment by Clement VI (1345) and Innocent VI (1356). While in prison he wrote *Visiones seu revelationes* (1345) and *Vade mecum in tribulatione* (1356).

JOHN DE SACROBOSCO, (*fl.* early 13th cent.) English mathematician and astronomer. He was born in Holywood or Halifax, hence the epithet, ''Sacrobosco.'' His most influential writing was *Tractatus de sphaera*, an astronomical work which was printed in at least 25 editions by the end of the 15th century. Also influential was his *Algorismus* (arithmetic), a practical account of reckoning which was important in the diffusion of Hindu (''Arabic'') numerals. He also wrote a treatise on the calendar. BIBLIOGRAPHY: *The ''Sphere'' of Sacrobosco and Its Commentators* (ed. and tr. L. Thorndike, 1949); *idem,* NCE 7:1069.

[V. L. BULLOUGH]

JOHN OF SAHAGÚN, ST. (1429–79), Spanish preacher and reformer. Benedictine-educated, ordained in 1445, he renounced his Burgos benefices, studied canon law, did parish work, then entered the Augustinians at Salamanca (1463). Novice master, prior (1471–75; 1477–79), visionary, peacemaker, wonder-worker, he reformed Salamanca singlehandedly. After several attempts were made on his life, he died, probably of poisoning. BIBLIOGRAPHY: J. M. F. Catón, BiblSanct 6:899–901; Butler 2:526–527.

[R. I. BURNS]

JOHN DE SAINT-POL (*c.* 1295–1362), archbishop. Born in Yorkshire, England, of a family that had come from France, his ordination was first postponed on the grounds of illegitimacy; but the Pope dispensed him and he was later cleared of this charge. He held important positions in various dioceses and served for a while as Master of the Rolls. King Edward II imprisoned him for a time but he was released and appointed abp. of Dublin. There he also served as chancellor of Ireland, enlarged Holy Trinity Cathedral (Christ Church), and played a part in certain liturgical changes.

[R. T. MEYER]

JOHN OF SAINT-SAMSON (John du Moulin; 1571–1636), Carmelite mystic. Blind from the age of 3, he was nevertheless well educated. In 1606 he entered the Carmelites at Dol as a lay brother, but in 1612 transferred to the monastery at Rennes which was inaugurating the *Touraine Reform. Influenced by the mystics of the Rhineland and especially of the Low Countries, he gave to the reform his own spiritual doctrine based on his own personal experience. He maintained that the mystical life, attained through love and detachment in conformity to Christ, is necessary to Christian perfection and is available to all, at least at the end of life. His writings, largely notes drawn from his many lectures and conferences, comprise about 60 treatises and were published by Donatien de Saint-Nicolas (1658–59). BIBLIOGRAPHY: S. M. Bouchereaux, *La Réforme des Carmes en France et Jean de St. Samson* (1950); P. W. Janssen, NCE 7:1070.

[J. C. WILLKE]

JOHN OF ST. THOMAS (1589–1643), Dominican philosopher and theologian, a Thomist of the first rank, and an author of predilection for those close to Jacques *Maritain. Born in Lisbon, of Austrian, Hungarian, and Portuguese blood, he studied under the Jesuits at Coimbra and the Dominicans at Louvain, taught with acclaim at the University of Alcalá, was influential in the counsels of the Spanish Habsburgs, being confessor to Philip IV, and died of a camp-fever caught at the siege of Lérida. He was a devout and tranquil religious, a father to the poor and prisoners, courteous in debate with Suarezians, and protective toward Belgian professors accused of Jansenism on insufficient evidence. In moral theology he is regarded as a *probabilist. His compendium of Christian doctrine was translated from the Spanish into Italian, Latin, Gaelic, and Polish—a sidelight on the international history of the day. His *Cursus philosophicus* (7th ed., 1883) is a systematic exposition of Aristotelianism; it may be thought of as conducted in a vacuum, not altogether unfairly, at least with respect to contemporary streams of thought in natural philosophy. His great work, the *Cursus theologicus,* an extended and sometimes diffuse commentary on the **Summa* (8 v. 6th ed., 1931–51), is notable for its study of the operation of the *gifts of the Holy Spirit in the life of contemplation, a basic theme in mystical theology. BIBLIOGRAPHY: J. T. Ramirez, ed. *Cursus theologicus* (1931) 1:iii–xciii, "Preface."

[T. GILBY]

JOHN OF SALERNO, BL. (*c.* 1190–1242), Dominican preacher. Having received the habit from St. Dominic at Bologna where he was studying, he founded S. Maria Novella in Florence *c.* 1230. Gregory IX used him on missions against the Patarines and confided the reform of the Diocese of Chiusi to him. He was beatified in 1783. BIBLIOGRAPHY: G. de Agresti, BiblSanct 6:896–897.

[L. E. BOYLE]

JOHN OF SALISBURY (*c.* 1115–80), English philosopher, historian, humanist. A native of Salisbury, he studied in Paris under Peter *Abelard, at Chartres under *William of Conches, and again at Paris under *Gilbert de la Porrée. After some time spent as tutor, J. became attached to the papal court for several years, but in 1154 he returned to England and entered the service of Theobald, abp. of Canterbury. He became acquainted with Thomas *Becket, then chancellor of England, and served on a number of important diplomatic missions. In 1159 royal displeasure, incurred by his defense of the rights of the Church, forced him into retirement and gave him leisure to write his two most important works, *Policraticus* and *Metalogicon,* both dedicated to Becket. He left England in 1163 and spent 6 years with his friend *Peter of Celle in Reims. He returned to England with Becket in 1170 and was in Canterbury when Becket was assassinated. In 1176 he was made bp. of Reims where he spent the rest of his life. Although he was a man of broad interests and activities, J. was primarily a philosopher. He was the first important medieval philosopher acquainted with the whole *Organon* of Aristotle. His *Policraticus* is the classic of medieval political philosophy; his *Metalogicon,* a philosophical defense of the study of grammar, dialectic, and rhetoric (the trivium) against certain obscurantists he called "Cornificians." He was a leading figure in the literary revival of the 12th cent., the best Latin stylist of his time. He wrote two biographies, one of St. Anselm of Canterbury, and the other of Becket. The latter biography and his letters provide an intimate portrait of Becket, and are a primary source for the history of the conflict between Becket and Henry II. They contain much valuable information about contemporary society in general. His *Historia pontificalis,* drawn largely from his personal experience, is an important source for the history of the papacy from 1148 to 1151. Works: PL 199:1–1040; critical editions, ed. C. C. J. Webb, *Policraticus* (2 v., 1909), *Metalogicon* (1929); *Historia pontificalis* (ed. R. L. Poole, 1927). For translations see N. M. Haring, NCE 7:1071–72, bibliog. BIBLIOGRAPHY: C. C. J. Webb, *John of Salisbury* (1932); H. Liebeschütz, *Medieval Humanism in the Life and Writings of John of Salisbury* (1950).

[M. S. TANEY]

JOHN OF SAN GIMIGNANO (*c.*1265–after 1333), Dominican of Siena, author of several collections of sermons and a more celebrated book of *exempla* for the use of preachers. He is called J. ''of S. Gemignano'' because he founded a convent of his order in that place. BIBLIOGRAPHY: A. Walz, EncCatt 6:605–606; Quétif-Échard 1:528–530.

[M. J. SUELZER]

JOHN SCOTUS ERIGENA (John the Scot; Eriugena; *c.*810–*c.*877), foremost religious thinker of the early Middle Ages. The names Scotus and Erigena both refer to his Irish origin. The history of his earlier as well as his later years is obscure, but *c.*845–847 he accepted the invitation of Charles the Bald to teach grammar and dialectics at the palace school at Quierzy, near Laon, in France. His first doctrinal work, *De praedestinatione* (851) was written because Hincmar of Reims requested J.'s intervention in the controversy with Gottschalk on double predestination. The work pleased no one, because of its philosophical and untraditional approach; it was condemned by the Council of Valence in 855, which makes reference to J.'s doctrine as ''Scots porridge'' (D 633). In the next phase of J.'s career Charles the Bald commissioned him to provide a better translation from Greek to Latin of the works of Pseudo-Dionysius; the translation had considerable influence on the medievals. J. also translated writings of Gregory of Nyssa, Maximus the Confessor, and Epiphanius. This contact with Greek theology stimulated and shaped J.'s own independent works, the most important of which is *De divisione naturae.* Composed between 862 and 866, it was set in the form of a dialogue between a master and a disciple concerning J.'s well-known division: (1) nature which creates and is not created; (2) nature which is created and also creates; (3) nature which is created and does not create; (4) nature which is not created and does not create. The first is God, the second is the Platonic ideas as found in the Word, the third is the world of creatures, and the fourth is God as the end of all things. The work was apparently used by Amalric of Bene and David of Dinant in the 13th cent. as an aid in the interpretation of Aristotle. It was condemned at the 1210 Council of Paris, and in 1225 Honorius II ordered all copies to be burned. The edition printed at Oxford in 1681 was put on the Index.

J. extolled the use of reason and emphasized philosophy, but the once prevalent readiness to classify him as a rationalist was an anachronism that ignored his own insistence that reason only functioned soundly under faith and grace. While there were deviations from the orthodoxy of Latin theology in his writings, he cannot be classified as a heretic. Within the context of his interpretation of the ways of knowing God—by affirmation, negation, and supereminence—the charge of pantheism is at least questionable. BIBLIOGRAPHY: Gilson HCP 113–128; F. Vernet, DTC 5:402–434; L. E. Lynch, NCE 7:1072–74.

[T. EARLY]

JOHN DE SECCHEVILLE (Sècheville; d. betw. 1279 and 1292), English scholastic philosopher and diplomat. Probably of noble Exeter family, he studied at Oxford and Paris, where he was rector in 1256. He took part with *William of Saint-Amour in the struggle against mendicants. His chief work, *De principiis naturae,* was written in Paris, *c.*1263 (ed. R. M. Giguère, 1956). He was one of the outstanding representatives of the Averroist movement. BIBLIOGRAPHY: T. C. Crowley, NCE 7:1075; Emden Ox 3:1661–62; J. C. Russell, *Dictionary of Writers of 13th Century England* (1936) 76–77.

[J. A. WEISHEIPL]

JOHN OF SEVILLE (Hispalensis; d. 1157), author of Latin treatises, esp. on astronomy, and translator of many works from Arabic. He is to be distinguished from *John of Spain.

[T. C. O'BRIEN]

JOHN THE SILENT, ST. (454–558), Armenian monk, bishop. Although he entered the monastery while still young (18), he was soon after consecrated bp. of Colonia in Armenia. He remained for a time there but left to fulfill what was for him a deeper vocation—the call to the monastery of St. Sabas where he led a life of silence and sacrifice. He faced the dilemma of having to admit that he was already consecrated as bp. when the patriarch expressed a desire to ordain him. BIBLIOGRAPHY: Butler 2:298–299.

[J. R. RIVELLO]

JOHN OF SPAIN (d. 1166) translator of Arabic works at Toledo, who collaborated with both *Dominic Gundisalvi and *Gerard of Cremona. His identity is obscure (he has been confused with John of Seville), but he was apparently a Jewish convert. BIBLIOGRAPHY: D. Cabanelas, NCE 7:1075; Gilson HCP 235.

[T. C. O'BRIEN]

JOHN OF STERNGASSEN (Korngin; 14th cent.), Dominican theologian, brother of *Gerard of Sterngassen. J. was regent of studies at Cologne (1320) and a friend of Meister *Eckhart. His teaching substantially followed that of St. *Thomas Aquinas, but on the distinction between essence and existence he preferred the position of *Henry of Ghent. J.'s commentary of the *Sentences,* which exists only in MS is a series of discussions occasioned by the text. Works: *Predigten* and *Sprüche* in W. Wackernagel, *Altdeutsche Predigten und Gebete* (1876) 163–210; 544–548. BIBLIOGRAPHY: Gilson, HCP 746; A. Landgraf, "Johannes Sterngasse OP und sein Sentenzenkommentar," DivThomF (1926) 40–54; 207–214; 327–350; 476–480; A. Walz, EncCatt 7:609–610.

[T. C. O'BRIEN]

JOHN STRATFORD (d. 1348), abp. of Canterbury from 1333; chancellor of England, 1330–40. J. was educated at Oxford where by 1312 he was a doctor of civil and canon law. His legal skill obtained for him many benefices. He had part in the deposition of King Edward II, whose abdication he obtained. During the years 1330–40 he was the most trusted advisor of Edward III, whom, however, he opposed on some occasions. There was a breach between the two that began in 1340 and ended in reconciliation the following year. BIBLIOGRAPHY: D. Nichol, NCE 7:1075–76; Emden Ox 3:1796–98.

[J. A. WEISHEIPL]

JOHN OF THORESBY (d. 1373), English ecclesiastic and diplomat; bp. of St. David's (1347); bp. of Worcester (1349); abp. of York from 1351. Edward III used J. on several important diplomatic missions and in civil offices of great responsibility. J. is chiefly due the credit for the settlement of the ancient dispute between York and Canterbury concerning primatial privileges; each abp. was to be permitted to have his cross carried erect in the province of the other, and, as Pope Innocent VI directed in his confirmation (1354) of the compromise, the abp. of York was to be called Primate of England and the abp. of Canterbury, Primate of All England. BIBLIOGRAPHY: Emden Ox 3:1863–64.

[M. J. SUELZER]

JOHN TWENGE, see JOHN OF BRIDLINGTON.

JOHN UTHRED, see UTHRED OF BOLDON.

JOHN OF VALENCE, ST. (d. 1145) bishop. Born in the Diocese of Lyons, he was ordained a priest and served as a canon of the Lyons cathedral. His resolution to enter Cîteaux was put aside in favor of a pilgrimage to the shrine of Santiago de Compostela. Upon his return he dreamed of his destiny and in 1114 entered Cîteaux. Four years later he was sent to found the monastery of Bonnevaux, from which he established four daughter houses. In 1141 John was elected bp. of Valence and fulfilled his office with vigor, alleviating the needs of widows, orphans, and the poor, and promoting social justice. BIBLIOGRAPHY: J. R. Sommerfeldt, NCE 7:1076.

[J. D. LOUGHLIN]

JOHN OF VERCELLI, BL. (*c.* 1205–83), sixth master general of the Dominican Order. He was a secular priest and canonist who was attracted to the Dominicans by Bl. *Jordan of Saxony, from whom he received the habit *c.* 1230. He served as local and provincial superior before being elected general in 1264. During the next 20 years he traveled on visitation to supervise observance in the provinces of the order throughout Europe. He was a participant in the Council of Lyons IV (1274). Among the minor works of St. Thomas Aquinas is a set of responses to J. on theological questions. J. is regarded as the founder of the Holy Name Society because of his promotion of reverence for the name of Jesus. He was formally beatified in 1803.

[T. C. O'BRIEN]

JOHN OF VIKTRING (d. before 1347), Cistercian abbot and chronicler from Carinthia. Elected abbot of Viktring in 1312, J. became chaplain to Albrecht II in Vienna in 1341 and later to Patriarch Bertrand of Aquileia. The former may have suggested the subject matter for J.'s treatise, *Liber certarum historiarum,* which begins as a world chronicle and ends with a history of the house of Austria. BIBLIOGRAPHY: H. Wolfram, NCE 7:1076.

[M. J. FINNEGAN]

JOHN, ACTS OF, see APOCRYPHA (NT), 27.

JOHN, ACTS OF (PROCHORUS), see APOCRYPHA (NT), 28.

JOHN, APOCRYPHON AND SECRET BOOK OF, see APOCRYPHA (NT), 29.

JOHN, EPISTLES OF ST., three of the Catholic Epistles, the doctrine and the style of which are very close to those of the fourth Gospel. They are traditionally ascribed to its author, but 2 and 3 Jn were placed by Eusebius among the *antilegomena* and are not in the Syriac Peshitta. Some modern scholars ascribe the three Epistles to some other writer. BIBLIOGRAPHY: R. E. Brown, NCE 7:1078; EDB 1181.

[A. VIARD]

JOHN, GOSPEL ACCORDING TO ST., the fourth book in the NT canon. The church tradition of Asia Minor, recorded by St. Irenaeus (A.D. 180), attributed the fourth Gospel to John the Apostle, an early disciple of Jesus (Mk 1.19) and one of the more prominent members of the Twelve (Acts 1.13; 3.1). Christian writers of the late 2d and 3d cent. followed the same tradition. The Alogoi in the late 2d cent. rejected John's authorship because of their doctrinal objections to the Gospel, but they did not attempt to adduce an alternative tradition in defense of their viewpoint. With the rise of modern critical scholarship in the 19th cent., John's authorship was again contested, principally on stylistic and theological grounds. For many modern scholars both the ancient tradition concerning the Gospel's origin and the modern critique of this tradition carry their own weight. Since much of the material of the Gospel gives evidence of having passed through a lengthy tradition, John the Apostle cannot be simply accepted as the literary author of the canonical Gospel. An unknown literary author must be postulated. On the other hand the ancient concept of author ascribed more importance to the person who originally inspired the ideas and spirit of a work than to the literary author, or authors, of the final product. Consequently, it is reasonable to accept John's authorship of the Gospel in this broader sense, while admitting a final literary author for the Gospel in its canonical form.

The fourth Gospel is noteworthy for its forthright presentation of the divinity of Jesus, set forth from the very beginning of the work in a prologue (1.1–18), the famous "logos-hymn"; for its emphasis on the sacraments of baptism and the Eucharist; and for its realized eschatology, which insists upon the presence of the gifts of salvation in the Christian Church. It is particularly distinctive for its style. Though simple, the style has great dramatic power, developing its episodes with skill to confront the reader with the religious meaning of Jesus. BIBLIOGRAPHY: R. E. Brown, *Gospel according to John* (1966) 1:88–102; 135–136; R. Schnackenburg, *Gospel according to St. John* (tr. K. Smyth, 1968) 1:75–104; 111–118.

[C. P. CEROKE]

JOHN STREET UNITED METHODIST CHURCH situated at 44 John Street, New York City, the oldest American Methodist Society in continuous uninterrupted service; a national shrine of the United Methodist Church. Organized Sept. 1766 by Philip Embury, a Methodist immigrant from Ireland, the Society first met in Embury's home on Augustus Street from where it moved to a rigging loft at 120 William Street. Here Captain Thomas *Webb visited the Society and became an active leader. On March 30, 1768, the present site on John Street was purchased for 600 pounds. The original deed is still in possession of the John Street Church. The church is marked by numerous distinctions, including the fact that it hosted the first delegated general conference of the *Methodist Episcopal Church in 1812. In 1817 the original chapel was demolished and a larger edifice erected. In 1841, as the result of a street widening project by the city, the second building was replaced by the present structure. The church not only contains a museum of Methodist memorabilia but also continues to function as a church with both weekday and Sunday services. BIBLIOGRAPHY: J. B. Wakeley, *Lost Chapters . . . From the Early History of American Methodism* (1858); *Encyclopedia of World Methodism* (1974).

[F. E. MASER]

JOHN VINCENTIUS, ST. (also called John of Celle; d. 1012), hermit. Called in his epitaph a disciple of St. Romuald, J., though a bp., retired to a hermitage on Mount Caprasio and gathered about him a group of hermits, a community that came to be known as Santa Maria delle Celle. The chapel he built on Mount Pirchiriano in honor of St. Michael grew into San Michele di Chiusa abbey (*c.* 1000). As to his alleged identification with Bp. John Angelopte of Ravenna, BIBLIOGRAPHY: G. Lucchesi, BiblSanct 6:1064–65.

[R. I. BURNS]

JOHN OF WALDBY (d. *c.* 1372), Augustinian friar and author. Prominent among English Augustinians and probably provincial of the Order in England (1366), he wrote a series of homilies on the Apostles' Creed, the Pater Noster, and the Ave Maria, and two collections of popular sermons for Sundays and Holy Days. BIBLIOGRAPHY: Emden Ox 3:1957–58.

[C. D. ROSS]

JOHN OF WALES, (d. 1285), Franciscan theologian and moralist. He taught at Oxford (1257–1258), at Paris (1282) and was one of those appointed to examine the writings of Peter John Olivi. His best-known works are *Communiloquium, Breviloquium, Monoloquium, Legiloquium.* Though rambling, these works are of great interest for moral and social teaching; some were translated into Catalan and Italian, and were printed more than once. The best treatment of these writings is W. A. Pantin's in *Studies Presented to Aubrey Gwynn* (1961) 297–319.

[L. E. BOYLE]

JOHN WALWAYN (d. *c.* 1326), historian and treasurer of England. Trained in civil law at Oxford, J. was confidential clerk in the retinue of Humphrey de Bohun, Earl of Hereford. As a civil servant he had a double and difficult allegiance, viz., to the Earl of Hereford and to the Crown. His importance to English history resides in his possible authorship of the *Vita Edwardi secundi* (ed. and tr. N. Denholm-Young, 1957). BIBLIOGRAPHY: Emden Ox 3:224–225.

[J. A. WEISHEIPL]

JOHN WELLES (d. 1388), English theologian and Benedictine monk of Ramsey Abbey. He studied at Oxford (Gloucester College), and served as head of the college for many years. An active and bitter opponent of John *Wycliffe, this "Hammer of Heretics" was one of 12 masters who examined the writings of Wycliffe at Oxford in 1380 and helped suppress Wycliffite teachings in 1382. He was appointed by the English Black Monks in 1387 to plead for the release of Card. *Adam Easton from the papal prison in Rome. He died the following year in Perugia. BIBLIOGRAPHY: Emden Ox 3:2008; J. A. Weisheipl, NCE 7:1078.

[J. A. WEISHEIPL]

JOHN AND PAUL, SS., according to the legendary *passio,* brothers, officials in the imperial household, who were martyred in Rome under Julian the Apostate and buried in their home on the Caelian Hill, over which a basilica was constructed by the new Emperor Jovian. Their cult led to the inclusion of their names in the Roman Canon. Today the *passio* is considered a plagiarism from the Acts of SS. Juventinus and Maximinus. The basilica, which dates from the 5th cent., may have been dedicated to John the Baptist and the Apostle Paul, while the extensive excavations beneath it reveal a large pagan dwelling apparently used for Christian services. BIBLIOGRAPHY: Butler 2:645–646; G. De Sanctis, BiblSanct 6:1046–49; L. Kenney, *The Saints of the Canon of the Mass* (2d ed., 1963) 139–145.

[F. J. MURPHY]

JOHN XXIII CENTER, an ecumenical center for Eastern Christian studies, founded in 1951 at Fordham University, New York, as "Russian Center" by Jesuits driven from Russian works in China. Activities include courses in Oriental theology, an institute granting the master degree, lectures, publications including quarterly *Diakonia,* the Icon and Book Service, and an information center on Eastern Christianity.

[F. WILCOCK]

JOHNSON, GEORGE (1889–1944), priest and educator. After studying at St. John's Univ., Toledo, and St. Bernard's Seminary, Rochester, J. completed his studies and was ordained (1914) in Rome. Graduate study at The Catholic Univ. of America in Washington, D.C. led to a doctorate in education (1919) and his appointment to the faculty there (1921). He served as director of the Department of Education of the National Catholic Welfare Conference (1928–44), secretary general of the National Catholic Educational Association (1929–44); and at Catholic Univ. was director of the Campus School (1935–44), a member of the executive committee of the Commission on American Citizenship (1938–44), and director of that commission (1943–44). He also served on several presidential committees. His *Better Men for Better Times* (1943) is the statement of principles of the Commission on Citizenship. His writings include a study of curricula in Catholic elementary schools, several textbooks, and a number of periodical articles and pamphlets. BIBLIOGRAPHY: E. Kevane, NCE 7:1089.

[M. B. MURPHY]

JOHNSON, LIONEL PIGOT (1867–1902), poet and critic. J. was another in the considerable group of English converts to Catholicism in the late 19th century. A classicist and Oxonian, he wrote both poetry and prose with classic restraint. His *Art of Thomas Hardy* (1894) and collected essays in *Post Liminian* are excellent examples of prose. *Poems* (1895) reveal a man of deep spirituality and agonizing problems. He was an alcoholic, but his Catholicism served as an anchor of stability, as his finest poem, "The Dark Angel," shows. BIBLIOGRAPHY: L. P. Johnson, *Poetical Works* (1915).

[J. R. AHERNE]

JOHNSON, LYNDON BAINES (1908–73), 36th president of the U.S., 1963–69. Born near Stonewall, Texas, J. attended school in nearby Johnson City, named for his grandfather. After graduation from Southwest Texas State Teachers College (now STS University) at San Marcos in 1930, he taught school briefly and then began a lifelong career of government service. He was elected to the House of Representatives in 1937 as a champion of the Roosevelt New Deal, and to the Senate in 1948. Unsuccessful in his campaign for the Democratic presidential nomination in 1960, he became John F. Kennedy's running mate and was elected vice president. In that campaign J. worked vigorously to win over those Protestants, particularly in the South, who held reservations about supporting a Catholic for president. After Kennedy's assassination in 1963, J. set forth as the keynote of his administration a pledge to continue the work of his predecessor. During the remaining months of Kennedy's unexpired term and, after a landslide victory in 1964, the first part of his own, J. led Congress to pass a vast body of domestic welfare legislation. This included the Civil Rights Act of 1964, the Voting Rights Act of 1965, aid to education, medicare and other measures to further the "war on poverty" and build the "great society." In securing passage of an education bill, J. was able to break a long-standing impasse regarding aid to parochial schools. Though the bill did not aid them directly, it established programs in which they and their students could share. J.'s domestic policies brought him widespread support in the religious community, particularly the more liberal sector, and in 1964 many church leaders went further than usual in presidential elections to declare support for him and condemn the stand of his Republican opponent, Senator Barry Goldwater, on such issues as civil rights and aid for the poor. However, much of J.'s support in the religious community also came from a perception of him as the less hawkish candidate on foreign affairs. Many 1964 supporters grew increasingly critical of J., therefore, on the Vietnam issue, and controversy over the war dominated the latter part of his administration. Vietnam was a principal topic of discussion when J. stopped off at Rome in 1967 to meet with Pope Paul. In March 1968, with the nation torn by dissension over Vietnam, and with Senators Robert Kennedy and Eugene McCarthy challenging for the 1968 Democratic nomination, J. announced that he would not seek reelection. During his retirement years, he lived at his Texas ranch.

A member of the Christian Church (Disciples of Christ), J. attended churches of various denominations and maintained close friendships with many church leaders, including evangelist Billy Graham. His wife Claudia Alta Taylor, known as Lady Bird, was an Episcopalian, and their daughters, Lynda Bird and Luci Baines, were reared in the Episcopal Church, though Luci became a Catholic. BIBLIOGRAPHY: L. B. Johnson, *Vantage Point* (1971).

[T. EARLY]

JOHNSON, SAMUEL (1696–1772), American Anglican rector, philosopher. Born in Guilford, Connecticut, graduated from Yale in 1716, he was ordained a minister for the Congregational Church. He became convinced of the necessity of ordination by a bishop, however, and embraced Anglicanism, sailing for England to receive orders in 1722. His conversion, along with that of Timothy Cutler, formerly president of Yale, caused a great stir in the New England colonies. J. established the first Anglican parish in Conn. at Stratford in 1724. His influence was responsible for a high-church tradition in the Protestant Episcopal Church well into the 19th century. He helped in the foundation of the Univ. of Pa. and King's College (Columbia Univ.), of which he was first president (1754–63). As a philosopher and as a friend and disciple of Bp. Berkeley, J. sought to establish a union between religion and science. His *Elementa philosophica,* published in 1752 by Benjamin Franklin, was the first philosophical textbook to be published and used in the United States. BIBLIOGRAPHY: EncPhil 4:290, with bibliog.; Olmstead 58–60.

[M. A. GARDNER]

JOINVILLE, JEHAN DE (1224–1317), nobleman and author, intimate and biographer of Louis IX (St. Louis). Though admiring Louis' piety, and his companion on the Seventh Crusade (1248–54), J. held back from the quixotic Eighth Crusade (1268–70) which took the king's life. The conversational biography of Louis contrasts with J.'s *Credo,* a book of prayers, which Louis copied for his son's education. Text of the biography: *Life of St. Louis* (tr. R. Hague, 1955).

[J. P. WILLIMAN]

JOINVILLE, TREATY OF, formal agreement (December 31, 1584) between Philip II of Spain and the Holy League in France. The death of Francis, Duke of Alençon and Anjou, on June 10, 1584, which made it apparent that a Protestant, Henry of Navarre, was to succeed to the throne, prompted Philip II to support the efforts of the revived Holy League. A meeting was arranged between the representatives of Philip II and such important Leaguers as Henry of Guise, Charles of Mayenne, and Francis of Mayneville, at Joinville, traditional seat of the Guises. Some provisions of this treaty include: no Protestant was to be recognized as the king of France; Charles of Bourbon was made the legitimate heir; heresy was to be eliminated not only in France but also in the Netherlands; Philip II agreed to financially support the League; and, finally, after the Protestant threat had been ended, Spain and the Holy League pledged to remain allies. The agreement did not commit Philip II to sending Spanish troops to aid the League. The Treaty of Joinville was significant because it formed the basis of the relations between the Holy League and Spain until 1593. Later Spain militarily intervened in France. BIBLIOGRAPHY: D. Lamar Jensen, *Diplomacy and Dogmatism* (1964).

[C. T. EBY]

JOLENTA OF HUNGARY, BL. (*c.*1235–98), widow, Poor Clare nun. She was the daughter of King Bela IV of Hungary and married Duke Boleslas VI the Pious. After his death J. became a Poor Clare and was elected abbess of the monastery she and her husband founded at Gniezno. Her cult was approved in 1827. BIBLIOGRAPHY: Wadding Ann 5:77; 485; W. Forster, LTK 5:1111–12.

[H. DRESSLER]

JOMMELLI, NICCOLÒ (1714–74), Italian composer of operas and sacred music. Among the positions he held were assistant *maestro di cappella* at St. Peter's in Rome (1749–54) and *Kapellmeister* for the Duke of Württemberg at Stuttgart (1754–69). His first opera was *L'Errore amoroso* (1737); others followed and he had great success in Venice; in 1745 he was in Vienna for performance of his operas. He wrote about 50 in all. Both his operatic and sacred music—Masses, motets, oratorios, Offertories, Sequences—underwent a change during his German period, esp. by a quality of style, "germanization," marked by subtler harmonies and orchestration. His later music is regarded as richer and superior.

[T. C. O'BRIEN]

JÓN ÖGMUNDSSON, ST. (1052–1121), bp. of Hólar, Iceland. His work influenced Iceland in two ways: in education and in ecclesiastical administration. He brought Saemund the Learned from Rome to found the famous school at Oddi; he started a school for future priests at Hólar, the see to which he was assigned when Iceland was divided into two dioceses. His cult survives in his native land. BIBLIOGRAPHY: J. C. F. Hood, *Iceland's Church Saga* (1046); D. C. C. Pochin Mould, NCE 7:1093.

[M. E. DUFFY]

JONAH BEN JIṢHAQ, JEHUDAH (Giovanni Battista; 1588–1668), Galilean Jewish convert to Catholicism (Poland, 1625). His rabbinical training enabled him to teach Hebrew and Aramaic at Pisa and Rome, where he also made Hebrew translations of the Christian catechism, *Limmud ha-Meshihim* (1658), and of the four Gospels (1668), dedicated to Clement IX, who wrote a preface. J. assisted his student, G. *Bartolocci, in that scholar's *Bibliotheca magna rabbinica de scriptoribus et de scriptis hebraicis* (4 v., 1675–94).

[R. J. LITZ]

JONAH MARINUS (Ibn-Janaḥ; Abū'l Walīd Merwān Ibn-Janaḥ; (*c.*990–*c.*1050), Spanish Hebrew philologist. His *Book of Criticism (Kitāb al-Mustalhaq),* written in Arabic like many of his works, elaborated on the grammatical work of Judah ibn Ḥayyuj and criticized it closely and carefully; a number of subsequent works were replies to critics of his *Mustalhaq*, particularly to the criticism of Samuel ha-Nagid ibn Nagdala, a former student of Ḥayyuj. J.'s most important work, his last, *The Book of Minute Research (Kitāb al-Tankiḥ),* the oldest work of Hebrew philology to be entirely preserved, contains an extensive grammar and a complete lexicon of biblical Hebrew that includes exegesis on difficult passages. For centuries his influence on biblical philology and exegesis was considerable.

[R. J. LITZ]

JONAH, BOOK OF. This late post-Exilic book is unique among the "writing prophets" in that it consists not of a collection of prophetic oracles but of a fictitious moral tale or novel, which falls into two main episodes. In the first Jonah is thrown into the sea by hostile sailors while attempting to sail to Tarshish in defiance of Yahweh's command to go to Nineveh. But Yahweh sends a "great fish" which swallows him and after 3 days vomits him up on the shores of Nineveh. In the second episode Jonah does preach repentance with such effect that the entire population of Nineveh from the King downwards does penance and actually averts the threatened destruction of that city. Jonah complains angrily that his predictions have not come true and that he has been discredited as a prophet, but Yahweh teaches him a lesson by sending a worm to kill the gourd that shelters him from the sun. Just as Jonah himself loved the gourd, so Yahweh loves the city and does not wish it destroyed. Thus the axiom that the Lord has ". . . no pleasure in the death of the wicked but that the wicked should turn from his way and live" (Ezek 33.11) is reapplied to the worst and most ferocious of the enemies of the Jewish people, the Assyrians. The miracles which abound in the story all lead to this point. Yahweh miraculously overcomes the reluctance of his Prophet and all other obstacles in order to bring this gentile city its chance of salvation. BIBLIOGRAPHY: A. Feuillet, DBSuppl 4 (1948) 1104–31; A. R. Johnson, "Jonah 2:3–10, a Study in Cultic Phantasy," *Studies in Old Testament Prophecy Presented to T. H. Robinson* (ed. H. H. Rowley, 1950); J. G. Aalden, *Problem of the Book of Jonah* (1948).

[D. J. BOURKE]

JONAH, SIGN OF. When Jesus was asked for a sign (Mt 12. 38–42; 16. 1–4; Lk 11.29–32; partial parallel in Mk 8.11–12), he gave the Sign of Jonah. His meaning seems to be that just as Jonah and his preaching were a sign to the Ninevites, so Jesus and his preaching will be sign enough (Mt 12.41; Lk 11.32). In Mt 12.40 a different explanation is given paralleling Jonah in the whale and Jesus in the tomb. This latter explanation would be from the Evangelist or the early catechesis. The first explanation would seem to be from Jesus himself, although a few exegetes think that the original logion was as in Mt 12.39; 16.4; Lk 11.29 with no explanation of the sign. BIBLIOGRAPHY: J. Howton, *Scottish Journal of Theology* 15 (1962) 288–304; R. B. Y. Scott, *Interpretation* 19 (1965) 16–25. *SIGN.

[E. J. CROWLEY]

JONAS OF BOBBIO (*c.*600– after 665), hagiographer. Entering the monastery of Bobbio in 618, J. was secretary to abbots Athala (d.626), Bertulf (d.639), and perhaps St. Eustace of Luxeuil. J. spent the years 639–642 as a missionary in N France with St. Amandus. Toward the middle of the 7th cent., he traveled extensively and probably never returned to Bobbio. J. is the author of the lives of St. Columban, St. Vedast and St. John abbot of Réomé, and of the Book of Miracles of St. John. The life of Columban in two books is an outstanding work of its kind for the Middle Ages. The first book contains the material J. compiled from available records and the remembrances of those who knew Columban. He did the same in the second book for SS. Athala, Eustace, and Bertulf. J. is a genuine biographer who strove to obtain trustworthy information and refrained from an excessive dependence on miracle stories. Yet the faults of the times are manifest: little regard for chronology except where dates had a particular relationship to cult, a style inclined to verbosity and involved sentences, an unevenness in his narrative and errors. BIBLIOGRAPHY: H. Leclercq, DACL 7.2:631–641; M. L. W. Laistner, *Thought and Letters in Western Europe A.D. 500–900* 135–137.

[J. M. O'DONNELL]

JONAS (*c.*780–843), bp. **of ORLÉANS,** theologian and trusted adviser of Louis the Pious. He proved to be a zealous bp. and promoter of monastic reform. Among his writings are *De institutione laicali,* a treatise on morality and *De cultu imaginum,* a reply to the iconoclasm of *Claudius of Turin. Works: PL 106:121–394. BIBLIOGRAPHY: É. Amann, DTC 8:1504–08.

[R. B. ENO]

JONAS, JUSTUS (Jodocus Koch, Jobst Koch; 1493–1555), German Reformer. He studied law at Erfurt and Wittenberg, and was ordained in 1516. He became professor of law at Erfurt in 1518, then, encouraged by *Erasmus, studied theology at Wittenberg, where he became the friend and follower of Martin Luther. J.'s contribution to the Reformation started when he accompanied Luther to the Diet of *Worms, 1521. He participated in the Marburg Colloquy with the Zwinglians, 1529 (see MARBURG ARTICLES) and in the preparation of the *Augsburg Confession, 1531. He introduced the Reformation in Halle, prepared several important *church orders for other German cities, and contributed to Lutheran hymnody in his revision of the liturgy. He collaborated in Luther's translation of the Bible. He himself translated many Reformation documents, among them Luther's *De servo arbitrio* and Melanchthon's theological text, *Loci communes,* into

German. He preached at the funeral service held at Eisleben when Luther died there in 1546. BIBLIOGRAPHY: M. E. Lehmann, *Justus Jonas, Loyal Reformer* (1963).

JONATUS, ST. (d.*c.*690), abbot. Disciple of St. Amandus, apostle of the Belgians, he was called from Elnor to be abbot of monks at the double monastery of Marchiennes near Douai; he later returned to Elnor as abbot (*c.*652–*c.*659). After an interval he retired to spend his remaining years as a simple monk. BIBLIOGRAPHY: Zimmermann 2:523; D. Misonne, BiblSanct 6:504–505.

[A. CABANISS]

JONES, BOB, SR. (1883–1968), evangelist, founder of Bob Jones University. Born Robert Reynolds Jones in Dale Co., Ala., where his father was a farmer, he was licensed to preach at 15 by the *Methodist Episcopal Church, and after attending Southern Univ., Greensboro, Ala., began preaching in evangelistic campaigns. Noted for his *fundamentalism and militant attacks on those he considered modernists, he left the Methodist Church in 1939 in protest against its liberal trends and had no church affiliation during the latter part of his life. To further his principles, he founded his university (originally a junior college) in 1927 near Panama City, Fla., moving it to Cleveland, Tenn., in 1933, and to Greenville, S.C., in 1947, when he was succeeded as president by Bob Jones, Jr. The enrollment in the university was 4,265 in 1975; it rejects accreditation as interference of the State in its commitment to Christian education. One of the foremost American evangelists, J. preached in every state of the U.S. and in many foreign countries; he also conducted a widely broadcast radio program of evangelism.

[T. EARLY]

JONES, ELI STANLEY (1884–1973), a Methodist missionary in India, world evangelist and author. Born at Baltimore, Md., and educated at Asbury College, Ky., he was sent to India. It is said that conversions took place every week of his 3-year pastorate in the historic Lal Bagh Methodist Church at Lucknow. In 1924 he wrote his first of numerous books, *The Christ of the Indian Road,* a religious best seller that gave him an international reputation. He was elected by the Methodist Episcopal Church as a bp. in 1928 but resigned before being consecrated in order to continue evangelistic work. He was the recipient of the Ghandi Peace Prize in 1961. BIBLIOGRAPHY: *Encyclopedia of World Methodism* (1974).

[F. E. MASER]

JONES, GRIFFITH (1684–1761), Anglican divine. He was born at Kilredin, Wales, and educated at Carmarthen. Rector of Llanddowror (1716), he was an eloquent preacher and revivalist. His greatest work was the founding of the Welsh Free Schools in 1730, in which traveling teachers strove to reduce illiteracy among the poor and provide them with religious instruction. Supported by subscriptions and offerings, the schools numbered 3,000 at J.'s death and included 158,000 scholars. He also induced the *Society for Promoting Christian Knowledge to publish two inexpensive editions of the Welsh Bible for the benefit of the poor. BIBLIOGRAPHY: T. Kelly, *Griffith Jones, Llanddowror* (1950).

[F. E. MASER]

JONES, INIGO (1573–1652), English architect, 50 years ahead of his time in classical design. His models were admired equally with Palladio's. His notable buildings include the Queen's House at Greenwich, the Banqueting House in Whitehall, and St. Paul's, Covent Garden. Surveyor of the works and chief theatrical designer to the court under the Stuarts, a collaborator with Ben Jonson, with whom he had famous quarrels, he was a RC and suffered under Cromwell. BIBLIOGRAPHY: J. Lees-Milne, *Age of Inigo Jones* (1953).

[T. EARLY]

JONES, JOHN, ST. (alias John Buckley; 1559–98), Welsh Franciscan martyr. After joining the Franciscans at Rome he was sent to the English mission (1592) and worked chiefly in London. During his imprisonment, which began in 1597, he reconciled to the Catholic Church a layman, John Rigby, who had conformed to Protestantism for a time, and who was himself to suffer martyrdom later (1600). J. was found guilty of returning to England after being ordained abroad and was executed at St. Thomas Waterings in 1598. He was beatified in 1929, and canonized in 1970. BIBLIOGRAPHY: N. Del Re, BiblSanct 7:1023–24; Butler 3:7

JONES, RUFUS MATTHEW (1863–1948), liberal Quaker leader, and author. He was a native of Maine, graduated from Haverford College, studied at Heidelberg and Harvard. From 1904–34 he was a professor at Haverford. J. was a leading advocate of liberal and mystical thought within the Society of *Friends, and worked for Quaker unity. He helped to form the American Friends Service Committee (1917), serving as chairman until 1928 and as honorary chairman until his death. J. wrote more than 50 works, many of them devoted to mysticism. His *Studies in Mystical Religion* (1909), *Quakers in the American Colonies* (1911), *Spiritual Reformers in the 16th and 17th Cent.* (1914), and *Later Periods of Quakerism* (2 v., 1921) along with W. C. Braithwaite's *Beginnings of Quakerism* (2d ed., 1955), and *Second Period of Quakerism* (2d ed., 1961) comprise the Rowntree series of Quaker history. BIBLIOGRAPHY: D. Hinshaw, *Rufus Jones, Master Quaker* (1951); *Rufus Jones Speaks to Our Times* (ed. H. E. Fosdick, 1951); E. G. Vining, *Friend of Life* (1958).

[T. C. O'BRIEN]

JONES, WILLIAM AMBROSE (1865–1921), bp., missionary. A Philadelphian, J. was ordained in the Augustinian Order in 1890. Answering an appeal for Americans to work in Cuba after the Spanish-American War, he went to Havana where he took charge of the old churches of San Augustín and El Christo and opened Colegio San Augustín. In 1906 he was named bp. of San Juan, Puerto Rico.

[J. R. AHERNE]

JONG, JOHANNES DE (1885–1955), Dutch church historian, abp. of Utrecht, 1936–51, cardinal from 1946. He was professor of church history at the seminary of Rijsenburg, 1913–35, rector from 1931; he published *Handboek voor de Kerkgeschiedenis* (2 v., 1929–31; 5th rev. ed., 1962). His episcopacy was marked by his staunch resistance to the persecution of Christians and Jews during the Nazi occupation (1940–45). On his retirement he was succeeded by Card. Bernard Alfrink.

[T. C. O'BRIEN]

JONGHELINCK, JACQUES (1530–1606), Flemish sculptor. Commissioned by Philip II of Spain, J. created the tomb of Charles the Bold (1558) in Notre-Dame, Bruges, eight allegorical figures for the town hall of Antwerp, and other works.

[M. J. DALY]

JONSON, BEN (1572–1637), poet, playwright. The great classicist of the Elizabethan and Jacobian age ranks with Shakespeare and Milton as a writer. While in prison for killing an actor in a duel J. became a Catholic in 1598 at the height of the Elizabethan persecution. After his release from prison he studied Catholic theology in some depth. The publication of his play *Sejanus* in 1603 brought an indictment for "popery." There is no question that for 12 years J. lived as a Catholic recusant and endured more than one accusation therefor. In 1606 he and his wife were brought to court for habitual absence from his (Anglican) church. There is no question that the influence of his faith is evident in many poems from 1598 to 1610. It would seem equally apparent that his embracing Catholicism was utterly sincere. What happened to diminish his practice of the faith is not clear. The Gunpowder Plot with its ill-advised attempt on the government seems to have dismayed J. as it did many of his Catholic contemporaries. BIBLIOGRAPHY: L. I. Guiney, *Recusant Poets* (1939); *Works of Ben Jonson* (ed. C. H. Herford and P. Simpson, 11 v.,1925–1952).

[J. R. AHERNE]

JOPPA (JOPPE), a city of Palestine on the coast of the Mediterranean Sea which served as the only port city S of Tyre and Sidon in ancient times. It has been inhabited since prehistoric times and is mentioned several times in ancient Egyptian and Assyrian texts. Although mentioned as belonging to the territory of the tribe of Dan (Jos 19.46), the Philistines always controlled it even though the cedars of Lebanon for the Temples of Solomon (2 Chr 2.15) and Zerubbabel (Ezra 3.7) came through Joppa. It changed hands frequently from the Maccabees (144 B.C.) until the Jewish revolt of 67 A.D. Peter came to Joppa to restore life to Tabitha (Acts 9.43), where he saw the vision of clean and unclean food and was called to visit Cornelius in Caesarea.

[S. MUSHOLT]

JORDAENS, HANS (JEAN) III ("Lange" Jordaens; 1595–1643), Flemish painter of religious subjects. Pupil of his father Hans Jordaens II, becoming a master in 1620, J. painted *The Passage of the Jews through the Red Sea* (1624) and other works in a strong "Rubensian" manner.

[M. J. DALY]

JORDAENS, JACOB (1593–1678), Flemish painter. Dean of the Guild of St. Luke (1621), J. did decorations (1635) for the entry of Card. Ferdinand, assisting Rubens, after whose death J. was rated Flander's first painter. Though professing Protestantism after 1655, J. continued to produce altarpieces for Catholic churches. Notable works are *Susannaei Vecchioni* (1651) and *Gesù fra i dottori* (1663). He disdained the aristocratic, mythological address of Rubens and Van Dyck, expressing in colorful, coarse technique a Caravaggesque mannerist image related to P. Brueghel the Elder's typically Flemish temper.

[M. J. DALY]

JORDAN FORZATÈ, BL. (*c.* 1158–1248), a Camaldolese monk, prior of San Benedetto Novello in Padua, who served as an examiner in the canonization process for Anthony of Padua. He took an active role in the struggle between Frederick II and the popes. He was imprisoned by Ezzelino III of Romagna and finally found refuge in Venice, where he died. BIBLIOGRAPHY: M. Csáky, NCE 7:1099.

[M. A. WINKELMAN]

JORDAN OF GIANO (*c.* 1195–*c.* 1262), Franciscan chronicler. J. entered the order in Italy in 1217. Between 1221 and 1239 he served in Germany and became provincial vicar of Poland and Bohemia (1241). In 1262 he collected his reminiscences of the founding of the order in Germany; these remain an important source of Franciscan history. BIBLIOGRAPHY: E. J. Auweiler, *Chronica fratris Jordani a Giano* (1917).

[B. F. SCHERER]

JORDAN OF OSNABRÜCK (d. after 1283), author of the brief treatise *De prerogativa Romani imperii* (composed between 1256 and 1273). The longer *Memoriale de prerogativa Romani imperii* (1281), once ascribed to him, is actually, as Schraub has demonstrated, the work of Alexander von Roes. BIBLIOGRAPHY: W. Schraub, *Jordan von Osnabrück und Alexander von Roes* (1910).

[M. F. MCCARTHY]

JORDAN OF QUEDLINBURG, BL. (d. 1380), German Augustinian preacher and writer. After serving as lecturer in several Augustinian houses, J. became provincial of Saxony (1341–51) and helped in adapting the Augustinian Order to a mendicant status. His ascetical and mystical sermons and treatises were widely influential, and his *Vitasfratrum* is of historical value. He is venerated as a blessed in his order. BIBLIOGRAPHY: W. M. Plöchl, NCE 7:1100; F. Baumann, BiblSanct 6:508.

[M. J. FINNEGAN]

JORDAN OF SAXONY, BL. (d. 1237), second master general of the Dominican Order and one of the finest embodiments of its ideal. As bachelor of theology and deacon (ordained at the advice of St. Dominic), he entered the order in 1220. He attended the first general chapter at Bologna in that year, was appointed first provincial of Lombardy in June, 1221, and was elected master general in 1222. Under his able leadership the order completed its organization, developed its provinces, sent the first friars to Greece and Palestine, obtained two chairs of theology at the Univ. of Paris, entered the papal service, and increased its membership. He himself gained hundreds of recruits, esp. at the Univ. of Paris, Bologna, and Oxford. His *Libellus de principiis ordinis Praedicatorum* is a prime source for the life of Dominic and the order's first days; his letters to Diana d'Andalo are a spiritual classic. His possible identification with *Jordanus de Nemore has been discussed but most scholars reject it. BIBLIOGRAPHY: M. Aron, *Saint Dominic's Successor* (1955); H. C. Scheeben, *Beiträge zur Geschichte Jordans von Sachsen* (*Quellen und Forschungen zur Geschichte des Dominikanerordens in Deutschland* 35, 1938).

[W. A. HINNEBBUSCH]

JORDAN, EDWARD BENEDICT (1884–1951), educator. Ordained in 1909 he taught at Mt. Saint Mary's College in Emmitsburg, Md. 1910 to 1921. For the next 30 years he was at The Catholic Univ. of America as faculty member, dean and vice rector. He is known for his translation of two key works on a Catholic philosophy of education by Franz de Hovre, *Philosophy and Education* (1931) and *Catholicism in Education* (1934).

[J. R. AHERNE]

JORDAN, FRANCIS MARY OF THE HOLY CROSS (1848–1918), German founder of the *Salvatorians. Ordained in 1878, he founded the Society of the Divine Savior in Rome in 1881 to offset the effects of the Kulturkampf in his native land. Under his direction as superior general the congregation spread to other countries; he established it in the U.S. in Wisconsin, 1896. J. founded a community of nuns which became the Franciscan Sisters of the Sorrowful Mother in 1885. In 1888 he was instrumental in founding the Sisters of the Divine Savior as an adjunct to the Salvatorians. His cause was introduced in Rome in 1956.

[J. R. AHERNE]

JORDAN, the only significant river in Palestine. The river runs from N to S, rising in Lebanon from a series of streams fed by the melting snows of the Lebanon and Anti-Lebanon Ranges. The more important of these streams are the rivers Hasbani, Leddan, and Banias. These streams combine to become the Jordan River at an altitude of nearly 500 feet above sea level, and after flowing for only 7 miles the river becomes the marshy area of Lake Huleh where the altitude is only 10 feet above sea level. The river leaves Lake Huleh and falls nearly 700 feet in 10 miles to form the Sea of Galilee which is 690 feet below sea level. The major portion of the Jordan River lies between the Sea of Galilee and the Dead Sea, a straight-line distance of about 65 miles, but as the river twists and turns, it travels 200 miles, while it drops another 600 feet to the level of the Dead Sea, lying 1290 feet below sea level. The depth of the river is from 3 to 12 feet with seasonal variations; the current is swift, but the river affords many fording places.

The Jordan River is actually part of a larger deep cut in the earth's surface beginning in N Syria and running southward for more than 3,000 miles through the Jordan Valley, the Dead Sea, the Araba, through the Gulf of Aqaba and the Red Sea, all the way to Lake Nyasa in E Africa. The deep, wide valley of the river, becoming as much as 12 miles wide in the area of Jericho, makes a very striking impression on anyone who views it. The Arabs call this valley el-Ghor which nearer the river is almost imaginary moon-like terrain with mounds and valleys of whitish-gray marl and clay, so saturated with salt that there is no possibility of vegetation. The Arabs call the area immediately adjacent the river ez-Zor. This is a strip up to several hundred yards deep along the river that is dense jungle with wild life which Jeremiah referred to when he said, ''like a lion coming up from the jungle of the Jordan'' (Jer 49.19).

This is the formidable river that the Bible mentions more than 200 times and that divided Palestine into its two parts. Lot chose the Jordan Valley for his territory (Gen 13.8–13). Under the leadership of Joshua the Israelites miraculously crossed this river on dry land (Jos 3.7–17). The Midianites crossed the Jordan as they fled from Gideon (Jg 7.24). It was along the banks of the Jordan that Elijah was taken up to heaven and left his spirit upon his disciple Elisha (2 Kg 2.6–15). In the NT John the Baptist preached in the region of the Jordan (Lk 3.3), and he baptized Christ there (Lk 3.21). Today at a point on the river not far from Jericho is a small Christian shrine commemorating Christ's baptism in these waters. BIBLIOGRAPHY: N. Glueck, *River Jordan* (1946); C. Kopp, *Holy Places of the Gospels* (1963) 99–103.

[S. MUSHOLT]

JORDAN, HASHEMITE KINGDOM OF, a constitutional monarchy of the Near East (37,737 sq mi; pop. [1973 est.] 2,560,000). In the Ottoman Empire Jordan constituted an independent emirate. The majority of the inhabitants are Arabic in race, language, and religion. Christianity was planted in what is now Jordan after the dispersion of the Christian community of Jerusalem (A.D. 70) and achieved a splendid growth in the 5th and 6th cent. but perished with the Islamic invasion (636). After 1869 efforts were made in preaching the gospel by French and Italian missionaries. Catholics of the Western rite are under the abp. of Jerusalem. Existing Orthodox groups and the Vatican have made gestures toward union. In 1932 Pius XI restored the Melkite Diocese of Pera. No fewer than 16 Protestant denominations are at work in Jordan. The most influential is the Jerusalem Society of Berlin.

[P. DAMBORIENA]

JORDANIS (fl. *c.*550), chronicler and historian of the Goths. The chronicle, *De summa temporum vel origine actibusque gentis Romanorum,* was commissioned by Pope Vigilius, and is a mere compilation of earlier works. But J.'s *Getica* or *De origine actibusque Geticae gentis* is a primary source on the history of the Goths; it summarizes *Cassiodorus's lost *Historia Gothica*.

[T. C. O'BRIEN]

JORDANUS DE NEMORE (fl. first half of the 13th cent.), mathematician. He was taken to be the Dominican *Jordan of Saxony, to whom J.'s works were also ascribed, until the identification was disproved by H. *Deniflé. The works were in wide use in the medieval study of mathematics; J. also developed in mechanics his own theory of statics.

[T. C. O'BRIEN]

JØRGENSEN, JENS JOHANNES (1866–1956), Danish poet, man of letters, and convert to Catholicism from atheism (1896). He is best known in the U.S. for the translation of his biographies of St. Francis of Assisi and St. Catherine of Siena.

[H. JACK]

JORIS, DAVID (Jan Jorisz, Jan Joriszoon, David George; *c.*1501–56), Flemish visionary, preacher of *millenarianism. As a youth J. accepted the teachings of the Reformation and in 1533 became an Anabaptist. But in 1536 he gathered adherents to his own revelations: he was the new messiah (a third David); he and his followers were so spiritualized as to be beyond sin or the need of moral restraint (see ANTINOMIANISM). Jorists survived until the 17th cent. in Friesland and N Germany. Some allege that J. influenced H. *Niclaes. In 1538 J. was pursued as a heretic and stopped preaching. The bizarre *'t Wonderboeck* (Book of Wonders) belongs to the period of his preaching but was published anonymously in 1542. Many of his more than 200 writings were composed at Basel, where he lived from 1544 under the alias Jan van Brugge, pretending to be a Lutheran. Three years after his death his true identity was detected; the Protestant authorities exhumed his body and burned it, along with his writings. BIBLIOGRAPHY: A. Ingold, DTC 4:152; R. M. Jones, *Studies in Mystical Religion* (1923) 442.

[T. C. O'BRIEN]

JORNET E IBARS, TERESA, ST. (1843–97), foundress. Of Spanish birth, Teresa became a Poor Clare but was forced by poor health to leave. She founded, establishing the motherhouse at Valencia, and was until her death, superior general of the Little Sisters of the Poor and Aged, which in her lifetime grew to 103 houses. She was beatified in 1958 and canonized in 1974.

[J. R. AHERNE]

JOSAPHAT KUNCEVICZ, ST. (baptized John; 1584–1623), abp. of Polotsk, martyr. Born of Catholic parents at Vladimir in Volhynia, J. was apprenticed to a merchant of Vilna. Finding himself more inclined to study and books than to trade, he entered the monastery of the Holy Trinity in Vilna in 1604 and there he was associated with Velamin Rutsky, the future cardinal and metropolitan of Kiev. Living the austere life of a monk, J. laid plans for the extension of the recent Union of Brest-Litovsk. In 1614 he became archimandrite of his monastery; he was made bp. of Vetbsk in 1617 and abp. of Polotsk a few months later. With the help of some fellow monks he began a reform of his archdiocese and worked zealously to win over those who distrusted union with the Catholic Church. His efforts met with considerable success, but the patriarch of Constantinople sent emissaries into White Russia and Ukraine to encourage resistance to the Council of Florence and the Synod of Brest-Litovsk. As a result of their machinations, J. was set upon by a mob outside the cathedral of Vitebsk; he was slain and his body was thrown in the Dvina. The orthodox abp. of Polotsk, Cyril Smotritsky, who bore some of the responsibility for J.'s death, was later converted to the cause of the union. BIBLIOGRAPHY: Butler 4:337–340.

[A. WALKER]

JOSCIO, BL. (d. 1163), monk of St. Bertin, near St. Omer, France. According to legend, five roses sprouted from his head at death, each bearing a letter of the name *Maria*. His grave was under the small choir altar at St. Bertin. BIBLIOGRAPHY: Zimmermann 3:375–376.

[M. R. P. MCGUIRE]

JOSEPH, ST., the husband of Mary and the legal father of Jesus. Aside from the *genealogies of Jesus and the *infancy narratives, J. is mentioned in the NT only as the reputed father of Jesus (Lk 2.5; Jn 1.46; 6.42). His name was common among the Jews, and honored the Patriarch *Joseph. There is a variation between Mt's and Lk's genealogies (Mt names Jacob as Joseph's father and traces his Davidic ancestry through Solomon; Lk has Heli as Joseph's father and traces the Davidic line through Nathan), although the purpose of both genealogies, to indicate the Davidic ancestry of the Messiah, is clear. The necessity of journeying from Nazareth to Bethlehem for the census indicates that J. was a native of Bethlehem or at least owned property there. He seems to have been an artisan, probably a carpenter (Mt. 13.55). There is no reason to suppose that he was an old man at Christ's birth. John 6.42 implies that he was alive during the public ministry, although the Synoptics are silent about him. His manner of betrothal to Mary was customary among the Jews (see MATRIMONY, IN THE BIBLE); it was a formal contract but did not include cohabitation. The best interpretation of his attitude upon learning of Mary's pregnancy is that he was completely baffled. Because he was a just man, i.e., a conscientious observer of the law that forbade him to consummate marriage with an adulteress, he would have sought to divorce Mary without publicly revealing his reasons. In view of the angel's explanation, J. did take Mary into his house although Christian tradition is quick to affirm that she remained a virgin.

The infancy gospels further show J. as providing for Mary at the Nativity, a participant at the Presentation of Jesus, and warned in a dream to circumvent Herod's plan to kill Christ by fleeing into Egypt. He shares Mary's wonder when they find Jesus in the Temple, and also participates in the parental authority exercised over Jesus (Lk 2.51). Five NT apocrypha mention J., notably the *Coptic History of Joseph the Carpenter* and the *Protoevangel of James,* in which J. is presented as a widower with children, chosen by lot to marry Mary, and respectful of her virginity. BIBLIOGRAPHY: F. L. Filas, NCE 7:1106–08; U. Holzmeister, *De Sancto Joseph quaestiones biblicae* (1945).

[T. M. MCFADDEN]

JOSEPH, DEVOTION TO ST. Although Joseph, the husband of Mary and the putative father of Jesus, was honored in early Christian literature as the chaste guardian of Mary's virginity and Jesus' safety, and although his virtues were extolled by such saints as Bernard of Clairvaux, Thomas Aquinas, and Gertrude, there was no feast set aside for his reverence until 1324 on March 19. In the 15th and 16th cent., John Gerson, St. Bernardine of Siena, and St. Teresa of Avila further promoted his veneration, until Gregory XV in 1621 established St. Joseph's feast as a holy day of obligation. Pius IX declared St. Joseph the Patron of the Universal Church in 1870; then Pius XI named him the guardian of the spiritual battle against Communism; while Pius XII instituted the feast of St. Joseph the Patron of Workers to compete with the Communists' celebration of May Day. John XXIII called on him to protect Vatican Council II and had his name inserted next to Mary in the Roman canon of the Mass in 1962. Popular devotion to St. Joseph is now very widespread among Catholics and has led to a more thorough description of his role as Jesus' surrogate human father as it is found in infancy gospels of Matthew and Luke. In Matthew's view Joseph is chosen by divine fiat to be the Jewish father of Jesus, who passes on to him all his prerogatives as the final Son of David, the Messiah of the Lord, who was to establish God's final reign. Joseph is divinely commissioned to name Jesus, and thus he enters into the economy of Jesus' saving his people from their sins. The view of early apocryphal infancy gospels that Joseph was an old man when he married Mary is surely a naive invention that aims at preserving Mary's virginal integrity after Jesus' birth and at explaining how Jesus could have brothers and sisters living in Nazareth—the offspring of his foster father's previous marriage. Modern devotees of Joseph prefer to picture him as a strong, young man, capable of protecting and providing for his family and quite capable through God's grace and strength to live a chaste life as the husband of Mary to whom he was truly married by divine decision and will and his own obedience. The problem of the the Lord's brothers and sisters may be explained in other ways than by identifying them as Joseph's children. In many ways Joseph's role as the father of Jesus, in every real sense except natural generation, and this because of divine vocation, sets him parallel to Mary, his wife, in the economy of the Incarnation of Jesus that included growth to maturity. Such a principle as this has led some to aver that the grace of God that Joseph received was relatively on a par with Mary's, and that he too now enjoys total resurrected happiness with Jesus, who still remains his son as much as he remains Son of David, and with Mary, his dearest friend and his wife.

[J. F. FALLON]

JOSEPH II, (1741–90), **HOLY ROMAN EMPEROR** from 1765, from whose efforts to control the Church in his domain Josephinism took its name. Eldest son of Maria Theresa and Francis I, J. was elected Holy Roman Emperor upon his father's death in 1764 and was made coregent with his mother in Austria. During his coregency, he participated in the partition of Poland (1772). Unlike his mother, J. was deeply imbued with the philosophy of enlightened despotism. After her death (1780), he immediately began to initiate his long-desired reforms. Over a period of 10 years he published 6,000 decrees and more than 1,100 new laws. The key to his reform was his desire for greater administrative centralization, including the subordination of the Church to the State. He welcomed the dissolution of the Jesuits, forced the Pope to grant him the special privilege of nominating the bps. of his Italian provinces as well as those of other parts of his empire. He suppressed contemplative orders, and drastically interfered with the administration of other orders. He made the clergy civil servants and assumed jurisdiction over their education. His edict of toleration and the abolition of serfdom are considered to be the most enlightened of his reforms. His arbitrary methods aroused the hostility even of the beneficiaries of his decrees. Harassed by revolution, he was obliged to rescind many of his decrees before his death. BIBLIOGRAPHY: G. P. Gooch, *Maria Theresa and Other Studies* (1951) 1–118; M. C. Goodwin, *Papal Conflict with Josephinism* (1938).

[A. WATHEN]

JOSEPH I (*c.* 1200–83), **PATRIARCH OF CONSTANTINOPLE** from 1267–1276; 1282–1283. J. owed his appointment to Emperor Michael VIII Palaeologus, who had deposed Arsenius and Germanus III in quick succession. A moderate who opposed the fanatical Arsenites in the internal affairs of the Byzantine Church, J. took the lead among the Orthodox clergy in repudiating the union with the Latin church that Emperor Michael negotiated at the Council of *Lyons II in 1274. The emperor's sister Eulogia, quarreling with her brother, influenced the patriarch to some degree. J. resigned his office rather than change his attitude. In 1282 a new emperor, Andronicus II, repudiated Michael's reunion policy and restored J. to the patriarchate. He died shortly thereafter. BIBLIOGRAPHY: D. J. Geanakoplos, *Emperor Michael Palaeologus and the West, 1258–1282* (1959); B. Roberg, *Die Union zwischen der griechischen und der lateinischen Kirche auf dem II. Konzil von Lyon (1274)* (1964).

[R. H. SCHMANDT]

JOSEPH II, (*c.* 1359–1439), **PATRIARCH OF CONSTANTINOPLE** from 1416. A very religious and strong-willed person, at about the age of 80 he accompanied the Emperor *John VIII Palaeologus to the Council of *Florence. Although theologically somewhat naive, he was efficient and kindly in managing the Greek bps. and was intensely devoted to the cause of union. After affirming his acceptance of the Roman belief, he died shortly before the proclamation of the union and was buried in Florence. BIBLIOGRAPHY: J. Gill, *Personalities of the Council of Florence* (1964).

[G. T. DENNIS]

JOSEPH, SON OF JACOB, one of the 12 Patriarchs. J. is sold by his brothers to slave traders and taken to Egypt (Gen ch. 37), where he staunchly resists the attempt of his master's wife to seduce him and meekly endures imprisonment because of her false accusation. Later, as a result of his marvelous capacities as a diviner and interpreter of dreams and as a sage counselor, he wins favor in Pharaoh's eyes and is set as administrator over the whole kingdom. In this capacity he saves the land from famine by his wisdom and foresight, and eventually also forgives and rescues his own brothers (Gen ch.44–45), bringing them and his father to live in prosperous and honorable circumstances in the land of Goshen (Gen 46.1–47:12). G. von Rad has argued convincingly that the story of J. reflects the values of a new humanism that began under Solomon and was a result of Egyptian influence. J. is the ideal of the *kaloskagathos,* a young man, wise, modest, prudent, and virtuous in all circumstances and outstripping the Egyptians in those very humanistic virtues that they so much cultivated.

[D. J. BOURKE]

JOSEPH OF ARIMATHEA, wealthy Jew, member of the Sanhedrin, who became a Disciple of Jesus, obtained his body from Pontius Pilate after his Crucifixion, and buried it in his own tomb (Mt 27.57–60; Mk 15.43–46; Lk 23.50–54; Jn 19.38–42).

[D. J. BOURKE]

JOSEPH CALASANCTIUS, ST. (1556–1648), educator; founder of the Piarists. Born in Peralta de la Sol in Aragon he attended the Univ. of Lérida, obtaining a doctorate in law, then studied at Valencia and Alcalá before being ordained in 1583. After serving as vicar general of Trempe, he resigned in 1592 and journeyed to Rome, where he received the guidance of Card. Colonna. J. labored mightily among the poor in Rome, esp. during the plague year of 1595. In 1597 he founded Europe's first free school in the belief that the destitute children of Rome could be saved only through the opportunity for education. As the number of pupils increased in the succeeding years, Pope Clement VIII pledged his support and, in 1617, Pope Paul V gave the congregation its first official recognition. In 1621, the Clerks Regular of the Secular Schools (Piarists) were granted full recognition as a religious order. By 1630, the order had opened schools in Tuscany, Germany, Poland, and Moravia. The congregation became subject to internal power struggles and plots against J.'s authority. Distorting his ideas on humanistic education and his friendship with Galileo, the insurgents persuaded Innocent X to depose him and disband the order in 1646, 2 years before his death. The Piarists were reinstituted by Alexander VII, who gave them simple vows, and confirmed by Clement IX in 1669. J. was canonized in 1767 and declared Patron of the Christian Schools in 1948 by Pius XII. BIBLIOGRAPHY: Q. Santoloci, BiblSanct 6:1321–30; Butler 3:413–416.

[R. J. BRADY]

JOSEPH OF CUPERTINO, ST. (1603–63), Conventual Franciscan whose celebrated flights of ecstasy resulted in his being called by some "the flying friar." Dismissed from the Capuchins, he entered the Franciscans, first as a tertiary, then as a cleric, and was ordained in 1628. In Grotella he began experiencing ecstasies and his levitations became an embarrassment to authorities, who sought to exclude him from public gatherings and services. At Naples (1638), he faced the Inquisition but was released and sent to Rome where he went into ecstatic flight in the presence of Urban VIII. He was sent to Assisi where, after 2 years of abatement, the powers returned and attracted curious pilgrims; the Duke of Brunswick was converted when he witnessed J.'s ecstasies. After Assisi J. was sent to Pietrarubbia and Fossombrone to live with the Capuchins; in 1657 he was allowed to return to his own order at Osimo, where he remained until his death. He was canonized in 1767. BIBLIOGRAPHY: N. Del Re, BiblSanct 6:1300–03; Butler 3:587–591.

[R. J. LITZ]

JOSEPH OF EXETER (*fl.* 1180–90), English Latin epic poet. Educated at Exeter, England, he was a friend of *Guibert de Gembloux; some of their correspondence has survived. His fragmentary poem *Antiocheis* commemorates the Third Crusade on which he went as far as Acre. *De bello Troiano,* his only surviving complete work, an epic of the Trojan War, reveals him as a good Latinist and rhetorician but as a mediocre poet.

[F. D. BLACKLEY]

JOSEPH OF THE HOLY SPIRIT (1609–74), Portuguese Discalced Carmelite, theologian. His *Cadena mistica* (1678), the first systematic exposition of the spiritual theology of St. *Teresa of Avila, is equally important for its documentation from sources no longer extant. J. is not to be confused with the Andalusian Discalced Carmelite of the same name.

[T. C. O'BRIEN]

JOSEPH THE HYMNOGRAPHER (*c.* 810–886), brother of St. *Theodore of Studius, and a major liturgical poet of the 9th century. A native of Sicily, he lived at monasteries in Thessalonica and Constantinople, fled Constantinople during the iconoclastic persecution, fell into the hands of pirates and spent many years on Crete, and finally returned to Constantinople to establish a monastery in connection with the Church of St. John Chrysostom. He managed to stand in the good graces of both the Patriarch Ignatius and his rival Photius. He composed more than 1,000 hymns, 200 of which are contained in the **Menaion*. His Canon of the Ascension is very majestic and probably the finest extant hymn on the Ascension. BIBLIOGRAPHY: J. Julian, *Dictionary of Hymnology,* (2 v., 1957).

[M. F. MCNAMARA]

JOSEPH OF LEONESSA, ST. (1556–1612). Born to a noble family in Leonessa, Umbria, and baptized Eufranio, he received much of his early education from an uncle, Battista, in the town of Viterbo. When he returned to Leonessa, he decided, at the age of 18, to become a Capuchin, a decision opposed by his family, which sought political alliances through his marriage. Eufranio persevered and changed his name to Joseph as a Capuchin. In 1587, he was sent as a missionary to Constantinople, where he worked among the prisoners of Turkish prisons. After attempting to convert the Sultan Murad III, J. was imprisoned and tortured, then banished from Turkey. Returning to Italy, he cared for the poor in Venice and his native Leonessa. Stricken with cancer, he underwent several operations holding only a crucifix. Until his death J. accepted his suffering with patience and dignity. He was canonized by Benedict XIV in 1746. BIBLIOGRAPHY: C. Da Langasco, BiblSanct 6:1305–07; Butler 1:253–254.

[R. J. BRADY]

JOSEPH OF METHONE (John Plusiadenus; *c.* 1429–1500), Cretan-born Byzantine scholar, bp., and advocate of the union achieved at the Council of *Florence. He defended the Greek-Latin church union in his *Defensio synodi Florentinae* (after 1455, often under name Gennadius), and was named by Card. Bessarion as head of the churches in the Orient and vice-Protopapas (*c.* 1466–*c.* 1481). Until 1492, when he was elected bp. of Methone, he served as a copyist in Italy. Visiting Venice (1497), Rome (1498), en route to Crete, he was told of the expected Turkish attack on his see. He returned to Methone and died in the battle.

[R. J. LITZ]

JOSEPH OF VOLOKOLAMSK, ST. (*c.* 1439–1515). Noted for his uncompromising personality and intellectual ability J. was made abbot of Borovsk, but his strict discipline caused so much discontent that he left to found a new monastery at Volokolamsk. He believed the monasteries needed to possess property, and he also felt that the Church should make concessions to the State. This brought him into conflict with St. Nil Sorsky. A synod in Moscow in 1503 supported the "possessors," as Joseph's followers were known.

[G. T. DENNIS]

JOSEPH AND ASENATH, the father and mother of Manasseh and Ephraim, eponymous heroes of the Joseph tribes who led the Israelite conquest of Canaan. The patriarch Joseph was the favorite son of Jacob, and firstborn of Rachel. Asenath was his Egyptian wife, daughter of the priest of On. Joseph and Asenath are the subject of a Jewish and Christian romance which can be traced back at least to the 5th cent. A.D., in which Asenath renounces her false gods before her marriage with Joseph. In the biblical record, however, the marriage reflects rather the rank Joseph attained in Egyptian society, marrying as he did the daughter of Potiphera, one of the outstanding dignitaries of the realm, priest of the national temple of the Sun at On (or Heliopolis). The Hebraized name Asenath probably comes from an Egyptian name meaning "belonging to (the goddess) Neith," the goddess of Saïs. This type of name was prevalent during the Late Period (*c.* 1075–663 B.C.). Neith was an especially popular component in names during the 26th, or Saïte, Dynasty (*c.* 663–525 B.C.).

[E. J. DILLON]

JOSEPH THE CARPENTER, HISTORY OF, see APOCRYPHA (NT), 30.

JOSEPHINE, EMPRESS (1763–1814), wife of *Napoleon I Bonaparte. Born on Martinique in the W Indies, J. was married in Paris to Viscount Alexandre de Beauharnais, also from Martinique; she bore two children, Eugène and Hortense, but her husband disclaimed the daughter as his. In 1794 he was executed as an aristocrat and J. also was imprisoned for a short time. She married Bonaparte in a civil ceremony in 1796, after having been his mistress. She was notoriously unfaithful. The irregularity of their marriage was corrected at the insistence of Pius VII on the eve of his crowning Bonaparte as emperor (1804). The religious ceremony was performed without witnesses, Card. Fesch, uncle of Bonaparte officiating. The defect of witnesses became the grounds on which the French matrimonial tribunals annulled the marriage in 1809, when Bonaparte blamed J. for their lack of children (Rome did not recognize the annulment). She lived comfortably for the remainder of her life near Paris. BIBLIOGRAPHY: F. Mossiker, *Napoleon and Josephine: The Biography of a Marriage* (1964).

[R. H. SCHMANDT]

JOSEPHINISM, the name given to the close control exercised by the State over the RC Church in Austria from the late 1760s to the early 1850s; it also implies a liberal policy toward non-Catholic minorities. The system was primarily devised by Wenzel von Kaunitz, chancellor of Empress Maria Theresa. However, her piety and Kaunitz's own judgment set limits to state interference with church life and the ties with Rome. Joseph II (d. 1790) exercised no such restraint, and from him the system takes its name. An apostle of the *Enlightenment and imbued with *Febronianism, he sought to make the Austrian Church autonomous and to create of it an instrument of progressive government. He suppressed purely contemplative orders, severed ties between monasteries and their foreign superiors, subjected church correspondence to government control, and placed seminaries under bureaucratic direction. The Pope was largely ignored in the planning and execution of these changes. Josephinism did bring some gains to the Church, since Joseph II built many new parishes; non-Catholics also benefited from his policies. The system itself remained in being until 1850, when Franz Josef I decided that political conditions dictated more respect for the Church's own conception of its mission and rights within the State; the effects of Josephinism, however, lingered for another century. BIBLIOGRAPHY: *Der Josephinismus* ... (ed. F. Maass, 5 v., 1951–61); M. C. Goodwin, *Papal Conflict with Josephinism (1938).*

[J. K. ZEENDER]

JOSEPHITE FATHERS (St. Joseph's Society of the Sacred Heart; SSJ),a religious community of priests and brothers, which originated in the society founded in 1866 at Mill Hill, London, England by H. *Vaughan. In 1871 Vaughan and the Missionary Society of St. Joseph (MHM) were called to work among the 4 million emancipated U.S. Negroes, in response to the appeal for priests of the Second Plenary Council of Baltimore. It was found that missions to the blacks could better prosper with an American community; thus the Josephite Society was founded in 1893 in Baltimore, Md. in which city is their generalate. The Josephite leads a common life without vows, but makes a promise of obedience to the superior; papal approval was given the Society in 1932.

Josephite missions have spread through 4 archdioceses and 12 dioceses of the U.S., esp. in the South; in 1954 they entered the foreign mission field and minister in the Bahamas. Of their number is Bp. J. L. Howze who in 1976 became in this century the first black ordinary in America. In 1976 they had 109 houses and 245 members, 190 of whom were priests. They publish *The Josephite Harvest,* a quarterly that, begun in 1888, records their activities among the blacks. The Catholic Board for *Negro American Missions is likewise in their apostolate. BIBLIOGRAPHY: J. T. Gillard, *Catholic Church and the American Negro* (1930); *idem*, *Colored Catholics in the United States* (1941).

[M. R. BROWN]

JOSEPHISTS (Josepins), an obscure sect that appeared in parts of France, Germany, and Italy in the late 12th century. "Josepins" were condemned by Lucius III in 1184 (see D 760) and by Gregory IX in 1231, but their distinctive teachings are not known. Because it was alleged that adherents spurned marriage but allowed full indulgence of the passions outside that state, the sect is often listed as a branch of the *Cathari; this relationship, however, has not been established by any historical documentation and is doubted by historians. BIBLIOGRAPHY: É. Amann, DTC 8:1547–48; DE 2:207.

[C. J. LYNCH]

JOSEPHUS FLAVIUS, (*c.*37–100 A.D.), Jewish historian who was born Joseph ben Matthias of an aristocratic, priestly family in Jerusalem, received an excellent education, joined the party of the Pharisees, and went to Rome (63) to plead before Nero for the release of several Jewish priests. On his return he attempted to stem the growing revolt against Rome, but later joined the insurgents. Appointed governor of Galilee by the Sanhedrin (66), he was taken prisoner by Vespasian but later freed when his prophecy that Vespasian would become Emperor came true. He was present at the siege of Jerusalem (70) with Titus, whom he afterwards accompanied to Rome. As the protégé of Vespasian and Titus, he assumed the name Flavius in their honor. His time in Rome until his death there was spent on the composition of his works. These, in Greek, include the *Jewish Antiquities,* a history of the Jews from the creation to 66 A.D. , and the *History of the Jewish War,* a record of Jewish history from the revolt of the Maccabees, for much of which he was an eyewitness. Other works are an autobiography and an essay defending his *Jewish Antiquities* against Apion. In these works J. is both historian and apologist. As historian he is both uncritical and incomplete, and in his use of Scripture, given to additions, omissions, and variations. Nevertheless, he is the most important source for the history of Judea in his own time. Although pro-Roman politically, he was a defender of Jewish culture, but had no sympathy for extreme Jewish nationalism. BIBLIOGRAPHY: H. St. J. Thackeray, *Josephus the Man and the Historian* (1929).

[F. J. MURPHY]

JOSETSU (fl. 15th cent.), Japanese priest and official painter to the Ashikaga shogun, who illustrated the "life questions" posed for the meditation of Zen priests, in delicate lines and subtle values, evidencing the influence of Sung, China's ink (*sumi*) painting. J. worked in the Shōkokuji of Kyoto.

[M. J. DALY]

JOSHUA, BOOK OF. The events recorded in Joshua fall approximately within the period 1250–1180 B.C. , but the book itself could hardly have acquired its existing form before the 6th cent., when the numerous independent traditions it contains would have been reedited and reinterpreted by the Deuteronomist history writers, and so incorporated into their great historical saga extending from the last discourse of Moses to the downfall of the Judahite monarchy in 587.

In terms of content the book falls unmistakably into the following three main parts: (1) The conquest of Canaan, including the crossing of the Jordan (ch. 3), circumcision at Gilgal (5.2–9), the proclamation of the law at Mount Ebal (8.30–35), and the pact between Israel and the Gibeonites (9.3–27). Clearly a number of independent units of tradition have here been blended (at the cost of some inconsistency) into a single saga of conquest, and a far greater number of victories have been ascribed to Joshua's personal leadership than he would have attained in historical fact. Certain of the tradition strata incorporated in the Pentateuch can plainly be discerned extending into this book also. (2) The tribal territories are defined and tribal cities recorded, including the Levite "cities of refuge" (ch. 13–21). (3) The ceremony of the renewal of the covenant is presented as Joshua's last act as leader of the assembled tribes. The manner in which this story is told is widely held to reflect the successive stages of an alleged autumn festival of covenant renewal as celebrated by the tribal confederation in premonarchist days. The ceremonies and traditions associated with this festival are held to have left a deep impress on many areas of the Old Testament. BIBLIOGRAPHY: F. M. Abel, *Le Livre de Josué, Book of Joshua* (2d ed., 1958); K. Gutbrod, *Das Buch vom Lande Gottes, Josua und Richter, B. A. T.* (2d ed., 1957); M. Noth, *Buch Josua* (rev. ed., 1965); N. H. Snaith, "The Historical Books," *Old Testament and Modern Study* (ed. H. H. Rowley, 1951) 84 ff.; L. Roussel, *Le Livre de Josué, ch. 1–12* (1955); J. Garstang, *Joshua and Judges* (1931); Y. Kaufmann, *Biblical Account of the Conquest of Palestine* (1953) (the two last named to be read with caution). Cf. also J. Bright, *History of Israel* (1959) and M. Noth, *History of Israel* (2d ed., 1960).

[D. J. BOURKE]

JOSHUA ROLL, 7th-cent. Byzantine illuminated MS expressive of the "Macedonian renaissance" in an amalgamation of the pictorial tradition of the Alexandrian school (figures delicate and graceful of form and modeling set against architectural and landscape backgrounds) with the Eastern tradition of rich ornamentation.

[M. J. DALY]

JOSIAH, King of Judah *c.*640–609 B.C. (2 Kg ch. 22–23; 2 Chr ch. 34–35). At the age of 8 he succeeded his father Amon, who had been murdered (2 Kg 21.23–26). A major event of his reign was the national religious reform based on "the book of the law" found during repairs on the Temple. Scholars usually identify that work with Deuteronomy, which many of them think was likely written in Josiah's time. A principal feature of the reform was centralizing worship in Jerusalem and destroying the *high places (see Dt ch. 12). J. was killed at Megiddo by Pharaoh *Neco, and was succeeded by his son Jehoahaz. He was praised by Jeremiah for his justice to the poor (22.15–16).

[T. EARLY]

JOSIPPON (Josephon; Yosephon), medieval Hebrew chronicle of Jewish history from Adam to the end of the first Jewish revolt in 70 A.D. The term means little Josippus (Josephus). The work is based largely on *Hegesippus*, a free Latin version of Josephus's *Jewish War*, but also draws on the OT and other sources. It possibly originated in S Italy, where it was known *c.*950. Popular in medieval Europe and translated into the European languages, it was also used by Muslims in an Arabic version and by the Ethiopic Church in an Ethiopic version. BIBLIOGRAPHY: G. Strugnell, NCE 7:1124.

[T. EARLY]

JOSQUIN DES PREZ, see DESPREZ, JOSQUIN.

JOSUE, SON OF JOSEDEC (Joshua in Hag and Zech; Jeshua in Ezra and Neh; *c.*560–490 B.C.), high priest. He was the son of a Jew taken captive in 586 B.C. (1 Chr 6.15), and his name heads the list of those who returned with Zerubbabel (Ezra 2.2; Neh 7.7). With the encouragement of Haggai and Zechariah, J. and Zerubbabel rebuilt the Temple (Ezra 5.1–2; Hag 1). J. appears in several of Zechariah's visions. In one, his "filthy garments" were replaced with clean, presumably confirming his right to the office of high priest (3.1–5). In another, he and Zerubbabel are the "two anointed" (4.14). His name has perhaps displaced Zerubbabel's in 6.11.

[T. EARLY]

JOSUE, SON OF NUN (Joshua), successor of Moses and leader of the conquest. Moses changed the name from

Hoshea (Num 13.16) to Josue, which means Yahweh is salvation and is the Hebrew equivalent of Jesus (Mt 1.21). J. is first mentioned as a military leader (Ex 17.8–13); he also served with Moses in the tent of meeting (Ex 33.11). Representing the Josephite tribe of Ephraim, he was one of the 12 spies sent into Canaan (Num 13.8). He and Caleb were the only ones advising immediate invasion (Num 14.6–10). Moses commissioned J. as his successor (Dt 34.9), with the task of leading the conquest; the activity is described in the Book of Josue.

[T. EARLY]

JOSUE, BOOK OF, see JOSHUA, BOOK OF.

JOUARRE-EN-BRIE, ABBEY OF, French convent of Benedictine nuns near Meaux which was founded in the 7th cent. as a double monastery for both nuns and monks, the latter coming from Luxeuil. The abbess had extraordinary powers of jurisdiction from the 13th to the 17th century, e.g., appointment of pastors in the parishes within the boundaries of the convent property. Suppressed in 1791, the convent was revived in 1837. BIBLIOGRAPHY: H. Thiercelin, *Le Monastère de Jouarre* (1861); L. J. Lekai, NCE 7:1130.

[L. J. LEKAI]

JOUFFROY, JEAN (*c.* 1412–73), cardinal, diplomat. He is most noted for his role in the negotiations between Louis XI and Pius II (1461) concerning the abrogation of the Pragmatic Sanction of Bourges. Already bp. of Arras (1453), he was given the cardinal's hat in 1461 as a reward for his services. BIBLIOGRAPHY: Pastor 3:135–157.

[J. MULDOON]

JOÜON, PAUL (1871–1940), Jesuit grammarian and lexicographer. After a short teaching career in Beirut and at the Pontifical *Biblical Institute, J. was totally involved in scientific research. He wrote extensively on Oriental languages, OT textual criticism, and biblical exegesis as well as a well-known grammar of biblical Hebrew and a translation and commentary on the Gospels for the *Verbum salutis* series. BIBLIOGRAPHY: S. Lyonnet, DBSuppl 4:1141–43.

[T. M. MCFADDEN]

JOURNET, CHARLES (1891–1975), Swiss theologian, cardinal, and from 1965 titular archbishop. Ordained in 1917, J. spent most of his life teaching at the Grand Séminaire and Univ. of Fribourg. He was also devoted to the preaching ministry, esp. in retreat work. He was throughout his life devoted to the study of apologetics, ecclesiology, and ecumenism; he consequently was an important contributor to the conciliar discussions of Vatican II. His best known, single work in English is *Church of the Word Incarnate* (tr. A. H. C. Downe, 1955); other translated works include: *Dark Knowledge of God* (tr. J. F. Anderson, 1948); *Wisdom of Faith* (tr. R. F. Smith, 1952); *Primacy of Peter* (tr. J. Chapin, 1954); *Meaning of Grace* (tr. A. V. Littledale, 1960); *Meaning of Evil* (tr. M. Barry, 1963). His writings were marked by a thorough knowledge of the Fathers and of St. Thomas Aquinas, and by his own personal insight.

[T. C. O'BRIEN]

JOUVANCY, JOSEPH DE (1643–1719), French Jesuit, classicist, poet, educator. Professed in 1677, J. taught for 20 years at the Collège Louis-le-Grand in Paris. Called to Rome he began work on the history of the Society, to which he devoted the rest of his life. A poet who wrote precise Latin and Greek, he was author of a number of school editions of Latin writers, among them Terence, Horace, Cicero, Martial, and Ovid. For the Society he published a pedagogical work *Christianis litterarum magistris de ratione discendi et docendi* (1691), which the Jesuits adopted for their courses in classical studies. He continued N. Orlandini's *Historia Societatis Jesu* for the period 1591–1616; his work was condemned in 1715 by the French Parliament because it opposed the doctrine of the divine right of kings, and put on the Index in 1722 for its discussion of the Chinese Rites Controversy.

[J. R. AHERNE]

JOUVENET, JEAN BAPTISTE (Jean III; 1644–1717), French painter and decorator who studied with his father and with Charles Le Brun to whose style he added a baroque expressiveness and strong naturalism seen in the ceilings of chapels at Versailles and *Les Invalides* and in the painting *Miraculous Draught of the Fishes* (Louvre).

[M. J. DALY]

JOVIAN (*c.*331–364), **ROMAN EMPEROR** from 363. The day after the death of Emperor Julian, the army in the field elevated the young, gay-spirited Flavius Claudius Jovianus, a prominent member of the imperial household. In order to reach Rome to strengthen his rule, Jovian needlessly capitulated to Persia, surrendering the five Roman provinces beyond the Tigris as well as a strip west of the river that included Nisibis, Singara, and other important cities. Jovian was careful in his choice of officials and governed with energy and shrewdness. In his brief reign he removed all of Julian's edicts against the Christians, prohibited public pagan sacrifices, and destroyed or closed many pagan temples. He showed tolerance, however, in his treatment of individual pagans, punishing only witchcraft and attempts at prophecy. A few days before his death he added to his private patrimony the landed property belonging to the temples he had closed. BIBLIOGRAPHY: O. Seeck, PW 9.2:2006–11.

[M. J. SUELZER]

JOVINIAN (d. *c.*405), adversary of St. Jerome. After living for some time as an ascetic, J. appeared in Rome *c.*385 in vigorous opposition to the monastic-ascetical ideals that were currently being advocated in some circles. He taught, according to Jerome, that there was no difference in value between the married, celibate, and widowed states: all are equally meritorious to the baptized, nor will there be any difference in heaven based upon earthly states. In this connection he also denied the perpetual virginity of Mary. Jovinian and his doctrines were condemned by synods at Rome (390) under Pope Siricius and at Milan (391) under St. Ambrose. After these rebuffs J. and a few followers withdrew to Vercelli. In 393 Jerome published his *Adversus Jovinianum,* and St. Augustine also refuted J.'s doctrine in his *De bono coniugali* and his *De sancta virginitate.* BIBLIOGRAPHY: Jerome, PL 23:221–352; F. Froget, DTC 8:1577–80; P. J. Healy, CE 8:530.

[R. B. ENO]

JOVITA, ST., see FAUSTINUS AND JOVITA, SS.

JOVIUS, PAULUS (Paolo Giovio; 1483–1552), historian, litterateur, bishop. An Italian physician who was employed as a diplomat by several popes, J. was named bp. of Nocera in 1528, an assignment that did not occupy much of his time. His writings include *Commentaries* (1531), which demonstrate his shrewd awareness of the Turkish danger, and a major work *Historiarum sui temporis libri XV* (1550–52), a work on which he spent 30 years.

[J. R. AHERNE]

JOWETT, BENJAMIN (1817–93), English scholar. He entered Balliol College, Oxford in 1836 and became a fellow while still an undergraduate. Ordained an Anglican priest in 1845, he held a succession of offices at Balliol until elected master in 1870. He was renowned for his classical learning; among his published translations, the works of Plato (4 v., 1871), became widely used. His *Commentaries on the Epistles of St. Paul* (2 v., 1855), and "Interpretation of Scripture" in *Essays and Reviews* (1860) by their liberal interpretations of Christian dogmas, esp. the Atonement, raised doubts about his orthodoxy, and he ceased from further theological writing. BIBLIOGRAPHY: G. Faber, *Jowett* (1957).

JOY (Lat. *gaudium*), the delight which is the healthy complement of intelligent and willed activity when appetition is actively at rest in a good really possessed (ThAq ST 1a2ae, 31–34). In classical moral theology it is a quality of a rightful act. Pleasure or delight (*delectatio*) is a wider term which applies also to emotional activity; it is morally neutral, and its rightness or wrongness depends on the deed from which it results. Even *voluptas* as such is not to be looked at askance, though in most contexts it is colored with the sense of overindulgence in sensual gratification. Much will depend on whether a moralist's philosophy is *Stoic or *Epicurean or, preferably, neither, but *Eudaemonian instead. Joy itself is not a virtue, but the effect of virtue which has reached its achievement, above all of *agapē* or charity (*op. cit.*, 2a2ae, 28). And so St. Paul (Gal 5.22) counts it among the fruits of the Spirit. Enjoyment or fruition, *frui,* is a key-notion with St. Augustine who contrasts it with using, *uti;* as the proper response to an object too good and final to be used, it should characterize our relations with God. BIBLIOGRAPHY: ThAq ST 1a2ae, 11 and 16 (esp. in Lat-Eng, v. 17, ed. T. Gilby, 1970).

[T. GILBY]

JOYCE, JAMES (1882–1941), an Irish author, born in Dublin, on which his work was to be focused, and in no mere topographical sense. He was Jesuit-educated at Clongowes Wood and Belvedere, devout to begin with, but he formally renounced Catholicism in 1903. At University College, Dublin, he specialized in modern languages and displayed a range of interests—musical, medical, theatrical—which were later combined with utmost variegation. He left Ireland in 1903, returning twice for brief periods, never after 1912. Dogged by ill-health, suffering from near blindness, he earned a meagre livelihood, often by teaching when he was able, in Trieste and Zurich. After the appearance of the *Dubliners* (1914), a collection of 15 stories, his reputation was made. It was enhanced by the long banned but clandestinely circulated novel, *Ulysses* (1916), a luxuriant fugue on the transition from religion to art, and confirmed by *Finnegans Wake* (1939), which invests a cyclic theme of theocracy and chaos with captivating and baffling mergings and echoings of meaning and allusion. For 20 years he lived in Paris, and escaped the German occupation to die a year later in Zurich. BIBLIOGRAPHY: R. Ellmann, *James Joyce* (1959).

[T. GILBY]

JOYEUSE, HENRI, DUC DE (1562–1608), Capuchin, political and religious leader of French Catholicism in the late 16th century. J. possessed a unique personality. In his early years he was part of that intimate and boisterous group of friends surrounding Henry III known as the *mignon*. Yet after his wife's death in 1587 he abandoned this worldly way of life and entered the Capuchin monastery as Frère Ange at St. Honoré in Paris, and was ordained in 1589. Circumstances, however, occurred that necessitated J.'s return to active politics. His family, the Joyeuse, were influential leaders of the Holy League and enthusiastic royalists in S France. In 1587 his famous brother, Anne, Duc de Joyeuse, was killed; another, Anthony Scipion, was drowned in 1592 and a third, Cardinal Francis, abp. of Narbonne refused to become involved. Leadership of the Holy League in the region of Languedoc, therefore, fell to J., who reorganized the League forces and held them together until Henry IV's abjuration. From 1596 to 1599 he served as Henry IV's governor in Languedoc. He returned to the Capuchin Order in 1599 and served in various administrative posts until his death. He was esteemed as a preacher and counselor. BIBLIOGRAPHY: P. de Vaissière, *Messieurs de Joyeuse, 1560–1615* (1926); Father Cuthbert, *Capuchins* (2 v., 1929).

[C. T. EBY]

JOYS OF MARY, a form of Marian piety, antedating the Seven Sorrows, which gradually emerged in the 12th cent. as the Rosary and the Litany of Loreto developed. This devotion was furthered by Franciscans in the 15th cent., esp. by St. *Bernardine of Siena, whose popular, but controversial, Mariological sermons depended on the earlier works of Peter John Olivi (d. 1298) and *Ubertino of Casale (d. 1330). Eventually the joys were fixed at seven: the Annunciation, the Visitation, the birth of Jesus, the visit of the Magi, the finding in the Temple, the Resurrection, and the Assumption. The biblical root of this devotion is seen in the astounding message brought to Mary (Lk 1.35) and in her joyful response to the grace of the Holy Spirit (Lk 1.47). BIBLIOGRAPHY: H. C. Graef, *Mary: A History of Doctrine and Devotion* (2 v., 1963–66) v.1.

[P. J. ROSATO]

JUAN, see also JOHN.

JUAN DE BADAJOZ (fl. 1499–1549), Spanish architect who designed the monumental lantern at the Cathedral of Orense (1499–1505), combining Gothic and Mudejar styles (probably derived from the lantern of Burgos Cathedral), and the vaultings of walks in the cloister of S. Marcos at León.

[M. J. DALY]

JUAN DE LA ANUNCIACIÓN (family name Llanes Campomanes; 1633–1701), Discalced Carmelite theologian. His *Collegii Complutensis . . . cursus ad breviorem forman collectus* . . . (5 v., 1670) was the definitive edition of the work of the *Complutenses, superseding all previous editions and supplements. He contributed the treatises *De gratia, De iustificatione et merito, De virtutibus theologicis, De Incarnatione, De sacramentis in communi,* and *De Eucharistia* to the *Cursus Salmanticensis,* and left in MS the first portion of the treatise *De poenitentia* for that same work. BIBLIOGRAPHY: S. Corazon, *Los Salmanticenses* (1955).

[P. K. MEAGHER]

JUAN OF AUSTRIA, DON see JOHN OF AUSTRIA, DON.

JUANA INÉS DE LA CRUZ, see CRUZ, JUANA INÉZ DE LA.

JUANES, JUAN DE (*c.*1523–79), Spanish painter of religious works showing fluid, manneristic poses in a *Last Supper* (Valencia), and *The Mystical Marriage of the Venerable Agnesto,* and scenes from the life of St. Stephen, both in the Prado.

[M. J. DALY]

JUÁREZ, BENITO PABLO (1806–72), Zapotec Indian, president of Mexico, constitutional reformer. He left his native mountains at the age of 13 and reached the city of Oaxaca, acquired an education, first in the seminary, then in the Institute of Arts and Sciences. He became a lawyer and a teacher, but early was involved in politics and by the age of 41 was governor of the State of Oaxaca. His policy in that office for impartial application of law and elimination of privilege, based on a positivist philosophy, characterized his whole political career. After being exiled in uprisings of 1850–51, he returned in 1855 to join the federal government of Juan Álvarez as minister of justice and church affairs. J.'s *Ley Juárez* suppressed the privileges of the Church and the army. He became president of Mexico in 1857 and held office until his death. In keeping with his convictions he enacted the Reform Laws of 1859 that expropriated all ecclesiastical property, suppressed all religious orders, radically secularized the schools, and enjoined complete separation of Church and State. The Church in effect ceased to have legal existence. He weathered a civil war and the exploitation of the Habsburgs, seeing the overthrow of Maximilian in 1867. Mexico regards J. as a hero for his constitutional reform, but his presidency marked the beginning of the Church's bitterest days in Mexico; he is credited also with enhancing the nation's sense of identity and sovereignty.

[T. C. O'BRIEN]

JUBILEE YEAR, in the OT (Lev 25.8–55, 27.17–21; Num 36.4), the seventh Sabbath year, completing a cycle of 49 years. The name derives from the ram's horn blown at its beginning or from its character as a year of release and liberty. As an instrument of social justice, the jubilee proclaimed God as the world's owner with human beings as his stewards; alienated lands were restored, Hebrew slaves set free, debts forgiven. It is questionable whether this was ever observed; it seems more a social blueprint expressing values of family, personal rights, and individual human dignity (see JBC: 83–84). Medieval popes applied this spiritually, beginning with Boniface VIII in 1300, who made the first year of each cent. a year of special indulgences for those visiting certain Roman basilicas. The interval for jubilee years was progressively reduced to 50 years (1342), 33 years (1389), and 25 years (1470). The jubilee or holy year begins with the opening of the Holy Door of St. Peter's on Christmas Eve. During it, Catholic pilgrims from around the world visit Rome in large numbers. The 1975 Holy Year returned to the biblical roots by placing strong emphasis on social justice and reconciliation.

[J. DALLEN]

JUBILEES, BOOK OF, a work attributed by some to a Pharisaic author and dated in the reign of John Hyrcanus (134–103 B.C.); by others, ascribed to an Essene of the Qumram community and dated 150–125 B.C. Because it purports to be an account of saving history revealed to Moses on Mt. Sinai by an angel, it is sometimes called the Apocalypse of Moses; because whole sections reproduce the contents of Genesis almost verbatim, though with variations of order, it is also called Little Genesis. The text of this apocryphon was discovered in a 6th-cent. Ethiopic version; fragments of Latin and Greek versions also exist; all of these go back to a Hebrew original, of which fragments were found at Qumram. The Book of Jubilees relates the events from creation to the institution of the first Passover, i.e., from Gen 1 to Ex 12. A Qumram origin is suggested by the anti-Hellenistic insistence on the solar calendar. The time span covered is divided into periods of 49 years, the jubilee period defined in Leviticus 25. Each jubilee is further divided into 7 ''weeks'' of years and each ''week'' subdivided into years of 364 days, i.e., according to the solar calendar. Special prominence is given to the priestly tribe of Levi. Still more important, however, are the haggadic and halakic expansions and additions to the story as presented in Genesis and Exodus. Haggadah seeks to draw edification, consolation, guidance, and admonition from the sacred events as recorded, while halakah draws precepts and norms for practical living from the text. For instance, it takes occasion of the reference to the Sabbath in Gen 2.1–3 to lay down the rules for Sabbath observance.

This work is esp. concerned with preserving the traditions of Judaism pure and intact by avoiding all contaminating contact with the gentiles and their customs. Only the strictest observance of the Law in all its details can ensure this, and accordingly the patriarchs are presented as models of strict observance. BIBLIOGRAPHY: Charles APOT 2:1–82; H. H. Rowley, *Relevance of Apocalyptic* (2d ed., 1947) 60–63; C. O. Torrey, *Apocryphal Literature* (1945); M. Testuz, *Les idées religieuses du Livre des Jubilés* (1960); R. E. Brown, JBC 2:538–539.

[D. J. BOURKE]

JUBILUS, in plainchant a long melisma on the final *a* of *alleluia*. The *alleluia* is sung by the soloist (or soloists); the choir repeats this and continues with the *jubilus;* the soloist then sings the verse, with the choir joining on the last phrase, after which the entire *alleluia* with *jubilus* is sung by the chorus. The name refers to the joyous quality of the music.

[M. GRANAHAN]

JUDAEO-CHRISTIAN STUDIES, INSTITUTE OF, see INSTITUTE OF JUDAEO-CHRISTIAN STUDIES.

JUDAEO-CHRISTIANS, generally, those in the early Church who counted themselves Christians while continuing to be Jewish in some sense, usually through descent or by certain practices (circumcision, sabbath observance, food laws). The issue is complicated by the great variety of available ways of being ''Jewish'' (Jewish Christians of Judaea and Syria differing as much from Alexandrian Jewish Christians as would Jews of the two areas differ); by the fragmentary (and polemic) nature of our sources; and by the near total disappearance of any Jewish-Christian writings, although there may remain some traces in certain *apocryphal gospel fragments and in the *Pseudo-Clementine literature (thus our knowledge comes almost completely from their adversaries).

In the first decades of the Christian movement, two groups of Jewish Christians (the original and dominant groups in the movement) must be distinguished, largely by their reaction to the crisis of the admission of gentile converts and the concomitant disputes about table fellowship and the conditions under which gentiles might enter: (1) those who simply continued in their Jewish observances but did not demand circumcision of gentile converts (Gal 2; Acts 15), and (2) those who believed that gentiles, too, were to be circumcised (Gal 2.12; Acts 15.1). For the next century, as the Christian communities became predominantly gentile, as the mission to Jews became frustratingly less successful, and as most Christians, Jewish and gentile, increasingly took pains to distinguish themselves from the three Jewish revolts against Rome, Jewish Christianity became less acceptable in many places, even though several originally ''Jewish'' practices continued fairly commonly among Christians (sabbath observance until well into the 4th cent. in some areas). In the latter half of the 2d cent. Justin Martyr (*Dialogue* 47) differentiates between two kinds of Jewish Christians: (1) those who accept Jesus as Messiah, yet observe ''the commandments of the Mosaic law'' (these, Justin believes, can be saved and may associate with other Christians; he admits that others disagree and will have nothing to do with them); and (2) those who (further) believe that observance of the Mosaic law is necessary and try to influence others (of these Justin does not ''approve''). Later Christian writers (Irenaeus, Hippolytus, Eusebius, Epiphanius) are unanimous in their negative polemical attitude toward Jewish Christian groups (usually referred to as *Ebionites, but also as Nazoreans and *Elkesaites), whom they consider ''heretical.'' Their objections to these groups center around their Jewish practices and their (alleged) emphasis on the humanity of Jesus. After the catastrophe of Jerusalem's fall there is no evidence of later Palestinian Jewish Christianity; the rabbis' strong reaction to Christianity in the 2d cent. prevented any further large-scale conversions to Christ among Mishnaic Jewry. Remarkably, a small but vital charismatic Judaeo-Christian community arose in the 1960s: they claim Jesus as their Messiah and Lord, while retaining their Jewish identity and many Jewish traditions. In the new state of Israel there are some RC parishes that use Hebrew as their sacred language for prayer and worship and whose members retain their identity as Jews in culture and politics. BIBLIOGRAPHY: J. Fitzyer, *Essays on the Semitic Background of the NT* (1974) 271–303; 435–480; H. J. Schoeps, *Jewish Christianity* (1969); *Recherches de science religieuse* 60, n. 1 (1972); A. F. J. Klijn and G. J. Reinink, *Patristic Evidence for Jewish-Christian Sects* (1973); E. Hennecke and W. Schneemelcher, *New Testament Apocrypha* (1963) 1:117–165; (1965) 2:88–166; 532–570; for contemporary Judaeo-Christians, see M. Evans and B. Summers, *Young Lions of Judah* (1974).

[D. P. EFROYMSON; J. F. FALLON]

JUDAH (Juda), name of: the fourth son of Jacob and Leah (Gen 29.31–35); one of the 12 tribes of Israel (Num 1.27); the southern part of Israel, which was a separate kingdom before and after the united monarchy (2 Sam 2.10–11; 1 Kg 12.16–20).

Judah, son of Jacob, played a leading role in the Joseph stories (Gen 37.26–27; 43.3, 8; 44.14–18; 46.28), and in Jacob's blessing he was to have the scepter (Gen 49.10), a reflection of the position achieved by the Judah tribe in Israelite history. According to the biblical account, Judah was the ancestor of the tribe of that name, which settled in the southern part of Palestine (Gen ch. 38; Jos ch. 15). It was frequently mentioned first in lists (Num 2.3; 7.12). Moses' second census gave it a strength of 76,500 people (Num 26.19–22).

During the time of Samson, the people of Judah were subordinate to the Philistines (Jg 15.11), but they grew in strength, and under David, who was of the tribe of Judah, achieved dominance over all Israel as well as the Philistines and other peoples of the area. After the death of Solomon, however, the northern tribes rebelled against David's grandson Rehoboam and established a separate kingdom, which endured until 722 B.C. The northern kingdom was called Israel, while the southern was named Judah. Judah survived until 587 B.C. when Nebuchadnezzar destroyed it and took its people into exile. A form of national life continued after the Exile, though the people no longer had their own king. Under the Roman Empire, beginning in 63 B.C. , the name of the area took the Greek form *Judea.

The genealogy of Christ makes him a descendant of Judah and the royal house of David, born in the city of David (Lk 2.11; see also Heb 7.14 and Rev 5.5).

[T. EARLY]

JUDAH AL-HARIZI (*c.*1170–*c.*1230), Spanish Jewish translator from Arabic into Hebrew of works of Moses Maimonides; author of a Hebrew epic poem *Tahkᵉ-Mōnī,* on God, man, and the world. The poem is a source of information on Jewish life in the Near East during the Middle Ages.

[T. C. O'BRIEN]

JUDAH BEN SAMUEL HA-LEVI (Hallevi; *c.*1080–*c.*1145), major medieval Hebrew poet, also author of a classic prose work on faith and reason. He was a physician who lived and wrote in Spain, chiefly in Andalusia; he died on a journey to the Holy Land. Adopting rules of poetry from Arabic and writing in classic Hebrew, he expressed a mystical love of God and the Jewish aspirations for the land of Zion. His religious and national verses became part of Jewish liturgy. Written in Arabic, his theological prose work, generally referred to as *The Khazar* (the proper title meant Book of Argument and Proof in Defense of the Humiliated Religion), utilized Platonic dialogue form, to tell of the conversion of the *Khazar king to Judaism. The work, reacting against contemporary Jewish attempts at a natural theology, argues that Jewish religious truth transcends any philosophical knowledge about God, and emphasizes Israel's historical and living experience of God, who has chosen this people for a prophetic mission to the world. BIBLIOGRAPHY: L. Husik, *History of Medieval Jewish Philosophy* (pa. 1958).

[T. C. O'BRIEN]

JUDAH HA-NASI (*c.*135–*c.*220), the prince or patriarch (Nasi) of Palestinian Jewry, who codified the *Mishnah. He was a lineal descendant of *Gamaliel and Hillel, and a man of wealth, wisdom, and holiness, acknowledged as leader even by the Romans. He is known simply as Rabbi, the teacher par excellence. Before J.'s codification, the rabbinic law, handed down orally, had grown into a mass of conflicting and confusing opinions. His text provided the authoritative and consistent norm that became the basis for the formation of the *Talmud.

[T. C. O'BRIEN]

JUDAISM, an equivocal term, here taken to mean the religion and culture of the Jewish people, as they developed in the Judean ethnarchy and the Diaspora of the Persian period (539–333 B.C.) and as they evolved through the Greek (333–63 B.C.), Roman (63 B.C.–70 A.D.), Rabbinical (70–*c.*400 A.D.), Medieval (East 7th–12th cent., West 12th–16th), and Modern Emancipation (18th–20th cent.) periods.

Although Jewish credal and ethical traditions began to develop with Abraham in the early 2d millennium B.C., Judaism as a religion and culture centering around the cult practised in the second Temple and the written and codified Mosaic Law (the *Torah) may well be considered as having begun with the reforms of the priestly scribes of whom Ezra is the best known (*c.*400 B.C. ; see 1 and 2 Chr, Ezra, and Neh); they preserved, organized, and definitively determined the corpus of Jewish Sacred Scripture, the Law, the Prophets, and the Writings. The Jews thereafter became the People of the Book, whose life and customs were enlightened and guided by loyal belief and worship of the one God of Israel, Yahweh. Such exclusive worship of one God as the sole creator and governor of all men and of the universe was unique to Israel, Jewry's more ancient name, among all peoples. Yahweh had chosen them as his special possession and was their savior and redeemer who would bring them the full culmination of all blessings, peace, and freedom, when he came to establish his final reign over all men in a renewed world, after he had condemned those who refused to accept his unique, divine dominion. This unalterable belief in and submission to the one, personal, and loving master of the universe was, and is, the essence of Judaism, which Christianity and Islam have inherited from it. The adamant legalism and exclusivity of this postexilic period assured Judaism's preservation among so many larger nations and throughout so many attempts at its destruction.

In the 2d cent. B.C., the Seleucid king Antiochus

Epiphanes tried to assimilate all Jews in his kingdom, desecrated the Temple, and evoked a courageous reaction in the Maccabean revolution that won a hundred-year respite of freedom from gentile dominance (165–63 B.C.) and strengthened Jewish longing for God's final kingdom, to be inaugurated by his anointed king, the Messiah, the successor of the great king David (see: 1 and 2 Macc; Dan). During the same era the expansion of synagogal Judaism outside Palestine led to populous Jewish communities in Mesopotamia, Syria, Asia Minor, Egypt, and the whole Mediterranean basin.

The center of Judaism in the Roman era remained Jerusalem and its Temple, the place where God's mysterious presence was most real. To Jerusalem all Jews looked with longing and they often returned there on the pilgrimage feasts of *Passover, *Pentecost, and *Booths (Tabernacles). When John the Baptist began to preach the nearness of the Messiah and God's final Kingdom (15th year of Caesar Augustus, i.e., 27 A.D., Lk 3.1), Judaism was composed of many different elements all accepting the essential monotheism but dividing into groups with varying beliefs. The Sadducees, nobles of the priestly clans, enjoyed whatever rule the Romans permitted, held only the first five books of the Bible to be authoritative, and so, refused to believe in angels, spirits, and the resurrection of God's just ones. They seem to have been most influenced by Hellenism. The Pharisees were strict observers of the written Law as the oral traditions of previous rabbis adapted it to new situations. They were devoted lay students of the whole Bible and believed in angels, the spirit world, and the final resurrection; but they also had factions: the devotees of the Rabbi Shammai were strict in observance and harsh in interpretation; those of Rabbi Hillel were more benign, considerate of human weaknesses, and confident in God's providence. The Essenes and/or Qumranites were sectarians withdrawn from ordinary Jewish life and cult, who practised repeated ritual baptisms, severe asceticism, celibacy, and a cenobitic way of life in desert areas. They were preparing for God's final kingdom, which they thought was destined for them alone. The Zealots were armed revolutionaries, with the nickname "dagger men", who engaged in guerrilla activity against the Romans to hasten Israel's independence. Apart from these Palestinian factions, worldwide Jewry included learned Greek-speaking Jews who read the Bible in Greek translation (LXX and others) and acted as channels for Hellenistic influences on Judaism (e.g., *Philo of Egypt and the author of *Wisdom of Solomon*). Hellenistic Jews maintained well-established synagogues in Jerusalem and probably in Greek areas of Palestine. Finally, there was the mass of ordinary Jews, in Palestine and in the Diaspora, who were basically unlearned in the Law and followed as best they might the scribes who had enthroned themselves "on Moses' seat" (Mt 23.1). These people of the land were held by the learned to be accursed, "a contemptible crowd, ignorant of the Law" (Jn 7.49); yet, they formed the main audience when John the Baptist and the Rabbi Jesus preached conversion from sin to prepare for God's final kingdom. The early Christians were part of the Judaism of the 1st cent., believing the resurrected Jesus to be Israel's Messiah, this "Israel of God," and identified themselves as the inheritors of all the promises that God had given his chosen people. Only a few years before Jerusalem's fall (70 A.D.) did the Christian mother Church of Jerusalem emigrate *en masse* to the Transjordan.

From among all this complexity of Judaism in the 1st cent., only the Pharisaic, rabbinical Judaism, in itself a complexity, remained in existence. The great rabbis, the Tannaites and the Amoraim, from the 2d to the 5th cent. in Palestine and Babylonia, preserved, molded, and added to, mainly, the Hillel traditions for all subsequent Judaism in the *Mishnah (completed *c.*200), *Talmud (*c.*400), and other haggadic writings. This vast, holy literature was basically a collection of diverse, often contrary, rabbinical opinions regarding the Mosaic and traditional Law (Halakah). Judaism in its learned core thus became a casuistic mulling over religious legal texts by lay scribes who were ingenious in differing with one another. However, many rabbis did comment on biblical narratives and the prophets with reverential wisdom (see *HAGGADAH; MIDRASH). The cult of tradition also preserved the Hebrew text of the Bible for later generations (see MASSORAH) and important Aramaic paraphrases and loose translations of the Bible (Babylonian and Palestinian Targums). However, many Jewish holy writings, revered by the more complex Judaism of the 1st cent., were excluded from the Jewish Bible by the rabbis, whereas the Christian Church retained these writings as they had received them from 1st cent. Judaism.

In the East, medieval Judaism was influenced by Islamic theology that had borrowed a great deal from Greek thought traditions. A violent reaction within Rabbinic Judaism against the *Karaite Judaism that denied the value of Mishnaic and Talmudic traditions and concentrated solely on the Bible, led to the strengthening of the Mishnah and Talmud as fundamentally normative and the main subject matters of Jewish religious schools. The opinions of the rabbis became more normative than the Bible itself.

In the West, Arabic, Neoplatonic, and Aristotelian influences led to the development of vigorous Jewish medieval theologians, esp. *Moses Maimonides, a great Talmudist and profound Aristotelian philosopher, who tried to reconcile revelation and reason. Judah Halevi reacted to too much human reason by emphasizing mystery and the choice of Israel, its sacred land, and the obligation to make others aware of God's glory. Further mystical and esoteric developments led to the codifications of *Cabala in the *Zohar*. All this time the population of Jews in Italy, Eastern Europe, Germany, and Spain had greatly increased, and more and more contact was made with the Christian world. Frequently cruel persecutions occurred, the worst in Spain, leading to the expulsion of Jews in 1492 and the resettlement of many in Islamic countries where they were allowed to practise their religion in freedom.

Jewish emancipation in the Christian world came gradually in the 17th and 18th cent.; ghettos were opened and

Jews began to play their role in the Enlightenment through their ancient heritage of literacy and devotion to study. In Eastern Europe a mystical renewal related to Cabala emerged in *Hasidism; it produced many influential spiritual leaders among poverty stricken Jews. Yet, like Christianity, Judaism suffered in its spiritual development from the rationalism, idealism, and scientism of modern times until now Jews can no longer be identified automatically as belonging to a united religion, to a religious people who believe the same things and act according to established custom and ritual. Present-day Jews may be Orthodox, faithful observers of Mishnaic and Talmudic traditions of pure and impure, sabbath observance, a liturgy of daily and holy day prayer (in Hebrew and in the synagogue), and prayerful longing for the Messiah as a real person; Conservative-Reformed, believers in the essentials of Judaism, but making some adaptions to modern times in dietary rules, prayer language and life, and messianic hope; Reformed, who may or may not believe in the revelational validity of Judaism, but nevertheless revere and honor their Jewish heritage, practice communal good works by social action as a pragmatic messianism, and conduct religious services in the vernacular. There is a mass of Jews, esp. in the U.S., who never or seldom go to any synagogue but take pride in their Jewish heritage and identity, whatever their belief about the supernatural. Remarkably, there are small but growing groups of Messianic Jews, who accept Jesus as their Messiah and Lord, read the NT as part of their Bible, but retain their identity as Jews, in fact, as completed Jews, who pray in Hebrew and follow many other traditions of their ancestors. (See M. E. Evans and B. Summers, *Young Lions of Judah,* 1974.)

The Judaism in the new state of Israel is as complex as worldwide Judaism, although the Orthodox tradition insists upon giving Israel an external religious form, despite the fact that Judaism is not the state religion. There are in Israel a few Catholic Hebrew parishes that use Hebrew as their liturgical language and whose members consider themselves Jews and loyal Israelis. Zionism itself comes as much from 19th-cent. romantic nationalism as from religious Judaism.

[J. F. FALLON]

JUDAISM, WORLD UNION FOR PROGRESSIVE, see WORLD UNION FOR PROGRESSIVE JUDAISM.

JUDAIZERS, a heretical sect that originated in NE Russia (Novgorod and Pskov) in 1470, partly in consequence of Western influence connected with this area's appeal to Poland-Lithuania for support in its struggle with Muscovy. Within a decade the heresy had spread to Moscow where it found extensive support. The movement was formally condemned by a church council in 1504, and many of the more prominent figures accused of being Judaizers were burned at the stake.

Because the only extant sources concerning the beliefs of the heretics are the polemical works of their opponents, estimates of the convictions and organization of the sect vary widely. Bolshakoff, relying solely on the works of the group's enemies, contends that the heretics were actually converts to Judaism, but this seems unlikely, given the large numbers of prominent nobles and clergymen involved. Other commentators have likened the movement to W European popular movements of socio-religious dissent, such as Hussitism, which they claim penetrated Russia via Novgorod and Kiev. This view overlooks the fact that the Judaizer heresy was limited to the intellectual elite of Muscovy. Fennell contends that a combination of cultural and political factors lies at the bottom of the phenomenon: the centralization of political power under Moscow, the growth of autocracy at the expense of the boyars or nobles, the subjugation of the Church to the State with the multiplication of the privileges of the former, the struggle with Russia's western neighbors for hegemony in the borderlands, and the conservative reaction of the Church to free-thinking echoes of the Western Renaissance. Indeed, despite the catalogue of heresies with which those suspect were charged (rejection of the Trinity, the divinity of Christ, the Resurrection, denial of the authority of Scripture and the efficacy of the sacraments, etc.), it seems unlikely that they shared any sharply defined body of theological opinion. Works of Judaizer literature which have survived are mostly translations of "scientific" works (astrology, divination, logic) from Hebrew, Arabic, and W European sources, as well as parts of the OT not previously translated (the Pentateuch). Such material was proscribed by the Church, the more so because those involved were the boyars who protested the Church's amassing of property (often at the expense of the nobility). Given the nature of the heretics' intellectual interests, the Russian tradition of anti-Semitism, and possibly even the Church's apprehension at the large influx of Jews into NE Europe after their expulsion from Spain, it is not surprising that the label "Judaizer" would be applied to the dissenters, partly in hopes of arousing popular hostility against them. The view that the main issue involved was not theological, but rather the struggle of the boyars to maintain their position, gains credence when one notes that the heresy was suppressed at precisely the time when the boyar party suffered a serious and decisive defeat. BIBLIOGRAPHY: J. H. Billington, *Icon and the Axe* (1967); S. Bolshakoff, *Russian Nonconformity* (1950); Cizevskij, *History of Russian Literature* (1960); J. L. I. Fennell, "Attitude of the Josephites and the Trans-Volga Elders to the Heresy of the Judaisers" *Slavonic and East European Review* 29 (1957) 486–509.

[R. H. MARSHALL]

JUDAS ISCARIOT, the 12th Apostle, treasurer and alms dispenser in Jesus' closest entourage, but secretly a thief and Jesus' adversary (Jn 12.6; 6.70). He was the betrayer, leading temple officers to arrest Jesus privately, apart from the crowds. According to Matthew he regretted his act. After he learned Jesus had been condemned, he returned the betrayal price and hanged himself. Acts reports that he fell headlong and split open his abdomen. Both stories are etiological, i.e., giving popular, early Christian reasons why a burial place S of Jerusalem, called Akeldama, Aramaic for "field of blood," had been given such a name (Mt 27.3–10; Acts 1.18,19).

In the Gospels, Judas' betrayal became a didactic symbol of how one who is intimate with Jesus could still betray him and, if not truly repentant, incur divine rejection. It was contrasted with the accounts of Peter's denials followed by true sorrow—an example of how a Christian should repent after having denied Christ (Mk 14.66–72). Jesus' startling saying with regard to Judas (Mt 26.24; Mk 14.21) is also didactic rather than a definitive judgment of the truth of Judas' destiny: it is Semitic hyperbole, accentuating the crime of using intimacy with the Lord Jesus as a mask for evil. Such symbolism continued in Christian tradition, esp. in the now altered Holy Thursday liturgy.

[J. F. FALLON]

JUDAS MACCABEE, third son of Mathathias and renowned leader of the Jewish revolt against the Seleucid kings (166–160 B.C.). Judas inherited the leadership of the rebellion from his father, defeated Apollonius, Seron, and Lysias, took Jerusalem and rededicated the temple. He died in battle after he had set the stage for independence and the Hasmonaean dynasty (1 Macc 1–9). BIBLIOGRAPHY: P. Ellis, *Men and the Message of the Old Testament* (1963) 491–505; P. Ellis, NCE 8:16.

[E. CABEY]

JUDDE, CLAUDE (1661–1735), French Jesuit, master of the spiritual life. A Jesuit from 1677, he became renowned as a preacher before dedicating most of the remainder of his life to the spiritual formation of Jesuit tertians and novices: as master of tertians at Rouen (1709–13); and rector of the novitiate at Paris (1713–21). His spiritual teaching was in the line set by L. *Lallemant. From notes taken during his conferences, J.'s doctrine was published as *Oeuvres spirituelles du P. Judde* (last ed. 5 v., 1898–1910).

[T. C. O'BRIEN]

JUDE THADDAEUS, ST., the Apostle Jude, the brother of James, who figures in the lists of the Twelve in Lk 6.16; Acts 1.13. In the lists of Matthew and Mark, the name Jude has been replaced by that of Thaddaeus, though the same individual is clearly intended. This Jude is widely held to be a distinct figure from Jude, the relative of the Lord (cf. Mt 13.55; Mk 6.3), to whom the Letter of Jude is traditionally ascribed. The apocryphal work entitled "The Passion of Simon and Jude" records the missionary activity and martyrdom of Jude Thaddaeus and Simon as missionaries in Persia. The 14th-cent. *Revelations* of St. Bridget of Sweden speaks of Christ's urging her to invoke St. Jude with confidence; this is the basis for his cult as the patron of hopeless causes.

[D. J. BOURKE]

JUDE, LETTER OF, NT book, traditionally attributed to Jude, one of the "brothers of the Lord" (Mt 13.55; Mk 6.3), who is probably not the same as Jude the Apostle (Lk 6.16; Acts 1.13). One of the *catholic epistles, this one, like that of James, is cast in the form of Hellenistic homily and is written in good Greek. Unlike the Letter of James, however, it does not seem to be specifically Jewish in outlook or to be addressed to Jewish Christians. The most probable date of its composition is the late 1st century. Its canonicity was rejected by a number of Eastern Churches, but it is included in the canon of *Muratori and was accepted as canonical in the Western Church from the 4th cent. onwards. This epistle has as its primary aim to combat the evil influence of false teachers in the Church. These seem to have been libertine in tendency, and both by their example and their teaching to have represented the freedom of the gospel as license for immoral behavior grave enough in character to amount to a practical denial of Christ (cf. v. 4). Their punishment for this is assured (v. 5–16). A striking feature of this epistle is that in developing this argument, the author quotes extensively from the apocryphal books of the *Apocalypse of Enoch (v. 14–16), the *Assumption of Moses (v. 9), and the *Testament of the Twelve Patriarchs (v. 7), though his use of these is illustrative and does not imply an affirmation of the historical truth of their contents. BIBLIOGRAPHY: C. Bigg, *Epistles of St. Peter and St. Jude* (2d ed., 1910); R. Leconte, "Épître de Saint Jude" DBSuppl 4:1285–98; B. Reicke, *Epistles of James, Peter and Jude,* Anchor Bible 37 (1964) 187–219; T. W. Leahy, JBC 2:378–380.

[D. J. BOURKE]

JUDEA, a term used in the latter biblical period to describe a geographical area. It is first used for the Persian province between Samaria and Idumaea where the Jews of Judah and Benjamin settled after the Babylonian exile. At that time it comprised Jerusalem and its environs, but in the course of time it extended to more territory, according to a list of villages Nehemiah mentions as inhabited by its people (Neh 11.25–36). Later, under the Maccabees it grew to include Joppa and the coastal plain, Idumaea, and both sides of the Jordan valley. In the Roman period and in the NT, the term Judea is used in different ways. Sometimes it refers to all of Palestine as in the accusation against Jesus before Pilate, "He stirs up the people, teaching throughout all Judea, from Galilee even to this place" (Lk 23.5); and in Peter's speech, "the word which was proclaimed throughout all Judea, beginning from Galilee" (Acts 10.34–37). At other times the term indicates the territory governed by the Roman procurators between the Plain of Esdraelon and the Sinai Peninsula (cf. Lk 3.1). In this sense it is distinguished from Samaria, Galilee, Peraea, and Idumaea. The terrain of Judea has an extreme amount of variation. The central portion lies along Palestine's central limestone ridge slightly lower than the altitude of Samaria. The N part of this central ridge in Judea is the plateau of Benjamin, slightly less than

3,000 feet altitude; the area around Jerusalem is lower, a little more than 2,000 feet, and then the ground rises to the 3,370–foot peak near Hebron. To the south is the Negeb where the ground is lower. The E slope descends from the high ridge to the Jordan Valley and the Dead Sea area. Here lie the dry, rocky hills that make up the biblical Judean desert. It is used mainly for grazing sheep and goats with an occasional plot for fruit or vegetables. This area has been neglected and abused by man for centuries. It is believed that at one time it was much more fertile and really contained the forests mentioned in the OT. The slope of the ridge to the west receives more rainfall and has a greater amount of vegetation. The foothills in this area south of Jerusalem are called the Shephelah and are separated from the central ridge by a trough. This has always made it difficult to attack Judea from the west.

[S. MUSHOLT]

JUDGE, THOMAS AUGUSTINE (1868–1933), religious founder, missionary in the South. Ordained a Vincentian in 1899, he demonstrated from the beginning his avid concern for the lay apostolate. Establishing in 1900 the foundations for the Outer Missionary Cenacle which grew to 1,000 members in succeeding years, J. turned to the South as a missionary field. In 1920 he founded the Missionary Servants of the Most Holy Trinity, congregations of both men and women, to work in home missions. He was a man of great spiritual depth, if sometimes unorthodox methods. J. served the poor and the blacks of the South himself; his congregations grew and now serve in many areas of the U.S. and Puerto Rico. He suffered under the criticism of many clergy, the financial burdens of his work, and his own poor health. BIBLIOGRAPHY: R. Purcell, DAB Suppl 1:456.

[J. R. AHERNE]

JUDGE, a public officer lawfully appointed or elected to decide litigated questions according to law. The Bible commands judicial integrity and condemns the vices of judges. It also teaches us to obey authority and commends those in authority to our prayers. The complexity of modern life creates new duties and poses new moral obligations for the judiciary. Nevertheless, the general moral obligations are for the most part well expressed in the canons of judicial ethics and the statutes. The common good requires that respect for the judicial office be supported by the qualities and deeds of the judge. The office requires many virtuous acts: impartial justice and fairness; patience and fortitude; good example; diligence and promptness joined with humility and genuine respect for the persons before the court. The judge must perform administrative duties and render decisions in a wide variety of matters. Some cases require a development of the law to fit social change; others are decided according to precedents. Judges must participate in judicial reform. Therefore the judge is obliged to have a thorough knowledge of the law and his duties. The unjust judge is bound to restitution. BIBLIOGRAPHY: ThAq St 2.2a, 67.

[R. H. DAILEY]

JUDGE, THE, a title used of Christ only twice in the NT (Acts 10.42; 2 Tim 4.8). Yet it is clear that this divine prerogative of judging men is seen as a messianic function given to Jesus (Acts 17.31; 2 Tim 4.1; 1 Cor 4.4; Rom 9.9; 2 Cor 5.10). In John, judgeship is connected with the Son of Man theme (5.27). The same Gospel speaks of judgment as already taking place (9.39). This judgment is the decisive separation made among men by their confrontation with the word. Thus John also insists that the Son was not sent to judge the world (3.17; 8.15), but the rejected word stands in judgment of men (12.48). BIBLIOGRAPHY: L. Sabourin, *Names and Titles of Jesus* (tr. M. Carroll, 1967); V. Taylor, *Names of Jesus* (1962).

[J. J. CUNNINGHAM]

JUDGES (IN THE BIBLE), charismatic military leaders who delivered Israel from oppressors; rulers of the people in the period between Joshua and Saul. The Book of Judges describes the period of the judges. When neighboring states oppressed one or the other of the loosely confederated Israelite tribes, Yahweh would inspire a ''judge'' to deliver them, just as he had delivered them from Egypt. The judges also governed the people and decided disputes. Samuel, the last of the judges, paved the way for a more stable form of government by instituting the monarchy with Saul (1 Sam 1–13). Judges in other texts were officials who administered justice by trying cases in law as magistrates (Ex 18.15; Num 11.16–17; 2 Sam 15.2–3; 2 Chr 19.5–6). The ruler—later the high priest—was the supreme judge. BIBLIOGRAPHY: De Vaux AncIsr 142–163; C. U. Wolf, InterDB 2:1012–1013.

[E. CABEY]

JUDGES (CANON LAW), officials of a court of canon law whose function is to settle legal questions presented to him. The terms are applied to the members of the diocesan tribunal, as well as the auditors of the Rota and the magistrates of the Apostolic Signatura, the Congregation for the Doctrine of the Faith, and the Sacred Penitentiary. In a diocese the judge of the common law of the Church is the bp., and for this reason every bp. must have obtained at least a licenciate in canon law or in theology. Ordinarily, however, the bp. delegates his judicial function to a tribunal of between four and twelve appointed judges, who must also be in Holy Orders. These judges are appointed at a diocesan synod and hold office until the next synodal meeting or for ten years; they may be reappointed, but may not be removed by the bp. without serious reason or without the counsel of the diocesan consultors or cathedral chapter. The judge's duties entail the certification of his own competence, to make sure that the case falls within his jurisdiction and that there is no conflict of interest involved. He is obliged to make a decision on cases presented to him usually within a month. When the law is silent on a particular point, he must base his decision on the principle of equity and on precedents in similar cases. The ethics of his office bind him to secrecy concerning cases under his consideration, whether past or present, and forbid him to accept any gifts from interested parties. Every judge, except the bp. himself, takes an oath on entering office that he will fulfill its obligations. The judge who presides over a tribunal is responsible also for deciding the order of the agenda of the court, for keeping order, and for overseeing judicial procedure.

[R. A. ARONSTAM]

JUDGES, BOOK OF. The "judges" whose triumphs are recorded in this book are a series of charismatic champions raised up by Yahweh during the period between Josue and the first of the kings to lead his people to victory over foreign oppressors. The authority of the judge usually extended over a large part of the tribal confederation, and, once his particular victory had been gained, seems to have lasted for the remainder of his life. The book comprises the stories of seven major judges (counting Deborah and Barak as one) and five minor ones.

In addition to these stories the book also contains the following elements: (1) a variant account of the conquest of Canaan (1.1–36); (2) the Canticle of Deborah celebrating the victory of Deborah and Barak and constituting one of the earliest known instances of Hebrew poetry (ch. 5); (3) the story of the migration of Dan (ch. 17–18) and the holy war against Benjamin (ch. 20–21).

The moral and religious state of Israel reflected in the book of judges is one of considerable laxity, in which religious syncretism and even idolatry abound. The confederation is extremely loosely knit, and the tribes largely independent. The original theological message conveyed by the earlier traditions is that of the power of Yahweh's spirit working through the individual judges. Superimposed upon this by the Deuteronomist editors of the 6th cent. B.C. is a further interpretation according to which each successive episode reproduces the pattern of sin, chastisement, repentance, and deliverance. BIBLIOGRAPHY: C. F. Burney, *The Book of Judges* (2d ed. 1920); C. A. Simpson, *Composition of the Book of Judges* (1958); E. Iaübler, *Biblische Studien I. Die Epoche der Richter* (ed. H. J. Zobel, 1958).

JUDGES, SYNODAL, priests-canonists, members of the diocesan *curia, having power delegated by the bp. to act in litigations, canonical investigations, matrimonial cases, and other judiciary matters. They may not be more than 12 in number. Judges appointed for special cases, and not members of the curia, are called "prosynodal judges" (CIC c.1574).

[T. C. O'BRIEN]

JUDGMENT, DIVINE, the direction by God of the world toward its consummation and of all history toward its completion at a final end determined by him. It is God's initiative effectively carrying out his providential plan through the freedom of creatures. This activity of God may be viewed from different points of view. The individual's response to God's plan is disclosed in the particular judgment when all that the individual has become through past free choices and his resultant relationship with God and creation are made clear to him. The totality of God's plan will be disclosed in what is called the general (involving all men) or final judgment (terminating history). In this disclosure all men will recognize their relationship to God, to one another, and to creation as well as the part their actions have played in the total design of history. BIBLIOGRAPHY: A. Winklhofer, *Coming of His Kingdom* (tr. A. V. Littledale, 1963); J. H. Wright, NCE 8:30–40.

[J. CORDOUE]

JUDGMENT, PRIVATE, see PRIVATE JUDGMENT.

JUDICAËL OF QUIMPER ST. (d.*c.*647–658), king of Brittany. From legendary reports about Judicaël, the last independent king of Brittany, only a few facts can be gleaned. He relinquished his throne, became a monk, and died with a reputation for sanctity. His cult was well established by the 10th century. BIBLIOGRAPHY: U. Turck, LTK 5:1178; H. Dressler, NCE 8:40.

[H. DRESSLER]

JUDICATORY, another term for the courts characteristic of Presbyterianism. *CHURCH SESSION; *PRESBYTERY; *SYNOD; *GENERAL ASSEMBLY.

[T. C. O'BRIEN]

JUDICIAL COUNCIL (Methodist), a kind of supreme court of the Methodist Church since 1939. Members are elected by the *General Conference, which also determines their number, qualifications, terms of office, and method of election. The Council decides the constitutionality of any act of the General, Jurisdictional, or Central Conferences and passes on questions of law raised in the Annual Conference and on the legality of any actions of the boards and agencies of the general Church. Its rulings are decisive and final. BIBLIOGRAPHY: *Doctrines and Discipline of the Methodist Church* (1964); HistAmMeth 3:464.

[F. E. MASER]

JUDITH, biblical name: (1) the Hittite wife of Esau (Gen 26.34); (2) the heroine of the Book of *Judith who gained entrance to the tent of Nebuchadnezzar's general Holofernes and decapitated him.

JUDITH, BOOK OF, composition of the 2d-1st cent. B.C. which has hardly any connection with historical fact;

this book has as its heroine a young and beautiful widow of an unidentifiable Jewish city called Bethulia, which is besieged and almost reduced to surrender by an immense Assyrian army under Holofernes. Judith deliberately uses her charms to inveigle herself into Holofernes' tent, succeeds in making him drunk, cuts off his head, and returns in triumph to Bethulia. As a result the Assyrian army, deprived of its leader, is routed. Achior, an Ammonite who had initially warned Holofernes that it was impossible to defeat the Jews unless they had sinned against their God, is converted to Judaism. Judith celebrates the triumph in a canticle (ch. 16) and subsequently lives on, still a widow, to the age of 105. The fact that by modern standards Judith's action is morally indefensible should not blind us to the essential message of this story, which is that Yahweh, the protector of the weak and poor, can overthrow the mightiest of worldly powers even through a weak woman working alone, provided she has sufficient faith and trust. BIBLIOGRAPHY: J. Steinmann, *Lecture de Judith* (1953); J. M. Grintz, *Book of Judith* (1957); A. M. Dubarle, "Les textes divers du livre de Judith. À propos d'un ouvrage récent," RevBibl 66 (1959) 514–519.

JUDITH, CANTICLE OF, hymn of thanksgiving with which the Book of Judith concludes (ch. 16). The structure, and much of the language of the poem, is that of the hymn as found in the Book of *Psalms. After an invitatory (v. 1) the main theme of the hymn (thanksgiving for deliverance from enemies) is announced (v. 2). Then follows a development of this motif of thanksgiving (v. 3–9), and this leads on to more general themes for praising God (v. 10–15). Finally, in v. 16–17, lessons are drawn from the facts referred to and a general warning is given to the gentiles. BIBLIOGRAPHY: A. Dubarle, *Judith: Formes et sens des divers traditions* (1966); E. Haag, *Studien zum Buche Judith* (1963).

[D. J. BOURKE]

JUDITH OF NIEDERALTAICH, BL.,(8th or 12th cent.?) widow and recluse. She and her cousin Salome were said to be of royal English ancestry. According to one account they lived before 800 in Oberaltaich-am-Donau as recluses under Abbot Walther. Another record locates them *c.* 1100 in Niederaltaich, where, after a pilgrimage to the Holy Land, Salome became blind and leprous and was befriended by the abbot of Niederaltaich, who built her a cell. Here after an eventful life Judith found her and tended her, and both women worked as servants in the monastery. They are venerated in monastic martyrologies and in art but have no liturgical cult. BIBLIOGRAPHY: G. Spahr, NCE 8:43–44.

[M. J. FINNEGAN]

JUDSON, ADONIRAM (1788–1850), Baptist missionary. While a student at Andover Theological Seminary in Newton, Mass., J. participated in the plan that led to the formation of the *American Board of Commissioners for Foreign Missions. Ordained a Congregationalist minister in 1812, he was sent immediately by the Board to India; on shipboard he, like L. *Rice, came to accept *believers' baptism, and in India, with his wife, he was rebaptized as a Baptist. From 1813 on he spent the rest of his life in Burma as a missionary, suffering adversity and hardship, including 17 months of imprisonment. He published (1840) a Burmese translation of the Bible. BIBLIOGRAPHY: life by C. Anderson (1956).

[T. C. O'BRIEN]

JUGAN, JEANNE (1792–1879), foundress of the Little Sisters of the Poor. A native of France, devoted to care of the poor and the elderly, she joined with two other women who elected her superior in 1842. The sisters supported their work of charity by begging daily. In 1843 J. was replaced by Marie Jamet as superior upon direction of the moderator Father Le Pailleur. Though in 1845 the French Academy recognized J. for her heroic labors for the poor, she was assigned by her superiors to live in obscurity from 1852 until her death. Only posthumously was she revered as foundress. BIBLIOGRAPHY: F. Trochu, *Jeanne Jugan* (tr. H. Montgomery, 1950).

[J. R. AHERNE]

JUGIE, MARTIN ÉTIENNE (1878–1954), Orientalist. Born in France, J. joined the Assumptionists and was ordained in 1901. His career was spent as a professor of Oriental theology in Turkey, Rome, and Lyons. One of the most eminent scholars in his field, he served as consultor to the Congregation for the Oriental Church from 1935 to 1954. His published works include *Theologia dogmatica Christianorum Orientalium ab Ecclesia Catholica dissidentium* (5 v., 1926–36), *Le Schisme byzantin* (1947), and, with Louis Petit, *Oeuvres complètes de Georges Scholarios* (8 v., 1928–36). The work *La Mort et l'Assomption de la Sainte Vierge* (1944) prepared the way for the definition of the dogma of the Assumption in 1950.

[J. R. AHERNE]

JULIAN THE APOSTATE (Flavius Claudius Julianus; 331–363), **ROMAN EMPEROR** from 361. After the murder of his father, Julius Constantius, in 337, he and his elder brother Gallus were kept under a certain amount of surveillance by the Emperor Constantius II. In 351 Constantius, who was lacking an heir, made Gallus his Caesar, but then had him put to death in 354. The following year he appointed Julian to the same position and gave him his daughter Helena in marriage. After a series of brilliant campaigns in Gaul, Julian was hailed as emperor by his troops in Paris in 360. The death of Constantius in 361 on his march against Julian precluded an actual contest of arms. Julian, while making an ill-advised attack on Persia, was slain after being forced to withdraw from Ctesiphon.

Julian possessed literary as well as military talents and has left some important essays and satires and a considerable number of letters, but he was of a somewhat erratic temperament. He was baptized and educated as a Christian and may even have been a lector in the Church in his youth, but his hostility to the Christians who had murdered his father, his high esteem for Greek culture, his pagan tutors such as Libanius and Maximus, and his interest in theurgy made him secretly apostatize *c.*351. As Emperor he tried to revive the moribund pagan priesthoods, forbade the teaching of pagan classics by Christians, and acquiesced in the popular uprisings against the Christians in various cities. The reputation which he gained after his death as a bloodthirsty tyrant was not deserved. BIBLIOGRAPHY: G. Ricciotti, *Julian the Apostate* (1960); A. Amore, EncCatt 6:740–744.

[M. J. COSTELLOE]

JULIAN OF CUENCA, ST. (*c.*1113–1208?), included in the Roman Martyrology in 1589. He taught philosophy and theology in Palencia before he became bp. of the frontier see of Cuenca in 1196; *c.*1200 he compiled a constitution for his cathedral chapter. Hagiographical data are of obscure origin; but he was an exemplar for bps. of the Spanish Reconquest and Repopulation, and cures attributed to him made Cuenca a shrine.

[E. P. COLBERT]

JULIAN OF ECLANUM (*c.*385–454), bp. of Eclanum (near Beneventum, Italy) and Pelagian opponent of St. Augustine. He attacked the condemnation pronounced upon *Pelagianism by Pope Zosimus, and was in consequence deposed and driven from Italy. He traveled to the East in search of support and protection from Theodore of Mopsuestia and Nestorius, among others. Instead of helping his cause, his efforts led only to involvement in further trouble. He was condemned by the Council of Ephesus as well as by various local councils. He is said to have died in Sicily. His controversy with Augustine was carried on in the four books to Turbantius and the eight to Florus. These works are lost, but much of what he wrote can be gathered from Augustine's rejoinders, *Contra Iulianum* and the *Opus imperfectum*. J., who also commented extensively on Scripture, was one of the few followers in the West of the school of Antioch. His polemic was bitter and his dialectic skilled in pointing up the weak spots in Augustine's doctrine of grace. But if Augustine can be said to have exaggerated the depravity of human nature, J. certainly erred in the opposite direction. BIBLIOGRAPHY: A. Vaccari, EncCatt 6:744–745; Altaner 442–443; F. Refoulé, ''Julien d'Éclane, théologien et philosophe'' RechSR 52 (1964) 42–84, 233–247.

[R. B. ENO]

JULIAN OF HALICARNASSUS (d. after 518), monophysite bp. of Halicarnassus in Caria. Driven from his see *c.*518 by the Emperor Justin I, Julian fled to *Alexandria. *Severus of Antioch had also taken refuge there earlier, and the two soon became embroiled in a controversy over the question of whether or not the body of Jesus during his earthly life was essentially incorruptible and impassible. J. maintained that it was; his party became known as the ''Aphthartodocetists.'' During the controversy, he wrote four treatises against Severus, but these are now lost except for some 150 fragments, mostly in Syriac. Three of his letters have been found in the 20th century. BIBLIOGRAPHY: Altaner 612; R. J. Schork, NCE 8:48.

[R. B. ENO]

JULIAN OF LE MANS, ST. (dates unknown), first bishop of Le Mans (?). Indirect sources indicate that he flourished probably in the 4th century. His biography, found in *Actus pontificum Cenomannis in urbe degentium* (composed betw. 840 and 857), is completely falsified, obviously written by someone bent upon defending the rights and possessions of Le Mans at that time. He was named patron of the Cathedral of Le Mans in 1158. BIBLIOGRAPHY: J. Cambell, NCE 8:48; H. Platelle, BiblSanct 6:1199–1201.

[F. D. LAZENBY]

JULIAN OF NORWICH (1342–1416/1423), English mystic and anchoress, author of *Sixteen Revelations of Divine Love*. Her anchorhold was attached to the church of SS. Julian and Edward at Conisford, Norwich. What is known of her is derived chiefly from her *Revelations*. She states that when she was 30 years of age and very ill, she received 14 ''shewings'' about the Passion of Christ and other spiritual matters. Two visions took place a few days later. Julian left two versions of her *Revelations,* both in the first person and following the chronological order of the visions. The short account was probably written soon after her experience; the longer version embodies 20 years of meditation on what had been revealed to her. She says that she had prayed for three things: ''bodily sight'' of the Passion, sickness, and suffering, and three ''wounds''—sorrow for sin, suffering with Christ, and longing for God. She tells simply how these were granted to her. The charge of deluded imagination or hysteria has been refuted by Paul Molinari (*Julian of Norwich,* 1958). Her thought centers on God's love and her puzzlement as to how this can be reconciled with evil and sin and with Christ's words to her, ''All shall be well.'' Text: Long version—*Revelations of Divine Love* (ed. and tr. J. Walsh, 1961); shorter version—A. M. Reynolds, *A Shewing of God's Love* (1958). BIBLIOGRAPHY: C. Pepler, *English Religious Heritage* (1958); D. Knowles, *English Mystical Tradition* (1961); *Pre-Reformation English Spirituality* (ed. J. Walsh, 1965).

[M. M. BARRY]

JULIAN SABAS, ST. (*c.*300–*c.*380), hermit commemorated. His famed spirit of asceticism moved him to live for many years in a cave by the river Euphrates in Mesopotamia. Even here he was not sufficiently removed from the world to be able to avoid the controversy with the Arians. He acceded to requests for him to return to his city of Antioch in defense of orthodoxy. His intervention apparently was effective and has been linked in Greek hagiography with many miracles worked on that occasion. He went back to solitude in Mesopotamia where he died. BIBLIOGRAPHY: Butler 1:110–111; R. Janin, BiblSanct 6:1226.

[E. J. DILLON]

JULIAN OF SPEYER (d. *c.* 1250), chapelmaster at French court, Franciscan musician and poet, known also as Julianus Teutonicus. He was author of the text and composer for the rhymed offices of St. Francis and of St. Anthony of Padua. Both were widely imitated, although the former is the more distinguished. BIBLIOGRAPHY: L. J. Wagner, NCE 8:49 (excellent bibliog.).

[V. BULLOUGH]

JULIAN OF TOLEDO, ST. (*c.*642–690), abp. of Toledo from 680, theologian and canonist. He was a member of a family converted from Judaism. His extant theological works include apologetics, *De sextae aetatis comprobatione* addressed to Jews, and *Apologeticum de tribus capitulis,* against *Monothelitism; a systematic theological treatise, in the style later perfected by Abelard, *Antikeimena seu liber de contrariis;* and a much-read devotional work, *Prognosticum futuri saeculi.* In canon law he revised the * *Hispana collectio.* He also wrote concerning the study of the classics for education. Under his episcopacy the Councils of Toledo XII-XV were convened, and the Mozarabic liturgy was revised.

[T. C. O'BRIEN]

JULIAN, JOHN (1839–1913), author of the *Dictionary of Hymnology* (1892), a work of more than 400,000 hymns. Among the most important are Ken's Morning Hymn, "Awake, my soul" (1695), Watt's "When I survey the wondrous cross" (1707), Charles Wesley's "Hark the herald angels sing" (1739), and Toplady's "Rock of Ages" (1775). The Hymn Society of Great Britain and Ireland is undertaking a revision of the Dictionary.

[M. GRANAHAN]

JULIAN CALENDAR, the calendar which Julius Caesar as *Pontifex Maximus* promulgated with the aid of the Alexandrian astronomer Sosigenes in 46 B.C. to replace the lunar calendar. It was drawn up because of dissatisfaction with the adjustments needed to keep the lunar year in line with the seasons. In effect, the Roman lunar year had 13 months: 4 of 31 days; 7 of 29; 1 of 28; and an *intercalaris,* a month of 22 or 23 days inserted after February 23. This *intercalaris* was so much longer than the approximately 10 days needed, that the civil year was at times 2 or 3 months ahead of the solar and had to be subjected to periodic correction. Caesar introduced instead the solar year of 365 days used at Alexandria and provided for an extra day after February 28 every four years to take care of the nearly six additional hours in the true solar year. The *intercalaris* fell out entirely. To bring the 12 months to a total of 365 days, he increased the length of some of them. December, January, and *Sextilis* (later called August in honor of Augustus) were increased to 31 days; April, June, September, and November, to 30. Four of the months: October, March, May and Quintilis (renamed July for Caesar) kept their original 31 days; and February remained at 28. The slight annual excess of the Julian year over the solar, known to at least some astronomers but not resolved by them, was corrected in 1582 by the Gregorian calendar. BIBLIOGRAPHY: H. J. Rose, OCD 155–156.

[M. J. SUELZER]

JULIANA OF LIÈGE, ST. (1191 or 1192–1258), promotor of the feast of Corpus Christi. J. was prioress of the Canonesses Regular at Mont-Cornillon (1222). After a vision in 1229 she became an ardent protagonist for a feast of the Blessed Sacrament. Her zeal earned her many enemies, forcing her to leave Cornillon. She was taken in by the Beguines of Namur. Six years after her death Urban IV, a former archdeacon at Liège, incorporated the Feast of Corpus Christi into the liturgy for the whole Church. J.'s cult is local. BIBLIOGRAPHY: Butler 2:37–38; A. D'Haenens, BiblSanct 6:1172–76.

[J. J. SMITH]

JULIANISTS, a heretical sect which took its name from Julian, bp. of Halicarnassus (d. after 527). They are also known as the Aphthartodocetae (holding the incorruptibility of the body of Christ) or Phantasiastae (holding a merely phenomenal body of Christ). Julian defended his position on the grounds that Christ was not subject to the effects of original sin. In the mid-6th cent. Julianism was widespread in Egypt, Ethiopia, Mesopotamia, and Armenia. However, following the opposition of the patriarchs of Antioch, Alexandria and Jerusalem together with the death of the sect's supporter, Emperor Justinian I, the heresy came to an end. BIBLIOGRAPHY: R. Draguet, *Julien d'Halicarnasse et sa controverse a vec Sèvère d' Antioche sur l'incorruptibilité du corps du Christ* (1924); R. Draguet, DTC 8.2:1931–40.

[P. FOSCOLOS]

JÜLICHER, ADOLF (1857–1938), prominent liberal Protestant NT scholar and church historian, who taught church history at Berlin (1882–89) and ancient church history and NT exegesis at Marburg (1889–1923). His two-volume work on the parables of Jesus made him famous and paved the way for the later work of the form critics, in recovering the life situations that occasioned the parables and the dynamics of the life of the primitive Church that gave the parables their final form in the Christian writings. According to C. H. *Dodd in *The Parables of the Kingdom* (1935), it was J. who taught us to mistrust the allegorical applications of the parables as made even by the

Evangelists, and to take the first step towards understanding the parable as the dynamic teaching method that it is. With the greatest possible economy of words, the teacher in parables depicts a real life situation and urges his hearers to form a judgment about it. This method at which Jesus excelled places him in line with the aims of the Pharisees and the rabbis in attempting to make the prophetic tradition real to the lives of ordinary people. BIBLIOGRAPHY: C. H. Dodd, *Parables of the Kingdom* (1935; rev. ed., 1961).

[E. DILLON]

JULIOT (JULYOT) FAMILY (fl. 16th cent.), French sculptors. **Jacques J. I** created the alabaster tomb of the Abbot of Montier-la-Celle, the famous retable for the Abbey of Larribour, and an altar for St. Nizier in Troyes where **Jacques J. II** did the retable for St. Urbain. The J.s' style was a mannerist modification of the *imagier* tradition of Troyes.

[M. J. DALY]

JULIUS I, ST. (d. 352), **POPE** from 337. J. took a leading role in the defense of orthodoxy against *Arianism in the 2d quarter of the 4th century. He assisted both *Marcellus of Ancyra and *Athanasius after they had been deposed by the Arians (339). In 340 he convened a Roman council of some 50 bps. who condemned these depositions as unlawful. The Council of *Sardica (343) united the Western Church in favor of Athanasius and supported the Pope's contention that any bishop deposed by a synod of his own province had a right to appeal to Rome. In 346 Athanasius, en route back to his rightful see, stopped at Rome and there received a letter from the Pope to the Church of Alexandria. J. built two basilicas in Rome and three churches outside the walls. Two of his letters are extant in Greek in Athanasius' *Apology against the Arians* (PG 25:247–410). Three heretical treatises by *Apollinaris of Laodicea were circulated under J.'s name. BIBLIOGRAPHY: Altaner 364, 413; Bihlmeyer-Tüchle 1:251–252, 390; E. Weltin, *Ancient Popes* (1964) 176–190.

[R. B. ENO]

JULIUS II (Giuliano Della Rovere; 1443–1513), **POPE** from 1503. He was nephew of Pope Sixtus IV, who sent him to be educated by the Franciscans. Numerous benefices were conferred upon him; he was bp. of Carpentras and of Bologna, abp. of Avignon, and cardinal by 1471. He served as legate to France (1480–81) and gained influence with the College of Cardinals and the new Pope, Innocent VIII. His constant rivalry with Rodrigo Borgia compelled Della Rovere to spend most of his time away from Rome during Borgia's pontificate (Alexander VI, 1492–1503). But with the death of Alexander VI, he returned to Rome and was instrumental in the election of Pius III, who died a month later. Thereupon Della Rovere succeeded in securing the papal throne for himself, winning support by bribery and promises. J. was apparently sincere in his hope to repair the damage done to the Church during the Borgia papacy. He wanted to recover lost territories and consolidate the Papal States, strengthen administration and finance, and eliminate simony and nepotism. He regained Perugia and Bologna from Venice by forming the famous League of Cambrai, which united Spain, France, and Germany with the papacy. He then took a position against France, and, by forming Venice, Spain, and the papacy into the Holy League, succeeded in forcing the French to withdraw from Italy. He sought to strengthen papal authority in the territory of the Church. He issued bulls denouncing simony in papal elections, forbade dueling, and effected some monastic reforms. He was spurred to convoking Lateran Council V to effect much needed reforms by the uncanonical and conciliarist assembly of Pisa-Milan. J. was distinguished as a patron of the arts and employed the best artists of the age (among whom were Raphael and Michelangelo) to aid in his plans for the beautification of Rome. The construction of the Basilica of St. Peter began in his pontificate. BIBLIOGRAPHY: D. R. Campbell, NCE 8:52–54.

[D. G. NUGENT]

JULIUS III (Giovanni del Monte; 1487–1555), **POPE** from 1550. A canonist and copresident during the first period, beginning in 1549, of the Council of Trent, he was excellently qualified for the papacy. He brought the Council back into session in 1551 but could not prevent the outbreak of the war that soon disrupted it again. J. tried to remain neutral in the quarrels of Charles V and Henry II; consequently, both of them distrusted him. J. worked for disciplinary reform in the Church and encouraged the Society of Jesus. Nepotism was his most obvious weakness. He was patron to many artists and scholars of the Renaissance.

[R. H. SCHMANDT]

JULIUS AFRICANUS, SEXTUS (*c.* 170–after 240), Christian chronographer. A native of Jerusalem, not of Africa, J. possibly acquired his title ''Africanus'' from military service. His friendly relations with Roman emperors and with the royal house of Edessa suggest that he came of a prominent family. At Alexandria he attended the lectures of Heraclas, successor to *Origen in the catechetical school. At Rome he was commissioned by the Emperor Alexander Severus to set up a public library near the Pantheon. He was probably not a cleric, despite the later tradition that he became a bishop. His chief work was his *Chronicles* in five books, the first Christian synchronistic history of the world, in which he correlated the pagan and Judeo-Christian dates from creation until 221 A.D. This chronology influenced *Hippolytus as well as *Eusebius. J. also wrote for the Emperor Alexander Severus an encyclopedia of general knowledge called the *Kestoi* in 24 books. Of his two works only fragments have survived. Two of his letters are also preserved, one of which, addressed to Origen, discusses the canonicity of the Susanna story in the Book of Daniel. Works: PG 10:63–94. BIBLIOGRAPHY: Quasten 2:137–140; LexAW 1443–44.

[R. B. ENO]

JUMIÈGES, ABBEY OF, former Benedictine abbey near Rouen. Founded in 654 by Clovis II, it was originally established under the Luxeuil observance, became Benedictine at the end of the 8th century. The abbey's commercial port was established on the Seine. During the 11th cent. a scriptorium was organized and a school of miniature painting developed. An extensive manuscript collection was assembled. The abbey was restored in the 15th cent. after it had fallen into decline during the Hundred Years War. The Reform of Chezal-Benoît was introduced in 1516, but in 1562 the abbey was pillaged by Protestants. In 1616 the *Maurist Reform was introduced and many outstanding Maurist scholars were educated there. The monastery was suppressed during the French Revolution, its buildings left to fall into ruins. BIBLIOGRAPHY: P. Cousin, NCE 7:56.

[M. A. MCFADDEN]

JUNG, CARL GUSTAV (1875–1961), formulator of *analytic psychology. Born at Kesswil, Switzerland, he studied at Basel (1895–1900), and at Zurich, became an M.D. (1902), and an assistant professor in psychiatry. His association with S. *Freud, begun in 1906, ended in 1913 with their disagreement over psychoanalytic theory. J. was founder and first president (1911–14) of the International Psychoanalytical Association. He ceased teaching in 1913 to concentrate on clinical practice and research. He traveled widely to lecture and to pursue his investigation into the mythology of primitive civilizations. J. called his own approach analytical psychology, as distinguished from Freud's psychoanalysis. He differed from Freud in his view of the libido as including, besides the sexual, other drives, esp. the will to live; in explaining the unconscious not only by the personal history of the individual but by the collective history of the race; in a different form of psychotherapy that emphasized the future possibilities of an individual rather than the neurotic repetitions of a past childhood. The most widely accepted element of J.'s ideas is his classification of personality types, under the general heading of introvert and extrovert. In connection with his theory of archetypes present in the collective unconscious, he investigated common symbols in mythology and religion. He regarded religious beliefs, not as objectively verifiable, but as a necessary part of man's recognition of the collective unconscious. J.'s *Collected Works,* planned for 17 volumes, was begun in 1953. BIBLIOGRAPHY: C. G. Jung, *Modern Man in Search of a Soul* (1933); *idem, Psychology and Religion* (1938).

[T. C. O'BRIEN]

JUNG CODEX, one of the 13 Gnostic papyri discovered at the Egyptian village of Nag Hammâdi (near ancient *Chenoboskion) *c.* 1945. This document became separated from the other 12 and was eventually purchased for the Jung Institute at Zurich in 1952. Dating probably from the 4th cent. A.D., it comprises the following treatises: a pseudepigraphical *Letter of James, The Gospel of Truth, Letter to Rheginos, A Treatise on the Three Nations,* and some much damaged fragments of the *Prayer of the Apostles.* These appear to reflect that brand of *Gnosticism known as Valentinian, and it has been suggested that the *Gospel of Truth* and *Epistle to Rheginos* may well have been written by Valentinus himself. BIBLIOGRAPHY: M. Malinine, H. C. Puech, and G. Quispel, *Coptic Text of the Evangelium Veritatis* (1956); *Jung Codex* (ed. and tr. F. L. Cross, 1955).

[D. J. BOURKE]

JUNG-STILLING, JOHANN HEINRICH (pseudonym of J. H. Jung, 1740–1817), German writer, physician (known for successful operations for cataracts), and economist. Part one of his autobiography, published by Goethe in 1777 under the title *Heinrich Stillings Jugend,* portrays, in a style reminiscent of the *Volksbuch,* the pietistic ethos of J.'s youth. To the work he added numerous sequels. Of his other writings, the best is the novel *Das Heimweh* (4 v., 1794). BIBLIOGRAPHY: W. Kosch, *Deutsches Literatur-Lexikon* (1963) 203–204.

[M. F. MCCARTHY]

JUNGMANN, BERNARD (1833–95), German theologian, seminary professor, and professor of church history at the Univ. of Louvain (1871–80); author of an apologetics text, *Demonstratio christiana* (1864); of a manual of sytematic theology, *Institutiones theologiae dogmaticae specialis* (1868) and . . . *generalis* (1874); and of a manual of church history, *Dissertationes selectae in historiam ecclesiasticam* (7 v., 1880–87).

[T. C. O'BRIEN]

JUNGMANN, JOSEF ANDREAS (1889–1975), Austrian Jesuit, historian and theologian of liturgy and catechetics. He was ordained as a diocesan priest in 1913 and did parish work in the Diocese of Brixen, S Tirol, before entering the Society of Jesus in 1917. Most of his professional life was spent in the theology faculty of the Univ. of Innsbruck, where, from 1923, he taught pastoral theology, liturgy, and catechetics. From 1926 until retirement in 1963 he was editor of the prestigious *Zeitschrift für Katholische Theologie*.

J.'s complete bibliography comprises more than 300 books and journal articles. Among the most influential works translated into English are the following: *Liturgical Worship* (tr. by a monk of St. John's Abbey, Collegeville, Minn., 1941); *Mass of the Roman Rite* (tr. F. Brunner, 1950, 1955; 1 v., abridged ed., tr. C. K. Riepe, 1959); *The Eucharistic Prayer* (tr. R. L. Batley, 1956; American ed. 1964); *The Sacrifice of the Church* (tr. C. Howell, 1956); *Public Worship* (tr. C. Howell, 1957); *Handing on the Faith: A Manual of Catechetics* (tr. A. N. Fuerst, 1959; 5th ed. 1968—tr. of 2d ed. of *Katechetik; Aufgabe und Methode der religiösen Unterwesung*, 2d ed. 1955); *Early Liturgy up to the Time of Gregory the Great* (J.'s Univ. of Notre Dame lectures, tr. F. A. Brunner, 1959); *Pastoral Liturgy* (tr. R. Walls, 1962); *The Good News Yesterday and Today* (tr. W. A. Huesman, with appreciative essays, ed. J. Hofinger, 1962); *The Place of Christ in Liturgical Prayer* (tr. A. Peeler, 1965); *The Liturgy of the Word (tr. H. Winstone, 1966); Announcing the Word of God* (tr. R. Walls, 1967); *The Mass: An Historical, Theological, and Pastoral Study* (tr. J. Fernandes, ed. M. E. Collins, 1976). One significant work, *Die lateinischen Buszriten* (1932), a study of the history of the sacrament of penance, has yet to be translated.

J. participated in the work of Vatican II as a member of the preparatory commissions, a *peritus* at the Council, and then as a member of the Consilium for the Implementation of the Constitution on the Sacred Liturgy. The title of the volume published shortly after his death in English reads "Josef A. Jungmann: A Life for Liturgy and Kerygma" (see bibliog. Fischer and Meyer). There can be no doubt of the magnitude and heroic dedication of his life to both causes in the life of the Church. The classic *Missa sollemnis (Mass of the Roman Rite),* his masterwork composed during the period of Nazi closure of the Innsbruck theology faculty (1st ed. 1948; 5th ed. 1962), was preceded by numerous published particular studies on the origins and developments, sound and distorted, of the parts of the Mass. The pastoral commitment, inspired by his early parochial experience, was visionary—so much so that the original German publication of *Good News Yesterday and Today* (*Die Frohbotschaft und unsere Glaubensverkundigung*, 1936) had to be quickly withdrawn from circulation to escape ecclesiastical censure. The impact of J.'s dedication to both liturgical renewal and pastoral preaching and catechesis cannot be measured. Two points, however, can be made. Underlying all of his work there was a deep theological conviction or rather a conviction that the theological and the Christological are the central elements in the life and worship of the Church and of the Christian. He perceived that the meaning of grace, the theological life of faith, hope, and charity, the living presence of Christ were not integrated into the devotions, the awareness, even the worship of people. To make possible renewal along these lines he pursued indefatigably his historical research. That same perception made his name the most prominent in the movement for kerygmatic theology and for preaching and catechesis as the proclamation of the good news and the communication of the realities of Christ's presence and person. The second remark about J.'s work is implicit in the chronology of his writings. Certainly they had influence before Vatican II; yet many appeared in English in the era of the Council and afterwards. Written for the most part before the Council, they yet can be read as commentaries on the Council documents and their implementation. The liturgical renewal and its subsequent revisions endorsed and promoted by the Council are illumined by his work. The pastoral spirit of the Council, and its permeation of the current life of the Church, may well be described by the title of J.'s first published book, *The Place of Christ in Liturgical Prayer,* which appeared in German (*Die Stellung Christi im liturgischer Gebet*) in 1925 (rev. ed. 1962). For it is the sense of Christ's presence, the Church's own sense of being the Sacrament of Christ, that makes its life pastoral and a proclamation of the good news in every expression of church life and ministry. BIBLIOGRAPHY: *J. A. Jungmann, Ein Leben für Liturgie und Kerygma* (ed. B. Fischer and H. B. Meyer, 1975) with J.'s complete bibliog., 156–207; J. Hofinger, "J. A. Jungmann," *Living Light* 13 (1976) 35 359; ZKT 91 (1969) 249–516, complete issue.

[T. C. O'BRIEN]

JUNI, JUAN DE (1506–77), Spanish sculptor and architect working in High Renaissance, mannerist, and protobaroque styles in stone, wood, and terra cotta. Though heavy in proportions, J. attained mystical effects in highly emotional figures (*St. Matthew,* León), and used dramatic, undulating walls foreshadowing Borromini by a century (altar of the Benavente Chapel, Medina del Rioseco, 1557).

[M. J. DALY]

JUNILIUS AFRICANUS (fl. 6th cent.), imperial official under the Emperor Justinian I, but notable for his *Instituta regularia divinae legis.* This is a work of exegesis showing the author's familiarity with the method of Theodore of Mopsuestia; it was written as a free translation into Latin of an earlier Greek work by Paul of Persia. J.'s work was known to early medieval writers in Europe.

[J. R. RIVELLO]

JUNIORATE, in a religious community, the school for the education and religious formation of candidates intending to enter the community's novitiate; such candidates are usually of high-school age. Current thought on religious vocations favors accepting candidates at a more mature age. The term is also used in some communities of religious women for the training period following novitiate and first profession.

[T. C. O'BRIEN]

JUNIPER, BROTHER (d. 1258), Franciscan laybrother. A biography of him, attributed to Brother Leo, is contained in the *Fioretti,* and there is also mention of him in most lives of St. Francis. A Franciscan from 1210, he is known to have been in Assisi, Spoleto, Viterbo, Foligno, and Alviano. Among the various things recorded of him are that he was an ecstatic and an exorcist, that he was remarkable for eccentricities that caused him to be taken for a fool, and that he pilfered from his house to provide alms for the poor. St. Clare called him God's jongleur and wished him to be near at her death. He has had no cult in the Franciscan Order. BIBLIOGRAPHY: P. Willibrord de Paris, *Catholicisme* 4:1832.

[M. J. SUELZER]

JUNKER, JOHANN (fl. 1598–1623), German sculptor active in Würzburg, Mainz, and at Aschaffenburg Castle. His ecstatic, mystical interpretations in varicolored marbles—the earliest Baroque work in S Germany—are seen in the altar for the castle chapel and the Altar of the Magdalen in the Stiftskirche, both in Aschaffenburg.

[M. J. DALY]

JUPITER TEMPLE OF, see BAALBEK.

JUPITER CAPITOLINE, TEMPLE OF, ROME, earliest and most magnificent ancient Roman temple on the Capitoline Hill, begun by Tarquin I and completed by his son in 509 B.C. Hexastyle with six peristyles, it was decorated (according to Pliny) with terra cotta, sculpture by an Etruscan artist, Vulca, from Veii, and had a quadriga on its pediment. Burned and restored many times, its representation exists on a relief fragment from a lost Arch of Marcus Aurelius.

[M. J. DALY]

JUPPE, LUDWIG (1465–fl. until 1538), German sculptor. J., who executed the tomb of Wilhelm II (1516; Elisabethkirche, Marburg), was the most important Renaissance tomb sculptor of the Middle Rhine region.

[M. J. DALY]

JURA, FATHERS OF, monastic community, founded in the French Jura region by St. Romanus (d.*c*.464) and his brother, St. Lupicinus (d.*c*.480). The two became hermits at Condat (now Saint-Claude), and attracted many followers. Later they established a monastery at Leuconne (now Saint-Lupicin) and a convent for cloistered nuns, La Beaume. Prayers, reading, and manual labor characterized the original rule. BIBLIOGRAPHY: Butler 1:438–439; L. Duchesne, "La Vie des Pères de Jura" *Mélanges d'archéologie et d'histoire* 18 (1893) 3–16.

[G. E. CONWAY]

JURISDICTION (CANON LAW), the spiritual authority of government given to the Church by Christ for the purpose of building up the Christian community. The authority may be exercized judicially, executively, or legislatively; there is no separation of jurisdictional powers in the government of the Church. The *magisterium*, or teaching authority, of the Church is also part of its binding jurisdiction. Prelates are those leaders in the Church like the pope, patriarchs and bishops, whose offices entail jurisdiction. When they themselves exercize the power to govern conveyed by their office, they are said to employ ordinary jurisdiction; when others are commissioned either by law or by an ecclesiastical superior to exercize this power, the term delegated jurisdiction is used (CIC c.197.1). The Church's jurisdiction can be exercized either in the external, or public, forum, if the matter concerned can be legally proved, or in the internal, or private, forum (including sacramental penance), if legal proof is not possible. Ordinarily, the exercize of jurisdiction within the Church is limited to clerics.

[R. A. ARONSTAM]

JURISDICTION, ECCLESIASTICAL, the power to rule and govern that is vested in the Church in the persons of certain of its officials. Although in its present sense, as distinguished from the power of order and differentiated from purely administrative function, the term is hard to find before the 13th cent.; the reality that it expresses arises from the nature of the Church as established by Christ. It is clear from the ordinary teaching of the Church that it considers itself a society completely master of its own social action and that it consequently possesses jurisdiction, the power for direction of social life in a juridically perfect society.

The source of such social power, as of all other powers of the Church, the Catholic theologian finds in the intention of Christ himself in founding the people of God as a visibly organized unity with the Twelve under Peter as his surrogates. All power had been given to him (Mt 28.18), and he sent them as he had been sent by his Father (Jn 17.18; 20.21). The Pauline Epistles and the Acts of the Apostles testify to the consciousness, shared by the Apostles and the first Christian communities, that within the new Israel direction was vested in the Apostles.

The conviction that those who gathered in Christian communion were subject to authority derived by succession from the Apostles (and without dependence on any other human authority) is attested to by the earliest postapostolic writers from the days of Clement of Rome and Ignatius of Antioch.

This power of directing ought, of course, always be exercised in a spirit of charity for the good of sons and daughters who are deeply cherished. Thus understood, jurisdiction and the juridical order need not appear incompatible with a religion that essentially involves community life and common worship, in which differences of view and disagreements inevitably occur; nor need it be distasteful to one who admits that the juridical order is part of the moral order and not a thing of mere force and violence. BIBLIOGRAPHY: E. Valton, DTC 5.2:1711–16; M. Schmaus, LTK 5:386–387; D. E. Heintschel, *Mediaeval Concept of an Ecclesiastical Office* (CUA CLS 363, 1956).

[S. E. DONLON]

JURISDICTIONAL CONFERENCE (Methodist), a large geographical region of the Methodist Church in the U.S., and the administrative agency for that region. *CONFERENCE METHODIST.

JURISPRUDENCE, a term used for the science of law, the philosophy of law, the art of interpreting and applying law. The ambiguities in use are explained to a degree by the American law tradition itself, in which the dominant trend has been positivistic, an emphasis on what the actual law and, above all, case law is. Thus discernment in interpreting law and applying it and a theory of law can easily be seen as identical. In one philosophical and theological understanding of law, however, there is a basis for identifying the theoretical meaning jurisprudence has. It is a function of the virtue of "regnative" prudence, the kind of prudence necessary to those who have ruling responsibility over a political community, whether civil or ecclesiastical. This legislative prudence (ThAq ST 2a2ae,50.1) is concerned with the direction of the community to the common good through appropriate means. Its counterpart, supporting and effecting its decisions, is *legal justice (*ibid.*, 80.1 ad 4). The rule over a community, governance, whether invested in one person or many, includes the distinct powers making up the U.S. form of government: the legislative, the judiciary, the executive. The virtue of jurisprudence is required for each. Right laws require right judgment about what truly promotes the common good (see LAW); right exercise of executive power requires right judgment in enforcing the law; right exercise of judiciary power requires right judgment in cases at law. As jurisprudence is more commonly understood, it has special reference to the judiciary act of interpreting the law (see LAW, INTERPRETATION OF), as is clear from the function of the U.S. Supreme Court. The philosophy or science of law as an academic discipline includes a study of jurisprudence because the judiciary exercise of jurisprudence establishes certain principles and sets precedents that become the basis for studying rules of interpretation. When, however, it comes to identifying what jurisprudence actually consists of in any concrete meaning, generalizations are difficult. The interpretation of law as well as legislation itself are expressions at least de facto of a philosophical concept of law, of political science, often of sociology, ethics, and a philosophical or even theological conception of man. As these are in fact all historical and cultural variables, what right judgment is—legislative, executive, or judiciary—becomes also a historical and cultural variable. In its convictions about man and about justice, however, Christian theology can and does formulate generalities that allow for an evaluation of the exercise of the governing function.

[T. C. O'BRIEN]

JURORS, members of a jury, sworn to declare the facts of a case as they are proven from the evidence placed before them. Citizens selected for jury duty are bound in legal justice to serve unless legitimately excused. Before trial they are bound to reply truthfully to questions bearing upon their qualifications and competence. They are bound to pay close attention to the evidence and the instructions of the judge during the trial. After the trial they are bound to render a fair and impartial verdict according to the evidence presented and admitted. The issue of fact is decided according to the preponderance of the evidence in civil cases. In criminal proceedings the juror cannot render a verdict of guilty unless he is convinced by the evidence beyond a reasonable doubt of the guilt of the accused. An unjust juror is bound to restitution. BIBLIOGRAPHY: R. H. Dailey, NCE 8:66.

[R. H. DAILEY]

JUST PRICE, in a sales transaction, the monetary value that reflects the real value or utility of what is sold and bought. Commutative justice requires that in the contract implicit in buying and selling, an objective *equality be respected: the buying and selling serve the purpose of benefiting both parties, and justice is not observed where one party is benefited, the other harmed. Since the value and usefulness of commodities are measured by money, the price set on them must serve an equally balanced benefit for both parties. What such a price is, however, is not simple to determine. Prices are in fact almost completely controlled by economic theory and practice: moral theology can only indicate guidelines that justice requires economics to respect (see ECONOMIC JUSTICE). A primitive criterion of the just price is the worth of a commodity to satisfy human need. That worth may be determinable according to the general assessment of a populace or a region; or be determined by law. A second determinant of worth is the seller's right not to suffer loss in a transaction; thus what the object sold is worth to him and what surrendering it entails enter into settling a price. Usefulness to the buyer is a further index; that should be based on the real, intrinsic value of the object bought; a utility arising from some personal and peculiar condition of the buyer is not a right reason for increasing the price demanded. Particularly when it comes to the basic necessities of life, a seller with an abundance would be unjust in fixing a higher price on the basis of scarcity alone. Profit is a further index to setting a price; it is legitimate since per se it repays the seller for his investment in a product. In modern commerce, of course, profit is the primary determinant of price; in the free enterprise economies the conditions of the free market and of competition are assumed to be effective economic determinants of price and profit. Precisely because such economies are managed and represent an art, they call for an equally reasonable and positive intent of justice, of responsibility to the public or common good. Clearly, price-fixing, gouging, monopolies, cartels are violations of justice. But a positive will towards justice would also require questioning excessive profits and relating prices to the general good of society. "Whatever the traffic will bear" is not a moral principle. As to buyers, paying a price far below the worth of a product by taking advantage of the seller is also unjust. Finally, with respect to articles of pure luxury or of artistic value, the mutual agreement between buyer and seller is really the sole basis for settling a just price.

[T. C. O'BRIEN]

JUSTICE, the moral and *cardinal virtue that consists in a settled intent of will to honor every form of indebtedness. Indebtedness is a relationship to another person; the relationship justice intends to preserve or to establish is that of *equality. These are the implications of a definition of justice that captures the classical Graeco-Roman thought on the subject, the definition of the Roman jurist Ulpian (d.228

A.D.) incorporated in the Justinian code of Roman law: "the constant and steadfast willingness to give to everyone what is his by right" (see ThAq ST 2a2ae, 58.1). Among the many ways human beings interact, there is one whose rightness is determined by an objective fact: certain objects or ways of acting belong to one person, and everyone else has an indebtedness to respect that fact. The respect consists in preserving or creating equality, i.e., a balance in which one gives exactly what the other is entitled to receive, and, negatively, refrains from taking what the other is entitled to have. If the exactness of this equality is arithmetical, or quantitatively calculable, the kind of justice involved is called "commutative," for which the paradigm is the exchange characteristic of buying and selling. When the parties interact as private persons, commutative justice is called "particular" or "individual"; when the party to which one is indebted is a whole community, i.e., a moral person, the justice is called "legal" or "general." If the exactness is not quantitative but proportionate, i.e., matching the relative merits or even needs of the recipient, the justice involved is called "distributive." Virtues that are analogously forms of justice and called parts of the cardinal virtue respond to other kinds of indebtedness, which is either not fully acquittable or is not objectively calculable (see RELIGION: PIETY: TRUTHFULNESS: GRATITUDE).

There is no moral issue about which there is such human consensus as the need for justice. There is, however, no consensus on the basis of justice nor on means to achieve its intent. Certain generalities in the thought of Aristotle and Aquinas touch on the complexities of the problem. Justice as an ideal is often invested with greater expectations than are warranted. Equality as sought by justice does not consist in an immediate, interpersonal relationship between human beings. Aristotle refers to a commonplace in Greek thought on the point: "If men are friends there is no need of justice between them, whereas to be merely just is not enough" (*Ethics* 8.1. 1155a 25). St. Thomas gives one interpretation of this: a friend regards a friend as another self, and there is no justice properly speaking toward oneself (*In Ethic.* 8, lect.1n.1542–43). The ideal in human relationships is at the least a friendliness that expresses the common share in humanity; even issues of justice in law are tempered by *equity, by a kind of friendliness; and the ultimate objective of law and governing is concord in the community. Friendship, even friendliness, tries to create among men the attitude of oneness, of belonging to each other. But justice stresses the otherness of the one to whom it is shown: the other's autonomy and status in his own right; liking him does not come into it. Justice is basically impersonal and impartial, bent on observing equality through the external media of human contact. The reason St. Thomas gives for the need of the will to be trained, as it were, by the virtue of justice is that the will connaturally seeks what is good for the self, but not, without virtue, what is good for others (ThAq ST 1a2ae,56.6). Justice is a developed attitude that respects others as other; that prevents self-seeking from conflicting with the legitimate interests of others: it is the virtue that protects human beings from one another. More cannot be expected of it: in essence it is not benevolence, brotherhood, friendship, or love; it is the antecedent condition for any of these. Its motivation is exclusively the objective way that things are, not the way one person feels toward another. The sphere and the spirit of justice are not the same as those of charity toward neighbor. If there is a basis simply in being human for a universal brotherhood, it is not justice that expresses or achieves it. Whether there can be, abstractly speaking, any natural analogue of the theological virtue of charity may certainly be questioned. But the meaning of justice cannot be interchanged with the counsels of the Sermon on the Mount that call for love, even of enemies. As for the impartial objectivity of justice and equality, their recognition presupposes recognition of some proportionate basis: that is the issue of *RIGHT AND RIGHTS.

BIBLIOGRAPHY: ThAq ST (Lat-Eng v. 27, ed. T. C. O'Brien) 99–105; (v. 41, *idem*) 316–320.

[T. C. O'BRIEN]

JUSTICE, COMMUTATIVE, that moral virtue which governs an exchange (Lat. *commutatio*) requiring an exact and arithmetic *equality between the parties, as in buying or selling. It is distinguished from distributive justice in which the giving and receiving are measured by the proportionate status of the parties, as in the conferring of honors or the imposing of burdens. *JUSTICE.

[T. C. O'BRIEN]

JUSTICE, DISTRIBUTIVE, see DISTRIBUTIVE JUSTICE.

JUSTICE, ECONOMIC, see ECONOMIC JUSTICE.

JUSTICE, GENERAL, see GENERAL JUSTICE.

JUSTICE, ORIGINAL, see ORIGINAL JUSTICE.

JUSTICE, RACIAL, see RACIAL JUSTICE.

JUSTICE OF GOD. Etymologically speaking, the word *sedakah* (usually translated justice in English) often has the force of genuine, true. A person or thing is *sedek* when he or it genuinely is what it purports to be. Thus there are just or true weights, "just" rain (i.e., rain which comes at the right time and in the right measure to conform to the established pattern). If we apply this general notion to human behavior, we find that a just man is one who fulfills the personal obligations arising (a) from his blood ties with other members of his family, tribe or clan; (b) from his position in the community as a whole; (c) from the personal commitments such as vows, covenants, etc., which he has voluntarily entered into. Thus justice demands that a blood relative shall support and sustain those nearest to him in their time of need, avenge wrongs done to them, etc. Again, the head of a family, tribe, or even nation incurs special obligations in virtue of his position to protect the poor and the defenseless among those subject to him, to act as their champion, defend them from oppression, and avenge wrongs done to them. He must do this without fear or favor toward the more powerful members of the community, and without thought of personal gain to himself. From this aspect honorable or even chivalrous sometimes seems a more appropriate rendering of *sedek* than the English word just. The Hebrew concept of justice also demands that a man shall be true to his word once he has pledged himself in vow or covenant, and this often demands a profound and all-pervasive personal loyalty to another, so that here unswerving loyalty or even devotion in all circumstances to another is demanded. In such cases loyalty or even faithfulness may sometimes be a better rendering of *sedakah* than justice. Correspondingly, injustice consists in personal disloyalty, treachery, or failing to fulfill one's promise to another, failing, therefore, in the obligations of one's personal relationships. This is why von Rad strongly insists that for the Hebrew, righteousness consists, not in conformity with an abstract norm, but in loyal fulfilment of personal obligations. From this aspect *sedakah* is closely related to *hesed*, which essentially and primarily signifies the loyal devotion of one covenant partner to another. As A. R. Johnson remarks, it is this virtue of loyal devotion that ". . . knits society together." The personal obligations which this virtue entails can be defined in terms of laws and so applied in concrete detail. But it is only in this secondary and subordinate sense that justice can be considered as conforming one's behavior to a norm or rule of conduct.

This, then, is what it means for Yahweh to be just. Essentially and primarily it implies that he faithfully fulfills his own decrees in relation to his creatures. His word is not "false." It does not fail. "He spoke and it *was so*. He commanded and *it stood*" (Ps 33.4–6). This word "endures for ever" (Is 40.8), and once uttered it is never recalled, never fails in its purpose. This is supremely true of his word of self-commitment to his elect, the promise to the patriarchs; and his covenant promises. He is totally and unswervingly faithful to these in spite of the sins of his people and the temporary chastisements which these entail. And he is also chivalrous in his attitude towards them, angry when they are oppressed or injured, ready to vindicate their wrongs, and above all, to *save* them. First and last, therefore, Yahweh's justice is exercised in his act of *salvation*. All this pertains to Yahweh's justice in the sense of his "honor" and to his covenant "devotion" to his people. But his decisions and decrees in their regard are also just in another sense. They bring about the maximum possible harmony, well-being, and prosperity for the people themselves. They are designed to make the people secure, happy, and respected in the eyes of other nations. They conduce to the *salom (shalom),* the basic peace and well-being of the people. On a larger scale this applies to the order of creation and of nature, too. Yahweh's ordering of the cosmos is supremely wise and right in the sense that it conduces to the harmony of the whole. Thus, *ḥesed,* loyal devotion, *sedakah,* justice, and *salom,* peace, are concepts which are so closely interconnected that no one of them can be explained without constant reference to the other two.

In the NT, justice is righteousness or justice in this sense, therefore, the chivalry, honor, integrity, faithfulness, loyalty, and mercy implied in the word *sedakah,* which Jesus fulfils in a new and unheard of degree (cf. Mt 3:15), of which he convinces the world by his death and resurrection (Jn 16.8,10) and which he inculcates in the Sermon on the Mount as a program of life for his disciples (cf. Mt 5.20). Here, too, peace and justice go hand in hand (cf. Heb 12.11), the first issuing from the second (cf. Jas 3.8). The justice of God that is *saving* becomes identified with the redeeming death of Jesus (cf. Rom 5.18). The righteousness of Christ himself is appropriated by the Christian through faith (cf. Rom 1.17; 3.28; 4.5; 5.1; 9:50–51, etc.), but that faith must be made fruitful in works of righteousness. Otherwise it lacks that integrity which is an essential part of righteousness and is vain (cf. Jas 2.14). The Christian, therefore, becomes righteous through the righteousness of Christ's redeeming death, made his own by faith and baptism. For in them he himself dies to the flesh in the Spirit which he receives from Christ (cf. Rom 6.7; 1 Cor 6.11). Thus, where the man of the OT became just by steeping himself in the Law and so uniting himself with God, the man of the NT becomes just by uniting himself with Christ, the righteous one par excellence, and living by his grace under the divine protection.

[D. J. BOURKE]

JUSTICE OF MEN. The Hebrew concept of justice, as we have seen (*JUSTICE OF GOD) must be defined primarily and essentially in terms of the obligations of loyalty, devotion, faithfulness, and integrity, which arise from personal relationships. Now the specific kinds of loyal service which Yahweh demands as covenant God of the people as a whole and of each individual Israelite are defined in his laws. Hence in this secondary and derived sense, human justice consists in hearkening to and obeying Yahweh's laws, though always with this underlying sense of thereby fulfilling one's debt of personal devotion, loyalty, and faithfulness to himself. Legalism arises only when this essential and primary sense of personal loyalty is lost and the laws are hypostatised into abstract norms instead of being thought of as personal claims of the lawgiver upon his covenant people. Nevertheless, human righteousness does consist in conforming one's life and actions to the personal will of Yahweh as defined in law, and so in loving and reverencing the law as something that is one and continuous with himself. By steeping oneself in the law, by allowing one's every thought and action to be possessed by it, one unites oneself to Yahweh himself, and can confidently count on him faithfully and loyally to uphold one's interests.

Righteousness for the Hebrew, therefore, consists in allowing his mind and heart to be pervaded by Yahweh's laws in this way. But clearly it also involves fulfilling one's personal obligations toward one's fellows, being true to what one is by nature or by one's position in the community, and to what one has committed oneself to be in their regard by human decision. Essentially, the ideal of justice toward one's fellow men consists in acting toward them with the same honor, chivalry, and integrity which Yahweh has shown toward oneself. This comes out very clearly in the so-called motivation clauses in the law codes, e.g., "A sojourner you shall not oppress: for you know the heart of a sojourner, seeing you were sojourners in the land of Egypt" (Ex 23.9, etc.).

[D. J. BOURKE]

JUSTIFICATION, a term standing for man's passage from sin to justice or righteousness. The common elements of this doctrine, shared by the various Churches, have been greatly underestimated because of the serious controversies that have arisen, esp. from the time of the Reformation. An initial distinction of emphasis can be made, however. Luther affirmed that the doctrine of justification is the *articulus stantis et cadentis ecclesiae* (the article upon which the Church stands or falls). For this reason, the doctrine is at the center of the doctrinal corpus of the Churches of the Reformation, esp. the Churches of the Lutheran confessions. In the RC doctrinal system, however, the doctrine of justification is viewed with what might be called great circumspection. Thus, e.g., in the *Summa theologiae* of St. Thomas Aquinas, it stands in a peculiar but significant place in the treatise on grace (ThAq ST 1a2ae, 113).

The terminology employed by St. Paul is commonly agreed upon to describe the process in virtue of which the sinner is justified: rebirth, regeneration, and becoming an adopted child of God. Justification is also called the sanctification of the inner man, and all hold that the righteousness of the just man is derived from the justice or righteousness of Jesus Christ. The manner in which this derivation takes place, however, is a point upon which there does not seem to be full agreement, even though ambiguities of language make it possible to construct a concordance of Protestant and RC views. In the RC tradition, justification is seen to be the work of God, who because of his mercy and through the merits of Christ declares man to be just. To this declaration, however, there corresponds the free response of man, to which is given the technical name "consent," and which consists in an act of living faith, i.e., faith enlivened by love of God. With this consent righteousness becomes inherent.

The Protestant tradition, which stems directly from the thought of Luther and hardly needs to be distinguished according to particular confessions, puts emphasis upon justification as the work of God. As regards man, the view is that justification consists in his getting a new heart through faith, while God counts him to be just for the sake of Christ. With extreme literalness this may be interpreted to mean that man is not inherently just at the term of the process and that his "justice" is really a fiction. There is no doubt that some Protestants have tended to think of justification in this way. Luther, however, makes the following statement in his lectures on Galatians, which appears to temper the position a good deal and to reduce the point of controversy: "To be outside of us means to be beyond our powers. Righteousness is our possession, to be sure, since it was given to us out of mercy. Nevertheless, it is alien to us, because we have not merited it." BIBLIOGRAPHY: S. Pfürtner, *Luther and Aquinas on Salvation* (tr. E. Quinn, 1964); W. Dantine, *Justification of the Ungodly* (tr. E. W. Gritsch and R. C. Gritsch, 1968).

[M. B. SCHEPERS]

JUSTIFICATION, DISPOSITIONS FOR. The preparedness on man's part for his changeover from the state of sin to the state of justice (or grace), can be either negative, i.e., not constituting an obstacle, or positive, i.e., influencing and inviting or deserving somehow the grace of justification. If a sinner happens to do any naturally good acts, these would be a negative disposition for his justification. Positive preparedness for justifying grace comes from acts done with the help of (actual) grace, as taught by the Council of Trent (D 1526): acts of faith, sense of sin, hope, initial love of God leading up to repentance. All these acts are a more or less remote preparation. The ultimate disposition on man's part, namely, the voluntary acceptance of sanctifying grace (see D 1528) is made possible and actual by sanctifying grace itself. It is contrition perfected by charity, i.e., the sinner's repentance made perfect by theological love of God above all things, that makes his renouncement of sin into a full actual giving up of sin (before that, it was only attrition, or incomplete renouncement of sin, in which the will remains partly attached to sin). Thus man's voluntary acceptance of justifying grace is itself a gift of God's grace. BIBLIOGRAPHY: J. M. Scheeben, *Mysteries of Christianity* (tr. C. Vollert, 1946) 635–641.

[P. DELETTER]

JUSTIFICATION BY FAITH, to gain one's righteousness from believing in Jesus Christ, not from one's own works. This doctrine corresponds to the demand Jesus Christ made upon his disciples to believe in him but is more immediately derived from Pauline literature, in which the Apostle works out the consequences of this demand (esp. in Galatians and Romans).

Always integral to Christian tradition, this doctrine stands at the very heart of the Reformation controversy. Thus, the RC position was stated in more ample fashion in some of the documents issuing from the Council of *Trent (esp. in the Decree on Justification). The Council clearly taught that faith is the first step in a possibly gradual process of justification in the sense that man is freely moved to believe when faith is conceived from the hearing of the

Gospel, so that he believes to be true that which is revealed and promised by God, namely, that God does justify unregenerate man by his grace (D 1526). Furthermore, the "formal" cause of justification is the righteousness of God himself, in virtue of which he makes man to be righteous, i.e., by a righteousness which each man receives, according to the measure of the Spirit and his own peculiar disposition and cooperation (D 1529). This disposition and cooperation can scarcely be understood unless they somehow include faith.

The Lutheran position, as worked out by Luther himself, is stated succinctly in the *Schmalkaldic Articles: "What I hold concerning justification is . . . that through faith, as Peter says [Acts 15.9], we acquire a new and clean heart, and that God, for his part, and for Christ's sake . . . reputes us as just and holy" (Art. 13). Furthermore, Luther held that the faith which justifies man is not a *good work, but rather a laying hold of the merits of Christ. Thus faith is not to be counted among the items in a catalogue of meritorious works. "Faith alone is the means and instrument whereby we lay hold on Christ the Savior, and so in Christ lay hold on that righteousness which is able to stand before the judgment of God" (*Formula of Concord, Art. 3). The *Reformed position on justification by faith is not easy to distinguish from that of the Lutherans. "We receive righteousness, not by any works, but by the faith in the mercy of God and in Christ. Thus do we teach with the Apostle that man, the sinner, is justified solely by faith in Christ, not by any works." (Second *Helvetic Confession, Ch. 15; cf. *Westminster Confession, Ch. 11.)

In this controversy (insofar as it is a controversy) the Protestant position tends more to the "justification by faith alone" idea. It would appear that this is based on a reading of St. Paul according to which "law" would stand for any work on man's part by which he intends or attempts to gain God's good pleasure. Protestants generally eschew any tendency in this direction, yet all agree that faith does not remain alone but that the just man does act righteously. BIBLIOGRAPHY: *Doctrine of Justification by Faith* (ed. G. W. H. Lampe and tr. T. Collins et al., 1964).

[M. B. SCHEPERS]

JUSTIN I (*c.*450–527), **BYZANTINE EMPEROR** from 518. Justin came from the W Balkans, of peasant background. His education, though not considerable, was sufficient. Arriving in Constantinople, he entered the elite Palace Guard, the *Excubitores,* and after a successful military career became its commander. When Anastasius I died, in 518, Justin, at the age of 68, was elected emperor. During his rule, the empire was endangered in the East through struggles with the Persians, contacts in Mesopotamia and Ethiopia and in the North by Slavs invading the Balkan provinces. Justin's religious policy promoted a return to orthodoxy and re-established relations with Rome, thereby ending the Acacian Schism of 484–519. Toward the end of his reign, he spoke out so strongly against Arianism that he provoked reactions from Theodoric in Italy and involved Pope John I in unsuccessful mediation. J. was ably assisted in the administration of the empire by his brilliant nephew, Petrus Sabbatius, who became Justinian I (527–565) and was officially proclaimed as co-emperor shortly before Justin I died. BIBLIOGRAPHY: M. R. P. McGuire, NCE 8:93–94; L. Bréhier, Fliche-Martin 4:423–436.

[M. G. SCHUMACHER]

JUSTIN II, BYZANTINE EMPEROR from 565–578. Before becoming emperor, J. and his domineering wife Sophia had inclined toward the Monophysite heresy, but they changed back to the orthodox or Chalcedonian view before their accession. J. opened his reign with overtures along the lines of Zeno's **Henoticon* to the leading Monophysites, but the heretics rejected his attempts at a compromise. Only the Armenians were for a time reconciled to Orthodoxy. In 571 J. then reverted to more forceful measures and decreed the imprisonment of all Monophysite clergy and monks. His persecution only exacerbated the situation. With Syria and Egypt in a state of schism and rebellion, J. left the Monophysite problem unresolved. He became insane in 574 and Tiberius I took power.

[R. H. SCHMANDT]

JUSTIN THE GNOSTIC, 2d-century author of the Book of Baruch. All that is known of J. is reported by Hippolytus in his *Refutation of All Heresies*. For J., Baruch is the angel of revelation who appeared to Moses, the Israelite prophets, Heracles, and Jesus. The book reinterprets Jewish ideas, particularly those from Genesis, from a gnostic point of view. For example, Gen 2.8, "God planted a garden in Eden," is read as a reference to the primal intercourse between two of the three major uncreated principles, Elohim and Eden, which initiated the complex gnostic drama of fall and salvation. The third and highest principle, Priapus, is known simply as the Good. BIBLIOGRAPHY: R. M. Grant, *Gnosticism: An Anthology* (1961) 93–100; E. Haenchen, "Das Buch Baruch," *Zeitschrift für Theologie und Kirche* (1953) 123–58.

[E. V. GALLAGHER]

JUSTIN MARTYR, ST. (*c.*100–*c.*165), foremost Christian apologist of the 2d century. Born of pagan parents in Flavia Neapolis in Palestinian Syria, J. received a good education in philosophy as expounded in the various leading schools, from all of which he drew some inspiration, but esp. from *Stoicism and *Platonism. He was converted to Christianity when a discussion with a mysterious old man led him to see that the soul cannot arrive through purely human knowledge at the idea of God. He then devoted himself to the propagation and defense of Christianity, first in Asia Minor, then in Rome, where he taught philosophy and had *Tatian among his students. Seized by the civil authorities (probably on his denunciation by a philosopher whom he had attacked), J. and several of his pupils were condemned, scourged, and beheaded. The account of his trial and martyrdom, based on court records, is indubitably authentic. J. was a prolific writer but only three of his works have survived, though certain other extant works have been wrongly attributed to him. His genuine works include an apology addressed to the Emperor Antoninus Pius and his sons; a second apology, perhaps an appendix to the first, written later and addressed to the Roman Senate; and a dialogue with Trypho the Jew. His writings are of interest as an early effort toward a synthesis of Christian and Hellenic thought. He saw the philosophers in partial possession of the seminal Logos (*Ogos Spermatikos)* that is wholly manifest only in Jesus Christ; and in Judaism also he noted a truth needing, and indeed, essentially pointing to, completion in Christ. His Christology is imperfect and he proposed a form of *Millenarianism but at a time when orthodoxy in those matters had not yet been clearly established. He is important as a witness of 2d-cent. Christianity in its faith, life, and worship, e.g., in what he has to say about the Eucharist, the baptismal liturgy, and the observance of Sunday. Particularly valuable is his witness to the doctrine of the Real Presence (*Apol.* 65.3). Works: PG 6; (tr. T. B. Falls, FathCh 6, 1948). BIBLIOGRAPHY: G. Bardy, DTC 8:2228–77; Butler 2:88–91; C. C. Martindale, *St. Justin the Martyr* (1923); L. W. Barnard, *Justin Martyr: His Life and Thought* (1967).

[R. B. ENO]

JUSTINA FRANCUCCI BEZZOLI, BL. (d. 1319), Benedictine nun of the monastery of Santa Maria del Ponte in Arezzo. For many years she lived as an anchoress in a cell at Civitella. She was forced by blindness to return to the convent. Because of her patient bearing of her condition for 20 years, she is invoked in cases of eye diseases. She was beatified officially in 1890. BIBLIOGRAPHY: Butler 1:578–579.

[T. C. O'BRIEN]

JUSTINIAN I (Flavius Anicius Iulianus Iustinianus; 483–565), **ROMAN EMPEROR** of the East from 527, one of the most remarkable rulers of all time. Born of a peasant family in Illyricum, he was brought to Constantinople, given an excellent education, and adopted by his maternal uncle Justin, an illiterate member of the imperial guard who had risen to become a *comes excubitorum* and later (518), Emperor as Justin I. Succeeding his patron in 527, Justinian set about restoring the political and religious unity of the Empire in the East and West. In 532 he concluded a peace with the Persians, who had been repelled by his able general Belisarius. He then turned his attention to the West, and in a brief campaign, again under the direction of Belisarius, he conquered the Vandals and restored the whole of North Africa to imperial rule. He then moved against the Ostrogoths, taking as an excuse the murder of Theodoric's daughter, who had placed herself under his protection. Belisarius occupied Sicily in 535, captured Naples and Rome in 536, and Ravenna in 540, which was then made the exarchy of the West. In subsequent years the Franks and Alemanni were driven from the N of Italy, and even a part of Spain was made subject to Constantinople.

Shortly after his accession, Justinian established a commission for the codification of Roman law. Under the direction of Tribonian, this was completed in a relatively short time (530–534), but it was the greatest achievement of his reign (see CORPUS IURIS CIVILIS). Intelligent, energetic, and autocratic, Justinian chose able administrators but at the same time concentrated the powers of the state in his own hands. He checked abuses in the collection of taxes, but his own heavy exactions to pay for his wars and extensive building programs were deeply resented. Among the many churches he erected was the great basilica of St. John the Evangelist at Ephesus and in Constantinople, SS. Sergius and Bacchus and the *Hagia Sophia, both still standing.

An ardent champion of religious orthodoxy, Justinian closed the philosophical schools at Athens in 529, harassed the Monophysites, and practically exterminated the Montanists. He summoned the Fifth General Council (Constantinople II), in 553 for the condemnation of the writings of Theodore of Mopsuestia, Theodoret of Cyrrhus, and Ibas, bp. of Edessa. In his political and religious reforms, Justinian was ably assisted by his wife Theodora, a woman of strong character, intelligence, and piety, who had been a dancer in the circus before her marriage to the future emperor. Since their only child died in infancy, Justinian was succeeded by his nephew Justin II. BIBLIOGRAPHY: A. M. Schneider, EncCatt 6:834–841; F. X. Murphy, NCE 8:96–101.

[M. J. COSTELLOE]

JUSTINIAN II, BYZANTINE EMPEROR, reigned 685–695, 705–711. He convoked (691) the *Quinisext Council (also known as "in Trullo II"; see CONSTANTINOPLE III, COUNCIL OF) to impose disciplinary canons not enacted at the Councils of Constantinople II and III. He was fiercely concerned with religious unity in the Empire, and to achieve it even tried to have Pope Sergius I arrested and brought to Constantinople; some compromise was reached in 711 when Pope Constantine voluntarily visited the imperial city. J. was a harsh but able ruler; he was deposed by force in 695, regained power in 705, then was killed in a mutiny against his taxation policies.

[R. H. SCHMANDT]

JUSTINIAN CODE, the name given to a code of law published by the Emperor Justinian in 529. After the promulgation of later books of laws (Institution, Digest) discrepancies appeared in the texts. Justinian then ordered a revision of the original code which was published under the title *Codex Repetitae Praelectionis* (534). This revision abolished the first code and is the one transmitted to us. The revised edition brought some changes here and there in the text of the laws. This code was built up of excerpts and parts of imperial laws decreed by Justinian and his predecessors and is divided into 12 chapters. The Institution, Digest, and Code formed a body of laws called the *Corpus Iuris Civilis,* which abrogated other laws previously in force. Justinian in this work used the work of previous jurists of the Univ. of Constantinople and Beirut. He was ably assisted by a legal genius named Tribonian.

[P. K. MEAGHER]

JUSTINIANUS, ST. (Stinian; fl. 6th cent.), Celtic hermit and martyr. Probably of noble Breton birth, he journeyed to Wales and then to either the Isle of Ramsey or the Isle of Man, where he became a hermit and was later murdered. Disagreements between sources and paucity of material render the details of his life almost wholly obscure. BIBLIOGRAPHY: J. Stephan, BiblSanct 7:10.

[R. W. HAYS]

JUSTUS OF CANTERBURY, ST. (d. 627), archbishop. With Mellitus and Laurentius, J. was sent from Rome by Pope Gregory to assist Augustine who consecrated him first bp. of Rochester (604). Because of a resurgence of idolatry, J. spent a year in Gaul. He returned to his diocese and succeeded to the See of Canterbury at the death of Mellitus. He was granted the right to consecrate his successor Romanus at Rochester. BIBLIOGRAPHY: W. Hunt, DNB 10:1120; AS November 4:532–537.

[A. WARDLE]

JUSTUS OF GHENT (Joos van Ghent, Joos van Wassenhove; 1430 or 1435–1476?), major painter at Ghent after the death of Hubert van Eyck. In Italy J. was employed (1472–75) by Federigo da Montefeltro, duke of Urbino. Probably teacher of Hugo van der Goes, J. in his pre-Italian works—*Adoration of the Magi* (N.Y.) and *Crucifixion* triptych (Ghent)—was influenced by R. van der Weyden, D. Bouts, and the Master of Flémalle. Unlike other Flemish masters, J. reduced details and integrated planes in backgrounds. Work from J.'s Italian period, though simple and monumental, shows an eclecticism of Flemish, Italian, and Spanish styles (*Communion of the Apostles*, Urbino).

[M. J. DALY]

JUSTUS OF LYONS, ST. (d. *c.* 390), bishop and monk. As bp. of Lyons J. was present at the Synods of Valence (374) and Aquileia (381). Conceiving himself to be unworthy of the episcopate because of his inability to fulfill a guarantee of safety given to a criminal who had sought sanctuary in his church, J. left Lyons and went to live unrecognized in a monastery in Egypt. His whereabouts becoming known by chance, the Lyonese sent *Antiochus, a priest, to bring him back. The emissary, however, was won over to J.'s point of view and would have stayed, had he been permitted, to share the monastic solitude. BIBLIOGRAPHY: Butler 4:108–109; AS Sept. 1:373; H. Leclercq, DACL 10.1:191–193.

JUSTUS OF TIBERIAS (fl. 1st cent. A.D.), Jewish historian. Since none of his writing remain, knowledge of J. is totally derived from citations in Flavius *Josephus and in some of the early Church Fathers. According to Josephus, J. participated in the anti-Roman revolt of A.D. 66, was imprisoned at Beirut by Agrippa II whose favor he won, but was later expelled. He is said to have written a *History of the Jewish War,* a *Chronicle of the Jewish Kings,* and (according to Jerome) a commentary on the Bible. BIBLIOGRAPHY: H. Luther, *Josephus und Justus von Tiberias* (1910); R. Krinsky, NCE 8:101–102.

[T. M. MCFADDEN]

JUSTUS OF URGEL, ST. (d. after 546), one of four brothers listed by Isidore as Spanish bishops. His short allegorical commentary on the Song of Solomon, addressed to his metropolitan in Tarragona, is one of the first works written in Spain after the barbarian invasions (PL 67:961–994). BIBLIOGRAPHY: H. Quentin, RevBén 23 (1906) 257–260; 487–488.

[E. P. COLBERT]

JUTTA, BL. (*c.* 1090–*c.* 1136), sister of Count Meginhard of Spanheim. J. became a recluse near the monastery of Disibodenberg. In time, she attracted a number of noble women to her foundation, among them St. Hildegarde. J. presided as abbess until her death. BIBLIOGRAPHY: W. Böhne, LTK 5:1230–31; Butler 4:597–598.

[B. F. SHERER]

JUTTA OF SANGERHAUSEN, ST. (d. 1260), a patroness of Prussia. After her husband's death, J. gave her property to the poor and engaged in charitable works. The last 4 years of her life she spent as an anchoress, nursing the sick, particularly lepers. Like Bl. John Lobedau, her director, she was devoted to the Sacred Heart. BIBLIOGRAPHY: D. Andreini, NCE 8:102; Butler 2:239–240; W. Lampen, BiblSanct 1033–36.

[M. J. FINNEGAN]

JUVARA, FILIPPO (1678–1736), Italian architect from Messina, pupil of Carlo Fontana in Rome (1703–14). Traveling to Turin, Portugal, London, and Paris, J., internationally recognized, designed royal palaces and gardens and the façade of S. Ildefonso, Segovia, for Philip V; and for the King of Turin extensive city plans, palaces, the basilica churches of S. Filippo Neri (1715), Sta. Croce (1718), Chiesa del Carmine (1732–35, destroyed in World War II but restored 1950–53), and two centralized churches. His plans are brilliant restatement of the leading architectural stylists of his day (Palladio, Alberti, Borromini, and Bernini), showing castles of unprecedented scale in which Italian architecture merges with other European forms.

[M. J. DALY]

JUVENAL (d. 458), bp. of Jerusalem from 420, patriarch from 451. Until his episcopate, Jerusalem was a see suffragan to Caesarea in Palestine and under the patriarchal authority of Antioch. The Council of *Nicaea (325) had granted its bishop a place of honor after the patriarchs of Rome, Alexandria, and Antioch, but juridically he was left subordinate to Caesarea. Discontented with this status, J., beginning *c.*425, consecrated several bps. on his own authority as though he were a metropolitan. At the Council of *Ephesus he sided with *Cyril of Alexandria in the hope of having his see elevated above, not only Caesarea, but even Antioch, a see then in disfavor with Cyril because its bp. supported Nestorius. Cyril, however, refused to countenance J.'s claims. Switching back to an earlier attitude of favor toward the Monophysites, J. backed their cause at the *Robber Synod of Ephesus (449), but 2 years later at *Chalcedon, he made another about-face and signed the *Tome of Leo. As a reward, the Council made Jerusalem a patriarchate, taking some territory from Antioch (Palestine and Arabia), but allowing that see to retain its precedence over Jerusalem. When J. returned from the Council he had to face the rebellion his change of opinion had stirred up among the Monophysite monks. BIBLIOGRAPHY: A. Fortescue, CE 8:358–359.

[R. B. ENO]

JUVENCUS, GAIUS VETTIUS AQUILINUS (4th cent.), Spanish priest who *c.*330 ingeniously paraphrased the Gospel, esp. Matthew, into 3,211 Virgilian hexameters (CSEL 24). His effort to free Christians from pagan models for Latin grammar and prosody had great success in the Middle Ages and to 1700. He used pre-Jerome versions of the NT and the Greek; Medieval Latin, German, Irish, and Frankish glosses are extant.

[E. P. COLBERT]

K

KAABAH, the holy shrine in the Great Mosque in Mecca toward which all the faithful turn in prayer. The direction is indicated by the *kibleh* (*qibla*) in the mihrab or niche of all mosques.

[M. J. DALY]

KAAS, LUDWIG (1881–1952), German ecclesiastic and political figure. He was ordained in 1909, appointed a domestic prelate in 1921, and an apostolic prothonotary in 1930. After Hitler's assumption of power in Germany K. went to Rome and was subsequently named Secretary of the Congregation of the Fabric of St. Peter's, a post that made him responsible for the excavations under the basilica. His political career began in 1920 when he was elected as a delegate from the Center Party to the postwar Reichstag. He became leader of the party in 1928 and remained a key figure in Weimar politics until 1933. Although he had supported Brüning, he led the Center Party closer to a coalition with Herman Hugenberg and the German Nationalists and, in the hope that he could bargain with Hitler, voted for the Enabling Act of March 23, 1933. He participated in the negotiations preceding the Concordat of 1933, but he seemed unworthy of complete trust in some matters because of the ambiguity of his position. BIBLIOGRAPHY: E. Alexander, ''Church and Society in Germany,'' *Church and Society* (ed. Moody, 1953); E. Eyck, *History of the Weimar Republic* (v. 2, 1963); G. Binder, *Irrtum und Widerstand* (1968).

[M. A. GALLIN]

KACHINA, term for Pueblo Indian spirits of nature and of the dead. Dancers dressed as *kachinas* summon these supernatural beings. *Kachina* cults among Zuñi and Hopi have persisted from prehistoric times, their ceremonies, masks, and accessories preserved in *kachina* figurines and costumes: highly symbolic in organic and geometric designs in brilliantly colored wood, horsehide, feathers, and cloth.

[M. J. DALY]

KACMARCIK, FRANK T. (1920–), graphic designer and church architecture consultant, active in the post-World War II renewal of religious art in the United States. He studied at the Minneapolis School of Art, Académie de la Grand Chaumière (1947–48) and the Centre d'Art Sacré (1948–50), Paris. With a distinctive purity and strength of line K. created forms—graphic and plastic—exquisite in shape, elegant in precision and economy of technique. As consultant to building projects (St. Patrick's, Oklahoma City) and as designer of liturgical books he has helped form a critical consciousness on religious art in the United States. BIBLIOGRAPHY: *U.S. Catholic* (Nov., 1968) p. 21–28.

[R. J. VEROSTKO]

KADDISH, a Jewish doxology exalting and glorifying the holy name of God, and usually recited in Aramaic at the end of synagogue services. Its name derives from the Aramaic word for ''hallowed,'' as in its opening phrase: ''Hallowed be the great Name of the Lord''; and may have originated with the Jewish community in Babylonia, where it served as a closing doxology to end haggadic discourse. The ancient core of the prayer is from Ezek 38.23. Other sections were added through the centuries, and its theme is echoed in the Lord's Prayer of Christians. At the end of the prayers in synagogue, the congregation responds with: ''May His great Name be praised forever to all eternity.'' There are five forms of Kaddish (Qaddish) for differing occasions. That for Renewal is recited at gravesides after burial. The Mourner's (or Orphan's) Kaddish is recited for 11 months and a day after the death of a parent or close relative, in conformity with the rabbinical injunction to praise God even in time of deepest mourning.

[E. J. DILLON]

KAGAWO, TOYOHIKO (1889–1960), Japanese Christian minister, author, social reformer. A convert at age 15 from Shintoism to Protestantism, he gave up his wealth and lived in the slums of Kobe to work with the poor. After receiving his divinity degree from Princeton Univ. (1916), he returned to Japan to organize a section of the Japanese Federation of Labor. K. campaigned for universal suffrage for men and women. In 1923 he was appointed to Japan's National Reconstruction Commission. He pursued a plan to build 1,000 small church and community centers in farmlands and fishing villages. He opposed the war with China in 1936 and was imprisoned for his pacifist opposition to World War II. In 1946 he was appointed to the house of peers, and he had an important place in Japanese reconstruction. Author of 100 books, the royalties from which were given to the poor, K. was spiritual writer, poet, and novelist. Among his published works were *Crossing the Deathline* (1921), *Love, the Law of Life, Challenge of Redemptive Love,* and *Christ and Japan.*

[J. R. AHERNE]

KAHLE, PAUL ERNST (1875–1964), German OT textual critic. His studies to distinguish various Masoretic and non-Masoretic Hebrew textual traditions revolutionized modern textual criticism. Because of Nazi persecution he left the Univ. of Bonn in 1939, and continued his career in England. Important works were *Der hebräische Bibeltext seit Franz Delitzsch* (1961); *Cairo Geniza* (2d ed., 1960). BIBLIOGRAPHY: J. Steinmann, *Biblical Criticism* (tr. J. R. Foster, 1958) 71–72, 74. *MASORA.

[T. C. O'BRIEN]

KAHRIE-DJAMI (CHURCH OF THE CHORA), ISTANBUL (12th-14th cent.), Byzantine church of central plan originally known as the Church of St. Saviour in Chora, with large central square nave (*bema*), carrying a dome on pendentives, a narthex at the W end and triple apses at the E extension, with additions of N aisle and narthex (1331). The interior is rich in marble and in mosaics depicting lives of the Virgin and of Christ, subtle in color and rich in decorative pattern, executed in the 14th cent. under the patronage of Theodore Metochites. BIBLIOGRAPHY: A. Grabar, *Byzantine Painting* (1953.)

[M. J. DALY]

KAIKEI, (d. *c.*1240), Japanese sculptor. He was trained by Kōkei, Unkei's father, his quiet, gentle figures of the Amida Buddha are distinguished from the dynamic forms of Unkei by a delicacy seen in the *Miroku* (1189, Boston).

[M. J. DALY]

KAILASA, in Hinduism the paradise of Siva, in Buddhism, Kuvera's abode. K. is a mountain in the Himalayas, N of Mānasa Lake. There Siva, the great Yogī, sits deep in meditation in mystical stillness maintaining the world, his long hair in a topknot where the crescent moon is fixed and from which flows the sacred waters of the Ganges.

[M. J. DALY]

KAILASA TEMPLE, ELLORA (757–783), rock-cut Hindu temple built by Krishna II, King of the Rāṣṭrakūta dynasty. Cut out and isolated from the mountain and carved profusely, it embraces a main shrine of Siva, a pillared hall, and small shrine for Nandi, Siva's bull vehicle. Cloisters were cut in cliffs to the sides.

[M. J. DALY]

KAILĀSANĀTHA TEMPLE. See KANCHIPURAM.

KAISANDŌ (1352?), Japanese Zen Buddhist memorial chapel to the founder of the Eihōji, Buttoku Zenshi, pupil of the Zen master Musō Soseki (1275–1351), who established the Kannon Hall (1314). The Kaisandō, the oldest example of its kind, having a sanctuary at the rear connected by a passageway to a forehall for memorial services, was a model for Zen monasteries in Japan.

[M. J. DALY]

KAISARIANI, MONASTERY CHURCH OF, late 10th-cent. Greek church of the Byzantine domed cross-plan, near Athens. Upon four columns at the crossing rests a slender octagonal drum supporting the dome. Three aisles terminate in apses, and rich frescoes decorate the interior.

[M. J. DALY]

KAKUBILLA, ST. (Cacucabilla, Cacucilla, Cucacilla, etc.), a popular legendary saint of the late Middle Ages. Represented in some regions as male, in others as female, K. was invoked against rats and mice. In Germany and Sweden pictures labeled with some form of the name portray a female saint holding two mice. Those representing her as an abbess apparently confuse her with another protectress against rodents; St. Gertrude, abbess of Nivelles. BIBLIOGRAPHY: V. H. Redlich, NCE 8:113; W. Stammler, LTK 5:1254–55.

[M. J. FINNEGAN]

KALĀM, a term in Muslim theology that evolved from its earliest literal meaning of "word" or "speech" to mean "discussion," and finally came to indicate dogmatic theology, and, in particular, the substance of a discourse. *Kalām* is often associated with the Mu'tazilite and Mutākallimūn schools of theology, which emphasized rational, polemical or apologetical arguments to support theological doctrines.

[R. J. LITZ]

KALAMAZOO CASE, a precedent-setting decision of the Supreme Court of Michigan in 1874, affirming the right of the state to levy taxes for public schools from the elementary to the university level. A group of citizens in Kalamazoo had brought suit against the school district to enjoin it from taxing in support of a high school. The decision affirmed that under the laws and constitution of Michigan the state had the right to provide for education beyond the elementary level because such education was not a luxury but a practical service to pupils.

[J. R. AHERNE]

KALAŚA, a rain vase symbolizing the exilir of life. The *Kalaśa* is the finial of the sikhara of the Hindu temple.

KALI, Indian goddess who, from alternate points of view, is both one of *Siva's consorts and one of his principal manifestations as his energy or "other self." She is usually depicted in black, frequently with a sword and bedecked with skulls or severed heads, symbolizing the destructive aspects of her activity as personification of death or time. Sometimes, however, emphasis lies on her destruction of the elements of an "enslaved" human condition; in this sense she is a liberating force, personifying the path to liberation, enlightenment, *moksha. BIBLIOGRAPHY: A. Danielou, *Hindu Polytheism* (1964) 253–273.

[D. P. EFROYMSON]

KĀLIDĀSA (late 4th–early 5th cent. A.D.), Hindu poet and dramatist, the most illustrious name among the writers of the second period of Sanskrit literature. He wrote vividly about the seasons, penetratingly of human love, engagingly about legends and history. A Brahman, he believed in a transcendent God of the universe, the evidences for whose existence are in the heart and conscience of man and an ordered world. BIBLIOGRAPHY: S. A. Sabnis, *Kalidasa, His Style and His Times* (1966); M. Mansinha, *Kalidasa and Shakespeare* (1968).

[H. JACK]

KALOGEROS (*kaloyer*), Gr. for "good old man," a term used by Greeks to designate a monk.

[G. T. DENNIS]

KALOGRIA, Gr. for "good old lady," a term used by Greeks to designate a nun.

[G. T. DENNIS]

KĀMA, Hindu god of love and lord of nymphs (*apsarases*). Armed with a bow and arrow (the Indian bow of sugarcane strung with a row of bees), K. was earlier honored in the Festival of Spring, when people paraded streets scattering red powder on one another, probably a survival of a primitive bloody fertility rite—now but a kind of merrymaking.

[M. J. DALY]

KAMARES WARE (2200–1580 B.C.), pottery from the neolithic sacred cave Kamares on the S slope of Mt. Ida, Crete, of the Middle Minoan period. Fine Kamares ware, richly decorated with geometric, floral and marine designs, is a very early glazed pottery of artistic excellence.

[M. J. DALY]

KAMILAFKION (Gr., of camel hair; also spelled *kalymavchion, kamelavkion, kamelaukion,* etc.; Sl. *kamilavka*), the ordinary headdress of Byzantine clergy in sacred orders, worn during divine service or outside the church. It is black in color and cylindrical in shape, perfectly plain among the Russians but with a small brim at the top among the Greeks. It is not to be confused with the *skouphos,* which is shorter, always brimless, and is the headdress of monks and clerics in minor orders. Monks, bishops, and dignitaries wear a long black veil called the **epanokamilafkion* over the kamilafkion. The patriarch of Moscow and Russian metropolitans wear a white kamilafkion with matching white veil bearing a small diamond cross on the front. Russian archpriests wear a purple velvet kamilafkion without a veil. The Syrian and Ethiopian clergy also make use of a similar headdress. The kamilafkion is generally worn from the beginning of the liturgy until the Great Entrance, but it is removed at the initial doxology of the liturgy, at the Little Entrance, and during the singing of the Gospel. It is not used during the Anaphora and Communion, but after the Communion of the Faithful and the transfer of the holy gifts to the prothesis table it is taken up again and worn till the end of the liturgy.

[A. J. JACOPIN]

KAMISION, in the Byzantine Churches a vestment similar to an *alb, but with wider sleeves, worn by minor clerics or acolytes.

[T. C. O'BRIEN]

KANCHIPURAM, city in the E Deccan, Madras State, India, early cultural center before being the seat of Pallava rulers (575–600). The Chinese pilgrim Hsiian-tsang visiting the city (640) remarked its splendor. Here in 700 Rajasimhavarman built the Kailāsanātha temple of Siva and Parvati with sikhara (tower), *maṇḍapa* (hall), wall of cells topped by cupolas, and caryatids of rampant lions—some with riders. A larger temple of Vaikuntha Perumal was built 10 years later in mature Pallavan style.

[M. J. DALY]

KANDINSKY, WASSILY (1866–1944), Russian painter, one of the greatest innovators in modern purely abstract, nonfigurative, or nonobjective art. After early periods in Italy, Russia, and Paris (1896) K. determined to study painting in Munich. He traveled extensively in the Near East and Europe, showing with *Die Brücke* in Dresden and establishing the Munich *Blaue Reiter* group. Moving from naturalism through Russian religious themes, using color as the *Fauves, K. introduced purely abstract, freely brushed work (*Composition I,* or *Improvisations*), often with musical connotations. He was successful in Russia during the war (1914), member of the Bauhaus (1925); his work was later labeled degenerate by the Nazis (1937). K. made valuable contributions as theorist and writer of the work *Über* *das Geistige in der Kunst . . .* (*Concerning the Spiritual in Art,* 1912), which, translated widely, influenced Klee, Marc, Macke, Von Jawlensky, and other associates.

[M. J. DALY]

KANISHKA RELIQUARY (2d cent. A.D.), important cylindrical bronze, covered and inscribed, from Shāh-jī-kī-Dherī, Gandharā (Peshawar). On the cover in relief is a seated halved Buddha flanked by Brahmā and Indra, with garland-bearing yakshas, a Buddha and a royal figure around the body. The inscription upon cleaning referred not to Kanishka I (as thought) but to an unidentified monastery.

[M. J. DALY]

KANSAS, a midwestern state admitted to the Union in 1861 as the 34th state. A Spanish expedition under Francisco Vásquez Coronado crossed the territory in 1541, and later expeditions under Juan de Onate, Charles Claude du Tisne, and Sieur de Bourgmont also visited the area. After the region was acquired by the U.S. as part of the Louisiana Purchase in 1803, it was explored by Meriwether Lewis and William Clark, Zebulon Montgomery Pike, and Stephen Harriman Long. The Santa Fe, Oregon, and similar trails provided an early means of passage through the area. In 1824 Presbyterians established a mission and school among the Indians in what is now Neosho County. Methodists, Baptists, and Quakers also set up missions during the 1830s, the time when the first major Catholic mission was established among the Kickapoo Indians. Jesuits were responsible for much of the Catholic missionary activity in Kansas. Since 1952 Kansas City has been a metropolitan see with the Dioceses of Dodge City, Salina, and Wichita as suffragans. Edward J. Hunkeler was named as the first archbishop.

Kansas' population of 2,279,000 (over 50% urban) makes it the 30th most populous state in the Union. In 1976 Catholics numbered 320,991 or 13% of the total state population. Major Protestant bodies are the Methodist Church (12.9% of the population in 1971) and the United Presbyterian Church (3.7%). Other Protestant denominations comprised 22.2% of the population. The Jewish population (1968) was 3,515 (0.16%). There are 15 church-related colleges in Kan., 6 of which are Catholic and enroll 3,959 students. There are 7,093 students attending 18 Catholic high schools. Some 19,264 pupils are enrolled in 100 Catholic elementary schools. BIBLIOGRAPHY: W. F. Zarnow, *Kansas: A History of the Jayhawk State* (1957, repr. 1971); P. Beckman, *Catholic Church on the Kansas Frontier, 1850–*1877 (1943); D. W. Wilder, *Annals of Kansas: New Edition, 1541–1885* (1886, repr. 1975).

[J. L. MORRISON; R. M. PRESTON]

KANSAS CITY STATEMENT, document adopted by the Congregational Churches. The National Council of the Congregational Churches that met in Kansas City in 1913 was outstanding in the many important constitutional changes it effected. The Statement it adopted, setting forth "the things most surely believed among us concerning faith, polity and fellowship," was simple, brief, and forward-looking in its declaration of faith. In polity it emphasized the right of private judgment, the autonomy of the *local church, and "our representative democracy." Mainly, however, it affirmed and promised to cooperate in achieving "the unity and catholicity of the Church of Christ." BIBLIOGRAPHY: Schaff Creeds 3:915–916. *CONGREGATIONALISM.

[R. F. G. CALDER]

KANT, IMMANUEL (1724–1804), German philosopher, founder of the school of critical idealism. Born in Königsberg, East Prussia (now Kalingrad, U.S.S.R.), he spent the major part of his life there, receiving his doctorate from the university and remaining there to teach. His parents were of an evangelical and pietistic bent, and K. remained a firm believer, though not in their mode. A lifelong bachelor, he enjoyed the esteem and affection of his townsmen and colleagues as a charming guest, an affable host, and a brilliant lecturer.

K. is a major figure in the history of thought. He has been described as "the first professional philosopher." Certainly no philosopher since his day remains unaffected by him. His philosophical formation had been that of Continental rationalism, most immediately in terms of Leibniz and Christian Wolff. He was well-read, even expert, in the sciences, and this was to prove an important factor in his method of philosophizing, for he had a grasp of the empirical, lacking in the rationalist school. He tells us that Hume "woke him from his dogmatic slumber [of rationalism]." His writings until 1770 show a preoccupation with the sciences, esp. physics and mathematics, and with the rationalist mode of thought. Thereafter until his death he was engaged in the reconstruction of philosophy. He sought to give to metaphysics the clarity and certitude that he found in the mathematical physics of Newton.

K. began as an idealist. Faced with the impasse produced by the conflict of empiricism and rationalism, he put the problem: How are synthetic a priori judgments possible? That is to say: How can we have knowledge, known to be true, through judgments whose content concerns the sensible and contingent (synthetic), but whose subject and predicate are necessarily connected (a priori)? In answer to this he proposes a distinction. Outside the knowing subject there exist *noumena*. The *noumenon—das Ding an sich,* the thing-in-itself—is unknowable. Our knowledge is of *phenomena*. The *phenomenon* represents extramental reality, and it is the product of our knowing faculties (sense, understanding, reason)—but it is considered apart from these notes in K.'s analysis. The raw data of sensation give the matter of our knowledge, but this matter is known only under the forms of space and time. These forms or categories are innate and present before any sense experience. They are a priori.

The sensible intuition under the forms of space and time is the matter for the understanding. To be true and certain, a judgment must be universal and necessary. These notes of universality and necessity are given by concepts or categories of the understanding. As in the sense order, so here these are a priori forms. At this point in his analysis K. has established, to his satisfaction, the validity of scientific knowledge—say, the conclusions of mathematical physics. But this knowledge is phenomenal only. It does not reach to the thing-in-itself, the reality outside the mind. Noumenal knowledge is achieved by the faculties of understanding (*Verstand*) and reason (*Vernunft*). A further set of innate, a priori forms is invoked. These are the regulative ideas of God, the soul, and the material world. These give the end product of "pure reason." But even this is not enough, and K. sees this clearly, for such knowledge is hypothetical, not necessary. It is knowledge of what can be. The ideas of pure reason are, in themselves, devoid of phenomenal content.

The gulf is bridged by an act of faith. The faculty of reason is not only "pure," it is "practical." K.'s examination of the process of knowledge has established the validity of the sciences, but such knowledge is restricted to space and time. It is not yet a metaphysics. Practical reason employs the conceptions of God, the immortality of the soul, the freedom of the will. The validity of these conceptions, the very existence of what they represent, cannot be established by the noumenal–phenomenal critique. They must be accepted by what K. calls "faith." It might be clearer to say they are values which the knowing self (by the practical reason) imposes upon experience.

In the course of his critique of knowledge, K. examines the proofs for the existence of God. He reduces all proofs that men have offered to three: the ontological (Anselm, Descartes, Leibniz), the cosmological (arguing from contingent to necessary being), and the physico–theological (from order in the universe). He rejects all of them as inadequate, for (in his system) they are based on a sort of knowledge that cannot transcend space and time. Our notion of God (as those of the soul and of the totality of the universe) must be attained by the regulative concept of the practical reason.

K.'s ethical thought strikes a new note. Ancient Greek thought was concerned with the nature of the good (read "happiness"). Man rationally should so act as to achieve happiness. Stoic philosophers added the note of motivation. Christian thinkers, accepting God as a benevolent lawmaker, saw right conduct as the following of a common law issued by an all-knowing and all-powerful Father. Imbued with this Christian ethic, K. places duty at the center of his system. But as a philosopher and a man of his times, he makes reason rather than God the source of the moral law. Man's reason, which makes him unique in the created universe, has as its function the perception of the moral law. A good will in man enables him to follow the law thus seen. A good man is one who does his duty, and duty is defined as "the necessity of acting from respect for the law." Every good act of man must be from principle and not be simply a means to an end, even the end of happiness. The fundamental moral principle that regulates all particular ones is the categorical imperative: so act that the maxim or principle regulating your particular action could serve as a universal law for all men.

K.'s notion of duty as central leads him to the assertion of the freedom of man's will. If a man must act rationally to act morally, he can act rationally. However, the necessity imposed by duty cannot be the necessity of causality in the material world. Man must be autonomous. K. further derives (in the order of practical reason) the existence of God from this concept of duty: the will of man acting for duty's sake seeks a supreme good that cannot be achieved without the help of a Supreme Being acting by intelligence and will. It involves, therefore, a practical acceptance of God's existence as a fact. Finally, K. proves the immortality of the soul from the notion of duty: man cannot be perfectly in accord with the moral law at any given instant. Such perfection requires infinite duration and the endless existence of the moral personality, that is, of the individual.

Intricate, subtle, difficult as it is in concept and vocabulary, K.'s system remains a monument. His reexamination of philosophy, the questions he asked, even more than the answers he gave, influence men today. BIBLIOGRAPHY: W. H. Walsh, EncPhil 4:305–323, with excellent bibliog.; A. W. Wood, *Kant's Moral Religion* (1970); J. Collins, *Interpreting Modern Philosophy* (1972); H. J. Paton, *Categorical Imperative; A Study in Kant's Moral Philosophy* (pa. 1971).

[W. B. MAHONEY]

KAPILAVASTU, capital city of Kosala, sacred as the birthplace of the Buddha, who delivered in the Lumbinī grove of sāl trees near Kapilavastu, by Mahāmāyā, chief queen of Śuddhodhana, King of the Śākyas, was named Prince Siddhārtha on the fifth day after his birth, with the *gotra* name Gautama, one of the legendary seers from which the brāhman caste claimed descent, and so is called the Gautama Buddha.

[M. J. DALY]

KARAISM (from qārā'i, Scripture), a religious movement originating with an 8th-cent. Jewish sect, founded by Anan ben David, denying authority to the Talmudic-rabbinical tradition of Judaism, recognizing Scripture as the only source of religious belief and practice. Though Karaites claim to have begun in the time of Jeroboam and some scholars suggest a connection between the Dead Sea sect and the Karaites, the sect emerged among Jews living outside Babylonia. Anan's basic advice to his followers was to search the Torah personally and not rely on his nor anyone else's opinions. After Anan's death the sect splintered into numerous transient subsects. During the 9th cent. Benjamin ben Moses Nahavendi began consolidating Karaism. Though occasionally borrowing precepts from Rabbinites which were not binding on Karaites, he made private independent study of Torah, Prophets, and Hagiographa a fundamental principle. He also alleviated anti-Rabbinite hostility. Using *Philo's notion of *logos,* he sought to eliminate anthropomorphism from the Bible. Daniel ben Moses al-Qumisi, late 9th-cent. scholar in Jerusalem, objected to Benjamin's hermeneutics and stressed adherence to the literal sense of Scripture. During the 10th cent. Karaism blossomed in literature, scholarship, masoretic and grammatical exegesis, and theology, their literature mainly written in Arabic. The Karaite community at Jerusalem was destroyed in 1099 when the First Crusade under Godfrey of Bouillon took the city and burned the synagogue where members of the Jewish community had sought refuge. Karaite activity shifted to Byzantium and Turkey. During Suleiman the Magnificent's reign Karaism again flourished, its scholars adding the secular sciences to their religious study. A rapprochement between Karaite and Rabbinite scholars occurred during the 15th and 16th centuries. Following persecution of the Jews during the 17th cent., Christian interest in the sect grew, resulting in a number of works' being written (1690–1720) about the sect. When Russia gained control of Lithuania and the Crimea, where Karaite activity had shifted during the 17th and 18th cent., Empress Catherine II legally distinguished between Jews and Karaites in 1795, relieving members of the sect from the double tax and allowing them to own land. By early 19th cent. the rift between the groups had enlarged; Karaites had Rabbinites expelled from Troki (1835), and they officially designated themselves as Russian Karaites of the OT Faith, not Jews-Karaites. By 1863 Karaites had all the rights of native Russians. The 20th cent. saw the decline in the number of Karaites. Those in the Middle East resettled in Israel when the state was established. But there are few organized Karaite communities in the world.

[R. J. LITZ]

KARDEC, ALLAN (Hippolyte Léon Denizard Rivail; 1804–69), pseudonym of the early French investigator of psychic phenomena and exponent of Spiritism. After early experiments with hypnosis and mesmeric magnetism, he began (1854) working on the phenomenon of a table that danced under the resting hands of seated persons. He concluded that some other extracorporeal agent, a spirit with intelligence and physical potency, not the presence of the people or animal magnetism, caused the distinctive movements of the table. Communications with these spirits, in particular with the souls of the dead, were designated by Kardec as Spiritism. Through Spiritism he believed he could answer man's many religious and moral questions. He founded the *Revue Spirite* (1857) and the Society of Spiritual Studies (1858). His *Le Livre des esprits contenant les principes de la doctrine spirite* (1857), over 1,000 questions with answers dictated by evoked spirits, became the basis for formal Spiritism. His other works include guides for evocators or mediums and spiritist tracts on religious topics, all of which were put on the Index in 1864.

[R. J. LITZ]

KARIYE DJAMI (ISTANBUL), a Byzantine church (11th to 14th cent.) now a museum. Its mosaics and wall-paintings were executed *c.*1305–20 under the patronage of Theodore Metochites. Most striking masterworks of the Paleologan period the frescoes in the Parecclesion—full-length portraits of Church Fathers and Saints, Christ framed in a white *mandorla* and extensions in vaults are unique in Byzantine art—in this final century of its expression. Outstanding in their completeness and quality, they exemplify the late Byzantine Style in its most resourceful period, imaging things not seen. BIBLIOGRAPHY: P. A. Underwood, *Kariye Djami* (3 v. 1967).

[R. C. MARKS]

KARLE (KARLI), site of a great Hinayana Buddhist rock-cut **caitya hall* (*c.*75 A.D.) near Bombay. Important are the façade screen of rock and two free-standing lotus columns supporting addorsed lions in the Indian-Persian stylistic synthesis of the Mauryan era. Later Buddha figures are in the Mahayana tradition.

[M. J. DALY]

KARLOVCI, CHURCH OF, a former autonomous Orthodox Church made up of Serbs who were given refuge from the Turks in the late 17th century. Emperor Franz Josef granted the metropolitan of Karlovci the personal title of patriarch in 1848, but from an ecclesiastical viewpoint the abps. of Karlovci were considered exarchs of the Serbian patriarch. Serbia was incorporated into Yugoslavia in 1918, and in 1920 the patriarchate of *Serbia was reestablished with the Church of Karlovci joining the three metropolias of Belgrade, Bosnia, Montenegro and the diocese of Dalmatia. The head of the Serbian patriarchate is titled abp. of Pec, metropolitan of Belgrade-Karlovci, and patriarch of Serbia. BIBLIOGRAPHY: J. Mousset, *La Serbie et son Église (1830–1904)* (1939).

[F. T. RYAN]

KARLOVCI, SYNOD OF (1921), a *sobor of exiled Russian Orthodox composed of 12 bps., 30 to 40 priests and about 100 laymen who met in Sremski Karlovci, Serbia, from Nov. 21 until Dec. 3, 1921, with the approval of Patriarch Dimitrije of Serbia. Headed by Metropolitan Antony Khrapovitsky of Kiev, those present passed resolutions condemning the Bolshevik regime, proclaiming their wish for the restoration of the Romanov dynasty, and appealing to the European Economic Council at Genoa for armed intervention against the rulers of Soviet Russia. The members of the sobor based the legitimacy of their actions on a ukaz or decree (no. 362) of Patriarch *Tikhon of Moscow, but the latter disavowed his approval and officially disbanded them. The Soviet government, however, used the Synod's statements as a pretext for suspecting Tikhon and his Church, accusing him of counter-revolutionary tactics. The *Russian Orthodox Church Outside Russia (formerly the Russian Church Abroad) considers the Synod as its first council, but divergent interpretations of the ukaz have led to subsequent divisions. The Moscow patriarchate considers the meeting as uncanonical.

[F. T. RYAN]

KARLSTADT, ANDREAS RUDOLF BODENSTEIN VON (*c.* 1480–1541), German Reformer. He used the name of his place of birth, Karlstadt or Carlstadt. After study at Erfurt, Cologne, and Wittenberg, he began to teach Thomistic philosophy at Wittenberg in 1505. Three years later he became canon of the collegiate church and subsequently doctor of theology (1510). It was he who advanced Luther to the rank of doctor of theology in 1512. The same year K. was sent to Rome for a doctorate in canon and civil law, which he acquired in a few months. On his return to Wittenberg he attacked the abuses of the papal court, and scholastic philosophy as well. He was J. *Eck's first opponent at the *Disputation of Leipzig until the critical intervention of Luther himself (1519). K. was mentioned by name in *Exsurge Domine,* the bull that excommunicated Luther (1520). While Luther was in hiding at the *Wartburg (1521), K. put through many reforms: the marriage of priests, the abolition of private Masses, the discarding of vows. He gave communion under both kinds into the hands of his followers and celebrated the Lord's Supper in secular clothing. His attack upon the externals of worship contributed to the Wittenberg riots of 1521 (see ZWICKAU PROPHETS). Expelled from the city (1524), he wandered for a time in Germany and then received a post at the Univ. of Basel. Mainly through him the Zwinglian doctrine of the *Real Presence was adopted in Switzerland. In the resultant controversies with the Lutherans K. tried vainly to be a conciliator. BIBLIOGRAPHY: E. G. Schwiebert, *Luther and His Times* (1950); C. Crivelli, EncCatt 3:867–889.

[M. J. SUELZER]

KARLSTEIN, important Czechoslovakian castle of Charles IV, built (1348–65) by Mathieu d'Arras and Peter Parler and renowned for many magnificent chapels, with semiprecious stones, gilded plaster, portrait frescoes (*King and Queen in the Chapel of St. Catherine*), with strong Italian influence in the Chapel of the Virgin (*c.*1357), in frescoes of the apocalypse and the life of Charles IV. The important Chapel of the Holy Cross was painted (1357–67) by Theodoric of Prague, who embodied the style of Tommaso da Modena in a broad second Bohemian idiom that strongly influenced Master Bertram of N Germany.

[M. J. DALY]

KARMA (Sanskrit, action, deed), in Indian belief, the metaphysical-moral law (analogous to a ''law'' of physics) of actions and their consequences, or ''fruits.'' Accordingly, each action is a result of forces set in motion by previous actions, and in turn has its own consequences that will take effect (or ripen) later, either in this life or in a subsequent incarnation (according to the belief in *samsara, or reincarnation). The focal point is that karma accounts for both fortune and misfortune in the life of each being. One's station in life, one's *caste, is thus determined by previous karma; similarly, one's caste duty (*dharma: what is appropriate to one's status) dictates whether actions will have ''good'' or ''bad'' karma as their inevitable consequence. Modern Hindu philosophers deemphasize the apparently fatalistic aspects and lay stress on human responsibility: humans fashion their own lives. In the *Jain tradition, karma is conceived as an almost physical substance that adheres to the *jiva (soul, spirit) as it transmigrates. Early *Buddhism stressed the oppressive elements of the doctrine and sought release in *nirvana. BIBLIOGRAPHY: T. Organ, *Hinduism* (1974); M. Spiro, *Buddhism and Society* (1970) 66–139.

[D. P. EFROYMSON]

KARMATIANS (Carmathians; from Arab. *Qarâmiṭa,* sing., *qarmaṭî*), a branch of the Ismaili *Shiites. The sect is named for one of its earliest leaders, Ḥamdân Qarmaṭ. Through its egalitarian propaganda, the movement was able to attract wide support against the Abbasid government. The open activity of Ḥamdân Qarmaṭ was begun in 890 A.D., but from the earliest beginning the movement was run as a highly organized secret society and its true leaders have never been known. In 894 a Karmatian agent, al-Jannâbî, established a base of power in al-Aḥsâ' and Bahrein and from 900 another, Dhikrawaih, opened a major revolt in Syria. This revolt, carried on with terrible cruelty, was put down in 906 but al-Jannâbî continued to cause havoc in S Iraq and Arabia. In 390 the Karmatians succeeded in carrying off from *Mecca the Black Stone which was returned in 915 through intervention of the *Fatimid caliph. Their esoteric doctrine is heavily influenced by Gnosticism and late Neoplatonism and may in part have influenced Fatimid theology. The Karmatians are thought to have had considerable influence on later secret societies in Islam and perhaps on the Freemasons in Europe. BIBLIOGRAPHY: L. Massignon, EncIslam[1] *idem,* bibliog. in Gibb-Kramers SEI.

[R. M. FRANK]

KARNAK, site of a complex of ruins among which is the Great Temple of Amon, the largest enclosure in Egypt, growing by accretion (2060 B.C.–7th cent. B.C.), the courtyards and pylons added by successive Pharaohs. K. is noted for the magnificent Hypostyle Hall (338 by 170 feet), having two rows of papyrus columns (69 feet high) in the nave and 122 smaller bundle-bud columns in the aisles, with a sacred lake S of the earliest structures. A Festival Hall with clerestory, set transversely to the axis of the Temple of Amon, built by Thutmose III, served later as a Coptic church. Important are the Karnak Table carrying a list of Pharaohs and a room with reliefs of Syrian plants and animals. An avenue of sphinxes leads to temples of Amenhotep III and Rameses II. Colossal architecture at Karnak is not marred by deterioration in later styles.

[M. J. DALY]

KĀRTTIKEYA, Hindu god of war, son of Siva and Parvati, also called Skanda or Kumāra (youth).

KASCHAU, MARTYRS OF, three Jesuits slain September 7–8, 1619, in Kaschau, Hungary, now Košice, Czechoslovakia; beaten to death by the army of G. Rákóczy, acting at the instigation of the Calvinist leader, Bethlen Gabor. Beatified in 1905, their relics are in Strzegom and Trnava. Mark Crisin (Körösy) was born in Croatia in 1588, studied at the Germanicum in Rome, was professor and rector of the Trnava seminary and canon of Strzegom before coming to Kaschau in 1619. Stephen Pongracz was born in 1582 in Transylvania, of Hungarian royal lineage, and taught in Ljubljana, Klagenfurt, and Graz before coming to Kaschau to teach in 1618. Melchior Grodecz was born in Silesia in 1584, a Czech of Polish extraction, and came to Kaschau as chaplain to the imperial troops in 1619. BIBLIOGRAPHY: E. Páztor, BiblSanct 3:927–928 s.v. "Cassovia, Martiri di."

[E. J. DILLON]

KÄSEMANN, ERNST (1906–), Lutheran theologian and NT scholar. Born in Bochum-Dahlehausen, Westphalia, he studied in Bonn, Marburg, and Tübingen and was for some years pastor of the parish of Gelsenkirchen-Rotthausen in Westphalia. From 1946–51 he was professor of NT at Mainz, and from 1951–59 at Göttingen. From 1959 he has been professor at Tübingen. His dissertation *Leib und Leib Christi* appeared in 1933 and was followed in 1939 by his study of the Epistle to the Hebrews, *Das wandernde Gottesvolk*. Selections from his *Exegetische Versuche und Besinnungen* (1960, 1964) have appeared in English under the titles *Essays on NT Themes* (1964), and *New Testament Questions for Today* (1972). His *Paulinische Perspektiven* (1969) also has been translated (*Perspectives on Paul,* 1971). He is also the author of a commentary on Romans, *An die Römer* (1973).

[T. J. RYAN]

KASHKULL, East Syrian liturgical book containing in full certain ferial texts abbreviated in the **ḥûḏrā*. BIBLIOGRAPHY: J. Mateos, *Lelya-Ṣapra* (1959) 14.

[A. CODY]

KASPER, KATHERINA (1820–98), religious foundress. A native of Bavaria, K. founded in 1848 a community of women religious, Poor Handmaids of Jesus Christ, dedicated to nursing the sick, and later also to teaching. As Mother Maria she saw her community grow to 2,000 members by the end of the 19th century. The first house in the U.S. was established in 1868. Her cause for beatification was introduced in 1946.

[J. R. AHERNE]

KASTENBANER, BOIUS, see AGRICOLA, STEPHEN.

KASTL, ABBEY OF, monastery founded in 1098 as a Benedictine abbey in the Diocese of Eichstädt on the Lauter River. It was placed under papal jurisdiction in 1102, and imperial protection in 1163. Advocating the Hirsau Reform, it played an important role in Benedictine monastic and liturgical reforms. The Peasants' War and the Reformation brought about decline and Kastl's eventual suppression in 1563. Kastl was restored and placed under Jesuit jurisdiction from 1636 to their suppression in 1773. For a short period until its final suppression in 1808, it was under control of the Knights of St. John of Jerusalem. BIBLIOGRAPHY: C. Wolff, LTK 6:14–16.

[M. A. MCFADDEN]

KASUGA SHRINE, NARA (8th cent.), Japanese Shinto shrine of the Fujiwara clan founded to house their four guardian gods. The present building (1863) preserves the original form, duplicated precisely every 20 years. The wood is painted bright orange-red in Buddhist style because of connection with the nearby Buddhist temple of Kōfukuji, also of Fujiwara patronage.

[M. J. DALY]

KĀŚYAPA (Chin., Chia-yeh-po), most famous disciple of Buddha Sākyamuni. In early sculpture and painting K. is paired with Ananda in attendance upon the Buddha. K., wrinkled for age and status, appears with Ananda in early Chinese Buddhist art, notably at Tun-huang.

[M. J. DALY]

KATERKAMP, JOHANN THEODOR HERMANN (1764–1834), church historian. Ordained 1787, K. was tutor to the princely family of *Droste Vischering and a member of Princess Amalia Gallitzin's Münster circle. Provisional professor of church history at Münster Univ. (1809), and ordinary professor (1819), he wrote the pioneering *Kirchengeschichte,* (1819–34). BIBLIOGRAPHY: H. Rumpler, NCE 8:135 (bibliog.).

[R. I. BURNS]

KATHENOTHEISM (Gr. *kat'hena,* one after the other; *theos,* god), classification for a stage between polytheism and monotheism, i.e., the stage in which one of many gods is conceived as supreme. *HENOTHEISM.

[T. C. O'BRIEN]

KATHISMA (Gr., sitting), a division of the Psalms in the Byzantine Divine Office, the 150 Psalms being distributed into 20 kathismata or sessions. The term owes its origin to the custom of standing for the singing or recitation of the Psalms and of sitting only during certain interruptions in the psalmody for scriptural readings, troparia, or canons. The intervening periods of sitting, called kathismata, separated one group of Psalms from another, and the term came later to be applied to the group of Psalms so marked out by a kathisma. The 20 kathismata are in turn divided into three *staseis* (or standings, stations) consisting of from one to five Psalms each and ending with the doxology.

[R. K. GOLINI]

KATHOLIKON, see CATHOLICON.

KATHOLIKOS, see CATHOLICOS.

KATSCHTHALER, JOHANNES (1832–1914), Austrian theologian, prince abp. of Salzburg from 1900, cardinal from 1903. He was a seminary professor at Salzburg and at Innsbruck before being appointed auxiliary bp. of Salzburg in 1891. He published a text, *Theologiae dogmaticae specialis* (5 v., 1877–88), as well as works on church music. As abp. he led resistance to the *Los-von-Rom movement.

[T. C. O'BRIEN]

KATTERBACH, BRUNO (1883–1931), Franciscan paleographer and archivist. After entering the Franciscan Order in 1901, he studied theology in Fulda and was ordained in 1909. At the Antonianum in Rome he studied history and was trained in paleography and diplomatics at the Vatican where he held the chair in those studies (1913–16; 1920–31) and also the position of Vatican archivist. BIBLIOGRAPHY: A. Kleinhans, *Antonianum* (1932) 7:281–283; O. J. Blum, NCE 8:135.

[O. J. BLUM]

KATZER, FREDERICK FRANCIS XAVIER (1844–1903), Austrian-born third abp. of Milwaukee from 1891. As a seminarian he volunteered to come to the U.S. and was ordained for the Diocese of Milwaukee in 1866. He taught there at St. Francis Seminary, then became vicar general of Green Bay, Wis., in 1875 and its bp. in 1886. His strong intervention achieved repeal of a state law requiring instruction in English in all schools of the state. On similar grounds of German cultural loyalty he became identified with the German Catholic side in the controversies that divided the American Church at the time. His nomination as abp. of Milwaukee in 1890 was therefore opposed by the liberal, more "Americanizing" bps., but K. was appointed by Rome over their protest. During his episcopacy the strain continued, with K. siding against Ireland, Gibbons, and other American bps. on all issues concerning the schools and the retention of the German language. He also welcomed Leo XIII's *Testem benevolentiae* (1899), and assured the Pope of the widespread existence of the *Americanism it condemned.

[T. C. O'BRIEN]

KAULEN, FRANZ PHILIPP (1827–1907), theologian, biblical exegete, and editor. K. taught at the Univ. of Bonn (1863–1903) and was a member of the *Pontifical Biblical Commission. He published a widely used introduction to Scripture, a grammar and history of the Vulgate, and edited the 2d edition of the *Kirchenlexikon* (12 v., 1886–1901; 3d ed. renamed *Lexikon für Theologie und Kirche*). K.'s erudition was undeniable, but his exegetical judgments were often excessively conservative. BIBLIOGRAPHY: J. Starcky, DBSuppl 5:3–4; F. J. Schaefer, CE 8:611.

[T. M. MCFADDEN]

KAUNITZ, WENZEL ANTON VON (1711–94), Austrian chancellor from 1753 to 1792 and president of the imperial council for many years. K. was the guiding force behind much of the legislation of Maria Theresa and Joseph II. His views on Church-State relations reflected the secularistic trends of the Enlightenment, the prevailing practices of royal absolutism, and the theory of Church subject to State known as *Febronianism. All these combined as *Josephinism in Austrian history. K. advocated state control of all ecclesiastical affairs except dogma. When the Austrian government applied K.'s theories, great turmoil resulted in the Church in Habsburg lands, esp. under Joseph II (1780–1790). BIBLIOGRAPHY: *Der Josephinismus* (ed. F. Maass, 5 v., 1951–61) v. 1–2.

[R. H. SCHMANDT]

KAUTZSCH, EMIL FRIEDRICH (1841–1910), liberal OT scholar and philologist. K. taught OT at several German universities, notably at Halle (1888–1910). He made scholarly contributions both to OT study, in which he was generally sympathetic to the school of J. *Wellhausen, and to Hebrew philology. He published seven revised editions of W. *Gesenius' Hebrew grammar, two studies on biblical Aramaic, and collaborated in producing a German translation of the OT. BIBLIOGRAPHY: J. de Fraine, DBSuppl 5:4–6; J. Trinquet, *Catholicisme* 6:1382–83.

[T. M. MCFADDEN]

KAWK^{e}B̲Ō, (West) Syrian equivalent of the Byzantine **asteriskos*.

[A. CODY]

KAYE-SMITH, SHEILA (1887–1956), English novelist. Determined as a child to be an author K. wrote several novels of 22,000 words each while still at school and published two novels before she was 21. One of the most prolific of English novelists of the time, she eventually published 31 books, chiefly novels, a number of which became best sellers in England and America. Her fiction reveals her deep love for her native Sussex: she did for Sussex what Thomas Hardy did for Wessex. K.'s first encounter with Catholicism was an evening spent at the home of Alice Meynell where she was deeply impressed by the artistic, cultured atmosphere. In 1924 she married an Anglo-Catholic clergyman, R. T. Penrose Fry. Both were weary of the constant disputes between the Anglo-Catholic Church and the Church of England and turned to Roman Catholicism. In 1928 they went to Italy and became convinced more than ever of the merely national and provincial character of Anglicanism. After returning to England her husband resigned and both were received into the RC Church (1929). They settled on a farm in Sussex where they arranged to have a visiting priest celebrate Mass for the scattered Catholics in the area, the first time since the Reformation that Mass was celebrated publicly there. After her conversion she published *Superstition Corner,* her first really Catholic novel, one which increased her literary fame. Her religious autobiography, *Three Ways Home,* is characterized by great sincerity, simplicity, and power. BIBLIOGRAPHY: P. Braybrooke, *Some Catholic Novelists* (1931); F. Delteil, *Catholicisme* 6:1383–84.

[S. A. HEENEY]

KAYSIEWICZ, JEROME (1812–73), Polish Resurrectionist. After a short career as a soldier, K. went to France, where under the influence of A. Mickiewicz he returned to the practice of his religion. He became one of the first members of the Congregation of the Resurrection. In 1843 he began an apostolate in Poland. Later he returned to France to combat the teaching of A. Towiánski, the Polish messianist. He was superior of his congregation (1850–73) and founded the Polish College in Rome (1866). BIBLIOGRAPHY: E. G. Borghese, DE 2:540.

[M. J. SUELZER]

KAZAN, OUR LADY OF, Russia's most venerated icon. In 1579 it was miraculously found in the ground on a spot revealed to a girl and caused many cures, esp. of the blind. The army took it to defeat the Poles in 1612, and a cathedral was built for it in Moscow. In all crises it was invoked, and Russia's salvation from Napoleon is attributed to it. Sold by the Soviets, it is now in private hands.

[F. WILCOCK]

KEANE, JOHN JOSEPH (1839–1918), abp., a founder and first rector of The Catholic Univ. of America. Of Irish birth, he was brought to the U.S. by his parents when he was 7 years old. A keen student he taught himself Latin and Greek before entering the seminary at Baltimore, where he was ordained for that diocese in 1866. From the first days as a curate at St. Patrick's, Washington, D.C., he was a friend of Card. Gibbons, a friendship that had both good and bad results, since he also acquired Gibbons' opponents. At the age of 39 K. was named bp. of Richmond, Va., where he won the respect of his people and of Protestants alike. One of the vigorous promoters of the notion of a national Catholic university, he became a member of the committee appointed in 1884 at the Third Plenary Council of Baltimore to set up such an institution. With Spalding of Peoria, Ireland of St. Paul, and Card. Gibbons, he battled strong opposition to the university on the part of many other American bishops. He resigned his see in 1888 and when The Catholic Univ. of America opened in Washington, D.C. (1889), K. was named a titular bp. and first rector. A striking personality and genuine intellectual, he did much to represent the Church in the academic world of the United States. Unhappily there were powerful conservative elements in the American Church still hostile to his views, considered to be liberal. When a term was set for the rectorship, Leo XIII in 1896 removed K. from office, appointed him to Rome to serve on two papal congregations (Studies and Propaganda) with the title of archbishop. K. served in Rome with some disappointment, but intent on vindicating himself and the causes he supported from suspicion. In 1899 he returned to assist in fund raising for Catholic University. He was appointed abp. of Dubuque in 1900 and labored therre until ill health forced retirement in 1911. He felt that his appointment and service there were testimony enough to his orthodoxy. K. was a celebrated orator and a regular contributor of articles to the *American Catholic Quarterly Review* and *The Catholic University Bulletin*.

[J. R. AHERNE]

KEBLE, JOHN (1792–1866), poet and divine, leading figure in the *Oxford movement. A Cotswold man, after brilliant studies at Corpus Christi College, Oxford, and receiving an Oriel fellowship at a very early age, K. retired to assist his father, a clergyman of the *high-church school, in a country parish. There he wrote a well-known cycle of poems, *The Christian Year* (1827). Appointed professor of poetry at Oxford in 1831, he retired again and was vicar of Hursley, on the edge of the New Forest, from 1836 until his death; his winning beauty of character continued to exert an influence out of proportion to the diffidence of his personal manners and the modesty of his office. The start of the Oxford movement is counted from his assize sermon on national apostasy (1833), directed against a proposed suppression of 10 Irish bishoprics by a government backed by reforming and liberalizing forces that were regarded as threats to the Establishment. He contributed to *Tracts for the Times* and published a learned edition of the works of Richard *Hooker, and also was an editor of the *Library of the Fathers,* for which he prepared the translation of the works of St. Irenaeus. He remained a firm associate of E. *Pusey after 1845, when, to their sorrow, J. H. Newman had left them. He stressed the Real Presence in his work *On Eucharistic Adoration* (1857). Keble College, Oxford (1870), is his monument, and the Butterfield vigor of its architecture symbolizes how confidently the movement freed itself from the imputation of archeologism and boldly developed from the delicate strength of its progenitor. BIBLIOGRAPHY: G. Battiscombe, *John Keble: A Study in Limitations* (1964); J. C. Shairp, *Studies in Poetry and Philosophy* (1868, repr. 1970).

[T. GILBY]

KEDERMYSTER, RICHARD (d. 1531), Benedictine, abbot of Winchcombe in Gloucestershire. He became abbot in 1487 and until his resignation in 1525 was a staunch promoter of monastic discipline and learning. He was a renowned preacher, often preaching before Henry VIII. K.'s sermon against a 1512 act of parliament depriving minor clerics of exemption from trial by secular courts (benefit of clergy) provoked controversy and anticlericalism. He published (1521) a treatise attacking M. Luther's teaching.

[T. C. O'BRIEN]

KEEGAN, ROBERT FULTON (1888–1947), administrator. Ordained in 1915, K. was appointed (1919) the first executive director of New York Catholic Charities, which under his direction became the largest voluntary charitable organization in the U.S. He unified the work of the agency, cooperated with non-Catholic welfare groups, and placed charitable service on a professional basis. His work made the New York agency a model for other dioceses in the United States.

[J. R. AHERNE]

KEHR, PAUL FRIDOLIN (1860–1944), Protestant historian of the papacy. After working as a collaborator on the *Monumenta Germaniae historia,* K. was nominated to the chair of medieval history at Göttingen in 1895. In this capacity he set about collecting papal documents from the time preceding the reign of Innocent III. K. was financially aided in this work by Pius XI. BIBLIOGRAPHY: O. Vasella, LTK 6:102–103.

[B. F. SHERER]

KEITH, GEORGE (*c.*1639–1716), early Quaker dissident. Born in Aberdeen, Scotland, K. became a Quaker in 1662 and a colleague of G. *Fox, whom he accompanied, together with R. *Barclay and W. *Penn, to Holland (1671). After immigrating to America (1688), K. expressed a recurrent problem within Quakerism by his resistance to emphasis on the *Inner Light at the expense of traditional Christian beliefs. He called himself and his followers "Christian Quakers" and observed baptism and the Lord's Supper. K. wrote against Penn, *The Deism of William Penn and His Brethren* (1699), and against Barclay, *The Standard of the Quakers Examined* (1702). BIBLIOGRAPHY: E. W. Kirby, *George Keith, 1638–1716* (1942) with complete bibliog.

KELLEY, FRANCIS CLEMENT (1870–1948), bp., founder of the Extension Society. Canadian by birth and education, K. was ordained for the Detroit Diocese in 1893. He founded the Catholic Church Extension Society as an aid to needy parishes and home missions in 1905 and led the Society for 20 years. *Extension,* the magazine he established and edited, grew to a paid circulation of 3 million copies. K. was active in diplomatic representation, serving the Mexican bps. at the Peace Conference following World War I, making the first overtures to settle the *Roman question, and conducted a mission for the Vatican to England. In 1924 he became bp. of Oklahoma City and Tulsa where he succeeded in offsetting the influence of the Ku Klux Klan. He wrote a number of popular books, including novels and a very readable autobiography, *The Bishop Jots It Down* (1939).

[J. R. AHERNE]

KELLISON, MATTHEW (*c.*1560–1642), fourth president of the English College, Douai. He replaced Thomas Worthington at Douai in 1613 and presided there for 27 years. He appointed qualified professors and tried to remove Jesuit influence from the college. He was a respected man, a brilliant scholar, and an effective controversialist. BIBLIOGRAPHY: Gillow BDEC, 3:677–685.

[V. SAMPSON]

KELLNER, HEINRICH (1837–1915), German patrologist and liturgist whose classic *Heortologie oder das Kirchenjahr und die Heiligenfeste in ihrer geschichtlichen Entwicklung* (1900) appeared in English translation as *Heortology: A History of Christian Festivals* (tr. a priest of the Westminster diocese, 1908).

[N. KOLLAR]

KELLS, ABBEY OF, an Irish monastery founded in 804, which became the head of the Columban league of churches in 807. About 848, the Pictish king, Kenneth MacAlpin seems to have tried to withdraw the churches in Scotland from the primacy of Kells. In the 12th cent. the primacy did pass from Kells to Derry; and at Kells the Columban Rule was replaced by that of the Canons Regular of St. Augustine. Kells was frequently sacked by the Vikings. To it belonged the **evangeliarium* called the Book of Kells (now at Trinity College, Dublin). A modern Protestant church occupies the site of the original monastic foundation. BIBLIOGRAPHY: M. Archdall, *Monasticon hibernicum* (1786); J. F. Kenney, *Sources for the Early History of Ireland* (1966); C. McGrath, NCE 8:145.

[C. MCGRATH]

KELLS, SYNOD OF, a name erroneously applied by some older writers to the Council of *Mellifont. The error is traceable to Mansi.

[P. K. MEAGHER]

KELLY, GERALD ANDREW (1902–64), Jesuit theologian and writer. Born in Denver, he studied with the Jesuits in Missouri and was ordained in 1933. K. taught moral theology at the Jesuit seminary, St. Mary's Kansas for 26 years. He was managing editor of the *Review for Religious* for 18 years. A moral theologian of great merit, he published a number of books: *Modern Youth and Chastity* (1941), *Medico-Moral Problems* (1957), and with J. C. *Ford, *Contemporary Moral Theology* (2 v., 1958–63).

[J. R. AHERNE]

KELSO ABBEY. In 1113 Earl (later king) David I of Scotland founded a monastery for Tironian monks on his lands at Selkirk, Roxburghshire, but in 1128 he removed it to nearby Kelso, where he further enriched it with lands and gifts. The vigorous community there quickly established daughter houses at Lindores, Arbroath, and Kilwinning, but the abbey suffered much by its close proximity to the border and was badly damaged by the English in the later Middle Ages. Finally suppressed at the Scottish Reformation in 1560, it is now a ruin. BIBLIOGRAPHY: G. W. S. Barrow, ''From Queen Margaret to David I: Benedictines and Tironians,'' *Innes Review 11* (1960) 22–38; *Liber S. Marie de Calchou* (1846).

[L. J. MACFARLANE]

KEMBLE, JOHN, ST. (1599–1679), Welsh martyr. He was ordained at the English College, Douai (1625) and then returned to his native district of Herefordshire where he labored as a missionary for more than 50 years. With the help of the Jesuits, he established mission centers throughout Herefordshire and Monmouthshire. During the Oates Plot, he was arrested, tried, and sentenced at Hereford to be hanged, drawn, and quartered as a seminary priest. In April 1679 he was brought to London for examination by Titus Oates who was unable to find any charge against him or, by promise of pardon, to exact any details from K. regarding the supposed plot. K. was returned to Hereford and executed. He was beatified in 1929, and canonized in 1970. BIBLIOGRAPHY: Butler 3:383–385; N. Del Re, BiblSanct 7:1040–41.

[V. SAMPSON]

KEMÉNY, ZSIGMOND (1814–1875), Hungarian journalist and novelist. Of a noble Transylvanian family, he studied at Nagyenyed and at Vienna. Combining politics with journalism, he supported Kossuth in 1848 and was exiled for 3 years after the failure of the revolution. BIBLIOGRAPHY: O. J. Egres, NCE 8:148.

[H. JACK]

KEMP (KEMPE), JOHN (1380?–1454), English ecclesiastic and statesman; bp. of Rochester (1419), Chichester (1421), London (1421); abp. of York (1425), Canterbury (1452); cardinal priest (1439); cardinal bishop of Santa Rufina (1452); chancellor of Normandy (1417–22), of England (1426–32). Educated at Merton College, Oxford, he practiced in ecclesiastical courts. His cardinalate gave him precedence over Abp. Henry Chichele, but Kemp was more politician than churchman. He undertook diplomatic missions for Henry V and Henry VI, including fruitless attempts to negotiate peace with France; served on Henry VI's council; sided with Henry Beaufort against Humphrey, Duke of Gloucester, and with Lancastrians against Yorkists; and subdued rebellion in Kent(1450). BIBLIOGRAPHY: W. Ullmann, NCE 8:148–149; Emden Ox 2:1031–32.

[R. W. HAYS]

KEMP, THOMAS (*c.*1414–89), bp. of London. After taking his M.A. and B. Theol. at Oxford, he became canon of Lincoln (1433), of York (1435), archdeacon of York (1436–42), of Richmond (1442–48), of Middlesex (1449), and bp. of London (1448–49). K. was a notable benefactor of Merton College, Oxford, and the university, helping to finance the building of the Divinity School and the library. BIBLIOGRAPHY: EmdenOx 2:1032–34.

[C. D. ROSS]

KEMPE, MARGERY (*c.*1374–*c.*1440), reputed English mystic. Born at Lynn, Norfolk, she married a well-to-do burgess to whom she bore 14 children, then turned to a life of prayer and penance after an attack of madness and the failure of her business ventures. Separating from her husband, she devoted herself to a religious life in the world. A great traveler, she visited *Julian of Norwich, made pilgrimages to the Holy Land, Italy, Spain. Unable to write herself, she dictated a vivid and frank account of her life:—her ''boystrous'' spells of crying, her temptations, her visions, her love of God, and compassion for sinners. The oldest autobiography in English, the book has great value as a human document and picture of medieval life, but little value as a spiritual treatise. K. is today more often considered a victim of religious mania than a true mystic. BIBLIOGRAPHY: *Book of Margery Kempe* (ed. H. E. Allen and S. B. Meech EETS, 1940); D. Knowles *English Mystical Tradition* (1961, 1964) 138–150; L. Collis, *Memoirs of a Medieval Woman* (pa. 1971).

[M. N. MALTMAN]

KEMPER, JACKSON (1789–1870), first missionary bp. of the Protestant Episcopal Church. Born near Poughkeepsie, N.Y., after finishing Columbia College (now Univ., 1809), he studied for orders under the bp. of New York. Ordained in 1814, he spent 20 years as assistant to Bp. W. *White at Christ Church, Philadelphia. He made missionary journeys into Pennsylvania, Virginia, Wisconsin, and Ohio. Consecrated as missionary bp. of the Northwest (Missouri and Indiana) in 1835, he found only one Episcopalian priest in his territory. In 1854 Iowa and Wisconsin came under his care; the same year he became diocesan of Wisconsin, devoting full time to his diocese after 1859. He opened Kemper College, Boonville, Mo., as well as Nashotah House and Racine College, both in Wisconsin, seeing to it that these institutions had a full Anglo-Catholic religious life. BIBLIOGRAPHY: G. White, *Apostle of the Western Church* (1900).

[M. A. GARDNER]

KEMPTON, ABBEY OF, former Benedictine monastery in Bavaria. Founded by Sankt Gallen *c.*725, it soon became a royal Benedictine monastery favored by Charlemagne. Following the destruction of the abbey in 926, the monks moved to a new site nearby. After its abbot was made a prince of the Empire in the 14th cent., only nobles were allowed to be monks at Kempten. In 1593 Kempten established a printing press. Although the original church was begun in the 10th cent., it was not completed until the 18th century. Kempten was dissolved in 1803 and its property (some 18 square miles) was taken over by the state of Bavaria. BIBLIOGRAPHY: G. Spahr, NCE 8:149.

[M. A. MCFADDEN]

KEN, THOMAS (1637–1711), bp. of Bath and Wells. K. was born in Hertfordshire of Somerset stock and educated at Winchester and New College, Oxford. A friend of Izaak Walton, who married his half sister, he manifested an equal peacefulness and piety; a Wykehamist, he well exemplified the founder's motto, ''Manners makyth man.'' No timeserver, he disobliged Nell Gwyn (the mistress of Charles II, who referred to him as ''the little black fellow that refused his lodging to poor Nelly'') and roundly told James II that he had seen enough at Rome to keep him from changing his religion. The two Stuart kings respected him, and he was faithful to them. Though K. was one of the seven who refused to read James II's *Declaration of Indulgence, he was dispossessed of his see as a *nonjuror under William III. He wrote the *Practice of Divine Love* (1685), a classic of Laudian devotion, and died in the C of E ''as it stands distinguished from all Papal and Puritan Innovations.'' BIBLIOGRAPHY: H. A. L. Rice, *Thomas Ken: Bishop and Non-Juror* (pa. 1958).

[T. GILBY]

KENCHOJI (1253), Japanese Buddhist temple in Kamakura. Established by a Sung Chinese missionary Tao-lung, it was the first true Zen monastery in Japan. Modeled on Ch'an (Zen) headquarters in Hangchou, China, K. became a model for later Japanese Zen monasteries.

[M. J. DALY]

KENITES, see CINITES.

KENNEDY, JOHN FITZGERALD (1917–63), 35th president of the U.S.; educated at Choate School and Harvard Univ.; member of prominent Boston Irish family with strong proclivities for public service; grandfather a celebrated mayor of Boston; father ambassador to the Court of St. James; brothers Robert and Edward members of U.S. Senate; K. a congressman from Massachusetts 1947–52; senator from 1952 to 1960; president from 1960 to 1963; assassinated in Dallas, Texas, November 22, 1963. K. brought to the presidency wit, intelligence, and grace. Above all else, he gave the nation a leader, a rallying point to which Americans responded with enthusiasm. Martyrdom for his country was merely the capstone of the edifice his statesmanship wrought. To those who in retrospect see only the boyish charm and the attractive personality, a look at his record in the presidency should give an entirely different appraisal. With the Alliance for Progress he gave concrete substantial support to Latin America. The Peace Corps was an inspired instrument to channel young idealism into constructive aid for underdeveloped nations. The Civil Rights Act of 1964 is almost entirely his effort. His vigorous steps to bolster a failing economy and to fight inflation prevented a serious recession. The nuclear test ban was won after years of delicate negotiation with the Soviet Union. His courageous support of Berlin in the face of Soviet and East German pressures won the love of Berliners and all of Western Europe. K. faced the most crucial moment in modern American history occasioned by a Soviet missile buildup in Cuba, a direct threat to American security. Cautiously, but with determination, he faced the possibility of nuclear war and won the battle for peace. Such a diverse assortment of political figures in Europe as Khrushchev, Macmillan, and De Gaulle came to admire him as a tough, thoughtful, and resilient leader of his country. Millions of Americans cherished him as the personification of the grace and strength befitting one who holds the most powerful position in the world. BIBLIOGRAPHY: T. C. Sorensen, *Kennedy* (1965).

[J. R. AHERNE]

KENNETH OF DERRY, ST. (*c.*521–*c.*600), Irish monastic founder and missionary. His first foundation was at Aghaboe, County Laois, and he probably also had a foundation at Kilkenny which became the principal church in the County Ossory; he established another in the Hebrides, near Iona. He was a friend of St. Columba, whose preaching mission in Scotland K. shared. There he was revered as St. Kenneth; in Ireland he is called St. Canice. BIBLIOGRAPHY: Butler 4:86–87.

[T. C. O'BRIEN]

KENNEY, JAMES FRANCIS (1864–1946), Canadian archivist and historian. He received the Ph.D. in history at Columbia Univ. in 1910. His primary field of interest was medieval Irish history, and he acquired a good knowledge of Old, Middle, and Modern Irish to enable him to do independent research in this field. In 1912, he took a position in the Dominion of Canada Archives and from 1926 until his death he was Director of Historical Research, Public Archives of Canada. While he made some contributions to Canadian history, his most important work is his epoch-making *Sources for the Early History of Ireland: An Introduction and Guide*. v. 1: *Ecclesiastical* (1929). A 2d volume, *Secular Sources,* was in progress at the time of his death. He did much to promote Catholic historical scholarship in the U.S. as well as in Canada. BIBLIOGRAPHY: M. R. P. McGuire, NCE 8:153–154.

[M. R. P. MCGUIRE]

KENNICOTT, BENJAMIN (1718–83), Anglican biblical scholar. Born at Totnes, Devonshire, he entered Wadham College, Oxford, in 1744 and remained at Oxford till his death, serving as fellow of Exeter (1747–71), librarian at Radcliffe (1767–83), and canon of Christ Church (1770–83). He set forth the difficulties in the received Hebrew text in his *State of the Printed Hebrew Text of the OT*

Considered (2 v., 1753–59). His *Vetus Testamentum hebraicum cum variis lectionibus* (2 v., 1776–80), a critical Hebrew text of the OT with alternate readings from over 600 MSS, demonstrated that the variants were too slight to present the establishing of the correct text of the OT. BIBLIOGRAPHY: W. P. Courtney, DNB 9:10–12; E. Michels, DB 3.2:1887–89.

[T. EARLY]

KENOSIS, a Greek word meaning "emptying," used to express the abasement of the Son of God in the Incarnation. The origin of the term is an early Christian hymn, probably borrowed by Paul from the Palestinian Church and quoted by him in Phil 2.6–11. The pertinent verses are 6–7: "His state was divine,/yet he did not cling/to his equality with God/but emptied (*ekenosen*) himself/to assume the condition of a slave,/and become as men are. . . ."

This emptying did not involve a temporary abandonment of his divine nature, but a concealment of the divine attributes under the weakness of his assumed humanity. The word used for "equality" does not denote the abstract attribute. It is a neuter plural form meaning literally "equal things": divine glory, power, brilliance, such as he manifested in his risen state. Paul is urging his readers to develop deeper humility and presents Jesus as the perfect model of this virtue. As God, he could have enjoyed and exercised all of the prerogatives of divinity even in his incarnate state. But in deference to the Father's will, he relinquished this right and became obedient even to death on a cross, the death of a slave. Paul goes on to speak of Jesus' resultant glorification in which his divinity shines forth and is acknowledged, as far as this is possible in time and space: "But God raised him high/and gave him the name/which is above all other names/so that all beings/in the heavens, on earth and in the underworld,/should bend the knee at the name of Jesus/and that every tongue should acclaim/Jesus Christ as Lord,/to the glory of God the Father" (9–11).

[J. J. CASTELOT]

KENOTIC THEORIES, explanations which interpret the Incarnation to mean that in becoming man the Second Person of the Trinity, the Logos, emptied himself of his divine attributes. The term is taken from the Greek **kenosis* in Phil 2.7 which states that Christ "*emptied* himself, taking the form of a servant, being born in the likeness of men" (RSV). The general concept of a *kenosis* connected with the Incarnation occurs in theologians from patristic times, but as a specific theory it derives from G. Thomasius and other German Lutherans of the 19th century. It was advocated by several Anglican theologians, notably Bp. C. *Gore (1853–1932) in his Bampton lectures: *The Incarnation of the Son of God* (1891). Kenotic theories have become less influential in recent decades. Interest was in part a result of the "Jesus of history" movement which sought through historical criticism of the Gospels to "rediscover" a supposed human Jesus beyond the Christological dogmas of the Church. Accordingly, kenotic theories held that by an act of self-limitation Christ at his Incarnation totally gave up his divine attributes and lived a life fully human in every way. Opponents of this approach hold that it "seems more like a pagan story of metamorphosis than like the Christian doctrine of Incarnation, which has always found in the life of Jesus on earth God and man in simultaneous union—the Godhead 'veiled in flesh' but not changed into humanity." BIBLIOGRAPHY: D. M. Baillie, *God Was In Christ (1956)* 96–97; T. F. Torrance, *Space, Time and Incarnation* (1969).

[T. EARLY]

KENRAGHTY, MAURICE (d. 1585), Irish priest and martyr. Chaplain to the rebels during Desmond's rebellion, he was captured (1583) and imprisoned at Clonmel. His jailer was bribed to release K. for one night during Passiontide to administer the sacraments. Betrayed, K. fled but surrendered himself in exchange for Victor White who had bribed the jailer. Charged with high treason and refusing to acknowledge the Queen's spiritual supremacy, K. was executed. BIBLIOGRAPHY: R. D. Edwards, *Church and State in Tudor Ireland* (1935).

[R. J. LITZ]

KENRICK, FRANCIS PATRICK (1796–1863), abp. of Baltimore. After ordination (1821) and a period as professor of theology at Bardstown, Ky., he went to Philadelphia (1830) as coadjutor bp. to H. *Conwell. Soon given full jurisdiction, K. put an end to the *trusteeism that had plagued Philadelphia for some time. His ministry during the cholera epidemic of 1832 was heroic. His spirit of moderation in the agitations of the Irish controversy was spread through the *Catholic Herald,* the diocesan newspaper founded in 1833. K. convened frequent diocesan synods, fostered parochial schools, and was a friend to Villanova and St. Joseph's Colleges. His calm and wise leadership during the *Nativist riots in 1844, which destroyed St. Augustine's church, restrained his people from reprisals and won the respect of sensible non-Catholics. In 1851 K. was named abp. of Baltimore; he presided as apostolic delegate over the First Plenary Council of Baltimore (1852). He continued to support Catholic higher education and charitable institutions. Devoted to the Union, he received much criticism from pro-Southern Marylanders. He continued his scholarly interest throughout his life and published: *Theologia moralis* (3 v., 1843), *Theologia dogmatica* (4 v., 1840) and between 1849 and 1862, 10 studies on OT and NT subjects.

[J. R. AHERNE]

KENRICK, PETER RICHARD (1806–96), abp. of St. Louis, Mo., missionary. Educated in Ireland and ordained there in 1821, he went to Philadelphia, invited by his brother F. P. *Kenrick, then bp., and became rector of the seminary and vicar general. In 1841 K. was named coadjutor bp. of St. Louis, succeeding Bp. J. *Rosati as ordinary in 1843. The diocese was heavily in debt and K. devised a banking and real estate venture that relieved the debt. He visited the vast diocese that included Missouri, Arkansas, and half of Illinois at that time. He brought in the Vincentians and Jesuits and recruited many secular clergy. As first abp. when St. Louis became an archdiocese in 1847, he saw five new sees created out of his territory, and the number of Catholics in St. Louis itself increase dramatically. During the Civil War K. refused to have the U.S. flag flown from his cathedral, and he was in general a friend of the Confederacy. At Vatican Council I he was an anti-infallibilist, and at Naples published his *Concio,* a pamphlet against both the opportuneness of the definition and against the doctrine itself. While in Rome he secured appointment of Patrick J. *Ryan as coadjutor, and for 12 years until Ryan was named abp. of Philadelphia, K. was in virtual retirement. He became active again from 1884 until 1893, when the St. Louis pastors petitioned Rome for appointment of an administrator. In 1895 K. was replaced, receiving a titular archiepiscopacy. Evidence is lacking to explain K.'s latter decades.

[T. C. O'BRIEN]

KENSIT, JOHN (1853–1902), English Protestant propagandist. He gained prominence as an abrasive opponent of Anglo-Catholic trends in the Church of England. He opened the City Protestant bookshop in London in 1885 and in 1890 became secretary of the newly established Protestant Truth Society, which disrupted services and employed other controversial tactics. From 1898 he directed his efforts largely against "ritualism" in the Dioceses of London and Liverpool.

[T. EARLY]

KENT, MAID OF, see BARTON, ELIZABETH.

KENTEMA, in *Byzantine chant notation, the sign indicating a note two scale steps higher than the previous note. *DYO KENTEMATA.

[A. DOHERTY]

KENTIGERN, ST. (fl. 6th cent.). K.'s alternate name, Mungo, is Celtic for "my dear one," which his protector said on first seeing him. After K. was educated at Culross, he became a missionary in what is now Scotland. Here he was consecrated but after several years of severe persecution, he withdrew to Wales where he founded a monastery (St. Asaph's). After the Christian party assumed power in the north, K. eventually returned to Glasgow and devoted himself to strengthening the faith and converting pagans among the Strathclyde Britons. His biographer, Jocelyn, relates many miracles. BIBLIOGRAPHY: J. Stéphan, BiblSanct 3:1185–86; Butler 1:83–85.

[A. WARDLE]

KENTUCKY, a S state admitted to the Union (1792) as the 15th state. Because of conflict between the French and English, white men were not generally attracted to Kentucky until 1769, when Daniel Boone and a party of hunters crossed the Cumberland Gap. The first permanent settlement was made by James Harrod at Harrodsburg, about 8 miles S of the Kentucky River. Using Boone's Wilderness Road, large numbers of Baptists and Methodists had settled in Kentucky by the end of the 18th cent., while a group of Shakers appeared in the 19th century. The first Catholics came to Kentucky from Maryland in the last decade of the 18th century. Settling at Harrodsburg, they were served between 1793 and 1819 by Stephen Theodore *Badin, the first priest to be ordained in the United States. By 1808, when the Diocese of Bardstown was erected, there were about 1,000 Catholic families and 10 Catholic churches in Kentucky. The first bp., Benedict Joseph *Flaget, a Sulpician, exercised jurisdiction from the Alleghenies to the Mississippi River and from Canada to Tennessee. Flaget opened the first seminary in the state, brought the Jesuits and Trappists to Kentucky, and erected numerous schools and churches. In 1841, Flaget's see was transferred to Louisville, which had become a major port and commercial center on the Ohio River.

After Flaget's death (1850), Martin J. *Spalding became the 2nd bp. of Louisville. During his episcopacy, some 30 churches were established, the St. Vincent de Paul Society was organized in the diocese, and the Ursuline nuns and Christian Brothers began their labors in Louisville. After Spalding's transfer to Baltimore (1864) and the brief administration of Bp. Peter Joseph Lavialle, William George *McCloskey began his long and controversial episcopacy in 1868. McCloskey managed to irritate his secretary and chancellor, John L. *Spalding, as well as the Jesuits, Trappists, Ursulines, Dominican Sisters, Sisters of Mercy, Sisters of Loretto, and others. Many of these religious left Kentucky before McCloskey's death (1909), but the continued growth of the diocese was indicated by the presence of 150,000 Catholics and 200 priests. Denis O'Donaghue, who succeeded McCloskey in 1910, was responsible for such further advances as the organization of the Clerical Aid Society and the Catholic Orphans Society. John A. Floersh was consecrated as the sixth bp. in 1924 and became the first abp. in 1937 when Louisville was raised to the status of a metropolitan see. Louisville now has three suffragan dioceses: Covington and Owensboro, Ky., and Nashville, Tennessee.

Kentucky's population of 3,401,469 (one-third urban) makes it the 23rd most populous state in the Union. In 1976 Catholics numbered 350,364, or 10.3% of the total state population. The major Protestant sects are the Southern Baptist Convention with 25.5% of the total population in 1972 and the Methodist Church with 6.7%. Other Protestant denominations comprised 2.1% of the population. The Jewish population (1968) was 11,200, or 0.35%. Kentucky has 8 Catholic colleges with a total enrollment of nearly

5,129 students. There are 32 Catholic high schools attended by 23,691 students, and 161 Catholic elementary schools with 38,366 pupils. BIBLIOGRAPHY: T. D. Clark, *History of Kentucky* (1961); C. McMeekin, *Old Kentucky Country* (1957); M. R. Mattingly, *Catholic Church on the Kentucky Frontier* (1937); M. Spalding, *Sketches of the Early Catholic Missions of Kentucky* (1844, repr. 1972).

[J. L. MORRISON; R. M. PRESTON]

KENTUCKY REVIVAL, a frontier outburst of highly emotional religion that began in 1800 at Gasper River, Ky., N of Nashville, Tenn., and reached its peak at Cane Ridge, Bourbon Co., Ky., in mid-Aug. 1801. Although Kentucky's population was then only 221,000, of whom no more than 10,000 were church members, the crowd that camped at Cane Ridge in Aug. 1801 was estimated at 20,000 to 30,000. The meeting went on for 6 days and nights, until provisions gave out. Called by Presbyterian ministers, 18 of whom attended, the revival also drew active participation from a number of Methodist and Baptist ministers; denominational distinctions were ignored. From stands set up in various parts of the grounds and even from stumps and fallen tree trunks, as many as five or six ministers preached simultaneously to crowds forming, dispersing, and reforming within the camp. Spontaneous singing, praying, shouting, and strange "religious exercises" punctuated day and dark. Preaching, which emphasized the bliss of heaven somewhat less than the terrors of hell, described salvation in strictly individualistic and otherworldly terms. Scores of hearers "under conviction" fell into catatonic trances, jerked in nervous spasms, attempted running flight only to be cast to the ground in trance, danced, sang, and laughed in "holy myrth." It was a kind of excitement suited to the raw and sparsely settled frontier against a background of lawlessness and repressed religiousness. From Cane Ridge the revival spread to North Carolina, Virginia, Pennsylvania, and as far south as Georgia, retaining much of its zest into 1803 but waning by 1805. Evidently Methodist camp meetings with their hundreds of campgrounds derived from this origin. *SECOND GREAT AWAKENING.

[D. E. STEVENSON]

KENYON, FREDERIC GEORGE (1863–1952), English biblical scholar and papyrologist, who was director of the British Museum (1909–30) and president of the British School of Archeology at Jerusalem (1920–52). He edited many Greek papyri, including Aristotle's *Constitution of Athens* (1891), and the *Chester Beatty Papyri (8 v., 1933–41).

[T. C. O'BRIEN]

KEOGH, FRANCIS PATRICK (1891–1961), bp. of Providence, R.I., from 1934; abp. of Baltimore from 1947. Ordained for the Diocese of Hartford, Conn., in 1916, he served in diocesan administration and was secretary to the bp. before being named to Providence. There he became beloved for his gentle and unfailing kindness, and did much to diminish the Franco-American animosities toward the diocese that had arisen during his predecessor's episcopacy (over allocation of diocesan funds for schools). As abp. of Baltimore he earned by his charity the title, "archbishop of the poor." Under his management the archdiocese grew in numbers, a new cathedral was built, numerous schools, orphanages, and other institutions added. He became a leading member of the National Catholic Welfare Conference (now U.S. Catholic Conference), and esp. in the formulation of the 1958 episcopal condemnation of racism. K.'s final years from 1954 were marked by ill health.

[T. C. O'BRIEN]

KEOGH, JAMES (1834–70), theologian and editor. Ordained in 1856, K. served the Dioceses both of Pittsburgh and Philadelphia. He was professor of dogmatics, then president (1863) at St. Michael's, the Pittsburgh diocesan seminary, and editor of the *Pittsburgh Catholic*. He resigned both posts over policy disputes in 1865, then joined the faculty of St. Charles Seminary in Philadelphia, and was briefly editor of the newly founded *Philadelphia Catholic Standard*. He acted as a secretary at the Second Plenary Council of Baltimore (1866). Ill health forced his early retirement.

[J. R. AHERNE]

KEOGH, JOHN (1740–1817), Catholic leader in Ireland. In a time when Catholics were despairing and apathetic about the injustices of their condition under the British, K. emerged as their vigorous spokesman. In 1790 he was elected to the Catholic Committee; in 1791 he brought the case for Catholics to the government in London and won a favorable response. K. successfully opposed the inactivism of some of the Committee; through his labors the Catholic convention met in Dublin in 1792 and appointed a deputation, with K. as head, to present Catholic grievances to the King. The outcome was the Relief Act of 1793. Opposed to violence, he would not join the United Irishmen, yet was arrested and imprisoned with members of that movement. He took no part in the uprising of 1798 and gradually withdrew from active participation in Irish affairs.

[J. R. AHERNE]

KEPLER, JOHANN (1571–1630), a founder of modern astronomy, born at Weil in Württemberg, the son of Lutheran parents. A childhood attack of smallpox left his eyesight permanently impaired. He studied theology but turned to mathematics and astronomy, becoming acquainted with the heliocentric system of Copernicus at the Univ. of Tübingen. He lectured on mathematics at Graz and also, at the request of the university, on Virgil and rhetoric. In 1600 he began work as assistant to Tycho Brahe near Prague, and after Brahe's death succeeded him as court mathematician to the Austrian Habsburgs. In 1612 he was appointed mathematician to the states of upper Austria and in 1628 he moved to

Silesia. His last years were spent at Ulm and Sagan under the glittering patronage of Wallenstein, but vainly seeking the money owed to him by the imperial treasury. His many contributions to mathematics, optics, physics, and astronomy include the discovery of the three laws of planetary motion called Kepler's laws. By his offices he was not immune from some of the astrological preoccupations of the period. He was supported by the political forces of the Counter Reformation, but himself continued to subscribe to the Augsburg Confession. He gave a religious interpretation to some astronomical phenomena such as the 1604 nova and the 1607 comet. He attempted to explain the star of the Magi as the unusual conjunction of Mars, Saturn, and Jupiter, calculated by him to have occurred in 6 B.C. BIBLIOGRAPHY: Baumgardt, *Johannes Kepler: Life and Letters* (1952); A. Koyre, *Astronomical Revolution* (1973).

KEPPLER, PAUL WILHELM VON (1852–1926), German theologian, bp. of Rottenburg from 1898. Ordained in 1875, after first doing parochial work he taught NT studies at the Univ. of Tübingen, 1883–89, then at Freiburg (Breisgau). His episcopacy was spent in coping with the problems of World War I and rebuilding his diocese afterwards. His works include: *Das Johannes-Evangelium und das Ende des I christliche Jahrhundert* (1883) and *Mehr Freude* (1909).

[T. C. O'BRIEN]

KERALA, a federal state on the SW coast of the Republic of India. This region contains the greatest number of Christians in all of India. Of its approximately 14 million inhabitants more than 25% (about 4 million) are Christians, as compared with 2% for the rest of India. Of the 9 million Catholics in India more than 3.6 million (40%) live in Kerala. Three rites are represented: Malabar, Malankar, and Roman. The *Malabar rite is the original Christian tradition of India and originated with the missionary activities of the Persian (Chaldean) Church. The Malankar rite is used by those who in the 17th cent. accepted the Antiochene traditions as a result of difficulties with the Portuguese missionaries. Those Catholics converted since the 16th cent. have followed the Roman rite. BIBLIOGRAPHY: E. Tisserand, *Eastern Christianity in India,* (tr. E. R. Hambye, 1957).

[J. MEIJER]

KERBY, WILLIAM JOSEPH (1870–1936), pioneer in Catholic social thought and action. Ordained in Dubuque in 1892, after thorough study in his field in the U.S. and abroad he began a teaching career at The Catholic Univ. of America in 1897 that covered 39 years. Amid the divisions within the hierarchy over the issue of *Americanism, K. labored to promote social reform, without opposing papal directives, but with whatever collaboration of non-Catholic social forces the cause required. He took an early and influential part in the support of the labor movement and throughout his career called for laws establishing minimum wages and other legislation beneficial to labor. In the field of Catholic charities he brought about a unification of efforts as a leader in the establishment of the National Conference of Catholic Charities in 1910. He inaugurated the *Catholic Charities Review* in 1916 and helped organize the National Catholic School for Social Service at Catholic Univ. in 1921. Through teaching and writing he strove to awaken the Catholic social conscience and to emphasize the scientific and theological rationale for Catholic social work.

[J. R. AHERNE]

KERLE, JACOBUS DE (de Kirl; *c.* 1532–91), Flemish Renaissance composer who went to Italy, where he served as carillonist, organist, and *Kapellmeister* at Orvieto cathedral (1555). He was commissioned (1561) to set 10 Latin poetic prayers by theologian Pietro de Soto to music for the Council of Trent; his polyphonic settings of the prayers, *Preces speciales pro salubri generalis concilii successu* (1562), sung at processions of the Council, so impressed their auditors that they reversed the Council's prevailing feeling against polyphonic music. He traveled with his patron Otto von Truchsess, cardinal archbishop of Augsburg, to Spain and elsewhere. He also composed 6 Masses (1562) and a book of 14 motets (1571).

[R. J. LITZ]

KERLL, JOHANN KASPAR VON (Kerl; Cherll; Kherl; 1627–93), German baroque organist and composer, *Kapellmeister* to the Munich court (1656–74); famous for his improvisation at the coronation of Leopold I (1658) at Frankfurt-am-Main. After Munich, he went to Vienna (1674) to teach, serve as organist of the cathedral of St. Stephen (1677) and court organist (1680); he returned to Munich in 1684. His novel stylistic introduction of discord marks him as a predecessor of Bach. K. composed numerous operas of which only the librettos are extant. His sacred works include Masses, motets, a Requiem, and numerous organ compositions, the best known being *Modulatio organica super Magnificat octo tonis* (1689). His castrato duet, *O bone Jesu,* is accompanied solely by ground bass passing through every key; his *Missa nigra* was composed exclusively in black notes.

[R. J. LITZ]

KERN, MICHAEL (1580–1649), German sculptor, who executed many Würzburg altars, tombs, portals, and other religious works in the weighty style of the German Renaissance (as Portal at Dettelbach, 1612–13).

[M. J. DALY]

KERSUZAN, FRANÇOIS MARIE (1848–1935), bishop. Born in France, K. was ordained in 1871, became auxiliary bishop of Port-au-Prince, Haiti, in 1884 and in 1886 was named to the See of Cap-Haitien. A man of pastoral vigor he was for years the only Catholic bp. in Haiti.

An effective opponent of *voodoo he began the paper *La Croix* to fight it. K. established a number of primary parochial schools and a secondary school. During the continual upheavals and civil disorder in Haiti in the early years of the 20th cent. he protected citizens and political suspects. In 1918 and in 1921 he came to the U.S. to testify concerning the state of the Church in Haiti and to represent the people of that land.

[J. R. AHERNE]

KERYGMA (Gr., *kērygma,* preaching, proclamation), central content of the biblical proclamation. The term refers to the basic elements of the earliest Christian message as seen, e.g., in the sermons of the early chapters of Acts—Christ's birth, suffering, death, and Resurrection. It is contrasted with *didachē,* teaching, particularly ethical teaching, which is considered by exponents of *kerygmatic theology to be secondary and derived from an acceptance of the kerygma. The term is translated ''preaching'' by the RSV in Rom 16.25: ''the preaching of Jesus Christ,'' and ''what we preach'' (to distinguish it from the act of preaching) in 1 Cor 1.21: ''it pleased God through the folly of what we preach to save those who believe.'' The New English Bible translates it as ''gospel'' in 2 Tim 4.17: ''that I might be his instrument in making the full proclamation of the gospel.'' Behind the emphasis on the distinction between kerygma and *didachē* is a conviction that the Christian message should be first an announcement of what God has done to accomplish man's salvation, rather than the ethical requirements that are laid upon man. It also corresponds to the OT emphasis on the events of the Exodus in which God acted to give deliverance to his people. In the NT kerygma is generally equivalent to gospel and is a message delivered not on the preacher's own authority but as a messenger of God. BIBLIOGRAPHY: C. H. Dodd, *Apostolic Preaching and Its Developments* (1937); Kittel TD 3:714–717.

[T. EARLY]

KERYGMATIC THEOLOGY, a description of theology as receiving its origin, form, and purpose from the preaching of the good news of salvation. In the Gr. of the NT, *kērygma* refers to the proclamation of what God has done in Christ for the salvation of men. *Dialectic theology, or *crisis theology, has been called kerygmatic because of an exclusive concern, chiefly inspired by Karl *Barth, for the proclamation of God's word and self-revelation in Christ, the only saving knowledge for man. This intent includes opposition to any intrinsic function of philosophy within theology. The beginning of RC kerygmatic interest at Innsbruck in the 1930s was partly a reaction to scholastic, or systematic, theology. Kerygmatic theology was first proposed as a distinct discipline, a preaching theology in contrast to an academic or school theology. The point was controversial; ensuing discussions led to agreement by the major theologians that theology is a science, is one, but is both theoretical and at the same time ordained to Christian decision and living. Thus kerygmatic theology denotes the approach and pedagogy necessary to theology as rooted in God's saving word and actions. The kerygmatic emphasis has directed the efforts of RC theologians to a systematization, necessary to theology as science, corresponding to the historic order in God's saving revelation and a presentation directly related to man's need of salvation. Theology must have kerygmatic aspects that are Christocentric, shaped around Christ life, work, and Church, and stated through biblical themes, rather than philosophical categories. BIBLIOGRAPHY: J. A. Jungmann, *Good News Yesterday and Today* (ed., abr., and tr. W. A. Huesman, 1962); J. MacQuarrie, *Twentieth Century Religious Thought* (1963).

[T. C. O'BRIEN]

KETCHAM, WILLIAM HENRY (1868–1921), missionary and promoter of Indian missions. A convert as a college student, K. was ordained in 1892 and sent to the N Indian territory of Oklahoma where he worked among the Choctaws. In 1901 he was appointed director of the Catholic Indian Mission Bureau which he headed for 20 years. K. fought the legislation that denied federal funds to Catholic missions, carrying the case successfully to the U.S. Supreme Court. President Taft named him to the Commission of Indian Affairs in 1912. In the succeeding 10 years he was responsible for the betterment of Indian schools and hospitals.

[J. R. AHERNE]

KETTELER, WILHELM EMANUEL VON (1811–77), German bp. and social reformer. Born in Münster and ordained in 1844, he was consecrated bp. of Mainz in 1850. He participated in the Frankfurt Parliament in 1848 and the Reichstag in 1871–73. His career as a social reformer began with a series of public addresses in Frankfurt in 1848. *Die Arbeiterfrage und das Christentum* (1864) is his most programmatic book, based on principles of Christian justice, particularly as derived from Aquinas. K. was the first Catholic bp. anywhere to recognize fully the legitimacy of proletariat complaints and to call for a Christian response in opposition to extreme economic individualism and to Marxism. He has been called the most important German bp. of his century; he was not simply a theorist but by his intervention promoted passage of enlightened social legislation. Leo XIII regarded him as the inspirer of the encyclical *Rerum novarum.* During the Kulturkampf K. strove to protect the rights of the Church in Hesse and succeeded without any major confrontation. BIBLIOGRAPHY: W. E. Hogan, *Development of Bishop Wilhelm von Ketteler's Interpretation of the Social Problem;* A. M. Birke, *Bischof Ketteler und der deutsche Liberalismus* (1971).

[R. H. SCHMANDT]

KEVENHOERSTER, JOHN BERNARD (1869–1949), first vicar apostolic of the Bahamas. German-born, he was ordained as a Benedictine in Minnesota in 1896. From 1907 he served as pastor at St. Anselm's Church, Bronx, N.Y.; from 1929 until the end of his life he was in the Bahamas and there established many parishes and schools. He was consecrated bp. in 1933.

[J. R. AHERNE]

KEVIN, ST. (Coemgen; 498–618), Irish abbot. The sources of information on him all date from 300 to 400 years after his death. The legends are many and doubtful. It is certain that K. was a solitary who ultimately founded (*c.* 570) a community of monks at Glendalough (the tower of the monastery still stands). He is said to have lived to the age of 120. BIBLIOGRAPHY: N. Del Re, BiblSanct 4:71–72; Butler 2:463–465.

[J. R. AHERNE]

KEYS, POWER OF, a traditional expression, developed from the statement of Our Lord to St. Peter "To thee I will give the keys of the kingdom of heaven" (Mt 16.19). This text has long been employed in proof of the divine authority committed to the Church and those who direct it. As found in the famous Petrine text, "the keys" is the second of three metaphors (rock, keys, binding and loosing) employed by Christ in his promise to Peter. Both in ancient Jewish and non-Jewish usage the surrender of keys or the delivery of keys was a natural symbol for the transfer or cession of power. Peter, possessing the keys of the kingdom, will open and close the kingdom as vicar and steward of Christ himself. The parallel between this metaphor and the other two in the same passage makes it sufficiently clear that the keys are to be employed here on earth during the present phase of the kingdom of heaven, the economy inaugurated by the coming of the Messiah.

Although the text on which the expression is based concerns itself primarily with the exercise of public social direction of the community, the phrase "power of the keys" has long been employed also of the power exercised in the sacrament of penance, where the authority of the Church intervenes sacramentally for the reconciliation between God and the individual. BIBLIOGRAPHY: J. Jeremias, Kittel TD 3:744–753; F. A. Sullivan, NCE 8:172; H. Vorgrimler and L. Hödl, LTK 9:422–425.

[S. E. DONLON]

KEYSER, HENDRIK DE (1565–1621), head of a Netherlandish family of architects and sculptors in the late 16th and early 17th centuries. K. as chief city engineer introduced the Italian Renaissance style to Amsterdam. Working at first on small objects (wooden model for the goblet of St. Martin), K. began construction of the Zuiderkerk (1606), visited London (1607), returning with N. Stone as assistant sculptor. From 1614 K. worked on the tomb of William I and on his masterpiece, the Westerkerk, Amsterdam (erected 1620–38).

[M. J. DALY]

KHAJURAHO (950–1050 A.D.), in N Madhya Pradesh, India, capital of tolerant Chendella Rajputs and site of a magnificent group of Hindu and Jain temples, of which 20 of the original 85 remain, and some prior Buddhist art. Typically the same, the Khajuraho temple, high on a plinth, has three main parts: entrance portico, assembly hall, and cella (shrine); the last may have vestibule, transepts, and processional path, the exterior walls profusely carved in triple friezes with multiple-domed roofs rising toward the graceful sikhara above the cella. The interior columns and ceilings—elaborately carved—are renowned for dynamic gestures and beauty of form.

[M. J. DALY]

KHANDAGIRI AND UDAYAGIRI, hill sites in Orissa, India, where Jain monasteries (1st and 2d cent. A.D.) show cells on three sides of inner court and façades with religious sculpture.

[M. J. DALY]

KHARIJITES (from Arab. *ḫârijî,* pl. *ḫawârij*), a heterodox Islamic sect. One of the earliest dissident sects in Islam, the Kharijite movement originated in the violent opposition of a number of the followers of the *Caliph 'Alî to his submission to arbitration with Mu'âwiya at the battle of Siffin in 657. Because of this they declared 'Alî to be a sinner and his caliphate to be void. The movement, which soon divided itself into a number of opposing groups, was a source of widespread and violent insurrection against the Umayyad government for many years. Common to all Kharijite groups is a highly puritanical moral doctrine according to which any Muslim who commits grave sin is no longer a believer and therefore may be killed or enslaved. The most extreme form of this doctrine was held by the Azraqites (founded by Nâfi 'ibn al-Azraq) who held virtual control over some of the E provinces for a number of years until they were finally overcome in 699. According to their teaching, a Muslim who commits even one serious sin (including the failure to adhere to their doctrine and join in open rebellion) is an unbeliever and must be killed. Less extreme was the doctrine of the Najadât (founded *c.* 682 by Najda ibn 'Âmir) who held that only the habitual sinner is an unbeliever. Another "moderate" group the Ṣufrîya, was powerful in parts of N Africa for many years. The most important Kharijite sect is that of the Ibâḍites, founded *c.* 685 by 'Abdallâh ibn Ibâd in direct opposition to the extremism of the Azraqites. Ibâḍite communities are known to have existed from Spain to Sind, though they flourished most in N and E Africa where a number remain to this day. BIBLIOGRAPHY: H. Laoust, *Les Schismes dans l'Islam* (1965) 36–47.

[R. M. FRANK]

KHAZARS, a people, probably of Turkish origin, who from the 7th to the 11th cent. established a strong kingdom in the lower Volga Valley, N of the Caucasus between the

Dnieper River and the Caspian Sea. At the height of its power the Khazar State extended its rule as far W as Kiev. The Russians brought an end to this power in 1083; as a people the Khazars disappeared by the early 13th cent., although traces remained until the 15th century. Religiously, the Khazar lands became a crossroads of Christianity, Judaism, and Islam. Dynastic ties with Constantinople led in the 8th cent. to some spread of Christianity, and later St. *Cyril made further attempts at conversion. During the most flourishing Khazar period, the King and many of his nobles embraced Judaism (*c.*786–805), and the kingdom became a center of Jewish scholarship (see JUDAH HA-LEVI). The Judaic element remained a strong minority until the end; many Eastern European Jews are thought to have been of Khazar origin. Islamic influences became strong in the 10th cent., as the Khazar King appealed to Muslim neighbors for help against the Russians. BIBLIOGRAPHY: P. Dunlop, *History of the Jewish Khazars* (1954); K. Hruby, NCE 8:173.

[T. C. O'BRIEN]

KHIRBET QUMRAN, see QUMRAN, KHIRBET.

KHLYSTY, flagellants, so called from Khlyst, a whip; also known as Disciples of Christ and Men of God. This sect originated in Vladimir in 17th-cent. Russia. It stressed personal inspiration, often aroused by scourgings and whirling dances.

[F. WILCOCK]

KHMER REPUBLIC (CAMBODIA), formerly a constitutional monarchy in SE Asia (69,866 sq mi; pop. *c.*6,750,000 [1975 est.]). The language of the country is Thai; 60% of its people are illiterate. The Khmers, forebears of today's Cambodians, developed a Hindu-Buddhist civilization that flourished from the 1st to the 8th cent. A.D. ; the influence of Angkor, its capital, extended to Vietnam, Burma, and even as far as Malaysia. Its great temples with their striking wall sculptures were disclosed by discoveries made in the mid-18th century. After 1863 the territory formed part of the French Protectorate of Indochina. The Japanese Army took control of the country during World War II and granted independence to the monarchy established (1945) under its auspices. France resumed control of Cambodia's defense and foreign affairs after the war, but the monarchy continued as an associated state in the French Union. Complete independence was achieved in 1955 in consequence of the Geneva Conference. The state religion, as well as that of the vast majority of the people, is Buddhism of the Hynayana type, blended with animistic practices imported from Burma and Ceylon. Monasticism is highly esteemed, and many youths live for a period in a monastery, of which there are some 3,000 in the country. Religious freedom is permitted to those of other faiths. Christianity has not enjoyed an encouraging history in Cambodia. Beginning in the 16th cent., attempts were made by Dominicans, Jesuits, and priests from the Paris Mission Society to evangelize the country. But the missions were not well planned, the number of missionaries was small, and Buddhist resistance, accompanied at times with bloody persecution, was strong. In 1844 there were only four churches and 222 Catholics in the country. The territory was made a vicariate apostolic in 1924, but it was not until 1957 that the first Cambodian was ordained priest. In 1970 several thousand Catholics of Vietnamese origin were forced to flee the land. Missionaries work among the small community, with religious sisters and brothers doing the work of pre-evangelization and operating various schools and charitable institutions. The principal Protestant denominations engaged in missionary activity are the Christian and Missionary Alliance (Holiness) and the Seventh-Day Adventists. Since the Khmer Rouge takeover in 1975, the status of the RC Church (members, approximately 17,000) has been uncertain. BIBLIOGRAPHY: J. Pianet, *Histoire de la mission du Cambodge* (1929).

[P. DAMBORIENA]

KHOMYAKOV, ALEXIS (1804–60), noble, army officer, landowner, poet, philosopher, theologian, called the father of Russian lay theology. Many of his views were banned by the Orthodox Church in his own day, only to be accepted and developed after his death. He is known for his theological notion of *sobornost* or conciliar spirit involving both hierarchy and laity as opposed to papal infallibility in the Catholic Church. Real freedom, K. felt, is found only in the Church, outside of which there is only ignorance and sin. As a leader in the Slavophile movement K., besides supporting the supremacy of Russian autocracy among the Slavic States, characteristically exaggerated Russia's role in world history, notably it mission to save the ''rotten'' and ''dying'' West from its prisons of individualism and materialism. BIBLIOGRAPHY: P. K. Christoff, *Introduction to Nineteenth-Century Russian Slavophilism* (1961); N. Zernov, *Three Russian Prophets: Khomiakov, Dostoevsky, Soloviev* (1973, repr. 1974).

[D. DIRSCHERL]

KHRAPOVITSKIĬ, ALEKSEĬ PAVLOVICH (Antoniĭ; 1864–1936), theologian and metropolitan of the Russian Orthodox Church. Ordained in 1885, he became teacher and rector of theological academies in Moscow and St. Petersburg. Named bp. of Volhynia, Ukraine, in 1902 he was an inveterate enemy of the Catholic Church in Ukraine. From 1914 to 1917 abp. of Kharkiv, he became metropolitan of Kiev in 1918. With the coming of Bolshevism he fled to Yugoslavia. A controversial theologian accused of heresy, he wrote a number of works, *Dogma of Redemption* (1917) creating a considerable stir.

[J. R. AHERNE]

KICHIJOTEN, Japanese goddess of fecundity, and incarnation of feminine beauty. Painted on hemp cloth, the K. in

Yakushiji, Nara (8th cent.), with plump face and richly decorated costume in the court fashion of T'ang China, reveals the delicate elegance of the Japanese. The K. in Joruriji, near Nara, a wood sculpture (*c.* 1212) shows a Fujiwara noblewoman resembling the former painting in T'ang style.

[J. R. AHERNE]

KIDDUSH, Jewish prayer and ceremonial ritual. At the meal on the eve of Sabbath or festival the head of the household chants the *kiddush* (prayer of sanctification of the day, *kiddush ha-yom*), while holding a cup of wine in his right palm; on the table in front of him are two loaves of *hallah,* bread covered with cloth, symbolizing the two portions of manna gathered on the eve of Sabbath during Israel's wilderness wandering. Those present either join in the recitation or answer *amen* before drinking the wine or in some cases eating only the bread. Preceding the two benedictions of the prayer—one to sanctify the bread or wine, the other to sanctify the Sabbath or feast—there is a recitation of the scriptural account of the Creation Sabbath (Gen 1:31; 2:1–3). The scriptural warrant for the ceremony is Ex 20:8 (Talmud, Pes. 106a). The word *kiddush* is Hebrew for sanctification and derives from *kaddesh,* to sanctify. The ceremony is maintained in Orthodox, Conservative, and Reform Judaism. The *Kiddusha Rabbah,* actually a minor *kiddush* and subordinate to the evening ceremony, is recited before the first meal of the Sabbath after the Morning Service.

[R. J. LITZ]

KIDRON (CEDRON), the name given to the wadi (stream and its valley) flowing S between Jerusalem and the Mt. of Olives. It is known today as Wadi Sitti Maryam; in 2 Sam 18.18 it is called King's Valley. The lower course of the Kidron (Wadi en-Nar) runs through the wilderness of Judah to the Dead Sea, about 6 miles S of Qumran.

[J. E. LUSSIER]

KIERKEGAARD, SOREN AABYE (1813–55), Danish philosopher and religious thinker; first important existentialist. K. reacted against the prevailing Hegelianism of his day, which he saw as a static, unreal system robbing man of his individuality. K.'s alternative was a subjective and passionate Christian faith. He refused to organize his own thought systematically but continually reflected upon the theological themes of faith, sin and forgiveness, ethics and religious commitment, and the nature of the Church. In all of his works, he presents a dialectic of his own experience rather than an abstract philosophy.

K.'s thought was significantly influenced by his personal relationships. His early years were dominated by his father's anxiety-ridden and melancholy piety. In 1835, K. experienced a shattering ''earthquake,'' occasioned by his father's revelation of a childhood curse against God. Thereafter, K. was beset not only by his own melancholy but by a continual awareness of human sinfulness. After obtaining a theological degree from the Univ. of Copenhagen, K. became engaged to Regina Olsen; he broke the engagement after 1 year, convinced that his inability to react spontaneously and accept the intimacy of marriage would destroy Regina. His love for her remained throughout his life and became the symbol of Abraham's faith in being willing to sacrifice Isaac. In 1846, a disreputable but popular paper, the *Corsair,* launched a vitriolic personal attack upon him. He became even more withdrawn from society and devoted himself to religious writing on specifically Christian themes. The last 2 years of his life were spent in severe criticism of the established Church in Denmark as a mockery of Christianity.

K. argued that a philosophical system, by which he meant that of Hegel, cannot fulfill its promise to explain the human situation. The ''system'' deals with abstractions and considers individuality as only a passing moment in a necessarily evolving Spirit. But K. refused to reduce the individual as such to any category. The experience of reality and not the concept of it must constitute the basis for reflection. Truth cannot be attained by an objective, logical process. Primacy must be given to subjectivity, i.e., the passionate appropriation of objective uncertainty. It is only when I choose to be related to reality that I reach truth. To be without passion (subjectivity) is not to exist. Hence K.'s notion of faith: a passionate commitment to God in the midst of objective uncertainty. This free choice of faith can alone assure me of authentic existence.

The three stages of life form an important part of K.'s thought. Each stage (aesthetic, ethical, and religious) has its own dynamism and is totally different from the others. Man is faced with a radical choice between God and the world. The aesthetic life is one of pleasure, cultivated humanism, and refusal to limit life's infinite possibilities by permanent choices. In the ethical stage, man chooses duty and responds to general principles of moral conduct. But it is only in the religious stage that the individual through faith makes the ultimate leap beyond despair and dread to a true realization of himself before God. K.'s thought was one of the principal influences that changed the direction, method, and interest of theology in the 20th century. Among K.'s work in English translation are *Either/Or* (v. 1, tr. D. F. and L. M. Swenson, 1941; v.2, tr. W. Lowrie, 1944) and *Concept of Dread* (tr. W. Lowrie, 1944). BIBLIOGRAPHY: L. Dupré, *Kierkegaard as Theologian* (1963) with complete list of Kierkegaard's works; J. Collins, *Mind of Kierkegaard* (pa. 1965); W. Lowrie, *Short Life of Kierkegaard* (1942); A. Shmueli, *Kierkegaard and Consciousness* (1971); M. C. Taylor, *Kierkegaard's Pseudonymous Authorship: A Study in Time and Self* (1975).

[T. M. MCFADDEN]

KIESLER, FREDERICK JOHN (1892–1965), Austrian-American architect, member of de Stÿl (1920) at Juilliard School of Music, New York and director of the

Architectural Laboratory at Columbia University. K. was an experimenter, his most significant conception being *La Cité dans l'Espace* (Paris, 1925), a suspended Cartesian space grid. K.'s last poetic major work was the Shrine of the Book, housing the Dead Sea Scrolls, in Jerusalem.

[J. R. AHERNE]

KIEV (ARCHITECTURE), capital of the Ukraine, oldest city in the Soviet Union preserving Russia's earliest architecture (before 10th century). Major architectural form is the Sta. Sophia and its monastic complex (1037), built under Yaroslav the Wise, evidencing the affinity of early Russian to Byzantine style. The interior is rich in mosaics, frescoes of saints and of the family of Yaroslav; 18th-cent. reconstruction in brick and stucco in Russian Baroque is brightly colored under gilded onion domes.

[M. J. DALY]

KIEV, ACADEMY OF, theological center, founded as a college in 1631 by Peter *Mogila at the Monastery of the Crypts, where a school had existed since 1589. In 1701 Tsar Peter I raised the college to the rank of ecclesiastical academy; in the 19th cent. the Kiev theological journal *Trudy* (*Works*) specialized in Russian translations of the Latin Fathers. The Kievan Academy was modeled by Peter Mogila on the Polish Jesuit colleges. The theology texts and courses were in Latin, scholastic in content and method. This Westernization of Russian theology sacrificed many of the themes and viewpoints traditional to Orthodoxy. After 1667 the Kievan influence was extended, when the Moscow Academy was established and staffed by theologians from Kiev. With the Revolution of 1918 the Kiev Academy ceased to exist.

[T. C. O'BRIEN]

KILDARE, ABBEY OF, a monastery in County Kildare, Ireland, founded by St. Brigid (*c.*460–520), who persuaded the hermit-bishop Conlaed to take up residence beside the abbey, thus originating the only double monastery in Ireland. Its abbesses exercised jurisdiction, with the approval of Armagh, over a large part of the province of Leinster. Kildare became an episcopal see in 1111. The Book of Kildare (which seems to have been comparable to the Book of Kells) is lost. BIBLIOGRAPHY: J. F. Kenney, *Sources for the Early History of Ireland* (1966).

[C. MCGRATH]

KILEY, MOSES ELIAS (1876–1953), archbishop. A Canadian, he was ordained for the Archdiocese of Chicago in Rome (1911). K. became the first director of Catholic charities in Chicago. He was named bp. of Trenton, N.J., in 1934 and abp. of Milwaukee, Wis., in 1940.

[J. R. AHERNE]

KILHAM, ALEXANDER (1762–98), chief founder of the Methodist New Connexion. He was born of Methodist parents at Epworth, England. He experienced a conversion at 19 and helped Robert Brackenbury found Methodism in the Channel Islands. An effective evangelist, K. wrote tracts urging Wesleyan Methodists to separate from the C of E. Because of his vehement writing he was expelled in 1796, and with some others founded the Methodist New Connexion (Aug. 9, 1797). BIBLIOGRAPHY: *New History of Methodism* (ed. W. J. Townsend et al., 2 v., 1909) 1:489–497).

[F. E. MASER]

KILIAN OF AUBIGNY, ST. (d. 670), hermit. He was a native of Ireland, possibly of royal descent. It is said that while K. was returning from a pilgrimage to Rome he met St. Faro of Meaux who persuaded him to settle in Artois. K. established a hermitage at Aubigny, preached in the area, and reputedly worked many miracles. BIBLIOGRAPHY: G. M. Fusconi, BiblSanct 3:1235–37; Butler 4:330–331.

[G. M. COOK]

KILIAN OF WÜRZBURG, ST. (*c.*640–86), bp. and martyr. K. (apparently already a bp.) and 11 companions left Ireland (*c.*689) to evangelize Franconia and East Thuringia. Tradition relates that K. converted Gozbert, Duke of Thuringia, whom he persuaded to renounce Geilana, his brother's widow. K. and two of his missionary companions were beheaded at the order of Geilana. BIBLIOGRAPHY: T. Ó Fiaich, NCE 8:179, good bibliog.

[M. F. MCCARTHY]

KILMER, JOYCE AND ALINE MURRAY, husband and wife, poets. **Joyce** (1886–1918) was educated at Rutgers and Columbia Univ., and achieved a considerable popularity with three volumes of poetry and a volume of essays. He became a Catholic in 1913, enlisted in the army in World War I, and was killed in action in France. His wife **Aline** (1888–1941) became a Catholic with her husband and after his death lectured on literary topics, publishing four books of poems, a volume of essays, and two books for children. BIBLIOGRAPHY: H. Cargas, *I Lay Down My Life* (pa. 1964).

KILPATRICK, WILLIAM HEARD (1871–1965), American educator, founder of the project method of teaching, and popularizer of J. Dewey's educational theories. Following graduate work at Johns Hopkins Univ. and the Univ. of Chicago, he taught in the Georgia public schools and at Mercer University. In 1909 he joined the faculty of Teachers College, Columbia Univ., received his doctorate there (1912), and taught philosophy of education. Guided, like Dewey, by a purely naturalistic and pragmatic philosophy, K. saw education as life itself, continued growth its essence and end, and purposeful activity its proper method. Among his works are *Education for a Changing Civilization* (1926) and *Philosophy of Education* (1951). BIBLIOGRAPHY: *Bertrand Russell, A. S. Neill,*

Homer Lane, W. H. Kilpatrick: Four Progressive Educators (ed. L. Perry, pa. 1968).

[M. B. MURPHY]

KILPECK, CHURCH OF (*c.*1170), English church, square in nave and choir, having an amazing array of Norman ornamental sculpture in arch of chancel, S door and corbel tables—in local Herefordshire style.

[M. J. DALY]

KILWINNING, ABBEY OF, former Benedictine monastery at Kilwinning, Ayrshire, Scotland. Founded originally as a church in the 12th cent., it became known as an abbey in the 13th century. Well-endowed by benefactors, it was a daughterhouse of Kelso Abbey. Plundered by Reformers in 1561, it was given to William Melville in 1592, and stands now in ruins.

[T. M. MCFADDEN]

KIM, ANDREW, BL. (Kim-tai-ken; 1821–46), martyr. A Korean of a Christian family, his father a martyr in 1839, K. was the first native Korean priest, ordained in Shanghai in 1845. Since Christianity was proscribed in Korea, K. made another secret entry into the country (a first attempt in 1843 had failed and a second had as its object to prepare the way for Bp. Ferreol to live in Seoul). Each entry was filled with incredible hardship and danger of death from Korean authorities. The third and final penetration of his native land occurred after his ordination. With Ferréol and Father Daveluy, K. embarked on a small ship from China, and after near disaster at sea the party landed on the Korean coast. Within a year K. was captured and beheaded. He was beatified in 1925. BIBLIOGRAPHY: C. Testore, BiblSanct 4:176–177 s.v. "Corea, Martiri della"; Butler 3:611–613.

[J. R. AHERNE]

KIM, HELEN (1899–1970), Methodist Korean educator and World Christian leader. She was educated at Ewha College, Seoul, Korea, Ohio Wesleyan Univ., Boston Univ., and Columbia Univ. Teachers College where in 1932 she became the first Korean woman to receive a doctorate. Returning to Korea she became vice-president and in 1938 president of Ewha College. During her career she was a delegate to 40 international gatherings of which 10 were related to the International Missionary Council and the World Council of Churches. Other organizations included World Council of the YWCA, International Committee on Red Cross, World Convention on Christian Education, and Twelfth UNESCO Conference. She served her government for many years as director of public information on the Korean mission to the United Nations, and as ambassador-at-large. She retired as President of Ewha College in 1961 and in 1963 received the Order of Cultural Merit of the Republic of Korea and the Ragsaysay Award (Philippines). BIBLIOGRAPHY: *New York Times* (Feb. 12, 1970); *Encyclopedia of World Methodism* (1974).

[F. E. MASER]

KINDEKENS, PETER (d. 1873), church administrator and founder of the American College, Louvain. Born and educated in Belgium, he was ordained for the Diocese of Detroit in 1842, and became vicar general to Bp. P. *Lefevere. Included in K.'s career were parish ministry, rectorship of St. Thomas Seminary, the designing of a new cathedral. Without success he proposed in 1856 establishment of an American college for seminarians in Rome; but his plans for Louvain were accepted. He personally arranged purchase of the buildings and acted as first rector. He returned to Detroit in 1860.

[J. R. AHERNE]

KINDĪ, 'ABD AL-MASIH AL- (*c.*9th cent.), an Arabic author and Nestorian Christian to whom is attributed an apologetic work on the Christian faith. K.'s writing was in reply to a letter from a Muslim, 'Abdallah ibn Ismā'īl al-Hāshimī, who apparently had a knowledge of Christians and their practices and was appealing to K. to convert to Islam. The work is considered a record of a controversy held before the Caliph al-Ma'mun (813–833) about 819, on the worth of Christianity and Islam. This controversial treatise was known and used by scholars of medieval Europe and was first printed in London in 1880. BIBLIOGRAPHY: L. Massignon, EncIslam[1] 2:1080.

[R. A. TODD]

KINDĪ, ABŪ-YŪSUF YA 'QŪB IBN ISHĀQ AL- (*c.*801–*c.*873), scholar and philosopher. Of noble Arab descent, he studied at Basra and Baghdad and held court positions to the Caliphs al-Ma'mūn (813–833) and al-Mu'taṣim (833–842). Honored with the title Faylasūf al-'Arab (the philosopher of the Arabs), al-Kindī was the first in a notable line of scholars and translators of the Greek philosophers. His influence and authority were strongly felt a century after his death, though the works of later Arab philosophers as, *al-Fārābī and Ibn-Sīnā (*Avicenna) far surpassed his writings. A few of al-Kindī's basic principles concerned with the divinely created world and divinely inspired prophecy were unacceptable to his Muslim successors. Considered mainly a natural philosopher, he believed that between God and the world of matter lay the world of the soul. Al-Kindī sought primarily to clarify the harmony that existed between the views of Plato and Aristotle. Some of his philosophical works give evidence of Neoplatonic and Neo-Pythagorean influence. Besides many translations, al-Kindī wrote over 250 treatises on such subjects as mathematics, physics, optics, medicine, astrology, geography, music, logic, poetry, and theology. Only several works on medicine and astrology are extant. It is possible that many of his writings were lost during the rule of conservative-minded al-Mutawakkil (847–861), who confiscated his entire library. It was probably through the Toledo school of translators and medieval Christian scholars, such as *Gerard of Cremona and *John of Seville, that the knowledge of al-Kindi reached the Latin world. BIB-

LIOGRAPHY: al-Kindī, *Rasā' il al-Kindī afalasafiyyah* (2 v., ed. 'Abd al-Hādī Abū Rīdah, 1950–53); M. Fakhry, *History of Islamic Philosophy* (1970) 82–112.

[R. A. TODD]

KING, MARTIN LUTHER, JR. (1929–68), American clergyman and civil rights leader. Born in Atlanta, Ga., the son and grandson of Baptist clergymen, he graduated from Morehouse College in Atlanta (1948), from Crozer Theological Seminary, Chester, Pa. (1951), and earned a doctorate from Boston Univ. (1955). Ordained in 1947, he became pastor of a Baptist church in Montgomery, Ala., in 1954, and there came to national prominence through his leadership of a strike against the segregated bus system. In 1960 he moved to Atlanta, where he was associated with his father as minister of a church, but gave most of his time to civil rights activities as president of the Southern Christian Leadership Conference, which he founded in 1956. He was noted for his oratorical gifts and for his philosophy of nonviolence, in part derived from Gandhi, which he considered the appropriate way of advancing the rights of black Americans. He received the Nobel Peace Prize in 1964. He was assassinated in Memphis, Tenn. on April 4, 1968. BIBLIOGRAPHY: W. R. Miller, *Martin Luther King, Jr.* (1968); L. G. Davis, *I Have a Dream* (1969, repr. 1973); A. Westin and B. Mahoney, *Trial of Martin Luther King* (1975); C. S. King, *My Life with Martin Luther King, Jr.* (pa. 1970).

[T. EARLY]

KING JAMES VERSION, the name generally used in the U.S. for the *Authorized Version of the Bible. The AV was published under the authority of King James I in 1611.

[T. C. O'BRIEN]

KINGDOM OF CHRIST, an expression that may designate (1) *kingship of Christ; (2) *kingdom of God; (3) the *millennium of Rev 20.4–6. In the first sense, the concrete collective noun kingdom is used as an archaism for the abstract kingship; thus Jn 18.36 probably refers to Christ's ruling power rather than to the realm he established. In the second sense, the kingdom of Christ is practically equivalent to the kingdom of God. Both expressions designate the realm set up by God's saving work—a realm revealed as a mystery by Christ (Mk 4.11): an eschatological reality (Mt 8.11–12) already inaugurated by Christ's coming (Lk 17.20–21). God's work in Christ has established this kingdom which in a broad sense embraces the universe (1 Cor 15.27) but comprises esp. redeemed mankind (Col 1.13) with Christ at its head (Eph 1.10, 20–23). One may get the impression in 1 Cor 15.25, 28 that Christ's kingdom is temporary: that it was based on his Resurrection, was inaugurated at his Ascension, and will end when he turns it over to his Father on the last day. This is not the case. The kingdom was eternally decreed to be Christ's by the Father's good pleasure (Eph 1.4, 22–23) so that it must be said to be his from the first moment of the Incarnation. Likewise, Christ will come at the end of time "with his kingdom" (Mt 16.28) which is his forever (Lk 1.33; 2 Pet 1.11) and is forever to be shared with his faithful followers (Mt 19.28; Lk 12.32). Paul's meaning in 1 Cor 15 is not that Christ's kingdom is provisional, but that through the perfect fulfillment of Christ's mission the kingdom will be perfectly subject in Christ to God (cf. Rev 21.22–23, 22.3). In the third sense, the kingdom of Christ is the 1000-year reign beginning with the chaining of the dragon and ending with the dragon's release (Rev 20.4–6). An excessively literal interpretation of apocalyptic symbolism led some early Christians to profess belief in a reign of Christ on earth for the 1000-year period beginning with his second coming in 1000 A.D. This teaching can be traced to Christian interpretations of the apocryphal Jewish book, *Secrets of Enoch,* according to which each of the 7 days of creation (Gen 1.1–2.4) stood for 1000 years.

Christ's birth inaugurated the 6th millennium, and his return the 7th. Cerinthus, the Ebionites, and Nepos professed a crude version of this teaching, according to which the millennium would afford the opportunity for unrestricted physical pleasure. A more spiritual, or mitigated type was held by several Fathers of the Church: e.g., St. Justin, St. Irenaeus, Tertullian, and St. Methodius. This view, also called *chiliasm is rejected by the Church; cf. the Decree of the Holy Office, confirmed by Pius XII in 1944 (see D 3839). BIBLIOGRAPHY: ThAq, *In 4 sent.* 43.1.3; H. Lesêtre, "Millénarisme," DB 4:1090–97; E. G. Ladd, *Presence of the Future: The Eschatology of Biblical Realism* (pa. 1973). *MILLENARIANISM.

[M. D. MEILACH]

KINGDOM OF GOD, an expression that may designate either (1) the reign or royal power of God as almighty and supremely free agent in history; or (2) the realm gradually constituted by God's saving work, a realm essentially transcendent and eschatological but in process of formation throughout history. The kingdom theme is rare in the OT, though its use becomes more frequent in the later books. It can be traced to the Davidic period, when it was mainly functional and expressed God's actual exercise of kingly power on behalf of Israel (Ps 24.8). It also had a nationalistic aspect: liturgical celebrations stressed God's choice of Sion as his people (Ps 29.10–11) and the ark as his throne (Ps 99.1). In the Prophets (Is 35.1–10; Dan 7.9–28) and in later Judaism (4 Esdras 12.32, Syriac Apocalypse of Baruch), Israel is the seat of God's rule over the nations. Messianism pervades the theology of the kingdom, and the kingdom itself becomes explicitly universal and eschatological (cf. esp. Is 60).

In the NT the kingdom of God is presented as the heart of the Good News preached by the Baptist as well as Jesus himself. (Note that in Matthew "kingdom of heaven" replaces "kingdom of God" 34 times in accord with the Jewish reluctance to use the divine name). Christ's contemporaries expected the future vindication of God's royal rights, but his message startled them because of the imminence he attributed to the kingdom's advent. He saw God's rule as already universal (Mt 5.34–35) but as about to be manifested in a unique way in his ministry (Mt 12.28). Indeed, that ministry is a sign of the kingdom's arrival (Lk 16.16), and yet he asks his disciples to pray for its coming (Mt 6.10). No one knows when its full realization will take place. The parables of the sower, the darnel, the mustard seed, and the yeast (Mt 13.4–43) make it clear that the kingdom has come but will not be fully established until the end of time. The kingdom belongs especially to the poor (Lk 4.18) and the righteous (Mt 5.1), and entrance into it brings salvation (Lk 3.6). Thus the early Christians regarded themselves as a "royal priesthood" (1 Pet 2.9) because they were given a place in the kingdom (Col 1.13). The Eucharist was their sign of unity in it and the pledge of their share in its fulfillment (1 Cor 11.25–26).

With few exceptions (e.g., St. Justin, *Dialogue* 31) the theme of God's kingdom was not developed in patristic writing because its Hebrew character was alien to Greek thought. In theology it differs only slightly from the notion of the Church: whereas the two are practically synonymous in most contexts, the kingdom is in a sense presupposed by the Church, which both results from its revelation and awaits its full establishment. BIBLIOGRAPHY: R. Schnackenburg, *God's Rule and Kingdom* (1963); H. Ridderbos, *Coming of the Kingdom* (1962); C. H. Dodd, *Parables of the Kingdom* (1961); G. Harkness, *Understanding the Kingdom of God* (1974).

[M. D. MEILACH]

KINGS, BOOKS OF. The existing division of these books into two is artificial, and for purposes of interpretation should be disregarded. The treatise as a whole probably acquired substantially its present form during the reign of Josiah (640–609 B.C.) and is the work of Deuteronomist reformers, who combined a number of earlier sources and reinterpreted them from their own distinctive standpoint so as to produce a strongly "slanted" version of the history of Israel and Judah extending from the death of David (*c.*961) to the final collapse of the Judahite monarchy (587). The work falls unmistakably into three main parts: (1) an elaborate account of the glories of Solomon's reign (961–922), and summary histories of (2) the divided kingdoms up to the overthrow of Israel, the northern kingdom in 721 and (3) of Judah alone up to the downfall of the monarchy in 587. Of the earlier sources subsumed into this Deuteronomist history three are explicitly mentioned: the "Acts of Solomon" (cf. 1 Kg 11.41), the Chronicles of the kings of Judah" and of Israel. These were probably court histories of a more or less official kind recounting the achievements, glories, and triumphs of the kings involved. Manifestly other and more important sources were drawn upon, notably a detailed account of the building and dedication of the Temple (cf. 1 Kg ch. 6–7) and the "tradition cycles" of the prophets, above all of Elijah (1 Kg 17–2 Kg 1) and Elisha (2 Kg 2–10 and 13.14–21), but of other prophets too, such as Ahijah of Shiloh (cf. 1 Kg 11.26–39), Micaiah (1 Kg 22), and Isaiah (2 Kg ch. 19–20). A number of stories of anonymous "men of God" and prophets clearly derive from a similar source or sources (cf., e.g., 1 Kg 13 and 16.1–4; ch. 20 and 22). The central theme of the treatise as a whole is in fact a condemnation of all the kings of Israel and most of the kings of Judah for refusing to obey Yahweh's word as delivered to them by the prophets. The court histories of the kings have been combined in such a way that the reigns of Israelite kings are synchronized with those of the kings of Judah for the relevant period. All these records have been made to conform to a stereotyped pattern superimposed by the Deuteronomists themselves. Thus in the case of the kings of Judah the names of the king's father and mother are recorded, and also the length of his reign and the year of the reign of the contemporary king of Israel in which he acceded to the throne. In the case of the kings of Israel a similar, though less full pattern has been superimposed. The most significant element in this is the brief moral evaluation supplied in each case from the Deuteronomists' own standpoint. All the kings of Israel are condemned, and of the kings of Judah only Asa (1 Kg 15.9–15), Jehoshaphat (1 Kg 22.41–51), and Josiah (2 Kg ch. 22–23) are unreservedly praised. The final downfall of the kingdom is attributed to the fact that despite the persistent warnings of the prophets so many kings obstinately led the people into sin. The whole work underwent a final revision and completion during the Exile, and at this time it was recorded that the king of Babylon showed favor to his captive, the exiled Jehoiachin of Judah, thus providing a ray of hope for the future restoration. BIBLIOGRAPHY: J. Montgomery and H. S. Gehman, *Books of Kings* (1951); E. R. Thiele, *Mysterious Numbers of the Hebrew Kings* (1951); J. Gray, *I and II Kings* (1964).

[D. J. BOURKE]

KINGS, DIVINE RIGHT OF, the doctrine that monarchic sovereignty is neither derived from the people nor reposes on their consent and is to be exercised without check by any other human agency. Generically a doctrine of political absolutism, such as was supported by Thomas *Hobbes (d. 1679), though with the proviso of an implied contract in the transference of power, its specific difference was that sovereignty had been indefeasibly granted by God and, moreover, in virtue of the monarch's genealogy. On neither count was it deeply rooted in Western history. Some sort of theocratic function was allowed to rulers in the Middle Ages, but absolute power could not prevail so long as they were confronted by the Church as a rival center of authority and needed its blessing for popular acceptance. Then, too, the politico-theological doctrine that government of a family by a father was the true exemplar of all government and effectively transmitted in the rightful line of succession, though adumbrated under the Tudors, was not prominent until the Stuarts, when it was espoused as a cause by leading

Anglican divines during the Great Rebellion of Parliament against Charles I. It scarcely lasted the century, however, since it had virtually to be scrapped by accommodation to the needs of the Protestant succession. Its classical statement is the *Patriarcha, or the Natural Power of Kings Asserted,* by Sir Robert Filmer (d. 1653), a work posthumously published in 1680, and influentially criticized in the *Two Treatises of Government* (1690) by John Locke (d. 1704), who was, however, too Whig to treat the paternalism and priesthood of princes at depth. BIBLIOGRAPHY: J. N. Figgis, *Theory of the Divine Right of Kings* (2d ed., 1914); M. Bloch, *Les rois thaumaturges* (1924).

[T. GILBY]

KING'S BOOK, or *A Necessary Doctrine and Erudition for Any Christian Man,* published May 1543, a revision of the *Bishops' Book of 1537 in a more conservative direction following the standard of the *Six Articles of 1539. Prepared by a commission of the two English abps., six bps., and twelve scholars, it received the approval of *Convocation and contained a preface by King Henry VIII. The work was preceded by a survey of the answers to 17 questions on the nature and number of the sacraments. It remained the official standard of doctrine of the C of E until the death of Henry (1547). The most recent edition of *The King's Book* is by T. A. Lacey (1932). BIBLIOGRAPHY: *Works of Thomas Cranmer* (1846) 2:115–117.

[M. H. SHEPHERD]

KING'S CHAPEL, BOSTON, designed (1749–58) by Peter Harrison and completed (1787) with Ionic porch. Though the edifice is rooted in James Gibbs' designs, its scale, space, and carving render it one of the finest American Georgian churches.

[M. J. DALY]

KING'S COLLEGE CHAPEL, Cambridge, England. Named for Henry VI who laid the first stone in 1446, this Gothic chapel is of extremely simple interior but magnificently decorated in repetitive window tracery and fan-vaulting, beautifully combining a simple practical spirit with mystery and rich ornament.

[M. J. DALY]

KING'S CONFESSION, an anti-Roman appendix to the *Scots Confession; sometimes called the Second Scots Confession. It was written by John Craig (d. 1600), a friend of John *Knox, and received its name from the fact that it was signed by King James VI of Scotland. It became part of the *Scottish National Covenant of 1638.

[T. C. O'BRIEN]

KING'S EVIL, medieval name for scrofula because of the legend that the kings of France and England had power to cure the disease. The power, according to legend, was given the kings of France by St. Remigius of Reims (d. *c.*533). In England record of its use dates to the reign of St. Edward the Confessor (d. 1066). The touching was accompanied by prayers and conferring of a medal of St. Michael the Archangel on the sufferer. Cures seem to have occurred. The last record of the practice in England was in the 16th cent.; in France in the 19th.

[T. C. O'BRIEN]

KINGSHIP OF CHRIST, the ruling power that Jesus Christ, considered in his human nature, exercises in relation to all other creatures. Prefigured in the prophecies of Isaiah (9.5–6) and Daniel (7.13–14), the kingly power of Christ is said by Luke (1.31–33) to have been revealed to Mary at the Annunciation. Royalty as such was repudiated by Christ during his public ministry (Jn 6.15) and admitted symbolically (Jn 12.14–15) and explicitly (Jn 18.37) only in close connection with his impending death. It forms an important aspect of the Christology of Revelation (2.27; 19.16).

Patristic development took several forms. Some apologists, to stress Jesus' Jewish background, presented him as David's royal descendant. The Alexandrian theologians, influenced by Philo, related Christ's kingship to his status as divine Logos. The school of Antioch (Marcellus of Ancyra in particular) linked that kingship to the Incarnation as such. Athanasius, in opposition to Arianism, fused these traditions into a doctrine of dual kingship: Christ was said to be King both as God and as man. The Middle Ages fostered devotion to Christ as King by preaching and art, rather than by theological development. It was similarly a pastoral, rather than theological, movement to which Pius XI acceded when he instituted the Feast of Christ the King (**Quas primas,* 1925). Asking men to submit their minds, wills, and hearts to the royal dominion of Christ as man (his theology here is Antiochene), the Pope spelled out the benefits that would thereby result for every level of society.

It is possible, esp. in light of much contemporary Protestant theology, to regard the attribution of kingship to the man Christ as owing more to human political structures than to revelation. The revealed truths of Christ's *primacy and unique mediation might then be expressed better in terms of service than of royalty. Such a view would be a reemphasis of Alexandrian theology, stressing Christ's absolute power as God and attributing less autonomy to his human nature. BIBLIOGRAPHY: L. Cerfaux, "Le Titre 'Kyrios' et la dignité royale de Jésus," *Recueil Lucien Cerfaux* [1] (1954) 3–64; P. Beskow, *Rex Gloriae: The Kingship of Christ in the Early Church* (1962); W. Zimmerli and J. Jeremias, *Servant of God* (1957).

[M. D. MEILACH]

KINGSLEY, CHARLES (1819–75), Anglican novelist and Christian Socialist leader. Ordained in 1842, K. devoted much of his time to writing, producing a number of well-known novels, among which were *Alton Locke* (1850) and *Westward Ho!* (1855). In his earlier life, as a follower of F.D. *Maurice, he became a Christian socialist in London and served the cause as its leading pamphleteer; but he was disillusioned with it in later life. In his views of church life he tended toward a *broad-church interpretation of Anglicanism. His strong anti-Roman animus led him to publish an incautious statement reflecting unfavorably upon the attitude of the Roman clergy and J.H. *Newman toward the truth. This evoked a shattering rebuttal in Newman's *Apologia pro vita sua*. Works: 19 v., 1901–03. BIBLIOGRAPHY: U. Pope-Hennessy, *Charles Kingsley* (1949); G. Kendall, *Charles Kingsley and his Ideas* (1937, repr. 1972). *CHRISTIAN SOCIALISM.

[R. B. ENO]

KINKAKUJI (1397), Japanese temple in Kyoto; originally a grand villa for the Ashikaga shogun Yoshimitsu; upon his death converted into a Zen monastery (Rokuonji) or Kinkakuji (Temple of the Golden Pavilion), the last remaining structure until 1950 when it, also, was destroyed by arson. An exact replica now stands—three-storied, covered with gold leaf, facing a reflecting pond in the garden.

[M. J. DALY]

KINNARA, mythical figure with human body and horse's head in Buddhist and Hindu art, one of the celestial choristers and musicians attending Kuvera, Lokapāla of the N, dwelling on Mt. Kailāsa.

[M. J. DALY]

KINO (CHINO), EUSEBIO FRANCISCO (1644–1711), Jesuit missionary, explorer, and pioneer of the Pacific Coast missions. Born at Segno di Val di Non, Italy, K. entered the society's province of Upper Germany, taught mathematics at Ingolstadt, and volunteered for the Mexican mission in 1678. With the Atondo expedition K. crossed Lower California in 1683. Later he worked at Pimería Alta in modern Sonora and Arizona. For 25 years he traveled extensively, founded numerous mission stations, built chapels and churches, baptized thousands of Indians, and became one of the greatest missionaries in history. K. was also a cartographer and furnished proof that California is not an island. BIBLIOGRAPHY: H. E. Bolton, *Rim of Christendom: A Biography of Eusebio Francisco Kino, Pacific Coast Pioneer* (1936); J. Bannon, *Frontier Mission in Sonora* (1946); *Kino Reports to Headquarters* (ed. E. J. Burrus, 1954).

[P. DAMBORIENA]

KINSHIP, see CONSANGUINITY.

KIRBY, LUKE, ST. (1549–82), English martyr. He was probably educated at Cambridge, became a Catholic at Louvain, prepared for the priesthood at Douai, and was ordained at Cambrai (1577). In April 1580 he set out for the English mission with Edmund *Campion and several others. As soon as they landed at Dover, they were arrested and taken to prison in London. In November 1581 they were tried and condemned on the spurious charge of plotting against the Queen. K. was executed in May 1582, and was beatified in 1886, and canonized in 1970. BIBLIOGRAPHY: N. Del Re, BiblSanct 7:1050–51; Butler 2:415–416; Gillow BDEC 4:50–52.

[V. SAMPSON]

KIRCHENORDNUNG, German, meaning *church order. The church orders for the *territorial churches are frequently cited sources in Reformation history.

KIRK, mainly Scottish form of the word church, with which it is used interchangeably in literature and in documents of the Church until the 17th century. It is still used popularly, often to distinguish the Church of Scotland from other religious bodies. The *Westminster Assembly (1645–48) gave official sanction to the title Church (rather than Kirk) of Scotland.

[J. A. R. MACKENZIE]

KIRK, KENNETH ESCOTT (1886–1954), born in Sheffield, fellow of Trinity College, Oxford, Regius Professor of moral and pastoral theology, and bp. of Oxford. An Anglo-Catholic in the liberal tradition of Charles *Gore, K. wrote much on traditional Christian spirituality and, at home with the Dominican authors and *Caroline divines, promoted the study of systematic moral theology in the Church of England. His *Bampton Lectures for 1928 produced a work of lasting value, *The Vision of God,* the Christian doctrine of the *summum bonum*. See life and letters, by E. W. Kemp (1959).

[T. GILBY]

KIRK-SESSION, the *church session in the Church of Scotland.

KIRKSTALL, ABBEY OF, English Cistercian monastery in Yorkshire near Leeds which was founded by monks of Fountains (1147) and prospered throughout the Middle Ages with its successful sheep farming, wool trade, and pottery making. After its suppression (1540), Abbot John Ripley and his monks were pensioned. Its building program continued up to that time with the completion of the great tower in Tudor Gothic. At the present time, its ruins, representative of Norman Gothic style of the 12th cent., are maintained as national monuments. BIBLIOGRAPHY: D. E. Owen, *Kirkstall Abbey* (1955); W. H. Hope, *Architectural Description of Kirkstall Abbey* (repr. 1907).

[L. J. LEKAI]

KIRLIN, JOSEPH (1868–1926), parish priest, writer. A Philadelphian, he was ordained in 1892 and served in a number of parishes in the Philadelphia Archdiocese. He was a friend of the poor, a celebrated preacher, and an influence in the temperance movement. In 1903 he wrote *A Life of the Most Rev. Patrick Ryan* and in 1909 published a model diocesan history, *Catholicity in Philadelphia*. He was a frequent contributor to devotional periodicals, and wrote a series of meditations published as *Christ the Builder* (1929) as well as several books on eucharistic devotion.

[J. R. AHERNE]

KIRSCH, JOHANN PETER (1861–1941), church historian and archeologist. A native of Luxembourg, where he made his theological studies and was ordained, K. developed a considerable interest in advances then being made in the fields of history and archeology. He studied in Rome as a young priest (1884–90). From 1890 to 1932 he was professor of patrology and Christian archeology at Fribourg, and from 1926 until his death, rector of the Pontifical Institute of Christian Archeology in Rome. In addition to his writings in the fields of patrology and ancient church history, he also published learned studies on the finances of the medieval papacy; he contributed many articles for the *Catholic Encyclopedia*. BIBLIOGRAPHY: E. Molitor, NCE 8:206; A. Schuchert, LTK 6:307.

[R. B. ENO]

KIRTTIMUKHA, stylized head in Indian art lacking lower jaw, appearing over windows or niches as at Ajanta, Ellora (Cave 19), and on doorways of Javanese medieval monuments at Barabudur.

[M. J. DALY]

KISHON (CISON), a stream in N Palestine. It was the scene of Barak's victory over the Canaanites (Jg 5.21) and of Elijah's slaying of the prophets of Baal (1 Kg 18.40).

[F. J. MONTALBANO]

KISMET, Turkish adaptation of an Arabic word, *qismah* or *qismat,* meaning portion, lot, or destiny and having to do with the fate that befalls or is allotted each individual in life. More poetic and popular than philosophical in origin, the word does not appear in the Koran in the sense it later acquired, though the concept is traditionally associated with the attitudes of resignation or submission to fate found among Islamic peoples during the centuries of their decline. The term relates specifically to an individual's destiny in this life, not to the punishments or rewards apportioned him in the hereafter, and as such is not the Islamic concept of predestination. In its acceptance of inevitability and stress on the power of the irrational, kismet implies the idea of divine arbitrariness, even of divine injustice. It is to be distinguished both from the Calvinist doctrine of predestination and from the more general religious belief that the universe is guided by a divine intelligence or purpose.

[E. M. GATES]

KISS, HOLY (The Kiss), (1) a practice among Mennonites to express Christian love (cf. Rom 16.16;1 Cor 16.20). Exchange of a kiss by brethren at baptism, at the Lord's Supper, or as a salutation was common among most early Swiss and Dutch Mennonites. Withholding of the kiss from the wayward was part of church discipline. In Europe the practice has almost completely ceased. In N America only the more conservative bodies, such as the Old Order Amish, still observe it. See MennEnc 3:181–186

(2) In some countries, as in Ireland, the term is used for a kiss given to parents by children who have just received their first holy communion.

[T. C. O'BRIEN]

KISS OF PEACE, or Pax, the liturgical action by which the faithful greet one another as a symbol of their love and union. The kiss of peace is most commonly associated with the Eucharistic Liturgy, although it can and has occurred in other rites, baptism, penance and confirmation. It is probably of apostolic origin, and is definitely mentioned as a liturgical act already in the 2nd cent. by Justin. In the Eucharistic Liturgy the kiss originally took place before the Offertory whereas now it is attached to the Communion. Through the centuries, the manner of giving the kiss has varied: sometimes with the mouth, at other times as an embrace. The sign of peace is now exchanged by all the faithful present at the Eucharistic Liturgy. BIBLIOGRAPHY: B. J. Mullahy, NCE 8:207; J. Miller, *Fundamentals of the Liturgy* (1959) 287.

[B. ROSENDALL]

KISSANE, EDWARD (1886–1955), OT exegete. After studies at the *Pontifical Biblical Institute in Rome, K. taught OT in Toronto and at St. Patrick's College, Maynooth (1917–1955). He published numerous articles, as well as translations and commentaries on OT books. He was a critical scholar and knowledgeable Hebraist. BIBLIOGRAPHY: J. Trinquet, *Catholicisme* 6:1449–50.

[T. M. MCFADDEN]

KITTEL, surname of two German biblical scholars, father and son.

Rudolf (1853–1929), professor of OT at Breslau from 1888, and at Leipzig from 1898. In his writings on the history of Israel he stressed the primacy of revelation against the evolutionary interpretation of J. *Wellhausen. He also opposed the *Panbabylonianism of F. Delitzsch (1850–1922). He published numerous works on the OT, but is esp. known for his edition of the Hebrew Bible, *Biblia Hebraica* (1905–06).

Gerhard (1888–1948), son of Rudolf, he taught at Tübingen (1926–39) as well as at other universities. He was a NT scholar; his main idea was that Jewish rather than Hellenic thought was dominant in NT literature. He was the inaugurator and editor of the first four volumes (1932–39) of the incomparable *Theologisches Wörterbuch zum Neuen Testament,* known familiarly as "Kittel" (Eng. tr. and ed. G. W. Bromiley, *Theological Dictionary of the New Tes-*

tament 9 v. 1964–1973). His anti-Semitic writings under the Nazi regime led to his imprisonment by the Allies in 1945. He died at his home in Tübingen. BIBLIOGRAPHY: W. F. Albright, "Gerhard Kittel and the Jewish Question in Antiquity," *History, Archeology, and Humanism* (1964).

[T. C. O'BRIEN]

KITTIM, Hebrew name for Cyprus (Num 24.24). It was derived from the city-state Kition on the SE coast of the island. According to the Table of Nations (Gen 10.4), it descended from Japheth's son Javan (Ionia, and by extension Greece). The name Kittim was also used for other lands beyond the seas.

[T. EARLY]

KIVA, Hopi Indian underground ceremonial chamber containing altars, masks. A small round hole in the floor, the sipapu, communicating with the underworld, symbolized the ancestral tribes' place of emergence and final departure.

[M. J. DALY]

KJELD, ST. (d. 1150), Danish noble whose cult is confined to Denmark. At an early age K. became a canon regular at the cathedral in Viborg. Later as its provost he was considered excessively generous and removed from office. He was reinstated by Pope Eugene III but died while planning to become a missionary. Pope Clement III refused to canonize him but allowed Abp. Absalon of Lund to establish Kjeld's cult in his own see in 1189. BIBLIOGRAPHY: L. Musset, NCE 8:208.

[F. G. O'BRIEN]

KKK, see KU KLUX KLAN.

KLEIN, FÉLIX (1862–1953), French author, translator. K. was ordained in Paris in 1885. A teacher at the *Institut Catholique,* he became a well-known writer; his work fills 50 volumes. K. translated a number of works by such American Catholic writers as Abp. John Ireland and Bp. John Lancaster Spalding. When W. Elliott's *Life of Father Hecker* appeared (1891) K. was asked to translate it into French. Published in 1896, the translation was an immediate success, but provoked a famous controversy when conservatives in Europe saw in it what they termed the heresy of *Americanism. K. withdrew the book when Leo XIII's letter to Card. Gibbons (*Testem benevolentiae*) condemned certain errors supposedly reflected in the book. Other books by K. are *Nouvelles tendences en religion et en littérature* (1893) and his seven-volume autobiography, *La Route de petit Morvandiau* (1946–52).

[J. R. AHERNE]

KLEINSCHMIDT, BEDA (1867–1932), Franciscan liturgist and art historian. Ordained in 1892, K. served as provincial in Saxony (1913–19), and from 1925 was professor of liturgy at Paderborn. He founded these important reviews: *Monumenta Germaniae Franciscana, Franziskusstimmen,* and *Franziskanische Studien.* He is well-known for his works dealing with sacred art, esp. Franciscan art. BIBLIOGRAPHY: R. Spirito, DE 2:552; L. Hardick, NCE 8:210.

[F. D. LAZENBY]

KLEIST, HEINRICH VAN (1777–1811), German dramatist and author of *nouvelle.* From the study of Kant, he derived the theme that is recurrent in his works—the relativity, and consequent fallibility, of human knowledge. Despite the romantic element in most of his works, his style is realistic. Of his dramas, the best is *Prinz Friedrich von Homburg* (1810). A one-act comedy in verse, *Der zerbrochene Krug* (1808), is counted among the few great comedies in German literature. His *Erzählungen* (2 v., 1810–11) includes the masterpiece *Michael Kohlhaas.* BIBLIOGRAPHY: W. Silz, *Heinrich von Kleist, Studies in His Works and Literary Character* (1961). R. E. Helbling, *Heinrich Von Kleist: The Major Works* (1975).

[M. F. MCCARTHY]

KLEIST, JAMES (1873–1949), Jesuit classicist, biblical scholar and translator. Born in Silesia, K. taught Latin, Greek, and Scripture in the U.S. at Campion College (1908–17), John Carroll Univ. (1917–28), and St. Louis Univ. (1928–49). He published a number of books on NT topics, but is best known for his collaboration with J. *Lilly on a modern English translation of the NT (1952). K. produced an accurate translation of the Gospels in an intelligible and contemporary style.

[T. M. MCFADDEN]

KLENOVSKY, JOHANN (*c.*1431–98), Moravian lay leader. Able, learned, but without degrees or orders, he entered the *Unitas Fratrum apparently before 1467 and led the group that sought a compromise between the ideals of perfection of the first Brethren and the demands of reality. In the critical years following the death of Brother Gregory (1474) he created the framework for reorganizing the Unity according to the principles worked out by the Great Party. BIBLIOGRAPHY: E. Peschke, RGG 3:1659.

[M. J. SUELZER]

KLEPTOMANIA, an obsessive urge to steal objects that offer little or no material gain to the individual who takes them. The objects may be different, though related, or they may be the same type. The stolen items are sometimes hoarded, and other times the items are disposed of almost immediately regardless of their market value. The moral culpability depends upon the degree of moral freedom present at the time of the theft. The limitations of moral freedom on this issue are psychological. Kleptomania is generally considered to be a form of what are called obsessive-compulsive reactions. In other words, the agent attempts to alleviate his repression-caused anxiety through acts that he is unable to control. Hence, by the compulsive act of stealing the agent receives symbolic satisfaction. There are various opinions as to the cause of the underlying anxiety. Generally psychologists see it as displaced sexual gratification in which the stolen object symbolizes some unconsciously desired sex object. Other opinions stress the fact that, since the agents are usually embarrassed and repentant when caught, this stealing symbolizes the unconscious desires of the agent to be apprehended, punished, and eventually forgiven. Nevertheless, the exact degree of moral limitation present in each act of stealing varies. Sometimes the agent retains enough self-control either to refrain from stealing or at least to be partially culpable for his actions. Other times, however, it seems that the agent loses all, or almost all ability to resist the urge to steal and hence loses his moral freedom in the situation.

[C. NEELY]

KLEUTGEN, JOSEPH (1811–83), Jesuit scholastic theologian. K. lived in Rome from 1843 where he held several responsible positions, helped formulate the dogmatic constitution *De fide catholica* of Vatican Council I, and reportedly made the first draft of the encyclical **Aeterni Patris*. He was a constant opponent of the philosophical and theological rationalism prevalent in Germany (see HERMESIANISM), and is credited with restoring scholastic theology there through his books, *Die Theologie der Vorzeit* (3 v., 1853–60) and *Die Philosophie der Vorzeit* (2 v., 1860–63). BIBLIOGRAPHY: J. J. Toohy, CE 8:667; P. Bernard, DTC 8.2:2359–60; A. Kerkvoorde, *Catholicisme* 6:1456–57.

[T. M. MCFADDEN]

KLOPSTOCK, FRIEDRICH GOTTLIEB (1724–1803), poet. The religious fervor and intensity of expression that characterize the first three cantos of the *Messias* (1748) inspired changes in German poetry that anticipated *Sturm und Drang* and Romanticism. K.'s *Odes* (1771) reveal his mastery of lyric form. He is also author of *Geistliche Lieder* (2 v., 1758, 1769), of three dramas on biblical themes, and of the *Bardiete,* a trilogy of lyrical dramas about the national hero Hermann (Arminius). BIBLIOGRAPHY: F. G. Klopstock, *Klopstock, Friedrich Gottlieb: Werke und Briefe, Historisch-Kritische Ausgabe* (36 v., ed. H. Gronemeyer et al., 1974).

[M. F. MCCARTHY]

KLOSTERNEUBURG, MONASTERY OF, Austrian monastery of Augustinian Canons on the Danube in the Archdiocese of Vienna. Established *c.* 1100 with secular canons, it was transferred to Augustinians in 1133. Margrave St. Leopold III (*c.* 1075–1136) richly endowed the monastery, which was always one of the most important spiritual, scientific, and artistic centers of the Austrian Church. Monastic discipline declined during the Reformation, but revived in the 17th century. In 1730 Emperor Charles VI began a gigantic (still unfinished) monastery-residence modeled after the Escorial. In 1918 the popular liturgical movement was begun at Klosterneuburg by Pius Parsch. During World War II the Nazi regime suppressed the monastery (1941–45) and executed Canon Romanus Scholz.

Klosterneuburg has a theological academy, founded in 1768, a choir school, and editorial and publishing facilities. It is the greatest producer of wine in Austria. The interior of the Romanesque church (1114–36) with Gothic towers was rebuilt in 17th-cent. Baroque. Its shrine of St. Leopold includes the famous enamel altar by Nicholas of Verdun (1181) and beautiful Gothic glass paintings. The library contains *c.* 170,000 volumes; the archives, the famous treasure containing the Austrian archducal crown (1616), and a gallery with many Gothic paintings are of great value BIBLIOGRAPHY: F. H. Röhrig, NCE 8:213–214; *idem, Der Verduner Altar* (3d ed., 1965); *Jahrbuch des Stiftes Klosterneuburg* (9 v., 1908-20, NS from 1961).

[F. H. RÖHRIG]

KLUBERTANZ, GEORGE P. (1912–72), American Jesuit philosopher at St. Louis University (1949–71). A graduate of the Pontifical Medieval Institute, Toronto, he developed in his teaching and writing the Christian existential philosophy inspired by the work of É. Gilson. Among K.'s works were his important study on the *vis cogitativa* or ''particular reason'' in the teaching of St. Thomas Aquinas, published as *The Discursive Power* (1952), a course in metaphysics, *The Philosophy of Being* (1952, 2d ed. 1963), and a personal interpretation, *Saint Thomas Aquinas on Analogy* (1960).

[T. C. O'BRIEN]

KLUG, IGNAZ (1877–1929), professor of moral theology at Passau from 1916, author of studies on the psychological influences limiting freedom of will, esp. in his *Willensfreiheit und Persönlichkeit* (1932) and *Kriminalpädagogik* (1936). He also published popular apologetical works.

[T. C. O'BRIEN]

KLUPFEL, ENGELBERT (1773–1811), German Augustinian, theologian. After teaching in houses of his order, he became professor at the Univ. of Freiburg-im-Breisgau, 1767–1805. In his writings he defended the teaching of H. *Noris on the intrinsic efficacy of grace through attraction of the will. He also showed a marked preference for theology based on patristic sources rather than on scholastic categories. He published *De statu naturae purae* (1768), *De eximiis dotibus humanae naturae ante peccatum* (1769). His *Institutiones theologiae dogmaticae* (1789) rejects papal infallibility, in keeping with the *Josephinism of the times, and was one of the official texts imposed on the Austrian government-sanctioned seminaries.

[T. C. O'BRIEN]

KNABENBAUER, JOSEPH (1839–1911), Jesuit biblical commentator. K. taught Scripture at the Jesuit houses at Ditton Hall, England, and Valkenburg, Holland. He was one of the founders of the noted series, *Cursus Scripturae Sacrae,* to which he contributed 17 volumes of commentary on various OT and NT books. He was a moderately conservative exegete, intentionally dependent upon traditional interpretations. BIBLIOGRAPHY: A. Bea, DBSuppl 5:188–189; F. X. Weiser, NCE 8:214; J. Trinquet, *Catholicisme* 6:1560.

[T. M. MCFADDEN]

KNEELING, a natural gesture or posture externally manifesting or expressing certain interior sentiments, feelings, or attitude of a human person toward another. In primitive cultures it symbolized or expressed inferiority, dependence, submission; in Graeco-Roman ceremonial it was the posture of supplication. It is the posture of mourning or of urgent petition, or humility in the OT; and in the NT Christ "fell on his knees and prayed" (Lk 22.41), while with St. Paul to "bow the knee" before the Father (Eph 3.14) or "at the name of Jesus" (Phil 2.10) is synonymous with prayer and adoration. From the 4th cent. kneeling is the common posture of private prayer in Christianity, first, it seems, as symbolic of a penitential attitude, later as simply expressing the reverence, humility, submission proper to petition and all forms of prayer. Related to kneeling, in liturgical observance, are genuflection, prostration, and the profound bow. BIBLIOGRAPHY: F. T. Bergh, CE 6:423–427; A. E. Crawley, Hastings ERE 7:745–747. *PRAYER, POSTURE AT.

[W. J. READ]

KNEIPP, SEBASTIAN (1821–97), German priest, promoter of water therapy. Cured of a lung ailment with the help of Johann Siegmund Hahn's treatise on the medicinal power of water, K. was able to fulfill his wish to become a priest (1852). He was named chaplain at a convent in Wörishofen and later, the town's pastor. He improved Hahn's methods, supplementing them with the use of sunlight, fresh air, and herbs, including the famous Kneipp malt. Physicians who worked with him in caring for the thousands who flocked to him in the cholera year 1854 built sanatoria elsewhere, esp. in the Black Forest. K.'s first work, *Meine Wasserkur* (1886), was soon translated into many languages. It was followed by *So sollt ihr leben!* (1889) and *Mein Testament* (1894). Royalties were used to build hospitals and orphanages. Critical examination of K.'s books reveals little knowledge of diagnostic theory, errors in interpretation of symptoms, and an unscientific dependence on intuition. The undoubted cures obtained by his methods are the result of hygienic living, a tranquil environment, and the uplift that comes from the personal interest of physicians. K. is also recognized as a pioneer in the field of modern dietetics. BIBLIOGRAPHY: C. Robert, *Catholicisme* 6:1461–62.

[M. J. SUELZER]

KNIGHT, WILLIAM (1476–1547), English diplomat. As secretary to Card. Wolsey, he was sent to Rome to make arrangements for Henry VIII's divorce. He returned to England (1527) to find that the concessions he obtained were inadequate for Wolsey's purposes. After lesser ecclesiastical appointments, he finally (1541) became Bp. of Bath and Wells.

[V. SAMPSON]

KNIGHTS OF ALCÁNTARA, Spanish military order, known as Knights of San Julián del Pereiro (from *c.* 1167) and approved by Pope Alexander III (1176). The order followed the Benedictine Rule and was a Cîteaux dependency. It affiliated with the Knights of Calatrava (before 1187), and acquired a new name by the acquisition of the Alcántara fortress on the Tagus near Portugal (1218). The knights wore a white mantle with a scarlet cross. After helping reconquer Extremadura and Andalusia, they became embroiled in intramural fighting and peninsular politics until Ferdinand and Isabella assumed control (1494,1523). Alcántara soon declined into an aristocratic association and, after 1875, became a decoration. BIBLIOGRAPHY: J. F. O'Callaghan, NCE 8:215; S. Mattei, EncCatt 1:721.

[R. I. BURNS]

KNIGHTS OF COLUMBUS (K of C), a fraternal benefit organization for Catholic men. Nearly 1,220,600 men belong to its 6,018 councils. It was organized by Rev. Michael J. McGivney in New Haven, Conn. and received a charter from the state in 1882. Like the Masonic lodges, which Catholics were forbidden to join, the K of C devised a three-degree system of initiation. Members do not take oaths. A fourth degree was introduced in 1900. Members of this degree wear plumed hats, evening clothes, a cape, sword, and baldric in religious processions and parades. Knights may purchase insurance, although those who do not take policies may be initiated as associate members. Men who are over 18 years of age and practicing RCs, regardless of race, are eligible for membership. There are councils in every state of the union as well as in Canada, Puerto Rico, Mexico and the Philippines. The K of C engage in various religious and charitable projects; they provide scholarships at The Catholic Univ. of America where they also established a chair. The organization contributed $1 million for the campanile at the National Shrine in Washington, D.C. and a substantial sum to the Pius XII Memorial Library at St. Louis University. The K of C place advertisements in daily and weekly newspapers offering instruction in the Catholic faith. This has led to more than 600,000 enrollments in courses in the Catholic faith. The only official auxiliary organization is the Columbian Squires for young men which was founded in 1925. Insurance assets of the K of C exceed $590 million while insurance in force on members exceeds $3 billion. The society publishes a monthly magazine *Columbia*. BIBLIOGRAPHY: W. J. Whalen, *Handbook of Secret Organizations* (1966); E. D. Klerr, EncCatt 3:1198–99.

[W. J. WHALEN]

KNIGHTS OF DOBRIN, a military order of knighthood of German origin. The order was founded by Duke Conrad of Masovia and Bp. Christian of Prussia (1228), and was modeled after the Knights of the Sword of Livonia. They were given Dobrin castle on the Drweca River. The order encountered the animosity of the Teutonic Knights and was absorbed by them in 1235. BIBLIOGRAPHY: M. Tumler, *Der Deutsche Orden im Werden, Wachsen und Wirken bis 1400* (1955; 2d ed. 1965).

[B. F. SCHERER]

KNIGHTS OF LABOR, a labor organization founded in 1869 at Philadelphia by a group of garment workers, headed by Uriah S. Stephens. He gave it the character, oath, and ritual of a *secret society; but these elements were dropped in 1881. An enlightened philosophy of labor was advanced by the Knights, including the fair share of workers in profits, equal pay for women for equal work, restriction of child labor, arbitration, and the right to unionize an industry. By 1881, under the leadership of Terence V. *Powderley, the organization numbered nearly 700,000 members. Financial losses in cooperative ventures, factionalism, clumsy administrative structures contributed to the decline; by 1890 the craft-centered American Federation of Labor had superseded the Knights; they formally disbanded in 1917. The Knights of Labor belong to an episode important to the relationship between the Church and the worker. The Canadian bps. condemned the Knights in 1884 as a secret society; many American bps. and clergy, regarding the Knights as socialistic and revolutionary, favored the same action. But Card. *Gibbons saw the need for an enlightened social policy in the Church and succeeded in persuading Leo XIII against condemning the Knights. The issue contributed to the Church's championing of labor, as signaled by Leo XIII's *Rerum novarum* (1891).

[J. R. AHERNE]

KNIGHTS OF MALTA (Sovereign Military Order of the Hospital of St. John of Jerusalem, of Rhodes, and of Malta), a religious and knightly order that traces its origin to a society founded by Bl. Gerard (d. 1120) to operate hospitals in the Holy Land for the care of pilgrims. Pope Paschal II approved the society as the Hospitallers of St. John in 1113. Its members lived under an adaptation of the Rule of St. Augustine, but during the 12th cent. the order assumed a military-chivalric character. Expelled from Jerusalem by the Saracens in 1187, the knights (known then as the Knights of St. John of Jerusalem) retreated to Acre and then to Cyprus. Wresting control of Rhodes from pirates in 1310, they established a sovereign republic there with its own flag, mint, navy, and diplomatic corps, and became known as the Knights of Rhodes. They were driven out of Rhodes by the Sultan Süleyman I in 1522, and in 1530 were given the island of Malta by Charles V of Spain. When Malta was lost to Napoleon in 1798 the knights sought the protection of Czar Paul I of Russia, who assumed the grand mastership. With his death in 1801 membership dwindled until the order was nearly extinct. It revived, however, under Leo XIII who restored the grand mastership in 1879; and headquarters were established in Rome. New constitutions were adopted in 1957 and 1961. The affairs of the modern Knights of Malta are subject to the Holy See, the Sacred Congregation of Religious, and the Vatican Secretariat of State. Because of its history the order's sovereignty is recognized by a number of nations and it maintains diplomatic relations with the Holy See and with certain other countries of both hemispheres. The order now engages in the operation of hospitals, clinics, and relief units in Europe, Africa, the Middle East, and South America.

Other organizations have also used the name of this ancient Christian fraternity. The second degree conferred in a commandery of the Masonic Knights Templar is called the Knights of Malta. The incongruity of a degree named after the chief rivals of the Knights Templar has been pointed out by Masonic scholars. The Masonic lodge has no connection with the Knights of Malta, either medieval or modern.

A Protestant society organized in England in 1830 is called the "Grand Priory in the British Realm of the Venerable Order of the Hospital of St. John of Jerusalem." This society engages in hospital and relief work.

An American secret society noted for its nativism and anti-Catholicism has also appropriated the name. It calls itself the Ancient and Illustrious Order of Knights of Malta; it was founded in 1870 and reorganized in 1889. It reported 75,000 members in the 1920s but membership has since declined to a fraction of that number. Only Protestants are eligible for initiation. BIBLIOGRAPHY: J. H. Van der Veldt, *Ecclesiastical Orders of Knighthood* (1956); *Constitutional Charter of the Sovereign Military Hospitaller Order of St. John of Jerusalem, of Rhodes, and of Malta* (1961); O. P. Sherbowitz-Wetzor and C. Toumanoff, NCE 8:217–220.

[W. J. WHALEN]

KNIGHTS OF MONTESA, a military order established in 1317 by Pope John XXII at the request of King James II of Aragon. The new order was given the properties of the Templars and Knights of Malta in Valencia, with its chief center at Montesa. The Knights of Montesa were bound by the rule and customs of the Order of Calatrava. The Cistercian general chapter of 1321 incorporated Montesa into the Order of Cîteaux, and the abbot of Santas Creus was authorized to send monks to care for the spiritual needs of the new knights. In 1400, Pope Benedict XIII, at the request of King Martin of Aragon joined the Order of San Jorge de Alfama to that of Montesa. In 1587 Pope Sixtus V annexed the mastership of the Order of Montesa to the crown. BIBLIOGRAPHY: J. F. O'Callaghan, NCE 8:220.

[M. R. P. MCGUIRE]

KNIGHTS OF PETER CLAVER, a fraternal organization founded by four Josephite priests and three laymen in 1909 for black Catholic men, the established Catholic lodges being unwilling at that time to admit nonwhites. The founders chose as their patron St. *Peter Claver (1581–1654), the Jesuit missionary who had labored among the blacks of South America. The objectives of the organization are to promote parish activities, civic improvements, and Catholic Action; to provide benefits for sick members and to beneficiaries of deceased knights; to award scholarships; to develop recreational facilities; and to offer social and intellectual fellowship. There are four degrees in the society, and there is provision for the admission as associate members of applicants over the age of 55. Associated with the main organization are the Junior Knights (for boys under 18), the Ladies Auxiliary, and the Junior Daughters (for girls under 18). The society reports over 17,000 members and maintains national headquarters in New Orleans, La. It publishes the bimonthly *Claverite*.

[W. J. WHALEN]

KNIGHTS OF RHODES, see KNIGHTS OF MALTA.

KNIGHTS OF ST. JAMES, or of Uclés, Spanish military order founded at Cáceres by Peter Fernández (1170), with help from Ferdinand II of Léon and the abp. of Santiago de Compostela, and approved by Alexander III (1175). The knights observed the Augustinian Rule and wore as a badge a scarlet cross terminating in sword and pilgrim's cockleshell. They had a life-term master, priors for Castile (Uclés), Léon, and Aragon (Montalbán), and commanders for local *encomiendas*. The Reconquest made them more extensive and wealthy than the Alcántara and Calatrava Knights combined, inviting aristocratic exploitation and eventual control by the crown (1493, 1523). BIBLIOGRAPHY: J. F. O'Callaghan, NCE 8:220–221; D. Lomax, *La orden de Santiago* (1965).

[R. I. BURNS]

KNIGHTS OF ST. JOHN, see KNIGHTS OF MALTA.

KNIGHTS OF THE FAITH, secret royalist society of French Catholics. It was founded in 1810 by Ferdinand de Bertier, whose father had been killed by a revolutionary mob in 1789. He held Freemasonry responsible for the Revolution and his father's death, and decided to oppose it with a similar society. It helped prepare the way for the Bourbon restoration, but after exerting some influence, particularly under Charles X, the society developed internal conflicts and dissolved in 1826.

[T. EARLY]

KNIGHTS OF THE SWORD (called also Brothers of the Sword, Livonian Knights, Brothers of the Militia of Christ), a military order founded by Bp. Albert I of Riga in 1201 and confirmed (1204) by Pope Innocent III. They were assigned the rule of the Knights Templar, put under obedience to the bp., and allowed to wear the insignia of a sword and a cross on their clothing. Their purpose was to convert the heathens and to protect missionaries in the Baltic regions. The Knights became, in fact, a permanent army of occupation in the newly conquered area. In the last years of Albert's life, they were merged with the Teutonic Knights, which led to further invasions of Baltic lands by knightly mercenaries. These Germans were paid by land grants, becoming founders of an aristocracy, or as later in Estonia, creators of an intellectual elite. They were instrumental in attaching these regions to the Hanseatic League. The brotherhood lost its individual character through absorption into the Teutonic Knights. Henry of Livonia, a medieval chronicler, incorrectly attributes their foundation to Abbot Theodoric of Treiden. BIBLIOGRAPHY: *Chronicle of Henry of Livonia* (tr. J. A. Brundage, 1961) *passim*.

[N. F. GAUGHAN]

KNIGHTS TEMPLAR, see TEMPLARS.

KNOLL, ALBERT (1796–1863), Tyrolese Capuchin theologian, author of *Institutiones theologiae dogmaticae generalis* (1852) and *Institutiones theologiae theoreticae* (6 v., 1853–59), both having multi-editions. His *Exposito regulae Fratrum Minorum* (1850) holds a high place in Capuchin tradition.

[T. C. O'BRIEN]

KNÖPFLER, ALOIS (1847–1921), German church historian. K. studied at Tübingen and was ordained in 1874. After serving as pastor and teacher, he succeeded Döllinger at Munich, where he founded the renowned church history seminar. His *Lehrbuch der Kirchengeschichte* (1895) shows the influence of Hefele. BIBLIOGRAPHY: M. Csáky, NCE 8:222–223; A. Bigelmair, LTK 6:359–360.

[F. D. LAZENBY]

KNOWLEDGE, a gift of the Holy Spirit. It is explained theologically by analogy with the *epistēmē* of Greek philosophy, which, properly speaking, means the scientific knowledge of demonstrated conclusions and is one of the intellectual virtues. Thus the gift is seen to focus on God's effects as such. Its judgment, however, is not that of a spectator; it is rather a love-knowledge that comes from living with and not just knowing about those effects. Based on faith, it is a bittersweet appreciation of what creatures are, real in themselves, yet no substitutes for God, from whom they wholly derive and whom they anticipate. It discerns between them and knows its way among them. Its burden is found in the poetry of Gerard Manley *Hopkins, its sadness in the thought that so much good may keep us away from God. Accordingly St. Augustine matches it with the third Beatitude, "Blessed are those who mourn, for they shall be comforted." St. Thomas Aquinas contrasts this gift with no special vice, but just with plain ignorance of what the world is about, and with the practical mistakes at the root of sin. The science of Christian theology (*sacra doctrina*) though able to survive without it, should be ideally and normally animated by this gift. BIBLIOGRAPHY: ThAq ST (Lat-Eng v. 1 and 32, ed. T. Gilby).

[T. GILBY]

KNOWLEDGE, AFFECTIVE, cognition markedly toned by appetition, usually that of desire and of enjoyment. The use of the term hinges on the distinction between the true, the object of mind, and the good, the object of will, which distinction is not to be pressed to suggest that there are two manikins engaged with two different things. The person is a single substance, and so also is what ultimately engages him, yet he has the power of knowing it under the aspect of truth, and of loving it under that of goodness. As true he takes it somehow into his mind; as good he goes out to it: this is the systole and diastole of man's response to reality. The analysis then proceeds to the interaction. In knowledge which is purely theoretic and detached, or which is practical yet cool, the mind acts on the will in the manner of a formal cause, the will acts on the mind in that of an efficient cause. Yet when the person is committed and in love, when, in other words, the will really only begins where the mind leaves off, then it enters into the condition of the object known and works on the mind in the manner of a formal cause. Such is the knowledge by connaturality, also called experimental, and not least when there is an infusion of emotional love. Classical exponents are two great 17th-cent. divines, *John of St. Thomas and G. V. de *Contenson (*Theologia mentis et cordis*). The term tends to be engrossed by the theology of spirituality; but it signifies what is common in life. BIBLIOGRAPHY: ThAq ST (Lat-Eng, v. 10, ed. T. Gilby) app. 10. *KNOWLEDGE, CONNATURAL.

[T. GILBY]

KNOWLEDGE, CONNATURAL, a term applied by the scholastics to a knowledge too deep for words, unlike that of science which can be articulated in its own proper medium. Among the several senses of the word "natural" (Lat. *naturale*; Gr. *phusikon*), there is one in which, as implying activity, it is contrasted with the willed (*voluntarium*; *thelēmon*), or, better, with the deliberated (*consiliatum*; *boulēton*); consequently experience that works at levels below and beyond our own decisions and choices, or at least not in their fashion, is called knowing "by connaturality," and is contrasted with knowing "by judgment." It is also called knowing by kinship *(affinitas)*, bent (*inclinatio*), and sympathy (*compassio*), for in it, as Dionysius says, the subject undergoes rather than learns about the object. Since "habit" becomes second nature, knowing by training (*habitus*; *hexis*) induces a certain spontaneous ease and assurance which verges on the condition of connaturality. So does affective knowledge. The term applies in particular to the type of knowledge proper to the operation of the *gifts of the Holy Spirit. *KNOWLEDGE, AFFECTIVE.

[T. GILBY]

KNOWLEDGE, INFUSED, knowledge imparted (Lat. *infundere*, to pour forth) as a gift of God, not acquired by a natural cognitive process. Angelic knowledge is regarded to have been imparted at the moment of their creation (ThAq ST 1a, 55, 2). From the medieval theological tradition such knowledge is ascribed to the first man, in order that he might fulfill his place of primacy (*ibid.* 94. 3 & ad 1), and to Christ's human mind as he is the first revealer of the meaning all creation has in the Word (*ibid.* 3a, 9. 3). St. Thomas excludes infused or innate ideas from the connatural manner of human knowing, since it would run counter to the naturalness of the soul's union with the body, which serves the acquisition of the mind's knowledge through the senses (*ibid.* 1a, 84. 3). In principle infused knowledge is recognized also as a charismatic gift (*ibid.* 1a2ae, 111. 2), and many saints are considered to have been given such knowledge (see REVELATIONS, PRIVATE) because their teaching so far surpassed their education.

[T. C. O'BRIEN]

KNOWLES, DAVID (1896–1974), English Benedictine, foremost modern historian of monasticism. Baptized Michael Clive Knowles, he took the name David on becoming a monk of Downside in 1914, where he was solemnly professed in 1918. He studied at Cambridge, a member of Christ's College from 1919 until ordination in 1922. After a year's study at Sant' Anselmo in Rome, he began to teach theology at Downside and became editor of its *Downside Review*. The first book he published was *The American Civil War: A Brief Sketch* (1926). K.'s mentor in many ways was Abbot Cuthbert *Butler, upon whose death he personally wrote and published a whole issue of the *Downside Review* (1934) that stirred some controversy.

The center of K.'s study and devotion was authentic Benedictine monasticism. It was that passion that moved him to petition the abbot of Downside, then, when refused, the Congregation of Religious for the right to establish a monastery of more primitive observance. When the permission was denied by Rome in 1934 he separated himself from Downside, never to return. For the next several years K. was in a canonically irregular state and during that period suffered a nervous collapse. Through the intervention of Abbot Christopher Butler an indult of exclaustration was granted and Father David, as he was always known to his friends and students, lived the remainder of his life in good standing as a Benedictine. In 1944 he began his illustrious professorial career at Cambridge, becoming a fellow of Peterhouse and the next year University lecturer. He was named professor of medieval history in 1947 and from 1954 until his retirement in 1963 was Regius Professor of Modern History. He also was editor of *Cambridge Studies in Medieval Life*. After retirement age he continued to lecture periodically at Cambridge and right up to the time of his death continued those writing projects on monastic history that permitted a recent biographer rightly to call him a "Maurist of today" (see Egan).

The same biographer with equal justice points out the importance of K.'s work to an understanding of the Church today, since so much of the Church's life and spirit can be measured by the vitality of monasticism as index. One dominant concern of Fr. David's later years was reverence for religious traditions in the Church, a reverence guided by a sense of history. He was an unforgettable person once met, because of his manifest goodness, gentleness, kindness, and dedication. His works possess that rare quality, masterful learning expressed with clarity and grace. Perhaps the best evidence of this is his *Evolution of Medieval Thought* (1962), a work not really in his field, yet unrivalled by any work of professional philosophers or theologians. His great renown, of course, rests on his studies of monasticism, esteemed not simply for their history but for the author's powers to interpret the influence of monasticism. The chief studies are: *The Monastic Order: A History of Its Development from the Time of St. Dunstan to the Fourth Lateran Council, 940–1216* (2d ed. 1963); with R. Neville Hadcock, *Medieval Religious Houses of England and Wales* (new ed. 1971); *Religious Orders in England* (3 v., 1956–59); a separate and abridged ed. of v. 3 was published posthumously as *Bare Ruined Choirs: The Dissolution of the English Monasteries* (1975). A mark of K.'s own character as well as an indication of his view of the historian's task is his view that the historian's function is search for goodness, wisdom, and justice in the lives of those he studied (see his *Saints and Scholars,* 1962). He also had an abiding interest in mysticism and published *The English Mystics* (1927); *The Mystical Tradition* (1961), and *The Nature of Mysticism* (1966). BIBLIOGRAPHY: for K.'s works, to 1963, see D. Knowles, *The Historian and Character, and Other Essays* (1963); for works to 1974, A. Stacpoole, "Making of a Historian III," *Ampleforth Journal* 80 (Autumn 1975) 48–55; life, K. J. Egan, "Dom David Knowles OSB," ABR 27 (1976) 235–246.

[T. C. O'BRIEN]

KNOW-NOTHING PARTY, a secret, political society in the United States. Fear of growing Irish and German immigration led to the formation of the Know-Nothings during the 1850s. It grew out of an oath-bound fraternity, the Order of the Star-Spangled Banner, and other nativist organizations. Initiates were instructed to answer all questions about the movement with "I know nothing," from which it received its popular name. The Know-Nothings opposed "foreign influence, Popery, Jesuitism and Catholicism" and sought to exclude all Roman Catholics and "foreigners" from public office. The party tried to establish a period of 21 years of residence before citizenship, after which such naturalized citizens still could not hold public office. After 1854 the Know-Nothing movement abandoned most of its secret apparatus and called itself the American Party. Its constitution stated: "The object of this organization shall be to resist the insidious policy of the Church of Rome, and other foreign influence against the institutions of our country by placing in all offices in the gift of the people, or by appointment, none but native-born Protestant citizens." A Know-Nothing had to be a native-born citizen, a Protestant born of Protestant parents, reared as a Protestant, and not married to a Roman Catholic. In 1854 the American Party elected governors in Massachusetts and Delaware and gained control of several state legislatures. Former President Millard Fillmore joined the American Party and ran for president on its ticket in 1856. In that election the party won 25% of the popular vote but carried only one state, Maryland. The Know-Nothings entered a disastrous alliance with proslavery Southerners and faded into obscurity in a few years. BIBLIOGRAPHY: A. R. Billington, *Protestant Crusade, 1800–1860* (1938); J. Highman, *Strangers in the Land: Patterns of American Nativism* (1955); L. F. Schmeckebler, *History of the Know-Nothing Party in Maryland* (1899, repr. 1973).

[W. J. WHALEN]

KNOX, JOHN (1515?–72), leader of the Reformation in Scotland. In his *History of the Reformation of Religion within the Realm of Scotland* (modern ed., W. C. Dickinson, ed. 2v., 1949), K. records an epoch in which he was the dominant figure. Born near Haddington and perhaps ordained, he early fell under the influence of George Wishart (d. 1546) and his *Reformed ideas. On Wishart's death K. fled to Saint Andrews, where his work as a Reformer began; but he was captured by the French and deported to France. After his release K. spent 5 years in the service of the C of E, becoming royal chaplain in 1551. Persecution under Mary Tudor drove him to the Continent, where he ministered successively in Frankfurt and Geneva. In 1558 he wrote *The First Blast of the Trumpet against the Monstrous Regiment of Women,* a bitter attack upon women as rulers. On his final return to Scotland in 1559, K. at once took over direction of the reforming cause, and despite Queen Elizabeth's reluctance to aid any who disapproved of feminine rule, the Treaties of Edinburgh and Leith were ratified in Feb. and July 1560, and French forces were withdrawn, though K.'s clash with Mary Stuart was still to come. In Aug., K. and his colleagues produced the *Scots Confession. The first *Book of Discipline, largely the work of K., is an application of his reforming ideas to the whole life of the nation. In 1562 the *Book of Common

Order was approved for use by the General Assembly. His one theological work was a *Treatise on Predestination* (1560). Knox represents a sacramental evangelicalism that differs widely from later Scottish Calvinism. A figure who aroused controversy and violent emotion, he was fearless, opinionated, yet deeply sensitive and profoundly influential. BIBLIOGRAPHY: P. H. Brown, *John Knox* (2 v., 1895); E. Percy, *John Knox* (1965); J. S. McEwen, *Faith of John Knox* (1961); H. Cowan, *John Knox: The Hero of the Scottish Reformation* (1905, repr. 1970).

[J. A. R. MACKENZIE]

KNOX, RONALD ARBUTHNOTT (1888–1957), wit, scholar, translator of the Bible, spiritual writer. K. was educated at Eton and Balliol; with his friend, Harold Macmillan, he was one of a brilliant company decimated on the Somme and in Flanders, and haunted by a lasting sense of bereavement. His father, Bp. of Manchester, was an evangelical; he himself moved to Anglo-Catholicism, and was closely associated with the publishing house of SS. Peter and Paul, which looked for its embellishments from the Baroque rather than the Gothic. He was a pungent critic of modernism and latitudinarianism, and his parodies in the style of Dryden and Swift hold a lasting place in satirical literature. Throughout his life he was fertile with epigrams, limericks, clerihews, and squibs, never ill-natured, and became a legend like Talleyrand, so that pieces were fathered on him that were not his own. He applied the methods of biblical criticism to Sherlock Holmes, and proved that *In Memoriam* was written, not by Tennyson, but by Queen Victoria. The *Spiritual Aeneid* (1918) gives his account of why he became a Roman Catholic. Gently but doggedly he embraced the ideals and to some extent the manners of the English secular clergy; he always kept their trust and affection, later enlarged by that of Scots, Irish, and American priests. During his years as chaplain to Catholic students at Oxford, it was felt that the Church had no need to be defensively apologetic in that critical and sophisticated society. Yet personally he was shy and retiring, diffident and modest, at ease only with close friends, at home in the Catholic households of the Frasers at Beauly, the Actons at Aldenham, and the Asquiths at Mells. He was a man of great generosity, about which he was reticent; much of his lighter writing was to earn money for lame dogs or to maintain the functions to which he had been appointed with insufficient funds. Above all he was a man of prayer and a priest of great regularity, in great demand as a giver of retreats, particularly to the clergy, religious, and children. He was not so sorry for himself as his biography by Evelyn Waugh (1959) might suggest. After his retirement from Oxford he was commissioned to translate the Vulgate anew; the complete work appeared in 1955, and was adopted for public use. Though often regarded as over-mannered for the times, the Epistles were gratefully accepted. His own work of predilection was *Enthusiasm* (1950), a careful and classical study of post-Reformation deviations from and suppressions of the established forms of Church order. Others, more burdened by the apparatus of technical philosophy and systematic theology, admired his gift for never putting a foot wrong in the most tangled religious topics. BIBLIOGRAPHY: E. Waugh, *Monsignor Ronald Knox* (1960); Y. Congar, *Catholicisme* 6:1464–65.

[T. GILBY]

KNOX VERSION, Bible translation by R. *Knox, commissioned by the English hierarchy and completed in 1949. It is based on the Vulgate, though reference has constantly been made to the original texts. The version is chiefly remarkable for the author's attempt to produce a "timeless English" suitable to all ages. This has appealed to many, though others find it mannered and artificial, esp. in the Old Testament. As a guide to what the original authors wrote or meant, its value is somewhat limited.

[D. J. BOURKE]

KNUDSON, ALBERT CORNELIUS (1873–1953), Methodist theologian. K. was professor of OT exegesis (1905–21) and systematic theology (1921–43) at Boston Univ., and through his teaching and writings, which were used in many Methodist seminaries, had widespread influence. His major works in systematic theology were the *Doctrine of God* (1930) and the *Doctrine of Redemption* (1933). K.'s thought was characterized by a liberal and naturalist interpretation of theology, inspired by the personalist idealism of B. P. *Bowne. K. regarded this form of personalism as the only sound basis for theology and believed that thought, the ultimate principle in all reality, is in man the capacity for the reception of grace. The primary Christian doctrine for K. is the Trinity, which he explained as a threefold manifestation of God's being. His ethical theory stressed the absoluteness of human freedom as the condition of all morality and fellowship with God. BIBLIOGRAPHY: HistAmMeth 3:276–280.

[F. E. MASER]

KNUTSON, KENT SIGVART (1924–73), president of *American Lutheran Church 1970–73. Born in Goldfield, Iowa, K. received a B.S. (1947) in chemical engineering from Iowa State Univ., and then after a short period with an oil company left to study for a B.D. (1951) at Luther Seminary, St. Paul. Following graduate study at Union Theological Seminary (N.Y.) and Columbia Univ., from which he received a Ph.D. in 1961, he was ordained (1954) in the Evangelical Lutheran Church, later to become part of the American Lutheran Church. K. spent 4 years in a N.Y. pastorate, then taught theology at Luther Seminary and had served 1 year as president of Wartburg Seminary, Dubuque, Iowa, when he was elected ALC president. During a 1972 world tour that included mission fields in East Asia, he developed symptoms of a rare nerve disorder, Jakob-Creutzfeldt disease, which proved fatal.

[T. EARLY]

KOCH, JOSEPH ANTON (1768–1839), Tyrolean painter in Strasbourg (1791), Switzerland (1792–94), and finally in Rome. K. bridged the classicist and romantic traditions, and as a friend of Thorwaldsen and the Nazarenes, collaborated on the *Dante Frescoes* (1825–28) at the Villa Giustiniani-Massimo in Rome. He greatly influenced the romantics Richter, Fries, and others.

[M. J. DALY]

KODÁLY, ZOLTAN (1882–1967), composer, musicologist. Without doubt the most important figure among modern Hungarian composers and musicologists, K. was the bridge between the romantic tradition of the 19th cent. and the modernist direction of the 20th. His best work shows the profound influence of his Catholicism. His first attempts at show of interest in music occurred at the Catholic gymnasium of Nagyszombat. The library of the cathedral led him to the study of musical MSS. Attending the Univ. of Sciences in Budapest, K. was influenced by French Impressionism and Latin humanism, two major sources of his later work. He studied composition (1902) at the Budapest Academy of Music. Among other compositions of this period was an *Assumpta est Maria* for voices and orchestra. Interested in what constituted Hungarian (Maygar) music, he began research in the field in 1905. A significant development in 1906 was his friendship with Bela Bartók, with whom he collaborated to publish *Magyar Népdalok* (1907), a collection of folk tunes. In 1907 he went to Paris where he met Debussey and learned to admire Impressionism. The composition *Meditation* for pianoforte and several other works resulted from the Paris visit. K. was appointed a teacher at the Budapest Academy of Music in 1907. He continued to collect folk music and to compose during his teaching years.

With Bartók, K. planned a major musicological study on folk music in 1913 but two World Wars delayed publication of *Maygar Népzene Tára* (*Corpus musicae popularis Hungaricae*) until 1951.

The years 1907 to 1910 saw a number of K.'s compositions performed, esp. outside Hungary, and his reputation abroad surpassed the recognition received in his own country. He was a founder of U.M.Z.E., a Hungarian association for new music. In 1923 he composed a choral work, *Psalmus hungaricus,* honoring the 50th anniversary of the union of Buda and Pest. The work was a complete success with the public and became an international favorite. The fairy tale *Hariy Janos* was written for the stage, was performed in Budapest in 1926 and enhanced further K.'s reputation. The year 1932 saw performances of K.'s work in every section of Hungary in honor of his 50th birthday; the 1930s, the appearance of the *Budavara, Te Deum,* the *Organ Mass* (later expanded as *Missa brevis*). In his choral music K. shows the influence of Palestrina and polyphony of the 16th century.

The genius of K., whose music blends the Oriental Magyar folk themes with the best in Western technique, appears in choral work, music for the stage, orchestral works such as the *Variations* and the *Concerto,* and church music, forming an output of singular brilliance.

[J. R. AHERNE]

KODI (East Armenian, *goti*), the cincture, made of the same material as the *shourtchar*, worn by Armenian eucharistic celebrants. It buckles in front and is worn over the pendants of the *pororar*.

[A. CODY]

KOENIGSFELDEN: ABBEY OF SS. CLARA AND FRANCIS, double cloister founded by Elizabeth, wife of Albert I, in 1311 and governed by her daughter Agnes (d. 1364). It was completed (1320–30) in strict Franciscan style, the polygonal apse boasting magnificent stained-glass windows donated by dukes of the family, the red St. Francis window the most elegant example of Upper Rhine workmanship.

[M. J. DALY]

KŌFUKUJI, NARA, Japanese Buddhist temple, originally a monastery (669) under the Fujiwara clan. Its site often changed, the temple was transferred and rebuilt in Nara (746) as the prestigious family temple Kōfukuji. Three Golden (Buddha) Halls (since rebuilt), many excellent Nara sculptures, and noteworthy works—by the great Japanese carver Unkei and his school—adorn the temple.

[M. J. DALY]

KOGH (*Qogh*), in the Armenian liturgy, (1) a veil for covering the chalice and paten (*dzadzkotz*); (2) a veil placed over a bp.'s head during his consecration, then traditionally carried before him in certain solemn processions.

[A. CODY]

KOHLMANN, ANTHONY (1771–1836), Jesuit missionary, teacher. A native of Alsace where his familiarity with German and French prepared him for future work, he was ordained in 1796. After some years spent in hospital work and in teaching, he joined the Society of Jesus (1804). He came to Georgetown College, Washington, D.C., in 1806; from there he did considerable missionary work among the Germans in Pennsylvania. Abp. Carroll appointed him administrator of the Diocese of New York in 1808. There K. became (1813) the center of a lawsuit threatening the seal of confession; the case was decided in favor of the confessional privilege and this decision became state law. K. returned to Georgetown (1815) and served for 2 years as its president. His last years (from 1824) were spent as a teacher of theology at the Gregorian Univ. in Rome.

[J. R. AHERNE]

KOIMESIS CHURCH, NICAEA, church in Nicaea (Iznik), Turkey, of provincial domed Byzantine plan, prototype of the architecture of the Macedonian revival. Renowned for excellent mosaics of the 8th and 9th cent., it was destroyed in the Greco-Turkish War (1921–22).

[M. J. DALY]

KOINONIA, Gr. term meaning communion, association. (1) Throughout Aristotle's moral philosophy, as seen in his *Ethics* and *Politics*, a community of interest; it is a general term for the community's sense of solidarity, founded on a common interest (*koinon sympheron*) and expressed in common action (*koinon ergon*). *Koinonia* has special prominence in *Ethics* 8, 11–14, Aristotle's classic discussion of *friendship. The language of Aristotle there is reflected in St. Thomas Aquinas's treatise on *charity: as a form of friendship, charity is based on the *koinonia,* the *communicatio,* that God by his grace establishes between himself and man (ThAq ST 2a2ae, 23.1). (2) In the NT *koinonia* is esp. a Pauline term that describes the fellowship, the community in mutual sharing, of those united to each other because each is united to Christ, the source of their shared life; the Eucharist is the sign and sustaining force of that *koinonia* (see 1 Cor 1.9; 10.16–17; 2 Cor 13.13; Rom 15.26; cf. 1 Jn 1.3). Such are the meanings, so far removed from an induced bonhommie, that define the Christian community. BIBLIOGRAPHY: T. Gilby, *Political Thought of Thomas Aquinas* (pa. 1973) 261–263.

[T. C. O'BRIEN]

KOINONIA FARM, interracial Christian community founded in 1942 at Americus, Ga., by Clarence Jordan, a Southern Baptist clergyman. The object of intense hostility from segregationists, it has been highly applauded by many Christians working for an end to racial discrimination.

[T. EARLY]

KOKOSCHKA, OSKAR (b. 1886), Austrian painter, poet, and graphic artist. K. studied at the school of Applied Art in Vienna (1904–07), joined (1910) *Der Sturm*group in Berlin, and lived in Dresden until 1924, teaching at the Academy. Traveling through Europe, North Africa, and the Middle East, K. painted his powerful "portraits of cities." His art was condemned as "degenerate" by the Nazis in 1937. In London during World War II, K. expressed destruction and despair (1942), afterwards visiting the United States. Influenced by the "Wiener Sezession", K. developed his highly personal, expressionistic style, making remarkable portraits, emphasizing psychological aspects of the model, and landscapes. In 1947 his work was hung in the International Venice Biennale. BIBLIOGRAPHY: O. Kokoschka, *Schriften, 1907–55* (ed. H. Wingler, 1955); H. M. Wingler, *Oskar Kokoschka, Das Werk des Malers* (1958).

[P. H. HEFTING]

KOLBE, MAXIMILIAN, BL. (1894–1941), Polish Franciscan (OFM Conv), founder of the Militia Immaculatae (MI), the Militia of Mary Immaculate, charismatic apostle of Mary, victim of the Nazis at Auschwitz, beatified in 1971. He was baptized Raymond, took the name Maximilian (so M.) at religious reception at Liepoli, Poland, 1910. Professed in 1911, he was sent the next year to complete his studies of philosophy and theology at Rome, where he received a doctorate in each discipline. He was ordained in 1918 at the Church of San Andrea della Valle. The foundation of MI, canonically a *pious union, dates from 1917, the first members being M.'s confreres in Rome. First ecclesiastical approval was received in 1922; MI was made a *pia unio primaria* in 1927. M.'s still-extant Latin memorandum on the foundation (see Ricciardi, p. 61) expresses its nature as a crusade against the forces of evil in society and the conversion of the Church's enemies; members were to consecrate themselves to Mary Immaculate as her "knights"; devotion to the Miraculous Medal was a symbol of their dedication. The apostolate to which M. particularly devoted his vision was that of what today would be called the media of social communication. Thus his great foundations, Niepokalanów (near Warsaw) and Mugenzai No Sono, Nagasaki, Japan (Cities of the Immaculate), had as their main work the apostolate of the printed word. Editions of the magazine *Knight of the Immaculate* appeared in Polish, Japanese, the main European languages, English, and Latin (for seminarians and clergy). The Niepokanalanóv foundation by 1930 numbered over 800 members, many professionals from the press and radio; growth of the Nagasaki foundation was proportionately astonishing. Most of the members became Franciscans and of these most were content to serve as brothers. The influence of M. was truly an evidence of special charisms; work is being done on collecting and publishing his doctrine on Marian theology and spirituality from his conferences and correspondence, and it is expected to provide a rich witness to his own theological and spiritual depth.

During his apostolate his work was frequently interrupted by illness (he had been diagnosed as tubercular while still a student and that he could accomplish as much as he did was a source of amazement). His first assignment was in Poland. The foundation of Niepokalanóv, canonically established (1927), climaxed his early efforts to promote MI with the blessing of his religious and ecclesiastical superiors (the first issue of the Polish edition of *Knight of the Immaculate* (in Polish [*Rycerz Niepokalanej*] appeared in 1922). In 1930 he was assigned to the missions in Japan and made his foundation there of the "City of the Immaculate" in 1932. During this period he also spent time in India and started the Marian work there. With some time spent in Poland in 1933, M.'s missionary work in the Orient lasted until 1936, when he was recalled to be superior at Niepokalanóv because of his failing health. The assignment became a sentence to death because when the Nazis overran Poland in 1939 he soon became a target of their barbarity. From Sept. to Nov. 1939 he was imprisoned at Amtitz. On his liberation he was allowed to return to the City of the Immaculate. His last year or so there was spent in caring for refugees, among them many Jews, with the few brothers who were not expelled by the Nazis. But he was arrested in Feb. 1941, on a false charge of political interference. He was put into a prison hospital in Warsaw for a time because of lung failure. In May 1941 he was transferred to Auschwitz; out of hatred for priests his captors assigned him to the hardest labor and abuse. His death came because of his own heroic act; he volunteered to substitute for a fellow prisoner chosen to die with nine others in reprisal for a single prisoner's having escaped. M.'s offer was accepted; he and his companions were entombed in a bunker to die of starvation. Still alive after two weeks, because the space was needed for further executions, he was killed by an injection of poison; his body was burned in the Auschwitz crematorium. Testimony for his beatification indicates that during the ordeal he sought to sustain his fellow victims' faith and courage. He died with tranquility. BIBLIOGRAPHY: A. Ricciardi, *Beato Massimiliano Maria Kolbe* (rev. ed., documents, bibliog. 1971); M. Winowska, *Our Lady's Fool* (tr. T. Plumereau, 1952); J. Burdyszek, *Father Maximilian Kolbe: Fire Enkindled* (1954).

[T. C. O'BRIEN]

KOLDE, DIETRICH (Dederick Coelde van Münster; *c.*1435–1515), a Franciscan held in great esteem by J. *Trithemius and Erasmus of Rotterdam. He wrote the first Low German catechism (*Kerstenspieghel,* 1470) and religious hymns, some of them published in the oldest printed hymnal (1508); also meditations in Latin on Christ's Passion, and daily spiritual exercises (1500). BIBLIOGRAPHY: K. Zuhorn, "Neue Beiträge zur Lebensgeschichte Dietrich Koldes" in FranzStud 18(1941); J. Goyens, "Le Bx. Thierri Coelde de Münster, OFM. Biographie et documents sur ses reliques," AFH 19 (1926) 3:1–13.

[S. A. SCHULZ]

KÖLLIN, CONRAD (1476–1536), German Dominican theologian. He was a student, then professor at the Univ. of Heidelberg, but the major part of his career was at the Univ. of Cologne (1511–36). He was also inquisitor for a time (1527–33) for the dioceses of Mainz, Cologne, and Trier, and wrote several anti-Lutheran polemics. K.'s chief importance is his contribution to the 16th-cent. restoration of Thomism. He introduced into Germany as the text for theology lectures St. Thomas Aquinas's *Summa theologiae*. His commentary on the ST 1a2ae (1512) for at least a century was a standard citation and source for Thomist theologians; for its fidelity to, and clear penetration of, the thought of St. Thomas it remains superior to many later works. BIBLIOGRAPHY: J. Wilms, *Der Kölner Universitätsprofessor Konrad Köllin* (1941).

[T. C. O'BRIEN]

KOLPING, ADOLF (1813–65). RC priest and founder of the Katholische Gesellenvereine in 1849, an association designed to keep the working class close to the Church while achieving goals of social justice. K.'s ideas were similar to those of von *Ketteler, and he successfully organized journeymen into units in which they received vocational training and spiritual guidance. By 1865 there were 420 branches of the organization and about 60,000 members. BIBLIOGRAPHY: *Biographisches Lexicon zur Deutschen Geschichte* (1967); K. Pinson, *Modern Germany* (rev. 1966) 181–182.

[M. A. GALLIN]

KOLPING SOCIETY, CATHOLIC, see CATHOLIC KOLPING SOCIETY.

KOLYBA (sometimes *kalyva*), a word of uncertain origin signifying a cake of boiled wheat with almonds, pistachios, and raisins mixed with sugar and spices. It is blessed and dedicated to the dead and distributed to the faithful on the first Saturday of Lent. At a funeral a similar cake is brought to the church by the family of the deceased during the last office celebrated for his soul, *i.e.,* after the liturgy and vespers. Often three lighted candles are placed in it; it is blessed by the priest and then distributed to all present, each one saying as he receives it, "May the memory of the dead be joyous." The custom is a form of a funeral meal and perhaps had its origin in the pagan practice of leaving food offerings for the deceased.

[R. K. GOLINI]

KONARAK (KONARKA; 1238–64), site in Orissa State of Sūrya Deul, a Hindu sun temple designed as the divine chariot, the most impressive ruin of N India's finest architecture, with sikhara (collapsed), and *maṇḍapa* (hall), the outer walls covered with magnificent figure carvings of musicians, dancers, and loving couples.

[M. J. DALY]

KÖNIG, EDUARD (1846–1936), Hebrew scholar and OT exegete. During a teaching career at the Univ. of Leipzig, Rostock, and Bonn, K. contributed scholarly works on Hebrew and Aramaic, hermeneutics, and OT commentary. He is best known for his classic study on the structure of the Hebrew and Aramaic languages, *Historisch-kritisches Lehregebäude der hebräischen Sprache* (3 v., 1881–97). K. opposed the Wellhausen school for its evolutionary interpretation of Israelite religion, and stressed a more conservative explanation based upon supernatural revelation. He was one of the most eminent Protestant scholars to oppose the rationalistic interpretation of the Bible at the turn of the century. BIBLIOGRAPHY: J. Coppens, DBSuppl 5:189–192.

[T. M. MCFADDEN]

KONIJNENBURG, WILLEM A. VAN (1868–1943), prominent Dutch painter. K. abandoned the realism of The Hague for symbolic themes, publishing *Die ästhetische Idëen.* (1916), and executing theological paintings, such as the *Triumph of St. Thomas Aquinas* (1924–38; Dominican Monastery, Zwolle), designs for stained-glass windows, tapestries, and other works.

[M. J. DALY]

KONRAD VON SOEST (fl. *c.*1400–25), painter of the famous *Wildungen Altar* (1404) said to have the oldest "signature" in northern European painting, K.'s most important works include the *Virgin Mary Altar* (1420). This evidences his style—a love of ornamentation, delicate modeling of elegant, elongated figures, with landscape and animal forms, and relates his work to that of the Limbourg brothers, establishing K. as a leading master and, with Master Francke, most important exponent of the International Gothic style in Germany.

[M. J. DALY]

KONTAKION, a liturgical poetic form created by Romanus Melodus, the foremost Byzantine liturgical poet of the late 5th and early 6th centuries. It consists of 18 to 30 troparia or stanzas that are in turn joined by an acrostic or by the letters of the alphabet in sequence. A melodic homily, it celebrated the Nativity, Epiphany and other events of the Gospels. As a liturgical form it was succeeded in the liturgy by the *kanon* in the 7th century.

[F. H. BRIGHAM]

KOPPERS, WILHELM (1886–1961), German ethnologist, priest (from 1911) of the Society of the Divine Word. He taught at the Univ. of Vienna from 1924, where he was professor from 1928 and director of the university's institute of ethnology from 1929. He did field work in India (1938–39) and went into voluntary exile in Switzerland during World War II because of his opposition to Nazism. He followed W. *Schmidt's *Kulturkreis* postulate, but by 1952 admitted that the concept needed radical revision. K. wrote more than 200 treatises, edited *Anthropos* and *Wiener Beiträge zur Kulturgeschichte und Linguistik,* and for many years coedited *Mitteilungen der Anthropologischen Gesellschaft in Wien.*

KORAH (CORE), DATHAN, AND ABIRAM, rebels against Moses and Aaron. Korah and 250 Israelites rebelled against the religious authority of Moses and Aaron; the brothers Dathan and Abiram rebelled against the civil authority of Moses; Korah and 250 Levites protested the priestly privileges of Aaron. A bolt of lightning killed Korah and his followers; Dathan and Abiram were swallowed alive in an earthquake (cf. Num 16.1–35 which conflates Priestly, Yahwistic, and Elohist traditions).

[F. J. MONTALBANO]

KORAN (Arabic, *al-Qur'ân*), the holy book of *Islam. The word is from the verbal root *qr',* to read, recite, and is probably borrowed from Christian Aramaic *qeryânâ,* a recitation from Scripture. The Koran, which according to Muslim belief, contains verbatim the word of God revealed to the Prophet *Mohammed through the intermediary of the Angel Gabriel, consists of 114 chapters known as suras (Arab. *sûra;* pl. *suwar*), ranging in length from 3 to 286 verses and arranged (with the exception of the opening sura) roughly in decreasing order of length. According to tradition, parts of the Koran were quite early reduced to writing on such materials as were available: sherds, scraps of leather, etc. At *Medina, tradition reports, Mohammed undertook some systematic editing of the revelation and it is plain that lengthy suras such as No. 2, which is mentioned by name in a number of traditions from this period, could only have maintained their integrity in written form. Although at the death of the Prophet (632) there existed no universally accepted text, a number of complete copies of the Koran existed, most importantly those of Ubay ibn Ka'b and Abdallâh ibn Mas'ûd, whose variant readings continue to be cited. Under pressure of growing disputes concerning the text of the revelation, *Caliph 'Uthmân (d. 656) appointed, towards the middle of his 12-year reign, a commission headed by Zayd ibn Thabit, one of the Prophet's former secretaries, to produce an official text. The basis of their work was a collection of suras that had originally belonged to Caliph 'Umar (d. 644), which they supplemented with other written documents and oral sources. This work, despite strong opposition in various circles, came soon to supplant all other recensions, and forms the present vulgate text.

The chronological development of the Koran is to be discovered only with difficulty; the individual suras contain, in most cases, elements widely disparate in both date and content and the process that determined the building of the suras from shorter, primitive elements is not known. Even though there is some tendency for single suras to contain mostly material from approximately the same period of the Prophet's career, the artificial ordering of the suras by length jumbles even this rough chronological grouping. The earliest material (generally contained in the shorter suras) consists in impassioned appeals to belief in God and the coming judgment, exhortations to a moral life, and vivid portrayals of damnation and beatitude. Later, stories of the trials of past prophets (mostly biblical) and of God's judgment against those who refused to heed them are introduced to support the message. Attacks on the blindness and intransigence of the idolators *(mušrikîn)* and those who refuse to believe (*kâfirîn*) become more bitter as hostility towards Mohammed and his message continued to increase. Following the emigration (see HEGIRA) of the small community of Muslims from *Mecca to *Medina, the content and style of the Koran changes notably, as the Prophet's task became one of directing the activities of a political community. In these parts of the Koran one finds much legislation aimed at regulating both the social and religious life of the Muslims, together with passages reflecting the community's struggles and the growth of Mohammed's power until the final triumph of Islam over all opposition. It is in the suras of this period that one finds explicit rejections of Jewish and Christian religious doctrines.

The Koran is the central and predominant element in the religion of Islam. It proclaims itself to be inimitable and the Muslims regard it as the unique miracle of Mohammed by which the truth of his mission is preeminently verified. According to orthodox Muslim teaching, the Koran is the uncreated word of God: God's self-revelation "in clear Arabic." Translations: A. J. Arberry, *Koran Interpreted* (2 v., 1955); R. Bell, *Qur'ān* (2 v., 1937–39). BIBLIOGRAPHY: A. Jeffery, *Qur'ān as Scripture* (1952); J. Jomier, *Bible and the Koran* (tr. E. P. Arbez, 1964); R. Paret, *Der Koran, Kommentar und Konkordanz* (1971); W. M. Watt, *Bell's Introduction to the Qur'ân, . . . Revised and Enlarged* (*Islamic Surveys* 8, 1970); L. As-Said, *Recited Koran: A History . . . .* (ed. B. Weiss, tr. M. Berger et al., 1975).

[F. M. FRANK]

KOREA, a country located on a peninsula extending S from Manchuria on the E coast of Asia. It is now divided by the 38th parallel into the Republic of Korea in the south (38,452 sq mi; pop. [1976 est.] 34,000,000) and the (Communist) Democratic People's Republic of Korea in the North (46,540 sq mi; pop. [1974 UN est.] 15,440,000). Koreans are a blend of Mongolian and indigenous stock with a culture dating from the 1st millennium B.C. Korea was first opened to foreigners in 1876 and was occupied by Japan 1907–45. Buddhism was brought to Korea from China in the 4th cent. and became the state religion in the next cent.; but from 1392 until 1910 Confucianism was the official religion. Korean Christianity owes its origin to Japanese Christians and the influence of Jesuit missioners in Peking. Peter Ni-Shun-hun was baptized at the Chinese court in 1784 and became instrumental in establishing the Catholic Church in Korea. The first Christian community elected a bp. and a number of priests, who exercised sacerdotal function without being ordained. To remedy the situation a priest was sent from China, but persecution claimed his life and that of 300 of his flock in 1801. Korea became a vicariate apostolic in 1831. By 1865 there were two bps. and about 8,000 Catholics; but these also became victims of persecution. When religious freedom was proclaimed in 1882 Catholics numbered about 16,000. Unfortunately, missioners were too few to minister to all who wished conversion; but by 1931 membership had risen to 110,000.

North Korea has two dioceses, but its bps. have been expelled, its priests imprisoned, and an incalculable number of Catholics have fled to the South. No Catholic statistics are available for North Korea. In South Korea Christianity is progressing rapidly. There are 3 archdioceses with 10 sees. Catholics number 987,197 (2.9%).

Protestantism entered Korea in 1865. In the first 3 decades of the 20th cent. leadership lay with the Presbyterian Church. Methodists, Pentecostals, Southern Baptists, the Evangelical Mission Alliance, and several other churches now have flourishing congregations. In 1968 the Protestant membership was reported as 1,873,122. BIBLIOGRAPHY: *Bilan du Monde* 2:280–287; *Korean Annual* (12 ed., 1975).

[P. DAMBORIENA]

KOREA, MARTYRS OF, 79 Catholics martyred in Korea between 1839 and 1846, and beatified in 1925. They constituted a cross-section of Christianity in *Korea: a bp. and two priests all of the Paris Foreign Mission Society, a Korean priest, and a variety of laymen and laywomen. Laurent Imber entered Korea in 1837 as vicar apostolic, the first prelate to make his way there where Christianity and foreigners were proscribed. He was preceded by two priests, Pierre Maubant and Jacques Chactan. Working in secrecy all three fell victim to the persecution of 1839 and were executed in Seoul. Andrew Kim, the first Korean priest, was executed in 1846. Two sisters, laywomen, Columba and Agnes Kim, were beheaded after torture. Peter Ryou, a boy of 13, was strangled in prison. The catechist Charles Hyon was beheaded in 1846. BIBLIOGRAPHY: C. Testore, BiblSanct 4:176–178; Butler 3:611–613.

[J. R. AHERNE]

KOREA, ORTHODOX CHURCH IN. Missionaries were sent from Russia from the 1890s until the revolution of 1917, and the Orthodox Church in Korea was governed by the Russian Church until 1949, when hostilities broke out between North and South Korea. During the Korean War Orthodox chaplains attached to the Greek military forces under United Nations command began to conduct Orthodox services for the local population; subsequently the Greek Orthodox Archdiocese in America assumed support for the mission. BIBLIOGRAPHY: R. Stephanopoulos, *Encyclopedia of Modern Christian Missions* (1967) 236.

[T. BIRD]

KOREAN RELIGION. The most primitive indigenous religion of Korea was characterized by *animism, a belief in spirits, and *ancestor worship. The early Koreans worshiped natural phenomena such as the sun, moon, some stars, high mountains, and wide rivers; they venerated good spirits and propitiated evil ones. Equally pervasive was a recourse to magic, esp. through the shaman or witchdoctor (see SHAMANISM). Women acted as sorceresses, after resorting to dancing dervishes or trances to communicate with occult powers. In some rural communities, these sorceresses or *mudang* still exercise a considerable influence. Ancestor worship was prevalent, and the choosing of the grave site, the mourning and burial rites, the various prayers and sacrifices to the ancestor's spirit were meticulously performed. But despite all their beliefs in a multitude of good and evil spirits, the ancient Koreans held the idea of a Supreme Being. Known as *Hananim,* a name derived from the words for heaven and master, he was the Supreme Ruler of the universe and of the spirit world. There were no idolatrous rites in his worship, but no personal devotion either, since the worship of this awesome deity was entrusted to the king alone.

Buddhism was introduced into Korea from China in A.D. 372. It was the courier of Chinese civilization as well as the harbinger of eternal hope to the primitive Koreans. It became so well entrenched that many Buddhist monasteries were established and much Buddhist-inspired art, sculpture, and architecture proliferated. Buddhism became the state religion from 527–1392. In 1097 a meditative sect called Son (Chan in Chinese; Zen in Japanese) was introduced from China, and eventually became the most powerful Buddhist sect in Korea. Confucianism entered Korea earlier than Buddhism and has always influenced Korean ethics. Near the end of the Koryo Dynasty (935–1392), the Neo-Confucianism of the Chinese philosopher Chu Hsi (1130–1200) had a great impact on the country. It combated some decadent features of Buddhism and provided valuable ethical norms. In the Yi era (1392–1910) which followed, Chu Hsi Confucianism became the state philosophy and the basic pattern for the court and local governments. Christianity was introduced into Korea in 1784 by the Koreans themselves, who brought it from China, but it could not be freely professed until 1882. During that interim there were four violent anti-Christian persecutions, but these failed to prevent its spread (see KOREA, MARTYRS OF). After the Korean-American treaty of 1882, the first American Protestant missions were opened in Korea by the Presbyterians and Methodists. Similar treaties with other Western countries brought additional missionaries. By 1890, at least 10 other Protestant mission Societies were at work in the country. Roman Catholicism also spread quickly, and has increased at a rate of about 40,000 annually since 1950. Today, Christianity, Confucianism, and Buddhism are the major religions with Shamanism and Chondo-kyo (or Eastern Learning, which emerged as a reaction against the 19th-cent. spread of Christianity) also widely practiced. BIBLIOGRAPHY: L. Hong-Ryol Ryu, *History of Catholicism in Korea* (1962); Duk-Hwang Kim, *Religious History of Korea* (1963); C. A. Clark, *Religions of Old Korea* (1932).

[V. T. JOHNSON]

KORMCHAIA KNIGA (Sl. for navigator's chart), a Slavonic version of the chief Byzantine collections of canon law, including also much civil law and some ascetical and polemical works. The Kormchaia formed the basis of ecclesiastical law in medieval Russia and its importance lasted into the 19th century. It effected a striking unity of church legislation in Russia and the preservation there of a very early church discipline, which was due largely to the unswerving adherence of the bps. to its prescriptions. BIBLIOGRAPHY: I. Žužek, *Kormčaja Kniga: Studies on the Chief Code of Russian Canon Law* (OrChrAnal 168, 1964).

[G. T. DENNIS]

KOROLEVSKY, CYRIL (1878–1959), Orientalist. Ordained in the Catholic Byzantine rite in 1902, he came in 1909 under the jurisdiction of Metropolitan A. Szeptycky but was joined to the Russian eparchy of Kamenets-Podolsk. Most of his life was spent in Rome where he was commissioned to do research into the history of the Ruthenian Church. He was attached 1919–29 to the Vatican Library on behalf of the newly formed Pontifical Institute for Oriental Studies. His scholarship led Pope Pius XI to send him with E. Tisserant, the future cardinal-secretary of the Congregation of the Oriental Church, on a special mission in Eastern Europe. After K.'s second report on Bulgaria, Abp. Roncalli, the future Pope John XXIII, was sent as apostolic visitor. K. was responsible for inspiring *L. Beauduin to enter the ecumenical movement and to found the Monastery of *Chevetogne. K.'s magisterial work, *Histoire des patriarchats melkites depuis le schisme monophysite du 6ème siècle jusqu'à nos jours* (1911), has done much to open Western eyes to the Eastern Churches as did his controversial brochure *L'uniatisme* (1927). BIBLIOGRAPHY: D. Stiernon, *Catholicisme* 6:1477–78.

[S. QUITSLUND]

KOŚCIUSZKO, TADEUSZ ANDRZEJ (1746–1817), Polish patriot and American Revolutionary War general. Educated at the Jesuit College at Breese and the Royal School at Warsaw, K. graduated as an army captain. A year of engineering study in Paris followed. Hearing of the American Revolution he came to Philadelphia (1776) and was engaged by the Pennsylvania Committee of Defense. His engineering work brought him a commission as colonel in the Continental Army. With General Gates in command he chose the battlefield and erected the fortifications that led to the victory of the American forces over General Burgoyne at Saratoga. When General Nathaniel Greene made his strategic retreat before Cornwallis, K. was in charge of transportation. In 1783 he was made a brigadier general. In 1794, once more in Poland, he led the uprising against the Russians. After several victories he became dictator and issued a number of liberal reforms. Defeated and imprisoned by the Russians, he was pardoned by the Czar and revisited America (1797), where Congress made him a grant of 500 acres in Ohio. His last years were spent in France, devoted to unsuccessful efforts for Polish freedom.

[J. R. AHERNE]

KOSHER (KASHER), a biblical term used to identify objects, usually food, fit, proper, or ritually correct (Est 8.5; Ec 10.10; 11.6). The detailed dietary laws, the context of this term's most ordinary use, have been explained by some as an ancient guide to nutritional hygiene; others have disagreed, claiming that these laws are designed to distinguish Jews from others and to promote self-discipline and thus holiness. In the rabbinic literature, the term has been extended to include proper handling of scrolls and to designate competent witnesses in judicial proceedings.

[R. J. LITZ]

KOSHO (fl. mid-13th cent.), sculptor. Son of the Japanese master sculptor Unkei, K. assisted in the reconstruction of the *Kōfukuji, Nara, carving the Amida Buddha of the Golden Hall of the Horyuji (1232) and a portrait of the priest Kūya in Kyoto.

[M. J. DALY]

KŌSŌ (East Syr., *Kāsā*), Syriac word for the chalice.

KOSTKA, STANISLAUS, ST. (1550–68), patron of Poland. K. was born of a noble family in the castle of Rostkova, Poland. In 1564, accompanied by his older brother Paul, he attended the Jesuit college in Vienna. After that institution was closed by Maximilian II, the two brothers received their education from Dr. John Bilinsky. During this period, Stanislaus' life of piety brought only derision from Paul. After recovering from an illness in 1565, K. decided to join the Jesuits. When the Jesuit provincial in Vienna would not accept him, he walked to Dillingen, Germany, where he met Peter Canisius, who instructed him to petition the Jesuit general, Francis Borgia. Traveling on foot, K. arrived in Rome in Oct. of 1567 and entered the novitiate under the guidance of Francis Borgia. After taking simple vows in 1568, he was overcome by illness and died, as he predicted he would, on the Feast of the Assumption in 1568. Since his death, K. has been declared patron saint of Poland, patron of the dying, and patron of religious novices. BIBLIOGRAPHY: J. Warszawski, BiblSanct 11:1369–73; Butler 4:335–336; J. E. Kerns, *Portrait of a Champion* (1957).

[R. J. BRADY]

KOUDELKA, JOSEPH MARIA (1852–1921), Bohemian-born American bishop. After parish work in Cleveland, where he was pastor of St. Michael's Church, he was appointed (1908) auxiliary bp. with specific jurisdiction over the care of non-English–speaking immigrants of Central Europe; his was the first such appointment. In 1911 he became auxiliary bp. of Milwaukee, and in 1913, bp. of Superior, Wisconsin. He was a renowned preacher, published textbooks in German for the instruction of immigrant children, as well as prayer books and devotional works.

[J. R. AHERNE]

KOUPHISMA, in *Byzantine chant notation, one of the *somata, or signs indicating a note one scale step higher than the previous note. It is very rarely used.

KRAFT, ADAM (*c.* 1455–1509), preeminent German late-Gothic sculptor in Nürnberg (1490–1509). For the Schreyer-Landauer family K. carved on the outside of the choir of St. Sebald a relief triptych of many levels. His dramatic power is further seen in the great tabernacle of St. Lorenz (1493–96)—a Gothic tower reaching to the vaults, with portraits of K. and his assistants supporting tiers of the *Passion* and *Crucifixion*. K.'s sandstone Stations of the Cross for the Cemetery of St. John (1505–08) are characterized by torturous rhythms.

[M. J. DALY]

KRALIK, RICHARD VON (1852–1934), Austrian author, representative of Austrian traditional Catholicism with Neoromantic, Germanic-Christian ideas. A deeply religious convert, K. took his material from the Middle Ages as the great era of Catholic culture. Apart from some religious lyrical poetry, his impact was as critic and essayist and as founder of the *Gralbundes* (1905), a circle of Catholic writers in Vienna modeled after the Görres circle in Munich. Their journal, *Der Gral* (1906–) was later continued in Germany by F. Muckermann, SJ. Influenced by Calderon and R. Wagner, K. promoted the idea of the festival. However, his dramas are considered unproducible. Of Bohemian origin, K., after juridical studies, became an independent scholar in Vienna. Works: *Osterfestspiel* (1894); *Das Deutsche Götter- und Heldenbuch* (1904). BIBLIOGRAPHY: W. Hug, LTK 6:581.

[B. F. STEINBRUCKNER]

KRAMP, JOSEPH (1886–1940), German Jesuit theologian and liturgist, influential in his support of the German Catholic youth movement. He was among the first to advocate the active participation of student groups in the Mass. Interested esp. in pre-Tridentine theology, K. produced several works that won international recognition, among them *Eucharistia* (1924; Eng. tr. W. Busch, 1926); and *Messliturgie und Gottesreich* (1922–23) which appeared in Eng. as *Liturgical Sacrifice of the New Law* (tr. L. F. Miller, 1926).

[N. KOLLAR]

KRATEMA, in Middle Byzantine musical notation, a subsidiary sign prolonging the note.

[M. T. LEGGE]

KRATTMANN, HERMAN (d. 1704), Danish Dominican. K. left Denmark in 1665, became a Catholic, and entered the Dominicans in Paris. He devoted himself with some local success to the conversion of Scandinavians to Catholicism. BIBLIOGRAPHY: A. Otto, LTK 6:595.

[M. J. SUELZER]

KRAUS, FRANZ XAVER (1840–1901), church historian; historian of art. Ordained in 1864, K. studied in Freiburg and Bonn before taking the post of professor of Christian art at Strassburg in 1872. From 1878 he was professor of church history at Freiburg. His scholarly writing through the years contributed much to the study of early Christian art and archeology. His books in this field include *Geschichte der Christlichen Kunst* (2v., 1896–1900) and *Roma Sotteranea* (1873). Theologically K. was a liberal in the sense that he was opposed to *Ultramontanism and defended the rights of the State against the Church in an attempt to find a middle way during the *Kulturkampf. The government made an unsuccessful effort to secure his appointment to a bishopric.

[R. B. ENO]

KRAUS, KARL (1874–1936), Austrian essayist, poet, and dramatist, a representative of Expressionism. Through brilliant essays in his controversial journal *Die Fackel* (1899–1936), K. sharply criticized modern society and the decay of culture as expressed in the decay of language. He called for high ethical and aesthetic standards and for a period embraced Catholicism. Born in Bohemia, K. studied law for several semesters in Vienna, then tried unsuccessfully an acting career until he discovered his talent for writing. In his monumental drama, *Die letzten Tage der Menschheit* (1918), he revealed his pacifism. The work is regarded as one of the literary masterpieces on the tragedy of World War I.

[B. F. STEINBRUCKNER]

KRAUTH, CHARLES PORTERFIELD (1825–83), Lutheran theologian. Born in Martinsburg, W. Va., K. was educated at Gettysburg College and Seminary. After a succession of pastorates in Maryland, Virginia and Pennsylvania, he became (1860) editor of a Philadelphia weekly, *Lutheran and Missionary*. He brought his broad historical and theological knowledge to the service of the paper's interest in Lutheran doctrinal tradition, and labored in opposition to the emergence of a so-called American Lutheranism under Samuel Schmucker, which was anticonfessional and influenced by non-Lutheran elements. *The Conservative Reformation and Its Theology* (1871), K.'s masterwork, was a powerful incentive for American Lutherans to study and retain their specific doctrinal identity. The work particularly stressed the need for a return to the positive spirit and confessional documents of the Reformation, and for a strong eucharistic and liturgical life in Lutheranism. BIBLIOGRAPHY: A. Spaeth, *Charles Porterfield Krauth* (2 v., 1898; repr. 1969); Smith-Jamison 1:275–279.

[T. C. O'BRIEN]

KREIN, ALEXANDER (1883–1951), Russian composer. He studied at Moscow Conservatory before composing his *Hebrew Sketches* (1909–10) for string quartet and clarinet; in 1913, his *Salome* for orchestra was completed. His music was influenced by Russian and Jewish folklore. Later it also developed a revolutionary content. His most famous work is "Threnody", a funeral ode he wrote for Lenin. Composer of operas, symphonic and chamber music, K. also wrote music for the Jewish theater.

[M. GRANAHAN]

KREMLIN (Russ., citadel), administrative center of Russia and the Soviet Union. Located on the left bank of the Moscow River and adjacent to Red Square, the traditional symbol of power has walls of red brick which measure more than 7,000 feet in circumference and enclose 20 towers, several squares, cathedrals, churches, the world's largest bell (200 tons in weight and 20 feet in height), and a cannon weighing 40 tons. Until 1712 when Peter the Great moved the capital to St. Petersburg, the Kremlin was the residence of the czars. The Bolsheviks returned the capital to Moscow in 1918, and today the Kremlin surrounds the Council of Ministers and Presidium of the Supreme Soviet buildings. The Kremlin Palace, the largest in the complex, is the site of party congresses and conventions. BIBLIOGRAPHY: D. D. Duncan, *Kremlin* (1960).

[D. DIRSCHERL]

KREMSMÜNSTER, ABBEY OF, Austrian Benedictine abbey on the Krems River, in the Diocese of Linz. It was established in 777 by Duke Tassilo III of Bavaria, probably with monks from Mondsee. Its missionary activity was terminated by Magyar invasion in the beginning of the 10th century. Afterwards the monastery was under the authority of the bps. of Passau. During the Middle Ages its scriptorium was far-famed, and humanism acquired early influence (gymnasium founded 1549). The baroque period was the golden age of the abbey: all buildings were renovated, an observatory constructed, an academy for young noblemen founded, and many activities in music and liturgical drama were cultivated. Even today the abbey's gymnasium is one of the best schools in Austria, and many monks are occupied in the sciences. The abbey's museum contains the famous Tassilo chalice (8th cent.) and other rare objects. BIBLIOGRAPHY: *Festschrift zum 400-jährigen Bestand des öffentlichen Obergymnasiums Kremsmünster (1949); A. Kellner, Musikgeschichte des Stiftes Kremsmünster* (1956); *ibid. Professbuch des Stiftes Kremsmünster* (1968).

[F. H. RÖHRIG]

KRENEK, ERNST (1900–), Austrian composer whose most famous work is *Jonny spielt auf* (1927), a jazz opera. Having studied under Franz Shreker, in his first works he was a neoromantic along the lines of his father-in-law, Gustav Mahler. After a neoclassical period of sharply atonal, contrapuntal, and rigidly rhythmic works, K. began integrating jazz elements into his work during the 1920s. Association with the Viennese circle of Schoenberg, Berg, and Webern, reinforced his experiments in serial music and guided him into 12-tone composition. He emigrated to the U.S. in 1938. His *Studies in Counterpoint* (1940) is an essay on dodecaphonic technique. K.'s corpus includes a number of liturgical choral works, the most significant of which musicologically is his *Lamentatio Jeremiae Prophetae* (1940–41), the first use of a "principle of rotation" in serial composition.

[R. J. LITZ]

KRISHNA (KṚṢṆA), most popular and celebrated Hindu hero and god, eighth and most important avatar of Viṣṇu.

Kṛṣṇa and his elder brother Balarāma were preserved from death by hiding as children of the cowherd Nanda. During his youth K. performed many miracles for the cowherds and was worshipped later as K. Govinda (Lord of Herdsmen). K. is the divine lover seeking the beautiful Rādhā (symbol of the soul of man), playing on his flute a mystical Song of Songs. In Indian MSS K. is distinguished by the blue coloring of his figure.

[M. J. DALY]

KRIST, see EVANGELIENBUCH.

KRIŽANIĆ, JURAJ (Juris; *c.*1617–83), Croatian missionary and writer. Ordained 1642, he took his doctorate in theology before beginning his mission to Croatia (1645). He then went to Poland and Russia where he sought converts to Catholicism. Returning temporarily to Rome (1652), he wrote about Russia and Russian Orthodoxy. He worked as a translator for Czar Alexis' government (1659–61) until his identity as a Catholic priest was discovered. Exiled to Siberia, he wrote several books dealing with Pan-Slavic themes, his best known work, *Politika*, advocated Pan-Slavic resistance to the Germans. Released (1676), he joined the Polish Dominicans at Vilna and as chaplain to the Polish army died in the Turkish siege of Vienna. He is sometimes called the Father of Pan-Slavism.

[R. J. LITZ]

KRIŽEVCI, Byzantine rite Catholic diocese in Yugoslavia. With the northern advances of the Turks in the 15th cent., Eastern Orthodox Serbs and Vlachs migrated from the central region of the Balkan Peninsula into the Kingdom of Croatia. Their bishop, Simeon Vratanjić, had resided since 1606 in the Monastery of Marča; he joined the Catholic Church in Rome (1611). He and his successors were the ecclesiastical superiors of the faithful who had found refuge S of Zagreb in the region of Žumberak. Bishop Paul Zorčić founded a seminary in Zagreb (1685) that is still in existence. The bps. were treated as suffragans of the Latin rite bp. of Zagreb until in 1777 a bishopric of their own was established in Križevci (Croatia). Following political changes, the jurisdiction of the bp. was extended to all Yugoslavia, and includes several nationalities: Croats, Ruthenians from Slovakia, Ukrainians from Galicia, Macedonians who joined the union *c.*1860, and Romanians. the bp.'s residence is now in Zagreb, although his official title is that of Križevci. The diocese had (1975) 46,876 faithful with 59 priests in 57 parishes.

[V. J. POSPISHIL]

KROMER, MARTIN (Cromer; 1515–89), Polish historian, writer, diplomat, bishop. He served as government secretary and ambassador during the years he was preparing his two most important works: *De origine et rebus gestis Polonorum* (1555), which covers the early history of Poland up to 1506; and *Polonia sive de situ, populis, moribus, magistratibus et republica regni Poloniae* (1577). Coadjutor of Ermland (1569), he became its bp. in 1579, in which position he opposed the efforts of Lutheran and Calvinist Reformers, gave support to the Jesuits, and wrote liturgical and pastoral works in his native Polish.

[R. J. LITZ]

KRONSTADT CATHEDRAL, Russian neoclassic church of St. Andrew by Adrian Dmitrievich Zakharov (1761–1811), leading architect of imperial St. Petersburg.

[M. J. DALY]

KRSTJANI (Sl., Christians), name used by medieval dualist heretics of Bosnia, an offshoot of the Bogomil sect of Bulgaria. They appear in Bosnia first toward the end of the 11th cent., and then suddenly increased in the second half of the 12th cent. after the cruel persecution of the Bogomils in Serbia under Prince Stefan Nemanja (1168–96). With the access of Prince (Ban) Kulin of Bosnia (1180–1204), the Krstjani sect became the established Church of the country. They were the object of persecution and crusades by both Latin and Eastern Christians. After the Turkish conquest of Bosnia in 1463 most of the Krstjani accepted Islam and form the bulk of the Muslim population of present-day Yugoslavia. There is a complex literature about the theological tenets and ecclesiastical allegiance of the Krstjani in the Middle Ages, but more recent evidence seems to prove that the Church of Bosnia was a Bogomil Church, holding the typical doctrines of Manichaean dualism, elaborated by the Bulgarian Bogomils of the 10th century. A still-intriguing archeological feature of the medieval Krstjani is the widely scattered tombstones with strangely distorted smiling figures. BIBLIOGRAPHY: M. Miletič, *I krstjani di Bosnia alla luce dei loro monumenti di pietra* (1957); D. Mandič, *Bogomilska Crkva Bosanskih Krstjana (1962)*.

[G. ELDAROV]

KRUMBACHER, KARL (1856–1909), modern restorer of Byzantine studies; professor at the Univ. of Munich from 1892; founder in 1892 of the journal, *Byzantinische Zeitschrift*. His *Geschichte der byzantinischen Literatur* (1891; rev. 1897) became a standard for the study of Byzantine theology, liturgy, and church history.

[T. C. O'BRIEN]

KU KLUX KLAN (KKK), the name of three distinct racist secret societies, the second of which played a major role in American life. All three Klans worked out a similar ritual, employed common symbols and vocabulary, and opposed Negroes, Catholics, Jews, and the foreign-born.

The original KKK was founded by six Confederate veterans in Pulaski, Tenn., in 1865. The name was devised by adding alliterative embellishments to the Greek word *kuklos* (circle). The Klansmen rode about the countryside in white sheets and masks to terrorize the recently freed slaves. In their view they were merely fighting carpetbaggers, radical Republicanism, and the threat to Southern life posed by the emancipation of the Negroes. Gen. Nathan Bedford Forrest lent prestige to the KKK when he became Grand Wizard in 1869, but in the face of ample proof that Klansmen employed lynching, torture, and floggings, the general agreed to direct the dissolution of the KKK, and within 4 years it had disappeared.

An unfrocked Methodist minister and professional fraternalist, William J. Simmons, resurrected the KKK in Atlanta, Ga., in 1915. The glorification of the KKK by T. Dixon's *The Clansman* and by the film *Birth of a Nation* had prepared the way. Two public relations specialists helped Simmons recruit members by the thousands, and in the mid-1920s the KKK had enrolled as many as 5 million men. The Klansmen belonged to local Klaverns, paid Klectokens (dues), followed the ritual presented in the Kloran, and joined in prayers led by the Kludd (chaplain). Between 1921 and 1925 the KKK elected governors in Indiana, Maine, and Colorado; controlled legislatures in five states; sent senators and congressmen to Washington; and took over numerous city halls and courthouses. The KKK fought the nomination and election as governor of N.Y. of Alfred E. Smith, a Catholic and antiprohibitionist. This second KKK claimed to be defending Protestantism from the threat posed by Catholics, Jews, Communists, Negroes, foreigners, and bootleggers. It posed as the expression of 100% Americanism. In fact it was probably more anti-Semitic and anti-Catholic than racist. The conviction for rape and murder of D. C. Stephenson, Grand Dragon of Indiana, and the exposure of the low moral standards of other Klansmen led to a decline of the KKK that was almost as rapid as its rise; by 1930 membership had dwindled to 35,000.

After World War II several groups in southern states took the name of the KKK and enrolled members in a crusade to preserve racial segregation. Taken together, these rival Klans could muster fewer than 40,000 members, most of them in Georgia, Alabama, and Mississippi. The major Protestant Churches completely repudiate the objectives and methods of the present KKK. It was branded in 1965 by Pres. Lyndon B. Johnson as "a hooded society of bigots." BIBLIOGRAPHY: D. M. Chalmers, *Hooded Americanism: The First Century of the KKK* (1965); W. P. Randel, *KKK: A Century of Infamy* (1965); A. W. Trelease, *White Terror: The KuKluxKlan Conspiracy of Southern Reconstruction* (ed. K. B. Clark, 1971).

[W. J. WHALEN]

KUDARA KANNON OF HORYUJI, Japanese wood sculpture of the 7th cent., slender, tall, with delicately carved drapery, a figure of utmost gentleness, expressive of the *Kannon (Avalokiteśvara)*—most compassionate of bodhisattvas.

[M. J. DALY]

KUGLER, FRANZ XAVER (1862–1929), astronomer, Assyriologist. German-born, he became a Jesuit in 1886, already a doctor in chemistry, and was ordained in 1893. As a professor at Exaeten in the Netherlands, he was associated with two Jesuits who pioneered in the field of Babylonian astronomy. K. furthered their work and became an accepted scholar in the field of Babylonian astronomy. His writings include *Sternkunde und Sterndienst* (3 v., 1907–35) and *Im Bannkreis Babels* (1910).

[J. R. AHERNE]

KUHN, JOHANNES (1806–87), German philosopher, theologian. Ordained in 1831, he taught at the Univ. of Giessen (1832–37) when he was appointed to the Univ. of Tübingen, holding there the chair of dogmatic theology until his retirement in 1882. A theologian of the first rank, K. wrote an important philosophical work in 1834 entitled *Jacobi und die Philosophie seiner Zeit.* He published numerous articles on NT topics in the *Jahrbucher für Theologie und christliche Philosophie.* Outstanding is his work *Katholische Dogmatik* (4 v., 1846–68) even though it was not completed. K. was often engaged in theological and philosophical controversy with the Hermesians and the Neo-Scholastics. Out of one dispute came K.'s important work *Die christliche Lehre von der göttlichen Gnade . . .* (1868). BIBLIOGRAPHY: F. Lauchert, CE 8:703.

[J. R. AHERNE]

KULMBACH, HANS SUSS VON (Hans Suess; 1480–1522). With Hans Baldung-Grien K. was a most important student of Dürer, strongly influenced by the master in important works: *Scenes from the Lives of St. Peter and St. Paul* (1511), *Adoration of the Magi* (1513), the famous *Tucher Altar* (1514), and the *St. Katharine Altar* (Cracow, 1516). K.'s work is less plastic than Dürer's, with a Venetian landscape style that distinguishes it from German 16th-cent. painting.

[M. J. DALY]

KULTURKAMPF (Ger., struggle for civilization), the name given by the pathologist and liberal Rudolf Virchow to the struggle going on between several German states, esp. Prussia, and the RC Church in the 1870s. He first used the term in the Prussian Landtag in Jan. 1873 and then repeatedly, as did his colleagues in the Progressive party, as a campaign slogan in elections. German liberals, moderate and radical alike, believed that Pope Pius IX's *Syllabus of Errors* (1864) and the proclamation of papal infallibility (1870) confirmed their opinion that the RC Church was the foe of free thought and progress; they also attributed to unpatriotic motives RC opposition to German unification under Prussian leadership. Some liberals, Progressives included, rejected the Kulturkampf, but most helped to provide either legislative materials or parliamentary support. The Kulturkampf became a possibility and then a harsh reality when Otto von *Bismarck, Prussian Minister-President and German Chancellor, decided in the early summer of 1871 to align the Prussian state with the anti-Catholic liberals. His motives were political and essentially derived from his fear of the new Catholic Center party, which he thought hostile to the new Reich for combined ecclesiastical and particularist reasons. Three of the Kulturkampf statutes were national in scope: the Pulpit Law ("Misuse of the Pulpit for Political Ends") of Dec. 1871; the "Jesuit Law" of June 1872, which prohibited the maintenance of Jesuit institutions and permitted expulsion of individual Jesuits; and the Civil Marriage Act of Feb. 1875. The major theater of the Kulturkampf was Prussia, where it became intense after the appointment of Adalbert Falk as minister of education and public worship in Jan. 1872. He insisted on state control of all lower and secondary education in the School Inspection Law of March 1872; he then made a massive attack on the bps.' disciplinary and administrative powers in the *May Laws of 1873. Additional legislation a year later provided for severe penalties against churchmen violating the May Laws and for the administration of vacated bishoprics. New laws in May and June of 1875 dissolved numerous religious orders and established communal lay associations to administer church properties. By 1877 eight of the twelve Prussian bps. were either imprisoned or exiled, and about 990 regular parishes were without priests. In the state of Baden, earlier the site of a lesser Kulturkampf, the government tried to impose a state examination on candidates for the priesthood, closed seminaries, introduced interconfessional schools, and insisted on state approval of all clerical appointments. A more moderate government carried on a milder Kulturkampf in Hessen-Darmstadt. By the time Pius IX died in 1878, Bismarck had become weary of a struggle that had stimulated the growth of the Center party, made conservative Protestants wary, and led to the Prussian and Imperial governments' dependence on the liberal parties; he was also concerned about the new socialist movement. After fitful gestures and negotiations throughout the period 1879–86, the Prussian government and the Vatican negotiated a compromise settlement in 1886–87, which led in turn to settlements in several other German states. BIBLIOGRAPHY: E. Eyck, *Bismarck after Fifty Years* (1950).

[J. K. ZEENDER]

ḲUMMUṢ (also *Ghomos*), the abbot of a Coptic monastery, derived from the Greek word **hēgoumenos*; also the honorific title of a Coptic archpriest or dean who has jurisdiction over several churches. The monastic office requires a special form of ordination, and a patriarch or bp. must receive this order before he can be consecrated.

[D. W. JOHNSON]

KUNDIG, MARTIN (1805–79), Swiss born priest, church leader in the Midwest. Ordained in 1829 for the Diocese of Cincinnati, he labored in Ohio, Michigan, and Wisconsin. Because of his interest in public education he was appointed a regent of the Univ. of Michigan; in Wisconsin he established over 20 parishes; he served as vicar general for the first bp. of Milwaukee, and in 1845 at Kenosha opened the first free public school. He also worked on behalf of immigrants, aiding them to become citizens and to purchase land; he was a leader as well in other civic projects.

[J. R. AHERNE]

KÜNG, HANS (1928–), controversial RC theologian. Ordained in 1954, K. studied at the Gregorian Univ. in Rome and the Institut Catholique in Paris and has held the chair of fundamental theology at the Univ. of Tübingen since 1960. K. served as an official theologian (*peritus*) at Vatican Council II. His central theological concerns have been ecclesiology and ecumenics. He has defended the fundamental agreement between Barth and contemporary RC notions of justification, called for radical renewal in the Church, and proposed the idea of papal indefectibility rather than verbal infallibility. The Congregation for the Doctrine of Faith has called K.'s teaching into question in 1973 and in 1975; K. has maintained that the curial procedures violate the principles of due process. BIBLIOGRAPHY: *Justification* (1964); *Church* (1968); *Infallible? An Enquiry* (1971); *On Being a Christian* (1977).

[T. M. MCFADDEN]

KUNIGUNDE, BL. (*c.* 1224–*c.* 1292), patroness of Poland and of Lithuania. Daughter of royalty who married Boleslas V, she is alleged to have lived in continence and to have spent her life in doing charitable works. After her husband's death she became a Poor Clare at Sandeckcz. There she lived until the Tatars' invasion forced her to withdraw to the castle once again. The Tatars pursued, but with K.'s prayer they left. Clement XI named her patroness of Poland and of Lithuania in 1715. BIBLIOGRAPHY: Butler 3:178.

[J. R. RIVELLO]

KUNIGUNDE, ST. (*c.* 980–1033), German empress of the Emperor Henry II. They were married *c.* 998, crowned as king and queen in 1002, and received the imperial crown at Rome from Benedict VIII in 1014. She was counsellor to the Emperor, shared in his good works, and become renowned for her own sanctity and miracles. Widowed in 1024, she entered the monastery she had herself founded at Kaufungen. She was entombed in the cathedral of Bamberg next to her husband. She was canonized in 1200. BIBLIOGRAPHY: G. D. Gordini, BiblSanct 4:393–397.

[T. C. O'BRIEN]

KUNO OF TRIER, ST. (1016–66), archbishop. K. became cathedral provost under his powerful uncle, Abp. Anno II of Cologne. Emperor Henry IV named and invested K. abp. of Trier against the wishes and rights of the city. He was captured and killed at Ürzig June 1, 1066, on his way to his enthronization. His body was brought to Tholey monastery where he was venerated as saint and martyr in a local cult. BIBLIOGRAPHY: L. Falkenstein, BiblSanct 4:209 s.v. "Corrado."

[S. WILLIAMS]

KÜRNBERGER, FERDINAND (1821–79), Austrian writer, essayist, representative of German literary realism whose *feuilletons* were widely read in the middle of the 19th century. In 1848 he participated in the Revolution in Vienna, and in 1849 also in Dresden. From 1867 to 1870 he was secretary general of the German Schiller Foundation. His novel *Der Amerikamüde* (1855), a biography of N. *Lenau, is a criticism of the capitalistic system in America.

[B. F. STEINBRUCKNER]

KURTH, GODEFROID (1847–1916), Belgian historian. Born at Arlon, Luxembourg of German-Belgian descent, K. attended the State College at Arlon and the Univ. of Liège, with training in the classics, philology, and literature. After 3 years' teaching, he was appointed professor of medieval history and history of modern literature at Liège in 1872. In 1874, on his own initiative, K. established a scientific course of history at the Univ. of Liège. This included paleography, epigraphy, diplomatic history, and auxiliary sciences. In 1877 this method succeeded, leading to other courses at Brussels, Ghent, and Louvain. K. earned the title of founder of the scientific teaching of history in Belgium. He authored over 28 volumes, among which are *Church at Turning Points in History* and *St. Boniface*. As director of the Belgian Institute of History at Rome during World War I, he suffered great agonies of spirit because of the conflict.

BIBLIOGRAPHY: F. Neuray, *Une Grande figure nationale, Godefroid Kurth* (1931); H. Nelis, RHE 17 (1921) 656–665.

[N. F. GAUGHAN]

KÛSHĀPĀ, a prayer which the East Syrian celebrant is directed to say in a low voice and kneeling. In practice, the Nestorian celebrant says it rather with his knees bent in such a way that he is almost sitting on his heels.

[A. CODY]

KÛSSÎṮŌ, nonliturgical hat worn by Jacobite bps. in public and in processions entering or leaving a church on solemn occasions. It is black, formed like a bulging turban curving to a point on top, and is commonly called in Arabic *tabyeh* or *arf*. Syrian Catholic bps. have abandoned it, wearing instead a Greek-style *kalymafkion* surmounted by a tiny crown. The word is also used sometimes for the West Syrian monastic hood.

[A. CODY]

KÛTÎNŌ (East Syrian, *kôtînā;* Arab., *kîtûnah* or *qamûs*), the Syrian equivalent of the Western alb. Among the West Syrians it is either white or colored, the alb of deacons and lesser ministers usually being decorated with embroidery. It is regularly white among the Maronites, and among the East Syrians (who often call this vestment the *sudrā*).

[A. CODY]

KUTNA HORA: ST. BARBARA, late Gothic cathedral in Bohemia begun by Peter Parler in 1380 and continued by Benedikt Rejt (Ried) in the 15th cent. with richly varied vaulting, frescoes, and baroque altar paintings by I. J. Raab and P. Brandl.

[M. J. DALY]

KUTSCHKER, JOHANN RUDOLPH (1810–81), canonist, prince abp. of Vienna from 1876, cardinal from 1877. From his career as professor of moral theology at Olmütz came his: *Die gemischten Ehen* (1838); *Die Lehre vom Schadenersatz* (1851); *Das Eherecht der katholische Kirche nach seiner Theorie und Praxis* (5 v., 1856–59). In Vienna K. served in the ministry of education from 1857 until becoming abp., and from 1862 was suffragan bp. and vicar general.

[T. C. O'BRIEN]

KUVERA (KUBERA), god of wealth, appearing in later Vedic literature, well-known in Buddhism, lord of precious jewels and metals, guardian (lokapāla) of the North, living in the jeweled city of Alakā, near Mt. Kailāsa, commanding gnomes (*guhyaka*) and fairies (*yakṣa*). The many-jeweled K. rides a lion or horse, and with fierce expression exerts power over the nagas who guard the earth's treasures.

[M. J. DALY]

KUYPER, ABRAHAM (1837–1920), Dutch Reformed theologian, church leader, member of parliament in the lower chamber 1874–77 and 1894–1901, when he became minister of the interior, serving until 1905. He was a strict orthodox Calvinist, advocating absolute adherence to the classic Reformed confessions of faith, and leading in the formation of the Gereformeerde Doleerende Kerk in 1886 and the Gereformeerde Kerk in Nederland in 1892, in protest against the liberal theology of the official Reformed Church. K.'s *Calvinism* (1899) was a publication of lectures given at Princeton Theological Seminary in 1898. His political, antirevolutionary position was published in *Ons Program* (1879). In addition to his *Calvinism* English translations of many of his other works appeared in the *Encyclopedia of Sacred Theology: Its Principles* (1898).

[T. C. O'BRIEN]

KYD, THOMAS (1558–94), English dramatist, author of the sensational and popular revenge play, *The Spanish Tragedy,* written *c.* 1589. Much of his writing has probably been lost. He was sent to prison for a blasphemous paper against religion, which he swore was C. Marlowe's. When Marlowe was killed in a brawl, K. was released. *The Spanish Tragedy* combines the Senecan demand for revenge as a duty with Christian opposition to this idea and with the Renaissance code of personal honor in the struggle within Hieronymo, the father of the murdered Horatio. The revenge plays of this period reveal the Renaissance glorification of the natural man, but support the moral law in the tragic death of the avenger, who has usurped God's right.

[M. M. BARRY]

KYLISMA, see QUILISMA.

KYRIE ELEISON, in the Roman Mass, a Greek litany-acclamation addressed to Christ. It translates literally as "Lord, have mercy" but is more an expression of joy and confidence in the risen Lord than a penitential plea. Originating in the East as a congregational response to the deacon's litany, it came into use in the West by the late 5th century. By the time of St. Gregory the Great (d. 604) the invocations of the litany (corresponding to today's Prayers of the Faithful) were ordinarily omitted, leaving only the responses (Lord, have mercy and Christ, have mercy). Prior to the 1969 liturgical reforms the chant (Kyrie, three times; Christe, three times; Kyrie, three times) served as an introduction to the priest's opening prayer; since 1969, whether in Greek or in the vernacular, it has been incorporated into the penitential rite of the Mass.

[J. DALLEN]

KYRILLOS (CYRIL) VI (1902–71), patriarch of the Coptic Orthodox Church (1959–71). Born at Damanhur in the Nile Delta, after his theological studies he entered the Baramus monastery in Wadi el Natrun. Later he spent a number of years as a hermit. He succeeded Patriarch Yousab—after a 3-year vacancy—and under K.'s leadership the Coptic Church developed more extensive contacts with other Churches. In 1968 he secured the return of relics of St. Mark from Venice. He was succeeded by Shenouda III.

[T. EARLY]

KYRION, see CYRION.

KYUNGJU, old capital of the Silla dynasty (668–918), in Korea near which the Pulguksa temple and rock-cut cave chapel (Sokkulam) house some of the greatest examples of Korean sculpture.

[M. J. DALY]

L

LABADIE, JEAN DE (1610–74), founder of a small communal group called *Labadists. L. entered the Society of Jesus in 1625 and was ordained in 1635. An excellent preacher, but with an unquiet temperament and reforming spirit, he left his order at his own request in 1639 because of illness and stayed for a while with the Fathers of the Oratory. As a diocesan priest in 1644 he founded at Amiens conventicles for prayer, meditation, and Bible study; he stressed the direct inspiration of the Holy Spirit on the believer. Apparently because he distributed *communion under both kinds, he was moved by Card. Mazarin to Southern France. L.'s preaching soon became suspect, and in 1749 he had to ask hospitality of the Carmelites at Bazas to escape arrest. In 1650 he went over to the *Reformed Church. While pastor at Montauban (1652–57), his reforming innovations led to conflict and he moved to Orange in 1657 and to Geneva in 1659. In 1666 he became a pastor in the Netherlands. At first he was well received as a zealous and able preacher. The authorities put a watch on him, however, and when he refused to retract unorthodox statements, the Dutch Synod exiled him. In 1670 he was able to establish his own community at Herford in Westphalia. He gathered 55 followers, but he was forced to leave Herford in 1671. He and his disciples went first to Bremen and then to Altona, where he died. L. left 30 treatises, almost all of them written after he had entered the Reformed Church. BIBLIOGRAPHY: G. Frank, EncRelKnow 6:390–392; M. Schmidt, RRG 4:193; B. D. Dupuy, *Catholicisme* 6:1511–12.

[M. J. SUELZER]

LABADISTS, members of the Reformed sect founded in Herford, Westphalia, *c.* 1670 by Jean de *Labadie. They believed that the Bible could be understood only by the immediate inspiration of the Holy Spirit, denied the Real Presence, rarely celebrated the Eucharist, and held that marriage with an unregenerate person was not binding. Their communal life resembled that of the Moravians; in their devotional practices they foreshadowed *Pietism. In 1690 they numbered about 300. Anne Marie Schürmann, who reestablished the group in West Frisia after Labadie's death, looked forward to founding missions in Surinam and along the Hudson River in North America; but the sect dwindled, and after the death of their last preacher in 1732 its remaining members scattered. BIBLIOGRAPHY: B. D. Dupuy, *Catholicisme* 6:1511–12; F. E. Stoeffler, *Rise of Pietism* (1965); B. B. James, *Labadist Colony in Maryland* (1899, repr. 1973).

[M. J. SUELZER]

LABAN, the brother of Rebekah (Gen 24.29,50) and uncle of Jacob, who contrived to make Jacob work for 14 years in order to marry his two daughters Leah and Rachel. The "trickster" stories of Gen ch. 29–31, in which Laban defrauds Jacob of his true wages and initially fobs him off with the wrong daughter, but in which Jacob, by the power of Yahweh, finally outwits and overcomes Laban (cf. Gen 31.24,42), are full of details which are paralleled in the Hurrian records of *c.* 1500 B.C. BIBLIOGRAPHY: G. Stano, EncCatt 7:769–770.

[D. J. BOURKE]

LA BARRIÈRE, JEAN DE (1544–1600), founder of the Feuillants, a congregation of reformed Cistercians. As a young man he had been granted the Abbey of Les Feuillants *in commendam* and afterwards, fired by the spirit of reform, completed his studies in Paris, joined the Cistercians, was ordained, and became regular abbot, and superior general of the congregation. He was deposed for political reasons and spent 8 years in confinement in Rome. He bore his humiliation with patience and was rehabilitated shortly before he died through the intervention of St. Robert Bellarmine. BIBLIOGRAPHY: M. B. Brard, *Catholicisme* 6:1516–18.

[H. JACK]

LABARUM, from the time of *Constantine I, the banner of the imperial Roman legions, bearing a cross crowned with the monogram of Christ, *Chi Rho,* and the motto, ''In this sign you will conquer.'' *IN HOC SIGNO VINCES.

[T. C. O'BRIEN]

LABASTIDA Y DÁVALOS, PELAGIO ANTONIO DE (1817–91), abp. of Mexico City. First a professor of theology and rector at the Univ. of Mexico City, he was named bp. of Puebla in 1855. A year later he was expelled for resisting anti-Catholic laws; he returned to Mexico in 1863 as abp. of Mexico City, and held posts in the French government under Emperor Maximilian. Again L. left the country after protesting the failure of the government to repeal laws that permitted confiscation of church property. Invited to Rome in 1867, he remained there because of the collapse of the French venture, until 1871, after participating in Vatican Council I.

[T. C. O'BRIEN]

LABAT, JEAN BAPTISTE (1663–1738), French Dominican missionary and author. L. entered the Order of Preachers (1683), was professed (1685), and volunteered for missionary work among the Indians of the Lesser (French) Antilles. Active participation in island life—including initiating resistance to the third unsuccessful British invasion of Guadeloupe (1703)—earned him a reprimand and a 10-year exile from the French government but occasioned for posterity voluminous descriptions of Spain, Italy, Syria, West Africa, and North Africa. L.'s most widely read work is *Nouveau voyage aux Isles de l'Amérique* (6 v., 1722). BIBLIOGRAPHY: A. Redigonda, EncCatt 7:773–774; J. Galopeau, *Catholicisme* 6:1520–22.

[H. P. ANNAS]

LABBE, PHILIPPE (1607–67), French Jesuit savant. A Jesuit from 1623 and for a time a teacher at Bourges, he devoted most of his life to historical and antiquarian research and writing; he published over 80 titles. His contributions to scholarship include his most valuable work, *De Byzantinae historiae scriptoribus* (1648); *Aristotelis et Platonis graecorum interpretum typos hactenus editorum* (1657); *L'Abrégé royal de l'alliance chronologique de l'historie sacrée et profane* (1651); and *Sacrosancta concilia ad regiam editionem exacta* (8 v., 1671–72).

[T. C. O'BRIEN]

LABERTHONNIÈRE, LUCIEN (1860–1932), French Modernist philosopher and theologian. L. joined the Oratorians and was ordained in 1886, then taught philosophy at the College of Juilly. He was editor of *Annales de la philosophie chrétienne* (1905–13). This, along with six other works, was placed on the Index because of L.'s immanentist views. The influence of Blondel can be seen in L.'s writing. His two principal works, *Le Réalisme chrétien et l'idéalisme grec* (1904) and *Essai de philosophie religieuse* (1903) evince his view of Christianity as essentially practical truth. He saw it as a choice to be made in preference to a speculative world view and rejected any reasoned support surrounding faith. He remained faithful to the Church throughout his life. BIBLIOGRAPHY: C. Testore, EncCatt 7:775–777.

[H. P. ANNAS]

LA BIGNE, MARGUERIN DE (1546–89), patrologist. In refutation of the work of the *Centuriators of Magdeburg, L. collected and published more than 200 patristic writings arranged systematically according to subjects (1575–79). In its edition of 1677 this was called the *Maxima bibliotheca sanctorum patrum* (27 v.), and it is important as an early effort to provide a comprehensive collection of patristic literature. BIBLIOGRAPHY: R. Bäumer, LTK 6:720; E. Peterson, EncCatt 7:777–778.

[R. B. ENO]

LA BOÉTIE, ÉTIENNE DE (1530–63), French humanist writer. Close friend and colleague of *Montaigne at the Parliament of Bordeaux, L. shaped Montaigne's interest in the late neo-Stoic revival in vogue among the magistracy. His works include *Discours de la servitude volontaire* or *Contr'un* against monarchical tyranny and *Mémoire sur l'édit de janvier 1562,* advocating nonviolent Catholic reform. BIBLIOGRAPHY: E. de La Boétie, *Oeuvres complètes* (ed. P. Bonnefon, repr. 1967) introd.; J. Fenouillet, *Catholicisme* 6:1533.

[R. N. NICOLICH]

LABOR AND THE CATHOLIC CHURCH (19th and 20th cent.). The struggle of labor in mid-19th cent. to organize and thereby cope with the often ruthless regimen growing out of the industrial revolution in Europe and the U.S. presents a complex history. No less complicated is the record of the Catholic Church in relation to the labor movement. It is an unfortunate fact that Socialism, with its materialists and antireligious philosophy, dominated efforts to protect the workingman. Because of this bias, Catholics distrusted any movement to improve the lot of labor. The first and most influential Catholic voice on behalf of workers was that of Wilhelm von Ketteler, bp. of Mainz, Germany. In 1864 Von Ketteler published *Christianity and the Labor Question,* expanding principles drawn from St. Thomas Aquinas and making a detailed analysis of the Socialist philosophy. In later addresses and in his position in the Reichstag, the bp. developed a philosophy and program of social action. Pope Leo XIII acknowledged that much in the encyclical *Rerum novarum* derived from Von Ketteler. From his impetus the pro-labor campaign grew and was furthered by Catholic leaders in 19th-cent. Germany.

In England Card. Manning spoke and acted with great force on behalf of labor, and his influence was widespread. In Switzerland the work of Card. Mermillod focused on the economic situation, and specifically the labor question, thus anticipating Pope Leo's stand on these matters. Card. Gibbons should be credited with significant contribution to the labor movement in the United States. His championship of the Knights of Labor, against bitter hostility on the part of many American and Canadian bps. who feared it a secret society, brought a new era in Catholic relationship with organized labor and drew the approval of Leo XIII. Involvement by churchmen and laymen in promoting the rights of labor made great strides in France, Belgium, and The Netherlands in the late 19th and early 20th centuries. One force that slowly grew to importance was the association of Catholic workers in an organization. Later this concept would be enlarged to include non-Catholics and the result was the International Confederation of Christian Trade Unions (1920). It has strong national groups in Germany, France, Italy, Belgium, and The Netherlands.

The teaching Church has spoken clearly on the rights of labor. Pioneering in that area was the encyclical of Pope Leo XIII, *Rerum novarum,* issued in 1891.; the principles there enunciated were reiterated by Pius XI in *Quadragesimo anno* (1931), which took note of developments in the social order since *Rerum novarum* and expanded the Leonine doctrine. The third great papal document was Pope John XXIII's encyclical *Mater et magistra* (1961). It discussed the pronouncements of Leo XIII, Pius XI, and Pius XII and added a new section on the social problems of the world of the 1960s. All three encyclicals call for recognition of the rights of workers as part of the reconstruction of the social order. The exploitation of workers was strongly condemned in Vat II Ch Mod World 67–68. The American bps. currently are expending great efforts in behalf of migrant workers and farm laborers.

A 20th-cent. movement, originating in Belgium, played a major role in Christianizing the labor movement. Canon (later Card.) Cardijn founded the *Young Christian Workers (JOC) who borrowed organizational elements from the highly successful Communist worker groups and used them, though the JOC was thoroughly Catholic in philosophy. Two towering leaders in the labor question in the U.S. in the 20th cent. were Msgr. John A. Ryan and Bp. Francis Haas. Each wrote important works: Ryan, *A Living Wage: Its Ethical and Economic Aspects* (1906), *Socialism: Promise or Menace*? (1914), and *Distributive Justice* (1916); Haas, *Shop Collective Bargaining* (1922) and *Man and Society* (1930). Both men wielded considerable influence as professors at The Catholic Univ. of America and in the administration of Franklin D. Roosevelt. Ryan was part of the National Recovery Administration and played a key role in the acceptance of the Fair Labor Standards Act. Haas was a member of Roosevelt's Labor Advisory Board and served with the Works Progress Administration. He founded the Catholic Conference on Industrial Problems. BIBLIOGRAPHY: L. Watt, *Handbook to Rerum Novarum* (1941); *Challenge of Mater et Magistra* (ed. J. Moody and J. Lawler, 1963); J. Moody, *Church and Society* (1953); G. Jarlot, "Christian Trade Unions: the European Scene," Social Order 9 (1959) 75–80, 108–116; J. Laux, *Christian Social Reform: Program Outlined by Its Pioneer, William Emmanuel, Baron von Ketteler* (1912); J. T. Ellis, *Life of James Cardinal Gibbons* (2 v., 1952); F. Broderick, *Right Reverend New Dealer: John A. Ryan* (1963).

[J. R. AHERNE]

LABOR UNIONS, associations of wage earners organized for the purpose of improving their wages, working conditions, and job security. An interchangeable term is trade union, which originally had the stricter meaning of an association of workers from a single trade.

Labor unions constitute the workingman's response to the Industrial Revolution. As such, unions have enjoyed the strong support of modern papal teaching beginning with the encyclical *Rerum novarum* (1891). Forty years later, Pope Pius XI reaffirmed this support in *Quadragesimo anno.* Many Catholic employers resisted this papal teaching, however, forcing Pius XI to ask in 1937: "What is to be thought of the action of those Catholic employers who in one place succeeded in preventing the reading of our encyclical *Quadragesimo anno* in their local churches? Or of those Catholic industrialists who even to this day have shown themselves hostile to a labor movement that We Ourselves recommended?" (*Divini Redemptoris,* 50).

In economic theory, labor is human effort directed toward producing income; it is one of the factors of production. In quite a different sense, labor means the organized labor movement.

Broadly speaking, the labor movement in Europe has been politically oriented and socialistically inspired. In Great Britain the original impetus to unionism was less an ideological than a bread-and-butter concern. But by the turn of the cent. British unions shifted to a non-Marxist socialist ideology and provided the political base for the Labour Party. In the U.S., however, unions have been and continue to be much more concerned with wages, working conditions, and other short-term objectives than with ideological conflicts in the political arena.

The first American unions, in the sense of continuous associations of workingmen, appeared *c.* 1800 and organized skilled tradesmen. As the impact of the Industrial Revolution hit America *c.* 1850, the need to organize was felt by broader groups of less skilled workers, but employer resistance hardened and the movement declined.

No real legal support existed for unionism in the U.S. until the Wagner Act was passed in 1935 and upheld by the Supreme Court in 1937. This encouraged an increase in both the size and influence of labor unions. Employers could no longer legally avoid collective bargaining with a duly constituted union chosen by the workers to represent their interests.

The organizational structure of most unions rests on the local union of which there are about 74,000 in the U.S. today. The local's territory rarely extends beyond an easy commuting distance for its members. Hence there may be a dozen locals of a single union in a large city. In the case of industrial unions, a local's entire membership may work in a single plant. In some parts of the country, membership in locals is decided on ethnic or racial lines. Locals are normally affiliated with a national union or, if the union has locals in Canada, an international union. National or international unions can consolidate into a federation. The two dominant labor federations, the American Federation of Labor (AFL) and the Congress of Industrial Organizations (CIO) merged in 1955 to form a single federation, the AFL-CIO, which is not itself a union but an umbrella organization whose purpose it is to promote the good of unions and unionism.

Less than one-fourth of those who work in the U.S. belong to labor unions. The movement is suffering a relative decline in both numbers and influence at a time when the American worker is better off economically than ever in the past. This affluence, together with widespread insensitivity on the part of union members to the issues of race, poverty, and peace might well point to the continued decline of unions as a force for social change in the 1970's. BIBLIOGRAPHY: S. and B. Webb, *History of Trade Unionism* (rev. ed., 1920); D. C. Bok and J. T. Dunlop, *Labor and the American Community* (1970).

[W. J. BYRON]

LABORDE, VIVIEN (1680–1748), French Oratorian, theologian, and controversialist. L. was instructor and later director (1708–16) at the seminary of St. Magloire. His opposition to the bull *Unigenitus* and to the ecclesiastical politics of Louis XIV created some stir. His books reflect his polemics; but he grew milder and apparently accepted *Unigenitus* at the end of his life. He held important posts in his congregation. BIBLIOGRAPHY: J. Carreyre, DTC 8:2388–90; M. Join-Lambert, *Catholicisme* 6:1534.

[M. J. SUELZER]

LABORS OF THE MONTHS, personifications of the months of the year appearing in early Christian art, Carolingian MSS, medieval relief carving on cathedrals (Amiens) and treated realistically in the illuminations of Books of Hours (*Très riches heures du Duc de Berry* by the Limbourg brothers).

[M. J. DALY]

LABOURÉ, CATHERINE, ST. (1806–76), apostle of devotion to Our Lady of the Miraculous Medal. Zoë, her baptismal name, entered the Sisters of Charity of St. Vincent de Paul, at Rue de Bac in Paris, in January 1830 and received the first vision of Our Lady on July 18 of that year. A second apparition took place on Nov. 27, during which Mary revealed to L. the design of the medal she was to have struck, and the devotion she was to promote. There were further apparitions in 1830 and 1831. Within a few years there were millions of medals in circulation and accounts abounded of their miraculous efficacy. L. herself spent the remaining 46 years of her life in obscurity, caring for the aged poor at the Hospice d'Enghien in Paris, never highly regarded by her superiors, but continuing to be blessed with mystical experiences. She was canonized in 1947. The devotion of the Miraculous Medal and the authenticity of L.'s visions were subjected to an official ecclesiastical inquiry and in 1836 the abp. of Paris, Monseigneur H. L. de Quélen accepted their authenticity. In 1894 Rome gave formal approval with the establishment of a liturgical feast commemorating the Apparitions of Our Lady of the Miraculous Medal. The chapel at the Rue de Bac continues to be a center permeated with a deep spirit of devotion, visited by praying pilgrims; L.'s body is enshrined there. BIBLIOGRAPHY: O. Engelbert, *Catherine Labouré and the Modern Apparition of Our Lady* (1959).

[J. R. AHERNE]

LABRE, BENEDICT JOSEPH, ST. (1748–83), poor man of God. Of middle-class parentage in France, L. was ushered toward the clerical state by his parents through the mediation of a priest relative. Unsuccessful in their attempt, they refused him permission to join a monastic order but subsequently relented. However, L.'s six attempts to become a Cistercian or Carthusian were failures. Three times he was denied admittance and three times illness forced his superiors to dismiss him, but not before seeing to his recuperation. L. now realized his vocation was to be a wandering monk whose cell was the open air. Thereafter L. visited all the notable shrines in Italy, Switzerland, Germany, France, and Spain all the while joyfully enduring abject poverty, homelessness, and humiliations. L. settled in Rome (1776), used the Colosseum as his lodging, and spent his days in the city's churches, esp. those having the Forty Hours Devotion. Recognized as a saint by the common people, L. was unable to hide his great gift of holiness beneath the covering of bodily repulsiveness he adopted. Leo XIII canonized him in 1883. BIBLIOGRAPHY: G. Jacquemet, *Catholicisme* 1:1453–54; H. Claude, BiblSanct 2:1218–20.

[H. P. ANNAS]

LABRIOLLE, PIERRE DE, (1874–1940), French patrologist and literary historian. A member of the *Académie des inscriptions et belles lettres,* L. taught patrology and classical languages at universities in Montreal (Canada), Rennes, Fribourg, Poitiers, and Paris. To him is credited the revival of patristic studies in French universities. His early research was into the history of Montanism. In 1910 he published his *Histoire de la littérature latine chrétienne* (3d ed., 2 v., 1947 by G. Bardy), which was acclaimed for its scholarship, clarity of style, and orderly arrangement and was translated into several languages. He founded in 1910 the *Bulletin d'ancienne littérature et d'archéologie*. For the Budé collection he edited and translated several works of Augustine, notably the *Confessions* (2 v., 1925–1926), and established definitive texts of Vincent of Lérins, Jerome, and Ambrose. Portions of Volumes 3 and 4 of the Fliche-Martin *Histoire de l'Eglise* are also from his pen. BIBLIOGRAPHY: C. Testore, EncCatt 7:781; A. Hamman, LTK 6:721; G. Jacquemet, *Catholicisme* 6:154–42.

[M. J. SUELZER]

LABROUSTE, HENRI (1801–75), French architect, pioneer in cast-iron construction, best-known for his Bibliothèque Ste. Geneviève (1843–50) and the reading room in the Bibliothèque Nationale (1862–68). L. used an advanced technique of exposed ironwork and original details of exterior masonry. His emphasis on polychromy was rooted in Roman archaeological studies and the theories of Hittorff.

[M. J. DALY]

LA BRUYÈRE, JEAN DE (1645–96), French moralist, member of the French Academy (1693). Of bourgeois ancestry which had supported the Catholic Holy League in the 16th-cent. religious wars, L. was probably raised at the Paris Oratory, studied law, and was recommended by Bossuet as a tutor (1684–86) for Louis, duc de Bourbon. He won literary fame with his *Les Caractères de Théophraste traduits du grec, avec les caractères et les moeurs de ce siècle* (1688–89), which satirically exposes hypocrisy on every level, including religious, as exemplified by Onuphre, the *faux dévot* (Ch. 13, "On fashion"), inspired by Molière's Tartuffe. In the preface to his *Discours à l'Académie,* L. explains the work as leading up to its last chapters (15, "On preaching" and 16, "On freethinkers") which are an assertion of religious orthodoxy and a Christian conclusion, but this has been interpreted as a veil for his biting satire. Seen as a precursor of the Enlightenment and Revolution, he accepted, instead, all institutions while criticizing abuses. In favor of the ancients in the "Quarrel of the Ancients and Moderns," he sided with Bossuet against quietism in *Dialogues sur le quiétisme* (ed. E. Du Pin, 1699). BIBLIOGRAPHY: F. Tavéra, *L'Idéal moral et l'idée religieuse dans les 'Caractères' de La Bruyère* (1940); J. Fenouillet, *Catholicisme* 6:1543–45; E. Bottasso, EncCatt 7:781–782. *BOSSUET, JACQUES BÉNIGNE.

[R. N. NICOLICH]

LABYRINTH, an intricate building or system of passageways, rooms, doorways, etc., so constructed as to make access to a central place or escape to the place of exit difficult. Such, e.g., was the labyrinth in Greek myth built by Daedalus to confine the Minotaur. The term came to be applied also to intricate mazes made of shrubs, bushes, etc., in gardens, and to printed, carved, or inlaid representations of such mazes. In medieval churches labyrinths were often traced out in mosaic patterns on the floors, in paintings on the walls, or in the decorative carvings on pilasters. These were sometimes used by the faithful for the purpose of devotion. To follow the devious route of ingress or egress with one's steps, or to trace it with one's finger, could be viewed symbolically as a sort of pilgrimage. BIBLIOGRAPHY: H. Leclercq, DACL 8:973–982; W. H. Matthews, *Mazes and Labyrinths* (1922, repr. 1969).

[P. K. MEAGHER]

LA CAVA (SS. TRINITÀ), ABBEY OF, Benedictine monastery near Salerno, Italy. Founded in 1011 by St. Alferius, it was involved in Mediterranean trade. During the 13th cent., La Cava fell into decline, became entangled in hostilities between the houses of Anjou and Aragon. Finally in 1282 La Cava was forced by Pope Martin IV to turn over its holdings in Sicily to Aragon. The monastery was closed (1807–15) and then suppressed in 1866, but the monks remained as "custodians." Several of La Cava's abbots were made saints. La Cava maintains a library of historical significance. BIBLIOGRAPHY: I. De Piccoli, NCE 8:302–303.

[M. A. MCFADDEN]

LA CHAIZE, FRANÇOIS DE (1624–1709), French Jesuit, for 35 years from 1675, confessor to Louis XIV. A Jesuit from 1639, he taught philosophy and theology and held office as rector and as provincial in Lyons. As confessor to the King he brought about Louis's renunciation of an adulterous relationship; was counsellor in the appointment of bps. and the assignment of benefices; aided the cause of the Society against the Jansenists. The celebrated cemetery of Père La Chaise [*sic*] in Paris bears his name because it is on the site of his garden.

[T. C. O'BRIEN]

LACHAT, EUGÈNE (1819–86), bp. of Basel, Switzerland, 1863–84. For upholding papal infallibility at Vatican Council I and censuring priests of his diocese who refused to accept the dogmatic definition, he incurred the wrath of the Swiss press, and the Protestant governments of five of the cantons in his diocese declared him deposed; in 1873 he had to go into exile from Basel, ruling his diocese from Lucerne. He resigned at the request of Leo XIII and was named a titular bp. and apostolic administrator of Ticino. L. built seminaries at Lucerne and at Lugano.

[T. C. O'BRIEN]

LA COLOMBIÈRE, CLAUDE DE, BL. (1641–82), Jesuit preacher. Born at Saint-Symphorien d'Ozon, he attended the Jesuit college at Lyons and, in 1658, entered the Jesuit novitiate at Avignon. From 1661 to 1666, he taught the humanities at Avignon and in the latter part of 1666 was sent to Paris to study theology. He was ordained in 1669 and in 1675 was appointed superior of the college at Paray-le-Monial. Here L. met St. Margaret Mary Alacoque and as her confessor supported her efforts toward devotion to the Sacred Heart. In 1676, L. journeyed to London at the request of Mary, Duchess of York and wife of James, future king of England. A renowned orator, L. converted many English Protestants to Catholicism. However, in 1678, he was falsely accused and imprisoned on the pretext of a papal conspiracy against England. In 1679, through the aid of Louis XIV, L. was released from jail and returned to France. Imprisonment had caused irreparable damage to his health and he died at Paray. He was beatified in 1929. BIBLIOGRAPHY: C. Testore, BiblSanct 7:1065–67; Butler 1:346–348.

[R. J. BRADY]

LACOMBE, ALBERT (1827–1916), Canadian missionary. After ordination (1849), he began his missionary labors in North Dakota and then cared for both Indians and white settlers along the Red River. He joined the Oblates of Mary Immaculate (1856) and established a mission at Edmonton, Alberta (1858). His work was primarily with the Cree Indians and among the métis, a seminomadic people of mixed French and Indian ancestry. He played a major part in restoring peace after the Red River Rebellion (1869–70). He became pastor at Winnipeg (1874) and developed parishes in other new settlements. He had a considerable following in Quebec, where he was well-known as a pulpit orator and spokesman for Catholic causes, notably in his opposition to the 1890 legislation establishing a religiously neutral public school system in Manitoba. BIBLIOGRAPHY: P. E. Breton, *The Big Chief of the Prairies: The Life of Father Lacombe* (1956); G. Rommerskirchen, EncCatt 7:792; N. Kowalsky, LTK 6:724.

[R. K. MacMASTER]

LA COMBE, FRANÇOIS (1643–1715), Barnabite priest who served as the spiritual director of M. Jeanne Marie Guyon, the controversial quietist and writer. In Rome L. had been influenced by the quietist teachings of Miguel de *Molinos. He became M. Guyon's director in 1681 at Gex, near Geneva, where she had helped establish a group of converted Huguenots, called *Nouvelles Catholiques*. Through her independently developed quietism, L. was exposed to even deeper quietistic doctrines and practices. They went to Paris in 1686. Suspected of doctrinal and moral turpitude, L. was imprisoned for life (1687) and M. Guyon put in a Parisian Visitation convent. In prison, L.'s mental capacities deteriorated and his letter (1698) confessing a sexual relationship with M. Guyon was almost certainly a forced confession that is generally doubted.

[R. J. LITZ]

LACOMBE, GEORGE (1886–1934), historian. Ordained in San Francisco, he studied at Stanford Univ. and the École des Chartes. L. resided in Paris, was active in philosophical-historical circles, stimulated basic research and publication in the history of medieval philosophy, and catalogued the medieval Latin MSS of Aristotle. BIBLIOGRAPHY: J. Corbett, LTK 6:725.

[R. I. BURNS]

LACORDAIRE, JEAN BAPTISTE HENRI (1802–61), French Dominican preacher, member of the Académie Française. After pursuing legal studies at Dijon, L. was converted in 1824 to the faith he had abandoned as an adolescent, and was ordained in 1827. His liberal views in politics led him to help Lamennais in founding *L'Avenir*. Gregory XVI's condemnation of the movement caused his break with Lamennais and his criticism of *L'Avenir* in *Considérations sur le système philosophique de M. de Lamennais* (1834) and *Lettre sur le Saint-Siège* (1838). L. revitalized pulpit oratory by his sermons at Notre-Dame and promoted the renewal of the French Church through religious orders. In 1839 he entered the Dominicans in Rome and founded many priories of the order in France, becoming provincial in 1850. He fought for adaptations to contemporary situations in the Dominican rule, and for Church freedom in education. After Napoleon III's *coup d'état* L. retained his liberal Catholic views and devoted himself primarily to education. He founded a Third Order of Practicing Teachers and organized a private school for boys at Sorèze (1854). His *Oeuvres complètes* in nine volumes were published in 1911 and 1912. He is esp. noted for his sermons and correspondence, particularly *Lettres à des jeunes gens*, published posthumously in 1863. BIBLIOGRAPHY: L. C. Sheppard, *Lacordaire: A Biographical Essay* (1964); J. Peyrade, *La Conversion de Lacordaire ou le baptême du romantisme* (1966).

[G. E. GINGRAS]

LACROIX, CLAUDE (1652–1714), Jesuit moral theologian, professor at Münster and Cologne. His *Theologia moralis* (8 v., 1707–14) went through multiple editions, the last, 4 v., 1874. The work is a commentary on the probabilist H. *Busenbaum's *Medulla theologiae moralis* (1650). The works of both authors were condemned and publicly burned at Toulouse (1757) and Paris (1763), in political agitation over their lenient justification of tyrannicide (see TYRANNY).

[T. C. O'BRIEN]

LACTANTIUS (Caecilius Firmianus; *c.*250–*c.*320), Christian writer. L. was an African, a disciple of *Arnobius the Elder, and a teacher of Latin rhetoric at Nicomedia, until deprived of his post after his conversion (*c.*300). Near the end of his life (*c.*317) he was tutor to Crispus, son of *Constantine, at Trier. Of his surviving works (PL 6 and 7) the *Divinae institutiones* (304–313) are the first attempt in Latin at a synthesis of Christian teaching and view of life. The *De opificio Dei* (*c.*303) is a purely philosophical treatise on divine providence, as proved through the structure of the human body and the working of the mind. The *De ira Dei* (*c.*313) is a defense of God's justice against Epicurean and Stoic denials. The authenticity of two other works, *De mortibus persecutorum* and *De ave Phoenice* is now generally acknowledged; the first describes the horrible fate of imperial persecutors of the Christians and the second is a long poem devoid of Christian content. L.'s loyalty to Christianity, like that of Arnobius, far surpassed his theological grasp of its teaching; on the Trinity, he is completely confused, his interpretation of creation is *dualistic, his *eschatology is *chiliastic. His chief contribution was his Latin prose style; the humanists called him the Christian Cicero. BIBLIOGRAPHY: Altaner 208–212; M. Pellegrino, EncCatt 7:951–954; Quasten 2:392–410, with bibliog. and list of L.'s works; P.-T. Camelot, *Catholicisme* 6:1581–83.

[R. B. ENO]

LACTICINIA, such foods as butter, or cheese, that derive from milk (*lac*) and were at times forbidden according to some ecclesiastical or monastic rules.

[T. C. O'BRIEN]

LACUNZA, MANUEL (1731–1801), Chilean Jesuit theologian and author, noted esp. for his millenarian doctrine. During his pastoral work L. had read many times the apocalyptic passages in Dan and Revelation. The expulsion of the Jesuits brought him from Chile to Italy, where in seclusion he began to see in contemporary events in the Church the sure signs of the end of the world and of the imminent second coming of Christ. Under the pseudonym of Juan Josafat Ben-Ezra he wrote *Venida del Mesias en gloria y majestad,* published posthumously in Cadiz in 1812 and translated into several languages. The work, condemned by the Holy Office in 1824 and again in 1941, has become a standard treatise for Seventh-Day Adventists and other millenarian groups. BIBLIOGRAPHY: A. F. Vaucher, *Une célébrité oubliée: Le Padre Manuel de Lacunza y Díaz* (1941); A. Piolanti, EncCatt 7:796–797.

[P. DAMBORIENA]

LACY, EDMUND (d. 1455), doctor of theology, University College, Oxford, *c.* 1398–1401; bp. of Hereford 1417–20, of Exeter 1420–55. Dean of the chapel royal, Windsor, 1414, L. attended Henry V on the Agincourt campaign. Active in his diocese and interested in liturgical observances, he composed a new office in honor of St. Raphael. BIBLIOGRAPHY: Emden Ox 2:1081–83.

[C. D. ROSS]

LADEUZE, PAULIN (1870–1940), orientalist, exegete, rector of Louvain Univ., titular bishop. A specialist in Oriental patrology, L., after finishing his studies at Louvain in 1898, joined the theological faculty there and taught until 1909. In that year he became rector of the university and guided it through the Modernist crisis. In his years as rector, he saw the university ravaged by World War I and supervised the reconstruction of its great library. He had an active part in inaugurating two important scholarly enterprises, the *Revue d'histoire ecclésiastique* of which he was cofounder (1900), and the *Corpus scriptorum christianorum orientalium,* which he helped to organize (1913), and he encouraged the foundation of a number of scholarly journals. BIBLIOGRAPHY: J. Coppens, EncCatt 7:797–798; F. X. Murphy, NCE 8:309; R. Aubert, *Catholicisme* 6:1587–90.

[R. B. ENO]

LADIES OF CHARITY, the first group founded by St. Vincent de Paul for his apostolate to the poor, at Châtillon les Dombes, Lyons, in 1617. The success there led him to establish similar confraternities wherever he and the Congregation of the Mission (Vincentians) labored. The decline brought on by the French Revolution was overcome by a renewal under Jean Baptiste Étienne, CM, superior general, in 1840. The association, blessed with spiritual favors to the members made by many popes, is spread throughout the world; headquarters are in Paris under supervision of the Vincentians and the *Daughters of Charity. A parish unit may be instituted with the permission of the pastor and approval of the bp., who obtains a charter from the superior general of the Vincentians. The Ladies of Charity exist in parishes throughout the world and continue their work under the inspiration of the founder.

[T. C. O'BRIEN]

LADIES OF ST. MAUR, women religious, better known as the Sisters of the Child Jesus, founded in France in 1666 by Nicholas Barré, OMinim (1621–86), who established and directed institutions of free popular teaching. There were two separate branches of the Institute of the Sisters of the Holy Infant Jesus: one originated in Rouen in 1662, named The Institute of Providence; and the other in Paris, referred to as The Institute of the Dames of St. Maur, named after the house of the foundation. The Paris foundation under the title Soeurs de l'Instruction charitable du Saint-Enfant Jésus dites de St.-Maur, had a total membership of 1,617 sisters and 105 houses in 1974.

[R. A. TODD]

LADISLAUS, KING OF HUNGARY, ST. (*c.* 1040–*c.* 1095) who ruled Hungary from 1077. He was a strong king who united his kingdom, expanded its borders, and consolidated its Christian organization. Although he was not deeply committed to the Hildebrandine Reform, being too occupied with problems peculiar to Hungary, he sided with the Pope in the investiture struggle. He worked zealously for the spread of Christianity among his subjects, esp. in Croatia and Bohemia (annexed in 1091). At the Synod of Szabolcs (1092) he introduced a new civil and religious code for his kingdom which, among other things, safeguarded private property and forbade priests to remarry. According to his legendary vita, which is not altogether reliable, he was canonized by Pope Celestine III in 1192. BIBLIOGRAPHY: E. Pásztor, BiblSanct 7:1068–71; Butler 2:654–655; T. Z. Garab, *Catholicisme* 6:1590–91.

LADISLAUS OF GIELNIÓW, BL. (*c.* 1430–1505), Franciscan missionary. L. became a Franciscan in 1462 and served twice as provincial. Known for regular observance and devotion to the Bl. Virgin, L. was a forceful preacher and composer of religious songs in the vernacular. BIBLIOGRAPHY: K. Kantak, AFH (1929)22:444–451; W. Malej, BiblSanct 7:1067–68.

[H. DRESSLER]

LADY ALTAR, a side altar dedicated to the Blessed Virgin Mary, and often under one of her particular titles, e.g., Our Lady of Mount Carmel, of the Rosary, of Lourdes.

[T. C. O'BRIEN]

LADY CHAPEL, particularly in the great medieval cathedrals a chapel dedicated to the Blessed Virgin Mary, often an impressive structure in its own right. Many beautiful lady chapels were destroyed or their decorations disfigured during the English Reformation, or by Cromwell's armies.

[T. C. O'BRIEN]

LADY AND THE UNICORN, THE, one of the greatest series of 16th-cent. Gothic enigmatic allegorical tapestries. Acquired by the Musée de Cluny from the Chateau de Boussac in the 19th cent., the tapestry with beautiful rose ground covered with exquisitely delicate flower and animal forms in wealth and accuracy of detail, is soberly elegant in composition and mysterious in meaning (allegory of the senses). Reference to the betrothal of Jean de Chabannes and Claude le Viste appears on each piece, in arms supported by a lion and a unicorn. Allegorically the unicorn—rare and inaccessible, with the miraculous power of saving from death, symbol of love and purity visible only to virgins—is often identified with Christ, and the lady with the cult of the Virgin Mary, sublime expression of chivalric love. A second series, *Hunting the Unicorn,* in magnificent condition today (Morgan and Rockefeller collections, Cloisters, New York) was mentioned in the La Rochefoucauld inventory (1728) as a "well-worn" five-piece tapestry in the Chateau de Verteuil. The pursuit of the unicorn is also the theme of German tapestries in which the cult of the Virgin Mary is inferred. BIBLIOGRAPHY: J. Jobé, *Great Tapestries* (1965).

[M. J. DALY]

LAESTADIANS, participants in a mid–19th-cent. revival movement inspired by L. L. *Laestadius. The movement began in 1844 with the preaching of Laestadius in Swedish Lapland, and was carried to N Norway and esp. to Finland by lay preachers he commissioned. The Laestadians were Lutheran in basic doctrine, but they rejected baptism and the Eucharist. Their gatherings were marked by ecstatic manifestations and by absolution from sin through the laying on of hands, a practice introduced by J. Raattama (1811–99). Many of the early Laestadians were unlettered people, and some interpreted the message of their election and salvation as a call to take bloody vengeance upon the unconverted. In time three kinds of Laestadians emerged: Old Laestadians, who were antinomian; Newer Laestadians, who accepted both law and gospel; and the Firstborn, a small circle who believed that Christianity only came into being with the preaching of Laestadius. The Laestadian revival continues as a factor in the life of the Church in Finland. In 1866 some Finnish Laestadians immigrated to the U.S. and formed what is now called the Apostolic Lutheran Church of America. BIBLIOGRAPHY: U. Saarnivaara, *History of the Laestadian or Apostolic Lutheran Movement in America* (1947).

[J. FANG]

LAESTADIUS, LARS LEVI (1800–61), Swedish Lutheran pastor, founder of the *Laestadians. After studying at Uppsala, L. was ordained (1825) and became pastor in Swedish Lapland. He had an interest in botany and became a recognized authority on northern flora. At the death of his infant child and under the inspiration of the simple gospel testimony of a Lapp girl named Maria, L. experienced a religious conversion and became a revivalist preacher. His emotional, vivid sermons stressed justification by faith alone and the need of rescue from sin. He sent out lay preachers to spread his revival. During his latter years he was forced to restrain the violence of some of his unlettered followers. L. published some of his evangelical ideas in Swedish; his sermons were delivered in Finnish (Eng. tr. 1960). The Laestadian revival continues to be a factor in church life in Finland; the Apostolic Lutheran Church in America was established by Laestadian Finnish immigrants. BIBLIOGRAPHY: T. A. Kantonen, EncLuthCh 2:1242–43.

[T. C. O'BRIEN]

LAETARE MEDAL, an honor bestowed annually on Catholic laymen in the U.S. by the Univ. of Notre Dame. Established in 1883 the medal honors Catholic men and women who have achieved distinction in their respective fields. John Gilmary Shea was the first in the long roll of distinguished recipients, President John F. Kennedy among them (1961).

[J. R. AHERNE]

LAETARE SUNDAY, the fourth Sunday of Lent, so called from the opening words of the entrance song of the Latin Mass, "Rejoice (*Laetare*) Jerusalem" (Is 66.10). On this Sunday the liturgy of the Western Church encourages the faithful, then in the midst of their Lenten observance, with the joyful thought of the victory to be won. Since the 13th cent. the celebrant at Mass has been permitted to wear rose-colored vestments on this day. One of the Sundays in mid-Advent is observed in a similar way (see GAUDETE SUNDAY).

[P. K. MEAGHER]

LAETENTUR COELI, the bull of reunion with the Greeks promulgated July 6, 1439 at the Council of *Florence. It affirms agreement on the *filioque, purgatory, the use of either leavened or unleavened bread in the Eucharist, papal primacy, the traditional order of precedence among the patriarchates—Rome, Constantinople, Alexandria, Antioch, Jerusalem (D 1300–08).

[T. C. O'BRIEN]

LAETUS, ST. (fl. mid-6th cent.), monk at Micy and then a hermit in the forest N of Orléans. The source for his life is a largely legendary vita composed in the 10th century. The place where he died was later called Saint-Lié in his honor. He was venerated in the last cent. of the Middle Ages especially at Laon, Paris, and Orléans. BIBLIOGRAPHY: BHL 2:4672; Zimmermann 3:264–265; A. Poncelet, ''Les Saints de Micy,'' AnalBoll 24 (1905) 1–104, esp. 61–71, 98–103.

[M. R. P. MCGUIRE]

LA FARGE, JOHN (1835–1910), American painter, stained glass artist, writer, lecturer. He attended St. John's College (Fordham Univ.) and graduated (1853) from Mount St. Mary's College, Emmitsburg, Maryland. Abandoning a law career, he studied art under Thomas Couture in Paris (1856). Inspired by William Morris Hunt, L. designed murals and revived the art of stained glass, emphasizing the harmony between architecture and decoration (Trinity Church, Boston; St. Thomas Church, New York (destroyed); Church of the Ascension, New York City). A significant group of watercolors resulted from a trip with Henry Adams to the South Pacific and Japan (1886). L. stated his philosophy of art in *Considerations on Painting* (1895). **Christopher Grant** (1862–1938), John's eldest son, architect. He designed St. Matthew's Cathedral, Washington, D.C.; St. Paul's Church, Rochester, N.Y.; the Fourth Presbyterian Church and the Cathedral of St. John the Divine (early stage), both in New York City. **John Louis Bancel** (1865–1938), painter, stained glass and mosaic artist, second son of John, with whom he was associated. His work includes the *Coronation of the Virgin Mary* mosaic in Trinity College Chapel and mural decorations for the National Shrine of the Immaculate Conception, both in Washington, D.C. BIBLIOGRAPHY: *John La Farge, a Memoir and a Study* (1911), R. Cortissoz, *John La Farge* (1911). See his Jesuit son in article below.

[F. S. GRUBER]

LA FARGE, JOHN (1880–1963), Jesuit editor and journalist, founder of the Catholic interracial movement. Educated at Harvard and Innsbruck, Austria, L. was ordained in 1905 and shortly afterwards became a Jesuit. After 15 years service in rural Maryland he began the great work of his life, the apostolate for interracial justice, by founding the Catholic Laymen's Union, a group of Catholic Negro men, who under L.'s direction engaged in a program of spiritual formation and a study of race relations. The Union expanded throughout the U.S. into the Catholic Interracial Councils, which in 1958 combined into a national organization, the National Catholic Conference for Interracial Justice. L. also interested himself in many other causes; he was associated with *America* in an editorial capacity from 1926 until his death, and in its pages and those of other periodicals, and in his many books he proved himself a tireless as well as an extremely able journalist and religious leader. BIBLIOGRAPHY: J. La Farge, *Manner Is Ordinary* (1954), an autobiography.

[M. J. BARRY]

LA FAYETTE, MARIE MADELEINE PIOCHE DE LA VERGNE (1634–93), French novelist whose psychological masterpieces revolutionized the French novel. Married (1655) to François Motier, comte de La Fayette (1616–83), L. bore him two sons (1658 and 1659). A pupil of Gilles Ménage and Père *Rapin, she had many prominent friends and acquaintances including the Cardinal de *Retz, Henrietta of England, Mme. de *Sévigné and esp. the duc de *La Rochefoucauld to whom she was bound in intimate friendship, and with whom, it is thought, she formed a literary partnership as she did with Segrais. During her later years she acted as diplomatic intermediary between France and the Duchess of Savoy, and her last days were spent piously under the spiritual direction of the abbots de Rancé and Duguet. Her works include: numerous letters; her *Histoire de Madame Henriette d'Angleterre* (written c.1670–75, pub. 1720), and *Mémoires de la cour de France pour les années 1688 et 1689* (1731), both historical writings; and her novels, *La Princesse de Montpensier* (1662), *Zaïde* (1670), *La Princesse de Clèves* (1678)—considered her ''classic'' masterpiece, and *La Comtesse de Tende* (1724). These offer penetrating psychological analyses of passion and examinations of conscience which reflect the influence of pessimistic Jansenism on L.'s approach to love, reminiscent of *Racine's tragedies. BIBLIOGRAPHY: B. Pingaud, *Mme. de La Fayette par elle-même* (1959); J. C. Rémy, *Madame de La Fayette: L'Esprit et les lettres* (1967); F. Mars, *Catholicisme* 6:1598–99; E. Battasso, EncCatt 7:801.

[R. N. NICOLICH]

LAFAYETTE, MARQUIS DE (Marie Joseph Paul Yves Du Motier; 1757–1834), French statesman and figure of the American Revolution. Born of an ancient French family with a military tradition, L. as a very young man inherited his father's title and estates as well as considerable wealth from his grandfather. His marriage to Marie Adrienne de Noailles in 1774 allied him to one of the most powerful families of France. L. served as an officer in the French army, but he was an enthusiastic follower of the social reformers of the day who sought to create a new world. When the struggle of the American colonies against Britain began, he decided to offer his services to the rebels. The Continental Congress was slow to accept him but when L. offered to serve without pay he was commissioned in 1775, a major-general but without a command. L. began a lifelong friendship with Washington, on whose staff he served. He took part in the battle of Brandywine, where he was wounded. Congress finally made him commander of a division of Virginian light troops. In the harsh winter at Valley Forge, L. shared the privation and earned respect for his solicitude for the men. Placed in charge of an abortive plan to invade Canada he was bitter about the absence of support. When the French alliance brought his countrymen to join the Americans, L. performed great service as liaison between the two groups. In 1778 L. visited France on furlough and was greeted as a popular hero. His efforts to obtain increased help from France were only partially successful. When Rochambeau sailed for America, L. returned with him. Resuming his command in Virginia, he was instrumental in preventing Cornwallis from retreating southward. He showed himself a military commander of great skill as the war ended.

L. on his return to France continued to help the new American republic and his help, especially in commercial matters, was invaluable. As a republican enthusiast he took part in the French Revolution but was imprisoned from 1792 to 1797. His exile ended in 1799 when he returned to an estate near Paris. Always a believer in representative government, his last political involvement was in the July Revolution of 1830, which failed. Meanwhile in 1824 L. made a triumphant tour of the U.S. and was received as a national hero. A man of considerable ability and great generosity, L. often demonstrated the impractical dreamer when he should have been the man of practical action.

[J. R. AHERNE]

LA FERTÉ, ABBEY OF, former Cistercian abbey, the first foundation of Cîteaux. On this land bordering the Grosne and given by the count of Châlon and his son William, St. Stephen Harding installed Abbot Philibert and 12 monks on May 17, 1113. The abbot ranked immediately after the abbot of Cîteaux in the order and enjoyed special prerogatives. There were 16 foundations from the monastery of La Ferté. The abbey was sacked by roving bands of mercenary troops after the treaty of Brétigny (1360), and by the Calvinists (1567); it was later transformed and reconstructed by Abbot Claude III the Small (1677–1710), who set up an important library. The last abbot, Antoine Louis Desvignes de la Cerve (1730–93), died while en route to Paris to be executed. BIBLIOGRAPHY: Cottineau, 1:1134–35; M. A. Dimier, NCE 8:318.

[J. DAOUST]

LAFITAU, JOSEPH FRANÇOIS (1681–1746), French Jesuit missioner, writer. He was sent to Canada in 1711 where he worked among the Iroquois for 6 years. Returning to France he devoted his life to the Jesuit periodical, *Mémoires de Trévoux,* and additionally wrote several notable works. The two-volume *Moeurs des sauvages Américains comparés aux moeurs des premiers temps* (1724) is important to anthropology. His *Histoire des découvertes et conquêtes des Portugais dans le Nouveau Monde* (1733) is devoted to the Orient rather than Brazil. BIBLIOGRAPHY: Koch JL 1056–57.

[J. R. AHERNE]

LAFITTE, JEAN (1780–1824?), adventurer and pirate. With his brother Pierre, the French-born L. owned a blacksmith shop in New Orleans which was a cover for goods and slaves brought into Louisiana by smugglers. In 1810 L. became chief of a group of pirates on the island of Barataria. He dispatched a fleet of privateers to prey on Spanish ships in the Gulf. He was an astute businessman who contributed to New Orleans prosperity in spite of unorthodox activity. L. gave valuable information about the British plans to attack New Orleans in the War of 1812, but in spite of this an American naval and military expedition attacked L.'s establishment in Barataria and destroyed it. L., from hiding, nevertheless offered the service of the Baratarians, who fought on the American side in the battle of New Orleans. Because of this, President Madison pardoned the group. The Lafittes turned to Galveston and founded a new settlement. L. became governor of Galveston in the short-lived republic established by the American James Long. From there he sent out a fleet of privateers under the flags of countries in revolt against Spain. A raid on the coast of Louisiana and the scuttling of an American merchantman caused reprisals by the U.S. L. burned his establishment and went into hiding. Soon after, both brothers died. L. became a legendary hero in the tradition of Captain Kidd.

[J. R. AHERNE]

LAFLÈCHE, LOUIS FRANÇOIS (1818–98), Canadian missionary and bishop. Ordained in his native province of Quebec (1844), he was assigned to missionary work in the Canadian Northwest Territory, where he quickly mastered the Indian languages. In 1866 he became coadjutor bp. of Three Rivers, and in 1870 succeeded to that see. He distinguished himself as a spokesman for the teachings of the Church and traditional French-Canadian ways. He was a staunch advocate of government aid for Catholic education and an outspoken critic of Canadian liberalism. BIBLIOGRAPHY: R. Rumilly, *Monseigneur Laflèche et son temps* (1938).

[R. K. MACMASTER]

LA FONTAINE, JEAN DE (1621–95), French poet. After spending 18 months in the Paris Oratorian seminary, L. left or was dismissed (1641). Passing most of his time in Paris in literary pursuits he won fame for his *Contes et nouvelles en vers* (1665, 1666, 1671), licentious tales presented without coarseness, inspired mainly by Boccaccio; but he is best known for his *Fables* (bk. 1–6, 1668; bk. 7–11, 1678–79; bk. 12, 1693), stylistic masterpieces in a much-enriched Aesopic tradition, with penetrating psychological analyses. One can detect in L.'s complex moral insight, as a result of his contacts in Mme. de La Sablière's salon, various influences from the realm of metaphysics and moral philosophy: the Christian Stoicism of Guillaume du Vair; Epicureanism inspired by Bernier, disciple of the Epicurean *libertin,* Gassendi. In his later fables L. attacked the Cartesian theory of animals as machines, relying on Gassendi's theory of the soul, an attempted reconciliation between Lucretius' materialism and orthodox Christianity. Close to death (1692) after a life of religious indifference, L. returned to Catholicism and solemnly condemned his *Contes,* but lived to translate a number of psalms and hymns, including the *Dies irae* (1693). Among his other works, generally of uneven quality, are his *Adonis* (1658), *Les Amours de Psyché* (1669), and a Christian poem inspired by St. Jerome, *La Captivite de Saint Malc* (1673). BIBLIOGRAPHY: M. Guiton, *La Fontaine, Poet and Counterpoet* (1961); P. Clarac, *La Fontaine* (1959); F. Hamel, *Jean De La Fontaine* (1911, repr. 1970); F. Mars, *Catholicisme* 6:1605–07.

[R. N. NICOLICH]

LA FRESNAYE, ROGER DE (1885–1925), French Cubist painter. L. was influenced by Maurice Denis and P. Sérusier at the Académie Ranson (1908). After travel he was associated with the founding of the Section d'Or producing (1914) important, though weaker, Cubist works of decorative quality. L. illustrated Paul Claudel's *Tête d'Or*.

[M. J. DALY]

LAGARDE, PAUL ANTON DE (1827–91), Orientalist and political writer. L. taught Oriental languages at Göttingen (1869–91), and was a prolific scholar, drawing upon his expertise as an Orientalist for valuable textual criticism of the Bible. His critical edition of the Septuagint was never completed and is now outdated. L. also wrote highly conservative, nationalistic political treatises. BIBLIOGRAPHY: L. Schmid, LTK 6:730–731; J. E. Lazur, NCE 8:320, F. R. Stern, *Politics of Cultural Despair: A Study in the Rise of the Germanic Ideology* (1974).

[T. M. MCFADDEN]

LAGNY-SUR-MARNE, ABBEY OF, former royal Benedictine abbey, Meaux, France. Founded *c.* 644 by an Irishman, St. Fursey, it was destroyed by the Normans and rebuilt in the 10th century. Its abbots were the counts of Lagny. The abbey was attacked by the Huguenots in 1562; followed the *Maurist reform in the 17th cent., but was suppressed by the French Revolution. Today the abbey church is a parish church; other buildings are used by the municipal government. BIBLIOGRAPHY: H. Tardif, NCE 8:321.

[M. A. MCFADDEN]

LA GORCE, PIERRE DE (1846–1934), French historian. After attaining a doctorate in law (1869), L. built up a practice culminating in the acquisition of the office of magistrate in Saint Omer (1872–80). He resigned when the Third Republic banned congregations of religious teachers. *Histoire religieuse de la Révolution française* (5 v., 1905–23) ranks first among L.'s works. His writings won him the Gobert prize, election to the French Academy and the academy of Moral Sciences, and membership in the Legion of Honor.

[H. P. ANNAS]

LAGRANGE, MARIE-JOSEPH (1855–1938), French Dominican biblicist, the chief initiator of the revival of biblical studies in the RC Church. Baptized Albert, he took the name Marie Joseph when he entered the Dominican Order in 1879 at St. Maximin, Toulouse; he was ordained in 1883 at Zamora, Spain. He first took up Oriental studies at Vienna in 1888, having previously taught history and philosophy at Salamanca and at Toulouse. In 1890 he opened the École Pratique d'Études Bibliques at Jerusalem (see ÉCOLE BIBLIQUE), and was the leader in its program of biblical studies for 45 years. He established the *Revue biblique* in 1892, a biblical quarterly to which he contributed nearly 200 articles, including one on the authorship of Genesis that appeared in the issue announcing his death. His monumental commentary on the Book of Judges (1903) was the first of the *Études bibliques,* the superb series of studies that has developed (more than 50 volumes to date) under the auspices of the École Biblique. In papers delivered at Fribourg in 1897 and at Toulouse in 1902, he manifested his positive attitude toward the methods and findings of higher criticism with regard to the sources of the Pentateuch, and provoked accusations of *Modernism against him. In 1912 a decree of the Sacred Consistorial Congregation warned against ''certain of the works of Père Lagrange,'' without specifying which of his works were to be considered dangerous. For a year he withdrew from teaching, but returned in 1913. The more positive effect of the opposition was that he concentrated primarily on NT studies. His classic and irreplaceable commentaries on the four Gospels as well as on Rom and Gal appeared between 1911 and 1929; the *Gospel of Jesus Christ,* a work synthesizing his critical studies for the general reader, appeared in 1928 (Eng. tr. 1939). Other writings of lasting importance are his three articles on biblical inspiration in *Revue biblique* (1895–96); *Études sur les religions sémitiques* (1903); and three parts of what he intended as a complete introduction to NT studies, *Histoire ancienne du canon du N.T.* (1933), *Critique textuelle. La Critique rationelle* (with R. P. S. Lyonett, 1935), and *Critique historique. Les Mystères: l'orphisme* (1937). Because of ill health he spent the last 3 years of his life at St. Maximin; his remains were returned to Jerusalem in 1967. All agree that the program, spirit, and work of L. were vindicated and consecrated officially with the encyclical *Divino afflante Spiritu* (1943). BIBLIOGRAPHY: F. M. Braun, *Work of Père Lagrange* (tr. R. T. A. Murphy, 1963); R. De Vaux, *Catholicisme* 6:1617–20.

[T. C. O'BRIEN]

LA GUERRE, ELIZABETH JACQUET DE (1659–1729), French composer, organist, and harpsichordist. Born to a family of professional musicians, she was presented at an early age at the court of Louis XIV. She was educated by Mme. de Montespan and later married organist Marin de La Guerre. Her first book of harpsichord pieces (1687) was followed by the opera *Céphale et Procris* (1691), a ballet (1691), and Italianate sonatas, harpsichord pieces, and cantatas. The subjects of 12 of her cantatas were taken from the Bible, setting works by poet Houdar de La

Motte. She also wrote vocal religious pieces including a *Te Deum* (1721).

[R. J. LITZ]

LA HAYE, JEAN DE (1593–1661), French Franciscan, biblical scholar, editor, preacher. Returning to France from Spain, where he had become a Franciscan, around 1620, he became preacher to the court of Louis XIII. Noted for his learning, he edited over 40 folio volumes, including works of SS. Francis of Assisi, Anthony of Padua, and Bernardine of Siena. He also prepared two mammoth commentaries on the Bible, the five-volume *Biblia magna* and the 19-volume *Biblia maxima,* of vast but undisciplined erudition.

[R. J. LITZ]

LAICISM, an attitude that passes beyond the reaction of *anticlericalism to a positive and explicit interference into areas regarded as the monopoly of the clergy's influence and competence. Although the term is of fairly recent origin—French Revolution—and has seen its full development in contemporary life, lay intrusion into the doctrinal and sacramental preserves of the clergy is as ancient as the Church's division into the people and their ministers. Such a society in unstable equilibrium is almost bound to result in tensions. *Montanism, e.g., early accorded greater authority to the "charismatic," putting prophet above priest. The Church had hardly emerged from the catacombs when the emperors, esp. Eastern, tried to use their civil power to shape dogmatic definitions and church order; St. Ambrose had to remind Theodosius that the emperor is in, not above, the Church. This was but the beginning of the long struggle, hardly over even now, between lay rulers and church authorities. It reached a peak in the early Middle Ages, a chapter in ecclesiastical history justly named, "the Church in the power of the laity." But the investiture struggle that made the mitre the gift of the crown was but one phase of continuing conflict between an overweening clericalism and a sacristan concern for lay-power even in pulpit and sanctuary. However, it was Luther who, in his *Open Letter to the Christian Nobility* (1520), attacked the very distinction of clergy and laity as oversubtle and hypocritical. Anticlerical feeling had been seething for some time; during the late Middle Ages the quantity of clergy was conspicuously greater than their quality. In his time a St. Bernard took a prophetic stance; and Chaucer indulged in laughing at clerical pretensions. As the *Cathari and *Waldenses gave authority only to the "spiritual," *Wycliffe, and *Hus recognized it only in the predestined. In the era of the Reformation, Erasmus, Rabelais, and St. Thomas More used satire for correction to such an extent that anticlerical literature became almost a genre of its own. One of the key doctrinal positions of Luther was the *priesthood of all believers; Calvin confined NT priesthood to Christ. Protestant secular rulers in large measure ruled the ecclesiastical life. Roman Catholic rulers also profited from the changed climate, and laicism assumed the shapes of *Febronianism and *Josephinism. A new wave of laicism is observable in the post-Vatican II era; the collegiality of bishops and particularly the emphasis on the Church as the people of God rather than as hierarchical society gives the laicist a strong lever.

All this was within the structures of the Churches; the *Enlightenment and the French Revolution produced what was essentially an anti-Christian laicism; Voltaire may resemble Erasmus in his mockery of clerics, but the underlying motive of his program is not that of a believer. A positive plan for de-Christianization began with the French Revolution, and the laws against religion in Spain, Portugal, and Piedmont of the 19th cent. continued the general attack. France particularly developed a laicist politic that in its most extreme form in the 20th cent. admitted that it was an attempt to destroy the Church and the idea of God. Similarly, Pius XI in the encyclical *Quas primas* (1925) denounced the laicism of totalitarian states as "the plague of our epoch."

BIBLIOGRAPHY: B. du Chesnay, NCE 8:323–325; A. Manaranche, *Catholicisme* 6:1643–66.

[U. VOLL]

LAICIZATION, in general a juridic process leading to a rescript that allows one in holy orders to return to the lay status in the Church. Since minor orders and the subdeaconate were abolished in the Latin Church by Paul VI's apostolic constitution *Ministeria quaedam* (1972), the term laicization applies to one who is a deacon or a priest, whether diocesan or religious. In current usage the term usually connotes the contemporary phenomenon whereby a priest's resignation from the priesthood is canonically accomplished. The process of laicization of priests until the Vatican II era did not envision dispensing from the obligation of celibacy. Since 1964, however, the Church has dealt with the problem of men leaving the priesthood by allowing petition for and granting dispensation from all obligations connected with holy orders, including that of celibacy. The process from being a juridic inquiry has moved toward a pastoral approach that seeks to deal both with the crises of those seeking laicization and also to safeguard the common good of the Church and the sacredness of the institution of the priesthood. The most recent instructions were issued by the Sacred Congregation for the Doctrine of the Faith, Jan. 13, 1971, and were accompanied by a circular letter explaining the norms; a further interpretation of these norms was issued June 26, 1972, by the same Congregation. The petition is presented by a diocesan priest through his bishop; by a religious priest, through his major superior. If the petition is granted, the effect is that the recipient cannot lawfully exercise any form of ministry in the Church (he is bound, of course, to administer the sacraments in a case of emergency). Once canonically married he may never be readmitted to the exercise of the priesthood. He is also barred from teaching theology in seminaries or ecclesiastical faculties of theology; he may not teach religion courses. There are some attempts on the part of Catholic learned societies and other groups concerned with the Church's ministry to make it possible for the laicized priest to contribute more to church life than simply living as an upright Christian.

[T. C. O'BRIEN]

LAINEZ, DIEGO (1512–65), second general of the Jesuits, prominent at the Council of Trent. As a student at the Univ. of Paris, he became one of a group of six who in 1534 joined with St. *Ignatius of Loyola to form the first company of Jesuits. L. was ordained in 1537, at the invitation of Paul III taught in Rome at the Sapienza, then was sent on missions of reform to Parma and Piacenza. On the death of Ignatius in 1556, he became vicar general, then at the general congregation of the Society in 1558 was elected to succeed the founder. In 1561 Pius IV set aside the triennial term for the generalate that Paul IV had imposed, and L. remained in office for the remainder of his life. At Trent in the first two periods he participated as papal theologian; in the third period he was a conciliar father in virtue of being general. His interventions in both capacities were notable for their prolixity, sometimes for the vehemence of his language, and for his extensive knowledge of church fathers as well as of Protestant authors. In the discussions concerning *justification he spoke at length Oct. 26, 1546, opposing G. *Seripando's *double justice theory, and favoring certitude about being in the state of grace. It is an exaggeration to attribute to L. the decisive part in the formulation of the decree on justification. In the twenty-first session of the council (1562) he was a vigorous opponent of communion under both kinds by the laity.

[T. C. O'BRIEN]

LAISSEZ-FAIRE (Fr. "let do"), the reply, according to the story, of a manufacturer when asked by Colbert how the government could help. It became a maxim with 18th-cent. free-traders, a principle of economics with Adam Smith and David Ricardo, and of political economy with the two Mills, Jeremy Bentham, and the Manchester School during the first half of the 19th century. Insofar as it defended individual freedom in industry and trade against bureaucratic interference, it was a legitimate protest; insofar as it supposed that there was a natural order in the powers of nature such that the best interests of the community and the working of the economy could be left to the enlightened self-interest of producers and consumers, and to the play of free competition, it rested on an unreal abstraction that did not work out with success, but on the contrary produced great social wretchedness. Were human beings like machines, a balance might possibly be struck—though many economists might deny it—between exchange, distribution, and consumption. As it is, they are both better and worse; and particularly as worse, namely as overconsuming, overhoarding, overexploiting, and overfouling the land, waters, and air, they have shown the need of community action to check the inevitable abuse of individual ownership of large units. *Laissez-faire* has been condemned in the social encyclicals from **Rerum novarum* (1891) onwards, by the World Council of Churches (1948), and has been abandoned with differences of degree by every state since World War I. In 1927 J. M. Keynes entitled his famous work, *End of Laissez-faire*.

[T. GILBY]

LAITY, the body of Christian people who have received the sacrament of baptism (and, eventually, confirmation) but not ordination of any kind. The origin of the word is the Greek term *laos tou theou,* "the people of God," a widely used synonym for the Church. As the people of God, the Church has been set apart from the rest of humanity. The fundamental distinction, therefore, is not the one between clergy and laity but the one between the *laos* of God and the world: to be of the laity means to belong to the former rather than to the latter. Yet the NT also distinguishes within the people of God between Apostles and other believers; not every 1st-cent. Christian was an Apostle. After the death of the Apostles, that distinction was carried over into the organized life and developing structures of the Church, and by the 3d cent. there was some such differentiation between clergy and laity.

Whenever the Church has been dominated by some variety of *clericalism, the laity have been thought of as the passive recipients of the grace dispensed by the clergy. Such a conception was prominent in the Middle Ages, as in the bull *Clericis laicos* (1296) of Pope Boniface VIII; this is understandable in the light of social and political conditions, but it has been carried over into other situations as well. The demeaning of the laity ignored both the gratuitous nature of the gifts bestowed upon the clergy and the special form of ministry entrusted particularly to the laity. That ministry is a ministry in the world and to the world. Because the grace given to the Church is not meant as a possession to be hoarded but as a gift to be shared, those Christians whose life is in the world are charged with a special responsibility for proclaiming and carrying out the rule of God beyond the present borders of the Church. Clergy and laity together, each performing its unique ministry, can thus articulate the ministry of Jesus Christ, who at one and the same time was a "layman," being of the tribe of Judah rather than of the priestly tribe of Levi, and a "priest forever, after the order of Melchizedek" (Heb. 5.6). The concept of the laity, far from being negative, can be seen as a special form of Christian existence, with its own privileges, duties, and sacred vocation, as well as its own dignity and promised reward.
BIBLIOGRAPHY: Vat II ApostLaity; H. Kraemer, *Theology of the Laity* (1958); C. P. Hall, *Lay Action: The Church's Third Force* (pa. 1974); M. Ivens, *Theology of the Laity* (pa. 1975).

[J. PELIKAN]

LAKE, KIRSOPP (1872–1946), biblical scholar. Born and educated in England (Lincoln College, Oxford) and ordained to the priesthood in the C of E (1896), L., after serving two curacies in England, was professor of early Christian literature and exegesis (1904–14) at the Univ. of Leiden, Holland, and professor of history at Harvard Univ. (1914–38). His scholarly work was in textual and historical criticism and in archeology. In the first field he published *Text of the New Testament* (1900; 6th ed. rev., 1928), *Codex I of the Gospel and Its Allies* (1902) and, with his wife, a photographic facsimile of *Codex Sinaiticus Petropolitanus: The New Testament, the Epistle of Barnabas and the Shepherd of Hermas* (2 v., 1911–22). His works of historical criticism include *Historical Evidence for the Resurrection of Jesus Christ* (1907), *Earlier Epistles of St. Paul* (1911), and, with F. J. Foakes-Jackson, *Beginnings of Christianity* (5 v., 1920–23), a monumental study of Acts. BIBLIOGRAPHY: A. Vaccari, EncCatt 7:822; J. Schmid, LTK 6:751–752.

[H. H. GRAHAM]

LAKHU MARA (''Lord of All''), opening words of a hymn of the East Syrian liturgy preceding the *Trisagion and recited alternatively by the priest and the congregation; the hymn is also recited at baptisms.

[J. MADEY]

LAKSHMI (LAKSMI; SRI). Hindu goddess of beauty and fortune, L. clothed in jewels stands in the *tribhanga* (three-bendings) pose, carrying her symbol—the lotus flower. *Sri* may be used also as prefix and for highly esteemed personages and books.

[M. J. DALY]

LALANDE, JOHN, ST. (d. 1646), lay missionary and martyr. Born in Dieppe, he went to Canada as a lay missionary and worked with the Jesuits in Quebec. He accompanied Isaac *Jogues on a missionary trip to the Iroquois; the two were captured by Mohawks. Lalande was tomahawked and beheaded Oct. 19 at Ossernenon, N. Y. BIBLIOGRAPHY: J. Despont, *Catholicisme* 6:463–464; F. Baumann, BiblSanct 6:1033. For bibliog, see NORTH AMERICAN MARTYRS.

[P. K. MEAGHER]

LALANDE, MICHEL RICHARD DE (1657–1726), French composer who served as Music Master in the court of Louis XIV and director of the Royal Chapel. His 42 motets for orchestra and chorus, distinguished by their clarity and brightness even in five-part polyphony, composed for use in the Royal Chapel at Versailles, are the basis of his enduring fame. Three other occasional pieces of church music are worthy of mention—his *Symphonies des Noëls*, a solo *Miserere*, and three *Leçons de tenèbres*.

[R. J. LITZ]

LALEMANT, GABRIEL, ST. (1610–49), Jesuit missionary, martyr. Born at Paris, he became a Jesuit in 1630 and went to Canada on the Huron mission in 1646, assisting John de *Brébeuf at St. Ignace mission. March 16, 1649, the settlement was destroyed by Iroquois who immediately massacred all but the priests. After torture, Brébeuf died the same day; Gabriel, the following day. BIBLIOGRAPHY: F. Baumann, BiblSanct 5:134–142; U. Milliez, *Catholicisme* 4:1690. For bibliog. see NORTH AMERICAN MARTYRS.

[P. K. MEAGHER]

LALIBELA, pilgrimage town 200 miles N of Addis Ababa, Ethiopia. Located there are 11 churches hewn out of solid rock as monolithic structures—outer walls, façade, and interior. The interiors are hollowed out into naves and vaulted ceiling. Their monolithic structure makes these churches unique among all rock sanctuaries.

[T. C. O'BRIEN]

LALLEMENT, JACQUES PHILIPPE (1660–1748), French Jesuit polemicist against the Jansenists, esp. in his *Jansenius condamné . . .* (1705) and *Le Véritable esprit des nouveaux disciples de Saint-Augustin* (4 v., 1705). Against P. *Quesnel he wrote *Réflexions morales avec des notes sur le N.T. traduit en français* (12 v., 1713–25), and *Entretiens au sujet des affaires présentes par rapport à la religion* (7 v., 1713–25).

[T. C. O'BRIEN]

LALLEMENT, LOUIS (1587–1635), French Jesuit, spiritual guide. A Jesuit from 1605, he spent most of his priestly life in charge of the spiritual formation of novices or tertians. Notes from his instructions and conferences were edited posthumously and, along with a biography, published by P. Champion, SJ, as *La vie et la doctrine du Père Louis Lallement de la Compagnie de Jésus* (1694); the first English translation was made by F. *Faber, *The Spiritual Doctrine of Father Louis Lallement, SJ* (1883); a more recent edition is that of A. McDougall, ed., *The Spiritual Teaching of Father Louis Lallement, Preceded by an Account of His Life by Father Champion* (1946). Another work published is *Réflexions morales sur le N.T. traduit en français* (2 v., 1838). Main spiritual themes in L.'s teaching are purity of intention, dependence on the Gifts of the Holy Spirit, and the mutual relationship between contemplative prayer and apostolic action.

[T. C. O'BRIEN]

LALOR, TERESA, MOTHER (1769–1846), foundress of the Visitandine order in the U.S. She was born Alice Lalor in Ireland. Under the direction of Rev. I. *Neale she established a religious community, first at Philadelphia then at Georgetown (Washington, D.C.); she was given the Visitation rule for her community in 1816. She resigned as superior in 1819 and lived the rest of her life as a simple subject.

[J. R. AHERNE]

LA MADELEINE, see MADELEINE, LA.

LAMAISM, special designation for Tibetan Buddhism; a religion marked by syncretism of the indigenous Bon (Boen) religion, which featured magic, healing, sacrifice to local deities, and a cult of royal dead, with Hindu Tantric practices and Mahayana Buddhism imported from India. The official practitioners of Bon opposed the arrival of Mahayana into the court (*c.*620–649 A.D.) of King Srong-tsan-Gam-po whose Nepalese and Chinese wives were both devout Buddhists. During the 8th cent., Padmasambhava (Son of the Lotus), an Indian guru mystic of questionable historicity, is said to have come by royal invitation to Tibet where he taught Tantrism and established a monastery at bSamyas which became the center for the rÑinmapa, the Red Lama or Red Hat sect. Santarakshita, however, is probably responsible for founding the monastery and sect as well as for ordaining the first Red monks. Atisa, a Bengali master from the Univ. at Vikramashila, was invited and went (1042) to Tibet bearing his message of the Kalasakra or Mahayana Pala (Wheel of Time). Atisa's disciple, Brom-ston (1008–64), founded the strict bKagdamspa (Bound by Command) order at his monastery of Rva-sgreng. Marpa (1012–96) was a scholar traveller whose most famous disciple was Mila Ras-pa and whose disciple sGam-po-pa (1079–1153) founded the bKa-rgyud-pa (Transmitted Word) order that, in opposition to traditional Buddhism, justified marriage as compatible with ascetic practices and yoga. Most of the six schools of sGam-po-pa's order chose their lamas or superiors by a reincarnation system in which the soul of a deceased lama, having taken refuge in another creature, is then sought out among the infant population as the newly incarnated lama. The title "lama" originally designated only monks of the highest grade, but gradually became applied to every Tibetan monk, much in the way "Father" is used in Catholic terminology. Ordinary monks are usually called grva-pa or ge-slong; below lamas and monks in the Tibetan hierarchy are the Ge-tsu (deacons), Gen-ye (novices), and Ge-snen (laity). The effective spread of Lamaism among the Mongol Khan invaders of the 13th cent. brought power to the lamas, particularly Psags-pa, abbot of Sa-skya, who became vassal-ruler of Tibet (1275) when he converted Kublai Khan. Reformation of Lamaism under Tsong-kha-pa (1357–1419) resulted in the dGe-lug-pa (Model of Virtue) school, also called the Yellow Hat sect, which forbade marriage and generally opposed the worldliness of the Red Hats, advocating a strict monasticism and encouraging philosophical study. The Yellows gradually replaced the Reds, who survived only as sorcerers. In 1575, the Mongols bestowed the title of Dalai ("sea," measureless, profound) on the chief lama of the Potala convent in the Tibetan capital of Lhasa. This Dalai Lama, who exercises temporal power, is considered to be an incarnation of Avalokiteśvara, a Bodhisattva (one who resides on the border between this life and nirvana). A Tashi Lama ("jewel"), the second highest lama, exercises spiritual powers and resides at the Ta-shi-lhum-po monastery. In recent decades the Tashi Lama has sided politically with the Chinese, the Dalai Lama, with Britain and the West. In the 18th cent., the Yong-ho-Kong or Temple of the Lamas in Peking was built by the Manchus to serve the Lama cult. Tantric recitation of mantra spells, especially "*Om mani padme hum,*" the manual or mechanical revolving of devotional wheels containing prayers (improperly called prayer-wheels), and use of visual devices called mandalas as protection against evil are all fundamental to Tibetan Buddhist practice. Emphasis is placed on an awareness of the essential identity of the human being and the universe, related as microcosm to macrocosm. The scriptural canon of Lamaism assumed its present shape in the 13th and 14th cent. through the work of the scholar Bu-ston (1290–1364); it comprised the *Kanjur* (Translated Word), the canon proper of 100–108 volumes, and the *Tanjur* (Translated Treatises) in 225 volumes. The Perfection of Wisdom texts, *Prajñā Pāramitās,* in 18 volumes and found in every temple, provides the philosophical foundation of Lamaism. BIBLIOGRAPHY: L. Petech, EncCatt 7:826–832.

[R. J. LITZ]

LAMB, THE. In Israelite religion the lamb appears to have been the dominant sacrificial victim, the sacrifice of which was prescribed for the major feasts (Num 28.26–27; 29.7–8, 13–16), the daily offerings (Ex 29.38–42), and other occasions (Lev 3.6; 4.27,32; 5.6). The central symbol and sacrifice in the Passover (Ex 12.11–12), the lamb also symbolized innocence (2 Sam 12.3) or evoked sympathy as in the consoling words addressed to exiled Israel (Is 40.11). Threatened with death by his persecutors, Jeremiah compared himself to a lamb led to slaughter (Jer 11.19) and the same comparison was applied to the Servant of Yahweh, whose suffering has an expiatory character (Is 53.4–7). Influenced by the Servant texts of Isaiah and the Passover-Exodus typology, early Christianity in the NT employed the image of the lamb (*amnos, arnion*) to stress the dispositions of Jesus during his Passion (Mt 26.63; Jn 19.9; Acts 8.32); the effect of Jesus' mission and sacrifice (1 Pet 1.19; Jn 1.29; Rev 5.6; Heb 9.12–15) or the qualities of Jesus as sacrificial victim, innocent and without blemish (1 Pet 1.19; Jn 8.46; 1 Jn 3.5; Heb 9.14), redeeming mankind through his precious blood (1 Pet 1.18; Rev 5.9f; Heb 9.12–15). The fourth evangelist most clearly emphasizes the coincidence between the immolation of the prefigurative paschal lamb and the hour when Christ's mission is accomplished (18.28; 19.14,31). The Book of Revelation elaborates the present and future function of Christ as the now exalted lamb who executes the decrees of God against the impious (Rev 6.1–17), leads the heavenly army in eschatological warfare against the powers of evil (17.14), and shepherds the faithful to the living water of heavenly blessedness (Rev

7:17). BIBLIOGRAPHY: R. Brown, *Gospel of St. John* (1966) 1:58–63.

[T. J. RYAN]

LAMB OF GOD, a title given to Jesus in several books of the NT (Jn, Acts, 1 Pet, Rev) and used in the Christian liturgies. The title evokes the twofold idea of the Servant of Yahweh, who is compared to a lamb (Is 53.7; cf. Acts 8.32), and the paschal lamb. In the Johannine corpus, the theme of Jesus as the true paschal lamb is very important. This is indicated by enclosing the Gospel between two references to the lamb (1.29 and 19.34–36) and by emphasizing the coincidence between the immolation of the ritual lamb and "the hour" of Jesus' glorification (18.28; 19.14, 31). The passover lamb is sacrifice in its immolation, and Jesus is forever the sacrificial lamb of God. Consecrated for sacrifice from the beginning, he becomes fully sacrifice only in death. Risen and glorified, he remains eternally "the Lamb standing, as if slain" (Rev 5.6). Here the unending reality of his sacrifice is suggested: he never ceases to be the one who has died in suffering expression of perfect, saving worship. In resurrection he is always the *Christus passus* (ThAq ST 3a, 73.6); his sacrifice is an eternally present sacrifice. Just as the paschal rite of Israel was a sacrifice of communion—the meal being essential to it—so Jesus' sacrifice is one we share only by communion with him. Only thus is the sin of the world destroyed. Mankind must be washed in the blood of the Lamb (Rev 7.14), follow the Lamb (Rev. 14.4), and share his wedding feast (Rev 19.7). The sacraments and sacrifice of the Church are the privileged points of saving communion with the Lamb immolated. BIBLIOGRAPHY: F. X. Durrwell, NCE 8:338–342; EDB 1297–99.

[C. REGAN]

LAMBACH, ABBEY OF, Austrian Benedictine abbey on the Traun River in the diocese of Linz. Established *c.* 1040 as a chapter of secular canons, it was transferred (1056) to Benedictine monks by Bp. Adalbero of Würzburg. In a short time the abbey became a prominent monastic and cultural center and influenced other monasteries, including Melk. In 1664 all its monastic buildings were rebuilt. Suppressed during the Nazi regime (1941–1945), the abbey today conducts a middle school and a school of agriculture. In the oldest part of the church, there are splendid romanesque frescoes (11th cent.). BIBLIOGRAPHY: Cottineau 1:1542–43; W. Luger, *Die Benediktinerabtei Lambach* (1952); S. Leidinger, *900 Jahre Lambach* (1956); N. Wibiral et al., "Die Freilegungsarbeiten im ehemaligen Westchor der Stiftskirche von Lambach," *Oesterreichische Zeitschrift für Kunst und Denkmalpflege* 14 (1960) 1–24.

[F. H. ROHRIG]

LAMBECK, PETER (1628–80), German librarian, bibliographer. Like his uncle and tutor, Lucas Holstenius (1596–1661), a papal librarian, L. was a convert to Catholicism (1664). As librarian and historian of the imperial library in Vienna he prepared and annotated a catalogue of its MSS resources, *Commentarii de bibliotheca caesarea Vindobonensi* (1665); his major work was a history of literature, *Prodromus historiae literariae* (1659).

[T. C. O'BRIEN]

LAMBERT (LAMPERT) OF HERSFELD (*c.* 1025–*c.* 1085), Benedictine annalist. L.'s enthusiasm for the Cluniac reform and opposition to Emperor Henry IV motivated his move from Hersfeld to the Abbey of Hasungen in 1077. His principal work, the *Annales,* is a world history beginning with Genesis. The period 1040–68 contains original matter and is covered in considerable detail. Lambert is a valuable source for contemporary Church thought, though inaccurate at times and often biased. BIBLIOGRAPHY: C. E. Boyd, NCE 8:342–343; G. Marié, *Catholicisme* 6:1694.

[M. S. TANEY]

LAMBERT OF MAASTRICHT, ST. (d. *c.* 705), succeeded his uncle Theodard as bp. in 672. In the chaos following the assassination of King Childeric II of Austrasia, L. was forced into exile. Pepin II of Herstal restored him. In a dispute over church immunity, or possibly, as was claimed in a later biography, for having disapproved the adultery of Count Dodo's sister with Pepin, Dodo had him slain. L. is the patron of the city of Freiburg im Breisgau, Baden, Germany. BIBLIOGRAPHY: W. Lampen, BiblSanct 7:1079–80; Butler 3:579–580.

[J. E. LYNCH]

LAMBERT DE LA MOTTE, PIERRE (1624–79), founder (1658), with F. *Pallu of the Paris Missionary Seminary, the base of the *Paris Foreign Mission Society. The foundation was made in pursuance of the Congregation for the Propagation of the Faith's program for a more direct control over missions than was possible with Spanish or Portuguese missionaries (see PATRONATO REAL). L. was made a titular bp. in 1659, and as vicar apostolic for Cochin China established missions in Indochina and Thailand and ordained native clergy. The directive for missionaries sent to Rome by L. and Pallu became a standard guide.

[T. C. O'BRIEN]

LAMBERT OF ST. BERTIN (*c.* 1060–1125), monastic reformer and scholar. A monk of the abbey of St. Bertin, St. Omer, France, he became abbot in 1095 and introduced the *Cluniac Reform. He was a teacher in the monastery school and there are records of his having written on natural science and on questions of grace; his correspondence with St. Anselm of Canterbury survives (PL 158:1083; 159:72, 171). He is sometimes confused with *Lambert of St. Omer.

[T. C. O'BRIEN]

LAMBERT OF ST. OMER (d. *c.* 1125), canon of St. Omer, known only as the author of *Liber floridus,* an encyclopedic compilation on a wide variety of academic disciplines (PL 163:1003–31).

[T. C. O'BRIEN]

LAMBERT OF SPOLETO, GERMAN EMPEROR (d. 898), son of Guido III of Spoleto and co-emperor with him (892–894). When Guido died in 894, L. became sole ruler. By 897, his conflicts with Arnulf, whom Pope Formosus had crowned emperor in 896, and with Berengar I of Friuli, were at an end. The Synod of Ravenna ratified his royal power in 898. BIBLIOGRAPHY: C. E. Boyd, NCE 8:342; L. Duchesne, *Beginnings of the Temporal Sovereignty of the Popes, A.D. 754–1073* (tr. A. H. Mathew, 1908) 195–203.

[M. F. MCCARTHY]

LAMBERT, LOUIS ALOYSIUS (1835–1910). Ordained for Alton, Ill., Lambert eventually worked in New York and Rochester. He was a fiery but able editor of the *Freeman's Journal* (1895–1910) and a polemicist. His *Notes on Ingersoll* (1887) constitute a refutation of the famous agnostic Robert Ingersoll.

[J. R. AHERNE]

LAMBERTENGHI OF COMA, GEREMIA, BL. (1440–1513), Franciscan ascetic. At the age of 20, L. decided to join the Third Order of St. Francis and entered the Franciscan hermitage of St. Donato. After his ordination, L. was assigned to Montebello where he began a life of extreme mortification. In 1489, he was sent to Piratello, where he supervised the construction of a new convent. In 1508, L. became vicar of Sta. Maria of Valverde, where he remained until his death. His body lies in the church at Valverde. L. was beatified in 1941. BIBLIOGRAPHY: F. Provenzano, AnalTOR (1953)6:47–71, 107–129, 210–223; *idem,* BiblSanct 7:1075–76.

[R. J. BRADY]

LAMBESIS, ruins of a Roman camp and town that became headquarters for the Legion III Augusta between 123 and 129 A.D. and capital of the Province of Numidia during the reign of Septimius Severus (193–211 A.D.); located 80 miles S-SW of Constantine in Algeria, it is N of the present Algerian village Tazoult. The praetorium built in 268 A.D. is the center of what is left of the camp. Lambesis was the execution site of a number of Christian martyrs. BIBLIOGRAPHY: P. Canivet, NCE 8.344; E. Josi EncCatt 7:840–841; CAH 12:20; PW 12.1:539–541.

[F. H. BRIGHAM]

LAMBETH ARTICLES, nine propositions affirming a rigid Calvinist doctrine of *predestination, adopted at Lambeth Palace, Nov. 20, 1595. There John Whitgift (*c.* 1539–1604), Abp. of Canterbury, summoned a synod to deal with a minority opposition to unconditional predestination that had arisen at the Univ. of Cambridge. The Articles affirmed God's absolute predestination of the elect, excluding foreseen faith or good works. The Lambeth statement reflected the prevalent Calvinism of the Puritan era, but never was adopted as a doctrinal standard in England. BIBLIOGRAPHY: Schaff Creeds 1:658–661; G. Böing; LTK 6:760.

[G. RUPPEL]

LAMBETH CONFERENCES, meetings to which the abp. of Canterbury invites bps. of the *Anglican Communion, and at which he presides. Until 1968, those gatherings, generally held every 10 years, were at his London residence, Lambeth Palace, hence their name. They are informal meetings rather than synods or councils, and their reports and resolutions have no official authority, except as they are implemented by the individual member Churches. However, the influence of the Conferences on the life and witness of the Churches of the *Anglican Communion is substantial, and they play a unique role in expressing the viewpoint of these Churches on contemporary issues. The first Conference was held in 1867, at the request (1865) of the metropolitan and bps. of the ecclesiastical province of Canada, made to the abp. of Canterbury, C. T. Longley (1794–1868). In their request, however, the Canadian bps. were giving voice to a wish widely held in the younger Anglican Churches outside the British Isles—a wish arising from the nature of the Anglican Communion itself. Lacking any central government or single worldwide organization, national Anglican Churches were coming into vigorous existence in every part of the world. The American and New Zealand Churches were already autocephalous; the rest were well started on that road. In consequence of this swift, largely uncoordinated growth, it was becoming clear that the unity expressed in their "full communion" with the C of E required articulation and embodiment in order to develop beyond sentimentality. This need was sharpened by the contemporary political and doctrinal tensions symbolized by the trial for heresy of Bp. Colenso of Natal, in which the judgment of the church court in South Africa had been reversed by the Privy Council in England. The Colenso incident raised vivid questions as to both the Church's doctrine and the freedom of the younger Churches from English domination. The phrase "Anglican Communion" was only then coming into use; the reality that lay behind the phrase needed to be developed, and this development, in turn, depended on the way Anglican unity and diversity were to be reconciled and expressed within some central body.

The hope of the Canadians, and many others, was for a worldwide synod or council of the Anglican Churches. But the possibility of such a supranational authority, which might even override the authority of the established C of E, aroused grave questions within that body itself. Only a minority of English bps. were to attend the first meeting;

and the Conference was not permitted to hold official services either in Westminster Abbey or in St. Paul's Cathedral. Abp. Longley, however, recognized the need for such a gathering and accordingly issued an invitation to all the diocesan bps. of the Anglican Communion to attend a 5-day "Conference" at his official headquarters. The use of the word "conference" clearly indicated that the gathering was not conciliar or synodical; and the meetings, during the 100 years since the first, have amply demonstrated their informal, consultative nature. With the growth in the Anglican Communion, the number of bps. attending has steadily increased from the 76 present in 1867. The invitations to the 1968 conference were, for the first time, sent to every bp. in active service, whether diocesan or otherwise; and the number responding was close to 500. Successive Lambeth Conferences (1878, 1888, 1897, 1908, 1920, 1930, 1948, 1958, 1968) have dealt with many of the issues in ecclesiastical life as well as in social and political matters. Notable among the Conferences was that held in 1920, memorable for its concentration on the unity of the Church, chiefly in the "Appeal to All Christian People," which established a new level of responsible Anglican ecumenical concern. The 1958 report on "Family in Contemporary Society" established a broad new Anglican approach to the theology of human sexuality and marriage. Every conference, however, devotes a fair amount of attention to the internal problems of the Anglican Communion and its member Churches as well as to wider issues.

The Tenth Lambeth Conference (July 25-August 25, 1968), called by the Abp. of Canterbury, Dr. Michael Ramsey, opened with a service in Canterbury Cathedral at which he was the preacher, and the apostolic delegate to Great Britain was a special guest. At the opening session at Church House, Westminster, London, where, because of the large attendance the month-long meetings were held, greetings were read from the Pope and the Ecumenical Patriarch. In attendance were 467 of the 740 bps., metropolitans, and primates of the worldwide 47-million-member Anglican Communion. Lambeth '68 was the first Conference to be open to the press and the first to have consultants (25 Anglican specialists in various fields) and some 50 official observers from other denominations, who participated actively in the discussions. The latter included the RC Church, Orthodox and other Eastern Churches, Old Catholic, and all major Protestant bodies, represented by many distinguished religious leaders. The theme was Renewal of the Church, in Faith, Ministry and Unity, with the three sections headed respectively by the primate of Canada, the archbishop of York, and the metropolitan of India. Its 32 subcommittees dealt with subjects ranging from theological questions and social and moral issues to world problems of race, poverty, and war. The most controversial issues were those concerning the ordination of women, and *intercommunion between Anglicans and other baptized Christians, in order to meet special pastoral needs, and between Churches committed to and awaiting full organic union. Such intercommunion involves the Anglican principle of episcopacy (the fourth point of the *Lambeth Quadrilateral) and the question as to whether intercommunion should be a means to unity or the expression of its fulfillment. Robert Cecil Mortimer, Bp. of Exeter, England, was chief spokesman for the traditional Anglo-Catholic position, and their contention that in some of the current unity schemes under consideration the essentials of Anglicanism are in danger of being lost or compromised.

While the leadership of the Anglican Communion is still predominantly Anglo-Saxon, the native Asiatic and African bps. carried great weight at this conference. Abp. Lakdasa de Mel, Metropolitan of India, pushed through the resolutions endorsing full communion with the *Church of South India and with other uniting Indian Churches upon their inauguration, and the highly controversial Anglican-Methodist unity scheme in England, though not without heated debate and sizable dissent. Lambeth '68 produced a notable statement on prayer, but no radical theology. It proclaimed that the Church of today will be renewed only insofar as it pursues its role as the Servant Church. It stressed the ministry of the laity, encouraged the expansion of the perpetual diaconate and part-time ministries where needed, and recommended that deaconesses be considered to be within the diaconate. The final amended resolution on women and the priesthood stated that arguments on both sides were inconclusive but urged further study by the member Churches and canonical provision for women to preach, baptize, read the Gospel and Epistle, and distribute the elements at the Eucharist.

The bishops authorized the resumption of talks with the Orthodox Church, the continuance of Anglican-Roman conversations, and support for the Anglican Center in Rome; initiation of talks with world Lutheranism; and close cooperation with the World Council of Churches and the establishment of an Anglican Center in Geneva. A total of some 75 resolutions were debated in plenary session and acted upon. One important structural step was the proposed 50-member Anglican Consultative Council composed of bps., priests, and laity meeting every 2 years, to provide a representative central organization for common action. Another was the Wider Episcopal Fellowship, scheduled to meet in 1969, which will include bps. in full or partial communion with the Anglican Churches. Also proposed was a summit meeting of Christian and non-Christian leaders, to speak in the interest of humanity on behalf of world peace. Other resolutions pressured the governments for relief of social ills; outlawed the use of nuclear and bacteriological weapons; upheld the rights of conscientious objectors; called for the involvement of youth in the Church; denounced racism as a blatant denial of the Christian faith; and reaffirmed the stand of Lambeth '58 that birth control is a matter of individual conscience. At an outdoor Eucharist at London's White City Stadium, 15,000 church men received communion, concelebrated by overseas bps. from five continents in thanksgiving for the spread of the gospel. Two other great conference services were held at Westminster Abbey and St. Paul's Cathedral, with consultants and observers present. In addition to its balanced emphasis on spiritual renewal and social action and its prime thrust toward church unity, Lambeth '68 may be chiefly notable for its ecumenical impact.

Increasingly, debate goes on in Anglican circles as to the future place and nature of the Lambeth Conference. As full communion is established by the Anglican Churches with other non-Anglican bodies such as the Old Catholic Churches, and as particular Anglican Churches become more involved in schemes of church unity in their own countries, the concept of unity expressed in the Anglican Communion is more and more sharply tested and questioned. Yet the need for a worldwide expression of the Church's unity remains unsatisfied by anything less than full sacramental communion; and it may be argued that the Lambeth Conference will have a significant part to play in the divided Christian world until fuller and deeper manifestations of unity in the Body of Christ are possible. BIBLIOGRAPHY: A. N. C. Stephenson, *First Lambeth Conference: 1867* (1967); W. R. Curtis, *Lambeth Conferences: The Solution for Pan-Anglican Organization* (1942); B. D. Dupuy, *Catholicisme* 6:1705–06.

[S. F. BAYNE]

LAMBETH QUADRILATERAL (Chicago-Lambeth Quadrilateral), a statement of Anglican principles worked out by the American Episcopalian William Reed *Huntington in *The Church-Idea, An Essay toward Unity* (1870). In the Quadrilateral Huntington offered a basis for organic church unity within American *denominationalism; he attempted as well a redefinition of Anglicanism by means of the proposal in the belief that neither the *Thirty-Nine Articles nor the *Act of Uniformity of 1662 was relevant to the American religious scene in the 19th century. The Quadrilateral suggested four points as a basis for the reunion of the Churches: "first, the Holy Scripture as the Word of God, second, the Primitive Creeds as the Rule of Faith, third, the two Sacraments ordained by Christ himself, and fourth, the Episcopate as the key-stone of Government Unity." These points were accepted by the *General Convention of the Protestant Episcopal Church meeting at Chicago in 1886 and by the *Lambeth Conference of 1888. While Huntington's wording (above) underwent changes over the years, the general principles were reiterated by the later Lambeth Conferences of 1920 and 1930 and by the General Conventions of the Episcopal Church of 1949 and 1961. Commentary and interpretation have tended in a catholic direction, particularly with reference to the troublesome fourth point dealing with the *historic episcopate. Claims respecting the *apostolic succession of bishops (*to*, not *of*, the Apostles) were reintroduced however much Episcopalians sought to distinguish between the episcopate as doctrinally understood, as historical fact, or as function. Far from being a source of unity both within and without the *Anglican Communion, the Lambeth Quadrilateral has proved to be something of a focal point for party debate. While Huntington's proposals initiated unity conversations between American Episcopalians and other Protestant Churches, none of these has resulted in organic union. The Quadrilateral, however, must be seen as an expression of the desire of liberal Christians in the U.S. in the late 19th cent. for reconciliation.

The term "Quadrilateral" comes from the system of fortress-cities in Lombardy comprised of Mantua, Verona, Peschiera, and Legnano, important in the Napoleonic wars and in the Austrian occupation of Italy, 1815–59. Huntington's allusion implied that within such a fortress as his four points the Church might stand secure. BIBLIOGRAPHY: *Documents of Church Unity* (1962); J. A. Hardon, *Spirit and Origins of American Protestantism* (1968) 188–191; B. D. Dupuy, *Catholicisme* 6:1706.

[J. F. WOOLVERTON]

LAMBILLOTTE, LOUIS (1796–1855), French Jesuit composer of church music, organist, author, and editor. Chief among his works on plainsong is *Clef des Mélodies Grégoriennes* (1851). He edited *Musée des Organistes* (2 v., 1842–44). He also composed other sacred music, 4 Masses, organ pieces, and fugues.

[R. J. LITZ]

LAMBIN, DENYS (Dionysius Lambinus; 1516–72), French classicist. L. was born at Montreuil-sur-Mer. After studying at Amiens, he traveled to Rome with the card. of Tournon in 1549. L. spent much of the next decade in Italy and enjoyed a rich assocation with many of the leading scholars of the period. In 1560 he gained a position at the Collège de France in Paris and in 1561 he was named Royal Professor of Greek. L. was much troubled by the persecution of the Huguenots, and he was so dispirited by the death of his friend Peter Ramus in the St. Bartholomew's Day Massacre in 1572 that he died shortly afterward. His most significant writings include a study of Horace's *Ars poëtica* (1561), an edition of Lucretius' *De rerum natura* (1563) that is still regarded as definitive, and an edition of the works of Cicero (1566). BIBLIOGRAPHY: J. E. Sandys, *History of Classical Scholarship* (3v., 1958) 2:188–191.

[R. J. BRADY]

LAMBING, ANDREW ARNOLD (1842–1918), historian. A priest of the diocese of Pittsburgh, Lambing wrote widely popular devotional works but is important principally for his publications on the history of Catholicity in western Pennsylvania. *A History of the Catholic Church in the Diocese of Pittsburgh and Allegheny (1880)* and the editing of the first Catholic historical quarterly, *American Catholic Historical Researches,* were highlights of a career in critical historical scholarship. BIBLIOGRAPHY: M. Hammill, *Expansion of the Catholic Church in Pennsylvania* (1960).

[J. R. AHERNE]

LAMBRUSCHINI, LUIGI (1776–1854), Italian Barnabite, archbishop, cardinal, and papal secretary of state. Ordained in 1799 he taught philosophy and theology in Barnabite houses until 1814, when he began his long service in the Roman curia. He was a consultor for curial congregations and for the secretariat of state; abp. of Genoa from 1819; nuncio to Paris (1826–31). Recalled to Rome, he was created cardinal (1831), became prefect of several congregations, then secretary of state to Gregory XVI until that pope's death in 1846; Pius IX made L. a member of the Congregation of State. In both latter capacities L. was staunchly conservative in resistance to the forces of liberalism and Italian nationalism, and the defender of all challenges to the papal temporal power; he was Pius IX's counsellor during the Pope's exile at Gaeta. L. also had a major influence on the proclamation (1854) of the dogma of the Immaculate Conception.

[T. C. O'BRIEN]

LAMENNAIS, HUGUES FÉLICITÉ ROBERT DE (1782–1854), the real founder of the Ultramontanist party in France, he popularized and organized the ideas of de Maistre and de Bonald. After the July Revolution he became a great leader in the episode of liberal Catholicism, a movement eventually persecuted and crushed by the Church. Ultramontanism, in triumphing, drove out Lamennais. In 1808 L. published his *Reflection on the State of the Church in France* and in 1817, an *Essay on Indifference in Matters of Religion,* which put him in the forefront of Catholic apologists. Like *Chateaubriand, he emphasized primarily the utility of religion, its moral value as a cohesive social force. Men need the certainty of religion because they have a personal longing, they must believe (here, echoes of Pascal), in order to avoid the horror of skepticism. As de Maistre maintained, religion is necessary for social peace. Harmony and intellectual peace are to be found only in the great tradition, in the embodied universal reason men accept by common consent.

In 1824 L. began to move toward defiance of ecclesiastical authority. His work *On Religion* (1826) supported a theocracy, in which political power should be submitted to the natural law, as interpreted by the Church. *The Progress of the Revolution and the War against the Church* (1829) was censured by the religious authorities; in it L. demanded freedom to defend the Ultramontanists. In 1830 he founded *L'Avenir* as the organ of a liberal Catholicism, supporting the political revolt of the Belgians, Poles, and Irish. For L. the *vox populi* had become the *vox Dei.* With *Lacordaire, L. made a pilgrimage to Rome, where he hoped to enlist the approval and perhaps support of the Pope. Instead, the editors of *L'Avenir* were reprimanded by Pope Gregory XVI and came away from Rome greatly disappointed. Liberal Catholicism found even less favor there than it had among L.'s conservative foes at home. Embittered and intransigent, he reiterated the principles of a free Church in a free State in the powerful *Words of a Believer* (1836). Rome's condemnation was swift and unequivocal. Thenceforth outside the Church L. preached his revolutionary combination of democracy and Christianity, joining those pioneers of a heterodox new Christianity which evolved later in the century into what came to be called Christian socialism.

L.'s ambition had been to awaken the Church to two great modern issues, liberalism and the social movement. He saw the Restoration, in its cynical use of religion as an instrument of the regime, as leading Catholics to miss entirely the opportunity to come to terms with what he sensed to be the wave of the future. The Church was supporting the wrong cause and L. was most afraid lest its spiritual power be compromised by blunders in the temporal sphere. He returned again and again to the problem of the industrial proletariat. In these respects, however inconsistent and heretical on fundamental issues of faith, L. was far ahead of his time. BIBLIOGRAPHY: *Catholic Political Thought* (ed. B. Menczer, 1962); W. Gibson, *Abbé de Lamennais and the Liberal Catholic Movement in France* (1896); A. R. Vidler, *Prophecy and Papacy, A Study of Lamennais, the Church, and the Revolution* (1954).

[J. P. REID]

LA MENNAIS, JEAN MARIE ROBERT DE, VEN. (1780–1860), founder. A Frenchman ordained in 1804, La Mennais spent some time in retirement at his parents' home because of ill health. He collaborated with his brother Hugues Félicité on *Réflexions sur l'état de l'Église en France au XVIIIe siècle* (1808) and *Tradition d l'Église sur l'institution des évêques* (1814). Named vicar-general of the diocese of Saint-Brieuc in 1814 he served also as the bishop's secretary. In 1818 he joined with Marie Cartel in establishing the Daughters of Providence of Saint-Brieuc. He was cofounder (1819–20) of the Brothers of Christian Instruction of Ploërmel, a community which he headed until his death. In 1822 L. became vicar-general to the grand almoner of France in Paris. In later years he aided in founding the Holy Cross Brothers and reorganizing the Marist Brothers. His cause was introduced in Rome in 1911 and the antepreparatory congregation convened in 1946. BIBLIOGRAPHY: A. Lavelle, *Jean-Marie de La Mennais (1780–1860)* (2 v., 1903).

[J. R. AHERNE]

LA MENNAIS BROTHERS, see BROTHERS OF CHRISTIAN INSTRUCTION OF PLOËRMEL.

LAMENTABILI, a decree of the Holy Office (approved by Pope Pius X, July 4, 1907) listing 65 condemned propositions without affixing any determined theological censure. While the decree was aimed at the movement later called *Modernism (**Pascendi,* Sept. 8, 1907), it mentions no names. Condemned as erroneous are certain views relating to the interpretation, inspiration, and inerrancy of Scripture, the meaning of revelation and of dogmas, certain beliefs about Christ, about the origin of the Church and of the sacraments, and about the immutability of revealed truths. BIBLIOGRAPHY: ASS 40 (1907) 470–478; D 3401–66; V. A. Yzermans, *All Things in Christ* (1954). *MODERNISM.

[J. H. ROHLING]

LAMENTATIONS, BOOK OF, part of the Bible, grouped among the Writings (Ketûbîm) in the Hebrew Bible; in the LXX and Vulgate traditions, attached to Jeremiah. Lamentations consists of five poems written in the form of the laments of the Psalms, and contains the following themes: the desolation and destruction of the holy city, here personified as a female figure; Yahweh's indignation and judgment against Jerusalem; lamentation and hopeful entreaty for deliverance; Zion's past glories compared with her present miseries; the sufferings of the conquered. The style and language of these poems suggest that at least two of them were written shortly after 587, and the others rather later. The ascription to Jeremiah is probably based on 2 Chr 35.25, where mention is made of dirges composed by Jeremiah on the death of King Josiah in 609. The most likely explanation of their provenance, however, is that they are liturgical poems, some composed by an unknown author or authors, recited in the course of an annual day of mourning commemorating the destruction of Jerusalem in 587. In Jewish liturgy, this usage continues; in the Christian Holy Week, Lamentations are recited in commemorating Christ's Passion. BIBLIOGRAPHY: A. B. Albrektson, *Studies in the Text and Theology of Lamentations* (1963); N. K. Gottwald, *Studies in the Book of Lamentations* (1954); G. F. Wood, JBC 1:609–613; R. Gordis, *Song of Songs and Lamentations* (1974).

[D. J. BOURKE]

LA METTRIE, JULIEN OFFRAY DE (1709–51), French physician and philosopher. In his *Histoire naturelle de l'âme* (1745) and other works, he taught that man's soul is material; that human life is to be completely explained in terms of bodily organisms and their natural laws; that the highest ethical good is sense pleasure. BIBLIOGRAPHY: J. Fenouillet, *Catholicisme* 6:1733.

[T. C. O'BRIEN]

LA MORICIÈRE, LOUIS CHRISTOPHE LÉON (1806–65), French general, supreme commander of papal army. He was born in Nantes of a noble family, but fought for the Republic. An outstanding soldier, he fought in the Algerian campaign of the 1830s and in the revolution of 1848. After being wounded, he was chosen as Russian ambassador and war minister. With the ascent of Napoleon III, however, he was exiled for 9 years, during which time he reembraced Catholicism and renounced republicanism. He was chosen as commander in chief of the papal army defending the Papal States in 1860, but was defeated by the Piedmontese army at Castelfidaro and Ancona, after which he resigned.

[P. J. HENNESSEY]

LAMORMAINI, WILHELM (1570–1648), Jesuit confessor of Emperor Ferdinand II. Coming from a peasant family in Luxembourg, he began his education at the Jesuit College in Trier. Later he studied at Prague, Vienna, and Brünn (Brno). He had a wide knowledge of languages, in particular, German, French, Italian and Czech, which later served as an invaluable diplomatic aid. After holding various teaching positions from 1624 to 1637 he was the confessor of the religiously scrupulous Ferdinand II. It was during these crucial years of the Thirty Years War that L. acquired his reputation. Traditional historians often picture him as the evil Jesuit genius who made himself the absolute ruler of Ferdinand. This picture was heightened by L.'s lean physical appearance and noticeable limp. Perhaps this interpretation is exaggerated; while he was certainly influential, he did not make the final decisions. In general his policies were motivated by his desire to protect the Church and the Emperor in Germany, as shown in his support of the *Edict of Restitution in 1629. At other times his loyalty to Ferdinand became passionate. He had earlier liked Wallenstein, but when the general became a threat to Ferdinand L. turned against him. BIBLIOGRAPHY: L. Koch, *Jesuiten Lexikon* (2 v., 1962); G. Pagès, *Thirty Years War, 1618–1648* (tr. D. Maland and J. Hooper, 1970).

[C. T. EBY]

LAMPSTAND, in biblical references, the lampstand of the tabernacle and temple (Ex 25.31–40; 26.35). A specific Hebrew term, *mênōrāh*, refers to the lampstand. The menorah became a symbol of Judaism, particularly after the fall of Jerusalem (A.D. 70); the menorah of Herod's temple is depicted on the Arch of Titus in Rome. In Rev. 1.12–20 lampstands are symbols of the Churches (see also Mt 5.5).

LAMY, BERNARD (1640–1715), French Oratorian, philosophical and theological writer. In philosophy he was a follower of R. *Descartes and N. *Malebranche. L.'s attempt to apply Cartesian philosophical ideas to the doctrine of the *Real Presence led to his dismissal from the faculty of the Univ. of Angers. His *Harmonia sive concordia evangelistarum*, which proposed a novel chronology of Christ's life, also provoked controversy. Among his other works, on a wide range of topics, the most significant is his *Démonstration de la vérité et de la sainteté de la morale chrétienne*.

[T. C. O'BRIEN]

LAMY, FRANÇOIS (1636–1711), Benedictine, prior of the Abbey of St.-Faron-de-Meaux; polemicist, esp. against the philosophy of Descartes and N. Malebranche, notably in *De la connaissance de soi-même* (1694). Other works include *Vérité de la religion chrétienne* (1694); *Lettres théologiques et morales* (1708); *L'incrédule amené à la religion par la raison* (1710).

[T. C. O'BRIEN]

LAMY, JOHN BAPTIST (1814–88), first abp. of Santa Fe, New Mexico (1875). One of the most remarkable of missionary bps. in the U.S. and the prototype of the central figure in Willa Cather's great novel *Death Comes for the Archbishop*, L. was a native of France, where he was ordained in 1838. He came to the U.S. and in 1850 was appointed vicar apostolic of New Mexico, a territory comprising what is now New Mexico, Arizona and eastern Colorado. The Hispanic clergy of the territory were hostile to a French vicar-general but L. secured the cooperation of Bp. Zubiria of Durango, the former ordinary, and gradually gained acceptance. His prodigious journeys through his vicariate, his recruitment of priests and religious and the founding of parishes and schools created a strong vicariate, and in 1853 Santa Fe became a diocese. L. brought the Sisters of Loretto, Sisters of Charity, Brothers of the Christian Schools, and the Jesuits to Santa Fe. He was a beloved figure not only among Catholics but among Protestants and Jews as well. He is regarded as one of the pioneering leaders of the Southwest. BIBLIOGRAPHY: P. Horgan, *Lamy of Santa Fe* (1975).

[J. R. AHERNE]

LAMY, THOMAS JOSEPH (1827–1907), biblical scholar and Orientalist. L. taught at the Catholic Univ. of Louvain (1858–1900), and was president of the Collège de Marie Thérèse there. He wrote a popular but now out-of-date introduction to Scripture; he also wrote commentaries on Gen and Rev, and edited a valuable collection of St. *Ephrem's sermons as well as the *Chronicon Ecclesiasticum* of *Bar-Hebraeus. BIBLIOGRAPHY: G. Marsot, *Catholicisme* 6:1755.

[T. M. MCFADDEN]

LANCE, LITURGICAL, in the Byzantine rite a small knife which is used to cut the Prosphora (altar bread) into particles for use at the Divine Liturgy. It usually has the shape of a lance in order to recall the instrument used to pierce the side of Jesus on the cross.

[P. MORLINO]

LANCE, THE HOLY, the spear claimed to be that mentioned in Jn 19.34 which pierced the side of Jesus. According to legend this lance was discovered at the time of the finding of the holy cross. From the 6th cent. there is ample record of the veneration of such a lance at Jerusalem. The point of the Jerusalem lance was broken off and taken to Constantinople in 614 and was followed by the rest of the lance in the late 7th or early 8th century. In 1241 some relic of the lance was sold by Baldwin II to Louis IX of France and this was preserved in the Sainte Chapelle at Paris until its destruction in the Revolution. The Constantinople lance, or the part of it that remained, was given to Innocent VIII by Sultan Bayazid in 1492 and has since been kept at St. Peter's in Rome. Other lances have been preserved, such as the holy lance of St. Maurice (Constantine's lance) at Vienna, but their origin and history are uncertain. A Feast of the Holy Lance and Nails has been observed in some places since 1353.

[N. KOLLAR]

LANCELOT, popular name for the *romances concerning the love affair between Guinevere, wife of King Arthur, and Lancelot du Lac, Arthur's most valiant knight. The most famous version, by *Chrétien de Troyes, is entitled *Knight of the Cart,* referring to Guinevere's humiliation of Lancelot for his one hesitation in her service. Her dominance indicates a voluntary acceptance of the rules of *courtly love moving beyond the magic-induced adultery of *Tristan,* a folkloristic romance. BIBLIOGRAPHY: T. P. Cross and W. N. Nitze, *Lancelot and Guenevere* (1922, repr. 1970); L. A. Paton, *Sir Lancelot of the Lake* (1929).

[J. P. WILLIMAN]

LANCICIUS, NICHOLAS, VEN. (LECZYCKY; 1574–1653), Jesuit writer and administrator. Born in Vilna to Calvinist parents, in his youth L. became a scholar in Greek and Hebrew studies. In 1590, he converted to Catholicism and in 1592 entered the Jesuit novitiate at Cracow. Later in that same year he began his studies at the Jesuit college in Rome. After his ordination (1601), he assisted N. Orlandini in the compilation of a history of the Society. Orlandini died in 1606 and L. was assigned to Cracow the following year. He taught theology at Lwów and then in 1621 became rector of the college at Cracow. In 1630, L. was appointed provincial in Lithuania, a post he held for 5 years. Following this he instructed young Jesuits at Gitschin (1637–40) and at Neswiesz (1643–49). He spent his last years teaching at the college of Braunsberg (Prussia). In addition to the work he contributed to Orlandini's *Historia societatis Iesu*, L. wrote *Gloria s. Ignatii fundatoris*. He also wrote many works on the individual's search for spiritual progress, the best known of which is *De indiciis et gradibus profectus in virtutibus* (1641). BIBLIOGRAPHY: A. Massimini, *Study of the Antinomy of Humility and Self-Esteem according to the Writings of N. Lancicius* (1963); A. Liuima, DSAM 9:180–186; P. Bernard, DTC 8:2556–57.

[R. J. BRADY]

LAND REFORM, in the cause of social and economic justice, the more equitable and fruitful distribution and use of the land for cultivation. Vatican Council II reiterated the general principle of Catholic social teaching that private ownership of property by its nature has a social quality, deriving from the law of the communal purposes of earthly goods (Vat II ChModWorld 71). The Council applies this norm to the abuses of ownership by those who in underdeveloped areas either maintain huge estates that are left fallow for personal profit or who use tenant farmers in a manner equivalent to serfdom. The Council states flatly that "insufficiently cultivated estates should be distributed to those who can make these lands fruitful" (*ibid.*). Respect for the right of legitimate ownership calls for compensation when such distribution is carried out; but social justice requires that the more equitable distribution actually be carried out. The issue of agrarian reform is not new; Gladstone's government fell over the issue in Britain's policy towards Ireland, agrarian reform was central in the Russian and Chinese revolutions. The Church's direct and concrete involvement in the cause of land reform is, however, if not new, at least more explicit and emphatic as part of its espoused ministry of justice and peace. Land reform is an issue in the developing countries of the Third World; in Latin America it is an esp. burning issue for the Church. Since Vatican II the Latin American bps. and leaders, both clerical and lay, have clearly championed the cause of social justice and taken the side of the poor and deprived. There have been efforts to resist exploitation of Indian lands and to secure fairer distribution of land to the people. Because the right of private property is at stake, land reform has been equated by some as evidence of Marxism. There are Marxist influences on Christian thinking in Latin America and elsewhere; in some forms of liberation theology these influences are quite explicit. But land reform itself is not a proprietary teaching of Marxism; it is a matter of social justice, a cause to which the Church of today has dedicated its teaching and its action.

[T. C. O'BRIEN]

LANDA, DIEGO DE (1524–79), Spanish Franciscan missionary. In 1541 he joined the Franciscans and in 1549 went to Yucatán under the leadership of Nicolas Abalate. When the Franciscan general chapter made Yucatán a separate province, L. became the first provincial in 1561. Since there was no bp. present in Yucatán, L. as provincial was the chief ecclesiastical authority in the land and as such began an Inquisition in 1562 concerning the renewal of idolatry among the Mayan Indians. This investigation was marked by much inhumane conduct toward Mayan prisoners and was condemned by Francisco Toral, who was consecrated bp. of Yucatán in the latter part of 1562. Toral ended the Inquisition and charged that L. had exceeded his authority in conducting such an investigation. L. sailed for Spain in 1564 and in 1565 argued his case before Pedro de Bobadilla, provincial of Castile. He contended that various papal bulls granted provincials a wide range of powers, among them the authority to undertake religious investigations. In 1569, Bobadilla's successor, Antonio de Córdoba, found him innocent and in 1571, L. was named bp. of Yucatán. He arrived in Mexico in 1573 and died in Mérida. While in Spain in 1566, L. wrote his *Relación de las cosas de Yucatán,* which contained invaluable information on all aspects of Mayan culture. This work remained unknown until Abbé Brasseur de Bourbourg discovered it in Madrid in 1684. BIBLIOGRAPHY: D. de Landa, *Relación de las Coasas de Yucatan* (tr. A. Tozzer, 1941); F. Scholes and R. Roys, "Fray D. De Landa and the Problem of Idolatry in Yucatán," *Cooperation in Research* (Carnegie Inst. of Washington, 1938).

[R. J. BRADY]

LANDELIN, SS. (1) **St. Landelin of Ettenheim** (7th-8th cent.), missionary, hermit, and martyr about whom little is known. He settled in the Black Forest region, where he lived an eremitical life. An account of his life written between the 10th and 12 cent. tells the story that hunters in the area confronted him one day, alleging that he was destroying their hunting grounds and thereupon killed him. On the site where St. Landelin had built a small monastery—probably the first one in that area—Bp. Eddon of Strasbourg founded the abbey of Ettenheim, where the memory of St. Landelin has been kept alive. His tomb at Ettenheimmünster continues to attract many pilgrims, and even today numerous miracles are attributed to him.

(2) **St. Landelin** (*c.*625–*c.*686), abbot. He was born at Vaux of noble Frankish parents who left him in the care of St. Autbertus, bp. of Cambrai. In his youth L. was influenced by evil companionship but later repented and returned to the bishop. His renewed spiritual life drew many followers. This small group of disciples led him to establish the abbey of Lobbes and later on, that of St. Crespin. BIBLIOGRAPHY: M. C. Celletti and A. D'Haenens, BiblSanct 7:1090–91; P. Rouillard, *Catholicisme* 6:1760–61.

[R. A. TODD]

LANDÉVENNEC, ABBEY OF, a monastery founded *c.*480 in the Diocese of Quimper (Finistère, France) by St. Guénolé, its first abbot, on a piece of land situated on the estuary of the Aulne. The monastery adopted the Benedictine Rule in 818, but was abandoned from *c.*878 to 935 by the monks, who had fled in fear of the Normans. In the second half of the 11th cent. the abbey church was rebuilt. The abbey fell into decay from 1350 to 1600 and was frequently sacked and looted. When Abbot Jean Brient (1608–30) arrived, he found only two monks at Landévennec. He restored the monastery and imposed on it the statutes of Chezal-Benoît (1614). These were soon replaced by the reform of Dom Noël Mars, founder of the Society of Brittany (1617), which was absorbed by the Congregation of Saint Maur in 1632. In the 18th cent. all the monks were among the "appellants" of the bull *Unigenitus.* Suppressed during the Revolution, the monastery was restored in 1958 by the monks of Kerbénéat, and the first stone of the new abbey church was blessed in 1962. The abbey in the late 1960s had about 45 monks. Some ruins of the church (11th cent.), of the cloisters, and of the palace (1630) are still standing. BIBLIOGRAPHY: Cottineau, 1:1549–50; G. Ollivier, NCE 8:358–359; R. Gazeau, *Catholicisme* 6:1762–64.

[J. DAOUST]

LANDGRAF, ARTUR MICHAEL (1895–1958), bp. and historian. He studied at Eichstätt, Innsbruck, and Rome. Ordained in 1918, he taught in Bamberg, lectured at The Catholic Univ. of America (1929, 1937–1939), and became Bamberg's auxiliary bp. (1943) and cathedral dean (1950). L. won acclaim for studies and critical editions, esp. in the history of medieval theology. BIBLIOGRAPHY: L. Ott, LTK 7:775–776; F. Dressler, NCE 8:359; H. Chirat, *Catholicisme* 6:1764–65.

[R. I. BURNS]

LANDINI, FRANCESCO (Landino; 1325–97), Italian composer, virtuoso organist, and instrumentalist. Blind from childhood, he was famous in Florence for his poetry and his public performances on the portable organ. His dance songs, madrigals, and a spirited *caccia,* mark the peak of Italian *ars nova* music, a style of which he was one of the most famous Florentine masters.

[R. J. LITZ]

LANDÍVAR, RAFAEL (1731–93), Guatemalan Jesuit poet. Born in what is now Santiago de los Caballeros, L. attended the Univ. of San Carlos and entered the Society at Tepotzotlán near Mexico City. He was rector and teacher of rhetoric at the seminary in Guatemala. During his exile he lived with other Jesuits at Bologna, Italy, where he died. L. is best known for his *Rusticatio mexicana,* a poem of 5,000 Latin hexameters published in 1781. It describes the landscape, animal life, and agriculture of Mexico along with the customs of its people. The merits of his poem placed L. in the front rank of Latin-American writers; his name has been given to the new Catholic Univ. of Guatemala. BIBLIOGRAPHY: *Rusticatio mexicana: Mexican Country Scenes* (ed. and tr. G. W. Regenos, 1948); C. Testore, EncCatt 7:885; Sommervogel 4:1456–57.

[P. DAMBORIENA]

LANDMARKISM, a Baptist movement that stressed the independence of local churches, denied that the NT refers to a universal Church, and claimed that the Baptist Church is the only true Church. It originated in Nashville, Tenn., in 1850 with James B. Graves and James M. Pendleton. Of signifance in understanding the movement is the individualism of the frontier and the fact that in the same period arose Old-School Presbyterians and Baptists, high-church Episcopalians, and German Reformed and Lutheran movements, which sought to counteract the tendency in *revivalism to water down theological distinctions of particular denominations. The movement took its name from Pendleton's *An Old Landmark Reset* (1854). Believing that a succession of properly baptized persons is essential to a true gospel ministry, the Landmarkists maintained that there had been an unbroken succession of Baptist churches, practicing *believer's baptism by immersion, since the time of Christ. Since Baptists alone had such a succession, all baptism by others was held to be invalid; there could be no other gospel Church; and theirs was the only valid ministry. Exchanging pulpits with non-Baptists was condemned, and communion was restricted to the members of each particular congregation (see OPEN COMMUNION). Graves publicly attacked the Methodists in *The Great Iron Wheel* (1856) and the Presbyterians in *The Tri-lemma: or Death by Three Horns* (1860). His comprehensive statement of Landmarkist principles was *Old Landmarkism: What Is It?* (1880). Separately organized in 1905 as the Baptist General Association (since 1924, American Baptist Association), the movement had widespread influence on other Baptists, especially in the South. BIBLIOGRAPHY: R. G. Torbet, "Landmarkism," *Baptist Concepts of the Church* (ed. W. S. Hudson, 1959).

[N. H. MARING]

LANDO (d. 914), **POPE** for about 6 months from mid-913. Little is known of him apart from the fact of his brief occupation of the Chair of Peter at a time when the papacy was under the control of the family of *Theophylactus. It is conjectured that he was the instrument of that family. Nothing is recorded of his acts. BIBLIOGRAPHY: Mann 4:147; P. J. Mullins, NCE 8:360.

[P. F. MULHERN]

LANDOALD, ST. (d. 668), missionary priest of Lombard parentage, commissioned along with others by Pope St. Martin I, to assist with the evangelizing of the territory now known as Holland and Belgium. L.'s missionary activities centered at Wintershoven, where he built a church, dedicated by St. Remaclus (*c.*659), supposedly a monastic bp. in that area. The small community at Wintershoven was frequently supported by royal gifts from Childeric II, King of Austrasia. L.'s remains were transferred to Ghent in 980. BIBLIOGRAPHY: BiblSanct 7:1095–96.

[R. A. TODD]

LANDOWSKI, PAUL MAXIMILIEN (1875–1961), French sculptor who effected monumental, linear works. He is best known for the large statue of Christ in Rio de Janeiro Harbor (1931).

[M. J. DALY]

LANDRY (LANDRICH), SS. Two saints bore this name. (1) L., bp. of Paris (650–657), according to tradition is credited with great concern for the poor during the famine of 651 and with the foundation of Paris's first real hospital, later the famous Hôtel-Dieu. (2) L. (d. 690?), abbot of Soignies (Belgium) and of Hautmont (France), and a missionary in the region of Brussels. BIBLIOGRAPHY: G. Mathon, BiblSanct 7:1092–93; P. Rouillard, *Catholicisme* 6:1770–71.

[G. M. COOK]

LANDSHUT: HEILIG-GEIST-SPITALKIRCHE, 15-cent. German church and greatest work of H. Stethaimer. It is noted for elegant proportions and rich ornament comparable to the work of the Parler school in Bohemia.

[M. J. DALY]

LANDULF OF ÉVREUX, ST. (*c.*614), bishop. Very little is known about the saint beyond the fact that he became bp. of Évreux *c.*600 and found the body of St. Taurinus, in whose honor he erected a basilica. The veneration of Landulf is a predominantly local cult. BIBLIOGRAPHY: H. Platelle, BiblSanct 7:1096.

[H. DRESSLER]

LANE, RAYMOND ALOYSIUS (1894–1974), Maryknoll Missioner and bishop. In 1913 when the American Society for Foreign Missions was in its first stages, L. joined the group, which was later to be known as Maryknoll Missioners. Ordained in 1920, he spent most of his life on the missions of Manchuria. Just before the outbreak of World War II he was consecrated vicar apostolic of Fushun. Taken prisoner by the Japanese he spent almost 4 years in various internment camps. In 1946 he was elected superior general of the Maryknoll Missioners; his term—until 1954—was one of expansion in Formosa, East Africa, and in the U.S. BIBLIOGRAPHY: R. Lane, *Early Days of Maryknoll* (1951).

[J. R. AHERNE]

LANFRANC (*c.* 1005–89), abp. of Canterbury. A native of Pavia in Italy, and educated there in civil law, L. went to Tours to study dialectics and theology, and in 1039 opened his own school at Avranches in Normandy. He entered the Benedictine abbey of Bec in 1042, and became head of the monastic school that had an important influence on the growth of scholasticism; St. Anselm of Canterbury was one of L.'s students. L.'s theological writing included a defense of the Real Presence against the symbolic interpretation of Berengarius of Tours. Excelling in dialectics, L. nevertheless reproached Anselm for arguing theologically without the use of Scripture. L. became the adviser of William Duke of Normandy, who made him abbot of St. Stephen at Caen (1063) and who, as William I of England, the Conqueror, had him consecrated abp. of Canterbury (1070). In this office L. revitalized English ecclesiastical and monastic life through the reform measures of Gregory VII. BIBLIOGRAPHY: B. W. Scholz, NCE 8:361–362; G. Mathon, *Catholicisme* 6:1775–78.

[T. C. O'BRIEN]

LANFRANCO, GIOVANNI (1582–1647), Italian painter in Parmaand Rome, combining the influences of Annibale Carracci and Correggio in a lyrical *Magdalen* (1605) and a later monumental fresco, *Joseph Interpreting Dreams*. In the cupola of S. Andrea della Valle (1625–28) and that of the Cappella di S. Gennaro (1641–43) L. introduced the baroque to Rome and Naples respectively.

[M. J. DALY]

LANG, ANDREAS (*c.*1450–1502), Benedictine abbot of Michelsberg in Bavaria. L. revitalized religious observance in his abbey and reorganized the administration of its temporalities. The abbot is esp. known for having gathered materials for the history of his abbey and of the diocese of Bamberg, and for the lives of Benedictine saints. BIBLIOGRAPHY: F. Dressler, LTK 6:782.

[H. DRESSLER]

LANG, ANDREW (1844–1912), Scottish-born folklorist, anthropologist. A journalist by choice he made numerous contributions to the study of mythology as folklore. His works were often controversial because his era was one in which the framework of studies in these areas was rigidly evolutionary. He maintained a defense of the monotheistic tradition among primitive peoples and defended the authenticity of Genesis and its miraculous events. Not always thorough in his scholarship, he was nevertheless courageous in affirming views which supported orthodox Christianity. A prolific writer, he wrote fairy tales, biography, history, did important translations of Greek classics, including the *Iliad* and *Odyssey*. His best works, however, are in the field of folklore and myth, beginning with a pioneering article "Mythology and Fairy Tales" in the *Fortnightly Review,* (1873). This was followed by *Myth, Ritual and Religion* (1887) and *Making of Religion* (1898).

[J. R. AHERNE]

LANG, MATTHÄUS (1468–1540), imperial diplomat and cardinal. Son of an Augsburg burgher, L. studied law at Tübingen and followed a chancery career. He became the most trusted and influential adviser of Emperor Maximilian I, participated in negotiations leading to the League of Cambrai against Venice in 1508, and helped to draw up an alliance between the Emperor and Pope Julius II (1512). At this time Lang was created cardinal and accredited to the Fifth Lateran Council. He was ordained and consecrated only after being named abp. of Salzburg in 1519. L. resisted the Lutheran Reformation while striving to reform the Church in his jurisdiction. He was a friend of humanists and a patron of the arts.

[J. E. LYNCH]

LANGDON, JOHN (d. 1434). Benedictine monk, bp. of Rochester (1421–34), royal councilor (1422). On a university commission to examine the errors of Wycliffe (1411), and later on heresy trials, he was appointed English envoy to the Council of Basel (1432) and Constance (1434), but it is unlikely that he attended either. BIBLIOGRAPHY: Emden Ox 2:1093–94.

[C. D. ROSS]

LANGGÄSSER, ELISABETH (1899–1950), German poet and novelist. A convert to Catholicism, half Jewish by blood, L. was harassed by the Nazi government from 1936. Under the influence of surrealism she developed a narrative style saturated with natural mysticism. She was fascinated by the mystical and quasi-magical and wrote powerfully of the demonic powers that drive men to salvation or damnation. BIBLIOGRAPHY: J. Bourgeois, NCE 8:364–365; J. Ancelet-Hustache, *Catholicisme* 6:1790.

[I. MERKEL]

LANGLAND, WILLIAM (*c.* 1322–*c.* 1392), generally held to be the author of all three versions of **Piers Plowman*. L. was born in Ledbury, Herefordshire; he lived in London. He was in minor orders, was married, and earned a meager living singing the Office of the Dead for wealthy patrons. No respecter of persons, L. dressed like a beggar, brooded all his life on man's relationship to God, and kept on writing and rewriting his great poem—the A text in his youth, the B in middle age, and the C when he was 65. See bibliog. for *Piers Plowman*.

[M. O'CONNOR]

LANGRES, COUNCILS OF. Langres in NE France was the site of provincial synods in the 9th and 12th centuries. One such council held in 830 is mentioned in a donation charter. BIBLIOGRAPHY: R. Kay, NCE 8:365.

[B. L. MARTHALER]

LANGTON, STEPHEN, see STEPHEN LANGTON.

LANGUAGE, LITURGICAL, the language used by a religious group for its cultic acts (see CULT). The type of language used generally reflects basic attitudes toward the meaning of *religion itself, i.e., the relationship between the *sacred and *profane, the place of *tradition, and the use of *magic. In many religions, the desire to establish a distinct realm for all hieratic forms contributes to significant differences between the vernacular and liturgical language, even when the same language is used for both the sacred and profane spheres. Thus liturgical language employs older, even archaic, constructions and vocabulary; it avoids slang and idiomatic phrases in favor of more conservative modes of expression, even though they often become elaborate and ornate. Frequently it is the language of the religion's scriptures, its sacred texts; and it preserves the religious heritage of an exiled or conquered or scattered people. Quite often the liturgical books of a religion date from the time of its most intense vitality and tend to remain stable even in the midst of succeeding changes in the secular tongue. Such cultic languages as biblical Hebrew, Vedic Sanskrit, Homeric and patristic Greek as well as Koinē, Latin, Syriac, Coptic and Ethiopic, the German of Martin Luther, Armenian, Old Slavic, and Georgian are all distinguished from the profane languages of the contemporary practitioners of the religion and reflect each cult's origins and traditions. In those religions that stress magic in their cultic rites, the liturgical language is intentionally elaborate and often incomprehensible. Sacred languages can be misused as curses or preserved in imperfect form as oracular pronouncements.

The history of liturgical language in Christianity is quite varied. The first Christians used vernacular *Aramaic in their worship and did not attempt to impose it upon later Greek-speaking Christian communities who used the common, or *Koinē Greek. This seems to have been the custom throughout the East: where there was a sufficiently developed vernacular, no effort was made to establish a uniform cultic practice. By *c.*370, the above considerations prompted the change from Greek to Latin in the West. There were several reasons for this: Latin's unique status as the language of culture and learning throughout the West; the underdeveloped dialects of the barbaric peoples; the stylistic beauty of liturgical Latin; the later emphasis on tradition, sacramental efficacy **ex opere operato*, and a common language as a sign of ecclesial unity. The 16th-cent. Reformers, however, formulated their liturgical services in the vernacular to avoid the "magicism" and clerically oriented liturgies which they believed to be present in RC worship. Vat II SacLit inaugurated decisive changes in RC liturgical language. In accordance with the principle that liturgical texts should express clearly the holy things that they signify so that the Christian people might easily understand and participate in them, an extended use of the vernacular was permitted. Subsequent decisions of territorial episcopal bodies have, as a general rule, authorized the vernacular throughout the liturgy. BIBLIOGRAPHY: E. Cassirer, *Language and Myth* (tr. S. Langer, 1946); A. De Marco, *Rome and the Vernacular* (1961); C. Korolevsky, *Living Languages in Catholic Worship* (ed. and tr. D. Attwater, 1957); D. B. Stevick, *Language in Worship: Reflections on a Crisis* (1970).

[T. M. MCFADDEN: R. J. LITZ]

LANGUEDOC, CHURCHES OF. Under the counts of Toulouse (11th and 12th centuries), Languedoc in SW France, on the pilgrimage routes from Arles and Le Puy to Santiago de Compostela, boasted important churches and beautiful abbeys: Ste. Foy Conques, St. Sernin, Toulouse, Beaulieu-sur-Dordogne. With Burgundy, Languedoc was a most important school of French Romanesque sculpture with significant and impressive portals and cloisters at Moissac and Souillac.

[M. J. DALY]

LANIGAN, JOHN (1758–1828), Irish church historian, his chief work being *An Ecclesiastical History of Ireland from the Introduction of Christianity among the Irish to the Beginning of the Thirteenth Century* (4 v., 1822). Because he had been something of a protégé of P. *Tamburini while a professor of theology at Pavia, L. was barred by the bp. of Cork from seminary appointments in both Cork and

Maynooth. L. had in fact refused to take part in the Jansenist Synod of *Pistoia, but was accused, unjustly it is thought, of being a Jansenist. He succeeded in obtaining an appointment as assistant librarian of the Royal Dublin Society and spent his life writing on Scripture and theology as well as on history. In the last years of his life he suffered a mental breakdown.

[J. R. AHERNE]

LANSPERGIUS, JOHANNES JUSTUS (1490–1539), Carthusian writer on ascetical and mystical theology. A leading member of the Charterhouse of St. Barbara at Cologne, he preached the love of Christ as the only way of combatting the evils against which the Reformation was directed. L. wrote, preached, and was spiritual director for both the learned and the simple. His *Omnia opera* were published in a modern edition in 1890. He was important to the theology of and the spread of devotion to the Sacred Heart.

[P. J. HENNESSEY]

LANTERI, PIO BRUNONE (1759–1830), Italian religious founder. Ordained *c.* 1782, he devoted himself to apostolic work in Turin, associating himself with Amicizia Cristiana, an organization which emulated the secret activity of the Freemasons but on behalf of Catholicism. L. had great influence on students, soldiers, and workers and has been called the precursor of Italian Catholic Action. In 1815 he cofounded a congregation of priests, the Oblates of the Virgin Mary. His cause was introduced in Rome in 1952.

BIBLIOGRAPHY: P. Frutaz, EncCatt 7:897–898.

[J. R. AHERNE]

LANTERN OF TODAIJI, NARA (8th cent.), bronze octagonal lantern in front of the Great Buddha Hall, with 8 panels in shallow relief showing flowers and musician-bodhisattvas in the style of T'ang China. The lighting of lanterns was a penitential act.

[M. J. DALY]

LANTERNE DES MORTS, a small stone tower in the French graveyard of the 11th and 12th cent., holding a lamp lit at evening for the dead.

[M. J. DALY]

LANTRUA, GIOVANNI OF TRIORA, BL. (1760–1816), Italian Franciscan martyr. A Franciscan from 1777 and ordained in 1784, after working in various houses of his order in Italy he went to China in 1800. He labored on the missions in the provinces of Hupeh, Hunan, and Kiangsi. In 1815 he was arrested and after 6 months in prison was executed by strangulation. He was beatified in 1900.

[J. R. AHERNE]

LAO TZU, ancient Chinese sage of dubious historicity; also the title of a work purportedly written by that sage which by the 2d cent. A.D. came to be known as the Tao-te Ching. The view that Lao Tzu was a late contemporary of Confucius (551–479 B.C.) is based on Ssu-ma Ch'ien's *Shih chi* (1st cent. A.D.), China's earliest general history, in which a meeting between Confucius and Lao Tzu is narrated. Such stories however were of a popular genre, describing encounters between Confucius and hermits, and are not historical. The name Lao Tzu (Old Man) was often given to 4th and 3rd cent. B.C. anthologies of wise sayings collected by members of particular schools of thought. *Lao Tzu* is an anthology compiled by one or more persons with passages that reflect the common Taoist views of different schools. Some are associated with the Chi Hsia of *c.*350–250 B.C. when the work was gathered; they are presented without identification of sages or schools in the text itself. The work, often referred to as "the book of 5000 characters," has 81 chapters divided into two books of 37 and 34 chapters at some point before the late 2d cent. A.D. Tao, which is usually translated as "way," a concept fundamental to all branches of early Chinese thought, is pointed to in the *Lao Tzu* but never named or defined, "for Tao that can be named or defined is not really Tao." Yet it is apparent that it is Tao that provides metaphysical support for the universe it produced. In *Lao Tzu* Tao replaces the concept of *t'ien,* Heaven, as creator, the term found in other philosophies of the Warring States Period (480–222 B.C.). Opposite attributes, e.g., strong and weak, are simultaneously applied to Tao, since Tao expresses all forces in the universe. All should model their lives on the Tao. There is a politico-moral emphasis about the *Lao Tzu*: the principles of submission and noncontention provide a practical means of survival for common folk during that turbulent, violent era. A ruler who lives the Tao will govern little, keeping his hands off the State, keeping his subjects ignorant while satisfying all their basic human needs, and the people in turn ought to become childlike. The *Lao Tzu* has had continued philosophical and religious influence ever since its compilation. The Wang Pi version is the standard Chinese text, and Chiang Hsi-ch'ang's *Lao tzu chiao ku* (1937) remains the most convenient reference for variant readings. New translations and commentaries are still being written, D. C. Lau's (1963) being the best recent English version.

[R. J. LITZ]

LAODICEA, modern Eskihisar, an important city of ancient Phrygia in W central Asia-Minor. It already had a large Jewish colony when a Christian community was established there by Epaphras and Nymphas (Col 1.7; 4.12ff). Paul wrote a letter for these Laodiceans, which was either lost or is identical with that to the Ephesians. At an unknown date (betw. 343 and 381), a synod in Laodicea enacted some 60 canons, which were circulated in all Churches, repeated by ecumenical councils, and thereby exerted a great influence on the subsequent development of discipline and liturgy. Among matters decreed by these canons are: admission of the remarried to the sacraments (c. 1); exclusion of neophytes from ordination (c. 3); exclusion of catechumens from ordination rites (c. 5); total separation from heretics and Jews in regard to marriages or ritual, prohibition of clerics from unbecoming professions or entertainment; and exclusion of the appointment of women "presiders" (*presbytides*, c. 11); prohibition of lay appointment of priests (c. 12); prohibition of sending the Eucharist to other places (c. 14); determination of the rights of clerics and prohibition of holding agapes in churches or sleeping there (c. 28); prohibition against exaggerated worship of angels (c. 35); mandatory attendance of bps. at synods (c. 40); required permission of bps. for clerics to travel (c. 41); barring of women from the altar (c. 44); replacement of chorbishops by *periodeuts,* circuit superiors (c. 57); proscription of marriages during Lent (c. 52); determination of the OT and NT canon, but with omission of Rev (c. 60).

[V. J. POSPISHIL]

LAODICEANS, EPISTLE TO THE, see APOCRYPHA (NT), 31.

LAON, CATHEDRAL OF (*c.*1150–1205), French church of inspiring silhouette with its seven "mystic" towers—pairs at the W front and transepts and one at the crossing, decorated with magnificent forms of oxen, beasts which hauled the stones for building. At Laon the early Gothic architect timidly eschewed the solid Romanesque plan for a sweeping uninterrupted interior space W to E, and reflected the interior in divisions of the façade with deep embrasures of doorway and windows—and open towers—the Gothic reduction of mass for framed voids. Laon influenced the Cathedral of Notre-Dame in Paris and its deeply set W porches determined the transept porches at Chartres. Sculpture at Laon destroyed in the French Revolution was restored in the 19th cent., yet much rich original carving from the 12th and 13th cent. remains. With Chartres and Paris, the mid-12th-cent. School of Laon surpassed others in theology and dialectics. E. Panofsky identifies the extended *disputatio* of dialectics with the open *manifestatio* of the "new Gothic" structures, in *Gothic Architecture and Scholasticism* (1951).

[M. J. DALY]

LAOS, a monarchy in SE Asia (91,429 sq, mi.; pop. [UN est. 1971] 3,030,000, formerly part of French Indochina. Laotians belong to three racial groups: Thai, Idonesian, and Chinese. Official languages are Lao and French. Originally tribal, Laos was unified in the 16th cent., became a French protectorate in 1893, achieved independence as a constitutional monarchy within France in 1947, and gained full independence in 1954. Since then the pro-Communist Pathet Lao faction has been active. More than 85% of the Laotians are Buddhists, whereas the mountain tribes adhere to animism. The Jesuit Father Liera reached Laos about 1630. Later, Bp. Pallou, the first vicar apostolic of Siam, sent several missioners, but with no success. In the 19th cent. a more systematic mission was launched from Siam. A pronounced interest in Christianity developed at the end of the cent. but lack of missionary personnel prevented its being exploited. Laos and Thailand together became a vicariate apostolic in 1899. The N of Laos was opened to missioners in 1929. Ten years later evangelization there was entrusted to Oblates. Now there are vicariates in Luang Prabang, Thakkek, and Vientiane. Catholics number 32,303 (almost all foreign), cared for by 85 priests and 90 religious, but persecution in the N has resulted in the death of several priests. Protestantism has been represented for more than 50 years by Swiss Christians in Many Lands and by the Christian and Missionary Alliance, but it counts only a few hundred members. BIBLIOGRAPHY: J. Guennou, NCE 8:381–382; T. A. Dooley, *Dr. Tom Dooley's Three Great Books* (1960).

[P. DAMBORIENA]

LAPIDARY, pertaining precisely to the cutting of gems, it also refers to medieval books, supplements to bestiaries containing allegorical interpretations of various precious stones.

[M. J. DALY]

LAPIDE, CORNELIUS A (1567–1637), Flemish Jesuit exegete, a professor first at Louvain (1596–1616), then at Rome (1616–36). Between 1614 and 1645 he published commentaries on every book of the Bible except Job and Psalms. His most famous work is the *Commentaria in omnes Divi Pauli Epistolas* (1614). A scholar well-versed in the classical philosophers, his thought seems to have been esp. influenced by Aristotle. He had a thorough knowledge of the original languages of Scripture. In his interpretations he drew heavily on the Fathers, and he often expounds not only the *literal sense, but the *spiritual senses as well. He also shows a lively awareness of the special problems of his own time. His commentaries were regarded as standard reference works by Catholics well into the 19th century. BIBLIOGRAPHY: J. Schmid, LTK 3:58.

[D. J. BOURKE]

LAPINI, ANNA MARIA (1809–60), foundress of the Poor Daughters of the Holy Stigmata of St. Francis (Stigmatine Sisters). After enduring 9 years of matrimonial unhappiness, she was widowed (1844) and enabled to realize her premarital desire to become a religious. Founding her own community in her native Florence (1848), she devoted her efforts to the education of poor and homeless girls. However, suffering followed her in her new life in the form of physical ills and hostility. Her beatification process began in 1918.

[H. P. ANNAS]

LAPLACE, PIERRE SIMON DE (1749–1827), French theoretical astronomer and mathematician. His systematic presentation of celestial mechanics, *Traité de mécanique céleste* (4 v., 1799–1805; 5th v., 1825; Eng. tr. N. Bowditch, 1829–39), is the classic statement of Newtonian astronomy, refined and clarified. It provided further support for the deistic notion of God as creator-architect who set the heavens in order and motion and then left them alone. All perturbations in orbit were periodic and would correct themselves with time, the average path remaining constant. In his *Exposition du système du monde* (1796), L. presented a nebular hypothesis for the formation of the earth's solar system—whirling orbiting gases gradually condensing into rotating planetary bodies. His numerous contributions to astronomy, pure and applied mathematics, and physics include: an analytical theory of probability (1812), the Laplace equation still used in mathematical physics; theoretical treatment of questions of planetary- and moon-satellite formation and movement. Honored in his own time by his peers and admirers in science, university, and government, he was named a member of the Académie Française (1816), a rare honor for a scientist.

[R. J. LITZ]

LAPSED CATHOLICS, those who, while presumably not rejecting the faith (see APOSTASY), have fallen away from the practice of their religion, particularly from attendance at Mass and fulfillment of the Easter precept of at least annual reception of the sacraments. The number of nonpracticing Catholics, judged on the basis of a drop in Sunday Mass attendance, has increased during the 1970s.

[T. C. O'BRIEN]

LAPSI (Lat., those who have fallen or failed), description applied to Christians who apostatized under the persecution of Decius (249–251). Some offered incense in pagan rites (the *thurificati*), some sacrificed to the Roman gods (the *sacrificati*). The question of reconciling the numerous *lapsi* was the occasion of the *Novatianist schism, which in turn raised the *rebaptism issue. Cyprian of Carthage (d. 258) received the *lapsi* back into communion after due signs of repentance. Novatianists insisted that the *lapsi* be excluded from communion. *LIBELLATICI.

[T. C. O'BRIEN]

LA PUENTE, LUIS DE, VEN. (1554–1624), Jesuit. L. was born at Valladolid, Spain. He received a bachelor's degree from the Univ. of Valladolid (1572) and studied theology at the Dominican college of St. Gregory. In 1574 L. entered the Jesuit novitiate at Medina del Campo. From 1576–78 he studied under Francisco Suárez and in 1579 he first met Baltasar Alvarez. L. was ordained in 1580. He taught philosophy at the college of León (1582–85) and then served as master of novices at Villagarcia (1585–89). He was chaplain at Salamanca (1590) and Valladolid (1591) master of novices at Medina (1592–93), rector of the Univ. of Valladolid (1594–96), and chaplain once again at Salamanca (1596–99). In 1601 he was reappointed rector of Valladolid but resigned in 1602 because of poor health. During the remaining years of his life he served several colleges as a visiting lecturer. L. was declared venerable by Clement XIII in 1759.

As a spiritual writer of the first order L. grounded all his work on a thorough knowledge of Scripture, the writings of SS. Gregory, Basil, John Chrysostom, and Thomas Aquinas. In 1605 L. published perhaps his most important work, *Meditaciones de los misterios de nuestra santa fe,* a study of the life of Christ and meditations on divine perfection. In 1609 he wrote *La Guia espiritual,* a study of prayer and contemplation. From 1612–16 he published the *Tradato de la perfección en todos los estados de la vida del cristiano,* which describes the attainment of perfection in the various states of life (laity, religious, priesthood). L. wrote a life of B. Alvarez (1615) and an explanation of the Canticle of Canticles. BIBLIOGRAPHY: M. Nicolau, DSAM. 9:265–276; A. Fonck, DTC 13:1159–61.

[R. J. BRADY]

LARDNER, NATHANIEL (1684–1768), English Protestant preacher and apologete. He refused Presbyterian ordination and became an *Independent minister in Leyden in 1709. He served as a private chaplain and preacher in England, in spite of recurrent illness and worsening deafness. His chief publication was a richly documented defense of the Gospels, *Credibility of Gospel History,* consisting of 14 volumes and a three-volume supplement (1727–57).

[J. R. AHERNE]

LARES, benevolent gods, protectors of the Roman family, household, public buildings, and state to whom offerings were made daily and on festivals. The small niche or shrine for the *lares* in the Roman house was termed the *lararium.*

[M. J. DALY]

LARIVEY, PIERRE DE (*c.* 1540–1619), French comic dramatist and canon of Saint-Étienne de Troyes. His free translations of Italian comedies influenced the development of French comedy and esp. of *Molière. His other translations include *Les Facétieuses nuits* by Straparoa (1572); Alessandro Piccolomini's *La Philosophie et institution morale* (1580); and Aretino's *L'Humanité de Jésus-Christ* (1604). BIBLIOGRAPHY: L. Morin, *Les Trois Pierre de Larivey: biographie et bibliographie* (1937).

[R. N. NICOLICH]

LA ROCHE, ALAN DE, see ALAN DE LA ROCHE.

LA ROCHEFOUCAULD, FRANÇOIS DE (1613–80), French moralist and writer. Descended from an illustrious noble family who, after embracing the Protestant cause during the French religious wars, had converted to Catholicism. L. participated actively on the rebel side in the Fronde, of which he gives an account in his *Mémoires* (1662). His *Maximes,* originally entitled *Réflexions ou sentences et maximes morales* (1665), for which he is best known, are classic examples of the intensely concise, impersonal French epigram. However, L.'s pessimistic and cynical view of man is ascribed, in part, to Jansenistic influences: his key word, *amour-propre,* as used in Mme. de Sablés salon where he discussed his *Maximes,* had acquired definite theological overtones through Jansen's *Augustinus* and the Port-Royal moralists who opposed the secular Cornelian ethic of "glory." BIBLIOGRAPHY: M. Bishop, *Life and Adventures of La Rochefoucauld* (1957); A. Levi, *French Moralists: Theory of the Passions, 1585 to 1649* (1964) ch. 7–8. *CORNEILLE, PIERRE; *JANSENISM.

[R. N. NICOLICH]

LA ROCHELLE, CONFESSION OF, another name for the *Gallican Confession, used because it was revised and adopted in La Rochelle in 1571 at the seventh national synod of the *Reformed Church in France.

[T. C. O'BRIEN]

LARRAGO, FRANCISCO (d. 1723), Spanish Dominican moralist, author of a compendium on moral topics, a modern edition of which was published in 1919; his *Panégyrique de Ste. Catherine de Sienne* (1697) is a treatise on the spiritual life.

[T. C. O'BRIEN]

LARRAÍN, GANDARILLAS, JOAQUÍN (1822–97), Chilean churchman and educator. L. was named rector of the seminary of Santiago where he introduced the new programs he had observed during a European tour. He founded the *Revista Católica* and became a staunch defender of religious uniformity in Chile. L. devoted much time and money to the foundation of the Catholic Univ. at Santiago and became its first president. He took no salary for his work, and much of his personal fortune was spent in helping educate young men from poor families. Toward the end of his life L. was made a bishop. BIBLIOGRAPHY: A. M. Escudero, NCE 8:387.

[P. DAMBORIENA]

LARRAÑAGA, DÁMASO ANTONIO (1771–1848), Uruguayan churchman and patriot. He had been destined for medical studies, but preferring theology, he studied at the seminaries of Córdova and Buenos Aires and was ordained at Rio de Janeiro. L. sided with the revolutionary movement in Buenos Aires in 1810 and was expelled by the Spaniards. But, after the victory, he was made a member of the congress. In 1818 he was named vicar apostolic and distinguished himself with his charitable works. He advocated the restriction of the death penalty and the abolition of slavery. His knowledge in the fields of botany, zoology, and paleontology was extensive. BIBLIOGRAPHY: A. D. González, NCE 8:387.

[P. DAMBORIENA]

LA RUE, PIERRE DE (Petrus Platensis; Pierchon; 1460–1518), Flemish composer and contrapuntist. He may have been a pupil of Okeghem. He was attached to the court of Burgundy (1477) and the chapel of Archduke Maximillian (1485); he was canon of Mechlin (1501) and Courtrai (1503) and attached to the court of Margaret of Austria, the Netherlands regent (1512). Despite his great reputation and favor, very little of his music was printed. His religious and secular works include some 40 Masses and motets, a Requiem, and a Kyrie, and chansons.

[R. J. LITZ]

LA SALETTE, a village in Grenoble, France, where the Blessed Virgin Mary is said to have appeared on September 19, 1846 to two children, Melanie Mathieu-Calvat (15) and Maximin Giraud (11). The children saw a beautiful woman in the midst of a brilliant light; she was weeping and entrusted them with the message that unless men repented from their sins she would let fall the arm of her Son in judgment. The children were not believed at first, but a number of miraculous cures at the site of the apparitions convinced many. A canonical inquiry was begun by Bp. Philibert de Bruillard, the apparitions declared credible, and devotion to Mary under this title authorized. In spite of continuing disputes about the genuineness of the vision, recent popes have approved the cult, and a proper Mass and office have been established (1942). BIBLIOGRAPHY: J. S. Kennedy, *Light on the Mountain* (1953); H. M. Gillett, NCE 8:388–389.

[T. M. MCFADDEN]

LA SALETTE, MISSIONARIES OF OUR LADY OF, religious institute of priests and brothers dedicated to the preaching and missionary apostolate. The congregation traces its origins to a group of diocesan priests set apart by Bp. Philbert de Bruillard in 1852 for ministry in the church at the mountain of La Salette in France, scene of a Marian apparition in 1846. The formal foundation date is 1858, when the first religious vows were made by the earliest members. The work of Revs. Sylvain *Giraud and Pierre Archier was important to the shaping of the congregation: Giraud setting forth its spirit and form of life; Archier, on being elected general superior in 1876, clearly pointing the congregation to the apostolic, rather than the simply contemplative life. First Roman approval was granted in 1879; final approval, in 1926. In France the La Salettes lost all their houses in 1901 because of secularist legislation and it was not until 1943 that they returned to serve the sanctuary of La Salette. Missions and provinces of the congregation, however, spread throughout the world. In N America, ministry to Polish immigrants gave rise to the first province, beginning in 1895. A province with ties to French Canada dates from an apostolate in the New England states, beginning in 1927; the province was formally instituted in 1945. Another province, covering the western part of the U.S. and Canada, dates from 1958. The work of the La Salettes includes foreign missions, the care of parishes, preaching missions and retreats, and maintaining centers of Marian devotion. The general motherhouse is in Rome. In 1975 worldwide there were 209 houses with 868 members of whom 693 were priests.

[M. T. REILLY]

LA SALLE, JOHN BAPTIST DE, ST. (1651–1719), founder of the Brothers of the Christian Schools, pioneer in pedagogy. In spite of his aristocratic family background and his ecclesiastical dignity as a canon of Reims, after ordination (1678) he became involved in charity schools for poor boys and felt called by God to this work as his mission in life. He put aside all his possessions, resigned his canonry, gathered 12 school masters together, and with them in 1684 made a vow of obedience for one year in order to give stability to their apostolate. By 1694 he was convinced that the work could only be accomplished by a religious congregation with a mission throughout France; with his confreres at Paris he pronounced a perpetual vow of obedience and so formed the Institute of Brothers of the Christian Schools. It was his strongly held view that the community should be made up of and be led by brothers alone; his wish was realized when Brother Bartholomew was elected to succeed him as superior general in 1717. Realizing that the existing religious rules in the Church needed mature adaptation to the brothers' apostolate, he drew up his *Règles communes de l'Institut des Frères des Écoles Chrétiennes* only after long experiment and deliberation; they were first published in 1705, then in revised form in 1717–18. As L. made daily study of the catechism part of the brothers' religious life, so, too, he made the teaching of religion the central lesson of each day in their schools. The curriculum was also designed to make religious instruction permeate the whole educational program. He was a pedagogical genius. His innovations included care for an education that would fit the actual lives of the poor youth who were his primary concern. Thus he abandoned the classical mode of education, substituted lessons in the vernacular for the study of Latin and Greek, and perfected a method for class, rather than individual, instruction. He established the first normal schools for the training of teachers in a way appropriate to their pupils' needs. He also led in the establishment of schools to rehabilitate delinquent and troubled boys. The spiritual program for the brothers' own religious life he set forth in his *Method of Mental Prayer*. His pedagogical ideals and practices are contained in his *La Conduite des écoles chrétiennes* (1720). His work on Christian religious instruction, *Duties of a Christian* has been through more than 250 editions. After his death L.'s institute received papal approbation, granted by Benedict XIII in 1725. L. was canonized in 1900 and declared patron of all Christian teachers in 1956. BIBLIOGRAPHY: E. Fitzpatrick, *La Salle, Patron of All Teachers* (1951).

[T. C. O'BRIEN]

LA SALLE, ROBERT CAVELIER DE (1643–87), explorer. After trying religious life among the Jesuits at Paris, L. sailed to Canada (1667). There he acquired land which he soon sold to finance an expedition (1669) that may have taken him to the Ohio River. In 1672 with official approval he erected Fort Frontenac on Lake Ontario and made it a center of trade; later he created a new base on the Niagara River and established Fort Crèvecoeur near Peoria, Illinois. Despite serious setbacks in his grandiose plans for a commercial empire, he descended the Mississippi (1682) to the Gulf of Mexico, claiming Louisiana for France. He sailed for the West Indies (1684) and from there began a fruitless effort to reach the mouth of the Mississippi from the sea. He landed in Texas at Matagorda Bay, where he established a temporary base. An attempt (1686) to bring supplies from Canada by way of the Mississippi failed; on a second attempt he was murdered by members of his party. BIBLIOGRAPHY: F. Parkman, *Discovery of the Great West* (1962); L. V. Jacks, *La Salle* (1931); H. Joutel, *Journal of the Last Voyage Perform'd by Monsr. De La Salle, to the Gulph of Mexico* (1714, repr. 1966); R. S. Weddle, *Wilderness Manhunt: The Spanish Search for LaSalle* (1973).

[R. K. MacMASTER]

LASANCE, FRANCIS XAVIER (1860–1946), priest of the Archdiocese of Cincinnati who was forced into semiretirement at the age of 30 by ill health. He put his time to good use by writing spiritual books, esp. for religious and children, and devotional works on the Mass and Eucharist, and by compiling and editing a number of prayer books and missals.

[N. KOLLAR]

LASCARIS, CONSTANTINE (1434–1501), Greek scholar and bibliophile. An exile from Constantinople after its capture by the Turks (1453), he settled in Italy and taught at Milan, Rome, Naples, and Messina, where he finally settled. At his death he left to the city of Messina the rich library he had collected (it is now in Spain at the Escorial). L.'s *Grammatica Graeca* (1467) served the intense humanist desire to study the Greek classics.

[T. C. O'BRIEN]

LASCARIS, JOHN (*c.* 1445–1534), Byzantine humanist. Following the capture of Constantinople in 1453, he went to Crete and later to Venice. Through the help of Card. Bessarion he was able to study at the Univ. of Padua and to acquire a good knowledge of Latin. At the invitation of Lorenzo de' Medici (*c.* 1490), he taught Greek in the *studium* at Florence. He took an active part in building up the Medici library and was sent to the East to acquire new Greek MSS. After the expulsion of the Medici from Florence (1495), he was brought to Paris by King Charles VIII and became one of the first teachers of Greek in France. Under King Louis XII he served as French ambassador to Venice. In 1513 Pope Leo X made him director of the papal institute of Greek studies at Rome and employed him on several diplomatic missions. In 1518, he was asked by Francis I to collaborate with Guillaume Budé in setting up the royal library at Fontainebleau. He played an important role as a patron of Greek scholars in the West, was an influential teacher, and the editor of important Greek texts, among them the *Greek Anthology,* Lucian, Sophocles, and the *scholia* of Homer. BIBLIOGRAPHY: D. J. Geanakoplos, NCE 8:394; *id., Greek Scholars in Venice: Studies in the Dissemination of Greek Learning from Byzantium to Western Europe* (1962).

[M. R. P. MCGUIRE]

LAS CASAS, BARTOLOMÉ DE (1474–1566), colonial reformer and ''Apostle of the Indies.'' Born in Seville, he went to the Spanish Antilles (1502), where he served as government adviser and was ordained priest in Hispaniola (1510). Under the influence of the Dominican, Antonio de Montesinos, the first publicly to denounce Spanish injustice to the Indians, he began his life-long campaign, in season and out of season, to put an end to the system of expropriating their land and making them serfs. He found a patron in the great Ximénez, cardinal regent of Spain. But his own settlement on the Venezuelan coast, using only free labor, was not a success; his suggestion that slaves should be imported from West Africa who were better fitted than the natives for heavy labor he lived to regret bitterly. He withdrew from public life and in 1523 joined the Dominicans at Santo Domingo. After deepening his theology and writing his monumental *History of the Indies,* he was ready to plan a renewed campaign. Expelled from Nicaragua by the Spaniards, he was successful in northern Guatemala in pacifying and converting the Indians. In 1540 he returned to Spain where his stubborn fight reached its climax in the ''New Laws'' that reorganized the Council of the Indies and prohibited unjust exploitation. However, in large measure they were not adopted, even in Chiapas, Guatemala, of which he had been made bishop (1544) and where he met constant opposition. He left America for the last time 3 years later, but it was to continue the fight at close quarters with the court of Spain. Though well in his 70s the indefatigible old man continued to lobby, to protest, and in no measured terms, and to appeal to the public conscience with his pen. The best known of his writings is *A Short Account of the Destruction of the Indies* (1552). His statesmanship, but not his devotion to the cause of the oppressed, remains a matter of controversy. BIBLIOGRAPHY: L. Hanke, *Spanish Struggle for Justice in the Conquest of America* (1949); F. A. McNutt, *Bartholomew De Las Casas* (1909, AMS Pr.)

[T. GILBY]

LASCAUX (B.C. 379), prehistoric cave sanctuary of hunting magic in the Dordogne region, France, discovered in 1940 by five youths rescuing their dog. The Great Hall of the Bulls, 60 ft by 30 ft, is named for large paintings of black bulls, with horses and bison on a smaller scale. Two passages lead out from the Great Hall: the smaller Painted Gallery, with three red-and-black bovids, and bistre-and-black horses on a vaulted ceiling, more consciously composed, and a Lateral Passage with faint traces of painted animals in a maze of incised lines, which leads to the Chamber of Engravings with overlapping of incised and painted animal forms, giving access to the long, narrow Main Gallery (80 ft long, 3 to 9 ft wide) with the major friezes of horses, ibex, bison, and famous deer heads. A steep slope leads to the Chamber of Felines. A shaft of the Dead Man, adjacent to the Chamber of Engravings, carries an image of a man between a rhinoceros and bison. The vast areas of painting in outline or wash are still brilliant in color due to a calcite film deposit. Dating as middle Upper Paleolithic is deduced from lamps, charcoal, and spears with a radiocarbon date 15,000 years ago, the second half of Abbé Breuil's Aurignacio—Périgordian age, with Extensions into proto-Magdalenian. BIBLIOGRAPHY: A. Leming, *Lascaux, Paintings and Engravings* (1959).

[M. J. DALY]

LAS HUELGAS, CONVENT OF, founded for Cistercian nuns near Burgos, Spain (1187), the church by Master Ricardo, with Angevin vaulting, and a chapel of the Assumption in Mudejar style, enshrines the bodies of the 13th-cent. kings of Castile.

[M. J. DALY]

LASKI, family name of a Polish abp. and his Reformer nephew. **Jan** (1456–1531), abp. of Gniezno, chancellor, and primate. As chancellor from 1503 he edited the first official codification of Polish law (1505) and pursued a policy of opposition to the Teutonic Knights, whose territories he sought to have annexed to Poland. He received the archbishopric of Gniezno, primatial see of Poland, in 1510. He was zealous in promoting ecclesiastical discipline and education. When the Reformation came he was a staunch opponent of Lutheranism and instituted the Counter Reformation in his country. **Jan** (**À Lasco**; 1499–1560), the nephew, educated under his uncle's auspices at Cracow, Bologna, and Rome. Ordained in 1521, he visited Basel in 1524, stayed with Erasmus for a year, and made contact with the Swiss Reformers. On a second visit to Western Europe he became a Calvinist in 1538, married at Liège, and by 1542 was church superintendent in Emden. There he introduced a Genevan discipline and edited (1546) the

Emden Catechism, on the model of the *Geneva Catechism*. Through his friendship with J. *Hooper L. visited England in 1548 as an advisor on church reform to Abp. Cranmer. He was in England again in 1552 as pastor in London for a group of continental Augustinians turned Protestant. He is thought to have had a part in preparing the BCP of 1552. When Mary Tudor became queen, he left England and by 1556 was back in Poland, seeking to introduce Calvinism and acting as leader of the Polish Calvinists.

[R. J. LITZ]

LASSO DE LA VEGA, RAFAEL (1764–1831), bishop in Gran Colombia during the independence period. Bp. of Mérida from 1815, L. is noted for his opposition to then active participation in the independence movement of Colombia as legislator, senator (1823–24), and vice president of the Congress. His communication to Pope Pius VII (October 20, 1821) brought about Vatican recognition of the new republic. Under Leo XII L. became bp. of Quito in 1828.

[H. P. ANNAS]

LAST ADAM, THE. Christ is specifically termed "the last Adam" (*ho eschatos Adam*) by Paul in 1 Cor 15.45–55 to explain to the Corinthians that the model of the "spiritual body" (*sōma pneumatikon*) is the body of the risen Christ. Just as the first Adam is the source and model of natural life, so the last Adam is the source and model of spiritual life. Comparisons between the two Adams are also to be found in Rom 5.12–21 and Eph 5.22–24. In these comparisons, Adam and Christ are representatives of the whole human race; each fulfills the function of a head and is related to the many represented by him as the head is related to the body; every person bears the image of one or the other. Some commentators see in the comparison the influence of such Hellenistic pagan materials as the Hermetic writings, which speak of a primordial man, made in the image of God, who fell into the realm of materiality by falling in love with the created world (*Poimandris*). Others, on the other hand, stress the influence of Hellenistic Jewish references to Adam such as those found in Philo (*Leg-All.* 1.31–42; 53–55; *De opificio mundi* 134) or in apocalyptic literature (2 Esdras 3.21; 4.30–32, 7.116–31; 2 Bar 54.15–19). Yet if Paul had any of these Hellenistic concepts in mind, his presentation is such as to reject them, for he insists that the opposite of these interpretations is the truth. First came Adam, formed from earth, and long afterward came the second head of humanity, the risen Christ. From the first Adam mankind inherited a mortal and corruptible body; from the glorified Christ, the believer inherits life and glory, for through his Resurrection, Christ became a "life-giving Spirit" (1 Cor 15.45) who sends the Holy Spirit to make believers sharers in his risen, glorified life. By the action of the indwelling Spirit whom the last Adam sent to them, Christians are being transformed more perfectly in his image (2 Cor 3.18), until at the parousia their bodies will become like Christ's risen body, incorruptible and glorious. BIBLIOGRAPHY: J. Fitzmyer, JBC 51:86 (274); R. Scroggs, *Last Adam: A Study in Pauline Anthropology* (1966); R. H. Fuller, *Foundations of New Testament Christology* (1965).

[T. J. RYAN]

LAST JUDGMENT, see JUDGMENT, DIVINE.

LAST SACRAMENTS, the term used to designate those sacraments (*penance, *anointing of the sick, and the Eucharist as *viaticum) which are received by a person near death. The phrase, last rites of the Church, is often used equivalently. Penance and anointing of the sick are administered conditionally if the recipient is unconscious. Included with the administration of the last sacraments is a prayer invoking a plenary indulgence upon the sick person. The Vatican II document *Constitution of the Sacred Liturgy* 74 requires that viaticum be received after penance and the anointing of the sick. Although not generally understood as such, baptism, confirmation, and matrimony can be classified as last sacraments insofar as they may be administered to a person near death, e.g., when a priest witnesses a sacramental marriage to convalidate a civil marriage when one partner is dying. BIBLIOGRAPHY: N. Halligan, *Administration of the Sacraments* (1962).

[J. J. FLOOD]

LAST SUPPER, the term employed to describe the last meal that Jesus ate with his Disciples before his Passion and death, at which he instituted the Eucharist. The importance of the Last Supper for Christians through the centuries has centered in the institution of the Eucharist on that occasion. The Last Supper is related by the Synoptic Gospels (Mt 26.17–30; Mk 14.12–26; Lk 22.7–38) and by Paul (1 Cor 11.23–26). The meal is mentioned by John (Jn 13.2ff) without precise reference to the institution of the Eucharist, which is treated in the discourse appended to the account of the feeding of the multitude (Jn 6.51–56). The synoptic accounts mention the preparation for the meal, the prophecy of Judas' betrayal, and the institution of the Eucharist. Luke alone places the betrayal prophecy after the institution, and adds a farewell discourse (Lk 22.24–38), which can be found substantially in the other Gospels (Mt 20.25–28; Mk 10.42–45). The fourth Gospel lacks the story of the preparation of the meal, and the eucharistic words of Jesus over the bread and the wine, but reports a footwashing (Jn 13.1–20) and a long last discourse (Jn 13.31–17.26), neither of which is found in the Synoptic Gospels. Luke's account of the institution (22.15–20) has been handed down in several different forms, but these can be traced back to two original sources, the shorter text of the Gospel (22.15–19a) and the longer form (22.15–20). It is possible to view Lk 22.15–18 as the fragment of an old account of the feast of the Passover in which the paschal lamb is replaced by the Eucharist. The two types that underlie the Synoptic and Pauline accounts are those of Mark, upon which Mt depends, and the tradition behind Paul and Luke. The Paul-Luke tradition is regarded by some as older than the tradition behind Mark, and certain features of the Lucan version may show that it is closer to the original tradition than Paul's account. The accounts of the institution of the Eucharist have been transmitted as the standard forms for its celebration in the early Christian communities, and their character was to a great extent determined by the current form of worship of the community. The accounts are concerned, not with providing a historical report of the Last Supper, but with setting out the celebration of the Eucharist on the basis of Christ's own actions. Thus, "for many" (Mk 14.24) appears in the Paul-Luke tradition as the liturgical acclamation "for you" (1 Cor. 11.24; Lk 22.19). The Pauline and Lucan accounts explicitly designate the covenant in blood as "new" (1 Cor 11.25; Lk 22.20). The words of consecration as pronounced by Jesus have not been handed down verbatim, but show legitimate development in this form while maintaining essential fidelity to the intention of Jesus as understood by the Christian community.

According to the Synoptics (Mk 14.12), Jesus ate a Passover meal with his Disciples on the night before he died. Old Testament legislation (Lev 23.5) prescribed the eating of the Passover meal on the evening that concluded the 14th of Nisan and began 15th of Nisan. For the Synoptics the evening on which the Last Supper was eaten, together with the next morning and afternoon on which Jesus was crucified, constituted the 15th of Nisan, the feast of Passover. Mark 15.42 specifies that the afternoon of the Crucifixion preceded the Sabbath, and thus 15th Nisan ran from sundown on Thursday to sundown on Friday. John's Gospel gives a different picture, in which the Last Supper is set in the period before the Passover, the condemnation and Crucifixion of Jesus are clearly dated to Passover eve (14th Nisan), with the Passover falling at a time when Jesus' body was already in the tomb. To reconcile this dating conflict between the Synoptics and John, various theories have been proposed. Some have proposed the Johannine dating as valid, but believe that it was permitted for sufficient reasons, e.g., the proximity of the Sabbath, the great number of pilgrims, to anticipate the meal. Others believe that John altered the dating to show Jesus, the true Passover lamb, dying at the time when the lambs were being sacrificed in the Temple (Jn 19.36). A recent theory, based upon the solar calendar used by the Qumran Essenes, attempts to show that Jesus ate the Last Supper on a Tuesday evening (15th Nisan), was arrested the same evening, and put to death on Friday. But for such an elaborate reconstruction there does not seem to be sufficient biblical evidence, and it is highly unlikely that Jesus would have followed an Essene calendar.

No complete agreement exists as to whether the Last Supper was in fact a Passover meal. Opponents of the Passover interpretation have marshaled a formidable series of objections to the Synoptic presentation, most notably the absence of the Passover lamb, to show that Jesus was celebrating a Chaburah, a fellowship meal, rather than a Passover. Yet in the Synoptics and John there can be found numerous pointers to the fact that this festive meal has the stamp of the Jewish Passover (Mk 14.26; Mt 26.30). While the question may never be definitively settled, many scholars hold that Jesus celebrated a meal with his Disciples that had Passover characteristics. There can be no doubt that one of the prime theological motifs of the Last Supper is the anticipation of the messianic banquet that Jesus would share with his Disciples in the coming kingdom. The image of the banquet was a common Jewish symbol for the life of the age to come (Ps 23.5; Is 25.6ff; 55.1ff; 65.13) and was a figure Jesus had employed in his teaching (Mt 8.11; 22.2; 25.10; LK 14.16; 22.29–30) and applied in his ministry by eating with sinners (Mt 9.10–12; Mk 2.15–17). Furthermore, the Jewish Passover celebrations in Jesus' day were linked with the final deliverance of the people from bondage and oppression. Also prominent in the theology of the Last Supper event is the sacrificial character of Jesus' death, as shown in Jesus' words identifying the bread and the wine at the supper with his own flesh and blood, about to be separated in his approaching death (1 Cor 11.24–25; Mt 26.28). Both the eschatological and sacrificial connotations are unified in the reference to "covenant." Through the eucharistic words Jesus defines the meaning of his forthcoming death as a sacrificial shedding of blood, the means of inaugurating a new covenant between God and man (Mk 14.24), fulfilling the prophecy of Jeremiah (31.31–34), and offering to those who later share in the Eucharist the means of participating in the atoning effects of his death and in the blessings of the new covenant it inaugurates. The teaching that St. Paul transmits shows that the liturgical remembrance of the Last Supper makes present this covenant sacrifice of the body and blood, nourishes the hope of the Lord's return, and communicates the blessings which the early Church associated with being "in Christ" and "members of his body" (1 Cor 11:23–26). BIBLIOGRAPHY: H. Schürmann, *Der Paschalmahlbericht Lk 22: (7–14), 15–18.* (1953); *idem, Die Abendsmahlbericht Lk 22:7–38* (1957); *idem, LTK* 3.1159–62; J. Jeremias, *Eucharistic Words of Jesus* (1966); J. Coppens, DB Suppl 2:1146–92; A. Jaubert, *La Date de la Cène: Calendrier biblique et liturgie chrétienne* (1957); M. H. Shepherd, InterDB 3:72–75; C. Bernas, NCE 8:397–399.

[T. J. RYAN]

LATAE SENTENTIAE. An ecclesiastical penalty may be imposed according to the Code of Canon Law, c. 2217, either automatically at the moment when the crime is committed *(latae sententiae),* or at the time when a qualified judge should proclaim it *(ferendae sententiae).* When the law specifies a *latae sententiae* penalty, the simple fact of the criminal action *ipso facto* subjects the delinquent to the legislated discipline; he does not have to stand trial in a court of either the external or the internal forum, nor is proof of guilt necessary. If the penalty would involve the defamation of the delinquent, however, he is not bound by the external penalty unless a declaratory sentence, stating that the penalty has been incurred, has been issued (CIC, c. 2232).

[R. A. ARONSTAM]

LA TAILLE, MAURICE DE, see DE LA TAILLE, MAURICE.

LATEAU, LOUISE (1850–83), Belgian stigmatic. In 1863 she was injured and became a semi-invalid. Beginning on April 24, 1868, she experienced bleeding wounds in her hands, feet, and side on each Friday for the next 13 years. She was reputed to have visions and other mystical experiences. From 1876 she was completely bedridden and seemed to have eaten nothing except the host at Holy Communion. The authenticity of her experiences has been doubted by some, by others admitted to be inexplicable through natural causes.

[T. C. O'BRIEN]

LATERAN, THE, ROME, Italian palace (museum), church, and baptistery complex across the Tiber from, and part of Vatican City according to the 1929 Lateran Pact. The Palace of the Laterani was the first donation of Constantine (313) to his new faith—as site of the first major Christian church which continued in its early Christian form until the fires of 1308 and 1361. The current baroque structure is the work of F. *Borromini (1646–49). Old drawings, frescoes, and archeological investigation show the early five-aisled basilica with large E apse and clerestory, and arcade of columns with Corinthian and Ionic capitals. Pope Innocent X having insisted upon preserving the old basilica, the baroque church as designed by Borromini encased alternate columns within colossal pier-units containing sculpture niches. The ceiling (not vaulted as planned) is a wooden coffered structure (1564–72) by Daniele da Volterra. Dark and light marble contrasts enrich the interior. The monumental façade (1733–36) by Alessandro Galilei, though related to Maderno's façade at St. Peter's, is more severe, and heavily contrasted between columns and darkly recessed arcades. *San Giovanni in Fonte, the Lateran baptistery, retains its original Early Christian character, though restored. The interior has two concentric naves separated by eight porphyry columns, and supporting an architrave, with an inscription from Sixtus III (5th cent.), from which rise smaller columns supporting a cupola. The circular pools at the center was used for baptism by immersion. BIBLIOGRAPHY: R. Wittkower, *Art and Architecture in Italy, 1600–1750* (1958).

[M. J. DALY]

LATERAN COUNCILS. The basilica of St. John Lateran was the traditional site for the Roman synods in the Middle Ages. Four of the councils, summoned to deal with crises of the times, are of enduring importance because of the major contributions they made to Church law. No aspect of Christian society, ecclesiastical or civil, escaped their attention. Latern Council V was of a different character and accomplished very little.

Lateran I (1123). Pope Callistus II summoned a council in 1123 to ratify the agreement which had settled the Investiture Controversy the previous year. Its 25 canons deal with the protection of Church property, clerical mores, with the crusades and with counterfeiting, among other issues.

Lateran II (1139). A contested election in 1130 resulted in two popes, Innocent II and Anacletus II. The latter died in 1138 and in the following year Innocent convened a Council to heal the schism and punish his rival's supporters. The Council also condemned the followers of Arnold of Brescia and Peter de Bruys, social reformers with heretical views. Lateran II pushed the cause of reform forward. It published 30 canons which included a prohibition of usury, tournaments, and the study of law and medicine by monks. Canon 7, a landmark in the history of celibacy, declared marriage of clerics in major orders null and void; previously it had been considered only illicit.

Lateran III (1179). Another schism caused by rival claimants to the papacy led Pope Alexander III to summon a Council. Some of the norms formulated in the 27 canons promulgated by Lateran III continue in force: e.g., it required that a two-thirds majority of votes cast is necessary in papal elections; a candidate for a bishopric must be at least 30 years of age. Injunctions against some of the worst abuses of the time were repeated and strengthened. The Council is reported to have received a delegation from the "Poor Men of Lyons," followers of Peter Waldo. They sought approbation for their translation of Scriptures and their way of life, but without success. At Lateran Council IV they were condemned because they presumed to preach without a canonical mission (D 809).

Lateran IV (1215). By far the best attended and most important Lateran Council was the fourth. Carefully planned by Pope Innocent III, it took up every major political and spiritual issue of the time: it promoted a new crusade; drew up procedures to deal with heretics, specifically the Albigenses and Waldenses; declared the Magna Carta invalid; and restricted the establishment of new religious orders. Much of the legislation dealt with the sacramental life of the Church: it spoke of the Real Presence in terms of transubstantiation, and enjoined all Christians to receive the sacraments of penance and the Eucharist at least once a year. In all, 70 canons were promulgated.

Lateran V (1512–1517). Although he had agreed at the time of his election to call a council, Pope Julius (1503–13) procrastinated for one reason or another. Finally, threatened by an antipapal council at Pisa in 1511, he convoked Lateran V the following year. Attended almost exclusively by Italian prelates, it met intermittently into the reign of Pope Leo X. The Council Fathers called for some much needed reform. Although their decrees were published as papal bulls, the new legislation made little impact on the policies of Julius and Leo, neither of whom recognized the urgency of reform. The last session was held March 16, 1517. BIBLIOGRAPHY: R. Foreville, *Histoire des conciles oecuméniques. Latran I, II, III, et Latran IV.* (1966); H. Jedin, *Ecumenical Councils of the Catholic Church* (tr. E. Graf, 1960); C. Duggan, NCE 8:406–410.

[B. L. MARTHALER]

LATERAN PACTS, the treaty, financial agreement, and concordat signed between the Holy See and the Kingdom of Italy (Feb. 11, 1929). The formal negotiations to end the Roman Question were begun in 1926 and were conducted by Domenico Barone for Italy and Francesco Pacelli (brother of the later Pius XII) for the Vatican. The treaty settled the Roman Question once and for all, with the Pope recognizing "the Kingdom of Italy under the dynasty of the House of Savoy with Rome as capital of the Italian State." In return, Italy recognized the Pope's absolute sovereignty and independence over Vatican City, an area of *c.* 109 acres. Under the financial settlement, Italy agreed to compensate the Holy See for the loss of the States of the Church by paying 750 million lire in cash and 1 billion lire in 5% negotiable government bonds. The concordat regulated the status of religion and the Church in Italy. It guaranteed to the Church free exercise of its spiritual power and freedom for its associations such as Catholic Action. Members of the hierarchy were to be appointed by the pope after their names had been presented to the government for possible objections. Catholic religious instruction was to be given in elementary and secondary public schools. Article 7 of the Constitution of republican Italy gave recognition to the Lateran Pacts. For text of Lateran Pacts, cf. *Treaty and Concordat between the Holy See and Italy: Official Documents* (Washington, 1929).

[E. A. CARRILLO]

LATERAN UNIVERSITY, THE PONTIFICAL, in Rome the *Pontificia Università Lateranense,* which also incorporates several important institutes: the Pontifical Pastoral Institute; the Pontifical Institute *Jesus Magister;* Pontifical Medieval Institute John XXIII; the Institute of Moral Theology (*Accademia Alfonsiana*); the Institute of Patrology *Augustinianum*; the Pontifical Leonine Institute of Letters; the Pontifical Institute *Ecclesia Mater*. The title of Pontifical University was granted to the Lateran by John XXIII in the motu proprio *Cum inter* May 17, 1959. The origins of the Lateran as a center of higher ecclesiastical studies dates from 1773 when the work of the Jesuits at the Collegio Romano, interrupted by the suppression of the Society, was entrusted to the Roman diocesan clergy. Leo XII in 1824 (after the Jesuit restoration) decreed the continuation of the Lateran, at the Palazzo S. Appolinare. The Lateran became esp. celebrated for its *faculty utriusque iuris* (canon and civil law) established by Pius IX in 1853 and formally constituted as the Pontifical Institute *utriusque iuris* of the *Ateneo Lateranense* by Pius XI's apostolic constitution *Deus Scientiarum Dominus* (1931). Besides the institutes noted above, established in the pontificates of Pius XII and John XXIII, the philosophy faculty has a special chair of St. Thomas Aquinas, dating from 1962, and the "Swiss Foundation," a chair of Christian anthropology (1970).

LATHROP, ALPHONSA, MOTHER (1851–1926), foundress, writer. Daughter of Nathaniel Hawthorne, she married George Lathrop in 1871. In the years when her husband was an editor for the *Atlantic Monthly,* Rose Hawthorne wrote stories and poetry for leading American magazines. With her husband she wrote *A Story of Courage* (1894), the account of the Visitation nuns at Georgetown. Because of his intemperance, the couple were separated. Rose Hawthorne in New York saw the plight of the poor who were afflicted by cancer and determined to devote her life to their care. She worked on the East Side, dependent on charitable support; she also published in those years *Memories of Hawthorne* (1897). When her husband died Rose became a Dominican tertiary and in 1900 established the Dominican Congregation of St. Rose of Lima to care for the poor with cancer, a work which her magazine *Christ's Poor* helped to support. BIBLIOGRAPHY: K. Burton, *Sorrow Built a Bridge* (1937).

[J. R. AHERNE]

LATIMER, HUGH (*c.* 1485–1555), English Reformer. L. was a Leicestershire man of yeoman stock. He became a fellow of Clare Hall, Cambridge, and was early suspected of Lutheranism, which he disowned; he later admitted indiscretions, but not errors, in doctrine. He approved Henry VIII's divorce and marriage to Anne Boleyn, and was favored by Thomas *Cromwell, being appointed bp. of Worcester (1535). He resigned (1539) over the *Six Articles. He applauded the sacrifice of Cardinal Pole's family to the King's vengeance, and was a scoffer at shrines of Our Lady. He continued as a famous court-preacher throughout the reign of Edward VI. Though ill and worn, "as meet to discuss theology as to be captain of Calais," L. was indomitable when, under Mary, he was called to defend himself against charges of heresy. He was condemned to the stake at Oxford, together with Nicholas Ridley. They were allowed to have bags of gunpowder fastened round their necks by friends. Latimer's words still ring: "Be of good cheer, Master Ridley, we shall light such a candle, by God's grace, in England as I trust shall never be put out." BIBLIOGRAPHY: A. G. Chester, *Hugh Latimer, Apostle to the English* (1954), with bibliog.

[T. GILBY]

LATIN (IN THE CHURCH). The Latin language was used in the Western Church's liturgy and official communiqués. It was the official language in the Western Church and its mission territories until Vatican Council II. The policy today is to use the vernacular. The principal developments of the Western Church's Latin usage were during four periods: 1) from the 2d to the 4th cent.; 2) 4th to the early medieval; 3) medieval; 4) post-Reformation.

Latin was used by the Church because Latin speakers became Christians, first in Northern Africa (end of 2d cent.) and then in Rome (beginning of the 3d century). Latin became the official papal language after mid-4th century. Christian Latin depended upon the popular Latin which was malleable to foreign influences. New words were coined, e.g., *salvare,* and others were borrowed from Greek and Hebrew, e.g., *apostolus, ecclesia, gehenna.* The 3d cent. saw the consolidation of the linguistic form of Christian Latin, a solid beginning of a theological terminology, and the standardization of the style and language of the Latin Bible.

Because such solid foundations were laid in the 3d cent., the 4th and subsequent centuries developed a liturgical Latin that was sacred and hieratic in character. Two main features of this Latin were its predilection for Roman religious terminology, e.g., *preces* for *oratio,* and its imitation of the ancient Roman prayer style. At the same time a curial Latin that was technical, juridical, and artificial rose up. Both these specialized uses of the language were separate from popular speech.

In the Middle Ages, what might be called the scholastic innovation was added. The language was transformed into a specialized instrument for the formulation of abstract philosophical and logical ideas. It was at this time that the vernacular grew up as the language of literature.

There were few additional influences on the language until after the Reformation when, as a result of the influence of the Jesuit schools, the Latin of the classics, e.g., Cicero and Vergil, became the normative Latin.

At present, Latin is still part of the Western Church, mainly in official Vatican correspondence and documents and church law. BIBLIOGRAPHY: C. Mohrmann, NCE 8:412–417 (extensive bibliog).

[N. KOLLAR]

LATIN AMERICA, CHURCH IN. Until fairly recent times the history of the Church in Latin America was obscured by legends, suppositions, and extreme misinterpretations, both anti- and pro-Catholic. A common and mistaken supposition assumed that there was one history for all of Latin America. The authoritarian Spanish empire did decree a uniform approach, but the implementation of royal policy differed greatly from one section to another and of course Spanish policy does not cover the history of a vast and sprawling country like Portuguese Brazil. The effect of the Church on Latin America has to be understood against the origins of Spain's and Portugal's missionary and Christianizing influence. Seldom in history have mixed motives produced such, on the whole, beneficial results. The greed—royal and private—that in great measure prompted the efforts at colonization, the rigid structure of Iberian Catholicism, the mixed bag of conquistadors, missionaries, governors, and settlers are all variable components in one of the most remarkable chapters in the history of civilization.

The Colonial Era (1493–1810). The 1493 decrees of Alexander VI (see ALEXANDRINE BULLS) in granting Spain the vast, relatively unknown land of the Indies enjoined on Queen Isabella the evangelization of the natives. There would be times when the search for wealth and trade would seem paramount, but a consistent effort to Christianize and to civilize a savage people remained. Alexander's decrees and their confirmation by Julius II in 1508 also made the Church subject essentially to the Crown (see PATRONATO REAL): it operated with considerable independence in the New World, in spite of periodic setbacks by the civil authorities. The early days of missionary activity saw the religious orders in almost complete command of the situation. The friars, whether brothers or priests, were given sweeping faculties by Adrian VI's bull, the *Omnimoda* of 1522. In the earlier period there was no hierarchy, and there were few diocesan clergy in Latin America. Franciscans, Augustinians, Dominicans, Mercedarians, and Jesuits were present in increasing numbers during the 16th cent. and established the Church in Latin America. They taught the civilized arts to the people: agriculture, animal husbandry, crafts. Schools, hospitals, care of the aged—all that would today be called welfare—were introduced and maintained by missionaries. Above all it was the religious who protected the Indians from exploitation and destruction by the colonists. Even the Holy Office of the Inquisition, watchdog of orthodoxy established in Mexico City, Lima, and Cartagena, had no jurisdiction over the Indians. The first obligation of the missioner was to lead the Indians to baptism and the practice of the faith. Extreme care was exercised not to condone forced conversion. Efforts were made to instruct the neophytes. These were, understandably, not always fully successful. Large segments of the Indian population were given to superstitions and a low moral code. The multiplicity of dialects and languages constituted a serious obstacle to the missioner. The influx of exiled prisoners and unscrupulous adventurers from Spain and Portugal brought scandalous behavior by so-called Christians. The ultimate control of the New World was in the hands of the Council of the Indies, the right arm of the monarchy. The viceroys exercised commanding power over the clergy in Latin America. Some were bent on interference with ecclesiastical matters, but most were a support as long as the Church served their political ends. Then as now there was much criticism of the wealth of the Church in the Indies, but the monarchy as well as the faithful in the New World made generous grants to the missions, and the Church performed all welfare services for millions of natives and thus needed funds for that work. The early years of the friars' dominant power of the Church in Latin America ended in 1568. In 1574 the King replaced the regular clergy under the direction of the viceroy and this gave the secular clergy a new dominance, by then as well, normal diocesan organization and establishment of a hierarchy were in order. Only the Franciscans retained the early vitality. Rivalry between diocesan and religious order clergy continued for centuries and the ousting of the Jesuits in 1767 was a final crippling blow. The population of Catholic Latin America comprised Spanish, Creoles i.e., Spanish Americans of pure blood, mestizos (half-breeds), Negroes (esp. in Brazil), and Indians. The bps. and diocesan clergy continued to be European as did the religious superiors, but the Orders admitted Creoles, mestizos and some Indians to their ranks, although by the end of the 16th century they were barred by law from religious orders and holy orders.

The conquest of various areas of Latin America varied as did the subsequent treatment of the Indians. A distinguished line of religious struggled to assure better treatment for the Indians, with Bartholomé de las Casas, a Dominican, leading the crusade as early as 1516. A major target of reforming churchmen and humanitarians was the **encomienda*, a system that permitted a Spanish colonist to assume control of a number of Indians, ostensibly for their religious instruction, but often who became, in effect, a de-facto enslavement. In spite of Cortés in New Spain (Mexico) and the unruly elements under his command, Christianity came to flourish among the conquered Aztecs. The notable Franciscan Bp. Juan de *Zumárraga, first bp. of New Spain, established an Indian court and did yeoman labor as educator and apostle to the Indians. Franciscans, Augustinians, and Dominicans in New Spain became leaders of many Indian communities and conversions to Christianity by 1550 were numerous. In Peru the ruthless and mindless assaults of Pizarro alienated the Incas so that their resistance to Christianity was fierce and lasted for many years. By contrast the conciliatory and (for his times) kindly Quesada paved the way for ready acceptance of the faith in New Granada (Colombia). In Chile the long-sustained opposition of the Araucanian Indians made Christianization a slow process (see VALDIVIA, LUIS DE), Argentina in early years was an unimportant colony and the progress of the Church there was slow. The most extraordinary story is that of Paraguay and the Jesuits. The Crown turned over Paraguay, part of Argentina, and a corner of Brazil to the Society in an experiment to see whether or not a mission-dominated colony could develop. The venture was a great success, in spite of slave-hunting raids by settlers in Brazil. Hundreds of thousands of docile Indians were gathered in "reductions" or settlements entirely controlled by the Jesuits. They were educated, instructed in the faith, taught agriculture and useful crafts, and lived peaceably. If the effort was paternalistic, it was a model of successful Christianization and civilization (see REDUCTIONS OF PARAGUAY). Brazil, the Portuguese colony, had a character very different from that of the Spanish colonies. Discovered early, Brazil developed slowly; the coming of Tomé de Sousa as captain-general in 1549 began a new era, for with him came the first Jesuits, led by the brilliant Manoel de *Nóbrega. The Jesuits were very successful in converting the Indians and in protecting them from the slavery Portuguese settlers attempted to impose. The Society also sent José de *Anchieta, who did as much as Nóbrega in southern Brazil. The worst feature of Portuguese colonization for 300 years was its traffic in the slave trade. Millions of Africans were forcibly sold into slavery in Brazil. Curiously, the missionaries whose resistance prevented Indian slavery did not do the same for the Africans.

Truly magnificent architecture, cathedrals, churches, monasteries, was a unique creation in colonial Latin America. Designs may have been started in Spain or Portugal but the execution lay in the hands of local inhabitants. It is remarkable that such a rich variety of styles and designs could have come to fruition in the limited civilization of the colonies. They constituted a totally original development in the history of architecture. In Ecuador the city of Quito became the center of arts for Latin America. Under the aegis of the Church, a fusion of European concepts and Indian tradition gave the world from 1550 to the 1800s a whole new school of art, comparable in influence to that of Florence. Equally amazing was the growth of universities of colonial Spain. The Univ. of Mexico in 1553, Lima in 1571, and in rapid succession universities in Santiago de Chile, Caracas, Quito, Havana, and Santa Fe de Bogatá were respectable centers of learning. Modern history owes a debt likewise to the missionaries: as anthropologists, philologists, historians, grammarians, topographers, they gave an accurate account of Latin America as it was long before the coming of the Europeans.

The Era of Nationalism (1810–1890). The years 1810 to 1824 saw both the Spanish and Portuguese colonies in Latin America rebel or secede from the mother countries. Though the hierarchy and superiors of Orders were for the most part loyal to the Crown, many of the secular and religious clergy joined or supported the liberation movement. With the establishment of the new order, conflicts in Church-State relations arose. Most of the new States accepted Catholicism as the national religion but demanded a continuation of the *patronato real* that in the colonial period had given civil authority wide powers over the Church. The organizational disruption produced by the wars of independence resulted in a decline of clergy and a hierarchy weakened by vacancies lasting many years. The spirit of reform also touched the Church. Throughout the 19th cent. a bitter conflict divided Latin America into two camps; conservatives, who favored moderate and slow change, and liberals, usually anticlerical, who sought to restrict the Church simply to conducting religious service. The bps. were uniformly conservative and often even royalist. The chief questions in the conflict concerned the preferred status of Catholicism, the privileged state the Church had enjoyed in the colonial period, the custody of education, civil enforcement of church law, the very existence of the religious orders, and perhaps most crucial of all, autonomy of the Church in its internal government. The seesawing of conservative and liberal dominance occupied the 19th century.

Era of Modern Latin America (1890 to the present). The diversity of nations, cultures, and 20th cent. developments in Latin America are as varied as those in contemporary Africa or Europe. Summaries do not distinguish sufficiently one Latin American country from another, but can point only to some discernible general phenomena. Both over the continent as a whole and within individual Latin American nations social changes and the role the Church should play in their regard are matters of widespread disagreement. The terms majority and minority are suspiciously simple. It can be said that in those countries that most clearly demonstrate the ferment characteristic of the post-Conciliar Church, the ideology of those seeking change varies remarkably; the one constant, shared conviction centers on the need for change; how and why change should come is a matter of violent disagreement.

Internal Problems of the Church. Since the parish is the fundamental unit in the life of the Church, a reasonable ratio of priests to people is imperative. In Latin America the combination of population explosion and decline in priestly vocations has created a situation in which the parish priest as administrator of the sacraments and pastoral guide faces a task made hopeless by overwhelming numbers of souls for which he is responsible. Parishes that at least theoretically number 40,000 or more people cannot be cared for by one priest. In addition, the geographical spread of rural parishes makes frequent contact impossible. Even the considerable influx of priests from countries outside Latin America has not redressed the imbalance.

A second factor in the alienation of many Catholics from their Church is historical. The hierarchy generally and numbers of Catholic intellectuals traditionally sided with conservative elements which ostensibly supported the Church and were hostile toward social change because it was espoused by radicals and liberals with a strong anticlerical, if not antireligious, bias. Needed reforms were not supported by bps. and intellectuals because they came from the enemy camp. As a result the deprived who constitute the majority in Latin America saw the Church as indifferent to their plight. The protests of a small group of bps., clergy, and laymen were not sufficient to alter the Church's basic image in the 19th cent. and the first half of the 20th.

The issuance of Leo XIII's encyclical *Rerum novarum* in 1891 marked the beginnings of a new age. Slowly and against much opposition from church officials themselves, a new sense of the social mission of the Church began. In time both clerics and laymen were less involved with political matters and more with the social question. Increased evangelizing by Protestant groups, esp. Pentecostals, and the rise of communism both required positive Catholic reaction. Vatican Council II and the documents emanating from it, together with the encyclicals *Mater et magistra, Pacem in terris,* and *Populi progressio*—all issued in mid-20th cent.—have had major influence on the involvement of the Church in seeking a new order in Latin America. A Christian Democracy movement in Chile in the 1930s, and the writings of its leader, Eduardo Frei, gave Latin America not only a theoretical invitation to Christianize the revolution but as a political party made some progress in bringing about such a peaceful revolution. More recently, impatience with the concept of Christian Democracy, a slow process, has stimulated the rise of the New Christian Left, a far more radical reform group, drawing support particularly from the young, both Catholic and Protestant. It is anti-Marxist but socialistic. Unhappily its more radical clerical members, notably Camila Torres, have abandoned nonviolent action for violence.

It would be difficult to exaggerate the importance of the Latin American Episcopal Council (CELAM). Organized in 1955, it has permanent headquarters in Bogotá, Colombia. Operating through a permanent secretariat, CELAM meets annually and in addition conducts many specialized conferences. Each Latin American country's Episcopal Conference is represented by one delegate. There is an elected president with two vicepresidents plus a secretary general and five sub-secretaries. The influence of national episcopal conferences, an outgrowth of Vatican Council II, varies with the nation represented, but has been of great significance for both internal and external development of the Church in Latin America. The mechanism makes possible united and rapid action within each country. While each nation, to some degree, has taken new initiatives, the Big Five: Chile, Mexico, Brazil, Argentina, and Colombia show most rapid and vital development. Among those developments, not realized to the same extent in each of the five, are the following: a tendency to maintain separation from government and to feel free to criticize political leaders, a spirit of cooperation with secular influences on society, a massive effort toward education—religious, political, and social—of the hitherto neglected lower classes, a clear identification of the Church with the social and economic problems of Latin America. Among the more liberal episcopates there is a new willingness to assign religious women to church functions and to invoke the laity in meaningful sharing of ecclesiastical responsibility.

Some areas of Latin America have been blessed with the vigorous presence of outstanding bps. who have gone far beyond their more conservative colleagues. Outstanding examples are Bps. Helder Câmara and Eugenio Sales in Brazil, Manuel Larrain of Chile, Carlos Maria Jurgens, Raúl Silva Henriquez, and José Dammert Bellido in Peru. The Medellín Documents published by the Latin American Episcopal Conference in 1968 after its meeting in Medellín, Colombia, have been seen as a firm declaration of the Church's intent to put itself on the side of human rights and of the poor.

No picture of the forces of change among Latin American Catholics would be complete without reference to centers and organizations. They cover a broad spectrum from tradition-based to avant-garde. The Christian Democratic movement enjoyed great success in earlier years and is still a force. Two movements associated with students and young people generally are Ação Popular in Brazil and the emerging radical organization Juventude Universitaria

Catolica (JUC), also in Brazil. Two concomitant centers deserve mention: The Jesuit Centro Belarmino supporting the Christian Democratic movement in Chile and the Catholic Univ. of Rio de Janeiro, center of JUC. BIBLIOGRAPHY: J. Fagg, *Latin America: a General History* (1963); *Roman Catholic Church in Colonial Latin America* (ed. R. Greenleaf, 1971); *Roman Catholic Church in Modern Latin America* (ed. K. Schmidt, 1972; J. Rippy, *Latin America* (1968); I. Vallier, *Catholicism, Social Control, and Modernization in Latin America* (1970); *Church and Social Change in Latin America* (ed. H. Landsburger, 1970); F. Turner, *Catholicism and Political Development in Latin America* (1971); the Medellin Documents, USCC publication v-170b, *Church in the Present-Day Transformation of Latin America . . .* (1968).

[J. R. AHERNE]

LATIN AMERICA, PONTIFICAL COMMISSION FOR, see PONTIFICAL COMMISSION FOR LATIN AMERICA.

LATIN-AMERICAN ART. Art of the Latin American countries may be divided into three periods: Pre-Columbian, Colonial, and Modern.

Pre-Columbian cultures flourished from 1200 B.C. to the Spanish conquest in two major areas—Mesoamerica to the N and highlands of Peru to the S. The Northern civilizations built majestic urban centers in stone at Teotihuacán, Monte Albán, Tenochtitlán, Chichén-Itzá, Uxmal, and Tikal, devoted to mythical gods and characterized by a ''Pyramid'' base on which rested the temple of sacrifice. Sculpture consisted of a rhythmic repetition of expressive and decorative elements, either geometric or figurative.

Inca art and architecture, as we know them, existed then between the years 500 and 1530. Among the Incas' remarkable public works, the most famous was the fortress-city of Machu-Picchu, built on top of a mountain in the heart of the Andes.

Colonial art and architecture remained essentially Iberian and were only occasionally and superficially modified by climatic conditions and existing local cultures. Throughout the 16th cent., Franciscan, Dominican, and Augustinian Orders built some 400 Augustinian monasteries in Mexico alone, using a variety of European styles: Gothic, Romanesque, Mudejar, and Plateresque. In the 17th cent., Peru, Bolivia, and Ecuador became centers of the Mestizo style which introduced native Indian decorative elements. In Mexico, the mid-18th-cent. baroque style reached an incredible degree of lavishness in the ''Churrigueresco'' period (Sta. Prisca in Taxco; the Monastery of Tepotzotlán).

Brazilian style followed the Portuguese baroque of the same period, with most famous examples in and around Ouro Preto, where the renowned sculptor Antonio Francisco Lisboa, ''O Aleijadinho'' worked.

Painting remained essentially didactic and conventional except in the Quito and Cuzco schools where traditional religious subjects by mestizo painters show strong native influences.

The 19th cent. marked a decline in Latin American architecture. In the 1930s, functional architecture, introduced by Le Corbusier, was influenced by local conditions of climate, available building materials, and cultural traditions. In Brazil, the design of the Ministry of Education and Health (1939) marked a golden period of architecture, continuing into the 1960s under the leadership of Lúcio Casta and Oscar Niemeyer, in an original style full of elegance, exuberance, and poetry. Brasília, the new capital, built in a virgin area in the interior of the country—the supreme architectural achievement—is an apotheosis of creative imagination and engineering prowess. In Mexico alone architects tried to establish a continuity of spirit between the Pre-Columbian heritage and modern conceptions. University City, Mexico (1953) boasts a Juan O'Gorman mosaic on the exterior walls of the Library showing Aztec, Colonial, and modern historic and didactic symbols and a *Stadium* mosaic by Diego Rivera expressing the Indian and Spanish fusion in the Mexican race, evidencing the collaboration between artists and architects in Mexico. Latest buildings of elegance and refinement by engineer Félix Candela, Church of the Miraculous Virgin (1954), Chapel of the Missionaries of the Holy Ghost (1956) based on hyberbolic paraboloid shell concrete forms in a modified functionalism, are remarkable.

Elsewhere, particularly in Venezuela and Colombia, the influence of the U.S. is strong, and architecture is close to the International style.

Painters attaining international renown are Candido Portinari, Roberto Matta, and Rufino Tamayo. The outstanding achievement was the mural movement in Mexico (1922) which, led by Rivera, Siqueiros, and Orozco covered the walls of old and new buildings with monumental, expressive paintings of political and historical significance to the new social order. They repudiated the dealers' gallery and sophisticated clientele, desiring to bring art into the lives of the people and glorifying monumental art as a public possession.

Since the late 1950s, Latin American artists have turned toward the U.S. and have been greatly influenced by Abstract Expressionism, Pop Art, and Op Art and successive styles. BIBLIOGRAPHY: P. F. Damaz, *Art in Latin American Architecture* (1963).

[P. F. DAMAZ]

LATIN CHURCH, part of the Catholic Church that follows the Latin rite in the liturgy, has its own canon law, and is subject to the bp. of Rome as the patriarch of the West. Compared with the other section of the Catholic Church, i.e., the Eastern Churches or patriarchates, the Latin Church forms the great bulk of the Catholic Church: 705,028,000 Catholics, about 20,271,979 belong to Eastern Churches. The chief reason for the development of the W patriarchate is that Rome is the see of the pope, the head of the entire Church. From the time of St. Leo the Great (440–460), Rome initiated a progressive centralization in the administrative and disciplinary order. Later with the conversion of England, begun under St. Gregory I (590–604), the influence of Rome increased. It did so still more when the pope took direct action in erecting dioceses in Italy and Gaul; this became the regular practice sanctioned by canon law. With the codification of canon law under Gregory IX (1227–44), the entire Latin Church was strictly subjected to the discipline of Rome. Much of the Church's missionary activity was carried on by the Latin Church. Attempts at latinizing other rites has occurred in the history of the Church. Forbidden by modern popes, it was also forbidden by Vatican II's *Decree on Eastern Catholic Churches,* 5–6. BIBLIOGRAPHY: A. Caron, NCE 8:520–522.

[P. DELETTER]

LATIN EMPIRE OF CONSTANTINOPLE, the state established by the leaders of the Fourth Crusade on the ruins of the Byzantine Empire in 1204. Individual nobles and the Venetians shared the lands they conquered under a feudal structure of government, with Baldwin of Flanders as emperor. Thomas Morosini and a succession of other Venetians secured the patriarchal throne, over the initial protests of the popes. The schism between the Greek and Latin Churches did not end, however, despite pressure on the native population. Several parts of the Byzantine Empire escaped Latin conquest and from one of these, Nicaea, *Michael VIII Palaeologus recovered Constantinople and ended the Latin Empire in 1261. The incident proved a serious stumbling-block impeding reconciliation of the Greeks with the Latins. BIBLIOGRAPHY: J. Longnon, *L'Empire Latin de Constantinople* (1949); R. L. Wolff, ''Organization of tte Latin Patriarchate of Constantinople,'' *Traditio* 6 (1948) 33–60; *idem,* ''Latin Empire of Constantinople, 1204–1261,'' *History of the Crusades* (ed. K. M. Setton, 3 v., 1955–75) 2:187–233.

[R. H. SCHMANDT]

LATIN FATHERS. The four great Fathers of the Western Church are: SS. *Ambrose of Milan, *Augustine of Hippo, *Gregory the Great, and *Jerome; these were the first officially designated *Doctors of the Church as well by Boniface VIII in 1295. More broadly used to include other premedieval writers, the term would include SS. *Bede the Venerable, *Cyprian of Carthage, *Hilary of Poitiers, *Isidore of Seville, and *Leo I the Great. *FATHER OF THE CHURCH.

[T. C. O'BRIEN]

LATIN LITERATURE, MEDIEVAL. For 1000 years, from A.D. 476 to the Renaissance, Latin continued as the language of educated men and the official language of the Western Church. Historians, theologians, and philosophers have always read this Latin literature for its content, but humanists have generally neglected it. The beginnings of medieval Latin literature in Africa came even before the fall of Rome in the writings of Tertullian (*c.* 160–230) and Cyprian (*c.* 200–258). These men expressed their Christian ideas in vigorous and effective Latin enriched by new and varied vocabulary. The positive and practical tradition they began in Africa reached its zenith in the greatest of the Latin Christian writers, St. Augustine (d. 430).

In Europe the beginnings of medieval Latin were later. Two factors may account for this: the Church in Europe was Greek-speaking for the first centuries, and the curriculum of the schools was dominated by the ideals of Greek rhetoric. This tradition of learning, so entrenched and rigid, did not encourage creativity. As a result, most of the European Latin Fathers put their energies into transmitting to the West theological and philosophical speculation of Eastern scholarship. There were exceptions; Jerome (*c.* 342–420) studied Scripture and even learned Hebrew to revise his Latin translations of the Bible. Gradually, as the Church prevailed over paganism, its writers became less apologetic and theological. Their interests at this point shifted to sermons and scriptural exegesis.

Undoubtedly, the greatest European contribution to Latin literature was Christian poetry. Ambrose (333–397) was usually considered its founder. His scansion frequently iambic dimeter, was still quantitative rather than accentual, and occasionally he used rhyme. Prudentius (348–405), the master of complex classical meters, however, was the greatest of the Christian poets. Hymns joined to music and shaped to the new poetry with accentual rhythm and rhyme unknown to classical poetry were among the achievements of this medieval literature.

Growth of Western monasticism came at a most opportune time, providing cells of Western culture in a world overrun by barbarian hordes. The Irish and English monasteries esp. contributed to this work of preservation and transmission of Christian and classical culture. In addition, they sent to the continent eminent missionaries such as SS. Columban and Boniface.

After the Arabs had conquered Africa and Spain in the 7th and 8th cent., the restoration and revival of Latin culture came from Charlemagne. He gathered to his court from all over Europe such scholars as Einhard, Alcuin, Rabanus Maurus, and Strabo. Although unlettered himself, Charlemagne was completely devoted to the work of restoring learning and raising the standard of education throughout his realm. This renaissance of classical and patristic traditions centered in the school of the palace and was diffused throughout the empire from monastic and episcopal centers.

Learning declined after the Carolingian Age because during the 10th and the 11th cent. the Church was concentrating on problems of Church and State and trying to recover the Holy Land from Islam. Prominent in these struggles were the Cluniac monks who paid little attention to scholarship. From the aesthetic point of view, the greatest prose of the time was the liturgy of the Church, rhythmic Latin chanted to the accompaniment of ceremonial. During this time and concurrent with the growth of the university, there was a great increase in secular poetry. This poetry, known as Goliardic, used many metrical innovations and more rhyme. The Goliards, students who wandered from one university to another, showed they had been influenced by classical poetry, but chiefly expressed personal joys and griefs.

Before the 12th cent., nearly all writing was in Latin. The 13th cent. saw the climax of medieval intellectual development and the 14th saw the last and the greatest revival of Latin literature. The vernaculars, begun in the 10th cent., were well beyond the formative stage. But the vernacular literature that began to appear continued to reflect the influence of Latin. Its models of style and standards of criticism were those of the classical tradition. BIBLIOGRAPHY: M. L. W. Laistner, *Thought and Letters in Western Europe* A.D. 500–900 (new ed., 1957); F. J. E. Raby, *History of Christian Latin Poetry from Beginnings to the Close of the Middle Ages* (2d ed., 1953); C. F. Curtiss, *European Literature and the Latin Middle Ages* (tr. W. R. Trask, 1973); *Oxford Book of Medieval Latin Verse* (ed. F. J. Raby, 1959).

[M. F. MCNAMARA]

LATIN PATRIARCH, see PATRIARCH, LATIN.

LATIN RITE, one of the 18 canonical rites recognized in the RC Church (the other 17 are Oriental). Canonical rite means not only the liturgical rite but also the canonical discipline and spiritual heritage of a Church. In this canonical sense the Latin rite coincides with the Latin Church. Liturgically, however, there are other Latin rites besides the Roman: the particular rites of religious orders (e.g., Carthusian, Cistercian, Dominican) and the rites of primatial sees, such as those of Lyons (Gallican), of Milan (Ambrosian), and of Toledo (Mozarabic). The obvious characteristic of the Latin rite is the use of Latin in official Church law and communications and prior to Vatican II in the liturgy. Yet, before and after Trent decreed the use of Latin in the Mass (D 1749, 1759), the Slavonic language was used in parts of Croatia and Czechoslovakia, Vatican Council II, while maintaining the principle of Latin for the Latin rite, allows the use of "the mother tongue in the Mass, the administration of the sacraments, and other parts of the liturgy" (Vat II SacLit 36). The postconciliar period has witnessed a rapid vernacularization of the liturgy the world over. Special features of the Latin rite in canonical sense are the celibacy of priests, use of unleavened bread for the Eucharist, communion under one kind (this last ruling was modified after Vatican II by special concessions of communion under both kinds when practical and on special occasions) and with approval of the Holy See, the practice of in-hand reception of Holy Communion in regions and countries where it had the approval of the appropriate bishops' conferences. BIBLIOGRAPHY: A. Caron, NCE 8:520–521; A. A. King, *Liturgies of Religious Orders* (1955); *idem, Liturgies of Primatial Sees* (1957); W. D. Maxwell, *Outline of Christian Worship: its Development and Forms* (1939).

[P. DeLETTER]

LATINIZATION, the imposition of Latin ecclesiastical, theological, and liturgical forms and usages upon non-Latin Christians. It stems from a distorted view of the Church, a view that is non-Catholic in the strict sense inasmuch as it contradicts the catholicity of the Church. If given conscious expression, it would certainly seem to be heretical. This view tends to restrict Christianity to its Western European form and to regard other Christian traditions, particularly the Eastern ones, as inferior and suspect. Although the tendency to impose Latin, esp. Roman, forms and usages is most apparent in the liturgy, it has entered into almost every phase of the structure and life of the Eastern Catholic Churches. The very real fear of such latinization is still one of the major obstacles to reunion between the Catholic and the Orthodox Churches.

While instances of latinization and a latinizing mentality are found earlier, they became more widespread after the Crusades, and from the 13th cent. to the present have been prevalent in the Western Church. During the Crusades the legate of Pope Urban II insisted that the Greek Patriarch of Antioch retain his jurisdiction and had Latin bps. consecrated by him; but after his death the crusaders established the anomalous Latin patriarchate of Jerusalem to which the Eastern Christians were subjected. Before the schism, diversity of rites within the one Church occasioned no serious difficulty. Later when the Roman rite became practically coterminous with the Western European Church, it was perhaps understandable that people came to regard the Roman or Latin rite as the only truly Catholic one. In the 12th cent. papal letters first speak of ritual uniformity as the ideal. Moreover, once the Greeks were regarded as schismatics and heretics, it was a simple step to look upon their practices with suspicion. The Latin conquerors of Constantinople in 1204 set up a Latin patriarch and bishops, a situation unfortunately approved of by Pope Innocent III. He and his successors insisted that Roman canonical and liturgical usages be observed in Greek lands. The Latin rite was held to be superior, and the Greek reluctantly tolerated. The explicit recognition by the *Council of Florence (1439) of the equality of the rites had no real effect, and even in its own *Decree for the Armenians, the Council forgot its own principles. It also admitted "all the privileges of the Eastern patriarchs," but it is doubtful whether either side understood what the other meant by "privileges." The general attitude of the late medieval popes was that the Eastern Churches were basically inferior as well as heretical. Union meant simply bringing the Easterners back into the same belief, discipline, and rite as the West. With few exceptions latinization was the rule well into the 19th century. The Roman notion of unity had become confused with that of uniformity. Owing largely to European missionary activity in the Near East, there developed by the end of the 17th cent. a general respect for the Eastern rites. Groups entering into union were assured that their ties would not be altered, although in other matters they had to submit to Rome. Yet, many Eastern Churches themselves adopted Latin usages, sometimes out of ignorance, sometimes in order to appear equal to Latin Catholics.

In 1742 Pope Benedict XIV clearly stated that the Latin rite was superior, although the Eastern rites should be respected and preserved. The first real change in attitude was that of Pope Leo XIII; in his letter of 1894, *Orientalium dignitas,* he saw the Eastern rites as an expression of the Church's catholicity and forbade missionaries to convert Orientals to the Latin rite. But both the missionaries and Rome continued to latinize. With the establishment of the Congregation for the Oriental Church in 1917 the situation has improved somewhat, but far-reaching changes must be made before the Congregation will be fully accepted by the Eastern Churches. The same may be said of the Codification of Oriental Canon law made under Pope Pius XII. The precedence accorded cardinals over Eastern patriarchs as well as the granting of the cardinalate to the patriarchs are sufficient evidence that latinization has not yet entirely disappeared. BIBLIOGRAPHY: W. de Vries, *Rom und die Patriarchate des Ostens* (1963).

[G. T. DENNIS]

LATITUDINARIANISM, a word used derisively in the latter part of the 17th cent. for a school of thought within the C of E that tended to regard formal expressions of doctrine, worship, or government to be of little importance as compared with man's inner, rational, or mystical experience. England was emerging from a century of sharp and often bitter controversy marked by strong, sectarian loyalties. With the final religious settlement of 1661, the way seemed open to new horizons of scientific and philosophical inquiry and a new spirit of liberty and tolerance. At the least, the nation was weary of ecclesiastical quarrels and theological hairsplitting. More deeply, many needed and sought a recovery of respect for reason and for the deep mystical knowledge of God. One significant group usually identified as latitudinarian was the *Cambridge Platonists, who reacted against formalism and sectarianism and led the way toward a rediscovery of Greek mystical thought. But latitudinarianism as a whole tended toward liberalism without mysticism, even toward the sterile *deism of the 18th cent. (see ENLIGHTENMENT). The movement became identified largely with the rise of Whig politics and finally disappeared in the face of the Evangelical Revival and the *Tractarian movement. The *broad-church adherents of the 19th cent. were in some ways the successors of the latitudinarians, but without the political affiliations of the earlier group. BIBLIOGRAPHY: *Rational Theology and Christian Philosophy in England in the Seventeenth Century* (ed. J. Tulloch, 1874, repr. 1972).

[S. F. BAYNE]

LATOMUS, BARTHOLOMAEUS (Steinmetz; *c.* 1490–1570), humanist and polemicist. He was a friend of *Erasmus, taught at Trier, Cologne, and the Royal College of France, and became counselor to the Elector of Trier. He wrote treatises against the Reformers Jakob Andreä and M. *Bucer as well as an analysis of the errors of the *Augsburg Confession.

[T. C. O'BRIEN]

LATOMUS, JACOBUS (Masson, Jacques; *c.* 1475–1544), theologian and, from 1534, rector at the Univ. of Louvain. He attacked Erasmus on the position that the theologian must be learned in the biblical languages in *De trium linguarum . . . dialogus* (1519). He wrote *Articulorum doctrinae F. Martini Lutheri* (1521) in support of Louvain's condemnation of Luther, and *De primatu Romani pontificis* (1525). L. also wrote against other Reformers. Luther referred to L. as the ablest of all the authors who had opposed him.

[T. C. O'BRIEN]

LA TOUR, GEORGES DE (1593–1652), French painter of religious and genre scenes achieving a monumental visual reality of great reserve. In religious works L. expresses transcendent truth in lucid stucture and absolute quietude. Noble of birth, master painter (1620), L. employs a style that moves from an early Baroque, echoing Caravaggio, through the plasticism of Dutch realism (*St. Jerome, c.* 1621) to the final drama of night-lighting from Terbrugghen and Honthorst (*The Magdalen with an Oil Lamp,* 1635; *Christ and St. Joseph in the Carpenter Shop,* 1645). His final style (*St. Sebastian Being Ministered to by St. Irene*) records only geometric essentials, grand and grave in the strong light of torch or candle, in utter stillness. L.'s works are in museums throughout the world. BIBLIOGRAPHY: F. G. Pariset, *Georges de la Tour* (1948).

[M. J. DALY]

LA TOUR DU PIN, CHARLES HUMBERT RENÉ (Marquis de la Charce; 1834–1924), Catholic sociologist, theoretician of "corporativism," which opposed economic liberalism as well as state control, repudiated the exploitation of the worker, and espoused the socially responsible right of private property and the ordered contribution of all ranks to the social good. He was an opponent of Leo XIII's policy of **ralliement.* In 1871 L. founded *L'Opera dei cercoli cattolici dei operai* and in 1884 the Union of Fribourg, which became the International Union of Social Catholics.

LA TOUR DU PIN, PATRICE DE (1911–75), poet and essayist, born of a French father and a mother of Irish descent, whose work defines in personalist terms man's relationship to himself, his fellows, and God. Of aristocratic lineage, he studied political science, was a prisoner during World War II, and afterward lived as a country squire. He was reared in a Catholic milieu (his sister Phyllis became a Dominican nun), originally contemplated taking orders, and made frequent monastic retreats an integral part of his spiritual life. Following Vatican Council II he served on the commission charged with translating liturgical texts into French. He evolved from a spiritual lyricism toward more dramatic forms, increasingly employing medieval symbolism and allegorical figures. Segments of his work appear in translation: *The Dedicated Life in Poetry* and *The Correspondence of Laurent de Cayeux* (tr. 1948 by G. S. Fraser with an introduction by S. Spender). BIBLIOGRAPHY: E. Kushner, *Patrice de La Tour du Pin* (1961).

[G. E. GINGRAS]

LATOURETTE, KENNETH SCOTT (1884–1968), ecclesiastical and Oriental historian, missiologist. He was born in Oregon City, Ore., and graduated from Linfield College, McMinnville, Ore., in 1904. At Yale his graduate work was in Oriental languages and history; he received the doctorate in 1909. Through work with the YMCA and the Student Volunteer Movement, he became interested in missions; he went to China in 1910, but ill health forced his return to the U.S. in 1912. He remained devoted to missions, esp. in the Far East, throughout his life. He was ordained a Baptist minister in 1918, but spent his whole active life in the academic world. He was a professor of history at Reed College, Portland, Ore., and Denison Univ., Granville, Ohio, before his appointment as professor of missions at Yale in 1921. He became chairman of the department of religion at Yale in 1938, and from 1946 until his retirement in 1953 was director of graduate studies of the Yale Divinity School. He also served as visiting lecturer at many other universities and at schools of theology. He was president of the American Baptist Convention, 1951–52, a member of the board of several mission organizations, and of the committee for the drafting of a constitution for the World Council of Churches at Utrecht in 1938. Several of his more than 80 books dealt with the political and cultural history of the Far East, esp. China. His works on church history are regarded by many as the foremost 20th-cent. contributions to the field. The two major works are *History of the Expansion of Christianity* (7 v., 1937–45) and *Christianity in a Revolutionary Age* (5 v., 1958–62); the one-volume *History of Christianity* (1953) is a remarkable accomplishment. His work has been recognized not only for its scholarship but for its freedom from sectarian bias. He exercised as well a wide influence through his own personality, and his dedication to Christian causes, esp. Christian unity. BIBLIOGRAPHY: K. S. Latourette, *Short History of the Far East* (4th ed., 1964).

[T. C. O'BRIEN]

LA TRAPPE, ABBEY OF, Cistercian abbey, Notre Dame de la Trappe, in the present diocese of Sée, France, founded in 1122 by Rotrou III, Count of Perche. In 1147 the Benedictines of the congregation of Savigny, who occupied it, became Cistercians affiliated with Clairvaux. The relaxation of observance that occurred in the 16th cent. was reformed in 1664 by Abbot Armand-Jean le Bouthillier de Rancé, who introduced heavy manual labor, perpetual silence, and other bodily austerities. At the time of the French Revolution, the religious of La Trappe took refuge in Switzerland at La Valsainte. They returned in 1816 and in the course of the cent. reconstructed the monastery buildings. In 1847 the French Cistercians separated into two congregations—of the old and of the new reform, the monasteries of Sept-Fons and La Trappe being their respective centers. In 1892, however, the groups reunited under a general superior resident in Rome. BIBLIOGRAPHY: Cottineau 2:3201–02.

[J. DAOUST]

LATRIA (Gr. *latreia*, service, servitude), the adoration offered and due to God alone (see COUNCIL OF NICAEA II,D 601); thus the primary concern of the virtue of *religion In the NT *latreia* occurs a few times with the meaning of service to God (Jn 16.2; Rom 9.4; 12.1; Heb. 9.1.6). St. Thomas Aquinas uses *latria*, first, as an equivalent for *religio* in discussing the virtue that respects the indebtedness of man to God (ThAq ST 2a2ae, 94.1 ad 2); thus *latria* includes all the inner and outward expressions of this reverence. In a narrower sense, *latria* is a specific act, the primary outward manifestation of the inner virtue, namely adoration (*ibid.*, 84.1.). That act above all is a sign of interior reverence and submission to God as Lord, and it is these sentiments that, in keeping with human need for symbols and gestures, bowing, kneeling, etc., represent. Because God's eminence surpasses and is uniquely distinct from that of any creature, *latria* differs from **dulia*, the veneration offered to the saints. See IMAGES, VENERATION OF.

[T. C. O'BRIEN]

LATROBE, BENJAMIN HENRY (1764–1820), Anglo-American architect and engineer. Arriving in Norfolk, Va. in 1795, L. became, under Jefferson, the most influential architect of Federal Neoclassicism. He conceived master plans for the neo-classical Bank of Pennsylvania (Philadelphia, 1801; destroyed), the Gothic Sedgelen-Crammond house (Philadelphia, 1799), and the impressively grand old Catholic Cathedral of the Assumption, Baltimore (1805), to this day treasured as one of the finest architectural forms in the United States. Its exterior, resembling Soufflot's Panthéon (the bulbous crowns of the towers are not L.'s work), and its distinguished interior, with exquisitely suppressed Roman details heightening the spatial quality to a grandeur vast, pure, and sublime, evidence L.'s genius. Surveyor of public buildings (1803–12 and 1815–17), L. completed the Senate and House chambers of the U. S. Capitol, Washington, D. C., exerting a profound influence for excellence on American architecture. BIBLIOGRAPHY: T. F. Hamlin, *Benjamin Henry Latrobe* (1955).

[M. J. DALY]

LATROCINIUM, see ROBBER SYNOD OF EPHESUS.

LATRONIANUS, Spanish poet executed in Trier with Priscillian in 385. None of his works, written in a variety of meters, are extant. Jerome compared him with the ancients (*De vir. ill.* 122).

[E. P. COLBERT]

LATTER-DAY SAINTS, CHURCH OF JESUS CHRIST OF (known as the Mormon Church, founded 1830) in Fayette, N.Y., by Joseph *Smith, Jr. He reported that a heavenly personage, the Angel Moroni, led him to discover a set of golden tablets, on which were inscribed characters in Reformed Egyptian, and a set of spectacles called the Urim and Thummim, to be used for translating the plates. The **Book of Mormon* is the translation; it describes the aboriginal people of the Western Hemisphere and the establishment of a Church in North America by Jesus Christ after his Ascension. The book covers a period from 600 B.C. to A.D. 421. Smith declared that all existing Christian Churches were apostate and without authority to preach or baptize. He said that John the Baptist had conferred the powers of the priesthood of Aaron on him and that Peter, James, and John had given him the priesthood of Melchizedek. The Church he founded was to succeed the Christian Churches that had apostatized in the Eastern Hemisphere and died out in the Western.

Smith and his followers built their first temple in Kirtland, Ohio, and then moved to Missouri. Driven out of that state, they purchased land on the banks of the Mississippi and founded the city of Nauvoo, Ill. which grew and prospered so greatly that it aroused the envy of others. Rumors that Smith had introduced polygamy into his Church began to spread, and some of his followers turned against him. An opposition newspaper appeared, but followers of Smith destroyed the printing plant. Smith was arrested on charges of sedition and imprisoned at Carthage, Illinois. A mob stormed the jail and murdered the prophet and his brother Hyrum in 1844. The question of succession caused dissension; some groups broke away from the majority, which followed the leadership of Brigham *Young, senior member of the Council of the Twelve Apostles. Continuing antagonism in Nauvoo culminated in mob violence that compelled the Mormons to leave that city in 1846. Under Young's leadership the first of the Mormons made the difficult journey to the valley of the Great Salt Lake in 1847. In Utah the Mormons established a theocracy and openly practiced polygamy from 1852 to 1890, when the president of the Church declared plural marriage a suspended doctrine.

The accepted Scriptures of the Mormon Church are the Bible, the *Book of Mormon, *Doctrines and Covenants,* and the *Pearl of Great Price*. The Church also believes in a continuous revelation from God expressed through the president of the Church. In Mormon theology God and Jesus Christ are personages of flesh and bones. God is a polygamist who has countless spirit children. Man has the potential of becoming a god on his own planet with his own spirit children. The Mormon belief is succinctly expressed in the phrase: "What man is now, God once was; what God is now, man may become." The God of this world was once a man himself and is now only one of many gods in the universe. Man has preexisted with God from eternity but is given the opportunity of achieving godhood himself by undergoing the experiences of mortality. Those who wish to reach the highest of the three states of exaltation in the next life must be Mormons who receive their temple endowments, marry in the temple, obey the priesthood, and lead good lives. Lukewarm Mormons and non-Mormons will enjoy a lower form of bliss, and a small number of men will be condemned as sons of perdition for such sins as adultery and apostasy. *Millenarianism has always been a part of Mormon teaching. Original sin is denied.

Mormons worship in nearly 4,000 local congregations, known as wards. These are grouped in 420 stakes, which correspond to dioceses. Pastors of wards are called bishops and support themselves with secular jobs. Only the top officials of the Church receive salaries. The Sunday sacrament meeting always includes a communion service, at which bread and water are served. Young Mormons are baptized by immersion at the age of 7 or 8. Mormons also believe in *baptism for the dead. Great care is taken to compile genealogies of deceased ancestors, who are baptized by proxy in the dozen Mormon temples. Since 1890 Mormons no longer practice polygamy, although deviationists at times have defied both the State and the Church by taking additional wives. Two qualified Mormons may marry "for time and eternity" in a temple; this is a celestial marriage. The bonds of such a union are believed to last throughout eternity.

The Church is governed by the *First Presidency (composed of a president, elected for life and known as the Prophet, Seer, and Revelator, and his two counselors) and by the *Council of the Twelve Apostles. Almost every male adult in the Church holds some rank of priesthood of Aaron or of Melchizedek: deacon, teacher, priest, elder, member of the seventy, or high priest. Negro Mormons may not be ordained or be allowed to enter the temples, because they are thought to have been cursed by God in their previous lives. A Mormon in good standing will tithe his income, observe the Word of Wisdom (no tobacco, liquor, coffee, or tea), attend church regularly, and participate in the secret temple rites known as endowments. The Church promotes education, recreation, a strict sexual code, honesty in personal relations, respect for civil authority, mutual assistance, and large families. The Mormon Church owns many profitable commercial enterprises and it assists any Mormon who is unemployed or sick and maintains warehouses for storing food, clothing, and household goods.

Brigham Young University in Provo, Utah, has become the largest church-related university in the nation, with more than 20,000 students. The Church also staffs colleges in Idaho and Hawaii. Mormons in public schools and state universities receive religious instruction in nearby seminaries and institutes of religion. By 1967 the Church of Jesus Christ of Latter-Day Saints had grown to 2,400,000 members, mostly in the U.S.; Mormons predominate in Utah but make up large communities in Ariz., N. Mex., S Calif., and Idaho. They maintain a corps of about 12,000 young missionaries around the world who devote 2 years to spreading the "restored gospel." BIBLIOGRAPHY: K. J. Hansen, *Quest for Empire* (1967); T. F. O'Dea, *Mormons* (1957); W. J. Whalen, *Latter-Day Saints in the Modern World* (1964); R. B. West, Jr., *Kingdom of the Saints: The Story of Brigham Young and the Mormons* (1957). *LATTER DAY SAINTS, REORGANIZED CHURCH OF JESUS CHRIST OF; CHURCH OF CHRIST (FETTINGITES); CHURCH OF CHRIST (TEMPLE LOT); CHURCH OF JESUS CHRIST (BICKERTONITES); CHURCH OF JESUS CHRIST (CUTLERITES); LATTER-DAY SAINTS (STRANGITES), CHURCH OF JESUS CHRIST OF.

[W. J. WHALEN]

LATTER PROPHETS, also called Later Prophets, the Books of Isaiah, Jeremiah, Ezekiel and the 12 *minor Prophets, according to the division of the Hebrew Bible. *FORMER PROPHETS.

[T. C. O'BRIEN]

LATTER RAIN MOVEMENT, a description used of Pentecostalism, esp. during its early years. Joel 2.23 refers to a former and a latter rain; for Pentecostals the former is the outpouring of gifts on Pentecost and the latter rain is the new outpouring of the same gifts of the Spirit that ushers in a new premillenial dispensation. In 1947 the New Order of the Latter Rain was formed in North Battleford, Saskatchewan, to protest the loss by the organized Pentecostal Churches of the original Pentecostal insights and direction. BIBLIOGRAPHY: G. Schwartz, *Sect Ideologies and Social Status* (1970).

[T. C. O'BRIEN]

LATTEY, CUTHBERT CHARLES (1877–1954), Jesuit biblical scholar. L. taught Scripture at St. Beuno's College and Heythrop College, England. He wrote several NT commentaries and edited the *Westminster Version of the Sacred Scriptures* (1913–1935; OT only partially completed). BIBLIOGRAPHY: D. Hoy, NCE 8:527.

[T. M. MCFADDEN]

LATVIA, republic of the U.S.S.R., located between Estonia and Lithuania, with capital at Riga. Lutherans form the largest religious group, but Latvia also has a substantial Catholic population and a smaller number of Orthodox. The area became Christian after Meinhard of Holstein established a church at Ikskile, near modern Riga, in 1180, and Bp. Albert established Riga in 1201 and made it his see, suffragan to Bremen until 1214. In 1202 Albert founded the Knights (Brothers) of the Sword, merged with the Teutonic Order in 1237, and they ruled Livonia, German name for modern Estonia-Latvia, until 1561. Lutheranism was introduced into Latvia *c.* 1530. From 1561 Poland ruled Latvia, but the NE part was taken by Sweden in 1629. This was lost in 1721 to Russia, which took the rest of Latvia in the 1772 and 1795 partitions of Poland. German merchants, established in Latvia by the Hanseatic League, remained dominant under Polish and Russian rule, and German remained the official language until replaced by Russian in 1885. Latvia experienced a national revival in the 19th cent. and in 1918 became independent. But it was retaken by the U.S.S.R. during World War II.

[T. EARLY]

LATVIA, ORTHODOX CHURCH IN. This Church proclaimed its autonomy during the revolution of 1917 and in 1936 was recognized by the Patriarchate of Constantinople as an autocephalous metropolitan headed by the abp. of Riga. With the absorption of Latvia into the U.S.S.R. in 1940, it became a simple diocese within the Patriarchate of Moscow.

[T. BIRD]

LATVIAN CATHOLIC ASSOCIATION, AMERICAN, (ALCA) an organization founded 1954 whose members are American Latvian Catholic mission parishes, groups of Catholics, cultural organizations with pronounced Catholic character, and individual Catholics who are not affiliated with any Latvian parish or group that is a member of ALCA. The aims of the Association are to unite American Catholics of Latvian descent, to preserve and foster Latvian Catholic traditions, ethnic culture, and principles of Christian democratic traditions, and to give them spritual, moral, and material assistance. Latvian immigrants came comparatively late to the U. S., because there were no compelling reasons to leave their home country until the beginning of this century, when the Russian tzarist oppression against non-Russian peoples who were ruled by the Russian empire became intolerable. The wave of the first immigrants contained few Latvian Catholics, because the majority of the population of Latvia were Protestants. During the years of the independence of Baltic States, there was no emigration to the U. S. and none was possible during World War II. Toward the end of the war, when Russian armies were invading the Baltic States, there was a mass exodus to the W of Baltic peoples fleeing the Communist reign of terror.

Starting in 1949, many Latvians immigrated to the U. S., among them a considerable number of Catholics.

The first years in the U. S. were spent in building a new life. Latvian mission parishes were established. They were esp. needed for the people whose lack of knowledge of the

English language prevented them from participation in Catholic parishes of their neighborhoods. The coordinating functions were performed by the Latvian bp. in exile—Joseph Rancans and by Msgr. E. Stukels. Under their initiative, on Aug 13-14, 1954, convened a Latvian Catholic conference in Grand Rapids, Michigan. Participants were 9 Latvian clergymen and 20 lay representatives. The conference decided to found the ALCA, drew up the charter which was later amended and completed. Its first president was Msgr. E. Stukels.

There have been 10 ALCA conventions in Chicago, New York, Grand Rapids, Indianapolis, and Milwaukee. In these participated American Latvian Catholic clergy and lay representatives of parishes, groups of Catholics and Catholic student organizations, as delegates.

The principal work of ALCA has consisted in promoting human rights and religious freedom in Latvia by calling public attention to the persecution of religion in Latvia and of the Latvian Catholic Church in particular. American Latvian Catholic Association publishes a bulletin called "ALCA's News" (ALKA's Zinas).

[B. BAGINSKIS]

LAUD, WILLIAM (1573–1645), abp. of Canterbury who so dominated pre-Commonwealth Anglicanism that both it and the ideals that survived it are called Laudian. Intransigent in upholding *episcopacy and the sacramental order, he bore severely on those, mainly Puritans, who did not conform. Undergraduate and fellow of St. John's College, Oxford, and later its head, he devoted himself to the restoration of a Catholic liturgy in the C of E and defended the great high road, the *via media*, of its theology against Calvinism; it was the noble period of the *Caroline Divines. Elected bp. of St. Davids (1621), he engaged in controversy with the Jesuit John Percy (a *Relation* of which L. published in 1639), in which he maintained that the RC and Anglican Churches were both parts of one Church Catholic. Translated to Bath and Wells (1626), then London (1628), and appointed chancellor of Oxford Univ. (1629), he was consecrated abp. of Canterbury in 1633. He was a notable patron of learning. Growing hostility and the attempt to enforce his reforms in Scotland led to his impeachment, imprisonment in the Tower of London (1641), a trial conducted with little regard for justice, and his execution (1645) at the block on Tower Hill. He left a remarkable diary of his last years, published among his works in the Library of Anglo-Catholic Theology (7 v., 1847–60). BIBLIOGRAPHY: E. C. E. Bourne, *Anglicanism of William Laud* (1947); *Archbishop Laud Commendation, 1895* (ed. W. E. Collins, 1895, repr. 1969). *ANGLICANISM.

[J. P. WHALEN]

LAUDABILITER, the papal bull (*c.* 1159) in which Adrian IV expressed his concurrence in the English King Henry II's proposal to invade Ireland in order to effect a needed reformation of morals and religion in the island; often referred to as the Donation of Adrian. The Pope also tried to define the King's rights there and thus protect the rights of others. The document does not exist in the original nor in a copy in the papal or the English archives, but only as recorded in *Giraldus Cambrensis' chronicle *Expugnatio Hiberniae*. Its authenticity has been intensely debated, but the most informed view now accepts *Laudabiliter* as genuine. BIBLIOGRAPHY: M. P. Sheehy, "Bull *Laudabiliter:* A Problem in Medieval Diplomatics and History," *Galway Archaeological and Historical Society Journal* 29 (1961) 45–70.

[R. H. SCHMANDT]

LAUDES DOMINI, a short, anonymous early-Christian poem, written between 316 and 323, composed in 148 hexameters, and preserved in one lone 9th-cent. Parisian manuscript. It is the work of a rhetorician of Autun, following such classical models as Virgil and Ovid. The miracle of a widower being greeted by his long-dead wife as he himself is being laid to rest, gives occasion for the poet to speak of imminent judgment and to deliver a panegyric in honor of Christ. BIBLIOGRAPHY: Erik Peterson, EncCatt 7:957; PL 19:379–86.

[E. J. DILLON]

LAUDOMAR, ST. (var. Lomer, Launomar; d. *c.* 590), hermit and abbot. As a priest he served as a pastor at Chartres and then became a hermit in the solitude of La Perche. Later, he left La Perche and founded the monastery of Curbio (*c.* 570), becoming its first abbot. The monastery of Saint-Lomer in Blois was built in 924 and named in his honor. BIBLIOGRAPHY: M. R. P. McGuire, NCE 8:531; BHL 2:4733–40; Zimmermann 1:104.

[M. R. P. MCGUIRE]

LAUDS, the morning prayer of the Liturgy of the Hours (formerly the Divine Office until its revision in 1971). Its name derives from the Lat. *laudare* (give praise) from which the theme of praise becomes its predominant characteristic. The "Morning Praises" is considered with Evening Prayer (see Vespers) to be one of the two "hinges" of the Hours and except for serious reason should not be omitted. If said as the first hour of the day, after the Invitatory, otherwise after the introductory verse, Lauds now consists of a hymn, psalm, OT canticle, psalms with their antiphons, short reading, short response, antiphon with Zechariah's canticle (the Benedictus), intercessions, Lord's prayer, and the concluding prayer. BIBLIOGRAPHY: P. Regan, NCE 16:261–263.

[C. KEENAN]

LAUDUS, ST. (Lô; d. *c.* 568), French bp. born at St. Lô, Normandy. Besides administering his see, he was also present at the synods (held 533, 538, 541, 549) in Orléans.

[J. R. RIVELLO]

LAUGHTER. Since laughter is an outward manifestation of an inner attitude, its morality is derivative. In its first meaning, laughter has been taken by philosophers to be a sign of the power distinctive of man, reasoning; as the sign of a sense of humor, it indicates power of comparative knowledge, the perception of the incongruous. As an expression of humor or of good spirits, it can be related to the meaning of virtuous *leisure or the various forms of human joy and pleasure. Where these are right, so is the laughter expressing them. Laughter can also be a sign that communicates contempt for another person, specifically as the external act of *derision or ridicule (both from the same Lat. root, *ridere*, to laugh). Then laughter signifies a special form of injustice, namely a contempt for another so great as to treat the other's defects or misfortune as a joke. Because it is a sign of contempt, scornful and belittling laughter is a worse sin according as the person deserves instead respect and reverence or mercy and compassion. BIBLIOGRAPHY: ThAq ST 2a2ae, 75.1 & 2.

[T. C. O'BRIEN]

LAUNOY, JEAN DE (1603–78), French theological writer. L. was a master of theology from the College of Navarre in Paris and was ordained in 1603. Deeply concerned with the authenticity of authorship and legend, he claimed that Gersen of Vercelli, not Thomas à Kempis, wrote *Imitation of Christ*. He argued against the identification of Denis of Paris with the Areopagite and publicly doubted St. Magdalen's presence in Sainte-Baume. He edited and published the works of *Nicholas of Clamanges. He defended *conciliarism and challenged the doctrine of papal infallibility. He also participated in controversy over the universal divine influence on human action, a debate that arose from discussion of the works of Durandus of Saint-Pourçain. In his *Regia in matrimonium potestas* (1674), L. maintained that marriage is a secular civil contract. His 10-volume *Opera omnia* was published in 1731–33.

[R. J. LITZ]

LAURA (var. lavra; from a Gr. word meaning lane or alley), a term that came into use in 4th-cent. Palestinian monasticism to denote a colony of monks who lived in separate huts grouped around a church where they assembled for Divine Liturgy and other services and who were subject to a common spiritual father. This type of monasticism spread into many countries of the East and West. The best-known example of a monastery of this type was that established by St. Sabbas in Palestine near Jerusalem and known as the Great Laura. In later centuries the term denoted any large monastery whose importance was widely recognized, e.g., the Great Laura on Mount Athos. Other well-known examples are Russian Orthodoxy's leading monastic and spiritual center, the Holy Trinity-St. Sergius Laura at Zagorsk, the Pechersky Laura at Kiev, and the Pochaev Laura in Volynia.

LAURANO, FRANCESCO (*c.*1425–1502), Italian sculptor, medalist, architect. Medalist in the court of René I in Anjou (1461–66), L. carved the signed marble Madonna for Sta. Maria della Neve, Palermo (1471), decorated the Chapel of St. Barbara in the Castel Nuovo, Naples (1474), completing both Chapel of St. Lazare, Marseilles, and the altar carving, *Carrying of the Cross*, Avignon, in 1481. L.'s work unites French late Gothic with a strong Florentine Renaissance style in a personal idiom. His renowned, exquisitely delicate marble portrait busts of women may be seen in museums throughout the world. (*Baptista Sforza*, Florence; *Beatrice of Aragon*, Vienna). BIBLIOGRAPHY: J. Pope-Hennessy, *Italian Renaissance Sculpture* (1958).

[M. J. DALY]

LAURENTIUS, ANTIPOPE, Roman archpriest and intermittent claimant to the Roman See (498–506), following the death of Anastasius II in 498. His name is given to the Laurentian schism which briefly divided the early 6th-cent. Roman Church over the issue of reconciliation with the East. L. approved Anastasius's attempt at conciliation and for this reason a minority of the Roman clergy favored him to succeed Anastasius. The majority, however, supported Symmachus, who had opposed conciliation. The Ostrogothic king, Theodoric the Great was called in as arbiter and decided in favor of Symmachus in view of the majority vote. L. already consecrated in St. Mary Major's, submitted to the decision and was appointed bp. of Nocera in nearby Campania. His partisans did not rest, however, and soon there was bloody strife again, resulting in the Laurentians' installing their man as pope (501). When the Roman synod (501–502) could not resolve the matter, Theodoric intervened again, at the advice of the Alexandrian deacon Dioscorus, and declared Symmachus the legal pope. L. retired safely under the protection of the patrician Festus. Only a small faction of his partisans remained in schism. BIBLIOGRAPHY: G. Schwaiger LTK 6:829; Duchesne 1:46.

[E. J. DILLON]

LAURENTIUS ANDREAE, see ANDERSON, LARS.

LAURIER, WILFRID (1841–1919), Canadian statesman. After graduating from McGill University in Montreal, L. settled in the Eastern Townships region of Quebec Province (1866) and became a spokesman for French Canadians there. He represented constituencies of that area in the Canadian House of Commons (1874–1919). L. found no conflict between his Catholicism and his support of the Liberal Party, although the hierarchy often opposed him on specific issues, while he on his part was opposed to the idea of a Catholic party and to clerical domination in politics. In 1887 he emerged as the leader of the Liberal Party and served as prime minister (1896–1911). His handling of the Manitoba school issue brought charges from the bishops that he had compromised the rights of the French Catholic minority by leaving the public school system religiously neutral. His defeat in 1911 turned on his Naval Service Act of 1910 establishing a separate Canadian Navy and his advocacy of reciprocal trade agreements with the U.S. His opposition to conscription in World War I cost him much of his national popularity. He was knighted in 1897. BIBLIOGRAPHY: *Laurier and a Liberal Quebec* (ed. B. Neatby, pa. 1973); J. S. Willison, *Sir Wilfrid Laurier and the Liberal Party* (rev. ed. 1926); *Imperial Relations in the Age of Laurier* (ed. C. Berger, pa. 1969).

[R. K. MACMASTER]

LAURIN VON KLATTAU (fl. *c.*1400), leading Bohemian MS illuminator in Prague. L. executed (1403–11) the magnificent initials and border designs of the Missal for the Abp. of Hasenburg (National Library, Vienne).

[M. J. DALY]

LAUSANNE CATHEDRAL, Swiss cathedral built 1175–1275 and "restored" by Viollet-le-Duc (1873–79), with structures from the 8th, 9th, and 11th cent. discovered in excavations, and showing influences in ground plan and elevation from Laon Cathedral and Notre-Dame, Dijon. Noteworthy are the S portal carvings (*c.*1240) and the rich W portal added (1516–35). The polychromed S transept, with rose window (*c.*1230) mentioned by Villard de Honnecourt depicts allegorical and zodiacal motifs with influence from Picardy.

[M. J. DALY]

LAUSANNE CONFERENCE, first world conference of the *Faith and Order movement, held at Lausanne, Switzerland, Aug. 3–21, 1927. Over 100 Protestant and Orthodox Churches were represented. The idea for the meeting came originally from the Protestant Episcopal Church under the influence of Bp. C. H. *Brent. The purpose of the conference was to find bases for doctrinal unity among Christian Churches, starting from their common belief in Christ and the Gospel and their deep distress at disunity. The subjects considered were: (1) the call to unity; (2) the Church's message to the world: the Gospel; (3) the nature of the Church; (4) the Church's common confession of faith; (5) the Church's ministry; (6) the sacraments; and (7) the unity of Christendom and the relation thereto of the existing Churches. There was wide disagreement on many points, esp. the nature and number of the sacraments and the positions on *episcopacy, *apostolic succession, and *ordination. The statements voted by the conference were therefore largely limited to defining areas of agreement and disagreement. The conference issued a rather general but fervent statement (the only one accepted by the Orthodox) on the Gospel as the Church's message to the world and as the "source for social regeneration." BIBLIOGRAPHY: *Faith and Order: Proceedings of the World Conference, Lausanne* (ed. H. N. Bate, 1928).

[D. CODDINGTON]

LAUSIAC HISTORY (PALLADIUS), a history of the Desert Fathers, written *c.*420 by Palladius, bp. of Helenopolis, who dedicated it to Lausus, chamberlain at the court of Theodosius II. It gives a description of the monastic movement in Egypt, Palestine, Syria, and Asia Minor in the 4th cent. and is a primary source for the history of early monasticism, despite the vast amount of legend it contains. BIBLIOGRAPHY: Quasten 3:177–179; R. T. Meyer, ed. and tr. (ACW 34, 1965).

[P. FOSCOLOS]

LAVABO, the first word of the Latin Vulgate version of Ps 26.6, which was recited by the priest in the Roman Mass as he washed his fingers after the Offertory. The ceremony continues in the revised form of the Mass, but the prayer is shortened to a brief petition for purification from sin. Originally practical after the priest's handling and incensing of the people's gifts, the rite is now symbolic of the spiritual cleansing needed to participate worthily in the Eucharistic celebration.

[T. C. O'BRIEN]

LAVAL, FRANÇOIS DE MONTMORENCY, VEN. (1623–1708), first bp. of Quebec. Born in France and educated by the Jesuits at La Flèche and Clermont, L. was ordained in 1647 and stood staunchly with the Jesuits in their opposition to the Gallican current in his native land. He was consecrated as vicar apostolic of New France in 1658. He established a major (1663) and a minor (1668) seminary to train a diocesan clergy, gradually replacing regulars with secular priests and assigning each priest to a group of churches to make the most effective use of his manpower. Indian mission fields were consolidated under the Jesuits. He was strongly opposed to the brandy trade, which debauched Christian Indians and left the frontiers exposed. Frequently at odds with governors and fur traders, L. built up a strong missionary program in Canada. In 1674 he was named Quebec's first bishop. Ill health caused him to resign from his see (1688), but he continued to influence the Canadian Church until his death. BIBLIOGRAPHY: G. E. Demers, *Mgr. de Laval* (1951); É. Bégin, *François de Laval* (1954); C. A. Liederbach, *Canada's Bishops from 1120 to 1975 . . . from Allen to Yelle* (pa. 1975).

[R. K. MACMASTER]

LAVAL, MARTYRS OF, 19 victims of the French Revolution martyred at Laval, Mayenne, France, in 1794 and beatified on June 19, 1955. This group, 15 priests, 3 women religious, and one lay woman, refused to subscribe to the *Civil Constitution of the Clergy. Fourteen priests were guillotined (Jan, 21, 1794) after refusing the oath; one other priest was ambushed and shot (Oct. 17, 1794) while ministering secretly to nonjuring Catholics. The three sisters were guillotined for refusing the oath; two in March, one in June;

the laywoman, a teacher, captured while caring for wounded soldiers, was guillotined in Feb. for being a nonjuror.

[H. P. ANNAS]

LA VAL SAINTE, ABBEY OF (Valsainte) ancient Carthusian monastery in the canton of Fribourg, Switzerland, where, because of the French Revolution, Dom Augustine de *Lestrange established a Trappist abbey in 1791 rigorous monastic discipline, sterner than that of Abbot de *Rancé. Upon Napoleon's invasion of Switzerland (1798), the monks fled, (by then almost 250 in number) only to return in 1802. After the fall of Napoleon (1815), the group abandoned the abbey and returned to La Trappe. *TRAPPISTS.

[T. M. MCFADDEN]

LAVAL UNIVERSITY, a coeducational Catholic institution of higher learning in Quebec, Canada, modeled on the Univ. of Paris. The oldest Catholic univ. in Canada, it traces its origin to the Quebec Seminary, founded in 1663 by François Xavier de Laval-Montmorency, first bp. of Quebec, and later (1765) combined with the *Collège des Jésuites*, established in 1635. In 1851 a council of Canadian bps. requested the seminary authorities to assume the responsibility for an institution of higher learning in Quebec City. In 1852 Queen Victoria issued a royal charter for the new institution, which took the name of Laval to commemorate the original founder; in 1853 Pius IX conferred certain canonical privileges upon it, including the right to award degrees in theology and canon law; and in 1876 the university was granted a pontifical charter. In the same year, at the request of I. Bourget, bp. of Montreal, the Sacred Congregation of Propaganda enjoined Laval to establish a branch in Montreal. Laval of Montreal was erected in 1878 and gained full independence as the Univ. of *Montreal in 1920. Laval Univ. which in 1856 integrated 11 French classical colleges, together with Montreal, now includes about 90.

Government is vested in the board of trustees and in the administration in the senate or university council. The presiding officer is the rector, who is appointed by Rome. The abp. of Quebec is the apostolic chancellor and royal visitor. The university, which grants the baccalaureate, licentiate or master's degree, and the doctorate, comprises the faculties of theology, agriculture, arts, administrative and commercial sciences, education, forestry and geodesy, law, letters, medicine (which affiliated with the Royal College of Surgeons of London in 1870), philosophy, sciences, and social sciences. It offers adult education noncredit courses and programs for farm and labor leadership, and operates Camp Laguenoc jointly with McGill Univ., Montreal. The teaching staff numbers about 1,345; enrollment, approximately 14,442 full-time and 4,636 part-time students. The library, established in 1852 and containing holdings from the library of the Collège des Jesuites, houses 689,500 volumes, 12,100 periodicals, and 28,000 maps. Since the end of World War II the university has been located on two campuses: one in historic old Quebec; the other, University City, in St. Foy on the outskirts of Quebec. BIBLIOGRAPHY: International Handbook of Universities (1967).

[M. B. MURPHY]

LAVALLIÈRE, ÈVE, (1868–1929), a vivacious, sensitive, and unconventional actress, who for 20 years before the outbreak of World War I was a brilliant ornament of the Parisian theatre and then suddenly abandoned that life completely to spend the last 15 years of her life in seclusion and prayer. Born at Toulon in the Midi, she abandoned her family name Eugénie Fenoglio and chose for herself the stage name Ève Lavallière. Apparently she was aware of the duality of her nature, since Lavallière was the name of the near-legendary favorite of Louis XIV who centuries earlier had suddenly forsaken gay court life for a Carmelite cloister. L. married and divorced the director of the Variétés and was a member of a remarkable company associated with that theater. Her last success was playing a boy's part in "Les Petits" at the Théâtre Antoine. She retired to a mountain village with a single servant, was received into the Church by Abbé Chasteigner, but was unable, despite determined efforts, to take Carmelite vows, because of ill health. She did missionary work among the Arabs of Africa as Sister Ève Marie du Coeur de Jésus of the Third Order of St. Francis. She died with the reputation of sanctity. BIBLIOGRAPHY: È. Lavallière *Ma conversion* (1930); P. Claudel, *Trois figures saintes pour le temps actuel* (1953).

[E. J. DILLON]

LAVANOUX, MAURICE (1894–1974), American artist, critic, and editor. After studying architecture in France and Canada, L. organized and led (1928) a group of laymen incorporated in New York as the Liturgical Arts Society to foster a renewal of religious art in the Church. For over 40 years he single-handedly managed and edited the Society's prestigious magazine *Liturgical Arts* (1931–49). L. traveled extensively throughout the world, documenting and recording with unerring aesthetic judgment his contacts and experiences which he published in diary form as a regular feature in *Liturgical Arts*. He thus provided the forum and means of communication among artists, architects, and ecclesiastics concerned with religious art. He was instrumental in raising the consciousness of the modern Church to artistic values in the liturgy and was a visionary and authoritative force in directing the Church toward a renewed religious art. BIBLIOGRAPHY: M. Lavanoux, "Editor's Diaries in Liturgical Arts," *America* (Nov. 1975).

[R. VEROSTKO]

LAVATER, JOHANN KASPAR (1741–1801), Swiss Protestant theologian. He developed a novel method of character interpretation, through study of a person's facial and bodily structure, which won him some renown; he published his theory in *Physiognomische Fragmente zur Berförderung der Menschenkenntnis und Menschennliebe* (1775–78). His theology was marked by an intense devotion to Christ and an emphasis on the experiential, but at the cost often of a balanced correlation with a reasoned theological position. He died of wounds received while serving as a stretcher–bearer near Zurich during the Napoleonic wars. His works include: *Christliche Lieder* (1776–80); *Aussichten in die Ewigkeit* (4 v., 1768–78); *Pontius Pilatus oder die Bibel im Kleinen* (4 v. 1782–85).

[T. C. O'BRIEN]

LAVELLE, MICHAEL JOSEPH (1856–1939), educator, and administrator. Ordained for the archdiocese of New York in 1879, he spent his entire life as a priest at St. Patrick's Cathedral and as rector he completed the building. L. was vicar-general of the New York archdiocese for 21 years under three archbishops. He founded Cathedral High School in 1905, was cofounder of the Catholic Summer School at Plattsburg, N.Y., established the Catholic Institute for the Blind, and organized the forerunner of the National Catholic Welfare Conference.

[J. R. AHERNE]

LA VÉRENDRYE, PIERRE GAULTIER DE VARENNES DE (1685–1749), Canadian explorer. The decline in the fur trade around Lake Superior and the competition from the Hudson's Bay Company led him to set up a series of new trading posts (1728). Moving W from Lake Nipigon, he financed his expedition by establishing control of the trade in the Manitoba Basin (1731–34). In 1738 he extended his efforts to the Mandans on the bend of the Missouri and discovered the Saskatchewan River, adding extensively to France's empire in North America. BIBLIOGRAPHY: N. M. Crouse, *La Vérendrye: Fur Trader and Explorer* (1956, repr. 1971).

[R. K. MACMASTER]

LA VERNA, see ALVERNIA.

LAVIGERIE, CHARLES MARTIAL ALLEMAND (1825–92), cardinal, religious founder. A native of France and ordained at St. Sulpice in 1849, L. taught at the Sorbonne for several years and as chaplain to Catholic students exercised great influence. He collected sums of money for the persecuted Christians of Syria and went there to supervise their distribution. In 1861 he was appointed to the Roman Rota and in 1863 was named bp. of Nancy, where his organizational genius produced much good for his diocese. Appointed abp. of Algiers in 1867, he founded the White Fathers and White Sisters to evangelize the Muslims in Africa. With his congregations he opened orphanages, industrial schools, hospitals, and agricultural colonies for the Arabs. In 1868 as Apostolic Delegate of W Sahara and the Sudan, he ventured into Central Africa, where he was instrumental in establishing missions in an area hitherto untouched. L. was responsible for the restoration of Carthage as the primatial see of Africa and held the title of archbishop there as well as at Algiers. In an effort to bring the Eastern and Western Churches closer, he founded in 1878 a Melchite seminary in Jerusalem. In Vatican Council I, L. served as mediator between the opposed groups who differed on the definition of papal infallibility. Leo XIII named him cardinal in 1882. He was a strong voice urging French Catholics to rally to the support of the Republic; his stand, symbolized by his Algiers Toast (Nov. 12, 1890) brought bitter attacks from Catholic monarchists (see RALLIEMENT). When Leo's encyclical *Inter innumeras* appeared in 1890 it completely vindicated L.'s position on the Republic. When Leo XIII appealed for an end to the African slave trade, L. made vigorous efforts. The Brussels Conference, at which the great powers all agreed to end slavery, was the triumph of L.'s efforts. The Paris Congress, called by L., confirmed the anti-slavery resolution. L. was one of the outstanding churchmen of the 19th cent., and any one of his great projects would have given him a secure place in history. BIBLIOGRAPHY: L. Baunard, *Le Cardinal Lavigerie* (1896).

[J. R. AHERNE]

LAVIN, MARY (1912–), Irish short-story writer. If the short story is in some ways an Irish achievement, L. is one of its exquisite creators. From 1938 to the present, this farm-dweller from outside Dublin has fashioned a dozen books of short stories and two novels. Her early collection, *Tales from Bective Bridge,* won the coveted James Tait Black Memorial Prize in 1944. For the book *The Great Wave and Other Stories* she won the Katherine Mansfield Prize in 1962. L. writes lucidly, with quiet compassion and remarkable insight into character. She shares the Irish instinct to create large canvases with small people, to convey a human message in terms of simple lives.

[J. R. AHERNE]

LAVRA, see LAURA.

LAW, WILLIAM (1686–1761), Anglican apologist and spiritual writer. L., who was educated and ordained at Cambridge, lost both his ecclesiastical and academic position because he was a *nonjuror (1712). The rest of his life he spent quietly in tutoring, spiritual direction, and writing. His *Three Letters to the Bishop of Bangor* (1717) is a defense of Anglican principles, and his *Case of Reason* (1732) is a skillful reply to M. Tindal, a deist. L.'s most famous work, however, is a *Serious Call to a Devout and Holy Life* (1728; many eds. since). The work, which relied heavily on Catholic spiritual writers (Tauler, Ruysbroeck, Thomas à Kempis) was the most effective Protestant spiritual book in English after **Pilgrim's Progress,* exercising in particular a strong influence upon John *Wesley and upon evangelical revivalism generally. It stresses the individual ascetical life through the cultivation of the virtues. In his later years L. became interested in J. *Boehme and developed a theory of mysticism similar to that of the *Inner Light, which alienated Wesley. L.'s mystical works are *Spirit of Prayer* (1749–50) and *Spirit of Love* (1752 and 1754). BIBLIOGRAPHY: E. W. Baker, *Herald of the Evangelical Revival* (1948); J. B. Green, *John Wesley and William Law* (1945); S. Hobhouse, *William Law and Eighteenth Century Quakerism* (1927); L. Stephen, DNB 32 (1892) 236–240.

[R. B. ENO]

LAW, an ordinance of reason for the common good, by whoever has charge of the community, and promulgated (ThAq ST 1a2ae, 90.4). Thomas Aquinas' classical definition of law is situated within his theological synthesis, wherein he views law as a unity. He writes *de lege,* not *de legibus*. Human experience begins with the multiplicity of laws: civil and ecclesiastical, natural and positive, human and divine. The unity of law derives from the unity of reason, the common good, and authority.

The formal element in the definition is reason: law is a construct of reason. As a rule and measure of human conduct, law is practical, not speculative (1a2ae, 90.1 ad 2), and is always moral, for man's good is to live reasonably (1a2ae, 18.5; 19.3). As man devises order for his conduct, he is creative only within limits. His moral knowledge, like all human knowledge, is specified and measured by what is known. Only God's creative knowledge is an unmeasured measure. Thus, the divine reason, as directive of all creatures (the eternal law), is the fundamental law. Other laws are such only in conformity with it. Natural law, as man's understanding of the intelligiblity of creation, is at the base of the created moral order. Upon this foundation, human legislators construct laws and institutions that embody natural law demands. The rights of man outlined in **Pacem in terris* reflect man's self-understanding in an industrial society; new demands will arise in a technological society.

Giving meaning to this hierarchy of laws is a parallel hierarchy within the *common good. God as the beginning and end of all creation is both its law and common good. Man's vocation to full participation in God as the goal of his existence is fully known only through God's self-manifestation. Yet man's reflection upon his experience as finite spirit does reveal his openness to transcendence.

The obligatory force of law derives from its relationship to reason and the common good. Moral and legal *obligation is a hypothetical necessity predicated upon choice of an end, together with its necessary demands. In this the voluntarist school disagreed with Aquinas and preferred to root law's obligatory character in the will of the legislator.

Man recognizes that his freedom implicitly affirms certain a priori conditions. As K. Rahner has indicated, such conditions are known a posteriori only when they are made known concretely in external laws. Such laws, framed and promulgated by the authority of the Church and the State, instruct men in their search for their human destiny. They also contain coercive sanctions to be exercised against those whose actions would deflect the course of society's movement toward its goal. Using these ideas of reason, common good, and authority, Aquinas divides law.

God formulates the eternal law, which he executes by his governance and providence. Creatures share the eternal law by their subjection to it; nonrational creatures by natural necessity; rational creatures by choice. Man's participation in the eternal law is the natural law. On the basis of what he knows of his nature and personality, man derives moral norms to direct his conduct. Men gathered in civil and ecclesiastical societies give specific content to the guidelines indicated by natural law in human laws. Bills of rights, independent judiciaries, and procedures guaranteeing due process of law insure that man's fundamental, natural rights will not be lost in the process of political organization.

The Christian must also recognize in the natural law the content of his normal norms. In accepting redemption by Christ and justification by God's grace, he knows himself incapable of fulfilling the moral demands by himself. At the same time he accepts the divine invitation to self-transcendence through accepting Christ in faith. He will strive to fulfill the obligations of law even as he avoids a self-righteous sense of self-justification because he has kept the law.

Historically, some Christians attempted to circumscribe the good news and the freedom of God's sons within narrow legal confines, while others envisioned a community without structure, law, or authority. Both deny in practice the incarnational character of the present economy of salvation. The difficulty emerges because specific laws can demand only the minimum morality necessary for society's peace and order. The Christian ideal, like the ideal of natural law, invites men to maximum possibilities. The destiny of man cannot be realized simply by conformity to an external law. Yet even as man internalizes laws and values, he requires the instruction of law and the support of a structured society. Thus, law has a necessary, albeit secondary, role in the achievement of man's human and Christian destiny. BIBLIOGRAPHY: T. E. Davitt, *Nature of Law* (1951); J. M. Aubert, *Loi de Dieu, lois des hommes; (Le Mystère chrétien, théologie morale,* 1964).

[R. P. STENGER]

LAW, CIVIL, a body of rules governing the conduct of a people in temporal, as distinguished from spiritual, matters. It may be statutory or customary; it may originate with king or parliament or courts. It may be defined in terms of its relationship to government (positive, imperative conception), to societal institutions (historical, sociological conception), or to ideals and values (philosophical conception). In the course of history it has often been difficult to separate civil from ecclesiastical (or canon) law. Justinian's Code begins with a title on the Trinity; church councils and popes made their own the prevailing customs and laws of the times.

Church-state or *sacerdotium-imperium* struggles during the Middle Ages did not center around the right of the civil power to legislate. Even though certain Fathers of the Church found the origin of civil authority in Adam's fall, and later writers gave the pope widespread power to judge sin even in rulers, the obligation of obeying just civil laws was not questioned. The NT makes clear the Christian's duty of obeying tax laws (Mt 17.22–26; 22.17–21) and of respecting all authority as from God (Rom 13.1). Peter counseled obedience for the Lord's sake (1 Pet 2.13) even as he insisted upon obedience to God before men (Acts 5.29).

Thomas Aquinas rooted the obligation to obey civil law in man's social nature and his need to share in the civil common good. (*De regimine principum,* 1.1). Because of sin, paternal training alone is insufficient to lead all youths to virtue; the coercion of civil law becomes necessary for some (ThAq 1 ST 1a2ae, 96.4). But even if all men were virtuous, civil law would be necessary for directing a multitude to a common good (2a2ae, 47.10 ad 2). Civil authority has two functions: one, substitutive, for those who cannot or will not rule themselves; the other, essential, for those who need unity and direction to achieve common purposes. Aquinas recognized the inherent limitations of civil law. Man is totally subordinate only to God, never to the government (1a2ae, 21.4 ad 3). No human law can direct man to his divine, transcendent destiny, nor can any human legislator totally encompass the contingencies of human conduct and the motives of the human heart (1a2ae, 91.4).

As man's understanding develops and as human situations change, it is necessary for civil law to change. Too rapid changes can disrupt the unity of society, for they disturb the people's customs, which are the strongest support of law (1a2ae, 97.2). Because of his concern for order in society, Aquinas was cautious about sanctioning sedition (2a2ae, 43.2). Civil disobedience must be justified by achieving some good which compensates for the disruption of society.

Because civil law, like all law, must be made for the common good of all, the obligation to obey springs from the objective requirements of that common good and not from the will of the legislator to oblige subjects. The Thomistic tradition finds little room for a ''purely penal law'' because this idea tends to make part of man's political activity nonmoral.

Aquinas mentions several means for alleviating the harshness of civil law: contrary custom introduced by free citizens (1a2ae, 97.3); dispensation (1a2ae, 97.4); interpretation of the law by individuals in special situations (1a2ae, 96.6); and **epikeia,* the virtue whose exercise realizes the highest form of justice (2a2ae, 120.1).

Recent papal social encyclicals place much reliance upon government intervention and civil law for the realization of social justice in today's technological societies. BIBLIOGRAPHY: Y. Simon, *General Theory of Authority* (1962); T. E. Davitt, *Nature of Law* (1951); H. A. Rommen, *State in Catholic Thought* (1945). H. L. Hart, *Concept of Law* (1961).

[R. P. STENGER]

LAW, DIVINE, most generally, the plan by which divine Wisdom directs all things to their appropriate goals. In this definition Thomas Aquinas makes the Eternal Law the measure, exemplar, and source of every law (ThAq ST 1a2ae, 93.1). More specifically, it is any law whose immediate origin is God, either by way of special revelation (many OT laws) or creation (natural law). Most properly, it is the law directing man to his proper transcendent destiny. The knowability and goal of this law exceeds man's native capacities, hence his need for special instruction (ST 1a2ae, 91.4).

Confusion reigns when this divine law is denominated by positive law, for positive law is composed of specific precepts for a particular human society. Now in history man's true destiny was only gradually revealed to him. Before Christ, God's people lived by faith in his coming and by laws ascribed to Moses. Jesus came to fulfill the law and the prophets (Mt 5.17–18), not by adding new or different precepts, but by his life, death, Resurrection, and the sending of his Spirit. The grace of the Holy Spirit, given through faith in Christ, is primary in the new law (ST 1a2ae, 106.1). The Christian has a new life (Rom 6) and performs the works of the Spirit (Gal 5). As the grace of the Holy Spirit possessed by man, the new law justifies man. (ThAq ST 1a2ae, 106.2).

Secondarily, the new law includes the Scriptures, which inspire man's faith, and sensible signs by which man comes to and lives in grace. As the new law was inaugurated by Christ, so it continues in the signs or sacraments that he instituted. The actions required by the new law are those necessarily connected with faith operative in love, such as confession of faith. Thus, under the impulse of the Spirit, God's people are left free by Christ to determine the specific forms which the Christian life takes in the course of history. (ST 1a2ae, 108.1, 2). BIBLIOGRAPHY: B. Häring, *Law of Christ* (v.1, 1961); D. Wilkerson, *Commandments and Promises of Jesus Christ* (pa. 1974).

[R. P. STENGER]

LAW, INTERNATIONAL, the body of general principles and specific rules binding upon the international community in their mutual relations. International law has grown as legal theories developed with changing political realities.

While Greek philosophers recognized the existence of laws different from those of their city-states, it was the Roman jurists who encompassed these different laws within a conceptual framework. **Ius gentium,* a law common to many peoples, was located between *ius naturale,* common to all men, and *ius civile,* proper to a particular people. The legal theory of imperial Rome proved to be an effective vehicle for continuity even as it was amalgamated with various barbarian customary laws. Revived study of Roman law and the formation of the *Corpus iuris canonici* provided medieval authors with a comprehensive legal structure. This was effective as long as Christendom could be considered one universal society.

With the emergence of stronger local autonomy, the late Middle Ages saw the end of effective papal and imperial hegemony in Europe. J. Bodin (*Six livres de la république,* 1576) provided a theory for the legislative sovereignty which individual rulers were exercising. The 16th cent. was the golden age for scholastic writers on natural and international law. The discovery of the Americas broadened narrow European horizons to new lands and new peoples. A number of writers, mostly Spanish, wrote treatises *De iustitia et iure.* B. de las Casas and F. Vitoria wrote of the rights of peoples, including the rights of American Indians. F. Suárez and St. Robert Bellarmine extended their treatises on law beyond the outlines of Aquinas.

Hugo *Grotius is considered the father of international law for his *De iure belli ac pacis* (1625). His theory of natural law was independent of papal sanction and promulgation. He considered the *ius gentium* both in the Roman sense of a law common to several peoples and as a law between states. Although the work of Grotius had enduring importance, it was the Treaty of Westphalia (1648) that decisively shaped international law. Recognition was given to the reality of territorial sovereignty, which remains one of the cornerstones of international law and international relations.

Theories of corporate personality and the spirit of the people have made nationalism the most potent political reality. With the importance of national sovereignty, peace came to mean a balance of power. In the realities of politics, only a balancing of sovereign powers could insure that no power could become strong enough to render ineffective another's sovereignty.

The immediate origins of contemporary international law are the multinational conventions that followed various 19th-cent. alliances. The most important of these were the two peace conferences at The Hague (1899, 1907), which called for general limitations of armaments and the principle of compulsory arbitration of disputes.

After World War I the Treaty of Versailles (1919) called for the establishment of the League of Nations. In 1920 the Permanent Court of International Justice was established for the arbitration of international disputes. The court has had limited success, for nations are free to submit their disputes or to regard them as matters of national interest. In the formation of the United Nations Organization (1945), several structural weaknesses of the League were avoided. The World Court was included in the UN Charter, as were agencies concerned with health, welfare, economics, culture, and education. As Paul VI taught in *Populorum progressio* (1967), the maintenance of peace cannot be separated from the economic, social, and cultural development of peoples.

The basic question in international law remains the source of obligation behind the rules. Historically, the rules acquired their binding character from the consent of sovereign states to be obliged by them. There is also adherence to the traditional principle, *pacta sunt servanda.* Yet conflict remains between national sovereignty and supranational obligatory laws. International law will reach maturity only when involvement in international associations is understood to be an exercise of, and not an abandonment of, sovereignty, and when resort to war is no longer an expected method of diplomacy.

John XXIII called for "a public authority with worldwide power and endowed with the proper means for the efficacious pursuit of its objective, which is the universal common good in concrete form" (*Pacem in terris,* 1963). The existence of this worldwide common good and the increasing interdependence of nations create the moral demand for a corresponding worldwide authority. The endorsement of John XXIII and Vatican II and the visit of Paul VI have given moral authority and approval to the UN quest for peace. BIBLIOGRAPHY: J. L. Brierly, *Law of Nations* (5th ed., 1955); C. G. Fenwick, *International Law* (1948); W. L. Gould, *Introduction to International Law* (1957); *World Justice* 4 (1962).

[R. P. STENGER]

LAW, INTERPRETATION OF, a declaration or explanation of the fact or the manner of a law's applicability. The need for interpretation of all human law rests on its inherent limitation: the legislator can only envision and formulate a law on a level that is universal and on the basis of what is usually the case; the law itself, of course, is also subject to the vagaries of human language (ThAq ST 1a2ae, 96.6). One way of interpretation is covered by the meaning of *epikeia; this strictly is not an interpretation of the law itself, but a judgment that in a particular instance the good intended by a law would be thwarted by observance of the letter of the law (*ibid.,* 2a2ae, 120). In its more usual meaning, interpretation deals with the law itself. Because the function of interpretation coincides with the function of law, the right to interpret law authentically belongs to the one who has the power to legislate. In American civil law that power is so divided into the three functions of governing, that much of the interpretation of the law belongs to the Supreme Court and to other lower courts. Moral theology considers the question of interpretation in regard to the legislative power of the Church. Fundamental is the distinction: authentic interpretation, interpretation by use, theoretical or academic interpretation. Authentic interpretation belongs to the supreme legislator in the Church, the pope or the pope in concert with the bps., when it is a question of divine law, and the interpretation can engage the Church's solemn magisterium in matters of Christian morality. The supreme legislative power obviously also has competence to interpret authentically purely ecclesiastical law. Benedict XV in 1917 established the Commission for the Authentic

Interpretation of Canon Law. An authentic interpretation has the force of law itself; it may be declaratory or clarifying; it may restrict or extend the law. Interpretation by use refers to the way that actual observance and customs that are not contrary to the law make clear the law's force. "Custom is the best interpreter of law" is an old adage of the jurists. Among its implications is the principle that use indicates the legislator's agreement with the way the law is being observed. An academic or theoretical interpretation is that given by experts in the study of law, and for this there are classical and established principles of interpretation and jurisprudence followed by canonists and moral theologians.

[T. C. O'BRIEN]

LAW, PENAL, theoretically, a law that does not impose moral obligation, but solely a penalty for transgression. Examples sometimes cited are city ordinances imposing fines for traffic violations, customs laws, or even tax laws. The theoretical possibility of laws that are purely penal rests on the fact that if a law can be binding morally, a law can also bind to something less, namely, merely penalty. But sound moral theology views law, all law, as a principle guiding the positive orientation of the will towards good, not as a mere restriction on a will indifferent to either good or evil. Ideally, law is interiorized by those subject to it; they accept it along with their own moral judgment as a guide to right human action. The responsiveness to law includes not only obedience, but *justice in all its forms, and in a society particularly, *social justice and other forms of respect for authority. The purpose of law and of the virtues responsive to it is the common or public good. The theory of a purely penal law abstracts from or ignores such considerations and isolates the transgression of law from the full human context. The human legislator, it is true, does not legislate virtuous compliance but simply compliance; that does not take the issues of law for the subject out of the realm of morality. An interiorized attitude towards law does not require legalism, scrupulosity over the jot or tittle; the same such attitude includes prudence and taking into account legitimate grounds for nonobservance of the letter of the law and whether custom, dispensation, or the accepted intent of a law permits latitude in the manner of compliance.

[T. C. O'BRIEN]

LAW, POSITIVE, a law that is "placed" (Lat., *posita*) to make explicit the provisions and more determinately achieve the purposes of a higher law. The eternal law is conceived of as expressing the purposiveness of divine wisdom; divine positive law, e.g., the Decalogue or the NT itself, expresses the concrete ways of salvation (see LAW, DIVINE). Natural law consists in the connaturally apprehended imperatives (see SYNDERESIS) consonant with human nature's drives towards self-fulfillment; positive civil law has its radical grounding in natural law, but makes determinations that fit the concrete, socio-cultural ways in which the members of a society live together. Positive ecclesiastical law, e.g., canon law, regulates the communal life of the Church in its externals and in ways that are meant to serve the fundamental law of the Church's life, the grace of the Holy Spirit conjoining its members to Christ and to one another. In any of its forms, positive law consists in both affirmative precepts enjoining certain acts, and negative precepts prohibiting others.

[T. C. O'BRIEN]

LAW, ROMAN, see ROMAN LAW.

LAW AND GOSPEL, a basic distinction made in many kinds of Christian theology between the two principal modes of God's relation to man. Both the distinction and the close connection between the gift and the command of God are evident as early as the fundamental statement of the Decalogue (Ex 20.2–3): "I am the Lord your God, who brought you out of the land of Egypt, out of the house of bondage. You shall have no other gods before me." The gospel in this declaration is the remembrance that it was God, the Lord of the covenant, who had brought the people of Israel out of captivity. This was the historical basis for any requirement that he would lay upon them. And the requirement was correlative to it, namely, the acknowledgment of his sole claim to deity, together with the refusal to ascribe such deity to anyone or anything less than the Ultimate, who had brought about the Exodus of the people from Egypt. As is evident already in the story of Abraham and in the other patriarchal narratives, the initiative of God in creating a relationship between himself and his chosen ones was always the presupposition for the rule of conduct that he enunciated. The law was grounded in the gospel; the two were inseparable, but they were in a real sense distinct from each other throughout the history of biblical religion, whether in the OT or in the NT.

With the coming of Christianity, however, this distinction took on new meaning. Although Jesus described his mission as one of fulfilling, not of destroying, the law and the prophets, he made clear again what the adherents of the law and the prophets were in danger of forgetting: that the deeds of God, not the works of men, were the foundation for the relation between them. It was esp. in the epistles of the Apostle Paul—and specifically in those to the Romans and to the Galatians—that the distinction between the law and the gospel was developed most fully. God's covenant with Abraham preceded the giving of the law. Therefore "the law, which came four hundred and thirty years afterward, does not annul a covenant previously ratified by God, so as to make the promise void. For if the inheritance is by the law, it is no longer by promise; but God gave it to Abraham by a promise" (Gal 4.17–18). In the gospel of Jesus Christ, therefore, "the righteousness of God has been manifested apart from law . . . the righteousness of God through faith in Christ Jesus for all who believe" (Rom 3.21–22). Other parts of the NT do not work as explicitly with this distinction, but it is implied wherever the primacy of the divine gift over the divine demand is asserted.

In the 2d cent. Marcion laid such emphasis upon the distinction of law and gospel as to separate rather than merely distinguish them. His opponent, Tertullian, said that "the separation of law and gospel" was "Marcion's special and principal work." But now it was a matter, not of differentiating between two modes of God's relation to men, but of differentiating between two Gods: one God of the law, the Jewish deity of wrath and punishment portrayed in the OT; the other, the God of the gospel, the Father of our Lord Jesus Christ, revealed in the NT. It is probably correct to see Marcion's teaching as a protest against a tendency already evident in the Church of his time, to depress Christianity into a religion of conduct rather than a message of salvation. But the cure he proposed was no less dangerous than the disease he diagnosed, and the Church was obliged to reject any interpretation of the relation between the law and the gospel that would threaten the unity of God.

Luther, too, protested against the blurring of the distinction between the promises of God and the demands of God, and he made the relation between the law and the gospel a dominant theme of his theology. In his *Lectures on Galatians* (1535) he used this relation as the touchstone by which to identify true and false doctrine in Christianity. Thus, e.g., the Christian doctrine of the sacraments was distorted when they were seen as holy works that we perform in order thereby to become worthy of the favor of God, rather than as means of grace, by which God bestows his gratuitous favor. Lutheran theology since the 16th cent. has continued to lay great emphasis on the proper relation between the law and the gospel. The *Formula of Concord declared this relationship in Art. V, and in Art. VI discussed the "third use of the law," namely, as a reminder to the regenerated of their remaining sinfulness and their need of grace (see ANTINOMIANISM). *Pietism came to be condemned because it taught that the proper preparation of the heart would make a man ready to receive grace. Various forms of 19th-cent. *liberal theology were interpreted as a relapse into the moralistic distortion of the gospel as a "new law." Many of the debates within the Lutheran theological tradition were, in one way or another, discussions of the proper relation between law and gospel.

The theme of law and gospel is prominent in the *Reformed tradition as well (e.g., *Westminster Confession, ch. 19–20; Second *Helvetic Confession, ch. 12–13). The relationship has a different emphasis, with obedience to law being stressed as a mark of election. The distinction between law and gospel, however, is not a denominational label but an issue to which Christian doctrine in every denomination has been obliged to address itself. BIBLIOGRAPHY: G. Forde, *Law-Gospel Debate* (1969); C. F. W. Walther, *Proper Distinction Between Law and Gospel* (1897); ThAq ST 1a2ae, 106.1 and 2; C. H. Dodd, *Gospel and Law* (1951).

[J. PELIKAN]

LAW OF ASSOCIATIONS, legislation passed by the French Assembly in 1901 which severely restricted the rights of religious congregations in France by making foundations—both new and established—subject to the state's prior authorization. Theoretically, the law affected the legal status of all associations, political, social, and commercial as well; but practically its primary target was the regular orders of the RC Church whose influence anticlericals saw as detrimental to the welfare of the Republic. Introduced by Prime Minister Waldeck-Rousseau in the wake of the Dreyfus affair, the law was directed in the first instance against the reactionary policies of the Jesuits and Assumptionists, and more generally against the prodigious growth of religious orders in France throughout the 19th century. According to the law, religious congregations which had enjoyed state recognition in the past were permitted to continue, provided they complied with certain administrative regulations; even so, their authorization could be rescinded by cabinet decree at any time. However, those that had not been authorized, a category embracing all the most prominent teaching, preaching, and contemplative orders, were declared dissolved and their members disqualified from any teaching activity, a section of the law formalized in 1902 by the closing down of 2500 schools run by unauthorized orders. Under these circumstances, the men's orders were virtually compelled to leave the country, while the women's orders thereafter generally directed themselves to nursing.

[E. M. GATES]

LAW OF CONSCIOUSNESS, phrase formulated by *Teilhard de Chardin to describe the evolution of consciousness as the specific effect of organized complexity. According to Teilhard, there is a direct proportion between the exterior complexity of matter and the inner psychism or consciousness of matter. To the extent that matter in its measurable exterior structure has become more complex or more intensely knit, its interior psychism becomes more intensely conscious. Man stands on the evolutionary scale of matter as the most closely knit and the most intensely conscious. From the very beginning, matter in its most primal state had both an exterior structure or complexity and an interior psychism or consciousness. In the evolution of matter, the process of complexification in which the simple moves to the complex is at work. Involved in this process is the law of consciousness in which the inner psychism of matter moves from the less intensely conscious to the more intensely conscious. Moving backward and downward from man, both consciousness and complexity dwindle until the interior element of consciousness is no longer measurable, but this non-measurability does not argue for its nonexistence. BIBLIOGRAPHY: Teilhard de Chardin, *Phenomenon of Man* (1959); *Future of Man* (1964); A. M. Young, *Reflexive Universe; Evolution of Consciousness* (1976).

[W. J. DUGGAN]

LAW OF GUARANTEES, the legislation enacted by the Italian Parliament (May 13, 1871) which separated Church and State in the Kingdom of Italy but guaranteed to the pope his dignity and independence. The principal provisions of the law were: (1) the pope's person was declared sacred and inviolable and attempts against him were to be considered as serious as those against the king; (2) the Holy See was to receive in perpetuity an annual, tax-exempt grant from the Italian government; (3) the pope was to have the use of the Vatican and Lateran Palaces and the villa at Castel Gandolfo, and state officials would not be permitted to enter these areas; (4) foreign envoys to the Holy See were to enjoy all the rights and privileges accorded to ambassadors by international law. The Law of Guarantees was rejected by Pope Pius IX in his encyclical *Ubi nos*. The Lateran Pacts (1929) formally abrogated the Law of Guarantees.

[E. A. CARRILLO]

LAWRENCE OF BRINDISI, ST. (1559–1619), Capuchin theologian, diplomat. Born Cesare de Rossi in Naples, L. lost his parents at an early age and joined the Capuchin novitiate in Verona. He studied at Padua and at St. Mark's in Venice, earning a reputation as a scholar of the Scriptures and biblical languages. Ordained in 1582, he was named provincial of Tuscany in 1589. In 1592, he was appointed by Pope Clement to work for Jewish conversions. In 1599, he was sent to Prague, then part of the Holy Roman Empire. In 1601, while still assigned to Prague, he rallied the troops of the empire against the Turks at Albareale in Hungary. Returning to Italy (1602), L. was elected vicar general of the Capuchins and, in that post, traveled throughout Europe renewing the Capuchin Order. Returning to Prague (1606–09), L. was successful in persuading Philip III of Spain to join the Catholic League with the Holy Roman Empire against Henry IV of France. From 1610 to 1613, L. represented the Holy See at the court of Maximilian, Duke of Bavaria. In 1616, L. mediated peace talks between Peter of Toledo, Governor of Milan, and the Duke of Savoy on the question of Monferrato, and after initial setbacks, was able to produce an accord in the year 1618. L. completed (1619) his last mission when he persuaded Philip of Spain to remove the tyrannical Duke of Osuna from his position as viceroy of Naples. Many of L.'s major works were not published until after his death. His two most important works are *Explanatio in Genesim,* and *Lutheranismi hypotyposis,* an examination of the theology of Luther. L. was canonized in 1881. BIBLIOGRAPHY: M. A. da Carmignano Di Brenta, BiblSanct 8:161–179; Butler 3:172–173.

[R. BRADY]

LAWRENCE OF CANTERBURY, ST. (d. 619), one of the band accompanying Augustine to Britain. L. was later sent to report to Gregory and seek advice. He returned to Britain with the pallium for Augustine. L. was then consecrated by Augustine to succeed him as abp. of Canterbury. He remained in his see when other bishops fled during a hostile reversion to paganism. He died in 619 after converting the pagan king. BIBLIOGRAPHY: Bede, *Ecclesiastical History* 1:27; 2:4, 6, 7; F. M. Stenton, *Anglo-Saxon England* (1947); Butler 1:241; G. D. Gordini, BiblSanct 8:129–134.

[A. WARDLE]

LAWRENCE OF DURHAM (d. 1154), English–Latin poet and prior of Durham (1149). The details of his life and of many events at Durham come from his *Dialogi*. He also wrote a popular account of scriptural history in elegiac verse, the *Hypognosticon*. BIBLIOGRAPHY: M. L. Mistretta, NCE 8:567.

[F. D. BLACKLEY]

LAWRENCE JUSTINIAN, ST. (1381–1455), bp., patriarch of Venice. Born to a noble Venetian family, at 19 years L. joined the Augustinian Canons Regular at Alga. This convent became the new Congregation of Secular Canons of Boniface IX (approved 1404). L. was ordained probably in 1405. This new congregation opened houses in 1409, 1413, and 1418, and in 1424 L. became the first superior general. In 1433, Pope Eugene IV appointed him bp. of Castello, although L. protested his unworthiness. In 1451, after the death of the patriarch of Grado, the Pope merged the Dioceses of Grado and Venice and named L. first patriarch of Venice. He refused the princely trappings of his office and dedicated himself to working among the poor. He died at the age of 74 and was canonized by Alexander VIII in 1690. L's writings centered on two broad areas: the ascetic life (*De perfectionis gradibus; De casto connubio Verbi et animae;* 1425) and church administration (*De institutione et regimine praelatorum; c.*1450). BIBLIOGRAPHY: G. Di Agresti, BiblSanct 8:150–156; Butler 3:489–492.

[R. J. BRADY]

LAWRENCE O'TOOLE, ST. (1128–80), abp. of Dublin from 1162, taken under the dominion of the English king. He was under the care of the bp. of Glendalough from boyhood, became a monk there, and was elected abbot in 1148. As abp., L. worked for reform of church discipline in his see and reformed the canonry of his cathedral, Christ Church. Much of his time was given to defending the Church against the English Crown; he was able to secure from Pope Alexander III protection of his churches while assisting at the Lateran Council III in 1179. L. died in Eu, Normandy, where he had followed Henry II of England in order to defend Irish interests. He was canonized in 1226. BIBLIOGRAPHY: Butler 4:341–343; BiblSanct 8:159–60.

[T. C. O'BRIEN]

LAWRENCE OF THE RESURRECTION (1611–91), Discalced Carmelite lay brother. Born Nicholas Herman, he became a Carmelite at Paris in mid-life after an army career. After his death some of his spiritual maxims and letters were found and published by Joseph de Beaufort, vicar general of the Paris archdiocese. They were used by Mme. de *Guyon and republished (1710) by P. *Poiret. Because she used them to defend her theories, they lost popularity and were not widely read by Catholics. L.'s chief spiritual counsels concerned the practice of the presence of God. BIBLIOGRAPHY: N. Herman, *La Pratique de la présence de Dieu* (mod. ed., 1934); *Practice of the Presence of God* (tr. D. Attwater, 1962).

[T. C. O'BRIEN]

LAWRENCE OF RIPAFRATTA, BL. (1373 or 74–1456), Italian Dominican, counselor of St. *Antoninus, Abp. of Florence; professor and preacher, promoter of the reform of his order. There is no proof for the claim that L. was the novice master of St. Antoninus and Bl. Fra *Angelico.

[T. C. O'BRIEN]

LAWRENCE OF SPAIN (d. 1248), bp. of Orense in Spain from 1218 or 1219, canonist. He taught at the Univ. of Bologna and composed the *Apparatus* and glosses on Gratian's *Decretum* that had great influence on the development of medieval canon law. BIBLIOGRAPHY: A. Garcia, NCE 8:569–570.

[T. C. O'BRIEN]

LAWRENCE OF VILLAMAGNA, BL.. (1476–1535), preacher. Born to the noble Mascoli family in Abruzzi, L. entered the Franciscan monastery at Sta. Maria delle Grazie. After his ordination, he achieved a reputation as a renowned preacher and was said to possess the gift of prophecy. L. died in Ortona and was buried in the friary church there. He was beatified in 1923. BIBLIOGRAPHY: Butler 2:491–492; EncCatt 7:1552–53.

[R. J. BRADY]

LAWRENCE, ROBERT, ST. (d. 1535), English Carthusian martyr. He joined the London Charterhouse and succeeded Bl. John Houghton as prior of Beauvale (1531). He appeared with Houghton and Bl. Augustine Webster before Thomas Cromwell to discuss a modification of the oath required by the Act of Supremacy (1535). With the two others, he was imprisoned, tried, and found guilty of treason, and executed. He was canonized in 1970 by Pope Paul VI. BIBLIOGRAPHY: S. Mottironi, BiblSanct 3:1140–42; Butler 2:277–280; Gillow BDEC 4:159–161.

[V. SAMPSON]

LAWRENCE, THOMAS (1769–1830), a prodigy, one of England's great portrait painters working in the grand manner of Sir Joshua Reynolds, enriched by his own personal romantic elegance. Early phenomenally successful, painter to the King (*Portrait of George IV*, Vatican) and to the society of his day, L., commissioned (1818) to paint European leaders, executed the sophisticated portrait of *Pope Pius VII*—one of his finest works (Windsor Castle). In 1820 L. succeeded the American Benjamin West as president of the Royal Academy, London.

[M. J. DALY]

LAWS, CONFLICT OF, the imposition of one law that contradicts another. The rightness of a law as an ordinance of reason is its conformity to the requirements of justice. That in turn requires that the law be truly promotive or protective of the common good; that its enactment be within the competence of the legislator; that the law itself respect the just and proportionate conditions within the social unit of those whom it obligates. A conflict of true laws, therefore, is an anomaly. The whole order of justice is hierarchic: there are levels of the "common good" as its stands for the common good of man's destiny, natural and supernatural; the common good of a nation; the common good of a narrower civil unit. Accordingly, there are levels of competence among legislators as they are responsible for a higher or lesser common good. True conflict is a contradiction, for it is not between equal laws but between a higher law and an infringement by a lower and spurious law. Thus a civil law that imposes an obligation contrary to divine law is not a law but a usurpation. Historically, conflicts of law have existed and still exist. Often the way of prudence must be to avoid worse upheaval by avoiding confrontation. But this attitude does not legitimize an unjust law nor does it mean that nonresistance or the avoidance of a showdown is moral compliance.

[T. C. O'BRIEN]

LAWS, PROMULGATION OF, the official, public proclamation by the competent legislator that a law is in force. The term "promulgation," of unknown etymology, comes into the medieval and later discussion of law from *Gratian's *Decretum*: "Laws are instituted when they are promulgated" (Decr.1.4). Law in essence is the ordinance of the legislator's mind and enactment, but since it binds reasoning beings it must be made known to them. With civil law the passage and signing of a law usually includes the determination of the time it comes into operation and the official publication of the law. In church law, the laws of the popes in antiquity were promulgated by being posted on the doors of the Roman basilicas. Benedict XV promulgated the CIC on Pentecost, 1917, and made Pentecost 1918 its date of effectiveness. Subsequent laws are to be published in the official organ of the Holy See, the *Acta Apostolicae Sedis,* and to be binding three months after publication there (CIC,c.9). A whole history of government interference is reflected in Pius IX's *Syllabus of Errors* condemning the proposition that bps. do not have the right to promulgate apostolic letters (D 2298), and in Vatican Council I's rejection of secular approval as a condition required before enactments of the Holy See have force (D 3062).

[T. C. O'BRIEN]

LAWYER, ideally a defender of rights before a civil or ecclesiastical court; actually one whose licensed profession is to conduct suits for clients or to advise on rights and obligations before courts. His moral obligations are defined, not only by the statutes proper to his profession, the principles of professional ethics, but above and underneath all, the moral law. The most general of these are to possess both knowledge of the law and art in its applications, diligence for his clients, and lawful conduct. While the lawyer's immediate attention is focused on his client's business, he has other obligations to serve the courts, the community, and even his own professional colleagues. To the client he owes diligent service in pursuing his just aims but should not so identify himself with the client that he loses his own objectivity or violates his own conscience. As counselor, the lawyer should not participate in the furthering of enterprises that are illegal or actually harmful to the community. Nor should he pursue his clients' unjust claims or allow just claims to be established by unjust means. As advocate and counselor, he will recognize the doubtful justice of some projects, but may accept them when he is able to form a probable opinion of their justice and has candidly advised his client about chances of success. In personal injury cases he should seek only what he honestly believes the client deserves. Tax lawyers, however, may generally take advantage of loopholes left by the legislator. In advocacy, the lawyer must be truthful and diligent, neither seeking nor allowing undue delay. Therefore, he himself must not accept more business than he can conveniently handle. Where justice is equally served, he should negotiate rather than litigate. When he has begun work on a case with belief in its justice, but later discovers it to be unjust, he must admonish the client to desist or dissociate himself from it.

Defense of the criminally accused is permitted and even necessary lest the common good be imperiled by denial of rights. Thus the attorney may use every defense permitted by law, but must not allow witnesses to lie or to cast suspicion on innocent persons. Nor should he attack the reputation of hostile witnesses unless their faults are related to the issues. He is bound by the *professional secret. This obligation may force him to refuse employment when the business of a new client would involve disclosure or abuse of knowledge imparted by a former or present client. While the lawyer is entitled to a just fee, he is also bound to restitution for any injustice he perpetrates. The lawyer assists the court by pleadings which are well prepared and by learned criticisms of judicial decisions. Since the community needs legal aid for the indigent, a lawyer should willingly accept his share of this burden. He should also conduct himself in a way casting credit upon his profession, and participate in associations which improve its ethics and proficiency. BIBLIOGRAPHY: R. H. Dailey, NCE 8:572–573;ThAq ST 2a2ae, 68 and 71; H. S. Drinker, *Legal Ethics* (1953); Roberti Palazzini, 41–44; E. Cahn, *Moral Decision: Right and Wrong in the Light of American Law* (pa. 1955).

[R. H. DAILEY]

LAWYERS GUILDS, CATHOLIC, organizations of Catholic lawyers established for the purpose of applying Christian principles to the practice of law. France organized a lawyers guild in 1945 and several years later in Rome one was established by the name of Unione Giuristi Cattolica Italiana. Among the flourishing lawyers guilds of England, the most prominent ones are: the Newman Association, the Edmund Plower Society, the Thomas More Society, and the Langhorne Society. In America, the Guild of Catholic Lawyers (GCL) was founded in New York in 1928.

The *Red Mass, dating from 14th-cent. England and named for the scarlet of the Lord Justices robes, is celebrated annually with the attendance of Catholic lawyers' guilds.

[R. A. TODD]

LAXISM, A *moral system never theoretically proposed as such, but implied in certain solutions of some 17th-cent. moral theologians that went to extremes in favoring the liberty of the individual against any but the most certain demands of law. The system was diametrically opposed to tutiorism; it was probabilism carried to the ultimate extreme. Its *reflex principle was: in moral doubt it is prudent to act on any opinion, however tenuously probable. This principle was proscribed by Innocent XI in 1679 (D 2103). A number of practical opinions that were laxist in inspiration were also condemned (D 2021–65; 2101–67). Now, even in the rare instances in which reflex principles are held to be important, no moralist of repute would think of approving recourse to the legalist calculation of this system to escape from responsibilities that are practically certain. BIBLIOGRAPHY: H. L. Hart, *Law, Liberty, and Morality* (1963).

[C. WILLIAMS]

LAY APOSTOLATE, the participation proper to the laity in the mission of the Church for the salvation of men "designed to manifest Christ's message by word and deeds and to communicate grace to the world" (Vat II ApostLaity, n.6). Such an apostolate exists "for by its very nature the Christian vocation is also a vocation to the apostolate" (*ibid.*, n.2). As Christians, the laity "share in the priestly, prophetic, and royal office of Christ and therefore have their own role to play in the mission of the whole People of God in the Church and in the world" (*ibid.*). The laity derive the right and duty with respect to the apostolate from their union with Christ their Head. Incorporated into Christ's mystical body through baptism and strengthened by the power of the Holy Spirit through confirmation, they are assigned to the apostolate by the Lord himself. They are consecrated into a royal priesthood and a holy people (1 Pet 2.4–10) in order that they may offer spiritual sacrifices through everything they do and may witness to Christ throughout the world (Vat II ApostLaity, n.3). The font of the apostolate is the inner life of charity (see LAY SPIRITUALITY), nourished and expressed in the Eucharistic liturgy.

The living of the Christian life, with prayerful communion at its center, is itself apostolic; it is the witness to a living faith, hope, and charity that makes Christ's gospel message manifest. But the laity have certain, actively undertaken missions as well. The first is their sustaining the work of the pastors in the Church; without lay cooperation the pastoral duties of teaching, sanctifying, and governing cannot be carried out effectively. The Council particularly stresses the peculiar scope given to the laity by their situation "in the world." That in itself gives special opportunities for leading others to the gospel by word and by example and for practicing in every walk of life the spiritual and corporal works of mercy. Perhaps the greatest "mercy" the Christian can show to his brethren in society is to promote the causes of justice in all its forms. That is at once the recognition of true and integral temporal values, above all the value of the human person, and the search to further the kind of human existence that will allow people the time and attitudes needed to search for God. This mission is open to every phase of the laity's existence. The active lay apostolate is made more effective by participation in associations with others for common apostolic purposes. Because of the emphasis of the Council on the universal apostolic call, there is in the Church both increasing awareness of, and a more willing participation in, programs of theological and spiritual formation that make lay response to the apostolic vocation more effective. *APOSTOLATE:*APOSTOLATE AND SPIRITUALITY.

[T. C. O'BRIEN]

LAY ASSOCIATIONS, in canon law pious associations of the faithful that include: third orders secular, archconfraternities and confraternities, "primary" pious unions, and other pious unions (CIC c.701,§1). The laws proper to each kind are set forth in CIC for c.702–725. By general definition, lay associations are groups of the faithful bound together for the promotion of the Christian life, for the practice of works of charity and devotion, or for enhancing public worship (c.685). The law stresses that such groups require the approval and exist under the control of ecclesiastical authority, and that membership is open only to Catholics in good standing; associations of a secret, seditious, or unsupervised character are forbidden societies. The existing legislation reflects the experience of the Church in earlier ages with uncontrolled lay groups that often took the path of anticlericalism and unorthodoxy (e.g., the *Humiliati). The legislation also reflects, however, an attitude that made a sharper distinction in the Church between the clergy or religious and the laity. The spirit of Vatican Council II has stressed the mutual goals and the cooperative spirit uniting clergy and laity. There is more initiative, more autonomy, more cooperative responsibility encouraged and expected on the part of the laity in their contribution to the Church's life and apostolate. Consultation of the laity because of their specific competencies and gifts is also recommended. It is also true that there is diminishing stress on lay associations of the type mentioned because of an increased stress on the parish itself as the center of church life and of the cooperation between clergy and laity in the intensification of the pursuit of holiness and of apostolic objectives.

[T. C. O'BRIEN]

LAY BROTHER, Lat. *conversus,* originally a member of a monastic community who was not a choir monk, but devoted himself principally to manual labor. The status was historically that of one presumed to have been turned (*conversus*) from a worldly life or secular occupations to a monastic life. The term lay brother also gained the connotation in some monastic and mendicant orders of a nonclerical religious. In more recent times, esp. since Vatican Council II, the term has fallen into disuse in favor of a term such as cooperator brother. Such religious also have been given more rights of active participation in community governance and business and a more direct share in ministry. The former distinction in religious garb is also being dropped.

[T. C. O'BRIEN]

LAY CONFESSION, the acknowledgment of one's sins to a layman in order to obtain forgiveness. This practice has appeared at various times and under various circumstances in the Church's history, although no theologian has ever claimed that a layman possessed the power to absolve sacramentally. In the Early Church, confessing slight faults to another Christian was an optional but well-regarded practice, and certain laymen notable for their sanctity regularly heard confessions and absolved. Even during this time, however, grave sins were confessed publicly to the bp. or later to a priest. In the East, the emphasis upon the confessor's holiness continued, and monks, even those who had not been ordained, were often sought out for confession and spiritual direction. The case was different in the West, where lay confession was revived in the 11th cent. mainly to fulfill the requirement of auricular confession when a priest was unavailable. Of major importance was an apocryphal work *De vera et falsa poenitentia*, attributed to St. Augustine, which clearly states the position of most medieval theologians: "So great is the power of confession that if a priest be wanting, one may confess to his neighbor . . . Although the confession be made to one who has no power to loose, he who confesses his crime to his companion becomes worthy of pardon through his desire for a priest." Peter Lombard regarded this lay confession as sacramental; Thomas Aquinas saw it as sacramental in some way (*quodammodo sacramentalis, In 4 sent*. 17.3.3. sol. 2); but Duns Scotus rejected it. As the nature of sacramental absolution came to be better understood, lay confession began to disappear, and the Council of Trent defined that sacramental absolution must be administered by a priest.

BIBLIOGRAPHY: P. Anciaux, *Sacrament of Penance* (1962);

B. Poschmann, *Penance and the Anointing of the Sick* (tr. F. Courtney, 1964); J. A. Spitzig, NCE 8:576–577. *PENANCE, SACRAMENT OF.

[J. J. FLOOD]

LAY CONGRESSES, AMERICAN, CATHOLIC. The idea of bringing the laity into closer understanding of, and cooperation with, the hierarchy was largely the concept of Abp. J. *Ireland and led to the first Congress at Baltimore in 1880. Card. Gibbons was not an ardent advocate but participated. The son of Orestes *Brownson was leader of the lay participants. The Congress heard papers and passed resolutions on many areas of Catholic concern. In 1893 a second lay Congress was held in Chicago. The Vatican favored both the Congresses. Vatican Council II has revived the idea as an expression of the common interest of clergy and laity. BIBLIOGRAPHY: J. T. Ellis, *Life of James Cardinal Gibbons* (2 v., 1952).

[J. R. AHERNE]

LAY MISSION HELPERS ASSOCIATION, THE, a foundation having the objective of recruiting and training laity for a 3-year, volunteer term of mission service either in the U.S. or abroad. The founder and first director was Msgr. Anthony J. Brouwers (d. 1964), with the endorsement (1956) of Card. J. F. McIntyre, Abp. of Los Angeles. Those accepted as members usually bring professional or practical skills to their service, and receive a 9-month training program of studies appropriate to mission work. The bishop or ecclesiastical superior of the mission they serve provides transportation and support. Members serve in groups of at least three and follow a simple rule of life. The Association has succeeded in providing service to missions in Africa, Latin America, the South Seas, and to home mission territories.

[T. C. O'BRIEN]

LAY MISSIONARIES, nonindigenous laymen or laywomen engaged in apostolic activity sponsored by a missionary organization or by the local bishop of a mission area. The direct participation of the laity in missionary action goes back to Apostolic times, although emphasis on the sacramental aspects of Christian living and the consequent need for priests to effect a sacramental life in the local community has, until recent times, tended to make lay participation in missionary action appear useful only to a minor degree. This previous lack of appreciation is also explained by the lack of theological clarity regarding the lay apostolate in general. But recently the situation has radically changed, and the lay missionary movement has grown extensively, esp. since the encouragement of Pius XII (*Evangelii praecones* and *Fidei donum*) and John XXIII (*Princeps pastorum*), and their appeal to Europe and North America for volunteers for Latin America. Today in the U.S. vigorous programs of recruitment, selection, training, and placement exist in such movements as the *Grail, *Papal Volunteers for Latin America, *Extension, the Lay Mission Helpers Association, and others. Involvement of the laity in missionary action is not to be regarded as a stopgap measure or an unavoidable situation resulting from the shortage of missionary priests and religious. The laity have a positive call to be missionaries, and their role in the missionary apostolate is both distinct and important. Vatican Council II frequently speaks of the laity as having a coresponsibility for the mission of Christ in the Church and the world and, when speaking of mission lands, calls for laymen to teach in schools, administer temporal goods, cooperate in parish and diocesan activities, and assist in institutions which touch on the basic structures of social life. BIBLIOGRAPHY: S. Brechter, "Decree on the Church's Missionary Activity," Vorgrimler 4:87–183; Y. Congar, *Lay People in the Church* (rev. ed., 1965); L. S. Vaughan, "Layman in the Apostolate," *Modern Mission Apostolate* (ed. W. J. Richardson, 1965); F. Klostermann, "Laity," SacMund 3:258–268.

[L. J. LUZBETAK]

LAY PREACHING, public proclamation of the word of God by the nonordained. Acts and the Epistles of Paul attest that lay persons shared in preaching. The charisms of the word, of evangelization, and of prophecy were given to ministers and laymen alike (see Acts 13.1; Rom 12.6–7; 1 Cor 12.10, 28). Preaching was charismatic and not necessarily connected with office or orders. In the patristic era, the period of the organization of church life, lay preaching decreased. As a layman, Origen was invited by the bps. of Caesarea and Jerusalem to preach and explain the Scriptures. Such a practice did not last beyond the 3d century. Lay preaching came to depend on the initiative and control of the bishops. The *Apostolic Constitutions* (4th cent.) still referred to lay teaching; The *Statuta ecclesiae antiquae* (6th cent.) severely restrict teaching by lay persons and women. Pope Leo the Great ruled that preaching belongs to the priestly order. The Middle Ages witnessed a revival of lay preaching in the spiritual movements of the 12th and 13th centuries. *Waldo and companions were allowed by Alexander III to preach "at the request of priests." The *Humiliati of northern Italy, forbidden to preach in 1179 and 1184, were allowed by Innocent III to preach with the bishop's permission, but only the *verbum exhortativum,* i.e., on the Christian life and virtues, and not *de articulis fidei et sacramentis,* i.e., on dogmatic questions. The *Waldenses did not obey such directives; the Humiliati did. In Milan in 1216, 50 communities of these preached in churches and public squares. In the 13th cent. the mendicant orders were given the same faculty for their lay members, and St. Francis of Assisi confirmed it in his rule. Their preaching was to be restricted to exhortation to a Christian life; it was to avoid doctrinal questions.

In 1418, Martin V in the bull *Inter cunctas* repudiated the practice of the followers of John *Wycliffe and Jan *Hus and their contention that lay persons of either sex can freely preach the word of God (see D 1277–78). To Luther's mind, in principle all believers were ministers of the word of God no less than pastors. The enthusiasm of lay preaching, however, led to disorder and the Peasants' War; thus the *Augsburg Confession restricted the right of public preaching to the *rite vocati,* pastors and ministers (Art. 14). The same restrictive policy was followed in the *Reformed Churches (see, e.g., Second *Helvetic Confession, c. 18). Lay preaching was part of the very nature of the Anabaptist and Quaker origins. Mennonite preachers are ordained; but many Quaker bodies do not have an ordained ministry. Methodists have, beside ordained preachers, institutional lay preachers (see LOCAL PREACHERS). The Protestant Churches generally restrict preaching to ordained ministers but make exception for specially qualified laity, theologians, or professors, and for the laity generally at (nonliturgical) Bible services. The question of women preachers still is controverted; but there is wide acceptance of women to the ministry. While most Pentecostal bodies have ordained ministers, the charismatic nature of Pentecostalism essentially includes the testimony and prophecy of all members.

For the RC Church, the Council of Trent ruled that preaching is the function of bishops and priests. The present canon law (CIC *c.* 1354) grants the right to preach to priests and deacons and excludes other clerics and laity (even lay religious). Vatican Council II has reopened the question of lay preaching by its teaching on the lay apostolate. The question is: do the right and the duty of the laity to take their part in the apostolic mission of the Church and its prophetic function comprise lay preaching? Vatican II decreed that "the hierarchy may entrust to laymen some functions more closely connected with the pastoral office, e.g., teaching Christian doctrine . . ." (Vat II ApostLaity 24). According to one commentator, F. Klostermann, this extends not only to "catechetical instruction for children but also preaching to adults, preaching in the course of non-liturgical divine services which do not require the presence of a priest, and sometimes the function of preaching in other types of divine service" (Vorgrimler Vat II 382). BIBLIOGRAPHY: Y. Congar, *Jalons pour une théologie du laïcat* (2d ed., 1964) 414–426; H. Day, *Layman in the Pulpit* (pa. 1973); M. J. Dirks, *Laymen Look at Preaching* (1972). *PREACHING.

[P. DELETTER]

LAY PRIESTHOOD. The Apostles and their successors in the Christian ministry are never called priests in the NT period. The term priest is applied to Christ as high priest of the new covenant in the Epistle to the Hebrews (*passim*), and the whole Christian people is graced with the title "a holy priesthood" and "a royal priesthood" in 1 Pet 2.5 and 2.9. This has led most Protestants to conclude that all Christians without distinction are priests, and to agree with Luther's interpretation of Rom 12.1 that the sacrifice of Christians consists solely in offering themselves as holy victims (cf. *On Abrogating the Private Mass, Luthers Werke,* Weimar ed., 8:420). Without minimizing this subjective and personal element so essential to the true meaning of sacrifice, Christian tradition agrees with Augustine, who also comments on Rom 12.1, but who concludes that "the whole redeemed city . . . is offered as a corporate sacrifice through the great priest," and that this sacrifice "the Church continually celebrates in the Sacrament of the Altar, which is known to the faithful. In it the Church learns that, in the offering which it makes, the Church itself is offered" (*Civ.* 10.6). Accordingly, the sacrifice of Christians is a liturgy in which the whole Christ, head and members, offers and is offered to the Father through the sacramental ministry of the ordained priest.

From the time of St. Thomas Aquinas, and influenced by his teaching, Catholic theologians have founded the layman's privilege of offering the Eucharistic Sacrifice on the sacramental character of baptism, which, according to the encyclical of Pius XII on the sacred liturgy *Mediator Dei,* "sets aside the faithful for divine worship, with the result that they share according to their own status in the priesthood of Christ" [AAS 39 (1947) 555]. BIBLIOGRAPHY: Y. Congar, *Lay People in the Church* (tr. D. Attwater, 1957); P. F. Palmer, *Sacraments and Worship* (v. 1, *Sources of Christian Theology,* 1955); "Lay Priesthood: Real or Metaphorical?" ThSt 8 (1947) 574–613.

[P. F. PALMER]

LAY READER, a title with two principal uses. (1) In the early Church, as Tertullian and the *Apostolic Constitutions* attest, the lector was a minor officer of the Church empowered to read or chant the lessons at Mass. The lectorate was continued in both the Eastern and the RC Churches as a minor order received by clerics in the course of their theological studies. With the liturgical reform instituted by Vatican Council II, the exercise of the office has been revived in such a way that laymen and laywomen normally read the lesson and lead the congregation in other prayers of the Mass. The Council calls this a "genuine liturgical ministry" (Vat II SacLit 29). Paul VI's *motu proprio, Ministeria quaedam* (Aug. 15, 1972) abolished minor orders and established the offices of acolyte and reader as lay ministries. Women may exercise the office of reader, but not receive institution in this ministry. (2) Lay reader is a title applied throughout the *Anglican Communion to an unordained person licensed by the bp. to read some public services. The extent of the authorization varies in different jurisdictions, but it usually includes the reading of Scripture, such services to the BCP as are not restricted to priests, and authorized sermons. In some dioceses, lay readers regarded as having sufficient preparation are licensed to preach. Provision for their admission was made in the 1550 Ordinal of Edward VI, and their duties were defined by Convocations in 1559. Their licensing was discontinued in England in 1775, but resumed in 1866. They performed esp. important work in the expansion of the Anglican Communion in new countries, where there was always a shortage of ordained ministers. BIBLIOGRAPHY: H. B. Restarick, *Lay Readers* (1894); *Regulations for Readers in the Anglican Church* (1915); J. M. Staudacher, *Laymen Proclaim the Word* (pa. 1973).

[R. B. ENO]

LAY SISTER, one who performed domestic work in a religious community. According to Vatican Council II, there should be only one class of sisters in communities of women, no matter in what types of work they are engaged.

[M. T. REILLY]

LAY SPIRITUALITY. Christian spirituality or the *interior life in its essence can be but one: it is the life of grace through the theological virtues, above all of charity. The term "lay spirituality" can contain an unfortunate distortion, a disparagement of the lay Christian, and a description of spirituality by negative comparison with the religious or priestly life. Contemporary thought and attitudes are remedying such misconceptions (*laos* in the NT means all believers). Historically St. Francis de Sales, e.g., in his *Introduction to a Devout Life,* is credited with at least extending the ideal that Christian perfection and a deepening of the spiritual life are open to all Christians. His labors can be understood in a measure as a reaction to Reformation teaching, which in its positive emphasis sought to summon all Christians to an intense life of grace (see PRIESTHOOD OF ALL BELIEVERS). The term "lay spirituality" is acceptable in a secondary and relative sense. The secondary and supportive elements in the religious' pursuit of perfection are, in general, the three vows of poverty, chastity, obedience, and in particular the rule of life proper to each religious community. The spirituality of the priest is describable through the requirements of those offices for which he is set apart by ordination. On the same level of secondary characteristics, the laity's Christian life is describable by the general index of the duties of their station in life. Vatican Council II also points to a special lay function in the Church, a contribution to its life by "services and charisms" (Vat II ConstChurch, n.30) through which the apostolate of the laity is fulfilled. The Council sees the condition precisely of being secular, i.e., in the world, as the basis for the witnessing and service peculiar to the laity (*ibid.* n.31). But as to the primary and the essential, to speak of spirituality at all means for priests, religious, laity alike, one reality: the life of charity, therefore of faith and hope, lived as an adoptive child of the Father through Jesus Christ (cf. *ibid.* n.30). The Church itself is the community of faith, hope, and charity (*ibid.* n.7). For all in the Church, life as part of that community is above all the life of prayer, i.e., in which the love of God is active in the light of faith and pressing onward through the strength of hope (cf. *ibid.* n.42). The keeping of the commandments, the active and ascetical performance of virtuous ways of living, the apostolate in all its forms—these rest on and have as their final purpose the inner life of loving God. That inner life becomes possible for all and has its character from Christ, as it is a new life initiated by baptism and quickened above all by the Eucharist. All Christians are called to seek and to grow in that inner life of holiness (*ibid.* n.39–40). Lay spirituality is one with the life of holiness to which all in the Church are committed. Thus the Council points out that in the Eucharist, the sacrament of charity and union, the act of Christ's own priesthood, holiness is expressed and strengthened. "All the faithful join in the offering of the Eucharist by virtue of their royal priesthood. They likewise exercise that priesthood by receiving the sacraments, by prayer and thanksgiving, by the witness of a holy life, and by self-denial and active charity." (*ibid.* n.10).

[T. C. O'BRIEN]

LAYAMON (Laweman or Lawman; fl. 1200), English poet and priest, author of **Brut,* a long alliterative poem on the legendary and actual history of Britain from Brutus to Cadwalader. L. declares that he used many sources, among them Bede's history and Wace's *Roman de Brut.* He also gathered together many stories not otherwise known, and tells them with spirit and power in the vernacular of the West Midlands. His work has historical importance as the first English account of such kings as Arthur, Lear, and Cymbeline. His Arthur as compared with Geoffrey of Monmouth's is more knightly, more generous and courteous, and a lover of law and order. Layamon retains much of the Old English tradition while making use of new French materials. BIBLIOGRAPHY: R. Blenner-Hassett, *Study of the Place-Names in Lawman's Brut* (1950).

[M. M. BARRY]

LAYING ON OF HANDS, also called the imposition of hands, the placing of the hands by one person on the head of another, a gesture or rite with many Christian uses. In the NT it is a gesture of blessing (Mk 10.16) or of healing (Mt 9.18); it is also used as a sign of the Holy Spirit's being received (Acts 8.15–17; Heb 6.2), or of conferring a special mission (Acts 6.1–6; 1 Tim 4.14; 2 Tim 1.6). In the RC Church the laying on of hands by the bp. is an essential part of the sacrament of holy orders to symbolize the reception of the Holy Spirit. Pius XII in 1947 (see D 3860) declared that the "matter," i.e., the essential external action in the ordination of bps., priests, and deacons, is the laying on of hands. It is also included as a subsidiary rite in the exorcism of catechumens before baptism, and as a blessing for healing and pardon in the anointing of the sick. The raising of the confessor's hand before the imparting of absolution is also a trace of the laying on of hands as a symbol of reconciliation. Outside of the ritual of the sacraments, it is part of the blessing of monks, and abbots, and of the consecration of virgins. In the Anglican *Book of Common Prayer, the laying on of hands by the ordaining bp. is essential in the rite of ordination of bps., priests, and deacons. In the Reformation era the laying on of hands was regarded as one of the *adiaphora, acceptable as a sign of blessing, prayer, or conferring a special function in the Church. The most universal Protestant use of the practice has been in the ordination of ministers. But the laying on of hands is also used in invoking the Holy Spirit and in prayers for the sick or those in grave spiritual need. It is an esp. prominent feature in *divine healing, one of the essentials of Pentecostalism.

[P. DELETTER]

LAYMAN (WOMAN). The terms lay, layman, and laity are all derived from the Greek *laos,* the people. To the laity belong all baptized persons who are not members of the hierarchy and who therefore are not in the clerical state. According to canonical legislation, the laity have a right to receive from the clergy spiritual goods and benefits and esp. the necessary means of salvation (CIC 682 and ClerSanc c. 527). Canon 528 defines the role of the laity in the apostolate of the Church.

Present understanding of laymen's role in the Church can be traced directly to Vatican Council II when the Fathers presented in *Lumen gentium* on Nov. 21, 1964, a more vital and dynamic vision of the entire nature of the Church. In ch. 4, a new and creative approach to the role of the laity is explicitly developed. This is supplemented in ch. 2 and 5, which point out the dignity and responsibility of lay Christians. *Lumen gentium* affirms that all the faithful constitute the Church, the people of God, made one body with Christ by baptism, as well as sharers in his priestly, prophetic, and kingly mission.

In this *Dogmatic Constitution on the Church,* the apostolate of the laity is clearly delineated. "Whoever they are, they are called upon, as living members, to expend all their energy for the growth of the Church and its sanctification" (33). As participants in the saving mission of the Church, through their baptism and confirmation, all are commissioned to that apostolate by the Lord himself." Particularly in their own environment, laymen are "called in a special way to make the Church present and operative in those places and circumstances where only through them can she become the salt of the earth" (33).

The very sanctification of the People of God depends on the mutual communication by all members of those gifts that they have received for individual and community holiness. The total communion of charity, the bond of perfection, can be attained in a priestly people striving for Christian maturity only when the layman recognizes his proper role, spelled out hopefully for a whole Church anticipating resurrection. "They must assist one another to live holier lives. . . . In this way the world is permeated by the spirit of Christ and more effectively achieves its purpose in justice, charity, and peace. The laity have the principal role in the universal fulfillment of this purpose" (36).

Regarding the common priesthood of the faithful and the ministerial or hierarchical priesthood, the same document (10) states that each in its own special way is a participation in the one priesthood of Christ. The laity "exercise that priesthood by receiving the sacraments, by prayer and, thanksgiving, by the witness of a holy life, by self-denial, and active charity."

Finally, 41 summarizes the role of the laity: "All of Christ's faithful, therefore, whatever be the conditions, duties, and circumstances of their lives, will grow in holiness day by day through these very situations . . . if they cooperate with the divine will by showing every man through their earthly activities the love with which God has loved the world."

[J. MORGAN]

LAYMANN, PAULUS (1574–1635), Jesuit canonist and moral theologian. Ordained in 1603, he taught philosophy at Ingolstadt (1603–09), theology in Munich (1609–25), and canon law at Dillingen (1625–32). His *Theologia moralis in quinque libros partita* (1625), which was used as a seminary text for over a cent., and his *Jus canonicum seu commentaria in libros decretales* (3 v., 1666–98) are the most important of his 35 works. A work on witchcraft and the trial of witches sometimes attributed to L. is not his.

[R. J. LITZ]

LAZARISTS, in France, a popular name for the Congregation of the Missions, or Vincentians. Their motherhouse until the French Revolution was Saint-Lazare, former priory of the Canons Regular in Paris, given to St. *Vincent de Paul, the founder, in 1632.

[T. C. O'BRIEN]

LAZARUS, in the Gospel of Luke (16.20), a fictional character in the parable of Dives and Lazarus. In the Gospel of John (chs. 11–12) a real person, brother of Martha and Mary of Bethany. Jesus raised him from the dead after he had been entombed for 3 days.

[J. J. CASTELOT]

LAZARUS THE CONFESSOR, ST. (968–1054), monastic founder. He became a monk at Saint Sabas monastery near Jerusalem and was also ordained priest there. He founded three monasteries near Ephesus, where he himself adopted the stylite existence, living in a hut at the top of a column next to the church. He composed a rule for his monasteries.

[T. C. O'BRIEN]

LAZINESS, see ACEDIA.

LEA, HENRY CHARLES (1825–1909), historian. Born at Philadelphia, Pa., L. was vaguely Episcopalian, but in later life became a Unitarian. He entered the family publishing business (1843), retired a millionaire in 1880, and devoted his later life to the study of the medieval Church. A self-taught historian, L. wrote extensively on celibacy, confession, indulgences, Morisco expulsion from Spain, and the Inquisition. His broad conceptions, industry, thoroughness, and liberal passion won acclaim from Acton and Maitland, but his bigotry alienated most Catholic historians. BIBLIOGRAPHY: H. Thurston, "Dr. Coulton and Dr. Lea," *Month* 169 (1937) 51–61.

[R. I. BURNS]

LEADE, JANE (1623–1704), mystic, spiritual leader of the Philadelphians. Born in England, L. early dedicated herself to religious contemplation. A study of the German mystic J. *Boehme impressed her. She experienced daily visions, which from 1670 she set down in a diary entitled *A Fountain of Gardens*. Two books, *The Heavenly Cloud* (1681) and *The Revelation of Revelations* (1683), made considerable impression when translated into Dutch and German. Francis Lee, whom she adopted as her son and adviser, was commissioned to seek other writings. He took down her statements and edited them.

[J. R. AHERNE]

LEADER OR AUTHOR (Gr. *archēgos*), title of Jesus in the NT; the Gr. term means beginner or founder of something. In Acts 3.15 Jesus is called "the author of life" in contrast to the murderer released by pleas of the mob who shouted for Jesus' death. Or, the contrast is between the murderer's pardon and the death of "the leader" who leads men to the life revealed by his Resurrection. Either meaning or both may be intended. In Acts 5.31 Jesus is called "the leader" or "prince" and savior, raised from the dead to, or by, the right hand of God, so that he may grant Israel repentance and forgiveness of sins—the ambiguity of the "he" is present in the Greek. Jesus would then be the author of a salvation consisting in sins' forgiveness. In Heb 2.10 the focus is on God's intention through Christ to lead many sons to glory through his death, willed by God's grace: He made "the one who leads" them to salvation perfect by his sufferings. In Heb 12.2 the title comes at the end of a long enumeration of examples of faith in salvation history: Jesus is identified as "the author, instigator, leader, or pioneer" of the highest faith and trust, because he accepted death in view of the glory he knew God would give him. He thus became also the perfecter of all faith.

[J. F. FALLON]

LEADERSHIP CONFERENCE OF WOMEN RELIGIOUS (LCWR), a national organization of administrative officers of all institutes of women religious in the U.S. and its territories. It was first organized in 1956 in Missouri, under the title of Conference of Major Superiors of Women Religious (CMSW), and in 1971, when it was incorporated in the District of Columbia, it became known as the Leadership Conference of Women Religious. In 1959, it was decreed as an ecclesiastical organization by the Sacred Congregation for Religious and Secular Institutes. The members of LCWR aim "to develop creative and responsible leadership" and to collaborate with other sisters in undertaking those services that foster and develop the life and mission of women religious, in response to the gospel message in the contemporary world. In view of this objective, LCWR plans and conducts at national, regional, and local levels, programs that benefit the members, ensuring communication among them; supports and assists in the study and research of topics concerning women religious; and organizes programs in which the Church and society are enabled to collaborate and communicate in support of the members. The conference operates by means of a national assembly, a national board, an executive committee, national officers, and national committees or commissions. Headquarters are in Washington, D.C. BIBLIOGRAPHY: H. Jessup, "Nuns revise structure to gain interdependence," *National Catholic Reporter* 12, no. 6 (Sept. 1976); J. Chittister, "Interdependence and revitalization"; (address given to the Leadership Conference of Women, Aug. '76, *Sisters Today* 48 (1976) 41–47.

[R. A. TODD]

LEAGUE, THE HOLY, see HOLY LEAGUE, THE.

LEANDER OF SEVILLE, St. (*c.*549–*c.*600), bp. of Seville from *c.*577, elder brother of *Isidore of Seville. Born in Cartagena, L. early in life became a monk. As bp. he was the foremost ecclesiastical figure in Spain. He was influential in the conversion of the two sons of the Arian Visigothic King Leovigild, *Hermenegild and *Reccared. Suspected of having incited Hermenegild's revolt, L. was exiled for a time. In Constantinople he met and became a close friend of Gregory I (The Great), then papal *apocrisiarius* in that city. Under King Reccared, L. succeeded in leading the Arian Visigoths back to the Church, the conversion being sealed at the Council of Toledo of 589, over which L. presided. Of his works only a rule for nuns (*De institutione virginum*) and his sermon on the occasion of the Council of Toledo have survived. Works: PL 72:869–898. BIBLIOGRAPHY: Butler 1:432–433; J. Madoz, EncCatt 7:1000–01; C. W. Barlow, FathCH 62:175–299.

[R. B. ENO]

LEAVEN, in biblical times usually a piece of fermenting dough from an earlier batch mixed into the new dough. Leaven, therefore, was considered a symbol of corruption (Lk 12.1; 1 Cor 5.6–8). Jesus also used the symbol in the good sense, of the insignificant origin yet sure development of the Church (Mt 13.33). Food sacrificed to Yahweh could not be leavened (Ex 23.18; Lev 2.11; 6.17) except that eaten by the people (Lev 7.13; 23.17).

[T. EARLY]

LEAVEN, HOLY, in the *Nestorian Church an element used in the preparation of the eucharistic bread. When the bread is baked before every Liturgy, it is leavened, not only with some dough from the last baking, but with the "holy leaven" which has been passed on from age to age. A baseless legend claims that the holy leaven derives from a second loaf given to St. John the Apostle at the Last Supper and mixed by him with the water from Christ's baptism and the blood and water that flowed from his side at the Crucifixion. This leaven is made anew each Holy Thursday with the addition of dough, salt, and olive oil. A small fragment of it is included in the bread to be consecrated at every Liturgy and is sometimes numbered among the Nestorian sacraments. An addition to the legend claims that the Western Church anathematized Nestorius because when he fled Constantinople, he took all the holy leaven with him, leaving the rest of the Church without it. The tradition reflects the Nestorian emphasis on the continuity of the Eucharist through the unity of the bread used. BIBLIOGRAPHY: G. P. Badger, *Nestorians and their Rituals* (2 v., 1852); Attwater CCE 2:229.

[F. T. RYAN]

LEBANON, Near East republic (4,015 sq mi). Ruled by Turkey for many centuries and occupied by France in 1860, Lebanon became independent in 1941. It is one of the most advanced countries of the Near East, with a literacy rate of 90%. Christianity was introduced in apostolic times. In the Middle Ages relations with Rome were friendly; in 1254 the Pope recognized the title of the Maronite patriarch of Antioch. In the 19th cent. Lazarists, Sisters of Charity, and Jesuits entered Lebanon. In 1977, of a total population of 3,300,000, the number of Catholics was estimated to be 900,000. The country is the center of the Maronite rite. There are 17 ecclesiastical jurisdictions in Lebanon serving the following rites: Armenian (1 diocese); Chaldean (1 diocese); Roman (1 vicariate apostolic); Maronite (3 archdioceses, 3 dioceses); Melkite (3 archdioceses, 5 dioceses); the Syrians are served by a patriarchal vicar. The patriarchs of Antioch of the Syrians and Antioch of the Maronites reside in Lebanon. The Church has been outstanding in educational and hospital work. The many Lebanese Catholics who have migrated to other parts of the world remain as a rule staunch Christians. Protestantism came to Lebanon in 1825 with the American Board. At present most of the work is carried on by the United Presbyterian Church, which operates American University, Beyruth College for Women, and the Near East School of Theology.

Although Lebanon remained neutral in the Israeli-Arab wars of 1956, 1967 and 1973, it suffered severely from a civil war that erupted in 1975. The conflict involved an effort by Muslims, particularly Shiites from the South, and Palestinian refugees to dislodge the Maronites from their dominant position. It was widely viewed as a Christian-Muslim war, but some Christian groups remained neutral and others, including Christian Palestinians, fought against the Maronites, who had the sympathy of some Muslims and of Israel. The war subsided after Syria sent in troops in 1976. However, continued raids on Israel by Palestinian refugees brought an Israeli invasion of southern Lebanon in 1978 and subsequent introduction of United Nations troops.

LEBBE, FREDERIC VINCENT (1877–1940), Belgian Vincentian missionary. L. joined the Congregation of the Missions (1895), was ordained in Peking, China (1901), and lived completely as a Chinese the rest of his life. He sought to propagate the faith through the press—establishing in turn a weekly and a daily newspaper—public lectures, and the formation of lay associations. He founded religious communities for men and women in China and mission-support societies in Europe. His efforts were directed also to forming a native clergy, and six Chinese bps. were consecrated (1926) at his suggestion. L.'s innovative influence on missionary methodology can be seen in Benedict XV's letter *Maximum illud* (1919). During the Chino-Japanese War Chinese Communists inflicted sufferings on L. that caused his death.

[H. P. ANNAS]

LEBRETON, JULES (1873–1956), Jesuit church historian and theologian. After his ordination in 1903 he taught at the Institut Catholique de Paris and was professor of the history of Christian origins until his retirement in 1943. With L. de Grandmaison he founded the review *Recherches de science religieuse* (1910). L. published many works on the history of the doctrines, most notably his *History of the Doctrine of the Trinity,* a work combining sound scholarly criticism and strict orthodoxy, and the first two volumes of Fliche-Martin, *Histoire de l'Église* (with J. Zeiller). BIBLIOGRAPHY: DTC *Tables générales* 2:2925–27; M. R. P. McGuire, NCE 8:596.

[R. B. ENO]

LE BRUN, PIERRE (1661–1729), French Oratorian writer and liturgist. His *Histoire critique des pratiques superstitieuses . . .* (1696) is an enlarged and revised version of his earlier *Lettres . . .* (1693); but his most important work, which strove to consolidate two antagonistic views of the Mass, symbolic vs. functional interpretations of rubrics, was his *Explication littérale, historique et dogmatique des prières et des cérémonies de la Sainte Messe . . .* (4 v., 1716–25). Controversy over his position that epiclesis was an essential element of the Consecration in the Mass followed publication of this work.

[R. J. LITZ]

LEBRUN, RICO (Federico; 1900–64), American painter from Naples (1924). In a Baroque style, he painted the sufferings of war-ravaged man of the 20th cent. in an intensive emotional series of crucifixion studies (1947–50), and a large triptych *Crucifixion* (1951, Syracuse Univ.), combining the Gothic of Grünewald with Picasso's cubist constructions.

[M. J. DALY]

LEBUFFE, FRANCIS PETER (1885–1954), American Jesuit writer. Ordained in 1915, he spent a lifetime in writing, largely for periodicals. He served as regent of the

School of Law at Fordham Univ. (1920–22) and as dean of its School of Social Service (1923–26). He was for many years a member of the staff of the Jesuit weekly *America* and managing editor of the quarterly *Thought*.

[J. R. AHERNE]

LEBUINUS (LEBWIN), ST. (d.*c.*780); Anglo-Saxon monk at the monastery of Ripon sent *c.*754 by St. Gregory of Utrecht to preach the gospel to the Frisians and Saxons in the vicinity of Westphalia. Though fairly successful among the Frisians, L. failed to convert the Saxons until, at the yearly meeting of their chieftains at Marklo on the Weser, he threatened them with divine retribution. The angered chieftains were dissuaded from killing him by one Bute, who urged that, as they heeded messengers from the Normans, Slavs, and Frisians, so they should heed the messenger from God. After L.'s death, the Saxons burned the church he had built at Deventer. It was rebuilt by St. Ludger, but destroyed again in 882 by the Normans. L. is probably to be identified with the St. Livinus who is honored at St. Bavo in Ghent. BIBLIOGRAPHY: M. E. Collins, NCE 8:597; *Anglo-Saxon Missionaries in Germany* (tr. and ed. C. H. Talbot, 1954)20:228–234; K. Van Den Berg, BiblSanct 7:1163; Butler 4:324.

[M. F. MCCARTHY]

LE CAMUS, ÉMILE PAUL (1839–1906), bp. and scripture scholar. L. worked as a parish priest, founded a school at Castelnaudary, France, and became bp. of La Rochelle in 1901. He collaborated with F. *Vigouroux on the *Dictionnaire de la Bible,* wrote a highly regarded life of Christ and an extensive history of the apostolic Church, *Origines du christianisme* (2 v., 1905). He restored scripture studies to a prominent place in his diocesan seminary and was a prudent opponent of *Modernism. BIBLIOGRAPHY: R. Leconte, DBSuppl 5:348–350.

[T. M. MCFADDEN]

LE CAMUS, ÉTIENNE (1632–1707), bp. of Grenoble, cardinal from 1686. Under the influence of J. *Bossuet he had a personal conversion from his dissolute life as almoner at the royal court. He was appointed abp. of Grenoble in 1671; he lived in great austerity and holiness. His gentleness towards Protestants in contrast to the harsh measures against them at the time, led many of them to become converts.

[T. C. O'BRIEN]

LE CLERC, ALIX, BL. (1576–1622), foundress of Canonesses Regular of St. Augustine of Our Lady. At age 20 she met Peter Fourier at Mattaincourt and exchanged ideas on the education of the poor. On Christmas day 1597, L. and a few friends formed a group pledged to free public education. In 1598 this group founded its first school at Poussay. In 1599 they opened a convent at Mattaincourt and L. resisted attempts by the Franciscan Recollect friar F. Boulengier to place the newborn congregation under the auspices of the Poor Clares. In 1601, L. with the help of Fourier, opened a convent at Saint Mihiel. In 1603, the card. legate of Lorraine offered the first official approval of the new congregation. In 1616 Paul V gave papal recognition to the congregation, but limited it to one convent, at Nancy. In 1617 the first official monastery was opened for the training of the Augustinian Canonesses of the Congregation of Our Lady. L. took the name Maria Teresa of Jesus and served as superior of the order from 1617–21. When De Lenoncourt, the primate of Lorraine, took control of the order, he forced L. to resign as superior. Her last years were also saddened by the extravagant claims of Fourier as to his own importance in founding the congregation. She was beatified in 1947. BIBLIOGRAPHY: A. Amore, BiblSanct 7:1165; Butler 1:59–63.

[R. J. BRADY]

LE CLERC, JEAN (1587 or 1588–1633), French religious painter and etcher. After study in Rome, L. brought to Nancy a Caravaggesque light and shadow that influenced J. Callot and particularly G. de La Tour, though his dynamic nudes witness to the anatomical strain of Pollaiuolo.

[M. J. DALY]

LE CLERC, JEAN (1657–1736), Calvinist theologian. A native of Geneva, he turned away from strict *Calvinism to *Arminianism, publishing his ideas in *Epistolae theologiae* (1679) under the pseudonym Liberius de S. Amore. He taught at the *Remonstrant seminary in Amsterdam, where he also published his edition of the Apostolic Fathers and three encyclopedias of literature.

[T. C. O'BRIEN]

LE CLERC DU TREMBLAY, FRANÇOIS (Father Joseph of Paris; 1577–1638), Capuchin, the *éminence grise* (grey was the color of the habit at that time) of Card. *Richelieu. L. became a Capuchin in 1599 at Orléans, was ordained in 1604. Besides his prominence in the political history of Europe as counselor to Richelieu, whose service he entered in part to promote the welfare of the Church, L. has importance for his purely religious activities. He was a champion of reform in his own order; the founder and director of a reformed congregation of Benedictine nuns (the Calvariennes); he was a spiritual director and the author of *Introduction à la vie spirituelle* (1626); he was the promoter of Capuchin missionary work and of the French missions in the Near East.

[T. C. O'BRIEN]

LECLERCQ, HENRI (1875–1945), archeologist and historian. A native of Belgium, L. became a French citizen and made his profession as a Benedictine in the abbey of Solesmes. He then transferred to Farnborough, England, along with his mentor Dom Fernand Cabrol, prior-elect of the monastery projected there, and was ordained in 1898. In 1914 he took up residence in London. He was incardinated into the Archdiocese of Westminster in 1924 but kept his Benedictine ties as an oblate. Serving as chaplain of the Sisters of Sion in London, he spent his days in the British Museum at work on the great editions begun by Dom Cabrol. He personally wrote most of the articles in the 15 volumes of the *Dictionnaire d'archéologie chrétienne et de liturgie* (1907–53, the final volume prepared by H. I. Marrou). He also published *Les Martyrs* (15 v., 1902–24) and *Monumenta Ecclesiae liturgica* (4v., 1904–12). Besides, he translated and revised C. J. von Hefele's *History of the Church Councils* (19 v., 1907–49). L.'s writing is marred at times by prejudice and inaccuracy, but his volumes are invaluable for the study of Church antiquities. BIBLIOGRAPHY: F. X. Murphy, NCE 8:599; E. Josi, EncCatt 7:1013–14.

[M. J. SUELZER]

LECOMTE, FÉLIX (1737–1817), French sculptor and student of Falconet. L., an academic classicist, executed portraits, mythological works, the tomb of Stanislas I Leszczynski of Poland and the Bons-Secours Church, Nancy (1774).

[M. J. DALY]

LECONTE DE LISLE, CHARLES MARIE (1818–94), French writer, chief poet of the Parnassian movement. Influenced by Lamennais, Saint-Simonism, and Fourierist communalism, L. advocated social reform under a republic, but disillusioned after the 1848 Revolution he channeled his idealism into art. His poetry reflects 19th-cent. humanism's hostility to Christianity, to which L. opposed classical paganism's cult of beauty and reason (*Hypatie*) and a pessimistic philosophy derived from Indian thought (*La Maya; La Vision de Brahma; Bhagavat*). He exalted man's revolt against an authoritarian God (*Qaïn*), depicted a romantic Christ rejected by the Father, and at odds with institutionalized Christianity (*Le Nazaréen; L'Agonie d'un saint*), and finally proclaimed the death of God (*La Paix des dieux*). He satirized the medieval Church's institutions (*Les siècles maudits*) and wrote (1870–72) three anticlerical, republican tracts including the *Catéchisme populaire républicain*. He was less antagonistic toward religion in his last years and was buried with Church rites. BIBLIOGRAPHY: H. Elsenberg, *Le Sentiment religieux chez Leconte de Lisle* (1909); I. Putter, *Pessimism of Leconte de Lisle* (1954–61).

[G. E. GINGRAS]

LE CORBUSIER (CHARLES-ÉDOUARD JEANNERET-GRIS; 1887–1965), renowned innovator in contemporary architecture. Swiss born, he studied at La Chaux-de-Fonds, then worked with A. Perret (Paris, 1908), and studied with W. Gropius and Mies van der Rohe under P. Behrens (Berlin, 1910). After 1917 he worked professionally in Paris, signed the manifesto *Après le cubisme* (1918), initiated the journal *L'Esprit nouveau* (1920–23), and published his theories in 1923, *Vers une architecture*. His earlier conceptions included the Dom-ino houses (1914) and a model city for 3 million people (1922). His contributions to modern city planning are seen in his *Cité Radieuse* at Marseilles (1946–52) and the new city of the Punjab at Chandigharh, India (1950–57). Church architecture received an impetus from his designs for the shrine chapel at Ronchamp (1955) and the Dominican monastery at Arbresle, Ste. Marie de la Tourette (1957). BIBLIOGRAPHY: *Le Corbusier: Oeuvre complète* (ed. W. Boesiger, 5 v. 1952–55; 1975); C. Jencks, *Le Corbusier and the Tragic View of Architecture* (1975); *Le Corbusier: My Work* (tr. J. Palmes, 1974).

[R.J. VEROSTKO]

LECOT, VICTOR LUCIEN SULPICE (1831–1908), French cardinal. L. was made bp. of Dijon (1886) and abp. of Bordeaux (1890), where he arbitrated a builders' strike, opened workers' kitchens, and aided all movements to improve conditions among the laboring class. It was to him that Pope Leo XIII directed a letter urging French Catholics to forget their old differences and to give loyal support to the constitution. *RALLIEMENT.

[M. J. SUELZER]

LE COURRAYER, PIERRE FRANÇOIS (1681–1776), French RC defender of Anglican Orders. A native of Rouen, C. became a canon regular at Paris. Beginning with his *Dissertation sur la validité des ordinations des anglais et sur la succession des évêques de l'Église Anglicane*, published anonymously in 1723 at Brussels, he devoted all his efforts to defending the validity of Anglican Orders and episcopal succession. He was welcomed in England when he went there (1732) to spend the rest of his life. In France C.'s work provoked a series of episcopal condemnations. Always protesting his RC orthodoxy, he engaged in literary controversy with those who assailed his thesis. He also published a French translation of Paolo Sarpi's *History of the Council of Trent* (2v., 1736; 3v., 1751), with his own historical and theological notes. This work of C. was itself translated into English, German, and Italian, was explicitly at variance with RC teaching, and provoked further polemical exchanges with his adversaries. BIBLIOGRAPHY: J. Carreyre, DTC 9:112–115; E. Predein, *L'Union des Églises gallicane et anglicane* . . . (1928).

LECTERN, a stand to hold books used for readings in the liturgy. In a cathedral or monastic choir there is a lectern, often ornate, for the use of cantors or lesson readers. The lectern is also found in a parish church's sanctuary for the readings in the Eucharistic Liturgy. The lectern derives from the ambo, which in early basilicas (e.g., S. Clemente in Rome) was a stone platform used for the same purpose.

[T. C. O'BRIEN]

LECTIONARY, a liturgical book introduced in 1970 of scriptural readings and psalm responses for the celebration of the Liturgy. In the early days of the Church lessons were read directly from the Bible. The celebrant chose the lessons with a view to their appropriateness to particular occasions, but the choices were becoming stabilized by the 5th century. The customary selection of readings was fixed in the liturgical books called *capitularia,* which were lists of the Gospels or the Epistles. A book which was much used was the *comes* in which the Gospel or Epistle pericope was written out in full. These were very popular. Another book, the full lectionary (*lectionarium plenarium*) in which both the gospel and epistle pericopes were written in full, was not popular until the division of liturgical roles became less marked. By the time this happened, the *Missal, which contained all the readings, was in fairly common use. The 1970 Lectionary is a book separate from the Sacramentary, in keeping with the distinction of liturgical ministries

[N. KOLLAR]

LECTIONARY OF LUXEUIL, Merovingian illuminated MS in the Bibliothèque National, Paris.

LECTOR, a person who proclaims scriptural readings and other selections at Mass and other services of worship. Originally, any competent Christian could perform this function, but by the 2d cent. it was reserved to those ordained to the minor order of lector. Gradually this task was taken over by the deacon or subdeacon at Mass, and the order lost its importance. It was retained, however, as the second of the now abolished minor orders for a candidate for the priesthood. In the present day the ministry of lay reader has been revived and is open to men, women, and children. *COMMENTATOR. BIBLIOGRAPHY: J. Tate, *Manual for Lectors* (pa. 1975).

[T. M. MCFADDEN]

LEDESMA, MARTIN DE (d. 1574), Dominican theologian from Salamanca, professor at Coimbra for more than 30 years. His commentary on the *Sentences* was published, but not that on the *Summa theologiae*.

[T. GILBY]

LEDESMA, PEDRO DE (d. 1616), Dominican theologian and one of the Thomist masters of Salamanca. In the debates on efficacious grace, he held to the position of *Báñez. The evidence is slight that he was a precursor of *probabilism.

[T. GILBY]

LEDÓCHOWSKA, MARIA TERESA (1863–1922), sister of W. *Ledóchowska, foundress. A countess and member of the court of the Grand Duchess of Tuscany at Salzburg, L. through the influence of Card. *Lavigerie, became an advocate of the abolition of slavery and the Christianizing of Africa. She founded the Sodality of St. Peter Claver for African Missions in 1894, a congregation she directed until her death. L. also founded the magazine *Echo of Africa* which ultimately was published in 11 languages. Her many printing houses turned out catechetical works in 140 native languages. She is a candidate for beatification. BIBLIOGRAPHY: G. Papàsogli, *Maria Teresa Ledóchowska* (1950).

[J. R. AHERNE]

LEDÓCHOWSKI, MIECZYSŁAW HALKA (1822–1902), Polish abp., cardinal, diplomat. He was the uncle of Maria Teresa *Ledóchowska and Wladimir *Ledóchowski. Ordained in 1845, he served in the papal nunciature of Lisbon, as apostolic delegate (1855–60) to Colombia and Chile, and as nuncio to Brussels (1861). In 1866 he was named abp. of the sees of Gnesen and Posen (Gniezno and Poznań). He was sent to Versailles to ask the aid of Prussia for reestablishing the Papal States and to offer the mediation of Pope Pius IX between Prussia and France, but the mission failed. A long struggle in the time of Kulturkampf ensued between L. and the Prussian government. The abp. ordered teachers of religion to ignore the government decree against religious instruction in the schools and the imposition of the German language. When all teachers complying with his order were dismissed from state schools by Prussia, L. created private schools. A decree forbade pupils in higher education to attend these classes and L. was ordered (1873) to resign. He refused and was imprisoned (1874). While in prison he was created cardinal (1875). Exiled, L. directed his sees from Rome. In 1885 he resigned as abp. in the interests of settlement of the Kulturkampf crisis, served in curial work in Rome, and in 1892 was appointed prefect of the Congregation for the Propagation of the Faith. BIBLIOGRAPHY: M. Ott, CE 9:111–112.

[J. R. AHERNE]

LEDÓCHOWSKI, WLADIMIR (1866–1942), Jesuit superior general, brother of Maria Teresa *Ledóchowska and nephew of Card. M. *Ledóchowski. Austrian-born, he studied for the secular priesthood but entered the Society of Jesus in 1889 and was ordained in 1894. Provincial of the Province of Galicia in 1902 and German assistant to the superior general from 1906, in 1915 he was elected to the lifetime office of superior general of the Society. L. was a remarkable leader; during his tenure the mission labors of the community increased dramatically, the number of missioners rising from 971 to 3,785. The Jesuit membership grew from 17,000 to more than 26,000. He revised the constitution of the Society and the *Ratio studiorum,* improved Jesuit institutions of higher education in Rome, esp. the Pontifical Oriental Institute and the Russian College, and gave strong direction for intensifying Jesuit spirituality in the inner life of the Society.

[J. R. AHERNE]

LEE, ANN, founder of the United Society of Believers in Christ's Second Appearing, commonly known as *Shakers. Born in Manchester, England, she received no education, but worked as a factory hand and later as a cook. In 1758 she was converted in a revival led by two Quaker tailors, Jane and James Wardley, who had been influenced by some French Prophets or *Camisards then active in England. The Wardley group came to be known as the Shaking Quakers because of a shaking motion, supposedly the result of divine influence, that took place at their meetings. Lee married A. Standerin (sometimes given as Standley or Stanley) in 1762. By 1766 she had borne four children, all of whom died in infancy. Coming to believe that concupiscence was the source of all evil, she began teaching celibacy. Becoming increasingly zealous, she was imprisoned for her religious activities. After her release, she assumed leadership of the Wardley group, who called her "Mother Ann." She claimed to have received a vision of Christ giving her great authority and called herself "Ann of the Word." After another imprisonment, she migrated to America in 1774, accompanied by six men and two women. Sometime thereafter she separated from her husband, and in 1776 established her community at a place near Albany, N.Y., with the Indian name of Niskayuna and the Dutch name of Watervliet. She spent her remaining years in work with the community, and in preaching tours of New England. BIBLIOGRAPHY: *Shakers: Testimonies of the Life, Character, Revelations, and Doctrines of Mother Ann Lee* (1888, AMS repr. 1975).

[T. EARLY]

LEE, EDWARD (1482?–1544), abp. of York. Boyhood friend of Thomas More, fellow of Magdalen College, Oxford, L. took his M.A. at Cambridge. His quarrel with Erasmus (1519–20) over Erasmus's translation of the NT is the basis of characterizations of L. as an opponent of the new learning. During the 1520s he served as a diplomatic agent of Henry VIII and was rewarded with the chancellorship of Salisbury (1529) and prebends (1530) at York and St. Stephen's Chapel, Westminster. In 1531, the year L. became abp. of York, he tried to persuade Catherine to withdraw her cause in the royal divorce. Finally approving (1535) the King's actions, L. promised to obey his ruler's will and stated that the Pope had no more power in England than any other foreign bishop. Taken prisoner by the northern rebels during the Pilgrimage of Grace (1536), he swore support of the rebellion under duress. In parliament (1539) he defended the *Six Articles. In York (1541) he issued new statutes governing his diocese. Throughout his public life he was always, if somewhat falteringly, loyal to Henry and thus helped to establish the principles of royal supremacy in the Tudor Church.

[R. J. LITZ]

LEE, FREDERICK GEORGE (1832–1902), English theological writer, who wrote voluminously also in history and archeology. He was a partisan of the Anglo-Catholic cause, poet, editor of Tory and High Church newspapers, founder and editor of various periodicals. Born at Thame, Oxfordshire, he matriculated at Oxford, but did not graduate. Ordained an Anglican priest in 1856, he helped found the Association for Promoting the Union of Christendom in 1857 to achieve union of the Churches of Rome, England, and Russia; started the *Union Review* in 1863 to promote union between Rome and the C of E; wrote in 1870 the estimable "The Validity of the Holy Orders of the Church of England maintained and vindicated"; and, when he began to doubt the validity of Anglican orders, collaborated in founding the Order of Corporate Reunion to restore valid orders. He apparently had himself secretly consecrated bp. *c.* 1877 at or near Venice by some prelate whose credentials were acknowledged by Rome and took to himself the title of bp. of Dorchester. From 1867 to 1899 he was vicar of All Saints', Lambeth and was known as an impressive Anglican preacher. At the same time he was ordaining and consecrating others who shared his view of Anglican orders, in what must have been considered a secret episcopal mission. A year before his death he was received into the Catholic Church by his old friend Father Best of the Oratory. BIBLIOGRAPHY: W.G.D. Fletcher, DNB Suppl 1901–11, 2:440–443.

[E. J. DILLON]

LEEMING, BERNARD (1893–1971), Jesuit sacramental and ecumenical theologian. He was born in the U.S. and joined the Society of Jesus there in 1911, but did his theology in England and Rome, which became the chief center of his teaching career. He taught theology at the Gregorianum in Rome, 1931–37; in England after World War II. L. was master of novices at the English Jesuit novitiate, then taught theology at Heythrop College for the remainder of his life. Among the ecumenical areas in which his views won respect were the issues of corporate Anglican-Roman Catholic reunion, and then recognition of each others' orders by the practical gesture of a mutual imposition of hands. His work in sacramental theology is marked by his *Principles of Sacramental Theology* (1956), grounded on St. Augustine and St. Thomas Aquinas. In the field of ecumenics he published *The Church and the Churches* (1961), *Vatican Council and Christian Unity* (1966), and *Towards Christian Unity* (1966).

[T. C. O'BRIEN]

LEEN, EDWARD (1885–1944), Irish Holy Ghost Father, educator, administrator, conference master, spiritual director, and spiritual writer. He is known principally for the spiritual writings that appeared within the last decade of his life. These present a spiritual doctrine that is thoughtful, realistic, and Christ-centered. Noteworthy among them are: *Progress through Mental Prayer* (1935), *In the Likeness of Christ* (1936), *Why the Cross?* (1938), *The True Vine and*

Its Branches (1938), *The Holy Ghost* (1939). BIBLIOGRAPHY: M. O'Carroll, *Edward Leen* (1953).

[W. J. READ]

LEEUW, GERARDUS VAN DER (1890–1950), Protestant theologian. A professor at the Univ. of Groningen, Holland, (1918–50), L. was a prominent phenomenologist in theology. The history of religions, with emphasis on the description of the phenomenon of religion, was his chief interest. Among his writings are *Religion in Essence and Manifestation* (tr. J. E. Turner, 1938) and *Sacred and Profane Beauty* (tr. D. F. Green, 1963).

[J. R. AHERNE]

LEFEBVRE, GUILLAUME (WILLIAM; fl. 1431–76), Flemish copper and brass caster of Tournai. L. executed four copper angels for the cathedral of Cambrai and a masterwork—the baptismal font of Notre-Dame (1446; Hal, St. Martin) with numerous figures of saints and donors in mid-15th-cent. style.

[M. J. DALY]

LEFEVERE, PETER PAUL (1804–1869) bp. and missionary. A native of Belgium, he was ordained in St. Louis, Mo., in 1831. He presided over a parish in Missouri which included eight stations in that state, four in Illinois, and two in Wisconsin. Becoming coadjutor bp. of Detroit in 1841, he demonstrated exceptional ability as an administrator, establishing discipline through diocesan statutes (1843) and a diocesan synod (1859). With John Lancaster *Spalding he established the American College at Louvain. He was responsible for marked growth of the Church in Michigan during his tenure. BIBLIOGRAPHY: R. Clarke, *Lives of the Deceased Bishops of the Catholic Church in the U.S.* (4 v., 1887–89).

[J. R. AHERNE]

LEFÈVRE, PIERRE, see FABER, PETER, BL.

LEFÈVRE D'ÉTAPLES, JACQUES (Jacobus Faber Stapulensis; 1455–1536), French humanist, biblical and patristic scholar. He was born at Étaples in Picardy. He was ordained a priest and became a master of arts at the Univ. of Paris. Visits to Italy led to his first interest, the study of Aristotle. As professor at Paris (1492–1507), he became the center of a circle of men who became eminent scholars. In 1507 St. Germain des Prés, under Abbot Briçonnet, afterwards bp. of Meaux, became his home; there L. lectured and turned his efforts to the study of the Scriptures, the Fathers, and the mystics, esp. Raymond Lull and Jan van Ruysbroeck. In commentaries on the Psalms (*Quintuplex Psalterium,* 1509), on St. Paul (1512), and on the Gospels (1522) he developed his ideas on justification, the Christian life, and reform of the Church. He participated in the reform movement of Bp. Briçonnet at Meaux, contributing a French translation of the NT (1503) and of the Psalms (1524). The reform at Meaux and L.'s own writings became suspect in the reaction of the Sorbonne and Parlement to the first penetration of Luther's writings into France. L.'s commentary on the Gospels was condemned for doctrinal errors by the Sorbonne faculty in 1523. Called before Parlement to face charges of heresy, he fled to Protestant Strassburg (1525). He was able to return to France in the next year to the post of librarian and tutor for the royal family at Blois. His translation of the whole Bible was published in 1530. The last years of his life were spent at the court of Margaret of Navarre, in writing and editing, esp. works of the Christian mystics, and on mysticism. L. had among his pupils G. *Farel, Calvin's companion in the reform of Geneva; personally or through his writings he influenced Erasmus, Reuchlin, and other humanist Reformers. His ideas on justification and reform of the Church have been regarded as congenial to those of Luther. But L., however, worked for reform within the RC Church and did not break with the old tradition or institution. BIBLIOGRAPHY: E. F. Rice, NCE 8:604–605; Léonard HistProt 1:20–21.

[M. J. SUELZER]

LE FORT, GERTRUD VON (1876–1971), German poet and novelist. Born of a Protestant family of noble rank, which had left France and settled in Germany for religious reasons, she studied at Heidelberg where she came under the influence of E. *Troeltsch. After his death she edited his *Glaubenslehre* (1925). She was converted to Catholicism in 1927 and became a prominent figure in the Catholic literary revival. Her *Hymnen an die Kirche* presents the dominant theme of her writings: the all–embracing reality of the Church, mother of all the children of this world. This was also the theme of her great novel *Veil of Veronica* (tr. C. M. R. Bonacina, 1936). Among her other writings that have been translated into English are: *Pope from the Ghetto* (tr. C. M. R. Bonacina, 1934); *The Eternal Woman* (tr. P. Jordan, 1962); *The Judgment of the Sea* (tr. I. and F. McHugh, 1962); *The Song at the Scaffold* (tr. O. Marx, 1961). BIBLIOGRAPHY: N. Heinen, *Gertrud von Le Fort* (1960); A. Focke, *Gertrud von Le Fort* (1960).

[I. MERKEL]

LEFORT, LOUIS THÉOPHILE (1879–1959), Coptic scholar. Ordained in 1901, he taught at the Univ. of Louvain most of his life and was named chief of the Oriental Institute in 1936. L. published many studies on the Coptic Church. From 1921 to 1959 he was editor of the periodical *Le Muséon,* a journal specializing in Orientalist studies. In 1936 he established Le Centre de Documentation Copte at Louvain. His works include: *S. Pachomii vita bohairice scripta* (CSCO, ser. 3, v. 7, 1925); *Les Pères apostoliques en copte* (CSCO, v. 135, 136, 1952); *Oeuvres de Saint Pachome et ses disciples* (CSCO v. 159, 160, 1956).

[J. R. AHERNE]

LEFRANC, FRANÇOIS, BL., (1739–92), French priest and vigorous polemicist, put to death during the September massacres of the first Reign of Terror, September 2–3, 1792, and beatified in 1926 as one of the 191 Martyrs of Paris. Born in Normandy he studied there and entered a small society of priests called the Congregation of Jesus and Mary (CJM) and popularly, Eudists, after their 17th-cent. founder, St. John Eudes. Named superior of their house at Caen, L. combatted revolutionary ideas by his numerous writings. He came to Paris in 1791 with partisans of the monarchy, was incarcerated in August 1792 in the Carmelite monastery, and was one of the first victims of the massacre. At the time he was assistant to the superior general and one of three Eudists to die. They had been imprisoned for refusal to support by oath the Civil Constitution and were victims of a panic of insurrection which led to summary executions. L.'s writings reflect the view that the Freemasons were at the heart of a conspiracy against the monarchy and the Catholic religion. His works, reprinted in Liège in 1827, purport to be a history of Freemasonry, and indict it for numerous plots. BIBLIOGRAPHY: *Nouvelle Biographie Générale* (1862) 30:362–363.

[E. J. DILLON]

LEFT AND RIGHT (IN THE BIBLE). The symbolism which associates "right" side with that which is good, propitious, true or "lucky" and the left with that which is bad, unpropitious, false, or "sinister" is archetypal. While the elaborate mythologies that have grown up around this symbolism are absent from the Bible, it is still that the right, and esp. the right hand of Yahweh, is associated with blessing (Gen 48.13); deliverance (cf. Ex 15.6,12; Ps 20.6; 138.7, etc.); consecration (cf. Lev 14.14–28); oaths, skill in craftsmanship or arms (cf. Ps 137.5); and in general with that which is powerful, good, and morally right. Conversely the left hand seems often to symbolize a lesser blessing (cf. Gen 48.13–14); deviations from the course prescribed by Yahweh (cf. 2 Sam 14.19; Is 30.21); or condemnation (cf. "He will place the sheep on his right hand and the goats on his left" Mt. 25.33). This general symbolism should be borne in mind in interpreting the positions of the two thieves in relation to the crucified Lord (cf. Lk 23.33).

[D. J. BOURKE]

LEGAL JUSTICE, also called "general justice," the kind of *justice bent upon preserving, respecting, and furthering the common or public good. It is called legal (not legalistic) because it looks to laws (*leges*) to be kept or to be enacted as guides, and *law by definition has the common good as its objective. It is called general, first, in distinction from particular justice that regulates one-to-one relationships between persons, whereas legal justice belongs to a person as part of a general or collective whole; secondly, because it prompts and calls into its service acts of other virtues to achieve its purpose (see ThAq ST 2a2ae, 58.6). Legal justice includes in its interests the meanings of *social justice, *economic justice, *racial justice, even punitive justice; and the term civic virtue well describes its place in human life. Because civic society is composed of those who govern and those who are governed, legal justice belongs to the first as planners and legislators for the common good, and as its guardians; to the second, as carrying out, by the observance of justice, what is rightly determined by those who govern. The status of legal justice as a *virtue emphasizes that to live as a member of civil society in a morally responsible way is to interiorize what belongs to that life. Legal justice implies an attitude of positive acceptance that a societal life is necessary: there is one kind of human good or wellbeing that can be achieved only by mutual assistance, interaction, and cooperation. That is the public good, and it means the providing of the maximum advantages to the members of the community through life in the community. The positive intent of legal justice includes the willingness to harmonize actions having a social bearing with the wellbeing of other members of the community. Laws are guidelines for the same purpose; in themselves they are extrinsic guides: the human legislator cannot legislate virtue nor elicit internal assent or obedience. But in legal justice a citizen interiorizes these laws, i.e., makes them positive moral norms for his actions as a citizen. The interiority in question is perhaps best underlined by the meaning of *epikeia in its original use by Aristotle and St. Thomas: it is a higher form of justice, acting for the sake of the common good when observing a law to the letter would in fact frustrate the purposes of law and justice (ThAq ST 2a2ae, 120). The interiority of legal justice can be seen as implicit in Christ's coupling two obligations: of rendering to Caesar the things that are Caesar's, and to God the things that are God's (Lk 20.25). In the Christian life the civic or public good is one particular human good: the "common good" that is truly all-sufficient and fulfilling is God, the object of *charity. But charity itself calls for legal justice as respect for truly human values: those derived from and increased in the civic community.

[T. C. O'BRIEN]

LEGALISM, as a religious attitude, strong reliance on, and strict adherence to, laws. It has been interpreted as "belief that observance of the Ten Commandments or of humanly established laws will gain merit and eternal life" (Mayer RB 566). In this strict sense, it is doubtful that any Christian body can properly be described as legalistic. Mayer applies the term to several Protestant bodies and to Roman Catholics, because of his own views on *law and gospel. None of those to whom he imputes legalism, however, would accept the charge in the sense in which he defines it. To others legalism means excessive emphasis upon conformity to codes of ritual or ethics, and in this sense many groups have a tendency toward legalism. Puritans in England and America were considered legalistic because they opposed recreation or unnecessary work on Sundays (see SABBATARIANS). Many American Protestants have insisted that genuine Christians do not indulge in dancing, card playing, smoking, or drinking. Seventh-day Adventists are often said to be extreme legalists, because of their views of the Sabbath, dietary regulations, advocacy of tithing, and prohibition of drinking and smoking. Denying that they are legalistic, they insist that out of thankfulness to Christ, by whose grace they have been saved through faith, they obey his will as the Scriptures reveal it (see *Seventh-day Adventist Encyclopedia,* 1966). The question of legalism is bound up with the perennial problem of faith and works, which began with Paul's controversy with Judaizers (Galatians and Acts ch. 15). The relationship is a problem that continues to perplex Protestant and RC theologians; many deplore past emphasis on precepts and prohibitions as legalism that neglects the primacy of charity in Christian life. *ANTINOMIANISM.

[N. H. MARING]

LEGARDA, BERNARDO (fl. *c.*1700), Spanish colonial sculptor in Ecuador. A mestizo with studio in Quito, L. executed polychrome wood sculpture of remarkable energy and dignity in the baroque style of Seville (*Tota pulchra*, Monastery of S. Francisco).

[M. J. DALY]

LEGATE, BARTHOLOMEW (*c.*1575–1612), Seeker, executed as a heretic. L. was a cloth merchant and traveled to Holland, where he was in contact with Mennonites. In England he became a spokesman for Seeker expectation of a new revelation. For his Arian views (because of which Seekers were sometimnes called "Legatine Arians") he was arrested (1611, condemned, and became the last person to be burned in London for religious belief. BIBLIOGRAPHY: R. M. Jones, *Studies in Mystical Religion* (1923) 454–455; R. F. Jones, *Mysticism and Democracy in the English Commonwealth* (1965). *SEEKERS.

[T. C. O'BRIEN]

LEGATES, PAPAL, representatives sent by the pope throughout the world to a nation, civil ruler, international conference, or even a local Church to act in his behalf. The custom is quite old, and traces of this representation can be found at the imperial court of Constantinople. From the 9th cent., legates or envoys on special and temporary missions occur more and more frequently. In some cases the legate was chosen from the local Church and in time the metropolitans of important sees automatically became papal legates, endowed with special papal powers in canonical matters. Permanent papal envoys do not appear until the end of the 15th cent., coinciding with the development in Europe of regular diplomatic missions. The system was regularized by Pope Gregory XIII (1572–85), with the papal envoys bearing the title of apostolic nuncio. They ranked as ambassadors and enjoyed precedence over all the other ambassadors at the courts of the Catholic princes. The papal representative known as internuncio ranks as a minister plenipotentiary. In recent years a new category, the pronuncio, has come into use in those countries where the papal envoy has the rank of ambassador but where his automatic deanship in the diplomatic corps is not recognized. The nuncio, pronuncio, or internuncio has a double mission. He is accredited to the civil authorities but also deals directly with the national hierarchy. Where there are no diplomatic relations, an apostolic delegate is appointed with the sole mission of serving the local clergy and faithful. At Vatican Council II, suggestions were made by some bps. that the papal envoys be chosen from the local clergy and be of the nationality of the country, or that the nuncio be a layman. BIBLIOGRAPHY: R. A. Graham, *Vatican Diplomacy* (1959); E. L. Heston, "Papal Diplomacy: Its Organization and Way of Action," *Catholic Church in World Affairs* (ed. W. Gurian and M. A. Fitzsimons, 1954); J. A. Abbo, NCE 8:607–609.

[R. A. GRAHAM]

LEGATIONS, the civil provinces or administrative divisions of the *states of the Church before their incorporation into the Kingdom of Italy (1870). These divisions or papal states emerged in the 8th cent. when the popes began to exercise temporal, territorial power. The legations were generally governed by cardinal legates assisted by lay counselors who also served as governors of territorial subdivisions or delegations. The number and boundaries of the legations changed repeatedly under the impact of war and political events. The restoration of papal temporal power after the Napoleonic period witnessed a number of governmental reforms: Pius VII established (1816) five legations with 21 delegations; Leo XII reduced the delegations to 13; and a final reorganization provided for only four legations (Bologna, Urbino, Perugia, and Velletri). BIBLIOGRAPHY: D. D. Waley, *Papal State in the Thirteenth Century* (1961); P. Partner, NCE 8:609.

[T. M. MCFADDEN]

LE GAUDIER, ANTHONY (1572–1622), French Jesuit, spiritual writer, and religious director. After teaching Scripture at Pont-à-Mousson, moral theology at Le Flèche and Verdun, he served as master of novices and tertians, then rector at Liège and later at Paris (1618–21), where he wrote his works on the spiritual life: *De sanctissimo Christi Jesus Dei et hominis amore paraeneticum* (1619); *De vera Christi Jesus Dei et hominis imitatione* (1620); *De Dei praesentia* (1620), a commentary on St. Ignatius of Loyola's Spiritual Exercises (1620), and *De natura et statibus perfectionis* (1643).

[R. J. LITZ]

LEGENDA AUREA, see JAMES OF VORAGINE.

LEGENDS, CHRISTIAN. The word legend is derived from the Lat. *legenda*, meaning "things to be read." It was used in the Early Church as a name for works of edification, esp. accounts of the trials and executions of the Christian martyrs, which were read at liturgical functions. The primary purpose of these stories was to edify, and their role as historical records became relatively unimportant. Often they were built around some kernel of fact, but this was commonly so overlaid with imaginative embroidery that the total story was fictional rather than historical in character. From this circumstance the term legend in modern times is applied to any unauthentic story handed down by tradition, with or without a kernel of historical truth, esp. when it is illustrative of a group of people and its moral ideals. Every civilization or culture has legends dealing with its primitive origins, and just as pagan Rome had its tales concerning the founding of Rome by Romulus, son of Mars and Rhea Silvia, and the defense of the city by such figures as the Horatii, so Christian Rome developed its own romantic tales to fill in the gaps in its authentic history.

Legends of Christian Rome. Many of the NT apocrypha, most of which were composed in the East, contain legends that concern Rome, e.g., the *Acts of Peter, Acts of Paul* (see APOCRYPHA [NT], nn. 40, 43, 44, 51, 52, 56). Another source of early Christian legends with respect to the Apostles are the *Pseudo-Clementines.

Possibly because of the severity of the persecutions at Rome, but also because the veneration of the martyrs in that city might have been a relatively late development, authentic accounts of Roman martyrdoms are few; none are known except the accounts of the trials of Ptolemaeus, Lucius, and a third unnamed Christian (Justin 2 *Apol.* 2), of Justin Martyr and his companions, and of Apollonius, though the acts of the last named have been considerably embellished. The names and burial dates of a number of Roman martyrs, however, were preserved in the Roman Calendar of 354 A.D., and the tombs of a considerably larger number were known and venerated. In order to fill up the lacunae, hagiographers of the 4th, 5th, and 6th cent., making use of fragmentary bits of information, but frequently also of their own fertile imaginations, composed extensive accounts of the lives and deaths of SS. Cecilia, Agnes, Susanna, Felicity and her seven sons, Sebastian, Lawrence, John and Paul, Cosmas and Damian, and other popular saints. It was obvious, even in those times when historical criticism was an undeveloped art, that the authenticity of many of the stories was open to question. The *Gelasian Decree forbade the reading of them in church, "lest even slight occasion be given for ridicule" (D 353)—a prohibition that was either forgotten or ignored in later centuries.

Among the legends that sprang up concerning emperors and popes may be mentioned that of the baptism of Constantine by Pope Sylvester (5th cent.) and the *Donation of Constantine, an 8th- or 9th-cent. forgery that probably originated in France.

Many of the sites of Rome are associated with Christian legends. St. Peter is said to have been imprisoned in the *Mamertine and to have converted his two jailers, Processus and Martianus. A miraculous fall of snow is supposed to have marked out the site for the Liberian Basilica, St. Mary Major's, built by Pope Liberius on the Esquiline. The Scala Sancta is purported to be the stairway of Pilate's praetorium.

Despite the fantastic character of many of the popular Roman legends, they reflect a popular piety that nourished the devotion of countless pilgrims during the Middle Ages and more recent times, and they have been a constant inspiration for Christian art. A proper respect for historical fact need not blind a man to the importance of other types of truth than that with which the historiographer is primarily concerned. Like parables, allegories, and fables, legends too can have their value. BIBLIOGRAPHY: H. Leclercq, DACL 8.2:2309–2460; H. Delehaye, *Les légendes hagiographiques* (1927); J. E. Vaux, *Church Folklore* (1894, repr. 1974).

LÉGER, ANTOINE (d. 1662), Calvinist pastor. In 1628 he accompanied the Dutch ambassador to Holland and collaborated in publishing the fateful confession of faith of *Cyril Lucaris. On his return he was pastor at St. John's in the Vaudois from 1637 to 1643, when he fled to Geneva to escape prosecution for promoting Protestantism BIBLIOGRAPHY: C. Crivelli, EncCatt 7:1038.

[M. J. SUELZER]

LÉGER, FERNAND (1881–1955), French cubist painter of distinctly personal style, designer of the film *Ballet mécanique,* 1924, and illustrator of Eluard's *Liberté* (1953), chiefly known for his "mechanical cubism" (*Nudes in the Forest*, 1909–10) involving human and machine forms (*Three Women*, 1921). L.'s work ranged from acrobats, cyclists—in earlier modeled volumes to flat patterns of brilliant color floating freely over dynamic black linear statements. Living in New York from 1940, L. returned to France in 1946 and engaged in architectural decorations, executing for the churches at Assy (1946) and Audincourt (1951) colored glass, a portable mural and mosaics which are among the finest examples of contemporary religious art in the abstract style. BIBLIOGRAPHY: K. Kuh, *Léger* (1953); R. Rosenblum, *Cubism and Twentieth Century Art* (1960).

[L. A. LEITE]

LÉGER, JEAN (1615–70), Calvinist historian. As pastor of St. John's in the Vaudois, he opposed the House of Savoy and was forced to flee from France. He was restored to his post through the intercession of Cromwell and took part in the negotiations that led to a general amnesty, but he fomented further uprisings and was retired to Geneva. L. is best known for his controversial history of the evangelical churches of Piedmont (1669). BIBLIOGRAPHY: C. Crivelli, EncCatt 7:1038–39.

[M. J. SUELZER]

LEGES ROMANAE BARBARORUM, a general term referring to all the legal codes issued after the mid-5th cent.

governing Roman subjects of Germanic kings. In keeping with German legal tradition, even under a single king each tribe or people had its own laws, thus the Goths were governed by *Leges Barbarorum* and the Romans in Germanic lands by *Leges Romanae*. As Romanization of the West progressed, these distinct but often similar codes began to merge until all subjects were governed by one legal code. The Roman law of these codes, drafted by clergy and laity trained in Roman law, lacked the systematic precision of classical jurisprudence and was considered ''vulgar law.''

[R. J. LITZ]

LEGIO MARIA (Maria Legio; Legion of Mary Church), a Church in western Kenya which, when formed in 1963, was the largest such body ever to have seceded from the RC Church in Africa. Various attempts had been made since 1953 by a Catholic woman of the Nilotic Luo tribe, Mariam Ragot, to form a new religious protest movement *Dini ya Mariam* (Religion of Mary), but on three occasions incipient risings under her leadership were thwarted and suppressed by the colonial administration. By 1963 there was a considerable body of disaffected and lapsed Catholics in the Dioceses of Kisumu and Kisii. At this point a 20-year-old Luo Catholic girl, Gaudencia Aoko, claimed to have had a physical experience similar to death and resurrection followed by a prophetic call from God to form an African Catholic Church free from European interference and control. Her magnetic preaching attracted some 60,000 former Catholics; because of the surge of malcontents into the new body, political disturbances broke out, and led to police action and prison sentences for several leaders. Initially almost all adherents were of the Luo tribe, but during the next 5 years membership grew increasingly multitribal and spread also to neighboring Uganda and Tanzania. No RC priests joined the new movement, hence numbers of laymen were ordained; by 1967 some dozen bishops, a cardinal, Carolus Mumbo, and a pope, Simeon Ondeto, known also as *Baba Mtakatifu* (Holy Father), had been designated. After initial troubles with the newly independent Kenya government authorities, the movement asserted its loyalty to the administration and by 1967 had been permitted to register as a legal society claiming 10,000 adult members in East Africa. Early on, Legio Maria made contacts with the 160 Churches of the African independent church movement in Kenya, and joined their militantly antimission federation, the East Africa United Churches and Orthodox Coptic Communion. In 1967 all these Churches abruptly swung in an ecumenical direction by applying for membership to the All Africa Conference of Churches, which is linked with the World Council of Churches.

In doctrine Legio Maria is conservative, stressing orthodox Catholic teaching but inserting a strong element of African culture and world view; the right of Africans to run their Church without European interference is constantly stressed. Practice is conservative and ritualistic; Latin is retained in full as an essential ritual language, and the Mass and sacraments are performed with punctilious ceremonial. Colorful robes based on monastic garb and priestly vestments are worn by all members, with white, black, and mauve especially popular, and members festoon themselves with rosaries, crucifixes, and other Catholic insignia. Services emphasize ex tempore prayer and *glossolalia, mass prayer for the sick, and healing rites. As with many other African independent Churches, Legio Maria soon suffered from the recurrent problem of secession. Shortly after its founding in 1963, 300 Luo members in North Mara across the border in Tanzania seceded to form the African Catholic Church under Marcellianus Orongo. In 1967 several small Legio Maria factions in Kenya were discussing further secessions, although the bulk of the movement had settled down as a stable body recognized by a number of other Churches. BIBLIOGRAPHY: D. B. Barrett, *Schism and Renewal in Africa* (1968); *idem*, *African Initiatives in Religion* (1971). *AFRICAN INDEPENDENT CHURCH MOVEMENT; *AFRICAN CHRISTIANITY (CONTEMPORARY).

[D. B. BARRETT]

LEGION OF MARY, a lay association founded in Dublin, Ireland, in 1921, to assist the clergy in the sanctification of souls and spread of the Christian faith. It was begun by a small group of lay people and based on the principles of the mystical body and on the *True Devotion to the Blessed Virgin Mary* of St. Louis *Grignion de Montfort. The movement spread very rapidly throughout Ireland, Great Britain, the U.S., the Philippines, Brazil, and Africa. It now numbers more than one million active members. Any practicing Catholic over 18 years of age is eligible for full admission. A member is required to lead an exemplary Christian life; attend a weekly Legion meeting consisting of prayer, spiritual reading, and instruction by a priest director; and spend at least two hours a week in apostolic work. This work is quite varied and includes almost every form of social service and Catholic Action except collecting money and dispensing material relief. The Legion has a distinctive organizational structure, borrowing the title for its various divisions from ancient Roman military nomenclature. A praesidium is the smallest unit; the curia, a group of two or more praesidia; the senatus, a regional governing body; and the concilium, the supreme governing body. This precise organization and the universal use of the Legion handbook have made the Legion an extremely effective force in the intensification of the Christian life. The Legion makes a significant contribution to evangelization by its Peregrinatio pro Christo, a program of home visiting and Bible study. BIBLIOGRAPHY: L. J. Suenens, *Theology of the Apostolate of the Legion of Mary* (1954).

[T. M. MCFADDEN]

LEGIPONT, OLIVER (1698–1758), Benedictine of the Abbey of Great St. Martin, Cologne; cataloguer of monastic libraries; editor of *Monasticum Moguntiacum* (1746), of *Dissertationes philologico-bibliographicae* (1747), and of

M. *Ziegelbauer's *Historia rei literariae Ordinis S. Benedicti* (4 v., 1754).

[T. C. O'BRIEN]

LEGISLATION, ECCLESIASTICAL. The Church, having been established by Christ to promote the salvation of mankind, seeks to fulfill this purpose not only by teaching and the administration of sacraments, but also by establishing laws for the governance and guidance of its members. The power to make law was transmitted to the Apostles, who in turn entrusted it to the pope and to the college of bishops, when they act as a group. The canon law of the Church is the end result of this legislation. Specific precepts may become part of the law of the Church in several ways. They may be tacitly accepted by the papacy rather than specifically prescribed; in this way, many biblical and patristic texts have been incorporated. Even maxims of Roman and other civil law have been in the past admitted as valid in canon law courts for this reason. Such precepts must, however, be consistent with the Church's perception of the unchanging and eternal law of God, the primary legislator. The pope is the only individual invested with legislative power over all the Church, not solely in matters of faith and morals, but also in all matters of ecclesiastical discipline and government. This authority may be exercised personally, in the form of constitutions, bulls, *motu-proprio* etc. (see DOCUMENTS, PAPAL), or it may be delegated to a Roman Congregation, Tribunal or Office. The Code of Canon Law was itself promulgated by means of the apostolic constitution *Providentissima Mater Ecclesia* of Pope Benedict XV. New laws of the Holy See are now promulgated through the publication *Acta Apostolicae Sedis* (see LAW, PROMULGATION OF). The legislative authority that the pope bears for the entire Church is exercised with his diocese by every bishop. An ecumenical council of the Church also has the authority to legislate for the entire Christian community. Through this organ the entire college of bishops, under the presidency of the pope, exercises its collective pastoral mission over the whole Church.

[R. A. ARONSTAM]

LE GOBIEN, CHARLES (1653–1708), French Jesuit who, as procurator for the China missions, published extensively to attract interest and support for the missions. Most notably he began (1702) and was first editor of the annual *Lettres édifiantes* from Jesuit missionaries, a rich source of mission history.

[T. C. O'BRIEN]

LEGRENZI, GIOVANNI (1626–90), Italian conductor, composer, and teacher. Appointed to St. Mark's, Venice, as vice-master (1681) and master (1685), he served there for the rest of his life. His numerous works for the church orchestra, which he expanded to 34 members, and church choir, include motets, Masses, sonatas, psalms, and other occasional compositions. L. instructed Gasparini, Caldara, and Lotti.

[R. J. LITZ]

LEGROS, PIERRE I AND II, French sculptors. **Pierre I** (1629–1714) worked at Versailles (1670–92); **Pierre II** (1666–1719) worked mainly in Roman churches and at the Abbey of Montecassino. His altar *Religion Overthrows Heresy* (1695–99), Il Gesū, Rome) eschews the French classicism of his father for a rococo quality.

[M. J. DALY]

LE HIR, ARTHUR MARIE (1811–68), Scripture scholar. L. taught theology, Scripture, and Hebrew at the Seminary of Saint-Sulpice (Paris). A collection of his articles, entitled *Études bibliques,* as well as several commentaries on OT books, was published posthumously. His *Résumé chronologique de la vie du Sauveur* was edited by F. *Vigouroux. BIBLIOGRAPHY: L. Bertrand, DB 4:162.

[T. M. MCFADDEN]

LEHMANN, PAUL (1884–1964), Protestant medieval scholar. He taught at the Univ. of Munich most of his career. Author of many studies on the libraries, MSS, and literature of the Middle Ages, L. published, among other works, *Die Parodie im Mittelalter* (1963); *Eine Geschichte der alten Fuggerbibliotheken* (2 v., 1956–59), and *Erforschung des Mittelalters* (5 v., 1959–62).

[J. R. AHERNE]

LEHMKUHL, AUGUST (1834–1918), German Jesuit moral theologian, author of the many-times edited *Theologia moralis* (2 v., 1883). In line with the Jesuit tradition in moral theology, he also published *Probabilismus vindicatus* (2 v., 1906). Other writings include *Casus conscientiae* (2 v., 1906), works in the interest of the social betterment of workers.

[T. C. O'BRIEN]

LEHODEY, VITAL (Alcime Jude; 1857–1948), Trappist ascetical writer. Of French origin, L. was ordained a diocesan priest in 1880 but entered the Trappist monastery at Bricquebec in 1889. Even before his solemn profession he was elected abbot in 1895 and served in that capacity until 1929. L. was a modern master of Cistercian spirituality, his writings offsetting the pessimism which befell that ascetism in Jansenist days. His chief works are: *A Spiritual Directory for Religious* (1932), *The Ways of Mental Prayer* (1912), and *Holy Abandonment* (1934). BIBLIOGRAPHY: N. Kinsella, *Flight and Pursuit: The Mission of Dom Vital Lehodey* (1962).

[J. R. AHERNE]

LEI-WEN (thunder pattern), Chinese decorative design on ritual bronzes of the Shang and Chou dynasties (*c.*1500–256 B.C.). Used as a fret or "meander" in background and borders, in variants—curved, angular, and at times, with hook-like projections, the "thunder pattern" in an agricultural civilization was a beneficient symbol harbingering rain.

[M. J. DALY]

LEIBNIZ, GOTTFRIED WILHELM VON (1646–1716), German philosopher and universal genius. His learning embraced mathematics (he was, along with Newton but independent of him, the inventor of the calculus); law, history, and logic. His long career in the service of the dukes of Hanover showed him to be an able diplomat. Diplomatic missions and voluminous correspondence made him an intimate of the best and most inquiring minds of his day. He displayed an early interest in developing a universal language of argumentation, his *ars combinatoria,* an effort of interest to semanticists and logicians even today. L. was one of the first thinkers to investigate the logic of probabilities. Protestant by persuasion but educated in the scholastic tradition, he strove, by a kind of philosophical ecumenism, to unite the thinking of Protestants and Catholics. L. combined two of his interests in a work on the Council of Trent in which, by application of the law of probabilities, he attempted to show the decrees of that council as acceptable to Protestants.

L.'s writings reveal a brilliant series of philosophical insights, often profound, rather than an integrated and completely coherent system. His basic pattern of thought derives from Cartesian rationalism, but he found the monism and pantheism Spinoza developed from it distasteful. Taking the Cartesian dichotomy of thought and extension as a point of departure, accepting with Spinoza, the Cartesian definition of substance as that which stands alone, but rejecting Spinoza's monism, L. developed his monadology. Monads are the elemental substances of the physical world, psychic in nature but the source of the extension characteristic of matter. L.'s is a metaphysics of the impossible: by the principle of sufficient reason, all is possible that does not involve a contradiction; all that is actual comes to be by the creative act of God.

L.'s notion of God is developed most fully in his *Theodicy*. God's existence can be proved a posteriori from the principle of sufficient reason, and it can be imperfectly demonstrated, a priori by a variation of the ontological argument, in which he sought to infer God's real existence from the fact (only imperfectly established) that he is possible. L.'s optimism, the assertion so viciously caricatured in Voltaire's *Candide* that this is the best of all possible worlds, is widely misunderstood. The divine intelligence can know an infinity of possible worlds and remains free to create one or another of them. The one chosen is relatively, not absolutely, the best. L. sought to reconcile the mechanical and psychological determinism of created things with the freedom of God and man. His neglect of the empirical element in thought left him with a sterile rationalism. BIBLIOGRAPHY: B. Russell, *Critical Exposition of the Philosophy of Leibniz* (2d. ed., 1937); Copleston 4:264–332, 344–346; L. J. Russell, EncPhil 4:422–434, esp. for the bibliography, including sources, works, revisions, commentaries, translations, biographies, and interpretations.

[W. B. MAHONEY]

LEIDRADUS OF LYONS (d. 817), archbishop. As a young cleric L. was invited to Charlemagne's court by Alcuin. He subsequently became abp. of Lyons. Noted for rare ability, good sense, and virtue, he took a stand against the heresy of Adoptionism at the Council of Urgel (799). At Lyons he dealt with the sad conditions resulting from the Muslim occupation and from subsequent confiscations by Charles Martel. L.'s achievements were solid. Fearing death would interrupt his long-range programs, he recounted them in a letter to Charlemagne so that the Emperor might carry them out. He restored chant, rebuilt churches, and organized his clergy. Added to his letter to Charlemagne was a summary account of each church and monastery, giving the number of its inhabitants and their social rank. During the final years of his life he retired to the monastery of Saint-Médard at Soissons. BIBLIOGRAPHY: C. M. Aherne, NCE 8:622.

[F. G. O'BRIEN]

LEINBERGER, HANS (1480?–1535?), a leading German Renaissance sculptor. L. executed the *St. James* and *St. George* (both 1525, Munich), altars at Moosburg and at Polling, and the bronze figure of Albert IV for the tomb of Maximilian I at the Hofkirche, Innsbruck. L.'s wood carvings express an intense late-Gothic emotional realism in monumental forms.

[M. J. DALY]

LEIPZIG, DISPUTATION OF, see DISPUTATION OF LEIPZIG.

LEIPZIG INTERIM, see INTERIMS.

LEIPZIG, UNIVERSITY OF (Karl Marx University), an institution of higher learning in East Germany, founded by Frederick IV and his brother Wilhelm II, landgraves of Meissen, who, with the approval of Pope Alexander V (1409), invited a group of German students and professors, disturbed by the Hussite conflict and political inequality at the Univ. of Prague, to establish a *studium generale* in Leipzig. Modeled on Prague, the university, composed of faculties of arts, philosophy, canon and civil law, and medicine, was divided into four nations: Meissen, Saxony, Bavaria, and Poland. The masters of arts were lodged with their students in two houses: the *collegium maius* and the *collegium minus,* which were both residences and lecture halls. The bp. of Merseburg was chancellor *ex officio*. The university soon became a German center of scholasticism and humanistic studies, only to be later overshadowed for almost a century by the Univ. of Wittenberg (1502). The statute of 1559 that suppressed the Reformation movement precipitated the withdrawal of a large number of professors and students. Although strong in orthodox Lutheran scholasticism in the 17th cent., in the 18th cent. Leipzig became a rich cultural center, counting among its students Goethe, and among its professors J. P. Richter, the novelist, C. Fürchtegott, poet, and J. S. Bach, the composer, whose leadership contributed largely to the establishment of the famous conservatory of music. Reorganized and expanded in 1830, the university became one of the largest in Germany. It was greatly damaged during World War II but was later restored. In 1953 it was renamed the Karl-Marx Univ. by the Communist government. BIBLIOGRAPHY: H. Rashdall, *Universities of Europe in the Middle Ages* (ed. F. M. Powicke and A. B. Emden, 3 v. 1936).

[M. B. MURPHY]

LEISURE, the condition of one who, being unengaged in work or other compulsory activity, is free to do as he pleases. In contemporary usage the term differs from rest, which implies a withdrawal from activity, generally for the purpose of overcoming physical or mental fatigue, whereas leisure is often filled with activity. In earlier times leisure, so understood, was commonly the privilege of the few whose wealth put them above the need to toil. In modern times mechanization has put leisure increasingly within the reach of ordinary people, and at the same time the monotony of specialized labor in industrialized society has enhanced its desirability. The OT found no special value in leisure as distinct from necessary rest, and it stressed rather the dignity of labor, which it saw as the fulfillment of God's commission (Gen 1.28). The day from dawn to dusk was given to man to work (Ps 103 [104] 22; Job 8.4). Even the happiness of man's original state did not exclude work (Gen. 2.15), which only became burdensome after the Fall (Gen 3.17–19). Only the Lord's day, the Sabbath, and certain feasts were to be free from toil. However, though the sacred holidays were instituted to honor the covenant with God, they did provide for man's rest, and this appears to have been intended by the law. According to the Epistle to the Hebrews, the succession of work and rest in its own way reflects the image of God (3.7–4.11). From the eschatological perspective of early Christian preaching it could be truly said that man was made for rest and at the end of time God will admit him to that rest—a rest, however, not to be confused with a state of inertness, for it is filled with intense spiritual activity (1 Cor 13.12–13).

The broader opportunity for leisure in contemporary industrial civilization gives rise to problems of social, moral, and religious significance. The opportunity should be justly distributed, and this calls for continuing negotiation between workers and employers to extend the progress that has been made. Second, the possibility of using leisure time to the enrichment of human life needs further expansion. Third, the opportunity of leisure requires conversion to a thing of religious value. If leisure is looked upon not simply as inactivity or idleness but rather as re-creation, it can be, just as work is, a way of sharing in God's creativity. Work and leisure will not then be opposed to each other as action and inaction. Both can be centered on the complete fulfillment of the person and thus converge toward a unification of life's object. A theology of leisure will then complete the theology of work in the sense that both reveal to man, each in its fashion, the dignity of a creature made to God's image. Leisure and work have their own peculiar demands and their special opportunities for union with Christ. The workday is the time for an implicit union in the construction of the world in preparation for the glorified Lord. Leisure provides the occasion for explicit union by prayer and fellowship in worship. BIBLIOGRAPHY: J. Pieper, *Work and Leisure* (1955); D. Riesman, *Lonely Crowd* (1950); H. Marcuse, *One Dimensional Man* (1967).

[R. SCHÜRMANN]

LEITGEB, JOSEF (1897–1952), Austrian poet, essayist, whose work combines formal beauty and enjoyment of the senses with the ideals of a Christian humanism. After military service in World War I, L. studied law and eventually became a teacher and school superintendent in Innsbruck. He founded the literary periodical *Wort im Gebirge* (1948). Works: *Vita somnium breve* (1943), collected poems; *Trinkt, o Augen* (1943), essay.

[B. F. STEINBRUCKNER]

LE JAY, CLAUDE (Jajus; 1504–52), Swiss-born Jesuit theologian. At Paris he took vows when St. Ignatius and his first companions renewed theirs in 1535, on the anniversary of their first profession. With *Salmeron and St. *Peter Canisius L. received a doctorate in theology at Bologna in 1542. At the Council of Trent he was the theologian for Card. O. *Truchsess von Waldburg and was commissioned to prepare the conciliar decree on Scripture and tradition. L. was a strong defender of papal primacy.

[R. J. LITZ]

LEJAY, PAUL, (1861–1920), classical and patristic scholar. After completing his seminary studies, Lejay attended the École des Hautes Études. He was ordained in 1890 and appointed to the Institut Catholique of Paris where he taught Latin philology till his death. Though his contributions to classical studies are well known, his greater fame rests on *Textes et documents pour l'étude historique du Christianisme,* which he and H. M. Hemmer began and directed (18 v., 1904–12). He was a member of the Académie des Inscriptions and contributed numerous studies to the *Dictionnaire de théologie catholique* and scholarly journals.

BIBLIOGRAPHY: DTC *Tables Générales* 2946 (1965); M. R. P. McGuire, NCE 8:625.

[H. DRESSLER]

LEJEUNE, JEAN (1592–1672), French Oratorian preacher. L. studied theology at Dôle, was a canon at Arbois, but entered the Oratory (1611) under the influence of P. de *Bérulle. After serving in the Langres seminary, L. began his lifework of preaching and quickly became famous for his ardent popular, though academically structured, sermons and lectures. Blinded at Rouen (1629), he continued to preach, acquiring the name Le Père Aveugle (the Blind Father), and living a life of holiness. He published *Le Missionaire de l'Oratoire* (1662; 1825–27), a collection of 362 sermons, and a selection of his sermons was translated into Latin and published as *Johannis Junii deliciae pastorum* (1667).

[R. J. LITZ]

LE LIGET, CHAPEL OF ST. JOHN OF LIGET, small, circular chapel added to the Carthusian monastery of Liget (founded 1176–89) by Henry II of England to expiate the murder of Thomas à Becket. An important cycle of Romanesque frescoes remains on the interior (*c.* 1197–1201) showing below a frieze of patriarchs and Prophets, grand scenes of the *Nativity, Presentation in the Temple, Descent from the Cross, Holy Women at the Tomb, Dormition of the Virgin,* and *Tree of Jesse*.

[M. J. DALY]

LE LOUP, JEAN, 13th-cent. French architect and second master at Reims Cathedral, succeeding Jean d'Orbais. Between 1231 and 1247 L. altered the N transept façade with a triple portal.

[M. J. DALY]

LELOUTRE, JEAN LOUIS (1709–72), French missionary. He was ordained in 1737 as a member of the Paris Foreign Mission Society. Most of his career was spent as a missioner to the Micmacs of Acadia (Nova Scotia). In 1754 he was named vicar general of Quebec. Taken prisoner by the British and deported in 1758, after the Treaty of Paris he returned to France where he worked for the resettlement of the deported Acadians. BIBLIOGRAPHY: N. Roger, "Abbé Le Loutre," *Canadian Historical Review* 11 (1930).

[J. R. AHERNE]

LEMAISTRE, ANTOINE AND ISAAC LOUIS, two sons of Catherine Arnault, who became leaders at the Jansenist center, *Port-Royal.

Antoine (1608–58) was a brilliant lawyer, and a counselor of state when he renounced the world (1638) and under the advice of the Abbé de *Saint-Cyran became one of the first *solitaires* of Port-Royal. He collaborated in Isaac Louis' translation of the NT and began his own *Vie des saints*. With skillful eloquence he defended Saint-Cyran against Cardinal Richelieu: *Apologie pour feu M. l'abbé de Saint-Cyran* (1642); *Apologie pour Jean Duvergier de Hauranne* (1645). The *Lettre d'un avocat,* 19th of Pascal's *Provincial Letters, is sometimes ascribed to him.

Isaac Louis (1613–84), better known as Lemaistre de Sacy (anagram of Isaac), was under the spiritual direction of Saint-Cyran when he was ordained (1649). He became director first of the other *solitaires,* then of the nuns at Port-Royal. During a period of anti-Jansenist persecution, he was imprisoned in the Bastille (1666–69), where he began an edition of the Bible, *La sainte Bible en latin et en français* (32 v., 1687–1702). His translation of the NT published in 1667, known as the "de Mons" edition, was quite popular, but was condemned (1669) by Clement IX for its Jansenism. He also translated the *Imitation of Christ* (1662), the Psalms, sermons of St. Augustine, as well as Phaedrus's Fables and Terence's comedies. In addition he left many letters of spiritual direction, and *Poème sur l'eucharistie* (1695). His writings helped circulate Jansenist ideas in France. BIBLIOGRAPHY: G. Delassault, *Le Maistre de Sacy et son temps* (1957); bibliog. for Jansenism.

LEMAÎTRE, JULES (1853–1914), French academician and a versatile author of fiction, drama, and esp. literary criticism. In his attitude toward religion he typifies many conservative intellectuals of the time. He wrote sympathetically of the priesthood, defended religious institutions, and considered Catholicism part of the national patrimony. Although he frequented the same circles as Anatole France and, like him, cultivated an antidogmatic and impressionistic critical method, the authenticity of his philosophical skepticism and emancipation from Christian ethics was doubted. The Dreyfus affair accentuated the differences between them, and he came to support the Action Française movement. Though he insisted he was not a believer, his royalist, nationalist, and patriotic activities brought him closer to Catholics holding kindred views and eventually to Catholicism. In his testament he stated, "I die a Catholic"; his deathbed conversion was described by the attending priest. BIBLIOGRAPHY: M. Harry, *La Vie de Jules Lemaître* (1946); P. Gisell, *Anatole France and His Circle* (1922).

[G. E. GINGRAS]

LE MASSON, INNOCENT (1627–1703), general of the Carthusians from 1675. He promoted valuable research into Carthusian history through his own *Disciplina Ordinis Cartusiensis*, reconstructed archives of the Grande Chartreuse after a fire in 1675; and by encouraging the work of others that led to editions of the annals of the order and of the lives of Carthusians renowned for holiness. He governed with a strong hand; defended his order against criticism by the Abbé de *Rance and against the incursion of Jansenism and *quietism.

[T. C. O'BRIEN]

LEME DA SILVEIRA CINTRA, SEBASTIÃO (1882–1942) cardinal, political force. One of the most influential church leaders in modern Latin America, L. was ordained in 1904 for São Paulo, Brazil. In 1911 he was named bp. of Olinda, Pernambuco, and in 1916 he set an example of vigorous pastoral concern. Founder of the Catholic Confederation embracing all Catholic Action groups, L. issued a famous pastoral on religious ignorance and recommendations to ameliorate it. In Rio de Janeiro as coadjutor bp. he founded the Catholic Confederation of Rio de Janeiro and its manual *Acão Católica* (1923). L. was appointed abp. of Rio de Janeiro in 1930 and named a cardinal. His leadership drew support from Catholic intellectuals who exercised considerable influence throughout Brazil. After the overthrow of President Vargas in 1932, L. obtained concessions from the Constitutional Assembly to abolish anti-Catholic laws, was instrumental in gaining the right of women to vote, and brought the influence of Catholicism to the Constitution of 1934. He organized the Brazilian Plenary Council of 1939 and founded the Catholic Univ. of Rio de Janeiro (1941.)

[J. R. AHERNE]

LEMERCIER, JACQUES (*c.*1580–1654), French architect. L. absorbed the Italian style in Rome, extended Lescot's wing of the Louvre, executed the Sorbonne chapel and added to François Mansart's Church of Val-de-Grâce "the most dramatic and impressive 17th-cent. dome in Paris."

[M. J. DALY]

LEMIRE, JULES (1853–1928), French priest, social activist in the Chamber of Deputies from 1893 until his death. He identified himself with the cause of the worker, and contributed significantly to legislation that began family benefits in France. He was suspended by the abp. of Cambrai for seeking and winning reelection in 1914, but the suspension was lifted by the Pope in 1916. L.'s inspiration and objective were to spread the social teaching of Leo XIII's *Rerum novarum*.

[T. C. O'BRIEN]

LEMKE, PETER HENRY (1796–1882), missionary. A Lutheran pastor in Germany, he converted to Catholicism in 1824 and was ordained a priest in 1826. He came to the U.S. in 1834 and worked with D. *Gallitzin at Loretto, Pa.; he founded Carrolltown, Pa., in 1853. Becoming a Benedictine at Latrobe, Pa. (1853), he worked in the Kansas territory for several years. He spent his last years, from 1877, in retirement at Carrolltown. BIBLIOGRAPHY: R. Bechman, *Kansas Monks: A History of St. Benedict's Abbey* (1957) 9–43.

[J. R. AHERNE]

LEMMENS, LEONHARD (1864–1929), historian of the Franciscan Order. Ordained priest in 1888, L. taught at Fulda and at Ottsberg. He became professor of ecclesiastical history at the International College of Rome (1901) and prefect of the College of Quaracchi (1903). Widely traveled, he was named general archivist of his order in 1921. He wrote more than 90 works dealing with the history of the Franciscans. BIBLIOGRAPHY: S. Cipriani, DE 2:633; O. Bonmann, LTK 6:942.

[F. D. LAZENBY]

LEMNIUS, SIMON (*c.*1511–50), humanist and polemicist. He studied at Wittenberg where Melanchthon was forced to expel him because of his publication (1538) of two books of *Epigrams* which aroused Luther's anger. The incident occasioned two other provocative works. L. also wrote poetry, a translation of the *Odyssey*, and other Latin writings. BIBLIOGRAPHY: B. M. Peebles, NCE 8:629.

[G. E. CONWAY]

LE MOITURIER, ANTOINE (MAISTRE ANTHONIET; *c.*1425–97), French sculptor. M. completed the tomb of John the Fearless (1466–70) started by Jean de la Huerta, and probably that of Philippe Pot—where massive figures bearing the effigy of the deceased continue with a gentle restraint the monumental tradition of Claus Sluter.

[M. J. DALY]

LEMOS, TOMÁS DE (*c.*1546–1629), Spanish Dominican, who, with D. Alvarez, was appointed to present at Rome his order's position on grace and free will in the **Congregatio de auxiliis* (1602–06). His own work, *Panoplia gratiae* (4 v., 1676) is a masterly presentation of the Dominican theological tradition on grace. His collection of the *Acta* of the *Congregatio de auxiliis* was published in 1702.

[T. C. O'BRIEN]

LE MOYNE, PIERRE (1602–72), French Jesuit poet. His *Saint Louis ou la Couronne reconquise sur les infidèles* (1653) was an attempt to give France a national epic; in 18 chants, it expresses Counter Reformation tastes. L. is also author of: *La Galerie des femmes fortes* (1647); *La Dévotion aisée* (1652), criticized by Pascal in his 11th **Provincial Letter*; *Peintures morales*; and *Le Triomphe de Louis XIII*. BIBLIOGRAPHY: H. Chérot, *Étude sur la vie et les oeuvres de P. Le Moyne* (1887).

[R. N. NICOLICH]

LE MOYNE DE BIENVILLE, JEAN BAPTISTE, see BIENVILLE, JEAN BAPTISTE LE MOYNE DE.

LE NAIN BROTHERS, French painters of genre, religious panels, and portraits. **Antoine** (1588–1648), **Louis** (1593–1648), and **Matthieu** (1607–77) having left works signed without their Christian names, and frequently evidencing collaboration, have confused attributions. Antoine, master painter of St.-Germain-des-Prés, excelled in miniatures and small portraits. Louis called "le Romain" is the greatest of the brothers working in larger scale, with subdued cool palette and atmospheric perspective, his figures standing in monumental classic reserve in surrealistic airless spaces(*Adoration of the Shepherds*, Louvre). Matthieu was more prosperous and pretentious, showing lively figures in sentimental, courtly attitudes, though still reserved. Works by the Le Nain brothers are in France, England, the U.S., and Russia.

[M. J. DALY]

LENAU, NIKOLAUS, (real name, Franz Nikolaus Niembsch von Strehlenau; 1802–50), Austrian poet of German-Hungarian ancestry, whose pessimistic **weltschmerz* lyrical works have a place among the greatest of German poetry. He is sometimes called the "German Byron." His profound melancholy and unfulfilled search for happiness is reflected in his haunting lyrics of nature, love, and loneliness. His epic poems *Faust* (1836), *Savonarola* (1837), and *Die Albigenser* (1842) reveal religious and political idealism outside the established CHurch. He began to write under the influence of the Swabian school (L. Uhland, J. Kerner). An attempt to settle as a farmer in the U.S. (1832–33) ended in failure and he returned to Vienna. From 1844 L. was confined in an institution for the care of the insane. BIBLIOGRAPHY: L. Spuler, NCE 8:631.

[B. F. STEINBRUCKNER]

LENDINARA, CRISTOFORO DA (fl. 1449–91), Italian wood intarsist working with his brother Lorenzo. L. inlaid *The Evangelists* (Modena cathedral), showing Piero della Francesca's forms and a masterful perspective.

[M. J. DALY]

LENIN, N. (VLADIMIR ILLICH ULYANOF; 1870–1924), from 1900 pseudonym of the founder of the Russian Communist Party, the Soviet Union, and the Communist International, the man who was to become the most influential theoretical political thinker and statesman of the 20th century. Reared in a cultivated family of professionals, L. attended the Kazan Univ. as a law student but was expelled for participating in illegal student activity. He read Marx's *Das Kapital* and became a Marxist in 1889. Despite opposition L. was finally admitted to the bar. As a lawyer he met with dissident Marxists in St. Petersburg. With others he founded the Union for the Struggle for the Liberation of the Working Class. He was jailed for 15 months and then exiled to Siberia for 3 years. In his great work, *Development of Capitalism in Russia* (1899) L. argued that half of the peasants in Russia constituted a proletariat to join with industrial workers and thus formed the basis of a collectivist society. In a second work, *What Is To Be Done?* (1902), he formulated the concept of a disciplined central party which would make the working class aware of its true interests. He called for a corps of revolutionaries who would lead the way and overturn Russia. L. headed the Bolsheviks (those in the majority) of the party which stood opposed to and finally separated from the Menshevick (those in the minority) group, which favored a bourgeois rather than a proletarian revolution. Russia in the disaster of World War I provided the conditions needed for a revolution. L. plotted against the Kerensky moderate Provisional Government after the ouster of the Czar and drove it from power. With consummate skill he defeated the White Russians and the Western Allies. His Bolshevik party became the sole party in Russia, and L. was elected chairman of the People's Commissars, in effect, the ruler of Russia. He concluded the treaty of Brest-Litovsk, fought off the Whites in a civil war, and made concessions to the peasantry. In 1919 he formed the Third International which demanded the allegiance of Communist parties in all countries. Opposed to Stalin's views on centralized authority, he could not prevent the election of Stalin as general secretary of the party. L.'s illnesses from 1922 to 1924 made it impossible for him to stem the rise of Josef Stalin. BIBLIOGRAPHY: L. Fischer, *Life of Lenin* (1964); A. Meyer, *Leninism* (1957); B. Wolfe, *Three Who Made a Revolution: A Biographical History* (1964).

[J. R. AHERNE]

LENINGRAD THEOLOGICAL ACADEMY, formerly Ecclesiastical Academy of St. Petersburg; before the revolution of 1917 one of the four major centers (besides Moscow, Kiev, and Kazan) for the education of clergy, for theological studies, and for publications. After the revolution all activities were discontinued. With the restoration of the patriarchate of Moscow in 1945, there commenced a limited renewal of theological studies in the two ecclesiastical academies, that of the celebrated monastery of St. Sergious in Zagorsk, not far from Moscow, and that of Leningrad. Theological articles are published, many up-to-date and, in general, of somewhat conservative bent. Scholars of the Academy publish in the *Messenger* for Western Europe and more recently in a review edited in East Germany. The publication of theological works in the Soviet Union has been limited extremely to only a few volumes.

[L. PEANO]

LENITY, a quality of the virtue of *clemency; mildness of spirit that inclines to tempering the redress of grievances or the infliction of punishment (ThAq AT 2a2ae, 157.4 ad 3). This quality may apply either in the case of a judge's passing sentence, or of a private person's redressing a wrong done him (see REVENGE). In either case, as belongs to virtue, lenient mitigation still observes the requirements of what is right, but in the given circumstances rightly forgoes severity.

[T. C. O'BRIEN]

LENNERZ, HEINRICH (1880–1961), theologian. L. was born in the Rhineland, entered the Jesuits, and spent a long career on the theology faculty at the Gregorian University. He sought to shed light on contemporary theological problems by an exegesis of the documents of the Church's magisterium, esp. those of the Councils of Trent and Vatican I. He wrote numerous theological manuals used by students at the Gregorian for over 30 years. BIBLIOGRAPHY: Anon., "In Memoriam. P. Henricus Lennerz, S.J.," *Gregorianum* 43 (1962) 87–88.

[T. M. MCFADDEN]

LENORMANT, French archeologists and historians. (1) **Charles** (1802–59), whose primary interest was in the study of the origins of Christian civilization. He taught at the Sorbonne and filled several important administrative posts when not engaged in missions to Egypt and Greece. He was elected to the French Academy in 1839. (2) **François** (1837–83), son of Charles. His interests ranged over ancient civilizations and numismatics. He occupied the chair of archeology of the Bibliothèque National, and was elected to L'Académie des Inscriptions et Belles-Lettres.

[P. J. HENNESSEY]

LE NOURRY, NICOLAS DENIS (1647–1724), Maurist patristic scholar. Educated by the Oratorians in his native city of Dieppe, he joined the Benedictines and made profession July 8, 1665, at Jumièges. He collaborated with J. Garet in editing Cassiodorus, and with J. Duchesne and J. Bellaise in preparing an edition of the works of St. Ambrose. His own chief work is: *Apparatus ad bibliothecam maximam veterum patrum et antiquorum scriptorum* in two volumes (1703 and 1715). In 1710 he edited *De mortibus persecutorum* and made the first modern attempt to prove that it is not the work of Lactantius. BIBLIOGRAPHY: J. Baudot, DTC 9.1:217–218.

[H. DRESSLER]

LENT, a penitential season extending from Ash Wednesday until Holy Saturday in preparation for the Easter feast. This period of preparation appears originally to have consisted in a 1- or 2-day fast in anticipation of the admission of catechumens to baptism. The period varied from time to time and place to place, but by the end of the 4th cent. it began at Rome on Quadragesima Monday and lasted until Holy Thursday. To make the period correspond to Christ's 40-day fast, the beginning of Lent was moved back to Ash Wednesday in the 7th century. In the East, where neither Saturday nor Sunday was observed as fast days, Lent began during Sexagesima week. With the constitution *Poenitemini* of Pope Paul (Feb. 17, 1966), major changes in the penitential observance in the RC Church were introduced, and, in the U.S., in line with provisions of the constitution and a 1974 decision of the NCCB, Ash Wednesday and Good Friday are days of fast and abstinence, and all Fridays of Lent are days of abstinence with fast and abstinence encouraged on all other days. However, the Lenten season retains its penitential character and the substitution of other forms of penance is recommended for those who do not choose to observe the fast.

In the early Church the Eucharist was celebrated only on Sundays during the Lenten period; by the 5th cent. it was also celebrated on Wednesdays and Fridays, and the following century saw the introduction of the Eucharist on Mondays, Tuesdays, and Saturdays; it was not until the early part of the 8th cent. that the Thursdays of Lent became days of Eucharistic Celebration. The stational observance at Rome began during the 5th century.

Two chief characteristics of the Lenten season played a part in the formation of its liturgy: its penitential significance and its relation to baptism. In its earlier development the notion of Lent as a preparation for baptism was more dominant. The liturgy reflects this esp. on those days given over to public scrutinies: the 3d, 4th, and 5th Sundays, and later the weekdays to which these scrutinies were moved, the Friday of the 3d week, the Wednesday and Friday of the 4th week. The penitential aspect is reflected in the exclusion of penitents on Ash Wednesday—before the 7th cent. this took place on the Monday after Quadragesima Sunday. The whole community became involved with penance with the introduction (10th cent.) of imposing hands and sprinkling ashes on everyone instead of simply upon public penitents.

With the reformation, the Lutherans did not immediately abandon the observance of Lenten discipline, although after a time fasting as an imposed practice was given up. But the tendency to regard Lent as a season closed to the solemnization of marriage, and certain liturgical vestiges of ancient observances have been retained among some Lutherans. In the C of E the observance of Lent continued after the Reformation and it is provided for in the BCP. The observance entailed fasting, abstention from festivities, and the devotion of more time to religious practices. Observance slackened considerably during the 18th cent., but it revived with the Tractarian Movement and has become widespread since that time. BIBLIOGRAPHY: N. Hordern and J. Otwell, *Lent* (pa. 1975); W. J. O'Shea, NCE 8:634–636; N. M. Denis-Boulet, *Christian Calendar* (1960).

[N. KOLLAR]

LENTEN VEIL, in medieval Europe, particularly the Low Countries, a veil hung between altar and congregation during Lent, a sign of the people's penitential status and a symbolic exclusion from the altar, like the actual exclusion of the penitents of the ancient period. The term is sometimes used to refer to the veiling of crucifixes and statues during Passiontide, a practice begun when crosses depicted the risen Christ or were richly jeweled to proclaim the Resurrection; the veiling was done to center attention on the Passion. The practice was continued even after crosses began to depict the crucified Christ. It is now optional.

[J. DALLEN]

LENTULUS, LETTER OF, a brief document that purports to be an account sent to the Senate in Rome by Lentulus, a Roman official in Palestine at the time of Tiberius Caesar. It describes Christ as "a man of stature middling tall and comely, with a venerable countenance . . . hair of the hue of an unripe hazelnut . . . a brow smooth and very calm . . . a face without wrinkle or blemish . . . a full beard of the color of his hair . . . eyes gray and clear; in rebuke terrible, in admonition kind and lovable; . . . sometimes he has wept but never laughed." In some MSS this account appears not as a letter, but as an entry in an annalistic record. In either form it dates from probably the 13th or 14th century. BIBLIOGRAPHY: E. von Dobschütz, *Christusbilder in Texte und Untersuchungen zur Geschichte der Altchristlichen Literatur* (1899) 308ff; M. R. James, *Apocryphal New Testament* (1945) 477–478; W. Eltester, RGG 4.317.

[H. DRESSLER]

LENZ DESIDERIUS (PETER; 1832–1928). German architect, sculptor and painter. L. opposed naturalism, reviving a religious art rooted in ancient Egyptian canons of proportion and form, erecting (without mortar) and decorating with fresco (1868–71) the St. Maur Chapel, Beuron. Becoming a Benedictine monk, L. founded (1878), with Wüger, the Beuron School of art (1894) and directed the decoration of Montecassino in fresco and mosaic (1876–1913). The formal art of Beuron influenced Jan Verkade and P. Sérusier.

[M. J. DALY]

LEO I, ST. (*c.*400–461), **POPE** from 440, declared Doctor of the Church by Benedict XIV. L. is known to have been a deacon in the service of the Church at Rome before being elected by the Roman people after the death of Sixtus III. L. Merited the honorific, "St. Leo the Great" both for his doctrinal contribution to the Church and for his governance. Doctrinally before becoming pope he is thought to have had a part in opposing Nestorianism and in the anti-Pelagian appendix to Pope Celestine's letter to the bps. of Gaul (431), so important to the Western theology of grace (D 238; PL 51:202–212, among the works of Prosper of Aquitaine). As pope L. sent legates to preside over the Council of Chalcedon (451), the *Tome of Leo to Flavian became the standard of orthodoxy, and L. approved the decrees of the Council against *Monophysitism. He also took measures against other heresies. His preaching throughout the liturgical year as a truly pastoral bp. had great influence on Western theology and spirituality. The sermons cover the major tenets of Catholic teaching on the Church—including an emphasis on the primacy of the successor of Peter—the mystery of salvation, the sacraments, particularly the Eucharist, and the life of grace. His spiritual doctrine describes the need to strive against the effects of sin and to practice the evangelical virtues. The sermons were particularly effective in written form because of their clarity and vigor of expression; they were incorporated into the Liturgy of the Hours and became prominent in medieval theology. His rule as pope put into practice his convictions about the primacy of the See of Rome. He exercised supervision over the choice and consecrations of bps. in Italy. He reproved every sign of challenge to his authority as Peter's successor. He reproached the Patriarch Flavian for delaying to refer the Monophysite errors to Rome. He refused to accept c. 28 of Chalcedon, the assertion that Constantinople was the New Rome. He termed the pseudo-council at Ephesus in 449, the "Robber Synod" (*Latrocinium*). He also urged liturgical and canonical uniformity throughout the Church. His defense against the Huns in 452 is a famous incident; when the Vandals did take Rome in 455 he was able to secure some concessions from their leaders. BIBLIOGRAPHY: Works: *Leo I, Letters* (tr. E. Hunt, *Fathers of the Church* 34, 1957); *Sermons* (ed. J. Leclercq, tr. R. Dolle SC 2 v., 1949, 1973); Sermons: *Sancti Leonis Magni tractatus septem et nonaginta* (A. Chavasse, tr., CCL 138–139, 2 v., 1973); Studies: T. Jalland, *Life and Times of St. Leo the Great* (1941); W. J. Halliwell, *Style of Pope St. Leo the Great* (1939); M. M. Mueller, *Vocabulary of Pope St. Leo the Great* (CUA PatrSt 67, 1942). M. B. de Soos, *Le Mystère liturgique d'après Léon le Grand* (1958); L. J. McGovern, *Ecclesiology of St. Leo the Great* (1957); F. Bajcer, *Ecclesiologia S. Leonis Magni ex epistulario desumpta* (1957); Y. M. Duval, *Sacramentum et mysterium chez Saint Léon le Grand* (1959).

[T. C. O'BRIEN]

LEO II, ST. (d. 683), **POPE** from 681. His brief pontificate was marked by his confirmation of the acts of the Third Council of Constantinople which condemned *Monothelitism. In so doing, he also condemned his predecessor, *Honorius I, for failing to take a firm stand against the heresy and its proponent, *Sergius. L. seems to have been of Sicilian origin. BIBLIOGRAPHY: Butler 3:10.

[R. B. ENO]

LEO III, ST. (d. 816), **POPE** from 795. A Roman of humble origin, L. held various posts in the papal service and eventually became cardinal priest of S. Susanna. From the time of his election to the papacy he was the victim of plots and attacks instigated by relatives of his predecessor, *Adrian I. After a violent physical assault that showed L. the extent of his peril, he fled to the court of *Charlemagne at Paderborn for protection. Received with honor, he stayed several months and was escorted back to Rome. Charles appointed envoys to investigate the situation at Rome, but seeing that the defamatory charges against the Pope continued, he went to Rome himself to settle the affair. At a synod held in the Vatican Basilica, the assembled bps. declared they had no right to judge the Pope, but L. of his own free will avowed under oath his innocence of the charges. This solemn statement was accepted by Charles, and the leaders of the hostile faction were sentenced to death; but at Leo's plea the sentence was commuted to exile. Shortly thereafter, on Christmas Day, L. crowned Charlemagne at

St. Peter's, and the assembled crowd acclaimed him as Emperor of the Romans. Whether L. planned it so without Charles' knowledge, or whether it was done by a prearranged agrreement between the principals, is disputed by historians. None, however, question the epoch-marking character of the event. It meant, in effect, the revival of the Empire in the West and the cooperation of spiritual and temporal powers in a Western world becoming conscious of its unity. Despite troubles to come as emperors and popes came into conflict over ambiguities regarding their respective spheres of authority, both Church and State benefited by the arrangement. Some of the advantages to the Church were apparent from the beginning. Charlemagne, esp. through his system of inspectors (*missi*), improved the administration of church affairs, along with civil affairs, throughout his vast territories; he fostered the education of the clergy and the reform of clerical life. Imperial protection enabled the Pope to consolidate his control of the patrimony of the Roman Church and strengthened his hand in dealing with ecclesiastical disorder in distant places, as e.g. *Adoptionism in Spain. But *caesaropapism, to which the door was opened, also made an early appearance. Charlemagne often directed religious affairs in his empire without consulting the Pope, and he pressed for the insertion of the **filioque* in the Creed (which the Pope refused to sanction). BIBLIOGRAPHY: Bihlmeyer-Tüchle 2:49–53; H. K. Mann, CE 9:157–159; W. Ullmann, *Growth of the Papal Government in the Middle Ages* (1962); Butler 2:531–532. *HOLY ROMAN EMPIRE.

[P. F. MULHERN]

LEO IV, ST. (d. 855), **POPE** from 847. A Roman and a Benedictine monk, L. was called into the papal service by Gregory IV and made a cardinal priest by *Sergius II whom he succeeded as pope. The urgent need for a strong leader after the sack of Rome by the Saracens probably accounts for his consecration without the approval of the Frankish Emperor. L. immediately undertook the fortification of the district around St. Peter's, which has since been known as the Leonine City. By his diplomacy he was able to assemble an Italian fleet which helped to save Rome by breaking up another Saracen expedition off Ostia in 849. Although L. maintained an attitude of deference toward the Frankish authorities, this did not prevent him from taking a strong and independent position on issues that fell under the jurisdiction of the Church. A number of highly placed ecclesiastics felt the sting of his sharp rebuke, among them. Abp. John of Ravenna and Abp. Hincmar of Reims, the most powerful prelate in the Frankish Church. He summarily excommunicated *Anastasius the Librarian, a priest whom the Emperor Lothair I was openly grooming as his candidate to succeed Leo. Despite the disturbed times, L. found means to improve church buildings and he did much to encourage the development of church music. Alfred, later king of England, appears to have been brought to Rome as a boy of 4 during L.'s pontificate and to have been invested by the Pope with the honorary dignity of a Roman consul. BIBLIOGRAPHY: Mann 2:258–307; Hughes HC 2:184–185; Butler 3:128–129.

[P. F. MULHERN]

LEO V (d.903), **POPE** from July to Sept. in 903. Nothing certain is known about his election and almost nothing about his reign. He was probably sympathetic to the Formosan party. His reign was brought to an end when Christopher, cardinal priest of S. Damaso, imprisoned L. and took over the papacy for himself. Even the details of L.'s death are not known. Some have thought that he was put to death by Christopher; according to other authorities Sergius III (904–11), on his accession, liquidated both L. and Christopher; but it is possible that L. died a natural death in prison. BIBLIOGRAPHY: O. J. Blum, NCE 8:641; Mann 4:111.

[P. F. MULHERN]

LEO VI (d. 929), **POPE** during the latter half of 928. He was a Roman, whose father had been a highly placed official in the reign of *John VIII. He probably owed his election to the party headed by *Marozia which had deposed his predecessor. Of his reign nothing is known except that he concluded the settlement, begun by John X, of a jurisdictional dispute in Dalmatia. BIBLIOGRAPHY: Mann 4:188.

[P. F. MULHERN]

LEO VII (d. 939), **POPE** from 932, a Benedictine monk raised to the pontificate through the influence of *Alberic II, who had wrested control of Rome from his mother, *Marozia, in 932. Despite his dependence on Alberic, L. appears to have been an energetic pope, seriously interested in promoting ecclesiastical and moral reform. He brought St. *Odo, founder of *Cluny, to Rome, hoping thereby to give impetus to a spiritual revival. L. used Odo as an arbitrator between Alberic II and his stepfather Hugh, King of Italy, and made him vicar for all the monastic houses in the vicinity of Rome in an effort to restore religious fervor. L. also encouraged reform in France by bestowing privileges on the growing chain of Cluniac houses, and in Germany by appointing Frederick of Mainz his vicar with the charge of raising the level of clerical and monastic discipline. He instructed Frederick that Jews were not to be baptized by force, but he sanctioned the banishment to the countryside of those who refused to become Christians. Letters: PL 132:1065–68. BIBLIOGRAPHY: Mann 4:205–207.

[P. F. MULHERN]

LEO VIII (d. 965), **POPE** from 963. He was a Roman and a lay official of the papal court when he was designated (963) by Otto I to replace the deposed John XII. The election was dubious from a canonical point of view and L. was not even a cleric. He was hastily ordained and in 2 days consecrated. Bloodshed resulted even while Otto remained in Rome and, once he had departed, L. was obliged to flee after him for protection. The deposed John was reinstalled on the papal throne (964). When John died within a few months, the Romans elected as his successor Benedict V, paying no heed to Otto and ignoring Leo. The Emperor, determined to have his way, returned to Rome, saw to Benedict's removal and the reestablishment of L. as pope. These tumultuous circumstances overshadow whatever L. may have accomplished; nothing positive is known of his brief reign. Even the documents ceding territories to Otto and attributed to L. are now recognized as forgeries of the following century. The question of the legitimacy of L.'s claim to the papacy remains. He was long dismissed as an antipope, but the revised list of popes in the *Annuario pontificio* includes him. It may have been that Benedict V, rightfully elected by the people, accepted his deposition by the synod of 964 and thus left the papal chair vacant. BIBLIOGRAPHY: Mann 4:260–281; Hughes HC 2:194–196; A. Mercati, "New List of the Popes," MedSt 9 (1947) 71–80.

[P. F. MULHERN]

LEO IX, ST. (Bruno of Egisheim; 1002–54), **POPE** from 1048. His reign marks the beginning of papal reform and of the disengagement of the Church from the domination of both the Roman nobility and of German imperial policy. After serving as bp. of Toul for 21 years, he was elected pope through hs cousin, Emperor Henry III, with whom he worked harmoniously as imperial vicar for Italy. An experienced administrator, he introduced fresh policy into the papal curia, implementing his ideas with young reformers from Lorraine, among them his "secretary of state," Card. Humbert of Silva Candida. Spending all but 6 months of his pontificate in travel through Italy, France, and Germany, he secured the Church's position against simony and clerogamy in a dozen synods at which he issued decrees. In 1053, on his own initiative, he opposed in battle the Normans of Robert Guiscard, and suffered defeat at Civitate and imprisonment near Bari. During the last months of his life he sent the ill-starred mission to the Byzantine Emperor, Constantine IX, that led, after L.'s death, to the disastrous confrontation of Humbert and the Patriarch Michael Cerularius and to the eventual denouement of 1204. BIBLIOGRAPHY: A. Michel, *Humbert und Kerullarios,* (2 v., 1924–30); Mann 6:1–182; O. J. Blum, NCE 8:642–643; J. Choux, BiblSanct 7:1293–1301.

[O. J. BLUM]

LEO X (Giovanni de' Medici; 1475–1521), **POPE** from 1513. As second son of Lorenzo the Magnificent, he was early destined for high service in the Church and was educated at his father's court by Ficino, Pico della Mirandola, and other humanists. Before the age of 20 he was a cardinal and had received many rich benefices. When the Medici were expelled from Florence (1494), Giovanni took the opportunity to travel N of the Alps and upon his return began to rise to power. After the death of Julius II he was elevated to the papacy as Leo X. The problems he inherited from his predecessor included preserving the papal patrimony, delivering Italy from the control of foreign powers, healing the Pisan schism, and resolving the disunity in the French Church. Lateran Council V, convoked by Julius II and concluded under L., was intended to counteract the Council of Pisa. Its main objectives were peace within the Christian world, a Crusade against the Turks, and ecclesiastical reforms. The council, lacking unity, failed to achieve these goals. Meanwhile, L. was confronted with a French threat to the peace of Italy. France's interest in the peninsula was based on Charles VIII's claims to Naples, and Charles' successor, Louis XII, attempted to gain control of Milan as well as Naples. L., allied with Emperor Maximilian I, Ferdinand I, and Henry VIII of England, defeated the French (1513), and peace was reestablished. In 1516 L. agreed upon a concordat with Francis I, successor of Louis XII, regulating relations between the Church in France and the papacy. Like many popes of the period, L. was a brazen nepotist and elevated members of his family to high church offices. He was also a great patron of the arts and made Rome the center of European culture. But his lavishness depleted the papal treasury, and when he desired to press forward with the construction of St. Peter's, he authorized the preaching of an indulgence. This became the occasion of Luther's Ninety-five Theses. L.'s involvement in international diplomacy and his troubles in Italy partially explain his failure to do anything effective about the Protestant revolt. L., though a popular pope and a capable person, was unable to recognize the desperate need for church and papal reform. BIBLIOGRAPHY: Pastor v. 7 and 8.

[D. G. NUGENT]

LEO XI, (Alessandro Ottaviano de' Medici; 1535–1605), **POPE,** April 1–27, 1605. Ambassador to Rome of Grand Duke Cosimo of Tuscany for 15 years, he became bp. of Pistoia (1573), abp. of Florence (1574), and cardinal (1583). In 1596 Clement VIII, concerned about Catholics under Henry IV, sent him to France as papal legate. He was elected over Robert Bellarmine and Caesar Baronius in the conclave of 1605. In his short pontificate he introduced changes in the system of voting for a pope.

[R. J. LITZ]

LEO XII (Annibale della Genga; 1760–1829), **POPE** from 1823. Ordained priest in 1783, he carried out many diplomatic missions for the Holy See. In 1816 he was named cardinal priest of Sta. Maria Maggiore and appointed to the see of Sinigaglia. Conservative cardinals secured his election as pope in the conclave of 1823, thereby repudiating the policies of *Consalvi. Within the States of the Church he pursued extremely conservative policies. Members of secret societies and Jews were subjected to harassment or penalties. L.'s foreign policy produced concordats which were favorable to the Church.

[E. A. CARRILLO]

LEO XIII (Gioacchino Vincenzo Pecci; 1810–1903), **POPE** from 1878. After his education in theology and law in Rome, where from 1832 he was enrolled in the Accademia dei Nobili Ecclesiastici, he was ordained (1837) and immediately entered the papal diplomatic service. He gained experience in both the ecclesiastical and civil administration of the States of the Church before his assignment as nuncio to Belgium in 1843. His opposition to liberals seeking to gain secularistic state control over education led to the government's demanding his recall in 1846. From then until 1878 he lived in relative obscurity as abp. of Perugia. But the intellectual concerns for a revival of Thomism and pastoral concern that the Church confront modern problems, both developed and were carried out in his See during these years. He was named cardinal in 1853; papal camerlengo in 1877. In the conclave following Pius IX's death he was elected as a moderate and with the expectation that at 68 he would have a brief, transitional pontificate. But it is perhaps only in the post-Vatican II era that it has become clear how his pontificate has shaped the life of the modern Church. Many immediate causes he championed met defeat: union with the Orthodox Churches; bettering of relations with the Anglican Communion (see ANGLICAN ORDERS); checking secularistic liberals; resolution of the *Roman question; protection of the Church in France (see RALLIEMENT). Yet the principles and the goals of his policies and their articulation in his great encyclicals were taken up into the life and thought of the Church and are obvious in the contemporary Church. In the intellectual sphere his *Aeterni patris* (1879) restoring Thomism, and *Providentissimus Deus* (1893) on biblical studies invigorated pursuit of the sacred sciences. Even if the revival of Thomistic philosophy was in part reactionary, and *Providentissimus Deus* precautionary against rationalist criticism, their positive force promoted the intellectual life of the Church. The encyclicals on Church and State and their respective rights as societies (*Diuturnum,* 1881; *Immortale Dei,* 1885; and *Sapientiae christianae,* 1890) began a line of both ecclesiology and of the Church's consciousness of her own nature and existence in a pluralistic society that led to the developments of Vatican II on the nature of the Church, religious freedom, the Church in the modern world. Catholic social teaching as the Church entered into the modern world on the side of the oppressed traces its lineage back to *Rerum novarum* (1891), from which derive the series of great papal encyclicals on social justice in the 20th cent. and the Church's mission of justice and peace. During L.'s pontificate the conflict of the *Kulturkampf was resolved; in spite of setbacks in France and Belgium he was able to guide Catholics to an acceptance of legitimate regimes in political matters and even to encourage the formation of Catholic political parties. In the inner, spiritual and devotional life of the Church he encouraged devotion to the Sacred Heart (*Arcanum,* 1899); he issued repeated encyclicals on Mary, esp. on her rosary. Perhaps only with the contemporary charismatic renewal in the Church are the full force and value of his great encyclical *Divinum illud munus* (1897), on the Holy Spirit in the Christian life and the life of the Church, appreciated. BIBLIOGRAPHY: M. C. Carlen, *Dictionary of Papal Pronouncements, 1878–1957* (1958); E. Soderini, *Pontificate of Leo XIII* (tr. B. B. Carter, 1934) v. 1.

[T. C. O'BRIEN]

LEO I, OF ARMENIA (d. after 1140), prince of Lesser Armenian Cilicia (1129–38). In league with the Crusaders against the Byzantine Empire, he built upon the power base in the Taurus Mountains established by his predecessor Ruben *c.*1071, and seized fortresses in Cilicia. He was finally captured by the forces of Emperor John II Comnenus, and taken with his two sons to Constantinople, where he died. Byzantine rule was reestablished in Lesser Armenia.

[E. J. DILLON]

LEO II, THE GREAT, OF ARMENIA, ruler of Cilician Armenia (1187–1219). The decline of the neighboring Byzantine and Latin states offered opportunity for the Armenian prince to attain a significant status. Having unified the Cilician Armenians, L. acknowledged the sovereignty of the Holy Roman Emperor and the religious supremacy of the Roman Church. Emperor Henry VI and Pope Celestine III concurred in his coronation as king in 1198. The Pope seems to have been satisfied about the orthodoxy of the Armenian Church. Despite some political controversy with Innocent III, L. enjoyed the favor and protection of the papacy. He established numerous ecclesiastical and eleemosynary institutions. BIBLIOGRAPHY: C. A. Frazee, "The Christian Church in Cilician Armenia: Its Relations with Rome and Constantinople to 1198," *Church History* 45 (1976) 166–184; S. Der Nersessian, "The Kingdom of Cilician Armenia," *History of the Crusades* (ed. K. M. Setton, 2d ed., 3 v., 1969–75) 2:630–659.

[R. H. SCHMANDT]

LEO I (*c.*400–474), **BYZANTINE EMPEROR** from 457. The Monophysite heresy was L.'s chief problem. At his accession the Monophysites in Egypt murdered their Chalcedonian patriarch Proterius and installed Timothy Aelurus. Surprised at the strength of Monophysite sentiment, L. inclined at first towards summoning a new council to reexamine the Chalcedonian decision. Pressure from Pope Leo I and the nearly unanimous opinion of the Greek clergy convinced him to uphold Chalcedon's definition of the two natures in Christ. He also moved against the Arians and legislated against disciplinary abuses within the Greek Church. BIBLIOGRAPHY: T. Jalland, *Life and Time of St. Leo the Great* (1941).

[R. H. SCHMANDT]

LEO III, BYZANTINE EMPEROR (*c.*675–740), called "the Isaurian." He served the Emperors Justinian II and

Anastasius II before taking over the imperial throne himself in 717. L. defeated the Arabs at Constantinople (717) and at Acroninon, thus preserving the empire. He published a new legal code, the **Ecloga,* and from 726 to 729 issued a number of edicts against the veneration of images, thus provoking the controversies of *iconoclasm that disturbed the Church for over a century. L. also annexed Sicily, Calabria, and Illyricum from papal jurisdiction, placing them under the Byzantine patriarchate, a move that added to the rift between East and West. BIBLIOGRAPHY: Ostrogorsky 133–147; A. A. Vasiliev, *History of the Byzantine Empire* (1964, repr. 1968) 234–271.

[F. T. RYAN]

LEO V (d. 820), **BYZANTINE EMPEROR** from 813. L. repudiated the policies of his predecessor Michael I and reopened the iconoclastic controversy, the second stage of that dispute. L. apparently was convinced of a relationship between recent military disasters and divine displeasure, supposedly caused by the iconodule stance of Michael I. L. deposed Patriarch Niceophorus, exiled Theodore the Studite, and persecuted certain bps., all defenders of icons. Under a new patriarch, Theodatus Melissenus, a synod met in 815, repudiated the Council of *Nicaea II (787), and reaffirmed the iconoclastic council of 754. Yet L. found it difficult to stimulate enthusiasm for the old heresy. He died by assassination. BIBLIOGRAPHY: P. J. Alexander, *Patriarch Nicephorus of Constantinople* (1958).

[R. H. SCHMANDT]

LEO VI (866–912), **BYZANTINE EMPEROR** from 886, called "The Wise." A student of Photius, he was noted for his literary interests and activities. He dealt with the Arab and the Bulgarian threats more by diplomatic than by military means. More enduring were his reforms of the legal and administrative machinery of the empire. He encountered severe opposition from many of the clergy because of his four successive marriages into which he entered in the hopes of begetting an heir. After deposing the Patriarch Nicholas Mysticus, he named his confessor Euthymius to his place and obtained the approval of Rome for his fourth marriage. This conflict, referred to as the Tetragamy, resulted in a long-lasting division in the Church. BIBLIOGRAPHY: G. Ostrogorsky 213–231; G. Moravcsik, *Byzantinoturcica,* 1 (1958) 400–409.

[G. T. DENNIS]

LEO OF ASSISI (BROTHER LEO; d. 1271), secretary, confessor, and constant companion of St. *Francis of Assisi. L. was called *Frate pecorella di Dio* by Francis because of his simplicity and tenderness. The only extant holographs of Francis (a letter and the *Laudes Creatoris*) were written for Leo. After the death of Francis, L. spent much of his time writing in defense of what he believed were the authentic ideas of Francis regarding poverty.

[F. G. O'BRIEN]

LEO OF CAVA, the name of two abbots of the Benedictine abbey of La Cava near Salerno, Italy, whose cults have been approved by the Holy See. (1) **Leo I** (d. 1079), a native of Lucca, whom the abbey's founder, St. Alferius, chose as his successor. He ruled the monastery from 1050 to 1079 and was greatly venerated for his humility, his simplicity of life, and his charity to the poor. BIBLIOGRAPHY: G. Mongelli, BiblSanct 7:1231–32; Zimmermann 2:441–444. (2) **Leo II, Bl.** (d. 1295), abbot from 1268. He attended the Council of Lyons II (1274), developed the scriptorium, and built the chapel of San Germano. BIBLIOGRAPHY: G. Mongelli, BiblSanct 7:1282–83; Zimmermann 2:592–593.

LEO DIACONUS (*c.*950–after 992), Byzantine historian. He published a history covering the years 959–976 in 10 books. As a historian of contemporary events, he was able to use the reports of eyewitnesses as well as his own personal observations. His work is the only contemporary Greek source for the military campaigns of Nicephorus II Phocas and John Tzemisces, and it furnishes valuable information on early Russian history. BIBLIOGRAPHY: M. C. Hilferty, NCE 8:652; F. Dölger, LTK 6:693.

[M. R. P. MCGUIRE]

LEO LUKE, ST. (*c.*885–*c.*980), a Sicilian monk, who had a part in the establishment of Byzantine monasticism in S Italy.

LEO MARSICANUS (*c.*1046–1115), monk of Monte Cassino, librarian, chronicler. L. was created cardinal bishop of Ostia in 1101. Owing at least in part to Monte Cassino's importance in the Middle Ages, his reliable account of the monastery from the days of St. Benedict to 1057 is an important source work for medieval history. BIBLIOGRAPHY: V. Gellhaus, NCE 8:652.

[M. A. WINKELMANN]

LEO OF OCHRIDA (fl. 1025–53), a writer who contributed to the developing breach between Eastern and Western Churches in the 11th century. L. was chartophylax of Hagia Sophia when *c.*1025 he was made autocephalous abp. of Bulgaria with his see at Ochrida. The Byzantine Emperor Constantine IX Monomachus was trying *c.*1053 to establish better relations between Eastern and Western Churches in the hope of making an alliance with Pope Leo IX and the German Emperor to fight against the Norman invaders in S Italy, a policy in which he was opposed by Michael Cerularius, patriarch of Constantinople. At the instigation of Cerularius, L. wrote a letter to John, abp. of Trani in Apulia, and through him to all the Frankish bps. and the Pope, dealing with points in controversy between Eastern and Western Churches, e.g., the use of unleavened bread for the Eucharist, fasting on Saturdays, the dropping of the *alleluia* during Lent. In reply Card. *Humbert of Silva Candida wrote a strong and somewhat biased treatise (PL 143:744–769). Two other letters of Leo on the question of unleavened bread are extant. BIBLIOGRAPHY: G. Hofman, EncCatt 7:1134.

[V. VON FALKENHAUSEN]

LEO OF ST. JOHN (1600–71), French Carmelite theologian and mystical writer; born Jean Macé. A Carmelite from 1616, he became prior of several convents, provincial, preacher at the courts of Louis XIII and Louis XIV, confessor to Card. Richelieu, at whose deathbed he assisted. Among his writings are included works in theology, philosophy, and history; books of sermons; works on the mystical life. He stressed a Christian life that in its development should normally lead to contemplation.

[T. C. O'BRIEN]

LEO THAUMATURGUS, ST. (d. *c.*785), bp. and wonderworker. He was bp. of Catania in Sicily, a Greek archbishopric under the patriarch of Constantinople. Universally respected, L. was twice invited to the imperial court at Constantinople, once during the reign of Emperor Leo IV (d. 780), and again during that of Constantine VI (d. 797). BIBLIOGRAPHY: A. Amore, BiblSanct 7:1223–25.

[G. M. COOK]

LEO TUSCUS (*c.*1110–after 1182), Tuscan Greek scholar who, with his elder brother, *Hugh Etherian, served at the imperial court of Constantinople under Manuel I Comnenus. He remained, as interpreter and translator of Latin letters, longer than Hugh, but left before the massacre of Latins there in May 1082, since he wrote about it to Pope Lucius III in December of that year. L. is important esp. for two of his works: one a Latin translation of the Liturgy of St. John Chrysostom, which gives evidence of the practice of concelebration in the Byzantine rite of that time; the other his *De haeresibus et praevaricationibus graecorum*. In this he attacks the liturgical and penitential practices of the Greeks, and also discusses the causes of the East-West schism; the work is also important for the history of Photius.

[T. C. O'BRIEN]

LEO OF VERCELLI (d. 1026), bishop. After studying law, perhaps in his native Hildesheim, L. was ordained and, together with Gerbert (later Pope Sylvester II), served in the chapel of Otto III. His unswerving loyalty to Otto and to his successors, Henry II and Conrad II, and his enthusiasm for the empire contributed to the success of their reigns, esp. to the amicable relations between empire and papacy. BIBLIOGRAPHY: MGHSPoetae 5.2:476–489; C. E. Boyd, NCE 8:653.

[M. A. WINKELMANN]

LEO, LEONARDO (Lionardo Oronzo Salvatore de Leo; 1694–1744), Italian Neapolitan teacher and composer of serious and comic operas, church music, and works for harpsichord and organ. L. became organist at the Royal Chapel in 1717 and returned as organist in 1725 after work in comic opera. His famous *Miserere* was composed in 1739 for use in the Royal Chapel. His Mass in D major for five voices and orchestra is his best known work in that genre. He instructed Pergolesi, Piccinni, Jommelli, Sacchini, and Traetta.

[R. J. LITZ]

LEOBARD, the name of two saints: (1) a Benedictine recluse and confessor (d. 593). He lived for 22 years in a cell near Marmoutier. His spiritual guide was Gregory of Tours, who also wrote his vita; (2) a Benedictine abbot (d. 618), also known as Liuberat, who founded the abbey of Maursmünster. BIBLIOGRAPHY: J. Lahache, BiblSanct 7:1183–84; DE 2:635–636.

[F. D. LAZENBY]

LEOBIN OF CHARTRES, ST. (bp. of Chartres 544–*c.*556). Owing to his zeal for strict enforcement of monastic discipline, he was forced to leave the monastery of St. Hilary at Chartres. Later, St. Avitus of Vienne made him abbot of Brou. In 544 he was elected bp. of Chartres and did much to develop its episcopal school. He participated in the synods of Orléans (549) and Paris (552) and was one of the judges who deposed Saffaracus, bp. of Paris. BIBLIOGRAPHY: M. R. P. McGuire, NCE 8:654; DACL 3.1:1021–25; A. Poncelet, ''Les Saints de Micy,'' AnalBoll 24 (1905) 1–104, esp. 25–31.

[M. R. P. MCGUIRE]

LEODEGAR OF AUTUN, ST. (Léger; d. *c.*679), bishop. He was abbot of St. Maixent and (*c.*656) was called to the Neustrian court by Queen Bathildis, through whose influence he was made bp. of Autun (*c.*663). Caught up in current political intrigues and rivalries, L. was party to the revolt that defeated Ebroin, the Neustrian mayor of the palace, exiled him to Luxeuil, and brought Neustria under Childeric II of Austrasia. Later Leodegar, accused of plotting against Childeric, was himself exiled to Luxeuil, but on the assassination of the King (675) was released and restored to his see. Ebroin, also freed, proclaimed Clovis III king and laid seige to Autun. To prevent the sack of his city, L. gave himself up. Accused of having been party to the assassination of Childeric, he was blinded and subjected to other tortures. In 678 he was degraded by a synod and beheaded. After the death of Ebroin (681), and assembly of bps. cleared L.'s name and declared him a martyr. BIBLIOGRAPHY: C. Boillon, BiblSanct 7:1190–93; Butler 4:9–11.

[G. M. COOK]

LEON, LUIS DE (1527–91), theologian, philosopher, poet, teacher. Educated at Salamanca, he entered the Augustinian Order in 1544 and held a chair at Salamanca as a distinguished lecturer until denounced to the Inquisition for criticising the Vulgate text of the Bible (1572). He was exonerated, returned to the university (1576) after nearly 5 years in prison, and opened his lecture with the famous statement: "Yesterday we were saying . . ." He was denounced again in 1582 but the charge was dropped. In 1585 appeared the prose masterpiece of 16th-cent. Spain, *De los nombres de Cristo*, on the various names given Christ in Scripture, a work that epitomizes classical Spanish writing. His translations from Greek, Latin, Hebrew, and Italian of OT books with commentary establish him as a classic translator. L. is perhaps the greatest lyric poet of Spain and such poems as "Noche serena" made him a model for the later generations of Spanish classicists who fought to keep a native, rather than Latin, flavor in their literature. In spite of the ecclesiastical and academic, bitter conflict of his era he maintained a moderation singular for a man who could do battle when such action was called for. It would be difficult to exaggerate his influence on the course of Spanish literature. With St. John of the Cross and St. Teresa of Avila, he is one of the great Spanish mystics; his mystical teaching is contained in his commentary on the Song of Songs (1580–82).

[J. R. AHERNE]

LEON PINELO, ANTONIO DE, Spanish writer and historian. L.P. was born in Peru near the end of the 16th century. After studying at the college of Lima, he journeyed to Spain to work for the Council of the Indies. In 1623 he undertook a definitive study of the myriad laws governing each Spanish colony in the world. He gathered thousands of documents from every settlement in the Spanish New World and published his *Recopilacion general de las leies de las Indias* in 1628. (This edition was a shortened version of the four-volume study that was published in 1680, after his death.) In 1629 he published his *Epitome de la Biblioteca orientali occidental,* a compilation of existing Spanish colonial literature. L. also wrote many works on religious issues, being particularly interested in the subject of the Virgin Mary (e.g., *Bibliotheca seu catalogus Marianus*). In addition, he produced works on the history of Peru, Chile, and Mexico. In his range of subjects and his thoroughness of scholarship, he proved himself one of the major authors of the 17th century. BIBLIOGRAPHY: *Decripcion bibliografica de las impresas de Antonio de Leon Pinelo (Biblioteca hispanoamericano* v.6 1898–1907).

[R. BRADY]

LEONARD OF NOBLAC, ST. (6th cent.), Frankish nobleman. The oldest record about him is from the 11th century. He was converted by St. Remigius and lived for a time at the monastery of Micy where he made vows. A gift of land from Clovis gave him the opportunity to build a monastery, which he called Noblac. Later for greater solitude, he lived in Limoges in a hermit's cell. BIBLIOGRAPHY: Butler 4:273–274.

[J. R. RIVELLO]

LEONARD OF PORT MAURICE, ST. (d. 1751), renowned preacher and ascetic. L. was educated by the Jesuits at Rome; he later became a Franciscan. He spent 40 years in the apostolate of preaching. Though declared blessed in 1796, he was not canonized until 1867. L. was given the title of patron of popular missionaries in 1923. BIBLIOGRAPHY: S. Gori, BiblSanct 7:1208–21; Butler 4:429–432.

[F. G. O'BRIEN]

LEONARDI, JOHN, ST. (1543–1609), founder of Clerks Regular of the Mother of God. L. studied under the Franciscans and was ordained after giving up a lucrative career as a pharmacist. He organized a lay group (Company for Christian Doctrine) to implement the teachings of the Council of Trent. L. was devoted to caring for the poor and the ill, and to that end he organized a group of priests in 1574 to live in community, but not according to the traditional monastic way of life. In spite of some opposition the new Clerks Regular of the Mother of God (as they would be officially named in 1614) continued to increase, receiving recognition from Gregory XII in 1583. In 1594 the college of cardinals in Rome lifted L.'s sentence of exile, and in 1595 Clement sent him on a mission to Montevergine to reform the monastery there. In 1603 Card. Baronio became protector of the Clerks Regular and L. was elected superior general. He was canonized in 1938. BIBLIOGRAPHY: G. Gordini, BiblSanct 6:1033–39; Butler 4:65.

[R. J. BRADY]

LEONARDO DI SER GIOVANNI (fl. 1350). Florentine goldsmith. L. assisted Francesco di Niccolo on the left wing of the S. Jacopo Altar in the Pistoia cathedral and in 1366 executed the silver altarpiece for the Baptistery, Florence, revealing the influence of A. Pisano.

[M. J. DALY]

LEONARDO DA VINCI (1452–1519), Florentine painter, sculptor, engineer, stage designer, musician, architect, naturalist, inventor. An epitome of the "myriad minded" man of the Renaissance, L. worked chiefly in Florence, Rome, Milan, and in his last two years in France. His accomplishments made him a legendary figure even in his life time. L. covers a variety of fields, many immediately related to his study of the arts of drawing and painting which he so advanced that they became, in his hands, perfect means for representing nature accurately and for investigating and describing its processes and elements. Much of the immediately subsequent development of the visual arts as well as the high repute in which they are commonly still held are due to his work and thought. Many of his observations are preserved in his Notebooks. Among them are drafts of the major portions of a treatise on painting (see J. P. Richter, *The Literary Work of Leonardo da Vinci,* London, 1939). The best collection of his drawings, including many of his famous caricatures, is at Windsor Castle. L. took much trouble with the completion of his works and finished only a few. These are, however, distinguished by an air of serene and effortless perfection. His most famous paintings are *The Last Supper* (Milan), which presents the extreme dramatic tension of the momentous event in a beautiful order that in itself is a celebration of the subject, and the *Mona Lisa* (Paris), a *tour de force* in psychological, enigmatic portraiture with a landscape background which seems to encompass the whole world. Among L.'s many inventions was a submarine. He recorded in his notes that he did not intend to make it known "by reason of the evil nature of men who would use it for assassinations at the bottom of the sea." BIBLIOGRAPHY: L. Heydenreich, *Leonardo da Vinci* (1954); J. P. Richter, *Literary Work of Leonardo da Vinci* (1939).

[P. P. FEHL]

LEONI, POMPEO (*c.*1533–1608), Italian sculptor and medalist, son and pupil of L. Leoni. In Spain from 1556, L. executed his masterpiece for the main altar of the Church of the Escorial—15 saints and 12 Apostles of gilded and enameled bronze (1579–81), the tomb of the Inquisitor Don Fernando de Valdés, and the Habsburg tomb statues flanking the altar of the Escorial (1593–98).

[M. J. DALY]

LEONIDES, ST. (d. *c.*202), teacher at Alexandria, Egypt, father of *Origen. When Emperor Septimius Severus (193–211), an African who in the beginning of his rule was rather benevolent towards the Christians, changed his policy in 202, persecution broke out, esp. in Africa and Egypt. Eusebius (*Hist. eccl.* 6.1–5) reports that among the first victims at Alexandria were L. and some of Origen's catechumens.

[J. MADEY]

LEONIN (LEONINUS; 12th cent.), composer of liturgical music. Chapel master of Notre Dame de Paris, L. was the creator of the Notre Dame school of composers. He was author of *Magnus liber organi de graduali et antiphonario* . . . (1160–80), a cycle of *organa* composed for Masses and Offices of the liturgical year. His method was to set plainchant against a contrapuntal free melody. They may move together note by note or the plainchant be written in very long notes with the organal part in free rhythm. The *organum* was a musical form seemingly influenced by troubadour music.

[J. R. AHERNE]

LEONINE CITY, that part of Rome on the right bank of the Tiber including Vatican Hill and St. Peter's Basilica protected with a wall erected by Pope Leo IV (847–855 A.D.), known as the Leonine Wall after the destruction of Rome by the Saracens. BIBLIOGRAPHY: R. E. Sullivan, NCE 8, 640–641; Fliche-Martin, 6:281–288.

[F. H. BRIGHAM]

LEONINE COMMISSION AND EDITION. The Leonine Commission is an entity established (1879) within the Dominican Order by Leo XIII to provide a critical edition of the works of St. Thomas Aquinas; thus the Leonine Edition. The Commission's work began in 1880; the first volumes produced (commentaries on Aristotle's *Organon*) were issued in 1886. The *Summa theologiae,* in eight folio volumes, was completed by 1906. Between then and 1965, because of the two World Wars and other adversities, the only other volumes issued were the *Summa contra gentiles* (1930) and an index to the extant volumes (1948). From 1965, however, work has proceeded apace: commentaries on Job, Isaiah; opuscula on the spiritual life; commentaries on the Ethics and Politics of Aristotle; the *quaestio disputata, De veritate*. An American section of the Commission has been in existence since 1966, first at Yale Univ. and from 1977 at the Catholic Univ. of America; its first project, the extremely difficult text of the commentary on Aristotle's *Metaphysics* is ready for press; subsequent texts to appear under the American section are parts of the Commentary on the *Sentences* and on Pseudo-Dionysius, *De divinis nominibus*. Since Oct. 30, 1977, W. A. Wallace, OP has been Director General of the Commission and head of the American section. The Canadian section, at Ottawa, continues its work on the biblical commentaries. Future work of the Commission must include a revision of the *Summa theologiae,* at least of the earlier parts, which were issued in haste and without the benefit of the massive resources for critical establishment of texts developed since the Commission's early work.

[T. C. O'BRIEN]

LEONINE PRAYERS, the prayers once recited by the priest and congregation after low Mass in the RC Church by order of Leo XIII (1884). The Hail, Mary was said three times, then the Hail, Holy Queen, with a versicle and response, followed by a prayer for the conversion of sinners and the liberty and exaltation of the Church. A prayer to St. Michael the Archangel was added in 1886, and Pius X recommended the addition of an ejaculatory prayer to the Sacred Heart. The prayers were originally offered for relief from the situation imposed on the Church by the loss of the Papal States. After the *Lateran Treaty (1928), Pius XI ordered that they be offered for Russia. They were suppressed in 1964. BIBLIOGRAPHY: R. E. Brennan, "The Leonine Prayers," AER 125 (1951) 85–94.

[N. KOLLAR]

LEONINE SACRAMENTARY (Verona Sacramentary), earliest surviving collection of Roman Mass formularies, a single, incomplete MS from the beginning of the 7th cent. found in Verona in 1713. The formularies themselves are from the 4th–6th centuries. Once attributed to Pope Leo I, they are now regarded as probably a private collection, never in official use. Formularies (often several for each feast and occasion) are arranged according to the civil calendar, with no Ordinary and with the first 3 months missing. Many of the texts are found in the Roman Missals of Pius V and Paul VI and in the Book of Common Prayer. BIBLIOGRAPHY: Text, *Sacramentarium Veronense,* ed. L. C. Mohlberg, (1956); Commentary, D. M. Hope, *Leonine Sacramentary* (1971).

[J. DALLEN]

LEONIUS, BL. (d. 1173), Benedictine abbot of Lobbes and St. Bertin. L. was noted for his charitable works. He adopted the ideals of the Cluniac reform and as abbot established a school of higher religious studies. With his friend Bernard of Clairvaux he took part in the Second Crusade.

[F. G. O'BRIEN]

LEONTIEV, KONSTANTIN NIKOLAYEVICH (1831–91), Russian philosopher, critic, essayist. After a year at the monastery on Mt. Athos, L. rejected the aesthetic amoralism of his earlier works and became a conservative Orthodox Christian. In 1891, he secretly took monastic vows. His essays, collected under the title *The East, Russia, and Slavdom* (1885–86), warn Russia that orthodoxy and autocracy can preserve her from the disintegration inherent in Western democracy. His thought influenced Solovyov and Berdyayev. BIBLIOGRAPHY: N. Berdyayev, *Leontiev,* (Eng. tr. C. Reavey, 1940); *Russian Philosophy* (eds. J. M. Edie et al., 1965) 2:267–270.

[M. F. MCCARTHY]

LEONTIUS OF ARLES, bp. of Arles from 462–491, succeeding Ravennius. The bp. of Arles at that time was a leading ecclesiastical personage, second only to the bp. of Rome in influence among the emerging barbarian Christian Churches. There are letters extant addressed to L. from his contemporary Pope Hilary, which point to a much larger correspondence between the two. In 475 L. convened the Council of Arles, which gave its authority to the views of *Faustus of Riez in his opposition to the predestinarian views of the priest Lucidus. L.'s attention had been drawn to Lucidus in a letter written by Faustus. Later, at a council at Lyons (474), Faustus had to defend himself against the charge of semi-Pelagianism because of a book dedicated to L. in which Faustus commented on the acta of the earlier council.

[E. J. DILLON]

LEONTIUS ARMENIUS (d. *c.*790), also known as Ghevond, Armenian priest, author of the only source book for a description of the Arab invasion of Armenia (662–789). BIBLIOGRAPHY: P. Hamelian, EncCatt 7:1168; T. E. Dowling, *Armenian Church* (repr. 1970).

[J. R. RIVELLO]

LEONTIUS OF BYZANTIUM (*c.*500–543), monk of the New Laura in Palestine, active at Constantinople (531–536) in defense of Chalcedonian Christology, and again in 540 as a defender of the *Origenism condemned in 543 under Justinian I. His term *enhypostaton* to indicate the union of two natures in one person was developed in later Eastern Christology. BIBLIOGRAPHY: D. B. Evans, NCE 8:660–661.

[T. C. O'BRIEN]

LEONTIUS OF FRÉJUS, ST. (d. *c.*432), bishop. He encouraged his friend St. Honoratus of Arles to establish a monastery at Lérins, which became illustrious because of the bps. and writers it has given to the Church. BIBLIOGRAPHY: P. Viard, BiblSanct 7:1315–16.

[G. E. CONWAY]

LEONTIUS OF JERUSALEM, 6th-cent. monk at Constantinople known only as a strict adherent of the Christology of St. Cyril of Alexandria from two extant works, against Nestorianism and against Monophysitism.

[T. C. O'BRIEN]

LEOPOLD III OF AUSTRIA, ST. (*c.*1075–1136), margrave of Austria from 1095. By his marriage (1106) with Agnes, widowed daughter of Emperor Henry V, he became the father of the historian *Otto of Freising and Abp. Conrad II of Salzburg. Instrumental in arranging the Concordat of Worms (1122), L. also refounded the monastery of Klosterneuburg and founded Heiligenkreuz and Kleinmariazell. In 1125 he refused an offer of the imperial crown. His reign marks the beginning of Austria's greatness and of ecclesiastical provincialism as well. Canonized in 1485, L. is the patron saint of Austria and his feast (Nov. 15) is a national holiday. BIBLIOGRAPHY: Butler 4:350; J. Baur, BiblSanct 7:1340–42.

[M. S. TANEY]

LEOPOLD I OF BELGIUM (1790–1865) **KING OF THE BELGIANS** from 1831. Born at Coburg, George Christian Frederick, eighth child of Francis, the heir to Saxe-Coburg, married in 1816 the heir to the British crown, the princess Charlotte, who died only months later. In 1831 he was elected king of the Belgians by the National Congress; and in 1832 married the princess Louise-Marie d'Orléans, daughter of King Louis-Philippe of France. L. is considered to have been a model constitutional monarch, a Protestant king well-loved by a Catholic people. His cabinet ministers were chosen alternately from the Liberal and Catholic parties. Among his children are to be found the future King Leopold II and Charlotte, who was to be the wife of Maximilian, archduke of Austria and emperor of Mexico.

[E. J. DILLON]

LEOPOLD OF GAICHE, BL. (1733–1815), Italian Franciscan preacher. L. entered the Franciscan Order in 1751 and was ordained in 1757. His life was one of pastoral care and preaching. Provincial of his order, he was appointed papal missioner to the Papal States in 1768. Imprisoned during the French occupation of Italy for refusing to take the oath of allegiance to Napoleon, he later returned to the work of preaching missions. In 1893 he was beatified.

[J. R. AHERNE]

LEOPOLDINEN STIFTUNG (LEOPOLDINE SOCIETY), an Austrian society for support of missions, founded in 1828 by F. Résé, German missionary to the U.S. with imperial and papal approval. The society was made up of members who were under obligation to pray for the U.S. missions and contribute weekly to their support. Almost three quarters of a million dollars were contributed between 1828 and 1921, when the society ceased to exist. Equally important were the Austrian missioners sent by the society to America, most notable being St. John *Neumann of Philadelphia. BIBLIOGRAPHY: T. Roemer, *Ten Decades of Alms* (1942).

[J. R. AHERNE]

LEOPOLDINISM, a movement that took its name from Leopold I, (1747–92), Grand Duke of Tuscany, afterwards Leopold II Holy Roman Emperor on the death of his brother, Joseph II. He was an able and enlightened prince whose ideals were expressed in the Synod of *Pistoia held in his territory. That a hygienic and paternal state despotism should clean up some of the unsanitary consequences of political ecclesiasticism and curb the pretentions of Roman curialism was admitted, even by many clerics of the day; the real point of criticism was the threat of secular intrusion into the sacred. However, the dispute was conducted with a Florentine humor, sunnier than prevailed elsewhere; in general, the Habsburgs seemed to have been more genial than the Bourbons in the matter.

[T. GILBY]

LEOVIGILD OF CÓRDOBA (fl. mid-9th cent.), a highly respected cleric who probably took part in affairs of state. His treatise *De habitu clericorum* (*c.*850) describes the symbolic meaning of tonsure, dress, and celibacy and seeks to revive the zeal of clergy who were demoralized in consequence of physical abuse and a special tax to which they were subject under Muslim rule. BIBLIOGRAPHY: E. P. Colbert, *Martyrs of Córdoba* (1962).

[E. P. COLBERT]

LEPANTO, Oct. 7, 1571, one of the decisive naval battles of the world. After the fall of *Constantinople the West lay open to the Ottoman Turks who during the 2 following centuries developed a two-pronged assault, one by sea across the Mediterranean, the other by land across the plains of Hungary; the only powers that could be relied on to fight them were the *Habsburgs and the Papacy. The Turks were eventually beaten back, and Christendom is happy indeed in its heroes and the literature which has sung them; De La Vallette of the Knights of Malta, Don John of Austria at Lepanto, King John Sobieski at Vienna, and Prince Eugene, *der edle Ritter,* at Belgrade are the types of thousands of others whose monuments remain throughout the Catholic lands from the Vistula to the Tagus. The campaign which led up to Lepanto was launched by the Christian League of Powers formed by *Pius V. Its fleet, composed mainly of Spaniards and Venetians, but including flotillas from Genoa and the Papal States, about 300 ships in all, met an equal number of Turks, who had been raiding in the Adriatic, in the Gulf of Lepanto, or Corinth (W coast of Greece), and after a ding-dong fight, smashed into the center of their crescent and utterly defeated them. It was the last great mêlée between galleys, but six great galleasses of Spain turned their gunnery to powerful effect, a presage of future naval actions for 3 cent. or more. Cervantes took part and was wounded three times. The victory, for which the church bells rang all over Europe, even in Protestant countries, was esp. associated with the Rosary devotion, and, until recent changes, was commemorated in the liturgy. It is also the subject of a well-known poem by G. K. Chesterton.

[T. GILBY]

LEPER WINDOW (Leper's Squint), small aperture in the outside wall of some medieval churches that gave a view of the altar. It allowed anchorites, lepers, and others to view the liturgy without mingling with the general congregation. *HAGIOSCOPE.

[T. EARLY]

LÉPICIER, ALEXIS HENRI MARIE (1863–1936), French theologian, cardinal. L. entered the Servites in England, and was ordained there in 1885. Appointed professor of dogmatic theology by Leo XIII at the Propaganda Fide in Rome in 1892, he filled that post for 21 years before he became superior general of the Servites (1913). As a writer, L. made important contributions to Thomistic theology. His masterwork was *Institutiones theologicae dogmaticae ad textum S. Thomae concinnatae* (25 v.), the culmination of a lifetime of scholarship. His *De beata Virgine Maria Matre Dei* is a fundamental work in Marian theology. His life was busy also with many important assignments to Roman Congregations. In 1924 he was consecrated a titular abp. and was named cardinal in 1927. He became prefect of the Congregation of Religious in 1928. BIBLIOGRAPHY: A. M. Lépicier, *Le Cardinal Lépicier, des Servites de Marie* (2 v., 1946).

[J. R. AHERNE]

LEPIDI, ALBERTO (1838–1922), Dominican philosopher. Born in the Abruzzi, he taught at Louvain and Rome and was made master of the sacred palace by Leo XIII. The ordinary run of Thomists were disposed to regard him as somewhat of an eccentric at some points. His main interest lay in the theory of knowledge; he admitted St.

Anselm's ontological argument for the existence of God. He wrote a penetrating study of Kant's *Critique of Pure Reason*.

[T. GILBY]

LEPORIUS (5th cent.), priest of Gaul, promoter of a Christological error. John *Cassian in his *De incarnatione Christi* reported that L. maintained Christ to be merely a man who merited divine honor and power by his heroic human life and death. This interpretation of L.'s teaching may have been Cassian's own construction. It actually seems that L., intent on defending the divine transcendence as well as Monophysitism, explained the Incarnation as a juxtaposition of the divine and human nature in Jesus, an explanation which destroys true unity of person. L. was condemned by the bps. of southern Gaul. His retraction *Libellus satisfactionis* (PL 31:1221), made for the Gallic bps. and endorsed by African bps., is important as an orthodox Christological statement in the Latin Church anterior to the Nestorian divisions. BIBLIOGRAPHY: É. Amann, DTC 9:434–440.

[E. A. WEIS]

LEPROSY, a disease that induced ritual uncleanness in Israel. Today the term leprosy is used to designate Hansen's disease, which is not the same as leprosy in the Bible. Hansen's disease is caused by mycobacteria similar to that of tuberculosis, infecting the skin and peripheral sensory nerves. It is curable and is transmitted by direct person-to-person contact, not through heredity. The Hebrew term *zara'at* (Gr. *lepra*) included milder skin diseases and even signs of decay in clothing or on walls. This induced ritual uncleanness. Lev. ch. 13–14 codifies the priestly rules for diagnosing and treating it. Jesus cured many lepers, which was one of the messianic signs (Mt 11.5), and dined with "Simon, the leper." BIBLIOGRAPHY: R. Brown, NCE 8:667–672; R. G. Cochrane, "Biblical Leprosy—A Suggested Interpretation," *Life of Faith* 80 (1956).

[E. CABEY]

LE PUY CATHEDRAL, important Romanesque church of the pilgrimage route to Santiago de Compostela. Built in 11th and 12th cent., in its striations of native black and red granite the edifice shows strong Moorish influence. Especially interesting is the disposition of elements in the beautifully proportioned E tower, the octagonal vaulted lantern, older bays of the nave covered with domical vaults on squinches, and an impressive open porch. Cusped arches at portals and windows confirm the Moorish elements from Spain.

[M. J. DALY]

LE QUIEN, MICHEL (1661–1733), French Dominican scholar on the Eastern Church. He was librarian at the priory of St. Honoré in Paris. Among his works are a pseudonymous *Panoplia contra schisma Graecorum* (1718), in which he denied the validity of *Anglican orders; an edition of the works of St. *John Damascene in 1712 (the text incorporated in PG 94–96); and a history of the Eastern patriarchates, *Oriens Christianus* (3 v., 1740).

[T. C. O'BRIEN]

LERCARO, GIACOMO (1892–1976), abp. and cardinal. Noted for his aid to anti-Fascist partisans when he was a parish priest in Genoa during World War II, L. was named in 1952 abp. of Bologna, over which he presided for 16 years. L. created the so-called flying friars to take part in rallies against the Communist city government. A liberal, he was a staunch defender of the reforms of Vatican II. L. spoke out strongly for a new policy in the Church toward Africa and other non-European areas of the world. After the Council he directed the work of liturgical reform, esp. revision of the liturgical books.

[J. R. AHERNE]

LERCHER, LUDWIG (1864–1937), Austrian Jesuit, professor at the Univ. of Innsbruck, author of a dogmatic theology text, *Institutiones theologicae* (4 v., 1924–34).

[T. C. O'BRIEN]

LÉRIDA CATHEDRAL. The Old Cathedral (Seo Antigua) of Romanesque and Gothic design begun by Pedro of Aragon in 1203, consecrated in 1278, is distinguished by the octagon over the crossing, a single campanile (15th cent.), Gothic cloister of delicate tracery, and a doorway of impressive geometric carving. Lérida was partially destroyed in 1717 and was a military citadel until 1948.

[M. J. DALY]

LÉRINS, ABBEY OF, one of the earliest monastic establishments in Europe. It was located on the island of St. Honoratus off the S coast of France, opposite Cannes, and was founded by Honoratus *c.*410. The first monks lived as hermits until *c.*600, when they adopted the Rule of St. Benedict. Destroyed by the Saracens in 732, it was restored in 975. Its medieval prosperity came to an end in 1464 under commendatory abbots. Suppressed by royal order in 1786, the property was sold in 1791. In 1869 Lérins was again resettled by Cistercians of Sénanque. BIBLIOGRAPHY: A. Cooper-Marsden, *History of the Islands of the Lérins* (1913); C. Falk, NCE 8:673–674.

[L. J. LEKAI]

LERMONTOV, MIKHAIL YURIEVICH (1814–41), Russian poet and novelist. His lyric and narrative poems are characterized by an immediacy and intimacy of expression that are purely romantic. Their melodiousness has its source in his constant experimentation with new verse forms and rhythms and even with new sentence structures. His melancholy introspection and injured sense of futility and alienation give new dimensions to the repeated theme of rebelliousness not only against his own bitter fate, but against the society that made it inevitable. This theme is present, too, in his single great prose novel, *A Hero of Our Time* (1840), whose hero, Pechorin, continues the tradition of the "superfluous man." L. became famous in 1837 with the publication of the poem *The Death of a Poet,* in which he blamed the regime of Nicholas I for the death of the poet Pushkin. His other great works include the lyric poems "The Angel" and "The Sail," both written in 1832; the narrative poems *The Demon* (1839) and *Mtsyri* (1840); and the heroic poem *The Song of the Merchant Kalashnikov* (1837). BIBLIOGRAPHY: *Michael Lermontov* (tr. C. E. L'Ami and A. Welikotny, 1967); J. Lavrin, *Lermontov* (1959); L. Galdi, *Quelques aspects du style poétique de Lermontov* (pa. 1974).

[M. F. MCCARTHY]

LEROQUAIS, VICTOR MARTIAL, (1875–1946), French priest and specialist in liturgical manuscripts. He gave up a pastoral career to devote his life to investigating the sources of the liturgy. He worked principally at the Bibliothèque Nationale at Paris and published a series of inventories of the Sacramentaries, Breviaries, Pontificals, and Psalters found in the French public libraries. BIBLIOGRAPHY: N. Huyghebaert, NCE 8:674.

[N. KOLLAR]

LE ROUX, ROLAND (ROULLANT; d. 1527), master French sculptor succeeding his uncle at Rouen cathedral. L. did 261 statues and the grand portal (1509–30) and worked on the Tomb of Card. Georges d'Amboise (1520–25). He remains a significant figure among French sculptors.

[M. J. DALY]

LESAGE, ALAIN RENÉ (1668–1747), French novelist and dramatist. L. is best known for three works: *Turcaret* (1709), *Le Diable Boiteux* (1707), and *L'Histoire de Gil Blas de Santillane* (1715–35). *Turcaret,* a comedy, is a scathing satire of the tax collector of the Old Regime; *Le Diable* and *Gil Blas* are narrative fictions; the first, an adaptation of a Spanish work; the second, his masterpiece, a novel of manners in the Spanish picaresque tradition. In both fictions, the action takes place in Spain and the characters are Spanish, but the real target is French society of the early years of the 18th century. BIBLIOGRAPHY: E. Lintilhac, *Lesage* (1893).

[A. S. CRISAFULLI]

LESBIANISM, see HOMOSEXUALITY.

LES DUNES, ABBEY OF, Cistercian monastery near Coxyde, Belgium, which was founded by the hermit Léger (1107), who with his followers joined the Benedictine Congregation of Savigny (1122) and the Cistercians in 1138. By the end of the 13th cent., the abbey had more than 400 monks, maintained a system of dikes, and engaged in extensive sheep farming. Repeatedly attacked by Protestants in the 16th cent., the community moved to Bruges. Suppressed during the French Revolution (1797), the buildings now accommodate the diocesan seminary. BIBLIOGRAPHY: J. de Vincennes, *L'abbaye des Dunes* (1956); P. Schittekat, *Sous les dunes de Coxyde* (1960).

[L. J. LEKAI]

LESEUR, ELIZABETH (1866–1914), French spiritual writer, mystic. Her *Spiritual Journal,* published posthumously in 1917, records her own passage from unbelief to an intense interior life and her prayer for her husband's conversion, and prophecy that he would become a priest. He was Félix Leseur, an unbeliever whose effort to draw his wife to share in his irreligion resulted instead in a reawakening of her faith. She drew many to the pursuit of Christian perfection simply by her example and serenity, but it was only after her early death of cancer that her prayers for her husband were fulfilled. He experienced a spiritual conversion, became an intense Catholic, and joined the Dominican Order in 1917. He lived to be 90 years old, and as Père Leseur preached and lectured on the interior life, using his wife's *Spiritual Journal.*

[T. C. O'BRIEN]

LESKOV, NIKOLAY SEMYONOVICH (1831–95), Russian novelist, master of the short story, gifted stylist. Though himself an Orthodox Christian, he was fascinated by religious sects, esp. the Old Believers, who often figure in his works. His novelle, modeled on the Russian *skaz* (short story told by a narrator), are remarkable for their use of folk etymology and dialectical expressions to distinguish personalities. His best works include *A Lady Macbeth of the Mtsensk District* (1865); *Cathedral Folk* (1872), and *The Enchanted Wanderer* (1873). BIBLIOGRAPHY: J. Lavrin, *From Pushkin to Mayakovsky* (1948, repr. 1971); D. S. Mirsky, *Contemporary Russian Literature* (1926) 29–39.

[M. F. MCCARTHY]

LESLIE, JOHN (1527–96), Scottish bishop. From his ordination (1558), L. opposed the Reformation. He visited Mary Queen of Scots in France (1561) and was her ambassador to Elizabeth I (1569). He became bp. of Ross in 1566 but was imprisoned in 1571 for aiding Mary. Two years later he was permitted to go into exile and became bp. of Rouen (1579) and Coutances (1593). The latter portion of his *De origine, moribus, et rebus gestis Scotorum* (1578) is important for the history of his age. BIBLIOGRAPHY: T. F. Henderson, DNB 33:93–99.

[M. J. SUELZER]

LESLIE, SHANE (John Randolph, 1885–1971), author of notable and numerous literary works. An Irish baronet of Castle Lesley, Glaslough, Ireland, L. was born in London of Irish-American parentage. He was cousin to Winston Churchill through his mother Leonie Jerome. Intellectually active and spiritually questing, L. visited Tolstoy in Russia in 1907 and became a RC the following year. He studied in Paris, tramped through England and Ireland, and visited the U.S. His varied works might be classified as monumental, touching as they do historical periods and revealing biographical thoroughness. Recognized as a competent lecturer, he gave, under the Rosenbach Fellowship, a series on Jonathan Swift at the Univ. of Pennsylvania (1935). The Univ. of Notre Dame conferred an L. L. D. on him at this time. A cross section of his work includes *The Oxford Movement, Henry Edward Manning. His Life and Labors* (1921). *The Irish Issue,* and the autobiography *The Film of Memory* (1938). Intellectual, scholarly, cosmopolitan, brave, and loyal to his religion, L. seems a Renaissance figure in a latter-day setting.

[R. M. FUNCHION]

LESMES, ST., see ADELELM, ST.

LESORT, PAUL-ANDRÉ (1915–), French writer who has used the subjectivist techniques of the phenomenologically orientated new novel in formulating a neo-Christian, personalist response to the dilemma of the human condition. Viewing the modern Christian not as a man with redemption in his grasp but as a witness living amidst evils created by capitalism, he refuses to be called a "Catholic novelist" and eschews any apologetical aim. BIBLIOGRAPHY: P. Cogny, *Sept romanciers au delà du roman* (1963).

[G. E. GINGRAS]

LESSER LITANIES, traditional days of prayer and penance, with a procession and blessing of spring crops on the 3 days before the solemnity of the Ascension. They were also known as the Minor Litanies or *Rogation Days. They originated in Gaul, when Bp. Mamertus of Vienne decreed their annual observance in 470 during unusual spring calamities. They were adopted by Rome in the 9th cent. but have recently been dropped, as such, from the Roman calendar. BIBLIOGRAPHY: F. X. Weiser, *Handbook of Christian Feasts and Customs* (1958).

[N. R. KRAMER]

LESSING, GOTTHOLD EPHRAIM (1729–81), German critic and dramatist. His critical works include contributions to *Briefe, die neueste Literatur betreffend* (1759–65), esp. the 17th letter, which attacks pseudoclassicism; *Laokoon, oder Über die Grenzen der Malerei und Poesie* (1766); and the *Hamburgische Dramaturgie* (1767–68). His best dramas are *Minna von Barnhelm* (1767), the first great German comedy; *Emilia Galotti* (1772), a political tragedy; *Nathan der Weise* (1779), a plea for religious tolerance. BIBLIOGRAPHY: H. B. Garland, *Lessing: The Founder of Modern German Literature* (2d ed., 1962); M. F. McCarthy, NCE 8:678; V. A. Rudowski, *Lessing's Aesthetics in Nuce* (1971).

[M. F. MCCARTHY]

LESSIUS, LEONARD (Leys; 1554–1623), Belgian Jesuit, theologian. A Jesuit from 1572, he taught philosophy at the Jesuit college of Douai, was ordained in 1581. At the Collegio Romano (1581–84) he studied theology under both F. Suárez and St. Robert Bellarmine. From 1584 at the Jesuit college in Louvain, he taught theology, substituting for Peter Lombard's *Sentences* the *Summa theologiae* of Aquinas as the text, a practice already begun at Rome. L.'s teaching on grace was attacked by M. du Bay (Baius), and the controversy reached the attention of Sixtus V; when L. published his *De justitia et jure* (1605), his name was already well known. This, his greatest work, went through 12 editions during his own lifetime. In 1600 he stopped teaching to devote himself exclusively to research and writing. His *Defensio potestatis Summi Pontificis* (1613), dedicated to Paul V, was highly esteemed. His *De gratia efficaci* . . . (1610) contained an appendix on *predestination subsequent to foreseen *merit that provoked a controversy (the memory of the *Congregatio de auxiliis was still fresh) that turned him away from dogmatic to moral and ascetical studies, the fruits of which were his *De summo bono* (1616) and *De perfectionibus moribusque divinis* (1620). He died with a reputation for holiness and was the object of a cultus before the French Revolution.

[T. C. O'BRIEN]

LESSON (from the Lat. *legere,* to read), a section of the Bible, patristic writings, life of a saint or historical narrative designated to be read in the Liturgy of the Hours or, in the case of biblical passages, proclaimed at Mass. The Latin *lectio* is now translated as "reading," a term preferable to "lesson" in English usage.

[T. M. MCFADDEN]

LESTONNAC, JEANNE DE, ST. (1556–1640), foundress of the Company of Mary. A Frenchwoman of strongly Catholic background from a region of Bordeaux where Calvinism was flourishing, L. married but was left a widow with seven children in 1597. After rearing the children she entered (1603) a Cistercian convent but had to leave because of ill health. She devoted herself to works of charity in Bordeaux and ultimately founded the Order of Notre Dame, approved in 1607 with L. as first superior. The order was popularly called the Company of Mary, since it was intended to be a counterpart of the Company of Jesus, the Jesuits, dedicated to educating girls. In 1622 one of the nuns conspired to depose L. as superior and succeeded. L. bore with the persecution patiently and in 1624 was proved innocent of accusations made against her. She spent her life fostering growth of her order. She was canonized in 1949. BIBLIOGRAPHY: P. Hoesl, *In the Service of Youth* (tr. J. Carr, 1951); G. Mathon, BiblSanct 6:587–588.

[J. R. AHERNE]

LE SUEUR, EUSTACHE (1616–55), French painter of religious and mythological scenes and portraits. Student of S. Vouet, L. early filled his master's commission for tapestry cartoons, and painted *Presentation of the Virgin* (1640–45), and panels (1646–47) showing the influence of Poussin and of Raphael, his mature style appearing in a *Life of St.*

Bruno series, combining a French international Baroque as in Zurbarán, with Poussin's classicism, Raphael's simple grandeur, and a Carracci chiaroscuro. In his last years *St. Paul at Ephesus* (1649) is again eclectic, whereas the *Mass of St. Martin* is more individually mature.

[M. J. DALY]

LE SUEUR, JEAN FRANÇOIS (Leseure; 1760–1837), self-taught French composer who served in churches at Seéz, Paris, Dijon, Le Mans, and Tours; in 1786 he became Master at Notre Dame de Paris where he used the full orchestra and choir to achieve dramatic effects in his motets and Masses. After turning to opera during the 1790s, he was appointed chapel master to Napoleon in 1804, retaining his position under Louis XVIII. L. was a noted teacher and Hector Berlioz was one of his more illustrious students. Over 30 Masses, ten oratorios, psalms, motets, and a *Stabat Mater* comprise his sacred works.

[R. J. LITZ]

LESYNGHAM, ROBERT (fl. 1350), English architect who designed Exeter cloisters (1377–78) with W front, screen and E window (1389–90), and probably the earlier Gloucester cloisters.

[M. J. DALY]

LE TELLIER, family name of two prominent figures in French history, father and son. **Michel** (1603–85), the father, war minister under Card. *Mazarin and King Louis XIV. He arranged the marriage treaty between Louis and Maria Theresa of Spain and carried out the king's policy of military conquest. **Charles Maurice** (1642–1710), son of Michel, abp. of Reims. Ordained in 1666 and a royal favorite, he became abp. in 1670. He was a competent administrator of his see, a friend of Bossuet, and a supporter of St. John Baptist de *La Salle, founder of the Christian Brothers. In the general assemblies of the clergy in 1681 and 1682, L. sided with Louis XIV against the papacy. He was a strong advocate of *Gallicanism; he wrote against the Jansenists, but was also anti-Jesuit.

[J. R. AHERNE]

LE TELLIER, MICHEL (1643–1719), French Jesuit, confessor to King Louis XIV. A member of the Society of Jesus from 1661, L. taught at Paris for 28 years before beginning his service to the King in 1708. He published *Histoire des cinq propositions de Jansenius* (1689) and *Observation sur la nouvelle édition de la version française du Nouveau Testament* (1672), a work directed against P. *Quesnel's *Reflexions morales*. In his official position L. was able to intensify his anti-Jansenist campaign: he had a main hand in having the bull **Unigenitus* condemning Quesnel promulgated in France and was largely responsible for the King's ordering the razing of the abbey of Port Royal, the Jansenists' center. Because he earned their enmity, L. was often portrayed in a distortedly harsh way by historians of the period.

[T. C. O'BRIEN]

LE THORONET, ABBEY OF, Cistercian monastery in Provence, France, founded in 1136 by monks of Mazan. Its most famous abbot was Bl. Fulk (Foulques) of Marseille, celebrated troubadour, who became a Cistercian in 1196, abbot in 1201, and bp. of Toulouse in 1205. The abbey declined under commendatory abbots, was sacked in the wars of religion and was suppressed (1790). The church and cloister, completed *c.* 1190, are beautiful examples of Cistercian architecture, and are maintained as national monuments. BIBLIOGRAPHY: F. Cali, *Architecture of Truth* (1957); A. Dimier, *L'art cistercien* (1962) 185–212; *idem,* NCE 8:680; F. Pouillon, *Stones of the Abbey* (tr. E. Gillott, 1970).

[L. J. LEKAI]

LETI, GREGORIO (1630–1701), Italian writer. An adventurer and libertine, L. became a Calvinist in Geneva after various wanderings in middle Europe. He wrote many obscene but widely read books against the Catholic Church. His biography of Elizabeth I of England and of Pope Sixtus V are typical of the novelistic historiography of his age. BIBLIOGRAPHY: M. Petrocchi, EncCatt 7:1208.

[M. J. SUELZER]

LETTER (NT), the literary form and title of several NT writings, also called epistles. A distinction is sometimes made between the letter and the epistle. *EPISTLE.

[T. C. O'BRIEN]

LETTERS, ANONYMOUS, see ANONYMOUS LETTERS.

LETTERS, DIMISSORIAL, see DIMISSORIAL LETTERS.

LETTERS, PASTORAL, see PASTORAL LETTERS.

LETTERS OF PEACE, see LIBELLI PACIS.

LEUBUS, ABBEY OF, Cistercian monastery in Silesia near Breslau, which was founded by Polish Benedictines (1150) and later taken over by Cistercians from Pforta (1163). The abbey served as a major center of the arts and learning throughout the Middle Ages. Destroyed by the Swedes (1632), it was rebuilt in splendid Baroque. After it was secularized (1810), its buildings were used as a mental hospital until 1945. The abbey is presently unoccupied. BIBLIOGRAPHY: A. Schneider, NCE 8:681; J. Gottschalk, LTK 6:989–990.

[L. J. LEKAI]

LEUCIPPUS OF MILETUS (fl. *c.* 440 B.C.) **AND DEMOCRITUS OF ABDERA** (*c.* 460–*c.* 370 B.C.), the founders of Atomism. They must be treated together, since the ancients did not distinguish their respective contributions. It would seem that Leucippus was the pioneer and that Democritus elaborated or supplemented his doctrine, which may be considered a logical development of the philosophy of Empedocles of Acragas (*c.* 493–*c.* 433 B.C.) and its embryonic teaching on particles. Leucippus and Democritus held that reality is composed of an infinite number of individual corporeal units or atoms of varying size and shape, and of the unreal, but existent, void or space in which they move. These atoms move in all directions, collide, and by a vortex process combine in groups to form bodies. The movement of the atoms was apparently explained or taken for granted in accordance with necessity or cosmic law. Epicurus attributed the perpendicular fall of the atoms to their weight, but there is no reference to weight in the theory of Leucippus and Democritus. Soul and mind are considered to be identical and composed of small fiery atoms. The soul is mortal and there is no place for God as an active or controlling force in the system. All that happens, happens on some account and by necessity. Sense qualities such as color, taste, sound, etc., are explained as existing by convention and as resulting from the difference in the shape, arrangement, and position of the atoms. The atomist theory of knowledge is based on a transformation of the "effluences" of Empedocles into atoms, which are regarded as images that objects are continually shedding. On the ethical side, Democritus seems to have considered happiness as the end of conduct. "The best thing for a man is to pass his life so as to have as much joy and as little trouble as may be" (Fragment 189). Democritus was a voluminous writer, but only scattered fragments from his works are preserved. He was much admired by Aristotle. The Atomism of Leucippus and Democritus is the foundation for the philosophy of Epicurus; and in addition to its continued influence in antiquity, it has enjoyed a great revival in the materialistic philosophies of modern times. BIBLIOGRAPHY: OCD 498; LexAW 1714–15, 715–716; Copleston 1:72–75, 124–126; Guthrie 2:382–507.

[M. R. P. MCGUIRE]

LEUCIUS CHARINUS, a shadowy figure whose existence can be doubted, yet whose name has some importance. In apocryphal tradition there is a Leucius who is a companion of St. John the Evangelist on the Isle of Patmos. Epiphanius refers to the two of them as refuting heretics together. There is some irony then in the fact that this same Leucius (called Charinus by Photius many centuries later) came first to be credited with collecting and later even with writing the entire corpus of apocryphal Acts of various Apostles. This corpus became known as the Manichean corpus because of the docetic Christ who figures in them (see DOCETISM), and because of the harsh asceticism throughout with a pervasive hostility to sexuality and marriage. Thus the name of the friend of the Evangelist had acquired by the 6th cent. the epithet "disciple of the devil" in the Latin Church. *APOCRYPHA, NT.

[E. J. DILLON]

LEUTFRED (LEUFROY), ST. (d. 738), Benedictine abbot. He studied at Chartres under renowned teachers. Leaving his native Évreux (Normandy), he went to Rouen where he received the religious habit. He returned to Évreux in 690 and founded a monastery and a hospital for the poor. He is credited with miracles before and after death. BIBLIOGRAPHY: P. Rouillard, BiblSanct 7:1351–52; É. Brouette, NCE 8:681.

[F. D. LAZENBY]

LE VACHER, JEAN (1619–83), Vincentian missionary, and French consul in N Africa. In 1647 he was sent by St. Vincent de Paul to the Christian slaves in Tunis, and was later prefect apostolic of Tunis (1648), vicar apostolic of Tunis (1650), vicar general of Carthage (1651), and vicar apostolic of Algiers, Tunis, Tripoli, and Morocco (1668). He was French consul in Tunis (1648–53, 1657–66); and French consul in Algiers in 1677. His close identification with the French government paved the way for his brutal murder by Algerian forces during the French bombardment of Algiers in 1683.

[E. J. DILLON]

LEVADOUX, MICHAEL (1746–1815), French missionary to the U.S. A Sulpician, he was sent to Baltimore in 1791 to aid in the founding of St. Mary's Seminary. In subsequent years he served as a missionary in Ohio, Indiana, and Michigan among Indians and whites. BIBLIOGRAPHY: A. E. Jones, CE 9:204–205.

[J. R. AHERNE]

LEVELERS (Levellers), a religious, political party of Puritans. The name, applied from 1647 onward, was intended as a term of derision. The Levelers sought to abolish the monarchy, all class privileges, and any *established Church and to create a democratic republic with complete political and religious equality for all. Their chief strength was drawn from the rank and file of the army; J. *Lilburne was their spokesman and pamphleteer. In 1649 Oliver Cromwell took strong measures against the movement; the Levelers had disappeared by 1660. Their ideas influenced Quaker emphasis on human equality. BIBLIOGRAPHY: J. Frank, *Levellers* (1955).

[T. C. O'BRIEN]

LEVI, SON OF JACOB, the third son, born to Leah, Jacob's first wife (Gen 29.34). He gave his name to the tribe of Levi. The harsh revenge that L. and Simeon instigated against the rapist of their full sister, Dinah, evoked from Jacob a severe rebuke (Gen 34.30), and, later, in his testament, a curse that they would never have any territory of their own among the tribes of Israel (49.7). In fact, the sons of Levi labored as ministers of various shrines scattered throughout Israel and never possessed any territory of their own. In the post-Exilic era, when there was only one sanctuary, the *Levites who remained were reduced to the level of minor temple officials and servants of the priests of Jerusalem.

[J. F. FALLON]

LEVIATHAN, mythological monster of chaos, Lothan, slain by Baal in the Ugaritic epic and conquered by Yahweh in Is 27.1; Ps 74.14 (vaguely in Job 3.8). In Job 41.13 and Ps 104.26, Leviathan is nonmythological. BIBLIOGRAPHY: J. L. McKenzie, "Note on Psalm 73(74).13–15," ThSt 11(1950) 275–282; H. Wallace, "Leviathan and the Beast in Revelation," *Biblical Archaeologist* 11 (1948) 61–68.

[E. J. CROWLEY]

LEVIRATE MARRIAGE (Lat., *levir,* brother-in-law), marriage between a widow and the brother of her deceased husband. In the Bible the law of levirate made such a marriage obligatory in certain circumstances. This was required of the brother of the deceased (Dt 25.5–10) when the brother lived on the same land and the dead man had had no son. The purpose was to keep property in the family, and to keep the family name alive. Refusal to obey this law was punished by publicly disgracing the guilty man. (It is to be noted that the levirate law in Dt conflicts with Lev 18.16.) In the Book of Ruth (3.12–4.17) the law is extended to other male relatives in order of their relationship to the deceased. Jewish speculation on the meaning of the law is reflected in Mt 22.23–28. Levirate marriage has been practiced in other cultures and religions.

[T. C. O'BRIEN]

LEVI-STRAUSS, CLAUDE (1908–), French anthropologist, leading exponent of structural analysis. Though he has done field work among several SA tribes, his overriding interest is in the universal structures of the human mind rather than the peculiarities of particular societies. He seeks structure not on the level of superficial facts, but in the unconscious framework of the logical relations underlying them. His point of departure is the structural linguistics of Roman Jakobson and others. The fruits of the focus on structure are perhaps most accessible in L.'s *Totemism* (tr. R. Needham, 1963) and *The Savage Mind* (1966), in which he examines the "logic" of a variety of systems of classification. He characterizes "primitive" thought by its demand for order and contends that "classifying, as opposed to not classifying, has a value of its own, whatever form the classification may take." It is the task of the observer to uncover the principles on which that system is founded, since for L. mythical thought differs from modern science not in the quality of its intellectual processes but in the nature of the things to which it is applied. The concern for structure, order, and systems of classification also informs the four volumes of *Mythologiques* in which he pursues the "logics of myth." He claims to show there "not how men think in myths, but how myths operate in men's minds without their being aware of the fact." There is much that is penetrating in L.'s writings, but there is also much that is obscure and overly allusive. Nevertheless, his work, which represents only one strand of structuralist thinking, has exerted wide-ranging influence on contemporary scholarship. BIBLIOGRAPHY: C. Levi-Strauss, *Structural Anthropology* v.1 (tr. C. Jacobson and B. G. Schoepf, 1963) and v. 2 (tr. M. Layton, 1976); *Mythologiques: The Raw and the Cooked* (tr. J. and D. Weightman, 1969); *From Honey to Ashes* (tr. J. and D. Weightman, 1973); *L'origine des manières de table* (1968); *L'homme nu* (1971); E. Leach, *C. Levi-Strauss* (1970); J. Piaget, *Structuralism* (tr. C. Maschler 1970).

[E. V. GALLAGHER]

LEVITATION, a phenomenon in which a material object, usually the human body, is suspended in the air without any visible means of support. In some cases the body has moved rapidly from place to place; in others it has remained stationary or been subject to the surrounding air currents. It is a phenomenon reported in the lives of many saints, e.g., SS. Catherine of Siena, Francis of Assisi, Francis Xavier, John of the Cross, Joseph Cupertino, Peter Alcántara, Philip Neri, Teresa of Avila, and others. While it cannot be explained by natural causes, it is thought to be not beyond the power of angels or devils and therefore can be *preternatural. When it is supernatural, levitation may be considered as anticipation of the agility that will be enjoyed by the glorified body. Sometimes there are simulations of it in hysterical seizures. BIBLIOGRAPHY: A. Royo, *Theology of Christian Perfection* (tr. J. Aumann, 1962); H. Thurston, *Physical Phenomena of Mysticism* (ed. J. H. Crehan, 1952). *MYSTICAL PHENOMENA.

[M. B. PENNINGTON]

LEVITES, remnants of the secular tribe of Levi who continued as a priestly caste that gradually spread throughout Israel as dedicated servants of cultic sanctuaries. They seem to have migrated northward from their native association with Judah and Simeon in the practice of their profession. The Levites of the Jerusalem sanctuary eventually became dominant and advocated centralization of worship in their temple, thus forcing local shrines to be abandoned and the local Levites to become impoverished. In the post-Exilic era, when there was only one center of Jewish worship, the Jerusalem Temple, non-Jerusalemite Levites became second-class ministers relegated to minor tasks. The preservation of much of Israel's traditional doctrine and law was their major contribution to history.

[J. F. FALLON]

LEVITICAL CITIES, the 48 towns in Jos 21, some of them important ones such as Hebron, David's first capital, listed as having been allotted to priests and Levites—a distinction that did not occur until post-Exilic times. The text is obviously an idealized view that enhances the glory of the period of the conquest of Canaan, a major Deuteronomic theme of the book of Joshua. However, there may have been an ancient pre-Exilic core to the list: since none of the cities is near Jerusalem or Bethel, the two most important shrines of Judah and Israel, the towns may represent populous centers of Levites at a distance from the central sanctuaries after they were established. But, as the text stands now, the obvious intent is to give a theological, idealistic, and symbolical picture of Levitical inheritance in the Promised Land.

[J. F. FALLON]

LEVITICUS, BOOK OF, the name first given to the third book of the OT by the Septuagint translators to indicate that its contents deal almost wholly with levitical or priestly concerns. The laws and regulations are only very rarely interspersed with narrative material (e.g., the ordination of Aaron and his sons in ch. 8–9; the punishment of Aaron's sons for a ritual sin in 10.1–5), and even these have a legal or liturgical purpose. There is general agreement, therefore, among the scholars that the entire book came from Priestly circles and that the definitive editing of it took place after the return from the Babylonian Exile, when the Priestly influence was at its height. It is also agreed that the various sections came from different circles at different periods of Israel's history, some of the laws being very ancient. There is no general agreement on the precise determination of the circles and the periods. The following division is proposed: 1–7, the laws for sacrifice; 8–10, ordination ritual; 11–15, purification ritual; 16, the Day of Atonement; 17–26, the Holiness Code; 27, appendix on vows and tithes. The Holiness Code was recognized early as a distinctive collection within the book; it is marked by its introduction (17.1–2) and conclusion (26.46), by the repetition of the command to be holy as God is holy (e.g., 19.2; 20.7–8) and by the frequent use of the divine First Person (e.g., 17.10; 18.2, 4). Behind the ritualism of the book can be discerned a profound conviction of divine transcendence and of Israel's high destiny by reason of the divine election. BIBLIOGRAPHY: EDB 1332–33; J. A. Seiss, *Holy Types: The Gospel in Leviticus* (1972); W. G. Heslop, *Lessons from Leviticus* (pa. 1975).

[E. H. MALY]

LEWES PRIORY, former Benedictine monastery in Sussex, England, located in present-day Lewes. The earliest Cluniac foundation in England—the original community having been sent by St. Hugh of Cluny—it was founded, 1078/81 by William of Warenne, Earl of Surrey, and his wife, Gundreda, daughter of William the Conqueror, and dedicated to St. Pancras. Lewes eventually laid claim to a dozen dependent monasteries. In 1537 it surrendered to Henry VIII and was demolished the following year. Its lands were given to the family of Thomas Cromwell.

[E. J. DILLON]

LEWIS, C. S. (full name Clive Staples Lewis; 1898–1963), literary historian, critic, novelist, Christian apologist. Born in Belfast, L. was brought up in Ulster Protestantism, went through a period of agnosticism, and discovered Catholicism, which he found embodied in the C of E without feeling the need of pursuing juridico-theological questions of religious authority. He tells his own story in *Surprised by Joy* (1955). A distinguished academic, fellow of Magdalen, he was a man of Oxford, living there and commuting weekly when he was appointed professor of English at Cambridge. *The Allegory of Love* (1936) opened up the study of the conflict between *courtoisie* and the moralism of medieval Latin Christianity; later researches have tended to close the gap. It was followed by *A Preface to Paradise Lost* (1942) and *English Literature in the Sixteenth Century* (1958). He stood for values not congenial to analytically nominalist groups, but his scholarship, logic, and energy made him a formidable controversialist. He became most widely known by a series of defenses for Christianity published in the 10 years from 1942. These included three works of space-fiction, *Out of the Silent Planet, Perelandra,* and *That Hideous Might*. The approach was less allegorical in the *The Problem of Pain, Christian Behaviour, Mere Christianity;* the *Screwtape Letters* (of an elderly devil to a young disciple). These get down to the occupational diseases of "churchy" religion. He had a far-ranging imagination well tempered by philosophical and theological reason. As a conversationalist he was the delight of his many friends; like Dr. Johnson he spoke with authority and humor, but he was never crushing. BIBLIOGRAPHY: T. Corbishley, NCE 8:686; G. L. Greene and W. Hooper, *C. S. Lewis: A Biography* (1974); *Letters of C. S. Lewis* (ed. W. H. Lewis, 1975).

[T. GILBY]

LEWIS, DAVID, ST. (1617–79), Welsh martyr. L. was reared as a Protestant in Wales but converted to Roman Catholicism in 1632 while serving as a tutor in Paris. He was ordained in 1642 at the English College in Rome and joined the Jesuits 2 years later. After spending a short time as spiritual director at the English College, L. returned to S Wales (1648) where he labored as a parish priest for 28 years. He seems sometimes to have used the names Charles Baker. His charity and pastoral concern earned him the title of Father of the Poor. He was seized during the Titus Oates plot and found guilty under the Elizabethan statute 27, which made it treasonous to be ordained abroad and then return to England and celebrate Mass. L. was hanged, drawn, and quartered at Usk, Wales. He was beatified in 1929 and canonized in 1970. BIBLIOGRAPHY: Butler 3:424–426; N. Del Re, BiblSanct 7:1355–57.

[T. M. MCFADDEN]

LEWIS, EDWIN (1881–1959), Methodist theologian. Born in Newbury, England, he was educated in Canada, the U.S., and Europe, and in 1916 became a member of the faculty of Drew Theological Seminary, where he taught systematic theology for 35 years. His early publications marked him as a liberal theologian of the personalist-idealist school of B. P. *Bowne, but, influenced by Karl *Barth, he became the champion of *neo-orthodoxy through his later articles and books, particularly *A Christian Manifesto* (1934), *A Philosophy of the Christian Revelation* (1940), and *The Creator and the Adversary* (1948). His greatest work was as editor of the *Abingdon Bible Commentary* (1926–29). BIBLIOGRAPHY: D. W. Soper, *Major Voices in American Theology* (1953, repr. 1969) 17–36; HistAmMeth 3:284–287; 304–307; 311–315.

[F. E. MASER]

LEX ORANDI, LEX CREDENDI (the rule of prayer is the rule of faith), an adage pointing out the liturgy as a source of data for theological reflection and proof. It goes back to Pope St. *Celestine I (d. 432), and to *Prosper of Aquitaine (D 246) and *Augustine in their arguments against *Pelagianism. Augustine taught that the Church at prayer does not essentially falsify its faith, and therefore that the general prayers of the Church, starting with the Lord's Prayer, furnish a reliable guide for understanding the faith. The argument is basically an appeal to tradition where, in the liturgy, tradition may be expected to be at its most vital. BIBLIOGRAPHY: K. Federer, LTK 6:1002; H. Schmidt, *Introductio in liturgiam occidentalem* (1960) 134; H. E. W. Turner, *Pattern of Christian Truth* (1954) 319. *LITURGY AND DOGMA.

[P. MISNER]

LEX ROMANA BURGUNDIONUM, a code of Roman Law issued (*c.*500) by King Gundobad (Gombette), one of the last Burgundian kings, for Roman subjects of the Burgundian kingdom. Burgundian subjects were governed by the *Lex Burgundionum* in keeping with the Germanic practice of independent legal codes for separate tribes and peoples. (see LEGES ROMANAE BARBARORUM). The provisions of the code were not new but were presented by Gundobad as a manual of those Roman laws which were in effect and would be enforced in his kingdom. This code was displaced by the superior *Lex Romana Visigothorum.*

[R. J. LITZ]

LEX ROMANA VISIGOTHORUM (Breviary of Alaric), a law code and book of statutes drafted by legal specialists, passed by civil rulers and bps., and issued by King Alaric II in 506 for Roman subjects of the West Gothic kingdom, rescinded by King Recceswind in 654. The code remained in effect for the Latin people and the Church in S France until the 12th century. Much of the Law of Alaric was borrowed from the Gregorian and Hermogenian codes, the *Institutes* of Gaius, the *Sentences* of Paul, and most importantly from the code of Theodosius (438). It is an important source for the history of Roman law.

[R. J. LITZ]

LEX SALICA (Salic Law), the most important though not the oldest Barbarian legal code containing the customs and laws of the Salian Franks, a Teutonic people who conquered Gaul during the 5th century. Issued under the Merovingian Clovis (*c.*507–511) and written in Latin but only slightly influenced by Roman law, the code was primarily penal with certain civil-law provisions. Its major effect was to moderate blood-feuds among Frankish families. Its duration as the law of the Carolingian and Merovingian rulers and its connection with the origins of feudalism make this body of law extremely important historically. One provision concerning the succession of females to the crown, wrongly supposed to derive from Title 62 of the Salic Law, *De Alode,* by which females were excluded from inheriting landed estates, is often separately referred to as the "Salic Law."

[R. J. LITZ]

LEX TALIONIS, the law of equivalence in retaliation against an offending party, e.g., the OT "eye for an eye, tooth for a tooth" (Dt 19.21). In groups where the talion is accepted as law, the offended party may with group sanction exact justice on the principle of proportion. The custom prevailed in ancient Israel and is found in most primitive societies, historical and contemporary. It usually marks a point of transition from savage personal revenge to group-approved methods of punishment. BIBLIOGRAPHY: R. Hirzel, "Die Talion," *Philologus,* Suppl. 11 (1907–10) 407–482; Hastings ERE 2:720–735; 4:251; 6:76–77.

[P. K. MEAGHER]

LEYDEN, LUCAS VAN (*c.*1489–1533), Dutch painter and engraver. An infant prodigy, L. studied with his father and C. Engebrechtsz, mastering stained glass and engraving (*Mahomet and the Monk Sergius,* 1508). Engravings of the Netherlandish masters and of Dürer influenced L. in *The Raising of Lazarus* (1508), 9 prints in *The Circular Passion* (1509), and *Ecce Homo* (1510). An Italianate style marks later works after contact with Dürer, Gossaert, and engravings of Marcantonio Raimondi. L. painted an early *St. Anthony* (1511), and a mature *Virgin and Child with Magdalen and Donor* (1522) related to Gossaert. BIBLIOGRAPHY: M. J. Friedländer, *Early Netherlandish Painting* (tr. H. Norden, 1967); C. D. Cuttler, *Northern Painting* (1968).

[M. J. DALY]

LEYSER, POLYCARP (1690–1728), literary historian. A German Lutheran, L. was a professor of philosophy, history, and poetry all his life. Of his copious publications in the field of history, particularly literary history, the masterly work is *Historia poëtarum et poëmatum medii aevi* (1721), which treated 700 Latin medieval poets, most of them hitherto unpublished.

[J. R. AHERNE]

LEZANA, JUAN BAUTISTA (1586–1659), Spanish Carmelite theologian, religious superior. L. taught philosophy and theology, was a prior and provincial of his order, and secretary to several superiors general. He was a consultor to the Congregation of the Index and the Congregation of Rites in Rome where he lived and taught from 1625 until his death. L. wrote a history of his order, including its "prehistory," up to 1513, *Annales sacri* . . . (4 v., 1645–56). He also wrote a number of theological works, among them *Liber apologeticus pro Immaculata Deiparae Virginis Mariae Conceptione* (1616); *Summa quaestionum regularium* . . . (1634–47); and *Summa theologiae sacrae* (1651). BIBLIOGRAPHY: Espasa 30:396.

[J. R. AHERNE]

L'HERMITE, FRANÇOIS (*c.* 1601–55), French poet and dramatist of the Louis XIII period, and member of the French Academy (*c.* 1648). L.'s works include: *Plaintes d'Acante* (1633), *Les Amours de Tristan* (1638), *La Lyre du sieur Tristan* (1641), and *Les Vers héroiques* (1648), all collections of poetry; as well as *Le Page disgracié* (1642), an autobiographical novel. Of his plays, including *Penthée* (1637), *La Mort de Sénèque* (1645), *La Mort de Crispe* (1645), *Le Parasite* (1653), and *La Mort du grand Osman* (1656), his first tragedy, *Mariamne* (1636), was the most successful, rivaling P. *Corneille's *Le Cid*. It is based on an episode from Flavius Josephus' *Antiquities* (Bk. 15), as retold in *La Cour sainte* by the Jesuit, Nicolas Caussin. Sometimes considered an atheist, L. gives proof of his Catholic faith in his *Les Heures de la Sainte Vierge* (1646). BIBLIOGRAPHY: F. Lachèvre, *Tristan L'Hermite, sieur du Solier, poète chrétien et catholique* (1941).

[R. N. NICOLICH]

L'HÔPITAL, (L'HOSPITAL), MICHEL DE (1505–73), chancellor of France (1560–68). His fame as a statesman rests on the part he played in the deliberations that granted religious freedom to the Huguenots. He maintained that the only way to assure peace lay in having confessional differences regulated by the crown. In 1568 he retired from court to devote himself to humanistic studies. BIBLIOGRAPHY: W. J. Steiner, NCE 8:692.

[M. J. SUELZER]

LHOTE, ANDRÉ (1885–1962). French critic and painter, L. exerted lasting influence through his important writing, example, and teaching, indoctrinating generations of students in cubism, in his own work, expressing space through flat surfaces and seeking the absolute through intelligence and sensibility. He raised major questions in writings for *Nouvelle revue français*, in "Treatises on the Figure and Landscape" and "Egyptian Painting in the Valley of the Kings," painted several murals, and illustrated works of Cocteau, Claudel, and others.

[M. J. DALY]

LIBANIUS (314–*c.*393), rhetorician. During a 5-year (343–348) tenure as public teacher in Nicomedia, L. met the future St. *Basil the Great and the future emperor, *Julian the Apostate. A spurious correspondence exaggerates the first acquaintance; L. was more closely associated with Julian. L. shared the emperor's deep interest in a pagan revival, but as official sophist (teacher) of Antioch (a post he assumed in 354), he was forced to speak for the city in a controversy with Julian. At Antioch L. was also the teacher of St. *John Chrysostom. Later, because of his close ties with Julian, L. suffered in the religious reaction that followed the emperor's death. L.'s writings (some 1600 letters survive) show him to be a keen observer and critic of Roman society. BIBLIOGRAPHY: A. F. Norman, *Libanius' Autobiography (Oration I)* (1965); A. F. Norman, *Libanius: Selected Works* (1969); P. Petit, *Libanius et la vie municipale à Antioche* (1955).

[E. V. GALLAGHER]

LIBATION (Lat., *libatio* or *libamen*), a sacrificial offering made to the gods or to the dead by the pouring out wholly or in part of some liquid such as wine, milk, honey, oil, or a mixture of these. A libation could be of a private or of a public character; it could be employed alone or in conjunction with other sacrifices; it could be used to solemnize an oath, to seal a treaty, or simply as an offering at the beginning of a meal. In the early Church the taking of wine during a *refrigerium* at the shrine of a martyr was substituted for the earlier libations poured out at family tombs. During the 4th cent. the practice was proscribed in some places such as Milan because of the abuses that arose from it. BIBLIOGRAPHY: A. Stuiber, LTK 6:1004–05.

[M. J. COSTELLOE]

LIBELLATICI, a term used to describe those Christians who, during the persecution of Decius (249–251), used a questionable strategy to evade the penalties imposed by the imperial government on those who refused to offer sacrifice or to give other indication of their adherence to the pagan gods and their loyalty to the Emperor. They used bribery to obtain from local officials certificates (*libelli*) falsely testifying that they had offered sacrifice. After the persecution church authorities condemned the subterfuge, but with less severity than the apostasy of those who had offered the required sacrifice (*sacrificati*). The controversy and events connected with the reconciliation of the *libellatici* can be traced in the letters of St. Cyprian and in his treatise *De lapsis*. BIBLIOGRAPHY: Jedin-Baus 222–226.

[R. B. ENO]

LIBELLI PACIS (Letters of Peace), letters obtained from Christian martyrs while they were still in prison, urging that one who had apostatized during the persecution of Decius (249–251) be received for reconciliation (see LAPSI). Belief that the martyrs' suffering gave them special powers of forgiveness seems to have been involved. St. *Cyprian of Carthage (Ep. 12, PL 4,259) recognized the intercessory power of the martyrs, but rejected any laxity in accepting the *lapsi* for reconciliation. The *libelli pacis* are sometimes confused with the certificates obtained by bribes from pagan officials, falsely attesting that the Christian bearers, **libellatici*, had offered sacrifice to the gods.

[T. C. O'BRIEN]

LIBER CENSUUM, a book listing the taxes, contributions, rents, and diverse kinds of payments due to the Holy See from individuals and institutions of all kinds. The papal chamberlain, Card. Cencio Savelli (*Honorius III) compiled it in 1192 to facilitate the work of his office. The *Liber censuum* lists the various sorts of income according to diocese or church province, and includes copies of some documents in which the grants were originally made, as well as other historical data. Thus it resembled the contemporary medieval cartulary. The *Liber censuum* gives evidence of the complexity yet rudimentary state of papal finances as well as of the bureaucratic growth of the Roman Curia (see CHURCH PROPERTY). BIBLIOGRAPHY: *Le Liber censuum de l'Église romaine* (ed. M. P. Fabre and L. Duchesne, 3 v., 1889–1952); P. Partner, *Lands of St. Peter* (1972).

[R. H. SCHMANDT]

LIBER DE CAUSIS (Book on Causes), a short anonymous treatise that exercised a great influence on later medieval philosophy. It was translated from Arabic into Latin by *Gerard of Cremona (d. 1187). It was first quoted by *Alan of Lille (d. 1203) and then by a whole series of Latin authors, including *Albert the Great, *Thomas Aquinas, *Bonaventure, and Roger Bacon, each of whom composed a commentary on the work. For some 70 years it was assumed to be a treatise of Aristotle and was listed among Aristotle's works at the Univ. of Paris as late as 1255. When Thomas Aquinas read William of Moerbeke's translation of Proclus' *Elements of Theology* shortly after 1268, he recognized its Neoplatonic character, and suggested that *Proclus was its ultimate source, and that its author was some Arabian philosopher intimately acquainted with Proclus. An analysis of the work's content indicates that the author may have lived as early as the 9th cent., that he derived his knowledge of Creation from divine revelation, but for the rest composed his book on the basis of Arabic versions of Proclus' *Elements of Theology,* and probably portions of the *Enneads* of Plotinus. He has not been identified with any certainty. BIBLIOGRAPHY: L. Sweeney, NCE 8:693–694 (with bibliog.); Gilson HCP 236–238, 637 n. 3.

[M. R. P. MCGUIRE]

LIBER EVANGELIORUM, see EVANGELIENBUCH.

LIBER PONTIFICALIS, "Book of the Popes," a collection of the popes' lives from St. Peter to Pius II (d. 1464). Because of its wide distribution and claims to authenticity it was extremely influential in shaping the medieval thought about the papacy. It may be divided into two sections: (1) from the 1st to the 5th cent., wherein canonical and liturgical discipline are arbitrarily assigned to various popes; (2) from the 5th to the 15th cent., wherein semi-official accounts are kept of each papal reign. This latter section is indispensable for an appreciation of the history of the papacy and the city of Rome. BIBLIOGRAPHY: J. Chapin, NCE 8:695–696.

[N. KOLLAR]

LIBER SEXTUS, the collection of papal and conciliar legislation promulgated in the bull, *Sacrosanctae* by Boniface VIII, March 3, 1298, and abrogating any legislation it did not include. It was intended to bring the **Decretals* of Gregory IX up to date; thus its name as the Sext, i.e., a sixth book added to the *Decretals,* in order to remedy confusion about intervening papal legislation. Boniface dropped the decretals of many of his predecessors since Gregory; formulated his own in 251 of the Sext's 359 chapters. This collection formed part of the **Corpus juris canonici* of 1582.

[T. C. O'BRIEN]

LIBERA, former absolution rite at the coffin or catafalque in Requiem services; so named from the first word of the responsory beginning the rite; the text is no longer part of the funeral rites since the 1969 revision. The responsory was also that recited after the ninth lesson in the office of the dead: "Deliver us O Lord from eternal death on that dread day when the heavens and earth shall be moved and thou shalt come to judge the world by fire."

LIBERAL THEOLOGY, a complex theological movement in the 19th- and 20th-cent. Europe and the United States. The character and development of the movement can best be examined by considering separately its manifestations in Protestant and RC thought.

In Protestantism. In the Reformed Churches liberalism's features included the view that Christian teaching is simply the expression of natively human religious affectivity; a doctrine of God's immanence in the world; the blending of Jesus' work into the history of human development; optimism with regard to human goodness and social progress; and attention to moral ideals and religious experience rather than doctrine. The remote background for liberal theology, esp. in Germany, was the philosophy of the *Enlightenment, and particularly the idealism of G. *Hegel (1770–1831) and his identification of religion with philosophy. F. *Schleiermacher (1768–1834), the father of Protestant liberal theology, formulated the viewpoint universal to the movement: religion is a basic human sense of total dependence, and Christianity is simply the highest expression of religion. The liberal attitude was formed, as well, by 19th-cent. biblical higher criticism, the development of evolutionary theory, and the sense of confidence in progress through science.

The center of German liberalism was the Protestant theological faculty at Tübingen. There F. C. Baur (1792–1860) formulated a theology that in a pantheistic interpretation of world history included Christianity as the last state of the "evolving God." Influencing liberal attitudes toward the Bible and the historical Jesus were B.

Bauer (1809–92), who denied the historical basis of the NT, and D. F. Strauss (1808–74). Strauss's *Life of Jesus* (1835) represents the NT narratives as "mythical," originating in the poetically inspired reflection of the early Christian community. A. *Ritschl (1822–89) contributed to the movement in the realm of ethics, attempting to relate the gospel to the "secular" aspects of human life. His espousal of the theology of the history of religions, however, called into question the objectively unique character of the Christian religion. In *Das Wesen des Christentums (What is Christianity,* tr. T. Saunders, 2d ed., 1903), A. von *Harnack (1851–1930) defined Christianity as man's consciousness of God's Fatherhood; the dogmas of the Christian Church were a conceptualization (beginning with St. Paul) into Greek thought patterns of this simple consciousness and were a distortion. The *Social Gospel aspect of liberal theology was personified in the bp. of Uppsala, N. *Söderblom (1866–1931), initiator of *Life and Work, the theme of which ("service unites but doctrine divides") reflected the liberal viewpoint.

Horace *Bushnell (1802–76) is called the father of liberalism in the U.S., where the movement came fully into being after the Civil War. The influence of philosophic idealism on religious thought was represented particularly in the "personalistic" idealism of Borden Parker *Bowne (1847–1910). The impact of the higher criticism was fully evident in the *Outline of Christian Theology* (1898) of William Newton *Clarke (1841–1912). The names of Walter *Rauschenbusch (1861–1918) and Washington Gladden (1836–1918) came to represent the broad influence of the Social Gospel in the United States. Liberal theology had many more exponents and came to dominate numerous theological faculties, esp. in the North. By reason of the so-called fundamentalist-modernist controversy, intradenominational disputes, and the liberal tendency to minimize any special sacred function of the Church, the movement had its effect on the denominational pattern in the United States.

Liberal theology may be said to linger wherever the reality of the supernatural in interpreting Christianity is set aside as either inconceivable or at best irrelevant to modern technological man. The pervasive influence it had in the first third of the 20th cent. (in spite of strong high church, confessional, and revivalist counteraction) has ceased. *Crisis theology was initiated just after World War I in reaction against liberalism (see BARTH, KARL). In the U.S., the two *Niebuhrs, both of liberal background, by their writings contributed to the move away from liberal theology and to the rise of *neo-orthodoxy. BIBLIOGRAPHY: J. Dillenberger and C. Welch, *Protestant Christianity in the Light of its Development* (1954); Smith-Jamison 1:279–316; *Liberal Theology* (ed. D. E. Roberts and H. P. Van Dusen, 1942); K. Cauthen, *Impact of American Religious Liberalism* (1962).

In Roman Catholicism. Liberalism in a religious context is in RC thought a somewhat chameleon-like term that takes its color from its context; it is often best defined by the opposite it protests against. Here we leave aside the term's political variations, which may allow a man to feel flattered with the epithet "liberal," yet resentful under the implication of being "a liberal," and consider the term simply in its religious, or rather ecclesiastical implications in Roman Catholicism. It is a 19th-cent. phenomenon, the spirit of which trails into modern times, of opposition to *absolutism, *clericalism, ultramontanism, and the too stiffly official and vested-interest application of traditional forms, both administrative and ideological. It inherited the temper of the Enlightenment and took to heart some of the lessons of the French Revolution. It came to mean something very definite and condemnable to Pius IX after his unhappy love-affair with the *Risorgimento,* namely the rejection of authority not transmitted nor exercised with the agreement of subjects, the exaltation of freedom as a sort of absolute value, and the exclusion of the Church from political life. Whereas to a then contemporary movement among Catholics, represented by *Montalambert and *Lacordaire, who "would die," he declared, "an impenitent liberal," it meant the Church's openness to the fresh winds of democracy, free inquiry, and the social reform then blowing in from the "secular" world.

Rigid lines cannot be drawn. A liberal spirit in theological thought did not necessarily go with a liberal spirit in social and political affairs, or conversely: *Newman and *Manning respectively are cases in point. Nor was the tension finally resolved in favor of one side or the other. Pius IX was followed by Leo XIII, Pius X by Benedict XV, and with a more corporate type of effect, Vatican I by Vatican II: the modernism of yesterday becomes the antimodernism of today. It still healthily continues between those who stress the need for the adaptation of ecclesiastical institutions, discipline, doctrinal formulations, and procedures to contemporary conditions, and those who stress the need for stability and continuity with the past. The opposition is rather between contraries than contradictories: authentic liberals have always been concerned that changes should be made in an orderly and constitutional fashion and above all, with respect for the freedom and worth of individual persons, for which they are derided by more violent, and sometimes more callow exponents of revolution. Hooligans, however high-minded their pretentions, do not qualify for the title. Liberalism, it has been said, can be maintained only when it is protected by the use of enlightened force, and, more cynically, that it tends to disappear with old age and responsibility. What is sometimes called liberalism among contemporary Catholic theologians to some extent reenacts the crisis that faced the Reformation Churches, particularly in Germany nearly a century ago and shook their philosophism, pietism, and revivalism. It may be considered as part of the backwash of the modernist movement, or as among the results of biblical criticism not easily reconcilable in detail with old securities, or as a reaction against Hellenic rationalism and Roman legalism which perpetuates a somewhat facile antithesis of law and liberty, or as an accompaniment to the specialization and decentralization of the religious sciences, or as a heightened emphasis on the command to love coupled with lessened attention to full range of particular demands that love may make, or as a disposition to be content with intellectual agnosticism, or as a prophetic and charismatic response to a kerygma that ventures out into an unknown outside our control and unratified by authority. All this is the parallel in the religious field to the romantic and radical rather than to the classical and whig wings of historical political liberalism.

[T. GILBY]

LIBERALE DA VERONA (*c.*1445–betw. 1526 and 1529), Italian painter and miniaturist in Verona (1467–76) and in Siena where his music MSS survive (Chiusi cathedral and Piccolomini Library, Siena). Late works are *St. Sebastian, Berlin Altarpiece, Adoration of the Shepherds,* damaged frescoes and other smaller works with strong influence of Mantegna in line, and Girolamo da Cremona's rhythmic movement.

[M. J. DALY]

LIBERALISM, POLITICO-SOCIO-ECONOMIC, a term that may stand for a temper, for general policies, or for particular programs. As for the first, respect for and promotion of free, not servile, conditions is thoroughly congenial to Christian social philosophy, which will be neutral about the third when the supposition is verified that purely political and economic measures are directed to the morally permissible. It is on the second sense that we pause to look at its historical setting. It appears early in the 19th cent.: at first few were inclined to disavow it because of its laudatory ring, but soon it came to mean a reforming radicalism that advocated constitutional changes, in contrast to conservatism. In continental Europe and Latin America it went with an attack on old privileges, and in particular on those of the Church. By force of circumstances it was associated with the cause of an open mercantile economy, shaped by the play of competition with the minimum of State control (**laissez-faire* economics), in which prosperity would come by producing as cheaply as possible and selling as dearly. It was all very well for the few; they grew richer and richer with the growth of industrial capitalism and concentration on large units of production, but the many grew poorer, reaping nothing but a wage, and then only when they could get work, while it was an advantage to the system to keep a large pool of the unemployed. The evils were sufficiently obvious before the middle of the century, and the Christian protest against them culminated in the series of social encyclicals that began with Leo XIII and continued with Paul VI.

[T. GILBY]

LIBERALITY, see GENEROSITY.

LIBERATORE, MATTEO (1810–92), Italian Jesuit prominent in the 19th-cent. restoration of Thomism. His *Institutiones philosophicae,* which went through 11 editions, reflected his own intellectual conversion from eclecticism to the thought of St. Thomas Aquinas. He was also a founder (1850) and editor of the influential periodical *Civiltà cattòlica.*

[T. C. O'BRIEN]

LIBERATUS OF CARTHAGE (fl. 535–566), archdeacon and antiheretical writer. As a member of an African mission to Rome and of the African delegation to the East (Constantinople and Alexandria), L. was closely involved in the Western opposition to the imperial condemnation of the *Three Chapters from 535 on. During all this time he was gathering materials for his *Breviarium causae Nestorianorum et Eutychianorum* (555–566), a history of the Christological controversies from *Nestorius to the Three Chapters episode. The work is valuable for the historian inasmuch as it is based on reliable sources. Liberatus provides the first Western testimony to the writings of the *Pseudo-Dionysius. Works: PL 68:969–1050. BIBLIOGRAPHY: F. X. Murphy, NCE 8:713; E. Peterson, EncCatt 7:1259–60; H. Rahner, LTK 6:1012.

[R. B. ENO]

LIBERIAN BASILICA, church built by Pope Liberius (352–366) in the form of a Roman basilica on the Esquiline Hill of Rome. It was rebuilt by Pope Sixtus III (432–440) in honor of the Bl. Virgin Mary and is now known as Sta. Maria Maggiore. The basilica was to honor Mary's divine maternity, just defined at the Council of Ephesus (431). The majestic nave and the mosaics (432–440) are outstanding examples of early Christian art and are the earliest surviving example of the use of an OT cycle for architectural decoration: 29 of the original 44 scenes have been preserved. The Pope is mentioned on the triumphal arch: *Xystus Episcopus Plebi Dei* (Sixtus the Bishop to the People of God). The basilica is the largest of the 88 churches in Rome dedicated to Mary. It is one of the four patriarchal basilicas in Rome that pilgrims are supposed to visit. In the Middle Ages the legend arose that a Roman patrician had a vision of Our Lady who ordered him to build a basilica in her honor on a plot that would be designated by snowfall in August. This is the origin of the feast formerly Our Lady of the Snows (now August 5, dedication of St. Mary Major). The basilica has also important mosaics in the apse of the church dating from 1290 to 1305 in the Italo-Byzantine style found also in Venice's St. Mark and in the Sicilian cathedrals from the Norman time.

[J. MADEY]

LIBERIAN CATALOGUE, a list of the popes from the beginning down to Liberius (352–366) contained in a collection of documents compiled by the *Chronographer of 354. The Liberian Catalogue derives its data from Hippolytus and gives the reign of each pope in years, months, and days. The order of names differs from that found in

Eusebius, who lists: Peter, Linus, Anacletus, Clement, Evaristus; whereas the Liberian Catalogue has: Peter, Linus, Clement, Cletus, Anacletus, Evaristus. Errors such as the Cletus-Anacletus doublet in the Liberian Catalogue have influenced later listings such as that of the *Liber pontificalis*. BIBLIOGRAPHY: F. X. Murphy, NCE 8:714.

[R. B. ENO]

LIBERIUS (d. 366), **POPE** from 352. A Roman and successor to St. *Julius I, L. was the builder of the Liberian Basilica, St. Mary Major. The chief concern of his pontificate was the attempt of *Constantius II to impose *Arianism in the West. After L. had rejected condemnations of *Athanasius extracted by the emperor from councils at Arles (353) and Milan (355), this emperor exiled the Pope to Beroea in Thrace, and put the antipope *Felix II in his place (355). By his own admission in four letters to Eastern bps. (D 138, 141–143) L. acknowledged that during his exile from Rome he capitulated: he excommunicated Athanasius, and signed a Semi-Arian doctrinal formula, the First Formula of *Sirmium (D 139–140), which deliberately omitted the *homoousios of *Nicaea, expressing that the Son was one in substance with the Father. The authenticity of the four letters is certain. In 358 L. was allowed to return to Rome and, Felix being removed, spent the rest of his pontificate defending orthodoxy and the Roman primacy. L. was blamed by contemporaries for his fall, as is clear from accounts in Athanasius (PG 25:741), *Sozomen (PG 67:1152), *Hilary of Poitiers (PL 10:688–695), and the *Collectio Avellana*. The argument, raised again at the time of *Vatican Council I, that L.'s capitulation disproved papal infallibility, is not strong. His signing of the doctrinal formula was not an **ex cathedra* teaching, but the personal act of a weakened man. In spite of its tainted origin, the formula in its literal wording could be understood in a sense short of, but not contradictory to, the teaching of Nicaea. BIBLIOGRAPHY: P. T. Camelot, NCE 8:714–716; E. Weltin, *Early Popes* (1964) 190–206.

[R. B. ENO]

LIBERMANN, FRANÇOIS MARIE PAUL, VEN. (1802–52), religious founder. He changed his name from Jacob when he was converted from Judaism and baptized in 1826 at Paris. He entered the seminary the next year but his ordination was delayed, because of epilepsy, until 1841 in Rome. He had gone there in 1840 seeking papal approval for the Congregation of the Holy Heart of Mary, a congregation he had founded for the apostolate to the blacks. The society accepted missions in Africa and in Haiti, but it merged at the Holy See's direction with the Holy Ghost Fathers. L. became superior general of the revitalized congregation and was responsible for inaugurating its great missionary history. BIBLIOGRAPHY: H. W. Homan, *Star of Jacob* (1959); A. L. van Kaam, *Light of the Gentiles* (1962, pa. 1963).

[T. C. O'BRIEN]

LIBERTAS, Encyclical letter, June 22, 1888, of Leo XIII on human liberty. The encyclical was directed against the rationalistic position that denied the existence of divine law and asserted the supremacy of human reason as the norm of individual and social behavior. Because he is an intelligent being man enjoys a moral freedom, but since intellect and will are imperfect, law is needed to assure objective morality. All law derives from divine law. Liberty in the moral order requires submission to the divine authority. In part of the encyclical Leo speaking primarily to French Catholics, asserts that the Church is not tied to any one form of government, and that her adherents should participate in public affairs. BIBLIOGRAPHY: ASS 20:593–613.

[J. R. AHERNE]

LIBERTINES, a name with a variety of uses in religious history. (1) Antinomian sects have often been called Libertines (see ANTINOMIANISM). (2) In 16th- and 17th-cent. England *Nonconformist, particularly subjectivist, groups (Seekers, Familists, Quakers) were so designated. (3) The term was applied erroneously to the party in Geneva that opposed (1541–1555) Calvin's theocracy. (4) It was used derogatorily of a sect originating in 1525 at Lille. The leaders were a tailor named Quintin (d. 1546) and a priest, Antonin Pocquet (d. *c.* 1560). These Libertines resembled the *Picardians, and are known solely through Calvin's writings against them (esp. *Contre la secte . . . des libertins qui se nomment spirituelz,* 1545). The basis of their teaching was a pantheistic understanding of God's presence and action in men. In consequence they claimed that man was above the law and the Bible and that the only threat to his innocence was any concern over the difference between right and wrong. There is no evidence that this sect was given to immoral excesses. BIBLIOGRAPHY: W. Niesel, RGG 4:356–357. (5) In 17th-cent. France the term *libertin* came to be used in a sense equivalent to *freethinker (e.g., by Pascal in *Apologie de la religion chrétienne*).

[T. C. O'BRIEN]

LIBERTY, SPIRITUAL, see FREEDOM, SPIRITUAL.

LIBIDO, Lat. term for lust (from *libet,* it is pleasing) often in a lewd or wanton sense. In old authors it can be taken as synonomous with "concupiscence" particularly as a sexual urge. In Freudian psychology it signifies specifically one of the two basic instinctual drives, namely the sexual or erotic drive, as opposed to the aggressive or destructive drive. Yet it is applied to so many different manifestations of love and desire that it should not be narrowed to a genital reference. For instance, a person's love of himself is considered as the attachment of libidinal drive to the self (ego-libido or narcissistic libido). When a person loves someone else, this is understood as a transfer of ego-libido to an object (object libido), even if this other person is a parent, child, friend, political leader and not a prospective sexual partner. The fact that a person's love for others in these former categories is not explicitly sexual is explained as a partial deflection or suppression of the libidinal drive, i.e., as a kind of desexualization. Similarly, the energies put into creative and productive works of all kinds are considered as desexualized libido. In this view, the libidinal drives are said to be sublimated, i.e., channeled into substitute activities that are socially and morally more acceptable than direct sexual expressions. Accordingly, libido can be considered as the psychic energy of all positive (as opposed to destructive) drives in general.

This broad use of the terms libido and sexual drive has aroused criticism by moralists and academic psychologists on the grounds of pansexualism now generally rejected. In fact Freud did not go so far as to claim that all positive motivation is libidinal. Nevertheless his theory does see unconscious sexual motivation in many apparently nonsexual spheres of human behavior. BIBLIOGRAPHY: J. Nuttin, *Psychoanalysis and Personality,* (1953).

[M. E. STOCK]

LIBRI CAROLINI, four learned but labored books compiled *c.* 791, purporting to be Charlemagne's answer to a defective account of the Council of Nicaea II (787), which repudiated iconoclasm. Variously attributed to Theodulf of Orléans and Alcuin, they received their final editing from the latter. Although they acknowledged that pictures and images are useful as memorials or decorations in churches, they denied that they may be adored. (The council had indeed refused to representations the degree of worship reserved for God alone, but that seems not to have been clear to Westerners.) The books criticized the role played by Empress Irene at the council; expressed regret that ''double procession'' of the Holy Spirit had been ignored; virtually asserted that general synods were unnecessary, that local synods sufficed; employed many *argumenta ad hominem;* exalted veneration of relics over representations. They did not fail, however, to give evidence of great deference to the Holy See. BIBLIOGRAPHY: L. Wallach, *Alcuin and Charlemagne,* (1959, repr. 1968); A. Freeman, NCE 8:729.

[A. CABANISS]

LIBYANS, ANCIENT, a people living near the N coast of Africa, W of Egypt; the biblical Lubim. In Egyptian documents, allusions to war with the Libyans run through the entire course of Egyptian history. They are mentioned on lists of defeated enemies by Thutmose III, Amen-hotep III, and Merneptah. An Egyptian prophecy from the Middle Kingdom predicted Libya's defeat. They were among the ''peoples of the Sea'' whose invasion was repelled by Ramses III in 1187 B.C. The impoverished nomads of Libya were a traditional source of mercenary soldiers for the Egyptian armies. This dubious tradition provided the occasion for one such Libyan military chieftain in Egyptian service to seize the Egyptian throne with the idea of reestablishing Egypt as an imperial power. His name was Sheshonq, the biblical *Sesac (Shishak), first king of Egypt's 22d Dynasty (935–914 B.C.). Biblical texts mentioning Libya postdate this event and therefore refer to Libya and Egypt as neighbors and allies. Sesac's imperial designs probably explain the giving of asylum to Jeroboam, a potential threat to the Solomonic kingdom. This was a likely tactic for regaining control of Palestine, and part of a strategy that culminated in the Egyptian sack of Jerusalem in 918 B.C., during the reign of Rehoboam.

[E. J. DILLON]

LICCIO, JOHN, BL. (*c.* 1430–1511), Dominican. L. was born near Palermo. His mother died shortly after his birth, and his father abandoned him to the care of an aunt. In his adolescent years, L. was influenced by Peter Geremia in deciding to enter the Dominican Order. After his ordination, L. worked among the poor in Lombardy, Venice, Naples, Rome, and above all, Sicily. In 1487, L. opened a new Dominican house at Caccamo, dedicated to Sta. Maria of the Angels. L. served as vicar of the Sicilian province (1488–89), and in 1494 he was appointed prior of the Caccamo monastery. Throughout his life, L. demonstrated a spirit of humility and a total dedication to the service of the poor. He was beatified by Benedict XIV in 1753. BIBLIOGRAPHY: S. M. Bertucci, BiblSanct 8:33–36; Butler 4:344.

[R. J. BRADY]

LICENTIATE, an academic degree, considered equivalent to a Master's degree, in the fields of theology, philosophy, or canon law.

LICINIANUS OF CARTAGENA, bp. of Carthage towards the end of the 6th cent., apparently a contemporary of Pope St. Gregory I. Little is known of this figure beyond the brief allusions to him found in the writings of St. Isidore of Seville. In his ''Book of Famous Men,'' Isidore mentions a certain Lucinianus (sic), bp. of Carthage, learned in Scripture, and author of many letters: one on the sacrament of baptism and many to an abbot named Eutropius, later bp. of Valencia. After noting that L. flourished in the times of ''the august Maurice,'' and died of poisoning at Constantinople, Isidore concedes that scant remainder of his zeal and labor survived. In a note, the editor of Isidore in PL 83 adds that he himself had come across a letter of Licinianus to St. Gregory.

[E. J. DILLON]

LICINIUS (250–324) **ROMAN EMPEROR** from 307. Of Illyrian peasant origin, he was named Augustus by Galerius (307) and after Galerius's death (311) became joint ruler of the Eastern half of the Empire with Maximinus. In 313 he married Constantine's half-sister Constantia, and made himself master of the East by defeating Maximinus in battle. From Nicomedia he published a letter granting complete freedom of belief to Christians, and jointly signed with Constantine the Edict of Milan. But by 314 the two rulers of the Empire were at war. L. was defeated near Adrianople and forced to cede all the Balkans except Thrace. He gradually returned to a policy of repression of the Christians, the outward sign of his alienation from Constantine. After 9 years of uneasy peace the civil war reached its climax: in 324 L. was completely defeated in a series of battles at Chrysopolis (present Üsküdar) near Chalcedon, and executed the following year. BIBLIOGRAPHY: H. Parker, *History of the Roman World from A.D. 138–337* (1935) 257, 307.

[F. J. MURPHY]

LICINIUS OF ANGERS, ST. (d. *c.*606), bishop. His anonymous biography states that he was born of a wealthy family and was made count of Anjou by Clotaire II. He was engaged to be married, but when the woman he was to marry contracted leprosy, he took this as an indication that God willed him to abandon the world. He became a cleric and was elected bp. of Angers, an office he accepted with reluctance, but he became a zealous pastor and a strong advocate of frequent communion. He erected a monastery near Angers but was forbidden by the king to retire to a hermitage. BIBLIOGRAPHY: AS Feb. 2: 678–682; J. Levron, *Les Saintes du pays Angevin* (1943) 73–84; J. Lahache, BiblSanct 8:40–41.

[P. K. MEAGHER]

LIDANUS, ST. (*c.*1026–1118), Benedictine abbot. Having entered the abbey of Monte Cassino at the age of nine. L. was later permitted to use a portion of the patrimony that came to him to found a monastery with an adjoining church at Sezze. He became its first abbot, and there he lived for the remaining 72 years of his life. He is credited with having drained the Pontine marshes in the region of Sezze. BIBLIOGRAPHY: AS July 1:302–309; V. Venditti, *La leggenda medievale di Lidano d'Antena* (1959); *idem,* BiblSanct 8:41–42.

[P. K. MEAGHER]

LIDDON, HENRY PARRY (1829–90), Anglican theologian. Educated at Oxford, L. was successively vice-principal of Cuddesdon Theological College (1854–59) and of St. Edmund's Hall, Oxford (1859–62). At Oxford he helped to restore the flagging fortunes of the Oxford Movement badly shaken by *Newman's conversion. His Bampton Lectures on the *Divinity of Christ* (1866) enhanced his reputation as a theologian, and in 1870 he became both a canon of St. Paul's and Dean Ireland Professor of exegesis at Oxford. His influence brought some restraint to the spread of liberal opinions. Toward the end of his life he was saddened by the publication of *Lux mundi* (1889) in which some of his younger followers indicated their acceptance of much of modern biblical criticism. His other writings include several volumes of sermons (much admired and liberally borrowed from by other preachers) and a four-volume life of E. B. *Pusey (published posthumously, 1893–97).

[R. B. ENO]

LIDGETT, JOHN SCOTT (1854–1953), English Methodist reformer, editor, and advocate of Methodist union. L. became a Wesleyan Methodist minister in 1876. Together with W. F. Moulton, he founded Bermondsey Settlement for the poor in 1891 and was its warden for 58 years. L. was for 11 years editor of the *Methodist Times* and later joint editor of the *Contemporary Review*. He was a leader in, and first president of, the reunion that brought together (1932) all Methodists except the Calvinistic Methodists into the Methodist Church.

[F. E. MASER]

LIÉBANA, BEATUS OF, see BEATUS OF LIÉBANA.

LIEBERMANN, BRUNO FRANZ LEOPOLD (1759–1844), Catholic pastoral theologian and leader of progressive reform in priestly formation. Ordained priest in 1783, he combined seminary work in Strassburg with pastoral ministry in Ernolsheim. In 1792 he fled with the entire seminary to All Hallows (Allerheiligen) in the Black Forest. From 1795 to 1801 he resumed pastoral ministry in Ernolsheim and was made cathedral preacher of Strassburg in 1801. In 1804 he was imprisoned in Paris until freed by Napoleon, and was then invited by Bp. J. L. Colmar to be rector of the new seminary of Mainz, which he eventually made a model of progressive priestly formation (1805–23), with more emphasis on a pastoral biblical theology than on scholasticism. In 1828 he became vicar general in Strassburg. BIBLIOGRAPHY: L. Lenhart LTK 6:1045.

[E. J. DILLON]

LIEBERMANN, MAX (1847–1935), German painter, studying at the Art School at Weimar (1868–72), and influenced by Munkáscy. Working in Paris (1873–78), L. was impressed by the paintings of Millet, Ribot, and Courbet. After 1875 in regular visits to Holland, he was influenced by Josef and Isaac Israëls. His *Christ in the Temple* (1878, Munich)—considered irreverent in its coarse realism—caused a furor. L. left Munich for Berlin (1884) where he remained for the rest of his life, painting the depressed folk. After an early period of dark palette, L. worked with bright tones in an impressionistic technique (1890), establishing this French style in Germany. Revolting against the established order, he became president of the Secession (1899). BIBLIOGRAPHY: K. Scheffler, *Max Liebermann* (1923).

[M. J. DALY]

LIECHTENSTEIN, predominantly Catholic principality of 157 sq. km., located on the upper Rhine between Austria and Switzerland. Formed in 1719 by a union of Vaduz county with Schellenburg barony, it was part of the Holy Roman Empire until it gained independence in 1866. Allied with Austria till 1919, it now uses Swiss currency and Switzerland handles its foreign affairs. The Catholic Church is established, but the constitution grants religious freedom to all. Referendums of 1971 and 1973 reaffirmed Liechtenstein's status as the only Western country denying the vote to women. German is the national language.

[T. EARLY]

LIENDO Y GOICOECHEA, JOSÉ ANTONIO (1735–1814), Franciscan natural scientist, botanist, and promoter of pure and applied science, who introduced experimental physics into the universities of Central America. Born in Costa Rica he entered the Franciscans in 1748. He was ordained in 1759 and was eventually (1802) elected provincial of the Franciscan province of Guatemala. Early in his career he taught philosophy and then "philosophia recentior" (including optics, geometry, astronomy, and geography) at the Univ. of San Carlos de Guatemala. In 1780 he was appointed president of a commission to investigate the cure of smallpox.

[E. J. DILLON]

LIESBORN, ABBEY OF, Benedictine monastery in the Diocese of Münster, Westphalia, founded in 1131 (originally a convent founded *c.* 815). Influential and rich but not known for its religious life, it became a retreat for nobles. But in 1465, it became a center for intellectual life after is joined the Bursfeld Union. It fell into decline and was suppressed in 1803.

[M. A. MCFADDEN]

LIESSIES, ABBEY OF (*Laetiae, Lesciense*), former monastery founded in the Diocese of Cambrai (Nord, France) in honor of St. Lambert by Count Wibert and his wife Ada in the 8th century. Sacked by the Normans it was restored in 1096 by Thierry, count of Auvesnes, and his wife, Ada of Roussy. With the aid of Bp. Baucher they replaced the canons with Benedictines. The most famous abbot of Liessies was Louis of Blois, author of such spiritual works as *Speculum monachorum* and *Spiritualis vitae documenta.* He governed the monastery from 1530 to 1566 and established a regular observance which lasted until the Revolution. Only the abbey church (16th cent.) remains standing; the body of St. Hiltrude, a 7th-cent. recluse, is preserved there. BIBLIOGRAPHY: Cottineau 1:1607–08; H. Platelle, NCE 8:733.

[J. DAOUST]

LIETBERT OF CAMBRAI-ARRAS, ST. (Liébert; d. 1076), bp. of Cambrai. In this office L. worked for the good of his people and attempted to protect them from Hugo, and from Jean of Cambrai who had L. exiled, L. afterwards returned to Cambrai and led a pilgrimage to the Holy Land (1054). The Saracens had, in the meantime, ordered the Holy Sepulcher closed and this together with misadventures at sea discouraged L. from pursuing the pilgrimage. He is noted for his establishment of a monastery and basilica of the Holy Sepulcher (1063) and the construction of the churches of Ste. Croix and St. Vaast in Arras. BIBLIOGRAPHY: H. Platelle, BiblSanct 8:28–29; Butler 2:621–622.

[J. R. RIVELLO]

LIETZMANN, HANS (1875–1942), German Protestant church historian. He taught at Jena and at Berlin, where he succeeded A. *Harnack. L.'s many works include: *Geschichte der alten Kirche* (4 v.); *Handbuch zum N.T.; Petrus und Paulus in Rom* (1915). From 1920 he was editor of *Zeitschrift für Neutestamentliches Wissenschaft.*

[J. R. AHERNE]

LIFE. Though natural life as such is not the immediate object of theology, it is only by analogy with the natural life that we see around us that we are able to speak of the living God, of Christ our life, of man's supernatural life, and of the eternal life to which man is called. Natural life, as we know it, consists essentially in a self-determination in act, an independence in operation. In the living beings we know this quality is limited, but it is realized so perfectly in the living God, who is pure act, that we cannot simply say that He has life: we must say that He is life. So the OT proclaims the living God, source of all life, ever living to save and to deliver, to love and to punish—the exact opposite of the lifeless and "vain" gods of the gentiles. The NT revelation of the Trinity leads us further into the richness of the mystery of divine life, and this revelation is made that we may know Christ as the one who is sent that we may have life (Jn 10.10), that eternal life that is our communion with the life of the Blessed Trinity, by grace now and in glory hereafter. In his exaltation Christ is "life-giving spirit" (I Cor 15.45): he sends the Holy Spriti to give life to the Church and to his members.

Thus the very terms in which Scripture speaks of man's new life, new birth, etc., justify us in applying to man's supernatural state, necessarily by analogy, the fundamental ideas that we draw from the life we see around us. In this sense life, a share in the divine life, is the very center and core of the Christian mystery: "Anyone who has the Son has life" (1 Jn 5.12). BIBLIOGRAPHY: R. L. Stewart, NCE 8:738–739.

[R. L. STEWART]

LIFE, EXTRA-TERRESTRIAL. The notion that man is not alone in space, that there are other intelligent creatures inhabiting other planets throughout the universe, is not a recent one. Classical Greek philosophy dealt with the possibility, and the scientific revolutions which followed the Copernican speculative shift reawakened interest in extraterrestrial life. In the first two decades of this century the American astronomer Percival Lowell stirred up much popular interest by proposing that Mars is inhabited. Beginning about 1947 there were increasingly frequent and widespread reports of "unidentified flying objects" (UFOs), identified by many people as alien spacecraft. But an intensive scientific study, headed by a distinguished physicist, Dr. Edward U. Condon, discredited this interpretation. The frequency of these reported appearances diminished after about 1962. From the late 1960s forward numerous books were written contending that many artifacts from antiquity were constructed by, or under the direction of, visiting extraterrestrials. Scientists tend to regard such claims as unconvincing.

Paradoxically, despite their skepticism about UFOs and earlier visits to earth, many scientists now regard the search for extraterrestrial life as worthwhile for two basic reasons. First, astronomical studies are leading to the conclusion that there well may be many planets associated with stars in Earth's galaxy which have physical properties suitable for supporting some sort of life form. Estimates as large as 1,000 million such planets have been made. Secondly, there is a growing suspicion among some biochemists that life may arise spontaneously wherever physical conditions are "suitable." Although this has not been demonstrated in the laboratory, experiments have shown conclusively that certain fragments of proteins are spontaneously formed in mixtures of sterile primordial gases. Indeed, many organic molecules have been detected in interstellar space. Some scientists feel that the further evolution to living matter is possible, even inevitable. Scientific searches are being made. The two "Viking" spacecraft sent by the U.S. to Mars in 1976 contained fully automated biological analysis systems. Results to date are inconclusive. Pursuing another avenue, some scientists are pointing radio telescopes toward "likely" stars in search of signals which show signs of intelligence.

Christian theologians have recently speculated on the implications of extraterrestrial life. Questions have centered on whether such intelligent life would be in need of Redemption or could it be in a state of natural perfection; whether it would share in any supernatural vocation; and the relationship between such life and Jesus of Nazareth. No consensus concerning the need or the means of Redemption has been reached. BIBLIOGRAPHY: I. S. Shklovskii and C. Sagan, *Intelligent Life in the Universe* (1966); *Extraterrestrial Intelligence* (ed. J. Christian, 1976).

[J. R. HOUSTON]

LIFE, PROLONGATION OF, see PROLONGATION OF LIFE.

LIFE, RISKS TO. The virtue of *courage has as one of its functions the restraint of recklessness in the face of mortal danger; to risk life needlessly and recklessly is morally wrong (see HEALTH, CARE OF). The meaning of a needless risk is sometimes quite clear, e.g., smoking. But sometimes the case for prudential judgment is not so clear. The primary Christian norm for such a judgment is the hierarchy of human goods: the good of the soul before that of the body; the spiritual good of another person before one's own physical well-being (see ThAq ST 2a2ae, 26). A further criterion for the avoidance of risks is that ordinary means be taken to prolong life (see LIFE, PROLONGATION OF).

[T. C. O'BRIEN]

LIFE AND WORK, branch of the modern ecumenical movement directed toward achieving unity of action among the Christian Churches in the social, economic, and political spheres, without regard for doctrinal differences; also known as Practical Christianity. The movement owed its origin largely to the Lutheran Abp. Nathan *Söderblom of Uppsala, Sweden, who during World War I became convinced that the Churches must unite to work for peace. The first conferences called to that end, in 1917 in Uppsala and in 1919 in The Netherlands, were unsuccessful; national feelings were still too high in the Churches of the countries that were, or had been at war. The first truly international conference of the movement met in Stockholm in 1925 for study and discussion of the Church's place in politics, international relations, education, and economics and industry. The reports of the conference were inconclusive, but it established a Permanent Committee on Practical Christianity, which set up commissions to continue studies on social issues, and an International Christian Social Institute.

The worldwide depression that soon followed, and the rise of National Socialism in Germany, with its far-reaching effects on the German Lutheran and other Churches, presented pressing challenges to the movement, and it soon became apparent that the doctrinal bases for Christian social action could not be ignored. The split within the Church in Germany especially focused attention on the nature of the Church, as a starting point for consideration of Church and State relations. By the time the Life and Work movement held its second international conference, in Oxford in 1937, it was moving closer to the *Faith and Order movement, and many members were about to attend the *Edinburgh Conference. At Oxford a merger of the two movements as a first step toward an international ecumenical council was proposed and approved. The Life and Work movement was absorbed into the *World Council of Churches that sprang from this merger, losing its separate identity but not its influence, which has lived on esp. in the Church and Society division of the World Council. BIBLIOGRAPHY: E. Duff, *Social Thought of the World Council of Churches* (1956); P. Bock, *In Search of a Responsible World Society: The Social Teachings of the World Council of Churches* (1974). *STOCKHOLM CONFERENCE; *OXFORD CONFERENCE.

[D. CODDINGTON]

LIFE PHILOSOPHIES, a term sometimes used to designate the thought of several French, German, and English philosophers who emphasized a surging vibrant principle of life that abstract concepts, scientific theories, and metaphysics tend to belie and ignore. Their biological explanation of life tends toward vitalism, an alternative to materialism and organicism that holds for a substantial entity present in living things, fundamentally distinguishing them from inanimate things. Henri *Bergson and Hans Driesch are the two most explicitly vitalistic of these philosophers. Hans Driesch (1867–1941), a biologist and Aristotelian in philosophy, admitted the operation of physical and chemical laws in biological processes but criticized all reductions of life to physico-chemical explanations. He asserted that there exist entelechies or vital principles in every living organism. Other philosophers whose concerns were less strictly biological and scientific yet whose philosophical concerns focused on some distinctive life-identifying characteristic in human existence include such thinkers as Wilhelm *Dilthey, Oswald *Spengler, Arnold *Toynbee, Ernst *Troeltsch, Édouard *Le Roy, and Maurice *Blondel.

[R. J. LITZ]

LIGAMEN (Lat., bond), short designation for the matrimonial *impediment of an already existing valid marriage that bars any subsequent marriage (CIC, c. 1069).

[T. C. O'BRIEN]

LIGHT, LITURGICAL USE OF. In almost all religions light is made to serve some cultic purpose because of its symbolic value. As a natural sign, light conveys a sense of joy, festiveness, and life. Accordingly, religion uses light to signify solemnity, purity, joy, and esp. the presence of God. Undoubtedly, light has also had a practical function in the liturgy, but in modern times symbolic value has been attached to various uses of it that were originally of practical import. Jewish ritual uses light extensively. The Mosaic Law prescribed that a seven-branched candlestick be erected in the Temple. A perpetual light was burned in the Temple sanctuary, a custom that was later interpreted as an act of reverence for the Torah. The Jewish Feast of the Dedication (Hanukkah) employs candles extensively as symbols of joy and festivity. Pagan religions at the time of Christ also used lights in their ceremonial and as signs of honor before images of their gods. Similarly the Roman emperors had the right to be preceded by torches in court processions.

The Christian significance of light depends largely upon the association of light and God in the OT. Yahweh is the source of light, and it becomes the symbol of his nature (Is 60.19) and presence (Ex 13.21; 1 Sam 3.3; 2 Chr 4.7; 13.11). This identification is carried into the NT and applied to Christ (esp. Jn 1.9; 8.12; 9.5; 12.46). The Nicene Creed calls Christ the "light from light". Subsequent liturgical use centers almost exclusively around this application of light to Christ. The Easter Vigil ceremonies graphically present the risen Lord as the light who dispels the darkness of sin. The paschal candle stands for Christ who brings light to men because of his Resurrection. Baptism, esp. within the setting of the Easter Vigil, emphasizes that the Christian life should resemble the pure flame of a candle. The *Christmas liturgy celebrates the coming of Christ as a light shining in the darkness. The feast of Candlemas (Feb. 2), built around the words of Simeon that the infant Jesus would be a light of revelation to the gentiles (Lk 2.32), obviously employs the theme of light.

Lights are also used in Christianity to convey dignity and reverence, e.g., during processions, on the altar at Mass, at the chanting of the Gospel during solemn Mass, before statues of the saints, and in the sanctuary lamp. Finally, lights were used from about the 5th cent. to show respect for martyrs and other deceased Christians. This custom seems to form the basis of the contemporary practice of burning candles at the coffin during burial services. BIBLIOGRAPHY: D. Dendy, *Use of Lights in Christian Worship* (1959). *LIGHT OF GLORY; *CANDLES.

[T. M. MCFADDEN]

LIGHT, WEEK OF, in the Byzantine Church the name given to the week after Easter Sunday. During this time the royal doors and the deacon's doors of the iconostasis are left open and the veil is not drawn. The Divine Liturgy is celebrated each day exactly as on Easter Sunday itself.

[A. J. JACOPIN]

LIGHT OF GLORY, (*Lumen gloriae*), the created grace which, according to RC teaching, is necessary for the *beatific vision (D 895). Its necessity rests upon the doctrine that the immediate vision of God transcends the natural potentiality of the knower. This supernatural gift is needed to experience the vision of God so that the intellect is elevated and strengthened, much as a habit perfects one of man's powers enabling it to act more perfectly. By means of it, the blessed know God as he is, although none can know him completely since he is incomprehensible. The individual's vision of God is deeper through the *lumen gloriae* according to the intensity of *charity reached in life. The greater the participation of the blessed in the light of glory the greater their vision of God (ThAq ST 1a, 12.6). BIBLIOGRAPHY: K. Rahner, SacMund 1:151–153.

[J. CORDOUE]

LIGHT OF THE WORLD. While almost all religions quite appropriately associate light with goodness and divinity, darkness with wickedness and spiritual evil, it would be a mistake to reduce the biblical imagery of light to a mere figure of speech. Throughout the Bible, God's appearance, his will, his work, his word and at times his very being are described in terms of light. While on one level of interpretation (1 Jn 1.5–7), means that God is altogether good, without any hint of evil, at another level the words were also true for their author in their literal sense: in his very essence God is light, light in the simple physical sense of the word. Hence it is not possible often enough to distinguish clearly between the literal and figurative senses of light in biblical usage. For biblical man, light possesses something of an ontological status because of its intimate association with the Father of lights (Jas 1.17), who "dwells in light inaccessible" (1 Tim 6.16). The creation of light stands at the beginning of the universe and of man according to the priestly account (Gen 1.2–5). God's interventions in human history are surrounded by light, fire, lightning (Ex 3.2; 19.16; Deut 33.2; Ps 17.15; 49.2; Is 30.27; 66.15). Yahweh's glory shines with a brilliant light (Ezek 10.4); he is robed in light (Ps 103.1–2). Light is the sign of the divine presence (Ex 13.21; 1 Sam 3.3), and God's very nature is compared to light (Is 60.19; cf. Ps 35.10; Wis 7.26). Light and darkness possess ethical meaning; they are used in the Bible to describe conflicting ways of life, and hence they are names used to delineate good or evil conduct. Both Testaments of the Bible contain such formulae as "children of light," "to be in darkness," "to walk in darkness," and "deeds done in darkness" (Is 9.2; Ps 82.5; Pr 2.13; 16.15; Sir 23.18; 1 Th 5.5; Eph 5.8–9). Similar phraseology may also be found in the sectarian writings of the Qumran community (IQS 1.9; 2.16; 3.3, 13, 24–25). In 1 Pet 2.9 redemption is depicted as a call from darkness into the light, and in Col 1.13 it is described as a rescue from the powers of darkness.

Light is given in the Bible what may be termed "existential" meaning. Its presence signifies life, redemption, reconciliation, joy to man, and the effects of these gifts: vitality, freedom, honor, peace, security, gladness, well-being. When Yahweh bestows his favor upon mankind, he is said to let his countenance shine upon it (Num 6.25; Ps 4.7; 88.16). Jesus as the Son of God is presented as the bringer of the divine light into a sinful world (Lk 1.79; 2.32; Acts 26.23; 2 Cor 4.6), and this light shines through the glorified humanity of Christ (Mt. 17.2–5; 28.3; Acts 9.3; 22.6–11; 26.13). In the Synoptic Gospels, the imagery associated with light is used by Jesus to depict the revelation and teaching he has brought into the world (Lk 11.33). Those who believe in Jesus are said to participate in this light insofar as their lives reflect their faith in him (Mt 5.14–16; Lk 16.8; Acts 13.47; 2 Cor 3.18; Eph 5.8; 1 Th 5.5). In both Testaments then, a "child of the light" is more than just a knowledgeable and ethical person, but one who experiences a divinely sent happiness because of liberation from evil (Ps 27.1; Job 22.28; Est 8.16–17). The Johannine corpus most consistently and thematically employs the light-darkness contrast to reveal the true identity of Jesus and his mission. Jesus indeed is the "light of the world" (Jn 8.12; 9.5; 12.46), "the true light which enlightens every man who comes into the world" (Jn 1.9). In Jn 8.12, Jesus proclaims himself to be the "light of the world" even as in Jn 7.37–38 he proclaimed himself to be the source of living water. Both of these proclamations seem to have been prompted by the ceremonies of the Feast of Tabernacles (cf. Zech 14.7–8). The illuminations used during Tabernacles, symbolizing the divine presence and the light of the Mosaic Law, may have suggested the specific use of this figure. It must also be remembered that the Exodus account of the wanderings that supplied the imagery of the water from the rock also provided the imagery of a flaming pillar which guided the Israelites through the darkness of the night (Ex 13.21). Also, Wis 18.3–4 witnesses to the tradition which identified the pillar with "the imperishable light of the Law." The meaning of the imagery in both Jn 7.37–38 and 8.12 is that Jesus is the divine revelation of the Father come into the world. This meaning is confirmed in the dramatic action of Jn 9 when as the light (9.5) Jesus opens the blind man's eyes to faith (Jn 9.35–38). Thus, with the Incarnate Word, light and life have definitively entered the world (Jn 1.4–5; 3.19) to dispel the darkness of sin once for all, since those who come to believe in him do not remain in darkness but become children of the light (Jn 3.19; 5.35; 12.46). Shining forth in Jesus as incarnate revealer, God's light illuminates human existence, giving mankind knowledge of the purpose and meaning of life that surpasses that found in the Mosaic Law, and offering a consummation realized in the heavenly Jerusalem of which Christ himself is the light (Rev 21.23–24). BIBLIOGRAPHY: E. R. Achtemeier, *Interpretation* 17 (1963) 439–449; M. Barth, *Ephesians 4–6* (1974) 598–603; R. Brown, *Gospel According to John* (1966).

[T. J. RYAN]

LIGHTFOOT, JOSEPH BARBER (1828–89), Anglican bp. and biblical and patristic scholar. Educated at Trinity College, Cambridge, he was appointed Hulsean professor of divinity there in 1861 and Lady Margaret professor in 1875. He became bp. of Durham in 1879. He is renowned for his commentaries on Galatians (1865), Philippians (1868), Colossians and Philemon (1875), and for his studies of Clement of Rome, Ignatius, and Eusebius of Caesarea. BIBLIOGRAPHY: *Lightfoot of Durham* (ed. G. R. Eden and F. C. Macdonald, 1932).

[T. EARLY]

LIGHTFOOT, ROBERT HENRY (1883–1953), Anglican NT scholar. After ordination in 1909 he was a curate for 3 years; then taught at Wells Theological College (1912–19) and Lincoln (1919–21) and New Colleges (1921–50), Oxford. From 1941 until his death he also edited the *Journal of Theological Studies*. His scholarly works, beginning with his Bampton Lectures, *History and Interpretation in the Gospels* (1935), relied heavily on German form criticism. BIBLIOGRAPHY: *Studies in the Gospels: Essays in Memory of R. H. Lightfoot* (ed. D. Nineham, 1955).

[T. EARLY]

LIGHTS, FEAST OF, see DEDICATION OF THE TEMPLE, FEAST OF.

LIGUGÉ, ABBEY OF (*Locogiacum*), the first monastery established in France, founded by St. Martin *c.*360 on the bank of the Clain, where he lived for about 15 years before being made bp. of Tours. Benedictines later lived in the priory, which depended on the abbey of Maillezais. In the 17th cent., Ligugé was joined to the college of the Jesuits of Poitiers. Suppressed during the Revolution, it was restored in 1853 by Dom Guéranger, abbot of Solesmes, at the request of Card. Pie and was erected as an abbey. Besides the church (late 15th cent.), some old buildings of the former priory still remain, as well as a tower where Rabelais is said to have stayed. Since the 19th cent. many monks of Ligugé have distinguished themselves in the field of history, among them Dom Chamard, Dom Besse, and Dom Charvin. The famous writer Joris Karl Huysmans was an oblate of the monastery. The abbey publishes the scholarly *Revue Mabillon* and the volumes of the collection, *Archives de la France monastique*. BIBLIOGRAPHY: Cottineau 1:1613; H. Rochais, NCE 8:755–756.

[J. DAOUST]

LIGUORI, ALPHONSUS, ST., see ALPHONSUS LIGUORI, ST.

LILBURNE, JOHN (*c.*1614–57), English political agitator, pamphleteer for the *Levelers. In 1638 L. was fined for distributing pamphlets against the hierarchy. In *England's Birthright* (1645, often repr. as *An Agreement of the People*) he set forth the program of the Leveler movement, including religious equality; he wrote many other pamphlets urging constitutional reform. He was tried for treason in 1649, but was acquitted; further political agitation led to exile and then confinement until 1655, in which year he became a Quaker. BIBLIOGRAPHY: M. A. Gibb, *John Lilburne, the Leveller: A Christian Democrat* (1948); L. V. Hodgkin, *Shoemaker of Dover* (1943) 44–52; P. Gregg, *Free-born John* (1961, repr. 1974).

[T. C. O'BRIEN]

LILIENFELD, ABBEY OF, Austrian Cistercian abbey in the diocese of St. Pölten, founded by Duke Leopold in 1202 and settled by monks from Heiligenkreuz. It prospered steadily till the 14th cent., declined during the Reformation, but was revitalized in the 17th century. The great early Gothic church remains, but the monastery was rebuilt in Baroque. The abbey has a fine library and serves 19 parishes. BIBLIOGRAPHY: S. Brunner, *Ein Cisterzienserbuch* (1881) 138–205; M. Matschik, *Stift Lilienfeld* (1952); N. Mussbacher, NCE 8:756.

[L. J. LEKAI]

LILLY, JOSEPH (1893–1952), biblical scholar. Ordained a Vincentian in 1918, he taught Scripture at The Catholic Univ. of America, and became general secretary of the Catholic Biblical Association of America (1942–48). He is coauthor of the Kleist-Lilly version of the New Testament (1954) made from the Greek text.

[J. R. AHERNE]

LILY, WILLIAM (1468?–1522), English grammarian, headmaster of Colet's school for boys at St. Paul's, London. He graduated from Oxford, made a pilgrimage to Jerusalem, stayed at Rhodes, then studied in Italy, chiefly Roman antiquities, while he perfected his Latin and Greek. Teaching in London, he became a friend of Thomas More, with whom he translated Greek epigrams into Latin elegiacs, showing great command of both languages. When Colet established his school, he asked L. to be headmaster and to write a short work on Latin grammar. This was prefaced by Colet's introduction. The text remained in use in England, changed and enlarged, and, under the title *Eton Latin Grammar,* was made compulsory in schools in 1758. L. ranks with Grocyn and Linacre in Greek scholarship. BIBLIOGRAPHY: J. H. Lupton, DNB 11:1143–45.

[M. M. BARRY]

LIMBO (Lat. *limbus,* border, edge). In medieval theology the "limbo of the fathers" meant the waiting place or condition in which the just who had died before Christ's Passion remained until his opening of the gates of heaven. The "limbo of the infants" meant the destination of the unbaptized who died innocent of personal sin. *INFANTS, UNBAPTIZED.

[T. C. O'BRIEN]

LIMBOURG BROTHERS (fl. 1399–*c.*1439). Most noted Franco-Flemish illuminators working for the great patron of the arts, Jean, Duc de Berry. The brothers Paul (Pol), Hermann, and John (Jehannequin) Malouel from the Lowlands, apprenticed (before 1399) to a goldsmith in Paris, were early attached to the court of Burgundy, producing the *Heures d'Ailly* (*c.*1403, Rothschild Collection) for the Duc de Berry, showing the influence of the *Boucicaut Master, *Jacquemart de Hesdin, and Melchior *Broederlam. Most important was the Italianate quality of Hesdin to which the brothers added their finesse of line and execution, and attention to details deriving from the goldsmith art. Their major work is the *Très riches heures du Duc de Berry,* the epitome of late medieval illumination, begun 1413, and completed after the Duke's death by Jean Colombe—combining with the Hours of the Virgin, a Calendar of the *labors of the months, the Zodiac, and compositions related to Florentine panels of T. Gaddi and Brunelleschi's *Isaac.* From such contributions to the illuminator's art early Flemish panel painting developed.

[M. J. DALY]

LIMINA APOSTOLORUM, see AD LIMINA VISIT.

LIMITED ATONEMENT, the theological position that Christ died only for the elect. The point is implicit in any theology of *predestination that restricts God's will and plan of salvation to include only some, not all, men. In its specific reference limited atonement is one of the five points of Calvinism as defined by the Synod of *Dort (1619) in rejecting *Arminianism. The Arminians taught that Christ died for all men, and that the saving effects of his redemptive act are available to all. The Canons of Dort (Second Head of Doctrine), condemned this position and affirmed that Christ died not for all but only for the elect. One of the propositions ascribed to C. *Jansen's work **Augustinus* and condemned by Pope Innocent X (1653) affirmed a similar teaching (D 2005; cf. D 523).

[T. C. O'BRIEN]

LINACRE, THOMAS (1460–1524), English humanist and physician. A scholar and man of learning, he was one of the first Englishmen to study Greek in Italy and to bring back the "new learning" to Oxford, where as friend of John Colet, William Grocyn, and William Lily and teacher of Erasmus and Thomas More he formed part of a brilliant group of Oxford humanists. Though royal physician of Henry VIII, he seems to have avoided political involvements and devoted most of his energy and fortune to the establishment of the Royal College of Physicians in London. Ordained late in life he spent his last years mainly in priestly duties. His literary works can be divided into grammatical and medical, the latter consisting chiefly of very accurate and elegantly phrased translations of Galen and other Greek scientists. BIBLIOGRAPHY: J. F. Payne, DNB 11:1145–50; G. N. Clark and A. M. Cook, *History of the Royal College of Physicians of London* (3 v., 1964–72).

[M. J. BARRY]

LINCOLN, CATHEDRAL OF, superb 13-cent. English Gothic, built (1074–93) by Bp. Remigius, with additions by Alexander the Magnificent (1123–48). The earthquake of 1185 destroyed all but the magnificent Norman W towers and W front. A new Gothic cathedral was begun (1192) by Bp. St. *Hugh of Lincoln, under the master of works, Geoffrey de Noier, whose brilliantly inventive style in the "bizarre" choir with its asymmetrical vaulting and elaborate patterning of nonstructural ribs culminated in England's distinctive and dramatically decorative, gossamer lierne, fan, and star vaultings. In the English square-ended E chancel, the rays of light fall on the altar, through the 8–59-ft high traceried windows, a paean to the sun significantly expressive of the philosophy of *Robert Grosseteste, bp. of Lincoln, whose treatise on optics extolled light as the "noblest of natural phenomena . . . the mediator between bodiless and bodily substance—the spiritual body and the embodied spirit. . . ." Lincoln's famous Angel Choir (1256–80) named for figures with outstretched wings filling the spandrels of the triforium, is among the finest achievements of English Gothic in serene proportions and exuberant but controlled decoration. The elegant clerestory windows derive from Reims via Westminster Abbey. Geoffrey's central tower having collapsed, the new tower (1238–55) by Master Alexander, carrying his characteristic diagonal lattice or trellis pattern and raised in the 14th cent. by Richard of Stowe to 271 ft, is England's highest and finest central tower. Wooden needle spires covered with lead extended the towers to a soaring 524 feet. Lincoln was fortunate in her many reforming bps., among whom were Hugh of Wells (1209–35), Robert Grosseteste, O. Sutton (1280–99), and John Dalderby (1300–20). The beautiful Angel Choir enshrines the tomb of St. Hugh of Lincoln, a place of pilgrimage.

[M. J. DALY]

LINDAU BOOK COVER, a 9th-cent. metal casing of the Lindau (Ashburnham) Gospel Book from the Monastery at Lindau, Austria, made on the Continent under strong Anglo-Saxon influence. The cover, which has later additions and repairs, is a masterpiece of the goldsmith's art, ornamented completely with reliefs and interlace, in frames studded with enamels, and semiprecious stones raised on claw feet so that the light may penetrate beneath—effecting full brilliance. It is now in the Pierpont Morgan Collection, New York.

[R. L. S. BRUCE-MITFORD]

LINDAU, CONVENT OF, a Benedictine nunnery in Tirol, founded *c.*,817. Known as St. Marien, the convent was prosperous. The nuns adopted the Rule of St. Augustine in the 12th cent. and in the early 13th cent. founded a hospital. Disregarding pressure, Lindau did not accept Protestantism. The convent was secularized in 1805, and its church—rebuilt after a fire—still serves as a parish church.

[M. A. MCFADDEN]

LINDISFARNE, ABBEY OF, a monastery on Lindisfarne Island (or Holy Island) founded by St. Aidan *c.*635. Aidan was succeeded by SS. Finan, Colman, and Cuthbert, all abbot bishops. It was the center of missionary activity in Northumbria and Mercia, and the first abbey to suffer from Viking attacks (793), which eventually caused the monks to flee to Chester le Street *c.*883. The see was transferred to Durham in 995. The abbey was taken over by Benedictines of Durham in the 11th cent. and in 1536 by the Dean and Chapter of Durham. The Lindisfarne Gospels are now in the British Museum. BIBLIOGRAPHY: E.N.O. Gray, "Notes on the History of Lindisfarne and its Place in the Conversion of England to Christianity," *History of the Berwickshire Naturalists' Field Club*, 31 (1948) 98–109; H. H. E. Craster, "Red Book of Durham," EHR 40 (1925) 504–532; Knowles-Hadcock.

[C. MCGRATH]

LINDISFARNE, BOOK OF (7th cent.), Vulgate Gospel Book, with prefatory matter, written and splendidly decorated at Lindisfarne by Eadfrith *c.*698. A masterpiece of Hiberno-Saxon art, it is disciplined, showing strong Mediterranean influence. The interlinear translation into Anglo-Saxon added in the 10th cent., one of the longest extant Old English texts, is of great linguistic importance. The binding by Aethelwald of Lindisfarne, enriched with gold, silver, and gems by Billfrith, was lost. The codex is now in the British Museum. BIBLIOGRAPHY: R. L. S. Bruce-Mitford, NCE 8:771. *ANIMAL STYLE.

[R. L. S. BRUCE-MITFORD]

LINDORES, ABBEY OF, former Benedictine monastery in Fifeshire, Scotland. Founded in 1191, its congregation was formed with monks from Kelso. Although the abbey survived the wars of independence, the monks were expelled by reformers in 1543. In 1559, John Knox and his followers plundered the abbey. It is now a ruin.

[M. A. MCFADDEN]

LINDSEY, THEOPHILUS (1723–1808), English Unitarian. He was educated at St. John's College, Cambridge. As vicar at Catterick from 1763, he began to accept Unitarian views, esp. through his friendship with J. *Priestley. He joined in an appeal to Parliament, the Feathers Tavern petition (1772), against obligatory subscription to the *Thirty-Nine Articles; when the appeal was rejected, he gave up his Anglican ministry and from 1774 preached Unitarianism in London. Among his works was *Historical View of the State of the Unitarian Doctrine and Worship from the Reformation to Our Own Time* (1788).

LINDWORSKY, JOHANNES (1875–1939), German Jesuit psychologist, who integrated experimental with theoretical psychology on thought and volition. His own training was influenced by J. *Fröbes and O. Külpe. L. taught at Cologne (1920–28), then at Prague. His translated works include: *Experimental Psychology,* (tr. H. De Silva, 1931); *Theoretical Psychology* (tr. *idem,* 1932); *Psychology of Asceticism* (tr. E. A. Heiring, 1936); *Training of the Will* (tr. A. Steiner and E. A. Fitzpatrick, 1955).

[T. C. O'BRIEN]

LINE, ANNE, ST. (*c.*1565–1601), English martyr. Although reared as a Calvinist, Anne Heigham became a Catholic and married Roger Line, also a convert. Shortly thereafter, Roger was arrested for assisting at Mass (1586). He was released and exiled to Flanders where he died (1594). For some time she acted as the head of a house in London organized by John Gerard, the Jesuit missionary, as a refuge for priests; she managed the housekeeping and financial affairs, taught children, and answered inquiries. After Gerard's escape from the Tower (1597) she fell under suspicion and moved to a safer location. Here she and others were arrested after Mass (1601). She was tried and executed on the charge of harboring a priest. She was canonized in 1970. BIBLIOGRAPHY: N. Del Re, BiblSanct 8:55–56; Gillow BDEC 4:247–251; Butler 1:436.

[V. SAMPSON]

LINGARD, JOHN (1771–1851), historian. Descendant of an old English Catholic family, L. studied for the priesthood at the English College in Douai, France. In 1793 he was forced to flee by the revolutionary mob and returned to England. Completing his theological studies he was ordained in 1795. Prefect of studies at the college of Crook Hall, he taught philosophy there, and published *The History and Antiquities of the Anglo-Saxon Church* (2 v., 1806). When the college moved (1808) to Ushaw, L. taught there. In 1811 he was appointed to Maynooth but refused the appointment because the chair had been held by a cleric who apostatized. At a small mission near Lancaster, he led a secluded scholarly life the remainder of his days. In 1817 he went to Rome where Card. Consalvi opened to him the Vatican archives. The first three volumes of L.'s monumental *History of England* appeared in 1819, the fourth volume in 1820, and by 1830 the eighth and final volume, bringing the history to the Revolution of 1688. L.'s objectivity, which irritated overzealous Catholics, was a revelation to Protestants. In addition, the work was a needed corrective to the biased histories of England then in vogue. The reception of the work was enthusiastic and today the sections on the 14th and 15th cent. and the Reformation are still highly regarded.

[J. R. AHERNE]

LINGUISTIC ANALYSIS, the philosophical method of analysis or description of linguistic function as a means of removing conceptual difficulties and the internally quite diverse philosophical tradition that regards such procedure as the primary or even the only method of philosophy. The use of the investigation of language is not new in philosophy, being employed notably by Socrates and the Sophists, and is compatible with widely diverse doctrinal positions. But the philosophy of the English-speaking universities of the 20th cent. has been dominated by a novel and deliberate conception of philosophy's role: the function of philosophy is not the acquisition of new knowledge, but the clarification and elucidation of what is already known by the analysis or description of the meaning of propositions.

Linguistic analysis began with the work of G. E. Moore (1837–1958). Moore sought to vindicate the truisms of common-sense belief, e.g., that breakfast comes before lunch, against the extravagances, e.g., the belief that time is unreal, of the metaphysical idealism dominant at the time. Moore, thinking that the meaning and truth of much of ordinary discourse were obvious, sought only to provide the analysis necessary to make their truth unmistakably clear. In general, his analysis consisted in replacing a word or sentence normally used by some other expression both exactly equivalent and less puzzling. He provided neither a metaphysical theory of the real, although he did not rule one out, nor a systematic theoretical basis for his method of analysis.

Having once been initiated by Moore, linguistic analysis has passed through three stages of development. The first was that of Bertrand Russell (1872–1970) and Ludwig Wittgenstein (1889–1951). It was indeed strictly analytic, holding analysis, the reduction or translation of the complex into its ultimate constituents, to be the proper method of philosophy. But it was less strictly linguistic in that, while linguistic in method, its professed goal was to discover the true structure of the real. Rather than relying on conventional linguistic tools, Russell's program of "logical atomism" was inspired by the mathematical logic of which he was one of the principal developers. By using this logic to analyze compound or "molecular" propositions into simple or "atomic" ones, he hoped to arrive at that ultimate atomic proposition which would correspond to the ultimate atomic fact. This procedure is clearly based upon the assumption of the rationalist thesis that the structures and relations of the real are the same as those of the human conceptual and linguistic apparatus, an assumption equally evident in Wittgenstein's aim of making every statement an adequate picture of the reality it describes. Both Russell, with his famous theory of descriptions, and Wittgenstein proposed analysis as a linguistic transformation that could reveal logical form, rather than the misleading grammar of natural languages. Starting from ideas derived from Wittgenstein's classic *Tractatus logico-philosophicus* and from mathematical logic, the group of philosophers known as the Vienna Circle began the next movement, logical positivism. Now chiefly to be found in the U.S., this point of view adds to the positivist tradition the analytic concern for logic and meaning. Logical positivists divide meaningful sentences into the empty tautologies of logic and mathematics that say nothing about reality, and factual propositions that are meaningful only insofar as they are empirically verifiable; this is the celebrated "verification principle." For the logical positivist, then, despite the ultimately metaphysical nature of his positivism, all metaphysics and all theology are meaningless. The task of the philosopher can be but to establish a logically impeccable foundation for empirical science. Rudolph Carnap (1891–) and A. J. Ayer (1910–) are logical positivism's most important spokesmen.

The third stage of linguistic analysis, drawing inspiration from, once more, Wittgenstein and his *Philosophical Investigations* (1952), has been heavily critical of the reductionism of logical atomism and logical positivism. In this stage it is more rigorously linguistic, deriving its criterion of meaning from an examination of the structure of language and of what can be said in language. Rather than being analytic, it is expressly descriptive, seeking to find how language actually works, not how it should. Prominent among the school of "ordinary language analysis," as it is known, are John Wisdom (1904–), Gilbert Ryle (1900–76), John Austin (1911–), and P. F. Strawson (1919–).

[R. E. HENNESSEY]

LINGUISTICS, MISSIONARY CONTRIBUTIONS TO. Although the contributions of missionaries to the science of language have had as their goal the advancement of the Gospel rather than the advancement of linguistic theory, missionary accomplishments have been numerous and universally acknowledged. Christian missionaries have consistently recognized that the faith must be proclaimed within the accepted patterns of each culture, and that language is both an important component of any culture and an essential tool in communicating the faith. Early European mission history attests to the deep cultural impact that missionaries had on the written languages of the nations which they evangelized, e.g., the early apostles to the Germanic, Slavic, Irish, and Anglo-Saxon peoples. This missionary commitment to linguistics continued even more vigorously in the colonial period. Dictionaries, grammars, and catechisms were produced everywhere that missionaries were sent. In North America, grammars in 86 languages and catechisms in 77 languages were produced by 1699. Similar studies in over 200 African languages were accomplished by missionaries by 1940. Equally extensive work has been characteristic of the missionary effort in India, Japan, Korea, Indochina, the Philippines, and the South Pacific.

The 20th cent. saw a continuation and intensification of missionary interest in language study. Two separate movements have been responsible for this intensification in quantity and quality, the one Catholic and European, and the other Protestant and American. Father Wilhelm Schmidt, SVD (d. 1954), known esp. for his anthropological studies, began the journal *Anthropos* and the ethnological and linguistic research center Anthropos Institute, now located near Bonn, Germany. The center encourages and trains missionaries to do ethnological and linguistic field work and has published countless articles and books of linguistic interest. The American Protestant counterpart is the Summer Institute of Linguistics founded by W. C. Townsend. The Institute gives courses to some 500 missionaries annually, and is engaged in analyzing and describing languages, Bible translating, and literacy work. The statement of Vat II MissAct (26) constitutes an apt mandate for this characteristic missionary activity, "Let missionaries learn languages to the extent of being able to use them in a fluent and polished manner. Thus they will find more easy access to the minds and the hearts of men." BIBLIOGRAPHY: Streit Dindinger; *Bibliography of the Summer Institute of Linguistics 1935–1968* (ed. A. C. Wares, 1968); D. Crystal, *Linguistics, Language, and Religion* (1965); A. Burgmann, NCE 8:776–781. *MISSIONS; *ADAPTATION, MISSIONARY.

[L. J. LUZBETAK]

LINUS, ST. (d. 76 or 79), **POPE,** first successor of St. Peter. Almost nothing is known of L., but he is accepted as the undoubted 2d bp. of Rome on the testimony of St. *Irenaeus (*Adv. haer*. 3.3, 2; PG 7.849), who also identified him as the Linus mentioned by St. Paul (2 Tim 4.21). L.'s pontificate lasted 12 years. The claim that he was a martyr seems false, as there is no mention of any persecution of the Roman Church at the time of his pontificate. His burial place is unknown. A record of the martyrdom of SS. Peter and Paul attributed to L. is apocryphal. His name is in the Canon of the Mass. BIBLIOGRAPHY: A. Amore, BiblSanct 8:56–57; Duchesne LP 1:121.

[P. F. MULHERN]

LIOBA, ST. (d. 782). A relative of St. Boniface, she was professed in Wimborne Abbey, from which, in company with 29 other nuns, she was later sent to aid him at Mainz. She became abbess of Bischofsheim and founded other convents in Germany. Highly regarded by the Carolingian rulers, she was buried at Fulda at the specific behest of Boniface. BIBLIOGRAPHY: "Life" by Rudolf of Fulda in Talbot's *Anglo-Saxon Missionaries in Germany;* her letters in MGH Ep. Sel., I, nn. 29, 67, 96, 100; J. Stéphan, BiblSanct 8:60–61.

[J. DRUSE]

LIPCHITZ, JACQUES (1891–1973), leading 20th-cent. Lithuanian American sculptor. Largely self-taught in the Louvre, L. carved Cubist forms (1914) influenced by Picasso. With J. Gris he worked interlocking forms (*Man with Guitar,* 1916) and polychromed reliefs (1918). A one-man show in Paris followed (1920) and a commission from Albert Barnes of Merion, Pa. for five reliefs (1922). Forms of increased scale and dramatic voids mark the group *La Joie de vivre* (1927), for the garden of Vicomte Charles de Noailles (reworked for Whitney Museum, New York, 1960). L. was preoccupied with the embrace—for life or death—*Jacob Wrestling with the Angel* (1932) and the repeated *Prometheus,* symbol of man's triumphal struggle in life. With a first exhibition in the U.S. (1932) he continued sensuous, full-bodied, baroque shapes (*Mother and Child, Return of the Prodigal*) and multiple images (*Benediction,* 1942), then began a *Sacrifice* series, from primitive worship to the Virgin Mary (*Prayer,* 1943). In 1941 L. fled to the United States. Commissioned by Fr. Couturier to carve a baptismal font (aborted as a sculpture piece) for the church of Notre-Dame-de-Toute-Grâce, Assy, L. created the unique *Notre Dame de Liesse* (1948) one of the most remarkable religious sculptures of our age (casts for Philip Johnson, Indiana; monastery, Iona). His *Government by the People* (1976) is in Penn Plaza, Philadelphia. L., in works of drama and depth, attained greatness in modern sculpture. His works are numbered in private collections and museums throughout the world. BIBLIOGRAPHY: A. M. Hammacher, *Jacques Lipchitz, His Sculpture* (1961).

[M. J. DALY]

LIPPERT, PETER (1879–1936), German Jesuit theologian and writer. Collaborator on the *Stimmen der Zeit,* impressive orator, and radio preacher, he combined clarity wth wisdom and compassion, and influenced both the style and substance of spiritual dialogue. Many of his works exist also in English translation. BIBLIOGRAPHY: F. Hillig LTK 6:1070.

[E. J. DILLON]

LIPPI, FILIPPINO (*c.*1457–1504), Italian painter. Son of Fra Filippo Lippi; pupil of Botticelli. He completed Masaccio's frescoes in the Brancacci Chapel, Florence; other frescoes in Florence and Rome. His altarpieces have great sweetness and devout feeling. The *Esther* series (1478), the *Adoration of the Magi* (*c.*1475–80), and the *Adoration* (*c.*1480) are Botticellian. The *Apparition of the Virgin to St. Bernard* (1486) prepares the way for the late works, in which monumental qualities gradually give way to increasing agitation of form and neurotic expression, prefiguring Florentine mannerism.

[K. B. NEILSON]

LIPPI, FRA FILIPPO (1406–69), Italian painter, born in Florence. L. was professed as a Carmelite (1421). The Medici were among his patrons. His altarpieces, reflecting the scientific discoveries of the Renaissance, have uniquely appealing human qualities. L. painted important frescoes in Prato (1452–60) where he was convent chaplain. Through the intervention of Cosimo de' Medici, Pope Paul II released the painter and the nun Lucrezia Buti, his model, from their vows (1461). To them was born the painter son Filippino Lippi. L. died in Spoleto after designing for the cathedral frescoes, which, because of his illness, were likely executed by his shop, L.'s early works show massive figures in the style of Masaccio, (*The Madonna and Child of Corneto Tarquinia,* 1437), but his reputation was established by the *Barbadori Altarpiece* (*c.*1437) in which he added his own heightening color to Florentine space and sculptural form, the richer and more complex *Coronation of the Virgin* (*c.*1441–47) with inferences of Fra Angelico, and the *Annunciation* (*c.*1438) in which he shows mastery of perspective and composition. The *Adoration of the Magi* roundel (*c.*1445–47) shows decorative qualities foreshadowing Botticelli, with Florentine mystic and pietistic qualities in the 1450's. L. remains an artist of importance, bridging a gap between Masaccio and his contemporaries, and through his own innovations shaping the style of Botticelli, Filippino Lippi, and many other artists.

[K. B. NEILSON]

LIPPOMANO, LUIGI (Aloysius Lippomanus; 1500–59), Italian bp. and cardinal, one of the presidents at the Council of Trent in 1551–52. Nuncio to Poland in 1555, he aided the cause of resistance against Protestant incursions into that country. In 1558 he became bp. of Bergamo.

LIPSIUS, JUSTUS (1547–1606), humanist. A Belgian by birth, he taught at Louvain, Jena, Leyden, and again at Louvain, accepting whichever form of Christianity —Catholic, Lutheran or Calvinist—was official at the place. His chief scholarly works were editions of Tacitus and Seneca; he also influenced a renewal of interest in Stoic philosophy by his *De constantia* (1584). Like *Erasmus his aim was to treat Christianity as an ethical program in which doctrinal differences were inconsequential.

[T. C. O'BRIEN]

LIPSIUS, RICHARD ADELBERT (1830–92), German Lutheran professor at the Univ. of Leipzig, Kiel, and Jena; exponent of *liberal theology; active in the missionary endeavor of the Lutheran Church.

LIQUEFACTION. (1) a change from a dry to a liquid state in the relic of a saint's blood, as with the relic of St. Januarius at Naples; (2) the melting of the affections, a metaphor for one effect of love as it expands and opens the heart to the one loved; like "fervor" it may describe an effect of *charity as well (ThAq ST 1a2ae, 28.5).

[T. C. O'BRIEN]

LISBOA, ANTONIO FRANCISCO, see ALEIJADINHO.

LISBOA, CRISTÓVÃO DE (*c.*1590–1652), Portuguese Franciscan missionary to Brazil; noted literary figure, preacher, and natural historian; champion of the rights of the Indians. He was sent to Brazil with 18 friars by the Portuguese King, after 1621; was the first custos (guardian) of the Franciscan vice province of Maranhão-Pará in N Brazil, with quasi-episcopal authority. He was the foremost champion of the rights of the Indians in the area of his jurisdiction, although he enjoyed limited success on their behalf, esp. in Pará. He returned to Portugal in 1636 in broken health. BIBLIOGRAPHY: M. C. Kiemen, NCE 8:785.

[E. J. DILLON]

LISMORE, ABBEY OF, a monastery in County Waterford, Ireland, founded apparently by St. Mo-Chutu in 638. It became the religious center of the Déissi clan. Although sacked six times by the Scandinavians, it flourished as a center of learning. Many of its community were venerated as saints, and it became one of the strongholds of the Culdees. Its later history is that of the origins of the Dioceses of Lismore. BIBLIOGRAPHY: C. McGrath, NCE 8:788.

[C. MCGRATH]

LISZT, FRANZ (1811–86), pianist, composer. The many-sided genius of L. shows itself in his virtuoso performance on the pianoforte, his compositions, and in his towering influence on music and musicians in the 19th century. Hungarian by birth, he was a true cosmopolitan, becoming a center of musical attraction in Paris, London, Rome, and Weimar. The virtuoso period began at Vienna in 1822 with his first public appearance. There he enjoyed public acclaim and the respect of Beethoven and Schubert. Going to Paris in 1823 where he continued studying and playing in public, L. became a friend of Chopin and Berlioz and was influenced by the literary masters Victor Hugo, Lamartine and George Sand. A liaison with the Countess d'Agoult lasted from 1833 to 1869.

The years of whirlwind concert tours from 1839 to 1847 made L. a renowned figure all over Europe. In 1848 he settled at Weimar where he was to remain for 13 years. There he married Princess Carolyn von Sayn-Wittgenstein. Their home became the center for the modern trends in music. As permanent conductor of the Weimar Symphony, L. encouraged young and unknown composers by performing their work. This was part of the essentially generous nature of the man. His contributions, whether to aid victims of disaster or erect a statue of Beethoven, were a lifelong witness to his concern for others. Among works performed or revived on the Weimar stage were Wagner's *Tannhäuser, Lohengrin,* and *The Flying Dutchman; Benvenuto Cellini* by Berlioz and many others. Weimar became a European capital of music. The firm friendship between L. and Wagner belongs to this period.

The transition from virtuoso to composer began in 1847. L. continued to teach at Weimar until 1858 when he left for Rome and again after his return. Here in a kind of retreat, he turned to the devout life, taking minor orders and wearing clerical garb (hence the name Abbé Liszt). Without a question his espousal of the new life was genuine.

The last triumphs were in Paris (1886) and London (1886), where he attended a performance of two great works *Graner Mass* and *The Legend of St. Elizabeth.* The English visit was a royal progress, a fitting capstone to the brilliant career; he died after returning to Weimar.

The amazing diversity of L.'s compositions includes as major categories music for the pianoforte, transcriptions orchestral and operatic, symphonic poems, choral works, songs, music for the organ, and works for pianoforte and orchestras. The *Apparitions* and *Transcendental Studies* are original and sensitive mood pieces for the pianoforte. With the Paganini studies they laid the foundation for modern piano technique. Justly famous are the numerous Hungarian Rhapsodies. At Weimar L. wrote the best-known of his piano compositions, including *Harmonies poétiques et religieuses.* L.'s transcriptions of operas such as *Don Giovanni* are brilliant compositions. In orchestral composition L. developed the symphonic poem, a work designed to convey the prevailing mood of the subject. *Faust* and *Dante* are examples. L.'s tone-coloring greatly influenced that of Wagner. In the area of music for pianoforte and orchestra the most brilliant is *Tolentanz,* variations on the Gregorian *Dies Irae.* The *Christus* and *St. Elizabeth* exemplify the category of choral music.

[J. R. AHERNE]

LITANY, a form of responsorial prayer in which a leader speaks or sings a series of petitions and/or invocations, and the congregation answers with a set response. The term also refers to a procession with accompanying petition, e.g., the *Greater Litanies of April 25 and the *Lesser Litanies on the 3 days before the *Ascension. As a prayer form, the litany is known in most religions. The *psalms contain several litanies, e.g., Ps 135. The early Christian Church seems to have employed a litany with the response **Kyrie eleison* (Lord have mercy) which was incorporated into the Mass and subsequently shortened to the response alone. In the Eastern liturgies, this response occurs very frequently. The **Agnus Dei* (Lamb of God) of the Roman rite Mass may also be considered a litany. The *Prayer of the Faithful now used at Mass is actually a restoration of an ancient litany. Most significant is the *Litany of the Saints, comprising a lengthy invocation of holy persons, a list of petitions, Psalm 69, and several concluding orations. Many other litanies have been approved for public recitation: *Litany of Loreto (1587), Holy Name (1862), Sacred Heart

(1899), St. Joseph (1909), and Most Precious Blood (1960). BIBLIOGRAPHY: E. J. Gratsch, NCE 8:789–790.

[T. M. MCFADDEN]

LITANY OF LORETO, prayer composed of a series of invocations, titles given to the Blessed Virgin Mary, expressed by a leader to which the congregation replies, "pray for us." The litany dates from the early Middle Ages and is perhaps influenced by Eastern practices of compiling such lists of titles of Mary. The name comes from the litany's association since the mid-16th cent. with the Marian shrine at Loreto. It is the only Marian litany in common use in the Catholic Church of the West.

[J. DALLEN]

LITANY OF THE SAINTS, prayer consisting of a series of saints' names read by a leader, to each of which the congregation responds, "pray for us," followed by a series of invocations and petitions addressed to Christ with appropriate responses. The second part is the more ancient and forms the basis of the Litany in the Book of Common Prayer. In the Roman rite there was no uniformity in the catalogue of saints in the prayer until Pius V. The 1969 revision of the litany provides both a long form and a short form (the latter for use at rites during Mass, such as ordinations, dedications of churches, and the blessing of the baptismal font at the Easter Vigil); it also makes provision for variations both in the list of saints and in the petitions, according to the occasion.

[J. DALLEN]

LITERAL SENSE OF SCRIPTURE, the meaning of a biblical book or text intended by the author and conveyed by his words. This sense is called literal not as opposed to figurative, since metaphor, allegory, and other figures of speech are part of the biblical idiom; but as distinguished from possible senses beyond the meaning intended by the author, the so-called spiritual senses, the *sensus plenior* or the typical sense (see SENSES OF SCRIPTURE). In modern biblical studies, the absolute primacy of the literal sense in the interpretation of Scripture is universally accepted. With few exceptions, exegetes maintain that there is only one literal sense for any given passage. This does not mean, however, that the literal sense is always a plain or easy sense. Hermeneutics in determining rules of interpretation, and exegesis in applying them must rely on the resources of modern scholarship in investigating the language, literary forms (see LITERARY GENRES, BIBLICAL), and the purposes and environment of the author. The diversity of the biblical books, which evolved over a 2,000-year period, indicate the complexity of determining the literal sense. Since the Bible is regarded as divinely inspired, Christians generally have regarded the traditional understanding of any text to be a norm for determining the literal sense. The Protestant principle referred to as private interpretation does not reject this norm, but presupposes that there is a right understanding of the Bible guaranteed to the believer. For RCs the authentic interpretation of the Bible by the *magisterium is a principle of determining the literal sense. In practice, however, the interpretation has been applied in very few instances. While the Church, as well, points to the Fathers of the Church as an important witness to Christian tradition, modern RC exegetes regard the actual patristic exegesis to be of limited value. BIBLIOGRAPHY: R. E. Brown, JBC 2:606–610, 619–621, bibliog. 605.

[T. C. O'BRIEN]

LITERALISM, adherence to the letter of a statement, ignoring in the assessment of its meaning the context of the statement or its use of figures of speech. Such literalism is a feature of *fundamentalism in the interpretation of Scripture. Sometimes it arises from a misunderstanding of the varied types of literature present in the Bible. Genesis 1, e.g., was long interpreted as a descriptive account of the divine work of creation in six days. The Bible itself can succumb to literalism, as is clear from Heb 11.4–7. In these instances literalism may place the Bible in apparent conflict with science, to the detriment of religious faith itself. In other cases the simplistic acceptance of a biblical dictum, e.g., Mt. 5.39, may offend against common sense. The antidote to literalism in the interpretation of the Bible is the awareness of literary form, i.e., the particular kind of literary vehicle the inspired author has chosen to convey his thought or reflection. Jesus himself used the traditional rabbinic method of teaching in parables, which, however, were sometimes taken in the early centuries of Christianity as true stories. In the 20th cent. much progress has been made in identifying the various literary forms in the Bible, thus opening the way to a clearer understanding of the true literal meaning of Scripture, i.e., what the inspired writer actually intended to say in his employment of the type of writing current in his time. Literalism may also result from a false principle of biblical interpretation known as *biblicism.

[C. P. CEROKE]

LITERARY GENRES, BIBLICAL, the predocumentary sources involved in the composition of the books of the Bible. The phrase is associated with the method of biblical interpretation called *form criticism (*Formgeschichte*), originated by H. *Gunkel, and acknowledged by both Protestant and Catholic exegetes as valid and necessary. The 19th-cent. historical criticism of the Bible limited itself to the analysis of the sources from which the actual biblical books derived (see DOCUMENTARY THEORY). The study of literary genres goes further, recognizing that the contents of both OT and NT existing in fixed written form often had passed through numerous and complex oral traditions over a long period before becoming written literature. In many cases, also the literary forms do not reflect the creation of one individual, but are the product of the collective mind in Israelite society. Comparison with the literature of other ancient Near Eastern people, in the case of the OT, and with Roman and Hellenistic literature in the case of the NT, indicates how the biblical literary genres were drawn from culturally more advanced peoples and adopted and modified. The form critic's task, which is essential to questions of historicity and authorship of the biblical books as well as to interpretation of the meaning of the text, is to establish basic and original types of the oral traditions and the process by which the original units were combined until the book stage was reached. The study recognizes that some books in the later Hebrew tradition were literary productions in the usual sense. It also recognizes that oral and written forms often developed side by side over long periods; but the larger units of written tradition, which became entire books, belong to later stages of the development of the traditions now contained in the Bible.

Sitz-im-Leben or "life situation" has been a key phrase in the study of literary genres. The form critic seeks to reconstruct the setting in which a particular type of tradition unit evolved, recognizing that this has a vital bearing on the meaning of the actual tradition units of this type. The values, interests, and ideas of Israelite society varied from age to age and from group to group. The form critic recognizes that the total combination of circumstances in which life was lived at a given time or in a given milieu had a determining effect upon the modes of expression in which a speaker or writer would seek to communicate his ideas.

By way of concrete example the following literary genres have been suggested as typical for the OT writings: in the poetic sections, drinking songs such as the ones apparently cited in Is 22.13 and 56.12; working songs such as the "Song of the Well" in Num 21.17–18 (an incantation sung while a well was actually being dug); funeral songs, e.g., the Lament over Saul and Jonathan, 2 Sam 1.19–27; songs of victory, e.g., 1 Sam 18.7, etc. The most important genres of Hebrew poetry, however, are unquestionably the psalm categories, the hymns, laments, thanksgivings, royal psalms, songs of Zion, etc. Of the prose types the novel, etiological story (purporting to explain some natural or historical phenomenon, e.g., the pain of childbirth in Gen 3.16, or a pillar of salt near the Dead Sea, in Gen 19.26); ancestor stories (explaining the origins of a people, e.g., the birth of the Ammonites and Moabites from Lot's incestuous and drunken union with his daughters in Gen 19.32–38) may be instanced as representative of early genres of oral tradition. The study of literary genres has also to show how these most basic units are progressively combined into cycles and become more complex, the larger cycles subsuming smaller and more localized complexes of tradition, and how the great pan-Israelite traditions emerge to become the nucleus of all these complexes and so of the actual books of the Old Testament.

In the case of the NT an initial distinction is usually drawn between discourse and narrative. Discourse may include such types as wisdom sayings (e.g., Mt 5.3–9), community rules (e.g., Mt 18.15–22), parables, and allegories. The narratives are divided into miracle stories, historical narratives, etc. In establishing and interpreting these and numerous other genres, it is important to retain openness and flexibility of mind, and to remember that much work still remains to be done in establishing the traditional forms of Semitic expression. BIBLIOGRAPHY: A. Robert, "Littéraires (genres)" DB Suppl 5:405–421; L. Alonso-Schökel, "Genera Litteraria," *Verbum Domini* 38 (1960) 3–15; *idem,* NCE 8:803–809; *idem, Understanding Biblical Research* (tr. P. J. McCord, 1963); A. Suelzer, JBC 2:598–600.

[D. J. BOURKE]

LITERATURE, EROTIC, see EROTIC LITERATURE.

LITHUANIA, republic of the U.S.S.R.; located between Latvia and Poland, with capital at Vilnius. The predominant religion is Catholicism. In 1251 Grand Duke Mindaugas and many of his people accepted Christianity, Pope Innocent IV recognized Mindaugas as king, and a Teutonic Knight, Christian, became the first bp. of Lithuania. However, the murder of Mindaugas in 1263 was followed by a pagan reaction, lasting until 1386 when Grand Duke Jagiello accepted baptism in Cracow so that he could marry Jadwiga, heiress to the Polish throne, and become King Ladislaus II. The combined Lithuanian-Polish state constituted one of the strongest powers of medieval Europe, in 1410 inflicting a historic defeat on the Teutonic Order. But after Russia freed itself from the Mongols, it began expanding and by 1815 had incorporated all of Lithuania. At the Reformation, many leading families of Lithuania became Protestant, but a Catholic effort led by the Jesuits reversed the tide. Later efforts of the czars to convert Lithuania to the Orthodox faith intensified nationalistic resistance. In the 19th cent. Catholic clergy led in a national revival, and in 1918 Lithuania became independent. But in World War II it was incorporated into the U.S.S.R. A Lithuanian Jewish community was almost totally exterminated during the years of German occupation (1941–44). After World War II, Soviet oppression of the Churches was severe, but it eased to some extent following the death of Stalin (1953).

[T. EARLY]

LITHUANIAN NATIONAL CATHOLIC CHURCH, This church was started in 1914 with the help of F. *Hodur, founder of the Polish National Catholic Church of America. The Lithuanian National Catholic Church existed exclusively among Lithuanian emigrants in the U.S., and had no basis in the home country in Europe. It became independent in 1923 but merged again with the Polish National Catholic Church in 1964. There is one congregation existing today, the Divine Providence Church in Scranton, Pennsylvania. It has a few thousand adherents.

[J. MADEY]

LITTA, ALFONSO (1608–79), cardinal. Of a famous Milanese family, L. became abp. of Milan in 1652 and a cardinal in 1666. He was a vigorous administrator and reformer of his clergy and defended the rights of the Church against the King of Spain.

[J. R. AHERNE]

LITTA, LORENZO (1756–1820), cardinal, diplomat. Of the same Milanese family as Card. Alfonso Litta, he was ordained in 1789. Named a titular abp. in 1793, he was sent to negotiate with Kościuszko better observance of the rights of the Church in Poland, a goal he achieved. In 1796 L. was appointed legate to St. Petersburg. There he influenced Czar Paul to restore confiscated Catholic Church property and to allow reorganization of Latin rite and Ruthenian jurisdictions. In 1799 L. had to leave Russia, became papal treasurer, and was created cardinal in 1801. A foe of Napoleon, he was exiled from Rome (1809–14). In this period he wrote *Lettres diverses,* a refutation of Gallicanism. In his last years he was cardinal vicar of Rome.

[J. R. AHERNE]

LITTERAE LUNARES, the first 20 letters of the alphabet as used in the Julian calendar to indicate the age of the moon on any day of the year. These letters in ancient times were of some use in the determination of the date of Easter.

LITTLE, ANDREW GEORGE (1863–1945), British historian. After leaving Balliol, L. went to Göttingen and Dresden, where he gained proficiency in methods of research. His extensive knowledge of Franciscan MSS aided him in producing his now-famous *The Grey Friars in Oxford* (1892). In that same year L. was made a Fellow of the British Academy. He taught history at Cardiff and was reader in paleography at Manchester. He founded the *British Society of Franciscan Studies* and was its general editor until its demise in 1937. His *Initia operum latinorum* (1904) is an essential reference for MSS of the 13th, 14th, and 15th centuries. BIBLIOGRAPHY: D. L. Douie, NCE 8:853; F. Powicke, *A. G. Little (1863–1945)* (1947).

[F. D. LAZENBY]

LITTLE BROTHERS OF JESUS, religious congregation founded (1933) in South Oran, Algeria, by Father René Voillaume in Algeria. The brothers form a diocesan congregation with simple, perpetual vows. For liturgical purposes some few are ordained. However, all receive philosophical and theological training. Their work of ''preevangelization'' through a witness of presence was inspired by the ideals of Charles de *Foucauld. Living in small communities, they work with and among the people, doing manual labor in factories and fisheries; and they also serve lepers and primitive people. In 1975 there were 232 members in 75 houses. BIBLIOGRAPHY: M. Carrouges, *Le Père de Foucauld et les fraternités d'aujourd'hui* (1963).

[M. T. REILLY]

LITTLE BROTHERS OF MARY, see MARIST BROTHERS.

LITTLE CHURCH OF UTRECHT (OBC, Kerk der Oud-Bisschoppelijke Clerezie), the Church originating in the 18th cent. with the *Schism of Utrecht, in 1899 entering into the Old Catholic communion, and now called the Old Catholic Church of the Netherlands. The Church of Utrecht became formally separated from Rome with the election (1723) of Cornelius Steenoven as abp., and his consecration (1724) by a suspended French missionary bp., Dominique Varlet. The latter also consecrated Steenoven's three successors, the third of whom, P. J. Meindaerts (1739–67), provided for episcopal succession by reviving the Sees of Haarlem (1742) and Deventer (1758). The formal schism was the culmination of protracted disputes with Rome, arising from the Utrecht clergy's defense of the right to elect its ecclesiastical superior (the province was under a vicar apostolic from 1592 because of the disruption of the hierarchy caused by the Reformation) and from accusations of *Jansenism against the Dutch clergy made at Rome, esp. by the Jesuits. These causes were embodied in the case of the deposition in 1704 of the vicar apostolic, Pieter Codde, who had been summoned to Rome (1699) on charges of Jansenism and had refused to sign the anti-Jansenist formula imposed by Alexander VII. The Utrecht Church, which became known also as the Jansenist Church of Holland, refused to accept the pro-vicar apostolic appointed by Rome, Theodorus de Cock, and ultimately chose Steenoven. During the above-mentioned Meindaert's episcopacy a synod held (1763) at Utrecht gave hope of reunion by its rejection of Jansenist teachings; but neither this nor subsequent attempts at reconciliation with Rome in 1823 and 1827 succeeded. By its rejection of the dogmatic definition of the Immaculate Conception (1854) and papal infallibility (1870), and esp. by acceptance of the *Declaration of Utrecht (1889), which rejected the Council of Trent, the OBC became clearly separated in teaching from Rome; in 1950 it also rejected the definition of the Assumption. In discipline, the Church did away with obligatory clerical celibacy in 1923 and imposed a vernacular liturgy. It was from Bp. H. Heykamp of the OBC that the first Old Catholic bp., J. H. Reinkins, received episcopal consecration (1873). In 1889 the *Union of Utrecht bound the OBC in communion with Old Catholic Churches of Germany and Switzerland. In 1968 the OBC had about 7,500 active communicants in three dioceses. The OBC maintains close relations with many Protestant bodies; it is also an active member of the World Council of Churches. Consecration by the abp. of Utrecht has been the source of *apostolic succession for some Churches and is important in the question of the so-called **Episcopi vagantes*.

[T. C. O'BRIEN]

LITTLE COMPANY OF MARY (LCM), the Blue Nuns, a community for nursing the sick, founded in 1877 at Nottingham, England, by Mother Mary Potter. She based their spiritual life on the teaching of St. Louis de Montfort. The community gradually spread to N and S America, Australia, New Zealand, Korea, Scotland, Malta, Ireland, S

Africa, and Italy. The motherhouse is in Rome where, as in many other cities, they operate a hospital. In 1893 the Sisters opened their first house in the U.S. in Chicago and thence in 1930, went to Evergreen Park, Ill., which is the headquarters for five foundations in the U.S. and one in Argentina. In 1975 the community maintained 48 houses and had 746 members.

[M. T. REILLY]

LITTLE FLOWER, THE, see THÉRÈSE DE LISIEUX, ST.

LITTLE GIDDING, home of Nicholas *Ferrar in Huntingdonshire, 18 miles from Cambridge, an establishment in 17th-cent. England that bore some resemblance to a religious community. It was essentially a household, its personnel either family members, schoolmasters, or servants. Mary Wodenoth Ferrar purchased Little Gidding in 1625. Sharing in the restoration of manor house and chapel were: her son Nicholas, ordained deacon in 1626; an older son John, his wife, and children; and a daughter, Susannah Collett, her husband, and their 16 children. Schoolmasters and servants rounded out the group, for Little Gidding was school and dispensary for the neighborhood. Its chapel, according to Izaak Walton, attracted "many of the Clergy that were more inclin'd to practical piety, and devotion, than to doubtful and needless Disputations. . . ." The "constant and methodical service of God" which Walton praised included private and liturgical prayer (Psalms, Scripture, hymns), night vigils, and reading at table from the Bible or Foxe's *Book of Martyrs*. Nicholas *Ferrar's sojourn in Italy influenced the richly decorated chapel and the practice of the art of bookbinding; two illustrated harmonies of the gospels allegedly made by Ferrar himself are in the British Museum, one, dated 1635, said to have been made for Charles I, who visited Little Gidding in 1633 and 1642 (also 1646?). In his later years Ferrar reassured a visitor that he held as seriously as any part of his creed the general Protestant conviction that the Pope was antichrist, but the Anglo-Catholic household attracted the animosity of Puritans; in 1641 an anonymous pamphlet was addressed to Parliament, entitled *The Arminian Nunnery; or, A Brief Description and Relation of the late erected Monastical Place, called the Arminian Nunnery at Little Gidding in Huntingdonshire*. In 1647 house and chapel were despoiled by adherents of Parliament and the little community dispersed; the church was restored in 1853. T. S. Eliot called the last (1943) of his *Four Quartets* "Little Gidding:" "Here, the intersection of the timeless moment/Is England and nowhere. Never and always." BIBLIOGRAPHY: I. Walton, *Life of Mr. George Herbert* (1670); H. C. White, *Metaphysical Poets* (1936, repr. 1972).

[M. S. CONLAN]

LITTLE LABYRINTH, see LABYRINTH.

LITTLE MISSIONARY SISTERS OF CHARITY, the Piccole Suore Missionarie della Carità (PMC), founded at Tortona, Italy by Don *Orione in 1915 as part of his apostolate of mercy (see SONS OF DIVINE PROVIDENCE). The Sisters labor in many countries of Europe and S America. They came to the U.S. in 1949, and their American headquarters are in East Boston, where they staff a home for the aged. The motherhouse is in Rome. In 1927 Don Orione organized a group of the blind as the Perpetual Adorers of the Most Blessed Sacrament, the cloistered and contemplative branch of the community. In 1977 they numbered 882 members worldwide in 50 houses.

[T. C. O'BRIEN]

LITTLE OFFICE OF THE BVM, a shortened version of the Roman rite's Common Office of the BVM. It probably originated as a votive office in the 9th century. By the 12th cent. it was widely used, and its recitation, in addition to the Divine Office, was regarded as obligatory for some regular and secular clergy. It also formed a principal part of Books of Hours and primers used by devout lay folk. Pope Pius V (d. 1572) abolished all general obligation to recite it, but in some monastic orders its use continued as a matter of constitutional obligation. After the Council of Trent it was adopted by many modern congregations of religious women for choral use rather than the Divine Office. Vatican Council II declared that the recitation of such an office in accordance with a religious institute's constitutions is part of the public prayer of the Church (Vat II SacLit 98). There were few seasonal variations in the Little Office, but these were increased in 1952 when a number of new lessons, little chapters, and collects were added for different periods of the year.

[N. KOLLAR]

LITTLE ORATORY, BROTHERHOOD OF THE, a lay auxiliary attached to each house of the Congregation of Priests of the Oratory. The members, called brothers, meet weekly for prayer and instruction, and undertake corporal works of mercy. The Little Oratory was St. Philip *Neri's first foundation; the congregation developed out of it.

[M. T. REILLY]

LITTLE SISTERS OF JESUS, founded in 1939 in Algeria by Sister Madeleine of Jesus. Like the *Little Brothers of Jesus, they are inspired by the spirit of Charles de *Foucauld. The spirituality of the sisters centers on the Blessed Sacrament and on the hidden life of Jesus. Their apostolate is one of witness and example. They earn their living by manual labor on farms, in hospitals, factories, etc. They live mostly among Islamic peoples. Their motherhouse is in Rome. In 1975 there were 1,032 members in 209 houses. In the U.S. the central house is in Washington, D.C.; they are also established in Boston, Chicago, and Fairbanks, Alaska.

[M. T. REILLY]

LITTLE SISTERS OF THE ASSUMPTION, religious community founded (1865) in France by E. *Pernet and

Marie Fage (1824–83) to minister to the sick poor in their homes. The institute was approved by Leo XIII (1897). The sisters follow the Rule of St. Augustine. As of 1975, the community included about 1,888 members in 176 houses. The community has been in the U.S. since 1891 and has houses in New York, Massachusetts, Pennsylvania, and North Carolina.

[M. T. REILLY]

LITTLE SISTERS OF THE HOLY FAMILY, a congregation founded in 1880 in Canada for the purpose of providing domestic help in kitchens, laundries, and sacristies of colleges, seminaries, and episcopal residences. Alodie Virginie Paradis (d. 1912), a Sister of the Holy Cross, assigned for 20 years to domestic work at St. Joseph's College, Memrancook, New Brunswick, found that there were many young women who desired to do this work. Mère Marie Léonie, as she was called in religion, with the help of Camille Lefebvre, CSC, formed the new community, whose motherhouse now is in Sherbrooke, Quebec. The work of the congregation extends throughout Canada, the U.S., Brazil, Italy and Central America. In 1975 there were 80 houses and 885 members.

[R. C. CLIGGETT]

LITTLE SISTERS OF THE POOR, community founded in France (1839) by a peasant, Jeanne *Jugan, and called until 1847 Servants of the Poor; papal approval, 1854. Besides the three standard vows, they add a vow of hospitality. They are mendicants, depending on God's providence for support of their work. Their apostolate is to provide homes and care for men and women, 60 years of age or over and without means. The sisters since 1958 have been assisted by oblates who follow a rule of life and wear a uniform garb but take no vows, and by auxiliaries who donate their time and resources. The first American house was opened in 1868 in Brooklyn, N.Y. There and in Baltimore and Chicago are provincial houses subject to the motherhouse in St. Pern, France. In 1975 worldwide membership consisted of 4,890 sisters in 280 houses.

[M. T. REILLY]

LITTLE SISTERS OF THE POOR AND AGED, community founded by Bl. Teresa *Jornet e Ibars in Spain about 1870. The general motherhouse was established in Valencia, Spain, in 1873. The community received papal approbation in 1876 as Little Sisters of the Poor, but the title was changed in 1882 to avoid confusion with another congregation. Their work spread to Italy, Germany, Portugal, and to South America. In 1975 there were 2,985 members in 214 houses.

[M. T. REILLY]

LITTMAN, ENNO (1875–1958), German Oriental scholar. A master of languages, L. took active part in expeditions to the Middle East from the time he was 24. He edited inscriptions in Latin, Greek, Ethiopic, and Arabic. In 1921 L. was appointed professor of Semitic languages and literature at the Univ. of Tübingen, Germany. Among many publications was his translation from the Arabic of the *Thousand and One Nights* (1921–28).

[J. R. AHERNE]

LITURGICAL BLESSINGS, see BLESSINGS, LITURGICAL.

LITURGICAL BOOKS, EASTERN, listed by rite, include only books in actual use.

(1) Byzantine: the *Typikon*, regulating the structure of the Offices, with an introductory section on more general prayers and ceremonies, regulations for days of fixed date and of movable date, an appendix on special ceremonies, and a table of occurrence and concurrence for feasts from Jan. 11 to May 25 (the period when such a table is required); the *Leitourgikon*, also called the *Hieratikon* or the "Little" *Euchologion*, with the prayers of the priest for Vespers and *orthros* (absent in older editions), the three Liturgies, and the rites of the sacramental *mysteria* except those of ordination; the "Great" *Euchologion*, containing all that is in the *Leitourgikon* along with the complete ritual for ordinations, funerals, monastic ceremonies, blessings, and functions proper to particular days; the *Evangelion* and the *Apostolos* containing, respectively, the readings from the Gospels and those from the Epistles and Acts, for Liturgies and Offices throughout the year; the *Psalterion*, with the Psalms (divided into liturgical sections) and the nine canticles ("odes") for *orthros*; the *Horologion* with the ordinary of the canonical Hours and the *troparia* and *kondakia* for each day of the month and some supplementary material; the *Oktoēchos* with eight sets of Sunday Propers, one for each of the eight musical tones; the *Paraklētikē* (or "Great *Oktoēchos*") with eight sets of Propers for each day of the week; the *Triōdion* with the Propers of the temporal Office from the 10th Sunday before Easter until Holy Saturday, inclusive; the *Pentēkostarion* with the Propers of the temporal feasts from Easter until the Sunday after Pentecost; the *Mēnaion*, or Proper of all feasts of fixed date for the entire year, in 12 volumes (one per month). Certain parts of this Byzantine library exist in extracts. There is no equivalent of a Latin Missal nor Breviary, although Catholic editions of the *Leitourgikon* are expanded in the direction of a Missal, and compressed collections for the Office, called *Anthologia* have been published in various forms by both Orthodox and Catholics. The Catholics also have, in Greek and Arabic, a single, much abbreviated volume called a *Horologion*, not be confused with the authentic liturgical book of the same name.

(2) Armenian: the equivalent of the Byzantine *Typikon* is the *Tonatzoytz*. The texts for use at the altar in the Eucharistic Liturgy constitute the *Khorhrdatetr*. The common of the Office is found in the *Zhamakirq*, which also often includes diaconal material for the Liturgy not found in the *Khorhrdatetr*. The biblical readings for both the Liturgy and the Office are in the *Djashotz*. The variable hymns of the Liturgy are contained in the *Tagharan*, those of the Office in the *Sharagan*. The *Zhamakarguthiun* in the Gregorian Armenian Church is the *Zhamakirq* with the full Psalter; in the Catholic Armenian Church it is a sort of breviary, combining the *Zhamakirq* with elements of the other books necessary for the Office. The *Yaysmavourq* contains the homilies and the lives of the saints to be read daily at the beginning of Vespers.

(3) East Syrian: the Chaldean Catholics have a Missal, a Lectionary, a three-volume Breviary, a Ritual, and a Pontifical, all provided with a Latin title page in addition to the Syriac one. The Nestorians have a printed book containing the three anaphoras with their *ordo communis* and the rite of baptism, a printed edition of the *K^e^t̲āb̲â d̲-q^e^d̲ām wad̲-b̲āt̲ar* of use in the Office, and booklets for marriages and funerals. The *Ḥud̲râ, Gazzâ,* and *Kashkul* for the Office and other liturgical texts remain in MS among the Nestorians.

(4) West Syrian and Maronite: the Catholic Syrians have a Missal, a Diaconal, a ferial Breviary, a seven-volume festive Breviary, an ordinary Ritual, a Pontifical, and a Psalter. The Jacobites have a printed ferial Office and printed Diaconals, but all else remains in MS, the contents of different MSS varying considerably. Indian Jacobites have printed a collection of some anaphoras with the *ordo communis* (*Ṭak̲sô d-qûrrōb̲ô),* some festive Offices, a ferial Office and parts of the Ritual. The Maronites have a Missal, Ritual, ferial and festive Offices, and an Pontifical, all printed.

(5) Coptic: the book called *Euchologion* or (Arabic) *Khūlag̅ī* contains the three Liturgies with the Morning and Evening Offices of Incense, and the "Book of the Seven Prayers of the Night and the Day" contains the ordinary of the monastic cycle of the Divine Office. Everything else —Lectionaries, ritual books, Propers for the Offices of Incense, etc.—is published in parts, with varying bases of division and combination.

(6) Ethiopic: the national (non-Catholic) church has, for Eucharist: the *Qeddāsē* containing the anaphoras and their *ordo communis*, and the *Zemmārē* with the various chants; for the Office: the *Deggua, Ṣoma Deggua,* and *Mawāšē'et,* all containing Propers for various days and seasons of the year (each differing in both content and arrangement), and the *Me'erāf* containing the common of the Office. Ritual texts are contained in separate booklets or grouped differently in various MSS. The *Qeddāsē* and some ritual texts have been printed. The Ethiopian Catholics also have a printed *Qeddāsē* and some parts of the Ritual, as well as a book entitled *Masafā Sa'atat* containing extracts of the old office books arranged to make a kind of *horologion* for private recitation. BIBLIOGRAPHY: S. Salaville, *Introduction to the Eastern Liturgies* (tr. J. M. T. Barton, 1938) 185–207 for Byzantine and Armenian books; A. Baumstark, *Liturgie comparée* (3d ed. 1953) 237–259, surveys the material of each rite that has been published either in liturgical books or in scholarly works, but does not always state clearly what a given book contains.

[A. CODY]

LITURGICAL BOOKS (ROMAN RITE), the official books used in liturgical services conducted in accordance with the Roman rite. Such books may be published only by the authority of the Holy See or by competent or local authority with the approval of the Holy See. The general revision of service books was entrusted to the Consilium established by Paul VI in 1964 to implement the liturgical reform prescribed by Vatican Council II, and with the Consilium's dissolution, to the Congregation of Sacraments and Divine Worship in 1969. Some of the principal books at the present time are: (1) The Roman *Ritual published under Paul V in 1614, revised in 1952 by Pius XII, with further revisions having taken place under Paul VI. Those rites already revised are the Rites of Christian Initiation of Adults; Baptism for Children; Confirmation; Holy Communion; and Worship of the Eucharist outside of Mass; Reconciliation; Matrimony; Anointing and Pastoral Care of the Sick; Religious Profession; and Funerals. (2) The Roman *Missal with its divisions: the Sacramentary, containing the celebrant's part of the Mass, the first revision published since 1570; and the Lectionary, containing a 3-year cycle of scriptural Readings for Mass on Sundays and solemn feasts; a 2-year weekday cycle; and a 1-year cycle for the commemorations of saints; in addition to Readings for a great variety of Masses, Ritual Masses, and Masses for various needs. There are also Responsorial Psalms to follow the First Reading and verses to precede the Gospel. (3) The Roman *Pontifical promulgated by Clement VII in 1596 with current revisions of Part I completed under Paul VI. The Pontifical contains rites whose ordinary minister is the bp., such as the Rites for the Institution of Readers and Acolytes; Admission to Candidacy for Ordination as Deacons and Priests, the Ordination of Deacons, Priests, and Bps., the Blessing of Oils and the Consecration of the Chrism, the Blessing of an Abbot or Abbess, and the Consecration to a Life of Virginity. (4) The *Liturgy of the Hours, formerly the Roman Breviary promulgated in 1568 by Pius IV, reformed by Pius X, Pius XII, John XXIII, and its present form and structure by Paul VI. Translations of these rites prepared by the International Commission on English in the Liturgy and approved by Rome have been issued by decree of the English-speaking episcopal conferences (the last, the Pontifical scheduled for 1978), and use of these official translations is obligatory. (5) The Ceremonial of Bishops, published under Clement VII in 1600 and currently under revision according to the liturgical reform of Vatican Council II. (6) The Roman Calendar, which consists of an arrangement throughout the year of a series of liturgical seasons and feasts of saints for purposes of divine worship, revised and approved by Paul VI in 1969. The future offers plans for the revision and publication of all ritual books.

[C. J. NOONE]

LITURGICAL CONFERENCE, an association composed primarily of RCs whose purpose is to promote a full, active, and knowledgeable participation in the Church's worship. It began in 1940 as the Benedictine Liturgical Conference and became, in 1943, the National Liturgical Conference. The conference is a private organization. Although approved by the bps., it is not an agency of the hierarchy. Its present offices are in Washington, D.C., and it has a membership of about 7,000. BIBLIOGRAPHY: W. Leonard, ''Liturgical Movement in the United States,'' *Liturgy of Vatican II* (ed. W. Baraúna, 2v., 1966) 2:302–310; *Liturgy in Transition* (*Concilium* 62, ed. H. Schmidt, pa. 1971).

[N. KOLLAR]

LITURGICAL DANCING, see DANCING, RELIGIOUS.

LITURGICAL DRAMA, a play or drama on a religious subject conceived as an amplification of a liturgical text or Scripture reading and performed during the course of a service. Medieval liturgical dramas, popular from the 11th to the 13th cent., originated as outgrowths of *tropes, esp. those in the form of dialogue which served as an introduction to the *Introit. Typical was the *Quem quaeritis* trope to the Easter Introit, based on the conversation between the women come to anoint the body of Christ and the angel at the tomb. The development into actual drama, i.e., with staged actions, did not take place until the tropes were moved from the beginning of Mass to the end of *Matins, just before the singing of the **Te Deum*. At this less solemn moment there was greater freedom for artistic development and the dramas grew into quite elaborate productions with several scenes. The separation from the liturgical chant which the trope preceded also permitted many new musical forms to be introduced, and both text and music were frequently new compositions. Eventually the whole range of medieval literary and musical forms was employed together with costumes, pageantry, and instruments, in plays about Christmas, Easter, and biblical personages such as Noah, Daniel, and Herod. Although liturgical dramas were certainly meant to be instructive as well as entertaining to the congregation, their importance was, like the liturgy itself, greatest for the participants. The popular outdoor mystery play was an independent development and not an outgrowth of the liturgical drama; it, and eventually secular drama, quickly won over both participants and spectators, however, and liturgical drama declined rapidly from the 14th cent. on. A revival of interest in these plays in recent years has resulted in productions by both professional and amateur groups of medieval dramas, most notably the 13th-cent. *Play of Daniel* from Beauvais, as transcribed by R. *Weakland and edited by Noah Greenberg (1959), undoubtedly the greatest of the medieval plays. In recent years there have been a number of plays and operas on religious subjects either written for or at least readily adaptable to performance in church, such as T. S. Eliot's *Murder in the Cathedral* on the martyrdom of St. Thomas *Becket, also composed as an opera by Ildebrando Pizzetti, and the operas of John La Montaine. Such performances have been accepted by many Protestant Churches as worship services (thus liturgical drama in the strict sense); liturgical reform in the Catholic Church since Vatican II has led to speculation and even experimentation in the direction of expanded liturgical forms, in which an appropriate dramatic presentation might serve as the Liturgy of the Word at Mass. BIBLIOGRAPHY: R. Brandel, ''Some Unifying Devices in the Religious Music Drama of the Middle Ages,'' *Aspects of Medieval and Renaissance Music* (ed. J. LaRue, 1966) 40–55; K. Young, *Drama of the Medieval Church* (2v., 1933).

[P. MURPHY]

LITURGICAL EXPERIMENTATION, the use of certain adaptations and modifications of liturgical practices permitted in order to test their effectiveness. After 4 cent. of rigidly codified liturgy, the Churches following the Roman rite have reverted after Vatican Council II to an earlier tradition of living liturgy that adapts itself to changing human conditions and cultures. Liturgical experimentation, according to the council's *Constitution on the Sacred Liturgy* (40), is the tool required for valid adaptation. In this strict sense, liturgical experimentation is an authorized, public, scientifically measurable effort to draw from the experience of a concrete congregation rites and modes, and styles of worship meaningful in and congenial to its culture. Historically, liturgy evolved by means of a less formal kind of experimentation and adaptation. Contemporary tools of research and measurement as well as a quickened tempo of cultural change make possible and desirable a more rapid adjustment of liturgical action to the human situation.

Among the Churches in communion with Rome, territorial authorities (national or international conferences of bps.) are charged with responsibility for liturgical experimentation and adaptation, subject to confirmation by the Holy See. The U.S. Bishops' Committee on the Liturgy has formed a subcommittee on liturgical adaptation whose task is to stimulate, receive, and organize proposals and requests for experimentation, to study them and to submit them to the bps. for approval. This structure is new and primitive and in serious need of additions in order to facilitate actual experimentation, e.g., research centers (in connection, perhaps, with university liturgy programs) with structural and financial means for engaging the services of social scientists and experts in other relevant disciplines, a suitably representative and various number of places and groups designated for experimentation, etc.

Liturgical experimentation is concerned with changing, modifying, eliminating, or adding to elements in the liturgy that are presently prescribed or mandatory, on the basis of data collected in a specific cultural situation. This is the basic and strict meaning of the term. However, it is used more broadly to refer to at least three other types of activity. It is used to describe the testing in selected places of rites or services purified and restructured by the Holy See's post-conciliar liturgical commission (*Consilium*). As that commission proceeds in its work of restoring each rite according to the rules of liturgical science, it releases individual rites for purposes of testing and report. Territorial authorities or their agencies authorize representative churches and communities for this type of experimentation.

Popularly, liturgical experimentation may also be used to describe a kind of adapting which is quite licit under present laws and options and which therefore requires no authorization by a conference of bishops. Any bp., e.g., is free to found or recognize a new community of worship, a new church, based on a kind of association distinct from the territorial parish—communities of common interest or common vocation. Any priest is free to opt for the "Supplementary Weekday Lectionary" for scripture readings at Mass, and the number of his other options in celebration grows with each step of liturgical renewal. Contemporary music and accompaniment by instruments other than the organ are not excluded from the liturgy by current law.

Structures of church authority are slow to implement the conciliar approval of liturgical experimentation, so the early stages of renewal are marked by instances of an unofficial and illicit type of "underground" experimentation. Since it is private in character and unpublished, the Church as a whole cannot share in its discoveries. The advantage of public and authorized experimentation are obvious. BIBLIOGRAPHY: *Liturgy in Transition* (*Concilium* 62, ed. H. Schmidt, pa. 1971). *LITURGICAL RENEWAL.

[R. W. HOVDA]

LITURGICAL FORMATION, the process by which the Christian community, clergy and laity alike, are instructed in the purpose and meaning of the liturgy and of the various liturgical rites. The aim of this formation is to promote liturgical understanding, full and active liturgical participation, and the integration of the liturgical spirit into the spiritual lives of all the faithful. The need for liturgical formation arises from the liturgy's role as the primary and indispensable source of a true Christian spirit. Responsibility for the liturgical formation of the faithful rests primarily with the hierarchy and clergy. But to ensure that they are properly equipped to determine and impart this liturgical instruction, Vat II SacLit 14–20 sets forth a number of norms for the liturgical education of the clergy. These norms provide for the professional formation of professors of liturgy, the liturgical instruction and formation of clerical candidates, the continuing in-service liturgical education of those already engaged in the pastoral ministry, and the application of this training to the liturgical education of the faithful and the promotion of their full and active participation. The directives for liturgical formation can only be set down in general terms since the rate of progress in individual liturgical assemblies will vary. Nevertheless, liturgical formation is a continuing process, to be undertaken at all times, and not restricted to periods of liturgical reform. BIBLIOGRAPHY: A. G. Martimort, *Signs of the New Covenant* (1964); G. S. Sloyan, *Worship in a New Key* (1965); F. R. McManus, "Constitution on Liturgy, Commentary, Part One," *Worship* 38 (1964) 324–332; *Church and the Liturgy (Concilium* 2, ed. J. Wagner, 1965).

[B. ROSENDALL]

LITURGICAL FORMULAS, ROMAN, the set patterns of prayer, invitation, and responses which are said or sung by the congregation, the deacon, or the president of the community. They are directed to the Father when it is a matter of prayer; to the president of the assembly or the assembly itself when it is a matter of invitation and response. These are not spontaneous formulas, for by their very nature they are of set style and are to be repeated. Formulas used by the congregation are those of acclamation and joy such as "Alleluia," "Thanks be to God"; those of response such as "and with your spirit," and assent such as "Amen." A directive such as "Go, the Mass is ended," is a formula reserved for the deacon. The presidential prayers such as the Canon of the Mass or presidential invitation such as "The Lord be with you" are also examples of liturgical formulas. Liturgical prayer is always expressive of the Church's structure; thus the priest leads the prayer, with the active participation of the deacon and the congregation according to their respective functions. BIBLIOGRAPHY: E. J. Gratsch, NCE, 8:893–894.

[N. KOLLAR]

LITURGICAL GESTURES, the ritual bodily expressions of Christians gathered together in a liturgical act which convey the love of God. In ritual these may be seen as actions that are merely functional, e.g., washing one's hands after receiving the Offertory gifts; or as an interpretative expression of a person's wish to convey a specific attitude, such as prayer, greeting etc.; or as something purely symbolic, such as the former custom of giving a child a taste of salt at his Baptism. The following are some standard gestures: standing, which is a normal prayer gesture expressing one's dignity as a child of God; sitting, which is the customary position for a teacher or one listening to a reading or talk; kneeling, which shows sorrow, supplication, and adoration; genuflection, which primarily is an act of worship and adoration; raising of the hands and eyes to express an acknowledgment of the transcendence of God; the folding of hands as a mark of fidelity to God's will. Besides these individual gestures there are community gestures such as processions. BIBLIOGRAPHY: B. I. Mullahy, NCE 8:894–897; P. C. Whyman, *Worship with Hands* (pa. 1974).

[N. KOLLAR]

LITURGICAL GOSPEL, see GOSPEL (LITURGY).

LITURGICAL LANGUAGES, see LANGUAGE, LITURGICAL.

LITURGICAL MINISTERS, those who function in an official capacity in the worshiping community. Liturgy itself is an action of the entire existing community which is composed of people with various functions. The ministers function as leaders of the community or perform actions in the name of the community that the whole body cannot do together. There are a variety of ministers, officers, or functionaries in the celebration of the Liturgy, chief among whom are the priest celebrant who presides over and leads the liturgical action, aided on occasion by the deacon. Other auxiliary ministries may include the master of ceremonies, lector, cantor, schola and choir, organist and other musicians, acolytes, commentator, those who form the entrance and/or offertory processions (carrying the Missal, cross, and gifts), and ushers.

[N. KOLLAR]

LITURGICAL MOVEMENT, the renewed interest in the liturgy, and esp. in the full participation of Christians in the liturgical celebrations. In the 20th cent. the movement has developed in both the Protestant Churches and the RC Church and is closely related to the ecumenical movement.

Protestant Liturgical Movement. Many Protestant Christians are striving to bring about the corporate worship of their respective communities in such a way that there is active, intelligent, and salutary worship by all present. The response of the various Protestant Churches to the liturgical movement depends upon their historical background and theological emphasis. Although the Reformers reacted against the abuses of the Middle Ages, they also accepted some of its presuppositions. One of these presuppositions was the dominant and almost exclusive role played by the minister in the worship service. The liturgical movement therefore has attempted to reinstate the active role of the faithful. The roots of this movement are the historicism and romanticism that developed in the mid-19th century. The Anglican *Oxford movement with its emphasis on the sacraments, Eucharist, ceremony, and chant produced scholars and prayer books. The Lutherans lead by Wilhelm *Löhe (1808–72) and Theodor Kliefoth (1810–95) paved the way for the revision of the Common Service. The *Reformed Churches' recognition of the values of the liturgical movement came through the formation of the Church Service Society (1865) and produced the Book of Common Order (1928), with its subsequent revisions. These standardized liturgies have influenced the prayer forms of the *free Churches. Slowly but surely those with a less structured liturgy have adopted some of the recent structures. The principal agent for the promotion of liturgical reform has been the ecumenical movement, which has had to face the major problems separating Christians. The agreement among biblical theologians and exegetes regarding the meaning of worship in the NT and the Fathers has laid the basis for the introduction of newer communal forms of worship into the Protestant Churches. In many communions the present is a period of liturgical experimentation.

RC Liturgical Movement. In the RC Church there is an organized activity and trend directed toward the awakening of the Christian to his rightful role in liturgical functions and toward their more fruitful celebration. Such a concern has always been present in the Church, but it became more necessary as the liturgy became a work of the clerics. Various individuals attempted to get the people involved in the celebration. Alcuin (9th cent.) demanded that the clergy be instructed in the meaning of the liturgical acts and the people learn to sing the parts proper to them. It was only after Trent (17th-19th cent.), however, that the movement obtained the scholarly tools needed for a profound renovation of liturgical attitudes. The fruition of this scholarship and desire was first evident in the Benedictine Prosper Guéranger (1805–75), who brought liturgy back into esteem and raised the standards for its celebration. At the same time he was limited by his neo-Gothic romanticism and his philosophical traditionalism. Yet the estheticism and juridicism of Guéranger led to the popular liturgical movement of Pius X, as found in *Tra le Sollecitudini* (1903), and the works of L. Beauduin. The primary aim of the modern liturgical movement is the active, intelligent, salvific participation of the people in the liturgy of the Church. It is this aim that has produced the scholarship of such men as Probst, Duchesne, Battifol, Baumstark, Jungman, Leclercq, and others. Vatican II's *Constitution on the Liturgy* (1963) and the Consilium for its implementation are the foundations for the movement as it now exists. BIBLIOGRAPHY: K. G. Phifer, *Protestant Case for Liturgical Renewal* (1965); M. H. Shepherd, "Liturgical Movement in American Protestantism," YBLS 3 (1962) 35–61; M. J. Taylor, *Protestant Liturgical Renewal* (1963); E. B. Koenker, *Liturgical Renaissance in the Roman Catholic Church* (2nd ed., 1966); The Sacerdotal Communities of Saint-Severin of Paris and St. Joseph of Nice, *Liturgical Movement* (tr. L. Sheppard, 1964).

[N. KOLLAR]

LITURGICAL MUSIC, see MUSIC, LITURGICAL.

LITURGICAL PARTICIPATION, the fulfillment of one's designated role in community worship. One is involved externally, internally, and sacramentally in the act of worship. The right to participate in the Church's worship is obtained through baptism, confirmation, and orders. According to one's role in the Church, as affected through the reception of these sacraments, he has a specific function in the liturgical act. This function was not always recognized. In the early Church there was little difficulty. But for a number of reasons the spontaneity and communal awareness of the early times gave way to inactivity and disinterestedness. Some reasons are: (1) the separation of the liturgical language from the people's language; (2) the overelaborate ceremonial; (3) a false sense of the sacred which set aside certain people for the Liturgy; (4) a mechanistic view of the sacraments that required little active participation. Until the beginning of the modern *liturgical movement (19th cent.) the people's participation was seen as a passive devotional attendance at the performance of worship. The encyclical *Mediator Dei* (1947) and the *Constitution on the Liturgy* (1963) ask for the interior, exterior, active, and conscious participation of all in the worship of the Church. BIBLIOGRAPHY: Vat II SacLit, esp. 1–20; P Murray, NCE 8:906–908; J. H. Miller, "Distribution of Roles in the Liturgy according to the Constitution" YBLS 5 (1964) 47–56; W. S. Pregnall, *Laity and Liturgy: A Handbook for the Parish Worship Committee* (pa. 1975).

[N. KOLLAR]

LITURGICAL REFORM, the twofold movement arising from the Church in general on one hand and the magisterium on the other, resulting in an authorized form of worship. Some of the most influential reforms occurred during the reigns of Popes Damasus I (d. 384), Leo the Great (d. 461), Gregory the Great (d. 604), Gregory VII (d. 1084), Innocent III (d. 1216), Pius V (d. 1572). The Council of Trent (1545–65) gave the mission of reform to the popes. They accomplished the reform through the publication of definitive and official books of worship. The publication of these books and the establishing of the Congregation of Rites (1588) resulted in the suppression of abuses and excessive diversity; on the other hand, this centralization produced a stable and rigid liturgy. There were only feeble attempts at reform after Trent. The 20th-cent. liturgical reform was brought about during the reigns of Pius X, Pius XII, John XXIII, and Paul VI. The reforms that these popes and Vatican Council II effected have been very extensive. Every aspect of the Church's life has been affected. These reforms are guided by three principles: that the rite be clear in what it signifies, that it be intelligible, and be capable of full communal participation (Vat II, 21). Innovations are invited into the liturgy, but they must be for the good of the Church and grow organically from existent forms (*ibid.*, 23). Three important factors are to be kept in mind in liturgical reform: (1) the hierarchical and communal nature of the liturgy; (2) its didactic and pastoral nature; and (3) the culture in which it is celebrated. BIBLIOGRAPHY: F. R. McManus, NCE 8:908–910; L. Mitchell, *Liturgical Change: How Much Do We Need* (pa. 1975). *LITURGICAL BOOKS, *LITURGICAL MOVEMENT.

[N. KOLLAR]

LITURGICAL RENEWAL, the contemporary movement toward a revivifying reform in the Church's liturgical life. Liturgical renewal in the late 20th cent. is the heir and successor of periodic reform movements in the history of the Church and of many more recent prophetic pioneers. Because the liturgy is the chief realization and actualization of the Church, any effort to return to the sources, to purify the Church's life, to achieve a kind of rejuvenation must deal with the liturgy. This is true of church reform movements since the 4th cent., including the extensive reformation, advanced, recognized, and approved by Vatican Council II. The *Constitution on the Sacred Liturgy* was the first of that Council's teaching documents and was clearly influential in its subsequent work. That document teaches that liturgical renewal must be a permanent and constant part of the Church's work, because as man and society change the liturgy must adapt itself to them, must be able to speak to them and for them.

The ideal of a changeless liturgy, which had gained some currency in the Churches in communion with Rome during the rigid post-Reformation centuries, was exposed in the council's teaching as indefensible both theologically and historically. But, because of those centuries, the early stages of liturgical renewal are a somewhat complicated and multilevelled process. One part of the process is the work of uncovering or restoring rites and rediscovering valid primitive practices. Tradition is an important factor in liturgy, so the most authentic tradition must be ascertained. This is a kind of purification, a clearing away of historical accidents, so that the genuine development and structure of each rite can be seen clearly. The beginnings of this century's renewal under Pius X and Pius XII involved this kind of activity, and Vatican Council II mandated the same restoration for all liturgical rites, a work carried on by the postconciliar liturgical commission in Vatican City.

Another part of the process of renewal is the practical pastoral work of adult education and total community involvement in the liturgy. Because of the communal and hierarchic nature of liturgy, everyone present in a liturgical assembly is an actor—each with his own role—and there is no audience. A liturgical tradition in the West which has ignored this fact adds a special urgency to the educational effort and to the work of soliciting everyone's active engagement and participation in liturgical celebrations.

*Liturgical experimentation is still another, important aspect of the renewal process. Liturgy is for man. It orientates man to God, but it is for man. It is itself, education, not merely rational or intellectual, but an experience meant to touch the human person on every level of his existence, including the levels of his physical senses and his emotions. Because its nature is to be instructive and formative, to be an effective sign language or symbol language, it is subject to measurement by the criteria of communications. Changing man and changing cultures require experiments to determine contemporary effectiveness and to discover new and useful elements which liturgy can incorporate. When liturgical experiments, places of experiment, and research centers analyzing and measuring the results of experiment achieve an established place in the various national Churches, then the part of the renewal process which the council fathers called "adaptation" can begin. This is the work of modifying or elaborating on the restored normative services in the liturgical books of the Roman rite, according to the results of liturgical experimentation in each country. While restoration is a part of the process that can be completed, the work of experimenting and adapting is open-ended and will be characteristic, presumably, of the Church's life and activity in the future. BIBLIOGRAPHY: F. R. Mc Manus, NCE 8:908–910; G. Devine, *Liturgical Renewal* (pa. 1973). *LITURGY; *LITURGY, HISTORY OF; *LITURGICAL MOVEMENT; *LITURGICAL PARTICIPATION; *LITURGICAL FORMATION.

[R. W. HOVDA]

LITURGICAL RITES, those fixed patterns of ceremonial movement, sounds, and verbal formulas which have been fixed by law and tradition and are expressive of Christianity as it exists in specific areas of the world. The two great families of liturgical rites in the Church are the Eastern and Western rites. For the first 4 cent. the ritual of these respective liturgies were not as detailed as they are today. In the 4th cent., because of Arianism, apocryphal literature, and the ignorance of many clerics, the ritual became more uniform. Liturgical books evolved, along with standardized forms of celebration which centered around the local metropolitan or patriarchal see.

In the E there are the Syrian liturgies of West Syria and East Syria. The East Syrian centers around Edessa. It is Semitic in tone and survives in the liturgies of the Nestorians, Chaldeans, and Malabar Christians of India. The West Syrian liturgy evolved from the liturgies of Jerusalem and the primitive rite of Antioch. The result was the so-called liturgy of St. James, which survives among the Jacobites, Melchites, and Maronites. Its vigils, singing, and magnificent processions are some of its outstanding characteristics. The Byzantine rite, whose center is Constantinople, received its primary liturgical impetus from Antioch in the 4th century. By the 9th cent. it was the rite used throughout the Eastern Empire. The tradition of Alexandria, the rival of Antioch, is still found in the Coptic and Ethiopian rites.

The Western rites are generally divided into two principal families: the Gallican and Roman. The origin of the Gallican rites is disputed; four general types can be enumerated: Old Spanish (Mozarabic), Celtic of Ireland and Scotland, Milanese, and Gallican properly so called, which merged with the Roman rite at the time of Charlemagne. The Roman rite's origin is also difficult to ascertain. But the essential formularies of the rite were developed by the 5th, or at the latest, the 7th century. The present Roman rite is an amalgam of Gallican, Eastern, and Roman traditions. BIBLIOGRAPHY: J. A. Jungmann, *Mass of the Roman Rite* (tr. F. Brunner, 2 v., 1950); A. A. King, *Rites of Eastern Christendom* (2 v., 1950); *idem., Liturgies of the Past* (1959).

[N. KOLLAR]

LITURGICAL VESSELS, various utensils used in the official worship of the Church. Originally, almost all were common household articles. Once adapted for ecclesial use they were treated with reverence and, in time, were blessed or in some cases consecrated. Some of the more important sacred vessels of the Roman rite are: the chalice (cup) and paten (plate) used to hold the Eucharistic elements at Mass; the ciborium, a vessel used from the 13th cent. to hold the consecrated hosts for distribution to the faithful at the communion of the Mass and for reservation of the hosts in the tabernacle; the *intinctorium,* a vessel used for the distribution of communion to the laity under both kinds; the *monstrance or ostensorium, a portable receptacle so made that the sacred host, when enclosed therein may be clearly seen as at Benediction or during extended exposition of the Blessed Sacrament; the luna, lunula, or lunette, a small receptable which holds the sacred Host in an upright position in the monstrance; the *pyx, a watch-shaped vessel used in carrying the Eucharist to the sick; and oil stocks, usually cylindrical shaped containers used for chrism, the oils of catechumens and of the sick. Among other vessels are the *thurible, a small pot-like container, suspended from one or more chains, used for the burning of incense; and the cruets, the two vessels containing the water and wine to be used at the Eucharistic Liturgy.

[N. KOLLAR]

LITURGICAL VESTMENTS, the articles of attire worn by the pope, bishops, priests, and other ministers in the exercise of their liturgical functions. Until the 5th cent. those who presided over public prayer were accustomed to wear their best clothes, but these did not differ in style from those worn by the rest of the congregation. When, between the 5th and 9th cent., the mode of dress of ordinary people changed substantially, the clergy continued to wear in the liturgy the same basic types of garment that were used in older times, although these underwent considerable development for practical or artistic purposes. The texture and art of the vestments reflect the specific time in which they were made and the attitude of the Church toward the arts at that time. The principal liturgical vestments in the Roman rite are: the *amice, a rectangular linen cloth generally worn around the neck and shoulders; the *alb, a long white robe reaching from the neck to the ankles; the *cincture, a cord tied around the waist to hold in the alb; the *stole, a narrow length of material that is hung around the neck and reaches to the knees; the *chasuble, the outer liturgical garment of varying shape and design visible to all during the Eucharistic Celebration; the dalmatic, the outer vestment worn by a deacon. The minimal vestments required for a priest celebrating Mass are the alb, stole, and chasuble. In addition to the above vestments worn by the priest, the bp. wears the signs of his office known as the pontificals. These include: *buskins, gloves, and sandals are now optional, *crozier, *miter, *pectoral cross, and ring. The falda, *fanon, and

**subcinctorium* (*subcinculum*) are vestments reserved to the pope. Apart from the Eucharistic Celebration, various other vestments are worn in the celebration of the liturgy, among which are the *surplice, the *cope, and the *humeral veil. These are worn in various combinations depending upon which liturgical function is being celebrated.

[N. KOLLAR]

LITURGICAL YEAR (BYZANTINE). The Byzantine liturgy has no cycles corresponding to those of the Roman Church. Owing to a highly developed spirituality of each Eucharistic celebration, the theology of the Church year as a re-presentation of the life of Christ never developed to the degree that it did among the Latins. However, some parts of the year stand out over others, the Easter season, extending from the Sunday of the Publican and the Pharisee (10 weeks before Easter) to All Saints Sunday, the Sunday after Pentecost. Some of the most beautiful ceremonies of the Byzantine liturgy occur in this season: the triumph of Orthodoxy, commemorating the victory over the iconoclasts; the Sunday of the Holy Cross; and the beautiful services of Great Week and New Week. The Sundays of the year are often named after the Gospel of the day, e.g. the 9th Sunday before Easter is the Sunday of the Prodigal Son. There is no formal Advent celebration, there being the 18 weeks of the Paschal season and 34 weeks after Pentecost. The Theophany (Epiphany, January 6th) receives much emphasis in Byzantine spirituality.

The Sanctoral cycle begins on September 1st and continues to August 31st. The feasts are divided into three classes: great, simple, and commemorations. The dates of the feasts may vary. Some have borrowed Latin feasts (e.g., Corpus Christi and St. Teresa among the Melkites). An interesting feature of the rite is the Synaxis, a celebration commemorating individual saints involved in a prior celebration of another feast or mystery. For example, the day after Christmas is the Synaxis of the All-Holy Mother of God. The days of the week are also devoted to commemorating particular saints or mysteries. Sunday is dedicated to the Resurrection, Monday to the Holy Angels, Tuesday to John the Baptist, Wednesday and Friday to the Holy Cross, Thursday to the Apostles and Nicholas of Myra, and Saturday to all the Saints and the faithful departed.

Four Lents or fasts occur during the year: the Christmas fast from November 14th to December 24th; the Great Lent, the 7 weeks preceding Easter; the Apostles' Fast from after Pentecost to June 29th; and the Lady Fast from August 1st–14th. The Great Lent is the most severe. The celebration of the liturgical year is augmented by a series of eight tones, one for each week in succession starting from St. Thomas Sunday. The use of the Julian calendar is common, so most feasts are celebrated 13 days after their observance in the Western Church. However, the Gregorian calendar is being employed more and more, esp. by the Greeks and Syrians. All Churches celebrate Easter after the Passover, except the Catholic rites and the Orthodox Church of Finland.

[P. MCGHEE]

LITURGICAL YEAR (WESTERN CHURCH), the pattern in which the celebration of the liturgy, the official prayer of the Christian community, is carried out annually. Commemoration of the martyrs and later saints, of Mary, but above all of the mysteries of Christ's redemptive work began in the earliest years of Christianity. Calendars were followed in Rome and many other localities, all different in detail but having a common theme of the redemptive cycle and the cycle of the saints. From the beginning and throughout all local variations the liturgical year had a common purpose: to commemorate but in a deeper sense to re-enact the mystery of our Redemption. For this reason "year of grace" is perhaps a more meaningful term than "liturgical year." The Christian follows a calendar which not only conveys remembrance of the Redemption but in a very real fashion makes the effects of that redeeming work of Jesus Christ operative in his own soul.

The calendar of the liturgical year has undergone many variations in the history of the Western Church, though central themes have remained constant. In earlier cent. the Roman rite, now the prevalent one in the Western Church, was one of many and each had its calendar. In the 16th cent. Pope Pius V established a universal calendar, essentially the Roman. From the 16th to the 20th cent., there was a multiplication of feasts of the saints which later reforms have moderated. Milestones in liturgical reform include the encyclical *Mediator Dei* of Pope Pius XII, *Codex Liturgiarum* of 1960, and the *Constitution on the Sacred Liturgy* of Vatican Council II. The major effect of all the reforms has been to emphasize the celebration of the mystery of Redemption (as had been prevalent in early cent. of the Church) and reduce the prominence of feasts of saints.

Pre-Vatican II. It is convenient to make Vatican Council II the major turning-point in change of the liturgical year, as well as more fundamental changes in the liturgy of the Eucharist and what used to be called the Divine Office (now Prayer of Christians or Liturgy of the Hours). It must be noted, however, that the direction of change antedated the Council by 10 years. As the liturgical year was observed from the 16th cent., the celebration of the Christian mystery centered on Easter and Pentecost, with a second focal point in Christmas and Epiphany. Lent was a 40-day preparation for celebrating the Paschal event, including the Passion and death on the Cross. Easter to Pentecost (50 days) was one paschal festival. Sundays from Pentecost to Advent revolved around the public life of Christ. The liturgical year began with Advent, approximately 4 weeks before Christmas (It is of interest to note that the liturgical year follows, for the most part, the lunar calendar). Following Christmas were commemorations of the childhood and early ministry of Christ and several ancient feasts of Mary. Three Sundays

(70th, 60th, and 50th days before Easter) linked the Christmas cycle to the Easter cycle. Immediate preparation for Easter was the 40-day season of Lent. Though Easter and Pentecost were the true culmination of the year, in later cent. the Feast of the Holy Trinity was placed just after Pentecost week. Weaving in and out of the great redemptive cycle were feasts of the saints, as well as a variety of festivals honoring the Blessed Virgin, both on fixed days (here the solar rather than lunar calendar was followed).

Post Vatican II. The primary impact of reform has been to reduce the importance of feasts of saints, to give less place to "idea" celebrations (e.g., Christ the King), and to stress the primacy of Sundays as celebrations of Christ. Weekdays also have assumed new emphasis in contrast to the previous emphasis on the saints. What were designated before as Sundays after Epiphany, Septuagesima time, and Sundays after Pentecost are now combined under the title Sundays in Ordinary Time. The elaborate classification of feasts of the saints has been simplified, many of dubious historical background having been eliminated from the calendar. In summary, it may be said that the reforms of the liturgical year in the second half of the 20th cent. have stressed the centrality of the redemptive mystery and the primacy of Christ in the history of salvation.

[J. R. AHERNE]

LITURGIES, EASTERN. From what little is known of the liturgical practice of the primitive Church, the liturgy seems to have had a nucleus that was essentially the same everywhere, with differences reflecting local cultures and the creativity of different men. When historical documentation brought developed liturgies to light, one found clear differentiation between the liturgical usages of the first patriarchal centers, Alexandria, Antioch (with Jerusalem), and Rome. Eastern liturgies fall, accordingly, into two great families: the Syrian (Antioch-Jerusalem) and the Alexandrian (Egypt and Ethiopia).

The Syrian family contained from the outset a potential cause of division, because within the Antiochene patriarchate was a Hellenized urban element in W Syria, Cappadocia, and Palestine, and an Aramaean element, both in rural areas within the Roman Empire and, above all, in those communities lying across the frontier in the Persian Empire. In the 5th cent. the Church in Persia at first became autonomous, then schismatic with respect to Antioch and the rest of Christendom, and its East Syrian liturgy developed independently. The Antiochene patriarchate within the Roman Empire was also divided by the 6th cent. into the orthodox Churches remaining in communion with Constantinople and the Monophysite Church of Syria with its West Syrian liturgy. The liturgy of orthodox Antioch and Jerusalem was supplanted by that of Constantinple in the Middle Ages. Cappadocian Caesarea, lying within the patriarchate of Antioch but with liturgical creativity of its own, was influential in forming the liturgies of Armenia and of the patriarchate of Constantinople, so much so that the Byzantine and Armenian liturgies can be said to form a Cappadocian, or Asian, subgroup in the original Syrian family. Thus of the Syrian family there are today five types.

(1) The *East Syrian liturgy, used by the Nestorians of Iraq and Persia and their Chaldean Catholic counterpart, and, in a somewhat hybrid Latinized form, by the Malabar rite Catholics of India. The principal anaphora is that of the apostles Addai and Mari (to which the Chaldeans and Malabars have added the words of institution) with an *ordo communis* into which two alternate anaphoras can be inserted.

(2) The *West Syrian liturgy used by the Syrian (Jacobite) Church and the large group of formerly East Syrian Malabar Christians who broke with Rome in the 17th cent. to avoid further Latinization of their rite and entered the Jacobite communion. It is also used by the Syrian rite Catholics and the Malankar Catholics (Indian Jacobites reunited with Rome since 1930). The principal anaphora is that of St. James, with its properly Syrian *ordo communis* and a large number of alternate anaphoras.

(3) The *Maronite liturgy, close to that of the West Syrians, but with some affinities to that of the East Syrians and with considerable Latin influence in details.

(4) The *Byzantine liturgy, used throughout the vast Orthodox communion and in Byzantine Catholic rites, with its liturgies of St. John Chrysostom, St. Basil, and of the Presanctified, developed from original Cappadocian-Antiochene elements.

(5) The *Armenian liturgy, a single liturgy "of St. Athanasius," used by Gregorian and Catholic Armenians. Its original Cappadocian-Antiochene basis evolved less than in the Byzantine liturgy, from which it was independent until the Middle Ages, when the developed Byzantine liturgy and the Roman Mass made some influence.

The patriarchate of Alexandria, like that of Antioch, was culturally divided into an urban Hellenistic element and a rural national element that grew into an ecclesiastical division of Egypt: an Orthodox patriarchate, whose liturgy was eventually supplanted by that of Constantinople, and a Coptic patriarchate with its own further development. The Ethiopian Church was originally evangelized from Syria; but it always belonged to the patriarchate of Alexandria, remained with the Copts after the schism, and has a basically Alexandrian liturgy but national in its spontaneous development, and retentive of some Syrian elements. Thus of the Alexandrian family there are today:

(1) The *Coptic liturgy, used by non-Catholic and Catholic Copts in Egypt, with a form of the ancient liturgy of St. Mark, one of St. Gregory, and a Coptic form of the liturgy of St. Basil. The anaphora of the latter is normally used in the two other liturgies as well.

(2) The *Ethiopian liturgy, used by both the non-Catholic and Catholic groups, with many anaphoras, of which about 15 are in use today. The most common, that of the Apostles, is derived from the anaphora found in the Apostolic Tradition of Hippolytus.

The meaning and significance of liturgical rites, prayers, and ceremonies in the various Eastern Churches can be considered in the realm of theory and in the realm of practice. The theory, with variations of emphasis in different times and places, insists upon the sacramental rites as mysteries in which divine grace is given to man by making mystically present the saving actions of Christ: in liturgy, heavenly and earthly realities meet. The theory stresses common prayer as a corporate means of glorifying God and his saints, and of begging pardon for sins and grace for all in the Church. Some liturgical theologies are centered on the attributes of God, others on the realization of the divine plan for the universe. Much traditional liturgical commentary and exposition is heavily symbolic or allegorical, comparing liturgical action with the actions of Christ or other biblical persons, or with the activity of angels. Charitable social work is important and evangelical, but its nature is such that it can also be done by pagans; the principal work of the Church precisely as the Church is the sanctifying activity of sacraments and other rites, of the Eucharistic gatherings, and of common prayer. In the realm of practice, some Churches have seen the emergence of private devotions apart from the canonical forms of prayer, but Eastern piety expresses itself normally in the liturgy, and forms of prayer said privately—particularly those said in the home—are for the most part derived from the liturgical orders. The liturgy, too, is a basis for catechetical instruction of the faithful; and the ancient catechetical tradition evident in the homilies of Cyril of Jerusalem, Theodore of Mopsuestia, and John Chrysostom continues today, with many young Eastern Christians studying the substance of their religion in books largely concerned with the expressions of faith found in the Eucharistic and sacramental rites, with their biblical readings. The Church is also a sociological phenomenon, and liturgy in the East has a vital sociological role to fulfill: it is the rallying point and center of sociological identity which has enabled the Eastern Churches to survive at least as a remnant in the now largely non-Christian Orient.

Liturgical style goes hand in hand with cultural style, and the place of the liturgy in the lives of the people takes different shapes in different Churches. Today's Syrian rites, East and West, are markedly different from one another in tone: the East Syrians retaining the frugality of expression and action characteristic of their Semitic Mesopotamian origins, the West Syrians reflecting in popular form the somewhat florid way Hellenistic Antioch had of expressing its sense of transcendent mystery; but both rites, and the Maronite rite too, were formed in the Syriac-speaking towns and countryside; and all three have remained close to the people. Perhaps in no other rites are the people (in the non-Catholic Churches) so assiduous in attending the morning and evening prayers of the Office in church. The more elegant style of urban Antioch itself, newly expressed in the magnificent forms of the Byzantine imperial court, live on in the Byzantine rite, which manages to emphasize the awesome character of sacred mystery with a religious pageantry from which the people are in some ways excluded, but in which at times they can participate with great exuberance. The Slavs have used music and decoration to give the Byzantine rite in their lands a quieter, more introspective expression suiting their own religious temperament. Liturgy for the Copts means an austere and lengthy type of liturgy marked by use in the desert monasteries; but the high enthusiasm with which the entire congregation takes part is a characteristic note of Coptic piety. The Ethiopians, by filling their rites with narrative pieces, movements, and gestures drawn from native folklore, have achieved what is perhaps the most authentically popular type of liturgical expression in Christendom. The Armenian religious spirit expresses itself in liturgical forms that are elegant but sober, enhanced in performance by a discriminate artistic sense that knows how to adapt the style of music, declamation, and gesture to the moods of different texts and actions. For all the Eastern Churches the ideal condition for the prayer of those forming the Church is had when two or more are gathered together, that Christ may be among them. The condition is realized even when the individual, unable for some reason or other to take part actively in the singing or action of a given moment, prays in his own way, in the communal liturgical context of which he is a part.

In the Catholic Eastern rites some modification of the meaning and significance of liturgy has taken place. In these rites the formation of both clergy and people has for centuries been in the hands of priests and religious from the West. The Roman theology of the Mass has been applied to the Eastern liturgies. The oblivion of the public celebration of the Divine Office in the Latin West has led to its great neglect in the Catholic East, and Latin private devotions like the rosary, Way of the Cross, Marian devotions, have been introduced with great conviction by Latin missionaries. Religious instruction, far from being liturgically and biblically oriented, has conformed in the Near East to the catechetical practices of France and Italy; in Eastern Europe, to that of Austria and Poland. In recent decades, however, a reaction against this process has set in, at least in parts of the Near East. BIBLIOGRAPHY: A. Hanssens DTC 11:1434–87; S. Salaville, *Introduction to the Study of the Eastern Liturgies* (tr. J. M. T. Barton, 1938) 9–30; A. Raes, *Introductio in liturgiam orientalem* (1947); A. Baumstark, *Liturgie comparée* (3d ed., 1953); I. H. Dalmais, *Eastern Liturgies* (tr. D. Attwater, 1960); F. E. Brightman, *Liturgies Eastern and Western* (1896).

[A. CODY]

LITURGIOLOGY, that branch of theology concerned with the scientific study of rites, texts, symbols, and actions that make up the worship of the Church. It studies the liturgies of past and present in order to help the celebrations of the future. BIBLIOGRAPHY: W. O'Shea, NCE 8:919–927; J. M. Neale, *Essays on Liturgiology and Church History* (1863, repr. AMS).

[N. KOLLAR]

LITURGY, a term used in the Eastern Church to refer to the Eucharistic Celebration; in the Western Church it has had various meanings. The *Constitution on the Liturgy* avoids a definition of the liturgy yet describes it as: (1) an exercise of the priestly office of Christ as it is present in his Body, the Church (Vat II SacLit 2), (2) a foretaste of the heavenly liturgy (*ibid.* 9), (3) the supreme activity and source of strength of the Church (*ibid.* 10), (4) something the regulation of which depends upon the Holy See and the bps. (*ibid.* 22), (5) composed of sensible signs through which the sanctification of man is signified and brought about in a way proper to each (*ibid.* 5–7). Originally liturgy (*leitourgia*) in the Greek-speaking world referred to a voluntary work done for the people such as a play, road building, or the outfitting of warships. In the Greek Septuagint the term generally refers to priestly worship in the temple services. The NT seldom uses the term, and when used it generally refers to OT practice. The usage of the early Fathers and that of the NT, where the context is properly Christian, would describe the liturgy as a service of worship where each member of the Christian community according to his role offers to God within and on behalf of the community. The word vanished from use in the West. Words such as *munus, servitus, officium* took its place. The Renaissance saw the reappearance of the word, which now was used to describe the Church's worship. The term usually conveys the meaning of public worship performed in a place that serves as a church according to the circumstances of time and place. Liturgy has the characteristics of being: Christian, for the ability to function in the liturgy is founded upon one's baptism; hierarchical, because according to one's sacramental character he performs a work for the community; communal, because it is a public ecclesial act; sanctifying, because it is a means of being caught up into Christ's paschal mystery; didactic, because it is expressive of and speaks to the faith of those celebrating. BIBLIOGRAPHY: J. D. Cloud, "Meaning of Liturgy" *Liturgy* (1967) 63–73; J. H. Miller, NCE 8:928–936; C. Davis, *Liturgy and Doctrine* (1960).

[N. KOLLAR]

LITURGY, ALLEGORICAL, a form of commentary on the liturgy based upon a purely arbitrary symbolism which is usually extraneous to the original significance of the rite, e.g., when one says that the priest washing his fingers at the *Lavabo is a symbol of Pilate washing his hands. There have been many allegorical interpretations of the liturgy. The most famous, and tenacious, is that of Amalarius (d. *c.*853), for whom every vestment, motion, and word said by the priest is a reminder of some historical event in the Old or New Testament. Such interpretation neglected the fact that many things in the liturgy are there simply because they are necessary; e.g., one washes his hands because they are soiled after receiving the gifts. It also neglects true symbolism in which there is a likeness between the symbol and what is symbolized. BIBLIOGRAPHY: H. A. Reinhold, NCE 8:937–938; J. A. Jungmann, *Mass of the Roman Rite* (tr. E. Brunner, 1950).

[N. KOLLAR]

LITURGY, HISTORICAL DEVELOPMENT OF, the story of the positive growth, atrophy and stagnation, and the restructuring of the public worship in the Church. The historical evolution generally involves these steps: (1) new usages become more popular than the older ones; (2) the primitive elements tend to shrink away before the more recent ones; (3) the more archaic elements are preserved on the more important days; (4) there is a tendency to fill in silent parts; (5) there is development from diversity to uniformity. The original liturgical structure was spare and lacked luxuriance of any kind. The Jewish heritage and the message of Christ were the principal controlling factors of the early liturgy. By the 4th cent. the structure became more ordered because of its public character, the current controversies, and the beginning of a liturgical year. Between the 4th and 9th cent. the structure and many details within the structure were formulated so that from the 10th cent. onward only minor variations in the ceremonies and texts of the rite were made. After Trent even these minor variations were prohibited. With the reform of the liturgy after Vatican II room has once more been made for some local and personal variations. BIBLIOGRAPHY: A. Baumstark, *Comparative Liturgy* (tr. F. L. Cross, 1958); G. Dix, *Shape of the Liturgy* (1945); J. A. Jungmann, *Mass of the Roman Rite* (tr. E. Brunner, 2 v., 1950); R. X. Redmond, NCE 8:938–939.

[N. KOLLAR]

LITURGY, STRUCTURAL ELEMENTS OF, those external, visible, sensible forms of public worship which are the efficacious symbols of Christ's presence within the worshiping community. These symbols are words, actions, things, and persons involved in the rite. Each ritual has a different structure. The sacrament of baptism, e.g., is structurally different than Eucharist. In general one always finds a call to worship, prayer, scripture reading, and the sacramental action, e.g., anointing, which specifies the way the resurrected Christ meets man for his salvation at this time and place. BIBLIOGRAPHY: L. Bouyer, *Rite and Man: Natural Sacredness and Christian Liturgy* (1963); F. A. Brunner, NCE 8:939–942.

[N. KOLLAR]

LITURGY OF THE HOURS, in RC worship the name given to a revision of what was formerly referred to as the Divine Office. It is a communal prayer of praise and thanksgiving distributed throughout the day as the sanctification of the day and a complement to the Eucharist. The reformed Liturgy of the Hours differs from the Divine Office primarily in its being intended for communal celebration by the Christian community rather than for private recitation by clergy and religious.

History. Rooted in Jewish daily prayer, nonsacramental Christian prayer services took two directions after the legalization of Christianity: cathedral or parish liturgy (rather simple and with emphasis on morning and evening prayer) and monastic liturgy (longer and more complex, with several services at set times throughout the day, and with established formulas). The complex services of the Roman basilicas, served by "regular" clerical communities, eventually became those used throughout most of Europe. By the mid-8th cent. the idea of communal celebration was weakened and the notion of clerical obligation to these "Offices" (from the Latin *officium,* duty or responsibility) was being emphasized. The Offices continued to become longer and more elaborate. Despite 11th- and 12th-cent. reform attempts, public celebration gradually declined and the obligation became a private, individual one for those clergy who were not members of religious orders with the obligation of choral recitation of the Offices. Eventually the Office of the papal curia, collected into a single book called the Breviary, was adopted throughout most of Europe, largely because of its adoption and popularization by the Franciscans. This was somewhat reformed and simplified by the reform of Pius V (1568).

Reform. Reforms during this century began under Pius X (1911), who restored the precedence of Sunday and redistributed the psalms. Pius XII provided a new version of the psalms (still in Latin) and John XXIII simplified the office and its rubrics.

By the time of Vatican Council II the complexity and quantity of Latin prayers that the priest was required to recite in the course of the day militated against both prayer and pastoral responsibilities. The conciliar call for reform suppressed Prime, the first of the daytime Hours, permitted the omission of two of the remaining three daytime Hours, and provided for a complete reform. The *Liturgia horarum* (1971; Eng. tr., *Liturgy of the Hours,* 1975) simplified and shortened the Office, giving emphasis to the scripture readings and the psalms, distributing the psalms over a 4-week cycle (rather than the former 1-week cycle), and providing for a certain adaptability.

In the course of history the Liturgy of the Hours, intended as the public prayer of the Christian community, was individualized and clericalized. The intention of the reform is to restore this communal prayer of the Church, the prayer of Christ in the Spirit, as a prayer of praise consecrating time and extending the Eucharist.

Structure. Structurally, the Liturgy of the Hours is made up of hymns, psalms, scripture readings, prayers, and some readings from the Fathers and saints. Prior to the reform the individual Hours were Matins (a long vigil Office, originally prayed during the night, which contained several readings), Lauds (Morning Prayer), Prime (the first daytime Hour, prayed before beginning the day's work), Terce (about mid-morning), Sext (at noon), None (mid-afternoon), Vespers (Evening Prayer), and Compline (Night Prayer, before retiring). In the present format, Morning and Evening Prayer are the hinges: that in the morning (formerly Lauds) is a prayer of resurrection-praise sanctifying the day; that in the evening (Vespers) is a prayer of thanksgiving for the day. Other Hours include the Office of Readings (formerly Matins), a Daytime Prayer, and a Night Prayer (formerly Compline).

The Future. The reform calls for the restoration of the Liturgy of the Hours to parish life, but little attempt has yet been made to implement this. The fact that the reform failed to make a clear choice between the cathedral (parish) and monastic models and maintains a clerical orientation with a rather cumbersome structure makes this difficult, unless the provision for adaptation is taken seriously. Ideally, if properly implemented, the Liturgy of the Hours could come to occupy the same place in Catholic devotional life as former nonliturgical devotions did, a much more sound and biblically rooted source of spirituality. Anglican experience perhaps has a great deal to offer here, as Cranmer's Morning Prayer and Evening Prayer, modeled on the medieval offices, have been the staple of their worship. Perhaps the blending of their experience with Catholic eucharistic emphasis holds promise for both communions. BIBLIOGRAPHY: P. Salmon, *Breviary through the Centuries* (1962); *Worship* (April 1972); *Liturgy of the Hours,* with commentary by A. M. Roguet (1971).

[J. DALLEN]

LIUTBIRG, ST. (d. *c.*880), virgin, anchoress. L. was enclosed (*c.*824) by Bp. Thiatgrim of Halberstadt in a hermitage near the church of Wendhausen. Here she prayed, taught church music and handicrafts to young girls, and advised those who sought her counsel, among them Bp. Haimo of Halberstadt and Bp. Ansgar of Bremen. BIBLIOGRAPHY: M. B. Ryan, NCE 8:942; BiblSanct 8:70.

[M. F. MCCARTHY]

LIUTPRAND OF CREMONA (*c.*920–*c.*972), bp., diplomat, historian. A member of a noble family long active in the political life of the Lombard kingdom, L. served as King Berengar II's ambassador to Constantinople (949). Upon his return he quarreled with Berengar and joined the court of Emperor Otto I (the Great), where he remained for the rest of his career. When Otto invaded Italy (962–63), he secured for L. the See of Cremona and employed him in negotiations with the papacy. Later (968–69) Otto sent L. to Constantinople, this time to secure a Byzantine princess as a bride for his son and heir. L.'s historical works: the *Antapodosis*, the *Historia Ottonis*, and the *Relatio de legatione Constantinopolitana*, provide the best available sources for the history of Germany and Italy in the 10th century. BIBLIOGRAPHY: *Works of Liutprand of Cremona* (tr. F. A. Wright, 1930); C. Brooke, *Europe in the Central Middle Ages 962–1159* (1964).

[J. MULDOON]

LIVARIUS OF METZ, ST., martyr. Although some accounts place the martyrdom of Livarius at Lyons, and others made him a martyr in 451 during the incursions of the Huns around Marsal, S of Metz in Lorraine, if there is any historical basis at all for his legend he is more likely to have been a martyr of the 9th or 10th century. His relics are known since the 10th cent. and are venerated now in the church of St. Livarius in Metz. BIBLIOGRAPHY: H. Leclercq, DACL 11.1:810–817.

[W. A. JURGENS]

LIVING STANDARD, see STANDARD OF LIVING.

LIVING WAGE, payment for labor sufficient to furnish workers and their dependents with the means to develop their material, social, cultural, and spiritual life in a way worthy of human dignity (Vat II ChurchModWorld 67). The actual payment will vary according to each worker's type of labor and productivity, the regional economy and culture, and the common good. While the concept of a living wage may appear to be a new term, it is founded on traditional principles of Catholic teaching. The essential point of that teaching is that "individual men are necessarily the foundation, cause, and end of all social institutions" (John XXIII, *Mater et magistra,* 219). Thus civil authority is obliged to promote the common good, and members of society and their institutions must contribute to the common good. Building upon criteria established by Leo XIII and Pius XI, John XXIII elaborated on his predecessors' contributions to the notion of a just or living wage by stressing that the norms of equity and justice require that workers receive a wage sufficient to lead a life worthy of a man and properly fulfill family responsibilities. In determining what constitutes an appropriate wage, the following must be considered: the contribution of individuals to the economic effort; the economic status of the enterprises wherein workers are employed; the requirements of each community; the common good of all peoples. These criteria are extremely complex and difficult to achieve in a balanced manner in the concrete situation. In the attempt to apply such standards in practice, social justice demands that the acquisition and presentation of a living wage can only be reasonably achieved if each individual contributes whatever is necessary for the common good.

[F. T. RYAN]

LIVINGSTONE, DAVID (1813–73), Protestant missionary, explorer of Africa. A Scottish member of an independent Christian Church, self-educated, dedicated to work of the missions, L. was accepted by the London Missionary Society in 1838. Bent on serving in China, he was forced by war there to shift to Africa and after ordination in 1840 landed in Cape Town in 1841. A firm believer that Christianity, commerce, and civilization would transform Africa, L. began a series of explorations into areas no white man had ever seen. The determination and physical stamina his journeys required are incredible. In 1849 L. aided in the discovery of Lake Ngami, for which he was honored by the Royal Geographic Society, with which he thus began a lifelong association. Plunging into the uncharted interior of Africa, he explored the Zambezi River area and in 1855 discovered the great falls which he named Victoria Falls. Returning to England as a national hero, he wrote *Missionary Travels and Researches in South Africa* (1857), which became a great popular success. A second book, *Dr. Livingstone's Cambridge Lectures* (1858), brought the foundation of the Universities' Mission to Central Africa. On his return to Africa with several others, an expedition up the Zambezi was a disaster. L. had to work alone. It would be 30 years before the British realized how valuable the Zambezi expedition had been and established the British Central Africa Protectorate (now the republic of Malawi). Again in England in 1864, L. published *Narrative of an Expedition to the Zambesi and Its Tributaries* (1865). The third and most important expedition began in 1866 and in addition to spreading the gospel and abolishing the slave trade, L. set out to discover the source of the Nile. Again dissension was a problem and added to it, L.'s failing health. The arrival of the American journalist, H. M. Stanley, with food and medicine was only a temporary boost. With Stanley he explored the N vein of Lake Tanganyika and pushed 200 miles eastward, still seeking the Nile source. On May 1, 1873 L. was found dead in his quarters. On April 18, 1874 his remains were entombed in Westminster Abbey. L. was the individual who opened up the continent of Africa and promoted belief that Africans could take their place in the modern world. BIBLIOGRAPHY: G. Seaver, *David Livingstone: His Life and Letters* (1957).

[J. R. AHERNE]

LIZÁRRAGA, REGINALDO DE (1540–1615), Dominican missionary, bp., and writer. Born in Medellín in the province of Cáceres, Spain, he was taken by his parents to the New World. He entered the Dominicans in Lima (1560), served his order as provincial, founded new convents in Chile, and was made bp. of Imperial. Prevented from occupying his see by an Indian uprising, he was assigned to the See of Asunción in Paraguay (1608). He wrote a number of works, only two of which have survived. The more important of these is his *Descripción y población de las Indias*. BIBLIOGRAPHY: A. M. Escudero, NCE 8:944.

[P. DAMBORIENA]

LLANCARFAN MONASTERY, earlier known as Nant Carfan, a Celtic monastery founded by St. Cadog in the 6th cent. in the Cantra of Penychen (between the Thaw and the Taff), Wales. It was the head of an extensive monastic parish with foundations in Anglesey, Scotland, Brittany, Cornwall, and possibly in Ireland. To it belonged churches with dedications to Gwynllyw and Gwladus (reputedly the parents of St. Cadog). It ceased to function as a monastic house *c.* 1100. BIBLIOGRAPHY: J. E. Lloyd, *History of Wales* (2 v. 1948); A. W. Wade-Evans, *Welsh Christian Origins* (1934).

[C. MCGRATH]

LLANDAFF MONASTERY, a Celtic monastery near Cardiff, Wales. It is supposed to have been founded in the 6th cent. by St. Oudoceus (d. *c.* 552–562). Some form of Welsh monasticism may have survived in it until *c.* 1108. It became a diocesan seat. BIBLIOGRAPHY: A. W. Wade-Evans, *Welsh Christian Origins* (1934); J. E. Lloyd, *History of Wales* (2 v. 1948).

[C. MCGRATH]

LLANDELLO FAWR MONASTERY, a Celtic monastery in Carmarthenshire, Wales, founded by St. Teilo in the 6th century. It contains his body. This monastery was the center of a large monastic parish extending to its E and W, and to Monmouthshire. The monastery later claimed to have inherited the parish of St. Dyfrig, and it became the most important ecclesiastical center in the Cantraf Mawr (the country to the N of the Towy), but was extinct *c.* 1220. BIBLIOGRAPHY: A. W. Wade-Evans, *Welsh Christian Origins* (1934); J. E. Lloyd, *History of Wales* (2 v. 1948).

[C. MCGRATH]

LLANDOUGH MONASTERY, a Celtic monastery 4 miles SW of Cardiff, Wales, founded by St. Dochau in the 6th century. It was one of the three great monasteries of SE Glamorgan. It had houses in Monmouthshire, Cornwall, and possibly in Anglesey. Its later history is unknown. BIBLIOGRAPHY: A. W. Wade-Evans, *Welsh Christian Origins* (1934); J. E. Lloyd, *History of Wales* (2 v. 1948).

[C. MCGRATH]

LLANTHONY, MONASTERY OF, a monastic house in Monmouthshire, Wales, which had its origin in the hermitage of William de Lacy, an ex-knight, *c.* 1103, but soon became Augustinian. In 1136 a new priory, Llanthony Secunda, was founded near Gloucester. A new Llanthony Prima was also begun at the end of the 12th cent. and completed by 1230. In the meantime the two priories had become independent (*c.* 1205); but Llanthony Prima declined during the 14th and 15th cent. and became a cell of Llanthony Secunda in 1481. Llanthony Secunda was dissolved in 1539. BIBLIOGRAPHY: O. E. Craster, *Llanthony Priory* (1963); Knowles-Hadcock.

[C. MCGRATH]

LLANTWIT MAJOR MONASTERY, (Welsh, Llanilltud Fawr), a Celtic monastery in Glamorganshire, Wales. Founded either by St. Germanus (d. 448) or by St. Illtud (d. *c.* 525–540), it gave shape to Welsh monasticism in the 6th century. From its famous school came Samson, Gildas, Paul Aurelian, and probably David (Dewi) and Maelgwn Gwynedd. It had a large monastic parish, mainly in Glamorgan; but was extinct *c.* 1100. BIBLIOGRAPHY: J. E. Lloyd, *History of Wales* (2 v. 1948); A. W. Wade-Evans, *Welsh Christian Origins* (1934); G. H. Doble, *Saint Iltut* (1944).

[C. MCGRATH]

LLORENTE, JUAN ANTONIO (1756–1823), historian. Of Spanish birth, L. was ordained in 1779 and in 1782 was named vicar general of the Diocese of Calahorra. A Jansenist, he was yet made a commissioner of the Inquisition. His work promoting a return of the Church in Spain to the disciplinary framework it had in the 6th and 7th cent. was used for a planned schismatic group. Siding with the French when they involved Spain, he administered the church property confiscated by the French. When the Napoleonic forces were driven out, L. migrated to France. His chief work was *Histoire critique de l'Inquisition d'Espagne*. . . . (4 v. 1817–18).

[J. R. AHERNE]

LLOYD, JOHN, ST. (*c.* 1630–79), Welsh martyr. After studying at Valladolid, he was ordained in 1653. For 25 years he labored on the mission in his native Wales. With the outbreak of the Oates persecution, he was arrested on the charge of saying Mass and imprisoned at Cardiff Castle. He was tried and found guilty of high treason simply on the basis of his priesthood. He was executed on July 22, 1679, beatified in 1929, and canonized in 1970. BIBLIOGRAPHY: N. Del Re, BiblSanct 8:79–80; Gillow 4:289–290; Butler 3:166–167.

[V. SAMPSON]

LO, GREGORY (López, Gregorio; 1611–91), first native Chinese bishop. L. became a Catholic as an adult, studied for a time in Manila, and in 1651 entered the Dominican Order there. He was ordained in 1656, the first Chinese priest. After refusing bishoprics several times, he was consecrated bp. of Canton in 1685. He was later named to the new See of Nanking but died before taking possession. BIBLIOGRAPHY: Quétif-Échard 2:708–709.

[M. J. SUELZER]

LOAYSA, JERÓNIMO DE (1498–1575), Dominican missionary in S America, first bp. and abp. of Lima. After completing his studies in Spain, L. was sent to the American missions but was recalled to Spain, where he took a strong position in favor of the missions and denounced abuses of the colonists. He was made bp. of Cartagena (1537) but in 1541 was transferred to the new Diocese of Lima, which soon thereafter was raised to the status of an archdiocese. He presided over the first two provincial councils of Lima (1551 and 1567). BIBLIOGRAPHY: F. De Armas Medina, NCE 8:946–947.

[P. DAMBORIENA]

LOBBES, ABBEY OF (*Laubiense, Laubacense*), Benedictine monastery founded in 654 in the Diocese of Cambrai (now Tournai, Hainaut, Belgium). Lobbes' second abbot, St. Ursmer (d. 713), was able to complete the buildings through the generosity of Pepin, and it became one of the richest abbeys of the country, famous as an intellectual center. Destroyed by the Hungarians in 954, the monastery was magnificently reconstructed. When it was given to Franco, bp. of Liège, by Arnoul of Carinthia, 153 villages were included in its property. After a fire in 1546 the monastic structures were rebuilt. The monastery was destroyed in 1794. BIBLIOGRAPHY: Cottineau 1:1632–33.

[J. DAOUST]

LOBO, JERÓNIMO (1593–1678), historian of the Portuguese mission to Ethiopia. A Coimbra Jesuit, he was posted to India (1622) and later (1625) to Abyssinia where he remained for 9 years. After the Catholic king died, the mission was expelled, and he returned to Europe to report to Lisbon and Rome before being assigned to Goa as rector and provincial. His history was not published until 1728. He, after Father Pero Páez (1603), was the first to reach the source of the Blue Nile, which he called the "Father of Waters."

[H. JACK]

LOBOTOMY, see PSYCHOSURGERY.

LOCAL CHURCH, a group of Christians who regularly meet for worship, fellowship, and instruction and to plan their corporate activities; distinguished from the universal Church or from a national or regional organization. In NT language the term Church oftens signifies the local church, the community of Christians under their bishop. In the language of Vatican Council II the phrases, "local congregation" and "particular churches" are used in this same sense, and the statement is made that "the Church of Christ is truly present in all legitimate congregations of the faithful, which, united with their pastors, are themselves called churches in the New Testament" (Vat II ConstCh 26; see also 27). The phrase may be similarly used of Churches belonging to the *Anglican Communion. In a narrower sense, the local church refers to the congregation or parish, although the latter term strictly implies a connection between residential community and church membership, which the phrase local church does not. As meaning the particular congregation, the local church is esp. important in the *gathered-church theory and in *congregational polity.

[N. H. MARING]

LOCAL PREACHER, a layman licensed to preach in a Methodist *quarterly conference. Being so licensed is usually a step preliminary to ordination to the ministry. The use of lay preachers was initiated by John *Wesley. At first he was willing for laymen only to exhort, but not to preach or interpret the gospel. The rapid growth of the Methodist *societies, however, influenced him to change his policy. In 1740, strongly influenced by his mother, he allowed Thomas *Maxfield, who was not ordained, to preach; subsequently Wesley used laymen regularly in his work. He exercised control, however, by granting a license to preach only to one who met requirements he himself prepared. Most of the early Methodist preachers, both in England and in the U.S., were licensed either by Wesley himself or by a recognized Methodist preacher. The survival and early growth of Methodism in the U.S. largely depended on lay preachers. The modern local preacher preaches at the request and direction of the pastor or district superintendent. He is not salaried, or supported by the Church. BIBLIOGRAPHY: R.D. Urlin, *Churchman's Life of Wesley* (n.d.) 137–146; N. B. Harmon, *Understanding the Methodist Church* (1961). *LAY PREACHING.

[T. C. O'BRIEN]

LOCATION (UBI), one of the Aristotelian *categories of being: the ambience or surface surrounding by reason of which the surrounded body is in a place (*locus*). The meaning of location enters into the theological discussion on God's *omnipresence, and on the mode of Christ's *Real Presence in the Eucharist; neither involves presence by location.

[T. C. O'BRIEN]

LOCCUM, ABBEY OF, the greatest Cistercian abbey in Lower Saxony, established near Nienburg in 1163 by monks from Volkenrode. It maintained its prosperity to the Reformation, enjoying the privileges of an independent imperial monastery. Toward the end of the 16th cent. it was taken over by the Lutherans who, however, continued monastic life and customs. The title of abbot was held henceforth by prominent Lutheran clerics of Hanover. One of them, G. W. Molanus (1633–1722), worked for reconciliation with Catholics. Since 1815 Loccum houses a Lutheran seminary. Most recently it has become a center of the ecumenical movement. BIBLIOGRAPHY: H. Lilje, *Loccum* (1952); O. Karpa, *Kloster Loccum 800 Jahre Zisterzienser Abtei* (1963); H. Engfer, LTK 6:1109; A. Schneider, NCE 8:948–949.

[L. J. LEKAI]

LOCHNER, STEFAN (*c.*1410–51), leading painter of Cologne in the 15th cent., whose art reflects German mysticism of the late Middle Ages. Stylistically his works show the influence of Netherlandish painting (*Last Judgment Altar*) as well as the Soft Style characteristic of the International Gothic in Germany. L. added a unique rhythm effecting masterly compositions vividly portrayed in the *Altar of Patron Saints* (1447, Cathedral of Cologne). A *Crucifixion with the Virgin, St. John and Four Saints* (1435–40,

Nürnberg), *Virgin with the Violet* (1433, Cologne), and *Presentation in the Temple* (1447, Darmstadt) can be dated with certainty though many works present problems. BIBLIOGRAPHY: O. H. Förster, *Stefan Lochner, ein Maler zu Köln* (1952).

[R. E. FLEISCHER]

LOCI THEOLOGICI, a term used in theological methodology and epistemology, meaning: first of all, principal truths, points of view affecting content, or principal subdivisions of the revealed faith, according to which it is possible to construct a coherent system of theological knowledge, e.g., grace, sin, faith etc. This predominantly Protestant view dates from the 16th cent. (see Melanchthon's *Loci communes rerum theologicarum seu hypotyposes theologicae* [Wittenberg 1521]). It means, second, sources and different methodological and epistemological possibilities of theological knowledge that help to discover and evaluate the revealed truths of faith and to establish certain formal theological principles and rules that must be observed in elaboration of theological conclusions and systematic reflection on the Christian faith. This view has been generally accepted in Catholic theology since the *De locis theologicis libri duodecim* (Salamanca 1563) written by Melchior Cano, OP. He enumerated 10 theological *loci:* (1) the Scriptures; (2) apostolic traditions; (3) the Catholic Church; (4) the councils; (5) the Roman Church; (6) the saints (church Fathers); (7) scholastic doctors; (8) natural reason; (9) philosophers; and (10) human history. The first two are constitutive theological *loci*, 3 to 7 declarative, 8 to 10 are alien rather than proper to theology as are 1 to 7. Both views rely on *Topics* of Aristotle, who distinguished between general principles or laws governing logical categories and concepts (common *loci)* and norms governing each of the fields of knowledge (proper *loci*). Precursors of Melanchthon and Melchior Cano were: medieval theologians with their *regulae theologicae* (e.g., Gilbert of Poitiers, Alan of Lille); St. Thomas Aquinas (ST 1a, 1.8 ad 2) and Rudolphus Agricola, *De inventione dialectica* (1480, Cologne 1539). Critique: The first view of *loci theologici* was supplanted by the ideal of a theological system, and the term itself was lost. The second view exaggerated argumentation from the principles and led to the codification and dissection of theology. BIBLIOGRAPHY: A. Gardeil, DTC 9.1:712–747; A. Lang, LTK 6:1110–12; P. B. Bilaniuk, *De magisterio ordinario summi pontificis* (1966) 120–133; A. Lang, *Die Loci theologici des Melchior Cano und die Methode des dogmatischen Beweises* (1925).

[P. B. T. BILANIUK]

LOCKE, JOHN (1632–1704), English philosopher and most influential of the empiricists. Educated at Oxford, he acquired a distaste for the rigid formalism of the scholastics but was marked by the prevailing Ockhamist nominalism. In his later years there L. read Descartes and also developed an interest in the positive sciences and medicine. He served as personal physician and secretary to the Earl of Shaftesbury, an association that involved him in politics. Following his patron into exile in Holland (1683), L. came to know the House of Orange. He returned to England after the Revolution of 1688 that placed William of Orange on the throne.

L. is not a system-building philosopher. His interest lay in the process of knowledge and even there more in the psychological (How do I know?) than in the epistemological (How do I know that what I know is true?) question. He wrote as well on the natural sciences and in moral and political philosophy. L.'s characteristic English bent for the empirical and the practical led to a broad, common sense body of thought, comfortably tolerant of internal inconsistencies.

An Essay concerning Human Understanding, his chief work, was published only after 20 years of revision. He sets out to examine the origin, content and extent of our knowledge. He argues from, though he does not state, the Cartesian distinction of thought and extension, of spirit and matter. The human mind is aware of its own states, which represent the world external to it. L. argues cogently against what he regarded as the position of his Oxford mentors that man possesses innate ideas. For him the human mind begins as a blank sheet, a *tabula rasa*. All ideas, simple or complex, have their origin in experience, either the experience of sensation or that of the mind's reflections on its own activities. The mind is capable of establishing relations among its own ideas.

By force of his assumptions, L. was obliged to affirm that we can know only our ideas, a position that would lead to solipsism. Like Descartes, however, he held that we can know three sorts of existent reality: ourselves, God, and other selves and substances. We know ourselves by intuition, God by demonstration, other things by sensation. Though he was not explicitly writing metaphysics, L. nevertheless faced the metaphysical problems of substance, accident, and causality. With Galileo, Descartes, and Newton, L. distinguished between primary and secondary qualities in extended things. For L., bodies have primary qualities which produce ideas that resemble them (solidity, figure, motion) and secondary ones which produce ideas that do not (sweet, blue, hot). There is a substance, a thing-in-itself, which accounts for these qualities. Substance and causality are linked for him. His argument for God's existence rests on causality.

L. held that moral philosophy is a demonstrable science. Man's will is free and he acts for motives of pleasure. That is good which gives rational pleasure, that evil which produces pain. Man is led to seek the good and avoid evil by conforming his will to some law imposing reward and punishment. The law of opinion is the common consent of men in a "state of nature"; civil law comes into existence when men have established a commonwealth; divine law is made known to man by reason or revelation. The two first are to be judged true and valid insofar as they conform to the third.

In his political thought, L. holds that state best which is most likely to promote civil law in conformity with divine law. All men are equal before the law in certain rights: "life, health, liberty, and possession." Sovereignty lies radically with the people; the state is formed by their consent. Concretely, L. defended constitutional monarchy in which the legislative power lies with a parliament, the executive and (residually) the judicial power with the prince.

L.'s political theory, if not always his spirit of tolerance, has had wide influence in Western thought. Many of his phrases appear verbatim in the American Declaration of Independence and Constitution. BIBLIOGRAPHY: M. Cranston, *John Locke, a Biography* (1957); R. I. Aaron, *John Locke* (rev. ed. 1955); J. W. Yolton, *Locke and the Compass of Human Understanding* (1970).

[W. B. MAHONEY]

LOCKOUT, in labor-management disputes, strictly speaking, the step taken by employers who close their places of business against their employees until these accept the terms offered them. However, the work lockout is frequently used in a broad sense, esp. by workers, for those occasions when the employer attempts to worsen the conditions of employment and the workers refrain from work in protest. Before the 20th cent. lockouts took place when an employer or group of employers attempted to stop union membership and employment by barring workers who would not sign a promise not to join a trade union. Later, lockouts occurred when a group of employers retaliated against a strike by closing all factories until strikers returned to work. A lockout in its wider sense, is difficult to distinguish from a strike. Hence, what workers will describe as a lockout, employers will call a strike. Hence, the two types of action are categorized under work stoppages or labor disputes.

[F. T. RYAN]

LOCRIAN, one of the two impracticable modes, the other being the Hypolocrian, which has a final note on B, mentioned by Henricus *Glareanus in his *Dodecachordon* (1547). Glareanus argued that there should be 12 instead of the traditional 8 modes of church music. In theory he held that there were 14, but two of these, the Locrian and its plagal Hypolocrian were impracticable.

[R. J. LITZ]

LOCULUS (pl. *loculi*), diminutive form of the Lat. *locus*, meaning a place, a term with two meanings in Christian usage. (1) The horizontal rectangular niches cut into the walls of the catacombs to contain bodies of the dead were called *loculi*. After the entombment of a body (or bodies) in a *loculus*, it was sealed off with a slab of stone which was generally marked with some suitable inscription. In Christian archeology the *loculus*, a simple grave, is distinguished from the *arcosolium*, which was larger and designed to receive a sarcophagus. (2) The cavity cut in the mensa of an altar or in an altar stone to contain the relics is also called a *loculus*, or sometimes a "sepulcher."

[R. B. ENO]

LOCUTIONS, mystical phenomena in which a person becomes aware of words or statements directed to him from some supernatural source. Locutions are customarily divided into three types: auricular, physically heard by the ear; imaginative, perceived directly in the imagination either in dreams or while awake; and intellectual, understood by the mind without any auricular or imaginative experience. The experience often directs a person to a specific, virtuous action and usually imparts a sense of understanding and certitude. Locutions are distinguishable from psychogenic states or satanic deception by their beneficial effects. Scripture contains numerous examples of supernatural locutions.

[T. M. MCFADDEN]

LOD, see LYDDA.

LODGE, THOMAS (1558–1625), poet, prose master. With the publication of *Rosalynde* in 1590 L. became a leading practitioner of English prose in an age of giants. With Robert Greene he produced a satirical work, *A Looking Glass for London and England*, a blend of history, Scripture, and social satire. The marriage of L. to his second wife, who was a friend of Anne, Countess of Arundel, brought him close to many recusants. The year 1591 is conjectured as the date of his conversion to Catholicism. Much of his writing thereafter was devotional and indicates a new resolution "to paint fair things in the light of my meditations." In 1602 L. was incorporated at Oxford as a doctor of physic and practiced medicine in London thereafter. Twice he was indicted for rescusancy but escaped conviction, dying of the plague. BIBLIOGRAPHY: L. I. Guiney, *Recusant Poets* (1939).

[J. R. AHERNE]

LOENING, EDGAR (1843–1919), canonist, church historian. L. taught at a number of German universities, principally at the Univ. of Halle from 1888 till his death. His major work is *Geschichte des deutschen Kirchenrechts*, a study of the rights of the Church that appeared in part in 1878. The first volume is an extensive study of Church and State in the era of Constantine and Clovis; the second covers the subject in the Merovingian period. Though L.'s approach is that of a canon and civil lawyer, he writes with lucidity and charm. He with other German historians brought new awareness of the institutions of the Church as seen through their historical development. BIBLIOGRAPHY: L. Falletti, DDC 6:619–635.

[J. R. AHERNE]

LÖFFLER, KLEMENS (1881–1933), German Catholic historian. In 1918 he became the director of libraries for the Univ. and the city of Cologne. He is known principally for his *Papstgeschichte von den Anfängen bis zur Gegenwart* (1933), which he wrote in cooperation with Franz Xaver Seppelt. His other contributions are in the area of cultural history and the history of the Church in Germany. BIBLIOGRAPHY: M. Csáky, NCE 8:953–954 (excellent bibliog.); R. Baumer, LTK 6:1115.

[J. J. SMITH]

LOGIA OF JESUS, a hypothetical source for the Synoptic Gospels. It is commonly held that Matthew and Luke depended on Mark. They have in common, however, about 235 verses which do not turn up in Mark. These verses are almost exclusively of the "sayings" (*logia*) type. Accordingly, the so-called Two-Source Theory opines that at the time Matthew and Luke wrote, there was in existence a fixed collection of Jesus' sayings. This is antecedently probable; the early Christians would have treasured the Master's words. However, the material shared by Matthew and Luke as against Mark is not limited to sayings; it includes narrative as well. This would indicate not just a collection of *logia*, but a sort of proto-gospel. Called Q (from *Quelle*, German for source), the elusive document has been the subject of much speculation, both as to its contents and its form. One suggestion is that it is an early Greek version of Aramaic Matthew. Others, while admitting such a version or versions, insist that the *logia* source is different from it. *SYNOPTIC PROBLEM.

[J. J. CASTELOT]

LOGICAL POSITIVISM, a name devised in 1931 by A. Blumberg and H. Feigel to identify the philosophical movement developed by the Vienna Circle (*Wiener Kreis*) in the 1920s. The same system and movement has been called logical empiricism, scientific empiricism, and the Unity of Science Movement. Logical positivism proposes experimental or empirical verification as the sole criterion of the meaning of propositions concerned with reality, and it rejects traditional philosophy and its problems as meaningless in all matters in which this approach is not possible. Like earlier forms of empiricist philosophy it rejects metaphysics, but it goes beyond them in its concern to prove by logical analysis that any metaphysical statement whatever is nonsensical. The Vienna Circle was made up of physicists, mathematicians, historians, sociologists, economists, and others well schooled in scientific methodology and mathematical logic. Logical positivism rejects the claim of religious thought to be expressive of reality, yet it also rejects atheism, for the denial as well as the affirmation of religious truth is meaningless in its understanding of the term. It does not reject ethics, although it denies cognitive value to ethical concepts and propositions. Such concepts and propositions simply indicate feelings of approval and disapproval and are used by individuals to prevail upon others to share their own emotional attitudes. BIBLIOGRAPHY: M. F. Griesbach, NCE 8:964–966; J. Passmore, EncPhil 5:52–57; A. J. Ayer, *Logical Positivism* (1959); G. Bergmann, *Metaphysics of Logical Positivism* (2d ed. 1967).

LOGOS (Gr. for Word), a name given to Christ in the Gospel of St. John. By calling Christ the Word made flesh (Jn 1.14) the Gospel pronounced the NT's last word concerning the mystery of Christ. In St. John's mind the concept did not refer to the Logos of Hellenistic philosophies with its rational and speculative overtones but to the concrete and dynamic *dabar* of the Jewish revelation. The Word stood for God's efficacious action in history, not for intelligibility immanent to the world. St. John's intuition consisted in perceiving how all that the OT had attributed to the Word of God was verified eminently in the Person of Jesus, the Son of God. Through him God had created the world (Jn 1.3), given life to men (Jn 1.12; 1 Jn 1.1) and revealed himself to them (Jn 1.18); he would at the end exterminate all his enemies (Rev 19.11–16).

Christ had revealed himself as the Son of God; John saw in him the Word of God (Jn 1.1). This meant that God had not only spoken words to mankind, had not only spoken to men through his Word; he had sent into the world to speak to men and save men the Word whom he utters eternally in secret. This insight laid the fundamental principle for much of the later reflection on the mystery: Jesus Christ is revealer and Savior because he is the Word uttered by God eternally. Centuries of Christian reflection were also to dwell on the identification of God's Son and of his Word: in God, generation takes place by way of self-consciousness; the Father knows himself in the Son whom he begets. BIBLIOGRAPHY: D. M. Crossan and C. J. Peter, NCE 8:967–972; C. J. Peter, *ibid.* 14:1012–13 s.v. "Word, The."

[J. DUPUIS]

LOGOS-SARX CHRISTOLOGY, derived from the use of *Word-flesh* in Jn 1.14, the characteristic framework of the school of Alexandria. The underlying analogy compares the Word-flesh union to the soul-body union. An obvious problem results: if the Word is united to the flesh as soul to body, there is no place nor need for a human soul; but without a human soul, Christ would not be man. Despite this inadequacy many orthodox theologians, including St. Athanasius, used it without drawing heretical conclusions.

Two representatives of this Christology, however, were condemned in the early Church. Arianism in viewing the *Logos* as a created soul that took the place of the human soul, denied to Christ both divinity and humanity. Apollinarianism, in opposing the Arian denial of divinity, coincided in denying the human soul. Both of these heresies were thus victims of the weakness of *Logos-sarx* framework.

The *Logos-sarx* pattern was most popular in the 4th century. It lost ground to the Antiochene approach of *Logos-anthropos* (Word-man) after the condemnation of Apollinarianism in 381. Most important was St. *Gregory of Nazianzus, who applied the principle "What is not assumed is not healed" to prove the need for a human soul in Christ. An even stronger attack on the one-sidedness of the *Logos-sarx* theology came from *Theodore of Mopsuestia.

In summary, the weakness of the *Logos-sarx* framework was its failure to provide for the human soul of Christ. Its strength was that it emphasized the unity of subject in the Word Incarnate. BIBLIOGRAPHY: A. Grillmeier, *Christ in Christian Tradition* (tr. J. S. Bowden, 1965); J. M. Carmody and T. E. Clarke, *Christ and His Mission* (*Sources of Christian Theology* 3, 1966).

[J. J. MEGIVERN]

LOGOS SPERMATICOS (Gr., the germinal word), a philosophical term, used by the Stoics, for human reason or intelligence as the cause of union, knowledge, and similarity between God and man. The term was adopted by *Justin Martyr to explain how men from all times could come to know God and even be called Christians: every human being possesses in his reason a seed of the perfect divine Logos, or Christ. BIBLIOGRAPHY: Quasten 1:209.

[T. M. MCFADDEN]

LÖHE, JOHANN KONRAD WILHELM (1808–72), German Lutheran pastor. Except for several vicarates (1831–37), L. spent all of his adult life as pastor in the insignificant village of Neuendettelsau. He sent hundreds of emergency pastors to the U.S. to care for German Lutheran immigrants there. The Missouri Synod, the Franconian colonies in Michigan, and the Iowa Synod all claim him as founder. For the evangelization of Australia and the Americas he organized the Neuendettelsau Foreign Mission Society and established a *deaconess motherhouse for *inner missions. After almost seceding from the Bavarian state Church, he petitioned the general synod to promote strict adherence to the church symbols and to free itself from state control. Chief among his 60 writings are *Drei Bücher von der Kirche* (1845) and a number of prayer-books. BIBLIOGRAPHY: J. L. Schaaf, *Wilhelm Löhe's Relation to the American Church* (1962); E. H. Heintzen and F. Starr, *Love Leaves Home* (1973).

[M. J. SUELZER]

LOHELIUS, JOHANN (1549–1622), Abp. of Prague. L. was born into a poor family and as a youth he worked as a servant in the Premonstratensian abbey at Tepl. He began to study at the abbey and received the habit in 1573. In 1575, he went to Prague to study philosophy. After his ordination he worked in Bohemia to counteract the growing influence of Lutheranism. In 1579, L. was appointed prior of the abbey of Strahov and in 1586 was elected abbot. Later, he was appointed vicar general of the Premonstratensians and in that capacity visited abbeys in Austria, Hungary, and Poland. In 1604, he was named bp. of Sebaste and auxiliary to Abp. von Lamberg of Prague. When von Lamberg died in 1612, L. was appointed abp. of Prague. Along with many of his followers, he was soon forced to flee when the Calvinists took control of Prague. In 1620, after the Catholic victory in the battle of White Mountain, L. returned to Prague and oversaw the reconstruction of the cathedral. He was buried in the church at Strahov. BIBLIOGRAPHY: K. Pichert, AnalPraem 264–283 (1927); R. Seton-Watson, *History of Czechs and Slovaks,* (1943) 113.

[R. J. BRADY]

LOHMEYER, ERNST (1890–1946), NT scholar. L. taught at the Univ. of Breslau (1920–35), but his anti-Nazi stand caused his transfer to the Univ. of Greifswald, Prussia. In 1946 he was arrested there for unknown reasons, and it is assumed that he died in Russia in September of that year. He is a noted NT commentator who used the latest hermeneutical methods and is regarded as one of the leaders in the Redaktionsgeschichte school, moving from an extreme *form criticism to an emphasis upon the creative contributions of the Evangelists. His commentaries on Matthew (1962) and Mark (1959) for H. Meyer's *Kritisch-exegetische Kommentar über das Neue Testament* are esp. noteworthy. BIBLIOGRAPHY: L. A. Bushinski, NCE 8:972.

[T. M. MCFADDEN]

LOISY, ALFRED FIRMIN (1857–1940), French priest, theologian, principal proponent of *Modernism in France. Born in Ambrières in Lorraine, he studied at the Grande Séminaire of Châlons-sur-Marne, and was ordained in 1879. He served as a parish priest for 2 years before graduate studies under Abbé L. Duchesne at the Institut Catholique in Paris. From 1882 to 1885 he attended the lectures of E. Renan at the Collège de France to learn Renan's position so it could be refuted. Upon completion of his studies at the Institut in 1884 he joined the faculty as professor of Hebrew and OT exegesis, although his doctoral thesis was refused publication because of ''relativism'' regarding revelation. He was dismissed in 1893 over the question of the inerrancy of the Bible in an article ''La Question biblique et l'inspiration des Écritures.'' The dismissal was bitter and at least partly political, to save Msgr. D'Hulst, the rector, from embarrassment; it resulted in hostility toward ecclesiastical authority on L.'s part. He continued his writing while chaplain to a Dominican convent in Neuilly, 1894–99, even though his faith in Catholicism had disappeared as early as 1886. Five of his works were condemned in the 1903 publication of the Index of Forbidden Books. These were a paper, ''La Religion d'Israel,'' and five books: *L'Évangile et l'église, Études évangéliques, Autour d'un petit livre,* and *Le Quatrième Évangile*. His reaction was ambiguous and unacceptable to the Holy Office in Rome, and he was formally excommunicated on March 8, 1908. He publicly renounced Christianity and joined the faculty of the Collège de France as professor of church history (1909–30), the position previously held by Renan.

During the period just before his excommunication and after the publication of the encyclical *Pascendi* (1907) L. published extensively. His books included *Simples Rélexions* (1908), on the events leading to his excommunication, and in the same year a major work entitled *Les Évangiles synoptiques*. Later at the Collège de France he published *Les Mystère païens et le mystère chrétien* (1914), *La Religion* (1917), *Les Livres du Nouveau Testament* (1922), the lengthy *Mémoires pour servir à l'histoire religieuse de notre temps* (1930–31), and a summary of his final teachings on the NT called *Naissance du christianisme* (1933). L. was a man without faith in traditional RC teaching for most of his creative years and was yet dedicated to making the Churcn modern from within. He was the central figure in French modernism and its principal spokesman. He died without reconciliation with the Church. BIBLIOGRAPHY: A. Vidler, *Modernist Movement in the Roman Catholic Church* (1934); J. Ratté, *Three Modernists* (1967).

[J. P. WHALEN]

LOKA-PĀLA, guardian of one of the four cardinal points or quarters of the world. Kuvera (N), Virūdhaka (S), Dhṛtarāṣṭra (E), and Virūpākṣa (W) dwell on Mt. Sumeru (Kailāsa).

[M. J. DALY]

LOKEŚVARA, Indochinese Buddhist form of Avalokiteśvara. Lokeśvara, Lord of the World, has 1 to 16 heads and 1 to 16 pairs of arms. His four faces crown each of the 51 towers of the Bayon in Angkor Thom, Cambodia.

[M. J. DALY]

LOLLARDS, in England followers of the teaching of John *Wycliffe. In the Low Countries from the early 14th cent. the Alexian Brothers were called by this name (Low Ger. *lullen,* to sing softly), because of their chanting in a muted tone. In England John Wycliffe's "poor priests" and later all his followers in general were called Lollards, the term being used first by the Oxford Cistercian, H. Cromp, in 1382 and in a condemnatory document by the bp. of Worcester in 1387. The name was derisive, having the sense of idler or mumbler. Lollardy in the last 20 years of the 14th cent. was mainly centered at Oxford, among theologians. A document presented to Parliament in 1395, *The Conclusion,* contains the Lollard teaching. Wycliffe's doctrines were pushed to extremes: Lollards rejected the *Real Presence, church authority, auricular confession, all sacramentals, and vows, esp. chastity. They extolled the sufficiency of Scripture and private interpretation. The Lollards also propagated Wycliffe's ideas on lordship and advocated primitive evangelical poverty and a kind of communism. Abuses of ownership by ecclesiastics fostered this sentiment, which is reflected in the creed of **Piers Plowman* (1395). Even after the *De haeretico comburendo* of 1401, the continuance of Lollardy among theologians prompted the repressive measures of the abp. of Oxford, Thomas Arundel, in 1408, and the philosophic apologetics of Reginald Pecock, in 1455. By the early 15th cent. Lollardy was more and more a social movement of the lower classes; a popular rising in 1414 was put down and the Lollard leader, Sir John Oldcastle, was executed in 1417. Thereafter, Lollards gathered in secret, scattered groups, which, however, maintained contact with each other. Periodic legal reprisals continued down through the reign of Henry VIII. The term Lollard came to be applied to all manner of religious dissenters; but the true Lollards were of little significance when the English Reformation came to pass. BIBLIOGRAPHY: J. Gairdner, *Lollardy and the Reformation in England* (4 v., 1908–13); R. Hedde, DTC 9:910–925; Hughes RE 1:100, 126–127; J. A. F. Thompson, *Later Lollards 1414–1520* (1966); bibliog. for J. Wycliffe.

LOMAS RISHI (RSI) CAVE. Cut into the living rock of the Barābar Hills, Bihar State, India *c.*250 B.C. in Aśoka's reign (Mauryan period), its domical interior and highly polished portal reflects prototypes in wood with thatched roofs and overhanging eaves. The portal's ogival frame echoes architecture in pliable wood and is probably a prototype of the rock-cut chaitya hall. BIBLIOGRAPHY: P. Brown, *Indian Architecture* (1959).

[M. J. DALY]

LOMBARD LEAGUE, an alliance formed in 1167 by the merger of the Leagues of Verona and Cremona to resist Frederick Barbarossa. Sixteen northern Italian cities comprised the original, unified League, but its membership fluctuated. It espoused Alexander III's cause against the Emperor's antipope Paschal III. Alexander in turn used papal resources, financial and spiritual, to support the League; esp. important was his encyclical *Non est dubium* (1170). The League defeated the Germans at Legnano in 1176. Barbarossa approached Alexander in separate treaties (Anagni in 1176, Venice in 1177), in which the Pope protected the League's interests. After a 6-year truce, the League came to terms with Barbarossa by the Treaty of Constance in 1183. It disbanded thereafter. BIBLIOGRAPHY: M. Pacaut, *Frederick Barbarossa* (1970); W. Baldwin, *Alexander III and the Twelfth Century* (1968); W. Butler, *Lombard Communes* (1906).

[R. H. SCHMANDT]

LOMBARDS, Germanic tribe that migrated from Sweden to the Danube during 5 cent. and then entered Italy in 568. They conquered most of the Po Valley from the Byzantine Exarch and established Pavia as their capital. Individual Lombard chieftains seized parts of central and S Italy. By the 590s the Lombards threatened Rome; Pope Gregory I alternately opposed and negotiated with them. Some had become Arian Christians before 568; others remained pagan. The influence of their new environment, reinforced by the Catholic Bavarian Theodelinde, wife of King Agilulf (590–616), gradually brought them into Catholicism. Adaloald (616–625) was the first Catholic king. Aggressive leaders in the 8th cent. threatened Rome and threw the popes into alliance with the Franks. Charlemagne in 774 annexed the Lombard state. BIBLIOGRAPHY: E. Schwarz, *Germanische Stammeskunde* (1956); T. Hodgkin, *Italy and Her Invaders,* (8 v. in 9 1892–1899) v. 5–7.

[R. H. SCHMANDT]

LOMERS, COUNCIL OF. In 1165 the bp. of Albi in France convoked an assembly of bps. and nobles at Lombers where for the first time the Cathari were examined and accused of heresy in Languedoc. BIBLIOGRAPHY: R. Kay, NCE 8:975–976.

[B. L. MARTHALER]

LOMÉNIE DE BRIENNE, ÉTIENNE CHARLES DE (1727–94), French abp., cardinal and minister of state. His orthodoxy was suspect even while he was a student at the Sorbonne. He was ordained in 1752 and as a member of a prominent family achieved quick preferment and became abp. of Toulouse in 1763. He was responsible for civic improvement, but was suspected of being an atheist. His policies in the general assembly of the clergy wreaked havoc with the religious orders of France. He became minister to Louis XVI in 1787 and received rich monastic benefices. In 1788 at Rome he was created card., but for subscribing to the Civil Constitution of the Clergy in 1791 was expelled from the college of cardinals. During the Revolution he renounced his ecclesiastical titles and ministry, he did not, however, escape arrest and is thought to have died of a stroke while being interrogated.

[T. C. O'BRIEN]

LOMONOSOV, MIKHAIL VASILYEVICH (1711–65), Russian poet, grammarian, member of the Russian Academy of Sciences in St. Petersburg, and one of the founders of Moscow Univ. (1755). His scientific studies embraced astronomy, chemistry, mineralogy, economics, and mathematics. But he is best known as the ''father of modern Russian literature,'' a title conferred on him because of the many linguistic and literary reforms that he propounded in such works as the ''Letter on the Rules of Russian Versification'' (1739), *Rhetoric* (1748), *Russian Grammar* (1755), and the famous ''Theory of the Three Styles'' (1757). L. is also the author of sonorous and solemn odes in the classical style, notably the deistic ''Morning Reflections on the Majesty of God'' (1751). BIBLIOGRAPHY: B. N. Menshutkin, *Russia's Lomonosov, Chemist, Courtier, Physicist, Poet* (tr. J. E. Thal and E. J. Webster, 1952).

[M. F. MCCARTHY]

LONDON CHARTERHOUSE, the Carthusian monastery in London, 18 of whose monks suffered martyrdom for refusing Henry VIII's Act of Supremacy. The prior, John *Houghton, was first to be hanged, drawn, and quartered on Tyburn Hill, May 4, 1535; the other monks were executed in the interim before final suppression in 1537. London Charterhouse, founded in 1370, was noted for its vitality and faithful observance. St. Thomas More lived 4 years there as a young man, and even tried his vocation. After suppression the monastery became an almshouse and private school (the latter, Charterhouse School, now moved to Surrey).

[T. C. O'BRIEN]

LONDON CONFESSION, see SECOND LONDON CONFESSION.

LONDON MISSIONARY SOCIETY (LMS), an agency for foreign missions founded in 1795 by members of many Churches. The distinguishing feature was its evangelical, interdenominational character, its ''fundamental principle'' being that the Society was committed to spreading the ''glorious Gospel of the blessed God'' and no particular church form. While still adhering to this principle, it became and has remained an agency of Congregationalism, since its *independency encouraged support of Congregational Churches throughout the British Empire. In 1966 the LMS united with the Commonwealth Missionary Society to become the Congregational Council for World Missions. The first missionaries were sent out to Tahiti in 1796; missions fields have included India, South Africa, China, Madagascar, Central Africa, Papua, S Pacific, and Malaya. The rolls of the Society's missioners include John Williams, David Livingstone, Robert Moffat, Robert Morrison, and James Chalmers. BIBLIOGRAPHY: M. Goodall, *History of the London Missionary Society, 1895–1945* (1954).

[R. F. G. CALDER]

LONERGAN, BERNARD J. F. (1904–), Canadian philosopher and theologian. L. entered the Society of Jesus (1922), studied philosophy at Heythrop College in Oxfordshire, England (1926–29), and was graduated from the Univ. of London with a degree in economics (1930). Later he studied theology at the Gregorian Univ. in Rome where he received his licentiate and then his doctorate (1945). From 1940 to 1953 he taught at Jesuit seminaries in Montreal and in 1953 was assigned to the Gregorian as a professor of dogmatic theology, remaining there until 1965 when he was forced to leave because of ill health. He was Stillman Professor of Theology at the Harvard Divinity School (1971–72) and is presently research professor of systematic theology at Regis College, Toronto.

L. refers to himself as an intellectualist in Thomistic thought. His doctoral dissertation, *Gratia operans* (published in 1971 as *Grace and Freedom–Operative Grace in the Thought of St. Thomas*), is an historical and psychological analysis of the teachings of Aquinas on grace. Articles on the concept of *Verbum* in St. Thomas were first published in five parts (1946–49) and later brought out in *Verbum: Word and Idea in Aquinas* (1967). His works on Christology and the Trinity were published while he was in Rome: *De constitutione Christi ontologica et psychologica* (1956); *Divinarum personarum conceptionem analogicam*

(1957); *De Verbo incarnato* (1961), and *De Deo trino* (2 v., 1964). L.'s major work, *Insight: A Study of Human Understanding* seeks to understand what it is to understand. L. deals with the organizing intelligence that operates on a set of incomplete, then complete, insight in areas of mathematics, philosophy, psychology, and other sciences. Insight is regarded as the controlling event in the appropriation of all knowledge, although the zenith of knowledge is the activity of the rationally self-conscious subject who gives order to the set of heuristic notions that finally leads to a threefold conversion in the subject: moral, religious, and intellectual. A second major work, *Method in Theology* (1972), outlines a methodology for philosophers and theologians dealing with functional specialities: research, interpretation, history, dialectic, foundations, doctrines, systematics, and communications. It is an ample glossary for theology that also provides a dynamic corpus in other fields of human investigation. *Method* imposes on those who seek authenticity the obligation of the triple conversion implied in *Insight*. *The Subject* was published in 1968, and *The Philosophy of God, and Theology* in 1974. Papers delivered at the first (Tampa, Fla., 1970) of several national and international Lonergan conferences and workshops were published in *Foundations of Theology* (v. 1, 1971) and *Language, Truth and Meaning* (v. 2, 1972), both edited by Philip McShane. L.'s papers, unpublished and published works have been collected by Frederick E. Crowe, SJ and organized into the Lonergan Centre, a research facility for scholars at Regis College. Searching the mind of Aquinas through rational inquiry has brought L. to new manifestations of Thomistic thought, esp. in the areas of knowing and intelligent subjectivity. L. moves from the experience of knowing to the transcendent horizon toward which all conscious activity is unthematically directed. What is grasped intelligently and affirmed reasonably also yields proportionately the contents of ethics and ultimately ethics made explicit by moral living. BIBLIOGRAPHY: F. E. Crowe, ''Introduction'' in *Collection, Papers of Bernard Lonergan* (1967) 7–35; D. Tracy, *Achievement of Bernard Lonergan* (1970); W. J. Hill, *Knowing the Unknown God* (1971) 79–88.

[J. R. RIVELLO]

LONGFELLOW, HENRY WADSWORTH (1807–82), poet and translator, the most popular American poet of the 19th cent., both at home and abroad. Educated at Bowdoin College, Maine, he was offered a professorship of modern languages there. To prepare himself for the position, he traveled and studied in France, Italy, Spain, and Germany. Later he was to occupy the same chair at Harvard University. For additional grounding in European literature, he visited the Scandinavian countries and Holland. L.'s increasing familiarity with the body of foreign literature provided him with a knowledge of the RC Church, whose beauty and moral grandeur—but not doctrine—he admired. Sympathetic treatment of Catholic themes is found in many of his works. L. contributed significantly to a growing national literature with, among other works, three famous narrative poems: *Evangeline; Hiawatha* which was based on Indian legends and became an immediate success; and his narrative of colonial days, *The Courtship of Miles Standish,* which was even more popular. Among his notable short poems are his sonnets, a supreme achievement that ranked L. with the best of his British contemporaries. Six of them are prefixed to cantos of his translation of Dante's *Divina Commedia*. L. also wrote some prose works, e.g., *Outre-Mer,* a book of travel sketches, and *Hyperion,* a romantic novel, but his forte was poetry—lyric and narrative. It is upon this that his reputation rests. The adverse critical reaction that set in after his death and jeopardized for a while his deserved eminence, could not withstand his touch of poetic genius, which is still appreciated by the discriminating. BIBLIOGRAPHY: H. W. Dans for the bibliog. in *Cambridge History of American Literature* 2:425–436, R. P. Hickey, *Catholic Influence on Longfellow* (1928).

[S. A. HEENEY]

LONGHENA, BALDASSARE (1598–1682), the church of S. Maria della Salute (begun 1630) is the best example of his unmatched ability for taking advantage of a church structure's surrounding environment to produce a strikingly pictorial work of total architecture. He also designed two remarkable palaces, the Rezzonico and the Pesaro, both in Venice. BIBLIOGRAPHY: C. Semenzato, *L'Architettura di Baldassare Longhena* (1954).

[L. P. SIGER]

LONGINUS, ST., by Christian legend identified as the soldier who lanced Jesus' side (Jn 19.34), and was converted through the cure of his faulty vision by a drop of Jesus' blood. Later, as a monk in Caesarea of Cappadocia, in a persecution, he had his tongue cut out, but continued to talk clearly. On the point of being decapitated he prayed for the executioner, who later became a sincere believer in Christ. The legend, although not authentically historical, has edified Christians down the ages.

[J. F. FALLON]

LONGINUS, JOHANNES, see DŁUGOSZ, JAN.

LONGLAND, JOHN (1473–1547), bp. of Lincoln. L. was educated at Magdalen College, Oxford, and ordained in 1500. He was appointed dean of Salisbury and confessor to Henry VIII (1514). He strongly upheld the royal supremacy and supported Henry's divorce proceedings against Catherine of Aragon, serving as an assistant judge to Thomas Cranmer in the divorce hearings at Dunstable Priory (1533). L. was a noted preacher and humanist to whom Erasmus dedicated several works.

[T. M. MCFADDEN]

LONG-SUFFERING, the Douai translation of the Vulg *longanimitas,* one of the *fruits of the Holy Spirit in Gal

5.22. St. Thomas Aquinas explains it as a forbearance, prompted by charity, in waiting to receive the final fruition of charity, amid the experiences of evils besetting life (ThAq ST 1a2a, 70.3). It is also a quality that characterizes Christian patience as this requires endurance over a long period of time (*ibid.* 2a2ae, 136.5).

[T. C. O'BRIEN]

LOOFS, FRIEDRICH (1858–1928), Lutheran pastor and church historian at the Univ. of Leipzig (1882–87) and Halle (1887–1926); his chief works, both books and numerous entries in the *Realenzyklopädie für protestantische Theologie und Kirche,* were dedicated to the history of dogmas.

[T. C. O'BRIEN]

LOOS, CORNELIUS (*c.* 1546–95), Flemish theologian, professor at Mainz and Trier, chiefly notable for his opposition to the witch-burning craze of the era. For this he had to undergo several trials and even imprisonment; his book on the subject, *De vera et falsa magia* was proscribed by church authorities.

[T. C. O'BRIEN]

LOPEZ, CARLOS ANTONIO (1792–1862), Paraguayan statesman. A lawyer in Paraguay, he was an opponent of the dictator José Gaspar de Francia. After the fall of de Francia, a general congress established the Consulate and L. was named one of two consuls in 1841. The national congress in 1844 named L. first president of the republic. He served as president from 1844 to 1854, was re-elected and served from 1854 to 1857 when he was again re-elected to a 10-yr. term. L. was a defender of the rights of the Church and a talented and progressive leader.

[J. R. AHERNE]

LÓPEZ, GREGORIO, see LO, GREGORY.

LOPEZ, LUDOVICO (d. 1595), theologian. A Spanish Dominican, L. taught theology in Spain and Colombia. He was a strong advocate on behalf of the Indians against the plantation owners. An important work is his *Instructorium conscientiae* (1585).

[J. R. AHERNE]

LOPEZ DE MENDOZA GRAJALES, FRANCISCO, missionary. L. has provided a firsthand account of the Spanish expedition which founded St. Augustine, the first permanent settlement in the U.S. He was the chaplain of the fleet of Menendez de Aviles which sailed from Spain on June 28, 1565. Eleven ships left Cadiz but half were lost to the stormy Atlantic. The expedition reached Puerto Rico on August 9 and L. was offered the chaplaincy of that port but declined it. The fleet continued on toward Florida and sighted land on August 28, the same day that a French expedition under Ribault reached the river May. Menendez de Aviles conquered the French at Fort Carolin and then savagely executed every Huguenot as an enemy of King Philip. L. remained in Florida and named himself vicar general. BIBLIOGRAPHY: B. F. French, *Historical Collections of Louisiana and Florida* (second series) 2:191–234.

[R. BRADY]

LÓPEZ Y VICUÑA, VINCENTA MARÍA, ST. (1847–90), foundress. Daughter of middle-class Spanish parents, L. was attracted to work on behalf of young working girls in Madrid. She lived a common life there with a small group for 5 years. In 1876 she established the Daughters of Mary Immaculate for Domestic Services, a community to conduct hospices for working girls and to teach domestic arts. In 1888 the congregation received papal approval and spread through Europe and Latin America. Beatified in 1950, she was canonized in 1975.

[J. R. AHERNE]

LORAS, JEAN MATHIAS PIERRE (1792–1858), first bp. of Dubuque, Iowa. Ordained for the archdiocese of Lyons in 1815, he was a seminary professor and superior, then a parish missioner before volunteering for work in Mobile, Ala., at the invitation of Bp. M. Portier in 1828. In Mobile, L. was pastor, vicar general, and head of Spring Hill College from 1830. He was named and consecrated bp. of Dubuque in 1837, took possession of his see in 1839, after a European recruiting visit. He undertook visitation of his then vast diocese, encouraged religious foundations, notably the Cistercian Abbey of New Melleray in 1849. The foundations he laid for what is now one of the most flourishing of American archdioceses include Loras College, Mount Saint Bernard's Seminary, the Dubuque establishment of the Sisters of Charity of the Blessed Virgin Mary, the cathedral, the cathedral school for girls and for boys. He attracted many Irish immigrants to the diocese and dealt with tensions that grew up between them and the predominantly French clergy. L. is buried in the crypt of the cathedral of Dubuque.

[T. C. O'BRIEN]

LORBER, JACOB (1800–64), German theosophical mystic. L. was influenced chiefly by Jakob *Böhme and Emanuel *Swedenborg. While a teacher of music in 1840, he heard the command, "Write!" For the rest of his life he expounded in treatises that fill 25 volumes the millenarian-gnostic cosmological ideas his voices dictated. According to his teaching, God has filled the universe from all eternity. He is in essence love (Father), wisdom (Son), and will (Holy Spirit). In time, God separated from himself a world of primeval spirits, some of whom fell away. Through the love of the rest arose the material world, including man, in whom lives a spark of divinity. God then united his full essence with matter in Christ. Through baptism, the Lord's Supper, and fulfillment of moral and charitable requirements, a fraction of mankind reaches perfection here on earth; but with the aid of the primeval spirits all will be saved in the end, after long probation. L. established a group called the New Salem Society and founded his own press at Bietigheim (now the Lorber Verlag). His association dissolved in 1937 but was reconstituted in 1945 as the Lorber Gesellschaft. Its members, who need not separate from confessional Churches, eschew church buildings and meet instead in the prayer rooms of charitable institutions in about 25 locations in Austria, Switzerland, France, and Brazil. BIBLIOGRAPHY: K. Algermissen, LTK 6:1140.

[M. J. SUELZER]

LORD, THE, the Hebrew title *Adonai* (My, or the Lord) for Israel's God, Yahweh. It meant that he had redeemed his chosen people and by the covenant of Sinai became their master and they, his servants. He was also Lord of all the earth, since he created it and its fullness. The title frequently preceded his proper name, Yahweh, and eventually became another, less sacred, proper name. When Yahweh was no longer pronounced out of reverence (*c.*3d cent. B.C.), *Adonai* became its most frequent substitute. The Greek translations of the 2d cent. B.C. used *Kyrios* most frequently for the Yahweh of the Hebrew text. In the NT this Greek usage perdured: God was called Lord or the Lord as if that were his proper name, while only infrequently was the lordship meaning of the title emphasized (e.g. Acts 17.24). But, the title was much more often applied to Jesus and expressed his lordship and rule over those who accepted him as their Lord and master. The simplest and most basic Christian creed was: Jesus is Lord (Acts 2.36; 1 Cor 12.3; Rom 10.9–13; Jn 20.28). In the Gospels the Evangelists sometimes anachronistically used *Kyrios* for Jesus, although his lordship was not revealed until his Resurrection (Mk 5.20; 11.3; Lk 2.11; 7.13; Mt 7.21,22; Jn 6.23; 11.2). Even the vocative form *Kyrie,* used in addressing Jesus, although it could mean simply, "Sir," had a deeper meaning for the Christian authors and their readers, who believed in his postresurrectional identity as Lord (Mk 7.28; Mt 8.2,6 etc.; Lk 5.8 etc.; Jn 4.11 etc.). The most significant usage was when Bible texts, in which *Kyrios* stood for Yahweh, were applied to Jesus (Mt. 3.3 and parallels with Is 40.3; Rom 10.13 with Jl 3.5, cf. Acts 2.21,38; 1 Cor 1.31 with Jer 9.22, 23; Heb 1.10 with Ps 102.26; etc.). Thus, the title was the most important expression of Christian NT belief that Jesus was not only man but God—the first step in the development of the doctrine that God is three distinct Persons but only one God, the doctrine of the Trinity.

[J. F. FALLON]

LORD, DANIEL ALOYSIUS (1885–1955), American Jesuit writer, leader of the Sodality movement. He was ordained in 1923. His great vehicle was the sodality movement, which by his genius was turned into an effective instrument nationally to draw young people to the Church. He was national director of the Sodality from 1925 to his death. With fellow Jesuit E. *Garesché he edited *The Queen's Work* from 1913. A technical adviser to filmmakers, he coauthored the Motion Picture Code and was instrumental in creating the Legion of Decency. L. in 1928 organized the first national Leadership School and in 1931 the Summer School of Catholic Action, which attracted hundreds of thousands over the years. His writing output was incredible: 30 books, 300 pamphlets, 66 booklets, 50 plays and 12 musicals. In addition he prepared 900 radio presentations. BIBLIOGRAPHY: J. McGloin, *Backstage Missionary* (1958).

[J. R. AHERNE]

LORD OF HOSTS, an abbreviated form of the original Yahweh, the God of the Armies of Israel (1 Sm 17.45; Am 3.13; Jer 35.17), in which *Adonai* (Heb. Lord) has been substituted for Yahweh, the name of God too sacred to be pronounced. As used in early texts it meant that God is the general of Israel's battle array and leads it to victory. Its later frequent use by the Prophets connoted God's power over all creation, the armies of earth (history's governor) and of the heavens (stars and angels).

[J. F. FALLON]

LORD OF THE DANCE, see NATARĀJA.

LORD'S DAY, THE (Gr., *kyriakē hemera*), the first day of the week on which Christians celebrate Christ's Resurrection, in distinction from the Jewish Sabbath. The phrase occurs once in the NT (Rev. 1.10) as the day on which the seer "was possessed by the spirit." In early Christian literature the Lord's Day refers to the Christian observance of Sunday (*Didache,* 14.1). The first day of the week was emphasized as the day on which Christ rose (Mt 28.1; Jn 20.1), and become prominent as the day on which there was preaching and the commemoration of the Lord's Supper (Acts 20.7–11; Lk 24.1,30–35). Each Lord's Day was an Easter festival. Soon the Lord's Day replaced the Jewish Sabbath as the day of rest appointed by God, and in 321 Constantine made Sunday a public holiday. BIBLIOGRAPHY: W. F. Dicharry, NCE 8:990–991; O. Cullmann, *Early Christian Worship* (tr. A. S. Todd and J. B. Torrance, 1962) 9–12; W. Rordorff, *Sunday: The History of the Day of Rest and Worship in the Earliest Centuries of the Christian Church* (1968).

[E. CABEY]

LORD'S DAY ALLIANCE of the United States, a group organized as the American Sabbath Union in 1888 and incorporated in New York State under its present name in 1909 to secure Sunday as a day of rest and worship for the working man and to work for legislation to that end. At a time when the 7-day working week was common, the Alliance campaigned to secure Sunday closing, or compensatory time off for necessary Sunday work, esp. for federal and state employees, and fought for laws to curb commercialization of the Sunday by theaters, professional baseball games, and other amusements. BIBLIOGRAPHY: *American State Papers Bearing on Sunday Legislation* (ed. W. A. Blakely, 1911, repr. 1970). *SABBATARIANS.

[D. CODDINGTON]

LORD'S SUPPER, sacrament of the Eucharist. In 1 Cor 11.20 St. Paul refers to the Lord's Supper. The Reformers, rejecting RC eucharistic teaching and the name "Mass" connoting it, substituted Lord's Supper for the eucharistic celebration; the name appears in all of the main *confessions of faith, continental and English. Along with baptism, the Lord's Supper is recognized by most Protestant bodies as a true sacrament. Although the name still commonly excludes by connotation any sacrificial note from the Eucharist, its positive meaning varies among the Churches (see EUCHARIST; REAL PRESENCE). Recent RC reemphasis on the Eucharist as a meal has taken away the former Protestant flavor of the term Lord's Supper; Vatican Council II refers to the Eucharist as the Lord's Supper in discussing ecumenical dialogue with the Protestant Churches (Vat II Ecum 22). BIBLIOGRAPHY: C. O'Neill, *New Approaches to the Eucharist* (1967); E. Lussier, *Getting to Know the Eucharist* (1974).

[T. C. O'BRIEN]

LORENZANA, FRANCISCO ANTONIO DE (1722–1804), Spanish churchman, abp. of Mexico and later cardinal of Toledo. L. was bp. of Plasencia when he was appointed to the archbishopric of Mexico (1766). In his new see he labored to extirpate superstitition, improve the training of the clergy, and ameliorate the social conditions of the people. He published the acts of the first three Mexican provincial councils and himself presided at the fourth (1771). L. was recalled to Spain and made abp. of Toledo in 1772. Among his other activities he published the writings of the Spanish church fathers, edited the Gothic Missal and Breviary, and helped hundreds of exiled French priests out of his own resources. As a cardinal L. was envoy to Pius VI in his exile and he facilitated the holding of the conclave at Venice (1799) that elected Pius VII by taking upon himself the expenses of the cardinals who were without funds. Renouncing his see in 1800, he settled in Rome. BIBLIOGRAPHY: M. de Camillis, EncCatt 7:1533.

[P. DAMBORIENA]

LORENZETTI, Sienese painters. **Ambrogio** (fl. 1319–47), notably original, painted *Madonna and Child* (1317), another dated 1319, and a Cathedral *Maestà* (*c.*1330). His extensive and famous allegorical frescoes—*Good Government* and *Bad Government* in the Palazzo Pubblico, Siena (1338–39)—are eloquent in characterization, boldly realistic and experimental in depicting panoramic distance. A *Presentation in the Temple* (1342) is noted by E. Panofsky as significantly innovative. Damaged frescoes in S. Francesco, Siena, survive. Ambrogio moved from Duccio toward Giotto in space and composition, anticipating the Renaissance in Siena. **Pietro** (fl. 1320–44), brother of Ambrogio, moving (as did Ambrogio) from Duccio toward Giotto. He painted a *Madonna and Child with Saints* (1320, Arezzo) and an altarpiece in S. Ansano a Dofana (1329), a *Virgin and Child Enthroned* (Philadelphia Museum of Art) and many frescoes in the Lower Church, S. Francesco, Assisi. A style monumental and severe, with evidences of sculptural form beneath the drapery in the manner of Giotto, marks many later works (*Man of Sorrows, St. Lucy, St. Catherine,* and *Crucifixion* fresco in S. Francesco, Siena). Most remarkable of his last works is the triptych, *Nativity of the Virgin* (1342, Opera del Duomo, Siena), foreshadowing Mantegna's *S. Zeno,* Verona, in illusion of space. Though Pietro had many followers his influence was not as great as that of Ambrogio. BIBLIOGRAPHY: G. Rowley, *Ambrogio Lorenzetti* (1958); E. T. De Wald, *Pietro Lorenzetti* (1930).

[M. J. DALY]

LORETO, a small town in the marshes near the Adriatic Sea, site of the Holy House of the Virgin. The first mention of it is in an account by Pietro di Giorgio Tolomei of Teramo (*c.*1472). Tradition has it that the house is Mary's and that it was taken to Loreto by angels. The move to Loreto was its fourth. Popes *Boniface IX (1389) reorganized it as a shrine and Paul II (1470) so alludes to it. It was established as a parish in 1482, taken under papal protection in 1484; in 1507 the account of it was recorded in a papal bull. It was established as a minor basilica in 1728. For a time control over it was taken by the Italian government, but it was restored to the Church in 1929. BIBLIOGRAPHY: H. M. Gillett, *Famous Shrines of Our Lady* (2 v., 1949).

[J. R. RIVELLO]

LORETTO, LADIES OF, (Institute of the Blessed Virgin Mary), a religious community founded in 1609 in Belgium by Mary Ward, an English woman; therefore they were often called the English Ladies. The community, following the Rule of the Society of Jesus, was uncloistered in order to devote itself to the instruction of youth. During the 17th cent. a house was established in England (the first convent there after the Reformation), from which foundations were made in Bavaria and Italy. In the next century the institute spread to Ireland, Australia, Canada, and Spain, and now has houses on every continent. In 1975 worldwide membership consisted of 5,454 sisters in 279 houses.

[M. T. REILLY]

LORETTO, SISTERS OF, also known as Sisters of Loretto at the Foot of the Cross, were founded in Kentucky in 1812 by Reverend Charles *Nerinckx, a Belgian. Mary Rhodes and her two companions became interested in religious life while they were teaching catechism to students enrolled in their school. They founded the first community of the congregation at Hardin's Creek, Ky., which was later moved to St. Stephen's Farm, Ky. In 1907 Pius X gave papal approval to the constitution of this American sisterhood, whose purpose was the Christian education of youth. They labored in China from 1923 till 1952 when they were expelled by the Communists. In 1960 they began missionary work in La Paz, Bolivia. Their motherhouse is in Nerinx, Kentucky. In 1975 membership consisted of 804 sisters in 76 houses.

[R. C. CLIGGETT]

LORICA, see BREASTPLATE OF ST. PATRICK.

LORRAIN, CLAUDE (CLAUDE GELLEÉ; CLAUDE; 1620–82), one of the greatest masters of all time in ideal landscape, second only to Poussin in 17th-cent. French painting. After study with Tassi in Rome (1613?–20), L. returned to Lorraine, painted the ceiling in a Carmelite church (destroyed), but finally settled in Rome (1627). Friend of Poussin, L. painted frescoes, and friezes of landscapes (*c.*1630) that established his reputation. He worked in other media—etching, painting (on copper) *The Rest on the Flight into Egypt* (1631), *The Judgment of Paris* (1633), and other mythological works. By 1638 L. was the leading landscape painter in Italy, with commissions from the pope., cardinals, and the King of Spain (*The Temptations of St. Anthony,* 1638). Unlike Poussin who was rooted in the Venetians, L. followed the Northern tradition in a style less heroic but more poetic, effecting an atmosphere and light with a sublety unknown in his time, a brilliance emanating from the horizon permeating all with radiance, moving forward and outward, and connecting foreground and background. *The Marriage of Isaac and Rebekah* (1648), paintings of *Magdalen, SS. Serapia and Paula,* and *Tobias* (1640) are idyllic and pastoral in mood. Occasionally the figures were added by assistants (Giovanni Desiderii) as in *Jacob the Angel* (1672). L. was prince of landscape painters until the 19th-cent. masters of the Romantic and Impressionist schools extended his expression. BIBLIOGRAPHY: M. Rothlisberger, *Ein Nachtrag Zu Claude* (1962); *Wildenstein Album* (1962): E. Knab, "Stylistic Problems of Claude's Draughtsmanship" (*Acts of the 20th International Congress of the History of Art* (1963).

[M. J. DALY]

LORSCH, ABBEY OF, a Benedictine abbey and later a Premonstratensian monastery in Hesse, Germany. Founded in 764, it was given royal protection by Charlemagne. Very influential, with an outstanding library, it fell into decline in the 12th century. In 1229, Archbishop Siegfried II of Mainz obtained jurisdiction over Lorsch. In 1244 Premonstratensian canons were introduced, but in 1461 it was turned over to the Count Palatine. Destroyed (1621) during the Thirty Years' War, the territory was given in 1803 to the state of Hesse-Darmstadt. Its crypt, where two Carolingian rulers were buried, has been restored.

[M. A. MCFADDEN]

LOSSKY, VLADIMIR NIKOLAEVICH (1903–58), Orthodox dogmatic theologian, leading advocate of the Western rite in Orthodoxy, and a founder of the Confraternity of St. Photios. Son of the philosopher, Nicholas Lossky, L. specialized in the study of Palamism, mysticism, sophiology, and the Latin Middle Ages. He was dean and professor at the Orthodox Institute of St. Denis in Paris. His most important works are *Mystical Theology of the Eastern Church* (1957) and *Vision of God* (1963). He opposed Bulgakov's sophiology and sought points of contact between Orthodox and Western theology.

[T. BIRD]

LOST PROPERTY AND OWNERSHIP. Finding is one of the ways of acquiring *ownership, but it is a way hedged round by the restriction that in *justice a possession "calls out for" its rightful owner (*res clamat domino*). The simple fact of finding an object is not a just title of ownership. The finder, therefore, who makes no attempt to discover the true owner and to restore the found object is a *possessor in bad faith. Obviously this presumes that the object is of some value, and that its loss means *damage to the owner. The finder who makes every reasonable effort but fails to learn the true owner may then himself become the owner, whether because civil law determines so or on the presumption of *occupancy, i.e., the object becomes de facto abandoned and the possession of no one. (There has been disagreement among moralists on the precise way finding becomes a title of ownership.) In case of doubt about the true owner, the problem has to be resolved on the principles governing possessors in doubtful faith. Finally, the finder of a lost object has no obligation in justice to take it into his custody and to seek out the owner, but such a course may be dictated by charity where the loss represents serious harm to the rightful owner. A finder who has taken a lost object into his charge must take reasonable care of it; he has a right to reimbursement for any expense incurred once the owner is discovered, but not per se to a reward, unless one has been promised.

[T. C. O'BRIEN]

LOS-VON-ROM MOVEMENT, the concerted attempt made by German nationalist organizations to promote a secession of Austrian Catholics from their Church in the late 19th and early 20th centuries. The expression was first used by a student at a nationalist rally in 1897 and then by Georg von Schönerer, the leader of the Pan-German party, in his manifesto of Nov. 1898, when he called for the conversion of Catholics to the Old Catholic Church or to Protestantism. The movement partly reflected the resentment of German nationalists in Austria against the RC Church for its support of the Habsburg government, which after 1892 tried to provide parity for the Czech language in its mixed German-Czech provinces. It was also a reaction to use of Czech RC priests in some German parishes. Nationalist Protestant organizations from the German Reich, e.g., the Evangelische Bund, provided assistance to the movement. From 75,000 to 85,000 Catholics left the Church between 1897 and 1914. The movement fell far short of its objectives, however, and was not a serious factor in Austrian affairs after World War I. Adolf Hitler, a warm admirer of Schönerer, later wrote in *Mein Kampf* (1925) that the Pan-German leader had made the mistake of waging major campaigns against two foes, the Austrian monarchy and the RC Church, at the same time.

[J. K. ZEENDER]

LOT, son of Haran and nephew of Abraham. Lot migrated with Abraham from Ur to Palestine, separated from him when their herdsmen quarrelled, and settled outside Sodom (Gen 11.27–13.13). With regard to Abraham, Lot is made to appear selfish, perhaps to emphasize the magnanimity of Abraham (Gen 14). With regard to his wife and daughters, Lot appeared more obedient and the victim of his daughters' machinations which made him the ancestor of Israel's enemies, the Moabites and Ammonites (Gen 19). BIBLIOGRAPHY: L. Hicks, InterDB 3:162–163.

[E. CABEY]

LOTBINIÈRE, FRANÇOIS LOUIS CHARTIER DE (1716–84). Born of a reputable Canadian family, L. became a Franciscan Recollect and was ordained in 1741. His life was spent under a succession of canonical clouds. He left the Recollects, was in and out of several orders, was repeatedly under censure in Canada, France, and Martinique for misconduct, and spent extended intervals of time in a state of apostasy. When the American colonists invaded Quebec (1775–76) he supported their cause and was a chaplain with Col. Moses Hazen's Canadian volunteers. For a time he exercised an independent ministry in N New York.

[R. K. MACMASTER]

LOTHAIR I (795–855), **GERMAN EMPEROR** from 840. Crowned co-emperor in 823, he twice (830 and 833–834) led unsuccessful revolts against his father. In 834, deprived of title, he retreated to Italy. At his father's death (840) he became emperor. Outmaneuvered by his brothers at Fontenoy (841) and Verdun (843), he accepted a tripartite division of the empire. Assigning Italy to his son Louis II, he devoted himself to the N part of his realm (called the "middle kingdom"). Shortly before dying he retired to Prüm, succeeded by his son, Louis II as Emperor and by his other sons Lothair II and Charles in the "middle kingdom." BIBLIOGRAPHY: J. F. Böhmer, *Regesta imperii* (2d ed. 1908) 1:412–482; A. Cabaniss, NCE 8:1003–04.

[A. CABANISS]

LOTHAIR II (*c.*825–869), **GERMAN KING** from 855. Second son of Lothair I and Irmengard, he acquired in 855 the northern portion of his father's realm which thereafter bore his name: Lotharingia, Lothringen, Lorraine (*Lotharii regnum*). He suffered constant harassment by his uncles, Louis the German and Charles the Bald. When he died, they divided his land between them (treaty of Meersen, 870). He also suffered marital and ecclesiastical misfortunes when he divorced his childless wife Theutberga to marry his concubine Waldrada. That action provided his uncles an excuse to press upon his frontiers and evoked condemnation by Hincmar of Reims and Pope Nicholas I. BIBLIOGRAPHY: J. F. Böhmer, *Regesta imperii* (2d ed. 1908), 1:524–557; A. Cabaniss, NCE 8:1004.

[A. CABANISS]

LOTHAIR III (1075–1137), **HOLY ROMAN EMPEROR** from 1133. In 1106 he succeeded to the duchy of Saxony. When Henry V died childless, his nephew, the head of the Hohenstaufen house, was passed over for king in favor of Lothair. Thus did the elective principle become established in fact as well as in theory. L. married his daughter to Henry the Proud of Bavaria, thereby uniting that dukedom with Saxony against the Hohenstaufen. L. did not achieve complete victory until 1135. Persuaded by St. Bernard, he recognized Innocent II over Anacletus as rightful pope in 1130 and was himself crowned emperor in 1133. He died upon returning from an Italian campaign against the Normans. BIBLIOGRAPHY: H. Wolfram, NCE 8:1004–05.

[J. E. LYNCH]

LOTI, PIERRE (pseud. of Julien Viâud; 1850–1923), French novelist and naval officer. His novels, which were very well received, are notable for their accurate and exotic descriptions. In their pessimistic tone they resemble the romantics. In its simple gravity, L.'s style reflects that of the realists. His many novels include his most famous one, *Pêcheur d'Islande* (1886; Eng. tr. *An Iceland Fisherman*), a tale of Breton fishermen. Of his travel books, *Vers Ispahan* (*Toward Ispahan,* 1904) is highly esteemed. He was considered a highly talented and original writer of the second half of the 19th century. BIBLIOGRAPHY: E. B. D'Auvergne, *Pierre Loti* (1926, repr. 1970).

[S. A. HEENEY]

LOTTIN, ODON (1880–1965), historical theologian. L. was a Benedictine monk at the monastery of Mount César, Louvain. His lifetime of research into the medieval sources of moral theology were compiled and published in his monumental *Psychologie et morale* (4 v., 1942–60). The work is esp. important for the study of the fundamentals of moral theology, and of the background to moral treatises in St. Thomas Aquinas' *Summa theologiae*. The author's own doctrinal interpretations as set forth, e.g., in *Principes de morale* (2 v., 1947) are less reliable than his superb historical documentation.

[T. C. O'BRIEN]

LOTTO, LORENZO (*c.*1480–1556), Venetian painter of the High Renaissance, whose early works show intense color, strained poses, and hard surfaces (*Madonna with St. Peter Martyr,* 1503; *Bishop Bernardo de' Rossi,* 1505; *The Assumption,* 1506), which somewhat softened after his trip to Rome (*Entombment of Christ*). Altarpieces of the Bergamo period introduce fluttering forms and night light. *Christ Taking Leave of His Mother* (1521) and the *Mystical Marriage of St. Catherine* (1523) are his best works. His last paintings are pious (*Madonna of the Rosary,* 1539). L. is a painter of interest though he exerted no influence on other artists. BIBLIOGRAPHY: B. Berenson, *Lorenzo Lotto* (1956).

[M. J. DALY]

LOTZE, RUDOLF HERMANN (1817–81), German philosopher and physician, professor of philosophy at Leipzig, Göttigen and briefly, Berlin. L.'s thought developed against the background of German idealism, but was strongly influenced by his own knowledge of the positive sciences. Philosophy, he held, since it requires a basis of science, cannot be frozen into a system but must remain open. The world is psychical; men have individual souls. The world below man follows mechanistic laws, but the laws of the soul are teleological. The existence of a personal God is known from the existence of souls and of ends. Reality is always in flux, but it flows according to a fixed order, a preestablished harmony between God and the multitude of spirits. He emphasizes the importance of feeling in man's full development, natural as well as religious. Knowledge of nature leads to the concept of God, social life to the concept of ethical living. The feeling for the holy leads man to seek truth as it is fused with goodness and beauty. L. left no school of followers, but his influence is seen in such thinkers as F. Brentano, E. Husserl, and in America, G. T. Ladd and Josiah Royce. BIBLIOGRAPHY: Copleston 7:376–381; R. Gotesky, EncPhil 5:87–89; G. Santayana, *Lotze's System of Philosophy* (ed. P. G. Kuntz, 1971).

[W. B. MAHONEY]

LOTZER, SEBASTIAN (*c.*1490–after 1525), in the German *Peasants' War, author of the Twelve Articles. L., who was a furrier at Memmingen in Bavaria, was well read in the Bible and the new Reformation literature, as is evident from his five pamphlets on the layman's right to interpret and expound the word of God. In 1525 he put the demands of the peasants into writing, giving the Twelve Articles, the manifesto of the Peasants' War, a strong biblical base. After the peasants' defeat he escaped to St. Gall, and thereafter disappears from history. See bibliog. for Peasants' War.

[T. C. O'BRIEN]

LOU-TSENG-TSIANG, CELESTINE (1871–1949), Benedictine monk at the abbey of Lophem, Belgium, noted for his contributions to missiology. He wrote to bridge the gap between Christianity and Confucianism. BIBLIOGRAPHY: Lokuang, EncCatt 7:1583–84.

[J. R. AHERNE]

LOUGH DERG, see ST. PATRICK'S PURGATORY.

LOUGHLIN, JAMES F. (1851–1911), educator, writer. Ordained a priest in 1874, he served in Philadelphia as a seminary professor, then as a pastor and diocesan leader. He was a founder of the Catholic Summer School of America. As a writer on historical subjects he was a popular rather than scholarly contributor. L. served as editor of the *American Catholic Quarterly Review.* BIBLIOGRAPHY: W. Lallou "Monsignor James F. Loughlin, D.D." RACHS 25 (1914) 277–284.

[J. R. AHERNE]

LOUGHLIN, JOHN (1817–1891), first bp. of Brooklyn. A native of Ireland he was brought as a young man to the U.S., where he studied for the priesthood and was ordained in 1840. Vicar general of New York he was named first bp. of Brooklyn in 1853. In his new diocese L. faced many problems, but his work paved the way for the future development of the jurisdiction. He was a participant in all 3 Plenary Councils of Baltimore. BIBLIOGRAPHY: J. Sharp, *History of the Diocese of Brooklyn* (2v., 1954).

[J. R. AHERNE]

LOUIS VI (1081–1137), **KING OF FRANCE** from 1108. Son of Philip I and Bertha of Holland, L. was educated at St. Denis where he met Suger who was later to become his biographer. Crowned king at Orleans, he was supportive of the clergy and also of Innocent II in the latter's battle against the antipope Anacletus. BIBLIOGRAPHY: D. J. A. Matthew, NCE 8:1008; Suger, *Vie de Louis VI le Gros* (ed. and tr. H. Waquet, 1929).

[J. R. RIVELLO]

LOUIS VII (1120–80), **KING OF FRANCE** from 1137. The son of Louis VI and Adelaide of Maurienne, L. was married to Eleanor of Aquitaine (1137) and upon the annulment of this marriage (1152) married Constance of Castile and later, Adela of Champagne. His divorced wife Eleanor married Henry Plantagenet, Duke of Normandy, who 2 years later became Henry II of England. Henry laid claim to Aquitaine as Eleanor's inheritance and thus began the recurrent struggle between Louis and Henry. L. participated in the second Crusade (1147–49) and in pilgrimages to Santiago de Compostela (1154–55), to the Grande Chartreuse (1162–63), and to Canterbury (1179). He was buried at the Cistercian monastery which he founded at Barbeaux. BIBLIOGRAPHY: Fliche-Martin 9:188–197.

[J. R. RIVELLO]

LOUIS VIII (1187–1226), **KING OF FRANCE** from 1223. Son of Philip II and Isabella of Hainault, married (1200) to Blanche of Castile. L. fought for the French monarchy in the guise of a Crusader. In 1213 he took the cross to enforce Innocent III's excommunication of John of England but did not invade England until 1216–17, for which he was himself excommunicated. L.'s successes came in Languedoc during the Albigensian Crusade. He conducted a reconnaissance in 1215, and returned in 1219 for the siege of Toulouse. He was consecrated king at Reims in 1223. In 1226 he made his major effort and reaffirmed his rights to the de Montfort lands, thus annexing Languedoc to the French royal domain. BIBLIOGRAPHY: R. Fawtier, *Capetian Kings of France* (1960); Z. Oldenbourg, *Massacre at Montsegur* (1961).

[R. H. SCHMANDT]

LOUIS IX, ST. (1214–70), **KING OF FRANCE** from 1226. The son of Louis VIII and *Blanche of Castile, he was indebted to his mother for effective government during his long and troubled minority (to 1234). He married Marguerite of Provence and was the father of 10 children.

Once Louis assumed control of France in his own right, he ruled with wisdom and authority, achieving order at home and peace abroad. He kept close control over the royal officials, frequently sending others to investigate their conduct and to hear complaints against them (*enquêteurs de justice*). In a series of royal ordinances, he attempted to regularize the customary law, extend royal justice, and establish closer control over the city of Paris. He tried to replace trial by battle with examination of witnesses. It was during his reign that certain sessions of the *curia regis* (the king's traditional feudal court) began to specialize; some of its sessions were reserved to judicial affairs (*curia in parliamentum*) and others to finance (*curia in compotis*). Louis's reputation for sanctity and fairness brought him appeals for arbitration from all parts of Europe, and this fact in addition to difficulties in England and the Holy Roman Empire made France the dominant power in Western Europe. He successfully used his influence and reputation to settle the difficulties between France and England and between France and Aragon. Though Louis was noted for his piety, he kept firm control over episcopal appointments, and held a very high conception of the right and duties of a king (*la royauté mystique*). He also refused to intervene in the struggle between the Pope (*Innocent IV) and Emperor (*Frederick II), although he gave the Pope asylum in France.

Louis is probably best known for his two Crusades, and on the first he was accompanied by his biographer, Sire de Joinville. Neither of his Crusades, however, was particularly successful. On the first (1248–54) he captured Damietta in Egypt, which he had intended to exchange for Jerusalem. However, he was defeated and captured when he was forced by his brother's imprudence to change his plans and move against Cairo. His second Crusade concentrated on Tunisia, which Louis hoped to use as a base for attack on Egypt. He died during this campaign. L. was canonized by Pope Boniface VIII in 1297. BIBLIOGRAPHY: J. de Joinville, *History of St. Louis* (ed. N. de Wailly, tr. J. Evans, 1938); C. Petit-Dutaillis, *Feudal Monarchy in France and England from the Tenth to Thirteenth Century* (tr. E. D. Hunt, 1936); D. J. A. Matthew, NCE 8:1010–12; J. Levron, *St. Louis ou L'apogée du moyenne âge* (1957); H. Platelle, BiblSanct 8:320–338; Butler 3:394–398.

[V. L. BULLOUGH]

LOUIS XI (1423–83); **KING OF FRANCE** from 1461, son of Charles VII and Mary of Anjou. The treaty of Arras (1482), which brought the Duchy of Burgundy under royal control, climaxed his struggle to subdue France's feudal nobility and to centralize the government of France. BIBLIOGRAPHY: P. Champion, *Louis XI* (tr. W. Whale, 1929).

[J. MULDOON]

LOUIS XII (1462–1515), **KING OF FRANCE** from 1498, son of Charles, Duke of Orléans and successor to his childless cousin, Charles VIII. As a participant in the Italian wars Louis conquered Milan and Genoa (1499–1500); failed in his efforts in Naples; invaded Venice (1509) as a member of the anti-Venetian League, but was expelled later (1513) by Maximilian I and the Swiss. He was a patron of the arts in France and sponsor of the schismatic Council of Pisa (1511–12), called to depose Julius II, his political antagonist in the Italian wars. BIBLIOGRAPHY: J. A. Néret, *Louis XII* (1948); R. Doucet, CModH² 1:292–315.

[J. J. SMITH]

LOUIS XIII (1601–43), **KING OF FRANCE** from 1610. Son of Henri IV and Marie de Médicis, he became king in 1610 and spent his early years under the regency of his mother and her Italian favorites, the Concini family. The many court intrigues were gradually mastered by Card. *Richelieu; L. recognized the cardinal's ability to rescue France from anarchy and bring it to a foremost role in European politics. He thus supported Richelieu's anti-Habsburg policies and allied France with the German and Swedish defenders of Protestantism against the anti-Gallican Spanish and Austrian monarchies. Within the country he vigorously opposed the Huguenots and destroyed their fortified cities, particularly La Rochelle in 1627. Finally, in an effort to strengthen royal power, L. accepted Richelieu's plans to crush the power of the nobility. L.'s final share in Richelieu's policies was the prosecution of the war against Spain, begun in 1635 and continued after the cardinal's death in 1642. BIBLIOGRAPHY: O. Ranum, *Richelieu and the Councillors of Louis XIII* (1963).

[I. M. KASHUBA]

LOUIS XIV (1638–1715), **KING OF FRANCE** from 1643, whose unprecedented 72-year reign witnessed the triumph of monarchical absolutism at home and of French cultural and political dominance abroad. As he was only four when he inherited the throne from his father Louis XIII, his mother Anne of Austria, became regent. Real power during L.'s minority was exercised by Card. Mazarin who, as first minister, had to put down the quasi-feudal uprising of nobles, known as the Fronde (1648–53), against the growing power of the monarchy. Their subjection freed L. thereafter from internal threat. Before retiring (1660), Mazarin also arranged L.'s marriage to Maria Theresa, daughter of Philip IV of Spain. This gave the French king an interest in the Spanish inheritance, which included the southern Netherlands, important parts of Italy, and the New World. Once L. took command, the *parlements* were turned into rubber stamps for the registration of royal edicts; a modern police system, centering on Paris, spread its tentacles into the provinces; a program of economic reform dramatically increased the royal revenues. L. now had on call a strengthened navy, a powerful, well-knit army and a diplomatic corps in size and energy second to none. The foundations were thus laid for the pursuit of *gloire* through foreign military ventures to which L. dedicated himself for the better part of 45 years. His first bid for aggrandizement was based on his wife's supposed inheritance rights to the Spanish Netherlands. This brought on the War of Devolution (1667–68) with Spain, from which L. gained some Flemish territory along his N frontier, including the city of Lille. He next conspired with Charles II of England to smash their trading rival Holland as a commercial power, but the Dutch War (1672–78) instead bogged down in a costly, rather inconclusive series of campaigns. Nevertheless, by the Peace of Nijmegen, L. won back Franche-Comté, on his E frontier, from Spain as well as additional territory in Flanders. By 1683, after bloodlessly acquiring the cities of Strasbourg and Colmar on his NE frontier, L. stood at the peak of his power and prestige. But his apparently insatiable appetite, together with the ruthless means he employed, inspired his enemies to unite at the next threat to European security. Thus, when L. laid claim to, then invaded the Palatinate, he was opposed by a coalition that included the Holy Roman Emperor, the German princes, Holland, and England now led by his old enemy, William of Orange, who in 1688 became William III. In the course of his struggle against the League of Augsburg (1688–97), L. lost a substantial part of his fleet, and by the Treaty of Ryswick was forced to abandon his territorial conquests. This time the war's expenses had caused misery in France too. The War of the Spanish Succession (1701–14) was brought on by L.'s stubborn refusal to assure the powers that the Spanish throne (left to Louis' grandson Philip of Anjou by the dying Charles II of Spain) would never be united with the French. France was thus faced by a reanimated Grand Alliance, which under the Duke of Marlborough's brilliant leadership won every important engagement. Though the Peace of Utrecht (1713–14) confirmed L.'s grandson as Philip V of Spain, France otherwise lost large stretches of Canada to Great Britain, was forced to accept the transfer of Gibraltar to England and of Belgium to Austria, and to restore the right bank of the Rhine. With this prolonged effort, the country's resources were exhausted, its people tired and impoverished. L. lacked a sense of proportion. By the early 1680's, he not only reigned over the strongest state in Europe but at Versailles had created a personal monument which for sheer splendor, pomp, and the brilliant artists it attracted was the envy of the civilized world. It was not enough. Even as L.'s foreign policy both taxed the tolerance of his neighbors and ultimately consumed the substance of France, so his religious policy also strained relations abroad and exacerbated differences at home. Throughout the 1670s, he quarreled with the popes regarding the extent of the crown's power over the Church in France, and when Innocent XI came close to excommunicating him in 1679 had an Assembly of the Clergy (1680) declare its unswerving allegiance to the monarchy. This was followed in 1682 by the promulgation of the Four Gallican Articles, which affirmed the traditional privileges of the French Church and defined relations between pontiff and sovereign in terms of disadvantage to the Holy See. Though L. himself compromised on the issue in 1693, a total break with Rome was only narrowly averted. L.'s handling of the Protestant question involved far more serious consequences and was even less necessary in view of the loyal stance maintained by the Calvinist minority during the Fronde. The repression started in 1682: a warning to the Huguenots to relinquish their faith was followed by the destruction of many Reformed houses of worship and the unscrupulous imposition of *dragonades* on Protestant families to encourage their conversion. Finally, in 1685, L. revoked the Edict of Nantes, by which Henri IV in 1598 had granted toleration to the Huguenots. The upshot of this shortsighted policy was the loss to France of nearly a quarter-million Protestant subjects, together with their skills, and the growth of anti-French sentiment in the Protestant countries of Europe. L. was little disposed to countenance the revival of Jansenism, which broke out in 1693 with the publication of Quesnel's *Réflexions morales*. Interpreting it as a threat to his authority and to the religious conformity he wished to prevail, he procured the Pope's formal condemnation of the movement in 1705 and 1713, and in 1710 ordered the destruction of the convent at Port-Royal, which had been the center of the theological controversy for 70 years. Those who refused to recant were imprisoned. L.'s religious intolerance and the formal piety he embraced in his later years may have resulted from his secret marriage in 1683, following the queen's death, to Mme. de Maintenon. This ended his long-term relationship with Mme. de Montespan, mother of seven of his children and the most famous of his many mistresses. Of his legitimate male heirs, four had died so that at the end L. had to turn to his great-grandson to succeed him. His passing found France still superficially strong but bearing within the seeds that in time would shake the Old Regime to its foundations.

[E. M. GATES]

LOUIS XV (1710–74), **KING OF FRANCE** from 1715. Only son of the Duke of Bourgogne and great-grandson of Louis XIV, he began his reign under the regency of Philippe, Duke of Orléans. The regency period

(1715–23) is noted for its immoral character and lack of political order and control. L.'s former tutor, Card. André *Fleury, directed the government from 1726–43, and succeeded in stabilizing the government and the economy. He also tried to maintain peace in Europe, but could not prevent France's involvement in the War of Austrian Succession on behalf of L.'s father-in-law, Stanislas Leszczynski. He did succeed however in making peace between the king and the Jansenists. The death of Fleury in 1743 marked a turning point in L.'s reign. Weary of his wife Maria Leszczynski, the mother of seven children, he turned his attention to his mistresses and a life of frivolity, costly both to the economy and to his reputation. Mme. de Pompadour, upon whom L. conferred the title of Marquise, was his principal favorite. Although she favored culture and the arts, she also involved France in the Seven Years' War (1756–63), which led to the loss of Canada, Louisiana, and colonies in India. Mme. de Pompadour supported the philosophes and their work, though L. himself mistrusted and suspected them. In 1764, the Jesuits were expelled from France, as a gesture of reconciliation toward the Gallican party through the efforts of Choiseul, L.'s very able financial minister. Upon the death of Mme. de Pompadour, Mme. du Barry, less cultured and more limited than her predecessor, became the King's favorite. Choiseul was dismissed, but parliamentary reforms were begun. Improved economic conditions toward the end of L.'s reign were not able to efface the memory of his overwhelming love of pleasure and apparent indifference toward the State; and his death in 1774 was welcomed with relief and hope. BIBLIOGRAPHY: P. Gaxotte, *Le Siècle de Louis XV* (1961); F. P. G. Guizot, *Histoire de la civilisation en France* (1830).

[I. M. KASHUBA]

LOUIS XVI (1754–93), **KING OF FRANCE** from 1774. The grandson of Louis XV, whom he succeeded under difficult political circumstances. He was a man of intelligence and integrity, though lacking in imagination. He began his reign with public favor and several humanitarian reforms, among them abolition of torture and the restoratioan of civil rights to the Protestants. Financial problems, complicated by the resistance of the *parlements* to all reforms, led to the downfall of the notable ministers Turgot, Necker, and Calonne. Because the treasury was empty and the power of the liberal bourgeoisie was increasing, L. convoked the Estates-General in 1789, its first sitting in 175 years. He was at first favorable to their demands, but refused to sign the *Déclaration des droits de l'homme*. Later the *Civil Constitution of the Clergy, (1790), which led to serious repercussions among French Catholics, troubled him greatly and he not only opposed the Revolution, but attempted to flee with his family in 1791. He was arrested and forced to remain under surveillance until his public execution on Jan. 21, 1793, during the Reign of Terror. BIBLIOGRAPHY: J. Bainville, *History of France* (1926); A. Goodwin, *French Revolution* (1962).

[I. M. KASHUBA]

LOUIS XVIII, (1755–1824), **KING OF FRANCE** from 1814. Brother of Louis XVI and Count of Provence, L. took an active part in antirevolutionary activity both in France and abroad after his flight in 1791. He was particularly active in the Catholic Resistance in the Vendée. Although he considered himself Regent after the execution of his brother in 1793, and assumed the title "Louis XVIII" in 1795, he did not come to power until 1814, when the Bourbons were recalled after Napoleon's abdication and exile following the Hundred Days. Less attentive to political affairs than to court etiquette, L. nevertheless accepted the Charter of 1814, which limited the monarchy by establishing a legislative body and incorporating many Napoleonic reforms. During his short reign of 10 years many exiled nobles returned and tried in vain to reestablish the *Ancien Régime*. Although L. seemed unaware of rapidly developing liberal movements, he did succeed in maintaining peace and order in a country recovering from the Revolution and Napoleonic wars. BIBLIOGRAPHY: P. A. Gagnon, *France since 1789* (1964); J. Bainville, *History of France* (1926).

[I. M. KASHUBA]

LOUIS I, THE PIOUS, (778–840), **GERMAN EMPEROR** from 814. Son of Charlemagne and Hildegard, he was the only legitimate son to outlive his father. He was crowned King of Aquitaine (781) by Hadrian I. About 794 he married Irmengard by whom he had Lothair, Pepin, and Louis (the German). At Charlemagne's death, L. succeeded as Emperor. When Irmengard died (818), he married Judith. His reign was troubled by factionalism: a baronial, constitutional party favoring the sons of Irmengard and a centralizing, royalist party favoring Judith and her son, Charles (the Bald). Open revolt broke out (830 and 833–834), but L. emerged successfully because of fissiparous tendencies among the rebels. Under him European Jewry experienced a "golden age," and seeds of a cultural renaissance, sown by his father, came to flower. Despite ability to maintain the empire in his lifetime, he prepared its dissolution by leaving it to his three sons, Lothair, Louis, and Charles the Bald. BIBLIOGRAPHY: *Son of Charlemagne* (ed. and tr. A. Cabaniss, 1961).

[A. CABANISS]

LOUIS II (*c.*822–875), **GERMAN EMPEROR** from 855. Oldest son of Lothair and Irmengard, he was married to Engelberga, but left no legitimate issue. As his father's lieutenant in Italy, he became emperor on his father's death (855). Embroiled in bitter altercation with the Pope and the Byzantine Emperor, and having lost Lotharingia, he left only an empty title. BIBLIOGRAPHY: J. F. Böhmer, *Regesta imperii,* (2d ed. 1908), 1:482–524; A. Cabaniss, NCE 8:1019.

[A. CABANISS]

LOUIS THE GERMAN (*c.*804–876) **KING OF GERMANY** from 840. Youngest son of Emperor Louis I the Pious and Irmengard, he governed the eastern portion of the empire. His wife Hemma was sister of his stepmother, Judith. Twice he joined his brothers, Lothair and Pepin, in revolt against their father. His dual relation to the imperial household made him an undependable link in the conspiracy. But he was estranged from his father when the latter died. He then allied with Charles the Bald against Lothair and later against Lothair II whose land they divided after his death. Pursuing German interests in Slavic lands, he encountered opposition from Cyril and Methodius. BIBLIOGRAPHY: J. F. Böhmer, *Regesta imperii* (2nd ed. 1908) 1:561–646; A. Cabaniss, NCE 8:1019.

[A. CABANISS]

LOUIS IV, THE BAVARIAN (1287?–1347), **HOLY ROMAN EMPEROR,** son of Duke Louis of Bavaria and Matilda, daughter of Emperor Rudolph I, laid claim to the German throne at the death of Henry VII in 1314. The Ghibellines and Luxemburgs supported him but the Guelfs and the Habsburgs backed Frederick the Fair of Austria. Civil war ensued and at the battle of Mühldorf (1322) L. defeated and captured his rival. When Pope John XXII refused him recognition, Louis countered by issuing the Sachsenhausen Appelation (1324) which accused the Pope of heresy for having condemned the doctrine of absolute poverty. John reacted to this move by excommunicating L. and condemning him as a usurper. In 1327 L. invaded Italy, and the following year had himself crowned emperor by Sciarra Colonna acting as representative of the Roman people. John then deprived L. of his fiefs, absolved his vassals from their oaths of fealty, invalidated his coronation, and branded him a heretic for having defended the doctrine of absolute poverty. L. next declared John deposed and set up as antipope a Franciscan Michaelist, Peter Rainalducci of Corbara (Nicholas V). After John's death L. sought reconciliation with the papacy but his efforts were frustrated by Philip VI of France. In 1338 he issued the decree *Licet juris* which stated that the imperial title was conferred by majority vote of the electors independent of papal confirmation. With the encouragement of Clement VI the German nobility elected Charles of Bohemia emperor in 1346, but L. vigorously defended his claim until his death 2 years later. BIBLIOGRAPHY: G. Mollat, *Popes at Avignon, 1305–78* (tr J. Love, 1963) 190–228; Gebhardt-Grundmann 1:427–455.

[C. J. LYNCH]

LOUIS D'ALEMAN, BL. (*c.*1390–1450), theologian, canon lawyer, abp. of Arles (1423). He was a leading figure at the Council of Basel which elected the antipope Felix V, but when Felix abdicated (1449), he also recanted and was restored to his previous position. BIBLIOGRAPHY: J. Gill, *Council of Florence* (1959).

[J. MULDOON]

LOUIS OF ARNSTEIN, VEN. (1109–85), Premonstratensian lay brother. Count of Arnstein and married, L. and his wife mutually decided to enter the Premonstratensian Order at Arnstein in 1139. He transformed the castle into an abbey of his order and established two other houses for men and three for women. Buried in St. Margaret's Church in Arnstein, he was venerated in his order immediately after his death; there are no documents for his formal beatification. BIBLIOGRAPHY: G. B. Valvekens, BiblSanct 8:307.

[M. E. DUFFY]

LOUIS OF BESSE (Alphonse Eliseus Chaix; 1831–1910), French Capuchin devoted to the social interests of the worker; spiritual writer. His social apostolate was inspired by the example of Bl. Bernardine of Feltre, whose biography he published (2 v., 1902). L. also was the author of *Éclaircissement sur les oeuvres de S. Jean de la Croix* (1893; tr., *Light on Mount Carmel*, 1926), and *La science de la prière*.

[T. C. O'BRIEN]

LOUIS OF CASORIA, VEN. (Arcangelo Palmentieri; 1814–85), founder, social worker. A Franciscan priest in Italy, L. established a society for Catholic intellectuals and the periodical *Carità*. His charitable enterprises throughout Italy included hospitals, refuges, homes for handicapped children and the elderly. In 1859 L. founded the Brothers of Charity and in 1862 the Gray Sisters of St. Elizabeth. His cause was introduced in Rome in 1907.

[J. R. AHERNE]

LOUIS OF GRANADA (1504–88), Spanish Dominican spiritual writer. He became a preacher first in Cordova, then in Portugal (1547), where he was called to be confessor to Queen Catherine (1551) and was elected provincial in 1556. He was the author of many works on the spiritual and mystical life (tr. J. Aumann, *Summa of the Christian Life,* 3 v., 1954–58) that came to be esteemed by many saints. But in his own lifetime some of L.'s writings were put on the Index in 1559, but later approved by Pius IV; his teaching on prayer brought charges by the Inquisition, but he was exonerated (1568). However, his position that all Christians are called to strive for spiritual perfection was condemned by the Inquisition. He was the biographer of the Dominican nun Sor Maria de la Visitación, a reputed stigmatic, but the claims and documents on which he based his book proved to be fraudulent. His teaching is Christocentric and based on the main themes of St. Thomas Aquinas's spiritual theology.

[T. C. O'BRIEN]

LOUIS-PHILIPPE (1773–1850), **KING OF FRANCE** 1830–48. A member of the Orléanist branch of the Bourbons, he was active in revolutionary circles and activities and had served in the revolutionary army in the north under Biron. Until his return to Paris in 1815, where he was well received by the Bourbon rulers, he traveled abroad extensively. In July of 1830, after the revolution overthrowing Charles X, he was summoned to power as king. Not a legitimate heir, he considered himself "King of the

French,'' was not crowned, and accepted the Charter of 1814. His reign is known as the ''bourgeois monarchy,'' and his advisers and supporters were wealthy bourgeois. Although relations with the Church were peaceful, he tried to limit the privileges of the clergy and the nobility. He was however not aware of the rising working class and its problems, nor of the power of public opinion, journalism, and socialistic trends. These factors, coupled with financial difficulties, provoked the revolution of 1848, which obliged him to renounce the throne and to flee to England, where he died shortly afterwards. With him the French monarchy also saw its final defeat. BIBLIOGRAPHY: P. H. Beik, *Louis-Philippe and the July Monarchy* (1965); G. Duveau, *1848: The Making of a Revolution* (1967).

[I. M. KASHUBA]

LOUISE OF FRANCE, VEN. (Thérèse de St. Augustine; 1737–87, daughter of King Louis XV of France. L. entered the Carmelite convent at St. Denis in 1770; she exercised considerable spiritual influence as novice mistress and prioress. She wrote a series of meditations on the Eucharist and a spiritual testament, both published after her death. Her cause was introduced in 1873.

[J. R. AHERNE]

LOUISE DE MARILLAC, ST. (1591–1660), cofoundress of the Daughters of Charity. L. was born to a noble Parisian family and began her education in the Royal Monastery. When financial difficulties beset the family after the father's death in 1604, L. left school. She applied for admission to the Capuchin house at St. Honoré but was refused because of her poor health. In 1613, L. married Anthony Le Gras. When Anthony's health began to deteriorate, L. experienced depression that was assuaged only through the counseling of Francis de Sales. Shortly before Anthony's death (1625), Vincent de Paul enlisted her aid in forming the Daughters of Charity. Together they structured a noncloistered order of women whose mission would take them among the poor of Paris and rural France. L. became the first director, overseeing the opening of a hospital in Paris and also an orphanage. In 1655 the Daughters of Charity received formal recognition from Rome. L. was canonized in 1934 by Pius XI. BIBLIOGRAPHY: L. Chierotti, BiblSanct 8:366–371; Butler 1:598–601.

[R. J. BRADY]

LOUISE OF SAVOY, BL. (1462–1503), widow, Poor Clare. She was the daughter of Bl. Amadeus of Savoy and Yolanda of France, granddaughter of Charles VII, and niece of Louis XI. After 9 years of happy married life, her husband, Hugh of Orléans died. Two years later Louise dispersed her fortune and entered the Poor Clare monastery at Orbe, Switzerland. Admirable in her religious life, she was an inspiring abbess. Her cult was approved by Gregory XVI in 1839. BIBLIOGRAPHY: D. Stöckert, LTK 6:1202; M. G. McNeil, NCE 8:1024; Butler 3:518–519; G. D. Gordini, BiblSanct 8:297.

[J. M. O'DONNELL]

LOUISIANA, a southern state, admitted to the Union (1812) as the 18th state. Cabeza de Vaca probably visited the area (1530), as did later expeditions led by H. de Soto (1541), and by J. *Marquette and L. Jolliet (1672). Robert de *la Salle claimed Louisiana for France (1682). Except for a period of Spanish rule (1763–1800/02) the territory remained in French hands until acquired by the U.S. as part of the Louisiana Purchase (1803). The first chapel was erected in 1700 when Paul du Ru, SJ began to work among the Indians. Among the early missionaries were F. de Montigny and A. Davion, as well as J. F. Buisson de St. Cosme, who was killed by the Indians (1706). Besides the Jesuits, Carmelites and Capuchins were active in the missionary field, the latter building numerous churches and founding the first school for boys in New Orleans (1725). The Acadians from Nova Scotia brought a notable increase to the Catholic population and the Diocese of Louisiana and the Floridas was established in 1793. With New Orleans as his see, the first bp., Louis Ignatius *Peñalver y Cárdenas presided over a flock of 11,000 Catholics. When Peñalver was transferred to Guatemala (1801), a period of ecclesiastical confusion followed that lasted until the consecration of W. *Dubourg (1815). Dubourg, who died in 1830, was succeeded by A. *Blanc in 1835, during whose episcopacy the number of churches and priests greatly increased. A seminary, two colleges, numerous schools, orphanages, and a hospital were established, and various communities sent sisters to help with the work.

New Orleans was made a metropolitan see in 1850, with Blanc as its first archbishop. Blanc, who died in 1860, was succeeded by J. M. *Odin, who served through the difficult time of the Civil War and the occupation of New Orleans by the federal troops. After the war he was able to bring in many religious to resume and expand the educational and charitable work that had been disrupted by the disorders. At Odin's death (1870) his coadjutor, N. J. Perché, became abp. and continued his predecessor's program of expansion, but in doing so built so extensively that when he died (1883) the archdiocese was burdened with a staggering debt. He was succeeded by F. X. Leray (d. 1887) whose major concern during his brief incumbency was to reduce the debt. Leray was followed (1887) by F. Janssens, who established parishes for Negroes, but on a temporary basis, for he deplored racial segregation. Janssens' successor was P. L. Chapelle (1898–1905), whose measures to reduce the debt and whose absences on diplomatic missions for the Holy See caused some disaffection among the clergy. The next abp., J. H. Blenk, SM (1906–17) zealously promoted education and Catholic lay organizations. At his invitation Mother Katherine *Drexel, foundress of the Sisters of the Blessed Sacrament for Indians and Colored People, opened a normal school in New Orleans (1917) which later developed into Xavier Univ., the first Catholic university for Negroes in the United States. J. W. Shaw, Blenk's successor (1917–34), established a major seminary (1923), encouraged education, provided for the reorganization of social services and charities, and promoted Catholic Action. J. F. *Rummel succeeded Shaw in 1935 and until 1962 presided over the archdiocese. Expansion and efficiency were the keynotes of his tenure. The number of parishes increased by 40%, and the number of priests by 25%. Building construction at the cost of more than $100 million was undertaken, most of it for schools. Many new communities entered the archdiocese. Rummel was, often in the face of bitter opposition, a leader in the field of social justice, as an opponent of right to work laws and of racial discrimination. Abp. (later, Card.) John P. Cody, Rummel's coadjutor, became apostolic administrator of the archdiocese in 1962 at Rummel's request, and in 1964 when Rummel died, became Abp. of New Orleans. His tenure was brief, however, for he was transferred to Chicago in 1965; and P. M. Hannan replaced him in New Orleans. New Orleans has three suffragan sees: Alexandria (1910), Lafayette (1918), and Baton Rouge (1961). In 1976 the state's Catholics numbered 1,309,185 or 35.1% of the total population. The major Protestant denominations are the Southern Baptist Convention with 16.6% of the population and the Methodist Church, with 3.4%. Other Protestant bodies account for 9.8% and the Jewish population (as est. in 1968) for 15,630 or 0.43%. There are four Catholic colleges in Louisiana, with a total enrollment of 8,121, all in the Archdiocese of New Orleans. Of the 63 Catholic high schools attended by 32,312 students in the state, 31 are in the archdiocese and enroll 19,056. There are 194 Catholic elementary schools, with enrollments totalling 79,732. About 49,680 of these pupils attend the 105 Catholic elementary schools in the archdiocese. BIBLIOGRAPHY: G. W. McGinty, *History of Louisiana* (1951); T. L. Smith and H. L. Hitt, *People of Louisiana* (1952); R. Baudier, *Catholic Church in Louisiana* (1939). B. W. Johnson, et al., *Churches and Church Membership in the U.S.* (1974).

[J. L. MORRISON; R. M. PRESTON]

LOUISMET, SAVINIEN (1858–1926), Benedictine missionary, writer. A monk from 1877 and ordained in 1882, L. served on the Benedictine missions in Oklahoma territory for 13 years. Ill health forced his return to Buckfast abbey in England, where he taught and wrote on mystical theology. Among his works, which were very popular but not always theologically accurate, were *The Mystical Knowledge of God* (1917) and *Divine Contemplation for All* (1922).

[J. R. AHERNE]

LOURDES, town in SW France at the foot of the Pyrenees, site of one of the most frequented shrines of Our Lady. The pilgrimage place commemorates the 18 appearances to St. Bernadette of Mary from Feb. 11 to July 16, 1858, identifying herself in one of them as the Immaculate Conception. The Lourdes spring that now flows at the rate of 32,000 gal. per day began to flow miraculously during the apparition of Feb. 25. There was civil and ecclesiastical opposition to the popular cult that sprang up, but by 1862 the bp. of Tarbes gave approval and building of the first church began. It was consecrated as a minor basilica in 1876. A second church, the Rosary Basilica, was built 1883–1901; the underground Church of St. Pius X was completed in 1958. The feast of Our Lady of Lourdes was approved for the whole Church in 1907 for celebration on Feb. 11. Pilgrimages to Lourdes began to be immense from 1872, in the wake of the Franco-Prussian War; in the average year pilgrims now number about 2 million. Miraculous cures of organic illnesses have been claimed since the beginning; they occur during Eucharistic processions, during other prayer services, and during baths in the Lourdes spring. Since 1882 a group of physicians at the shrine have examined cases of claimed cures; then the International Medical Commission of Lourdes, located in Paris, reexamines the claims. When they seem to be valid, the cures are reported to the bp. of the person cured for official recognition. The most widely attested phenomenon, however, is the increase of faith, love, and patience experienced by pilgrims to Lourdes.

[J. R. AHERNE]

LOURDES, BROTHERS OF OUR LADY OF, a congregation also known as the Brothers of Good Works, founded at Ronce, Belgium, in 1930 by Rev. E. M. Glorieux. The work of the brothers is the education of youth, the care of the sick and the poor. The motherhouse is in Oostakker near Ghent, Belgium. In 1975 they had 57 houses and 565 members.

[R. C. CLIGGETT]

LOUVAIN, CATHOLIC UNIVERSITY OF, the oldest Catholic univ. in the world which has remained Catholic throughout its history and has retained the full range of higher studies—theology, medicine, and canon law. Established in 1425 by a bull of Martin V as a university, comparable to those in other European countries, it was designed to serve the scholars and students of the Lowland countries which were then being reunified as an independent and distinct region. The student body was international; the first professors came from the Univ. of Cologne and Paris. Approving Louvain's resources to maintain a faculty of theology, Eugene IV authorized its foundation in 1432. Among the notable figures associated with the university in the 16th cent. were: Adrian VI, who had studied, taught, and then served as rector at Louvain before becoming pope; Erasmus of Rotterdam, who was associated with the university (1517–21) and who established the Trilingual College (1517) for comparative study of the Latin, Greek, and Hebrew Bibles; Justus Lipsius, whose pioneer work in classical philology helped establish modern textual criticism; Gerardus Mercator, the cartographer; Rember Dodoens, creator of the first scientific herbarium (1583); and the investigator of human anatomy, Andreas Vesalius. Members of the theological faculty took an active role in the Council of Trent, as did their modern counterparts in Vatican II. Following the *acte de visite* (1617), a law requiring a university degree to practice law or medicine, the size of the enrollment grew quickly. During the 17th cent. the faculty of law at Louvain, focusing attention on national as well as Roman law, became prominent in Europe. Political unrest, in particular the War of Spanish Succession, the successful invasion of the Lowlands by France (1794), and the two World Wars, seriously interfered with the university's historical and institutional continuity. It was during World War I that the library and its priceless holdings were wantonly burned by the invaders. Under Honoré Van Waeyenbergh, rector 1940–64, the university recovered and grew in the wake of World War II's devastations. Throughout the 19th and early 20th cent., the university adapted to the changing needs of the scholarly community, in particular to the need for improved scientific training. In 1882, the teaching of Thomist philosophy in higher education was organized by Constant Piéraerts, with D. *Mercier and led to establishment of the Higher Institute of Philosophy (1893). The American College at Louvain, founded in 1857, originally designed to prepare priests for the American missions, became a school for the training of American students. The College was officially affiliated with the university in 1899.

[R. J. LITZ]

LOVE. The wisdom of man has tirelessly pondered the many-sided problem of love; only God's word in Christ could reveal its mystery, which theology has synthesized.

Philosophy. In its broadest meaning, love is an affective tendency towards a "value," culminating in an active communion with it (ThAq ST 1a, 20.1); it is an essentially relational and unitive force.

In man, this tendency either is passively attracted by an object which enriches it as its good (interested love), or it manifests actively its gratuitous generosity by self-communication (disinterested love).

Characteristic of the first type is man's sensible love connected with his biological functions. It reacts to the sense stimuli and seeks its pleasurable fulfillment; but unlike the animal's compelling reaction, it normally leaves man free to follow or resist the subjective attraction, impregnated as it is with spiritual or rational love. It is man's basic "passion" (ST 1a2ae, 25.27). It is love only in a lower and analogical sense. Rational love is the free answer of the person's will to the intellectual perception of an objective worth, mostly a personal one, in which he recognizes a partial presence of the absolute good: God, his ultimate personal end. A fundamental dynamism of spiritual love for God (natural love) is thus implicitly at work in all human activities; these specify that necessary striving towards God.

This personal response, however, is not merely an interested love, an *eros* (Plato) tending to the perfection of the lover as a finite being; but it is—or should be—even more a disinterested self-surrender, an *agape,* since the very striving towards the perfecting of a "participation" or "image" of God is ultimately actuated by a deeper dynamic relatedness to God's own lovableness and to his manifold presence in others (St. Thomas, *In 4 Sent.* 49.1.2.1 ad 3) whose good is promotes. In man, every self-gift is also self-perfecting.

To love is actually "to will good to someone" said Aristotle (*Rhetor.* L. 2, c.4) and St. Thomas comments: "man has a love of concupiscence for the good that he wishes to another, and a love of friendship for the person to whom he wishes good" (ST 1a2ae, 26.4); the former is obviously subordinate to the love of friendship, which is a reciprocal form of the love of benevolence.

Starting from man in his present sinful condition, philosophy alone would probably never have discovered the ultimate nature of love: Plato's longing for the immutable Good does not exceed an exalted *eros* (*Symp.* 210 A–E) and Aristotle's generous "friendship" is finally subordinate to one's own search for perfection (cf. *Eth. Nic.* 1166a 1–2). Moreover, left to itself, human love is often perverted by selfishness. The Christian revelation, by disclosing and communicating God's inner life, has not only revealed human love to itself and redeemed it, but has brought forth a revaluation of all the values connected with it (cf. Max Scheler's *Umwertung der Werte*). If men of other religions, like great Indian bhaktas (Kālidās) and alvars (Śathakopa) or Muslim sūfis (Al-Hallāj) have discovered the divine meaning of love, it was through the invisible influence of Christ's love at work in the whole world (Ohm, esp. 371–422).

Theology starts from God's revelation. By delivering his Son unto death and by imparting to us the Spirit, the Father, "God of love" (2 Cor 13.11), reveals the inner mystery of the divinity: "God is *agapē*" (1 Jn 4.8,16). He communicates everything he has to his Son (cf. Jn 16.15; 17.10) and both together breathe forth their personal love, the Spirit: in its transcendent source, love is thus an eternal act of totally generous communion *(koinōnía)* among the Divine Persons (cf. St. Thomas, *In 1 Sent.* 10.1.3; *De Pot.* 9.9, arg. 6, sed contra): "God is love, because the Father, the Son and the Holy Spirit are one" (St. Aug., *In Epist. Ioh.* 10.5; PL 35:2057). The Divine Being is eternally possessed in an interpersonal communication. All created are "participants" in that Being.

Of men, it is revealed that God created them in his own image (Gen 1.27), not only as free creatures whose basic driving force is love (cf. ST 1a, 20.1), whose fundamental duty is to surrender to God in love (Dt 6.4–9), and as members of a human community whose cohesive force is an interpersonal love; but even more so as adopted sons introduced into the inner circuit of the triune *communio* by being incorporated into Christ's body (Eph 1.1–14).

Thus God's progressive manifestation appears in all its unity as an unfolding design of gratuitous and merciful love:

from the beginning, creation is meant for man (Gen 1.28–30), man for Christ (Col 1.16; 1 Cor 3.23), and Christ returns the whole universe to the Father (1 Cor 15.24–28), thanks to His act of self-sacrifice (Lk 23.46), which is the greatest proof of love (Jn 15.13) and the supreme gift of the Father (Rom 8.32; 1 Jn 4.9–11), eternalized as it is in the Resurrection and made sacramentally present in the sacrament of love (cf. Jn 13.1; Th Aq ST 3a, 73.3 ad 3) flowing from his open heart (Jn 19.37).

The Father, who manifested himself as the almighty Creator and Lord (Ps 147–148), is recognized as the shepherd (Gen 48.15; Is 40.11), the father (Ex 4.22), the spouse (Hos 2.18–21; S of S) in a growing intimacy. He freely elects a people (Dt 7.8; 29.12; Is 44.2,24) and binds it to himself by a covenant, in order to make of it a son (Jer 3.19; Hos 11.1), or rather the body of his Son (1 Cor 12.27; Eph 1.23), that he may love it with the love he has for his Only Begotten (Jn 15.9,12) and make it live of his Spirit of love (Rom 5.5; Eph 4.4). This love brings with it the indwelling of the three Divine Persons (Jn 14.16–18,23). Our supernatural love for both God and men is thus truly theological (from God to God); it extends and shares in the disinterested generosity of God's *agapé* (1 Cor 13.4–7) and excludes selfishness. Because all men are meant to be this body of Christ, they must be united among themselves with one *agapé:* the love we have for the invisible Father must be manifested in the loving service of our visible brethren (1 Jn 4.20–21). For man, then, the "greatest commandment" (Mt 22.38–40; cf. 25.31–46), which summarizes (Rom 13.8–10) and fulfills the law (Gal 5.14) as the bond of perfection (Col 3.12–15), is love for God and for men: this charity constitutes our Christian being and action; without it "I am nothing at all" and can do nothing definitively valuable (1 Cor 13.2–3). Such a love is not content with the strict minimum of obligation, but freely strives to do better, in the spirit of the counsels.

We see why the inspired writers have chosen, not the word *eros,* but *agapē* to express these nuances of predilection, of beneficent goodwill and of lasting attachment to the one loved (Spicq).

The living members of the Son thus participate in Christ's filial charity (cf. D 1530–31; 1546) by which their will is divinized. This supernatural love, therefore, animates from within as their ultimate "form" of perfection all their virtues and all the good moral acts which proceed from that will (ST 2a2ae, 23.8). In all their good actions charity is at least implicitly at work. Their virtuous acts are participations and expressions of charity (*De Ver.* 14.5 ad 3) and the test of its sincerity (Jn 14.15; 15.10; 1 Jn 3.17–19; 2 Jn 6). Though remaining specifically what they are (justice, temperance) with their own laws, these acts receive from the virtue of charity, which they diversify, their intrinsic meritorious value (*De Malo* 2.5 ad 7; Gilleman, pt 2).

Flowing from Christ's love, our supernatural love brings with it an inner drive to pattern our lives on Christ's mysteries (cf. Gal 2.20), primarily the paschal mystery of His death-Resurrection (Rom 6.3–11). It is normally lived in his body, the Church, and the community of charity (cf. Acts 2.44–45; 4.32–35) is a witness to Christ's mission in the world (Jn 13.35; 17.21): brotherly love is the image of the triune *agapē* (Jn 17.22–23). This love embodies itself in deeds (Mt 25.35–45); it extends to all, even to enemies (Mt 5.44) and may demand the supreme sacrifice (1 Jn 3.16).

Sexual love as such is not *agapē,* but a particular and specific human love, both spiritual and sensible, proper to our earthly condition (Mt 22.30). As redeemed and sanctified by a sacrament (Matrimony) and thus assumed into charity, it symbolizes, though imperfectly (1 Cor 7.28–35) the life-giving union of Christ with his Church in *agapē* (Eph 5.25–33).

Virginal love is a charism and a special vocation (Mt 19.11–12; 1 Cor 7.7) meant to unite man undividedly (1 Cor 7.32–35) with Christ beyond the symbols as an anticipation of, and a witness here on earth of the heavenly *agapē* (1 Cor 7.29–31). As realizing the evangelical fulness of man's consecration to God, it stands above married love (D 1810; 3911–12).

The supernatural love will never fade away (1 Cor 13.8). The face to face of the vision (Jn 17.3; 1 Cor 13.12) will make God's triune *agapē* "present to the will" (ST 1a2ae, 3.4) and to the love of the adopted sons in an eternal act of fruitive communion with the three Persons.

In its Christian fulness, love is the core of God's communication to man and of man's response to the offers of his *agapē,* in faith and hope. BIBLIOGRAPHY: G. Gilleman, *Primacy of Charity in Moral Theology* (tr. W. F. Ryan and A. Vachon, 1959) pt 2, ch. 2.; T. Ohm. *Die Liebe zu Gott in den Nichtchristlichen Religionen* (1940); C. Spicq, *Agape in the New Testament* (tr. M. A. McNamara and M. H. Richter, 1963); V. Warnach, *Agape* (1951) esp. pt 2.

[G. GILLEMAN]

LOVE, PLATONIC, see PLATONIC LOVE.

LOVE, PURE, see DISINTERESTED LOVE.

LOVE FEAST, a technical meaning given to the word for Christian, mutual love, *agapē.* This is the clear meaning only in Jude 12 and there the love feast is censured. It was used for a friendly table fellowship by 2d cent. and later Christians. The Eucharist may often have been celebrated as part of a full, community meal in the Churches of NT times (1 Cor 11.17–34), but the practice ceased because of abuses and because of a deepening awareness of the sacredness of the Lord's Supper in its liturgical aspects and in its mystical reliving of the Church's unity with the Lord Jesus through faith, love, and holy communion. Thus the social aspects of a communal, fellowship meal gradually disappeared from a more solemn Eucharistic Celebration. By St. Augustine's time such feasts had become occasions for feeding the poor.

[J. F. FALLON]

LOVINER, JOHN FOREST (1896–1970), American Franciscan who founded St. Anthony's Guild (1924) and was its director until his death. He published materials for the Confraternity of Christian Doctrine (CCD) and was a key participant in the production of the *New American Bible*.

[C. KEENAN]

LÖW, JOSEPH (1893–1962), Austrian Redemptorist and liturgical scholar. From 1935 until his death he was an official in the historical section of the Congregation of Rites. He helped prepare the restored Easter Vigil (1951) and the Code of Rubrics (1960). His published works are on the history of the liturgy, archeology, and Redemptionist history. BIBLIOGRAPHY: A. Sampers, EphemLiturg 77 (1963) 39–45.

[N. KOLLAR]

LOW CHURCH, originating in 18-cent England, a phrase denoting an attitude tending to minimize the importance within the Church of *episcopacy, priesthood, sacraments, and ceremonial richness as against the more biblical and personal notes of individual conversion, the preaching of the gospel, and salvation by faith. "Low" refers to the slight importance attached to the historical and sacramental claims of the Church. The designation has been applied to proponents of *latitudinarianism, to *Nonconformists generally, and is the opposite of both *high church and *broad church.

[S. F. BAYNE]

LOW MASS, a term to indicate a simplified form of the former Tridentine Mass in the Roman rite, less elaborate than a *solemn or a *high Mass. In origin it goes back to the Middle Ages when it became customary for each priest to offer Mass daily, thus requiring a minimum of external ceremony. Prayers were recited rather than sung. There were no assistants to the celebrant save an acolyte and on occasion a deacon. With the revision of the liturgy of the Mass by Vatican Council II, calling for singing and other forms of participation by the congregation, such distinctions as solemn, low, or high Mass are no longer applicable. BIBLIOGRAPHY: J. Miller, NCE 9:414–426, esp. 416–418.

[R. B. ENO]

LOW SUNDAY, former title of the first Sunday after Easter; its liturgical designation in Latin **Dominica in albis*. Why this Sunday was called "low" in English is not altogether clear. Some suggest that it was so designated in contrast to Easter. The whole week following Easter was sometimes called Low Week. Probably the adjective in its application both to the Sunday and to the week was used to indicate that the entire period was considered to pertain to the Easter feast, but in lower degree than Easter Sunday itself.

[P. K. MEAGHER]

LOWE, JOHN (*c.* 1380–1467), an Austin friar and theologian who vigorously combated heresy. He served as provincial, first at Northampton (1428), then at York (1430). In 1433 he was made bp. of St. Asaph, Wales. Eton College and King's College were assisted in their foundation by him. L. was transferred to Rochester in 1444. At his death, his important library went to the London convent of his order. BIBLIOGRAPHY: Emden Ox 2:1168–69; F. Roth, *History of the English Austin Friars* (2 v., 1961).

[A. WARDLE]

LOYALTY, the moral quality of faithfulness included in the meaning of several moral virtues connected with *justice. It can be associated with *devotion, the primary inner response of the virtue of *religion, a readiness of will for the service of God, which includes allegiance and dedication to God's honor and to the causes that attest to his sovereignty and goodness. Loyalty may also be taken as part of familial *piety, a dedication to family as the source of the being and development of its members; or as *patriotism, a devotion to honoring the land of one's birth and opportunities. Loyalty also enters the meaning of *truthfulness, as this virtue includes fidelity to one's word, promises, pledges, or commitments; as the note of honorableness connoted by use of the term indicates, loyalty in this sense honors a *debt owed in decency. The moral uprightness and nobility of true loyalty have nothing to do, of course, with bigotry, blind or fawning allegiance to a political regime, brutal *nationalism, favoritism, or collusion in evil-doing. BIBLIOGRAPHY: ThAq St Lat-Eng (v. 41, ed. T. C. O'Brien, *Virtues of Justice in the Human Community).*

[T. C. O'BRIEN]

LOYALTY OATHS, in U.S. law, a sworn disavowal of any intent or advocacy of the violent overthrow of government, or of membership in organizations, particularly the Communist party, promoting subversion. A loyalty oath is not simply the oath to uphold the Constitution, but one concerned with the specific issue of national security, and required of some public employees. The moral justification for such a requirement rests on the meaning of *legal justice, which dictates taking precautions to safeguard the public or common good; and of distributive justice, which dictates that one with subversive intent be denied an office of public trust. The courts have both upheld the legality of loyalty oaths, and sought to constrain indiscriminate and punitive interpretations of their meaning and purpose.

[T. C. O'BRIEN]

LOYSON, CHARLES (1827–1912), French priest, founder of the schismatic L'Église catholique gallicane. He was first a Sulpician at Paris, then entered the Dominicans in 1859, but 5 months later became a Discalced Carmelite. In religion Père Hyacinthe, L. became a forceful and well-received preacher at Notre Dame de Paris. In 1868, however, he left the Church in protest over the proposed definition of papal infallibility. He was excommunicated in

1869, in 1872 entered a civil marriage with Emily Meriaman, an American convert of his, then became pastor of the Old Catholic Church at Geneva, 1873–74. He founded his own schismatic body at Paris in 1879; the venture was a failure. Among his writings were: *La société civile dans ses rapports avec le christianisme* (1867) and *Les principes de la réforme catholique* (1893).

[J. R. AHERNE]

LSD (LSD-25), D-lysergic acid diethylamide, a potent synthetic hallucinogenic drug. First used as a psychotomimetic drug in research projects to mime or mimic a psychotic reaction, it was thought to be useful in the study of schizophrenic psychosis. It derives from the ergot alkalides found in grain deformity and the toxic infectant of flour caused by the fungus of grasses. It is called an ''indole hallucinogen'' because of the indole ring system in its molecule that can block the action of serotonin (which transmits nerve impulses) in brain tissue. More recently it is used in smaller doses as an adjunct to psychotherapy: to relax the patient, lower his defenses, make him more communicative, and facilitate insight. It can be absorbed readily from any mucosal surface, even from the ear. It acts within 30 to 60 minutes and its effects usually last for 8 to 10 hours. The danger of prolonged or even permanent psychotic reaction led to the severe restrictions on its availability and use by the Drug Abuse Control Amendment of 1965. Still the euphoria and the mystical hallucinatory state it induces has insured its steady popularity in the black market. Since LSD causes suspension of control over human faculties, therapeutic use is justified morally only in a way proportionate to achieve a truly greater good; frivolous use is immoral.

[E. J. DILLON]

LUBAC, HENRI DE (1896–), the erudite and prolific French Jesuit theologian whose literary output to date (forty volumes and innumerable scholarly articles) has been characterized by a colleague as ''an eminently successful attempt to present the spirit of Catholic Christianity to contemporary man'' (H. Ur von Balthasar). Born in Cambrai, L. became professor of fundamental theology and the history of religions at the Institut Catholique in Lyons (1929). On the occasion of his recent 80th birthday, the *Zeitschrift für Katholische Theologie* republished L.'s address given as the inaugural of his teaching career; it still seems progressive. His first major work was *Catholicisme* (1938), a seminal work that set the tone and orientation of all that followed, revealing his fundamental decision in favor of fullness, letting the total tradition speak to counter the catastrophic abandonment of the ''catholic'' viewpoint for the sake of a narrow or rigid particular standpoint. He presents sympathetic treatments of victims of the politically Catholic, but the spiritually anti-Catholic. His heroes were Origen, Erasmus, Fénelon, Blondel, Teilhard de Chardin, and most recently, Pico della Mirandola. He even defends Proudhon against the Catholic integrism of the Restoration. He himself was under official censure after *Le Surnaturel* (1946), but was vindicated at Vatican Council II, where he was one of the most influential French theologians. His alarm at the chaos following the Council is expressed in such recent works as *L'Église dans la crise actuelle* (1969). BIBLIOGRAPHY: H. Ur von Balthasar, ''Achievement of H. de Lubac,'' *Thought* 51 (1976) 7–49. H. de Lubac, ''Apologetics and Theology,'' Theol Dig 25 (1977) 144–148.

[E. J. DILLON]

LUCARIUS, CYRIL, see CYRIL LUCARIUS.

LUCAS, HENRY S. (1890–1962), historian of the late Middle Ages. A native of the U.S. with Dutch background, Lucas taught at the Univ. of Washington for 38 years. He was a convert to Catholicism in 1947. L. wrote a large number of historical studies, notable among them being *The Renaissance and Reformation* (1934) and *Netherlanders in America: Dutch Immigration to the United States and Canada, 1798–1950* (1955). He served as president of the American Catholic Historical Association in 1949.

[J. R. AHERNE]

LUCERNARIUM, the ancient Christian blessing of lights at the beginning of evening services, derived from the Jewish lighting of the sabbath lamp. The famous hymn *Phos Hilaron* in the Byzantine liturgy comes from this service. It is also the basis of the light service at the beginning of the Easter Vigil.

[J. DALLEN]

LUCHESIUS OF POGGIBONSI, BL. (d. 1260), first Franciscan tertiary. Once a greedy Tuscan merchant, he underwent a change of heart *c.* 1213. With his wife, Buona dei Segni, he was among the first to be enrolled by Francis of Assisi in the Third Order Secular. He distributed his wealth to the poor and undertook an apostolate of charity, setting a pattern for other tertiaries to follow. BIBLIOGRAPHY: C. R. Hallack and P. F. Anson, *These Made Peace* (rev. and ed. M. A. Habig, 1957); R. Volpini, BiblSanct 8:230–234.

[O. J. BLUM]

LUCIAN OF ANTIOCH (*c.* 240–312). A native of Samosata, L. came to Antioch during the episcopacy of *Paul of Samosata. It is uncertain whether or not he was a pupil of Paul. L. is considered the founder of the *Antiochene school of exegesis. He numbered among his pupils *Arius and *Eusebius of Nicomedia; his subordinationist (see SUBORDINATIONISM) teachings can be considered the proximate source of *Arianism. He did valuable work on the LXX and NT as a textual critic. In the persecution of *Diocletian L. died as a martyr, although for some time before the persecution, he appears to have been a member of a schismatic group loyal to the deposed Paul. BIBLIOGRAPHY: Quasten 2:142–144; Quasten Init 2:168–170.

[R. B. ENO]

LUCIAN OF KAPHAR GAMALA, presbyter of the church of Caphargamala (alternate spelling), near Jerusalem, mentioned in the Roman Martyrology on August 3 as the one to whom it was divinely revealed that the relics discovered in that vicinity *c.* 415 A.D. were indeed the relics of St. Stephen Protomartyr. A letter attributed to the priest Lucian and treating of the reputed discovery is also extant. BIBLIOGRAPHY: W. M. Sinclair DCB 3:749.

[E. J. DILLON]

LUCIAN OF SAMOSATA (*c.* 120–after 180), Greek satirist and one of the most brilliant representations of the Second Sophistic. In dialogue or epistolary form he satirizes popular religion and practices, human vanity, and literary and philosophical pretensions. His "True Story" (*Alēthēs historia*) ridicules the extravagances of the contemporary novel or tale of adventure. His *Alexander* is a savage attack on the wonderworker *Alexander of Abonoteichos, whom he pictures as a charlatan of the worst kind. His *Death of Peregrinus* has a special interest, because Peregrinus at one stage in his career was a Christian. L. praises the fraternal charity of the Christians but regards them as religious fanatics and worshipers of the crucified Sophist. He does not attack Christianity with any marked vehemence, but it would be a mistake to think that he was really sympathetic toward it. He was a superficial thinker, who, in a Voltairesque and pessimistic vein, tended to ridicule men and institutions without being concerned about obtaining a deeper understanding of the objects of his satire. L. was a favorite author of the Renaissance humanists and of European writers in general of the 16th, 17th, and 18th centuries. BIBLIOGRAPHY: G. Lohse, LexAW 1776–78; P. De Labriolle, *La Réaction païenne* (6th ed., 1942) 97–108 (excellent on the *Death of Peregrinus*); B. Baldwin, *Studies in Lucian* (1974).

[M. R. P. MCGUIRE]

LUCIĆ, IVAN (Lucius, Lucio; 1604–79), Croatian historian. He studied law at Padua and Rome, receiving the doctorate (1633). Working in the Dalmatian and then the Vatican archives, he wrote the first scholarly history of the Croatian people up to 1420, *De regno Dalmatiae et Croatiae* (1666), and other historical writings on the Illyrian provinces of Dalmatia and Trogir (both 1673).

[R. J. LITZ]

LUCIFER, a Latin word that as a substantive means the morning star, and as an adjective, "light-bearing." In its formation it is analogous to the Greek *phōsphóros,* which it translates into Latin. It has been adopted into English unchanged. In the sense of "morning star" the word was used in the Wycliffe Bible in the translation of Job 38.32 and in some religious poetry. It is used in this sense also in the *Exsultet* of the Latin Holy Saturday liturgy in figurative reference to Christ. But as a proper noun it is most commonly used as a name for the devil or Satan. This usage is based on the patristic interpretation of the morning star mentioned in Is 14.12, "How you are fallen from heaven, O Day Star [in the Vulg, *Lucifer*], Son of Dawn!" The Fathers took this to mean the devil. The Lucifer of the Vulg survived in all English versions down to 1611, and the word has passed into wide use in English and in other languages as a synonym for Satan. BIBLIOGRAPHY: OED 6:485.

[E. A. WEIS]

LUCIFER OF CAGLIARI (d. *c.* 370), anti-Arian bp. of Cagliari, Sardinia. At the Council of Milan (354–355) he steadfastly refused to accede to the wishes of the Emperor Constantius and condemn Athanasius. His vehement resistance to the Emperor led to his banishment to the East, where, in exile, he persisted in his denunciations of Constantius, writing several violent diatribes against him. Taking advantage of an amnesty in 362, he went to Antioch and became embroiled in the conflict raging there in consequence of the efforts of Melitius, the bp., to reconcile repentant Arians. Accusing the bp. of Semi-Arianism, L. consecrated Paulinus, a priest of Antioch, as bp. for those who would not submit to Melitius, thus cooperating in the creation of a schism that lasted many years. He then returned to Sardinia. Reference by Augustine, Ambrose, and Jerome to his followers as Luciferians suggests that Z. was excommunicated and the leader of a schismatic group. Writings: PL 13:767–1038. BIBLIOGRAPHY: É. Amman, DTC 9:1032–44; Altaner 429–430.

[R. B. ENO]

LUCIFERIANS, a term with two usages: (1) followers of *Lucifer of Cagliari; (2) a name for supposed medieval sects of devil worshipers. Reports of such sects began in the 10th cent. and continued throughout the Middle Ages. The *Cathari did honor to Satan; it is doubtful, however, that there were Luciferians who practiced the blasphemies and obscenities reported in popular tales or in the charges of zealous inquisitors. BIBLIOGRAPHY: É. Amman, DTC 9:1044–56; Bihlmeyer-Tüchle 2:307; Knox Enth, 101.

[T. C. O'BRIEN]

LUCILLA (fl. first half of 4th cent.), described by R. Knox as Lady Bountiful of Donatism. A wealthy and devout woman, L. took offense at *Caecilian for rebuking her for her exaggerated veneration of confessors and martyrs. She generously supported the cause of the Numidian bps. whose election of Majorinus as a rival to Caecilian in the See of Carthage started the *Donatist schism. BIBLIOGRAPHY: Knox Enth 54–61.

[P. K. MEAGHER]

LUCIUS, ST. (fl. 2d cent.), legendary king and evangelist of Britain. He was reported to be in correspondence with Abgar IX, King of Edessa and with Pope Eleutherius. Possibly the core of the legend is a South Welsh prince, Lleuer the Great. L. is confused also with a Swiss evangelist of the same name. BIBLIOGRAPHY: C. J. Godfrey, *Church in Anglo-Saxon England* (1962) 10.

[J. L. DRUSE]

LUCIUS I, ST. (d. 254), **POPE** from 253. L. was sent into exile under the Emperor Gallus shortly after he was elected to succeed St. Cornelius, but an abatement of persecution soon made it possible for him to return to Rome. St. *Cyprian of Carthage saluted him as a confessor and congratulated him on his release. Writing to L.'s successor, St. Stephen I, Cyprian declared that L. continued the papal opposition to the Novatianists' denial of pardon to the **lapsi* who had apostatized during persecution. L.'s pontificate lasted less than a year. He apparently died of natural causes, for there is no satisfactory evidence to support the claim of the *Liber pontificalis* that he was martyred in the persecution of Valerian. A part of his epitaph has been discovered in the catacomb of Callistus, from which his relics were taken at an early date and later transferred to the church of St. Cecilia. BIBLIOGRAPHY: E. G. Weltin, *Ancient Popes* (1964); J. P. Kirsch, CE 9:411–412; Butler 1:479–480.

[P. F. MULHERN]

LUCIUS II (Gerardo Caccianemici; d. 1145) **POPE** from 1144. He was made a cardinal priest by Honorius II and served frequently as a papal legate. During his pontificate reactionaries under Jordan Pierleoni occupied the Capitoline. The Pope may have died of a wound received in trying to restore peace in Rome. BIBLIOGRAPHY: Duschesne LP 2:385–386.

[H. DRESSLER]

LUCIUS III (Ubaldus Allucingolus; *c.* 1097–1185), **POPE** from 1181. Admitted to the Cistercians by St. Bernard, he was created a cardinal priest by Innocent II. Because of troubles in the city most of Lucius' pontificate was spent away from Rome. He obtained a promise for a new Crusade to the Holy Land from Frederick Barbarossa. The most far-reaching act of L. was the issuing of the decretal letter *Ad abolendam* at Verona, Nov. 4, 1184. This document, which specifically mentions the Cathari, Humiliati, and the Poor of Lyons, established the canonical procedure for dealing with heretics, ecclesiastics, and laymen, which was followed in subsequent centuries. BIBLIOGRAPHY: CorpIurCan 10:5.7.9 (1922); É. Amann, DTC 9.1:1058–262; G. Schwaiger, LTK 6:1176–77.

[H. DRESSLER]

LUCIUS OF ALEXANDRIA, an Arian priest of Alexandria who was consecrated bp. of that city by Euzoius, bp. of Antioch, after the death of Athanasius in 373. Realizing that Arianism would not prevail without the approval of the monks, he began a cruel persecution of these "Homoousians." He was expelled from the city and fled to Constantinople after Peter, the brother and lawful successor of Athanasius returned from Rome with letters of approbation from Pope St. Damasus. BIBLIOGRAPHY: Socrates, *Eccl. Hist.* 4.21; Sozomen, *Eccl. Hist.* 6.5; Theodoret, *Eccl. Hist.* 4.18, 19.

[M. J. COSTELLOE]

LUCIUS LEGEND. The story that recounts that King Lucius of Britain wrote to Pope Eleutherius requesting baptism (174–179) for himself and his people is traced to a reference in the *Liber pontificalis,* mentioned by Bede (*Hist. eccl.* 1.4; 5.24). In later versions, this king is alleged to be the son of Simon of Cyrene, a convert of St. Timothy, and martyred at Chur in Switzerland, whose patron is St. Lucius. Most recent opinion suggests that he was mistaken for Lucius Aelius, Septimus Megas Abgar IX (a Christian king of Edessa in Asia Minor) through a scribe's incorrect reading of Britannio for Britio. BIBLIOGRAPHY: H. Le Clercq, DACL 92:2061–63.

[F. H. BRIGHAM]

LUCK, an unforseeable and unintended outcome following on a free agent's action. This Aristotelian notion of luck (*tychē*) contrasts with an occurrence incidental to the activity of a nonvolitional agent (Aristotle, *Physics* 2.6–7). The discussion of fate, chance, or fortune and luck is prominent in early ecclesiastical writers, who opposed non-Christian fatalism and determinism, i.e., that human actions or events affecting human beings are of spiritual *demons, entirely the result of the inexorable influence of the stars and planets. Medieval theology was particularly influenced in this matter by *Boethius's reflections on divine *providence in his *The Consolation of Philosophy* and by St. *Augustine's *City of God*. The basic theological teaching is that luck, fate, or fortune exist in the sense that events occur outside the expectable patterns of created causality. That does not mean in the case of human beings a subjection to the "forces of destiny," as though the stars or some other unseen influence determined human choices and the course of life. All such terms refer to events unforeseeable on the basis of the created actions on which they are attendant. At the same time such events do not escape God's providence: any reality that occurs in creation is dependent on his causality, and the divine causality is ordered in God's mind and in God's purpose, above all to the salvation of man. Wishing for "good luck" or hoping against "bad luck" do not usually mean that a person excludes the events of life from God's care.

[T. C. O'BRIEN]

LUCRETIUS (*c.* 98–55 B.C.), Roman poet and philosopher. He was an Epicurean and his great didactic poem, *De rerum natura* was primarily ethical in purpose. He wished to banish all fear based on superstition and the fear of death, and thus to give man that tranquility of soul which was the Epicurean ideal. In his interpretation of man, nature, and the universe, he adopted the atomic theory of Epicurus, which was itself derived from the atomists Leucippus and Democritus. He did not deny the existence of the gods, but maintained that they lived in happiness apart from mankind and were not concerned with human affairs. As an Epicurean, he rejected magic and other forms of superstition that had found a haven in Middle Stoicism. He was a man of true poetic genius and his *De rerum natura* is one of the great masterpieces of world literature. While his outlook and teachings were repugnant in principle to early Christian writers, both Arnobius and Lactantius put him to good use in their polemic against paganism. St. Jerome reports that he was intermittently insane and that he commited suicide. However, St. Jerome was writing 4 cent. later, and we do not know how reliable his source was in this respect. BIBLIOGRAPHY: H. Hagendahl, "Apologists and Lucretius," in *Latin Fathers and the Classics* (1958); A. J. Festugière, *Epicurus and His Gods* (tr., 1956); E. E. Sikes, *Lucretius, Poet and Philosopher* (1936, repr. 1971).

[M. R. P. MCGUIRE]

LUCY, ST. (d. 304), martyr at Syracusa, Sicily, in the reign of Diocletian. Her cult is traceable at least to the 5th cent.; there is a 5th- or 6th-cent. *passio;* St. Gregory the Great introduced her name, along with that of St. Agatha (who appeared in a vision, encouraging L.) into the Roman Canon of the Mass. Devotion to her spread throughout Europe in the Middle Ages (as is evident from the festival of light observed esp. by Scandinavian Lutherans on her feast, Dec. 13). She is the patroness of eyes, her martyrdom having included hers being plucked out. BIBLIOGRAPHY: Butler 4:548–549; P. Toschi, EncCatt 7:1618–23; M. C. Celletti, BiblSanct 8:241–257.

[T. C. O'BRIEN]

LUDANUS, ST. (d. 1202), a Scottish pilgrim who was venerated in the Middle Ages in the Diocese of Strassburg. According to a 14th cent. vita, L. was born of noble family in Scotland and after founding a hospital with his inheritance, went on pilgrimage to Rome; he died in Alsace on the return journey. His tomb, at Hipsheim, became a popular shrine and center of pilgrimage. BIBLIOGRAPHY: G. MacNiocaill, BiblSanct 8:289.

[R. W. HAYS]

LUDGER OF MÜNSTER, ST. (*c.*745–809), first bp. of Münster (804), missionary to Frisia and Westphalia. A deacon and missionary in Deventer, L. was ordained in 777 and after 7 years in West Frisia was sent to Deventer to rebuild the church which had been destroyed during a Frisian uprising. He was forced to flee during the Saxon rebellion against the Franks. After more than 2 years in Rome and Monte Cassino, L. was recalled by Charlemagne and sent to re-Christianize the Frisians. His destruction of pagan places enraged the Frisians, who ravaged the missions and drove L. out. Charlemagne then sent L. to Münster (Westphalia), which he organized into 40 parishes. He also founded the abbeys of Helmstedt and Werden and a convent for women at Nottuln. BIBLIOGRAPHY: Butler 1:686–688; J. Lieball, BiblSanct 8:290–292.

[M. S. TANEY]

LUDMILLA, ST. (*c.*859–921), martyr, patroness of Bohemia. A Slav princess and wife of Boriwoj, first Christian Duke of Bohemia, L. was baptized by St. Methodius and became a zealous promoter of Christianity in Bohemia. Her grandson St. Wenceslaus, whom she had reared in the Christian faith, ascended the throne as a minor and thus fired the opposition of the already militant pagan faction. Exercising the regency in his stead, Wenceslaus' mother Drahomira favored the pagan cause, but it is not known for certain that she instigated L.'s murder. BIBLIOGRAPHY: Butler 3:570; J. Polc, BiblSanct 8:293–296.

[M. S. TANEY]

LUDOLF OF CORVEY, ST. (d. 983), abbot of Corvey from 965. Under his care the abbey prospered, esp. the monastic school. L. is said to have had the power of extrasensory perception. His cult began *c.*1100. A baroque statue of Ludolf stands in the abbey church. BIBLIOGRAPHY: Baudot-Chaussin 8:217–218; R. Van Doren, BiblSanct 8:296.

[B. F. SCHERER]

LUDOLF OF RATZEBURG, ST. (d. 1250), bp. of Ratzeburg 1236–50. An ascetic and canon of Prémontré, L. as bp. set his rule as a guide for his cathedral chapter and for a convent of Benedictine nuns which later became a Premonstratensian monastery. He courageously struggled for ecclesiastical rights with Duke Albert of Sachsen-Lauenburg. The imprisonment, banishment, and tortures he endured have caused him to be regarded as a martyr. Canonized in the 14th cent. his cult is observed at Wismar in Mecklenburg. BIBLIOGRAPHY: Butler 1:702; *Book of Saints* (comp. by the Benedictine Monks of St. Augustine's Abbey, 1966); G. B. Valvekens, BiblSanct 8:297.

[M. E. DUFFY]

LUDOLF OF SAXONY (*c.*1295–1377), Carthusian spiritual writer. Born in Strassburg, he was for 30 years a Dominican, then from 1340 a Carthusian. He relied heavily on allegory and moral prescription in his writing. His works, esp. the *Vita Christi,* influenced Ignatius of Loyola and Theresa of Avila, among others. The complete title of the work is *Vita Domini nostri Jesu Christi ex quattuor Evangeliis;* the first printing was in 1474; it was subsequently translated and reprinted in many languages. It is a treatise on the whole Christian moral and spiritual life.

[J. R. RIVELLO]

LUDOVISI, LUDOVICO (1595–1623), cardinal. At the age of 26, L. was made cardinal by his uncle Gregory XV. He was also invested with many benefices which he used in favor of his relatives, in collecting art, and in largesse to the poor. BIBLIOGRAPHY: G. Auletta, EncCatt 7:1647–48.

[M. J. SUELZER]

LUDWIG, FRIEDRICH (1872–1930), German musicologist, specialist in 13th and 14th-cent. music. After studying at the Univ. at Marburg and Strassburg, he served as lecturer in musical science at Strassburg (1905–11), and after 1911, professor of music and rector at Göttingen. He published numerous articles in the *Sammelbände der internationalen Musikgesellschaft* and the *Festschrift* for Hugo Riemann, noted music historian.

[R. J. LITZ]

LUDWIG MISSIONVEREIN (Ludwig Mission Society), a society founded in Munich in 1838 by F. *Résé for support of missionary activity in the U.S. and Asia, named for King Ludwig of Bavaria. The scope of aid to the U.S. eventually focused on German-American projects such as aid to religious orders working among German immigrants and help for St. Francis Seminary in Milwaukee. The American College at Louvain was also a beneficiary. Archives of the Society in Munich are valuable historical sources for mission history. BIBLIOGRAPHY: T. Roemer, *Ludwig Missionverein and the Church in the United States 1838–1918* (CUA StAmChHist 16, 1933).

[J. R. AHERNE]

LUEGER, KARL (1844–1910), Austrian political leader, mayor of Vienna. After briefly practicing law, he turned to politics and the liberal party as a means of achieving social justice for the lower middle class. When the liberals failed to work towards this goal, L. left the party and helped organize the Christian Social Party in 1889. Although suspect to the Austrian hierarchy, and to the crown, the party and its program were favored by Pope Leo XIII. L.'s party merged with the Catholic *Volkspartei* in 1907 and became a strong voice in Austrian politics. As mayor L. promoted the urban development and modernization of Vienna.

[H. P. ANNAS]

LÜFTHILDIS, ST., (fl. 9th cent.), virgin whose name, or a form of it, is widely dispersed topographically in the Archdiocese of Cologne, and whose popular cult has her invoked for relief from earache, headache, and dog bite. The earliest literary references to her are in Caesarius of Heisterbach, 1222. Her bones were translated in 1623, and again in 1902 were honored with a marble tomb. BIBLIOGRAPHY: AS Jan. 2:1146–48; F. Baumann, BiblSanct 8:315–316.

[S. WILLIAMS]

LUGDUNUM (earlier, Lugudunum) was a common Gallic place name, meaning perhaps "bright hill." The most famous city of this name was at the juncture of the Rhone and Saône on the site of modern Lyons. A Roman colony was founded there in 43 B.C. and, because of its central location became the financial center of Gallia Comata. In 15 B.C. it received the main mint for imperial coinage; in 12 B.C. Drusus erected there an altar to Rome and Augustus, thus making it a center for the imperial cult; in 10 B.C. the Emperor Claudius was born there. A theater, aqueduct, and *exedrae* attest the prosperity of Lugdunum in the 1st and 2d cent. A.D. It became the center of a flourishing Christian community, made up originally of merchants and workers from the East. St. Pothinus, its first bp. was probably a native of Asia Minor and a disciple of St. Polycarp. With 47 others he was put to death for the faith in 177 A.D., during the reign of Marcus Aurelius. He was succeeded by St. *Irenaeus. During the Middle Ages, in 1245 and 1274, the 13th and 14th ecumenical councils were held here. BIBLIOGRAPHY: Cramer, RAC 13:1718–23.

[M. J. COSTELLOE]

LUGO, FRANCISCO DE (1580–1652), Spanish Jesuit theologian, brother of J. de *Lugo. A Jesuit from 1600, he first taught theology in Mexico, then in Spain, and in Rome; his last post was as rector of the Jesuit college at Valladolid. L.'s commentary on Aquinas's *Summa* was lost on the voyage back to Spain from Mexico; his published works are: *De principiis moralibus actuum humanorum* (1642); *Theologica scholastica* (1647); *De septem ecclesiae sacramentis* (1652).

[T. C. O'BRIEN]

LUGO, JUAN DE (1583–1660), Spanish Jesuit theologian, created cardinal by Urban VIII in 1643. Brother of F. de *Lugo, he became a Jesuit at Salamanca in 1603. His early teaching was at Valladolid, beginning in 1616; from 1621 or 1622 he taught for 20 years at the Collegium Romanum in Rome. He wrote voluminously; many of his philosophical and theological treatises exist only in MS form; his published dogmatic and moral works were issued in an eight-volume modern edition (ed. J. B. Fournals, 1891–94) under the title *Disputationes scholasticae et morales*. L.'s most celebrated work, dedicated to Urban VIII, is *De justitia et jure* (1642); highly prized also is his *Responsorum moralium libri VI* (1651). He advocated a moderate reaction towards the Jansenists, a stand unpopular at the time in the Society of Jesus. He represented King Philip IV's exercise of the right of exclusion (veto) against Card. Sacchetti in the papal conclave of 1655.

[T. C. O'BRIEN]

LUINI, BERNARDINO (*c.* 1480–1532), Milanese painter of charming Madonnas in the Lombard tonal tradition, relating to Leonardo (*Madonna with Rose Hedge, Madonna with Kerchief,* both in Milan). L. painted unusual secular frescoes (*c.* 1520), followed (1525) by a vivacious cycle of the life of Christ in Sta. Maria dei Miracoli (Saronno).

[M. J. DALY]

LUKAS OF PRAGUE (*c.* 1460–1528), bp. and outstanding leader of the *Unitas Fratrum. Completing his education at the Univ. of Prague, he left the *Utraquists to join the Brethren. His learning and native gifts soon brought him into prominence as administrator and writer. His catechism, liturgies, and theological works decisively shaped the development of the Brethren from a sect withdrawn from the world to a Church including in its membership a cross section of society and recognizing the need for a learned clergy. The hymnal he edited for his Church in 1501 is looked upon as the first Protestant hymnal. He initiated colloquies with Luther and brought the Brethren into the mainstream of Protestantism. BIBLIOGRAPHY: P. Brock, *Unity of Czech Brethren* (1957).

[J. R. WEINLICK]

LUKE, EVANGELIST, ST. (Gr., *Loukas*), a companion of Paul, a physician, and traditionally considered the author of the Gospel of Luke and the Acts of the Apostles. The name Loukas (Luke) appears in Col 4.14; 2 Tim 4.11; Philem 24. He was a gentile by birth (Col 4.10–14). Church tradition and his information about Antioch point to Antioch of Syria as his native country. However, the "we" sections of Acts (beginning 16.10), with their emphasis on Philippi in Macedonia suggest this city. Paul evidently left his companion there until their reunion on his final trip to Jerusalem (Acts 20.6). Acts mentions a certain Lucius of Cyrene at Antioch (13.1). Paul refers to a kinsman, or fellow countryman Lucius in Rom 16.21. However, it is less probable that these refer to the Evangelist. BIBLIOGRAPHY: J. Jervell, *Luke and the People of God: A New Look at Luke—Acts* (1972).

[J. A. GRASSI]

LUKE OF ARMENTO, ST. (d. 995), Sicilian monk. From his hermitage in Calabria, where he was under the tutelage of St. Elias of Reggio, he fled away to escape the Saracens in 959. He then established a monastic community at Noa in Lucania and restored the monastery of San Giuliano near the Agri River. Fleeing from the Saracens again in 969, he settled at Armento where he remained until his death. BIBLIOGRAPHY: AS Oct. 6:337–342; G. Robinson, *History and Cartulary of the Greek Monastery of St. Elias and St. Anastasius of Carbone* (2 v. in 3, 1928–30); F. Russo, BiblSanct 8:187–188.

[W. A. JURGENS]

LUKE BELLUDI, Bl. (*c.*1200–86), the son of a rich family near Padua who at the age of 20 was received into the Friars Minor by St. Francis. He was a close companion of St. Anthony at whose death he was present. L. became provincial minister and was effective in erecting the basilica which enshrines the remains of Anthony in Padua. He is buried in Anthony's first tomb. BIBLIOGRAPHY: Butler 1:359–360; A. Blasucci, BiblSanct 2:1085–1086.

[A. WARDLE]

LUKE, GOSPEL ACCORDING TO ST., the third book in the NT canon, written after A.D. 70, perhaps toward A.D. 80, by Luke, a physician and companion of Paul (Philem 24; Col 4.14; 2 Tim 4.11) and, as may be inferred from Col 4.10–14, a gentile convert to Christianity. Luke's authorship is contested by a minority of NT scholars, esp. in Germany, on the ground that Acts (certainly written by the same person as the Lukan Gospel) presents a portrait of Paul and his teaching that does not harmonize with the Pauline letters. The majority of NT scholars are not convinced that this argument is sufficiently weighty to overthrow early Church tradition that unhesitatingly ascribed Lk-Acts to Luke the physician and companion of Paul. Further study of Acts may eventually determine whether the differences between Lukan and Pauline theology are due to Luke's ignorance of Paul or to the objectives he had in view in writing Acts.

The third Gospel cannot be fully appreciated except in the light of the significance of Acts. Alone among the Evangelists Luke chose to follow up his Gospel with a second work that recounts, from a theological standpoint, the origin and development of the Christian community, particularly under the influence of Peter and Paul. He was responding to second-generation Christians who needed to be informed of the origins of the Christian community and of its key traditions and teaching. This need of Christians of the 70s is traceable to the change of perspective in the Church's thought that was the result of the Roman capture of Jerusalem and destruction of the Temple in A.D. 70. Prior to this date Christians expected the parousia of Jesus and the end of human history as a possible proximate event (cf. 1 Th 4.13–18; 1 Cor 1.7; Mk 13.14–26). But when the parousia did not materialize in conjunction with Jesus' prophecy of the destruction of the Temple, the previous orientation away from worldly concerns (cf. 1 Cor 7.29–31) had to be reexamined. The Acts reflects the growing awareness that the Church was a real part of history, and that its destiny was inescapably associated with the Roman Empire. It is reasonable to assume that this shift away from emphasis on the nearness of the parousia toward a keener historical consciousness influenced Luke in the writing of his Gospel. Supporting evidence for this assumption is found in Lk 2.1–2; 3.1–2, where the Evangelist places the birth of Jesus and the prophetic message of the Baptist in the setting of the Roman Empire and the political and religious governments of Palestine. The gospel message is thus placed on a par with the major events of world history.

Luke's portrait of the ministry is esp. weighted in the direction of Jesus' human concerns. The Galilean ministry (4.14–9.50) begins on the note of universalism: Jesus' teaching is directed to the spiritually poor, captive and blind, whether Jew or gentile (4.16–30). The gentile also was able to perceive his unique religious authority and purpose, and to rise to faith in him (7.1–10). When the people responded favorably to this sympathy with their plight (4.37,42; 5.1), he chose disciples to expand his work

(5.1–11; 6.12–16; 10.1–2). But he did not aim only to alleviate human suffering; he demanded a response to his teaching as God's word that affected the very core of man's relationship to his fellowman (6.20–49; 8.21; 11.28). Practicing his own preaching, he was tolerant of those who did not fully accept him (9.49–50), and refused violence against those who rejected him (9.51–56). But conscious of the eternal importance of his prophetic message, he accepted violence against himself as the inevitable outcome of the prophet's lot (9.51,62; 12.35–48; 13.31–33). He left behind a legacy of teaching that warned the wealthy of their responsibility toward the poor (16.19–31; 19.1–10), that objected to the toleration of a system of social outcasts (15.1–10; 17.11–19), and that welcomed the service of women as integral to the well-being of society (7.36–50; 8.1–3; 10.38–42).

The third Gospel abounds in the confidence that the person and teaching of Jesus must inevitably prove attractive to many in the gentile world, symbolized by Theophilus, "God's friend," to whom Lk-Acts are addressed (Lk 1.3; Acts 1.1), because of its emphasis on love and justice among men and its clear and authoritative teaching on human destiny that provides balance for the conduct of human affairs. As has often been remarked, while Luke greatly stresses the gentleness of Christ, he is no less emphatic in urging the moral demands made upon men by the word of Jesus that are not only a leaven within society, but lie at the heart of the fulfillment of man's true destiny. BIBLIOGRAPHY: G. B. Caird, *Gospel of St. Luke* (1964); H. Conzelmann, *Theology of St. Luke* (1960); A. Hastings, *Prophet and Witness in Jerusalem* (1958); A. R. C. Leaney, *Commentary on the Gospel according to St. Luke* (1958).

[C. P. CEROKE]

LUKEWARMNESS, a lack of *fervor in living the life of charity. It is a classic term taken by spiritual theology from Rev 3.16, "So, because you are lukewarm *(tepidus)* and neither hot nor cold, I will spew you out of my mouth." This tepidity or languor is not itself a sinful state of soul, but a lethargy in responsiveness to what love for God calls for. Deliberate venial sins may be the symptoms of lukewarmness; they are retardants to spiritual progress and can even be dispositive to a loss of charity through grave sin. Lukewarmness is a characteristic of the vice of *acedia, which is not physical laziness, but an indifferent or reluctant response to the love of God, and by no means a rare spiritual failing.

[T. C. O'BRIEN]

LULL OF MAINZ, ST. (d. 768), abp., missionary companion of St. Boniface. A native of Wessex, he became a Benedictine at Malmesbury. After a pilgrimage to Rome, he joined Boniface's missionary work in Germany. Consecrated coadjutor to Boniface (752), L. succeeded him as bp. of Mainz (754). He founded the monasteries of Hersfeld and Bleidenstadt and was made the first regular metropolitan of Mainz (780). BIBLIOGRAPHY: F. Baumann, BiblSanct 8:372; Butler 4:129–130.

[G. M. COOK]

LULL, RAYMOND (*c.* 1235–*c.* 1316), theologian, missionary, and mystic. L. served King James I of Aragon at his S court in Majorca, where he learned Arabic and was influenced by Oriental mysticism. He became a Franciscan tertiary *c.* 1265, and devoted himself to converting the Muslims. He traveled widely in Asia and Africa as a missionary; tried to enlist support for his projects throughout Europe; established a school of Oriental languages at Miramar; and probably died as a martyr, stoned by the Muslims in North Africa. L.'s major literary work is the *Ars magna,* the principles of which pervade all of his thought. He believed that even the deepest Christian mysteries can be demonstrated by reason, and that all possible knowledge can be shown to be logically dependent upon certain evident first principles. These first principles, really divine attributes such as goodness and infinity, were applied to every strata of creation so that a comprehensible order in the universe became evident. By this method, L. hoped to show the unity of all knowledge and to bring both Muslims and Jews to Christianity. As a mystic, L. sought to contemplate the divine perfections from which all truth and love were derived. He was in the Franciscan spiritual tradition, but was strongly influenced by Sufi mysticism (see SUFISM) and medieval Augustinianism. BIBLIOGRAPHY: E. A. Peers, *Raymond Lull: A Biography* (1929); F. A. Yates, NCE 8:1074–75 with bibliog.; J. N. Hillgarth, *Ramon Lull and Lullism in Fourteenth Century France* (1971).

[T. M. MCFADDEN]

LULLY, JEAN BAPTISTE (Lulli; 1632–87), Italian-born composer in France. Rising from social oblivion to a high position in the court of Louis XIV, L.'s abilities as a musician, composer, dancer, and courtier eventually gained him the favor and patronage of the French court. He gained permission to form his own band of "violinists of the King" and with its success he later became Instrumental Composer to the King (1653), Composer to the King's Chamber Music (1661), and the Royal Family's Music Master (1662). L. began to collaborate with Molière in 1664, a partnership that culminated in *Le Bourgeois gentilhomme* (1670). L. began his compositions for the stage toward the new form of Italian opera and after 1763 he held and maintained a royally enforced monopoly on operatic productions in France. L.'s influence dominated French opera for nearly a century after his death. For church he wrote five motets for two choirs, five Grands Motets, and a dozen Petits Motets which were published by Ballard in 1684, the most praised of which is his *Miserere.*

[R. J. LITZ]

LUMEN CHRISTI (the light of Christ), the versicle intoned three times in the course of the solemn procession of light during the *Easter Vigil liturgy, and from which the entire procession takes its name. The appropriate response is ''Thanks be to God.'' During the procession the light from the *Paschal candle, image of the Risen Christ, is spread throughout the whole assembly. The ceremony had its origins at Jerusalem. BIBLIOGRAPHY: J. Gaillard, *Holy Week and Easter* (2d and rev. ed., tr. W. Busch, 1957) 117–120. *HOLY WEEK.

[B. ROSENDALL]

LUMEN GLORIAE, see LIGHT OF GLORY.

LUNA PIZARRO, FRANCISCO JAVIER DE (1780–1855), abp. of Lima, statesman. Born in Peru, L. was ordained in 1806 and spent some time in Spain where he developed his liberal political views. Returning to Lima, he was made a member of the Metropolitan Assembly in 1812. When Peru broke away from Spain, L. became presiding officer of the first constituent congress of Peru. His career in politics was admirable in its support of civil liberties. Named auxiliary bp. of Lima in 1838, he became abp. in 1845. He promoted church discipline and supported restoration of the seminary.

[J. R. AHERNE]

LUNAR CALENDAR, originated by the Chaldean astronomers of the Seleucid period (beginning in the 4th cent. B.C.). Fundamental units of the calendar were the day and the month. The day began with sunset, and the month began on the day when the new moon's crescent was visible. A difficulty in this reckoning was that months varied between 29 days and 30 days. A second problem was that a 12-month year did not keep pace with the sun. The solution of 4th-cent. Chaldean astronomers was to arrange the lunar calendar so that 7 years in every 19 contain 13 months, a device that keeps the lunar and solar cycles relatively the same. The liturgical calendar is based on this calculation.

[J. R. AHERNE]

LUND CONFERENCE, the third World Conference on *Faith and Order, held at Lund, Sweden, Aug. 15–28, 1952. The subjects considered were (1) Christ and his Church; (2) continuity and unity; (3) ways of worship; and (4) intercommunion. The Conference marked a change from the *Lausanne and *Edinburgh Conferences, which had endeavored to compare the doctrinal positions of the Christian Churches in the hope that greater understanding of the differences would remove obstacles to unity. At Lund the emphasis on tradition and Scripture as expressed in worship was more effective. Continued efforts were made to define the nature of the Church. In its eschatological aspect the Church was viewed as the ''pilgrim People of God,'' and a strong desire was manifest for greater unity in worship based on an essential unity in faith. At Lund, for the first time, authorized RC observers took part in the discussions, a fact reflecting the RC development of ecumenical theology that followed the 1949 Vatican document *De motione oecumenica*. BIBLIOGRAPHY: *Third World Conference on Faith and Order* (ed. O. S. Tomkins, 1953). *WORLD COUNCIL OF CHURCHES; *ECUMENICAL MOVEMENT.

[D. CODDINGTON]

LUNDENSIAN THEOLOGY, a theological school represented by a number of 20th-cent. Lutheran scholars at the Univ. of Lund In Sweden. Their main contribution has been the development of *motif research. To a great extent the Lundensian theology has been the reaction to two previous influences affecting Swedish Lutheran theology: *Pietism, with the revivals of the 19th cent.; and the Kantian metaphysical critique of Christianity. Pioneers were E. Billing, with his insistence on the centrality of forgiveness in the theology of Luther, and N. *Söderblom's historical and psychological approach to the Reformer's thought. G. *Aulén found in the eros-agape theory the ground motif to distinguish Christianity from all other religions. A. *Nygren, while accepting Luther's ''Copernican Revolution'' of a sovereign and gracious God, a concept that had been blurred by the eros motif in medieval scholasticism, denied the right of the school of Lund to regard as the central theme of theology the question, ''What is the Christian faith?'' when in truth it is ''How can the sinner find peace with God?'' More recently G. Ljunggren and R. Bring have studied Luther's anthropology; A. Runestam has expressed fear that the Reformer's concept of God's sovereignty might lead to determinism; others have gone to the roots of his dualism. The Lundensian contribution has been outstanding for the contemporary Luther renaissance. BIBLIOGRAPHY: E. Carlson, *Reinterpretation of Luther* (1948); N. Ferré, *Swedish Contribution to Modern Theology* (1938); G. Wingren, *Theology in Conflict* (1958).

[P. DAMBORIENA]

LUNETTE (Lat., *lunula*), a part of the *monstrance which is used to hold the host. It usually slides into a fitting which holds it firm and makes the host visually accessible to all. It should be gilded and blessed for use.

[N. KOLLAR]

LUNG-MÊN (''dragon-gate''), the site of black limestone caves of important Buddhist sculpture (*c.*453–550 A.D.), located 8 miles S of Lo-yang, second capital of the Wei dynasty (494 A.D.), whose rulers (444 A.D.) persecuted the Buddhists. Ending the persecution (453 A.D.) they, in propitiation for the evils of their forefathers, initiated the carvings, with special reference to the Suvarnaprabhasa Sutra of sin and repentance. Some 40 caves were carved through the Six Dynasties period into T'ang, with stylistic modifications. The Pin-yang-tung Cave (523 A.D.) is the finest with a procession of gracefully attenuated donors in exquisite linear patterns (a section of these donors is in the William Rockhill Nelson Gallery, Kansas City), and a great Buddha attended by disciples and Bodhisattvas against a mandorla ornamented with delicate leaping flames. The T'ang cave (670–675) shows a Vairoçana (universal) Buddha, 50 ft tall and full-bodied—a Sino-Indian symbiosis in heavy T'ang style—secular and baroque. Wei figures at Lung-mên are elegant and elongated in contrast with the soft sandstone forms at Yün-Kang, site of earlier Buddhist cave carving. BIBLIOGRAPHY: S. Mizuno and T. Nagahiro, *Study of Buddhist Cave Temples at Lung-Mên, Honan* (1941).

[M. J. DALY]

LUNN, SIR ARNOLD (1888–1974), Catholic apologist. L. was a leading figure in the sport of Alpine skiing; creator of the slalom race, he won acceptance of it as an Olympic sport; he was knighted in 1952. His interest in religion began as an undergraduate at Oxford; he afterwards described it as a wish to be anti-Catholic, rather than to be an apologist. His approach took the form of "correspondence controversy," conducted as a rational challenge to religious claims. The form, he thought, would engage an otherwise indifferent reader's interest because it was a contest between adversaries. Two such controversies before his conversion were, *Difficulties* (1932) with Ronald Knox the adversary, *Is Christianity True* (1933), the opponent being C. E. M. Joad; after his conversion there was *Science and the Supernatural* (1935), with J. B. S. Haldane. Knox, whose influence was critical to L.'s acceptance of Catholicism, received him into the RC Church in 1933. L.'s apologia appeared in *Now I See* (1934) and *Within the City* (1936). He had satisfied himself that there was a satisfactory answer to the worst that could be said against the Church. He was appointed assistant professor of apologetics at the Univ. of Notre Dame in 1937; he also lectured at Harvard. Along with his many secular interests, L. remained active in defense of Catholicism throughout his life. His works on apologetics are now rather period pieces.

[J. R. AHERNE]

LUPERCALIA, ancient Roman festival observed every year on February 15. It had three purposes–expiation, purification of the Palatine City and its environs, and fertility for fields, livestock, and citizens. As symbols of fertility, goats and a dog were sacrificed and their blood put on the forehead of two young men and removed by wool saturated with milk. Festival participants then circled the walls of the Palatine beating all whom they met with thongs made from the skin of the sacrificed animals. By this they hoped to bring fertility to women.

[F. H. BRIGHAM]

LUPOLD OF BEBENBURG (*c.* 1297–1363), canonist and bp. of Bamberg 1353–63. Born in Germany, educated at Bologna where he earned the doctorate in canon law, he was concerned principally in his specialty and its implications for secular polity. During the Avignon papacy, he favored the German emperor without being antipapist. In his works (written before he became bp.) L. tried to distinguish the roles of the secular and the spiritual in Christian society: *Tractatus de iuribus regni et imperii* (1340), followed (1341) by a rimed tract: *Ritmaticum querulosum et lamentosum dictamen de modernis cursibus et defectibus regni ac imperii Romanorum*. The *Tractatus* influenced the constitutional law (Golden Bull of 1356) affecting German emperors and princes until 1806. As bp. he advised the Emperor Charles IV and worked for understanding between emperor and pope.

[M. E. DUFFY]

LUPUS OF FERRIÈRES (Servatus Lupus; *c.* 805–*c.* 862), abbot, theologian, writer, humanist. He entered the abbey of Ferrières at an early age, and *c.* 829 went to Fulda where he studied under *Rabanus Maurus, and met *Gottschalk of Orbais, whom he later defended against heresy charges. In 836 he returned to Ferrières and in 840 was made abbot there. A leading figure in the Carolingian renaissance, he made his abbey an important center of learning. His letters addressed to famous personages are a primary source for the history of his era. BIBLIOGRAPHY: E. S. Duckett, *Carolingian Portraits: A Study in the Ninth Century* (1962); C. H. Beeson, *Lupus of Ferrières as Scribe and Text Critic* (1930).

[M. S. TANEY]

LUPUS OF SENS, ST. (Loup, Lew; *c.* 573–*c.* 623), French bishop. Born in Orléanais, apparently he was known for his holiness even at an early age, since he was chosen to replace the bp. of Sens in 609. He was later exiled to the village of Ausne near Lyons, where he worked diligently at converting the pagans. In 614 Chlothar II, who had exiled him, granted a pardon, and L. returned to rule his diocese. He was buried in the monastery at Sens which he had founded. His intercession is sought for epileptics. BIBLIOGRAPHY: Butler 3:459–460; P. Viard, BiblSanct 8:388–389.

[J. R. RIVELLO]

LUPUS OF TROYES, ST. (*c.* 383–479), bishop. L. and his wife, the sister of St. Hilary of Arles, agreed to separate in the 7th year of their marriage to devote themselves to religion. He entered a monastery at Lérins in 426 but the following year became bp. of Troyes. He is credited in his earliest vita with fending off an attack of the Huns upon Troyes. But he was obliged to accompany Attila as a hostage for a time, a circumstance that brought him into temporary disfavor with his people, who thought he had been too compliant to the invader. For 2 years, while the feeling against him lasted, he lived in the mountains as a hermit. BIBLIOGRAPHY: P. Viard, BiblSanct 8:390–391; Butler 3:207–208.

[M. J. SUELZER]

LUQUE, CRISANTO (1889–1959), abp. of Bogotá, and cardinal. Ordained priest in 1916, L. was made bp. of Tunja in 1932, where he became one of the main promoters of the mass educational enterprise known as *Escuelas Radiofónicas de Sutatenza*. He was made abp. of Bogotá in 1950 and helped in the foundation of the *Consejo Episcopal Latinoamericano (CELAM). His main pastoral work was the promotion of a parochial system in the new barrios of Bogotá, then flooded by poor people who had fled from the bandit-infested interior. Although he had recognized the Rojas coup that overthrew the conservative government in 1953, he disliked the dictatorial policies of the Rojas regime and his sympathies were with the students and the people when they ousted the dictator. BIBLIOGRAPHY: R. Gómez Hoyos, NCE 8:1079.

[P. DAMBORIENA]

LURÇAT, JEAN (1892–1966), French painter, foremost contemporary tapestry designer in the world, who restored that form of weaving to its initial magnificence in the Middle Ages—re-establishing its solemn, public character for palaces, embassies, concert halls, the liturgy of churches, emphasizing its purely decorative quality as a ''mural'' object, filling architectural demands—wedded to the wall—deadening noise, satisfying intimacy. L. experimented alone (1916) in stitches, wool, and dyes, met (1933) François Tabard, master weaver at Aubusson, and was overwhelmed (1938) by the *Apocalypse of Angers*—foreshadowing his own *Apocalpyse* at Assy (1948). L. designed *Forêts* in 1937 and was commissioned to execute *Les Illusions d'Icare*—presented by the French nation to Queen Juliana of the Netherlands. In 1939, settling at Aubusson by invitation of the Ministry of National Education, L. began his famous *Jardin des coqs*. In 1945 the Association of Tapestry Cartoon Painters was established. Artists recognizing that weaving as a transcription of pictures had caused the decline in that magnificent art into the 19th cent., advocated reduced color, simple design, and carefully numbered color cartoons. 1946 saw the impressive Paris show of historic French tapestries, followed by L.'s publication on beasts and other designs of the Middle Ages (1947). In 1948, he designed his own tremendous Apocalypse (15 ft x 14 ft) for Notre Dame de Toute Grâce at Assy, in the Haute Savoie, France, beginning in 1957, his last series *The Song of the World*. L. designed more than 1000 tapestries, restoring the art to magnificence, and through his work and writing influenced two generations of artists over all the world. BIBLIOGRAPHY: J. Jobé, *Great Tapestries* (1965); C. Roy, *Jean Lurçat* (1956). **Apocalypse of Angers; *Apocalypse of Assy.*

[M. J. DALY]

LURIA, ISAAC BEN SOLOMON (De Luria; R. Isaac Askenazi Luria; Ha-Ari, ''sacred lion''; 1534–72), Jewish cabalist (see CABALA), mystic. He passed his early years in Jerusalem, then at age 7, went to Egypt where he began esoteric studies, seeking seclusion on the island of Jaziratal-Rawda in the lower Nile. He studied the **Zohar*, and other early Cabalistic works. He taught his disciples orally about Cabala and communion with righteous souls through mystical meditations. There is some evidence that L. thought of himself as the Messiah. The details of his life are found in the writings of his disciples, esp. those of Vital, but within a few decades, legend had transformed fact and a mystique veiled history. The chief source of L.'s teachings is Vital's *Eẓ Ḥayyim* (Tree of Life, written *c.*1573–76; published 1850–98, 1960–63), which includes all of L.'s extant writings and theosophical teaching, comments on the Bible, metempsychosis, meditative practices, an apology for religious precepts, atonement, and mystical unifications. L.'s introduction of messianic eschatology into Cabala altered subsequent thinking, anticipating the messianic Shabbatean movement. The task of redemption through restoration of inner and outer cosmos to original purity lies with the entire Jewish people, not with the Messiah who will appear when the people are restored.

[R. J. LITZ]

LUST, desirous love or *concupiscence, Lat. *concupiscentia,* which even as emotional desire bears no pejorative meaning as such in moral theology, but only when, which is usually the case, it connotes a disorderly appetition against living according to Christian reason, or the libidinous rebellion in our loins which to St. Augustine, though not to St. Thomas Aquinas, was original sin. Here it is treated, in accordance with common usage, as the equivalent of lechery, or *luxuria*.

This, which is one of the *capital sins, so named because they are the heads of a wide range of other sins, is placed by systematic theology as a sin against *chastity, which is part of the virtue of *temperance. Temperance is here taken, not in its Stoic sense as a general condition of all virtue, nor is chastity taken in its metaphorical sense according to which ascetical writers refer to any sin as spiritual fornication and, with biblical warrant, to unfaithfulness to God as spiritual adultery, but in its more specific Aristotelian sense as one of the four cardinal virtues, namely that which controls the human appetites for sensuously pleasurable objects. With regard to sex objects it is called chastity, which in its most specific sense is concerned with climactic activity, yet in a broader sense includes in the surroundings to this, thoughts, words, and deeds, that are more accurately the concern of *pudicitia,* which in this connection is commonly rendered as *purity or *modesty. The immoderate pursuit of sexual gratification may lead to complete unchastity or lechery, or it may stop at impurity or immodesty.

As types of heterosexual unchastity Gratian's *Decretum* enumerates simple *fornication, *adultery, *incest, *seduction, and *rape. The division arises from the historical exigences of canon law, not from any interior logic in lust; the same applies to additional types, namely *sacrilege, *prostitution, and *concubinage. Nonheterosexual unchastity includes auto-erotic, contraceptive, and homosexual practices, para-organic congress, and also bestiality. A similar division applies to sins of impurity or immodesty, which may be committed by thoughts (which may be idle fancies or may be dwelt on, *delectatio morosa*), or by words (pornography, obscene speech), or by deeds, whether in private or for public show.

All types are wrong in themselves, though their culpability may be lessened in various degrees according to the lack of deliberation and consent. Some occurrences of immodesty are not to be overloaded too censoriously, and some, of course, are matters of sentimentality rather than of sexuality: a moralist is precipitate if he reads a genital reference into all romantic fancies or indeed into all overfamiliarities. The condemnation of lust is clear in the Scriptures (cf. Mt 19.3–9; Rom 1.24–28; 1 Cor 6.9–20; Gal 5.19–20; Eph 5.25–33); the wrongfulness of its various forms can be inferred with different degrees of immediacy from the commands of natural law; and the Christian position in general has been unwaveringly maintained, allowances being made for differences of custom according to region and period about what is and what is not immodest, and also, outside the Roman Church, for differences of mentality about the derivative conclusions to be articulated and applied.

It may be remarked that to a classical Catholic moral theology there is nothing wrong with the intensity of *pleasure as such, or with the enjoyment of pleasure; that is what pleasure is for, indeed the phrase is almost a tautology. If wrong is present, that hinges on what is done, namely that it is out of place; that it is pleasurable adds to the incitement, but not to the wickedness. Intemperate men do wrong because they treat pleasure as an object in practice; moralists, unless they are deontologists, get confused when they treat it as an object in theory. If we are to judge from its effects, lust is a vice, not because it is high-spirited and fun, but because it is ungenerous and sad. BIBLIOGRAPHY: J. Fuchs, *De castitate et luxuria* (1963); ThAq ST 2a2ae, 141–145, 151–154, esp. in ed. Lat-Eng, (v. 43, *Temperance,* ed. T. Gilby, 1968).

[T. GILBY]

LUSTRATION, a ceremonial purification of a group of people, a piece of land, a city, or some other object employed by the Romans to ward off a potential disaster that might result from some known or unknown crime or guilt. A lustration, which could be of a public or private nature, was frequently carried out before the sailing of a fleet or the departure of an army; and every 5 years the city of Rome itself was purified through the solemn lustrum of the censors. The rite usually entailed a procession and sacrifice. The ancient lustration of the fields on April 25, the feast of the Robigalia, to ward off rust *(robigo)* from the wheat, was transformed by the early Christians into the Rogation Days. BIBLIOGRAPHY: Boehm, PW 13:2029–39.

[M. J. COSTELLOE]

LUTGARDIS, ST. (1182–1246), Cistercian mystic and stigmatic. Born at Tongres (then Netherlands), she was placed in the Benedictine convent of St. Catherine at St. Trond, in 1194, because her dowry was lost by her father. She was professed in 1200, and after being elected prioress in 1205, she sought out the stricter Cistercian rule at Aywières (near Liège), even though it was a French-speaking house and she spoke only Flemish. She had great humility, refused offices, and had many mystical experiences, esp. showing devotion to the Sacred Heart. She lost her sight in 1235; long fasts preceded her death, which she predicted. Thomas of Cantimpré wrote an account of her life. BIBLIOGRAPHY: T. Merton, *What Are These Wounds?* (1950); M. De Somer and A. M. Raggi, BiblSanct 8:396–400.

[N. F. GAUGHAN]

LUTHER, MARTIN (1483–1546), Protestant theologian and German Reformer. He was born at Eisleben in Saxony, the son of a miner, Hans Luther, and his wife Margaret. Despite later legends of extraordinary strictness in his parental home (some of them repeated by Luther himself), his relations with his parents do not appear to have been abnormal. His early education was received in Mansfeld, Magdeburg, and Eisenach; at Magdeburg his teachers belonged to the *Brethren of the Common Life. In 1501 he entered the Univ. of Erfurt, where he became Master of Arts in 1505 and undertook the study of law. These plans were interrupted in July 1505 by a severe personal and religious crisis. The occasion was a thunderstorm, during which L. vowed to St. Anne that he would become a monk. He fulfilled the vow on July 17, entering the Order of Augustinian Hermits at Erfurt. He was ordained in 1507 and during the following years pursued a program of theological study and theological teaching, receiving the degrees of Bachelor in Bible (1509) and of Doctor of Theology (1512). This obligated him to undertake lectures on Scripture, and it was out of these lectures that his historic transformation came. From 1513 to 1515 he occupied himself with the exposition of the Psalms *(Dictata super Psalterium),* which was followed by lectures on Romans, Galatians, and Hebrews. Although it seems impossible to date it with any precision, his "discovery of the gospel" occurred as he struggled with the meaning of the term "righteousness" *(justitia)* in these texts. How could the righteousness of God be revealed in the gospel, as Rom 1.17 declared, if this righteousness was the quality by which God demanded of man that he keep the law? The "new and wondrous definition of righteousness" that enabled him to answer this question—which was above all a personal religious question for him, and only secondly a theological one—was that this righteousness was not what God demanded, but what he conferred as his free gift in Christ. This discovery changed L.'s life—and the history of the Church.

Yet the issue that made him a public figure and precipitated the Reformation was not justification but the practice of indulgences. On Oct. 31, 1517, he issued his *Ninety-Five Theses against the indulgence that had been issued as part of the arrangement between Pope Leo X, Albert of Brandenburg, and the banking house of Fugger. L.'s objections, in which many faithful Catholics concurred, attacked not only the financial corruption of the practice but above all its distortion of the true nature of penance. The notoriety evoked by the Theses brought him into other debates that touched more closely the central concerns of his new theology. Of these, probably the most important in its consequences was the encounter with John *Eck at the*Disputation of Leipzig in July 1519, where L. was moved to voice his opposition to the infallibility of councils and the primacy of the pope. After Leipzig events moved even more swiftly. Various efforts to make the Saxon monk recant failed. On June 15, 1520, in the bull **Exsurge Domine,* he was ordered to recant in 60 days, under threat of excommunication. He burned the bull. In April 1521 he appeared before the imperial Diet of *Worms and was given another opportunity to recant. He declared instead that here he stood and could not do otherwise.

Now he was both an outlaw before the Empire and an apostate before the Church. Yet none of this kept him from his work as a theologian. To protect him from the consequences of the Diet's action against him, the elector of Saxony spirited him off to the *Wartburg. One fruit of this exile was his translation of the NT into German—his most influential achievement culturally, and perhaps also religiously. But this was also the time when Luther came into conflict with other advocates of reform, who for one or another reason were dissatisfied with either the pace or the scope of the changes. The fierce *Karlstadt wanted the Reformation to move faster toward the abolition of various medieval practices and toward the restoration of the chalice to the laity. The Anabaptists claimed to be drawing the logical consequences of L.'s attack upon the sacramental system when they repudiated *infant baptism. Similarly, J. *Oecolampadius and esp. *Zwingli attacked his retention of the doctrine of the *Real Presence as a remnant of *scholasticism. And Desiderius *Erasmus, whose lampoons against corruption and superstition in the Church had been far more acrid than Luther's, nevertheless could not follow him either in his defiance of authority or in his doctrine of the bondage of the will. The rebellious peasants claimed his support, but he repudiated their revolution (see PEASANTS' WAR).

These developments set the pattern of his thought and of his reformatory movement for the rest of his life. Although, as an outlaw, he himself did not attend the Diet at Augsburg in 1530, the *Augsburg Confession presented there was a faithful, if rather irenically phrased, summary of his doctrine. Most of what his Reformation meant historically had already been determined by this time, and the movement in many ways passed out of his hands. Personally and intellectually, however, he was far from finished. In 1529 he wrote his catechisms, which formed and still form the basis of Lutheran religious instruction (see CATECHISMS, LUTHER'S). In 1525 he married Catherine von Bora, thus founding the Protestant manse. His commentary on Galatians (1535) was a mature statement of the central themes of *justification, the distinction between *law and gospel, and the nature of faith. Students from many parts of Europe came to Wittenberg to hear his lectures, and his correspondence extended his influence far and wide. One of the great disappointments of his life was the fragmentation of the reform movement into warring factions. Neither the attempts to reconcile these factions nor the repeated efforts to reopen the dialogue with Roman Catholicism were successful. When he died on Feb. 18, 1546, he had laid the foundations for the history of Protestantism, but had also seen it move in directions that he found dangerous.

These and other disappointments aggravated the profound depressions of spirit that repeatedly came over him throughout his mature years; his German word for them was *Anfechtungen,* "trials." They were compounded of profound reverence, nagging guilt, and persistent doubt. He combined in an unusual measure the self-confidence and self-doubt characteristic of prophetic men in Israel and in the Church. Neither the muckraking of his RC detractors (who have portrayed him as an adulterer, a suicide, a drunkard, a foul-mouthed liar, and a psychopath) nor the idealizing of his Lutheran biographers (who have seen in him the fulfillment of the prophecy in Rev 14.6–7) does justice to the complexity of his character. He was a man of deep contrasts, capable of massive candor about himself and his faults but also given to towering rages and petty grudges. His kindness toward his inferiors was matched by his harshness toward those whom he regarded as deliberate perverters of the word of God. It is characteristic of the man that, in the 20th cent. as in the 16th, almost no one is neutral toward him. From his faith and thought have come some of the most powerful theological insights in Christian history, and he continues to fructify Christian doctrine beyond the borders of the communion that bears his name. BIBLIOGRAPHY: *Luther's Works: The American Edition* (ed. J. Pelikan and H. Lehmann, 1955–); R. Bainton, *Here I Stand* (1951); E. G. Rupp, *Luther's Progress to the Diet of Worms* (1951); EncLuthCh 2:1356–57, bibliog.; J. M. Todd, *Martin Luther* (1964); J. McSorley, *Luther: Right or Wrong (1969);* J. Wicks, *Man Yearning for Grace* (1968).

[J. PELIKAN]

LUTHERAN CHURCH—MISSOURI SYNOD, a Lutheran church body in North America comprising approximately one-third of the total membership of American Lutheranism. The Lutheran Church—Missouri Synod was formed in 1847 by immigrants from Germany who had begun to arrive in the U.S. in 1839. From its beginnings in such states as Missouri, Michigan, and Ohio, it has expanded and is now represented in all the states and provinces. Its greatest strength, however, continues to be in the Middle West. Of the three largest *synods—the other two being the *American Lutheran Church and the *Lutheran Church in America—the Missouri Synod has traditionally been the most conservative in doctrine. Although all Lutherans adhere to the doctrines of the *Augsburg Confession of

1530, the Missouri Synod has insisted upon a stricter interpretation of this confessional standard and has added to it a demand for theological orthodoxy also in doctrines not explicitly set forth there. Of special importance has been the doctrine of biblical inspiration and the corollary doctrine of inerrancy, against both the RC understanding of *tradition as the authentic interpreter of Scripture and the modern critical approach to Scripture. The last has led to a schism with the formation of the Association of *Evangelical Lutheran Churches. The issue also threatens synod fellowship with the American Lutheran Church.

In church practice also the Missouri Synod has emphasized a strict enforcement of the ban against membership in secret societies and has opposed *unionism, i.e., pulpit and altar fellowship without agreement in doctrine.

The Lutheran Church—Missouri Synod has at the same time accepted and even taken the lead in developing modern techniques for the work and mission of the Church. The Lutheran Hour was the first evangelistic program to be broadcast regularly on a national scale. "This Is the Life" has played a similar role in the field of religious television. Concordia Publishing House in St. Louis, the official press of the Missouri Synod, has been a leading religious publisher, first in German and now in English, since its establishment in 1869. The theological seminaries of the Missouri Synod, both named Concordia, are in St. Louis, Mo., and Springfield, Illinois. The church body also maintains two teachers' colleges (in River Forest, Ill., and Seward, Neb.) to staff its parochial school system, the largest such school system outside Roman Catholicism. In 1976 the Lutheran Church-Missouri Synod numbered 2.8 million baptized souls.

[J. PELIKAN]

LUTHERAN CHURCH IN AMERICA, the largest of the three Lutheran bodies in North America. The Lutheran Church in America, formed in 1962, united the former United Lutheran Church, Augustana Lutheran Church (Swedish), Finnish Evangelical Lutheran Church (Suomi Synod), and American Evangelical Lutheran Church (Danish). The United Lutheran Church, by far the largest of these uniting bodies, included those sections of American Lutheranism whose origins go back to colonial days (see MUHLENBERG, H. M.). The ethnic variety suggested by the composition of the bodies which formed it has its counterpart in other aspects of the Lutheran Church in America. Thus it combines theological emphases of greater heterogeneity than either of the other two Lutheran groups, the American Lutheran Church and the Lutheran Church—Missouri Synod. It has also taken the lead among American Lutherans in ecumenism, having participated in interdenominational councils and conferences, both national and international, almost since the inception of these ecumenical programs. Significantly, the Churches that formed the Lutheran Church in America were among the earliest Lutheran congregations to make the transition from German or Scandinavian to English and to move from an immigrant status into the mainstream of American Protestantism. The headquarters of the Lutheran Church in America are in New York City. Its theological seminaries are: Hamma School of Theology (part of Wittenberg Univ.), Springield, Ohio; Lutheran School of Theology at Chicago; Lutheran Theological Seminary at Gettysburg, Pa; Lutheran Theological Seminary at Philadelphia, Pa.; Lutheran Theological Seminary at Saskatoon, Saskatchewan, Canada; Lutheran Theological Southern Seminary, Columbia, S.C.; Northwestern Lutheran Theological Seminary, Minneapolis, Minn.; Pacific Lutheran Theological Seminary, Berkeley, Calif.; and Waterloo Lutheran Seminary (part of Waterloo Lutheran University), Waterloo, Ontario, Canada. It also operates 19 colleges. In 1976 the Lutheran Church in America numbered 3.2 million baptized members. BIBLIOGRAPHY: T. G. Tappert et al., EncLuthCh 2:1366–1408; *Lutheran Church of America Yearbook* (pa. 1975).

[J. PELIKAN]

LUTHERAN-ROMAN CATHOLIC DIALOGUES, discussions by Lutheran and Catholic theologians to explore the possibilities for overcoming differences. The dialogues began in Germany, the land of Luther, in 1946. There the Lutheran-RC Ecumenical Working Group has met twice annually, but has not issued joint statements. Lutheran-RC dialogue began in the U.S. in 1965, with representatives of all three major Lutheran Churches involved. This group has issued joint statements indicating areas of consensus and of continuing difference. At various times it has announced substantial areas of agreement on baptism, the Eucharist, and the ministry. A joint 1974 statement said that papal primacy "renewed in the light of the Gospel need not be a barrier to reconciliation." The group then turned to the subject of papal infallibility, which proved more difficult. Dialogue on the international level was begun in 1967 with the formation of a Joint Lutheran-RC Study Commission, under the auspices of the Lutheran World Federation and the Vatican Secretariat for Promoting Christian Unity. This commission, meeting annually, produced a statement on "The Gospel and the Church" *(Malta Report)* in 1972 that subsequently served as a basis for discussion in the Churches. A report from the commission's 1976 meeting indicated that responses to the statement were diverse, but that most respondents welcomed the dialogue. In Oct. 1976 a delegation of top Lutheran World Federation leaders held talks with Christian Unity Secretariat members and met with Pope Paul.

[T. EARLY]

LUTHERAN SYNODICAL CONFERENCE, a unitive body of strongly confessional Lutheran synods formally established in Milwaukee, Wis., in 1872. The founding members were the Ohio, Missouri, Wisconsin, Minnesota, Illinois, and Norwegian Synods. The original name was

Evangelisch-Lutherische Synodal-Conferenz (Evangelical Lutheran Synodical Conference). The history of the Synodical Conference has been marked by a desire to maintain strong doctrinal unity and fellowship only with those Lutherans and non-Lutherans who met the standards of the Conference. The composition of membership, however, has changed constantly, as new bodies joined and others withdrew, usually over doctrinal disagreement. In 1963 both the Evangelical Lutheran Synod and the Wisconsin Evangelical Lutheran Synod withdrew. A close relationship continued between the Lutheran Church—Missouri Synod and the *Synod of Evangelical Lutheran Churches, but the Synodical Conference ceased to exist. BIBLIOGRAPHY: G. T. Mueller, *History of the Synodical Conference* (1948); E. L. Lueker, EncLuthCh 3:2316–17.

LUTHERAN WORLD ACTION (LWA), cooperative aid program of U.S. Lutherans. It began in 1940 with a campaign to raise funds for needs related to the war situation in Europe. The outbreak of the war created difficulties for missionaries and mission programs that had been supported by Lutherans of Germany and Scandinavia. U.S. Lutherans sought to assist with these needs, as well as to aid the Lutheran refugees who began coming from Europe to America. As the U.S. became involved in the war, LWA funds were also used for ministries to service personnel. LWA was established as an agency of the National Lutheran Council, a cooperative body of eight Lutheran Churches that subsequently merged to form the American Lutheran Church (ALC) and the Lutheran Church in America (LCA). In 1956 the Council became the USA National Committee of the Lutheran World Federation, and in 1977 Lutheran World Ministries. Following World War II, LWA collected food, clothing, and medicine, as well as funds, for relief and reconstruction in war-devastated areas. Later, more aid went to development and church-assistance projects in mission areas of Asia, Africa, and Latin America. LWA funds have also gone for continuing ministries to armed-forces personnel, study projects, and various other needs. Funds have been distributed primarily through the U.S. agency Lutheran World Relief, the Lutheran World Federation and the National and World Councils of Churches. In the early 1960s the ALC and LCA began budgeting funds for the LWA, and fund-raising promotion ceased in 1977.

[T. EARLY]

LUTHERAN WORLD FEDERATION, a free association of Lutheran Churches throughout the world to act "as their agent in such matters as they assign to it." It was organized at Lund, Sweden, in 1947 to supersede the Lutheran World Convention, which had been in existence for 23 years, seeking not only closer harmony and understanding among Lutheran Churches throughout the world but also cooperation in relief and mission work with special consideration for the weaker Churches, for unity of action and utterance among Lutherans, and for exchange of students, professors, and literature. Lutheran World Conventions were held at Eisenach in 1923, at Copenhagen in 1929, at Paris in 1935, and at Lund in 1947. At Lund a constitution was adopted that changed the Convention into the Lutheran World Federation. The key figure in the formation of the new organization was S. C. Michelfelder of the American Lutheran Church, who had been sent to Europe in 1945 by the American Section of the Lutheran World Convention for relief and reconstruction work. The functions of the organization are: to further a united witness before the world to the gospel of Jesus Christ as the power of God for salvation; to cultivate unity of faith and confession among the Lutheran Churches of the world; to develop fellowship and cooperation in study among Lutherans; to foster Lutheran interest in, concern for, and participation in, ecumenical movements; to support Lutheran Churches and groups as they endeavor to meet the spiritual needs of other Lutherans and to extend the gospel; and to provide a channel for Lutheran Churches and groups to help meet physical needs. BIBLIOGRAPHY: A. R. Wentz, EncLuthCh 2:1425–30; D. P. Scaer, *Lutheran World Federation Today* (pa. 1971).

[F. E. MASER]

LUTHERANISM, the largest of the Protestant bodies in Western Christendom. As its name indicates, Lutheranism traces its historical origin to the work of Martin *Luther. He did not, however, intend to found a new Church; nor was he pleased that the movement that emerged from his work as a Reformer was baptized with his name. Before his death there were Lutheran Churches not only in various lands of Germany but in Scandinavia and in eastern Europe. Although these countries still account statistically for the largest part of its membership, Lutheranism has spread to most of the inhabited portions of the earth. Beginning already in the early colonial era, Lutherans immigrated to North America and gained converts there once they had settled, with the result that by the late 1960s the U.S. had almost 10 million Lutherans. In Latin America, Canada, Australia, the Union of Soviet Socialist Republics, Africa, Asia, and the islands of the sea, the combination of various immigrations and several missionary societies planted the Lutheran name.

The international character of Lutheranism and its adaptation to many different cultures are symbolized by its heterogeneity in church organization. There is no Protestant congregationalism more extreme than that of some Lutheran groups, esp. in the U.S.; at the same time, even under the terms of **Apostolicae curae,* the *apostolic succession of the Lutheran Church of Sweden may be more nearly valid than that of any except Eastern Orthodox communions. Lutherans themselves are characterized by considerable indifference to questions of *polity; such questions are neither constitutive of the life of the Church nor, in and of themselves, an adequate basis for separation from other Christians. For the first generations of Lutheranism, even the papacy was not such a ground, provided that it could be accepted as *jure humano*. This indifference to polity is combined with a great regard for the office of the ministry. Sociology and theology join in various Lutheran traditions to make the pastor a figure of authority and respect, often to a degree exceeding the regard in which the clergy are held by traditions that, theoretically at least, exalt the office far more.

Lutheran liturgy is no more uniform than Lutheran polity. The "high Mass" of the Church of Sweden has retained some elements of the Western rite that have been discarded by Roman Catholicism, and the liturgical revival of various Lutheran Churches, including those of North America, has involved the recovery of various practices (such as the Elevation) lost since the 16th century. Yet within some of the very same Lutheran bodies there are devotional traditions (such as prayer meetings) of an unmistakably Protestant cast. The most distinctive feature of Lutheran worship is its hymnody. The Lutheran chorale, which owes its origins to Luther himself and reached its climax in the work of Paul Gerhardt (d. 1676), epitomizes both the continuity of Lutheranism with the RC tradition (as in the hymn "O Sacred Head Now Wounded," based on the *Salve caput cruentatum*) and its special forms of faith and life (as in Luther's "A Mighty Fortress Is Our God"). It is neither in its polity nor in its liturgy but in its theology that Lutheranism has defined itself most clearly. For Luther himself, the "doctrine of the gospel" was the decisive point on which the Church was not permitted to yield, while on the Christian life it had to recognize the frailty of men and the variations in their capacity. Lutheranism codified this position in its confessional statements, beginning with the *Augsburg Confession (1530) and concluding with the *Book of Concord (1580). Even when, as in *Pietism, Lutheran spokesmen denounced an exclusive preoccupation with doctrine as intellectualism, their very denunciation took theological form. As a consequence, the training of the ministry in the Lutheran tradition has traditionally emphasized the need for a learned clergy. Greek, Hebrew, and Latin, together with church history, exegesis, and dogmatics have made up the curriculum of both the theological faculties in the European universities and the theological seminaries in America. This emphasis upon humanistic erudition in the equipment of the minister has helped to give Lutheranism, esp. German Lutheranism, a dominant position in international theological scholarship, particularly during the 19th century. With its base as much in the university as in the Church, Lutheran theology has frequently manifested a spirit of intense controversy and a tendency toward rapid and radical shifts. Nevertheless, certain common and continuing themes document a unity beyond these fluctuations. Almost without exception, the parties and schools of Lutheran theology have taken the exegetical task with great seriousness, devoting themselves to the biblical text with learning and care. Even in the heyday of Pietism, with its emphasis upon conversion, most Lutheran theologians stressed the primacy of grace over merit and the *monergism of the divine initiative. Thus justification by grace through faith (a more accurate formulation than the usual *justification by faith) has united Lutheran theologians of diverse positions. On other doctrinal questions unity has been less substantial, esp. in the 19th and 20th centuries. Biblical criticism and the new study of the Gospels have made the formal adherence of confessional Lutheranism to the Christology of Chalcedon quite ambiguous; these and other factors have been responsible for a fundamental recasting of the traditional Lutheran views of such issues as the sacraments, the inspiration of Scripture, the Atonement, and even the Trinity.

These characteristics of the Lutheran Church have shaped its participation in the ecumenical movement, which has included some of the movement's most inspired leadership (notably Nathan *Söderblom) and some of its sharpest critics. When ecumenism was almost exclusively a Protestant matter, the attitude of various Lutheran groups toward it was determined by their understanding of Lutheran distinctiveness on the questions that set it apart from bodies other than the RC Church, such as the *Real Presence. But with the growth of RC ecumenism in the decades after World War II, Lutheran participation took a different form. Always prominent in ecumenical discussions, Lutherans now began to play a mediatorial role between RCs and Protestants. Centuries of living in separated communities meant that, in vocabulary and interest, Lutherans and RCs could not communicate with each other as simply and directly as they had supposed. It is significant that the most effective communication took place in those areas, e.g., portions of Germany and the U.S., where both communities were strongly represented and had at least some theological sophistication.

The distinctive genius of Lutheranism cannot be understood from its confessional statements alone but must be seen in the light of its piety, hymnody, social history, and liturgy; the character and thought of Martin Luther have also continued to be a powerful force in shaping Lutheranism to the present day. As the Lutheran participation in the ecumenical movement makes clear, this legacy determines Lutheran thought also in the 20th century. At the same time, the commitment of Lutheran theology to authorities beyond itself—Scripture, but also the Catholic tradition and, sometimes in tension with this, the implications of an unfettered theological scholarship—has given it the special accent in which it speaks. BIBLIOGRAPHY: *Book of Concord: Confessions of the Evangelical Lutheran Church* (ed. T. G. Tappert, 1959); W. Elert, *Structure of Lutheranism* (tr. W. A. Hansen, 1963); *Church in Fellowship* (ed. C. H. Lytkens et al., v. 1, 1963; v. 2, 1969); H. Fagerberg, *New Look at the Lutheran Confession* (tr. C. J. Lund, 1972).

[J. PELIKAN]

LUTHER'S CATECHISMS, see CATECHISMS, LUTHER'S.

LUX MUNDI (1889), a collection of Anglican "Studies on the Religion of the Incarnation," to which H. S. Holland, E. S. Talbot, R. C. Moberly, and F. Paget contributed, under the editorship of Charles *Gore, then principal of Pusey House. Their purpose was "to put Catholic faith into its right relation" to intellectual and moral questions of the time. It was Gore's study, *The Holy Spirit and Inspiration,* that shocked and distressed Anglo-Catholics of the conservative school; he was a freethinker, in the best sense of the term, with a mind open to the new critical problems raised by OT study. In fact his convictions on the fundamental articles of belief were not shaken, and, as his leadership of the Anglo-Catholic party during the next 40 years was to prove, his allegiance was not in doubt.

[T. GILBY]

LUXEMBOURG, predominantly Catholic grand duchy of W Europe, surrounded by Belgium, Germany, and France. It became an independent entity in 963. Its count in 1312 became Henry VII of the Holy Roman Empire; and his grandson Emperor Charles IV made Luxembourg a duchy in 1354. It was ruled by Burgundy from 1443 until 1482, when the Habsburgs acquired it. In 1714 it passed to the Austrian Habsburgs, and Austria ceded it to France in 1797. The Congress of Vienna (1815) made Luxembourg a grand duchy under the Netherlands crown. It also became a part of the German Confederation, remaining until the Confederation dissolved in 1866. In 1830 Luxembourg joined the Belgians in revolt against William I of the Netherlands. After gaining independence, Belgium claimed Luxembourg and got the largest part, now a Belgian province. But the present state of Luxembourg, though securing autonomy in 1848, remained under the Netherlands crown until 1890. Christianity came to Luxembourg in the 5th and 6th cent., with consolidation continuing until the 8th century. Echternach monastery, founded by Willibrord in 698, became an important mission center and was later famous for its production of MS copies. Ecclesiastically most of the area was under Liège and Trier until modern times, but Luxembourg has been a separate diocese since 1870. The capital is also called Luxembourg.

[T. EARLY]

LUXEUIL, ABBEY OF, Celtic monastery in east central France, founded *c.*590 by St. Columbanus, which soon became an important religious and cultural center. Its scriptorium originated a distinctive script; and among its more important productions is the Lectionary of Luxeuil (7th century). During the abbacy of Waldebert (3d in succession to Columbanus), Luxeuil adopted the Benedictine Rule. The abbey suffered during the Arabic invasion (732), was restored by Charlemagne, but was again sacked by the Normans in 888. From the 10th cent. its abbots were princes of the Empire. In 1631 it was reformed by Abbot Philip of Baume and incorporated into the Benedictine community of St. Vanne. It was suppressed during the French Revolution, in 1790. BIBLIOGRAPHY: T. Scott Holmes, *Origin and Development of the Christian Church in Gaul during the First Six Centuries of the Christian Era* (Birkbeck Lectures, Cambridge, 1907 and 1908 [1911]); J. F. Kenney, *Sources for the Early History of Ireland* (1966).

[C. MCGRATH]

LUXOR, site of the famous ancient Egyptian temple of Amen-Mut-Khons built (*c.*1390 B.C.) by Amenhotep III with pylon, pillared halls, colonnaded court. Rameses II added pylons, court, Colossi, and two obelisks (*c.*1290 B.C.), and the sanctuary was remodeled by Alexander the Great. The columns are remarkable for beauty and variety of form and capital. Decorations show low relief scenes of ritual, the birth of Amenhotep from the gods, a wall by Tutankhamen, and a hypostyle hall transformed into a chapel by the Copts (4th cent.) remarkable for murals (over the Egyptian reliefs). BIBLIOGRAPHY: A. Schwaller de Lubicz, *Le Temple de l'homme* (1958).

[M. J. DALY]

LUZARCHES, ROBERT DE, master mason of the cathedral of Amiens, which in High Gothic style derives from Chartres, though it is perhaps more elegant in proportion.

[M. J. DALY]

LUZZATTO, SAMUEL DAVID (1800–1865), Italian Jewish scholar. A native of Trieste, L. was a biblical scholar, poet, and philosopher, a member of a Jewish family with a long tradition of scholarship. In 1829 he was appointed professor at the rabbinical college of Padua where he remained the rest of his life. His correspondence (700 of his letters published) with Hebrew scholars of his time shows his astounding erudition. His work on the Bible includes the five-volume commentary on the Pentateuch (1871–76), on Isaiah, Jeremiah, Ezekiel, Proverbs, Job, and Ecclesiastes. L. was critical of the school of Maimonides and Ibn Ezra. He himself was a traditionalist in the manner of *Rashi. As a poet, he revived interest in medieval Hebrew poetry. L. was an opponent of Hellenism and medieval moral rationalism but more vigorously of the 19th-cent. doctrine of "progress." He believed in the election of Israel as the inheritor and carrier of a revealed nationalist religion, which Hebrew language and literature helped to foster. BIBLIOGRAPHY: *Encyclopedia Judaica* 11:604–607.

[J. R. AHERNE]

LWANGA, CHARLES, ST., AND THE MARTYRS OF UGANDA. In the late 19th century a foothold of Christianity had been gained through the work of the White Fathers and of Protestant missionaries. Under the chieftain, Mwanga, however, a fierce persecution broke out. The ruler was a homosexual who abused the pages of his court. A Catholic, Joseph Mukasa, reproached the ruler who put him to death to deter other Christians. L. was in charge of the boys kept by Mwanga and converted many to Catholicism. Fifteen young men were told to abjure Christianity or die. They chose death. On June 3, 1886 they were immolated on a huge funeral pyre. Their execution created a vast increase in converts to Catholicism. L. and 21 other *Uganda martyrs were beatified in 1920, canonized in 1964. BIBLIOGRAPHY: AAS 12:272–281; A. E. Howell, *Fires of Namugongo* (1948); N. DelRe, BiblSanct 12:746–748.

[J. R. AHERNE]

LYDDA (LOD), a Palestinian town, about 11 miles SE of Joppa, head of a Samaritan district (1 Macc 11.34). Lydda had an early Christian community (Acts 9.32–35). BIBLIOGRAPHY: EDB 1393–94.

[J. A. GRASSI]

LYDIA, DISTRICT OF, a region in W Asia Minor. From 133 B.C. it was a part of the Roman province of Asia. It had three of the seven Churches of the Apocalypse. BIBLIOGRAPHY: EDB 1394–95.

[J. A. GRASSI]

LYDIAN (also *quintus modus,* fifth mode), in Gregorian chant, the *mode or scale equivalent to a white-key scale beginning on F. Its *plagal form is termed hypolydian (*sextus tonus,* sixth mode).

[A. DOHERTY]

LYING, as traditionally defined, speech contradicting what is in one's mind. For this definition to be acceptable to modern theological thought, "speech" must be taken in a formal sense, limited to situations in which all observable circumstances indicate that the speaker intends to communicate what is in his mind. At times, circumstances indicate that what one says is not necessarily intended to communicate one's real thoughts; e.g., an actor in a play does not lie even though the words he speaks contradict what he himself thinks. So too, if one is questioned about secrets the questioner should realize that the answers do not mean to communicate information which is legitimately secret. Lying in this restricted sense is always sinful. It is an abuse of the function of speech and militates against trustful communication between human beings. The sin in lying is of itself generally venial. It becomes objectively grave matter for mortal sin only inasmuch as it does serious harm to another person, either gravely damaging his reputation or causing loss of an important job or of valuable assets, or causes intense suffering to anyone. Untrue statements made to protect legitimate secrets are labeled lies by some; if so, they could be licit lies. All recognize that statements can convey the truth without being literally true, as in the use of figures of speech or conventional language, as "The sun rises in the East." Likewise expressions demanded by politeness, such as "I enjoyed the dinner" to a hostess, or "You look fine" by a hospital visitor are hardly taken as serious statements of one's judgment. Embellishment of such statements beyond the requirements of politeness would be lies if not truly expressing the speaker's judgment.

Lies are sometimes classified as pernicious when they are harmful to others, officious when told to gain some advantage or avoid embarrassment, and jocose, when told to be pleasant or amuse. According to the stricter definition of lying, an obviously tall story is not a lie. A jocose lie would be an untruth told in such a way that there was no indication that the speaker did not intend to communicate what he believed. "White lie" is a term often used of any untruth which does no harm to anyone, and includes statements which would not be lies according to the stricter definition.

It has been debated in the past whether or not an intention to deceive is essentially a part of the definition of lying. The question is not of much importance. Such an intention will always be present in a lie but is not the sole constituent of a lie. One may legitimately intend to deceive for various reasons without telling a lie. BIBLIOGRAPHY: D. Hughes, NCE 8:1107–10; J. A. Dorszynski, *Catholic Teaching about the Morality of Falsehood* (1948).

[J. J. FARRAHER]

LYLY (LILLY), JOHN (*c.*1554–1606), English dramatist and novelist. After graduating at Oxford L. went to London to write and to establish himself at court under the patronage of the Earl of Oxford. He became famous for his novel *Euphues* (1578), written in an affected jargon, full of the conceits and extravagances used by young gallants of Elizabeth's court. L. took part in the Martin *Marprelate war of pamphlets in which Puritans attacked certain aspects of discipline of the Church of England. L. and other court writers defended the Church in the same ranting style the attackers used. L. also wrote prose comedies for the court, to be played by the choir boys of St. Paul's Cathedral. BIBLIOGRAPHY: J. W. Houppert, *John Lyly* (*English Authors* 177, 1975).

[M. M. BARRY]

LYNCH, BAPTISTA, MOTHER (1823–87), foundress of the Ursuline community of Columbia, South Carolina. She was professed as an Ursuline at Cincinnati in 1850. At the invitation of her brother Bp. Patrick Lynch of Charleston, she brought a band of Ursulines to Columbia, and there established the Convent and the Academy of the Immaculate Conception in 1858. The foundation flourished until devastated by the Civil War. L. was finally able to return and reopen the convent in Columbia in 1887. The community amalgamated with the Ursulines of Kentucky in 1937.

[J. R. AHERNE]

LYNCH, JOHN (1599–1673), Irish scholar, historian. Educated in France, L. was ordained in 1621 and returned to Ireland to teach. Because he opposed the uprising of 1641 he had to flee to France, where he spent most of the rest of his life. A classical scholar he was also a notable historian, his work *Cambrensis eversus* being a refutation of the anti-Irish work of Geraldus Cambrensis in the 12th century. A second study dealt with Ireland during the reign of Elizabeth.

[J. R. AHERNE]

LYNCH, JOHN JOSEPH (1816–88), missionary, abp. of Toronto. An Irish-born Vincentian, L. was ordained in 1843. He was sent to the U.S. in 1847 and made president of St. Mary's of the Barrens in Missouri. In 1856 he founded Our Lady of the Angels Seminary, Niagara, New York. Named coadjutor bp. of Toronto in 1859, he became bp. of that see a year later. L. was a proponent of definition of papal infallibility at Vatican Council I. Elevated to the rank of abp. in 1870, he convened the First Provincial Council of Canada and helped achieve passage of the Separate School Bill in 1863. BIBLIOGRAPHY: H. C. MacKeown, *Life and Labors of Most Rev. John Joseph Lynch, D. D., Cong. Miss, First Archbishop of Toronto* (1886).

[J. R. AHERNE]

LYNCH, PATRICK NEISON (1817–82), bp. of Charleston. An Irish immigrant ordained at Rome in 1840, he worked in Charleston, S.C., and edited *The United States Catholic Miscellany,* the diocesan weekly. He directed the building of the cathedral of St. John and St. Finbar. In 1857 he was named bp. of Charleston. Near the close of the Civil War L. was sent by the Confederate government to plead the Southern cause before Pius IX, but the collapse of the Confederacy made his visit pointless. The Civil War destroyed much church property and his postwar years were devoted to continuing efforts to rebuild. He attended Vatican Council I (1869–70) and wrote accounts of its proceedings for the *Catholic World*.

[J. R. AHERNE]

LYNDWOOD, WILLIAM (Lyndewode, Lindwood; 1375–1446), English canonist, diplomat, bishop. Fellow of Pembroke Hall, Cambridge, he took his Ll.D. from Oxford. He became an official of Abp. Chichele's Canterbury court (1414) and participated in persecution of the Lollards William Claydon and William Taylor. From 1417–41 he served Kings Henry V and VI as ambassador, envoy, and negotiator, and became bp. of St. David's (1442). He helped in founding both Eton and King's College, Cambridge. The *Provinciale* or *Provincial Constitutions,* Lyndwood's great compendium of canon law (begun in 1422, completed 1430) is a principal source work on the medieval canon law of England. It is a five-book digest of the synodal constitutions of the Canterbury Archdiocese from the time of Stephen Langton (1222) to Henry Chichele, commented upon in Latin, and providing lawyers with a way of intelligently and systematically coping with a large body of law. First printed in the late 1480s, it was printed repeatedly until 1679, an edition that includes John of Acton's glosses, and the *Constitutiones* of the papal legates to England.

[R. J. LITZ]

LYNSKEY, ELIZABETH MARY (1896–1954), educator. A teacher of political science at Hunter College in New York for 27 years, L. was a founder and officer of the Catholic Association for International Peace and liaison representative for the Association to the U.S. Mission to the United Nations. She was a contributing editor to *Commonweal* magazine, and also wrote *The Government of the Catholic Church* (1952).

[J. R. AHERNE]

LYONESE RITE, the manner of worship proper to the Archdiocese of Lyons. From the 4th to the 7th cent. Lyons used the Gallican rite. In the 1st decade of the 9th cent. the monk Leidratus (d. 814), under the direction of Charlemagne, introduced the rite in use at Aachen, which had followed Metz in adopting the Roman liturgy. Local customs were retained and the rite of Lyons thus became a Carolingian variant of the Roman rite. In the 17th and 18th cent. this traditional rite suffered in the neo-Gallican trend that resulted from the anti-Roman feeling prevalent in the French hierarchy. The traditional rite has been partially restored in the 19th and 20th centuries. The Mass is basically Roman with a number of distinctive variations. BIBLIOGRAPHY: A. A. King, *Liturgies of the Primatial Sees* (1951); R. X. Redmond, NCE 8:1112–14.

[N. KOLLAR]

LYONNET, STANISLAS (1902–), Jesuit NT exegete and theologian; sometime dean of faculty at the Pontifical Biblical Institute, Rome; consultor to the Sacred Congregation for the Doctrine of the Faith. He was born at Saint-Étienne (France) and entered the Society of Jesus in 1919. After teaching classical philology at Izeure, he embarked on his long and fruitful career as professor of NT, teaching Scripture at Lyon-Fourvière from 1938–43, and from 1943 at the Pontifical Biblical Institute. His doctoral dissertation *Les Origines de la version arménienne de la Bible et la Diatesseron* was published in 1950, followed by a series of articles, reviews, and books including, *De peccato et redemptione* (1957), which appeared in English under the title, *Sin Redemption, Sacrifice* (1972, with L. Sabourin); *Les Épitres de Saint Paul aux Galates et aux Romains* (1959); *Il dialogo della chiesa col mondo* (1967); *Les Étapes de l'histoire du salut selon l'Épitre aux Romains* (1969). Perhaps his most widely read article in English, published in many collections, is his now classic *St. Paul: Liberty and Law*.

[T. J. RYAN]

LYONS I, COUNCIL OF, the general council convened in June 1245 by Pope Innocent IV. The purpose was defense of the papacy against the encroachment of Emperor Frederick II, including the imprisonment in 1241 of 100 bishops. Although Frederick was summoned to face charges of heresy, he did not attend. His ambassador, Thaddeus of Suessa, supported the Emperor's right to a defense against the charge of heresy. After a 12-day delay, the Emperor failed to present himself. Innocent thereupon excommunicated and deposed him and the majority of the bps. signed the censure. Other matters on the agenda were aid to the Holy Land and several disciplinary matters, including condemnation of usury and restricting use of excommunication. It was Robert Bellarmine who first numbered Lyons I among the general Councils. Frederick appealed "to a future general council." BIBLIOGRAPHY: O. McKenna, NCE 8:1116–18; F. Dvornik, *Ecumenical Councils* (1961).

[F. H. BRIGHAM]

LYONS II, COUNCIL OF, In 1274 Pope *Gregory X convoked a council in Lyons to organize a crusade to aid the Latin states in Syria and Palestine and to effect the union of the Greek and Latin Churches. The union was encouraged by the Byzantine Emperor *Michael VIII Palaeologus largely for political reasons. He addressed a letter to the council affirming his full acceptance of the Roman faith and the papal primacy, asking that the Greeks retain their own creed and rites. The Greek representatives at the council voiced no objection to the *filioque and other controverted points. Union between the two Churches was then proclaimed, but although the Emperor tried to enforce its acceptance, it had no meaning and died with the Emperor. The Council also dealt somewhat unsuccessfully with clerical reform and the raising of funds for the crusade. It established stricter rules for the papal conclave to avoid a long vacancy of the Holy See. BIBLIOGRAPHY: O. McKenna, NCE 8:1118.

[G. T. DENNIS]

LYONS, THE FATHERS OF, diocesan missionary priests, members of an institute better known as the Society of *African Missions (SMA), founded in 1856 in Lyons, France, by Bp. Melchior de *Marion-Bréssillac.

LYONS AND VIENNE, MARTYRS OF, victims at Lyons of the persecution under Marcus Aurelius in 177 A.D. Their martyrdom is recorded in one of the earliest and best authenticated of the *Acts of the Martyrs, a letter sent by survivors of the persecution to the Churches of Asia and Phrygia and preserved in the *Ecclesiastical History* of Eusebius (bk. 5, ch. 1). It is a document of importance not only for its illustration of the heroic faith of those who suffered, but also for the information it provides about the Christian community in Lyons in the mid-2d cent. and its connection with the Churches of the East. The persecution appears to have begun with a popular feeling of outrage against the Christians who were accused of eating human flesh and other abominations, but it was soon taken up officially by the civil authorities and prosecuted with savage atrocity. Forty-eight Christians were slain, half of whom, to judge by their names, were of Greek or Asiatic, and half of Gallo-Roman, origin. Among them were SS. *Pothinus (first bp. of Lyons) and *Blandina. BIBLIOGRAPHY: Butler 2:454–458; H. Leclercq, DACL 10:78–121; A. Amore, BiblSanct 8:61–65.

[P. K. MEAGHER]

LYSERGIC ACID DIETHYLAMIDE, see LSD.

LYSIAS, the regent appointed by the Seleucid ruler Antiochus IV Epiphanes to rule Syria (166–165 B.C.). L. was to carry on the campaign against the Jews in Palestine while he (Antiochus) devoted his energies to the Parthians. L., whose name is a shortened version of the Greek name Lysanias meaning "freeing from sorrow," was a constant scourge to the Jews, and the relentless enemy of Judas Maccabeus. L.'s exploits are narrated in some detail in 1 and 2 Maccabees. First he sent a large army under feared leadership into Palestine, only to have them soundly rebuffed. Next he came himself to attack Judas. The resulting peace treaty, approved by Antiochus Epiphanes, took away restrictions on Jewish worship, paved the way for the cleansing of the Temple from the worship of Zeus, and inaugurated the Hanukkah feast. At the death of Antiochus Epiphanes, L. again invaded Judea, taking with him the boy-king Eupator (Antiochus V) and claiming to be acting as regent on the latter's behalf. He defeated Judas this time, and laid siege to Jerusalem, but had to make terms quickly with the Jews and hurry back to Antioch to confront a rival claimant to the regency. He overcame this rival only to be murdered along with his boy-king patron by a later successful claimant to the throne.

[E. J. DILLON]

LYSTRA, the city of Lycaonia visited by Paul and Barnabas after their forced leave of Iconium. When Paul cured a crippled man the citizens wanted to worship them as Zeus and Hermes, and only with difficulty did they prevent it. The same people were quickly turned against them by Jews from Antioch and Iconium so that Paul barely escaped with his life from a stoning (Acts 14.5–19). Paul visited the community on his second missionary journey (Acts 16.1). Lystra was the home of Timothy (Acts 16.2).

[S. MUSHOLT]

LYTTLETON (LITTLETON), THOMAS (d. 1481), English jurist. Educated at the Inns of Court, he became serjeant-at-law 1453, king's serjeant 1455, and justice of the court of common pleas 1466–81. A respected judge, he wrote a learned treatise on the land law, *Tenures,* nowadays best known through Sir Edward Coke's famous commentaries thereon. BIBLIOGRAPHY: DNB 33:373–376.

[C. D. ROSS]

M

MA'APRĀ, the outer garment of the East Syrian eucharistic celebrant, like a Western cope in form; today it is also called *painā* by the Chaldeans.

[A. CODY]

MABILLON, JEAN (1632–1707), French Benedictine (Maurist Congregation) and church historian. Although ordained at the Abbey of Corbie in 1660, M. spent most of his subsequent life in the monastery of Saint-Germain-des-Prés in Paris. He began his career as a scholar by editing with Jean Luc d'Achéry the works of St. *Bernard (1667). Following this, in collaboration with T. *Ruinart, he published documents pertaining to the lives of the Benedictine saints (9 v., 1668–1701). During this same period (1672–85), he and Ruinart journeyed through France, Italy, Switzerland, and Germany in search of manuscripts. In controversy with the Bollandist D. von *Papebroch, he produced *De re diplomatica,* an exposition in six volumes of the principles of documentary criticism. His treatise on monastic studies defended the intellectual life in the monastery against the attacks of A. de Rancé. M. was among the greatest scholars and most learned men of his day. BIBLIOGRAPHY: P. Roche, NCE 9:1–2; G. Heer, LTK 6:1254–55.

[R. B. ENO]

MABUSE, JAN, see GOSSAERT, JAN.

MACAO, Portuguese overseas province in S China (6 sq mi; pop. [U.N. est., 1974] 270,000). Occupied by the Portuguese in 1557, Macao became the base for their expansion in the Far East. It is now flooded with refugees from Communist China. Macao played a prominent part in early mission work, becoming a diocese in 1575, with jurisdiction over China and Japan. Its influence faded with the expulsion of the Jesuits (1762). In spite of its long history, missionary effort has had slight success. In 1976 there were only 41,000 Catholics; but churches, convents, and other buildings remain as monuments of a glorious past. Groups of Catholics from Macao have done apostolic work in Shanghai and Hong Kong and more recently among Chinese refugees. BIBLIOGRAPHY: H. Bernard-Maitre, *Aux portes de la Chine* (1937).

[P. DAMBORIENA]

MACARIUS (1482–1563), **METROPOLITAN OF MOSCOW,** 1542–63. His reforms helped to consolidate the new ideology of Tsar Ivan IV the Terrible, whom he crowned in 1547. In his work with Russian annals, legends, and histories, M. presented the Empire as having a special, divinely ordained place in God's salvation history. He convoked an important synod for reform in 1551.

[R. J. LITZ]

MACARIUS OF ALEXANDRIA, ST. (d. *c.*394), an Egyptian hermit, sometimes called the Younger to distinguish him from Macarius the Egyptian (the Elder). M. retired first to the Thebaid to learn the rudiments of the eremitical life and then to the desert of the Cells where he lived for many years a life of great austerity. Some of the feats and miracles attributed to him are recorded by Palladius in the *Lausiac History*. BIBLIOGRAPHY: Butler 1:19–21; Quasten 3:168–169.

[R. B. ENO]

MACARIUS OF ANTIOCH, Patriarch deposed by the Council of *Constantinople III on March 28, 681 for his *Monothelitism. It was M. who quoted Pope *Honorius I as a proponent of the same heresy; the council's condemnation of Honorius (D 550) figured in the debates on papal infallibility at Vatican Council I. After his deposition M. was confined in a Roman monastery.

[T. C. O'BRIEN]

MACARIUS CHRYSOCEPHALOS (*c.*1300–82), Greek bp., hagiographer, and exegete. M. became a monk (1327) and bp. of Philadelphia (1336); later (1340s) he was named metropolitan judge of the empire by John V Palaeologus. M. wrote a life of Meletius Galesiotes. He advocated continued separation of the Eastern Church from Rome. He compiled a collection of secular maxims and proverbs, but his major works were exegetical texts of Genesis, Matthew, and Luke.

[R. J. LITZ]

MACARIUS THE EGYPTIAN (the Great; *c.*300–*c.*389), one of the Desert Fathers, referred to in the *History of the Monks of Egypt,* he influenced monasticism throughout Christendom. Having become a monk at the age of 30, he lived in the desert of Scete for 60 years. His reputation was great among his contemporaries, who named him "the young old man" because of his wisdom. When he was 40 years old, he received the grace to exorcise demons and to foretell the future. He was ordained a priest (340), died at the age of 90, and is venerated as a saint by the Coptic and the Byzantine Churches. The Coptic St. Macarius Monastery in the Nitrean Desert is named for him. The sources of his life do not mention any literary activity, and the homilies, letters, prayers, attributed to him in later MSS are not genuine. He won fame for the spiritual guidance he gave by his talks and instructions; some of his sayings appear in the **Apophthegmata patrum*. The writings going under his name, and perhaps expanded by disciples from his conferences, were appreciated by a number of Lutheran writers and by John Wesley, the founder of Methodism. BIBLIOGRAPHY: Quasten 3:161–168.

[J. MADEY]

MACARIUS OF JERUSALEM, ST. (fl. 312–334), bishop. An anti-Arian, M. participated in the Council of Nicaea I as bp. of Jerusalem. M. contributed to the restoration of the newly discovered sacred places in Jerusalem. Tradition associated him with the finding of the True Cross. BIBLIOGRAPHY: R. Janin, BiblSanct 8:421–425; Butler 1:544–545.

[J. R. AHERNE]

MACARIUS MAGNES, Christian apologist who *c.*400 wrote the *Apocriticus,* a work only partially extant today. Originally written in five books, it reports an alleged 5-day disputation carried on by the author and a pagan philosopher, probably Porphyry. Most of Porphyry's attacks on Christianity are criticisms against passages selected from the Gospels, Acts, and the Pauline Epistles. The chief merit of the *Apocriticus* is the clarity with which it presents the pagan viewpoint; it is not very cogent as an apology. Of the ten fragments of *Homilies on Genesis* ascribed to Macarius only the one on Gen 3.21 is authentic. BIBLIOGRAPHY: G. Bardy, DTC 9.2:1456–59; Quasten 3:486–488.

[H. DRESSLER]

MACARIUS OF MOSCOW (1482–1564), metropolitan of the Russian Orthodox Church. A product of the famous monastery of St. Paphnutius, M. became archbishop of Novgorod in 1526 and in 1542, metropolitan of Moscow and All Russia. He was the architect of the union of Church and State in Russia and the plan to make Moscow replace Rome and Constantinople as the divinely approved center of Christianity. From the time of his crowning Ivan the Terrible as Tsar in 1547, M. became a powerful influence in both state and church matters. He established the first printing press in Russia, canonized 40 Russian saints, and wrote a 12-volume work of meditation on the Russian saints. He wrote also the *Book of Generations,* a history of Russian ruling families. The Council of the Hundred Chapters held in Moscow approved his revision of Russian canon law, administration, and liturgy.

[J. R. AHERNE]

MACARIUS SCOTTUS, BL. (d. 1153), a Benedictine monk who went from Scotland to Germany, where he became first abbot of the Benedictine monastery of St. James. He was a holy, prayerful man through whom God apparently worked many miracles, even after death. He wrote *De laude martyrium;* two other Latin works are also ascribed to him. BIBLIOGRAPHY: K. Kunze, BiblSanct 8:432.

[A. WARDLE]

MACARIUS OF PELECETE, ST. (*c.*750–829), opponent of *iconoclasm. He was a monk, then abbot, of the monastery of Pelecete in Bithynia. He was renowned for his holiness and miracles, coming to be called Macarius Thaumaturgus, the Wonderworker. For opposing the iconoclastic emperor, Leo V the Armenian, M. suffered torture and imprisonment. Though released by Michael II, he was exiled for still refusing to accept the heretical teaching; he died in exile.

[T. C. O'BRIEN]

MACAULAY, THOMAS BABINGTON (1800–59), English historian, essayist, and statesman. After serving with distinction in Parliament and on the Supreme Council of India, he retired from public life in 1847 to devote himself to his historical work, *The History of England* (5 v., 1849–61) which when published won instant and tremendous popularity and was translated into many languages. Among his other well-known literary works are *Lays of Ancient Rome* (1842) and *Essays* (1843). M.'s writings show surprising limitations: no interest in philosophical speculation, ecclesiastical history, nor even in the scientific discoveries which were arousing such enthusiasm in his contemporaries; a tendency to exaggerate; and an inability to balance evidence calmly. Yet they also display his vast literary and historical background and his fine practical understanding of government affairs and administration. BIBLIOGRAPHY: R. C. Beatty, *Lord Macaulay, Victorian Liberal* (1938, repr. 1971).

[M. J. BARRY]

MACAULAY, ZACHARY (1768–1838), Anglican evangelical and philanthropist. At 16 M. was manager of an estate in Jamaica where slave labor was used. The experience led him to become an ardent abolitionist. A member of the *Clapham Sect, he edited its *The Christian Observer* (1802–16). He was the father of Thomas Babington Macaulay.

[M. J. SUELZER]

MACCABEES (MACHABEES), BOOKS OF THE (1 AND 2), late OT books classified as *deuterocanonical. These two works independently describe Jewish resistance to Syria's attempts at Hellenizing Jewish life and religion (the Maccabean Wars, 175–135 B.C.). The term Maccabee probably derives from Hebrew *maqqābāh* (hammer)—a nickname given to Judas Maccabee, later applied to his brothers and their descendants.

Book 1 was written *c.* 100 B.C., most probably in Hebrew (but preserved only in Greek). Its anonymous author, a devout, educated Jew, knew well the times and events of which he wrote, and had access to many documentary sources. Despite fictional dialogue and prayers and occasional hyerbole, his work is a remarkably accurate historical book covering Jewish history from 175–135 B.C. Sympathetic to the Maccabean dynasty, the author tended to equate religion and patriotism. He never mentioned God by name, probably from over-scrupulous reverence. He did show a profound consciousness of the divine transcendence (3.18–22; 4.30–33), had great attachment to the Torah (2.68), and to Mt. Zion and its sanctuary (3.43–45; 7.33–38).

Book 2, also written *c.* 100 B.C., is an anonymous compendium in Greek of a five-volume earlier work written by Jason of Cyrene (2.23). Covering about 15 years of Maccabean history (1 Macc 1–7), it was written to edify Jewish coreligionists in Alexandria. Much more florid and imaginative than 1 Macc, 2 Macc stresses the feats of Judas Maccabee in particular, and abounds in miraculous and supernatural events. The book is noteworthy for belief in a resurrection of the body (7.9; 14.46), intercession of the saints (15.12–16), and the famous "purgatory" text (12.41–46).
BIBLIOGRAPHY: W. H. Brownlee, InterDB 3:201–215; C. Dimier, *O. T. Apocrypha,* (tr. S. J. Tester, 1964).

[E. MAY]

MACCABEES (MACHABEES), BOOKS OF THE (3 AND 4), two apocryphal books that have some relation to *deuterocanonical 2 Maccabees.

Book 3, also called the Ptolemaica. The events it recounts belong to the reign of the Egyptian king, Ptolemy IV Philopator (221–203 B.C.) and therefore antedate the Maccabean revolt by at least 40 years. The work was composed in the 1st cent. A.D. by a Jew writing in Greek. The book presents three attempts of Ptolemy IV to suppress the Jewish religion and to violate the sanctuary. He is prevented by fantastic happenings that bring him to recognize the sacredness of the Jews to a powerful God, and to repent. Similarities with 2 Macc and Est serve to define the essential character of 3 Maccabees. While the author evidences some historical basis, it is a largely legendary account that draws upon a story widely circulated among Hellenistic Jews to convey one essential message: the need for steadfastness by the Jews of the diaspora against calumny, malice, even persecution by the Gentiles, who will be taught by God that the Jews are a people holy and inviolate to him.

Book 4. This book, known also under the title *On the Supremacy of Reason,* is essentially a philosophical work probably composed by a Jew of the Alexandrine or Antiochene diaspora early in the 1st century A.D. It aims at showing that right reason as informed by true religion (i.e., the Torah) can rise above all human passions and sufferings. The supreme example of this is held to be the martyrdom of Eleazer, and of the seven brothers and their mother under *Antiochus IV Epiphanes as recounted in 2 Macc 6.18–7.42; (cf. 4 Macc 1.8–12; 5.1–18.24). The author also adduces examples from the OT such as Joseph's conquest of passion when Potiphar's wife attempts to seduce him, Moses' victory over anger, etc.; but he constantly returns to the martyrdoms of the period of the Maccabees.

It is evident that he has drawn extensively on 2 Macc (perhaps also on Jason of Cyrene, the principal source of 2 Macc) to provide himself with instances with which to substantiate his basic thesis, but his ideas appear to represent an attempt to absorb what he can approve of in Stoic philosophy into the framework of traditional rabbinical teaching. Thus the fourfold division of the emotions into desire, joy, fear, and grief is reminiscent of Stoic teaching, while the innate inclination to evil as he envisages it *(hē kakoēthēs diathesis)* is in reality the *yēṣer hā-ra'* of the rabbis, which is counterbalanced in each individual by the *yeṣer hā-tôb,* the "inclination to good." Again the author rejects the Stoic ideal of immunity to all passion, *apatheia,* in favor of the specifically Jewish ideal of emotion made subordinate to reason as informed by true religion (2.21–23). The author evinces a clear idea of the immortality of the soul and of man's ultimate destiny to eternal punishment or eternal reward. More surprisingly he also seems aware of the value of vicarious suffering to atone for the sins of others and to purify them (1.11; 6.29; 17.21–22). This according to him is the significance of the sufferings of the Jewish martyrs on behalf of the Jewish people as a whole. The tyranny to which the people are subjected is a punishment for their sins, but it is dissolved by the blood of the martyrs. At the same time this blood, like that of Abel, calls down the vengeance of God upon him who sheds it (cf. 11.22; 12.17–18). Finally, the heroism and endurance of Eleazar and the seven martyr brothers (here taken as prototypes of Jewish virtue sustained by Jewish faith) are superior to any of the noble qualities of which the Gentiles can boast. They demonstrate that "The Hebrews alone are invincible in virtue's cause." By contrast, Antiochus, the representative of all that is ignoble in human nature, is an upholder of hedonism and opportunism of the basest kind (5.6–12; 8.5–10; 12.3–4). These sentiments had an influence on the Christian cult of martyrs. BIBLIOGRAPHY: C. W. Emmett, *Third and Fourth Book of Maccabees* (1918); M. Hadas, *Third and Fourth Books of Maccabees* (1953); P. Riessler, *Altjüdisches Schrifttum ausserhalb der Bibel übersetzt und erklärt* (1928) 682–699, 1312–13 (3 Macc); 700–728, 1313–14 (4 Macc); J. Cohen, *Judaica et Aegyptiaca. De Maccabaeorum Libro III. Quaestiones Historicae* (1941).

[D. J. BOURKE]

MCCAFFREY, JOHN HENRY (1806–81), educator. A native of Maryland, who as a deacon became vice president of Mt. St. Mary's College, Emmitsburg, Md., he was ordained in 1838 and served as president of that institution for 34 years. Mt. St. Mary's acquired national recognition during this time as an institution which provided the American Church with 26 bishops and archbishops. M. participated as a theologian in several of the Councils of Baltimore and his catechism formed the basis for the famous Baltimore Catechism.

[J. R. AHERNE]

MCCLELLAN, WILLIAM HILDRUP (1874–1951), OT exegete. M. was ordained an Episcopalian minister, but became a Catholic (1908) and later a priest. He taught OT at the Jesuit theologate in Woodstock, Maryland, and was a frequent contributor to scholarly periodicals. His study of the Latin Psalter was serialized in the first 22 issues of the CBQ. BIBLIOGRAPHY: J. B. Donnelly, NCE 8:6.

[T. M. MCFADDEN]

MCCLOSKEY, JOHN (1810–85), abp. of New York and cardinal. Born in Brooklyn, N.Y., of Irish immigrant parents, he attended Mt. St. Mary's College and Seminary in Emmitsburg, Md., was ordained (1834), and studied at the Gregorian Univ. in Rome (1834–37). In addition to pastoral work in New York, he served as first president (1841) of St. John's College (later Fordham Univ.) and was consecrated (1844) coadjutor, with right of succession, to Bp. John Hughes. Although he resigned his right of succession when he was made ordinary (1847) of the new Diocese of Albany, N.Y., he later (1864) reluctantly accepted the appointment as New York's second archbishop; in 1875 he became the first U.S. cardinal. A mild and peace-loving man, he was successful in handling the problem of *trusteeism and in settling a long-standing dispute Bp. Hughes had had with the Jesuits. M. gave particular support to the new *Paulist community and to the social reforms of L. S. *Ives and the Rev. J. *Drumgoole. After 1880 age and ill-health caused him to turn over most of the active management of the archdiocese to his coadjutor Bp. M. A. *Corrigan. BIBLIOGRAPHY: J. M. Farley, *Life of John Cardinal McCloskey* (1918).

[M. CARTHY]

MCCLOSKEY, WILLIAM GEORGE (1823–1909), bp. of Louisville, Kentucky. Born in Brooklyn, N.Y., he was ordained in 1852. He became the first rector of the North American College in Rome where he served from 1859 to 1867. Named bp. of Louisville in 1868, he was a zealous and competent administrator, though he engaged in controversies both with his own clergy and with religious in the dioceses. Under his direction the diocese grew in numbers of Catholics as well as in churches and institutions.

[J. R. AHERNE]

MCCOLLUM *V.* BOARD OF EDUCATION (333 U.S. 203), a case decided by the U.S. Supreme Court that has had wide ramifications in juridic consideration of Church-State relations. The case originated in Champaign, Ill. and its target was the released-time concept as carried out in the public schools of that city. The released-time program in the U.S. was the project of Protestant organizations, beginning in 1913. The movement spread from Indiana to most of the states in the U.S. by 1947. Essentially it provided for various denominations to supply at their own expense teachers of religion one hour a week in public schools, for which instruction pupils were released from other classes. Parents who chose not to have their children participate indicated the fact in writing. Mrs. McCollum, an avowed atheist, sued the Board of Education of Champaign to stop the practice. Eventually the case went to the U.S. Supreme Court. Justice Hugo Black ruled that the practice was unconstitutional, since public schools were furthering religion, the program being a breaching of the "wall of separation" between Church and State. Justice Felix Frankfurter concurred, adding that the meaning of separation of Church and State must be ruled on by individual case rather than appeal to an abstract principle. He cited the experience of the American people, rather than the intention of the framers of the Bill of Rights as the norm. Frankfurter saw released-time as a divisive influence in public education which was intended to foster unity among citizens. The dissenting opinion was written by Justice Stanley Reed who argued that a metaphor (wall of separation) was not a basis for constitutional judgments. He added that Jefferson and Madison did not oppose religious education at the Univ. of Virginia, and that many other practices accepted as not in conflict with separation of Church and State (e.g., provision of chaplains to the armed forces) proved that such relations were part of the understanding of the people. It should be noted that the opposition to the McCollum appeal came chiefly from Protestant sources (as did some of the support). After the decision the U.S. Catholic hierarchy and many Protestant groups as well as constitutional authorities subjected it to severe criticism. Criticism cited an earlier case (Pierce *v.* Society of Sisters—268 U.S. 510) in 1925 when the Court upheld the right of parents to place children in religious schools and thereby fulfill requirements of the compulsory attendance law. The Court was accused of falsifying history and damaging freedom of religion. It contradicted long-accepted practices such as tax-exemption for religious bodies. BIBLIOGRAPHY: R. Drinan, *Religion, the Courts and Public Policy* (1963); L. Pfeffer, *Church, State and Freedom* (1953); J. O'Neill, *Religion and Education under the Constitution* (1949).

[J. R. AHERNE]

MCCONNELL, FRANCIS JOHN (1871–1953), Methodist bp., social reformer. Born in Trinway, Ohio, and educated at Boston Univ., he became a Methodist minister in 1894. He was made president of De Pauw Univ. in 1909, and elected bp. in 1912. His theological views were influenced by the personalism of Borden Parker *Bowne. In the steel strike of 1919 his work led to the abolition of the 12-hour working day in the industry. His *John Wesley* (1939), a popular biography, was marked by a realistic evaluation of the man, and a critical judgment of Wesley's relationship to Reformation traditions. M. was president of the Federal Council of Churches and active in the programs that led eventually to the formation of the World Council of Churches. BIBLIOGRAPHY: F. J. McConnell, *By the Way: An Autobiography* (1952); HistAmMeth 3.

[T. C. O'BRIEN]

MCDONALD, BARNABAS EDWARD (1865–1929), youth worker. A native of New York State, he entered the Brothers of the Christian Schools (FSC) in 1885. In 1902 he founded St. Philip's Home for boys working in urban areas and in 1909 Lincoln Agricultural School in Lincolndale, N.Y. He was instrumental in the establishment of the National Conference of Catholic Charities (1909). Director of Catholic Charities in Toronto, Canada, from 1919 to 1922, he later organized the Columbian Squires of the Knights of Columbus. He pioneered at the Univ. of Notre Dame a program to train youth workers, the first of its kind in the U.S.

[J. R. AHERNE]

MACDONOUGH, THOMAS (1878–1916), Irish poet and patriot. Like his friend Padraic Pearse, M. was a teacher and exponent of the Gaelic language. He joined Pearse in the bilingual school, St. Enda's, Dublin. Between 1902 and 1913 M. published five volumes of poetry full of lyric intensity and philosophic reflections. His work is characteristic of the Celtic Renaissance. He joined the Irish Volunteers in 1913 and was made a member of the commanding group. In the Easter Rebellion in 1916 he was taken prisoner with Pearse and executed by a British firing squad. M. was an engaging personality and shared the mystique of the Easter martyrs. His *Poetical Works* were published in 1917.

[J. R. AHERNE]

MCDOUGALL, WILLIAM (1871–1938), Anglo-American psychologist and physician largely responsible for establishing experimental psychology in Great Britain. He was invited to Harvard Univ. in 1920, and in 1927 was appointed head of the psychology department at Duke Univ., a post he held until his death. He rejected both mechanistic and intellectualistic accounts of human behavior and emphasized purposive striving. In this hormic (purposive) psychology, biologically purposive energy intimately joined innate psychophysical dispositions (instincts) and their cognitive, affective aspects (emotions) in pursuit of certain goals utilizing socially acquired patterns. Character growth and personality integration involve a hierarchical arrangement of these pursuits around a master, self-regarding sentiment. A breakdown of this integration accounts for psychopathology. His American period was one of immense literary productivity in which he applied his hormic theory to national mind and character. Persuasive, he had great temporary influence; his weaknesses were his preference for speculative solutions to empirical problems and his penchant for premature systemization. Among his works are *An Introduction to Social Psychology* (1908), *Psychology, the Study of Behaviour* (1912), *Modern Materialism and Emergent Evolution* (1929), *The Riddle of Life* (1938).

[J. MCFADDEN]

MACE, originally a weapon with a studded, loaded head for striking; then a symbol of authority, first as a wooden staff, then gradually a more ornate metal rod with engraved heraldic devices (e.g., the drum major's baton); it is borne at the head of processions in some cathedrals; also used by the marshall in an academic procession.

[T. C. O'BRIEN]

MACEDO COSTA, ANTÔNIO DE (1830–91), Brazilian bp., defender of the rights of the Church. Ordained in 1857, M. became bp. of Pará, Brazil in 1861. He was the leader in protesting the interference of the emperor in ecclesiastical affairs and in publicly condemning the influence of Freemasonry. Arrested in 1874 and imprisoned, he issued a famous pastoral letter from prison on the Religious Question. In 1875 he was released from prison on orders of Emperor Pedro II, returned to Pará to continue his opposition to regalism, a course which earned the hostility of the emperor. When the republic brought down the empire in 1889, M. wrote the pastoral for the Brazilian bps. accepting the new order. In 1890, named abp. of Baía and primate of Brazil, he presided at the meeting of the Brazilian hierarchy. Pressing needs of his involvement in the new government prevented his assuming the responsibility of his primatial see, and he shortly died of ill health and exhaustion, without having officially entered into office.

[J. R. AHERNE]

MACEDONIA, region north of Achaia. Under Philip II (359–336 B.C.) and his son Alexander the Great (336–323 B.C.) it became the center of a wide empire. Conquered by Rome in 168 B.C., it was under Roman government during NT times. Paul sailed to Macedonia in response to a vision and won his first European convert there at Philippi (Acts 16.10–15). He later made other visits, and the NT includes his letters to the Churches of Philippi and Thessalonica, the

Macedonian capital (see also 2 Cor 8.1–5). BIBLIOGRAPHY: N. G. Hammond, *History of Macedonia.* (v.1, 1972).

[T. EARLY]

MACEDONIAN ORTHODOX CHURCH. Slavs penetrated Macedonia in the 7th and 8th centuries. Greek culture and language were assimilated by those who settled in urban centers, but the rural population developed a language that shows relationship to Bulgarian (grammar and syntax) and Serbian (vocabulary). After a brief period of cultural flowering, the result of the work of the disciples of SS. Cyril and Methodius in the 10th cent., and of political glory under Tsar Samuel (980–1014), Macedonia came permanently under Greek ecclesiastical influence (with the exception of the short-lived Serbian archiepiscopate of 1219 and patriarchate of 1346–75). The Greek autocephalous major abp. of Ohrid (Achrida) attempted to continue the heritage of Justiniana Prima, the ancient city and autocephalous Church founded by Emperor Justinian I near Ohrid, but the independence of the see was abolished in 1767 by order of Sultan Mustapha at the request of the patriarch of Constantinople. Slavic Macedonia came under the patriarch of Constantinople and was incorporated into Yugoslavia (1918) and the Serbian Patriarchate (1920). Communist Yugoslavia (1945) recognized the existence of a separate Macedonian nation and language, which compelled the Serbian Patriarchate to grant autonomous status to the Macedonian Orthodox Church (1958). The bps. of this Church, unable to obtain the consent of the Serbian Patriarchate to the reestablishment of the archiepiscopate of Ohrid, assumed by a unilateral declaration (July 1967) the status of autocephaly or total independence, as yet not recognized by any other Orthodox church union. The Macedonian Orthodox Church comprises the metropolitan see of Skopje and the dioceses of Zletovo, Bitola, Debar, and one for the U.S., Canada, and Australia with seat in Toronto (Canada), and is headed by His Beatitude the Abp. of Ohrid and Metropolitan of Skopje. In 1961 the number of Macedonians (presumably Orthodox) was 893,000 or 64% of the population of Macedonia.

When the Greek patriarch of Constantinople refused to grant the Bulgarians and Macedonians a native hierarchy, a movement towards union with Rome started in Macedonia in 1859. A group of 4,600 Catholics remained a part of the Byzantine-rite Eparchy of Križevci, but are now under the Latin-rite bp. of Skopje-Prizren as apostolic visitor. BIBLIOGRAPHY: D. Ilievski, *Macedonian Orthodox Church. The Road to Independence* (1973).

[V. J. POSPISHIL]

MACEDONIAN STYLE, see BYZANTINE ART.

MACEDONIANS, 4th-cent. opponents of the Holy Spirit's full divinity. The name is taken from Macedonius, abp. of Constantinople, who was deposed by the Arians in 360, although there is no clear evidence that he himself held the position. The Council of *Constantinople (381) declared the Macedonian doctrine a heresy since it taught that the Holy Spirit was subordinate to the Father and to the Son, being different in substance and therefore a creature. *PNEUMATOMACHIANS.

[A. MORHBACHER]

MACEDONIUS, ST. (d. *c.*430), Antiochene hermit, called *Critophages* because he subsisted on barley. He is known through the account of his life by *Theodoret of Cyr; Theodoret's mother attributed his birth, after 13 years without children, to M.'s prayers. M. was sought out by the people in his cave-dwellings because of his holiness and miraculous powers. BIBLIOGRAPHY: Butler 1:161.

[T. C. O'BRIEN]

MACEDONIUS II (d. 511), **PATRIARCH OF CONSTANTINOPLE** from 495. Emperor Anastasius I installed him as successor of the deposed Euphemius. Having first signed the **Henotikon,* M. later became a defender of the Council of Chalcedon (451). The Emperor wished to have a synod condemn Eutyches and Nestorius, along with Chalcedon, but M. opposed him and instead called for a general synod under the pope's presidency. He also signed the compromise Acacian formula (see ACACIAN SCHISM), but soon after reaffirmed the faith of Chalcedon. Deposed and exiled to Euchaita in 511, he fled to Gangra, where he was assassinated, according to rumors at Anastasius' request.

[J. MADEY]

MCELROY, JOHN (1782–1877), Jesuit missioner, founder of Boston College. Born in Ireland but coming to the U.S. in 1803, he was a Jesuit brother, then a student for the priesthood in the Society, and was ordained in 1817. For 23 years he served in Frederick, Md., where he built a church, a boy's school, an orphanage, a convent, and a free school for girls, as well as the Jesuit novitiate. From Frederick he served 10 Maryland parishes. In 1846 he accompanied Gen. Zachary Taylor's army to Mexico as chaplain. Made pastor of a parish in Boston (1847), M. founded in 1863 Boston College and served as pastor of the college church.

[J. R. AHERNE]

MACEVILLY, JOHN (1818–1902), abp. and biblical scholar. M. taught Scripture at St. Jarlath's College, Tuam, and held several ecclesiastical posts in Ireland, notably bp. of Galway and abp. of Tuam (1881–1902). His commentaries on the whole NT, except Apocalypse, were widely used but are now out of date. BIBLIOGRAPHY: K. O'Sullivan, NCE 9:16.

[T. M. MCFADDEN]

MCGARRY, WILLIAM JAMES (1894–1941), Jesuit educator. M. taught Scripture and theology at Weston College, Massachusetts; was president of Boston College

(1935–37); and the first editor of the periodical *Theological Studies* (1937–41). He published several articles on philology and theology, and three devotional Scripture studies. BIBLIOGRAPHY: J. B. Donnelly, NCE 9:17.

[T. M. MCFADDEN]

MCGARVEY, WILLIAM (1861–1924), writer, convert to Catholicism. A Philadelphian M. was ordained in the Episcopal Church in 1886. An adherent of the high church group, he served in several parishes favoring ritual. He became master of the Companions of the Holy Savior, a congregation of Anglican priests, and was chaplain to the Anglican Sisters of Mary. In 1908 during the open pulpit controversy, he entered the Catholic Church, studied for the priesthood, and was ordained in 1910. He served in parishes in Philadelphia and Bethlehem, Pa. M. wrote much both as an Anglican and as a Catholic. Among his works were *The Council of Nicaea* (1894); *The Doctrine of the Church of England and of St. Thomas on the Real Presence* (1900); and *The Ceremonies of Low Mass* (1905).

[J. R. AHERNE]

MCGILL, RALPH EMERSON (1898–1969), journalist, editor, publisher, spokesman for liberalism in the Southern states, champion of human and civil rights. Of Scottish and Welsh descent and a native of Tennessee, M. studied at Vanderbilt Univ., began his career as a reporter in Nashville, moved up to sports editor and in that capacity was employed by the *Atlanta* (Ga.) *Constitution* in 1929. He became executive editor of that paper (1938), editor (1942), and publisher (1960). A Presbyterian by upbringing, M. became an Episcopalian. Although he was a man of broad interests and accomplishment, he is esp. remembered for the important part he played in awakening the conscience of the South by his forceful and courageous advocacy of civil rights. He won the Pulitzer prize for editorial writing in 1959 and was awarded the Presidential Medal of Freedom in 1964. BIBLIOGRAPHY: H. H. Martin, *Ralph McGill, Reporter* (1973).

[P. K. MEAGHER]

MCGIVNEY, MICHAEL JOSEPH (1852–90), founder of the Knights of Columbus. Ordained in 1877, M. served in Connecticut. As a young priest he founded a benevolent Catholic society, dedicated to charity, fraternalism, unity, and patriotism, and named the organization the Knights of Columbus, incorporated in Connecticut in 1882. He devoted much of his remaining few years to the work of the Knights. In 1957 the society he had established erected a monument to McG. in Waterbury, Connecticut.

[J. R. AHERNE]

MCGLYNN, EDWARD (1837–1900), priest and social reformer. He was born in New York City of Irish immigrant parents. After study at the Urban College in Rome, he received a doctorate in divinity and was ordained (1860). As pastor of St. Stephen's, a large New York City parish, he became concerned with the problem of poverty and eventually accepted Henry George's single tax remedy. M. was censured (1887) by Rome for disobedience after he failed to desist from active support of H. George and his theory. Reinstated in the ministry (1892), he was given a pastorate in Newburgh, N.Y. (1894), where he continued to defend the single tax theory without interference from his superiors. He was the first president of the Anti-Poverty Society which he helped to found. His unconventional views included support of public over parochial schools. BIBLIOGRAPHY: S. Bell, *Rebel Priest and Prophet: A Biography of Dr. Edward McGlynn* (1937, repr. 1975); J. T. Ellis, *Life of James Cardinal Gibbons* (2 v., 1952) 1:547–594.

[M. CARTHY]

MCGOWAN, RAYMOND AUGUSTINE (1892–1962), labor expert. A native of Missouri, M. was ordained in 1915. Assigned to the National Catholic War Council (later the National Catholic Welfare Conference), he worked as assistant director of the Department of Social Action under the director John A. Ryan and became director at the latter's death in 1945. He served in that capacity until 1953, when he retired. M. was a leading authority on labor and industrial relations. He founded the Catholic Conference on Industrial Problems and held conferences between labor and management across the U.S. In 1933 he was appointed to the Latin American bureau of NCWC and was named in 1943 by Pres. Franklin D. Roosevelt to a commission to study the organic law in Puerto Rico. Later he acted as labor consultant to Gov. Marín of Puerto Rico. M. founded the Catholic Association for International Peace and the American Catholic Social Action Confederation. He was a frequent contributor to journals and his *Towards Social Justice* was published in 1933.

[J. R. AHERNE]

MCGRATH, JAMES (1835–98), Oblate missionary. An Irish Oblate of Mary Immaculate, he was ordained in the U.S. in 1859. A celebrated preacher he conducted parish missions in New England, Pennsylvania, Ohio, New York, and Illinois. In 1883 he became provincial of the newly created American Province of the Oblates, with foundations from Massachusetts to Mexico, a position he held for 10 years.

[J. R. AHERNE]

MAC GREGOR, JAMES (*c.* 1480–1551), Scottish folklorist and dean of Lismore. He and his brother Duncan collected the 178 Irish and Scottish poems of what is called the *Book of the Dean of Lismore*. Many of these poems, transcribed from oral recitations of wandering bards and minstrels, are not found elsewhere, and they reveal one aspect of life in medieval Scotland.

[R. J. LITZ]

MCGROARTY, JULIA (1827–1901), superior, foundress of Trinity College in Washington, D.C. Born in Ireland, she was professed in the Sisters of Notre Dame de Namur in the U.S. in 1848. One of her early achievements was her school for blacks in Philadelphia. She was appointed in 1886 superior of the Sisters of Notre Dame east of the Rocky Mts. and later of the California houses. An able administrator, she founded 14 convents. In education she was a vigorous leader and sound academician. In 1897 at the request of the administration of The Catholic Univ. of America, which at that time did not admit women, she founded Trinity College for their education.

[J. R. AHERNE]

MCGUIRE, MARTIN R. P. (1897–1969), American patristic scholar, historian, linguist, encyclopedist. M. spent his boyhood on a farm in Whitinsville, Mass. and attended Holy Cross College, Worcester, Mass., from 1916 through 1921, with an interruption to serve in the U.S. Army. He taught at Georgetown Preparatory School, Washington, D.C., from 1921 through 1927 and at the same time took graduate studies leading to the Ph.D. awarded in 1927 at The Catholic Univ. of America. He was appointed instructor in the Department of Greek and Latin there in 1927, and there he remained for the rest of his life, advancing through academic grades to the ordinary professorship (1946) and serving as department head as well as Dean of the Graduate School of Arts and Sciences (1937–1947). He read with facility 12 languages, wrote *An Introduction to Classical Scholarship* (1961), *Introduction to Medieval Latin Studies* (1964), *The Political and Cultural History of the Ancient World* (1961), and with others he edited the *Confessions of St. Augustine* (1931), *A Concordance of Ovid* (1939), and did an English translation of *Guide to the Bible* (ed. A. Robert and A. Tricot, 1960). M. served as a member of the President's Commission on Higher Education, the United States Advisory Commission on Educational Exchange, and the Fulbright Board of Foreign Scholarships. He served as a member of the board and sometime officer of Medieval and Renaissance Latin Translations and Commentaries. He was on the editorial board of *The Fathers of the Church* and was co-editor of "The Catholic University of America Patristic Studies" and "The Catholic University of America Studies in Medieval and Renaissance Latin Language and Literature." He was associate editor of CHR, and senior editor of the NCE as well as its editor for Non-Christian Religions. He was a member of the original board of directors of Corpus Instrumentorum, was its first president, as well as special editor for Non-Christian Religions. He was the first layman to receive the Catholic Theological Society of America's annual Cardinal Spellman Award for the outstanding theologian of the year (1968). Although he had no children of his own, he and his wife Florence (née Mattimore) adopted seven children. He had a significant impact on the intellectual development of the Church in the U.S. for two full generations. He was a very retiring man, and of the many honorary degrees offered him he accepted only one, a degree from Holy Cross College. Another from The Catholic University of America was awarded posthumously.

[J. P. WHALEN]

MÁCHA, KAREL, HYNEK (1810–36), Czech baroque poet. Though his life was tragically short, M. achieved a high level of poetic power and became one of the great exponents of Slavic poetry in the 19th century. His theme was God's grandeur and man's insignificance except where he is placed in relationship to his Creator. His chief work, *Maj* (1836), is a Slavic classic.

[J. R. AHERNE]

MACHABEES, see MACCABEES.

MACHADO Y RUIZ, ANTONIO (1875–1939), Spanish poet. He was a keen student of philosophy, esp. of Henri Bergson. Most of his life was spent as a teacher in Spain. A Castilian, he reflects the landscape of that area and its people. The great theme of his poetry is God and time, love and death. A gentle melancholy pervades his work, beginning with *Soledades* in 1903. His most characteristic poetry is gathered in *Campos de Castilla* (1912). Love of his wife, who died a few years after their marriage, and his reflections on the marriage and her loss are vital elements of his work. An important collection, *Nuevas Canciones* (1924) reveals his continued philosophical bent but shows a modification of style in favor of brevity and simplicity. A Loyalist sympathizer in the Spanish Civil War, he went into exile in France, where he died.

[J. R. AHERNE]

MACHAERUS, a desert fortress in ancient Palestine, some 5 mi E of the Dead Sea (modern *Khirbet el-Mukawer*). Built originally by Alexander Jannaeus *c.* 90 B.C. to guard SE Juda against the Nabateans, it was destroyed by the Romans in 57 B.C. but rebuilt by Herod the Great *c.* 25–13 B.C. Machaerus is not mentioned in the Bible. According to Josephus, Herod Antipas imprisoned and beheaded John the Baptist there. As a strong center of Jewish resistance, Machaerus was finally destroyed by the Romans A.D. 71–72. BIBLIOGRAPHY: Josephus, *Wars* 7:6; L. Hartman, EDB 1410–11.

[E. MAY]

MACHALE, JOHN (1791–1881), Irish abp. and patriot. He was drawn to the Irish cause by the outcome of the Rising of 1798. Ordained in 1814, he taught theology at Maynooth until 1825. Using the pen name of Hieropolis, M. published a number of letters on the plight of Catholics in Ireland, a series that brought him into alliance with Daniel O'Connell in the struggle for Catholic emancipation. Named coadjutor bp. of Killala, he fought proselytism by Protestants in Ireland. In letters and in person he presented the Irish grievances to the British Prime Minister Grey. In 1834 M. was appointed abp. of Tuam, where he continued his attacks on British policy. A Gaelic scholar, he fostered the use of that language in the schools and churches, preaching in Gaelic himself. It was his leadership among the Irish bps. that caused them to condemn mixed schools that excluded the teaching of religion, and to formally reject the plan in 1869. Though M. favored the founding of a Catholic university in Ireland, his hostility towards Card. Cullen of Dublin (where M. was known as the "Lion of the West") and his lack of support for J. H. *Newman, first rector (1851), contributed to the initial failure of the project and Newman's resignation. At Vatican I M. was of the minority opposed to the definition of papal infallibility. In the years after mid-century, his influence as a major force in the hierarchy declined. He concentrated on being a kindly, hard-working leader of his diocese. M. translated the Pentateuch (1861) and Homer's *Iliad* (1841–71) into Gaelic and wrote a number of religious works in that language. BIBLIOGRAPHY: N. Costello, *John McHale, Archbishop of Tuam* (1938); W. Ward, *Life of John Henry Newman* (2 v., 1912) 1:344–389.

[J. R. AHERNE]

MACHAUT, GUILLAUME DE (*c.* 1300–77), French poet and **ars nova* composer, secretary to the King of Bohemia and later *canon of Reims Cathedral. He achieved renown for his secular chansons, lays, ballades, and rondeaux, for the remarkable structure of his *motets, and esp. for the design of his *Messe de Nostre Dame,* the earliest known complete polyphonic setting of the Mass Ordinary by a single composer. The motets, because of their isorhythmic *tenors and long-held notes, recall the earlier techniques of *organum, but in rhythmic subtlety and harmonic interest they are forward-looking. In his Mass M. unified the Kyrie, Sanctus, Agnus Dei and Ite Missa Est by a skillful use of *isorhythm, while the Gloria and Credo are set in declamatory style. His poetry was influenced by Ovid and Bede and in turn became a source for Chaucer, Deschamps, and Villon. In style it moved from the romanticism of the medieval troubadour and trouvère to the beginnings of a Renaissance concept of poetry. BIBLIOGRAPHY: D. Stevens, NCE 9:30; Reese MusMA; Reese MusR.

[P. MURPHY]

MACHEBOEUF, JOSEPH PROJECTUS (1812–89), missionary, bishop. Born and educated in France, M. was ordained in 1836. Coming to the U.S. in 1839, he served as missionary and pastor in Ohio until 1851 when he went to Sante Fe, New Mexico, to work with Lamy, vicar general and later abp. of Sante Fe. (The place and times are the setting for Willa Cather's novel, *Death Comes for the Archbishop.*) Sent to Denver, Colo., in 1860, M. was missioner to the mining towns. He became vicar apostolic of Colorado (including Utah and Wyoming) in 1868 and bp. of the newly created diocese of Denver in 1887. As ordinary M. founded schools and parishes, the first hospital in Denver, charitable institutions, and the first Catholic college for men (now Regis College).

[J. R. AHERNE]

MACHEN, JOHN GRESHAM (1881–1937), Presbyterian biblical scholar, opponent of *modernism. He completed his studies at Johns Hopkins, Princeton, and Marburg and Göttingen in Germany, and was ordained in 1914. As professor of NT exegesis at Princeton Theological Seminary from 1916, he became known for his conservative views. In the name of fidelity to the *Westminster Confession he opposed the *Auburn Affirmation (1924). His stand led to his resignation from Princeton in 1929; he founded Westminster Theological Seminary at Philadelphia, Pa., and taught there until death. His opposition to liberal policies in the Presbyterian Church in the U.S. brought about suspension from the ministry (1933). He helped found (1936) the conservative body later named the Orthodox Presbyterian Church. M. was not a fundamentalist but a vigorous conservative apologist, whose clearly expressed writings, esp. *Christianity and Liberalism* (1923), came to the aid of conservatives of many denominations. BIBLIOGRAPHY: E. H. Rian, *Presbyterian Conflict* (1940).

[J. H. SMYLIE]

MACHIAVELLI, NICCOLÒ (1469–1527), Renaissance political theorist and writer. Born of a Florentine middle class family steeped in republican traditions, M. had in effect two careers. The first was as a man of public affairs. In 1498, 4 years after the collapse of Medici rule, M. was named chancellor of the republic, an important secretarial position. He held several posts under this republic and was sent on special diplomatic missions to Rome, France, and the imperial court. This broadened his horizons for his second career, which was that of political thinker and writer, a change of activity thrust upon him by the return of the Medici to Florence in 1512. M. was tortured, tried, and forever exiled from the city. The rest of his life was spent at his modest villa outside Florence. There he wrote *The Prince,* the *Commentary on Livy* (the *Discorsi*), *The Art of War, Mandragola* (a bawdy play), and *History of Florence.* The most important of these works was *The Prince,* a treatise celebrated for its proposal of a politics separated from all ethical considerations and for advocating the principle that in politics the end justifies the means. As much as anything, this can be seen as a comment on the cynical political practices of the late Renaissance. But in fact *The Prince* sorts ill with the republican spirit of M.'s background and other writings, and it is not impossible that the author's intention was, in part at least, satirical. M. was an "essential Christian" (Ridolfi). BIBLIOGRAPHY: R. Ridolfi, *Life of Niccolò Machiavelli* (tr. C. Grayson, 1963); D. L. Jensen, *Machiavelli: Cynic, Patriot or Political Scientist?* (pa. 1960), including G. Mattingly's essay on the satire theory; P. E. Bondanella, *Machiavelli and the Art of Renaissance History* (1974).

[D. G. NUGENT]

MCHUGH, ANTONIA, SISTER (1873–1944), educator. A Nebraskan, M. entered the Sisters of St. Joseph of Carondelet at St. Paul, Minn., which was to be the center of her activity for a lifetime. As teacher, dean, and president of the College of St. Catherine, 1911–37, she contributed much to the development of that institution. A genuine academic leader she created one of the outstanding Catholic colleges in the U.S., the first to merit having a chapter of Phi Beta Kappa. As a builder she added a chapel, a science building, and a center for physical education and medical care. During her last 7 years at St. Catherine's she served also as religious superior.

[J. R. AHERNE]

MCHUGH, JOHN AMBROSE (1880–1950), American Dominican theologian. With C. J. *Callan he was coauthor of many scriptural, theological, and liturgical works, and coeditor of the *Homiletic and Pastoral Review*. The two were for many years professors at Maryknoll Seminary, Maryknoll, New York.

[T. C. O'BRIEN]

MACINTOSH, DOUGLAS CLYDE (1877–1948), Baptist theologian. Canadian-born, M. received his B.A. from McMaster Univ. in Ontario, and his Ph.D. from the Univ. of Chicago; he taught theology at Yale Divinity School, 1909–42. His thought marked a new direction in American *liberal theology. His main theme, as seen in his own work *Theology as an Empirical Science* (1919), and in a collection he edited, *Religious Realism* (1931), was that metaphysics and theology could and must be empirically grounded. He moved away from the subjective idealism of earlier liberalism, toward what he termed "Religious Realism." He held that belief in God must be grounded in the objective experience of a God immanent in the processes of history. He would grant no authority to historical revelation as the basis for belief. He affirmed as well that scientific generalizations about the values of Christianity were to be verified through the experiences of the lives of those who will accept the gospel. M.'s last important work was *The Problem of Religious Knowledge* (1940). Already, however, *neo-orthodoxy had begun to supplant liberal theology and "Religious Realism." BIBLIOGRAPHY: K. Cauthen, *Impact of American Liberalism* (1962); Smith-Jamison I:309–312; 469–470.

[M. J. SUELZER]

MCINTYRE, JAMES FRANCIS ALOYSIUS (1886–), cardinal. A New Yorker who began his adult life on Wall Street, M. entered the seminary at the age of 29 and was ordained for New York in 1921. Soon after, he was given a position in the chancery office of the archdiocese and in 1934 became chancellor. From 1945 to 1948 M. was one of two vicars general of New York. He early demonstrated strong views on the right of parents to educate their children as they chose. In 1948 M. was appointed archbishop of Los Angeles, a responsibility he carried for 22 years. His background in financial management, both on Wall Street and in the New York Chancery proved a needed boon to Los Angeles. A sprawling diocese along the Pacific coast, it became in M.'s time an area of phenomenal growth, calling for the building of hundreds of churches and parochial schools. Under his leadership a diocesan secondary school system was created; he was an able administrator of a mushrooming jurisdiction where charitable and social service institutions kept pace with parishes and schools. M.'s prudent financial vigilance over his diocese prevented the incurring of excessive indebtedness while providing for a vast building program. Both in New York and Los Angeles, M., like his friend and mentor Card. Spellman, was not averse to controversy, esp. where the rights of Catholics to maintain their own schools were concerned. In 1951 he denounced the federal government as "devoid of principle," a condition traced to the influence of Justice Oliver Wendell Holmes. That same year, M. questioned the fitness of Mrs. Franklin D. Roosevelt to be chairman of the UN Human Rights Commission. He played the leading role in defeating an antiparochial school tax measure in California. In 1953 M. was created cardinal, the first to be named from the West coast.

[J. R. AHERNE]

MACK, ALEXANDER (1679–1735), founder of the *Brethren Churches. By trade M. was a miller, from Schriesheim near Heidelberg, Germany. Separating from the *Reformed Church, he associated with Pietists who gathered at Schwarzenau in the Palatinate, and led a number of other separatists in search of the apostolic faith, practices, and manner of life. In the summer of 1708 he was chosen leader of a group that covenanted together in forming a new fellowship, which he declared to be "the old Church which Christ instituted through his blood." Because of persecution, M. migrated with his group to Friesland in the Netherlands about 1720, and likewise with them, in 1729, to Germantown, Pennsylvania. There he served the Brethren as minister until his death.

[A. T. RONK]

MACKAY, ALEXANDER MURDOCH (1849–90), missionary in Uganda, whose engineering skills and mechanical aptitude greatly enhanced his chances of survival in what was often an extremely hostile environment. He was the last survivor of the original band sent by the Church Missionary Society (an Evangelical missionary organ of the Church of England) in 1876, on a proposed mission to Victoria Nyanza. The son of the Free Church minister of Rhynie, Aberdeenshire, he studied engineering at the Univ. of Edinburgh; was a draughtsman with an engineering firm in Berlin (1873); learned enough German to translate into English advanced German mathematical writings; and constructed an agricultural machine which earned first prize at the Breslau Exhibition. His missionary band arrived in Zanzibar in May 1876. Only a remnant survived sickness and massacre en route to Uganda, which they reached in November 1878. Despite the opposition of Roman Catholics and Muslims, the band gained the protection of King Mtesa. M.'s engineering skills won for him the friendship of native tribesmen, so that he was allowed to stay even under the hostile Mwanga. When M. was finally expelled in 1887, he settled at Usambiro on the southern end of what the colonialists called Lake Victoria. He translated the Scriptures into the vernacular of Uganda. He died there of malaria.

[E. J. DILLON]

MCKENNA, BERNARD A. (1875–1960), first director of the National Shrine of the Immaculate Conception, Washington, D.C. A Philadelphian, McK. was ordained for the archdiocese in 1903. Appointed national director of the Shrine of the Immaculate Conception in 1915, he served in that capacity until 1933. As director, in association with Bishop *Shahan, founder of the Shrine, McK. helped plan the edifice and raise funds for its buildings. Though the plans for the entire shrine were completed in his time as director, only the crypt was finished when he left the assignment to return in 1933 to Philadelphia, where he served as a pastor until his death. McK. held a chair at The Catholic Univ. of America from 1918 to 1929. He served as president of the American Catholic Historical Society of Philadelphia, 1941–43. Among his writings was *Memoirs of the First Director of the National Shrine of the Immaculate Conception* (1959).

[J. R. AHERNE]

MCKENNA, CHARLES HYACINTH (1835–1917), Dominican parish missioner, promoter of the Holy Name Society. A native of Ireland, he came to the U.S. in 1851. He worked as a stonecutter for 6 years before entering the Dominicans, first as a brother, but later as a cleric; he was ordained in 1867. A remarkable preacher, he operated out of St. Vincent Ferrer Church in New York, in a long career of 44 years of missions and lectures to Catholics and non-Catholics. He wrote a number of devotional works, including the *Manual of the Holy Name* (1871), *The Rosary, the Crown of Mary* (1900). M. spent much time promoting Catholic societies; and popularized the Holy Name Society as a parish society for men that became almost universal in the United States.

[J. R. AHERNE]

MACKENZIE, EDWARD MONTAGUE COMPTON (1883–1972), convert to Roman Catholicism, novelist, founder of the Scottish nationalist party. He published over 100 novels, the most acclaimed being the five-volume *Four Winds of Love* (1937–41); notable as well are his first major work, *Sinister Street* (2 v., 1913), on his undergraduate days at Oxford; *Sylvia Scarlett* (1918), and a ten-volume autobiography written in his old age. One of his memoirs, on the days of his service in British intelligence during World War I, *Greek Memories,* had to be withdrawn from publication (it was reissued in 1939), and led to his being fined for violation of military secrets, and to temporary financial ruin. He became very early interested in religion; by 1908 he had become an Anglican layreader licensed to preach; he was converted to Roman Catholicism and received into the Church at Capri in 1914. Thought to be the story of his own religious experience is the trilogy: *The Altar Steps* (1921), *The Parson's Progress* (1924), *Heavenly Ladder* (1924). He was the first Catholic elected as rector of the Univ. of Glasgow (1931) since the Reformation. His strong espousal of Scottish nationalism is reflected in his writing as well as in his political activities. He was a devout adherent to Catholicism from 1914 on and in his old age daily trudged up the hill to Edinburgh cathedral for morning Mass.

[J. R. AHERNE]

MCKILLOP, MARY (1842–1909), Australian religious foundress. With Father Julian Woods she established the Sisters of St. Joseph of the Sacred Heart in 1866, when she took religious vows and the name Mother Mary of the Cross. The society met with strong opposition and in 1871 the bp. of Adelaide suppressed the community and excommunicated M. She appealed to Pope Pius IX who reinstated the congregation. Her record of achievement includes creation of 160 convents and over 100 schools; in her lifetime her community grew to 1,000 members.

[J. R. AHERNE]

MCKINNON, WILLIAM DANIEL (1858–1902), U.S. Army chaplain. A Canadian by birth, he studied for the priesthood in California and Baltimore, Md. and was ordained in 1887. A foe of the bigoted American Protective Association, he defended the civic loyalty of Catholics, recruiting 600 of his coreligionists for the First California Volunteers in the Spanish-American War (1898). He served as chaplain with distinction at the siege of Guam. His most remarkable achievement was at Manila, the Phillipines; alone and at great risk he made his way to the headquarters of the Spanish in that city and persuaded the commander to surrender, thus saving thousands of lives. Worn out by constant labors in Manila after the peace, M. died in that city. A statue of M. stands in Golden Gate Park, San Francisco, California.

[J. R. AHERNE]

MACKINTOSH, HUGH ROSS (1870–1936), Scottish theologian, professor of systematic theology at Edinburgh from 1904. He strove to make the thought of liberal German theology, which he had learned as a student in Marburg, more influential in England and Scotland. His most important work was *Doctrine of the Person of Christ* (1912); in which he espoused a modified form of kenotic theory. BIBLIOGRAPHY: D. M. Baillie, DNB (1931–40) 581–582.

[M. J. SUELZER]

MCLAREN, AGNES (1837–1913), Scottish medical missionary. She studied medicine in France and was licensed for practice in the United Kingdom. A convert to Catholicism in 1898, she became a Dominican tertiary. M. founded a women's hospital in Pakistan staffed by women. Hoping to found a community of women for medical mission work she made five attempts to have Holy See approval, but at the time canon law was opposed to religious being engaged in medicine. Her dream was realized after her death when Anna Dengel, whom she sponsored as a doctor, founded the Medical Mission Sisters.

[J. R. AHERNE]

MCLOUGHLIN, JOHN (1784–1857), pioneer, settler of Oregon. A licensed physician, he was a native of Quebec who early abandoned practice to become a fur trader with the Hudson Bay Company. At Fort Vancouver he was a strong leader, an early conservationist, and one who maintained peace with the Indians. In 1842 he became a convert to Catholicism. He was a pioneer in promoting the settlement of Oregon and founded Oregon City. In 1846 when the Oregon Question was settled, he established a town at Willamette Falls, against the opposition of the U.S. After his death his claim was recognized.

[J. R. AHERNE]

MACLOVIUS, ST. (Machutus, Malo; d. *c.*640). He was educated in the monastery of Llancarfarn, Wales. Becoming a monk against his parents' wishes, M. was ordained and went as missionary to Brittany. The monastery at Saint-Malo (Aleth) was named for him. He may have known both Sts. Columbanus and Brendan. BIBLIOGRAPHY: R.T. Meyer, NCE 9:39 Butler 4:349–350; H. Leclercq, DACL 10.1:1293–1318.

[R. T. MEYER]

MCMAHON, EVER (1600–1650), Irish bp. and patriot. Educated for the priesthood on the Continent, he became vicar apostolic of Clogher. An ardent patriot, he enlisted troops for Owen McNeill's regiment in Flanders. Appointed bp. of Down and Connor in 1841, he took part in the insurrection and was a member of the Supreme Council of the Confederation of Kilkenny. After O'Neill's death he was named commander of the Ulster Army; he was defeated in 1650 at Scariffholis and executed.

[J. R. AHERNE]

MCMAHON, JOSEPH HENRY (1862–1939), librarian. A native of New York City, he was ordained in 1886. His career from 1887 centered on the Cathedral Free Library, which he turned into a library for the general public in 1892. He added 11 branch libraries. In 1896 the library was granted a state charter. The largest Catholic library in the U.S., Cathedral Library was absorbed in 1904 by the newly formed New York Public Library.

[J. R. AHERNE]

MCMAHON, THOMAS JOHN (1909–56), American mission director. Ordained for the Archdiocese of New York in 1933, he was named national secretary of the Catholic Near East Welfare Assn. in 1943. Six years later he was appointed president of the Pontifical Mission for Palestine, established by the Holy See to give help to Palestinian Arab refugees. The difficult task weakened his health and in 1954 he resigned to return to parish work in New York City.

[J. R. AHERNE]

MCMANUS, JAMES E. (1900–76), bishop. Ordained in 1927, he earned a doctorate in canon law from The Catholic Univ. of America (1937). He served as bp. of Ponce, Puerto Rico (1947–63) where he took public issue with the government of Luis Muñoz Marín on such controversial subjects as birth control. He then served as an auxiliary bp. of New York (1963–70).

[M. A. MCFADDEN]

MCNABB, VINCENT (1868–1943), English Dominican theologian and preacher. Of Ulster stock, son of a sea-captain, he studied at Louvain (1891–94) and after his return to England taught at houses of his order at Woodchester and Hawkesyard (1894–1906; 1914–20) and for the last 23 years of his life was stationed in London where he became one of the city's best-recognized figures. His life was one of evangelical poverty; he slept on the floor and tramped everywhere in army boots and homespun habit. He preached the gospel with compassion and a characteristic pungency that attracted the crowd at Hyde Park and other open places. He was held in great if sometimes exasperated affection by his brethren and was revered by thousands, esp. from the top and bottom social levels. M. was a prophetic figure in the causes of social reform and Christian reunion. His was the theological inspiration of *Distributism, yet he was a close friend of G. B. Shaw and the Fabians, as he was of Randall Davidson, Abp. of Canterbury and other religious leaders. He was often regarded as an *enfant terrible* by the RC establishment, both clerical and lay, but his technique was too assured and angular for his orthodoxy to be safely impugned; his loyalty to his order and the See of Peter was rarely reticent. He was full of contrasts: rigorous with himself, yet warm and gentle with others; his ideal of truth was generous and his notion of the limits of religious authority exact, yet in controversy he could press hard, the more so with deviators from his own party-line than with people from quite another background. As a young lecturer he had read widely in English literature and German philosophy, but for the last 30 years he confined himself to the Bible, the *Summa* of St. Thomas, papal documents, and official Blue Books. Works: *Oxford Conferences on Prayer* (1903); *Oxford Conferences on Faith* (1905). BIBLIOGRAPHY: *Father Vincent McNabb.* (1955), a somewhat slanted biography by F. Valentine.

[T. GILBY]

MCNEIL, NEIL (1851–1934), Canadian archbishop. M. was ordained in 1879. He taught at St. Francis Xavier Univ., Antigonish, Nova Scotia, and served as rector there from 1884 to 1891. In 1881 he founded the weekly *Aurora* and served as editor. Named vicar apostolic of the W coast of Newfoundland in 1895, M. became first bp., when the area received the status of a diocese (1904), then abp. of Vancouver (1910), and was appointed abp. of Toronto in 1912. He gave strong backing to St. Michael's College there and the Pontifical Institute of Medieval Studies.

[J. R. AHERNE]

MCNICHOLAS, JOHN TIMOTHY (1877–1950), Dominican, abp. of Cincinnati, Ohio. Of Irish birth, M. was brought as a child to the U.S. by his parents. Entering the Dominican Order in 1894, he was ordained in 1901. When the Dominican House of Studies was opened in Washington, D.C. in 1905, M. became regent of studies there. From 1909 he was the national director of the Holy Name Society. Named an assistant to the general of his order in 1917, he spent a year in Rome; then he was appointed bp. of Duluth, Minn., where he served from 1918 to 1925, when he was named abp. of Cincinnati. M. was a vigorous and intelligent administrator; his long tenure was marked by his special efforts to care for blacks, to attract non-Catholics, to support labor, and esp. to promote Catholic education on the elementary, secondary, and college levels. He established the Athenaeum of Ohio for the supervision of educational institutions in the archdiocese, founded a teachers' college to train priests, sisters, and lay teachers. A postgraduate center for study of philosophy, science, and theology, the Institutum Divi Thomae, reflected his own outlook on the need for higher learning. M. exercised national influence in offices held for the NCWC as chairman of the education department for 8 years, chairman of the episcopal committee on motion pictures for 10 years, chairman of the administrative board for five terms, and shaper of the annual statements of the American bishops. BIBLIOGRAPHY: M. Reardon, *Mosaic of a Bishop* (1957).

[J. R. AHERNE]

MCPHERSON, AIMEE SEMPLE (1890–1944), evangelist, founder of the *International Church of the Foursquare Gospel. A Canadian by birth, Aimee Kennedy in her public life used the names of the first two of her three husbands. In 1907 she experienced a religious conversion at a revival conducted by Robert Semple, whom she married in 1908. The two worked as missionaries in Hong Kong until his death in 1911. She continued to travel, fulfilling what she regarded as her divine commission to preach. A second marriage, to Harold McPherson, ended in divorce. Her evangelistic campaign carried her to Los Angeles in 1918, and in 1921 she built her Angelus Temple, with a seating capacity of 5,300; she was ordained in a Baptist church in 1922. She organized her Church in 1927, and later established the Lighthouse of International Foursquare Evangelism (LIFE) Bible College, and a radio station. Lawsuits, an escapade in which she claimed to have been kidnapped, a third marriage in 1931 to David Hutton (a singer in the Temple choir) which ended in another divorce, brought her great notoriety. Sister Aimee was able to use even this, as well as her pleasing appearance and eloquence, to make herself the foremost woman evangelist in the United States. She preached a pure *fundamentalism and *Pentecostalism. She died leaving 35,000 followers; her son Rolf K. McPherson succeeded her. Her autobiography, *Story of My Life,* was published posthumously (1951).

[W. J. WHALEN]

MCQUAID, BERNARD JOHN (1823–1909), bishop. Orphaned at the age of 9, he was cared for by the Sisters of Charity. He was ordained to the priesthood in 1858 and labored in New Jersey, becoming rector of the Newark cathedral in 1853. A vigorous and determined man, M. faced a mob attacking the German Catholic Church in 1854, was responsible for establishing two orphanages and the cathedral school, was a founder of Seton Hall College. As a staunch supporter of the Union in the Civil War he went to Washington in 1864 to see to the care of Catholic soldiers and served as chaplain to the wounded at Fredericksburg. As vicar general to Bp. James R. Bayley of Newark, he supplied the firmness the bp. lacked. Named first bp. of Rochester in 1868, M. alienated many priests by his autocratic rule. He was opposed to the definition of papal infallibility and voted against it at Vatican Council I, but submitted to the final decision. Content to remain in Rochester, he refused larger sees offered to him and gave his energies to building churches, schools, and charitable institutions. He sponsored the Sisters of St. Joseph already in Rochester and entrusted to them the well-organized parochial school system. He was rigid in his opposition to Catholics attending public schools and nonsectarian or public colleges, denying absolution to parents who sent children to public schools when a parochial school was available. In the numerous battles that flared among American bps. in the 19th cent., he was the constant adversary of Card. Gibbons and Abp. Ireland (He was reprimanded by Rome for publicly denouncing Ireland's policies; the two were reconciled in 1905). M. applied the canonical ban on secret societies to the *Knights of Labor and the Ancient Order of Hibernians, in contrast to the policy of Gibbons. However conservative he may have been, he brought Rochester to a point of admirable organization and service to its faithful. St.

Bernard's Seminary, which he built, became a major institution for training clergy. He was responsible for many charitable institutions as well as for the gradual acceptance of chaplaincies at state institutions. He was a fighter not always tolerant of his opposition but a man who left a strong diocese behind him at his death. BIBLIOGRAPHY: F. Zwierlein, *Life and Letters of Bishop McQuaid* (3 v., 1925–27).

[J. R. AHERNE]

MACRINA, ST. (*c.*327–379), known as M. 'the Younger', was the elder sister of St. Basil the Great and St. Gregory of Nyssa. Their paternal grandmother, Macrina the Elder (d. *c.*340), had deeply influenced the Christian upbringing of the famous grandchildren. M., after the death of her fiancé, with her mother Emmelia and her household lived on the family estate near the river Iris in Pontus, where she established a flourishing community and dedicated herself to a life of prayer, contemplation, and penance. By her spiritual gifts and strength of character, she exercised a deep influence upon her brothers, esp. in winning Basil from a promising secular career to the sacred priesthood. St. Gregory of Nyssa's *Vita Macrinae Junioris* offers valuable details of her spirituality and a vivid account of their meeting at her deathbed. He also gives testimony of her competence as a theologian (*Opera*, ed. V. W. Callahan 8.1:370–414). For M.'s vita see PG 46:959–1000 (tr., introd. W. K. L. Clarke, 1916).

MACROBIUS, AMBROSIUS THEODOSIUS (fl. *c.*400 A.D.), Latin author of Neoplatonist outlook. His *Saturnalia* is a symposium in seven books covering a wide variety of miscellaneous lore, but with Vergilian criticism as its critical theme. The work gave him an undeserved reputation for universal knowledge in the Middle Ages. His *Commentarii in Somnium Scipionis* has come down to us in the MS tradition of Cicero's *Somnium Scipionis*. It is Neoplatonic in tone and content, emphasizing the Neoplatonic theories of emanation. He seems to have drawn upon Porphyry's commentary on Plato's *Timaeus* as his main source. This work exercised considerable influence on medieval writers from the Carolingian Age to the end of the 12th century. BIBLIOGRAPHY: R. G. Austin, OCD 527; J. R. O'Donnell, NCE 9:45–46; D. Fehling, LexAW 1804; T. Whitaker, *Macrobius* (1923).

[M. R. P. MCGUIRE]

MACROCOSM AND MICROCOSM. The terms are Greek. Aristotle, e.g., refers to man as the *mikros cosmos,* (*Phys.* 8.2.252b), but the concept of a corresponding connection between the great external world and the little world or life of man is very ancient and widespread. In the mythologies of numerous peoples a cosmogonic connection is made between the universe regarded as a living entity and man as an individual. There is a close relation between the macrocosm and the *World-Soul in respect to its nature and operation. Among the Babylonians and the Hindus, the macrocosm-microcosm concept enters into all phases of public and religious life. In the Hindu Upanishads, the All-Soul, Brahman, is identified with the individual soul, Ātman. The temple frequently symbolizes the cosmic mountain or serves as an *imago mundi*. The concept is found among the Greeks; beginning with Old Pythagoreanism, it is developed by Plato, and then by the Stoics. It occupies a central place in the Hermetic literature and in the Neoplatonists of theurgic bent like *Porphyry, *Iamblichus, and *Proclus. According to Plato's *Timaeus* (73b) man is constituted out of the cosmic elements fire, air, water, and earth. In Manicheism the body is regarded as having been made according to the model of the cosmos. The idea was widespread that on death the constituent elements of man returned to the cosmic elements whence they came, or that individual souls were united with the All-Soul. Since the stars and other celestial bodies comprising the macrocosm were considered living beings and as maintaining a fixed and eternal order in the universe, they were believed to have a direct influence on man's life and actions. Religious festivals reflected cosmic cycles, and the New Year feast in particular was a symbolic repetition of an ever-recurring cosmic renewal. By magic, esp. by astrology and divination, man tried to ascertain the attitude of the powers of the macrocosm toward him. There was a definite tendency to ascribe the course of one's life an actions to the stars and to give a major role to Fate. The Stoics never resolved completely the problem of the dominant role of necessity in their cosmology and the possibility of human freedom of action. The Christian Fathers had to develop an effective polemic against the pagan acceptance of fate as an explanation of and excuse for aberrations of conduct. It is to be noted also that in Chinese thought, as presented in the teachings of Confucius and Taoism, Heaven plays a major role in determining human conduct.

With the renewal of full-scale contact with Greek literature and learning in the Renaissance, which included an exaggerated esteem for Hermetic and Oracular literature, there was not only a revival of the concept macrocosm-microcosm, but also elaborate development and application of the concept, culminating in the thought of *Paracelsus (1493–1541). BIBLIOGRAPHY: D. Levy, EncPhil 5:121–125 (with copious bibliog.); M. Schmidt, RGG 4:624–626; R. Allers, "Microcosmus from Anaximandras to Paracelsus," *Traditio* 2 (1944) 319–408 (excellent); A. J. Festugière, *La Révelation d'Hermès Trismegiste* (4 v., 1944–54); *idem, Le Dieu cosmique* (1949).

[M. R. P. MCGUIRE]

MACRORY, JOSEPH (1861–1945), Scripture scholar and cardinal. M. taught Oriental languages and NT exegesis at St. Patrick's College, Maynooth (1889–1915); was appointed bp. of Down and Connor (1915); abp. of Armagh (1928); and cardinal (1929). He helped found the *Irish Theological Quarterly,* published many scriptural articles for scholarly periodicals, and wrote widely-used commentaries on St. John's Gospel and Corinthians 1 and 2. BIBLIOGRAPHY: K. O'Sullivan, NCE 9:46.

[T. M. MCFADDEN]

MADAURA, MARTYRS OF, claimed by some to be the protomartyrs of Africa. What is known of them is derived from a letter of a pagan grammarian, Maximus of Madaura, written to *Augustine *c.*390. According to Maximus, the four martyrs, Namphano, Miggin, Sanam, and Lucitas died in the year 180 (therefore just prior to the *Scillitan martyrs). The obviously Punic origin of the names of these martyrs, to whom much popular veneration was being extended, was seized upon by Maximus as an indication that Roman civilization was being overthrown by barbarians. The historical existence of these martyrs and the fact of their martyrdom seems well assured, but the date of their death, as asserted by Maximus, is open to question, although the claim of some that they were *Donatist martyrs of a much later time is not well founded. BIBLIOGRAPHY: J. Gavigan, NCE 9:47; A. Amore, EncCatt 7:1788–89.

[R. B. ENO]

MADELEINE, LA (Church of Ste. Marie Madeleine, Paris), French church conceived as a strong architectural feature at the end of the Rue Royale. After attempts by Contant d'Ivry (1764) and Couture, Napoleon in 1806 commanded P. Vignon to transform it into a temple of glory to the victorious French army. The peripteral Corinthian temple was transformed into a church by Vignon (1842), with works of Rude and Barye adding sculptural richness.

[M. J. DALY]

MADELEINE SOPHIE, ST., see BARAT, MADELEINE SOPHIE, ST.

MADELEVA, SISTER MARY, see WOLFF, SISTER MARY MADELEVA.

MADER, ANDREAS EVARISTUS (1881–1949), archeologist. A German Salvatorian ordained in 1903, M. taught at the seminary in Tivoli beginning in 1909. He spent 3 years in archeological research in Palestine. A chaplain in World War I, he was badly wounded. Director of the Oriental Institute of the Görresgesellschaft in Jerusalem from 1926 to 1932, he discovered the ancient Church of the Multiplication of the Loaves at Tabgha and the sanctuary of Mamre. Two pivotal archeological works by M. were *Altchristliche Basiliken und Lokaltraditionen in Südjudäa* (1918) and *Mambre* (1957).

[J. R. AHERNE]

MADERNO, CARLO (1556–1629), leading architect of his generation in Rome, unjustly criticized for the nave he added to St. Peter's, Rome (1607–29), and justly famous for the superb early Baroque façade of Sta. Susanna, Rome (completed 1603), with its successful marshaling of plastic and structural elements focusing on the portal. M. was active in villa designs (Aldobrandini, Frascati) and completed works of others (S. Giovanni dei Fiorentini and S. Andrea della Valle). BIBLIOGRAPHY: R. Wittkower, *Art and Architecture in Italy: 1600–1750* (1958).

[L. A. LEITE]

MADIANITES, see MIDIANITES.

MADONNA (Ital., my lady), a title of the Blessed Virgin Mary par excellence; commonly also refers to an image or statue of Mary.

[T. C. O'BRIEN]

MADONNA HOUSE APOSTOLATE, a Catholic rural apostolate founded by Catherine de Hueck at Combermere, Ont., Canada, in 1947. The apostolate is made up of two pious unions, one of men and one of women, moving toward the status of secular institutes with vows of poverty, chastity, and obedience. The members wear no religious habit. By the 1960s there were some 150 members, some of them priests, working in Canada, the U.S., the W Indies, and E Pakistan. BIBLIOGRAPHY: C. de Hueck–Doherty, NCE 9:51.

[D. CODDINGTON]

MADOZ, JOSEPH (1892–1953), Spanish Jesuit patrologist. After completing his studies in Rome, M. returned to Spain in 1930, where he taught theology at Oña until his death, with the exception of the years 1932–38 when he taught at Merneffe, Belgium. His scholarly work in patrology centered around *Vincent of Lérins and the figures of Visigothic and Mozarabic Spain. BIBLIOGRAPHY: I. Onatibia, NCE 9:51; J. Alfaro, LTK 6:1264.

[R. B. ENO]

MADRIGAL, an Italian name that describes a type of Italian lyric poetry: in the 14th cent., the form consisting of one to four 3-line stanzas and a refrain of one or two lines; in the 16th cent., a lyric poem, a polyphonic song with or without instrumental accompaniment. Spiritual madrigals are songs with a religious text or prayer in a musical setting. Madrigals—among the finest lyrics of the Elizabethan Age—flourished in England in the late 16th and early 17th cent. and were preserved in splendid songbooks of great musical composers of the period. Notable collections are Nicholas Yonge's *Musica Transalpina* (1588) and five books of lyrics of literary importance by Thomas Campion. BIBLIOGRAPHY: E. H. Fellowes, *English Madrigal Verse* (1929); *idem, English Madrigal Composers* (1948); E. Einstein, *Italian Madrigal* (tr. A. K. Krappe et al., 1949).

[S. A. HEENEY]

MAḎRŌSHŌ (East Syrian, *maḏrāshā*), long expository metric composition, accompanied by an *'ûnnōyō,* of which several are sung in East and West Syrian festive Night Offices.

[A. CODY]

MADRUZZO, a powerful family of Trent in the Italian Tyrol, members of which were bps. of Trent from 1539 to 1658. **Cristoforo** (1512–78) served in numerous ecclesiastical and diplomatic positions, was ordained and consecrated bp. (1542), named cardinal by Paul III, and left Trent (1567) to serve as cardinal bishop of Sabina, Palestrina, and Porto. Cristoforo managed the details of the Council of Trent's first convocation (1545–47), insisting upon discussion of theological issues in conjunction with matters of reform. **Ludovico** (1532–1600), Cristoforo's nephew, was made cardinal (1561) after serving as ambassador to France. He took part in the third session of the Council (1562–63), at which he advocated the principle of residency for bishops. He replaced his uncle as bp. of Trent in 1567. **Carlo Gaudenzio** (1562–1629), nephew of Ludovico, succeeded his uncle to the See of Trent (1600), and became cardinal (1604). He opposed trials for witchcraft and later opposed Cardinal Melchior Klesl at the Diet of Regensburg (1613). **Carlo Emanuele** (1599–1658) succeeded his uncle Carlo Gaudenzio as bp. of Trent (1629), and frightened by the absence of legitimate heirs, he scandalously sought to legitimize his own natural children in order to preserve the Madruzzo line.

[R. J. LITZ]

MAES, ADRIEN, see EXUPÉRIEN, FRÈRE.

MAES, BONIFACE (1627–1706), Flemish spiritual writer. A Franciscan Recollect, M. was a teacher of theology and an official of his order—provincial of the Flemish province (1677–90), commissar of the Belgian, German, French, and Irish provinces, and definitor general of the order. He is best known as a writer on mystical and ascetical theology. He wrote with compassion and understanding for the less perfect among Christians but maintained a high standard of expectation. Among his writings were *Mystieke Theologie of te verborgen Godts-gheleertheyt* (1668; Eng. tr. B. Whelan, *Mystical Theology,* 1928) and Consolatorium piorum (1672).

[J. R. AHERNE]

MAES, CAMILLUS PAUL (1846–1915), bishop. A Belgian ordained for the Diocese of Detroit in 1868, he became chancellor of the diocese in 1880. Named bp. of Covington, Ky., in 1885, M. labored to bring the inhabitants of Appalachia into the Church. He founded two diocesan weeklies, *New Catholic Chimes* and the *Christian Year.* An early promoter of The Catholic Univ. of America, he served as secretary to its board of trustees from 1900 to 1915. M. was for many years president of the board of bps. of the American College at Louvain. M. was an advocate of the publication of *The Catholic Encyclopedia* and the *Catholic Historical Review.* First president of the Priests' Eucharistic League, he founded its magazine *Emmanuel* (1895).

[J. R. AHERNE]

MAESTRO DI CAMERA, the highest among the *papal chamberlains, in charge of the personal service of the pope, custodian of the *fisherman's ring, and in charge of arranging papal audiences.

[T. C. O'BRIEN]

MAESTRO MATEO (Matheus). Main sculptor of the Glory Portal at Compostella, Spain, identified by an inscription also giving the date of 1188. Although Spanish elements are present, the use of jamb statues and other motifs shows that Mateo was trained in the traditions of N French Early Gothic portal sculpture. BIBLIOGRAPHY: G. Gaillard, ''Le Porche de la Gloire à S. Jacques de Compostelle'', *Cahiers de civilisation médiévale* I (1958). *PORTICO DE LA GLORIA.

[R. C. MARKS]

MAFFEI, noble Italian family of the Renaissance period. Many Maffei held positions of importance in the Church and in cultural life in Italy. In the Canons Regular of the Lateran were Paolo (d. 1480), Timoteo (d. 1470) and Celso (d. 1508). Cardinal Bernardino (d. 1553) was close to Pope Paul III; his brother, Abp. Marcantonio (d. 1583), served Pius IV and Pius V in several capacities. Giampietro (d. 1603) was a political figure in Genoa before becoming a Jesuit; he wrote, among other works, a life of Ignatius Loyola. Francesco Scipioni (d. 1755) produced 21 volumes of collected poetry and prose. Raffaele, of the Volterran branch of the family (d. 1522), a scholar, composed a polemic against Luther; his brother Bp. Mario (d. 1537) belonged to Pope Leo X's circle. BIBLIOGRAPHY: J. F. D'Amico, ''A Humanist Response to Martin Luther: Raffaelle Maffei's Apologeticum,'' *Sixteenth Century Journal* 6 (1975) 37–56.

[R. H. SCHMANDT]

MAGDALEN ALBRICI, BL. (d. 1465), Augustinian abbess. Orphaned, M. entered St. Andrew convent near her home. Her piety and gentleness soon commended her to the office of abbess. She is said to have been a visionary. She was beatified in 1907. BIBLIOGRAPHY: A. M. Confalonieri, *La beata Maddalena Albrici, badessa del convento di S. Andrea in Brunate* (1938).

[B. F. SCHERER]

MAGDALENS (Penitents, White Ladies), religious order of women instituted to protect or reform women and girls. Rudolf of Worms founded the congregation at Metz and became its first general prior. Gregory IX confirmed it in 1227. After 1232 a Dominican form of the rule of St. Augustine replaced the original Cistercian rule in most houses of the order. A male branch was attached to the Magdalens for direction and government. Each house had a prior, three priests, a prioress, and laymen. The order spread rapidly not only in Germany but also in France, Italy, Spain, and Portugal. In 1286 the Magdalens were placed under the direction of the Dominicans but became independent in 1291. After 1370 the order declined. It also lost many houses at the time of the Reformation. Various small communities were originally connected with the order but later developed independently. BIBLIOGRAPHY: A. Condit, NCE 9:57–58.

[M. J. FINNEGAN]

MAGDEBURG CATHEDRAL (1208–1520). The Church of SS. Maurice and Catherine, erected (1208) on the site of a Benedictine abbey, the earliest Gothic structure in Germany, with polygonal choir, E towers and bays (1208–30), the nave (1363), W towers (1310–1520), is French in the two-storied ambulatory and chapels of the choir, but German in many details. The N transept porch shows the famous *Wise and Foolish Virgins* (1300) related to Strasbourg. Within is the tomb of Abp. Ernest by P. Vischer the Elder (1495).

[M. J. DALY]

MAGDEBURG CENTURIES (*Ecclesiastica historia secundum singulas centurias* . . .). Protestant-inspired, documentary ecclesiastical history. It was a monumental work in 13 volumes, published in Basel, 1559–74. The authors, often called the Centuriators, were seven in number, but the work was planned and supervised by the disputatious M. *Flacius Illyricus (1520–75). The popular title derives from the place of editing and from the division of content by centuries. The work was projected up to the 16th cent., but the last three volumes were not published. This first real Protestant church history, an effort to vindicate the Reformation, is apologetic and partisan. Its thesis is that the Roman Church has progressively corrupted the true gospel. Though based on sources gathered throughout Europe, the work uses them uncritically and with distortions. The myth of Pope Joan is incorporated, and the pope is always designated as anti-Christ, whose empire is the RC Church. Though the *Magdeburg Centuries* represents a break with the often more critical spirit of the Renaissance, it did stimulate historical research as a reaction, beginning with the *Annales ecclesiastici* of C. *Baronius.

[D. G. NUGENT]

MAGDOL, see MIGDOL.

MAGEDDO, see MEGIDDO.

MAGELLAN, FERDINAND (Fernão de Magalhães; *c.*1480–1521), Portuguese explorer, commander of the first expedition to circle the globe. In 1505 he set sail for India in the party of Francisco d'Almeida, the beginning of 7 years' service and exploration in the East. There he participated in Afonso de Albuquerque's capture of Malacca (1511) and accompanied Antonio d'Abreu to the Spice Islands (the Moluccas) before returning to Europe. He was disabled in battle while fighting in Morocco. It was only after his idea for a westward voyage to the East Indies was rejected by the Portuguese king, into whose disfavor he had fallen, that M. offered his services to Charles I of Spain (1517), who agreed to back and outfit his expedition. Thus, with five ships and some 270 men, M. set forth on his great voyage of discovery from the port of San Lúcar de Barrameda on Sept. 20, 1519. Sailing southward, they reached the Brazilian coast by late Nov., entered the Río de la Plata in Jan. in search of a westward passage, then explored the E. coast of South America down to Port St.-Julián, where they wintered until late August 1520. There in Patagonia, M. had to suppress a mutiny brought on by privations. It was on Oct. 21 that with his three remaining ships M. discovered the hidden entrance to the long and perilous strait (now called after him) which led 38 days and some 360 mi later to the Pacific Ocean; this, along with Tierra del Fuego, the explorer named. The passage across the Pacific took a further 98 days during which the expedition was a prey to starvation and every form of sickness. But finally on March 6, 1521, it reached Guam and 10 days later the Philippines. Here M. made an alliance with the king of Cebu Island who recognized Spain's sovereignty, but M. met his death while attempting to conquer the neighboring island of Mactan. The survivors of the expedition journeyed on to their original destination, the Moluccas, where they loaded cargoes of spices and other precious goods. February 11, 1522, reduced to one ship, the *Vittoria,* captained by Juan Sebastián del Cano, they commenced their homeward voyage via the Indian Ocean and Cape Verde Islands. When they landed in Spain on Sept. 6, 1522, the crew numbered only 18, or a fifteenth of those who had set forth 3 years earlier. The cost of the lengthy expedition was more than recovered by the sale of cloves brought back. But this small vindication was the least of M.'s achievements. With only a few primitive instruments to guide him, he had found the westward route to the Indies sought in vain by Columbus; explored a large portion of South America; discovered Guam and the Philippines; gauged the vastness of the Pacific; and established the circumference of the earth.

[E. M. GATES]

MAGER, ALOYSIUS (1883–1946), theologian, psychologist. An Austrian Benedictine, M. was a teacher of philosophy, mystical theology, and experimental psychology at Salzburg, Austria. One of the founders of the Catholic intellectual study group, *Hochschulwochen,* in Salzburg, M. was a celebrated authority in his fields. In addition to frequent periodical writings, he published several books, among them *Vorlesungen über experimentelle Psychologie* (1929) and *Mystik als seelische Wirklichkeit* (1946).

[J. R. AHERNE]

MAGI, a Median tribe and Persian priestly class. Herodotus has given us a vivid account of their customs.

They did not bury their dead, but exposed corpses to be eaten by birds of prey. They practiced consanguineous marriage and were specialists in the interpretation of dreams, in astrology, and in magic, the art of magic itself being named after them. They forbade the killing of certain animals, but made the killing of certain others a duty. Their cosmic outlook was dualistic. Although the revolt of the Magus Ganmata was put down by Darius I (521–486 B.C.) and an annual feast instituted, "The Killing of the Magi," the religious influence of the Magi steadily increased. Even before the end of the 5th cent. B.C., they possessed a monopoly in the religion of the State. The religion of the Avesta is actually a fusion of Zoroastrian and Magian elements, although it would seem that Zoroaster's teaching in its purist form was opposed in many respects to Magian practices. The Magi identified themselves with Zoroaster and his doctrines. Hence it was assumed by many Greek and Roman writers that Zoroaster himself was a Magus. Under the Sassanids the head of the state religion had the title *magupat* (chief of the Magi). BIBLIOGRAPHY: J. Duchesne-Guillemin, NCE 9:60–61; *id., La Religion de l' Iran ancien* (1962) *passim.*

[M. R. P. MCGUIRE]

MAGI (IN THE BIBLE). In Mt 2.1–12 the Magi were experts in astrology who recognized by the appearance of his star that an important king of the Jews had been born, and so they traveled from "the East" to pay him homage. The story supports a Matthean theological theme: the Gentiles, and creation itself have honored God's anointed King, Jesus Christ, with joyful acceptance and precious gifts in fulfillment of Sacred Scripture (Gen 49.10; Num 24.17; Ps 72.10,11,15; Is 60.6), while the King's own people, although beneficiaries of God's prophetic word (Mt 2.6), through their evil and jealous leaders, have rejected him and opposed his reign. For Matthew, the star and the astrologers' mysterious knowledge were, obviously, divine wonders that escape human investigation. The midrashic aura of the account indicates that the author's intent was theological rather than historical. *MIDRASH.

[J. F. FALLON]

MAGI PLAYS, liturgical dramas featuring the visit of the Wise Men to the infant Christ. These plays were highly spectacular productions because of the splendid pageantry of the Magi and their retinues, together with the ostentation of Herod's court. The latter figure became the dominant character of these plays in his role of angry and jealous tyrant, a part coveted by a talented actor aand applauded by the spectators, who expected him to "out-herod Herod," in Hamlet's phrase.

[E. C. DUNN]

MAGIC, the attempt to control human actions, natural events, and, in some instances, the will of the gods by the use of certain incantations, rites, or objects such as fetish figures or *amulets. Magic has been present in every type of culture, although in different forms. Basically, it strives to achieve objectives by means that are incongruent to their character.

As such, magic may be regarded as directly contrary to man's fundamental effort to deal with the world in a realistic way. Religion is a process of realizing life according to the ultimate transcendental terms of an intelligible world; magic appears as the reification of these terms in such a way that the transcendental is manipulated within the empirical framework of cause-effect relations. Man tries to achieve security in and domination over empirical reality by means other than those provided by this reality. Thus, whenever it is believed that life can be made livable by the mechanical deployment of meta-empirical symbols at the expense of person and reason, the belief involves magic phenomena. In this view, magic is not a preliminary although barren stage leading to religion (see J. G. Frazer). Nevertheless, as the symbolic background of magical techniques as well as their deployment in official ceremonies shows, the transition between magic and religion is very fluid. Since religious symbols are always a synthesis between the visible and the invisible, they may be looked upon as signposts in the search for religious meaning, or misinterpreted as ends in themselves. In this sense each ritual may be either religious or magical, conditional upon the intention of the participants.

Distinctions can be made, as precise as the symbols and principles employed allow, among various types of magic. *Substitute magic* is based upon the idea that a part substitutes for the whole, thereby reversing the transcendental principle that the part may represent the whole. Man seizes power over someone else by possessing parts of him, e.g., bones, hair, nails, etc. *Contagious magic* obtains when the substitution of the part for the whole is only partially realized and integrated into a scheme of causal connections. By touching or wearing power-laden objects such as relics, fetishes, sacred stones, amulets, etc., or even by assimilating them as in the case of cannibalism, man integrates himself and his deeds into the efficacy of an invisible power structure. *Sympathetic magic* deals with symbols and their supposed unity or sympathy with that which is symbolized. It differs from substitute magic by the ideational character of the substitution. Examples are the anticipation of a successful hunt by striking a picture of the animal; the manipulation of pictures and figures in general; the use of curse figurines or dolls; the deployment of arcane formulas, both in connection with pictures and statues or independently from them. In this latter instance, the practice of subjecting the godhead, a ghost, or an individual to one's will by means of a name or proper formula should also be mentioned. *Gnoseological magic* appears as a more or less autonomous type when the instrumental function of knowledge and reason becomes an end in itself. The knowledge of the right time, the right setting, the godhead proper in a given situation, is in itself sufficient reason to achieve the desired goal. The world of the sacred as a means of orientation for the growth and meaning of the person turns into a state of impersonal and mechanically effective anonymity. Ascetic technique becomes its own end, effective by its very deployment.

As a technique of reaching goals by means different from those required by these goals, magic is of particular significance for the social life of a community. In this regard we have to distinguish between official and private magic. Official magic obtains when public affairs are treated by help of magical techniques, e.g., when a drought is counteracted by the imitative act of sprinkling water, or when the office of a *shaman is a generally recognized institution. Private magic on the other hand is a matter of individuals and/or exclusive groups who, often in deep secrecy, use their knowledge and techniques in order to pursue their particular goals. Such magic very often proceeds at the expense of others; for instance, by destroying the vitality of those who are believed to be an obstacle to success. In distinction from white magic of official institutions, it is called black magic. BIBLIOGRAPHY: R. R. Marett, et al., ERE 8:245–321; W. Dupré, NCE 9:65–67; *idem, Religion in Primitive Cultures* (1970); G. B. Vetter, *Magic and Religion* (1958); B. Malinowski, *Magic, Science and Religion* (1955). *RELIGION, COMPARATIVE STUDY OF.

[W. DUPRÉ]

MAGISTERIUM, the teaching authority of the Christian Church, held by Roman Catholics to pertain by divine right to the pope and bishops as the successors of the Apostles. This authoritative teaching office in the Church was originally conferred by Jesus himself in a special way on Simon Peter as leader of the twelve Apostles (Lk 22.31; Mt 16.19; Jn 21.15–17) and upon the Apostles themselves (Mt. 18.18; 28.18–20). The Apostle Paul received the same mandate (1 Cor 9.1; Gal 1.15–16). As a group the Twelve were not only personally familiar with Jesus and the events of his ministry but were also the divinely constituted witnesses to his person and teaching, understood by them in the light of his Resurrection (Acts 1.21–22; 10.39–42; 13.31). Thus their teaching authority was exercised on the prophetic level (1 Thes 2.13). Insofar as their authority derived from personal experience of Jesus, and was endowed with a prophetic charism, their apostolic witness was not transferable. But authority to safeguard the content of their witness was transferred by them to the presbyters (elders) and *episkopoi* (overseers), as Luke indicates (Acts 14.23; 20.17–35). This tradition of authoritative teaching authority over apostolic doctrine appears in 1 Tim 6.20 and 2 Tim 1.14, where it is considered to be a key function of the *episkopoi*. They are the chief and authoritative witnesses to the content of faith, i.e., to its meaning and to its implications for conduct ("faith and morals").

In the course of time RC theologians have come to distinguish between the extraordinary magisterium and the ordinary magisterium. The former occurs when the pope alone teaches solemnly, i.e., in a formal, definitive, and public way that addresses itself to the whole Church and declares a precise meaning of God's word as binding in faith upon the Church; and when in the same manner a teaching comes from the bishops together with the pope (as in an *ecumenical council). The ordinary magisterium is exercised when the pope or bps. formulate and express the meaning of God's word in the normal course of the performance of their pastoral teaching responsibility. Both these exercises of the magisterium are authoritative and require religious assent from Roman Catholics. The extraordinary magisterium is believed by Roman Catholics to be infallible, i.e., protected from error by the assistance of the Holy Spirit, since its very aim is to articulate the meaning of God's Word in a definitive fashion; thus the extraordinary magisterium shares in the quality of *infallibility characteristic of the divine Word. The ordinary magisterium may also be infallible when the pope and bishops teach with moral unanimity, though in practice the fact that such unanimity exists is difficult to ascertain. The teaching of the ordinary magisterium, whether of the pope or bishops, is subject to revision, as the history of papal teaching on such questions as interest-taking, freedom of conscience, and the relationship of Church and State reveal. BIBLIOGRAPHY: J. R. Lerch, NCE 13:959–965; D. C. Maguire, "Moral Absolutes and the Magisterium," *Absolutes in Moral Theology* (ed. C. Curran, 1968).

[C. P. CEROKE]

MAGISTRI COMACINI, name, the first record of which is from *c.*643, for the medieval lay cathedral builders. The name refers to the region of Lake Como in Lombardy, famous for its skilled builders, many of whom were actually architects. The builders formed themselves into tightly knit organizations, keeping close the secrets of their trades, and working throughout Europe. The movement of *Freemasonry traces its origins and lore to the lodges of Italian masons and stoneworkers. BIBLIOGRAPHY: E. Carli, EncCatt 4:35–36; A. K. Porter, *Lombard Architecture* (4 v., repr. 1967).

[T. C. O'BRIEN]

MAGLIABECHI, ANTONIO (1633–1714), Florentine librarian. A goldsmith, uneducated until taught Latin, Greek, and Hebrew at age 40 by the librarian of Card. de'Medici, M. became in 1673 librarian of the Palatine. His service to scholars of Europe was astounding and he became a leading influence in the intellectual life of Florence. At his death he left his own great collection to the poor. This with the Palatine was later the basis of the National Library of Italy.

[J. R. AHERNE]

MAGLIONE, LUIGI (1877–1944), Italian cardinal and papal diplomat. Ordained in 1901, he taught at the papal diplomatic academy and worked in the secretariat of state

1907–18. During the 1920s M. was nuncio in Switzerland and France. As papal envoy in France, he supported the ban against Action Française. In 1935 he was named a cardinal, and in 1939, secretary of state—a post he held until his death. With Pius XII, M. sought to avert the outbreak of World War II. In 1940 he protested to the German government against actions in German-held foreign territories that were inimical to the Church. BIBLIOGRAPHY: R. Leiber, NCE 9:69.

[E. A. CARRILLO]

MAGLORIUS, ST. (d. *c.*595), abbot, bishop. A 9th- or 10th-cent. biography, largely legendary, makes him a pupil of *Illtud in a Welsh monastery school, and later a companion of Samson of Dol, whom he accompanied to Brittany and succeeded as abbot and bp. of Dol. He spent his last years as abbot of a monastery on the island of Sark. BIBLIOGRAPHY: Butler 4:192–93; J. Evenou, BiblSanct 8:534–536.

[G. M. COOK]

MAGNA CARTA, a charter issued by King John of England in 1215. At Runnymede, Surrey, June 15, 1215, barons, clergy, townsmen, Scots, and Welsh combined to force John to put his seal to what was later called Magna Carta, the Great Charter. New versions were drawn up (1216, 1217, 1225) and the charter was entered in the Statutes of the Realm (1297). It reaffirmed the underlying principle of the feudal contract, that the king has obligations under the law and is not above it, and included a guarantee of the liberties of the Church; provisions concerning services and incidents of feudal land-tenure; provisions, some of them highly important, concerning administration of justice; and miscellaneous provisions concerning towns and trade, debts and estates, forests, abuses by local officials, and correction of the King's past wrongs. A long provision for enforcement proved ineffective. Often appealed to in the later Middle Ages, the charter was largely forgotten in Tudor times: Shakespeare's *King John* nowhere mentions it. Its revival came with protests by Sir Edward Coke and others against 17th-cent. Stuart tyranny. Given interpretations not originally intended, the charter was dubbed ''cornerstone of English liberties.'' Its influence spread with the British Empire, proving esp. strong in nations, such as the U.S. and Australia, whose governments are based on the principle of separation of powers. BIBLIOGRAPHY: E. John, NCE 9:69–70; A. E. Dick Howard, *Magna Carta: Text and Commentary* (1964), and other ''Magna Carta Essays'' published for the Magna Carta Commission of Virginia; Sir Ivor Jennings, *Magna Carta and Its Influence in the World Today* (1965).

[R. W. HAYS]

MAGNANIMITY, the virtue, recognized by Aristotle and other philosophers of antiquity, that regulates and controls a man's appetite for honor and glory. The virtuous man will not strive for a greatness that is beyond his powers, but neither will he allow timidity or disinterest to discourage the attempt to make his accomplishment measure up to the greatness of his potential. Judaism and Christianity saw no value in honor or glory except to the extent that it serves the interest of the honor and glory due to God; ''Not to us, O Lord, not to us, but to thy name give glory'' (Ps 113 [115] .1). Nevertheless, when the Aristotelian classification of moral virtue was taken over in Christian theology it was found possible to make room for this virtue along with the others, although some adaptation was necessary. A Christian could not see the honor and glory that come to a man from his fellow mortals as things worthy of pursuit on their own account. The desire that Christian magnanimity moderates must have as its object excellence itself and not the honor and glory with which its achievement is sometimes rewarded. A Christian can rightly aspire to excellence; indeed he is commanded to be perfect as his heavenly Father is perfect (Mt 5.48). A spirit of magnanimity is needed therefore to accompany, inspire, and animate the practice of all the virtues. Superficially magnanimity may seem to be in conflict with humility, but on closer inspection the two virtues are revealed as complementary to each other. Without the dynamism of the desire for excellence, humility would be a paralyzing thing; without humility's evaluation of excellence as the work and gift of God, pride would corrupt what magnanimity achieves. BIBLIOGRAPHY: ThAq ST 2a2ae, 129–133; A. Gauthier, ''Fortitude,'' TL 4:489–532, esp. 493–505, 521–524.

[P. K. MEAGHER]

MAGNASCO, ALESSANDRO (1667–1749), Genoese painter active also in Milan and Florence, using nervous, splintery brush strokes and exaggerated proportions. He depicted peasants, mountebanks, and religious themes (*Baptism of Christ*, Washington, D.C.), violent activity on stormy seacoasts, or among ruins; monks in agonized penitential prayer, their religious fervor and grotesque anatomy sometimes approaching caricature (*Landscape with Wandering Monks*, Milan). M.'s flickering surfaces give, at one instant, a sense of intense mysticism (*S. Carlo Borromeo Receiving Oblates,* Milan), and again, a sense of the grotesque (*Inquisition Scene,* Vienna). M.'s style invigorated Venetian 18th-cent. painting.

[K. B. NEILSON]

MAGNERICUS OF TRIER, ST. (d. 596), abp. of Trier. M. was associated with Abp. Nicetius of Trier, whom he accompanied into exile when Nicetius was banished by Clotaire I. Six years after they returned from exile M. succeeded Nicetius. He founded the monastery of St. Martin of Tours and several churches. He was a friend of Saint Gregory of Tours. BIBLIOGRAPHY: Butler 3:188–189.

[J. R. RIVELLO]

MAGNI, VALERIANO (1586–1661), Bohemian Capuchin, diplomat and missionary, active during the

Thirty Years' War. Born in Prague, he entered the Capuchin Order in 1602 and won almost instant recognition for his preaching. As a teacher of philosophy at Vienna and Prague, he also wrote philosophical works; later in his career he participated in the controversies with the Protestants through his theological writings. He is better known, however, for the role he played in the affairs of the Holy Roman Empire throughout the religio-political crisis of the 17th century. In 1616 he became head of the Capuchin mission to Poland during the reign of Sigismund III. In 1629 he was appointed apostolic missionary to Bohemia by Urban VIII, with the task of restoring the faith to that area, and a year later served as papal delegate to the Diet of Ratisbon. In 1634 he mediated between the emperor (Ferdinand II), the pope, and General Wallenstein. Again named apostolic missionary in 1643, M. succeeded in reestablishing the Church in Saxony and Hesse by 1652. A man of his times, he was involved in disputes with the landgrave of Rheinfels and the Jesuits, which led to his imprisonment in 1655.

[E. M. GATES]

MAGNIEN, ALPHONSE (1837–1902), educator. A French diocesan priest ordained in 1862, M. joined the Sulpicians. In 1869 he came to St. Mary's Seminary, Baltimore, Md. As teacher and for 33 years rector of the seminary, he created a prestigious institution. The Sulpicians took over the direction of seminaries in New York, Boston, and San Francisco. He brought the Sulpicians to The Catholic Univ. of America. M. was a principal adviser to Cardinal Gibbons for 25 years.

[J. R. AHERNE]

MAGNIFICAT, see CANTICLE OF OUR LADY.

MAGNIFICENCE, a virtue described by Aristotle as controlling the expenditure of money on works befitting great wealth (*Ethics* 5.2); one of the virtues required, then, for the honorable use of riches. *Generosity or liberality guards against the demeaning attitudes of *avarice or against the irresponsibility in *prodigality. Magnificence is more concerned with external works accomplished by the honorable use of money. Its exercise presumes wealth; its purpose is that the rich man seek uses for his wealth in projects of grandeur, taste, elegance, without vulgar display or meanness, and with style appropriate to the work intended. Such a virtue may show itself in building a home appropriate to station in life; in supporting the arts; in subsidizing public buildings of architectural merit; in the quality of hospitality or gift-giving. Because of Aristotle, St. Thomas Aquinas includes magnificence among the virtues, and allies it to *courage, on the grounds of its concern for great deeds. But like Aristotle's *magnanimity, this virtue has to be Christianized; its purpose is given, therefore, as honoring and glorifying God (ThAq ST 2a2ae, 134.2 ad 3). It can be thought of, at least hopefully, as the ideal of those who have enriched Christian and humane civilization by patronage of art and architecture.

[T. C. O'BRIEN]

MAGNOBOD OF ANGERS ST. (*c.*574–after 635), bishop. His aptitude for studies and love of prayer moved Bp. Licinius to ordain him to the priesthood. About 610 Magnobod succeeded Licinius as bp. of Angers and proved himself a zealous bp. and capable administrator. BIBLIOGRAPHY: J. Campbell, LTK 6:1286; H. Dressler, NCE 9:74; G. Mathon, BiblSanct 8:558–559.

[H. DRESSLER]

MAGNUS, SS., the name of several saints. (1) St. Magnus of Orkney (Magnus Erlingsson; d. 1116), the son of one of the two brothers (Paul and Erling) who ruled the Orkney Islands in the second half of the 11th century. He led a life of penitence and prayer to repent for the excesses of his youth, and was murdered for political reasons by his cousin Haakon on the island of Egilsay. He is revered as a martyr, and many churches in the area are named in his honor. (2) St. Magnus of Füssen (d. 772), apostle of the Algäu, patron of Füssen and Kempten; popular folk saint honored under the name St. Mang in S Germany, Tirol, and Switzerland. He is invoked against snakes, vermin, and mice. He was called from Sankt Gallen by Bp. Wichpert of Augsburg to evangelize the Algäu; and with the aid of King Pepin he converted the heathen and cleared the land for cultivation. (3) St. Magnus, martyr commemorated August 19, is sometimes called M. of Fabrateria (now Ceccano). He is thought to have been bp. of Trani in Apuleia, and to have died under Decius. In another legend he is M. from Caesarea in Cappadocia, who died under Aurelian. BIBLIOGRAPHY: Butler 2:103; D. Andreini, NCE 9:74; F. Zoepfl, LTK 6:1286–87; A. P. Frutaz, LTK 6:1286

[E. J. DILLON]

MAGNUS OF SENS (fl. early 9th cent.), abp. of Sens, consecrated at Rome by Leo III (801) while accompanying Charlemagne to the Holy See. A close confidant of Charlemagne, M. wrote his *Libellus de mysterio baptismatis* in response to the Emperor's treatise on baptism, *De ordine baptismi,* which had been dedicated to M. and which the latter circulated among his suffragans. Both documents shed light on the reality and the theory of the 9th-cent. catechumenate. G. Bareille, DTC 2:1894; S. A. Bennett, DCB 3:784.

[E. J. DILLON]

MAGNUS, JOHANNES (1488–1544) and **OLAUS** (1490–1558), Swedish brothers, both of whom were churchmen and historians. After serving as a diplomat in Rome, Johannes was elected abp. of Uppsala in 1523, but was deprived of the post by Gustavus I following the latter's conversion to Protestantism. J. was the author of the posthumously published *Historia de omnibus Gothorum Sveonumque regibus* (1554), a patriotic but uncritical work, and of *Historia metropolitanae ecclesiae Upsaliensis* (1560). Out of loyalty to Catholicism, both brothers exiled themselves after the triumph of the Reformation in Sweden, eventually settling in Rome. On the death of Johannes, Olaus succeeded him in the then purely titular archiepiscopal see of Upsala and in 1546 was commissioned by Pope Paul III to attend the Council of Trent. He is better known, however, for his contributions to humanistic learning. As a mapmaker, he greatly extended the cartographer's knowledge of Scandinavia with his *Carta marina,* published in Venice in 1539; while his lively and wide-ranging *Historia de gentibus septentrionalibus,* a compendium of Scandinavian history, folklore, and customs, published in Rome in 1554, had a fundamental impact on historiography and long remained an authoritative guide to the peoples of northern Europe.

[E. M. GATES]

MAGRATH, JOHN MACRORY (Eoghan Mac Ruadhri Mac Craith), Irish historian of the 15th century. Born at Munster of a literary family, M. became noted poet and historian of the Dal Cais in Thomond and wrote of the wars of Turlough (1194–1318), the *Cathreim Thoirdhealbhaigh,* a work fashioned on the *Cath Catharda,* the Middle-Irish prose version of the *Bellum civile* of Lucan. BIBLIOGRAPHY: R. T. Meyer, NCE 9:75.

[R. T. MEYER]

MAGUIRE, CATHAL MACMAGHNUSSA (1439–98), Irish priest-scholar and historian. M. was rector of Inishkeen. He collected MSS and compiled the *Annals of Ulster (Annala Senait),* covering the period 431–1498. After his death the annals were extended to 1541 and were used later by the Four Masters. BIBLIOGRAPHY: R. T. Meyer, NCE 9:75.

[M. J. FINNEGAN]

MAGUIRE, CHARLES BONAVENTURE (1768–1833), missionary. An Irish Franciscan, M. worked among the Germans in the Netherlands, then came to the U.S. in 1817. He was assigned to the Pittsburgh area where he enjoyed great success in pastoral work. He built the church that later became the cathedral of the new Diocese of Pittsburgh. M. published *A Defense of the Divinity of Jesus Christ and of the Mystery of the Real Presence* (1825).

[J. R. AHERNE]

MAGUSAIOI, a Greek word coined to designate the Hellenized Magi, to whom a copious literature in Greek dealing with astrology, magic, and Oriental occult lore is attributed. While definite contacts were made between Greek and Iranian thought esp. in Asia Minor in the Hellenistic Age, there is very little evidence that the writers of such pseudo-scientific works had any real knowledge of Iranian religion or cosmic speculation. Under the influence of this literature the term *magus* among the Greeks after Alexander, and among the Romans, came to designate an astrologer, magician, or sorcerer. BIBLIOGRAPHY: J. Duchesne-Guillemin, *La Religion de l'Iran ancien* (1962) 245–246; *id.,* NCE 9:61; J. Bidez and F. Cumont, *Les Mages hellénisés* (1938).

[M. R. P. GUIRE]

MAGYARS, ethnic name of the nation commonly referred to as Hungary. In the language of the Hungarians, Magyar is the name both of the nation and the language. Magyar belongs to the Uralic language family which includes Finno-Ugric and Samoyed. Closest to Magyar are the Vogul and Ostyak languages; other members of the family are Cheremis, Mordvin, Lettish, Lappish, Estonian, and Finnish. Of the distant origins of the nation and its language little can be said with certainty, although in recent years striking similarities between Hungarian and Sumerian have come to light. Both are agglutinative—form new words by adding numerous suffixes to the root; both are predicative—the predicate tends to absorb the functions of all the rest of the sentence; both lack grammatical gender, etc. Legends and heroic myths of the Magyars have traditionally placed their ancestral homeland in the region of the Black Sea; myths of their close kin, the Finns, show remarkable affinity to Sumerian myths, and Magyar folklore lends support to a need for further research in this area, with the Magi as a promising link between the two cultures. In historical times, the Finno-Ugric family resided on the European side of the Ural mountains up to about the time of the birth of Christ. At this time, the Finnish branch of the family moved to their present homeland, while the ancestors of the Magyars crossed the Urals into Asia. After 8 centuries of wandering, they recrossed the Urals and settled in their present homeland in A.D. 896. During their wanderings, they added Turkish and Iranian loan-words to their vocabulary and adapted a runic alphabet, scattered use of which survived until recently. The Roman alphabet is used; a clear distinction is maintained between long and short vowels, making Hungarian one of the most phonetic languages. Spelling and pronunciation are consistent with each other; there are no silent letters or slurred syllables. The accent of every word always falls on the first syllable, and vocal harmony prevails. In a person's name, the family name precedes the Christian name. BIBLIOGRAPHY: J. Lotz, *Das ungarische Sprachsystem* (1939); M. Zsiray, *Finnugor rokonságunk (Our Finno-Ugric Relationships,* 1937); I. Bobula, *Sumerian Affiliations* (1951); C. A. Macartney, *Magyars in the Ninth Century* (1930, repr. 1969). *HUNGARY; *FINNO-UGRIC RELIGION.

[D. H. BRUNAUER]

MAHABHARATA, great (Sanskrit, *mahā*) Indian epic of the Bharata clan, originally centering on the wars of succession between the two lines of descendants, the Pandavas (esp. the sons Yudisthira, Bhima, and Arjuna) and the Kurus or Kauravas (esp. the son Duryodhana). During the long history of retelling and rewriting the basic narrative (from 400 B.C. to 400 A.D.), the saga became the center of cycles of additional legends, poems, hymns, and lessons, eventually growing to its present massive size (nearly 100,000 double lines of verse). The epic's most famous and important inclusion is the **Bhagavad Gita* [Song of God] the occasion for which is *Krishna's urging on of Arjuna, who is reluctant to fight. Among the *Mahabharata's* many significant, though sometimes inevitably inconsistent, teachings are its emphasis on *dharma, or duty, and its presentation of Krishna as warrior. BIBLIOGRAPHY: J. A. B. van Buitenen, *Mahabharata* (v.1, 1973); R. C. Zaehner, *Hinduism* (1966).

[D. P. EFROYMSON]

MAHANAIM, city of Gilead in the area assigned to Gad (Jos 13.24–30; 21.38). Meaning two camps, the name is said to have been given by Jacob when he saw angels there (Gen 32.3). Ish-bosheth and his army took refuge there (2 Sam 2), as did David later (2 Sam 17.24). The site has not been identified with certainty.

[T. EARLY]

MAHAYANA (Sanskrit *mahā,* great; *yāna,* vehicle), originally the self-designation of a Buddhist tradition developing in NW India (100 B.C.–600 A.D.). It opposed what its adherents called the self-centered and limited teaching of their opponents (whom they called the *Hinayana). The term has come to be used more inclusively to refer to northern Buddhism generally (in China, Korea, Japan, Tibet), which developed from the Indian tradition; here it is distinguished from the *Theravada, the form of Buddhism prevalent in SE Asia. Mahayana's hallmark is its distinctive literature (the "Perfection of Wisdom" or *Prajnaparamita, Lotus,* and *Vimalakirti* treatises or sutras being important). The most significant teachings include: the Bodhisattva (the "enlightened being" whose unsurpassed wisdom and compassion lead him to work for the salvation of all, rather than the elite few) as the ideal for all Buddhists; a mythological doctrine of many Buddhas and heavenly Bodhisattvas who help humans to salvation, the most famous being Amitabha (Jap., *Amida*), the Buddha of infinite compassion, the center of devotion in *Amidism or "Pure Land" Buddhism; a mystical-metaphysical doctrine on "emptiness" *(sunyata),* an absolute, transcendent reality beyond the grasp of intellect or verbal expression which, as the focus of meditation, leads to an attitude of perfect even-mindedness (this is the teaching of the Madhyamika school, esp. of Nagarjuna). BIBLIOGRAPHY: E. Conze, *Buddhist Thought in India* (1967); D. T. Suzuki, *On Indian Mahayana Buddhism* (1968); K. K. Ch'en, *Buddhism in China* (1964); E. D. Saunders, *Buddhism in Japan* (1964).

[D. P. EFROYMSON]

MAHDĪ, AL- (Arab. *al-mahdī,* the rightly guided one), a term sometimes employed as an honorific title for important religious persons, but also used from an early period in orthodox Islam, esp. in popular religion, to designate an eschatological figure who will come, after a period of complete moral and religious decline, to restore the true faith to its original purity and to establish a final era of justice and plenty. The Mahdi is not infrequently identified with Jesus (Arab. *'Îsà*), though most commonly it is held that Jesus, whose chief function in the popular eschatology is to destroy the antichrist *(al-dajjâl),* will follow the Mahdi. Among the *Shiites the term is frequently applied to the *Imam, particularly in reference to the return of the "hidden Imam." The title has been assumed by a number of would-be reformers, including Mohammed Ahmad, who initiated the Mahdist revolt in the Sudan in 1881. BIBLIOGRAPHY: D. B. Macdonald, EncIslam[1].

[R. M. FRANK]

MAHER, MICHAEL (1860–1917), Irish Jesuit, philosopher, psychologist. Ordained in 1894, M. taught philosophy at Stonyhurst and became superior of the seminary. His study, *Psychology: Empirical and Rational* (1890) was widely used as a text in Catholic institutions for 30 years. He served as examiner at the National Univ. and the Royal Univ. (Dublin); he also spent years in charge of students at the Univ. of Edinburgh. Among other books, M. wrote *English Economics and Catholic Ethics* (1912); he was a contributor to the CE.

[J. R. AHERNE]

MAI, ANGELO (1782–1854), Italian cardinal and paleographer. As a young Jesuit, M. became famous for his discoveries of lost works of pagan and early Christian authors in the Ambrosian Library of Milan of which he was a scriptor. Many of his discoveries were in the form of palimpsests. In 1819, M. left the Jesuits to become the prefect of the Vatican Library and was made a cardinal in 1838. In his work at the Vatican Library, he arranged and catalogued its MSS and continued to bring lost works to light. M. is credited with the discovery of 359 such works in the course of his career. BIBLIOGRAPHY: F. X. Murphy, NCE 9:79; C. Testore, EncCatt 7:1851–52.

[R. B. ENO]

MAILLA, JOSEPH ANNE MARIE MOYRIA DE (1669–1748), missionary, Chinese expert, mapmaker. A French noble, M. entered the Jesuits in 1686 and went to China in 1701. He became proficient in Cantonese and made a number of translations of religious works into Chinese. One of three Jesuits selected by the emperor to map a number of Chinese provinces, M. was rewarded by being named a Mandarin. Mastering the Mandarin language M. translated the history of the empire into French, a work included in Grosier's *Histoire générale de la Chine* ... (1777–85). At his death M. received a state funeral in Peking.

[J. R. AHERNE]

MAIMBOURG, LOUIS (1610–86), historian, polemicist. A French Jesuit, M. was noted esp. for his works against the Jansenists and Protestants. His publications, despite their intent to defend Catholicism, frequently ended on the *Index*—because of their Gallicanism—*Histoire du grand schisme d'occident* (1678) and *Histoire du pontificat de St. Grégoire le Grand* (2v., 1686) among others. Such other works as *Histoire de l'arianisme* (2v., 1673) and *Histoire du schisme des Grecs* (2v., 1677) escaped condemnation. In 1682 Pope Innocent XI expelled him from the Jesuits and he was given a pension by Louis XIV; he spent his last years at Saint-Victor in Paris working on a history of Anglican orders, but died before its completion.

[J. R. AHERNE]

MAIMONIDES (Moses ben Maimon; 1135–1204), the most renowned Jewish philosopher of the Middle Ages, known to the Arabs as Ibn-Maymun and to rabbinic writers as Rambam, the acronym for Rabbi Moses ben Maimon, 'Maimonides' being the Latinized cognomen. Born at Cordova, Spain, of an illustrious Jewish family, he received a comprehensive education in Hebrew literature from his father, Maimon ben Joseph, a distinguished Talmudist. In 1149, an anti-Jewish persecution under the Muslim rule forced the family to emigrate to Morocco where M. wrote his *Epistle on Apostasy* to strengthen his coreligionists against Islamic beliefs. In 1165, the family settled in Palestine and shortly thereafter in Fostat, a suburb of Cairo, where M. became the *nagid,* or accepted leader, of Egyptian Jewry.

Gifted as a scholar, he acquired a knowledge of theology, philosophy, mathematics, astronomy, and medicine, becoming court physician to Saladin and producing writings of importance in various of these fields. His greatest work in rabbinic scholarship is his *Mishneh Torah* (Second Law) also called *Yad Ḥazakah* (Strong Hand). Written in Hebrew in 1180, it sets forth a systematic presentation of the whole of the rabbinic tradition, a Talmudic codification of 14 books. All of his other publications were in Arabic including his famous *Commentary on the Mishnah* (1168), called *Siraj* (Luminary), a notable contribution in exegesis. But because of the *Mishneh Torah,* M. was and is esteemed as a commanding authority on Jewish religious law.

From youth, M. was attracted by Aristotelian philosophy as taught by the renowned Islamic philosophers, al-Farabi (*c.*873–950) and Avicenna (980–1037), so much so that at the age of 16 he composed *Treatise on the Terminology of Logic* (1151). But this interest in Aristotle is reflected principally in his major opus, *Guide of the Perplexed* (1190), or *Moreh Nebuhim* which set forth his mature philosophic thought and had a considerable influence upon both Jewish and Christian scholarship in the Middle Ages. Seeking to interpret rabbinic theology within the context of Neoplatonic Aristotelianism, it aimed basically at a harmony between faith and reason by achieving a practical synthesis of Jewish revelation and the philosophy of Aristotle. Among other items of a similar nature, it deals with man's concept of God, arguments for his existence, the problem of evil, Divine Providence, and knowledge, and the world of spirits. In some important respects, M.'s philosophical system resembles that of Averroës (*c.* 1126–*c.* 1198), the Muslim philosopher of Cordova. Among its more significant positions, it recognizes both human freedom of will and the rule of Divine Providence over humanity, emphasizing the place of natural laws to which man is subject. Only the soul of man is immortal so that the beatitude of the just is an incorporeal one. It is impossible to define or describe God's essence but existence is implied in it. The use of negative theology is quite prominent in M. since he holds that it is impossible for man to know anything positive about God's essence in that it has nothing in common with other beings. M. proves the existence of God with the arguments of the Unmoved Mover and necessity-contingency. He accepts Aristotle's cosmology in broad outlines but rejects his doctrine of the eternity of the world. Moreover, M. maintains that religious revelation does not give any knowledge of truth which cannot be acquired by the human intellect. Man's purpose is that of loving God and resembling him insofar as that is possible.

M.'s writings have been reprinted repeatedly since 15th cent., but there is no collected edition. The principal edition of *The Guide* (Arabic text) is that of S. Munk with a French translation and valuable notes (3 v., 1856–66); Eng. tr. by M. Friedländer, (3 v., 1881–85). The *Mishneh Torah* exists in Eng. (incomplete) by J. Rabinowitz, et al, (Yale Judaica Series, ed. J. Obermann, 1949–).

[J. T. HICKEY]

MAINAGE, THOMAS (1878–1931), French Dominican scholar; professor of the history of religions at the Institut Catholique in Paris. Born at Caen, he entered the Dominicans in 1898 and was professor of Scripture at Le Saulchoir before coming to the Institut. His books include a major study of Buddhism, a critical analysis of theosophy and the occult, a collection of essays on the problem of life after death, and a study of the religion of cavemen and prehistory. His special interest seems to have been the psychology of conversion and apostasy, about which he wrote three major works between 1913 and 1919. BIBLIOGRAPHY: H. D. Gardeil, DTC Tables générales, 3065.

[E. J. DILLON]

MAINE DE BIRAN, FRANÇOIS (1766–1824), French philosopher and psychologist. After college studies at Périgueux, M. entered the Royal Life Guards in 1785, defended Louis XVI (1789), and then retired to his estate at Grateloup (1793) to avoid the turmoil of the Revolution. In his retirement he gave himself to the study of philosophy, psychology, and mathematics. He became a member of the Council of the Five Hundred (1797), of the Corps Legislatif (1809), and opposed the rule of Napoleon (1813). After the Restoration he was appointed treasurer to the Chamber of

Deputies. M.'s philosophy is marked by a perceptive interest in the inner life of man. First identified with the French ideologues who amplified the empiricism of J. *Locke, he gradually became disillusioned, and his writings show a growing appreciation of the prominence of the human will in the development of thought. Typical of this trend is his first significant essay, *The Influence of Habit on Thought* (1802). Later works stress the analysis of self and the secondary function of sensation in thinking, e.g., *The Analysis of Thought* (1805), which won him membership in the Institute of France. M. cites the experience of willing the movement of the human body as the basic instance of causation known in man's awareness. In this he sees the foundation of human liberty of action. He rejects Cartesian dualism and all deterministic arguments, contending that the will is capable of rejecting any desire or motivation. Works: *Oeuvres de Maine de Biran,* (ed. P. Tisserand and H. Gouhier, 14 v., 1921–42). BIBLIOGRAPHY: G. Boas, *French Philosophies of the Romantic Period* (1925), F. C. Moore, *Psychology of Maine De Biran* (1970).

[J. T. HICKEY]

MAINE, a New England state admitted to the Union as the 23d state in 1820 as part of the Missouri Compromise. The area was probably explored by John and Sebastian Cabot, 1498–99, and numerous English and French adventurers landed on its rocky coasts during the early 17th century. French colonists led by Sieur de Monts made the first permanent settlement on St. Croix Island in 1604. George Popham and Raleigh Gilbert founded the first English settlement at the mouth of the Sagadahoc (now Kennebec) River in 1607. Jesuit and Anglican missionaries accompanied their European compatriots in order to labor among the Indians; the first Jesuit mission in North America, at Mount Desert, was founded in 1613 to further this work. After Massachusetts obtained control over Maine in 1677, however, the Congregational Church became the major denomination, a status it retained until the end of the 19th century. Three Shaker settlements were also established during this century, at Alfred, Gorham, and New Gloucester. The major impetus to Catholic growth was afforded by 19th-cent. French and Irish immigration. In 1853 the Diocese of Portland was created as a suffragan of Boston and given jurisdiction over all of Maine. By 1860 the Catholic population reached 35,000 in a state population of 628,000. Maine's population has grown slowly. Ranking 38th among the states, it showed (1970 U.S. Census) 993,663 people, more than half of whom resided in urban centers. In 1976 Catholics numbered 265,620, or approx. 26.7% of the total state population. The major Protestant sects are the American Baptist Convention, with 4.2% of the total pop. in 1971, and the United Church of Christ with approximately 3.9%. Other Protestant denominations comprised 9.4% of the population. There are two Catholic colleges in Me. with a total enrollment of 931 students. Some 1,246 students attend the state's 4 Catholic high schools, and almost 6,702 are enrolled in 23 Catholic elementary schools. BIBLIOGRAPHY: L. D. Rich, *State o' Maine* (1964); W. L. Lucey, *Catholic Church in Maine* (1957); E. C. Helmreich, *Religion and the Maine Schools: An Historical Approach* (1960).

[J. L. MORRISON; R. M. PRESTON]

MAINTENON, FRANCOISE D'AUBIGNE DE (1635–1719), wife of Louis XIV, educator. She was baptized a Catholic, brought up as a Huguenot by an aunt, then was converted to Catholicism. M. spent years of privation until her marriage in 1651 to the literary figure Paul Scarron. M. became a favorite in literary circles and through the influence of the King's mistress was chosen to educate his illegitimate children. She was widowed in 1660 and became part of the royal court in 1674 and was given the title Marquise de Maintenon. She became a favorite of the King and in 1683 was secretly married to him. Her influence on Louis XIV was powerful, though she has suffered in history from the slander of political foes. M. esp. influenced Louis and the court in moral and religious ways. She gave its character to the famous Institut de Saint-Louis at Saint-Cyr, a school for girls of which she was the planner and sometimes administrator. She was the author of essays on education. BIBLIOGRAPHY: J. Cordelier, *Madame de Maintenon* (1955).

[J. R. AHERNE]

MAINZ CATHOLIC CONVENTION, a meeting of Catholics in Germany that convened in 1848, simultaneously with the Frankfurt Assembly. Though suppression engulfed the work of the Assembly, the fruits of this first German Catholic convention were lasting. It was the first coming together of Catholics, clerical and lay, to discuss issues of social reform and of proletarian distress. Ritter von Buss and Emmanuel von Ketteler, later bp. of Mainz, were the principal speakers. The first, more conservative, stressed the need for caritative institutions and gave impetus to their development, so notable an aspect of German Catholic life since that time. Ketteler, who had left the Prussian Civil Service for the priesthood, was a man of experience, profound insight into the problem of poverty, and an advocate of social justice. The Convention did not immediately endorse his views but his influence on subsequent German Catholic thinking is undeniable. Accordingly, the Mainz Catholic Convention may not unrealistically be considered a first step toward Leo XIII's Encyclical, *Rerum Novarum*. BIBLIOGRAPHY: *Church and Society* (ed. J. N. Moody, 1953).

[G. N. SHUSTER]

MAIR, MARTIN (*c.* 1420–80), German jurist and diplomat who studied at Heidelberg. M. served as chancellor of the newly founded Univ. of Ingolstadt under Louis of Bavaria. In the employ of several German princes, in 1457 he listed the *gravamina* (complaints) of the Germans against the Roman Curia. He sought to set up King George Poděbrad, the Czech Hussite, as a partner and real ruler with Emperor Frederick III, but sided with the papacy when Poděbrad was excommunicated for heresy.

[J. E. LYNCH]

MAISON-DIEU, see HOTEL (MAISON-DIEU).

MAISONNEUVE, LA, see HÉROET, ANTOINE.

MAISONNEUVE, PAUL DE CHOMEDEY (1612–76), founder of Montreal. M. first went to Canada (1641) as the leader of the party sent by the Société de Notre Dame de Montréal to plant a colony at the site of Montréal. Except for brief visits to France (1645; 1651–53), M. directed the struggle of the Montreal settlers for survival against Iroquis raids and natural calamities until his recall to France (1665). He died in obscurity in Paris. BIBLIOGRAPHY: R. Le Blant, "Les Derniers jours de Maisonneuve et Philippe de Turmenyes," *Revue d'Histoire de l'Amérique Française* 13 (1959–60) 263–280.

[R. K. MacMASTER]

MAISTRE, JOSEPH MARIE DE (1753–1821), statesman and ultramontane apologist. Uprooted by French Revolutionary armies (1792), he went into exile, later serving as Sardinian minister plenipotentiary to Russia (1803–17). Jesuit-educated, M., though originally influenced by illuminism, Freemasonry, and liberalism, reacted against republican ideology, and defended legitimacy, autocracy, and religious authority. His political philosophy rests on (1) the principle that authority is divine; (2) Burke's notion that the body of national tradition guarantees the organic continuity of the State; and (3) the postulate that man's fallen nature makes democratic government unrealizable. His affirmation of both papal infallibility in spiritual matters (relegating Church councils to an advisory role) and papal supremacy over secular authority, which in turn is absolute in its own domain, is expounded in his masterpiece, *Du pape* (2 v., 1818–19). BIBLIOGRAPHY: *Works of Joseph de Maistre* (tr. J. Lively, 1965); A. Caponigri, *Some Aspects of the Philosophy of Joseph de Maistre* (1945); F. Bayle, *Les Idées philosophiques de J. de Maistre* (1945).

[G. E. GINGRAS]

MAITANI, LORENZO (before 1270–1330), Sienese architect and sculptor, remembered as most important for his work as *capomaestro*, on the façade of Orviete Cathedral (1310–30), including the documented bronze symbol of St. John the Evangelist, in a style showing the direct influence of Giovanni Pisano's *Symbols of the Evangelists,* Siena, and indirectly that of northern Gothic linear sculpture in certain details of M.'s *Scenes from Genesis* and *Last Judgment*. BIBLIOGRAPHY: J. White, *Art and Architecture in Italy: 1250–1400* (1966).

[L. A. LEITE]

MAJELLA, GERARD, ST. (1726–55), Italian Redemptorist lay brother, mystic. An orphan, M. led a wretched life under two masters. In 1749 he was admitted to the Redemptorists as a lay brother. The 6 years remaining in his life were marked by mystical phenomena and miraculous works. M. was canonized in 1904. He is invoked as patron of mothers.

[J. R. AHERNE]

MAJESTAS (MAESTÀ), representation of Christ in Majesty in an aureole (mandorla) surrounded by the four evangelical symbols, a frequent subject of Romanesque architectural sculpture (St. Trophime, Arles; St. Pierre, Moissac; St. Sernin, Toulouse). The term is applied also to the *Virgin Enthroned* surrounded by angels—as seen in early Italian works (Duccio's *Maestà* now in the Cathedral Museum, Siena).

[M. J. DALY]

MAJOLUS OF CLUNY, ST. (*c.*910–994), Benedictine abbot. M. was esp. renowned for his energetic direction of Cluny. Availing himself of close personal relations with contemporary sovereigns, M. traveled widely to spread the Cluniac reform. He was a great promoter of studies and exercised powerful influence on his contemporaries. BIBLIOGRAPHY: J. Hourlier and M. C. Celletti, BiblSanct 8:564–567; S. Hilpisch, LTK 6:1307.

[F. D. LAZENBY]

MAJOR, GEORG, see MAJORISTIC CONTROVERSY.

MAJOR ORDERS, see HOLY ORDERS.

MAJOR PROPHETS, Isaiah, Jeremiah, Ezekiel, and Daniel. The distinction between major and *minor prophets goes back to St. Augustine (*City of God* 18.29) and is based simply on the longer length of the books ascribed to the four prophets called major. Daniel is included on the basis of the Septuagint and Vulgate tradition.

[T. C. O'BRIEN]

MAJOR SUPERIORS, in canon law: an abbot primate; abbot general of a monastic congregation; abbot of a monastery; the general superior of a religious order or congregation; the provincial superior; the vicars of all of these; any other superiors having rank equivalent to that of provincial (CIC c. 488, n.8).

[T. C. O'BRIEN]

MAJORDOMO, formerly (until 1929) a member of the papal court charged with overseeing the papal household.

[T. C. O'BRIEN]

MAJORISTIC CONTROVERSY, the Lutheran dispute over *good works (1552–77), named for Georg Major (Maier; 1502–74) a polemicist and professor of theology who, influenced by Philipp Melanchthon's ideas, advanced the thesis that good works are necessary to salvation, at least in the sense of being required to preserve it. The position was bitterly attacked as in opposition to Luther's *justification by faith alone (see FLACIUS ILLYRICUS, M.; GNESIOLUTHERANISM). N. Amsdorf (1483–1565) went so far as to assert that good works are a danger to salvation. Major sought to defend himself against charges of Pelagianism or Romanism, and refrained from using the expression "necessary for salvation" after 1558, but the controversy continued. The *Formula of Concord (1577) settled the matter (Art. IV), affirming that good works will be done by the regenerate freely and spontaneously in testimony to the presence of the Holy Spirit; they neither cause nor merit salvation or its preservation; nor are they detrimental. *GOOD WORKS.

[P. DAMBORIENA]

MAKARA, fabulous sea animal, appearing in Hindu art as the vehicle of Varuna, is a composite beast with head and forelegs of an antelope, body and tail of a fish—with some resemblance to a crocodile or dolphin.

[M. J. DALY]

MAKARII, METROPOLITAN OF MOSCOW, see BULGAKOV, MAKARII.

MAKEMIE, FRANCIS (d. 1708), Presbyterian clergyman and pioneer organizer of the denomination in America. Born in Ireland, M. served in Barbados as a minister until he moved to Maryland, where he organized one of the first American Presbyterian congregations in 1684 at Snow Hill. Marriage brought him the status and leisure of a gentleman, and he was able to go about preaching throughout Virginia and the Carolinas. He was so successful that with other ministers he was able to organize the first *presbytery in Philadelphia in 1706; he became its moderator. In 1707 he won the sympathy of colonial Dissenters when he was imprisoned for preaching in New York without a proper license; he was acquitted under the 1689 *Toleration Act.

[J. H. SMYLIE]

MAL DU SIÈCLE, term describing the sense of ennui, melancholy, revery, and unrealizable yearnings for the infinite characteristic of Romanticism. A state of moral crisis rooted in the late 18th-cent. reaction against the Enlightenment, it was diagnosed by Chateaubriand as religious in origin, studied respectively from a metaphysical and psychological point of view by Senancour and Constant, and analyzed by de Musset as a generation-wide moral malady. Expressed in countless variations by numerous authors, it was given final embodiment in the Baudelairean notion of spleen with *Les Fleurs du mal* (1857). BIBLIOGRAPHY: A. Hoog, "Who Invented the Mal du Siècle?" *Yale French Studies* 13 (1954) 42–51; I. Babbitt, *Rousseau and Romanticism* (1919), esp. the ch., "Romantic Melancholy."

[G. E. GINGRAS]

MALABAR CHRISTIANS, see ST. THOMAS CHRISTIANS.

MALABAR LITURGY. Persian or Chaldean missionaries brought the Gospel to the Malabar Coast of India (see ST. THOMAS CHRISTIANS) and with it their own liturgical traditions. Under the influence of Portuguese missionaries, however, this liturgical tradition underwent much Latinization (see MALABAR RITE). In 1962 a purified Malabar Qurbana (sacrifice or liturgy) restoring fully Eastern traditions of the Malabar liturgy (including Eastern vestments, fermented bread, communion under both species, etc.) was promulgated. In the pastoral renewal initiated by Vatican Council II, further adaptations and reforms were considered necessary. This resulted in 1968 in the promulgation of another Malabar Qurbana for experimental use. This is the This is the Liturgy here described, although it has not met with universal satisfaction because of the evidences of Latinization and the obvious influence of the liturgical renewal of the Roman rite.

After the vesting of the priest (during which one of the canonical Hours may be sung) the Liturgy opens with an invocation of the triune God and the solemn recitation of the Our Father. A few psalms and prayers in dialogue between priest and congregation precede the Liturgy of the Word with the Epistle and Gospel. The Creed is solemnly recited, the gifts are prepared upon the altar, and the priest invites all the faithful to join him in praising God. Then follow the solemn antiphons—commemorations of the Blessed Virgin, of St. Thomas, and other saints, and of the living and the dead—and the eucharistic prayer (Canon) opens with the Kiss of Peace and the traditional dialogue. As in all Eastern Liturgies, the narration of the institution (Consecration) is followed by the anamnesis and the invocation of the Holy Spirit (epiclesis). The anaphora (Canon) is concluded with two psalms recited by priest and congregation together. In the rite of Elevation the new order of 1968 dropped the traditional kissing of the host. After the Pauline salutation, "The grace of Our Lord Jesus Christ, the charity of God the Father, and the fellowship of the Holy Spirit be with you all" (which occurs in all Eastern Liturgies and in the new Roman Mass), the community again intercedes in prayer for the great needs of the Church and the world, and concludes with the Our Father. Then, after the Kiss of Peace is given a second time and the faithful are reminded that holy things are for holy people, the congregation is invited to communicate under both species. A postcommunion prayer and a last farewell prayer conclude the Liturgy. BIBLIOGRAPHY: G. Varanikunnel and J. Madey, "A 'Reform' of the Restored Syro-Malabar Qurbana?" *Osterkirchliche Studien* 18 (1969) 172–181.

[J. MEIJER]

MALABAR RITE, one of the 18 Eastern Catholic rites; its use was centered around the coastal part of S India known as Kerala. Before the 14th cent. little is known about these Indian Christians. It seems they never had been actively involved in Nestorian controversies but accepted their bps. from Persia both from the Nestorian and the Jacobite sides. When the Portuguese came in 1498 this situation did not change at first, since the new rulers had then no doubts about the orthodoxy of these Malabar Christians, but they later became suspicious. The Chaldean bp. Mar Joseph Sulaga, sent by his brother, the Catholic patriarch of the Chaldeans, was pressed to introduce Latin practices. This was very much against the will of the people, but the Portuguese were obsessed with the idea that everything that differed from the Latin rite must be somewhat heretical. This was due to their unfamiliarity with the liturgy and the Syriac language, and to their misguided zeal for uniformity. When in 1597 Chaldean Bp. Mar Abraham died, the Portuguese refused his successor admission to the country and submitted the people to the jurisdiction of the Latin hierarchy. At the Synod of *Diamper (1599) further changes were imposed in defiance of the will of Rome. This attitude on the part of Portuguese church and civil authorities proved disastrous. In 1653 the majority of the Malabar Christians decided to throw off the yoke of the Latin bishops. They consecrated the leader of this movement, Thomas Parambil, bp., and established a separate community (see MALANKAR RITE). This act was not directed against Rome but against the Portuguese missionaries, esp. the Jesuits. A few years later in 1662 many of them came back when the Carmelites took over the jurisdiction. Portuguese influence diminished when the Dutch became the rulers of Malabar. The reason the schism did not totally disappear is that the Malabar Catholics still did not have their own bishops. This difficulty severely damaged this community and resulted in a series of little schisms (esp. when the Protestant influence of the English was felt in 1790) and fragmented their unity with Rome. Finally in 1896 the Malabar Catholics received their own bishops and in 1923 a fully separate Malabar hierarchy was established. The Malabar Catholics enjoy a great spiritual strength, and there are many vocations to the priesthood and religious life. In 1962 the Pope entrusted to them a vast territory in central India (Chanda) for missionary work, and again in 1969 three new exarchates were given to the Malabar Catholics, in Jagar, Satna, and Ujjaim. In these central provinces of India with their Hindi-speaking population, the gospel has had hardly any influence. It is a challenge for the Malabar Christians to show the apostolic spirit of the past is still alive. At present the Catholic Malabar Church is organized under two metropolitan sees, Ernakulam, with the eparchies Kothamangalam, Tellicherry, and Trichur, and Changanacherry with the exarchates Kottayam, Palai, Chanda, Jagar, Satna, and Ujjaim. The faithful number around 2,117,000 (1975). BIBLIOGRAPHY: E. Tisserant, *Eastern Christianity in India* (tr. E. R. Hambye, 1957); J. Thaliat, "The Synod of Diamper," OrChrAnal 152 (1958); OrientCatt 379–392.

[J. MEIJER]

MALACHI, BOOK OF. This book, which belongs to the period after the completion of the second temple in 515 B.C., but before the reforms of Nehemiah which began in 432, is dominated by the idea of an occasion in the near future, the "day of Yahweh," when Yahweh will come in person to his temple (3.1–5), divide the wicked from the good, condemn and punish the former according to the covenant curses, but deliver and renew the latter with the abundant blessings of the messianic age. Malachi accuses the priests of failing to instruct the people properly (2.6–9) and the people of failing to pay their temple tithes (3.6–12), as well as of marrying foreign wives (2.10–16). In a later addition the coming of Elijah is predicted as a prelude to the "great and terrible day of Yahweh" (4.4–6, or 3.22–24 in the Heb.), and this is taken up in the NT and applied to John the Baptist (cf. Mt 17.10–13). BIBLIOGRAPHY: A. von Bulmerincq, *Der Prophet Maleachi,* (v. 1, 1926, v. 2, 1932); C. C. Torrey, "Prophecy of Malachi," JBL 17 (1898) 1–15; T. Chary, *Les Prophètes et le culte à partir de l'exil* (1954) 160–189; O. Holtzmann, "Der Prophet Maleachi und der Ursprung des Pharisäertums," *Archiv für Religionswissenschaft* 29 (1931) 1–21.

[D. J. BOURKE]

MALACHY, ST. (*c.*1094–1148), abp. of Armagh. He was born at a time when Ireland was being plundered by invasions, particularly of the Danes, and when civil authority had neither the physical stamina nor moral rectitude to lead Ireland out of the chaos. He was educated first by his father and after his death, by St. Celsus (Ceallach), bp. of Armagh, who also ordained him. M. learned the Benedictine life at Lismore. He reformed the abbey of Bangor and was named bp. of Down in 1123, of Connor in 1124. It was at Connor that he had one of his hardest tests; i.e., the conversion of the Christians who were that in name only, and he retired to become abbot of Iveragh, Co. Kerry. St. Celsus dictated on his deathbed that M. was to be his successor. With that, several years of turmoil ensued between the supporters of Malachy and those of Murtaugh, and later, Niall. Finally peace was restored (1137) but M. left Armagh and lived as bp. of Down in a monastery at Bangor. He also introduced Roman liturgy into Ireland. He was appointed papal legate by Pope Innocent II while he was on a visit to Rome. As a result of his stopping at Clairvaux and meeting St. Bernard, the first Cistercian foundation in Ireland, the abbey of Mellifont, was established in 1142. In 1148 on a second journey to Rome to request the pallium for the bps. of Armagh and Cashel, M. died at Clairvaux. He was canonized in 1199. The so-called Prophecy of St. Malachy, on the succession of future popes, is a forgery fabricated in the 16th century. BIBLIOGRAPHY: Butler 1:249–253.

[J. R. RIVELLO]

MALAGRIDA, GABRIEL (1689–1761), Italian Jesuit and missionary. He joined the Jesuits in 1711 and from Portugal set out in 1721 for Brazil, where he became a celebrated preacher and missionary. In 1751, after conferring with King John V in Lisbon, M. returned to Brazil with the title of royal councilor for the Portuguese overseas missions. Back in Lisbon in 1754 he was confessor to Queen Mariana of Austria. After the earthquake of 1775 he earned the enmity of the minister *Pombal and was exiled. In 1758 M. was wrongly accused of plotting against the life of Joseph I and jailed. His mind broke; on the basis of two works written after his mental breakdown he was denounced to the Inquisition, which condemned him as a heretic and he was executed.

[J. R. AHERNE]

MALANKAR LITURGY. The rite of the Qurbana (sacrifice), as the Malankar liturgy is called, is basically the rite of Antioch that was accepted in Kerala in the 17th cent. by a part of the Malabar Christians (see MALANKAR RITE). The veil that separates the altar from the nave of the church is one of the many elements in the Malankar liturgy that recall the liturgical traditions of the OT. In the center of the altar a tablet of wood (*tablitho*) represents the cross on which Christ died. It is consecrated by the bishop, who inscribes it with the name of the Holy Trinity. Only one liturgy a day is celebrated on the *tablitho*. In a special service called "of Melchizedek," priest and people prepare themselves for the liturgy; the altar is venerated and the gifts are prepared. "At your door, O Lord, I knock and ask for mercy. At what door shall I knock if not at yours, compassionate Lord?" There follows the service known as "of Aaron," in which, while lessons from the OT are read, the priest vests himself and puts on special shoes.

The Liturgy proper opens by recalling the memory of Mary and John the Baptist, and by singing a hymn of praise to the Incarnation. The veil is opened, and the people are incensed. After the *Trisagion three readings follow, one from the Acts of the Apostles or from the Catholic Letters; one from St. Paul; and one from the Gospels, which is proclaimed with great solemnity. Priest and congregation join in praise of God and ask him for mercy and compassion, a prominent feature in this liturgical tradition. Altar and people are incensed again, bells are rung, and fans are waved in the solemn confession of the Holy Trinity, which is followed by the Creed and the kiss of peace. The eucharistic prayer or Canon, of which the Antiochene tradition has about 70 forms, is begun by the dialogue found in all liturgies and is interrupted by the Sanctus. As in all Eastern liturgies, the narration of the institution (Consecration) is followed by the anamnesis and the invocation of the Holy Spirit (epiclesis). A long prayer of intercession precedes the breaking of the bread. After the Our Father the gifts are elevated in adoration and are brought in procession into the church as a solemn invitation to holy communion, which the faithful receive under both kinds. Two prayers of thanksgiving follow and the priest dismisses the people with a threefold blessing. The Qurbana is concluded behind the veil when the priest completes his communion and says the postcommunion prayers. BIBLIOGRAPHY: *Order of the Holy Qurbana of the Syro-Malankara Rite* (1964).

[J. MEIJER]

MALANKAR RITE, one of the Eastern Catholic rites proper to those Catholics of South India who use the Syro-Antiochene ritual and are distinguished from the Indians of the *Malabar rite. Syrian tradition prevailed in Christian India until the 16th cent., when the Portuguese arrived and tried to impose the Latin rite and to establish a Latin hierarchy. Because of this suppression of their traditions, the majority of the Malabar Christians refused further obedience to the Latin hierarchy. In 1653 their leader, the archdeacon Thomas Parambil, received "consecration" through the imposition of hands by 12 priests claiming to act in the name of the pope as a sign that their action was not directed against Rome. During the next 12 years 84 congregations reunited with Rome. The others, aware of their irregular position, unsuccessfully approached the Nestorian patriarch to receive a bishop. They then appealed to the Jacobite Patriarch of Antioch, and in 1772 they received a valid hierarchy with the consecration of the fifth successor of Thomas Parambil as Dionysius I. They call themselves Syrian Jacobites. Their submission to the Jacobite patriarch of Antioch was not taken too seriously at times and several attempts at reunion were made. The coming of the English in 1790 brought a strong Protestant influence, esp. through the activities of the Anglican Church Missionary Society. A reaction against this in the 19th cent. resulted in another division, the foundation of the Jacobite Anglican Church, which is now a member of the *Church of South India. Another Protestant Church which keeps the Antiochene liturgical usages was formed in 1875 under the name of Mar (St.) Thomas Jacobite Church. In this same year the Jacobite patriarch of Antioch, Peter Ignatius XXIII, consecrated Dionysius IV with six other bishops and established an indigenous hierarchy for the Syrian Jacobites of India.

The 20th cent. brought another discussion between the patriarch of Antioch, Abdullah Sattuf, and Metropolitan Dionysius V. At stake was the independence of the Indian Jacobites, under their *catholicos. This split the church into two groups, one in obedience to the patriarch, the other in favor of their own catholicos. In order to overcome their state of isolation after excommunication by the Antiochene patriarch, the "catholicos" faction opened official discussions with Rome in 1925 which resulted in the reunion of two bps., Mar Ivanios and Mar Theophilus, a few clergy, and laity. The conditions had been full preservation of the Antiochene tradition and retention of Ivanios and Theophilus as bishops. This was agreed upon, and in 1932 Pope Pius XI erected the separate Malankar Rite province of

Trivandrum. Soon other bps. and laity followed, esp. the members of the Order of the Imitation of Christ which Mar Ivanios had earlier founded. Those who did not decide to unite with Rome continued their fight for independence, and in 1957 the two parties were reconciled. The Jacobite patriarch of Antioch recognized the title of catholicos and gave the South Indians a great degree of autonomy. The Malankar Catholics follow the Antiochene Liturgy, which has undergone relatively few Latinizations, though the influence from the West and also of the Malabar brothers cannot be totally denied. In 1975 there were about 207,650 Malankar Catholics in two jurisdictions, and the efforts for full reunion of Indian Christians continue. BIBLIOGRAPHY: S. G. Potham, *Syrian Christians of Kerala* (1963); E. Tisserant, *Eastern Christianity in India* (tr. E. R. Hambye, 1957); OrientCatt 135–144.

[J. MEIJER]

MALASPINA, GERMANICO (d. 1604), papal nuncio. As nuncio to Prague, seat of Emperor Rudolf II, M. was instrumental in having the emperor carry out Tridentine reforms. In 1582 M. was made nuncio to Poland where he brought an end to the conflict between King Sigismund III and his chancellor. His hopes of restoring Catholic supremacy to Sweden were dashed when the Protestant Charles usurped the throne there claimed by Sigismund. M. played a major role in the reunion of the Ruthenian Church with Rome in 1595.

[J. R. AHERNE]

MALATESTA, important ruling family in Rimini during the Renaissance. In 1237 Giovanni was named *podestà*. His son, Malatesta da Verucchio, ruled until 1312. He sired four sons: Malatestino; Giovanni, immortalized by Dante (*Inferno* 5.73–142) for having killed his wife, Francesca, and her lover Paolo, his brother; and Pandolfo. Out of the subsequently divided lines of the Malatesta sprang eminent *condottieri* and *litterati:* Pandolofo II; Carlo; and Pandolfo III, father of Galeotto (Bl.); Sigismondo; and Novello. To Sigismondo, notoriously profligate but erudite patron of the arts, Rimini owes its renown. One of his illegitimate descendants sold the family rights in Rimini to Venice in 1503. BIBLIOGRAPHY: L. Spitz, NCE 9:107–108.

[F. D. LAZENBY]

MALAVAL, FRANCESCO (1627–1719), French contemplative. He was blind. While in the French diplomatic service in Rome, he was in contact with M. *Molinos. M.'s own life was marked by true signs of holiness. He entered the clerical state in 1674, but did not receive major orders. His *Pratique facile pour élever l'âme à la contemplation* (2 v., 1664, 1670) was condemned for suspicion of *Quietism by the Holy Office in 1688.

[T. C. O'BRIEN]

MALAYALAM, the language spoken by the *Malabar Christians in Kerala, India. Ethnically they are of Dravidic-Arian origin. For some years the Malabar and Malankar rite Catholics have been using this language in the liturgy.

[J. MEIJER]

MALAYSIA, an elective constitutional monarchy in Asia formed in 1963 by 11 states of the former Federation of Malaya together with Sabah (North Borneo) and Sarawak (128,000 sq mi; pop [1974 Govt. est.] 11,700,000). Malaysia is a member of the Commonwealth of Nations. Malay and English are the official languages. Islam is the dominant religion. The new constitution guarantees religious freedom, but does not permit the evangelization of aborigines under the age of 18. Christianity was brought to the area by the Portuguese when they conquered Malacca in the 16th century. St. Francis Xavier preached for some years along the coasts. The bishopric at Malacca dates from 1557. When the Dutch captured the territory in the 17th cent., the Christian communities were razed. A fresh start was made in 1807 by the Paris Foreign Mission Society. Malacca became a vicariate apostolic in 1841. Mission personnel has been reinforced by Redemptorists, Salesians, Jesuits, and Christian Brothers, but work has been limited to the cities. Malacca-Singapore was created an archdiocese in 1953, with suffragans at Kuala Lumpur and Penang. The Catholic population numbers about 333,000 (1974).

Anglicans, Presbyterians, and several other denominations were active in Malaysia. In 1968 their combined membership was 197,295, including secessionist Singapore. BIBLIOGRAPHY: B. Mathews, *Unfolding Drama in Southeast Asia* (1944); N. J. Ryan, *Making of Modern Malaysia and Singapore: A History from Earliest Times to 1966* (pa. 1969).

[P. DAMBORIENA]

MALCHION, priest who was in charge of a school at Antioch in the middle of the 3d century. He convicted Paul of Samosata of his errors at a synod held in 268. The synodal letter and the disputation are known only in parts.

[J. MADEY]

MALDERUS, JOHN (Jan van Malderen; 1563–1663), professor at the Univ. of Louvain from 1596, rector in 1604; bp. of Antwerp from 1611. He was first incumbent in the chair of St. Thomas Aquinas endowed by Philip II of Spain. He published commentaries on the major treatises of the *Summa theologiae*. His main episcopal concern was for Christian instruction—he prepared an excellent catechism in the vernacular—and for the proper training of his clergy.

[T. C. O'BRIEN]

MALDONATUS, JOHANNES (Juan de Maldonado; 1534–83), Spanish Jesuit, biblical commentator. He became a Jesuit in 1562 after the completion of his theological studies and was ordained in 1563. His professorial career at Paris ended in 1574 because of controversy over his teaching on the Immaculate Conception. M. devoted most of his remaining years to writing on Scripture. One of the mainstays of RC study of the Gospels until recent times was his *Commentarii in IV Evangelistas* (2 v., 1596–97). He also published other biblical and theological works (*Opera,* 1677), and at Rome from 1581 collaborated in a papally commissioned revision of the Septuagint.

[T. C. O'BRIEN]

MÂLE, ÉMILE (1862–1954), French art historian. He was the first to establish medieval iconography as a scholarly discipline, using medieval writers Isidore, Bede, etc., to identify and interpret imagery. M.'s books on French 12th- and 13th-cent. religious art remain the standard works on the subject. A member of the Académie Française, M. was professor of medieval art at the Sorbonne and director of the French Archaeological Institute in Rome. BIBLIOGRAPHY: E. Mâle, *L'Art religieux du XIIe siècle en France* (1922); *idem, L'Art religieux du XIIIe siècle en France* (4th ed. 1931); *idem, La Fin du paganisme en Gaule, et les plus anciennes basiliques chrétiennes* (1950); M. Aubert, *Monuments et mémoires* 48.2 (1956) 1–7.

[R. C. MARKS]

MALEBRANCHE, NICOLAS DE (1638–1715), French philosopher of the Cartesian school usually ranked second to Descartes himself. Born in Paris, he studied theology and philosophy at the Collège de La Marche and the Sorbonne, after which he became an Oratorian and was ordained in 1664. Apart from his formal studies, he was versed in mathematics, physics, optics, and architecture. But his principal lifelong interest lay in the formulation of a highly original mystic idealism, rooted in the thinking of both Augustine and Descartes, that sought to harmonize the latter with the former in a new synthesis. M.'s thought, the essence of which appears in his work *Search after Truth* (1674–75), is regarded by some as the philosophic link between Descartes and Spinoza. M.'s fundamental concept is a philosophic application of St. Paul's statement that in God we live and move and have our being. From this flow M.'s two chief tenets: (1) vision in God, and (2) occasionalism. According to (1), individual material realities as known by man are but ideas representative of the objects we behold. But these idea-objects are actually eternal essences existing in the mind of God, and thus not dependent upon us for their existence but only as objects of our thought. In themselves, they are the archetypes of all reality, together constituting Divine Reason known eternally by God contemplating all things in himself. God's mind thus embraces the ideas of all things ever possible for man to know, and insofar as we are aware of them in our own cognitions, we see all things in God as the nonspatial seat of the immutable archetypal ideas. Point (2) is the metaphysical counterpart of the epistemological view expressed in (1); and whereas M.'s doctrine of occasionalism does not deny human free will or moral responsibility, it regards God as the one true cause. Hence, the known object and the knowing subject do not interact in a causal manner since there are no natural causes, but rather does God take these occasions to intervene directly, causing a perfect coincidence of the two. BIBLIOGRAPHY: *Oeuvres complètes de Malebranche,* directed by André Robinet (1958–65); *Dialogues on Metaphysics and on Religion* (tr. M. Ginsberg, 1923).

[J. T. HICKEY]

MALÈGUE, JOSEPH (1876–1940), French teacher and lawyer who became a writer in middle age. His literary reputation rests on *Augustin ou le maître est là* (1933), a novel describing religious faith lost during the Modernist crisis through intellectual pride and regained through yearnings for sanctity and mystery, a theme M. further developed in the posthumously published *Pièces noires* (1958). M. also authored a theological tract, *Pénombres* (1939), two works showing strong Marianist and liturgical influences: *De l'Annociation à la Nativité* (1935), and *Petite suite liturgique* (1938); studies in hagiography, *Vie de Saint Vincent de Paul* (1939); and numerous articles concerning the role of the Catholic novelist, the priest in the contemporary social order, and religious art. BIBLIOGRAPHY: G. Varin, *Foi perdu et retrouvé dans "Augustin"* (1953); E. Michel, *Joseph Malègue, sa vie, son oeuvre* (1957).

[G. E. GINGRAS]

MALEVEZ, LÉOPOLD (1900–73), modern Jesuit theologian of transcendence and incarnation. Born at Saint-Marc, Namur, he entered the Society of Jesus at an early age and was ordained priest 1927. From 1931 he taught fundamental and dogmatic theology at the Jesuit scholasticates at Louvain and Heverlee. He was a disciple of P. Joseph Maréchal; his main theological concern was the reason-faith, nature-grace dialectic, in dialogue with such as K. Barth, E. Brunner, R. Bultmann, O. Cullmann, and H. Duméry. He is best known for the two works: *Le Message chrétien et le mythe; La Théologie de Rudolph Bultmann* (1954), and *Transcendance de Dieu et creation des valeurs; L'Absolu et L'Homme dans la philosophie de Henry Duméry* (1958). BIBLIOGRAPHY: NRT 95 (1973) 353–366, 1057–89, 1090–93 (bibliog. with critical reviews); L. Malevez, "Diverse Expressions of the One Faith," TheolDig, 22 (1974) 57–61.

[E. J. DILLON]

MALHERBE, FRANÇOIS DE (1555–1628), French poet. Of an old noble family with Protestant sympathies, M. received a Protestant education at Caen, Paris, Basel (1571), and Heidelberg (1573) before converting to Catholicism. His first published poem, *Les Larmes de saint*

Pierre (1587), was an imitation of L. Tansillo's *Le Lagrime di San Pietro,* an example of the early Counter Reformation genre of spiritual poetry on the penitential tears of saints. Its mannerist style was later repudiated by M. who had matured at Aix-en-Provence mainly through his friendship with the Christian neo-Stoic, Guillaume du Vair, and the scientist Peiresc who along with Card. du Perron supported M. to become court poet to Henry IV in Paris (1605). M.'s work consists of: occasional verse; state poems including his *Prière pour le Roi allant en Limousin* (1607); love poems; and "consolations," including his often-cited *Consolation à M. Du Périer sur la mort de sa fille,* a curious mixture of Christian neo-Stoic moralism and classical mythology. His Stoical tastes are also seen in his translations of Livy and Seneca. Among his religious poems are paraphrases of the Psalms, esp. his well-known *Paraphrase du Psaume CXLV* (1627). His influence on the development of 17th-cent. French classical poetry was considered enormous, particularly concerning the rules and restrictions he advocated for poetic technique. BIBLIOGRAPHY: R. Fromilhague, *La Vie de Malherbe, 1555–1610* (1954).

[R. N. NICOLICH]

MALICE, a cause of sin on the part of the will: its fixed sinful intent either as present in a single act or as a habitual disposition towards a sinful way of acting. Sins described as being "from set wickedness or malice" (*ex certa malitia*) are distinguished against sins of *weakness or from lack of knowledge (*ignorance). Since malice means resolute wilfulness, sins of malice indicate a more voluntarily disordered will, and so are more serious. The disorder in particular is a preference for some earthly good to the exclusion of the goods to which grace is ordered. Particularly, though not exclusively, designated as sins of malice are *sins against the Holy Spirit; sins that are the indulgence in a cultivated, unretracted vice are also described as sins of malice (see ThAq ST 1a2ae, 78.1–3). The term malice may also be used in a less restricted sense as an abstract word, the badness in the disordered moral act; or for an effect of *original sin, the diminution of the will's positive bent upon the good (ibid 85.3). Spiteful or malevolent acts towards other persons are also described as prompted by malice.

[T. C. O'BRIEN]

MALINES, CONGRESS OF (1909), a Catholic congress held at Malines (Mechelen), Belgium, a turning point in the modern liturgical renewal. With this congress the movement turned away from the monastic ethos toward a definitive parochial and pastoral emphasis. A paper given at the congress by L. Beauduin, a monk of Mont-César, Louvain, articulated the needed change.

[E. J. DILLON]

MALINES CONVERSATIONS, a series of discussions between certain prominent Roman Catholics and Anglicans at Malines (Mechelen), Belgium between 1921 and 1926. The appeal of the *Lambeth Conference of 1920 for efforts toward church unity moved Lord *Halifax to approach his friend F. *Portal, the French Vincentian, with the proposal that they appeal to Card. D. J. Mercier to sponsor and be host to a series of Roman Catholic–Anglican meetings. The first of these was held in Dec. 1921, with Halifax, W. H. Frere, and J. A. Robinson representing the Anglican position and Mercier, J. E. van Roey, and Portal, the RC side. After the first meeting the Holy See and the abp. of Canterbury expressed interest and approval, although the private and unofficial character of the meetings was not changed. Further meetings were held in 1923, 1925, and 1926. At the conversations of 1923, C. Gore and B. J. Kidd joined the Anglican representatives and P. Battifol and M. H. Hemmer the RC participants. The last of the meetings (Oct. 1926) took place without two of the principal participants, Mercier and Portal, both of whom had died earlier that year. The conversations were viewed with suspicion by many evangelically minded members of the C of E and by many English RCs as well. They were not resumed after 1926. While it must be admitted that they ended without immediate tangible result, their importance as a start in the serious exploration of the possibilities of accord and their contribution to the development of a climate more favorable to ecumenical effort cannot be denied. BIBLIOGRAPHY: J. G. Lockhart, *Charles Lindley Viscount Halifax* (2 v., 1935–36); Lord Halifax, *Conversations at Malines, 1921–25* (1930); J. de Bivort de la Saudée, *Anglicains et Catholiques* (2 v., 1949).

[R. B. ENO]

MALKĀ (Syrian, king), the Nestorian leaven, traditionally handed down from SS. Addai and Mari, added to the dough used in making eucharistic bread; it is renewed on Holy Thursday by adding to the remaining *malkā* of the previous year. The term is also applied to that part of the baking actually used for consecration.

[A. CODY]

MALLARMÉ, STÉPHANE (1842–98), French symbolist writer whose hermetic verse and theory of the poet's sacerdotal role have influenced modern literature. Holding secondary-school posts in the Provinces and after 1871 in Paris, M. began to be an important figure in French literary circles through his Tuesday gatherings at which young writers were introduced to an antirealistic and intuitive aesthetics. M. was reared a Catholic, married at the Brompton Oratory in London (1863), then underwent a spiritual crisis in which the "light of science" overwhelmed his faith yet left his sense of the transcendent untouched. By the age of 24 M. had fashioned his own religion. Although he did not allow for a personal God, he saw the cosmos as the reflection of the divine attribute of Beauty, and he claimed that poetry was its perfect expression. He wanted poetry to furnish an orphic explanation of the universe and toward that end he tried unsuccessfully to create a great poem of synthesis. His poetry embodies a nontheological quest for the Absolute crystallized in the anguished act of literary creation, and it restates through recurring symbols that express emptiness, the void, absence, and annihilation, the effort to pass from nothingness to being, from contingency to necessity, from appearance to reality, and from the object to its essence. Although he rejected Catholicism, M. valued the "ceremonious aesthetic of the Church" and held that poetry must also create a sacred ritual analogous to the hieratic language of the liturgy. Works: for English translations, see *Poems*, tr. R. Fry with commentaries by C. Mauron (1951); *Selected Poems*, tr. C. F. MacIntyre (1959). BIBLIOGRAPHY: W. Fowlie, *Mallarmé* (1953); J. P. Richard, *L'Univers imaginaire de Mallarmé* (1962); G. Michaud, *Mallarmé* (1953; Eng. tr. M. Collins and B. Humes, 1965); H. M. Block, *Mallarmé and the Symbolist Drama* (1963).

[G. E. GINGRAS]

MALLINCKRODT, VON, family name of two prominent German Catholics. **Hermann** (1821–74), political leader, a founder of the Catholic Center Party, and, as a member of the Reichstag (1871–74), a staunch opponent of Bismarck's *Kulturkampf and its infringement of the rights of the Church. **Pauline** (1817–81), sister of Hermann, foundress of the Sisters of *Christian Charity, a community devoted at first to the care of blind children then to the teaching apostolate. After failing, because of the *Kulturkampf, to have the school for blind children she had founded at Paderborn (1842) entrusted to the French *Sacred Heart Sisters, M. founded her own community in 1849. As superior general, and in spite of the obstacles placed by the antireligious policies of the Kulturkampf, she succeeded in expanding the membership and the foundations of the community. She visited both North and South America and established the first community in the U.S. at New Orleans in 1873. Her cause for beatification has been introduced.

MALLING, ABBEY OF, formerly a Benedictine nunnery, located in W. Malling, Kent, England, founded by Gundulf, bp. of Rochester, at a date probably between 1078 and 1106. Destroyed by fire in 1190, it was soon rebuilt. During the English Reformation it was necessary for the abbess, Dame Vernon, and her 11 nuns to sign the surrender of the abbey with its lands. Cranmer came into possession of it. Though comparatively little of it has survived, some of its remains make up part of a modern building. The chapel of the chapter house was restored to use, and the Early English cloisters were rebuilt in the 14th century. In private hands since its dissolution in 1583, it became the property of an Anglican community in 1893. BIBLIOGRAPHY: P. Brookfield, CE 16:60; F. H. Crossley, *English Abbeys* (1935).

[S. A. HEENEY]

MALLON, ALEXIS (1875–1934), archeologist and Coptic philologist. M. taught Coptic at Cairo, Beirut, and at the *Pontifical Biblical Institute (Rome). He established and was the first director of that institute in Jerusalem (1927), directed excavations at several prehistoric sites in Palestine, and discovered the highly significant archeological traces of a Chalcolithic civilization in the desert at Teleilat-Ghassoul, NE of the Dead Sea. M. published a Coptic grammar, a study of the Hebrews in Egypt, and many articles on the results of his archeological findings. BIBLIOGRAPHY: S. Lyonnet, DBSuppl 5:751–753.

[T. M. MCFADDEN]

MALMÉDY, ABBEY OF (*Malmundariense*), Benedictine monastery founded *c.* 650 in what is now the diocese of Liège in Belgium by Sigebert II, king of Austrasia, at the request of St. Remaclus (who also founded Stavelot) three miles from Malmédy. After 1126 one abbot governed the two monasteries. Malmédy was destroyed many times (1244, 1441, 1521, 1587, and 1689). It was rebuilt for the last time in simple style in the years 1701–08 and was closed in 1797, although it remained an abbatial principality until the peace of Lunéville in 1801. The abbey church now serves the local parish. BIBLIOGRAPHY: Cottineau 2:1719–20.

[J. DAOUST]

MALMESBURY, ABBEY OF, a Benedictine monastery in Wiltshire, England. Aldhelm, first abbot (*c.* 672) was a pupil of Maidulf, a Celtic monk who established a school there (*c.* 635) from which the monastery grew. It became renowned as a center of learning and enjoyed the patronage of numerous English kings. Among many famous men, it produced *William of Malmesbury, considered after St. Bede the greatest medieval English historian. Last in the area to submit to suppression under Henry VIII, it stands with but nave and aisles remaining of the once vast, magnificent Norman structure, used today as a parish church. BIBLIOGRAPHY: Knowles-Hadcock; Knowles MOE; S. Sitwell, *Monks, Nuns and Monasteries* (1965).

[S. A. HEENEY]

MALONE, SYLVESTER (1821–99), missionary, pastor, social reformer. Of Irish birth he studied for the priesthood in the U.S. and was ordained for the Diocese of New York in 1844. The pioneer pastor of what is now Brooklyn, N.Y., he headed the celebrated parish of SS. Peter and Paul, out of which grew 25 new parishes in his time. An abolitionist and a liberal, he worked for the rights of blacks after the Civil War. M. supported Edward *McGlynn in the single tax controversy. He was elected to the New York Board of Regents in 1894. M. was a strong supporter of public schools and of the school position of Abp. Ireland. At his death he had completed over 50 years as pastor of SS. Peter and Paul.

[J. R. AHERNE]

MALORY, SIR THOMAS (*c.* 1410–71), author of the English prose *Morte d'Arthur*, written while he was in prison, and completed *c.* 1469. Caxton printed it with his own preface in 1485. Scholarship today has revealed that M. wrote eight individual romances, which Caxton assembled into a single volume. It now seems that the moral purpose of teaching true chivalry and virtuous deeds, which Caxton asserts is M.'s intention, is not M.'s primary aim. He was interested in telling a good story, and used English and French sources which were available to him. He presents in the final breakup of Arthur's court a sympathetic view of the moral struggles of his major characters. In this sense of inner conflict M.'s narrative is far above the ordinary medieval romance. Works: ed. E. Vinaver, 3 v. (1947). BIBLIOGRAPHY: E. Vinaver, *Malory* (1929); *Concordance to the Works of Sir Thomas Malory* (ed. T. Kato, 1974).

[M. M. BARRY]

MALOUEL, JEAN (fl. 1396–1415), artist of the Dijon School. He was commissioned (1398) to execute five large pictures for the Chartreuse de Campmol and assisted in the painting and gilding of Sluter's Well of Moses. His *Pietà* (*c.* 1400) combines the Trinity theme with the Lamentation and Crucifixion in a work of emotional intensity.

MALRAUX, ANDRÉ (1901–1976), French writer, statesman. He led a life of high adventure and was involved in military and political conflicts most of his years. He was a mysterious participant in the Chinese Civil War (1924–27), active as a soldier on the Republican side in the Spanish Civil War, and a prominent member of the Resistance in France in World War II. A friend and associate of General de Gaulle, he served as Minister of Propaganda and as influential Minister of Culture in the Gaullist regime. A violent anti-Fascist, though never a Communist, M. was associated with Marxist movements before the De Gaulle years. He was a voluminous writer, perhaps one of the best French writers of the 20th century. In 1933 he won the Goncourt Prize with his most celebrated novel, *Man's Fate*. Almost equally praised was *Man's Hope*. *The Voices of Silence* (1953) showed Malraux as a philosopher of art.

[J. R. AHERNE]

MALTA, republic consisting of the island Malta and associated smaller islands S of Sicily. The population of 315,756 (1974 Govt. est.) is almost totally Catholic (91.7%). Because of its central Mediterranean location, Malta has played a role in world history from antiquity. It was occupied successively by Phoenicians, Greeks, Carthaginians, and Romans, who were ruling when Paul spent three months there (Acts 28). It was taken by the Saracens in 870 and by the Normans of Sicily *c.* 1090. In 1530 Charles V gave it to the Knights Hospitallers (consequently called Knights of Malta). They surrendered it to Napoleon in 1798, but Britain took control in 1800. Malta became independent in 1964 and a republic in 1974, but retained its ties with the British Commonwealth. From 1154 to 1831 the Malta diocese was suffragan to Palermo. It then became immediately subject to the Holy See.

[T. EARLY]

MALTHUS, THOMAS ROBERT (1766–1834), English political economist. His father was one of the executors of Rousseau. A contemporary of S. T. Coleridge at Jesus College, Cambridge, M. was elected to a fellowship, took orders, and served as curate in Surrey for a short time. In 1798 he published *An Essay on the Principle of Population as it Affects the Future Improvement of Society, with Remarks on the Speculations of Mr. Goodwin, M. Condorcet, and Other Writers,* which ran though six editions during his lifetime. With great felicity of style it argues that when unchecked, population increases in a geometrical ratio, whereas the means of subsistence increase only in an arithmetical ratio. As a preventive check he proposed "moral restraint," by which he understood strict sexual continence and the postponement of marriage. M. was also an economic theorist of some note, the close friend and correspondent of David Ricardo.

MALTHUSIANISM, the birth control movement as it developed from the social diagnosis of Thomas *Malthus. It came to advocate contraception rather than the sexual abstinence Malthus had proposed as a means of checking the population explosion. Originating in England, the movement drew on French knowledge of techniques and spread to the U.S. and other countries. Despite legal obstacles it attracted increasing support, which resulted in the foundation of the Malthusian League in 1878.

MALTRET, CLAUDE (1621–74), classical scholar. A French Jesuit who entered the Society in 1637, he was appointed rector of Montauban in 1662. There he published his critical edition of the Latin translation by Alemannus of the works of Procopius of Caesarea.

[J. R. AHERNE]

MALVENDA, TOMÁS (1566–1628), Dominican historian, exegete. M. worked with C. *Baronius on his revision of the *Annales Ecclesiastici*, revised the Dominican Breviary, annotated Brasichelli's *Index Expurgatorius*, and prepared an annals for the Dominican Order. His most important work is an uncompleted literal translation of the Hebrew OT into Latin. The translation is so literal that it is sometimes unintelligible, but was of significant use at the time. BIBLIOGRAPHY: DB 4.1:624–625.

[T. M. MCFADDEN]

MALVERN, ABBEY OF, a former Benedictine monastery in Worcester, England, whose church was built in Norman and Perpendicular styles, and dedicated to the Blessed Virgin Mary and St. Michael. Founded by Aldwyn, a monk of Worcester, at the suggestion of St. Wulstan, bp. of Worcester, it dates from 1085 and was rebuilt magnificently *c.* 1460. It shared the fate of other monasteries in the dissolution by Henry VIII and was suppressed in 1540. Local people bought the church to serve the needs of their parish. It was notable for its beautiful stained glass and its tile, which was made at the priory. BIBLIOGRAPHY: W. Dugdale, *Monasticon anglicanum* (1836) 3:440–454; R. Cram, *Ruined Abbeys of Great Britain* (1905).

[S. A. HEENEY]

MAMACHI, TOMMASO (1713–92), Dominican church historian and archeologist. M. taught first in Florence and then at the Propaganda in Rome. His chief work, of value even today, was *Origines et antiquitates christianae* (5 v., 1749–55). He also edited the works of St. Antoninus, abp. of Florence (2 v., 1741–56), and collaborated on the first volume of the annals of the Dominican Order (1756). BIBLIOGRAPHY: U. M. Fasola, LTK 6:1338.

[M. J. SUELZER]

MAMALLAPURAM (MAHABALAPURAM) VILLAGE, S of Madras, India, port of the Pallave Dynasty (7th cent.), site of seven monolithic *rathas* (''chariot''-temples), each quarried from a single boulder (*c.* 30′ high) with many stone variants of wood prototypes, śikharas, barrel roofs and thatch-roofs. Sculpture is of the sensuous Amarāvati, Pallavan, and Ceylonese types. Impressive is a huge cliff carving, the *Descent of the Ganges*, with channel for falling water, showing life-size worshipers, animals, and deities. BIBLIOGRAPHY: P. Brown, *Indian Architecture* (1959).

[M. J. DALY]

MAMAS, GREGORY, see GREGORY III MELISSENES, PATRIARCH OF CONSTANTINOPLE.

MAMBRES, see JANNES AND JAMBRES.

MAMELUKES (from Arab., slave), Muslim military caste. From the 9th cent. Muslim rulers used slaves, primarily Turks and Mongols, as bodyguards and soldiers. In 1250 the chief Mameluke officer of Egypt, Aibek (Eibek), succeeded the last Ayyubite sultan, marrying his widow. Baibars, who seized power in 1260, was the principal founder of Mameluke power. The first dynasty, called Bahrites, ruled till 1382. The Burjites, chiefly Circassians, then ruled till 1517, when the Turks captured Cairo, making it the center of Muslim civilization. Among Mameluke military exploits was the expulsion of the Crusaders from Palestine (1291). Resting economically on the spice trade, Mameluke power declined after Portugal mastered the ocean route to the East. But they continued to exist under Turkish rule. Although they regained some independence in the 18th cent., their power was ended by Mohammed Ali in 1811.

[T. EARLY]

MAMERTINE PRISON, the name of Carcer Tullianum the oldest prison in Rome, located on the E side of the Capitoline Hill. Built, according to tradition, by Ancus Marcius, 4th king of Rome (640–616 B.C.), the prison, including a small underground circular section and a spacious rectangular section above ground, was last renovated during the reign of Tiberius. Among those who were imprisoned or died there were Jugurtha, Lentulus, and Vercingetorix. An early Christian tradition claims that SS. Peter and Paul were also detained there.

[F. H. BRIGHAM]

MAMERTUS CLAUDIANUS, see CLAUDIANUS MAMERTUS.

MAMERTUS OF VIENNE, ST. (d. *c.* 475), bp. of Vienne, France, known to be the originator of the *rogation day processions that were adopted for all of Gaul in 511 by the Council of Orléans.

[T. C. O'BRIEN]

MAMMON (transliterated from Aram. *māmōnā'*, riches), a biblical term. The Hebrew equivalent was used in Sir 31.8 and often in rabbinical literature. In the NT Christ alone used the term (Mt 6.24; Lk 16.9,11,13). The conclusion of the parable about the Unjust Steward (Lk 16.13) seems best rendered: ''You cannot serve God and gold'' (i.e., riches as opposed to God).

[E. MAY]

MAMRE, area N of the site later occupied by *Hebron. Abraham camped at Mamre (Gen 13.18), and Yahweh appeared to him there (Gen ch. 18). East of Mamre Abraham bought a field for a burial place (Gen 23.17–20). The person, Mamre, was an Amorite and presumably the owner of the area of that name (Gen 14.13–24).

[T. EARLY]

MAN. Man is universally acknowledged to be body and soul, or (in biblical terms) body, soul, and spirit. The precise content of these terms is much discussed. Theological anthropology must incorporate philosophical anthropology. It is usual to see man as a psychosomatic unity rather than a combination of spirit and matter in a Platonist or Cartesian sense, the soul being neither imprisoned in the body nor ''the ghost in the machine.'' The body is identified with man's self; his bodily mode of existence is essential to him; his bodiliness is involved in all his activities of whatever sort, not always helpfully; man as mind must be identified with man as body. Man as a totality is not self-subsistent but oriented upon "the other" (see C. A. Van Peuren, *Body, Soul and Spirit,* 1966). Theology speaks of man in his relationship to God as being less than the angels (Heb 2.7) yet superior to animals (Gen 1.28), having by God's creation a spiritual and a material aspect; in spite of his sinfulness God's call, with which he must freely cooperate, destines him to abiding union in his totality with the triune God.

It is common teaching that man is made up of body and soul, the soul being immaterial and therefore immortal, so that when man dies the body corrupts and the soul lives on. This way of putting the matter is probably too concrete. It opens body and soul to the possibility of being too readily thought of as separate. Man is a true psychosomatic unity: to look at a person bodily present is to look at not a body but a soul-informed body, i.e., the body is such only when the soul is present. The definition of the Council of Vienne (1312) that the soul is of its nature essentially the form of the human body (D 902) makes precisely this point; it is not teaching a particular philosophical view but, in terms borrowed from Scholastic philosophy (which was then the language most generally intelligible), it is stating man's unity to the exclusion of dualism.

Creationism. The spiritual nature of the soul has been understood to involve creationism, i.e., the immediate creation of the soul by God whenever a human being comes into existence. Creationism is opposed primarily to pantheistic emanationism, which regards the soul of each person as part of God (condemned, D 190, 201, 455, 685, 977); it is opposed also to the Platonist teaching that souls exist before their union with their bodies, a teaching that stems from Origen (D 403, 456). It is further opposed to the view that the soul is produced by the parents, either materially (Tertullian) or spiritually (St. Augustine); the former (traducianism) is commonly disproved by arguing that the parents' bodies cannot be the cause of a spiritual reality such as the soul is, the latter (generationism) by arguing that the parents' souls—being indivisible—cannot provide a portion of themselves as their child's soul. This however may be too crude a refutation of generationism, esp. in the light of something that creationism does not take into account, namely, that there is an a priori case for the parents being the adequate cause under God of their offspring. It may be possible to find the truth partially represented both by creationism and generationism. The argument for creationism is drawn from the spiritual character of the soul which cannot be adequately caused by the generative action of the parents; the parents' action does, however, entail God's production of the soul, as was commonly stated by the Scholastics. Yet creation of its nature is subject to no physical conditions and is completely God's free action. What in fact happens when a human soul is "created" would seem to be more properly an act by which God does not so much create as concur with the parents' action: God enables the generative act of the parents to issue forth in a new human being, whose production is thus totally due to the action of God as first cause and of the parents as secondary causes. Theologians have generally regarded the immediate creation of the soul by God as certain; Pius XII (in *Humani generis*) stated it is a truth that Catholic faith imposes on Christian belief. The essential affirmation seems to be the special activity of God in the production of a new human being.

Monogenism. *Humani generis* cautiously allowed the adoption of evolution but excluded a polygenistic origin of mankind; this by reason of the Church's traditional proposition of the doctrine of original sin. Of itself the precise way in which man appeared and grew in numbers on this earth is a matter for natural science; one may even regard it as unlikely that God would make man's understanding of his need of salvation (and therefore of salvation itself) dependent on a scientific finding; one must allow, however, that theology could thus incidentally offer guidance to science. Most scientists are led by purely scientific considerations to accept the view that humanity originated from more than one male-female pair, possibly in more than one place on the earth, though they can never offer strict proof of this point. They do not have any lawful comment to make about man's fall from grace, though they would regard first man as very primitive and would presume the progress of man toward fuller human life to be a more or less continuous process, a slow one, and a continuation of the evolution that enabled him to emerge from the higher animals.

Catholic teaching on original sin has traditionally regarded man as having originated from one pair because it has taught that all mankind subsequent to Adam has derived original sin from him by physical descent. Adam is thus seen as the representative head of mankind because he is its biological head. Various attempts are now being made to explain how a polygenistic origin may be allowed while the human race still has a unity in the sinfulness, rightly described as a Fall, that necessitated the redemptive Incarnation of Christ. The essential core of the dogma would seem to be that men are in need of a redemption by Christ and this need for redemption is derived from sin that introduced evil into a world God created good.

Salvation in Christ. Whatever explanation be given of the need for Christ's salvation, man finds his fulfillment in Christ, who is the "firstborn of many brothers" (Rom 8.29; cf. Col 1.18), who by his paschal mystery passed over from the unregenerate state of sinfulness in which mankind existed to the state of salvation, of humanity transformed by the Spirit. This passover Christ made in the name of humanity so that when he passed over, all men in principle did likewise, although their transformation is gradually effected by the Spirit working through the Church, to be complete only at the second coming, when the just will reign with Christ in glorified bodies. Meanwhile man lives in a world that his free activity, empowered by God's grace, must strive to include in this transformation. His human nature is designed for fulfillment not merely by human values but by human values related to his close union with the Trinity. All that goes to make up man's earthly life has a place in the plan of salvation; terrestrial realities are thus seen in their theological context. The eschatological fulfillment of man, of all men, is centered on the glorified Christ, from whom the Father receives the transformed world as his kingdom (1 Cor 15.24–28). Man finally fulfilled in body and soul takes his place in the reconstituted universe, eternally happy in his intimacy with the Blessed Trinity. BIBLIOGRAPHY: *God and His Creation* (ed. A. M. Henry, tr. C. C. Miltner, 1955); J. Mouroux, *Meaning of Man* (tr. A. H. G. Downes, 1948); L. Roberts, *Achievement of Karl Rahner* (1967) ch. 5 and 6; R. North, *Teilhard and the Creation of Man* (1968).

[B. FORSHAW]

MAN, ELEVATION OF, see ELEVATION OF MAN.

MAN, RIGHTEOUSNESS OF, see RIGHTEOUSNESS OF MAN.

MANA, a term native to the Pacific South Seas region, important in the comparative study of religion. The concept of mana is found in Polynesian and Tongan religions, but also among the Indians of N America, e.g., the Algonquin *manitou*. Mana is a power or influence, mysterious or supernatural, not physical, but showing itself in physical force and in any kind of power or excellence. Mana is not fixed in anything, but can be communicated in almost anything. Spirits, whether disembodied souls or supernatural beings, have it and can impart it. To be its source essentially belongs to personal beings, but it may act through a medium, e.g., water, a stone. Its influence is varied, for good and for evil. Members of a tribe are anxious to possess or control it. Success in warfare is not due to the warrior's personal resources but to the mana or spirit of a deceased hero empowering him through mana, communicated in an amulet worn round the neck, or a tuft of leaves in the belt, or a verbal formula; these bring supernatural assistance to the warrior. Mana has similar influences in other areas of life. In the study of comparative religion various interpretations of the idea have been advanced. Mana and *taboo have been coupled as the basic perceptions of the forces of good and evil structuring primitive religion. More recently both have been viewed more simply as means for explaining and trying to control the unknown or unusual in the forces and phenomena of nature.

[M. T. HANSBURY]

MĀNASĀRA SILPAŚĀSTRA (6th cent.), Gupta Indian treatise on architecture given by the gods to rishis (inspired poets, sages), called *Mānasāra*.

MANASSEH, the patriarch Joseph's oldest son by his Egyptian wife Asenath (Gen 41.50–52), and reputed ancestor of one of the 12 tribes of ancient Israel. Jacob adopted M. and his younger brother Ephraim (Gen 48.5), but in blessing them gave preference to the younger Ephraim (Gen 48.14–20). The Tribe of M. had territory on both sides of the Jordan River. BIBLIOGRAPHY: EDB 1430.

[E. MAY]

MANASSEH, KING OF JUDAH, the son of King Hezekiah, *c.*687–642 B.C. (2 Kg 20.21; 2 Chr 32.33). At age 12 he succeeded his father on the throne of Judah. Whereas Hezekiah had instituted genuine religious reform, the long reign of M. is depicted as fostering idolatry, bloodshed, divination (cf. 2 Kg 21.1–17)—probably influenced by Assyria to which Judah was vassal at the time. According to 2 Chr 33.11–20, M. was taken captive to Assyria (perhaps for rebellion), had a change of heart (cf. the apocryphal prayer of M.), and on his return to Jerusalem inaugurated a religious reform. Modern authors tend to question the historicity of this conversion, because of passages like 2 Kg 21.10–17; Jer 15.4. BIBLIOGRAPHY: EDB 1430–32.

[E. MAY]

MANASSES I OF REIMS (b. *c.*1040), abp. of Reims. Of a noble family of the Champagne, M. was raised to the important archiepiscopal See of Reims just as the reforms of Gregory VII were advancing in France. When M. refused summons to present himself at synods for examination, he was first suspended, then in 1077 deposed, and finally in 1080 excommunicated. Last mentioned in 1081 by Benzo of Alba—another royalist—M. disappeared from history. BIBLIOGRAPHY: S. Williams, NCE 9:142; LTK 6:1342; J. R. Williams, *American Historical Review* 54 (1948–49) 804–824.

[S. WILLIAMS]

MANASSIA (1407–18), Serbian monastic site, center of book production, but most famous for a cycle of murals from the Morava period, depicting the miracles and parables of Christ, probably the most remarkable achievements of their time. Closely related to Italo-Greek art of the Adriatic, the iconography and style are Palaeologan of Constantinople.

[M. J. DALY]

MANAZKERT, SYNODS OF (Manazgerd; Manzikert; Turkish, Melazgerd), synods of the Armenian Church held in the town of that name in the 7th and 8th centuries. The only one of lasting historical importance is that convoked by the catholicos John IV of Odzoun ("the Philosopher") in 726, attended by 20 Armenian bps. and a dozen Armenian priests, as well as by the Syrian Monophysite patriarch with some of his clergy. Doctrinally, the formula of St. Cyril, "one nature, incarnate, of the Word," was reiterated as normative and interpreted in a Monophysite sense, but the Aphthartodocetism of Julian of Halicarnassus (accepted by the Armenians in the Synod of Dvin of 555) was abandoned, the Armenian Church thereby coming closer to the Monophysitism of Severus of Antioch, normative in the other Monophysite Churches by that time. The practices of using unleavened eucharistic bread and of not adding any water to the chalice were confirmed. BIBLIOGRAPHY: F. Tournebize, DHGE 4:305.

[A. CODY]

MANCE, JEANNE (1606–73), French founder of the Hôtel Dieu, Montreal, Canada. After early hospital efforts in war-devastated Champagne, she came to Canada (1641) with the pioneers sent out by the Société de Notre-Dame de Montréal to establish a new colony. In 1642 she founded the Hôtel Dieu hospital at Montreal and was closely identified with the struggle of the Montreal colonists for survival. BIBLIOGRAPHY: M. C. Daveluy, *Jeanne Mance* (2d ed., 1962).

[R. K. MACMASTER]

MANCHURIA, a region of the People's Republic of China roughly coterminous with the three provinces of NE China before the Communist take-over (about 400,000 sq. mi; pop. est. of more than 51,500,000). Manchuria was long a part of the Chinese Empire. Its modern development began *c.*1900 with Russian penetration, followed by Japanese. The Chinese Nationalist government maintained a tenuous hold on Manchuria until 1949 when the Communists took control. Though attached to the diocese of Peking, it was practically neglected as a mission field until the 19th century. The vicariate apostolic of Liatung was erected in 1832 and entrusted to the Paris Mission Society. Despite difficulties progress was made and in 1898 the territory was further divided into two vicariates. The missions suffered heavily from the Boxer Rebellion (1900), the Russo-Japanese War (1904), and endemic banditry after 1911. Most of the foreign missioners were expelled during World War II. After 1945 Maryknollers, Austrian Capuchins, Benedictines, and Columban Fathers entered Manchuria. In 1946 there was an archdiocese at Mukden, with suffragan sees at Kirin, Yenki, Fushun, Szepingkai, and Yingkow; and a vicariate at Kiamusze. The Catholic population had increased from 57,000 in 1920 to about 300,000 in 1948, but the Communist takeover in 1949 brought ruin to the missions. Irish and Scotch Presbyterians entered Manchuria in 1869. By 1900 their community numbered 27,000. Then came Baptists, Lutherans, Methodists, Mennonites, the United Church of Canada, Adventists, and Pentecostals. It is not possible to ascertain Protestant membership at the present time. BIBLIOGRAPHY: T. Morton, *Today in Manchuria. Young Church in Crisis* (1928).

[P. DAMBORIENA]

MANDAEANS (from Aram. *mandā'*, i.e., knowledge), also called Sabaeans (baptizers) and, incorrectly, Johannine Christians, are Arab-speaking adherents of a sect comprising a few thousand members in S Iraq and Iran. They have a copious literature in an Aramaic dialect that was committed to writing in the 7th or 8th century A.D. Among the chief works are the *Ginza* (Treasure) and the *Book of John*. Mandaean religion comprises Jewish, Iranian, Babylonian, Gnostic, and Christian elements. It reflects an underlying dualism of light and darkness. There is a supreme being, Great Life or Lord, and an evil holy Spirit. Souls come down from the Kingdom of Light and are caught in the bonds of matter. The "Gnosis of Life" was sent by God as a bringer of divine revelation. The means of salvation for the soul, that is, return to the Kingdom of Light, are baptism in running water, knowledge, moral living, and practice of cult. The Mandaeans claim John the Baptist as their master but reject Jesus as a false prophet. The leaders of the community are the priests (Nasoraeans, i.e., observers), who possess a secret doctrine and conduct sacred rites in windowless huts of clay. Cult consists in liturgical prayers, distribution of bread and water, baptism (*mosiqtā*), and a ritual for the dead including a sacred meal. The Mandaeans seem to have had their beginning as an offshoot of a heretical Jewish baptist sect, under Gnostic influence. The sect is pretty clearly from the 4th or 5th cent. A.D. and may go back to the 1st century. BIBLIOGRAPHY: G. W. MacRae, NCE 9:145; J. Schmid, LTK 6:1343–47; J. Colpe, RGG 4:709–712; E. S. Drower, *Mandaeans of Iraq and Iran* (1937; repr. 1962).

[M. R. P. MCGUIRE]

MANDALA, in Hindu or Buddhist art a spiritual plan of the universe. It may be used as the basic design of temple (Java) or as painting or carving on ceilings, walls, hangings, or pavements.

[M. J. DALY]

MAṆḌAPA, the open assembly hall before the shrineroom *(garbhagṛha)* in the Hindu temple, simplest and most beautiful examples of which were in the 10th and 11th cent. at Khajurāho.

[M. J. DALY]

MANDATE, see FREEDOM OF CHRIST.

MANDATUM, the ceremonial washing of the feet which occurs during the Mass of the Lord's Supper on Holy Thursday. It is done by the liturgical celebrant for several members of the worshiping community in imitation of Christ's washing of the Apostles' feet at the Last Supper (Jn 13.4–16). The name comes from Christ's words contained in the opening words of the first antiphon sung in conjunction with the rite: *Mandatum novum* (I give you a new commandment). Maundy Thursday, a common English name for Holy Thursday, is derived from this rite. The intent of the rite is to illustrate the precept of fraternal charity that is the theme of the Scripture readings for this day. The practice is ancient, but dates from only about the 6th cent. as a Western liturgical rite. After the 14th cent. it was performed apart from the eucharistic celebration. In 1955 Pius XII restored it to its traditional position after the homily. BIBLIOGRAPHY: J. Gaillard, *Holy Week and Easter* (2d and rev. ed., tr. W. Busch, 1957) 71–74. *HOLY WEEK.

[B. ROSENDALL]

MANDE, HENDRIK (*c.*1360–1431), Dutch mystic. M. was a secretary in the court of the Duke of Holland before he entered the Brothers of the Common Life through the influence of a sermon preached by Gerard *Groote. In 1392 M. transferred to the Augustinians at Windesheim but did not take orders. He suffered from ill health and was given to ecstasies and to visions that were more original than his treatises. M.'s most important work is *De tribus statibus hominis conversi*. He also wrote 12 mystical treatises in Dutch, replete with excerpts and paraphrases of mystics, esp. of Jan van *Ruysbroeck. BIBLIOGRAPHY: E. Barnikol, RGG 4:712.

[M. J. SUELZER]

MANDER, KAREL VAN (1548–1604), Flemish painter, poet, and biographer. After study in Ghent, M. began 10 years of travel (1573–83), founded an Academy in Haarlem, and moved to Amsterdam (1604). In *The Martyrdom of St. Catharine* (1582–83) M. reflects N mannerist qualities. Later work (*The Preaching of St. John the Baptist,* 1597) returns to the Flemish tradition. M., a "northern Vasari," is best known for his *Schilderboek* (*Book of Painters*, 1604), chief source for the lives of N artists.

[M. J. DALY]

MANDEVILLE, BERNARD (1670–1733), English philosopher and physician. M. was born in the Netherlands, took his medical degree at Leyden and settled in England. He is best known for the *Fable of the Bees; or, Private Vices Made Public Benefits*, a political satire on the state of England in 1705. M.'s main thesis is that the vices, that is, the self-regarding actions of man, are the means of inventions and thus the basis of the development of society and of civilization. His ironical paradoxes are a criticism of Shaftesbury's idea of natural goodness in man. The work aroused great protest because it viewed all virtue as a delusion, and the higher life of man as a fiction introduced by philosophers and rulers to simplify government and social relationships. M.'s thesis foreshadowed utilitarianism. BIBLIOGRAPHY: E. Sprague, EncPhil 5:147–149; the account of M.'s life in the introd. essay by F. B. Kaye to his modern ed. of M.'s *Fable of the Bees* (2 v., 1924).

[M. M. BARRY]

MANDEVILLE, SIR JOHN (*c.*1290–?), supposed author of one of the best-known books of the Middle Ages, his *Travels*. But this work is believed to be actually a compilation from other authors. There is hardly a page in the book that does not have its share of marvels: the gigantic race with one eye in the middle of the forehead; people with no heads but eyes in their shoulders; the fountain of youth; anthills of gold dust, and so forth. Its aim was to be a guide to pilgrims to the Holy Land. It is quite an admirable work, expressing with remarkable fidelity the English craze for traveling, and it supplied romantic inspiration for generations. Sir John began to travel in 1322 and journeyed in the East for over 30 years. Having returned home, he produced his book, originally written in French (1356), and translated into English and Latin. The work is, as far as it is known, the first considerable example of prose in English and the first book of *belles lettres* in English prose. It is of special interest, too, because it was the first time that the subject and the author produced between them a style. The sentences are mostly short; the vocabulary is simple and rather modern, with few obsolete or archaic words. It contributed to the rise of a literary prose style in English. BIBLIOGRAPHY: J. W. Bennett, *Rediscovery of Sir John Mandeville* (1954).

[S. A. HEENEY]

MANDONNET, PIERRE (1858–1936), French Dominican pioneer in critical historical studies of Thomism and of the origins of the Friars Preachers. He joined the Dominicans in France, but spent a good part of his career (1891–1918) as church history professor at the Univ. of Fribourg, Switzerland. He was the founder of the *Bulletin thomiste* and the *Revue thomiste*. His *Des écrits authentiques de St. Thomas d'Aquin* became a standard for the bibliography of Aquinas, although later scholarship sorted out as spurious some works M. classified as authentic. His study of Latin Averroism (*Siger de Brabant et l'averroisme au xiiie siècle,* 2v., ed. 1908–11) was also a fontal work, though, again, later scholarship, particularly a work of F. Van Steenberghen on Siger, replaced some of M.'s positions. In Dominican history M.'s *St. Dominic and His Work* (tr. M. B. Larkin, 1944), published in French posthumously (M. H. Vicaire ed. 1938) was notable for its interpretation on the basis of contemporary documentation of St. Dominic's intent for the life, the governance, and the mission of the Friars Preachers. M.'s work on Dante, *Dante le théologien* (2d ed. 1935) is also highly regarded, although K. Foster's *The Two Dantes and Other Studies* (1977) shows that the Thomism of the great Florentine has been exaggerated.

[T. C. O'BRIEN]

MANDYAS (Gr. for cloak; Sl. *mantiya*), the name of two types of garment in the Byzantine Church. (1) A black, hoodless monastic cape, part of the angelic habit of the advanced Byzantine monk and worn on solemn occasions. (2) The choir mantle of bps. in the Byzantine Church. It is made of purple or blue silk, open in the front but fastened at the neck and again beneath the knees. Four richly embroidered squares (Gr. *pomata*, potions; Sl. *skrizhali*, tables) sometimes depicting pictures or symbols of the Evangelists are found at the fastenings. Horizontal stripes of red and white come forth from these squares to symbolize the life-giving streams of true doctrine. The mandyas is also worn by prelates such as the archimandrite or hegumenos of a monastery but is black in color. The episcopal mandyas usually has a long train which is carried by a train bearer and may be ornamented at the bottom with tassels or little bells reminiscent of the decoration of the ephod of the Jewish high priest.

[A. J. JACOPIN]

MANDYLION OF EDESSA, icon of Christ. According to the Syriac "Doctrine of Addai" (6th cent.) the portrait, the only one of Jesus, was painted by Hannan, a secretary and envoy of king Abgar V Ukkama of Edessa (today Urfa, Turkey) A.D. 9–46. He had been sent to Jerusalem with a letter of the king and had taken back a reply of Our Lord. He had also painted Jesus, and this icon, Mandylion, was later believed to have been painted by Jesus himself. It was venerated in Edessa till 944, when it was seized by the Muslim conquerors, who ceded it to the Byzantine emperor in return for a heavy ransom and the liberation of Muslim captives. A Jacobite writing in Arabic states that he saw the mandylion at Constantinople in the Hagia Sophia in 1058. It was taken to the West by the Crusaders, probably after the Fourth Crusade, and was lost.

[J. MADEY]

MANEGOLD OF LAUTENBACH (*c.* 1030–*c.* 1103), canon regular, teacher, and writer. Although he was previously married, M. entered the monastery of Lautenbach before 1084. Known as a theologian and Augustinian jurist, he founded a convent at Raitenbuch (1086) and one at Marbach (1090). He participated in the investiture controversy between Gregory VII and Henry IV, and wrote against the latter *Manegoldi ad Gebehardum liber*. His works also include *Opusculum contra Wolfelmum Coloniensem*. BIBLIOGRAPHY: F. Courtney, NCE 9:148; E. Maccagnolo, EncCatt 7:1951–52.

[J. R. RIVELLO]

MANESSIER, ALFRED (1911–), French abstract artist, avant-garde religious painter, living in Paris, first studied architecture, turning to painting (1935) under R. Bissière. Religious themes dominate M.'s work after 1943. He designed stained glass windows for churches at Breseux in Doubs, at Basel, and Arles, and mosaics for the chapel of Ste. Thérèse at Hem, France (1958), having won the Carnegie International award, 1955. M.'s paintings show shapes in patterns broken as in glass or mosaic. The religious content is implied, not represented, the spiritual and mystical import deriving from light and color (*For the Feast of Christ the King*, 1952, and *Crown of Thorns*, 1955).

[M. J. DALY]

MANETHO, Egyptian priest and historian who wrote in the era of the first Ptolemies (*c.* 300 B.C.). He wrote in Greek, translating several Egyptian annals and providing a history of Egypt (*Aegyptiaca*). Much of his work is lost, but some has been preserved by Josephus (esp. in *Against Apion I*, at least in abridged form) and by Christian chronographers (Julius Africanus; Eusebius). M.'s work seems to have been frequently used by Jewish and Christian authors to establish biblical chronology. One notable legend he recorded attributes the origins of the Jews to an alleged banishment from Egypt as lepers; this becomes a standard Egyptian counter-tale to the Israelite account in Exodus, and a staple of pre-Christian anti-Semitism. BIBLIOGRAPHY: W. G. Waddell, *Manetho* (1940); R. Laqueur, PW 14.1:1060–1101; M. Stern, *Greek and Latin Authors on Jews and Judaism* (1976) 1:62–86.

[D. P. EFROYMSON]

MANETTI, GIANNOZZA (1396–1459), Italian statesman and humanist. Born in Florence of a noble family, he became active in political and ecclesiastical affairs. After successfully defending himself against accusations of treason he went into exile in 1453, and taught himself Greek and Hebrew. He was appointed apostolic secretary by Pope Nicholas V. Eventually, he composed Latin translations of the Psalter and NT from the original languages. Other works are: *Chronicum Pistoriense; De illustribus longaevis; Contra Judaeos et Gentes libri X; De Liberis educandis*. M.'s *De dignitate . . . hominis* (1532), written against the *De miseria hominis* of Innocent III, was put on the Index in Spain in 1584. BIBLIOGRAPHY: K. H. Oelrich, LTK 6:1349; H. Barron, *Crisis of the Early Italian Renaissance: Civic Humanism and Republican Liberty in an Age of Classicism and Tyranny*.

[J. R. RIVELLO]

MANFRED (*c.* 1232–66), **KING OF SICILY** from 1258. A legitimized natural son of Emperor Frederick II, M. served as regent of Sicily for his half-brother Conrad IV and his nephew Conradin. As leader of the Italian Ghibellines, he incurred the opposition of the papacy and was defeated and killed at Benevento by a coalition between Urban IV and Charles of Anjou. Dante places him in Ante-Purgatory (*Purg.* iii, 112–146). BIBLIOGRAPHY: J. M. Powell, NCE 9:149–150.

[M. A. WINKLEMANN]

MANFREDA OF PIROVANO (d. 1302), a heretical nun, a disciple of *Wilhelma of Bohemia. According to M., Wilhelma was the incarnation of the Holy Spirit, who would rise from the dead and ascend into heaven. M. saw herself as Wilhelma's vicar, just as Peter was vicar of Christ. Members of the sect wore costly garments in their expectation of Wilhelma's resurrection. The new era to which they looked forward would be announced in new gospels, and it would be characterized by the passing of dominion into the hands of women. M. celebrated Mass clad in the liturgical dress of a priest. She and a priest who was one of her followers were condemned by the Inquisition and burned at the stake. BIBLIOGRAPHY: L. Oliger, EncCatt 6:1251–52 s.v. "Guglielmiti."

[P. K. MEAGHER]

MANGENOT, JOSEPH EUGÈNE (1856–1922), Scripture scholar. M. taught at the seminary in Nancy (1883–1903), and at the Institut Catholique in Paris (1903–22). He was an important collaborator with F. *Vigouroux on the *Dictionnaire de la Bible* (DB), contributed innumerable articles to the *Dictionnaire de la théologie catholique* (DTC) of which, upon the death of A. *Vacant, M. became the director (1901). In addition to his articles on textual criticism, general introduction to Bible study, exegesis, and biblical theology, M. published significant treatises on the Mosaic authorship of the Pentateuch, the Resurrection, and the Synoptic Gospels. BIBLIOGRAPHY: É. Amann, DTC 9.2:1830–41; A. Clamer, DBSuppl 5:789–793; A. Cousineau, NCE 9:150.

[T. M. MCFADDEN]

MANGER, place where Mary laid the infant Jesus (Lk 2.7,12,16). The Greek term (*phatnē*) properly meant a trough for cattle fodder, but sometimes its meaning was extended to include the stall or cattle enclosure. In NT times, the manger proper was generally carved out of stone, forming a kind of box that would sit on the floor. Caves also served as stables, and in them mangers were often carved out of the walls. The tradition that Jesus was born in a cave is traceable to the time of Justin (*c.* 150).

[T. EARLY]

MANICHAEISM, a religious system and Church, once believed to be a Christian heresy, but now more accurately seen as a world religion quite distinct from all others. It rose in the 3d cent. A.D. and its founder was Mani (Manes, Manichaens). It centers on a *gnōsis* (revelation to an elect) and drew elements from Babylonian, Hindu, Judaic, and Christian sources. The great prophets are Buddha, Zoroaster, Jesus, and the culminating teacher, Mani. Manichaeism spread from Babylonia into much of Asia, Europe, and North Africa. It was essentially a missionary religion and the elect were called to devote their lives to propagating it. Complex and esoteric, it had great appeal to both East and West. Duality is its fundamental concept: there are two uncreated principles, Light (goodness) and Darkness (Evil). Creation is the result of interpenetration of the two principles. The Father of Light and the Prince of Darkness are at war, and the created world is the battleground. Knowledge, spirit, and the soul are manifestations of light. Ignorance, matter, and the body are parts of darkness and evil. The faithful undergo redemption through awareness and moral practices which include abstinence from meat, wine, all sexual contacts and work. Man must liberate the particles of Light within him and be a corner of the revelation to those around him. The present state of man makes him a victim of the Evil which created the world. His purpose is to rise above a basically evil creation by sharing in the redeeming light even in this time of struggle on earth. The Manichaen Church had two classes of followers: the Elect (liberators of the Light) who were fully initiated into the mysteries and practiced the abstentions required by Manichaen morality. The Auditors were more numerous and practiced an imperfect version of the moral code. They required a purgatory of transmigration before entering paradise, whereas the Elect entered immediately.

The early history of Manichaeism was one of persecution. From its beginnings it was proscribed in the Roman Empire by a succession of emperors. The Fathers of the Church (notably St. Augustine, once a Manichaen himself) wrote against it for centuries. It was the target of pagan critics. Nevertheless Manichaeism continued in many places. In China, for example, it persisted until the time of Ghengis Kahn (13th century). Later forms of gnostic religion such as the Cathari and Albigensian heresies carried much of the Manichaen doctrine in the 13th cent. in the West. BIBLIOGRAPHY: G. Bardy, DTC 9:1841–95.

[J. R. AHERNE]

MANIERA, term for a style of late 16th-cent. Italian painters who translated mannerist intellectuality into a decorative aestheticism with distortion. Notable are F. Primaticcio and T. Zuccari.

[M. J. DALY]

MANIPLE, an oblong strip of cloth which hangs over the wrist or forearm in equal folds. Its use in liturgical services is no longer obligatory. It began as a linen cloth which was much like a handkerchief, became stylized as a formal item of dress, and after Constantine (d. 337) was a symbol of rank. It spread throughout Europe between the 7th and 9th centuries. In the 12th cent. it became a badge of the subdiaconate. *LITURGICAL VESTMENTS.

[N. KOLLAR]

MANITIUS, MAX (1858–1933), medieval historian, philologist. He was associated (1822–84) with the *Monumenta Germaniae historica*. Although M. edited several medieval Latin texts and published monographs in medieval history, his greatest contribution was in medieval Latin literature. In this area he published the *Geschichte der Christlich-lateinischen Poesie bis zur Mitte des 8. Jahrhunderts* (1891) and the three volumes of the *Geschichte der lateinischen Literatur des Mittelalters* (1911, 1923, 1931) in the series *Handbuch der klassischen Altertums-Wissenschaft*. These three volumes extend from Boethius to the first quarter of the 13th century. There is a biographical treatment of each author, citation of sources on which the vita is based, discussion of the specific contribution, MSS and editions. BIBLIOGRAPHY: F. Brunholzl, LTK 6:1357; A. Ziegler, NCE, 9:163.

[J. J. SMITH]

MANN, HORACE (1796–1859), American educator and reputed ''Father of the American Public School.'' A graduate of Brown Univ. (1819) and admitted to the Massachusetts bar (1823), M. was elected to the state legislature (1827), made senate speaker (1835), and first secretary of the state board of education (1837). In this last capacity he agitated for better schools, higher salaries for teachers; teacher-training institutes; and improved methods based on the Pestalozzian system he had observed abroad (1843). M., who rejected dogma and any ''man-made'' religion, set a national pattern of religious formation by allowing only the basic religious and moral principles of the Bible to be taught in school, a compromise that favored only some religious groups. Defeated for Massachusetts governor (1852), M. became first president of Antioch College, Ohio (1853). His works include his 12 *Annual Reports* and the *Common School Journal*. BIBLIOGRAPHY: L. H. Tharp, *Until Victory: Horace Mann and Mary Peabody* (1953).

[M. B. MURPHY]

MANN, THOMAS (1875–1955), novelist and essayist. M.'s psychological novels and stories reflect Schopenhauer's and Nietzsche's views applied to the decadence of the German bourgeoisie, as well as the painful yet desirable isolation of the artist in bourgeois society. Later M. reinterpreted mythological and biblical themes in his highly polished narrative style. His essays deal with a variety of aspects of the cultural, literary, political, and philosophical life in Germany and Europe. M.'s first great novel *Die Buddenbrooks* (1901) describes the gradual decline of an energetic patrician family in Lübeck. His most profound work, *Doktor Faustus* (1947) shows man falling into barbarism and chaos. He received the Nobel prize for literature in 1929. BIBLIOGRAPHY: I. Feuerlicht, *Thomas Mann* (1968).

[S. A. SCHULZ]

MANNA, a substance which the Israelites ate during their wilderness wanderings. Num 11.7–9 describes it simply as resembling coriander seed, which the people ''ground in mills or beat in mortars, and boiled in pots, and made into cakes. It tasted like cake made with oil.'' This description suggests the sweet resinous excretions of scale insects feeding on the tamarisk trees in the Sinai desert. The Bedouins still call it *man* today. Compared with their Egyptian diet, this was worthless food and the Israelites murmured against it, arousing the anger of Yahweh (Num 11.4–34). Later traditions describe the manna theologically as a wonder which reveals Yahweh's marvelous power in providing for the people, and a sign to teach them complete reliance on God (Ex 16.10–30). This symbolic meaning of the manna is further developed in Dt 8.3,16; Wis 16.20–23 and Ps 78.25. The tension between the material reality of the manna and its deeper significance forms the OT background of Jn 6, the Bread of Life discourse. Like Yahweh Jesus provided food for the people. The Jews saw this as a wonder similar to the manna and alluded to it (Jn 6.31). But like their ancestors in the desert they did not recognize the deeper significance of the bread: a sign to teach them complete reliance on Christ; the physical bread was the sign that Jesus was the bread of life. Salvation now lies in accepting Christ as the genuine life-giving bread from heaven (Jn 6.32–58). ''The manna in the desert, the multiplication of the loaves, the eucharistic meal were all related signs of the great banquet in the Kingdom of heaven.'' BIBLIOGRAPHY: J. Plastaras, *God of Exodus* (1966) 286–292; R. Brown, *Gospel according to John I–XII* (1966) 231–304.

[E. CABEY]

MANNERISM, a debated style in art (*c.* 1520–1580), originating in Italy as a perversion, some say, of the rational ideals of the High Renaissance, and noted for its pronounced emotional aestheticism accompanied by a disturbing combination of distortions such as the crowding of compositions, attenuation of figures, exaggeration of poses, ambiguity of space, and acidity of color.

[L. A. LEITE]

MANNERS, see POLITENESS.

MANNING, HENRY EDWARD (1808–92), second abp. of Westminster, 1865–92, cardinal from 1875. After reading classics at Balliol College, Oxford, from 1830 M. worked briefly as a civil servant, but was drawn to the Church and in 1832 became a fellow of Merton College and was ordained in the Church of England. In 1833 he received his first parish, and married Caroline Sargent. (Her death 5 years later was a great blow and he observed her anniversary till the end of his life.) From the beginning of his ministry he gave himself to causes he would espouse all his life: educational opportunity, social reform, opposition to *rationalism. In 1840 he became archdeacon of Chichester and two years later select preacher at Oxford. Under the influence of the *Oxford Movement he published *The Unity of the Church* in 1842, a statement of the Anglo-Catholic position. These views, the Gorham Judgment in which the State approved as vicar a minister who held heretical views on baptism (M. wrote a letter in protest to the bp. of Chichester), and a tour of Catholic Europe (during which he visited Pius IX) brought to a conclusion M.'s leanings towards Rome. He was received into the Catholic Church April 6, 1851 and the same year ordained priest by Card. Wiseman, abp. of Westminster. For 3 years, at the request of Pius IX, M. studied in Rome at the Academy for Noble Ecclesiastics. In this period he published *The Grounds of Faith* (1852), arguing that Roman Catholic teaching alone could effectively oppose rationalism. Returning to England he set up a system of archdiocesan primary schools, and the Westminster Diocesan Education Fund to promote them. In 1857 he was named provost of the Westminster chapter of canons, and in the same year founded the *Oblates of St. Charles, a community for diocesan priests which he directed until 1865. M. continued apologetical writing: his article "Workings of the Holy Spirit in the Church of England" prompted E. *Pusey's famous letter to J. *Keble, . . . *an Eirenicon* (1865). Others of M.'s polemical essays appeared in *England and Christendom* (1867). As successor to Wiseman he founded schools, orphanages, homes for the needy. In 1872 he published *National Education and Parental Rights,* which stimulated the growth of Catholic schools; in 1890 he was the vigorous opponent of the Education Act, an attempt to legislate civil control over education, and as a member of a royal commission on education achieved by his statesmanship the compromise of 1891. His zeal for labor was evidenced in his pamphlet, "The Dignity and Rights of Labor" (1887) and it was his intervention that brought about a settlement favorable to workers of the Dock Strike of 1889. He strove to end child labor and to stop the East African slave trade. In church affairs he was the champion in England of papal infallibility and played a key role in bringing about the definition at Vatican Council I. After the Council, which caused a furor in England, M. published a powerful answer to W. E. *Gladstone's attack: "The Vatican Decrees in their Bearing on Civil Allegiance"—picking up Gladstone's own wording and giving a lucid exposition of the ultramontane version of the Church-State relationship. M. also wrote works of devotion that were widely read, esp. *The Eternal Priesthood* (1883; repr. 1950). The tension between M. and the other giant of 19th-cent. English Catholicism, J. H. *Newman, is well known. They shared similar backgrounds and theological views as Anglicans; both were affected in their conversion by the Oxford Movement; Newman's *Development of Christian Doctrine* was a principal influence on M.'s drift to Catholicism. But there was a sharp contrast in temperament and personality, in social outlook, in method of thinking and theological assessment that caused painful barriers to their collaborating as Catholics. M. was a man of virtue, compassion, and integrity; it is tragic that he could not share Newman's warmer, more intuitive perceptions of the Catholic approach to the rationalist or skeptic. But it was M. who was the most influential of all activist figures in the Catholicism of 19th-cent. England. BIBLIOGRAPHY: V. A. McClelland, *Cardinal Manning, His Public Life and Influence* (1962).

[J. R. AHERNE]

MANNIX, DANIEL (1864–1963), Irish abp. of Melbourne. M. was often the center of controversy for his outspoken opposition to Britain. A teacher at Maynooth, Ireland, after his ordination in 1890, he headed the famous seminary from 1903 to 1912 and brought the college to great prominence as a newly constituted constituent of the National Univ. of Ireland. Named coadjutor bp. of Melbourne, Australia in 1912, he became abp. in 1917. M. was a defender of Irish independence and successfully opposed conscription in Australia during World War I. Enroute to Rome in 1920, because of the Irish troubles his ship was stopped by British warships off the coast of England and M. was removed, the government refusing to allow him to speak in England. M. was an extraordinary administrator of his diocese, building hundreds of churches and schools, founding two colleges and a seminary, and becoming a leader in Catholic Action, social action, and the liturgical movement. BIBLIOGRAPHY: F. Murphy, *Daniel Mannix, Archbishop of Melbourne* (1948).

[J. R. AHERNE]

MANOGUE, PATRICK (1831–95), American bp., missionary. Born in Ireland, he came to the U.S. in 1848. In 1850 he began studies for the priesthood; but to help his family he interrupted them by several years' work in the gold fields of California. He resumed his studies at Saint-Sulpice in Paris and was ordained there in 1861. He was pastor of N Nevada and from Virginia City, Nev., carried out extraordinary missionary activity among whites and Indians. In 1870 M. became vicar general of the Diocese of Grass Valley, Nev. and was named coadjutor bp. in 1881. He became first bp. of Sacramento, Cal., in 1884, when it was made the seat of the diocese. He built a magnificent cathedral and became a major public figure and a leader among miners and mine operators.

[J. R. AHERNE]

MANRESA, name often given to retreat houses of the Society of Jesus. After his conversion St. *Ignatius of Loyola, the Jesuit founder, spent 11 months in prayerful seclusion at Manresa, near Montserrat, the Benedictine mountain abbey outside of Barcelona. At Manresa Ignatius composed the greater part of his *Spiritual Exercises, which became the basis for the Jesuits' promotion of what has become the spiritual retreat in the Church.

MANRÍQUES Y ZÁRATE, JOSÉ DE JESÚS (1884–1951), bishop. A native of Mexico ordained in 1907, M. as pastor in Guanajuato established parochial schools, two secondary schools, one for higher studies, the Ketteler Workers Circle, and the League for Catholic Social Action in the years 1912 to 1922. He was a vigorous administrator, reaching the Indians, founding schools and promoting social action. M. became the most militant of the Mexican bps. in opposition to the persecution of the Church by President Calles, who sentenced him to 1 year in prison and then exiled him (1927). In the U.S. M. became the spokesman for the persecuted Church in Mexico. M. resigned as bp. in 1939 and in 1944 was permitted, by reason of failing health, to return to Mexico. There he engaged in a vigorous campaign of preaching until 1949 when he was named vicar general of Mexico City. His funeral was a triumph of popular acclaim.

[J. R. AHERNE]

MANSE, in Scotland, and elsewhere in Presbyterian parishes, the minister's residence (Lat. *mansio*); more generally, any clergyman's dwelling.

[T. C. O'BRIEN]

MANSI, GIOVANNI DOMENICO (1692–1769), historian, scholar. At an early age M. entered the Congregation of the Mother of God. Later he taught moral theology at Naples. Called to Lucca to be the abp.'s theologian, M. founded an academy for the study of the history of the Church and the liturgy. In 1765, Clement XIII appointed him abp. of Lucca. M.'s outstanding work is his collection of the acts of the councils down to 1440: *Sacrorum conciliorum nova et amplissima collectio*. This work, based on the previous collections of Labbe, Cossart, and Coleti, needs to be redone. It lacks critical spirit and contains numerous errors. However, the *Amplissima collectio* is still useful by reason of its comprehensive coverage. BIBLIOGRAPHY: H. Rumpler, NCE 9:173; R. Bäumer, LTK 6:1365; J. Carreyre, DTC 9:1915–16; Hefele-Leclercq 1.1:111–114.

[J. M. O'DONNELL]

MANSIONARIUS, Roman name for the porter of a church.

MANSLAUGHTER, in civil law the unlawful taking of another's life in a manner other than by murder; it is classified in law as either voluntary or involuntary. Moral theology considers the meaning of manslaughter in discussing *homicide and the ways in which taking another's life is not fully or directly intended.

[T. C. O'BRIEN]

MANSO DE NORONHA, JUANA, PAULA (1819–75), educator, writer. An Argentinian, daughter of a family that fled to Uruguay because of political persecution, she founded there, as a girl in her teens, the Ateneo de Señoritas, a school for girls. In Rio de Janeiro she published an important poem *Una Armonîa* (1844) and several other books. On a visit to the U.S. she found a friend in Horace Mann. After the death of her husband, the Brazilian violinist F. Saa de la Noronha, she returned to Buenos Aires where, in 1854, she established a magazine *Album de señoritas*. A proponent of women's rights, M. was appointed by the government director of a coeducational school. Among published works of this period was *Compendio de la historia de las provincias unidas*. From 1868 to 1874 she was in the Department of Education of Argentina.

[J. R. AHERNE]

MANTEGNA, ANDREA (1431–1506), master painter of the northern Italian school. Working in Padua and Mantua, M. painted the Ovetari chapel ceiling (*c.* 1450) in the Eremitani church, Padua (bombed, 1944). M.'s famous altarpiece in S. Zeno, Verona (1456–59) with the renowned predella *Crucifixion* (Louvre) shows spatial arrangement anti-Florentine and Venetian, rooted in G. Bellini (whose daughter M. had married, 1454). M. was court painter to L. Gonzaga in Mantua (1457), and visited Florence and Rome between 1466 and 1489. His heroic figures exquisitely arranged in classical settings attest to the Paduan worship of the antique. In severe foreshortening (*The Dead Christ*, 1489, Milan) M. challenged Tuscan masters, and anticipated 17th-cent. Baroque work in the dramatically recessive planes of his ceiling in the *Camera degli Sposi* (Ducal Palace, Mantua). Master engravings by M., attaining his usual monumentality, were guides for Dürer. BIBLIOGRAPHY: R. Cipriani, *All the Paintings of Mantegna* (1964).

[M. J. DALY]

MANTELLETTA, a sleeveless garment, fastened at the neck but open in front, worn liturgically by cardinals, bishops, abbots, and papal prelates. Round in form, it reaches to just below the knees and is of the same color as the individual's cassock. It seems originally to have been a mantle or cape, covering the rochet.

[J. DALLEN]

MANTELLATE SISTERS (OSM: Servants of Mary Servites; Filippine), religious women of the Third Order Servites. Founded originally by St. *Juliana Falconieri in 13th-cent. Florence, "documentation is practically nonexistent" for the early period (see Ryska, bibliog.). By the mid-1900s worldwide there were 24 congregations and 4 independent convents of women, 11 pontifical and 13 diocesan; the present article is concerned chiefly with those who came to the U.S., all but one branch being of pontifical right. The earliest (1893) was made with Mother Mary Gertrude as superior, first at Mt. Vernon, Ind. but later at Blue Island, Ill. That at Ladysmith (Wis., diocesan) was made in 1912. Sisters at Sublimity, Ore. stem from Vienna-Mauer, Austria. The Omaha group (1916) originated in the French-English branch centered in London and has a motherhouse in Rome. The Mantellate teach (elementary through college), care for the aged and sick, and engage in parish visiting and social work. Members numbered (1976) 2,786 in 286 houses (of pontifical right). Some 2500 both pontifical and diocesan are presently in the U.S. apostolate. BIBLIOGRAPHY: J. M. Ryska, NCE 13:130–135 s. v. "Servants of Mary" and "Servites"; P. J. Griffin, CE 13: esp. 737 s. v. "Servites"; J. P. Kirsch, *ibid.* 8:556 s. v. "Julia Falconieri"; A. Pugliese, EncCatt 7:1985; Kapsner 244–245; M. F. De Mato, NCE 9:174.

[M. R. BROWN]

MANTOVA, BENEDETTO DA (fl. 1549), Italian Benedictine connected with Juan de Valdés's circle in Naples. His treatise on the benefits of Christ's death (1542–43) was widely circulated and translated before its condemnation by the Inquisition. BIBLIOGRAPHY: W. Göbell, RGG 4:730.

[M. J. SUELZER]

MANTRA, in the Hindu, Buddhist, and perhaps esp. the Tantric traditions, a series of sounds or words (sometimes a scriptural verse; most often the sounds are meaningless to all but the initiated) imparted by a guru or teacher to his disciple as part of initiation. Its recitation is used psychologically as support for meditation and concentration; it is further believed to possess a metaphysical or cosmic power enabling the devotee to be united with, or at least interiorly "in tune" with, a universal force, a divine being, or ultimate reality. BIBLIOGRAPHY: A. Bharati, *Tantric Tradition* (1970) 101–63.

[D. P. EFROYMSON]

MANTUAN WAR OF SUCCESSION (1527–31), struggle for Italian supremacy between France and the Habsburgs of Spain and Austria. Mantua, in the Po Valley, was a strategic and wealthy buffer between the Duchy of Milan and the Republic of Venice. When Vincenzo Gonzaga died in 1527, his niece Maria held claim to the Mantuan fief of Montferrat and his cousin, the Duke of Nevers, appeared the logical male heir to Mantua itself. Nevers improved his position by having his son, the Duke of Rethel, marry Maria and then he immediately moved into Mantua. However, Nevers was a Frenchman, an ally of Louis XIII, and his presence in northern Italy threatened the Habsburgs and the Duke of Savoy. France desired a route of access to Italy through the territory of Carlo Emanuele, Duke of Savoy. In opposition to the French, Carlo allied himself with Spain and claimed Montferrat. Although Savoy experienced an initial victory in his war with the French, a second, larger French army defeated him in 1629 while Nevers occupied the Spanish forces of Milan. Savoy signed a treaty which guaranteed France a route into Italy but almost immediately allied with the Habsburg army that was invading Italy. The imperial army besieged Nevers and his Venetian allies at Mantua. Louis XIII led a French army that again defeated Carlo Emanuele's army. The Austrian army of 35,000 soldiers held Mantua under seige while the plague swept the city, killing at least 70 percent of the population. Finally, the Imperial army under Aldringhen entered, and sacked Mantua. The treaty of Ratisbon between France and the Holy Roman Empire (1630) allowed Nevers to regain possession of Mantua. In 1631 France negotiated a settlement with Carlo Emanuele's successor in Savoy. This treaty acknowledged French territorial possessions in Italy. The Habsburgs, once predominant in Italy, could not contest the French intrusion because its troops were needed to meet the Swedish threat in the north. BIBLIOGRAPHY: S. Brinton, *Gonzaga–Lords of Mantua* (1927); K. D. Vernon, *Italy 1494–1790* (1909); C. V. Wedgwood, *Thirty Years' War* (1939).

[R. J. BRADY]

MANUAL MASSES, those that are to be celebrated in fulfillment of the obligation incurred by acceptance of a *stipend from someone offering it out of devotion or to satisfy the terms of a will (CIC c. 826, §1). Classified like manual Masses (*ad instar manualium*) are those offered, as allowed by the terms of a *pious foundation or by indult of the Holy See, in a place or by a priest other than the place or priest stipulated by the terms of the foundation (*ibid.*, §2).

[T. C. O'BRIEN]

MANUAL OF DISCIPLINE (*Serek ha-Yaḥad*), the rule of the *Qumran community. Several MSS have been discovered; the document has been dated from *c.* 100–75 B.C. The rule is inspired by Jer 32.37–41. Like the Jews in the desert, the members must withdraw and live according to the spirit of light and truth in order to become a new Israel and enter into the new covenant promised by God. BIBLIOGRAPHY: M. Burrows, *Dead Sea Scrolls* (1955).

[T. EARLY]

MANUAL OF THE MOTHER CHURCH, also called *Church Manual of the First Church of Christ, Scientist,* the fundamental law of the Church of Christ, Scientist, establishing in minute detail the polity, form of worship, and other particulars of the Christian Science movement. It is composed of a series of bylaws, which cannot be in any way altered or repealed since the death of Mary Baker Eddy and which are binding and normative for all branch Churches of Christ, Scientist. The Christian Science Board of Directors, as Mrs. Eddy's representatives and legal successors, are permitted to act only within the scope of the *Manual,* and its terms are as binding on them as on any other member. The *Manual* was first published in 1895 and was periodically revised until 1906; it has preserved Mrs. Eddy's legislation intact since that time and prevented alteration or dissension within the Christian Science movement.

[R. K. MACMASTER]

MANUEL I COMNENUS (1120–80), **BYZANTINE EMPEROR** from 1143. An outstanding general and statesman, M. maintained very close ties with western Europe. He forced the Latin states in the Near East to submit to him, but was unsuccessful against the Turks. BIBLIOGRAPHY: Ostrogorsky 337–350.

[G. T. DENNIS]

MANUEL II PALAEOLOGUS (1348?–1425), **BYZANTINE EMPEROR** from 1391. He devoted his energies to calming the civil strife within the empire as well as to resisting the attacks of the external foes, particularly the Turks. In a futile effort to obtain Western aid, M. visited Paris and London. He was also genuinely interested in theology and literature, composing an impressive number of works himself. He encouraged the work of Byzantine humanists who played an important role in the beginnings of the Italian Renaissance. BIBLIOGRAPHY: G. Dennis, *Reign of Manuel II Palaeologus in Thessalonica, 1382–1387* (1960); J. Barker, *Manuel II Palaeologus (1391–1425): A Study in Late Byzantine Statesmanship* (1967).

[G. T. DENNIS]

MANUEL II (d. 1254), **PATRIARCH OF CONSTANTINOPLE** from 1244. In residence at the temporary Byzantine capital of Nicaea, Patriarch M. was involved in negotiations concerning possible union with the Roman Church, and union between the Armenian and Byzantine Churches.

[G. T. DENNIS]

MANUEL CALECAS (d. 1410), Byzantine theologian and rhetorician. A native of Constantinople, M. felt called to the religious life but did not become a monk because he opposed *hesychasm. He opened a school, which proved unsuccessful. About 1391 he became a disciple of Demetrius Cydones, who introduced him to Aristotelian philosophy and Thomas Aquinas. Largely owing to his opposition to hesychasm, which brought the wrath of the Orthodox Church upon him, he became a Catholic in 1396. He journeyed throughout the Byzantine Empire, engaged in theological controversy, and after a few years in Italy settled on Lesbos where he entered the Dominicans. His writings, imbued with scholasticism, include theological and polemical treatises and Greek translations of Latin theological works. BIBLIOGRAPHY: R. J. Loenertz, *Correspondance de Manuel Calécas, ST* 152 (1950; *idem*, "Manuel Calécas: Sa vie et ses oeuvres", AFP 17 (1947) 195–207; Beck 740–41.

[G. T. DENNIS]

MANUEL-DEUTSCH, NIKOLAUS (1484–1530), Swiss painter and wood-engraver, influenced by Dürer, Baldung-Grien and Grünewald. M. painted panels for the *Mary Altar* for the Dominican cloister, Bern (1515), showing a *Beheading of St. John the Baptist* and the *Temptation of St. Anthony*, an important mural—*Dance of Death* (1515–20) and a noteworthy woodcut series—*The Wise and Foolish Virgins*. His figures in elaborate costume, restricted within the narrow front area of the picture, are strongly animated in gesture. As councilman in Bern (1528) M. espoused the Reformation, propagating it through woodcuts which attacked the Church.

[M. J. DALY]

MANUELINE STYLE, Portuguese architectural style in the time of King Manuel I (1495–1521)—a combination of Islamic, Flamboyant Gothic and some Renaissance elements with luxurious decoration. (Portal of Batalha Abbey by Mateus Fernandes and the nave of the abbey church, Tomar, by Di Ogo and Francisco Arrudas exemplify the best of the style).

[M. J. DALY]

MANUSCRIPT ILLUMINATION, term applied to many types of decoration of MS pages. Beginning in the 6th cent., Byzantine artists, adapting the methods used in Hellenistic illumination of ancient Greek classics, provided a rich counterpart to Byzantine church painting and mosaic. In Europe from the 7th to the 9th cent., Anglo-Irish art produced masterpieces in the Lindisfarne Gospels and the Book of Kells, remarkable for a complex, intricate fantasy of decorated initials. On the continent great Carolingian MSS include the *Vivian Bible* from the school of Tours, and the 9th-cent. *Utrecht Psalter* whose illustration consists of extraordinary lively and expressive drawings without color.

German MSS of the Ottonian period, chiefly from the island of Reichenau, are characterized by lavish use of color and gold appropriate to their regal style. Outstanding examples are the 10th-cent. *Codex Egberti* and the 11th-cent. *Evangeliary of Otto III*. The flowering of monasticism during the Romanesque period helped to spread the art of illumination. The work of high medieval artists on the MS page complemented—in inventiveness and subtlety—Gothic stained glass and sculpture, culminating in *Les Très riches heures du Duc de Berry* by the Limbourg brothers. BIBLIOGRAPHY: D. Miner, *Illuminated and Illustrated Books* (1949).

[M. J. DALY]

MANZ, FELIX (1500–27), Swiss Anabaptist martyr. M. was a humanist and at first a close associate of Zwingli, but broke with him and accepted *Anabaptist ideas. After the ceremony of rebaptism in Jan. 1525, expressive of Anabaptist belief (see GREBEL, C., and BLAUROCK, G.), and in spite of persecutions and imprisonment, M. won many converts in the N and E of Switzerland. In order to suppress the movement, the city council of Zürich had him drowned in the Limmat River on Jan. 5, 1527.

[T. C. O'BRIEN]

MANZÙ, GIACOMO (1908–), major Italian sculptor. From Bergamo, in art school, Verona (1928), carving in the Catholic Univ. of Milan (1930). M. admired Donatello, Rodin, Maillol; winning prizes (1934), engaging in his famous series of 49 *Cardinals*—monumental, classic expressions of mitre and cope, in pure pyramidal form (1938–59), censured by the Church and Fascists for powerful, unique *Crucifixion* reliefs (1939–43) followed by *Cardinal and Deposition* (1941–42). Commissioned to do a pair of bronze doors for St. Peter's, Rome (1949), M., at the request of Pope John XXIII, hastened to complete the *Door of Death* (1964). He carved the bust of the Pope, and earlier executed his bronze coat-of-arms. M.'s art, endowing all things with poetry and mystery, remains provocative, stripping man of his defenses and leaving him exposed to the horrendous realities which are M.'s concern. BIBLIOGRAPHY: M. Seuphor, *Sculpture of This Century* (1960).

[M. J. DALY]

MAPHRIAN (Mafrian), a title in the *Syrian Jacobite Church, now of the Metropolitan of Jerusalem and the bp. of the Jacobites of S India, as delegates of the Patriarch of Antioch. The term means "fructifier" and has the force of indicating that the bearer as delegate is the source of authority; the title was borne originally by the metropolitan of the Jacobite Church in Persia, who was empowered to choose and consecrate bps. and to consecrate the holy chrism.

[T. C. O'BRIEN]

MĀR (mār(y), a word meaning "(my) Lord" in Syriac. It is used in that rite as a title of Christ, and is prefixed to the names of patriarchs, bishops, and saints (fem., *mārt*[y]).

[A. CODY]

MARABOUT, a Muslim holy man or saint, a term used particularly in N Africa. It is derived from the Arab. *murâbit* (see ALMORAVIDS), one who lives in a ribat or (generally fortified) monastery and dedicates his life to asceticism and the spread of *Islam by means of the sword (see JIHAD). Such communities were particularly common in N Africa where all too often jihad served as little more than a pretext for slaving (see ISLAMIC SLAVERY). Nonetheless, the heads of such communities are esp. revered by the people for their sanctity and are commonly believed to have some supernatural gifts (*baraka*). The term marabout is used in French and thence English to designate a solitary Muslim ascetic.

[R. M. FRANK]

MARAN, PRUDENTIUS (1683–1762), Benedictine biblical and patristic scholar. He was professed in the Maurist abbey of Saint-Faron de Meaux (1703), and studied oriental languages under Abbé Renaudot. At Saint-Germain-des Prés in Paris he assisted Dom Touttée in the edition of the works of St. Cyril of Jerusalem, and then produced a critical edition of the works of St. Cyprian and the letters of St. Basil. In his several treatments of the development of the doctrine of the divinity of Christ, M. was irenic in his treatment of the semi-Arians. At one point he won the praise of Benedict XIV. When he opposed the bull *Unigenitus*, he was forced to leave Saint-Germain (1734). From 1737 he lived in the Paris cloister of the White Friars (Blancs-Manteaux). BIBLIOGRAPHY: D. Misonne, LTK 6:1370; J. Baudot, DTC 9:1933–36.

[E. J. DILLON]

MARANATHA, the transcription into Greek of an Aramaic phrase meaning either "Our Lord, come!" or "Our Lord has come." It is a closing greeting in 1 Cor 16.22. In the first sense, imperatively, it expresses a longing for the return of Jesus as in Rev 22.20, "Amen, come Lord Jesus." In the second sense, declaratively, it can express a warning or curse. It appears to be used in this sense in the *Didache* 10.6. BIBLIOGRAPHY: R. Kugelman, NCE 9:184–185.

[J. A. GRASSI]

MARBACH, ABBEY OF(*Marbacum*), monastery of Augustinian canons founded in 1089 either by a noble woman named Guta or by Burchard de Bebeleswibre in honor of St. Irenaeus or St. Augustine (commune of Vögtlinshoffen, diocese of Basel, and at present Strasbourg, Haut-Rhin, France). The monastery was attached in 1463 to the Congregation of Windesheim. Laid waste several times in the course of the 16th-cent. wars, looted by the Swedes in 1632, Marbach disappeared at the time of the French Revolution. BIBLIOGRAPHY: Cottineau 2:1735–36.

[J. DAOUST]

MARBECK, PILGRAM (Marpeck; *c.* 1495–1556), Anabaptist leader in S Germany. M. was a mining engineer in Rattenberg in the Austrian Tyrol when he turned from Catholicism, first to Lutheranism then to Anabaptism. As an Anabaptist he lost both position and property and was forced in 1528 to seek refuge in Strassburg. At first well received by M. *Bucer and others, he was ordered from the city in 1532 because of his repudiation of infant baptism and his doctrine of a pure, spiritualized Church. Historians have discovered that he spent time in Germany, Switzerland, and Moravia before settling permanently in Augsburg in 1544. Modern research into his life and writings, including his controversies with C. *Schwenkfeld and the *Taufenbüchlein* (baptism booklet), has shed new light, not only on his own highly developed *free church theology, but also on the history and nature of the early Anabaptist movement. BIBLIOGRAPHY: W. Klassen, *Covenant and Community* (1908); MennEnc 3:491–502.

[T. C. O'BRIEN]

MARBOD OF RENNES (*c.* 1035–1123), bp. and poet. M. received his education at the cathedral school at Angers where he later became master. He served as chancellor of the same diocese and in 1096 was appointed bp. of Rennes in Brittany by Urban II, from which see he resigned at the age of 88. As a poet, his skill is manifested in a wide range of subject matter (*Carmina varia*). Among his other writings, largely didactic, are: *Passio S. Laurentii* and *De ornamentis verborum*. BIBLIOGRAPHY: PL 171:1451–1780; Anal Hymn 50:388–403; V. Battezzati, EncCatt 8:6–7; D. D. McGarry, NCE 9:185–186; F. J. Schmale, LTK 6:1372–73.

[J. R. RIVELLO]

MARBURG, ST. ELIZABETH CHURCH (1235–83). The first pure Gothic structure in Germany, Marburg became (1249) pilgrimage shrine of the bones of St. Elizabeth. The architecture combines the German triple-apse and French basilica-plan with elaborate interior ornamentation in the high altar (1290), the shrine of St. Elizabeth, and numerous tombs.

[M. J. DALY]

MARBURG ARTICLES, a statement of Reformation doctrine drawn up by Martin *Luther for the Marburg Colloquy, Oct. 1–3, 1529. This conference was summoned by Philip of Hesse with a view to uniting German and Swiss

Reformers. Luther was accompanied by P. *Melanchthon; the Swiss side was represented by *Zwingli, M. *Bucer, and J. *Oecolampadius. In 14 of the 15 articles the participants agreed concerning the Trinity, the Person of Christ, faith and justification, good works, confession, infant baptism, and human traditions. The 15th article, however, widened the gap between the two parties, since Zwingli could not accept Luther's doctrine of the *Real Presence. The revision of the Articles made by the Lutheran theologians a few days later, the *Schwabach Articles, formed the basis for the first part of the *Augsburg Confession. BIBLIOGRAPHY: Schaff Creeds 1:212–213. *TETRAPOLITAN CONFESSION.

[P. DAMBORIENA]

MARC, CLEMENT (1831–1887), French Redemptorist. He taught and wrote on moral theology, his best-known work being *Institutiones morales Alphonsianae*, which became a standard seminary text (last ed., 1933–34) and was a principal authority on St. Alphonsus Liguori's moral opinions.

[P. J. HENNESSEY]

MARC, FRANZ (1880–1916), German expressionist painter from Munich, in Paris (1903) teaching anatomy (1907–10). After 1909, M. expressed creation and the mystery of nature through abstraction which he considered the spiritualization of art. Though he never abandoned the recognizable subject, as member of the Blue Rider group (1911) M.'s religious approach was as a pantheistic mystic. His rhythms of form mesh with the background (Blue Horses) expressing his philosophy that animals—not man—live harmoniously in nature. The mystery of color was expressed symbolically: blue was male, yellow—gentle, female. Dark premonitions of destruction prevail in 1913–14. M. was killed in the war in 1916.

[M. J. DALY]

MARCA, PIERRE DE (1594–1662), abp. of Toulouse; abp-elect of Paris. Of a family prominent in the magistracy, M. studied first at the Jesuit college, France, then law at the Univ. of Toulouse. Councillor at Pau (1615) and president of its parlement (1621), *intendant* at Béarn, he became a member of the council of state at Paris (1639). His wife M. de Forges, by whom he had four children, had died; he prepared for the priesthood and was ordained 1642. M. served the Crown as governor of Catalonia (1644–51); consecrated bp. of Conservans in Catalonia (1648), at instance of Card. J. Mazarin he was named abp. of Toulouse (1652), serving as minister of state from 1659. Named to succeed Card. J. de Retz at Paris (1662), he died on June 19 in Paris. He wrote a scholarly *Histoire* of his native Béarn (1650) and an account of Catalonia, *Marca Hispanica seu limes hispanicus* (1688); his *De la Concorde du Sacerdoce et de l'État,* had historical merit but was Gallican and placed on the Index. He accepted the censure (1646). M. wrote other historical and theological works: a dissertation, *De primatu Lugdunensis et aliis primatibus* (1644) helped to retrieve his reputation; he directed against *Jansenism his *Rélations des déliberations du clergé de France,* published the year before his death. His influence against Jansenism was recognized by a letter of 1656 from Pope Alexander VII. His subservience to Louis XIV in the arrest of Card. de Retz shadows, however, the memory of this canonist, jurist, and historian.

[M. R. BROWN]

MARCAN HYPOTHESIS, in general, the agreement among scholars that Mark is one of the primary sources of Matthew and Luke. All but about 50 verses of Mark turn up in Matthew; more than half of Mark (about 350 verses) was taken over by Luke. This priority of Mark is, however, variously explained. The theory proposed by L. Vaganay questions this priority, at least in the absolute sense. For him, the basis of all three Synoptics was a Greek translation of the original Aramaic Matthew. But the more general opinion is that Mark is a literarily original and independent work on which the other two drew, each adapting the Marcan material in accordance with his individual style and purpose. A hypothesis similar to that of Vaganay's suggests that Mark was preceded by a smaller proto-Mark. This suggestion is made with a view to explaining the omission of a great deal of the Marcan material by Luke and of at least a part of it by Matthew. Were these omissions purposeful or were the passages in question not included in the version of Mark on which they depended? In one attempted reconstruction, that of Bussmann, there were three different forms of Mark: proto-Mark, which would stand behind all three Synoptics and was used specifically by Luke; an expanded version of this original, used by Matthew; a final edition, identical with our canonical Mark, which would thus be the latest instead of the earliest of the Synoptic Gospels in their present form. This hypothesis has not won many adherents, and while no single system is free of difficulties, the most satisfactory one remains that which accepts the canonical Mark as an original, independent literary work which was utilized in the composition of both Matthew and Luke, with modifications of the Marcan material peculiar to each. BIBLIOGRAPHY: *Introduction to the New Testament* (ed. A. Robert and A. Feuillet, 1965); V. Taylor, *Gospel According to St. Mark* (1957); B. Vawter, *Four Gospels* (1967); A. Wikenhauser, *New Testament Introduction* (tr. J. Cunningham, 1958).

[J. J. CASTELOT]

MARCEL, GABRIEL (1889–1973), French philosopher and playwright. M. was reared by his father and aunt, both agnostics, after his mother's death. His father had rejected Catholicism earlier, yet M. was influenced by the ethic of his aunt as well as by the aesthetics of his father. Some attribute Marcel's later religious-oriented philosophy to the logical extension of the tension between the contrasting influences in his life. The demands for achievement in academic life at the expense of personal growth frustrated M. in his earlier life. The recognition of these frustrations contributed to his understanding of the larger disorientations man experiences in contemporary society as a result of bureaucratization and technology. During World War I he served as a Red Cross official (after rejection by the army because of poor health), his responsibility being to notify the relatives of deceased soldiers about their deaths. This brought him face to face with the horror of man's alienation and the loss of what he termed "the ontological self." In 1929 his friendship with Charles Dubois and with François Mauriac led him at first to recognition, then acceptance, of faith. Finally, it was a challenge of Mauriac's which moved him to convert to Catholicism; this was viewed by some as the external fulfillment of what he already accepted interiorly. Known both as dramatist and musician, he found in the latter sphere, symbolically represented, the harmony and unity he sought in the drama of living.

For M. modern man's disorientation is seen, symptomatically, in the "metaphysical dis-ease" that encapsulates him in a world torn between the possibility of enormous promise and the potentiality for terror and destruction. The greatest harm to man is one coming, not just from technology as such, but from the development of a technology that robs man of his dignity by viewing him solely in the flux of history, rather than as an entity with a permanence that transcends the accidents and events of history. Such a view leads one to reductionism and abstractionism, says Marcel. Like other existentialists, his philosophy found form in the dramatic representation of the effects of an excessive abstractionism which ignores the concrete realities from which we abstract; unlike such existentialists as Sartre, however, he believed that such abstraction is futile since it reduces man to a "useless passion" (Sartre's term). For M., man was, rather, "*homo viator*."

The recurring themes of Marcel's philosophy are "metaphysical dis-ease", availability, transcendence, and limitation. The ethical consequences involved in the development of such thought make little sense unless one views man qua man, as existential, transcendent subject, and not in the roles he assumes in his functional living. His major works are: *Metaphysical Journal* (1952); *Being and Having* (1965); *Creative Fidelity* (1964); *Homo Viator: Introduction to a Philosophy of Hope* (1951); *The Philosophy of Existence* (1949); *The Mystery of Being* (1950); *Men Against Humanity* (1952); *The Existential Background of Human Dignity* (1963); *Three Plays* (1958). BIBLIOGRAPHY: K. T. Gallagher, *Philosophy of Gabriel Marcel* (1962); R. Vernaux, *Catholicism,* 4:919–931; Cornelo Fabro, EncCatt 5:589–91; H. B. Acton, EB 8:968–968B s.v. "Existentialism."

[J. R. RIVELLO]

MARCELLA, ST. (*c.*335–410), illustrious Roman widow and ascetic of the wealthy Marcelli family, friend of St. Jerome. His account of her life (Ep. 127) is the main source of information concerning her. Through Athanasius, while he was an exile in Rome, M. came to know of the Egyptian ascetical tradition. In the year 374, having lived as a widow many years, she became the first in Rome to adopt the Egyptian monastic ideal, giving away her wealth and living in stark simplicity. She continued to live with her mother in their house on the Aventine, with her mother thus able to help her avoid the extremes of asceticism not uncommon in the Egyptian tradition. When Jerome came to Rome in 382, M.'s house became a gathering place for devout women to study Scripture under his guidance. He wrote for her 15 treatises on difficult passages of Scripture. She did not accompany him on his return to Palestine in 385, as did others of her group, but remained in Rome where she is credited with personally persuading Pope Anastasius to condemn the teaching of Origen. She suffered personal violence at the hands of the Goths during their sack of Rome under Alaric in 410 and died shortly afterwards. BIBLIOGRAPHY: B. Signitti, BiblSanct 2:904–905.

[E. J. DILLON]

MARCELLINA, ST. (*c.*332–*c.*398), the older sister of St. Ambrose. Born probably at Trier where her father was prefect of the Gauls, M. outlived her famous brother and probably died in Milan. She lived also in Rome, where she was consecrated a virgin by Pope Liberius on the feast of the Epiphany. It was to her that Ambrose addressed his writings on the excellence of virginity. The brother and sister remained in close correspondence throughout their lives. BIBLIOGRAPHY: A. Rimoldi, BiblSanct 8:646–648.

[E. J. DILLON]

MARCELLINE SISTERS, a congregation founded by Msgr. Luigi Biraghi and Sister Marina Videmari at Arnusco sul Naviglio, near Milan, in 1838 to teach girls. It received papal approval (1897 and 1910), and later extended its endeavors to hospital service, mission activity, and social work. The community has spread to England, France, Switzerland, Brazil, and Canada. In 1975 membership consisted of 1,283 sisters in 45 houses.

MARCELLINUS, ST. (d. 304), **POPE** from 296. The life and pontificate of M. is clouded in obscurity, and even the fact of his existence has been questioned by some, who identify him with Marcellus I, his successor as pope (308–309). Much of the obscurity seems to stem from the charges circulated by the Donatists at the end of the 4th cent. that he had offered incense and given up the sacred books during the persecution of Diocletian. This accusation was sharply disputed by Augustine. But the Donatists persisted in their claim, and some Catholics in later times appear to have accepted the story and to have tried to restore him to good repute by claiming that he atoned for his sin by dying a martyr's death—as in, e.g., the *Liber Pontificalis.*

There is, however, no satisfactory early evidence that he did die as a martyr, which itself suggests that he did not, esp. since it appears that he was venerated in Rome before the Donatists made their accusations. BIBLIOGRAPHY: A. Amore, BiblSanct 8:651–653; *idem*, "Il preteso 'lapsus' di papa Marcellino," *Antonianum* 32 (1957) 411–426; Butler 2:163–164.

[P. F. MULHERN]

MARCELLINUS COMES (d. *c.* 534), chancellor of Justinian I, author of *Annales*, a continuation down to 534 of Eusebius's *Chronicon*, distinguished only for its chronology of consuls in the Eastern Roman Empire. BIBLIOGRAPHY: Altaner 281.

[T. C. O'BRIEN]

MARCELLINUS FLAVIUS, ST. (5th cent.), African martyr, praised by Jerome, and by Augustine who dedicated his *De civitate Dei* to M. and may even have undertaken the work at the latter's suggestion. Having attained the military rank of tribune, and being also a notary, M. was apparently secretary of state to the emperor Honorius. He was caught in the middle of controversy when he was sent to Carthage to preside and act as judge over a conference of Catholic and Donatist bishops. He decided against the Donatists and ordered them to resign their offices and return to the Catholic communion. The Donatists retaliated by accusing M. of complicity in a treasonous rebellion. Cast into prison and executed without a trial, he was afterwards vindicated by the emperor. His name was added to the Roman martyrology by Baronius. BIBLIOGRAPHY: A. Rimoldi, BiblSanct 8:650; Butler 2:40.

[E. J. DILLON]

MARCELLINUS AND PETER, SS., Roman martyrs, invoked in the Roman Canon of the Mass (Eucharistic Prayer I) since the time of Pope Vigilius (d. 555). A church in their honor stands on the site of their reputed burial on the Via Labicana, Rome, where in modern times a 5th-cent. crypt honoring them was discovered. Marcellinus was a priest, Peter an exorcist.

MARCELLUS, SS., several saints bear this name. **Marcellus, of Chalon-sur Saône,** martyred during the persecution of Marcus Aurelius *c.* 178. He escaped martyrdom once, but was murdered by his host when the latter learned that M. was a Christian. M.'s *passio,* however, is legendary. **Marcellus, St., bp. of Die** (d. 510). After his consecration he was imprisoned and exiled for opposing Gundiok, King of the Burgundians. When M. returned he became noted for his holy life. His cult was approved by Pius IX for the diocese of Valence. **Marcellus, St., Bp. of Paris** (fl. early 5th cent.), whose reputation for holiness was widespread even while he was still young. He succeeded Prudentius as bp. of Paris and was renowned as a miracle worker. See: Butler 4:238. **Marcellus, St., the Centurion,** martyr who was decapitated in Tingis (Tangier) in 298 when he repudiated paganism and imperial military service. See: Butler 4:220–221.

[J. R. RIVELLO]

MARCELLUS I, ST. (d. 309), **POPE** from 308. A vacancy of 3 years in the papacy, due to the violence of the persecution of Diocletian, preceded his election. M. is credited with doing much to overcome the chaotic conditions that resulted from the persecution. Serious conflict arose in consequence of M.'s insistence that those who had defected do proper penance as a condition of readmission to the Church. The violence of the ensuing turmoil led the Emperor Maxentius to send him into exile, and he died shortly thereafter. This is cited as one of the earliest examples of imperial interference in internal affairs of the Church. His body was returned to Rome and buried in the catacomb of Priscilla. BIBLIOGRAPHY: E. G. Weltin, *Ancient Popes* (1964) 148–149; J. P. Kirsch, CE 9:640–641.

[P. F. MULHERN]

MARCELLUS II (Marcello Cervini; 1501–55), **POPE** from April 9, 1555 to May 1, 1555. He was born in Montepulciano, studied at Siena, and then assisted his father, Ricciardo, who had begun structuring a new calendar under an assignment of Leo X. The Cervinis completed the task during the reign of Clement VII, in the year 1525. At this time M. went to Rome to continue his education, which focused on classical studies. M. spent the next few years away from Rome because of the German invasion but returned in 1531 under the patronage of Card. Alessandro Farnese. In 1534 Farnese was elected Pope Paul III and in 1538 he appointed his young nephew, Card. Farnese as Vatican Secretary of State. As counsellor and educator of the young Farnese, M. actually conducted the diplomatic missions of the papacy. In 1539 Cardinal Farnese was the papal legate to Francis I of France and Emperor Charles V but M. actually handled the delicate negotiations between the two monarchs. That same year he was assigned the administration of the Diocese of Nicastro and was named a cardinal. In 1540 M. was appointed bp. of Reggio, and in 1544 bp. of Gubbio. In February 1545 M. was chosen by Paul III to preside over the Council of Trent in association with Cardinals Del Monte and Pole. At the Council M. became a leader in the debates on dogmatic matters. M. also concerned himself with ecclesiastical reform and did not hesitate to protest against nepotism in the administration of Paul III or his successor, Julius III. In addition to the work of the Council of Trent, M. was also given charge of the Vatican Library in 1548. In that capacity, M. actively searched for Greek and Latin MSS, pursued the study of archeology, and opened the resources of the archives to the 16th-cent. scholars. In short, M. became one of the leading contributors to the greatness of the Vatican Library. When Julius III died in 1555, M. was clearly the leader of the reform party in the College of Cardinals. Despite the many maneuvers of Card. Este, M. was elected pope on April 9, 1555 and chose the name Marcellus II. In the simplicity of his coronation, in his political neutrality, in his merit system of ecclesiastical appointments, M. chartered a course of reform for his papacy. However, he had never enjoyed good health and he died after only 22 days in the papacy. BIBLIOGRAHY: Pastor 14:1–55; Jedin Trent v. 1.

[R. J. BRADY]

MARCELLUS ACOEMITUS, ST. (Akimetes; d. after 469), abbot. Born in Apamea, Syria, of a wealthy family, M. studied theology in Antioch and lived the monastic life in Ephesus before going to the monastery of Eirenaion on the Bosporus across from Constantinople. This was a monastery of *Acoemetae (unsleeping) monks, who recited the divine office night and day in relays. He soon became an abbot and led his monks to new heights of zeal and devotion, insisting upon strict observance of poverty, stressing manual labor, and encouraging apostolic activities. M. also played a role in the doctrinal disputes of his day; he was one of those who signed the condemnation of *Eutyches in 448, and he took part later in the Council of *Chalcedon. BIBLIOGRAPHY: Butler 4:638–639; A. Stephenson, NCE 9:191.

[R. B. ENO]

MARCELLUS OF ANCYRA (d. *c.*374), bp. of Ancyra (modern Ankara) in Galatia. M. took part in the Synods of Antioch and Ancyra that preceded *Nicaea, and at Nicaea itself he was present as an outspoken opponent of *Arius. Writing against *Asterius the Sophist (*c.*330), he appeared to incline toward *Sabellianism, and this put him under attack from both sides, but esp. from the anti-Nicene party. A synod of Constantinople in 336 condemned his book and expelled him from his see. This began a series of expulsions from and restorations to his diocese that ended with his final expulsion by Constantius in 347, after which time little was heard of him. He was condemned by the first canon of the (ecumenical) Council of Constantinople I in 381. Only fragments of M.'s work remain, chiefly preserved in citations by Eusebius. These show his Monarchianist beliefs and a rather primitive theology. For M., the Son and Spirit are merely modalistic functions of the one God; they will disappear again into the Godhead at the end of time when their tasks are done. For this reason there was added to the Creed the phrase: "And of his [i.e., Christ's] Kingdom there will be no end." BIBLIOGRAPHY: V. DeClercq, NCE 9:191; Quasten 3:197–201; ODCC 853.

[R. B. ENO]

MARCHANT, JACQUES AND PIERRE, Flemish brothers born at Couvin in Namur province, both of whom became theologians. **Jacques** (*c.*1585–1648), parish priest and pastoral theologian. He is best known for his *Hortus pastorum sacrae doctrinae* (3 v., 1626–27). **Pierre** (1585–1661), Franciscan theologian, prolific writer. He filled several offices including that of commissary general for Germany, Belgium, Holland, England and Ireland, where he became involved politically in the affairs of the Kilkenny Confederation. His best-known work is *Tribunal sacramentale* (3 v., 1642), a treatise on moral theology according to the probabalist system. He also published (1655) a manual of casuistry, and works on Franciscan history.

[P. J. HENNESSEY]

MARCHETTUS OF PADUA (Marchetto; 1280–1325), Italian musical theorist. He authored two treatises on notation: *Lucidarium in arte musicae planae* (*c.*1309), noted for its chromaticism and the division of the whole tone into fifths, and *Pomerium artis musicae mensurabilis* (1318), which demonstrates the transition from the Franconian notation system to the *ars nova* of Philippe de Vetry and his followers. The treatises were published in the third volume of Gerbert's *Scriptores*. A system of notation designed by M. was too complex and later was replaced by the simpler *ars nova*.

[R. J. LITZ]

MARCHI, GIUSEPPE (1795–1860), Italian Jesuit archeologist. From 1838, the year of his appointment as director of the Museum Kircherianum, M. began a systematic investigation of the catacombs and other ancient burial places in and around Rome. When he was appointed in 1842 by Gregory XVI to the new post of curator of the sacred cemeteries of Rome, he saw his office as a commission to restore the catacombs and to preserve them from further depredations. In 1854, M. was made director of the Lateran Museum. His careful, scholarly work marked the beginning of a new era in Christian archeology. M.'s most ambitious project was the publication of a corpus of ancient Christian inscriptions and monuments, but of this he was able to complete only the first part: *Architettura cimiteriale* (1844–47). BIBLIOGRAPHY: R. Fausti, EncCatt 8:31–32; P. Roche, NCE 9:192.

[R. B. ENO]

MARCIAN, BYZANTINE EMPEROR (*c.*392–457). He married Pulcheria, the sister of Emperor Theodosius II, after the latter's death and thus became emperor himself (450–458). An orthodox Christian like his wife, he convoked the Council of Chalcedon (451), which upheld the doctrine that Christ had two natures, divine and human. He supported also canon 28 of Chalcedon that gave the patriarch of Constantinople (New Rome) rank second only to the pope's and jurisdiction over all the East. After the Council, M. strongly defended the doctrine of Chalcedon against the Monophysites.

[J. MADEY]

MARCIAN OF ARLES (fl. 254–257), bishop of Arles. Not much is known of him, not even the dates and extent of his episcopate, nor even the manner of its termination. It is certain that he was bp. of Arles in the opening year of the 3-year tenure of Pope St. Stephen I (254–257). M. was an adherent of *Novatian's rigorist approach to the **lapsi*, those who denied their faith under pressure of persecution. M. refused to admit them back to communion even after repentance, putting himself in opposition to Faustinus, bp. of Lyons, and the other provincial bps., who first unsuccessfully appealed to Stephen to excommunicate the rigorist, and then appealed to St. *Cyprian, bp. of Carthage. This occasioned the famous correspondence between Cyprian and Stephen, studied by scholars in their analyses of the evolving role of the bp. of Rome within the college of bishops. Cyprian's letter to Stephen all but ordered him to intervene decisively as his predecessors had, and not to let M. continue to insult "our college." Cyprian characterized M. as opinionated, proud, the enemy of divine piety and of the health of his brothers. It was clear to Cyprian that M. did not possess the Holy Spirit, because he had not the same attitudes as the others. Cyprian directed Stephen to send a letter to Provence and to the faithful of Arles that would effectively remove M. from office so that another could take his place and heal the wounds in the scattered flock. This, Cyprian noted, is the way such things are handled. Asserting that those who possess the one Spirit cannot follow different opinions, Cyprian also directed Stephen to let him and the other bps. know M.'s successor at Arles, so that they would know to whom to refer their brothers, and to whom they must write. BIBLIOGRAPHY: Fliche-Martin 2:197–199.

[E. J. DILLON]

MARCIAN OF CYR, ST. (*c.*300–*c.*387), monk and hermit. Born in Cyr (Cyrrhus) in Syria of a patrician family, he withdrew to the desert of Chalcis between Antioch and the Euphrates; there he built himself an austere cell within an enclosure. His goal was to live a life of prayer and manual labor in solitude, subsisting on a daily diet of bread in small quantities. However, his reputation for holiness spread and people came to him for spiritual conversation or seeking miracles. He was abashed by both kinds of seekers. On one occasion the patriarch of Antioch came in company with other bps. and begged him to give them a spiritual conference. Alarmed by their dignity, he stood facing them in awkward silence. When they kept urging him to speak to them, he managed to say that since God speaks every day through the wonders of creation and through the Gospels, what more could he say that would be useful? He would not listen to requests for miraculous intercession. One time when he emphatically refused to bless oil for a sick daughter of a visitor, the daughter was still reportedly recovered that very hour. He was eventually prevailed upon to accept his first two disciples: Eusebius and Agapitus. When his followers increased, he appointed Eusebius their abbot. Eusebius promised to bury M. secretly to avoid human scavengers who had severally built chapels to house his remains. He is commemorated in the Roman Martyrology on November 2. The writings of Theodoret are the only source of knowledge of M.'s life. BIBLIOGRAPHY: Butler 4:242–243; J. M. Sauget, BiblSanct 8:689–690.

[E. J. DILLON]

MARCION (*c.* 85–*c.* 160), founder of an early separatist sect. A wealthy shipowner of Sinope in Pontus, M. went to Rome *c.* 140 and affiliated himself with the Christian community of that city. The claim of Hippolytus and of Epiphanius that he was the son of a bishop excommunicated for violating a virgin vowed to God, was probably intended in an allegorical sense. M. developed a system of religious ideas and gathered disciples. When finally expelled from the orthodox community (*c.* 144), he established a rival Church of his own, which spread to many places in the empire and continued to exist for several centuries, though many of its communities merged in time with the Manichaeans. His thought can be described as Gnostic in its dualism, but it is not marked by the mythological tendencies characteristic of Gnosticism. He considered the God of the OT, the creator God or demiurge, to be different entirely from the God revealed by Jesus. The OT God was a God of Law as opposed to the God of Love of the NT; Christ came to liberate men from the tyranny of the Creator God. He insisted that all Judaizing tendencies be resisted and excised from Christianity and esp. from the NT writings. He rejected all the OT and much of the NT as well. He accepted only the Pauline Epistles (except for the Pastoral Epistles and Hebrews) and a revision of the Gospel of St. Luke that omitted all mention of the infancy of Christ. The repudiated sections of the NT were corrupted for him by remnants of Jewish influence. This rejection of sacred writings, by calling attention to the question of canonicity, probably exercised some influence upon the development of the canon of the Scriptures in the Church. Marcion's writings, among which was the *Antitheses,* which stated the Marcionite creed, have been lost except for the fragments cited by his opponents. BIBLIOGRAPHY: Quasten 1:268–272; E. Blackman, *Marcion and His Influence* (1948); A. Stephenson, NCE 9:193–194.

[R. B. ENO]

MARCION, GOSPEL OF, see APOCRYPHA (NEW TESTAMENT), 33.

MARCIONITE PROLOGUES, introductory paragraphs prefacing the Epistles of St. Paul in many Vulgate manuscripts. They are called Marcionite because they are generally considered to be the work of *Marcion, whose phraseology and ideas they reflect, e.g., the exaltation of Paul at the expense of the other Apostles and the abomination of "Jewish" teachings. They appear to have been written originally in Greek. The Pastoral Epistles, which Marcion rejected as noncanonical, also have prologues, but these betray no heretical ideas and are probably the work of another hand. BIBLIOGRAPHY: G. Bardy, DBSuppl 5:877–881.

[R. B. ENO]

MARCIONITES, followers of Marcion, the most powerful adversary of the official Church in the 2d century. The Marcionites represent an extreme version of Pauline teaching. They utterly opposed Christian faith to Judaism, rejecting the OT with its God, its revelation, and its tradition of piety and worship, and accepting from the NT only a corrected version of the writings of Luke and most of the Pauline letters. Apparently the only writing of Marcion himself was his book of *Antitheses,* no longer extant, but refuted in detail by *Tertullian, through whom this controversial figure is known. Marcion was a leader and a man of action, who established well-structured church communities, tightly bound to one another. His followers practised an austere asceticism and did not shrink from martyrdom in confessing their faith. Marcion, born in Pontus, was active in Rome in the mid-2d cent., contemporary with Irenaeus, Polycarp, and Justin. By the beginning of the next cent., Tertullian could say that Marcion's teachings had filled the whole earth. He was opposed by Denis at Corinth, Irenaeus at Lyons, Theophilus at Antioch, Philip in Crete, Tertullian in Carthage, Hippolytus in Rome, and Bardesanus at Edessa. Beginning with the 3d cent., the Marcionites seem gradually to have been assimilated into the Manichaean movement, but in the 4th cent. Epiphanius could note that they were still widespread, to be found in Rome and Italy, in Egypt and Palestine, in Arabia, Syria, Cyprus, Persia, and elsewhere. BIBLIOGRAPHY: Fliche-Martin 2:26–35.

[E. J. DILLON]

MARCO POLO (1254–1324), Venetian traveler in the Far East. The son of Niccolò Polo, a fairly prosperous merchant, M. at 17 accompanied his father and uncle on their second trip to the Orient, where they were representatives of the Pope and the Holy Roman Emperor to Kublai Khan. During 17 years at the Mongol court, M. was sent on confidential missions throughout the empire, learning much about India, Persia, and Japan. He returned home (1292) and was captured (1295) during a war between Venice and Genoa; he dictated the famous account of his travels to a fellow prisoner. Later travelers verified his account, incredibly fantastic to his contemporaries. BIBLIOGRAPHY: J. A. Brundage, NCE 9:194; H. H. Hart, *Marco Polo: Venetian Adventurer* (1967); L. Olschki, *Marco Polo's Asia,* (tr. J. A. Scott, 1960).

[G. E. CONWAY]

MARCONI, GUGLIELMO (1874–1937), inventor of the wireless. A physicist educated in N Italy, M. experimented in early years with wireless communication both in Italy and England. His first experiments transmitted signals for only a few miles, but continued work made it possible to transmit and receive messages for long distances. In 1901 M. proved the long range capacity of wireless by receiving in Newfoundland, messages originating in Cornwall, England. Further work enabled him to send the first radio message from England to Australia in 1918. By 1923 he had perfected short-wave communication, now the basis of most long-distance communication. In 1932 the inventor installed a radio station in the Vatican. BIBLIOGRAPHY: W. Baker, *History of the Marconi Company* (1970).

[J. R. AHERNE]

MARCUS AURELIUS (121–180), **ROMAN EMPEROR** and Stoic philosopher. Born M. Annius Verus, son of a noble family of Latin origin in Spain, M. enjoyed the favor of Emperor Hadrian, who took a special interest in his education, putting him under the best teachers of rhetoric, philosophy, and law. With Lucius Verus, he was adopted by the Emperor Antoninus Pius as Marcus Aelius Aurelius Verus in 138. He ruled the Empire in a joint principate with his adoptive brother, Lucius Verus, from 161 until the latter's death in 169, and thereafter as sole emperor. Despite his devotion to philosophy, which he had made the central personal interest of his life from 146, he had to face formidable difficulties and calamities, esp. in the period of his own principate. There were revolts and invasions from Britain to Mesopotamia, but esp. in the Danubian region, and the empire was devastated by a great plague that broke out in 166 and did not abate until some years after his death. He showed poor judgment in the choice of Lucius Verus as joint-princeps and of his son Commodus as his successor. His internal administration of the empire was conscientious but tended to be rather routine. He did not come to grips with the danger of military donations and inflation. His policy toward Christianity reveals a mixture of devotion to the imperial cult as mark of loyalty to the State and of Stoic condemnation for what he regarded as Christian obstinacy. There was no general persecution during his principate, but he must be regarded as a persecutor. A number of Christians suffered martyrdom, including St. Polycarp. M. composed his *Meditations* in 12 books in Greek, the language of philosophy, in the course of his campaigns. His Stoicism, like that of Epictetus, whom he greatly admired, and of Seneca, is deeply religious. He stresses the close bond that should exist between man and God and love for one's fellow men. "Love mankind, follow God" (*Med.* 7.31). While adhering to Stoic monism in theory, under Platonic or Aristotelian influence he tends to separate the *nous* from matter. He regards the *nous* as the *daimōn* which God has given to every man for his guidance. M. has a firm belief in Stoic teaching on world-conflagration and admits immortality of the soul to a limited degree only. Pagan philosophical, religious, and ethical thought reaches one of its highest points in the *Meditations,* and the work well deserves to be considered one of the masterpieces of world literature. BIBLIOGRAPHY: C. H. V. Sutherland, OCD 124–125; CAH 11 (1936) 325–393; Copleston 1:435–437; P. De Labriolle, *La Réaction païenne* (1934) 71–79.

[M. R. P. MCGUIRE]

MARCUS, EUGENICUS (*c.* 1392–1445), Greek monk who opposed the addition of the *filioque in the decree of union of the Greek and Latin Churches at the Council of Florence. He was chosen metropolitan of Ephesus and procurator of the Patriarchate of Alexandria. Because of his opposition to the filioque, he became a staunch antiunionist, writing prolifically to support his stand. He was canonized in 1734 by the Greek Orthodox Church.

[P. J. HENNESSEY]

MARDECHAI, see MORDECHAI.

MARDUK, local city-god of Babylon; hence, the national god of Babylonia. Although M. was not originally a high or cosmic god, Babylonian theological construction justified his exalted divine rank by explaining that he was the son of a cosmic god, Enki or Ea (god of the cosmic ocean), honorifically identified with Ea, and given sovereignty over the universe by two other cosmic gods, Anu (god of heaven) and Enlil (god of terra firma). From his father, Ea, M. inherited supremacy in magic and the arts and crafts, a supremacy reflected in his cosmogonic role as the god who vanquished the forces of chaos and proceeded to create man. A tendency already evident in the Bablonian epic of creation *(Enuma Elish),* with its honorific identification of M. with Ea and its attribution to M. of qualities expressed, by word-play, in various minor divine names, reached its culmination in the Neo-Babylonian period, with other gods of the Mesopotamian pantheon reduced largely to aspects of Marduk. From M.'s universal sovereignty, the earthly sovereignty of the kings of Babylon was derived, and it was the king—at least in the later periods of Babylonian history—who assumed the personality of M. in the annual cultic drama of the battle between M. and the forces of chaos, intended to assure order in the world for the coming year. Bel-Marduk (Lord-Marduk) provides both the Bel and the Merodach of the Bible. BIBLIOGRAPHY: E. Dhorme, *Les Religions de Babylonie et d'Assyrie* (1945) 139–50.

[A. CODY]

MARÉCHAL, AMBROSE (1764–1828), abp. of Baltimore, Md., missionary. A French Sulpician ordained in 1792, M. came to Baltimore, in the same year. After some years of pastoral work in Maryland, he taught at St. Mary's Seminary in Baltimore and at Georgetown College. Recalled to France in 1803, M. taught at various seminaries until 1811 when the Sulpicians were expelled from seminary teaching. Returning to the U.S., he was named coadjutor to the abp. of Baltimore in 1817. The abp. died the same year and M. succeeded him. He visited his vast jurisdiction, which included Maryland, Virginia, the Carolinas, Georgia, and the territory W to the Mississippi. He solved problems of *trusteeism, succeeded in persuading the Holy See to accept nominations for American bps. from the bps. of the U.S., and completed the Baltimore cathedral.

[J. R. AHERNE]

MARÉCHAL, JOSEPH (1878–1944), Belgian Jesuit psychologist and philosopher. M. taught experimental psychology and philosophy at the Jesuit scholasticate in Louvain (1919–35) and during this time composed his principal works: *Études sur la psychologie des mystiques* (2 v., 1924, 1937, tr. in part by A. Thorold, 1927, under the title *Studies in the Psychology of the Mystics*); and *Le Point de départ de la metaphysique* (1922–23, 1926, 1947). After 1935 ill health caused him to discontinue writing and teaching. The fifth volume *(cahier)* of *Le Point de départ* is regarded as the most important statement of his position on the epistemological question; it is a consideration of Kant's critical philosophy in the light of Thomistic principles, presenting by implication a defense of St. Thomas's moderate realism. The problem and its solution, however, is stated in Kantian terms, and M. unfortunately did not survive to write a sixth volume in which he planned to expound his position in his own terms. M. sought to resolve the antinomy of the understanding and reason, and to justify the objectivity of knowledge by stressing the dynamic role of the intellect in the process of knowledge. BIBLIOGRAPHY: J. I. Conway, EncPhil 5:157–159.

[J. T. HICKEY]

MAREDSOUS, ABBEY OF, Benedictine monastery founded in 1872 at Denée (Diocese of Namur, Belgium) by Benedictines from Beuron, Germany, at the initiative of the Desclée firm, the famous printers of Tournai. Placidus Wolter was the first abbot. The monastery was built (1873–81) in neo-Gothic style of local granite; it dominates the picturesque valley of the Molignée. Maredsous helped restore the Benedictine congregation in Brazil; its monks also founded the Irish abbey of Glenstal and the priory of Gihindamuyaga in Ruanda. A number of Maredsous monks have distinguished themselves as scholars, e.g., Germain Morin, Donatien de Bruyne, Ursmer Berlière, Bernard Capelle, and the monastery's third abbot, Columba *Marmion, well known for his spiritual writings. The abbey publishes several scholarly journals, e.g., the learned *Revue bénédictine,* and the *Bulletin d'ancienne littérature chrétienne latine.* BIBLIOGRAPHY: Cottineau 2:1744.

[J. DAOUST]

MARENZIO, LUCA (1553–1599), Italian composer, best known for his madrigals. Born near Brescia, he was choirmaster of that city's cathedral (1586–89). Both before and later, he enjoyed the patronage of some of the leading figures of the Renaissance, including Card. d'Este (1579–1586), Card. Aldobrandini (1591–95), King Sigismund III of Poland (1596–98), and Ferdinand de' Medici, for whose wedding to Cristina of Lorraine he composed the intermezzo, "Il combattimento di Apolline con il serpente." In 1595 he was named cantor of the Pontifical Chapel in Rome. A prolific composer, he wrote both secular and sacred works. Included in the latter category are a book of *Sacri concerti* for five to seven voices, a Mass for eight voices, and innumerable books of madrigals and motets. The full development of the madrigal form in Elizabethan England can be attributed to his influence.

[E. M. GATES]

MARESCOTTI, HYACINTHA, ST. (1588–1640). She was born Clarice Marescotti to a noble family in Vignanello. Her early life was distinguished for its self-serving petulance and greed. When she was 20, her parents sought to becalm their household by placing her in the Franciscan convent of S. Bernadino at Viterbo. M. took the name Hyacintha and for approximately 15 years she totally ignored her religious vows, living the life of a secular noblewoman within the convent. After a serious illness took her near death, M. altered her life completely. She exhibited great habits of mortification and penance. When the plague swept over Viterbo, she worked tirelessly for the sick, creating an organization (the Oblates of St. Mary) to aid the poor and the dying. M. also attempted to foster devotion to the Blessed Sacrament in the wake of the Jansenist philosophies that had spread to Italy from France. In her later years, she had several mystical experiences and was said to possess the gift of prophecy. She was beatified in 1726 and canonized in 1807. BIBLIOGRAPHY: G. Mariani, BiblSanct 6:322–24; Butler 1:206–207.

[R. J. BRADY]

MARET, HENRI LOUIS CHARLES (1805–84), French theologian, professor, and from 1853 dean of the theology faculty at the Sorbonne. After Rome refused to confirm his nomination to the see of Vannes because he was considered to incline too much toward Gallicanism, he was made titular bp. of Sura. In his strong opposition to pantheism and atheism he became a proponent first of traditionalism and later of ontologism. He sought to dissuade Pius IX from publishing the Syllabus of 1864, and in his best-known work, *Du concile général et la paix religieuse: Le Pape et les évêques* (1869), he opposed the definition of papal infallibility. After the definition, he disavowed, at the request of Pius IX, whatever the book contained that was contrary to the dogma. BIBLIOGRAPHY: C. Butler, *Vatican Council* (1930); G. Bazin, *Vie de Mgr. Maret* (3 v., 1891); Hocedez v. 2, *passim;* É. Amann, DTC 9.2:2033–37.

[J. P. REID]

MARGARET, ST. (1046–93), Queen of Scotland. Born in Hungary of an Anglo-Hungarian royal marriage, reared in England and Scotland, M. married (1070) Malcolm III of Scotland. She brought up a family of eight children, softened the native roughness of her husband's character, and helped make him one of Scotland's best and greatest rulers, sharing with him the burden of government. She promoted (with Lanfranc's help) reforms in Church and court aimed at bringing Scotland under Roman and English influence, yet found time and energy also to have great care for the poor. Canonization came in 1249; in the calendar of the saints she barely qualified for the status of widowhood, since the death of her husband came but 4 days before her own. BIBLIOGRAPHY: Butler 2:515–517; D. McRoberts, BiblSanct 8:781–786.

[P. K. MEAGHER]

MARGARET, SS., 18 saints or blesseds cited in Butler's *Lives of the Saints,* most of them dating from medieval times, and coming from various countries of Europe. This attests to the enormous popularity both of the name and of the supposed original St. Margaret. Unfortunately, the entire corpus of legend, folklore, and miracle story associated with this original Margaret stems from a mistaken identity of Margaret of Antioch with a penitent described in a sermon of one of the early Church Fathers. This penitent probably had, in fact, only a homiletic existence and yet so appealed to creative imagination that she effectively obliterated any authentic cultus of the blessed Margaret, virgin and martyr of Antioch, who is nevertheless still commemorated in the Latin Church on July 20, and by the Greeks on July 17.

[E. J. DILLON]

MARGARET, LADY, see BEAUFORT, MARGARET.

MARGARET OF ANGOULÊME (Marguerite de Navarre; 1492–1549), queen of Navarre from 1527, French Renaissance writer, and humanist patroness. Daughter of Charles d'Orléans and Louise de Savoie, M. married Charles, duc d'Alençon (1509), and became the center of court life when her brother Francis I became king (1515). Widowed (1525), she was remarried (1527) to Henry d'Albret (Henry II of Navarre). Interested in such great movements of her time as humanism and the Reformation, M. protected, esp. at her courts at Nérac (Gascony) and Pau (Béarn), numerous men of letters and reformers, including *Rabelais, *Marot, Bonaventure des Périers, *Lefèvre d'Étaples, and Calvin. M.'s most important literary work, the *Heptameron* (publ. 1558–59), imitating the plan of Boccaccio's *Decameron* and containing strong satires of licentious monks and clerics, offers a good example of the intellectual and religious ideals of the period, and reveals a Christian, even mystical, conception of love. M.'s *Miroir de l'âme pécheresse* (1531) is a devotional poem, reflecting her intense, mystical faith which is evident in her correspondence with Guillaume Briçonnet. The rest of her poetry is collected in *Les Marguerites de la Marguerite des princesses* (1547) and in her *Dernières poésies* (containing "Le Navire" and "Les Prisons"), which again offer examples of her mystical pietism. M. also wrote plays. While sympathetic toward Lutheranism because of her personal religious inclinations, it would appear that she never embraced Protestantism, but wanted reform within the Catholic Church. If she defended those persecuted as heretics, it was because of her desire for tolerance. M.'s Calvinist daughter (by Henry II), Jeanne d'Albret (1528–72), became the mother of the future Henry IV of France. BIBLIOGRAPHY: J. Gelernt, *World of Many Loves: The Heptameron of Marguerite de Navarre* (1966); P. Jourda, *Marguerite d'Angoulême, duchesse d'Alençon, reine de Navarre (1492–1549)* (2 v. 1930); A. Lefranc, *Les Idées religieuses de Marguerite de Navarre d'après son oeuvre poétique*

(1898); H. Sckommodau, *Die religiösen Dichtungen Margaretes von Navarra* (1954).

[R. N. NICOLICH]

MARGARET OF COLONNA, BL. (d. 1280), mystic. Daughter of Odo of Colonna and Margaret Orsini, M. was the first cousin of Pope Nicholas III. She refused all marriage proposals and adopted the life of the Poor Clares without entering that order. She spent herself and her fortune on the sick and the poor. Her life, written by her brother Giovanni, reports mystic visions and miracles. Her second brother, Card. Giacomo Colonna, promoted her cause for canonization, but the case foundered during the family struggle with Boniface VIII. BIBLIOGRAPHY: G. Colonna, *B. Margherita Colonna* (ed. L. Oliger, 1935); Leo of Clary, *Lives of the Saints* (4 v., 1887) 4:70–73.

[O. J. BLUM]

MARGARET OF CORTONA, ST. (d. 1297), Franciscan tertiary, penitent. Rejected by her stepmother, she became the mistress of Arsenio of Montepulciano with whom she lived for 9 years. The discovery of her lover's murdered corpse shocked her into conversion and a life of austere penance. She later founded a congregation of tertiary sisters, called the Poverelle, devoted to the care of the poor. Benedict XIII canonized her in 1728. Her incorrupt body is interred in St. Margaret's Church, Cortona. BIBLIOGRAPHY: F. Mauriac, *Margaret of Cortona* (tr. B. Wall, 1948); A. M. Hiral, *Revelations of Margaret of Cortona* (tr. R. Brown, 1952); A. Blasucci and M. Liverani, BiblSanct 8:759–773.

[O. J. BLUM]

MARGARET OF HUNGARY, ST. (*c.* 1242–70), Dominican nun. Daughter of Béla IV, King of Hungary, Margaret refused three offers of royal marriage; entered St. Mary of the Isle, a monastery built by her father; pronounced her vows and also asked for the solemn ceremony of the consecration of virgins. Contemplative and ascetic, charitable toward the poor, M. suffered with them, determined to have no respect shown her rank. Although she has been venerated at Budapest since her death, she was not canonized until 1943. BIBLIOGRAPHY: M. Catherine, *Margaret: Princess of Hungary* (1945); H. Roeder, *Saints and their Attributes*, (1955); Butler 1:176–178; *Book of Saints* (compiled by the Benedictine Monks of St. Augustine's Abbey, 1966).

[M. E. DUFFY]

MARGARET OF LORRAINE, BL. (1463–1521). Born in Vaudemont, Lorraine, she was the grandchild of René, King of Sicily, and the sister of Margaret of Anjou, who would marry Henry VI of England. In 1488 M. married the Duke of Alençon and dedicated herself to alleviating the poverty of her subjects in the duchy. When the Duke died in 1492, M. took her three children to Mauves, Normandy in order to avoid plots against their lives. (Her daughter Francesca would become the grandmother of Henry IV of France.) M. worked for the well-being of the entire community at Mauves. She came under the influence of the asceticism of Francis of Paola and undertook a life of poverty. In 1513, she began to care for the sick at Mortagne and in the years following, opened convents of the Poor Clares at Alençon, La Flèche, and Chateau Gontier. She took vows as a Poor Clare in 1520 and declined the honor of becoming an abbess. She was beatified in 1921. BIBLIOGRAPHY: M. O. Garrigues, BiblSanct 8:776–777; Butler 4:281–282.

[R. J. BRADY]

MARGARET MARY ALACOQUE, ST., see ALACOQUE, MARGARET MARY, ST.

MARGARET OF METOLA, BL. (*c.* 1287–1320), Dominican tertiary. Deformed and blind, she was abandoned by her parents at the age of 16 in Città del Castello. She became a tertiary and spent her short life in caring for prisoners and the infirm poor. Many miracles were attributed to her after her death and she was beatified in 1609.

[T. C. O'BRIEN]

MARGARET OF PARMA, (1522–1586), illegitimate daughter of Charles V and regent-governess of the Netherlands. The wife of Ottavio Farnese, Duke of Parma, she was appointed regent by Philip II from 1559 to 1567. While initially subordinated to Philip's favorite, Lord Granvelle, she assumed an active role when resentment in the Netherlands forced his dismissal in 1564. She has sometimes been criticized for her lack of political insight, but she—more clearly than Philip II—understood that the Netherlands would not tolerate political centralization and religious persecution. Unlike Philip, she involved the local nobility in governmental decisions and practiced a moderate religious policy. Yet Calvinism grew, and in November 1565 Philip sent his famous ''Letters from Segovia'' which demanded that the edicts against heresy be strictly enforced. Anti-Spanish feelings flared. The ''Beggar Petition'' was presented in April 1566, Calvinist preaching intensified and, finally, the iconoclastic riots broke out. The outrage prompted by the riots favored M.; she rallied support and rapidly crushed the rebellion. Perhaps she would have achieved a reconciliation; however, the arrival of Duke Alva on August 22, 1567, signaled the end of her moderate policies and a turning point in the Dutch Revolt. BIBLIOGRAPHY: P. Geyl, *Revolt of the Netherlands* (1958); J. H. Elliot, *Europe Divided, 1559–1598* (1968).

[C. T. EBY]

MARGARET OF SAVOY, BL. (*c.* 1382–1464), widow, abbess. Her father was Amadeus of Savoy, and her mother, a sister of Clement VII, the Avignon claimant to the papacy. In 1418 her husband died and Margaret retired to her estate at Alba in Piedmont. She resisted the insistent offers of marriage by Philip Visconti of Milan and took the habit of the Third Order of St. Dominic. Later M. established the

Monastery of St. Mary Magdalen. Pope Eugenius IV permitted her and her associates to be professed in the Second Order of St. Dominic. She was a competent abbess. Her cult was sanctioned by Pius IV in 1566 and confirmed by Clement IX in 1669 BIBLIOGRAPHY: M. E. Casalandra, NCE 9:203; Butler 4:603–604; A. Ferrua, BiblSanct 8:793–796.

[J. M. O'DONNELL]

MARGERY KEMPE, see KEMPE, MARGERY.

MARGIL, ANTONIO, VEN. (1657–1726), missionary. A Spanish Franciscan ordained in 1682, he went to Mexico in 1683. He developed the missionary college of Santa Cruz de Querétera for training missionaries to the Indians. He founded also Cristo Crucificado in Guatemala City (1701) and Our Lady of Guadaloupe at Zacatecas (1708) for the same purpose. An active missioner himself, M. worked in what is now Central America, Mexico, and southern areas of the present U.S. He was declared venerable in 1836.

[J. R. AHERNE]

MARGOUNIOS, MAXIMOS (*c.* 1549–1602), Greek theologian and humanist. Born in Crete, M. studied in Padua, then became a monk in Crete, and in 1584 was named bp. of Cythera. But with a generous subsidy from the ducal government M. spent the rest of his life in Venice, devoting himself to the study of philology and theology, both Eastern and Western. M. carried on a voluminous correspondence, compiled a large number of theological works, particularly on the questions dividing the Roman and the Greek Churches, for whose union he ardently strove. BIBLIOGRAPHY: D. Geanakoplos, *Byzantine East and Latin West* (1966) 165–193.

[G. T. DENNIS]

MARGUERITE DE NAVARRE, see MARGARET OF ANGOULÊME.

MARI, ST., see ADDAI AND MARI, SS.

MARIA ANGELICA OF JESUS, a discalced Carmelite nun (1893–1919) known primarily through the book *Sponsa Christi* (1926 Herder), based on her notes, and written by Msgr M. J. von Waltendorf.

[E. J. DILLON]

MARIA BERTILLA, ST., see BOSCARDIN, MARIA BERTILLA, ST.

MARIA CRISTINA OF SAVOY, VEN. (1812–36), queen. A princess of the Bourbon family she gave up her wish to become a religious and married Ferdinand II, King of Naples. Her life was exemplary and her influence on King and court profoundly spiritual. She died at age 24 in childbirth and was declared venerable in 1937.

[J. R. AHERNE]

MARIA FRANCESCA OF THE FIVE WOUNDS, ST., see GALLO, MARIA FRANCESCA OF THE FIVE WOUNDS, ST.

MARIA LAACH, a Benedictine monastery in the Rhineland near Andernach; founded 1093 by Count Palatine Henry II and his wife and settled by monks from St. Maximin in Trier and from Affligem. The Romanesque church was consecrated in 1156 by Abp. Hillin of Trier in honor of Our Lady and St. Nicholas. The monastery flourished during the Cluniac reform and later joined the Bursfeld Union (1474), in which it played a leading role after the Reformation. Suppressed during the French Revolution and secularized (1797–1802), it was acquired by the Jesuits in 1862. After they were expelled in the Kulturkampf, they sold it to the Benedictines of Beuron (1892). The following year, the titles and rights of the old abbey were restored, and since then it has become a center of liturgical renewal and reform. BIBLIOGRAPHY: E. von Severus, NCE 9:205; *idem,* LTK 7:45–46; Cottineau 1:1533–34.

[E. J. DILLON]

MARIA LAURENTIA LONGO, VEN. (1463–1542), foundresss of the Capuchinesses. She was the wife of the Catalan Juan Llone, royal chancellor in Naples, who died in 1507. M. then became a participant in the Oratory of Divine Love of St. Cajetan. She founded a convent of nuns in 1535, which first followed the rule of St. Clare; later statutes were based on the consitutions of the Franciscan Capuchins. Pope Paul III approved the order in December 1538. The order spread to Rome (1576) and to Barcelona (1599). The rule is indicative of Maria's spirit: personal sanctification through work of the apostolate, especially in charitable institutions; poverty and humility. M. founded a hospital for incurables in Naples (1519). The process for her cause was introduced in 1892. BIBLIOGRAPHY: J. A. De Harsberg, *Die Maria Laurentia Longo Stifterin der Kapuzinerinnen* (1903); CollFran (1953) 23:166–228; J. Pérez de Urbel, NCE 9:206.

[J. J. SMITH]

MARIA-MODINGEN (also Medingen), **CONVENT OF,** former house of Dominican nuns founded before 1239 near Dillingen, Bavaria, and protected by Count Hartmann IV. Affiliated to the Dominicans in 1246, it became one of the notable convents of southern Germany and the home of the 14th-cent. mystic, Margaret Ebner, whose tomb is enshrined in the present 18th-cent. church. After a 14th-cent. decline, the convent was restored in 1468, only to be confiscated in 1546. It was restored to the Dominicans by Duke Wolfgang Wilhelm of Pfalz-Neuburg, and reconstituted in 1616 by nuns from St. Catherine's in Augsburg. Suppressed after 1802, it was finally given to Franciscan teaching sisters in 1842. BIBLIOGRAPHY: J. A. Doshner, NCE 9:206; F. Zoepfl, LTK 7:47–48.

[E. J. DILLON]

MARIA THERESA OF AUSTRIA (1717–1780), Habsburg empress. Daughter of Emperor Charles VI, she benefited from her father's law, the Pragmatic Sanction, which permitted females to succeed to the Habsburg kingdoms (though not to the empire) and with her husband, Francis Stephen of Lorraine, inherited the Habsburg monarchy on the death of Charles (1740). In 1745 she managed to have her husband, Francis, elected emperor. Her determined efforts created a new and powerful army, reformed the administration of her realm, introduced social changes, linked Austria with Russia and France instead of England, and generally proved her to be an autocratic but shrewd ruler. Among her children, whom she continued to advise as long as she lived, was Marie Antoinette of France. She wept when her son and coregent, Joseph II, took part in the partition of Poland. M. has place apart in European church history, because it was she who effectively began the dominance of State over Church called *Josephinism after her son and successor, Joseph II. Tension with the papacy marked the very outset of her reign. Under the policy of her chancellor Wenzel Anton von *Kaunitz, she claimed the right to tax the Austrian clergy without papal agreement. In 1763 she had a new canon law drawn up and enacted for Austria. New laws of domination over the Church were decreed in 1767 for Lombardy, then under Austrian control; they impeded free contact of the hierarchy with Rome, interfered with episcopal jurisdiction and the Church's power to acquire property. In 1768 these laws were effectively extended to the whole empire, in defiance of the protests of the Holy See. Under M., religious houses were suppressed; the only seminaries allowed were those under government administration, and their syllabus and antipapal textbooks were state-imposed (see RAUTENSTRACH, F. S.). In spite of her professed friendship for the Jesuits, she suppressed them in 1773 in order, it is thought, to win Bourbon acceptance of Marie Antoinette as queen of France.

[J. R. AHERNE]

MARIAM, see MIRIAM.

MARIAM (MIRIAM), CANTICLE OF, see CANTICLE OF MIRIAM.

MARIAN ANTIPHONS, texts for alternate utterance to honor the Mother of God and her Son, though not necessarily with the psalms in the restricted sense of later origin. The O Antiphons of Advent inspired a like Marian series; the most favored one of the medieval profusion, *O Virgo Virginum quomodo fiet,* was retained in the Roman Breviary for Dec. 18, Expectation of the Blessed Virgin Mary, with the *O Adonai* following it. The four great Marian antiphons originated in the 11th and 12th cent. and are recited, or preferably sung, at Compline in accord with the liturgical season; first prayed as antiphons connected with the psalms, the Antiphons of Our Lady became (since 1239) independent chants or hymns, their beautiful though simple melodies intended to be sung by the entire congregation present at the Marian celebration. The Advent antiphon, *Alma Redemptoris Mater,* composed *c.* 1054, is often attributed to Herman the Lame *(Contractus);* the *Salve Regina,* last in the cycle, to Bernard of Clairvaux. Their authorship is, however, highly doubtful, while none is known for the second or third seasonal texts, the *Ave Regina Caelorum,* prayed for the Presentation of Our Lord in the Temple (formerly in the West, the Purification) and the *Regina Coeli,* whose tones lift the hearts of Christians at Easter. The *Salve Regina* is perhaps the most popular of Marian Antiphons. BIBLIOGRAPHY: G. Suñol, EncCatt 1:1442–43; H. Graef, *Devotion to Our Lady,* (1963) 55–56.

[M. R. BROWN]

MARIAN CLERKS REGULAR OF THE IMMACULATE CONCEPTION, an order founded in Poland in 1673 by Stanislaus of Jesus and Mary Papczynski to honor Mary's Immaculate Conception, to teach the poor, and to pray for the souls in purgatory. King John III Sobieski granted them permission to establish houses throughout his dominion after 6 years from the time of their founding. In 1699 the rule and constitutions were approved and the order was granted permission to take solemn vows. They were forced out of their foundations in Lithuania, Portugal, Italy and Rome by religious persecutions. They were saved from extinction by two Lithuanian diocesan priests who asked to be admitted secretly to their order. In 1913 they settled in Chicago and spread throughout other states. In 1976 they numbered 249 priests, 97 brothers and 43 houses.

[R. C. CLIGGETT]

MARIAN FATHERS (Clerks Regular of the Immaculate Conception of the B.V.M.; **MIC** or **SM**), congregation of priests and brothers founded (1673) as an order by S. Papczynski (1631–1701) in Poland (papal approval 1699, 1787). They engage in parochial and mission work, and in education, and publish extensively. In Poland the order, approved by Innocent XII and with solemn vows, made foundations in Lithuania, Portugal, and Italy; harassment, exile, and subsequent absorption of many by the diocesan clergy had by 1864 all but extinguished the order. Pius X in the crisis permitted two Lithuanians, the later Abp. G. Matulaitis-Matulewicz (1875–1927) and a priest F. Bucys, in Russia to be admitted secretly into the order; the Pope in the restoration permitted the change from solemn to simple vows (*Constitutions* 1910, rev. 1930). In the persecution in Russia, the St. Petersburg novitiate was sent to Fribourg, Switzerland. Presently the motherhouse is in Rome; membership (1975) was 346 (249 priests) in 43 houses. Two provinces are in the U.S.: St. Casimir (1930, Chicago) and St. Stanislaus Kostka (1948, Stockbridge, Mass.), with total membership of 81. The former are in 2 archdioceses, 3 dioceses, and in Argentina; the latter in one archdiocese and one diocese, with a Melkite apostolic exarchate in Boston.

In the U.S. they staff two seminaries, 13 parishes and other places of worship; conduct retreats; and publish two religious magazines. Several minister in the Byzantine-Slavonic rite. The Marian Fathers came to Chicago in 1913, and have spread to Connecticut, Massachusetts, Michigan, New York, Wisconsin, and Washington, D.C.

[M. R. BROWN]

MARIAN FEASTS. The Blessed Virgin *Mary is honored by a number of liturgical feasts commemorating various aspects of her life, intercesssion, or attributes. The oldest feast in her honor followed the early Church practice of remembering a saint on the day of his martyrdom; Mary's feast commemorated her return to God as the new Eve and emphasized her role in salvation as the Mother of God. It seems to have originated in the 5th cent. and was first celebrated as part of the Christmas liturgy; it was later transferred to January 1. The third Mass of Christmas retains this earliest commemoration of Mary's role in redemption. It was not until the 7th cent. that additional Marian feasts were introduced into the Latin liturgy. At that time, four feasts of the Oriental Church were brought to the West: (1) The Purification (February 2)—originally a feast honoring the *Presentation of Christ in the Temple, its Marian connotations gradually prevailed. The 1960 liturgical reforms reinstated its dominical significance. (2) Annunciation (March 25)—this feast also was originally a feast of the Lord and was celebrated in Advent, but it came to be considered a Marian feast and its date fixed at 9 months before Christmas. (3) Assumption (August 15)—this feast first arose in Jerusalem and honored the divine maternity. It then spread throughout the Byzantine Empire as the *Dormition of Mary, and finally into Rome as the Assumption. A new formulary was composed after the solemn definition of the Assumption in 1950. (4) Nativity of Mary (September 8)—the object of this feast is not so much Mary's birth as her designation, from all eternity, to be the Mother of God.

The emphasis upon Mariological devotion in the West occasioned the multiplication of her feast days in the 12th century. These feasts usually commemorate some attribute of Mary (Immaculate Heart; Holy Name of Mary; Our Lady of Mercy, etc.), or a miraculous intervention (Our Lady of Lourdes, Guadalupe, or La Salette). The most important of these later feasts is the Immaculate Conception (December 8), which appeared in England during the 12th century. The designation of Saturday as Mary's day grew up in Carolingian times and was esp. promoted by Alcuin (d. 804). Many of these latter feasts duplicate other celebrations and are limited to local devotion, or commemorate only legendary events in Mary's life. Recent liturgical reform has sought to reduce their number or restrict their celebration to particular areas in order to place proper liturgical emphasis on the Mass as the celebration of man's redemption. BIBLIOGRAPHY: B. Capelle, "Les fêtes mariales," *L'Église en prière* (ed. A. Martimort, 1961) 747–765; Miller 419–423; P. Rouillard, NCE 9:210–212.

[T. M. MCFADDEN]

MARIAN PRIESTS, those ordained in England during the reign of *Mary Tudor, as distinct from priests ordained on the Continent, the *seminary priests.

[T. C. O'BRIEN]

MARIANA, JUAN DE (1536–1624), Jesuit theologian. Born in Spain, he is best known for a treatise, *De rege et regis institutione,* in which he defended regicide in the case of tyrants. The treatise provoked a violent reaction against the Jesuits when Henry IV of France was coincidentally assassinated in 1610. An anti-Jesuit work published a year after his death and attributed to him has not been proved to be his, but he is recognized as a divisive force within the Society during his life.

[P. J. HENNESSEY]

MARIANIST SISTERS (FMI; Daughters of Mary Immaculate), pontifical congregation founded (1816) by William Joseph Chaminade (1761–1850) and Adèle de Trenquelléon (1798–1828) at Agen, France. A complement of the *Marianists, they share with the men their Marian heritage. Their constitutions were approved (1888). The motherhouse was established at Sucy-en-Brie, Diocese of Versailles; and the generalate in Rome. The sisters teach on all levels through college, catechize, assist working girls, and sponsor retreats. They have spread to Italy, Spain, Japan, and have African missions. In the U.S. since 1948, presently 29 are in the Archdiocese of San Antonio, Texas (1977). Total membership numbers 421 in 47 houses (1975). BIBLIOGRAPHY: G. J. Ruppel, NCE 9:214; *Directory of Religious Organizations in the U.S.A.* (Consortium Book; ed. J. V. Geisendorfer, 1977) 104; ODCC 857.

[M. R. BROWN]

MARIANISTS (SM; Society of Mary), pontifical association of men religious that in the aftermath of the French Revolution originated (1800) in a sodality of the BVM, and was erected (1817) into a congregation in Bordeaux (1817); papal approbation (1865). It was founded by William Joseph *Chaminade (1760–1850) who the year before had founded also the *Marianist Sisters. The priests "fight religious indifference" by engaging in sacred ministry, and with the Brothers teach, give retreats, write and publish esp. on the Virgin Mary. To the usual vows of religion, they add a fourth of stability in the service of Mary. They spread to Alsace, Belgium, Germany, Hungary, Spain, Switzerland, and in America to the U.S., Canada, and South America (Argentina, Chile); to Africa (Kenya, Nigeria, Nyasaland); to Lebanon and to the Orient (Japan, Korea, and the Pacific). At Nivelles, Belgium, from 1904, the motherhouse moved to Rome (1949). Provinces are: Cincinnati (1849), St. Louis (1908), Pacific (1948), New York (1961). In France they had assumed care of the state college of Gray and Collège Stanislaus and by 1834 were at Colmar. St. Mary's Institute, Cincinnati (1851) developed into Dayton Univ. where is located their Marian Library, largest collection of books on the BVM in the world, and the Marianist

Training Network (MTN). Membership (1975) was 2,368 in 210 Houses, 618 of them priests. BIBLIOGRAPHY: For MTN and *Marian Library,* see p. 257, *Directory of Religious Organizations in the U.S.A.* (Consortium Book; ed. J. V. Giesendorfer, 1977) 257; K. Burton, *Chaminade: Apostle of Mary* (1946, 1949); G. J. Ruppel, NCE 9:214–216; *idem* 3:440 s. v. "Chaminade . . ."

[M. R. BROWN]

MARIANITES OF THE HOLY CROSS (MSC), pontifical congregation of women religious, complement of Brothers of Holy Cross and the Fathers. Founded by B. A. *Moreau, CSC and Leocadie Gascoin (Mère Marie des Sept-Douleurs; d. 1900) at LeMans, France (1841), they came to the U.S. (1843) and to Canada (1847). Intended first for domestic assistance in the seminaries and schools of the male Holy Cross congregations, the sisters soon undertook also teaching, nursing, care of the orphans and of the elderly. *Constitutions* were approved 1885 by Pius IX. They teach on all levels through college (see bibliog. Wolff), care for orphans and the elderly, nurse, staff and maintain hospitals, write and publish. They share the interest of the whole congregation in the missions of India, esp. of Bengal where they went first in 1853–73, returning in 1946; missions were opened likewise in East Pakistan and in Haiti. Membership (1975) was 438 in 65 houses; in the U.S. are two provinces: Louisiana (at New Orleans) and New York (at Princeton, N.J.) with their motherhouse in France (now at Sarthe). The Indiana province became autonomous (1867) and that of Canada (1883). BIBLIOGRAPHY: A. Pugliese, EncCatt 8:148–149; M. L. Dorsey, NCE 9:216; M. M. Wolff, *ibid.* 12:919 s. v. "St. Mary's College." *WOLFF, SISTER M. MADELEVA.

[M. R. BROWN]

MARIANNHILL FATHERS (CMM or RMM; Congregation of the Missionaries of Mariannhill), a mission community of priests and brothers, for work esp. among the pagans. Stemming from the Trappist foundation in Natal, South Africa in 1882, they were founded by Franz (Wendelin) *Pfanner, later named abbot (1885). Work was first among the Zulu natives, who were trained in agriculture and other skills by the priests and brothers; they were aided in this by the Missionary Sisters of the Precious Blood (CPS) whom Pfanner had formed (1885). It was realized that the mission work and Trappist monasticism could not be sustained; the Holy See thus separated the Mariannhill group from the Trappist Order, forming (1909) the Congregation of the Mariannhill Missionaries. Dedicated to the BVM and St. Anne they formed their name; their *Constitutions* were approved (1936). Establishments were made in Europe, in England, the U.S. (1920), and Canada. Missions spread throughout Africa, and (1961) the New Guinea field was opened to them. Mariannhill Fathers encourage an indigenous clergy and sponsor formation of a native religious order of priests and brothers, and another of women religious. Mariannhill Missionaries were (1975) 551, of whom 315 were priests. The generalate is in Rome; U.S.-Canada headquarters at Dearborn Heights, Michigan. BIBLIOGRAPHY: T. Mock, NCE 9:216, bibliog.; J. Bouchaud, *ibid.* 1:172–186, esp. 182 and bibliog.; R. Kneipp, LTK 51–52.

[M. R. BROWN]

MARIANO DEGLI AMATORI, see CUNILIATI, FULGENZIO.

MARIANUM, the name of 1) a Mariological institute in Rome; and 2) the scientific quarterly published by its faculty. The pontifical theological faculty "Marianum" was established by decree of the Sacred Congregation of Seminaries and Universities in 1955; and is located on the Viale Trenta Aprile in Rome. Staffed by members of the Servite Order, it is authorized to grant diplomas in Mariology and doctorates in theology. The review *Marianum* published by this faculty is a quarterly specializing in Mariology, and was founded in Rome in 1939 by G. Roschini, OSM.

[E. J. DILLON]

MARIANUS SCOTUS, name for two Irish monks. **Marianus Scotus of Mainz** (1028–*c.* 1083) left Ireland for Cologne some time after entering the monastery *c.* 1052. After his ordination (1059) at Würzburg he lived in a cell walled up in the church of St. Kilian and then at the abbey of St. Martin. After his death his rich chronicle on the Irish monks in Germany during the 10th and 11th cent. was found; the MS is preserved in the Vatican Library. **Marianus Scotus of Regensburg, Bl.** (d. 1088), founder of monasteries in Germany. Born in Donegal, he became a monk and in 1067 on a pilgrimage to Rome, stopped at Bamberg and was so impressed with the monastery of Michelsberg that he resolved to remain there as a recluse. He established two monasteries near Regensburg, one at Weih Sankt-Peter and the other nearby. He devoted himself to copying MSS of the Bible and other sacred works; only a MS of St. Paul's letters (with the apocryphal Epistle to the Laodiceans included) survives. BIBLIOGRAPHY: C. M. McGrath, NCE 9:216–217; L. E. Boyle, BiblSanct 8:1149–50.

[J. R. RIVELLO]

MARIASTEIN, ABBEY OF, Swiss Benedictine monastery near Basel, founded (1085) as a daughter-house of Einsiedeln Abbey. It is one of the abbeys united in 1602 to form the Swiss congregation. Political upheavals in the late 18th cent. drastically reduced the number in this congregation. Mariastein survived but suffered later dissolution and relocation several times. Members were dispersed during the French Revolution (1798) but reunited in 1804. Suppressed again (1875) they settled in Delle, France. Dispersed once more (1902), they moved to Durnberg, Austria; in 1906 they relocated in Bregenz. Expelled by the Nazis (1941) the monks returned to Mariastein. A shrine there with an old statue of the Blessed Virgin, famous for its miracles, has been a popular attraction for pilgrims. Bibliography: M. Furst, LTK 7:54.

[S. A. HEENEY]

MARIÁTEGUI, JOSÉ CARLOS (1894–1930), Peruvian journalist and sociologist, active proponent of socialism. M. founded the Peruvian Communist Society in Rome in 1920. Returning to Peru, he edited a review, *Amauta,* for radicals of the younger generation. M.'s most important work was *Siete ensayos sobre la interpretación de la realidad peruana* (1928), which soon became Latin America's manual of socialism. M. advocated an autonomous socialism based on the communal ownership of the Inca system. His influence continues to be strong among radicals of the left wing. BIBLIOGRAPHY: J. Baines, *Revolution in Peru: Mariátegui and the Myth* (1972).

[P. DAMBORIENA]

MARIAVITES, since 1906, a separate denomination in Poland, named from the motto, *Mariae vitam imitantes* (imitators of Mary's life). A community of sisters was founded in 1888 at Płock, then Russian Poland, by Felicja Kozlowska (1862–1921); and of priests, by Jan Kowalski in 1892; both groups lived according to the Franciscan rule and were dedicated to the cult of Mary and to the Eucharist. Rome regarded their doctrines and practices, partly based on the visions of Kozlowska, as extravagant, and the two founders were excommunicated in 1906. In the same year the Russian authorities recognized the Mariavites as a separate Church. They were received into communion with the Old Catholic Church in 1909, Kowalski being consecrated abp. over the approximately 200,000 members. The Old Catholic Church severed the relationship in 1925, esp. because of the cult of Kozlowska as the "Bride of the Lamb" and of Kowalski as a second Michael the Archangel, and because of the mystical marriages between priests and nuns, which were to lead to "immaculate conceptions," children of a new and sinless race. In 1935 a majority rejected Kowalski. He died at Dachau during World War II, and all the Mariavites were severely persecuted by the Nazis. A small group in the Kowalski line remains; the majority of Mariavites, however, numbering about 25,000, with three episcopal sees and about 40 parishes, have entered into cooperative association, but not communion, with the Old Catholic Church. Mariavite teachings agree basically with those of the Old Catholics, esp. in the rejection of papal primacy and infallibility; the practice of auricular confession and the veneration of relics, however, are forbidden. BIBLIOGRAPHY: P. F. Anson, *Bishops at Large* (1965); J. Peterkiewicz, *Third Adam: the Mariavite Experiment in Mystical Marriage* (1975).

[T. C. O'BRIEN]

MARIE ANTOINETTE, QUEEN OF FRANCE (1755–1793), the daughter of Empress Maria Theresa of Austria and recipient of endless letters from her mother which, if heeded, might have forestalled M.'s tragic end. M. was married in 1770 to the Dauphin of France, who later became King Louis XVI. As an Austrian she was not popular in France. As queen she was extravagant; as a sister of Emperor Joseph II of Austria, she made errors in supporting his policies and aroused French hostility. She alienated those who would have accepted a constitutional monarchy. Much stronger than the King, she nevertheless lacked tact and diplomacy. In 1792 she was imprisoned; and her strength of character, patience, and strong Christian faith edeemed whatever past failings she may have had. Condemned by the Revolutionary Tribunal, she went to her death in noble resignation at the age of 38. BIBLIOGRAPHY: A. Castelot, *Queen of France: A Biography of Marie Antoinette* (1957).

[J. R. AHERNE]

MARIE DE FRANCE, earliest French woman poet whose works are extant. Three works are known; *Lais* (*c.* 1170), *Ysopet* (1180), and the *Espurgatoire Saint Patrice* (*c.* 1190). Twelve episodes in octosyllabic rhyming couplets, narrating an unrelated series of fairy tales and marvelous adventures, comprise the *Lais*. A collection of 75 fables, each having a moral climax expressing a feudal ideal, is entitled *Ysopet*. The *Espurgatoire Saint Patrice* embroiders an Irish legend about St. Patrick with details borrowed from a monastic literary source. These works are excellent examples of Western Europe's chivalric attitudes toward the close of the 12th century. BIBLIOGRAPHY: A. Adler, NCE 9:218–219.

[J. E. WRIGLEY]

MARIE DE L'INCARNATION, BL. (1566–1618). Born Barbara Avrillot in Paris, she desired to join the Franciscans, but her father married her to Peter Acarie, Viscount of Villemor. Because Peter was a supporter of the Catholic League, he was banished when Henry of Navarre came to the throne in 1593. M.'s defense of her husband resulted in Peter's return to Paris. In time she gained the complete confidence of the King. She was a friend of Francis de Sales and in 1601 began to explore the philosophy of Teresa of Ávila. With her cousin Pierre de *Bérulle, she undertook the establishment of the Carmelites in France. In 1603, a papal bull issued by Clement VIII granted approval to the project and in 1604, Marie opened the first convent of Teresa's Carmelites in France. When Peter Acarie died in 1613, Marie joined the Carmelites, entering at Amiens. She made vows in 1615, taking the name Marie de l'Incarnation. As a nun, she worked among the sick and the dying at Amiens and later at Pontoise. M. had several mystical experiences in the contemplation of the life of Christ. She was beatified by Pius VI in 1791. BIBLIOGRAPHY: G. de Gesú Maria, BiblSanct 8:1013–15; Butler II: 124–126.

[R. J. BRADY]

MARIE OF THE INCARNATION, VEN. (1599–1672), foundress of the Ursulines in Canada. Born Marie Guyart, she was married to Claude Martin, widowed, and for some time operated a mercantile business at Tours, supporting herself and her son. After joining the French Ursulines (1632), M. went to Canada (1639) to establish an Indian school at Sillery, and in 1641 began the Quebec Ursuline convent. She mastered three Indian languages and devoted herself to the education of both Indian and French children. BIBLIOGRAPHY: D. Mahoney, *Marie of the Incarnation* (1964); D. G. Oury, *Marie de L'Incarnation* (2 v., 1973).

[R. K. MACMASTER]

MARIE DE MÉDICIS (1573–1642), queen regent of France for *Louis XIII. The daughter of Francesco de' Medici, Grand Duke of Tuscany, she was married to Henri IV of France in 1600—an alliance depicted by Rubens in a famous series of paintings. A difficult and ambitious woman, she had herself crowned queen in 1610, on the very eve of her husband's assassination, and thereafter acted as regent for her son Louis XIII, then only nine. Under the influence of the papal nuncio, the Spanish ambassador, and her favorite the courtier Concini, she renounced France's traditional foreign policy in favor of rapprochement with Catholic Spain, arranged through the marriages of two of her children to Habsburg heirs. The combined arbitrariness and laxness of her rule led to discontent and rebellion on the part of the great nobles. In 1617, after having had Concini murdered, Louis XIII imprisoned his mother, then exiled her to Blois and later to Angers, where she organized an armed rebellion against the king, who repulsed it in 1620. Through the agency of Card. *Richelieu, mother and son were reconciled and by the following year Marie again had a place in the royal council. But her intrigues against Richelieu, originally her confederate, but since 1624 the king's prime minister, eventually led to her downfall in 1630. She was exiled to Compiègne in 1631 but soon left for the Spanish Netherlands and then for England, where her daughter Henrietta Maria was Charles I's queen. Unable to abandon her intriguing, she was forbidden ever to return to France and died in obscurity in Cologne.

[E. M. GATES]

MARIENBERG, ABBEY OF, Romanesque Benedictine abbey of St. Joseph in Burgesio, north central Italy. Its founding is traceable to Charlemagne, who established a Benedictine monastery between 780–786 in Graubunden, Switzerland. It was dissolved after 880 and 2 cent. later reorganized in Schuls, Switzerland (1090), was destroyed by lightning and rebuilt. Shortly after its consecration in 1131 it was made an abbey. It was relocated in Vintschgau in 1146 and finally, in 1150, in its present site near Burgesio, retaining its name, Marienberg. Subsequent years brought dissolution by Bavaria, destruction by fire, and reconstruction by Emperor Francis of Austria (1816). In the 19th cent. the abbey produced numerous renowned scholars. The apostolate of the monks includes education and parish work.

[S. A. HEENEY]

MARIENKLAGE (Lament of Our Lady), a special genre of poetry (often chanted) with words supposedly uttered by Mary at the foot of the Cross and during the burial of her Son; it is based on the sequence *Planctus ante nescia*. Mary represents mankind. Later dramatized by dialogues between Mary, Christ, Mary Magdalene, and John, the laments became part of the Passion plays. The most accomplished Marienklage is probably the *Bordesholmer Marienklage* (from the Augustinian monastery in Holstein) of the late 15th century. It shuns all realistic form, even Christ's words, and uses allegory and symbol to bring Mary's grief and suffering to mind. BIBLIOGRAPHY: *Die deutsche Literatur des Mittelalters, Verfasserlexikon* (ed. W. Stammler, 1955) 5:655–665; *Reallexikon der deutschen Literatur* (1965) 2:285–288.

[S. A. SCHULZ]

MARIGNY, ENGUERRAND DE (1275–1315), royal councillor of Philip IV. M. became Philip the Fair's most influential financial adviser. Although he achieved a reconciliation of France with the Holy See and was skillful as a peacemaker, he aroused the hatred of Philip's brother, Charles of Valois, who succeeded in having him hanged during the reign of Louis X (1314–16). BIBLIOGRAPHY: J. R. Strayer, NCE 9:221.

[J. E. WRIGLEY]

MARIJUANA, see DRUG ADDICTION.

MARÍN-SOLA, FRANCISCO (1873–1932), Spanish Dominican theologian. M. was born in the Philippines; taught there and at the Dominican house of studies in Avila, Spain; founded the Dominican College in Rosaryville, La.; taught at the Univ. of Notre Dame (Indiana); and held the chair of theology at the Catholic University of Fribourg (Switzerland) 1918–1927. He is primarily known for his work on the development of doctrine. M. taught that *theological conclusions (conclusions arrived at by positing a truth of faith and a truth of reason as the major and minor premises of a syllogism) are doctrines of faith if the predicates applied to Christian doctrines belong to them essentially and not accidentally. Some contemporary critics claim that he holds an overly propositional conception of revelation and faith. BIBLIOGRAPHY: F. Marín-Sola, *L'Évolution homogène du dogme catholique* (1924); F. D. Nealy, NCE 9:221–222.

[J. MCGLYNN]

MARINHO, JOSÉ ANTÔNIO (1803–53), Brazilian educator, politician, and priest. Of a multi-racial background and the son of poor working people, he was involved in the revolution in Pernambuco in 1824; but was a man of considerable culture by the time he was ordained priest in 1829. He obtained the chair of philosophy in Ouro Prêto, served two terms in a provincial assembly, was substitute deputy and twice regular deputy in the imperial legislature, and then abandoned formal politics to become a pastor in Rio de Janeiro. He was a notable preacher, founder of a school named after himself, and no stranger to the imperial chapel. He was the author of two works of historical import.

[E. J. DILLON]

MARINUS, SS., two different saints of the early Church. The first was martyred *c.*262 in the time of Gallienus, in spite of the edict of Toleration, probably because of the rebel command of Macrianus, who had revolted and taken possession of Egypt, Palestine, and other Eastern provinces. Eusebius narrates the circumstances of the martyrdom. Born of a noble family of Caesarea in Palestine, M. had served with distinction in the army. When he was about to be honored as centurion, a rival objected that since he was a Christian he would not sacrifice to the emperor and should be disqualified. Marinus professed his faith to the governor Achaeus and was given three hours to reconsider. After reaffirming his faith, he was led away to execution. Both the Roman Martyrology and the Greek Menaion commemorate M.'s friend Astyrius as a martyr along with him. But Eusebius merely notes that Astyrius was a senator in high favor with the emperor; that he was present at the martyrdom; that he wrapped his own cloak around his friend's dead body, and carried him away to give him honorable burial. Nothing but beautiful legend is known of the second St. Marinus. He is Marinus the Deacon and may have lived in the 4th century. He is patron of the little, independent Italian republic of San Marino. He is named in the Roman Martyrology on September 4. BIBLIOGRAPHY: Butler 1:466–467; 3:484.

[E. J. DILLON]

MARINUS I (d. 884), **POPE** from 882, long erroneously called Martin I, M. had spent his life in the service of the papal curia. As a deacon he was legate of Adrian II to the fourth Council of Constantinople, after which he became archdeacon and treasurer of the Roman Church, and then bp. of Caere in Etruria. After the assassination of *John VIII, M. was elected pope, the first occupant of another see to be elevated to that office. Such translation was considered uncanonical at that time. M. recalled from exile the opponents of John VIII's Frankish policy, among them *Formosus, who was restored to the See of Porto and was to succeed to the papacy in 891. As John VIII's legate to Constantinople, M. had been strongly opposed to Photius, and both Photius and the Emperor used the canonical irregularity of M.'s election as an excuse for not recognizing him as legitimate pope. However, M. made a gesture toward reconciliation by conferring the office of papal librarian upon Zachary, a personal friend of Photius and leader of the Greek party in Rome. BIBLIOGRAPHY: Mann 3:353–360; V. Gellhaus, NCE 9:222.

[P. F. MULHERN]

MARINUS II (d. 946), **POPE** from 942, sometimes mistakenly called Martin III. A Roman and a priest of the ihurch of St. Cyriacus at the time of his election to the papacy, M. owed his elevation to the influence of Alberic II, to whose control of temporal affairs M. offered no challenge throughout his pontificate. But the few records of his reign indicate a concern to promote discipline in monasteries and to protect religious houses from greedy bishops. In the interests of clerical and religious discipline, he reappointed Frederick of Mainz as legate in Germany. BIBLIOGRAPHY: Mann 4:218–233; M. Mulholland, NCE 9:223.

[P. F. MULHERN]

MARINUS (scholarch from 484 A.D.), Neoplatonic philosopher, pupil of Proclus, and his successor as head of the Platonic Academy at Athens. M. commented on works of Plato and Aristotle and was accused of being too favorable to the latter. He was esp. interested in mathematics. However, in keeping with the teachings of his master Proclus, of whom he wrote a biography, M. gave great weight to theurgy. He placed the theurgic virtues at the summit of his scale of virtues. BIBLIOGRAPHY: H. Gericke, LexAW (1851); Ueberweg 1:631–633.

[M. R. P. MCGUIRE]

MARIOLATRY, giving to Mary the worship due to God. It is sometimes used as a term of reproach by Protestants contending that the honor Catholics pay to Mary is improper and should be directed only to God. Catholic theology, however, distinguishes **latria*, worship paid to God, from **dulia*, honor given to saints, and **hyperdulia*, veneration given to Mary. Controversy has centered around whether common devotional practices directed toward Mary violate the prohibition against honoring her with *latria*, particularly among uneducated worshipers who may be unaware of the theological distinctions. BIBLIOGRAPHY: T. A. O'Meara, *Mary in Protestant and Catholic Theology* (1966); J. Haran, *Mary, Mother of God* (pa. 1973). *MARY, BLESSED VIRGIN, DEVOTION TO.

[T. EARLY]

MARIOLOGICAL SOCIETIES, national Marian organizations founded in five countries of Europe and four countries of the Americas for the purpose of promoting research and theological studies on Mary. Besides furthering Mariological research, the societies conduct lectures, discussion groups, and hold annual conventions. The Mariological Society of America was founded in 1949 and has its offices in St. Petersburg, Florida. Its U.S. publication is called *Marian Studies*.

[R. A. TODD]

MARIOLOGY, the study of the Blessed Virgin Mary in Christian Churches, in the RC Church especially. More particularly it is that part of the theological study of the Incarnation of Christ and the redemption of mankind that analyzes the role of the Blessed Virgin Mary. It concerns itself mainly with the few defined dogmas about Mary—her divine motherhood, virginity, Immaculate Conception, and

Assumption. It dates from the 16th cent., when this study was distinguished and more or less separated from the rest of theology. Scriptural Mariology limits itself to the study of the NT texts that refer to Mary—Mt 1.16–2.23; 12.46–50; 13.55; Mk 3.31–35; 6.3; Lk 1.26–2.52; 8.19–21; 11.27–28; Jn 1.14; 2.1–12; 19.25–27; Rom 1.3; Gal 4.4. (Despite its legitimate use in the liturgy as a description of Mary, Rev ch. 12 is more generally considered to be a figure of the Church than to be a description of Mary.) In a looser sense, OT "figures of Mary" like Sara, the sister of Moses, Ruth, the Temple, the ark, Jacob's ladder—and their allegorical treatment by some of the Fathers—are part of the concern of scriptural Mariology. Until the Council of Trent (1545–63) Marian attributions of Scripture texts were relatively restrained; the magisterium, the teaching authority of the Church, had proclaimed as dogma only the divine motherhood (Ephesus, 431) and the virginity (Lateran, under Martin I, 649). Protestant attacks on Mary caused a proliferation of Mariologies during the 16th and 17th cent.—more chronicles than theologies. The outstanding Mariological event of the 19th cent.—otherwise considered the doldrums of Marian writings—was the carefully reasoned proclamation and definition by Piux IX (1854) of the doctrine of the Immaculate Conception. In a similar theological vein was the definition of the Assumption by Pius XII (1950).

Twentieth-century Mariology was shaken from some of its straining, more emotional than theological, and put into a posture that was at once more biblical, patristic, ecclesial, and ecumenical. The occasion was the controversy between the Marian minimalists and maximalists at Vatican Council II. The fathers of the Council eventually (1964) published the dogmatic Constitution of the Church. Its final chapter (8) was the first official Mariology of the RC Church. It recognized the centuries-old appreciation of Mary and Eve, each as a mother of the living. The parallel, suggested by St. Paul's parallel of Christ and Adam (Rom 5.12–21, 1 Cor 15.44–49), was developed by SS. Justin, Irenaeus, Jerome, Augustine, and others. Thus Mary is an image, prototype, and exemplar of the Church. She is even Mother of the Church as the Popes of the Council, John XXIII and Paul VI, called her. These conciliar events brought Mariology back into the theology of the Incarnation and of the Church and indicate that Mary's motherhood of Christ correlates her in a unique manner—evidently as a creature, dependent on Christ—to the Trinity on the one hand and to the people of God on the other. Of this group she is the first and holiest member. BIBLIOGRAPHY: E. R. Carroll, NCE 9:223–227; Carol Mariol; *Marian Studies,* (Annual Proceedings of the Mariological Society of America (1950–); C. Vollert, *Theology of Mary* (1965).

[J. W. LANGLINAIS]

MARION-BRÉSILLAC, MELCHIOR MARIE JOSEPH DE (1813–1859), founder of the Society of the *African Missions. A native of France, he was ordained priest at Carcassone (1838) and joined (1841) the *Paris Foreign Mission Society. On mission in India (1842–54) he advocated a native priesthood and showed strong disapproval of the *caste system. Superior of the Pondicherry seminary (1844), at Coimbatore he was provicar (1845) and vicar apostolic (1850). He resigned (1854) because of opposition to his views. Attracted to the African mission field, with Joseph Planque he founded (1856) in Lyons the Society of the African Missions. Named vicar apostolic of Sierra Leone (1858), he left for Africa. At Freetown, Liberia, he and his band of four were stricken with yellow fever and died. His vision—a native clergy and adaptation of culture—continued to inspire, to bring success to his society's missions both in Africa and the Bahamas. With 52 houses, the Society of African Missions had (1977) 1,510 members of whom 1,434 were priests. BIBLIOGRAPHY: J. M. Todd, *African Mission* (1962); R. M. Wiltgen, *Gold Coast Mission History, 1471–1880* (1956) 127–154.

[M. R. BROWN]

MARIST BROTHERS (FMS), also known as the Little Brothers of Mary, a pontifical congregation of lay religious with simple vows, founded in France in 1817 by Bl. Marcellin *Champagnat of the Society of Mary (Marist Fathers) for the Christian education of the young. It was the original intention of Champagnat that the brothers become part of his congregation, but the Holy See considered such a union impractical and kept the two separate. Over the years the Marist Brothers absorbed many other communities of brothers, viz, in 1842 the Brothers of Saint-Paul-Trois-Châteaux in France; in 1844 the Brothers of Christian Instruction of Viviens, France; in 1956 the Brothers of St. Peter Claver of Nigeria; and in 1959 the Brothers of St. Francis Regis in Canada and France. The Marist Brothers staff about 700 schools in Europe, Asia, Africa, and the Americas. Forming a single province with Canada they operated schools in the U.S. from 1886. In 1911 the U.S. became an independent province; this province was in turn divided in 1959. The general Motherhouse is located in Rome, Italy. In 1975 the brothers maintained 882 houses and had 7,767 members.

[M. T. REILLY]

MARIST FATHERS, the Society of Mary (see also MARIANISTS), a community of priests and brothers founded by Jean Claude Courveille and J. C. M. *Colin, engaged in the parochial, educational, and missionary apostolate. The foundation can be traced to 1816 at the seminary of Lyons, where the two founders and four other newly ordained priests consecrated themselves to Mary. But Colin gave the Marist family its actual existence when he composed and received approval in 1822 of a rule for Marist priests, sisters, and tertiaries. From that point originate the four distinct religious branches: Marist Fathers, Marist Brothers; Marist Sisters, Marist Missionary Sisters, and the Marist Third Order. The Marist Fathers received final approval in

1836 with their acceptance of missions in the South Sea; since then they have been prominent in that mission field. The congregation has provinces or vice provinces in France, Belgium, Spain, England, Ireland, Mexico, Canada, and the United States. The Marist foundations in the U.S. began in 1863; there are provinces centered in Massachusetts, Washington, D.C., and California. The inspiration of the spirituality and apostolate of the Marists is imitation of Mary. The generalate is located in Rome. In 1976 there were 366 houses, with 1,640 priests, and 374 brothers.

[T. C. O'BRIEN]

MARIST MISSIONARY SISTERS (SMSM; Missionary Sisters of the Society of Mary), pontifical congregation, founded at Saint-Brieuc, France (1845–1857) by Ven. Jean Claude Marie Colin (1790–1875). Of the Marist Family, they are international: from France they spread to Italy, where their generalate was established at Castel Gondolfo; the American province is at Waltham, Mass., and other provinces are in Australia, New Zealand, Oceania, and France (Euro-Africa). They came to the U.S. first at Boston (1922); many from America labor there or in the missions in the SW Pacific; diocesan congregations were formed in Fiji, the North and South Solomons in the area where they have pioneered. They are in Australia and New Zealand; the West Indies; in Peru; in India, and Bangladesh. They conduct schools, dispensaries, maternity centers, and leprosaria. Membership (1975) was 807 in 135 houses. *MARIST SISTERS.

[M. R. BROWN]

MARIST SISTERS (MS; Sisters of the Holy Name of Mary), pontifical congregation founded *c.* 1817–24 by Ven. Jean Claude Marie *Colin (1790–1875) and Jeanne Marie Chauvoin (Mère St. Joseph) at Cerdon, E of Lyons, France. They are of the Marist Family (see bibliog., J. L. White, esp. 229), and dedicated to the education of girls and young women, and the care of orphans. Papal approval came in 1884 (revised 1958); the motherhouse is in Anzio, Italy; membership (1975) was 691 in 76 houses. Marist Sisters teach in elementary and secondary schools; engaged early in Catholic Action, they work with the young, do social work, and serve in parishes; they are missioners in the South Pacific and in Senegal, Africa. Some 25 sisters are in the U.S. apostolate, where they staff two Michigan schools, Dearborn Heights (1956) and East Detroit (1958); in Wheeling, W. Va. they opened another (1962), and Chauvoin House (1967). BIBLIOGRAPHY: E. Leonard, *Enriching Many: Jeanne-Marie Chauvoin* (1956); J. L. White, NCE 9:229–230; G. Goyau, *Life of Colin* (1910).

[M. R. BROWN]

MARITAIN, JACQUES (1882–1973), foremost 20-th cent. exponent of the metaphysics and moral philosophy of St. Thomas Aquinas. With his wife Raïssa Oumansoff, a Russian Jewess whom he married in Paris in 1904, M. passed from a practical atheism to reception into the Catholic Church in 1906. The Maritains' conversion developed out of their friendship with Léon Bloy. An appreciation of the life and work of both Maritains requires recognition that their conversion was motivated by a profound longing for contemplation and union with God; that commitment antedated their "conversion" to Aquinas. Their first living of Catholicism was an intense pursuit of prayer and sanctification, and they came under the spiritual direction of P. Humbert *Clérissac, OP, whom they met in 1908. With his approval, after long deliberation, the couple made a mutual vow of chastity in 1911 (see Kernan 46–47).

During an illness in 1908 Raïssa received from P. Clérissac for spiritual reading St. Thomas's *Summa theologiae;* fittingly its gripping effect on Raïssa was the occasion of Jacques' introduction to St. Thomas the following year. He had received his *agrégé* in philosophy from the Sorbonne in 1905; the two had lived in Heidelberg (1906–08) while he studied biology at the university there. On their return to Paris he was employed by Hachette, the publishers, as an editor of reference works. His study of St. Thomas, however, revived his interest in philosophy; it also turned him from his earlier attachment to H. *Bergson's thought, and an article criticizing Bergson in the *Revue de philosophie* in 1909 was M.'s first philosophical publication. That led to the beginning of his teaching career, first at the Collège Stanislas, then at the Institut Catholique (1913) where he continued to teach until 1939. Early in this period he came into contact with and was guided by P. R. M. *Garrigou Lagrange and P. Pierre Dehau, both Dominicans. As his knowledge of the Thomistic tradition deepened, from his own works and words it is apparent that the commentator par excellence for M. was *John of St. Thomas (see *The Peasant of the Garonne* [tr. 1968] p. 175). During this phase of M.'s teaching life, the couple established at Meudon near Versailles a center for the study of St. Thomas and a group that was dedicated to the combination of the intellectual and the spiritual life. M.'s *Art and Scholasticism,* first published in 1920, a perennially valuable work on aesthetics, resulted from the Maritains' contacts with friends from the arts and drew new friends to them. These years also brought controversial involvement in politics: on the Church's relationship to the State (see ACTION FRANÇAISE) and M.'s unpopular anti-Franco stance during the Spanish Civil War.

M.'s first visit to North America occurred in 1939 when he lectured at the (Pontifical) Institute of Mediaeval Studies in Toronto. Because of World War II the Maritain's were stranded in New York in 1940 until the war's end (they suffered in anguish over the fall of France and the slaughter of the Jews); he taught at Columbia and lectured at Princeton. The North American phase of his career also included lecturing frequently at Notre Dame and at the Univ. of Chicago. When the Maritains did return to France, he was appointed ambassador of France to the Vatican, where he presented his credentials in May 1945. This was a period of close friendship at the Secretariat of State with Card. G. B. Montini, who had earlier translated into Italian M.'s work, *Three Reformers: Luther, Descartes, Rousseau* (Eng. tr. 1929), and who, as Pope Paul VI, frequently referred to M. simply as "my teacher." Resigning in May 1948, M. accepted an appointment at Princeton and there finished his teaching career. (The Maritain home there was bequeathed to Notre Dame.) In 1961 Raïssa died in Paris, and he retired to live with the Little Brothers of Jesus in Toulouse, finally joining the community in 1970.

M.'s bibliography, including some 50 books, is evidence of his constant dedication to study; a Maritain Center was established at Notre Dame in 1959 for preservation and translation of his writings and for research. A complete bibliography to 1962 was published in that year: D. and I. Gallagher, *The Achievement of Jacques and Raïssa Maritain.* His last book at Toulouse, was *On the Church of Christ: The Person of the Church and Her Personnel* (tr. 1973). There are three works—besides *Art and Scholasticism* (tr. 1962) and its special interest (see also *Creative Intuition in Art and Poetry,* tr. 1953)—that are fundamental to the two primary concerns of M.'s intellectual labors: on the philosophy of knowing, *The Degrees of Knowledge* (2d. Eng. tr. and ed.—the first tr. of 1937 was a disaster—under G. B. Phelan 1959, from the 4th French ed. of *Distinguer pour unir* 1946; on the philosophy of being, *Preface to Metaphysics: Seven Lectures on Being* (tr. 1939 of *Sept leçons sur l'être,* 1934); on moral philosophy, *The Person and the Common Good* (tr. 1947 of *La Personne et le bien commun,* 1947). Also to be recommended because of current church interests in social justice is J. W. Evans and L. R. Ward, *The Social and Political Philosophy of Jacques Maritain* (1955; pa. 1965), which gives a selection of reading on key topics from M.'s many works on the subject.

In the Peasant of the Garonne, in which M. exercises the right he had earned to its irony and the arguments of which on certain contemporary philosophical and theological positions cannot be dismissed as merely querulous, he says, after a description of St. Thomas: "Why have I begun to go on about his character and personality? Because I love him" (152). The reason for this love and its lineaments (besides the simple, personal communion with the lovable man who gives himself to those who come to know the *Summa*) M. states thus: ". . . because that faithful servant, human wisdom, instrumentally used—the *metaphysics of St. Thomas* (not that of Aristotle)—had the intuition of being and saw in *esse* her chief object, the higher wisdom—*the theology of St. Thomas*—was able to contemplate in the transluminous obscurity of the mysteries of Faith, the Uncreated Cause of Being as *Being itself subsisting by itself* . . . to which the handmaid had already lifted her eyes as toward her ultimate end" (*ibid.* 158). M. loved St. Thomas for the great vision of being and its relationship to the higher vision of God through grace: hence his *Degrees of Knowledge*—a philosophy of transcendent knowing, of knowing as a way of being, traced from its humblest roots to the lights of mystical windows;—and his *Sept leçons sur l'être*—a philosophy of being that separates false from true metaphysical coin" to show the possibility of a human wisdom that yet lies open to a higher wisdom. Fittingly M. shares St. Thomas's fate of being read only by a few. When, however, there is a return to a more balanced appreciation of the Catholic tradition, whoever wishes help in reaching Aquinas—for Aquinas needs to be read within a tradition and with a guide—M. will be one to depend on; to read him is to read St. Thomas (for whatever can be read out of St. Thomas *is there*); he is a much more reliable interpreter than the great historian with whom his name is coupled, É. Gilson (see *The Peasant of the Garonne,* 160–161).

At the close of Vatican Council II, Dec. 8, 1965, in St. Peter's, dressed in the habit of the Little Brothers, M. received the Council's letter addressed to intellectuals from the hands of his friend Paul VI. One impact of the Council has continued to intensify in the years since: the Constitution on the Church and the World. Of M.'s work in moral and political philosophy it can simply be said that they are the best possible commentary on *Gaudium et spes*, even as their ideas are clearly part of the background of that marvellous document. Two quotes suggest central themes of M.'s thought:

"The common good of the body politic is . . . the good *human* life of the multitude, of the multitude of persons; it is their communion in good living. It is therefore common *to the whole and to the parts:* it flows back to the parts and the parts must benefit from it . . . The common good is something ethically good. Included in it as essential element is the maximum possible development here and now of human persons, of persons making up a united multitude to the end of forming a people organized not by force alone but by justice. . . . The end to which [social life] tends is to procure the common good of the multitude in such a way that each concrete person gains the greatest measure possible, i.e., compatible with the good of the whole, of real independence from the servitudes of nature—an independence assured alike by the economic guarantees of work and ownership, political rights, the moral virtues, and the cultivation of the mind" (Evans, Ward 88–89, the section on "the Person and the Common Good").

"The horizontal movement of civilization when directed towards its authentic temporal aims, helps the vertical movement of souls. And without the movement of souls toward their eternal aim, the movement of civilization would lose the charge of spiritual energy, human pressure, and creative radiance which animate it toward its temporal accomplishment. For the man of Christian humanism has a meaning and a direction. The progressive integration of humanity is also a progressive emancipation from human servitude and misery as well as from the constraints of material nature. The supreme ideal which the political and social work in mankind has to aim at is thus the inauguration of a brotherly city, which does not imply that all men will some day be perfect on earth and love each other fraternally, but the hope that the existential *state* of human life and the structures of civilization will draw nearer to their perfection, the standard of which is justice and friendship. . . . Against the deceptive myths raised by the powers of illusion a vaster and greater hope must rise up, a bolder promise must be made to the human race. The truth of God's image as it is naturally impressed on us, freedom, and fraternity are not dead. If our civilization struggles with death, the reason is not that it dares too much or that it proposed too much to men. It is that it does not dare enough or propose enough to them. It shall revive, a new civilization shall come to life on condition that it hope for, and will, and love truly and heroically, truth, beauty, and fraternity'' (*ibid.* 168–169, section on ''Christian Humanism''). Nothing could be more appropriate than the singular distinction of his name's being included among the Fathers and Doctors in Paul VI's *Populorum progressio* esp. in this age of the laity in the Church's life. BIBLIOGRAPHY: An intimate portrait of the life ''behind'' the scholar is J. Kernan's *Our Friend Jacques Maritain* (1975). Two important studies are the ''Maritain Volume'' of the *Thomist* 5 (1943) on the occasion of his 60th birthday; and the Winter 1972 issue of *New Scholasticism* honoring his 90th. Also J. W. Evans NCE 16:275–277, good bibliography; J. J. Sikora, *The Christian Intellect and the Mystery of Being: Reflections of a Maritain Thomist* (1966).

[T. C. O'BRIEN]

MARITAIN, RAÏSSA OUMANSOFF (1883–1960), French poet and philosopher. She was born in Rostov, Russia, of a Jewish family that later emigrated to France. She married Jacques Maritain (1904) and was converted with him to Catholicism (1906). Her spiritual memoirs, translated as *We Have Been Friends Together,* (1942) and *Adventures in Grace,* (1945), describe the stages of their mutual conversion, that of her sister Vera, and of her parents; they note also the religious progress of friends like Péguy, Psichari, and Massis. Her breadth of mind can be gauged by the range of her works: four volumes of poetry, essays on poetics in her husband's *Situation de la poésie* (1938); art criticism; and philosophical and religious essays. Her diary, *Le Journal de Raïssa,* was published posthumously (1963). BIBLIOGRAPHY: D. A. and I. Gallagher, *Achievement of Jacques and Raïssa Maritain. A Bibliography 1906–61* (1962).

[G. E. GINGRAS]

MARIUS OF AVENCHES, ST. (*c.*531–594), French bishop and chronicler, important for his *Chronicle* covering the years 455–581 which rendered, somewhat flatly, accounts of events in Italy and in the Orient. There are indications that later writers borrowed from this work. Before he died he had moved the seat of his diocese to Lausanne and he is buried there. BIBLIOGRAPHY: É. Brouette, LTK 7:88; B. D. Hill, NCE 9:230; Altaner 281

[J. R. RIVELLO]

MARIUS MERCATOR (d. *c.*451), Latin ecclesiastical writer. A native of Africa, M. was in Rome *c.*417 when he wrote and sent to St. Augustine two anti-Pelagian treatises, both of which have been lost. After 429 he was in Constantinople where he continued his attack upon Pelagianism and was instrumental in securing the condemnation of Julian of Eclanum and Caelestius at Ephesus (431). He also wrote against the Nestorians, but most of his writings are compilations or translations of Greek works into Latin made for the benefit of the Latin-speaking monks of Thrace. Works: PL 48. BIBLIOGRAPHY: Altaner 534–535.

[R. B. ENO]

MARIUS VICTORINUS, GAIUS (betw. 275 and 300–after 362), professor of rhetoric, Neoplatonic philosopher, and African convert to Christianity. M. wrote commentaries on the rhetorical and philosophical works of Cicero, translated *Isagoge* of Porphyry, and other Neoplatonic treatises, including very probably some of Plotinus. Of his philosophical works, the *De definitionibus* is extant. About 355, his conversion to Christianity stunned pagan circles and brought special joy to Christians (cf. St. Augustine, *Conf.* 8.2.4). Under Julian, M. was forced to resign his professorship. He was not only a translator of Greek philosophical works, but, as a Christian Neoplatonist, he wished to employ Aristotelian logic and Neoplatonic philosophical concepts in the elucidation of the Christian doctrine of the Trinity. M. engaged also in the controversy against Arianism, and 12 of his treatises *Adversus Arium* are preserved. He lacked adequate training in Christian theology and on the theological side he did not exercise any marked influence on his contemporaries. However, M.'s translations of Neoplatonic writings made these works accessible to a West in which the knowledge of Greek was in rapid decline. It is certain that St. Augustine owed much to these translations. BIBLIOGRAPHY: P. Hadot, NCE 9:231; P. Henry and P. Hadot, *Marius Victorinus: Traités théologiques sur la Trinité,* SC (1960) 68–69.

[M. R. P. MCGUIRE]

MARK, EVANGELIST, ST., the author of the second Gospel. Mark, known also as John, was an assistant to Paul and Barnabas (Acts 12.12,25; 13.5,13; 15.37,39; Col 4.10; Philem 24; 2 Tim 4.11). Papias calls him an interpreter of Peter's preaching. The author of 1 Pet sends a greeting from ''my son Mark'' (5.13). BIBLIOGRAPHY: EDB 1448–49.

[J. A. GRASSI]

MARK, ST. (d. 336), **POPE** for a little less than 9 months in 336. According to the *Liber Pontificalis,* M. began (or possibly confirmed) the custom of having the bp. of Ostia (upon whom he conferred the *pallium) consecrate a newly elected pope, but this claim is supported by no corroborative evidence, and the pallium is not known to have been used until a later time. An alleged letter of M. to St.

Athanasius is a forgery. BIBLIOGRAPHY: J. Chapin, NCE 9:233; J. P. Kirsch, CE 9:674; Butler 4:51–52.

[P. F. MULHERN]

MARK OF ARETHUSA, ST. (d. *c.*364), bishop. M. was a participant in the Arian controversies of the 4th cent., and was usually ranked among the Semi-Arians. He attended the Councils of Antioch (341) and Philippopolis (343). He drafted the Homoean creed adopted at Rimini (359). During the reign of *Julian, he was tortured for his part in the destruction of a pagan temple (362) and died not long afterwards. St. Gregory of Nazianzus and Theodoret praised him after his death, and the Greek Church honors him as a martyr. His cult was confirmed by Clement VIII in 1598. BIBLIOGRAPHY: A. Amore, EncCatt 8:38; J. van Paasen, NCE 9:233.

[R. B. ENO]

MARK EUGENICUS (*c.*1392–1445), metropolitan of Ephesus, theologian, a canonized saint in the Orthodox Church. Regarded as a leading theologian, M. was the chief spokesman for the Greeks at the Council of *Florence. The most obdurate opponent of union, he showed himself absolutely impervious to argument. Every statement of the Latin position, particularly on the **filioque*, he simply brushed aside as heretical and went to the extent of asserting that all the citations from the Greek Fathers which spoke of the procession of the Holy Spirit "through the Son" were Latin interpolations. Yet this obstinate, narrow-minded ascetic was given full freedom of speech at the Council by the Emperor. His actions alone should put an end to the myth that the Greeks at Florence were forced to vote for union. Alone among the Greek prelates, M. refused to sign the decree of union. Back in Constantinople he was the center of opposition to union, and his influential writings combined serious theological reasoning with the most vulgar pamphleteering. Perhaps more than any one individual, M. was responsible for the failure of Florence. BIBLIOGRAPHY: J. Gill, *Personalities of the Council of Florence* (1964); Beck 755–758.

[G. T. DENNIS]

MARK THE GNOSTIC (2d cent.). According to the reports of Iranaeus, Hippolytus, and Epiphanius, M., a disciple of Valentinus and representative of the Oriental school of Gnosticism, taught in Asia Minor. His teachings are characterized by strange speculation about names and numbers. Irenaeus met his disciples (known as *Marcosians) propagating their doctrines in the Rhone valley. Rich women seem to have been a special target of their efforts. BIBLIOGRAPHY: T. Camelot, LTK 7:13; E. Peterson, EncCatt 8:49–50; Quasten 1:266.

[R. B. ENO]

MARK THE HERMIT (d. *c.*430), monk and theologian, a disciple of St. John Chrysostom. He is known through the *Hist. eccles.* of Nicephorus, Callistus, and Photius as an important witness to Orthodox teaching on Christology and grace. He wrote against the Nestorians; he defended the reality of original sin, the efficacy of baptism, personal reponsibility for actual sin, and the sanctifying effect of grace. He carefully distinguished between the essence of grace and extraordinary mystical gifts. BIBLIOGRAPHY: Quasten 3:504–509.

[J. R. RIVELLO]

MARK OF THE NATIVITY (1617–96), French reformer of the Carmelite order (O.Carm.). He participated in the Touraine Reform, which emphasized the contemplative ideal and which in its effects shaped subsequent Carmelite history and legislation. He was the author of guides on the spiritual life that were incorporated into the *Directorium Carmelitanum vitae spiritualis* (1940; *Carmelite Directory of the Spiritual Life,* 1951).

[T. C. O'BRIEN]

MARK, GOSPEL ACCORDING TO ST., the second book in the NT canon; chronologically, the first of the canonical Gospels. Many scholars date Mk A.D. 65–70, since early Church tradition indicates that it was written after Peter's martyrdom in A.D. 64–65; and since ch. 13 of Mk seems to envision the Temple in Jerusalem, destroyed by the Romans in A.D. 70, to be still standing. It remains possible, however, as other scholars of Mk maintain, that the Gospel was written shortly after A.D. 70. Early Church tradition unhesitatingly ascribed the Gospel to Mark. Such a person is mentioned under the name of John Mark in Acts 12.12,25 and 13.5,13 as originally a companion of Paul, and elsewhere in the NT as associated with Paul and Peter (Philem 24; 1 Pt 5.13). Early tradition also understood Mk as reflecting the preaching of Peter.

Modern study of Mk has established that it is a combination of traditional material existing for decades before Mark wrote, at least in oral, if not partly in written, form, and of its author's editorial work, which wove the material into a unified literary composition. Generally speaking, Mark had at his disposal traditional materials concerning John the Baptist, Jesus' miracles, his parables, his disagreements with the religious authorities, and a considerably developed Passion narrative. But his Gospel is much more than the mere artificial linkage of these materials. It is shot through with the Christian community's developed faith in Jesus as Messiah of OT promise and the Son of God (Mk 1.1), and the Redeemer of mankind (10.45). Writing out of this realization of the community's faith, Mark focuses attention on Jesus' teaching authority and miraculous power (1.22,27; 2.10; 5.30; 6.2–14). He thereby creates a sense of the mystery of Jesus' person as it impinged itself upon his audiences. He portrays Jesus as popular with the masses (1.32–34,45; 3.7–10), but as misunderstood by his relatives (3.20–21), fellow townsmen (6.1–6), Herod's court (6.14–16), and as repudiated by the religious authorities

(2.1–3.6; 11.27–12.27). His Disciples have the greatest insight into him, but their view is tainted by their messianic preconceptions and proves unacceptable to him (8.27–30). He prophesies his own violent death as the divinely willed outcome of his ministry, designating himself Son of Man who must suffer and die before he rises to reign in glory (8.31,38).

For Mark, the identity of Jesus and the true significance of his ministry are determined by the prophetic word of the Christian community that originated in the preaching of the Twelve (cf. Acts 2.14–36), not by human speculation about him and his work. This word of understanding in faith had its beginning in the teaching of Jesus himself and was completed in principle by the fulfillment of his prophecy of Resurrection (Mk 16.1–8). To reenforce the position that the understanding of Jesus and his ministry derives from prophetic light, Mark uses the messianic secret. He depicts Jesus as imposing silence upon those, including evil spirits, who attempt to identify him out of rational resources (1.24–25,34; 3.11–12), or who would take advantage of his healing power without due recognition of its relationship to his message (1.44; 7.36; 8.26,30). Thus Mark shows that the community's faith in Jesus as Messiah and Son of God, although resulting from prophetic light, is an explanation of him that accords with the striking features of his ministry and of his own self-understanding.

Stylistically, Mk is distinctive among the Gospels for vivid, concrete detail in many of its narratives. This feature hardly seems explainable as due to Mark's literary ability; it was rather imbedded in the traditional materials he utilized, and is indicative of eye-witness testimony, presumably that of Peter. BIBLIOGRAPHY: A. Jones, *Gospel according to St. Mark* (1963); D. E. Nineham, *Gospel of Mark* (1963); V. Taylor, *Gospel according to St. Mark* (1966); E. Troome, *Formation of the Gospel According to Mark* (tr. P. Gaughan, 1975).

[C. P. CEROKE]

MARK, LITURGY OF ST., a specifically Alexandrian liturgy, originally in Greek. Parts of its early Greek text have been found in three MSS of the 4th to 6th cent., but its full Greek text is found only in MSS showing evidence of Byzantine or Syrian influence, none of them earlier than the 12th century. Among details that distinguish it from non-Alexandrian liturgies are the location of the long intercessory prayer immediately after the opening dialogue of the *anaphora, a short Sanctus without Benedictus, and an *epiclesis both before and after the words of institution. A. Baumstark and H. Lietzmann have held that the early Liturgies of the Alexandrian family contained a single epiclesis, before the words of institution (instead of after them, as in the Antiochene liturgies), but from the more recent work of B. Capelle and H. Engberding it appears that the early evidence points to the existence of two epicleses, one before and the other after the words of institution, as a distinguishing mark of the Alexandrian liturgies. The Liturgy of St. Mark in Greek remained in use in the Orthodox patriarchate of Alexandria until the 12th cent., when it was definitively replaced by Byzantine liturgies. The Coptic Church has retained a modified form of St. Mark, called the Liturgy of St. Cyril, as one of its three liturgies, but it is almost never used. An attempt has been made recently to revive it. BIBLIOGRAPHY: A. Raes, EncCatt 1:769–773; H. Engberding, "Neues Licht über die Geschichte des Textes der ägyptischen Markusliturgie," OC 40 (1956) 40–68; F. E. Brightman, *Liturgies Eastern and Western* (1896) 1:113–143 (an eclectic Greek text); *ibid.*, 1:144–188 (Eng. tr. of the Coptic Liturgy of St. Cyril); Orthodox Eastern Church, *Liturgies of Sts. Mark, James, Clement, Chrysostom, Basil* (1859, repr. 1969).

[A. CODY]

MARKS OF THE CHURCH. "This is the unique Church of Christ, which in the Creed we avow as one, holy, catholic, and apostolic" (VatII ConstChurch 8). Unity, holiness, catholicity, and apostolicity are the most generally accepted qualities or "properties" of the Church's being and identifiability. The history of theology and apologetics, however, attests to the proposal of many other characteristics as both defining the nature of the Church and as "motives of credibility," i.e., evidence that can prepare a person for belief (see Thils). Particularly in the era between the two Vatican Councils Catholic apologetics was guided by the declaration of Vatican I that the Church, being manifestly one, holy, catholic, and apostolic, is itself a "moral miracle," an abiding and irrefutable witness to its own divine commission (D 3013). The context of the conciliar statement is that to the Catholic Church alone do so many and such wondrous elements belong, divinely disposed to establish the evident credibility of the Christian faith.

The significance and status of the principal marks of the Church of Christ, however, have undergone a subtle shift in Vatican II and post-Vatican II ecclesiology. A "mark" as understood in the present usage is an index, a sign. The sign can be understood as evidence both proceeding from and pointing to an inner reality. Perhaps the description of the Church most typical of Vatican II ecclesiology is this: "By her relationship with Christ the Church is a kind of sacrament or sign of intimate union with God and of the unity of all mankind" (*ibid.* 1). The chapter that contains that statement ends by quoting St. Augustine: "The Church like a pilgrim in a foreign land presses forward amid the persecutions of the world and the consolations of God. . . . By the power of the risen Lord she is given strength to overcome patiently and lovingly the affliction and hardship which assail her from within and without, and to show forth to the world the mystery of the Lord, in a faithful, though shadowy way, until at last it will be revealed in total spendor" (*ibid.* 8).

The implication of these two texts is that as the sacrament of Christ, therefore of intimate union with God the Father, the Church is itself always a "mark," a sign in process of achieving the full reality her being and life signify. The four primary marks of the Church are specific expressions of her sacramentality and so of her nature. It is the belief of the Church that by reason of Christ's institution, his Church is meant to be one, holy, catholic, and apostolic. The belief of the Church is also, as the Council so carefully expressed it, that Christ's unique Church "subsists in the Catholic Church" (*ibid.*). The phrase *subsistit in* connotes by its choice two points of Vatican II ecclesiology. The first concerns the inner life of the Church itself. The marks of the Church subsist in the Church in the same way that the Church itself exists; they are not static "achievements" to be historically or theologically proved, then triumphantly claimed. They are as much ideals and goals to be achieved as qualities already present. The pilgrim Church as sacrament is an as yet incomplete sign of the ultimate reality toward which she tends. All that belongs to the Church is also imperfectly realized. The one mark that may be singled out also as typical of Vatican II ecclesiology is that of holiness. This holiness is one of both community and of individual union with Christ. To the extent that the community and the individual respond to the universal call to holiness (*ibid.* 39–42), there will be church unity, for the unity of the Church is as communion of faith, hope, and charity vivifying the visible structure (*ibid.* 8). To the extent that there is holiness, the Church will be catholic, universal in its effective communication of the Gospel to all peoples. To the extent that the Church is holy, it will be apostolic, faithful in witnessing as the Apostles witnessed in teaching and in service.

The second implication of the chosen phrase, *subsistit in* is the affirmation that elements of holiness and truth—as they come from Christ—are present not simply in individual Christians who are not Catholics, but in other Christian Churches and ecclesial communities as such (*ibid.* 15). The program that has been fostered by that acknowledgment and by *Unitatis redintegratio*, the decree on Ecumenism, has led to Catholic share in the affirmations of the ecumenical movement. More and more there has emerged a mutual recognition of, and a striving together to bring to greater realization, the nature and marks of the Church that Christ intends it to have. Greater and greater is the evidence that these are shared ideals. The consensus has been expressed in common statements on church unity, apostolic succession, holiness; the ecumenical movement by definition is an attempt to make the Church truly universal, to achieve catholicity. The significance of the marks of the Church, therefore, is less as proofs to establish claims, than as signs of common yearning to make the Church more clearly the sacrament of Christ. BIBLIOGRAPHY: G. Thils, NCE 9:240–241.

[T. C. O'BRIEN]

MARLEY, MARIE HILDA (1876–1951), educator, child guidance authority. Of English birth, M. became a Sister of Notre Dame de Namur. In 1931 she founded the Notre Dame Child Guidance Center in Glasgow, a pioneering Scottish institution. After her teaching career closed, M. lectured throughout Europe. In 1951 she was vice president of the International Congress of Catholic Psychotherapists.

[J. R. AHERNE]

MARLOWE, CHRISTOPHER (1564–93), English poet and first major dramatist, graduate of Cambridge, a professed atheist, a government agent killed in a tavern brawl, perhaps because of political activities. His major plays, *Tamburlaine* (1587), *Dr. Faustus* (1588), *The Jew of Malta* (1589), and *Edward II* (1593), show the rise and fall of exultant individualism and despairing fatalism in the Renaissance. M. lived in an age of revolt in which intellectuals were making a claim of self-sufficiency. His heroes show his understanding of the disastrous effects of a false humanistic ideal, which led in the end to a denial of human spirituality and greatness and even of life itself. M. combined knowledge of the London theater and London public with classical university training, and his work marks the beginning of great drama in England. BIBLIOGRAPHY: F. S. Boas, *Christopher Marlowe: A Biographical and Critical Study* (1940); G. B. Harrison, NCE 9:242–243; *Critics on Marlowe* (ed. J. O'Neill, 1970).

[M. BARRY]

MARMION, JOSEPH COLUMBA (1858–1923), Benedictine, from 1909 abbot of Maredsous, Belgium; spiritual writer. He was a priest and professor of philosophy in his native Ireland before entering the Benedictine order in 1886. Before being elected abbot he taught at the order's house of studies at Mont-César, Louvain. He became an esteemed spiritual director and retreat master in Belgium, Ireland, and England. His many translated works include: *Christ the Life of the Soul* (1925): *Christ in His Mysteries* (1925), which follows the liturgical year; *Christ the Ideal of the Monk* (1926): *Sponsa Verbi* (1939): and *Christ the Ideal of the Priest* (1953). All his writings reflect his own integration of the most solid traditional components of Christian spirituality: the teachings of the Gospel, St. Pauls' gospel of grace, the liturgical texts, sound patristic and medieval theology, esp. that of St. Thomas Aquinas. M.'s cause of beatification was introduced in 1954. BIBLIOGRAPHY: R. Thibaut, *Abbot Columba Marmion* (tr. M. St. Thomas, 1949).

[T. C. O'BRIEN]

MARMION, SIMON (*c.*1420–1489), Northern French painter and illuminator, who executed the *St. Bertin Altarpiece* (1459). A *St. Jerome as Cardinal* in the Johnson Collection, Philadelphia, Pa. is attributed to M. by J. J. Friedländer, who has researched his work. Called "prince d'enluminure" by Lemaire, M. is credited with numerous illuminations showing affinities to the St. Bertin work.

[M. J. DALY]

MARMÎTĀ (East Syrian), a division of the Psalter. It signifies one of two, three, or four subdivisions of the **hullālā*. *Marmîtō* among the West Syrians, one of the 15 principal divisions, each subdivided into four *shûbbōhē* or *shûbhē*. Among the Maronites it is the name given to a prayer, perhaps originally meant to accompany a division of the Psalter in the Office.

[A. CODY]

MARMOUTIER *(Maius Monasterium),* former monastery, founded by St. Martin on the Loire near his See of Tours. The Benedictine rule was later adopted there; but by the time of the abbey's destruction by the Normans in 853, it was in the possession of canons. Later the monastery was reestablished by the collegial canons of St. Martin of Tours. In 982 Eudes, count of Blois, gave it to St. Mäieul, abbot of Cluny. Marmoutier gave rise to more than 120 priories, 10 affiliated in England. Marmoutier was pillaged by the Calvinists in 1562 and joined to the congregation of St. Maur in 1637. It was secularized in 1792 and the buildings razed. BIBLIOGRAPHY: Cottineau 2:1762–66.

[J. DAOUST]

MARO OF CYR, ST. (fl. 4th–5th cent.), Syrian monk, known also as Maron or Maroon, and patron of the Maronites. (see MARONITE RITE). He lived an ascetical life as a hermit on a mountain near Apamea, the capital of Syria Secunda. His saintly example drew many disciples who imitated his way of life, such as SS. James of Cyr, Limnaeus, and Zebinas. The exact theological position of the Maronites on *Monothelitism is not entirely clear, but the orthodoxy of M. is affirmed by his biographer, Theodoret, bp. of Cyr (PG 52:630). After his death a church was built over his tomb and a monastery established by his disciples. BIBLIOGRAPHY: P. Dib, DTC 10.1:1–2; P. Sfair, BiblSanct 8:1194–96.

[F. T. RYAN]

MARONITE CHURCH, an Eastern Catholic Church. The name is from a monastery built in the valley of the river Orontes in the neighborhood of Apamea in Syria upon the tomb of a St. Mar. of Cyr. This monastery was among centers of resistance to Monophysitism (5th cent.), but it remains unclear whether the monks embraced *Monotheletism. When after the Arab conquest the patriarchs of Antioch took up residence in Constantinople, the monks of St. Maron and some neighboring bps. elected a patriarch of their own. Thus the Maronite patriarchate came into existence, and was continued even after the Greek patriarchs had returned to Antioch. The Maronites were recognized as a separate community for the first time by Caliph Marwan II (744–748). In the 9th cent. the monks and their faithful fled from the Muslim enmity to Lebanon where they enjoyed a state of semi-independence in the mountains. The authority of their patriarch was everywhere accepted as that of an *ethnarch. During the Crusades they entered into communion with the Latin patriarch of Antioch (1182). Patriarch Jeremias II took part in Lateran Council IV (1215), confirmed by Pope Innocent III, who influenced the Maronites toward Latinization. Originally the Maronite community constituted one diocese and the bps. acted as vicars of the patriarch. The Synod of Mt. Lebanon (1736), while strengthening the organization of the Church, advanced even more Latinisation, though the liturgical language has remained unchanged, namely, Syriac (Aramaic); now Arabic is also used. It is the only Catholic Oriental Church with no Orthodox counterpart, and is ruled today by the Patriarch of Antioch and All the East who has residence in Beirut, with dioceses in Lebanon, Syria, Egypt, Australia, Brazil, and the United States. The faithful, estimated at more than one million, are found also in Argentine, France, Canada, Central and South America, and in parts of Africa. A return to their genuine tradition is now in progress in the aftermath of Vatican II.

[J. MADEY]

MARONITE CHURCH IN THE UNITED STATES. Toward the end of the 19th cent., large numbers of Maronites from Lebanon emigrated to the United States. But restrictive immigration laws after World War I limited the quota of Lebanese and Syrians to 925 per year. In general, the Maronites settled in the larger cities of the U.S. where parishes for them were established. At present they number approximately 200,000 with some 50 parishes. In 1961 at Washington, D.C. a major seminary was established for the formation of Maronite clergy, and the following year it was dedicated by the Maronite Patriarch Paul Meouchi. In 1966 an exarchate was erected for the Maronites in the U.S. with F. M. Zayek as its first exarch; he became first bp. of the Diocese of St. Maro, which was established in 1972 at Detroit and includes parishes and missions in all 50 states.

MARONITE LITURGY, a form of Eastern Christian worship derived from the Syro-Antiochene rite. The oldest anaphora, called Sharar, has some affinities with the East Syrian (Chaldaean) anaphora of the Apostles Addai and Mari. The anaphoras used are those of the Twelve Apostles, of James the Apostle, of John the Evangelist, of Mark the Evangelist, of Pope Sixtus, of John Marun, and that of the Holy Roman Church. The usual Liturgy is celebrated with the anaphora of St. Peter. There is also a Liturgy of the Presanctified Gifts. The synod of 1596, convoked by Jerome Dandini SJ, the envoy of Pope Clement VIII, intensified the Latinization, which was then executed by Patriarch Joseph Rizzi (ar-Ruzzi, 1599–1608): confirmation was separated from baptism; components of the holy chrism *(murun)* were conformed to the Latin chrism; leavened bread was forbidden, and substituted with the unleavened host; only bps. were permitted to bless the oil for the sick; the forms of sacraments were changed to those of the Roman Church; communion had to be given only under one kind, etc. This Latinization, which had been initiated by

Pope Innocent III in 1215, was then continued through the zeal of the graduates of the Maronite College in Rome, founded in 1484. Vatican II has inaugurated a return to the original tradition of the Maronite Church. The liturgical languages are Arabic and Syriac.

[J. MADEY]

MAROT, CLÉMENT (1496–1544), French poet. In the service (1519–27) of Marguerite d'Angoulême, wife of the duc d'Alençon. M. succeeded his father as *valet de chambre* to Francis I (1527), and his poetry won him court favor. Accused, however, of having eaten meat during Lent and suspected of Protestantism, M. was imprisoned in the Châtelet (1526), which inspired his satire, *L'Enfer,* and where he wrote his famous *Épître du lion et du rat,* addressed to his friend Léon Jamet. After a second imprisonment for less serious charges (1527), he was again accused of having eaten meat in Lent (1532) but was saved by the intervention of Marguerite, now become queen of Navarre. In the aftermath of the *Affaire des Placards* (Oct. 1534), M., suspected of heresy, was forced to seek refuge first with Marguerite de Navarre at Nérac, and then in Ferrara (1535) at the court of Renée de France, protectress of French Lutheran refugees, including Calvin. Suspected there by the Inquisition, M. fled to Venice (1536), received permission to return to France, and publicly abjured Protestanism at Lyons (Dec. 1536). He then dedicated himself to translating in verse 30 Psalms (1541) with the assistance of the noted Christian Hebraist François Vatable, but his work was condemned by the Sorbonne. He fled to Geneva, where his Psalms were welcomed by Calvin (1542) as the beginning of a French Protestant Psalter; but finding life difficult there, M. left for Savoy and then Turin, where he died. His poetry, published in such collections as *Adolescence Clémentine* (1532), *Suite de l'adolescence* (1534), and *Poésies complètes* (1544), had great influence on the French Renaissance, for while his early works are in the fixed medieval style of the *rhétoriqueurs,* his late works are inspired by classical antiquity in theme, imagery, and in such genres as the epigram, the eclogue, the elegy, and the *épître.* His complete works, put on the first Index (1557), offer numerous instances of satire directed against the institutions and dogmas of the Catholic Church: against monks and monasticism *(De frère Lubin, D'un gros prieur, Le Second chant de l'amour fugitif);* and against the papacy, Lent, and purgatory *(La Seconde épître du coq-à-l'âne).* In his *Déploration de Florimond Robertet,* he defends his belief in justification by faith alone, while in his *Épître au Roi, du temps de son exile à Ferrare* he defends freedom of conscience. BIBLIOGRAPHY: P. Leblanc, *La Poésie religieuse de Clément Marot* (1955); C. A. Mayer, *La Religion de Marot* (1960).

[R. N. NICOLICH]

MAROZIA (*c.*892–*c.*937), woman prominent in the "pornocracy" that dominated Roman and papal politics in the early 10th century. The Pope *Joan legend may have been built out of popular tales concerning her influence and activities. The daughter of *Theophylactus, leader of the Roman nobility, and *Theodora the Elder, M. married three times: Alberic I of Spoleto, Guido of Tuscany, and Hugh of Provence. The second marriage was opposed by John X, so she resolved to eliminate him; he was imprisoned and died probably by assassination. She had herself proclaimed "Senatoress and Patrician" *(senatrix et patricia)* of Rome, and secured the election of her son as John XI; he was probably the fruit of her illicit relations with Pope Sergius III. Her son by her first marriage, Alberic II, affronted during the celebration of her third nuptials, roused the people. Her husband was forced to flee, and M. was clapped into Sant'Angelo, where she died 5 years later—how is unknown. BIBLIOGRAPHY: Fliche-Martin, 7:29–38.

[T. GILBY]

MARPRELATE TRACTS, a series of polemical pamphlets published in England (1588–89) under the pseudonym of Martin Marprelate. They were a Puritan attack upon *episcopacy, and their brilliant satire caused alarm among the defenders of the *established Church. However, they appear to have overshot their mark, for their violence inspired renewed adherence to the C of E and brought an increase of suspicion upon the Puritans. Their authorship has never been established beyond doubt, though J. Penry was believed guilty and was hanged in 1593 on the charge of inciting rebellion. A modern edition of the seven pamphlets that survived was published with historical notes by William Pierce in 1911; he also wrote *Historical Introduction to the Marprelate Tracts* (1908). BIBLIOGRAPHY: Hughes RE 3:212–214.

[P. K. MEAGHER]

MARQUESAS ISLANDS, a group of 11 islands, part of French *Polynesia (492 sq mi; est. pop. [1970] over 4,900). Picpus missionaries reached the islands in 1838 but were not successful in evangelization because of the unusual fierceness of the natives. A vicariate, however, was established in 1848; and after the French gained political control, the mission gradually took hold. By the 1960s all but 5% of the inhabitants were Catholic. In 1966 the Diocese of Taiohae was created. The London Missionary Society was the first Protestant group to send missioners to the Marquesas. They maintained their mission from 1785 until 1825. Congregationalists and the American Board attempted to work on the islands on several occasions but were refused permission. French Protestant missionaries are now settled there, but converts are few. BIBLIOGRAPHY: B. Mathews, *Unfolding Drama of Southeast Asia* (1944).

[P. DAMBORIENA]

MARQUETTE, JACQUES (1637–75), French-born Jesuit missionary and explorer. He entered the Jesuit novitiate in 1654 and was ordained (1666) in France shortly before he left for missionary work with the Indians in Canada. He was assigned to Three Rivers on the St. Lawrence, where he set about learning the Indian languages, becoming fluent in the Huron dialects particularly. He founded the mission of St. Ignace (1671) at Mackinac Straits in present-day Michigan, and with Louis Joliet, he followed the Wisconsin River to the Mississippi, descending it as far as the mouth of the Arkansas River (1673). On the return trip he had to winter at the Jesuit mission at Green Bay on lower Lake Michigan; and for 2 years he continued working in Illinois, because the Indians asked him to stay. He died from illness while on a return voyage to Mackinac for additional supplies, after having begun a new mission at Kaskaskia. BIBLIOGRAPHY: E. J. Burrus, ''Father Jacques Marquette, SJ . . .'' CHR 41 (1955) 257–271; F. B. Steck, *Joliet-Marquette Expedition, 1673* (1928, repr. AMS).

[R. K. MACMASTER]

MARQUETTE LEAGUE, a lay missionary association whose purpose is the evangelization of native American Indians of the U.S., and preservation of the faith of RC Indians; it provides the needful support, spiritual and material, for chapels, missions, mission schools and catechists. Founded in New York City in 1904 by the Rev. H. G. *Ganss, chaplain (1890–1910) of the government Indian School at Carlisle, Pa., it was organized under direction of a 25-member board, chosen originally from the councils of the St. *Vincent de Paul Society. Widely spread throughout the nation are the members who honor the spirit of Père *Marquette (1637–75). Offices are maintained not only in New York City and Brooklyn, but in Washington, D.C., Worcester, Mass., and Philadelphia. The League is associated with the *Bureau of Catholic Indian Missions. BIBLIOGRAPHY: T. F. Meehan, CE 9:691; C. Testore, EncCatt 8:186–187 s. v. ''Marquette, Jacques''; M. McDonnell, NCE 9:255, bibliog.

[M. R. BROWN]

MARRANOS, organized secret Jews in Spain and Portugal as distinguished from openly practicing Jews. Current use, however, applies the term to anyone connected with Judaism either by blood or practice. Since 1917 Jews have been proselytizing in northern Portugal among a backward group of Christians that, though without known ties with Judaism, may be a relic of the Marranos who from 1600 to 1800 formed a rich merchant league with centers in Constantinople, Salonika, Venice, Ferrara, Livorno, Antwerp, Amsterdam, Hamburg, London, Recife (Brazil), and Mexico. By 1800 most European countries permitted the open practice of the Jewish religion; in Spain and Portugal the Inquisition had by then eliminated Marranism. Early modern Marranos were given to intermarriage, discriminated against other Jews, kept Spanish and Portuguese as official and cultural languages, and at times acted as diplomats abroad for Spain and Portugal. Crypto-Judaism goes back to antiquity. What complicated the issue in Christian times was the conviction that baptism *accepted* against one's belief was valid. Even so, neither Spain nor Portugal (the lands of classic Marranism) acted against first generation pseudoconverts. It was later generations, baptized in infancy, raised with secret Jewish practices, and making public use of the sacraments in a blasphemous way that raised the specter of the Inquisition. Unable for years to maintain anything more than a clandestine tradition, Marranos clung to basic tenets: salvation through the law of Moses, not the law of Christ; observance of the Sabbath; iconoclasm; expectation of a Messiah. Their beliefs and practices are known chiefly through the records of the Inquisition.

Ironically, Spain's radical position toward Marranos derived from its great medieval tolerance of Jews. Forced or insincere conversions of Jews had occurred in the 5th and 7th cent.; but in the 13th cent. Christian Spain welcomed Jewish along with Mozarab refugees from Muslim persecution in southern Spain and soon became the world center of Judaism. Anti-Jewish riots in Spain (rooted in religious, political, and financial animosities) culminated in an outbreak that occurred in some 70 towns in 1391. A good number of Jews accepted baptism to save their lives, but many others either responded to Christian missions in the aftermath or opportunistically joined the new Christians (*conversos*), whose lot was so much better than that of open Jews. Religious feeling among the *conversos,* who numbered more than 200,000, was generally no stronger for Christianity than it had been for Judaism. *Conversos* were accepted into all levels of Spanish society, dominating professions, and marrying into the noblest families. By 1429, however, the concern of old Christians over the reputed insincerity of the *conversos* and the resentment of the old aristocracy against loss of power to the new bureaucrats resulted in a reaction against *conversos,* some of whom were crypto-Jews. The uprising of 1467–68 was worse than that of 1391, there being now no escape via baptism. The Church could not sanction open return to Judaism, even had *conversos* desired it. In 1478, after Ferdinand and Isabella won the civil war, a papal bull revived the Inquisition in Seville, center of crypto-Judaism. The Inquisition, eventually based in 15 cities, worked secretly, carefully, and without haste, dealing out penalties of burning at the stake, confiscation, and lesser penances. The number of victims, Judaizers and others, has been exaggerated. Few were burned alive; most were burned in effigy while their goods were confiscated. The great majority suffered minor penances; others were released without penalty. Confiscated properties at first accrued to the king, later to the Inquisition. Political and personal vengeance probably did work through the Inquisition.

The expulsion of Jews from Spain in 1492 left crypto-Jews isolated from Judaism, and after 1550 almost all crypto-Jews in Spain had entered from Portugal. Jewish exiles from Spain in 1492 went mostly to Portugal, but in 1496 Spain obtained their expulsion from that country also. Rather than lose his rich, new subjects, however, Manoel of

Portugal (1495–1521) forcibly baptized Jewish children under 14 years and then exempted Marranos from Christian observance. Portuguese Marranos had left Spain rather than give up Judaism and were never regarded as true Christians. Crypto-Jews now fled Spain for the security of Portuguese Marranism. Anti-Marranism arose in Portugal in 1504; the Inquisition was established there in 1531 and suspended 1544–47; confiscations accrued to the crown from 1579. By 1547 Portuguese Marranos, wealthy and controlling trade, were second generation and extended throughout society, clerical and secular. Activity by the Portuguese Inquisition, which dealt almost exclusively with crypto-Jews, increased after the Spanish-Portuguese union of 1580; of 40,000 cases, 30,000 were condemned, fewer than 1,200 died at the stake. Refugees from the Portuguese Inquisition, usually identified as "Portuguese merchants" abroad, caused a diaspora of Marranos that lasted until the French Revolution. Portugal deported Marranos to Brazil, where they allied themselves with the Dutch in war against Portugal. The Portuguese victory in 1654 caused an exodus of Brazilian Marranos through the Caribbean and to New York. After a purge in Mexico and Peru (1634–49), crypto-Judaism all but disappeared from Spanish colonies. BIBLIOGRAPHY: E. H. Flannery, NCE 9:256–258; C. Roth, *History of the Marranos* (1932, repr. 1975).

[E. P. COLBERT]

MARRIAGE (EASTERN CHURCHES). Eastern Orthodox theology does not differ in its teaching on the notion and number of the sacraments from the doctrine of the RC Church, and it therefore recognizes marriage as a sacrament. The Eastern Orthodox Churches, like the Roman Church, do not recognize the jurisdiction of the State over the marriages of their members but claim for themselves absolute authority over such marriages. The officiating priest is considered the minister of the sacrament of marriage, whereas the Roman Church considers the contracting parties the ministers. Hence in the Orthodox Churches marriage is regarded as impossible if no priest is available. The Eastern Catholic Churches, however, do not differ from the Roman Church in their dogmatic teaching. The most remarkable difference between Catholic and Orthodox teaching on marriage is that the latter permits the remarriage of divorced persons. This detail of Orthodox teaching renders other points of Orthodox marriage law of lesser importance, e.g., the grounds for annulment. The canonical rules concerning marriage have been set down in the decrees of synods and in the writings of the Fathers. Some Eastern Orthodox Churches have codified their marriage laws, e.g., the Serbian Patriarchate *(Bračna Pravila,* 1934). The marriage law of Eastern Catholic Churches has been codified in *Crebrae allatae* (1949), but is now undergoing a general revision. BIBLIOGRAPHY: V. J. Popishil, *Law on Marriage* (1962).

[V. J. POSPISHIL]

MARRIAGE, IMPEDIMENTS TO, circumstances disqualifying a person from contracting a valid or a lawful marriage. Impediments arising from natural, divine-positive, or ecclesiastical law are of two types: diriment or prohibitive; the first prevent valid marriage; the second render a marriage unlawful but not invalid. The prohibitive impediments are: *Simple Vows* of virginity or perfect chastity, not to marry, to receive sacred orders, or to embrace the religious state; *Legal Relationship,* resulting from adoption where the civil law declares such marriages unlawful; *Mixed Religion* when one party is Catholic and the other is a validly baptized non-Catholic. The law constitutes the following as diriment impediments: *Lack of Age,* which is 16 years completed for males, and 14 completed for females; *Impotence* that is antecedent and perpetual, rendering a person incapable of performing the marital act; *Bond, i.e. an existing and valid marriage; Disparity of Cult* when one party is a baptized Catholic and the other is nonbaptized; *Sacred Orders* received by priests and deacons destined for the priesthood (permanent deacons are not included under this impediment); *Solemn Vows* or vows which by special provision of the Holy See are endowed with the power of invalidating marriage (such as the simple vows taken by Jesuits); *Abduction* with the intent to marry, this impediment endures as long as the woman remains unwillingly in the power of the abductor; *Crime* which admits of three degrees (first, when adultery is committed with the promise of or attempt at marriage; second, adultery with conjugicide perpetrated by one of the adulterers; third, conspiracy of conjugicide with an intent of marriage); *Consanguinity,* or blood relationship, in all degrees of the direct line and up to the third degree inclusive in the collateral line; *Affinity,* which arises from a valid marriage and exists between one spouse and the blood relative of the other; *Public Propriety,* which springs from an invalid marriage or concubinage and exists between one partner and the blood relatives of the other; *Spiritual Relationship* resulting from baptism and existing between the person baptized and either the sponsors or minister of the sacrament; and *Legal Relationship* arising from adoption where the civil law constitutes such as invalidating. No one can dispense from impediments which have the natural or divine-positive law as their basis (impotence, existing bond of marriage, consanguinity in the first degree of the direct line). While the Holy See can dispense from all others, local ordinaries may dispense only from those not reserved to the Holy See. Such are the defect of age exceeding one year, sacred orders and solemn vows, crime in the second and third degree, consanguinity in the direct line and in the collateral line up to the second degree mixed with the first, and affinity in the direct line. However, in cases of danger of death, the local Ordinary, or the priest assisting at marriage when the local Ordinary cannot be reached, can dispense from all impediments except those arising from the sacred order of priesthood and affinity in the direct line. BIBLIOGRAPHY: T. Bouscaren, A. Ellis, F.

Korth, *Canon Law* (1966); Paul VI, *De episcoporum muneribus, AAS* 58 (1966) 467.

[R. W. KUTNER]

MARRIAGE, INDISSOLUBILITY OF, the position taken in Catholic theology and canon law that a valid sacramental marriage which has been consummated cannot be dissolved except by death. The doctrine, founded on Scripture, while apparently not solemnly defined as a dogma of faith, has been institutionalized in canon law and defended in Catholic theology, although in recent years the Church's official position has been questioned by both canonists and theologians.

Scripture. Jesus' words in Mk 10.2–12 and Lk 16–18 clearly uphold the permanence of marriage. Although exegetes argue whether this is presented as norm or as ideal, the placement in Mk suggests that this standard is considered part of the cost of discipleship. The exceptive clause in Mt 5.31–32, apparently added by the Matthaean community, has been taken by the Eastern Churches and many interpreters to allow divorce and remarriage in the case of adultery. (Other interpretations of the *porneia* given as an exception are, apart from adultery, concubinage, an unlawful union, or a woman's premarital intercourse with another man.) In Mt 19.3–12, when Jesus is asked to choose between the Jewish schools of Shammai (which allowed divorce and remarriage for adultery) and Hillel (which allowed it for any reason), he refuses and instead appeals to God's plan in creation: the two are to be one flesh. (Some interpreters suggest this means that the goal is to be so completely one that divorce would be unthinkable.) Paul emphasizes the eschatological framework of marriage in 1 Cor 7.10–16, but he admits an exception: separation is permitted because of irreconcilable religious differences so that ''peace'' may be achieved. While Jesus does not speak of exceptions or mention failure or restrict his teaching only to certain marriages, the Church, beginning with Paul and Matthew, has had to deal with these realities.

Dogmatic Teaching. Historically, no definitive position was established prior to the 6th century regarding the possibility of divorce and remarriage. Even in subsequent cent. a good deal of ambiguity remained. The Eastern Churches allowed it in some cases, particularly because of adultery; the Western Church also tolerated it at some times and in some places. By the mid-13th cent. in the West, however, indissolubility was no longer an ideal but rather a law to be adhered to and was accepted by most scholastics as a doctrinal norm. The *Decretum pro Armenis* of the Council of Florence (1439; D 1327) allowed for separation but no remarriage, yet Pope Eugene IV did not consider the contrary Eastern position a barrier to reunion. Interestingly, the Council of Trent (D 1807) framed its teaching carefully so as not to condemn the differing teaching and practice of the East, stating that the Western position is not contrary to the Gospel and apostolic teaching. (Only the Orthodox Churches still uphold the traditional Eastern position as the Catholic Eastern Churches have been heavily Latinized.) Jesus speaks of marriage in general, harkening back to creation; while the Church has consistently upheld the ideal of permanence, it has not dogmatically defined indissolubility and has in fact in its laws restricted indissolubility to certain classes of marriage.

Canon Law. Canonists and theologians struggled for centuries to identify the nature and effects of Christian marriage and precisely what rendered it indissoluble. From Augustine's time the sacramental character and indissolubility were seen as closely related, but the origin of the ''bond'' was disputed. An eventual compromise between the school of Paris (which saw the bond established through mutual consent to the marriage contract) and the school of Bologna (which considered sexual relations necessary to form the bond), particularly during and after the pontificate of Alexander III (1159–81), led to the general acceptance of the position that marriage is essentially constituted by the consent and that subsequent sexual intercourse renders it indissoluble, making it a complete sign of Christ's union with his Church (cf. Eph 5.21–32). The contention has been that it is in this way that the ''two become one flesh.'' The 1918 Code of Canon Law thus stated that a valid marriage between baptized persons (*matrimonium ratum*) which has been consummated or completed by sexual union (*consummatum*) cannot be dissolved except by death (CIC c. 1118) because of its sacramental character (CIC c. 1013). But church law and practice do dissolve some marriages, e.g., a nonconsummated marriage, by religious profession or papal dispensation (CIC c. 1119); a lawful marriage between two unbaptized persons, in favor of the faith (Pauline Privilege, CIC c. 1120.1, based on 1 Cor 7); a lawful marriage where only one person is baptized, in favor of the faith (*Privilege of the Faith or Petrine Privilege). The question is thus what is a valid sacramental marriage.

Annulments—declarations that a true sacramental marriage does not and has not existed (see NULLITY, DECLARATION OF) between the parties—are given for various reasons; e.g., because of an invalidating or diriment impediment prior to the marriage (e.g., age, impotence, crime, close relationship); because of a defect in consent, particularly with regard to sexual relations, procreation, or permanence, or because of a lack of due discretion (psychic incapacity or emotional immaturity) at the time of marriage; because of a defect in the required canonical form (presently for a Catholic the required form is the exchange of consent before two witnesses and a properly delegated priest, unless a dispensation has been given).

Theology. From Augustine's time theologians have emphasized three dynamics as vital elements in marriage: mutual fruitfulness (*bonum prolis* or children, although contemporary thought gives more emphasis to mutual completion and growth through sacrificial self-giving); faithfulness (*bonum fidei*—an exclusiveness in self-giving that precludes marital affection for another); and lastingness (*bonum sacramenti*—the consequence and condition of fruitfulness and faithfulness). The enduring bond of marriage is seen as sacramental sign of the enduring union between Christ and his Church (cf. Eph 5), which is the primary reason for its indissolubility (see GOODS OF MARRIAGE). Indissolubility is also seen as necessary to uphold the ends of marriage (the one end being the procreation and education of children and the other mutual love, aid, and companionship).

Contemporary Questions and Practice. In recent years both theologians and canonists have questioned the legal framework within which marriage has been situated. Some claim that the law looks only at the wedding ceremony and the first night, yet most questions concentrate on the consent necessary to establish sacramental marriage (annulments are increasingly being given for lack of requisite discretion or psychic capacity) and consummation (is a single act of intercourse sufficient to render a marriage indissoluble, or is "becoming one flesh" more than this?). Recent simplification of marriage tribunal procedures and a closer attention to psychological factors have greatly increased the number of annulments. Where an annulment cannot be granted, many advocate the so-called "good conscience solution," whereby the remarried who are convinced that they are in good conscience are permitted to receive the sacraments. Similarly, some writers advocate that those who repent their violation of the divorce prohibition but who are in new marriages which cannot be abandoned without grave spiritual or psychological harm should be permitted the Eucharist.

Others go further. Some writers ask if the fact the two are baptized is itself sufficient to make their marriage sacramental and if the Church should not permit some sort of "catechumenal" or nonsacramental marriage. Others contend that while a valid sacramental marriage cannot be dissolved, it can die, and that only the parties concerned can make the judgment as to whether this is the case and whether they are thus free to remarry.

While the Church continues to uphold the permanence of marriage proclaimed by Jesus, it must, like Paul and Matthew, face the realities of its situation and ask when and how marriage is, in fact, indissoluble.

BIBLIOGRAPHY: *Bond of Marriage* (ed. W. Bassett, 1968); S. J. Kelleher, *Divorce and Remarriage for Catholics?* (1976); J. T. Noonan, *Power to Dissolve* (1972); *Divorce and Remarriage in the Catholic Church* (1973). Bibliographical surveys of recent literature include C. E. Curran, "Divorce: Catholic Theory and Practice in the United States," AER 168 (1974) 3–34; 75–95; R. A. McCormick, "Divorce and Remarriage," ThSt 36 (1975) 100–117.

[J. DALLEN]

MARRIAGE, MIXED, see MIXED MARRIAGE.

MARRIAGE, MYSTICAL, a term used to describe the spiritual state of a person intimately united to God. Here the term is considered as employed in mystical theology (for its scriptural basis and application to consecrated virgins, see MARRIAGE, SPIRITUAL). Mystical marriage is the culmination of man's intersubjective communion with God. It is also called a transforming union and is the summit of infused *contemplation. In the writings of St. *John of the Cross (*Spiritual Canticle* 12.27) and St. *Teresa of Avila (*Interior Castle,* Seven Mansions, 2), the state is characterized by three elements: a continual sense of God's presence, a consciousness of participation in the divine life through the supernatural acts of intellect and will, and a habitual awareness of the Trinity or some divine attribute. In this state, man's cognitive and affective tendencies do not incline to any unreasonable object, but are God-directed even unconsciously. Experiencing an undisturbable peace and habitual delight, the person has no problem with sinful attractions, but is confirmed in grace. The virtues are heroic, penetrated with love, devoid of ordinary weakness. Even the senses are spiritualized and share in the delight of the spirit. BIBLIOGRAPHY: C. Baumgartner, DSAM 2.2:2171–2193; A. A. Bialas, NCE 10:170–171; A. Poulain, CE 9:703.

[T. DUBAY]

MARRIAGE, NULLITY OF, an ecclesiastical declaration that an ostensible marriage never in fact came into being because one (or more) of four requirements for validity was lacking at the time of the nuptials. The four essential conditions are these: (1) Each partner must be free of any mental or emotional disorder that would inhibit the ability to enter the intimate marital union of minds and hearts. (2) Each partner must be free of all diriment impediments (see MARRIAGE, IMPEDIMENTS TO), since these preclude valid matrimonial consent. (3) Each partner must give and accept consent to marriage in its constitutive meaning, as a life of true partnership of mutual, unitive, and exclusive love and that is open to the begetting and education of children (cf. VatII ChModWorld 50). (4) In the case of Catholics, marital consent must be exchanged in the presence of an authorized priest and two witnesses, a requirement called the "canonical form" of marriage (CIC c. 1094).

An ecclesiastical annulment is a declaration of nullity and differs from a civil divorce. Civil divorce terminates existing rights and obligations before the law; ecclesiastical annulment declares that, for want of one of the above conditions, no marriage ever existed. All children born of a marriage declared null are legitimate in canon law. Contemporary canonical jurisprudence allows greater latitude in interpreting grounds for a declaration of nullity, taking into consideration the psychological complexities that have bearing on free and mature consent to the perduring, intimate, and child-oriented commitment that makes up the essence of the marriage union. BIBLIOGRAPHY: L. Wrenn, *Annulment* (1978).

MARRIAGE, SACRAMENT OF, the abiding union of a man and woman, committed to each other and expressing that committment through sexual relations, thus providing for the birth of children and their upbringing within a familial structure. Marriage is an essential component of every society, although its forms (e.g., monogamy, polygamy, polyandry) are numerous and societal attitudes toward it have varied greatly. In the RC tradition, marriage is regarded as a perpetual and exclusive bond, one of the seven sacraments with its proper redemptive significance. The OT attitude toward marriage was generally naturalistic, although that attitude underwent significant development. Marriage was seen as providing for the continuity of the man's clan; the woman became the man's property, and he was obliged to protect and provide for her. Social needs largely determined marriage practices and attitudes: children were seen as a great blessing, childlessness was a curse, perpetual virginity was regarded as unnatural, and certain types of polygamy and concubinage were permitted. Yet the creation account in Gen 2, as well as other OT sections, underlines also the intimacy and completion of the individual that strongly colors the OT notion of marriage. Thus, at the time of Jesus, polygamy had been almost completely abolished, and one rabbinic school regarded adultery and moral misconduct as the only acceptable grounds for divorce. In the NT, Jesus raises the Jewish conception of marriage by emphasizing its intimacy (referring to Genesis 2 in Mt 19.3–6) and rejecting divorce. Protestant and RC interpretations of Mt 5, 32 and 19, 9 vary ("Whoever divorces his wife, except for unchastity, and marries another commits adultery."), although earliest church practice seems to have allowed separation after adultery but not remarriage. Jesus' eschatological expectation gives focus to his attitude toward marriage: compared to the kingdom of God and its demands, marriage has only secondary importance and can even be an evil when it restricts a person from seeking full participation in the kingdom. Thus for some, including Jesus and John the Baptist, abstinence from marriage on account of the kingdom is upheld. Paul extends this teaching of Jesus and interprets Christian marriage as a sign of Christ's loving union with the Church (Eph 5.21–33). Just as Christ has totally and singly loved and sacrificed himself for humankind, so husband and wife must totally and singly dedicate themselves to their spouse, thus reflecting in their relationship the great mystery of salvation. Nevertheless, Paul also regards marriage as of secondary importance in light of the coming parousia (1 Cor 7. 25–35).

An ambivalent attitude toward marriage dominates most patristic thought, especially insofar as that period was dominated by Augustine of Hippo. The linchpin of Augustine's thought was the pervasive influence of original sin from which Christ alone could save humankind. Sex, too, was seen as so influenced; indeed, human sexuality is an animal function that can overwhelm the human spirit. The principal reason why sexual actualization in marriage is tolerated is because of childbearing, although Augustine also praised the bond of love that joins husband and wife to the degree that it clarifies the meaning of faithfulness and spiritual commitment. Marriage has a place within the economy of salvation, not because of its inherent value, but because of its good results, *viz.,* the birth of children (see GOODS OF MARRIAGE). The Hellenistic valorization of ascetic self-control and Gnostic notions of a matter/spirit duality undoubtedly contributed greatly to these ideas, although the fundamental goodness of marriage was never denied. This negative attitude was mitigated in the scholastic period. Thomas Aquinas and others understood the realization of sex in marriage as valuable in itself and not as an evil which could be merely tolerated because of the birth of children. Nevertheless, a narrowly sexual, and later legalistic, view of marriage came to dominate Christian moral theology. The decisive standard of matrimonial ethics came to be the sexual act properly ordered to the conception of children. The physiological process itself, too often separated from the entire context of the marriage and the relationship between the partners, was regarded as morally normative. Contemporary theology eschews this one-sided view and seeks to formulate a matrimonial ethics grounded in the full, human purposes of marriage. This ethic does not deny the generative dimension of human sexuality but seeks to place the sexual within the total context of marital love: the mutual completion of the spouses, the development of their children, and their responsibility for the total social and ecological order. Contemporary theology has also long broken with the Augustinian toleration of marriage as an evil excused by the need to beget offspring. Recent popes have insisted upon marriage as a true vocation and Vatican II noted, "Furthermore, married couples and Christian parents should follow their own proper path (to holiness) by faithful love" (Vat II ConstChurch 41). The Christian perfection of the married couple will be achieved only in and through their marriage. By means of self-denying love, husband and wife are led to the holiness that is proper to them and signify to the community that unselfish mutuality that is at the core of the Christian message. This loss of self in the marital union mirrors the paradox of every Christian vocation: that through self-denial the person is brought to his highest personal realization. This realization in marriage will be specifically sexual and mutual.

The Ends and Properties of Marriage. Christian thought has always linked sexual actualization to the birth and education of children. In RC theology especially, this procreation/education of children has been regarded as the primary finality of marriage. The secondary ends of marriage have been seen to be the mutual love and support that the spouses extend to each other. Thus the Holy Office decreed in 1944 that this primary end of marriage cannot be denied and that the secondary ends are subordinate to it (AAS 36 [1944], 103). This hierarchical ordering sought to safeguard a responsible, nonhedonistic attitude toward sex, especially in this century when much of Western culture seemed to adopt a more casual, pleasure-centered view. More recently, however, many moral theologians prefer to avoid any prioritizing of purposes. The finalities of marriage are regarded as mutually dependent and harmonious. The fruitfulness of marriage cannot be divorced from the sexual completion and realization of the partners, nor can their sexual completion and personal realization in marriage exclude an acceptance to the birth of children. Vatican II assiduously avoided the terminology of primary and secondary ends of marriage while insisting upon the natural ordering of conjugal love to procreation (VatII ChurchModWorld 48 and 50). These natural ends of marriage establish its two central properties: unity and indissolubility. Unity means an exclusive relationship between one man and one woman; indissolubility signifies that this union is lifelong. The exclusivity of marriage follows from the meaning of commitment to another human being: a complete dedication in love to another is possible only through the security and single-mindedness of an exclusive bond. Even though polygamy has been practiced in many cultures, the optimal situation for acknowledging and fostering the value of each individual would be a monogamous union. Marriage is also indissoluble for similar reasons: the realization of the partners optimally entails a lifelong commitment. The emotional well-being of children also postulates a permanent union so that the constancy, security, and example of dedicated love necessary for the child's development be present. Separation may be tolerated, however, when a continued common life would be destructive of either partner or detrimental to the children.

Sacramentality of Marriage. Early Christianity, especially through the writings of Augustine of Hippo, regarded marriage as a *sacramentum,* i.e., a sacred, indissoluble obligation and also a religious sign of the unity between Christ and the Church. But this meaning of *sacramentum* should not be anachronistically confused with the developed theology of seven specific Christian sacraments as that theology emerged from the 11th to the 13th centuries. Partly as a reaction against the Catharist and Albigensian sects of the 12th cent., theologians came to an increasingly explicit awareness of marriage as an effective sacred symbol. Gradually, stricter definitions distinguished sacraments from sacramentals, and marriage was included among the seven sacraments because of its importance for Christian life. Alexander of Hales, Albert the Great, and Thomas Aquinas all contributed to the complete doctrine that marriage was not only a sign of the more sublime union of Christ and the Church, but possessed also a distinctive power of grace. This full sacramentality was defined at the Council of Florence (1438–1445) and Trent (1545–1563). The ministers of the sacrament are the spouses themselves; the priest is only the Church's official witness. The sacrament does not impart a permanent character, but a character permanent until the death of either spouse. Thus, through the sacramental rite whereby two baptized and legally competent persons express their agreement to marry, the conjugal bond becomes the symbol of the union between Christ and the Church. Sacramental grace is also conferred, thereby increasing sanctifying grace and the actual love of God conducive to the partners' living in accordance with their vocation. Marriage makes effectively present those graces which will enable the partners to fulfill the natural purposes of marriage as well as symbolically present the self-sacrificing love that is at the heart of Christ's Redemption.

Canon Law. Insofar as the marriage of two baptized persons is a sacrament and also insofar as the Church has traditionally been involved, especially in the West, with the good order of society, certain ecclesiastical regulations dealing with marriage have developed. This legislation for Catholics of the Latin rite is found in the Code of Canon Law, cc. 1012 to 1143, and in Pius XII's motu proprio *Crebrae allatae,* cc. 1 to 131, for Catholics of the Eastern rites. Variations from the CIC as well as in the interpretation of its canons have been significant in recent years and a new body of legislation is presently being discussed. The present CIC notes the sacramentality of marriage, its effects (a perpetual and exclusive bond), and sets forth the requirements for a valid marriage between baptized persons. An inquiry into the freedom of both parties to marry, partially fulfilled through the publication of the banns of marriage, must be made so that any impediments might be uncovered. This inquiry is also directed to the knowledge, psychological ability, and intention of the partners to enter into a valid marriage contract. Since marriage is a contract, the primary requisite for its validity is the consent of the partners to enter into a perpetual and exclusive union with the right to acts apt for the conception of children. This consent must be freely willed and informed about the nature of the contract. Mere lack of information or simple error (an error of the intellect that never led to an act of the will) does not invalidate the contract. A marriage would be invalid, however, if either party consciously excluded any of the specific ends or properties of marriage as discussed above. Canons dealing with the form of marriage are concerned with the proper conditions for the celebration of marriage. The Council of Trent in 1563 declared marriages invalid unless contracted before a bishop or his delegate and two witnesses. Pius X extended this decree in 1908, postulating that for validity all Latin rite Catholics must be married before a priest, even when marrying a non-Catholic. Non-Catholics are not held to this canonical form. The provisions of Pius's X's decree (*Ne temere*) were adopted by the CIC, although dispensation from canonical form is now generally granted so that a mixed marriage may be officially witnessed by a non-Catholic minister.

Restrictions on the natural right to marry are called impediments. Some impediments, e.g., impotence or prior marriage, stem from the very nature of marriage (divine law). Other impediments stem from ecclesiastical law and affect only the baptized. Two types of impediments to marriage occur: prohibitive, making a marriage unlawful; and diriment, making a marriage null (see MARRIAGE, IMPEDIMENTS TO). Thus a marriage could be null and void for three reasons: a diriment impediment, defective consent, and lack of ecclesiastical form. A declaration of nullity is an ecclesiastical procedure operative in these cases. Marriages that are null and void may also be convalidated, either simply or radically (see VALIDATION OF MARRIAGES).

A legitimate, consummated marriage between two unbaptized persons may be dissolved through the *Pauline Privilege. Distinct from the Pauline Privilege are cases ''in *favor of the faith.'' BIBLIOGRAPHY: G. H. Joyce, *Christian Marriage: an Historical and Doctrinal Study* (1933); M. Oraison, *Harmony of the Human Couple* (1967); E. Schillebeeckx, *Marriage: Human Reality and Saving Mystery* (1965); S. Kelleher, *Divorce and Remarriage for Catholics?* (1975); E. Kennedy, *What a Modern Catholic Believes About Sex and Marriage* (1975).

[T. M. MCFADDEN]

MARRIAGE, SPIRITUAL, a term used in Scripture to describe God's relationship with his people, and the bond uniting Christ and the consecrated virgin. In the OT, Yahweh speaks of being wedded to Israel (e.g., Is 54.4–5; 62.4–5; Jer 2.2; 3.20; Hos 2.19), and Paul writes in a similar vein regarding Christ and the Church (2 Cor 11.2; Eph 5.21–33). There is also a biblical basis for seeing the consecrated virgin as a bride of Christ, since Paul places his teaching on virginity in a marriage context and relates the virgin to Christ as a wife is related to her husband (1 Cor 7). Patristic literature continues this imagery, viz, Ambrose's remark, ''A virgin is a women wedded to Christ'' (*De virginibus*). The liturgy uses these texts in the various Masses for virgins, and the theme appears throughout the profession Mass of religious women. BIBLIOGRAPHY: EDB 1446–50; C. Marmion, *Sponsa Verbi: Virgin Consecrated to Christ* (tr. F. Izard, 1925). *MARRIAGE, MYSTICAL; *VIRGINITY.

[T. DUBAY]

MARRIAGE, VALIDATION OF, the canonical procedure that rectifies an invalid marriage. The procedure takes two forms. (1) Simple convalidation (CIC c. 1133–37) amounts to a renewal of matrimonial consent that had not been given or not rightly given. A valid marital consent, which is of the essence of the sacrament, must be one that is exchanged without the influence of grave fear, force, or moral pressure on either party, and without error or deception regarding the constitutive meaning and conditions of marital union. Convalidation in this case is the exchange of marital consent free of any such nullifying elements. A valid marital consent cannot be given where a diriment (invalidating) impediment affects either partner. Convalidation of a marriage so invalidated involves removal of the nullifying impediment—either (a) *de facto*, e.g., in the case of the impediment of insufficient age, by the passage of time or, in the case of one bound to a previous spouse the bond of a prior valid marriage, by the death of the previous spouse; or (b) *by dispensation* from the impediment. Once the impediment is removed, valid marital consent can be given. Marital consent is also invalid for a Catholic who does not observe the ''canonical form'' of marriage, i.e., in the presence of an authorized priest and two witnesses (CIC c. 1094). Convalidation of a marriage invalid for failure to observe this requirement consists in again giving consent according to the due form. When the invalidity of a marriage is not publicly known, simple convalidation in any of the circumstances outlined may require only that the partner who is aware that the union needs convalidation renew consent, provided there is no reason to think that the consent of the other partner does not perdure.

(2) Extraordinary validation is called in law a *sanatio in radice* (a healing at the root; CIC c. 1138–41). Such a validation does not involve renewal of consent; it is a juridic act of the Church correcting any diriment impediment and is retroactive, constituting the marriage a true sacramental marriage. It presupposes that the marital consent was given, rightly given, and never revoked; the partners were unaware of the invalidating impediment that is ''healed'' by this procedure.

[R. F. HURLEY]

MARRIAGE COUNSELING, a general term used to describe attempts by a third party, usually a paid professional, to help partners experiencing difficulties in their relationship to identify and resolve them. Married partners may present problems ranging from general disharmony to specific sexual disfunctioning. Couples usually come voluntarily for counseling, although some states now require pre-divorce counseling. Marriage counseling may be offered by psychologists, psychiatrists, pastors, social workers, sociologists, general physicians, or paraprofessionals. Methods and goals differ according to the counselor's training. Most frequently the counselor works with both partners and often with the entire family (an approach generally termed ''family counseling'') and attempts to remain an objective outsider rather than a partisan of one partner or the other. Most often the modern counselor uses a variety of techniques, including interviews (both individual and joint and often videotaped), personality and interest tests, and even structured games to help couples identify their marital difficulties, decide whether they have sufficient incentive to work through their problems, and to help plan either a course of therapeutic action or the least traumatic separation.

Intervention approaches differ greatly according to the theoretical orientation of the counselor. In the past, many counselors (especially those with psychoanalytic training) assumed that marital difficulties stemmed mainly from unresolved individual (and early childhood) conflicts and often recommended separate therapy for each partner. A more current approach views a couple as members of a group, even a group of two, and draws upon advances made in understanding group dynamics and social learning. This approach focuses on the couple as an interdependent unit in which a change in one brings about a change in the other; it attempts to help the couple to understand their own, often unique, patterns of interaction, and to learn to modify their behavior so as to effect greater compatibility. The counselor may employ a variety of techniques for the couple or family designed to change their patterns of interaction, increase honest communication, and modify destructive behavior. Marriage counseling thus may combine individual, couple, family, or even multicouple group counseling. Duration may be either moderate or long-range (i.e., from 6 months to several years), depending on the type and severity of the couple's problems, their commitment to change, and the counselor's methods. Traditionally, parish priests have filled some of the functions of the marriage counselor. More recently, however, there has been recognition of the need for specialization in this area. Most dioceses in their Catholic charities services include professional family and marriage counseling. There are both clerical and lay specialists available who integrate into the theological and religious approach to marriage problems the techniques developed in the behavioral and social sciences. *MARRIAGE ENCOUNTER.

[C. B. REGAN]

MARRIAGE ENCOUNTER, is a movement begun and developed by Father Gabriel Calvo and 28 Spanish Christian Family Movement couples in Barcelona, Spain, in 1958, which senses the need for husbands and wives to deepen their own relationship in order to realize the tremendous apostolic potential that is present in every Christian marriage. Marriage Encounter presents a way of life, open to all, that begins with a weekend where methods of communication between couples are taught with the goal of achieving physical, mental, and spiritual unity through reflection and dialogue, creating couples who are living Christian love. Offering postweekend activities, Marriage Encounter's purpose is to motivate couples to dialogue daily and to grow as a couple in love, confidence, and unity. In 1965 Marriage Encounter was brought to Mexico and Latin America and spread to Spanish-speaking groups in the U.S. The first English-speaking Marriage Encounter took place in Miami under the direction of Robert and Mary Munson in January 1968. It was not until the summer of that year that the real roots of Encounter took place in the U.S. when the founders of the Christian Family Movement, Pat and Patty Crowley, brought 50 teams of couples and priests, some bilingual, from Spain to conduct the weekends throughout the country. Donald Hessler, MM, an American priest who had worked with the Spanish couples, soon began to promote a national organization of Marriage Encounter. At his urging, a weekend in January 1969 was set aside for a meeting at Villa Stella Maris, in Elbaron, New Jersey, for all couples and priests who were known to have presented two or more Marriage Encounters in English. From this meeting emerged the National Executive Board for the Marriage Encounter movement with Jamie and Arline Whelan, who arranged the meeting, being chosen Executive Couple. The board was to be a clearing house for information, communications, and national publicity and was to promote the growth of the movement in the U.S. and Canada. This meeting and the establishment of the executive board marked a break with the structure of the Christian Family Movement, but at the suggestion of Pat and Patty Crowley both movements were to maintain close, cordial, mutually supportive affiliations. The growing pains of the Marriage Encounter movement began to surface in 1970, evolving very differently in various parts of the country. While keeping the central program, two organizations resulted on the basis of different emphases, National Marriage Encounter and the New York-centered Worldwide Marriage Encounter. A division between the Christian Family Movement and the Marriage Encounter also developed. In the summer of 1973 a group of couples and priests with background in both movements joined their talents to produce The Encountering Couple, a followup program for couples who had made the Marriage Encounter. In August 1973 the First National Marriage Encounter Conference was held at Notre Dame Univ. in conjunction with the CFM National Conference. Such cooperation between the two groups continues and is highlighted by the sharing of the publication, *Agape,* as the national voice of both movements.

Various programs have evolved from the National Marriage Encounter such as Engaged Encounter, Beginning Encounter for divorced and widowed persons, and various family weekend programs, parish enrichment programs, and marriage education programs for the Confraternity of Christian Doctrine. One of the most significant programs developed by Father Calvo is the *Retorno,* which is a weekend for couples to encounter God through scriptural prayer together. It is a program separate from the Worldwide Marriage Encounter and National Marriage Encounter and is coordinated in such a way that it is open to all who have experienced Marriage Encounter.

From 1967 to 1975 the Marriage Encounter in the U.S. began, grew, developed, suffered disillusionment, strife, and misunderstanding within and without but still endeavors, as it continues its growth and development, the creation of couples who are living Christian love.

[C. J. NOONE]

MARRIAGE OF CLERGY, see CLERGY, MARRIAGE OF.

MARRIAGE OF CONSCIENCE, a marriage which the diocesan bp. permits to be celebrated without *banns and with the marriage rites performed in secret. The usual marriage rite is celebrated in the presence of a priest and two witnesses; all participants, however, are bound to the obligation of secrecy. This obligation ceases if there is possibility of grave scandal arising or of children born of the union not being rightly baptized. Such marriages may be performed without permission by a priest ministering to one in danger of death. Record of such marriages is kept, not in the parish register, but in the diocesan archives (CIC, c. 1104–07). A procedure similar to the marriage of conscience is observed in the case of a laicized priest who is given permission to marry.

MARROQUÍN, FRANCISCO (1477–1563), bp. of Guatemala and protector of the Indians of Central America. As Bishop Zumárraga's vicar general in Mexico City, where both had landed in 1528, M. put his life in jeopardy by excommunicating members of the royal court for their cruelty to the Indians. He was thereafter dispatched to Central America; he learned the native languages, later teaching them to the Dominicans, Mercedarians, and Franciscans who came under his jurisdiction. Created bp. of Guatemala by Zumárraga in 1537—the first to be consecrated in the New World—M., in addition to founding churches and the Colegio de Santo Tomás, devoted his life to promoting the welfare of the Indians. A proponent of conversion solely by peaceful means, he struggled against the enslavement and exploitation of the indigenous population and worked to integrate them fully into Spanish colonial life.

[E. M. GATES]

MARROW CONTROVERSY, a dispute in the Church of Scotland. The republication in 1718 of an old Puritan work, *The Marrow of Modern Divinity,* originally published in 1646 and recommended for its evangelical doctrines by Thomas Boston and others, marked the beginning of the so-called Marrow controversy. The question of the doctrinal orthodoxy of the *Marrow* increasingly divided the evangelical party from the more accommodating moderates, and in an act condemning the work (1720), the *General Assembly of the Church declared itself against the teachings of the *Marrow* and forbade its ministers to preach or advocate its views. Twelve ministers, including Boston and Ebenezer and Ralph Erskine, signed a representation addressed to the Assembly of 1721 in protest against the condemnation, but the ''Marrow men'' were themselves rebuked and admonished by the Assembly. The controversy died down, but the bitterness it created was partly responsible for the later secession of the Erskines.

[J. A. R. MACKENZIE]

MARSHALL, DANIEL (1706–84), Baptist revivalist. Reared a Congregationalist in Conn., he experienced conversion through the influence of George *Whitefield. About 1752, he went to preach to Indians in western New York and Pennsylvania. By 1754, he had reached Opeckon, Va., where he became a Baptist. In 1755, with his brother-in-law, Shubael *Stearns, he moved to Sandy Creek, N. C., where he was ordained a Baptist minister. His revivalistic preaching led to the establishment of several churches, and he moved to South Carolina, where he preached for about 10 years. In 1771 he settled in Columbia Co., Ga., where he formed the Kiokee Baptist Church and thus helped to lay the foundations of Baptist work in that state. BIBLIOGRAPHY: J. D. Mosteller, *History of the Kiokee Baptist Chuirch in Georgia* (1952).

[N. H. MARING]

MARSILIUS OF PADUA (Marsiglio; *c.*1275–1342), physician, scholar, and author of the antipapal *Defensor pacis* (1324), his major work, written with some assistance from Jean de Jandun. The *Defensor pacis* had a direct bearing on the contemporary dispute between the Pope and the Emperor, already broadening out into projects for the control of the Church by the State. It was acridly antipapal; when his authorship was discovered (1326), M. had to leave Paris. Siding with Louis of Bavaria, afterward proclaimed emperor in defiance of the Pope, M. was made Imperial Vicar of Rome (1328). Thrown out by a mob after a few months, he remained for the rest of his life at Louis's court in Munich.

The *Defensor pacis* is composed of three books, the third being a brief summary of conclusions. The first is a philosophy of the State in the sober line of the studies on Aristotle's *Politics* initiated by Thomas Aquinas and Peter of Auvergne. The second book is strikingly different. Had it developed the ideals of Dante's *Monarchia,* no great dust would have risen nor would odium have been aroused. But it was a theology of the Church that advocated a radical secularism and allowed the spiritual power no coercive jurisdiction of any kind, not even in ecclesiastical affairs, but subjected the Church to civil control. The whole conception of a divinely ordered hierarchical structure, one moreover that was centered in the primacy of Peter, was attacked, and in a temper that far exceeded contemporary anticlericalism. It was for this reason that the work was condemned as heretical in 1327 and 1378. It was studied by Thomas *Cranmer, and translated into English to provide support for the religious policies of Henry VIII. BIBLIOGRAPHY: A. Gerwith, *Marsilius of Padua, Defender of the Peace* (2 v., 1951, 1956).

[T. C. O'BRIEN]

MARTÈNE, EDMOND, (d. 1739), French Benedictine scholar of the Congregation of St. Maur, known for his work in editing liturgical sources and in thus helping lay the foundations for the history of liturgy and the science of liturgiology. He collected rituals and ordinals from every part of Europe and in particular provides information on usages of French dioceses. He is best known for *De antiquis ecclesiae ritibus* (1700–02), in collaboration with J. *Mabillon.

MARTENSEN, HANS LASSEN (1808–84), Danish Lutheran theologian, bishop. He taught theology at Copenhagen from 1838 to 1854. A romanticist, M. sought to bring together Christian and humanist elements. From 1854 to 1884 he was bp. of Seeland, Denmark, chief Lutheran diocese of the country. He engaged in several controversies with Kierkegaard. Among his published works were *Katholicisme og Protestantisme* (1874) and *Den kristelige Ethik* (3 v., 1871–78).

MARTHA OF BETHANY, see MARY AND MARTHA OF BETHANY.

MARTÍ, JOSÉ (1853–95), Cuban patriot and writer. Born of Spanish parents, M. joined the independence party in 1868 and in consequence of his political ideas was obliged to spend most of his life in exile, but he never ceased to carry on with his work for Cuban independence. He became one of the foremost figures in Hispano-American literature. In 1895 he joined the Cuban patriots and died in the battle of Dos Ríos. The contribution he made to Cuba's liberation by his eloquence and dynamic leadership was such that he has been accounted the father of the Cuban nation. BIBLIOGRAPHY: J. Manach, *Martí: Apostle of Freedom* (tr. C. Taylor, 1950); R. B. Gray, *José Martí: Cuban Patriot* (1962).

[P. DAMBORIENA]

MARTÍ, MARIANO (1721–92), Spanish bp., first of Puerto Rico (1761), then of Caracas, Venezuela (1769). He was a native of Tarragona and vicar general there when appointed to Puerto Rico. His episcopal visitations of both Puerto Rico and Guiana, then part of the Puerto Rico Diocese, as well as of the Caracas Diocese, built up the Church in Hispanic America. His reports on his journeys are a rich source of historical information.

[T. C. O'BRIEN]

MARTIAL (BISHOP), see BASILIDES AND MARTIAL.

MARTIAL (MARTYR), see FAUSTUS, JANUARIUS, AND MARTIAL, SS.

MARTIALL, JOHN (Marshall; 1534–97), English Catholic controversialist. Educated at Winchester and New College, Oxford, he received a degree in civil law in 1556 and in 1560 began studying at Louvain (Belgium) together with other English Catholic exiles. In 1568 he received a degree in divinity at the Univ. of Douai, where Bp. W. *Allen was just forming the new English College for Catholics. M. is best known, however, for his *Treatise of the Cross* (1564), which he dedicated to Queen Elizabeth. From 1579 he lived in the canonry of Lille, France.

[E. M. GATES]

MARTIANUS CAPELLA (fl. later 4th cent. and early 5th cent. A.D.), Latin author of Neoplatonic outlook. He composed a work on the liberal arts in nine books under the title, *De nuptiis Mercurii et Philologiae*. It is written in a mixture of prose and verse and in an inflated style reminiscent of Apuleius. The arts are represented as the bridesmaids of *Philologia*, and the elaborate allegory is sustained through the larger part of the composition. Despite its artificial and superficial character, the work had a great influence on medieval education. Commentaries on it by John Scotus Erigena and Dunchad are extant.

MARTIN I, ST. (d. 655), **POPE** from 649, martyr. As a deacon of the Roman Church, M. served as legate of his predecessor, *Theodore I, at Constantinople. Early in his pontificate M. presided over a Lateran synod that condemned the **Typos* of the Emperor Constans II as well as the **Ecthesis* of his predecessor, Heraclius. The Pope was seized by imperial forces and taken to Constantinople where he was subjected to insult and brutal treatment. He was charged with responsibility for the loss of Sicily to the Muslims, but it was evident to all that he was being persecuted for his refusal to approve the *Typos*. He was sent in exile to Cherson in the Crimea, a place then in the grip of famine. In the sufferings of his exile, he complained that even the Church of Rome had abandoned him, but he prayed publicly for Eugene I who had been installed as Pope. This action on the part of M. had been construed as an equivalent resignation and an approval of the choice of his successor. He was buried in Cherson, where he had an immediate cultus. Most of his relics are thought to have been translated to the church of San Martino ai Monti in Rome. He is the last of the popes to be venerated as a martyr. BIBLIOGRAPHY: Mann 1.1:385–405; C. M. Aherne, NCE 9:300–301; Butler 4:319–320; PL 129:591–604; 87:204; 111–120.

[P. F. MULHERN]

MARTIN IV (Simon de Brion; d. 1285), **POPE** from 1281. Little is known of his life and career before he became a priest at Rouen and, sometime later (*c.*1255), a canon at Tours. His ecclesiastical career was aided by royal patronage, and Louis IX of France eventually (1260) appointed him to the office of chancellor of the kingdom. After being made a cardinal, 1261, he took a leading role in the negotiations between the papacy and the French concerning the claims of Louis's brother, Charles of Anjou, to the throne of Sicily. As pope, Martin continued to support the French in Sicily until the Sicilian Vespers (1282), which eventually led to Aragonese control of the kingdom. French political aims played a major role in shaping papal policy throughout his reign. The planned reunion of the Eastern and Western Churches, begun at the Council of Lyons (1274), was ended when he excommunicated Emperor Michael VIII Paleologus at French instigation. BIBLIOGRAPHY: Mann 16:167–356; S. Runciman, *Sicilian Vespers* (1958); D. J. Geanakoplos, *Emperor Michael Palaeologus and the West, 1258–1282* (1959).

[J. MULDOON]

MARTIN V (Oddo Colonna; 1368–1431). **POPE** from 1417. In 1405 Innocent VII created him cardinal deacon. He participated in both the Councils of Pisa and Constance. When the two antipopes, John XXIII and Benedict XIII, were deposed and excommunicated by the Council Fathers, Oddo Colonna was elected pope and assumed the name of Martin V. In 1418 when the Council of Pisa was dissolved, M. left for Rome but was detained in Florence and did not reach Rome until 1420. Energetic, adroit, and politically talented, M. set about reconstituting the Papal States, restoring basilicas, roads, and buildings. He took action against the Hussites, sent legates to mediate between France and England, and acted as patron to Bernardine of Siena, who aided him in religious reform. He was guilty of nepotism for the Colonna clan and of delaying reform in the Church desired by so many, for he feared limitation of papal power and the overturn of the Church constitution. This unfortunate delay definitely paved the way to Protestant Reform. But with M., the Western Schism, which had lasted for 40 scandalous years, came to an end; for this he was called *temporum suorum felicitas*. BIBLIOGRAPHY: G. Mollat, DTC 10.1:197–202; K. A. Fink, NCE 9:301–302; *idem*, LTK 7:114–115.

[F. D. LAZENBY]

MARTIN OF ALNWICK (*c.* 1270–1336), Franciscan, master at Oxford *c.* 1303, author of works on logic; a participant at Avignon of his order's defense against the Spirituals (see SPIRITUALS, FRANCISCAN).

[T. C. O'BRIEN]

MARTIN OF BRAGA, ST. (*c.* 515–*c.* 580), missionary to the Suevians in the NW Iberian peninsula (modern Galicia and northern Portugal); founding abbot of a monastery at Dumio (550); and first bp. of Dumio (557). He probably entered monastic life in the East, perhaps as a consequence of a pilgrimage to Palestine. His writings reflect a broad theological culture, a knowledge of Greek, and a decided pastoral bent. He drew on such diverse traditions as the Egyptian Fathers, Seneca, John Cassian, and St. Caesarius of Arles. BIBLIOGRAPHY: M. R. P. McGuire, NCE 9:303; É. Amann, DTC 10:203–207.

[E. J. DILLON]

MARTIN OF LEÓN, ST. (*c.* 1125–1203), Spanish Augustinian ascetic. His cult was authorized in 1632 and then suppressed. A vita records his early life in a monastery in León followed by a long pilgrimage through the Middle East and Europe. Wealthy patrons and clerks enabled him to compile 58 lengthy sermons in a *Concordia* full of quotations from both OT and NT (PL 208–209), begun in 1185 for fellow canons. Several hard arguments against Jews and heretics may be interpolations.

[E. P. COLBERT]

MARTIN OF TOURS, ST. (d. 397), bp. of Tours, founder of the first monastery in Gaul (Ligugé), and patron of France, hailed as the glory of Gaul and the light of the Western Church. His burial place was a main pilgrimage center for well over 1,000 years. Born in Sabaria, a town of Pannonia (modern Hungary), of pagan parents, he was reared in Pavia, Italy, where his father was an officer in the Roman army. He became a catechumen at Pavia while a young boy and joined the army at an early age. How long he was a soldier and a catechumen is the subject of dispute, as is the substance of so many legends including the famous one of his dividing his cloak for a beggar while still a catechumen and soldier at Amiens. He became a disciple and friend of St. Hilary, bp. of Poitiers, who gave him land for his community of hermits. Despite his own resistance, and that of some ecclesiastics, M. was made bp. of Tours (371) by acclamation of the people. He continued the hermit life outside town with many disciples, and gave himself to a rural apostolate, traveling the pagan countryside by foot. He unsuccessfully opposed the death penalty for the heretic Priscillian and, although he opposed their heresy, he intervened with the emperor Maximus to save the Priscillianists from deadly persecution in Spain. His biography was written by a contemporary, Sulpicius Severus, who visited the saint at Tours. St. Gregory of Tours, a successor as bp. 1½ cent. later, wrote another account which, however, differs much from the former one. BIBLIOGRAPHY: J. Lahache, BiblSanct 8:1248–79; Butler 4:310–313.

[E. J. DILLON]

MARTIN OF TROPPAU (*c.* 1200–after 1278), Dominican archbishop. Also known as Martin of Poland, M. was papal chaplain, apostolic penitentiary, and finally (1278) abp. of Gnesen, but he died before taking possession of his see. He is best known for his compendious though uncritical chronicle of history, canonical writings, and sermons all composed as an aid to preaching. BIBLIOGRAPHY: H. Wolfram, NCE 9:304; Quétif-Échard 1:361–370; B. Stasiewski, LTK 7:119.

[J. A. WEISHEIPL]

MARTIN, GREGORY (*c.* 1540–82), biblical translator. M. studied classics at St. John's College, Oxford (1557–69); escaped anti-Catholic persecution by fleeing to *Douai; was ordained a Jesuit (1573); and assisted William *Allen in establishing the English College in Rome. From 1578 to 1582, he taught Scripture at Reims and proceeded to translate the *Vulgate into English. The NT was published at Reims in 1582; financial difficulties postponed publication of the OT until 1609–10 at Douai. M.'s Douay-Reims version is most faithful to its Vulgate source and, until new versions began to appear in the 20th cent., was the standard Catholic translation of the Bible into English. BIBLIOGRAPHY: B. Ward, CE 9:727–728.

[T. M. MCFADDEN]

MARTIN, KONRAD (1812–79), bp. of Paderborn, Germany, from 1856. Before his episcopacy he was professor of moral theology at the Univ. of Bonn. He worked as bp. toward the reunion of Christians and published dialogues with German Lutherans. As a conciliar at Vatican Council I he shared in the formulation of the dogmatic constitution *Dei Filius*, on faith, and *Pastor aeternus*, in which papal *infallibility was defined. Because of his resistance to state interference during the *Kulturkampf he was deposed, jailed for a year in 1874, and then was an exile in Belgium for the remainder of his life.

[T. C. O'BRIEN]

MARTIN, PAULIN (1840–1890), Orientalist and NT textual critic. After studies in Paris and Rome, M. held the chair of Sacred Scripture and Oriental languages at the Institut Catholique in Paris (1878–90). Best noted for his Syriac studies, M. also published many articles on NT textual criticism. BIBLIOGRAPHY: O. Rey, DB 4.1:828–829; W. Drum, CE 7:729–730.

[T. M. MCFADDEN]

MARTIN, RAYMOND JOSEPH (1878–1949), French Dominican theologian and historian of theology. He was professor at the Univ. of Louvain from 1909 until 1940. His primary work of historical scholarship was *La Controverse sur le péché originel au debut du XIVe siècle* (1930); he also edited *Oeuvres de Robert de Melun* (3 v., 1932–41), and *Pierre Mangeur, De sacramentis* (1937). With J. Lebon and J. de Ghellinck he founded (1921) the journal *Spicilegium sacrum Lovaniense*.

[T. C. O'BRIEN]

MARTIN, VICTOR (1886–1945), planner and organizer with A. *Fliche, of *Histoire de l'Église* (26 v., 1934–). Ordained in 1910, he spent most of his career on the theology and canon law faculty of the Univ. of Strasbourg (1921–45) and was dean from 1923. He is recognized as the prime authority on the history of *Gallicanism, esp. in his *Le Gallicanisme politique et le clergé de France* (1929), and *Les Origines de gallicanisme* (2 v., 1939).

[T. C. O'BRIEN]

MARTINA, ST. (fl. 3d. cent.), virgin and martyr. According to her legend, M. was the orphaned daughter of a former consul and a deaconess of the Roman Church. She was tortured and decapitated for the faith under the Emperor Alexander Severus (222–35). The earliest mention of her known to history is in the *Liber pontificalis*, which states that Pope *Adrian I presented gifts in her honor to a chapel near the Forum. The *acta* of her martyrdom are of late origin and appear to be modelled on the *passio* of St. Tatiana. They are preposterously extravagant and untrustworthy in every respect. BIBLIOGRAPHY: A. Amore, BiblSanct 8:1220–21; Butler 1:203.

[R. B. ENO]

MARTINDALE, CYRIL CHARLES (1879–1963), English Jesuit writer. A convert to Càtholicism as a young man, he entered the Society of Jesus, finished his studies at Oxford, and embarked on a career of popular writing, preaching, and pastoral work which was to span more than half a century. Equally at home among the young toughs of his East End club and the aristocracy of London's Mayfair, M. was a remarkable preacher whose speaking obligations carried him to Australia, Africa, and South America. He wrote much on the saints which was illuminative but not always of the highest quality. His biography of Robert Hugh *Benson is worthy of note. Other works include *The Risen Sun* (about Australia and New Zealand) and *African Angelus,* written after visiting South Africa. A pioneering work was the BBC series *What Are Saints?*, one of BBC's most impressive religious series. M. was an early leader in the movement for a university apostolate and was a force in the international *Pax Romana*. Anticipating Vatican II, he labored for liturgical change that would look to the pastoral rather than the merely historical. His observation of missionary fields made him an advocate of adaptation of the Western Church to native cultures. In spite of lifelong ill health, his prodigious efforts—and above all, his winning character—made M. one of the great English Catholic influences for half a century. BIBLIOGRAPHY: I. Evans, "C.C. Martindale, SJ" *America* (April 6, 1963).

[J. R. AHERNE]

MARTINEAU, JAMES (1805–1900), English Unitarian, theologian, philosopher. He was a Presbyterian when a profound disturbance at the premature death of a relative who was a Unitarian minister produced his conversion to Unitarianism and determination to enter the ministry. He was ordained a Unitarian minister in 1828 and worked in Dublin until 1832, when he accepted an associate pastorship in Liverpool. M. became known as a brilliant thinker, esp. with the publication of *Rationale of Religious Enquiry* (1836). As a philosophic thinker he was a naturalistic theist, but he maintained at the same time a rather mystical spirituality. In 1840 he published *Hymns for the Christian Church and Home,* which became a standard collection for the 19th century. In addition to pastoral work, he accepted an appointment as professor of mental and moral philosophy at Manchester New College in 1840, continuing to lecture when the institute moved to London, and remaining with Manchester New College until 1887. A prodigious writer, he contributed to the *London Review,* the *London and Westminster Review,* and the *National Review*. Among his books, all widely circulated, are *Endeavors after the Christian Life* (1843), *Study of Spinoza* (1883), and *Types of Ethical Theory* (2 v., 1885).

[J. R. AHERNE]

MARTÍNEZ, GREGORIO (1575–1637), Spanish Dominican, theologian at Segovia and Valladolid, author of a prolix commentary on the *Prima secundae* of the *Summa* of St. Thomas (3 v., 1617–37), a work reflecting the rising acceptance at that time of *probabalism.

[T. C. O'BRIEN]

MARTÍNEZ, JUAN DE PRADO (d. 1668), Spanish Dominican, Thomist philosopher and theologian. He taught at Avila and at Alcalá, where he held the "chair of Vespers'' from 1642 and the ''chair of Prime'' from 1660. He became provincial of the Province of Spain in 1662. M. is the author of a superb text in metaphysics, *Controversiae metaphysicales s. theologiae ministrae* (1649). Among his many moral theology treatises are: *Theologiae moralis quaestiones praecipuae* (2 v., 1654–56); *Dubitationes morales de sacramentis in genere et in specie* (1660), and *De poenitentiae sacramento* (opus posthumous, 1669).

[T. C. O'BRIEN]

MARTÍNEZ, LUIS MARÍA (1881–1956), Mexican abp., spiritual writer, diplomat. He was associated with the Instituto del Sagrado Corazón for over 20 years. Named prefect before his ordination in 1904, he became vice-rector in 1905 and rector in 1919. His influence on the formation of clerics was great. Apostolic administrator of Chilapa (1922), auxiliary to the abp. of Morelia (1923), he administered the diocese when government persecution drove Abp. Ruiz y Flores into exile in 1925. M.'s ability to deal with the hostile government saved much church property. Appointed coadjutor of Morelia in 1934, he became abp. of Mexico in 1937. M.'s tact and diplomacy effectively brought an end to the era of persecution, and he became a close friend of President Alemán. His writings earned him membership in the Academia Mexicana de la Lengua; among them were *El espíritu santo* and *La pureza en el ciclo litúrgico*. The first, translated as *The Sanctifier* (tr. M. Aquinas, 1957), is a work rich in patristic thought and profound in its exposition of the role of the Holy Spirit in the Christian life.

[J. R. AHERNE]

MARTÍNEZ COMPAÑON Y BUJANDA, BALTASAR (1737–97), bishop, social activist. Of Spanish origin, M. was ordained in 1761. He went to Lima, Peru, became rector of the seminary there. Named to the see of Trujillo in 1779, he launched on a remarkable career as bp. and social reformer. His grasp of the great problems of society in Peru as well as what his clergy should represent was profound. In addition to providing churches and schools, he established villages, built roads and sewage systems, improved mining conditions and agriculture. M. wrote a valuable study, *Historia natural, civil y moral de Trujillo por mapas, planos y estampos con sus memorias para ella* (1780–85), a model history of the region and a repository of folklore and natural science. In 1788 M. became abp. of Bogotá.

[J. R. AHERNE]

MARTÍNEZ DE ALDUNATE, JOSÉ ANTONIO (1730?–1811), Chilean bp., educator. He was ordained in 1756. Much of his career was spent as professor, then rector, of the Univ. of San Felipe. In 1804 he was named bp. of Guamanga in Peru. The first native government of Chile named him to the ruling junta in 1810.

[J. R. AHERNE]

MARTÍNEZ DEL RÍO, PABLO (1892–1963), Mexican archeologist, historian. Educated in England, M. returned to Mexico City in 1914, serving as a distinguished teacher at the Univ. of Mexico and the Instituto Nacional de Antropología e Historia, of which he became director in 1944. His important works include *Los orígenes americanos* (1936) and *Alumbrado* (1937), a compassionate study of a Jewish mystic of the 16th cent. in Mexico. M. played a major role in the study of Tlatelolco, a section of Mexico City, the history of which he put together by using archeology, native documents, and records of the civil and ecclesiastical authorities.

[J. R. AHERNE]

MARTINI, GIOVANNI BATTISTA (Giambattista; Padre Martini; 1706–84), Italian composer, musical theorist, scholar, educator, and historian. As a young man he played violin and harpsichord, and learned counterpoint from Antonio Riccieri, a Vincenzian soprano and composer. M. was ordained in 1722 and became *maestro di cappella* in Bologna in 1725. Many European musicians sought his advice, including Mozart. M.'s most important works are the *Storia della musica* (3 v., 1757–81), an unfinished history of music, and *Esemplare ossia saggio . . . di contrappunto* (2 vs., 1774–75), a treatise on counterpoint. His church music includes *Litaniae,* Op. I (1734); *XII Sonate d'intavolatura,* Op. 2 (1741); *VI Sonate per organo e cembalo* (1747); *Duetti di camera* (1763), and requiems, oratorios, Masses and intermezzi.

[R. J. LITZ]

MARTINI, SIMONE (1284–1344), Italian painter of the Sienese School, gifted pupil of Duccio, his earliest work (1315) a great *Majestas* in the Palazzio Pubblico, Siena. In 1317 M. painted for Robert of Anjou in Naples *St. Louis of Toulouse Crowning Robert of Anjou,* later executing a cycle of frescoes in the Lower Church of S. Francesco, Assisi (1320–25) and the outstanding equestrian portrait of Guidoriccio da Fogliano (1328). M. developed a distinctive style, at times essentially conservative, producing highly decorative art with an intense interest in sumptuously patterned and textured fabrics. He introduced progressive elements, particularly the use of formal relationships to portray another level of meaning as in the active-receptive relationship between Gabriel and the Virgin in *The Annunciation* (1333; the Uffizi, Florence), the peak of his achievement and one of the greatest works of the Sienese School, its elegant and expressive linearity equaled only by master painters of the Orient. M. is also a key link between Gothic art in Siena and in France owing to his residence at Avignon in his last years. BIBLIOGRAPHY: B. Paccagnini, *Simone Martini* (1967).

[S. CONWAY]

MARTINSBERG, ABBEY OF, see PANNONHALMA, ABBEY OF.

MARTINUZZI, GYÖRGY (1482–1551), cardinal, statesman. A Croatian, M. joined the Paulites. For many years he was adviser to King John I of Hungary. Named bp. of Nagyvárad in 1534, M. was architect of the Treaty of Nagyvárad in 1538, an agreement that provided for succession of the Habsburgs on the death of John. King John rescinded the treaty and made M. governor of Transylvania, responsible for the succession of the infant Prince. With the aid of the Turks M. followed the King's wishes but reverted to the treaty provision after the Turks conquered Buda in 1541. For his labors M. was created cardinal and abp. of Esztergom. Suspected of complicity with the Turks, M. was assassinated.

[J. R. AHERNE]

MARTYRDOM. In the OT and frequently in the NT the Greek *martus* means witness; but St. Paul uses the term to designate Stephen at the precise moment of his death: "When the blood of Stephen thy *witness* was shed, I also was standing by and approving" (Acts 22.20). The suffering of Jesus in his Passion is the martyr's model; in fact, the early Church popularly called Christ himself the first martyr. In the *Epistle of Clement* the indifference to pain that characterizes many martyrs is ascribed to their confidence in Christ rather than to their belief in the truth of his teaching. It is in the passion of Polycarp, however, that the full meaning of "witness" comes through: the martyr testifies to the fact that Jesus is the Son of God. Augustine gives the classic formulation: "The cause, not the suffering, makes genuine martyrs" (*Epist*. 89.2). A question arises when unconscious persons or those who have not the use of reason are killed by enemies of the Church. Tertullian calls martyrdom a second baptism, and Clement of Alexandria asserts that martyrs gain immediate entrance into glory. Readiness to suffer death rather than to deny the faith was not confined to antiquity. Religious conflicts particularly in the 13th and 16th cent. have given rise to numerous martyrs as have various mission fields in later times.

Theology defines martyrdom as the voluntary undergoing of death to bear witness to a cause, most properly speaking, to Christ's truth. How extensive is this truth will vary according to different views on the universality of grace; some will see instances of it in those who have laid down their lives for any righteousness, thus Socrates and St. John the Baptist; others will require a more explicitly Christian certificate to be attached to this heroism, and this, quite understandably, will be expected for official commemoration in the ecclesiastical calendar. The cause for which they died may have been the simple gospel tidings, such as we may imagine to have been the case with St. Thomas the Apostle, or for order in the Church (thus St. Thomas More), or the Church's freedom (thus St. Thomas of Canterbury). The hatred of the faith (*odium fidei*) from which they were killed normally is surrounded by a host of other pressures, and for similar biographical reasons their precise motive and deliberateness should not be unduly isolated: the feast of the Holy Innocents has been celebrated since the 5th century. Martyrdom is an act of the virtue of courage pushed to its utmost in facing the ultimate of death and embracing it. Where sacramental baptism has not been already received, its gracious effects are equivalent, and it is called baptism of blood. BIBLIOGRAPHY: ThAq St 2a2ae, 124 (Lat-Eng v. 42, ed. A. Ross and P. G. Walsh; A. P. Frutaz and J. Beckmann, LTK 7:127–133; E. E. Malone, *Monk and the Martyr* (1950).

[M. J. SUELZER; T. GILBY]

MARTYRIANS, a group of *Euphemites. Epiphanius (*Panarion 80*) reports that several Euphemites were put to death by the magistrates for their beliefs. Their coreligionists buried those executed, held religious services at the burial places, and referred to themselves and their buried dead as Martyriani. BIBLIOGRAPHY: É. Amann, DTC 10:792–795.

[L. G. MÜLLER]

MARTYRION, (Gr., pertaining to a witness or martyr), a word applied to (1) a book containing the account of the life and death of a martyr; (2) a martyr's tomb or a church built over it, or occasionally even a church built in honor of a martyr; also called a *martyrium; (3) the Constantinian basilica built E of Mount Calvary and reputedly enshrining the well where the True Cross was discovered.

[R. K. GOLINI]

MARTYRIUM, a church built over the tomb or the relics of a martyr, or a side chapel housing them, or even an entire cemetery. Originally the Greek word signified the repository of a martyr's remains; but by metonymy its Latin equivalent came to be used of entire edifices built over the bodies of martyrs and even of churches erected in places connected with the life of Christ or his Apostles. The martyrium was not intended for the regular celebration of the Sunday liturgy but arose from the need of shelter for the crowds that thronged the resting place of martyrs on special days. By the time of Ambrose, additional remains were interred in side chapels of martyria and in the next cent. in parish churches as well, where tombs were often combined with altars. Members of the imperial family sometimes erected martyria so that they might after death lie *ad sanctos*—near the holy ones whose intercession they sought. BIBLIOGRAPHY: A. Grabar, *Martyrium,* 2 v. and album (1943–46).

[M. J. SUELZER]

MARTYROLOGIES, strictly speaking, are official catalogs listing the names in chronological order of those who have died for the faith. More generally they are, like the Eastern menologies and synaxeries, expanded ecclesiastical calendars giving brief descriptions of the feasts of the Blessed Trinity, of Christ, and of the saints and martyrs martyrs which are commemorated or celebrated in the liturgy of the day. The early Christians, like the Jews and pagans of the Greco-Roman world before them, found it advantageous to create their own religious calendars. Originally these were of a local nature, but with the passage of time they were expanded to take in the feasts commemorated in other churches as well. The earliest extant calendars of this type, either whole or in part, are those from Rome (4th cent.), a Gothic calendar from Thrace and one from Tours (both 5th cent.), and the calendars of Carmona (near Seville), Carthage, and Oxyrhynchus (all of the 6th century). The Roman calendar, known as the Chronographer of 354 or the Philocalian Calendar, is of particular importance. It contains two lists of depositions or burials, one for bishops and one for martyrs. The former contains the names of 12 popes, that of Lucius (253–254) being the earliest, each preceded by the date of his anniversary and followed by the name of the cemetery in which he was buried. The martyr-popes are given in the other list, that of the martyrs, the earliest pope being Callistus (217–222). Besides recording the dates, names, and places of burial for the Roman martyrs honored in the Church, the *Depositio martyrum,* as this list is called, includes the names of martyrs from Ostia, Porto, and Albano, and also three martyrs of Carthage, SS. Perpetua and Felicitas on March 7, and Cyprian on Oct. 14. This is already an indication of how the early local calendars would develop into more universal ones. The earliest extant calendar of this more general type is the *Breviarium Syriacum* of 411. This is a translation and synopsis of a lost Greek calendar compiled in Antioch between 362 and 381 which included early and late martyrs from both the East and the West. It is of great importance as one of the prime sources of the so-called *Martyrology of St. Jerome composed in Northern Italy at the middle of the 5th century.

From the 8th cent. on it became the custom to read the martyrology of the day at Prime during the public recitation of the Office. At this time the practice began of adding brief biographies to the names of the saints commemorated, giving rise to the so-called historical martyrologies. The best-known of these were compiled by Ven. Bede (8th cent.) and Rabanus Maurus, Florus, Ado, Usuard, and Erchembert (9th century). The added biographical details were taken as a rule from Scripture, the acts and legends of the martyrs, the *Ecclesiastical History* of Eusebius, and various writings of the Fathers. The martyrology of Ado, however, was of a different type. He claimed that it was based upon that of Florus and an old Roman martyrology, the *Martyrologium Romanum vetus,* which he discovered at Ravenna. H. Quentin has proved quite satisfactorily that this old Roman martyrology was in fact a forgery of Ado's own invention. His work is particularly unfortunate in that it was used extensively by *Usuard of St. Germain in compiling his own martyrology, which in turn became the basis for the Roman *Martyrology. BIBLIOGRAPHY: R. Aigrain, *L'Hagiographie* (1953) 11–106.

[M. J. COSTELLOE]

MARTYROLOGY, ROMAN, the official calendar of the feasts celebrated or commemorated in the Church of Rome and read at Prime in the public recitation of the Divine Office. During the Middle Ages various *martyrologies were used throughout the Church, but the most popular was that of *Usuard (9th cent.). In 1582, Gregory XIII, as a corollary to his reform of the Julian calendar, formed a commission under the presidency of Cardinal Sirleto to revise the martyrology of Usuard, then used in Rome, so that it could be given official approbation for the whole Church. After two preliminary texts had been published, a final edition was printed and approved by the Pope in his bull *Emendatio* of Jan. 14, 1584. The revisions and additions to the basic text were from Bede, Florus, Ado, the Greek menologies, and the calendars of individual churches. Two years later, under Sixtus V, the text was reprinted with some slight corrections and additions by Baronius. He also included a discussion of the martyrology and notes on the sources for the entries. In 1598 Baronius also supervised a republication of the martyrology. Since then, though remaining fundamentally the same, it has been frequently revised, notably under Urban VIII (1630), who introduced the names of recently canonized saints, Clement X (but not published until 1681, after his death), and Benedict XIV (1748). Researches made at the end of the 19th cent. and at the beginning of the 20th have shown that the Roman Martyrology is in need of radical revision. An attempt in this direction known as the *prima post typicam* edition made under Benedict XV but not published until 1924 under Pius XI was severely criticized by H. Quentin. It was approved by neither Benedict XV nor Pius XI. A general revision of the Roman Martyrology is in process at the present time. BIBLIOGRAPHY: R. Aigrain, *L'hagiographie* (1953), 91–99.

[M. J. COSTELLOE]

MARTYROLOGY OF ST. JEROME, a calendar of feasts celebrated in Rome, Africa, and the East compiled in the second half of the 5th cent. in northern Italy and revised *c.*600 in southern France, probably at Auxerre. All the extant MSS of this martyrology, in four different recensions, are from this Gallican revision. At the head of the mss are found two spurious letters, one addressed to, and the other from, St. Jerome. These were added to give authority to the work, and from them it has derived its name. In composing this work, the unknown author drew upon the local martyrology of Rome, a general martyrology of Africa, a general martyrology of the East much like the *Breviarium Syriacum,* some other local martyrologies, and a few literary sources, including Eusebius. The work was intended for use in the liturgy, but whether it was actually employed is unknown. It was certainly read later in monasteries as a book of edification. In addition to the feasts of the martyrs it includes notices on the dedication of churches and the consecration of bishops. The *Martyrologium Hieronymianum* is of great importance, not only because it has incorporated within it the most important early ecclesiastical calendars, but because it served as the foundation for the later historical martyrologies and thus eventually of the *Roman Martyrology still used in the Church. BIBLIOGRAPHY: R. Aigrain, *L'Hagiographie* (1953) 32–50.

[M. J. COSTELLOE]

MARTYRS, CULT OF. The veneration of those who voluntarily underwent death for their belief in Christ developed only slowly, a sublimation of the pagan cult of the dead coupled with a desire to retain communion with the martyrs and to obtain their intercession. Early victims of persecution seem to have been buried with only the observances customary for other Christians, including the ceremonial meal at the tomb common to pagan ritual. The earliest extant record of what was to become a universal custom is the account written at Smyrna *c.* 175 of the death of *Polycarp: ''We took up his bones . . . and interred them in a decent place. There the Lord will permit us . . . to assemble in rapturous joy and to celebrate his birthday—his martyrdom'' (18). This *dies natalis* assumed the importance originally attached to the anniversary of birth into this life. To accommodate the throngs that gathered to celebrate it when persecution was in abeyance, the faithful began to build churches over the tombs. Frequently the remains of the martyr were disposed directly under the altar, an arrangement that brought into relief the relation of the martyr's sacrifice to that of the altar and foreshadowed the decree of 1596 that every altar used for the Eucharistic Liturgy contain the relic of a martyr. At times the church was built in a safer or more populous place and the martyr's remains were transferred to it. Since Roman law forbade the disturbing of corpses, cloth that had been touched to the martyr's body was sometimes preserved with cultic honor instead of the actual remains. Other manifestations of the cult of the martyrs were the adornment of their tombs and churches with flowers and perfume; the burning of perpetual lamps; the insertion of their names into martyrologies; and in doubtful cases the affirmation by legal process of their right to the honors of martyrdom (*vindicatio*). With the rise of pilgrimages, veneration of the martyrs lost its provincial character. Ex-votos were disseminated widely along with the passions of the martyrs, the panegyrics of the great orators, and the poems of Prudentius and Paulinus of Nola so that by the 6th cent. the cult had become everywhere a component of the liturgy and continues so to the present time. BIBLIOGRAPHY: H. Leclercq, DACL 10.2:2359–2512; T. Klauser, *Christlicher Märtyrerkult* (1960).

[M. J. SUELZER]

MARTYRS, NORTH AMERICAN, see NORTH AMERICAN MARTYRS.

MARTYRS OF CÓRDOBA, see CÓRDOBA, MARTYRS OF.

MARTYRS OF ENGLAND AND WALES, those clergy and laity who sacrificed their lives for the Faith during the period 1535–1684 and who have been recognized by the Church for their heroic response to persecution. In England, the Crown began to move against the Catholic Church during the reign of Henry VIII. Henry did not break with Rome because of deep theological differences (he himself had attacked the teachings of Martin Luther) but rather because he desired to augment the strength of the monarchy. He dissolved his marriage to Catharine so that through union with Ann Boleyn he might secure a male heir to the throne. In 1534 he influenced Parliament to pass legislation declaring him supreme ruler in all matters, temporal and spiritual. In 1535 he seized 500 religious houses (the majority of which, contrary to popular myths, were not nests of decadence and corruption) and spread the wealth among the nobles and gentry whose gratitude might one day prove useful to the Crown. Henry's plan for the assimilation of Catholicism into royal jurisdiction encountered difficulty in 1535 when he sought from his subjects an oath declaring the King to be their spiritual, as well as temporal, leader. John Houghton, prior of the Carthusian monastery at Charterhouse, refused to recognize the authority of the king in spiritual affairs and thus became the first Catholic to go to the gallows, being drawn and quartered on May 4, 1535. During this early period of persecution Bp. John Fisher and Sir Thomas More, former Lord Chancellor, were perhaps the two most distinguished men to be martyred. In its rites, Henry's C of E did not differ radically from Catholicism but the state continued to execute men and women who could not with clear conscience follow the king's rule in religious affairs.

When Edward VI succeeded to the throne in 1547 he was but a child and consequently, his reign witnessed the de facto rule of the nobility. During this period (1547–53), the Anglican Church developed a character quite apart from traditional Catholicism, rejecting the doctrines of clerical celibacy and transubstantiation among others. The nobles were sympathetic to Catholics who still refused the oath of supremacy. The list of martyrs continued to grow.

When Mary became Queen in 1553, she sought to reestablish Catholicism. She repealed the Act of Supremacy and initiated a purge of Protestants in ranking positions. Of the 300 she executed, some were individuals who played lifelong at opportunistic politics and had at last erred as to the drift of the political tides. Others who were put to death were victims of religious intolerance and they suffered with firm conviction in the justness of their Protestant cause.

Mary reigned an unpopular monarch, even among Catholics, largely because she married the Spanish king, Philip II. When Elizabeth came to the throne in 1558, she enjoyed widespread support that allowed her to follow a relatively moderate path. Although she reenacted the Act of Supremacy in 1559, Elizabeth did not execute anyone for reasons of religion during her first decade on the throne. However, after Pius V excommunicated her in 1570, Elizabeth began an active campaign to destroy Catholicism in England. In that year she made it treasonous to bring any papal communications into the country; in 1581 she forbade the saying of the Mass; in 1585 she declared all foreign-trained priests in England to be traitors. Deteriorating relations with Spain during the decade of 1580 led to spurious charges of treason against various individuals (most notably Edmund Campion and the Welsh poet Richard Gwyn) who willingly acknowledged the sovereignty of Elizabeth in affairs of state. The Spanish threat culminated with the execution of 31 Catholics in 1588.

During the reign of the Stuart Kings (1603–84), Catholics suffered because of pressure on the Anglican Church from the right. Puritans, Calvinists, and Anabaptists found in the Church of England too many vestiges of Roman Catholicism. In order to assuage these sects, which exerted a political threat, the Crown oppressed the "papists" in the land. After Charles II was restored to the throne in 1660 he evidenced sympathy for the plight of the Catholic population, even to the point of issuing a declaration of religious freedom in 1672. However, a strong Parliament retained anti-Catholic beliefs and forced Charles to repeal the measure. Anti-Catholic propaganda reached its zenith in 1678 with the conspiracy of Titus Oates. With substantial evidence, Catholics throughout the land were accused of participating in this plot to destroy the government and the incidence of execution grew significantly.

The most famous martyr of this period was Oliver *Plunket, abp. and primate of Ireland, who was charged with plotting with the French and was executed in 1581. Even Charles II believed in his innocence but the King felt powerless to halt the execution.

An investigation into the lives and character of the men and women who died for the Faith during the period 1535–83 was initiated by Card. Manning, who sent a list of 353 names to Rome in 1874. The Congregation of Sacred Rites added six names to the petition. In 1886, the Congregation pronounced 54 of the individuals under examination had in effect been declared martyrs by Pope Gregory XIII, who had bestowed the honor upon them in 1584. In addition to the 54 already beatified, the Congregation announced in December 1886 that 261 were adjudged venerable and 44 had their cases resubmitted for further study. In 1889 a second list, containing 242 names was sent to Rome and the investigation broadened to include the period 1535–1684. In 1920 Abp. Plunket was beatified and canonized in 1975. In 1929 136 more were declared blessed. Sir Thomas *More and John *Fisher were canonized in 1935. In 1970 Pope Paul VI canonized 40 additional martyrs: John *Almond, Edmund *Arrowsmith, Ambrose *Barlow, John *Boste, Alexander *Briant, Edmund *Campion, Margaret *Clitherow, Philip *Evans, Thomas *Garnet, Edmund *Genings, Richard *Gwyn; John *Houghton, Philip *Howard, John *Jones, John *Kemble, Luke *Kirby, Robert *Lawrence, David *Lewis, Ann *Line, John *Lloyd, Cuthbert *Mayne; Henry *Morse, Nicholas *Owen, John *Paine, Polydore *Plasden, John *Plessington, Richard *Reynolds, John *Rigby, John *Roberts; Alban *Roe, Ralph Serwin, Robert *Southwell, John Southworth, John *Stone, John *Wall, Henry *Walpole, Margaret *Ward, Augustine *Webster, Swithun *Wells and Eustace *White. BIBLIOGRAPHY: R. Challoner, *Memoirs of Missionary Priests* (1741–42); J. H. Pollen, *Acts of the English Martyrs* (1891); C. Tigar, *Forty Martyrs of England and Wales* (1961); E. Waugh, *Edmund Campion, Jesuit and Martyr* (1946).

[R. J. BRADY]

MARTYRS OF THE COMMUNE, see COMMUNE, MARTYRS OF THE.

MARUCCHI, ORAZIO (1852–1931), Italian, Christian archeologist at Rome, follower of G. de *Rossi. He himself was the discoverer of the crypt of St. Valentine in the Via Flaminia. He was the director (1898–1922) of the *Nuovo bollettino de archeologia cristiana*; a professor at the Univ. of Rome, the College of the Propaganda, and at San Anselmo dei Sulpiziani. His courses there were published in *Éléments d'archéologie chrétienne* (3 v., 1900–03) and *Manuel d'archéologie chrétienne* (1906). While his claims were sometimes extreme, he did prodigious work and published extensively on both Christian and classical Roman archeological sites.

[T. C. O'BRIEN]

MARULIĆ, MARKO (1450–1524), Croatian literary figure. A pioneer in Croatian literature, M. wrote both in Latin and his native language. His approach was didactic in both prose and poetry. The Latin works esp. were widely read throughout Europe. Among them were *De institutione bene vivendi per exempla sanctorum* (1506) and *De humilitate et gloria Christi* (1519). In such vernacular works as *Istorija svete udovice Judit u versih hrvacki složna* (1521), an epic poem of classical structure, M. invokes the history of Judith as a symbol of opposition to the Turks. Another epic poem was *Istorija od Suzane*. N. set the style for Croatian literature with the elements of Christian inspiration, classical form, and the ever-present dread of the Turks.

[J. R. AHERNE]

MARUTHAS, ST. (d. before 420), bp. of Martyropolis (Maiferkat) in Mesopotamia. M. appealed to the Emperor Arcadius to use his influence with the Persian monarch in the interests of the Christians of Persia who had suffered grievously in the persecution under Shapur II (d. 380). As ambassador from the emperors Arcadius and Theodosius II to the Persian court in 399 and again in 408, he won the esteem of King Yezdigerd by his saintly life and also, reputedly, by his knowledge of medicine. He was permitted to return to his episcopal see with the relics of so many martyrs that it came to be called Martyropolis. His writings include *Acts of the Persian Martyrs* and a number of hymns. Some doubt exists as to the authenticity of certain works attributed to him. BIBLIOGRAPHY: Butler 4:489–490; J. M. Sauget, BiblSanct 8:1305–09.

[R. B. ENO]

MARUTHAS OF TAGRIT (*c.*565–649), Monophysite (Jacobite) maphrian (abp.) and delegate of the patriarch for the Jacobite Church in Persia. Born at Surzag near Baladh, he became a monk in 605 and taught at Mar Mattai Monastery near Mossul. Patriarch Athanasius I Gammala of Antioch consecrated M. in 628 or 629 as maphrian. To the existing 12 suffragan metropolitan sees he added three for Azerbaijan, Herat, and Segestan. One of the Syriac anaphoras is named after him. Fragments of his homilies have been preserved.

[J. MADEY]

MARVILLE, JEAN DE (d. 1389), Flemish sculptor who worked at Rouen for King Charles V, and at Dijon, for Philip the Bold of Burgundy. On his death Claus Sluter, one of Jean's former pupils, continued his work on the ducal tomb at the Chartreuse, Champnol, near Dijon, a key monument in the development of Burgundian sculpture. BIBLIOGRAPHY: A. Humbert, *La Sculpture sous les ducs de Bourgogne (1913)*.

[S. D. MURRAY]

MARX, KARL (1818–83), economic and social theoretician. Although M. was baptized in 1826 when his father became a Protestant, and he was sent to religious instruction classes, there is no evidence that religion ever played a positive role in his life, even before he became a professed atheist. He studied at the Univ. of Bonn and Berlin, giving special attention to philosophy and history, although he matriculated officially in the faculty of law. In 1841 M. submitted a doctoral dissertation comparing the materialist philosophies of Epicurus and Democritus. In a supplement to his thesis he defended the atheism of Epicurus. M. wanted a post as lecturer in philosophy but had to turn instead to journalism. In 1842 he became editor of the *Rhineland Gazette of Cologne*. Fiery editorials got him into frequent trouble with censors, and in 1843 he was dismissed and moved to Paris where he entered upon a lifelong collaboration with F. *Engels. Criticism of the Prussian government resulted in his expulsion in 1845 to Brussels. In 1848, the *Communist Manifesto* was published. Expelled again from Germany in 1849, he settled in London where he lived in reduced circumstances on a meager income from occasional writings and a pension from Engels. His later years were devoted to publishing, research, and efforts to organize workers. His chief works were: *Das Kapital* (3 v.—1, 1867; 2 and 3, ed. F. Engels, published posthumously, 1885–94); *Holy Family* (with Engels, 1843); *Economic and Philosophic Manuscripts* (1844); *German Ideology* (with Engels, 1845); and *Contribution to the Critique of Political Economy* (1859), all regarded as the classics of communism. BIBLIOGRAPHY: I. Berlin, *Karl Marx: His Life and Environment* (1948); J. Y. Calvez, *La Pensée de Karl Marx* (1956); H. P. Adams, *Karl Marx in His Earlier Writings* (1940); F. Conklin, "Marxian Philosophy of God," New Schol (Jan. 1954) 38–57.

[J. P. REID]

MARXISM, the philosophical system elaborated by Karl Marx, developed by Soviet theoreticians as *dialectical and historical materialism, and adopted as the official doctrine of world communism. Marxism's view of religion is an integral and important component. Marx entered the socialist movement already a confirmed atheist and when preparing to take over the Communist League, one of his first acts was to eliminate all who maintained an affinity to Christianity and socialism. Marxists have consistently enforced this rejection of all religious belief and practice. In the classics of Marxism, religion is mentioned only casually and nearly always in reference to some other problem. Yet the religious question is at the center of Marxism, which in this respect is quite Hegelian. The Marxist critique of religion, closely bound up with revolutionary practice, is extremely radical and at times impassioned. In its espousal of the Promethean attitudes to deity, Marxism seeks to promote man's dynamic self-sufficiency in nature. Reality is reduced entirely to this relationship to nature, in which human labor assumes a transforming power. The Hegelian absolute is replaced by society which is immersed in an evolving historical process. Marxist dialectics imparts a wholly this-worldly meaning to history; all social revolutions tend inevitably toward the realization of the whole of man-laboring-in-nature. Only the timid or insincere naturalist or humanist would allow any divine actuality beyond nature or distinct from human intelligence and labor.

For Marx, L. A. Feuerbach had completed in principle the antitheist critique, hence it would be a waste of time and energy to mount a full-scale attack on religion. M.'s relatively few allusions to arguments for the reality of God fault these proofs on several counts: the *ontological argument is logically fallacious, a mere tautology or definitional assertion; every such proof is only a reflection of human consciousness, a proof rather of the nonexistence of God. Man projects an illusory idea of himself and infers from the emptiness and evil of this world to a divine Being, the guarantor of a better existence. In order to posit the question of creation, the questioner must contradict himself, either annihilating himself or dissolving the premises, which are the real and existing beings that constitute the universe. Marxism affirms the completely finite character of human intelligence, a function of man's finite condition, but understands this in terms of Feuerbach's concept of abstraction. Religious alienation is central to Marxist thinking and is criticized on two levels. Every sort of religious attitude, however private or subjective, is an illusion and a sickness and is exposed as false and unrealistic. Feuerbach's critique is inadequate, however, for he failed to see religion as the ideological expression of an underlying and more pervasive socioeconomic alienation. Marxism is antitheistic as well as antireligious, although atheism is here incorporated into the wider context of opposition to all forms of alienation. Antireligion and antitheism merge into a critique of political economy. Only radical social change will render religion finally meaningless. BIBLIOGRAPHY: A. G. Meyer, *Marxism: The Unity of Theory and Practice* (1954); R. N. Carew-Hunt, *Marxism: Past and Present* (1954); L. Dupré, *Philosophical Foundations of Marxism* (1966); A. Schaff,

Marxism and the Human Individual (1970); D. A. Drennan. *Karl Marx's Communist Manifesto* (1972); *Guide to Marxist Philosophy; An Introductory Bibliography* (ed. Boehenski et al., 1972).

[J. P. REID]

MARY, BLESSED VIRGIN, the mother of Jesus Christ. She is here considered from the viewpoints of biblical witness and RC theology.

In the Bible. Although the thrust of OT messianism is Christological, some passages refer also to the mother of the Messiah: the 'almâ-mother of Emmanuel (Is 7.14; cf. Mt 1.23); the woman who is to give birth (Mic 5.1–3; cf. Mt 2.4–6); the woman whose offspring crushes the serpent's head (Gen 3.15; cf. Jn 19.26–27 and Rev 12). Modern scholars do not agree on the precise biblical sense in which such passages refer to Mary.

Facts about Mary in the NT are relatively few but usually significant. Most of the material is concentrated in the independent gospel traditions of Mt 1–2 and Lk 1.26–2.52. Mary, a virgin living at Nazareth, is espoused to Joseph. He certainly, she possibly, is of Davidic descent (Lk 1.26–27; cf. Rom 1.3). The couple were not yet living together (Mt 1.18–25) when Mary's consent to become the mother of the Messiah, "Son of the Most High," is solicited by an angelic messenger. She is puzzled; she has resolved (vowed?) to remain a virgin. When assured that the conception would be effected by God, she humbly agrees (Lk 1.26–38; cf. Jn 1.13). Joseph's subsequent predicament concerning the pregnancy is also resolved by an angelic messenger (Mt 1.18–23). After the Annunciation Mary visits her relative Elizabeth and gives voice to the Magnificat (Lk 1.39–56). In response to a census decree, Joseph takes Mary to Bethlehem, where she brings forth Jesus "her firstborn son" (Lk 2.1–7). Neighboring shepherds visit the newborn child, and Mary ponders the significance of all that is happening (Lk 2.8–20). Forty days after the birth, Mary and Joseph take the infant to the Temple for her rite of purification and his presentation to the Lord. Mary receives from aged Simeon the prediction that the infant would be a sign of contradiction (Lk 2.22–38). Later, Magi from the East visit the child and Mary, and offer gifts in homage (Mt 2.11). Then, to protect the boy from harm at King Herod's hands, Joseph takes him and Mary to Egypt until notice of Herod's death (Mt 2.13–15), after which they return to Nazareth, where they settle down (Mt 2.19–23; Lk 2.39,51). When Jesus is 12 years old he visits Jerusalem at Passover with Mary and Joseph but remains there unknown to them as they begin the return trip. After searching several days they find him with the teachers in the Temple but do not comprehend the reasons he gives for his actions (Lk 2.41–50).

Further references to Mary are infrequent. During the public ministry of her son, she is responsible for his first miracle, the changing of water into wine at a wedding feast in Cana (Jn 2.1–11), after which she accompanies him to Capernaum (v. 12). People know her as the mother of Jesus (Mk 3.31; 6.3). In two enigmatic passages she is apparently praised by her son as a model of faith (Lk 11.27–28; cf. 8.19–21). She stands beneath the cross on Calvary and is entrusted by her crucified son to the care of the beloved Disciple (Jn 19.25–27). She is last found in the community at prayer in the Upper Room after the Ascension (Acts 1.14). Paul's writings contain but one passing reference to her (Gal 4.4). Many scholars find a final significant reference to Mary in the "woman" of Rev 12.

From her actions, mainly at Bethlehem, Jerusalem (Temple, Calvary, Upper Room), Nazareth, and Cana, from the only words recorded of her (Lk 1.34,38,46–55; 2.48; Jn 2.3–5), and from the remarks made about her by others (e.g., Lk 2.19,33–35; 11.27–28), Mary is shown explicitly as the mother of Jesus the Messiah, Son of God, and as having conceived and borne him virginally by the power of God. Explicitly or implicitly, the Bible also shows Mary as closely associated with Jesus in the Redemption and as maternally related to the members of his kingdom, the Church. She is a woman of piety, kindness, humility, obedience, and of deep faith, despite the unusual sorrows associated with her unique vocation in life.

Nevertheless, the wealth of devotion to the Blessed Virgin that developed from the 4th cent. onward is in such striking contrast to the unmistakable reticence of the NT about her, despite the references cited above, that some explanation of this seems called for. Recently it has been argued that this reticence would have been necessary so long as the kinsmen of Jesus were still alive. Not only James, the "brother of the Lord," but several more of these brethren of the Lord (cf. Mt 13.55; Mk 3.31–35) would have become Christians (cf. Acts 1.14), and may have claimed special privileges or authority in the Church on the grounds of their physical relationship with him. They may even have formed a "party of Christ" such as that alluded to by St. Paul (cf. 1 Cor 1.12). To counteract these false claims the early Christian preachers, the initiators of the traditions now enshrined in the NT, would have insisted that not physical kinship but faith and obedience were the basis for true union with Christ (cf. Lk 8.19–21). This would also explain the reticence with regard to his personal relationship with his mother, and in particular the strange form of address, "woman," which he is represented as using to her (cf. Jn 2.4; 19.25), a form which, though certainly not disrespectful, is without parallel as between a son and his mother at the ordinary human level. At all events, the two basic tenets of Christian belief about Mary, namely that she became mother of God and that this took place while she was still a virgin, are asserted unequivocally in the New Testament. The fact of the virgin birth is brought out very clearly in the infancy narratives of Matthew (cf. 1.18–25) and Luke (cf. 1.26–38), and this is manifestly the point of explaining in such detail the circumstances of her marriage or, more probably, betrothal, to Joseph, and her rejoinder to the angel at the Annunciation, etc.

With regard to her understanding of the significance of what was taking place in and through her two somewhat different traditions appear to lie behind the existing NT narratives. The first, which is probably closer to the literal historical facts, represents her as incompletely aware of the significance of the events. This is brought out in the story of the finding in the Temple (cf. "Son, why have you done this to us? Behold your father and I have been looking for you anxiously." Lk 2.41–52), in the episode at Cana (Jn 2.1–5), and perhaps too in the fact that she seeks Jesus and is unable to divert him even momentarily from his mission (cf. Mk 3.31–35; Lk 8.19–21). This incomplete awareness may also be indirectly reflected in Luke's statement that she "kept" and "pondered" the events in her heart, and that her relationship with Jesus seems to have been regarded as completely natural by her fellow villagers and others at Nazareth (Mt 13.55).

In the other tradition (in which the element of theological interpretation has probably played a stronger part) her inspired utterances are recorded, expressing the messianic significance of the events, and these events are related in such a way as unmistakably to bring out their messianic meaning. This applies to the visit to Elizabeth (Lk 1.39–45) and Mary's own Magnificat, to the actual accounts of the birth at Bethlehem (cf. Mt 1.18–25; Lk 2.1–20), the visit of the Magi (Mt 2.1–12), the purification and canticle of Simeon (Lk 2.22–35), the flight into Egypt (Mt 2.13–15), and return to Nazareth (Mt 2.19–23). In this tradition, therefore, she is first and foremost the mother of the Messiah, and she and others who "wait for the consolation of Israel" recognize this as the significance of her own virginal motherhood.

Finally, Jn 19.25–27 records her presence at the Crucifixion, when Jesus gives her to John, while Acts 1.14 informs us that she remained with the Disciples in the days leading up to the bestowal of the Spirit.

In RC Theology. In his encyclical *Munificentissimus Deus* of Nov. 1, 1950, Pius XII aptly summarized RC doctrine about Mary: "The revered Mother of God, from all eternity joined in a hidden way with Jesus Christ in one and the same decree of predestination, immaculate in her conception, a most perfect virgin in her divine motherhood, the noble associate of the divine Redeemer who has won a complete triumph over sin and its consequences, was finally granted, as the supreme culmination of her privileges, that she should be preserved free from the corruption of the tomb and that, like her Son, having overcome death, she might be taken up body and soul to the glory of heaven where, as queen, she sits in splendor at the right hand of her Son, the immortal King of the ages." He stresses the four great privileges of Mary that have been formally defined: her divine maternity—that she is truly the mother of God, because mother of Jesus Christ, who is true God and true man; her Immaculate Conception—that from the first moment of her own conception she was preserved free from all stain of original sin; her perpetual virginity—that she was a virgin before, during, and after the birth of Christ; and her Assumption—that after the completion of her earthly life she was assumed body and soul into the glory of heaven. The Pope also referred to other Marian beliefs not formally defined, e.g., that Mary is queen of heaven and earth, sharing her Son's dominion in a real but analogous, subordinate way; and that she is associated with her Son in the Redemption.

Catholic tradition sees Mary's role in the Redemption as twofold. She is coredemptrix, in that she cooperated indirectly and subordinately with her Son in the objective Redemption, willingly devoting her whole life to the service of her Son, and suffering and sacrificing with Him beneath the cross. She is mediatrix of all graces because of her cooperation in subjective Redemption, using her maternal intercession in the application of Redemption's grace to mankind. Tradition likewise attests to Mary's spiritual maternity: in becoming Christ's physical mother she also became the spiritual mother of all Christians, Christ's brethren. The theme of Mary as a type of the Church in virginal motherhood and faith has been emphasized in recent decades (see Vat II ConstChurch ch. 8). Because of her dignity as mother of God, the Church encourages special devotion to her (hyperdulia)—essentially less than the adoration due her Son, but uniquely superior to the veneration given to other saints. BIBLIOGRAPHY: S. Garofalo, *Mary in the Bible* (tr. T. J. Tobin, 1961); K. Rahner, LTK 7:25–28; J. de Fraine, EDB 1462–72; B. Rinaldi, *Mary of Nazareth, Myth or History?* (tr. M. F. Ingoldsby, 1966); DBT 297–303; C. P. Ceroke, NCE 9:335–347; E. Dublanchy, DTC 9:2339–2474; C. Friethoff, *Complete Mariology* (1958); E. Schillebeeckx, *Mary, Mother of the Redemption* (tr. N. D. Smith, 1964); C. Vollert, *Theology of Mary* (1965); Carol Mariol.

[D. J. BOURKE; E. MAY]

MARY, BLESSED VIRGIN, DEVOTION TO. As described in Vatican II ConstChurch ch. 8, Catholic devotion to Mary is based upon her role in the history of salvation as Mother of the Incarnate Word and thus Mother of God. Devotion to her (hyperdulia) has traditionally been carefully distinguished from worship offered to God (latria) and devotion shown the other saints (dulia). The Council warned against both exaggeration and indifference. Acknowledgement of her divine motherhood historically led to recognition of her unique role, invocation seeking her prayer and assistance, and the effort to imitate her prompt obedience to God's will and intimacy with her Son. The foundations of Marian devotion are thus soundly based in Scripture.

Patristic writers frequently presented Mary as the "new Eve," closely associated with her Son, the New Adam, in humankind's redemption (Justin, Irenaus; 2nd century). She was also noted as an example to dedicated virgins (Athanasius, Ambrose; 4th century). But the most important of her titles is that ascribed in the dogmatic definition of the Council of Ephesus in 431, calling her *theotokos* or "God-bearer." It is this role which accounts for her mention in the early creeds. Central, then, to Marian devotion in the first 7 cent. is her holiness as Mother of God; the devotion from its beginnings was thus Christocentric, as was the definition at Ephesus.

The liturgical cult, likewise Christocentric, began in the East, with the oldest feast that of the "remembrance of Mary" patterned on the martyrs' "birthdays" (from the 5th century?); this formed part of the Christmas cycle and came to be celebrated on January first. The feast of the Annunciation, first celebrated in Advent and then on March 25 as the liturgy came to be historicized, dates from the mid-6th century; the feasts of the Dormition (later the Assumption) on August 15, the Nativity on September 8, and the Presentation on February 2 are all from the late 6th century.

These Marian feasts were brought to the West by Oriental monks in the 7th cent., but Mary was already mentioned in the Roman Canon (the *Communicantes* prayer) in the 6th century. Marian devotion grew rapidly in the medieval West, with Mary coming to be regarded as queen, spiritual mother, and intercessor. In the 15th century the scapular devotion became popular, the Hail Mary took on its present form (the rosary is earlier, though not in its present form), and various litanies (esp. that of Loretto) came into being. It was during the High Middle Ages with emphasis on the saints (based on Christian community, the "communion of saints") that Marian devotion sometimes seemed to eclipse the role of Christ, the unique mediator, often regarded as crucified redeemer and distant judge. Mary's own suffering and compassion at the Crucifixion became a favorite artistic subject and her role as heavenly intercessor was emphasized. Numerous liturgical feasts were added to the calendar and spurious relics received much attention.

Neither Luther nor Calvin rejected devotion to Mary, but both insisted upon scriptural simplicity, with an emphasis on her humility and obedience and her role as first of believers. But the Reformers' rejection of prayer to the saints, Trent's defense of the practice, and subsequent polemics led to Marian devotion's being a hallmark of the difference between Catholicism and Protestantism and to frequent exaggeration of the devotions during the 17th and 18th centuries.

Nineteenth-century devotion often centered on shrines built to mark apparitions of Mary: LaSalette (1846), Lourdes (1858), Knock (1879). In the 20th century Fatima (1917) also became an important center of pilgrimage. While all of these have been approved by the Church as fostering prayer, penitence, and sacramental participation, Catholics are not required to believe in any such "private" revelations. The dogmatic definitions of the Immaculate Conception (1854) and the Assumption (1950) further fostered devotion to Mary. But in his encyclical on the liturgy, *Mediator Dei* (1947), Pope Pius XII proposed the liturgy as the ultimate norm for Marian devotion and in *Ad caeli reginam* (1954) he called for correct balance in such devotion. Both of these points have been repeated by Vatican II and by Pope Paul VI (*Ecclesiam suam,* 1964) who calls Mary "Mother of the Church." Recent years have seen declining interest in many formerly popular Marian devotions which were once the primary form of vernacular communal prayer. But the contemporary scriptural, pastoral, and ecumenical reassessment of Marian devotion has only strengthened its foundations while showing the need for more authentic contemporary expressions of that devotion. Attention has also been given to Mary as a model for contemporary women, as a pattern for Christian attitudes on sexuality, and by some as revealing the "feminine" aspects of God. BIBLIOGRAPHY: H. Graef, *Mary: A History of Doctrine and Devotion* (1963); A. Greeley, *Mary Myth* (1977); R. Laurentin, *Mary's Place in the Church* (1965); E. Schillebeeckx, *Mary, Mother of the Redemption* (1964); O. Semmelroth, *Mary Archetype of the Church* (1963).

[J. DALLEN]

MARY, BLESSED VIRGIN, MOTHERHOOD OF, see MOTHERHOOD OF MARY, SPIRITUAL.

MARY, BLESSED VIRGIN, QUEENSHIP OF, the RC teaching that in the kingdom of Christ's grace, Mary, mother of Jesus Christ the King, shares her Son's dominion in a real but subordinate and analogous way. Sacred Scripture at times implicitly favors this role of Mary (e.g., Gen 3.15; Lucan Nativity account, esp. Lk 1.32–33,42–43; Jn 2.1–11; Rev 12.1–18). Tradition from ancient times has addressed her in terms like Patroness, Lady, Queen. The liturgy honors her as queen of heaven and earth, as have the popes repeatedly, esp. Pius XII. Mary's titles to queenship are her divine maternity (mother of Christ, the King, who is God and man), and "right of conquest" (the intrinsic role she played, esp. on Calvary, in her King-Son's work of Redemption). Her queenly power is coextensive with, yet subordinate to, the royal power of her Son. She is traditionally described as the sovereign suppliant, the royal dispenser of grace and mercy, ruling with a mother's love. Theologians discuss whether Mary's queenship is like Christ's kingship mainly because of her role as coredemptrix, or because of her maternal power over the heart of her King-Son through universal intercession. In any case her vast involvement in the kingdom of grace adds new dimension to her other titles of Spiritual Mother and Mediatrix. BIBLIOGRAPHY: E. R. Carroll, NCE 9:386–387; *idem, Marian Studies* 4 (1953); C. Friethoff, *Complete Mariology* (1958) 270–282.

[E. MAY]

MARY, DAUGHTERS OF (ESCOLAPIAS), (SP; Piarist Sisters or Religious of the Pious Schools), pontifical congregation, international in character, founded (1847) at Barcelona, Spain (Diocese of Gerona) by Paula Montal (d. 1889). Leo XIII gave approval (1887). With the Piarist Augustin Casanovas, she adapted to women the *Constitutions* of the *Piarists (Clerks Regular of the Pious Schools [Escolapios]) founded by St. *Joseph Calasanctius (1617) for the education of the poor. The Daughters spread through three European countries, and South America: Argentina, Brazil, Chile, Colombia; and went also to Cuba and Japan. The motherhouse is in Rome; membership (1975) was 1,004 sisters in 83 houses. BIBLIOGRAPHY: M. P. Moriones, NCE 9:393, A. Pugliese, EncCatt 5:1276–77.

[M. R. BROWN]

MARY, GOSPEL OF THE BIRTH OF, see APOCRYPHA (NT) 34.

MARY, ST., MARTYR, see ARIADNE, ST.

MARY DE CERVELLÓ (1230–90), Spanish foundress of the Mercedarians (Sisters of Our Lady of Ransom). Born at Barcelona into nobility and educated at home, she took a vow of chastity at 18 and imposed on herself the obligation of wearing the habit of the Mercedarian friars. After she founded the Mercedarian nuns, she became renowned for service to the poor and afflicted. She was known as *Sor María del Socors* because of her kindness to the sick and her reported miraculous appearances to seamen in peril. (She is often depicted holding an oar or a ship.) Her body was displayed for public veneration (1904 and 1939) after having been found incorrupt. BIBLIOGRAPHY: C. M. Aherne, NCE 9:387; V. Ignelzi, BiblSanct 8:1044–45.

[J. R. RIVELLO]

MARY OF EGYPT, ST. (5th cent.), penitent. The earliest account of M. is found in the life of St. Cyriacus by *Cyril of Scythopolis. Later Byzantine hagiographers developed a more elaborate version of the legend according to which M. as a young woman had led a life of sin in Alexandria. Going on a pilgrimage to Jerusalem out of curiosity, she was converted and went into the wilderness beyond the Jordan, where for 47 years she lived in solitude doing penance for her sins. After these many years of penance, she crossed the river by walking on the water to receive communion from a priest called Zosimus, and on the evening of the same day she died. BIBLIOGRAPHY: A. Amore, EncCatt 8:120–121; Butler 2:14–16; J. M. Sauget, BiblSanct 8:981–991.

[R. B. ENO]

MARY OF JESUS, see ÁGREDA, MARY OF.

MARY MAGDALENE, ST., a native of the village of Magdala on the western side of the Sea of Galilee. Luke identifies her with one out of whom Jesus had cast seven demons, but this need not be interpreted to mean she had been a sinner; even if she had been truly possessed, this could have been without fault of her own, and the expression may well have meant no more than that she had been the victim of some serious mental disorder. In gratitude for her cure, she ministered to Jesus as he moved about preaching. She accompanied him on his last journey to Jerusalem, witnessed the Crucifixion, and followed his body to its entombment. She saw the empty tomb and, according to Jn 20.11–18, was the first to see the risen Christ. Western piety has confused her with the repentant sinner, whose name Luke did not mention (Lk 7.37–50) and also with Mary of Bethany, sister of Lazarus and Martha. A legend unsupported by any reliable evidence has it that she was transported with Lazarus and Martha to S. France where they engaged in the evangelization of Provence. BIBLIOGRAPHY: Butler 3:161–163; EDB 1472–74; V. Saker, BiblSanct 8:1078–1104; for iconography, M. C. Celletti, BiblSanct 8:1104–07; J. E. Fallon, NCE 9:387–389; for a critical view of her presence in Provence, H. Leclercq, DACL 8:2038–86.

[M. A. MCNAMARA]

MARY MAZZARELLO, ST., see MAZZARELLO, MARIA DOMENICA, ST.

MARY OF OIGNIES, ST. (1177–1213), Flemish Beguine and mystic. Married when she was 14, by mutual agreement she and her husband lived poorly, in continence, and in charitable service esp. to lepers. Later she went to the Beguinage at Oignies to avoid the attention aroused by report of her visions and miracles. Her spiritual director there, James de Vitry, an Augustinian canon, attests to her sanctity. BIBLIOGRAPHY: G. Geenen, BiblSanct 8:1018–25; Butler 2:623–626.

MARY OF ST. JOSEPH SALAZAR (1548–1603), Spanish nun, known chiefly for her association with St. St. Teresa of Ávila. Born of a noble family in Toledo, M. accompanied the great mystic and reformer to the new Carmelite foundation of Beas in 1565 and the following year went with her to Seville. In 1571 M. took her vows in the order. She was responsible for founding the Lisbon house in 1588, but in 1603 was transferred to the new establishment at Talavera. Her writings, published more than 3 cent. after her death, are valuable primarily for the further light they shed on St. Teresa.

[E. M. GATES]

MARY OF ST. THERESA PETIJT (Sister Mary of St. Teresa; 1628–77), Carmelite mystic and exponent of the Marian life. After two experiences with religious communitarian living, she took the vows of the Carmelite Third Order Secular and submitted her devotional life to a spiritual director. From 1657 to her death she lived in Malines (Belgium) as a recluse under the strictest Carmelite regimen. Constant contemplation of the Virgin Mary's virtues led her to view Mary as a means through which God himself could be known and in whom he was actually reflected. The progress of her spiritual growth can be traced in her autobiography, begun in 1668.

[E. M. GATES]

MARY STUART, QUEEN OF SCOTS (1542–87). Born in Scotland the heir of James V, who died soon after her birth, M. was sent to France to be raised by her mother's family, the prominent Guises, while her mother remained in Scotland as regent. A beautiful young girl, highly educated, full of charm, she became the ideal princess at the French court. She was married at 16 to the Dauphin, son of Henry II of France, whose death in 1559 made her Queen Consort. Her husband King Francis died a year later, leaving Mary a widow at 18. When Elizabeth ascended the English throne in 1558, Mary Stuart was next in line, and to Catholics, who regarded Elizabeth as illegitimate, the rightful ruler of England. This circumstance determined Elizabeth's lifelong enmity and conspiracy against Mary. She returned to Scotland as queen in 1561 and thus embarked on a reign of turbulent conflict with the Scottish nobles and John *Knox who hated her for her Frenchness and Catholicism. From the beginning, M. had two primary objectives: to rule strongly and to restore the old faith to Scotland. She was doomed to fail in both, largely because of the betrayal she encountered on every side. Her marriage to Lord Darnley was foolish; he plotted her death, murdered her friend and secretary David Rizzio, and was despised by all his contemporaries. M. turned to the Earl of Bothwell, a Protestant but friendly to the Queen. There is no real evidence that they were lovers or that she was implicated in the murder of Darnley. Foolishly she married Bothwell within 3 months of Darnley's death and this was ultimately her downfall. They were parted forever by the agitation of the jealous Scottish nobles in 1567. Bothwell went into exile and imprisonment and M. to prison, where she was deposed. Again through fatal imprudence, she sought refuge in England and protection by Elizabeth. She was imprisoned for 18 years by her cousin, tried by an English court in flagrant violation of her rights as a royal person and rightful Queen of Scotland. Her son, James V of Scotland, who was to become James I of England, raised no objection. On February 8, 1587, she was executed at Fotheringay Castle, Northants. Her motto "In my end is my beginning" sums up the tragic fate of a passionate, if wilful, and beautiful woman of great grace, who except for a brief wavering with Bothwell, was an ardent champion of Catholicism, and who died with unsurpassed dignity and courage. BIBLIOGRAPHY: A. Fraser, *Mary, Queen of Scotts* (1969).

[J. R. AHERNE]

MARY TUDOR (1516–58), **QUEEN OF ENGLAND** from 1553. Daughter of King Henry VIII and Catherine of Aragon, M. was only 12 when her father began divorce proceedings, and she incurred his disfavor by her allegiance to her mother. In 1533 she was pronounced technically illegitimate after Abp. Cranmer declared Henry's marriage to Catherine invalid. Upon the birth of her half-sister, the future Elizabeth I, M. was also denied the title Princess of Wales. In 1536, under compulsion, she signed a statement acknowledging that her deceased mother's marriage had been unlawful and that the Pope had no authority. When her half-brother became King, as *Edward VI, in 1547, his advisers attempted to make M. conform to the reformed Church of England, but without complete success. In 1553 they were able to persuade the dying Edward to set aside M.'s right to the throne for fear it would lead to a Catholic restoration. Accordingly, Lady Jane Grey was treasonably proclaimed Queen after Edward's death. Within a fortnight, however, M. marched on London with heavy support and made good her claim to the throne. Her principal adviser, Card. Pole, urged her to overcome schism and heresy at all costs; but she proceeded slowly. In her first year as Queen she induced Parliament to nullify the religious legislation of Edward's reign. In 1554 Henry's legislation was also revoked. She then set out to revitalize Catholicism. Though lenient by nature, she caused 300 persons to be executed for opposition to Catholicism during her reign. Her unhappy marriage to Philip II of Spain, the loss of Calais, and the Pope's dismissal of Card. Pole saddened her final days. BIBLIOGRAPHY: J. J. O'Connor, NCE 9:391–393, with bibliog.; W. C. Richardson, *Mary Tudor: The White Queen* (1969).

MARY AND JOSEPH, DAUGHTERS OF (DMJ), pontifical congregation founded at Olost-Gand, Belgium (1817) by Canon Constant Wilhem Van Crombrugghe (1789–1865). International, they came to the U.S. (1926), where the American provincialate is at Rancho Palos Verdes, Calif., with (1977) 88 professed and 2 novices; they serve in the Archdioceses of Los Angeles and San Francisco, and the Dioceses of New Mexico and San Diego. The *Constitutions* were approved (1891); the generalate is in Rome, total membership (1975) was 1,102 in 119 houses. They also have houses in Canada, Mexico, Brazil, Africa, Ireland, and England. They teach primary classes through high school and conduct boarding schools, staff hospitals, engage in social work, and conduct a retreat house. BIBLIOGRAPHY: M. C. Cotter, NCE 4:654; A. Pugliese, EncCatt 5:1274.

[M. R. BROWN]

MARY AND MARTHA OF BETHANY, two sisters who received Jesus into their home (Lk 10.38–42), whose brother Lazarus Jesus raised from the dead (Jn 11.5). Jesus praised Mary because she preferred to sit at his feet (the attitude of a disciple). Martha, however, kept to the traditional role of a woman which was to provide hospitality. Martha's confession of faith (Jn 11.27), like that of Peter (Mt 16.16), is a pattern for Christians. BIBLIOGRAPHY: J. E. Fallon, NCE 9:393–394.

[J. A. GRASSI]

MARY, HELP OF CHRISTIANS, DAUGHTERS OF (FMA: Salesian Sisters of St. John Bosco), a pontifical missionary congregation, international in character, founded by St. John *Bosco (1815–88) and St. Maria Domenica *Mazzarello (1837–81) in Italy (1872). Established in the U.S. (1908), they have here (1977) 341 sisters. World membership was (1975) 17,957 in 1,429 houses. Their mission is principally with youth, in the educational, catechetical, and missionary apostolates, to bring them to God "through religion, reason, and loving kindness." They teach in elementary schools through college, conduct recreational centers and hospices for working girls, staff orphanages, and sponsor retreats. They serve in 57 countries on 6 continents; their generalate is in Rome. Five years after their founding they went to South America. In the U.S. a provincialate is at Haledon, New Jersey. BIBLIOGRAPHY: S. Mattei, EncCatt 5:1274; T. P. McCarthy, *Challenge for Now* (1974) 192–193.

[M. R. BROWN]

MARYLAND, a Middle Atlantic state, admitted to the Union (1788) as the 7th state. The area was given to George *Calvert, first Lord Baltimore, who died before a charter could be granted. He was a RC as was his son Cecil, to whom a proprietary charter was granted (1632). A group of about 200 persons, including both Catholics and Protestants, sailed for Maryland where they landed after a voyage of 4 months (1634). St. Mary's became the first settlement in Maryland and its capital until 1694. Among the early laws adopted in the colony was the famous 1649 Act Concerning Religion, which guaranteed religious toleration to all but non-Trinitarians. After large numbers of Puritans, mostly from Virginia, settled around the present-day capital city of Annapolis, conflicts between Protestants and Catholics developed into a civil war. The Puritans were victorious (1654) and succeeded in repealing the Toleration Act. Following the Glorious Revolution of 1688, Maryland became a royal colony and the Anglican Church was established.

Jesuit missionaries served Maryland from the start. They founded the first church in Baltimore, St. Peter's, where John *Carroll, vicar apostolic and first bp. of the U.S., maintained his residence (1786–1815). By that date there were three parishes and about 10,000 Catholics in Maryland. Baltimore was the only see in the U.S. until 1808, and the only metropolitan see until 1846. Its preeminence was reflected in the numerous provincial councils held there (1829–69). Three other Councils of *Baltimore (1852, 1866, and 1884) were legally plenary.

Carroll's more notable successors included F. P. *Kenrick, who became the sixth abp. of Baltimore (1851). After presiding over the First Plenary Council (1852), Kenrick encouraged parish schools, promoted education generally, and won a reputation as a moral theologian. He died (1863) and was followed by M. J. *Spalding. Remaining neutral during the Civil War, Spalding supplied chaplains for both Federal and Confederate troops. He completed Baltimore's cathedral, promoted the St. Vincent de Paul Society, and presided over the Second Plenary Council (1866).

In 1877 James *Gibbons became the eighth archbishop. Until the creation of the office of apostolic delegate (1893), Gibbons served as the central official of the American Church. In this capacity he presided (1884) over the Third Plenary Council, which created The *Catholic Univ. of America. Once he became cardinal (1886), Gibbons, in addition to his duties as abp., was involved in handling all the major problems involving the American Church. He died in 1921 and was succeeded by M. J. *Curley, a champion of education, who opened more than 65 new schools and supported such new institutions as St. Mary's Seminary and St. Charles College, Catonsville, Maryland. F. P. *Keough became the 11th abp. of Baltimore (1947). During his episcopacy he served the NCWC as head of its education, legal, and social action departments. To serve the half-million Catholics of his archdiocese, he built a home for the aged (Stella Maris), a residence for deprived children (Villa Maria), and supported the beginning of an infant home (St. Vincent's). He also oversaw construction of Baltimore's Cathedral of Mary Our Queen. After years of declining health, Keough died (1961) and was succeeded by L. J. Shehan, a native of Baltimore. A cardinal 1965–74, Abp. Shehan involved himself in problems of social reform and has supported ecclesiastical renewal in the spirit of *Vatican Council II. Abp. William Borders succeeded to the see after Card. Shehan's resignation in 1974.

In 1976 Maryland's Catholics numbered 454,414, or 19.2% of the total state population. The major Protestant denominations are the Methodist Church, concentrated heavily in the Eastern Shore region, with 8.5% of the total pop. in 1971; the Episcopal Church, with 1.9%; and the United Lutheran Church in America, with the same percentage. Other Protestant groups comprised 11.4% of the population. The Jewish pop. (1968) was 177,115, or 4.5%. There are 4 Catholic colleges in Maryland, with a total enrollment of 7,144 students. More than 13,326 students attend the state's 25 Catholic high schools, while 34,543 pupils are enrolled in 94 Catholic elementary schools. BIBLIOGRAPHY: J. T. Ellis, *Life of James Cardinal Gibbons* (2 v., 1952); R. Walsh and W. L. Fox, *Maryland: A History, 1632–1974* (1974); G. Petrie, *Church and State in Early Maryland* (1892, repr. 1973).

[J. L. MORRISON; R. M. PRESTON]

MAS, ADRIEN, see EXUPÉRIEN, FRÈRE.

MASACCIO (1401–28), Florentine painter. As first major artist to continue Giotto's tradition, he is regarded as one of the founders of modern painting and celebrated for his paintings at the Brancacci Chapel, Sta. Maria del Carmine, Florence (1425), the famous *Expulsion from Paradise, Tribute Money* with self-portrait; and the *Trinity with Donors* (1425, Sta. Maria Novella, Florence). His style, which heralds the High Renaissance, is characterized by a solid three-dimensional form, monumentality of figure, a single source of light, and spatial recession in linear and aerial perspectives. M.'s works have power, tremendous emotional expressiveness (Shivering man in *St. Peter Baptizing*) in a generalized concept that gives universal significance to his statements. Adding grace of posture to figures, and atmospheric distance, M. extends Giotto's conceptions. BIBLIOGRAPHY: C. Gilbert, *Masaccio* (1969).

[L. A. LEITE]

MASAMUNE, HAKUCHŌ (1879–1962), Japanese critic, novelist. A Buddhist, M. came under the influence of Protestant Christianity and was baptized in 1897, but abandoned Christian practice 4 years later. As novelist, critic, and student of culture M. showed Christian influence even after he abandoned Christianity. Among his novels were *Kotoshi no aki* (1959), dealing with death; *Umare zarishi naraba* (1924), which seeks the meaning of life; and *Doko e* (1908), a study of anxiety. An essay on Christianity was *Kanzō Uchimura* (1950).

[J. R. AHERNE]

MASARYK TOMÁŠ GARRIGUE (1850–1937), statesman, intellectual. Of a Catholic Czech family, M. early abandoned Christian practice. Professor at the Czech Univ. in Prague, he became an influence in Czech intellectual life. Founder of the periodical *Athenaeum* (1883), he achieved fame for his position against anti-Semitism. M. was a liberal who believed the Catholic Church out of step with the modern age and politically rightist. He sat in the Austrian Reichsrat from 1891 to 1899 and again from 1907 to 1914. Convinced of the need of a Czech state, he drew support from groups in the U.S. and formed a National Council. In 1918 on his return to Prague he was elected first president of Czechoslovakia, retaining that office until 1935. An important work of M.'s is *The Making of a State: Memories and Observations, 1914–1918* (1927). BIBLIOGRAPHY: K. Capek, *President Masaryk Tells His Story* (1934, repr. 1970); P. P. Salver, *Masaryk. A Biography* (1940, repr. 1970).

[J. R. AHERNE]

MASCARON, JULES (1634–1703), French preacher and bishop. Entering at an early age the Oratorian congregation, M. taught rhetoric at the Oratorian college of Le Mans and began to preach at Saumur, whence his reputation spread. He was summoned to Paris to preach the Advent sermons of 1666 and the Lenten sermons of 1669 at the court of Louis XIV. He delivered the funeral orations for the Queen Mother (1666) and Henriette d'Angleterre (1670), this last being now forgotten since it was far surpassed by Bossuet's. After being named bp. of Tulle (1671) and then Agen (1679), M. reappeared only three times at Versailles to deliver Advent and Lenten sermons (1683, 1684, 1694). In 1695, he gave the opening address at the Assembly of French Clergy. To M. are attributed the conversions of numerous Calvinists in his diocese as well as a role in the conversion of Turenne, for whom he delivered a funeral oration (1675), considered his masterpiece, which is seen as rivaling the oration pronounced by Fléchier (1676). BIBLIOGRAPHY: L. Le Honneur, *Mascaron d'après des documents inédits* (1878).

[R. N. NICOLICH]

MASEN, JAKOB (1606–81), German Jesuit, author of several Baroque works: an epic (*Sarcotis*), one extant tragedy (*Mauritius Orientis Imperator*), and several comedies (e.g., *Rusticus imperans*). In *Palaestra eloquentia ligatae* (1654–57), M. provides the best contemporary statement of the theory of Jesuit drama. His theory, which regards drama as the artistic expression of reality, is based on Aristotle and, to some extent, anticipates French classicism in its interpretation of catharsis. BIBLIOGRAPHY: G. Müller, *Deutsche Dichtung von der Renaissance bis zum Ausgang des Barock* (1927) 223–226.

[M. F. MCCARTHY]

MASÍAS, JUAN, BL. (1585–1645), Dominican lay brother. A humble, illiterate shepherd known for his piety, M. left Spain in 1620 for Peru, where 2 years later he entered the Convent of Santa María Magdalena in Lima. Exercising the office of porter in the convent for the rest of his days, he continued his practice of prayer and penance and became widely known for his exemplary virtue, particularly his charity to the poor. He was beatified and his cult approved in 1837 by Pope Gregory XVI.

[E. M. GATES]

MASIUS, ANDREAS (Maes; 1515–73), Belgian classicist. M. was born in the province of Brabant and studied Greek and Hebrew at Louvain. After gaining his doctorate, M. worked as secretary to Jean de Weze, bp. of Constance. Following the death of de Weze M. traveled to Rome (*c.* 1548) where he associated with the leading Italian classicists. M. left Rome in 1558 to become counselor to the Duke of Cleve. His major writings are *Grammatica linguae syricae* (1571), the first European study of the Syriac language, and *Josue imperatoris historia* (1574) which examined the Book of Josue. BIBLIOGRAPHY: G. Coppens, EncCatt 7: 1801–02.

[R. J. BRADY]

MAṢNAPHTHŌ, the hood, made of the same material as the **phainō*, worn by West Syrian episcopal celebrants. Among the Jacobites it is supple and very ample and is raised or lowered at several points in the rite; among the Syrian Catholics it is stiffened slightly and kept lowered on the back of the *phainō* and omophorion. The term is applied to Maronite Latin-style amice, also called *manṣafah* in Arabic.

[A. CODY]

MASO DI BANCO (fl. 1325–50), Florentine painter, gifted pupil of Giotto, whose main works are five frescoes of the legend of St. Sylvester with a three-dimensional quality anticipating Masaccio, in the Bardi Chapel, Sta. Croce. Other works are a *Coronation of the Virgin* (Sta. Croce Museum), *Madonna and Child with Saints*, and other panels. Sienese and Florentine in style, Maso, elegant as Simone Martini and eloquent as A. Lorenzetti, was a distinguished master of his day. BIBLIOGRAPHY: J. White, *Art and Architecture in Italy, 1250–1400* (1966).

[M. J. DALY]

MASOCHISM, the abnormality of seeking sexual gratification in submitting to pain, torture, debasement; the term deriving from the name of the Austrian writer, Ritten von Sacker-Masoch (1836–95). In its proper, pathological meaning, such behavior cannot be morally imputable. Simply experimenting with masochistic practices for sexual variety, a phenomenon of the contemporary sexual revolution, may well be a moral, not a psychic perversion (see SADOMASOCHISM). In a wider sense, masochism can mean a morbid desire for any kind of suffering or humiliation based on self-loathing. Where it is morally controllable, such self-depreciation is in conflict with true Christian self-esteem, a moral balance between *humility and *magnanimity; and more importantly in conflict with theological hope and the proper self-love warranted and sustained by the reality of *charity.

[T. C. O'BRIEN]

MASOLINO (TOMMASO DI CRISTOFORO FINI; 1383–1447?), Florentine painter associated with Masaccio (1423), vacillating from the 14th-cent. International Gothic of G. da Fabriano to Florentine form and space; with final relapse into the International style. In 1425 M. painted frescoes in the Brancacci Chapel of S. Maria del Carmine, Florence, showing the influence of Masaccio. Two *Annunciation* panels (Washington, D.C.) date from 1430. Late frescoes in S. Clemente, Rome, and altarpiece for S. Maria Maggiore, Rome (section in Philadelphia) were started by Masaccio and finished by Masolino whose weak adoption of Masaccio's mastery resulted in a variant of the International style.

[M. J. DALY]

MASON, LOWELL (1792–1872), American composer, conductor, and organist. *The Handel and Haydn Society's Collection of Church Music,* a collection of M.'s psalm tunes based on sacred melodies by Gardiner was published in 1822. M. established the Boston Academy of Music (1832) with G. J. Webb, taught in the Boston schools, and worked with the Massachusetts Board of Education. After examining teaching methods in Germany, he wrote *Music Letters from Abroad* (1853). He composed such well-known hymns as "Nearer My God to Thee," "My Faith Looks Up to Thee," among others, and juvenile song books including the *Juvenile Psalmist* (1829), *The Juvenile Songster* (1837), and other song books for church and popular audiences. He arranged the music for "Joy to the World." M.'s hymnal library is now at Yale University.

[R. J. LITZ]

MASORA (Massora; Heb., tradition), a system devised to preserve with rigorous exactitude the full purity of the Hebrew text of the Bible in accordance with the traditions of the *Talmud. The Masoretes were Jews of Palestine and Babylonia who, beginning in the 7th cent. A.D.. when Hebrew had become a dead language, began developing this system. Previously the text had been written in consonants alone, the Hebrew alphabet containing no vowel signs in the true sense. The Masoretes, therefore, devised a system of points or vowel signs to be placed around the consonantal text without disturbing its traditional form. They based their work on the pronunciation traditional in the synagogues and rabbinical schools. Several different systems of points were produced, but the Tiberian one, named after the town of Tiberias in Galilee, completed by the *ben Asher family *c.*930 A.D., survived and appears in most MSS and in modern Hebrew Bibles. Masoretic points were also devised to indicate variations in the pronunciation of certain consonants which could be hard or soft, stressed or unstressed. The "great Masora" at the end of each book recorded the number of verses, words, and even letters in each book, and so helped the scribe to check his accuracy. BIBLIOGRAPHY: P. Kahle, *Cairo Geniza* (2d ed., 1959) 51–188; *idem,* "Masoretic Text of the Bible and the Pronunciation of Hebrew," *Journal of Jewish Studies* 7 (1956) 133–153; M. H. Goshen-Gottstein, "Rise of the Tiberian Bible Text," *Lown Institute for Judaic Studies* 1 (1963) 79–122.

[D. J. BOURKE]

MASPHA, see MIZPEH.

MASS, see EUCHARIST.

MASS, ATTENDANCE AT, term with several connotations. It may refer to the obligation (CIC c. 1248) binding Catholics to be present with a degree of attention sufficient to make that presence a human act and not merely bodily, at the Eucharistic Liturgy on Sundays and holydays (see SUNDAY AND HOLYDAY OBSERVANCE). There has been in recent years in some quarters a dismissal of this obligation as imposing mere extrinsic compliance. Such a dismissal ignores the nature of obedience as an interior choice to follow the injunctions of lawful authority. A second meaning of the term may be taken as in contrast with liturgical participation, so that Mass attendance has the implication of passivity, as the old Catholic idiom of "hearing Mass" suggests. The whole emphasis in the postconcilar Church has been on active participation in the liturgical action by the gathered community. This of course has always been the law's objective in imposing the Sunday Mass obligation. Simply attending Mass and not participating in the liturgy is still characteristic of some Catholics, but it is diminishing; the liturgical renewal has had a noteworthy effect even though there is still much progress to be made. The future development of closer and smaller communities in place of the huge churches of an earlier era and greater liturgical education will make "passive" Mass attendance a thing of the past and "hearing Mass" an archaism; grudging compliance and indifference will of course always remain. A third connotation of Mass attendance is its use as an index of church membership. Since obligatory church attendance has been historically peculiar to the RC Church, it has been taken to be a mark of the "practicing Catholic." Statistical surveys in recent years have shown a decline in Sunday Mass attendance (e.g., a 1977 survey set attendance at only 45% of Catholics). The reasons assigned have been in part sociological—the upward social movement of Catholics and the American Church's transition away from being an immigrant Church—partly an authority crisis in the Church since the 60s; partly, it has also been suggested, a loss of faith. The 1977 Synod of Bishops and the 1977 meeting of the National Conference of Catholic Bishops both stressed evangelization. The American bps. in particular pointed to the need to evangelize Catholics. The objective would not be to fill the churches on Sunday but a personal interiorization of faith that would make attendance at Mass an active witness to and formative participation in the mystery of Christ.

MASS, DIALOGUE, a manner of celebrating the Eucharistic Liturgy in which the congregation recites some of the Mass prayers aloud. Before Vatican Council II, the dialogue Mass was a specific way of celebrating a low Mass. Several distinct forms of dialogue Masses were recognizable, measured by the degree of participation of the faithful: (1) the recitation of only those responses ordinarily made by the server; (2) in addition to the former, the recitation in Latin of the parts of the Ordinary of the Mass normally sung: *Gloria, Credo,* etc.; or (3) along with all the preceding, the recitation of the sung Proper parts of the Mass: Introit, etc. The intent of the dialogue form of Mass was to foster an active participation of the people in the Eucharistic Liturgy and to give expression to its communal nature. The modern practice can be traced back to the Belgian Abbey of Maredsous in 1880, but the idea follows from the nature of the Mass itself. Vatican Council II gave recognition to the dialogue nature of every Mass and designed its liturgical reforms to promote full and active participation of the faithful. The dialogue form of the Mass is now acknowledged to be the usual, not a specific, type of Eucharistic Celebration. BIBLIOGRAPHY: W. J. O'Shea, NCE 9:413–414; J. Miller, *Fundamentals of the Liturgy* (1959) 248–249; J. M. Champlin, *Mass in a World of Change* (pa. 1973).

[B. ROSENDALL]

MASS, DRY, a prayer service which utilizes all the Mass texts and actions except the Offertory, Consecration, and Communion. It was a devotional form prevalent in the Middle Ages, used for funerals, afternoon weddings, or at any service when liturgical regulations forbade celebration of another Mass. The blessing of palms on Palm Sunday in the Roman rite was given a place in such a service until Pius XII promulgated his *Holy Week Ordo* in 1956. COMMUNION OUTSIDE OF MASS.

[N. KOLLAR]

MASS, HIGH, see HIGH MASS.

MASS, OFFERINGS FOR, see STIPENDS.

MASS, ROMAN. In the Roman rite, the combined celebration of the Liturgy of the Word and the Liturgy of the Eucharist. Though in early times the two were often celebrated separately, they came very early to be united and the term "Mass" (derived from the late Latin *missa,* meaning "dismissal," which was applied to any public assembly) was given to the joint celebration. The Roman rite has always been characterized by simplicity of structure: "soberness and sense" (E. Bishop). But the Liturgy of the Word (formerly called the "Mass of the Catechumens") came to have an introductory or preparatory rite attached to it and the Liturgy of the Eucharist (formerly called the "Mass of the Faithful"), a concluding rite; both of these were added as the primitive nucleus was expanded in the 4th through 8th cent. as Christianity adjusted to the new legal and public situation which followed official toleration. The expansion of the rites, however, did not totally obscure the earlier simplicity which centered, respectively, on the reading of the scriptures and the celebration of the sacrament of the Eucharist.

The Gallican rites, however, did develop a complexity (often derived from the Eastern rites) which eventually came to affect the Roman Mass. In the late 8th cent. Charlemagne introduced the Roman liturgy as a means of unifying his dominions. In the following years a hybrid of the Roman and Gallican liturgies developed; this returned to Rome in the 10th cent. and was adopted there. Medieval elaboration then led to a further obscuring of the simple lines of the Roman liturgy, particularly in the so-called "offertory," an introduction to the Liturgy of the Eucharist which anticipated the actual offering that takes place during the Eucharistic Prayer. The reforms called for by the Council of Trent and introduced by the *Missale Romanum* of Pius V in 1570 imposed the developed Mass of the Roman Curia on most of the Western Church, doing away with some of the more complex (often superstitious and theologically erroneous) practices prevailing in various areas. But the Mass of 1570 was not the *Roman* Mass but rather an overlay of Gallican elements on the Roman outline. This was particularly true in the case of the introductory rites, the offertory, and the concluding rites.

Four hundred years later, the reforms called for by Vatican Council II in 1963 in its Constitution on the Liturgy (*Sacrosanctum Concilium*) were implemented by the *Missale Romanum* of Paul VI (1970). The intent of the reform was the restoration of the Roman liturgy, although numerous Gallican elements, hallowed by a millenium of usage, were retained. However, the centrality of Word and of Sacrament are much clearer in the contemporary Roman Mass. Perhaps one of the most outstanding characteristics of the Roman Mass, at once its greatest strength and its greatest weakness, is its emphasis on offering (sacrifice). In earlier

ORDINARY OF THE MASS: MISSAL OF PIUS V (1570)	**ORDER OF MASS: MISSAL OF PAUL VI (1970)**
MASS OF THE CATECHUMENS	Introductory Rite and LITURGY OF THE WORD
OPENING OR ENTRANCE RITE	Introductory Rite
Asperges (sprinkling rite)	Entrance Song (or antiphon)
Veneration of the Altar	Veneration of the Altar & Kiss
	Incensing of Altar
Prayers at the Foot of Altar	
Sign of the Cross	Sign of the Cross
	Greeting *and Introduction* (alternate forms of greeting)
Antiphon and Psalm 42	
	Blessing and Sprinkling Holy Water or Penitential Rite (three forms)
Confiteor of Priest	
Confiteor of Servers	
Versicles and Responses	
Prayer while ascending steps	
Prayer while kissing altar	
Incensing of Altar	
Introit	
Kyrie	Kyrie (if not in penitential rite)
Gloria	Gloria
Kiss of Altar	
Greeting	
	Invitation to Prayer and Silent Prayer
Collect	Opening Prayer
SERVICE OF READINGS	LITURGY OF THE WORD
	First Reading: Old Testament
	Responsorial Psalm and Antiphon
Epistle	
Gradual	
	Second Reading: Epistle
Alleluia	Alleluia
Prayer before Gospel	Prayer before Gospel (quiet)
Gospel	Gospel
Sermon	Homily
Creed	Creed/Profession of Faith
	General Intercessions
MASS OF THE FAITHFUL	LITURGY OF THE EUCHARIST and Concluding Rite
	LITURGY OF THE EUCHARIST
OFFERTORY	PREPARATION OF ALTAR AND GIFTS
	Procession

Offering of Bread	Presentation of Bread *(aloud)*
Preparation of Chalice	Preparation of Chalice (quiet)
Offering of Chalice	Presentation of Chalice *(aloud)*
Prayer for acceptance	Prayer for acceptance (quiet)
Prayer for blessing of sacrifice	
Incensing of offerings, altar, priest, and people (several prayers)	*Incensing of offerings, altar, priest, and people (silent)*
Washing of Hands and Psalm 25	Washing of Hands (quiet)
Prayer for acceptance of sacrifice	
Invitation to Prayer and Response	Invitation to Prayer and Response
Secret Prayer	Prayer over the Gifts
PREFACE, SANCTUS, CANON	EUCHARISTIC PRAYER (four forms) with congregational acclamations
	COMMUNION RITE
The Lord's Prayer (priest)	The Lord's Prayer (congregation)
Embolism	Embolism and Doxology
	Sign of Peace, preceded by prayer
Breaking of Bread	Breaking of the Bread; Lamb of God
Lamb of God	
Private Preparation of Priest (three prayers)	Private Preparation of Priest (one prayer; quiet)
	Communion
	Invitation and Response
Communion of the Priest (several prayers)	Communion of the Priest
Communion of the People (several prayers)	Communion of the People (with song)
Ablutions (two prayers)	*Cleansing of Vessels* (may be after Mass; one quiet prayer)
	Period of Silence or Song of Praise
Postcommunion Prayer	Prayer after Communion
	Concluding Rite
	Announcements
Greeting	Greeting
Dismissal	
Prayer of Priest	
Blessing	Blessing (alternate forms)
	Dismissal
Last Gospel	

Explanation: type, size, indention shows relative importance
------ correspondence but changed form/position
______ changed position
italics indicates optional element

centuries a diversity of roles also characterized its celebration; this was lost when the communal dimension disappeared during the early Middle Ages and the priest became sole minister and celebrant. While the emphasis on sacrifice (somewhat better balanced, however) remains in the Missal of 1970, other roles have once more been brought to the fore. For an adequate understanding of the contemporary Roman Mass, the Apostolic Constitution promulgating the new Missal, the Foreword to the Missal, and its General Instruction (more thoroughly pastoral than the previous *De defectibus*) need to be carefully studied. Numerous elements of the Mass structure have been renamed (with earlier terminology often revived) in order to clarify the meaning and purpose of the structural elements as well as their interrelation; e.g., the "offertory" is now the "preparation of the altar and gifts." In general, the reform has been a matter of restoring the Roman liturgy with its simple and clear outline. For convenient comparison, a parallel outline of the Mass of 1570 and the Mass of 1970, see pages 2290–91. BIBLIOGRAPHY: J. A. Jungmann, *The Mass of the Roman Rite* (2v; 1951); J. A. Jungmann, *The Mass* (1976); A. King, *The Liturgy of the Roman Church* (1957).

[J. DALLEN]

MASS, SACRIFICE OF THE, see EUCHARIST.

MASS FOR THE DEAD, see DEAD, MASS FOR THE.

MASS FOR THE PEOPLE, in the RC Church, the obligation of pastors to celebrate Mass for the intentions of the people of their parishes on certain specified days, currently all Sundays and holydays of obligations but formerly a number of other days as well. They are forbidden to accept a stipend for this Mass, in view of the fact that their support is derived from the parish.

[J. DALLEN]

MASS OF THE CATECHUMENS, the first part of the Mass—now generally known as the Liturgy of the Word consisting of prayers, scripture readings, and instruction (homily or sermon). The name derived from the dismissal of the catechumens (those preparing for baptism) at its conclusion, but the term is inaccurate: the term did not come into use until the 11th century, long after the catechumenate had disappeared, and the catechumens were dismissed before the prayers of the faithful (general intercessions) and sometimes even before the Gospel reading. The Latin word *missa* (dismissal) became the name for any public assembly and is the source of the English "Mass." BIBLIOGRAPHY: J. A. Jungmann, *Mass of the Roman Rite* (tr. F. A. Brunner, 2 v., 1951–55), 1:261–271.

[J. DALLEN]

MASS OF THE FAITHFUL, see FAITHFUL, MASS OF THE.

MASS MEDIA, see MEDIA.

MASSA CANDIDA, the name given to a group of African martyrs whose number is placed by legend at 300, and who probably suffered in the persecution of Valerian (*c.* 257–260). St. Augustine refers to them in his writings. He once preached in a basilica in Utica named after them. He gives no description of their martyrdom. The Carthage Calendar, the Jerome Martyrology, and Florus of Lyons all cite August 18 as their *dies natalis,* i.e., date of martyrdom. BIBLIOGRAPHY: Butler 3:392–393; G. D. Gordini, BiblSanct 9:4–6.

[E. J. DILLON]

MASSACHUSETTS, a New England state admitted to the Union (1788) as the 6th state. Several expeditions had come to the Massachusetts coast in search of fish and trade prior to the first permanent settlement by the Pilgrims (1620). Religion was a major force in the Plymouth Colony, which was Separatist, and in the Massachusetts Bay Colony, where Puritans sought to create a Bible Commonwealth. Since Congregational church polity became the basis of Puritan political thought, each town developed an autonomous status similar to that of each Church. The political system was highly theocratic and restrictive, however, prompting the excluded or otherwise-minded to move elsewhere and found other New England settlements. Puritan zeal also produced expansionism, and it led to difficult relations with the Indians that culminated in King Philip's War. An exception was John Eliot, a Puritan "Apostle to the Indians" whose life was devoted to missionary work. Massachusetts legally excluded Catholic missionaries throughout the 17th century. Since religious freedom was not granted until adoption of the Massachusetts Constitution of 1780, Catholicism grew slowly, and by 1803 there were only 1,000 Catholics in the state. When the Diocese of Boston was erected (1808) as a suffragan of Baltimore, it included all of New England and was headed by Bp. J. L. de *Cheverus. Because of the Napoleonic Wars and the War of 1812, Cheverus accomplished little until 1820, when the first Ursuline nuns began to arrive. Recalled to France in 1823, he was succeeded by B. J. *Fenwick, SJ, who had served as president of Georgetown College. Fenwick's main concern was to meet the needs of a population rapidly swollen by immigration. At his death (1846) there were 70,000 Catholics, 39 priests, and 48 churches in the diocese.

The third bp., J. B. Fitzpatrick, a native Bostonian, provided improved social services, notably orphanages and almshouses, and promoted the establishment (1863) of Boston College. In 1866 he was succeeded by J. J. *Williams, whose episcopacy extended over a period of 40 years. During Williams' administration Boston became an archdiocese; St. John's Seminary, Brighton, was opened; and many religious communities came to help with the educational, charitable, and religious activities of the archdiocese. After Williams' death (1907), W. H. *O'Connell became the second abp. of Boston. During his episcopacy, the *Pilot* became the archdiocesan newspaper; the administrative powers of the chancellor were broadened; and annual retreats were provided for the clergy. In addition, O'Connell released J. A. *Walsh to found the Maryknoll Order. By the time of O'Connell's death (1944), there were 375 churches, 322 parishes, 1,582 priests, 5,469 nuns, and 21 religious communities. R. J. Cushing (1895–1970) became the third abp. of Boston (1944). Born and educated in Boston, he expanded educational facilities, increased the number of Catholic colleges from three to six, opened a seminary for delayed vocations at Weston, Mass., sponsored missionary work in Latin America, and exerted leadership in the ecumenical movement. He resigned and was succeeded (1970) by Humberto Medeiros, cardinal from 1973. Suffragan to the Boston archdiocese are the Dioceses of Worcester, Springfield, and Fall River, Mass.; Portland, Maine; Burlington, Vt.; and Manchester, N.H. In 1976 the Catholics of Massachusetts numbered 3,037,815, or 40.5% of the total state population. The major Protestant denominations are the United Church of Christ, 3.3% of the pop. in 1971, and the Episcopal Church, with 2.7%. Other Protestant Churches comprised 5.5% of the population. The Jewish pop. (1968) was 259,635, or 4.56%. More than 29,191 students attend the state's 9 Catholic colleges, half of which are in the Archdiocese of Boston. There are 84 Catholic high schools in the state, with a total enrollment of 37,970 students. More than 25,636 attend the 62 Catholic high schools in the archdiocese. There are 86,521 pupils in the state's 280 Catholic elementary schools, 177 of which are in the archdiocese and enroll 54,495. BIBLIOGRAPHY: *Commonwealth History of Massachusetts* (ed. A. B. Hart, 5 v., 1927–1930, repr. 1967); R. H. Lord, et al., *History of the Archdiocese of Boston in the Various Stages of Its Development, 1604 to 1943* (3 v., 1944).

[J. L. MORRISON; R. M. PRESTON]

MASSAJA, GUGLIELMO (Lorenzo; 1809–89), Italian Capuchin missionary, cardinal. M. was ordained in 1836. He taught philosophy and theology for the succeeding 10 years, then was made a bp. and sent to be first vicar apostolic of Galla, Ethiopia. Unable to go to his vicariate at once, he labored on the missions in E Africa, Egypt, and the Sudan. In Ethiopia he made thousands of converts, introduced medical missions and developed a native clergy. He was a friend of Nejus Menelik, but was exiled by that emperor's successor. Leo XIII made M. a cardinal in 1884. He wrote a valuable history of his years in Ethiopia, *I miei trentacinque anni di missione nell'alta Etiopia* (12 v., 1885–95). He had earlier also published African grammars and other books in African languages.

[J. R. AHERNE]

MASSENET, JULES (Émile Frédéric; 1842–1912), composer. Brilliant, if limited, M. who was to become one of the most popular operatic composers of France, was a Parisian by both residence and character. A student in composition of Ambroise Thomas at the Paris Conservatory he won the coveted *Prix de Rome* in 1863, enabling him to do 3 years' study at the Villa de'Medici. Returning to Paris he saw his first opera *La Grande Tante* produced in 1867. M. composed a number of songs, the best known being *Élégie* and a series of song-cycles (e.g., *Poème d'Avril*). To this prolific period belongs the oratorio *Marie Magdeleine* (1873). The memorable operas began with *Hérodiade* in 1881, slow to win favor but from 1903 a popular work. M.'s masterpiece *Manon* was first performed in 1884 and remains today one of the staples of the operatic theater. Not only is it notable for dramatic repetition of its themes but for the innovation of spoken prologues to each act and *recitativo* spoken against orchestral accompaniment. M. was appointed to teach at the Paris Conservatory in 1878 and in the same year was elected to the Académie des Beaux-Arts, the youngest member ever elected to that body. His opera *Le Cid* was performed first in 1885, *Thaïs* in 1894, and *Werther* in 1892, all of them became favorites of operagoers; he wrote nearly a score of other, less popular operas.

M. was perhaps too facile an operatic composer, possibly more dependent on popular taste than one expects of genius—but the same criticism could be lodged against Shakespeare. The lyricism of his work and its dramatic power are undeniable. The Wagnerians have sneered at M. for generations but it must be admitted that M.'s work is free of the arid stretches one finds in Wagner. BIBLIOGRAPHY: A. Bruneau, *Massenet* (1935).

[J. R. AHERNE]

MASSIGNON, LOUIS (1883–1962), Orientalist and historian whose main scholarly concern was Islamic culture and civilization and who became one of the greatest authorities on Muslim mysticism. His doctoral dissertation at the Sorbonne (1922) was an exposition of the spirituality of Al-Ḥallaj, the martyred mystic of Islam, but it also illuminates every aspect of *Sufism and of the entire religious life of the early Muslim community. A companion study of the vocabulary of the Sufis provides the basis for his conviction that the origins of Sufism are to be found within the dynamics of Islam, without recourse to Christian and Neoplatonic roots. His love for Islam explains his leadership role in the push for Algerian political prisoners in the French-Algerian conflict. He was professor at the Collège de France and a member of the national academies of seven European countries, as well as of Iraq, Afghanistan, and Egypt. In later life he became a Catholic priest of the Byzantine rite.

[E. J. DILLON]

MASSILLON, JEAN BAPTISTE (1663–1742), French preacher and bishop. Educated in the colleges of the Oratorians in Hyères and Marseilles, M. entered the congregation (1681), taught in its colleges, and was ordained at Vienne (1691). Here he was commissioned to deliver his first two funeral orations, for M. de Villars, abp. of Vienne, and Villeroy, abp. of Lyons. Named director of the St. Magloire Seminary in Paris (1696), M. became known for his Lenten sermons at Montpellier (1698) and at the Paris

Oratory (1699). His Advent sermons at Versailles (1699) and his Lenten sermons before Louis XIV (1701, 1704), established his reputation, which was sustained by his Lenten and Advent sermons in important Paris churches and in the Advent of 1715 at the court of Stanislas of Lorraine. His celebrated funeral orations are those he delivered for the Prince de Conti (1709), the Grand Dauphin (1711), and Louis XIV (1715), which begin with the famous line: "God alone is great, my brethren." Under the Regency M. was nominated bp. of Clermont (1717; consecrated 1718), and preached before the young Louis XV the 10 Lenten sermons known under the title of *Le Petit carême,* considered once to be his masterpieces, whereas his sermons *On Final Impenitence, On Death,* and *On the Fewness of the Elect* (1704) are cited now. After assisting at the coronation of Louis XV and preaching the funeral oration for the Regent's mother, the Duchesse d'Orléans (1723), M. retired to his see. Greatly admired as a preacher by his contemporaries Voltaire and D'Alembert, he was also a model pastor. BIBLIOGRAPHY: A. Chérel, *Massillon* (1943); I. Champomier, *Massillon* (1942).

[R. N. NICOLICH]

MASSIS, HENRI (1886–1970), French academician. M. made his debut as a writer while still a student, publishing works on Zola, Barrès, and skepticism. His conversion to Catholicism (1913) was influenced by Bergson's antipositivism and by contact with Péguy, Psichari, and Maritain. He rallied to the cause of French classical culture, and moved politically to the right. Though not officially associated with the newspaper *L'Action française,* M. was influenced by Charles Maurras. If M. rejected Nazism on patriotic and religious grounds, he found at least a degree of spiritual and intellectual affinity in the Latin Fascist movements of Mussolini, Salazar, and Franco. A spiritual heir of De Maistre and a rigid neo-Thomist, M. saw the Reformation, the Revolution, and Romanticism as forces inimical to the intellect, Western tradition, and Catholicism. A major literary critic, he has evaluated modern literature from stringent Catholic moral and dogmatic norms. BIBLIOGRAPHY: G. de Catalogne, *Les Compagnons du spirituel* (1945); A. Rousseaux, *Litérature du 20e siècle* (v. 1, 1938); L. Christophe, "Regards sur Henri Massis," *La Revue générale belge* (1961) 17–41.

[G. E. GINGRAS]

MASSON, ANDRÉ (1896–), French painter, cubist (1918–20), with Miró-organic surrealist (1930) and illustrator of his own *Bestiaire* and books by A. Malraux, G. Bataille, and De Sade.

[M. J. DALY]

MASSOULIÉ, ANTONIN (1632–1706) French Dominican theologian. A Toulousain, M. wrote effectively to show that Bañez on divine premotion truly represented the thought of St. Thomas Aquinas, and to disprove the accusation that it was anything like Jansenism. He held high office in the administration of his order and was a consultor in Rome, notably on quietism and the Chinese rites. His judgment on *Fénelon was unfavorable. BIBLIOGRAPHY: Quétif-Échard 2.2:769–770, 827–829.

[T. GILBY]

MASTER BERTRAM (1345–fl. 1415; Meister Bertram von Minden), German painter and sculptor whose name is determined by the signed *Grabow Altar* (1379), but disputed in the *Buxtehude Altar* (both in Hamburg). A *Passions Altar* and *Harvestehude Altar* are ascribed to his workshop. Carved details of the *Grabow Altar* are also by Master Bertram. His works, plastic, naturalistic, and emotional, showing a Bohemian interest in animals, exerted a strong influence on Master Francke. BIBLIOGRAPHY: A. Dorner, *Meister Bertram von Minden* (1937).

[M. J. DALY]

MASTER OF CEREMONIES, the person who coordinates a religious ceremony and sees that it is properly enacted. He is usually dressed in a cassock and surplice.

MASTER E. S., German engraver and goldsmith, whose monogram appears 1451–68. He was the creator of 500 unique impressions, including two sets of playing cards of which some are still extant. His unusual subjects include an alphabet of grotesque human and animal forms, a design for a monstrance, 11 plates of *Ars moriendi*, many Madonnas, Nativities, Apostles, with Gothic conventions and Netherlandish solidarity of form. He was surpassed by Martin Schongauer, whose art is rooted in that of E.S.

[M. J. DALY]

MASTER OF FLÉMALLE (*c.*1406–44), called after paintings in Frankfurt which are stylistically related to the Mérode altarpiece, New York (therefore, also called Master of Mérode), he is now identified with Robert Campin from Tournai. He is the first to create religious scenes in the tangible world of bourgeois interiors with considerable perspective, and invest Gothic symbols with unidealized still-life features. Together with Eyck and R. vander Weyden (perhaps his pupil), he initiated early Netherlandish painting and determined its course. BIBLIOGRAPHY: R. Campin and E. Panofsky, *Early Netherlandish Painting* (1953).

[R. BERGMANN]

MASTER FRANCKE (fl. *c.*1400–35), painter of the important German 15th-cent. *Altar of the Englandfahrer* or *Thomas Altar* (1424, Hamburg) in the French Burgundian MS style. Commissioned by the Hansa merchants trading with England, and carrying the legend of St. Thomas à Becket, the *Thomas Altar* is distinguished by M. F.'s dynamic space and dramatic realism. The *St. Barbara Altar* (Helsinki *c.*1410) shows details from *Revelations* to the

14th-cent. Swedish mystic St. Bridget. M.F.'s style is not naive, like that of Master Bertram, but elegant in the manner of International Gothic (details relate to miniatures in the *Très Riches Heures* of the Limbourg brothers). His Netherlandish *Man of Sorrows* (two panels) though Burgundian is an **Andachtsbild* of German pathos distinctive of M.F., who exerted an overwhelming influence for several decades, with his union of French elegance, mystic expression, and Netherlandish realism. BIBLIOGRAPHY: C.D. Cutler, *Northern Painting* (1968).

[M. J. DALY]

MASTER HONORÉ OF PARIS (fl. 1250), MS illuminator of *La Somme le Roy* (before 1295) and of the *Breviary of Philippe le Bel* (before 1296); an example of the work of the new urban workshops of laymen of that day. The modelled larger figures overlapping the frame effect a new spatial concept derived from the earlier *Psalter of St. Louis* (*c.*1260). His unique style influenced the master Jean Pucelle. The MSS are in the Bibliothèque Nationale, Paris.

[M. J. DALY]

MASTER OF MÉRODE, Flemish painter, named after a small, devotional, richly symbolic triptych of the Annunciation (*c.*1426) with devout donors in a spring garden with enclosing wall—symbol of the Enclosed garden of the Song of Songs, and St. Joseph, as carpenter, making mousetraps in the wing—a most recondite symbol of St. Augustine's statement that the Incarnation was a trap set by God to catch the Devil. The masterpiece belonged to the Belgian Mérode family before it entered the Cloisters, New York. Stylistic similarity with a group of other early 15th-cent. panels points to the Master of Flémalle as artist—now identified with Robert Campin, traceable in Tournai (*c.*1406–44). BIBLIOGRAPHY: M. Frinta, *Genius of Robert Campin* (1966).

[R. BERGMANN]

MASTER OF MOULINS, outstanding French anonymous painter, named after a major work, the *Moulins* triptych (*c.*1498). The painting's central Virgin as the apocalyptic woman in its formal clarity, precise figure and space construction is truly Renaissance in spirit. Although Hugo van der Goes' influence is discernible, in many details of works (*Nativity of Cardinal Rolin*, Autun), M.'s style in delicate color and restrained elegance relates directly to the central French heritage, esp. to Fouquet. BIBLIOGRAPHY: A. Châtelet, "A Plea for the Master of Moulins", Burlington Magazine 114 (1962) 517–524.

[R. BERGMANN]

MASTER OF NOVICES, the religious (in clerical institutes, a priest) in charge of a religious community's novices during the period of their noviceship. It has always been considered desirable that an individual appointed to this office should be a person of relatively mature years, well schooled in the traditions and spirit of the institute, and capable of giving sound direction to his charges in their study of rule and constitutions and in their formation in virtue and the practice of prayer. In contemporary religious life, which lays stress on the postulancy and the prolongation of formation through an extended period of commitment and the fuller integration of the novices into the professed community, novices tend to be exposed to a wider range of formative influences, and the responsibility is concentrated less exclusively in the novice master than in the past. BIBLIOGRAPHY: B. Steidle, *Rule of St. Benedict with a Commentary* (tr. U. Schnitzhofer, 1966).

MASTER OF THE HOUSEBOOK (HAUSBUCH; fl. 1475), S German engraver unique in wit and free drawing of religious and genre subjects. M. caught expressions and gestures, in a gentle feeling second only to that of Schongauer in the 15th century. Known as Master of the Sketchbook and of the Housebook of Prince von Waldburg-Wolfegg—though of disputed provenance, M. in some 91 engravings shows occasional influence from the Master E.S. BIBLIOGRAPHY: A. H. Strange, *Der Hausbuchmeister* (1958).

[M. J. DALY]

MASTER OF THE ROHAN HOURS (fl. 1410–30), French illuminator of impressive creativity, famous for *Les Grandes Heures de Rohan* (Paris), a masterpiece (1420–25), large, rich, and expressionistic in the International Gothic style. Porcher states it was owned by the Rohan family but designed for the House of Anjou. Its origin is disputed.

[M. J. DALY]

MASTER OF THE SACRED PALACE, in the *papal household, the official theologian of the pope; the title (*Magister sacri palatii*) was changed by Paul VI's *motu proprio*, *Pontificalis domus*, March 28, 1968, revamping the papal household to "theologian of the pontifical household" (*Pontificalis domus doctor theologus*). Legend makes St. Dominic the first to hold the office and by immemorial custom it is assigned to a Dominican (at present Card. Luigi Ciappi). The incumbent has advisory functions in theological matters for the pope and the secretariat of state; he also serves in the Curia Romana.

[T. C. O'BRIEN]

MASTER OF THE SENTENCES, a title commonly applied to *Peter Lombard (*c.* 1095–1160) because of the central place that his **Sentences* held in scholastic theology.

[T. M. MCFADDEN]

MASTRIUS, BARTHOLOMAEUS (1602–1673), well-known Scotist theologian, who coauthored (with Bonaventura Bellutus) many works designed to elucidate the Scotist teaching on divine grace, with its attempt to reconcile human freedom and divine foreknowledge. He entered the Franciscan Conventuals in 1617, was dean of studies at Cesena, Perugia, and Padua (from 1628), and was provincial of Bologna (1647–50), BIBLIOGRAPHY: V. Heynek, LTK 7:160; J. C. Willke, NCE 9:437–438.

[E. J. DILLON]

MASTURBATION, also called, with slight difference in connotation, self-abuse, pollution, solitary sin, autoeroticism, or "ipsation," means arousing oneself sexually, whether by physical stimulation, by phantasies or daydreaming, or by any other means. The full act is to the point of orgasm or release, accompanied in the male by seminal emission and in the female (at times) by glandular secretions. A similar experience happening involuntarily during sleep is usually called a nocturnal emission. Many religions, Christian and non-Christian, have considered deliberate masturbation objectively sinful, without going into the question of the gravity of the sin. Many secular humanists, atheists, and even some Catholic proponents of situational ethics have held that deliberate masturbation to relieve tensions is not evil at all. Traditional Catholic moral theology has always maintained that a deliberate act of masturbation is a misuse of the sexual function and objectively serious matter. On the other hand, if the arousal and orgasm are involuntary and spontaneous even when awake, there is no sin. Even if one foresees that the experience will result from something else one is doing, if one truly does not intend the arousal and orgasm, and what one is doing is good in itself like legitimate study, then there will be no sin if the reason is proportionately good, according to the principle of the indirect voluntary or *"double effect." If it is truly not intended and what one is doing is not evil in itself, but there is not a proportionately good reason for allowing the bad effect, there might objectively be venial sin. For any deliberate action to be a mortal sin, there must of course be full realization of what one is doing and a fully free and deliberate choice of the will to perform the action. Often it is difficult to determine with any accuracy, both for the person himself and for his confessor or counselor, whether and to what extent there was a fully free and deliberate choice of the will. A semideliberate or partially deliberate act, even when directly voluntary, can never amount to more than venial sin. And such experiences can happen as indirectly voluntary or as spontaneous reactions to natural stimuli. Most theologians agree that regret immediately after an act as well as resistance to previous temptation are good signs that there was not a fully free choice of the will. When one is falling into sleep or has just awakened, he is not generally held to be in a state in which his acts are fully voluntary. Anyone who is trying to love God and keep his commandments, and is in doubt about his full voluntariness after such an experience, can safely presume that he is not guilty of formal mortal sin.

So much has been written on psychiatric problems connected with masturbation as a symptom of deeper disorders that many counselors and confessors tend to judge that experience of masturbation is either mortally sinful or a sign of psychiatric trouble. But semideliberate or indeliberate experiences are far more common than serious psychiatric problems, which explains why some psychiatrists have written that masturbation should not be considered a serious problem unless other signs of disturbance are present. Even then the psychological problem can range from mere anxiety about what the subject deems serious sin to full-blown neuroses. Such signs can include excessive frequency (daily or oftener); obsession about sexual matters at all waking times; patterns of seemingly deliberate preparation combined with a sincere habitual attitude of wanting to love God and avoid sin; and other more easily recognizable signs of mental or emotional agitation. Mere excessive frequency beyond the normal expectancy, which ranges from an average of about once a month to twice a week, may simply be the result of worrying about such experiences, thinking that they are mortally sinful. Anxiety of this kind, esp. on retiring, can call forth by contrast the feared phantasies and start the whole process. Realizing that there is no formal mortal sin, when circumstances permit such a judgment, can often help reduce excessive frequency.

So far as pastoral treatment by counselor or confessor is concerned, various possibilities are suggested. The proper diagnosis is of greatest importance. To treat a penitent or counselee as though he were guilty of mortal sin or as though he had a habit of sin, when in truth his experiences were normal semi-deliberate or indeliberate experiences, can easily lead the subject into despair. To suggest to a similar subject that he needs the professional help of a psychiatrist can cause him unnecessary fear and embarrassment. On the other hand there are some individuals who do need psychiatric help and others, esp. adolescents, who have contracted a real habit of masturbation, can profit from the usual pastoral helps for overcoming habits. Where masturbation is a fully deliberate act, it will rarely be the only serious sin on the subject's conscience, and in any case what he will need will be ordinary pastoral help to realize his need for genuine contrition and commitment to the love of God. BIBLIOGRAPHY: J. J. Farraher, NCE 9:438–440.

[J. J. FARRAHER]

MATER ECCLESIA, a patristic designation for the Church as the spiritual mother of Christians. Although the general concept is found earlier, e.g., the *Second Epistle of Clement* (*c.* 160) which speaks of the Church as previously barren but finally given children by the Spirit's action (2.1), the title itself is first used by Tertullian. He employs it as an expression of reverence and love (*Ad martyras*, 1) and compares Eve, the physical mother of mankind, to Mary who is the "true mother of the living" (*De anima*, 43). More significant is the use to which St. Cyprian puts the title. Since he was principally concerned with church unity in the midst of schisms, he refers to the Church as the mother who joins all her children into one family. Cyprian seems to have coined the adage, it is impossible to have God as Father except we have the Church as mother (*De *unitate*, 6). The phrase has continued in use to the present as a general title for the Church. Vat II ConstChurch 64 speaks of the Church becoming a mother of men, asserting that the Church like Mary becomes a mother by accepting God's word in faith. Theologically the title emphasizes that the Church is the bearer of Christ's salvation, establishing an intimate, living, and unified community analogous to that of a family. BIBLIOGRAPHY: K. Delahaye, *Erneuerung der Seelsorgsformen aus der Sicht der frühen Patristik* (1958).

[T. M. MCFADDEN]

MATER ET MAGISTRA, social encyclical of John XXIII on "Christianity and Social Progress," issued in 1961 on the anniversary of Leo XIII's *Rerum novarum*. The encyclical reviewed the social doctrines of previous popes, reaffirmed their teachings regarding private property, socialism, union organization, and other subjects, and extended the application of these principles to the changed conditions that followed World War II. The improved condition of industrial workers was recognized but attention was drawn to the special needs of small business and artisans, and the organization of cooperatives to safeguard their rights was urged. The encyclical stressed the need for technological improvement and declared that workers should be aided to acquire the higher skills and qualifications that this necessitated. Reasserting the responsibility of the State to promote social and economic justice, the encyclical also noted the need for a balance between state-regulating activity and freedom of individual and group enterprise. Aspects of the world situation treated in the encyclical include the condition of agriculture and of rural workers and the relations between rich and poor nations. The Pope, recognizing that gains for industrial workers had outpaced those for rural workers and small farmers, urged that these form associations for mutual aid comparable to the unions of industrial workers; and he declared that national economic policies, to be productive of the true prosperity (which he defined as a matter not of the total national wealth but of its just distribution), must make special provision for such needs as social security, price protection, credit, insurance, and technological innovation in agriculture.

The international imbalance between wealthy industrialized nations and underdeveloped ones was noted. Reiterating the words of a 1960 allocution, "We all share responsibility for the fact that populations are undernourished," the Pope praised programs of scientific, technical, or financial aid to developing areas by governments, private business, or other organizations. But he warned that economically developed nations, in giving such aid, must not try to impose their way of life on other nations or attempt to use such aid for political advantage; this, he declared, is "another form of colonialism." In conclusion, the Pope directed that serious attention be given to social teachings in schools and seminaries and in parish instruction. But, he added, "We do not regard such instructions as sufficient . . . unless some action follows upon the teaching." Accordingly he proposed a three-step application of Christian social principles, summed up as "observe, judge, act." He reminded the faithful that "if Christians are joined in mind and heart with the most holy Redeemer when they apply themselves to temporal affairs, their work is . . . a continuation of the labor of Jesus Christ, drawing from it strength and redemptive power." Text: AAS 53 (1961) 401–406.

[D. CODDINGTON]

MATERIAL CAUSE, in a composite, material being, the determinable, potential component, and the subject in a process of change; then any recipient, determinable subject from which something is derived or into which a determinate element is introduced. See HYLOMORPHISM.

[T. C. O'BRIEN]

MATERIAL PRINCIPLE, the central doctrine or doctrines of any Church; the correlative of *formal principle, i.e., the source or criterion for doctrines.

[T. C. O'BRIEN]

MATERIALISM, the doctrine that reality is coextensive with the kinds of stuff that compose the physical universe, their interrelations, and the laws that govern their behavior. Six cent. before Christ the earliest pre-Socratic Greek philosophers explored the origins and constitution of things in terms of various material elements and compounds. Materialism emerges as well-defined and conscious of its implications, however, only when the distinct reality, and something of the character, of spirit is sufficiently recognized. Materialism takes on significance essentially in terms of a rejection of spirit, which is metaphysical materialism, a radical monism. The main principles of this theoretical materialism are: the uniformity of law, the denial of teleology, and the denial of any form of existence other than those envisaged by the physical sciences. A close connection appears between materialism, scientism, and positivism. The modern materialist establishes a uniformity in nature, which remains absolute within the experience of man. Purpose in the universe is vigorously excluded, along with ulterior motives or goals toward which events might be striving. All events are attributed to the interaction of matter and motion operating by blind necessity in accordance with those invariable sequences to which the name of law is given. Marxism is an esp. powerful and attractive version of materialism, although its materialism is its least convincing component. In a crude sense, materialism denotes the needless, unrestrained pursuit of worldly goods and sense pleasures. BIBLIOGRAPHY: F. A. Lange, *History of Materialism* (tr. E. C. Thomas, 3d ed., 1957); H. Eliot, *Modern Science and Materialism* (1919); J. Wisdom, *Problems of Mind and Matter* (1934).

[J. P. REID]

MATERIALISM, DIALECTICAL AND HISTORICAL, see DIALECTICAL AND HISTORICAL MATERIALISM.

MATERNITY, DIVINE, see MOTHER OF GOD.

MATHER, surname of three Puritan clergymen who were prominent in the civil and ecclesiastical history of colonial New England.

Richard (1596–1669) was born in Lancashire, attended Oxford briefly, and became pastor at Toxteth Park Chapel. In 1635, because of his Puritan leanings, he was suspended from his ministry. He immigrated to Massachusetts in 1635, became pastor at Dorchester, and remained there until his death. He helped to shape New England's Congregational way, collaborating in preparing the Psalms in meter for the *Bay Psalm Book,* and wrote the original draft of the *Cambridge Platform (1648). He was also one of the men who were responsible for the *Half-Way Covenant, strongly advocating the plan against fierce opposition by those who insisted on the necessity of personal conversion experience.

Increase (1639–1723), son of Richard, born in Dorchester, Mass., he graduated from Harvard in 1656 and from Trinity College, Dublin, 2 years later. He preached in England for 3 years. Returning to Massachusetts in 1661, he was called to Second Church, Boston, remaining there until his death. While preeminently a pastor, he was involved in politics, served as president of Harvard (1685–1701), and organized a society to discuss scientific matters. He was one of four representatives who persuaded the English government to grant a new charter to Massachusetts (1691), but had to make some concessions, most important of which were granting suffrage to nonchurch members and allowing the king to appoint governors. Accused of fomenting the witchcraft troubles at Salem, he was one of those who cautioned against use of "spectral evidence," esp. in his *Cases of Conscience Concerning Evil Spirits* (1692), which influenced Governor Phips to cease carrying out sentences of convicted witches. He was a scholar and the author of numerous political and religious works.

Cotton (1663–1728), son of Increase, also grandson of John *Cotton. He was a precocious youth, entering Harvard at age 12; he graduated in 1678 and received the M.A. in 1681. Ordained at 22 and installed as assistant to his father at Second Church, Boston, he labored there until his death. Primarily a minister, he was active in public affairs, organized numerous humanitarian societies, and was an erudite scholar. Although he was caricatured by later generations as a bigot, such a portrayal does him injustice. While upholding traditional congregational ideals, he was open-minded and inquiring. Although sometimes charged with responsibility for the witchcraft affair at Salem, his role in the matter was small. His many learned writings included sermons, theological works, histories, biographies, scientific discourses, and even poetry. Probably his best-known work was the *Magnalia Christi Americana* (1702), a collection of miscellaneous works that formed a kind of history of New England. BIBLIOGRAPHY: B. Wendell, *Cotton Mather: The Puritan Priest,* with an introduction by Alan Heimert (new ed., 1963); K. B. Murdoch, *Increase Mather: The Foremost American Puritan* (1925).

[N. H. MARING]

MATHEW, ARNOLD HARRIS (1853–1919), bp. in Old Catholic orders. Baptized an Anglican, M. was ordained a RC priest in 1878, but after his marriage in 1892 he ministered in Anglican churches. In 1908 he was consecrated a bp. in the Old Catholic Church of Utrecht, which Church, however, repudiated the consecration in 1910 on grounds that it had been deceived as to the numbers of Old Catholics in England to whom M. had professed a desire to minister. He himself consecrated others and thus a number of irregular episcopal lines are traceable to him. BIBLIOGRAPHY: H. R. T. Brandreth, *Episcopi Vagantes and the Anglican Church* (2d ed. 1961); P. Anson, *Bishops at Large* (1965).

[R. B. ENO]

MATHEW, DAVID AND GERVASE, brothers, English clerics. **David** (1902–75), archbishop. Born at Lyme Regis, Dorset, he studied at Balliol College, Oxford, and then at Beda College, Rome. After ordination in 1929 he was assigned first to Cardiff cathedral, and then in 1934 began a 10-year period as chaplain to Catholic students at the Univ. of London. Meanwhile, he began a career of scholarly publication with *The Celtic Peoples and Renaissance Europe* (1933). In his later works he specialized in Tudor and Stuart England, though he also wrote naval history and even novels. In 1938 he became a bp., auxiliary to Westminster (titular, Aelia), and he was raised to abp. (titular, Apamea) after appointment as apostolic delegate to British Africa in 1946. From 1954 to 1963 he served as Catholic bp. to British military forces. He then retired but continued to write.

Gervase (1905–76), English Dominican scholar at Oxford. Born Anthony Mathew, after completing his studies in modern history at Balliol College, Oxford, he joined the English Dominican province in 1928. He spend most of his life at Blackfriars, Oxford, doing his own unique kind of pastoral work along with his lecturing and writing. The title of one of his principal works, *Byzantine Aesthetics,* reflects what was perhaps his major interest in life outside of his pastoral work. In 1947 he accepted appointment to a university lectureship at Oxford in Byzantine Studies and continued in this post until 1971. It has been said of him that he deserves to be thought of as having been the main creator of Byzantine studies at the University. A list of his writings may be found in the *Eastern Church Review* (1972) that appeared as a *Festschrift* in his honor. His broad understanding of history and culture was accompanied by a most engaging eccentricity. His considerable talent at organization in study and life was entirely invisible, masked over by a side of that same eccentricity. Among his close friends he counted Thomas Whittemore and C. S. Lewis.

[F. E. KELLEY]

MATHEW, THEOBALD (1790–1856), Irish Capuchin, "Father Mathew," the preacher of *total abstinence. He became a Capuchin in 1808; after ordination in 1813, the City of Cork became the base for most of his work. He was provincial from 1822 to 1851. His apostolate for temperance began in 1838 when he was asked to lead the Cork Total Abstinence Society. He preached in Ireland, Scotland, England, and in the U.S., from 1849 to 1851, where he was invited by both Catholic and Protestant groups, and was received by Pres. Zachary Taylor. He persuaded thousands to "take the pledge," but the practice often proved ineffective. M.s most successful accomplishment was simply the emphasis on the need for *temperance.

[T. C. O'BRIEN]

MATHEWS, SHAILER (1863–1941), Baptist theologian. A native of Portland, Maine, M. was professor of theology at the Divinity School, Univ. of Chicago (1906–33). Strongly influenced by historical and sociological studies, he held that theology is always the product of social environment. Notions such as the deity, atonement, and Resurrection of Jesus Christ are historically conditioned and therefore relative, but also are functional in helping men to adjust to life. His mature views included belief that in the universe are personality-producing forces that men conceptualize as a personal God and that the ideals and life of Jesus inspire men to maintain personal values and to live worthy lives. Despite his liberal, reductionist theology, he remained an active churchman, sharing in the organization of the Northern Baptist Convention (1907) and serving as its president (1916); he was also president of the *Federal Council of Churches (1912–16). He had widespread influence through his teaching and writings, among which were *Faith of Modernism* (1924), *Atonement and the Social Process* (1934), *Growth of the Idea of God* (1931), and *New Faith for Old: An Autobiography* (1936). BIBLIOGRAPHY: K. Cauthen, *Impact of American Religious Liberalism* (1962). *MODERNISM.

[N. H. MARING]

MATHIEU, FRANÇOIS DÉSIRÉ (1839–1908), abp. of Toulouse, card., member of the *Curia Romana. A pastor and canon of the diocese of Nancy, he was named bp. of Angers in 1893, then abp. of Toulouse in 1896. He was created cardinal in 1899 and called to Rome, where he served on several curial congregations and as a papal envoy. He was a man of letters, and from 1906 a member of the Académie Française. M. made particularly effective contributions to Leo XIII's policy of *ralliement, which called for Catholic political support for the Third Republic.

[T. C. O'BRIEN]

MATHIS, MICHAEL AMBROSE (1885–1960), American Congregation of the Holy Cross priest, liturgist, and missiologist, co-founder of the Medical Mission Committee (later, the Catholic Medical Board) and the Medical Mission Sisters. In 1947 he established the Notre Dame School of Liturgical Studies. BIBLIOGRAPHY: C. E. Schidel, "Never Too Much. In Memoriam: Rev. Michael Ambrose Mathis, C.S.C." YBLS 3 (1962) 3–34.

[N. KOLLAR]

MATHURINS (Mathurines), a name used in English as well as in French for the *Trinitarians. They probably received this name because their principal house in Paris was near the chapel of St. Maturin.

[T. C. O'BRIEN]

MATIGNON, FRANCIS ANTHONY (1753–1818), missionary. Born in France, M. was ordained in 1778. A teacher at the College of Navarre from 1786 to 1791, he was forced to leave France during the Revolution when he refused to accept the *Civil Constitution of the Clergy. In 1792 he came to the U.S. and was assigned to Boston, Massachusetts. His tact and diplomacy ended internal strife between French and Irish Catholics and won the respect of Protestants. With J. *Cheverus he labored in a mission field that covered all of New England. M. built the first Catholic church in Boston, raising the money himself from both Catholics and Protestants. In 1808 he refused to be considered for the office of first bp. of Boston and Cheverus was appointed.

[J. R. AHERNE]

MATILDA, QUEEN OF GERMANY, ST. (*c.*895–968), wife of Henry the Fowler (later King Henry I); foundress of several monasteries including Nordhausen and Quedlinburg. She was mother of: Otto I (the Great); Gerberga, wife of Louis IV of France; Hedwig, mother of Hugh Capet; Bruno, abp. of Cologne; and Henry, Duke of Bavaria. BIBLIOGRAPHY: Butler 1:592–593; M. Kornstedt, K. Kunze, BiblSanct 9:93–96.

[M. F. MCCARTHY]

MATILDA OF TUSCANY (1046–1114), ruler of Tuscany, friend and defender of Gregory VII in the *investiture struggle. Daughter of Count Boniface II of Tuscany, she inherited his large and strategically located territory in northern Italy at a time when Emperor and Pope were engaged in a power struggle. When Gregory VII excommunicated Emperor Henry IV in 1076, M. arranged the reconciliation at her castle in Canossa (1077). She led an army in defense of Pope Victor III. Twice her domain was devastated by the forces of Henry IV. His successor Henry V made peace with her and appointed her vice-regent of Liguria. Her vast holdings were donated to the papacy and became the nucleus of the *States of the Church. In the 17th cent. her remains were transferred to a tomb in St. Peter's, Rome, designed by Bernini.

[J. R. AHERNE]

MATINS, from the Latin *matutinum*, the morning hours. The term was first used for the morning prayer of praise, today called *Lauds. In church usage, Matins was the name for the night office recited in choir inasmuch as it was celebrated at the end of the night toward the hour of prayer at dawn, Lauds. For a long time priests have been allowed to anticipate Matins, i.e., to recite them the previous afternoon; however, with the revision of the Liturgy of the Hours Matins may be said at any time of the day and is now called the Office of Readings. According to the 1971 General Instruction on the Liturgy of the Hours, retaining the form of a nocturnal vigil service the Office of Readings, if it is said as the first hour of the day, begins with an antiphon with the Invitatory psalm (Ps 94); otherwise it begins with the introductory verse; then follow: a hymn, three psalms with their antiphons; verse; 1st Reading, biblical, with its Responsory; 2d Reading, Patristic or hagiographical, with its Responsory (if it is a longer vigil there is an added antiphon, three OT canticles, then the Gospel); the *Te Deum*, if prescribed; the prayer, proper to the day; and the conclusion. BIBLIOGRAPHY: Podhradsky 134–135.

[C. J. NOONE]

MATISSE, HENRI ÉMILE (1869–1954), distinguished 20th-cent. French painter and sculptor, leader of Fauvism—first expressed in the Paris Salon d'Automne, 1905. Studying (1890–91), M. finally joined the atelier of G. Moreau, where he met Rouault. At first a follower of old masters (1896), then a post-Impressionist (M. acquired a Cézanne, 1898), beginning to carve (1900), influenced by neoimpressionism (1905), African and Near Eastern decorative arts (*Odalisque,* 1923), M. executed boldly patterned, brilliantly colored works with free linear definition. He received the International Prize (1927) and a commission for murals at the Barnes Foundation, Merion, Pa. (1933). In Vence (1939) M. introduced his vivid cut-paper designs (1940s), and was given an impressive show at the Philadelphia Museum of Art, 1948. In 1948–51 he engaged in the entire decorative scheme for the Dominican Chapelle du Rosaire at Vence, designing innovative stations and other images in powerful black lines on white tile (related to the Dominican habit), stained glass, the altar and its appurtenances, and the vestments, executing last projects from his sick bed. He collaborated with Léger and others in Nôtre-Dame-de-Toute-Grâce at Assy. A museum in his honor was established at Le Cateau (1952) and large retrospective shows throughout the world followed his death.

M.'s sculpture in small bronzes (1899–1935) moved from rhythmic emphasis, through cubistic structures, to the nearly abstract elegant bronze crucifix at Vence, his last sculptured piece. M. ranks with Picasso as a most innovative 20th-cent. creative master of remarkable productivity in painting and graphics (drawings, lithographs), whose theories were widely influential. BIBLIOGRAPHY: A. H. Barr, *Matisse, His Art and His Public* (1951).

[M. J. DALY]

MATRIARCHY, a system of lineal descent based on female kinship, incorporating concepts of female inheritance and dominance. Also referred to as "matriarchate" and "matriliny," it denotes the custom of reckoning kinship, descent, succession, and inheritance in the female line. Rejected outright by some anthropologists (Lowie, *Primitive Society*, 1947), the concept is well established in cultural tradition. W. R. Smith (*Kinship and Marriage in Early Arabia*) calls the form of marriage in which the husband becomes part of his wife's tribe *sadica*, from the *sadac* or gift given to the wife. *Mota* marriage is restricted to occasional visits to her home (cf. Samson's marriage). Beena marriage incorporates the husband and children in the wife's clan. Genesis 2.24, Mt 19.5, Mk 10.7, etc. commemorate the principle in Hebrew tradition in what appears to be an ossified formula. Laban claims Jacob's wives and children as his own (Gen 31.31,43); other OT traces of matriarchy may be found in Ex 2.21, 4.18, Jgs 14,15,16.4, in the stories of the marriages of Moses and Samson. Among Trobriand islanders, children call their father "my mother's husband"; Agamemnon called his wife "daughter of Leda." Among Finno-Ugric tribes, the expression "slipper husband" refers to a dominated male, one who cannot leave the house without permission of the matriarch. The Witch of Lapland in *The Kalevala*, Finland's national epic, rules her country, calls councils, declares and fights wars in classical matriarchal fashion; the reader learns almost accidentally that her husband is alive and well, indoors. Géza Képes discusses the same motif among Ugric tribes living in Siberia today. In W. Schmidt's scheme, matriarchy is one of the three primary cultures —the other two being patrilineal-totemic and patriarchal-nomadic. He maintains that in matrilineal agrarian culture, because of their pioneering work in the cultivation of plants, women obtained a high economic and social position. The cult of Mother Earth, combined with worship of the moon as a female, is so widespread in ancient religion that Robert Graves declares, "Men feared, adored, and obeyed the matriarch; the hearth which she tended in a cave or hut being their earliest social center and motherhood their prime mystery." BIBLIOGRAPHY: R. Graves, *Greek Myths* (1955); W. Schmidt, *Origin and Growth of Religion* (tr. H. J. Rose, 1931); V. Diószegi, *Sámanok nyomában Szibéria földjén,* 1960. *MOON WORSHIP; *FINNO-UGRIC RELIGION; *ANCESTOR WORSHIP.

[D. H. BRUNAUER]

MATRICULA, an official list of members enrolled in a medieval university, after having taken their oath of obedience to the rector and paid their fee. Matriculation was originally a practice in student-universities, e.g., Bologna, since only in them did students acquire full university membership. In Paris and Oxford, where only masters enjoyed full membership, there was no student matricula.

[M. B. MURPHY]

MATRIMONY, see MARRIAGE.

MATTEO DA BASCIO (1495–1552), cofounder of Capuchin Franciscans. M. was born in Montefeltro. He joined the Franciscan Observants and was ordained in 1520. Since the 14th cent. the Observants had constituted the branch of the Friars Minor which sought strict adherence to the rule of St. Francis. However, M. believed that the Observants were losing the vigorous dedication to the life of poverty advocated by St. Francis. In 1525, M. journeyed to Rome and petitioned Pope Clement VII for permission to become a wandering preacher living the rule of St. Francis to the fullest and wearing a hooded garment similar to that of the founder. He was granted papal approval but soon came under attack from the Observant provincial Giovanni da Fano for the unauthorized trip to Rome and unauthorized preaching in the Marches of Ancona. Da Fano was unaware of Clement's concessions to M. and promptly imprisoned him. M. was freed through the efforts of the Duchess of Camerino, who was indebted to the friar for his work among her subjects during the plague. Lodovico da Fossombrone joined M. in leading the eremitical life and it was he who secured from Clement in 1528 the bull *Religionis zeleus* which recognized the existence of the Capuchins. In 1529 the first chapter, consisting of 12 members, met at Albacina and wrote a constitution for the emerging Order. M. was elected vicar general but soon resigned that post. He deeply desired to pursue the life of the solitary preacher and played a minor part in the administration of the Capuchins. M. spent the remainder of his life preaching in Italy and Germany. In his steadfast devotion to the principles of St. Francis, M. represented the archetype of a new order which would affect not only the Franciscan community but the entire Catholic Reformation. BIBLIOGRAPHY: Cuthbert, *The Capuchins* (v. 1, 1928); M. Pobladura, *Historia generalis Ord. Fr. Minor Capuccinorum* (v. 1, 1947).

[R. J. BRADY]

MATTER AND FORM. In scholastic philosophy, these are two of the first principles of mobile (material) being with privation being the third. These principles and their meaning are derived from a dialectical explanation of *motion or *change. Thus, in substantial change something new comes into being or passes away; in an accidental change the subject acquires or loses some attribute. Change is not from nothingness to being nor from being to nothingness; the stable "something" or subject which persists throughout the change is called matter. The aspect or attribute of matter which changes is called form. In substantial change is an essential change of the whole or mobile, material being. Thus, if the wooden table is destroyed by fire, the the substance or subject called secondary matter with respect to some accidental quality or form. In a similar way there is a corresponding accidental form and substantial form. Etymologically, matter once had the meaning of forest because wood is a common subject for man's making of things and, therefore, the term matter could be extended to include the subject of change or motion. While form originally had a geometrical significance, in the sense of shape, the term form could be broadened to encompass the culmination or completion of any change. The difference between accidental and substantial change may be illustrated by way of example. A wooden table may originally be its own natural color and a painter paints the table green. In this way, the table undergoes an accidental change, i.e., its color is changed but the table, the subject of change, remains. In other words, the table retains the matter and form of what makes a table a table, but one of its accidents, namely color, is changed. On the other hand, substantial change is an essential change of the whole or mobile, material being. Thus, if the wooden table is destroyed by fire, the table becomes ashes and a substantial change is effected. Briefly, in accidental change according to the example given, the color of the table is changed but remains a table whereas in substantial change, as exemplified, what was a table ceases to be a table.

In classical Catholic theology the principles of matter and form are employed in explaining the sacraments. Thus, in each of the seven sacraments there exist both material and formal elements constituting the one reality of the sacrament. See MATTER OF THE SACRAMENTS; TRANSUBSTANTIATION. In the sacrament of the Eucharist, the bread and wine are the matter whereas the consecration of this matter by the priest in the Eucharistic Liturgy constitutes the form (see TRANSUBSTANTIATION).

[F. T. RYAN]

MATTER OF THE SACRAMENTS, one of the two constitutive parts of the sacramental sign, the other part being the *form. Matter refers to the sensible objects used to produce the sacramental sign in conjunction with the form, i.e., the words and/or actions which specify the significance of the pertinent matter. The terminology, matter and form, is derived from Aristotelian cosmology; but the two-fold division of sacramental sign expressed in this terminology is rooted in the NT: baptism with water and the Holy Spirit (Jn 3.5); confirmation with prayer and imposition of hands (Acts 8.14–17); Eucharist with the words of Jesus, and bread and wine (Mt 26.26–28). Patristic writers, reflecting upon biblical data of this kind and upon the Church's liturgical practices, began to speak of a sacramental sign as composed of two complementary parts variously designated: heavenly and earthly elements, visible and invisible elements, or word and element as expressed in Augustine, "The word comes to the element and a sacrament takes place" (*In evan. Ioan.* 80.3). Just as the Divine Word assumed a human nature to constitute Christ, the Primordial Sacrament, so also within the Church, the Divine Word assumes to himself another portion of created nature, e.g., water, bread, wine, to constitute a sacrament, which as an efficacious sign prolongs his Incarnation. With the advent of Aristotelian philosophy in the West, the sacramental word became the form of the sacrament, and the sacramental element became the matter of the sacrament, thus expressing in hylomorphic terminology the biblical duality of a sacramental sign. BIBLIOGRAPHY: B. Leeming, *Principles* *of Sacramental Theology* (1960); E. Schillebeeckx, *Christ the Sacrament of the Encounter with God* (1963).

[J. J. FLOOD]

MATTHEW, APOSTLE AND EVANGELIST, ST., one of the 12 Apostles of Jesus (Mk 3.18; Mt 10.3; Lk 6.15; Acts 1.13), and traditionally held to be the author of the Gospel of Matthew. In Mt. 10.3, he is called the publican, or tax-collector. According to Mt 9.9–13, he was a revenue officer of King Herod in Capernaum when Jesus called him to be an Apostle. The story of his call is the same as that of Levi (Mk 2.13–17) with whom he is probably to be identified. M. was present at Pentecost (Acts 1.13) but little is known of his work in the early Church. BIBLIOGRAPHY: EDB 1479–80.

[J. A. GRASSI]

MATTHEW OF ALBANO (*c.* 1085–1135), monk, cardinal. After studying with *Anselm of Laon, he joined the Cluniac monks after his ordination. He was an important monastic reformer in N Italy. Honorius II made him cardinal bishop of Albano in 1125. M. was sent by Innocent II to reform monastic life in France (1127) and in Germany (1128). BIBLIOGRAPHY: D. S. Buczek, NCE 9:490 (bibliog.).

[V. BULLOUGH]

MATTHEW OF AQUASPARTA (*c.* 1238–1302), Franciscan theologian, cardinal. A native of Aquasparta in Umbria, he became a doctor of theology in Paris in 1273. As minister general (1287–89) he strove to heal the divisions in his order. He was created cardinal in 1288 by Nicholas IV, and served Boniface VIII in diplomatic missions. In his many theological writings, he opposed Thomistic departures from the traditional Augustinianism defended by St. Bonaventure and the Franciscans. BIBLIOGRAPHY: G. Gál, NCE 9:491.

[T. C. O'BRIEN]

MATTHEW OF ARRAS (d. 1352), French master architect of the Gothic style working in Bohemia, appointed master of the Gothic cathedral of St. Vitus of Prague in 1344 under King John of Bohemia and his son Charles IV. M. had been architect at Narbonne cathedral. After his death P. Parler continued the work at St. Vitus.

[M. J. DALY]

MATTHEW OF CRACOW (*c.* 1330–1410), theologian and bp. of Worms. He taught theology at Charles Univ., Prague, and at the Univ. of Heidelberg. In 1396 he became rector at Heidelberg and confessor to King Rupert. M. returned to Poland in 1397 to reorganize the Univ. of Cracow. He became bp. of Worms in 1405, cardinal in 1408, and papal legate to Germany in the same year. His most important theological work, *De squaloribus curiae romanae*, advocates the supremacy of the council over the pope.

[M. J. FINNEGAN]

MATTHEW PARIS (*c.* 1200–59), English Benedictine monk of St. Alban's, chronicler. Visitors to his abbey, esp. important people in Church and State, supplied much of his information, although he made short trips and went on a papal commission to Norway (1248). His *Chronica majora* was the first illustrated account of contemporary events (1236–59) by an Englishman. Though inaccurate, his narrative is a fascinating and valuable record of the gossip and attitudes of the men of his own time. His artistic skill was considerable, and his maps are a landmark in cartography. His works included lives of Abps. Stephen Langton and Edmund Rich. He opposed the granting of English benefices to foreigners and was critical of government spending. BIBLIOGRAPHY: V. H. Galbraith, *Roger Wendover and Matthew Paris* (1944); R. Vaughan, *Matthew Paris* (1958).

[F. D. BLACKLEY]

MATTHEW OF VENDÔME (fl. late 12th cent.), author. M. studied at cathedral schools in Tours, Orléans, and Paris, then settled in Tours. His best-known work, *Tobias* (*c.* 1185) is a version of the Book of Tobit in verse. He also wrote *Ars versificatoria* which dealt with rules of expression and their methods of practical application. He also produced a collection of model letters. Several poems are ascribed to him including the Milo, a kind of Latin fabliau. BIBLIOGRAPHY: W. C. Korfmacher, NCE 9:492–493.

[V. BULLOUGH]

MATTHEW, GOSPEL ACCORDING TO ST., the first of the four Gospels according to the traditional listing of the NT canon. The actual canonical Gospel was in fact written in Greek, after Mk, and its author was not the Apostle Matthew-Levi (see Mt 9.9–13; 10.3), but an anonymous Palestinian Jew, writing probably in Antioch *c.* 80 A.D., after the fall of Jerusalem (70 A.D.). *Papias, writing in 130 A.D., is the source for the tradition that Matthew wrote the first Gospel in Aramaic. In dealing with the *Synoptic problem some accept this tradition, seeing in Aramaic Matthew one of the sources of Greek Matthew as well as of Mk and Lk (see JB, "Introduction to the Synoptic Gospels"; this is the theory of P. Benoit). Others question whether Papias' statement is reliable; certainly Greek Matthew is not a translation from Aramaic (see J. L. McKenzie, JBC 2:62–66).

The basic and distinctive message of Mt is conditioned by those to whom it seems primarily to have been addressed: Jewish Christians who are to have the responsibility of instructing their fellows and receiving them into the Church. This message is epitomized in the closing words of the Gospel: "All power in heaven and on earth has been given to me. Go, therefore, make disciples of all the nations; baptize them in the name of the Father and of the Son and of the Holy Spirit, and teach them to observe all the commands I gave you. And know that I am with you always, yes, to the end of time." (28.18–20). In the mind of Mt this message is directed to those who are to be the teachers and instructors in the "true Israel" which is the Church. This true Israel, the predestined heir to the OT promises, now brought to their fullness in Christ, is henceforward to be extended to all the nations of the earth. It is distinguished from the false Israel of the Jews, who, by consciously and culpably rejecting the Messiah and seeking to destroy him, have shown themselves to be false and no true heirs to the blessings foreshadowed in the Law and the prophets. The true Israel, by contrast, fortified by the power and presence of her risen and glorified Lord, is to last all days and to embrace all nations. Those addressed by this Gospel are to make disciples of these by baptizing them and instructing them in all Christ's commands, and so inculcating that "higher righteousness" of Christ's new Law which extends beyond and is more perfect than the righteousness of the Old Law as interpreted by the scribes. By hearing Christ's word and keeping it and so becoming members of the true Israel of the Church these gentiles will inherit the blessings of the kingdom of heaven which include, yet go far beyond, the promises of the Old Law. All this has been and is being achieved in and through Christ as new Moses and Son of David in a manner that fulfills, yet surpasses the predictions of the OT prophets.

In order to convey this basic message the author has artificially schematized his material. This appears most clearly in the fact that he has assembled the words of Jesus into five great discourses which form the central part of the Gospel (Sermon on the Mount, 5.1–7.29; Missionary Discourse, 9.35–11.1; Parables of the Kingdom, 13.1–52; Sermon on the Church, 18.1–35; Eschatological Sermon, 24.1-25.46). To each of these a more or less appropriate section of narrative material is attached. To this central part has been prefixed the genealogy and infancy narrative, and the Gospel concludes with the Passion narrative, making seven main sections in all.

This Gospel presupposes a Church with some kind of hierarchical ministry already in being. It is above all the Gospel of OT fulfillment, and its focal point is not precisely the Resurrection of Christ as in Mk, not "repentance leading to the forgiveness of sins" as in Lk, but the commands of Christ which inculcate a higher righteousness, and which must steadfastly be fulfilled despite all persecutions for the sake of the kingdom of heaven. BIBLIOGRAPHY: K. Stendahl, *School of St. Matthew* (1954); W. Trilling, *Das wahre Israel* (3d ed., 1964); B. Rigaux, *Témoignage de l'Évangile de Matthieu* (1967); G. Bornkamm et al., *Tradition and Interpretation in Matthew* (tr. P. Scott, 1963).

[D. J. BOURKE]

MATTHEW, MARTYRDOM OF, see APOCRYPHA (NT), 35.

MATTHEWS, MARY BERNARDINA (1732–1800), religious superior. Of an aristocratic Maryland family, M. entered the Discalced Carmelites in Belgium in 1754. She became mistress of novices and later prioress. When Emperor Joseph II suppressed religious orders in the Low Countries in 1782, M. came back to Maryland and was named prioress of the new foundation at Port Tobacco. The convent she established there in 1790, was the first American Discalced Carmelite cloister.

[J. R. AHERNE]

MATTHEWS, WILLIAM (1770–1854), missionary, pastor, public figure. Of an old Maryland family, M. became the first American to be ordained to the priesthood (1800). He worked in Maryland for several years, but most of his career was spent in Washington, D.C., as pastor of St. Patrick's church. M. served briefly as president of Georgetown College; he was a founder and president for 13 years of Washington's first public library, a trustee of its public school system from 1813 to 1844. M. established an orphan asylum for girls, aided in the foundation of Visitation Girls' School and St. Joseph Orphanage for boys. He was a friend of such great national figures as Andrew Jackson and Henry Clay. M. refused the See of Philadelphia after serving there as administrator.

[J. R. AHERNE]

MATTHEW'S BIBLE, a patchwork of *Tyndale's and *Coverdale's versions, published at Antwerp (1537), dedicated to Henry VIII, and licensed for general reading. Thomas Matthew for whom the edition was named was an alias for John *Rogers; he contributed prefaces and marginal notes.

[T. GILBY]

MATTHIAS, APOSTLE, ST., the Disciple chosen by lot to take the place of Judas (Acts 1.23–26). He was one who had accompanied the Apostles from the baptism of Jesus until his Ascension. The early traditions concerning him found in the apocryphal books and in the Fathers are not reliable. For some unknown reason his name was esp. honored in Gnostic circles in Ancient Egypt, and a number of apocryphal writings have been attributed to him. BIBLIOGRAPHY: Butler 1:407–408; A. Sisti, BiblSanct 9:150–154.

[M. F. MCNAMARA]

MATTHIAS A CORONA (1598–1676), French Carmelite. M. was several times prior at Lüttich and general commissioner for Belgium. He wrote a kind of encyclopedia of Catholic theology (8 v., 1663–76), a portion of which brought him repute as a missiologist. BIBLIOGRAPHY: G. Mesters, LTK 7:180.

[M. J. SUELZER]

MATTHIAS CORVINUS (Mátyás Hunyadi; *c.* 1440–90), king of Hungary and of Bohemia. Over the opposition of Emperor Frederick III (d. 1493), M. was elected king of Hungary in 1458. He fought against the Turks, intervened in Bohemia against *George of Poděbrad at the urging of Pius II, and was made king of Bohemia by the pro-Roman faction (1469). Through alliances and through victories over Frederick III, M. extended his rule over most of central Europe. He introduced the Renaissance into Hungary, and at Buda built up a library, the Corvina, celebrated for its illuminated codices. His reign was also one of political stability and justice. BIBLIOGRAPHY: D. Sinor, *History of Hungary* (1959).

MATTHIAS, GOSPEL OF, see APOCRYPHA (NT), 36.

MATTHYS, JAN (Matthijsz, Matthyszoon, Matthiessen; d. 1534), Anabaptist fanatic. M., a Dutch baker, was the first ruler during the *Anabaptist reign at Münster, 1533–35. On April 5, 1534, picturing himself as a second Gideon, he led a reckless sortie against the siege laid by the bishop, F. von *Waldeck, and was slain. See bibliog. for Anabaptists.

[T. C. O'BRIEN]

MATTIAS, MARIA DE, BL. (1805–66), Italian foundress of the Sisters Adorers of the Most Precious Blood, a congregation of religious women with special devotion to the Precious Blood and dedicated to the education of youth. The congregation dates from March 4, 1834, with the opening of a school at Acuto at the invitation of Bp. Lais, who was also administrator of Anagni; she eventually founded 63 houses. M. enjoyed the generous patronage of a Russian widow, Princess Zena Wolkonska. Her lifelong spiritual advisor was Ven. John Merlini, disciple of St. Caspar del Bufalo of the Missioners of the Precious Blood. M. was beatified in 1950. Butler 3:368–369; F. Caraffa, BiblSanct 4:549–550.

[E. J. DILLON]

MATTIUSSI, GUIDO (1852–1925), Italian Jesuit, compiler of the 24 theses proposed as the fundamental principles and positions of St. Thomas Aquinas's philosophy, and issued by the Vatican July 27, 1914. He was a professor at the Gregorian Univ. in Rome; published his own commentary on the 24 theses: *Le 24 tesi della filosofia di s. Tommaso* (1917). M. also published several dogmatic treatises, a critique of I. *Kant, *Il veleno kantiano* (1907), and an attack on Modernism, *Il giuramento anti-modernista* (1909). BIBLIOGRAPHY: P. Dezza, EncCatt 8:502.

[T. C. O'BRIEN]

MATULAITIS-MATULECWICZ, GEORG (1871–1927), apostolic visitator. A native of Lithuania ordained in 1898, M. taught at the Catholic Academy of St. Petersburg. From 1918 to 1925 he served as bp. of Vilna and from 1925 to 1927 as abp. and apostolic visitator to Lithuania. W. was a strong promoter of RC-Russian Orthodox unity.

[J. R. AHERNE]

MATURIN, BASIL WILLIAM (1847–1915), spiritual writer. Born in Ireland, M. became an Anglican priest in England and in 1873 entered the Cowley Fathers. For 10 years M. served at St. Clement's in Philadelphia, Pennsylvania. A noted preacher and spiritual adviser, he entered the Catholic Church in 1897, was ordained in 1898, and did parish work in London. M. became a member of the Westminster Diocesan Missionaries, and was chaplain to the Catholic students at Oxford for a time. He was drowned in the sinking of the *Lusitania*. Among his books on the spiritual life were *Self-Knowledge and Self-Discipline* (1905), *Laws of the Spiritual Life* (1907), and *Fruits of the Life of Prayer* (1916).

[J. R. AHERNE]

MATURITY, in moral theology, minimally the capacity to make a responsible moral choice. In the whole span of the Christian life, the meaning of maturity is best expressed in the words of St. Paul, "And his gifts were that some should be apostles, some prophets, some evangelists, some pastors and teachers, for the equipment of the saints, for the work of the ministry, for building up the body of Christ, until we all attain to the unity of the faith and of the knowledge of the Son of God, to mature manhood, to the measure of the stature of the fulness of Christ; so that we may no longer be children. . . . Rather, speaking the truth in love, we are to grow up in every way into him who is the head, into Christ, from whom the whole body . . . makes bodily growth and upbuilds itself in love" (Eph 4.11–16; cf 2.19–22; 3.17–19). A minimal moral maturity can be described in an abstract view of human life as the power to be aware of self and to choose between what is genuinely perfective of self and what is beneficial to one appetite, but detrimental to the whole person. There is a theoretical moral point in which a first decision will express an evaluation of self either as ultimate and absolute or as perfectible and related to another, true good; that point will mark either a right or a wrong moral choice and orientation (see ThAq ST 1a2ae, 89.6). More concretely in a Christian context this minimal moral maturity will be a capacity to ratify or to contradict the identity a person has through baptism. Such maturity is sacramentalized in the ideal meaning and reception of confirmation. In the actual condition of any individual person it may coincide or not with the confirmation or with any given age. In contemporary Catholic life the preparation and judgment by parents on *first communion and first *confession, as well as formal religious instruction, are designed to lead children to a basic Christian maturity. But whatever the process or techniques a person's ratification of Christian identity is always, at least implicitly, involved where there is truly a Christian choice in acting rightly or a lack of such a choice in sinning. That is simply a question of choosing a moral good in conformity to the being that is conferred by baptism, or of failing to do so. It is altogether conceivable that a person's whole moral life may lack such maturity and be only a disposition for some moment or period of crisis in which a truly interior decision becomes the choice or the rejection of salvation. The fuller sense of Christian maturity expressed in St. Paul's words can also be described by a generality as growth in virtue. The theological meaning of faith, hope, and charity is that they are the resources for growth and progress in the spiritual life, of growth in union with God. That union never reaches full development until the beatific vision; faith is the beginning of eternal life, hope progress towards it, charity the measure of its attainment. The meaning of the moral virtues is that they keep the judgments of prudence about concrete moral choices in conformity with charity's love of God above all; the progressive appetite for the good and the amenability of all human faculties is necessary for right, mature moral judgment. More concretely St. Paul's imagery of the body vitalized and growing through Christ the head is the Christian meaning of maturing. The measure of growth is the stature of the fullness of Christ. The sign of growth is "speaking the truth in love." Maturity and growth can never end, because Christ is the measure who cannot be equalled. But Christ above all is the Son, and maturity means growing more like him in sonship. The source of that growth is the vital communication vivifying the spirit of filiation; it is a communication within Christ's body, the community of faith and love, so that it is a growth in the love of Christ's other members. Speaking the truth in love means the deepening of faith, above all in the meaning of all life as seen under God's Fatherhood of Christ and of Christ's brethren. Maturity as it means wisdom is a judgment of self, of others, and of the world inspired by love for the Father (see Rom 8.15–17).

[T. C. O'BRIEN]

MAUBUISSON, ABBEY OF, convent of Cistercian nuns near Versailles. Founded by Queen Blanche of Castile (1236), it was richly endowed and populated by French aristocracy. After a period of decline (15th–16th cent.) it was reformed by nuns of Port Royal, but was suppressed in 1791. Of the once magnificent Gothic structure only some ruins survive. BIBLIOGRAPHY: L. J. Lekai, NCE 9:505.

[L. J. LEKAI]

MAUNDY THURSDAY, the name given traditionally to the Thursday preceding Easter. The English "Maundy" derives from the opening word of the Latin antiphon at the ceremony of the washing of the feet, *mandatum novum do vobis*, "a new commandment I give to you," (Jn 13.34); the ceremony itself was called the *Mandatum peragendum*.

[S. A. HEENEY]

MAUNOIR, JULIEN, BL. (1606–1683), French Jesuit. In 1625 he joined the Society of Jesus with the hope of an assignment to a foreign mission. However, after his ordination he was sent to Brittany on what would be a lifelong mission. Initially, M. received counsel and support only from LeNobletz while the rest of the ecclesiastical community in the province remained neutral, if not hostile. He sought to strengthen Catholicism in NW France by using the cultural traditions of the Bretons as a vehicle. An excellent orator and poet, M. preached to the people in the richness of their own language. He wrote hymns in the Breton tongue and encouraged devotion to such native saints as Corentino. M. eventually won the support of the secular priests of the province as his revival of the faith swept the countryside. He was beatified by Pius XII in 1951. BIBLIOGRAPHY: R. de la Chevasnerie, *Le Tad Mad:Vie du bienheureux Julien Maunoir* (1951); Butler 1:193–95; Bremond 5:82–117.

[R. J. BRADY]

MAURIAC, FRANÇOIS (1885–1970), French novelist. Educated in part by the Marianist Fathers at l'École Grand-Lebrun near Bordeaux, M. was influenced to a greater degree by immersion in woman-dominated worlds at Château-Lange, St. Symphorien, and Malagar. Preoccupation with death, sin, suffering, and the impact of grace stamp his novels, in which frequent autobiographical skeins are discerned. Steeped in the French classics, M. reveals the influence of Pascal and Racine, as well as that of Baudelaire and Rimbaud, among others. His progress through the world of the novel to a comparative objectivity is marked by such works as *The Desert of Love, Thérèse Desqueyroux*. Lyrical undertones and rhythms balance and merge with a strong tendency toward objectivity. Despite a deeply personal and poetic cast, M. juxtaposes tormented and frustrated persons against a seemingly safe family framework. Such a milieu evokes the term Jansenistic as one more label for him. Gide, Proust, and Freud influenced him, though he disagreed basically with their views. The loss of many friends during World War I, during which he performed ambulance duty, aided no doubt his growing tendency toward a deeper and more pervasive melancholy. His "wonderful years" (*c.* 1920–*c.* 1930) produced such works as *A Kiss for the Leper* (1922), *Thérèse Desqueyroux* (1927), and *The Knot of Vipers* (1932). M. received the *Grand Prix du Roman* of the Academy (1925) and was offered a seat in the Academy itself in 1933. He was awarded the Nobel prize for literature in 1952. M.'s apologia for Christianity counters an awareness of the absence of grace with faith in a strange, lonely love, a quasi-negative statement of our need for God. BIBLIOGRAPHY: P. Stratford, *Faith and Fiction* (1964).

[R. M. FUNCHION]

MAURICE, ST. (d. *c.* 286), martyr. According to the legendary account of the martyrdom of this saint, together with that of Exuperius, Candidus, and their fellow soldiers, these men formed a Christian legion which had been recruited from the region of Thebes in Egypt. In a military campaign to put down an uprising, the legion was twice decimated and finally slaughtered to a man, either for refusing to offer sacrifice or for refusing to shed innocent Christian blood. There is no surviving contemporary documentary evidence of this event, though if the facts were as alleged, it could hardly have escaped attention. The earliest account of it was written by Eucherius, bp. of Lyons (434–450), whose record of it was variously interpolated by later scribes. Eucherius claimed that in 380 Theodore, bp. of Octodurum (Martigny), built a church to enshrine the relics of these martyrs. Excavations have given evidence of the existence of the church, which suggests that there may have been some core of fact to the story, although its details were probably greatly exaggerated. BIBLIOGRAPHY: R. Henggeler and M. C. Celletti, BiblSanct 9:193–205; Butler 3: 619–621.

[H. DRESSLER]

MAURICE (539–602), **BYZANTINE EMPEROR** from 582. His greatest religious problem was the Monophysite heresy. Until 598 M. tolerated the Monophysites but thereafter gave more support to the Chalcedonian cause. He promoted the spread of orthodoxy among the Arab neighbors of the empire. M.'s relations with Pope Gregory I were strained on three accounts. The emperor forbade military and governmental personnel to become clergy; he backed the Patriarchs John the Faster and Cyriacus in their use of the title "ecumenical patriarch"; he ordered the Pope to break off diplomatic negotiations with the Lombard invaders of Italy. Gregory's protests were in vain on the first two points as was M's on the third. BIBLIOGRAPHY: F. H. Dudden, *Gregory the Great* (2 v., 1905, repr. 1967).

[R. H. SCHMANDT]

MAURICE OF CARNÖET, ST. (*c.*1114–91), Cistercian abbot. He entered the abbey of Langonnet in 1143, and became abbot 4 years later. In 1171 he founded the abbey of Carnoët (later renamed St. Maurice) and became abbot in 1176. BIBLIOGRAPHY: M.A. Dimier, BiblSanct 9:205–206; Butler 4:105–106.

[V. BULLOUGH]

MAURICE OF SULLY (1120–96), bp. of Paris, theologian. Of peasant background, M. was educated at Paris, became professor of theology there, and (1160) bp. of Paris. He broke ground in 1163 for the cathedral of Notre Dame. He wrote the vernacular *Sermons on the Gospels*, a collection of models for young priests, and the oldest extant prose work in French literature. BIBLIOGRAPHY: J.A. Corbett, NCE 9:507

[V. BULLOUGH]

MAURICE, FREDRICK DENISON (1805-72), Anglican social reformer. An East Anglian, reared a Unitarian, M. read law at Trinity Hall, Cambridge, studied at Oxford, and was baptized and ordained in the C of E (1834). He was not personally acquainted with the leading Tractarians, and afterward he stood apart from the high- and the low-church schools; nor was he broad church, for that to him was but a *caput mortuum* that just abandoned disputed doctrines. Like his friend Charles *Kingsley, he was moved by the revolutions of 1848; he was convinced that the Church should enter into, and not merely patronize, social reform; both were among the founders of *Christian Socialism. M. started the Working Men's Colleges (1854), and was appointed Knightsbridge Professor of Moral Philosophy at Cambridge (1866). Gentle and courteous in conversation, he could be sufficiently caustic in controversy. BIBLIOGRAPHY: F. Higham, *Frederick Denison Maurice* (1948); C.J. Brose, *Frederick Denison Maurice, Rebellious Conformist 1805–1872* (1972).

[T. GILBY]

MAURIN, ARISTIDE PETER (1877–1949), radical writer and teacher instrumental in founding *The *Catholic Worker*. Born of a French peasant family near Oulet, in Languedoc, M. emigrated in 1909, after 11 years as a Christian Brother and some years of teaching. For the next 15 years he roamed the U.S. and Canada, teaching and working in industry and agriculture, before adopting a life of voluntary poverty based on his concept of labor as a gift rather than a commodity to be sold. *The Catholic Worker,* started at his instigation in 1933, disseminated his program of round-table discussions, houses of hospitality, and farming communes, embodied in his "Easy Essays"—a prose form divided into strongly rhythmic "sense lines" resembling free verse and marked by alliteration and plays on words. He died at the Catholic Worker farm at Newburgh, N.Y. BIBLIOGRAPHY: A. Sheehan, *Peter Maurin: Gay Believer* (1959).

[D. CODDINGTON]

MAURISTS, Benedictines of the French Benedictine Congregation of St. Maur. Pope Gregory XV on May 17, 1621 canonically established this congregation, which developed under the initiative of Laurent Benard from an earlier reform movement at the abbey of St. Vanne. Strict observance of the Rule of St. Benedict and emphasis on education, preaching, and scientific research were its objectives. Most French Benedictine foundations joined it. The high ideals of Grégoire Tarisse, superior general (1630–48), set the standard for the Maurists' work for almost 2 cent. in Sacred Scripture, dogmatic and moral theology, patrology, canon law, Christian and monastic asceticism, history and its auxiliary disciplines, liturgy, and hagiography. Jansenistic influences, desire to relax strict discipline, and the French Revolution led to their collapse. The congregation was dissolved in 1818 by Pius VII. A. Chevreux, the last superior general, and two fellow monks executed in 1792 were beatified in 1926. BIBLIOGRAPHY: J. Baudot, DTC 10.1:405–443; *Tables Générales* (1967) 3166–68; G. Heer, LTK 7:190–192.

[H. DRESSLER]

MAURO, SILVESTRO (1619-87), Jesuit philosopher and theologian. Born at Spoleto, died at Rome, M. was rector of the Roman College. His commentaries on all the extant works of Aristotle (6v., 1668) offer a careful, faithful, and informed presentation of their Thomist interpretation.

[T. GILBY]

MAURRAS, CHARLES (1868–1952), political philosopher, leader of *Action francaise*. Inheriting through his mother the royalist Catholic tradition, M. led a life of controversy espousing the return of the monarchy to France. A prolific journalist, he contributed innumerable articles to the newspaper *L'Action française,* organ of the movement that he headed. A Darwinian approach to political theory led him to promote the view that the ideal government for France was the monarchy, supported by the Catholic Church as a guarantee of obedience and morality. M. had no real understanding of the Church's supernatural character but saw only its contribution to social stability. He long enjoyed the support of French Catholic royalists but earned the condemnation of the Holy See which placed a number of his books on the Index in 1926. A lapsed Catholic most of his life, M. returned to the Church in the year of his death. BIBLIOGRAPHY: H. Massis, *Maurras et notre temps* (1960).

[J. R. AHERNE]

MAURUS OF SUBIACO, ST. (d. first half of 6th cent). Benedictine monk. He was the son of a Roman senator and pupil of St. Benedict at Subiaco, whose trusted friend and companion he became. He may have succeeded Benedict as abbot of Subiaco when the latter retired to Monte Cassino. BIBLIOGRAPHY: A. Lentini, BiblSanct 9:210–219; Butler 1:97.

[G. M. COOK]

MAURUS, SYLVESTER (1619–87), Italian Jesuit, philosopher and theologian, professor at the Collegio Romano (1668–87). In theology he left *Opus theologicum* (3 v., 1687) and *Quaestionum theologicarum libri 6* (6 v., 1676–79); but his greater renown is for his commentaries on Aristotle. He was expert in Greek, as is evident from the work, *Aristotelis opera quae extant omnia brevi paraphrasi ac litterae perpetuo inhaerente explanatione illustrata* (6 v.,1668; modern ed., F.*Ehrle et al., ed., 1885–87). He also published *Quaestionum philosophicarum libri quinque* 1658; modern ed., preface by by M.*Liberatore, 1876).

[T. C. O'BRIEN]

MAURY, JEAN SUFFREIN (1746–1817), cardinal from 1794, prominent in the French Revolution and in the disputes between *Napoleon Bonaparte and Pius VII. M., the son of poor parents, became a renowned preacher in Paris, a member of the Estates General, championing the side of the aristocracy. He became an emigré in 1791, and at Rome in 1792 was made titular abp. and papal nuncio to Frankfurt; in 1794 he was named bp. of Montefiascone. After Pius VII's election in 1800,M. returned to Paris to support Bonaparte's régime; he acted as administrator of the Paris archdiocese. This led to a rebuke by Pius VII. When Napoleon fell from power, M. fled to Rome; he was imprisoned for 6 months and spent the last years of his life in obscurity. He published one homiletic work, *Essai sur l'éloquence de la chaire* (1777).

[T. C. O'BRIEN]

MAUSBACH, JOSEPH (1861–1931), German moral theologian, apologete. A priest of the diocese of Cologne, he taught moral theology at the Univ. of Münster from 1892 until his death. His manual, *Katholische Moraltheologie* (3 v.,1915–18), remained in continuous use and had its 10th edition by G. Ermecke in 1961. The comparative study, *Die katholische Moral und ihre Gegner* was published in England as *Catholic Moral Teaching and Its Antagonists* (1914). M. also wrote an apologetics text, *Grundzüge der katholische Apologetik* (1916: 6th ed. 1934), and insightful studies of Augustine and Aquinas: *Thomas von Aquin als Meister christlicher Sittenlehre* (1925); *Die Ethik des hl. Augustinus* (1909; 2d ed., 2 v., 1929).

[T. C. O'BRIEN]

MAWTB̲Ā (session, sitting), in the East Syrian Office a series of ecclesiastic and psalteric texts sung at the end of the psalmody *(hûllālē)* in the Night Office. Also, by extension, the *hûllālē* plus the *mawt̲bā* in the narrower sense, hence, a division of the Night Office. BIBLIOGRAPHY: J. Mateos, *Lelya-Ṣapra* (1959) 491.

[A. CODY]

MAXENTIUS, JOHN (fl.520), ecclesiastical writer and monk who led the Scythian (Gothic) monks in their demand for acceptance of the theopaschite formula ("one of the Trinity suffered in the flesh") as part of the *Trisagion. His works, written in Latin but until recently considered Latin translations from the original Greek, include a handbook of faith (*Libellus fidei*), a dialogue against the Nestorians (*Contra Nestorianos*), and a reply to a letter of Pope Hormisdas *(Ad epistolam Hormisdae responsio)*. BIBLIOGRAPHY: É. Amann DTC 15:505–512.

[F. H. BRIGHAM]

MAXFIELD, THOMAS (*c.*1720–84), one of Methodism's first lay preachers. M. was converted by John *Wesley at Bristol (1739). Placed in charge of the Methodist *society at the Foundry Meeting House in London, he took it upon himself, though not ordained, to preach. Wesley at first objected, but then relented and in fact thereafter authorized lay preaching extensively. M. was eventually ordained; as one of the chaplains of the Countess of *Huntingdon, he became estranged from Wesley in 1763 over doctrinal differences. BIBLIOGRAPHY: R. D. Urlin, *Churchman's Life of Wesley* (n.d.) 137–146; E. Halevy, *Birth of Methodism in England* (tr. B. Semmel, 1971).

[F. E. MASER]

MAXIMIAN (*c.*240–310), **ROMAN EMPEROR** of the West (286–305); Maximian Herculius was uneducated but a good soldier. Diocletian appointed him Caesar in 285 and in

286 named him brother and Augustus, whereupon he took the name Marcus Aurelius Valerius Maximianus. When Diocletian divided the empire in 293, M. received Italy, Africa, and Spain. He abdicated against his will in 305, returned twice to the throne, but died in 310, reportedly a suicide, while imprisoned for plotting against Constantine. BIBLIOGRAPHY: W. Ensslin, PW. 14.2: 2486–2516; J. R. Palanque, *Church in the Christian Roman Empire* (tr. E. C. Messenger, 1949).

[M. J. SUELZER]

MAXIMIANISTS, followers of the Donatist Maximian, who as a deacon was excommunicated by Primian, the Donatist bp. of Carthage, in 392. Maximian received the support and approval of 43 bps. who met at Carthage toward the end of the year. He was further approved by some 50 more bps., dismayed by Primian's misdeeds, at Cebarsussa in June 393. He was consecrated a bp., but then was condemned by a council of 310 Donatist bps. held at Bagai in April 394. He and his 12 coadjutors were excommunicated, and his followers were abused. Throughout his controversy with Primian, Maximian showed himself to be of a much better character than his adversary. BIBLIOGRAPHY: W. H. C. Frend, *Donatist Church* (1952) 213–224. *DONATISTS.

[M. J. COSTELLOE]

MAXIMILIAN, ST., the name of two different martyrs of the 3d century. (1) He was the apostle of the Roman imperial province of Noricum, who founded the Church at Lauriacum (Lorch), became its first bp. and suffered martyrdom in 284. (2) He was a young African martyr, whose trial and death were chronicled with simple authenticity by an eyewitness. In the consulate of Tuscus and Anulinus (295), M. appeared before the pro-consul Dion. He refused to be inducted into the army and accept the emperor's badge. When the proconsul observed that other Christians served as imperial soldiers, he replied: "That is their business. . . . I cannot serve." When asked what harm soldiers do, his answer was: "You know well enough." He was beheaded in the presence of his father at Theveste in Numidia (now Tebessa in Algeria) on March 12. A matron named Pompeiana obtained his body, carried it to Carthage, and buried it close to St. Cyprian. On his day of martyrdom he was 21 years, 3 months, and 18 days old. BIBLIOGRAPHY: Butler 4:93; 1:571–573; K. Kunze, BiblSanct 9:23–25; A. Amore, *ibid*. 9:25–260

[E. J. DILLON]

MAXIMILIAN I (1459–1519), **HOLY ROMAN EMPEROR** from 1493. The "last knight" of Europe, chivalrous, intellectual, interested in progress, patron of the arts, M. also contrived to be political and to build up the vast expanse of the 16th-cent. Holy Roman Empire, which he was to pass on to his grandson, Charles V. He was the son of Frederick III (Habsburg) and husband, first of Mary of Burgundy through whom he acquired territory (Netherlands) bordering on France; then, after Mary's death, of Bianca Maria Sforza of Milan. Through the marriage of his son Philip to Joanna, daughter of Ferdinand and Isabella I of Castile, Spanish territory became part of the imperial domain.

Rebellion of the Flemish who preferred French alliances led to conflict with the Valois, a conflict lasting 200 years, and to various alliances until the treaty of Frankfurt (1489). Other treaties and pacts, usually anti-French, mark his reign as king of the Romans (1486) and emperor (1493): treaties with Henry VII of England; Ferdinand V of Castile; with Brittany (he tried to marry Anne of Brittany by proxy); the league of Venice (1495 and 1508). He signed the Treaty of Senlis with France in 1493.

Most of his diplomatic alliances were entered upon to further Habsburg interests, pitting European states and city-states against one another: a third treaty or alliance with France (1508) against Venice; then with the Holy League against France (1513); with Denmark and the Teutonic Knights against Poland (1514); against France (1516) over the invasion of Milan.

Maximilian tried to promote government reform at home and throughout the empire: a system of Roman law, poll tax, central financial administration, a standing army, new types of arms.

His efforts were too diverse to be completely successful, but he did firmly establish the Habsburg dynasty—the real goal of all his intrigues and treaties. BIBLIOGRAPHY: H. Holborn, *History of Modern Germany* (3 v., 1959-) v. 1.

[M. E. DUFFY]

MAXIMILIAN I OF BAVARIA (1573–1651), Duke of Bavaria from 1597, elector of the Holy Roman Empire from 1623. Thoroughly educated and raised in a strict religious environment, M. dedicated his life to the Counter Reformation. He was a conscientious administrator whose internal legislation included considerable moral and religious regulation. He zealously encouraged the Jesuits and Capuchins. Disturbed at the spread of Calvinism in Germany, M. protected the Catholics of Donauwörth in 1607 and founded the Catholic League in 1609. The Thirty Years' War (1618–48) occupied much of his reign, bringing devastation to Bavaria, but the title of Elector to himself. His military and financial assistance was essential to the Habsburg, Catholic cause. BIBLIOGRAPHY: K. Pfister, *Kurfürst Maximilian I. von Bayern und sein Jahrhundert* (1948); R. Bireley, *Maximilian von Bayern, Adam Contzen, S. J., und die Gegenreformation in Deutschland, 1624–1635* (1975); D. Albrecht, *Die auswärtige Politik Maximilians von Bayern 1618–1635* (1962).

[R. H. SCHMANDT]

MAXIMILLA THE MONTANIST (d. 179), disciple of Montanus, widely revered as a prophetess. Along with her codisciple Prisca or Priscilla, she delivered the most striking manifestations of what many considered to be divine energy under the dispensation of the Paraclete. Both of these women had been married. They left their husbands and were given by Montanus the title of virgin. The movement was centered in Phrygia and was characterized by frenzied ecstasy and utterances delivered in unconscious states (this argues for a pre-Christian and nonbiblical origin and dynamic). The neighboring bps. considered M. and other such prophets to be frenzied heathens and ascribed their ecstatic utterances to demons. The bps. asserted that real prophets remained in perfect possession of their faculties while obeying the divine impulse. The main sources on the Montanist phenomenon, Eusebius, Hippolytus, and Tertullian, are not without bias. There are echoes in the Pauline and Joannine writings that are sympathetic to the belief that the revelation of the Paraclete surpasses even that of Christ and the Apostles. The ultimate impact of the Phrygian movement, however, was to discredit the gift of prophecy, which was still held in high esteem in the Church of the 2d century. BIBLIOGRAPHY: Knox Enth 30–38.

[E. DILLON]

MAXIMOS III MAZLŪM (1779–1855), Melchite patriarch. Ordained in 1806, M. was elected metropolitan of Aleppo in Syria in 1810, but the Congregation for the Propagation of the Faith declared the election irregular in 1813. Later he was named titular bp. of Myra. M. returned to Syria with the approval of Pope Gregory XVI (1831). In 1833 he was elected patriarch, in which capacity he convoked the Council of 'Ain-Trāz. He worked to secure autonomy for the Melchites in the Ottoman Empire. A man of great zeal, he advanced the interests of the Melchites in his territory, but incurred the opposition of both Rome and his own bishops. He wrote and translated a number of works of theology and spirituality.

[J. R. AHERNE]

MAXIMUS IV SAYEGH (1878–1967), Melkite patriarch. Born in Aleppo, Syria, he entered, as Father Joseph, the Society of the Missionaries of St. Paul, founded by the Melkite bp. Germanos Mouaccad in 1904. Metropolitan of Tyre (Sur) from 1919 to 1933, during which period he was apostolic visitor for the Melkites in North America, and then metropolitan of Beirut from 1933 to 1947, M. was elected patriarch of Antioch, of Alexandria, and of Jerusalem in 1947. In spite of his age, he became one of those prelates who were the inspiration of Vatican II, where he advocated a vernacular liturgy, decentralization of church government, sharing of certain papal prerogatives to the episcopacy, collegiality in the governance of the Church, autonomy for the particular Churches, esp. those of the Christian East, recognition of the Orthodox as part of the one, universal Church. He died in Beirut.

[J. MADEY]

MAXIMUS OF ALEXANDRIA (d. *c.*282), bp. of Alexandria, known through Eusebius (*Hist. eccl.* 7.7). A council held at Antioch in 268 under Malchion addressed a letter to M. and to Pope *Dionysius, informing them of its deposition of *Paul of Samosata for his denial of Christ's divinity. M. was succeeded at Alexandria by St. Theonas.

[J. MADEY]

MAXIMUS THE CONFESSOR, ST. (Maximus of Chrysopolis; *c.*580–662), Father of the Church, last original theologian of the patristic era, conqueror of Monothelitism. Born of a high-ranking family of Constantinople, M. was first secretary of the Emperor Heraclius by 30 years of age, then forsook his very prestigious post to enter a monastery across the narrow Bosporus in Chrysopolis. Later he journeyed to Carthage, then resided in Rome. M. opposed Monophysitism; then, esp. in Rome, Monothelitism, which he defeated in a Lateran Synod (649, prelude to the Sixth Ecumenical Council, Constantinople III [680–81]), unmasking it as implicit Monophysitism. From 653 until his death, he suffered persecution and exiles because of the emperor's displeasure with his blow to the Monothelites, for their rejection by the Church had renewed the secessionism of the Monophysites on the political level. In 662 he forfeited the conjoined instruments of his offense, his tongue and right hand, a usual condign punishment for a condemned speaker and writer. He died of these tortures in the same year, in exile on the shore of the Black Sea. His quasi-martyrdom accounts for the title "Confessor" which tradition has accorded him. M. distinguished himself from the other late Fathers (compilers and eclectics) by an eclecticism of towering synthetic originality, in which doubtful and widely differing theologies such as that of Origen and Pseudo-Dionysius find both orthodoxy and self-consistent systematization. The center of M.'s theology of history is the Incarnation, its goal is *theosis. BIBLIOGRAPHY: Beck 436–442; C. Vona, BiblSanct 9:41–47.

[R. R. BARR]

MAXIMUS OF SARAGOSSA (d. *c.*619) Spanish bp. who wrote a chronicle used by Isidore of Seville. Although the work is not extant, 33 brief glosses (450–568) to the chronicle of Victor of Tunnuna seem to be from M.'s chronicle.

[E. P. COLBERT]

MAXIMUS OF TURIN, ST. (d. between 408 and 423), bishop. According to Gennadius, who refers to him as a great preacher, M. flourished during the reigns of the Emperors Honorius and Theodosius II. But a Bp. Maximus of Turin was alive at the times of the Councils of Milan (451) and Rome (465). It was formerly thought that Gennadius erred in putting M.'s death date so early. Later opinion accepts the early date and holds that there were two bps. named M. in the see of Turin in the 5th century. L. Bruni's edition of the writings of M. (1784, repr. PL 57) includes 240 sermons, homilies, and treatises. The later critical edition of A. Mutzenbecher (CCL, 1962), eliminating the manifestly inauthentic writings, reduces the number to 119, and not all of these can be confidently accepted as genuine. M.'s writings are of value for the information they give about the times in which they were written, and esp. about the survival of pagan customs and superstitions. His Lenten homilies are important for the history of the liturgy. BIBLIOGRAPHY: Altaner 545–546; Butler 2:640–641; A. Amann, DTC 10:464–466; E. Crovella, BiblSanct 9:68–72.

[R. B. ENO]

MAXIMUS OF TYRE (fl. 180 A.D.), rhetorician and Middle Platonist philosopher. He emphasizes the divine transcendence, admits inferior gods and demons, and holds that the chief cause of evil is matter. He considers that evil was necessary if good was to be produced—an idea also found in the Stoics and in Plotinus. BIBLIOGRAPHY: W. D. Ross, OCD 546; P. Merlan, LexAW 1874; CHGMP 81.

[M. R. P. MCGUIRE]

MAXWELL, WINIFRED (*c.* 1678–1749), countess of Nithsdale, famous for rescuing her husband from prison. After her husband was captured during the Jacobite uprising in 1715, she pleaded in vain with George I for his release. To the considerable annoyance of the King, she smuggled her husband, who was dressed in female clothing, out of the Tower, hid him in London until he could safely depart for the Continent, and joined him in exile after securing important family papers she had hidden in Scotland.

[V. SAMPSON]

MAY DEVOTIONS, a traditional Catholic devotional service during the month of May, generally consisting of the Rosary, the Litany of the Blessed Virgin, and Benediction of the Blessed Sacrament. The association of Mary with May seems to have been the result of efforts begun in Italy in the 18th cent. to replace the "Queen of the May" (a remnant of paganism prevalent throughout medieval Europe and still surviving) with Mary. The Jesuits in particular popularized the devotion.

[J. DALLEN]

MAY LAWS, four statutes promulgated by the Prussian government against the RC Church in May 1873, aimed at converting the Church into a state institution. They decreed: (1) a special civil court for ecclesiastical appeals; (2) restrictions on episcopal disciplinary powers; (3) state requirements in clerical education and rights of intervention in all clerical appointments; and (4) provision for any citizen, by a simple declaration before a magistrate, to withdraw from the Church in which he was registered and which he had to support by a tax (supposedly to provide relief for Old Catholics). In the peace settlement of 1886–87 the state abandoned the first two statutes but achieved a compromise on both parts of the third; the original May law on church withdrawals remained intact. *KULTURKAMPF.

[J. K. ZEENDER]

MAYA RELIGION, a distinctive variant of Mesoamerican religion associated with the cities and religious sites in the tropical forests of S Mexico and E Guatemala and on the Yucatan peninsula during the great age of the Maya, from the 2nd to 10th century A.D. It was the native religion at the time of the Spanish conquest, and human sacrifice was part of the ritual. The deep concern of the Maya with natural powers and an astrological-cosmological theology is reflected in their inscriptions, sculpture, pyramids, courtyards, and stelae. The major deities were: a frog-like Earth Mother; the death god of the North; the jade-bead skirted Goddess of the South; Kulkulkan of the East, who is equivalent to Quetzalcoatl; the Toltec fertility god and earth-king, sometimes represented as the planet Venus; and a mysterious Moan Bird. All are represented in stone monuments that also serve as markers of astral positions in the complicated Mayan calendar. The four directions of the universe are guarded by the Bacabs, massive gods who hold the sky-band, which is divided into 13 constellations, across their chests. Each day and period was under divine protection, the days were counted in periods of 20, and periods by Tuns equal to 360 days, further elaborated by multiples of 20 into millions of years and subdivided with reference to the 4 directions. Thus there were for the mathematically inclined astrologers a limitless challenge in making every new prediction. Information about the Maya, who were a physically and linguistically self-contained group, depends primarily on archeological investigations, decipherment of Mayan hieroglyphs, and study of the few remaining Codices or painted books of the Maya.

[R. J. LITZ]

MAYAKOVSKI, VLADIMIR VLADIMIROVICH (1893–1930), leading Soviet poet, "bard of the Revolution." Though he joined the Bolshevik Party in his youth and served the cause faithfully with political and propagandistic poems (e.g., *War and World,* 1916; *Khorosho,* "All Right," 1927), he was more interested in a literary than a political revolution. To this end, he signed the Cubo-Futurist manifesto (1912); edited the Futurist journals *LEF* (1923–25) and *New LEF* (1927); and published verses, which, while they did not reflect the Futurist concept that language should transcend meaning, were nonetheless attacked by orthodox Communists as too individualistic and formalistic because of their unpoetical and shocking imagery (cf. the poem "The Cloud in Trousers," 1915), distorted word order, and exaltation of form over content. His Futurist (and pseudo autobiographical) drama *Vladimir Mayakovski* (1914) and the dramatic poem *Mystery Bouffe* (1918; rev. 1921) use religious motifs to serve atheistic and materialistic ends. The plays *The Bedbug* (1928) and *The Bathhouse* (1929) employ hyperbole and grotesquerie to satirize Soviet bureaucracy. In the poem *150,000,000,* he prophesies the victory of the Russian people over the capitalistic West. BIBLIOGRAPHY: C. M. Bowra, *Creative Experiment* (1949) 94–127; M. Slonim, *Soviet Russian Literature* (1964) 19–31; V. Shklovsky, *Mayakovsky and His Circle* (tr. and ed. L. Feiler, 1972).

[M. F. MCCARTHY]

MAYBECK, BERNARD (1862–1957), American architect, born in New York, settling in California (1894) after study in Paris. M. gained renown for his use of natural woods and new spatial effects (*First Church of Christ Scientist,* Berkeley, 1910).

[M. J. DALY]

MAYFLOWER COMPACT, the agreement made by the Pilgrim Fathers aboard the *Mayflower* off Provincetown, Mass., Nov. 11, 1620. The Compact was an application of the principles of Congregationalism to the civil sphere; the signers sought to form a body politic in the way they held the visible Church to be formed, namely, by the covenant of believers to associate together. BIBLIOGRAPHY: A. A. Haxtun, *Signers of the Mayflower Compact* (1897, repr. 1968). *COVENANT THEOLOGY.

[T. C. O'BRIEN]

MAYNARD, THEODORE (1890–1956), Anglo-American poet, biographer, historian, and critic. Born in India of Protestant missionary parents, M. received his early education in England. After coming to the U.S., where he earned his three degrees, he lectured widely and taught at such universities as Fordham and Georgetown. In 1913 he became a convert to Catholicism largely through his reading of G. K. Chesterton. He ultimately became a naturalized U.S. citizen. He was a prolific writer on many subjects and published countless articles and poems in periodicals. He considered his main province to be the interpretation of American Catholic history; his aim, to be interesting. He wrote 30 odd books. M. rated *The Story of American Catholicism* (1941) as his greatest prose achievement. Some critics considered his biography *The Reed and the Rock* (1942) his best work. His autobiography *The World I Saw* (1938) has been described as "the most complete autobiography of a conversion since the *Apologia* of Newman." M. thought of himself as a poet although since 1929 he had been chiefly occupied in the writing of biography and history. M.'s biographies are chiefly of figures of Elizabeth I's reign and of such saints as Francis Xavier, Francis of Assisi, and Thomas More. His collections of poems *Exile and Other Poems* (1929), *Man and Beast* (1936), and *Not Even Death* (1941) contain his later and more individual poetry.

[S. A. HEENEY]

MAYNE, CUTHBERT, ST. (1544–77), protomartyr of the English colleges on the Continent. Destined by his family to succeed to the lucrative benefice held by his uncle, an Anglican priest, M. took Anglican orders at a very early age. His further education at Oxford brought him into friendship with Edmund Campion and Gregory Martin, who reinforced his doubts about the Anglican Church. Eventually, he joined them at Douai where he received RC ordination (1575). The next year he returned to England and began his ministry in Cornwall, living disguised as a steward in the home of Francis Tregian. He was apprehended there in June 1577 and thus began the first trial in England of a seminary priest. At Launceston he was found guilty of high treason on the circumstantial evidence of his priesthood. The case was referred to London by one of the participating judges who thought the verdict might be unjust, and opinion on the bench of judges was divided also. Ultimately, the Privy Council ordered the sentence to be executed as an example to the papists. Mayne was hanged and quartered, Nov. 30, 1577, beatified in 1886 and canonized in 1970. BIBLIOGRAPHY: E. S. Knox, "Blessed Cuthbert Mayne" in B. Camm, *Lives of English Martyrs* (1905) 2:204–221; E. Graf, BiblSanct 9:248–250; Gillow BDEC 4:553–557; Butler 4:447–448.

[V. SAMPSON]

MAYNOOTH, see IRELAND, NATIONAL UNIVERSITY OF.

MAYOL, JOSEPH (d.1709), French Dominican theologian, spiritual writer. M. was professed in the Order of Preachers, taught philosophy and theology in houses of his order, was a local superior, and provincial from 1701 to 1705. He published *Abrégé de la dévotion du Rosaire de la Mère de Dieu* (1679) and *Summa moralis doctrinae thomisticae circa decem precepta decalogi* (1704).

[J. R. AHERNE]

MAYR, ANTON (1673–1749), Bavarian Jesuit theologian who taught at the Univ. of Freiburg and the Univ. of Ingolstadt. He wrote extensively on philosophy and theology.

[J. R. AHERNE]

MAZARIN, JULES (1602–61), cardinal and chief minister of France. Born in the Abruzzi of a Sicilian father, M. studied at Rome, served the Colonna family, became an army officer, took deacon's orders, and entered the service of France at Paris in 1634. He confirmed Richelieu's trust in him and was created cardinal through the influence of Louis XIII. He succeeded Richelieu, who died in 1642, continued his policies, with greater suppleness and no less eventual success, of consolidating royal authority and the frontiers of France. He engineered the Peace of Westphalia. His relations with Innocent X and Alexander VII were uneasy, but he supported the papacy in the conflict with Jansenism. The great fortune he left founded the Collège Mazarin with its valuable library, and secured the marriages of his beautiful nieces into the greatest houses of France and Italy. BIBLIOGRAPHY: A. Hassal, *Mazarin* (1903).

MAZARIN BIBLE, the Latin Vulgate printed at the press of J. *Gutenberg at Mainz before 1456. It was named for the two-volume copy, now in the Bibliothèque Nationale in Paris, that was discovered in the Bibliothèque Mazarin (see MAZARIN, JULES) in 1760; this copy contains an inscription, by the rubricator Heinrich Cremer, dated Aug. 15, 1456. Of the 47 surviving copies of this, probably the first complete book printed in movable type in Europe, only two, at Munich and at Vienna, are integral; the Library of Congress copy is regarded as the most beautiful. The Mazarin Bible is also called the "Forty-two Line Bible," since its 1282 pages in folio are in double columns, each of 42 lines.

[D. J. BOURKE]

MAZDAISM, a term often employed to designate ancient Persian religion, and more specifically, the worship of *Ahura Mazda,* which is central in the teachings of Zoroaster and in Zoroastrianism. *AHURA MAZDA AND AHRIMAN; *PERSIAN RELIGION, ANCIENT; and *ZOROASTER.

[M. R. P. MCGUIRE]

MAZENOD, CHARLES JOSEPH EUGÈNE DE (1782–1861), bp. of Marseilles, founder of the Oblates of Mary Immaculate, whose members he sent to Canada, the U.S., S Africa, and Ceylon. Born in Aix-en-Provence, France, of the nobility of the robe, he emigrated to Italy with his family during the French Revolution, returned in 1802, was ordained in 1811, and began a lifelong apostolate to the poor, and esp. to young workers. He succeeded his uncle as bp. of Marseilles in 1837. In 1856 he was senator of the Second Empire. Although an ardent Ultramontanist, he supported De Lamennais in Rome to the end. BIBLIOGRAPHY: N. Kowalsky, LTK 7:218.

[E. J. DILLON]

MAZZARELLO, MARIA DOMENICA, ST. (1837–81), foundress. A dressmaker in Piedmont, Italy, she was placed in charge of a school for girls founded by St. John Bosco. She became the foundress of the Congregation, Daughters of Our Lady Help of Christians (Salesian Sisters), which gradually spread to France, Argentina, and other countries. She was canonized in 1951.

[J. R. AHERNE]

MAZZELLA, CAMILLO (1833–1900), Italian Jesuit, theologian, cardinal, and bishop. He was ordained in 1855 and became a Jesuit in 1857. After teaching in Italy (1860–67), he became a professor at Georgetown Univ. and at the Jesuit Theologate, Woodstock, Md. (1867–77). Leo XIII summoned him to a chair at the Gregorian Univ. to contribute to the Thomistic revival. M. was made a curial cardinal in 1886 and served in the Congregations of Studies and of Rites; he was named bp. of Palestrina in 1897. His publications include: *De Deo creante* (1880), *De religione et ecclesia* (1893), *De gratia Christi* (1892), and *De virtutibus infusis* (1894). He was also author of a work against the views of A. *Rosmini-Serbati, *Rosminianarum propositionum . . . trutina theologica* (1887).

[T. C. O'BRIEN]

MAZZINI, GIUSEPPE (1805–72), Italian nationalist and revolutionary. A leading figure of the Risorgimento that he promoted through literary and political activities, M. is best remembered for founding the secret society Young Italy, (Giovine Italia). In 1849 he was elected to the triumvirate that governed the Roman Republic after the revolution in the States of the Church forced the Pope to flee to Gaeta. An advocate of a united, republican Italy, he opposed Cavour and the House of Savoy. He was in exile a good part of his life. Even after the formation of the Kingdom of Italy, M. lived in exile, making only brief visits to Italian cities. Bitterly anticlerical, he advocated a new "religious synthesis," of "God and the people." BIBLIOGRAPHY: E. E. Y. Hales, *Mazzini and the Secret Societies* (1956); S. Barr, *Mazzini: Portrait of an Exile* (1971); P. Pirri, EncCatt 8:528–535.

[E. A. CARRILLO]

MAZZOCCHI, VIRGILIO (1597–1646), Italian composer of sacred music. He became *maestro di cappella* of St. John Lateran (1628) and St. Peter's in Rome (1629). He composed with Marazzoli, *Chi soffre speri,* the first comic opera, with libretto by Giulio Rospigliosi (later Pope Clement IX). The opera was produced in 1639. M.'s *Sacrae Flores* for two to four voices was published in 1640 and a set of Psalms was issued posthumously.

[R. J. LITZ]

MAZZOLINI, SYLVESTER (Sylvester Prierias; 1460–1523), Italian Dominican, theologian, best known for his opposition to Martin Luther. Born in Priero, Piedmont, M. entered the Dominican Order in 1475 and later taught at Bologna and Pavia. Vicar general of the province of Lombardy (1508–10), he was appointed by Leo X to the Dominican chair of theology at the Gymnasium Romanum in 1514 and the next year became master of the sacred palace. In this office he was instrumental in having J. *Reuchlin condemned and played the initiating role in combating the teachings of Luther, vigorously upholding the powers of the pope, esp. the view that in matters of faith and doctrine the pope was infallible. M.'s most complete argument against the German Reformer appeared in *Errata et argumenta M. Lutheri recitata, detecta . . .* (1520). Other works include the *Rosa aurea* (1510) on the Gospels; *In theoricas planetarum* (1513); *Summa summarum quae Silvestrina dicitur* (1516), a popular compendium of moral theology; the *Conflatum ex s. Thoma* (1519), and *De juridica et irrefragabili veritate Romanae Ecclesiae Romanique Pontificis* (1520).

[E. M. GATES]

MAZZUCHELLI, SAMUEL CHARLES (1806–64), Dominican missioner in the Midwest, founder of the Sinsinawa (Wis.) Dominican Sisters, architect. Born in Milan, he became a Dominican in 1823, and, after study in Rome, came to the U.S. and was ordained in Cincinnati in 1830. He went as a missionary to Mackinac Island and Green Bay, Wis., working alone among French Canadians and Indians. He learned the Indian languages, and composed a prayer-book and catechism in the Winnebago tongue. He then labored as the only priest in the region of Galena, Ill., and Dubuque, and when the latter was made a diocese became (1839) vicar general for Bp. M. *Loras. In 1843 M. visited the Mormon settlement at Nauvoo, Ill., to try to convert the leader, Joseph *Smith. During a convalescence in Italy, M. received Roman authorization to establish a new American Dominican province in his territory, and did set up a novitiate, but the venture failed and he turned over the foundation to the Dominican Province of St. Joseph. He founded the community of Dominican Sisters of the Most Holy Rosary at Sinsinawa in 1847 and directed it until his death. As architect, he designed the county courthouse at Galena, the bp.'s residence at Dubuque, and the first capitol at Iowa City. He also founded Sinsinawa Mound College and Benton Academy. He died at Benton, Wisconsin.

[J. R. AHERNE]

MEAGHER, PAUL KEVIN (1907–76), Dominician theologian, teacher, writer, and editor. He was born in Clarion, Pa., reared in Portland, Ore., and entered the Western Dominican Province in 1925. After study at River Forest, Ill. and Benecia, Calif., he was trained in theology at the Collegio Angelico in Rome, 1929–30, and Blackfriars, Oxford, 1930–33, where he was ordained in 1931. While in England he was influenced by Bede Jarrett, OP and met Thomas Gilby, OP and Gerald Vann, OP, with both of whom he enjoyed deep friendship and lifelong collaboration. He returned to California in 1933 to teach philosophy and moral theology at St. Albert's College, Oakland. In 1939–40 he was professor of philosophy and director of the Newman center at the Univ. of Washington, Seattle, where he also pursued graduate study in psychology. In 1940 M. became lector primarius at St. Albert's College and in 1946 he was the first Dominican of his province to receive the highest degree conferred by the Dominican Order, that of Master of Sacred Theology. He was named regent of studies when with his efforts St. Albert's in 1949 became a *studium generale;* he held this position until 1961.

During these years at St. Albert's, M. taught moral theology and supervised the academic training and assignments of the priests of the province. He was also professor of theology at the Dominican College of San Rafael. A man of unusual energy and dedication, he served not only as teacher and administrator but also as preacher, confessor, and spiritual director, consultant on moral problems to the local clergy, and as advisor to members of the hierarchy. He became a skilled Latinist and frequently spent weekends in parish work. In 1957 he coauthored with G. Vann *The Temptations of Christ*.

In 1961 M. went to England and at Blackfriars, Cambridge assisted T. Gilby in the early work of editing the new Latin-English edition of the *Summa theologiae* (60 v., 1964–76). In 1962 at the request of Card. Patrick O'Boyle, abp. of Washington, D.C., and Rev. J. P. Whalen, managing editor of the *New Catholic Encyclopedia* (15 v., 1967), M. returned to the U.S. to become its staff editor for moral theology. In 1967 he received from the American Catholic Theological Society the Cardinal Spellman award for his outstanding contributions to theological studies.

From 1966 to 1970, again associated with Fr. Whalen, he directed the dictionary division of Corpus Instrumentorum, Inc., assisting in the preparation of *Corpus Dictionary of Western Churches* (ed. T. C. O'Brien, 1970) and doing the major work of the present *Encyclopedic Dictionary of Religion*. The work was continued from 1970 to 1972 when M. was assistant pastor at St. Mary's Church, Oneonta, New York. It was accelerated when he returned to the Washington area in 1973 and intensive preparation of this *Dictionary* began anew with the support and collaboration of the Sisters of St. Joseph of Philadelphia, Pennsylvania. In spite of failing health, M. oversaw the reorganization of the *Dictionary,* updating earlier articles and writing and editing new ones. During this time he also served as assistant pastor at St. Mark's Church, Hyattsville, Md., supervising the CCD program there and teaching classes to high school students.

M. was a modern Thomist with a rich background in humanistic learning and a rare insight into human problems. He taught a clear adherence to moral principles and the Church's magisterium and showed the way towards compassionate pastoral practice. He was a gentle and unassuming priest, noted for his unfailing wisdom, subtle humor, quiet warmth, and moral strength.

[J. C. WILLKE]

MEAL, SACRED. The sharing of food and drink as (sign of) communion with the Holy, generally regarded as their source, based on the fact that food in human society is a symbolic reality as well as an object of consumption. Anthropologically, there are two major types: theophagy (god-eating), related to cannibalism (e.g., Aztecs), and theoxenia, community meals with the gods, perhaps derived from meals shared with ancestors. ''Sacred'' and ''ordinary'' meals are difficult to distinguish in the OT because of the interrelation of the ''sacred'' and ''secular,'' except that the former have a more elaborate ritual. The sacred meal, a dinner in God's presence to acknowledge him as source of blessings, takes various forms. Theophagy is unknown; only in some offerings and sacrifices is there an indication of a divine meal, food offered to God. Communion meals (God as participant) are common (e.g., Passover): part of the sacrifice is offered to God and the rest is shared by the participants. Covenant meals, signifying fellowship and solemnizing an agreement, celebrate God as the source of the bond of sharing and union. In the NT, a banquet often symbolizes the messianic age and Jesus' meals with sinners anticipate the kingdom-feast.

In Christian theology the meal provides a paradigm of sacramentality as an effective symbol of the invisible transcendent: a paradigm of sharing, concern, care, responsibility, solidarity, and thus a ritual impetus to communal living and social action. The Eucharist centers on bread and wine, already signs, but moves beyond the gifts of creation to celebrate salvation in an eschatological perspective, with the Eucharistic Prayer or Canon articulating the meaning of the community's experience. Thus a meal as sign of fellowship and participation in the mystery of life, acknowledged as God's gift, is context for Christian Eucharist. But since no meal focusses exclusively or even primarily on food, it is "conversation over food," with the participants sharing a common background (anamnesis of the faith-tradition), common communication and dialogue in the present (focus on community and companionship), and a common goal (the eschatological kingdom). The attitude of the host (ultimately, Christ in his sacrificial self-giving, because of the derivation of the Eucharist from the Last Supper) is thus determinant of the Eucharist's meaning and value.

[J. DALLEN]

MEAN, DOCTRINE OF THE. The reflection that virtue observes the mean (Lat. *medium;* Gr. *meson,* used as synonymous with *metrion* and rendered sometimes as *ison,* equal, also equitable) often arises in Greek and Latin moral philosophy. It is discussed by Aristotle in bk. 2 of the *Nicomachean Ethics*. Like the good helmsman who steers between Scylla and Charybdis, right living holds a steady course between opposite and blamable extremes. Hence the laudatory epithet, the golden or the happy mean. The usage which held this "mediocrity" in esteem is now rare, and "middling" is meant for disparagement; as less than the best, not positively holding off two contrary evils, it damns with faint praise. The analysis of the notion by the scholastics may help to counter this drift.

They regard the moderation of a moral virtue, not as though implying a psychological mixture of opposites or a moral compromise between them, e.g., as though *chastity were too cool for *lust and too warm for *apathy, but as a matching the measure set by right reason (Lat. *recta ratio;* Gr. *orthos logos*). This is the "mean of reason," (*medium rationis*), the rule proposed by practical wisdom or *prudence to be observed by all the moral virtues. In the case of the moral virtues which govern our emotions, e.g., courage, the rule will vary within limits from individual to individual; too strong for one may be too weak for another. Accordingly, it is largely determined by a man's internal dispositions. How can we make a flat regulation about the proper intensity and extent of pleasure, and how impertinent were we to appoint to each the more or the less?

With the moral virtue of justice, however, matters are different. This is concerned with rendering a due, a service or thing irrespective of our dispositions and external to our feelings. The rule of virtue here depends on the "mean of the thing" (*medium rei*), and admits of impersonal and dispassionate assessment; it can be fixed, and the debt of strict justice be rendered according to that amount, no bigger, no smaller.

Such measures apply to the moral virtues, both acquired and infused, but not to the theological virtues. "All bounty dwelleth in mediocrity," says Edmund Spenser, "yet perfect felicity dwelleth in supremacy." The moral virtues may be looked upon as human appetites which have been tamed. Not so the theological virtues. Faith reaches out to the sheerly true, hope commits itself to surpassing power and mercy, charity lives with boundless good. Their objects are final and unlimited, and strike no measure between opposites, unlike those of the moral virtues, which are intermediate and limited and allow of excess and defect. For instance, the value of temperance has to be balanced with other values, and measured according to a wider scene than it alone can set. To be temperate is not our total and ultimate condition: to be with God is. We cannot believe and hope in God or love him more than we should. The only measure or mean that can be applied is negative, incidental, and a matter of circumstances, as, for instance, when we judge that we are loving him less than we could. The extremes of credulousness and infidelity and of presumption and despair, which are customarily treated as threats to faith and hope respectively, do not relate to the objects of these virtues, but to human projections about them. BIBLIOGRAPHY: ThAq ST 1a2ae, 64.

[T. GILBY]

MEANS, those goods, objects of a *human act, chosen because they serve an intended *end or goal. Whether the structure of the human act be taken in regard to some single action or as outlining the general orientation of a person's moral life, the will-components are basically intention of an end and choice of means. For the human act is the expression of the will as the faculty of human striving toward fulfillment through some perfective good. Since such a good is to be reached, it is the end or purpose of an action. That intended end sets the measure and value on whatever is appropriate or conducive to attaining the end. In this kind of abstract analysis end is intended for its own sake; means are chosen for the sake of something else, the end. But concretely means are better described as intermediary or subordinate ends. The objectives of human choice have an intrinsic value as ennobling or as pleasurable; they are not, like bitter medicine, accepted purely as utilities. This becomes clearer upon reflecting that most choices involve some personal relationship; it would be perverse to react towards another person as a sheer pragmatic means. Thus charity loves neighbor out of love for God. But charity still values the individual worth of another person. The love of God above all calls for and includes this personal response towards others. The perception of a subordination of ends is a truer valuation of the moral life than the dichotomy, ends-means. Yet the dichotomy does have some usefulness in showing the falsity of the proposition, "the end justifies the means." Because a true end is a good, it can never give value to a means that is evil in itself; the only quality compatible with a true end is a good, never the lack of good that *evil is.

[T. C. O'BRIEN]

MEAUX (MELSA), ABBEY OF, English Cistercian monastery in Yorkshire. Established in 1150 by monks of Fountains, Meaux was hampered by chronic financial difficulties and the Black Death, which in 1349 carried away 40 of the 50 monks. It recovered under Abbots William of Scarborough (1372–96) and Thomas Burton (1396–99; d. 1437). The latter wrote the important *Chronicle of Melsa*. In the year of dissolution (1539) Meaux had 24 monks under Abbot Richard Stopes. BIBLIOGRAPHY: A. Earle, *Essays upon the History of Meaux Abbey*. (1906).

[L. J. LEKAI]

MECCA (Arab. *Makka*), a city in S Hejaz, the birthplace of the Prophet *Mohammed, and the *Holy City of Islam. Mecca has been a center of religious pilgrimage for the Arabs since ancient times, the chief object of veneration being the Black Stone, which is incorporated into the eastern corner of the Kaaba (Arab. Ka'ba), a cubical building some 50 feet in height. The shrine and the rites of pilgrimage (see HAJJ) were taken over by Islam. According to the *Koran the Kaaba was originally built by Abraham and Ishmael (2.127) and it was Abraham who first prescribed the pilgrimage upon the order of God (22.27). The Kaaba, many times rebuilt and restored, now stands in the center of the Great *Mosque of Mecca and it is toward it that Muslims throughout the world face when they pray. BIBLIOGRAPHY: H. Lammens and A. J. Wensinck, EncIslam[1]; A. J. Wensinck, *ibid.*, s.v. "Ka'ba."

[R. M. FRANK]

MECHTILD OF HACKEBORN, ST. (*c.*1240–1298 or 1299) Benedictine (or Cistercian?) nun, mystic. At the age of 7 she was entrusted to her sister, Gertrude of Hackeborn, a nun at Rodarsdorf, for her education. Gertrude, abbess from 1251, transferred the monastery to Helfta in 1258, where it became a center of learning and spirituality. M., as head chantress and directress of the cloister school became in 1261 the spiritual mother of St. *Gertrude the Great, who came under her charge at the age of 5. In her later years she made known to certain sisters the extraordinary graces she had received. These were noted down and Gertrude the Great, one of the confidantes, edited the accounts in a work known as *Liber specialis gratiae*. M. was disturbed to discover this, but when assured in a revelation that all had been done by the Lord's will and inspiration, she offered no objection and even corrected the manuscript. This work exercised a considerable influence upon the development of piety. Like Gertrude, M. is an early example of devotion to the Sacred Heart. It is not certain whether M. or Mechtild of Magdeburg is to be identified with the Donna Matelda of Dante's *Purgatorio*. M. was never formally canonized. Text of the *Liber specialis gratiae: Revelationes Gertrudianae et Mechtildianae,* (ed. Benedictines of Solesmes, 1875), v. 2; *Select Revelations of St. Mechtild* (tr. a secular priest, 1872). BIBLIOGRAPHY: Butler 4:351–353; M. F. Laughlin, NCE 9:545–546.

[M. S. TANEY]

MECHTILD OF MAGDEBURG, ST. (*c.*1209–*c.*83), German mystical writer. In 1230 she became a Beguine at Magdeburg, where she led a life of prayer and penance for 40 years. Her unusual experiences and her manner of expressing her mystical doctrine, together with her criticism of the clergy, aroused such opposition that she left Magdeburg in 1270 and sought refuge at Helfta, where SS. *Mechtild of Hackeborn and *Gertrude the Great welcomed her. Between the years 1250 and 1270 she wrote in her native Low German a work that came to be known as *Das fliessende Licht der Gottheit* (The Flowing Light of the Godhead) and has survived in Latin and Middle High German translations. The texts of the translations show signs of editorial mutilation due partly to misunderstanding and partly to an effort to soften the original text and make it more acceptable. The work is a mixture of prose and rhyming meters. It is filled with lyric outpourings on divine love and matters of mystical experience. She touches upon delicate themes such as the "annihilation" of the soul and deification but no reasonable doubt of her orthodoxy can be raised. She enjoyed a local cult, but has never been formally canonized. Text: *Das fliessende Licht der Gottheit* (ed. G. Morel, 1869; tr. L. Menzies, *Revelations of Mechthild of Magdeburg or the Flowing Light of the Godhead,* 1953). BIBLIOGRAPHY: E. Colledge, "Mechtild of Magdeburg," *Spirituality through the Centuries* (ed. J. Walsh, 1967) 159–170; J. Ancelet-Hustache, *Mechtild de Magdebourg* (1926).

[M. S. TANEY]

MECHTILDE DU SAINT SACREMENT, the religious name taken by Catherine de *Bar when she established the Benedictine Sisters of the Blessed Sacrament.

MEDALS, PAPAL, see PAPAL MEDALS.

MEDALS, RELIGIOUS, coin-like objects, made of metal or other solid material, bearing an image or inscription of Christ, Mary, a saint, a religious symbol, or a devout sentiment. In their earliest use by Christians they were probably an adaptation of pagan or secular custom to Christian practice. After the Empire was officially Christian, medals bearing the sign of Christ could easily be used as a sign of baptism and dedication. In the Middle Ages they served sometimes as souvenirs and badges of pilgrims to some great shrine. Sometimes they were struck to commemorate important events. Medals, along with other forms of images, were repudiated as idolatrous by the iconoclasts, and their use was considered superstitious by the Reformers. Although the simple may sometimes have employed them as magic amulets, their reasonable use was defended in principle by the Councils of Nicaea II (D 601) and Trent (D 1823) in their declaration of the lawfulness of venerating images. The modern usage of medals as blessed and indulgenced dates from the 16th cent., and they continue to be popular among Catholics and are even used by some non-Catholics, despite Protestant sentiment and sophisticated Catholic opposition. It is not claimed that medals, blessed or not, have any intrinsic value, but the prayer of the Church blessing them, the stimulation they provide to faith and piety, and their utility in helping human beings to think and communicate, gives them a value it seems priggish to disdain. BIBLIOGRAPHY: P. F. Mulhern, NCE 9:547–549.

[P. F. MULHERN]

MÉDARD OF NOYON, ST. (d.*c.*557), Frankish nobleman and bishop. Born in Salency where he studied, M. was ordained at 33. When made bp. (530), he moved the see to Noyon from Saint-Quentin. He is not, as was believed, the twin of St. Gildard. He was venerated in the Middle Ages; his relics are at Soissons. His intercession is sought in cases of toothache; he is also invoked to bring good weather. BIBLIOGRAPHY: Butler 2:502.

[J. R. RIVELLO]

MEDEBA, Moabite city on the Transjordan plateau conquered by Israel from the Amorites who had wrested it from Moab (Num 21.30). Assigned to Reuben's tribe, it was later retaken by Moab and eventually was ruled by Nabataea. One of its two extant Christian churches houses remnants of a mosaic map of *c.*6th cent. A.D. that contains important information on Palestinian topography of the Byzantine era.

[J. F. FALLON]

MEDES, an Iranian people who dominated a high plateau region of the ancient world called Media (modern NW and central Iran, bounded by the Elburz mountains on the S coast of the Caspian Sea; modern Kurdistan, parts of Kermanshad, and S Azerbaijan) from about the early 7th to the 5th cent. B.C. First mention of the Medes may be as early as 836–835 B.C. in conjunction with the campaigns of Salmanasar III. The Median tribes were probably confederated during the late 8th cent. under the tribal chief Dayakku (quite likely the Deioces mentioned by Herodotus) who ruled from Ecbatan, near modern Hamadan (see Ezra 6.2 and Tob 3.7). Cimmerians invaded Media from the N in about 700 B.C., followed by Scythian invaders who ruled the region later in that cent. (652–625). Another unification of Medes followed, and Cyaxares defeated the Scythians, reorganized his forces, captured the Assyrian city of Assur in 614 B.C., and allied with Babylonian King Nabopolasser to capture the Assyrian capital of Nineveh in 612. The Median kingdom under Cyaxares spread NW into Anatolia to the ancient Halys (Kizil) River where the boundary between the warring Medes and Lydians was settled in 585 B.C. Cyrus, a Persian vassal of the Medes, revolted in 553 B.C., and Astyages, the last Mede ruler, failed to suppress him. Cyrus established his Persian or Achaemenid kingdom on the Median foundation after capturing the Mede capital of Ecbatan in 550 B.C. The religion of the Medes, known to involve Magi, is poorly understood because of lack of documentary and archeological evidence. The Assyrian ruler, Saragon II, (r. 721–705 B.C.) exiled some Israelites to the cities of the Medes (2 Kg 17.6, 18.11).

[R. J. LITZ]

MEDIA OF SOCIAL COMMUNICATION, radio, television, films, the printed word. The term appears in Vatican II's Decree on the Instruments (*media*) of Social Communication, *Inter mirifica*. The force and sense of classifying these as media of ''social communication'' can be connected with the Council's Pastoral Constitution on the Church in the Modern World, esp. its statement that ''new and more effective media of social communication are contributing to the knowledge of events. By setting off chain reactions they are giving the swiftest and widest possible circulation to styles of thought and feeling'' (Vat II ChModWorld 6). In Part II, ch. 2, on culture, the same document refers to the impact of the media on cultural development and the possibility of a universal culture in the world (*ibid.* 61). The decree *Inter mirifica* was not a major or particularly impressive document, but it evidenced the Church's new self-assessment and its address to the world; it was the first time any statement on communications came from so major an official source as an ecumenical council. *Inter mirifica* addresses two major themes: the social and moral impact of the media; the Church's right to use all communications instruments to spread the gospel.

Social Import. The social and moral implications of the media are their service or their threat to genuinely human values. The instruments of communications serve the right to information necessary or helpful to human life and development. That right to information begets a freedom to present news and knowledge as completely and honestly as possible. The right and the freedom should preclude propagandistic or deceptive manipulation of the media. The same human right requires that information be disseminated in a spirit of respect for truth, justice, and charity. The media also serve the development and enjoyment of the arts. Art in all its forms is by essence communicative—created to be seen or felt or heard, understood, enjoyed. That requires respect for artistic integrity, i.e., the artist's genuine self-expression; but it also requires respect for genuinely human, therefore moral values. The intent to represent and to communicate moral evil as though it were a good is a distortion that is directed to appeal to the baser aspects of being human and that cannot claim artistic integrity as justification. Reflecting church concern present in *Inter mirifica* the 1971 Synod of Bishops in the document *Justice in the World* makes this statement: ''. . . contemporary consciousness demands truth in the communications systems, including the right to the image offered by the media and the opportunity to correct its manipulation. It must be stressed that the right, esp. of children and the young, to education and to morally correct conditions of life and communications media is once again being threatened in our days'' (USCC tr. p. 39).

As a result of the conciliar directives the former Vatican Secretariat for the Supervision of Publications and Entertainment became the Pontifical Commission for the Media of Social Communication. The Commission on Jan. 29, 1971, issued the pastoral instruction *Communicatio et pro-*

gressio, developing at greater length the principles of *Inter mirifica.* On the occasion of the World Day of Social Communications in 1977, Paul VI made an address that further elaborated similar themes. Of particular importance in both statements is the social impact of advertising and all that it means in the moulding of public opinion. Advertising itself may be a service to the community both as making known products and services and as an element in business competition that can be beneficial to consumers. But advertising also needs regulation as to its truthfulness, the appetitive appeal it makes, and the control it can exercise on media programming. The Church's concern for human dignity and well-being, even a material well-being, stands in opposition to the multiformed exploitation present in much advertising. The power it has obviously can and does create distorted values, consumerism, materialism. The devices it employs often appeal to unregulated sexual appetites. The control over media programming is frequently an affront to human intelligence and taste, to cultural and moral standards. As a result of Vatican II directives the Church has been more active in seeking to have the voice of decency heard. In the U.S. such agencies as the USCC Department of Communications and the international organization UNDA, exist to carry out church involvement. Initiatives include the USCC statement on Family Viewing Policy (Oct. 10, 1975), reviews of films and television programs, services to parishes and organizations on ways to achieve improvement in the media.

Evangelization. The second major church concern is the media and evangelization. The apostolic exhortation of Paul VI, *Evangelii nuntiandi* (Dec. 8, 1975) which reflected concerns of the 1974 Synod of Bishops, gave new force to the term ''evangelization'' among Catholics, and this new mode of viewing the mission of the Church. Paul VI's exhortation contains a penetrating statement of the significance of the media for evangelizing: ''Our century is characterized by the mass media or means of social communication, and the first proclamation, catechesis, or the further deepening of the faith cannot do without these means. . . . When they are put at the service of the Gospel, they are capable of increasing almost indefinitely the area in which the Word of God is heard; they enable the Good News to reach millions of people. The Church would feel guilty before the Lord if she did not utilize these powerful means that human skill is daily rendering more perfect . . . In them she finds a modern and effective version of the pulpit. Thanks to them she succeeds in speaking to the multitudes. Nevertheless the use of the means of social communication for evangelization presents a challenge: through them the evangelical message should reach vast numbers of people, but with the capacity of piercing the conscience of each individual, of implanting itself in his heart, as though he were the only person being addressed, with all his most individual and personal qualities, and should evoke an entirely personal adherence and commitment'' (n. 45). Thus the recognition of the effectiveness of the media requires also avoidance of seeing that use in the same way the advertising agencies view the mass media. Any concerted and supported form of evangelization through the media is practically nonexistent in the U.S. Catholic Church, esp. when measured against the efforts of many evangelical Protestant groups. The Fall 1977 meeting of the NCCB rejected the possibility of an annual collection in Catholic parishes to support media use. The formation of an ad hoc NCCB Committee on Evangelization and currently developing diocesan programs, however, may lead to a more significant Catholic effort in the future.

[T. C. O'BRIEN]

MEDIAEVAL ACADEMY OF AMERICA, scholarly association founded at Boston (1925) to promote ''research, publication, and instruction in mediaeval records, literature, languages, art, archaeology, history, philosophy, science, life, and all other aspects.'' Membership, currently more than 2200, is open to the public, with domestic and foreign Fellows elected. It sponsors projects like the Cluny excavations, a monograph series (75 v. since 1928), the Haskins book award, and *Speculum,* its quarterly journal. A constituent of the American Council of Learned Societies, it cooperates internationally with research institutes.

[R. I. BURNS]

MEDIATION, in general the interposition between persons at variance to pacify them; in Catholic theology: the process of reconciling God and man (J. B. Carol, ''The Theological Concept of Mediation,'' *EphemThLov* 14 [1937] 642–650). The role applies primarily to Christ, secondarily and by analogy to his mother and the Church. Christ's mediatorship has three phases: (1) Being God and man, he is in a middle position between the parties to be reconciled. (2) By his atoning and meritorious sacrifice on the Cross, he brought about man's Redemption, i.e., restored man to God's friendship lost through sin (Heb 7.27). (3) By interceding for man in Heaven, he now makes available the fruits (graces) of his Redemption (Heb 7.25). Christ's mediation is primary, self-sufficient, independent, of infinite value. In this sense he is the only mediator (1 Tim 2.5). The mediatorial role of all others is secondary, insufficient by itself, of finite value, drawing all its efficacy from Christ's Redemption. Hence, ''the unique mediation of the Redeemer does not exclude but rather gives rise among creatures to a manifold cooperation which is but a sharing in this unique source'' (Vat II ConstChurch 62). Mary has been hailed as mediatrix since at least the 8th century. The term first referred either to her exalted rank in the hierarchy of creation, owing to her divine motherhood, or to her influential prayer in man's behalf. In the 14th cent. she began to be styled Coredemptrix, a word widely used since, and found in papal documents (*D,* 31st ed., 1978a, note 2). According to most Catholic theologians, Mary is Coredemptrix, not merely because she gave man the Redeemer, but also because, in the restricted sense explained above, her lifelong cooperation with Christ, mainly through her sufferings, was accepted by God as having atoning and meritorious value for man's Redemption. Hence "it may rightly be said that she redeemed the world together with Christ" (Benedict XV, "Inter sodalicia," AAS 10 [1918] 182; cf. Pius XII, "Haurietis aquas," *idem,* 48 [1956] 352; Vat II ConstChurch 61). In heaven Mary continues her mediation by way of intercession. Most Catholics believe she is the "channel of all graces to all men," a teaching endorsed by recent popes (e.g., Leo XIII, "Octobri mense," ASS 24 [1891] 195–196. In virtue of the communion of saints, other members of the Church share in Christ's mediatorship. Unlike Mary, they contributed nothing to the Redemption itself (Pius XII, "Mystici corporis," AAS 35 [1943] 213), but they cooperate in the actual application of its fruits. This role is carried out, e.g., when priests administer the sacraments; when the saints in heaven intercede for man; when the faithful on earth pray for one another. BIBLIOGRAPHY: Carol Mariol 2:377–460; J. B. Carol, NCE 9:359–364.

[J. B. CAROL]

MEDIATION OF THE CHURCH, as conceived in RC theology, an element of God's plan for man's salvation. The mediation of the Church must be seen in light of the uniqueness of the mediation of Christ. In God's saving plan it is in and through the Church that the one mediation of Christ is now present tangibly, visibly, concretely among men. Thus the Church is indeed the sacrament of sonship in Christ, the body of Christ, the people of God. Any church mediation independent of Christ is rightly to be feared. A true incarnationalism, however, cannot limit the visible manifestation of mediation to the time of Christ's earthly existence. The mediation of the Church, in continuation and direct dependence on the mediation of Christ, is two-directional. In and through the communion of persons that is the Church, Christ now makes his grace visibly present in the human family, offering men salvation esp. through the symbols of word and sacrament. This descending grace of the Lord, which is indeed offered through created things, through persons, through human events, is esp. offered and more manifestly offered through the church community. On the ascending side, the response of man to God's saving grace is expressed tangibly and most explicitly in the faith-acceptance of creed in baptism, in sacramental and esp. Eucharistic Liturgy, in the full bonds of communion in church community. These expressions, divinely founded, concretize and polarize the total life response of man to God. They express the basic stance of man as person before God more clearly and explicitly than individual expressions or even other religious expressions. The Church, then, stands in the family of man as the efficacious sign of the presence of the Redemption of Christ. The Church community is called to the service of mankind by a mediation one with Christ's own that leads the human family to grasp explicitly its vocation to be God's family. Each Christian is called to mediate the saving grace of the Lord to his fellow men by his personal word of faith, service of love, suffering, and prayer. BIBLIOGRAPHY: Vat II ConstChurch 7–8; M. Eminyan, NCE 9:571; M. J. le Guillon, SacMund 1:318–319; K. Rahner, *Church and the Sacraments* (tr. W. J. O'Hara, 1963); E. Schillebeeckx, *Christ the Sacrament of Encounter with God* (tr. P. Barrett and N. Smith, rev. M. Schoof, 1963).

[J. F. GALLAGHER]

MEDIATOR. Biblical Hebrew contains no word that is really the equivalent of NT Greek *mesitēs,* despite Job 9.33. In the NT, *mesitēs* signifies an intermediary who in some way intervenes between two parties who are separated from each other (Gal 3.19; 1 Tim 2.5; Heb 8.6; 9.15; 12.24). The intervention may have the purpose of reconciling two parties who hitherto have been separated from each other (Rom 5.10; Col 1.21) or of engaging two parties in a compact or covenant without any implication of previous hostility between them. While the specific vocabulary is limited, the concept is essential not only to the biblical understanding of the relationship between God and man, but also to most forms of historical religious groups (e.g., Sumerian and Egyptian religion; Greco-Roman religion; Gnostic forms of Christianity). Mediators may be either supernatural beings (e.g., angels, mythological divine or quasi-divine beings), or human (king, prophet, priest). The exemplar of what may be called descending and ascending mediation in the OT is Moses. Called by God, he was the agent by whom God delivered his people and through whom the Law as the expression of the divine will was delivered (Ex 19–20). God dealt with the community of Israel by dealing with Moses as a friend (Ex 33.11; Num 12.6–8), and Moses approached God as the representative of the people, seeking on their behalf forgiveness of their wickedness (Ex 32.11–12, 31–34). At a later period, the ascending aspect of mediation came to be centered in the priesthood, and in formal prayer and sacrifice. With the exceptions of Saul and David (1 Sam 10.1, 6; 16.13), the role of the king as mediator is today problematic because of the mythologizing tendencies exhibited by most of the kings of Juda from the era of Solomon. On the other hand, the Hebrew prophet appears to be the genuine successor of Moses as mediator. Called by God, the prophets conveyed God's word to the people; his demands, his judgment on idolatry, and his promises to the faithful for the future. As watchmen of the people (cf. Ezek 33.1–9; 3.17–21), they implored God's mercy for an errant people (Amos 7.1–6; Jer 15.11; 18.20). The Servant of Second Isaiah (Is 40–55) brings a unique dimension to mediation, since the Servant not only communicates God's saving word, but by bearing the sins of many, intervenes for their redemption. Furthermore, by extension, such entities as the Law and wisdom exercise a mediatorial function according to the OT (Ps 19.7–11; Job 28.23–27; Pr 1.20–23), and Israel itself as a community acts as mediator for the individual Israelite who approaches God as a member of that community. Finally, the post-Exilic era marks a considerable development in the reliance on the intercessory activity of angels both in the OT (Zech 1.12–15; Dan 10.13, 21), the intertestamental literature (Enoch, Jubilees), and at Qumran.

The NT teaching is that all OT forms of mediation have been realized and fulfilled in the person of God's Son, Jesus Christ who is God's representative to man, and who as perfect man is man's representative to God. Jesus had been called to his mediatorial mission by the Father (Heb 5.5), and freely responded (10.7). He is greater than Moses (Jn 1.17), the guide of the new exodus, head of the renewed people of God. He is king (Jn 18.33–37), the Son of David (Mt 21.4–9), while at the same time the Servant of God (Mt 12.17–21) whose prophetic mission and sacrificial death has effected the forgiveness of sins (Mk 10.45; Lk 22.19–20). Not only is Jesus the prophetic communicator of saving revelation (Lk 4.17–21) but is himself God's Word (Jn 1.14), and hence his revelation is superior to that of the Law (Gal 3.19–23). His priestly intercession surpasses that of the old covenant because of the excellence of the sacrifice offered (Heb 8.6; 9.15; 12.24). The uniqueness of Jesus as mediator contrasts not only with the multiple mediators of OT religion but with the varied intercessors proposed by Gnostic forms of Christianity proliferating at the end of the first century (1 Tim 2.5). Hence the Church itself, its apostles, ministers and faithful can only exercise its earthly mission in complete dependence upon the one mediator for all humanity, Jesus Christ. BIBLIOGRAPHY: E. C. Blackman, InterDB 3:320–331; F. J. Taylor, "Mediator," *Theological Word Book of the Bible* (ed. A. Richardson, 1957) 141; DBT 344–348; A. Oepke, *Theological Dictionary of the New Testament,* 4.598ff.

[T. J. RYAN]

MEDIATOR DEI, an encyclical (1947) of Pius XII on the *liturgy and the liturgical movement. It was the first papal document to examine and propound in depth the basis of liturgical worship, and to encourage the renewal of the liturgy which was then taking place, esp. in N Europe. The Pope had reproofs for certain excesses and innovations, but in the main he elucidated the fundamental nature of the liturgy and the theological principles that should guide its celebration. Thus *Mediator Dei* became the Magna Charta of the liturgical movement, and marked the beginning of a new and more dynamic phase of its development. The encyclical defined the liturgy as the public worship of the whole Mystical Body, head and members, but emphasized the interior dispositions from which this public act flows. The Mass is the center of the Christian religion, and the laity, by virtue of their baptism, offer themselves with Christ through the ordained priest. Pius also suggested several pastoral practices that would make liturgical participation more extensive. Vat II SacLit indicates the extent to which *Mediator Dei* has been fruitful in preparing for further developments. See text in AAS 39 (1947) 521–595; Eng. tr. *On the Sacred Liturgy: Encyclical Letter "Mediator Dei"* (ed. G. Ellard, 1954). BIBLIOGRAPHY: W. J. O'Shea, NCE 9:571–572; E. Brunner, *Mediator.* A Study of the Central Doctrine of the Christian Faith (1949); K. Rahner, *Schriften zur Theologie,* v. 8 (1968).

[P. MISNER]

MEDIATRESS (MEDIATRIX) OF ALL GRACES, title given to the Blessed Virgin Mary and under which for a time, she was honored by a feast (May 31), discontinued in the new (1969) Calendar for the Roman rite. Vatican Council II expressed the precise understanding of the title by declaring that it is to be so understood as to take nothing away or add anything to the dignity and efficacy of Christ as the One Mediator (VatII ConstChurch 62;cf. also 8). The basis for use of the title at all (found in the Eastern Church in the works of St. Andrew of Crete in the 8th cent.; used by St. Bernard of Clairvaux and thereafter in the West) is Mary's divine maternity and her willed acceptance of being the one through whom Christ came into the world. The voluntary share in Christ's mission is signalled by her place in the Gospels at his birth, the beginning of his public life, and at the Cross. Mary's cooperative role is singular among all who follow Christ; it is that special role that the title of mediatress honors and sees as continued by her maternal care for the Church. Exaggerations have been preached, of course, among them that Mary mediates between Christ and his members in such a way that no one receives grace except through her. The truth of the matter is that in fact, i.e., in the divine plan itself, the economy of salvation, Mary is there and her share in Christ's mission a continuing one. That means the special effectiveness of her prayers and universal concern for those who follow Christ with her. *COREDEMPTION.

[T. C. O'BRIEN]

MEDICAL CARE, COMPULSORY, remedial or preventive medical treatment imposed by civil law or by a civil authority. Implicit in the theme is that the treatment overrides personal liberty either of the patient or of those having parental care of the patient. The justification can be considered on moral grounds and on legal grounds. The applicable moral norms are two. The first is that the obedience owed to civil law or authority suggests the limits of their jurisdiction over the individual. That competency does not extend to what belongs to the essential makeup of human nature itself: in that there is no relationship of superior to subject—all are equals in what nature bestows and so in what concerns maintenance of life or the power to beget children (ThAq ST 2a2ae, 104.5). Thus the State cannot justify morally the imposition of *sterilization, contraception, or abortion on citizens. The State, however, does have power over them as to external actions as they affect others in the community (*ibid.*). This leads to a second moral norm: in such externals the State has the right to legislate and to enforce measures that restrict dangers to the public good (*bonum commune*). That public good means not merely the general, collective well-being of the community, but also within the community the greatest possible benefit to each and all the members. Thus the State has the right to pass and enforce laws, first of all, that remedy or prevent contagion or an epidemic. Therefore such compulsory treatments as vaccination, inoculation against contagious diseases, premarital blood tests are morally right measures. The State does not interfere with internal beliefs; it can require measures with regard to the externals of civil life. In attending to the optimum welfare of each individual the State can legitimately protect the life of a person when those having parental care neglect or refuse to do so. Such a statement of principle, however, is a generality. Moral judgment about compulsory intervention that overrides a parental right must weigh several elements. The moral norm itself presupposes the rightness and obligation of taking ordinary means to care for the body and to prolong life. The moral consensus that underlies that presupposition implies that failure to take such means is a grave negligence and dereliction of duty, and justifies overriding parental objection, even when that is a conscientious opposition to any artificial healing or lifesaving means. Moral judgment, further, must be guided by an understanding of "ordinary means." In the present culture such measures as blood transfusions or routine, even if major, surgery must be reckoned ordinary means. Particularly with reference to medical technological expertise, however, not every life-sustaining procedure need be considered an ordinary means (see LIFE, PROLONGATION OF). In the U.S. courts all of these considerations have entered into legal decisions upholding or rejecting contested compulsory medical treatment. The basic jurisprudential principle in such cases, however, is that the U.S. Constitution guarantees personal liberty as a civil right; cases are argued and decided on that basis, not per se on the human and natural rights that moral theology looks to.

[T. C. O'BRIEN]

MEDICAL MISSION BOARD, CATHOLIC (CMMB), an administrative committee organized in 1928 by Dr. Paluel Flagg and the Jesuit Edward Garesché for the purpose of providing medical supplies and recruiting and assigning medical and paramedical personnel to overseas missions. During 1975 the board shipped $5 million in medicines to 1,961 mission-distribution centers in 56 countries and assigned 77 medical volunteers to 16 countries. In the first few months of 1976 an additional 23 volunteers received similar placement. CMMB publishes *Medical Missions,* a bi-monthly, and *Professional Placement News Notes,* a monthly guide and report of the medical services rendered in the mission fields. The headquarters are located in New York City.

[R. A. TODD]

MEDICAL MISSION SISTERS (SCMM: Society of Catholic Medical Missionaries, Inc.), the first community of women religious to enter the apostolate of professional care of the sick on the missions. They were founded (1925) by Mother Anna Dengel and the Rev. M. A. Mathis, CSC, with the aid of Dr. Agnes McLaren. The Society began as a pious union, since, until 1936 in *Constans ac sedula,* canon law did not permit women with public vows to practice medicine. Now international in scope, the Medical Mission Sisters have a generalate in Rome, the original Philadelphia foundation retained for administration with a novitiate nearby, *U.S. Resource Sector of the Medical Mission Sisters.* Work began in N India (now Pakistan), where they staffed the first of 24 hospitals, at Rawalpindi. They maintain clinics, dispensaries, maternity and social welfare centers and in the Orient, leprosaria: Pakistan, Vietnam, Burma, Indonesia; in Jordan; in Africa: Ghana and Uganda; in S. America, in Venezuela; in Europe: England, Holland, Germany, and Italy. In the U.S. they minister in slum areas, in nursing schools, and on Indian reservations. In 1977 they were in 25 nations. Final pontifical approval was received in 1959, and they were placed under direct supervision of the Congregation for the Propagation of the Faith. Membership in 1975 was 689 in 67 houses; in the American sector there are 134 sisters. BIBLIOGRAPHY: A. Dengel, *Mission for Samaritans* (1945); K. Burton, *According to the Pattern: . . . Dr. Agnes McLaren and the Society of Catholic Medical Missionaries* (1946); M. G. Demers, NCE 9:574–575; Note bibliog. in both: J. Morris, NCE 9:37–38 s. v. "McLaren, Agnes" and G. E. Schidel, *ibid.* 9:462 s. v. "Mathis, Michael Ambrose."

[M. R. BROWN]

MEDICAL MISSIONARIES OF MARY, SISTERS (MMM), Benedictine women of an international congregation for medical service on the missions. In answer to Pius XI's appeal in 1936 (see MEDICAL MISSION SISTERS) Mary Martin of Dublin founded the congregation, with several companions, at Anua, East Nigeria (1937). The following year they opened a house of studies in Dublin; in 1939 took over Our Lady of Lourdes Hospital, Drogheda, where they located a motherhouse. Presently the congregation, in 30 missions in Africa, 3 in Brazil, and since 1958 on Formosa, provides doctors, midwives, paramedics esp. for mothers and children; conduct dispensaries, marriage training centers, and domestic-service schools, engage in social work, and in Nigeria pursue leprosy research and control, caring for more than 12,000 lepers. They staff 18 hospitals and 16 resident health centers. In the Archdiocese of Boston, an American foundation was made in 1950; in Winchester, Mass. a novitiate and a training and promotion center were dedicated in 1952. They issue a quarterly for both the U.S. and Ireland. Members were 453 in 43 houses (1975), and in the U.S. 15 professed and 3 novices.

[M. R. BROWN]

MEDICAL MISSIONS, a general term covering the Christian missionary enterprises that seek to bring to the sick in mission lands the benefits of modern medical science. Medical missionary work has received special and increasing emphasis since the latter half of the 19th century. Jesus and his Apostles not only preached the gospel but also healed the sick, and the attempt to mitigate the suffering of those to whom missionaries of later times brought the gospel has never been completely dissociated from the work of evangelizing a non-Christian people. Christian charity and the example of Jesus require a concern for the afflicted; moreover, missionaries have always recognized the importance of the part played by the practical and corporal works of mercy in arousing people to take an interest in the gospel message.

As a specialized form of missionary endeavor, with trained personnel using the best available modern techniques and equipment, medical missionary work began with the establishment of a Medical Mission Association in London, England, in 1878 for the purpose of providing assistance to persons desiring to become medical missionaries. Still in existence and closely associated with many Baptist missionary societies, this organization continues to help students who need special training for the work; it also makes other grants helpful in furthering this aspect of missionary effort. Other denominations have developed comparable programs; hospitals, clinics, and outstation dispensaries are built and operated in missionary areas as frequently as schools and churches. Among Roman Catholics special emphasis on medical work was slower in developing because most RC missionaries were priests or religious or both, to whom their Church granted permission to practice medicine only reluctantly and in exceptional cases. Since the beginning of the 20th cent. the pioneering effort of Dr. Agnes McLaren and Dr. Margaret Lamont—both converts to Catholicism and both experienced in the medical missionary field while still Protestants—much organized effort has gone into the training of personnel and the operation of medical centers in connection with RC missions.

Not all medical missionaries have been associated with particular denominations. Some, like the celebrated Albert Schweitzer, have gone into the work without aid or support of a particular denomination. The development of specialized and skilled assistance to the people of mission lands has gone forward in such other fields as education, social work, and agriculture. All these have as their immediate aim the alleviation of human want and misery, but ultimately they prove an effective and impressive witness to Christian truth and values. They also serve the spreading of the gospel by making it possible for Christian missions to keep some foothold in many places where, were it not for this undeniable contribution to the public good, they would be unable to survive against the emerging spirit of anticolonialism. BIBLIOGRAPHY: J. J. Considine, *Missionary's Role in Socio-Economic Betterment* (1960); M. F. Hoefsmit, *Approach to the Meaning of Medical Missions* (1956); H. Schumacher, ''Rediscovery of the Original Christian Mission Method,'' *Medical Missionary* II (1937) 98–112; A. Schweitzer, *Out of My Life and Thought* (1933).

[P. K. MEAGHER]

MEDICI, family that dominated Florence from the 13th to the 18th centuries. The earliest Medici acquired wealth in commercial and banking enterprises. **Cosimo** (1389–1464) assumed an active political role and gained control of the republican city government. **Lorenzo the Magnificent** (1449–92), while not the first, was probably the greatest Medici patron of art and humanism. The Medicis and Florence were swept into the maelstrom of the Habsburg-Valois wars in Italy. In 1530 Charles V's army captured Florence and installed **Alessandro** (1511–37) as hereditary duke; in 1570 Pope Pius V made **Cosimo I** (1519–74) Grand Duke of Tuscany, a district which the family ruled until 1737. Popes Leo X, Clement VII, and Leo XI were Medicis, as was Catherine, wife of Henry II of France. BIBLIOGRAPHY: F. Schevill, *The Medici* (1949); H. M. M. Acton, *The Last Medici* (rev., 1959); C. Hibbert, *House of Medici: Its Rise and Fall* (1975).

[R. H. SCHMANDT]

MEDICI, LORENZO DE' (1449–92), politician, diplomatist, banker and patron of the arts in Renaissance Florence. While not a physically handsome man, Lorenzo, eldest son of Piero the Gouty, possessed a strength of character and keen intelligence that made him a natural leader. His humanist education stimulated his curiosity to become involved in every phase of human endeavor. Personally, he enjoyed not only philosophy, but also writing, poetry, architecture and music. Under his tutelage the Medici Palace became the showplace of the Italian Renaissance. Such figures as da Vinci, Botticelli, Ficino, Lippi and Michelangelo were indebted to his support. As a politician, M. successfully maneuvered through the maze of Florentine politics, particularly after his fortunate escape in the Pazzi Conspiracy, April 1478. His deep understanding of the diplomatic problems of Italy was largely instrumental in preventing a full outbreak of war. After his death, for example, his son Piero was unable to balance the rival Italian states, and in 1494 with the French invasion under Charles VIII the disastrous Italian Wars began. M.'s major failing was his lack of interest in the source of Medici power, namely, the Bank. Poor loans and gross mismanagement hastened decline. Yet it was his love of the Renaissance and his popularity which earned him the title ''the Magnificent.'' BIBLIOGRAPHY: C. Hibbert, *House of the Medici: Its Rise and Fall* (1975); C. M. Ady, *Lorenzo dei Medici and Renaissance Italy* (1955).

[C. T. EBY]

MEDICINE MAN, in many primitive societies primarily a healer, though his knowledge of sacred traditions may allow him a broader social role. One becomes a medicine man by inheritance, ''call,'' or personal quest; each aspirant must be initiated and receive instruction from the elder medicine men before he is recognized as one himself. Healers operate as individuals or as members of a "medicine society." In either case their activities are based on native theories of disease, that typically recognize both "natural" and "supernatural" (magic, witchcraft, violation of taboo, etc.) causes and appropriate remedies for each. BIBLIOGRAPHY: V. Turner, *Forest of Symbols* (1967) 359–393; J. R. Fox, "Witchcraft and Clanship in Cochiti Therapy, *Magic, Witchcraft, and Curing* (ed. J. Middleton, 1967), 255–284.

[E. V. GALLAGHER]

MEDIEVAL LATIN LITERATURE, see LATIN LITERATURE, MEDIEVAL.

MEDIEVAL STUDIES, PONTIFICAL INSTITUTE OF, see PONTIFICAL INSTITUTE OF MEDIEVAL STUDIES.

MEDIEVALISM. The term may be taken as a classification of the civilization, culture, and thought of the Middle Ages; or to designate a later preference for the architecture or thought of the Middle Ages (e.g., in Ruskin, Matthew Arnold, Henry Adams, Ralph Adams Cram). Most often, however, it is opprobrious, a label connoting ignorance, obscurantism, sacerdotalism, and repression of the human spirit. This sense reflects the humanists' categorization that gave origin to the term Middle Age(s) (*medium aevum*), meaning a barbaric interruption between classical antiquity and the new age of the Renaissance. Theologically the pre-Reformation period was considered in a parallel way: the period during which the understanding of the pure gospel of grace had been distorted and replaced by superstition, sacramentalism, and venality by the corrupt clergy and papacy.

Since the invention of the classification, historians of civilization, and of theology, have come to have a higher regard for the centuries between the fall of Rome and the rise of humanism. Use of "medieval" and "medievalism" continues, however, as a disparagement applicable to any idea, practice, or institution considered to be unenlightened. In a special sense within Catholic circles medievalism sometimes means the theology and conception of ecclesial life in the century before Vatican II. There is ample justification for seeing the Council as a turning point in the life of the Church, marking a renewal, a liberating fresh start, a catalyst for social thought and action. There is, however, room to regret that for some appreciation of a new era entails rejection of, or amnesia toward, the riches of the Catholic tradition.

[T. C. O'BRIEN]

MEDINA, BARTOLOMÉ DE (1528–80), Spanish Dominican theologian and author of a classical commentary on the moral part of the *Summa theologiae* of St. Thomas Aquinas. He became the disciple of Domingo de Soto and Melchior Cano, and himself taught, first from the chair named "of Durandus" and then from the principal chair of theology at Salamanca, where he gained a great reputation. His writing is limpid, the analysis profound, and sometimes original. He was well versed in Greek and Hebrew. He has been hailed as the father of *probabilism, because he took the sensible line that when a person hesitates before opposite courses of action he may follow one approved by wise men for well-founded reasons even though the other is safer and more probable. But in fact he was not admitting doubt into the practical decision, but thinking of St. Thomas's prudential certitude about the contingent and the individual which offer only probability to the theoretic reason, and it is likely that he would have been impatient with the debates over the reflex systems for settling a dubious conscience, which contested the field for the following 2 centuries. BIBLIOGRAPHY: Quétif-Échard 2.1:256–257; T. Deman, DTC 13.1:463–470.

[T. GILBY]

MEDINA, JOSÉ ANTONIO (1773–1828), priest, leader in the 1809 revolution in Bolivia against Spain. After failure of the revolution, he was imprisoned, escaped, and spent the rest of his life in the ministry in Chile.

[T. C. O'BRIEN]

MEDINA, JUAN (1490–1546), Spanish moral theologian. He was born and died at Alcalá, and taught at the university there, from the chair entitled *de los nominales*. He appears to have been a remarkable pedagogue, but he published nothing himself. In 1550 two works were printed on parts of his moral teaching, namely on commutative justice and sacramental penance. Two MSS in the Vatican Library give his courses on the *Sentences* with explanations in the manner of *Biel.

[T. GILBY]

MEDINA, MIGUEL DE (1489–1578), Spanish Franciscan Observant, theologian, controversialist. Born near Cordova, he lectured on Scripture at the Univ. of Alcalá; thence he went, at the invitation of Philip II, as royal theologian at the Council of Trent. He defended clerical celibacy against the Magdeburg Centuriators. His order named him definitor general at the chapter of 1571. But his last years brought him much grief. In 1558 he had crossed swords with Domingo de Soto when defending a confrère, John Wild, against charges of Lutheranism. In 1572 the Toledo Inquisition caught up with him, and despite his advanced years held him in prison for more than 5 years; he died 2 days after his release, having been carried out to his friary on a stretcher.

[T. GILBY]

MEDINA (Arab., *al-Madîna,* the city), a city in Hejaz (Arabia), *c.*210 miles N of *Mecca. Medina, originally called Yathrib, is the city to which *Mohammed emigrated from Mecca with his followers in 622 (see HEGIRA) and from which he gained control over most of the Arabian peninsula. It was also the center of Islamic government under the first four *caliphs. Because of its association with the Prophet, Medina is a major center of religious pilgrimage in Islam, and its *mosque, which contains his tomb, is one of the most important shrines in the Muslim world.

[R. M. FRANK]

MEDITATION, in current usage, a form of reflective mental prayer, usually called discursive in distinguishing it from other forms of prayer. Characterized by reasoning and reflection, it is a highly practical form of prayer that proceeds from an analysis of truths, or the comparison of realities, to their application to the one meditating. It differs from idle reflection by its methodical conduct; it differs from mere meditative study and is constituted a religious exercise by its prayerful content and religious aim: ''deeper insight into the will of God, so far as it concerns myself, and renewed purpose to fulfill his will'' (J. Lindworsky *Psychology of Asceticism,* tr. E. A. Heiring, [1950] 59).

Reflective prayer has always been practiced by the fervent (Lk 2.51), but the term meditation has had different meanings through the years. From the late Middle Ages it has denoted methodical mental prayer. At times the simple identification of mental prayer with meditation, or with the use of particular methods, has occasioned a depreciation of discursive prayer in favor of the greater spontaneity of a more affective prayer. In some of its disparagers this depreciation proceeded to the point of doctrinal error, as, e.g., among the quietists (D 2181–92). But it is normally impossible that faith take deep roots or a prayer life develop purposefully and solidly without some meditation. Hence, the insistence of canon law, religious rules, and spiritual directors on the necessity of meditation for clergy and religious. In the life of prayer, meditation will gradually yield to a simpler, more affective and contemplative form of prayer; yet there is always place (even with contemplatives) for prayerful reflection. Directors teach that the form and method of prayer must always be suited to the individual and subordinate to the influence of grace. Objections against meditation as a form of prayer (e.g., H. Bremond) fail to appreciate its contemplative content and religious aim (De Guibert); properly, meditation is replete with colloquy and communion with God. BIBLIOGRAPHY: J. deGuibert, *Theology of the Spiritual Life* (tr. P. Barrett, 1953), pt. 5; G. Lercaro, *Methods of Mental Prayer* (tr. T. F. Lindsay, 1957); A. Graham, *Contemplative Christianity* (1975); H. Slade, *Exploration into Contemplative Prayer* (pa. 1975). *PRAYER; *ASCETICISM.

[W. J. READ]

MEDIUM, according to the *Spiritualist Manual,* ''one whose organism is sensitive to the vibrations from the spirit world, and through whose instrumentality intelligences in that world are able to convey messages and produce the phenomena of Spiritualism.'' *Spiritualists do not maintain that the medium must be the recipient of extraordinary supernatural gifts; their view is rather that the medium acts in accordance with given laws of nature. They also feel that only certain individuals are naturally endowed with the necessary psychic powers and even they must carefully cultivate their sensitivity to spiritual impulses.

[R. K. MACMASTER]

MEDRANO, MARIANO (1767–1851), bishop. An Argentinian priest, M. became a celebrated teacher of philosophy at the Colegio de San Carlos in Buenos Aires. In 1822 as vicar general of Buenos Aires he opposed the reforms advanced by Rivadavia. M. was named bp. of Buenos Aires in 1832 by Gregory XVI but the State claimed that its right of patronage had been ignored. A commission of jurists and theologians paved the way for the acceptance of M. as bishop. In his tenure of the bishopric M. restored the hierarchy.

[J. R. AHERNE]

MEEHAN, THOMAS FRANCIS (1854–1942), editor, historiographer. A New Yorker by birth, M. was managing editor of the *Irish American* from 1874 to 1904 and served on the staff of the *New York Herald* for 2 years. He was assistant editor of the *Catholic Encyclopedia,* a member of the staff of *America* magazine, and contributed to a number of periodicals. Joining the staff of *Records and Studies* of the American Catholic Historical Society in 1905, M. was its editor from 1916 until his death. He edited also *Catholic Builders of the Nation* (1925).

[J. R. AHERNE]

MEEKNESS, a virtue allied to *temperance, in that its concern is restraining and tempering the emotion of *anger, the desire to retaliate (ThAq ST 2a2ae, 157.1). Meekness or gentleness differs from *clemency, which moderates actual punishing, in being concerned with the inner surge towards revenge. Because Our Lord both urges imitation of his own special meekness (Mt 11.29), and includes the meek among those who are especially blessed (see BEATITUDES), this virtue has become one of the distinctive traits of Christian holiness. Its restraint from wanting to inflict injury for injury received is its particular link with *charity as the intent to love and do good to others (ThAq ST 2a2ae, 17.4 ad 2). The meek are those who, relying on the Father's will, remain tranquil in the face of wrongs done them (*ibid.,* 1a2ae, 69.3). Their reward of ''inheriting the land'' means their security and stability in the possession of the eternal good, in contrast with the ephemeral victories of those who resort to violence (*ibid.,* 4).

[T. C. O'BRIEN]

MEERSCH, MAXENCE VAN DER (1907–51), French writer who interpreted the socio-economic matrix of the Franco-Belgian industrial belt from a neo-Christian perspective. He took degrees in law and letters and was a lawyer before turning to literature. Reared in an antireligious milieu, V. was converted, but his relationship to Catholicism remained complex, for he shunned its sacramental life and did not accept the contemplative ascetic life or clerical celibacy. His novels, in part autobiographical and neo-naturalistic in style, develop two themes: modern man's dechristianization and dehumanization in the secular ambience created by science and industrialization, and the drama of spiritual liberation and growth within such contexts. Most representative are *Car ils ne savent ce qu'ils font* (1933), *Le Péché du monde* (1934), *L'Empreinte de Dieu* (1936), which won the Prix Goncourt, *L'Élu* (1937), which narrates a conversion analogous to the author's, *Pêcheur d'hommes* (1940), based on the Jociste movement of Canon Cardijn, and *La Fille pauvre* (3 v., 1948), reflecting the influence of Léon Bloy. He has written hagiography, *La Vie du Curé D'Ars* (1942) and *La Petite Sainte Thérèse* (1947), criticism of the medical profession *(Corps et âmes,* 1943), and a war novel, *Invasion 14* (1935). BIBLIOGRAPHY: R. Reus, *Portrait morpho-psychologique de Maxence Van der Meersch* (1952); A. Jans, *À la rencontre de Maxence Van der Meersch* (1946).

[G. E. GINGRAS]

MEESTER, MARIE LOUISE DE, see DE MEESTER, MARIE LOUISE, MOTHER.

MEETING (Friends), a term designating Quaker organizational structure. The monthly meeting is a local congregation that meets weekly for worship and monthly for a business session. The quarterly and yearly meetings are broader geographical and administrative units. The whole corporate unit of some Quaker groups is called a meeting, e.g., the Friends United Meeting and the Ohio Yearly Meeting of Friends Church. The use of the term comes from G. *Fox, who, rejecting the organized Churches and their "steeple houses," designated the gatherings and groupings of his followers as meetings. *RELIGIOUS SOCIETY OF FRIENDS.

[T. C. O'BRIEN]

MEGALOSCHEMI, (Gr. meaning one who wears the "great habit"), in the Orthodox Church monks who have normally passed through the grades of rasophore and microschemos (Sl., stavrophore) and have accepted the highest state of monasticism which involves stricter fasting and prayer as well as a greater commitment to silence than is required of the other monks. In Russian practice the habit is given to the second grade of monks but in Greek practice it is reserved for the *megaloschemi* together with a special monastic headdress, the *koukoul* and the *analev,* signifying the mystic cross that the monk takes upon himself when he vows poverty, chastity, obedience, and a life of asceticism.

[S. SURRENCY]

MEGARIAN SCHOOL, one of the *Minor Socratic Schools, founded by Eucleides of Megara (*c.*450–380 B.C.), a disciple and friend of Socrates. An adherent of Eleatic Monism, he tried to harmonize the ethical teaching of Socrates with it by regarding virtue as a unity and by identifying the Good, God, and Reason with the One. He rejected the existence of a principle contrary to the Good, as this meant the acceptance of multiplicity, a concept alien to Eleatic doctrine. Among other representatives of the school may be mentioned: Eubulides of Miletus, a pupil of Eucleides, who is chiefly famous for his development of eristic arguments and for the systematic use of the *reductio ad absurdum* in his dialectic; Diodorus Cronus (*c.*350–early 3d cent.), who by ingenious arguments identified the actual and the possible; and Stilpo of Megara (*c.*380–300 B.C.), who, while maintaining the monism of the school, was concerned also, under Cynic influence, with ethics, emphasizing in this respect the doctrine of *apatheia*. Stilpo wrote a number of dialogues and as a teacher exercised a marked attraction through his own personality. The Megarians had considerable influence on Aristotle's logic, and on Pyrrhon of Elis; *Zeno of Citium, the founder of Stoicism, was a pupil of Stilpo. BIBLIOGRAPHY: Copleston 1:116–118; Ueberweg 1:155–158.

[M. R. P. MCGUIRE]

MEGERLE, JOHANN ULRICH, see ABRAHAM OF SANCTA CLARA.

MEGIDDO, Palestinian city overlooking the Plain of *Esdraelon. Extensive excavations have revealed that 20 cities were built on the site (today known as Tell el-Mutesellim), the earliest built *c.*3500 B.C. and the last inhabited until *c.*400 B.C. At the intersection of two important trade routes, the city had an importance exceeding its small size, and several of the *Amarna Letters were from its prince. It was in the area given to the tribe of Manasseh, though the tribe was not able to possess the cities of the area immediately (Jos ch. 17). The Song of Deborah says that Barak defeated Sisera "by the waters of Megiddo" (Jg 5.19). Solomon made it a royal chariot city (1 Kg 9.15, 19). Ahaziah died there, after he was shot by Jehu's forces (2 Kg 9.27), and Pharaoh Neco killed Josiah there (2 Kg 23.29). Some scholars interpret the name Armageddon (Rev 16.16) as the Mount of Megiddo. BIBLIOGRAPHY: Y. Yadin, *Hazor* (1972).

[T. EARLY]

MEGILLAT TA'ANIT, ancient list of Jewish feast days. The term means scroll of fasting, but the list was of days when fasting was forbidden. It commemorated some 35 events from the 2d cent. B.C. to the 2d cent. A.D. The first section, dating from the time of the last events covered, has one chapter for each of the 12 Hebrew months, describing the events that occurred in that month. One of the first postbiblical Tannaitic compositions, it was written by Hananiah ben Hezekiah of the Garon family and his son Eleazar, a general. The second section, dating from *c.*7th cent., contains Hebrew commentaries on the first section. The feasts commemorated esp. joyful or heroic events in Jewish history, 14 of them considered so important that even public mourning was forbidden (see Jdt 8.6). The festivals on the list have now all largely died out.

[T. EARLY]

MEHEGAN, MARY XAVIER, MOTHER (Catherine Josephine; 1825–1915), foundress. Born in Ireland she came to the U.S. in 1844 and 3 years later entered the newly formed Sisters of Charity of New York. She and another sister established a new branch of the congregation in Newark, N.J. in 1859. After the Civil War, the community grew rapidly spreading to New York, Massachusetts, and Connecticut. Under her administration, the College of St. Elizabeth at Convent Station was established, the first college for women in New Jersey. After 57 years as superior, her congregation numbered 1,200 sisters and operated almost 100 foundations—schools, hospitals, orphanages, nurseries, and homes for the aged.

[J. R. AHERNE]

MEHRERAU, ABBEY OF, a former Benedictine abbey on Lake Constance, Austria. Since the 19th cent., however, it has been the seat of the Cistercian abbey *nullius* of Wettingen-Mehrerau. At Mehrerau there is a secondary school as well as a theological and agricultural technical school. Its other interests include administering a sanatorium.

[M. A. MCFADDEN]

MÉHUL, ÉTIENNE NICOLAS (Étienne Henri; 1763–1817), French composer and organist. Born in poverty, he became an organist in a convent at the age of ten. His talent led him to Paris to study piano and composition with Edelmann. His early compositions were primarily church music; a cantata with orchestra composed to a sacred ode of Rousseau was particularly successful when produced at the Concert Spirituel in 1782. M. then studied with Gluck, who encouraged him to compose opera. He wrote over 30 pieces for the stage, his first in 1790, *Euphrosine et Coradin* and his most famous *Joseph* in 1807, a sacred opera. He also wrote patriotic songs, ballets, cantatas, an unperformed Mass for Napoleon's coronation, and several symphonies. M. is thought to have influenced Beethoven, Cherubini, and Paer.

[R. J. LITZ]

MEINONG, ALEXIS (1853–1920), Austrian philosopher and psychologist. He studied philosophy at Vienna under Franz Brentano and after obtaining his Ph.D. (1878) taught at the Univ. of Graz where he founded in 1886 the first laboratory for experimental psychology in Austria. Like Brentano's other disciple, E. Husserl, M. developed his master's ideas in an original way and strove for a philosophy as a strict science of the object. According to different psychical activities related to objects (representation, judgment, evaluation, desire) M. distinguishes various kinds of objects which he describes in great detail. His philosophy is thereby both a study of the objects and a psychology of the ways man deals with them. M.'s work has been influential, esp. in Austria. BIBLIOGRAPHY: J. N. Findlay, *Meinong's Theory of Objects and Values* (2d ed., 1963).

[B. A. NACHBAHR]

MEINRAD OF EINSIEDELN, ST., (d. 861), hermit, sometimes called a martyr. M. was educated at Reichenau, then taught at Babinchowa on Lake Zurich until his desire for solitude led him first to Mt. Etzel, then to what later became the site of the monastery of Einsiedeln (i.e., hermitage). In 861, he was murdered by two robbers. BIBLIOGRAPHY: Butler, 1:139–140; R. Henggeler, BiblSanct 9:273–277.

[M. F. MCCARTHY]

MEINWERK OF PADERBORN, BL. (often called Saint; *c.*970–1036), bp. of Paderborn from 1009, chosen for the post by Emperor Henry II, who hoped that the wealth of M.'s noble Saxon family would be used in restoring the see. The cathedral had been destroyed by fire in the year 1000. This M. rebuilt on a grander scale and with greater magnificence; he built a monastery of Abdinghof for a community of Cluniac Benedictines, and fostered other ecclesiastical projects at his own expense; he promoted clerical discipline and improved the quality of education at the cathedral school, and in general contributed so conspicuously to the cultural and administrative development of Paderborn, that he was accounted the see's second founder. He made Paderborn an outstanding center of the Ottonian renaissance. BIBLIOGRAPHY: J. E. Gugumus, BiblSanct 9:280.

MEIR, BEN BARUCH (Meir of Rothenberg; 1215–93), German born Talmudic scholar. He tried to flee Germany at a time of Jewish persecution; instead he was captured and imprisoned, but discouraged his followers from paying King Rudolph for his release so that other Jewish leaders would not be imprisoned for extortion purposes. Known as the "Light of the Exile," his works consist of the *Responsa* (answers to the questions of law), a commentary on the *Mishnah*, and liturgical hymns.

[M. A. MCFADDEN]

MEISTERMANN, BARNABAS (1850–1923), Franciscan archeologist and expert on the Holy Land. M. was first assigned to Assisi and as a missionary in China, but from 1893 devoted himself to history and archeological study in the Holy Land. He published several books on the Christian shrines there, notably his *Nouveau guide de Terre Sainte* (3d ed., 1936).

[T. M. MCFADDEN]

MeKAPRĀNĀ, East Syrian blessed bread distributed after Mass, the equivalent of the Byzantine **antidoron,* made from the same dough used for the bread to be consecrated.

[A. CODY]

MEKHITAR, religious name of Manouk Bedrossian (1676–1749), Armenian religious humanist and founder of the *Mekhitarists. Born a Gregorian Armenian at Sivas (Sebaste), M. was a monastic deacon at 15, subsequently becoming priest and *vartaped. The precise details of his movement to Catholicism are not known, but it is reasonably certain that contact with a French Jesuit in Aleppo was the decisive influence. He remained close to the Gregorians until his religious foundation in 1701, when Gregorian opposition led to his move, with his community, to the West. His role as awakener of an Armenian cultural renaissance is recognized by all Armenians, both Catholic and Gregorian. He was the author of many books on theology, Scripture, spirituality, and Armenian philology.

[A. CODY]

MEKHITARISTS, Armenian Catholic religious community founded by the *vartaped* Mekhitar in Constantinople in 1701. The nascent community met so much opposition that it moved to the then Venetian Peloponnesus (Morea) in 1702, until the advent of the Turks obliged them to leave in 1715. They settled permanently on the islet of San Lazzaro near Venice in 1717. In 1773 a number of monks displeased by a revision of the constitutions left San Lazzaro for Trieste, then under Austrian rule, forming a totally independent congregation in 1803; they transferred to Vienna in 1810. Both congregations follow the Rule of St. Benedict, but without specifically Benedictine traditions or spirituality, and profess simple vows of poverty, chastity, and obedience, plus a fourth of going to missions when sent. The Venetians have schools for Armenians in Venice, Sèvres, Aleppo, Alexandria, Buenos Aires, and Istanbul, with three parishes in France and Italy. The Viennese schools are in Beirut, Cairo (Heliopolis), and Istanbul, and their three parishes are in Hungary and the U.S. Both congregations have important publishing houses, and both have been influential centers of Armenian culture and learning. The scientific work of the Venetians has tended to be esp. literary and artistic, that of the Viennese esp. philological, both groups working in Armenian history and liturgy. In 1962 the Venetians numbered 54, the Viennese 32. BIBLIOGRAPHY: M. van den Oudenrijn, LTK 7:223–224.

[A. CODY]

MELANCHOLY, from Gr. "black bile," an extreme state of *sorrow or sadness, even manic depression. In this full sense, melancholy is not a moral, but a pathological disorder. In a looser sense it may have a moral quality, as a state of sadness unchecked by the virtue of *courage and so be an inordinate retardant to right moral action. It can also mean sadness contrary to the joy that should follow from charity because of the reality of God's loving goodness. *ACEDIA.

[T. C. O'BRIEN]

MELANCHTHON, PHILIPP (1497–1560), German humanist and close associate of Martin *Luther in the work of the Reformation. Born Philipp Schwarzert, he was something of a child prodigy, receiving the Bachelor of Arts degree at 14 and the Master of Arts at 16; he became Luther's colleague at Wittenberg in August 1518, at the age of 21. He was, however, a member of the philosophical rather than the theological faculty, which he joined as an adjunct member the following year. This joint appointment is representative both of his intellectual interests and of his historical significance. He was a biblical humanist, in the circle of *Erasmus and of his own kinsman, J. *Reuchlin. Many of M.'s university lectures and published writings dealt with texts of classical authors. He even contemplated the publication of a definitive edition of Aristotle, whom he wanted to rescue from the Thomists. In his work as a theologian, he applied many of the same interpretive methods to biblical texts, the meaning of which he believed to be accessible to sound philological investigation, untrammeled by scholastic apriorism. At the same time, he was more zealous than Luther in his cultivation of the Catholic tradition and in his desire to reconcile the Protestant-humanistic interpretation of the Bible with the teachings of the Fathers.

M.'s place in the history of the Reformation was determined by these factors. Thus his lectures on Romans became the basis for his composition, in 1521, of the first Protestant systematic theology, the *Loci communes,* which he revised several times, changing his theological position (Eng. tr. C. L. Hill, 1944). The controversy between Luther and Erasmus, his two heroes, was a source of personal anguish to him, and he tried unsuccessfully to mediate between them. In 1530 it fell to him to compose the *Augsburg Confession, and in the following year the *Apology of the Augsburg Confession. He was also the author of many textbooks that were used both in secondary schools and in theological instruction. His mediating spirit manifested itself also in his modifications of the Augsburg Confession (see VARIATA AUGUSTANA) to conciliate *Reformed theology, as well as in his repeated efforts to find a common ground with RC theology. After Luther's death in 1546, M. increasingly became a controversial figure, caught between the various parties and no longer able to depend on the support of his colleague-mentor. BIBLIOGRAPHY: *Melanchthon: Selected Writings* (ed. E. E. Flack and L. J. Satre, tr. C. L. Hill, 1962); C. L. Manschreck, *Melanchthon: The Quiet Reformer* (1958 repr. 1975); *Luther and Melanchthon in the History and Theology of the Reformation* (ed. V. Vajta, 1961). *ADIAPHORISTS; *CRYPTO-CALVINISM; *GNESIOLUTHERANISM; *MAJORISTIC CONTROVERSY; *PHILIPPISM.

[J. PELIKAN]

MELANDEZ, JUAN DE (d. 1684), Peruvian Dominican, author of *Tesoros verdaderos de las Indias* (3 v., 1681–82), a chronicle of Peruvian history, richly documented from archives at Madrid, Rome, and Lima.

[T. C. O'BRIEN]

MELANESIA, one of the three main divisions of *Oceania. It includes the Fiji, Loyalty, New Hebrides, Solomon, New Caledonia, Ellice and Gilbert archipelagoes, and some other islands. The name is derived from the dark skin of the inhabitants. Melanesians profess animism and practice ancestor worship. Masked impersonation of spirits and initiation into the spirit world are prominent features of their cult. BIBLIOGRAPHY: *History of Melanesia* (ed. K. S. Inglis, pa. 1971).

[M. J. SUELZER]

MELANIA THE ELDER (342–409), a Roman lady of the patrician *gens Antonia,* who, after being widowed at the age of 22, yielded to the urging of St. *Jerome and dedicated her life to prayer and asceticism in the East (372). With the help of her spiritual counselor, *Rufinus of Aquileia, she built a monastery for women in Jerusalem (*c.*378). She returned to the West (*c.*400–403) to visit her cousin, St. *Paulinus of Nola, and esp. to encourage her granddaughter, *Melania the Younger, in her resolve to dedicate her life to Christ. BIBLIOGRAPHY: F. X. Murphy, *Traditio* 5 (1947) 55–77.

[R. B. ENO]

MELANIA THE YOUNGER, ST. (383–439), Roman matron, ascetic, monastic foundress, conspicuous for her great benefactions. The granddaughter of *Melania the Elder, M. desired to devote her life to prayer and asceticism but was forced by her father to marry her kinsman, Valerius Pinianus, in 397. After the early death of their two children, Pinianus assented to her desire that they should live in continence. Despite the spirited opposition of family and the senate they distributed much of their immense wealth to the poor and the Church, and they liberated a vast number of slaves. Withdrawing from Rome before the oncoming invasion of the Goths, they visited *Paulinus of Nola (406) and *Rufinus of Aquileia (408) and for 7 years lived an ascetical life in North Africa, where they knew *Augustine and *Alipius. They then settled in Jerusalem, where after 14 years, M.'s mother died and the following year her husband. She buried the two on the Mount of Olives and nearby built a cell for herself. To this she added cells for other devout women, and thus grew up a monastery over which M. presided. In the East her cult is of great antiquity, but in the West it did not exist until after 1905, when M. Rampolla's discovery and study of the complete Latin text of her life drew attention to her. Life: SC 90 (ed. D. Gorce, 1963). BIBLIOGRAPHY: Butler 4:646–649; F. X. Murphy, NCE 9:625.

[R. B. ENO]

MELCHERS, PAULUS (1813–95), abp. of Cologne, cardinal. A native of Westphalia, M. was ordained in 1841 after having briefly practiced law. He became vicar general of Münster in 1852 and bp. of Osnabrück and vicar apostolic of the northern missions in 1857. He became abp. of Cologne in 1866. He was a leader of the anti-infallibilist party at Vatican I, but after the Council he disciplined theology professors who continued to oppose the definition. A leading foe of *Kulturkampf, M. was imprisoned in 1874 and forced to leave Prussia. In 1885 he resigned his see to clear the way for a settlement of the Prussian problem and was made a cardinal residing in Rome. The last 3 years of his life he spent as a Jesuit.

[J. R. AHERNE]

MELCHIADES, ST., POPE, see MILTIADES, ST., POPE.

MELCHIOR, according to a late tradition, one of the *Magi. Melkon is a variant form of the name. Tradition has commonly identified him as King of Persia, and sometimes also as brother of the other two, Gaspar (King of India), and Balthasar (King of Arabia). A very detailed account of him is given in the *Armenian Gospel of the Infancy*. A medieval legend asserts that the bodies of the three were brought by Empress Helena to Constantinople, then later transferred to Milan, and finally to Cologne.

[W. G. MOST]

MELCHIORITES, see HOFMANN, MELCHIOR.

MELCHISEDECHIANS, a name to classify those who taught that Melchisedek (Gen 14.18) was the Logos, or the Holy Spirit, or a power descending upon Christ. The name is found in Augustine (*Haer.* 34). Christ's inferiority to Melchisedek was a recurrent teaching among some Gnostics, but there is no evidence of a distinct body of Melchisedechians. BIBLIOGRAPHY: G. Bardy, DTC 10:513–516.

[L. G. MÜLLER]

MELCHITE RITE, see MELKITE CHURCH.

MELCHIZEDEK (Melchisedec), the king of Salem, i.e., Jerusalem (Gen 14.18–20), and high priest of its god El Elyon, "Most high God," who came to meet Abraham after his expedition against the four kings with offerings of bread and wine. He received a tithe of Abraham's booty and in return gave him a blessing. It has been argued that the real background to this story is to be found in the circumstances of David's conquest of Jerusalem. At this time he may have installed *Zadok, the reigning Jebusite high priest of El Elyon, as high priest of Yahweh. According to this theory, therefore, the story of Melchizedek blessing Abraham would contain a strong element of retrospective interpretation. El Elyon would have been regarded as in reality another name for Yahweh. Melchizedek himself would have been thought of as an adherent of the true religion of Yahweh, albeit only inchoately, and David's conquest of Jerusalem would have been interpreted as a fulfillment of the ancient blessing of Melchizedek. On this basis the words "You are a priest forever in the manner of Melchizedek" in Ps 110.4 can be interpreted as a solemn pronouncement by the newly enthroned Davidic king, whose first act would have been to install or to confirm his high priest in office. The form of the words would serve to emphasize the antiquity of the office, extending back to the time of Abraham. The interpretation of Melchizedek in Heb 5.7 involves rabbinical methods of exegesis which may seem artificial to the modern mind. Melchizedek prefigures Christ in that he has no genealogy, and therefore owes his priesthood to direct divine appointment and not, as with the Levitical priests, to physical descent. Moreover, at the time when Abraham recognized Melchizedek's priesthood by giving him tithes and receiving his blessing, the ancestor of these Levitical priests was still unconceived and "in Abraham's loins." Therefore in Abraham's gesture the Levitical priesthood was, in effect, recognizing the superiority of this other priesthood, the one that is a type of Christ's own. BIBLIOGRAPHY: A. Vaccari, "Melchizedek, Rex Salem proferens panem et vinum", *Verbum Domini* 18 (1938) 208–214, 235–243; cf. also J. Fitzmyer, CBQ 25 (1963) 305–321.

[D. J. BOURKE]

MELCHOM, see MILCOM.

MELETIAN SCHISM, a name given to two distinct schisms. (1) The first centered about Meletius, bp. of Lycopolis in Egypt (d. *c.*326). While Peter, bp. of Alexandria was in hiding during the Diocletian persecution (305–306), Meletius considered himself head of the Egyptian Church, and assumed to himself the right of ordaining clerics, excommunicating, etc. Later Meletius was himself arrested by the civil authorities. When the persecution subsided and Meletius was released, he was welcomed home as a confessor of the faith. He adopted a rigoristic attitude toward those who had lapsed or avoided arrest. He defied an order of deposition by a synod convoked by Peter of Alexandria, gained many adherents, and had a number of bishoprics under his control. These later became active in the Arian cause, and the sect survived until the 6th cent. BIBLIOGRAPHY: Hefele-Leclercq 1:488–503. (2) The other schism took its name from St. Meletius, bp. of Antioch (d. 381) and developed in the Church of Antioch in the confusion of an anti-Nicene reaction (360–418). BIBLIOGRAPHY: P. Canivet, NCE 9:631.

[P. K. MEAGHER]

MELETIANS, the Antiochian followers of St. *Meletius, who, out of fidelity to the decisions of Nicaea (325), became the leader of this orthodox, anti-Arian movement, centering on the proper terminology, designating God as one in nature in three Persons. After Meletius return from his first exile (362), Antioch had at once three bps. leading three communities. The Meletian counterpart were the Eustathians, followers of the deposed bp. of Antioch, deposed in 330. Both groups had a different understanding of the Nicaean term: the Meletians accused the Eustathians of Sabellianism. The latter taught that *ousia* and *hypostasis* are identical; in God there is one *ousia* or *hypostasis* in three *prosopa*. The Meletians were of the opinion that there is in God one *ousia* in three hypostases, a formula considered by the Eustathians to be Arian. This verbal difference continued till 398. At last a group of the Eustathians reunited with the Meletians in 413 and thus this schism came to an end.

[J. MADEY]

MELETIUS, ST. (d. 381), bp. of Antioch. He was born in Armenia Secunda, and he died as presiding officer at the Council of Constantinople I. Having become bp. of Sebaste, he took part in the synod of Seleucia in 359. One year later he became bp. of Antioch by election, both by the Eustathians, led by the presbyter Paulinus, and the *homoousion* majority lead by Bp. Euzoius. On account of the dissension caused by his preaching, Emperor Constantius II exiled M., but under Julian he returned in 362. He was exiled twice again, under Emperor Valens (365–367 and 371–377).

[J. MADEY]

MELETIUS OF LYCOPOLIS in Upper Egypt (d. *c.*325), bp. of Lycopolis. Accused of having performed ordinations illegally, he was excommunicated by a synod at Alexandria, under Patriarch Petros I of Alexandria. M., an opponent of Petros's mild stand with regards to the *lapsi*, organized the Church of Martyrs with 29 bishops. The Council of Nicaea did not succeed in eliminating the schism he created. The sect of the Meletians was in favor of the Arians and was encouraged by some monks. Its influence disappeared after the 5th century.

[L. PEANO]

MELETIUS PIGAS (1549–1602), patriarch of Alexandria. M. was born in Herakleion on the island of Crete. He studied at Padua and then at Alexandria (*c.*1572). M. became a monk at Ankarathos and was ordained by Jeremias II of Constantinople. He became the assistant of Silvester, patriarch of Alexandria, whom he succeeded sometime after the Council of Constantinople of 1591. During his patriarchate, M. tried unsuccessfully to maintain the important role of the Eastern Church in Poland against the increasing influence of Rome upon King Sigismund. M. administered the See of Constantinople while that patriarchate was vacant in 1597. M. brought a young relative to Alexandria, educated him, and ordained him; after M.'s death, this kinsman became the influential patriarch, Cyril Lucaris. BIBLIOGRAPHY: B. Kotter, LTK 7:258; E. Legrand, *Lettres de Meletius Pigas antérieures à son promotion au Patriarcat* (1902).

[R. J. BRADY]

MELFI, COUNCILS OF. The importance of Melfi in S Italy begins with the occupation of Puglia by the Normans.

Synods held there in 1059, 1067, 1100 and 1284 were primarily concerned with relations between Rome and the Norman kingdom which became a vassal state to the popes in 1059. BIBLIOGRAPHY: R. Kay, NCE 9:631.

[B. L. MARTHALER]

MELIORAMENTUM, the *Cathari rite in which the simple believers rendered a kind of worship to the *Perfecti.

[T. C. O'BRIEN]

MELITENIOTES, CONSTANTINE, theologian and diplomat. M. was archdeacon of Constantinople in 1270 when Emperor Michael VIII dispatched him aalong with the Patriarch John Bekkos to persuade Louis IX of France to participate in a joint Crusade to the Holy Land. The mission of the two envoys was unsuccessful because Louis died in Tunis before their arrival. M. represented Michael in negotiating an accord between the Eastern Church and Rome. At the Council of Lyons IV (1274), the Greek Church recognized the primacy of Rome, a concession which satisfied the political needs of the Emperor Michael but angered many powerful figures in Constantinople. When Michael died in 1282, his enemies regained control of the Church, repudiated the Lyons accord, and defrocked M. He and Bekkos were tried and imprisoned in 1285 for their support of the union between Constantinople and Rome. BIBLIOGRAPHY: S. Vailhe, DTC 3:1226–27; A. Vasiliev, *History of Byzantine Empire* (1961) 706–707.

[R. BRADY]

MELITO OF SARDIS, ST. (d. *c.*190), bishop, apologist. Among his more than 20 works, as listed by Eusebius, was an apology addressed to Marcus Aurelius (*c.*166). This, along with most of his other writings, has been lost. Apart from a homily on the Passion, discovered in modern times and published by C. Bonner in 1940, only fragments of his work have survived. M. was highly respected by Eusebius and other ecclesiastical writers, and various writings have been erroneously attributed to him. He is cited as favoring the *Quartodeciman practice and as an early exponent of orthodox Christology with a clear perception of the duality of natures in Christ. M. seems to have held the millenarian views of Irenaeus, and was accused (wrongly, it seems) of anthropomorphism by Origen. Works: *Homily on the Passion* (ed. O. Perler, SC 123, 1966). BIBLIOGRAPHY: Quasten 1:242–248; É. Amann, DTC 10:540–547; Butler 2:1.

[R. B. ENO]

MELK, ABBEY OF, Austrian Benedictine abbey on the Danube in the Diocese of St. Pölten. This world-known monastery was formerly a castle of the Austrian margraves. Here existed a chapter of secular canons who were relieved in 1089 by Benedictines from Lambach. Later the abbey was richly endowed and became one of the most important religious centers in Austria. In the beginning of the 15th cent. a monastic renaissance known as the "Reform of Melk," developed here. This renaissance touched all Benedictine monasteries in S Germany. During the Reformation the abbey declined but attained new prosperity since the 17th century. In 1702 Abbot B. Dietmayr began the new construction of the abbey's buildings. The baroque architect J. Prandtauer here erected one of the most beautiful buildings of the world in perfect accordance of nature and art. Today the monks are teaching in their famous liberal arts high school (*Gymnasium*) and in parish work. Many tourists visit the abbey with its incomparable baroque church, the famous library, and other sights. In the church St. Coloman (d. 1012), is venerated as one of the patrons of Austria. BIBLIOGRAPHY: A. Schramb, *Chronicon Mellicense* (1702); I. Keiblinger, *Geschichte des Benediktinerstiftes Melk,* 3 v. (1868–69); F. Klauner, *Die Kirche von Stift Melk* (1946); *Catalogue of exposition: Jakob Prandtauer und sein Kunstkreis* (1960).

[F. H. RÖHRIG]

MELKITE CHURCH, one of the most ancient Catholic Churches of the Byzantine rite in the Near East. The name is derived from the Aramaic title *melek,* king and was coined during the 5th-cent. theological and political dispute and applied to those Christians of Syria and Egypt who refusing Monophysitism and accepting the definition of faith of the Council of Chalcedon (451), remained in communion with Rome, and in that specific historical incident, with the imperial see of Constantinople as "king's men." A period of historically conditioned estrangement between Byzantine Melkites and the see of Rome followed.

In 1724, thanks to the initiative of Abp. Eftimios Saifi, the legitimate native Melkite Patriarch Cyril VI Tanas publicly reasserted the abiding communion of the Roman and Antiochene (Melkite) Churches. However the Greek Orthodox Church immediately installed a Greek bp. in the patriarchal see of Antioch, creating an Eastern Orthodox hierarchy for the so-called Syrian Antiochene Church. Cyril VI was exiled from Damascus to Lebanon where he established his residence.

Approximately one million people living in the Near East and throughout the world belong to the Melkite rite of the Catholic Church. Melkites follow the Byzantine rite, which is proper to the Church of Constantinople. Liturgical languages are basically Greek and Arabic but also any language of the local Melkite community. Since 1724 the Melkite Catholic Church has had as supreme ruler a single patriarch having ordinary jurisdiction over bps., clergy, and faithful. Today this group forms an entirely distinct community in the midst of the Oriental Church, having disciplinary and hierarchical autonomy, yet immediately subject to the Holy See. The present Melkite patriarch is Maximos V Hakim. His title is Patriarch of Antioch of the Melkites. He has also the personal title of Melkite Patriarch of Alexandria and of Jerusalem and has jurisdiction over 16 archdioceses and dioceses. The patriarchate of Antioch also has jurisdiction over Melkites in Egypt, Sudan, Jerusalem and Iraq. As an Eastern rite patriarch, Maximos is the head of the faithful belonging to his rite throughout the world. The Melkite Church in the U.S. was organized as an exarchate in the late 1960s and since 1977 has been organized as an eparchy under Abp. Joseph Tawil, with residence in West Newton, Mass. BIBLIOGRAPHY: L. Malouf, *Byzantine Melkite Thinking* (1972).

[L. PEANO]

MELKON, a variant form of the name *Melchior ascribed by tradition to one of the *Magi.

[P. K. MEAGHER]

MELL, MAX (1882–), Austrian dramatist. With his mystery plays set in his Alpine homeland, M. contributed much to the Catholic literary revival. His *Apostelspiel* (1923) attained great popularity; combining myth and reality, it tells of two men, who after entering a mountain hut with criminal intent, were converted by the pure faith of a girl seeing in them messengers of God. Other dramas: *Nachfolge-Christi-Spiel,* a mystical play of Christian forgiveness set in the times of the Turkish invasion; *Die Sieben gegen Theben* (1932) with the Antigone motif. He also wrote some lyrical poetry.

[B. F. STEINBRUCKNER]

MELLERAY, ABBEY OF, a monastery in Brittany, founded in 1145 by Cistercians from Pontron Abbey, Anjou. It declined after being given *in commendam* in 1544, and was suppressed in 1791. In 1817 the property was purchased by the Trappists of Lulworth, England. Abbot Eugene Achette (1875–1919), as vicar general of La Trappe, played a part in uniting the three Trappist congregations into the order of Reformed Cistercians. Melleray has two daughter houses. BIBLIOGRAPHY: A. Bernard, ''L'Abbaye de Melleray et les Trappistes,'' *Les Annales de Nantes,* 104 (1956).

[C. MCGRATH]

MELLIFONT, ABBEY OF, the first Cistercian house in Ireland. Founded in 1142 with the cooperation of SS. Bernard of Clairvaux and Malachy, abp. of Armagh, Mellifont was a highly successful establishment, the cradle of further Cistercian expansion in Ireland. In the 13th cent. it had over 100 monks. Declining discipline necessitated repeated reforms. In the year of dissolution (1539) the house had only 15 monks. In 1938 the abbey was revived by Trappist Cistercians of *Mount Melleray. BIBLIOGRAPHY: C. O. Conbhuidhe, *Story of Mellifont* (1958).

[L. J. LEKAI]

MELLIFONT, COUNCIL OF, sometimes called the Synod of Kells. In 1152 Card. Paparo, papal legate of Eugene III, presided over a national council at Mellifont. Its principal achievement was to divide Ireland into four ecclesiastical provinces: Armagh, Dublin, Cashel, and Tuam. Older works following Mansi, mistakenly call this the Synod of Kells.

[B. L. MARTHALER]

MELLITUS OF CANTERBURY, ST. (d. 624), archbishop. An abbot in Italy (possibly of St. Andrew's, Rome), M. was sent to England to aid St. Augustine. He became bp. of London by 604, and journeyed to Gaul and Rome. In the pagan reaction of 617 he fled to Kent and became abp. of Canterbury in 619, BIBLIOGRAPHY: Bede, *Hist. Eccl.* 1:29–30; 2:3–7; Butler 2:157; L. Boyle, BiblSanct 9:310–312.

[J. DRUSE]

MELLUSIANS. In the midst of the struggle of the Malabar Christians (see MALABAR RITE) to have their own bps., a group of priests under the leadership of Antonios Thondanatta looked to Rome for help. When nothing came of their appeal, they turned to the Chaldean Catholic Patriarch Joseph VI Ando (1848–78), who, acting on historical precedents, sent in 1860 the Chaldean bp. Thomas Rokos. Rome protested and Rokos was obliged to return to Mesopotamia. In 1874 Patriarch Joseph sent another bp., Mar Elias Mellus. When Rome demanded his return, he refused and established a small schismatic community that now numbers about 5000 members. It follows the liturgy and discipline of the Nestorians. They are called Mellusians, although Bp. Mellus himself later withdrew from the schism and died a Catholic in 1908.

[J. MEIJER]

MELO, FRANCISCO MANUEL DE (1608–66), diplomat, moralist, historian, and poet. Of a noble Portuguese family, M. served with Spanish troops in Flanders and Catalonia. Imprisoned and exiled by the King of Portugal, he was restored to favor by the later monarch, João IV and sent on diplomatic missions to England, France, and Italy. M. was one of the literary lights of 17th-cent. Portugal, his work encompassing a variety of forms in prose and verse. Among many books were *Historia de la guerra de Cataluña* (1645); the historical study *Epanáforas de vária história portuguesa* (1660); an essay on marriage *Carta de guia de casados* (1651); the play *Auto do fidalgo aprendiz* (1665); a series of religious reflections, *Obras morales* (1664); and collected poems, *Las tres Musas de Melodino* (1649). BIBLIOGRAPHY: E. Prestage, *Dom Francisco Manuel de Melo* (1914).

[J. R. AHERNE]

MELOZZO DA FORLI (1438–94), Italian painter of the Umbrian school, influenced by Piero della Francesca. M. executed the famous fresco in the Vatican Library (*Sixtus IV Names Platina Prefect of the Vatican Library,* now on canvas in Vatican), 1447, with mastery of perspective and foreshortening; a fresco in Sta. Maria in Trastevere (1483, lost), *Ascension of Christ, Angeles with Musical Instruments,* and many others. One of the important architectural painters of late 15th cent., M. influenced Signorelli and Bramante, and is an important precursor of the High Renaissance.

[M. J. DALY]

MELROSE, ABBEY OF, the first Cistercian house in Scotland. Established near the abandoned "Old Melrose" (an ancient Celtic monastery) in 1136 by monks of Rievaulx at the invitation of King David I, Melrose founded six other abbeys in Scotland. It was repeatedly sacked in wartimes but was rebuilt each time. In its final stage it was one of the finest examples of late decorated and early perpendicular Gothic. After 1541 commendatory abbots let the building deteriorate. The cloister disappeared but a portion of the magnificent church is now maintained as a national monument. *The Chronicle of Melrose,* compiled by the monks (new ed. by A. O. and M. O. Anderson, 1936) is an original source for events from *c.*1250–75. BIBLIOGRAPHY: D. E. Easson, *Medieval Religious Houses: Scotland* (1957).

[L. J. LEKAI]

MELVILLE, ANDREW, (1545–1622), greatest of the Scottish Reformers after John *Knox. M. was born at Baldovy, near Montrose. Educated at St. Andrews, Paris, and Poitiers, he was successively appointed professor of humanity (Latin) in Geneva (1569), principal of Glasgow Univ. (1574), principal of St. Mary's College, St. Andrews (1580), and rector of that Univ. (1590). Through his influence the *General Assembly of the Church of Scotland in 1580 found "the pretended office" of bp. to be unlawful, and in 1581 it ordered M.'s *Book of Discipline, setting forth Presbyterian polity, to be registered in the acts of the *Kirk. M.'s opposition to *episcopacy and royal supremacy brought him exile and imprisonment. On his release from the Tower of London in 1611 he accepted the chair of divinity in France at the Univ. of Sedan, where he remained until his death. Fearless, dogmatic, and even vituperative in his attacks on episcopacy and the Romanists, Melville is one of the stubborn giants of the Scottish Reformation, one of its most humane and distinguished scholars. BIBLIOGRAPHY: *Diary of James Melville* (1842); T. McCrie, *Life of Andrew Melville* (2 v., 2d ed., 1824).

[J. A. R. MACKENZIE]

MEMENTO (Lat., remember), in general a term indicating those moments in the Eucharistic Prayers of the Roman liturgy when all members of the Church, living and dead (specifically by name in Masses for the dead), are remembered and prayed for as sharers in the sacrifice being offered. Strictly speaking a term referring to the opening word of two commemorations in Eucharistic Prayer I (in Lat.) of the Roman liturgy when the living and dead are remembered. (1) The *memento* or commemoration of the living begins with the words, "Remember, Lord, your people." It was taken into the Roman liturgy in the 4th cent. as part of it; the names of those to be specially remembered were originally read from the *diptychs on which they were recorded. (2) The *memento* or commemoration of the dead begins with the words, "Remember, Lord, those who have died." This commemoration, observed in Ireland and Gaul from the 7th cent., was introduced into the Roman Mass in the 9th century, at first only in Masses offered specially for the dead.

[C. J. NOONE]

MEMLING, HANS (Memline, Jean or Jan; *c.*1440–94). Member of the painters' guild, Bruges, (1467), maintaining a large studio, M. enjoyed an international reputation being commissioned by patrons of England (Sir John Donne, *Virgin and Saints,* London), Germany (Greverade altarpiece, Lübeck), Italy (portraits of Tommaso Portinari and his wife, New York), and Spain (*Deposition* diptych of Isabella I, Granada). His most numerous commissions, however, came from the brothers and sisters of the Hospital of St. John in Bruges where many of his works are still housed: the *Floreins Triptych* (1479), *Reliquary of St. Ursula* (1489). The major painting found there, the *Mystic Marriage of St. Catherine,* demonstrates his command of the early Netherlandish technique, probably learned from Rogier van der Weyden. His figures are, however, much sweeter and gentler than those of Van der Weyden, his color softer and more harmoniously balanced. In addition to his religious paintings (The St. Christopher Altarpiece, 1485), the Virgin and Child being his most popular theme, Memling was also renowned as a portrait painter. (*Man with a Medal, c.*1475; *Diptych of Martin van Nieuwenhove,* 1487). BIBLIOGRAPHY: M. J. Friedländer, *Memling* (1950); E. Panofsky, *Early Netherlandish Painting* (1953).

[S. N. BLUM]

MEMMI, LIPPO (fl. 1317–56), Italian Sienese painter. He executed with his father a fresco for the Palazzo del Popolo, San Gimignano (1317), assisted his brother-in-law Simone Martini in the *Annunciation* (Florence, probably painting the SS. Ansanus and Margaret panels), another *Annunciation* for St. Francis, Avignon (1347), and many panels of the *Madonna and Child,* rather Byzantine, with long noses and close-set eyes, now in Orvieto, London, Boston, and elsewhere.

[M. J. DALY]

MEMORARE, a prayer to Mary, named according to its first word in the Latin original: "Remember . . ." Though it may be traced to the 15th cent., its author is unknown. The text may be found in the *Raccolta* and in many prayerbooks.

[J. DALLEN]

MEMORIA APOSTOLORUM, a place made holy through association with the martyr Apostles Peter and

Paul. It may have been in N Africa that the tradition originated of showing reverence to the place of martyrdom as a *memoria* of the martyr. Augustine was aware of this tradition of memorials, which expanded to include the tomb or grave of the martyr as well, and finally also any place that had contact with the remains of the martyr. According to an inscription of Pope St. Damasus I (d. *c.*305), the basilica attached to the catacombs of St. Sebastian contained a memorial of SS. Peter and Paul, which is an indication that the bodies of these two martyrs were at one time there. There was also a memorial of Peter on Vatican Hill under the ancient basilica there; and one of Paul at Tre Fontane, near the basilica of St. Paul-Outside-the-Walls. BIBLIOGRAPHY: H. Leclercq, DACL 11:296–324; H. Daniel-Rops, *Church of Apostles and Martyrs* (tr. A. Butler, 1960).

[E. J. DILLON]

MEMORIALE RITUUM, a liturgical book of the Roman rite providing materials for adaptation of ceremonies, esp. of Holy Week, for celebration in small churches. Benedict XIII drew up the book in 1725 while bp. of Benevento and as pope recommended it to the parishes of Rome in 1730. Pius X later recommended it for all parishes. The last typical edition (1920) has been made obsolete by recent liturgical reforms. Since new official liturgical books make provision for necessary pastoral adaptation, a revision is unlikely.

[J. DALLEN]

MEMPHIS (NOPH), in antiquity the premier city of Egypt. Standing at the junction of Upper and Lower Egypt, about 15 miles S of Cairo, it was the royal residence during most of the 3d and 4th dynasties and occasionally up to the 6th; it was rebuilt by the pharaohs of the 18th and 19th dynasties. It was a trading center and many crafts were carried on there under the auspices of the city god, the artificer Ptah. Its necropolis to the W extended over 25 miles from N to S, including the famous pyramids of Gizeh as well as the Sakkorah complex of tombs and pyramids close to Memphis. Easily open to invasion, it was captured by the Ethiopians, the Assyrians, and the Persians. It declined in importance after the foundation of Alexandria shortly after 332 B.C. When Cairo was founded by the Arab conquerors in 638 A.D., the ruins of Memphis were thoroughly exploited for building materials, leaving little evidence of the glorious past. Memphis is mentioned in Hos 9.6; Is 19.13; Jer 2.16; 44.1; 46.14, 19; Ez 30.13, 16. BIBLIOGRAPHY: T. O. Lambdin, Inter DB 3:346–347; J. A. Wilson, *Burden of Egypt* (1951) *passim*; H. Frankfort, *Kingship and the Gods* (1948) *passim*.

[E. J. CROWLEY]

MEMRĀ, homiletic poem in dodecasyllabic verse, sung in the East Syrian office.

[A. CODY]

MENA (MENA Y MADRAZO), PEDRO DE (1628–88), gifted student of baroque artist Alonso Cano (1652). M. executed 40 panels for cathedral choir stalls (1656–58). In an *Immaculate Conception, St. Joseph, St. Anthony, St. Francis,* M. moves from charm to powerful realism in grief, and mysticism (*The Penitent Magdalen, St. Francis in His Tomb*). There are examples from his workshop in many Spanish cities.

[M. J. DALY]

MENAHEM, king of Israel (745–738 B.C.), a ferocious ruler of the N kingdom who retained the throne by assassinating his predecessor Shallum. He is chiefly noted for the fact that he paid tribute to Tiglath-Pileser III of Assyria, thereby securing his throne for himself and his son Pekahaiah. A record of this tribute is to be found in the Assyrian annals.

[D. J. BOURKE]

MENAION, (Gr. *mēnē,* moon), a liturgical book which consists of 12 volumes, one for each of the months of the year in the Byzantine Rite. It contains the office for all the fixed feasts of the ecclesiastical year as well as that of the saints whose feasts occur on the calendar each day. The book was composed in rhyme by several holy persons. The Greeks also call this the Panthakete, which means all-inclusive.

[P. MORLINO]

MENANDERIANS, (MENANDRIANS), followers of the 2d-cent. Syrian Gnostic, Menander. According to St. Justin (*Apol.* 1.2656; cf. Augustine *Haer.* 2), he was a disciple of *Simon Magus and taught at Antioch. M. rejected the libertinism of his master; he claimed the power to confer immortality by his "baptism." BIBLIOGRAPHY: É. Amann, DTC 10:547.

[T. C. O'BRIEN]

MÉNARD, LÉON (1706–67), French historian, notably of *Histoire civil, écclésiastique, et littéraire de la ville de Nîmes* (1750–58). He also published on classical Greek civilization *Moeurs et usages des Grecs* (1743), and left an unfinished history of Avignon.

[T. C. O'BRIEN]

MÉNARD, RENÉ (1605–61), French Jesuit missionary, the first to enter the region of what is now Wisconsin. He was a Jesuit from 1624 and taught in France before being assigned to the Canadian missions in 1640. He began his missionary labors at Sainte-Marie-des-Hurons a year later and worked also among the Nipissing and Algonquin Indians. From 1651 to 1656 he was superior at Trois Rivières, P. Q., then worked among the Iroquois. In 1660 he reached modern Michigan, and in March 1661, while trying to reach some Hurons near the Black River in Wisconsin, died on the journey. Seven years later his breviary and soutane were discovered in the possession of the Sioux.

[T. C. O'BRIEN]

MENAS, ST. (also Mîna; fl. betw. 3d and 4th cent.), Egyptian martyr. The only certain facts about St. Menas are that he was martyred and that he was buried in his native village of Bu Mna SW of Lake Mareotis. This village, a popular place of pilgrimage, subsequently grew into a city with several churches, a monastery, and accommodations for pilgrim traffic. The city was excavated by C. M. Kaufmann (1905–08). Small phials for miraculous water inscribed with St. Menas' name and image are extant. BIBLIOGRAPHY: M. A. Murry, "St. Menas of Alexandria," *Proceedings of the Society of Biblical Archeology* 29 (1930) 25–30, 50–61, 112–122.

[D. W. JOHNSON]

MENCIUS, (Meng K'o; 372?–298? B.C.), Chinese philosopher who, succeeding Confucius, elaborated a Confucian theory of human nature and steered Confucian thought toward idealism. M. maintained that humans are innately good, born with four propensities which can develop into virtues: a sense of mercy grows to *jen* (humanity, benevolence); sense of shame to *i* (righteousness, justice); courtesy to *li* (ritual concern, decency); and a sense of right and wrong to *chih,* (knowledge). Practice of these virtues develops *ch'i,* a spiritual force or power that pervades the universe and in particular resides in and emanates from the perfect man. However, if the senses are not controlled by reason (*hsin,* both mind and heart), sense perception can mislead anyone into perversity and evil ways. The chaos and strife and suffering of society are due to the falling away of people from righteousness to greed for personal gain, yet M. did not flatly condemn profit or material well-being. In every political consideration, the material well-being of the people, "the roots of the nation," takes priority over State and king; M. advocated rule by benevolence and moral excellence not force, virtues which the people could imitate to the betterment of the whole society. He divided labor between the educated, who were suited to governing because they tend to be less affected by the threat of financial insecurity, and the uneducated, who were destined to toil manually. M.s' popular sympathies together with his social hierarchy made him available to both revolutionaries and imperialists in China's history as an ancient authority for their causes. He provided Confucianism with a more refined metaphysics. With him, Heaven came to be understood as a Supreme Being demonstrating moral will and order, the source and seat of virtue and righteousness. In practise, this translated: to become a perfect man, a *chun-tzu,* one must know Heaven.

[R. J. LITZ]

MENDEL, GREGOR JOHANN (1822–84), Augustinian prelate, biologist, founder of the science of genetics. A native of Moravia, M. entered the Augustinian Order and was ordained in 1847. Unaccountably, he failed in his efforts to become a secondary school teacher of science. His entire career was spent at the Abbey of Brünn (Brno in modern Czechoslovakia) as a researcher and superior. A man of prodigious patience and exhaustive research, he experimented with peas in the monastery garden, examining an incredible number of specimens. In addition to his painstaking observation M. had intuitive genius and was a brilliant statistician and mathematician, bringing both sciences to his work—itself a pioneering effort. M. stated that he set out to do three things: to determine the number of different forms under which the offspring of the hybrid appear; to arrange them according to their separate generations; to ascertain their statistical relations. Out of his work came the two basic laws of heredity, the law of segregation and the law of independent assortment. The story of M.'s subsequent publication of his researches and the total ignoring of his work by famous biologists is a sad one. It is interesting to speculate what light M.'s work might have shed on Darwin's work, had the latter ever heard of it. M. published "Experiments in Plant Hybridization" in the journal of the Brünn Scientific Society. No one outside of the area took up his conclusions. He sent the monograph to Naegali, a Swiss biologist, who urged the Augustinian to do research on the genus *Hieracium,* unfortunately an exception to the laws of heredity. M. wasted years on this foredoomed project. More disturbing was M.'s election as abbot and the long years of conflict with the government over taxation. M. won the case but at a terrible cost to his scientific research. He died without recognition by his fellow biologists. Sixteen years later his work was duplicated by a Hollander, a German, and an Austrian, who discovered that M. had anticipated them. From that time M.'s position in the scientific world as father of genetics has been secure. BIBLIOGRAPHY: W. Bateson, *Mendel's Principles of Heredity* (1913); H. Iltis, *Life of Mendel* (1932).

[J. R. AHERNE]

MENDELSSOHN, MOSES (Moses ben Menahem; 1729–86), German Jewish philosopher of the Enlightenment. Generally considered to be the first to distinguish between beauty, an aesthetic perfection limited by human understanding, and metaphysical perfection, the unity in multiplicity known only by God, a distinction which led to a theory of mental faculties that set the stage for Kant and others. In his *Morgenstunden* (1785), M. rationally defended a belief in God's existence, modifying both the *ontological argument and the proof from design. His *Phädon* (1767; Eng. tr., 1784), modernized Plato's dialogue on the immortality of the soul in light of contemporary psychology. In the wake of his dispute with J. C. Lavater, who sought either M.'s public conversion to Christianity or a thorough justification of Judaism, he wrote his most important work, *Jerusalem, or On Religious Power and Judaism*

(1783; tr., A. Jospe, 1969). He distinguished between Judaism and metaphysics and between religion and Judaism. Religion belongs to the realm of speculative metaphysics, but Judaism is a legislation not a religion, legal not philosophical, a divinely ordained system of laws for ethical behavior. *Torah, not speculative truths, distinguish Jews from other theists and the Law is a special dispensation of a universally Providential God to the Jewish people, all others being bound by the rules of natural religion. The Law defines a way which is particularly Jewish; it does not fall within the purview of rational inquiry; it is supranatural and so is not subject to historical adaptation to social and cultural change; law, being divinely given, is fixed. Yet, M. insisted that Judaism was his personal religion in that his Judaism shared with other natural religions a recognition of God's existence, God's providence, and the immortality of the soul; and that Judaism, in its special legal aspect, a Jewish way of living to God, was his heritage. ''Jerusalem'' was Mendelssohn's symbol of classic Judaism in which religion and law were unified in the State, but in diaspora, he advocated separation of Church and State, toleration of political and religious minorities, and he championed the political emancipation of Jews.

[R. J. LITZ]

MÉNDES, RAMÓN IGNACIO (1775–1839), bp., patriot. A Venezuelan, M. was ordained in 1797 and became vicar general of Mérida in 1802. Rector of the Seminary of St. Bonaventure in Mérida in 1805, he obtained for the institution the right to confer higher degrees in philosophy, theology, and canon law. M. worked for the independence of Venezuela from Spain. He was a deputy to the Constituent Assembly in 1811 and a signer of the Declaration of Independence. A trusted ally much admired by Simon Bolívar he served as chaplain in the revolutionary armies. A member of the Congress in Bogotá from 1823 to 1826 he advanced in the Church, being consecrated abp. of Caracas in 1828. Twice M. was in conflict with the State. In 1830 the new constitution abridged the rights of the Church and was opposed by the abp. who was exiled. Returning under a modification of the Constitution in 1832, he was soon in a second contest with the government which assumed the Law of Patronage without consulting the Holy See. M.'s refusal to accept this caused his second exile. He died in Bogotá. A hundred years later his remains were transferred to the National Pantheon in Caracas as a national hero. A prolific writer, M. published among other works *Exposición sobre el patronato eclesiástico* (1830) and *Observaciones, sobre el proyecto de constitución* (1830). BIBLIOGRAPHY: M. Watters, *History of the Church in Venezuela* (1933).

[J. R. AHERNE]

MÉNDEZ, ANDREAS (1608–84), theologian. A native of Spain who entered the Jesuits in 1625, he became teacher and the rector at Oviedo and the Irish seminary at Salamanca. A censor for the Spanish Inquisition and royal preacher, M. wrote on a variety of subjects in moral theology, including a work put on the Index for laxism.

[J. R. AHERNE]

MÉNDEZ PLANCARTE, GABRIEL (1905–49), Mexican humanist, writer. He was ordained in 1927. His short but notable career included teaching at the Seminario Conciliar de México and the National Univ., and lecturing in the U.S. and Canada. He was a member of the Academia Mexicana de la Lengua and a contributor to the newspaper *Novedades*. In 1937 M. founded the cultural journal *Ábside,* to which he contributed many articles. Among his works of poetry, criticism, and editing were *Primicias* (1927), *Nuevos salmos y odas* (1947), *Hildalgo, reformador intelectual* (1945), and *Humanismo mexicano del siglo XVI* (1946).

[J. R. AHERNE]

MENDICANT ORDERS (Lat. *mendicare,* to beg,), religious orders of men committed to an evangelical poverty that originally prohibited individual and in some cases even communal ownership of property. These orders emerged, mainly in the 13th cent., when clerical affluence was common enough to give scandal and various doctrinally suspect sects were intensely concerned with the practice of poverty (see WALDENSES, CATHARI, ALBIGENSES). In an effort to realize this ideal of Christian poverty, which was so highly esteemed in a cleric by the common people, and to unite it with obedience to the church hierarchy, SS. *Francis of Assisi and *Dominic Guzmán founded the Franciscans and Dominicans respectively. These orders grew very rapidly and from their beginnings exercised a considerable academic and pastoral influence. Other mendicant orders also appeared in the 13th cent., e.g., the *Carmelites and *Augustinians, and later the *Servites, *Minims, *Trinitarians, and *Jesuits. In the 15th and 16th cent. three independent branches of the Franciscans were formed, the Conventuals, Observants (or simply the Friars Minor), and the Capuchins. The mendicant orders' exemption from local episcopal authority was the cause of a notable 13th-cent. quarrel, led by *William of Saint-Amour; but the problem was solved, at least in theory, by Boniface VIII's bull *Super cathedram* (1300) in which the orders' relationship with the local ecclesiastical authorities was regularized. The absolute prohibition of communal ownership proved so impractical, however, that most of the mendicant orders have abandoned it or sought certain concessions in favor of individual poverty but community control of the order's resources. Under the impetus of Vatican Council II, the mendicant orders are seeking through new experimental constitutions to express the ideals of their founders. BIBLIOGRAPHY: H. Holzapfel, *History of the Franciscan Order* (tr. A. Tibesar, 1948); J. Canu, *Religious Orders of Men* (tr. P. J. Hepburne-Scott, 1960); L. E. Boyle, NCE 9:648–649. *POVERTY CONTROVERSY.

[M. B. PENNINGTON]

MENDIETA, JERÓNIMO DE, (1525–1604), Spanish Franciscan missionary in Mexico. Most of his life (after 1554) was spent in Mexico among the Indians, whom he idealized and defended against the exploitation of colonizers and the policies of Philip H. His *Historia eclesiástica indiana* was not published until 1870. BIBLIOGRAPHY: C. Crevelli, CE 10:185–186.

[E. J. DILLON]

MENDOZA, PEDRO GONZÁLEZ DE (1428–95), cardinal, chancellor of Castile. Fourth son of the Marquis of Santillana, he studied law at Salamanca and then became bp. of Calahorra (1453) and Sigüenza (1467). As cardinal and chancellor of Castile (1473), he switched from Henry IV to the rival Isabella, thereafter becoming abp. of Seville (1474), cardinal (1478), primate-abp. of Toledo (1482), and grand chancellor. "The Great Cardinal" and "Third King of Spain" took possession of conquered Granada (1492) and supported Columbus. Humanist, magnificent patron, brave on the battlefield, piously dedicated to his dioceses, generous to the poor, and a Renaissance worldling, he fathered two bastards and wrote a noteworthy catechism. BIBLIOGRAPHY: A. Merino Alvarez, *El Cardenal Mendoza* (1942).

[R. I. BURNS]

MENE-TEKEL-PERES, Aramaic names for various weights, which were awesomely written on the wall by a mysterious, disembodied hand during the banquet of Belshazzer (Dan 5.25). Only the Jewish seer Daniel could decipher the writing and explain its meaning: that Babylon was soon to be conquered by Medes and Persians. The interpretation (Dan 5.26–28) makes use of wordplay based on the roots and/or similarity in sound of the three words, a not uncommon device in prophetical and apocalyptical literature. The main intent of the theologically folklorish story was to comfort by entertaining with a great divine act the persecuted Jews of the Maccabean period, who were suffering from their own Belshazzers.

[J. F. FALLON]

MENÉNDEZ, JOSEFA, SISTER (1890–1923), mystic and member of the Religious of the Sacred Heart. Of humble Spanish background, she served as a kitchen aid with the Religious of the Sacred Heart in Poitiers, France. She fell ill and made her final profession of vows on her death bed. After her death, the details of her mystical experiences became better known through her notes. These experiences included both temptations by the devil and visitations from the Sacred Heart, the Blessed Virgin, and St. Madeleine Sophie.

[M. A. MCFADDEN]

MENESES, BEATRICE DA SILVA, ST. (1424–1490) religious foundress. Born of Portuguese nobility at Ceuta on the coast of Morocco, she was the sister of Bl. Amadeus IX of Savoy, who initiated the Franciscan "reform of Marignano," and she was brought up in the household of Princess Isabel, whom she accompanied to Spain for the latter's marriage to John II of Castile. After experiencing the hostile envy of court life, she retired to the Cistercian convent at Toledo. In 1484 she founded the Congregation of the Immaculate Conception of the Blessed Virgin Mary by adapting to their use the Cistercian Rule. After her death, the community, under the influence of Card. F. Ximénez de Cisneros, abp. of Toledo, adopted a modification of the rule of the Poor Clares. Her cultus was confirmed in 1926 and she was canonized in 1977. BIBLIOGRAPHY: Butler 3:350; F. Baumann, LTK 2:86.

[E. J. DILLON]

MENESES, JUAN FRANCISCO (1785–1860), Chilean educator, political figure. M. first practiced law and as a protagonist of Spanish dominance was rewarded by being made attorney general and secretary to two Spanish governors. When San Martin overthrew the Spanish regime, M. had to flee the country. After the death of his wife he returned to Chile and studied for the priesthood, being ordained in 1822. He became a noted preacher and dean of the cathedral of Santiago. He was deputy in the Chilean congress and a senator during a public life that spanned 26 years; he was a signer of the constitution of the republic in 1833. He also served as minister of the interior, of the treasury, and of foreign affairs at various times. He became rector of the National Institute, where he instituted sweeping academic reforms. In 1842 M. was named dean of the faculty of theology at the Univ. of Chile.

[J. R. AHERNE]

MENESTRIER, CLAUDE FRANÇOIS (1631–1705), French Jesuit savant who wrote voluminously in the fields of heraldry and musicology.

[T. C. O'BRIEN]

MENGARINI, GREGORIO (1811–86), Italian missionary in the U.S., philologist. A Roman, M. joined the Jesuits and was ordained in 1840. Volunteering for the U.S. missions he journeyed to Idaho with DeSmet in 1841. After serving the Flathead Indians in Montana, M. was moved to the Oregon mission at St. Paul. Later he was one of the founders of Santa Clara College in California, where he lived until his death. M. compiled *Salish or Flathead Grammar; Grammatica linguae Salicae* (1861), and *Dictionary of the Kalispel or Flathead India Language* (2 v., 1877–79).

[J. R. AHERNE]

MENGS, ANTON RAPHAEL (1728–79), German painter in Rome (1741). M. studied the antique, emulated Raphael, and with Winckelmann (1755) described antique statues of the Belvedere, becoming Europe's principal neoclassical painter before David. His eclectic art is contrived, lacking power. In 1761 M. worked with Tiepolo in Madrid, painted the *Lamentation* (1765–68) and walls of the Camera dei Papiri, Vatican, 1769–72, and died in Rome.

[M. J. DALY]

MENNAS, ST. (*c.*500–552) **PATRIARCH OF CONSTANTINOPLE** from 536. He first gained prominence as director of a pilgram hospice, St. Samson, in Constantinople. He was consecrated patriarch on March 13, 536, by Pope Agapetus in the Byzantine capital itself. The question of the *Three Chapters and of the *Judicatum* provoked a temporary conflict between M. and Pope Vigilius who was summoned to Constantinople by the Emperor (Jan. 25, 547). In the winter of 551, Vigilius, having broken relations with the patriarch and the Emperor Justinian, escaped from imperial custody into Chalcedon. M. was sent by Justinian to make due apology to the Pope and reconciliation was established on June 26. M. had been always an opponent of Nestorianism and Monophysitism. He nevertheless yielded to caesaropapism when he was a patriarch under Justinian's rule. He was quoted as stating: "It is proper that no question agitated in the Holy Church should be settled without the advice and command" of the emperor.

[L. PEANO]

MENNO SIMONS (*c.*1496–1561), religious leader from whom the Mennonites are named. Born in Witmarsum, Friesland, the Netherlands, he was called Simons (Simonszoon) from his father's Christian name. Ordained a priest, he began to read the writings of Luther and other Reformers when Anabaptism reached the Low Countries. His evangelical views led him to doubt the sacramental nature of baptism and the Lord's Supper; this led to his conversion to Anabaptism in 1536. He was called by Obbe and Dirk *Philips to gather the Anabaptists through preaching, counseling, and writing (*Foundation Book,* 1539) in the regions of Amsterdam, Danzig, and Cologne. Because of his successful leadership the Anabaptists soon became known as Mennonites. He had numerous debates with both Münster Anabaptists and Reformed opponents. He had to flee from Witmarsum, and lived in East Friesland and in Wüstenfelde near Oldesloe between Lübeck and Hamburg. He traveled and wrote extensively. His writings have been translated from the Dutch into German and English (*Complete Writings* [tr. L. Verduin, ed. J. C. Wenger, 1956]). BIBLIOGRAPHY: C. Krahn, "Menno Simons Research," *No Other Foundation* (1962).

[C. KRAHN]

MENNONITE CHURCH, the body that traces its origins in the U.S. to the original Mennonite settlement at Germantown, Pa. (1683). It is the largest Mennonite body in the U.S. (more than 100,000 members). Most members are descendants of Mennonites from Switzerland and S Germany; many Amish Mennonite groups have also become affiliated with this Church over the years. The Church holds to the essentials of Anabaptist, or Mennonite, doctrine, subscribing to the Dordrecht Confession of Faith and the Mennonite Confession of 1963. While maintaining the necessity of nonconformity to worldly manners and conduct and of strict church discipline, this Church has been more progressive than some Mennonite bodies. Local congregations are autonomous, but are joined together in regional conferences; there is also a consultative, biennial general conference of the Church. The membership is most numerous in the eastern part of the United States. Besides operating many charitable institutions and agencies, as well as a strong home and foreign mission program, the Church maintains Goshen College (Goshen, Ind.), Eastern Mennonite College (Harrisonburg, Va.), and the Mennonite Publishing House (Scottsdale, Pa.). BIBLIOGRAPHY: MennEnc 3:611–617.

[T. C. O'BRIEN]

MENNONITE CONFESSION OF 1963, a confession adopted by the General Conference of the Mennonite Church. Consisting of 20 articles, it is a modern adaptation of the *Dordrecht Confession of Faith. BIBLIOGRAPHY: J. Hardon, *Spirit and Origins of American Protestantism* (1968), 301–312.

MENNONITES, a name derived from that of *Menno Simons and applied to all who follow the essential religious teachings of the 16th-cent. Anabaptists. Melchior *Hofmann brought Anabaptism from Strassburg to Emden in 1530; mysticism and humanism created an atmosphere favorable to this teaching in the Low Countries, and the Anabaptists became the first organized Reformation movement there. Some 2,500 were martyred as Charles V sought to exterminate them. While some refugees became leaders in the violent episode of the theocratic kingdom at Münster (see ANABAPTISTS), others were gathered under the leadership of Menno, who stressed the spiritual content of Anabaptist doctrine. After the establishment of the *Reformed Church in Holland, they came to enjoy a degree of freedom in the cities and made notable contributions to industry, social and philanthropic work, and the fine arts. The Mennonites of the Netherlands were the first to organize into conferences, to establish a theological seminary, to open the pulpit to women, and to promote research into their own history and teaching.

In the 16th cent., some Dutch refugees had migrated to W Prussia, then followed the Vistula River into Poland, the Ukraine, and Russia. The first migrations of *c.*18,000 Mennonites from Russia to the western states and provinces of the U.S. and Canada took place 1870–80, after the Russian introduction of military conscription. The Russian Revolution (1917) and World War II were followed by further migrations to Canada, Brazil (*c.*21,000), and Paraguay (*c.*4,000). The approximately 150,000 Mennonites in Russia who survived the persecution of the Stalin era have to a degree been able to reestablish themselves.

Although there is mention of Dutch Mennonites in New York as early as 1643, the first permanent Mennonite establishment was in Germantown, Pa., in 1683. The settlers were descendants of Anabaptists from Switzerland and the Palatinate. Migration from the same source to Pa. continued into the 19th cent., then spread to Ohio, Indiana, Illinois, Virginia, and the Province of Ontario. Mennonites and Amish Mennonites from the East Coast to the Mississippi River are mainly of this Swiss and Palatinate lineage. The Mennonites of the prairie states and provinces have spread farther west, and have moved increasingly to urban areas. The conservative Mennonites of Manitoba have sent colonies to Mexico and Paraguay. The adjustment of their environment among the larger Mennonite groups in the U.S. was speeded up during and after World War I, by a process of acculturation away from German customs and language. Their views about *nonconformity to the world and *nonresistance have been altered considerably. Voluntary services for peace and social relief on a global scale sponsored by the *Mennonite Central Committee have awakened and challenged the Mennonites, whose forefathers were driven into isolated areas, but who are themselves now in the midst of a world in need.

Mennonites are not at all united organizationally. The reasons for the main divisions are numerous. From the beginning Anabaptists stressed a truly visible Christian Church, bound together by personal belief and discipleship, not by ecclesiastical structure. Emphasis on separation from the world has also led to numerous divisions (see AMISH MENNONITES). Coming to North America from various places and at different periods, Mennonites had diverse ethnic and linguistic backgrounds. Geographical separation often prevented various groups from becoming acquainted and entering into fellowship with one another. Challenges arising out of their secular environment, and religious influences such as *revivalism have also caused divisions. Some of these are disappearing under the influence of common Mennonite efforts to relieve spiritual, social, and economic hardships wherever they are found. The Mennonite World Conference aims to provide a platform on which all common and vital issues may be discussed. There are about 566,000 Mennonites in the world, with more than 250,000 in the United States.

Most Mennonite bodies subscribe to the *Dordrecht Confession of Faith, but creeds have never been strongly emphasized. The central teaching is still the Anabaptist doctrine of the personally accepted inner experience of Christ. Thus *believer's baptism, usually by pouring, is observed. Personal holiness through living the law of Christ is given greater prominence than traditional Christian trinitarian or soteriological doctrines. In some Mennonite Churches, however, evangelical Protestant influences have been introduced. Church discipline is aimed at making the visible Church, i.e., each congregation, match the invisible Church as a communion of the saints; the *ban and *avoidance of the ungodly have this purpose, but are strictly observed only by conservative groups. The Lord's Supper, footwashing, and the kiss of charity are observed as *ordinances. Mennonites have held steadfastly to nonresistance. They refuse to give service of a directly military nature, and they take no oaths. Local congregations are ordinarily autonomous, though joined in conferences with other congregations within the various Churches. Bishops or elders, ministers, and deacons are the officials and are often non-salaried. BIBLIOGRAPHY: C. H. Smith, *Story of the Mennonites* (1964). *ANABAPTISTS; *MENNONITE CONFESSION OF 1963.

[T. C. O'BRIEN]

MENOCHIO, GIOVANNI STEFANO (1575–1655), theologian and exegete. M. taught theology and Scripture at Milan, and held several important positions within the Jesuits. He is well noted for his *Brevis explicatio sensus literalis totius Sacrae Scripturae ex optimis quibusque auctoribus per epitomen collecta,* an exegetical study of the whole Bible. The work was printed in every country of Europe and went through many editions, the last of which appeared in C. F. Drioux's *La Sainte Bible* (1873). BIBLIOGRAPHY: P. Bliard, DB 4.1:973; T. T. Taheny, NCE 9:654.

[T. M. MCFADDEN]

MENOLOGY (MENOLOGION, Gr. *men* [month] and *logos* [discourse]), a term applied to a number of types of liturgical books used in the Eastern Church. It is at times used as the equivalent of *menaion,* one of the 12 volumes (one for each month of the year) that taken together correspond to the Proper of the Saints in the Roman Breviary, but with the addition of hymns and references to the saints honored on each day. More frequently the term is simply applied to a collection of the historical notices read in the daily liturgy. It may also be applied to lists for scriptural readings arranged according to the days of the months found at the beginning of MSS of the Gospels or other lectionaries. More properly it is used for long lives of the saints of the Greek Church arranged according to the months of the ecclesiastical year, which begins with September and ends with August. The most famous *menologion* of this type is that of Simeon Metaphrastes, compiled towards the end of the 10th century. The term was brought over to the West as *menologium* (English menology or menologe) to describe collections of short biographies of saintly individuals to be used for public or private nonliturgical reading. The earliest work of this kind may be the *Menologium Carmelitanum,* which was compiled by Saracenus and printed in 1627 at Bologna. BIBLIOGRAPHY: H. Thurston, CE 10:192–193; R. Aigrain, *L'Hagiographie: ses sources, ses méthodes, son histoire* (1953) 70–71.

[M. J. COSTELLOE]

MENORAH, a seven-branched candelabrum, part of the furniture of the Israelite Temple. It became a symbol for

Judaism in the 1st cent. A.D. and remains so today. The earliest depiction of the menorah is found on the Arch of Titus in Rome, built to celebrate the fall of Jerusalem in the year 70. The menorah of the feast of Hanukkah has eight rather than seven lamps and symbolizes the rededication of the Temple in 165 B.C., 3 years after Antiochus Epiphanes had profaned it.

[J. F. FALLON]

MENSA (Lat., table), a term with two usages: (1) the top plane of an altar; strictly speaking, the whole surface in the case of a consecrated altar; the altar stone in the case of other altars; (2) by metonymy, a *mensal fund.

[T. C. O'BRIEN]

MENSAL FUND, from about the 9th cent., the income from church or monastic lands set aside for the support of the clergy or the monks (in distinction from the abbot). When clergy or canons of a cathedral chapter ceased to live a common life, and the income was portioned out individually, the *mensa* or mensal fund was called a prebend or living. Another sense of the term appears in canon law's reference to the *mensa episcopalis,* i.e., diocesan income belonging properly to the support of a bishop (CIC c. 1356, §1).

[T. C. O'BRIEN]

MENTAL RESERVATION, in traditional RC moral theology, is the restriction by the mind of the meaning of words one speaks. It is called a strict mental reservation when there is no outwardly discernible indication that the speaker may be restricting the meaning; when, e.g., the speaker mentally inserts a negative in his mind to reverse the meaning of his spoken words. A broad mental reservation is a restriction by the mind to a less obvious but real meaning of the words spoken, e.g., if I wish to conceal from a caller the fact that Peter is in the house, I might say "He is not here just now," meaning that he is not in this place where I am standing, but hoping that the inquirer will take the more obvious meaning that he is away from the house. A strict mental reservation is always a lie. A broad mental reservation may be used to protect a legitimate secret. Older theologians insisted that the words spoken had to be true in some sense. Later theologians generally agree that as long as there is a legitimate secret which must be protected, or some discernible indication that the speaker does not necessarily intend to communicate what is in his mind, whatever he says will not be a lie. It may still be sinful if it causes unnecessary deception, since this would be causing the physical evil of error in one's neighbor. BIBLIOGRAPHY: D. Hughes, NCE 9:662–663.

[J. J. FARRAHER]

MEPHIBASHETH, name substituted for *Merib-baal in order that the name of the god Baal might not appear in the Bible text (e.g., 1 Chr 8.34).

[T. C. O'BRIEN]

M^{e}QABB^{e}LŌNÎṮŌ, a colored veil, usually red, attached to the hand-cross of West Syrian bishops. Among the Maronites it usually has the form of three long strips of cloth.

[A. CODY]

MERBECKE, JOHN (Marbeck; d. *c.*1585), English theologian and musician. Organist at St. George's, the royal chapel at Windsor, M. narrowly escaped (1544) execution for heresy, a crime of which he was found guilty through evidence taken from a concordance of the Bible he had written. This, the first to appear in English, was later published with a dedication to Edward VI. His *Book of Common Prayer Noted* was written to adapt plain chant to the Edwardian liturgy.

[V. SAMPSON]

MERBOT, BL. (d. *c.*1120), Benedictine monk whose legendary life identifies him as a brother of Bl. Diedo and Bl. Ilga, hermits, and a descendant of the counts of Bregenz (Austria). Pastor of the parish church of Alberschwende (near Bregenz), he was slain by some of his parishioners. The chapel built over his tomb became a center of pilgrimage. BIBLIOGRAPHY: J. Baur, BiblSanct 9:357–358; Zimmermann 1:346–347.

MERCADANTE (MERCADER), LORENZO (fl. 1453–70), Spanish sculptor. Working in Flemish realistic style, M. executed the *Sepulcher of Cardinal Cervantes* (1453–58) and in 1470 for the Nativity and Baptism doors of Seville cathedral, carved 12 innovative over-life-size polychromed terra cotta figures in which virtuosity and Eyckian realism are subordinated to the humanist ideal.

[M. J. DALY]

MERCADO, TOMÁS DE (d. 1575), Dominican of the Province of Santiago in Mexico, logician. He was sent back to Spain, his birthplace, to complete his studies. He taught at Seville, where he published his most esteemed works on the logic of *Peter of Spain and on *Aristotle's Organon: *Commentarii lucidissimi in textum Petri Hispani* (1571), and *In dialecticam Aristotelis cum opusculo argumentorum* (1571). He died in Mexico.

MERCANTON, JACQUES (1910–), Swiss author of short stories, essays, articles; convert to Catholicism. His novels include: *Thomas l'incrédule* (1942–43); *Ni le solect ni la mort* (1948); *La Joie d'amour* (1951); *De peur que vienne l'oubli* (1962). His *Poètes de l'univers* (1947) is a work of literary criticism.

[E. J. DILLON]

MERCATI, ANGELO (1870–1955), prefect of the Vatican Archives from 1925 until his death. He was ordained at Rome in 1893. He held responsible positions in the Vatican Library and Archives before he was made prefect. Under his direction notable accessions were made and greater accessibility became possible. He published nearly 200 works in many genres. BIBLIOGRAPHY: K. A. Fink, NCE 9:668–669; L. Santifaller, LTK 7:304.

[F. D. LAZENBY]

MERCEDARIAN MISSIONARIES OF BÉRRIZ (MMB), missionary institute developed (1930) from a cloister of the *Mercedarians or Order of Mercy. They were founded by Mother Maturana at Bérriz (Vizcaya), Spain. From Spain they spread to Italy, Mexico, Japan, Taiwan, and the United States. While yet cloistered they opened three missions: in China, and in the Mariana and Caroline Islands. In 1946 the U.S. vice-provincialate was established at Kansas City, Mo.: the sisters serve in the Dioceses of Albany, Hartford, Kansas City-St. Joseph; in the Vicariates of the Caroline-Marshall Islands and in the Diocese of Agana, Guam. In 1975 worldwide membership was 648 in 62 houses; membership (1977) in the U.S. was 44 in 13 houses. BIBLIOGRAPHY: P. Cody, NCE: 669.

[M. R. BROWN]

MERCEDARIANS (*Orden de Nuestra Señora de la Merced,* Order of Our Lady of Mercy for the Ransom of Captives), religious order of men, and later of women, still vigorous in the Church today. After the Virgin Mary appeared to St. *Peter Nolasco he founded (1218) in Spain "the Glorious, Royal and Military Order of Our Lady of Mercy or Ransom." Originally military, then clerical, it was approved (1235) by Gregory IX; it is now mendicant and missionary. Members, after a preliminary period of simple vows, make solemn ones and add a fourth vow to be a hostage for the captive's sake. Brothers assist the priests in their work esp. in hospitals; contemplative nuns and religious women are missionaries or in various active pursuits, esp. in Spain, South America, and elsewhere among the Spanish-speaking. The laity also received (1218–60) a rule of life. Flourishing are various branches: Mercedari and Mercedari Scalzi (barefoot) number (1975) 946 in 150 houses. Headquarters (ODM), whose generalate is in Rome, are in the U.S., at LeRoy, (N.Y.) where they have a seminary, and are in parishes in Cincinnati, Ohio. Mercedarian women religious (from 1265) total 3,738 and have a motherhouse in Rome, as well as in Córdova and Barcelona, and in Mexico. BIBLIOGRAPHY: S. Hartdegen, NCE 14:96 s. v. "Third Orders"; A. Morales, *ibid.* 9:669–670; V. Ignelzi, EncCatt 8:711–712; ODCC 887–888 esp. biblog.

[M. R. BROWN]

MERCERSBURG THEOLOGY, a theological position developed at the German Reformed Seminary in Mercersburg, Pa., as a response to the prevailing *revivalism of the early 19th century. It stresses a return to the faith of the Reformers, particularly as enunciated in the *Heidelberg Catechism. John Williamson *Nevin and Philip *Schaff were the leading exponents of this approach, and they made the *Mercersburg Review* its principal organ. In 1844 Nevin published *The Anxious Bench,* the first appeal of the Mercersburg theologians against the revivalist influence. Schaff sounded a similar note in his inaugural address as member of the Mercersburg faculty in 1844; his *Principle of Protestantism* stressed the ancient catholic and Reformation tradition as the dynamic force in Protestantism and explained his theory of doctrinal development. In 1846 Nevin published *The Mystical Presence,* an effort to present the Calvinistic understanding of the Lord's Supper as distinct from the prevailing Zwinglian view of his contemporaries. In 1847 Nevin published studies of the Heidelberg Catechism and of the Church. From the writings and teaching of Schaff and Nevin arose a strong tradition of doctrinal loyalty, liturgical renewal, and ecumenism, which had a marked effect on the Churches of the Reformed and Presbyterian tradition, although Mercersburg theology was never accepted in its entirety and did not lead to the reunion of *Reformed Churches. Its stress on the faith of the Reformers and on the centrality of Christ and his Church preserved an important heritage of Protestantism. In accord with the historical approach of J. A. *Neander, but controlled by a conservative orthodoxy, Schaff and Nevin taught a development of doctrine and polity that has important ecumenical implications. Modification of organization, teaching, and modes of worship are held to be valuable so long as Christ remains the center of the Christian life. In him men are regenerated and united in the spiritual organism of the Church. Sacraments are not mere acts of faith, but seals of God's covenant and channels of grace. Old modes of worship may be set aside, as in the Reformation, but through organic growth in Christ rather than through a series of new births, since there is only one rebirth, when God entered into history in Christ. BIBLIOGRAPHY: J. H. Nichols, *Romanticism in American Theology* (1961); L. Binkley, *Mercersburg Theology* (1952); Smith-Jamison 1:267–271.

[R. K. MACMASTER]

MERCIER, DÉSIRÉ JOSEPH (1851–1926), cardinal, philosopher, patriot, and pioneer ecumenist. A Brabant Walloon, M. studied and taught at the Univ. of Louvain, and, fired by *Leo XIII's revival of Thomism, was mainly responsible for the founding of the Higher Institute of Philosophy at Louvain (1894) and of the *Revue néoscolastique* (now the *Revue philosophique de Louvain*). The collaborators he enlisted were able, enlightened, and scholarly, and set a tradition that has been maintained. His own special interest was psychology; his school was firm on principle but not unadventurous in going out to meet scientific positivism and neo-Kantianism. Its critical and empirical spirit did not always match the academic party line in Rome; it was ironical that George Tyrrell, not unprovoked, was moved to reply to him in a book entitled *Medievalism.* In 1906 M. was made abp. of Malines and primate of Belgium; he was created cardinal the following year. His courage in defending his people during the German occupation in World War I made him a world-figure. Keenly alive to social problems, he founded the International Union of Social Studies and kept open house for its members. Between

1921 and 1925 he welcomed Anglican scholars to the famous *Malines Conferences, which though frowned on and abortive at the time, and cut short by his death, have proved an earnest of better things. He was a pastoral bishop and a man of prayer and deep piety: all in all, the most distinguished church leader of his age. BIBLIOGRAPHY: J. A. Gade *Life of Cardinal Mercier* (1935).

[T. GILBY]

MERCORI, GIULIO (Mercorus, Julius; d. 1669), Italian moral theologian and polemicist. A Dominican professor of philosophy and theology, first in Cremona, then in Naples, he became the censor of the Holy Office for Mantua, Pavia, and Milan sometime after 1650. His reputation rests on works written to counteract *probabilism and its opening the way to laxist moral theories. The most important (it appeared soon after the Dominican general chapter in 1656 had submitted and received approval from Alexander VII for a directive to the order to promote the sound moral theology of St. Thomas Aquinas in resistance to probabilism) is entitled significantly *Basis totius theologiae moralis . . . adversus nimis emollientes aut plus exasperantes jugum Christi* (1658). In defense of P. *Fagnani he also wrote a criticism of moral *laxism in the work of J. *Caramuel, *Apocrisis pro doctrina de probabilitate Prosperi Fagnani adversus apologiam Johannis Caramuel* (1664). M.'s *Solutiones trium nodorum. . . .* was written in 1563 to rebut the criticism of the Jansenist P. *Nicole against his *Basis*.

[E. M. GATES]

MERCURIALI, GERONIMO (1530–1606), Italian physician and early proponent of the therapeutic value of physical exercise. After studying medicine at Bologna and Padua, where he received his degree in 1555, he went to Rome and there devoted his attention to little-known ancient medical documents. From this study sprang his influential *De arte gymnastica* (1569). His works on practical medicine, on women's and children's diseases, and on melancholia also served as standard texts in both his own and the next century. During his lifetime he taught medicine at Italy's leading universities—Bologna, Padua, and Pisa—and enjoyed a brilliant reputation, enhanced by the favor of Emperor Maximilian II.

[E. M. GATES]

MERCURIUS, see JOHN II, POPE.

MERCY, the virtue that inclines one to compassion for those who suffer and inspires one to do what is possible to alleviate their misery. Already in the OT Yahweh is described as the God of mercy. Out of pity he frees the Israelites from the Egyptians (Ex 3.7). On Mount Sinai he reveals himself as the merciful one (Ex 34.6). The prophets continuously remind the people of this characteristic of their God (e.g., Hos 11.8) who wills the conversion of sinners. The mercifulness of Yahweh reaches out to all human beings (Is 58.6–11). The NT reveals the astounding dimensions of that mercy—the Son of God becomes man in order to share the misery of human lot and to rescue men from it. Jesus is the merciful and faithful high priest (Heb 2.17) who reveals to all mankind the Father of mercies (2 Cor 1.3). But the NT goes beyond the OT in its emphasis upon mercy as a divine quality in which men must share. Men are called upon to be merciful as their Father is merciful (Lk 6.36) and they are reminded that they will be judged according to their own mercifulness toward others (Mt 25.31–46). In St. Thomas Aquinas's scheme of the virtues, mercy is an effect of charity, but however intimate its association with charity, it is itself a virtue in its own right; it is a form of liberality and as such pertains as a potential part to the virtue of justice. Tradition arranges the most common works of mercy in two series of seven, one comprising spiritual and the other corporal works. The corporal works are to feed the hungry, to give drink to the thirsty, to clothe the naked, to harbor the stranger, to visit the sick, to minister to prisoners, and to bury the dead. The spiritual works are to convert the sinner, to instruct the ignorant, to counsel the doubtful, to comfort the sorrowful, to bear wrongs patiently, to forgive injuries, and to pray for the living and the dead. BIBLIOGRAPHY: W. S. Kissinger, *Sermon on the Mount: A History of Interpretation and Bibliography* (1975).

[V. DUCLOS]

MERCY, BROTHERS OF (FMM), a congregation of religious officially called Brothers of Mercy of Montabaur, founded in 1856 in Germany by Peter Loetschert (1820–86) and several companions. The members make simple, perpetual vows and are dedicated to the care of the sick, regardless of race or creed. Their apostolate spread from Germany into Holland, but during Hitler's regime the community suffered the loss of many houses. The first house in the U.S. was established at Buffalo, N.Y. in 1924. The motherhouse is located at Montabaur, Germany. In 1976 the brothers maintained 18 houses with 162 members.

[R. A. TODD]

MERCY, CONGREGATION OF PRIESTS OF (Fathers of Mercy), a society of priests, originally organized as a missionary community by the Rev. Jean Baptiste Rauzan in France in 1808. They were officially called the Congregation of the Priests of Mercy and received papal approval in 1834. The members are bound by religious vows. Since 1956 the society has undergone a reorganization by the Holy See. As a newly formed congregation (1960) of 10 priests, the first missionaries were sent to Ecuador. In the U.S. the first foundation was made in 1839 in Brooklyn, New York. Presently engaged in missionary work in the U.S., the congregation has houses in Kentucky, Maryland, Florida, and New York; their general motherhouse is in Cold Spring, New York.

[R. A. TODD]

MERCY, SISTERS OF (SM: RSM), religious women founded as a lay institute (1827) and a religious congregation (1831) in Dublin, Ireland by Catherine Elizabeth McAuley (1787–1841) with Elizabeth Harley and Anna Maria Doyle. Trained in the Presentation Convent, they made vows (1831), and the congregation of the Sisters of Mercy was approved (1841) by Gregory XV. First motherhouse was on Baggot St., Dublin; first of many pontifical and autonomous Mercy groups they are presently at Carysfort Park, Blackrock, In Dublin County, with 464 members in 29 houses. Mercy Sisters practice the spiritual and corporal works of mercy according to the Rule of St. Augustine, which was that of the Presentation Sisters. Before Mother Catherine McAuley's death she had directed formation of 12 houses in Ireland and 2 in England (1841), Bermondsey and Birmingham, and planned the first foreign mission to America (Newfoundland, 1842). Mother Francis Xavier Warde (d. 1884) left Carlow with six others for Pittsburgh in 1843). Mercy foundations were made in Chicago and New York (1846), Little Rock (1851), San Francisco (1854), Cincinnati (1858), Philadelphia, and Manchester, N. H. (1861), Bangor, Me. (1865), Middletown, Conn. (1872). Others were made in Australia (1846), New Zealand (1850), New South Wales (1859); Argentina (1856), the West Indies (1890), Mexico (1883); South Africa (1897). From the U.S. sisters went to Puerto Rico (1941). In the Pacific, U.S. sisters were on Guam (1946) and the Philippines; in the Peruvian Andes (1960), and first on the Asian continent at Jamshedpur, India. Innumerable others were on the continents of Africa, America, Asia, and on the Pacific and Caribbean islands. Their work is diverse: teaching (all levels through college), health services, care of the aged, handicapped, infants and orphans. Wars (they assisted in the Civil War, the Boer and Crimean, the two World Wars) and unfriendly government have in Mercy history impeded but not extinguished their zeal. Motherhouses show membership: in Ireland 1,287 in 111 houses; England 705 in 40; Italy 2,590 in 279; Australia 3,591 in 331; New Zealand 477 in 37; Africa 75 in 6; India (unknown); France 790 n 82; Canada 603 in 53; U.S. 11,179 in 1,137 houses. The wide diffusion caused the sisters to consider administrative union: in the Pacific (1907) Victoria and Tasmania amalgamated, the Australian Union developed, and in the U.S. (1922) those in the Dioceses of San Francisco, Monterey-Fresno, Los Angeles, and Tucson formed a union; in the East began (1929) a movement that culminated in the Roman Union, whose generalate is now at Bethesda, Maryland. U.S. motherhouses account for more than half the world membership of 20,694 in 2,023 houses. Sisters from Irish motherhouses continue to swell American ranks, with (1975) 617 in the U.S., 29 in Central America, 15 in South America and the West Indies. Seventeen autonomous Mercy congregations in the U.S. (1978) are in Pennsylvania (3), New York (4), California (2), and (each with one motherhouse) Connecticut, Iowa, Maine, Massachusetts, New Hampshire, New Jersey, North Carolina, and Vermont. BIBLIOGRAPHY: M. B. Degnan, *Mercy Unto Thousands* (1957); Bethesda Mercy Generalate, *His Mercy Endureth Forever* (pa. 1960); T. P. McCarthy, *Challenge for Now* (1974); M. McA. Gilgallon, NCE 9:674–676; R. B. Savage, *Catherine McAuley: The First Sister of Mercy* (1949, repr. 1955); *Letters of Catherine McAuley, 1827–1841* (ed. M. I. Neumann, 1969); *Directory of Religious Organizations in the U.S.A.* (Consortium Book; ed. J. V. Geisendorfer, 1977) 171–174; Kapsner, *Catholic Religious Orders* (1957) 433, no. 1269–88.

[M. R. BROWN]

MERCY OF GOD, the divine willingness to approach man in a loving, saving encounter. Mercy is generally used to translate the OT Hebrew *ḥesed,* although *ḥesed* is a much wider and more variable term than mercy. Most frequently, however, the *ḥesed* of Yahweh is his covenant love, proved by a saving presence among men (Ex 20.6). It is eternal (Ps 107.1) but related to historical events (Ex 3.7–10). The thought of the OT is summed up in the formula: "The Lord, the Lord, a God merciful and gracious, slow to anger, and abounding in steadfast love and faithfulness" (Ex 34.6). This mercy reaches its perfect manifestation in Messianic times when God performs the saving act which he had promised (Lk 1.72). This loving actualization is the person and saving presence of Jesus (Mk 5.19). In the NT, then, God's mercy is a manifestation of his love (Heb 2.17), revealed in and through Jesus (Heb 4.14–16). It is a historical actualization of God's freedom, so that he bestows his saving compassion on those who call upon him (Rom 10.12) and brings them into his divine presence (2 Cor 4.14).

The attribute of mercy, therefore, becomes most evident in the existential economy of salvation but it is also deducible from the divine nature itself since God is infinite in every perfection (D 1782). Since he is the source of all goodness, and mercy may be defined as the gratuitous bestowal of good gifts upon those in need, God may be said to possess mercy formally and properly. The communication of his own perfections upon sinful man is the supreme manifestation of the divine attribute of mercy. BIBLIOGRAPHY: G. Vann, *Divine Pity* (1945); ThAq ST (Lat-Eng, v. 5 *God's Will and Providence,* ed. T. Gilby, 1967); S. Kierkegaard, *Works of Love* (1961); B. Häring, *Law of Christ* (3 v., 1961–66); H. Worniecki, *Mystery of Divine Mercy* (1959).

[T. M. MCFADDEN]

MEREZHKOVSKI, DMITRI SERGEEVICH (1865–1945), Russian poet, novelist, and thinker; one of the founders of the Religious and Philosophical Society and its journal *The New Road* (1903–04). His essay *On the Causes of the Decline and on the New Trends in Contemporary Russian Literature* (1893) helped to prepare the way for Russian symbolism. Under the influence of Poe and Baudelaire, M. tried to popularize in Russia Western aesthetic concepts of art and literature. Under the influence of Hegel, he developed the view that the struggle of material and spiritual forces against each other and toward synthesis is the primary principle of cultural history. This view is reflected with particular effectiveness in his great trilogy *Christ and Antichrist* (1896–1905) and in the critical study *Tolstoy and Dostoyevsky* (1901–02). M. also wrote biographies of Christ, Dante, Napoleon, St. Paul, St. Augustine, and others. In his last years, his anti-Sovietism led him to hail the rise of Mussolini and Hitler, in whom he saw potential threats to Communism. BIBLIOGRAPHY: R. Poggioli, *Poets of Russia, 1890–1930* (1960) 71–73; O. A. Maslenikov, *Frenzied Poets: Andrey Biely and the Russian Symbolists* (1952) 128–145; C. H. Bedford, *Seeker: D. S. Merezhkovskiy* (1975).

[M. F. MCCARTHY]

MERGER, an ecclesiastical union in which, unlike *federated Churches, the participating bodies lose their separate identities and form a new corporate entity. Two congregations of the same denomination sometimes combine, drawing up new articles of incorporation. Two or more bodies of the same denominational family may merge. The Methodist Episcopal Church, the Methodist Episcopal Church, South, and the Methodist Protestant Church merged in 1939, to form the *Methodist Church in the United States. This in turn united with the Evangelical United Brethren in 1968 as the *United Methodist Church. In 1869–70, Old and New School Presbyterians formed a merger, and in 1958 the Presbyterian Church, U.S.A., combined with the *United Presbyterian Church. Three German Lutheran synods merged in 1918, forming the United Lutheran Church; a succession of mergers followed so that almost all American Lutherans belong to one of three major bodies, the *American Lutheran Church, the *Lutheran Church in America, the *Lutheran Church—Missouri Synod.

Mergers may also unite churches of different denominations; the United Church of Christ, for example, was constituted in 1957 out of the Evangelical and Reformed Church and the Congregational Christian Churches, each of which in turn had been made up of earlier mergers. One of the most interesting mergers outside the U.S. is the *Church of South India (1947), which combined Churches of Congregational, Presbyterian, and Anglican traditions. Numerous other mergers have been consummated, e.g., *United Church of Canada (1925); others are being contemplated. *CONSULTATION ON CHURCH UNION. BIBLIOGRAPHY: *History of the Ecumenical Movement, 1517–1948* (eds. R. Rouse and L. C. Neill, 2d ed., 1967).

[N. H. MARING]

MERIB-BAAL (Mephibosheth) biblical name. (1) Jonathan's son (1 Chr 8.34; 2 Sam 4.4). M. was 5 years old when his father was killed. He became lame through a fall while being hastily taken away by his nurse (2 Sam 4.4). After the assassination of his uncle Ishbosheth (2 Sam 4.7), M. was presumably the heir to Saul's throne. His claim was never pressed, however, and out of his regard for Jonathan, David brought M. to eat from his table and restored to him all of Saul's property (2 Sam 9). Later David gave half the property to M.'s servant Ziba in return for aid against Absalom (2 Sam 16.1–5; 19.24–30). (2) The son of Saul, handed over to the Gibeonites to avenge Saul's action against them (2 Sam 21.1–9).

[T. EARLY]

MERICI, ANGELA, ST. (1474–1540), foundress of the *Ursulines. M. was born in Desenzano (Lombardy). She was orphaned at the age of 10 and thereafter cared for by an uncle in Salo. Following the death of her sister, M. joined the Third Order of St. Francis. She returned to Desenzano (*c.*1494) and made her home into a small school for young girls. About this time M. had an ecstatic vision of one day organizing a religious community of teachers. In 1516 she was asked to establish a school in Brescia. She made a pilgrimage (1524) to the Holy Land and in 1525 her work was recognized by Clement VII. The war between the Habsburg Empire and France disrupted M.'s work until peace was restored by the Treaty of Cambrai (1529). In 1533 M. trained 12 girls to be her assistants and in 1535 M. and 28 others dedicated themselves to the service of God through the teaching of young girls. This loose confederation took St. Ursula as its patron, but it established neither formal vows nor habit. Although the 28 girls continued to live with their own families, 1535 marks the foundation of the Ursuline order, the first order of women teachers. M. was elected superior by the first chapter in 1537. After her death she was buried in the church of St. Afra in Brescia. Paul III formally recognized the Company of St. Ursula in 1544. M. was canonized by Pius VII in 1807. BIBLIOGRAPHY: B. O'Reilly, *St. Angela Merici and the Ursulines* (1880); S. Pedica, BiblSanct 1:1191–95; Butler 2:432–34.

[R. J. BRADY]

MÉRIDA, CARLOS (1893–), Mexican Mayan painter from Guatemala. Studying in Europe (1910–14) with Modigliani and Picasso, M. sought a synthesis of Indian and *avant-garde* art, painted murals with D. Rivera in a Mexican renaissance, published critical works (*Orozco's Frescoes in Guadalajara,* 1940) and illustrated Mayan books. M. experimented in ''Byzantine'' mosaics and the bark fiber of Indian codices, continuing public murals, denying the representational in brighter colors, evidencing Mayan and Tarascan influences in a uniquely personal style. BIBLIOGRAPHY: M. Nelkin, *Carlos Mérida* (1961).

[M. J. DALY]

MÉRIDA, FATHERS OF, bps. known by the names of Paulus, Fidelis, Masona, Innocentius, and Renovatus, who served successively in Mérida in SW Gothic Spain from about *c.*530 to *c.*633. Information on their lives has been attributed to Paulus, deacon and possible writer of the 7th cent. from *De vita et miraculis patrum Emeritensium.*

Paulus, a Greek physician, lived many years in Mérida before he served as bp. (530–560). He was succeeded by his nephew, Fidelis (560–571), whom he had trained for the sacred ministry. The bishop's palace was rebuilt and the church of St. Eulalia was restored, it is believed, during Fidelis's episcopate. From 571 to about 606, Masona, a well-known and noble Goth served as bishop. He built and supported many churches and monasteries and founded a hospital and a lending fund. Masona was exiled 3 years by the Arian King Leovegild, whose Catholic son and successor, Reccared, assisted in overcoming the uprisings of Arian bps., so that by 589 the Visigothic state became officially Catholic. Masona also presided over the Third Council of Toledo and signed the Acts of that famous conversion council. In *c.*606 the deacon Innocentius was consecrated bishop. He was known for his great sanctity. A decree of King Gundemar (610–612) that established the primacy of Toledo was signed by him. In 610 Renovatus succeeded Innocentius. He was a handsome and learned Goth who before he became bp. was an abbot of the monastery of Cauliana, 8 miles from Mérida. The last known bp. of Mérida was Stephen I, who signed the acts of the Council of Toledo IV (633). BIBLIOGRAPHY: *The Vitae sanctorum patrum Emerentensium* (ed. and tr. J. N. Garvin, 1946).

[R. A. TODD]

MERIT, in Catholic theology, broadly speaking, a good work worthy of reward; strictly speaking, that aspect of a good work by which it is deserving of reward. This is only one of the meanings of the term as it is used in English. The Catholic doctrine on merit, formulated at the Council of Trent (D 1545–49, 1582) against the Protestant rejection of good works as cause of men's justice, only means to express what the Gospel (e.g., Mt 5.1–12; 10.42) and St. Paul (e.g., 2 Tim 4.7–8) taught about the reward awaiting the followers of Christ. The juridical term "merit" is not biblical; "reward," its correlative term, is. The idea of merit was introduced into the Latin tradition by Tertullian (*De paenit.* 2, in which God is presented as debtor); its Greek counterpart, *axia,* is found, e.g., in Justin (*Apol.* 43, *axia tōn praxeōn).* St. Augustine developed the doctrine and explained that there can be no real merit of man before God without grace as its root; when rewarding man's merit, God crowns in man his own gifts (*Epist.* 194.5.19). Trent also explained that God in his love for man wants his own gifts to be man's merits; life eternal is both grace and reward, and so is growth in grace (D1545, 1576, 1582). The Council likewise stated that before justification there can be no strict merit without grace (D 1532). The object of theological merit of good works in the righteous is growth in grace (and in glory) and life eternal, to be obtained after death in grace (D 1582). Through their meritorious works the just advance toward life eternal; they do so by growing in sanctifying grace. The very increase in grace resulting from these good works constitutes the real expression of their merit of heavenly glory.

The concept of merit, juridical as it is, expresses the personalist aspect of the growth and fulfillment of the life of grace. By their good works the righteous increase their justice and grace, just as every agent grows in perfection by his proper activity. But the growth in the life of grace is not effected by the good works (as, e.g., knowledge is the fruit of study); it is only merited or striven for as a reward to be rendered by God. This is so because every increase in grace is given or effected by God alone, grace being essentially God's self-gift; it is rendered by God as a reward for the just man's good works. So is the fulfillment of grace in life eternal, viz., God's self-gift to the blessed in the glory of heaven. Thus the personalist aspect of the life of grace (constituted by the personal relationships between God-in-Christ and the just), of its growth and its fulfillment, of necessity entails a place for merit in the doctrine and theology of grace and glory. And because only works done in grace and under the influence of charity or love of God are meritorious in the proper sense, both growth in grace and life eternal, while truly being a reward for merit, are yet grace, or gratuitous gift, grace given for grace. Accordingly, the opposition between the RC doctrine of merit of good works and the Protestant denial of it may well be more verbal than real. It is not the just man's good works by themselves, but only as springing from grace, that have a causal influence in the life of grace. This influence regards, not the beginning of righteousness or of the life of grace, but only its growth and its fulfillment. Only grace, not the nature of man by himself, is the source of merit. The just man's merit springs from Christ's grace and merit, not from man's own power, and so it does not detract from Christ's merit. It rather allows Christ's merit to bear fruit in his members. Nor does the causality of meritorious works impair the relationships between God-in-Christ and the just man. God-in-Christ alone can make the divine self-gift in answer to man's striving for it through works of grace. This self-gift remains grace while being reward for merit. Protestant doctrine too requires good works as the necessary sign and fruit of man's justification. If this can be understood to mean a development of the life of righteousness, then this view approaches the RC doctrine on the merit of the growth and fulfillment of grace. The difference between the two is mainly one of conceptual formulation commanded by a different approach and problematic, e.g., following from different views on sin and justification.

Besides merit in the strict sense, or condign merit, RC theology knows a merit of congruity, in which the claim to a reward is not one of justice but of fittingness. This is insinuated in Trent (D 1532). It regards a gift of grace that has no direct connection with the good act that merits congruously but only a mediate connection, as, e.g., sufficient grace for new good acts needed by growth in grace. The idea of merit of congruity is based on the fittingness that God should bestow certain unpromised rewards on those whom he has made his friends by grace. BIBLIOGRAPHY: J. Rivière, DTC 10:574–785; C. S. Sullivan, NCE 9:683–686;

idem, Formulation of the Tridentine Doctrine on Merit (1959); P. De Letter, *De ratione meriti secundum s. Thomam* (1939); *idem,* ''Merit and Prayer in the Life of Grace,'' *Thomist* 19 (1956) 446–480; C. Ernst, *Theology of Grace* (pa. 1974).

[P. DELETTER]

MERK, AUGUSTIN (1869–1945), German Jesuit exegete, chiefly famous for his small critical edition of the Greek NT with parallel Latin translation. The volume first appeared in 1933 and has since passed through eight editions, the last of which was published in 1956. Initially M. based himself on volume 1 of H. von *Soden's classic work, *Die Schriften des Neuen Testaments in ihrer ältesten erreichbaren Textgestalt hergestellt auf Grund ihrer Textgeschichte*. But from the 4th and 5th ed. onwards he moved away from this, and more recent editions present an eclectic text established by M.'s own sound evaluation of the best MSS, ancient versions, readings of ecclesiastical writers, and critical studies. His work is remarkable, and almost unique in presenting as full a picture as possible of the early witnesses to the text of the NT within a concise volume. M. was a professor at the Pontifical Biblical Institute in Rome from 1928 until his death.

[D. J. BOURKE]

MERKELBACH, BENOÎT HENRI (1871–1942), Dominican theologian. Ordained in 1894 as a diocesan priest, he worked in a parish before becoming a seminary professor at Liège in 1905. He became a Dominican in 1917, taught in houses of his order at Louvain and at Rome (1929–36). His principal work *Summa theologiae moralis* (3 v., 1931–40), follows the order and inspiration of St. Thomas Aquinas's *Summa theologiae,* and stresses the theoretical principles of moral judgment. M. was also a noted Mariologist, publishing his *Mariologia* in 1939.

[T. C. O'BRIEN]

MERKLE, SEBASTIAN (1862–1945), Catholic church historian. In 1887 he was ordained priest, and he was professor, 1898–1933, in Würzburg, where he pioneered the way to a new Catholic valuation of, and approach to, Luther and the Enlightenment. He collaborated on the *Acta* of the Council of Trent, and edited for publication the three-volume *Diaries of the Council of Trent*. In church politics he, along with H. Schell and A. Ehrhard, was a prominent and harshly criticized advocate of progressive Catholicism. BIBLIOGRAPHY: R. Bäumer LTK 7:308.

[E. J. DILLON]

MERKS, THOMAS (Merke; d. 1409), bp. of Carlisle, prominent during the reigns of Richard II and Henry IV of England. A member of Richard's entourage, he became a bp. in 1397 at the King's behest and the same year was involved in the proceedings against the Duke of Gloucester. M. is chiefly remembered for his loyalty to Richard II in 1399 when the monarch was challenged and then overthrown by Henry Bolingbroke. Richard was forced to abdicate, but at Henry II's first Parliament, M. supposedly protested against the new King's treatment of his predecessor, while all his other former supporters remained silent. Whether M. actually delivered such a speech is disputed, but Shakespeare accepted the tradition in his dramatized history, *Richard II,* while Sir John Howard in his *History of Henry IV* (1599) turned the speech into a defense of monarchical rights, in which form it figured in the verbal struggles over the divine right of kings in the 17th century. Possibly for conspiring against Henry in late 1399, M. was sent to the Tower and at his trial in 1400 was found guilty; later he was deprived of his episcopal post. However, in 1401 he was fully pardoned by Henry and by 1405 had regained his influence and ecclesiastical functions.

[E. M. GATES]

MERLE D'AUBIGNÉ, JEAN HENRI, see AUBIGNÉ, JEAN HENRI MERLE D'.

MERLEAU-PONTY, MAURICE (1908–61), French philosopher. He studied at the École Normale Supérieure in Paris. After he took the *agrégation* in philosophy (1931), he taught at several lycées. During World War II he served as an officer in the army. He was appointed professor of philosophy at the Univ. of Lyons (1945), then at the Sorbonne (1949). In 1952 he was given a full chair at the Collège de France. For a time he was editor of *Les Temps modernes,* which he co-founded with *Sartre and Simone de Beauvoir.

The main thrusts of his philosophy are in psychology, in which he was influenced by the *Gestalt theories, and in phenomenology. His philosophical career really began in reaction to Cartesian thought. Much of his effort was directed toward a new interpretation of *Descartes, esp. his reduction of the world to perception. Unlike Sartre, whose phenomenology led him to reduce being to consciousness, M.-P. did not view consciousness as primary, however central to the method of phenomenology. For him, existence meant becoming conscious of our inviolable relation to the world, which is the true transcendental, and not consciousness, as Sartre holds. This world is the world that consciousness intends, not cosmologically, but existentially, as it is in relationship to man. The task of phenomenology is, then, to reveal the mystery of the world and the mystery of man interacting with it. In his first two works, *The Structure of Behavior* (tr. L. Fischer, 1963) and *The Phenomenology of Perception* (tr. C. Smith, 1962) he shows why he believes that questions about natural experience of the world must have answers provided from other disciplines besides Gestalt psychology and behavioral sciences.

With *Husserl he sees the role of philosophy as one that accounts for the structures of consciousness, yet he does not fully subscribe to the Husserlian ''bracketing'' of the world.

He rejects, as well, the theory that represents pure sensations as the primary level of experience—one that views these sensations without their referential transcendents. In his work on the phenomenology of perception he develops a theory about the role of the body in perceiving and another that deals with liberty and historical action. In other writings he deals with the subject of ethics, which for him is always associated with political action. One suspects, however, that the reduction of an ethical system to one of its components is just as blameworthy, philosophically, as the reduction of all human problems to economics. The latter reduction marked the Marxist relentless preoccupation with human history to which M.-P. subscribed. Yet, preoccupation with event and circumstance in man's life leads one to historicism rather than to an historical view of man. It furthermore contradicts the centrality of man's position in a world mediated by meaning—a centrality that is logically prior to event and circumstance, and one recognized by Merleau-Ponty. Other works include: *Humanisme et terreur* (1947); *In Praise of Philosophy* (tr. J. Wild and J. M. Edie, 1963); *Les Aventures de la dialectique* (1955); *The Primacy of Perception* (ed. J. M. Edie, 1964). BIBLIOGRAPHY: F. A. Olafson, EncPhil 5:279–282; A. De Waelhens, *Une philosophie de l'ambiguité: L'Existentialisme de Maurice Merleau-Ponty* (1951); *What is Phenomenology?* (ed. J. M. Edie, 1962).

[J. R. RIVELLO]

MERLIN, JACQUES (*c.*1480–1541), canon of Notre Dame de Paris, vicar general of Paris from 1530; editor of the works of *Durandus of Saint-Pourçain (1500–15) and of Origen (2 v., 1512); editor as well of a collection of councils of the Church, *Conciliorum generalium* (1524, 1530, 1535).

[T. C. O'BRIEN]

MERLINI, GIOVANNI (1795–1873), general of the Society of the *Most Precious Blood from 1847. An early member of the society (1820), he promoted devotion to and the liturgical feast honoring the Precious Blood of Christ. He was also the spiritual director of Bl. *Maria de Matthias in the foundation of the Sisters Adorers of the Most Precious Blood (1834). M.'s cause of beatification was introduced in 1927.

[T. C. O'BRIEN]

MERMILLOD, GASPARD (1824–92), Swiss cardinal, leader in the social movement. He was ordained in 1847. As a parish priest in Geneva, M. published two periodicals, *Les Annales Catholiques* and *L'Observateur Catholique*. Vicar-general for Geneva in 1857 and auxiliary bp. of Lausanne, he gave attention to education, being the co-founder of the Sister Oblates of St. Francis de Sales. When M. was named administrator of Geneva, a long conflict with the Protestant canton of Geneva ensued. In 1873 when M. was named vicar-apostolic of Geneva, he was expelled from Switzerland; he returned to Switzerland when appointed bp. of Lausanne in 1883. He was unrecognized by the canton until he was created cardinal in 1890. He worked effectively for social reforms with his *Union Catholique d'études sociales et économiques* established in 1885, which sponsored international conferences on social questions. M. was author of *Lettre à un protestant sur l'autorité de l'Église et le schisme*, widely circulated.

[J. R. AHERNE]

MERODACH-BALADAN (Babylonian name, Marduk-apal-iddina) ruler of the Chaldean tribe Bit-Yakin and twice king of Babylonia in rebellion against Assyria (721–710 and *c.*703 B.C.). Isaiah condemned Hezekiah for welcoming M.'s embassy, which was presumably seeking allies against Assyria (2 Kg 20.12–19; Is 39).

[T. EARLY]

MÉRODE, FRÉDÉRIC GHISLAIN DE (1820–74), French priest, secret papal chamberlain, and minister of the papal army. After a military career, he became a priest at Rome. When the French overcame antipapal rebels in 1849, M. celebrated Mass for the French soldiers at St. Peter's. In 1850 Pius IX made him his secret chamberlain, charged with works of reform in the Papal States. M. became minister of the papal army in 1860, and was with the army at the battles of Castelfidardo and Ancona. In 1865 because of differences with Card. *Antonelli, papal secretary of state, he resigned and became papal almoner and a titular archbishop. At Vatican Council I he opposed the opportunism of the definition of papal infallibility, but submitted to the decision of the council. M. remained the faithful friend and supporter of Pius IX until the end of his life.

[T. C. O'BRIEN]

MEROVINGIAN ART, an amalgam of Roman, Christian, and northern Germanic art styles flourishing under Clovis, King of the Franks. Objects often portable (fibulae, torques, etc.), cast in bronze—gilded and silvered, richly enhanced with glass, stones, enamels, and antique cameos—carry distinctive animal and geometric patterns. Elaborate decoration characterizes important MSS, the *Gelasian Sacramentary* (mid-8th cent., Vatican Library) showing words completely designed in bird and fish forms. Most noteworthy is the *Gellone Sacramentary* (late 8th cent., Paris), foreshadowing the Romanesque style in imagination, vigor, and humor, with rare examples of the human form (as in a Crucifixion on the letter T). With Byzantine and Coptic elements these MSS likely came from monastic centers at Luxeuil, Corbie, and Meaux.

[M. J. DALY]

MEROVINGIANS, the dynasty of Frankish kings who ruled from Childeric I (*c.*457–481) to Childeric III (743–751). Named for a legendary ancestor, the dynasty achieved a firm foundation through the vigorous efforts of Clovis

(481–511). His acceptance of Christianity facilitated the fusion of Germanic Franks with Gallo-Romans and assured Christianity a solid foundation among the Germanic peoples. After Dagobert (623–639) the dynasty weakened rapidly while the Arnulfing mayors of the palace emerged. With Pope Zachary's approbation, the last Merovingian was deposed in 751 by Pepin the Short, first of the *Carolingians. BIBLIOGRAPHY: Gregory of Tours, *History of the Franks,* (tr. O. M. Dalton, 2 v., 1927); J. M. Wallace-Hadrill, *Long-Haired Kings* (1962).

[R. H. SCHMANDT]

MERRICK, MARY VIRGINIA (1866–1955), social worker from Washington, D.C. Crippled when a youth, M. spent her life confined to a bed and wheelchair. But her interest in the poor led her to found the Christ Child Society in 1886. She served as president until her death and through chapters established across the country encouraged work in child welfare. She received national and papal recognition for her accomplishments.

[M. A. MCFADDEN]

MERRY DEL VAL, RAFAEL (1865–1930), cardinal and papal diplomat. He was born in England, the son of a Spanish nobleman and English mother. After his ordination (1888), he entered the papal diplomatic service and was named cardinal and papal secretary of state by Pius X in 1903. In 1904, he attracted much attention and unfavorable criticism when he protested against the visit of the French President to the King of Italy, who was unrecognized by the Holy See. An exponent of strict doctrinal orthodoxy, he worked well with Pius X in the campaign against Modernism. His influence declined after the death of Pius X. BIBLIOGRAPHY: F. A. M. Forbes, *Rafael, Cardinal del Val* (1932).

[E. A. CARRILLO]

MERSCH, ÉMILE (1890–1940), Belgian Jesuit, theologian on the doctrine of the mystical body of Christ. From 1920 to 1935 he taught at Namur, and at the outbreak of World War II was at Louvain. His major published works reflect a lifetime of research on the one theme; in English translation they are: *The Whole Christ* (1938), a compendium of scriptural and patristic teachings; *Morality and the Mystical Body* (1939); and his masterwork, *Theology of the Mystical Body* (1951), which contains his central theological synthesis, published posthumously as *Théologie du corps mystique* in 1944. M. had brought the third draft of his text with him into exile at the time of the German invasion; he was killed in the bombardment of Lenz, in France, while on a mission of mercy.

[T. C. O'BRIEN]

MERSEBURGER ZAUBERSPRÜCHE (Merseburg Charms), two charms in alliterative verse; one to effect the release of a captive, the other to cure the sprained leg of a horse. Both are bipartite: a narrative introduction followed by a magic incantation. Though found in a 9th-cent. MS now in Merseburg, the charms date from the 10th century. They are in Frankish dialect and almost certainly of pagan origin. For text, see K. V. Müllenhoff and W. Scherer, *Denkmäler deutscher Poesie und Prosa aus dem 8. bis 12. Jahrhundert* (3d ed. rev. E. von Steinmeyer, v. 1, No. 4 (1892); for commentary, see J. Knight Bostock, *Handbook on Old High German Literature* (1955).

[M. F. MCCARTHY]

MERTON, THOMAS (1915–68), convert to Roman Catholicism, American Trappist, writer. M. was a poet, social critic, and author of contemplative and monastic studies. He has been variously labeled as apologist for communist ideology as well as spokesman for authentic monachism. Of Anglican and Quaker parentage, he was born in France. His spiritual pilgrimages through aridities and temporary optimistic spas of hope are vividly recorded in *The Seven Storey Mountain* (1949), *New Seeds of Contemplation* (1961) and *Zen and the Birds of Appetite* (1968) among others. Education at Cambridge, Columbia, and theological studies at Gethsemani Abbey shaped a superb awareness of a need for religious dialogue in an aura of social consciousness. M.'s quest for contemplative reality is tinctured by easy literary reference to Dante, Blake, Gerard Manley Hopkins, Joyce, and others. His avant-garde vision of unity led him to Bangkok where he was accidentally electrocuted as he prepared notes for an Eastern ecumenical conference. BIBLIOGRAPHY: J. T. Baker, *Thomas Merton, Social Critic* (1971).

[R. M. FUNCHION]

MERULA, TARQUINIO (1590–1665), Italian composer and organist. He was *maestro di cappella* at Bergamo (1623). He held positions as court and church organist in Warsaw (1624); was organist, then *maestro di cappella* in Cremona (1628); returned to Bergamo in 1639 to become organist and *maestro di cappella;* in 1652 returned to Cremona Cathedral as *maestro di cappella*. M. composed canons and madrigals.

[R. J. LITZ]

MERULO, CLAUDIO (Merlotti; Claudio da Correggio; 1533–1604), Italian organist, composer, and teacher. Merulo was an organist at Brescia (1556), second organist at St. Mark's, Venice (1557), then first organist (1566). He composed and published madrigals and motets. His organ compositions were considered imaginative and bold by his contemporaries. His works include: *Sacrae cantiones* (2 v., 1579–80), a book of four Masses (1573), *Sacrorum concentium 8–16, lib. I* (1594), Masses and litanies published posthumously, an opera, *La Tragedia* (1574), and organ toccatas.

[R. J. LITZ]

MESCALINE, a crystalline alkaloid found in mescal buttons (dried top of the mescal cactus). It is an hallucinative substance which has been used especially by Mexican Indians in certain ceremonies. It has also been used in experimental psychiatry and some users claim that they have had unusual religious experiences under its influence.

[M. A. MCFADDEN]

MESCHLER, MORITZ (1830–1910), Swiss-born Jesuit, author of works on the spiritual life that emphasized the *following of Christ and liturgical prayer. Translations include: *Life of Jesus Christ* (1909), *Three Fundamental Principles of the Spiritual Life* (1912).

[T. C. O'BRIEN]

MESHA INSCRIPTION, stele of Mesha, king of Moab, inscribed with an account of his victory over the Israelites (2 Kg 3.21–27); it measures 44 by 28 by 14 inches. Called also the Moabite Stone, it was found at Dhiban (OT Dibon) in Transjordan, and first became known to the scholarly world in 1868. An impression of the slab had been taken before the Bedouin, hoping to get more money by selling many pieces, broke it into fragments. The Louvre recovered most of the pieces and reassembled them. The inscription has philological importance as the only major example of Moabite, a language closely related to Hebrew.

[T. EARLY]

MeSHAMMSHŌNŌ (East Syr. *meshammshānā),* Syriac word for deacon or minister. Among West Syrians today the word refers to the deacon proper, but also to the lesser ministers (cf. Arab. *shammâs).* Among the East Syrians it is used only of the lesser ministers. *SHAMMASHA.

[A. CODY]

MESMERISM, see HYPNOSIS.

MeSŌNÊ, liturgical slippers for wear in the sanctuary in Syrian churches, rarely used today.

[A. CODY]

MESONYTIKON, a Greek term (Sl., *Polunoshchnitsa)* meaning literally the midnight service, nocturns, or vigils. It is only celebrated in monasteries, since neither in structure nor content is it a parochial service. The service begins with the blessing of the one presiding and the usual *Trisagion prayers. Psalm 50 is then read, followed by Psalm 118 on weekdays, the *Kathisma* of Psalms 64–69 on Saturdays, and the Canon and Troparia of the Holy Trinity on Sundays. The Nicene Creed is then repeated, followed by the Trisagion and the Lord's Prayer (on Sundays, the *Hypocoae* is used instead). Several troparia, the prayer of the Hours, and other prayers follow. The second part begins with the reading of Psalms 120–133, followed by the Trisagion, the Lord's Prayer, more troparia and prayers. The service is concluded by the dismissal of the one presiding, a request for mutual pardon, and the final litany, i.e., the Irenica or Great Synapte.

[A. WALKER]

MESOPOTAMIAN RELIGION. The religion of the inhabitants of Mesopotamia in historical times, from the early 3d millennium B.C. down into the Persian and Hellenistic periods, shows a fundamental unity in continuity, despite modifications and differences of emphasis depending on differences of race (Sumerians, then the Akkadians and other Semites), on the shifting influences of local traditions, and on evolution in time. The matrix was Sumerian, and the waves of new Semitic inhabitants succeeding one another seem to have accepted the religious system already existing upon their arrival, modifying it slightly according to their own religious temperaments. While much of the practice and symbolism of the 3d millennium is known, it is only with the early 2d millennium that the religious thought clearly emerges. Gods and goddesses in the developed pantheon were of various types. Some were high gods, omnipotent but distant, like An (Anum), Enlil, and Enki (Ea). Others were numinous powers in natural phenomena; some of these, like the astral gods Sin and Shamash (Moon and Sun) or Naru (River), were confused with the phenomena themselves, while others, like Dumuzi or Tammuz, the power behind the fertile and infertile periods of the natural cycles, were personified without possibility of such material confusion. In the south the important gods were for the most part originally gods of particular cities; in the north they were rather nature-gods with cosmic functions. As Mesopotamian theology evolved, the attributes of various gods were often blended and transferred. West Semitic and other foreign gods tended to be absorbed into one or another of the local gods. The number of divinities, already high, was augmented by the throngs of anonymous gods called *igigi* and *anunnaki,* by various types of evil and good demons belonging to the divine world as ministering spirits, and by the personal gods, for the most part anonymous, one of whom aided every man as his protector and intercessor before the supreme gods. These latter groups of inferior divine beings are antecedents of the angels serving as heavenly courtiers and of the guardian angels, found in later Judaism and thence in Christianity. The high gods were responsible for the origins of the cosmic universe and for the continuing existence of that universe and its structures. The Babylonians regarded their divinities as somewhat quiet, orderly beings dwelling peacefully in their temples among the people. The more turbulent Assyrians regarded them as far more capricious and violent beings inspiring awe and dread, and performed cultic acts not only in temples but also on mountain tops, in sacred groves, and near the sources of streams, for the aspect of nature religion remained stronger in the Assyrian north. The personalities and actions of the gods, portrayed in narratives accounting for the reasons things are as they are—creation, cycles of fertility and infertility in nature, cultic practices—are the substance of Mesopotamian myth.

The tension between transcendence and immanence was not keenly felt in Mesopotamia. Just as a high god was lord and king in his heavenly palace, surrounded by ministering inferior divinities, so on earth he was lord and king in his temple (for which the Sumerian and Akkadian words, like the Hebrew word, were the same as those for the palace of an earthly king), surrounded by the ministering temple personnel, receiving homage from the people, receiving their petitions, appearing periodically in splendid processions, daily clothed, given food, and otherwise treated like an earthly king. His immanence in the temple was thus handled as a reflection of his transcendence in a higher world, where he was also a mighty lord in the palace of heaven. The notion of the earthly temple as an imitation of the heavenly one can also be found in the Bible (Ex 25.9,40; 26.30; 27.8; Heb 8.5), and the idea of the Temple in Jerusalem as a place where Yahweh holds court, listening to and acting upon the petitions of the people can be found in 1 Kg 8.10–51, with a corrective note in favor of transcendence in 1 Kg 8.27. It is in this context of the temple as the god's palace, where he is treated like an earthly king, that the Mesopotamian liturgical system must be understood. Hymns of praise differed from the laudatory songs sung by court musicians only in the matter of divine epithets and attributes; prayers of petition were analogous to the petitions of clients asking favors in the royal court. Incense perfumed the god's quarters, libations and sacrifices provided his daily food. There was no equivalent of the west Semitic holocaust, for part of the sacrificial food was always received by certain elements of the temple personnel; yet, there was no real equivalent of the Hebrew sacrifice of communion either, for participation in the god's meal was limited to the temple personnel and, upon occasion, the king—the ordinary people who offered sacrificial food having no share therein. There was no real sacrifice of expiation for sin, although the ritual for the Jewish Day of Atonement in Lev 16 has certain material parallels in Mesopotamian nonsacrificial, magic practice.

Mesopotamian religious practice was not limited to the strictly liturgical, however. It contained much apotropaic magical practice which, far from being condemned, entered the official cult itself and gave it much of its meaning. Sickness and misfortune were felt to depend upon the displeasure of the high gods, or, far more often, to be the result of the influence of evil demons. While prayer and sacrificial offerings often sought to assure divine good will, the ritual cleansings, exorcisms, and incantations that played so important a role in Mesopotamian life sought to turn away the harmful influences of demons in everything from toothache to marital problems. The Ancient Near Eastern mind's ability to envisage personal identity as a fluid thing explains such practices as transferring a sick man's personality (by ritual formula) to an animal, who was then killed, so that the besetting demon, transferring his animosity in all its fury from the sick man to the animal substitute, might leave the sick man in peace and the malady might depart; the killing of the animal was magical, not sacrificial. These magical practices, and divinitory practices too, formed part of the regular round of services available at a temple.

As in monarchical Israel, the temple, palace of the god, was associated with the palace of the earthly king, and the connection between temple and dynasty was close. The king, representative of god before the people and of the people before god, was ultimately responsible for the state cult, and in Assyria he was himself reckoned as the supreme member of the complex temple personnel. In ritual drama the king himself enacted the role of the god. The same notion of personal identity as a fluid thing which we have mentioned above was extended to the numinous, so that in ritual drama the king took on numinous power, activated it externally, and, since he also enjoyed fluid identification with the entire kingdom, made the numinous power effectively present throughout the land. Thus, in the rite of sacred marriage the king, representing Dumuzi, assured the powers of fertility throughout the land; representing Marduk in the battle drama of the Babylonian New Year festival, he vanquished chaos and assured cosmic order for the coming year; the people's lament for Dumuzi (cf. Ezek 8.13–14) associated the people themselves in the cycle of vanishing and reappearing fertility.

As for morality and ethics, the Mesopotamian people did indeed have a notion of sin as an offense against the divine will. A fairly exhaustive list of such offenses is contained in the *Shurpu* texts of the late 2d millennium. The list shows pronounced social concern for relatives, neighbors with their wives and possessions, and even for slaves with their families, and for captives; some of the sins are matters of ritual impurity like performing ritual acts with unwashed hands; others are unpropitious acts like swearing by Shamash, the sun god, at sunrise. Significantly, each sin in the list is followed by the incantation which can free the sick or troubled man from his sin (and hence from his sickness or trouble) by averting the influence of god or demon. Legal codes were seen as expressions of divine will. Moral life was devoid of mysticism and of love for the gods, who were looked upon as arbitrary and capricious in their dealings with the individual. Yet, there were cultivated and pious Mesopotamians who expressed a genuine reverence and affection for the gods—usually for a particular god, a point which suggests a certain occasional henotheism by individual choice in the midst of the full-blown Mesopotamian polytheism. BIBLIOGRAPHY: E. Dhorme, *Les Religions de Babylonie et d'Assyrie* (1945); S. N. Kramer and A. L. Oppenheim, *Forgotten Religions* (ed. V. Ferm, 1950) 47–62, 65–79; T. Jacobsen, *Bible and the Ancient Near East* (ed. G. E. Wright, 1961) 267–278; W. L. Moran, NCE 9:702–707; translations of important texts by S. N. Kramer, E. A. Speiser, A. Sachs, F. J. Stephens, R. H. Pfeiffer in *Ancient Near Eastern Texts Relating to the Old Testament* (ed. J. B. Pritchard, 2d ed., 1955) 37–119, 331–345, 383–392, 425–427, 434–440, 449–452.

[A. CODY]

MESPELBRUNN, JULIUS ECHTER VON, see ECHTER VON MESPELBRUNN, JULIUS.

MESROP, ST. (Mesrob, Mashtots; d. *c.*440), Armenian catholicos credited with inventing the Armenian alphabet. A student of Narses the Great, M. began his career as a soldier in the service of the King of Armenia, whose secretary he later became. After the division of the kingdom between Rome and Persia, M. became a priest. Finding his apostolic efforts hampered by the lack of a vernacular version of the Bible and the liturgy, M. constructed, with the help of other scholars, an alphabet based on the Greek which they used to translate the Bible into Armenian. M. himself is thought to have translated the NT and the Book of Proverbs. The liturgy was also translated, as were many Christian works gathered from afar. This provided Armenian literature at its start with a whole library of ecclesiastical authors. It is probable that 23 letters and homilies handed down under the name of *Gregory the Illuminator are the work of M. At the death of St. *Isaac the Great (St. Sahak), who had strongly supported his work, M. himself was elected catholicos, but lived to rule the Church of Armenia for only a short time. His life was written by his disciple Corium (Koriun, Goriun), who attributes to him the creation of the Georgian as well as the Armenian alphabet. BIBLIOGRAPHY: Altaner 409–410; Butler 1:374–375; N. M. Setina, NCE 9:713; M. Gianascian, EncCatt 8:757.

[R. B. ENO]

MESSALIANS, an ecstatic sect that appeared in the mid-4th cent. in Mesopotamia and spread to Syria and elsewhere in Asia Minor. Taking their name from a Syriac word meaning "praying people," they were also known as *Euchites from the Greek translation of the name, as Adelphians, from Adelphius, their first leader, and as Enthusiasts from their conviction that God dwelt in them. Many of them were monks, either vagrant or attached to monasteries. The sect is mentioned by Ephrem the Syrian in his homilies against heresy and by Epiphanius, but more reliable are the acts of the Synods of Antioch (376, under Bp. Flavian) and Side (388, under *Amphilochius of Iconium). They held that every man, in consequence of the sin of Adam, has a congenital demon that is not expelled by baptism but only by continued prayer and ascetical practices that achieve the extinction of all passion and desire in a state of **apatheia*. They claimed to come by this means to the vision of the Trinity in which the Spirit dwelt in them as sensibly as concupiscence dwells in a sinner. They neglected all forms of religious observance apart from prayer and asceticism, conforming only when that was necessary to avoid persecution. They were accused of immorality. The sect appears to have been influenced by lingering traces of Montanism and Gnosticism and in turn to have influenced the 9th-cent. revival of Manichaean sects in the Balkans through which it was linked with the medieval *Cathari. It bears a significant resemblance to *Quietism, not only in its view of prayer and *apatheia* but also in the charges of immorality leveled against it. BIBLIOGRAPHY: S. Runciman, *Medieval Manichee* (1947); Knox Enth; É. Amann, DTC 10:792–795; E. Peterson, EncCatt 8:841–842.

[R. B. ENO]

MESSENGER, a title used by Baptists for a delegate to their *conventions.

[T. C. O'BRIEN]

MESSIAEN, OLIVIER (1908–), contemporary French composer and organist. As professor of harmony at The Paris Conservatory since 1942 and organist at the Church of the Trinity since 1931, M.'s compositions and didactic essays have greatly influenced French religious music. Though known primarily for his organ works, (e.g., "The Celestial Banquet", "The Nativity of the Savior," and "The Mass of Pentecost") he has written choral, orchestral, piano, and vocal pieces. Centering on theological themes, his compositions exist to serve self-consciously Catholic dogmas and they constitute an exotic, personal expression of mystical Catholicism. Yet while serving tradition, M. has made use of many contemporary elements such as microtonal scales, bird song, Hindu rhythms, and the electrical keyboard instrument called ondes martenot.

[D. J. SMUCKER]

MESSIAH, biblical title from the Hebrew word meaning anointed. The complex of ideas normally grouped under the head of messianism is somewhat shifting and elusive, but broadly speaking it is concerned with the establishment of Yahweh's universal kingdom upon earth in and through his chosen people, with their king, the Messiah or anointed son of David, at their head. Although in later times the figure of the king sometimes almost disappears from messianic expectations, or else is replaced or duplicated by a priestly Messiah, the messianic idea originated from and developed around the idealization of the Davidic king. The initial inspiration of this idealization is undoubtedly the oracle of Nathan, which has survived in three heavily "edited" versions in 2 Sam 7.5–16, 1 Chr 17.4–14, Ps 89.20–38. It is not easy to recapture the terms of the original oracle from these texts, but the "constants" of the messianic idea which develop from it may tentatively be summarized.

The Messiah is a son of David (2 Sam 7.12–16; 1 Kg 8.25; 1 Chr 17.11; 28.5–21; 29.24–25; 2 Chr 9.8; 13.8; Is 9.7; 11.1,10; 16.5; Jer 23.5–6; 30.9; Ezek 34.23–24; 37.24–25; Amos 9.11, etc.). He is endowed more or less mysteriously with divine sonship (2 Sam 7.14; 1 Chr 17.13; Ps 2.7; 89.26–27, etc.), who, having in the power of the God of Israel subdued the nations of the world (Amos 9.12; Ps 2.8–12; 18.44; 110.1–2,5–6; 72.8–11, etc.), and extended the bounds of David's kingdom to the ends of the earth (Mic 5.3; Zech 9.10; Is 9.7; 11.14–16; Ps 2.8; 72.8; 89.25, etc.), rules over it forever with inspired justice and peace (2 Sam 7.11,13; Is 9.7; 11.4–5; Jer 23.5–6; Ezek 34.23; Zech 9.9; Ps 45.4,8; 72.2–4; 89.4,29, etc.), inaugurating thereby an age of Paradisal prosperity (Is 9.7; 11.6–9; Zech 9.10; Ps 72.6–7 etc.).

This concept of the Messiah is deeply conditioned by actual memories of David's own achievements, and, to a lesser extent, those of Solomon. David had been anointed by a prophet and thereby endowed in a more permanent form than his predecessor Saul with the charisms of the Spirit. He had been consecrated to Yahweh and filled with charismatic power. In this power he had conquered the Jebusite sacred city of Jerusalem and made it the shrine of the ark, the tangible symbol of Yahweh's covenant with Israel. Thereby he himself had become heir to the position of "covenant mediator," the position initially held by Moses. Again, as savior of Israel and conqueror of her enemies, "all the nations round about Judah," he had become heir to the charismatic "judges" and leaders in the holy wars of Israel who had gone before him, only now, once more, in a more permanent sense. Perhaps too he had inherited, in the idealized vision of his followers, some of the prerogatives of sacral kingship associated with the former Jebusite priest-kings of Jerusalem. He was intimately associated with Yahweh, and the mediator to his people of the divine blessings of harmony and justice, issuing in security, fertility, power over enemies, and prosperity in every sphere of life. Thus the ideal Davidic king is referred to as "the lamp of Israel" (2 Sam 21.17), "the breath of our nostrils" (Lam 4.20), an *elohim* (supernatural being) of more than earthly power (Ps 45.7), who is to "judge the poor of the people, save the needy, and break in pieces the rod of the oppressor" (Ps 72.4; cf. 21.9–13). "In his days the just shall flourish, abundance of peace to last while the moon endures" (Ps 72.7). In some sense he is to convey fertility in the natural order too: "He shall come down like rain on mown grass, like showers that water the earth" (Ps 72.6). In this way, and to an extent difficult to define, Israel seems to have drawn on the "king ideology" of the Canaanites and other neighbors in formulating her own messianic expectations. But these expectations were supremely influenced by the new note of permanency. The throne of David was to endure *forever*. Zion was to be Yahweh's resting-place *forever*. It is because Yahweh could not possibly fail in this promise, and because it had so manifestly not yet been fulfilled, that later generations looked forward to the future messianic age of bliss which was initially inspired by this idealized vision of the Davidic king.

This basic vision of the ideal messianic kingdom is retrospectively extended backwards so as to show it as part of God's plan and purpose from the creation onwards. Thus, for instance, the oracle of Gen 3.15, in which it is predicted that the seed of the woman shall strike the serpent's head, has a broadly messianic significance and points forward to the establishment of Yahweh's ideal kingdom on earth through an ideal charismatic mediator. Judah's blessing by Jacob (Gen 49.9–12) and certain other passages have also been retouched so as to give them a messianic significance. In the latter prophets, and above all in Isaiah (cf. Is 7.14–17), the birth of the Messiah is foretold in still more idealized terms (cf. also Is 9.1–7; ch. 11; Mic 5.1–6; Jer 30.9, 21; Ezek 17.22; 34.23; 37.24). In Exilic and post-Exilic times the concept of the Messiah underwent considerable transformations, perhaps as a result of attaching other motifs to the figure of the Davidic prototype. In the prophecies of Hag 2.20–23, and Zech 6.9–15, the messianic hope is attached to Zerubbabel, the representative of the Davidic house who returned from the Exile. Later still the figure becomes priestly in character, and in the *Qumran scrolls and other intertestamental writings two Messiahs are envisaged, one of Judah and one of Aaron.

It should be evident that these and other ideas of the messianic age had to undergo considerable revision and modification before it could be realized that Jesus was the true Messiah so long awaited. BIBLIOGRAPHY: L. Cerfaux et al., *L'Attente du Messie* (1954); J. Klausner, *Messianic Idea in Israel* (1946); E. Massaux et al., *La Venue du Messie* (1962); S. Mowinckel, *He That Cometh* (1956); H. Ringgren, *Messiah in the Old Testament* (tr. G. W. Anderson, 1956).

[D. J. BOURKE]

MESSIANISM, a term that, besides its proper sense as the biblical hope in the Messiah, is also used to describe: (1) belief that a person is a reincarnation of Jesus or a new divine emissary to the world; *Éon de l'Étoile, Anna *Lee of the Shakers, and Father Divine are examples of such a claim; (2) any urgent sense of divine mission to save or change the world, esp. through a new revelation or message. In both meanings messianism is associated with *apocalypticism and *millenarianism.

[F. E. MASER]

MESSIAS, DER, an epic by F. G. Klopstock (1724–1803) in 20 cantos and nearly 20,000 hexameters. Cantos I–III, published in 1748 in the *Bremer Beiträge,* produced in German poetry a new note of exalted individualism. The remaining cantos were published gradually (1751, 1755, 1768, 1773). Despite his indebtedness to Homer and Milton, Klopstock's treatment of his theme, viz., Christ's redemption of mankind, is not epic, but lyric, even rhapsodic. BIBLIOGRAPHY: J. G. Robertson, *History of German Literature* (4th ed., 1962) 223–228; E. A. Blackall, *Emergence of German as Literary Language, 1700–1775* (1959) 319–350 (the language of the *Messias*).

[M. F. MCCARTHY]

MESSINA, GIUSEPPE (1893–1951), Italian Jesuit, Orientalist, esp. on the history, language, and religion of Iran; professor at the Pontifical Biblical Institute in Rome; director of *Biblica et Orientalia*. He published his valuable research on the Persian version of *Tatian's *Diatesseron in that review in 1951.

[T. C. O'BRIEN]

MESSMER, SEBASTIAN GERHARD (1847–1930), educator, abp., canonist. Of Swiss background, M. was ordained in 1871, when he was invited to come to the U.S. and teach theology and canon law at Seton Hall College, South Orange, N.J. (1871–89). M. played a major role before, during, and after the Third Plenary Council of Baltimore. A brief time at The Catholic Univ. of America ended when he was named bp. of Green Bay, Wisconsin. His administration of that diocese was fruitful, although M. took the side of the German Catholics against the Irish. He was also a foe of labor unions, which he regarded as socialistic. He was appointed abp. of Milwaukee in 1903 and his 27 years there were a time of Catholic growth. M. promoted schools, colleges, and charitable institutions. He was a frequent contributor to periodicals, a translator and editor. Among his works were *Canonical Procedure in Criminal Cases of Clerics* (1886) and *Outlines of Bible Knowledge* (1910). M. edited *The Works of Rt. Rev. John England* (7 v., 1908).

[J. R. AHERNE]

MESSOS, APOCALYPSE OF, see APOCRYPHA (NT), 37.

MEŠTROVIĆ, IVAN (1883–1962), Yugoslavic sculptor and nationalist, internationally renowned, producing work in scale and power comparable to that of Michelangelo. M. was inspired as an apprentice by Roman sculpture at Split, and by medieval work. Student in Vienna, show in Paris (1910) where Rodin admired him as the ''greatest phenomenon'' of our day; winning international fame (1911), a London show (1915), offered but refusing seat in government (1919); becoming director of Zagreb Academy; after release from prison during World War II, M. in the U.S. taught at Syracuse Univ. (1947–55), becoming U.S. citizen (1954), and at the Univ. of Notre Dame (1955–62). Religious themes dominate his work; *Mary Magdalen* (1919), *Gregory, Bishop of Nin* (1926); *Cardinal Stepinac, Christ on the Cross* (1933), *Pope Pius XII* (1942) a *Pietà* and *Samaritan Woman at the Well* at Notre Dame. Early attracted to Egyptian and Assyrian reliefs, M. became a master in low-reliefs of magnificence and power (*The Annunciation* tympanum, and *Queen of the Universe* of the apse—in the National Shrine of the Immaculate Conception, Washington, D.C., 1959). M. is represented in great museums throughout the world. BIBLIOGRAPHY: N. L. Rice, *Sculpture of Ivan Meštrović,* 1948.

[M. J. DALY]

METAHISTORY, reflection on the nature of history and its meaning, and on the cause and significance of historical change. It relates to history in a way analogous to the way metaphysics relates to physics. As the Greek prefix *meta* would indicate, metahistory comes ''after'' the study of history, and seeks to get ''beyond'' a mere antiquarian focus. The questions and answers of the metahistorian are metaphysical, philosophical, and theological. They arise, however, out of a study of history and are colored by that discipline. The greatest historiographers are read for their overview, their metahistorical ideas: from St. Augustine to Karl Marx; including Voltaire, Gibbon, Spengler, and Toynbee. Even the denial of a world-view, or the denial of an overall meaning to history is a theological view in itself and just as apt to color investigation as any other. BIBLIOGRAPHY: M. R. P. McGuire, NCE 9:723–724; cf. C. H. Dawson *Dynamics of World History* (ed. by J. J. Mulloy, 1962), esp. Part II: ''Conceptions of World History,'' pp. 229–394).

[E. J. DILLON]

METANGISMONITES, from a Greek word meaning the putting from one vessel into another, a name given to certain heretics by Filaster (*Haer*. 51) and after him by Augustine (*Haer*. 58). During the Arian controversies, the text ''the Father is in me and I in the Father'' (Jn 10.38) raised the question of how the greater can be contained in the lesser. *Athanasius *(Or. 3 cont. Arianos)* replied that the question itself betrayed a material conception of God; one could not ask it without thinking of the persons of the Godhead as empty vessels, the one being filled with the other. There is, however, no evidence of any Arian use of this illustration, and much less of a distinct sect based upon it. BIBLIOGRAPHY: G. Salmon, DCB 3:908.

[L. G. MÜLLER]

METANOIA, Gr., a change in one's views; in Mt 3.2, Acts 8.22 and elsewhere, the NT word for repentance. It does not mean simply a vague remorse or regret, nor simply the juridic renouncement of wrongdoing. The point of Christian repentance is change, a conversion turning back to God and away from the sin that brought separation, and a reconciliation, the restoration of friendship with the Father. Metanoia refers to this willingness to change, to be submissive to the Father's loving will and to remove whatever is an obstacle to loving relationship with him. BIBLIOGRAPHY: ThAq ST 3a, 90.3.

[T. C. O'BRIEN]

METANY (from the Gr. *metanoia,* a change in one's views), a gesture of reverence in the Byzantine rite. In most of the Eastern Churches the Western genuflection is unknown but reverence is expressed by bows of various degrees. (1) The *proskynesis* or salutation bow is used when passing before a cross, icon, or altar, or when greeting a superior. This is made by an inclination of the head and shoulders often accompanied by a sign of the cross. It is also used at the mention of the Holy Trinity or at any doxology. (2) The lesser *(mikra)* metany is a profound bow with the hand brought down so as to touch the ground and accompanied by a sign of the cross. This metany, frequently made three times, is used often during the liturgy. Among the Slavs the sign of the cross is made first and this is followed by the deep bow. In Greek usage the bow precedes the sign of the cross. (3) The great *(megale)* metany is a complete prostration made on hands and knees by touching the forehead to the ground. This is often performed by the faithful in the middle of the nave when they enter the church. It is also used at the Royal Doors and during Lenten services and at the ceremonies of the Exaltation of the Holy Cross.

[A. J. JACOPIN]

METAPHOR, a name or expression belonging properly to one thing and applied to another, to which it does not so belong, through a pertinent similarity. Thus a fighting man may be called a tiger, by virtue of a ferocity approaching that of *Felis tigris,* or old age may be said to be the evening of life, as the relation of old age to life is similar to that of evening to day. The metaphorical application of an expression differs from the literal, be it analogical or univocal, in that the literal use does not involve application to something to which the expression does not belong. The simile differs from the metaphor in making explicit a comparison only implicit in the latter; thus it could be said that old age is like evening. Metaphor has not only poetical but also theological importance. Human concepts and, consequently, expressions of the perfections of God are derived from those of the perfections found in creatures. When concept and expression are such that reference to the creature is part of the very meaning of the expression, it can only be applied to God metaphorically. Such metaphors, both less demanding intellectually and more compelling emotionally than the technical terminology of scientific discourse, are of immense rhetorical value. But theology must sacrifice the emotional immediacy of metaphor, as in the "hidden God" of some thinkers, to the achievement of the literal, albeit but analogical, expression necessary to scientific rigor, as in the recognition of the God infinitely superior to the humanly intelligible.

[R. E. HENNESSEY]

METAPHYSICAL POETS, a group of 17th-cent. English poets, who were thoughtful and reflective, intellectual and analytical. They aimed to express the complexities and contradictions of life in religion, war, love, court-living and ordinary occupations, and they turned away from the conventions of Elizabethan love poetry and from Petrarchan language and figures toward a psychological analysis of the emotions. Striving to express the fullness of every experience with its opposing elements and ambiguities, they often use bold images from science and travel, conversational language, and rough rhythm. The term metaphysical was first applied to J. *Donne in 1693 by Dryden. Other major poets of the group are Herbert, Crashaw, and Vaughan. They have affected 20th-cent. poetry in the work of T. S. Eliot, John Crowe Ransom, Allen Tate, and others. BIBLIOGRAPHY: H. C. White, *Metaphysical Poets: A Study in Religious Experience* (repr. 1962); *idem,* NCE 9:725–727.

[M. M. BARRY]

METAPHYSICAL SCHOOL, art movement of the 20th cent., which surprises or shocks by the juxtaposition of the improbable or fantastic with ordinary experience. Ideal, mystical philosophies and theosophy (Kandinsky) led artists to seek inner realities—beyond the surfaces of things (Nietzsche). A popularized psychoanalysis intensified by the late 19th-cent. romanticism of the Munich School (A. Bocklin) resulted in panels of melancholy and loneliness, with an intense perspective—no longer descriptive but a vehicle of fear, isolation and threat of evil, and faceless mannequins within airless empty spaces of eerie luminescence. Founder and master G. de Chirico (1888–   ) in *Enigma of an Autumn Afternoon, Enigma of the Oracle, Nostalgia of the Infinite, Grand Metaphysical Interior,* reshaped Renaissance visual reality for future irrational or intuitive art movements in Europe and America.

[M. J. DALY]

METAPHYSICS, term with two meanings relevant to religion: (1) in the proper, philosophical sense, the study of being, its principles and causes; (2) in a transferred sense, an occult, esoteric or mental religious system, e.g., Christian Science and similar doctrines of mental healing are often described as metaphysical.

The origin of the term in its classic usage has been attributed both to Eudemus of Rhodes (3d cent. B.C.) and to Andronicus of Rhodes (1st cent. B.C.), editors of Aristotle's works. The group of treatises which both in subject matter and in the acquisition of learning came after his *Physics,* were designated as "Matters after the Physics" *(ta meta ta physica).* The books of the *Metaphysics* contained inquiries that went beyond the material and changeable in nature. Aristotle referred to this type of philosophical discourse as "first philosophy," because its subject matter is being as being, the ultimate, most universal aspect of reality. He also called it "theology" or "divine science," both because it considers the highest causes and because it terminates in a contemplation resembling the knowledge ascribed to divinity. While among the Greeks, beginning with Parmenides (5th cent. B.C.), there had been other suprasensible explanations of reality, notably Plato's theory of Ideas, Aristotle is called the Father of Metaphysics. His writings set the terminology and problematic that in Western thought came to be regarded as proper to metaphysics. (See also PLATONISM AND NEOPLATONISM).

The fullest and most enduring development of Aristotelian metaphysics was within *scholasticism. While their interpretations varied considerably, the scholastics did share a philosophical realism, i.e., a conviction that reality is the basis for objectively valid judgments and conclusions concerning being as substance and being as accident, being as actual and being as potential, being as dependent on a first cause. Metaphysics was accepted as a certain, transcendental, and absolute body of knowledge. Beginning with R. *Descartes a supra-experimental science of reality was sought through reflection on the ideas clearly present to the mind. (See IDEALISM). By his critique against the objectivity of the transcendental ideas of reason, I. *Kant sought to show that a valid metaphysics is impossible. For *positivism, and its contemporary continuation, *logical positivism, any nonempirical statement concerning reality is unverifiable and has no meaning. Against the widespread discrediting of metaphysics, *phenomenology and *existentialism have reasserted the primacy of being, of real existence, for genuine philosophical knowledge (see HEIDEGGER, M.).

Since Christian faith includes a view of the world that goes beyond appearances, that is transcendental and absolute, Christian theology has in many instances found classical metaphysics congenial to its purposes. Metaphysics has been regarded as a valid, if limited, expression developed by human reason of certain basic religious truths, for example, *Neo-Scholasticism in the RC Church involved such a view of metaphysics. Skepticism concerning the validity of metaphysics, however, has also had an effect on theology, both in 19th-cent. *liberal theology, and in the contemporary search for new thought categories to express doctrine or in the emphasis on ethical and kerygmatic approaches to theology. BIBLIOGRAPHY: For surveys and comprehensive bibliog. see G. F. McLean, NCE 9:727–731; G. F. Kreyche, *ibid.* 731–734; R. Hancock, EncPhil 5:289–300; W. H. Walsh, *ibid.* 300–307.

[M. R. P. MCGUIRE]

METAPHYSICS, EXISTENTIAL, see EXISTENTIAL METAPHYSICS.

METAPSYCHOLOGY, the term used by S. *Freud to designate the more general principles and concepts of psychoanalysis formulated in a series of papers written *c.*1915–17. The major concepts include those of instincts and their vicissitudes, repression, and the unconscious. Although these are key theoretical concepts for psychoanalysis, they were formulated fairly early in Freud's career and antedated other equally important ideas (e.g., *Id, *Ego and *Superego, *Anxiety theory) by several years. The metapsychological papers therefore can be considered as representing only part of Freud's metapsychological, i.e., theoretical, constructs. Metapsychology is also a term used at times for spiritism, in which sense it is closely related to *parapsychology.

[M. E. STOCK]

METEMPSYCHOSIS, see TRANSMIGRATION OF SOULS.

METEORA (Gr., raised from the ground), monastic establishments in the remote mountains of Thessaly in central Greece, thought to date from the 11th century. At one time there were 14 flourishing monasteries but now there are no more than 4: The Great Monastery, Holy Trinity, St. Barlaam's and St. Stephen's, each inhabited by only a small community. The bp. of Trikkis and Stagon has modernized the living facilities, introduced a number of educated monks into the monasteries, and has also founded a small convent for women. Some of the men observe the traditional monastic life and are training a new generation of monks; a second group lives in Trikkala where, like members of the Zoe Brotherhood, they engage in preaching and catechizing while maintaining an affiliation with the monasteries. The picturesque locale has made the houses of Meteora a chief tourist attraction. The Meteora stand as a symbol of past monastic strength and as a hope for future revitalization of Orthodox monasticism. BIBLIOGRAPHY: L. Heuzey and H. Daumet, *Mission archéologique de Macédoine* (1876).

[S. SURRENCY]

METHLEY, RICHARD (family name Furth; *c.*1451–*c.*1528), Cistercian writer, mystic. Called Methley from the village of that name, he became a Carthusian at the age of 25 at Mount Grace, England. This house had absorbed the old English spiritual teaching, mixed with the spirit of the Flemish mystics, and with traces of the *Devotio moderna.* M. left an autobiographical tract, *Refectorium Salutis,* a spiritual diary covering the days between October 6 and December 15, 1487. He also translated into Latin *The Cloud of Unknowing*. He was influenced by his predecessors, and his writing betrays echoes of Rolle, *The Cloud,* and Hilton, although in all there is a certain naïveté which betrays a youthful excess. There are no later writings, although he wrote a *Schola amoris languidi* in 1485, and last records show him alive at the end of 1491. He is said to have died as subprior (vicar) of Mount Grace in 1528. His memory seems to have been held in high regard by his contemporaries. BIBLIOGRAPHY: Knowles, ROE 2:224–226.

[N. F. GAUGHAN]

METHODISM, a name that now identifies the doctrines, polity, and discipline of several Protestant denominations tracing their origins to the 18th-cent. revival in England under John and Charles Wesley, and their friend George *Whitefield. While students at Oxford, these men experienced (*c.*1725) ''awakenings'' and, becoming intensely serious, decided to prepare for orders in the Church of England. Three or four other students united with them in their zeal for ''inward religion, the religion of the heart,'' and these members of the Holy Club, John Wesley wrote, ''by the exact regularity of their lives, as well as studies, occasioned a young gentleman of Christ Church to say, 'Here is a new sect of Methodists sprung up,' alluding to some ancient physicians who were so called. The name was new and quaint, so it took immediately and the Methodists were known all over the university.''

In 1735 the Wesleys and two of their friends accepted invitations from Gen. James Oglethorpe to cross the Atlantic to the Georgia Colony. On the voyage, and during their ministry in Georgia, these ''Methodists'' became acquainted with some Moravian settlers and were so favorably impressed by them as to accept some of their pietist peculiarities, particularly the felt assurance of justifying faith as the *sine qua non* of the Christian life (see PIETISM). Almost as appealing were the accounts of instantaneous conversions so frequently reported among the Moravians.

The effect of these associations on the Oxford missionaries was to intensify their search for "inward holiness" by the expectation of some kind of climactic experience in the achieving of it. Charles Wesley returned to England in Dec. 1736; John, in Feb. 1738. In the following weeks, when asked to preach in Anglican pulpits, John so stressed faith and Christian perfection in his sermons that several churches banned him. On May 24, 1738, he records the appropriateness of the anthem at St. Pauls', "Out of the depths have I cried unto Thee, O Lord," and in this mood, at a little religious *society in Aldersgate Street, London, that same evening he felt his "heart strangely warmed" and was convinced that he "did trust Christ, Christ alone for salvation." Significantly, he added, "I began to pray with all my might for those who had in a more especial manner despitefully used me and persecuted me." To John Wesley this undoubtedly was the inner witness or impression that he had been urged by his Moravian mentors to seek. Charles Wesley and others reported similar emotional experiences, and this type of religious conversion became a primary characteristic of the Methodist revival.

By 1739 revival excitement was high. Whitefield's emotion-charged sermons were swaying great crowds who came to see the novelty of an Anglican priest preaching in the fields. By 1744 most of the unique features of early Methodist life and organization had been adopted. Required membership in carefully controlled societies harnessed the enthusiasm of the converts. The only requirement for admission was a desire to seek inner holiness and to live a life of prayer, discipline, and fellowship in the Spirit. Large societies were divided into *classes of 10 or 12 members under an appointed class leader who was in charge of their weekly meetings for prayer, examination, and exhortation. *Field preaching, *itinerancy, the annual *conferences, "rooms" and chapels for worship and preachings, printed tracts and hymns, collections and funds—these and many other activities gave strength and order to the movement and, at the same time, encouraged among the Methodists a consciousness of independence. Legal status for the conferences was secured in 1784 by a Deed of Declaration that provided for the continuation of the work after Wesley's death.

Meanwhile, Methodism had spread to Ireland, Scotland, and Wales. In the 1760s lay preachers began to form societies in Maryland and New York; Virginia, New Jersey, and Philadelphia were at once included in the itinerants' circuits. In answer to their call to Wesley for help, the English Conference sent two local preachers in 1769 and additional pairs almost annually, until the American Revolution made English control impossible. F. *Asbury, who was sent by Wesley in 1771, remained after all the others returned, to become the greatest of the early leaders in America.

In spite of the Wesley brothers' devotion to the traditions and authority of the C of E, the Methodists drifted inevitably toward separation from their Anglican mother Church. A semblance of ecclesiastical dependence lasted as long as the Wesleys (and Asbury) could prevent the societies from having the sacraments and an ordained ministry, but when the situation demanded both of these for America as a practical necessity, John Wesley boldly took what he thought were the proper steps to supply them. On Sept. 1, 1784, believing that the early Church had regarded presbyters and bishops as the same order, he decided to perform an episcopal act himself, and he ordained two of his lay helpers, Richard Whatcoat and Thomas Vasey, as deacons and (on the following day) as elders. At the same time he ordained his fellow presbyter, Dr. Thomas *Coke, as "superintendent" over "the brethren in America." These men were joined by about 60 lay preachers at the *Christmas Conference in 1784. There the *Methodist Episcopal Church was organized; Asbury was ordained; he and Coke were elected "superintendents" (the title was changed to bishop in 1787); and a Ritual, a Sunday Service and Articles of Religion, all abridged by Wesley from the BCP and the *Thirty-Nine Articles, were adopted. No such formal acts of separation were made for English Methodists, although Wesley performed more than 20 ordinations for them in Great Britain before he died.

Methodists by tradition enjoy wide freedom in the interpretation of doctrines; at the same time they stress the central Protestant beliefs. This derives from John Wesley's strong dislike of theological controversy and reflects the pietistic *revivalism in which his followers were so prominent. By their larger interests in the Christian life, religious experience, and social issues, they appear to be less concerned with theology. But there has never been among them a theological vacuum. In general they try to maintain a mediating position by the avoidance of extremes. "As to all opinions which do not strike at the root of Christianity," said Wesley, "we think and let think." For doctrinal standards Methodists accept as guides the *Standard Sermons* of John Wesley, his **Notes on the New Testament,* and his **Twenty-Five Articles of Religion*. Their theology is fairly described as *Arminian because they stress an atonement for sin offered for all mankind, and freedom of the human will. A Calvinist minority in the following of Whitefield has been concentrated chiefly in Wales (see CALVINISTIC METHODISTS). The Apostles' Creed is commonly used in worship, but Methodists frequently prefer more modern confessions of faith. Their Social Creed, adopted by the General Conference of the Methodist Episcopal Church in 1908, has since been a model of its kind for many Churches. Heresy trials are almost unknown among Methodists, but several schisms have come from angry disputes over church polity, "worldliness," and social problems, such as slavery and race relations. Abstinence from alcoholic drink, associated with Methodism is based in part on the ideal of a Christian perfection, in part on a tradition of social concern dating from Wesley's own ministry to the victims of the Industrial Revolution. The *Discipline of the Methodist Church was modified in regard to total abstinence in 1968. (see UNITED METHODIST CHURCH [U.S.].)

Methodist church government, originally episcopal and

autocratically controlled by John Wesley through his preachers, has become fully representative through its many conferences. The pastoral charge (which as a *circuit may have more than one church) has its Quarterly Conference, and each church has its Official Board, both composed of laymen. The Annual, District, Jurisdictional, and General Conferences (all regional) have equal lay and ministerial representation. Bishops are the executive and general administrators of the Church's activities in the Annual Conferences assigned to them. They make the pastoral appointments, usually in consultation with the church members, and are elected for life by the Jurisdictional Conferences. Methodists recognize only the orders of deacon and elder; bps. are not a third order, but are elders set apart for administrative work, superintendents over the Church.

The language of the BCP is evident in the Sacraments and in the Ritual for ordination, weddings, and funerals. Sunday worship varies, and freedom in forms of prayer is encouraged, although the Methodist Hymnal and Book of Worship are provided. Two sacraments, baptism and the Lord's Supper, are observed; baptism is administered to both infants and adults, usually by sprinkling, but by another form if desired. Membership is on confession of faith or by letter of transfer from other Churches.

There are more than 20 separate Methodist bodies in the United States. Only a few of these, like the Free Methodists and the Fundamental Methodists, claim theological origins by insisting upon a return to Wesleyan standards in doctrine. A union in 1939 brought together the Methodist Protestant Church (which in 1830 opposed episcopacy and demanded lay representation), the Methodist Episcopal Church, South (which in 1845 had separated over slavery and polity), and the Methodist Episcopal Church into the *Methodist Church. In 1968 a union with the Evangelical United Brethren (originally German-Speaking "Methodists") created the *United Methodist Church, numbering more than 11 million members. Other large Methodist denominations are the African Methodist Episcopal (1816), the African Methodist Episcopal, Zion (1820), and the Christian Methodist Episcopal (1870) Churches, all Negro, and together numbering about 2½ million members. The *World Methodist Council, which meets at 5-year intervals, is composed of delegates from 42 countries, representing about 45 million Methodists. The Council meets for fellowship; it is without power to make laws for its constituent members. BIBLIOGRAPHY: N. B. Harmon, *Understanding the Methodist Church* (1955); W. W. Sweet, *Methodists: A Collection of Source Materials* (1946); R. Currie, *Methodism Divided* (1968); R. H. Short, *United Methodism in Theory and Practice* (1974).

[D. R. CHANDLER]

METHODIST CHURCH (ENGLAND), a body organized in 1933 with the merger of the Wesleyan Methodist, Primitive Methodist, and United Methodist Churches. British Methodists did not become a separate denomination until after the death of John *Wesley. By the Plan of Pacification prepared in 1795 the *Conference permitted societies to meet during the hours of service of the C of E, to have ministers authorized by the Conference, and to administer the sacraments in Methodist chapels. For years, however, many Wesleyan Methodists considered themselves to be Anglicans; and they still returned to the C of E to receive the sacraments. Final steps for separation were not taken until 1897. The various Methodist bodies prospered in spite of a series of divisive splits. At the beginning of the 20th cent. a change of temper, fostered in part by the Ecumenical Methodist Conferences, directed the Churches toward union. By a series of mergers beginning in 1907 the various bodies united, until by 1933 all but one or two had become part of the one Methodist Church. The doctrinal standards of the Church include the Scriptures as set forth in the historic creeds, Wesley's *Notes on the New Testament* and *Standard Sermons*. In polity, the Church is nonepiscopal and is organized in one Annual Conference. The Church maintains the Methodist traditions in stressing total abstinence, manifesting social concern, opposing war, and promoting ecumenism. With the Methodist Church in the U.S., it forms the core of the *World Methodist Council. On July 8, 1969, a plan for reunion with the C of E, 14 years in preparation, was defeated; the Methodist Church approved it, but because of the issue of the *historic episcopate, the plan failed to win a sufficient majority in the Anglican *Convocations. BIBLIOGRAPHY: R. Currie, *Methodism Divided* (1968); C. W. Keysor, *Our Methodist Heritage* (pa. 1973); E. Halevy, *Birth of Methodism in England* (tr. B. Semmel, 1971).

[F. E. MASER]

METHODIST CHURCH (U.S.), the largest Methodist body in the world, organized in 1939 with the merger of the Methodist Episcopal Church, the Methodist Episcopal Church, South, and the Methodist Protestant Church; 1968 membership was 10,300,000. In the early days of Methodism, followers of John *Wesley, both in England and in the American colonies, considered themselves still to belong to the Church of England. Following the American Revolution, Wesley himself helped to establish American Methodists as a separate denomination. He ordained T. *Coke as superintendent (bp.) of the American work and sent him to the U.S. with two other ministers, whom he had also ordained, with instructions to ordain F. *Asbury also as a superintendent. At the *Christmas Conference (1784) in Baltimore, Md., preachers were elected and ordained, and the Methodist Episcopal Church in America was organized. In the 19th cent., splits occurred among American Methodists over slavery, *episcopacy, and the doctrine of *entire sanctification. The Methodist Church represented a strong reunification; many Methodist bodies, however, continue in separate existence, and some have been born or strengthened in the 20th century. The chief subordinate doctrinal standards of the Methodist Church are the *Twenty-Five Articles of Religion; Wesley's **Notes on the New Testament* and *Standard Sermons* are regarded as guides rather than as actual standards. The Church is an episcopal body but regards *episcopacy as an office, not a distinct order, and makes no claim to *apostolic succession. The organization of church government is through a complex system of *conferences. American Methodist Churches were powerful forces in the passage of the 18th Amendment to the U.S. Constitution, and continue to favor total abstinence. The Church has strongly favored racial integration, open housing, and equal opportunity. The 1908 Social Creed of the Methodist Church is considered a classic expression for social justice. In the ecumenical movement, American Methodists have played a key role, with G. Bromley *Oxnam and J. R. *Mott prominent in the formation of both the National and World Council of Churches. In recent years the Methodist Church has been a part of the *Consultation on Church Union. The 1968 merger of the Methodist Church with the Evangelical United Brethren Church created the *United Methodist Church. BIBLIOGRAPHY: F. A. Norwood, *Story of American Methodism* (1974).

[F. E. MASER]

METHODIUS I, PATRIARCH OF CONSTANTINOPLE, ST. (d. 847). A native of Syracuse M. became a monk and vigorously supported the veneration of images, for which he was severely persecuted by the iconoclastic rulers. In 842 the orthodox Empress Theodora named him patriarch, and the following year he presided over a council which reaffirmed the legitimacy of venerating sacred images. BIBLIOGRAPHY: D. Stiernon, BiblSanct 9:382–393.

[G. T. DENNIS]

METHODIUS OF OLYMPUS, ST. (d.*c.*300), bp. and martyr. Not much is known about the place and manner of his martyrdom. He may have been decapitated during the persecutions of Diocletian, *c.*311 A.D. He was bp. first of Olympus, then of Patara. He was also a distinguished writer whose works were extensively quoted by Jerome, Epiphanius, Gregory of Nyssa, Theodoret, and Photius. There is thus ample evidence of the range of his theological interest, despite the fact that his only extant, complete work is a treatise in praise of virginity, written in a style apparently patterned after Plato's dialogues. M. wrote opposing Porphyry; he opposed Origen's views on the reality of the resurrection of the body; and defended free will against the Valentinians. BIBLIOGRAPHY: Butler 3:592.

[E. J. DILLON]

METHODIUS AND CYRIL, SS., see CYRIL AND METHODIUS, SS.

METHODOLOGY, THEOLOGICAL, the intellectual means by which the science of Christian theology can elucidate its proper object: the mystery of God which is present to man through faith, man's graced, yet free, response to God's self-communication in history in the person of Jesus Christ and in his Spirit. Due to the unique nature of its subject matter, theological methodology necessarily presupposes preliminary reflection on why and how this scientific discipline exists at all. This initial inquiry concerns man's very ability to know the mystery of God. Thus, the encounter of man's free nature with God's free self-disclosure to him in time constitutes the parameters of fundamental theology or apologetics. This basic approach to theology rests both on examining experience (inductions from empirical signals of the transcendent) and on hearing God's Word in the Scripture (deduction from privileged religious writings). Theological methodology, though unique, is still similar to all other scientific avenues to truth, which also rely on insight (discovery) and on authority (tradition). Faith in the graceful self-revelation of God is the goal of man's rational search to comprehend the divine mystery at the circumference and at the center of his existence. In order to find the fullest manifestation of this mystery in history, man comes to faith in Jesus of Nazareth whose words and actions, person and fate embody the free, loving and self-giving nature of the God whom man, himself the contingent possessor of all these qualities, seeks. Once one believes, he makes use of all possible human resources to gain a deeper understanding of the triune God and of the implications God's interpersonal nature has for his personal and social life in the world. Various theological methodologies were thus developed to deal with (1) biblical and historical and (2) dogmatic and practical aspects of the one totality which is theology. Biblical and historical theology employ a positive methodology based on exegesis and on literary criticism, in order to show how one faithfully explicates the origins and development of Christian faith. Dogmatic theology, by use of logic and philosophy, concerns itself with the ultimate intelligibility of and interconnection between the truths of revelation, in order to explain how God works the one mystery of salvation confessed in the Creed. Practical theology flows from the principles analyzed in dogmatics and can be further divided into: (a) moral theology, which delineates an individual's life of witness with the help of insights into the psychological development and ethical responsibility of the believer (ascetical and mystical theology) and (b) pastoral theology, which takes into account the whole community's attitude towards the diverse situations in which the Gospel must be preached (liturgiology, canon law, missiology, homiletics and catechetics). Today theological methodology is marked by awareness of the cultural changes that have influenced former theological formulations. While theology seeks to illuminate what has not yet been said, it is cognizant that a discrepancy always exists between the apparent clarity of its conceptions and the true brilliance of the mystery of God. BIBLIOGRAPHY: H. U. von Balthasar, *Science, Religion and Christianity* (1958); M. D. Chenu, *Is Theology a Science?* (1959); A. Dulles, *Survival of Dogma* (1971); B. Lonergan, *Method in Theology* (1972).

[P. J. ROSATO]

METHUSALAH, according to the *priestly tradition, the eighth of the antediluvian patriarchs descended from Seth, possibly to be identified with Methushael, the sixth of those descended from Cain in the *Yahwist tradition, and the grandfather or great-grandfather of Noah. The popular belief (for it is no more than this) that antediluvian patriarchs lived to enormous ages is also reflected in ancient lists of patriarchs in the literature of Mesopotamia, and here too lists of either eight or ten generations are recorded. The numbers of years ascribed to each patriarch probably had some symbolic value now lost to us. M. in particular has been taken by modern readers as the type of the antediluvian patriarch who enjoyed an enormous life span, in his case 969 years.

[D. J. BOURKE]

METOCHION (Gr., to live together), in Eastern monasticism this was originally a small dependency established by a monastery with a special purpose, usually to allow designated monks to practice a greater degree of asceticism than would ordinarily be possible at the main monastery. Sometimes this could be of a worldly nature such as managing an estate or serving as a trading center; at other times it was simply a means of relieving overcrowding in the main monastery. In contemporary practice a metochion may comprise fewer than six monks who share a common life, but whose asceticism may be akin to that of solitaries.

[S. SURRENCY]

METOCHITES, GEORGE, see GEORGE METOCHITES.

METROPHANES CRITOPOULOS (1589–1639), *Athanite monk, Byzantine theologian, and patriarch of Alexandria (1636–39). After embracing the monastic life on Mt. Athos where he met *Cyril Lucaris, he spent several years studying Protestantism and Anglicanism throughout Europe, esp. at Oxford and universities in Germany and Switzerland. He was consecrated bp. by 1633, becoming metropolitan of Memphis, Egypt, and was enthroned as patriarch of Alexandria in 1636. M. supported the anathemas against Cyril Lucaris because of the latter's Calvinist leanings. His own writings reflect a Protestant influence, esp. the *Homologia tēs anatolikēs ekklesias* (1624–25). He reduced the number of the sacraments to three, baptism, Eucharist, and penance, rejected the deuterocanonical books of the Bible, and refuted other specific points of RC doctrine. BIBLIOGRAPHY: V. Grumel, DTC 10.2:1622–27.

[F. T. RYAN]

METROPHANES OF SMYRNA, metropolitan from 857 to 880. Because he refused to recognize Photius as the legitimate patriarch of Constantinople, he was deposed by a Photian Synod and exiled to Cherson by the emperor Michael III. In 860 he met the Slavic Brothers, Cyril and Methodius, on their way to the Khazars. M. refused Photius's offer of reconciliation after the latter was reinstated as patriarch following Ignatius's death. He refused to appear at the union council (879–880) and was deposed and excommunicated. After Photius resigned in 886, he may have recovered the See of Smyrna. He wrote eulogies and biblical commentaries. BIBLIOGRAPHY: Mansi 16:54–73,178; F. Dvornik, *Photian Schism* (1948) 43–49,238.

[L. PEANO]

METROPOLIA, RUSSIAN (U.S.), see RUSSIAN METROPOLIA (U.S.).

METROPOLIA, UKRAINIAN (U.S.), see UKRAINIAN METROPOLIA.

METROPOLITAN, a word derived from the Gr. *metropolis* (mother city), as the capital of a province and certain other important cities were called in the late Roman Empire. The bps. of such cities were styled metropolitans (Nicaea, 325) and they enjoyed certain rights over other bps. in the province in which they were located. With the development of the patriarchate and improved means of communication, an intermediary hierarchical organization became superfluous, as happened also in the Latin Church. At the present time no Eastern Catholic or Orthodox patriarchate is subdivided into ecclesiastical provinces, with the exception of the Romanian patriarchate, which has five. But the title metropolitan is still preserved either for the bps. of important cities (as in the Russian patriarchate, the Serbian Church, and among the Melkites) or for all diocesan bps. (Greece, Bulgaria, Cyprus). Autocephalous and autonomous Churches are sometimes headed by metropolitans (e.g., the three Russian jurisdictions of the U.S.) Also the Eastern Catholic metropolitans who are not under the jurisdiction of a patriarchate can be regarded as heading independent jurisdictions or *metropolias. The Eastern Catholic canonical rules on metropolitans and metropolias are contained in *Cleri sanctitati* (cc. 315–339).

In the Latin Church a metropolitan is an abp. who exercises some degree of actual jurisdiction over the suffragan bps. of the designated province and is himself subject directly to the pope. Canon law of the Latin Church grants to the metropolitan power that is ordinary, not delegated, and proper, not vicarious, and this distinguishes him from an abp. whose title is honorary (e.g., most apostolic delegates). Latin metropolitans are superseded in honor and precedence by Latin patriarchs and primates (CIC c.280).

[V. J. POSPISHIL]

METSYS (MASSYS, MATSYS), QUENTIN (1466–1530), Flemish painter of unusual originality from Louvain, master in Antwerp (1491). M. combined a sensitive archaism with 15th-cent. Italian elements. *Legend of St. Anne* (1509) and *Lamentation over Christ* (1511) are symmetrical and tranquil. An earlier *Virgin and Child* relates to Rogier van der Weyden and Jan van Eyck, a *St. Christopher* to Dirk Bouts. The Louvre *Money Changer and His Wife* (1514) suggests borrowings from Van Eyck in composition and details. The *Ecce Homo* (1514–16) suggests Leonardo and Bosch grotesques effectively synthesized with notes of Renaissance "ideal." BIBLIOGRAPHY: M. J. Friedländer, *Die Altnederl, Malerei* 7 (1929).

[M. J. DALY]

METTEN, ABBEY OF, Benedictine monastery in Regensburg, S Germany, founded (766) by Bl. Gamelbert and Bl. Utto. In 1058 the monks were replaced by canons regular but returned in 1157. It suffered destruction by fire in 1236. After its collapse during the Reformation, the abbey was revived in 1596–1624. Suppression by Bavaria (1803) was followed by its restoration in 1826. In 1840 Metten regained the status of abbey. St Vincent Archabbey, Latrobe, Pa., was founded from Metten.

[S. A. HEENEY]

METTERNICH, KLEMENS WENZEL VON (1773–1859), Austrian statesman. Son of an Austrian diplomat, M. was born in Koblenz, Germany, studied at the Univ. of Strasbourg and Mainz, gained a position through marriage in Austrian aristocratic circles, served as Austrian envoy to Saxony (1801), ambassador to Berlin (1803) and to Paris (1806), and finally Austrian minister of foreign affairs (1809–48). A staunch conservative and a relentless foe of revolution, he skillfully used his influence at the Congress of Vienna (1815) to return Europe to the old order and to set up an alliance system to maintain it. He opposed the entrenched Josephinism of the Austrian government and valued the Church for its conservative influence. Despite his realization that discontent was strong and a new revolution was always imminent, M. held firmly to his reactionary position. When the revolution of 1848 broke out in Austria and he found himself practically deserted, he resigned his position and went into retirement, living first in England and Belgium (1848–51), and then spending his remaining years (1851–59) in Vienna. BIBLIOGRAPHY: A. J. May, *Age of Metternich, 1814–1848* (1933); G. Bertier de Sauvigny, *Metternich and His Times* (1962).

[A. WATHEN]

METZGER, MAX JOSEPH, (1887–1944) priest, pacifist, ecumenist. Born in Schopfheim in Baden, M. began the work of the World Peace of the White Cross which, after World War I, came to be known as the Peace Group of German Catholics. The name was later changed to the Society of Christ the King of the White Cross, a brotherhood with a threefold goal: (1) to foster Christian pacifism and peace among nations; (2) to do social welfare work and give spiritual aid; (3) to promote Christian union. The last aim was furthered by the foundation of the *Una Sancta* movement. From the beginning M. was seen as an enemy by the National Socialists. In 1934 he was imprisoned for 4 weeks; in 1939, for 11 weeks on charges of undermining their program. In June 1943 he was arrested once again, condemned to death on Oct. 14, 1943, and executed in Brandenburg on April 17, 1944. BIBLIOGRAPHY: *Dying We Live* (ed. H. Gollwitzer et al., 1956).

[M. A. GALLIN]

MEUNIER, CONSTANTIN (1831–1905). Belgian sculptor and painter of historical and religious subjects, M. was involved in the oppression of miners around Liège (1870), painted (1882) a copy of *Descent from the Cross* by Pedro de Campaña in Spain, and an original *Good Friday Procession in Seville* (1882–83). Humane, but not a socialist, M. carved a monument to Labor (Brussels), lauding the miners' heroism, or with the pathos of a Pietà (*Le Grisou,* 1893), treated the tragedy of their disasters.

[M. J. DALY]

MEURERS, HEINRICH VON (1888–1953), leader of the liturgical movement in Germany. He studied theology at Innsbruck and Rome, was professor of dogma at Trier (1923–35), vicar general of the diocese of Trier (1935–51), a founding member of the German liturgical commission (1940), first president of the Liturgical Institute of Trier (1947), and president of the first German liturgical congress at Frankfurt am Main (1950).

[E. J. DILLON]

MEURIN, SÉBASTIEN LOUIS (1707–77), French Jesuit missionary in America. M. came to the U.S. in 1746 by way of Canada and was assigned to the missions of Illinois. He worked first at Fort Vincennes, then moved to the French areas of Illinois. After the French and Indian War M. subjected himself to Bp. Briand of Quebec and was named vicar general of the French settlements W of the Mississipi. He was exiled by the Spanish commandant of the area, however, and went to English territory in Illinois, where he spent the rest of his life. During the earliest days of the settlement of St. Louis, Mo., he ministered to the people there. He labored as a secular priest after the suppression of the Jesuits in 1775.

[J. R. AHERNE]

MEXICO, a republic in N America, bordered on the N by the U.S. and on the SE by Guatemala and British Honduras (760,290 sq mi; pop [U.N. est. 1973] about 54,300,000). Of the pop., about 30% are Indian, 60% mestizo, and 10% white. The Indians are from many different ethnic groups, half of them with their own languages. Indian civilizations with a notable culture, esp. the Mayan and the Aztec, flourished in Mexico before the coming of the Spaniards. F. de Córdoba visited the coast (1517) as did Juan de Grijalva (1518). These were followed (1519) by Hernán Cortés who founded the city of Vera Cruz and proceeded within 12 years to take the Aztec capital, Tenochtitlán. The Aztec chiefs were captured and executed and the way was opened for the complete conquest of the land. In 1527 the *audiencia* of Mexico was set up; this was a court with executive powers and served as a curb upon the powers of Cortés. In 1535 the *audiencia* was superseded by a vice-royalty, with Antonio de Mendoza as first viceroy. Spanish rule lasted 3 centuries. Under it the Indians were Christianized, the great mineral wealth developed, agriculture and stock raising were encouraged, and a European culture was superimposed upon the people. Printing was introduced (1539) and Mexico had a university by 1553. But there were abuses that increased as time went on. The Indians were exploited; there was bad feeling between Spaniards of Mexican birth and those who came from the homeland to occupy the more lucrative positions in the government and the economy; there was much official corruption; and the wealth of the country was continually drained off to Spain. Under the influence of ideas of the Enlightenment, Spain effected some reorganization in the political and economic structure in the 18th cent. but not enough to put an end to the discontent with Spanish rule. An opportunity for successful revolt came with Napoleon's subjugation of Spain. The revolutionary period ended with separation from Spain and the brief attempt at an empire by A. Iturbide. In 1823 a republic was established. Between 1838 and 1848 Mexico lost half its territory to the U.S.

The evangelization of Mexico was the joint work of priests of various orders—Franciscans, Dominicans, Augustinians, Carmelites, Benedictines, and Jesuits. Among them were linguists, educators, preachers, builders, historians, and protectors of the Indians. Colonial Mexico was to a great extent, the work of their hands. Their literary output was impressive, their educational effort remarkably successful despite the difficulties that had to be faced. The provincial synods, the seminaries, colleges, hospitals were evidence of the activity of the Church. At the end of the 16th cent. there were 473 parishes in the country; later (1644) the number of priests was 6,000. During the 18th cent. there was a notable decline; vocations decreased and seminary training deteriorated. The bps. were shackled by their subordination to the representatives of the crown. Evangelization came to a standstill. Independence began under good auspices but the situation took an unfavorable turn. Rome was slow in providing bishops. Political leaders were antagonized by ecclesiastical opposition to reform measures, an opposition that stemmed in large part from the Church's dependence for the support of its institutions on a system of landholding that required readjustment. The constitution of 1857 and laws enacted in the years that followed decreed the separation of Church and State. Much church property was nationalized; many priests and religious were expelled. For long periods these laws were not rigorously enforced, but the Constitution of 1917 revived and extended them. Federal and state authorities were given power to regulate religious worship, to limit the number of priests and to control their activities. The enforcement of these laws, esp. under A. Obregón and P. Calles, led to bloody persecution, which abated somewhat during the presidency of L. Cárdenas (1934–40) and that of A. Camacho (1940–46), during which time many of the restrictions were lifted in practice.

At present Mexico is divided into 11 Archdioceses and 50 dioceses. There are 6,619 diocesan priests and 4,605 male religious, of whom 2,649 are priests. Female religious number 21,982. There is a religious revival among the laity, many of whom are active in the various lay movements of the time. Mexico has a Foreign Mission Society of its own. Catholic education is prospering; the Universidad Iberoamericana is its symbol. Among popular devotions, that to Our Lady of *Guadalupe retains its favored position. Among the obstacles to be overcome are remnants of superstition, the inadequacy of religious instruction, the appeal of spiritism, religious indifference among students and intellectuals, atheistic propaganda, and the impossibility of the priests taking part in the public life of the nation. Protestantism has been at work in Mexico since the time of Juárez. Among the bodies active there are the Iglesia Nacional Presbiteriana, the Convención Nacional Bautista, the Southern Baptist Convention, and the Svenska Fria Missionen. The eschatological and holiness bodies have been esp. active. Total national membership in Protestant denominations has passed the one million mark. BIBLIOGRAPHY: D. Olmedo, NCE 9:770–775, 775–783; R. E. Quirk, *Mexican Revolution and the Catholic Church 1910–1929* (1973).

[P. DAMBORIENA]

MEXICO CITY, CATHEDRAL OF. The old cathedral built on the ruins of an Aztec pyramid was begun in 1524, the present one begun (1563) to the west, in the area of the sacred precinct, the upper façade, with towers by Manuel Tolsá and crossing dome (1787–1813) in Spanish Herreran style, with Mexican notes in fluted pillars and arches, an 18th-cent. late-baroque façade, the interior rich in 17th- and 18th-cent. styles, the great gilded retablo and the enormous *Altar de los Reyes* (1718–37) by Gerónimo Balbas whose innovative *estípite* finally revolutionized Mexican church design—(into Texas and Arizona). The monumental retable façade is Mexico's spectacular contribution to art.

[M. J. DALY]

MEY, GUSTAV (1822–77), influential pastoral theologian and catechist, whose writings link catechetics to a living liturgy and a kerygmatic theology that invites active participation of the young in a vital response. He studied at Tübingen, was ordained in 1847, and exercised pastoral ministry at Schwörzkirch, Oberschwaben, from 1858. He had an effect on both the Munich school and the Vienna school of catechetics.

[E. J. DILLON]

MEYENBERG, ALBERT (1861–1934), Swiss theologian and teacher of homiletics, credited with raising the standard of preaching in his day, and influencing the liturgical movement. He was ordained priest in 1885 and taught at one time or another moral and pastoral theology, NT exegesis, pedagogy, catechetics, and homiletics. His experience prepared him well for restoring preaching to its roots in liturgy, Scripture, and sound theology. He was editor of the *Schweizer Kirchenzeitung* (1900–23). His principal writing is a life of Jesus. BIBLIOGRAPHY: J. Bondallaz, DTC 14:27–57.

[E. J. DILLON]

MEYER, ALBERT GREGORY (1903–65), cardinal abp. of Chicago. In the view of many observers, M. was the intellectual and moral leader among American bps. of the 20th century. While the two differed in many ways, M. can be compared to Card. Gibbons as a leader of American Catholicism. A native of Milwaukee, Wis., M. was ordained in 1926. Trained in biblical studies, he taught at St. Francis Seminary in Milwaukee and was rector from 1937 to 1946, a position from which he exerted great influence on the formation of clergy. In 1946, M. was named bp. of Superior, Wis., where he exercised pastoral concern. Promoted to abp. of Milwaukee in 1953 he embarked on a program which encompassed the building of over 30 churches, 70 parish schools, 40 convents, 3 hospitals, and 3 high schools. In addition he created a new college and aided 7 existing ones. He was president general of the National Catholic Educational Association (1956–57) and as chairman of the Department of Education of the National Catholic Welfare Association (1956–59) encouraged organization of Catholic laity. In 1958, M. was appointed abp. of Chicago and in 1959 was created cardinal. He served on Pontifical Biblical Commissions and the Commission for Revision of the Code of Canon Law, was a member of the Congregation for the Propagation of the Faith, of Seminaries and Universities, and of the Holy Office. As abp. of Chicago M. supervised a prodigious growth in Catholic churches, schools, high schools, and institutions. Perhaps his most notable achievements were in the spiritual realm, where he proved a great leader. Nothing in his career was more significant than his courageous fight for justice to blacks. He became a national force in this question and was one of the chairmen of the National Conference on Religion and Race convened in his archdiocese in 1963. As an influential participant in Vatican Council II M. was outstanding in innumerable presentations. Just to list the areas where his voice was heard is to gain an idea of the weight he exercised on the Council. He acted as one of the 12 presidents of the Council. He actively influenced the schema on the liturgy, on the Church, on the Church and the modern world, on ecumenism, on religious liberty, on non-Christians, on revelation, and on the priesthood. When there was a move to postpone the vote on the schema on religious liberty, M. led a group to appeal against the decision to Pope Paul VI. The Council demonstrated that M. was undisputed intellectual leader of the U.S. hierarchy. It may be said that he was the victim of the absorbing work of Vatican II, since he died prematurely in 1965.

[J. R. AHERNE]

MEYER, EDUARD (1855–1930), prolific, wide-ranging German Protestant historian, whose special interest was the origin of religions, esp. early Judaism and primitive Christianity. He taught at Halle (1879–1902) and Berlin (1902–23). He was a pioneer in relegating to the background the contributions of the Greeks, and he viewed Christianity as the product of the myth-making of the masses. His masterpiece is the 8-part, 5-volume *Geschichte des Altertums* (1884–1902).

[E. J. DILLON]

MEYNELL, ALICE CHRISTIANA (THOMPSON; 1847–1922). It is a judgment on the vagaries of literary fashion that M., justly famed in her time for her poetry—at once cerebral and passionate—and for essays that gleam like marble, should no longer command a wide audience. Of English birth she was educated at home in Italy, where the family lived during her childhood, by her father who was a charming dilettante. M. became a Catholic at the age of 20. Her friendship with the young priest who received her into the Church and who was a sympathetic critic of her early poetry was foregone, needlessly one would believe today, and that event became the inspiration of her many poems of renunciation. Praised for her work by Tennyson and Ruskin, she published the first small collection, *Preludes,* in 1875. In 1877 M. married Wilfrid Meynell, a journalist. The couple had 8 children. With her husband she shared the task of editing *The Westminster Gazette,* diocesan weekly of London and later the magazine *Merrie England*. Somehow she found time to contribute to the leading periodicals of her day such as *The Athenaeum* and the *Saturday Review*. A series of published essays appeared, *The Rhythm of Life* in 1893 (together with *Poems,* a revision of the first work), *The Colour of Life* (1896), *The Spirit of Place* (1899), *Ceres Runaway* (1909), *The Second Person Singular* (1921). New volumes of the poetry appeared: *Later Poems* (1902), *Poems* (1913), *A Father of Wonder* (1917), *The Poems of Alice Meynell* (1940).

Both her poetry and prose received praise from the critics of her age. In 1913 there was much support, popular and critical, for the movement to select M. as Poet Laureate. Some years before, the great satirist Max Beerbohm had complained good-naturedly that Mrs. Meynell was destined to become a sort of substitute for the English Sabbath. Both her multitudinous essays for newspapers and journals and her published books reveal a poet of restraint but great power and an essayist whose condensed and disciplined style demonstrated a perceptive observer of life. A major center of literary life in London, M. could well be termed the architect of the Catholic literary revival in England. BIBLIOGRAPHY: V. Meynell, *Alice Meynell, a Memoir* (1929).

[J. R. AHERNE]

MEYNELL, WILFRED (1852–1948), journalist, editor, an English Quaker who converted to Catholicism, M. married Alice Thompson (*Meynell) in 1877. Husband and wife founded a periodical *Merry England,* in 1883. Secretary to Card. *Manning, he edited the Westminster diocesan weekly, the *Weekly Register,* from 1881 to 1899. He contributed much to a number of periodicals including *The Dublin Review,* and frequently wrote under the pen-name, John Oldcastle. When editor of *Merry England,* he discovered the poet Francis Thompson, whom he rescued from despair and to whom he remained a lifelong friend. As managing director of the publishing house of Burns and Oates he published Thompson's poetry and essays. M. established the reference work, the Catholic *Who's Who*. With Alice he presided over the extraordinary salon at Palace Court where a brilliant group of writers gathered regularly. Among his published works are *John Henry Newman* (1890), *Benjamin Disraeli* (1903), *An Unconventional Biography* (written under his pseudonym), *Verses and Reverses* (1912), and *Rhymes with Reasons* (1918). He edited the collected works of Alice Meynell and Francis Thompson. M. was a man of great charm and abundant kindness, who encouraged young, beginning writers. In 1945 he was named a Commander of the British Empire for his contribution to letters. BIBLIOGRAPHY: V. Meynell, *Francis Thompson and Wilfred Meynell* (1953).

[J. R. AHERNE]

MEZGER, the family name of three brothers, Bavarian by birth, distinguished Benedictines, and luminaries of the Univ. of Salzburg. **Franz** (1632–1701) taught theology and made numerous translations from the *Maurists. **Josef** (1635–83) taught hermeneutics and polemics, and was an intimate friend and correspondent of Mabillon. He was succeeded as vice-chancellor by his younger brother **Paul** (1637–1702), whose *Theologia scholastica secundum viam et doctrinam d. Thomae* (4 v., 1695) is highly commended by Grabmann. All lived at the Abbey of St. Peter in Salzburg.

[T. GILBY]

MEZUZAH (Heb., doorpost), parchment on the front of which are written two Scripture passages, Dt 6.4–9 and 11.13–21, with the divine name Shaddai (Almighty) on the reverse. It is placed in a cylindrical container, which is attached to the right doorpost of a house in literal obedience to Dt 6.9 and 11.20. A Talmud tractate is devoted to regulations for the mezuzah.

[T. EARLY]

MEZZABARBA, CARLO AMBROGIO (*c.*1685–1741), unsuccessful envoy of Pope Clement X in 1719 to seek imperial support against Jesuit adoption of Chinese rites. M. afterwards became bp. of Lodi in Italy. *CHINESE RITES CONTROVERSY.

[J. R. AHERNE]

MEZZOFANTI, GIUSEPPE (1774–1849), Italian priest, teacher, Roman canon, Vatican librarian, curial cardinal, and linguist who spoke or understood 70 different languages. He was ordained priest in 1797 and taught various languages at the Univ. of Bologna for many years before being called to Rome in 1831 as a canon of the basilica of St. Mary Major. He was prefect of the Vatican library in 1833, canon of St. Peter's basilica, and finally cardinal (1838), after which he held various curial posts. He died in Rome.

[E. J. DILLON]

MICAH, BOOK OF. Very little is known of Micah except that he was a prophet of the southern kingdom, a contemporary of Isaiah (many of whose prophecies he probably knew), whose work probably dates from *c.*740–687 B.C.. If we assume (though this is still sometimes disputed) that the "weal" oracles as well as the "woe" oracles contained in his book are substantially authentic, it falls into two main parts each of which contains a section of "woe" or prophetic threats (ch.1–3; 6) followed by a shorter section of "weal" or prophetic promises (ch.4–5; 7). The sins he attacks are luxury, oppression of the poor, idolatry, listening to false prophets, superstitious reliance on the cult without true interior righteousness, and a general breakdown of morality among the people. Because of all this Jerusalem is to be destroyed (3.12). One of the outstanding characteristics of Micah is that he presents Yahweh's accusations against Judah as a cause at law in which witnesses are called, etc. (cf. esp. ch.1,6). In his "weal" oracles he depicts a restoration of Zion (4.6–10) and of the house of David to inaugurate the messianic age (5.1–6). BIBLIOGRAPHY: B. J. Copass and E. L. Carlson, *Study of the Prophet Micah* (1950); C. J. Lindblom, *Micha literarisch untersucht* (1929); A. George, "Le Livre de Michée," DBSuppl 5 (1952) 1252–63.

[D. J. BOURKE]

MICHAEL THE ARCHANGEL, ST., with Gabriel (Dan 8.16) and Raphael (Tob) one of the three angels whose name is given in the Bible. Michael is identified in Dan 10.13; 12.1 as an archangel, i.e., a chief prince, because he is deputed to be the guardian over Israel. (Because of this text *Pseudo Dionysius, who gave the West most of its angelology, assigns only groups or peoples to the tutelage of the angels; for him there are no personal angel guardians.) In the NT Jude 9, in a passage derived from a now-lost part of the *Assumption of Moses* (see APOCRYPHA), NT, alludes to a struggle between Michael and Satan over Moses' body. In Rev 12.7–12 he is the leader of the angels in victory over the dragon and the dragon's angels. Michael is the first of the archangels to have an individual liturgical cultus in the Church before the 9th century. His legenda recount an apparition at Gargano in S Italy (Monte Sant'Angelo); the great Abbey of Mont Saint-Michel in Normandy founded in 966 was built on the site of a shrine in Michael's honor dating from the early 8th century.

[T. C. O'BRIEN]

MICHAEL III (836–867), **BYZANTINE EMPEROR** from 842. A child when he first ascended the throne, M. had no part in the decision in 843 of his mother, the regent Theodora, to quash *iconoclasm. Later, however, M. himself took steps to assure the complete elimination of that heresy at the synod of 861, for which he requested papal aid. When Pope Nicholas I intervened in the Eastern Church's controversy about the validity of Patriarch Photius's accession, M., who consistently supported Photius, agreed to a rehearing of the case, but he refused to obey Nicholas's order to reinstate Ignatius. M. attended the synod of 867 that condemned the Pope, but he was assassinated before taking any action. BIBLIOGRAPHY: F. Dvornik, *Photian Schism* (1948).

[R. H. SCHMANDT]

MICHAEL IV, BYZANTINE EMPEROR 1034–41. A man of humble origin, M. became emperor through the efforts of Zoë, wife of Romanus III who died under suspicious circumstances. Zoë at once married M. and the patriarch Alexius performed the coronation. In church matters M. gave the patriarch a free hand, and he allowed his unscrupulous brother John Orphanotrophus to handle most of the domestic affairs of the government. M. devoted himself to military matters, successfully upholding the empire's authority in the Balkans. He suffered from epilepsy, and as his disease worsened he abdicated and entered a monastery that he had previously founded. BIBLIOGRAPHY: Ostrogorsky Charanis.

[R. H. SCHMANDT]

MICHAEL VII DUCAS (Parapinaces; 1059–78), **BYZANTINE EMPEROR** from 1071. Eight years old at his father's death, M. lived under the regency of his mother, who married the military commander Romanus Diogenes and proclaimed him coemperor. When Romanus was defeated by the Seljuk Turks in 1071, M. was proclaimed sole emperor. The 12-year-old emperor's rash call to the Turks to fight for the Byzantine cause in Asia Minor led to Turkish usurpation of that area. Under the influence of the eunuch Nicephoritzes and his disastrous policies, M. was forced to abdicate and became a monk in 1078, but soon died.

[J. R. AHERNE]

MICHAEL VIII PALAEOLOGUS (1224 or 1225–82) **BYZANTINE EMPEROR** from 1259. A prominent nobleman at the Byzantine court exiled at Nicaea, M. in 1259 usurped the throne, thus establishing the dynasty which would rule the empire until its end in 1453. By clever diplomatic maneuvering rather than by military means he strengthened the empire, recovered the capital from the Latins in 1261, and defeated the ambitions of the powerful Charles of Anjou to conquer Byzantium. In order to restrain Charles, M. sent envoys to the Council of Lyons II (1274) at which a union of the Roman and Byzantine Churches was proclaimed. The rejection of this union by the vast majority of his subjects caused serious internal problems, and the union died with him. BIBLIOGRAPHY: D. J. Geanakoplos, *Emperor Michael Palaeologus and the West* (1959).

[G. T. DENNIS]

MICHAEL I, THE SYRIAN (1126–99), **PATRIARCH OF ANTIOCH** from 1166, monk and historian. He was a monk and archimandrite of his monastery before becoming patriarch. He was noted as a reformer of his (Monophysite) Church. His writings include a chronicle in Syriac which spans the period from creation to 1199; it is valuable because it incorporates otherwise lost Syriac documents. The original Syriac version was found in 1888. BIBLIOGRAPHY: R. Browning, NCE 9:794.

[J. R. RIVELLO]

MICHAEL CERULARIUS, PATRIARCH OF CONSTANTINOPLE (1043–58). Trained for the civil service, Michael became a monk, apparently under political pressure, and on being named patriarch by Constantine IX, set out to assert the superiority of the spiritual power over the secular. He cleverly resisted the Emperor's attempts to effect a closer union with the papacy and, together with Card. *Humbert of Silva Candida, the papal envoy, is regarded as responsible for the schism of 1054 (see SCHISM, EAST-WEST). The power he wielded in political affairs made him unique among the patriarchs of Constantinople. Extremely popular with the crowds in the capital, he was able to force the Emperor to yield. He was no theologian and was vindictive, ambitious, and inflexible. Eventually in 1058 he was deposed and died the next year. BIBLIOGRAPHY: Beck, 535–538; F. Dvornik, CMedH² 4.1 ch.10; T. Niggl, LTK 7:396–397.

[G. T. DENNIS]

MICHAEL III, PATRIARCH OF CONSTANTINOPLE (1170–78), opponent of reunion with the Latin Church at the time of the westernizing emperor, Manuel I Comnenus. When Pope Alexander III, at Manuel's invitation, sent a delegation to Constantinople to discuss reunion of the Churches, M. composed his *Dialogues* (1171) strongly denouncing papal primacy. He declaimed against historical arguments as determinants of ecclesiastical jurisdiction and rank, insisting that circumstances dictated such matters. He declared that he preferred to be subjected to Muslim secular rule than to Latin spiritual authority. The patriarch's efforts succeeded; the Greek Church renewed its schism from Rome. M. also obstructed the emperor's efforts to restore the Armenians and the Jacobites to Orthodoxy. BIBLIOGRAPHY: V. Laurent, DTC 10.2:1688–74; S. Runciman, *Eastern Schism* (1955).

[R. H. SCHMANDT]

MICHAEL OF BOLOGNA, see AIGUANI, MICHELE.

MICHAEL OF CANTERBURY, important English architect developing a native style in St. Stephen's Chapel

(1292) and Cheapside Eleanor Cross (1291). M. was also leader of the London School of tomb masters (Tomb of Abp. Peckham, Canterbury Cathedral).

[M. J. DALY]

MICHAEL OF CESENA (*c.*1270–1342), Franciscan minister general, theologian. He entered the order *c.*1284 and, having just completed his doctorate in theology at Paris, was elected general in May 1316. At first working harmoniously with John XXII in ending the dispute with the Franciscan Spirituals, he led the order in its critical attack on that Pope in the contest over apostolic poverty. Under the protection of Louis of Bavaria, who in 1328 had been crowned emperor in Rome against the wishes of Pope John, he alienated most of his Franciscan support and left Italy for the safer climate of Germany. Other leading figures in his entourage were William of Ockham and Bonagratia of Bergamo. The general chapter in Perpignan (1331) expelled M. from the order. Until his death he continued to write in defense of his position. BIBLIOGRAPHY: D. L. Douie, *Nature and the Effect of the Heresy of the Fraticelli* (1932) 153–201; J. Campbell, NCE 9:797.

[O. J. BLUM]

MICHAEL OF MALEINOS, ST. (894–961), Byzantine hermit and monastic founder. A member of the imperial family named Manuel, he was brought up at the Byzantine court. In 912 he became a monk. In 918 he withdrew to solitary life on a cliff and, a year later, to a desert. In 921 he founded a monastery at Xerolimni in Bithynia. In the following year he founded the monastery of Maleinos on Mt. Kyminas and served as its *higoumen* (superior) until his death. He was the spiritual father of St. Athanasius the Athonite. BIBLIOGRAPHY: M. C. Hilferty, NCE 9:797; L. Petit, "Vie de s. Michel Maleinos," OC 7:543–603.

[M. R. P. MCGUIRE]

MICHAEL DE NORTHBURGH (d. 1361), English ecclesiastic and diplomat; bp. of London (1354). Pluralist, king's secretary, and keeper of the privy seal, he represented Edward III in France, Flanders, and Rome. Oxford-educated, he compiled a lost *Concordancia legum et canonum*. He bequeathed great sums to the London Carthusians and St. Paul's cathedral and scholarships to Oxford law students. BIBLIOGRAPHY: Robert de Avesbury, *De gestis Edwardi tertii,* Rolls S 43 (1889) 358–60, 367–69, for Michael's description of English military action (1346); C. L. Kingsford, DNB 14:632–633; Emden Ox 2:1368–70.

[R. W. HAYS]

MICHAEL DE SANTIS, ST. (1591–1625), mystic of Spanish birth. M entered the Trinitarian Order in 1607. After ordination he manifested extraordinary mystical gifts. From 1622 prior at Valladolid, he was a famous preacher. M. was canonized in 1862.

[J. R. AHERNE]

MICHAEL SCOT (d. 1235?), scientist, translator of Arabic scientific works into Latin. Born in Scotland, he was in Toledo in 1217 and Bologna in 1220, and may have taught at Paris. Elected abp. of Cashel (1227), he resigned unconsecrated. His last years were spent at Frederick II's court. The leading Western European intellectual of his day, M. helped to introduce and spread knowledge of Aristotle, Averroës, and Avicenna. M.'s own writings include *Liber introductorius,* on astronomy and astrology; *Liber particularis,* written to answer Frederick's questions; *De secretis naturae,* on physiognomy; and probably a commentary on John of Sacro Bosco's *Sphere*; a *Theorica planetarum*; and a treatise on alchemy. M. was primarily an astrologer at a time when astrology involved knowledge of astronomy, meteorology, and medicine; and theories of cosmology, sociology, and psychology. He had extensive knowledge of occult arts, but contrary to later legend, condemned magic as evil. BIBLIOGRAPHY: L. Thorndike, NCE 9:798 (bibliog.).

[R. W. HAYS]

MICHAELIS, JOHANN DAVID (1717–91), Bible scholar. M. studied Oriental languages at Halle, and taught at the Univ. of Göttingen where he published his German translation of the OT (13 v., 1769–83) and of the NT (2 v., 1788–92). He also wrote several other treatises on biblical philology and textual criticism.

[T. M. MCFADDEN]

MICHAELIUS, JONAS (1584–?), the first clergyman of the Reformed Dutch Church in North America. He was a graduate of the Univ. of Leiden and served as a pastor and as a chaplain of the West India Company before coming to New Amsterdam (now New York City) in 1628. The Dutch had practiced their religion there for several years without formal organization. M., in April 1628, summoned them to a convocation and, with about 50 Walloon and Dutch communicants, secured the organization of the Reformed Dutch Church, which worshiped in the Collegiate Church now famous in New York City. He returned to The Netherlands in 1632 and remained there. The *Reformed Church in America traces its American origins to his efforts. BIBLIOGRAPHY: E. Eekhof, *Jonas Michaelius* (1926).

[E. EENIGENBURG]

MICHAELMAS, feast day of *Michael the Archangel, which in the Middle Ages was a holyday of obligation. In England, Michaelmas was one of the legal quarter-days for paying rents and settling financial accounts. It was a festive holiday characterized by extensive hospitality. In the present liturgical calendar the feast of Michael, together with the Archangels Gabriel and Raphael, is celebrated on September 29th.

[T. M. MCFADDEN]

MICHAUD, JOSEPH FRANÇOIS (1767–1839), editor and historian. M. was a pioneer historian of the Crusades who urged interpretation of the Crusades as an historical force with far-flung consequences for the civilization of Europe, rather than as a religious experience. His great work is *Recueil des historiens des Croisades*. BIBLIOGRAPHY: A. S. Atiya, *Crusade: Historiography and Bibliography* (1962).

[B. F. SCHERER]

MICHEL, ANTON (1884–1958), historian. Ordained in 1909, he studied theology at Munich and taught at Freising Hochschule (1929–49). A self-taught historian, his method and substance in more than 50 books and articles on the Byzantine Church and the Eastern Schism helped revive interest in this field and in Byzantine studies generally. BIBLIOGRAPHY: B. Kotter, LTK 7:403.

[R. I. BURNS]

MICHEL, VIRGIL (1890–1938), Benedictine of St. John's Abbey, liturgist, and educator. While a student in Europe he became convinced of the importance of the liturgical movement which was already astir there and making notable forward strides. After returning to the U.S. he strove successfully to interest American Catholics in the movement. He founded the liturgical magazine *Orate Fratres* (later, *Worship*) in 1925 and a few years later he established the Liturgical Press. He also did important work in the field of religious education, planning and editing a series of books intended for graded instruction in religion from first grade through college. Some of these he himself wrote and others he coauthored. The eight volumes of the *Christ-Life Series in Religion* for the grades were published 1934–35. Of the *Christian Religion Series* for high school, only one volume appeared before M.'s death. Two volumes in the college series were published, *Our Life in Christ* (1934) and *The Christian in the World* (1937). In addition to these activities he was a leader in the Catholic social movement during the depression years. BIBLIOGRAPHY: P. Marx, *Virgil Michel and the Liturgical Movement* (1957); *idem*, NCE 9:800–801.

[N. KOLLAR]

MICHELANGELO BUONARROTI (1475–1564), Italian sculptor, painter, architect, poet. Apprenticed (1488) to the Ghirlandaio brothers, M. early evidenced his genius in sculpture, copying at the Medici gardens (1489) Lorenzo the Magnificent's antique carvings.

In Rome (1496–1501), M. received a commission for the *Pietà* (1499, St. Peter's, Rome), which proved to be one of his great masterpieces. Returning to Florence (1501) he executed the gigantic, magnificent *David* (1504), placed at the entrance to the Palazzo Vecchio, town hall of Florence.

In competition with Leonardo da Vinci he contracted to execute a battle fresco in the Chamber of the Great Council of the Palazzo Vecchio. Though never painted, M.'s cartoon of the *Battle of Cascina* established his reputation. He painted the ceiling frescoes of the Sistine Chapel (1508–12) for Pope Julius II, a monumental Renaissance work embracing Greek and Christian motifs in a concept of generic grandeur. M. later undertook the long and litigious assignment of the tomb for Pope Julius, carving for it his dynamic *Moses,* and the *Slaves*—a Neoplatonic concept of the soul captive in matter. He then completed his celebrated figures for the tomb of Giuliano and Lorenzo de'Medici (1519–34) in the New Sacristy, S. Lorenzo, Florence. During this time M. emerged as a poet, in powerful sonnets and madrigals which put him in the front rank of Italian Renaissance writers. He worked on *The Last Judgment* (1534–41) in which, 20 years after the exaltation of the ceiling painting, M., in a tortured baroque of grotesque and violent forms, expressed his soul's agony amid the turmoils and frustrations of a divided Christendom rushing toward the fearful Christ as Judge among hurtling, damned and awe-filled trumpeting angels.

With the expected virtuosity of the Renaissance, M. proved himself master architect. in his design for St. Peter's Basilica (1557). Respecting the original plan of Bramante, M. conceived a domed Greek-cross design, which, because of later modifications, can be seen today only from the W (apse) end, a "sculptured" architecture, moving dynamically, majestically to the most impressively beautiful dome in the world.

Further works are the *Bruges Madonna* (1501); a relief and a painting of the *Holy Family* (1506); *St. Matthew* (1506); the grand staircase, Laurentian Library, S. Lorenzo (1534–59); the *Medici Madonna*; frescoes in the Pauline Chapel (1542–50); the impressive piazza at the Campidoglio (1539); the Farnese Palace (1546); and others too numerous to mention, yet all too impressive to be overlooked.

Religiously M. was a man of profound piety, esp. in his later years, with a deep sense of human dignity that was heightened rather than diminished by his recognition of man's total dependence on his Creator. He moved from the idealized forms of an earlier Renaissance to the tortured baroque—a supreme genius transcending rules—in heroic, generic, cosmic concepts. Dying of fever in Rome, M. was buried at Sta. Croce, Florence. BIBLIOGRAPHY: J. A. Symonds, *Life of Michelangelo* (2 v., 1893); C. de Tolnay, *Michelangelo* (6v., 1943); L. Goldscheider, *Michelangelo: Paintings, Sculpture, Architecture* (4th ed., 1964); G. Brandes, *Michelangelo: His Life, His Times, His Era* (tr. H. Norden, 1967); A. Candivi, *Life of Michelangelo* (tr. A. S. Wohl, 1975).

[D. G. NUGENT]

MICHELET, JULES (1798–1874), historian of France. After a brilliant academic record, became professor at the École Normale. In 1833 he began the monumental *History of France* which led him to be critical of the Church. In 1851 he opposed the coup of Napoleon III and was exiled for a time. BIBLIOGRAPHY: G. P. Gooch, *History and Historians in the Nineteenth Century* (2d ed. 1952).

[B. F. SCHERER]

MICHELI, ROMANO (1575–1659), Italian composer and contrapuntist. He studied under Francesco Soriano. He was ordained a priest *c.*1610), became *maestro di cappella* at the Church of Concordia at Modena (1616), and at the Church of S. Luigi de'Francesi, Rome (1625). His works include canons, madrigals, Masses, psalms, and motets.

[R. J. LITZ]

MICHELOZZO (*c.*1396–1472), Italian architect and sculptor, working with Ghiberti and with Donatello collaborating on many tombs but influenced by Brunelleschi in his most important Palazzo Medici-Riccardi (Florence, 1444–60) which established the type of the Italian Renaissance palace, embodying principles of symmetry and mathematical arrangement with its rectangular groundplan, three-story elevation, courtyard, and antique cornice. M., under Cosimo de'Medici, restored the ruined Monastery of S. Marco, was chief architect at the Duomo, Florence (1446–51), and engaged in numerous other important projects. Though a close follower of Brunelleschi, his style is unique. BIBLIOGRAPHY: O. Morisani, *Michelozzo architetto* (1951).

[L. A. LEITE]

MICHIGAN, a Great Lakes state, admitted to the Union (1837) as the 26th state. The first permanent settlement was made at Sault Ste. Marie (1668), while Antoine de la Mothe Cadillac founded (1701) Fort Pontchartrain, now Detroit. In 1763 the area passed into the control of the British, who did not evacuate their garrison at Detroit until 1796, when the U.S. finally took control of the territory. The Jesuits C. Raymbault and I. Jogues, accompanied a French expedition into Michigan (1641) and were probably the first missionaries in the area. Thereafter the French maintained a series of missions in Michigan. Protestantism came to Michigan along with the British and Americans. State-wide denominational organization began (1836) with the establishment of the Michigan Conference of the Methodist Episcopal Church and of the State Baptist Convention. The Presbyterians founded the Synod of Michigan the following year, and the Lutherans established a Synod Conference in 1840. Leo XII created the Diocese of Detroit (1827), but F. Résé was not named as its first bp. until 1833. In addition to organizing parishes for Irish and German Catholics, Résé was chiefly concerned with caring for the poor. He was succeeded (1841) by *P. P. Lefevere, who constructed a new cathedral, SS. Peter and Paul, and sponsored two hospitals, including the first hospital in Michigan to care for the mentally ill. At the time of his death (1869), there were 150,000 Catholics, 88 priests, and 80 churches in the diocese.

Following the administrations of C. H. *Borgess (1870–87) and J. S. Foley (1887–1918), M. J. Gallagher served as fifth bp. of Detroit (1918–37). Of the 105 new parishes which he opened, almost one-third were national churches. Gallagher also founded Sacred Heart Seminary, and he supported colleges begun by Dominican Sisters and by Sisters of St. Joseph. The Archdiocese of Detroit, was created in 1937 with E. F. Mooney the first archbishop. Suffragan to Detroit were the Dioceses of Marquette in Wisconsin, and Grand Rapids, Saginaw, and Lansing in Michigan. Mooney concentrated upon charitable and educational work, beginning missionary work in inner city parishes and promoting the Catholic Youth Organization Home for Boys, the Kundig Center and Carmel Hall for the aged, and Our Lady of Providence School for retarded girls. Before his death (1958) he had doubled the number of Catholic elementary and high schools. Mooney's successor, Abp. J. F. Dearden, initiated day schools for retarded children, homes for the aged, and a student exchange program with Latin America. An outspoken advocate of racial justice, he organized the Archbishop's Committee on Human Relations (1960) and became one of the leading members of the American hierarchy. In 1976 Michigan's Catholics numbered 2,277,609 or 25.3% of the total state population. The major Protestant denominations are the Methodist Church, with 3.9% of the total population in 1971, and the Lutheran Church (Missouri Synod) with 3.2%. The Jewish population (1968) was 97,995 or 1.11%. There are 8 Catholic colleges in Michigan, with a total enrollment of 16,490 students. Five of these colleges, with an enrollment of 13,203, are in the Archdiocese of Detroit. Some 42,398 students attend the state's 71 Catholic high schools, 48 of which are in the archdiocese and enroll 26,887. There are almost 106,322 pupils attending the state's 350 Catholic elementary schools. This includes 65,649 pupils in the 166 Catholic elementary schools of the archdiocese. BIBLIOGRAPHY: F. C. Bald, *Michigan in Four Centuries* (1954); G. W. Pare, *Catholic Church in Detroit, 1701-1888* (1951).

[J. L. MORRISON; R. M. PRESTON]

MICON (fl. *c.*480–460 B.C.), great Athenian classical painter, less famous than his contemporary Polygnotus. M.'s greatest works were Amazonomachies in the Stoa Poikilé and in the Sanctuary of Theseus, Athens.

[M. J. DALY]

MICON OF SAINT-RIQUIER (Michon, Mico; d. 865), French monk and teacher esp. of prosody and grammar; poet. He contributed a unique *Florilegium* which has marginalia and alphabetical listings for major and minor classical poets. His own poetical works are not extraordinary; but are of historical worth. His works also include: *Exempla diversorum auctorum* and *De primis syllabis*. BIBLIOGRAPHY: E.R. Cortius, *European Literature and the Latin Middle Ages* (tr. W. R. Trask, repr. 1973);

[J. R. RIVELLO]

MICROLOGUS, a literary form of the Middle Ages presenting a précis or explanation of a topic. The *Micrologus de ecclesiasticis observationibus*, falsely attributed to Ivo of Chartres, should be ascribed to Bernold of Constance, a

Benedictine monk (d. 1100) who wrote during the Gregorian reform. By appealing to such ancient authorities as Leo I, Gelasius, and Gregory I, the author of this commentary on the liturgy sought to establish a liturgical uniformity based on Roman practice. The work as it has come down to us (PL 151:973–1022) is composed of three parts: the Sacrifice of the Mass. the four ember fasts, and the rest of the ecclesiastical year. It argues for a reduction and simplification of Mass prayers.

[J. E. LYNCH]

MICRONESIA, one of the three main divisions of *Oceania (*c.*300 sq. mi.; pop. 754,557). Its chief archipelagos are the Caroline, Marshall, and Mariana Islands. The Carolines were discovered in the 16th cent. and named in honor of Charles V. The Marianas (called also Marianne or Mariana Islands) were found in 1521 by Magellan, who named them Ladrone Islands. They were renamed in 1667 for Maria Ana of Austria. The Marshalls, discovered by Saavedra in 1529, take their name from the British navigator who together with Capt. J. Cook explored them in the 1780s. All the islands belonged to Spain from 1668 to 1898 and were administered from the Phillipines. Spain ceded Guam to the U.S. in 1901. About the same time Germany purchased the other islands, but lost them to Japan in 1914. They became a U.S. trusteeship in 1947. Spanish Jesuits reached the Marianas in 1668. Mission work continued until the expulsion of the Society in 1767, but by that date most of the natives had been baptized. The Carolines were first visited by Jesuits from the Marianas and then evangelized by Augustinian missionaries. The Carolines and Marshalls together form a vicariate. Guam was made a diocese in 1965, with Agaña its see city. The see is suffragan to San Francisco, California. The first native Micronesian bp. was ordained in 1970.

[M. J. SUELZER]

MICY, ABBEY OF, former monastery of St. Stephen and St. Mesmin (or St. Maximin: Lat. Maximinus) near Orléans, France. It perhaps dated from Euspicius, priest of Verdun (d. 510) and his nephew St. Maximinus, first abbot and patron saint (d. 520) and was founded on land given by Clovis (508) at the time of Bp. Eusebius. Destroyed by soldiers of Charles Martel in 732 and restored for Benedictines by Bp. Théodulf of Orléans with monks introduced by St. Benedict of Aniane (*c.*814), it was plundered by the Normans in 856 and 897, rebuilt in the 10th cent. under abbots Létald, Thierry, and Annon, suffered greatly during the Hundred Years' War, was largely destroyed by the English during the siege of Orléans (1428), and pillaged by the Huguenots in 1562. Abbot François de la Rochefoucauld introduced the Feuillant Cistercians in 1608; they stayed until the French Revolution, the abbey being totally destroyed in 1792. Its last abbot was executed during the September massacres. BIBLIOGRAPHY: Cottineau 2:1845–46.

[E. J. DILLON]

MIDDLE ACADEMY, The Platonic school founded by *Arcesilaus of Pitane, who emphasized extreme logical scepticism. *GREEK PHILOSOPHY 3 d.

[M. R. P. MCGUIRE]

MIDDLE PLATONISM, a term employed to designate a body of doctrines that go back in part to *Plato, *Speusippus, and *Xenocrates of Chalcedon and in part are borrowed from *Aristotelianism, *Stoicism, and *Neopythagoreanism. It flourished in the first 2 cent. A.D. and is marked furthermore by a preoccupation with theology and a religious way of life. Among its chief representatives it will suffice to mention *Plutarch of Chaeronea, *Albinus, *Apuleius of Madaura, and *Celsus. Middle Platonism is esp. important because, along with Neoplatonism, it is the form of Platonism that exercised the major Platonic influence on Early Christian philosophy and theology. BIBLIOGRAPHY: CHGMP 53-83. *GREEK PHILOSOPHY 4 c.

[M. R. P. MCGUIRE]

MIDDLETON, THOMAS COOKE (1842–1923), church historian. He belonged to a Philadelphia Quaker family that entered the Catholic Church in 1854. M. became an Augustinian and was ordained in 1864. His life as a priest was spent at Villanova College (Pa.) where for 58 years he functioned as teacher, vice-president, president, local superior, and secretary to the provincial. A founder of the American Catholic Historical Society of Philadelphia (1884) he served as its president from 1884 to 1890, director of its publication and editor of *Records of the American Catholic Historical Society* from 1899 to 1905. Much of M.'s writing was devoted to Augustinian history in the U.S.

[J. R. AHERNE]

MIDIANITES in the OT, an Arabic nomadic tribe reputedly kin to the Israelites (Gen 25.1–4), who lived E (and probably W) of the Gulf of Aqaba. They were at first friendly to Moses who had married one of their women (Ex 2.15–22), but later they aided Moab in battle against the Israelites (Num 22.4–6; 25; 31). At the time of the Judges they used camels in frequent raids against the Israelites until soundly defeated by Gideon (Jg 6–8; cf. Is 9.3; 10.26; Ps 83.9). BIBLIOGRAPHY: EDB 1411–12; G. M. Landes, InterDB 3:375–376.

[E. MAY]

MIDRASH (pl. Midrashim), Jewish method of searching (cf. the Heb. *daraš,* to search) the Scriptures with a view to discovering the deeper meaning held to underly the most minute details contained in the sacred text. The main characteristics of midrash are: (1) that it always takes as its starting-point an actual text or texts (often two quite different passages are combined) from the Bible itself; (2) that it is always homiletic, essentially designed to edify and instruct; (3) that it is based on a close and detailed scrutiny of the actual text, in which it seeks to establish the underlying reason for each word, phrase, or group of words (cf. the rabbinical method of systematically applying the question ''why?''); (4) that it is always concerned to apply the message thus established to the present age. Midrash is divided into *halacha* (oral law), midrashic investigation of the legal parts of the OT with the aim of establishing rules of conduct, and *haggadah*, a similar investigation of the nonlegal parts with a view to edifying or instructing. Numerous examples of midrash in most, if not all, of its various forms are held to be present in the New Testament. Thus Mt 2.1–12 (the first part of the Infancy Narrative) is held to be a midrash on Num 24.17. Mt 27.3–10 (the 30 pieces of silver) is regarded as a midrash on Zech 11.12–13 and Jer 32.6–15. Midrashic elements are also present in Paul (Gal 3.4; Rom 4.9–11; 2 Cor 3, etc.) and other areas of the New Testament. It is important, therefore, for the interpretation of the NT to understand the characteristic methods and approach of midrash. The term midrash is also used of the collections of midrashic expositions; or of a manner of religious teaching that follows the midrashic method. BIBLIOGRAPHY: R. Bloch, DBSuppl 5:1263–81; J. W. Doeve, *Jewish Hermeneutics in the Synoptic Gospels and Acts* (1954); J. Bonsirven, *Exegèse rabbinique, exegèse paulinienne* (1939); H. Strack, *Introduction to the Talmud and Midrash* (Eng. tr., 5th ed. 1945); B. Gerhardsson, *Memory and Manuscript: Oral Tradition and Written Transmission in Rabbinic Judaism and Early Christianity* (1961).

[D. J. BOURKE]

MIÈGE, JOHN BAPTIST (1815–84), Jesuit missionary and bishop. A native of Savoy, M. was ordained in 1847. Coming to the U.S. in 1848 he joined the Jesuit Missouri province. In 1850 he was named vicar-apostolic of a vast territory east of the Rockies embracing 500,000 square miles. M. lived with the Pottawatomi Indians at St. Mary's Mission. In 1855 he made his residence at Leavenworth, Kansas. M. brought several religious communities to his vicariate, built an academy, an orphanage, a hospital, a seminary and erected a cathedral. In 1874 he resigned his position. In 1877 he became the first president of Detroit College (now University). His last days were spent in retirement at Woodstock, Md., as spiritual adviser to his Jesuit colleagues.

[J. R. AHERNE]

MIELCZEWSKI, MARTIN (Mielcowski, Myltzewsky, Milchevsky; d. 1651), Polish composer. He was a member of the Warsaw court band (1638–44) and conductor of the band of the bp. of Plock (1645). M. composed 40 works in both traditional church style and in an expressive modern style. His works include *Cribrum musicum* (1643), a double canon; *Jesu hilf* (1659); and a concerto, *Deus in nomine tuo*. He was influenced by Italian composers Neri, Frescobaldi, Cazzati, Gabrieli, and Chiese.

[R. J. LITZ]

MIGDOL (Magdol), city of uncertain location in lower Egypt. The Semitic name meaning tower or fortress is found in three OT books; whether the references are to three separate places is unknown. A place on the route of the Exodus was called Migdol (Ex 14.2). Memphis, Tahpanhes, and Migdol were cities that had Jewish colonies during Jeremiah's time (Jer 44.1). Ezekiel used the phrase ''from Migdol to Syene'' to describe the extent of Egypt's territory (29.10).

[T. EARLY]

MIGETIUS (fl. 8th. cent.), teacher of unorthodox trinitarian doctrine at Seville about 780; followers were called Migetians. M. declared a gradual revelation of the Trinity in the persons of David (the Father), Jesus (the Son), and Paul (the Holy Spirit). Synods at Seville (782 and 785) condemned him. The replies of Elipandus, Bp. of Toledo, to M. gave rise to Spanish *adoptionism. BIBLIOGRAPHY: Bihlmeyer-Tüchle 2:81–82.

[T. C. O'BRIEN]

MIGNARD, brother artists of France. **Nicolas** (1606–68), religious painter and engraver. After study in France and Rome he worked in Avignon for 20 years. His portrait of Alfonse Louis du Pléssis de Richelieu (Avignon) is modeled harshly. Religious works (altarpieces at Aix, Sisteron, and Cavaillon) relate to Vouet, Poussin, and the Roman School. **Pierre** (*Le Romain;* 1610–95), pupil of J. Boucher and S. Vouet, and lifelong enemy of C. Le Brun. In Venice and N Italy in 1654, he settled in Rome (1636–57) knowing Correggio, A. Carracci, Reni, and Poussin. He executed altarpieces of the *Annunciation, St. Charles Borromeo Administering the Sacraments* (Narbonne); portraits of popes and of Roman society. In Paris (1657) he produced affectations (*Mignardés*) in court portraits insipid and cold in color (*Louis XIV as a Roman Crowned by Victory*) and continued his open opposition to Le Brun, upon whose death he assumed all his offices until his own death.

[M. J. DALY]

MIGNE, JACQUES PAUL (1800–75), French priest and ecclesiastical publisher. After his ordination in 1824, M. served as parish priest for 9 years. He then went to Paris and shortly thereafter founded his own printing and publishing establishment (Ateliers Catholiques) at Petit-Montrouge. This was destroyed by fire in 1868. Of his numerous publications the patristic series, *Patrologiae cursus completus,* is the most widely known. The Latin series, 221 volumes including indices (1844–55), covers Latin ecclesiastical writers from Tertullian to Innocent III. The Greek series, 166 volumes of Greek text, Latin translation, and indices (1857–66), contains the texts of Greek ecclesiastical writers from Clement of Rome to the Council of Florence. The best texts then available were used. In spite of its shortcomings this work is still indispensable. BIBLIOGRAPHY: L. Marchal, DTC 10.2:1722–40; A. Hamman, LTK 7:410–411.

[H. DRESSLER]

MIGNOT, EUDOXE IRÉNÉE (1842–1918), French abp. and essayist. Born at Brancourt (Aisne) and ordained in 1865, he was vicar general in Soissons in 1887, bp. of Fréjus in 1890, and abp. of Albi from 1899. In his essays he opposed the liberal Protestantism of L. A. Sabatier, favored critical historical studies, and opposed the vicious tactics of the *Integralists. While differing with A. *Loisy, he tried to prevent the latter's censure by Rome. He was one of the few bps. to support the Sillon of Marc Sangnier.

[E. J. DILLON]

MIGRANT WORKERS, farm workers who must change their location according to the area of agricultural needs during the different seasons. Because of this constant movement they are unable to establish permanent residence for their families. A Pontifical Commission for Pastoral Assistance to Migrants was instituted by Paul VI in 1970 under the general guidance of the Congregation of Bishops. In 1975 Paul VI expressed his concern for the "many problems that remain open involving the protection of the migrants' human dignity, the need for more equality in conditions of work, housing, protection and job training—not to mention their legitimate hopes for full enjoyment of civil rights, union rights, and educational rights." In the solution of these problems the American Church has been active, not merely because of the question of social justice and charity, but also because many of these workers, particularly in the Southwest, are Catholics. Most suitable to the migrant worker is an itinerant form of pastoral ministry in which opportunities are given them for attending Mass and receiving the sacraments, as well as services regarding health, instruction for children, etc. and for this purpose many Spanish-speaking centers for migrant workers have been established in more than 20 dioceses in SW United States. The Secretariat for the Spanish-Speaking of the U.S. Catholic Conference (USCC) is concerned with migrant workers and their pastoral needs along with their bilingual and bicultural religious and general education. This Secretariat acts as liaison for the Hispanics with the Church, civic and governmental agencies, and has regional offices in California, the Midwest, and the Southwest. The NE region of the country serves the Spanish-speaking through the NE Regional Pastoral Center for Hispanics, established in 1976 under the sponsorship of 35 bishops in 14 states from New England to Virginia. Among its activities is leadership training in the pastoral ministry. This Center has working relationship with the USCC Secretariat serving the same ethnical group. An apostolate serving about 100,000 migrant workers in metropolitan Miami has its headquarters at Centro Hispano Catolico in Miami, Florida.

[R. A. TODD]

MIGRATION COMMISSION, INTERNATIONAL CATHOLIC, see INTERNATIONAL CATHOLIC MIGRATION COMMISSION.

MIHAN, CHARLES, VEN. (d. 1679), Irish Franciscan martyr. When the edicts banishing bps. and regulars from Ireland were issued (1673–74), M. fled to the Continent. During his return voyage in 1678 his ship was forced onto the coast of Wales. He was arrested at Denbigh and imprisoned. During the Titus Oates Plot he was executed for being a priest.

MILAN, EDICT OF, an agreement reached early in 313 A.D. between Licinius and Constantine in Milan granting equal toleration to all religions in the Roman Empire and specifically recognizing the legitimacy of Christianity. The agreement climaxed earlier moves in this same direction: the edict of Galerius, Licinius, and Constantine issued at Sardica in April 311, allowing the Christians "again to exist" (Lactantius, *De mort. persec.* 34.4; Eusebius, *Eccl. Hist.* 8.17.9) and a letter written by Constantine to Maximinus Daia, after he had defeated Maxentius in 312, ordering him to stop persecuting the Christians. It is probable that at Milan the two emperors drew up general norms to be sent to various provinces. These have been preserved in a mandate sent by Licinius to the governor of Bithynia (Lactantius, *De mort. persec.* 48.2–13) and in similar instructions with some variations in detail to other governors (Eusebius, *Eccl. Hist.* 10.5. 4–14). The "edict" not only granted freedom of worship to Christians but the restoration of property to individuals and to the churches as corporations. It did not constitute Christianity as the state religion.

MILAN CATHEDRAL, Late Gothic structure in Italy begun 1386. Though nearest to a true Gothic cathedral in Italy it is actually through a succession of French and German architects a compromise between the *ad quadratum* of Master Jean Vignot of Paris and the *ad triangulum* of the German school, witnessing also, to the Italian rejection of dominant verticality, in a lack of height and absence of towers, yet in an abundance of delicate pinnacles, evidencing an Italian delight in the elaborate ornament of Late Gothic style. Milan's is the largest cathedral after St. Peter's, with five aisles and an aisled transept; the Baroque façade by Tibaldi (1607), is truly Italian in its alternating Greek pedimental and Roman arched window frames. The stained glass of the choir dates from the 19th century.

MILANESE (OR AMBROSIAN) CHANT, developed by St. Ambrose, one of several types of liturgical chant which evolved in the Western Church and later became absorbed by Gregorian chant.

MILANESE RITE, a non-Roman rite in the Western Church limited to Milan and some neighboring dioceses. Also called Ambrosian, after St. Ambrose, bp. of Milan (374–397); how much it owes to him is doubtful, but his name has been associated with it at least since the 8th century. The earliest such attribution is found in a short treatise on the various cursus or forms of the Divine Office used in the Church entitled *Ratio de cursus qui fuerunt ex auctores*, probably written by an Irish monk in France, with a clearer reference by Walafrid Strabo (d. 849) in *De rebus ecclesiasticis* 22. Discussion of the origins of the Milanese rite have raised questions that have not always received conclusive answers. Over the years three theories on its origin have been considered: (1) it is a development of the Roman rite; (2) it is an older Western rite which has survived only at Milan; (3) it is an Oriental rite introduced at Milan by the Greek Arian bp., Auxentius (or one of the other six Greek bps. who appear among the 10 predecessors of St. Ambrose), which, purged of heresy (it is suggested) by St. Ambrose, became the parent of the whole family of *Gallican rite. Given that all the Churches of the West received the faith and Scripture from Rome and given that these Churches must also have accepted from the same sources the first and essential liturgical formulas and rites, then with the widespread development of the liturgy during the 4th and 5th cent., as with other bps., the bps. of Milan, in order to meet the needs of the faithful, made adaptations and variations in the liturgy, and introduced new rites. Ambrose in *De sacramentis* (3.15), while affirming that his Church followed the leadership of Rome in all things by means of such conformity to the liturgy of Rome, defends the legitimacy of certain adaptations and variations in Milan. And so for practical purposes today the rite may be regarded as a use of the Latin liturgy, different from that of Rome in certain particulars.

In its development, with the exception of a few adaptations, probably adopted from Rome, a stability can be found in the rite during the 6th and 7th cent. with a revision probably taking place toward the end of the 8th century. The oldest extant evidence as to the nature of the rite is traceable to the 9th century. The traditions followed during the 10th to 14th cent. varied according to localities simply because during this period no typical edition of Milanese service books was made obligatory by the bishops. By the middle of the 15th cent. an episcopal decree regulating the calendar appeared. With the Roman Missal and Breviary becoming obligatory in the 16th cent., exceptions were made by Pius V for rites in existence for 200 years or more. With the assurance of its continuation the Milanese rite was in need of reform. A commission under the auspices of St. Charles Borromeo was established to bring about this reform and restore the rite to its original state. Although he removed the editing of service books from private initiative and creativity and published the first official calendar and Breviary, and although after his death a Ritual and Missal were published, the commission did not bring about a restoration but introduced changes not in accord with the ancient traditions of the rite. The end of the 19th cent. saw the beginnings of a new reform seeking such a restoration with the work continuing in this present age.

Although at present the rite is much like the Roman rite, particular differences exist in the Mass, Divine Office, and other services, e.g., at Mass the Offertory takes place before the Creed; there is different order of the ceremonies; baptism is by immersion.

[C. J. NOONE]

MILANTO, PIO TOMMASO (1689–1748) theologian. A Neapolitan, M. entered the Dominicans in 1704. His life was spent in the teaching of theology, from 1713 to 1743 at the Univ. of Naples. In 1743 he was named bp. of Castellamare. As a theologian M. sought a moderate position in moral theology. Among his works was *Theses theologico-dogmatico-polemicae* (1734).

[J. R. AHERNE]

MILCOM (Melchom), god of the Ammonites (1 Kg 11.5). The term is possibly a title meaning king (see Jer 49. 1, 3). The *high place Solomon built E of Jerusalem may have been for M. (1 Kg 11.7); the reference there to Molech may be a corruption of Milcom since Molech worship was in the valley of Hinnom (see 2 Kg 23.10, 13). A reference to *Chemosh as the god of the Ammonites is also perhaps a scribal error (Jg 11.24). Zepheniah protested against the worship of M. (Zeph 1.5). The Ammonite crown taken by David may have been from M. rather than the king (2 Sam 12.30).

[T. EARLY]

MILDRED, ST. (8th century), abbess of Minster-in-Thanet (England). She was the granddaughter of Penda, King of Mercia, educated in France. Her mother was St. Ermenburga whom she succeeded in office after many attempts had been made to marry her to various nobles. The date of her death is uncertain and for a long time both St. Augustine's and St. Gregory's at Canterbury claimed her relics. She was eventually buried in Holland. BIBLIOGRAPHY: Butler 3:91; L. E. Boyle, BiblSanct 9:479–482.

[R. T. MEYER]

MILESIAN SCHOOL, a school of Ionian pre-Socratic philosophers that flourished from the early 6th cent. B.C. until the fall of Miletus (494 B.C.). Its principal representatives were *Thales, *Anaximander, and *Anaximenes.

MILITARY CHAPLAINS, see CHAPLAINS, MILITARY.

MILITARY ORDINARIATE (U.S.), the canonically established nonterritorial diocese for those American Catholics and their dependents who are attached to, or affiliated with, the military forces. In addition, in those foreign countries where U.S. forces are stationed, all persons and their dependents who are employed by or engaged in diplomatic missions for the U.S. government belong to the Military Ordinariate. Since its members are found throughout the world, it is called a personal diocese or ordinariate, pertaining to certain classes of individuals. Patrick Hayes, then auxiliary of New York, was appointed as the first military ordinary in 1917. Previously, priests had served as chaplains but there was no military diocese. The present structure of the Military Ordinariate was established by a decree of the Consistorial Congregation (1957), and provides that the abp. of New York become Military Ordinary upon accession to his see. A chancery office is maintained in New York City where the baptismal, confirmation, and marriage records of Catholic servicemen are retained. The Military Ordinariate grants jurisdiction to those chaplains who receive permission to serve in the Armed Forces. Reserve unit chaplains are granted part-time spiritual jurisdiction over the Catholics in those units. BIBLIOGRAPHY: J. F. Marbach, NCE 9:847–848.

[W. J. TOBIN]

MILITARY SERVICE, see CONSCRIPTION.

MILL, JAMES, (1773–1836), Scottish utilitarian philosopher; ardent disciple of J. Bentham; close friend and mentor of D. Ricardo; and father of John Stuart *Mill. His early interest in the ministry and classical studies gave way to politics and writing. After years as a London writer for various reviews, he went on to become chief London administrator of the East India Company and was active in the formation of the Philosophical Radicals, who were influential in passing the Reform Bill of 1832. They had nine children. Mill's philosophy of education reflected a belief in the unlimited perfectibility of man through education. He put his theory to practice on his son, J. S. Mill, as narrated in the latter's *Autobiography*. M.'s writings include *Analysis of the Phenomena of the Human Mind* (1829) and several articles written for the *Britannica* (1816–23).

[E. J. DILLON]

MILL, JOHN STUART (1806–73), the most influential English philosopher of the 19th century. M.'s principal work, *System of Logic, Ratiocinative and Inductive* (1843), is a monumental presentation of empiricist thought and an attack on aprioristic intuitionism. In metaphysics, M. is a somewhat qualified follower of Berkeley; in political theory, a strongly modified follower of Bentham. M.'s publications were numerous and not yet collected, but his religious thought is to be found principally in the posthumous (1874) *Three Essays on Religion*. The first two show little regard for religion; the third, ''Theism,'' shocked his agnostic and atheist friends. M. states here that it is not unreasonable to hold that God exists, that the argument from design has merit. The human soul may be immortal. God is eternal, but not omnipotent; benevolent, but in need of man's help. Christianity is an inspiring and edifying belief that aids men to a grasp of the real, purely human, Religion of Humanity, or Duty. BIBLIOGRAPHY: Copleston 8:25–92, with bibliog. 529–531; J. B. Schneewind, EncPhil 5: 314–323.

[W. B. MAHONEY]

MILL HILL MISSIONARIES, a worldwide mission society of diocesan priests and brothers, officially named St. Joseph's Society for Foreign Missions, founded by Card. H. *Vaughan in 1866 at Mill Hill, London, England. The institute received papal approbation 1908 and is subject to the Sacred Congregation for the Evangelization of Peoples. Its apostolate is primarily to proclaim the gospel in unevangelized areas, and the activities of the society have spread through countries of Europe, Asia, Africa and the United States. The Josephite Fathers, now an independent community working among American blacks, originated in the U.S. when the Mill Hill Fathers established their first U.S. mission in 1871. Today Mill Hill has 1,086 members; 956 are priests. They maintain 26 houses with the general motherhouse located in London.

[R. A. TODD]

MILLAIS, JOHN EVERETT (1829–96), English painter, and child prodigy in the Royal Academy schools, M. was, with Rossetti and Hunt, one of the founders of the Pre-Raphaelite Brotherhood (1848) dedicated to the revitalization of art in an industrial society. His *Return of the Dove to the Ark, Christ in the House of His Parents,* and *Ophelia,* are masterpieces of Pre-Raphaelite expression. M. later became a fashionable academic artist enjoying contemporary acclaim, including a royal title and the presidency of the Royal Academy. BIBLIOGRAPHY: J.G. Millais, *Life and Letters of Sir John Everett Millais* (2 v. 1899); *Millais and the Ruskins* (ed. M. Lutyens, 1967); J. Maas, *Victorian Painters* (1969).

[F. S. GRUBAR]

MILLAN, PEDRO (fl. 1480 (?)–1520). Student of L. Mercadante whose work at Seville Cathedral portals was wrongly attributed to Millan, who, inferior to his teacher, did severely sharp images of a *Pietà* and *Virgin of the Pillar* in Seville Cathedral and a *Saintly Warrior* (U.S.).

[M. J. DALY]

MILLAR, MOOHOUSE I. X. (1886-1956), educator, writer. A member of an American family converted to Catholicism, M. entered the Jesuits in 1903 and was ordained in 1919. After assignment to several Jesuit institutions, M. joined the faculty of Fordham Univ., New York, where he served for almost 30 years. In collaboration with John A. Ryan he published in 1922 *Church and State.* In 1928 his *Unpopular Essays in the Philosophy of History* appeared. M. was associate editor and a frequent contributor to the quarterly review *Thought*.

[J. R. AHERNE]

MILLENARIANISM (Millennialism), a belief that Christ will establish a kingdom on earth for a 1,000-year period (Lat. *mille,* thousand; *annus,* year). Based upon a single passage, Rev. 20.1–10, this concept has given rise to varied speculation and hopes since the 1st century. According to the passage, Satan was to be bound for 1,000 years, and those who had not worshiped the beast or his image ''came to life again, and reigned with Christ a thousand years.'' Since this is an apocalyptic book and filled with imagery, there is need for caution about accepting literally the idea of a 1,000-year reign. Taken in context, the passage probably refers to the time between Christ's Resurrection and the end of the world, when Christ raises the dead, judges the world, and creates a new heaven and a new earth. Some early church Fathers (e.g., Justin and Irenaeus) shared the literal belief of a glorious millennial reign of Christ, but it was the *Montanists who not only taught this doctrine but predicted Christ's return at a particular date to establish his kingdom at Pepuza in Phrygia. Opposition of Alexandrian theologians, such as Origen, ended such literal views in the East, but they were preserved longer in the West. Augustine (*City of God,* 20.7–9) helped settle the question by identifying the Church with the Kingdom of God on earth. In the Middle Ages some briefly revived millennial hopes, and during and after the Reformation similar literal expectations were aroused. The *Anabaptists at Münster (*c.* 1534) expected the return of Christ to establish his kingdom there, and German *Pietism in the 17th and 18th cent. supported such ideas, as did the *Fifth Monarchy Men in 17th-cent. England. The *Plymouth Brethren in England (*c.* 1830) were millenarian and developed the basic ideas of *dispensationalism that were systematized and popularized by the *Scofield Reference Bible. Another independent millennial movement began in the U.S. when William *Miller worked out an interpretation of Daniel and Revelation, setting a date for Christ's return in 1843 or 1844. Out of this movement developed the *Seventh-day Adventists. The *Jehovah's Witnesses also hold millennial views but believe that the millennium has already begun. There are many millenarians in the United States. Some espouse premillenarianism, expecting a sudden return of Christ when certain conditions have been fulfilled. Postmillenarianism is the view that Christ's return, after the gospel has gradually permeated the world and after a Christian society has been established, will last 1,000 years, during which the Jews will be converted. Finally there will be an apostasy, a terrible conflict, and Christ will intervene to destroy the world after having raised and judged the dead. There are also amillenarianists, who do not take the idea of a millennium literally. BIBLIOGRAPHY: N. B. Baker, What Is the World Coming To? (1965); N. Cohn, *Pursuit of the Millennium: Revolutionary Millenarians and Mystical Anarchists of the Middle Ages* (rev. ed., 1970).

[N. H. MARING]

MILLENARY PETITION, an appeal, so named because it claimed the support of 1,000 ministers, made by Puritans in April 1603 to James I against ritual and ceremony. The petition led to the *Hampton Court Conference.

[T. C. O'BRIEN]

MILLENNIUM, a period of 1,000 years. In Rev. 20.4–6, a number of martyrs rise with Christ and reign with him 1,000 years until the second resurrection of all the faithful. In the original sense, if taken literally, the author may have looked to an indefinite peaceful reign of Christ after the end of a fierce persecution. If taken symbolically, it could mean that the first resurrection is Christian baptism, or Christ's victory through his death and Resurrection. The 1,000 years would be the period of the history of the Church until the second coming, or last judgment. The idea of a millennium is associated with Jewish hopes for the messianic era. Beginning with a number of the Fathers of the Church, various Christian groups have interpreted Revelation as predicting a literal 1,000-year terrestrial reign of Christ. BIBLIOGRAPHY: R. Kuehner and J. P. Dolan, NCE 9:854. *ADVENTISM; *JEHOVAH'S WITNESSES, *MILLENARIANISM.

[J. A. GRASSI]

MILLER, ATHANASIUS (1881–1963), Benedictine biblical scholar. Born in Wohlfartsweiler, Saulgau, Germany, he made his profession in the abbey of Beuron in 1902, was ordained in 1907, taught OT studies at Sant'Anselmo in Rome from 1922. He was appointed consultor to the Pontifical Biblical Commission in 1940 and its secretary in 1949. BIBLIOGRAPHY: DTC Tables générales: 3215.

[E. J. DILLON]

MILLER, WILLIAM (1782–1849), Baptist lay preacher, founder of modern *Adventism. The Seventh-day Adventists and other Adventist bodies ultimately trace their histories to his preaching and prophecies. M. received a sketchy education, took up farming in upstate New York, and served as a captain in the War of 1812. He became a religious skeptic but underwent a conversion in 1816 and began an intensive study of the Bible, esp. Daniel and Revelation, which led him in 1818 to the conclusion "that in about 25 years from that time all the affairs of our present state would be wound up.'' In 1831 he began to preach that Christ's second coming would occur in 1843 and was received in many Protestant pulpits. A Boston preacher, Joshua V. Himes (1805–95), became his patron and companion on lecture tours of New England, New Jersey, and New York. More than 700 Protestant ministers joined the movement and carried its message to W states; as many as 15,000 people attended Adventist rallies to hear M. expound his prophecies. He was licensed as a lay preacher in the Baptist Church, but his Adventist views began to trouble other clergymen, and he urged his followers to leave their Churches for the Adventist movement. When the end of the world did not come in 1843, Miller recalculated and set March 21, 1844, as the new date; he later revised it to Oct. 22, 1844. When that date also passed without incident, his followers became disillusioned. Between 50,000 and 100,000 Americans had expected the end of the world in 1844. Many Millerites returned to their former Churches or abandoned religion; a remnant remained convinced that the end was near. These small groups of Adventists organized the Adventist Churches, which survive and number more than 1,500,000 adherents around the world. M. never gave up belief in Christ's second coming, but ceased to try to fix its date. He took no active part in the new Adventist Churches and died in obscurity. BIBLIOGRAPHY: F. Nichol, *Midnight Cry* (1945).

[W. J. WHALEN]

MILLES, CARL (1875–1955), Swedish sculptor famous for numerous fountain groups in the U.S. where he settled (1929). In Paris (1897), M. was influenced by Rodin, Bourdelle, and Maillol, his figures in bronze moving toward elongated linear silhouettes with mannered gestures in *Jonah Fountain* (1940, Detroit), *The Hand of God* (1954, Sweden), *Trumpeting Angels* (1975, Philadelphia). BIBLIOGRAPHY: H. Cornell, *Millesgården: Its Garden and Art Treasures* (1960).

[M. J. DALY]

MILLET, JEAN FRANÇOIS (1814–75), French genre painter, most important member of the Barbizon school. M.'s romantic-realist paintings of peasants in monumental poses, endows them with a solemn grandeur. His denial of specific features through dramatically generalized forms (*The Sower, The Gleaners,* 1857) enhances them with universal significance, in serene compositions against landscapes filled with light and atmosphere, which strongly influenced later Impressionists. M.'s religious paintings (*The Angelus*, 1859) have been termed sentimental. His monumental work profoundly influenced Van Gogh and Seurat. BIBLIOGRAPHY: R. L. Herbert, *Barbizon Revisited* (1962).

[M. J. DALY]

MILLET, a Turkish word for ''religious community'' or ''people'' from the Arabic *millah,* the word in the Muslim Qur'an for the religion of Abraham and other prophets. In medieval Islamic states, it designated non-Muslim religious groups i.e. Christians and Jews. In the Ottoman Empire (1300 A.D.–1923 A.D.), millets were religious communities governed by an ecumenical patriarch (ethnarch, *millet-bashi*) who had responsibility to the central government for civil, social, and administrative matters including taxes and internal security. BIBLIOGRAPHY: G.A. Maloney, NCE 4:243–244; R. Janin, DHGE 13:626–728; G. Every, *Byzantine Patriarchate,* (2d. ed. London, 1962).

[F. H. BRIGHAM]

MILLS, SAMUEL JOHN (1738–1818), one of the founders of the *American Board of Commissioners for Foreign Missions (ABCFM). M., the son of a Congregationalist minister, while at Williams College, experienced a call to the mission during a famous ''haystack meeting'' in 1807. This experience led to the organization in 1810 of the ABCFM. As a licensed preacher M. made evangelizing tours of the Mississippi Valley in 1812 and 1815. After ordination (1815) he helped found the American Bible Society (1816). He also worked for the American Colonization Society, journeying to Africa to help purchase land that eventually became the Republic of Liberia. BIBLIOGRAPHY: P. J. Staudenraus, *African Colonization Movement* (1963).

[T. C. O'BRIEN]

MILMAN, HENRY HART (1791–1868), Anglican author, dean of St. Paul's. After holding a professorship of poetry at Oxford (1821–31) and serving as rector of St. Margaret's, Westminster (1835–49), M. was made dean of St. Paul's (1849). In his most famous work, the *History of the Jews* (1829), he gave offense to some by treating the OT Jews with the critical eye of the modern historian. His *History of Latin Christianity* (1855) is also well known and contributed notably to an increase of interest in the medieval period. BIBLIOGRAPHY: DNB 36 (1894) 1–4; C. Smyth, *Dean Milman* (1949).

[R. B. ENO]

MILNER, JOHN (1752–1826), vicar apostolic of the Midlands, England, titular bp. of Castabala. One of the most influential, if controversial, vicars apostolic in the days before the establishment of the Catholic hierarchy in England, M. attended the English College at Douai, France, and was ordained in 1777. Assigned to the parish at Winchester, he designed its striking Gothic church. An enthusiastic antiquary, he was elected to the Society of Antiquaries in 1790. His archeological study, *The History, Civil and Ecclesiastical, and Survey of the Antiquities of Winchester* (2 v. 1796–1801) is a standard reference. His life was so crowded with controversy and political activity, it is amazing that he found time to write. In addition to the above mentioned, he wrote extensively on theological and controversial issues. The great cause agitating English Catholics was the attainment of Catholic Relief Acts, from the first in 1778 until the final one in 1829, an effort for emancipation from the disabilities they had suffered since the time of Henry VIII. The precise form emancipation should take was a matter of long and bitter controversy. The Catholic Committee (made up chiefly of laymen led by C. *Butler) in 1791 agitated for Catholic Emancipation with a proviso that it include an oath of allegiance to the Crown in a form repudiated by the vicars apostolic. As their theological advisor M. offered vigorous opposition to the proposal. He went to London to press his opposition with such leaders of Parliament as Burke, Pitt, and Fox, and succeeded in killing the offensive proviso of the oath. In 1803 M. was named vicar apostolic of the Midland district. A new conflict arose from a proposal that the crown should have veto power over Catholic bps. appointed to the United Kingdom. M.'s opposition to this measure alienated him from the activist Catholic lay group as well as from the other vicars apostolic, but brought him the support of the Irish hierarchy. The Holy See was not in agreement with him on this question, but in a long stay in Rome in 1814 as agent of the Irish bps. he won tacit approval of his stand. (When the

Catholic Relief Act of 1829 was finally passed, the question of the veto was omitted.) In spite of public activity, M. was a zealous pastoral prelate. His introduction of devotional practices less cold and forbidding than those in vogue in England in his day, changed English piety. Cardinal Newman calls M. the ''Athanasius of England.'' His principal theological published work was *The End of Religious Controversy. . .* (1818), which ran through 11 editions.

[J. R. AHERNE]

MILTIADES, ST. (Melchiades, d. 314), **POPE** from 310 or 311, elected after a vacancy of some months owing to either the persecution under Galerius or to dissension in the Church over the reconciliation of those who had lapsed under its fury. The Edict of Toleration (311) led to the restoration of confiscated church property and M. arranged for its administration. Constantine made a gift of the Lateran Palace to the Church after his victory of 312, and it became the residence of the popes. From 313 the initiative in ecclesiastical affairs was assumed in large part by Constantine whose shadow obscures the role and activities of the Pope. It was Constantine who directed a commission of bps. under M.'s presidency to pass judgment on the claim made by the Donatists in Africa that Cecilian had been invalidly consecrated bp. of Carthage. The decision favored Cecilian. M. was buried in the cemetery of Callistus, the last of the popes to be placed in the catacombs. BIBLIOGRAPHY: A. Amore, BiblSanct 9:488–491; Butler 4:528–529.

[P. F. MULHERN]

MILTIADES (fl. 2d cent.), Christian apologist. Although all of his works are lost, some information about him is found in Tertullian and Eusebius. A native of Asia Minor, possibly at one time a student of St. *Justin, M. wrote many apologetical works. One, addressed to the Emperor, was in defense of the Christian faith; others attacked the Greeks, the Jews (two books), the Valentinian Gnostics, and the Montanists. BIBLIOGRAPHY: Quasten 1:228.

[R. B. ENO]

MILTITZ, KARL VON (1490–1529), German curial diplomat. After study at Mainz, Trier, and Cologne, M. obtained through his uncle the post of papal notary and titular chamberlain *c.*1514. In 1518 he carried the papal Golden Rose to Frederick the Wise of Saxony, an honor intended at least in part to persuade Frederick to consent to Martin Luther's extradition to Rome for trial. Unsuccessful in this, M. attempted to mediate with Luther at Altenberg; he proposed that Luther undergo trial before the abp. of Trier; but both the Reformer and his supporters mistrusted the offer. Two further conferences with Luther (Liebenwenda, Oct. 1519; Lichtenberg, Oct. 1520) were likewise fruitless. M. held benefices at Mainz and Meissen from 1523 to 1529, dying before his 40th year by accidental drowning. BIBLIOGRAPHY: F. Lau, RGG 4:954; J. P. Dolan, NCE 9:858.

[M. J. SUELZER]

MILTON, JOHN (1608–74), English scholar, poet, political and religious pamphleteer. After early private tutoring, M. attended St. Paul's School in London and Christ's College, Cambridge (1625–32). He early determined to dedicate himself to poetry and to this end devoted the years 1632–38 to intense private study, first in England and then in Italy. He abandoned an intention to take holy orders and gave his distaste for ritualism as the reason. He was strongly opposed to the episcopal form of church government and hence favored the Presbyterians in their efforts to reform the Church of England. These sympathies, however, did not prevent him from disclaiming the extremes of Calvinist theology. He rejected the view that the Fall of man was the result of God's predestination and held that it was the consequence of man's free choice. Neither would he admit that the Fall resulted in the total depravity of human nature: grace was available to all, and by means of it all could repent and find salvation. After his wife, Mary Powell, whom he married in 1642, left him that same year to return to her royalist family, he wrote against the indissolubility of marriage. His pamphlets caused the Presbyterians to attack him, and the case was carried to Parliament because M. had published his views without censorship. To this he reacted with his *Areopagitica* (1644), his best known prose work, which vigorously defended the freedom of the press. M.'s concern for freedom, civil and religious, was a passion that dominated much of his thought. He began to dissociate himself from the Presbyterians and to give his support to the Independents. In 1649 his *Tenure of Kings and Magistrates* defended the Puritans' trial and execution of Charles I, and he was rewarded by being made Latin Secretary to the Commonwealth. In later years he became disillusioned when it became apparent that O. *Cromwell did not share his interest in complete disestablishment. Still, M. defended the Commonwealth to the end and, after the death of Cromwell in 1658, wrote *Of Civil Power in Ecclesiastical Causes* as a plea for religious toleration, and he fiercely opposed the Restoration, even as it was taking place, in *The Ready and Easy Way to Establish a True Commonwealth*. He was briefly imprisoned after the Restoration, but was granted amnesty.

M. achieved his first important success in poetry in his *Ode on the Morning of Christ's Nativity* (1629). Other early poems include sonnets (English and Italian), the *Arcades* (a pastoral), and the companion poems, *L'Allegro* and *Il Penseroso*. After 1639 he did not pursue any secular theme in his poems. In *Comus* (a masque), he emphasized the theme of chastity; in *Lycidas*, an almost perfect elegy commemorating his drowned friend, Edward King, he traced the path from despair to hope. His greatest work was *Paradise Lost* (1667), in which the blind M. asserted ''eternal Providence'' and justified ''the ways of God to men.'' This great classical epic is a masterpiece of construction and expression; its epic majesty, the organ-tone power of its blank verse, its felicity of language, its magnificent imagery (particularly in the epic similes) make it the single greatest poem in the English tongue. *Paradise Regained* (1671), built about the temptation of Christ in the wilderness, lacks the grandeur of *Paradise Lost*. *Samson Agonistes* (1671) was his last great poem, a tragic drama, Greek in form and Hebraic in theme.

In M. one sees a blend of Reformation theology and humanistic culture, but the mixture was modified by strong individualistic convictions. His *De doctrina christiana*, published posthumously (1823), contained views that would commonly have been regarded as unorthodox in the Protestant tradition with which he was associated, e.g., his opinion that the Son was not coeternal and coequal with the Father, that the world was not created from nothingness by God. Editions: H. Darbishire ed., *Poetical Works* (2 v., 1955); F. A. Patterson, *Works* (18 v., 1931–40); D. M. Wolfe, *Complete Prose Works* (1953). BIBLIOGRAPHY: D. Masson, *Life of Milton* (7 v., 1962); H. Belloc, *Milton* (1935); J. H. Hanford, *Milton Handbook* (1946); C. S. Lewis, *Preface to Paradise Lost* (1959); E. M. W. Tillyard, *Miltonic Setting* (1938).

[M. M. WILLS]

MILVIAN BRIDGE, the ancient *Pons Milvius,* now the *Ponte Molle,* over the Tiber, a few miles N of Rome. There in 312 Maxentius, emperor of Italy and Africa, was drowned with a number of his troops when the bridge collapsed as they fled Constantine after defeat at Saxa Rubra. The battle, somewhat inaccurately called that of the Milvian Bridge, was pivotal in Constantine's fortune. It also made him favorable to Christianity since he attributed his success to the cross affixed to his military standard (*Labarum*). The following years as senior ruler of the Roman Empire he established religious toleration. BIBLIOGRAPHY: N. H. Baynes, *Constantine the Great and the Christian Church* (1930).

[M. J. SUELZER]

MIND-BODY, the question of how mind and body in man function in respect of one another in view of their different modes of existence, the one spiritual and the other material. Recognized and treated in every age of Western thought since Ancient Greece, it has importance for both theology and philosophy in that solutions offered bear upon human moral freedom and personal immortality. Since the 17th cent., it has had unusual prominence for two reasons: (1) the growing influence of natural science which tended to interpret the universe according to a theory of mechanistic and materialistic determinism, admitting of no freedom and no purpose but only blind obedience to unalterable laws; and (2) the dualism of René Descartes (1596–1650), French philosopher and mathematician, which divided man into two separate and independent substances, mind and body, each having a nature radically different from the other, the one spiritual and conscious, the other material and extended. Speculation since has centered upon the character of the relation between these entities, at times questioning whether a relation is even possible. The following express representative solutions of which others are but variations:

Spiritualism or Idealism: According to this extreme view, matter either does not exist or is at best a mere appearance, an externalization of mind as the primary reality. Only mental events exist, and these include such phenomena as sense perceptions, ideas, thoughts, consciousness, and volitions, depending upon specific interpretations. The subjective idealism of George Berkeley (1685–1753), Irish epistemologist, typifies this position in its denial of matter, and insistence upon ideas directly caused by God as the only realities. Spiritualism thus attempts to eliminate the mind-body problem by ignoring one of its members, thereby distorting the nature of man.

Materialism: In general, materialism disclaims the existence of the spiritual or mental, making of mind a mere phenomenon attributable to physio-chemical processes. Every human action is a bodily event wholly explainable by the mechanical laws of matter. Mind is but an aura or shadow produced by biological changes giving rise to sensations, ideas, images, and other happenings variously called mental. This was the position of Thomas Hobbes (1588–1679), English philosopher, and later of the English biologist Thomas Huxley (1825–95) in his theory of epiphenomenonalism. Materialism, then, evades the problem by disavowing one of its sides with grave import for man's freedom and immortality.

Interactionism: In its generic form, this is the widely accepted common sense position that admits of causal sequences in which bodily events cause bodily events and mental events cause mental events. It also recognizes that bodily events cause mental events, and vice versa, as when physical health affects one's disposition or when worry or fear precipitates glandular secretions. Descartes tried to save both mechanistic determinism for physics and freedom for morality by posing a clear-cut distinction between mind and body, and accounting for their admitted interaction by resorting to the pineal gland in the human brain. While all material things function blindly in keeping with fixed laws, man's body is an exception since it is moved by mental events. Hence the gland is needed as the point of causal exchange between mind and body in the moving of which the latter move one another. Descartes' account preserves neither mechanism nor freedom nor clarifies interactionism.

Parallelism: Broadly, this attitude repudiates any causal interaction between mind and body while accepting a causal sequence within each of the two areas. Mental causes produce mental effects and bodily causes issue in bodily effects, the twin systems operating along parallel and nonintersecting lines of action. For every mental occurrence there exists a corresponding bodily one, and vice versa, with no causal link between the two. Each of the two complexes is distinct from the other but in complete harmony, concomitance and correspondence with it. The German philosopher, Gottfried Leibniz (1646–1716), best represents this theory in his contention that God, in creating minds and bodies has so arranged it that the two will proceed always in accord with his plan of preestablished harmony. The latter is such that the two realms function perfectly together in a manner consistent with the laws of each, while never being causally related. For parallelism, mind and body are like two perfectly synchronized clocks, but no real proof is offered as to how this is done.

The Double Aspect Theory: In this account, neither mind nor body is literally real, nor a completely separate and independent entity, for both are appearances or modes of a reality which is a third something. Mind and body are thus similar in that they are both aspects, though different aspects, of the same unknown which is itself truly real. Benedict Spinoza (1632–77), Dutch-Jewish philosopher, exemplifies this trend, holding as a pantheist that only God or Substance is the real, whereas mind and body are but its attributes. The actions of both are not their own but rather the operations of Substance under two different appearances. Ideas or states of mind correspond to bodily processes, but the two do not causally influence one another. Thus, this theory, like the others, fails to solve the problem.

BIBLIOGRAPHY: T. Hobbes, *Human Nature and the Elements of Law* (1650); T. Huxley, *Collected Essays* (1894–1908); G. Berkeley, *Dialogues between Hylas and Philonous* (1723); R. Descartes, *Meditations on The First Philosophy* (1641); G. Leibniz, *Monadology* (1720–1840); B. Spinoza, *Ethics* (1677).

[J. T. HICKEY]

MIND OF THE CHURCH. (1) In regard to matters of divine faith the phrase, further illumined by Vatican Council II, refers to the living understanding in the Church of the deposit of faith, the content of divine revelation. The Council teaches, in its clarification of *tradition, that the existing understanding of the realities and the words handed down grows: in the contemplation and study of the *faithful and their own perception of the spiritual things they experience; and through the preaching of those who have received through episcopal succession the sure gift of truth (Vat II DivRev 8). The mind of the Church is the mind of the believers in the ecclesial community. For the very *faith that makes them believers rests immediately on God's own infallible word; faith can never be anything but a principle of right understanding (see ThAq ST 2a2ae, 1. 3); there exist as well enlightening the mind of the Church the Holy Spirit and his *charismatic gifts, including *infallibility. The reality of the living mind of the Church is well outlined in these words of Vatican II: "The words of the Church fathers witness to the living presence of this tradition, whose wealth is poured into the practice and life of the believing and praying Church. Through the same tradition the full canon of the sacred books becomes known to the Church, and the sacred writings themselves are more profoundly understood and unceasingly made active in her; and thus God, who spoke of old, uninterruptedly converses with the Bride of His beloved Son; and the Holy Spirit, through whom the living voice of the gospel resounds in the Church, and through her, in the world, leads unto all truth those who believe, and makes the word of Christ dwell abundantly in them" (Vat II DivRev 8). (2) in regard to matters pertaining to the implications of the truths of faith, or to actual circumstances of the life of the faithful, the "mind of the Church" connotes a guiding indicator, a point of reference for Christian prudence. The directives of official teaching are worthy of religious assent and obedience of the faithful. The *sentire cum Ecclesia,* a harmony of judgment with church directives, is an acceptance of the fact that the Church gives wise guidance, that essentials of the gospel message can be realized in the Christian life through such guidance. The fact of growth in understanding with regard to the deposit of faith is an indication that there is place for discussion and rethinking in the Church. But it is a mark of Christian docility and of responsible membership to allow the "mind of the Church" in this second sense the hearing and the function it should be presumed to deserve. (See VatII ConstChurch 25.)

[T. C. O'BRIEN]

MINDEN TREASURE. Magnificent German collection of religious art housed in the 12th-cent. north tower of the Cathedral of Minden, containing Romanesque and Gothic reliquaries, ritual vessels and ivory carvings dating from Ottonian times.

[M. J. DALY]

MINDSZENTY, JÓZSEF (1892–1974), abp. of Esztergom, primate of Hungary; card., confessor of the faith, indomitable foe of Communism. He became the symbol of Eastern European resistance to the Communist overthrow of many countries. Born József Pihm, he took the name Mindszenty because in 1932 the Fascist regime in Hungary attempted to enforce German names on Hungarians and in defiance he adopted the name of his village. Of peasant origin he returned from the seminary each summer to help in the fields. Ordained in 1915 he served as a parish priest. When in the aftermath of World War I Bila Kun headed a Communist government in Hungary, M. was imprisoned for his opposition. In the post-Kun era, he wrote a book full of concern for his people, *Zala Cries Out for Help* (1927). In 1934 he published the results of a long history of Catholicism in Hungary entitled *The Life and Times of Martin Padanyi Biro*. When the Nazi movement in Germany produced a Fascist movement in Hungary, M. joined the Small Holders Party in opposition to the Hitlerian Arrow Cross. In 1944 he was made bp. of Veszprem, and in the same year was imprisoned, mainly because of his defense of the persecuted Jews. After his release from prison in 1945, he was appointed by Pope Pius XII abp. of Esztergom and as such primate of Hungary; in 1946 he was made cardinal. An outspoken enemy of the Soviet-dominated Hungarian regime, M. was the object of a long program of vilification, and was finally put under arrest in 1948. Foreseeing the move, the cardinal wrote a statement that even if reports said he had confessed to crimes against the State, he had nothing to confess. His trial showed the world a man who had been tortured, brainwashed, and forced into a false confession. For 7 years M. was confined in various prisons, refusing conditions put on his release: that he leave the country or refrain from public statements. In the Freedom Fighters' Revolution of 1956, he was freed, restored as primate, and regarded as a rallying point of the revolution. When Soviet intervention drove out the liberal government, he took refuge in the American legation at Budapest. In 1971 he was allowed to leave Hungary and the Holy See requested that he live in exile in Vienna, and there he died, obedient but protesting to the last. There are many who believe that this concession to the Communists was a betrayal of a genuine martyr, no matter how expedient a course it may have seemed. BIBLIOGRAPHY: József Cardinal Mindszenty, *Memoirs* (tr. R. and C. Winston, 1974); J. Vecsey and P. Schlafly, *Mindszenty the Man* (1972); G. N. Shuster, *In Silence I Speak* (research assistant, T. Horanyi, 1956).

[J. R. AHERNE]

MINERVA MEDICA, TEMPLE OF (Rome; 350 A.D.). Probably a nymphaeum, the decagonal building is crowned by a dome upon pendentives, the ribs of which meet in a ring about an *oculus*.

[M. J. DALY]

MING, JOHN JOSEPH (1838–1910), sociologist. Born in Switzerland where he entered the Jesuits, M. was ordained in 1868. In 1872 he came to the U.S. and taught at St. Francis Seminary, Milwaukee, Wisconsin. The last 20 years of his life were spent at St. Louis University. M., a pioneer Catholic sociologist, wrote numerous articles for the *American Catholic Quarterly Review*. Among his books were *The Data of Modern Ethics Examined* (1894) and *The Morality of Modern Socialism* (1909).

[J. R. AHERNE]

MINGES, PARTHENIUS (1861–1926), German Franciscan theologian, considered the best Scotist of modern times. He made his Franciscan profession in 1881, was lecturer in dogmatic theology at Munich from 1891 until 1906, and again from 1914 until 1918, and was prefect of the college of Quaracchi in Italy from 1907 until 1914. BIBLIOGRAPHY: W. Forster LTK 7:428; cf. DTC Tables générales: 3216.

[E. J. DILLON]

MINIMAL ART. Also termed primary structure, minimal art is an antithesis to abstraction which emphasized the spiritual in art, the inner spirit or force which determined or directed the forms. Minimal art is not expressive, has no personal mystical overtones. The minimal work, often machine-produced, is simply and purely an object—nothing more than what the spectator sees. (It is difficult to forget that all art is fundamentally a concept—an intuition—determined—no matter the degree of consciousness—by an innate aesthetic sense and cannot escape personal overtones).

[M. J. DALY]

MINIMS, a mendicant order of men religious founded in 1435 at Paola in Calabria, Italy, by St. Francis of Paola. They are so called because of their dedication to becoming least of all, that they may die to self and live in and for God. The members lead an austere and penitential life observing a vow of abstinence from meat, eggs, and dairy products. Their rule, approved by Rome in 1474, is original in content and gives testimony that prayer and penance facilitate union with God. The Minims engage in parochial ministry, preaching, and teaching. The order flourished in the 17th cent., at which time it had 400 houses and 9,000 members, while during the 19th cent., their apostolate suffered a severe setback as a result of anticlerical persecution. Today the Minims have a total membership of 254, including 180 priests. The order maintains 40 houses in countries of Europe and South America. The generalate is located in Rome.

[R. A. TODD]

MINISCULE, a type of biblical *Codex, distinguished from the earlier *uncial type by being written in a cursive hand. The earliest miniscule goes back to 835 A.D. and the latest to the 17th or 18th century. Over 2,500 such MSS of the NT have been catalogued, and in the modern system of reference to the NT text are designated by the word Codex plus an Arabic numeral.

[D. J. BOURKE]

MINISTER, a person performing spiritual offices in the Church. In both RC and Anglican usage, one who administers a sacrament is called a minister; the term is also a general designation for anyone having a function at liturgical ceremonies, e.g., as celebrant, deacon, subdeacon, or acolyte. In *Reformed Churches the term generally means an ordained clergyman, particularly a pastor. The usage follows John Calvin's idea of the minister as one who preaches the word of God, administers the sacraments, and shares in governing the Church. During the Reformation, in the C of E the term minister was preferred to that of priest to designate an ordained clergyman, but many today reverse the preference. The *free Churches use "minister." Luther used both minister and pastor, but modern Lutherans usually prefer the latter. In the U.S., minister is the most widely used designation for an ordained clergyman. Some denominations have lay preachers, but usually only ordained ministers administer baptism and the Lord's Supper. Many American Protestants currently stress the total mission of the Church in which all members share. Thus all members of the Church are ministers, but some are ordained to specialized Christian vocations. BIBLIOGRAPHY: H. R. Niebuhr et al., *Purpose of the Church and Its Ministry* (1956). *MINISTRY.

[N. H. MARING]

MINISTERS OF THE SICK, see CAMILLIANS.

MINISTRY, any apostolic or evangelical activity, a body of clergy, or the total mission of the Church; most properly, the threefold office for which ordination is conferred: the conduct of worship and administration of the sacraments, preaching, the care of souls. Biblical scholars differ as to whether the NT provides a clear pattern of ministerial offices, but Protestants generally believe the ministry began as flexible and functional, becoming standardized in the 2d century. The RC Church holds that the threefold ministry is divinely prescribed, and requires the sacrament of orders, received within the line of *apostolic succession. Eastern Orthodox Churches refer rather to a communal succession, i.e., sacramental grace for the ministry is conveyed through the community, the ordaining bp. acting as its representative. For Luther the *priesthood of all believers meant that every baptized person carries out the priestly vocation in his own way, but some by a specialized ministry; the continuity of the Church and the ministry derived not from apostolic succession, but from accord in the apostolic gospel. Luther insisted upon the need for ministerial education. Calvin, whose teaching was adopted with modifications by the *Reformed Churches, held that the NT established a fourfold office in the Church, that of pastor, teacher, elder, and deacon. The pastor's ministry included preaching, the care of souls, and teaching; it required special education. Ordination was by other ministers, but with the civil magistrates and congregation having rights of approval. Some early English Reformers maintained that no particular *church order was indispensable, but that in fact *apostolic succession survived in the English Church. Ordination by a bp. came to be regarded as necessary for the ministry, and holy orders is now regarded by some as a sacrament. For the *free Churches generally, the ministry has been less clearly defined, and ordination has been regarded more informally. The Anabaptists put emphasis on individual faith and ethical standards; any member was capable of holding pastoral office; choice by lot from the congregation was common; education was lightly regarded. Congregationalists and Baptists also emphasized a spiritual succession, and each congregation had the power to choose its minister. In early Baptist practice, one who ceased to be a pastor ceased to be ordained; ordination now is regarded as permanent, although revocable, and the larger Baptist bodies require special education of ministers. The Friends, or Quakers, in the beginning denied the necessity of an ordained ministry, but in the U.S. some groups have a minister. John Wesley wished to retain the apostolic succession for the Methodists but by force of circumstances had to ordain bps. himself (see METHODISM). In the U.S. the Methodists retained the episcopacy but disregarded apostolic succession. Most Methodists require special education for the ministry. In Protestant Churches generally, women are eligible to participate in the ministry, although they have not received full acceptance by the Churches.

In recent years an increasing emphasis on the ministry of the laity has been evident among Protestants in the United States. Thus the Churches engaged in the *Consultation on Church Union regard the ministry as the total mission to which Christ called the Church, but they agree on the necessity of a ministry that is specialized and representative. Clergy differ from the rest of the people of God functionally, not in status or special grace. Ordination would mean a recognition of qualifications, the conferral of responsibility for the ministry, and a prayer for God's blessing. These Churches would recognize episcopacy as a symbol of continuity, but not as embodying any particular theory of succession. BIBLIOGRAPHY: H. R. Niebuhr and D. D. Williams, *Ministry in Historical Perspective* (1956); E. P. Y. Simpson, *Ordination and Church Unity* (1966); *Ministry and the Sacraments* (ed. R. Dunkerley, 1937); *Consultation on Church Union: A Plan of Union* (1970).

[N. H. MARING]

MINNE (MHG, love), usually signifies courtly love (*hohe minne*), i.e., the idealized conventional love of medieval German **Minnesang* (courtly lyric), as opposed to uncourtly love (*niedere minne*). BIBLIOGRAPHY: O. Sayce, *Poets of the Minnesang* (1967).

[M. F. MCCARTHY]

MINNESANG, (the medieval German courtly lyric). This reflected the highly stylized conventions of courtly love (*minne*), whereby a knight hoped through the service (*dienst*) of praise to win the favor (*genâde*) of his gracious, but inaccessible, lady (*frouwe*). The most common forms of *Minnesang* are the *Wechsel* (dialogue), the *Frauenklage* (woman's lament), the *Tagelied* (dawn song), the *Kreuzlied* (crusader's song). Four possible origins of the genre have been suggested: (1) Arabian poetry at the court of Andalusia; (2) medieval Latin or vernacular lyrics, including hymns in honor of Our Lady; (3) classical Latin poetry, esp. that of Ovid; (4) indigenous popular poetry. Among the most important *minnesänger* were: *Early Minnesang* (*c.*1150–80): Der von Kürenberg and Dietmar von Aist; *High Minnesang* (*c.*1180–1250): Heinrich von Veldeke, Hartmann von Aue, Wolfram von Eschenbach, Heinrich von Morungen, Reinmar von Hagenau, Walther von der Vogelweide; *Late Minnesang* (*c.*1250–1350): Ulrich von Lichtenstein, Neidhart von Reuenthal, Johannes Hadlaub. BIBLIOGRAPHY: O. Sayce, *Poets of the Minnesang* (1967); B. G. Seagrave and W. Thomas, *Songs of the Minnesingers* (1966).

[M. F. MCCARTHY]

MINNESOTA, a north central state admitted to the Union (1858) as the 32d state. The first white men to enter the region came from New France and included R. de *la Salle, S. de *Champlain, J. *Marquette, and L. Jolliet. The area remained a French possession until 1763, when the British acquired the portion of Minnesota E of the Mississippi in the Treaty of Paris. The Spanish acquired the area to the W of the river. Eastern Minnesota became a U.S. possession after the American Revolution, and the W portion was joined to it by the Louisiana Purchase (1803). Catholic families began to move into the territory during the 1820s, settling around Ft. Snelling and Mendota. In 1839 Bp. M. *Loras of Dubuque and Father Anthony Pelamourgues came to the Ft. Snelling area and ministered to the 185 Catholics there. The following year Father Lucien Galtier established Minnesota's first permanent mission at Mendota. The settlement that developed around this mission eventually became the city of St. Paul. The Diocese of St. Paul was established (1850), with J. *Crétin as first bishop. By the time of his death (1857), he had built 29 churches and 35 stations, and had acquired 20 priests to care for the 50,000 Catholics in his jurisdiction. Immigration increased the Catholic pop. of the diocese to 130,000 by 1884, and to meet their needs Bp. T. Grace, OP, opened 143 new parishes and secured the assistance of numerous religious orders.

John *Ireland, appointed third bp. (1884), continued to serve St. Paul for 34 years, becoming (1888) its first archbishop. Ireland furthered the work of numerous societies and advocated the Faribault School Plan, which provided for rental of parochial school buildings by the local school board, which would then pay the teaching sisters. Austin *Dowling, the second abp., expanded facilities for teacher education and secondary education. In 1930 Dowling was succeeded by J. G. Murray, who met growing urban needs by establishing 59 new parishes in the Twin Cities metropolitan area. He also built a large Newman center and chapel at the Univ. of Minnesota and established a Catholic labor school in Minneapolis. William O. Brady served as abp., 1956–61. Leo Binz (1962–ret. 1975) was succeeded by John R. Roach (1975–) the present abp. whose see has 9 suffragans: Bismarck and Fargo, N.D.; Rapid City and Sioux Falls, S.D.; Crookston, Duluth, St. Cloud, New Ulm, and Winona, Minnesota. In 1976 the number of Catholics had reached 994,809 and comprised more than 26% of the total state population. The major Protestant denominations are the American Lutheran Church, with 12.9% of the total pop. in 1971, and the Lutheran Church (Missouri Synod), with 7.4%. Other Protestant denominations comprised 19.8% of the population. The Jewish pop. (1968) was 33,565 or 0.88%. The nine Catholic colleges in Minnesota have a total enrollment of 11,981 students. There are 29 Catholic high schools in the state, with an enrollment of almost 13,960. More than 57,373 pupils attend 235 Catholic elementary schools. BIBLIOGRAPHY: T. C. Blegan, *Land Lies Open* (1949); J. M. Reardon, *Catholic Church in the Diocese of St. Paul* (1952).

[J. L. MORRISON; R. M. PRESTON]

MINO DA FIESOLE (1429–84), Italian sculptor who did the earliest Renaissance bust of Piero de'Medici (1453) and portrait of N. Strozzi (1454). In Rome (1463) M. collaborated on the Benediction pulpit of Pius II, and the tomb of Pius II in 1474. M. executed the less austere tomb of Card. Cristoforo della Rovere (1480) and a *Madonna and Child* tondo related to Rossellino in mannered delicacy. Though M. admired Donatello, his work is sentimental in charm, forecasting tendencies of the later Renaissance.

[M. J. DALY]

MINOAN RELIGION, see CRETAN-MYCENAEAN RELIGION.

MINOCCHI, SALVATORE (1869–1943), Italian biblicist, expositor of *Modernism. He was ordained in 1892, incurred suspension in 1907, and abandoned the priesthood the following year. He founded in 1901 the review *Studi religiosi* and in his writings showed the influence of A. *Loisy and G. *Tyrell. In works on the OT, he took a rationalist position. *PASCENDI DOMINICI GREGIS; *LAMENTABILI.

[T. C. O'BRIEN]

MINOR ORDERS, see HOLY ORDERS.

MINOR PROPHETS, the authors of the 12 shorter prophetic books in the OT as contrasted with the 4 *major prophets: Isaiah, Jeremiah, Ezekiel, and Daniel. The minor prophets are: Hosea, Joel, Amos, Obadiah, Jonah, Micah, Nahum, Habakkuk, Zephaniah, Haggai, Zechariah and Malachi. Jonah is included here presumably because of his identification with the Jonah of 2 Kg 14:25. In reality the book bearing his name is an edifying novel rather than prophecy in the true sense. The major-minor distinction goes back to St. Augustine (*City of God*, 18.29) and refers only to the length of the biblical books, not their relative importance. BIBLIOGRAPHY: K. Elliger, *Das Buch der zwölf kleinen Propheten* in Das Alte Testament Deutsch (3d ed. 1956); G. A. Smith, *Book of the Twelve Prophets* Expositors Bible (1898); E. D. Jacob, S. Amsler and C. A. Keller, *Les Petits prophètes* (1966).

[D. J. BOURKE]

MINOR SOCRATIC SCHOOLS, a term conventionally employed in Greek philosophy to designate several schools founded by men who had been, or claimed to have been disciples of Socrates and continuators of his teaching, although at most they emphasized only one of or another aspect of his doctrine, and often with distortion. The schools in question were: the *Megarian, *Elean-Eretrian, *Cynic, and *Cyrenaic. BIBLIOGRAPHY: Copleston 1:116–123; Ueberweg 1:155–178.

[M. R. P. MCGUIRE]

MINORITIES, RIGHTS OF. The phrase concretely connotes civil and *human rights that cannot be justly denied because a person belongs to a minority group in a society. It is not being a member of a minority that gives the rights but being human and being a member of society as a whole (see DISCRIMINATION; EQUALITY; LEGAL JUSTICE; RIGHT AND RIGHTS). A more difficult issue is the way to guarantee rights to those against whom discrimination has been or is being practiced. That is the purpose of "equal rights" laws or movements: equal employment opportunity; open housing; equal rights for women; hire the handicapped, etc. The political consensus seems to be that legislation and practices favoring minorities are needed in order to redress wrongs or to compensate for past deprival, and to achieve social justice and equality. Such a consensus is justified when it is based on an intent for the common good, and for genuine human rights. It is not clear, however, that e.g., a female minor has a human right, or a right as a member of a minority, to have an abortion without parental consent. The fact that civil law concedes such a right does not give it moral rectitude. The advocacy of the rights of minorities also creates at times a further dilemma, arising namely when minorities are favored to such an extent that a reverse discrimination is worked on other members of society.

[T. C. O'BRIEN]

MINSTER, monastery, the church of a monastery, church without a monastery and, at times, a large church attached to an ecclesiastical group: Beverly Minster, York Minster.

[M. J. DALY]

MINTON, SHERMAN (1890–1965), justice of U.S. Supreme Court. A native of Indiana, M. practiced law in several states. In 1934 he was elected Democratic senator from Indiana, serving as supporter of the New Deal until defeated in 1940. In 1941 he was named to the U.S. Circuit Court of Appeals with its center in Chicago, Ill. In 1949 President Truman nominated him associate justice of the Supreme Court where he served for 7 years. In 1961 M. became a convert to Catholicism.

[J. R. AHERNE]

MINUCIUS FELIX (fl. 260–300), a Roman lawyer, probably of African origin, who wrote the very literate *Octavius,* an apology for Christianity in the form of a dialogue between Caecilius, a pagan, and Octavius, a Christian. Caecilius represents a skeptic who seeks security in adherence to the ancient Roman traditions; Octavius attacks pagan mythology and sets forth the case for monotheism but avoids discussion of the most distinctive points of Christian belief and worship. Scholars have long debated the relationship of the *Octavius* to Tertullian's *Apology*. Similarities cannot reasonably be explained without supposing a dependence, but the question as to which drew from the other has never been satisfactorily resolved. Text, PL 3:193–652; text and tr., ed. G. Rendall (Loeb v. 250) 314–437. BIBLIOGRAPHY: Quasten 2:155–163.

[R. B. ENO]

MIRACLE, a religious sign whereby God testifies to his saving presence by an extraordinary event. In the OT, the Hebrew word *môpet* (wonder) is used for such a religiously symbolic act, but the implication of an event beyond the forces of nature is not necessarily present. This follows from the nature of ancient Hebrew thought which regarded all of nature as wonder-filled (Job 4.8–10). The world is radically open to God's influence and if an event is described as a wonder, it is because it reveals God's special presence with his chosen people. The plagues in Ex 7.14–11.10, for instance, are regarded as signs of God because they accomplished the deliverance of his people, not because they contradicted any set laws of nature. This attitude largely carries over into the NT where wondrous deeds were accomplished by Christ and the Apostles. The theological purpose of the miracle story tradition in the NT is varied, and several different interpretations have been proposed; but the following classification of Christ's miracles is helpful: (1) The healing miracles—the Gospels record 17 miraculous cures. They are recorded to indicate that the signs foretold by Isaiah have been fulfilled: the blind see, the deaf hear, and the lame walk. The fact that these signs are accomplished by Christ demonstrates that the Messiah is at hand. (2) The nature miracles—Christ is often described as exercising power over the forces of nature. This is consistent with the gospel proclamation that Jesus enjoys the fullness of Yahweh's power to which all creation is subject. (3) The exorcisms—in contemporary Jewish apocalyptic thought, the world was held under the power of *Satan until the day of deliverance would be achieved by the *Son of Man. In order that the new kingdom of God be established, the reign of the devil had to be broken. (4) Pronouncement miracle stories—narratives in which the miracle is attached to an important saying of Jesus and seems to illustrate that saying. The raising of Lazarus is the occasion for Christ's words on Christian death and resurrection; the multiplication of the loaves and fishes is a foreshadowing of the Eucharist. Thus the miracle story in the NT is not an invention of later Hellenistic Christians nor is it an extrinsic apologetical proof of Christ's divinity; rather, it is an intrinsic part of the gospel message and a vehicle for its proclamation.

This awareness of the nature of a miracle as a religious sign is evident in the patristic period and in early scholastic thought. Both St. Augustine and St. Thomas Aquinas defined a miracle primarily in terms of its religious significance, even though they also pointed out that the miracle goes beyond the power of nature. Gradually, this latter aspect received the greater attention of Christian theology.

Perceived from the perspective of Aristotelian thought, according to which all things move according to the determined laws of nature, the importance of the miracle was placed in its interruption or violation of the established world order. Moreover, when the Christian community accepted the missionary challenge of its discoveries in the New World, miracle came to have a primarily apologetic importance. Christ's claims to divinity were seen to be authenticated by his ability to perform actions that totally exceed human powers. An impasse was reached with the rise of *Rationalism and *Deism; these philosophies rejected even the possibility of miracles on the grounds that an almighty God should not have to intervene to correct those disorders in creation which he had originally established. Accepting the apologetic insistence on miracle as an extraordinary act to demonstrate divine power, the rationalists argued that for God to cure a man born blind seemed like a divine afterthought, correcting an earlier mistake. Thus *Voltaire considered the assertion of a miracle to be blasphemy.

This impasse continued into more recent times with some variations. Most Christian catechesis still emphasized the apologetic nature of miracles as events without natural explanation, although some sought to retain the NT message without any credence in miracles. In addition, the increasingly scientific and empirical attitude of modern man who, in the natural sciences, works on the methodological presumption that reality is fundamentally calculable, seemed to cause an irreparable rift between modern modes of thought and the gospel narratives. Indeed, it is the evidence of this rift that impelled R. Bultmann to launch his attempt to demythologize the New Testament. Contemporary theologians have sought to overcome this situation by a return to the sign value of the miracle. They insist on the historical rather than physical qualities of a miracle, i.e., on the miracle's connection with the revelation of God in Jesus and its place as an event calling for the free response of those involved. Emphasis is also placed upon man's fundamental openness to the miraculous; the world is not a closed system, totally determined by impersonal forces. Freedom, an intersubjective relationship between God and man, and the possibility within this relationship of a divine communication in historical events are seen as the basis upon which a contemporary explanation of miracle must be built. BIBLIOGRAPHY: R. H. Fuller, *Interpreting the Miracle* (1963); L. Monden, *Signs and Wonders* (1963); K. Rahner, "Theology of the Symbol," *Theological Investigations* 4 (1966) 221–252; J. Metz, SacMund 4:44–46; T. G. Pater, NCE 9:889–894.

[T. M. MCFADDEN]

MIRACLE, MORAL, represents the personalist dimension of the miraculous. While the physical miracle signifies God's special action in the world of things, and the intellectual miracle, prophecy, signifies God's special action in the world of knowledge, the moral miracle speaks of God's presence and action in the realm of human endeavor. Human behavior can be such that it manifests human talent, human genius, human striving. Certainly man's creator stands behind all such action. God is Lord of individual history as well as world history. Beyond this, man's action can be such that it manifests a special presence of God. Such special presence is clear from the unusual quality of the human activity, its extraordinary nature, its character as beyond the normal manner of human life.

Indeed, the physical miracle demands no more of God's power than the everyday. The daily giving of life is as truly great as the raising of the dead. But the unusual character of certain deeds impresses man and tells him of God in a special manner. Similarly, the moral miracle concerns human endeavor which, because it does exceed the normal pattern of human life, speaks to man of God in a special way. The morally miraculous, the human activity that exceeds man's normal powers and accustomed ways, speaks to men of God who enables man to accomplish what is truly extraordinary. It is a sign or symbol of God's presence. In the present moment of history, in which the Son has entered the human family to form a new family in God, a new humanity, his Church, it might be expected that his Spirit would be manifest in human action bearing the marks of his presence. And this is indeed the case. Life in the Church has been characterized by the presence of the charismatic not only of the physical order but of the moral order as well.

The morally miraculous, or the charismatic personal, can be found on the individual level and on the community level in the Church. The Spirit's presence is strikingly manifest in a sudden conversion, a total change of heart from selfishness to Christian sacrifice. A Francis of Assisi, an Ignatius of Loyola, a Vincent de Paul exceeds the normal pattern of human life. Less strikingly, but nonetheless truly, the presence of the Spirit is seen in the constant lifelong dedicated service of Christian parents, educators, doctors, priests, or religious. On the community level, the morally miraculous can be found in the total existence of the church community itself. The Church, in its complex reality, speaks of the Spirit's presence and is a sign of its own mission (D 3013). In its unity and catholicity, in its apostolicity and indefectibility, in its holiness, this communion of persons in Christ bears the marks of the presence of the Spirit. No merely human society could be such. This is not to deny or minimize its weakness. It is called precisely to represent man's human condition. It is its very participation in human frailty that clearly shows that the Church community exceeds the pattern of human community only because of the presence of the Spirit. Though less demonstrative than the physically miraculous, the morally miraculous is of great concern because it is not only charismatic but personal as well. It relates not to things but to persons. It is the Spirit's self-manifestation in and through the human. BIBLIOGRAPHY: A. Michel, DTC 10.2:1789–1859; S. E. Donlon, NCE 9:884. *MIRACLE, MORAL (THE CHURCH).

[J. F. GALLAGHER]

MIRACLE, MORAL (THE CHURCH). As a community of persons the Church manifests the power of the Spirit; it participates in the morally miraculous. Indeed, the morally miraculous is of great significance in the life of the Church precisely because the Church is a community of persons, and the morally miraculous, as distinct from the physically miraculous, concerns the charismatic human; it is the miraculous in the form of personal and community life and endeavor. The power of the Spirit is manifest in the Church community in its unity and catholicity, its apostolicity and indefectibility, and its holiness. From among men fully sharing in the human condition and of diversity in culture and nationality, the Spirit has called together a community that, despite inner lapses and outer attack, continues today the apostolic task of announcing Christ to men and inviting men to live the gospel.

The Church is one and catholic. One in its basic faith, its central liturgy, and in its leadership or ministry, the Church manifests diversity in its expression of faith, in its celebration of sacraments and in its exercise of ministry. Diversity flows from Catholic unity, for the one Church embraces all men by invitation, and many millions of men in fact, men of every age and culture. Such oneness and diversity, unity and catholicity, when seen in relation to the Church's apostolicity, indefectibility, and holiness, exceed the normal pattern of human events and communities.

The Church community of the present succeeds the primitive community gathered about Christ; the body of bps. today succeeds the apostolic college; the bp. of Rome holds the Petrine See. The centuries have witnessed great diversity in Christian life among laity, bps., popes; but the communion of persons with divinely founded leadership today stands in continuity with the primitive Christian community. It is indeed the apostolic faith we live, the apostolic liturgy we celebrate, the apostolic ministry we exercise. Even more significant than this horizontal apostolicity is that vertical apostolicity through which Christ himself continues to speak to his Church, to sanctify and lead it through the ministry of the bishops. Just as horizontal apostolicity does not exclude development but demands it, so vertical apostolicity does not exclude an active laity but rather presupposes and requires it.

Apostolicity involves indefectibility, for Christ's mission confided to the apostolic Church must reach all men of all ages. Such duration in continuity and development exceeds the normal pattern of human community. It manifests the presence of the Spirit.

The Spirit's presence is seen in the Church's holiness. Sharing in human frailty and bearing witness to the human condition itself, the Church announces Christ, celebrates his saving deeds, and leads mankind to Christian morality and holiness. Its entire mission is to lead men to the Christlife, the gracelife, the life of oneness with God that is holiness. The constant yearning for God, the constant striving for loving service of others, the everyday effort to make Christ live in the very human condition itself, manifest the presence of the Spirit. Not only the great saints, but also the dedicated, long-suffering, sacrificing parents, teachers, priests, religious manifest in life the power of grace.

The Church's unity and catholicity, apostolicity and indefectibility as well as its holiness are inner properties with exterior manifestations. To the extent of their outer manifestation they serve as identifying notes of the Church. To the extent that they, taken as a whole, exceed the normal pattern of human community, they speak of the Spirit and participate in the morally miraculous. All charism is given for the service of others. To see in the Church's charismatic quality a pretext for proud boasting instead of an invitation to loving service is to betray the nature of charism. The Spirit's manifestation in the Church, so clearly described by Vatican Council I (D 3013), enables the Church, as Vatican Council II points out, all the more effectively to be the servant Church, the community of service, ever present in the human family to lead it to Christ. BIBLIOGRAPHY: E. Dublanchy, DTC 4.2:2128–32; S. E. Donlon, NCE 9:884–886; Vat II ConstChurch 12–13, 18, 40; M. Grandmaison, *L'Église par elle-même motif de crédibilité. Histoire de l'argument: 1870–1960* (1961); C. Journet, *L'Église du Verbe Incarné* (1961) 2:888–903, 1253–89; R. Latourelle, *Theology of Revelation* (1966) 417–424.

[J. F. GALLAGHER]

MIRACLE DE THÉOPHILE, an old legend vividly updated *c.* 1265 by *Rutebeuf. Having refused a bishopric, Théophile is dispossessed by the cleric who accepts; disgraced, Théophile forms a diabolic compact but is rescued by the Virgin.

[J. P. WILLIMAN]

MIRACLE PLAYS, religious dramas having the lives of the saints as subject, and concentrated upon the marvelous works or the great sufferings credited to these heroic persons. The earliest surviving miracle plays are in Latin, and date from the 12th cent. Renaissance in France and Germany. Although the precise development of this genre is still uncertain, whether from tropes or directly from existing vitae, the materials are very similar to those in the lessons read on saints' days in the Office of Matins. A certain extravagant and exotic quality characterizes the incidents in the plays, because of the emphasis upon marvelous and miraculous events rather than upon the hidden work of grace. These medieval miracle plays have been plausibly regarded as the background of romantic Renaissance drama, particularly of Elizabethan England. The saint who appears earliest and most frequently in the Latin plays is Nicholas, whose cult was popular in Western Europe in the 11th and 12th centuries. He was known as a benefactor of the poor and distressed, particularly in the legend of the dowerless daughters (*Tres filiae*) for whom he tossed gold through the window as provision for their marriages. Vernacular plays also were written about him, as Jean Bodel's *Jeu de Saint Nicolas* proves. Many French miracles are concerned with the intercession and wonder-working of the Blessed Virgin, while surviving English representatives show more frequent choice of St. Anne and St. Mary Magdalene. In the latter case, it was the legendary story of her apostolate to France along with her brother Lazarus that served as focus, rather than the biblical account of her conversion from sin and her meeting with Christ on Easter morning.

[E. C. DUNN]

MIRACLES DE NOTRE DAME, general term designating the vast medieval genre recounting miracles of the Virgin, esp. in her role as intercessor. *Walter of Coincy assembled the best early group, though the cult continued until the Renaissance. Frequent themes are miraculous conversions, manifestations of favor, the Virgin substituting for sinners and condemned criminals.

[J. P. WILLIMAN]

MIRACLES IN THE BIBLE. These are primarily manifestations of God's power and revelations of his will. They are signs to God's people that he is present. In the OT the Israelites considered all that happened in nature and above nature to be the mighty works of God. They did not distinguish between natural and supernatural events. All happenings were God's mighty deeds (Dt 3.24; Ps 20.7). Biblically speaking, any unusual phenomenon was considered to be a sign of Yahweh's merciful providence. It was not a question of a work that transcended nature, but a revelation of God's activity. Quite natural phenomena such as the appearance of a new star would be recorded in the Scripture as miraculous not in the sense of a divine intervention, but in the sense of another sign of God's presence. Miracles are not signs of God's intervention, but reminders of God's constant activity in man's world. As signs of God's will miracles often coincided with the proclamations of the Prophets. Both the sign and the proclamation were invitations to faith. In this sense the miracles fulfilled two functions; they provoked the witnesses to faith and they intensified the sense of vocation on the part of the miracle worker. Basic to the biblical understanding of revelation is that God reveals himself to man not by ideas and concepts, but by mighty deeds. Biblical miracles should be understood then as revelations of God's power, his presence, his concern. They should not be considered signs apart from the proclamation of a Prophet, but part of that proclamation. The words of the Prophet and the deeds of God constitute the revelation. The mighty works of God need not always be accompanied by a proclamation, but when they are, they form part of revelation.

In the OT the mighty works of God surrounded the proclamations of the messianic Prophets. In the NT the preaching of Jesus was also surrounded by signs and wonders. It should be noted that in references to the miracles of Christ the Greek word *terata* is not used alone, but the Greek expression *sēmeia kai terata* (signs and wonders). The miracles that Jesus performed should not be considered ''proofs'' of his divinity. Rather they form a part of his proclamation that the Kingdom of God is at hand. The mighty work of Jesus—the exorcisms, the healings, the nature miracles—forms a unity with his preaching as a revelation of the presence of God, a revelation that invokes a faith response. Where faith was lacking, Jesus would not give a sign of God's presence. The gospel narratives are creatively embellished with miracle-stories. These miracle-stories are themselves basic insights into Jesus' mission as one who reveals God. The miracle-stories of Jesus are quite consistent with the miracle-stories of the Prophets. Miracles are not signs that the Prophets or Jesus are divine. They are signs that God is present, God is speaking, God is acting. To separate the miracles from the proclamation of Jesus as exterior signs of credibility is to misunderstand the basic biblical meaning of miracle as itself a sign of God's activity and part of the proclamation. In this context miracles cannot be used to establish the divinity of Christ nor can they be reduced to mere imaginative writing on the part of the biblical writers. Rather, they form an integral part of God's revelation of his activity in man's world. BIBLIOGRAPHY: A. Richardson, *Introduction to the Theology of the New Testament* (1958); Wikenhauser NTI.

[W. J. DUGGAN]

MIRACULOUS MEDAL, religious *medal honoring the Blessed Virgin. In 1830 St. Catherine Labouré, a Daughter of Charity of St. Vincent de Paul, received a vision of Our Lady in which the design of the medal was given and great graces were promised for those who wore it. Oval-shaped, the medal bears an image of the Virgin standing upon a globe, crushing a serpent beneath her foot, with rays of light symbolizing graces coming from her hands. Surrounding the image is the inscription: ''O Mary, conceived without sin, pray for us who have recourse to thee.'' On the reverse side is an **M,** a cross, and the hearts of Jesus and Mary. The medal is the badge particularly of the Children of Mary, and the devotion has been encouraged by indulgences granted by four popes, including Paul VI. BIBLIOGRAPHY: J. Dirvin, *Saint Catherine Labouré of the Miraculous Medal* (1958); *idem*, NCE 9:894–895.

[J. C. WILLKE]

MIRAEUS, AUBERT (Le Mire; 1573–1640), prolific church historian. He was born of a rich merchant family in Brussels. His history of religious orders and his history of Belgium are considered valuable source works for later historians. He studied in Douai and Louvain, was cathedral canon in Antwerp, secretary to the bp., palace chaplain, dean of the cathedral, and vicar general. Diplomatic assignments for Albert of Austria brought him to France and Holland. His writings reflect a zeal for strengthening papal authority, and a consistent post-Tridentine, Counter Reformation bias. BIBLIOGRAPHY: É. Amann DTC 10:1862–64; E. D. McShane NCE 9:895; É. Brouette LTK 7: 436–437.

[E. J. DILLON]

MIRARI VOS, encyclical letter of Gregory XVI, Aug. 15, 1832, aimed at the liberalism and religious indifferentism espoused by Félicité de *Lamennais. Without naming Lamennais, the encyclical's warnings against the evils of the day were obviously directed against *L'Avenir* and its editors. Lamennais drafted an act of submission, but 2 years later gave up his priestly functions and published his *Paroles d'un croyant* in defense of his position. Text of encyclical, *Acta Gregorii Papae XVI* (ed. A. M. Bernasconius, 1901) 1:169–174.

[J. P. REID]

MIRBT, CARL (1860–1929), German Protestant church historian. He was professor of church history in Marburg (1889–1912) and in Göttingen (1921–28). His historical contributions were primarily in the area of missiology and the history of the papacy. His most important work is: *Quellen zur Geschichte des Papsttums* (4th ed., repr. 1934) which is characterized by an anti-Catholic bias. BIBLIOGRAPHY: E. Strasser in *Evang.-luther. Missionsblatt* 44 (1931) 24–46; M. Csáky, NCE, 9:895–896.

[J. J. SMITH]

MIRIAM (Mariam), sister of Aaron and Moses (Num 26.59), and a prophetess (Ex 15.20) who led the inspired song of triumph after the Red Sea crossing (Ex 15.20–21). This figure may have played a more important role in Israelite history than the explicit mentions of her in the text suggest. As a result of her criticism of Moses' marriage with a non-Israelite she was struck with leprosy and expelled from the camp for 7 days (Num 12.1–16).

[D. J. BOURKE]

MIRIAM, CANTICLE OF, see CANTICLE OF MIRIAM.

MIRIAN (Meribanes, *c.*282–361), first king of Iberia (east Georgia). Converted to Christianity by the preaching of St. Nino (334). M. sent to the Emperor Constantine for priests and in 337 was baptized together with his people. The Church of Georgia was soon organized under the bp. John who was sent from Constantinople. M. is venerated as a saint by the Byzantine Georgian Church. BIBLIOGRAPHY: C. Toumanoff, *Studies in Christian Caucasian History*.

[L. PEANO]

MIRÓ, JOAN (1893–), Catalan painter, the "most surrealist" of all 20th-cent. masters, who working in Paris, produced greatly diversified works: nostalgic Catalan evocations of childhood, fantasy, phantasmagoria, collage, and abstracts of serene mystery. The Spanish Civil War drove M. to paint macabre, violent monsters; WW II, through contemplation, led to mystical, lyrical *Constellations*. In ceramic murals, M. executed *Night and Day* at UNESCO Headquarters (1958), walls at Harvard Univ. (1960), and at the Guggenheim Museum (1967). Cosmic explosions of suns and color-field paintings mark work in the 60s. BIBLIOGRAPHY: J. Lassaigne, *Miró* (1963).

[M. J. DALY]

MIROKU BOSATSU, in Kōryūji, Kyoto (mid-7th cent.), Japanese wood sculpture. The Miroku Bosatsu or Maitreya Buddha ("to come") sitting in serene, contemplative pose, of grace, gentleness, and purity, is said to have been the original icon (603) for the monastery built by Hata Kawakatsu of a clan of Koreans. There is an almost identical one in gilded bronze in Korea, and another in the Chugu-ji Nunnery, Horyu-ji, Nara.

[M. J. DALY]

MIRROR. In Chinese thought the mirror does not receive or absorb the image as in Western culture, but rather intercepts, arrests, and throws back the thing reflected. Therefore mirrors are protective. They are hung before houses at dead-end lanes or streets, turning away objects that might collide with them. Mirrors are placed in tombs to turn away evil or harm from the dead. Taoists placed mirrors to collect dew which they considered the Elixir of Life.

Chinese mirrors are objects of art, cast in bronze, the reverse sides magically or symbolically decorated with cosmological significance—the boss at center the dome of Heaven, the four directions inferred by animals or birds of the four quarters, confirming the yang-yin principles of Chinese thought. Mirrors range from simple, round early shapes, through Han "maps of the universe" often painted, and elaborate, silvered T'ang lotus-petal shapes with luxurious, exuberant decorations, through Sung 8-figure and twin-animal marriage mirrors, to the materialistic Ming and Ch'ing designs which lost magical significance. Scholarly literature on interpretation of these forms can be seen in Oriental collections throughout the world.

[M. J. DALY]

MIRROR OF PRINCES, a literary genre popular in medieval and Renaissance times that gave counsel on the proper conduct of kings, princes, and other rulers. Some of these were largely theoretical in the spheres of politics and ethics; others were more practical and gave advice on all phases of life. There are examples of this type of literature in classical Greek and Roman times, and these considerably influenced the medieval and Renaissance approaches to the subject. BIBLIOGRAPHY: L. W. Spitz, NCE 9:896–897.

[P. K. MEAGHER]

MISCEGENATION, literally racial interbreeding (Lat., *miscere,* mix; *gens,* race), but in usage, a racially-mixed marriage. In American law the term was applied to a marriage between a white and a black, proscribed by some states until quite recently. Currently the most notorious proscription of this kind is part of the *apartheid* system in South Africa. There, as also formerly in the U.S., the Scriptures have been invoked to justify the proscription. Roman Catholic teaching has never supported enforced racial separation; the teaching of Vatican II on the dignity and equality of all human beings and its rejection of any discrimination based on race, clearly indicate that there is complete freedom, certainly no moral objection, for a person to choose a marriage partner of another race. The essentials belonging to a marital union are personal rights that no human power has a right to infringe upon. The decision of the persons entering a racially mixed marriage, however, is one which, whatever the laws or guaranteed rights, often requires courage and therefore previous grave reflection, because of a social climate that may be alien to the partners and to their future children.

[T. C. O'BRIEN]

MISERERE SERIES (ROUALT), monumental, sublime series of etchings and aquatints, filled with tragedy, sorrow, and hope, expressive of the artist's sufferings from the horrors of World War I. These masterpieces of graphic compression were produced under the patronage and inspiration of the dealer A. Vollard by G. Rouault, one of the most authentic Catholic religious artists of the modern world. Born of moral, social, and religious passion and planned (1916–17) and (1920–27) as two volumes, *Miserere* and *Guerre*, of 50 plates each, (only 58 were finally completed), the drawings in India ink were worked and reworked on copper plates through 12 to 15 states to preserve R.'s plastic, dramatic effects. The *Miserere Series* was finally published in 1948.

[M. J. DALY]

MISERICORD, name for a small ledge or rest on the tipped-up seat of a choir stall for the "merciful" ease of the tired or ill monk when the choir was standing. Frequently misericords were decoratively carved.

[M. J. DALY]

MISHNAH, body of Jewish law transmitted orally by rabbis who were *tabbaim*, teachers. The term means repetition, the method by which it was learned. It differed from Midrash, which it partially replaced, in that it was not based directly on the Scripture text. Mishnaic law, with 63 treatises grouped into 6 main *seder* or orders (Seeds; Feasts; Women; Damages; Holiness; Cleanliness) was codified as early as the 1st cent. B.C. The principal collection was made by Rabbi *Judah Ha-Nasi *c.*135–217 A.D.), and this collection, written in a late form of Hebrew, with the *Gemarah, commentaries on the Mishnah, formed the *Talmud.

[T. EARLY]

MISRULE, LORD OF, see FEAST OF FOOLS.

MISSA ILLYRICA, an 11th cent. text for the order of celebration of Mass, edited (1557) by M. *Flacius Illyricus as a refutation of RC eucharistic teaching. He wrongly dated it c.700. The text is of interest to liturgists for its many liturgical apologies, i.e., prayers professing unworthiness.

[T. C. O'BRIEN]

MISSAL, ROMAN. In the RC Church it was the liturgical book containing the readings and prayers used in the celebration of the Mass. In the 1st cent. of Christianity the prayers and readings of the Eucharistic Liturgy were determined by each bp. for his own Church in accordance with its local tradition. Lessons were read directly from the Bible, and much of the prayer, imitating celebrated models, began to be adopted. During the 4th and 5th cent. collections of such prayers were made, from which developed the Sacramentaries. The selection of Bible readings for different occasions also became fixed toward the end of the 5th cent. and special books containing gospel and other texts came into use. The gathering of the readings and prayers into a single volume for convenient use at private Masses dates from the 10th cent.; such a collection was called a *Missale*. In the Missals used throughout Europe, largely as a consequence of the Carolingian liturgical reform, there was much similarity, but for various reasons there were also many differences. The Roman Missal (*Missale secundum usum Romanae curiae*), known everywhere in Europe through the mendicant friars and traveling officials of the Roman Curia, came into popular use or was closely imitated in many places. Pius V in 1570 published a revised edition in accord with the directives of the Council of Trent and prescribed its use in all dioceses, churches, and religious communities that lacked a Missal of their own in use for at least 200 years. A revision of the 1570 Missal appeared in 1961. Further adaptation and revision, in keeping with the liturgical reform proposed by Vatican Council II have been made under the direction of the Consilium in 1964 and subsequently in 1969 by the Congregation for Divine Worship established by Pope Paul VI to implement the liturgical reforms decreed by the Council. In 1970 the Latin text of the new *Missale Romanum*, replacing that of Pius V, was published by the Vatican Polyglot Press. Its use in English was made mandatory in the U.S. from Dec. 1, 1974 after the authorized translation, called the *Sacramentary*, was issued. The new Roman Missal contains the celebrant's prayers of the Mass (presidential prayers), along with general instructions on norms and forms of celebration and on the rites of the Mass. Readings and scriptural responsories formerly in the Missal are contained in the Lectionary.

[N. KOLLAR]

MISSIOLOGY, the branch of theology dealing with mission work, particularly the principles by which it is conducted. Despite the long history of mission work (see MISSIONS), missiology as a systematic discipline did not develop until recent times. It has its roots in German Protestant theology of the 19th cent. esp. in the work of G. Warneck (1834–1910), who is known as the father of modern missiology. RC missiology is likewise rooted in Germany, notably in the work of R. Streit (1875–1930), and J. Schmidlin (1876–1944). Despite its late development, however, the study has become well established through academic courses offered in most seminaries, the publication of numerous books and periodicals, and important missionary conferences. Twentieth-century popes have given extensive attention to the subject. The encyclical *Maximum illud* by Benedict XV (1919) is regarded as the Magna Charta of modern missions. At Vatican Council II the subject was treated in the *Decree on the Missionary Activity of the Church*.

Early missiology emphasized conversion of individual pagans. The emphasis later shifted to the establishment of the Church in all areas where it did not then exist. Since the Church is now established to some degree in nearly every part of the world, current emphasis is moving toward clarification of the basis of the Church's mission. Greater stress is now laid on its mission to transform society, rather than just win individual converts or establish itself institutionally. Study of the principles of mission work necessarily involves some auxiliary disciplines, particularly the history of missions, and the specialized studies that missionaries will use in their work. In the latter, attention is increasingly given to deeper analysis of the societies where the missionaries will serve and to the social sciences needed for solving the problems of those societies. BIBLIOGRAPHY: R. Hoffman, NCE 9:900–904.

[T. EARLY]

MISSION, CANONICAL, authorization given by competent ecclesiastical authority to preach and to teach (cf. CIC c. 1328). The term is not one with a long tradition of canonical interpretation. The canon cited above speaks of canonical mission with regard to preaching; Bouuaert applies it to teaching theology and to formal religious instruction, whether by clerics or laity. The entrusting of a religious community or other mission group with a mission field is called by instruction of the Congregation for the Evangelization of Peoples a mandate (*mandatum*; AAS 61:283). The current rethinking and expansion of the meaning of ministry in the Church will undoubtedly modify the concept of canonical mission. (See F. Claeys Bouuaert, DDC 6:890–892.)

MISSION DE FRANCE, a domestic missionary movement among the clergy of France devised to evangelize the de-Christianized masses of that country. Traditional diocesan structures insured that the dioceses that produced the most priests were the ones that needed them least. A special seminary was set aside in Lisieux, where priests were to be formed according to a new plan and new apostolic methods attributed to the vision of Card. G. C. Suhard of Paris. Created in 1941, it was the first step in a movement that eventually led to the *worker priest experiment, a dramatic attempt to make the Church present to the lives of workers and other classes of people to whom the Church was a bizarre, foreign anachronism. French conservative elements combined with Vatican curial forces to put an end to this aspect of the French domestic mission in 1954. The basic tension between the traditional clerical culture and the ethos of the new missionary consciousness has not been resolved.

[E. J. DILLON]

MISSION DOCTORS ASSOCIATION (MDA), lay organization founded at Los Angeles, Calif., in 1959. It aims to organize and support Catholic physicians, dentists, and other trained personnel in medical missionary work throughout the world. Working closely with the Society for the Propagation of the Faith and the Lay Mission Helpers Association, it selects recruits and prepares them by a 9-month program of courses including theology, missiology, the culture and language of the assigned area, and local medical problems. The MDA provides for the transportation, location, and financial assistance of medical missionary families who are expected to serve a minimum of 3 years in foreign fields.

[J. C. WILLKE]

MISSION SECRETARIAT, former agency under the National Catholic Welfare Conference for the coordination of the missionary affairs of the American Church. In 1970 its name was changed and its organization restructured into the establishment of the U.S. Catholic Mission Council.

[T. C. O'BRIEN]

MISSIONARY, a cleric subject to the jurisdiction of the Congregation for the Propagation of the Faith. This canonical definition came into being along with the canonical establishment of that Congregation, *c.*1622 A.D.., at a time when the RC Church alone was organized to send European apostolic workers into newly discovered non-Christian lands. The term missionary easily acquired a broader meaning to include anyone, cleric or lay, engaged in the establishment of the Church where it had not yet been established, esp. in those lands incorporated into the emerging Spanish, Portuguese, and French colonial empires. By the 18th and 19th cent. the Protestant Churches undertook similar efforts, and appropriated the term. It continued to evolve in meaning until, by the 20th cent., it applied to believers anywhere who attempted to bridge the gulf between the world of faith and a world largely estranged from Christianity. It now applies to Christians everywhere, in any walk of life, who by their work and lives are conscious of their involvement in transforming the world in Christ.

Vatican Council II in its Decree on the Missionary Activity of the Church opened the way to a fuller theological understanding of the term missionary. The Council refers to the sphere of the Church's missionary activity particularly as those regions where 2 billion people have scarcely heard of the gospel message (Vat II MissAct 10). The missionary—priest, religious or laic—is above all to be a witness, to be a sign and presence of the gospel to the people. The missionary is urged to become one with the people in respect for their cultures, in sharing their human aspirations for betterment, and in seeking to respect and adapt to their noble ideals and beliefs. Even in situations where the missionary cannot directly evangelize, the mission vocation is fulfilled by an evangelical and human presence among people estranged (*ibid.* 11–12). In view of this vocation the Council outlines the necessity of a missionary formation in the language, culture, history, and religions of missionary regions, as well as in effective means of catechizing and adapting gospel and liturgy to the requirements of the apostolate (*ibid.* 25–27).

[E. J. DILLON]

MISSIONARY APOLOGETICS, see APOLOGETICS, MISSIONARY.

MISSIONARY ASSOCIATION OF CATHOLIC WOMEN, founded in 1916 in the U. S., an organization, of laywomen who make altar linens and vestments for priests in Catholic foreign missions. The association has its national office in Milwaukee, Wisconsin.

[R. A. TODD]

MISSIONARY CENACLE APOSTOLATE (MCA), an association founded as a lay-apostolic movement in 1909 by Rev. Thomas A. *Judge in Brooklyn, New York. Its primary purpose is to assist the Church in performing various apostolic works by means of a Missionary Cenacle family, whose members belong to one of three groups. The Apostolate operates as an independent lay organization, directed by its own lay officials and assisted by two congregations: the priests and brothers of the *Missionary Servants of the Most Holy Trinity and the sisters of the *Missionary Servants of the Most Blessed Trinity. The members conduct local and regional workshops and institutes of Catholic action, and prepare and train lay apostles for leadership, catechetics, hospitals and prison work, home visiting, and youth activities in 8 archdioceses and 11 dioceses in the U.S. and Puerto Rico. The Apostolate has about 1,000 members and has headquarters in Philadelphia, Pennsylvania.

[R. A. TODD]

MISSIONARY CHILDHOOD, see HOLY CHILDHOOD, PONTIFICAL ASSOCIATION OF THE.

MISSIONARY CONFERENCES, the series of assemblies by which the Protestant missioners were able to transform the Protestant consciousness and inaugurate the modern ecumenical era. Local conferences, sometimes national event of this century (see EDINBURGH CONFERENCES). and Protestant missionary circles. But it was the series of 10 worldwide conferences undertaken by the Protestants which had decisive impact. First came the one in Liverpool in 1860; followed by London (1888); New York (1900); Edinburgh (1910); Jerusalem (1928); Tambaram, Madras (1938); Whitby, near Toronto, Canada (1947); Willingen, Germany (1952); Ghana (1958); and Mexico City (1963). The crucial one was in Edinburgh in 1910. It is considered, along with Vatican Council II, the decisive Christian institutional event of this century (see EDINBURGH CONFERENCES). It gave rise to movements that culminated first in the creation of the International Missionary Council (IMC), and then the World Council of Churches (WCC). Ecumenical currents made themselves present from the beginning, until they gradually brought to an end the missionary consciousness of the Western colonial Christian peoples. At the Jerusalem conference (1928), only one-fourth of attending members were from the Churches of Asia, Africa, and Latin America. At Tambaram (1938) over half the members were from such Churches. Even the shifting locus of the conferences is significant. The "six-continent view of mission" became normative. The need for unity, including organic union, among those professing to be Christians became paramount. On the Catholic side, such meetings of representatives of mission-sending societies as those generally held in the U.S. for Americans, under the sponsorship of the hierarchy's Mission Secretariat (now U.S. Catholic Mission Council), never were able to have a similar impact on the general Catholic consciousness. It was not until the convening of Vatican Council II that bps. from what were still termed mission lands were able to give a sustained presentation of their views of the role of the Church in the modern world. Never before had bps. from the "older Churches" (as the IMC and the WCC terms them) received such authentic firsthand input from the "younger Churches." In the wake of the Council there has emerged a pattern of dynamic episcopal conferences—an expression of collegiality which insures continuing mutual enrichment of the various Churches. BIBLIOGRAPHY: W. Richey Hogg, "Conferences, Missionary," *Concise Dictionary of the Christian World Mission* (ed. S. Neill et al., (1971) 131–133; "Conferences, World Missionary" *ibid.* 133–138; O. Barres, "Catholic Missions-Evaluation," *Encyclopedia of Modern Christian Missions* (ed. B. L. Goddard et al, 1967) 111–116).

[E. J. DILLON]

MISSIONARY COOPERATION, the phenomenon common to the Protestant and the Catholic experience of foreign mission, by which missioners learned to collaborate across denominational lines and overcome the isolation of particular religious traditions. On the Protestant side the missioners gave their special impetus to a series of missionary conferences that brought into being the modern manifestations of ecumenism, such as the International Missionary Council and the World Council of Churches. On the Catholic side, religious orders long used to living in isolation from one another learned to collaborate in apostolic work under the centralized leadership of the Congregation for the Propagation of the Faith in Rome. Protestants and Catholics were able to see how their estrangement from each other presented a grave obstacle to their credibility in mission lands. In the early centuries (16th to 18th) when the Catholics had the scene virtually to themselves, the tragic rivalry of approach between Jesuits and friars in China gave way to an informal collaboration in the Philippines, in which Augustinians, Dominicans, Franciscans, and Jesuits took part. In other areas there emerged an informal understanding by which specific areas were the exclusive ''turf'' of a particular religious group. Thus, in the Levant, N Mesopotamia and Armenia were considered Dominican territory; Baghdad and S Mesopotamia were the area of concern of the Carmelites; the Jesuits established themselves in Syria and Lebanon. It then became the custom for Propaganda to entrust certain areas to certain religious congregations or orders. That religious group was then committed to provide whatever staff and material would be necessary to evangelize the territory. Other religious groups might be invited in, but they would work subject to agreement as to what services were to be rendered, between the newcomers and the religious order in charge. The bp. of the area was normally chosen from the order in charge. Propaganda was able to form a structure of collaboration between congregations that would have been considered unheard of in the country of origin of these missionaries; an accomplishment all the more remarkable in view of the diversity of language and culture among the missionaries. The five leading mission-sending countries for Catholic missionaries are: Fr-France, Belgium, Holland, Ireland, and the United States. The five largest male missioner groups include the Jesuits (mostly in Asia), the White Fathers and Holy Ghost Fathers (all in Africa), the Oblates of Mary Immaculate (divided between Asia and Africa), and the Franciscans (60% Asia; 40% Africa). At the high point of Catholic missionary effort, during the 1960s, missionaries cooperated in maintaining 80,000 mission schools, 10,000 hospitals and dispensaries, 2,000 orphanages, 500 homes for the aged, and 400 leprosaria. BIBLIOGRAPHY: C. J. Armitage, ''Catholic Missions-Structure,'' *Encyclopedia of Modern Christian Missions* (ed. B. L. Goddard et al. 1967) 116–120.

[E. J. DILLON]

MISSIONARY FORMATION, the special preparation required for effective ministry in the mission apostolate. This notion has undergone considerable change and evolution in the course of the last 5 cent. or more. When Thomas Aquinas composed his *Summa contra Gentiles*, at the request of Raymond of Peñafort, he was aware of the high intellectual culture of the Muslim world. Missionary formation in those days seemed to be a question of having mastered arguments that would convince Muslims and Jews. In the 17th cent. the mission colleges of the Carmelites and Franciscans were considered to be models for others to emulate. The emphasis was on mission languages and spiritual survival in exile from Christendom. It was not until Benedict XV and Pius XI that unequivocal, authoritative teaching condemned colonialism, and the exaltation of Western and European culture as equivalent to Christian values. Two persons who enlarged and enriched the curricula of missioners were Joseph Schmidlin and Pio Maria de Mondreganes; insisting that missiology be the heart of the curriculum: including history and theory of missions, history of religions, ethnology, linguistics, national psychologies, literatures, legal traditions, and other such humanistic studies. Of late, voices are asking missioners to go even further and imitate the scrupulously reverent approach of the anthropologist. This would fundamentally change the missioner's perspective. Dialogue would replace proselytism. There would be listening as well as talking; learning as well as teaching. The document of Vatican Council II on the missions provided an opportunity for a breakthrough for these new approaches. The result is that alongside the Congregation for the Evangelization of Peoples there are now Curial mechanisms that deal with fostering dialogue with non-Christian religions and non-European cultures. There is even an honest openness to dialogue with nonbelievers. Much more care is given to education for sound emotional and mental health of the missioner. Just as Western man has learned to see the pathology of the colonialist mentality, so the missionary consciousness has come in for closer scrutiny. The psychological survival and growth of the missioner has turned out to be a more complex and challenging problem than was formerly supposed. As in so many other aspects, the progress made by missioners in so-called missionary formation has redounded to the deeper awareness of the entire Church concerning the religious formation of humankind in general. BIBLIOGRAPHY: J.A. McCoy, *Advice from the Field* (1962, with bibliog.).

[E. J. DILLON]

MISSIONARY SERVANTS OF THE MOST BLESSED TRINITY, a community of religious women dedicated to social work, esp. in the South of the U.S. It was founded by the Vincentian Father Thomas Judge as a counterpart to his congregation for men, which carries the same name. Arising from a group of lay associates, a group taking private vows was formed in 1912. They followed Father Judge to the missions of Alabama in 1916 when they opened a school for the poor and carried out a program of home visiting. In 1918 the group became a formal congregation, with Mother Mary Boniface Keasey as first superior. The sisters staffed missions, aided by lay associates, in the U.S., Puerto Rico, and the Virgin Islands. In 1958 the community was given pontifical status. In 1976 they had 425 members in 62 houses; their motherhouse is in Philadelphia, Pa.

[J. R. AHERNE]

MISSIONARY SERVANTS OF THE MOST HOLY TRINITY (ST or MSST), pontifical religious congregation of priests and brothers, for home mission work. Founded in the U.S. (1929; approved 1958) by Fr. T. A. *Judge, it is an outgrowth of his pioneer Missionary Cenacle Apostolate, for both men and women (from 1909), which formed the Missionary Servants of the Most Blessed Trinity. Papal social encyclicals have guided the Fathers' apostolate, chiefly with blacks and Latin Americans in the South and Southwest, and in Puerto Rico and the Virgin Islands. Preservation of the faith is the scope of the Congregation; to that end they work esp. among immigrants whose RC faith is endangered by proselytism. They have a generalate in Washington, D.C., and a house in Rome; in 41 houses (1976) were 215 members, 146 of whom were priests. BIBLIOGRAPHY: H. Marshall, NCE 9:921–922; L. Brediger, *ibid.* 8:18 s. v. "Judge, Thomas Augustine."

[M. R. BROWN]

MISSIONARY SISTERS OF NOTRE DAME DES ANGES (MNDA), a diocesan missionary congregation founded in 1922 in Sherbrooke, Canada, by Mother Mary of the Sacred Heart to train native sisters and catechists in the missions. This was the apostolate of most of the members of the community who were missioned in China until 1946 when they were compelled by the Communists to abandon most of their posts. Fields of their other labors of teaching, nursing, and social work, have included missions in the Far East, French Polynesia, Africa, and South America. The motherhouse is in Sherbrooke, Canada; in the U.S., the sisters are in Naugatuck, Conn., in the Archdiocese of Hartford. In 1975 there were 222 members in 25 houses.

[P. NEAL]

MISSIONARY SISTERS OF OUR LADY OF THE HOLY ROSARY (HRS), a community founded by Bp. Joseph Shanahan in 1924 in Killeshandra, Ireland. The community is engaged in educational, medical, and social work in Ireland, England, the Americas, and a number of countries of Africa. The motherhouse is in Kilmore, Ireland. In 1975 there were 435 members in 50 houses.

[P. NEAL]

MISSIONARY SISTERS OF THE MOST SACRED HEART OF JESUS OF HILTRUP (MSC), a pontifical institute founded in 1899 by Hubert J. Linckens, MSC, at Hiltrup, Germany, to assist the Sacred Heart Missionaries in the SW Pacific. The American province was established in 1908; the motherhouse in Reading, Pa., directs foundations in various parts of the United States. In 1928 the congregation was extended to Australia, in 1933 to China, and in 1938 to South America. The generalate was transferred from Hiltrup to Rome because of the worldwide area of apostolate—U.S., Peru, Germany, Italy, Spain, South Korea, SW Africa, S Pacific Islands, and China (until expelled by Communists in 1952). Under its motto, "May the Sacred Heart of Jesus be loved everywhere," the institute engages in all phases of hospital work, teaching, caring for the elderly and for dependent children. In 1975 there were 1,680 members in 131 houses.

[P. NEAL]

MISSIONARY SISTERS OF THE MOTHER OF GOD (SMIC), a congregation of cloistered origin, founded in 1910, at Santarém, Brazil, by Bp. Amanda Bahlmann, OFM (1862–1939) and Mother Maria Immaculata (Elizabeth Tombrock, 1887–1938). A branch of the contemplative Conceptionists at Rio de Janeiro, Brazil, who followed a modified rule of the Poor Clares, the new community of five sisters, released of papal enclosure, reorganized as active missionary sisters under the rule of the Third Order Regular of St. Francis. They were specifically founded for the sanctification of priests and the spreading of God's kingdom through missionary endeavors. As their work progressed, the apostolate extended first to S America and then to U.S. and Germany. After the first U.S. foundation (1922) at St. Bonaventure, near Allegany, N.Y., the congregation grew rapidly and has houses in the Archdiocese of Newark, the Dioceses of Austin, Buffalo, Galveston-Houston, Paterson, and San Angelo. There also are foundations in Africa, Brazil, Germany, and Taiwan. In 1975, there were 65 houses and 634 sisters engaged in educational, hospital, and social work. The general motherhouse is in Oradell, New Jersey.

[R. A. TODD]

MISSIONARY SISTERS OF THE PRECIOUS BLOOD (CPS), a religious congregation founded in 1885 by Abbot F. *Pfanner at Mariannhill, Natal, South Africa. The institute, whose motherhouse is now in Holland, is subject to the Congregation of the *Propagation of the Faith. It has accepted missionary assignments in countries throughout the world including the Netherlands, Germany, Austria, Denmark, Spain, Portugal, the U.S., Canada, the Congo, S and E Africa, and New Guinea. The first foundation in the U.S. was in 1925 in Princeton, New Jersey. The works of the community include teaching, nursing, caring for the handicapped, the aged, orphans, lepers, prospective mothers, and minority groups. Members are also engaged in catechetical, secretarial, and domestic work, art and daycare centers, and in the directing of native sisterhoods. In 1975 there were 1,373 members in 118 houses.

[P. NEAL]

MISSIONARY SISTERS OF THE SACRED HEART (MSC), a papal institute founded by St. Francis Xavier *Cabrini at Codogno, Italy, in 1880. Seven years later she requested papal approbation for her congregation and permission to open a house in Rome. Both were granted; but when she asked to establish missions in China, a work that had attracted her from early years, the reply of Leo XIII was, "Not to the East, but to the West." Thus she was directed to the U.S. to work to improve the religious and social conditions of large numbers of Italian immigrants. In 1889, with six of her sisters, she arrived in New York City where the U.S. provincialate is now situated; the general motherhouse is in Rome. St. Francis Cabrini also established many houses throughout Europe and Latin America, besides many in the U.S. stemming from the New York foundation. Her successors extended the congregation to China, Australia, and Canada. Characteristics of the institute are devotion to the Sacred Heart, a spirit of prayer and reparation, intense missionary activity, and obedience to the Holy See. The community is engaged in such works as schools, from nursery through college, foundling homes, orphanages, hospitals, nursing schools, catechetical instruction, retreats, and visitation to homes, hospitals, and prisons. In 1975 there were 993 members in 90 houses.

[P. NEAL]

MISSIONARY SOCIETY OF ST. JAMES THE APOSTLE, a society of diocesan priests founded in 1958 in Boston, Mass., by Card. Richard Cushing for the purpose of the parish apostolate in Latin America. Priests from 19 different dioceses in the U.S., Canada, and the countries of the British Isles have volunteered as missionaries of the society to serve the poorest parishes in Peru, Bolivia, and Ecuador. The goal is to make the parish the vital center of Catholic life. Headquarters of the society are at St. Stephen Church in Boston.

[R. A. TODD]

MISSIONARY UNION OF THE CLERGY, an association, also referred to as the Unio Cleri, organized to promote clerical efforts to enlist the missionary cooperation of the laity. The idea originated in 1908 with Father Paul Manna; he believed that to give impetus to missionary enthusiasm in the whole Church, it would first be essential "to organize the clergy for the missions." Fr. Paul's plan met with approval and Benedict XV recommended the establishment of the Missionary Union in all dioceses throughout the world. Pius XI encouraged all prelates to organize a Unio Cleri wherever there was none. In time, the Holy See depended upon it as an agency that, through universal concern, would assist the priests in their responsibility to disseminate missionary knowledge, further vocations, induce worldwide reconciliation, and motivate prayer and sacrifice among the faithful. The Missionary Union is comprised of an international council and general secretary; national councils and secretaries; and diocesan councils governed by local ordinaries. One of the organization's principal objects is to support and make known the three pontifical mission-aid societies of the Propagation of the Faith, the Society of St. Peter the Apostle for Native Clergy, and the Missionary Childhood. The Missionary Union of the Clergy in the U.S. publishes a quarterly called *Worldmission* and has its headquarters in New York City.

[R. A. TODD]

MISSIONS. A mission, as understood here, is the sending or going forth of a person to preach the gospel. From the beginning Christians regarded the gospel message as intended for all mankind and saw it as an important part of their duty to aid in carrying it to every creature (Mt 28.19; Mk 16.15). The Acts of the Apostles is the record of the earliest efforts of the Christian community to fulfill this mandate. In addition to the preaching of the good news by the Apostles and their coworkers, converts from every walk of life whose commercial, military, or other pursuits took them from place to place carried the Christian message abroad. In a remarkably short time there were small cells of Christianity in most of the important cities at the crossroads of the Roman Empire. Their bps. were established as leaders or pastors of the community, the faithful assembled for worship and instruction, and organized forms of a catechumenate developed. As time went on these pockets of Christianity grew and new ones were formed in other centers. By the time of the Edict of Milan (313), Christians in the Roman Empire already made up a substantial portion of the population—as high as 50% in some provinces. With the end of the persecutions the number of Christians increased greatly and began to include a larger proportion of people of wealth, education, and political importance. Missionary activity, which had in earlier times been chiefly confined to cities and large towns, gradually came to focus more upon the countryside, where zealous bps. and monks labored to drive paganism from its last refuge. In the outlying provinces of the Empire and beyond its limits the transition from paganism to Christianity was complicated by the introduction of a rival missionary thrust in the form of Arianism. Christianity in this form was taught by Ulfilas, apostle of the Goths, to his people along the lower Danube whence it spread to other German tribes, and when they invaded western Europe and established their kingdoms there, they brought Arianism with them and later took it into Spain, Africa, and Italy. By the time this threat was finally overcome, a new era of evangelization was already under way. Missionary bps. and monks were at work among Germanic and Slavic tribes, often with the support of civil rulers who were interested in consolidating their control and expanding their dominions. The phenomenon of mass conversion was not uncommon; this was in part because of the strong bond existing between chieftains and their people, but, in many instances, because of pressure and compulsion.

After the faith had been well established in Europe, the Western Church turned to mission activity among the Moslems in Spain, North Africa, and the Middle East, but this effort met with small success, except in Spain. In the latter part of the 13th cent. friars moved farther afield, traveling to Persia, Armenia, and Russia, a large part of which was then under Tartar occupation. An embassy under the Franciscan John of Monte Corvino bore letters from the Pope to the Great Mongol Kahn, then at Kahnbalik (Peking), and a missionary archdiocese was established at Kahnbalik by Clement V in 1307. But these and other efforts of the 13th and early 14th cent. bore no lasting fruit. In the mid-13th cent. the Black Death swept across Europe, and the spreading power of the Ottoman Turks cut the Western Church off from effective communication with either Near or Far East. The hospitality accorded the friars in China by the Mongol dynasty was not continued by the Mings, and troubles and disorders of various kinds in Europe diverted human and material resources from missionary enterprises. Western missionaries did not return to the East until the 16th century.

Missions of the Eastern Churches. The Church in the East was as vigorous in its missionary activity as it was in the West and accounted for much of the geographical spread of Christianity. By the 6th cent. missionaries had visited far places and there were Christian communities in India and Ceylon. Nestorian Christians penetrated along trade routes into Mongolia and China as early as the 7th century. From the 8th till the 10th cent. the Byzantine Church labored to evangelize the Slavs, an effort that culminated in the baptism of St. Vladimir *c*.988 and led to the conversion of his people. It was chiefly through the Russian Church that the missionary work of the East continued after Byzantium was overrun by Moslems and was no longer able to send out missionaries. The Russians, esp. in their monastic centers, took up the work with zeal. They evangelized their non-Slavic neighbors to the N and E and reevangelized the portion of their own land held by Mongol and Tartar invaders when these were finally overcome. Later, evangelization followed in the wake of the Siberian conquest and reached to China, Japan, and Alaska.

Roman Catholic Missions. A new period of intense missionary activity followed upon the voyages of Columbus and other explorers at the close of the 15th and during the 16th century. The first to take up the work were missionaries from RC Spain and Portugal. They were the earliest in the field because their countries were the first to become extensively involved in colonization and the exploitation of economic opportunities opened up by the new discoveries, and also because there was less internal religious strife in Spain and Portugal to preoccupy the attention of religious leaders. Under the system of royal patronage (*patronato real*) the apostolate was undertaken with great vigor in the West Indies, Mexico, Central and S America, Africa, India, the Malay Peninsula, and the Philippines. Later, French missionaries in Canada evangelized Indian tribes from the Atlantic to the Great Lakes and Mississippi regions. Much was accomplished, and the hope of greater achievement lay ahead. But a good part of the promise was frustrated by a variety of adverse circumstances. Recurrent war hindered communications and led to the diversion of resources from missionary to military uses. Religious and political developments in the homeland were reflected in shifts in policy regarding the promotion of the missions. There were bitter conflicts between missionary and government officials about the ill-treatment of native populations. There was conflict also between competing missionary orders and serious disagreement concerning the legitimacy of certain adaptations of Christian thought and practice to the native cultures of those to whom the gospel was being preached. These and other factors were already at work in the 17th cent., when the missionary movement was at its height. Moreover, the defects of the patronage system were even then becoming apparent. The Congregation for the Propagation of the Faith was founded, which would provide in time a framework in which the missions could operate independently of royal patronage. Civil governments, moving under the influence of the Enlightenment in the direction of secularism, began to lose interest in the work of the missions and to take an antagonistic view of the missionary activities of the religious orders. Toward the end of the 18th cent. the Jesuits, who were widely involved in mission work, were suppressed. These and other reverses led to varying degrees of decline and stagnation in different mission fields.

Various factors combined to bring about a notable revival of missionary effort in the 19th cent. from the pontificate of Gregory XVI (1829–46) onward. Popular support for the missions was stimulated by the activities of societies established for that purpose, e.g., the Society for the Propagation of the Faith, founded in France in 1822. New religious congregations were formed for missionary work (e.g., the Marists, founded 1836; the Pontifical Institute for Foreign Missions of Milan, 1850; the White Fathers, 1868), and the older orders, long engaged in the work, renewed their commitment. External circumstances also became more favorable. New explorations and discoveries aroused general interest; there was a renewal of colonial competition between European nations. With these developments, governments, however anticlerical at home, saw advantage in encouraging, or at least in not putting obstacles in the way of, missionary activity. In these more encouraging circumstances, the interior of Africa and Oceanica were opened to evangelization, and great gains were made. Nevertheless, much of the evangelical effort could appear too closely allied with colonial interests, and with the rising sense of nationalism in many mission lands it became evident that the work of the missions had to be increasingly dissociated from the politico-economic ambitions of the countries from which the missionaries came. Since the pontificate of Pope Benedict XV (1914–22) stress has been increasingly laid upon the fostering of a native clergy in the different mission fields and on the establishment at the earliest feasible time of local hierarchies with indigenous bishops. The desirability of adapting or accommodating the Christian message to the cultural and social conditions of the people to whom it was brought came to be insisted upon. This principle had suffered from some neglect after the unfavorable stand taken by the Holy See in the matter of the Chinese and Malabar rites, and where missions were too closely coupled with colonial ambitions there had been no strong movement toward its rehabilitation. However, during the 20th cent. the principle has been revived and restored to respectability, and it influenced the thinking of the conciliar fathers at Vatican Council II (see Vat II MissAct 19–22).

Other changing features in contemporary Catholic missionary effort include a new emphasis on education, medical and social work, and the use of lay workers with the specialized skills and training necessary in those fields. Not only does this development provide a practical and impressive example of Christian love, useful in disposing the nonbeliever to take an interest in Christianity, but it also establishes what is often the only basis upon which governments not well disposed toward Christian evangelization are willing to admit missioners and permit them to remain.

Protestant Missions. The Protestant Churches after the Reformation were slower to take up missionary work in the newly discovered regions of the world, chiefly because the countries in which Protestants were strongest were at that time less extensively engaged in colonial expansion and overseas commerce. Moreover, Protestant theological thought during the Reformation period was too preoccupied with other matters to develop the theme of the Christian's responsibility to labor for the spread of the faith. But in the 17th cent. there was already some attempt to evangelize the Indians near the Virginia and New England settlements. John *Eliot in New England translated the Bible into an Indian dialect and preached to the Indians of Massachusetts, and the Quakers also undertook evangelical work among the Indians. The *Society for Promoting Christian Knowledge (SPCK), founded in 1698, had for part of its objective the distribution in foreign places of Bibles and other religious literature, and in 1701 the *Society for the Propagation of the Gospel (SPG) was founded to supplement the SPCK's work in the foreign field. This led to an increase of missionary effort in all the British colonies. Dutch trading settlements in the West Indies in the 17th cent. opened the way for missionaries from The Netherlands. In Germany *Pietism aroused interest in the missions, and the Moravian Church, always conspicuous for its missionary zeal and perhaps esp. well-suited to the work because it did not see itself as a national Church in any sense, sent missionaries to many parts of the world and esp. to British North America. In 1792 the Baptist Missionary Society was established in England, largely through the influence of William *Carey, who himself went (1793) as a missionary to India. Other missionary societies were soon organized—the *London Missionary Society (LMS) for Nonconformist evangelicals (1795) and the *Church Missionary Society (CMS) for evangelicals within the Anglican Communion (1799). In 1804 the interdenominational *British and Foreign Bible Society was organized with the combined support of both Anglican and Nonconformist groups. Similar organizations were founded in the countries of continental Europe.

In the U.S., the *American Board of Commissioners for Foreign Missions was organized in 1810. It was an interdenominational agency but was principally supported by Congregational bodies. Other societies soon followed: the American Baptist Mission Union (1814), the American Bible Society (1816), the Methodist Board of Foreign Missions (1819), and the Presbyterian Board of Missions (1837). The formation of these organizations evoked by way of reaction an *antimissionary movement that was esp. strong during the years 1820–40. But the tide of missionary enthusiasm was too strong, and the feeling that results could best be achieved through national organization was too general for the opposition to overcome the trend. On the initiative of Robert Wilder, John Forman, and Robert Speer, the Student Volunteer Movement for Foreign Missions became active in 1886 and was formally organized in 1888. Its objective was declared to be "the evangelization of the world in this generation." John R. *Mott was associated with the movement from its beginning and long served as its chairman. The idea was taken up in other countries, and different national groups were linked, principally through the efforts of Mott, in the *World Student Christian Federation (founded 1895). Mott was chairman of the committee that called the first International Missionary Conference (Edinburgh, 1910). A continuation committee carried on the work of the Conference and this led to the establishment in 1921 of the *International Missionary Council, with which the missionary work of most Protestant bodies became associated, although some groups have preferred, mainly for doctrinal reasons, to operate independently of it. In 1961 this council was integrated into the World Council of Churches (WCC) and became the WCC's Commission on World Mission and Evangelism. The effect of the worldwide interdenominational organizations has been to reduce denominational rivalry in the missionary fields, to prevent overlapping of effort, and to develop more effective programs and methods of missionary work. There are many other missionary societies that are national, regional, or local in membership. Most of these are denominational, although they are in great part associated with broader interdenominational societies and ultimately with the WCC's Commission. Some, however, confine their interest to the promotion of their own denomination's missionary work.

Among those bodies that have kept apart from organizational association with other denominations, the Pentecostals are worthy of special mention. By themselves they account for as much as 10% of the total evangelical work being done by Protestants in the various missionary fields. Zeal to bear witness in foreign places has characterized the Pentecostal movement from its inception, and a substantial portion of the growth in membership of these bodies has been won in mission countries.

Through the years, new approaches to evangelization have been developed. As hostility toward colonialism gained strength in mission areas during the 20th cent., it became evident that missionary programs would be more effective if they included less direct preaching of the gospel by word and more indirect preaching through service, medical work, agricultural training, and education, with greater emphasis, esp. since World War II, upon helping backward countries to help themselves. More importance has been attached to the preparation of indigenous workers to take over and carry on the work of evangelization. Experience of the past and the realities of the present situation, esp. since the report of the Laymen's Commission which in 1932 published its findings in a volume entitled *Re-Thinking Missions,* have caused much stress to be laid on the need for the missionary to know the culture, religion, and customs of the people he encounters in foreign lands. BIBLIOGRAPHY: E. L. Murphy, NCE 9:924–928; W. J. Coleman, NCE 9:930–933; *Encyclopedia of Modern Christian Missions* (ed. B. L. Goddard, 1967); K.S. Latourette, NCE 9:938–941; *idem, History of the Expansion of Christianity* (7 v., 1937–45), esp. v. 3–7; *idem, Christianity in a Revolutionary Age* (5 v., 1958–62).

[P. K. MEAGHER]

MISSIONS, CALIFORNIA. This article treats the missions of Upper California (now the state of California); there was also extensive activity in Lower California (now the Mexican state of Baja California) which met with limited success. Jesuits, Franciscans, and Dominicans labored there in turn from 1683 to the secularization by Mexico in 1834.

Spain was intent on securing the N coast of California for itself and dispatched Captain Rivera with Father Juan Crespi, a Franciscan, in one group and Governor Portolá and Father Junípero Serra in another land expedition. Both arrived in San Diego in 1769, bringing provisions and livestock. While the governmental center was being established at Monterey in the north, Serra was struggling against odds to found the first mission, that of San Diego. Twenty-one missions in all would be established, each a day's journey on foot from its next neighbor, and stretching S from San Diego northward to Sonoma, a span of 500 miles. The great founder and *presidente* of missions was the heroic and brilliant Serra. His genius and that of his order created one of the most extraordinary mission cultures in the history of the missions throughout the world. The focal point of the mission compound was the adobe church, some examples of which constitute a new form of architecture (e.g., Santa Barbara) devised for the New World. Next to the church were the living quarters of the Franciscans. There were quarters for girls and women and in another area for boys and men. Around the patio, shops, storehouses, stables, and granaries stood. Indians who embraced Catholicism were drawn to live in the mission community. The missionary was both father and ruler of his Indians. He laid out daily regimen of work, prayer, and play. He taught them to build permanent structures, to raise livestock, to farm, and to acquire skill in crafts. Under his direction the Indians constructed irrigation ditches, many of great length, to bring in water so precious and scarce. The mission network brought the faith to 100,000 Indians but it also turned them from savages into an industrious people, farmers, herdsmen, carpenters, blacksmiths, and practicioners of many other useful occupations as well as craftsmen who created artifacts of great beauty. The missions were secularized by the New Republic of Mexico in 1834; the Indians were dispersed and gradually disappeared; the Franciscans, no longer reinforced from Spain, died out. Today the still active mission churches are largely diocesan parishes. A notable exception is Mission Santa Barbara, center of Franciscan life in California. BIBLIOGRAPHY: Z. Engelhart, *Missions and Missionaries of California* (4 v., 1929).

[J. R. AHERNE]

MISSIONS, DIVINE, the term missions here being understood in their Trinitarian sense. Paul's Epistle to the Ephesians (1.3–14) speaks of the Trinity's work in human sanctification. From eternity the Father predestined man to become conformable to his Son's image. This is effected in time by the Son and the Holy Spirit. Their activity in this world is clearly stated in Scripture, and from this the term "missions" is deduced. God "sent" his Son to redeem man (1 Jn. 4.9). This mission precedes that of the Spirit (Jn 16.17). After his Ascension the Son with the Father "sends" the Spirit (Jn 14.26; 16.7).

Further insight into the nature of these missions can be drawn from Scripture. They have a visible and invisible character. The Word was made flesh to reconcile man to God by his death. The Spirit manifests his presence to men by various signs, e.g., tongues of fire, wind, charismatic gifts. Such phenomena presage the inauguration of the messianic kingdom with all that implies regarding the life of the Church and its members.

In the patristic period the teaching on the divine missions developed. To the objection that if Christ was sent by his Father and descended from heaven, he was no longer with him, it was replied that the divine person, being God, was everywhere. Thus "to be sent" meant not to go where previously he had been absent but merely to exist there in a new way. The Word was sent to men in the sense that he showed his presence among them through the assumption of human nature. The Arian position that the one sending is more perfect than the one sent was countered by insisting that the the divine missions involved no subordination.

The early defenders of the faith also pointed out a difference between the two missions. In the person of the Son human nature was permanently united to the divine nature, but the various manifestations of the Spirit implied no union with his person.

From earliest times a connection between the missions and processions was recognized. Since the Father proceeds from no one, he has no mission. He does, however, come to men. The Son, proceeding from the Father, is sent by him. The Spirit proceeds from the Father and Son and is sent by them. BIBLIOGRAPHY: ThAq ST 1a, 43; J. Lebreton, *Histoire du dogme de la Trinité* (1928); B. Lonergan, *De Deo Trino* (1961).

[E. J. CARNEY]

MISSIONS, INDIAN, see INDIAN MISSIONS (U.S.).

MISSIONS, PAPAL LETTERS ON, the more than 30 mission-related letters written by the modern popes, beginning with the six such letters of Leo XIII (1878–1903). Leo's pontificate coincided with a period of expansion of European colonialism in Africa, Asia, and throughout the Pacific area. Many Christian missions were little more than spiritual colonies of the various European countries. Leo's letters brought to the fore the necessity of a native clergy and seminaries to prepare them. He had the vision and courage to cry out against slavery in Brazil and Africa. He supported Card. Lavigerie and his White Fathers in their complex and reverent approach to the peoples of Africa, coupled with their abolitionist campaign against slavery. But the Magna Charta of the modern missions is the crucially important letter: *Maximum illud* of Benedict XV issued on November 30, 1919. The letter minces no words in attacking the Europeanization of mission work, citing the tragedy of "attempts to increase and exalt the prestige of the native land (the missioner) once left behind." With principal reference to China, the Pope insisted that the chief aim of mission work is to make the missioner superfluous by promoting local clergy to full responsibility for the future of the Church in their land, stating that no country has ever been converted except by its own clergy. Benedict's letter comprises a synthesis of the progressive elements in previous papal teaching on the subject. The most comprehensive papal mission letter is *Rerum ecclesiae*, dated February 28, 1926, written by Pius XI. He called for renewed efforts to build a strong local clergy. He himself went from principle to practice by consecrating Chinese, Indian, and Japanese bishops. Pius XII carried on this emphasis with 10 mission letters. This emphasis made it possible for the Church to maintain an active and visible presence during the national struggles for independence from European and Western colonialism which have marked the last 2 decades and show no sign of abating. Paul VI's apostolic exhortation *Evangelii nuntiandi* (1976) marks a new understanding of universal evangelization as the mission of every believer, the need for inculturation of the Gospel, the freeing men from every form of oppression as part of the message of conversion and salvation. BIBLIOGRAPHY: *Catholic Missions: Four Great Missionary Encyclicals* (ed. T. J. M. Burke, 1957).

[E. J. DILLON]

MISSIONS, PAROCHIAL, parish missions; home missions; missions to the baptized on the domestic front, in accordance with canon law which urges every ordinary to see to it that at least every 10 years parish priests provide a structured mission for their parishioners (CIC c. 1349.1). This involved one or more weeks of having a special preacher, who used a plan for sermons for instruction geared to a renewal of faith and religious life, while providing the opportunity for confession to a special confessor. Basically this is a 17th-cent. form of apostolate, and in origin represented the same sort of movement to bring religion to the people as the Franciscan and Dominican movements had accomplished in the 13th century. It was the Jesuits and the Capuchins who led the way in the 17th cent., until they yielded preeminence to the Vincentians, who brought their retreats and missions to the most neglected. Many congregations were founded in the 18th and 19th cent. with emphasis on this kind of work: Redemptorists, Oblates of Mary Immaculate, the Passionists, and others; so that by the mid-19th cent. such missions were a staple of American Catholic parish life. In post-World War I Europe this strategy was seen as not making sufficient impact to reach the de-Christianized industrial masses. A more comprehensive and coordinated approach was instituted by various apostolic groups working and planning together, with a follow through. This pattern became common in post-World War II Catholic Europe. In the U.S., there has as yet developed no similar pattern, just as there is no general awareness of any similar alienation of the Catholic masses. Parochial missions have declined in popularity. The new emphases in parish life are on the liturgy and its formative function, on liturgical catechesis, on the homily centering on the scriptural readings, on new forms of parish retreats. For the "unchurched," those alienated from the Church, there is concentration on new forms of evangelization. Yet central to the parish mission was the indispensable place preaching has in Christ's mission; that central fact connects all contemporary developments with the inspiration of the parish mission.

[E. J. DILLON]

MISSIONS, SOCIAL ACTION OF, the labors of Christian missionaries in relief of human misery and in furtherance of social progress. This aspect of missionary endeavor has undergone an evolution analogous to that of the missionary endeavor as a whole. The Catholic missionaries who dominated the scene from the 16th to the 18th cent. were functioning under reactionary regimes. Even so they were able to act as protectors of the conquered peoples; to what extent can be seen by the disastrous impact on the native peoples of Latin America that the Bourbon-inspired suppression of the Jesuits had. Gradually, the emphasis among both Catholic and Protestant missioners in their social involvement was shifted from relief work to social empowerment. This did not happen overnight. During the 19th cent., few missionaries questioned radically the social impact of the schools, hospitals, and orphanages as to what extent they reinforced the colonial power and culture; to what extent they undermined traditional culture and autonomies. Even in the 20th cent., under native diocesan and other leadership, it has been difficult for the "younger Churches" to divorce themselves from colonial structures. Many missionaries resisted the divorce. So did heads of educational and benevolent institutions. Even the native clergy and Christian leaders were attached to a European identity and ethos, finding themselves estranged from their native cultures. The need to attack the roots of powerlessness is more easily honored in theory and in rhetoric than in persistent practice. Even so, the more progressive missionary groups, such as the American Maryknollers (the Catholic Foreign Mission Society of America, Inc, and the Congregation of Maryknoll Sisters) include among their social involvement, in Latin America and elsewhere, such empowering efforts as credit unions, various cooperatives, housing projects, better farming methods, cooperative factories etc.; and consciously seek to build indigenous leadership to whom the work can be transferred as soon as possible. Even in its less self-critical phase, missionary work was done with such self-sacrifice, and at such little economic cost, that it is hard to imagine social progress being made without them. Catholic social agencies have largely been run by clerics and were less hospitable to lay initiatives and leadership than their Protestant counterparts, but Vatican Council II has invited greater lay responsibility, esp. in areas of social concern.

[E. J. DILLON]

MISSISSIPPI, S Gulf state, admitted to the Union (1817) as the 20th state. The area was inhabited by Chickasaw, Choctaw, and Natchez Indians at the time Hernando de Soto discovered the Mississippi River (1541). French exploration was conducted by J. *Marquette and L. Jolliet (1673) and by Sieur de *la Salle, who claimed the mouth of the Mississippi for Louis XIV (1682). The first permanent settlement was established at Fort Maurepas (1699). The area came under British control (1763) and was ceded (1783) to the U.S., which organized it as the Mississippi Territory (1798). The first Mass was celebrated (1682) by Zenobius Membre, a member of La Salle's party. While Catholics have been a minority sect in Mississippi, their number had grown sufficiently by 1837 for the Holy See to establish the Diocese of Natchez. Renamed Natchez-Jackson (1956), it embraces the entire state of Mississippi, and is suffragan to the metropolitan See of New Orleans, Louisiana. In 1976 the Catholics of Mississippi numbered 86,773 or 3.7% of the total state population. The major Protestant sects are the Southern Baptist Convention, with 30.7% of the total population (1972), and the Methodist Church, with 9.7%. Other Protestant denominations comprised 7.0% of the population. The Jewish population (1968) was 4,015, or 0.18%. There are no Catholic colleges in Mississippi. More than 3,470 students attend the state's 12 Catholic high schools, and about 8,670 pupils are enrolled in the state's 39 Catholic elementary schools. BIBLIOGRAPHY: R. A. McLemore and N. P. McLemore, *Mississippi through Four Centuries* (1945); R. O. Gerow, *Catholicity in Mississippi* (1939).

[J. L. MORRISON; R. M. PRESTON]

MISSOURI, a central state, admitted to the Union (1821) as the 24th state. Traditionally regarded as the Gateway to the West, the area was first explored by J. *Marquette and L. Jolliet (1673) and by *La Salle (1682). Fur trading and lead mining brought the first immigrants to Missouri in the 17th and 18th centuries. The first permanent settlement was made at Ste. Geneviève *c.* 1735; St. Louis was founded in 1764 as a fur trading post. The U.S. acquired Missouri from France in the Louisiana Purchase (1803). Jesuits acted as the first missionaries in Missouri until their suppression (1773), after which the territory was served by the Franciscans. The Diocese of St. Louis was erected in 1827 and Joseph Rosati, CM, named its first bishop. Rosati was able to found a hospital, staffed by Sisters of Charity from Emmitsburg, Md., and to build a cathedral before his death in Rome (1843). P. R. *Kenrick, second bp. of St. Louis, worked to relieve the diocese of its debt and to quiet nationalistic rivalries between Irish and German immigrants. During his episcopacy, St. Louis was raised to the status of an archdiocese. Kenrick successfully carried to the U.S. Supreme Court his battle against provisions of the Missouri constitution which imposed censorship upon clergymen. Kenrick's successor was J. J. Kain (1895–1903), who reinvigorated the archdiocesan seminary and planned the new cathedral that was built by J. J. *Glennon, who succeeded him as abp. in 1903 and served in that capacity for 43 years. Glennon directed the opening of two Catholic colleges for women and promoted the expansion of St. Louis University. He also developed the parochial school system and a system of archdiocesan high schools. Glennon was created a cardinal less than a month before his death in 1946. J. E. *Ritter became the fourth abp. of St. Louis in 1946. Until his death (1967) he labored to integrate the school system and to increase the number of Catholic high schools. He favored significant participation of the laity in the affairs of the archdiocese. Bp. John J. Carberry of Columbus, Ohio, became abp. of St. Louis in 1968. The suffragan sees in Missouri are Jefferson City (1956); Kansas City (1880); St. Joseph (1868; sees united 1956); and Springfield-Cape Girardeau (1956).

Missouri's Catholics numbered (1976) 767,503, or 16.4% of the total state population. The major Protestant denominations are the Southern Baptist Convention with 13.4% of the total population, and the Methodist Church with 6.1%. Other Protestant bodies comprised 15.5% of the population. The Jewish population (1968) was 1.7% of the total. Of the seven Catholic colleges in Missouri, which enroll a total of 17,996 students, the archdiocese contains five whose total enrollment is more than 13,368. More than 26,847 students attend the state's 49 Catholic high schools; in the archdiocese itself there are 34 Catholic high schools with an enrollment of 19,985. Missouri's 288 Catholic elementary schools (181 in the archdiocese) have an enrollment of 73,135 pupils (51,429 in the archdiocese). BIBLIOGRAPHY: *Missouri, Its Resources, People, and Institutions* (ed. N. P. Gist et al., 1950); F. A. Culmer, *New History of Missouri* (1938); G. J. Garraghan, *Catholic Beginnings in Kansas City* (1920).

[J. L. MORRISON; R. M. PRESTON]

MIT BRENNENDER SORGE, (With Burning Anxiety), encyclical addressed to the German people in their own language by Pope Pius XI on Passion Sunday, March 14, 1937. The Pope began by referring to "much that is bitter and sad" reported to him "on his sick-bed" by visiting German bishops. He had despite "many serious misgivings" agreed to the Concordat of 1933 because he had hoped thereby to spare German Catholics "anxiety and suffering." The effort had been in vain. Not only had every concordat provision been violated and the persecution of the Church grown steadily more severe, but the German government had "deified" race and nation and fostered the apostasy of Christian youth. The Pope exhorted Catholics to resist the teachings of Nazism and to remain faithful to their Christian duties. The encyclical was banned by the Reich Minister for Ecclesiastical Affairs and became a source of increased tension between Church and State. BIBLIOGRAPHY: Pius XI, *Mit brennender Sorge,* English tr. *Catholic Mind* 35 (1937)186; *Documents on German Foreign Policy* 1918–1945 Series D, I.

[G. N. SHUSTER]

MITER (often, esp. in England, Mitre), a form of liturgical headdress worn by bps., abbots, and by certain other distinguished prelates. In its present form, its front and back are stiffened and are shaped like inverted shields; they are sewn together at the lower part of the sides, but above are separated by a cleft and the two parts are joined by folding cloth. Two wide lappets (*infulae*) hang down the back. The headdress may have developed from a cap originally worn by the pope during out-of-door processions. There is no satisfactory evidence that any headgear identifiable with the miter, even in its earlier forms, was in general use before the year 1000 A.D.. It seems to have been first used in Rome, and during the 11th cent. the right to wear it was gradually extended to prelates in other places. There are three forms of miter: the precious miter, which is adorned with jewels and made of gold or silver plate; the orphreyed miter, ornamented with gold cloth but without precious stones other than pearls; and the plain miter made of white silk or linen. The bp. always uses the miter when he carries the pastoral staff. It is not worn during the Canon of the Mass.

The term is also used for the liturgical headdress in several Eastern Churches. Besides *mitra*, it is sometimes called *korona* or *stephanos* in Greek; in Slavic *metra*. It is a dome-shaped crown made of metal or metallic cloth and richly ornamented with icons, stones, and embroidery and surmounted by a small cross. It is of comparatively late origin and is derived from the imperial crown of Constantinople. The miter is worn by all Byzantine bishops and by Coptic and Ethiopian prelates as well. Among the Russians it is also used by archimandrites and archpriests but often without the small cross on top. It is the normal headdress for all Armenian priests, the Roman miter being used by bishops. The Syrian Jacobite bps. use a small hood marked with crosses. In the Byzantine liturgy the crown is not worn during the preparation of the gifts, during the Gospel, at the great entrance, before and during the Creed, and during the anaphora and Communion.

[N. KOLLAR]

MITHRA AND MITHRAISM. Mithra (Gr. *Mithras*; Indic *Mitra*), is one of the old Indo-Iranian divinities. The name means "contract," but the full significance of the term in this connection is obscure. He was closely associated with *Ahura Mazda* and with light, and was early worshipped as a sun-god. Because of his role in the *haoma*-sacrifice and the bull-sacrifice, he was excluded from the religion of Zoroaster as described in the Gāthās. After the death of the prophet, however, he again appears as an important divinity in Persian religion, esp. among the masses. He is a warrior god with a white steed, and as a god of justice he is equated with the sun that sees all. In the Parthian period his popularity is attested by the frequency of personal names like Mithradates; and in Asia Minor he is identified with Apollo as sun-god and judge, with Helios as a sun-god, and with Hermes as a mediator between gods and men. In E Iran he supplanted *Ahura Mazda* or *Ormazd* as the chief god, and with the spread of Persian religion westward it was only natural the Greeks and Romans should regard him as the principal Persian divinity and that Iranian religion should be thought of as the cult of Mithra or Mithraism. This cult, as one of the Greco-Oriental mystery religions, spread throughout the Greco-Roman world, being esp. popular as a soldier's religion. Mithraic monuments are found even as far W as the Roman walls in N Britain. It was a man's religion in which women played no significant role. Contrary to views held at the beginning of the present cent., Mithraism was never a serious rival of Christianity.

The mysteries of Mithra are known to us through inscriptions but chiefly through archeological monuments. They were performed in caves, or in cave-like buildings called *Mithraea*—in general, in chapels rather than temples. On the chapel walls Mithra is depicted as wearing a Phrygian cap and killing a bull. The birth of Mithra was celebrated on Dec. 25, immediately after the winter solstice. There were seven degrees of imitation, each with its own symbols and each connected with a planet. The ritual included oaths, banquets of bread and wine, and a baptism of blood—a late rite borrowed from the cult of *Cybele (see TAUROBOLIUM). The followers of Mithra were promised a life after death. The soul passed through seven planetary spheres to a heaven that was beyond all things. It is possible that Mithraism was influenced in its ritual by contacts with Christianity. The cult of Mithra has a complicated history and in its fully developed form it reflects more and more the syncretistic tendencies of the last centuries of antiquity. BIBLIOGRAPHY: A. D. Nock, "Genius of Mithraism," *Journal of Roman Studies* 27 (1937) 108–113; J. Duchesne–Guillemin, *La Religion de l'Iran ancien* (1962) 172–175, 248–257; *idem*, NCE 9:982–983. *MYSTERY RELIGIONS, GRECO-ROMAN.

[M. R. P. MCGUIRE]

MITTARELLI, GIOVANNI BENEDETTO (1707–77), Camaldolese historian. M. entered the community in 1722 and was chancellor of the order in 1747. He became abbot of the abbey of S. Michele di Murano (1760) and abbot general at Rome (1765–70). Following Mabillon, M. compiled with Anselm Costadoni the *Annales Camaldulenses ordinis S. Benedicti 907–1764*. He also supplemented Muratori's *Rerum Italicarum Scriptores* with his *Accessiones historiae Faventinae*, and *Appendix de literatura Faventinorum*. BIBLIOGRAPHY: H. Rumpler, NCE 9:983–984; H. Kiene, LTK 7:493.

[J. M. O'DONNELL]

MITTY, JOHN JOSEPH (1884–1961), abp. of San Francisco. A New Yorker ordained in 1906, M. taught at the archdiocesan seminary from 1909 to 1917, when he became an Army chaplain and served in France. After World War I he was chaplain to the cadet corps at West Point for a time. In 1926 he was named bp. of Salt Lake City, Utah. Appointed coadjutor of San Francisco in 1932, he became abp. in 1935. As spiritual leader of a diocese experiencing phenomenal growth, M. proved vigorous and imaginative. His record as a builder is incredible: 85

parishes, 120 new churches, 119 parochial schools, 13 secondary schools, 28 youth centers, orphanages, and hospitals. M. pioneered schools of religion of the Confraternity of Christian Doctrine serving over 100,000 children. Among his innovative projects were counseling in social services, caring for migrant workers, making use of television, and permitting mixed marriages to be performed in church.

[J. R. AHERNE]

MIVART, ST. GEORGE JACKSON (1827–1900), biologist, evolutionist. A Londoner who converted to Catholicism in 1844, M. took a degree in law but worked all his life in biology. He became professor of comparative anatomy at St. Mary's Hospital, London, in 1862. A Fellow of the Royal Society, he contributed original and provocative papers to many scientific journals. His evolutionary theory was in opposition to the Darwinian view. M. wrote, perhaps too much, for such periodicals as the *Contemporary Review* and *The Nineteenth Century*. His attempts to reconcile evolutionary theory and Catholic philosophy and theology created a number of books: *Lessons from Nature as Manifested in Mind and Matter* (1876); *Philosophical Catechism* (1884); *On Truth: a Systematic Inquiry* (1889); *The Groundwork of Science: a Study of Epistemology* (1898). His Catholic thesis was further developed in such articles as ''Modern Catholic and Scientific Freedom'' (1885), ''The Catholic Church and Biblical Criticism,'' (1887), ''Catholicity and Reason'' (1887), and ''Happiness in Hell'' (1892). The last-named was placed on the Index. An article, ''The Continuity of Catholicism,'' together with one in the *Fortnightly Review* brought sentence of excommunication in Jan. 1900 from Card. Vaughan, Abp. of Westminster because M. refused to retract by a profession of faith. At his death the following April, M. was refused Christian burial but the intervention of friends allowed him to be buried later in the Catholic cemetery at Kensal Green.

[J. R. AHERNE]

MIXED LIFE is that chosen state which is an intermediate combination of both *contemplative and *active lives. While the expression is not used by the classical authors who considered the division into two lives adequate from the predominant concern of each, Augustine, Gregory the Great, and Thomas Aquinas did speak of those who were sometimes contemplative, sometimes active, because their particular function called for a fullness of contemplation as a condition for the active work of teaching and preaching. Perhaps a better expression for this ''mixed'' life would be *apostolic, since it is believed that not only the Apostles but Christ himself united filial prayer and contemplation of the Father with the active works of fraternal charity. This provided a pattern for the prelates of the Church. The traditional formula for this life is that expressed by St. Thomas: ''to give to others what has been contemplated'' (ThAq ST 2a2ae, 188.6). BIBLIOGRAPHY: I. Mennessier, ''Specific Aspects of Christian Life,'' TL 4:659–660; J. Aumann, *Action and Contemplation* (1966); E. Coreth, ''Contemplative in Action,'' Theol Dig 3 (1955) 37–45.

[U. VOLL]

MIXED MARRIAGE, ''marriages in which one party is a Catholic and the other a non-Catholic, whether baptized or not.'' (Paul VI, *motu proprio, Matrimonia mixta*, March 31, 1970). Mixed marriages are forbidden by ecclesiastical law (CIC c. 1060, 1070), while if there is danger to the faith of the Catholic or of the children, divine law itself forbids them, since ''the perfect union of mind and full communion of life'' to which married couples aspire can be more readily achieved when both partners share the same Catholic belief and life.

Although the Church greatly desires that Catholics marry Catholics and generally discourages mixed marriages, it recognizes the fact that mixed marriages do occur and upholding the principles of divine law makes special arrangements for them, relaxing (by dispensation) ecclesiastical discipline in particular cases. The Church recognizes however that . . . ''the canonical discipline on mixed marriages cannot be uniform and must be adapted . . .'' and ''the pastoral care to be given to the married people and children of marriage'' must also be adapted ''according to the distinct circumstances of the married couple and the differing degrees of their ecclesiastical communion.'' In such marriages pastoral care must emphasize concern and respect for the couples involved, with stress actively and positively on the holy state in which such couples are united; the conscientious devotion of the Catholic to the Catholic Church is to be safeguarded and the conscience of the other partner is to be respected. This is in keeping with the principle of religious liberty (cf. Vat II RelFreed 30). Therefore appropriate informational programs are to be established to explain both the reasons for restrictions upon mixed marriages and the positive spiritual values to be sought in such marriages when permitted. In addition to the customary marriage preparation programs, spiritual and catechetical preparations on a direct and individual basis are to be given, esp. in regard to the ''ends and essential properties of marriage which are not to be excluded by either party''; and most seriously in regard to the written or oral promise of the Catholic party concerning the obligation of preserving his or her own faith and as far as possible to see to it ''that the children be baptized and brought up in that same faith and receive all those aids to eternal salvation which the Catholic Church provides for her sons and daughters.'' Where serious difficulties are present in regard to observing the canonical form of marriage (before a competent priest and two witnesses) which is binding on the Catholic party, a dispensation by the ordinary may be granted for a just pastoral cause. According to the directive of the National Episcopal Conference, it is possible to obtain dispensation for the marriage to be performed in the Church of the non-Catholic party. It is then desirable for both pastors to participate in the service. *NCCB Statement on the Implementation of the Apostolic Letter on Mixed Marriages* (1971 [*Matrimonia mixta* AAS 62, 1972]) 257–263.

[C. J. NOONE]

MIXED MOTIVES, plurality of differing *intentions in a moral action. In general, both objectively and in moral self-evaluation, the primary good or evil of an action corresponds to the primary intention. The complexity of human nature and the versatility of perception with regard to the true or seeming good explain the possibility of a multi-intentioned act. But the phrase ''mixed motives'' should be understood of intentions regarding differing and gradated goods, since the intention of a false good vitiates any other good in an action. The mixture of goods means that there is present an opportunity for self-interest concomitantly with a higher, more altruistic good. That occasions questioning one's hierarchy of motives. Yet where true good is intended the lesser does not vitiate the higher. Nor does intensity of awareness of the lesser deny the objective value deriving to an act from the intention of the higher good. Striving in charity to achieve its ideals is to be accompanied not by morbid self-doubt, but by humility, and a sense of the room for growth through healing grace.

[T. C. O'BRIEN]

MIXOLYDIAN (also *septimus modus,* seventh mode), the *mode or scale equivalent to a white-key scale beginning on G. Its *plagal form is termed hypomixolydian (*octavus tonus,* eighth mode).

[A. DOHERTY]

MIZPAH (Mizpeh), name of several biblical sites. Since the term means lookout point, they were presumably on elevated spots and were probably cultic centers. One was an important gathering place for the Israelites (Jg 20.1; 1 Sam 7.5). See also Gen 31.49; Jos 11.3; Jg 10.17.

[T. EARLY]

MO TZU (Mo Ti; *c.*470–*c.*391 B.C.), Chinese philosopher, founder of Moism, one of the classical systems of Chinese philosophy, and first important critic of Confucianism. His thought survives in the *Mo Tzu,* of which only 53 of an original 71 chapters remain. He criticized the Confucianists for what he considered their atheism, their social elegance, their insistence on elaborate funeral rites and mourning that wasted the people's energy and wealth, their idle indulgence in music and literature, and their belief in fate (Ming), which he rather incorrectly claimed subverts the people's resolve to act. He shared with Confucians a high estimation of the virtues of *jen* (humanity) and *yi* (righteousness), though he reinterpreted these virtues in accordance with his own principle of all-embracing or universal love: Heaven (*T'ien*) loved all and it is Heaven's will that we love one another. He reaffirmed the existence of lesser spirits who could reward and punish good and evil. In the *Mo Tzu,* the authority of the State and its ruler originates in the will of the people and the Will of Heaven; the State described is to be totalitarian and the ruler absolute, rewarding the practice of universal love among his subjects, punishing their violations. Stressing method in all judgments, the *Mo Tzu* demands tests of all propositions for their compatibility with the best of recognized opinion, common sense and, on practical matters, for their utility in improving the lot of the poor, increasing population, eliminating danger, or alleviating disorder. M.'s sympathies always lay with the poor and with the *hsieh,* a lower class composed of warriors, whereas Confucius's sympathies remained with the literate upper and middle classes. M. was very influential during the Warring States Period (*c.* 480–222 B.C.). His movement, which attracted about 300 dedicated disciples, split into three factions after his death. During the Western Han Dynasty (206 B.C.–8 A.D.), Mo-ist thought fell into utter decline, and was not revived until the 18th cent., when Pi Yuan published the *Mo Tzu* with a commentary (1783). The Standard Chinese edition was edited by Sun I-jang (1894; rev. 1907).

[R. J. LITZ]

MOABITE STONE, slab (stele) of Mesha, King of Moab, inscribed with an account of his victory over the Israelites (2 Kg 3.21–27). It is the only major inscription in Moabite, a language similar to Hebrew. *MESHA INSCRIPTION.

[T. EARLY]

MOABITES, a people related to the Israelites through Lot (Gen 19.37). Their land lay E of the Dead Sea on a fertile plateau. Because of intermittent warfare with Israel over Moab's northern marches, claimed by the tribe of Reuben, the two peoples became bitter enemies, though in the post-Exilic period intermarriage with Moabites was a common Jewish practice. Moab was absorbed by Nabataea eventually.

[J. F. FALLON]

MOAK, IGNATIUS (1818–1901), bishop. An Austrian who after ordination in 1837 volunteered for the missions in Michigan, M. worked among the Indians for 13 years. He was appointed bp. of Sault Sainte Marie and Marquette in 1868. For 9 years he labored, never forgetting his first concern, the Indians. Ill health caused him to resign but did not prevent his return to the Indian missions.

[J. R. AHERNE]

MOCCAS, MONASTERY OF, a Celtic monastery founded in Wales in the 6th cent. by the abbot-bp. Dubricius or Dyfrig. It formed part of an important monastic parish located principally in the Romano-British kingdom of Erging or Archenfield. Dyfrig's first place was Hentland near the Wye, where he conducted a famous school. In the 12th cent. an unjustified attempt was made to make Dyfrig's parish the origin of the See of Llandaff. Its later history is unknown. BIBLIOGRAPHY: J. E. Lloyd, *History of Wales* (2 v. 1948); A. W. Wade-Evans, *Welsh Christian Origins* (1934).

[C. MCGRATH]

MOCQUEREAU, ANDRÉ (1849–1930), music scholar of the abbey of Solesmes, France. M. studied at the Paris Conservatory with Charles Dancla; he entered Solesmes in 1875, was professed in 1877, and ordained in 1879. M. continued the work of restoring Gregorian chant melodies and texts begun at the Abbey by Doms Guéranger, Pothier, Jausions, and others. This task led to the publication, beginning from 1889 of the *Paléographie musicale* (19 v.), a comparative study of medieval MSS gathered from all over Europe. This work and his two volume work *Le Nombre musical grégorien* (1908–27), have made a significant contribution to musicology and to subsequent study of both Eastern and Western chant. M.'s theory of the "free musical rhythm" of the chant, though not unchallenged even by M.'s master, Dom Pothier, became the basis for the new official Vatican edition of the liturgical chants. M. wrote several other important works, such as *Méthode de chant grégorien* (1899) and began the series *Monographies grégoriennes* in 1910 and the *Revue grégorienne* in 1911. He made two visits to the U.S., one in 1920 to preside at the International Congress of Gregorian Chant in New York and the second in 1922 to conduct a course in chant at the Pius X School of Liturgical Music. BIBLIOGRAPHY: "Liturgical Scholar Led in Restoration of the Gregorian Chant," *Catholic Choirmaster* 16 (1930) 8, 35; J. Ward, "Solesmes and a Centenary," *ibid.* 36 (1950) 108–111; C. J. McNaspy, "The Story of Solesmes," *Musart* (1955) 6.

[M. T. LEGGE]

MODALISM, a rigorous form of Monarchianism, known also as Sabellianism or Patripassianism. It is a heresy that emphasized the unity (*monarchia*) of God. Admitting a verbal but no real distinction in the Trinity, it maintained that the Father, Son, and Holy Spirit are merely aspects or modes of a single divine Person. Thus God, who is one from eternity, becomes three in time through different acts posited *ad extra,* or outside the Trinity. Through creation, he becomes Father, through Redemption Son, and through sanctification Holy Spirit. From the belief that God the Father suffered as the Son, it received the name of Patripassianism. The heresy arose in the early 3d cent., its chief proponents being Praxeas in the West and Sabellius in the East. BIBLIOGRAPHY: G. Bardy, DTC 10.2:2193–2209.

[M. J. COSTELLOE]

MODE, a particular arrangement of the successive notes of a musical scale, giving a distinctive quality to music written in that mode. The most familiar modes are the major and the minor, used in most music from *c.*1600 to *c.*1900. Mode refers to the type of scale, while key refers to the actual pitch of the scale. The same mode may be used at different pitch levels, i.e., in different keys (C major, D major), and different modes may be based on the same pitch (C major, C minor). The term refers particularly to the eight modes of *Gregorian chant, often called ancient, church, or ecclesiastical modes. Each has a distinctive psalm-tone, which epitomizes the mode. The reciting-note of the psalm-tone is the dominant note of the mode, and its *final (the usual beginning and ending note) is the tonic, the note on which the mode is built. The Gregorian modes are designated by ordinal numerals (tonus primus, first mode, etc.), and are grouped in pairs (1st and 2d, 3d and 4th, 5th and 6th, 7th and 8th) of an *authentic and a plagal mode sharing a common final (D, E, F, and G respectively) but having different reciting-notes and ranges, those of the plagal mode being lower than its respective authentic mode. The names of the modes of ancient Greek music were applied to the Gregorian modes (inaccurately, because of a misunderstanding of Greek theoretical treatises). The authentic modes on D, E, F, and G were named *Dorian, *Phrygian, *Lydian, and *Mixolydian respectively, and their plagals bore the same names with the prefix Hypo-. The Gregorian chant repertory shows a distinctive melodic style for each of the modes. Modes can also be built on A, B, and C. In chant, those on A and C were identified with those on D and F respectively, and that on B, musically closest to the one on E, was not used since a *tritone was formed between the final and the reciting note. In the 16th cent. the modes on A and C were named *Aeolian and *Ionian, and their pairs of authentic and plagal were numbered as the 9th and 10th, and the 11th and 12th modes (see *GAREANUS). The mode on B was eventually named *Locrian, but never gained acceptance. The rise of *polyphony in the late Middle Ages obliterated the distinction between authentic and plagal modes because of the increased melodic ranges employed; and the church modes themselves, whose characteristics are essentially melodic, lost their identities in the increasing emphasis on harmony from the 16th cent. on, and were absorbed by the modern major and minor modes. See also BYZANTINE CHANT.

[J. J. WALSH; A. DOHERTY]

MODENA CATHEDRAL. A most impressive Romanesque structure, the Cathedral of S. Geminiano by the Lombard Lanfranco was begun by Countess Matilda of Tuscany (1099), the later superstructure consecrated in 1184. A columned nave and two aisles support a triforium and ogival vaults, with compound arches in the bays. A campanile was added in 1319. The façade, boasting a handsome Lombardy porch with lion caryatids and balcony, is renowned for the important 12th-cent. portal reliefs by Masters Nicolaus and the famed Guglielmo da Modena.

[M. J. DALY]

MODERATOR, in *Presbyterianism the officer presiding over a *church session, *presbytery, *synod, or *general assembly. The moderator of the session is the minister; in the other Presbyterian courts the moderator is elected.

[T. C. O'BRIEN]

MODERATUS OF GADES (2d half of 1st cent. A.D.), Neopythagorean philosopher. He interpreted the Pythagorean theory of numbers as merely a symbolic way of expressing the basic concepts of a metaphysical system, which Plato had taken over from Pythagoras. Accordingly he maintained that there is a first, a second, and a third One. The first One is beyond all being and *ousia*. The second, what is actually being and intelligible, equals ideas. The third, namely the psychical, participates in the first One and in the ideas. These three are then followed by that which is sensible. The sensible comes into existence as cosmos—through the fact that the One and the ideas are reflected in the matter of the sensibles. The matter of the sensibles is a kind of shadow of the first nonbeing (CHGMP 93). BIBLIOGRAPHY: W. Burkert, LexAW 1975–76; CHGMP 90–95.

[M. R. P. MCGUIRE]

MODERN CHURCHMEN'S UNION, an Anglican society founded in 1898 for the advancement of liberal religious thought. Known until 1928 as the Churchmen's Union, its principal organ was *The Modern Churchman,* founded 1911 by H. D. A. Major (later principal of Ripon Hall, Oxford). It resisted both the High Church disciples of the Tractarians and the Low Church successors to the Evangelicals. It was in line with the Latitudinarian (Broad Church) emphasis on the comprehensive nature of the C of E, preferring to accept a wide spectrum of interpretations of Anglican formularies to accommodate communicants of divergent views. In general the MCU rejected belief in the miraculous and rigid adherence to the creeds of the ancient Church; it stressed moral rectitude, tolerance of heterodox views, and openness to scientific opinion; it minimized hierarchical organization and ritualism. It can be considered an expression of modernism in the C of E, with its insistence on the legitimacy of doctrinal restatement and liturgical reform.

[E. J. DILLON]

MODERNE, JACQUES (16th-cent.), Italian-born composer, *maître de chapelle* at Notre-Dame du Confort, Lyons, music printer and publisher (1532–67); works include motets and chansons.

[R. J. LITZ]

MODERNISM (Protestant), a designation for liberal Protestant thought. The term originally applied to a movement within the RC Church (see MODERNISM [ROMAN CATHOLIC]), but it became current in the C of E; then during World War I it came into use in the U.S. and was common during the 1920s in the Modernist-Fundamentalist controversy, e.g., J. G. *Machen declared that ''modern liberalism,'' which he equated with Modernism, was un-Christian, an entirely different religion from Christianity (*Christianity and Liberalism,* 1923). Many liberals, however, accepted it as an appropriate designation, because their aim was to accommodate Christianity to modern knowledge. Shailer *Mathews defined Modernism as ''the use of the methods of modern science to find, state and use the permanent and central values of inherited orthodoxy in meeting the needs of a modern world'' (*The Faith of Modernism,* 1924). Modernism was more a spirit or attitude than a particular system of ideas, and its representatives differed in their approaches to epistemology, metaphysics, traditional Christian affirmations, and attitude toward Christianity in relation to other religions. Despite their variety, modernist theologies all shared certain presuppositions as they faced the cultural changes reflected in philosophy, psychology, historiography, science and technology, and socioeconomic theory. Some of the factors that influenced the development of Modernism were: a scientific spirit that considered empirical method the only valid avenue to truth; the complete sufficiency of human reason; naturalism, or a tendency to account for everything in terms of natural causality; historical and literary criticism of the Bible; the authority of individual experience in religion; an emphasis upon practical ethics in religion; and an attempt to isolate the essential in Christianity from the accidental.

To a large extent the basic ideas in this process originated in Europe. In the U.S. they took on a distinctive shape as they were affected by *revivalism, with its stress upon religious experience and depreciation of dogmatic theology; by an emphasis on the practical and an impatience with the theoretical; and by the active spirit of reform that had flourished in American Christianity before the Civil War. Besides common influences, there were also common characteristics in theological content: emphasis upon the immanence of God; an optimistic view of human nature and of moral progress; acceptance of the Bible as a record of man's quest rather than a record of objective revelation; a deemphasizing of sin; an accent on the humanity of Jesus Christ that ignored or denied his deity and pictured him as the teacher and leader par excellence; and the elimination of miracles as superstitious accretions of a prescientific age.

Some Modernists might have accepted all of these viewpoints; others held only a few of them. In spite of common influences and tendencies in Modernist thought, there were also sharp differences respecting the extent to which they were willing to reinterpret Christianity. Kenneth Cauthen has suggested the categories of ''evangelical liberals'' and ''Modernistic liberals'' to distinguish two main types of liberal. The former made more effort to maintain continuity with historic Christianity and had a Christocentric emphasis. The latter were less concerned about the uniqueness of Christianity and considered Jesus Christ helpful, but not indispensable, to religious experience. During the 1930s liberalism in the U.S. came under heavy attack from within its own ranks, beginning with such works as Reinhold

Niebuhr's *Moral Man and Immoral Society* (1932) and Edwin Lewis's *Christian Manifesto* (1934). BIBLIOGRAPHY: J. Dillenberger and C. Welch, *Protestant Christianity Interpreted through Its Development* (1954); H. S. Smith, R. T. Handy, and L. A. Loetscher, *American Christianity: Interpretation and Documents* (v. 2, 1963). *FUNDAMENTALISM; *NEO-ORTHODOXY; *LIBERAL THEOLOGY.

[N. H. MARING]

MODERNISM (Roman Catholic), the ideological effort by a number of RC intellectuals to reinterpret the Christian faith in terms of contemporary historical, psychological, and philosophical positions that led to conclusions considered by the Church *magisterium as unorthodox and destructive of faith. The movement may be situated between about 1890 and 1910. Modernism was more a spontaneous orientation than an organized grouping. Three of the chief causes of the Modernist crisis were: (1) the backwardness of RC scholarship in its critical approach to the Bible; (2) the lack of a generally accepted philosophical anthropology and of an epistemology that could handle problems raised by Immanuel Kant; (3) the scholastic rigidity on the part of church officials as they addressed themselves to the newly emerging Catholic thought. Modernism found its chief center in France. M. Hébert in the article ''La dernière idole'' (1902) attacked the idea of personality in God. God, he held, is the category of the Ideal, immanent but unknowable. Abbé A. *Loisy in 1900 criticized the notion of inspiration as found in the encyclical *Providentissimus Deus* (1893). In 1902 and 1903 he wrote *L'Évangile et l'Église* and *Autour d'un petit livre* as a reply to A. *Harnack's thesis that the essence of the gospel was God and the soul, or the Fatherhood of God, and not a Christology or any other developed dogma. Loisy in rejecting this as an individualism foreign to the gospel insisted on the social aspect of the kingdom of God and the natural inevitability of development of dogma. He claimed, however, that Jesus erred in his teaching about the imminence of the kingdom and wrote: ''Jesus announced the Kingdom and it is the Church which came.'' As a result of subsequent condemnation by the Holy Office, Loisy made an ambiguous retraction of his positions in 1904. In 1902 and 1906 Abbé A. Houtin published a history of biblical criticism that was bitterly critical of RC scholarship. In 1905 E. Le Roy, a layman, asserted that dogma gives the believer a rule for practical conduct or a pragmatic stance rather than intellectual content about God.

In England G. *Tyrrell, who was endeavoring to reinterpret Catholic teaching, was dismissed from the Society of Jesus in 1906 for refusing to retract the ideas in his anonymous *Letter to a Friend, A Professor of Anthropology,* in which he greatly relativized the meaning of dogma. Gradually (esp. in *Through Scylla and Charybdis,* 1907) he worked out a theory of revelation in which he emphasized the immanent role of the recipient, accentuated the notion of religious experience in revelation, and gave dogma the secondary and totally relative function of protecting the ''prophetic truth'' of Scripture. Scripture itself was a record of an experience. The layman F. von Hügel generally supported Tyrrell. While pursuing his own work on mysticism, he made many contacts in Italy, France, and England, and came closest to being an organizer of Modernism. However he did not support all the ideas associated with the movement and was chiefly engaged in a crusade to gain for RC scholars the rights to a kind of academic freedom. In Italy the movement had a more social orientation. R. Murri, e.g., pushed for independence from the hierarchy in social and political areas and called for a reform of the Church's institutional structure. S. Minochi carried on the thought o Loisy and Tyrrell. A. Fogazzaro in his novel *Il Santo* (1905) painted a dark picture of the Church and called for reform of the four evil spirits of untruthfulness, domination, avarice, and immobility. E. Buonaiuti replied to the encyclical **Pascendi dominici gregis* with *Il programma dei modernisti* (1907), in which he demanded that Catholicism be reconciled with scientific findings and attacked scholasticism. In Germany the movement known as *Reformkatholizismus was concerned chiefly with disciplinary questions. It insisted on freedom in scientific religious work, called for the suppression of the Index, and was generally anti-Roman in tone. Out of this only a small Modernist group emerged, mostly after *Pascendi*. One of the leaders was J. Schnitzer, who supported Loisy. In the U.S. the most famous Modernist was W. L. Sullivan (*Letters to His Holiness Pius X, by a Modernist,* 1910), who left the Paulists and became a Unitarian. The scattered support for the movement in the U.S. was greater than has been generally realized, mainly among seminary professors. However, such tendencies in the U.S. died out rapidly. No one knows the number of Catholics throughout the world with strong Modernist tendencies. It seems that it was a moderate-sized group of intellectuals, who did not make a strong impact on the large body of faithful.

On July 3, 1907, the Holy Office in its decree **Lamentabili* condemned 65 propositions connected with biblical criticism and dogma. Pius X on Sept. 8, 1907, issued the encyclical *Pascendi dominici gregis*. Probably its chief target was the work of Loisy and Tyrrell. It condemned the theory of error on the part of Christ, theories relativizing dogma, and a biblical criticism in which it found agnostic, pure immanentist, and antiintellectualist bases. *Pascendi* condemned Modernism as ''the synthesis of all heresies.'' However, the encyclical presented a global picture of Modernism that was a theoretical construction dictated by contemporary neoscholasticism. It may have described the position of M. Hébert or perhaps even of the later Loisy, but Tyrrell, e.g., could never be described as a pure immanentist. The problems with which many of the Modernists were grappling were not handled in all their subtlety. In leveling its attack at *agnosticism and pure immanentism, *Pascendi* finds its permanent value; for many other issues the encyclical seems to have been a premature condemnation without solution. The encyclical set up Committees of Vigilance, which received strong support from simplistic conservative groups, one of which was the *Sodalitium pianum* directed by Msgr. U. Benigni in Italy. Attacks were leveled not only against theologians but against liberal positions in politics and even in literature. The result was a kind of paralysis with regard to broaching questions connected with subjects handled in the encyclical. The *Oath against Modernism (Sept. 1, 1910) sealed this mood upon the Church, a mood that was not totally relieved even by Benedict XV's *Ad beatissimi* in 1914, which was an attempt at checking the campaign of suspicion. Von Hügel alone of the leading characters in the movement escaped official condemnation. However, scholars like Lagrange, Batiffol, Grandmaison, and Rivière were destined to continue their work in an atmosphere of excessive constraint. It was only with *Divino afflante Spiritu* in 1943, which officially approved the use of literary forms as a key to understanding parts of the Bible, that a change began, a change that culminated in Vatican Council II.

In the overall view, Modernism was a challenge to the then prevalent analysis of the notion of official authority in the Church. Some magisterial action no doubt was called for in the face of the excessive challenges thrown out by some Modernist writers, or else the result might have been anarchy. Yet the Modernist crisis was a tragedy. On the one side there was the large body of the faithful unprepared for the new critical work and church officials who had little sense of the solidity of some of the recent scholarship. On the other side were scholars doing pioneer work who had little respect for the criticism of their often unprepared Catholic colleagues. The result of the condemnation was a temporary pastoral gain for the faithful at large. But the problems that were raised grew into a mountain of difficulties that the Church has had ultimately to face. Positively Modernism underlined the relation of revelation to human experience, the immediate orientation of dogma to practical action and prayer, the historically conditioned side of dogma, the need for thoroughly critical work in religious areas, the right to freedom in research, the need to restructure institutions in the Church, and the ultimate limitations to magisterial authority. BIBLIOGRAPHY: A. Vidler, *Modernist Movement in the Roman Church* (1934; repr. 1976; micro. 1978); J. Ratté, *Three Modernists: Loisy, Tyrrell and Sullivan* (1967); J. Heaney, *Modernist Crisis: Von Hügel* (1968); J. Rivière, *Le Modernisme dans l'Église* (1929).

[J. J. HEANEY]

MODERNISM, OATH AGAINST, see OATH AGAINST MODERNISM.

MODERSOHN-BECKER, PAULA (1876–1907), German expressionist artist at Worpswede (1899), painting peasants in a style related earlier to Bonnard and Vuillard, later to Van Gogh and Millet, finally in flat areas attesting to Gauguin's influence. M.'s figures convey a deeply introspective, moving presence. She died after childbirth without realizing her potential, but is honored in Bremen in the national museum, Becker-Modersohn Haus.

[M. J. DALY]

MODES, ECCLESIASTICAL, see MODE.

MODESTUS, ST., PATRIARCH OF JERUSALEM (d. 634). He rebuilt the holy places after the Persian invasion of 614. He was long thought to be the author of the earliest extant homily on the Assumption of Mary; but M. *Jugie proved that the ascription is false.

[T. C. O'BRIEN]

MODESTY (Lat. *modestia*), the quality of being moderate, of keeping to the proper mode, neither too much nor too little, and in moral theology that *virtue, a part of the cardinal virtue of *temperance, which maintains a certain reserve before the pleasures of holding oneself in esteem and of attracting the notice of others. As an attitude of mind and heart it is called *humility, but it extends also to outward show in comportment and dress. As implying a sense of what is decent and honorable, and an aversion from what is shameful, it has become synonymous with sexual humility, *pudicitia,* and the faithful commonly accuse themselves of immodesty in thought, word, or deed, when, though sinful, they have not proceeded to the lengths of complete unchastity. BIBLIOGRAPHY: ThAq ST 2a2ae, 160–169.

[T. GILBY]

MOECHIAN CONTROVERSY (Gr., *moicheia,* adultery). In 795 the Byzantine Emperor Constantine VI dismissed his wife and, with an Abbot Joseph officiating, married his mistress, whom he had crowned as empress. For this he was violently censured by the Studite monks, who also criticized Patriarch Tarasius for his lenient view of the matter. This resulted in a bitter division and actual schism in the Church between the rigorous, monastic faction and the patriarch, which lasted until the time of Emperor Michael I Rangabe (811–813). BIBLIOGRAPHY: Beck 491–494.

[G. T. DENNIS]

MOELLER, CHARLES (1912–), Belgian canon, theologian, and literary critic. Ordained to the priesthood (1937), he received a doctorate in theology from Louvain Univ. (1941) and was subsequently named to a professorship there (1956). As a *peritus* at Vatican Council II, he helped formulate decrees on the constitution of the Church, on revelation, and on non-Christian religions. One of the founders of the Ecumenical Institute of Theological Research in Jerusalem, he serves as assistant secretary of the Congregation of the Doctrine of the Faith and as consultant to the Secretariat for Unbelievers. His most ambitious work, *Littérature du XXe siècle et Christianisme* (4 v., 1953–1960), deals with the religious outlook of contemporary French and English authors and with theological questions posed by their writings. His other works inquire into Christianity's relationship to humanism and into pastoral approaches to atheism. They include *Humanisme et sainteté* (1946), *Sagesse grecque et paradoxe chrétien* (1948), *The Theology of Grace and the Ecumenical Movement* (1957; Eng. tr. 1961, coauthor, G. Philips), *L'Homme moderne devant le salut* (1965), *Modern Mentality and Evangelization* (1955; Eng. tr. 1967), and numerous articles in journals like *Irénikon*, the *Revue nouvelle,* and *Criterio*.

[G. E. GINGRAS]

MOFFAT, ROBERT (1795–1883), the father and pioneer of British missionary efforts in South Africa. The influence of Wesleyans drew him to mission work while he was still an apprenticed gardener. He eventually became a Congregationalist, was accepted by the London Missionary Society in 1816, and spent the years 1817–70 in South Africa, except for a brief interval spent in England (1839–43), during which time he managed to persuade David Livingstone (his eventual son-in-law) to go out to Africa. Staunch friend of the African tribesmen, tireless teacher and worker unafraid of manual labor, M. ventured extensively into areas of South Africa where few Europeans had entered and fewer had stayed. His wife Mary shared with him 50 years of missionary labors. Over a period of 3 decades, he translated the Bible and other inspirational works into the Sechwana language. His other publications include *Missionary Labours and Scenes in Southern Africa* (1842), and *Rivers of Water in a Dry Place* (1863).

[E. J. DILLON]

MOFFATT, JAMES (1870–1944), biblical scholar and church historian. Born in Glasgow and ordained for the ministry in the Free Church of Scotland, M. taught at Oxford (1911–15), Glasgow (1915–27), and at Union Theological Seminary in New York (1927–39). He is best known for his translation of the Bible into familiar modern language (NT 1913; OT 1924; rev. ed. of the whole, 1935). The popularity of this modern version led to a series of NT commentaries based on his text and edited by himself (17 v., 1928–49).

[R. B. ENO]

MOGILA, PETER (1596–1646), Russian Orthodox theologian. He studied in Phanariote schools in Moldavaia and the Univ. of Paris and Oxford. Ordained in 1626, he became grand archimandrite of the Monastery of *Caves, founded the Academy of *Kiev in 1631, and was metropolitan of that city from 1633 until his death. Because of the efforts of Latin-rite and Byzantine Catholics, and the Calvinistic tendencies of *Cyril Lucaris, Patriarch of Constantinople, M. felt the need to clarify Orthodox belief. This he attempted in his main work *The Orthodox Confession of Faith*. A synod at Kiev (1640) decided to submit the *Confession* to Constantinople and, after some modifications, it was accepted by the Synod of *Jassy (1642). M. later published a *Catechism* (at variance with the *Confession* on certain points), but both these works enjoyed great popularity. Many of M.'s writings were polemical attacks on Catholicism, and the influence that his work had on Russian theologians for 2 cent. has diminished as they now attempt a more creative theology. BIBLIOGRAPHY: J. Jugie and M. Gordillo, DTC 10.2:2070–76; 14.1:345–346.

[F. T. RYAN]

MOGROVEJO, TORIBIO ALFONSO DE, ST. (1538–1606), Spanish-born abp. of Lima. M. studied and taught law at Salamanca and, though a layman at the time, was made presiding judge of the Inquisition at Granada. At the request of King Philip II the Pope appointed him abp. of Lima. He accepted the office reluctantly, received minor and major orders, and was consecrated bp. in Seville (1580). In Peru he became a tireless missionary, visiting the whole of his vast see three times, despite the peril and hardship to which he exposed himself by his travels. He convoked and presided at a diocesan and a provincial council in Lima, erected the first seminary of the New World, enacted legislation to implement the Tridentine decrees, saw to the publication of catechisms suitable for the instruction of the Indians, reestablished discipline among the clergy and used his wealth unsparingly in works of charity. He personally baptized and confirmed many thousands, among whom were SS. Rose of Lima and Martin de Porres. He was canonized in 1726. BIBLIOGRAPHY: V. Rodriguez, *Santo Toribio de Mogrovejo, organizador y apóstol de Sudamerica* (1946); Butler 2:176–178.

[P. DAMBORIENA]

MOGULS, see MUGHALS.

MOHAMMED (Mahomet and other English adaptations of the Arabic Muḥammad; *c.*570–632), Prophet of *Islam. According to tradition M. was the son of a poor but respected member of the clan of Hashim, a leading branch of the tribe of Quraysh. His father, ʻAbdallâh had died shortly before his birth and following the death of his mother Amîna, not long afterward, his grandfather ʻAbd al-Muṭṭalib took charge of him, giving him to a Bedouin woman of the Banî Saʻd to nurse. In his early adolescence, at the death of his grandfather, M. was taken in by his uncle, abû Ṭâlib, a wealthy and important merchant whose son, *Ali was then quite young. Subsequently, in his early 20s he entered the service of a well-to-do, middle-aged widow, Khadîja, with whom he later contracted a very happy marriage and by whom he had several daughters, among them Fâtima, who was later to marry his cousin Ali. While in the service of Khadîja, M. is said to have made several commercial journeys to Syria and legend has it that on one of these trips he met an anchorite, Bahîrâ, who recognized him as a great prophet. These years of M.'s life are quite obscure. In the first decade of the 7th cent. he underwent a religious crisis and would, on occasion, retire to a cave on Mt. Ḥira, near Mecca, sometimes for lengthy periods of meditation. Influences upon him at this period are extremely uncertain; besides contacts he may have had with Christians or Jews, if the reports of his journeys to Syria and Yemen are true, there would have certainly been a few Christians and Jews at Mecca, mostly slaves, in addition to a small group of persons of monotheistic tendencies known as hanifs. Finally, in the month of *Ramadan, probably in the year 610, while at Mt. Ḥirâ, M. had a vision in which he was called to "Recite in the name of your Lord . . ." (cf. Koran 96.1–6). This vision and those that followed he communicated only to his wife and a small number of intimate friends, among them his cousin Ali, his adopted son Zayd, and abû Bakr and 'Uthmân, two respected men of the community who would later succeed the prophet as *caliphs. It was only later, after a lapse of perhaps more than 2 years, that M. began to preach publicly; at this time, he appears to have had no notion of founding a new religion. It is possible, indeed, that at the very beginning he felt called to do no more than to raise the moral level of life at Mecca and to proclaim the universal dominion of God as judge of human acts. The revelation given to him, he felt, was the same as that given to Abraham, Moses, and Jesus. The parts of the *Koran that come from the earliest period of M.'s ministry are written in short verses of heavily cadenced, rhymed prose of remarkable power, announcing in vivid terms the coming judgment against those who, self satisfied in their own wealth and prestige, neglect orphans, widows, and the poor and at the same time describing God's beneficence and the future beatitude of the righteous. For the most part the believers of the earliest period were persons of low estate, some of them slaves, and the attack on established paganism together with the call for social reform soon aroused strong opposition among the leaders of the city, including some of M.'s own kinsmen. He was mocked and variously accused of being a charlatan, a diviner (*kâhin*), and a poet possessed by a jinnî (see JINN). The idea of the resurrection was ridiculed and the notion of social and religious reform attacked as against ancestral custom. As time passed and new converts were made, opposition grew stronger. Hostility toward Muslims who were members of the Meccan clans was chiefly expressed in verbal abuse and, in some cases, economic pressure, for they were guaranteed physical protection by their clans, as M. was given the protection of the Hashemites through his uncles abû Ṭâlib and al-'Abbâs. However some of the Muslims who were slaves seem to have been subjected to severe physical persecution. Finally tensions became so great that 70 or 80 of M.'s followers, including a number of women, broke off their family ties and emigrated to Abyssinia where they sought the protection of the Negus. A year or so after this occurred the conversion of 'Umar ibn al-Khaṭṭâb, an important member of the clan 'Adî ibn Ka'b, who was to become the second caliph under whose reign the great expansion of Islam would be initiated. Moved in part perhaps by the recent conversion of such a notable member of the community, the majority of the Meccan clans instituted a boycott against the Hashemites, a boycott according to which they would neither deal commercially nor contract marriages with them, in the hope, evidently, of forcing the Hashemites to withdraw their protection from M. The boycott was unsuccessful, however, and lasted only a couple of years. Just after the termination of the boycott, in 619, both Khadîja and abû Ṭâlib, who had offered M. their strongest personal support died, and though he continued to receive some support from his own clan, his uncle, abû Lahab, violently opposed to Islam from the outset, soon withdrew his protection from the Prophet and the situation rapidly became intolerable for the Muslims. M. began to seek outside support, going first to Ṭâ'if, an oasis south of Mecca. There he was rebuffed, but during the pilgrimage of 620 he made contact with people from Yathrib (Medina) and in the following year a number of converts from Medina came to Mecca and pledged their obedience to the Prophet. In the following year, a group of over 70 Muslims came from Medina and met secretly with M. at al-'Aqaba, near Mecca, and pledged themselves to support him in every way. The tribes at Medina had for some time been engaged in a murderous feud, and an arbiter having religious authority and belonging to none of the warring parties was wanted. When, then, M. was invited to Medina and there offered protection for himself and his followers, he, together with about 100 of the Muslims of Mecca, severed all bonds with their clans and fled to Medina on July 16, 632.

At Medina M.'s position was completely altered; he was from the beginning recognized as the chief of a political community. Whereas traditional practice decreed that the immigrants from Mecca should be integrated as clients into the tribes of Medina, the Muslims, both immigrants (the *muhâjirûn*, i.e., those who made the *hegira) and those who were natives of Medina (the *anṣâr*, i.e., the helpers), formally constituted a separate community alongside the two Arab tribes (Aws and Khazraj) and the three Jewish tribes (Qaynûqâ', Naḍîr, and Qurayẓa) resident at Medina. Treaties drawn up by M. regulated the relations between them. The situation was not without difficulties, however; the *muhâjirûn* were at first taken in by the *ansâr* as guests, but as time passed this came to place an insupportable financial burden on the latter and a strain on the community as a whole. Among the non-Muslim Arabs there were also a number of persons, led by 'Abdallâh ibn Ubay, head of the Khazraj, who were hostile to the Muslims. Furthermore, the Jews, whose support M. had expected to receive, manifested from the outset undisguised contempt for his claim to be a prophet; whereas he felt that his message was identical to that of Abraham and Moses, they attacked his ignorance of biblical tradition and in doing so provoked an irremedial breach between themselves and M. that was signaled and sealed by the change of the *qibla* (the direction one faces in prayer) from Jerusalem to Mecca, early in 624. To ameliorate the deteriorating situation of the Muslims in Medina, M. turned to the ancient Bedouin custom of raiding. In March of 624, he, together with some 300 Muslims, intercepted the annual Meccan caravan in its return from Syria at Badr and, overcoming a quite superior force, made off with rich booty and a number of important prisoners. The Muslims saw the hand of God in this victory which became legendary in Islam. A month later M. turned on his new opponents and expelled the Qaynûqâ' from Medina, confiscating all their considerable possessions. In the spring of the following year the Meccans returned to seek vengeance. Battle was engaged at Uḥud, outside Medina, and in the end the Muslims were badly beaten and the Prophet wounded. His power within the city was not, however, impaired and again turning on his internal enemies he expelled the Naḍîr from the city. Again in March of 627 the Meccans set out against Medina to have done with M. once and for all, but failed to assault the city, stopped by a moat dug by the Muslims. The opposition within the city did nothing, and when the Meccans finally withdrew, M. expelled the Qurayẓa and became uncontested ruler of the city. From this point on Islam expanded aggressively as the power and prestige of M. grew unchecked. A treaty was signed with the Meccans at Ḥudaybiyya in April 628 according to which the Muslims would be allowed to make the pilgrimage the following year. Finally in the first days of 630, claiming that the treaty of Ḥudaybiyya had been violated, M. marched on Mecca, took the city without opposition, and subdued the environs. Paganism was forbidden henceforth, the idols destroyed, and the inhabitants given an amnesty of 4 months during which almost all became Muslims. Within the next 2 years most of the Arabian peninsula submitted to the authority of the Prophet. He died in June of 632 while preparing an expedition against the Byzantine borders to the north.

There can be no doubt that M.'s accomplishment is due to a number of factors, most significant among them his absolute faith in the validity of his mission and the truth of the revelation he proclaimed, an extraordinary strength of character and a remarkable understanding of men and human situations. To judge from the evidence of the *Koran* and the biographical tradition, he made no claim to any supernatural powers but rather regarded himself as simply a messenger called upon to transmit God's word. Tradition, however, esp. popular tradition, has invested him with all sorts of supernatural gifts and has filled his biography with prodigies and miracles. Orthodox doctrine recognizes that God granted M. absolute immunity (*'iṣma*) from all moral imperfections and sees him as the model of religious and moral perfection, whose intercession on the day of judgment will benefit all who have died in the faith of Islam. BIBLIOGRAPHY: T. Andrae, *Muhammad, the Man and His Faith* (rev. ed., 1955); W. M. Watt, *Muhammad at Mecca* (1953); *idem, Muhammad at Medina* (1956).

[R. M. FRANK]

MOHAMMED 'ABDUH (1849–1905), Muslim theologian and reformer. Born in Egypt, Mohammed 'Abduh received a traditional education in religion. In order to pursue higher studies in theology he went to the Univ. of al-Azhar where in 1872 he came under the influence of *Jamâl al-Dîn al-Afghânî and under his influence thenceforward devoted his greatest energies to the reform and modernization of *Islam. Despite difficulties with conservative officials he became editor of an important organ in 1880, increasing his influence considerably. He was exiled after the defeat of the revolt of 'Arâbî Pasha in 1882 and remained abroad until 1889 when, on his return to Egypt, he was made State *mufti. In 1894 he was appointed to the administrative council of al-Azhar and in this position was able to direct a thoroughgoing reform with a view to the modernization of the university. Through this, probably his most significant achievement, and through his numerous writings, esp. in the journal *al-Manâr* which he founded, he became one of the foremost figures in modern Islamic reform. Though the most important disciple of Jamâl al-Dîn al-Afghânî, he differed considerably in his basic orientation from his teacher, for while the latter was primarily an activist and revolutionary, Mohammed 'Abduh was far more concerned with religious and theological reform, feeling that no really significant social change could take place without the reformation and renewal of the religious consciousness of the Muslims. BIBLIOGRAPHY: L. Gardet and G. Anawati, *Introduction à la théologie musulmane* (1948), index.

[R. M. FRANK]

MOHAMMEDAN BLUE, valuable pigment made from cobalt oxide used in a distinctive underglaze by Muslim artists of Persia and Syria in Islamic pottery and tiles. The finest deposits of cobalt were in Baluchistan. Used in Chinese Yüan ware, it was brought to perfection in the blue-and-white porcelain of the Ming Dynasty.

[M. J. DALY]

MOHLBERG, KUNIBERT (1878–1963), German Benedictine liturgist. His interests were esp. centered upon the study of ancient Sacramentaries, i.e., the more developed liturgical books used by the celebrant at Mass after the earlier *Libelli missarum* and before the full Missals of later times had come into use. His scholarly editions of Sacramentaries are important contributions to the history of the liturgy of the Latin rite. Liturgical scholarship is also indebted to him for the system he devised for cataloguing liturgical manuscripts. BIBLIOGRAPHY: B. Neunheuser, EphemLiturg 78 (1964) 58–62; E. von Severus, NCE 9:1004.

[N. KOLLAR]

MÖHLER, JOHANN ADAM (1796–1838), RC theologian and church historian. Educated at Tübingen, M. was ordained in 1819 and after some experience in the parochial ministry became professor of church history at Tübingen (1828) and later transferred to Munich (1835). He was on friendly terms with Protestant theologians, among whom were F. *Schleiermacher and J. *Neander, and was strongly influenced, esp. in his earlier work, by the philosophical idealism of F. Schelling. Two of M.'s works in particular, his *Die Einheit in der Kirche* (1825) and his *Symbolik* (1832; Eng. tr. *Symbolism: Or Exposition of Doctrinal Differences between Catholics and Protestants As Evidenced by Their Symbolical Writings*, 1843) entitle him to a prominent place among the precursors of modern ecumenism, and to giving a new direction to *ecclesiology. He has been accused of being a forerunner also of *Modernism, but the charge appears to be unjust. BIBLIOGRAPHY: *L'Eglise est une: Hommage à Möhler* (ed. P. Chaillet, 1939); J. R. Geiselmann, *Johann Adam Möhler* (1940); R. H. Nienaltowski, *Johann Adam Möhler's Theory of Doctrinal Development* (1959); *idem*, NCE 9:1004–05.

[H. DRESSLER]

MOHR, JOSEF (1792–1848), Austrian priest, author of the words of "Silent Night" (*Stille Nacht*) at Obendorf, near Salzburg, on Christmas Eve, 1818; the music being by Franz Gruber (1787–1868). M. had been ordained only 3 years at the time. During the rest of his life, plagued by poverty and a weakness for alcohol, M. was pastor at Hintersee (1828) and Wagreun (1837).

[T. C. O'BRIEN]

MOINE, CLAUDINE (1618–*c.*55), French mystic. Born at Scey-sur-Saône, she went in 1642 to Paris to seek work and soon placed herself under the guidance of a spiritual director. The account of her spiritual journey in her *Relations spirituelles* is considered an important contribution to mystical literature.

[E. J. DILLON]

MOISSAC (ST. PIERRE), ABBEY OF, French church and cloister in Languedoc, its magnificent sculpture one of the highest achievements of Romanesque art. The old abbey founded in the 7th cent. by St. Amandus was thrice destroyed (732, 1030, 1042). A new church was consecrated (1063) with building continuing into the 15th century. Noteworthy are the S portal tympanum and cloister with magnificent sculpture begun under Abbot Anquêtil after 1085. The cloister (*c.*1100) boasts 50 historiated and 30 decorative capitals—a south gallery of "advanced" bold and complex forms, corner piers showing on each face a prophet, Evangelist, or disciple figure by a master hand. Stylistic skills in piers and galleries suggest four master carvers.

Most noted is the tympanum of the S portal (1115) showing Christ in Glory with the four Evangelist symbols, and the famous row of 24 Elders—carrying alternately their Spanish viols and goblets—iconographically identified by E. Mâle with those who worship the Lamb in glory in the famous Apocalypse of Beatus of Liébano. Decorative rosettes in a lower zone show the Eastern element in the rich amalgam of Romanesque art. Startling are the cusped jambs, the grotesque entangled beasts reflecting images of the barbaric mind, and the splendid Isaiah figure of the trumeau—twisted in a mystic dance of inspiration, the diaphonous, clinging drapery incised in calligraphic lines that derive from manuscript illumination (*Liber vitae*, 11th cent., British Museum) and evidenced again in the comparable St. Pierre at Souillac. BIBLIOGRAPHY: E. Mâle, *Religious Art from the 12th to the 18th Century* (1949); M. Schapiro, "The Romanesque Sculpture of Moissac," *Art Bulletin* (1931).

[M. J. DALY]

MOKSHA (Sanskrit *mokṣa*, release, freedom), Hindu term for liberation. Originally conceived as liberation from the oppressive weight of *karma (one's deeds and their consequences) and from the endless round of *samsara (rebirth), it later became synonymous with realization: liberation from a limited and conditioned human existence. It is conceived as the fourth and final goal (*varga*) of human existence, transcending pleasure (kama), wealth (artha), and even, at least for some, duty (*dharma). The positive content of moksha varies with diverse Hindu philosophies. The traditions generally agree, however, that some form of moksha may be achieved through any of the four paths (usually *margas*): knowledge or realization (jnana marga); love or devotion (bhakti marga); action (originally ritual actions but later through any deed, esp. one's duty, done with the whole of one's being: karma marga); and finally through *yoga, although here the goal is usually termed *samadhi, a consummate inwardness. BIBLIOGRAPHY: R. C. Zaehner, *Hinduism* (1966) 57–79.

[D. P. EFROYMSON]

MOLDOVITA, ABBEY OF (Vatra Moldovitci), a monastery established by the Moldavian Prince, Peter Rares, in 1532 for Orthodox monks. This monastery endowed with numerous territorial grants in addition to becoming a missionary and liturgical center for the Orthodox in Moldavia, was also an important outpost of defense. The many literary and artistic endeavors of the monks caused the abbey to be known as a cultural center of the time, with a library and a church painted in typical Moldavian-Byzantine style. So artistically executed are its numerous frescoes that it is still preserved as a tourist attraction. Since it no longer serves as a monastery today, the abbey stands as a national monument to a glorious past. BIBLIOGRAPHY: S. Bals and C. Nicolescu, *Mănăsteria Moldovita* (1958); *Enciclopedia României* (1936–40) 2:121.

[L. NEMEC]

MOLESME, ABBEY OF, former Benedictine monastery near Langres, France. Founded by St. Robert in 1075, it was meant to be a reformed Benedictine establishment, but in 1098 the dissatisfied Robert left Molesme and founded Cîteaux. Molesme eventually became the center of a monastic congregation of 64 priories and a number of nunneries. After declining in the 15th and 16th cent., the abbey was reformed as a member of the Maurist Congregation (1647), but was suppressed in 1791 during the Revolution.

[L. J. LEKAI]

MOLEYNS, ADAM (d. 1450), canonist, bp. of Chichester 1449–50. M. served at the papal court (1429–35) and was respected for his learning, esp. for his Latin style. He served as clerk to the Council of Henry VI (1436–42), and Keeper of the Privy Seal (1444–49); his association with an unpopular government resulted in his murder in 1450. BIBLIOGRAPHY: Emden OX 2:1289–91.

[C. D. ROSS]

MOLIÈRE (Jean Baptiste Poquelin, 1622–73), French dramatist, actor, director. Educated at the Jesuit Collège de Clermont, and in law at Orléans (1641), M. became an actor and founded, with Madeleine Béjart and her family, the financially unsuccessful *Illustre Théâtre* (1643–1645). After a 13-year apprenticeship in the provinces from which he emerged theatrical director and author, he returned to Paris (1658) and won royal patronage. His *Les Précieuses ridicules* (1659), with 28 plays in the following 14 years, was to change the nature of French comedy. The controversy over his *L'École des femmes* (1662) was one of several literary quarrels on aesthetic and moral issues in which M. was involved during his lifetime. He identified himself with liberal, naturalistic and humanistic values which angered Counter Reformation devout circles. They saw in *L'École,* in Arnolphe's sermon-like instruction of his pupil, Agnès, a parody of devotional literature and St. Paul, as well as a satire on convent education. The original version of M.'s *Tartuffe* was banned (1664) since the devout considered the hypocrite Tartuffe's duping of pious Orgon as an attack on religion. Only the third version was authorized (1669). M.'s *Dom Juan, ou le festin de Pierre* (1665), was withdrawn after 15 performances since it was suspected that M. was satirizing the religious man: despite the violent death of the liberal Dom Juan, the only defense of religion was made by the farcical Sganarelle. Some of M.'s other well-known comedies are: *L'École des maris* (1661), *Le Misanthrope (1666), L'Avare* (1668), *Les Femmes savantes* (1672); and *comédies-ballets: George Dandin* (1668), *Le Bourgeois gentilhomme* (1670) and *Le Malade imaginaire* (1673), after the fourth performance of which he died. Refusing to renounce his profession as actor which had incurred for him automatic excommunication, he was denied religious burial, but only at the intervention of Louis XIV was he interred, by night, in consecrated ground without religious service. BIBLIOGRAPHY: J. Cairncross, *New Light on Molière* (1956), on the first version of *Tartuffe*; L. Gossman, *Men and Masks* (1963); J. A. Calvet, *Molière est-il chrétien?* (1950).

[R. N. NICOLICH]

MOLINA, ALONSO DE (1512 or 1513–85), Franciscan missionary among the Aztecs in Mexico. He emigrated there from Spain with his parents, learned the Aztec language, Nahuatl, and served as interpreter for the first Franciscan missionaries in 1524. He became a friar himself in 1527, preached to the Aztecs, published a dictionary and a philological study of their language, and provided them with translations of liturgical books.

[T. C. O'BRIEN]

MOLINA, ANTHONY DE (*c.*1550–1612), Spanish Carthusian spiritual writer. He became a Carthusian in 1589 at Miraflores, after having been a member of the Augustinian Hermits since 1575. His chief work is on priestly piety, *Instrucción de sacerdotes,* which went through many editions and translations. He also wrote on lay spirituality and on prayer.

[T. C. O'BRIEN]

MOLINA, LUIS DE (1535–1600), Spanish Jesuit theologian. He studied the humanities for 4 years at Cuenca, law for a year at Salamanca, and entered the Jesuit novitiate at Coimbra in 1553. After completing his studies he taught philosophy at Coimbra until 1567, and theology at Evora until 1583, when he retired from teaching and thereafter devoted his time to writing. His first published work was *Concordia liberi arbitrii cum gratiae donis* (1588). An *Appendix ad Concordiam* appeared the following year and is bound with some editions of the 1588 *Concordia.* The *Concordia* is M.'s solution to the problem of the reconciliation of free will with efficacious grace, a reconciliation that he based upon *scientia media,* God's foreknowledge, anterior to any divine decree, of free choices that might be made by an individual (the free choices are called futuribles). The *Concordia* was originally written as part of M.'s *Commentaria in primam partem,* but it grew to such length that M. was advised to publish it as a separate work. Some of its contents are still to be found in the *Commentaria.* Although the work precipitated the controversy that culminated in the *Congregatio de auxiliis (1602–07), the solution it proposed became accepted by a great many theologians. M. also wrote *De justitia et jure,* one of the classic treatises on that subject. Three volumes of it were published during his lifetime, and the rest appeared posthumously—the first complete edition in 1613 (6 v.). M. is considered one of the primary authorities on moral probabilism, and a leading authority on the economic questions discussed in his time. Some of M.'s unedited writings were published by F. Stegmüller in *Geschichte des Molinismus* (1935). Text of the *Concordia:* ed. J. Rabeneck (1953). BIBLIOGRAPHY: Somervogel 5:1167–79; J. Rabeneck, "De Ludovici de Molina studiorum philosophiae curriculo," AHSJ 6 (1937) 291–302; *idem,* "De vita et scriptis Ludovici Molinae," AHSJ 19 (1950) 75–145; *idem,* "Antiqua legenda de Molina narrata examinantur," AHSJ 24 (1955) 295–326.

[F. L. SHEERIN]

MOLINISM, a system of theological thought based on the teaching of Luis de *Molina in his *Concordia* and further developed by his followers. It is concerned principally with the conciliation of efficacious grace and free will (see GRACE, EFFICACIOUS). The key to the Molinist solution of this problem is *scientia media.* Molinists have also characteristic doctrines on predefinition, predestination, and reprobation. In Molinism *scientia media,* or middle knowledge, is that knowledge by which God infallibly knows, before he makes an absolute decree creating the free creature, what choices it would make in any set of circumstances. This knowledge is called *media* because it is conceived of as partaking partly of the knowledge of simple intelligence, by which God necessarily knows all possible modes of existence, and partly of the knowledge of vision, by which God knows the things he freely ordains to exist.

The object known by *scientia media* is called the free futurible, i.e., a free choice or action that would take place in certain circumstances or conditions. Future events or choices that *de facto* will occur are known by God in knowledge of vision. The basis of this knowledge is the absolute decree to bestow that grace the acceptance of which was foreseen by *scientia media.*

Theology has always faced the problem of reconciling free will with efficacious grace and its infallible power to obtain human consent before that consent is given. Molinists unanimously teach that this power comes not from the intrinsic nature of efficacious grace but from three extrinsic sources combined. These sources are: first, the objective fact that a man would consent to a grace if it were given; second, from God's foreknowledge of that fact by *scientia media* before he makes any absolute decree about what shall take place; third, from the absolute, benevolent decree to give grace in the light of that foreknowledge. There is no efficacy to grace until this third point is reached. This grace, when given, takes away from man actual dissent, but not the power of consent or dissent, wherein lies freedom of the will.

Molinists, together with all other RC theologians, hold that all good human actions result from an absolute divine decree that a man shall perform a good act. But Molinists differ from other theologians in holding virtual predefinition: God simply wills to give a man grace to which he foresaw man would consent, thereby predefining the resultant good act. But he would give the same grace, even had he foreseen man's resistance, because there was no decree concerning a good action prior to *scientia media.* Molinists also hold that within the divine plan of salvation there is an absolute divine intention to give adults the reward of glory only after, and on account of, their absolutely foreseen future merits. This is the doctrine of virtual predestination. There is no place in the Molinist system for any kind of antecedent reprobation. In the divine plan there is only the positive consequent intention to reprobate the wicked on account of their foreseen death in the state of personal sin.

BIBLIOGRAPHY: A. C. Pegis, ''Molina and Human Liberty,'' *Jesuit Thinkers of the Renaissance* (ed. G. Smith, 1939) 75–131; H. Rondet, *Gratia Christi* (1948); G. Smith, *Freedom in Molina* (1966).

[F. L. SHEERIN]

MOLINOS, MIGUEL DE (1628–96), Spanish Quietist. After ordination he was sent to Rome to represent a beatification cause. Relieved of this office, he chose to remain in Rome, where he was esteemed as a confessor and spiritual director. In 1675 he published the *Spiritual Guide,* which was widely circulated and translated into several languages. The book soon gave rise to debate. Two Jesuits, Belluomo and Segneri, in defense of meditation, wrote treatises against M.'s doctrine. But M. had influential allies; after several years of debate, the works of Belluomo and Segneri were placed on the Index. In 1685 M. was arrested for reasons not clearly known; historians have conjectured about his moral conduct. The process against him lasted 2 years; seventy witnesses were called in and many letters examined. In 1687 he made a retractation of 68 propositions; he also admitted to certain charges against his morals. He was condemned to penitential imprisonment for the rest of his life. Whether he accepted the penalty because he admitted to its justice or as a humiliation sent by God is not clear. The list of M.'s errors contained in the bull *Coelestis pastor* (D 2201–69) is not taken from his book *Spiritual Guide.* The propositions selected and put in order by the Holy Office reflect a series of concrete applications deduced more or less accurately from principles. The principles in their theoretical formulation do not tend necessarily to lead astray; but the principles were in fact applied to sanction immoral practices in semisecret gatherings. The *Spiritual Guide* contains chapters with excellent doctrine that recent research has traced to St. John of the Cross. *QUIETISM.

[K. KAVANAUGH]

MOLITOR, RAPHAEL (1873–1948), German Benedictine musicologist. He studied philosophy and theology at the Benedictine monastery of Beuron, and he was ordained in 1897. He authored treatises on the Gregorian chants which led to a special advisory membership on the board of *Editio Vaticana* in 1904.

[R. J. LITZ]

MOLLOY, ALOYSIUS, SISTER (1880–1954), educator. The first woman to receive a Ph.D. from Cornell University (1907), M. was a native of Ohio. In 1907 with Sister M. Leo Tracy, OSF, she founded the College of St. Teresa in Winona, Minn., served as first dean of the college, and as president and dean from 1928 to 1946. In 1922 she entered the Sisters of St. Francis of the Third Order Regular of the Congregation of Our Lady of Lourdes. For 25 years a member of the Commission on Higher Education of the North Central Association, M. also was a pioneer member of the National Catholic Educational Association. Among her published books were *Catholic Colleges for*

Women (1918), *The Parochial Schools, School Organization and Teacher Training* (1919), *A Catholic Educational Directory* (1919).

[J. R. AHERNE]

MOLLOY, FRANCIS (fl. 1660), Irish Franciscan, theologian and grammarian. Born in County Meath, he entered religious life in Rome (1632), later taught theology there, and also represented the Catholics of his country at the papal court. Though he wrote several theological tracts in Latin and a catechism of Catholic doctrine in Gaelic, he is best known for his *Grammatica latino-hibernica* (1677), the first formal grammar of the Irish language to be printed. Dealing with the alphabet, etymology, prose, and verse, it was well respected for its breadth, though later found to be deficient on syntax.

[E. M. GATES]

MOLLOY, THOMAS EDMOND (1884–1956), bp. of Brooklyn. A native of New Hampshire, M. was ordained for the Diocese of Brooklyn in 1908. For a time he taught philosophy at St. Joseph's College for Women and later served as its president. Named auxiliary bp. of the diocese in 1920, he became the ordinary in 1921 (Pius XII conferred the personal title of abp. on M. in 1951). An able administrator in a growing diocese, M. expanded parishes, parochial schools, and high schools; founded a seminary, and encouraged the establishment of Molloy Catholic College for Women (1954).

[J. R. AHERNE]

MOLOCH (Molech), term associated with child sacrifice in the Bible. Some scholars interpret it as the name of a god, formed with the Hebrew consonants for the word king and the vowels for the word shame. Others consider it a technical term for child sacrifice. The RSV translates it as a proper name. The report of Solomon's building a *high place for Moloch identified him as "the abomination of the Ammonites" (1 Kg 11.1–8, where he is also called Milcom). Jephthah's speech to the Ammonites (Jg 11.24) indicated their god was the same as the Moabite Chemosh (see 2 Kg 3.27). Sacrifices to Moloch were associated with the valley of Hinnom (Jer 32.35), and Josiah defiled Topheth, place of the sacrifices in the Hinnom Valley (2 Kg 23.10). Child sacrifice was sometimes practiced in Israel (Jg 11.30–40; 2 Kg 16.3; 17.17), but it was condemned by the law (Lev 20.1–5) and the Prophets (Jer 7.31; Ezek 16.20; cf. Acts 7.42–43).

[T. EARLY]

MOLOKANS, literally "milk-drinkers," a Russian sect so called because its members drink milk during those times of the Orthodox Lenten season when milk products are forbidden. They were founded by Simeon Uklein in the early 18th century. They shared some convictions with the Doukhobors—e.g., pacifism, resistance to military service, and civil law when this contradicted the law of God as understood by Uklein, and a kind of communism of property. But unlike the Doukhobors, the Molokans did not reject the authority of the Bible; on the contrary, they professed to follow its teachings only. They worship by reading and commenting upon the Bible and singing hymns. Later, Mosaic dietary laws were introduced among them. Uklein proposed a subordinationist theology of the Trinity; he held that men would arise in bodies different from those they possess at present, and that after death true Christians go immediately to paradise, while the wicked go to eternal punishment. The Molokans spread rapidly in central Russia and were exiled to Caucasus and to Siberia. They soon split into numerous subsects. Their present number is unknown, but there is a large Molokan colony in Los Angeles, California.

[A. WALKER]

MOLYNEUX, ROBERT (1738–1808), missionary, religious superior. A native of Lancashire, England, M. entered the Society of Jesus in 1757, teaching at Bruges, Belgium, where he became a friend of John Carroll. Sent to the U.S. in 1771, M. was pastor of St. Joseph's and St. Mary's in Philadelphia, Pennsylvania. He founded the first parochial school in that city. He next worked in Maryland on the missions and was one of the founders of Georgetown College, Washington, D.C. and its president for two terms. When the Jesuits, suppressed in most countries, still existed in Russia, the American group was affiliated with the Russian and M. became the first superior of the revived Society in the United States.

[J. R. AHERNE]

MOMBAER, JOHN (Mauburnus; 1460–1501), monastic reformer and systematizer of ascetic principles. Born in Brussels, he entered the monastery of the Canons Regular at Mt. St. Agnes in the Netherlands in 1480 and in 1496 was invited to effect reforms in the monastic establishments of the same order in France. Imbued with the **Devotio moderna*, his spiritual writings set forth the steps by which Christian virtue might be attained and analyzed the practice of prayer. They include *Rosetum exercitiorum spiritualium et sacrarum meditationum*); *Exercitia utilissima pro horis solvendis et devota communione sacramentali*; and *Venatorium sanctorum ordinis canonicorum regularium*. In the last year of his life, he was elected abbot of Livry.

[E. M. GATES]

MOMBRITIUS, BONINUS (*c.*1424–*c.*1502), humanist, litterateur, hagiographer. After studying Greek and Latin, M. taught the classics at Milan where he won fame as a humanist. He remained single all his life and his deep spirituality was a source of admiration. His extensive literary output includes translations, editions of other authors, and poetry. He translated Hesiod's *Theogonia* (1474) and Eusebius of Caesarea's *Chronicle* (1474–76). He edited the

Collectanea rerum mirabilium of Solon, the *Chronicles* of Jerome and Prosper of Aquitaine, and the *Summulae* of Paul of Venice. His *Sanctuarium seu vitae sanctorum* in two volumes has the merit of exemption from the common faults of the hagiographers of the period who were rather free in emendating texts. M. preserved them as he found them. The problem of identifying the sources for these volumes has not been settled. M. also composed six books of poems, dedicated to Sixtus IV, *De dominica passione libri V*. Toward the end of his life he wrote *Thraenodiae in funere illustris quondam domini Galleazo-Mariae Sfortiae*. Some of his works are still unpublished. BIBLIOGRAPHY: J. Cambell, LTK 7:532; *idem,* NCE 9:1016–17; G. Eis, *Die Quellen für das Sanctuarium des Mailänder Humanisten B.M.* (1933).

[J. M. O'DONNELL]

MOMMSEN, THEODOR (1817–1903), German historian, jurist, and philologist. M. obtained his doctorate in law in 1843. After spending 3 years in Italy gathering ancient inscriptions for the Berlin Academy, he taught at Leipzig until dismissed for his liberal views. After some years at the Univ. of Zurich and Breslau he was named professor of ancient history at Berlin. A prodigious worker (his bibliography numbers 1,513 titles), he is best known for his Hegelian history of Rome and for his works on Roman civil and criminal law. New Testament study profited from his treatment of Roman law; church history, from his study of Church-State relations during the persecutions. He edited some of the works of Cassiodorus and the portion of the *Liber pontificalis* to A.D. 715. His powers of organization are evident in scholarly projects he developed: the *Auctores antiquissimi* of the *Monumenta Germaniae Historica* and the *Corpus inscriptionum latinarum,* of which he was editor for 25 years. Works: *Gesammelte Schriften* (8 v., 1905–13). BIBLIOGRAPHY: L. Wickert, *Theodor Mommsen* (1959–).

[M. J. SUELZER]

MOMMSEN CATALOGUE, list of the books of the Bible, sometimes known as the Cheltenham Canon, dating from *c.*350 A.D., discovered by T. *Mommsen in 1885 among the Phillipps MSS at Cheltenham, England and originally published in 1886. This list has certain peculiar features, notably the numbering of the Psalms (151 instead of 150), the order of the Gospels (Mt, Mk, Jn, Lk), the omission of Heb and of the Epistles of Jas and Jude. It agrees with the canons of Hippo (393), Carthage (397), and Innocent I (405) in including the *deuterocanonical books. It is generally agreed to be of N African provenance. For the list, see W. Sanday, *Studia biblica et ecclesiastica* 3.6 (1891) 217–325.

[D. J. BOURKE]

MONACO, principality of *c.*500 acres on the French Riviera, near Italy. It is a constitutional monarchy under French guardianship. Predominantly Catholic with a Catholic ruling family, it formed part of the Nice Diocese until separated in 1868. Perhaps settled by the Phoenicians, Monaco has lived under various political jurisdictions. The Grimaldi of Genoa became the ruling family in 1297, and when the male line died out in 1731, Monaco passed through a daughter to the French Goyon-Matignon family, which took the Grimaldi name and continues to reign. Monaco is noted as a resort, tax haven, and site of the Monte Carlo gambling casino.

[T. EARLY]

MONAD, one of the numberless individual simple substances constituting reality, according to Gottfried von *Leibniz (1646–1716), German philosopher and mathematician. Described variously as units of force, metaphysical points, and essential forms, monads are psychical or mental beings, and hence, spiritual rather than material. Not extended in space and having no quantitative mass, they have no parts and are thus not subject to either composition or destruction. God is The Supreme Monad and Creator of all other monads. Materiality is a mere appearance of aggregates of individual monads, all of which are alike in being essentially mental, but differing in degrees of consciousness. Each unit develops and progresses in accord with its own inner law—each a separate and independent world never altered or influenced by other monads, yet functioning in harmonious whole, wherein each mirrors the entire universe in its own unique manner.

[J. T. HICKEY]

MONAGHAN, JOHN PATRICK (1890–1961), priest pioneer in social work. He emigrated from Ireland, studied at St. Francis College, Brooklyn, N.Y., and St. Joseph's Seminary, Yonkers, N.Y., and was ordained for the New York Archdiocese. In 1957 he was made a domestic prelate. His program of worker education included the establishment of Catholic Labor Schools (1935) and the Association of Catholic Trade Unionists (ACTU, 1937) for the training of union members, Catholic and non-Catholic, in their social rights and responsibilities. He was also an early sponsor of youth programs, adult education, and liturgical reform.

[M. CARTHY]

MONARCHIA SICULA, a right claimed by the kings of Sicily to control the Church on the island. It was a subject of dispute for almost a thousand years. The oldest document upon which the claim was based is a bull of Urban II directed to Count Roger of Sicily and Calabria in 1098, wherein the Pope agreed not to appoint a papal legate to Sicily against his wishes. This made the king of Sicily himself vice legate of the Pope. (Sicily was at that time a vassalage of the Pope.) Later popes, e.g., Paschal II in 1117, sought to restrict the privilege; and Innocent III (1198–1216) repudiated it. The claim was revised during the Renaissance when Spanish kings assumed the crown of Sicily and it became part of their arsenal of arguments to support caesaropapist aims. This can be seen in the case of Ferdinand the Catholic (1469–1516) and Philip II (1556–98), who instituted a special permanent judge called *Iudex Monarchiae Siculae,* and forbade appeals from his decisions to the Holy See. Contention continued until the time of Italian unification. Garibaldi's claim was effectively repudiated by Pius IX in 1864 and the Italian government reluctantly renounced it in 1871. BIBLIOGRAPHY: I. J. Calicchio, NCE 9:1019; F. de Stefano, *Storia della Sicilia dal secolo XI al XIX* (1948).

[D. G. NUGENT]

MONARCHIAN PROLOGUES (Monarchian Arguments), introductory passages to the four Gospels found in many Vulgate MSS dating from antiquity and the Middle Ages. They were called Monarchian because they were thought to have originated in Monarchian circles during the 2d or early 3d century. Later scholarship inclines to attribute them to a later date and to Priscillianist influence. BIBLIOGRAPHY: LTK 1:839–840.

[R. B. ENO]

MONARCHIANISM (Gr., *monarchia,* one origin, rule), a 2d-cent. heresy that exaggerated the concept of the unity of God so as to deny the distinction between persons. Monarchianism has taken three forms: (1) Absolute Monarchianism denied any distinction of persons at all, so that the Father became incarnate and died on the cross, also known as Patripassianism; (2) Modalism or Sabellianism recognized a distinction in the Trinity not of persons but of energies or modes; (3) Subordinationism admitted a real and true distinction of persons in the Trinity but denied any equality between them.

[P. FOSCOLOS]

MONARCHY, from Gr. *monos,* alone, and *archein,* to rule), a political regime according to the undivided power of a single person. As a pure type it is a despotism or autocracy, which may be benign; as one element, the principle of executive unity, it enters, together with *aristocracy and *democracy, into the constitution of a well-ordered state. A despot becomes a tyrant when he governs as an absolute ruler unlimited by law for his own private benefit, not for the commonweal. Tyranny is the caricature, or deviation form of monarchy. In political history and political philosophy alike monarchy should not be identified with *kingship and kingdom, which often adds a mystique surrounding blood royal or the sacramental consecration of power, though in popular usage "monarch" often tends to mean a sovereign bearing a royal or imperial title, or the equivalent. In a strict sense, government is more extensively monarchical in the U.S. than in the United Kingdom. It is useful to distinguish between an absolute and a constitutional monarchy, and between an elective and an hereditary monarchy.

[T. GILBY]

MONASTERIES, DISSOLUTION OF THE, see DISSOLUTION OF THE MONASTERIES.

MONASTERY, originally the cell in which a hermit lived or a cluster of such cells; later, the dwelling of *cenobites or *monks who practiced a communal way of life under a specific rule and subject to a common authority. To some this is the proper sense of the term, but in popular and ecclesiastical usage, the designation has also been applied to houses of *canons regular and sometimes to the houses of friars and of other religious. It is used of the houses of female as well as of male religious. In fact so variously has the term been applied that further qualification must be added in order to convey anything specific about a particular religious house. In this diversity of application, however, a tendency can be noted to restrict the term to houses in which the religious lead a contemplative life and recite the Divine Office in common.

[P. K. MEAGHER]

MONASTERY, DOUBLE, see DOUBLE MONASTERY.

MONASTIC BISHOP, see BISHOP, MONASTIC.

MONASTIC SCHOOL, a place of instruction within a monastic foundation, initially necessitated by the practice of admitting young children to monastic life. Schools for these youths (*oblati*) who lived at the monastery and intended to become monks were common in both the East and West, and are provided for in the earliest monastic constitutions, e.g., the Rule of St. Benedict, 30, 59, 63. This remained the practice until the 6th cent. when *externi,* i.e., children living at home who were not preparing for monastic life, were also admitted. In this form, monastic schools flourished in England and Europe; were encouraged by Charlemagne; and became numerous in the 10th and 11th centuries. The course of study was generally the **trivium* and *quadrivium,* although there was no uniform curriculum. Discipline was strict, and the school master had total dominance over his pupils. From 1050 onwards, however, education came increasingly to be the responsibility of the *cathedral school. The *Cluniac Reform discouraged the education of *externi* in the monasteries and the Cistercian renewal rejected all kinds of schools, even those for children destined for monastic life, admitting no one to the novitiate under 16 years of age. Some contemporary monasteries have established schools at various levels similar to other ecclesiastical institutions, but these are not monastic schools properly so-called. BIBLIOGRAPHY: H. I. Marrou, *History of Education in Antiquity* (tr. G. Lamb, 1956); J. Leclercq, NCE 9:1031–1032.

[T. M. MCFADDEN]

MONASTIC THEOLOGY, a formula that designates the monastic approach to theology and not the study of the monastic life. It has been in current use since 1953, the 8th centenary of the death of St. Bernard of Clairvaux, but the type of theology it indicates existed long before. During the Middle Ages it was the business of contemplatives within the cloister, generally monks. Though distinct from scholastic theology as studied in the town schools, it was not opposed, but complementary, to it. In the 12th cent. it was exemplified by the writings of Benedictines, Cistercians, and Canons Regular. Because it was in fact the prolongation of the patristic thought of the ancient Church into the mid-13th cent., it may be called medieval patristics. Its value is not to be overestimated, yet it has been acknowledged by historians, including M. D. Chenu. It included the spiritual interpretation of the Bible as exposed by H. De Lubac in *L'Exégèse médiéval* (4 v., 1959–64) and by F. Vandenbroucke in *La Morale monastique* (1966), as well as in monographs on Aelred of Rievaulx, Bernard of Clairvaux, Bruno of Segni, Geoffrey of Admont, Gilbert of Hoyland, William of St. Thierry, Peter Damian, Peter the Venerable, Rupert of Deutz, and others. It was recommended, at least for monks, by the episcopal synod held at Rome in 1967. The stress it lays on the unity among Bible, patristic thought, and liturgy makes it akin to the theology of the Orthodox Church. Its emphasis on the union that should exist between reflection and spiritual experience gives it some relationship with certain trends of Protestant theology. It thus has ecumenical value. BIBLIOGRAPHY: J. Leclercq, *Love of Learning and the Desire for God* (tr. C. Mishrahi, 1961; pa. 1962) ch. 9; P. K. Meagher, NCE 9:1032.

[J. LECLERCQ]

MONASTICISM (Gr. *monos,* unique), an institution establishing and regulating the life of those in the service of the holy, whether in community or in solitude. Monasticism implies a separation from the secular to further an ideal based on celibacy, poverty, and obedience to a spiritual leader. It is a phenomenon observable in all the great religions of the world. Christian monasticism has been marked by distinguished service in education, scholarship, the arts, care of the needy and the sick, and mission work. Monasticism in the West was the instrument that preserved the achievements of Greco-Roman culture and Christianized Europe.

Early Western Monasticism. Organized asceticism began in the West somewhat later than in the East. Individuals who had gone on pilgrimages to the Desert Fathers in Egypt and to monasteries in other parts of the East brought back to the West ideals of abnegation which they followed at home singly or in small groups. An impetus was given to the movement by Athanasius, bp. of Alexandria, during his numerous exiles at the hands of the Arians. When he came to Rome in 339 to plead his case before a Roman synod, he was accompanied by two Desert Fathers. Marcella, a young Roman of high station, was so impressed by his reports of Egyptian monasticism that she and her companions made her house on the Aventine into a kind of convent. About 356 Athanasius wrote a life of Anthony of Egypt, which he intended as an ideal pattern of the ascetical life. The biography was soon translated into several languages. Augustine (*Confessions,* 8.6) testifies to the influence exerted by the Latin version of Evagrius of Antioch. Martin of Tours founded the first monastery in Gaul—at Ligugé in 361. When he had to leave this retreat upon his election as bp., he chose a cell near Tours in which to dwell. The influx of numerous disciples gave rise there in 372 to the famous monastery of Marmoutier (the word is a corruption of *maius monasterium*). In 388 Augustine, not yet ordained, founded a monastery at Tagaste. Later at Hippo he lived in common with his clergy under rule, a practice that had already been followed by Ambrose (d. 397) and Eusebius of Vercelli (d. 371), whose community may be regarded as the prototype of the secular canons of the Carolingian reform. This penetration of monastic life into the ranks of the clergy who served the local churches was a characteristic of Western monasticism in contradistinction to the forms it took in the East. At Lérins Honoratus established a monastery combining hermits and cenobites and continued to govern it after he became abp. of Arles, the first of a long line of monk bishops in that see.

Eastern ideas were freshly introduced into monasticism with the return of John Cassian from years spent studying Eastern institutions. His express purpose was the reform of Gallic monastic life. To this end he founded a double monastery at Marseilles in 415 and composed for his followers two books: *Institutes,* the foundation of many Western rules, and *Conferences,* purported conversations held with prominent Eastern ascetics. The earliest British monasteries date from about 430. At this time Patrick also founded his first community. The greatest of the Western founders was Benedict of Nursia, who drew upon Cassian and other sources to write *c.* 530–540 the first detailed piece of monastic legislation specifically for the West. In his firm outline of the liturgical, administrative, and spiritual life, Benedict provided for the essential autonomy of each house and incorporated a fourth vow of stability. Though the monastery founded at Vivarium by the pious layman Cassiodorus did not long survive his death in 580, his stress on intellectual pursuits gave rise to the tradition of scholarship in religious orders. The copying of MSS he fostered was imitated in other monasteries and helped in preserving the classical culture of Europe. The monasteries were important also to the conversion of the barbarians. Augustine of Canterbury, to cite one instance, was sent to England in 596 from a Benedictine monastery which Gregory the Great had founded in Rome. Monks from Gaul developed institutions in Ireland which were destined to bring Christianity and culture back to the Continent. After the arrival of the monk Finnian from Britain, Irish monasteries began to multiply. Finnian trained young monks at Clonard and sent them out to establish independent houses. Prominent among the founder-monks were: Columcille of Derry and Iona, Ciaran of Clonmacnois, Nessan of Mungret, Colman of Cloyne, Finbarr of Cork, Iarlath of Tuam, Ailbe of Emly, Comgall of

Bangor, Enda of Aran, Kevin of Glendalough, and Cronan of Roscrea. Greatest of the founder-nuns were: Brigid of Kildare, Ita of Killeedy, and Monenna of Killeavy.

Of the more than 20 Celtic rules only that of Columban is extant. It is characterized by severe bodily austerity and regards the interior spirit as vastly more important than external organization. For the Irish monks teaching was an important apostolate. In point of fact, the monks replaced the Druids as teachers of the young. Because of the lack of cities as centers of political life, abbots in Ireland became prominent as ecclesiastical rulers; and some bps. who were not monks were subordinate to the administrators of great monasteries. Irish monasticism was established in Luxeuil and Bobbio by Columban. From those centers some 50 other monasteries took their rise.

Later Western Monasticism. The Anglo-Saxon missioners who carried Christianity back to the Continent in the late 7th and the 8th cent. were Benedictines. It was only natural that the new centers they founded should be Benedictine also. In time the Benedictine rule became normative, sometimes with borrowing from older, more austere rules; and the legislation of Charlemagne (817) made it obligatory for all monks and nuns in the Carolingian domain. In Spain and the Celtic lands, however, other rules continued to be used for several centuries. As time passed, extramonastic activity grew. The rise of feudalism made abbeys into fiefs and abbots into feudal lords with accompanying obligations and privileges. Schools and scriptoria claimed much of the monks' time. The first attempt to reduce extramonastic interests was made by Benedict of Aniane. He presided over the monastic Synod of Aachen (817), which decreed the elimination of external work, the lengthening of the Divine Office, and many other changes; but only when Cluny adopted the Synod's legislation (910) did the reform come alive. Up to that time each monastery had been wholly autonomous, the rule being the only link among them. Now all Cluniac houses were made dependent upon a central policy administered by the abbot of Cluny. Reforms occurred also in other places: in S France and Flanders under John of Gorze; in England under the monk bishops Dunstan of Canterbury, Ethelwold of Winchester, and Oswald of York; and in Germany, Italy, and Spain. The 10th, 11th, and 12th cent. have come to be called the Benedictine centuries because of the monks who strove as bps. and popes to free the Church from secular control.

Some reforms among the Benedictines emphasized eremetic and contemplative ideals. Romuald inspired the movement that resulted in the Camaldolese (1012); John of Gualbert, the Vallambrosians (1036); and Bruno of Cologne, the Carthusians (1084). The most important reform of this century was the Cistercian Order (1098), founded by Stephen Harding and Robert of Molesme and brought to prominence by Bernard of Clairvaux. It was at first purely contemplative, given over to silence, poverty, and manual work. In time, however, the heavy labor was turned over to lay monks who developed the great Cistercian abbey estates. In 1120 at Prémontré, Norbert founded the Canons Regular, using as basis for his regulations the so-called Rule of St. Augustine. His canons are commonly called Premonstratensians or Norbertines. Other reform groups were the Williamites (1157), Sylvestrines (1231), Celestines (1235), and Olivetans (1313). Growths of a different sort also came from the Benedictine root as a result of needs arising during the Crusades: the Hospitallers and various military orders.

The ills attendant on commendation, the *Great Western Schism, wars, and the Black Death so weakened monasticism that Reformation attacks upon it were almost mortal. Yet renewal and reform continued. Two of the most notable reforms were those of the Maurists in 1621 and of the Cistercians at La Trappe in 1664, the origin of the Trappists. A characteristic of the reform movements of more recent centuries is a tendency to group monasteries into congregations with uniform observance and central government. In 1893 a loose federation of all Benedictine congregations was formed with headquarters at Sant'Anselmo in Rome. BIBLIOGRAPHY: J. Décarreaux, *Monks and Civilization* (tr. C. Haldone, 1964); J. Ryan, *Monasticism* (1931). *RELIGIOUS LIFE.

[M. J. SUELZER]

MONASTICISM, BUDDHIST, see BUDDHIST MONASTICISM.

MONCEAUX, PAUL (1859–1941), French historian and archeologist. Although his early career was devoted to the study of Greek antiquity and archeology, M.'s fame rests on his later studies of the literature and life of Christian North Africa, an interest he developed while teaching in the secondary schools of Algiers. After writing several smaller works in the field, he published his magnum opus: *L'Histoire littéraire de l'Afrique chrétienne depuis les origines jusqu'à l'invasion arabe* (7 v., 1901–23). This, the most thorough study of Christian literature of Africa, is particularly valuable for its contribution to the history of *Donatism. From 1907 M. was a professor at the Collège de France. BIBLIOGRAPHY: P. Roche, NCE 9:1050.

[R. B. ENO]

MONDRIAN, PIET (Pieter Cornelis Mondriaan; 1872–1944), Dutch painter. Pupil of his father and uncle, M. later studied at the Amsterdam Academy and worked in Amsterdam and Domburg (influenced by Jan Toorop), in Paris (1911–14 and 1919–38, influenced by Picasso and Léger), finally in London and New York, where he died. After a period of naturalistic landscapes in which his involvement with the interstices of trees and repeated rectangular shapes portend his later grids, he came via symbolism and cubism to simplified abstract forms and lines (horizontal and vertical) with metaphysical overtones, in primary colors within black grids, naming his abstraction neoplasticism. M. strove for a universal harmony and an absolute beauty. His rather dogmatic and orthodox ideas, expressed in *Le Néo-plasticisme* (1921), *Plastic Art and Pure Plastic Art* (1937), and other essays (1941–43, 1945) were partly influenced by theosophy. With Theo van Doesburg he founded the periodical *De Stijl,* where his ideas on the new abstract art could be published. M. strongly influenced modern architecture and the new structurist and constructivist painters and sculptors. BIBLIOGRAPHY: M. Seuphor, *Piet Mondrian, Life and Work* (1956); G. Beyeler, *Piet Mondrian* (1964).

[P. F. HEFTING]

MONDSEE, ABBEY OF, former Austrian Benedictine abbey on Mondsee Lake in the diocese of Linz. The monastery was founded in 748 by Duke Odilo II of Bavaria and passed (833) into the possession of the bp. of Regensburg. The abbey, an important center of religion and culture, had a famous scriptorium. Here was written the oldest German Bible translation. In 1791 the monastery was abolished, but the beautiful church and other buildings are preserved even today. BIBLIOGRAPHY: *Chronicon Lunelacense* (1748); C. Pfaff, *Scriptorium und Bibliothek des Klosters Mondsee im hohen Mittelalter* (1967).

[F. H. RÖHRIG]

MONE, FRANZ JOSEPH (1796–1871), German Catholic historian. M. taught history at Heidelberg (1819–27), when he was invited to the Univ. of Louvain. The Belgian Revolution caused his return to Germany in 1831. He served as director of the General State Archives in Karlsruhe until 1868. Much attracted by romanticism, his researches were very broad and varied, including the history of liturgy, German mythology, and heroic legends, and contributions which helped inaugurate Germanic philology. His *Lateinische Hymnen des Mittelalters* (3 v., 1853–55) is still highly regarded. He also published a four-volume work on the history of Baden. BIBLIOGRAPHY: H. Rumpler, NCE 9:1052; DE 2:1035.

[F. D. LAZENBY]

MONERGISM (Gr. *monos,* alone, *ergon,* work), the teaching that God is the sole cause of man's salvation; the opposite of *synergism. The term has been applied esp. to the *Gnesiolutheranism of those who invoked Luther's teaching on justification and the abiding sinfulness of man against P. *Melanchthon in the Synergistic Controversy (1550–77). *Calvinism, particularly as articulated in the Synod of *Dort (1618), may also be classified as monergistic in opposition to *Arminianism.

[T. C. O'BRIEN]

MONGOLIA, a geographical division of E Asia, divided by the Gobi Desert into Inner and Outer Mongolia. The Turks dominated Outer Mongolia in the 6th and 7th centuries. Later it gradually became the center of an immense empire under Gengis Khan (1206). It was a province of China from 1688 until it gained its independence in the 20th cent.; and in 1924 it became a Soviet satellite. Its official name is Mongolian People's Republic (604,247 sq mi; population [1974 est.] 1,400,000). Inner Mongolia became an administrative unit of China in 1947 and is now called Mongolian Autonomous Region (730,027 sq mi; population [1974 est.] 9,200,000). For hundreds of years the dominant religion in all of Mongolia was Lamaistic Buddhism, but it was suppressed in 1924. Christianity first came to the region in the 800s. Franciscans evangelized there in the 13th and 14th cent.; and in the 17th and 18th cent. Jesuits tried without success to renew mission work. Inner Mongolia became a vicariate apostolic in 1840, and missioners developed strong Christian communities among the Chinese. Suiyüan was made an archdiocese in 1946 with Ningsia, Siwantze, and Tsining as suffragan sees. Protestants entered Mongolia early in the 19th century. They translated the Bible into Mongolian and opened several medical centers; but their mission in Ulan Bator was forced to close in 1924.

[M. J. SUELZER]

MONGOLS, a group of Asiatic peoples who from *c.*1200 to *c.*1500 dominated large portions of the Asian and East European world. They were typical cattle-breeding and horse-raising nomads of the Asiatic steppes, centered originally in the regions S and E of Lake Baikal. They spoke Altaic dialects, lived in felt tents, and drank *kumiss*. They worshipped the Great Blue Sky, and shamanism played a vital part in their public and private life. The rise of the Mongols to a world-empire was meteoric and was due to the ability and achievement of the great leader Temuchin (1162–1227), who in 1206 received the title *Genghis (better Chingis) Khan. He united the Mongol clans and created an extraordinarily efficient and mobile army of mounted bowmen capable of covering 100 miles in a day, if necessary. By 1220 the Mongol armies had overrun N China, Azerbaijan, N Iran, and Transoxonia, and in 1223 they defeated the Russians and Cumans at the Battle of the Kalka River. Urban centers were not only captured but were ruthlessly destroyed by the Mongols, among them Khorasan, Merv, Kief, and Baghdad. Genghis Kahn was not only a great conqueror, but was an able imperial administrator with a deep interest in arts and crafts and in trade and commerce. He did not hesitate to employ foreigners in his service, and he adapted the Uighur script as a vehicle for writing his own language. Following his death, the Mongol empire was divided into four khanates, although in theory the empire was regarded as united under the Grand Khan, who finally established his capital at Khanbalyk, modern Peiping in China. In the West a Mongol state, the Golden Horde, was established on the lower Volga after the defeat of the Poles and Germans in 1241 and the subjugation of Bulgaria and the adjacent regions. It survived until 1502. The Mongols made two attempts to invade Japan but failed on both occasions. Apart from the short-lived world empire of Timur, Mongol political power in general was in rapid decline before 1350.

Timur (Tamerlane 1336–1405), a Muslim and the leader of Muslim Mongols, embarked on a career as a world conqueror. He made himself master of all Central Asia, including all Mesopotamia, defeated the Turks in Anatolia, and advanced into N India and looted Delhi. He was planning an attack on Ming China at the time of his death. His capital Samarkand became a great center of exchange between China and India, and SW Asia and the Mediterranean world. In spite of their terrible massacres and destruction of cities in the first stages of their conquests, the Mongols brought general peace and sound administration to much of the world they dominated. They welcomed contacts even with the Far West, and received the embassies of Pope Innocent IV and Louis IX in a friendly manner. Mongol envoys visited Italy, France, and England.

The Mongols, originally shamanists, were deeply influenced by the other religions with which they made contact through their conquests. In general, the Mongol khans pursued a policy of religious toleration. Some Mongols became Nestorian Christians, some Christians being found even in the imperial families; but throughout the Volga region, W Asia, and the Middle East, Islam was rapidly adopted by the majority of the Mongols as their religion. Buddhism in the Tibetan form of Lamaism was also adopted to a much smaller extent and much more slowly. The Franciscans and Dominicans attempted to spread Christianity among the Mongols in the late Middle Ages but their missions had very little success. The Mongols at the present time are largely concentrated in Outer Mongolia, the Mongolian People's Republic being one of the divisions of the Soviet Union. BIBLIOGRAPHY: D. Sinor, NCE 9:1059–61; B. Spuler, H. Motel, RGG 4:1097–98; W. Bingham, et al., *History of Asia* 1 (1964) 103–122; 409–448 (with bibliog.); K. Latourette, *History of Christian Missions in China* (1929).

[M. R. P. MCGUIRE]

MONICA, ST. (*c.*331–387), mother of St. *Augustine. Born of Christian parents, M. was married to Patricius, a pagan, to whom she bore at least three children, the eldest of whom was Augustine. By her prayers and good example she won not only her husband but also her difficult mother-in-law to the faith. After the death of Patricius (371) she was saddened by the waywardness of Augustine and his lapse into Manichaeism, but with courage and hope she besieged heaven with her prayers. She followed her son to Rome (383) and thence to Milan. Upon Augustine's decision to be baptized she withdrew to Cassiciacum with him and his friends and there took part in the conversations reported in the *Confessions*. She saw Augustine baptized by St. *Ambrose (387), and died soon afterward at Ostia as they were preparing to return to Africa. The record of her in the *Confessions* (esp. bk. 9) is a gem of hagiography and provides a credible picture of a great Christian wife and mother in no way dehumanized by eminent holiness of life. BIBLIOGRAPHY: Butler 2:226–229; A. Trapé, BiblSanct 9:548–558.

[R. B. ENO]

MONISM, a generic philosophical term used to designate any position in metaphysics that reduces all objective reality to a single principle which alone exists, or any position in epistemology that reduces all knowledge to one fundamental kind. The term is thought to have been coined from the Gr. *monos* (one) by the German philosopher C. *Wolff, who applied it to the opposing theories of idealism and materialism. Monistic views are usually contrasted with dualism, which admits two principles, and pluralism, which proposes more than two. Materialism, idealism, and pantheism are the principal varieties of monist philosophy, each of which involves its own unique ontological and epistemological commitments. Throughout its history, it has been characteristic of monism to emphasize a unity of reality in terms of time, space, and quality, so as to result in a view of the universe as immutable, indivisible, and undifferentiated. Monism appeared among the early pre-Socratic philosophers of ancient Greece. *Thales conceived water as the unifying principle; *Anaximander, the Boundless or Infinite; *Anaximines, air, vapor, or mist; *Heraclitus, fire; Xenophanes of Colophon, God, who is the one and all in whom everything is. Parmenides of Elea closed the cycle by opting for Being, the one, eternal, underived, and immutable. In modern thought monism has been represented in thinkers such as G. *Bruno, whose accent was upon spirit as the unique substance, and later in B. *Spinoza, whose pantheism identified God, nature, and substance as one, and accounted for seeming multiplicity in terms of attributes and modes of the sole reality. G. *Berkeley, proposed an epistemological monism that denied the existence of material things as distinct substances and reduced reality to an unknowable recognized as present by sense experience. G. *Hegel asserted Spirit or *Geist* to be the Absolute, the unitary ground of reality, possessing attributes of both substance and mind. British Idealism, inspired by Hegel and formulated in particular by F. H. *Bradley, stressed the radical unity of the universe and the role of the Absolute in causing it. Finally, psychical monism in the 19th cent., supported by idealists such as Lotze, Fechner, and Paulsen, took the view that matter is essentially an appearance, a shadow cast by thought, an externalization of mind, which is the true reality. In direct contrast to this, K. *Marx reduced everything to matter as the sole existent, with the spiritual or mental only one of its modalities. BIBLIOGRAPHY: A. Worsley, *Concepts of Monism* (1907); A. E. Taylor, *Elements of Metaphysics* (1902); A. Edel, "Monism and Pluralism," *Journal of Philosophy* 31.21 (1934); C. E. Joad, "Monism in the Light of Recent Developments in Philosophy," *Proceedings of the Aristotelian Society* 17 (1916–17).

[J. T. HICKEY]

MONITA SECRETA, short for *Monita secreta Societatis Jesu,* a set of forged instructions alleged to be from the Jesuit general C. *Acquaviva, and detailing unscrupulous and treacherous ways of gaining wealth, power, and influence for the Jesuits. The forgery was published in

Cracow in 1614 by Jerome Zahorowski, who had been dismissed from the Society in 1613. The spuriousness of the *Monita* was established almost immediately and confirmed by subsequent scholarship, yet the document went through numerous editions and translations by the end of the 18th cent., and has always been a favorite resource for the Jesuits' calumniators.

[T. C. O'BRIEN]

MONK, from the Gr. *monachos,* an individual member of a religious community of men that follows a monastic type of religious rule. The distinction of a monk from a friar or a male religious of other kinds is not simply historical, although all earlier religious of cenobitic communities can be referred to as monks, while the religious belonging to most communities that originated from the time of the first mendicant orders onward cannot be so classified, despite the loose application of the term sometimes encountered. Generally speaking, the monk is stably affiliated to a particular monastery that enjoys a certain independence of status, while the affiliation of friars and other religious is more commonly to an order or a province within an order that may embrace many houses. Another point of difference is the primacy of the monk's dedication to the worship of God and to a contemplative way of life.

[J. C. WILLKE]

MONK OF FARNE, spiritual writer of the 14th century. His name was John, a monk of Durham who died on Farne in 1371. He was the author of a series of meditations, the principal one on Christ crucified. The meditations are skillfully wrought and constitute a rare picture of a 14th-cent. monk and his interior life.

[J. R. AHERNE]

MONKS OF UNION, a group of Benedictine monks formed into a community in 1924 at the request of Pope Pius XI for the purpose of reuniting the Russian and other dissident Slav Churches with the RC Church. The community was formally founded in 1925 at Amay-sur-Meuse, Belgium, by Lambert *Beauduin. In 1928, it became a priory and in 1939 was moved to Chevetogne in the same country. The Benedictine Monastery of Union is divided into monks who celebrate the liturgy according to the Latin or the Byzantine rite. Much of the monks' time is devoted to studies in the history, spirituality, and theology of non-Catholic groups. They are dedicated to an apostolate of bringing about a corporate reconciliation between the Eastern Orthodox, esp. the Russian, and the Western Church. The monks publish a scholarly review called *Irénikon*. In 1964, they established an ecumenical training center at the monastery.

[R. A. TODD]

MONLUC (MONTLUC), BLAISE DE LASSERAN-MASSENCÔME, DE (*c.* 1502–77), French soldier, marshal of France (1574), and memorialist. After years of distinguished service with the armies of France in Italy (Pavia, 1525; Ceresole Alba, 1544; Siena, 1554–55), he fought in the French religious wars on the side of the Catholics, breaking Huguenot power in Guyenne and acquiring a reputation for severity towards heretics. Severely wounded (1570), he withdrew to write his *Commentaires* (1592), inspired by Caesar's *Gallic Wars,* generally considered a frank, autobiographical record of his campaigns, with a justification of his actions in Guyenne. Henry IV dubbed it *la Bible du soldat*. M. has, however, been accused of exaggeration concerning his own role. His brother, Jean (*c.* 1508–79), Dominican bp. of Valence and noted French diplomat, was condemned by the Roman Inquisition for his Protestant sympathies, but was spared with the protection of Catherine de Médicis. BIBLIOGRAPHY: J. Le Gras, *Blaise de Monluc, héros malchanceux et grand écrivain* (1926).

[R. N. NICOLICH]

MONNIKENDAM, MARIUS (1896–), Dutch composer. He studied with De Pauw in Amsterdam and with Vincent d'Indy in Paris (1924); later he taught music in Amsterdam and Rotterdam. His works include: *Missa nova* (1928), *Arbeid, Sinfonia sacra,* a symphonic setting of the *Te Deum,* and a commissioned work based on the Passion. He was influenced by Mahler and Tchaikovsky; his work most closely resembles the music of Delius.

[R. J. LITZ]

MONOGENĒS (Gr., only begotten), the opening word of the great dogmatic hymn in honor of the Incarnation of the Son of God and his redemptive economy, "O Only begotten Son and Word of God . . ." This hymn seems to have been originally the entrance hymn of the Byzantine Liturgy. The same hymn in expanded form is found in the liturgies of the Armenians, the Syrian Jacobites, and the Copts in an analogous position. The authorship of the hymn is doubtful. Some ascribe it to the Emperor Justinian, but most probably it was composed by *Severus of Antioch, patriarch of that see (512–536), and one of the ablest theologians of the Monophysite party. BIBLIOGRAPHY: F.E. Brightman, *Liturgies Eastern and Western* (1896).

[A. WALKER]

MONOGENISM, the belief that the human race stems from one original couple or that all men have Adam for their father. The word denotes a biological relationship whereby all men are blood-brothers; it connotes the spiritual fatherhood of the first man, whose legacy to his offspring was a fall from grace. Monogenism is deduced indirectly by theological argument from the doctrine of *original sin, rather than from explicit definitions of Scripture or the teaching Church. It is the prevailing opinion of biologists that the human race arose from one evolving group (not from a single pair), although some suggest that the existing races had separate origins. A monogenism consistent with biology is possible if hominization is equated with a unique mutation or change in one member of an evolving group, transmitted eventually to the whole group. Pius XII's encyclical *Humani generis* (1950) concluded that it was not apparent how *polygenism could be reconciled with church teaching on original sin. BIBLIOGRAPHY: P. De Rosa, *Christ and Original Sin* (1967); K. Rahner, *Hominization* (1966); J. De Fraine, *Bible and the Origin of Man* (1962).

[O. W. GARRIGAN]

MONOLATRY, worship of one god without denying the existence of others; *henotheism. The term was introduced *c.*1880 by J. *Wellhausen (1844–1918), to denote a stage supposed to exist between polytheism and *monotheism.

[T. EARLY]

MONOPHYSITISM, (from Gr. *monos*, one; and *phusis* (nature), the doctrine that Christ has no human nature. This is explained by saying either that his nature contains no human element at all, or that his human nature is totally swallowed up in the divine; or that his human and divine natures combine in something different from either. This doctrine was condemned at the Council of *Chalcedon (451).

*Eutyches (fl. *c.*445) in his effort to defend the concrete unity of Christ's being (in orthodoxy, the unicity of Christ's divine person) chose to deny his integral human nature and thus seemed to his adversaries to deny that Christ was in any way a human being. Condemned at Constantinople, Eutyches influenced Emperor Theodosius II to convoke the so-called *Robber Council of Ephesus which rehabilitated him and rejected Pope *Leo the Great's balanced and precise *Tome to Flavian, which condemned Monophysitism without lapsing into the opposite and symmetrical error of *Nestorianism. Theodosius died suddenly thereafter, and the orthodox ecumenical council of Chalcedon was convoked (451). Leo's Tome, the heart of the Chalcedonian creed, was approved, and the Robber Synod (Leo's term was *latrocinium,* an allusion to Eutyches' heterodox majority at Ephesus) was undone. But Monophysitism could not be stamped out. It continued to flourish esp. in the non-Greek East, probably more a cultural schism from Hellenism than a dogmatic heresy, using the term "one [divine] nature" of Christ probably much in the sense of the orthodox "one [divine] person." The Monophysites appropriated (posthumously) *Cyril of Alexandria as their patron saint, together with his formula "One nature, incarnate, of the Word of God" (by which the orthodox claim Cyril meant one person). Monophysitism became a kind of Egyptian national religion. Armenia, being anti-hellenist, was anti-Chalcedonian, and Monophysite. Ethiopia had been orthodox, but fell to the zeal of monophysite monasticism after Chalcedon. The Emperor Justinian had sent an orthodox mission to Nubia, but his Monophysite consort Theodora had it intercepted by a mission of her own, and Nubia became Monophysite. In Palestine, and esp. in Syria, orthodox and Monophysite communities existed side by side and fought pitched battles in the streets.

Severus of Antioch (fl. 522–538), the greatest theologian of Monophysitism, in an attempt to restore Monophysitism from a national or cultural chauvinism to a meaningful Christological position at odds with Chalcedonian orthodoxy, condemned the *Tome to Flavian* and Chalcedon's "two natures," and strengthened Monophysitism all over the non-Greek Christian East. His work was crowned by Jacob *Baradai, especially in Syria (see *JACOBITES). Paradoxically, modern scholars tend to see in Severus' terminological rejection of Chalcedon's "two natures" only a rejection of the heterodox Nestorian "two persons" and hence not theologically unorthodox. (Severus repudiated Eutyches). The *Monophysite Church endures today in Syria, Palestine, Egypt, Ethiopia, Armenia, and in the emigration in America, a few hundred thousand all told, surviving 14 centuries of persecution and internal strife.

[R. R. BARR]

MONOPOLY, a privilege or peculiar advantage vested in one or more persons or companies, consisting in the exclusive right or power to carry on a particular business or trade, manufacture a particular article, or control the sale of the whole supply of a commodity. A monopoly may also be viewed as a market wherein there are many buyers but only one seller having complete control over the price, and therefore the availability of a particular article or commodity. A monopoly is commonly contrasted with a competitive market wherein there are many buyers and sellers, each having such a limited control of a commodity that no one person or firm can control its price. Thus, monopoly and competition may be viewed from two different aspects: (1) as tools of economic theory in their differing impacts on market structures and; (2) as describing social situations either as goals for or as defects of the economy. From the latter viewpoint tations. Competition of some sort is normally preferred in the social order, whereas monopoly is almost universally socially undesirable. Where monopoly is inevitable, public supervision or control is necessary to provide the balance that competition would provide. This can involve regulation of prices, performance, and, to a degree, profits. Social policy needs to determine the extent to which competition can be a realistic goal and how monopoly can be adequately controlled when there is no alternative.

[F. T. RYAN]

MONOTHEISM, belief in the existence of a single God who is conceived as distinct from the universe of created being. In earlier Judaism some implicit recognition of the uniqueness of God can be inferred from the worship and experience of the Jewish people from the time of Abraham onward, but the explicit formulation of a monotheistic as distinguished from a henotheistic position first occurs in the Scriptures in Deutero-Isaiah (Is 44.6). Thereafter Judaism was staunchly monotheistic in the strictest sense (see GOD [IN THE BIBLE]), and this has also been the faith of Christianity and Islam. The question of whether monotheism has existed among primitive peoples, and to what extent, has been much debated. Although there is considerable evidence pointing to a widely diffused but implicit monotheism even in primitive cultures, the term in the precise sense it bears today can only be meaningfully applied to religions in which the idea of God has achieved considerable refinement. BIBLIOGRAPHY: W. Schmidt, *Der Ursprung der Gottesidee* (12 v., 1926–55); W.F. Albright, *From the Stone Age to Christianity* (2d ed., 1957); M. Eliade, *Patterns in Comparative Religion* (tr. R. Sheed, 1958); R. Pettazzoni, *All-Knowing God* (1956).

[P. K. MEAGHER]

MONOTHELITISM (Gk. *mono-thelēma,* one will) the heretical 7th cent. doctrine that Christ performed no human functions. Monotheletism issued from the attempt to reconcile the *Severian Monophysites to orthodox doctrine. Following the terminology of *Severus of Antioch (512–518), Monophysites in Syria and Egypt held that since Christ was but one individual, he had only one nature and functioned in a fully harmonious, integral manner in every action of his life. Their doctrine was, therefore, in at least terminological variance with the Council of *Chalcedon. In a conciliatory effort, Sergius I, Patriarch of Constantinople (610–638), proposed that although Christ had two natures, the human nature was without any independent operation or function, hence Christ had performed no purely human will acts or any other purely human operation. All Christ's activities were theandric. The Monophysites, judging that Christ's divinity had been sufficiently rescued from the Chalcedonian dual-nature doctrine, accepted Sergius' version of Chalcedon and were reunited with Constantinople and orthodoxy (633).

But Sergius' doctrine was susceptible of the interpretation that Christ's human will faculty did not function, or even that it was nonexistent. Sophronius, later patriarch of Jerusalem, immediately remonstrated with Sergius, whereupon Sergius wrote to Pope *Honorius I implying the unicity of Christ's will and the absence of an integral will faculty. Honorius, missing the implication, twice replied that Christ had indeed but "one will," since in him the human will and the divine will could never be in conflict. But what was at issue, for Sophronius as well as for the Monophysites, was whether Christ had two operating will faculties, the human and the divine, not whether they always acted in unison. At this point Emperor Heraclius published an *Ecthesis* to the same effect—that Christ had only one will. Honorius also intended the harmony of Christ's wills, but the *Ecthesis* was widely interpreted as meaning that Christ had no human will faculty or else that it was absorbed in the divine will. The *Ecthesis* was, therefore, condemned by Pope John IV (640–642); and in 647 Pope Theodore I excommunicated Paul, patriarch of Constantinople, for refusing to condemn Monothelitism. In the same year Emperor Constans II issued a *Typos* forbidding further discussion. In 649 Pope Martin I, seconded by *Maximus the Confessor, condemned Monothelitism and the *Typos*. Constans seized Martin, dragged him through the streets of Constantinople, and commuted his death sentence to exile only at the behest of the patriarch of Constantinople. Both Martin and Maximus soon died in exile.

A generation later Emperor Constantine IV and Pope Agatho convoked an ecumenical council (*Constantinople III, 680–681), where Christ was solemnly proclaimed to have both the divine will and an integral, free human will, which however always operated in harmony. BIBLIOGRAPHY: M. Jugie, DTC 10.2:2307–23; Fliche-Martin 5:103–179.

[R. R. BARR]

MONREALE, ART OF. Built for William II of Sicily (1172–89), the cathedral and monastery church of Monreale, near Palermo in Sicily, is a combination of Latin-basilica with Greek-cross-in-square plan. The mosaics in iconographic, hierarchical arrangement (Pantocrator in conch; Mary, archangels, Apostles and saints in apse; Old Testament cycle in nave, etc.) owe much to Cefalù, but are rather more florid in style. The cloister is magnificent: the paired marble columns with shafts exquisitely carved in Graeco-Latin and Byzantine styles, their storied capitals, individual or paired, evidencing French (Norman) influence. The bronze doors (1186) of the cathedral are the work of Bonannus of Pisa. BIBLIOGRAPHY: O. Demus, *Mosaics of Norman Sicily* (1950); E. Kitzinger, *Mosaics of Monreale* (1960).

[S. D. MURRAY]

MONROY É HIJAR, ANTONIO (*c.*1632–1715), Dominican master general, and bishop. Born in Mexico of a prominent family, M. entered the Dominicans in 1654. He taught theology for a time at the Univ. of Mexico. He was elected master general in 1667 and served until being named abp. of Santiago de Compostela, Spain, in 1685. He was distinguished for his zeal and the restoring of discipline in his see. Its considerable income went into building and charitable projects.

[J. R. AHERNE]

MONSABRÉ, JACQUES MARIE (1827–1907). French Dominican preacher. He was ordained in 1851 as a priest of the Diocese of Blois, and became a Dominican in 1855. His entire life was devoted to preaching, esp. preaching that reflected the theology of St. Thomas Aquinas. His collected sermons were published (35 v., 1901–04). His most celebrated tenure was as Lenten preacher at Notre Dame de Paris, 1870–90. He also was preacher at the Dominican church in Paris from 1867, and from 1897 to 1903 at Le Havre.

[T. C. O'BRIEN]

MONSIGNOR, an honorary ecclesiastical title; in the U.S. designates a *papal chamberlain, or the vicar general of a diocese, who ex officio is an honorary *prothonotary apostolic and a "reverend monsignor." Clerics of the papal household in the Vatican bear the title; in the European languages it is applied also to bishops. The title originated in France during the Avignon papacy.

[T. C. O'BRIEN]

MONSTRANCE, or ostensorium, a vessel used in exhibiting the sacred Host to public view. In its most common form it consists of a base surmounted by a stem in or on which a transparent glass or crystal container is fixed. Similar devices were used to display relics of the saints before the custom of exposing the consecrated Host arose. With the establishment of the Feast of Corpus Christi and the development of the eucharistic devotions associated with it, this type of vessel began to be used as early as the 14th cent. for the exposition of the Host. Because the piety of the early Middle Ages associated John the Baptist, who had proclaimed the Lamb of God, with the Eucharistic Sacrifice, some early monstrances were made in the form of a statue of John the Baptist holding the crystals that contained the Host. BIBLIOGRAPHY: A. King, *Eucharistic Reservation in the Western Church* (1964); J.H. Crehan, CDT 1:258.

[N. KOLLAR]

MONT-CORNILLON, MONASTERY OF, a double monastery of Liège, Belgium. The canons became Premonstratensians (*c.*1124); the nuns were Augustinian Canonesses. The men left in 1288 and established themselves at Beaurepart, a foundation that lasted until the French Revolution. Mont-Cornillon became Carthusian in 1360 and was suppressed during the French Revolution. A Carmelite convent exists on the site. Beaurepart is the diocesan seminary. BIBLIOGRAPHY: A. Versteylen, DHGE 7:245–246; F.M. Geudens, CE 4:379.

[T. C. O'BRIEN]

MONT-SAINT-MICHEL, ABBEY OF, Benedictine abbey dedicated to Michael the Archangel, in the Diocese of Coutances, France—a Romanesque Gothic architectural masterpiece crowning the massive rock of the same name and rising 240 ft from the sea—an apotheosis of topographic harmony in its marriage, indeed, almost identification, of site and architectural form—coupled with a daring engineering distinctively Norman. Its origin is traceable to an oratory founded *c.* 708, at the direction of St. Michael in a vision to Aubert, bp. of Avranches. The Benedictine monastery erected in 966 was endowed by Richard I, Duke of Normandy. Taking the first step in the seemingly impossible engineering of supports for a cluster of monastic buildings, Abbot Hildebert II, with the help of Richard II, undertook the construction of a new church at the summit *c.*1023. The four piers of the crossing and the central tower rising with Norman daring from the apex of the rock (1058) with a 200-ft expanse extended to an 80-ft wall of parapet dropping to the sea, were completed in 1135 in energetic, serious Romanesque style. One cannot overlook the fruitful alliance of abbots and royalty (1050–1122), and its harvest in the Norman cathedrals, the Chapel Royal in Palermo and at Monreale contemporaneous with Norman architectural daring at Mont-St.-Michel.

The choir having fallen (1421), was rebuilt (1450) in exuberant Late Gothic—a juxtaposition of self-conscious rhetoric against the quiet dignity of earlier Romanesque. The plan was finally realized in 1520. Subsequently given to the Maurists (1622), in 1776 the façade and seven nave bays were pulled down so that only four of the original sections remain.

Located in a highly strategic position for wartime and strongly fortified, the abbey was often assaulted, but never captured. Secularized during the French Revolution and used for political prisoners (1789–1863), it became a national monument in 1874, but since 1922 has functioned again as a place of worship. The extended drama of Mont St. Michel is its connection with the mainland by a narrow causeway inundated regularly by tides, which separate it completely from the continent. This, together with the precipitous rocky ascent through narrow medieval passes between ancient houses, is an allegory of the tortuous Christian journey to spiritual heights, where "on his Mount in peril of the sea" Michael keeps guard on the summit of the tower—the devil beneath his feet. Mont St. Michel is a major tourist attraction in Europe. BIBLIOGRAPHY: H. Adams, *Mont Saint Michel and Chartres* (repr., 1963).

[M. J. DALY]

MONT-SAINTE-ODILE, CONVENT OF (also called convent of Hohenburg, and Odilienberg—its German name), founded by St. Odilia (d. *c.*720) in Alsace and dedicated to Our Lady and St. Peter. Legends abound in the accounts of the life of Odilia, who was born blind and miraculously cured at her baptism at the age of 12. She established a fervent and flourishing community. Her shrine became a place of pilgrimage in the Middle Ages. In the 12th cent. when Herrad of Lansberg, author and compiler, was abbess, the convent was noted for its spirituality, culture, and scholarship. Fire and later the French Revolution took their toll of the foundation. Gradual reconstruction took place after the bp. of Strasbourg bought the property in 1853. The shrine and a hostelry still exist under the care of Sisters of the Holy Cross. BIBLIOGRAPHY: H. Leclercq, DACL 12:1921–34; A.M. Burd, LTK 7:1097; Butler 4:551–553.

[S. A. HEENEY]

MONTAIGNE, MICHEL EYQUEM DE (1533–92), French Renaissance writer and moralist, one of the creators of the modern literary genre of the "essay." M.'s father descended from a long line of rich Bordeaux merchants and his mother belonged to a converted Spanish-Jewish family which had fled to Toulouse from the Inquisition. His brother Thomas de Beauregard and sister Jeanne converted to Protestantism; his niece Jeanne de Lestonnac (1556–1640), foundress of the Company of Mary, was canonized a saint

(1949). After receiving a humanistic education and learning Latin as a native tongue, M. was sent to the Collège de Guyenne at Bordeaux, studied law at Toulouse (1546–50), and became *conseiller* at the Bordeaux parlement (1557) where he formed a close friendship (1558) with the stoic humanist Étienne de *La Boétie whose death (1563) greatly affected him and whose works he published (1570). Married (1565), M. published (1568) a French translation of Raymond Sebond's rationalistic *Theologia naturalis*. Retiring from public life (1571) after inheriting the family estate, he began writing the *Essais* (1st ed., 2 bks., 1580), his most important work, interrupted at intervals by his efforts as a moderate Catholic to act as intermediary between Henry of Navarre and the Catholic party. M.'s *Journal de voyage* (1774) describes the journey he next undertook through Germany and Italy (1580–81) in search of a cure for kidney stones. Summoned back to France upon being elected mayor of Bordeaux (1581–83, reelected 1583–85), M. discharged his duties well, diplomatically handling Protestants and Catholics, and foiling a Holy League plot. Back in retirement, he revised his *Essais* (new ed., including bk. 3, 1588), and while in Paris (1588), perhaps on a mission on behalf of Henry of Navarre's succession and conversion, he was arrested by the Ligueurs and imprisoned for a few hours in the Bastille. His last years were spent preparing a new edition of his *Essais*, published (1595) by his faithful companion, Marie de Gournay (1565–1645). He died after receiving all Catholic rites, while Mass was being said in his room. M.'s complex philosophical and religious thought is difficult to define. While his early essays reveal a stoic attitude, M. came to embrace skepticism, exposed principally in the "Apology for Raymond Sebond," the longest of the *Essais*, wherein appears M.'s motto, "Que sais-je?" (What do I know?). Casting doubt on almost all of man's beliefs, M. criticizes man's inability to find truth by feeble reason, and thus shows man's need to accept divine belief, which, being outside of reason, is outside of doubt. While his ideas were to influence the development of European thought in the following centuries, including such thinkers as *Descartes and *Pascal, M.'s beliefs have been seen as compatible with both Christian skeptical fideism and *libertin* freethinking. His skepticism, interpreted as an attack on the reasonings of the Reformers, make him part of the Counter Reformation, yet since no dogma is left secure, he is also seen as a forerunner of the critical spirit of the Enlightenment. Thus M. was put on the *Index* (1676) under Jansenist pressure. Looked at in respect to the 16th cent. religious wars, M. is seen as doubtful of radical proposals, opposed to fanaticism, advocating tolerance, and trusting in God. His conservativism is pragmatic. BIBLIOGRAPHY: P. S. Brown, *Religious and Political Conservativism in the Essais of Montaigne* (1963); H. Busson, *Le Rationalisme dans la littérature française de la renaissance (1533–1601)* (1957), viewing M. as freethinker; M. Dréano, *La Pensée religieuse de Montaigne* (1936), viewing M. as sincerely religious; L. Emery, *De Montaigne à Teilhard de Chardin via Pascal et Rousseau* (1965); D.M. Frame, *Montaigne's Discovery of Man. The Humanization of a Humanist* (1955); *idem, Montaigne: A Biography* (1965); C. Sclafert, *L'Âme religieuse de Montaigne* (1951). *CHARRON, PIERRE.

[R. N. NICOLICH]

MONTALEMBERT, CHARLES FORBES RENÉ DE (1810–70), champion of a Christian liberalism, member of France's parliament, historian. He was born in London son of an émigré father and an English mother (Eliza Forbes); his childhood and later English experiences influenced his political and social ideas. M.'s first political activities begin in 1830 as the associate of H. F. de*Lamennais and H. D. *Lacordaire in the publication of the review *L'Avenir,* dedicated to a Catholic liberalism. When *L'Avenir* was suspended (Nov. 15, 1831) the three went together to Rome to present their case to *Gregory XVI. Their program was effectively condemned by the Pope's *Mirari vos* (Aug. 15, 1832); M. separated from Lamennais, and by 1834 had become reconciled to the condemnation. He became a member of parliament in 1837, worked under Louis Phillippe, the Second Republic (1848–52), and under Napoleon III's Second Monarchy as a leader of the position for Christian solidarity against the egoism of pre-Revolutionary monarchy and against the egoism of materialistic economic liberalism. He succeeded to some extent in increasing Catholic participation in the political process; his single most important accomplishment was the passage of the Falloux law, establishing the rights of Catholics to their own schools. The rise of conservatism among Catholics in the face of the anticlerical forces of liberalism that were assailing the papacy in Italy, however, led to M.'s loss of his seat in parliament in 1857. The last major expression of his views came at the congress of Malines in 1863; particularly important was his advocacy of a practical acceptance by Catholics of religious freedom and pluralism in society. But he was also forced to reject C. *Cavour's interpretation of his own dictum: "a free Church in a free society." Most of his latter years were devoted to the publication of an historical work, reflecting an interest begun in his youth in medieval history, *Monks of the West* (Eng. tr. 1860; many repr. to 1912): *Les moines de l'Occident depuis St. Benôit jusqu'à St. Bernard* (5 v., 1860–68; 2 v., posthumous, 1877). M. took as repudiation of his views Pius IX's **Quanta cura* and *Syllabus of Errors* (1864). He was strongly opposed to the dogmatic definition of papal infallibility by Vatican Council I, but died before the dogmatic constitution *Pastor aeternus,* was approved. M also published biographies of St. Columba, St. Elizabeth of Hungary, H. D. Lacordaire, and a study (1865) of the Northern victory in the American Civil War (tr. *The Victory of the North in the United States,* 1867). BIBLIOGRAPHY: A. Trannoy, *Le Romantisme politique de Montalembert avant 1843* (1942); C. Constantin, DTC 19:523–610 s.v. "Libéralisme catholique."

[T. C. O'BRIEN]

MONTALVO, JUAN (1833–89), Ecuadorian writer and politician. At the age of 20, M. went to Europe as secretary of his country's legation in Paris. After returning to Ecuador he founded several papers, among them *La democracia,* in which he mercilessly attacked García Moreno and other presidents. His pamphlet, *La dictadura perpetua,* is said to have caused the assassination of Moreno. M. was bitterly anticlerical to the end of his life.

[P. DAMBORIENA]

MONTANA, a northern Rocky Mountain state, admitted to the Union (1889) as the 41st state. Originally the homeland of such Indians as the Blackfeet and Crow, the area was first crossed by white men, led by the sons of the famous trader Pierre Gaultier de *la Vérendrye, in 1642. The region was explored in the early 19th cent. by the Lewis and Clark Expedition, and fur traders soon moved in. The first major mission in the area was established (1840) by Pierre Jean De Smet, SJ. Jesuits continued to serve in Montana for a number of years, and in 1883 it was established as a vicariate apostolic. The following year the Diocese of Helena was created, its boundaries coextensive with Montana until 1904 when the Diocese of Great Falls was erected. Both dioceses are suffragans of the metropolitan See of Portland, Oregon. In 1976, Montana's Catholics numbered 131,294, or 18.9% of the total state population. The major Protestant denominations are the American Lutheran Church, with 7.0% of the population in 1971, and the Methodist Church with 4.1%. Other Protestant denominations comprised 16.0% of the population. The Jewish population (1968) was 615 or 0.09%. There are two Catholic colleges in Montana, with an enrollment of 2,550 students. Some 1,609 students attend the state's Catholic high schools, and 35,035 pupils are enrolled in 25 Catholic elementary schools. BIBLIOGRAPHY: J. K. Howard, *Montana, High, Wide and Handsome* (1943); L. B. Palladino, *Indian and White in the Northwest. A History of Catholicity in Montana, 1831–1891* (2d ed. 1922).

[J. L. MORRISON; R. M. PRESTON]

MONTAÑÉS, JUAN MARTINEZ (DE) (1568–1649), Spanish sculptor and architect of retables. A great genius of Andalusian carving, he was a student in Granada under Pablo de Rojas and in Seville. M.'s religious works of serene, ideal types embody the essence of holiness, his icons, theologically expressive and intimate, born of his subjective spirituality, avoid sentimentality. His polychromed wooden figures in Seville are innumerable (*Christ of Compassion, Christ Child Blessing, Immaculate Conception*). As architect of altars he collaborated with Juan de Oviedo (S. Isidoro del Campo). Figures in his altarpieces were often painted by F. Pacheco, Velasquez's father-in-law. Many of M.'s statues are in Peru.

[M. J. DALY]

MONTANI, NICOLA ALOYSIUS (1880–1948), American composer, conductor, church music reformer. He studied with Perosi in Rome (1903–05) and with Doms Mocquereau and Endine on the Isle of Wight (1906). To restore church music and the Gregorian chant, M. founded the Society of St. Gregory of America (1914) and edited its publication *Catholic Choirmaster* (1914–48). He composed church music, Masses and motets. He authored *Catholic Choir Book* (1920), *Essentials of Sight Singing, The Art of A Cappella Singing,* and *Cecilia* (1935). While serving as Newark's archdiocesan music director (1932–47) he created demonstrations of congregational singing that paved the way for the liturgical participation movements of the 1960s.

[R. J. LITZ]

MONTANISTS, members of a heretical sect founded in the 2d half of the 2d cent. by the Phrygian neophyte *Montanus. The movement spread rapidly and acquired a quasi-universal character. By 177 it had already been preached in Lyons and Rome. The Montanists, who did not entirely disappear until the 9th cent., soon broke up into various factions. Members of the sect came to be known as Phrygians, Cataphrygians, and Pepuzians from their place of origin (Pepuza in Phrygia). In Rome there were Montanists "according to Proclus" and others "according to Aeschines." In N Africa they were known as Artotyrites from their practice of using bread (*artos*) and cheese (*tyros*) in the celebration of the Eucharist.

Montanus and his two female companions, Priscilla (Prisca) and Maximilla, were subject to trances, which they took to be communications from the Holy Spirit. Collections of their prophetic oracles were gathered into "countless books" (Hippolytus, *Philos.* 8.19) and were regarded as being "new Scriptures" (Eusebius, *Hist. eccl.* 6.20.3) of equal authority with the Old and New Testaments. The revelation of the Spirit thus given was believed to be that which Christ had promised to his Disciples at the Last Supper; it announced the imminent end of the world and the dawn of the *millennium at Pepuza. Their millenary expectations induced the Montanists to lead a rigorously ascetical life. Prolonged fasts, virginity, and continence were held in exaggerated esteem. Their general flight from the world even found expression in voluntary martyrdoms. Later leaders, particularly *Tertullian, gave the movement a less charismatic and more dogmatic orientation. In his Montanistic period he taught, e.g., that second marriages were a kind of fornication, that flight from persecution was a form of apostasy, and that there are certain sins that cannot be forgiven by the Church. The emphasis that the Montanists placed upon the guidance of the Spirit caused them to reject episcopal authority. This rejection of the hierarchy and their conviction that the revelations given to the new prophets complemented those of the NT set them apart substantially from the Church.

The religious fanaticism of the Montanists had a powerful influence upon the less stable members of the Christian community. They were opposed by numerous writers, such as Apollinaris of Hierapolis, Miltiades, Melito of Sardis, the Roman priest Gaius, Eusebius, Epiphanius, and St.

Jerome. They also attracted the attention of less orthodox Christians, such as Origen and the patripassianist Praxeas. Montanism was condemned by Popes Soter (*c.*166–175), Eleutherius (*c.*175–189), and Innocent I (401–417), and by the Emperors Honorius I (407), Justinian I (530), and Leo the Isaurian (722). As the movement gradually lost its formal identity, its members returned to the Church or passed over to other sects, such as the Cathari and the Priscillianists. The last mention of the Montanists in antiquity is a petition of the 9th cent. that the patriarch Nicephorus of Constantinople made to the Emperor to repress the Phrygian heretics.

Montanism has been interpreted as an attempt to recover a primitive religious fervor in the face of a growing secularization. It is perhaps better to understand it as a particularly striking manifestation of a phenomenon that recurs within the Church—a craving for religious experiences to offset the difficulties of a life of faith. The ultimate defeat of Montanism marks the renunciation of the eschatological enthusiasm of the early Church, the affirmation of a hierarchy based upon an apostolic succession, the universality of the Church as opposed to individual propheticism, and the right of the Church to pardon the sins of all its members. BIBLIOGRAPHY: Epiphanius, *Adv. haer.* 2.48; P. de Labriolle, *Le Crise montaniste* (1913); A. Mayer, EncCatt 8:1343–47; H. Bacht, LTK 7:578–580; KnoxEnth 25–49.

[M. J. COSTELLOE]

MONTANUS (fl. mid-2d cent.), the founder of a widespread apocalyptic movement generally known as Montanism. He may have been a priest of Cybele before his conversion in 156 or 157 (Epiphanius, *Adv. haer.* 48.1) or, much more likely, in 172 or 173 (Eusebius, *Chronic.* 11, *Olymp.* 238). Soon after his baptism he began to preach at Ardabau on the boundary between Phrygia and Mysia and later in Pepuza. He claimed to be the organ of the Paraclete that had been promised by Christ and preached the proximate approach of the millennium. Among his first disciples were two ecstatic women, Priscilla (or Prisca) and Maximilla, who left their husbands to proclaim the "new prophecy." All three seem to have died before A.D. 179, but the ideas they had taught spread rapidly from Asia Minor into Syria, Thrace, and even to Lyons, Carthage, and Rome. M. is the prototype of the many apocalyptic preachers in church history. BIBLIOGRAPHY: P. de Labriolle, *Le Crise montaniste* (1913); A. Mayer, EncCatt 8:1343–47; H. Bacht, LTK 7:578–580. *MONTANISTS.

[M. J. COSTELLOE]

MONTANUS, ARIAS, see ARIAS MONTANUS, BENITO.

MONTCHEUIL, YVES DE (1900–44), French Jesuit theologian, teacher, and writer, hero of the French Resistance to Nazi occupation. He entered the Society of Jesus in 1917, was ordained 1932, was professor at the Institut Catholique of Paris (1935–44), during which time he also served as chaplain to Catholic Action. M. was shot by the Germans in August 1944 as he was visiting a group of students involved with the resistance. He had collaborated on some publications while he was alive (1932,1939), but it was after his death that most of his scattered theological writings came to light—most notably the two-volume collection gathered together by H. de Lubac, entitled *Mélanges théologiques* (1946). G. Mollat NCE 9:1080; DTC Tables générales 3248.

[E. J. DILLON]

MONTCHRÉTIEN, ANTOINE DE (*c.*1575–1621), French dramatist and economist. Although M. was killed in a Huguenot insurrection against Louis XIII, it is unsure whether he was reared a Protestant, or simply converted to Protestantism on making an advantageous marriage. He is the author of six influential tragedies, more poetic than dramatic: *Sophonisbe* (1596); *Les Lacènes* (1600); *Hector* (1604); *L'Écossaise* (1601), his best play, on the death of Mary Stuart, which M., exiled in England as the result of a duel, dedicated to James I; and *David* (1600) and *Aman* (1602), both religious plays. These last, along with his tragic epic *Susane ou la Chasteté* (1601), reveal deep biblical inspiration, the influence of Du Bartas' *Judith,* and Christian neo-Stoicism. His *Traité de l'économie politique* (1615) is considered one of the first of its kind. BIBLIOGRAPHY: *Traité de l'économie politique* (ed. T. F. Brentano, 1889) introd.; C. Willner, *Montchrestiens Tragödien und die Stoische Lebensweisheit* (1932).

[R. N. NICOLICH]

MONTE, PHILIPPE DE (Filippo di, Philippe de Mons; 1521–1603), Flemish composer. He spent his early years singing madrigals and composing throughout Europe. He served as *Kapellmeister* to Maximilian II and Rudolph II (1568–1603). M.'s church music dates from the year after his appointment to the Viennese court (1568). His works include over 1,000 madrigals and French chansons, 300 motets and 38 masses. Of these, the Requiem and the *Missa benedicta* are most renowned. In his secular music he was considered by contemporaries the equal of Lassus and Palestrina.

[R. J. LITZ]

MONTE CASSINO, ABBEY OF, cradle of the Benedictine Order, founded by St. Benedict in 529 within the citadel of ancient Casinum, midway between Rome and Naples. Destroyed by the Lombards *c.*581, it was restored in 720; by the Saracens in 884, it was restored in 954; by an earthquake in 1349, and built up during the centuries into a vast rectangular pile; looted by the French in 1799; sequestrated by the Italian government in 1866, though monks were allowed to remain as its guardians; bombed to bits by the English and Americans in 1944, it was defended by German paratroopers commanded by a general who was himself a Benedictine Oblate. Rebuilt, it was consecrated in 1964 by Pope Paul VI. Despite these vicissitudes the abbey has continued, the most venerable home of monasticism in the West. BIBLIOGRAPHY: R. Böhlmer, *Monte Cassino* (tr. R. H. Stevens, 1964); H. Bloch, NCE 9:1080–82 (bibliog.).

MONTE FANO, ORDER OF, see BENEDICTINES, SYLVESTRINE.

MONTE VERGINE, ABBEY OF, a historical shrine near Avellino, Italy. It was founded by St. William of Vercelli (b. 1085), who, desiring to live as a hermit, settled on a mount between Nola and Benevento called then Monte Vergiliano—perhaps for the Roman poet Virgil, believed to have stayed there. Having attracted disciples, William formed a community, the Hermits of Monte Vergine, and built a church (1124) dedicated to Our Lady. The site then became known as Monte Vergine. He founded other monasteries, delegating each one to the care of a prior. The only one remaining at present is Monte Vergine, which now belongs to the Benedictine congregation of Subiaco. It possesses a highly venerated picture of Our Lady of Constantinople and is a place of pilgrimage. BIBLIOGRAPHY: Butler 2:635–637; C. Rabasca, EncCatt 8:1372–73; G. Mongelli, LTK 7:589; P. Lugano, *L'Italia benedettina* (1929) 379–439.

[S. A. HEENEY]

MONTEFIORE, CLAUDE JOSEPH GOLDSMID (1858–1938), English theologian and leader of Liberal Judaism. Member of the notable Anglo-Jewish Montefiore family, he was educated at Oxford and Berlin. With Israel Abrahams, he founded and edited until 1905 *The Jewish Quarterly Review* (1888). He served as president of the Liberal Jewish Synagogue which emerged in 1911 from the Jewish Religious Union, a radical reform movement that he had founded in 1902. He was elected president of the World Union for Progressive Judaism in 1926. He and Baron von Hügel, a Catholic theologian, founded the London Society for the Study of Religion. M.'s sympathetic and scholarly understanding of Christianity never displaced his belief in Jewish theism yet it gained him the critical enmity of traditionalists. He found the distinctive feature of Judaism in its awareness of the immanence and transcendence of God, thus he saw Judaism as universal rather than narrowly national. He opposed Zionism and fought the Balfour Declaration (see BALFOUR, A.J.). He was attracted by Christian ethics and the mystical tone he found in the reading of the Gospels. He suggested that the NT be given an honored place in Judaism, yet he opposed any introduction of Christianity into Jewish practice or liturgy. His Hibbert Lectures (1892) were published as the *Origin and Growth of Religion As Illustrated by the Religion of the Ancient Hebrews*. His numerous historico-religious works deal primarily with biblical and Rabbinic literature and history; among them are: *The Synoptic Gospels* (1909); *Outlines of Liberal Judaism* (1912); and *A Rabbinic Anthology* (1938).

[R. J. LITZ]

MONTEIRO DA VIDE, SEBASTIÃO (1643–1722), influential Brazilian abp. and canonist. After brief careers in Portugal as a soldier, student of canon law at the Univ. of Coimbra, ecclesiastical judge, and vicar general of Lisbon, he was named bp. of Bahia, Brazil, in 1701. In that capacity he created many new parishes, held the first diocesan synod in Portuguese America, and published the famous *Constituições Primeiras* (Constitutions), which became the basic norm for governing the dioceses of Brazil until the 19th cent., replacing the constitutions of Lisbon.

[E. J. DILLON]

MONTEMAYOR, JUAN FRANCISCO (1620–85), Spanish jurist, writer, and priest, known also as M. de Cuenca, M. Córdoba de Cuenca, or simply Cuenca. He was first a jurist in Spain, at Huesca and Catalonia, before going to Santo Domingo in 1650, where, as virtual governor, he was responsible for recovering for Spain the island of Tortuga, N of Hispaniola. For 22 years he was judge of the *audiencia* of Mexico, during which period he was also ordained priest. On his return to Spain in 1672 he was a member of the Council of the Indies and an advisor to the Inquisition. His writings, among other things, show him to have been a theorist on the legalities of sea warfare. BIBLIOGRAPHY: H. Pereña NCE 9:1083–84.

[E. J. DILLON]

MONTENEGRO, ORTHODOX CHURCH OF, a former autocephalous Serbian Orthodox Church, now a part of the Serbian patriarchate of Yugoslavia. The Slavs of Montenegro (*Crna Gora*) had a Byzantine rite bp. appointed by St. Sava of Serbia in the 13th cent., although many of them were of the Latin rite and became estranged from the Catholic Church only in the 17th century. The bishops resided in the Mother of God Monastery in Cetinje, and after the extinction of the Crnojević family also became the political leaders of the region in the unceasing defense of their freedom against the Turks. The metropolitans acted as the secular rulers (ethnarchs), and between 1697 and 1851 were all taken from the family Petrović-Njegoš. The Church of Montenegro was recognized as independent and financially supported by Russia. Prince Danilo (1851–60), on succeeding his relative, the great poet Peter II Petrović-Njegoš, refused to accept priestly and episcopal ordination, and declared himself a secular prince. His nephew Nikola, (1860–1918), having enlarged Montenegro several times in territory and population, declared himself king (1910). The kingdom and the Church were incorporated into Yugoslavia (1918) and the Serbian patriarchate (1920). The Serbian Orthodox faithful are under the ecclesiastical care of the metropolitan of Cetinje.

[V. J. POSPISHIL]

MONTENSES, a name given to the small *Donatist community in Rome. It was composed of immigrants to the city and received Victor of Garba as its first bp. shortly after the origin of the schism in Africa. Since the Donatists had at first no church in Rome where they could assemble, they were forced to meet in a cave in a mountain (*in monte*) outside the city, and from this fact they received their name. Petilian and other Donatists appealed in vain to the existence of this small group as a proof of the universality of their Church. BIBLIOGRAPHY: Augustine, *Ep.* 53.2; A. Pincherle, EncCatt 8:1364.

[M. J. COSTELLOE]

MONTES PIETATIS (Monti di Pietà), in their inception, charitable lending agencies, making small loans to the poor in exchange for pawned objects. The term *pietatis* qualifies these funds (*montes*) as accumulated for beneficent purposes, not for speculation or usury. Although they had some antecedents, all inspired by the intent to make loans available to those in need from nonusurious sources, the first successful *mons pietatis* was established at Perugia in 1461 by the Franciscans, who soon established others; gradually such institutions spread throughout Europe. In due course the *montes pietatis* became more secularized, profit-oriented, and similar to modern savings banks. Theological opposition to the original idea, esp. by Dominicans, maintained that a charitable intent did not justify the basic immorality of lending at interest, i.e., of *usury. But at Lateran Council V Leo X's bull *Inter multiplices* resolved the controversy in favor of the defenders of the *montes pietatis*, with the proviso that interest be low and charged only for administrative expenses (D 1444). Thus these institutions were a step towards the moral acceptability of lending money at a legitimate rate of interest.

[T. C. O'BRIEN]

MONTESINO, ANTONIO (d. *c.*1530), Spanish Dominican, missionary to the New World. A Dominican from 1502, he worked in Española from 1510. He fought constantly against the enslavement and exploitation of the Indians, made journeys of protest to Spain in 1512, 1515, 1522, 1527, and published his *Informatio juridica in Indorum defensionem* (1516). He was part of the unsuccessful attempt to found a Spanish colony in Virginia in 1526. In the archives of San Estéban, the Dominican convent at Salamanca, his martyrdom is recorded, but without date or details.

[T. C. O'BRIEN]

MONTESINOS, LUIS DE (d. 1621), Dominican commentator on St. Thomas Aquinas. His only published work was *Commentaria in primam secundae S. Thomae,* (1622), but the work is highly regarded.

[P. J. HENNESSEY]

MONTESQUIEU, CHARLES DE (1689–1775), political theorist and man of letters, pioneer promoter of a critical, sociological view of the human condition, and the father of modern liberal political thinking. He was born near Bordeaux and his actual name was Charles Louis Joseph de Secondat; he inherited a barony (de la Brède) from his mother and another (de Montesquieu) from his uncle. He was an inveterate traveler and observer of the divergent customs, folk-ways, and traditions of peoples. Although always nominally a Catholic, he was closer in his views to the Deists and the later philosophers of the Enlightenment. His satirical *Persian Letters* (1721), critical of French life, esp. the court life of Louis XIV and that of the Church, made him the darling of the salons of Paris. Another major work gave his reflections on the causes of Rome's greatness and decline (1734); but it was his *De l'Esprit des lois* (1748) that brought him to the forefront of European social and political thought. His humanism, tinged with pessimism, led him to espouse a society made up of counterbalancing, mutually independent social forces, and a division of governmental powers into executive, legislative, and judicial branches, similar to the English tradition. He helped orient 18th-cent. thought toward liberty, rationalism, and tolerance; may have influenced the American Constitution, and prepared the way for the French Revolution's exalted view of the Republic and the required virtue of its citizens. His writings attempt to demonstrate how different political traditions evolve from differing moments in the evolutions of peoples. His special interest was in the interplay of such humble factors as geography, climate, terrain, and means of commerce with religion, custom, and political tradition. BIBLIOGRAPHY: W. Stark, NCE 9:1087–88; C. Constantin, DTC 10:2377–88; J. Wilhelm LTK 7:587.

[E. J. DILLON]

MONTESSORI, MARIA (1870–1952), Italian born educator and physician known for her unique concepts in educational theory which led to the development of schools around the world dedicated to the "Montessori method." A feminist and social reformer, M. was the first woman to graduate from the medical school of the Univ. of Rome. Her research in pedagogy led her to develop a method of teaching which was based on the child's natural interest in learning and radically challenged the accepted rigid methods of formal education. BIBLIOGRAPHY: R. Kramer, *Maria Montessori*, *A Biography* (1976). *MONTESSORI SCHOOLS.

[M. A. MCFADDEN]

MONTESSORI SCHOOLS, a system of pre-school and early childhood education based on the methods of child pedagogy developed by Maria *Montessori, Italian educator and physician (1870–1952). The methodology of the system emphasizes freedom of expression in a prepared environment with specially devised teaching materials designed to promote sense and muscular development, the teacher acting as trained observer or director rather than as formal instructor. Basic to Montessori methodology is recognition of the dignity of the child as a person endowed, even at an early age, with certain creative potentials that must be duly fostered. To achieve this there must exist between adult and child a close rapport stemming from the adult's recognition of the child's ability to respond creatively in an atmosphere of freedom and independent action to carefully devised and properly applied stimuli geared to his maturational level or readiness. Despite its emphasis on freedom, a prerequisite to interest and self-involvement, Montessori methodology insists on a certain order and routine to guarantee a pleasurable environment and preserve a sense of security indispensable to wholesome mental, social, and emotional development. The first Montessori school, the Casa dei Bambini, was opened in Rome in 1907. Others quickly followed in Europe and the U.S., but were later overshadowed by the progressive school. Since the 1950s there has been a widespread Montessori revival and Marquette Univ. and Boston College, among others, have introduced centers of research and teacher training. BIBLIOGRAPHY: N. M. Rambusch, *Learning How To Learn: An American Approach to Montessori* (1962).

[M. B. MURPHY]

MONTEVERDI, CLAUDIO (1567–1643), Italian composer of sacred music, a father of the modern opera. He spent over 20 years as court musician for Vincenzo Gonzaga, Duke of Mantua. In 1613 he became *maestro di cappella* at St. Mark's, Venice, and remained in that post for the remainder of his life. For many years a widower, he became a priest *c.*1632, a step probably taken during a period of social chaos and plague in N Italy. M.'s innovations in music mark the passage from the late Renaissance style to the early Baroque. On the basis of a conviction that the word, or poetic diction, should determine harmony, he flew in the face of the previous convention in polyphony that let harmony determine or overshadow the text. In his early opera, *Orfeo* (1607), he introduced the recitative, thorough-bass, and expressive *bel canto* style of singing. Though M. composed nothing solely for instruments, he influenced all later composition by introducing the *tremolo* and the *pizzicato* as musical expressions of the emotions. Two celebrated collections of his sacred works were published in his lifetime: in 1610 a Mass for five voices and a Vespers, with two *Magnificat* settings; in 1640, *Selva morale e spirituale*, which included a Mass and a series of Vespers, with multiple settings for the Psalms and the *Magnificat*. A posthumous work (1650) was M.'s *Messa a quattro voci e salmi*, again with many Vesper settings. His setting of Ps 1, *Beatus vir*, is most frequently heard.

[D. J. SMUCKER]

MONTFAUÇON, BERNARD DE (1655–1741), French Benedictine patrologist, paleographer, bibliographer, and archeologist. A member of the Maurists from 1575, he worked at their research center, St. Germain des Prés in Paris. His principal editions of Church Fathers are the works of St. Athanasius (3 v. 1690; PG 25–28) and St. John Chrysostom (13 v., 1718–38; PG 47–64); he also edited Origen's *Hexapla* (2 v., 1713). His *Paleographica graeca* (1708) was the foundational work on its subject; he also edited *Analecta graeca, sive varia opuscula graeca hactenus edita* (1688). From 1698 to 1701 he researched Italian libraries for their Greek MSS, and published a diary of his discoveries, *Bibliotheca bibliothecarum manuscriptorum nova* (2 v., 1739). In archeology he published, *L'Antiquité expliquée et répresentée en figures* (10 v., 1719), and *Monuments de la monarchie française* (2 v., 1729–33).

[T. C. O'BRIEN]

MONTFORT, LOUIS MARIE GRIGNION DE, see GRIGNION DE MONTFORT, LOUIS MARIE, ST.

MONTFORT FATHERS, priests and assisting brothers of the religious congregation called officially Missionaries of the Company of Mary (SMM), founded in 1715 in France by St. Louis Marie *Grignion de Montfort. The community received the rank of a pontifical congregation in 1853. The members take simple vows and their primary apostolate is to spread the reign of Christ through dedication to Mary. A work entitled *True Devotion to Mary*, written by the founder and his beatification in 1888 contributed greatly to the spread of the mission work. The Montfort Fathers preach and give retreats in countries of Europe, Asia, Africa, and the Americas. The congregation has a total membership of 1,525, with 1,166 priests, and maintains 74 houses. The superior general resides in Rome.

[R. A. TODD]

MONTGELAS, MAXIMILIAN (1759–1838), minister from 1799 to 1817 under Maximilian I Joseph of Bavaria; responsible for secularization of church property and repressive measures against the religious orders.

[T. C. O'BRIEN]

MONTGOMERY, JAMES ALAN (1866–1949), Orientalist and OT exegete. M. taught Scripture at the Philadelphia Divinity School (1899–1935), and Hebrew and Aramaic at the Univ. of Pennsylvania (1909–39). He was president of the American Schools of Oriental Research (1921–34), editor of the *Journal of Biblical Literature* (1909–13) and of the *Journal of the American Oriental Society* (1916–21, 1924). He published a large body of eminent scientific scholarship, notably *The Samaritans* (1907), a comprehensive and original study of this sect; *Hebrew Mythological Texts from Ras-Shamra* (1935), a compilation of Ugaritic texts; *The Origin of the Gospel according to St. John* (1923); and commentaries on Dan and Kg for the *International Critical Commentary*.

[T. M. MCFADDEN]

MONTHS, SPECIAL DEVOTIONS FOR, a nonliturgical Catholic practice of relatively recent development, by which the months of the calendar are dedicated to special devotions involving special prayers. Some, such as the dedication of May to Mary, and November to the Holy Souls, have been recognized and recommended by Rome and the Church. The dedication of October to the Most Holy Rosary was actually initiated by the Holy See. Others grew naturally out of popular feasts of a particular month: such as January being the month of the Holy Name or the Holy Childhood; March the month of St. Joseph; June, the Sacred Heart; July, the Most Precious Blood; August, the Immaculate Heart of Mary; September, the Mother of Sorrows; December, the Immaculate Conception. Secondarily, March is dedicated to the Holy Family, and October to the Holy Angels. Since Vatican II there has been emphasis on integrating all such devotional patterns with the course and content of the liturgical calendar itself.

[E. J. DILLON]

MONTH'S MIND, English term for a remembrance (''mind'') of a deceased person, usually 30 days after death. It is a Catholic custom to have Mass celebrated for the repose of the person's soul on that day. The old Roman Missal provided Masses for certain days after death as well as the *anniversary. Among the details on Masses for the Dead in the General Instruction of the Roman Missal (1969), special Masses for the Dead are allowed, even on days of obligatory 'saints' memorials, on the day news of a death is received, on the day of final burial, and the anniversary (nn. 335–337, 341). The month's mind as such is not singled out.

MONTLUC, BLAISE DE (1501?–77), French soldier and writer who served under several French kings and became marshal of France in 1574. He was harsh in his treatment of Huguenots. M. wrote commentaries on the various wars in which he was involved. His full name was Blaise de Montesquiou; Seineur de Mont luc his title.

[M. A. MCFADDEN]

MONTMAJOUR, ABBEY OF, former Benedictine abbey near Arles in S France. Although the actual date of establishment is uncertain, the abbey enjoyed widespread influence in SE France during the 11th and 12th centuries. In 1639 it joined the Maurist reform, but was suppressed in 1786. Today the abbey church and cloister still stand but the other buildings are in ruins.

[M. A. MCFADDEN]

MONTMARTRE, ABBEY OF, former Benedictine monastery for women on Montmartre (Paris; *Mons Mercurii*, later *Mons Martyrum*), the legendary site of the martyrdom of St. Denis and others. Oratories had been erected there very early, one of them becoming a priory for monks in 1098. Several others were united into a church for the Benedictine nuns established there in 1134. Beginning in 1560 the French kings appointed the abbess, a woman of noble birth who would hold office for life. The abbey was suppressed in 1794 and its abbess guillotined. BIBLIOGRAPHY: Cottineau 2:1964–66.

[J. DAOUST]

MONTPELLIER, UNIVERSITY OF, a state institution in the province of Hérault, one of the 19 comprising the National Univ. of France. It began as a school of medicine (1137), the first in Europe, to which a faculty of law was added (1160). It was approved by Honorius II (1220) and was recognized as a *studium generale* by Nicholas IV (1289). A faculty of theology, authorized by Martin V, was established in 1421. Until their suppression in the Revolution of 1789, the faculties of medicine and law were two distinct bodies, each with its own chancellor and rector. Restored under the Empire in 1808, the university was composed of faculties of medicine, pharmacy, and science, to which literature was added in 1810; the faculty of law was reopened in 1881. Associated with the faculty of law during its long history were many eminent jurists among whom were: Placentinus, Guillaume de Grimoard (Urban V), and Pietro de Licena (Benedict XIII). During the 12th cent., the university was one of the greatest European *studia*, on a par with Salerno, Bologna, and Paris, a position it retained, particularly in the field of medicine and surgery, throughout the 13th cent. and until the mid-14th cent. when it went into a period of decline. During the Renaissance it experienced a revival in medicine, theology, and the arts. Despite later fluctuations in the 18th and 19th cent., Montpellier continues to hold a place of distinction among French provincial institutions of higher learning, esp. for its school of medicine. The renowned Protestant theological faculty of Montarban was transferred to the Univ. of Montpellier in 1919 and its theologians have decisively influenced French Protestantism in the 20th century. A Centre Universitaire Protestant promotes an exchange of ideas with lay students. The faculty publishes the quarterly *Études théologiques et religieuses* (1926–). BIBLIOGRAPHY: J. Cadier, RGG 4:1124; H. Rashdall, *Universities of Europe in the Middle Ages* (ed. F. M. Powicke and A. B. Emden, 3 v., 1936).

[M. B. MURPHY]

MONTREAL, UNIVERSITY OF, a pontifical coeducational, French-language institution of higher learning, originally church-supported but now financed in large part by the province of Quebec. It began as a branch of Laval Univ. in 1878 with faculties of theology and law; in 1879 it incorporated a faculty of medicine that had been in existence from 1843; in 1887 it added a faculty of arts, composed of several affiliated classical colleges. In 1919 the univ. became independent of Laval and in 1920 was chartered by the legislature of Quebec as the Univ. of Montreal. Administration is vested in a board of governors and an academic senate, with the abp. of Montreal the university's *ex officio* chancellor. Since 1965 the rector, until then always a clergyman, has been a layman. In addition to the faculties named above, the univ. now has faculties of philosophy, letters, sciences, dental surgery, pharmacy, social sciences, arts, and music. It has schools of engineering, commerce, veterinary medicine, nursing, science of education, library science, town-planning, architecture, rehabilitation, public hygiene, optometry, and medical technology. Two institutes maintained by the faculty of philosophy—medieval studies and psychology—and others in the field of pedagogy, and the Institut Supérieur Des Sciences Religieuses have done distinguished work in matters of religious scholarship. The faculty of theology is identified with the Grand Seminaire of Montreal. The library, including the holdings of the affiliated colleges contains about 1 million volumes. The enrollment of full and part time students is about 28,000.

[M. B. MURPHY]

MONTREAL CONFERENCE, the fourth World Conference on *Faith and Order, held in Montreal, July 13–26, 1963. The topics presented for discussion were: (1) Christ and the Church; (2) tradition and traditions; (3) worship; and (4) institutionalism. The reports of the sections into which the Conference divided for consideration of the various subjects were presented to the participating Churches without a general vote of the Conference. The social implications of the doctrines studied were particularly strong in the reports entitled "The Church in the Purpose of God" and "The Process of Growing Together." The concept that the Churches were component parts of the one Church was rejected in favor of an emphasis on the union of all Christians in the body of Christ, the Church. A new approach to the question of the ministry of the Church was apparent: the ministry was seen as originating in and reflecting the threefold mission of Christ as prophet, as high priest, and as king. Notable at this Conference was the large representation from Eastern Orthodoxy and the participation of more than 20 RC theologians. BIBLIOGRAPHY: *Fourth World Conference on Faith and Order* (eds. P. C. Rodger and L. Vischer, 1964).

[D. CODDINGTON]

MONTREUIL, EUDES DE (d. 1289), French architect attached to the court of Louis IX. M. was one of the principal architects of his time; his buildings are considered models of the 13th-cent. Gothic style. In addition to several monuments in Paris, he designed the churches of the Cordeliers, Chartreux, Ste. Catherine du Val, the Hôtel Dieu, and Ste. Croix de la Bretonnerie. He also constructed the fortification of Jaffa during the Crusades of King Louis.

[T. MCFADDEN]

MONTREUIL (MONTEREAU), PIERRE DE (fl. *c.*1231–67). French master architect, pupil and later rival of the great Persian architect, pupil and later rival of the great the great Persian architect Jean de Chelles, M., called *Doctor Lathomorum,* was leading master of Rayonnant Gothic style in the 13th century. His most important works were the nave and chevet at St. Denis (1231–39), the south transept façade at Notre-Dame, Paris (1260), and refectory and chapel of the Virgin at St. Germain-des-Près, Paris (1245–55) where he is buried. BIBLIOGRAPHY: E. Panofsky, *Gothic Architecture and Scholasticism* (1951).

[M. J. DALY]

MONTREUIL, ABBEY OF, former Carthusian monastery in the Diocese of Arras, France, established in 1324 by Count Robert VII of Boulogne. It was pillaged intermittently in the 14th, 15th, and 16th centuries. After undergoing extensive rebuilding in the 17th cent., it was suppressed (1790) during the French Revolution. Though the Carthusians erected a new monastery between 1872 and 1875, which became an important center of their publications, it was closed (1901) when the French expelled religious orders. The community relocated in Parkminster, England, and its printing presses were transferred to Belgium. BIBLIOGRAPHY: R. Gazeau, *Catholicisme* 2:1008; G.R. Hudleston, CE 10:550.

[S. A. HEENEY]

MONTREUIL-LES-DAMES, ABBEY OF, convent of Cistercian nuns near Laon, France. Established in 1136 on the site of an ancient Benedictine monastery, it was famous during the Middle Ages as the custodian of the "Veil of St. *Veronica," an early replica of the one preserved in Rome. The house was suppressed in 1791. BIBLIOGRAPHY: Cottineau 2:1973–74.

[L. J. LEKAI]

MONTSERRAT, ABBEY OF, a Benedictine monastery near Barcelona, Spain, founded as a priory *c.*1025. Only ruins remain of the early church, a Romanesque portal (12th–13th cent.), and the 15th-cent. Gothic cloister. The 16th-cent. Renaissance edifice, extensively restored in the 19th and 20th cent., is the site of one of the holiest places in Spain, the shrine of Our Lady of Montserrat, the subject of both legend and history. The abbey was destroyed by Napoleon (1811); it was unused during the period of secularization and during the Spanish Civil War (1936–39). Through the centuries Montserrat was renowned for its remarkable and diverse contributions to culture and is famous for its liturgical and pastoral publications. The present church is a minor basilica. BIBLIOGRAPHY: C. Baraut, NCE 9:1101–02; A.M. Asbareda, *Historia de Montserrat* (1946).

[S. A. HEENEY]

MONUMENTS OF THE APOSTLES, see APOSTLES, TROPHIES OF THE.

MONZA, TREASURE OF, Italian treasure rich in early Christian art and iconography, housed in the Lombard Gothic cathedral of Monza (13th and 14th cent.), which was built on the site of the early Christian Church founded (595) by the Lombard queen, Theodolinda. Most important historically and iconographically are 16 Eastern Christian 5th-cent. lead ampullae for holy oil (given by Pope Gregory the

Great to Theodolinda), which carry earliest depictions of the Crucifixion—a palm branch cross beneath a bust of Christ, accompanied by two kneeling figures, the thieves on crosses, John and Mary, the sun and moon, and Marys at a tomb which is circular in the design of Constantine's Holy Sepulcher building. (These scenes are also found in the 6th-cent. Syrian Rabula Gospels). A small gold crucifix in rock crystal (also Eastern) from Pope Gregory, the famous iron crown of Lombardy monarchs, an 8th-cent. enamel pendant, the reliquary casket of gold, cloisonné enamel and jewels said to contain a tooth of John the Baptist, and many secular treasures from Theodolinda of 7th-cent. Lombard craftsmanship.

[M. J. DALY]

MOODY, DWIGHT LYMAN (1837–99), American revival preacher who applied business and advertising techniques to *evangelism and developed interdenominational revivals to reach urban audiences. M. had only a grammar school education in Northfield, Mass., and left home in 1854 to take a job in a Boston shoe store. The following year he experienced a religious conversion and joined the Congregational Church. Successful as a salesman, he devoted more of his time to religious work. Moving to Chicago in 1856, he formed the North Market Sabbath School in 1858 and was closely associated with the Young Men's Christian Association (YMCA). In 1860 M. became a full-time city missionary, and in 1863 he organized a nondenominational church in Chicago as a center for urban evangelism. The Chicago YMCA made him its president in 1866. He was little known outside Chicago until his 1873 evangelistic crusade in British industrial centers made him world famous. He conducted a series of interdenominational revivals in cities of the U.S. in 1875. His revivals were organized in minute detail and required the active support of all major Protestant Churches in an area. His sermons stressed evangelical "Bible Christianity" and were centered on Christ's redemptive love and call to repent. His preaching was simple, direct, and restrained. With the help of Ira *Sankey he succeeded in reaching audiences with simply worded gospel hymns. He toured the British Isles, 1881–84 and 1891–92, preaching in the U.S. and Canada in the intervening years. M.'s hope of reaching unchurched city-dwellers was only partially realized, but he sparked a notable revival among evangelical Protestants. His success among British students led to his founding of the Student Christian Movement. His young converts gave a new impetus to foreign missions and a new direction to campus religious life in the U.S. and in England. His Northfield Conferences for students had a marked influence on the ecumenism of the succeeding decades. The Chicago (now Moody) Bible Institute, which he founded in 1889 to train evangelists, has continued his work to the present day. BIBLIOGRAPHY: W. R. Moody, *Dwight Lyman Moody* (1930); W. M. Smith, *Annotated Bibliography of D. L. Moody* (1948); W. G. McLoughlin, *Modern Revivalism* (1958); R. K. Curtis, *They Called Him Mr. Moody* (1962); J. C. Pollock, *Moody without Sankey* (1963).

[R. K. MACMASTER]

MOON, PARKER THOMAS (1892–1936), American historian and internationalist, leading Catholic social theorist, promoter of the League of Nations and international justice. Born in New York, he was a convert to Catholicism from Methodism in 1914. He was instructor of history at Columbia Univ. in 1915, and full professor there from 1931. He was also editor of the *Political Science Quarterly* from 1921 until his death. Among his numerous writings are *Imperialism and World Politics* (1926) and a series of European history texts co-authored with Carlton Hayes. He also participated in the peace conference at Paris after World War I.

[E. J. DILLON]

MOON WORSHIP, a general name encompassing beliefs and rites of many kinds, found in all parts of the world from the remotest antiquity to the present time. The phases of the moon were already known in the Ice Age, as witnessed by Ice Age cultures in Siberia. The Hebrew word for moon is identical with month; in many languages moon also means "to measure." Is 1.13 shows traces of a moon-festival among the Jews; in Job 31.26–28 a salutation of the moon by kissing one's hand is mentioned, a practice still alive today. Finno-Ugric tribes bow down to "Old Man Moon" and cease work in honor of the new moon; French peasants sow at new moon, prune and harvest when the moon is on the wane; African pygmy women paint themselves white, dance and pray to the moon to keep away the dead and bring fertility. The only factor common to these heterogeneous practices is reverence accorded to the moon. Fr. Schmidt maintains that primitive cultures, when crossed with a matrilineal and agrarian culture, worship the moon as "the first man, the first mortal, risen from the dead." By contrast, in Schmidt's scheme, exogamous matrilineal lower agriculturists conceive of the moon as female; here the Great Mother may be either Mother Earth or the moon. M. Eliade stresses the universal aspects of moon worship: the moon waxes, wanes, and disappears, subject to the universal law of becoming: birth, death, and rebirth, in ever-recurring cycle. Paradoxically, it unites "being" and "becoming." It is the symbol and god of the rhythms of life: waters, rain, plant-life, fertility. Its connections with tides, female menses, and lunacy inspire reverence and fear. Its dual aspect is shown in the fact that as a giver of rain, it was worshiped, but as an agent of floods, it was feared. As a destroyer of old forms and agent of regeneration on a cosmic scale, it inspired Flood legends, in which a sinful generation violated the sacred rhythms of Nature, was destroyed, and replaced by a new race of men. After 11 centuries of Christianity, a Hungarian folk-charm retains still this dual aspect of moon worship, "New Moon, New King, Thee I greet; Thou art the Renewer, Thou art the Taker

Away . . ." BIBLIOGRAPHY: W. Schmidt, *The Origins and Growth of Religion* (1931); M. Eliade, *Patterns in Comparative Religion* (tr. R. Sheed, 1958); L. Kálmány, *A hold néphagyományainkban* (1894). FINNO-UGRIC RELIGION; *FOLKLORE; *ANCESTOR-WORSHIP.

[D. H. BRUNAUER]

MOONEY, EDWARD FRANCIS (1882–1958), first abp. of Detroit, Mich., and cardinal, leading Catholic churchman of the Great Depression era and World War II. Born in Mount Savage, Md., the youngest child of immigrants from Ireland, he went on to obtain doctorates in both philosophy and theology while studying at the North American College in Rome (1905–09). He was ordained there for the Diocese of Cleveland, Ohio in 1909; and later returned to Rome as spiritual director at his alma mater. In 1926 he was apostolic delegate to India. In 1931 he was delegate to Japan and in 1933 was named bp. of Rochester, New York. He served as chairman of the Social Action Department of the National Catholic Welfare Conference (NCWC) during the economic upheavals of the depression. By the time he was named the first abp. of Detroit (1937), he was already the leading Catholic churchman of the era, serving as chairman of the NCWC administrative board (1935–39, 1941–45). In Detroit he backed the unionization of the work force, insisting on the obligation of workers to join a union. He was a postwar backer of the United Nations. In 1946 he was named cardinal. During his 21-year tenure in Detroit, the Catholic population grew from 550,000 to 1,288,000. He died in Rome (1958) on the eve of the conclave that elected John XXIII. BIBLIOGRAPHY: F. X. Canfield NCE 9:1103–05.

[E. J. DILLON]

MOOR, MICHAEL (1640–1726), Irish-French priest and academician, first Catholic provost of Trinity College, Dublin. Born in Dublin, he was educated in France at Nantes and Paris, and upon his return to Ireland was ordained a priest by Bp. Wadding of Ferns (1684). A year later he was vicar general and virtual administrator of the archdiocese of Dublin. James II appointed him provost of Trinity College in 1689. He used his position to alleviate the suffering of Protestant prisoners in Dublin. Having fallen out with James II, M. fled first to France and then to Rome, where he was befriended by Pope Clement XI. After 1702 he held various administrative and teaching posts at the Univ. of Paris. He helped set up the Collège de Cambrai and to develop the Irish College, a Parisian school for poor Irish students. He died in Paris and was buried under the chapel of the Irish College. BIBLIOGRAPHY: P. S. McGarry, NCE 9:1105; G. LeG. Norgate, DNB 13:783.

[E. J. DILLON]

MOORE, EDWARD ROBERTS (1894–1952), priest, social worker. A native New Yorker, he studied at Fordham Univ. and St. Joseph's Seminary there, was ordained (1919), made a papal chamberlain (1941), and became a domestic prelate (1948). In addition to pastoral work at St. Peter's where he became pastor (1937–52), he served as advisor (1935) of the National Youth Administration, helped to establish a national Legion of Decency, and was a member of the New York Municipal Housing Authority. His *Roman Collar* (1950) relates his parish experiences.

[M. CARTHY]

MOORE, GEORGE (1852–1933), a versatile English novelist born in Ireland. Educated at Escott, M. went to Paris and studied art at various schools. Influenced by Zola and French realists, he turned to writing and published a novel, *A Modern Lover* (1883). He also attempted poetry in *Flowers of Passion* (1878) and *Pagan Poems* (1882). His novel *A Mummer's Wife* (1884) was a challenge to contemporary novels. Three great novels of his prime are *Esther Waters* (1894), *Evelyn Innes* (1898), and *Sister Teresa* (1901). These are a restoration of the Fielding tradition. He returned to Ireland (1901–10) where he was associated with Yeats, George Russell, and others active in the Irish Renaissance. This stay renewed his artistic youth. Once again in London he began publication of the autobiographical *Hail and Farewell* (1911–14) in three volumes. His interest in the story of Christ led him on a tedious journey to the Holy Land, as a result of which he wrote *The Brook Kerith* (1916). Having experimented with the novel, poetry, dialogue, and painting, M. turned to drama. In 1920 *The Coming of Gabrielle* was produced, but he had no success in the theater until *The Making of an Immortal* (1928). BIBLIOGRAPHY: G. N. Shuster, *Catholic Spirit in Modern English Literature* (1922, repr. 1928).

[S. A. HEENEY]

MOORE, GEORGE EDWARD (1873–1958), British philosopher. M.'s mother came from a Quaker family of merchants and philanthropists and his father from a family involved in medicine. M.'s earlier years were marked by a spirit of evangelical religion; he frequently preached and distributed literature on the Gospels. Gradually, he lost this fervor. In his later years he was thought, at least by some, to be an agnostic but this view is without serious foundation and is believed to stem from his opinion that the existence of God is indemonstrable. He began his studies of the classics at Cambridge (1892), later of philosophy, completing the requirements for moral philosophy in 1896. During a fellowship at Cambridge (1898–1904), he discussed his views with Bertrand *Russell. This was a productive period of his life, for he completed *Principia ethica* (1903), submitted papers to the Aristotelian Society, and published several articles and essays. He left Cambridge briefly but returned as lecturer in philosophy (1904) and remained there until his retirement (1939). He served as editor of *Mind* (1921–47). He received honorary degrees from Cambridge and from the Univ. of Saint Andrew, was elected a fellow of the British Academy in 1918, and appointed to the Order of Merit in 1951.

Up to 1903 his philosophy was marked by three separate positions. In 1897, his question about past and future time placed him on the side of Bradley's absolute idealism. M.'s denial of commonsense conclusions about internal relations and concrete universals outraged some philosophers. Later in an essay, "Freedom," M. softened considerably his thought on idealism and moved toward Kant, at least as far as his theory on synthetic necessary truth and transcendental exposition was concerned. His third position is seen in an article written in 1899: "The Nature of Judgment." This was a straightforward attack on psychology in philosophy and one with which Russell agreed. Not only does the essay mark a shift from M.'s first position but it also repudiates the idealism of that earlier work. M.'s *Principia ethica* marked a significant change in his thinking about the nature of concrete things and held for philosophers a base from which all subsequent patterns in his thinking could be traced. It is sometimes said of M. that he viewed all philosophical problems as pseudo-problems but this is not a fair evaluation of his method of philosophizing. What he did believe was that philosophers sometimes tend to obfuscate the issues by failing to clarify the questions that are asked of them or that they ask themselves. Most of M.'s published works are in article, paper, or lecture form. His major works include: *Principia ethica* (1903); *Refutation of Idealism* (1903); *Ethics* (1912); *Philosophical Studies* (1922); *The Philosophy of G. E. Moore* (1942) which contains "An Autobiography" and "A Reply to My Critics." BIBLIOGRAPHY: A. J. Ayer, *Russell and Moore, The Analytical Heritage* (1971); S. L. Mitchell, *George Moore* (1916, repr. 1973); I. A. Williams, *Bibliography of George Moore* (1974).

[J. R. RIVELLO]

MOORE, GEORGE FOOT (1851–1931), OT exegete and historian of religion. M. was an esteemed scholar of international repute who taught Hebrew at the Andover Theological Seminary (1883–1902), and Hebrew and the history of religion at Harvard (1902–28). He was president of several learned societies, editor of the *Andover Review*, (1884–93) and of the *Harvard Theological Review* (1908–14; 1921–31). Among his major publications are a critical commentary and translation of Judges; a collection of his exegetical positions in *The Literature of the OT*; an extensive *History of Religions* (2 v., 1913–19); and a pioneer study, *Judaism in the First Centuries of the Christian Era* (3 v., 1927–30). BIBLIOGRAPHY: J. H. Ropes, DAB 13:124–125; J. Trinquet, DBSuppl 5:1378–79

[T. M. MCFADDEN]

MOORE, HENRY (1898–), British sculptor from Yorkshire, one of the most innovative masters of the 20th cent., painter, draftsman, writer, trained in London (1919–21) travelling to France and Italy, 1925. With comprehension of all styles—primitive to modern, a sense of form comparable to the greatest of the Renaissance, with the "pure form" of Brancusi, and surrealistic overtones, M. exploited "voids" or "hollows" establishing the sculptor as carver,—not molder, in serenely monumental unique "pin-head" forms. M.'s drawings (underground shelters for the War Advisory Committee, 1940) are linear statements of *solid* masses in a sculptor's idiom. M. executed an impressive *Madonna and Child* (1944) for St. Matthew Church, Northhampton, huge reclining figures for UNESCO, Paris (1959–60) and Lincoln Center, N.Y. (1965). Latest gigantic boulder-like forms relate the sculptured piece to environment and landscape. M. established sculpture as one of the greatest arts of the 20th century.

[M. J. DALY]

MOORE, RICHARD CHANNING (1762–1841), Protestant Episcopal bp. of Va. from 1814. Born in New York, M. became a seaman after studying at King's College (now Columbia Univ.), then a physician before his ordination in 1787. For 20 years he was rector at Grace Church, Rye, N.Y., until his consecration as bishop of Virginia. Alarmed by the progress of the *Oxford movement, which he saw as a revival of the "Romish system," he set a *broad-church, or evangelical, tone, which remains characteristic of the diocese he headed. He gave his support to interdenominational projects, the *American Bible Society among them. He opened the Protestant Episcopal Theological Seminary in Alexandria, Va., in 1823.

[M. A. GARDNER]

MOORE, THOMAS VERNER (1877–1969), priest, monk, psychologist, and spiritual writer. He was a Paulist from 1896 (ordained, 1901); a Benedictine from 1924 and one of the founders of St. Anselm's Abbey, Washington, D.C.; from 1949, a Carthusian and founder (1950) of the first American Charterhouse (now at Arlington, Vt.). He received his doctorate in psychology from The Catholic Univ. of America in 1903 and became a faculty member there in 1910; he earned an M.D. at Johns Hopkins in 1913. After serving as a chaplain in World War I he left the Paulists and before making his Benedictine novitiate in Scotland studied under W. Wundt at Leipzig. He returned to the department of psychology at The Catholic Univ. and served there until joining the Carthusians at Miraflores, Burgos, Spain. He was department head from 1939, and through his leadership the department became the first Catholic faculty of psychology to receive recognition from the American Psychological Association. He also founded near the univ. St. Gertrude's School for girls in need of special education. Among M.'s works are: *Principles of Ethics* (1914–15; rev. ed., 1959); *Prayer* (1924); *Life of Man with God: An Introduction to the Spiritual Life* (1956); *Heroic Sanctity* (1959); there is as yet no complete bibliography of his numerous articles in journals of psychology and spirituality. A central theme in M.'s work was the integration of the religious dimension in the study of psychology. *BIBLIOTHERAPY.

[M. R. BROWN]

MORA, MIGUEL DE LA (1874–1930), underground bp. during the early 20th-cent. period of persecution in Mexico. Born in Ixtlahuacán del Rio, Jalisco, he was ordained priest in 1897, and was named bp. of Zacatecas in 1911. He fled before revolutionary forces in 1913. In 1922 he was named bp. of San Luís Potosí where he had to submit to increasingly harsh laws against religion. Subsequent years were spent in hiding or in self-imposed exile. He was bitterly disappointed when spokesmen for the Church agreed (1929) to submit unconditionally to the restrictive laws. He died soon after in San Luís Potosí. BIBLIOGRAPHY: A. Rius Facius NCE 9:1107; *New York Times* (July 16, 1930) 23.

[E. J. DILLON]

MORA Y DEL RIO, JOSÉ (1854–1928), first bp. of Tehuantepec, Mexico, later, primate of Mexico and foe of the revolutionary government. Born in Pajacuarán, Michoacán, he studied in Zamora and in Rome, was ordained in 1879, became the first bp. of Tehuantepec in 1893, was transferred to Tulancingo (1901) and to León (1907), then appointed abp. and primate of Mexico in 1908. He tried to live in peace with the revolutionary government, since he himself had long been in favor of many progressive reforms. He found himself in virtual exile from 1914 until 1919 and when the government campaign against the Church worsened to the point of forbidding public worship (1926), the bishop was eventually arrested (1927) and lived in exile in San Antonio, Texas until his death. BIBLIOGRAPHY: A. Rius Facius, NCE 9:1107–08; *New York Times* (April 23, 1928) 23.

[E. J. DILLON]

MORA Y PALOMAR, ENRIQUE DE LA (1907–), Mexican architect from Guadalajara, who built the Church of Mary, Monterrey (1947), the first modern structure in Mexico, Chapel of Nuestra Señora de la Soledad for the Missionaries of the Holy Ghost, Coyoacán (1956) with F. Candela, and some public works.

[M. J. DALY]

MORAL ABSOLUTES, see ABSOLUTES, MORAL.

MORAL CIRCUMSTANCES, see CIRCUMSTANCES, MORAL.

MORAL DOUBT, see DOUBT, MORAL.

MORAL MIRACLE, see MIRACLE, MORAL.

MORAL OBJECT, see OBJECT, MORAL.

MORAL ORDER, in an initial description, a coherent system of human rights and duties taking life as a whole, not merely in a provincial setting, and avoiding a suggestion either that it is enclosed or can be cast in a legal mold. It will be represented as an autonomous system by those, who may be called ethical formalists, who hold that it derives from an intuition of the ''right'' which sets up a categoric imperative demanding that duty be done for its own sake irrespective of consequences; but as a subordinate system by those who see the ''right'' as an inference from non-moral data, which sets up a hypothetic imperative, i.e., do this if you would achieve *x,* that is, right must be done if something beyond is to be achieved. What is to be achieved will be the general benefit for a social utilitarian, pleasure for a hedonist or epicurean, happiness for a eudaemonist, God for a Christian—these categories being understood as non-exclusive.

To a central Catholic tradition the moral order is the teleological arrangement of human acts, that is to say, their arrangement in the light of the true human purpose, which is to be with God. As such, the ''moral forms'' of human acting constitute an interest as specific and real, and rather more important, than ''musical forms'' in the field of sound. The moral order reposes on, but is not to be resolved into, the order of physical nature, and moral science cannot proceed without reference to the pre-moral sciences, physiological, psychological, metaphysical, and historical, which deal with its material: in brief the ''ought'' supposes the ''can.'' Nor should it fail to anticipate the post-moral sciences of contemplative theology and aesthetics, which are engaged with what is God and what is true joy. In fact it is a reasonable pattern of interim values constituted by responsible choices which aim at a nonmoral condition when the end is achieved and they are transcended. BIBLIOGRAPHY: ThAq ST (Lat-Eng v. 18, *Principles of Morality,* ed. T. Gilby, 1966) app. 2–13, pp. 131–175.

[T. GILBY]

MORAL RE-ARMAMENT (MRA), the spiritual revival movement called also First-Century Christian Fellowship and the Oxford Group. The present name was adopted in 1938. Members are often referred to as Buchmanites; MRA's founder was Frank *Buchman, a Lutheran minister, who sought to change the world by changing men. After a career as a youth worker and YMCA college secretary, Buchman experienced a religious conversion in 1908 at Keswick, England, and developed his distinctive evangelistic techniques, working with Oxford Univ. people. In the early Oxford Group period of the movement, concentration was on the moral perfection of the individual; by the time MRA was formally inaugurated, the movement had become a program to save society and the world. During World War II in the U.S. it took on the aspect of a morale-building patriotic organization; since then it has waged a strong anti-Communist campaign. Adherents test their lives by the standards of the Four Absolutes of purity, unselfishness, honesty, and love. The movement prescribes a strict sexual code, promotes racial and religious harmony, and opposes the Communist ideology. Individuals are invited to share their testimonies, to confess their sins publicly, and to change their lives by surrender to the will of Christ, by restitution for any past evil deeds, and by opening themselves to divine guidance. Buchman devised house parties, which resemble a cursillo, or informal retreat, to conduct this program, esp. among students.

Those who belong to MRA undergo no initiation, pay no set dues, and receive no membership card. They simply begin to model their lives after the principles of the movement. Adherents need not withdraw from their own Churches and may, in fact, become more active Protestants and Catholics. The 3,000 men and women who serve as full-time MRA workers receive room, board, and a small personal allowance. MRA is active in 100 nations and publishes literature in 20 languages. Headquarters in the U.S. are at the MRA center at Mackinac Island, Mich.; world headquarters are at Caux, Switzerland. There are also major centers in New York City, London, and Odawara, near Tokyo. The movement uses newspapers and magazines, advertisements, public rallies, television, motion pictures, books, youth organizations, and musical ensembles to spread its message.

Until recently RC authorities have been wary of Moral Re-Armament because they feared it fostered religious *indifferentism and *illuminism. On Aug. 8, 1951, the Holy Office (now Congregation for the Doctrine of the Faith) forbade priests and nuns from participating in MRA meetings and discouraged participation by lay Catholics. Individual national hierarchies and bishops have also banned RC participation, but this attitude has softened since the Vatican Council II. Some Catholics, such as Gabriel Marcel, Karl Adam, and Arnold Lunn, have warmly supported MRA and deny that the movement has the marks of a sect.

BIBLIOGRAPHY: W. H. Clark, *Oxford Group: Its History and Significance* (1951); T. Driberg, *Mystery of Moral Re-Armament* (1961); A. Lunn, *Enigma: A Study of Moral Re-Armament* (1957).

[W. J. WHALEN]

MORAL RELATIVISM, the theory that there are no lasting and universal objective standards for the ethics of human conduct, which instead are determined by the attitudes adopted by the cultural group to which an individual belongs or perhaps only by what his *conscience tells him to do in a particular case, a view that admits of differences of kind as well as degree, depending on the frame of reference. Moral relativism does not necessarily entail moral subjectivism, though this may easily result. For to individuals identified with their community, particularly if that be tribal or religious, the code will have a quasi-divine backing and will prevail over their personal inclinations, if any, though it may not be credited with relevance outside the group. Then, again, moral relativism does not necessarily entail the conclusion that all consciences are equally valuable. Ordinarily, however, it at least allows that what is right, not merely what is believed to be right, can take contrary forms in different periods and regions. This is an ethical position that goes beyond the descriptions by comparative anthropology and observations of the disagreements and variations among cultures. The contemporary fractioning of community loyalties tends to multiply these divisions in the lives of individuals taken both together and singly, so that vice for one man may be judged virtue for another, or what was wrong once may now become right, as when some think that in modern times contraception is a plain duty.

It would be tempting to contrast moral relativism with moral absolutism but for the fact that RC theologians, certainly those of the central tradition, do not picture the moral law as delivered to us complete and once and for all as on Sinai, and would not be quite comfortable under the term. For them a moral value is itself relational to human, created beginnings and divinely promised ends; it is so charged with personal and versatile intentions and modulated according to unique situations that it cannot be proclaimed as something fixed and unwinking except as an abstraction on which a deductively scientific moral theology may pause. At this point they will manifest some reserve about moral relativism, for their world view has been inherited from the Stoics; it sees a guiding *logos* running through the universe, and this concept has been complemented by St. Augustine's teaching on the *Eternal Law, by the developed Aristotelianism that for good or ill there are certain constant types of actions as there are of things, and even by the genius of the Roman and canon law which can be trenchant about causes without peering into idiosyncracies—all these have contributed to the approach exemplified in the moral teaching of papal encyclicals. It begins by uncovering the bones of a problem, which bones have been the same for human nature at all historic ages, and are likely to remain so. It springs from the conviction that we do not make up the basic rules for ourselves, but that they are given to all men by God. Accordingly moral judgments, though allowing for the paramount importance of personal intention and the infinite nuances of circumstances, are keyed to permanent moral meanings that cannot change. This, however, does not mean that all of their homogeneous developments can be easily defined, flatly applied, or intruded into human situations without economy. *SITUATION ETHICS; *CONTEXTUAL ETHICS; *ABSOLUTES, MORAL.

[T. GILBY]

MORAL SENSE, the ability to discern between right and wrong. It may be treated as a special faculty, as by some who hold that ethical practice is based on intuitions irreducible to the evidences implicit in common experience or that ethical science is a discipline proceeding from the categoric imperative of duty for duty's sake. Or it may be taken less specifically as the moral attitude formed by the settled disposition or *habitus* of assenting to the first general principles of practice, which was called *synderesis* by the medievals, together with the practical and particular conclusions drawn by the judgments of *conscience. The traditional view in Catholic moral theology is that moral apprehensions, judgments, reasonings, and choices are performed through the same powers of mind and will that are engaged with any other matter of human interest.

[T. GILBY]

MORAL THEOLOGY (moral from late Lat. *morale,* from *mores,* manners; theology originating from Gr. *theologia,* talk about God), the discipline that considers human conduct in relation to God. As a branch of theology it taps the same sources in revelation, faith-inspired reason, and the Church's tradition, and is subject to the same divisions, some of which will appear below.

The pedagogic distribution of a course of theological studies between "dogma" and "morals" has tended to make a rift between them, and with unhappy effects of formalism and legalism. Cut off from its roots and fruits proper to it when considered in a contemplative study of God and a non-ethical, theological anthropology, moral theology lost the self-sufficiency it enjoyed in that setting, was attracted to Canon Law, fell under its sway, and became in effect a catalogue of precepts, even predominantly of negative precepts. This has had a degenerative effect upon moral theology; for theology, as a unitary science, must maintain throughout all its ramifications a single-minded interest in God and the things of God as being from him and for him (ThAq 1a, 1.3). Although moral theology will take some of its shapes from human juridical patterns, both civil and ecclesiastical, and will be projected into *casuistry, its true life transcends them all.

The division between moral, ascetical, and mystical theology, prompted also by pedagogical considerations, should also be viewed with reserve, certainly when it makes the first concerned with keeping the Ten Commandments and not falling into grave sin; the second with the practice of virtue; and the third with quasi-miraculous states of prayer. The threefold way of perfection, which is classical in theology under various names, for those respectively who are beginning, getting on, and completing the course (cf. *op. cit.*, 2a2ae, 24.9; 184.2), represents three different emphases rather than three separate states: grace, which is the seed of glory, is continuous throughout, the end is in the beginning, the holiness Christ commands is in baptism, and is never such in this life that the *fear of the Lord disappears (*op. cit.* 2a2ae, 19.10). Above all, the main aim of a generous moral theology is seeking God, not avoiding the opposite; it is animated by the Sermon on the Mount and certainly will not resign itself merely to the Decalogue.

However, there is a narrow sense in which moral theology can be looked at as comparatively a humdrum affair, that is when it concentrates on its proper field, the *moral virtues. These, even when supernaturalized, arrive only at an adjustment to a creaturely environment. Dealing justly in the city of reason and the city of God, acting bravely amid tears and remaining temperate amid desires, all these are but modes of being in an earthly environment. But the *theological virtues break out from the scheme of things and go straight to God himself; in this manner they are trans-moral and supra-moral, and are not measured by the rule of right reason (*recta ratio; orthos logos*). By their genius they are already escaping from ethics, as are the gifts of the Holy Spirit, and following the gospel law of grace. Nevertheless it was by a sound instinct that the masters, notably St. Thomas Aquinas, treated them under moral theology, which was thereby saved from becoming scarcely more than a codification. A comparison between the Second Part of his *Summa theologiae* and a standard textbook of 50 years ago will serve to show the difference.

A difference will also be observed between moral theology as an art and as a science. The first includes simple statements without much discussion of the principles of Christian conduct, as well as popular homiletics, rhetoric, and the story-telling which have been part of moral instruction from early days. Systematic expositions *ad hoc* began with the great patristic theologians and developed into the comprehensive and compendious treatments of man's whole duty with the great *summae* of the 13th cent. and afterwards. In particular we should notice the standing of St. Thomas's moral theology as a science subordinate to the science of faith about what God is and what man is: only on the basis of acts that can be done may we settle the acts that should be done. In this it differs from autarchic systems of ethics.

Nevertheless Aristotle's teaching in the *Nicomachean Ethics* has been well heeded. Moral theology is not composed, like pure geometry, just of necessary relations between meanings, for it is concerned with human acts which in reality are individual and contingent. Moreover it is caught up in the history of revelation and the development of dogma. Consequently a severely abstract treatment of morals in the flat, so to speak, has to be rounded out by an appreciation of and practical adjustment to the facts of the situation: hence moral theory (*scientia; epistēmē*) needs the complement of moral practical wisdom (*prudentia, phronēsis*), and its auxiliary rules of casuistry. BIBLIOGRAPHY: ThAq ST 1a, 1 (Lat-Eng, *Christian Theology,* ed. T. Gilby, 1964); *idem,* v.18 (1967); R. C. Mortimer, *Elements of Moral Theology* (1947).

[T. GILBY]

MORAL THEOLOGY, HISTORY OF. The periods correspond to three methods—patristic, scholastic, and casuistic. However, impenetrable partitions are not to be set up between them, for some of the writers of the first period, notably Nemesius (later confounded with St. Gregory of Nyssa), St. Augustine, and St. John Damascene anticipated and influenced the scientific approaches of the second, while developments of the second flowered well into the third. The division is a convenient simplification, but it should not disguise the continuity and complexity of the tradition.

Patristic. The first and positive method consists in a simple statement, without much discussion, of Christian morals based on the Scriptures; it forms part of catechetics. It appears already in the 2d cent. in the **Didache* on the two ways, of life and of death, and in the *Shepherd of Hermas on the 12 mandates. It is more fully treated by St. Clement of Alexandria's *Paedagogus* to Christian life and manners, and is sustained in the ascetical writings of Tertullian and, less grimly, in those of the *Cappadocian Fathers; in the monographs of St. Cyprian on some of the virtues; and in the 24 ''catecheses'' of St. Cyril of Jerusalem. The tradition was summed up in the 25 books of morals, composed as an exposition on Job by St. Gregory the Great (d. 604), a man of a practical rather than speculative bent of mind. Philosophy at first had been distrusted, and when later it came to underlie moral instruction, it was that of the Latin Stoics, with their insistence upon reason and purpose in the universe and their suspicion of emotion, and particularly of pleasure. St. Ambrose modeled his *De officiis* on Cicero's. St. Augustine (d. 430), however, was an original thinker, and though he composed no synthetic work of moral theology, he was to prove the greatest single patristic authority for the later moral theologians, above all for his teaching on charity, which runs throughout his works and comes out esp. in the *Enchiridion* and *De moribus*.

Scholastic. The *Penitentials, who spread with the Celtic and Anglo-Saxon missions all over Europe and effected some degree of uniformity in Christian discipline, set the scene for the great work of constructing a comprehensive and systematic moral theology. This began with the *Sentences* of *Peter Lombard (d. 1160); his effort paralleled in theology that of Gratian, his contemporary—and half-brother according to legend—in making a harmony out of discordant canons: these two sources, of theology and law, lay close together, and the two streams were to spill over into one another, to the purity and health of neither. It went on in the *Summa* traditionally ascribed to Alexander of Hales (d. 1245), and achieved its fullest perfection in the Second Part of the *Summa theologiae* of St. Thomas Aquinas (d. 1274). He was the true founder of the science of moral theology. Three remarks must suffice here. He inherited Abelard's insistence on the importance of intention; he complemented this with his characteristic doctrine of types of action on the ground plan laid down by Aristotle and according to his teleology; and, a curious fact this, though he moved among men who were bringing canon law to the height of its power and was skilled in their métier, his discourse remains free of it; references are rare, and one of them is a protest, uncharacteristically sharp, against the intrusion of decretalism into moral theology. His confrere, St. Raymond of Peñafort (d. 1275), was a superb canonist and the precursor of later casuistry: his *Summa de poenitentia,* also called *Summa casuum,* exercised great influence for centuries.

Of particular note for its tackling of social and economic questions is the *Summa theologica moralis* of St. Antoninus, abp. of Florence (d. 1459). The authentic stream broadened out through Tommaso de Vio Cajetan into the work of the great divines of the Tridentine period and afterwards; it is enough to mention the Dominicans Francesco de Vitoria, Bartolomeo Medina, Domingo Bañez, and John of St. Thomas; the Jesuits Gabriel Vázquez and Francisco Suárez; and the Carmelite school of Salamanca, the Salmanticenses. Vitoria and Suárez are also great names in the history of jurisprudence, yet teleological morals still ran strong and was not yet choked by the codes; in England, where common law was to hold its own, the true temper of moral theology is found in Richard Hooker (d. 1600), Jeremy Taylor (d. 1667), and Robert Sanderson (d. 1663). There were to be few Protestant treatises on casuistry; that by William Ames (d. 1633) is perhaps the most notable.

Casuistic. The Roman Law had long been the Church's law, and by the 16th cent. it had been received in most countries. Code-thinking now made fresh inroads. The increasing frequency of sacramental confession and the growth of introspective schools of spirituality led to a preoccupation with right standing before the laws of God and the Church and the formulation of rules which, if they were dexterous in producing peace of conscience, tended to sap the robustness of the virtue of Christian prudence and to reduce moral theology to a shrewd application of law. This was the period of the moral systems, which attempted to steer between *rigorism on one hand and *laxism on the other. This is not the place to go into the *probabilism followed by the Jesuits, and attacked by Pascal, or the *probabiliorism favored by the Dominicans, though not by some of their greater theologians, such as Medina and John of St. Thomas, who caused head-shakings for being ''over-benign.'' It has been remarked that the systems were attempts to remedy conditions their own mentality had helped to bring about. They produced a copious literature and some handsome specimens of the printer's art; the authors are too numerous for individual mention, but we may sample them from two representative titles, *Praxis confessariorum* and *Resolutiones morales*.

In this medium of juridico-morals the author of the greatest eminence was St. Alphonsus Liguori (d. 1787), who combined a spirit at once legal and humane. The most widely consulted author in the 19th cent. was J. P. Gury (d. 1861). It was all a quite effective plumber's job, but it was not moral theology in the pure sense of the term. With the revival of philosophical and theological studies under Leo XIII, a reaction set in, and though manuals were multiplied which reproduced the spirit of the third period, the more considerable works took up their development from the second. BIBLIOGRAPHY: B. Häring, *Law of Christ (tr. E. G. Kaiser,* 1961) 1:3–33; T. Deman, *Aux origines de la théologie morale* (1951); *Le Traitement scientifique de la morale chrétienne selon Saint Augustin* (1957); DTC 13:417–619 s.v. ''Probabilisme''; O. Lottin, *Psychologie et morale aux XII*^{e} *et XIII*^{e} *siècles* (6 v., 1942–60); F. X. Murphy and L. Vereecke, NCE 9:1117–22.

[T. GILBY]

Contemporary Trends. Among the events which most influenced the work of moral theologians in the first half of the 20th cent. were the socio-economic encyclicals of Leo XIII (*Rerum novarum,* 1891) and of Pius XI (*Quadragesimo* *anno,* 1931). These two encyclicals occasioned a considerable amount of writings on the mutual rights and duties of labor and management. In this movement, John A. Ryan of The Catholic Univ. of America was esp. prolific. Pius XI popularized the term social justice, which has since then been used to describe all matters which in some way are concerned with society. In this same period, developments in medicine called forth a vast literature on medical moral questions. From the growth of the science of psychology came new realizations of the factors which affect the voluntariness of human actions.

The second half of the century has seen further developments in moral theology along several lines. From the encouragement of the ecumenical movement in the Catholic Church have come new applications of old principles on participation in the worship of other Churches. From the increase in rapidity and ease of nearly instantaneous long-distance communications by television and rapid transportation by jet planes to all parts of the world have come new considerations on the obligations toward those of other nations. These were esp. treated in papal encyclicals by John XXIII (*Mater et magistra,* 1961, and *Pacem in terris,* 1963) and Paul VI (*Populorum progressio,* 1967). Space exploration adds still another area to be considered. Further developments in medicine have raised new questions, esp. about death in the successful use of heart transplants. There has been more treatment of problems highlighted by historical events such as the race revolution; more demand for theological views on individual and corporate business matters, on the use of drugs, and on many facets of social justice not treated at all or treated inadequately in the manuals.

The spirit of renewal leading to and following from Vatican Council II called for changes in approach and attitude in the teaching of moral theology from the traditional form of most manuals. As a result, most moralists, at least in their periodical writings and lecturing in and out of the classroom, have tried to be much more theological and less philosophical, more biblical with less dependence on human authorities, more positive and less negative, more personalist and less abstract. Although a few new manuals, notably the three-volume work of Bernard Häring, have tried to work such changes into textbook form, practically none of the revisions of the older manuals have changed much. Great influence on much of modern moral writing must be attributed to existentialist philosophy and its moral counterpart, situational or personalist ethics. This influence was prominent in continental Europe in the 1950s and in the U.S. in the 1960s. The good effects of this influence were greater attention to the subjective or personal elements of morality, more consideration of the complexities of individual real situations, which too often in the past were considered solved by insisting on a universal negative precept. Bad effects include an over-emphasis on the emotional and a neglect of the theological aspects of morality, with very little reliance on revelation or on the Church's traditional interpretation of revelation. In some authors it has led to a denial of all moral absolutes other than the love of God. It has led some to become humanistic in a secular, almost atheistic way, considering only the values of personality development of the individual. This general influence seems to have contributed greatly to the widespread rejection of Paul VI's encyclical *Humanae vitae* (1968) on birth control, and even to a denial of Vatican Council II's teaching on the response due to papal and hierarchical teaching. Even those who willingly accept this teaching of Vatican II have become more cautious in citing papal teaching as a decisive argument for any point.

In the midst of all these changes of the early part of the second half of the 20th cent., the ideal would seem to be to keep what is good of the old and adopt what is of proven worth in the new: to be more theological and scriptural in accord with later exegesis; more ascetical with the moral and pastoral; more positive, more personal, but without eliminating the negative or abstract; redefining and perfecting former statements of principles and conclusions without denying all absolutes; ever trying to find the true message of Christ for our times. BIBLIOGRAPHY: J.J. Farraher, NCE 9:1122–23; P. E. McKeever, "Seventy-five Years of Moral Theology in America," AER 152 (1965) 17–32; the latter esp. for names and dates.

[J. J. FARRAHER]

MORALES, CRISTÓBAL DE (1500–53), Spanish composer of sacred music. In his native Seville, he was influenced and instructed by the prominent composers Peñalosa, Escobar, and Castilleja, chapel master at Seville cathedral. M. became *maestro de capilla* at Ávila (1526–30), was a member of the papal choir in Rome (1535), touring throughout Italy with Pope Paul III. He was *maestro de capilla* at the primatial cathedral of Toledo (1545–47), and at Malaga (1551–53). His music, including Masses, motets, madrigals, canons, *Magnificats* and Lamentations, was published throughout Europe in the 1540s and 1550s and was highly esteemed by contemporaries. M. was best known for his individuality, expressiveness, and mastery of the polyphonic style. Both Palestrina and Victoria based compositions on his work. M. personally instructed Francesco Guerrero and Juan Navarro.

[R. J. LITZ]

MORALES, JUAN BAUTISTA (1597–1664), Dominican missionary in China who successfully opposed the Jesuits in the Chinese rites controversy. Born in Andalusia, Spain, he was ordained in Mexico, and sent first to the Philippines, then to Cambodia and China; he is considered the second founder of the Dominican Chinese mission. He is the author of *Historia evangelica del reyno de la China;* and among other works, a Chinese grammar and lexicon. It was Jesuit practice to accept many Chinese customs in matters of religion, and not to impose European culture as a prerequisite to Christian faith. M. brought the matter to

Rome in 1645, where he secured the condemnation of Jesuit methods by Innocent X. Alexander VII rescinded the condemnation, only to have M. appeal the matter to Rome again in 1661. Clement IX again decided against the Jesuits in 1669. A final decision upholding M. and the Dominican position, and condemning the Jesuit practice was given in 1743. It is only in recent decades that sufficient appreciation is being given to the disastrous results of M.'s victory.

[E. J. DILLON]

MORALES, LUIS DE (EL DIVINO; 1510–86), Spanish painter, creator of many retables for Portugal. His personal style combines Flemish enameled surfaces, the compact composition, and sfumato of Leonardo, with oval patterns, elongated forms and tension in tightly bound figures (*Pietà, Madonnas, Ecce Homo*) relating to Italian mannerism.

[M. J. DALY]

MORALITY (from the Lat. *mos*, plural *mores*, manners, morals, character, the accepted rendering by Cicero of Gr. *ēthē*, whose adjectival form is *ēthikos*), the category according to which human conduct is judged according to a norm. In older usage it may be good, bad, or indifferent (whether a morally neutral type of act should be considered as coming with the moral frame of reference at all was debated among the 16th cent. scholastics); hence it was usually qualified, e.g., good morality, common morality. Gradually, however, the usage came in of treating "moral" and "ethical" as terms of approval, their opposites being denominated as immoral or unethical. Notice the distinction between the privative "immoral," which applies to embezzlers, and the merely negative "non-moral," which applies to dogs however admirable.

Morality is the subject matter of moral science or moral philosophy. Here the main division in the schools lies between those which treat the norm as pure duty, categorically imperative for its own sake, and those which relate it to an extra-moral good which gives to right conduct a hypothetical necessity. On both sides the differences are more pronounced than mere shades of difference; nevertheless, the first can be classed as non-naturalistic and deontological, whereas the second are naturalistic and referential to a wider anthropology and/or theology. The distinction roughly corresponds to that between ethical formalism, which isolates moral values, and ethical teleologism, which in its various manifestations—hedonism, refined and otherwise, utilitarianism, humane and otherwise, pragmatism, and eudemonism—sees them as productive.

A moral value is not necessarily thereby reduced to a non-moral good, but may be seen, as by St. Thomas Aquinas, as exhibiting its own proper though subordinate meaning. Thus an act of prayer is based on the appropriate psychological material and reaches out to the post-ethical being of God, yet is identified with neither; thus, too, an act of murder supposes a physiological event and results in juridical consequences, but its moral character is constituted by neither. The point calls for careful definition, particularly when the traditional triple determination of the morality of a human act is adopted, namely from intention, circumstances, and type of act performed. A moral theologian needs to be on his guard against explaining this last entirely in the physical, psychological, or sociological terms of the situation; for instance, against concluding that simply selling a contraceptive over the counter is intrinsically evil, though perhaps to be tolerated for outside reasons. The transaction in truth calls for a more moral inflection before this can be stated. BIBLIOGRAPHY: ThAq ST 1a2ae, 17–21 (esp. in Lat-Eng, v.18 *Principles of Morality*, ed. T. Gilby 1967).

[T. GILBY]

MORALITY, SEXUAL, see SEXUAL MORALITY.

MORALITY, SYSTEMS OF, in the history of RC moral theology, methods of guiding *conscience in case of moral *doubt. From the 16th cent. until quite recently allegiance to varying moral systems so dominated moral theology that it constituted its whole history, therefore indirectly shaped Catholic moral life; and not for the good. The actual systems developed ranged between two condemned extremes, *Tutiorism or Rigorism, and *Laxism (D 2303; 2103). The intermediary systems, within which there are sub-systems, are: *Probabilism; *Probabiliorism; *Equiprobabilism. While there are presages of the systems in medieval moral speculation, the issue itself of systematic norms for resolving moral doubt is postmedieval; it involved the moralists' borrowing rules from the jurists, and an emphasis on casuistry. The proponents of the systems all implicitly shared the view that both individual conscience and "the law" have prerogatives; their systems sought to determine the degree of liberty conscience has in the face of the exactions of law. The liberty presupposed is indeterminateness in the face of good and evil; law means an extrinsic constraint, narrowing legitimate alternatives. The systems differ according to the degree of liberty conceded to conscience; the degree of liberty, in turn, corresponds to the quality of opinion favoring it, required to outweigh the requirements of law. This kind of moral theology departs completely from a conception of *morality based on inner *finality, the natural orientation of the will toward the good; the rule of *prudence, and personal *conscience. BIBLIOGRAPHY: ThAq ST (Lat-Eng, v. 18, ed. T. Gilby), app. 1–6, 10–16; T. Deman, DTC 13:417–619 s.v. "Probabilisme"; *idem*, *Somme théologique* (ed. de la Revue des Jeunes) *Prudence* (2d. ed., 1949); S. Pinckaers, *Somme théologique* (ed. cited), *Les actes humaines* (2d ed., 1962) 215–276.

[T. C. O'BRIEN]

MORALITY PLAYS, a type of medieval religious drama presenting the struggle of the soul for salvation as a battle between forces usually portrayed as personified abstractions. The central character is Everyman or *Humanum Genus,* and the others are facets of his psyche (like Reason or Will); they may also be virtues and vices that affect his spiritual progress. The morality plays were the last major phase of medieval drama; they flourished on English soil in the 15th cent., although Continental dramas, particularly in France, show some of the techniques, without the central meaning, of the morality. The origin of this type is usually ascribed to the custom of illustrating a sermon on death by a solemn religious "dance," in which a skeletal figure designated as Death led away, one by one, a procession of representatives from the various ranks and professions of medieval life. The plays constructed on this theme (the *danse macabre*) often were a complex of several well-known themes from homiletic literature like the "pilgrimage of life" and the *psychomachia* (the latter referring to the struggle of virtues and vices for possession of man's soul). One of the devices or motifs was the besieged castle, as in *The Castle of Perseverance,* in which the soul took refuge from the attack of evil characters. The morality plays had an affirmative aspect that prevailed over the Gothic preoccupation with physical decay and disintegration. This positive note was the preparation for a happy death, regarded as an "art of dying well," a theme known as the *ars moriendi.* **Everyman,* the best of the English moralities, and a play related to the Dutch *Elckerlijk,* was built solidly on the materials of the *ars moriendi* literature. BIBLIOGRAPHY: M. E. Collins, NCE 4:1048–51.

[E. C. DUNN]

MORAN, PATRICK FRANCIS (1830–1911), Irish and Australian Catholic churchman, pioneer of Catholic social movements in the English-speaking world, abp. of Sydney, Australia and cardinal primate of that country. Born at Leighlinbridge, County Carlow, Ireland, he was the nephew of Card. Cullen of Dublin. M. attended the Irish College in Rome and was ordained there in 1853. He was vice rector of the Irish College (1856–66), then returned to Ireland and became professor of Sacred Scripture at Clonliffe College and founder of the *Irish Ecclesiastical Record.* In 1872 he was coadjutor bp. and then bp. of Ossory. In 1884 he succeeded Roger Bede Vaughan as abp. of Sydney, Australia, and became a cardinal the next year. He presided over three plenary councils (1885, 1895, 1905), established 2 seminaries, dedicated 500 churches, built numerous hospitals and schools, and acquired the right to state aid for Catholic schools. He encouraged the fledgling Australian Labor party and supported the strikers in the industrial conflicts of the 1890s. Among his more than 12 major published works is a 1,200-page *History of the Catholic Church in Australasia* (1895). Many of his other works reflect his keen interest in, and wide knowledge of, the age-long history of the Celtic Church. BIBLIOGRAPHY: J. G. Murtagh NCE 9:1134; S. E. Fryer DNB Suppl (1901–11) 2:645–646.

[E. J. DILLON]

MORANDI, GIORGIO (1890–1964), Bolognese genius and painter, of the metaphysical school, today considered the most important Italian artist since De Chirico. M's metaphysical philosophic statements seek to express the double loneliness of all things, the loneliness of separate, discrete essences, and the loneliness of things in the alien ambience of the visual art statement. His quiet, magical works, painted and etched, bestow on simple objects a near-human presence.

[M. J. DALY]

MORANDUS, ST. (d. *c.* 1115), Benedictine prior. He was trained in the episcopal school of Worms and ordained there. Following a pilgrimage to Santiago de Compostela in Spain, he became a monk at Cluny. Hugh of Cluny made him a prior in a monastery in the Auvergne and, later, of a new foundation at Altkirch in Alsace. His tomb became a center of pilgrimage, and Archduke Rudolf IV of Habsburg (1339–65) took a part of his head as a relic for the new cathedral of St. Stephen in Vienna. BIBLIOGRAPHY: Butler 2:466; M. R. P. McGuire, NCE 9:1134; F. Fues, *Vie de S. Morand* (1840); Zimmermann 2:262–263; P. Rouillard, BiblSanct 9:586–587.

[M. R. P. MCGUIRE]

MORAVIA, a region in what is now central Czechoslovakia; its inhabitants, who number about four million, are a homogeneous Slavic people. Its strategic location assigned it a unique role in Slavic civilization and it achieved national consciousness and political independence under Mojmir in the 9th century. It formed the nucleus for emerging Slavic states in Central Europe. From the West, Christianity penetrated through Irish and Scotch missionaries as early as the 8th cent. and from the East through SS. Cyril and Methodius in the 9th century. Both its provincial capital, Brno, and its historic archiepiscopal City of Olomouc claim notable universities. Recent archeological discoveries have focused attention on the Christian character of Moravia's past and provided a rich source of material for Slavic studies. BIBLIOGRAPHY: J. Bretholz, *Geschichte Böhmens und Mährens bis zum Aussterben der Przemysliden* (1912).

[L. NEMEC]

MORAVIAN CHURCH, a body first organized in Bohemia as the Unitas Fratrum in 1457 and refounded in Saxony under the impulse of *Pietism in 1722. During its early history the group was also commonly known as the *Bohemian Brethren. The term "Moravian" was first used after its refounding and is largely confined to the English-speaking world. In Germany the Church is better known as Die Brueder Gemeine (Brüdergemeine), or as Herrnhuters. The original name, Unitas Fratrum, is still used throughout the world. Through Count *Zinzendorf (1700–60), a Pietist of means, the virtually extinct Unitas Fratrum began its second phase of history, becoming what Moravians refer to as the Renewed Moravian Church. Refugee Brethren from Moravia and Bohemia founded the village of *Herrnhut on Zinzendorf's estate in E Saxony in 1722. Within a decade it had become a rallying place for Pietists and the center of itinerant evangelism at home and mission work abroad. In 1735 a surviving bishop of the old Church consecrated the first bishop of the renewed Church; this was followed by reestablishment of the three-fold ministerial orders: bishop, presbyter, and deacon. Under Zinzendorf the Moravians developed as a Pietist society within state Churches, and at the same time the desire of the refugees to perpetuate their Church prevailed. This gave Moravians in Europe the dual status of being both a denomination and a society, the latter known as the Diaspora. American development has been exclusively denominational.

The Church holds evangelical teachings common to Protestants and does not have a distinctively Moravian creed. Evidencing its Pietism, it emphasizes a life-centered, Christocentric faith. Guiding its members are doctrinal statements in its Book of Order, a catechism, and expressions of faith in its liturgies, esp. the one used at Easter (see EASTER LITANY). It has a liturgical form of worship, following to a modified degree the church year. German chorales have a prominent place in its hymnody. While the theological orientation of the Bohemian Brethren was *Reformed, that of the Church after Zinzendorf tends to be Lutheran. The Moravians pioneered missions and before the *Baptist Missionary Society (1793) had more missionaries than all other Protestants combined. They were indeed the first Protestant body to engage in missionary work unconnected with colonization and undertaken purely on its own account. They have specialized in missions to underprivileged peoples, Negroes, American Indians, and Eskimos. European centers are in Germany, Holland, Switzerland, Czechoslovakia, Denmark, Sweden, and England. The Church is divided into 17 geographic provinces with government by *synod and conference. The episcopal office is not administrative, bps. being primarily spiritual leaders whose function is to ordain and to serve the whole Church as pastoral advisors. Former mission fields are moving toward autonomy beside the provinces in the U.S. and Europe. A world synod convenes every 10 years. World membership in 1976 was 425,000 in 714 congregations. BIBLIOGRAPHY: G. L. Gollin, *Moravians in the Two Worlds* (1967); K. G. Hamilton, *History of the Moravian Church* (1967); J. R. Weinlick, *Moravian Church through the Ages* (1966).

MORAVIAN CHURCH IN AMERICA, a part of the worldwide Moravian Church, with headquarters in Bethlehem, Pa., and Winston-Salem, North Carolina. The causes that brought Moravians to America were missions to the Indians, Count *Zinzendorf's attempts at church union in Pa., and the threat of suppression in Germany. An unsuccessful settlement in Ga. (1735) was followed by the establishment of Nazareth and Bethlehem in Pa. (1740–41); settlement in N.C. began in 1753. During the colonial period, residence in Moravian communities was restricted to church members. These communities were characterized by religious nurture, music, missionary outreach, handicraft industries, and boarding schools for the education not only of Moravian children but also of those coming from outside the community. Control from Europe stifled growth, and not until the mid-19th cent. did the Church in the U.S. acquire the autonomy to launch an aggressive home-mission policy resulting in new Churches among German immigrants in the East and among Germans and Scandinavians in the upper Midwest. The modern Moravian Church is a representative American Protestant Church with congregations in 18 states and in the Canadian Provinces of Alberta and British Columbia. The transition to the use of English in worship was almost complete by World War II. It is one of the founding members of the National Council of Churches and of the World Council of Churches. The Church has two girls' preparatory schools, a parochial school, a coeducational college, a theological seminary in Pa., and a girls' preparatory school and a college for women in North Carolina. In 1978, it had 43,000 members in 145 congregations. BIBLIOGRAPHY: K. G. Hamilton, *History of the Moravian Church* (1967).

MORAX, RENÉ (1873–1964), Swiss dramatist and librettist. He was author of many works treating subjects from Scripture and national history and folklore; there are reflections of Calvinist theology in his early religious work; of Catholicism in the later mystery, *Job le vigneron* (1953), with music by A. F. Marescotti.

[T. GILBY]

MORDECAI (Mardochai), cousin and guardian of Esther (Est 2.5–7). Angered by M.'s refusal to bow to him, Hamaan sought to destroy him and all the Jews. With the aid of Esther, however, M. won the favor of the Persian king, Ahasuerus. He secured thereby the death of Hamaan and all enemies of the Jews, and instituted the Feast of Purim to celebrate the victory. He may have been the man of that name mentioned in Ezra 2.2.

[T. EARLY]

MORE, DAME GERTRUDE (1606–33), English Benedictine nun known for her meditational writings. Descended from St. Thomas *More, she became a postulant in the Benedictine Order at Cambrai in 1623 and before her death from smallpox acquired a considerable reputation for holiness. Her works, published posthumously in Paris, include *The Holy Practices of a Devine Lover, or, the Sainctly Ideot's Devotions* (1657) and *Confessiones amantis* (1658).

[E. M. GATES]

MORE, HANNAH (1745–1833), the prime analogate of all bluestockings, and the writer of poems, dramas, novels, and prodigiously best-selling tracts on elevated moral and religious themes, which brought her affluence. Her life falls into two periods. After schoolmistressing in Gloucestershire with her sisters, she moved to London into the circles of David Garrick and Dr. Johnson, who called her "little love" and "dearest," and even "the most powerful versificatrix in the English language," perhaps as an amend in kind for her flattery which sometimes irked him. Admirers held that she "blended the classick and the gothick"; she was versatile enough to be admired by Horace Walpole. She retired to the West Country in 1779, continuing her writing but devoting herself to schemes of educational improvement and deepening her religious impressions, and became a famous notability to be visited; she was on easy and familiar terms alike with high and dry churchmen and the Clapham Sect. Her fluent charm and vivacity, "as playful," noted a biographer, "as her conscience will permit," was interrupted when she was "tomahawked," as she put it, by charges of opening a conventicle: one abusive incumbent wrote under the name of the Rev. Archibald Macsarcasm. In fact she was no "enthusiast," but an evangelically-minded Anglican. In the phrase of the period, she was "respectful toward her superiors, affable towards her equals, condescending toward her inferiors." But she was too sensitively devout to believe that of such was the kingdom of God, as she was too genteel to have more than a faded appeal to later followers of muscular Christianity. BIBLIOGRAPHY: L. Stephen, DNB 38:414.

[T. GILBY]

MORE, HENRY (1614–87), a Lincolnshire poet and theologian. Born in a Calvinistic home, he grew up to make no secret of his attachment to the sacramental life of the C of E at a time when this required courage. A fellow of Christ's College, Cambridge, he refused all preferment "from a pure love of contemplation and solitude, and because he thought he could do the Church of God greater service in a private than in a public office." In character both modest and firm, he was much loved for his ease with his friends and for his corporal works of mercy. Perhaps the foremost of the 17th-cent. band of *Cambridge Platonists, he was kept from pursuing the contemporary vogue for the occult by his piety and conviction that holiness was a way of knowledge. He was a voluminous writer; his best-known work is *Divine Dialogues, Containing Sundry Disquisitions and Instructions concerning the Attributes of God and His Providence in the World* (1668).

[T. GILBY]

MORE, THOMAS, ST. (1487–1535), Lord Chancellor of England, writer, martyr. Son of John More, barrister and later judge, M. was born in London and given the best education Tudor England could supply. Sent about the age of 12 to learn good manners and the ways of the great in the household of Abp. Morton, he later spent 2 years at Oxford Univ. before taking up the study of law in London. A member of Lincoln's Inn, he married (1505) Jane Colt with whom he lived happily until her death (1511). His family life at Bucklersbury in London was made happier by the birth of his children and the visits of his many friends. Numbered among them were *Erasmus, T. *Linacre, J. *Colet, W. *Lily, W. Grocyn, pioneers of the study of Greek and fathers of the new learning. M. was eminent even among these men for his scholarship and the quickness of his mind. Married for the second time to Alice Middleton, he continued his practice of the law and became as eminent a lawyer as he was a scholar. For 8 years an under-sheriff of the City of London, he won enormous popularity among Londoners by his integrity and fairness. He left the city's service in 1518, invited or obliged to enter that of Henry VIII. During all these years, M. was producing works in Latin and in English; a life of Picus, epigrams and verses, *History of Richard III* and **Utopia* (1515–1516).

M.'s career in the King's service was distinguished. Promoted to positions of increasing power and responsibility, he served as speaker to the House of Commons, was sent on various embassies, and was high steward of the Universities of both Oxford and Cambridge. Henry and his Queen, Catherine of Aragon, valued him highly, but the King's affection for M. did not survive Henry's wish to divorce his wife. As early as 1527 Henry consulted M. as to the possibilities of persuading the Pope that his marriage to Catherine was invalid. In 1529 the Lord Chancellor, T. Wolsey, was disgraced because his efforts had failed to obtain a divorce, and Henry offered the chancellorship to M. who accepted the office. He fulfilled its legal duties so brilliantly, so rapidly, with such integrity and incorruptibility that his chancellorship became one of the wonders of 16th-cent. England. But by 1532 Henry had decided to reject papal supremacy and to create himself supreme head of the C of E, with a puppet Abp. of Canterbury to divorce him from Catherine and marry him to Anne Boleyn. The English clergy submitted to Henry and M. resigned the chancellorship.

He was allowed at first to live at home in Chelsea with his devoted family and household, peacefully retired though short of money, but in 1534 he was required to swear an oath recognizing Elizabeth, daughter of Henry and Anne, as heir to the throne. The preamble to this oath declared Henry's first marriage null from the beginning, and it could not conscientiously be sworn by anybody who upheld the Pope's supreme spiritual authority. M. refused the oath and was imprisoned in the Tower. He passed his time there in writing, mostly works of devotion, and kept silent as to his opinions on the supremacy.

By 1535 Parliament had formally conferred on Henry the title of supreme head of the Church, and it was now treason to dispute it. M. was brought to trial and found guilty of this treason on the evidence of Richard Rich, the solicitor general. M. denied the truth of Rich's evidence, which was almost certainly invented by Rich, but he was sentenced to death. He now spoke out strongly against the proceedings of

Parliament in making laws not in agreement with the general laws of Christ's Universal Catholic Church. He was beheaded on Tower Hill. Dying, he said: "The King's good servant but God's first." He was canonized in 1935. BIBLIOGRAPHY: R. W. Chambers, *Thomas More* (1935); J. D. Mackie, *Earlier Tudors* (1962); R. S. Sylvester, NCE 9:1136–40, esp. for bibliog.; Butler 3:49–55; R. J. Schoeck, 12:608–614.

[J. OGDEN]

MOREAU, BASIL ANTHONY (1799-1873), religious founder and educator. M. established the Auxiliary Priests of Le Mans in 1833 to assist parish priests in preaching and retreat work after the ravages of the French Revolution. In 1837, he united the Congregation of the Brothers of St. Joseph with the Auxiliary Priests, founding the Congregation of the *Holy Cross. M. regarded the reestablishment of religious education as the major task of his new congregation, started several colleges in France, and extended his congregation to five other countries. He also founded the *Marianites of the Holy Cross and is regarded as the founder of the *Holy Cross Sisters.

[T. M. MCFADDEN]

MOREAU, GUSTAVE (1826–98), French painter whose immense canvases with symbolic, enigmatic, morbid images, have the Eastern textural richness of Byzantine surfaces enamelled and jewel-encrusted with mysterious light, as in such "lush fantasies' as *L'Apparition* (*Dance of Salome*) *c.* 1876. Though engaged in *fin-de-siècle* "dreams" M. was the inspiring teacher who nurtured the genius of Rouault and of Matisse.

[M. J. DALY]

MORELL DE SANTA CRUZ, PEDRO AGUSTÍN (1694–1768), Cuban bp. and the first Cuban historian whose works are both preserved and published. His works cover political and religious events from the beginning of the Spanish involvement in Cuba. Born in Santo Domingo (Santiago de los Caballeros), he studied at the seminary of Santo Domingo, was ordained in Havana in 1718, and became vicar general that same year. Two years later he was dean of the cathedral of Santiago de Cuba. He was bp. of León, Nicaragua, 1745–50, then returned as bp. of Cuba in 1753. He suffered a brief exile in Florida in 1762, as decreed by the conqueror of Havana, Conde de Albemarle. M. died in Havana. BIBLIOGRAPHY: F. Dominguez-Company, NCE 9:1144–45.

[E. J. DILLON]

MORELLI, GIOVANNI (1816–1891), Italian Protestant patriot and art critic, formulator of the "Morellian method" whereby attributions in painting are determined by minor details (ears, fingers, etc.) uniformly painted through habit. The system, which powerfully influenced later connoisseurship, maintains that the direct evidence of the artifact itself is more reliable than documents or tradition.

[K. B. NEILSON]

MORELOS Y PAVÓN, JOSÉ MARIA (1765–1815), Mexican priest who assumed leadership of the Mexican independence movement after the execution of Miguel Hidalgo; between 1812 and 1815, his nomadic army controlled most of Mexico SW of Mexico City. He called the Congress of Chilpancingo which declared independence in November 1813 and drafted an egalitarian constitution in October 1814. At the last crucial confrontation with Royalist forces, M. fought a rear-guard action allowing most of his fellow insurgents to escape. He himself was captured, brought prisoner to Mexico City, unfrocked by the Inquisition, and executed before a firing squad at San Cristóbal Ecatepec. Born in Valladolid (now Morelia in his honor), Michoacán, Mexico, he was the son of a carpenter, was orphaned early, and was forced to work as a mule driver, putting off until full manhood his studies for the priesthood. Ordained priest in 1797 (at age 32), he was curate, successively, of Churumuco, Le Huacana, Carácuaro, and Nocupétaro, serving mostly Indians and Mestizos. After the insurrection of 1810 he was commissioned by Hidalgo to take Acapulco. He retired to the mountains with a small band of his parishioners for training and led the subsequent struggle leading to the capture of Acapulco in 1813. Throughout his life he was the ardent foe of slavery, poverty, social injustice, and ignorance.

[E. J. DILLON]

MORENO, JUAN IGNACIO (1817–84), abp. and cardinal. He was born in Guatemala but went to Spain in 1834 and obtained a doctorate in law before entering the seminary. Ordained in 1847, he was named bp. of Oviedo in 1857, abp. of Valladolid in 1864, then of Toledo in 1875. He was created cardinal in 1869, and was a strong infallibilist at Vatican Council I. In Spain he resisted government interference with the freedom of the Church and of the religious orders.

[T. C. O'BRIEN]

MORERUELA, ABBEY OF, former Benedictine abbey in Zamora, Spain, founded by SS. Froilán and Attilanus at the end of the 9th century. St. Froilán, a restorer of monasticism in Spain, was a hermit who, with his disciple, Attilanus, gathered their followers into a monastic community in Moreruela. The abbey was demolished by Muslim invaders (978–1002). Moreruela became almost certainly the first Cistercian abbey in Spain when refounded between 1130 and 1132. The abbey was in ruins in 1143 when Alfonso VII of Spain granted it to two monks, probably Benedictines. It was between 1143 and 1158 that Moreruela was affiliated with Cîteaux. It prospered for some years and founded other houses in several countries. The monastery was suppressed in 1835; its large church now serves a parish. Moreruela is notable for its Spanish Gothic architecture. BIBLIOGRAPHY: M. Cocheril, DHGE 15:944–948; Butler 4:18–19.

[S. A. HEENEY]

MORETTO DA BRESCIA (ALLESANDRO BONVICINO) (1498–1554), Italian artist in Brescia, deriving from Foppa and Raphael. An *Assumption Altarpiece* (1526) is Titian "prebaroque," a *St. Margaret Altarpiece* (1526) more personal in quietude. M. engaged in a long series of altarpieces showing gentle figures in a clarified mature style, *St. Nicholas Altarpiece* (1539), *Camaldolese Altarpiece* (1541), a late dated *Deposition* (1554), *Conversion of St. Paul,* a sketchy *Christ Among the Animals,* and several portraits. M. influenced Moroni and P. Veronese.

[M. J. DALY]

MOREY, CHARLES RUFUS (1877–1955), distinguished American art historian and educator, memorable chiefly for his part in establishing the *Index of Christian Art* (1917) at Princeton Univ., the most comprehensive iconographical card index systematically classifying all subjects in early Christian and medieval art up to A.D. 1400. Definitive works in the field are M.'s *Medieval Art* (1942) and *Early Christian Art* (1953).

[L. A. LEITE]

MORFI, JUAN AGUSTÍN DE (d. 1783), Franciscan chronicler who traveled extensively in Mexico, Texas, and New Mexico, kept valuable diaries of his journeys, and wrote important early histories of these regions. He was born in Asturias, Spain (date and exact place unknown), arrived in New Spain *c.*1756, made his Franciscan profession in 1761, and taught oratory and theology a the College of Tlaltecolco (Tlatelolco), originally the twin city of the Aztec capital of Tenochtitlán, now part of Mexico City. He died in Mexico City. BIBLIOGRAPHY: E. Gómez Tagle, NCE 9:1146.

[E. J. DILLON]

MORGAN, PHILIP (d. 1435), bishop, lawyer, administrator. He graduated in law at Oxford and was in the royal service by 1414; he became chancellor of Normandy (1418), member of the royal council (1422), bp. of Worcester (1419), and was translated to Ely (1426). BIBLIOGRAPHY: J. Tait, DNB 15:1057; Emden Ox 2:1312–13.

[J. L. GRASSI]

MORGANATIC MARRIAGE (very late Lat. *morganaticus*, from old High German *morgan*, morning), the marriage of a person of exalted rank to a person of a lower station, whereby the latter, together with their joint issue, are not entitled to be invested with the higher dignity or to succeed to its possessions, but only to receive "the morning gift." It was sometimes called a left-handed marriage, because the bridegroom gave his left hand, not his right in the ceremony. Regarded neutrally by the Church, it was a family arrangement adopted by the courts, some of them petty, in Middle Europe after the rise of sentiments about the special excellence of dynastic blood, and extended to royal families of German extraction.

[T. EARLY]

MORGENSTERN, CHRISTIAN (1871–1914), German poet, editor, writer, and dramatist, translator of H. Ibsen, A. Strindberg, and K. Hamsun, famous for the metaphysical humor of his nonsense verse. He was born in Munich, the grandson of Christian Morgenstern the painter (1805–67). He was influenced by Nietzche's *Also sprach Zarathustra* and by the anthroposophy of R. Steiner; he was also drawn to Buddhism and the mysticism of John's Gospel. In his lyrical nonsense, M. attempts to stretch the possibilities of language and get beyond the surface meaning of things. Even the titles of his various collections of verse defy translation, such as *Galgenlieder* (1905), *Palmström* (1910), *Palma Kunkel* (1916), and *Der Gingganz* (1919). He died at Meran (Merano), Italy, after a 20-year struggle with consumption.

[E. J. DILLON]

MORGOTT, FRANZ (1829–1900), German Thomistic philosopher/theologian; a Neo-Scholastic authority on the writings of St. Thomas Aquinas. He was ordained in 1853, taught philosophy (1857–69), then theology (1869–1900) at the Eichstätt seminary.

[E. J. DILLON]

MORIAH, the unidentified site where Abraham was to sacrifice Isaac (Gen 22.2). The ancient versions did not take Moriah as a proper name: Gr., "lofty"; Vulg, "land of vision"; Syr., "land of the Amorites." Genesis 22.14 gives a popular etymology. The Samaritan reading suggests a relation to the oak of Moreh (Gen 12.6). The site is a three-days' journey from Abraham's home (Gen 22.4), which is Beersheba in 22.19; but the latter connection may be redactional. The hill on which Solomon's temple was built is called Mount Moriah in 2 Chr 3.1; this identification is for theological purposes, but with some basis in Gen 22.14. It is possible that no real geographical site is intended. BIBLIOGRAPHY: G. A. Barrois, InterDB 3:438–439.

[E. J. CROWLEY]

MORIARTY, PATRICK EUGENE (1805–75), Augustinian missioner and religious superior. A controversial figure for the better part of his life, M. studied for the priesthood in the Augustinian Order in Ireland and Rome, where he was ordained in 1828. In 1835 he volunteered for the missions in Madras, India. In 1838 he refused the nomination of coadjutor bp. of Madras; instead he volunteered for the U.S. Sent to Philadelphia as pastor of St. Augustine's Church, he attended the Fourth Provincial Council of Baltimore as superior of the Augustinians in the U.S. A notable orator, M. soon attracted great crowds to St. Augustine's. Later he would become a preacher renowned from Savannah to Boston. In 1841 he purchased Belle Aire and laid the foundations for Villanova College for the education of candidates for the order. M. also became a vigorous spokesman for the Catholics of Philadelphia and for the Irish. The burning of St. Augustine's in the Nativist riots of 1844 drew him into controversy. Bp. F.P. *Kenrick advised him to leave the city for a while after the destruction of St. Augustine's; M. spent time in Ireland raising money to rebuild his church. A speech there accused Protestants of anti-Catholic hostility and caused a furore in the U.S. M. decided to remain in Europe. Named assistant general of the Order in 1847, he conducted a visitation in Ireland and aroused much opposition from the Irish Augustinians. The abp. of Dublin, upon investigation of the matter, decided in favor of Moriarty. Returning to the U.S., he worked for several years in Maryland, then again in Philadelphia as commissary general of American Augustinians. He was president of Villanova and pastor of St. Augustine's, attended the First Plenary Council of Baltimore in 1852, and increased his reputation as a preacher and lecturer. Named pastor of the newly founded parish of Chestnut Hill, M. resigned as commissary general. His last years were spent at Villanova. BIBLIOGRAPHY: J. Pejza, "Second Founder, Patrick E. Moriarty, O.S.A.," *Tagastan* 21(1960) 9–27.

[J. R. AHERNE]

MÖRIKE, EDUARD (1804–75), Protestant clergyman; greatest of the Swabian (late) Romantic poets; author of the *Bildungsroman* (psychological novel), *Maler Nolten* (1832), and the novella *Mozart auf der Reise nach Prag* (1856). His lyric poems (e.g., *Das verlassene Mägdlein, Er ist's, Septembermorgen*) and ballads (e.g., *Der Feuerreiter, Idylle vom Bodensee*) are simple and melodious, often melancholy, sometimes exuberant, but always reflecting the peaceful serenity that marked his life. His style contains elements of classicism, romanticism, and realism. BIBLIOGRAPHY: M. Mare, *Mörike, the Man and the Poet* (1957); W. Kosch, *Deutsches Literatur-Lexikon* (1963) 278–279.

[M. F. MCCARTHY]

MORIMOND, ABBEY OF (Morimundus), Cistercian abbey, the fourth foundation of Cîteaux, established in the valley of the Basigny, in the diocese of Langres (Haute-Marne, France) by Olderic of Aigremont, and his wife Adeline. Morimond's first abbot, Arnold, began his rule in 1115. About 200 monasteries were founded from Morimond, and several military orders were affiliated with it, e.g., Calatrava, Alcántara, Montera, Avis, the order of Christ in Spain and Portugal, and that of SS. Lazarus and Maurice in Savoy. The abbot of Morimond was recognized as the immediate superior of these religious soldiers. The monastery, which still had about 30 monks in 1768, was suppressed at the time of the Revolution. BIBLIOGRAPHY: Cottineau, 1:1985; M. A. Dimier, NCE 9:1148.

[J. DAOUST]

MORIN, GERMAIN (Léopold; 1861–1946), French Benedictine patrologist. Originally a monk of Maredsous, M. helped to found the *Revue Bénédictine* in 1884. From 1907, with the exception of the war years when he took refuge in Switzerland, M. lived in the Munich Abbey of St. Boniface. His scholarly research contributed greatly to monastic history, hagiography, and liturgy, but above all to patrology. In this last field, he published a critical edition of Caesarius of Arles (1937–42) and made important identifications of commentaries and sermons of St. Jerome, and sermons of St. Augustine. BIBLIOGRAPHY: F. X. Murphy, NCE 9:1148; P. Paschini, EncCatt 8:1415–16.

[R. B. ENO]

MORIN, JEAN (1591–1659), French orientalist, biblical theologian, and editor of the Samaritan Pentateuch. Brought up a Calvinist, he became a Catholic and an Oratorian under the influence of De *Bérulle. He was theological adviser to Urban VIII in the attempt to reunite East and West; he rejected the then widespread view among Latin theologians that the tradition of the instruments was an essential part of the matter for the sacrament of holy orders. His historical study on the development of the discipline of the sacrament of penance in the first 13 cent. (1651) was a work of considerable importance that exerted a salutary influence on polemical writing on that subject. BIBLIOGRAPHY: A. Molien, DTC 10:2486–89.

[T. GILBY]

MORISCOS, Spanish Moors who converted to Catholicism, from *c.*1492–1614. The Moriscos, like the Jewish community in Spain, were suspect because of their religious and racial differences. Although converts, their Christianity was doubted. Moreover, even though the Moorish kingdom fell in March 1492, they retained Islamic customs and language. Finally, with the resurgence of Turkish power in the 16th cent., the Spanish feared that the Moriscos were potential Turkish sympathizers. In 1568 several factors such as a decline in the silk industry, land losses, and renewed activities of the Inquisition prompted a Morisco uprising known as the Revolt of the Alpugarras. It was short-lived. In 1570 Philip II decided to scatter the Moriscos from the center of the rebellion, Andalusia, throughout Spain. The Moriscos remained an unsettled problem until the early 17th century. Between 1609 and 1614 they were finally systematically driven from Spain. Out of a population of nearly 300,000 Moriscos, 275,000 left the country. Partially, the expulsion was an attempt to salvage damaged Spanish pride, which had suffered at the hands of the Dutch. It was also indicative of the Spanish emphasis upon religious unity and purity of blood. BIBLIOGRAPHY: J. H. Elliott, *Imperial Spain, 1469–1716* (1964); and E. Spivakowsky, *Son of the Alhambra: Don Diego Hurtado de Mendoza, 1504–1575* (1970).

[C. T. EBY]

MORMONS, the members of the Church of Jesus Christ of *Latter-Day Saints. The *Book of Mormon is accepted by them as revelation.

MORNING PRAYER, service of worship based on the monastic offices of Matins and Prime and set forth in the Anglican BCP as "The Order for Daily Morning Prayer." Morning prayer with hymns and sermon became the principal service in many Anglican churches, with the communion service held perhaps once a month. Anglicans working for liturgical renewal have generally sought to overcome that tradition and have the communion service every Sunday, and at the hour of the principal service. BIBLIOGRAPHY: *ODCC* 876.

[T. EARLY]

MORONE, GIOVANNI (1509–80), card., bp., leading figure in the Council of Trent's final period. In M.'s career were exemplified both the need and the relative success of the Tridentine church reform. Without either theological or canonical training, he was appointed bp. of Modena at the age of 20 in fulfillment of a pledge made to his father by Clement VII. The episcopal sees M. held were: Modena (1529–50) and again (1564–71); Novara (1552–60); the *suburbicarian diocese of Ostia (1570–80). But early he became part of a circle of ecclesiastics genuinely devoted to a vital spirituality and zealous for disciplinary reform; Card. R. *Pole and G. *Contarini were prominent members. M. was nuncio to Germany from 1536 and came to an appreciative awareness of Reformation teaching, so that he became a counsellor of moderation in attempts at dialogue with the Protestants. He also developed the conviction that only honest church discipline could destroy the seedbed of heretical revolt in the Church. Thus he made provision even during his absences from his own diocese for the furthering of reform measures. In the unsuccessful effort to open the Council of Trent in 1542, he, along with Pole and Card. Parisi, were to be the papal legates. During Mary Tudor's reign in England he was intimately associated with Pole's efforts to restore the Church there, and with the accession of Elizabeth I, sought in the interest of the English Catholics to curb punitive measures against her. In June 1555 he was appointed legate to the Imperial Diet at Augsburg, but had to return to Rome in March for the conclave that elected his longtime enemy Gian Pietro Carafa, Paul IV. Long suspicious of M.'s orthodoxy and of Pole's as well, that pope instituted an investigation of M.'s alleged Protestant leanings; the Jesuit A. *Salmerón was a prominent accuser. By May 31, 1557, M. was a prisoner in Castel Sant'Angelo; he refused to accept a pardon from Paul, insisting on complete exoneration, and remained in prison until Paul's death, Aug. 10, 1559. M. was completely vindicated by the next pope, Pius IV. It was because of the sincere desire for reform demonstrated by M. and others that the Catholic powers agreed to the final resumption of Trent. When a crisis developed in spring of 1563, at the deaths of the legates G. *Seripando and E. Gonzaga, Pius IV appointed M. as president. M. saw the council through its final sessions, devoted esp. to disciplinary decrees, and by Dec. 1563 was in Rome to secure their papal approval. He spent his final years continuing in papal diplomatic missions and in carrying out the Tridentine program. BIBLIOGRAPHY: Jedin Trent (1961).

[T. C. O'BRIEN]

MORONI, the name of the angel who, according to Mormon teaching, led Joseph Smith, Jr., to the golden plates, the source of the *Book of Mormon. *LATTER-DAY SAINTS, CHURCH OF JESUS CHRIST OF.

[T. C. O'BRIEN]

MORONI, GAETANO (1802–83), self-educated author of the *Dizionario de erudizione storico-ecclesiastica* (103 v., 1840–61, with 6 index v., 1878–79). This astonishing compilation remains a source of ecclesiastical history, lore, politics. M. began as a barber; his encyclopedic interests started while he was chamberlain for Card. Cappellari and was assigned to transcribe the registers of the Congregation for the Propagation of the Faith. When the card. became Gregory XVI, M. was much involved in papal politics; he gained enemies, and when Pius IX became pope, retained his title only and was free to pursue his learned interests.

[T. C. O'BRIEN]

MOROSINI, noble Venetian family whose members were prominent in ecclesiastical and political affairs. Among them were **Tomaso,** first Latin patriarch of Constantinople (1205–11), two cardinals, and the historian, **Andrea Morosini** (d. 1618), as well as four doges of Venice. BIBLIOGRAPHY: V. Spretti, *Enciclopedia storico-nobilare italiana* (8 v., 1928–35) 4:713–716; V. L. Bullough, NCE 9:1157.

[V. BULLOUGH]

MOROSITY, as used in moral theology, the quality of being prolonged or lingering; from Lat. *moror,* to delay, to entertain. The term describes the quality that can make the experience of an inordinate emotion sinful. While this is most commonly discussed in connection with pleasurable emotions (as in the expression *delectatio morosa*), morosity may equally characterize feelings of anger, hatred, despair, and the like. The quality of being prolonged consists in a presence that the mind fails to check or the will to reject once a person adverts to such feelings. The morosity need not describe a calculable lapse of time, but simply an *advertence sufficient for moral evaluation and the failure to reject the feelings in question. BIBLIOGRAPHY: ThAq ST (1a2ae, 74.6 ad 3).

[T. C. O'BRIEN]

MORRIS, WILLIAM (1834–96), English artist and poet. Child of the Gothic revival and follower of Ruskin and Pugin, M. developed a school of art and crafts inspired by passion for beauty and love of pure color, admiration of the medieval guilds, and dislike of commercialism. He was interested in painting, architecture, metal work, weaving, and typography. His poetry, though exhibiting beauty, color, and music, lacks depth, tragic power, and real understanding of men. It portrays a dream world, which by its vivid contrast to the prim domesticity of early Victorian poetry, attracted many and exercised great influence on his age. Among his best known literary works are *Defense of Guenevere* (1858); *Life and Death of Jason* (1867); *Earthly Paradise* (1869); and *Sigurd the Volsung* (1876).

[M. J. BARRY]

MORRISON, ROBERT (1782–1834), missionary and translator who was the first Protestant missionary to be sent to China (1807). He was practically self-educated and when he went to China began at once to learn the language. M. translated Scriptures into Chinese and in 1820 established a college at Malacca. In 1821 his 6-v. Chinese Dictionary was published. He published also a Chinese tr. of the Book of Common Prayer. He died in China.

[M. A. MCFADDEN]

MORSE, HENRY, ST. (1595–1644), English Jesuit martyr. Born of Protestant parents, M. decided to become a Catholic while studying law in London. He was received into the Church at Douai (1614), was banished from England for refusing to take the Oath of Supremacy (1618), was ordained (1623), and returned to England as a missionary. There he worked for about a year before being imprisoned, first at Newcastle and later at York. During this time he made his profession as a Jesuit. After 4 years of imprisonment he was sent into exile. In 1633 he was back on the mission in London, and during the plague of 1636–37 converted many by his zeal in attending its victims. He was imprisoned again (1637) and convicted, but the queen's influence won him leave to go voluntarily into exile. Returning to England in 1643, he worked for about 18 months in the Durham district before he was captured, condemned to death, and executed at Tyburn. He was beatified in 1929 and canonized in 1970. BIBLIOGRAPHY: P. Caraman, *Priest of the Plague: Henry Morse, S.J.* (1957); Butler 1:231–232; N. Del Re, BiblSanct 9:599–601.

MORTALIUM ANIMOS, an encyclical letter of Pope Pius XI (Jan. 6, 1928), dealing with the *ecumenical movement as interpreted at that time by *Life and Work and *Faith and Order and explaining why Catholics could not take part in the *Lausanne Conference of 1927. The letter pointed out that Christian unity must be based on the acceptance of all revealed truths on the authority of God, that compromise in revealed doctrine is inadmissible, and that the one true Church cannot be composed of independent bodies holding conflicting doctrines. BIBLIOGRAPHY: AAS 20 (1928) 13ff.

[J. H. ROHLING]

MORTIFICATION, in religious, as contrasted with medical, chemical, and other usage, the lively action or practice of subjecting one's appetites to austere living, esp. by the self-infliction of bodily pain or discomfort. The idiom is old, based on the Pauline putting to death of the deeds of the flesh, and persists, not uncheerfully, in the RC practice of facing the frets of life by ''offering things up as a mortification.'' (Cf. Rom 8.13; Col 3.5.)

[T. GILBY]

MORTMAIN, in English law the transfer of property to any corporation, such as a church or monastery, which can never part with it again and is thus, in effect, a ''dead hand'' *(mort main).* Prohibition of transfers of this kind first appears in ch. 43 of the 1217 revision of Magna Carta; further legislation in 1279 and 1290 provided that land assigned in mortmain without royal license should be forfeit. BIBLIOGRAPHY: F. Pollock and F. W. Maitland, *History of English Law Before the Time of Edward I* (2d ed., 1898; repr. 1952) 333–334.

[L. E. BOYLE]

MORTON, JOHN (d. 1500), English cardinal; chancellor of Oxford and Cambridge, principal of civil law at Oxford. M. was bp. of Ely (1478–86), abp. of Canterbury (1486–1500), and cardinal (1493–1500). A Lancastrian exile in the 1460's, he was pardoned by Edward IV (1471) and rose rapidly in his service, becoming Master of the Rolls (1472–78). Imprisoned by Richard III, he joined Henry Tudor in exile and was chancellor of England (1487–1500). ''The Kynge put muche truste in his counsel, the weale publique also in a maner leaned unto hym,'' said St. Thomas More. BIBLIOGRAPHY: Emden Ox 2:1318–20.

[C. D. ROSS]

MORTUARY CHAPEL, an *oratory set aside for Masses for the dead or for repose of the corpse before the funeral rites, or for burial. A burial chapel belonging to a private family has special status in canon law governing oratories: the local bp. may permit regular celebration even of several Masses daily in them (CIC, 1194); unlike other private oratories, a burial chapel may serve any of the faithful for fulfilling the Sunday obligation to hear Mass (*ibid.*, c.1249).

[T. C. O'BRIEN]

MOSAN ART, art of the late 11th and 12th cent. in the valley of the Meuse River, centered at Liège and at the Benedictine abbey of Stavelot. From the 10th cent. Liège was renowned for ivory carving, but most noteworthy were Mosan MSS, metalwork, and enamels. The two-volume Stavelot Bible (1097) by monks Goderranus, Ernestus, and others, showing Carolingian and Byzantine influences is renowned. The magnificent *Reliquary Triptych of the Holy Cross* (1150) by Godefroy de Claire, in engraved gilded copper, with silver columns and *Émail brun,* set with precious stones, in bold and dynamic Romanesque style, and the *Portable Altar of Stavelot* (1150) in champlevé enamel, its legs in forms of the Evangelists—small but of Mosan monumentality—are masterpieces. An apotheosis of Mosan art from the Abbey of St. Bertin is the foot of a cross (1170) of gilded bronze, its domed base and pillar in champlevé enamel, with figural and symbolic sculpture evidencing a mastery of technique uniquely Mosan.

[M. J. DALY]

MOSCHUS JOHN, see JOHN MOSCHUS.

MOSCHOPHORUS. The archaic Greek sculpture (575 B. C.) of a man bearing a calf on his shoulder—a prototype of the later Christian Good Shepherd (*The Good Shepherd Sarcophagus,* Catacomb of Praetextus, Rome, late 4th cent. A.D.; *The Good Shepherd,* Lateran Museum).

[M. J. DALY]

MOSCOW AND ALL OF RUSSIA, PATRIARCHATE OF, the Orthodox Church of Russia. Christianity came to Russia *c.* 988 with the baptism of *Vladimir, Prince of Kiev. Since the early Church leaders and hierarchy were Greeks, Russia inherited Constantinople's separation from Rome, though not precisely in 1054. Metropolitan Isidore of Moscow participated in the Council of *Florence (1439) only to be deposed and imprisoned upon his return for attempting to implement the decrees of reunion. When Constantinople fell to the Turks in 1453, many Russians regarded this as divine punishment to the Greeks for their part in the union with Rome. As a result Moscow became the "third Rome." Thus the Russians felt that they alone were the real custodians of authentic Christianity. In the 16th cent. there was a dispute between Joseph of Volokolamsk and his followers, who supported close relations with the State and ownership of land, and Nil Sorsky who advocated the independence of the Church from the State and abstention from property. Joseph's victory resulted in closer ties with the State. The patriarchate of Moscow originated in 1589 when the metropolitan of Moscow, Job (1589–1605), was appointed by the Greek Patriarch Jeremias II despite the protests of the Greeks. Job was instrumental in Boris Godunov's successful rise to the throne by threatening his opponents with excommunication. In the mid-17th cent. schism broke out in the Church over the correction of liturgical books and rituals. Patriarch *Nikon (1652–66), who organized the needed reforms, was opposed by P. *Avvakum and his followers. This led to the formation of the *Old Believers. Nikon, haughty and despotic, was also engaged in a struggle for power with Alexis I (1645–76). The reforms were approved, but Nikon lost the power struggle which resulted in the further strengthening of state control over the church. Under Peter the Great (1682–1725), the Church suffered another setback when the Czar issued the Spiritual Regulation, under the inspiration of F. *Prokopovich. The patriarchate was abolished and replaced by the *Holy Synod of Russia, whose members were appointed by the Czar and presided over by a lay procurator. The plight of the Church was worsened, as it had been in the past, by the lack of a well-educated clergy and a want of social consciousness. Catherine II (1762–96) continued control over the Church by confiscation of land and putting the bps. under state salary. The dependence of the Church on the State was esp. strong in the 19th cent. when it became a more or less administrative arm of the czarist regimes. It reached its lowest ebb under Czar Nicholas II (1894–1917), his procurator Konstantin Pobedonostsev, and, the layman Rasputin whose disastrous influence reached into both ecclesiastical and secular affairs. Under the Bolsheviks the patriarchate was reinstated briefly in the person of *Tikhon (1917–25), formerly abp. of North America. Tikhon's opposition to the regime resulted in his arrest, "confession," and the formation of a rival group, the "Living Church." The Church was disestablished in January 1918 and separated from the State; it underwent savage attack by the Bolsheviks and various militant atheist groups which strove with fanatical zeal to wipe out all traces of religion. This was in contrast to orthodox Marxism. While Marx and Engels were admittedly hostile to all religions, they held that religion would die out of its own accord under the benefits and abundant blessings of communism. Under Lenin and Stalin, however, vicious campaigns were instigated to confiscate church property and to liquidate or deport anti-Soviet clergy and laymen. In 1929 alone, approximately 1400 churches were closed and religious education was restricted to the home. The assault was relaxed during World War II when the Soviets sought the support of the Orthodox Church. Orthodox faithful contributed more than 300 million rubles for the war effort, and after a meeting with Stalin and Molotov in September 1943, the patriarchate was allowed to be reinstated under the direction of *Sergius. After his death in May 1944, Metropolitan *Alexis of Leningrad became patriarch. Under Alexis, the 350-year-old Greek Catholic Church in the Ukraine and White Russia was forcibly annexed as the Vatican was branded fascist and anti-Soviet. Since World War II the battle against religion has persisted for the most part in more subtle forms, though no less than 10,000 churches were reportedly closed in the early 1960s. A new theme was introduced into the religious debate in 1965 and 1966 when two Orthodox priests wrote a 10,000-word letter of protest to the Soviet President and Patriarch Alexis, charging the regime with illegal interventions in the Church. Accurate statistics are unavailable, but there are approximately 50,000,000 faithful in 73 dioceses with about 14,000 priests serving 11,500 churches. Overseas, the Russian patriarch has jurisdiction over the exarchates of Western Europe, Central Europe, and the Americas. BIBLIOGRAPHY: F. Dvornik, *Slavs: Their Early History and Civilization* (1956); G.P. Fedotov, *Russian Religious Mind* (2 v., 1946, 1966); J. S. Curtiss, *Russian Church and the Soviet State (1917–1950)* (1953).

[D. DIRSCHERL]

MOSER KARL (1860–1936), progressive Swiss architect who studied at the Technischen Hochschule in Zurich and at the École des Beaux Arts in Paris. Although his early works reflect a dependence on historical styles, his church of St. Antonius in Basel (1925–27) the first reinforced concrete church in Switzerland is related to the work of A. Perret. BIBLIOGRAPHY: H. Vollmer, ed., *Künstler-Lexikon des Zwanzigsten Jahrhunderts* 3 (1956) 430.

[R. E. FLEISCHER]

MOSER, LUCAS (1400–50), German painter, known through the inscription on his only extant work, the winged *St. Mary Magdalen Altar* of Tiefenbronn, near Pforzheim (1431). It represents on several panels the story of St. Magdalen (Feast at the House of Simon, Miraculous Voyage to Marseille, Last Communion, etc.). The paintings are characterized by strong plasticity, naturalism and advanced spatial concepts that relate to Flemish art and to the International Gothic style. BIBLIOGRAPHY: W. Boeck, *Der Tiefenbronner Altar von Lucas Moser* (1951).

[R. BERGMANN]

MOSES, the man presented in the Bible as the leader of the Hebrew people at a critical juncture of their history. He leads them safely out of Egypt, mediates the covenant with Yahweh at Mt. Sinai, and continues to lead the people through the trans-Jordanian territory to the steppes of Moab. Here he dies before the entrance to the promised land. It is generally admitted that the figure of Moses was greatly enhanced in certain Israelite circles and that the many and complex roles attributed to him cannot all be accepted as historical. It is particularly in the late Deuteronomic and priestly traditions that the elaboration took place. The process was continued to a heightened degree in rabbinical and later Judaism. Some of this is reflected in the NT literature, although it is noteworthy that Jesus is contrasted with Moses (e.g., Jn 1.17). It is difficult to analyse the OT literature for precise historical information, but it would be extreme to consider Moses a total creation of a later period. Israel's pre-conquest history would be difficult, if not impossible, to explain without him. That he took a leading part in rescuing the Hebrews in Egypt and that he unified them under the aegis of a covenanting Yahweh, mediating in some form a basic code, can be accepted. This latter role would explain the attribution of all later laws and regulations to his Sinaitic mediation. BIBLIOGRAPHY: EDB 1558–60.

[E. H. MALY]

MOSES THE BLACK, ST. (*c.*330–*c.*405), Egyptian monk. Of Ethiopian origin and a man of legendary strength and ferocity, M. was converted from a life of brigandage by the monks of the desert of Scete. Through prayer, mortification, and the discipline of hard work, he learned to govern the fierceness of his passions. Self-mastery came slowly but so thoroughly that *Theophilus of Alexandria was impressed with his virtue and ordained him to the priesthood. With a number of companions he was slain in a Berber raid upon his monastery, refusing to permit any resort to violence in self-defense. BIBLIOGRAPHY: AS 6:199–212; Butler 3:435–436; E. D. Carter, NCE 10:13–14.

[R. B. ENO]

MOSES, ASSUMPTION OF. Written originally in Hebrew or Aramaic, and probably during the 1st cent. A.D., this work has survived only in a Latin translation of a Greek version. Moreover, since it breaks off abruptly in mid-sentence in 12.13, it is evident that a concluding section has been lost. It is probable, therefore, that the allusion to a struggle between Satan and Michael the Archangel over the body of Moses which we find in Jude v.9 refers to this lost concluding section, which would almost certainly have contained an account of the raising of Moses into heaven. Otherwise the title "Assumption of Moses" would be inexplicable.

The work purports to be Moses' testament to Joshua. In ch. 1 Joshua is told of the approaching death of Moses, while in the concluding ch. 11–12 he is depicted as hesitating to enter upon the heritage of Moses. Between these two is an apocalyptic section which takes the form of a prophecy of the whole history of Israel from the entry into the promised land to the inauguration of the final age of messianic bliss when Satan is to be destroyed, the gentiles judged, and Israel taken up into heaven. In 6.1 there is a reference to ungodly kings who are also high-priests and to an insolent king of non-priestly descent whose reign is to last 34 years, and who will punish these high-priest kings as they deserve. This clearly refers to Herod (37–34 B.C.), and the victims of his punishment are the Hasmoneans. There are also clear references to the events following upon the death of Herod, when Palestine was directly subject to the representatives of Roman imperial power. From this point onward, the prophecies become vaguer. There are allusions to the advent of false and hypocritical devotees (ch. 7), a terrible persecution of the Jews by a powerful king (ch. 8), the advent of a certain Taxo, a Levite, who, together with his seven sons is prepared for martyrdom (ch. 9), and the inauguration of the kingdom of God (ch. 10). It is clear that events belonging to the Maccabean period have been taken as types of what is to take place in the final age. BIBLIOGRAPHY: Charles APOT 2: 407–424; H. H. Rowley, *Relevance of Apocalyptic* (2d ed., 1947); C. Lattey, "The Messianic Expectation in the Assumption of Moses," CBQ 4 (1942) 9–21.

[D. J. BOURKE]

MOSES, CANTICLE OF, the classic song of victory, also known as the Song of Miriam or Song of the Sea, contained in Ex 15.1–18. By reason of its close affinities with Ugaritic triumphal poems of similar type, it has been held to be one of the earliest examples of Hebrew poetry in the Bible, and to date back to the 13th cent. B.C. BIBLIOGRAPHY: F. M. Cross and D. N. Freedman, "Song of Miriam," *Journal of Near Eastern Studies* 14 (1955) 237–250; M. Rozelaar, "Song of the Sea," VT 2 (1952)221–228; J.D.W. Watts, "Song of the Sea," VT 7(1957) 371–380.

[D. J. BOURKE]

MOSES' ORACLES, in Dt 33 a theophanic hymn that introduces and completes (2–5; 26–29) a collection of oracular blessings attributed to Moses as his final testament to Israel (6–25). The hymn is very archaic in language and symbol and may well predate the Monarchy—Yahweh is king of the assembled tribal chiefs (5) and he will help them complete their conquest (29). The blessings are quite early, too: Reuben is almost extinct—which occurred soon after the conquest; Judah is separated from the northern tribes—apparently pre-Davidic; Levi is no longer a tribe but a priestly caste—11th cent., but with later additions; Benjamin is still in favor—prior to Ju 20; Joseph's blessing is couched in archaic Canaanite symbols, and his tribe is still the most important and numerous—11th cent.; the other tribes are aloof and occupied with their own business and problems—pre-monarchy. The total complex may well have originated at a northern sanctuary (Shiloh?) but made a fitting climax to *Deuteronomy* for its editors and an apt introduction to Joshua, the next book of the Deuteronomic corpus.

[J. F. FALLON]

MOSHEIM, JOHANN LORENZ VON (1694–1755), renowned German Lutheran historian. First educated at the gymnasium at Lübeck, he attended the Univ. of Kiel, where he earned a master's degree in 1718. He taught at Helmstädt, and Göttingen. When the new Univ. of Göttingen was being formed, the authorities sought M.'s advice and in 1747 named him chancellor. A distinguished theologian, he also gained fame as a powerful preacher. With the publication of his *Institutiones historiae ecclesiasticae libri IV* (1726), M. became known as the founder of Protestant historiography. His exegetical writings display good style, erudition, and sound sense. BIBLIOGRAPHY: DE 2:1073; P. Meinhold, LTK 7:656–657.

[F. D. LAZENBY]

MOSQUE (Arab. *masjid*), a Muslim place of worship. The mosque building normally consists of a large open quadrangular court (*ṣaḥn*) surrounded by a portico supported by columns often arranged in many rows. The building is oriented so as to face the holy city of *Mecca, and in the wall at that side there is a niche called the *miḥrâb*, indicating the *qibla* or direction to face in prayer. Before it the *imam stands while leading the communal prayer. On the same side is the elevated pulpit (*minbar*) from which the Friday sermon is delivered. Attached to the building there is usually a tower, the minaret (Arab., *manâra* or *ma'ḏan*), from which the call to prayer (*iḏân*) is sung by the *muezzin five times a day. Although cities or administrative districts in large cities often have many mosques, each has a "cathedral mosque" *(masjidjâmi')* where the Friday communal services are held. From early times mosques have been centers of education in Islam, and major schools have grown up in association with many mosques. In larger mosques there are often rooms or apartments called *zawâyâ* (sing., *zâwiya,* literally a corner) set aside for the personnel of the mosque or as quarters for students or persons making a retreat. BIBLIOGRAPHY: J. Pedersen, EncIslam[1] 3:362–428.

[R. M. FRANK]

MOSQUERA, MANUEL JOSÉ (1800–53), Colombian prelate distinguished for his opposition to his government's claim to have succeeded to the Spanish crown's rights of patronage. Educated in Popayan and Quito, M. had already held important educational and ecclesiastical positions when at the age of 34, he was made abp. of Bogotá. He was a zealous and energetic archbishop, a forceful orator, and a leader in the promotion of education. His resistance to laws curtailing the Church's liberty caused the senate to decree his exile. He died in Marseilles en route to Rome.

[P. DAMBORIENA]

MOSSELMAN, PAUL (d. 1467), Flemish sculptor in Bourges who carved at the house of Jacques Coeur, completed the tomb of the Duc de Berry (1453) for the Sainte Chapelle (begun by Jean de Cambrai), and 48 figures of apostles and angels (1457–67) for choir stalls in Rouen Cathedral.

[M. J. DALY]

MOST HOLY REDEEMER, DAUGHTERS OF THE, see HOLY REDEEMER, SISTERS OF.

MOST HOLY SAVIOR, SISTERS OF THE (formerly Daughters of the Most Holy Savior), a congregation founded by Elizabeth Eppinger in Nieberbronn, Alsace, in 1849 and established as an independent branch in Slovakia in 1914. Suppressed after World War II by the Communists in East Germany, Czechoslovakia, and Hungary, the community survives in the Bavarian foundations of West Germany. The motherhouse is in Strasbourg. The works of the congregation are principally the care of the sick and the education of youth. In 1975 they had 4,418 sisters and maintained 514 houses.

[P. NEAL]

MOST REVEREND (Lat. *reverendissimus*), an honorific by which in the U.S. all bps. are addressed. It belongs also to a cardinal, to palatine prelates of the papal household, and to the general superiors of some religious orders of regulars.

[T. C. O'BRIEN]

MOSTAERT, JAN (1475–1556), Dutch artist, court-painter to the Archduchess Margaret of Austria, noted for young children in his religious works (*Ecce Homo*). M.'s landscape relates to Patinir, his architectural settings are Italian Renaissance derivations *(Portrait of a Man with the Sibyl of Tibur)*.

[M. J. DALY]

MOTA Y ESCOBAR, ALONSO DE LA (1556–1625), Mexican bp. of Guadalajara from 1597; of Puebla de los Angeles from 1608. He was a mediator who both calmed the Indian's rebelliousness and secured their better treatment by the Spanish. In Puebla he was the founder of hospitals, a college, and religious houses.

[T. C. O'BRIEN]

MOTHER OF GOD, the first among the titles of the Blessed Virgin *Mary, which points to the primary reason for the special privileges divinely given her, and the singular honor due her (see HYPERDULIA). The explicit dogmatic defense of this title came in the Council of *Ephesus (431) in opposition to *Nestorius. He denied that the title *Theotokos* (Mother of God) belonged to Mary; the denial was immediately bound up with his interpretation of the union of the divine and the human in Christ. For Nestorius, the Incarnation did not mean the substantial union of the divine and human natures in the one person of the Word; he meant that Christ, a human person, is joined to the divine by a union in dignity or power or holiness. There is no *hypostatic union. Any human attributes refer therefore only to the human person, not to the divine person of the Word; thus the human person was born of Mary; she is the mother of Christ, not of the Son of God. Ephesus taught that Mary is rightly called *Theotokos* because she begot in the flesh the one who is the Word of God made flesh (D 252). The theological reason for Mary's title is that the human nature of Christ was united from the moment of conception to the Word, so that the one Mary conceived is truly the Word of God (ThAq ST 3a,35.4). Just as the divine maternity in meaning is linked to the truth of the hypostatic union; so, too, this maternity, this proximity to the Word, is the reason for the *Immaculate Conception and the fulness of grace given to Mary. Because nearness to God is the reason for honoring the saints, Mary's unique nearness to her Son is the basis for the special veneration offered her, hyperdulia, and for the privileged intercessory power on which the faithful rely.

[T. C. O'BRIEN]

MOTHER OF THE CHURCH, a title of Mary, which, though never defined officially, played a significant role in patristic and medieval thought and gained prominence in Catholic theology since Vatican II (Vat II ConstCh ch. 8). Biblically rooted and ecumenically promising, this title emphasizes the role of Mary as the prototype of redeemed mankind, since, through the action of God's Spirit in her, Mary freely became the mother of those who believe in Christ, just as she was through her *fiat* his physical mother. Viewed as mother of the Christian community, Mary is not put on the same level as her Son, but on the level of those who knowingly share in the renewal of the cosmos accomplished by Christ and willingly witness to the gift of grace in the world. By placing Mary explicitly within a pneumatologically founded ecclesiology, the Church avoids the Protestant objection that Catholic Mariology conflicts with biblical Christology. Since salvation is a social rather than an individual event, Mary's incorporation into the Body of Christ through the Spirit foreshadows the solidarity of all men in Christ. All Mary's activity is thereby seen exclusively in the perspective of God's action in her through his Son and his Spirit. This is essentially the biblical image of Mary, who hears the word of God through Jesus and does it (Mk 3:31–35); believes in the spiritual power of her Son's ministry (Jn 2:3–5); and is present as the one to whom Jesus entrusts his community at his death (Jn 19:26–27). Mary is the sole figure in the Gospels who is overshadowed by the Spirit at Jesus' conception (Lk 1:35) as she is filled with the same Spirit at the inception of the Church (Acts 1:14). She is the woman who experiences the eschatological breakthrough of God's Spirit in time through the sending of the Messiah; she acts as the pivotal witness of the arrival of the kingdom among men, and attests to the unity of the second and third articles of the Creed. Thus Ambrose and Augustine understood Mary as the second Eve, who is the spiritual mother of all the faithful. This belief was stressed in the 12th cent. by *Berengarius of Tours. In the 13th cent. an anonymous writer described the Church as the mother of Mary, since she is full of grace through the Spirit of her Son, and Mary as the mother of the Church, since her openness toward the Spirit prefigures man's free participation in the advent of salvation. BIBLIOGRAPHY: J. Galot, *Mary in the Gospels* (1964); E. Schillebeeckx, *Mary, Mother of the Redemption* (1964); O. Semmelroth, *Mary, Archetype of the Church* (1963).

[P. J. ROSATO]

MOTHER CHURCH, the First Church of Christ, Scientist, in Boston, Mass., organized by Mary Baker Eddy in 1892. It was established as the Mother Church of Christian Science, and all other churches of the denomination are regarded as branches of the parent vine. The Christian Science **Manual of the Mother Church* declared that "In its relation to other Christian Science Churches, in its by-laws and self-government, the Mother Church stands alone." Each branch church is regarded as an independent body, even when several are located in the same city, so that later organizations are as directly attached to the parent vine as are any of the earliest foundations, and each congregation depends directly on the Mother Church, rather than on any local or regional association.

[R. K. MACMASTER]

MOTHER GODDESSES, female deities of fertility and sexual love esp. prominent in the Ancient Near East. The association of goddesses with the earth and its fecundity led some to be regarded as the sources of vegetation and as mates of a sky-god or other male deity; Gaia and Ouranos (Greece), Cybele and Attis (Anatolia), Ishtar and Tammuz (Mesopotamia), Isis and Osiris (Egypt), and Kali and Siva constituted such pairs. Female deities often acquired mythological functions outside the realms of sexuality and fertility. Ishtar and Ma (Anatolia) were both goddesses of war. Their connection with the earth also led several goddesses to become mistresses of the dead buried there. Though worshipped by the Greeks as a virgin, Artemis seems originally to have been a fertility goddess with strong ties to the earth, wild places, and wild animals. Cybele was also connected with the mountains and with animals. Individual deities rarely conform thoroughly to the "mother goddess" type; the coastal Incan worship of Mother Sea and the uncertain fertility aspect of the Roman Venus point up the imprecision of the category. The purported high antiquity of the mother goddess rests uncertainly on Paleolithic images of women with exaggerated sexual characteristics and on other remains that are difficult to assess. BIBLIOGRAPHY: M. Eliade, *Patterns in Comparative Religion* (tr. R. Sheed, 1958).

[E. V. GALLAGHER]

MOTHERHOOD OF MARY, SPIRITUAL, the relationship of the Blessed Virgin Mary with mankind that resulted from her being the mother of Jesus. Evidently Mary is the historical, physical mother of Jesus, the Son of God; in a different, spiritual sense she is mother of all men. The analogy of motherhood is derived from Mary's exceptional maternity of an exceptional Person. As mother of Jesus she gave all mankind "life" (Jn 1.4; 5.24; 11.25; 14.6) so that in a sense she is the spiritual mother of men. Spiritual motherhood is, then, a consequence of divine motherhood. The Scriptural texts adduced as directly or indirectly indicative of this relationship between Mary and all men are few. They are not given this Marian emphasis by all exegetes. "I will make you enemies of each other, you and the woman" (Gen 3.15). "You are to . . . bear a son and . . . name him Jesus. He will be called the Son of the Most High" (Lk 1.31–32). "Woman, this is your son. . . . This is your mother" (Jn 19.26–27). ". . . a woman, adorned with the sun, standing on the moon, and with twelve stars on her head" (Rev 12.1). Mariologists relate the spiritual maternity of Mary closely to other descriptions of her role in the economy of Christ's Redemption, for example, the new Eve, the exemplar of the Church, virgin and mother, coredemptrix, mediatrix and dispensatrix of grace. Relevant tradition extends from 2d cent. SS. Justin and Irenaeus, who compared and contrasted Mary and Eve; to 19th and 20th cent. popes, who called Mary mother of men, mother of the Church, etc. While the ancients elaborated the metaphor of Mary's resembling yet differing from Eve in the life that each gave, the popes speak most often of the adoptive motherhood described in Jn 19.26–27. It is debated whether the link between Mary and man's life of grace is really distinct or apart from her having given birth to Christ. Even her cooperation with Christ's lifework, e.g., visiting Elizabeth, attending to the miracle at Cana, being present at the Crucifixion and at Pentecost, could be said to be intrinsically bound to her divine motherhood rather than distinct from it.

The closing paragraphs (61–65) of Vat II ConstChurch (1964) are relevant: ". . . she cooperated . . . in the Savior's work of restoring supernatural life to souls. For this reason she is a mother to us in the order of grace. . . . This maternity will last . . . until the eternal fulfillment of all the elect." She "is invoked by the Church under the title of Advocate, Auxiliatrix, Adjutrix, and Mediatrix. These, however, are to be so understood that they neither take away from nor add anything to the dignity and efficacy of Christ the one Mediator. . . . Through the gift and role of divine maternity, Mary is united with her Son, the Redeemer, and with his singular graces and offices." BIBLIOGRAPHY: W. J. Cole, NCE 9:352–354; W. Sebastian, Carol Mariol 2:325–376; *Marian Studies* (1950–).

[J. W. LANGLINAIS]

MOTHERHOUSE, the generalate of a religious institute of women. A major abbey having dependent or daughter foundations is also sometimes so designated.

MOTHERS, ARCHCONFRATERNITY OF CHRISTIAN, see CHRISTIAN MOTHERS, ARCHCONFRATERNITY OF.

MOTIF RESEARCH, a theological method associated esp. with the Swedish Lutheran theologians Gustaf *Aulén (1879–) and Anders *Nygren (1890–). In keeping with 20th-cent. reaction against *liberal theology (see DIALECTICAL THEOLOGY), this approach stresses man's incapacity to initiate a true relationship to God. The task of theology is to discern the motif or distinctive themes in various religious and theological traditions in order to set out the essentials of Christianity. Aulén finds the properly Christian motif in God's spontaneous forgiving love expressed by Christ's atoning death. Through historical study he seeks to show that Luther rediscovered this theme after the scholastics had interpreted Christ's act as a human response to God's justice. Nygren finds the motif in Judaism to be *nomos,* the law; in Greek religion, *eros,* the anthropocentric search for God as fulfilling man's desire; in true Christianity, *agapē,* God's gracious, uncaused love reaching out to man. The Reformation reaffirmed *agapē* as the sole ground for man's fellowship with God, and for Christian living, after Christianity's misrepresentation in scholasticism and the Renaissance as a religion of *nomos* or *eros*. BIBLIOGRAPHY: G. Aulén, *Christus Victor* (1948); *idem, Faith of the Church* (rev. ed., 1961); A. Nygren, *Agape and Eros* (tr. P. R. Watson, 1953); G. Weigel, *Survey of Protestant Theology in Our Day* (1954).

[P. DAMBORIENA]

MOTION (Lat, *motus,* change) in the broad sense, any change or transition from one state to another. According to Aristotle (*Physics 3,* ch. 1.201a,10–12) it is the actuality of that which is in a condition of potentiality precisely as it is in potentiality. The Aristotelian definition embraces three concepts which need to be explained: motion is a kind of actuality: that which is undergoing motion was in potency, but is now in the process of becoming actualized (the green apple that is turning red is not merely in potency to be red; the act of becoming red is taking place). Second, motion is the act of the potential; only that which is in potency can be involved in motion, since to the extent that a potency is realized or fulfilled the corresponding motion is already completed. Thus, the apple which has reached the limit of redness has no more potency to become the color once it already possesses it. The third part of the definition refers to the fact that the motion being defined is not at its term and is still in process of reaching that term. For example, a piece of marble is in potency and also in act but in different ways. It actually is marble and is potentially a statue. The motion the marble undergoes in being shaped into a statue is the act of the marble, but insofar as it has the potency to become the figure being given it by the sculptor. The motion is the act of the marble not as it is marble but insofar as it is in potency to be a statue. In other words, it is the act of the subject, not as it already is, but insofar as it has a capacity to be something else. In Aristotelian thought, motion is found in all ten categories and the concept is interchangeable with the notion of change. In theology, St. Thomas employs the concept of motion as one of the five proofs for the existence of God by showing that motion is explained only by a mover not subject to motion.

[F. T. RYAN]

MOTIVE (late Lat. *motivum,* from *movere,* to move), a principle producing change in a subject whether by way of impulse or attraction. Under the first respect it is used of an *efficient cause initiating action, the motive power exerted by an agent; in this sense it occurs in natural and psychological philosophy, where by definition human willing and choosing, when given, are set in exercise only by God or the human will itself (see *FREE WILL). The most frequent use of the term, however, is under the second respect, in the psychological context of moral philosophy and theology; their motivation is discussed in terms of the objects of volitions and choices. These objects can be considered in a double light; first, of the moral purpose of the act considered in itself, which is called the aim of the deed *(finis operis),* second, of the moral purpose or aim of the doer *(finis operantis).* This is called the motive. Except when we are doing something just for its own sake these two purposes are not identical; indeed one may be right when the other is wrong, thus beneficence out of hypocrisy or murder out of mercy. For a human act to be morally good, it must not be lacking on either count.

Accordingly as such, a motive concerns an end rather than what is for an end. It can be of two types, substantial and incidental, and the latter can be numerous and mixed. The first is the main or root motive, and it is called the intention or resolve for an end *(intentio finis).* Every human act springs from such an intention, which may be and often is implicit, and is theologically resolved either into that of loving God or into that of loving something else instead—the "something else" is the self and the "instead" is the key term. Now though we cannot live on good intentions, without them whatever we do, however worthy and helpful to others, will be rather hollow from a personal point of view. From the time of *Abelard motives in this sense have been recognized as lying at the heart of a good morality that is a living response and not just a conformity to an objective pattern of reasonable and legal standards.

The second type of motive is more idiosyncratic and adventitious, and comes under the moral *circumstance, why, *cur.* We are now in the field of what are called the ulterior motives which can throng round an individual and historical act. They can be numerous and mixed; nevertheless, they can be roughly divided into those that enhance or alternatively fleck virtue and, correspondingly into those that mitigate or aggravate vice. So much the better if I go to church in order to worship God and to enjoy the music; not so good if I add, and to look stonily at the preacher whom I happen to dislike. Not quite so bad if I get drunk to be good company; much worse if also to preen myself on how much liquor I can carry. All our actions are meshed with such motives; they are so various and so fugitive that, except when clearly unworthy and somewhat habitual, they are scarcely worth pursuing: not all schools of spirituality advocate the introspective practice of "the purification of motives." The imputation of motives and "motive-mongering" can easily slip into the sins of *rash judgment and *detraction. BIBLIOGRAPHY: ThAq ST 1a2ae, 7,12,18–20; (Lat-Eng, v. 17 *Human Acts,* ed. T. Gilby 1970; v. 18, *Principles of Morality,* ed. T. Gilby 1967).

[T. GILBY]

MOTIVE, UNCONSCIOUS, a volition- or choice-determining factor that is not adverted to either because it is deliberately ignored or because it belongs to an inaccessible part of the psyche, or more properly, of the human organism. The two cases are quite different from the point of view of morals. As to the first, self-deception is a trick not uncommonly employed when we do wrong; we invent a creditable motive, and persuade ourselves that it is the one really operative: such inadvertence is a voluntary and culpable type of *ignorance.

As to the second, the causality of a *motive can be considered either as efficient or as final, that is, either as an impulse, which may be compulsive, or as an attraction, which may be obsessive. Let us take each in turn. The "exercise" of will-activity raises the question of its efficient cause; given that it takes place, then by definition of what the will is, and what is meant by *free will, only two causes are possible, God and itself as self-determining its own activity within its field. Divine causality operates at the very spring of our acting, and we are unconscious of it, but our own willing to deliberate and to come to a decision is as such a conscious process. This does not mean that it may not be largely in the grip of particular unconscious forces; it means only that to the extent it is, it is not a moral or *human act.

Next, the "specification" of will-activity, which is determined by its object or final cause. These are certainly unconscious drives from within the human organism according to a natural appetite it shares with mineral and vegetable; these are subsumed within its voluntary drives, which by definition are conscious at the level of sensation or of intelligence. Though a voluntary act as such has a conscious motive, it does not follow that this is the entire object of the act as it takes place, for it carries with it the burden of its non-voluntary elements and looks forward to a condition when deliberate consciousness is past. Indeed it is part of the dialectic of love that we can desire better than we may know. In this sense conscious motives should be seen as rising from the preconscious and aspiring to the postconscious.

It will not be denied that human ills arise from the attempts of the conscious to do *violence to the unconscious, and to remedy this moralists and depth psychologists should address themselves. Both can collaborate when their respective fields are defined, if only negatively. The first should not hold that man is entirely free, a purely conscious or purely volitional being autonomous with respect to unconscious forces, the second that he is entirely predetermined and that his apparent choices are but the rationalization of impulses toward what he is set on doing anyhow. BIBLIOGRAPHY: P. K. Meagher, NCE 10:40–43.

[T. GILBY]

MOTIVES OF CREDIBILITY, reasons for regarding a given set of phenomena as signs of a divine revelation. They are to be distinguished from the motive of *faith, i.e., the reason for actual belief in God which, in classical Christian theology, can only be the authority of God himself in his self-revelation. According to Vatican Council I, motives of credibility are external signs such as miracles and prophecies, but also the intrinsic appeal of God's revealed intentions and the inner promptings to believe which the hearer of the word may feel. A combination of these inward and outward indications points to a summons to believe in an inter-personal fashion. Protestant theology often prefers not to speak of any sort of reasons for believing, lest by insinuating some sort of objective basis for faith, it would cease to be faith. This is basically the same concern which leads Catholic theology to distinguish so sharply between the unique motive of faith and the manifold motives of credibility. BIBLIOGRAPHY: J. Alfaro, *SacMund* 2:322–324; K. Rahner, *Theological Investigations 5* (tr. C. Ernst, 1965); R. Bultmann, *Faith and Understanding* (1969); K. Barth, *Church Dogmatics I* (tr. I. W. Robertson, 1936). *PREAMBLE OF FAITH.

[P. MISNER]

MOTLEY, JOHN LOTHROP (1814–77), American diplomat and historian. His principal work, *The Rise of the Dutch Republic* (3 v. 1856), together with the later *History of the United Netherlands* (4 v. 1860–67), which continued the story until the truce of 1609, is a worthy Harvard pendant to the work of Prescott (who encouraged his historical writing) and displays similar characteristics.

MOTOLINÍA, TORIBIO DE BENAVENTE (1495–1565), Spanish Franciscan, missionary, and historiographer of Mexico. Arriving at the Aztec capital in 1524, he adopted the Indian word *motolinia* (poverty) as his proper name. He traveled much and served as guardian of Franciscan convents in Mexico, Guatemala, and Honduras. When he became provincial, M. was asked to write an account of the life and beliefs of the Indians before the conquest. This he did in his *History of the Indians of New Spain* (translated from the Spanish by F. B. Steck, 1951) which was published in 1541. This work is a classical source for information about the period with which he was concerned. He also published an attack upon Las Casas for the exaggerations contained in the *Brevísima relación de la destrucción de las Indias*.

[P. DAMBORIENA]

MOTT, JOHN RALEIGH (1865–1955), Methodist missionary leader and ecumenist. M. was born in Livingston Manor, New York. Educated at Upper Iowa and Cornell Univ., he became (1888) general secretary of student YMCA work and for 21 years was chairman of the Student Volunteer Movement for Foreign Missions. He also was chairman of the First World Missionary Conference at Edinburgh in 1910; this later became the *International Missionary Council, which he headed for many years. Spiritual father of the World Council of Churches, he was elected honorary chairman in 1948 and 1954. His addresses and papers were published (1946–47) in six volumes. Co-winner of the Nobel peace prize in 1946, he also received the Distinguished Service Medal from the U.S. and honors from 15 other countries. BIBLIOGRAPHY: G. M. Fisher, *John Raleigh Mott, Architect of Cooperation and Unity* (1952); HistAmMeth 3.

[F. E. MASER]

MOULTON, WILLIAM FIDDIAN AND JAMES HOPE, father and son of the erudite Moulton family of England. **William Fiddian** (1835–98), one of the foremost NT Greek scholars of his day. A Wesleyan clergyman, he was one of the revisers of the NT (1870–81), and served as the first head master of the Leys School, Cambridge. His elder son, **James Hope** (1863–1917) helped to produce a new understanding of NT Greek from evidence obtained from non-literary (*koinē*) papyri.

[M. A. MCFADDEN]

MOUNIER, EMMANUEL (1905–50), French philosopher. M. studied philosophy in Grenoble, completing his work for the *agréggation* in Paris (1928). He taught philosophy (1931–1932) and founded *Esprit* (1932). He held a teaching position in Brussels from 1933 until 1939 when he was called to active military duty. He was imprisoned in 1942 for a short time because of alleged subversive activity. From 1945 until his death in 1950, he wrote and again edited the resurrected *Esprit*, which had been suppressed (1941). M. is one of the most renowned philosophers in the personalist movement, which began for him with the publication of his work, *A Personalist Manifesto* (1938). The movement was not new, however, for its thesis about the person is traceable to Kierkegaard, Lavelle, and Le Senne, and in America, to Borden Bowne and William James. What was different in M.'s development was his view of the person responding to a vocation of moral excellence through his choices and self-conquest. M.'s Catholicism is clearly seen in his stress on the person as a spiritual being responding affirmatively to a hierarchal value system. For M. the real person is always in process of conversion. For both M. and the Protestant Denys de Rougemont, the person can only be so through fidelity to his vocation achieved in obedience to God's command and love of neighbor. It is unfortunate that the spiritual meaning of M.'s personalism was lost and the stress he placed on commitment and self-conscious moral choice, ignored in later personalist movements. In his early career M. was influenced by the writings of *Péguy whom he admired. He worked with a group who planned a compilation of Péguy's thought, which was published in 1931. Some of his major works, besides the Manifesto, include *La Pensée de Charles Péguy* (1931); *Personnalisme* (1952); *Révolution personnaliste et communautaire* (1935); *L'Affrontement chrétien* (1944); *Introduction aux existentialismes* (1946); *Qu'est-ce que le personnalisme?* (1947), and *Le personnalisme* (1949). BIBLIOGRAPHY: F. C. Copleston, *Contemporary Philosophy* (1956) 109–115; E. Cantin, *Mounier, A Personalist View of History* (1973). *PERSONALISM.

[J. R. RIVELLO]

MOUNT ANGEL ABBEY, a United States Benedictine abbey located in St. Benedict, Oregon. Some 100 monks and brothers are in the community.

[M. MCFADDEN]

MOUNT ATHOS, see ATHOS, MOUNT.

MOUNT MELLERAY ABBEY, a monastery in County Waterford, Ireland, founded 1832 by Trappists expelled from Melleray, France. They had been living since 1830 on a farm in County Kerry until Sir Richard Keane of Cappoquin offered them 500 acres of unreclaimed moorland. During the Great Famine of 1847, Mount Melleray aided thousands of starving people. It has six daughter houses. BIBLIOGRAPHY: A. J. Luddy, *Story of Mount Melleray* (1946).

[C. MCGRATH]

MOUNT OF OLIVES, a mountain ridge E of Jerusalem. Zechariah mentions it as a place of judgment (14.4). In the NT it is the site of Jesus' eschatological discourse (Mt 24.3), his agony of prayer (Lk 22.39), and of the apparition of his ascension into heaven (Acts 1.12). BIBLIOGRAPHY: EDB 1566–70.

[J. A. GRASSI]

MOUNT ST. BERNARD, MONASTERY OF, an abbey of Cistercian contemplatives of the Strict Observance (Trappists), in Leicestershire, England. It was founded in 1835 by the Trappists of Mount Melleray Abbey of Cappoquin, County Waterford, Ireland.

[M. A. MCFADDEN]

MOUNT SINAI, CHURCH OF, autocephalous Orthodox church whose abp. is the abbot of the Monastery of St. Catherine of Alexandria, on the slope of Mt. Sinai (present-day Jebel Mûsâ) on the Sinai peninsula. The Church is made up of only about 100 members, monks of St. Catherine's or its daughter houses and a few Christians living near the monastery. It has enjoyed independence from the patriarchate of Jerusalem since the 16th century. It is the smallest of the Orthodox Churches.

[T. C. O'BRIEN]

MOUNT TABOR, UNCREATED LIGHT OF, the light which the disciples saw when Jesus was transfigured before them on the mountain, which according to tradition, was Mt. Tabor: "And he was transfigured before them, and his face shone like the sun, and his garments became white as light" (Mt 17.2). Although the existence of the divine light of God's glory was always a part of the biblical revelation as well as of the Christian mystical tradition, the question of its nature, as created or uncreated, came to a point in the Hesychast controversy in 14th-cent. Byzantium when the monks of Mt. Athos claimed to have union with this divine light through their Hesychast method of contemplation and prayer. They identified this light with that which the Disciples saw at the Transfiguration, and the great question was concerning its nature and the meaning of its presence to men. St. Gregory *Palamas (d. 1359), the chief defender of the Hesychasts, whose doctrine has been officially adopted by the Orthodox Church, cited the patristic tradition before him in insisting that the divine light of Tabor, the same divine light of mystical contemplation, transcends all human thought and sense; that it is uncreated, immaterial, indescribable, ineffable, infinite, unlimited, timeless, eternal, inaccessible; the beauty, the glory, the grace, and the kingdom of God. The uncreated light is of God. It is not creaturely nor symbolic. It is not a contrived means of manifesting the presence of God which is different from the presence itself. It is, on the contrary, one of the expressions of the divine uncreated energies (see DIVINE ENERGIES) of God. This light is not seen by the physical eyes; it is not materially or sensibly visible. To behold it is only possible through an ascetical purification, in which, nevertheless, the body and the senses must participate together with the soul, the mind, and the heart, since the total transfiguration of the whole man by grace is the condition for this vision.

It is not the uncreated light that is changing, appearing and disappearing in revelation and mystical contemplation. On the contrary, it is the man who beholds the light who is changed. Thus, e.g., on Mount Tabor at the Transfiguration, it was not Christ who was essentially changed, who added to himself something which before was absent, or who became something which before he was not. It was the Disciples who were changed by the divine presence and who were granted to see Christ as he really was and is, in the light of the fullness of his divine glory. Thus, even in this world, by the purification of the Holy Spirit, men in the flesh can behold the uncreated light of God, the light of Tabor, which flows necessarily and naturally from the three persons of the Trinity, which will fill all creation at the divine parousia at the end of the ages, and which already now exists in and through all things and is already now visible to those whose hearts are pure and whose eyes are opened to see by the grace of the Spirit. BIBLIOGRAPHY: B. Krivosheine, *Ascetic and Theological Teaching of Gregory Palamas* (1938).

[T. HOPKO]

MOUNTAINS, SACRED. The mythology of most cultures and civilizations is replete with references to sacred mountains. They were considered the meeting place of heaven and earth, the inhabitation of the gods, and the highest spot on earth. Insofar as the gods dwelt in the sky and were the source of creation and life, the highest mountain of the region was regarded by the inhabitants as the point of initial contact with the sphere of the sacred. Its highest peak became the center of the universe from which sacrality and order spread to the chaos of unsacralized existence. Thus Moses ascended Mount Sinai to receive the Jewish law from Yahweh. Mount Tabor was also seen as the dwelling place of God in the OT, and Christ led his disciples to a high mountain at the Transfiguration (Lk 9.28–36). According to Muslim tradition, the Ka'aba was the highest place on earth. The Greeks had their deities enthroned on Mount Olympus, and the Shinto-Buddhist Japanese regard Mount Fuji as sacred. Mountains, therefore, are eminently hierophantic, i.e., expositors of sacred mysteries. Their peaks were as sacred as the sky itself, and every climbing of their heights was a transcending of the human status by placing the believer in a celestial sphere. BIBLIOGRAPHY: M. Eliade, *Patterns in Comparative Religion* (tr. R. Sheed, 1963); J. A. MacCulloch, ERE 8:863–868.

[V. T. JOHNSON]

MOURA, ANTÔNIO MARIA DE (1794–1842), Brazilian regalist, priest, canonist, and political leader; unsuccessful candidate of the Brazilian Empire for the office of bp. of Rio de Janeiro. Born in Vila Nova da Rainha do Caeté, Minas Gerais, he was left as a foundling at the door of Captain Caetano José Nascentes. M. was educated in the Regalist culture of Coimbra, Portugal, then returned as priest and lawyer to Brazil, where he was elected to the legislature (1830–37) and was professor of law in São Paulo. Rome gave avarice and drunkenness as reasons for its refusal to elevate him to the episcopacy, but must also have feared his complicity in a scheme to separate the Brazilian Church from Rome. BIBLIOGRAPHY: T. Beal, NCE 10:53–54.

[E. J. DILLON]

MOURNING. The 1969 revision of the rites for funerals expresses at many places the balance between grief at bereavement and Christian hope in the Paschal Mystery of Christ. The Introduction accompanying the rites states that "Christians should certainly affirm their hope in eternal life, but in such a way that they do not seem to neglect or ignore the feeling and practice of their own time and place (2)." The liturgical rites throughout are designed to foster hope, but also to offer solace to those who rightly grieve at the loss of one they love; the psalms especially are incorporated into the rites to express grief and to offer comfort (12). Emphasis in the new liturgy on Christ's resurrection does not mean insensitivity to mourning, not only as a genuinely human response to death, but also as mourning is part of the experience of being joined to Christ's suffering. Mourning is the experience of the power of death that Christ sustained and conquered; it is the setting for the affirmation of Christian hope.

[T. C. O'BRIEN]

MOURNING CUSTOMS (IN THE BIBLE). To die unmourned and unburied was considered a calamity by the Hebrews (Job 27.15; Jer 16.4–6). In common with other Near Eastern peoples, the Hebrews mourned their dead according to definite ritual. Burial was quick, usually on the day of death, since embalming was unknown to them. Lamentation began immediately after death. Relatives, friends, and others showed their grief by weeping (Lk 7.32; 8.52) and loud cries such as "Mourn for my brother! Mourn for my sister! . . . Mourn for his highness!" (cf. Jer 22.18; 1 Kg 13.30). Professional mourners, predominantly women, were also used (2 Chr 35.25; Jer 9.17–18). Accompanied by flutes (Mt 9.23) they wailed or sang stylized dirges in praise of the deceased (Am 5.16). Noteworthy are the dirges King David composed for Saul and Jonathan (2 Sam 1.17–27) and Abner (2 Sam 3.33–34). Generally speaking, expression of grief involved a conscious neglect of one's outward appearance. Thus Ezekiel (24.17) at the death of his beloved wife was forbidden by God to weep outwardly, to go bareheaded or unsandalled, to cover his beard or eat the common mourners' bread—all signs of sorrow. A mourner might tear his garment or wear sackcloth; he might throw dust on his head or roll in ashes (Ezek 27.30; Is 61.3). Fasting formed part of the ritual (1 Sam 31.13; Jdt 8.6). Though the Mosaic Law forbade self-mutilation as a sign of grief (Lev 19.28; Dt 14.1), it was not unknown for Hebrew mourners to strike their breasts (Lk 23.48) or thighs (Jer 31.19; Ezek 21.17), or even to pluck out their hair and gash their bodies (Jer 41.5; Ezra 9.3). Mourning did not stop with burial; it usually lasted 7 days (1 Sam 31.13; Sir 22.12), and occasionally 30 days as in the case of Aaron (Num 20.29) and Moses (Dt 34.8). BIBLIOGRAPHY: EDB 1571–73; E. Jacob, InterDB 3:452–454; De Vaux AncIsr 59–61.

[E. MAY]

MOURRET, FERNAND (1854–1938), French Sulpician priest and prolific church historian. After practicing law, he entered the seminary of St. Sulpice at Issy, near Paris, in 1879, was ordained 1883, and in 1902 began teaching church history at the Sulpician school on the Rue de Regard, Paris. His best known work is the nine-volume *Histoire générale de l'Église* (1914–27), which remains an authoritative work in its treatment of contemporary French history. The first eight volumes have been translated into English by Newton Thompson (1931–57). BIBLIOGRAPHY: DTC Table générales 3266.

[E. J. DILLON]

MOUTON, JEAN (1475–1522), French composer, contrapuntalist, student of Josquin des Prés, teacher of Willaert. M. was a court musician to Louis XII and Francis I, canon of Thérouanne and later of St. Quentin, where he remained till his death. Much of his work—Masses, psalms, canons, motets, and French chansons—was published and appreciated during his lifetime.

[R. J. LITZ]

MOUVEMENT RÉPUBLICAINE POPULAIRE (MRP) Catholic, political party in France. The MRP emerged after the French resistance movement during World War II. A young university student, Gilbert Dru, gave the movement its real direction even though Georges Bidault and other leaders had already thought of a Christian alliance. When Dru was executed by the Germans in 1944, Bidault carried on the work of the movement. The program of the movement was based on Catholic principles of ethics and social justice, opposed to the Communists, and critical of capitalist extremes. It endorsed the unification of Europe strongly and the post-war system of family allowances was in great part the work of the MRP. It was strongly in favor of government subsidies for Catholic schools. The party had its strongest showing immediately after the war; it declined from 1953 onward. But MRP members were in the De Gaulle government until 1962, when the party found itself in strong opposition to the nationalistic European policy of De Gaulle. This plus its opposition to the Communists weakened MRP and it has not been revitalized.

[R. C. CLIGGETT]

MOVEMENT FOR A BETTER WORLD (MBW), an international religious movement inspired by Pius XII and founded in 1952 by Riccardo Lombardi, SJ at Rocca di Papa, Italy. The cause was inaugurated primarily to renew the structure of society. Individuals and promoting groups of the movement include RC clergy, religious men and women, laity, all dedicating themselves to an ascetical practice of living in the spirit of mutual charity and unity that provides a climate for the social presence of Jesus. Groups of MBW are established on every continent, seeking to bring new life and unity to the Church and through the Church to the entire world. Retreats are conducted to stimulate Christian witness and motivate action towards the making of a better world. The U.S. national headquarters is located at Silver Spring, Maryland. Its publication is entitled *Atmosphere*.

[R. A. TODD]

MOYENMOUTIER, ABBEY OF, former Fr. Benedictine abbey founded *c.* 676 in the Vosges Mts. in E. France by St. Hidulf (Hidulphus, Hydulphe). Its name (lit. the middle moutier) derives from its location at the center point of four surrounding abbeys: Senones, Bonmoutier, Etival, and Saint-Dié. Hidwulf (d. 707) once auxiliary bp. of Trier having longed for the solitary life, finally settled in a hermitage in the Vosges. Many hermits were attracted to him and from this nucleus Moyenmoutier developed. It enjoyed a history of 11 cent., after which, during the Benedictine reform, it united (1601) with the abbey of Saint-Vanne at Verdun to form the Benedictine Congregation of Saint-Vanne et Saint-Hydulphe. During the French Revolution (1790) it was suppressed. BIBLIOGRAPHY: G. Allemang, LTK 7:666; G. Goyau, CE 13:344–345; Butler 3:72.

[S. A. HEENEY]

MOZARABIC ART, Christian art of Spain after the 8th cent., a synthesis of Christian and Muslim cultures effected by the penetration of Eastern and North African styles into Spanish Christian, Visigothic, and Roman styles, evidenced in architecture in the horseshoe arch (S. Miguel de Escalada, 920; Santiago de Peñalba, 937) decorative ceramic tiles, and saw-toothed moldings. Minor arts (textiles, pottery) show Oriental Persian and Coptic broad bands and flat figural work. Ivory carving remains highly ornate in old Visigothic, Celtic, or Carolingian modes. Most noteworthy is the MS of Beatus, monk of Liébana, whose 8th-cent. commentary on the Apocalypse was reproduced widely. The earliest (926) is in New York, with important copies from Távara and St. Sever. E. Mâle ascertained the Beatus Apocalypse as a source of tympanum carvings (Moissac). Later Mozarabic art is known as *Mudejar. BIBLIOGRAPHY: M. J. Daly, NCE 2:198 s.v. "Beatus of Liébana."

[M. J. DALY]

MOZARABIC CHANT, the liturgical *chant of the *Mozarabic rite. The medieval chant is preserved in approximately 20 complete MSS dating from the 9th through the 11th centuries. These melodies cannot be transcribed into modern musical notation, however, since the medieval notation indicates only approximate contours instead of specific pitches. Only 21 melodies were copied over in a more modern notation at about the time that the rite was suppressed in the 11th century. Barring the discovery of the new MSS with precise notation, these will remain the only medieval Mozarabic melodies which can be sung accurately.

The MSS transmit four distinct musical traditions, each with its own notational peculiarities. Two of these traditions correspond to the northern part of Spain and are quite similar to one another. The remaining two appear to have been associated with the city of Toledo and differ strikingly both from each other and from the northern traditions. One of the Toledan traditions is associated, furthermore, with a somewhat different liturgy. The historical relationship of the four traditions to one another is not clear. Nevertheless, an early MS without notation suggests that at least the core of the northern traditions was already formed by the time of the Muslim invasion of the Iberian Peninsula in 711.

Many features of *Gregorian chant are shared by the Mozarabic chant. Among these is the distinction between responsorial chants and antiphonal chants. In the Mozarabic chant, however, both types are characterized by the repetition following the verses of only the last part of the initial response or antiphon. The responsorial chants are the more elaborate and often include extensive melismas.

The responsories for the Office employ a system of psalm tones similar to those of the Gregorian great responsories. These suggest that the Mozarabic chant employed a scheme much like the Gregorian system of modes, but somewhat less elaborate. The antiphonal chants, too, make use of a set of psalm tones similar to those of Gregorian chant, but these tones rarely appear in the surviving manuscripts. Hence, it cannot be said with certainty how many tones there were or how many modes they represented. A single set of tones seems to have served for all of the antiphonal chants in both the Mass and the Office.

The following are the principal chants of the Mozarabic Mass with their Gregorian analogues given in parentheses: *antiphona ad praelegendum* (Introit), *psalmus* (Gradual), *laudes* (Alleluia), *sacrificium* (Offertory), *antiphona ad accedentes* (Communion).

When the Mozarabic rite was restored at the end of the 15th cent. new and different melodies were composed for the old texts. These melodies are preserved in MSS at the Cathedral of Toledo. BIBLIOGRAPHY: C. W. Brockett, *Antiphons, Responsories and Other Chants of the Mozarabic Rite* (1968); D. M. Randel, *Responsorial Psalm Tones for the Mozarabic Office* (1969); C. Rojo and G. Prado, *El canto mozárabe* (1929).

[D. M. RANDEL]

MOZARABIC RITE, ancient Iberian, Spanish, and Portuguese liturgical rite, named so after it had survived for the longest time in those Spanish provinces which were under the Arabs (from *mustarib,* i.e., arabized). It had its prime during the era of the Visigoths of the 7th cent. Pope Gregory VII, aiming for unity of liturgical practice, initiated its suppression by the synod of Burgos (1085) in favor of the Roman rite. After the fall of the Arabic rule, Card. Francisco Jiménez de Cisneros published the Mozarabic Missal (1500) and the Breviary (1502). Only six parishes in Toledo and some few monasteries were allowed to retain the Mozarabic rite. Today the Mozarabic liturgy is celebrated in a few churches of the diocese of Toledo, in the *Capilla Muzarabe* of the cathedral of Toledo, and a few times during the year also in the *Capilla de Talavera* in Salamanca. Originally this liturgy had a form quite different from the Roman one. Oriental influences seem to have played an important role. There was no fixed anaphora; some prayers of the priest are addressed to Christ and not to the Father. The Mozarabic liturgy influenced the Gallican liturgy, and from there some of the prayers found their way into the medieval Roman liturgy.

[J. MADEY]

MOZARABS, generic term for those who are Arabic in culture but not by birth, from the Spanish term *Mozárabe*. It is applied to Christians who lived among Muslims in such cities of Spain as Seville and Toledo. The ancient Mozarabic rite is the liturgy of these Christians.

[J. R. RIVELLO]

MOZART, JOHANN GEORG LEOPOLD (1719–1787) Austrian-born composer, violinist, father of Wolfgang Amadeus *Mozart. In 1762 M., having risen from the ranks of the orchestra, was appointed *Kapellmeister* and composer to the archiepiscopal court of Salzburg. After discovering the prodigious talent of his two children, Maria Anna (Nannerl) and Wolfgang Amadeus, he dedicated most his life to teaching, training, and managing their musical careers.

[R. J. LITZ]

MOZART, WOLFGANG AMADEUS (1756–91), Austrian-born composer and musician of the classical period. His virtuoso abilities on the keyboard instruments and his aptitude for the violin as well as for composition, became evident very early in his childhood. His father Leopold displayed him to audiences and royalty throughout Europe. M. began serving under Abp. von Schraftenbach of Salzburg in 1769, having been appointed Konzertmeister without pay. When Colloredo replaced Von Schraftenbach in 1772, he began paying M. a salary but in 1777, dismissed both M. and M's. father from his service rather than grant them leave to tour Europe once again. M. composed nearly all of his sacred music at Salzburg (1769 to 1781). There are 60 works in the Köchel listing of his complete extant works. His litanies, K. 109, K.125, K.195, K.243, his settings of the Vesper Psalms, K.321, and the *Magnificat*, K.339, are among his more important sacred works besides the Masses. Among these are the *Missa solemnis* K.139, with its large orchestral setting, the choral *Missa in honorem SSmae.*

Trinitatis, K.167, the *Missa brevis*, K.220, the so-called "Credo Mass," K.257; the "Coronation Mass" K. 317, and the great unfinished Mass in C minor, K.427, with its well known *Laudamus te* and other complex choral passages. Perhaps the best known of his sacred works is his last work, the *Requiem*, K.626, which M's pupil, F. Süssmayer, completed. M. composed a great many motets and minor compositions (Epistle sonatas) for liturgical use.

[R. J. LITZ]

MRA, see MORAL REARMAMENT.

MUARD, MARIE JEAN BAPTISTE (1809–54), founder. A French priest ordained in 1834, M. packed much activity into a career of only 20 years. His wish to join the Chinese mission having been blocked by his bp., M. founded a community of diocesan priests for the missions, the Society of St. Edmund (1843). For 5 years he directed the community at Pontigny. Two years after leaving Pontigny, M. founded the Benedictine monastery of Ste. Marie de la Pierre-qui-vire near Yonne, which became an abbey in 1884.

[J. R. AHERNE]

MUBARACH, BENEDICTUS, see AMBARACH, PETER.

MUCKERMANN, FRIEDRICH (1883–1946), German Jesuit writer and preacher who advocated a more effective participation by German Catholics in the solution of problems caused by the industrial age. From 1930 he strove as editor of the journal *Der Gral* (Grail) for a peaceful confrontation between modern culture and Christian religion. He fought, not only against communism, but also against National Socialism in Germany. His opposition to Nazi policy made it necessary for him to leave Germany in 1934 and he took refuge successively in Holland, France, and Switzerland. Works: *Der Mensch im Zeitalter der Technik* (1943); *Der deutsche Weg* (1946). BIBLIOGRAPHY: N. Herbermann, *In memoriam Friederich Muckermann* (1948).

[J. R. SCHULZ]

MUDEJAR (ART). The term "Mudejar" signified a Muslim who was subject to a Christian king and came to designate art of the Muslims under Christian patronage or direction after Spain's reconquest from the Arabs. The *Chapel of the Assumption,* Convent of Las Huelgas, the earliest example of Mudejar architecture in Spain, shows Muslim influence in the domical vault on carved stucco lambrequin arches and the horseshoe arches along five aisles in a synagogue, Toledo (*c.*12th cent.). In Seville (Alcazar, 1364), Toledo and Segovia, brick and glazed tiles of Arab origin (*azulejos*), elaborate ceilings, and slender towers reminiscent of minarets (San Gil, Sargossa) are Mudejar in style. Ceramics with metal glazes, and the decorative treatment of leather further signify Muslim tradition. After 1610 Moriscos (Moorish Christians) were expelled from Spain, but Mudejar work continued, spreading to the New World.

[M. J. DALY]

MUDRA, conventions of pose or gesture of hands in Buddhist and Hindu art having iconographic significance, among which are the *abhaya* (evil be far from you), *anjali* (worship), *dharmacakra* (teaching-turning the wheel of the law), *bhumisparsa* (earth-witness), *namaskāra* (praying), *varuda* (gift giving). The meanings derive from *jatakas* (tales) from the life of the Buddha or of the Hindu gods (Dance of Siva).

[M. J. DALY]

MUENCH, ALOYSIUS JOSEPH (1889–1962), cardinal, diplomat. A native of Wisconsin, M. was ordained for the Diocese of Milwaukee in 1913. He became a professor and later rector of St. Francis Seminary; he was named bp. of Fargo, N. Dak. in 1935. He was a competent administrator of his diocese and became a national spokesman for Catholics in rural areas as coeditor of *Manifesto on Rural Life* and president of the National Catholic Rural Life Conference. In 1946 M. condemned the Morgenthau plan, a primitive punitive project against defeated Germany. Appointed apostolic visitator to Germany that same year, M. was also religious consultant to the commanding American officer in occupied Germany and Vatican appointed administrator of papal relief in Germany. Named an abp. in 1949 and regent of the apostolic nunciature in Germany, he became papal nuncio in 1951 to West Germany. In 1959 Pope John XXIII created M. cardinal and assigned him to the Roman Curia, the first American to so serve.

[J. R. AHERNE]

MUEZZIN (Arab. *mu'a<u>d</u>din*), the one who calls out the *a<u>d</u>ân* or call to prayer for Muslims. The call is given from the minaret (see MOSQUE), often by loudspeaker, five times a day, when every Muslim is obliged to pray (see ISLAM). The *a<u>d</u>ân* of the *Shiites differs but slightly from that of the *Sunnites.

[R. M. FRANK]

MUFFAT, two musicians in Austria, father and son of Scottish descent. **Georg** (1653–1704), composer and organist. A student of Lully's style in Paris for 6 years, he later served as organist to the bp. of Salzburg (1678) and as organist (1690) and *Kapellmeister* (1695) to the bp. of Passau. His compositions include organ works, instrumental music, and orchestral suites. He developed the German concerto grosso. **Gottlieb** (Theophil; 1690–1770), son of Georg, composer of 72 fugues, 12 toccatas for organ and *Componimenti musicali* for harpsichord. He studied under Fux in Vienna, served as court and chamber organist to Charles VI in Vienna (1717), and became first organist (1741). His students included the Empress Maria Theresa and Wagenseil.

[R. J. LITZ]

MUFTI, In *Islam an expert in canon law who, at the quest of a judge or a private individual, issues an authoritative opinion on the application of the law to the particular case. This opinion, known as a *fatwâ*, is not based on the individual mufti's judgment but on the binding precedents and principles of the law. *ISLAMIC LAW.

[R. M. FRANK]

MUGHALS (Moguls), Muslim dynasty ruling India from 1526 to 1857. As the Arabic and Persian form of Mongol, the name is misleading since most of the rulers were Turks and Afghans. The dynasty, which claimed descent from Genghis Khan and Tamerlane, was founded by Babur (1483–1530) who gained control of Delhi and Agra. The empire was widely extended by Babur's grandson *Akbar (1556–1605) who followed a policy of religious moderation. The reign of Shah Jahan (1627–66), builder of the Taj Mahal, marked the high point of Mughal art and architecture. His son and successor Aurangzeb (1658–1707) tried to force a general conversion to Islam. The empire gained its greatest extent during Aurangzeb's reign, but he also prepared the way, particularly by his religious intolerance, for its later dissolution. Independent dynasties arose after his death, and the Marathas of the Deccan revolted. Despite the defeat of the Marathas in 1761, the empire was weakened and the British assumed control early in the next cent. though they maintained puppet emperors until 1857. Bahadur Shah II, last of the Mughal emperors, was involved in the *Sepoy Mutiny and condemned to exile. BIBLIOGRAPHY: S. M. Edwardes and H. L. O. Garrett, *Mughal Rule in India* (1930).

[T. EARLY]

MUHAMMAD, see MOHAMMED.

MÜHLENBERG, HENRY MELCHIOR (1711–87), commonly designated ''Patriarch of the Lutheran Church in America.'' A native of Eimbeck, Hannover, Ger., M. took up the study of theology in 1735 at the Univ. of Göttingen. After serving as a pastor at Grosshennersdorf, Upper Silesia (1739–41), M. accepted a call to the United Lutheran Congregations in Pennsylvania. He was officially recognized as the duly appointed pastor at Philadelphia in 1742. He traveled extensively through eastern Pa., preaching and administering the sacraments. After establishing and nurturing a large number of congregations, M. organized (1748) the Pennsylvania Ministerium, the first Lutheran *synod in the United States. In the years following he extended his work also into western Pa., N.J., and N.Y., and in later years visited the Lutheran churches in the South. He exercised a decisive influence on early Lutheranism all along the Atlantic seaboard. BIBLIOGRAPHY: W. J. Mann, *Life and Times of Henry Melchior Mühlenberg* (1911); T. G. Tappert and J. W. Doberstein, *Journals of Henry Melchior Mühlenberg* (3 v., 1942–58).

[R. BEESE]

MUHLENBERG, WILLIAM AUGUSTUS (1796–1877), priest and leader in the Protestant Episcopal Church. The great grandson of H. M. *Mühlenberg, M. was baptized a Lutheran but brought up as an Episcopalian. Graduating from the Univ. of Pennsylvania in 1815, he was ordained deacon in 1817 and priest in 1820. In his early career he became renowned as an educator through the schools he established on Long Island, New York. In 1846 he became rector of the Church of the Holy Communion, New York City. The parish had its own social agencies and initiated many practices that became general in the Episcopal Church, e.g., daily Offices, weekly Eucharist, emphasis on Holy Week. In 1850 he founded St. Luke's Hospital, and in 1852 a community of deaconesses, Sisters of the Holy Communion, to staff it. On a visit to England M. had come to know Pusey, Newman, and the *Oxford movement. He developed his own ideas of an ''Evangelical Catholicism,'' and his influence was important in lessening tension between *high-church and *broad-church parties within his Church. He presented the so-called ''Muhlenberg Memorial'' to the *House of Bishops in 1853; although controversial, it did lead to the formation of the Commission on Church Unity and to liturgical reforms. BIBLIOGRAPHY: Olmstead, 318–320; A. Ayres, *Life and Work of William Augustus Muhlenberg* (1894).

[M. A. GARDNER]

MULLANPHY, BRYAN (d. 1851), philanthropist. A son of Irish-born philanthropist John Mullanphy, whose family was responsible for establishing several religious institutions and orders in the St. Louis area, M. was elected mayor of St. Louis in 1847 and served as a judge. He left a sizable portion of his estate to found the Mullanphy Emigrant and Travelers' Relief Fund to aid needy travelers in the West. It became associated with the National Traveler's Aid Society in 1934.

[M. A. MCFADDEN]

MULLANY, AZARIAS OF THE CROSS, BROTHER (1847–93), well-known Catholic educator, Christian Brother, and essayist, much of whose wide-ranging literary output was posthumously compiled into *Essays Educational, Essays Philosophical, Essays Miscellaneous* (1896). Born Patrick Francis Mullany near Killenaule, County Tipperary, Ireland, he immigrated to Deerfield, N.Y., in 1857, was taught by the Brothers of the Christian Schools in Utica, and joined that congregation in 1862. He subsequently taught at Albany, New York City, and Philadelphia; was president of Rockhill College, Ellicott City, Md., and was a founder of the Catholic Summer School at Plattsburg, New York.

[E. J. DILLON]

MÜLLER, ADAM HEINRICH (1779–1829), German economist and political philosopher. A convert to Catholicism, he developed a romantic system of economics and political theory that foreshadowed national socialism.

[P. J. HENNESSEY]

MÜLLER, F. MAX (1823–1900), German orientalist and linguist. He was responsible for many of the early developments in this field; his major work was his editing of the monumental *The Sacred Books of the East*, in 51 volumes (1879–1904).

[P. J. HENNESSEY]

MÜLLER, GEORG (1805–98), German-born preacher whose work was chiefly in England. He had a conversion experience as a student at Halle in 1825, went to England for evangelical work in 1829 and there joined the Plymouth Brethren. He spent the rest of his life in Bristol, preaching and caring for orphans, relying solely on alms. The last 17 years of his life were spent in worldwide evangelization. He wrote *Narrative of the Lord's Dealings with George Müller* (2 v., 1837, 1841).

[T. C. O'BRIEN]

MÜLLER, JAN (1922–58), German expressionist painter working in the U.S. (1941). M.'s visionary studies of mutilated, distorted figures relate to the older German expressionist tradition, and even to German medieval painting (*Temptation of St. Anthony,* 1957).

[M. J. DALY]

MÜLLER, KARL OTFRIED (1797–1840), German Hellenic scholar. His *Geschichten hellenischer Stamme und Stadte* (1820) inspired widespread interest in the field of Hellenic studies.

[P. J. HENNESSEY]

MÜLLER, LUDWIG (1833–1945), Nazi *Reichbischof.* He played an important role in the consolidation of Nazi power in Germany. After M., a chaplain in E Prussia, had won over the chief of staff, Walther von Reichenau, to Nazi ideas, the two men exerted significant influence on their commander, Werner von Blomberg, who became defense minister at the same time Adolf Hitler became chancellor. Blomberg promptly assured Hitler of the army's cooperation with the new government. Hitler appointed M. plenipotentiary for negotiations with the various Lutheran church bodies in Germany, which were in the process of forming a united national body. The Nazi government favored such a union, since it might simplify control of the Church for political purposes; but the first national meeting elected a highly respected conservative pastor, Friedrich von Bodelschwingh, as *Reichsbischof* instead of Müller. The pro-Nazi *German Christians protested the legality of the election and appealed to the Prussian ministry of education, which took over the administration of the Lutheran Church in Prussia. When Bodelschwingh bowed to these pressures and resigned, M. proclaimed himself *Reichsbischof*-elect. With the obvious backing of the regime, he was elected *Reichsbischof* at the national synod at Wittenberg on September 27, 1933. In December M. merged the Lutheran youth movement with the Hitler Youth, and in January 1934 he persuaded most of the Lutheran bps. to sign a declaration of "unreserved loyalty to the Third Reich and its *Führer*." In spite of the use of threats of force and of illegal and arbitrary decrees, M. was an ineffectual administrator; he was unable to control the *Confessing Church established in 1934 to oppose the Nazi takeover of the Church (see BARMEN DECLARATION). The creation of a Nazi ministry of Church affairs in July 1935 left M. with little prestige and no authority. The Gestapo prevented him from preaching in public. M. returned to his home in Königsberg and oblivion; in July 1945 he committed suicide. BIBLIOGRAPHY: J.S. Conway, *Nazi Persecution of the Churches*, 1933–45 (1968).

[R. J. GIBBONS]

MÜLLER, OTTO (1874–1930), German Expressionist painter and printmaker. Among his best known works are *The Judgment of Paris* and *The Large Bathers*.

[P. J. HENNESSEY]

MULLINS, EDGAR YOUNG (1860–1928), Baptist clergyman and teacher. After serving pastorates (1885–99), M. became president and professor of systematic theology at Southern Baptist Theological Seminary, Louisville, Ky. His administration was marked by expansion of the school, and his teaching and writings strongly influenced Southern Baptists. Elected president of their Convention (1921–24), he also served as president of the *Baptist World Alliance (1923–28). Presiding over the seminary in an era when theological tensions were mounting in American Protestantism, M. sought to avoid the extremes of rigid conservatism or liberal reductionism. Although retaining a framework of supernaturalism, he was greatly influenced by the personalism of B. P. *Browne, and he made Christian experience central in his system. The objective facts of Christian revelation in history are corroborated by the Holy Spirit in the individual's experience, giving him a direct knowledge of God. *Christian Religion in Its Doctrinal Expression* (1920) was the fullest elaboration of his approach. Closely related to his emphasis upon religious experience was an individualistic strain, which is reflected in *Axioms of Religion* (1908). BIBLIOGRAPHY: W. A. Mueller, *History of Southern Baptist Seminary* (1959); Smith-Jamison 1:303–309.

[N. H. MARING]

MULRY, THOMAS MAURICE (1855–1916), American businessman and leading Catholic layman, a pioneer in influencing the Catholic charities movement in the U.S.; a founder of the National Conference of Catholic Charities, and elected its president in 1907. At first associated with his father as an excavation contractor, he went into banking, insurance, and real estate, becoming in 1906 the president of the Emigrant Industrial Savings Bank. He was first president of the Superior Council of the U.S. Society of St. Vincent de Paul (1915), helped establish the Fordham School of Social Work, and founded St. Elizabeth's Home for Convalescent Women and Girls. He is the author of *The Government in Charity* (1912). Among his 13 children four sons were Jesuits and one daughter a Sister of Charity.

[E. J. DILLON]

MULTSCHER, HANS (*c.*1400–67), German sculptor who carved the Wurzach Altar (1437) and the *Sterzing Altar* (*c.*1456–58), but likely did not paint the eight panels of the life of Mary and the Passion of Christ appearing in each work. M.'s sculptured *Schmerzensmann* (1430) and *Standing Madonna* (1440) blend the realism of Sluter and his Burgundian school with the German *Weicher Stil*.

[M. J. DALY]

MUN, ALBERT DE (1841–1914), pioneer in Catholic social thought and action in France, where, as a member of the Chamber of Deputies (1881–1914) his speeches and activities championed the cause of social legislation to benefit the worker. M. was an ardent Catholic and sought to bring Christian principles to bear on social problems.

[T. C. O'BRIEN]

MUNCH, EDVARD (1863–1944), Norwegian painter, in Paris (1889) influenced by Gauguin. M. sought to paint the human suffering of life as a sacred element. Through family experience with disease and death M. identified with unbearable tension, psychic anguish and an existentialist inescapable loneliness. His *Dance of Life* (1900), a counterpart of the medieval *Dance of Death,* examines the despair of life from innocence to the ravages of time. Friend of Kierkegaard, Strindberg, and Dostoievsky, M. by the drama of medium in his graphic work in woodcuts and lithographs added a new force to his tragic message.

[M. J. DALY]

MUNDELEIN, GEORGE WILLIAM (1872–1939), cardinal. A native of New York City, M. was ordained for the Brooklyn Diocese in 1895. Serving as associate secretary to the bp. of Brooklyn, he became chancellor in 1897 and in 1909 was named auxiliary bp. of his diocese. At the age of 43, M. was appointed abp. of Chicago (1915). Keenly interested in the training of students for the priesthood, he built Quigley Preparatory Seminary and the major seminary, St. Mary of the Lake, the latter becoming a place of many benefactions by the archbishop. M. never forgot the struggles he and his family experienced by reason of their poverty, consistently aiding the poor and laboring segment of Chicago. In 1918 he reorganized the charitable organizations of his archdiocese forming a central office of Catholic Charities.

Named a cardinal in 1924, M. made preparations for holding the 28th International Eucharistic Congress in Chicago in 1926, an event that became a landmark in such religious gatherings in the U.S. A major contributor to the newly erected Progaganda College in Rome, M. established the Colegio S. Maria del Lago for postgraduate studies in the Eternal City.

In 1937 he denounced the Nazi persecution in Germany and made the controversial reference to Hitler as an ''Austrian paperhanger,'' an allusion that drew rebukes from the Vatican and the U.S. State Department. M. became a close friend of President Franklin D. Roosevelt. BIBLIOGRAPHY: *First Cardinal of the West* (comp. P. R. Martin, 1934).

[J. R. AHERNE]

MUNDWILER, FINTAN (1835–98), second abbot of St. Meinrad's Abbey in Indiana. Born in Dietikon, Zurich, he studied at Einsiedeln, entered that monastery (1854), was ordained (1859), and sent to the newly founded St. Meinrad, where he was the first prior (1870) before becoming abbot (1880). He was the first president (1881) of the Swiss-American Congregation of the Benedictines and drew up that congregation's statutes.

[E. J. DILLON]

MUNGUÍA, CLEMENTE DE JESÚS (1810–68), Mexican bp., scholar, and prolific writer, defender of the traditional prerogatives of the Church against the 19th-cent. movement of Liberal reform. He practiced law in Morelia and Mexico City before ordination in 1841, was vicar general and vicar of the curia in Morelia and rector of the seminary (1843) before becoming bp. of Michoacán (1850). He was named president of the council of state by the dictator Santa Anna, was exiled briefly (1856) by President Comonfort, and again sent into exile after the victory of the Liberal reform and Benito Juárez (1861). With the French invasion of Mexico he returned as first abp. of Morelia (1863). Disillusioned with Emperor Maximilian, he went into final exile in 1865, ending his days in Rome.

[E. J. DILLON]

MUNICH, UNIVERSITY OF (Ludwig-Maximilians-Universität München), a state institution of higher learning, originally founded in Ingolstadt on the Danube (1472), but since 1826 located in Munich, West Germany. Approved by a bull issued by Pius II (1459) to Ludwig the Rich, Duke of Bavaria, the university did not open until 1472 because of political upheavals. Although modeled on the Univ. of Vienna and endowed with the same privileges, Ingolstadt was not divided into nations. Its chancellor was the bp. of Eichstätt, and the rector was chosen in turn from each of the four faculties (arts, theology, philosophy, and law) by vote. The then current philosophical controversy caused the faculty of arts to divide itself into two *viae*—nominalists and realists—until the duke ordered their reunion (1478). As required in the papal bull, each candidate for a degree was obliged to take an oath of obedience to the Holy See. This was the first time such a stipulation had been made by Rome in approving a university. The university became a center of humanistic studies with such outstanding scholars as C. *Celtis, Jakob Locher, *Aventinus, and Paulus Laymann. During the Reformation, esp. under chancellor Leonard von Eck, the university became a Catholic stronghold and later trained leaders of the German Counter Reformation. From 1594 until the suppression of the Society of Jesus (1773), there were Jesuits on the faculties of theology and philosophy. Among the first Jesuits named were Peter Canisius and Alfonso Salmerón. Throughout the 17th cent., Ingolstadt, despite the disturbances of the Thirty Years' War (1618–48), continued to be a center of learning. In the 18th cent. the university came under the influence of rationalism and the Enlightenment, mainly through the activities of Adam Weishaupt (1748–1830), who tried to make the university a center for the *Illuminati. Originally supported by church endowments and revenues, the university found itself in financial straits and in 1800 was transferred to Landshut, and in 1826 to Munich. Under teachers such as J. J. von *Görres, F. W. J. von *Schelling, and J. J. I. von *Döllinger, the university again became a center of Catholic scholarship. It was severely damaged during World War II, but has since been reconstructed. The faculty of theology (Catholic) was closed under the Nazis in 1939, but reopened in 1946, and confers the licentiate and doctorate. The library, founded in 1472, contains 870,000 volumes and 4,237 MSS. BIBLIOGRAPHY: H. Rashdall, *Universities of Europe during the Middle Ages* (ed. F. M. Powicke and A. B. Emden, 3 v., 1936); International Handbook of Universities (1967).

[M. B. MURPHY]

MUNICH METHOD IN CATECHETICS, an adaptation to catechetics of the psychology of learning as developed by J. F. Herbart and T. Ziller, considered an improvement over the prevailing method involving word analysis and rote memory. It is an expression of a pedagogy that appeals to the whole person, including senses, imagination, and the appetitive powers, with a view toward application, response, and action.

[E. J. DILLON]

MUNIFICENTISSIMUS DEUS (most bountiful God), first words of the apostolic constitution of Pius XII (1950), defining RC doctrine on Mary's Assumption into heaven. In addition to its content, the definition is significant insofar as it does not place the basis for its proclamation upon a scriptural argument but upon the common faith of the RC community, ascertained by Pius XII in an inquiry sent to all the bps. of the world. The definition reads: "We pronounce, declare and define it to be a divinely revealed dogma that the Immaculate Mother of God, the ever Virgin Mary, having completed the course of her earthly life, was assumed body and soul into heavenly glory." BIBLIOGRAPHY: Pius XII, "*Munificentissimus Deus,*" *AAS* 42 (1950) 753–771; Eng. *Catholic Mind* 49 (1951) 65–78; J. W. Langlinais, NCE 10:77. *ASSUMPTION OF MARY.

[T. R. HEATH]

MUNKACSY, MIHALY VON (1844–1909), Hungarian painter who settled in Paris, 1872, executing, within a broad range of subjects, a *Christ before Pilate* (1881, Philadelphia) with a romantic quality which distinguished him from the French realists of his day.

[M. J. DALY]

MUÑOZ, VICENTE (1699–1784), Spanish-born Franciscan, church architect in Argentina: the church of S. Francisco, Buenos Aires, the cathedral of Córdoba (Argentina), and the Franciscan church at Salta were of his design.

MÜNSTER, SEBASTIAN (1488–1552), Hebrew scholar and Bible translator. M. was ordained a Franciscan priest but converted to Lutheranism. He taught Hebrew at the universities of Heidelberg and Basel, and published a Hebrew text of the Bible together with a Latin translation (2 v., 1534–35). His illustrated works on geography and cosmology were used throughout Europe.

[T. M. MCFADDEN]

MÜNZER, THOMAS (*c.* 1489–1525), German radical Reformer. He was well educated and widely read in the mystics. Ordained a RC priest in 1513, he was a chaplain for nuns when he became acquainted with Luther *c.* 1519. He had already developed his own spiritualistic views of the Christian life and radical social theories. With Nicholas Storch he was one of the *Zwickau Prophets who caused turmoil at Wittenberg (1521–22) with the message of inner spiritual experience and the establishment of a kingdom of the just by force. Driven out of Wittenberg, he tried to establish a new "Church of the Spirit" at Prague, writing the "Prague Manifesto," his program of reform and social change. His efforts failed; he returned to Germany and served (1523–24) as priest at the small town of Allstedt. There he made a translation of the liturgy into German. He also began agitation for violent revolution to establish a new social order. He had to flee from Allstedt, and in Aug. 1523 became a preacher at Mülhausen in Thuringia. Between Feb. and May 1525 he was the chief agitator in the Peasants' War. When the peasants were defeated at Frankenhausen on May 15, he was captured; he was beheaded on May 27. He is said to have reaffirmed the RC faith before his death. M.'s theological position, never clear, is disputed by historians. Anabaptist scholars repudiate the title often given him, "Father of Anabaptism." Modern socialists have been interested in his radical theories. BIBLIOGRAPHY: R. Friedman, MennEnc 3:785–789, with complete bibliog.; E. W. Gritsch, *Reformer without a Church* (1969).

[T. C. O'BRIEN]

MURAT, JOACHIM (1767–1815), brilliant French cavalry leader whose name is linked with numerous victories of Napoleon Bonaparte. He was made a marshal of France, grand duke of Berg, and finally king of Naples (1808–15) in the Napoleonic Empire. He was the son of the manager of the estates of Talleyrand-Périgord and studied briefly for a career in the Church before entering upon his military career. As king of Naples he ended feudalism in his domain, broke up the vast landed estates, introduced the Code Napoléon, supported Napoleon's annexation of the States of the Church, condoned the arrest of Pius VII (1809), and set in motion currents that eventually played a major role in Italian unification and independence. He was betrayed by Metternich and his allies when he attempted to salvage his kingdom from the disintegrating empire of Napoleon. He was deposed, and in a futile, last attempt to regain his kingdom, captured and executed.

[E. J. DILLON]

MURATORI, LODOVICO ANTONIO (1672–1750), historian. Ordained to the priesthood (1695), M. began his life work at the Bibliotheca Ambrosiana in Milan. Pastoral obligations were assumed at Ferrara (1711) and Modena (1716), which he fulfilled with serious responsibility in addition to his prodigious literary and historical work. The quarrel between the papacy and the dukes of Este over the possession of the city of Commachio led to his writing *Antichità estensi*, which supported the house of Este. Then M. produced the three great source works important for the history of Italy: *Rerum italicarum scriptores, Antiquitates italicae medii aevi,* and *Novus thesaurus veterum inscriptionum*. His concern for religion unfettered by useless accretions was expounded in his *Regolata divozione*. Numerous publications on literature, theology, and philosophy attest to his versatility. His dedication to truth, to his ideals, and to historical inquiry incurred the wrath of contemporaries who resented his conclusions on the temporal power of the papacy, the need for reform in the Church, and the veneration of saints. Pius XII in 1951 gave public assurance of his submission to the Holy See. BIBLIOGRAPHY: H. Rumpler, NCE 10:81; H. Jedin, LTK 7:692; É. Amann, DTC 10 (2) 2547–56; E. Cochrane, "Muratori: The Vocation of a Historian," CHR 51 (1965) 153–172.

[J. M. O'DONNELL]

MURATORIAN CANON (Muratorian Fragment), earliest known list of writings (2d cent.) approved as Scripture for use in the Church at Rome, and with some omissions (Heb, 1 and 2 Pet, 3 Jn) and additions (Wis and the apocryphal Apocalypse of Peter) corresponding to the present NT canon. Discovered in 1740 in the Ambrosian Library in Milan by L. A. Muratori (1672–1750), the fragment is 85 lines of a longer, lost MS, written in the barbarous Latin of the 8th cent., but regarded as a translation of a 2d-cent. Greek document. Some, however, date this canon from the 4th century.

[T. EARLY]

MURBACH, ABBEY OF (*Murbachum, Florida Vallis, Vivarium peregrinorum*), former Benedictine abbey, dedicated to Our Lady and to SS. Michael, Peter, Paul, and Leger. It was founded. *c*. 727 on the banks of the Murbach in the present diocese of Strasbourg by St. Pirmin of Reichenau with the aid of Count Eberhard. Destroyed by the Hungarians in 929, it was rebuilt and was again damaged during the Thirty Years' War. In the 13th cent. the abbot of Murbach was made a prince of the empire; and in the 14th cent., only noblemen were admitted to the community. After vain attempts to restore common life, the abbey was secularized in 1764. It was suppressed in 1890. Still in existence are the transept, choir, and two towers of the church built *c*.1160 and containing the tomb of seven martyr-monks in the form of the Holy House of Loreto. They are the most significant pre-Gothic remains in Alsace. BIBLIOGRAPHY: Cottineau 2:2016–18.

[J. DAOUST]

MURDER, see HOMICIDE.

MURI, ABBEY OF, the title belonging to a Benedictine monastery in Gries, Bolzano, Italy, but formerly to the 1027 foundations at Aargau, Diocese of Basel, Switzerland. The monks were forced to leave Aargau because of secularizing policy in 1841. The original foundation was made from Einsiedeln, under patronage of the Habsburgs, but from 1139 was under papal jurisdiction. After the ravages of the Reformation, the monastery was revived by Abbot Johann Singeisen, and shared in formation (1602) of the Swiss Benedictine Congregation. By the time of the expulsion of the monks in 1841 it had become one of the richest abbeys in Switzerland. The abbey of Aargau is now an insane asylum; the church is still used by a parish.

[T. C. O'BRIEN]

MURIALDO, LEONARDO, BL. (1828–1900), founder, educator. A native of Turin, Italy, M. was ordained in 1851. His chief work became the education of poor boys. As rector of the Collegio Artigianelli in Turin he developed a respected school for the vocational training of young men. M. founded in 1873 the Pious Congregation of St. Joseph, of which he was first superior general. Active as promoter of Catholic labor movements, the Catholic press, and numerous other forms of what would later be called Catholic Action, M. became a national figure in Italy. He was beatified in 1963. BIBLIOGRAPHY: J. Cottino, BiblSanct 9:679–681.

[J. R. AHERNE]

MURILLO, BARTOLOMÉ ESTEBAN (1617–82), Spanish artist famous for painting *Inmaculadas,* Virgins, the Child Jesus, saints, and poor people. Studying with Juan del Castillo until 1639, M.'s *Vision of Fray Santerio,* though cold, is strongly painted. His *Holy Family* and *Adoration of the Shepherds* show the influence of Zurbarán; a series of 11 works for the Franciscans of Seville (1645–46) show M.'s genius for narrative through relating to Ribera Zurbarán, while *S. Diego of Alcalá Feeding the Poor* derives from Pacheco. Having surpassed Zurbarán, M. in

1655 painted *St. Leander, St. Isidore and the Birth of the Virgin, Christ Healing the Paralytic* (1671–75), the beautiful *Santiago Madonna* (New York), and the popular *Soult Inmaculada* (1678, Prado), swiftly brushed, lyrical and tender with an airiness almost rococo. He died of a fall while painting *The Mystic Marriage of St. Catherine* for the Capuchins in Cádiz. Famous in the 19th cent., in the 20th cent. considered insipid and oversentimental, M.'s works of virtuoso brushwork, flowing composition and rich color, though not profound, but full of charm and grace, do signal a decline in Spanish art until the advent of Goya.

[M. J. DALY]

MURJIITES (Arab., *al-murji'a*), an early Islamic theological school which, in opposition to the *Kharijites, held that works are not a part of faith or belief (*îmân*). The common doctrine (generally referred to as *al-irjâ'*) of the Murjiites, which is variously elaborated in its detail, is that faith, by which a person is a believer and so a member of the Muslim community, is not qualified or in any way dependent upon good works. Though nearly all later authorities explicitly reject *irjâ'*, as contrary to the teaching of several early theorists, in their basic contention that any one who professes to be a Muslim is to be considered a true member of the community and that legal political authority is to be obeyed as representing the will of God, the Murjiites represented, in fact, the great majority of the Muslim community in the early 8th century. Moreover, their doctrine is reflected by the Hanafites (see ISLAMIC LAW) and the traditionists (see HADITH). BIBLIOGRAPHY: Gibb-Kramers SEI, s.v. "Murdji'a."

[R. M. FRANK]

MURNER, THOMAS (1475–1537), German Franciscan, spokesman for German Catholics in the 16th cent.; prolific satirist and relentless critic not only of Luther and Fischart, but also of abuses in his own camp. Widely traveled, a learned and productive humanist, M. was chosen poet laureate by Emperor Maximilian in 1505, visited England at the invitation of King Henry VIII, represented the bp. of Strasbourg at the Nuremberg Diet, and received doctorates from the universities of Freiburg and Basel. He imitated and surpassed S. Brant. Driven from Strasbourg by insurgent farmers in 1525, he fled to Lucerne, but was soon expelled by followers of Zwingli. He died as pastor in his hometown of Oberehnheim (Alsace). Works: *Thomas Murner, Deutsche Schriften* (ed. F. Schultz, 9 v. 1918–31). BIBLIOGRAPHY: N. Scheid, CE 10:645–646.

[S. A. SCHULZ]

MÛRŌNÎTO̱, West Syrian episcopal staff, surmounted by two entwined serpents parting at the top to face each other over a globe surmounted by a small cross.

[A. CODY]

MURPHY, JOHN (1753–98), Irish rebel priest, born at Tincurry, County Wexford, Ireland. Having gained some instruction in a hedge school, he managed to acquire an education in Seville, Spain, then returned to Ireland a priest in 1785. He was assistant priest of the parish of Boulavogue, Diocese of Ferns, where his sincere piety won him the respect of all. He was probably driven to rebellion by outrages committed by the military against his parishioners. In May 1798 he initiated revolt in County Wexford and displayed considerable military ability in the battles that followed. He was probably captured near Kilcomney Hill, taken to Tullow, insulted and whipped, and finally hanged and beheaded, his body burned.

[E. J. DILLON]

MURRABA'AT, wadi about 15 miles SE of Jerusalem near the Dead Sea where some of the *Dead Sea Scrolls were discovered. In 1951 Bedouins of the Ta'amireh tribe, who had discovered the scrolls at Qumran, about 11 miles north, offered for sale new materials they had found in caves of Wadi Murraba'at; early in 1952 they led archeologists to the area. About half way up a 600-foot cliff, the explorers found four caves that had been used for refuge at various periods, including the Second Jewish Revolt (132–135 A.D.). MSS from the caves, dating from the 2d cent. A.D. included biblical texts of a Masoretic type and two letters signed by *Simon Bar Cocheba. Excavators at Murraba'at also found wooden utensils and rush mats, the first time perishable materials of such antiquity had been found in Palestine. BIBLIOGRAPHY: R. E. Brown, JBC 2:556.

[T. EARLY]

MURRAY, DANIEL (1768–1852), bishop. A native of Ireland ordained in 1792, M. served in and around Dublin until 1809 when he was named coadjutor with right of succession to the abp. of Dublin. Though reluctant to engage in politics he had little choice in the critical time for the Church in Ireland. He led the opposition to granting the British government the right to veto ecclesiastical appointments in Ireland and succeeded in defeating the proposal. Archbishop of Dublin from 1823 until his death, he cofounded the Irish Sisters of Charity and encouraged the coming of the Sisters of Mercy to Dublin as well as the Ladies of Loretto and the Irish Christian brothers, built schools and hospitals for the poor. Not an ardent nationalist, he frequently opposed the position taken on certain issues by Daniel O'Connell and the Irish bishops. M. was often called on to advise the British government on Irish affairs.

[J. R. AHERNE]

MURRAY, JOHN COURTNEY (1904–67), Jesuit theologian, author, ecumenist, and chief architect of the *Declaration on Religious Liberty* (*Dignitatis Humanae*) of Vatican Council II. M. was born in New York City; he entered the Society of Jesus (1920); studied at St. Andrew-on-Hudson, Poughkeepsie, N.Y. (1920–24); at Weston College, Weston, Mass. (1924–27); and at Boston College (1927). He spent 3 years teaching Latin and English literature in the Philippines and returned to Woodstock College, Woodstock, Md., to study theology in 1930. He was ordained in 1933 and pursued further studies at the Gregorian Univ. in Rome (1934–36). He was then assigned to the Jesuit theology faculty in Woodstock and remained on the faculty until his death. M.'s field of specialization in theology was the Trinity. During his studies, however, he became extremely interested in the problem of *Church and State and made himself an expert in this area. As early as 1945 he engaged in an extensive debate on the issue with two theologians at The Catholic Univ., Joseph C. Fenton and Francis J. Connell. The debate was epoch making in American creative theology but resulted in M.'s receiving direction not to publish further on the Church-State issue without first clearing his writings with his superiors in Rome. It is recognized, however, that his contribution to the Church-State issue was formative for later theological development and eventually culminated in his recognition as the outstanding American theological expert at Vatican Council II. He was not invited to the first session of the council since he was still somewhat under a cloud for his Church-State theories. However, Cardinal Spellman made him his personal theological expert at the remaining three sessions, and whatever suspicions may have lingered about M.'s orthodoxy were dispelled when he was chosen to be one of the concelebrants with Pope Paul VI of a Mass in the presence of the assembled council fathers.

In addition to his many articles in *Theological Studies*, of which he was the first editor-in-chief, a position he retained until his death, M. wrote several books, including: *We Hold These Truths* (1961); *The Problem of God: Yesterday and Today* (1964); and *The Problem of Religious Freedom* (pa., 1965). He edited *Freedom and Man* (1965) and *Religious Liberty: An End and a Beginning* (1966). For 2 years he was an associate editor of *America*, the weekly Jesuit magazine; he was twice visiting professor of medieval philosophy and culture at Yale. In his personal life, M. was a man of conservative habit who was known as the exemplar of what he liked to call the "tradition of civility." Of the *Declaration on Human Freedom*, M. himself wrote that it promised a new confidence in ecumenical relationships and a new straightforwardness in relationships between the Church and the world. BIBLIOGRAPHY: *Modern Theologians: Christians and Jews* (ed. Thomas Bird, 1967) 18–39; T. T. Love, *John Courtney Murray: Contemporary Church-State Theory* (1965).

[J. P. WHALEN]

MURRAY, PATRICK (1811–82), Irish theologian. He entered Maynooth (1829), was elected a Dunboyne scholar, was ordained, and served as curate in Dublin. In 1838 he was appointed to a chair in theology at Maynooth, which he occupied until his death. In 1879 he was made prefect of the *Dunboyne Establishment. His writings include the four-volume *Essays, Chiefly Theological* (1850–53); the three-volume *De ecclesia Christi* (1860–66); and *De gratia* (1877).

[E. J. DILLON]

MURRAY, PHILIP (1886–1952), labor leader. A Scot who emigrated to the U.S. at age 16, M. worked in the coal mines of W Pennsylvania. Here he learned from bitter experience the harsh treatment of the mining companies. He was unjustly discharged and forced to leave the company-owned town. Determined to work for better conditions for the miners, he was elected in 1912 to the executive committee of the United Mine Workers of America, became vice president in 1920, and served as such for 20 years. In 1936 M. headed the national effort to organize the United Steelworkers of America, and served as its president until his death. In 1940 M. was elected president of the Congress of Industrial Organizations (CIO) and remained president until his death. M. was the trusted adviser of Presidents Franklin D. Roosevelt and Harry S. Truman, a labor statesman imbued with the spirit of the papal statements on labor, a gentle but firm leader among labor-union giants.

[J. R. AHERNE]

MURRI, ROMOLO (1870–1944), Italian priest, sociologist, political leader, journalist, and writer, early leader of the movement toward social democracy among Italian Catholics. He was ordained priest 1893, studied at the Univ. of Rome, and founded the periodical *Vita nuova* (1895–97), which provided a basis for the Italian Catholic student federation. Later he founded the review *Cultura sociale* (1898–1906). When Pius X intervened to reshape Catholic Action in an antidemocratic spirit under the tight control of the hierarchy, M. struggled against this trend. He founded the National Democratic League, which was condemned by Pius X in 1906. M.'s name became linked with the Modernists. He was suspended *a divinis* in 1907 and excommunicated in 1909. He laid aside his clerical garb, married, entered the politics of the left, and was elected deputy. He wrote for the *Revista di cultura*, organ of the Church-condemned League, and later for such journals as *Il Corriere della Sera* and *La Stampa*. His numerous topical writings illumine the social and political struggles of those times. In 1943, a year before his death, he was reconciled to the Church. BIBLIOGRAPHY: F. Caraffa, EncCatt 8:1534–35; A. Martini, NCE 10:88; *idem*, LTK 7:697–98.

[E. J. DILLON]

MUSIC, BYZANTINE, see BYZANTINE MUSIC.

MUSIC, HEBREW, see JEWISH MUSIC.

MUSIC, LITURGICAL, music used in the public worship of the Church, i.e., in conjunction with the celebration of the Eucharist, of the other sacramental rites, of Benediction, and of the Liturgy of the Hours. Liturgical, or what is also called church music, is to be distinguished, therefore, from more general terms such as sacred, religious, or spiritual music. The Church, from her very beginnings, has been concerned with the music of worship and has exercised efforts to bar music that is inappropriate and to promote music of a kind that gives glory to God, to lift the worshiper up to God, and to create a real sense of community.

The early Christians in their gatherings for worship adopted Jewish psalmody. The music of those early centuries was monodic and strictly vocal in character, the early Church Fathers having rejected all musical instruments as being associated with pagan rites. This monody, or chant, varied greatly within the ever-widening Christian community. Families of chant developed in the East and in the West. Gregory the Great (d. 604) attempted to bring order into the liturgical chants, and the foundation of a *schola cantorum* eventually brought about a Roman chant tradition. By the end of the 9th cent. a vast and highly developed musical repertoire of Gregorian melodies had developed, to which were added freely composed texts and melodies. These latter gave birth to tropes and sequences, new responses, antiphons, and metrical processional hymns. Liturgical chants were grouped into books such as the *graduale* (Mass chants) and the *antiphonale* (Office chants).

The development of polyphony, a sign of profound change, occasioned division between ''modernists'' and conservatives. In response, Pope John XXII issued (1322) an instruction emphasizing the central position that the traditional chant melodies must retain but, at the same time, permitting the use of polyphony as a means of enhancing these melodies. Between the time of this pronouncement and that of the next major legislation by the Council of Trent, the Church enjoyed the flowering of sacred polyphony under Palestrina, Byrd, Victoria, and others. The Council of Trent (1545–63) called for the banning of secular texts and melodies and for greater intelligibility, and also gave its blessing to polyphony. The reform of the chant books decreed by the Council turned out to be little less than disastrous for the Gregorian melodies, and plainsong from this time began a temporary decline.

The operatic style of the Baroque era which followed, the orchestral emphasis in the Classic period, and the emotional and sometimes sentimental overtones of the Romantic school led to church music that often almost completely submerged the liturgy. Attempts to reform brought on a reintroduction of sacred polyphony, another effort to reform the chant, and the formation of the Caecilian Society by F. X. Witt in 1868—reforms that were formally approved in 1870 by Pope Pius IX. Whereas the Ratisbon editions of the chant following upon this reform proved to be unsound, the Benedictines of the Abbey of Solesmes took up, successfully, its final restoration, a task that continued into the 20th century.

Modern concern with liturgical music may be said to have begun with the motu proprio, *Tra le sollecitudini* (1903), of Pope Pius X, who laid down as norms for church music holiness, true art, and universality. Pius X recommended the use principally of Gregorian chant and of sacred polyphony, but approved modern compositions. These and certain other instructions, such as the encouragement of music instruction in schools and seminaries, and the high moral standards to be expected of persons involved in liturgical music were repeated in the documents *Divini cultus* (1928) of Pius XI and *Musicae sacrae disciplina* (1955) and the *Instruction on Sacred Music and Sacred Liturgy* (1958) of Pius XII.

Five years after this last instruction, the efforts at liturgical reform that had already been initiated were crystallized in the Vatican Council II's *Constitution on the Sacred Liturgy* (1963). Chapter six of this document, along with the *motu proprio* of Paul VI (1964), the Instruction of the Congregation of Sacred Rites (1964) and the directives of the U.S. Bishops of 1964, 1968, and esp. *Music in Catholic Worship* (NCCB, 1972) have been the catalyst of what will probably be considered the beginning of a new chapter in liturgical music history. The fathers of Vatican II ranked music as the first among the liturgical arts and declared it to be, when united with words, an integral part of the solemn liturgy. All of the instructions mentioned above exhort to active participation of the people by responses, songs, actions, bodily attitudes, and, at proper times, of a reverent silence. While they continue to encourage the preservation and development of the chant and of polyphony, the directives also urge expansion to include new forms and styles appropriate to diverse regions and cultures. While permission for the use of the vernacular has been given, new service music must be of high quality and appropriate in relation to its setting within the total celebration. The former categories of Proper (Introit, Gradual—Alleluia—Tract, Offertory, Communion) and Ordinary (Kyrie, Gloria, Credo, Sanctus, Benedictus, and Agnus Dei) are no longer the sole norms for determining what should be enhanced by music at Mass. New criteria are based on a deeper understanding of the function of the parts. The five acclamations of the Mass, for example, have top priority. Other directives in the instructions of 1974 advise as to the use of song at the entrance and at communion, the use of the responsorial psalm, the treatments of the ''ordinary'' chants, the use of supplementary music at the preparation of the gifts and at the recessional, and so on. The appendix to the *Sacramentary* (1974) contains the instructions on music for dioceses in the U.S.

The granting of great flexibility and freedom does not denote a change in the nature of the liturgy but rather reflects a keener perception of it and is intended to encourage 20th-cent. man to greater creativity and fuller participation in the mystery of faith. Although the post-Vatican years have witnessed the publication of much music that, if not downright poor, has, at best, been mediocre, the future holds more promise. The quality of hymnals is vastly improved, the International Commission on English in the

Liturgy, which includes musicians of international repute, is at work in forming suitable texts and melodies for the sacramental rites and has already completed the new Liturgy of the Hours, *Christian Prayer* (1976) with an excellent hymn section and settings for the different parts of the hours. The publication of a new *Graduale* (1974) by Solesmes and *Jubilate Deo*, a collection issued (1974) by the Congregation of Divine Worship are evidence that chant is still alive. A renewed interest in roots is sparking the young and holds the promise of restoring to them and to many in the Church, the beauty of chant and of polyphonic works. Trained musicians of wide repute such as Ernst *Krenek, Norman *Dello Joio, Lucien *Deiss, Alexander *Peloquin, Sister Theophane *Hytrek, and many others are joining the liturgical music forum and will give direction to the future. Acknowledgment of the fact that the sacred can very well find expression in a contemporary idiom has made admissible to the liturgy settings in twelve-tone and even in electronic music (Richard Feliciano's *Glossolalia* [1967], Joseph Doherty's *Psalm 28* [1969], and Ernst Krenek's *Missa duodecim tonorum* [1976]. What happens in the future will depend on the acceptance, not only by the musicians, but by all involved with the responsibility that mature freedom entails and on the working together of pastors, music ministers, and faithful to bring to the liturgy music that can, in the words of the Constitution on the Sacred Liturgy, "add delight to prayer, foster unity of mind, and confer greater solemnity upon the sacred rites" (n.112).

BIBLIOGRAPHY: C. J. McNaspy et al., NCE 10:97–131; A. Doherty, *ibid*. 16:306–309; Fellerer; E. E. Nemmers, *Twenty Centuries of Catholic Church Music* (1949).

[M. T. LEGGE]

MUSICA SACRA, PONTIFICO ISTITUTO DE, see PONTIFICAL INSTITUTE OF SACRED MUSIC.

MUSICAL INSTRUMENTS IN THE CHURCH. The use of musical instruments in church or more specifically, in the liturgy, has been from the earliest years of Christianity a matter of debate and concern and has been closely bound up with speculations on the "sacred" and the "secular." The Fathers of the Church, though mindful of the biblical exhortation to praise God with trumpets, harps, and lyres and all kinds of instruments (Ps 150), chose to exclude their use in Christian gatherings because of the inseparable connections musical instruments had, at the time, with idolatrous and immoral practices and with theatrical performances. Even the organ, now esteemed as the "king of instruments," was, for many centuries, positively excluded and then, eventually, only tolerated for limited purposes as its connections with things profane or specifically secular were severed. And so, in the Middle Ages, occurred the introduction, first, of instruments for the embellishment of the singing, such as bells and tambourines and, later, of instruments used in their own right—organs, vielles, rebecs, harps—to supply for or double voices in polyphony and sometimes to accompany processions. The organ, though never specifically prescribed for use by law, seems to have been in general use, in the Latin Church, by the 13th century. The perfecting of this instrument along with the development of a vast organ repertoire, particularly under the genius of J. S. Bach, gave it, by the time of the Reformation, preeminence of place in Christian worship. But the 17th and, esp. the 18th cent. witnessed the incursions, not to be contained, and domination of orchestral instruments, and a growing orchestral style. Legislation, such as that of Benedict XIV's encyclical *Annus qui* (1749), which asked, not that instruments be excluded, but simply that abuses be eliminated, remained somewhat ineffectual and, while composers like Haydn and Mozart and, later, Beethoven and Schubert produced sacred works of high caliber, liturgical considerations were often obscured by musical demands, vocal as well as instrumental. By 1870, reforms initiated by the Caecilian movement were ratified by Pius IX. His call for a restoration of Gregorian chant along with a renewed interest in sacred polyphony focused attention on purely vocal music. Official documents from the beginning of this cent. until Pius XII (Pius X's *Tra le sollecitudini*, 1903; Pius XI's *Divini cultus*, 1928; Pius XII's *Musicae sacrae disciplina*, 1955) showed, however, once again a growing esteem for the organ; while other instruments were not forbidden, their use was far from encouraged.

That the Church which uses the pipe organ does not represent the whole Church the Fathers of Vatican Council II acknowledged by admitting into divine worship the use of other instruments. The *Constitution on the Sacred Liturgy* (1963), while upholding the special privilege of the pipe organ, excluded no other instruments provided that they be "suitable for sacred use or can be made so, that they accord with the dignity of the temple and truly contribute to the edification of the faithful" (Vat II SacLit 120). The document takes into account other cultures and other musical traditions, deemphasizing uniformity so as to foster the creativity and development of talent of all races and peoples (*ibid.* 119).

An extension of the principles of the conciliar document may be found in the American bishops' instructions, *Music in the Liturgy* (1967) and *Music in Catholic Worship* (1972), both of which clarify the role of instruments and establish criteria for their use. Thus the debate over what is a "sacred" and what a "secular" instrument ends: the holiness of the instrument comes from how it is used in the liturgy. Any instrument which allows the congregation to perfect its ministerial function is admissible. Instruments, because they support the voices, render the parts easier and achieve a deeper union in the assembled congregation, may be used to accompany the singing; they should not be used in a way that would make it difficult to understand the text. Purely instrumental music may be used at appropriate times such as for preludes or postludes of song, as a background to a spoken psalm, at the preparation of the gifts, during portions of the communion rite and as a recessional.

All music, vocal and instrumental, is subject to the criteria of musical, liturgical, and pastoral judgment. In brief, therefore, it must be intrinsically good and well-performed, it must meet the needs of the liturgical celebration and it must be able to foster prayer for each specific group of worshipping people in each specific set of circumstances.

The 1972 instruction appeals to musicians and composers to "enhance the liturgy with new creations." It exhorts dioceses and parishes to establish policies for hiring musicians and for paying them living wages. One of the most challenging vehicles of creative expression, namely electronic music* is, thus, also admitted to church use. While its application in the liturgy has thus far been somewhat limited—Richard Felciano's *Glossolalia* (1967), Anthony Doherty's *Psalm 28* (1969), and John Eaton's *Mass* (1970) are some examples)—it is to be hoped that some dioceses and parishes, in which its use would be an acceptable enhancement of the liturgical celebration, will encourage the production of electronic music along with other new forms of art, so that the people of God may, in fact, be able to praise the Lord with a "new voice." BIBLIOGRAPHY: L. Deiss, *Spirit and Song of the New Liturgy* (tr. L. L. Haggard and M. L. Mazzarese, 1970); J. Gelineau, *Voices and Instruments in Catholic Worship* (tr. C. Howell, 1964); B. Huijbers, *Performing Audience* (2d ed., 1974); J. Ode, *Brass Instruments in Church Services* (1970); E. Routley, *Church and Music* (1950).

[M. T. LEGGE]

MUSLIM (MOSLEM), as an adjective, of or pertaining to the faith taught by the prophet Mohammed; as a substantive, one who professes that faith. To be a Muslim is considered in Islam both an obligation and a special grace. One becomes a Muslim by the willing acceptance of the tenets of Islam and by embracing the five pillars of religion: confession of faith; prayer five times a day in the prescribed manner; fasting during *Ramadan; almsgiving; and pilgrimage to Mecca (if that is possible). BIBLIOGRAPHY: A. S. Tritton, *Muslim Theology* (1947); A. J. Wensinck, *The Muslim Creed* (1932).

MUSLIM BRETHREN (Muslim Brotherhood; Arab. *ikhwân al-Muslimîn*), a radical religious and political movement in *Islam. The society of the Brethren was formally instituted in Ismailia, Egypt, by Hasan al-Banna (d. 1949) in 1929 as an Islamic revivalist and reform movement. The movement demanded a radical return to the primitive sources of Islam, namely, the *Koran and the *Hadith, as the sole valid principles of both private and public life; it attacked all forms of Western influence and condemned the established governments of Islamic countries for their domination by, or cooperation with, the European powers, insisting that a truly Islamic government was to be established that would eliminate the oppression of Islam by the West and, within Islam, that of the poor by the rich. By the mid-1930s the movement counted numerous branches in Egypt and soon afterwards spread abroad to Jordan, Lebanon, and the other Arab countries of the Near East. After the outbreak of war in 1939, the Brethren began an organized campaign of political action and were implicated in numerous political assassinations, among them that of King 'Abdullalh of Jordan. In 1945 they began to form and train paramilitary units, but their continued agitation brought about the suppression of the organization by the Egyptian government in 1948. Al-Banna was assassinated early in 1949 and was succeeded by Isma'il Hudaybi Bey. Though again suppressed by the Egyptian government in 1954, the society continues to exist. BIBLIOGRAPHY: I. M. Husaini, *Muslim Brethren* (1956); R. P. Mitchell, *Society of the Muslim Brothers* (1969).

[R. M. FRANK]

MUSONIUS RUFUS, GAIUS (*c.* 30–108 A.D.), a Late Stoic philosopher from Volsini in Etruria. Though of Latin origin, he lectured and wrote in Greek. After being banished from Rome under Nero and Vespasian, he returned under Titus and taught there for the rest of his life. Among his pupils were *Pliny the Younger and esp. *Epictetus. His instruction was eminently practical, and he exhibited the warm religious tone characteristic of Late Stoicism. Among the topics he is reported to have treated are: "That women also should engage in philosophy;" "That exile is not an evil;" "Whether parents are to be obeyed in all things;" "What is most important in marriage;" "Whether all children born are to be reared." M. was under Cynic influence also, and with Cynic fearlessness he did not hesitate to address the soldiers of Vespasian and Vitellius on the horrors of civil war. BIBLIOGRAPHY: LexAW 2031–32; Ueberweg 1:494–495.

[M. R. P. MCGUIRE]

MUSPILLI (an OHG word of uncertain etymology and meaning; perhaps "world destruction"); title given by its first editor (Schmeller in 1832) to a fragmentary poem in alliterative verse (104 lines; the beginning and end are missing) that had been copied (probably toward the end of the 9th cent.) onto the inside covers and blank end pages of a MS presented *c.* 830 to Louis the German. The poem, which is in Bavarian dialect, urges repentance by depicting the terrible events of the Last Judgment. For text, see K. Müllenhoff and W. Scherer, *Denkmäler deutscher Poesie und Prosa aus dem 8. bis 12. Jahrhundert* (3d ed., rev. E. von Steinmeyer, v. 1, No. 4 1892); for commentary, see J. Knight Bostock, *Handbook on Old High German Literature* (1955).

[M. F. MCCARTHY]

MUSSET, ALFRED DE (1810–57), French writer. A precocious, personal, and lyrical writer, M. embodied the genius of Romanticism while sharply criticizing its mannerisms. By the age of 35 he had created that movement's most original theater (the collections *Spectacle dans un fauteuil* (1833) and *Comédies et proverbes* (1840), elucidated its metaphysical *mal* (the autobiographical *Confession d'un enfant du siècle*, 1836), and written numerous short stories (e.g., *Mimi Pinson*, 1843). Having abandoned Catholicism, in which he saw only rigorous dogmatism and empty forms, M. reflected the Romantic's anguish at his loss of faith and insatiable quests for the absolute through the mystiques of deified love, heroic action (e.g., the drama *Lorenzaccio*, 1834), and the exotic life (*Contes d'Espagne et d'Italie*, 1830). Certain poems best reflect his religious views. *Rolla* (1833) anathematized Voltaire for having destroyed the conditions of belief, leaving modern man, who "came too late into a world too old" for faith, a prey to despair. However, both the *Lettre à Lamartine* (1836) and *L'Espoir en Dieu* (1838) see solace in the idea of God. The former expresses belief in Providence and the immortality of the soul. The latter, his only major lyrical poem treating exclusively a religious theme, was inspired by efforts to convert him and reflects, in its central section on the inscrutability of God, Lacordaire's Lenten sermons of 1836. M. distorts certain religious motifs, e.g., the pelican, symbol of Christ's immolation, represents the poet's soul destroying itself to objectify in the eternity of art the moment of suffering (*La Nuit de mai*, 1835); and suffering through love becomes a spiritual path to self-awareness. BIBLIOGRAPHY: P. van Tieghem, *Musset* (1945); C. Haldane, *Alfred: The Passionate Life of Alfred de Musset* (1960).

[G. E. GINGRAS]

MUSSO, CORNELIUS (1511–74), Italian Conventual Franciscan, theologian and bp. at the Council of Trent. He taught theology at the Univ. of Pavia and of Bologna before being named bp., first of Bertinoro (1541), then of Bitonto (1544). As a conciliar father at Trent, he preached at the solemn opening of the Council, 13 Dec. 1545. His interventions in the conciliar discussions were significant, esp. on June 5, 1546 against G. *Seripando on concupiscence and on July 7 and July 30, 1546, on justification. He was also the trusted liaison of the papal legates during the formulation of the decree on justification and deserves highest credit for the final form the decree took. After the Council he sought to implement Tridentine reforms; in 1572, however, he was forced to resign his see because of pressure against him from the court of Naples.

[T. C. O'BRIEN]

MUSSOLINI, BENITO (1883–1945), founder of the Italian Fascist Party and premier of Italy from 1922 to 1943. As a youth, M. was active in the left wing of the Socialist Party, but during World War I, he severed his connections with the socialists. After the Fascist "March on Rome" (1922), King Victor Emmanuel III appointed M. premier. During the Fascist regime, termed the "Corporate State," party and state organs were intermeshed, and all opposition to fascism was forbidden. One achievement of the regime was the settlement of the Roman Question through the Lateran Pacts. Foreign policy was expansionist, resulting in the alliance with Nazi Germany. Military defeat in World War II led to M.'s downfall in July 1943. On April 28, 1945, he was shot by Italian partisans in Dongo, near Lake Como. BIBLIOGRAPHY: L. Fermi, *Mussolini* (1961).

[E. A. CARRILLO]

MUSURUS, MARCUS (1470–1517), one of the most influential Greek scholars who came to the West. He came to Venice from his native Crete and *c.* 1486 he was studying Greek under John Lascaris in Florence. He later became one of the principal editors of the Aldine Press in Venice. In 1503 he was appointed professor of Greek at the Univ. of Padua and, as a teacher there and subsequently in Venice, he trained many of the leading Greek scholars of the age, including Erasmus. He prepared the *editio princeps* of Aristophanes (1498), and of the Greek text of Plato's Dialogues (1516), and nearly a dozen other first editions of Greek authors published by the Aldine Press. BIBLIOGRAPHY: D. J. Geanakoplos, NCE 10:143; *idem, Greek Scholars in Venice: Studies in the Dissemination of Greek Learning from Byzantium to Western Europe* (1962) 111–166.

[M. R. P. MCGUIRE]

MUTAZILITES (Arab. *al-Mu'tazila*), a major school of *Islamic theology. Taken from the verb *i'tazala,* the name originally meant the party that withdraws or stands aside. It was first applied to those who kept apart from the political turmoil dividing the Islamic community after the murder of the Caliph 'Uthmân (d. 655). The theological tradition to which the name was later applied was begun in Basra by Wâṣil ibn 'Aṭâ' (d. 749) and his son-in-law 'Amr ibn 'Ubaid (d. 762). The Mutazilites, who termed themselves *ahl al-'adl wat-tawḥîd* (those who uphold God's justice and unicity) are traditionally identified by their treatment of five theses concerned with their conceptions of: (1) God's unicity; (2) his justice; (3) "the threat [of hell] and the promise [of paradise]"; (4) "the intermediate status" [of the Muslim who commits a grave sin], in opposition to the positions of the *Murji'ites and the *Kharijites; and (5) the universal obligation to fraternal correction, which they carried into practice in the political sphere. The Mutazilites elaborated a number of theological systems that were quite divergent although they were in partial agreement concerning the treatment of the "five theses." These systems are grouped under the two major divisions of the schools of Basra and of Baghdad. With the end of the 12th cent. the Mutazila ceased to exist as a living school.

Customarily the theology of the Mutazilites is considered to be highly rationalistic because in comparison to that, e.g., of the *Ash'arites the Mutazilites gave an increasingly preponderant place to purely rational constructs in the interpretation of the canonical sources of faith and tended particularly to attribute little importance to much of the *Hadith. Typically, the Mutazilites tended to refuse to allow that God's essential attributes are ontologically distinct and to insist that the Koran is created; they also insisted on human freedom of the will and that man creates his own acts and held that, because injustice is evil, God will not (or cannot) do but what is most salutary for mankind. During the 1st cent. of the Abbasid dynasty, Mutazilism, though enjoying little popular support, was more or less the official theology of the rulers and, like many of the earlier Abbasid Caliphs, they showed a certain sympathy for the moderate Shi'a (see SHIITES). During the reigns of the Caliphs al-Ma'mûn (d.833), al-Mu'taṣim (d.842) and al-Wâthiq (d.847) the public confession of the createdness of the *Koran became official policy and during what is termed the *miḥna* (persecution) many notable and pious men suffered terribly at the hands of the Mutazilite-inspired inquisition. The official status of the Mutazila ended with the caliphate of al-Mutawakkil (847–861) who, inspired by Ibn Ḥanbal (see HANBALITES) gave his full support to traditional orthodoxy. The most important Mutazilite teachers of the Basra school are abû l-Hudhayl al-'Allâf (d. *c.*840), Ibrâhîm al-Naẓẓâm (d. before 845), al-Jâḥiẓ (d. 869), one of the greatest masters of Arabic literary prose, al-Jubbâ'î (d. 915) and his son abû Hâshim (d. 933) who gave definitive shape to the most important and enduring school of Mutazilite theology, among whose chief exponents were abû 'Abdallâh al-Baṣrî (d. 970), 'Abd al-Jabbâr al-Hamadânî (d. 1025), and abû Rashîd al-Nîsâpûrî (d. 1068). Among the chief masters of the Baghdad school, founded by Bishr ibn al-Mu'tamir (d. 826), were Thumâma ibn al-Ashras (d. 826) and Ibn abî Dû'âd (d. 855) both of whom had much influence in the Abbasid court and the latter of whom played an important role in the *miḥna,* al-Khayyât (d. *c.*900), and abû l-Qâsim al-Balkhî al-Ka'bî (d. 931). BIBLIOGRAPHY: H. S. Nyberg, EncIslam[1]; A. S. Tritton, *Muslim Theology,* (1947); W. M. Watt, *Islamic Philosophy and Theology (Islamic Surveys* 1, 1962).

[R. M. FRANK]

MUTH, CARL (1867–1944), journalist, critic, editor. Once a novice among the White Fathers in Africa, M. was (1893–95) director of the editorial staff of the daily *Der Elsässer,* and also editor of the periodical *Alte und Neue Welt* in Einsiedeln. In 1903 he founded *Hochland,* leading Catholic literary journal, and remained its editor until his death. In this position he directed the movement that succeeded in bringing Catholic literature and criticism out of its Kulturkampf ghetto, encouraging young writers and communicating to others his own conviction of the importance of a literature rooted in religious experience. After 1916 the *Hochland* enlarged its range of interest and became active in promoting Catholic participation in developments in the political and social fields. BIBLIOGRAPHY: O. B. Roegele, NCE 10:144–145.

[I. MERKEL]

MUTILATION, as understood by the moral theologian, the destruction, or removal of a part of a human being, or the suppression of a human function necessary to human completeness. In earlier times the term was generally restricted to crippling operations such as amputations. In current theological discussion it has been extended to mean any notable damage done to the living human body or its functions. The reason for the shift in meaning is historical. Surgery was not a well-developed art until recent times, and in the past the question of the lawfulness of mutilation tended to center about certain hazardous medical procedures and the use of mutilation as a punishment. To punish by mutilating is today regarded as too barbaric for serious consideration, although *sterilization as a punishment for certain sex offenses still has some advocates. The perfection of surgical techniques, the discovery of nonsurgical methods of suppressing human functions, the alleged desirability of eugenic sterilization, the use of pharmaceutical means to control ovulation and fertility, the success of certain organic transplants have, among other developments in medicine, posed new problems in moral theology. Moralists have in the main sought to cope with these by the application of principles first elaborated to deal with a kind of mutilation that was simpler in its concept. By some these principles were rigidly applied to situations of much greater complexity, and a few even questioned the legitimacy of blood transfusion and skin-grafts. Common sense prevailed, however, and it is now generally recognized that the privations incurred in such minor mutilations are morally negligible. The fundamental moral principle of relevance remains man's stewardship rather than outright ownership of his body (cf. Pius XII, AAS 44 [1952] 782). But if the use of the body is restricted by natural finality or openness to the Creator's rights, a second principle, that of *totality, is also pertinent. The person has such a right to the services of his total organism that he may allow an individual part to be destroyed to the extent needed for the good of his whole being. The application of this principle to *organic transplants has been denied, although it has been held that other principles, such as charity, may be invoked. BIBLIOGRAPHY: J. J. Lynch, NCE 10:144; G. Kelly, ''Morality of Mutilation: Towards a Revision of the Treatise.'' ThSt 17 (1956) 322–344.

[C. J. LYNCH]

MUTIS, JOSÉ CELESTINO (1732–1808), Spanish priest and scientist who worked 48 years in Colombia and became one of the leading botanists of his time. In Bogotá he founded an observatory, the first in Latin America, classified thousands of Colombian plants, studied the curative qualities of quinine, and drew the first botanical map of the country. He was ordained priest in 1774 when he was already well along in his career as a scientist. BIBLIOGRAPHY: G. Hernández de Alba, *La vida y obra de José Celestino Mutis* (1951); *idem,* NCE 10:146–147.

[P. DAMBORIENA]

MUZI, GIOVANNI (1772–1849), the first papal representative sent to the newly independent Spanish American republics. He had been theology professor at the Roman College and auditor of the papal nunciature in Vienna before heading the so-called Muzi Mission (1823–25) to Spanish America. This latter mission brought him to Chile, Argentina, and Uruguay, where he was empowered to recruit and consecrate bps. without further recourse to Rome; in his entourage was the future Pius IX. When M. returned to Rome to report on this short-lived and somewhat abortive diplomatic venture, the mission was much criticized and generally considered a failure. He remained a consultant on Spanish American affairs.

[E. J. DILLON]

MUZIO, GIROLAMO (1496–1576), Italian Renaissance writer and religious polemicist. A humanist whose patrons included Ferrante Gonzaga of Milan, the Dukes of Urbino, and Pope Pius IV, Muzio wrote poetry and interested himself in the linguistic and literary concerns of his day. Two works on chivalry, *Duello* (1550) and *Gentilhuomo* (1575), are characteristic. Of greater significance, however, were his religious polemics: against P. P. *Vergerio, apostate bp. of Capodistria (1549); against the Protestant, ex-Capuchin *Ochino (1551); and against the Swiss Zwinglian and Calvinist Reformer H. *Bullinger.

[E. M. GATES]

MYCONIUS, FRIEDRICH (1490–1546), German Reformer. Born in Upper Franconia, he attended Latin school in Annaberg and entered the Franciscan monastery there in 1510. Ordained in 1516 at Weimar, he was influenced by Luther to adopt Reformation views. In 1524 he became pastor at Gotha, where he helped to order affairs according to evangelical patterns. While pastor at Gotha he took part in church visitations of Thuringia, attended the Marburg Colloquy (1529; see MARBURG ARTICLES), and participated in the *Hagenau Conference (1540). In 1538, he was one of the Lutherans sent to England to effect a rapprochement with leaders of the Reformation there. His chief written contribution was *Historia Reformationis, 1517–1542*.

[N. H. MARING]

MYCONIUS, OSWALD (1488–1552), Swiss Reformer. Born at Lucerne, educated at Basel, he became a teacher in Zurich in 1516, where he was influential in having *Zwingli called as pastor. M. soon moved to Lucerne, where he taught until 1522. Teaching briefly at Einsiedeln, he returned to Zurich, where he was an ardent supporter of Zwingli's reform program. In 1531, he became a pastor at Basel, succeeding *Oecolampadius there a year later. Until his death, M. was chief pastor of the city and professor of theology at the university. He finished the First Confession of *Basel begun by Oecolampadius before his death, and was one of the drafters of the First *Helvetic Confession (1536). He was also Zwingli's first biographer.

[N. H. MARING]

MYERS, MYER (1723–95), foremost American silversmith of his day. M. executed unusual Torah ornaments (*rimonim*) for many synagogues in a delicate rococo style, and an alms bowl and baptismal font for two Presbyterian churches, New York. M.'s domestic silver embraces Georgian, rococo, and neoclassical designs.

[M. J. DALY]

MYRON (Gr., meaning ointment), a blessed oil which is used in the East to anoint the foreheads of the faithful on certain feasts. In the early days of Christianity, oil was a symbol of strength and the oil on the forehead symbolized the strengthening of the soul by the celebration of a particular feast of Our Lord, a saint, or of Our Lady. The priest greets the person with the words, "Christ is within," and he responds, "He is and will be." At Easter the greeting is "Christ is risen," and at Christmas is said "Christ is born."

[P. MORLINO]

MYSTAGOGY (from Gr.), a term originally used of initiation into the pagan mysteries or sacred rites of the Hellenistic world. When the early Church began to apply the word *mystērion* to the Christian rites in which divine power and grace are communicated to men, the word *mystagogia* came to be used of an initiation into those rites, often by the type of homiletic instruction represented in the *Mystagogical Catecheses* attributed to St. Cyril of Jerusalem. The term is used in the 1972 new rites of Christian initiation for adults as a synonym for the postbaptismal catechesis, ideally conducted in the Easter season.

[A. CODY]

MYSTÈRE D'ADAM, LE, an early (*c.*1150) French drama composed by clerics for lay performance and edification. Of its three divisions (The Fall; Abel's Murder; The Prophets), the first is distinguished by its dialogue between Eve and Satan.

[J. P. WILLIMAN]

MYSTERIES, SACRAMENTS AS. In Greek patristic writings from the time of Clement of Alexandria and Origen, the term *mystērion,* which designated esoteric religious rites, was also applied to the rites of Christian worship. In the Eastern Church, *mystērion* is equivalent in meaning to the Lat. *sacramentum*. But "mystery" has a universal appropriateness for expressing the meaning of a sacrament: St. Paul's use of the term to refer to the manifestation of the hidden plan of salvation. The sacraments are signs, manifestations that declare Christ's working out of the plan of salvation; they have their meaning and effectiveness only by their conjunction with Christ as the cause of grace and the conjunction of the recipient with Christ through faith in him as Savior. In being signs, they transcend time, as it were, in bringing the mystery of Christ's salvation into the present.

[T. C. O'BRIEN]

MYSTERIES, VILLA OF THE, POMPEII (*c.*50 B.C.), Roman villa named for the famous painted mural frieze (excavated and restored 1929–30), having as theme, mystical in subject, an exposition of the rite of initiation of brides before the god Dionysos and Ariadne. Executed in tempera by a Greek artist in the Second Style of Roman illusionistic painting, the figures conceived in dramatic perspective within the shallow space of a narrow green ledge, full of life, yet dignified, attain impressive grandeur.

[M. J. DALY]

MYSTERIES OF THE LIFE OF JESUS, the events through which Jesus worked out the divine plan of salvation, an expression used, e.g., of the events meditated on in the rosary. Theologically the expression indicates that the events described in the Gospels are mysteries in the sense of being events bound up with the hidden life of the Trinity and the divine plan of salvation (see MYSTERY). In the acceptance of these episodes as mysteries, faith, for one thing, assents to their truth. To treat them not as mysteries but as myth is to empty them of their truth content. *DEMYTHOLOGIZING.

[T. C. O'BRIEN]

MYSTERY, a reality whose intrinsic being involves or has reference to the three divine persons and whose proper, inherent truth is known only to divinity and accepted by others through grace. The primary mystery is the inner Trinitarian life itself; from that derives the reality and proper being of the economy of salvation, which consists basically in Christ as Incarnate Word and in the communion with divinity brought into being through the varied riches of Christ's grace shared by others. Because mysteries are the divine being itself or the wondrous grace-works of God, their proper truth and meaning are the connatural object of the divine mind alone. The power to accept their truth, the power by which they become known truths for the created mind, can only come as a grace-gift of God. That power is either the *light of glory given for the beatific vision, the immediate intuition of the divine reality, or it is the theological virtue of faith, as the power to adhere to God's word in belief that the unseen mysteries are true. Vatican Council I stated this strict meaning of mystery in its dogmatic constitution on faith (D 3016, 3041; see also DOGMA). In a wider usage, the term mystery is applied to a matter that of itself is not incomprehensible to the created mind but, because of its profundity and richness, leaves ever more to be penetrated; Maritain speaks of being as a mystery in this sense. He also separates mystery from problem, an issue of enormous complexity. BIBLIOGRAPHY: J. Maritain, *Preface to Metaphysics* (1962) 12–23.

[T. C. O'BRIEN]

MYSTERY PLAYS (or miracle plays), a form of medieval drama that reached its height in the 15th century. It was based on the liturgy. The French *mystère* distinguished those plays based on biblical stories (mysteries) from those about the lives of the saints (miracle plays). The development of the drama progressed in spite of some objection because it was in agreement with the medieval mind. The desire to establish in visible and popular form the revealed pattern of Redemption led to the production of mystery cycles in which the story of man was portrayed from the fall of Lucifer to the Last Judgment. Since a papal edict forbade the clergy to act on a public stage, the plays fell into the hands of the guilds. The increasing use of the vernacular instead of Latin resulted. By *c.*1220 performances were being given outside as well as inside the churches. What finally brought the mysteries out into the open air was their connection with the Corpus Christi processions. Based on the Scriptures, the plays were arranged into cycles and were given on church festival days, particularly the feast of Corpus Christi, which in England was probably established *c.*1318. The plays were usually performed on elaborately painted "pageants," platforms on wheels moving in order through the streets to prearranged places where an audience would have gathered. Acting became more dramatic as characterization and detail became more important. The four great collections of extant "miracles" or "mysteries" are known by the names of the towns where they were played: the York plays (1430–40), the longest, containing 48 plays; the Towneley or Wakefield plays (*c.*1450); the Coventry plays (1468); and the Chester plays (1475–1500). BIBLIOGRAPHY: E. K. Chambers, *Medieval Plays* (2v., 1903; repr. 1948); K. Young, *Drama of the Medieval Stage* (2v., 1933); E. C. Dunn, NCE 1043–46.

[S. A. HEENEY]

MYSTERY RELIGIONS (GRECO-ORIENTAL), secret cults of the ancient world which aimed at securing the salvation of an individual after death through an esoteric experience. These cults were in marked contrast with the ordinary family, tribal, and civic forms of worship, which were primarily concerned with the temporal well-being of the participants and openly practiced.

The principal mystery religions of the Greco-Roman world may be divided under three different headings: (1) an indigenous Greek worship of the grain goddess Demeter; (2) importations from Egypt and the Near East; (3) and mysteries created in historical times to resemble the others. Each of the primary mystery religions was centered about a mother goddess and her companion. In Syria, she was variously known as Astarte, Atargatis, or simply the Syrian goddess *(Dea Syria)*, and her consort was Adonis. In Phrygia, she was known as Cybele, the Great Idaean Mother *(Magna Mater Idaea)*, or the Great Mother *(Magna Mater)*, and her youthful lover is Attis. In Egypt, she is represented by Isis, and her partner is Osiris. In Greece, the mother goddess Demeter is not associated with a husband or lover but with her daughter Kore ("Maiden"), also known as Persephone.

In each of the myths pertaining to these deities, the companion of the mother goddess is involved in some disaster. In Syria, Adonis is slain by a wild boar during a hunt. In

Phrygia, Attis, grieved by his lack of fidelity to Cybele, emasculates himself. In Egypt, Osiris falls a victim to Seth. In Greece, Kore is carried off by Hades to the lower world. However, after each of these disasters there is a resurrection or return of the lost companion. Despite their variations in particular details, the myths obviously represent a common attempt to explain changes in the seasons of the year. The female deity, who is an evolved fertility goddess, grants the fruits of the earth to men while her companion is present with her but withholds them in an ever-recurring cycle when he or she is gone.

In Egypt and in Crete, there seem to have been few if any secrets connected with these cults, and this raises the question as to their origin on the Greek mainland and their continuance in the Greco-Roman world. Various explanations may be given. When the Indo-Europeans invaded Greece in pre-Homeric times, they brought with them their own religion, particularly the worship of the sky-god Zeus. In order to preserve their own beliefs, the conquered peoples could have surrounded them with a barricade of secrecy, a parallel to which could be found in the *Discipline of the Secret of the early Church. Another reason for secrecy could certainly have been the nature of the cult itself, the worship of a fertility goddess with its sexual overtones. Other reasons may have been the natural feeling of reverence and awe in the presence of what is deemed to be sacred and holy and the desire to exclude all hostile influences such as the presence of foreigners who might alienate the deity or even secure its favor to the detriment of the original worshipers.

Since those who were initiated into the mysteries bound themselves by oath never to reveal them, our knowledge of the rites connected with the mysteries and the knowledge communicated in them is rather limited. What we do know comes from scenes represented in works of art, from casual references in pagan authors, and the sometimes inaccurate or biased statements of early Christian writers. The *mysteria,* as may be seen from the etymology of the word (from *muein,* to keep [the mouth or eyes] shut) was a Greek rite that must be kept secret. Before this could be done, it had of course to be revealed, and this was done under the guidance of a hierophant (*hierophantēs,* a revealer of sacred things). According to Theon of Smyrna (*fl. c.* A.D. 115–140), there were four stages to this revelation: (1) a preliminary purification *(katharmos);* (2) a communication of secret knowledge *(teletēs paradosis);* (3) a revelation of sacred objects *(epopteia);* and (4) a crowning or garlanding of the mystic. The purification could involve abstinence from food and the use of sex, various types of penance, and a ritual bath. The initiation seems to have involved a ritual pageant *(drōmenon)* portraying the essence of the divine myth and an instruction or exhortation *(legomenon).* At Eleusis, the tradition of the sacred objects seems to have taken place a year after witnessing of the sacred drama. The formula recited by the initiates recorded by Clement of Alexandria gives some information on this rite: "I fasted. I drank the potion (*kukeōna,* a broth of barley, grated cheese, and wine). I took [the object or objects] out of the chest. After I had handled them, I placed them into the basket and from the basket into the chest" (*Protrepticus* 2.21). The object(s) given to the person may simply have been a stalk of wheat, but it seems more likely that they were sexual symbols, which would have been appropriate to a rite surrounding the worship of a deity that had originated as a fertility goddess. The knowledge communicated at the time of the initiation, whatever this may have been, was of relatively little importance, but the way in which it was communicated doubtlessly made a deep and lasting impression on many. As Aristotle observed with respect to the initiates, it was not so necessary for them to learn something but to experience something and receive a certain disposition (*ou mathein ti dei alla pathein kai diatethēnai*—preserved in Synesius of Cyrene, *Dio Chrysostom* 7).

In Greece and Italy, the best known of the mystery religions were the Eleusinian Mysteries in which the worship of Dionysius and of Demeter were combined (see ELEUSINIAN MYSTERIES). The worship of Dionysius had many other variations throughout Greece and Rome, many aspects of which resembled mystery religions (see CULT OF DIONYSIUS). Orphism, while distinct from these cults of Dionysius, included the god in its worship and shared other mystery religions' concern for the afterlife (see ORPHISM; AFTERLIFE). Of the several strictly Oriental mystery religions, the cult of Mithras was the most prevalent in the early Roman Empire and the most significant for its syncretism. (see MITHRAS AND MITHRAISM).

The mystery religions undoubtedly provoked different responses in the initiates. Some may have found them simply a source of sensual excitation. Others must have regarded them as a kind of magical guarantee of salvation. Those of a philosophical mind must have been led by them to speculate about the immortality of the soul. Still others must have found a deep religious experience in them and a desire to be united with the divinity. Artists found in them an endless source of inspiration, as may be seen from the numerous reliefs, particularly on sarcophagi, portraying some theme taken from the mysteries. BIBLIOGRAPHY: K. Prümm, NCE 10:153–164; R. Follet and K. Prümm, DBSuppl (1960) 6:1–225; W. K. C. Guthrie, *Greeks and Their Gods* (1954) 1–35, 145–182, 277–332; M. P. Nilsson, *Greek Piety* (tr. H. J. Rose, 1948) 150–161; E. R. Dodds, *Greeks and the Irrational* (1951) 270–282; Farnell, *Cults of the Greek States* (1906) v. 3.

[M. J. COSTELLOE]

MYSTERY THEOLOGY, a liturgical theology with a special orientation. Odo Casel (1886–1948), Benedictine monk of the Abbey of Maria Laach, strongly influenced by A. Vonier's work, *A Key to the Doctrine of the Eucharist* (1925), gave almost a lifetime of study to the theology of mysteries and the mystery character of the liturgy. For Casel, a mystery is a divine reality hidden but communicated to man. The main tenet of his theology of mysteries, which he garnered from Scripture (esp. Rom 6.2–11), the Church Fathers, and the Hellenistic mystery cults is that the saving work of Christ once uniquely, unrepeatably, and historically realized in the past, is sacramentally represented or re-actualized in the liturgy. Hence the liturgy is itself a mystery, enabling man to relive the mystery of Christ in his own life. The Caselian theory, though defended and refined by disciples of his, V. Warnach and B. Neunheuser, has fallen under the attack of K. Prümm, J. M. Hanssens, and J. B. Umberg, who criticized it particularly because it inferred too close a resemblance between pagan and Christian mysteries. Another question left open to debate is the mode of the re-actualization, namely, how Christ's saving acts are realized suprahistorically and supraspatially. E. Schillebeeckx, in his sacramental theology, has found the basic Caselian thesis congenial. BIBLIOGRAPHY: I. H. Dalmais, NCE 10:164–166; O. Casel, *Mystery of Christian Worship and Other Writings* (ed. B. Neunheuser, tr. I. T. Hale, 1962); T. Filthaut, *La Théologie des mystères, exposé de la controverse* (1954).

[J. FICHTNER]

MYSTICAL BODY. In accounts of St. Paul's conversion Jesus identifies himself as the one whom Paul persecutes by harassing Jesus' Disciples (Acts 9.1–4; 22.4–8; 26.9–15). This mysterious identification between Christians on earth and the resurrected Jesus became a major theme of Paul's doctrine, which he expressed in many ways. Christians live by Christ's life (Gal. 2.20; Rom 6.10,11; 7.6; 8.9–11; 14.8; Col 3.4). They are one in Christ (Gal 3.28,29; 4.6,7; 1 Cor 12.13; Col. 3.11). They exist "in Christ" or "in the Lord" (Gal 1.22; 1 Thes 2.14; 3.8; 1 Cor 1.30; 2 Cor 5.17; Phil 3.9; 4.1; Rom 8.1; 16.7,11; Col 1.28; 2.6; Eph 2.10,15,21; 5.8). Paul, however, describes the union most explicitly in his teaching about the body of Christ.

Christians' bodies are "members of Christ", and the body of believers, as a whole, is the sanctuary of the Holy Spirit (1 Cor 6.15,19,20; cf. 3.16,17, where they are called the sanctuary of God). Their sharing of the Eucharist makes them one body in Christ (10.16,17). In 1 Cor ch. 12, where Paul's concern is to strengthen the Church's unity through the proper use of spiritual gifts, he uses man's physical body as the pattern for the congregation's oneness in Christ (12.12–27). Christian unity comes from baptism into Christ's one body by the Spirit's action (v. 13). Every Christian is a member of Christ's body, no matter how lowly he is (v. 27). All positions, roles, and services must harmonize and not cause dissension. Love must knit together and govern the whole body (ch. 13). Communal gatherings must be orderly (ch. 14; see also Rom 12.4).

The epistles, Colossians and Ephesians, contain Paul's most elaborate development of this theme. Christ, the Creator, holds everything together, spirits and matter, and is the head of the body, the Church. The principal source and the firstborn from the dead, he holds the first place in all things. He has reconciled the whole of reality to God through the blood of his cross. Through his death and by the body of his flesh he has reconciled men, who were once sinners, to God and made them holy and blameless in his presence, as long as they continue to believe in the gospel (Col 1.12–23). Paul's suffering continues Christ's service for his body, the Church (1.24,25). By this union with his redeemed Christ is the ultimate mystery of God's eternal plan (1.27; 2.2,3). Christians have been filled up with the fullness of his divine reality and are now free from corrupt human nature that has been cut away by Christ's way of circumcising. They have been buried with him in baptism and have been raised to a new life by belief in God's power that raised Jesus from the dead. And so, Christians, once dead because of sin, have been brought to life to live with Christ and are participants in his triumphal procession over all opposition (2.9–15). Their way of life now is a holding on to their head as members of the body, for the head supplies the body with strength to grow into the full stature that God has planned (2.19). The true life of Christians is hidden with Christ in God, for Christ is their life, and, when he makes himself known, they, too, will appear with him in his glory (3.4). They lose their self-centered identities and Christ becomes everything in everyone (3.11). They are called to live, by the one body, in Christ's peace, which must govern their conscious lives. Their way of life is to praise the Father continuously in thanksgiving through Christ (3.12–17).

In Ephesians the teaching is essentially the same. The exalted Jesus is the head of the Church, his body, and the two, now one, have become the culmination of everything that God planned by his creative power (Eph 1.18–23). Christians live by grace in Christ, having been enthroned with him in heaven, and are the example of God's loving kindness for all ages. The Christian body is God's ultimate masterpiece, created in and by Christ, and is ordered to the accomplishment of the good works that God planned from eternity (2.5–10). In the one body the extreme elements of Jew and Gentile are reconciled to each other and to God by Christ's death, in order to form one new man, living at peace with all his parts. And all, together, have access in the one Spirit to the Father (2.11–18). They are being built up into the one living Temple of God in the Spirit (2.19–22). Paul, once the strictest of Jews, is amazed that the formerly so hated Gentiles now share the same inheritance, the same body, and the same promise in Christ Jesus (3.6). The manifold wisdom of God is proclaimed to all reality by this unity in the Church: it is the ultimate family, united in love by Christ dwelling in it and empowering it to become the total fullness willed by God Himself (3.11–19).

Paul constantly returns to this theme of unity: Christians' intense concern should be to protect "the oneness that comes from the Spirit and binds everyone together by his peace—there is only one body and one Spirit", one hoped for culmination of the common call, one Lord, one faith, one baptism, one God and Father of all, who rules over all, acts through all, and dwells in all (4.4–6). The multiple gifts meted out by Christ are ordered to one thing: the instrumenting of the loving service to be performed by all the "saints", i.e., all Christians, in their building up of the body of Christ to his full stature (4.9–16). Christians must put on this new man created according to God's plan in the uprightness and holiness that come from God's faithful fulfillment of his promises (4.24). Even the divinely created union between man and woman becomes a profound symbol of this union of Christ with his Church in the one body (5.23–32).

By such patterns St. Paul describes the central mystery of the Church: Christ's unifying power, active in the continuous life and growth of his members. By it he binds Christians together in his victory over sin and death and creates a mutual love in them that breaks through barriers of hostility and indifference to establish a harmonious continuity of life and growth through service offered to one another. The patterns are not allegories without meaning, but apt analogies that open up for believing human minds the hidden depths of the Lord Jesus' rule in the hearts and minds of his disciples. Paul's pastoral aim is clear. By the images he means to exhort and encourage his charges to live in accord with their identity with Christ in one spiritual organism and to advance to levels of greater love and holiness by a clarified awareness of their actual, though hidden, union with the exalted, all powerful Lord Jesus.

Although essentially an invisible reality, the union has visible effects in the human order. For Paul its effects are seen in the manifested gifts of apostleship, prophecy, evangelism, shepherding, teaching, and all the other gifts that create a system of service among the sanctified members of Christ for the building up of his body. But its visibility projects beyond what is seen to the final coming together of all the sanctified into the oneness of faith in, and knowledge of, the Son of God. They all will come together eventually into that one perfect image of God, that perfect "Adam", who is Christ in the fullness of his growth and age. With such a goal as this in mind, Christians living in the world must go on growing up into the new Adam in every possible way, but especially by repeating the truth of the goal to each other over and over again and by loving each other in accord with their mutual aim of oneness in the fullness of Christ. For, Christ *is* the head and it is from him, and from his conquest already attained, that the dynamic action of present growth takes place. He binds the whole body together and gives strength to every element of it. He accomplishes its labor of growth with an exuberance of supplemental gifts and with such a wealth of energetic power that each member, in his own turn and according to the grace he receives, keeps on growing up into the full growth of the one body. The final accomplishment of each member's growth will be the unique Adam, he who will exist eternally as the created and uncreated union of man and God. That final Adam, Christ in the fullness of himself with all his members, will be the perfect reflection of the Father's love.

So, the two terminals of the mystical body are invisible objects of faith. Christ, exalted by his salvific death, resurrection, and the rule he exercises through his Spirit, is the efficacious creator and sustainer of his body. Christ, in his full age, united with all his members, now made perfect, is the highest good to which all the members of the body are drawn. What is visible is gospel preaching, ministry, service, and all that tends to the building up of the Church through faith that works through love.

[J. F. FALLON]

MYSTICAL EXPERIENCE, in the language of RC mystical theologians, an infused, passive experience of God or of his divine activity in the soul. Called infused in order to designate its supernatural source, it is thus distinguished from an awareness of God produced by purely human effort or by an activity proper to the ascetical state. It is called passive because the experience is the result of God's operation, and the soul is more receptive than active during the experience. The authenticity of mystical experience, so understood, is verified by the testimony of innumerable Christian mystics. The possibility of mystical experience for all Christians is defended by those theologians (e.g., E. C. Butler, R. Garrigou-Lagrange, J. Arintero) who maintain that the mystical state is the normal development of the life of sanctifying grace, the virtues, and the gifts of the Holy Spirit. Many theologians identify mystical experience with infused *contemplation, which is an immediate contact with God through knowledge and love (e.g., J. Gerson, V. Lehodey, Butler, Gabriel of St. Mary Magdalene, J. de Guibert, A. Poulain, J. Maréchal). Others do not restrict it to infused contemplation, although some of these emphasize the function of intellect and will (J. V. Bainvel, A. A. Ribet, A. Saudreau, and A. Tanquerey). Modern Dominicans such as J. Arintero, Garrigou-Lagrange, and A. Royo hold that the constitutive element of mystical experience is the operation in the soul of the gifts of the Holy Spirit in such a manner that the soul is made aware of the divine activity. The experience may be delightful, as in the case of the various types of infused contemplation, or it may be painful, as in the case of the passive purgations. Jacques *Maritain is one of the modern theologians who have distinguished between mystical experience and infused contemplation; he also distinguished between the gifts of the Holy Spirit that are operative in mystics of the contemplative and active lives. BIBLIOGRAPHY: A. F. Poulain, *Graces of Interior Prayer* (tr. L. L. Yorke Smith, 1950); A. B. Sharpe, *Mysticism: Its True Nature and Value* (1910); E. Underhill, *Mysticism* (12th ed., rev., 1960); E. C. Butler, *Western Mysticism* (1922); A. Saudreau, *Mystical State* (1924); J. G. Arintero, *Mystical Evolution in the Development and Vitality of the Church* (2 v., tr. J. Aumann, 1949, 1951); R. Garrigou-Lagrange, *Three Ages of the Interior Life* (2 v., tr. T. Doyle, 1947, 1948); A. Royo, *Theology of Christian Perfection* (tr. J. Aumann, 1962); J. Maritain, *Degrees of Knowledge* (tr. under supervision G. B. Phelan,

1959); *idem, Prayer and Intelligence* (tr. A. Thorold, 1934). *MYSTICISM; *MYSTICAL STATE; MYSTICAL PHENOMENA.

[J. AUMANN]

MYSTICAL ILLUMINATION, a divine action whereby the intellect becomes united to divine truth, and the person experiences in some direct and absorbing, though still relatively obscure way, the essential beauty of God. In the early stages of the spiritual life, the action is usually quite transient; but, for those well advanced toward perfection, the experienced presence of divine truth may become an abiding reality that habitually absorbs the mind in contemplation. Ascetical theologians consider this to be the first stage of *mystical union, and they apply to it various names, e.g., the prayer of simplicity, prayer of quiet, infused recollection, infused contemplation, the prayer of simple regard. As this contemplative experience of God increasingly attracts, affects, and dominates the activity of the will and sensitive faculties, the mystical union becomes more complete. BIBLIOGRAPHY: J. G. Arintero, *Mystical Evolution in the Development and Vitality of the Church* (tr. J. Aumann, 2 v., 1949–51).

[M. B. PENNINGTON]

MYSTICAL PHENOMENA. Both words come from the Greek *mustēs,* an initiate, *muein* to close the eyes, and *phanein,* to be seen; their combination symbolizes a paradox that still continues in the treatment of the topic by science, theological and psychological, by popular hagiography, and by the middle discipline of a spiritual literature in which the classical pieces are vastly exceeded in number and bulk by job lots. These are often somewhat deficient in interest, whether that of the humane, the macabre, or the occult, and are of a sort to induce boredom even in the devout, who may dutifully attempt to read them. Mysticism refers to levels of experience above those attainable by ordinary human processes of reasoning and deliberating; and though this is controverted, is always implicitly Christian. Some of its associated phenomena can be greeted, however, only with some reserve. This outline may make matters clearer.

To start with the capital distinction between the supernatural, natural, and normal on one side and the preternatural, miraculous, and unusual on the other: the first of these categories comprises all that God does with us according to his blessed and ordinary *Providence, his cherishing of the natures he has created, and his effectively calling us, of his own good pleasure and generosity, and without any right on our side, to share his own life in friendship, *agapē*. ''Be ye perfect as your heavenly Father is perfect'' (Mt 5.48)—the call is addressed to all who are baptized in Christ, who is the way. It is pursued by faith, hope, and charity, and it may reach the heights without any extraordinary manifestations to arrest the attention or to startle the bystander. Such was the teaching of the Church, part of its response to Gnostic esotericism; it is found in the patristic and monastic masters (cf. E. C. Butler, *Western Mysticism,* 1922), and has been constantly maintained by the great theologians. Mystical phenomena lie only on the fringes of the devout life.

Yet this can be represented as rather an abstract view; human life in the concrete is sometimes much less uneventful. And so we are led to the second of the above categories. In the individual there are forces, scarcely scratched by depth psychology, of imagination and emotion, of glory and misery, of comedy and tragedy, even of farce and melodrama, and all are taken up into the life of grace. A person may love God with all his heart, yet that will not compose his spirit to the gravity of a Gregorian patrician. Moreover, the group psychology of a people, and that includes the people of God of a particular region and period, contributes vogues, prejudices, attitudes, memories, and ideals, all of which go to form what may be called the culture of mysticism. In addition, we are not alone, for there is about us a world of spirits, good and bad. We may be sure that few of these forces will be muffled when persons set out on their adventure in the life of the spirit, and it will not be surprising if the result is not always, as they say, in good taste.

Consequently, phenomena surrounding the mystical life are not to be judged only by the norms of a flattish civic theology. Some may be helpful, others not; some may look bizarre, others too dreary for words; others may turn out to be shams. Some may be permanently admirable; others, just period pieces; some may be of universal appeal. Let us classify them and sort some of them out. They fall into three main groups: (1) consequences or concomitants to sanctifying grace; (2) miracles granted for our profit; (3) mere prodigies.

Concomitant mystical phenomena, as they are sometimes called (R. Garrigou-Lagrange, *Christian Perfection and Contemplation,* 1937), are not physical phenomena in the strict sense of the word; that is, they are not verifiable to an outside observer; they are rather interior conditions, such as those described by theologians as the fruits of the Spirit, or the joy, peace, and compassion which are the effects of charity (cf. ThAq ST 1a2ae, 70; 2a2ae, 28–30). Insight into and experimental knowledge of divine things, purification of the senses, constant awareness of God's presence, passive purification of the spirit, death to self, heroic virtue, and zeal for souls—all these mark the different stages traced by the great mystical writers (e.g., St. Teresa of Avila, *Interior Castle* 4–7; St. John of the Cross, *Dark Night;* St. Francis of Sales, *Love of God,* 6–7). We may drag in, too, under this heading effects such as ecstasy (cf. ThAq ST 2a2ae, 175), which sometimes are signs of weakness, and regarded as such by a saint, in that divine knowledge and love proves, as it were, too great a charge for the organism, and produces alienation from the senses and even perhaps from the body.

Miracles. The *charisms to foster the apostolate of God's word are enumerated in 1 Cor 12; the next chapter is the paean about the charity that surpasses them all. Without prejudice to the special role of *prophecy, we treat them here as exceptional and miraculous graces, **gratiae gratis datae,* which do not flow from sanctifying grace or signify the holiness of the thaumaturge, but are given for the benefit of the people of God, *ad utilitatem,* as the Vulgate translates St. Paul's *pros to sumpheron.* The serious student will approach these manifestations of God's loving courtesies toward the vagaries of human nature in a proper spirit of gratitude, coupled with a balanced sense of history and anthropology, a decent modesty in applying the categories of his own subculture, a critical reverence for the facts, and an absence of credulity and addictive craving for signs and wonders. Miracles are meant to help belief, not to tax it. Even a brief account cannot fail to applaud the work carried out in this connection by the English Jesuit, H. Thurston *(The Physical Phenomena of Mysticism,* 1952). The procedure was established by Benedict XIV's classical instruction on the beatification and canonization of the servants of God (1757). One guiding rule is that no extraordinary event is to be publicly acclaimed as a *miracle until all natural explanations have been investigated and ruled out; these include those of paranormal psychosomatic science and demonology. The test of authenticity is not that it was all extremely odd, but that there is cumulative evidence for its helping us to love God the more, and our neighbor as well, for its effect should not be anti-social. Some mystical phenomena, of course, are not such as to commend themselves to a tidy-minded social worker.

Prodigies. There is no question of identifying mystical phenomena with the very life of grace, which is wholly supernatural. Mystical phenomena, however they come about, are physical or psychological facts. Apart from the expert yet cautious guidance of the Church in particular cases, the inquirer will do well to maintain a reserve that is respectful yet not too awed about the miraculous character of such events as the corporeal or imaginative vision of objects unseen by an onlooker, speaking in strange tongues, prevision of the future, telling another's secret heart, recognition of consecrated things, flames of love with scorching effects, resplendence of light, stigmata, bloody sweats, visible appearance in two places at once, levitation, impassibility to fire, abstinence from nourishment beyond the limits of nature, sweet perfumes from a corpse, and bodily incorruption. BIBLIOGRAPHY: ThAq ST 2a2ae, (esp. in ed. Lat-Eng, 171–178, v. 45, ed. R. Potter 1970); F. von Hügel, *Mystical Element in Religion* (1927); J. Dalby, *Christian Mysticism and the Natural World* (1950); A. Plé et al., *Mystery and Mysticism* (1956); R. Omez, *Psychical Phenomena* (1959); A. Wiesinger, *Occult Phenomena in the Light of Theology* (1957).

[T. GILBY]

MYSTICAL SENSE OF SCRIPTURE, another name for the spiritual sense. *SENSES OF SCRIPTURE.

MYSTICAL STATE, in the language of spiritual theology, a state in which the soul lives habitually, although not necessarily constantly, with an awareness of the presence of God as a result of the perfection of the virtues of faith and charity. Theologians commonly teach that the union of the soul with God is initiated substantially through sanctifying grace and is perfected to a mystical degree by supernatural knowledge and supernatural love. It is also common teaching that, as opposed to the ascetical state, the mystical state is characterized by the passivity or receptivity of the soul in relation to God.

For those theologians who identify the mystical act with infused contemplation, the essence of the mystical state consists in the operations of infused knowledge and love. Those, on the other hand, who identify the mystical act with the operations of the gifts of the Holy Spirit, hold that mystical state consists in the habitual predominance of the gifts of the Holy Spirit over the activity of the infused virtues, which operate in a human manner. The theologians who believe that infused contemplation, the mystical act, or the operation of the gifts of the Holy Spirit do not fall within the scope of the normal development of the life of grace, maintain that the mystical state is an extraordinary grace and in effect a *gratia gratis data.* Other theologians, on the contrary, teach that infused contemplation, the gifts of the Holy Spirit, and the mystical act and mystical state are not only the normal perfection of the life of grace, but that all Christians should strive for them. For those who deny the mystical state as the normal perfection of the life of grace and the infused virtues, there are two distinct perfections available to the Christian: ascetical perfection and mystical perfection, though the latter is rare and extraordinary. Those who consider the gifts of the Holy Spirit to be the perfection of the infused virtues, teach that there is but one path to the one Christian perfection and it passes from the ascetical to the mystical phase; hence the mystical state is the goal of all Christians. BIBLIOGRAPHY: J. G. Arintero, *Mystical Evolution in the Development and Vitality of the Church* (tr. J. Aumann, 2 v., 1949–51); R. Garrigou-Lagrange, *Three Ages of the Interior Life* (tr. T. Doyle, 2 v., 1947); *idem, Christian Perfection and Contemplation* (tr. T. Doyle, 1945); P. Barrett, *Theology of the Spiritual Life* (1953); C. Butler, *Western Mysticism* (1932); J. de Guibert, *Theology of the Spiritual Life* (tr. P. Barrett, 1953); J. Maritain, *Prayer and Intelligence* (tr. A. Thorold, 1934); *idem, Degrees of Knowledge* (tr. G. Phelan, 1959).

[J. AUMANN]

MYSTICAL THEOLOGY. As used in the 4th cent. by Marcellus Ancyranus, in the 5th cent. by Marcus Eremita, and later by the pseudo-Dionysius, mystical theology signified an experimental knowledge of God superior to that acquired by reason or faith. Later, the distinction was made between practical mystical theology (the result of infused contemplation) and speculative mystical theology (the scientific study of mysticism), as is evident in the writings of J. Gerson (d. 1429). In the treatises of H. Herp, OFM, Philip of the Holy Trinity, OCD, and T. Vallgornera, OP, speculative mystical theology covers the entire science of the spiritual life. But when Scaramelli, SJ, wrote his *Direttorio ascetico* and *Direttorio mistico* to defend his teaching that the ascetical life is no immediate predisposition for the mystical life and that infused contemplation is not a normal development of the lower grades of prayer, mystical theology was restricted to the study of infused contemplation and the extraordinary graces of the spiritual life. Since the time of J. G. Arintero, OP (d.1928), mystical theology is generally considered to be that section of the theology of the spiritual life at its higher levels, which treats of the operations and manifestations of grace in the souls of the just: passive purgations, contemplative prayer, habitual activity of the gifts of the Holy Spirit, and concomitant and extraordinary mystical phenomena. However, there is no unanimity among the theologians of the spiritual life regarding the mystical state and its operations. According to Murawski, de Journel, SJ, and Louismet, OSB the terms ascetical and mystical are used interchangeably to designate the entire scope of the spiritual life; according to Poulain, SJ, Farges, SS, Naval, CFM, Pourrat, SS, Zimmerman, SJ, mystical theology refers to the extraordinary operations which constitute infused contemplation and the *gratiae gratis datae* which sometimes accompany it. Tanquerey, SS, holds that mystical theology studies the spiritual life from the night of the senses to mystical marriage; Saudreau and Zahn restrict mystical theology to a study of the unitive way. For Arintero, OP, Garrigou-Lagrange, OP, Schrijvers, CSSR, and the modern Thomist school in general, mystical theology has as its field of study all those acts or states that are the result of the operation of the gifts of the Holy Spirit in the soul, which operations are considered to be the normal, full flowering of sanctifying grace and the infused virtues; Cayré, Mutz, and Valensin, while fundamentally in accord with the foregoing, stress the passivity and receptivity of the soul as the essential characteristic of the mystical life. The radical distinction between the various interpretations of mystical theology is that for one group the mystical state is within the ordinary development of the life of grace received at baptism; for the other, the mystical life is extraordinary, similar to a *gratia gratis data,* and is therefore given only to a few chosen souls; it is not to be desired by all since the normal terminus of perfection is the ascetical state. BIBLIOGRAPHY: A. Royo, *Theology of Christian Perfection* (tr. and ed. J. Aumann, 1962); R. Garrigou-Lagrange, *Three Ages of the Interior Life* (tr. T. Doyle, 1947); *Christian Perfection and Contemplation* (tr. T. Doyle, 1945). *MORAL THEOLOGY.

[J. AUMANN]

MYSTICAL UNION, an intense, intersubjective relationship between man and God. As distinct from acquired *contemplation, mystical union is intuitive, passive (the person is himself unable to produce or prolong the experience), and simple (usually with one dominant and strong affective consideration). The traditional division of mystical union follows from St. *Teresa of Avila's description of it in her *Interior Castle*. There are four stages or degrees, although some authors omit the first stage: incomplete mystical union, the prayer of union, ecstatic union, and transforming union. Incomplete mystical union is marked by a certain spiritual quiet but distractions are still present. In the prayer of union, the soul is fully given over to God, and aware of his presence; distractions are not present. The prayer of ecstasy entails the severance of all sense communication with anything but God. Voluntary bodily movements become impossible, and miraculous bodily phenomena sometimes take place. In the prayer of transforming union, also known as *mystical marriage, there is a total absorption of the mind and will into the divine life. This final union is permanent and consciously experienced. BIBLIOGRAPHY: Teresa of Avila, *Interior Castle,* in her *Complete Works* (ed. S. De Santa Teresa and E. A. Peers, 3 v., 1946); N. Lohkamp, NCE 10:174; A. Poulain, CE 4:325–326. *MYSTICISM.

[T. M. MCFADDEN]

MYSTICI CORPORIS, ecclesiological encyclical of Pius XII, issued June 29, 1943. The encyclical was cited by Vat II ConstChurch at many crucial points, and in fact it directed theological attention to many themes that are prominent in the post-Vatican II understanding of the Church. This positive expression of doctrine is the lasting value of the encyclical; most of the aberrant theological positions it sought to correct have faded from memory. *Mystici corporis* insists that the Church is neither exclusively hierarchic nor exclusively charismatic; it is made up of all the faithful together, all contributing to its life with their diverse functions, offices, and gifts. The Church on earth is not a community of saints alone, but is made up also of sinners. The encyclical notably emphasizes the theology of the local Church and the office of the local bp. as teacher and shepherd. The Church is Christ's body because it is Christ's vital communication of his grace and merits that gives it its life. The document develops the expression in Leo XIII's encyclical on the Holy Spirit, *Divinum illud munus* (1897) that the Holy Spirit is "the soul of the Church." It is the Spirit's sanctifying influence communicating the spirit of Christ that makes the body one "person"; the Church is not simply a moral person, constituted like a secular society only by a common goal; it is one by the Spirit that gives the members one shared life interiorly. The right understanding of the personal indwelling of the Holy Spirit in the souls of those in grace—another theme from *Divinum illud munus*—is also stressed. The universal call to holiness and the various forms of response, ideas so prominent since Vatican II, are also themes of the document. Finally, it clarifies the meaning of membership in the Church and in this sense prepared the way for the Council's clarification of ecumenical relations with other Christian communions. (It is noteworthy that Vat II ConstChurch in effect drops "membership" with its teaching on incorporation into the Church and recognition of the ecclesiality of other Churches and communions.) Vatican II proposed a variety of "models" that represent the mysterious nature of the Church; the model of the Church as Christ's body is but one of them, and it is now less exclusively stressed than in the era before *Mystici corporis*. But this encyclical in its positive teaching has contributed to an understanding of the realities that all the models, none adequate in itself, point to.

[T. C. O'BRIEN]

MYSTICISM, etymologically, from the Gr. verb *muo,* meaning to close the lips for silence and secrecy, in the context of the ancient mystery religions; in Christian tradition, the experience in which the believer arrives at a special kind of union with God. In this sense, Gerson defines mystical theology as a "knowledge of God by experience, arrived at through the embrace of unifying love." The knowledge arrived at in mystical experience has the same object as both natural and dogmatic theology, God. But whereas in "theodicy" the knowledge of God is achieved through the use of normal reasoning powers, and the knowledge of God is achieved in dogmatic theology by applying reasoning to the data of revelation, here the knowledge is more direct and less purely cerebral. Thus, a 13th-cent. commentator, Thomas Gallus, talks of a more profound and superintellectual manner of knowing God. The highest cognitive faculty, he says, is not the intellect; there is one far excelling this, called by him *principalis affectio,* which seems to mean the "high point of the soul" that is rather conative than cognitive. Sense-knowledge, imagination, and simple reasoning are all suspended. The mystic is drawn to God in a way analogous to, though immensely more spiritual than, the way in which a woman is drawn to her lover. Hence the frequency with which the language of human love is employed (e.g., by St. John of the Cross) to describe what is essentially an experience that is both unique and essentially incommunicable.

Non- Christian Mysticism. Although the present article is primarily concerned with Christian mysticism, it is necessary to recognize that there has been mystical experience outside that tradition. Indeed, if believing with Augustine that man is made for God and that his heart is restless until it comes to rest in God, one must expect to find evidence of such Godward striving in any authentic religious tradition. Thus in China an early teaching maintained that man's highest purpose was the quest for *Tao,* which was thought of as Ultimate Reality, source of all that is, pervading and harmonizing all natural phenomena. For man, *Tao* is the exemplar of moral perfection and man can realize himself only by some kind of identification with it. There are interesting parallels between the Chinese and Christian religions as to how this identification is achieved. In the words of Lao Tzu: "Only he who is forever free from earthly passions can apprehend the spiritual essence of *Tao.*" After this purgative phase comes the stage when the achievement of virtue is not a self-conscious, self-regarding effort but rather a connatural condition. Finally, man becomes the unresisting vehicle of *Tao,* so that he can rise above the limitations of matter and is no longer subject to the laws of the physical universe. At the same time in much Chinese speculation there is little sense of religion as understood today, no sense of a personal relationship with God, or, it would seem, of any obligation to him. In fact, the end of the Taoist mystical way seems to be the absorption into some pantheistic being. It is hardly surprising that to all intents Taoism became amalgamated with Buddhism. Of Hinduism it is unnecessary to mention more than the influence that Indian ideas had on the Greek tradition through Pythagoras, and hence on Plato and neoplatonism. Neoplatonic influence on the Christian tradition through Plotinus and Proclus, above all on Pseudo-Dionysius, who was the primary mystical authority for the medievals, is undeniable.

The Role of Grace. Christian writers agree that where genuine mystical experiences occur they are the direct result, not of the efforts of the mystics themselves, though they must prepare themselves by purification, but of a special grace, over and above the ordinary graces given to all Christians. The turning away from what is not God in order to arrive at God himself may be the effect of such ordinary graces. Yet, God's drawing to himself has already begun. Here one of the central problems in the whole discussion is encountered, cooperation between the soul and God. This is, of course, a special example of a larger problem.

Man is utterly dependent on God. This means that the roots of his being at a level deeper than consciousness are to be found in the being of God himself. Yet man's whole conscious life is passed in this space-time world. Moreover, because of original sin, the awareness of God that would seem connatural to man is fitful and obscure. It can be perfected, first by turning away from concentration on the space-time world and allowing the attraction of God to have its full effect. Precisely because so much of our conscious life is bound up with this world of sense-experience, the process of purgation is painful; hence the dark nights of senses and spirit in which the personality is detached from that total absorption in temporal and material reality that has become a permanent distraction from God. Hence the traditional insistence on the necessity for the *via negativa,* the attainment to some indirect knowledge of God by seeing him as the denial of all that is commonly felt or thought of by human beings in their normal cognitive processes. In this "cloud of unknowing" the mystic learns God by unlearning everything that is not God. Moreover, unlike the objects of normal thinking, God is not the passive object of the mystic's contemplative activity. Rather he is the active inspiration, the overwhelming Power to whom the mystic submits, freely and therefore not inertly. Surrender therefore becomes an immense enrichment simply because the knowledge and love of God are the consummation of man's purpose.

The Mystic's Knowledge of God. St. Thomas Aquinas developed what has become accepted as the classical explanation of what may be called the mechanics of the illumination that is an important element of the mystical experience. While human knowledge ordinarily begins with some sense-awareness, the intellect works to abstract from the colored shapes, sounds, feelings, scents, and tastes produced by chemical and physical interaction between an external object and the sense-organ, the idea, or "concept," that is the specific object of normal, rational activity. By linking together these abstract ideas, the mind makes judgments; it reasons and infers. St. Thomas suggests that in the state of innocence preceding the Fall there may have been a way of knowing that began with an immediate conceptual activity without a previous stage of sensation and abstraction. Only by special divine help would man be able to abide permanently in such a purely spiritual form of intellection. Having lost that preternatural endowment, he is no longer capable of that direct intellectual awareness of God that, to be adequate, must clearly be free from the distorting effects of imagery. God is pure spirit and cannot be described in language drawn from sense-experience. But there seems no reason why, in some cases and for special reasons, God should not confer a grace restoring a person temporarily to the state of perfection that man enjoyed before the Fall (see ThAq ST 1a, 94.1 and ad 3).

The foregoing remains nothing more than a theory, but it is as far as it goes a coherent explanation and a useful working hypothesis. It helps to understand why the mystic, after his experience, is invariably incapable of describing what has happened. Thus Augustine says: "Thy invisible things, understood by those that are made, I saw indeed but was unable to fix my gaze thereon. My weakness was beaten back and I was reduced to my ordinary experience" (*Conf.* 7.17). Recalling Gerson's definition, "knowledge of God arrived at through the embrace of unifying love," one might suggest that in the mystic's experience there is complete coordination of will and intellect directed toward God, who is the perfect and adequate end of their activity. Hence it can be seen why the effect of mystical contemplation is not primarily an illumination of the mind but is chiefly a deepening of the whole personality, an enriching of character, a development of virtue. BIBLIOGRAPHY: W. R. Inger, *Christian Mysticism* (1889); W. James, *Varieties of Religious Experience* (1902); A. F. Poulain, *Graces of Interior Prayer* (tr. L. L. Yorke, 1950); E. Underhill, *Mysticism* (12th ed. rev., pa., 1960); E. C. Butler, *Western Mysticism* (1922); F. von Hügel, *Mystical Element of Religion* (2v., 2d ed., 1923); R. Otto, *Mysticism, East and West* (tr. B. L. Bracey, 1932); D. Knowles, *English Mystical Tradition* (1961); F. C. Happold, *Mysticism: A Study and an Anthology* (1963), excellent bibliog.

[T. CORBISHLEY]

MYSTICS, those persons represented in almost every culture throughout history whose experience of the Absolute is direct, intuitive, and affective. The mystic is characterized by a type of consciousness in which the subject-object polarity is not sharply perceived. The mystic and the Absolute that he experiences tend to fuse into an undivided unity. The soul is vitalized with a new energy, liberated through an insight into pure truth, and filled with joy. Strictly speaking, there are no mystics among the Buddhists since they do not acknowledge an Absolute. Mystics have had great importance in Taoism (see LAO TZU), Islam (see SUFISM), and *Hinduism where the determined quest for an ultimate unity has readily lent itself to mysticism. In the Christian tradition, there have been innumerable mystics. Contemporary Christian theology emphasizes the possibility of mystical prayer for those strongly committed to the search for spiritual perfection, and points out that the mystic's intense experience of God is the ultimate goal for all mankind. BIBLIOGRAPHY: Hastings ERE 9:83–117; R. B. Zaehner, *Mysticism Sacred and Profane* (1957); *idem, Hindu and Muslim Mysticism* (1960). *MYSTICISM.

[T. M. MCFADDEN]

MYTH, a term derived from the Gr. *mythos* that in itself has a complicated history and numerous meanings. Probably originating from the Indo-European root, *mudh,* meaning to think, to reflect, *mythos* at first meant thought in the sense of the content of a speech or conversation. In early Greek it meant story or narrative with no connotation of truth or falsity. In Attic Greek it was used as a technical term for stories about the gods, which educated Greeks regarded as fictitious. Modern scholars have expanded this sense of myth to give it the general meaning of a story about the holy. For Aristotle and other Greek writers, *mythos* was equivalent to fiction. In this latter sense it is used in the Pastoral Epistles of the NT to repudiate religious speculations considered to be false (1 Tim 1.4; 4.7; 2 Tim 4.4) or practices judged to be false asceticism (Tit 1.14). It also appears in 2 Pt 1.16 in the sense of a fictitious story. Modern study of myth has thoroughly revised the concept, appreciating in it a method of religious thought and expression that performs the same function for religion that music and pictorial art perform for the aesthetic apprehension of reality. Ancient myths customarily deal in the form of a story with the principal cosmic themes that practically all cultures have reflected upon: creation, the divinity, the origin and end of the cosmos, the conflict between good and evil (in which savior myths appear). Myth in this sense is a nonscientific language that gives expression to man's religious awareness concerning his human situation. As such, it is a form of expression that cannot be simply made equivalent to falsity, for the myth's real aim is to convey man's sense of the mysterious universe that towers over and around him, and of which he as an individual is an important but very temporary being.

Many modern biblical scholars see this mythological way of thought and expression as entirely compatible with the dignity and truth of Sacred Scripture. They consider it appropriate and meaningful to designate certain biblical passages, such as the story of the Fall in Gen 3, the exodus of Israel from Egypt, and the redemptive death of Jesus on the cross as in some sense mythological in character. This use of myth in application to biblical passages is not intended to deny reality to the events about which the biblical myth speaks, but rather to focus attention upon the religious meaning the myth endeavors to draw from the event: the on-going realities of man's sinfulness (the Fall), of God's liberating power (the exodus) in and through Christ (his redemptive death). For modern man, whose habits of thought are strongly influenced by science and technology, the recognition of mythological thought patterns in Scripture as a legitimate and forceful expression of religiously significant realities is a valuable aid to the appreciation of the Bible and its message. Biblical scholars are not agreed on the extent to which mythical thought patterns are to be found in Scripture, nor are they in harmony on the point at which mythical thought and expression are to be distinguished from the reality of the event. It may confidently be anticipated that further research into biblical narratives from the standpoint of their mythological content, that is clearly much more restrained and meaningfully employed than in the case of their non-biblical counterparts, will contribute to a satisfactory solution of these problems. BIBLIOGRAPHY: B. Malinowski, *Mytn in Primitive Psychology* (1926); E. Cassirer, *Language and Myth* (tr. S. Langer, 1946); I. Henderson, *Myth in the NT* (1952); H. W. Bartsch, *Kerygma and Myth* (tr. R. H. Fuller, 1953).

[C. P. CEROKE]

MYTH, LITERARY, the use for literary purposes of stories associated with divinities and religious phenomena. Though distinctions are very difficult to draw, it seems possible to identify the use or invention of myth as the theme of a literary production that is distinct from an original, symbolic representation of mysterious phenomena in primitive consciousness. Epics and hymns of many peoples represent an early stage of the process, and within Homeric epic Demodocus's story of Aphrodite's adultery with Ares (*Odyssey* 8.266) is a clearly advanced example of the type. The close relation of myth both to folk-tale and to legend helps to explain its literary forms. Masters of Greek poetry, esp. Pindar and the Attic tragedians, used and interpreted inherited mythology as the framework in which to create new insights with a mythological sweep. Plato invented myths to provide a dramatic or epic force and a non-discursive dimension to his argument. With increased secularization in the Hellenistic period came increased use of mythology by poets merely as the theme of a story, particularly one explaining the origin of some name or custom (aetiological myth). This usage, already present in earliest epic, was adopted by the Romans, who had little or no inherited mythology of their own, and appears with particular prominence in Virgil, Propertius, and Ovid. Much of the compilation of myths in later antiquity was directed toward understanding of the poets rather than any religious interest. BIBLIOGRAPHY: H. J. Rose, *Modern Methods in Classical Mythology* (1930); *idem, Handbook of Greek Mythology* (6th ed., 1958).

[Z. STEWART]

N

NAAMAN, Syrian army commander cured of leprosy after following instructions of the prophet Elisha (2 Kg ch. 5). Told by his wife's maid, a captive Israelite, of a prophet in Samaria who could cure his leprosy, N. went first to the king of Israel and then to Elisha. After initial resistance, N. followed Elisha's instruction to bathe seven times in the Jordan and was cured, after which he acknowledged the God of Israel.

[T. EARLY]

NAASSENES, 2d-cent. *Gnostic sect (probably *Valentinian) described by Hippolytus (*Ref. haer*. 5), who claims their name derives from the Hebrew word for snake. Hippolytus's account is incomplete and somewhat unclear, but their teaching seems to have emphasized: human souls "fallen" into a material world; a complex account of the origin of this predicament (an emanation involving three principles: an unoriginated and hidden God; a self-originated primal divine Man; and a chaos-principle); and salvation as the reclaiming of one's true (spiritual or heavenly) identity through knowledge (*gnōsis*) and a rebirth through Jesus. BIBLIOGRAPHY: W. Foerster, *Gnosis* (1972) 261–282.

[D. P. EFROYMSON]

NABAL, Calebite who refused to make gifts to David and his men after they guarded his herds (1 Sam ch. 25). N.'s wife Abigail brought David the gifts as he came to take revenge. When she told N. of what David had intended, he was stricken and died 10 days later. David then made Abigail his second wife.

[T. EARLY]

NABATEANS, Arabian people who pushed N *c*.6th cent. B.C. and occupied a large area including Edom, Moab, the Sinai Peninsula, and an area extending N to Damascus. Their capital was at *Petra. They gradually achieved independence from Persia and remained free until the Roman Emperor Trajan annexed them in 106 A.D. Jason, a contender for the office of Jewish high priest, unsuccessfully sought refuge with Arestas I, king of the Nabateans, in 169 B.C. (2 Macc 5.8). Nabateans are not mentioned in the OT or NT, but Herod Antipas was married to the daughter of a Nabatean king before he married Herodias (Mk 6.17). The governor of Aretas IV of Nabatea sought to capture Paul at Damascus (2 Cor 11.32).

[T. EARLY]

NABER, JOSEF (1870–1967), pastor of Konnersreuth, Germany. N. was the first to tell of Theresa *Neumann's sufferings and was a witness to many of her phenomenal experiences, which contained controversial elements that initiated theological objections to their divine origin. He later became pastor emeritus and at the age of 92 was a bedside witness to her death in 1962.

[C. KEENAN]

NABIS (1889–99), term meaning "seers" or "prophets" for French symbolist poets and painters (M. Denis, P. Bonnard, E. Vuillard) with A. Maillot, and Jan Verkade named by P. Sérusier, scholar of Semitic literature with an interest in ideas occult and theosophic, who, adopting Gauguin's symbolist philosophy, added his own psychological and physiological reactions in a concept of art as universal communication expressed symbolically. To M. Denis art works were metaphors free of visual reality (red trees). "A picture—before it is a horse . . . is a flat surface of colors," Denis stated. In the exhibition (1891) Nabis showed their debt to Gauguin, Art Nouveau, and the Japanese print. The group disbanded in 1899, Bonnard and Vuillard alone pursuing their theories, becoming great painters.

[M. J. DALY]

NABONIDUS, see NABU–NA'ID.

NABOTH, citizen of Jezreel whose vineyard was coveted by Ahab (1 Kg 21). When N. refused to sell, Jezebel had him stoned to death on a false charge of cursing God and the King. Ahab then went to possess the vineyard, but Elijah met him and prophesied the death of both Ahab and Jezebel (1 Kg 22.37–38; 2 Kg 9.30–37).

[T. EARLY]

NABUCHODONOSOR, see NEBUCHADNEZZAR.

NABUCO DE ARAUJO, JOAQUIM (1849–1910), Brazilian writer and political figure who worked tirelessly for the abolition of slavery in his country. He also served as Brazilian ambassador to the U.S. and supported the development of Pan-Americanism.

[M. A. MCFADDEN]

NABU-NA'ID (Nabonidus), last king of Babylon (555–539 B.C.). He was not descended from his predecessors Evil-merodach (561–559), Neriglissar (559–555), and Labashi-Marduk (555), and it is not known how he came to the throne. Soon after he came to power, he left his capital for unknown reasons and made Teima in NW Arabia the center of his activity for several years. His son Belshazzar (called the son of Nebuchadnezzar in Dan ch. 5) was regent in his absence. N. lost support by favoring the moon god Sin and neglecting Marduk. Cyrus of Persia easily took control of Babylon, sparing N.'s life but exiling him.

[T. EARLY]

NABUSHAZBAN, Babylonian noble, perhaps the leading royal councilor, or the head chamberlain, who was a general in the army that in 587 B.C. captured Jerusalem (Jer 39.3,13).

[J. F. FALLON]

NABUZARADAN, the Babylonian general who in 587 B.C. destroyed Jerusalem and its Temple by fire (2 Kg 25.8,9), carried out the deportation of the middle and higher classes, freed Jeremiah from prison (Jer 40.1), and set up Gedaliah as governor at Mizpah.

[J. F. FALLON]

NACCHIANTI, GIACOMO (Nanclantus in contemporary Latin documents; *c.*1500–69), Dominican theologian. He was of the community of S. Marco, Florence, and afterwards was bp. of Chioggia. He took a spirited part during the early phases of the Council of Trent; vigorously maintained the supremacy of the Scriptures over ecclesiastical traditions—"What, accept the practice of praying eastwards with the same reverence as St. John's Gospel?" An awkward customer who took a line against that of the curia, and a man after Paolo Sarpi's own heart (who sometimes puts his discourses into the mouth of others), he would register his minority vote with "I will obey," rather than with the customary *placet* or *non placet*. Yet though he encountered animosity, and made the acquaintance of the Roman Inquisition, papal favor, if grudged, was not lost, and he zealously administered his diocese, in the Republic of Venice, to the end and applied the decrees of the Council. His writings, marked by a sober style not without elegance, enrich the systematic theology of St. Thomas Aquinas with much positive material, above all from St. Paul. BIBLIOGRAPHY: Jedin Trent v. 2.

[T. GILBY]

NADAB, the name of (1) one of Aaron's sons (Ex 6.23; Lev 10.1–2); (2) the king of Israel *c.*900 B.C. who succeeded his father Jeroboam I and was killed by Baasha (1 Kg 14.20; 15.25–31). The OT also mentions two others of the same name (1 Chr 2.28; 8.30).

[T. EARLY]

NADAL, GERÓNIMO (1507–80), Jesuit theologian and *alter ego* of St. Ignatius Loyola in organizing the Society. A Majorcan, N. studied with Ignatius at Alcalá and again at Paris, but refused to take the Spiritual Exercises, became a secular priest, and it was not until he was fired by a letter from Francis Xavier in India that he rejoined Ignatius 10 years later in Rome and became a Jesuit (1545). Henceforth he spent a life of travel promulgating the constitutions of the Society, acting as vicar general, visitator, and peacemaker. He took part in the Diet of Augsburg, was a papal theologian at the Council of Trent, and as a spiritual director was enlightened, particularly on the relationship of prayer to action. BIBLIOGRAPHY: J. Brodrick, *Progress of the Jesuits, 1556–79* (1947).

[T. GILBY]

NAG HAMMÂDI, village in Egypt near which Coptic Gnostic MSS were discovered in 1945. *CHENOBOSKION.

NAGELSCHRIFT (Hufnagelschrift; Ger *Nagel,* nail; *Huf,* hoof), a German variety of neumes used during the 14th and 15th centuries, so named because the characters resemble the type of nail used with horseshoes.

NAGLE, NANO (Honoria, 1728–84), Irish educator and foundress of the Society of the Charitable Instruction—later known as the Presentation Order. N. was educated in Ireland and Paris; during her postulancy in a French convent, she became convinced of her vocation to work with the poor in Ireland. She returned to Ireland, established a school for poor girls in Cork in spite of the English penal laws, founded the Presentation Order, and was the first to make formal education possible for the Irish poor since the Reformation. BIBLIOGRAPHY: M. R. O'Callaghan, *Flame of Love: Life of Nano Nagle* (1960).

[T. M. MCFADDEN]

NAGLE, URBAN (1905–65), Dominican dramatist, pioneer of the American Catholic Theater. Ordained in 1931, he devoted himself to the theater as an apostolate for 20 years. In 1932 he founded Blackfriars Guild, dedicated to Catholic influence in drama, which evolved in 1937 into the Speech and Drama School of The Catholic University. The Catholic Theater Conference, which he helped to found in 1937, gave intelligent stimulus to serious drama in the Catholic tradition. Blackfriars in New York became a pioneer off-Broadway theater. His play *Savonarola* (1938) was selected by the *New York Times* as one of the 10 best plays of the 1941–42 season. He was a delightful raconteur and his witty radio broadcasts about Uncle George and Uncle Malachy were enjoyed by a nationwide audience. Some of these broadcasts were later published (1946) in essay form under the title *Uncle George and Uncle Malachy*. BIBLIOGRAPHY: U. Nagle, *Behind the Masque* (1951).

[J. R. AHERNE]

NAGOT, FRANCIS CHARLES (1734–1816), Sulpician, a founder of St. Mary's Seminary, Baltimore, Md. A native of France, N. was ordained a Sulpician in 1760. Theology professor, superior of the Minor Seminary in Paris and vice-rector of the Grand Seminary of St. Sulpice in that city, he was sent to the U.S. to establish a seminary in the new Diocese of Baltimore. With three other Sulpicians he established in 1791 the forerunner of St. Mary's Seminary, the first seminary in the U.S. In 1809 Nagot became superior of Mt. St. Mary's Seminary in Emmitsburg, Md., where he resided until his death. BIBLIOGRAPHY: L. Bertrand, *Bibliothèque sulpicienne* (3v., 1900).

[J. R. AHERNE]

NAG'S HEAD FABLE, the story that M.*Parker (1504–75), named abp. of Canterbury by Queen Elizabeth in 1559, was not properly consecrated but merely went through a travesty of the rite at the Nag's Head Tavern at Cheapside, London. It was first put into circulation by the Irish Jesuit C. Holywood in 1604 and was widely used as late even as the 19th cent. in RC polemic against the validity of Anglican orders. The tale has been thoroughly discredited. BIBLIOGRAPHY: J. J. Hughes, *Absolutely Null and Utterly Void* (1968) 19–21.

[T. EARLY]

NAḤMANIDES (*c.*1195–1270), Spanish rabbi, scholar, biblical commentator, mystical philosopher, poet, and physician; a leading author of Talmudic literature in the Middle Ages. Born in the Jewish community of Gerona, Catalonia (Spain), he was known as Gerondi or Yerondi, after his place of origin. His Spanish name was Bonastrug da Porta, but his real name was Moses ben Naḥman. He was called Nahamani and RaMBaN (an acronym of *R*abbi *M*oses *B*en *N*ahman). His disciples included the leading halakhists of the following generation. He was referred to by subsequent Spanish rabbis as "the trustworthy rabbi," "the rabbi," or "the teacher." About 50 of his works are preserved. His halakhic works are among the masterpieces of Rabbinic literature. He also influenced decisively the subsequent course of Jewish mysticism. A descendant of Isaac ben Reuben, and a contemporary of Isaac ben Jacob Alfasi, he assimilated the tradition of the tosaphists of N France, and the methods of study of the yeshivot of Provence. He seems to have earned his livelihood as a physician, may have acted as chief rabbi of Catalonia and was consulted in Jewish matters by King James I of Aragon (1213–76). It was this same King who coerced him into the famous public disputation in Barcelona (1263) with the convert from Judaism Pablo Christiá, OP. Held in the presence of the King and leaders of the Dominicans and Franciscans, it turned out to be a momentous turning point in N.'s life. Despite the fact that he had been promised by the King freedom of speech and the fact that the book he wrote subsequently to summarize his views had been undertaken at the request of the bp. of Gerona, he seems to have roused the dangerous hostility of the Dominicans. Not even the King could protect him from their campaign, aided and abetted by Pope Clement IV, and N. escaped to Palestine for safety. He finished his life there, an exile in that diminished Jewish community. BIBLIOGRAPHY: E. Gottlieb, *Encyclopedia Judaica* 12:774–782; cf. E. A. Synan, NCE 10:197–198.

[E. J. DILLON]

NAHOR, name of (1) the father of Terah (Gen 11.22–24); (2) the son of Terah and brother of Abraham and Haran (Gen 11.27), who married Haran's daughter Milcah (Gen 11.29). Abraham sent his servant back to the city of N to find a wife for Isaac, and the servant brought back Rebekah, daughter of N.'s son Bethuel (Gen ch. 24).

[T. EARLY]

NAHUM, BOOK OF. The collection of oracles contained in this book, which was delivered shortly before the fall of Nineveh and the final overthrow of the Assyrians in 612, describes the approaching sack of Nineveh in a triumphal poem (2.1–3.13), the imagery of which ranks with the most powerful in the Old Testament. It is presented as the fury of Yahweh breaking out on these cruel oppressors of his people. The theophany and judgment of Yahweh are described in an acrostic psalm (unfortunately incomplete) in Nah 1.2–10. Apart from this, the book contains a number of shorter oracles containing threats against Assyria and promises to Judah. Nahum is above all the prophet of divine retribution. The cruelties Assur has perpetrated upon Yahweh's people in the past are now to be visited upon her in turn. BIBLIOGRAPHY: A. Haldar, *Studies in the Book of Nahum* (1947); W. A. Maier, *Book of Nahum: a Commentary* (1959).

NAILS, HOLY, the traditional term for those instruments by which Christ was nailed to the cross and therefore, the objects of Christian veneration for centuries. Support for their use by the Roman soldiers in the crucifixion of Jesus is found in John's description of the place of the nails in Christ's hands (Jn 20.25,27) and that of Luke which mentions the feet (Lk 24.39). Inconclusive evidence of the exact manner of Jesus' crucifixion has led to early iconography with no nails in the feet with both hands affixed to the cross to later versions with both one and two nails in the feet. While as many as 30 nails are venerated as the true nails throughout the world there is no historical authentication. BIBLIOGRAPHY: M. W. Schoenberg, NCE 10:199; H. Thurston, CE 10:672; C.E. Pocknee, *Cross and Crucifix in Christian Worship and Devotion* (1962).

[F. H. BRIGHAM]

NAIN, a town of Galilee, modern Nein, about 6 miles S of Nazareth. In this village, Jesus raised to life the only son of a widow (Lk 7.11–17). BIBLIOGRAPHY: InterDB 3:500.

[J. A. GRASSI]

NAJRAN, MARTYRS OF, those Christians who were martyred during a period *c.*520 in S Arabia, most of them in or around the town of Najran. Among the group are SS. Aretas and Elesbaan; Elesbaan is not one of the original martyrs but he later vindicated their deaths. Under Prince Dhū Nuwās, who had become a Jewish convert, thousands of others were martyred in the most cruel way for refusing to deny Christ's divinity. The murders are mentioned in the Koran. There is some evidence that many of those martyrs were Monophysites. BIBLIOGRAPHY: Butler 4:190–191; W.J. Burghardt, NCE 10:200.

[J. R. RIVELLO]

NĀLANDĀ, MONASTERY AND UNIVERSITY, most famous center of learning at Nālandā in ancient Magadha, Bihār, India. The vihara (monastery) erected by Aśoka and university by Sakrāditya (*c.*415–55), developed architecturally with stupas and shrines. Famous teachers under the saintly abbot Sīlabhadra, while advancing the doctrines of Buddhism, taught the Vedas, Hindu philosophy, logic, grammar, and medicine. Remains show an 8th-cent. colossal sculpture of Avalokiteśvara, and vigorous 9th-cent. bronzes. Vajrayāna and Hindu affinities mark the merging of Tantric schools.

[M. J. DALY]

NAMATIANUS, RUTILIUS CLAUDIUS (5th cent.), late Latin poet, a conservative pagan who wrote in the declining years of the Empire in the West. After holding office in Rome, he returned to his native Gaul *c.*416. In his poem *De reditu suo,* he describes this homeward journey and manifests his dissatisfaction with changes that were marking the evanescence of pagan glory. Works: Eng. tr. by J. and A. Duff in *Minor Latin Poets* (Loeb, 1934) 753–829. BIBLIOGRAPHY: J. Hammer, OCD 596; F. X. Murphy, NCE 10:200.

[R. B. ENO]

NAME, BAPTISMAL, a name given to a person at baptism. In the early centuries converts to Christianity sometimes changed their names, taking that of an Apostle, martyr, or using as a name some word associated with Christian belief. By the 14th cent. the taking of saints' names had become the almost universal custom. The name was thought of as conferred in baptism, which by that time was generally received in infancy. The practice was enjoined by the Council of Trent. The name thus given at christening is often called the Christian name by contrast with the surname, or with the new name taken in some religious communities at reception of the habit or at profession to mark an individual's separation from his former way of life. For Roman Catholics, the giving of a Christian name at baptism is required by the present Code of Canon Law (CIC c. 761), although the obligation is put more directly upon the pastor than upon the parents. The saint after whom an individual is named is often regarded as his special *patron saint. BIBLIOGRAPHY: H. Thurston, CE 10:673–675.

NAME DAY, also called "feast day," the day in the church calendar celebrating a person's patron saint. The custom of honoring a person on that day in a way like the celebration of a birthday still survives in some European countries; the custom is better known in the U.S. from its observance in religious communities.

NAMES, BIBLICAL. For peoples of Semitic cultures, names expressed more than simple identity; they connoted individual existence, qualities, and destiny. To name something was to have control over it. Hebrew personal names were mostly theophoric, being composed of a divine name and some predicate, e.g., Jonathan—a shortened form of *Jehu,* (God's proper name, fully written, Yahweh), plus *nathan* (has given), plus *ben* (a son). Place names expressed phenomena, e.g., Carmel, "orchard"; En-Gedi, "spring of the kid"; or, sanctuaries, e.g., Bethel, "house of the God, El." Sometimes kings received new names when enthroned, e.g., Elhanan, "God has been gracious" may well have been King David's original name (2 Sam 21.19). Isaiah gave symbolic names to his sons, e.g., Shear-jashub, "a remnant shall return." To call upon the name of God was to appeal to him in worship and to take upon oneself his security.

[J. F. FALLON]

NAMES, CHRISTIAN. The early Christians as a rule retained their former names after their conversion unless there was some special reason for changing them, as in the case of St. Paul, who changed his Hebrew name of Saul to the Roman Paul when he began his mission among the gentiles (cf. Acts 13.9). These Christian names, known from inscriptions and literary sources, thus retained the peculiarities of their Hebrew, Greek, or Roman origins. There are names taken from pagan deities (Apollo, Demeter), from pagan beliefs (Augustus, Faustinus), from numbers (Primus, Octavia), from colors (Flavius, Candida), from animals (Leo, Asella), from precious stones (Chrysanthus, Margarita), from the sea (Marina), rivers (Iordanus), and countries (Lydia), from physical and moral qualities (Formosus, Iustina), from the solar system (Phoebus), from months (Januaria), and from servile origin (Servulus). With the passage of time and a fuller appreciation of baptism as a rebirth, a new name was sometimes added to the former name. Ignatius of Antioch, e.g., added Theophoros (borne by God); Cyprian took that of Caecilian, after the priest who had instructed him; Eusebius, that of Pamphilus, out of reverence for this martyr. There are other names of Christian origin taken from the OT (Abel, Abraham) and NT (Thomas, Martha), from Christian dogmas (Anastasia, Redemptus), from Christian virtues (Agape, Elpidius), from Church feasts (Epiphanius, Pascasia), and from a divine gift or activity (Theodotus, Theotekne). Besides these, some Christians adopted bizarre and humiliating names to show their contempt for the pomp and pride of the world (Alogius, Contumeliosus, and even Stercorius). BIBLIOGRAPHY: H. Leclercq, DACL 12.2:1481–1553; F. X. Murphy, NCE 10:201–203, L.C. Hector, NCE 10:203–204; M. R. P. McGuire, NCE 5:470–475 s.v. "Epigraphy, Christian."

[M. J. COSTELLOE]

NAMES, MEDIEVAL. Whereas the Romans had developed an involved system of personal nomenclature (*praenomen, nomen, cognomen*), the barbarians of northern Europe were, at the time of the migrations (*c.*375–500), still using single names. After the migrations, the tendency to use single names spread even in Romanized areas. There were, in general, two sources of such names: (1) Indo-European stock elements, which yielded such names as *Siegfried, Gertrud, Adelbert,* etc.; (2) names with religious associations. As the medieval Church grew in importance, the latter gradually supplanted the former. Since there were relatively few given (or baptismal) names in common use, and since the custom had grown within families of giving the same name to more than one child, hypocoristic or diminutive forms were used to distinguish persons with the same name. In Latin documents, however, all forms of a given name, regardless of the national vernacular from which it came or the hypocoristic form in daily use, were standardized in one Latin form. To avoid confusion, surnames were introduced into legal documents in Latin, first in France toward the end of the 10th cent., then throughout Europe. Surnames were of four kinds: (1) patronymics or metronymics; (2) names denoting rank, occupation, or nationality; (3) toponymics; (4) names denoting personal traits. It was only after a long period of transition that surnames came into general use or were regarded as hereditary. BIBLIOGRAPHY: L. C. Hector, NCE 10:203–204; E. G. Withycombe, *Oxford Dictionary of Christian Names* (1950).

[M. F. MCCARTHY]

NAMES OF GOD, see GOD, NAMES OF.

NANNI D'ANTONIO DI BANCO (*c.*1384–1421), Italian sculptor. At Florence he carved reliefs for the Porta della Mandorla and figures of *Isaiah* and *St. Luke*. At Or San Michele the statues of *St. Eligius, St. Philip,* and *Quattro Santi Coronati* (four martyred sculptors) are attributed to N. He collaborated with Brunelleschi and Donatello on the cupola of the cathedral. While retaining Gothic vestiges, N. fully grasped the three-dimensional quality of the antique. In his last work, an *Assumption of the Virgin* (*c.*1414–21), the linear International Gothic is wedded to the dynamic *contraposto* of the Renaissance.

[M. J. DALY]

NANNI, JOHN, see ANNIUS, JOHN.

NANTES, EDICT OF, see EDICT OF NANTES.

NANTEUIL, ROBERT (1623–1678), French master graphic artist whose inimitable technique raised engraving to a major art. After a Jesuit education N., in Paris, studied portraiture with P. de Champaigne, and engraving with A. Bosse, his personal charm and ability gaining him a royal pension in 1659. In some 600 brilliant works he left an accurate record of the French court (portraits of Louis XIV, Colbert, Card. Mazarin) evolving his unique masterly technique of exquisite tonal effects.

[M. J. DALY]

NAOMI, wife of Elimelech of Bethlehem and mother-in-law of Ruth, who returned with Ruth from Moab to Bethlehem after the death of her husband and her two sons. She was instrumental in urging Ruth to seek marriage with Boaz, who was a remote kinsman of herself, and as a result of this took her grandson Obed, the ancestor of David, and became his nurse (Ru 4.16–17).

[D. J. BOURKE]

NAPHTALI (Nephthali), name of the second son of Jacob by Rachel's maid Bilhah (Gen 30.1–6), and also of one of the 12 tribes of Israel, supposedly descended from Jacob's son (Num 26.48–50; Gen 49.21; Dt 33.23). It settled in the N part of Palestine (Jos 19.32–39), an area taken by Benhadad (1 Kg 15.20) and later by Tiglath-pileser III (2 Kg 15.29). Barak was from Naphtali (Jg 4.6; 5.18), and members of the tribe were among Gideon's band (Jg 6.35). The prophecy of Is 9.1 concerning the tribe is cited in Mt 4.13–16.

[T. EARLY]

NAPOLEON I (BONAPARTE; 1769–1821), first emperor of the French, one of the greatest captains in history, and a statesman who has left a great and enduring mark on the map and political history of Europe. Here we are concerned only with his religious attitudes and influence, not with his civil and military achievements. Personally he was somewhat agnostic and certainly not devout, but he never lost his awe for his mother, who was pious and severe and who outlived him, and though he was a latitudinarian in the manner of the Enlightenment, his last testament expressed the desire to die in the Catholic faith of his forebears and with the last sacraments of the Church, which in fact he received through the solicitude of Pius VII, "the old imbecile" he had imprisoned at Savona and Fontainebleau. As a statesman he believed that religion was necessary for the people and the stability of the State. Already as First Consul he had provided for the freedom of religion and the restoration of worship in France (1799) and negotiated a concordat with Rome (1801), which ended the schism caused by the Civil Constitution of the Clergy. He sought the blessing of the Church at his coronation as emperor (1804), but probably for the same reasons that he removed the Pope from Rome and kept him in custody for nearly 5 years. Public religion was supported so long as it served the purposes of the empire; but when the papacy manifested a proper independence—or opened its ports to British ships—then it was to be kept in strict, if padded, confinement. So also his divorce from Josephine and second marriage with the Archduchess Marie Louise of Austria was prompted by the desire to have an heir with royal blood in his veins. The only clerics who emerged with credit from this affair, allowed by the decision of a diocesan tribunal, were the "black" cardinals who would not have anything to do with it. BIBLIOGRAPHY: J. Leflon, *La Crise révolutionnaire, 1789–1846* (1949).

[T. GILBY]

NAPOLEON III (1808–73), president (1848–52), then emperor of France (1852–70). Son of Louis Bonaparte and Hortense de Beauharnais, and nephew of *Napoleon Bonaparte, N. attained power and remained in office through the support of conservative Catholics. He in turn allowed the Church greater liberty than it had enjoyed under the previous regime. The Falloux law of 1850, reestablishing church schools, won him much praise. The journalist Louis *Veuillot was his vigorous advocate; the Count de Montalembert and Bp. F. *Dupanloup of Orléans represented the Catholic opposition. Even in foreign policy, Catholic interests shaped N.'s decisions as evident in his vacillating schemes supporting the *risorgimento but protecting the papacy with the French army, the Crimean War, and his intervention in Mexico and Indo-China. BIBLIOGRAPHY: J. Maurain, *La Politique ecclésiastique du second empire de 1852 à 1869* (1930); A. Dansette, *Religious History of Modern France* (2 v., 1961).

[R. H. SCHMANDT]

NARCOTHERAPY, treatment through use of psychoactive drug to facilitate the reemergence of an emotionally laden experience. The most commonly used drugs for this purpose are such short-acting barbiturates as sodium-amytal, although for a time in the mid to late 1950s lysergic acid diethylamide (LSD 25) was used for this purpose. Narcotherapy must be distinguished from chemotherapy in which a drug, by acting directly on the central nervous system, is used to correct a biochemical abnormality and thus normalize behavior or thought. While chemotherapy is frequently used in treatment of depression or schizophrenia, narcotherapy is used exclusively within the context of psychotherapy and then only to uncover buried unconscious memories or experiences that may contribute to neurosis. Narcotherapy has been most frequently used in treatment of "war neurosis" or "survivor syndrome" in which a surviving soldier may be helped to remember and reexperience a traumatic circumstance in which he participated but which he has repressed in order to escape the anxiety or guilt of the situation. BIBLIOGRAPHY: J. Cole and J. M. Davis, "Narcotherapy," *Comprehensive Textbook of Psychiatry* (1976); R. R. Grinker, and I. P. Spiegel, *War Neuroses* (1945).

[P. B. AMAR]

NARCOTICS, see DRUG ADDICTION; DRUG PEDDLING.

NARSES (NARSAI; *c.*400–*c.*503), Nestorian theologian, founder of the School of *Nisibis. After a brief period in the monastery of Kefar-Mari, N. went to Edessa as a student, and, when he had completed his studies, remained there as a teacher. He was elected rector of the school *c.*437 and continued in that position until he was deposed for his Nestorian teaching (*c.*457). He fled to Nisibis where, under the patronage of the bp., his friend Bar-Sumas, he reconstituted his school and directed it for the last 40 years of his life. His numerous commentaries on the OT have been lost, but 360 of his poems, hymns, and homilies have survived. Syriac text of works: ed. A. Mingana (2 v., 1905). BIBLIOGRAPHY: Altaner 407; PSO 107–110.

[R. B. ENO]

NARTHEX, a vestibule or portico stretching across the W end of some early Christian basilicas, divided from the nave by a wall, screen, or railing, and set apart for the use of catechumens and penitents, and sometimes women. It is also called an antenave.

[T. GILBY]

NARY, CORNELIUS (*c.*1660–1738), Irish priest, polemicist, historian. Ordained in 1684, he received a doctorate at the Univ. of Paris, and from 1700 was a parish priest in Dublin. He wrote *Case of the Catholics of Ireland* (1724), an influential defense of Catholic refusal of the oath abjuring James Stuart as pretender to the English crown, esp. because the oath included rejection of the temporal and spiritual power of the pope. He was also the author of: *Charitable Address to All Who Are of the Communion of Rome* (1724); *New History of the World* (1720); a popular catechism; a translation of the New Testament.

[T. C. O'BRIEN]

NAS, JOHANNES (1534–90), popular Franciscan preacher at Ingolstadt and later at Ulm and Innsbruck; auxiliary bp. of Brixen from 1580. A satirist in the tradition of Murner, N. attacked both Luther and Fischart, the prominent Protestant polemicist. Despite their Latin titles, most of N.'s works are in German. Among them are: *Sex centuriae* (evangelical truths, 6 v., 1565–70); *Examen chartaceae Lutheranorum concordiae* (1580). BIBLIOGRAPHY: G. Fussenegger, LTK 7:796.

[J. R. SCHULZ]

NASH PAPYRUS, Hebrew MS dating from *c.*150 B.C., containing the Ten Commandments, substantially in the form of Dt 5.6–21, and the *Shema (Dt. 6.4–5). Purchased in 1902 from an Egyptian dealer by W. L. Nash, it is now in the Cambridge Univ. Library. Before the discoveries at *Qumram it was the only known ancient biblical MS in Hebrew.

[T. EARLY]

NĀSIK, site of a small chaitya hall belonging to the Hīnayāna phase of Buddhist architecture with Mahāyāna superimpositions, the façades of the viharas (monasteries) in classical style with richly ornamented capitals.

[M. J. DALY]

NATALIS, HERVAEUS, see HERVAEUS NATALIS.

NATALITIA, Lat., birthday celebration, term used to refer to the martyr's day of death and its anniversary, the day of the martyr's birth into eternal life.

[J. DALLEN]

NATARAJA (Nateşvara; Lord of the Dance), aspect of Şiva in the "Cosmic dance" as Prime Mover or Eternal Energy, who creates, maintains, and destroys. Iconographic images show a four-armed Şiva holding in his upper right hand a small drum signifying sound or creation; the upper left hand, in the *ardhacandra* (half-moon) *mudra*, bears a tongue of flame—the final destruction; the lower right hand is raised in the *abhaya mudra* "fear not," the lower left hand, in the *gaja-hista* (elephant-trunk) gesture, gracefully points to Şiva's foot lifted from the earth, indicating release. Şiva dances in a ring of flames, with Apasmara–dwarf of "forgetfulness," beneath his foot. The Upanishads state "He (Şiva) stands behind all beings . . . and protects them, and rolls them up at the end of time."

[M. J. DALY]

NATHAN, prophet during the time of David and Solomon. The earliest known Israelite court prophet, he at first approved David's desire to build the Temple, but brought a later word from Yahweh that David should leave it for his son to build (2 Sam 7.1–17). N. condemned David for his adultery with Bathsheba (2 Sam 12.1–15), but he later helped Bathsheba secure the throne for her son Solomon (1 Kg 1). He reportedly wrote histories of David's and Solomon's reigns (1 Chr 29.29; 2 Chr 9.29). Other men of the same name are mentioned in 2 Sam 5.14; 23.36; 1 Kg 4.5; 1 Chr 2.36; and Ezra 8.16.

[T. EARLY]

NATHANAEL, according to Jn 1.47, a native of Cana and one of the first Disciples called by Jesus. He was summoned by Philip to "come and see" Jesus of Nazareth, the one foretold by Moses and the prophets. Jesus himself commends him for his guileless sincerity. A simple demonstration of the Lord's personal knowledge of himself prior to their meeting evokes from N. the profession of faith: "Rabbi, you are the Son of God! You are the King of Israel!" (Jn 1.49). After the Resurrection he is one of those who witness the apparition of Jesus at the Sea of Galilee (Jn 21.1). The absence of N.'s name from the lists of the Twelve recorded in the NT raises problems for exegetes. It is widely held that he is to be identified with Bartholomew in these lists, though some have suggested that he is the same figure as Matthias.

[D. J. BOURKE]

NATION, in its modern sense, a political and territorial unit of peoples having a common cultural tradition, often a common language, and a common purpose, self-determination; most properly, then, a nation-state. Classical Latin used *natio* to mean a race, tribe, or people, and usually in reference to the barbarians. The *nationes* of medieval universities were simply territorial groupings of scholars. The classical moral concept of patriotism as a virtue, however, did include loyalty to homeland as the source of being and betterment (ThAq ST 2a2ae, 101.1), a mutual bond and debt for the *compatriotes in natali solo* (ThAq *III Sent.* 33.3.4,i ad 2). That bond of loyalty enters into the modern meaning of nation; this, however, is not simply a unity of race or language, nor purely a geographical unit. Since the revolutions of the 18th cent., esp. in the U.S. and France, the political sense of citizenship, of sharing in rights, and in sovereign government is primary in the sense of nationhood. The sense of distinctness, sovereignty, self-determination is supported by common cultural traditions and language. These elements are all a basis for the virtue of patriotism. They have also led to exaggerated *nationalism; the wars of the 20th cent. were in part its result. The power of a sense of self-determination is evident in the emergence of the state of Israel and the new nations of Africa. The ever-present danger of wars and the earth's ecology indicate the need of restraint through cooperation in a world community of nations.

[T. C. O'BRIEN]

NATIONAL ASSOCIATION OF CONGREGATIONAL CHRISTIAN CHURCHES, Churches that declined to participate in the merger that was to form the *United Church of Christ. The proposal to unite the Congregational Christian Churches with the Evangelical and Reformed Church seriously troubled some Congregationalists, who saw in the move a danger to cherished spiritual freedoms. In 1947 an organization called Anti-Merger was formed. Its members united with others in 1949 to create the Committee for the Continuation of Congregational Christian Churches in the U.S.A. In 1955 the committee united with the League to Uphold Congregational Principles to form the National Association of Congregational Christian Churches of the U.S. Formed to protest against and prevent union, the association, once the United Church of Christ had been formed (1957), became a fellowship of continuing Congregational Christian Churches. It did not itself participate in the legal actions taken by some of its member Churches to contest local decisions to enter the United Church. With a simple nonauthoritarian organization, the National Association has no corporate legal existence. It works through an annual meeting to which a number of commissions (Missions, Ministry, Youth, Publications, Women, and Christian Education) are answerable. Its officers, who include one executive secretary, are likewise responsible to the annual meeting. Since its formation the National Association has grown to about 346 member Churches, some being new foundations. It also supports mission work overseas. It has no theological seminary and does not of itself accredit ministers. In 1962 the National Association applied for membership in the *International Congregational Council. The application was denied on the ground that its relationship to the United Church of Christ had not been legally clarified.

NATIONAL ASSOCIATION OF EVANGELICALS, an association of American Protestant evangelistic denominations, Churches, organizations, and individuals united by a commonly accepted creed for the purpose of national identification, fellowship, and service in the field of *evangelism. The term evangelical in this context signifies one who is fundamentalist, conservative, and often Pentecostal in outlook; who holds to *evangelicalism as the necessary doctrine of salvation in Christ; and who practices evangelism as the communication of the gospel by which a person is led to make a commitment to Christ, dedicate himself to a Christian way of life, and become a vital member of a local church. Typical evangelicals are the members of the Assemblies of God, a Pentecostal missionary denomination that grew out of the spiritual revivals of the 1900s. Protesting against what they considered the "liberal," unbiblical, and non-Protestant policies of the *Federal Council of the Churches of Christ (1905–50), approximately 40 denominations and Churches adopted (1943) a constitution forming an association without legislative or executive control but based upon the Bible as the supreme authority in all matters of belief and conduct. Headquarters of the Association are located in Wheaton, Ill., with field offices in seven regions covering the United States. An Office of Public Affairs in Washington, D. C., fulfills the tasks of keeping a watch on federal legislation, of protesting against the infringement of religious liberties, and of advancing the cause of evangelicalism. Other organizations of the Association include: the National Sunday School Association, the Evangelical Foreign Missions Association, and National Religious Broadcasters. A monthly magazine, *United Evangelical Action,* is the official publication. BIBLIOGRAPHY: J. D. Murch, *Cooperation without Compromise* (1956); C. F. H. Henry, *Evangelical Responsibility in Contemporary Theology* (1957).

[R. MATZERATH]

NATIONAL ASSOCIATION OF LAYMEN (NAL), an organization of Catholic laymen, now known as the National Association of Laity, founded in 1967 for the purpose of promoting a renewal in the Church that follows the decrees and spirit of Vatican II. It furthers the use of democratic processes at every level in the Church; encourages greater lay participation in decision and policy-making, and promotes man's efforts in overcoming poverty, war, racism and the like. NAL particularly allows for opportunities for Catholic laity to speak out on issues of concern to man and the Church. The association consists of 25 local groups and a national membership of approximately 25,000. It convenes annually and publishes a quarterly *Newsletter*. The national office is located in Bloomsburg, Pennsylvnia.

[R. A. TODD]

NATIONAL CATHOLIC CONFERENCE FOR INTERRACIAL JUSTICE (NCCIJ), a federation founded in 1960 for the purpose of promoting justice and favorable interracial relations. It serves 150 Catholic human relations and urban affairs groups. Member groups are autonomous and work in their own regions against discrimination. Their activities consist of community development and the improvement of housing, education, health care, and employment opportunity. NCCIJ not only aids the local groups in organizing programs, but trains leaders and assists member groups in forming staff professionally equipped to deal with interracial problems. The national office of the federation is located at Washington, D.C., where it publishes a bimonthly newsletter, *Commitment*, and has a library of about 600 volumes.

[R. A. TODD]

NATIONAL CATHOLIC EDUCATIONAL ASSOCIATION (NCEA), an organization originally established in 1904 as the Catholic Educational Association (CEA), under the direction of Msgr. (later Bp.) T. J. Conaty, rector of The Catholic Univ. of America, and Rev. F. W. Howard of Columbus, Ohio. Its purpose is to promote U.S. Catholic educational interests on all levels; to foster academic excellence and professional growth among clerical and religious teachers; to create mutual understanding by active participation in secular and religious educational associations; to stimulate educational research, and through its regional meetings, annual conventions, and publications, to interpret Catholic education to the public. The national office is in Washington, D.C.

[M. B. MURPHY]

NATIONAL CATHOLIC PHARMACISTS GUILD OF THE U.S. (NCPG), an organization established in 1962 with the aim of upholding the standards of the faith and the laws of the country in regard to the profession and practice of pharmacy. The members assist church authorities in dispensing knowledge of Catholic pharmacy ethics and encourage support of the needy through promoting donations of funds and supplies. In 1975 the association had approximately 325 members and had headquarters in St. Louis, Missouri. They publish a quarterly, *The Catholic Pharmacist*.

[R. A. TODD]

NATIONAL CATHOLIC RADIO AND TELEVISION APOSTOLATE FOUNDATION, an institution better known as the Catholic Communications Foundation (CCF), established in New York in 1968 by the Catholic Fraternal Benefit Societies. Its principal aim is to support and assist the Church in developing its apostolate of radio and television broadcasting. CCF has made financial grants of more than $475,000 from 1966 to 1975 for religious programs and programming services. It has also aided in the development of diocesan competence in communication and has funded scholarship programs at the Institute for Religious Communications at Loyola Univ., New Orleans. The foundation elects officers and has a board whose members are several U.S. bps., communications executives, and representatives of the fraternal societies. The national headquarters is in New York City.

[R. A. TODD]

NATIONAL CATHOLIC THEATER CONFERENCE, an association founded in 1937 in answer to an appeal by Emmet Lavery and which brought together three important movements to create a Catholic theater tradition. Loyola Univ. in Chicago under George F. Dineen, SJ, Les Compagnons de St. Laurent in Montreal, and the Blackfriars Guild in Washington, D.C., founded by Urban Nagle, OP, and Thomas Carey, OP, became three principal forces in the effort to create Catholic theater. In publications, conventions, and debate the Conference stimulated interest in theater. With the establishment of the Department of Speech and Drama in 1937 at The Catholic Univ. of America under the leadership of Gilbert Hartke, OP, Dr. Josephine Callan, Walter Kerr, and Ralph Brown, drama with Catholic overtones achieved national recognition. Other colleges and universities developed strong departments of drama, notably Fordham Univ., Loyola Univ., Boston College, and Immaculate Heart College, Los Angeles. Blackfriars Guild shifted to New York in 1940, and opened one of the first off-Broadway theaters, which continued until 1972.

[J. R. AHERNE]

NATIONAL CATHOLIC WELFARE CONFERENCE, see UNITED STATES CATHOLIC CONFERENCE, INC. (USCC).

NATIONAL CHURCH, a Church officially recognized by a State and independent of control from outside that State. This phenomenon existed in the Eastern Orthodox Churches prior to the modern era, but the rise of national states and the Reformation introduced this system in Western Europe. Foreshadowed in the Council of *Constance (1414–18), where representatives voted by nation, the national state idea was far advanced by 1500. Religious uniformity was considered requisite to political unity, and the Reformation offered a choice of religion. Hence there developed the principle of **cuius regio, eius religio,* allowing each prince to decide the religious character of his people. Consequently many national Churches supplanted the one visible Church of an earlier period. Instead of a single Lutheran Church, there were many autonomous Lutheran Churches in German territories and Scandinavian countries; regional *Reformed Churches existed in Switzerland, S Germany, and elsewhere. England had its own Church, as did Scotland. As political theory became more secularized, a spirit of toleration allowed for religious diversity within a particular State. National Churches have continued to be the rule in Western Europe, however, although relations between Church and State are generally not as strong as formerly. In a strict sense, the term "national Church" does not apply to the RC Church, since recognition of the primacy of the pope precludes national autonomy. The U.S. was first to experiment without a national Church, and many modern democracies have followed its example.

[N. H. MARING]

NATIONAL CONFERENCE OF CATHOLIC BISHOPS (NCCB), the episcopal conference of the U.S. bishops, established in 1966 in conformity with Vatican Council II's Decree on the Bishops' Pastoral Office (Vat II BpPastOff 38) and its implementation by Paul VI's *motu proprio, Ecclesiae sanctae* (1966). The NCCB superseded the National Catholic Welfare Conference. The membership of the NCCB, as of all episcopal conferences, is composed of local ordinaries and their associate bishops; decisions taken by the NCCB in matters committed to it by the Holy See (e.g., matters of liturgy and liturgical books) have the force of ecclesiastical law. In other matters the NCCB by its deliberations in full assembly, its executive committees promotes the internal interests of the American Church and gives expression to statements of public policy on political and social matters that are of concern to the Church in its ministry of justice and peace. In regard to the last the NCCB has exercised its influence in the prolife issue, in the Campaign for Human Development, in protecting against violation of human rights in Latin America, and in sponsoring, during the Catholic celebration of the U.S. bicentennial, consultations on justice that led to the Call to Action meetings of 1976. The areas of concern for church life have been particularly the reform and adaptation of liturgical rites, and translation of liturgical texts, the direction given to religious education and priestly formation. The NCCB has issued joint statements on Christian morality and medical ethics, and has given encouragement to scholarly research in the service of the Church. The chief executive officer is the general secretary. Allied to the NCCB is the *U.S. Catholic Conference. Headquarters for both are at 1312 Massachusetts Ave., NW, Washington, D.C.

[T. C. O'BRIEN]

NATIONAL CONFERENCE OF CHRISTIANS AND JEWS, an organization founded in the U.S. in 1928 to promote understanding, friendship, and cooperation among Jews, Protestants, and Roman Catholics. It grew out of a committee formed by the Federal Council of Churches to counteract the religious prejudice of the 1920s, esp. that of the 1928 presidential campaign. The Conference does not aim at religious *syncretism, nor does it approve of religious *indifferentism. Based on the Judaeo-Christian belief in the equality of all men, it aims at civic cooperation among men of varied religious, ethnic, and social backgrounds. The organization functions through three cochairmen—one Jew, one Catholic, and one Protestant. Its officers are a president and an executive vice president, a board of governors, and trustees. In 1966 it staffed 65 regional offices, each having three cochairmen and a mixed board. The Conference cooperates closely with schools and colleges, labor and management, the police, community leaders, and clergymen. One of its best-known observances is National Brotherhood Week. Prominent among its techniques are workshops, discussions, and clergy dialogues.

BIBLIOGRAPHY: J. E. Pitt, *Adventure in Brotherhood* (1955).

[M. J. SUELZER]

NATIONAL COUNCIL OF CATHOLIC MEN (NCCM), an organization of Catholic laymen founded in 1920 along with the *National Council of Catholic Women, representing the department of lay organizations in the National Catholic Welfare Conference (NCWC, renamed U.S. Catholic Conference USCC, 1966). It was established for the purpose of organizing lay groups into a federation under the guidance of the U.S. bps. for active participation in the mission of the Church. As an agency of the USCC, it acts as an informational service link between the Catholic hierarchy and laymen's organizations in the U.S. In fostering participation of the laity in the apostolate of the Church, the members engage mostly in the areas of religious activities, communications, civic and social action, legislation, family life, youth, public relations, international affairs and organizations and development of leadership among laymen. The federation consists of more than 9,000 Catholic organizations of men, which include parish and interparochial societies, diocesan federations, and state-wide and national organizations. NCCM has four regular publications: *Alert Catholic Men, Program and Training, Executive Newsletter,* and *Highlights*.

[R. A. TODD]

NATIONAL COUNCIL OF CATHOLIC WOMEN (NCCW), a federation of about 10,000 Catholic laywomen's organizations established in 1920 by the department of lay organizations of the National Catholic Welfare Conference, now the *U.S. Catholic Conference (USCC). As a service agency engaged in carrying out the programs of USCC, the NCCW acts as liaison between the bps. and the affiliated Catholic women's organizations in supplying information and material in the fields of education, family life, religion, social action, and international affairs. NCCW conducts national conventions, regional institutes, conferences, and workshops (from parish to diocesan and national levels). The members publish *The Catholic Woman* and have national headquarters at Washington, D.C.

[R. A. TODD]

NATIONAL COUNCIL OF THE CHURCHES OF CHRIST IN THE U.S.A. (NCC), an organization of U.S. Churches to facilitate unity in fellowship, witness, and service. Main offices are at 475 Riverside Drive, New York City. The NCC was established Nov. 29, 1950, in Cleveland, Ohio, as a successor to the Federal Council of Churches (founded 1908). It also incorporates and continues the work of several other organizations which had been established to further ecumenical cooperation in particular causes. The preamble to the constitution declares, "Under the providence of God, communions which confess Jesus Christ as Divine Lord and Savior, in order more fully to manifest oneness in Him, do now create an inclusive cooperative agency of Christian churches of the United States of America to show forth their unity and mission in specific ways and to bring the churches into living contact with one another for fellowship, study, and cooperative action." U.S. Churches were influenced by international developments in the *ecumenical movement, and many of their leaders had participated in it. The NCC developed as an independent organization, but in friendly cooperation with the *World Council of Churches.

The NCC currently has 30 member Churches, including all the larger bodies except the *Southern Baptist Convention, the *Lutheran Church—Missouri Synod, and the RC Church. The work of the NCC is directed by a triennial general assembly, composed of about 800 delegates from the member Churches, and by a General Board, composed of 250 members elected by the general assembly and meeting three times each year. The general assembly elects the officers of the NCC: president, several vice-presidents, treasurer, recording secretary, and general secretary. The general secretary, principal executive officer, directs the work of the full-time staff, which is organized into four divisions

(Christian Life and Mission, Christian Education, Overseas Ministries, and Christian Unity) and three staff offices (Planning and Program, Communication, and Administration).

The NCC has received criticism from conservatives because its leadership has included some they regard as too liberal, on both doctrinal and social questions. The NCC and groups under its sponsorship have taken positions on economic, social, and foreign policy issues which have been opposed by both conservative churchmen and conservative politicians. Some opponents of the NCC who nonetheless favor ecumenical fellowship and cooperation have formed the *National Association of Evangelicals (1942). Also the *National Council of Christian Churches has been formed under the leadership of C. McIntire (1941). Any communion which accepts the nature and purpose of the NCC as set forth in the constitution is eligible for membership. Approval of membership is by two-thirds vote at a general assembly. Various other organizations establish affiliate relationships with the NCC. The Constitution states, "The Council shall have no authority or administrative control over the churches which constitute its membership. It shall have no authority to prescribe a common creed, form of church government, or form of worship, or to limit the autonomy of the churches cooperating in it" (5.2).

The NCC sponsors conferences for study of various questions of Church and society, carries out projects of humanitarian service, including an extensive overseas ministry, publishes literature of various kinds, and seeks to develop a greater sense of unity and understanding among the Churches. It has adopted statements supporting the United Nations and the UN Universal Declaration of Human Rights, committing itself to "work for a nonsegregated church and a nonsegregated community," and affirming "the right of both employers and employees to organize for collective bargaining." It has pledged support to the public schools and to the separation of Church and State. It supports "the right and duty of the churches . . . to study and comment upon issues of human concern, however controversial." A 1968 policy statement recognizes civil disobedience as a "valid instrument for those who seek justice consonant with both Christian tradition and the American political and legal heritage." BIBLIOGRAPHY: A. W. Barstow, ed., *Christian Faith in Action* (1951) and the reports to the triennial assemblies.

[T. EARLY]

NATIONAL FEDERATION OF CATHOLIC PHYSICIAN'S GUILDS, a federation of U.S. Catholic physicians founded in 1927 for the purpose of furthering spiritual objectives and principles in the medical profession. The association has approximately 6,700 members in 88 independent guilds in the U.S. and Canada. Guild members participate on diocesan and parish levels by assisting in pre-Cana and family life instructions and in the general care of clergy and religious. The federation supports medical education and research programs, and fosters foreign mission service among its members. Its national headquarters is located at Milwaukee, Wisconsin, and the official journal is *Linacre Quarterly*.

[R. A. TODD]

NATIONAL FEDERATION OF PRIESTS' COUNCILS, an association established in Chicago in 1968 at a meeting of 233 delegates, representing 127 priests' organizations. Its objectives are to give priests' councils a voice in matters of concern to the Church; to facilitate better communication among priests throughout the country; to collaborate with the laity, religious, and bps. in addressing the needs of the Church. The organization consists of approximately 130 senates, councils, and associations, which together represent about 28,000 Catholic priests. The federation publishes a monthly called *Priests/U.S.A.* Its headquarters are located in Chicago, Illinois.

[R. A. TODD]

NATIONAL FEDERATION OF SODALITIES OF OUR LADY (NFS), a federation of diocesan sodalities in the U.S. established in 1956 by American bps. at the annual meeting of the National Catholic Welfare Conference, now known as the U.S. Catholic Conference. The NFS was organized to unify all sodalities in order to represent them on national and international levels with a view to their cooperating in the approved work of other associations. The apostolate of the Sodality, since it was founded in 1563, has involved a Christian way of life in the service of the Church under the patronage of Our Lady and the guidance of the bishops. In the spirit of renewal, advocated by Vatican Council II, the governing principles and norms of the Sodalities were revised and approved by Paul VI in 1971. Today, Sodalities of Our Lady are known as Christian Life Communities, which are groups of men and women, young and old, who join with others in living more fully their "Christian vocation and commitment in the world." The spirituality of these Communities is founded on the Spiritual Exercises of St. Ignatius. Christian Life Communities may be found in 42 countries. The U.S. Federation has about 150 communities and its national office is located in St. Louis, Missouri. The World Federation has its headquarters in Rome.

[R. A. TODD]

NATIONAL GUILD OF CATHOLIC PSYCHIATRISTS INC., an American organization of Catholic psychiatrists founded in 1949. Its objective is to support the principles of Catholic faith and morals in the practice of psychiatry. The guild meets annually at a convention with the American Psychiatric Association. In 1975 there were approximately 500 members. The *Bulletin,* a quarterly, is published at headquarters in Santa Monica, California.

[R. A. TODD]

NATIONAL LUTHERAN COUNCIL, an organization formed in 1918 for cooperation of several Lutheran bodies in missions, social welfare, and other projects. In 1966 it was succeeded by the Lutheran Council in the U.S.A., an agency of expanded membership and scope.

[T. C. O'BRIEN]

NATIONAL OFFICE FOR BLACK CATHOLICS (NOBC), an association of black priests, religious, and laymen of the Catholic Church, founded in 1970 for the purpose of promoting active and full participation of black Catholics in the life of the Church and to carry out more effectively the Church's apostolate in the black community. Specific objectives of NOBC are: representation and voice among those who are leaders and decision-makers in the Church; recognition of black culture; support of the Church in regard to human rights; recruitment for religious vocations; quality Christian education in the black community. Affiliated with the association are the three member-bodies: the National Black Catholic Clergy Caucus (1968), the National Black Sisters' Conference (1968), and the National Black Catholic Lay Caucus. NOBC is financially supported by the proceeds of Black Catholics Concerned collection, taken up annually in parish churches. A newsletter entitled *Impact* is published by NOBC, which has headquarters in Washington, D.C.

[R. A. TODD]

NATIONAL SHRINE OF THE IMMACULATE CONCEPTION in Washington, D.C. The cornerstone was laid Sept. 23, 1920 by Card. Gibbons on property adjoining The Catholic Univ. of America, but the Shrine was substantially completed only in 1959. On Nov. 20 of that year it was dedicated by Card. Spellman in the presence of the largest ecclesiastial gathering in U.S. church history. Bp. Thomas *Shahan, rector of Catholic Univ. initiated the project in 1914, with the approval of Pius X. The architectural firm of Maginnis and Walsh was engaged to design the edifice; the final design is chiefly the work of Charles Maginnis. For years only the crypt was worked on, but that alone is a gem of ecclesiastical architecture. The upper church was built in the 1950s. The Shrine is a combination of Byzantine and Romanesque styles, a design that aroused considerable controversy. The edifice is entirely built of masonry, without structural steel. A distinctive bell tower rising 329 feet is a striking feature. The church is the largest in the U.S. and seventh largest in the world. It can accommodate 6,000 in the upper church. Annually more than a million visitors view the Shrine. BIBLIOGRAPHY: T. Grady, NCE 10:238–239.

[J. R. AHERNE]

NATIONAL SOCIALISM, ideology underlying the activities of the National Socialist German Workers' Party (NSDAP), which governed Germany from 1933 to 1945. As a theory, it was expounded primarily in Adolf Hitler's *Mein Kampf* and in Alfred Rosenberg's *Myth of the XXth Century,* but as a movement it lacked cohesiveness and consistency. The principal theoretical tenets were these: the Aryan race, to which Germans belong despite some deplorable "mixing of blood," is alone qualified to lead and control humanity; the principal virtue of the Aryan is martial valor, to be inculcated through breeding and indoctrination; the Jew, author of capitalism and socialism alike, is pernicious and must be curbed and in particular restrained from marrying an Aryan; and the right to propagandize the masses is rooted in their inability to ward off the weaknesses of democratic society. God is seen as the abettor of the German people to live and triumph; Christianity is superstition fostering weakness. The origins of National Socialism are found in 19th-cent. racist literature, in ultra-rightist Pan-German theories, in resentment of Germany's defeat in 1918, the Peace Treaty that followed, and in the opportunism of a materialist society. Combined with the "leadership principle," it served as a vehicle for Adolph Hitler's totalitarian "Third Reich." BIBLIOGRAPHY: F. L. Neumann, *Behemoth: The Structure and Practice of National Socialism* (1944); R. Morsey, NCE 10:239–240.

[G. N. SHUSTER]

NATIONALISM, the sense of belonging to a *nation, with loyalty to its common heritage and conviction of its right to sovereign self-determination. Taken in a just and rightful sense, these attitudes amount to patriotism, the honoring of indebtedness to homeland, the source of physical, cultural, and spiritual values commonly shared, and cooperation in the well-being deriving to all from the bonds uniting compatriots. Historically, however, nationalism exaggerated has led to exclusivism, predatory colonialism, and unjust wars. The emergence of modern nation-states since the 18th cent. has included exploitation of national consciousness to exalt the State as an absolute value, and to justify totalitarianism and territorial rapacity. The cycle of dangers connected with nationalism is apparent in the emergence of new African nations. The moral need is a true patriotism, not blind loyalty to a political regime or to an ideology, but a dutiful honoring of homeland. The further need is for a sense of international *legal justice, a respect for the earth and its nations as a common homeland, with a commonly shared purpose, the general good of all mankind. That involves a genuine acknowledgement of subsidiarity, the recognition both of inner sovereignty and of heritages to be treasured, but also of cooperative responsibility towards the shared benefits of the community of nations.

[T. C. O'BRIEN]

NATIVISM, a recurrent feature of American life that has included an intense dislike and fear of the foreign-born and a particular hostility toward Catholics. By 1850 the RC Church in the U.S. had mushroomed to more than 1½ million, including about 700,000 immigrants who were the special target of nativist fury. Not infrequently the acrimony of anti-Catholic attacks by revivalistic preachers and nativist magazines, newspapers, pamphlets, and books overflowed into mob violence. Depredations were made against Catholic property and lives, as in the burning (1834) of the Ursuline Convent at Charlestown, Mass., and the riots (1844) in Philadelphia and New York City. Successive waves of popular hysteria swept many sections of the country over domestic issues, such as the Catholic protest against use of the Authorized (King James) Version of the Bible in public schools and the demand for public aid to parochial schools, and foreign developments, such as *Catholic emancipation in Great Britain and the restoration of the English hierarchy.

Nativism found political expression in the *Know-Nothing movement of the 1850s, which became a factor in national politics and enjoyed considerable success in some states and cities. The Civil War temporarily silenced these forces of bigotry, but in the 1880s increased immigration and concern over the growing political strength of Catholics led to a new wave of nativism. The *American Protective Association (APA), founded (1887) at Clinton, Iowa, by Henry F. Bowers and his associates, both fed upon and generated the old fear that Roman Catholicism was part of an international conspiracy to subvert the free institutions of America. Unsuccessful in influencing national politics, the APA gradually withered away after a decade of spreading religious intolerance. Xenophobia, however, continued to thrive in American society, and a revived *Ku Klux Klan grew rapidly, esp. in the South and West, viciously attacking Negroes, Jews, Catholics, and all foreign-born. Its program of terrorism not only spread fear among minorities but also enabled the Klan to gain political control in several states, notably Indiana. Its decline after 1925 was due largely to internal corruption. In 1921 nativist demands for the restriction of immigration were supported by the fear of an alien flood from war-devastated Europe, and Congress responded with a measure radically altering U.S. immigration policy. The quota system that ensued not only reduced immigration to a trickle but also discriminated against aliens from southern and eastern Europe. Thereafter, sporadic attacks by latter-day nativists were directed against internal minority groups, such as Catholics (until after the election of John F. Kennedy in 1960), Negroes, Jews, Communists, and during World War II, Japanese-Americans. BIBLIOGRAPHY: R. A. Billington, *Protestant Crusade, 1800–1860* (1938); D. L. Kinzer, *Episode in Anti-Catholicism: The American Protective Association* (1964); T. T. McAvoy, *Roman Catholicism and the American Way of Life* (1960).

[M. CARTHY]

NATIVITY OF CHRIST. It is probable that Jesus was born in 6 or 7 B.C. Certainly the formula used by *Dionysius Exiguus for fixing the beginning of the *Christian era is incorrect. Attempts to determine the exact year from the biblical evidence have been frustrated by its inadequacy. Matthew 2.1 states that Jesus was born in the days of Herod the Great, who died in 4 B.C. Luke places the nativity at the time of a census under Cyrinus, the governor of Syria, but the only known census under Cyrinus took place in A.D. 6–12. Perhaps Cyrinus had conducted an earlier census, but the silence of other sources makes a precise date impossible to fix. The Dec. 25th date was established later in opposition to the Roman winter sun festival on that day. The place of birth was *Bethlehem, a small town some 5 miles S of Jerusalem. The prophet Micah (5.1–2) foretold that the Messiah would be born in Bethlehem, and the Evangelists' designation of this town is seen as a confirmation of the Savior's Davidic ancestry since Bethlehem is the city of David. Although John implies that the birthplace of Jesus was unknown (Jn 7.40–42), there is nothing in the Gospels to indicate that Jesus was born elsewhere, and the tradition concerning Bethlehem seems worthy of acceptance. Jesus is described as the first-born son (Lk 2.7), a term which had significant Jewish overtones of patriarchal blessings and religious heritage. The word *prōtōtokos* bears no implication that Mary conceived other children. The caves in the hills around Bethlehem were often used as homes by constructing a wooden lean-to at the cave's entrance. The people slept and ate under this protection while the animals were kept inside. Because of the crowded conditions, Mary bore Jesus inside the cave, in the place reserved for the animals; wrapped him in the long strips of cloth customary in Palestine; and laid him in the feeding trough for animals. BIBLIOGRAPHY: EDB 232; 336–338; JBL 2:66–67; 124; B.G. Caird, InterDB 1:599–601.

[T. M. MCFADDEN]

NATIVITY OF MARY. Definite facts concerning Mary's birth are not known. Since Lk 1.26 says she was living at Nazareth at the time of the Annunciation, she may have been born there and was probably a descendant of David. A pious tradition concerning her parents, Joachim and Anne, sprang up very early, based largely on a 2d-cent. apocryphon entitled *The Birth of Mary: Revelation of James,* later called **Proto-evangelium of James* (see APOCRYPHA [NT], n. 24). Its unknown author writes to defend Mary against certain calumnies and to glorify her virtue and goodness. Her conception was miraculous: Joachim and Anne were very old and childless; they asked God for a child, and an angel appeared and assured them their prayer would be heard. Nine months later Mary was born. It seems clear that this tradition was taken from the biblical account of John the Baptist and adapted to Mary. BIBLIOGRAPHY: O. Cullmann, "Infancy Gospels" (tr. A. J. B. Higgins; *New Testament Apocrypha* Number 1, ed E. Hennecke and W. Schneemelcher, 1963) 363–414; A. Rush. "Mary in the Apocrypha of the NT," Carol Mariol 1:156–184; E. May, NCE 10:251.

[T. R. HEATH]

NATURAL LAW is a way of talking about morality, or more elegantly, a theory of ethical discourse. It has appeared in such diverse versions that any attempt to speak of "the" doctrine of natural law is misleading. Still a certain consistency in both languages and theme can be found throughout the history of Western ethics. The Ionic philosophers suggest the idea of nature as ordered cosmos. The Sophists of 5th-cent. Greece devise the "custom vs. nature" distinction; Plato provides the concept of an ideal law. Aristotle speaks of "natural" justice and introduces the notion of finality into ethics, but the Stoics were the first to fashion these themes into a comprehensive ethical doctrine. Cicero borrowed and modified their teaching and through the Fathers from Tertullian to Augustine, it entered Christian tradition. The Fathers tended to identify natural law with the Decalogue, the golden rule, and the double-love commandment of the Gospel. This tradition, together with the *jus naturale-jus gentium* distinction of Roman law, entered medieval canon law and theology, where it was stated most compendiously within Aristotelian perspectives by Thomas Aquinas. Attacked in the Reformation, revived in the Renaissance, and elaborated in the Enlightenment, the themes and language of natural law are today found principally in Neo-Scholastic Catholic ethics and as an alternative to legal positivism in jurisprudence.

The themes of natural law thinking are that universal standards for human behavior (1) exist; (2) are knowable and understandable by human beings; (3) stand in logical relation to facts about human beings; (4) serve as criteria of the morality of particular decisions and even of the statutes of civil law. In most versions of natural law, a relationship to an immanent and/or transcendent principle of the universe, God, is involved. Moreover, most versions indicate how these themes are interrelated and how in their interrelation they provide an adequate theory of ethical discourse, i.e., a coherent set of propositions proposing the logic and content for reasoning and argumentation about moral matters. The adequacy of such an ethical theory is to be judged by its ability to answer reasonably the theoretical questions and to provide practical guidance for decision.

In the light of these themes, natural law then might be defined as that theory of ethical discourse in which moral judgments are justified and moral principles grounded by reference to the radical exigencies and potentialities of the human person in community. Thus, any reason offered to justify a course of action is considered morally adequate if it can be shown, at least reductively, that this sort of action will fulfill the exigencies and actualize the potentialities constitutive of the human person in community. Actions that inhibit or prevent such realization are unjustified and hence wrong.

A natural law theory must determine what the radical exigencies and potentialities of the human person in community really are. It must further state how these, when formulated as imperatives, are related to the precise rules and values embodied in popular morality and positive civil law. The first task requires the metaphysical reflection on the nature of man; the second requires an ethical reflection on the nature of moral judgment. Metaphysical reflections must reveal the ineradicable characteristics of the human reality which constitute the inner ground and define the outer limits of human realization. They might be described in part as self-reflective consciousness, self-engaging commitment, historical and communal existence, consisting of interpersonality among men and before a transcendent Person. Human existence is unfinished; it can be promoted in accord with the inner possibilities and limitations of each constitutent characteristic as it reveals itself in a particular place and time. The first imperative of the natural law, according to the Stoics, is, "Follow nature!" This is implemented by imperatives to protect and promote the human characteristics of consciousness, commitment, communality, historicity, and interpersonality. Aquinas, e.g., states the primary precepts of the natural law command the preservation of personal and societal life and the search for truth and social order (ThAq ST 1a2ae, 94.2).

Ethical reflection does not deduce rules, but proceeds from these as absolute points of reference. It rather evaluates actual moral rules and practices in the light of the primary precepts of natural law. To the extent that practices and decisions protect and promote such "values" they can be called right, good, and in conformity with natural law. Practices dictated by customary morality or even enjoined by civil law which destroy such values are wrong, bad, and contrary to natural law. Thus, certain lines and directions of human behavior may be designated as "always and everywhere human" not because they are in fact practiced, but because they would, *if* practiced, contribute to a more human life. The actual realization of such lines of behavior must be continually reassessed both in the light of deeper insight into the radical exigencies and potentialities, and concrete conditions in which action takes place. Thus in natural law theory, moral judgments are justified insofar as the activities resulting from them are expected to contribute to the realization of the perceived values, not merely by prudential calculation of results (though this is involved), but by a metaphysical awareness of the radical exigencies and potentialities of man. Natural law then is not a morality in the sense of a full set of rules for behavior; it is an ethic, a system for the critique and development of morality.

This form of metaphysical and ethical reflection must be completed by a meta-ethics to explain and defend its procedures. Any modern natural law theory must explain how it moves from indicatives to imperatives about human behavior, how prudential calculation relates to values, in what manner values are perceived, etc. Lack of clarity on such meta-ethical issues has led many contemporary philosophers to doubt that natural law doctrines can shed light on the problems of moral life and ethical theory.

A final problem is the role of natural law thinking in Christian ethics. Since pre-Christian forms of natural law affirmed the relation between human morality and God, they were easily adopted, once purified of pantheism, into the Church's moral teaching. While the Reformation decreed natural law as an ethic more man than God-centered, the Church continued to claim the right to teach and interpret natural law. The theological task is to justify this claim and to indicate the compatibility of natural law with the law of the Gospel.

The radical needs and possibilities of the human person are open to human understanding and philosophical reflection. Nevertheless the man who possesses these needs and possibilities is revealed by God's Word to be created and redeemed in Jesus Christ. He is himself revealed as both perfect man and Eternal Son. The Church is the custodian and teacher of that revelation; it is charged as well with the task of leading all men to perfect manhood in Christ. For this teaching and task it draws from that understanding of human destiny revealed to it and from human understanding open to all. The revealed understanding offers a perspective from which human life can be viewed. This perspective is a pressure on human understanding to deepen itself; it is a challenge to men to realize their dignity as children of God and brethren of Christ. From this point of view teachers in the Church may perceive certain dimensions of human existence which might otherwise have gone unnoticed. They may declare that certain imperatives arising from these dimensions are necessarily involved in the formation of the Christian person and community. Thus the Church is guardian and interpreter of natural law insofar as she is charged with the task under the guidance of the Spirit of discovering and proclaiming forms of life and action which are truly human and hence in conformity with the dignity of man, created and redeemed in Christ. BIBLIOGRAPHY: Y. Simon, *Natural Law Tradition* (1965); H. A. Rommen, *Natural Law* (1947); J. Fuchs, *Natural Law* (1965); A. P. D'Entreves, *Natural Law* (1951); J. Messner, *Social Ethics: Natural Law in the Western World* (1965); *Natural Law Forum* (1956–) and *Proceedings of Natural Law Institute* (1947–1951); L. Fuller, *Morality of Law* (1964); H. L. A. Hart, *Concept of Law* (1961); S. Hook, *Philosophy of Law* (1964).

[A. JONSEN]

NATURAL ORDER, the disposition of reality that pertains to, arises from, or is comformable to nature. In theology, natural order is generally employed to distinguish what is meant by the supernatural. Five applications within this use of the term may be mentioned. (1) Natural sometimes designates all the beings comprehended in created nature as distinguished from the supernatural being which is God. (2) An effect is regarded as natural, in opposition to miraculous, when it proceeds according to the powers intrinsically present in its cause. (3) An act or the use of a particular faculty is natural when it is compatible with the essence of that faculty as a source of activity. In this sense it is possible to speak of a natural law or of unnatural acts. This use of the term also enables us to speak of Christian faith as a supernatural act insofar as it surpasses the faculties of intellect and will unaided by grace. (4) Most significantly, natural order is applied to the orientation of a being and the total complex of being toward its proper finality. It is in this sense that Thomas Aquinas writes of the natural order as the divine plan whereby all things work toward that goal in which their ultimate perfection is attained. (5) A later distinction, probably arising in the 16th-cent. commentaries on St. Thomas, employs the term natural order to designate the possible but nonhistorical state of being that would obtain if creation had not been granted its supernatural vocation.

The breakdown of the scholastic theological synthesis, the polemical need to maintain the gratuity of the supernatural in the face of philosophical naturalism and Modernism, and a rise of rationalism caused theologians to grant an unwarranted autonomy to the natural order. In the 19th cent., human nature came to be explained as a self-contained unit, finalized certainly in a return to the God of truth, but totally encompassed within a natural order to which the supernatural was an extrinsic fillip. The natural order began to be thought of as primary and fundamental, the order initially intended by the Creator. Finite natures were regarded as prior to the supernatural world order in the divine mind. The state of pure human nature, i.e., man without any preternatural or supernatural gifts, was regarded as that which was encountered in everyday experience. It became possible to speak of man as directed toward a finality that would be strictly proportionate to his capacities—God known through reason. The supernatural order, a superstructure lying beyond the range of experience, became an extrinsic gift for which man was disposed only by the principle of noncontradiction.

Many contemporary theologians have reacted strongly against such a presentation of the relationship between the natural and supernatural orders. Man's supernatural vocation is not just a juridical decree proceeding from the Divine Will, which affects man only when he consents to grace, but constitutes man in his very being. The act of creation which determines the essence of all created natures ordered man to the beatific vision. This determining creative act established within man a vital orientation toward his unique and supernatural finality. Nature has an affinity for its supernatural finality, not merely the absence of contradiction. This openness toward the supernatural is rooted in man's concrete, existential situation. As such, it does not contradict the gratuity of the supernatural but does engender a dynamic orientation toward the order of grace. BIBLIOGRAPHY: H. de Lubac, *Mystery of the Supernatural* (tr. R. Sheed, 1967); J. P. Kenny, ''Reflections on Human Nature and the Supernatural'' ThSt 14 (1953) 280–287; K. Rahner, *God, Christ, Mary and Grace (Theological Investigations 1,* tr. C. Ernst, 1961).*NATURE; *SUPERNATURAL EXISTENTIAL; *SUPERNATURAL ORDER.

[T. M. MCFADDEN]

NATURAL THEOLOGY, a philosophic inquiry leading to conclusions concerning the existence and attributes of God. Called ''natural'' from its sole reliance on the powers of unaided reason, it differs from theology in the ordinary Christian sense, which is based on revealed truths accepted by the grace of faith. Since the philosopher Gottfried Leibniz (1646–1716), natural theology has also been called "theodicy," i.e., a reasoned defense, or apologia, for the truth of God's existence and providence.

The highest speculations of ancient philosophers, esp. Plato and Aristotle, about a transcendent, divine being are cited as examples of natural theology. In Christian thought the basis for a natural theology was made explicit in the Middle Ages, when clear distinctions were drawn between nature and grace, between truths knowable by the unaided human mind and truths knowable only through divine revelation. St. Thomas Aquinas (*c.* 1225–74) drew these distinctions most precisely, defended the possibility of a conclusive proof of God's existence through reasoned reflection on facts of ordinary experience, and proposed such proofs in his *quinque viae*, or "five ways" (ThAq ST 1a, 2.1–3). While there has been a recurrent skepticism, even among the late medievals, e.g., William of Ockham (*c.* 1300–*c.* 1349), about any natural knowledge of God, there has been a strong RC natural theology tradition, aimed at showing that the findings of reason correspond to Christian belief in one God. In the 19th cent. Vatican Council I proposed as official church teaching, esp. against *fideism, the capacity of the human mind to acquire certitude about God's existence (D 3026). Beginning in the mid-19th cent. there was a renewed attempt at a natural theology based on Aquinas's indications; there were, however, widely diverse interpretations within Neo-Thomism. Since World War II and the growing abandonment of Thomistic metaphysics, new approaches, based upon contemporary philosophical viewpoints, have been sought.

Reformation teaching, while acknowledging the theoretical possibility of man's having some natural knowledge about God, minimized it and asserted that because of human depravity only the revelation that came through Christ will save man from turning away from all evidence of God (see TOTAL DEPRAVITY). Nevertheless, various forms of natural theology were developed by religiously inspired Protestant thinkers. For example, Christian Wolff (1679–1754), adapting the principles of Leibniz, produced a highly rationalistic system of philosophy, a key part of which was a natural theology. The Wolffian system became the target of Immanuel Kant (1724–1804), whose critique was directed against the possibility of any metaphysics and the validity of any reasoned proof that God exists. Kant's attack, and later that of linguistic analysis, led to a loss of confidence by many RC as well as Protestant thinkers in any empirically based knowledge about God. In the 20th cent., natural theology has been attacked most sharply by Karl *Barth (1886–1968) on theological grounds. As a reaction to *liberal theology, which naturalized all theology, Barth reasserted fundamental Reformation teaching. God is knowable and known only through the revelation given in Christ; man, because of his sinfulness, is totally incapable of knowing God by his natural powers. Barth's colleague, E. *Brunner (1889–1966), opposed him in this, holding that a limited place for a natural theology was allowed by both the Bible and Reformation teaching.

Two issues are involved for the Christian in the relevance of any natural theology. Its philosophical validity presupposes the capacity of the mind to know objective truth and to pass from immediate experience to a cause beyond experience. Its value to Christian life is limited; a natural theology may serve to show the reasonableness of theism, but it remains an indirect and inferential knowledge; only grace gives knowledge of God himself and a personal relationship with him. BIBLIOGRAPHY: D. Allen, *Reasonableness of Faith* (1968), with bibliog.; T. C. O'Brien, *Metaphysics and the Existence of God* (1960), with bibliog.

[T. EARLY]

NATURALISM, a term that has had a wide usage, esp. in theology, to categorize a number of philosophical or theological viewpoints; but that also designates a specific American philosophical position.

Among the forms of naturalism in its first sense are: (1) philosophies that in their view of reality exclude any nonnatural or transcendent being or cause; e.g., materialism, pantheism; (2) philosophies that limit their view of the world and of man to observable processes functioning according to fixed physical laws; e.g., positivism, empiricism, psychological and biological determinism that deny the spiritual in man; (3) theological positions that exclude the need of grace, e.g., Pelagianism; or the possibility of such divine supernatural interventions as revelation or miracles, e.g., rationalism; or that reduce the mysteries of Christianity to expressions of evolving consciousness of human needs or emotions, e.g., *liberal theology.

American naturalism as a distinct philosophical viewpoint had clearly emerged by the early 1930s, although its beginnings are traced to the work of G. Santayana, *Life of Reason* (5 v. 1905–06). The central figure in the history of naturalism, however, is John *Dewey (1859–1952); Sidney *Hook (1902–), Ernest Nagel (1901–), and John H. Randall Jr. (1899–) are other prominent representatives. Naturalists maintain that knowable reality consists in the natural objects of the world of space and time. These objects exist and change through processes totally explicable by natural causes. Philosophy acquires certitude by employing a scientific method, i.e., critical use of intelligence that is best exemplified in the empirical sciences. To seek an absolute or all-encompassing view of nature is a delusion because the philosopher cannot transcend natural processes to go "outside" nature; questions of the total origin or ultimate purpose of the universe are vain. Included in the naturalist viewpoint is the rejection of any nonnatural element as explanatory of natural objects: the nonnatural, the nonobservable, or nonverifiable by scientific method includes the existence of God, the immortality or spirituality of the soul, the supernatural in the theological sense, and the transcendent in the metaphysical sense. Naturalism has had its primary impact on ethics and social questions. What man does and how he acts are the evidence through which natural laws concerning his behavior can be known and formulated. Ethically, the pragmatic is primary: moral intuitions and absolutes are nonscientific. Moral values are not to be determined by inquiring what ought to be; but by learning what is, what is effective. BIBLIOGRAPHY: A. C. Danto, EncPhil 448–450, bibliog.; J. P. Dougherty, NCE 10:271–274; J. D. Collins, *Three Paths in Philosophy* (1962).

[T. C. O'BRIEN]

NATURE, according to Aristotle, the essential and intrinsic principle whereby a thing acts in a certain way. Aristotle sought a middle path between pre-Socratic philosophy, which maintained that matter alone is the ultimate principle of reality, and Platonism, which held that a being acts in accordance with an idea or principle distinct from that being's corporeal reality. Scholastic philosophy has generally adopted the Aristotelian concept of nature. Thus Thomas Aquinas defines nature as the essence of a thing precisely as it is the source of its life and activity. By stressing that nature is proper (not extrinsic or accidental) to everything that acts and that it is not materiality as such, Aristotelianism and Scholasticism allow for explanations of finality and order within the material universe, the intelligibility of a thing according to its acts, and a metaphysics based upon experience.

The concept of nature has been significant for the theology of the Trinity and Incarnation, esp. insofar as nature and person may be distinguished. Although the notion of nature varies in the development of a theological understanding of these mysteries, a consistency based upon a minimal definition of nature as that which constitutes the internal unity of anything, can always be found within this development. Hence, the affirmation that Father, Son, and Spirit are God indicates that each Person, distinct from the others because they are Persons, is truly divine because he possesses the divine nature as the constitutive principle of his essential unity. In regard to the Incarnation, Christ has both a human and a divine nature as principles from which human and divine acts respectively proceed. Christ does not, however, possess a human personality. The one person, the Word, possesses both natures.

The relationship between nature and supernature has also been an area of theological inquiry and divergent interpretation. The Pelagian controversies of the 5th cent., the various Reformation theologies, Modernism, and several contemporary theological questions center on this issue. Generally speaking, the problem has been one of steering a middle course between two extremes: an identity of nature and supernature which would eliminate the gratuity of the supernatural order, and radical separation between nature and supernature which would make the supernatural a type of divine after-thought, conveniently tacked onto a prior and autonomous natural state. In order to avoid these extremes, theologians have spoken of five states of nature: (1) pure nature, man without preternatural gifts or supernatural elevation; (2) integral nature, man with preternatural gifts only; (3) original justice, man with the preternatural and supernatural endowments he enjoyed prior to original sin; (4) fallen unredeemed nature, man after original sin but prior to any supernatural vocation; (5) redeemed nature, man saved by the grace of Christ. These states of nature must be understood, however, as rational constructs. The state of pure nature and of integral nature never existed, but emerge as ''remainder concepts'' logically derived from the gratuity of the supernatural. Since God's will to save man through Christ has been eternal, the state of fallen, unredeemed nature never existed, but may be deduced as an intelligible concept from man's existential state within the economy of salvation.

Contemporary theology has stressed this deductive quality of pure nature, pointing out that the human nature that we experience is suffused with the gift of grace. It is this supernatural state which alone is the object of experience. Man tends through his activity, not to a merely natural finality, but to a relationship with God that conforms to his elevation beyond his natural potentialities. The natural order in itself is, therefore, an insufficient explanation of the dynamism revealed in human action. This dynamic view of man's historical-social situation prohibits a static evaluation of human nature as a reality realized once and for all in any individual or at any stage of history. BIBLIOGRAPHY: S. O. Brennan, ''*Physis:* Meaning of Nature in the Aristotelian Philosophy of Nature,'' *Thomist* 24 (1961) 383–401; J. B. Hawkins, ''On Nature and Person in Speculative Theology,'' DownRev 80 (1962) 1–11; J. Somerville, *Total Commitment: Blondel's L'Action* (1968). *NATURAL ORDER; *SUPERNATURAL ORDER; *OBEDIENTIAL POTENCY.

[T. M. MCFADDEN]

NATURE DEITIES, revealers of sacred power rather than objects of worship in themselves. Sky, earth, star or planet, vegetation, and animal deities appear in a variety of guises, perform many functions, and achieve various degrees of self-definition. Tribal agriculturalists frequently worship a corn or rice mother who asexually reproduced food from her body, or who, after being slain by the tribe, produces crops from her dismembered remains. The Ancient Near Eastern ''dying-and-rising'' gods were closely connected with the rhythms of the agricultural year. The Greek myth of Demeter's search for her daughter Persephone (Kore) in the underworld may be an allegory of the sowing, harvest, and storage of seed-corn. In ancient Egypt many deities appeared in animal forms, and the steer and lion were royal symbols. Bear ceremonials are practiced widely by the circumpolar peoples of Asia, Europe, and North America, and may date to the Paleolithic period. In several traditions an animal or trickster in animal form secures various elements of culture for society. Among the Winnebago Indians of North America, for example, ''Hare'' functions as an intermediary between humans and the creator god in the acquisition of the important Medicine Rite; the origin myth of that rite features several nature deities and spirits. The natural realm also furnishes symbols of evil or chaos. Chaos beasts such as dragons frequently oppose creators or saviors; sorcerers and witches capitalize on their intimate familiarity with plants and animals to work harm; monsters are often associated with earthquakes and eclipses. BIBLIOGRAPHY: M. Eliade, *Patterns in Comparative Religion* (tr. R. Sheed, 1958); A. E. Jensen, *Myth and Cult Among Primitive Peoples* (tr. M. T. Choldin and W. Weissleder, 1963).

[E. V. GALLAGHER]

NATURE MYTHOLOGY, sacred tales concerning natural phenomena. Myths and legends about animals, plants, and other elements of nature provide people with a blueprint of the world in which they live. They detail the order on which life is founded, its sources, and the complex network of relationships whose fulfillment is necessary for social and biological survival. Though the content of a mythology of nature varies according to the character (hunting, agricultural, etc.) of the individual society, most myths and legends demonstrate acute powers of observation and classification. Classificatory grids distinguish the sacred from the profane, permissible activities from those proscribed (taboo), and one's own culture and identity from that of someone else. Creation stories (e.g., the subjugation of chaos in the form of a dragon or other monster), etiologies (e.g., stories about the discovery of fire, the origins of death, or the initial hunt), and sacred symbols (e.g., the cosmic tree that supports and nourishes the earth)—all contribute to the ordering of the natural world. At times order has been conceived as the equivalent of sacrality; conversely, power and knowledge may be obtained by the crossing of boundaries, as in the case of the *shaman who consorts with the gods and the dead, sometimes in animal form. A unifying thread in nature myths and legends is the concern with the proper "place" of human beings in the overall order of nature, gods, and society. BIBLIOGRAPHY: C. Levi-Strauss, *Savage Mind* (1966); M. Douglas, *Purity and Danger* (1966).

[E. V. GALLAGHER]

NATURE WORSHIP, attitude of reverence for manifestations of the sacred in natural phenomena. Max Müller proposed that all gods were personifications of natural phenomena, but his theories have been rejected. Greek polemics against Egyptian religion and Israelite polemics against the religions of their neighbors simplified their practices into "nature worship," and that judgment still influences Western scholarship. It seems, however, that elements of nature are not worshiped in themselves, but rather as manifestations of the sacred. As a sky-god Horus (Egypt) was represented by a falcon; gods of fecundity like Apis (Egypt), Rudra (India), and Vrthragna (Iran) were portrayed as bulls, but none is restricted to one particular manifestation. All religions deal in some way with natural things in their worship. Grains, dairy products, and meat are frequently sacrificed. Elixirs such as Soma (India) and Haoma (Iran) are thought to possess wondrous qualities; natural hallucinogens are used in the North American Peyote religion. In myth as well as cult the natural world plays a predominant role. An Indonesisan myth recounts that death came into the world because of a primordial choice between a stone (changeless and immortal) and a banana (the parent stem dies after producing offspring). The cultic iconography which tells the story of the Hellenistic god Mithras (Persia) focuses on his salvific slaying of a bull. In some representations wheat springs from the bull's wound; many animal and sidereal symbols also appear on the cultic reliefs. Nature, if not worshiped directly, is nonetheless an indispensable feature of worship. BIBLIOGRAPHY: M. Eliade, *Patterns in Comparative Religion* (tr. R. Sheed, 1958); A. E. Jensen, *Myth and Cult Among Primitive Peoples* (tr. M. T. Choldin and W. W. Weissleder, 1963).

[E. V. GALLAGHER]

NAU, FRANÇOIS NICHOLAS (1864–1931), French Orientalist and patrologist. He was a priest of the Archdiocese of Paris who taught mathematics and astronomy for many years at the Catholic Institute, becoming dean of the faculty of science 3 years before his death. He is chiefly remembered, however, for his editions of Syriac texts. N. had studied Syriac under R. *Graffin and with him edited the *Patrologia Orientalis* (10 v., 1903–15). He also served for a time (1911–60) as editor of the *Revue de l'Orient chrétien*. BIBLIOGRAPHY: L. Hartman, NCE 10:281; I. Ortiz de Urbina, EncCatt 8:1692.

[R. B. ENO]

NAUCLERUS, JOHN (*c.*1425–1510), humanist and historian. N. was instrumental in founding the Univ. of Tübingen, where he taught law and later acted as chancellor (1483–1509). He compiled the *Memorabilium omnis aetatis et omnium gentium chronici commentarii,* which Melanchthon later edited. Within 100 years, nine editions were published. BIBLIOGRAPHY: J. W. Thompson and B. J. Holm, *History of Historical Writing* (2 v., 1942) 1:426; H. Tüchle, LTK 7:845.

[J. E. LYNCH]

NAUMANN, JOHANN GOTTLIEB (1741–1801), German composer. N. was born and educated in Dresden, and studied music in Italy. In 1763 he was appointed court composer of sacred music by the Electress of Saxony, where he later became *Oberkapellmeister* (1786). He was a prolific composer of church music (13 oratorios, 21 Masses), as well as secular operas.

[T. M. MCFADDEN]

NAUMBURG CATHEDRAL, German Romanesque church (*c.*1200) with four distinctive half-Gothic towers, renowned for important sculptured figures of Uta, Ekkehard, and Willem von Camburg in the W choir, done under Bp. Dietrich von Wettin (*c.*1249) by the Naumburg master, who had worked in the Bamberg cathedral workshop. With an earlier St. John these carvings show Romanesque volume with indigenous German emotional expressiveness.

[M. J. DALY]

NAUMBURG MASTER (13th cent.), major German sculptor. His greatest works are the figures of Uta, Ekkehard, and Willem von Camburg in the W choir of the Naumburg cathedral, uniting a unique aristocratic realism, Romanesque plasticity and German psychological expressiveness.

[M. J. DALY]

NAUSEA, FRIEDRICH (Grau; 1490–1552), promoter of church reunion, bp. of Vienna. As secretary to the papal legate Card. L. *Campeggio, N. attended the Diet of Nuremberg. In 1525 he became a canon of Frankfurt am Main but was driven out by the Lutherans. Named preacher of the Mainz cathedral (1526) and court preacher to King Ferdinand (1534), he was appointed coadjutor to the bp. of Vienna (1538) and succeeded him as bp. 3 years later. N. worked actively for the reunion of the Lutherans and Catholics, joined with certain other prelates in petitioning Rome to permit the clergy to marry and the laity to receive *communion under both kinds, and helped in the preparations for the Council of Trent, where his attendance was cut short by death.

[R. B. ENO]

NAVARRETE, DOMINGO FERNÁNDEZ (1618–86), Spanish Dominican missionary to China. After his studies and ordination in Spain, N. worked as a missionary in the Philippines and China. He strongly opposed the Jesuit missionaries' position in the *Chinese Rites controversy and sought to implement uniform directives for all Christian missionaries there. He was named abp. of Santo Domingo in 1677.

[T. M. MCFADDEN]

NAVE (from the Lat. *navis,* a ship; until the 19th cent. used also in form of "nef"), the main body of a church, extending from the rear wall to the choir, chancel, or sanctuary, often between aisles.

NAVEL OF THE UNIVERSE, a place believed to be a fixed center around which the entire cosmos is arrayed in an orderly fashion. The navel is usually identified with the summit of a particular mountain or pyramid (human-built mountain), which is a sacred location, a place which acts as the umbilicus or *axis mundi* between the worlds of the gods, humans, and the inhabitants of the underworld. These central holy places, sites for sacred worship of the cult and the centers or foci for a people's world, are so common in the ancient (and in many ways the modern) world that some scholars consider it a religious universal. The Bible, for example, mentions Mount Garizim as the earth's navel (Jg 9.37); the Hebrew *tabūr* in Mount Tabor (Ezek 38.12) means navel. Jerusalem is considered a middle point and among Christians, Golgotha retains the function of navel. Pyramid and platform temples in Maya, Aztec, Greek, Roman, Islamic, Chinese, Japanese, Mesopotamian, Egyptian, and other world religions serve as navels, conduits to the other worlds, cult centers of this world. Modern basilicas and churches, even capitol buildings in some cases, have elements that suggest an affinity with this ancient concept.

[R. J. LITZ]

NAYLER, JAMES (*c.*1618–60), early Quaker leader. A retired soldier, N. met G. *Fox in 1651, embraced *Inner Light belief, and became Fox's friend and near peer as leader of the Quaker movement. Certain women in London from 1655 began to worship him as a new Jesus, and N. allowed them to stage his "triumphal entry" into Bristol (1656). He was arrested, and in a clamorous trial by Parliament, he was found guilty of blasphemy, sentenced to the cruelest punishments, and imprisoned. Throughout the episode, Fox sternly condemned N. as an enemy of the light; the two were not reconciled until 1660, a year after N.'s release. The affair led Fox to exercise greater control against the recurrence of misguided appeals to the Inner Light. BIBLIOGRAPHY: E. Foegelklou, *James Naylor, the Rebel Saint* (1931); Knox Enth 160-166; V. Noble, *Man in Leather Breeches* (1953) 108–143.

[T. C. O'BRIEN]

NAZARENE, translation of two different names given to Jesus: *Nazarênos* and *Nazôraios,* which may be considered as derivatives from Nazareth (Mt 2.23). It was also a name sometimes applied to Christians, "the sect of the Nazarenes" (Acts 24.5). BIBLIOGRAPHY: A. Le Houllier, NCE 10:284–285.

[A. VIARD]

NAZARENE, CHURCH OF THE, see CHURCH OF THE NAZARENE.

NAZARENES, Syrian Jewish Christians of the 4th cent. A.D., who still followed Jewish laws and customs, possessed an Aramaic Gospel, and seemed to be orthodox Christians.

[J. F. FALLON]

NAZARENES (BROTHERHOOD OF ST. LUKE), a group of 19th-cent. German and Austrian artists founded as the Lukasbund in Vienna, but finally centered (1810) in the abandoned cloister of S. Isidoro, Rome, as Nazarenes, advocating a return to pure elemental forms in religious art, particularly in mural painting. Influenced by the emotional ideas of W. H. Wackenroder and Friedrich von Schlegel, the Nazarenes included J. Friedrich Overbeck (1789–1869), Franz Pforr (1788–1812), Peter Cornelius (1783–1867), Gustav Heinrich Naecke (*c.*1786–1835), and Wilhelm von Schadow (1788–1862). BIBLIOGRAPHY: K. Andrews, *Nazarenes* (1964).

[F. S. GRUBER]

NAZARENES, GOSPEL OF THE, see APOCRYPHA (NT), 38.

NAZARETH, the town in Galilee in which Jesus grew to manhood. Although born in Bethlehem (Lk 2.4–7), Jesus grew up in Nazareth but was forced to leave because of opposition during the early period of his ministry (Lk 4.16–30). Excavations under the church of the Annunciation reveal a Crusader church, a 5th-cent. church, and a Christian structure from about 200 A.D.. BIBLIOGRAPHY: EDB 1616–18.

[J. A. GRASSI]

NAZARIUS OF LÉRINS, ST. (584?–629?), the 14th abbot of Lérins. Little is known of N. save that, like most of his predecessors, he sought to eradicate all traces of pagan worship. He is supposed to have turned a number of pagan shrines into Christian religious houses at Lérins. BIBLIOGRAPHY: P. Meyer, ''La Vie latine de saint Honorat et Raimon Féraut,'' *Romania* 8 (1879) 481–508.

[B. F. SCHERER]

NAZIRITES, persons set apart by special vows (Num ch. 6). The Nazirite was forbidden to consume any product of the grapevine, cut his hair, or go near a dead body. Samson was a Nazirite from birth (Jg 13.5). Paul perhaps took temporary Nazirite vows (Acts 18.18; see also 21.24). *RECHABITES.

[T. EARLY]

NCCB, see NATIONAL CONFERENCE OF CATHOLIC BISHOPS.

NCCM, see NATIONAL COUNCIL OF CATHOLIC MEN.

NCCN, see NATIONAL COUNCIL OF CATHOLIC NURSES.

NCCW, see NATIONAL COUNCIL OF CATHOLIC WOMEN.

NCWC, see UNITED STATES CATHOLIC CONFERENCE.

NE TEMERE, the title of a decree issued by Pius X in 1907 and which went into effect on Easter Sunday, 1908. It extended to the whole Latin Church the form necessary to the validity of a marriage prescribed by the Council of Trent in 1563. It also cleared up certain points that had caused difficulty in the interpretation and application of the council's legislation in special circumstances. *CLANDESTINE MARRIAGES.

NEA, CONSTANTINOPLE, ''New'' Byzantine church, erected by Emperor Basil I (881), now destroyed, a cross-in-square with five domes—prototype for St. Mark's, Venice and St. Sophia, Kiev.

[M. J. DALY]

NEA MONI (CHIOS), 11th-cent. Byzantine monastery church with a dome supported directly upon the outside walls on squinches. The transepts, forming eight niches in the corners, and transverse walls provide a fluted periphery to the interior, which is lavishly decorated with brilliant mosaics, marble paneling, and frescoes. BIBLIOGRAPHY: R. Krautheimer, *Early Christian and Byzantine Architecture* (1965); E. Diez and O. Demus, *Byzantine Mosaics in Greece* (1931); A. Grabar, *Byzantine Painting* (1953).

[S. D. MURRAY]

NEAL, DANIEL (1678–1743), Puritan historian. After studying for the dissenting ministry in Holland, N. began his lifelong care of the Independent congregation of Aldersgate Street in 1704. He was one of the ablest Puritan preachers. His *History of New England* (2 v. 1720) and *History of the Puritans, 1517–1688* (1732–38), though prejudiced, remain important. BIBLIOGRAPHY: J. B. Mullinger, DNB 40:134–136.

[M. J. SUELZER]

NEALE, JOHN MASON (1818–66), author and hymnologist. Scholar of Trinity College, Cambridge, he was an outstanding classicist. He joined the high-church movement in Cambridge and was one of the founders of the Camden Society for the study of ecclesiastical art, an organization important to the 19th-cent. liturgical life of the Church of England. From 1846 he was warden of Sackville College, East Grinstead, the only preferment he ever held; the diocesan exceeded his prerogatives and denounced the chapel ornaments as ''fripperies'' and ''spiritual haberdashery.'' N. founded (1854) the Sisterhood of St. Margaret, with a rule patterned on those of the Visitation nuns and the Daughters of Charity. A voluminous writer of theology, ecclesiology, and fiction, he won his greatest fame as a liturgiologist. By his contributions, both translations and original compositions, he exerted a lasting influence on Anglican worship. Among his other works were a *Commentary on the Psalms* (4 v., 1860–74) and *History of the Holy Eastern Church* (5 v., 1847–73), as well as several series of sermons, and devotional writings for children.

[T. GILBY]

NEALE, LEONARD (1746–1817), second abp. of Baltimore. Of an old Catholic family of Maryland, N. studied at St. Omer in Flanders and entered the Jesuits in 1767 with four of his brothers and was ordained some years later. When the Jesuits were suppressed he went on the English mission, then to British Guiana, and in 1783 to the U.S. He was a participant in the meeting which reorganized the American Church and though opposing an American bishopric, he supported John Carroll as vicar apostolic. In 1793 N. went to Philadelphia where he performed heroically during the yellow fever epidemic. As vicar general of that diocese he assisted in the founding of the Visitation Convent (see LALOR, TERESA). In 1799 he was made president of Georgetown, which he turned from an academy into a genuine college with a reputation for excellence. At Carroll's request N. was appointed coadjutor bp. of Baltimore with the right of succession and consecrated in 1800. On Carroll's death N. became abp. of Baltimore in 1815, but poor health prevented a vigorous administration and he died 2 years later. BIBLIOGRAPHY: P. Guilday, *Life and Times of John Carroll* (2 v., 1922).

[J. R. AHERNE]

NEAMTU, ABBEY OF, a 14th-cent. Romanian monastery established near Targu Neamt, Moldavia, which was an important fortress. One of the most famous monasteries in Romania, Neamtu had over 600 monks and 2 churches. Its benefactor, Stephen the Great, Prince of Moldavia (1457–1503) helped to make it a center for pilgrims and tourists.

[M. A. MCFADDEN]

NEANDER, JOHANN AUGUST WILHELM (1789–1850), German church historian. Until his conversion to Protestantism from Judaism, he was called David Mendel. His conversion and much of his intellectual formation were influenced by F. *Schleiermacher, whose colleague he became at Berlin in 1813. There he lectured for the remainder of his life on church history and NT exegesis. Besides works on Julian the Apostate (1812), St. Bernard of Clairvaux (1813), Gnosticism (1818), and Tertullian (1824), he published a major work, *Allgemeine Geschichte der christlichen Religion und Kirke* (6 v., 1825–52; Eng. tr. J. Torrey, *General History of the Christian Religion and Church,* 5 v., 1882). N. conceived of the history of Christianity as evidence of the intervention of the divine into the human, first fully in the life of Christ, then in the lives of individual Christians, which reflected the life of Christ. His portrayal minimizes doctrine and ecclesiastical institutions in favor of a Christianity that has developed as Christ animated the lives of individual Christians. BIBLIOGRAPHY: EncRelKnow 8:95–96.

[T. C. O'BRIEN]

NEBO, name of (1) mountain in Moab, possibly the modern Jebel en-Neba, where Moses viewed Canaan just before his death (Dt 34.1); (2) a town near Mount Nebo (Num 32.37–38); (3) a Babylonian deity for which the mountain might have been named (Is 46.1).

[T. EARLY]

NEBRASKA, a central Great Plains state, admitted to the Union (1867) as the 37th state. Francisco Vasquez Coronado explored the area (1541) and for the next 250 years it was visited periodically by Spanish and French explorers and traders. It became part of the U.S. (1803) through the Louisiana Purchase. There was little Catholic missionary activity in Nebraska during the period of Spanish and French control. When James O'Gorman, the first vicar apostolic, arrived in 1859, he found only a few hundred Catholic families. Attempting to develop Catholic educational facilities, he brought the Benedictine Sisters and the Sisters of Mercy to teach. After the Diocese of Omaha was established (1885), J. O'Connor and R. Scannell served as its early bishops. Following Scannell's death (1916) J. *Harty became bp.; during his episcopate Boys Town was started by Edward *Flanagan. Harty was succeeded (1928) by Joseph *Rummell, after whose transfer (1935) to New Orleans, J. H. *Ryan, Rector of The Catholic Univ. of America, became bishop. When Omaha became an archdiocese (1945), Ryan served as its first abp. until his death (1947). Under Gerald T. Bergan, abp. from 1948–69, the archdiocese expanded greatly. He saw to the construction of a seminary and a home for the aged, as well as doubling Catholic elementary school enrollment. He was succeeded by Daniel Sheehan, whose suffragan sees are the Dioceses of Grand Island and Lincoln.

In 1976 Nebraska's Catholics numbered 316,730 or 20.8% of the total state population. The major Protestant denominations are the Methodist Church, with 10.1% of the population in 1971 and the Lutheran Church (Missouri Synod), with 7.4%. Other Protestant Churches comprised 23.3% of the population. The Jewish population, as of 1968 was 8,100 or 0.5%. Both of Nebraska's Catholic colleges, which have a total enrollment of 5,294 students, are in the Archdiocese of Omaha. Nebraska's 34 Catholic high schools have over 11,876 students, 8,834 of whom are in the 21 Catholic high schools in the archdiocese. Of the 102 Catholic elementary schools in the state, with an enrollment of 23,344, 69 of these schools, attended by 18,666 pupils, are in the archdiocese. BIBLIOGRAPHY: J. C. Olson, *History of Nebraska* (1955); H. W. Casper, *Church on the Northern Plains* (1960); D. W. Johnson, et al., *Churches and Church Membership in U.S.* (1974).

[J. L. MORRISON; R. M. PRESTON]

NEBUCHADNEZZAR (Nebuchadrezzar), king of Babylonia 605–562 B.C. He succeeded his father Nabopolassar and was followed by his son Evil-merodach. As his father's general he defeated Pharoah Neco II at Carchemish (605 B.C.) and as king achieved dominance over all the area down to Egypt. Classical historians credited him with making Babylon one of the wonders of the world. N. was significant in biblical history as the ruler who brought the kingdom of *Judah to an end. He made Jehoiakim his vassal (2 Kg 24.1), and Jehoiakim's son Jehoiachin reigned only 3 months before N. took him and 10,000 leading citizens of Judah captive (2 Kg 24.8–16). He then put Zedekiah (Mattaniah) on the throne, and when Zedekiah rebelled, he brought the kingdom of Judah to an end (587 B.C.)—taking Zedekiah in fetters to Babylon, sending Nebuzaradan to burn Jerusalem, killing some of the Jewish leaders, and taking more captives to Babylon (2 Kg 24–25). Jeremiah contended that Yahweh had given N. his power, and despite charges of treason, he opposed Judah's rebellion against N. (Jer ch. 25 and 27–28). The N. in Dan ch. 1–4 is a fictitious king, meant to represent the Seleucids.

[T. EARLY]

NECESSITY: (1) a condition of need. The term in this sense has two notable occurrences in moral decisions. A person is bound to come to the assistance of another who is in dire physical need by using the resources superfluous to caring for his own and his family's needs according to his station in life. Where a person is in grave spiritual need, a priest is bound to administer the sacraments and may also absolve the person from some ecclesiastical *censures. (2) the condition or quality of a being or an action that cannot be otherwise than it is. Necessity in this sense can be explained on the basis either of inner constitutives or of external influences. On the grounds of its own make-up the necessary is that which has no inner element presupposing or leading to nonexistence. In this sense any being lacking matter as a component is a necessary being: the human soul, the angel, God. Necessity of this kind is also verified of the action of a will that is united to the object that totally fulfills its orientation to the all-good (see GOOD, SUPREME). Thus God's own self-love and the blessed's love for God are voluntary, yet naturally necessary will-acts. By reference to the external influence of an agent cause the necessity of a being is contrasted with contingency. Because the union of *essence and existence in any being other than God depends on the creative and sustaining free act of God's will, no creature has a necessary, but only a contingent existence. Necessity and contingency apply also to the effects of a created, agent cause: where the agent cause, e.g. the forces of nature, have a set and invariable way of acting, their actions and their effects are necessary, as distinct from both voluntary and chance acts or effects. Necessity with regard to the manner of acting proper to a voluntary agent has the meaning of coercion or force: an act done under duress is the opposite of a voluntary and free act. The meaning of necessity is further nuanced by reference to end or purpose. The willing of an object is absolutely necessary when the object coincides as end with the inner orientation of the will; such a necessity corresponds to necessity based on inner constitutives. The willing of an object is hypothetically necessary when a presupposed end is unattainable without the willing of that object. Thus presupposing that God wills eternal life to men, the willing of grace is necessary; but the presupposition itself depends solely on God's free will. Necessity deriving from end has a further variant: an action or means to an end may be necessary simply speaking when the action or means is the unique way of attainment of an end; it may be necessary in a relative sense (morally necessary) when it is the best, not the sole way of attaining the end or when, practically speaking, attainment of an end is so difficult as to be all but impossible. A further, allied distinction occurs with regard to the relationship of certain acts to salvation: moral theology speaks of a "necessity of means" and a "necessity of precept." Some acts are of their nature required for salvation, because without them man cannot be saved: thus faith; other acts are required by a necessity of precept, that is required because of a specific commandment of God or of the Church.

[T. C. O'BRIEN]

NECESSITY OF MEANS, in RC theology, a high and precisely specified degree of necessity. What is required as means to an end, without which the end cannot be attained, is said to be necessary by necessity of means. Such necessity stands in contrast to what is required because commanded. This is called *necessity of precept. Necessity of means may be absolute or conditional. In the former case, the means must be present in reality if the end is to be attained. In the latter case the reality of the means may be supplied by something that implicitly and by intrinsic tendency contains it. Through the graciousness of the Lord those things necessary for salvation by necessity of means absolutely (faith, love, grace) lie within the grasp of every person and contain implicitly and by intrinsic tendency the divinely instituted manifestations of these salvation realities (baptism of water, bond of faith, and communion in the visible Church), which are required by precept and by necessity of means conditionally. BIBLIOGRAPHY: Vat II ConstChurch 13–17; É. Amann, DTC 11.1:55–56.

[J. F. GALLAGHER]

NECESSITY OF PRECEPT, in RC theology a precisely specified degree of necessity. What is required because commanded is necessary by necessity of precept. The basis of such necessity is the free decision of authority, divine or human. Necessity of precept stands in contrast to *necessity of means, or the necessity of something related to the end as a means indispensable to its achievement. The human person can only fulfill those precepts of which he is aware and which fall within the limitations of his physical and moral powers. On the side of authority, the intention to bind only to what is known and can be done is reasonably presupposed. What is required of man for salvation by precept alone binds those only who have heard the word of God and in whose power it is to render explicit obedience. BIBLIOGRAPHY: Vat II ConstChurch 13–17; É. Amann, DTC 11.1:55–56.

[J. F. GALLAGHER]

NECHO (Nechao), a Pharaoh of the 26th Dynasty (609–594 B.C.), succeeding his father Psammetichus I. He killed Josiah at Megiddo (2 Kg ch. 23). N. was defeated by Nebuchadnezzar at Carchemish, but successfully resisted Babylonian invasion of Egypt.

[T. EARLY]

NECKER, JACQUES (1732–1804), French banker and periodic consultant to the French government in financial matters through the years leading up to the Revolution. His book published in London (1788), and later in Boston (1796) entitled *De l'importance des opinions religieuses* gives him a certain prominence as a religious thinker; but his overwhelming impact and interest was banking and finance, as the bulk of his prolific writing attests. Born in Geneva, of a family from Pomerania, he was cofounder of the foremost bank in France. Because of his Protestant religion, he was not able to have the royal title as finance minister, but he was often that in effect during a tumultuous career. He called into session the Estates General which led to the Revolution, and was held in favor for a time by the revolutionary Assembly, but finally had to flee Paris.

[E. J. DILLON]

NECROLOGY, a list of dead members of a community, particularly of a religious order. Originating in *diptychs, necrologies were made for special remembrance on the anniversaries of their deaths. Medieval necrologies are valuable historical sources.

[T. EARLY]

NECROMANCY (from the Gr. *necros,* a dead man, and *manteia* divination), a form of superstitious *divination which seeks to foretell the future by communicating with the souls of the dead, or to make use of them for magical purposes. The older form of the word in modern languages was close to the medieval Latin *nigromantia* and hence suggested ''black'' as opposed to ''white'' arts, but the proper etymological meaning of the term was known to the learned. A celebrated instance of necromancy is the witch of Endor calling up Samuel at the request of King Saul (1 Sam 28.3–19). The Mosaic Law forbids necromancy (e.g., Lev 19.31; 20.6; Dt 18.11–12); it was abhorred as a pagan abomination by early Christians (see e.g., Tertullian, *De anima* 57, PL 2:793), and has been repeatedly denounced by church authorities.

[T. GILBY]

NECTARIUS, ST. (d. 397), **PATRIARCH OF CONSTANTINOPLE,** who presided over the first Council of Constantinople in 381. His name heads the list of signatories to the canons of that council, among which is the one that places the See of Constantinople second only to the See of Rome in dignity. The account of his election as bp. resembles that of St. Ambrose in the West. When St. Gregory of Nazianzus resigned the see on the eve of the general council, the Emperor Theodosius invited the assembled bps. to submit names in nomination. The emperor selected the name of N., a senator and praetor of the city. His name had been submitted by the patriarch of Antioch, to whom it had been suggested by the bp. of Tarsus. Far from being involved in the ecclesiastical factions and intrigues, N., unknown to the emperor and the bps., was still a catechumen. Member of a noble family of Tarsus in Cilicia, he was an elderly man of admirable character and integrity. Even when it became known that he was not baptized, the Emperor held fast to his choice, and N. stepped at once to the presidency of the council. The people of the city were pleased with the choice. N. served as patriarch until his death, when he was succeeded by St. John Chrysostom. N. was active in defense of orthodoxy against Arian dissidents; his abolition of the office of priest-penitentiary belongs to the history of the sacrament of penance.

[E. J. DILLON]

NEDELLEC, HARVEY, see HERVAEUS NATALIS.

NEÉL, JEAN PIERRE, Bl. (1832–62), French missionary in China. N. was a member of the Paris Foreign Missions who worked in the Chinese province of Kwei-chou. He was beheaded there during the recurring persecutions of Christians in China at that time.

[T. M. MCFADDEN]

NEERCASSEL, JOHANNES VAN (1623–86), bp. of Castoria and vicar apostolic of Holland. N. studied at Louvain and Paris, became an Oratorian (1645), and taught at the Malines seminary before his appointment as vicar apostolic. His writings reflect a moral austerity and doctrinal stance similar to that of the Jansenists, and Antoine *Arnauld seems to have collaborated in N.'s most noted work, *Amor paenitens* (1682). That work was condemned by Alexander VIII as contrary to the Council of Trent's teaching on the forgiveness of sins.

[T. M. MCFADDEN]

NEGATION, WAY OF, a method of knowing God, called the *via negativa* by scholastics and *via remotionis* (way of removal) by Aquinas (ThAq ST 1a, 13). Accordingly, we deny all imperfections to God, and this amounts to a kind of valid knowledge concerning God. In addition, when we affirm in him perfections that admit of no defect (pure perfections), we deny the limitations which these perfections always entail when found in creatures. Many expressions used to designate perfections peculiar to God show by their very form their origin in the *via negativa*: *un*changeable, *un*caused, *in*finite, *im*mense, *in*effable. BIBLIOGRAPHY: C. N. Bittle *God and His Creatures* (1953) 191–193.

[E. J. DILLON]

NEGATIVE THEOLOGY, a description of theology as it is in part inherently apophatic (Gr. *apophēmē* to deny, to say no). Taken etymologically, theology is speech about God and therefore self-limiting: every positive statement made about God must be balanced by a negation. The negation is not a denial of the truth of what is thought or said, but a denial that the human thought or word is adequate to express how what is affirmed is true. Theology begins with the assent of faith to the reality, transcendence, and uniqueness of God. It also begins, therefore, with a self-evaluation: it is a human discipline that cannot transcend the power of human concepts to intend and to signify the realities about God that they seek to express. Thus what the "divine names" signify, e.g., God's goodness, power, justice, is true of the divine reality; the mode of being reflected by the names' manner of signifying is not because God exceeds any created mode of being (see INCOMPREHENSIBILITY; INEFFABILITY OF GOD). Recognition of the negative quality is part of the Christian theological tradition, esp. as it was vitally influenced by *Pseudo-Dionysius in his *The Divine Names*. The negative quality in theology is an essential of the theological epistemology of St. Thomas Aquinas (see ThAq ST 1a,13). But both those masters would take it as an extreme to regard God's word, as did K. *Barth until the late stages of his writing, as a divine NO to every human thought and word about the divinity. The communication of revelation through biblical thought and language is an assurance that however qualified as inadequate, the intelligibility of the divine reality that theology discovers is not irrelevant nor are its statements pure equivocations. *ANALOGY.

[T. C. O'BRIEN]

NEGEB, desert region of Palestine that was extensively settled and irrigated at various stages in history from 21st cent. B.C. to 7th cent. A.D., and is now being resettled and cultivated by modern Israel.

[J. F. FALLON]

NEGLIGENCE, lack of the care required for responsible moral action. Because the disorder in sin is a lack of the good that should be intended, negligence is a general characteristic of all sin: the failure namely, to attend to the subordination of the good sinfully chosen to the measure of full and true human goodness. In a more specific sense, negligence is also a sin contrary to the virtue of *prudence: the failure, namely, to make effective moral decisions about an act and the mode of its accomplishment. Negligence with regard to matters necessary for salvation can be a mortal sin, as can negligence that involves a slackness of will amounting to *contempt for the demands of charity. A frequent instance of sinful negligence is the failure to fulfill responsibilities required by one's state or position in life, esp. when the physical or spiritual well-being of others is involved. A milder form of negligence may be described as a lack of *fervor, and this is frequently the reason for *venial sin (ThAq ST 2a2ae, 54.3). Negligence in things of the spirit is a notable symptom of the vice of *acedia.

[T. C. O'BRIEN]

NEGRO AMERICAN MISSIONS, CATHOLIC BOARD FOR, formerly Catholic Board for Mission Work among the Colored People. An episcopal agency for raising funds for the education of blacks in the Southern United States, it was founded in 1906 at the request of Pius X to the U.S. Catholic hierarchy, and incorporated in 1907 under the laws of the state of Tennessee. In 1964 there was a staff of five, including two priests and three sisters, directing the solicitation for funds from a New York headquarters. The Official Catholic Directory of 1975 lists the Board as "The Catholic Board for Negro American Missions." Still headquartered in New York City it is described as engaged in the support of priests and sisters throughout the South; in monthly support of more than 401 sisters and 308 lay teachers teaching in the poorest schools. The director, a Josephite priest, is also the editor of the Board's publication *Educating in Faith*. This Board has no doubt been eclipsed by national organizations which express the growing autonomy of black American culture, such as the National Office for Black Catholics, in which black Catholic leaders seek to strengthen black participation in the Church, and to make the efforts of the Church more effective in black communities. A more comprehensive approach to the powerlessness of many black communities is also contained in the strategies of the various offices of the Campaign for Human Development.

[E. J. DILLON]

NEGRO MISSIONS IN THE U.S. The early American Church through the 19th cent. was hampered in its work for the blacks by a number of conditions. There were insufficient numbers of priests and religious; financial support was meager; the society was often hostile; and the great influx of Catholic immigrants was more than the Church could handle. As a result, though there were many individual efforts to care for Catholic blacks, there was no permanent and comprehensive effort. It must be remembered also that only a handful of Negroes were RCs before the 20th century. Two significant and lasting elements were communities of black religious: the Oblate Sisters of Providence (1831) and the Sisters of the Holy Family (1842). The Second Plenary Council of Baltimore (1866) considered a unifying program to be headed by a bp., but the plan was defeated largely through the opposition of Abp. P. *Kenrick of St. Louis, who feared divisive results. Pius IX in 1869 asked the Mill Hill Fathers, an English missionary society, to take charge of the Negro apostolate in the U.S. In 1893 the American Mill Hill Fathers with the encouragement of Card. Gibbons became an independent congregation (Josephite Fathers) for work among blacks in America. The Third Plenary Council of Baltimore (1884) established a Commission for Catholic Missions among Colored People and Indians and initiated an annual national collection in its support. In 1906 the hierarchy set up the Catholic Board for Work among the Colored People. In addition to the two congregations of black religious a number of other groups of sisters devoted their efforts to the blacks. The Mill Hill Sisters, the Mission Helpers of the Sacred Heart, Franciscans of Glen Riddle, Pa., the Sisters Servants of the Holy Ghost and Mary Immaculate, but, most important of all, Mother Katharine *Drexel and her Sisters of the Blessed Sacrament for Indians and Colored People, sparked by her indomitable spirit and vast fortune, gave powerful impetus to the Negro apostolate. A third community of black sisters, the Handmaids of Mary, was founded in 1917. Among communities of men the Holy Ghost Fathers, the Society of African Missions, and the Society of the Divine Word enlarged the missionary efforts for blacks. Another significant development has been the growth in the number of Negro priests, almost entirely a phenomenon of the past 40 years. The emergence of Catholic blacks as more than a missionary interest began in the last decade of the 19th century. Through congresses and organizations the Catholic Negro began to have some impact on American Catholicism. As awareness by Catholics of the situation of blacks sharpened, mission activity widened to programs for interracial justice and the civil rights movement. The Jesuit John LaFarge provided strong leadership in this area. In 1934 he was instrumental in forming the Catholic Interracial Council in New York City. A series of conferences of Catholic clergy to discuss the newly enlivened apostolate to the blacks was held in Northern and Southern cities and the Catholic Conference of the South (1940) began work for desegregation. During the Civil Rights agitation in the South priests and religious took active part. The need for coordination of the many programs led to the formation in 1960 of the National Catholic Conference for Interracial Justice. Meanwhile on a more personalist level Dorothy Day and her Catholic Worker movement and the Baroness De Hueck and her Friendship House program were demonstrating interracial living. Among the bps. who pioneered in the desegregation effort were Rummel of New Orleans, Lucey of San Antonio, Ritter of St. Louis, Sheil and Meyer of Chicago and O'Boyle of Washington. BIBLIOGRAPHY: J. Gillard, *Catholic Church and the American Negro* (1930); E. McManus, *Studies in Race Relations* (1961); J. Leonard, *Theology and Race Relations* (1963).

[J. R. AHERNE]

NEGRO MUSIC, see AFRO-AMERICAN MUSIC.

NEGRO SPIRITUAL, see SPIRITUALS, NEGRO.

NEHEMIAH, a Jew who had apparently attained a very high position in the civil administration of Artaxerxes I (465–425 B.C.), and was appointed governor of Judah (Neh 5.14); the rebuilder, defender, and religious reformer of Jerusalem, for whom one of the canonical books of the OT is named.

[D. J. BOURKE]

NEHEMIAH, BOOK OF, the fourth part of what is termed the Chronicler's history (1–2 Chronicles, Ezra, Nehemiah). Originally the Chronicler's history was a single work written either *c.*400 or *c.*200 B.C. by an unknown Levite author. The fourfold separation derives largely from the later Greek and Latin versions. In the Hebrew Bible, Ezra-Nehemiah appear before the books of Chronicles, since the canonicity of these books was not questioned and since *Ezra-Nehemiah provide information found nowhere else concerning the restoration period. The author had at his disposal a considerable number of historical sources: lists and letters; archival records; and specifically the personal memoirs of Nehemiah and Ezra. It appears that in transmission some of the Nehemiah material appears in the Book of Ezra and vice versa. As the Book of Nehemiah remains today, its contents are the following: (1) the narrative of the return of Nehemiah, an official at the court of the Persian King Artaxerxes I (464–423 B.C.) to the province of Juda; (2) an account of the work of Nehemiah and the people in rebuilding the walls of Jerusalem despite economic difficulties and the opposition of the Samaritan governor Sanballat and others; (3) the reading of the Law by the priest-scribe Ezra and the renewal of the covenant by the Jewish community; (4) the rehabitation of Jerusalem; (5) the return of Nehemiah to Jerusalem after an interval at the Persian court and his correction of abuses discovered upon his return. BIBLIOGRAPHY: A. Gelin, *Le Livre d'Esdras et Néhémie* (1960); J. M. Myers, *Ezra-Nehemia* (1965); R. North, JBC 24:1–114 (402–438).

[T. J. RYAN]

NEIGHBOR, every person who is to be loved in keeping with the second of the two great commandments of *charity (Mt 22.39, quoting Lev 19.18; see also Mt 19.19; Rom 13.9; Gal 5.14; Jas 2.8). Love of one another is given as Jesus' new commandment (Jn 13.34); the one to be loved is described as one's "brother," the motive for that love, "if God so loves us, we also ought to love one another" (1 Jn 4.11). The parable of the Good Samaritan (Lk 10.29–37) shows that Christ intends "neighbor" to embrace all human beings: the Samaritan's show of mercy indicates that charity transcends estrangement, even antipathy. The true basis for love of neighbor is its link with love for God: love for others expresses the union in love with the Father. By grace he wills all to be his children, and so to regard others as brothers, cosharers in the Father's love. Love of neighbor is the willing to all of what the Father wills them: their share in his life and in all that contributes to that (ThAq ST 2a2ae, 25.1). The minimal sense of treating others as neighbors is this: "The friendship of charity extends even to enemies, for we love them for the sake of God, who is the principal one in our loving" (*ibid.* 23.1, ad 2; see 27.8). Enemies and sinners are regarded as neighbors by charity, not by acquiescence in the evil they do, but by the intent that they come to share in grace and cast aside evil. The commandment of love also takes into the meaning of neighbor those bound together by the more personal, human ties of kinship and *friendship. In the scale of values that charity observes every personal quality for good endearing relatives and friends to each other is part of their full identity as children of the Father, therefore brothers through grace. Those closer by blood or affection are also closer "neighbors" with regard to the love of charity, since charity values in them with greater awareness and intensity all that God's love has made them to be (*ibid.* 26.6–8).

[T. C. O'BRIEN]

NEITHARDT (Nithardt), **MATHIS** (Mathes). See GRÜNEWALD.

NEKRASOV, NIKOLAY ALEXEYEVICH (1821–78), Russian poet, publisher and editor of the radical journals: *The Contemporary* (1846–66) and *Notes of the Fatherland* (1868–78). His poems of social protest and his love poems are inferior to the folk songs in which, by his imaginative rhythmical innovations, he created a new kind of national lyric. The ennobling power of suffering is a recurrent theme in his poems about the Russian peasant as, for instance, in the two narrative poems *Vlas* (1854) and *Frost the Red-Nosed* (1863). His masterpiece is the unfinished satirical poem *Who Can Be Happy in Russia?* (1873–76). BIBLIOGRAPHY: M. B. Peppard, *Nikolai Nekrasov* (1967); R. Poggioli, *The Poets of Russia 1890–1930* (1960) 40–43.

[M. F. MCCARTHY]

NEKTARIOS KEPHALAS, ST. (1846–1920), bishop. A great part of his life was devoted to restoring religious life among nuns, esp. in a convent on the island of Aegina. His advice was sought by many, and his tomb has become a place of pilgrimage. He was canonized by the Greek Orthodox Church in 1961.

[G. T. DENNIS]

NELL-BRUENING, OSWALD VON (1890–), German social theorist and educator. N. became a Jesuit in 1911, and has taught at the Jesuit seminary in Frankfurt/Main since 1928 as well as at the Univ. of Frankfurt (1956). He is one of the leading proponents of Catholic social and political ethics in Germany, where he has strongly supported the rights of workers. N. is a prolific writer, although only his *Reorganization of Social Economy* (1936) has been translated into English. BIBLIOGRAPHY: *Brockhaus Enzyklopädie* 13:287–288.

[T. M. MCFADDEN]

NELLI, OTTAVIANO DI MARTINO (fl. *c.*1400–44), Italian painter in Umbria and the Marches whose style, rooted in French and Italian MS illumination, shows exquisite taste, and refined color. N. executed the tempera polyptych, *Madonna and Child with Angels, Saints and Worshippers* (1403), frescoes of the *Life of the Virgin* (1424), and *Life of St. Augustine* (Gubbio).

[M. J. DALY]

NEMESIS, the Greek goddess of retribution. Though she was honored at various shrines, particularly at Rhamnus in Attica, and possessed a distinctive, even if at times, contradictory mythology, N. was most commonly little more than the personification of righteous indignation, the avenger of human pride and passion, and the equalizer of good and bad fortune. Psychologically she may be traced back to the innate sense of justice possessed by men and their respect for the punitive powers of the divinity. She was a favorite of moralists such as Herodotus and Pindar; her cult spread throughout the Greco-Roman world. She was usually portrayed as a virgin goddess accompanied by instruments of death and torture such as bridles, wheels, clubs, scourges, and swords. BIBLIOGRAPHY: H.J. Rose, OCD 601.

[M. J. COSTELLOE]

NEMESIUS (fl. *c.*400), probably bp. of Emesa, philosopher, about whom nothing is known except that he wrote a treatise *On Human Nature* (PG 40:504–817), a work regarded with much respect by the medieval schoolmen, who often erroneously attributed it to St. Gregory of Nyssa. In its basic contention that the soul is a substance complete in itself, the work is Platonic and Plotinist. However, its analysis of the human act, which greatly influenced the thought of the scholastics, is fundamentally Aristotelian (Eng. tr. ed. W. Telfer, LibCC 4, 1955) 201–466. BIBLIOGRAPHY: Quasten 3:351–355; Gilson HCP 60–64.

[R. B. ENO]

NEMROD, see NIMROD.

NENNIUS (9th cent.), born in North Wales, author of a history written in Latin but poorly preserved. An 11th-cent. Irish translation of the *Historia Brittonum* is our best guide. It is a sketch of British history from the earliest times to the 8th cent. followed by a list of the marvels *(mirabilia)* of Britain in which King Arthur is mentioned for the first time.

[R. T. MEYER]

NEOCAESAREA, SYNOD OF, a synod held in Bithynia between 314 and 325. Its 15 canons treated of the catechumenate and barred from the priesthood those who had received baptism while critically ill simply out of fear of damnation.

[E. EL-HAYEK]

NEO-CALVINISM, a description sometimes applied to the theological movement led by Karl *Barth. One aspect of this 20th-cent. reaction against *liberal theology was a return to Reformation sources and viewpoints, which in the case of Barth and others of the *Reformed tradition meant a return to John Calvin's thought. The term Neo-Calvinism also suggests that the renewal was not merely a repristination but a new interpretation in the light of the original Reformation insights, esp. regarding the word of God. *NEO-ORTHODOXY, *CRISIS THEOLOGY, *DIALECTICAL THEOLOGY.

[T. C. O'BRIEN]

NEO-GUELFISM, a 19th-cent. movement among Italian Catholic liberals in favor of the resurrection of Italy as a strong, united European power. This they expected to accomplish through the leadership of the popes, who had always been the defenders of liberty against destroyers of civilization. Under the leadership of Vincenzo Gioberti, a priest who looked to the Pope to initiate a patriotic program that would bring together the Italian states in a federation under his own presidency, the movement was strongest between 1843 and 1848. In his popular book, *Del primato morale e civile degli Italiani* (1843), Gioberti pointed out the reason why Italy had lost its former greatness: it had forgotten that Italian genius was built upon a religious foundation. When Pius IX, a liberal, was elected to the papacy in 1846, it seemed that the desired moment had arrived. After the failure of the Revolution of 1848, the idea of a federation and the spirit of Neo-Guelfism waned. BIBLIOGRAPHY: B. Croce, *History of Europe in the Nineteenth Century* (tr. H. Furst 1933); J. A. R. Marriott, *Makers of Modern Italy* (1931).

[M. A. WATHEN]

NEO-HEGELIANISM a designation indicating the rekindled interest in G. *Hegel's thought and method among philosophical groups in Germany, Italy, and Great Britain. In Germany, after it seemed that Hegel's abiding presence had been finally banished, Neo-Kantian philosophers around the turn of the century rediscovered aspects of his thought that seemed to fulfill patterns in the history of classical German philosophy; then Wilhelm Dilthey, in his *Der junge Hegel* (1905), presenting Hegel in an appealingly irrational and relativistic light, made Hegel's philosophy more congenial to "life philosophers" like Dilthey. Among the more significant German thinkers associated with this Neo-Hegelianism were E. Cassirer, H. Cohen, H. Glockner, N. Hartmann, R. Kroner, G. Lasson, P. Natorp, and E. Troeltsch. In Italy during the early 20th cent., the Neo-Hegelian movement took a decidedly historicist turn, primarily in the work of Benedetto Croce and Giovanni Gentile. Croce with his anti-Fascist temperament clashed with Gentile, who supported the emerging Fascist state on Hegelian grounds. Croce wrote widely for an international audience on philosophy of history and aesthetics. In Great Britain, following T. H. Green, a school of Neo-Hegelian thought had become firmly established by 1883 when a group including B. Bosanquet, J. S. Haldane, Lord Haldane, Sir H. Jones, A. S. Pringle-Pattison, D. G. Ritchie, and W. R. Sorley published *Essays in Philosophical Criticism*. Under the influence of F. H. Bradley and Bernard Bosanquet, Neo-Hegelianism became the dominant force in British philosophy until Moore and Russell. Only in a very general way can the American philosophers Josiah Royce and B. Blanshard be considered Neo-Hegelians.

[R. J. LITZ]

NEO-MALTHUSIANISM, a viewpoint in favor of contraceptive means of population control. Its originator was Francis Place (1771–1854), a London tailor, labor leader, and father of 15 children, who disagreed with the objection to contraception of Thomas Robert Malthus (1766–1834), who had advocated the limiting of birth by sexual abstinence and late marriage. Place and such reformers as Jeremy *Bentham argued that abstinence was not likely to be widely practiced and that earlier marriages with contraception were more appropriate than late marriages. With the increasing industrial poverty and overcrowding of the 19th cent., neo-Malthusianism became part of labor reform proposals, and in the 1860s George Drysdale started the Malthusian League, which despite continual attacks by the Churches and the medical profession, expanded into France, Germany, and Holland. Interest was also growing in the U.S. in feminist circles, but so was opposition, and in 1873, through the efforts of Anthony Comstock, Congress passed an act penalizing contraception. In 1912, Margaret Sanger began her writings and activities in support of birth control, a term she coined in 1914. Gradually, federal and state legal opposition were eliminated, and clinics and family planning associations expanded. What began as neo-Malthusianism ends as the modern *birth control movement.

[R. VAN ALLEN]

NEO-ORTHODOXY, a name given to a Protestant, and dominantly *Reformed, theological movement of the 20th century. Neo-orthodoxy embraces a range of teachings, which have in common the rejection of *liberal theology. The term has a particular reference to the thought of Karl *Barth (see CRISIS THEOLOGY, DIALECTICAL THEOLOGY), but it also applied to that of P. *Tillich, R. *Niebuhr, and others. Through translations of the works of Barth and S. *Kierkegaard, much theological effort in the U.S. after 1930 came to be called neo-orthodox. The movement is called "orthodoxy" in the sense that it marks a return to primary themes of the historic Reformation, esp. the impotence of man to attain God, the *total depravity of his nature, and the need for divine grace and pardon. The movement is "new" both in contrast to liberalism and in its reliance on modern thought and discoveries. Neo-orthodox theologians, for example, have not hesitated to employ methods of biblical criticism that were developed in a rationalistic context. BIBLIOGRAPHY: Smith-Jamison 1:309–317; J. Macquarrie, *Twentieth Century Religious Thought* (1963).

[M. B. SCHEPERS]

NEO-PATRISTIC SYNTHESIS, the return to the theological insights of the Fathers of the Church promoted by G. Florovsky and other Russian Orthodox theologians in France (Saint Serge Seminary, Paris) and the U.S. (St. Vladimir's Seminary, New York). It is also known as Neo-Traditionalist Orthodox Synthesis. Although its beginnings can be traced to the theological renewal of Russian theology at the time of Metropolitan Filaret of Moscow (1782–1867), it is largely a product of the Russian diaspora, its most convinced advocate being the archpriest Georges Florovsky (*Puty russkago bogoslovija* [1937]; "Westliche Einflüsse in der russischen Theologie," in *Procès-Verbaux du premier* *congrès de théologie orthodoxe à Athènes* [1939], 212–231; "Patristic and Modern Theology," *ibid*. 238–242). The return to the Fathers comprises three main steps. First, Orthodox theology must be freed from all non-Orthodox, mainly Western, superstructures, which distort the true image of Orthodoxy. In fact, according to this view, Orthodox theology ceased to exist as a genuine form of reflection on divine revelation soon after the time of the Fathers (8th-9th cent.), having come first under the influence of Latin nonpatristic thought, esp. scholasticism (Greek scholasticism of the 13th–14th cent.; Russian or Kievan scholasticism of the 16th–18th cent.), and then under the influence of Protestantism (Cyril Lucaris, 17th cent.). Scholasticism and Protestantism not only distort the true image of Orthodoxy; they also present the temptation of a theologically false and fundamentally rationalistic approach to revelation. The next step entails the complete elimination of this false theological, or rationalistic, approach from Orthodoxy if this is again to enjoy theological activity as in the patristic period. Finally, with the help of the Fathers, Orthodox theology will be put in a condition to overtake Western theological thought in its futile attempts to give a Christian answer to the modern world, and will itself supply the much-needed Orthodox answer.

The patristic character of this new Orthodox theology will appear in two aspects. First of all, it will be a conscious attempt to stay in theological communion with the Fathers, who, together with the Apostles, have been the true witnesses of a living tradition, still in the possession of Orthodoxy; and second, it will have recovered the fundamental theological intuition of the Fathers, the idea of a theology, or rather of a theological method or process, that is the expression of faith and life in Christ instead of the rationalistic, disincarnate theology of other schools. The Fathers, in fact, have given us a permanent model of theology, a theology that is the result of their believing reflection on the revealed mystery of Christ. They were able to accomplish this with the help of Hellenism, a most appropriate way of philosophical and human thinking, in which reality and symbol are perfectly integrated. Thus, the Christian Hellenism of the Fathers has become an essential feature of true Christian theology. To abandon Christian Hellenism, with the pretext of going, e.g., to the Scriptures alone, would mean going back to the OT, to the pre-Christian problematic, without Christ and the patristic synthesis of revelation, and the believing reflection of man.

This theological ideal, although critical of wide sections of Catholic theology, is not entirely alien to the Catholic mind. There has been a recurrent interest in the Fathers throughout the history of Catholic theology. In more recent years repeated appeals have been made for a return of Catholic theology to the "lost categories" of the age of the Fathers, esp. of those of the East, as is evident in the plan and purpose of the *Sources chrétiennes*. Vatican Council II employed many deep patristic insights, particularly regarding the Church. Even the assertion of the permanence of theological experience of the Fathers is quite congenial to Catholic theology. Theology does not go from one stage to the next by simply giving up former positions, but by developing and integrating every valuable theological element it already possesses. BIBLIOGRAPHY: Y. N. Lelouvier, *Perspectives russes sur l'Église* (1968).

[G. ELDAROV]

NEO-PENTECOSTALISM, the cultivation of the Pentecostal experience outside classical *Pentecostalism, by members of the historic Churches. This interest began among Protestants *c.*1955, occurring within Episcopalian, Lutheran, Baptist, Methodist, Reformed, and Presbyterian Churches, and has often met with official disapproval. Pentecostalism among RCs became widespread and publicized *c.*1967. Neo-Pentecostalism, unlike classical Pentecostalism, did not begin among the socially and culturally deprived. Its spread is regarded as a sign not simply of an interest in *glossolalia, or even in the charismatic rather than the institutional Church, but of a desire for the immediate experience of the divine promised by the Pentecostal experience. *FULL GOSPEL BUSINESSMEN'S FELLOWSHIP INTERNATIONAL.

[T. C. O'BRIEN]

NEO-PENTECOSTALISM IN THE RC CHURCH, a movement emphasizing the spiritual experience of the Holy Spirit's power inwardly sanctifying and outwardly manifested in *charismatic gifts; also called the Catholic Charismatic Renewal. Adherents take as a primary datum that the Holy Spirit's work of sanctification is a reality, and that the Christian's experience of this influence is to be expected. The recognizable history of the movement in the U.S. began in 1967 with charismatic manifestations in prayer groups, first at Duquesne Univ., Pittsburgh, Pa., then at the Univ. of Notre Dame, South Bend, Indiana. From then on charismatic prayer groups spread among Catholics throughout the U.S., and in Canada as well. Important occurrences in its public growth have been: the 1970 National Convention on Charismatic Renewal at Notre Dame, attended by over 1,000 members; the 1975 Third International Congress at Rome, attended by over 10,000 adherents from all parts of the world, and received by Pope Paul VI on May 19, 1975, with encouragement for the spiritual renewal through the Holy Spirit that the movement represents; the favorable doctrinal report on the movement made in 1969 to the National Conference of U.S. Bishops, and the supportive pastoral report made to the same Conference in 1975; finally, the 1976 Notre Dame Continental Conference, attended by 30,000 participants.

The movement has its name and distinctiveness from the charismatic activity in meetings of its prayer groups—what Paul VI spoke of as the miracle of Pentecost continued in history. As signs of spiritual renewal among the members, the Pope singled out their taste for prayer, for contemplation, for praising God; their attentiveness to the grace of the

Holy Spirit; their assiduousness in the reading of Scripture. While not stereotyped or highly structured, Catholic charismatic groups do share three common marks of identity. The first is that their meetings include *charismatic prayer as an integral and essential part. The second is the gift of tongues itself (see GLOSSOLALIA); this is taken as a gift of prayer, not of communication; it occurs mainly during prayer meetings; the tongue-speaker is completely self-possessed, not in an ecstatic state (once received, the gift can be used at will); the understanding given with the exercise of the gift is of the Spirit's real power and presence. At times the gift is used to convey "a message in tongues," but then the correlative gift of interpretation (not translation) is required. The third mark of identity is the *baptism in the Spirit, which often occurs after the communitary *laying on of hands upon one suppliant, and which consists primarily in an experience, manifest or hidden, of joy, peace, love as these come from the presence of the Holy Spirit. (Descriptions of this experience read like those in traditional theology on the workings of the *gifts of the Holy Spirit.) Particular effects of baptism in the Spirit are a sense of rebirth, of moral transformation, and of being filled with the Spirit. Participants in the charismatic renewal attest to certain general results in their spiritual life; a new sense of God's presence as Father; a more intense prayer life; love for the Scriptures; devotion to the Eucharist and to Mary; deliverance from sin; fidelity to the Church. Many Catholics remain, by temperament and by training, diffident towards the movement, esp. toward its specific features; firsthand experience of its prayer meetings, however, often dispels such reservation. As to "mainline," historical *Pentecostalism, there are many differences: Catholic Pentecostals adhere to the primacy of sacramental baptism, and reject any suggestion of "rebaptism"; retain a precise concept of the Church and its teaching office; do not profess *assurance of salvation; reject biblical fundamentalism or a rigid moralism. Theologians of the movement recognize the dangers of elitism, or of substituting specifics of the Pentecostal experience for essentials of life in the Church; but such dangers have not in fact prevailed. BIBLIOGRAPHY: K. McDonnell, "Catholic Pentecostalism: Problems in Evaluation," *Dialog* 9 (1970) 35–54; E. D. O'Connor, *Pentecostal Movement in the Catholic Church* (1971); *idem, Perspectives on Charismatic Renewal* (1975).

[T. C. O'BRIEN]

NEOPHYTE (transliteration of Gr. *neophutos,* from *neos,* new and *phuton,* plant), a new convert. In English the word was not in general use before the 19th century. When the Rheims NT adopted it, it was attacked as a ridiculous "ink-horn" term. But the word was prominent both in the mystery religions and in early Christianity. The Greek word occurs once in the NT in a warning against ordaining a recent convert as a bishop (1 Tim 3.6). The Council of Nicaea (325) extended the prohibition to include ordination to the priesthood, and the Council of Sardica (343) to the diaconate. Neophytes are to be distinguished from catechumens, i.e., those preparing for baptism. The term has also been applied to recently ordained priests and to novices in a religious order.

[T. EARLY]

NEOPLASTICISM, an important 20th-cent. art movement, precisely the personal extensions of De Stijl theories by the Dutch artist Piet Mondrian, rooted in the elimination of "baroque" accidents and the personality of the artist from the art work. Neoplatonic, ideal, Mondrian moved to the refined and rarified goal of primary color rectangles in an ordered relationship of black lines at right angles only. (Mondrian broke with T. van Doesburg when De Stijl used diagonals). Neoplasticism in balance and syntax offered a utopia to a modern world out of harmony with reality.

[M. J. DALY]

NEOPLATONISM (*c.*250–529, at Athens; until 642, at Alexandria), a term formally employed since the early 19th cent. to designate the comprehensive system of philosophy of Plotinus, the last great original Greek thinker, and its further development or modification by his successors. Plotinus himself regarded his philosophy as genuine Platonism, but he contributed something new himself—and the Platonism which he inherited was Middle Platonism with its liberal borrowings of Aristotelian, Stoic, Neo-Pythagorean, and Oriental elements. While he himself apparently ignored the **Chaldean Oracles,* they play an important role in the thought of Porphyry, but, above all, in that of Iamblichus. Separate articles cover the founders of Neoplatonism, Ammonius Saccas (teacher of Plotinus); Plotinus (205–270), Porphyry of Tyre (232–d. after 301) the pupil and editor of Plotinus, and the more significant subsequent representatives of Neoplatonism in its various phases. It suffices here to characterize briefly the chief Neoplatonic schools and to list by name only their founders and leading adherents. Following Ueberweg these schools and their representatives are grouped according to their main tendencies and interests. The metaphysical-speculative tendency is characteristic of the school of Plotinus and Porphyry, the Syrian school founded by Iamblichus (*c.*250–330), and of the Athenian school as continued and developed by Plutarch of Athens (*c.*350–433), Syrianus (scholarch *c.*431), Proclus (*c.*410 or 411), Marinus (scholarch 484), Damascius (*c.*458–after 533), and Simplicius (1st half of 6th cent.). The religio-theurgic tendency is characteristic of the Pergamene school represented by Aedesius (d. *c.*335), Secundus Sallustius (d. before 377), Julian the Apostate (332–363), and Eunapius of Sardes (*c.*345–414). The Pergamene school is so closely related to the Syrian school that these schools hardly deserve separate classification. The learned or scholarly tendency is characteristic of the Alexandrian school, as represented by *Hypatia (*c.*370–415), *Synesius of Cyrene (370/375–413), Hierocles of Alexandria (5th cent.), Ammonius Hermiou (*c.*445–517 or 520), Joannes Philoponus (d. *c.*570), and Olympiadorus (early 6th cent.), and of the Latin Neoplatonists Calcidius (fl. *c.*400), Macrobius (fl. 400), Marius Victorinus (fl. 2d half 4th cent.), and Boethius (*c.*480–524). Neoplatonism absorbed practically all the philosophical and religious thought of earlier schools into its own system and attempted to give a systematic foundation and a new vitality to traditional pagan beliefs and practices. Men like Porphyry and Julian were hostile to Christianity because they regarded it as a movement that threatened to destroy their Hellenic inheritance and cultural values. On the other hand, Christian philosophers and theologians were able to employ Neoplatonism effectively in their elaboration of Christian teachings and in particular in the development of mystical theology. Late Neoplatonism, at least at Athens, was definitely in a state of decline when Justinian closed the philosophical schools at Athens in 529. At Alexandria, however, learned and scientific work continued until the Arab conquest in 642. BIBLIOGRAPHY: Copleston 1:463–485; CHGMP 195–555; Ueberweg 1:590–655. *GREEK PHILOSOPHY 5.

[M. R. P. MCGUIRE]

NEO-PROTESTANTISM, a term used particularly by Karl *Barth to describe a type of Protestant thought exemplified by F. *Schleiermacher (1768–1834). In general it may be equated with Protestant liberalism and is distinguished from Reformation Protestantism and the succeeding *neo-orthodoxy by its shift from objective authority to subjective religious criteria. Barth traced it back to Lutheran and *Reformed theologians from *c.*1700 and saw its ancestors in *Arminianism and the humanists and radicals of the Reformation period. Later representatives include A. *Ritschl (1822–89) and A. *Harnack (1851–1930). The movement did not give rise to a separate denomination but cut across various Protestant groups. Barth's theology and the movement generally termed neo-orthodox or neo-Reformation theology was a 20th-cent. reaction, opposing Schleiermacher and his divergence from what is considered authentic Protestantism of Luther and Calvin. Barth particularly opposed liberalism's openness to natural theology, and therefore saw it as standing alongside Roman Catholicism in opposition to the biblical theology of the Reformation. BIBLIOGRAPHY: K. Barth, *Church Dogmatics,* 1.2 (1938). *LIBERAL THEOLOGY.

[T. EARLY]

NEO-PYTHAGOREANISM, a nominal revival of Pythagoreanism beginning in the 1st cent. B.C. at Alexandria, but in many respects a new movement. The Neo-Pythagoreans stressed their devotion to Pythagoras and his ascetical ideal and emphasized numbers and their mystical qualities. However, they borrowed elements from Platonism, Aristotelianism, and Stoicism, and showed a marked bent for the occult and for theurgy, embracing the *Hermetic Literature and the *Chaldean Oracles with enthusiasm. There is a wide range in the tenets held by those who called themselves Pythagoreans. Some maintained that all things are derived from the monad or point, while others stressed the opposition between the *monas* and the indefinite dyad, *aoristos duas*. Among the outstanding representatives of Neo-Pythagoreanism were P. *Nigidius Figulus (*c.*98–45 B.C.), the wonder-worker *Apollonius of Tyana (1st cent. A.D.), *Moderatus of Gades (2d half of 1st cent. A.D.), *Nicomachus of Gerasa (1st half of 2d cent. A.D.), and, above all, *Numenius of Apamea (2d half of 2d cent. A.D.). Neo-Pythagorean syncretism reached its high point in Numenius and definitely contributed to the development of *Neoplatonism. BIBLIOGRAPHY: Copleston 1:446–450; CHGMP 84–106. *GREEK PHILOSOPHY.

[M. R. P. MCGUIRE]

NEOROMANTICISM, 20th-cent. art movement to restore the human elements of figure, dreams, and feeling, in a restrained surrealism, by three artists C. Bérard, E. Berman, and P. Tchelitchew. Their poignant, lonely, isolated figures and classical settings, in the deep perspective space of De Chirico, influenced theatre and commercial art.

[M. J. DALY]

NEO-SCHOLASTICISM, the return, beginning in the 19th cent., to a study of philosophy patterned after medieval *scholasticism. The return began esp. among seminary professors who realized that the prevailing philosophy courses, generally Cartesian in their content, were not suited to preparing the students for the study of theology (see M. LIBERATORE; S. SCHIFFINI; C. SANSEVERINO; T. ZIGLIARA). The primary feature of the restoration was a presentation of philosophy "according to the mind of St. Thomas Aquinas." That was a direction championed by Leo XIII in the encyclical *Aeterni Patris,* Aug. 4, 1879. But Neo-Scholasticism includes the fact that the method of study and teaching followed the medieval method, and that great scholastics, other than St. Thomas, were studied intently, e.g., St. *Bonaventure, Duns Scotus. The term has been wrongly understood, even as the term scholasticism, to refer to a single, definable philosophical system, a so-called *philosophia perennis*. *NEO-THOMISM.

[T. C. O'BRIEN]

NEOT, ST. (d. *c.*900), monk of Glastonbury who became a hermit in Cornwall where he was venerated in the Middle Ages. Legend connects him with King Alfred the Great. Some authors think that the lives of two persons enter the legends about N., since a place in Cornwall and one in Huntingdonshire bear the name St. Neot. BIBLIOGRAPHY: Butler 3:227–228.

[T. C. O'BRIEN]

NEO-THOMISM, the revived study of the thought of St. *Thomas Aquinas, esp. in philosophy, that began earlier but was given official impetus by Leo XIII's encyclical *Aeterni Patris,* Aug. 4, 1879. This document and the later canonical legislation on seminary courses (see CIC, c. 1366 §2) had the effect of making *Thomism the quasi-official philosophy in RC schools. This official momentum carried the movement forward well into the 20th cent.; by the time of Vatican Council II, however, new currents of thought became dominant. Theological pluralism and interest in contemporary philosophical categories became characteristics of RC writings and academic courses. (See also TRANSCENDENTAL THOMISM). The motivation of Leo XIII was apologetic, esp. the intent to combat *rationalism with the supposedly most rational of Catholic Doctors of the Church. The pioneer ''Neo-Thomists'' often straitened the content and method of St. Thomas's works into alien epistemological and methodological frameworks. The official status of the ''principles and method of St. Thomas'' often led to a presentation both in philosophy and theology that devitalized his thought and often made the study of these disciplines a learning of rabbinical sayings. A further difficulty was that ''Thomism'' itself is an ambivalent term, even as is ''scholasticism.'' There were, however, many positive elements in the movement, and their fruit remains. Historical and textual studies of splendid scholarship emerged and led to an appreciation of the distinction between ''Thomism'' and the authentic ''mind of St. Thomas.'' Since his works stand, like those of St. Augustine, as a classical and precious heritage of the Catholic tradition, his extrication from the sterile and inauthentic ''St. Thomas says'' manner of teaching, as well as his quiet loss of official status have been a blessing. Excellent editions of his works have become available, including vernacular translations; an appreciation has been gained of the vitality of his ideas on creation, knowledge, morality, grace, and the theological virtues. Mention can be made of only a very few responsible for such gains: M.-D. Chenu, R. A. Gauthier, T. *Gilby, É. Gilson, J. Maritain, S. Ramirez.

[T. C. O'BRIEN]

NEPAL, independent kingdom of the Himalayas (54,662 sq mi; pop. [est., 1974], 12,320,000). The inhabitants of Nepal are of Mongolian stock with a considerable admixture of Hindu blood. In 1818 the British established a resident of the crown at the capital, Katmandu. Nepal's king proclaimed a constitutional monarchy in 1951 and a new constitution in 1962. Hinduism is the religion of the majority of the people, although there are many who practice Lamaist Buddhism. In 1661 Jesuits crossed Nepal on their way from China to India. The mission field was cultivated by Capuchins in the 18th century. Father Della Penna did pioneering work in translating the catechism into Newan, the language of Buddhism. In the 18th and 19th cent. Christianity was nonexistent in Nepal. Only in 1951 were American Jesuits of Patna, India, invited to open a school. Sisters provide a similar foundation for girls. The two institutions remain a living witness to Christ and his Church in the country, but conversions are forbidden by law.

Protestant Churches had long striven to enter Nepal. When freedom of religion was granted in 1954, they formed the United Mission to Nepal with 163 missionaries (78 Nepalese), who work in social, educational, and medical fields. In 1968 Protestants numbered 490. BIBLIOGRAPHY: H. Davis, *Nepal, Land of Mystery* (1942); *Bilan du Monde* 2:622–623.

[P. DAMBORIENA]

NEPHTHALI, see NAPHTALI.

NEPOS OF ARSINOË (fl. mid–3d cent.), bp. of Arsinoë, Egypt, the leading champion there of *Millenarianism. He wrote in refutation of the allegorists who could not accept the literal meaning of the vision in Revelation concerning the 1,000-year reign of Christ on earth. N. probably represents the enduring presence of the Jewish Christian tradition in Egypt, with its emphasis on a basically literal interpretation of the Scripture. Eusebius preserves the tribute paid by Dionysius of Alexandria, who did not concur with N.'s Millenarianist views, but still referred respectfully to his learning and piety, as well as to the many hymns with which he enriched the Church. N.'s disciples became schismatics. BIBLIOGRAPHY: Quasten 2:103–104.

[E. J. DILLON]

NEPOTISM, preferential treatment, usually in the form of appointment to office or benefices, given exclusively on the basis of kinship and by extension, of any other special claim other than qualifications or merit. The term is particularly associated in church history with the Renaissance popes, but plagued the Church from the 8th to the 17th cent. in its worst forms. The moral evil of nepotism consists in abuse of office to the detriment of church life and the violation of justice where one qualified or deserving is passed over. In politics cronyism, or dishonest patronage, is a form of nepotism.

[T. C. O'BRIEN]

NERESHEIM, ABBEY OF, Benedictine abbey near Aalen, Württemberg, founded 1095 for Canons Regular by Count Hartmann of Dillingen. The Benedictines took it over in 1106. They joined the Melk reform in 1497. In 1763 the abbey became imperial (Reichsabtei) and ruled its own territory. Its church, built at that time by Balthasar *Neumann, is famous. Though suppressed in 1803, the well-preserved buildings were given back in 1920 by the owner, the prince of Thurn and Taxis, to the Benedictine congregation of Beuron. BIBLIOGRAPHY: *Handbuchs der Historischen Stätten Deutschlands,* (1960–) 6:467.

[N. BACKMUND]

NEREUS AND ACHILLEUS, SS. (date unknown), martyrs whose tomb in the cemetery of Domitilla on the Via Ardeatina was a center of devotion from the 4th century. Probably because of their place of burial, legend has associated these saints with Flavia *Domitilla, making them eunuchs of her household who shared her banishment to the island of Terracina, where they were beheaded during the reign of Trajan. But they were in fact converted soldiers who died for the faith, as is indicated in the inscription composed for their tomb by Pope *Damasus I. Fragments of the slab with this inscription were discovered by G. B. De Rossi in the cemetery of Domitilla. BIBLIOGRAPHY: Butler 2:284–285; A. Amore, EncCatt 8:1764.

[R. B. ENO]

NERGAL, an Assyrian-Sumero-Babylonian god of the sun's hostile phases, particularly the fierce summer sun; thus often called Malik (Moloch) in the ancient Orient, and also lord of Arallu or king of the underworld (*Lugalmeslam*, king of Meslam) and judge of the dead. Also known as Girunugal, he is the source of war, death, disaster, and pestilence. He is represented as a lion (with two heads on monuments) or as a man with a sword in one hand and a decapitated head in the other. Chief cult-site was the temple *E-meslam,* in Cutha (Kutu), a Babylonian city (modern, Tell Ibrahim). When Sumeria fell to Assyria (721 B.C.), people from Cutha were removed to Palestine where they maintained the worship of N. (2 Kg 17. 24–30). The god is also mentioned in Jer 39.3,13. In a long, though incomplete poem, N. (as Irra) devastates the earth and Babylon in particular. A prophecy in the poem against the city and its king resembles Is 13–14. For the Babylonians N. represented the planet Mars, the name ur-ig-al meaning one fire.

[R. J. LITZ]

NERI DI BICCI (*c.*1419–1491), Italian painter and master of a thriving Florentine shop of painters and artisans (*c.*1450), having developed a highly decorative style of popular appeal but limited influence.

[M. J. DALY]

NERI, PHILIP, ST., see PHILIP NERI, ST.

NERIGLISSAR (Nergal-shar-usur), king of Babylon 559–555 B.C. According to Berosus, he was a son-in-law of Nebuchadnezzar and killed Nebuchadnezzar's son Evil-merodach in a rebellion. The Babylonian Chronicle reports that he carried out a campaign in Cilicia during the last year of his reign. His name is also found in legal texts of the time. He was possibly Nergal-sharezer (Nergal protect the king), one of the Babylonian officials who looked after Jeremiah (Jer ch. 39). Nergal-sharezer was called the Rab-mag, a term whose meaning is uncertain. N. was succeeded by his son Labashi-Marduk, who ruled only a few months before being killed by a conspiracy of Babylonian nobles. One of them, Nabonidus, then became the last Babylonian king.

[T. EARLY]

NERINCKX, CHARLES (1761–1824), missionary in Kentucky. Like many priests who became missioners in America, N. was individualistic, powerful physically, and restless. Ordained in his native Belgium in 1785, during the French Revolution he ministered to his parish from hiding and refused to accept the Napoleonic Concordat. He appealed to Bp. John *Carroll, who accepted him for the American mission in 1804. Most of N.'s career was spent in frontier settlements in Kentucky where his courage and strength won the admiration of all. He was hostile to the Dominicans in his area, whom he regarded as laxists, and who in turn regarded him as Jansenistic. He was a builder who literally erected log chapels with his own hands. He refused a bishopric in Louisiana. On journeys to Europe he brought back priests and nuns, as well as art treasures still preserved in the Diocese of Louisville. In 1812 N. founded the Sisters of Loretto at the Foot of the Cross, helped build their motherhouse at Loretto, and lived in a log cabin there. In a dispute about the modification of his rule for the Sisters of Loretto he left Kentucky and went to Missouri, requesting the neediest mission there, but he died before he could be assigned. BIBLIOGRAPHY: C. Maes, *Life of Rev. Charles Nerinckx* (1880).

[J. R. AHERNE]

NERO CLAUDIUS CAESAR (37–68 A.D.), Roman Emperor, son of Gnaeus Domitius Ahenobarbus and Agrippina the Younger, and adopted son and successor of Claudius in 54. The first years of his reign, when he was still under the influence of his tutors Seneca and Burrus, were good, but the murder of Britannicus in 55 and of his mother in 59 presaged the political murders of later years. To fend off the charge of arson after the great fire in Rome in 64, Nero ascribed it to the Christians and had many of them put to death. Of a vain, extravagant, and artistic temperament, he committed suicide after learning of the revolts of his generals and his own condemnation by the Senate. BIBLIOGRAPHY: J. Bishop, *Nero: The Man and the Legend* (1964); M. P. Charlesworth, OCD 603–604.

[M. J. COSTELLOE]

NEROCCIO DI BARTOLOMMEO LANDI (1447–1500), Sienese painter and sculptor, partner of Francesco di Giorgio. Linear and lyrical in the tradition of S. Martini, N. painted a triptych of the *Madonna and Child with SS. Michael and Bernardino* (1476), designed the *Hellespontine Sibyl* (cathedral of Siena 1483), an elegant *Annunciation* (Yale Univ.), a *Portrait of a Girl* and *Madonna and Child with SS. Sigismund and Anthony* (National Gallery, Wash., D.C.). N. modelled a terra-cotta *St. Jerome* (1468, lost), a wooden statue of *St. Catherine of Siena,* the marble tomb of Bishop Tommaso Testa Piccolomini (1483) and other notable works. BIBLIOGRAPHY: G. Coor, *Neroccio di Landi* (1961).

[M. J. DALY]

NERSES THE GREAT, ST. (*c.*333–373), a patriarch (*catholicos*) of Armenia. He came from Caesarea in Cappadocia. He used his time in office to renew religious life in Armenia and to build hospices for the sick and the poor. In the many legends concerning him it is difficult to separate the fact from the folklore. He seems to have been removed from office for chiding the King for living an unworthy life, then to have been reinstated by a later king. N. may even eventually have been poisoned because of some similar rebuke of a powerful personage. The beginning of N.'s episcopacy is given as either 338 or 351. He is variously described as the son of Athenagoras, the nephew of Hesychius, and the grandnephew of St. Gregory the Illuminator.

[E. J. DILLON]

NESHKAR, Armenian liturgical bread; round, thin, unleavened, and without salt. It is stamped with the image of a crucifix.

[A. CODY]

NESTLE, EBERHARD (1851–1913), German biblical scholar. He received his Ph.D. from Tübingen and from 1883 to 1898 taught both there and at Ulm. From 1898 he was professor and then superior at the Evangelical Seminary at Maulbronn. After early work on the LXX text, he turned to NT studies and in 1898 published an edition of the Greek NT, with critical apparatus. Wide use of this text spread a textual tradition at variance with that of the Erasmian **textus receptus*.

[T. EARLY]

NESTOR (*c.*1056–*c.*1114), important Russian hagiographer and chronicler who lived and wrote at the famous Cave Monastery of Kiev. Nothing certain is known of N.'s birth or death. Besides writing the lives of the Princes Boris and Gleb and a life of the Abbot Feodosii, he composed the *Tale of Bygone Years,* called also the *Primary Chronicle* and translated into English by S. H. Cross (1930). N. used many sources and eyewitness accounts. BIBLIOGRAPHY: N. K. Chadwick, *Beginnings of Russian History* (1946).

[S. WILLIAMS]

NESTORIAN CHURCH. The name Nestorian is applied by Monophysites to all supporters of the Dyophysite doctrine of two natures in Christ. Schism on this point arose in the first place between Armenians and Syrians in the Persian Empire, Christian communities culturally distinct, neither of which was effectively represented at the ecumenical councils of Ephesus (431), Chalcedon (451), or Constantinople (553), where Christological doctrines were defined for the Churches within the Roman Empire. Substantially the Armenians accepted Ephesus and Constantinople but not Chalcedon; the Syrians, Chalcedon but not the condemnation of Nestorius at Ephesus nor of the "three Syrian doctors," Theodore of Mopsuestia, Theoderet, and Ibas at Constantinople in 553. By that time their problems had been complicated by the presence of Monophysite refugees and a rival "Jacobite" Church in Persian territory, but they continued to regard the Greek and Latin Churches as orthodox and in substantial agreement with them, and in 629 their catholicos was received with honor at Constantinople at the conclusion of a long war between Rome and Persia. They were identified as Nestorians in Western terminology by the Armenian and Jacobite allies of the Crusaders, who were more sensitive to Mariological than to Christological errors. By this time the East Syrians from Babylon and Seleucia had spread along the trade routes to India and China and established missionary bishoprics in most of their caravan stations. The association of missions to Tartar tribes with trade no doubt gave rise to practices that could easily be represented as worse than they were, but the Franciscans and Dominicans who encountered them in the late 13th and early 14th cent. saw their missions in decay after the destruction of their Mesopotamian bases by Hulagu Khan in 1258. Their ruin was completed by Timur the Lame in the 14th cent., when Turkestan became a Muslim country. Henceforth the Nestorians were reduced to remnants in Iran, Iraq, and Kerala. At the present time there are more of them in North America than in any of their ancient centers. BIBLIOGRAPHY: E. Tisserant, DTC 11.1:157–323; P. T. Camelot, NCE 10:346–348.

[G. EVERY]

NESTORIAN MONUMENT, a marble monument discovered at modern Sian, China, in 1625 with the inscription "monument commemorating the introduction and propagation of the noble law of Ta Ts'in in the Middle Kingdom." Built in 781 in memory of the Nestorian Bp. Wang She-Cheng, it summarizes Christian doctrine and the history of the Nestorian Church in China from 635 when Alopen (Olopen), a Nestorian monk, first came from Syria or Palestine to Ch'ang-An, capital of the Middle Kingdom in the vicinity of the modern Sian to 781. BIBLIOGRAPHY: K. Krahl, NCE, 3:593; H. Bernard Maitre, DHGE 12:693–741; Y. Sacki, *Nestorian Documents and Relics in China* (2d ed. 1951)

[F. H. BRIGHAM]

NESTORIANISM, the heretical doctrine, condemned at the (third *ecumenical) Council of *Ephesus (431) that Christ is two persons, one divine and one human, and that Mary is the mother of the human person only, not "Mother of God" (in Greek, **Theotokos*). Fearing *Mariolatry among the faithful, *Nestorius impugned the propriety of the term *Theotokos* on grounds that it was one-sided at best, and forbade its use without the complementary *Anthropotokos,* mother of man. Nestorius in fact preferred simply *Christotokos,* Mother of Christ. (Later he reluctantly allowed *Theotokos* for the simple faithful.) In Christ, Nestorius explained, are two *prosōpa* (persons), one divine and one human. Mary bore only the latter; God can no more be born of a woman than die on a cross. The two persons are held together in a "*prosōpon* of union," which renders Christ one being in spite of his two persons. Nestorius admitted that Christ was not "two sons." His theology was a prolongation of the positions of *Diodore of Tarsus and *Theodore of Mopsuestia.

Reaction at Rome, Constantinople itself, and esp. *Alexandria was prompt and unfavorable. *Cyril of Alexandria argued, "If Christ is God and Mary is his mother, then how is she not God's mother?" and coined the expression *hypostatic union. He attacked Nestorius in letters addressed all over the Roman Empire. Pope Celestine I demanded Nestorius make a retractation through Cyril. Cyril demanded Nestorius retract precisely by subscribing to his own anti-Nestorian theology as expressed in his *Twelve *Anathematisms*. Nestorius, uncompromising and violent as was Cyril himself, refused. The Emperor called the Council of *Ephesus, where Cyril had Nestorius deposed and his teaching condemned before he could arrive to defend himself. The Emperor exiled Nestorius. Henceforward Nestorianism was and is officially unorthodox.

Theologians today tend to doubt whether *prosōpon* in Nestorius meant what the Church meant in defining at Ephesus that Christ had only one *prosōpon*. By "two persons" Nestorius may well have meant something much like the orthodox "two natures" (see CHALCEDON, COUNCIL OF). His nebulous "*prosōpon* of union," however, is considered to be too weak an attempt to preserve the concrete unity of Christ's being.

In spite of its condemnation Nestorianism endured and waxed, until in the 14th cent. a Nestorian Church with over 200 episcopal sees extended as far as India and China. Then the Mongols all but destroyed it. Internal strife, massacres by the Kurds and Turks, esp. during World War I, unions with Rome, and activity on the part of American Protestant and Russian Orthodox missioners further depleted their numbers. Today there are only about 200,000 Nestorians, mostly in and near Iraq. Their credal allegiance is really to the less extreme position of Nestorius's master, Theodore of Mopsuestia; and "Nestorianism" today is even less clearly heretical or "Nestorian" than was Nestorius himself. By "two persons" the Nestorians probably mean much what orthodoxy means by two natures.

[R. R. BARR]

NESTORIUS (*c.*381–*c.*451), heresiarch, patriarch of Constantinople. Of Persian parentage and born in Germanicia in Eastern Syria, N. studied in Antioch, possibly but not probably under *Theodore of Mopsuestia. He became a monk, was ordained priest, and acquired such renown as a preacher that he came to the attention of Emperor Theodosius II, who had him made patriarch of Constantinople in 428. As patriarch he proved zealous in the prosecution of heretics, but when his chaplain, in accordance with Antiochene theology, preached that Mary should not be called *Theotokos (Mother of God), N. supported his chaplain's position and a great controversy ensued. Eusebius of Dorylaeum, still a layman at the time, accused him of heresy and both parties appealed to Pope Celestine. *Cyril of Alexandria condemned N.'s teaching in a local synod, sending him a list of 12 anathemas and demanding his assent to them. N. in turn accused Cyril of *Apollinarianism. The Emperor convoked a council at *Ephesus in 431 under the presidency of Cyril, who acted as papal legate. N. was condemned, deposed, and banished to a monastery whence he was exiled, first to Petra (436) and finally to the Great Oasis in Upper Egypt where he died. Because of the imperial order of 436 demanding the burning of N.'s works, only fragments of his writings have survived. Some scholars attribute to him certain sermons contained among the works of *John Chrysostom. In 1895 N.'s *Bazaar of Heraclides* was discovered in a Syriac translation; this is an apologia composed in his last years in which he claims that his theology was in accord with the *Tome of Leo. Works: *Bazaar of Heraclides* (tr. G. Driver and L. Hodgson, 1925). BIBLIOGRAPHY: Quasten 3:514–519; T. Camelot, NCE 10:348; R. Sellars, *Two Ancient Christologies* (1940) 107–201.

[R. B. ENO]

NESTROY, JOHANN NEPOMUK (1801–62), Austrian playwright and actor, whose comedies satirize the Viennese social and political life of his time. He had acted on various European stages before he settled in Vienna in 1831, often performing in his own comedies. He has been called the "Viennese Aristophanes." Among his 83 plays, in which he used the Viennese dialect as a vehicle for his jest, are the popular *Lumpazivagabundus* (1835), the story of three vagabonds coping with unexpected prosperity; *Einen Jux will er sich machen* (1844), a parody of F. Hebbel. N.'s plays document the end of the Biedermeier era; they are still occasionally performed.

[B. F. STEINBRUCKNER]

NETHERLANDS (Holland), constitutional monarchy of NW Europe, with constitutional capital at Amsterdam and seat of government at The Hague. Prior to the independence of Belgium and Luxembourg, all three were termed Netherlands, or the Low Countries. Christianity came to the Netherlands during the Roman period, but after the Frankish conquest mission work began anew, and the Northumbrian St. *Willibrord (d. 739) became the first bp. of Utrecht. In the 10th cent. the Low Countries became part of the German kingdom. The bp. of Utrecht held extensive secular power and supported the emperors during the investiture controversy. The **Devotio moderna* arose in the Netherlands, led by such figures as Gerard Groote (1340–84) and Thomas à Kempis (*c.*1379–1471). Most of the Netherlands fell to the Dukes of Burgundy in the 14th–15th centuries, and the 1477 marriage of Mary of Burgundy to Maximilian gave the region to the Habsburgs. Under the Calvinist William the

Silent, Prince of Orange, the northern provinces rebelled against Spain and declared independence in 1581. These United Provinces became a wealthy commercial power, a development aided by accepting Jews, Huguenots, and other refugees—including the American Pilgrim Fathers for a time. The southern provinces, called the Spanish Netherlands (Austrian after 1714), remained Catholic. *Arminianism, originating at Leyden, was condemned at the Synod of *Dort (1618–19). The Church of Utrecht, Jansenists who separated from Rome in 1724, conveyed apostolic succession to Old Catholics. After the French Revolutionary Wars, the Congress of Vienna (1815) joined the United Provinces and Austrian Netherlands under William I of Orange. But a rebellion in 1830 led to the independence of Belgium and Luxembourg. The Protestant House of Orange has continued to reign over the Netherlands, and the country has been a principal center of Calvinism, though the Church was disestablished in 1848 and about 40 per cent of the population is Catholic. In the period of Vatican II and following, Dutch Catholics became noted for theological liberalism. BIBLIOGRAPHY: For the Reformation period and following see P. Geyl, *History of the Low Countries* (1964).

[T. EARLY]

NEUE SACHLICHKEIT, DIE (The New Objectivity), a form of social realism in post-war Germany (1920s and 1930s), exemplified in works of G. Grosz (1893–1959), Otto Dix (1891–) and Max Beckmann (1884–1950) whose uncompromising realism, "superrealism," or "magic realism" of exaggerated detail renders the horrors of their world so "unbelievably real" in ineluctable explicit statement that they appear fantastic. Grosz in forms macabre and sensual, expressed an intense hatred and disillusionment in the skeletal figure *Fit for Active Service* (1918). Dix in the overpowering horrors of *Trench Warfare* (1922–23) assaults us with fantastic demonic torture. Beckmann the principal artist of the group in *Descent from the Cross* and *Woman Taken in Adultery* (both 1917), striving at first to reconcile internal realities, finally through panels of torture, brutality, and sadistic realism in repulsive colors, expressed a Germanic "agony of the modern world" (not unrelated to Grünewald's tortured medieval agony of Christ) in monumental, symbolic works advocating freedom—the true salvation—possible only through *Departure* (1932–33)—the new start. All three artists suffered under the Nazis, Grosz and Beckmann fleeing to the U.S.; Dix, remaining in Germany, painted after the war mystical, religious works.

[M. J. DALY]

NEUMANN, JOHANN BALTHASAR (1687–1753), leading architect of S German Late Baroque, originally an artilleryman and military engineer, renowned for some of the most magnificent interiors of all time, such as the breath-taking Kaisersaal and staircase at the episcopal Residenz, Würzburg (1720–44), Bruchsal (1731) which is unparalleled in spatial organization, and Brühl (1743–48), all decorated in white, gold, and pastel shades with continuous ribbon molding, surfaces covered in a stucco lace and ceilings with illusions of figures and space in utter deceits. N. designed the monastery churches of Schöntal (1728) and Neresheim (1749–92), and the magnificent pilgrimage church of Vierzehnheiligen, (1743–72) which has one of the most complicated and delightful interiors of incomparable technique—composed of the interpenetration of elliptical and circular areas, a profusion of illusionistic carving enriching all surfaces, figures caught in a whirlwind of mannered gesturing, textures deceiving the eye. BIBLIOGRAPHY: E. Hempel, *Baroque Art and Architecture in Central Europe* (1965).

[L. A. LEITE]

NEUMANN, JOHN NEPOMUCENE, ST. (1811–60), missionary bishop. N. entered the diocesan seminary at Budweis, Bohemia (1831), and completed his studies at Prague (1835). His ordination was delayed since there were enough clergy in the Diocese of Budweis. N. decided to go to the U.S. and was accepted by the Diocese of New York where he was ordained (1836). After spending 4 years in the region of Buffalo, he entered the Congregation of the Most Holy Redeemer (CSsR) and became the first of the order to be professed in America (1842). N. served in parishes in New York, Baltimore, and Pittsburgh and later became vice provincial of the American Redemptorists. He was consecrated bp. of Philadelphia (1852) and immediately began to establish parochial schools into a diocesan system. Within a few years provisions for pupils increased twentyfold. He also raised the standard of study and discipline at the seminary of St. Charles Borromeo. During his episcopacy more than 80 churches were built. N., very humble in manner and noted for his sanctity during his lifetime, possessed great organizing ability and knew many Slavic dialects, numerous modern languages, as well as Latin, Greek, and Hebrew. He learned Gaelic so as to be able to communicate with the great number of immigrants arriving in Philadelphia at that time. He was the first American bp. to introduce the Forty Hours devotion on a diocesan basis and made yearly visitations to every parish and mission of his diocese, which comprised E Pennsylvania, W New Jersey and all of Delaware. He welcomed several communities of sisters as well as the Christian Brothers into the apostolate of education and founded the community of the Franciscan Sisters of Philadelphia, Glen Riddle, Pennsylvania. In the performance of his pastoral duties he collapsed on the street and died. N. received the title of Venerable (1896) and became the first bp. of the U.S. to be beatified (1963); he was canonized June 19, 1977. BIBLIOGRAPHY: M. J. Curley, *Venerable John Neumann, CSsR, Fourth Bishop of Philadelphia* (1952); N. Ferrante, BiblSanct 9:833–839.

[S. A. HEENEY]

NEUMANN, THERESA (1898–1962), Bavarian stigmatic. After a normal childhood, N. suffered various physical afflictions and intense psychological depression but was cured of all illness without medical help. In 1926, N. began to experience visions of Christ's Passion, states of ecstasy, and the stigmata. It is also reported that from 1928 until her death, she took no nourishment. While competent authority has never pronounced on her sanctity and capable theologians have shown opposition toward her mysticism, the stigmatization and ecstatic states are well substantiated. BIBLIOGRAPHY: H. C. Graef, *Case of Theresa Neumann* (1951); P. Siwek, NCE 10:365–366. *STIGMATIZATION.

[M. B. PENNINGTON]

NEUROSIS, a stable pattern of maladaptive or self-defeating behavior, often accompanied by high levels of anxiety, but one not impairing thought or producing the bizarre behaviors of psychosis. The most common forms of neuroses are those known as neuroses characterized by generalized anxiety and/or feelings of sadness and lack of personal worth. Next most common are those neuroses characterized by anxiety focused upon such specific events or situations as flying in airplanes and those involving relentless thoughts about a particular event or the performance of certain tasks in a repetitive routine. The first type are phobias and the second obsessions or compulsions. An additional group of neuroses consists of specific or generalized physical complaints, ranging from sudden loss of a physical function to vague but persistent complaints of pain or discomfort both without any physical abnormality being present. In the first, called conversion hysteria, function is lost; in the second, hypochondriacal neurosis, function is not lost, but discomfort and complaint are present.

There are two major theories on the origin of neurosis: one which derives from psychoanalysis and which has dominated the mental health field for the last half-century; another which grew out of the laboratories of learning psychology during the past 20 years.

The psychoanalytic approach to neurosis views the specific symptom or behavior as a symbolic representation of an unacceptable, hidden or repressed conflict. According to this view the individual engages in a series of defensive maneuvers in order to avoid the unpleasant experience of anxiety. To the extent that the defensive maneuver is successful in protecting the person from anxiety, a stable neurotic pattern is maintained. However, as anxiety builds, the person more and more diverts his available energy into the maintenance of the defense and thus drains his ability to cope with everyday life experiences. This diminished ability to cope with life distinguishes the neurotic from the normal person.

The learning theory approach suggests that rather than being a symbolic representation of hidden conflict, neurotic behavior is itself a learned response to anxiety-provoking situations. The individual, through a process of conditioning in which ordinary situations are coupled with fear-inducing situations, comes to experience fear or anxiety in what would otherwise be a nonfearful situation. Or, the individual learns a set of avoidance patterns that protect him from the anxiety-evoking situation. These may be simple avoidance patterns like not flying in airplanes, or not even leaving the house, or they may be complex rituals that prevent exposure to unpleasant anxiety.

Both theories have merit and may come to be understood as factors in a cognitive model of neurosis in which the crucial factor is what an individual tells himself about each situation and that then determines the amount of anxiety he will feel. Since both theories rest heavily upon anxiety as a key factor in neurosis, it should be noted that some modern researchers have postulated a biological predisposition to autonomic arousal which renders some individuals more vulnerable to the development of neurotic responses to the inevitable stresses of everyday life.

Neuroses are successfully treated in several different forms of therapy. In psychoanalytic therapy there is a process of uncovering the buried conflict that the neurotic behavior symbolizes. In behavioral therapy the individual is taught to reduce his anxiety through gradual exposure to the feared situation and to learn behaviors incompatible with anxiety and enhancing his sense of self-worth. Both of these major forms of treatment aim at producing an individual who can love, work, play, and face the future with a sense of optimism. BIBLIOGRAPHY: S. Freud, *Collected Papers* (tr. J. Riviere, 1959); S. Freud, *General Psychological Theory* (1963); O. H. Maurer, *Learning Theory and Behavior* (1960); J. Wolpe, *Psychotherapy by Reciprocal Inhibition* (1958).

[P. B. AMAR]

NEUROSIS (MORAL ASPECT). Neurotic behavior in any of its forms is not morally imputable, because of its lack of voluntariness; pastorally it requires professional therapy not simple counseling. Practically speaking, however, many people simply learn to live with a neurosis as part of the human condition and one element to be borne in the overall Christian pattern of their lives.

NEUTRAL TEXT, see BIBLE TEXTS.

NEVADA, a Rocky Mountain state admitted to the Union (1864) as the 36th state. The first European in the area (1776) was Francisco Tomás Hermenegildo Garcés, a Franciscan missionary and explorer. Nevada was acquired by the U.S. from Mexico in the Treaty of Guadalupe Hidalgo (1848). Catholicism was formally established (1868) when Hugh Gallagher founded the first Catholic congregation in Genoa. Patrick *Manogue, a pioneer priest who built the church of St. Mary's-in-the-Mountains in Virginia City, later became bp. of Sacramento, California. Although Catholicism grew slowly in Nevada, the number of Catholics had increased sufficiently by 1931 to necessitate the establishment of the Diocese of Reno. Thomas K. Gorman served as the first bp. and upon his transfer to Dallas-Fort Worth he was succeeded by Robert J. Dwyer. Bp. Dwyer was named abp. of Portland in Oregon and Joseph Green became bp. of Reno in 1967. He resigned in 1974 and was succeeded by Norman McFarland. In 1976 the title of the diocese was changed to Reno-Las Vegas. The Diocese of Reno is a suffragan of the metropolitan See of San Francisco.

In 1976 Nevada's Catholics numbered 95,000 or 17.3% of the total state population. The major Protestant denominations are the Church of Jesus Christ of Latter-Day Saints, with 9.7% of the total population in 1972, and the Southern Baptist Convention with 1.9%. Other Protestant denominations comprised 7.4% of the population. The Jewish population (1968) was 2,380 or 0.49%. There are no Catholic colleges in Nevada; two Catholic high schools have a total enrollment of 1,136 students. There are also 11 Catholic elementary schools in the state, attended by some 2,800 pupils. BIBLIOGRAPHY: R. G. Lillard, *Desert Challenge, An Interpretation of Nevada* (1942); H. L. Walsh, *Hallowed Were the Gold Dust Trails* (1946); T. K. Gorman, *Seventy-Five Years of Catholic Life in Nevada* (1935).

[J. L. MORRISON; R. M. PRESTON]

NEVILLE, GEORGE (*c.* 1432–76), brother of Warwick the Kingmaker; N. became bp. of Exeter (1456) while under age, and abp. of York (1465–76). Chancellor of England (1460–67, 1470–71), he fell into disgrace after Warwick's rebellion and was imprisoned (1472–75). A patron of scholars, he fostered the revival of Greek studies in England. BIBLIOGRAPHY: Emden Ox 2:1347–49.

[C. D. ROSS]

NEVIN, JOHN WILLIAMSON (1803–86), American theologian who, with P. *Schaff, developed the *Mercersburg theology. N. was a student of A. *Alexander and C. *Hodge at Princeton Theological Seminary and in 1830 became professor of biblical literature at Western Theological Seminary, Pittsburgh. He resigned in 1840 to accept a call to the German Reformed Seminary at Mercersburg, Pennsylvania. In 1844, N. published *The Anxious Bench,* which, with Schaff's *The Principle of Protestantism,* translated by N. in 1845, marked the beginning of the Mercersburg movement for a return to the true history of the Church and to the Reformation heritage, a reaction against the disregard of confessional traditions that was characteristic of *revivalism. In *The Mystical Presence* (1846) he stressed the central place in the life of the Church that Calvin had given to the Eucharist and that was unappreciated by the American denominations. N. also wrote on the *Heidelberg Catechism and on the nature of the Church. With Schaff in 1849 he founded the *Mercersburg Review*. In 1861 he accepted a professorship at Franklin and Marshall College, Lancaster, Pa.; he became its president in 1866. BIBLIOGRAPHY: T. Appel, *Life and Work of John Williamson Nevin* (1889); J. H. Nichols, *Romanticism in American Theology* (1961).

[R. K. MACMASTER]

NEVSKY, ALEXANDER (*c.* 1220–63), Russian grand prince of Vladimir, and hero of the Russian repulsion of German and Swedish invasions. He was the son of the grand prince of Vladimir, Yaroslav II Vsevolodovich, the foremost Russian ruler of his day. At age 19, he was married to the daughter of the prince of Polotsk. His name Nevsky derives from his defeat of the Swedes at the River Neva in 1240. He subsequently defeated the Teutonic Knights whom Pope Gregory IX instigated to attack Russia with an eye to implanting Latin Christianity. Both the Russian Orthodox Church and Alexander collaborated with the Mongols in imposing Mongolian rule in Russia, because it was believed that the anti-Mongolian elements were in league with the papacy. Soon after his death the shortlived unity he brought to the northern Russian principalities, with Mongolian aid, began to disintegrate. He was canonized by the Russian Church in 1547, and was the hero of a Russian epic film in 1938, which was intended as propaganda to rouse Russian feeling against the new German imperialist expansion into Russia.

[E. J. DILLON]

NEW ABBEY (SWEETHEART), former Cistercian abbey near Dumfries, Scotland. Founded in 1273 by the mother of the Scottish King, John Balliol (1292–96), the abbey was called Sweetheart (Dulce Cor) because the foundress (Dervorgilla) kept her husband's embalmed heart in her presence; it was buried with her when she died in 1289. Pillaged in the Anglo-Scottish wars of independence (1296–1306), the abbey came under Lord Maxwell's protection after the battle of Flodden in 1513. Maxwell later saved the abbey from being destroyed by the Reformers. But it was annexed to the English crown in 1587 and its last abbot, Gilbert Broun, who had defended the old religion, died in exile in 1612. The abbey became a temporal lordship for Robert Spottiswoode in 1624, but is now a ruin. BIBLIOGRAPHY: S. Cruden, *Scottish Abbeys* (1960) 73–74.

[M. A. MCFADDEN]

NEW ACADEMY, the Platonic School founded by *Carneades of Cyrene, who taught a doctrine of logical probabilism. The later members of the New Academy returned pretty much to the epistemology of the *Old Academy. See *GREEK PHILOSOPHY 3,d.

[M. R. P. MCGUIRE]

NEW AMERICAN BIBLE, a new RC translation of the Bible from the original languages into modern American English. Begun in 1944 at the request of American bps. in response to Pope Pius XII who called for translations from the original texts instead of traditional versions from the Latin Vulgate of St. Jerome (in the encyclical *Divino* *afflante Spiritu*), it appeared in complete first edition in 1970. The work, by members of the Catholic Biblical Association of America and some non-Catholic scholars, had as its aim publication of an accurate, readable version, representative of biblical styles without any attempt at uniform literary elegance. The OT translation is based on critical reading of the Massoretic text and Hebrew traditions underlying ancient versions, esp. the Greek Septuagint. The NT translation stems from most ancient MSS and critical editions of the original Greek. It has been criticized for unfamiliar wording by Catholics used to the Challoner recension of the Douay-Rheims version of the Vulgate and by devotees of the classical language of the King James' Bible. Generally, defensible are such changes as "favor" for "grace", "trust" for "faith", "kingship" and "way of holiness" for "kingdom" and "justice". But, how "John the Baptizer" is better than "John the Baptist" is not clear; nor that in Lk 12:35 "Let your belts be fastened around your waists . . ." is an English idiom for readiness. The "Be ready for whatever comes, dressed for action . . ." of the Good News Bible is more felicitous. A glaring omission in Rom 8.28 of "for those who love God" calls for correction in a subsequent edition. The explanatory footnotes are helpful and informative on the whole, but should not be definitive. The OT translation succeeds in its aim for accuracy and clarity, even if at times it rearranges verses, esp. in the Prophets, without the support of scholarly consensus. For bible study purposes the Revised Standard Version of the NT is to be preferred for its closeness to the original. However, the New American Bible has been well received and is a proof of North American Catholic scholarship's coming of age.

[J. F. FALLON]

NEW CALEDONIA, an island of the S Pacific, part of *Melanesia, forming with its dependencies a French Overseas Territory (7335 sq. mi.; pop. [1976] 131,665). Discovered by Capt. James Cook in 1774, New Caledonia became a French colony in 1853 and was soon converted into a land of deportation. Sixty percent of the inhabitants are illiterate. The first Marist missionary reached New Caledonia in 1839. More systematic evangelization began in 1843, but missioners were exiled during a revolt of natives against the colonists in 1847. On their return in 1851 the missioners encountered new difficulties, this time with the French authorities. In 1870 Gov. Guillain closed the mission schools and encouraged Christians to apostatize. Anti-Catholic furor developed again in 1892 and lasted until 1903, without forcing the withdrawal of the missionaries. Both World Wars interrupted mission endeavors. At the present time there is only one vicariate, directed by two bps., one residing on New Caledonia and the other on Wallis. In 1976 there were 84,500 Catholics, 56 priests, 215 sisters, and 102 brothers. Protestantism was introduced by the London Missionary Society in 1850, but the English were required to give place at the end of the century to the Evangelical Missionary Society of Paris. Adventists are also at work. The combined Protestant membership in 1964 was about 23,000.

[P. DAMBORIENA; M. J. SUELZER]

NEW CHURCH, a designation for the *Church of the New Jerusalem, often used in the title of its local congregations. The usage stems from the fact that the founder, E. *Swedenborg, was convinced that he was called upon to begin a "New Church."

[T. C. O'BRIEN]

NEW DELHI ASSEMBLY, third general assembly of the World Council of Churches (WCC), Nov. 19–Dec. 5, 1961, with 577 delegates representing 181 Churches, plus advisers, staff, observers, and visitors. The theme of the Assembly was "Jesus Christ, the Light of the World." The RC Church was officially represented for the first time at a WCC general assembly, sending five official observers. The membership of the WCC was enlarged with the addition of 23 Churches, including the Patriarchate of Moscow and two Pentecostal Churches of Chile. The doctrinal basis of the WCC was expanded from the *Amsterdam Assembly formula, "churches which accept our Lord Jesus Christ as God and Savior," to "churches which confess the Lord Jesus Christ as God and Savior according to the Scriptures and therefore seek to fulfill together their common calling to the glory of the one God, Father, Son, and Holy Spirit." This change was made to emphasize a more dynamic concept of faith (changing "accept" to "confess"), to evidence deeper roots in the Christian tradition (reference to the Scriptures and the Trinity), and to stress the mission of the Church ("calling"). Essentials to Christian unity were also enunciated. This was the first assembly to meet in the geographical area of the younger Churches, and the WCC became more conscious of their role. The *International Missionary Council merged with the WCC, becoming its Commission on World Mission and Evangelism. BIBLIOGRAPHY: *New Delhi Report)* ed. W. A. Visser't Hooft, 1962).

[T. EARLY]

NEW ENGLAND THEOLOGY, system of modified Calvinistic thought that originated from the works of Jonathan *Edwards, Sr., and flourished among New England *Congregationalists from the mid-18th to the late 19th century. Joseph Bellamy and Samuel Hopkins promoted, with variations, the themes of Edwards's major treatises, as did Jonathan Edwards, Jr. (1745–1801), Nathaniel Emmons (1745–1840), and Nathaniel *Taylor (see NEW HAVEN THEOLOGY). Edward A. Park (1808–1900) of Andover Theological Seminary was its last defender. The New England theology wrestled with the problems of human depravity, the freedom of the will, the nature of virtue, and immortality. The system centered in the sovereignty of God, a doctrine crucial to the senior Edwards's treatises on the freedom of the will, original sin, and true virtue. In denying freedom of choice, but not of action, stressing human depravity, and describing true virtues as the act of cordial consent of beings to Being in General, he had shown the complete dominance of God over all reality. His successors discussed the possibility of moral agents' exercising choice as to their fate in a world governed by, and expressive of, the divine will and attempted to prove that human responsibility remained. They sought to show how sin contributed to the good of the whole, and how benevolence was possible. The New England theology challenged the emerging liberalism of the Unitarians and Universalists. It also influenced the establishment of Andover, Hartford, and Yale Seminaries, and fostered foreign missions, antislavery sentiment, and other social reforms. BIBLIOGRAPHY: G. N. Boardman, *New England Theology* (1899); F. H. Foster, *Genetic History of the New England Theology* (1907).

[C. A. HOLBROOK]

NEW ENGLISH BIBLE, a completely new translation from the best available texts in the original languages into the contemporary idiom of British English. The work of four scholarly panels, it was first promoted by the Church of Scotland but was eventually sponsored by practically all of the United Kingdom's Christian denominations. Begun in 1947, it was completed *in toto* in 1970. The translation's aim was to break away from the traditional language and method of translating of the Authorized Versions, but, nevertheless, to retain some older English usages in formal prayers, e.g., "thou" and "thee." The translation is accurate without being awkward. The inclusion of the Apocrypha is praiseworthy as a trend away from the 3d-cent. rabbis and a return to the earlier church tradition.

[J. F. FALLON]

NEW EVANGELICALISM (Neo-Evangelicalism), movement to strengthen conservative Christianity in the United States. In 1954, H. J. Ockenga (*Bulletin of Fuller Theological Seminary*) pronounced *fundamentalism a failure and asserted that "new evangelicals" would combine traditional orthodoxy with social conscience and scholarship. J. H. Carnell, also of Fuller Seminary, was a proponent of New Evangelicalism. His colleague, C. H. F. Henry, left Fuller Seminary in 1957 to edit the newly founded fortnightly, *Christianity Today*; through this publication, as well as by lectures and books, he became a leading spokesman for *evangelicals (a term more often used than "Neo-" or "New"). Also associated with the movement have been Billy *Graham and numerous preachers, teachers, and business men. Emphasizing basic Christian doctrines, Evangelicals have stressed the authoritative and inerrant Scriptures as the word of God. They have tried to unite evangelicals of many denominations, to promote evangelism, to deal with social issues, to produce scholarly literature, and to deal with a wide range of theological concerns. BIBLIOGRAPHY: M. Erickson, *New Evangelical Theology* (1968); R. H. Nash, *New Evangelicalism* (1968).

NEW HAMPSHIRE, a New England state admitted to the Union (1788) as one of the original thirteen. The first permanent settlement was made at the mouth of the Piscataqua River (1623). Other early settlements included Hampton and Exeter, the latter founded (1638) by John Wheelwright, an Antinomian leader who had been banished from the Massachusetts Bay Colony. New Hampshire, under the jurisdiction of Massachusetts from 1641, became a royal province (1679) but continued to have the same governor as the Bay Colony until 1741. Through the 18th cent. Congregationalism was practically the established religion in New Hampshire, and until 1876 non-Protestants were excluded from high public office. Many denominations contributed to the state's history, however, including Anglicans in Portsmouth, Quakers in Dover, Scotch-Irish Presbyterians, and Baptists, who had over 40 churches in the state by 1800. The number of Catholics in New Hampshire was negligible before the Irish immigration of the 1840's; even as late as 1854 there were still only four Catholic churches in the state. Following the Civil War, French Canadians and Poles came to New Hampshire and added to the Catholic population. A number of national parishes were established after 1871 to provide for this polyglot population.

The Diocese of Manchester was established in 1884, with D. M. *Bradley as its first bishop. He was succeeded by J. B. Delany, G. A. Guertin, J. B. *Peterson, M. F. *Brady, E. J. Primeau, and O. J. Gendron (1974). Coextensive with state boundaries, the diocese is a suffragan of the metropolitan See of Boston, Massachusetts. In 1976 Catholics numbered 264,567 or 33.7% of the total state population. The major Protestant denominations are the United Church of Christ with 4.7% of the total population in 1972, the Episcopal Church, with 2.5% and the United Methodist Church with 2.4%. Other Protestant denominations comprised 4.7%. The Jewish population (1968) was 4,260, or 0.58%. Five Catholic colleges are in New Hampshire, with a total enrollment of 4,213 students. More than 2,613 students attend the state's 6 Catholic high schools, and 8,340 pupils attend 32 Catholic elementary schools. BIBLIOGRAPHY: J. D. Squires, *Granite State of the United States* (4 v., 1956); M. St. L. Kegresse, *History of Catholic Education in New Hampshire* (1955).

[J. L. MORRISON; R. M. PRESTON]

NEW HAMPSHIRE CONFESSION OF FAITH, a Baptist confession written in 1832 that soon superseded the *Philadelphia Confession. Originally drafted at the instigation of the New Hampshire Baptist Convention, it was recommended by the board of that body for use in the churches. In 1853, J. Newton Brown, who had helped draft the document, became editorial secretary of the American Baptist Publication Society, and he published the Confession with slight revisions in *Baptist Church Manual,* thus giving it wide circulation. Many Churches adopted it. In length it was a little over one-tenth that of the Philadelphia Confession, and its content reflected the modified Calvinism that was becoming prevalent. In accord with the revivalistic spirit of the Churches, it encouraged "the use of means in the highest degree." Reference to "eternal decrees" was omitted, as were other characteristic emphases of predestinarian theology. Very conspicuous was the absence of any reference to the "Universal Church." Because of this omission, it appealed to Landmarkists, whose churches and associations made it their standard (see LANDMARKISM). By the 20th cent. Baptists made less use of confessional statements than formerly. The Northern Baptist Convention voted against adoption of the New Hampshire Confession in 1922, claiming the NT as its only creed. The *Southern Baptist Convention (1925) published the Confession in modified form and recommended it to the churches. The General Association of *Regular Baptists, in 1933, adopted it with a premillennial interpretation of its article on eschatology. BIBLIOGRAPHY: *Baptist Confessions of Faith* (ed. W. L. Lumpkin, 1959).

[J. L. MORRISON]

NEW HAVEN THEOLOGY, also called the New Divinity, a view that developed at Yale Divinity School principally under N. W. *Taylor, and that modified traditional Calvinism on the crucial points of the *total depravity of human nature and man's freedom of choice. The *Second Great Awakening in Connecticut began with a revival at Yale in 1802 and a notable series of chapel sermons delivered by Timothy *Dwight. Under his leadership, Congregationalism moved imperceptibly into the revivalist camp. He had a marked influence on both Lyman *Beecher and N. W. Taylor. As the revival became accepted in New England Congregational circles, preachers sought to provoke a revival by utilizing means calculated to bring their hearers to a decision. The successful use of revivals as a means of bringing reborn Christians into the Church created problems for theologians in the Calvinist tradition and required the rethinking of key issues. In his 1819 sermon on "Salvation Free to the Willing," Taylor wrestled with fundamental problems of the Christian life. His more famous *Concio ad clerum* in 1828 brought a clear statement of Taylor's views on the depravity of human nature. He denied that it was a propensity in human nature, but said it was rather man's own act consisting of a free choice of some object other than God as his chief good. Taylor and his Yale associates believed that they were presenting the true meaning of the Calvinist tradition, but conservatives were scandalized. The New Haven school drew much of its inspiration from the *New England theology of Jonathan *Edwards and Samuel *Hopkins, as did its detractors. The New Divinity exponents sought to make a statement that would save both the fact that the work of regeneration was entirely God's work, and the fact that God could not be considered the cause of sin in his creatures. Their ideas were put into practice by Charles G. *Finney, whose *Lectures on Revivals of Religion* was grounded in the New Haven theology. The opposition of conservative Calvinists, esp. C. *Hodge and his Princeton colleagues, to the New Haven teachings was a contributing factor in the breakdown of the Congregational-Presbyterian *Plan of Union in 1837. The stress placed by Taylor and his school on disinterested benevolence as an effect of a true Christian conversion contributed to the growth of charitable, missionary, and social reform movements in 19th-cent. America. BIBLIOGRAPHY: S. E. Mead, *Nathaniel William Taylor* (1942); C. R. Keller, *Second Great Awakening in Connecticut* (1942); *Lectures on Revivals of Religion* (ed. W. G. McLoughlin, 1960); Smith-Jamison 1:254–260.

[R. K. MACMASTER]

NEW HEBRIDES, an archipelago of about 40 islands in the S Pacific, part of *Melanesia. Their combined area is about 5,700 sq mi; pop. 94,000 (1976). They were discovered by Pedro de Quiros in 1606 and were explored by Bougainville in 1768 and Cook in 1774. In 1906 they became the joint condominium of France and Great Britain. The first group of Marist missionaries to arrive on the islands was murdered in 1851. Methodical evangelization began in 1887 and a vicariate apostolic was erected in 1904. The Catholic population as reported in 1976 was nearly 15,304. In 1839 the London Missionary Society sent missionaries to the New Hebrides. Presbyterians, Anglicans, and Adventists are also at work. The total Protestant membership in 1966 was more than 40,000. BIBLIOGRAPHY: T. Harrison, *Savage Civilization* (1937); *Bilan du Monde* 2:650–651.

[M. J. SUELZER]

NEW JERSEY, a Middle Atlantic state admitted to the Union (1787) as the 3d of the original 13 States. The region was first explored (1524) by Giovanni da Verrazano, a Florentine who sailed under the French flag, and more fully later (1609) by Henry Hudson. Dutch settlers from New York came to NE New Jersey, and a Quaker colony was established in West Jersey by William *Penn and others in the 1670s. Anglicanism, however, became the dominant religion of New Jersey, esp. in the N portion, while Catholicism grew very slowly amid numerous legal obstacles. The early 19th-cent. Irish immigrants increased the Catholic population. The Diocese of Newark (1853) served as the administrative jurisdiction for the entire state until 1881. As an archdiocese it now has the suffragan sees of Trenton, Paterson, and Camden. The first bp. of Newark was J. R. *Bayley, who expanded Catholic institutions throughout the state, augmented the diocesan priesthood, and obtained the help of Benedictines, Passionists, Conventual Franciscans, and Jesuits. M. A. *Corrigan, who became the second bp. of Newark in 1873, devoted himself to stabilizing diocesan finances. His successors, W. M. *Wigger and J. J. O'Connor, initiated work on Newark's cathedral, and opened a major seminary at Darlington. T. J. Walsh, Newark's first abp. (1937), organized the Mount Carmel Guild to supervise social work, and began the archdiocesan newspaper, the *Advocate*. T. A. Boland, who became the second abp. (1953), consecrated the cathedral, introduced *Serra International and extended the work of the Mount Carmel Guild. He resigned in 1974 and was succeeded by Abp. Peter L. Gerety.

In 1976 New Jersey's Catholics numbered 840,483 or 37.1% of the total state population. The major Protestant denominations are the United Presbyterian Church in the U.S. with 3.1%; and the Methodist Church with 2.4% of the total population in 1971. Other Protestant denominations accounted for 7.5%. The Jewish population (1968) was 387,220, or 5.4%. There are 10 Catholic colleges in New Jersey, with a total enrollment of 17,610 students. Four of these schools, enrolling 16,039, are in the Archdiocese of Newark. Over 55,830 students attend the state's 96 Catholic high schools, 48 of which are in the archdiocese and attended by 24,819 students. There are 471 Catholic elementary schools in the state, with a total enrollment of 164,974 pupils. Some 72,189 of these pupils attend 217 Catholic elementary schools in the archdiocese. BIBLIOGRAPHY: *Story of New Jersey* (5 v.; ed. W. S. Myers, 1945); W. N. Jameson, *Religion in New Jersey* (1964); C. D. Hinrichsen, *History of the Diocese of Newark, 1873–1901* (1962).

[J. L. MORRISON; R. M. PRESTON]

NEW LEARNING, a term sometimes used interchangeably with Renaissance humanism. It is humanism translated into an educational program, as contrasted with the old learning, i.e., *scholasticism. Renaissance humanism begins effectively with Francesco Petrarch (1304–74), but its orientation toward education had its roots in the ancient Roman Quintilian. The Renaissance program of formal education was developed by such humanists as Guarino da Verona (1374–1460) and Vittorino da Feltre (1378–1446). This involved the revival of Cicero's *studia humanitatis,* i.e., the humanities, with a stress upon Greek and Latin literature and grammar, rhetoric, oratory, history, and moral philosophy. It was optimistic and practical, its objective being to train young men for service in Church and State. The New Learning had a profound impact upon education for centuries. BIBLIOGRAPHY: W. W. Woodward, *Vittorino da Feltre and Other Humanist Educators* (1912). *HUMANISM; *RENAISSANCE.

[D. G. NUGENT]

NEW MELLERAY, ABBEY OF, Cistercian (Trappist) foundation made in 1849 from Melleray, Ireland, on a site 12 miles SW of Dubuque, Iowa. Sixteen monks debarked from Ireland; six of them died of cholera en route from New Orleans to St. Louis. The community's numbers grew to 61 by 1860, but by 1917 there were only 17 monks. After World War II vocations became more plentiful; a new foundation was made in the S Missouri Ozarks—Our Lady of the Assumption Abbey. The resident community at New Melleray in 1976 was 73; that at Our Lady of the Assumption, 17.

NEW MEXICO, a SW state admitted to the Union (1912) as the 47th state. Its early history is closely associated with the development of Catholicism in the area. Discovered by Fray Marcos de Niza (1539) and explored by the Coronado expedition (1540), the area was the site of unsuccessful missionary efforts before the first permanent mission could be established (1598). Santa Fe was founded as a permanent capital for the region (1610). During the Pueblo Rebellion (1680) a number of Franciscans lost their lives, but missionary work was resumed in 1693 and continued during the 18th and 19th centuries. New Mexico became part of the U.S. (1846), and the Diocese of Santa Fe was created (1851) with J. B. *Lamy as first bishop. Welcoming French clergy to the diocese, he founded a seminary and helped to establish several schools. Before he resigned (1885), Santa Fe was made an archdiocese (1875), with Tucson (now a suffragan of Los Angeles, Calif.) and Denver (now an archdiocese) as suffragans; its present suffragans are Gallup, N.M. and El Paso, Texas. Lamy was succeeded by J.-B. Salpointe, who devoted himself to the education of the Indians, assisting the Sisters of the *Blessed Sacrament for Indians and Colored People in opening St. Catherine's Indian School. P. Bourgade (who became archdiocesan ordinary, 1897) continued missionary efforts with the aid of the Franciscans and of the Catholic Church Extension Society, which he helped to found. He was followed by J.-B. Pitaval, 1909–18, and A. T. Daeger, OFM, 1919–32, who invited to New Mexico such religious orders as the Missionary Catechists of Our Lady of Victory. Daeger was succeeded by Rudolph Aloysius Gerken (1933–43) and Edwin Vincent Byrne (1943–63) who emphasized educational development and established vigorous Newman Centers at the Univ. of New Mexico and its Las Vegas and Portales branches. He was succeeded by James Peter Davis (1964–74); Robert Sanchez is the present archbishop.

In 1976 New Mexico Catholics numbered about 351,000, or 36.4% of the total state population. The major Protestant denominations are the Southern Baptist Convention, with 11.5% of the total population in 1972, and the Methodist Church with 5.8%. Other Protestant denominations comprised 10.2%. The Jewish population (1968) was 3,645, or 0.36%. There are two Catholic colleges in New Mexico, with a total enrollment of 4,430 students. Almost 2,000 students attend the state's 6 Catholic high schools, while 3,769 pupils are enrolled in 32 Catholic elementary schools. BIBLIOGRAPHY: W. A. Beck, *New Mexico* (1962); A. Chávez, *Old Faith and Old Glory* (1946).

[J. L. MORRISON; R. M. PRESTON]

NEW MOON FEAST, HEBREW (*Rosh Hodesh*), observance marking the beginning of the month, a new period in the Hebrew luni-solar calendar. The New Moon was sighted, witnessed, and officially proclaimed by the Sanhedrin, announced by trumpet blasts and Musaf sacrifices (Num 28.11–15). Once the moon had been sighted, a prayer of thanksgiving called the *Kiddush Levanah* (''sanctification of the moon,'' dating from the time of the Second Temple) was recited. Festive meals, abstention from business, and calling upon the prophet were practices commonly associated with the feast. By the 4th cent. the calendar was fixed, thus eliminating the need for the reliable testimony of witnesses to the reappearance of the moon's crescent, eliminating also the beacon fires that had broadcast the announcement to Jewish communities throughout the Near East. The feast, still mentioned in the NT (Col 2.16), disappeared from Jewish observance.

[R. J. LITZ]

NEW MORALITY, name for a contemporary moral theory that has its roots in at least three major challenges to traditional thought. In metaphysics existentialism has challenged the assumption that human nature is a fixed datum. Contextual or situation ethics has challenged the assumption that certain moral actions are always and everywhere wrong. In moral theology personalism has challenged the assumption that morality is simply a matter of keeping a code. The combination of these three attitudes toward human activity has come to be known as the new morality. Existentialism sees each human being as a starkly given and irreducible complex. No man can generalize in abstraction from his own concrete aspirations and impulses, since from these he is continuously fashioning his own nature. Facing a moral decision challenges him to express his own authenticity. His act must be his own in the fullest sense. Situationalism takes its primary guidance from the circumstances in which the individual acts. Shall he tell a lie or tell the truth? Shall he kill or allow life? His answer depends not on recourse to an immutable moral law, but on the situation. Personalism emphasized the I-Thou dialogue between man and God, man and man. Love is the only norm in the light of which the human person must manage all the moral decisions of his life. A code, whether Jewish, Christian, Hindu, humanist, or whatever, may be acknowledged Situationalism takes its primary guidance from the circumstances in which the individual acts. Shall he tell a lie or tell the truth? Shall he kill or allow life? His answer depends not on recourse to an immutable moral law, but on the situation. Personalism emphasized the I-Thou dialogue between man and God, man and man. Love is the only norm in the light of which the human person must manage all the moral decisions of his life. A code, whether Jewish, Christian, Hindu, humanist, or whatever, may be acknowledged as a source of counsel, but it cannot be prescriptive. Charity, *agapē,* is the only precept.

One may reject these presuppositions as exclusive yet recognize much that is acceptable in the new morality. Psychology and psychiatry have shown how a man's childhood, his cultural milieu, and many other factors affect his adult decisions. One dare not presume to make sure moral judgments about the activity of any individual, no matter how unusual it may be, without profound personal knowledge of that individual and the influences that shaped him. The unique situation in which a moral action takes place is also crucial; no one acts in isolation; his decisions are shaped by circumstances and above all by people. Love certainly ought to be central. When traditional Christian morality loses that insight and goes over to the external keeping of the law as the critical norm, it needs to be purified and brought back to the clear message of the gospel. The new morality, however, assumes that men do not share in a common human nature, that no recognizably fixed values exist to guide men, that objectively wrong actions do not exist, or that Christian love observes no measure other than itself. Against this assumption it is argued that there are subordinate measures common to all men and expressing perennial values of which the violation is always wrong. Ovid, Dante, and T. S. Eliot display a common human characteristic in interpreting life through creative poetry. The evil men in the Bible and in Shakespeare look very much like those of our day. One can make valid statements applicable to all, recognize constant values and deviations from them and be assured that the way to authenticity is through respecting them. Christ set love as highest and best, but he also cited the other commandments as the way to life (Mk 10.19) and strongly condemned murder and adultery (Mk 7.22) with no hint that possible situations might permit them.

The whole subject of morality is one not open to simplistic statements. The conventional systems of moral theology have received insights from the new school, notably about natural law, historicity, conscience, and love. It would seem that the bridge of reconciliation between the old and the new will be built by a more profound study of the virtue of Christian prudence. It is there the complex elements of a moral decision meet, there that the rule of Christian living is consulted and its immediate and providential environment appreciated, together with all the extenuating, and sometimes excepting, circumstances. BIBLIOGRAPHY: *Norm and Context in Christian Ethics* (eds. G. H. Outka and P. Ramsey, 1968); ThAq ST (Lat-Eng), v. 18, ed. T. Gilby.

[T. R. HEATH]

NEW NORCIA, ABBEY OF, a Benedictine abbey *nullius* in Western Australia, suffragan of Perth, founded in 1846 by Rosendo Salvado, a Spanish monk, afterwards bp., for the evangelization of the nomadic aborigines and their instruction in farming. The social situation has now changed with the coming of white settlers, and the work has pushed in an upcountry direction, the main mission to the aborigines since 1908 being centered on the Drysdale River.

NEW OBJECTIVITY, see NEUE SACHLICHKEIT.

NEW PROPHECY, term used in reference to the *Montanists' practice of ecstatic utterance, inspired or prompted, as they claimed, by the Spirit. The term is found in Eusebius's selections from certain anti-Montanist writers (*Hist. eccl. 5.16 and 5.19),* but may have been the Montanists' self-designation. The resistance of some church leaders to the movement seems to have been based on the ecstatic (and therefore allegedly unintelligible) nature of their prophecy or preaching, as well as to its independence from (and sometimes criticism of) the growing institution of the episcopacy. The significant role of women prophets among the Montanists was also resisted (see MAXIMILLA THE MONTANIST). BIBLIOGRAPHY: R. M. Grant, *Augustus to Constantine* (1970) 131–44; P. de Labriolle, *La Crise montaniste* (1913); H. von Campenhausen, *Ecclesiastical Authority and Spiritual Power* (1969) 178–212; J. L. Ash, ThSt 37 (1976) 227–252.

[D. P. EFROYMSON]

NEW ROME (Second Rome), name given to Constantinople by the Roman Emperor Constantine I, the Great, after rebuilding the ancient city of Byzantium, changing its name, and deciding to adopt it as his personal city. The founding ceremonies took place on November 26, 328, a mix of permitted pagan rituals and prescribed Christian ceremonies. The dedication of the city in honor of the Christian martyrs was on May 11, 330. Seeking to provide his city with a Christian character, Constantine had the church of St. Irene constructed on the acropolis and plans were laid for the basilica of Hagia Sophia, even though certain traditional non-Christian practices were tolerated. The title New Rome was used to prove Constantinople's primacy of honor after Rome at the Council of Constantinople I in 381; that pride of place later came to mean equality in the schism between East and West.

[R. J. LITZ]

NEW SUBIACO, ABBEY OF, a Swiss-American Benedictine abbey in Subiaco, Arkansas, founded in 1878 by the monks of St. Meinrad Abbey, Indiana. It is part of a family of more than a dozen abbeys and priories, most of which are located in the United States, run by the Swiss-American Benedictines who were established by Pope Leo XIII in 1881. Governed both by the rule of St. Benedict and the Declarations and Constitutions of the Swiss-American Congregation, the monks are known for their liturgical interests and their missionary endeavors in the U.S. and Central America. They conduct a high school for lay students at Subiaco. BIBLIOGRAPHY: C. Gedert, *Swiss-American Congregation of Benedictines and Its Contribution to the American Catholic Church* (1956).

[M. A. MCFADDEN]

NEW TESTAMENT, division of the Christian Bible; the 27 books include the four Gospels, Acts, the Pauline and Catholic *Epistles, and Revelation (see BIBLE; TESTAMENT). These books are not arranged chronologically, but in correspondence to the Christian division of the OT into historical (the Gospels and Acts), didactic (the Epistles), and prophetic (Rev) books. (See BIBLICAL CANON.)

Development of the NT. The latest of the writings in the NT as it now stands is 2 Pet, written probably near the end of the 1st or the beginning of the 2d century. A period of 70–90 years of elaboration and adaptation lies between the first NT writing and the original spoken words of Jesus. Among the determining factors in the development of the NT message into its fixed written form were: adaptation to the division between Jewish and gentile Churches; the relationship between Church and Synagogue; the question of Jewish observances (circumcision, dietary laws, etc.); fulfillment of OT promises and the effectiveness of Christian Redemption; apologetic defense of the gospel convincing to the messianic-minded Jews and the philosophically-minded pagans; the implications, theological, liturgical, and moral, of the progressive realization that Christ's second coming was not imminent.

Like the strata of an archaeological tell, the levels of tradition in the NT have been superimposed one upon another, the later ones subsuming and absorbing but never obliterating the earlier ones, and the whole corpus deepening and broadening with the changing horizons and circumstances of the early Church. The earliest NT canonical writings presuppose and build upon many elements.

*(1) *Ipsissima verba of Jesus.* These sayings contained his ethical teaching and the messianic significance of his mission, death, and Resurrection. It has been argued (e.g., by B. Gerhardsson, *Memory and Manuscript,* tr. E. J. Sharpe, 1961) that Jesus would have taught these to his Disciples by rote, in rabbinic fashion, and that an oral *Torah would have thereby developed. While this may be exaggerated, it still is reasonable to believe that at least a substantial nucleus of Jesus' sayings and deeds would have been committed to memory and faithfully transmitted orally.

*(2) Pre-Easter *kerygma,* as it has been called. Even while not fully understanding the messianic significance of Jesus' words and deeds during his lifetime, the Apostles and Disciples would have reflected on them and pointed to his words and miracles as signs that he was the prophet and Messiah foretold in the OT.

(3) Post-Pentecostal kerygma, or primitive apostolic preaching. The essential content of the NT as a whole is made up of two virtually identical messages, the early apostolic preaching, as in Acts 2.14–39; 3.13–26; 4.10–12, etc., and Paul's gospel. The message is that God's plans and purpose for mankind, as recorded in the OT, have been fulfilled in Christ, the predestined Messiah and Son of David. This fulfillment has been by Jesus' ministry, attended by miraculous signs that accomplish the OT prophecies, and by his new, authoritative teaching of God's word and will. The fulfillment has been accomplished, secondly, by his redemptive death, his Resurrection, and glorification in heaven, where he is messianic head of the true Israel of God. The signs and wonders worked by the Holy Spirit are an assurance that the glorified Christ is still actively present in the Church. The messianic age inaugurated will reach its consummation in the second coming; mean-

while man must repent, believe, obey Christ's word, be baptized and so receive Redemption.

(4) Passion Narratives. Fuller eye-witness accounts of the climactic event, Jesus' Resurrection, and, as prelude, of his trial and death, would have been demanded. These narratives were among the earliest traditions to achieve fixed form in writing.

(5) Short collections of "words of the Lord". Traces of such collections for instructing converts are to be found in the early Fathers (e.g., First Letter of Clement 13.2; Didache 1.3) as well as in the NT itself. The development of a Christian apologetic led to a collection of "controversy stories" recording Jesus' disputes with the scribes and Pharisees in Galilee and in Jerusalem, and to collections of miracle stories, exorcisms, etc., designated to authenticate his messianic claims and divine sonship. Those who compiled or used these collections would have felt free to enlarge upon and adapt the sayings of Jesus so as to apply them to the specific needs of their hearers. Thus, e.g., J. Jeremias (*Parables of Jesus*, tr. S. H. Hooke, rev. ed. 1963) has shown that in the gospel *parables there are present not only the original as formulated by Jesus, but also the subsequent allegorizations, adaptations, and amplifications introduced by the authorized teachers of the primitive Church.

(6) Baptismal and eucharistic formulas. In this context primitive credal and confessional formulas, specifically Christian forms of blessing, invocations, doxologies, prayers, hymns, etc., would have become stereotyped and familiar to all Christians, or at least to those belonging to a particular Church or group of Churches. Many are quoted in fragmentary form in the NT writings and because of their familiarity, develop new ideas.

(7) Declarations of authority. The authority of the Apostles was challenged from a very early stage, and usurpers and heretical teachers constituted a real and persistent menace to the Church. The efforts of the true teachers to combat evil influence is vividly reflected in the Epistles, and less obviously, in the Gospels, notably in Mt and Jn. Active resistance to heresy became a major factor in the shaping of the NT message.

(8) Rules of conduct (Haustafeln). These are cited and enlarged upon in the Epistles, and the ethical principles underlying them are explicated and developed.

Relationship of the NT books. The earliest writings are not the Gospels but the Pauline Letters, designed, for the most part, to meet concrete needs of particular local Churches at particular stages in their developing awareness of the gospel and its claims upon them. In most cases the message of the Pauline Letters grows immediately out of such concrete local situations, and can be understood only in terms of them. By contrast the Catholic Epistles are, as their name suggests, addressed to the Church in general, and therefore less immediately related to local problems. Nevertheless their scope is also necessarily limited; they are concerned with the concrete problems entailed in living by the gospel in the contemporary Roman and Hellenistic world, amid an alien environment, false teachers, and persecution. The Gospels introduce a radical widening of perspective by viewing retrospectively the whole of Jesus' earthly life in its significance as "gospel." The Gospels also, in a sense, are composed from a more detached point of view; they do not deal *ex professo* with the immediate problems of the early Church, but rather propose the past words and deeds of Jesus as the basic light and strength by which all Christians must live in the present. In Mk the "gospel" extends from the ministry of John the Baptist to the apparition of the risen Christ. In Mt and Lk the span is widened so as to include the infancy of Jesus. Acts goes further, including the work of the Holy Spirit in the growth and formation of the Early Church. John also includes the pre-existence of the Lord in heaven. Finally in Rev the traditions of OT and Jewish apocalyptic writings have been drawn upon to develop the idea of the glorified Christ presiding in union with God over the whole of earth and heaven, and bringing all that takes place within them to the supreme climax of his second coming. BIBLIOGRAPHY: C. F. D. Moule, *Birth of the New Testament* (1962); Wikenhauser NTI; F. F. Bruce, *New Testament History* (1969); R. H. Fuller, *New Testament in Current Study* (1963); *idem, Critical Introduction to the New Testament* (1966); R. M. Grant, *Historical Introduction to the New Testament* (1963); *idem, Formation of the New Testament* (1965); M. C. Kee, and F. W. Young, *Understanding the New Testament* (1957).

[C. P. CEROKE]

NEW TESTAMENT LITERATURE. Christian preachers of the 1st cent. A.D. worked to spread the gospel among Jews and gentiles, to establish and confirm local churches, and to solve numerous problems, both moral and doctrinal. These preachers were the authors of the 27 NT books. Of less literary diversity than the much larger collection of writings received by the Church from Israel, the NT contains: epistolary writings—the Pauline corpus (13 Letters + *Hebrews*)—letters addressed to the whole Church, the Catholic or universal Epistles; a genre unique to the NT, the four Gospels; the Acts of Peter and Paul; and an Apocalypse (Rev), a visionary book about God's mysterious activity in the present and in the near future. None of these is the professionally produced work of a litterateur. Paul's early Letters, Gal, 1 & 2 Thes, 1 & 2 Cor, Phil, and Rom, appearing from 49 to 58 A.D., were the writings of a busy preacher, not polished, literary compositions but substitutes for doctrinal and exhortatory addresses that he would have preached, had he been able to be present in the liturgical gatherings of the Churches he addressed. Colossians, Eph, and Phil were sent from prison in Rome (61–63 A.D.) and, again, were substitutes for direct addresses (Eph was probably the work of a Pauline disciple). Hebrews was a written exhortation from a preacher steeped in the OT, someone other than Paul but of his entourage (Apollos?). The synoptic Gospels, Mk, Lk, and Mt, following the outline of the primitive Jerusalem accounts of Jesus' ministry, were based on oral and written sources that developed from the Church's preaching about Christ's life, death, and resurrection. These were arranged, edited, and published, with varying theological aims, for the needs of local Churches (Mk—Rome, *c.*65 A.D.), (Mt—Syria?, *c.*70–85), (Lk—Asia Minor?,*c.*70–85), after the original companions of Jesus began to die off. Luke's Acts appeared when his Gospel did, and carried on his theme that Christ's work was completed by the Spirit empowering preachers to broadcast God's Word, especially Peter and Paul. The Catholic Letters, Jam, 1 Pet, and Jude, were published anywhere from 60 to 100+, 1–3 Jn from 75–85, and were, again, the products of a preaching ministry prevented by time and distance from being exercised in person. Second Peter is pseudepigraphical, late (*c.*120), and was the only NT work that might have been intended to be a literary composition. John's Gospel, still again, the work of a preacher-teacher, who delved deeply into the mystery of the Word made flesh, appeared around 90–100 in its final editing. It followed a broader, probably, more historical, outline of Jesus' ministry, but its basic aim was theological propaganda to meet developing needs rather than history. The revelatory vision of John, the Elder, was apocalyptic in genre, contained the worst Greek of the NT, and was the product of Jewish-Christian prophets and liturgists confirming and exhorting their congregations to bear up under persecution in view of God's coming condemnation of evil and the final establishment of his new Kingdom.

The NT, therefore, is in no way belles lettres, but the record of the preaching of men and women, who from 30 to 100+ A.D., tramped the roads of the E Mediterranean basin, spreading and confirming the Good News of the eternal life offered by God through Jesus, the Lord, and the Holy Spirit. Their language was the common language of their day, interspersed with Hebrew and Aramaic turns of phrase and flavor, for all of them were Jews or under Jewish scriptural influences. Whatever vitality and attractiveness there was in their style and vocabulary came from the urgent, powerful content of the mystery they preached. Through their unpolished messages, delivered with no great, humanly devised skill, God was bearing witness to himself and his love, through Jesus, the crucified Messiah, the power and wisdom of God for those who believe (1 Cor 1.24; 2.1–5). And so, men believed them, not persuaded by flowing rhetoric, but by the pounding staccato of their own hearts, as God-power reached into them through stumbling words. This literature was and remains unique; it transmitted spiritual, eternal life, and still does, sermon after sermon.

[J. F. FALLON]

NEW THOUGHT, a mental healing movement, embracing a number of religious denominations and organizations and enjoying a wide influence outside of any formal organization. The followers of New Thought believe in spiritual healing, the creative power of thought, and mental and physical strength drawn from an inner source. The movement has strong Gnostic overtones. Inner power is generally available only to those who have been initiated into a new pattern of life. The insights available from New Thought are usually seen as a more perfect understanding of the Christian message than that recognized in the historical Churches. In its various forms and tendencies, New Thought has almost universally stressed the immanence of God and denied or ignored his transcendence. Sin, disease, and other human defects are errors of incorrect thinking, rather than realities. The immediate availability of God and the practical application of the force of spiritual thought to the solution of human problems are emphasized. This philosophical monism is drawn largely from Neoplatonic and Oriental thought. The doctrine of immanentism is in most cases avowedly pantheistic. While New Thought generally discusses God in impersonal terms as Life-Principle, it also stresses such personal qualities as his fatherhood and goodness. Although adherents often speak of the unreality of matter, they do not deny the reality of the physical body or other physical objects but maintain that all form is the manifestation of the energy of Mind. Man is regarded as a spiritual being with freedom of choice and with infinite possibilities through the power of constructive thinking in accord with the dictates of the Indwelling Presence in his inner self. While most New Thought groups believe in immortality, and some hold doctrines of reincarnation, the various kinds of New Thought sects are marked by a fundamental this-worldliness. The doctrine of salvation freely given has been transformed to mean assured happiness in the present life for those who are willing to take hold of God's promise. There is no need for repentance, since sin, evil, and suffering are illusory. Jesus Christ becomes simply a symbol of the divine spark in every man. He does not reconcile or redeem but points out that every man is an incarnation of God. His message is an awareness of the consciousness of inner harmony as a source of unlimited blessings. A New Thought group may make considerable use of the Bible, often interpreting its meaning in a secularist or non-Christian sense.

New Thought groups range from the *Unity School of Christianity, whose literature is widely distributed among Christians of different denominations, to such belligerently anti-Christian movements as the *I Am movement and *Psychiana. In origin, New Thought is a secularized *Arminianism. It arose in the U.S. in the decades following the Civil War, when material progress and popularly understood scientific teachings, such as evolution, had unsettled the faith of many Christians. Many of New Thought's most influential prophets, such as Myrtle and Charles *Fillmore, Nona Brooks, and Emma Curtis Hopkins, constructed their eclectic theology as members of the Methodist Church. Others brought to the movement a heritage of mesmerism, spiritualism, or mental healing. Phineas *Quimby, with whom Mary Baker *Eddy was early associated, was a 19th-cent. mental healer who developed some of the ideas later found in Christian Science and New Thought. By the 1880s there were a large number of New Thought groups and associations, some closely allied to Christian Science, others far removed from its teachings. In 1892 an attempt was made to unify these related movements in the International Divine Science Association. The International New Thought Alliance held its first convention at Boston in 1899. Among the many groups in the Alliance have been the Church of Divine Science, the Unity School of Christianity, the Church of the Healing Christ, the Church of Advanced Thought, and the Radiant Life Fellowship. New Thought has always extended beyond any form of organization, and many of its teachings can be found in groups and individuals never formally linked to the International New Thought Alliance.

[R. K. MACMASTER]

NEW YEAR (in ancient religion), the most important religious feast of the year in ancient Mesopotamia, and perhaps throughout the ancient Near East. This fact, verified by archeological discoveries in Mesopotamia, has led to a storm of controversy in biblical studies. Many scholars find copious hints leading to the conclusion that Israel also had its New Year Festival, and that it was the great festival of the year. The crux of the dispute is the explanation of what amounts to a conspiracy of silence in the OT concerning such a feast. In postbiblical Judaism, New Year's Day is an important feast, but it is only given cursory mention in Scripture (Lev 23.24f; Num 29.1–6) without being named. In Mesopotamia New Year was celebrated at the Spring equinox, and was a celebration of the creation: the renewed victory of the Lord of Creation over Chaos; the death and resurrection of the God of Creation. Connected with it was the celebration of the renewed fertility of the earth, the revitalizing of human sexuality; perhaps also the lordship of the Creator God, the enthronement of his anointed earthly vice regent (the king), and the celebration of the nation's history and destiny. Israel would have had a counterpart, according to theory, first in the Spring connected with Mazzoth; and then in the Fall, because of Assyrian or Tyrian influence. The three great feasts of Tishri (September/October): New Year's Day, Atonement, and Tabernacles, are fragments of the one great Israelite feast. The mysterious silence of the OT is offset by the numerous kingship psalms, celebrating the enthronement of Yahweh, with their refrain, ''Yahweh reigns''; the numerous psalms commemorating David, Yahweh's anointed, the covenant with David, and the choice of Zion. Then there are the creation stories placed at the very beginning of the sacred history, which would have played a major part in the Mesopotamian celebration; in Israel they contain an obvious polemic against such New Year's motifs as the tree of life and the fertility cult. The pervasive polemic of the prophets against fertility rites and sacred prostitution, and the generalized hostility toward feasts and festival days, becomes more comprehensible against a background in which pagan New Year's traditions had gained primacy. The efforts of priests and others in exile and later to reinterpret Israel's history and sacred traditions in sharp distinction from the universal nature mysticism may explain the systematic silence. The modern Jewish New Year feast retains the *shofar* and the reading of texts that allude to judgment and the kingship of Yahweh.

[E. J. DILLON]

NEW YEAR, HEBREW FEAST OF THE, see ROSH HA-SHANAH.

NEW YEAR'S DAY, a day that has been variously observed in Christian worship in the West. It was first kept as a day of prayer against pagan practices, probably because the day was marked by riotous pagan celebrations. Later it was established as one of the earliest Marian feasts, and was so celebrated until the Middle Ages. Then, from the time of the Gregorian and Gelasian sacramentaries it was observed as the octave day of Christmas. From this it developed into the Feast of the Circumcision in consequence of the fact that the Gospel read at Mass on the octave day was Lk 2.21. In 1961 the title Octave of the Nativity was restored, and in 1969 the ancient Marian character of the day was revived and its title was changed to Solemnity of Mary, Mother of God. *CHRISTMAS CYCLE.

[N. KOLLAR]

NEW YORK, a Middle Atlantic state admitted to the Union (1788) as one of the original Thirteen States. First explored by Verrazano, who sailed under a French flag (1524), settlement in the area awaited the voyage of Hudson (1609) and the creation of the Dutch colony of New Netherland (1623). The British gained control of the colony (1664) under the direction of the Duke of York, the future James II. The C of E then became the dominant religion, displacing the Dutch Reformed Church. Separation of Church and State did not occur until 1777. The first Catholic missionary in the area was probably Joseph d'Aillon, a Franciscan who visited the Niagara region (1627). Subsequently, the Jesuits served as missionaries to the Indian population. A number of missionaries suffered martyrdom, including René *Goupil (1642), Isaac *Jogues (1646), and John de *Lalande (1646). The Jesuits were forced to leave their Indian missions in 1709, however, and thereafter Catholicism could barely be found in all of New York until the Revolutionary era. By 1808, when the Catholic population had reached 15,000, the Diocese of New York was created. In addition to opening churches, notably St. Patrick's (1815), early bps. like J. *Connolly and J. *Dubois were faced with such problems as *trusteeism and *nativism. The skill of John *Hughes, a Philadelphia priest, in combating the nativist menace, led to his appointment as Dubois' successor (1842). Bp. Hughes continued to resist the nativists, notably during their attack on St. Patrick's Cathedral (1844), but other matters occupied his attention. To help the massive number of immigrants in New York, many of them Irish and German Catholics, he supported the founding of the Irish Emigrant Society and the Emigrant Industrial Savings Bank. He established numerous institutions to meet expanding population needs, including St. John's College and St. Joseph's Seminary. After his efforts to acquire public funds for Catholic schools failed, he opened 38 free schools and academies. Although he had earlier condemned abolition, Hughes publicly worked for the Union cause during the Civil War. He died in 1864, one of the best-known Catholics in America. During his long episcopate New York had been elevated to archdiocesan status (1850). Its suffragan sees are now the Dioceses of Brooklyn, Rockville Centre, Albany, Syracuse, Rochester, Buffalo, and Ogdensburg.

John *McCloskey, who succeeded Hughes, became the first U.S. cardinal (1875). He established 90 new churches, among them a national church for Italians, and formed the Holy Rosary Mission to serve immigrants at Castle Garden. He also opened St. Joseph's Provincial Seminary in Troy, welcomed 16 new religious communities, and supported the New York Foundling Hospital, which was staffed by the Sisters of Charity. McCloskey died in 1885 and was succeeded by Michael A. *Corrigan. The expansion of New York's Catholic immigrant population caused Corrigan to open national churches for the Italians and other non-English speaking Catholics. He doubled the number of Catholic schools in the archdiocese, but rejected such experiments as Abp. John *Ireland's Faribault-Stillwater Plan. Corrigan's conservatism was reflected in numerous conflicts, such as his controversy with Edward *McGlynn, a champion of Henry George's single-tax scheme. Corrigan died in 1902 and his successor, J. M. *Farley, opened Cathedral College as a preparatory seminary (1903) and established more than 100 new churches. During his episcopacy immigration continued; in 1907 alone, 1,285,349 persons, many of them Italian Catholics, came from Europe. Farley welcomed the establishment of the Catholic Foreign Mission Society of America (Maryknoll) in his jurisdiction, and during World War I he founded the New York Catholic War Council to aid in rehabilitation of war victims. At his death in 1918 he was succeeded by P. J. *Hayes. Hayes continued the work of institutional expansion and coordinated the charitable efforts of the archdiocese under the Catholic Charities of the Archdiocese of New York, a procedure imitated later by other dioceses. He also introduced the Catholic Youth Organization into New York (1936).

F. J. *Spellman became the sixth abp. of New York (1938). Considered by many as the major spokesman for the conservative element in the American Catholic Church, Spellman reorganized the archdiocese (esp. its fiscal policies) and supported further institutional growth by establishing more than 30 new churches and numerous schools. He created the office of Co-ordinator of Spanish-Catholic Action to meet the needs of New York's growing Puerto Rican population. As military vicar, Spellman became the superior chaplain to the U.S. armed forces. After Spellman's death, Terence Cooke became archbishop (1968).

In 1976 Catholics numbered 6,378,520 or 34.0% of the total state population. The major Protestant denominations are the United Methodist Church, with 2.9% of the total pop. in 1971, the United Presbyterian Church with 1.8%, the Episcopal Church, with 1.9%; other Protestant Churches comprised 4.8%. The Jewish population was 2,521,755, or 13.8%.

New York has 32 Catholic colleges, with a total enrollment of 51,656 students. There are 193 Catholic high schools in the state, with an enrollment of 120,150 students, 17,500 of whom attend the 75 archdiocesan high schools. More than 369,500 pupils attend New York's 988 Catholic elementary schools; this number includes the 109,223 pupils who attend the 290 Catholic elementary schools in the archdiocese. BIBLIOGRAPHY: D. M. Ellis, *Short History of New York State* (1957); J. T. Smith, *Catholic Church in New York* (2 v., 1905).

[J. L. MORRISON; R. M. PRESTON]

NEW ZEALAND, an autonomous parliamentary state in the S Pacific (103,736 sq mi; pop. [est. 1976] 3,100,000). The two principal islands that constitute New Zealand were annexed by Great Britain in 1840, proclaimed a dominion in 1907, and made an independent member of the British Commonwealth in 1947. Marist Fathers began evangelization in 1838, but the most important figure in the establishment of Catholicity in New Zealand was Thomas Poynton, an Irish layman. The territory became part of the Prefecture Apostolic of Great Oceania in 1829. Four years later there were two vicariates in New Zealand itself. The Diocese of Auckland was created in 1848, and in 1869 Wellington was made an archdiocese with Auckland, Dunedin, and Christchurch as suffragan sees. Mill Hill Fathers, Redemptorists, and several sisterhoods reinforced the Catholic missionaries. By 1910 the number of Catholics reached 130,376; in 1976 the total was 438,545 and these were served by 821 priests, 788 men religious, and 2,189 sisters. New Zealand is predominantly Protestant. In 1966 Anglicans numbered 901,701; Presbyterians 582,976; and Methodists, 186,260. Protestantism in New Zealand takes an active part in the ecumenical movement and in the World Council of Churches. BIBLIOGRAPHY: H. Wright, *New Zealand, 1769–1840. Early Years of Western Contact* (1960); *Bilan du Monde* 2:651–655.

[P. DAMBORIENA]

NEWBATTLE ABBEY, a Cistercian monastery in Midlothian, Scotland, founded in 1140. It was badly damaged in English raids in 1385 and 1548; its abbot subscribed to the Reformed religion in 1560 and secured the property for his son. Its remains have been incorporated into the present Newbattle Abbey College. BIBLIOGRAPHY: S. Cruden, *Scot-*

tish Abbeys (1960) 74–75; D. E. Easson, *Medieval Religious Houses: Scotland* (1957) 65.

[L. J. MACFARLANE]

NEWMAN, BARNETT (1905–). American painter, student at the Art Students League and Cornell Univ., represented in the New American Painting show, New York, N. executed 14 *Stations of the Cross* (1966, Guggenheim) in his geometric abstract style.

[M. J. DALY]

NEWMAN, JOHN HENRY (1801–90), historian, theologian, leader of the *Oxford movement, cardinal. N. was born into a London middle-class family, attended Trinity College, Oxford (1816), became fellow of Oriel (1822), a deacon in the Anglican Church (1824), priest (1825), and vicar of St. Mary's, the Anglican church at Oxford (1828–41). While vicar at St. Mary's N. became the outstanding preacher at Oxford, and his services were attended by students, faculty, and visitors from various parts of England. His carefully prepared sermons based on Scripture and the Church Fathers were later published in a multivolume work called *Parochial and Plain Sermons*. N.'s first significant exposure to RC institutions was in 1832, when he took a cruise with Hurrell Froude, a close friend and associate from Oriel, and became seriously ill in Sicily. During recovery he made several trips to RC shrines and came to know the customs of the RC Church. Returning from this trip, he wrote the famous "Lead Kindly Light." In England he found a lively debate going on in Parliament regarding the disestablishment of the Anglican Church. N. and his associates undertook the publication of a number of unsigned tracts, eventually 90 in all, of which N. wrote 26, called **Tracts for the Times*. They were designed originally to support the establishment of the Anglican Church and to rebel against what N. saw as growing popery in England. Eventually these tracts took a more ecumenical bent and ceased with the publication of the famous **Tract 90,* which was very pro-Roman Catholic, and was attributed to N. in the popular mind. He became general editor of the *British Critic,* a magazine published in London (1838–41). He resigned this post when he left St. Mary's as vicar and went to Littlemore with a group of associates to found a small community living according to a religious rule. His departure from St. Mary's was marked by the famous sermon "Parting of Friends." N. became more and more interested in the RC Church, and in 1845 he began preparations for the publication of his *Essay on the Development of Christian Doctrine,* one of the truly pioneering theological works of the past 300 years. With sadness he came to realize that the C of E had become a captive of that rationalism he opposed all his life. In 1845 he asked to be received into the RC Church, leaving Oxford with such agony as cannot be described. This action, undertaken only as a personal fulfillment, led to a movement to Catholicism by thousands over the ensuing 100 years.

It is essential to any understanding of N. to realize that his approach to the liberalism of England and Europe generally was based on a clear apprehension of the skeptical mind and an even clearer realization of how far from truth of mankind it was. Because he had gone through an evolution of thought from the excesses of intellectualism to profound faith, he was par excellence the fitting interpreter of what faith meant to the reasoning mind in the 19th century. It was this delicate balance between reasoning and faith which made N. so mysterious to the standard Catholic theologian of his day.

N. became a RC convert in 1845 and shortly thereafter his *Essay* on development was published. His group moved from Littlemore to the old Oscott College on the invitation of Card. Wiseman. In 1846 N. went to the College of Propaganda in Rome and there for less than a year was exposed to systematic RC theology. He was ordained a RC priest in 1847 and returned to Birmingham to found the first Oratory in England. Frederick W. Faber, a member of his community, later founded the Oratory at London. In 1852, upon the publication of *The Present Position of Catholics in England,* designed to calm the antipapal feeling that had been aroused by the restoration of the Catholic hierarchy (1850), N. was sued by a former Dominican priest, Giacinto Achilli, for libel since he was mentioned in the original publication of this work. N. lost the case and had court costs of approximately £12,000 which were paid by friends.

Newman was invited to establish a Catholic university in Dublin and worked for years on an undertaking doomed to failure because of the lack of support of the Irish bishops. Out of this time came a book, *The Idea of a University,* one of the most brilliant expositions of the nature of higher education in any language. Other attempts by N. to take his rightful place as a voice for English Catholicism were equally unsuccessful and N. resigned himself in great sadness to a life of frustration.

Two notable examples of the seeming effort to reduce him to impotence were the Oxford chaplaincy and his espousal of the liberal Catholic periodical *The Rambler*. N. as a long-time Oxonian realized that if Catholics were to maintain an intellectual parity with other Englishmen, they would have to attend Oxford or Cambridge. He believed it essential to establish a Catholic center at Oxford to offset the general irreligious thrust of that university. As happened so often, the project which N. saw as beneficial to the Catholics of England was judged harmful and the bishops condemned the presence of Catholics at Oxford and that ended the prospect of N.'s returning to his loved university. *The Rambler* was a liberal Catholic review that incurred the displeasure of many clerics and Catholic laymen under its lay editorship. N. reluctantly agreed to serve as editor but soon was forced to give up under pressure of Bp. Ullathorne and others who regarded the periodical as of dubious orthodoxy.

In 1863 the novelist Charles Kingsley unwittingly rescued N. by a gratuitous attack on his devotion to truth. The man who had given up everything and found only misunderstanding because he loved the truth answered in one of the great autobiographies of the language, *Apologia pro vita sua* (1864). It was a national success and brought both Anglicans and Catholics back to his side. He published his *Grammar of Assent* in 1870, during the time of Vatican Council I. N. was invited by Pope Pius IX to attend the council but received permission to stay in Birmingham and care for the problems of the Oratory. N. was not strongly in favor of the definition of papal infallibility at Vatican Council I because he thought it inopportune. After the definition, however, he gave it public support.

In 1874 the former Prime Minister, Gladstone, wrote a strong attack on the decrees of Vatican Council I in which he declared that they were an absolutist repudiation of moderate Catholic theology fatal to the organic life of the Church. The Gladstone charge, leveled at extremists in the Church, gave N. an opportunity to speak for moderates like himself. His ''Letter to the Duke of Norfolk,'' filled with a spirit of loyalty to Rome but critical of extreme statements by some Catholic writers, won N. the approval of most thoughtful Catholics.

Wearied and saddened by the vagaries of his experience as a Catholic, N. awaited death. In 1879, however, at the request of a number of Catholic laymen, Leo XIII created him a cardinal. When he received the news he exclaimed, ''The cloud has lifted from me forever.''

N. was a true religious genius who brought to RC theology a psychological and historical dimension that was lacking because of its strong scholastic, systematic orientation. The direction of the Church since Vatican Council II was outlined 100 years earlier by Newman. *The Development of Christian Doctrine, The Idea of a University, The Grammar of Assent* and N.'s position on papal infallibility have all been completely vindicated in the 20th century. He was an original thinker who produced many books and during the course of his life wrote more than 20,000 letters. His work has been appreciated more fully in Germany and France than in the English-speaking world, although his influence is constantly growing. BIBLIOGRAPHY: *Collected Works* (25 v., 1890–1927); *Letters and Diaries of John Henry Newman* (ed. C.S. Dessain, 1961–); M. Trevor, *Newman: The Pillar of the Cloud* (1962); *idem, Newman: Light in Winter* (1963); W. Ward, *Life and Times of John Henry Cardinal Newman* (1912, repr. 1970); P. Misner, *Papacy and Development: Newman and the Primacy of the Pope* (1976).

[J. P. WHELAN; J. R. AHERNE]

NEWMAN APOSTOLATE, now Catholic *campus ministry, an apostolate to the Catholic college and university community. The Newman Movement had a number of unique elements in the history of ministry and service of the Catholic Church in the United States: it was native to the Church in the United States; a new phenomena in the history of missionary activity in the Catholic Church; began and was developed through the initiative of young Catholic laymen. In 1893 a group of Catholic medical and dental students at the Univ. of Pennsylvania began to meet regularly under the leadership of James Harrington to discuss the Christian moral stance in their chosen professions and recruited priests in the Philadelphia area to meet with them and to direct their reading and study. Fr. P. J. Garvey of St. James parish actively helped them. Even though Card. J. H. *Newman had been dead only 3 years and was still the center of unresolved dissension and controversy, this group called themselves the Newman Society. Within the next decade a number of other groups came into existence, and applied the Newman goals to all academic disciplines. The Newman Society gradually created its own identity at non-Catholic colleges and universities, state and private. Most of the societies were in the Philadelphia and New York area, but extended to other schools along the East Coast. Some gained official, but most unofficial recognition from local chancery offices. They always were under the part-time guidance of a local pastor who volunteered and was recruited to serve as chaplain, spiritual advisor, and study director. As early as 1904 groups of similar nature were springing up in the Midwest and West. By 1906, Newman Society groups existed in the ''Big Ten'' area, e.g., at Purdue, Indiana, Wisconsin, Iowa Univ. and Iowa State Univ. and a number of others had formed themselves into a loose federation. They began to hold annual meetings to support each other, share problems, and give encouragement and direction. Newman groups spread to the West, to Colorado Univ. in 1908 and about the same time, to Univ. of California at Berkeley, Stanford, and a number of other schools along the West Coast. Diocesan, Paulist, Dominican, Benedictine priests were all involved in the development and growth of these groups, almost all on a part-time basis, with or without the expressed permission of the local ordinary.

Newman constitutions and by-laws had a number of common elements: their objective was to develop the spiritual, intellectual, and social activities of their members; membership was open to all Catholics, and also to non-Catholics willing to take part in and support the stated goals. Only Catholic members were eligible to hold major offices. The Newman Club movement existed in most of the larger non-Catholic colleges and universities by the mid 1920s. Through the 30s, they were either independent or related in a loose organization, sometimes recognized by the local chancery and sometimes not. They were always important to the question of Catholic attendance at non-Catholic schools.

In the early 40s, the Newman Movement was placed under the National Catholic Welfare Conference office of Catholic Youth and was recognized as the Newman Student Federation, with a part-time student executive secretary with a desk in the NCWC Youth Deptartment. The End of World War II brought a dramatic growth in college student population and a parallel growth in the Newman Movement. Equally dramatic was the gradual acceptance on the part of the Catholic hierarchy and the appointment of large numbers of full-time Newman Club chaplains. However, from 1946 through the 1950s, the stated vocation of the clerical Newman chaplains was the protection of the faith of the Catholic student and the protection of the Catholic student from the influence of the secular campus. During the 60s, a change gradually took place. The Newman Club chaplains formed themselves into the Newman Chaplains' Association and began to formulate and implement a philosophy of the "Ministry of Christian Faith to the Total Learning Community of the Secular Campus." Gradually the following five groups became identified: Newman Student Associations, Newman Alumni Association; John Henry Newman Honorary Society; The Newman Foundation (fund raising); Newman Chaplains Association. During this period, religious women joined the ranks of the Chaplains Association and were recognized as part of the ministry vocation of the Chaplains.

In 1969 and 1970, the current form of the apostolate of the Church to the secular campus took shape. The Newman Student Association ceased to exist. The inter-diocesan organization of 13 provinces gave way to a strictly diocesan organization of the apostolate under the leadership of diocesan directors appointed by the local ordinary; they are organized under the umbrella of the director of USCC Dept. of Education campus ministry and young adults in the office of the National Conference of Catholic Bishops in Washington, D.C. The Newman Chaplain Association was changed to the Catholic Campus Ministry Association with membership open to chaplains of Catholic colleges and universities; it has a working relationship with the National Campus Ministry Assoc., and with denominational associations of college and university chaplains.

[C. FORSYTH]

NIBELUNGENLIED, THE, most important medieval German heroic epic, composed *c.*1200 in the so-called *Nibelungenstrophe* by an unidentified author, probably an Austrian cleric. Though couched in Christian and courtly terms, the epic is more closely related, in content and ethos, to the heroic sagas of the migration period (*c.*375–500). Scholars conjecture, as the most probable source of its 39 *Âventiuren* (cantos), two alliterative lays of the 5th or 6th cent., a *Brünhildlied* and a *Burgundenlied*. *The Nibelungenlied* is preserved in 33 MSS, most of which also contain a sequel of later composition, *Die Klage*. For discussion and text in English, see *Song of the Nibelungs* (tr. F. G. Ryder, 1962); for bibliog., see W. Kosch, *Deutsches Literatur-Lexikon* (1963) 296–298.

[M. F. MCCARTHY]

NICAEA I, COUNCIL OF, the first ecumenical council (325), condemned *Arianism and promulgated the original *Nicene Creed. Disturbed by the turmoil in the empire caused by the controversy between *Arius and his bp., Alexander of Alexandria, Constantine sought to silence both principals. When these efforts proved unsuccessful, Constantine convoked a general synod of the most important bps. of the Roman world. He did all in his power to arouse the interest of the Western bps., but of the *c.* 300 who assembled there, all but three or four were Eastern. Pope St. Sylvester I was represented by legates, setting a common precedent. The majority needed to condemn Arius was easy to muster. Even the moderate subordinationists of *Origen's tradition were opposed to Arius's radical doctrine, and these were leagued with (1) conservatives opposed to any expression of dogma in nonbiblical terms, (2) Alexander, *Athanasius, and other doctrinaire antisubordinationists, and (3) ultrareactionary *Sabellianists. Arius and few followers, with their allies the *Syllucianists, were defeated, and Nicaea proclaimed Jesus Christ "true God of true God, begotten not made, consubstantial (**homoousios*) with the Father." Negatively, the Council unequivocally condemned Arianism; positively, it affirmed the Son's full divinity and equality with the Father, out of whose being he was derived and whose nature he consequently shared. But the crisis did not come to an end with the closing of the Council. Arianism was driven underground only to emerge in the form of *Semi-Arianism.

The Council also resolved the *Easter Controversy in favor of celebrating Easter on the Sunday following the first full moon after the vernal equinox, the formula still in use today. It also promulgated 7 canons and 20 disciplinary decrees, the most notable probably being cc. 6 and 7 granting bps. of certain very important sees some jurisdiction over bps. of less important neighboring sees, thus canonizing the antecedents of patriarchal jurisdiction (see PATTRIARCH). BIBLIOGRAPHY: Fliche-Martin 3:69–176; J. N. D. Kelly, *Early Christian Creeds* (2d ed. 1960).

[R. R. BARR]

NICAEA II, COUNCIL OF (787), the seventh ecumenical council of the Church and the last to be recognized by the Eastern Church. It condemned Iconoclasm and restored the veneration of icons. When Empress Irene assumed power in 780 in the name of her son Constantine VI, still a minor, she had already decided to restore the cult of images forbidden by the previous iconoclastic emperors. She appointed her secretary Tarasius as patriarch, informed Pope Adrian I that she was planning to convoke a general council, and requested him to send representatives. With two papal legates and some 350 Byzantine bps., the council began in Constantinople, but had to be transferred to Nicaea after some of the imperial guard broke into the church. The patriarch presided, and the legates signed all the documents first. Basing its argumentation on Scripture and the Fathers, the Council established the legitimacy of the veneration of icons and drew a distinction between the worship properly belonging to God alone and the attitude of reverent devotion that may be taken toward images. Twenty-two canons were appended to this dogmatic definition. The decree of faith was solemnly signed by the Empress and the Roman legates. The council was not recognized as ecumenical until

843. BIBLIOGRAPHY: G. Fritz, DTC 11.1:417–441; Fliche-Martin 6:107–120.

[P. FOSCOLOS]

NICARAGUA, a Central American republic reaching from the Carib. Sea to the Pacific Ocean between Honduras and Costa Rica (57,143 sq mi; pop. [est. 1974] 2,080,000; ethnic distribution: mixed 70%, white 17%, Negro 9%, Indian 4%). The Carib. coast of Nicaragua was discovered by Columbus on his fourth voyage (1502). It was explored by Gil González de Ávila (1552) and by Francisco Fernández de Córdoba (1523) who founded the town of León, which was to become the most important cultural center between Mexico City and Lima. In the 16th cent. the settlements were subject to attack, and sometimes to friendly visits, by Dutch, British, and French freebooters. British settlements on the Mosquito Coast along the Carib. led to England's claim until 1786 of the territory as a British protectorate. The country declared its independence in 1821 and was part of Iturbide's short-lived Mexican Empire (1821–23). From 1823 it was joined with its neighboring countries in the Central American Federation until 1838, when that union broke up and N. became fully independent. Great rivalry existed between the conservatives, centered at Granada, and the liberals whose stronghold was León. Managua was chosen as a compromise capital in 1855. There was much U.S. intervention in Nicaragua between 1912 and 1933. From 1936 until 1963 the chief political power of the country was the Somoza family. Nicaragua was evangelized by the Franciscans, Mercedarians, Hospitallers, and Dominicans. The first episcopal see (León) was created in 1526. Missionary effort on the Pacific Coast began in 1689 under Fray Margil de Jesús. In the 18th cent. the Church enjoyed its most prosperous era. Many parishes were developed, education went forward, a seminary was established. The educational program suffered much from the suppression of the Jesuits. In 1861 a concordat with the Holy See gave the State the power of episcopal presentation. During the period 1893–1904 much anti-Catholic legislation was enacted. The Church was disestablished, religious orders were suppressed, and many of the clergy were exiled. In 1912 Nicaragua was made an ecclesiastical province; the constitutions of 1911, 1939, and 1950 grant full freedom of religion and deny any official religion to the State, but *de facto* Catholicism is the religion of the majority. A certain amount of hostility still shows itself against the Church from time to time, most recently in restrictions and abuses of the Jesuits. The episcopal sees are Managua (archbishopric), Estelí, Grenada, León, Matagalpa. Bluefields is a vicariate apostolic and Juigalpa a prelacy *nullius*. In 1976 there were 299 priests, 110 of whom were diocesan; 288 male and 652 female religious. There is a Catholic univ. at Managua and progress is being made in secondary schools. Among the chief needs of the Church in Nicaragua are more native vocations, better religious instruction for the masses, and a quickening of interest in social problems. Among the Protestant bodies active in Nicaragua are the Moravians who have been working with the Mosquito Indians from 1849. The Central American Mission, the National Baptist Convention, and the Mormons are also represented. The total Protestant community numbers about 80,000, or 4% of the population.

[P. DAMBORIENA]

NICCOLÒ ALBERGATI, see ALBERGATI, NICCOLÒ, BL.

NICCOLÒ DELL'ARCA (Niccolò da Bari; 1435–94), Italian sculptor from Apulia active in Bologna (1463). His greatest work is a terra-cotta *Lamentation* group (1485–90) emotionally intense in drapery and gestures. N. is called ''Dell'Arca'' for his carving of the cover for N. Pisano's *Arca of St. Dominic,* and a unique series of statuettes (begun 1469) with their weighty drapery and expressive realism point to C. Sluter. BIBLIOGRAPHY: J. Pope-Hennessy, *Italian Renaissance Sculpture* (1958).

[M. J. DALY]

NICCOLÒ DA BARI, see NICCOLÒ DELL'ARCA.

NICCOLÒ DA CORTE (Corti, Curti; d. 1552), Italian sculptor, student in Milan, working in the cathedral of Genoa (1533–35) and on decorations of the Alhambra, Granada, Spain (1537).

[M. J. DALY]

NICCOLÒ (NICOLA) DA GUARDIAGRELE (Niccolò d'Andrea di Pasquale Galucci; 1395?–1462), Italian goldsmith and painter from Abruzzi. N. was a master of silver processional crosses (St. John Lateran, Rome, 1451) and executed an important altar panel in silver relief for Teramo cathedral (1433–48).

[M. J. DALY]

NICCOLÒ OF MODENA CATHEDRAL (fl. 1100), Italian sculptor known from inscriptions on Ferrara and Verona cathedral portals. He worked at Modena where he assisted and was influenced by his master teacher, Guglielmo da Modena, whose style derived from French Romanesque.

[M. J. DALY]

NICENE CREED, most properly the creed formulated by the Council of Nicaea (325), but in ordinary usage a later creed, the one used in the RC Mass and the liturgies of other Churches, called also since the 17th century the Niceno-Constantinopolitan Creed. The convention of designating the first as N and the second as C is followed in this article.

Creed of Nicaea (N). The Council was held to deal with Arianism. The creed is notable for being the first explicitly designed as a test of orthodoxy and for its application to Christ of the nonbiblical term *homoousion* (of one substance with the Father). It is the work of a commission of bps. who added anti-Arian, Nicene phrases to an extant Syro-Palestinian baptismal creed. The theory that N was based on a creed presented by Eusebius of Caesarea is no longer tenable. This creed ends with the simple phrase "And in the Holy Spirit," then anathemas against the Arians are added. N was also formally affirmed by the Councils of Ephesus (431) and Chalcedon (451). With C it is one of the rules of faith acknowledged by all of the Eastern Churches.

Niceno-Constantinopolitan Creed (C). The text of N was not literally the basis for the formulation of C; the two differ too much, not only by the addition in C of articles after that on the Holy Spirit and by the absence of the anathemas of N, but in language and style throughout. Doctrinally C is "Nicene," conformed to the faith of Nicaea, but elaborating the articles on the Son (against the Apollinarians) and on the Holy Spirit (against the Macedonians). It is called Constantinopolitan since the acts of the Council of Chalcedon (451), the primary source of the text, declare that it is the creed of the 150 fathers of the Council of Constantinople I (381). J. F. A. Holt (*Two Dissertations,* 1876) and A. Harnack (see EncRelKnow 3:256–260) denied this origin: the text of C antedated 381, and there is silence before Chalcedon on the promulgation of any symbol by Constantinople. Modern scholarship, however, is more inclined to accept the Chalcedonian tradition, while admitting that the Constantinopolitan fathers adopted C, as supplementing N against current heresies, from some existing baptismal formula (see Kelly; Bihlmeyer-Tüchle 1:258). With acceptance of Constantinople as an ecumenical council, C gained recognition in the East, both as authoritative teaching and as a liturgical formula in baptism and the Eucharist. It remains a primary rule of faith in the Eastern Churches, without, of course, the filioque, the affirmation that the Holy Spirit proceeds also from the Son, which was added in the West, where C came to be recognized in the 6th century. The Council of Toledo (589) ordered it sung at Mass. The practice spread from Spain and Gaul, but was not adopted at Rome until 1014. In the RC Church, as the profession of faith made at Mass, and as formally affirmed by the Council of Trent (D 1500), C is of the highest authority. The *Formula of Concord and the *Thirty-Nine Articles of Religion explicitly acknowledge it; the majority of Protestant Churches accept it, although liturgically it is used mainly by Lutherans and Anglicans. Of all creeds C alone is truly an *ecumenical creed accepted by East and West alike. Since the *Lambeth quadrilateral (1886) it holds a central place in modern discussions of Christian unity. BIBLIOGRAPHY: J. W. D. Kelly, *Early Christian Creeds* (2d ed., 1960); F. X. Murphy, NCE 4:434–437.

[T. C. O'BRIEN]

NICEPHORUS II PHOCAS (912–969), BYZANTINE EMPEROR from 963, great military emperor. He restored the imperial power in the Eastern Mediterranean and surrounding lands in the 10th cent. and inaugurated the Byzantine era in the East. A descendant of a distinguished Cappadocian family of soldiers and landowners, he was named commander-in-chief of the armies of the East (954–955) under Constantine VII, commander of the expedition to liberate Crete (960–61) under Romanus II, as emperor recovered Cilicia and Cyprus, and overran Syria. He was crowned by Patriarch Polyeuctus in Hagia Sophia and married Theophano, the widowed mother of, and acting regent for, Basil II and Constantine VIII. He proved to be no match for the political intrigue of Constantinople. He was murdered in the fortified palace of Boukoleion December 969 by agents of a conspiracy that included his wife and former friends. His name means "Bringer of Victory"; the Byzantines named him Kallinikos, artisan of good victories; the Arabs called him Nikfour, the Saracen Hammer. He was celebrated in poetry, beatified by the Church, and venerated by the monks of Mt. Athos as the martyred emperor, as well as their benefactor and founder; his sarcophagus bears the telling inscription: "You conquered all but a woman."

[E. J. DILLON]

NICEPHORUS I, PATRIARCH OF CONSTANTINOPLE (*c.* 758–828), Byzantine historian, theologian, and anti-Iconoclast. He served as imperial secretary and in that capacity attended the Council of *Nicaea II. In 806 he was appointed patriarch but shortly afterwards was coerced into reinstating Joseph, the priest who had approved the adulterous marriage of Constantine VI, son of the Empress *Irene. This brought him into disfavor with the Studite monks, but N. united with *Theodore of Studius in order to oppose Emperor Leo V ("the Armenian") over *Iconoclasm. N.'s resistance to Leo brought about his own exile in 815. His writings on the Iconoclast controversy include the *Apologeticus major* and *minor, Libri tres antirhetikoi*, as well as the Byzantine history, *Breviarium Nicephori*, covering the years 602–770. BIBLIOGRAPHY: P. J. Alexander, *The Patriarch Nicephorus of Constantinople* (1958); PG 100:201–850; *London Manuscript of Nicephoros "Breviarium"* (ed. L. Orosz, 1948).

[F. T. RYAN]

NICEPHORUS BLEMMYDES (1197–1272), Byzantine monk and theologian. He took part in theological discussions with the Latins, in which he argued against the union of the Churches so energetically that negotiations failed. Later, however, he took a more conciliatory position toward the Latins. His chief work is his autobiography (1264), in which he sets forth his theological views. He also wrote commentaries, scholia on the Psalms, an encomium of St. John the Evangelist, a dissertation on Johannine theology, and philosophical tracts. BIBLIOGRAPHY: V. Grumel, DTC 11.1:441–445; Beck, 671–673.

[P. FOSCOLOS]

NICEPHORUS CALLISTUS, see XANTHOPULUS, NICEPHORUS CALLISTUS.

NICEPHORUS GREGORAS (1295–*c.*1359), Byzantine historian. Born in Heracleia Pontica, he was educated in Constantinople, where he was an excellent student. He was imprisoned for some time because of his struggle against *Hesychasm. He is known mainly for his *Roman History* (modern ed., 3 v., ed. L. Schopen and I. Bekker, 1829–55) on the period 1204–1359, which contains information on the theology of that period.

[J. R. RIVELLO]

NICETAS CHONIATES (1140–1213), also called **ACOMINATOS,** Byzantine historian and theologian. He was the younger brother of Michael Choniates, metropolitan of Athens. He rose to high rank in the imperial service, becoming Grand Logothete under the Emperor Isaac II Angelus. Following the capture of Constantinople by the Crusaders (1204), he withdrew to the court of Theodore Lascaris at Nicaea and devoted himself to writing. His *History* or *Chronicle* in 21 books covers the period 1116–1206. In its reliability and brilliant description, it is second in quality only to the work of Psellus. His *Treasury of Orthodoxy* in 27 books deals with the history of heresies and the religious controversies of his age. It is in large part a new edition of the *Dogmatic Panoply* of Euthymius Zigabenes, but it incorporates much new material and is a valuable source for the history of Byzantine theology in the 12th century. Books 17–22 were apparently not composed by Nicetas, but are probably to be assigned to Theodore Skytariotes, a deacon of Cyzicus. BIBLIOGRAPHY: Beck 663–664; L. Pêtit, DTC 14.1:316–318.

[M. R. P. MCGUIRE]

NICETAS DAVID (fl. 913–963), anti-Photian writer. Nicetas of Paphlago, as rhetor at Constantinople, wrote his most important work, the life of the patriarch Ignatius, which attacked Photius for extreme political ambition. N. took the name David when he became a monk. His other writings include homilies and hagiographical works. BIBLIOGRAPHY: F. Dvornik, NCE 10:439–440.

NICETAS OF REMESIANA, ST. (d. *c.*414), missionary bp. and ecclesiastical writer. His friend, Paulinus of Nola, celebrated two of his visits to Italy in song and thus provided the principal source of information about N. that has survived. He became bp. (*c.*370) of Remesiana (Bela Palanka in Yugoslavia) on the Roman road between Belgrade and Constantinople and enjoyed great success in converting and taming the wild tribes. His writings, many of which were early attributed to Nicetas of Aquileia and Nicetius of Trier, have recently been made the object of closer study. The most valuable is a partially preserved manual of instruction for catechumens, with important chapters on faith, the Holy Spirit, and the Creed. He is among the earliest writers who gave specific witness to the doctrine of the Communion of Saints. At the end of the last cent., Dom Morin presented evidence that it was Nicetas and not Ambrose and/or Augustine who composed the *Te Deum*. This opinion is not accepted by all scholars. BIBLIOGRAPHY: M. R. P. McGuire, NCE 10:440; G. Bosio, BiblSanct 9:893–897; A. E. Burn, *Niceta of Remesiana, His Life and Works* (1901); *idem, Te Deum and Its Author* (1926).

[F. J. MURPHY]

NICETAS STETHATOS (the Lionhearted; *c.*1000–*c.*1080), Byzantine polemicist in the Eastern Schism, mystical writer. He was a monk of the monastery of Studion and became known as the Lionhearted because of his castigation of the licentious life of Constantine III. N.'s polemic included attacks against the Lat. use of the *filioque and unleavened bread in his *Dialexis, Antidialogus,* and *Synthesis against the Latins* (modern ed. by A. Michel, 2 v. 1924–30). His mystical writings consist of a life and collection of the works of *Symeon, the New Theologian, a treatise on the soul, and the *Spiritual Paradise*.

[T. C. O'BRIEN]

NICETIUS OF TRIER, ST. (d. 566), Benedictine abbot at Limoges; called to be bishop of Trier from *c.*525 by King Theodoric I. N. built up the diocese both materially and in discipline. He outspokenly censured the immorality of Kings Theodebert and Clotaire. There are extant letters both to the Lombard Queen Clodiswind and to Emperor Justinian I in Constantinople.

[T. C. O'BRIEN]

NICHOLAS I THE GREAT, ST. (d. 867), **POPE** from 858. Son of a civil official in the papal curia, N. himself was in the papal service under Benedict III, his predecessor in the papacy. The Emperor Louis II personally took part in N.'s election and assisted at his coronation. For his Greek secretary N. took *Anastasius the Librarian whom the Emperor had supported briefly as antipope in 855. N. was a strong pope who did much to establish the independent authority of the papacy. Early in his reign he renewed the decree of 769 which forbade non-Romans, including imperial envoys, to interfere in the papal election. John, abp. of Ravenna and friend of the Emperor, was deposed for misgovernment, and Louis's blandishments could do nothing to shake N.'s decision. He was equally firm with regard to the marriage of the Emperor's brother, Lothair II of Lorraine. He refused to yield to the wishes of the Frankish bps. and the council of Metz (863), and even a combined army led by both kings at the gates of Rome did not prevail upon N. to sanction the adulterous union. The siege was lifted and Lothair took back his defamed wife. N. was involved, perhaps less felicitously, in the beginnings of the Greek Schism. Ignatius, Patriarch of Constantinople, was deposed by the Emperor Michael III and Photius was appointed to fill his place. To N. the appointment appeared illegal, for he did not know of the resignation of Ignatius. N. anathematized Photius and declared Ignatius restored to his see (863). When the Pope encouraged the newly converted Bulgars who desired to be under the jurisdiction of Rome rather than Constantinople, relations between East and West suffered further deterioration (866). Photius responded by having N.'s name struck from the diptychs, an act tantamount to excommunication, and he declared the Pope deposed. N. replied with a famous letter on the primacy of Rome in which he declared the primatial rights of the Roman Church to be of divine origin (PL 119:926–962). The crisis was temporarily lulled when Photius himself was removed from office (867). N. took a great interest in the missionary work that was going forward in N Europe. He encouraged the preaching of St. *Ansgar, apostle to Scandinavia and sought to promote the conversion of the Slavs. BIBLIOGRAPHY: Mann 3:1–148; F. Dvornik, *Photian Schism* (1948); ''Patriarch Photius and the Roman Primacy'' *Chicago Studies* 2 (1963) 94–107.

[P. F. MULHERN]

NICHOLAS II (Gerard; d. 1061), **POPE** from 1058. Bishop of Florence from 1045, he was suddenly thrust by political circumstances into a struggle for the papal throne. At the death of Stephen IX in Florence (1058), the Tusculan family of Rome proclaimed Card. John of Velletri as Benedict X. Unacceptable to the reform curia and to the German court, Benedict's promotion was opposed by the election of Nicholas in Siena. Duke Godfrey of Tuscany's force installed him in Rome, where Nicholas was crowned in January 1059, after Benedict had fled. In April at a synod in Rome, Nicholas regularized the procedure of papal elections by placing them primarily in the hands of the cardinal bishops. The thrust of the election decree, authored in part by *Peter Damian, was leveled at the Tusculani and their candidate and not at the German court. Only some 30 years later was a spurious ''imperial'' version devised. Nicholas maintained the pace of papal reform begun by Leo IX by opposing simony, clerogamy, and lay influence in proprietary churches, and by normalizing marriage legislation regarding impediments. He reversed the anti-Norman policy of his predecessors, recognizing Robert Guiscard's conquests in exchange for his support of a reforming papacy. A legation to Milan in 1059, led by Peter Damian and Anselm of Lucca (later Alexander II), extended papal authority; but in 1061 Nicholas's synodal action was opposed by Anno II of Cologne, leading to further schism that broke out at his death. BIBLIOGRAPHY: A. Michel, *Papstwahl und Königsrecht* (1936); H. G. Krause, *Das Papstwahldekret von 1059* (1960); K. M. Woody, *Damiani and the Radicals* (diss. 1966); W. M. Plöchl, NCE 10:441–442, bibliog.

[O. J. BLUM]

NICHOLAS III, (Giovanni Gaetano Orsini; betw. 1210 and 1220, d. 1280), **POPE** from 1277. A member of the powerful Roman Guelf family, N. became a cardinal in 1244. His pontificate was occupied with attempts to resolve four major problems facing the 13th-cent. papacy: the schism between Rome and Constantinople; the division of the Franciscans into Conventual and Spiritual wings; the struggle between the Angevins and the Habsburgs for control of Sicily; and the creation of an adequate administrative structure for the papal lands. BIBLIOGRAPHY: Mann 16:57–166; D. P. Waley, *Papal State in the 13th Century* (1961).

[J. MULDOON]

NICHOLAS IV (Girolamo Masci; 1227–92) **POPE** from 1288. A Franciscan, N. had been minister general of his order (1274), cardinal (1278) and bp. of Palestrina (1281), before becoming the first Franciscan pope. He reflected his order's interests in his encouragement of missionary activities in Persia, China, and Ethiopia. His pontificate also saw the first attempt to create a coherent policy for administering the Papal States and to end the constant civil disorder caused by feuding political factions. BIBLIOGRAPHY: Mann 17:1–246; D. P. Waley, *Papal State in the 13th Century* (1961).

[J. MULDOON]

NICHOLAS V (Tommaso Parentucelli; 1397–1455), **POPE** from 1447. He was a Ligurian, for 20 years the factotum of the saintly Niccolò Albergati, bp. of Bologna, whom he succeeded in that see, and whose name he took on his election as pope. His election inaugurated a splendid period in the history of Rome, a Renaissance decorated with the frescoes of Fra Angelico, and not yet tarnished with later crimes and abuse. His project was to rebuild the Leonine City: he did strengthen the fortifications, restore the water supply, the Acqua Trevi, and founded the Vatican Library. He was served by legates of first-rate quality—Nicholas of Cusa in N Germany, St. John Capistran in S Germany, and William d'Estouteville in France. He crowned the Habsburg Frederick III, the last of the emperors to be crowned in Rome (1452). But all the glory of the reign was overshadowed by the fall of Constantinople to the Turks, and Nicholas died in gloom because of his failure to rally Christendom to its defense. BIBLIOGRAPHY: J. Toews, ''Formative Forces in the Pontificate of Nicholas V, 1447–1455,'' CHR 54 (1968) 261–284.

NICHOLAS V (Peter da Corbara; d. 1333), **ANTIPOPE** (r. 1328–30), an obscure Franciscan friar of the *Spirtuals branch that Pope John XXII, living in Avignon, was oppressing; associated with Emperor Louis IV the Bavarian who was also engaged in a controversy with the Pope. In 1328 Louis occupied Rome and on May 12 procured the irregular election of Peter as Pope Nicholas V. His cause was zealously promoted by Franciscan and Augustinian friars in a number of Italian cities, and with some success. When Louis left Rome after a few months, N. had to flee also. After some activity in N Italy he gave up his schism and submitted to John XXII on Aug. 25, 1330. He died in Avignon 3 years later. BIBLIOGRAPHY: G. Mollat, *The Popes at Avignon 1305–1378* (tr. J. Love, 1963).

[R. H. SCHMANDT]

NICHOLAS I, EMPEROR OF RUSSIA (1796–1855), r. from 1825. To strengthen Russia's hold over its W borderlands, N. continued earlier governmental policies of oppression of non-Orthodox peoples. In 1839 he dissolved the Union of *Brest and legally incorporated the Uniate or Greek Catholics into the Orthodox Church. The Latin Church in Russian lands saw its religious orders restricted, monasteries suppressed, and property confiscated. N. persuaded Pope Gregory XVI to censure Polish clergy who engaged in anti-Russian activities, thus giving N. a pretext for harassment of Polish Catholics. In 1847 he and the Pope signed a concordat reorganizing the Church's administration in Russian lands, but leaving fundamental problems untouched. BIBLIOGRAPHY: E. Winter, *Russland und das Papsttum*, (3 v., 1960–75); J. J. Zatko, *Descent into Darkness* (1965).

[R. H. SCHMANDT]

NICHOLAS I MYSTICUS, PATRIARCH OF CONSTANTINOPLE (852–925), son of an Italian slave, reared on the estates of Patriarch *Photius, he became secretary (*mysticus*) to Emperor Leo VI and appointed patriarch in 901. He attempted a conciliatory role in the *tetragamy dispute but was deposed in 907, possibly for opposing Leo VI's fourth marriage. Recalled *c.*912 N. became chief regent for the young Constantine VII Porphyrogenitus and took revenge on *Euthymius I who had been patriarch during his exile. The conflict divided the Byzantine Church into the opposing Nicholaite and Euthymian factions. Before Euthymius's death (917) N. brought about reconciliation, and in 920 published a decree of union that clarified Byzantine marriage law, viz, a second marriage was equivalent to a first, a third required dispensation, and a fourth was sinful. Another opposition faction turned to Rome for support against N., and Pope John X sent legates whose visit to Byzantium brought a final settlement to the Nicholaite-Euthymian conflict. BIBLIOGRAPHY: PG 111:9–392; K. Baus, LTK 7:995

[F. T. RYAN]

NICHOLAS III, PATRIARCH OF CONSTANTINOPLE from 1084 to 1111. He had been a monk at Prodromas. During his patriarchate he was active in internal church reform and also in reestablishing relations with Rome, but was unwilling to negotiate on the problems of Roman primacy, the *filioque, or use of unleavened bread.

[J. R. RIVELLO]

NICHOLAS OF AARHUS, BL. (*c.*1150–80), Ascetic. The illegitimate son of Canute V Magnusson of Denmark, he became known for his virtuous life, especially his chastity. A process for beatification was inaugurated in 1254, but N. was never formally beatified.

[J. R. RIVELLO]

NICHOLAS OF AUTRECOURT (of Ultracuria; *c.*1300-after 1350), French theologian and philosopher who lectured at the Sorbonne and the Univ. of Paris. N. was a leading opponent of Aristotelianism. He stood trial *c.*1340 for heresy and error under Popes Benedict XII and Clement VI and as a result was banned from further teaching and required to recant certain of his published teachings. His last known date is 1350 when he was serving as a deacon at the cathedral at Metz. His letters to the Franciscan, Bernard of Arezzo, and his treatise, *Exigit ordo executionis*, reflect the ideas that brought on his condemnation. As a disciple of *William of Occam (1280–1349), N. questioned the reasoned demonstrations of Aristotle and the Peripatetics, esp. the doctrines of causality and substance, denying the necessity of arriving at the existence of God as first cause, as final cause, and as the necessary most perfect being. Called the David Hume of the Middle Ages, he adopted an empirical attitude to knowledge that threatened to close the metaphysical approaches to God's existence, struck at the Aristotelian interpretations of matter and the soul, and sought to make faith the only source of knowledge of religious truth. For works see J. R. O'Donnell, "Nicholas of Autrecourt," MedSt, 1 (1939) 179–280, including the *Exigit*. BIBLIOGRAPHY: J. R. Weinberg, *Nicholas of Autrecourt* (1948); J. R. O'Donnell, "Philosophy of Nicholas of Autrecourt and His Appraisal of Aristotle," MedSt 4 (1942) 97–125.

[J. T. HICKEY]

NICHOLAS OF BASEL, (d. *c.*1395), layman, heretical Beghard. Claiming to be divinely inspired, N. first began teaching in the towns of the Rhine Valley. His teachings reflected the millenarian doctrines of the heretical Free Spirits. BIBLIOGRAPHY: E. W. McDonnell, *Beguines and Beghards in Medieval Culture* (1954).

[J. MULDOON]

NICHOLAS BONET, see BONET, NICHOLAS.

NICHOLAS BREAKSPEAR, see ADRIAN IV, POPE.

NICHOLAS OF CLAIRVAUX (d. *c.*1176), monastic author and courtier. Expelled from the abbey of Clairvaux in 1152, he lived at the courts of Adrian IV and of the count of Champagne. He later became prior of St. Jean-en-Châtel in Troyes, and perhaps eventually of Montiéramey. Some 19 sermons, 60 letters, 2 offices, and 10 sequences of his are extant. BIBLIOGRAPHY: I. F. Benton, NCE 10:448 bibliog.

[V. BULLOUGH]

NICHOLAS OF CLAMANGES (Nicholas Poillevilain; *c.*1363–1437), French humanist theologian who taught at Paris from 1381, was papal secretary at Avignon from 1397, and resumed teaching at Paris from 1425. He is noteworthy for the literary style of his theological treatises, the principal of which is his *De studio theologico*; he wrote also on church reform, and on spiritual theology, esp. in his *De fructu eremi* and *De fructu rerum divinarum*.

[T. C. O'BRIEN]

NICHOLAS OF CUSA (Nicholas Krebs or Kryfts; 1401–64), German theologian, philosopher, and mathematician. Born at Cues or Kues on the Moselle, N. studied philosophy at Heidelberg, canon law at Padua, and theology at Cologne. He rose to prominence through a mission to the Council of Basel, where his *De concordantia catholica*, which outlined a comprehensive program of reform for Church and Empire, won him favor because of the conciliarist views he had expressed in it. But his mission to the Council failed, and in disappointment at the Council's procedure and its ineffectiveness in bringing about union between East and West, N. abandoned conciliarism and became a supporter of the papal cause. For the rest of his life he served the Church in a succession of important offices and missions. He was sent by Rome as a commissioner to Constantinople, later served as papal legate to Germany, in 1448 was made a cardinal, and 2 years later became bp. of Brixen (Bressanone). Despite his diplomatic activities, N. retained a great interest in philosophy and theology and continued to write. His most famous work is his *De docta ignorantia* (1440) that sought to show that man's knowledge of God is at best learned ignorance. By that he did not mean to deny it all value but only to make clear its limitations. He had no patience with the Aristotelian logic and dialectic that had dominated Europe from the 13th century. In its place he wanted to substitute a universal synthesis, a Christian Neoplatonist type of structure that emphasized the unity of reality. To this end his works blend theology and philosophy in a manner highly original in content and style, and rich in symbolism, paradox, and mathematical insights and analogies. Although he was indebted to Plotinus for his inspiration, his thought was drawn chiefly from the Neoplatonist tradition in the Church—Augustine, Boethius, Anselm, Bonaventure, Meister Eckhart, and others.

At the core of his thinking is the notion of infinity as the fullness of positive being or perfection that is God—the absolute maximum in which is found the meeting and reconciliation of all the opposites occurring throughout reality. As the maximum, God is not the supreme degree of a finite series, for, as infinite, he is in no relation of proportion to the finite and must therefore be unknown to man because there is no basis for comparison. Not only is he the maximum but he is also the minimum, being at once all extremes and the being in which all opposition is resolved in perfect unity. N. rejected Aristotle's principle of contradiction as an illusion. The recognition of simultaneous contradictories was for N. the beginning of mystical theology. Reality is permeated with the presence of the infinite which is the coincidence of all opposites. Truth comes not through indulging the futility of conceptual distinctions but by means of a progressive overcoming of contradiction through mystical intuition. As the absolute maximum, God contains all things as their source, and all things are but so many moments in the unfolding and explication of the infinite; they are the limited and partial appearances of divine reality and add nothing to it but only reflect it in manifold ways. God transcends the universe but is immanent in it. In creating all things he is all things, whereas creatures, imitating God, participate in his being which they mirror. Yet N.'s position is not pantheistic. The creature is nothing without its mysterious sharing in its cause, yet the Creator transcends his creation.

Just as God is immanent in all reality, so every finite being is present in every other finite being. The entire universe exists in a contracted manner in every species of actual being. Individuals are further contractions of their species. Hence, all beings of creation exist in a unified manner and the universe itself in a state of unity is a contraction of the infinite. Works: Critical edition of the complete Latin works, *Nicolai de Cusa opera* (ed. E. Hoffman, 1936–37); *Vision of God* (tr. E. G. Salter, 1928); *Idiot* (tr. W. R. Dennes, 1940); *Of Learned Ignorance* (tr. G. Heron, 1954); *Unity and Reform; Selected Writings of Nicholas de Cusa* (ed. J. P. Dolan, 1962). BIBLIOGRAPHY: Copleston 3:231–247; K. Jaspers, *Anselm and Nicholas of Cusa* (ed. H. Arendt, tr. R. Manheim, pa. 1974).

[J. T. HICKEY]

NICHOLAS OF DINKELSBÜHL (1360–1433), German theologian. After completing his studies in arts and theology at the Univ. of Vienna, N. lectured there for more than 40 years. In 1405 he was made rector of the univ. and later served three terms as dean of its theology faculty. He has been called "the second founder of the university." He was canon of St. Stephen's and in 1425 became confessor to Duke Albrecht, whom he represented at the Council of Constance. He was also the German representative at the election of Martin V, which ended the Great Schism. As a member of the Holy Office N. showed a conciliating spirit and was appointed by the Pope to preach to the Hussites. He was a prolific writer of sermons and treatises on many subjects, among them monastic reform and conciliarism, which he favored. His scriptural commentaries follow scholastic tradition, but his comments on ecclesiastical polity show originality. BIBLIOGRAPHY: H. Wolfram, NCE 10:452.

[M. J. FINNEGAN]

NICHOLAS OF FLÜE, ST. (1417–87), "Bruder Klaus," patron saint of Switzerland, soldier, farmer, statesman. Father of 10 children, N. found himself unfitted for domestic life, but he was blessed with an understanding wife who gave him leave to go off and become a hermit. People in trouble flocked to his hermitage for his loving and wise counsel. He composed the quarrels of the cantons and brought them to peace at the Diet of Stans. He was canonized in 1947 and is venerated by Catholics and Protestants alike. BIBLIOGRAPHY: G. R. Lamb, *Brother Nicholas* (1955); Butler 1:660–663; P. M. Krieg, BiblSanct 9:913–917; R. Durrer, *Bruder Klaus. Die ältesten Quellen über* *den seligen Nikolaus von Flüe, sein Leben und sein Einfluss* (2 v., 1917–21).

[T. GILBY]

NICHOLAS OF GORRAN (1232–*c.*1295), Dominican biblical commentator at Saint-Jacques, Paris. He wrote glosses on the whole Bible; his *Commentaria in IV Evangelia* became esp. well known and was among the first printed books (1472).

[T. C. O'BRIEN]

NICHOLAS OF HEREFORD (d. *c.*1420), English priest excommunicated for preaching Wycliffe's doctrines. He probably recanted. Later he became chancellor and treasurer of Hereford Cathedral but resigned in 1417 to enter the Carthusian monastery in Coventry. He is said to have worked with J. Purvey on an English translation of the Bible.

[M. J. SUELZER]

NICHOLAS OF JESUS-MARY (1590–1660), Carmelite theologian. He taught at Salamanca and published (1631) a dictionary of the mystical terms used by St. John of the Cross. BIBLIOGRAPHY: L. Berra, DE 2:1135.

[M. J. SUELZER]

NICHOLAS OF LYRA (*c.*1270–*c.*1349), French Franciscan biblical scholar at the Sorbonne. N. is known as the foremost medieval biblicist because of his sound principles of exegesis—particularly his emphasis on the primacy of the literal sense of the text—and his knowledge of Hebrew and rabbinical scholarship. His *Postillae perpetuae sive Brevia commentaria in universa biblica* was the first printed scriptural commentary (1471–72).

[T. C. O'BRIEN]

NICHOLAS OF MYRA, ST. (d. *c.*350), bp. of Myra in Lycia. Legend records his imprisonment and release during the persecution of Diocletian and his attendance at the Council of *Nicaea. No Council register of bps. includes him. Justinian I named the Church of St. Priscus and St. Nicholas after him. Pope Nicholas I erected a basilica to honor him in Rome, *c.*860. In the West, Germany was introduced to his cult by the Byzantine princess Theophano, wife of Otto II *c.*973, and Italy received his remains at Bari in 1087. In German tradition, as patron saint of children, he brings them gifts on the eve of Dec. 6. English-speaking countries associate this legend with Christmas Eve and popularize his name as Santa Claus. BIBLIOGRAPHY: E. Crozier, *Life and Legend of St. Nicholas, Patron Saint of Children* (1949); Butler 4:503–506; N. Del Rey, BiblSanct 9:923–939; for iconography, M. C. Celletti, BiblSanct 9:941–948.

[F. H. BRIGHAM]

NICHOLAS ORESME (*c.*1320–82), French theologian, bp. of Lisieux from 1378, who proposed theories of astronomy, geometry, and economics that anticipated modern developments in these sciences. BIBLIOGRAPHY: Gilson HCP 515–516.

[T. C. O'BRIEN]

NICHOLAS PAGLIA, BL. (1197–1255), Dominican preacher. While a student of law at Bologna, N. joined Dominicans under influence of Dominic. He founded Dominican houses at Trani, Perugia, Orvieto, Naples, Brindisi and was twice provinical of the Roman province (1230–1235, 1255). He was beatified in 1828. BIBLIOGRAPHY: G. Cappelluti, BiblSanct 10:42–43.

[L. E. BOYLE]

NICHOLAS OF PRUSSIA, BL. (*c.*1379–1456), Benedictine. N. made his vows at the monastery of Santa Giustina in Padua; was sent to San Giorgio, Venice; then to San Benedetto di Polirone near Mantua; and, by 1430, had become prior and novice master at S. Niccolò del Boschetto near Genoa. He was distinguished for his faithful observance of the monastic rule. BIBLIOGRAPHY: F. G. Holweck, *A Biographical Dictionary of the Saints* (1924) 741–742; Zimmermann 1:247–249.

[M. F. MCCARTHY]

NICHOLAS OF STRASSBURG (fl. early 14th cent.), Dominican, prominent in the beginnings of the Thomist school in Germany. He was also a popular preacher of mystical piety, a friend and defender of Meister *Eckhart.

[T. C. O'BRIEN]

NICHOLAS STUDITE, ST., late 9th-cent. abbot. Born in Sydonia, Crete, of wealthy parents and educated at the monastery of Studion in Constantinople, he became a monk there. He gave aid to exiles who had come there after banishment by iconoclastic emperors. After iconoclasm subsided he became abbot of the monastery. During the controversy (858) between Ignatius and Photious over the patriarchate of Constantinople N. had to flee because of his opposition to Photius. He was later captured and forced to return to Studion. He lived to see the restoration of Ignatius by the Emperor Basil. BIBLIOGRAPHY: Butler 1:251.

[J. R. RIVELLO]

NICHOLAS OF TOLENTINO, ST. (1245–1305). Precocious in piety, N. was admitted to minor orders in early childhood and given a canonship. Later he entered the Augustinian monastery at Sant' Angelo, and in 1271 was ordained at Cinguli. The last 30 years of his life were spent at Tolentino. N. was canonized in 1446 and is the patron of the holy souls in purgatory. BIBLIOGRAPHY: AS Sept. 3:636–743; N. Concetti, *Vita di S. Nicola da Tolentino* (1932); Butler 3:524–527; D. Gentili, BiblSanct 9:953–968.

[W. A JURGENS]

NICHOLAS TREVET (*c.*1265–after 1334), Dominican theologian, historian, and humanist. N. studied at Oxford before 1300 and succeeded *William of Macclesfeld there as Dominican regent master (1303–07). Between 1307 and 1314 he lived in Paris, gathering materials for his *Annales sex regum Angliae* (1135–1307) and for his other chronicles. He developed a humanistic interest in ancient classics and commented on Seneca, Cicero, Vergil, and Livy. He also wrote the earliest commentary on St. *Augustine's *De civitate Dei* and outstanding glosses on the Bible. J. A. Weisheipl, NCE 10:452; Quétif-Échard 2:561–565.

[J. A. WEISHEIPL]

NICHOLAS OF VERDUN (1150?–1220?), greatest goldsmith and enameler of his time. N. inscribed the famous ambo (1181) in the Abbey Church of Klosterneuberg, engraving and enamelling its 59 plaques in gilt bronze and niello with Old and New Testament scenes, and at Tournai cathedral inscribed the reliquary of SS. Piatus and Nicasius (1205, badly restored, 1891). Probably in Cologne in the 1180's, N. may have worked on the reliquary shrines of the Three Kings in the Cathedral Treasury, St. Albanus in St. Pantaleon, and St. Anno in Siegburg. N.'s style is transitional, moving from late Romanesque toward Gothic linearism. BIBLIOGRAPHY: S. Collon-Gevaert, *Art Roman dans la Vallée de la Meuse aux XIe et XIIe siècles* (1963).

[M. J. DALY]

NICLAES, HENDRIK (Henry Nicholas; *c.*1502–*c.*1580), founder of the *Familists. N. was born in Münster and reared a Catholic, but at age 9 he claimed a revelation of an experiential religion. He established his sect in Amsterdam, at Emden where he lived, and in England, which he visited in 1552 or 1553. His teaching, influenced according to some by D. *Joris, proclaimed a personal revelation that he was a "begodded man," experiencing a divine spirit of love, which put him above Christ and Moses, as charity is above faith and hope. Those who shared in this inner spirit were divinized, righteous, and raised above dogma, liturgy, or law. N.'s teachings seem to have fostered pantheistic and antinomian excesses among the Familists. Some of N.'s works, such as *Glass of Righteousness* and *Evangelium regni,* were translated into English; all were placed on the Index (1570–1582). BIBLIOGRAPHY: R. M. Jones, *Studies in Mystical Religion* (1923) 428–448; Knox Enth.

[T. C. O'BRIEN]

NICODEMUS, described in John as a Pharisee, a teacher and leader of the Jews who questioned Jesus (Jn 3.1–21), later defended him (7.50–52) and assisted at his burial (19.38–42).

[M. A. MCNAMARA]

NICODEMUS OF THE HOLY MOUNTAIN, ST. (*c.*1748–1809). A native of Naxos, N. entered the monastery of Dionysiou on Mt. Athos in 1775, where he became an extremely influential spiritual writer. His most famous work was the *Philokalia,* a collection of passages from the ascetical writings of the Greek Fathers. This book, first published in Venice in 1782 and often reprinted, has had a profound and permanent influence among eastern Christians. He was canonized by the Greek Orthodox Church in 1955.

[G. T. DENNIS]

NICODEMUS OF MAMMOLA, ST. (*c.*900–990), Calabrian-Greek ascetic, monastic founder. N. became a Basilian monk at Mercurion and a strict ascetic on Mt. Celerano. Eventually his pious example led to still another foundation at Mammola. A life of Nicodemus exists (*c.*1200) as a principal source of information about him. BIBLIOGRAPHY: V. Zavaglia, *Vita del santo padre nostro Nicodemo* (1961); F. Russo, BiblSanct 9:908–911.

[B. F. SCHERER]

NICODEMUS, GOSPEL OF. This title has been given to a composite work, the first part of which had earlier been known as the *Acts of Pilate*. This earlier part may well have been intended as a Christian reply to the blasphemous "Acts of Pilate" circulated as anti-Christian propaganda by Emperor Maximin at the beginning of the 4th century. The Christian *Acts of Pilate* gives an account of the trial, death, and Resurrection of Jesus. In part it reproduces the gospel narrative word for word, but it also adds amplifications of its own designed to exculpate Pilate and to provide such overwhelming proofs of the Resurrection that even Annas and Caiphas are convinced. Nicodemus and Joseph of Arimathea figure prominently in this part. The second part of the work consists of a detailed account, cast in the apocalyptic genre, of Christ's descent into the underworld, his conquest of Satan and the powers of darkness, and the salvific effects of his advent on the souls which they have held captive there. Based on the text of 1 Pet 3.19, this second part purports to derive from the two sons of the aged Simeon, who have themselves been raised from the dead. BIBLIOGRAPHY: M. R. James, *Apocryphal New Testament* (1924) 94–146; R. A. Lipsius, *Die Pilatusakten kritisch untersucht* (1871); Quasten 1:115–118.

[D. J. BOURKE]

NICOLAITANS (Nicolaites), a sect condemned in the message of Rev 2.6, 14–15, to the Churches of Ephesus and Pergamum. They were accused of eating food sacrificed to idols and of practicing immoral behavior associated with Balaam (see Num 31.16). Beginning with Irenaeus, some Fathers spoke of a Gnostic sect of this name that originated with Nicolaus the deacon in Acts 6.5. There is no basis for this identification. In the Middle Ages the name was applied to opponents by defenders of clerical celibacy.

[T. C. O'BRIEN]

NICOLAS, JEAN JACQUES (1807–88), French apologete. He was a layman who served as a lawyer in various governmental posts from 1849 until his retirement in 1877.

His apologetic works were written at a popular level, on contemporary issues, and had a wide circulation. Among them are: a general apologia for Catholicism as the basis for hope, written on the occasion of a family tragedy, *Études philosophiques sur le Christianisme* (4 v., 1842–45; 26 editions during his lifetime); *Du Protestantisme et de toutes les hérésies dans leur rapport avec le socialisme* (1858), which sought to show that Protestant theology lay at the basis of socialist errors; *La divinité de Jesus Christ: démonstration nouvelle tirée des dernières attaques de l'incrédulité* (1864), against *Renan; *L'art de croire, ou préparation philosophique à la foi chrétienne* (2 v., 1866). He also wrote several works on cooperative relations between Church and State, as well as a defense of the temporal power of the papacy.

[T. C. O'BRIEN]

NICOLAUS (Nicholas), one of the seven deacons in Acts 6.5, where he is said to be a proselyte from Antioch.

[T. C. O'BRIEN]

NICOLE, PIERRE (1625–95), Jansenist theologian. N. studied theology at the Sorbonne, but was denied ordination by the bp. of Chartres. He was a constant companion of and collaborator with Antoine *Arnauld, leading Jansenist spokesman and spiritual director at Port-Royal. N. was a vigorous polemicist, defending a characteristically Jansenist attitude toward morality. His noted *Essais de morale* reached 14 volumes in its 1753 edition; N. also translated *Les Provinciales (Provincial Letters)* of his friend and supporter, Blaise *Pascal, into classical Latin.

[T. M. MCFADDEN]

NICOMACHUS FLAVIANUS (*c.*334–394), Roman statesman and scholar, champion of paganism. Like his close friend *Symmachus, he hoped to restore the old Roman religion and its institutions. His paganism, like that of his intellectual contemporaries, reflected the influence of Porphyrian Neoplatonism, being a syncretistic ensemble of various cults and practices. He translated Philostratus's *Life of Apollonius of Tyana* into Latin and was an expert in all forms of divination. In 392 he was an ardent supporter of the usurper Eugenius, who, he was confident, would overthrow Theodosius, destroy Christianity, and restore paganism. Even before the defeat and death of Eugenius in 394, Nicomachus seems to have committed suicide. BIBLIOGRAPHY: PW 6.2:2506–11; P. De Labriolle, *La Réaction païenne* (6th ed., 1942) 351–352.

[M. R. P. MCGUIRE]

NICOMACHUS OF GERASA (1st half of 2d cent.), Neo-Pythagorean arithmetician and philosopher. In his *Introduction to Arithmetic* he speaks of numbers as preexisting in the mind of God. This reflects a doctrine of the Platonic school that ideas are God's thoughts. In his *Arithmetical Theology* he identifies each number with a number of Greek and non-Greek divinities. This teaching will be taken up again and developed by *Proclus. N. maintains also that the number-gods are the causes of the being of beings. There are echoes of this doctrine in *Plotinus as well as in *Proclus. See Copleston 1:447; A. R. Armstrong, CHGMP 90–95.

[M. R. P. MCGUIRE]

NICOMEDES, ST., martyr. According to the historically unreliable *Passio* of SS. Nereus and Achilleus, N. was a Roman priest martyred for refusing to sacrifice. The date of this martyrdom is uncertain. N. is supposed to be buried in a cemetery on the Via Nomentana. BIBLIOGRAPHY: Butler 3:555; E. Josi, EncCatt 8:1863–64.

[R. B. ENO]

NICOMEDIA, city in ancient Bithynia; capital of the independent kingdom of Bithynia from *c.*264–74 B.C.; capital of the Roman province of Bithynia; favorite residence of Roman emperors; briefly the eastern capital of the empire under Diocletian; an important Christian center; a metropolitan see, two of whose suffragans included the sees of Chalcedon and Nicaea. It is located in NW Asia Minor near the Gulf of Izmit in the Sea of Marmara. Originally Nicomedia was a Megarian city called Astacus or Olbia, founded in the 8th cent. B.C. It is now called Izmit, the capital of Kocaeli province in modern Turkey. When it was an independent kingdom, Hannibal sought asylum there. In Roman times Origen lived there. Arius was granted asylum by the bp., *Eusebius of Nicomedia. It was a center of Arianism in the 4th cent., before being destroyed by a Gothic invasion, an earthquake, and fire. It was rebuilt by Justinian the Great and then destroyed by the Persian Shah Chosroes II. It declined during Byzantine times until it was captured by the Ottomans in 1326. No systematic excavations have as yet attempted to reconstruct its varied history.

[E. J. DILLON]

NIDER, JOHANN (Nyder, Neider; *c.*1380–1438), German Dominican theologian and religious reformer. In the life of his order he promoted the religious reform inaugurated by Bl. *Raymond of Capua and was vicar (1429–38) over all the priories of strict observance in Germany. He was a renowned preacher; he became professor of theology at the Univ. of Vienna from 1426 and dean from 1436. N. served as a theological consultant in the trial and condemnation of J. *Hus at the Council of *Constance (1418); he also attended the Council of Basel (1431). His *Formicarium* (1437) reflects his own experience of the religious history of his times; all his other works were published posthumously in 1500; they include *Praeceptorium divinae legis; Consolatorium timoratae conscientiae; De reformatione religiosorum; Manuale confessorum.*

[T. C. O'BRIEN]

NIEBUHR, BARTHOLD GEORG (1776–1831), statesman, historian of early Rome, and influential proponent of modern historiography. N. was extensively involved in government service: he helped direct the commercial interests of his native Denmark, contributed to the reconstruction of German finances after the collapse of the Prussian kingdom, and was in charge of the Prussian delegation to the Holy See dealing with the Catholic population in the Rhineland. During his academic career at the Univ. of Berlin (1810–13) and Bonn (1821–31), N. wrote a three-volume *Roman History* which combined a new empirical methodology with an emphasis on the evolution of legal and political institutions. BIBLIOGRAPHY: G. P. Gooch, *History and Historians in the Nineteenth Century* (1952) 14–23.

[T. M. MCFADDEN]

NIEBUHR, HELMUT RICHARD (1894–1962), Protestant theologian. The brother of Reinhold *Niebuhr, N. was born in Wright City, Mo.; he was educated at Elmhurst College (Ill.), of which he was later president. After studies at Eden Theological Seminary (Webster Groves, Mo.), N. was ordained in the Evangelical and Reformed Church in 1916. From Yale Univ. he received his Ph.D. in 1924. In 1931 he was appointed professor of Christian Ethics at the Yale Divinity School, where he remained until his death. His intellectual concerns ranged widely in the areas of sociological analysis, value theory, theological ethics, and the purposes of theological education. Although not a prolific author, he exhibited in his major works his interest in the dialogue between Christian faith and culture. His *Social Sources of Denominationalism* (1929) analyzed the secular forces that separate religious bodies in America. From the historical and theological aspect he traced the relation between Christianity and culture in *The Kingdom of God in America* (1937). *The Meaning of Revelation* (1941) set forth revelation as the intelligible event in the internal history of the Christian community, which provided guiding images for a coherent life. His typology of the relations that Christian faith has sustained with culture was expressed in *Christ and Culture* (1951). The theocentrism that ruled his theology was brought face to face with different aspects of modern culture in *Radical Monotheism and Western Culture* (1960), in which he stressed the center of ethics and value theory as residing on the principle of being-itself, the One beyond the many whence all beings derive their being and significance. His posthumous work *The Responsible Self* (1963) provided a truncated version of what might have become his systematic Christian ethics. N. came from a heritage of evangelical Christianity, which was dynamically theocentric yet toughly realistic about social problems. BIBLIOGRAPHY: *Handbook of Christian Theologians* (ed. M. Marty and D. Peerman, 1965); *Faith and Ethics* (ed. P. Ramsey, 1957).

[C. A. HOLBROOK]

NIEBUHR, REINHOLD (1892–1971), clergyman and teacher, influential in turning American Protestantism from liberalism toward Reformation and biblical theology. Born at Wright City, Mo., after studying at Elmhurst College (Ill.), Eden Theological Seminary (Webster Groves, Mo.), and Yale (B.D., 1914; M.A., 1915), he was ordained by the Evangelical Synod and was pastor of Bethel Church, Detroit, Mich., until 1928. He then moved to Union Theological Seminary, New York City, where he taught applied Christianity until his retirement in 1960. Having begun his ministry at the high tide of the Social Gospel movement, he shared much of the optimism that envisioned the kingdom of God on earth. Under his leadership, the small working-class church in Detroit increased in membership, erected a new building, and in addition to public services of worship and its church school program, held Sunday-evening forums to discuss crucial social issues. As he related in *Leaves From the Notebook of a Tamed Cynic* (1929), he became increasingly aware of the plight of the workingman in a depersonalized industrial society. He also became conscious of the illusory hopes of educators and moralists for curing the ills of the world. Basic to his ''Christian Realism'' has been a conviction that both individuals and groups are prevented from attaining perfection by a deep-rooted egotistic pride. His *Moral Man and Immoral Society* (1932) made a strong impact upon American Protestants, and his analysis of human nature was elaborated in his Gifford Lectures (*Nature and Destiny of Man,* 2 v., 1941–43). Reasserting the idea of original sin, he interpreted it as self-centered pride that leads men to absolutize their partial perspectives and to rationalize their own interests, incorporating them into their political, economic, and social structures. His view of human sinfulness was saved from sheer pessimism by his recognition of man's ability to transcend himself and to engage in self-criticism and by his awareness that man has a capacity for good as well as for evil. His provisional pessimism was also tempered by faith in the justifying grace of God, who is both transcendent and immanent. He continued to have a strong ethical concern and was active in reform movements but did not expect to establish a perfect society governed by love. Believing in working for the highest measure of justice possible in a given situation, he sought proximate solutions rather than idealistic ultimate goals. Moreover, he believed that group relations are political in nature and as such involve conflicting interests that cannot be resolved except by coercive power. Egoistic impulses of human groups cannot be restrained simply by appeals to reason and good will. Force must be countered by force, and even war may be necessary, if the alternative is brutal tyranny, such as Nazism under Hitler. Democracy must be preserved, not because men are wise and good, but because it is a safeguard against man's tendency toward injustice. As indicated in *Man's Nature and His Communities* (1965), some of his views underwent modification, but the major themes of his Christian Realism have remained basically unchanged. BIBLIOGRAPHY: *Reinhold Niebuhr: His Religious, Social and Political Thought* (ed. C. W. Kegley and R. N. Bretall, 1956); T. A. Kantonen, *Resurgence of the Gospel* (1948); P. A. Carter, *Decline and Revival of the Social Gospel* (1956).

[N. H. MARING]

NIEDERALTAICH, ABBEY OF, Bavarian Benedictine-congregation monastery on the Danube River near the Isar. Founded before 750, Niederaltaich colonized and evangelized not only the Bavarian forest, but Bohemia, Moravia, and Hungary as well. Ruined by the Hungarian wars, it later headed a reform and revitalization of several monasteries under St. Godard (d. 1038). There were several saintly women recluses at Niederaltaich. Losing its imperial status (857–1156), it was placed under episcopal authority. Rebuilt after the Thirty Years' War, the abbey and its library were destroyed by subsequent fires in 1659 and 1671. It was secularized in 1803, united to the Priory of Innsbruck Volders in 1927 and became an abbey again in 1930. Its Ecumenical Institute has been a leading influence in the ecumenical movement.

[M. A. MCFADDEN]

NIEDERMEYER, ABRAHAM LOUIS (1802–61), Swiss composer of sacred music and educator at the École de Musique in Paris, which now bears his name. After study in Vienna, Rome, and Naples, he composed sentimental songs to the poetry of Hugo, Lamartine, and Deschamps, and a number of unsuccessful operas in Paris. A work on plainsong, *Méthode d'accompagnement du plain chant* (1855) was poorly received by contemporaries. His sacred works still in use today include hymns, motets, and a fully orchestrated Mass.

[R. J. LITZ]

NIEDERMÜNSTER (ALSACE), CONVENT OF, former abbey of nuns founded *c.*710 by St. Odilia whose convent of Mont Sainte-Odile was located on a hill near the abbey. The saint's niece, Gundelinde, was the abbey's first abbess. For several cent. a relic, believed to be of the true cross, was kept at Niedermünster. Partially destroyed during the Peasant's Revolt (1525), the abbey did not survive after a fire in 1542. It is now a ruin.

[M. A. MCFADDEN]

NIEHEIM, DIETRICH OF, see THEODORIC OF NIEHEIM.

NIEMEYER, OSCAR (Niemeyer Soares Filho; 1907–), Brazilian master of 20th-cent. architecture working with Le Corbusier (1936); in 1937–42 on a team that designed the Ministry of Education, Rio de Janeiro, using Le Corbusier's sun-breaks (movable slats to filter the rays); the Brazilian Pavilion, New York World's Fair (1939); the controversial Church of St. Francis of Assisi—a parabolic concrete shell receiving light through vertical louvres. N.'s major achievement is Brasilia (begun 1956) where with 60 architect assistants he planned the sumptuous presidential palace, a cathedral with massive metal crown, houses of justice and fine arts, and a small chapel in imaginative, new forms magically engineered, in environs of reflecting pools, related to massive metal sculptures, all the apotheosis of contemporary design.

[M. J. DALY]

NIEMÖLLER, MARTIN (1892–), German Lutheran pastor. A career officer, he served as a U-boat commander in World War I. In 1919 he entered the seminary at Münster. After his ordination he became executive secretary for the Westphalian Council for Inner Missions. In 1931 he was called to the pastorate of St. Annen's in Berlin-Dahlem. Although originally a supporter of the National Socialist party, N. opposed at the very outset Hitler's attempt to control the Churches. He founded the Emergency Pastors' League (1933), helped write the *Barmen Declaration, and continued to preach against Nazism until his arrest in July 1937. Nine months later he was convicted on trumped-up charges and sent first to Sachsenhausen and then to Dachau. His wife kept the world press informed about him, and his reputation for resistance became legendary. The U.S. forces freed him in 1945 after 8 years of imprisonment, half of it spent in solitary confinement. For 15 years after his release N. traveled throughout the world in the interests of ecumenism and peace. He aroused controversy in 1953 by his letter to Chancellor Adenauer opposing rearmament and again in 1959 by his speech against the atom bomb. On the occasion of the All-German Church Day in Berlin in 1961 he denounced the gathering as "a complete blank in the history of the Evangelical Church." His action caused some former admirers to feel that the Communist regime of East Germany had made use of his prestige to help it sever East German Protestants from their brethren in the West. BIBLIOGRAPHY: C. S. Davidson, *God's Man; The Story of Pastor Niemöller* (1959).

[M. J. SUELZER]

NIEREMBERG, JUAN EUSEBIO (1595–1658), Spanish spiritual writer. N. became a Jesuit in 1614, was ordained in 1623, and taught at the Colegio Imperial in Madrid for 19 years. He was esteemed for his sanctity and capacities as a spiritual director. A prolific writer in ascetics, he is still read in Spain to the present time. Among his principal books are *Diferencia entre lo temporal y lo eternal* (latest Eng. tr. 1884), and *Del Aprecio y Estima de la Divina Gracia* (condensed Eng. tr. 1891). BIBLIOGRAPHY: Antonio Pérez Goyena, CE 11:72–73.

[T. M. MCFADDEN]

NIETZSCHE, FRIEDRICH WILHELM (1844–1900), German philosopher and poet. Son of a Lutheran pastor, he was educated at Pforta and the univ. of Bonn and Leipzig. His early brilliance in classical philology led to his appointment to the univ. of Basel, where he taught 1869–79. Plagued by ill-health all his life, he suffered a complete mental collapse in 1889. Schopenhauer is the greatest single influence on N.'s thought, for from him N. took his concept of the will, but not his pessimism. A brilliant, almost pyrotechnical style, abounding in irony and paradox, makes N.'s thought difficult to understand and easy to misinterpret. Seldom systematic, many of his writings are done in aphorisms that seem rather to be notes for a future philosophy.

N.'s philosophy is secular humanism and a paean to man. His key concept of the "will-to-power" is a hypothesis, not a postulate, and is offered in a psychological rather than an ontological context, although in some passages he extends the notion even to the inanimate. He offers it in opposition to Schopenhauer's blind will. N. would have repudiated the application made of the idea in 20th-cent. Fascism. Turning from the divine in human affairs (although it must be remembered that the oft-quoted "God is dead" passage from *Thus Spake Zarathustra* is placed in the mouth of a madman), N. embraced the ancient myth of the eternal return as the frame of being. Of no religion, he is not quite the thoroughgoing atheist. The dead God is the God of Christians, not of Christ, and had been killed by the liberal theologians N. knew.

N.'s distinctions between man and Superman (*Übermensch*) must be noted carefully. *Mensch* and *Übermensch* are not Darwinian species. Rather, Superman is the integrated man of this world, the antithesis to God. Man, once he acknowledges that he is stripped of supranatural status and dignity, must make himself by self-discipline and denial. N. writes as well of "slave morality," in which evil is the primary concept and good an afterthought, and "master morality," in which good is primary and bad an afterthought, designating what is undistinguished, unworthy. These again do not mark two different races of men and are found intermixed in Western culture. Despite the distortions of his words by National Socialism, N. does not seem a racist. His anti-German invective can be bitter. Controversial, hotly attacked and defended, N. yet remains influential in philosophy, in letters (e.g., Rilke, Yeats, Shaw), and in theology (death of God). BIBLIOGRAPHY: F. Copleston, *Friederich Nietzsche: Philosopher of Culture* (1942); W. Kaufmann, *Nietzsche* (rev. ed., 1956); *idem,* EncPhil 5:505–514, an excellent article.

[W. B. MAHONEY]

NIFO, AGOSTINO (Niphius; Suessanus; 1473–1538 or betw. 1545 and 1546), Italian Averroist philosopher (see AVERROËS; AVERROISM, LATIN). He taught at Padua, Salerno, Naples, and Pisa. His principal work, written in refutation of P. *Pomponazzi, was *Tractatus de immortalitate animae contra Pomponatium* (1518). N. also wrote commentaries on Aristotle (published in 14 v., 1654), and edited works of Averroës. It is thought that in his later life he became a Thomist. Quotations in his works are the sole source that suggest a now lost *De intellectu* of *Siger of Brabant, against whom St. Thomas Aquinas wrote his *De unitate intellectus*.

[T. C. O'BRIEN]

NIGEL WIREKER (*c.*1140–before 1206), English Benedictine satirist. John Bale (1557) first called him "Wirecker"; Longchamp may have been his contemporary appellation. N. was a monk at Christchurch, Canterbury, before the murder of Becket (1170), whom perhaps he knew. His best-known work, an elegiac poem which Chaucer knew, *Speculum stultorum* (Mirror of Fools), written between 1170 and 1187, uses an ass, Burnellus, who desires a longer tail, to depict the status-seeking monk, and satirizes those whom Burnellus meets at the Univ. of Paris, Salerno, and Rome. A prose treatise, *Contra curiales et officiales clericos* (Against Courtiers and Ecclesiastical Administrators), *c.*1200, attacks ecclesiastical families trafficking in benefices and often giving the cure of souls to unsuitable persons. His works were popular in 14th- and 15th-cent. Europe. BIBLIOGRAPHY: *Nigellus de Longchamp dit Wireker* (ed. A. Boutemy, v. 1, 1959); D. Nichol, NCE 10:465; R. A. Beals, *Nigellus Wireker* (1927).

[F. D. BLACKLEY]

NIGHT OF THE SENSES, the spiritual purification of sense faculties so that the person may be more completely directed toward God. This may be accomplished actively when an individual strives with grace and through various privations to use his senses in total conformity to God's will. On the other hand, the passive night of the senses is a product of purgative, contemplative prayer in which a man perceives his own unworthiness and God's infinite holiness, thereby accommodating his senses to the soul's spiritual *élan*. The night of sense is called dark because in it God transcends any concepts or symbols so that as the person grows in knowledge of him, this knowledge itself transcends the senses and is dark to them. This night is attested to by three classical signs described by St. *John of the Cross: the individual can no longer meditate discursively but rather seeks a simple communion with God; he finds no pleasure in his prayer and yet does not seek worldly diversions; he is concerned that he is not giving God enough. Many spiritual writers hold that man cannot be rid of all his defects without these passive purifications. BIBLIOGRAPHY: A. Rayo, *Theology of Christian Perfection* (tr. J. Aumann, 1962); K. Kavanaugh, NCE 11:1042. *PURIFICATION, SPIRITUAL.

[T. DUBAY]

NIGHT OF THE SOUL, the spiritual purification of the soul by which it is perfectly united with God through love. It is a phenomenon experienced only by those who are advanced in the spiritual life, and has been described most accurately by St. *John of the Cross (*Dark Night of the Soul,* bks. 2 and 3). This dark night follows from purgative contemplation in which the soul is aware of its own imperfections and God's perfect purity. The consciousness of this divergence between God and man in the night of the soul entails a loss of any spiritual satisfaction, intense *aridity of soul, and a sense of abandonment by God. This is darkness of pure faith in which the intellect is purified, of pure hope in which the memory is cleansed, of pure love in which the will is purified. Although it is a painful set of experiences, this night of the soul finally issues in a deep, passionate love for God, an habitual joy, and a view of reality transfused with God's presence. BIBLIOGRAPHY: G. Di Santa Maria

Maddalena, *St. John of the Cross, Doctor of Divine Love* (tr. a Benedictine of Stanbrook Abbey, 1946); P. De La Trinité, DSAM 4.1:911–925.

[T. DUBAY]

NIGHTINGALE, FLORENCE (1820–1910), founder of modern nursing. After training at the Protestant deaconesses' hospital at Kaiserwerth, Germany (1851), she reorganized the "London Institution . . . for Gentlewomen. . . ." Sidney Herbert, British Secretary of War and longtime supporter, obtained her help in improving sanitary conditions for soldiers during the Crimean War. *Notes on Matters Affecting the Health, Efficiency and Hospital Administration of the British Army* (1858) explained her findings. It has since gone through many editions. This and other studies made her a consultant on civil as well as military hospitals. She founded the Nightingale Training School for Nurses (1860), was given the British Royal Red Cross (1883), the Order of Merit (1907), and Freedom of the City of London (1908). BIBLIOGRAPHY: C. Woodham-Smith, *Florence Nightingale* (1963); L. Strachey, *Eminent Victorians* (1963).

[G. RUPPEL]

NIGIDIUS FIGULUS, PUBLIUS (*c.*98–45 B.C.), most famous of Roman neo-Pythagoreans. He wrote widely on grammar, natural science, and esp. on religion, magic, and the occult in general. He was an ardent devotee of astrology. He had a reputation for being an active practitioner in all kinds of magic arts, including necromancy. BIBLIOGRAPHY: A. Souter, OCD 608; W. Burkert, LexAW 2086–87; PW 17.1:200–212.

[M. R. P. MCGUIRE]

NIHIL OBSTAT, formula by which an ecclesiastical censor expresses the judgment that a work contains nothing detrimental to faith or morals (CIC c. 1393.4). The *nihil obstat* must precede the granting of an imprimatur, and although this is not required by law, is often printed with the imprimatur. *PRECENSORSHIP.

[T. C. O'BRIEN]

NIHILIANISM, a doctrine expressed in the Christological proposition "Christ as man is nothing" (*Christus secundum quod est homo, non est aliquid*); Christ's humanity has its whole reality from his divine being. The theory, developed out of certain inept passages in Peter Lombard (d. 1160), was taught by some 12th-cent. Parisian theologians and condemned by Pope Alexander III as a denial of the truth that Christ is truly man (D 749–750).

[T. GILBY]

NIHILISM, a 19th-cent. social and political movement, mainly Russian; it originally affirmed positive aims behind its destructiveness, but as a sort of philosophy it involves a total rejection of religious and moral values. More extremely it is a form of skepticism denying that anything is. However, this dogmatism can often be historically and sympathetically interpreted less as a subjectivist *solipsism than as a protest of appetite and will against an intellectualist rendering of being as a meaningful essence, or even of religious reverence against "explaining" God. As such it is associated with philosophies of naked will and of *existentialism, and even as the negative theology of a high mystical tradition that hesitates to speak of God's being (*ens*). Yet, as St. Thomas Aquinas notes, nothing (*nihil*) is not synonymous with non-being (*non ens*), and consequently exclamatory discourses against explanatory discourses should sometimes be called "non-beingism" rather than nihilism. After all, any true philosopher gets exasperated with philosophy, as a true theologian with theology, which is not to say that they can find a good reason for giving them up, unless of course they have reached a continuous state, whether natural or supernatural, of communion beyond conceptual thought.

[T. GILBY]

NIHILISTS, a radical group of materialistic positivists among the Russian intelligentsia of the 1860s. Under the leadership of Pisarev (1840–68), and strongly influenced by Chernyshevski (1828–89) and Dobrolyubov (1836–61), they rejected existing religious, social, and political institutions and advocated the methods of the natural sciences. The term first appeared in literature in the novel *Fathers and Sons* by Turgenev (1818–83). BIBLIOGRAPHY: E. Lampert, *Sons against Fathers* (1965).

[M. F. MCCARTHY]

NIKEL, JOHANNES (1863–1924), professor of OT at the Univ. of Breslau from 1897, consultant of the Pontifical Biblical Commission, advocate of Catholic critical scholarship, and opponent of extreme conservatism in biblical studies. He was also a founder of the journal *Biblische Zeitfragen* (1908).

[T. C. O'BRIEN]

NIKKO AND GAKKO BOSATSU (8th cent.), Japanese clay sculptures in the Todaiji, Nara, also known respectively as Lord of the World, and Chief of the Gods, are ideal examples of ancient Japanese sculpture expressing in the prayerful attitude of aristocratic forms a harmony of realism and spiritual idealism which served as models for the 13th-cent. works of the great master Unkei and his school.

[M. J. DALY]

NIKON, PATRIARCH OF MOSCOW, (1605–81). Born Nikita Minov, he first served as a parish priest, but after separating from his wife, became a monk and was *hegumenos of the Kozeozenskiĭ monastery. In 1649 Czar Alexis I appointed N. metropolitan of Novgorod and 3 years later he was elected patriarch of Moscow. His liturgical reforms brought Russian usage more into conformity with Greek and Ukranian. This antagonized the conservative element in the Church and gave rise to the formation of the *Old Believers (*raskolniki*). N.'s reforms were useful to the Czar since they led to the political absorption of the Ukraine, but he fell from imperial favor when he tried to gain complete Church independence. N. was deposed in 1667 and remained in exile until 1681 when he was recalled by Alexis' successor Feodor III. He died while traveling and was buried with patriarchal honors in the monastery of the New Jerusalem which he founded. BIBLIOGRAPHY: W. Palmer, *Patriarch and the Tsar* (6 v. 1871–76); J. Ledet, DTC 11.1:646–655.

[F. T. RYAN]

NIL SORSKY, ST., a Russian monk (*c.*1433–1508) who lived many years on Mt. Athos where he imbibed the Eastern Christian spirituality of the early Hesychastic Fathers. Returning to Russia, he established a hermitage or *skete* along the Sora River. His intense asceticism mingled with a loosely structured monastic order (described in his two works: *Predanie* and *Ustav*) that emphasized the freedom and intellectual development of the individual monk attracted followers who became known as the Trans-Volga elders. N. was responsible for introducing into the northern part of Russia a renaissance of the Hesychastic tradition of interior prayer and a love of solitude and poverty that clashed violently with the social monasticism of *Joseph of Volokolamsk.

[G. A. MALONEY]

NILLES, NIKOLAUS (1828–1907), liturgical scholar. After studies at the Gregorian University, N. became a Jesuit in 1858 and began in 1859 his lifelong career of teaching and research at the Univ. of Innsbruck. He was principally concerned with the historical development of liturgical feasts of both Latin and Eastern rites. His *Kalendarium manuale utriusque ecclesiae orientalis et occidentalis* (2 v., 3d ed., 1896–97) was highly praised for its accuracy and use of original sources.

[T. M. MCFADDEN]

NILUS (SS): the name of at least two and probably three saints of the universal Church, including St. Nilus the Elder and St. Nilus of Rossano, with the facts surrounding the former possibly being in reality a composite of two distinct historical persons. (1a) Nilus the Elder was a high court official at Constantinople, who first married and later became a monk at Sinai. It was his son whose capture by the Arabs gave rise to the many legends about N.'s experiences in trying to rescue him. (1b) Nilus, a monk of Ancyra in Galatia, was a writer of theological, spiritual, biblical, and ascetical works, many of whose letters are extant. (2) Nilus of Rossano (Nilus the Younger; *c.*905–1005) was a leading figure in the Greek monasticism of Italy. After some years of worldly if not sinful life in his youth, N. at the age of 30 became a Basilian monk. He lived for a time as a hermit, but when Saracen invaders made the support and companionship of others desirable, he established the monastery of S. Adriano near his native city, where he refused a later offer to become archbishop. When he needed further protection from Saracen harassment, he sought help from the Benedictines at Monte Cassino, who settled his community at Valleluce. Some years later they moved to Serperi near Gaeta, where N. urged the antipope John XVI to repent and warned Emperor Otto III. In 1004 he founded the monastery of *Grottaferrata near Rome, still the center of Greek monasticism in Italy. BIBLIOGRAPHY: E. S. Duckett, *Death and Life in the Tenth Century* (1967, repr. 1971) 114, 126–127, 186–187; Butler 3:654–656; *ibid.* 4:320–321; G. Giovanelli, BiblSanct 9:995–1008, R. Janin, *ibid.* 9:1008–09.

[C. J. NOONE]

NILUS THE ARCHIMANDRITE, see DOXOPATRES, NEILOS.

NIMBUS (HALO), in art the field of glory or light radiating from holy people, assuming a variety of shapes. The circular disk about the head, distinguished in a Christ-figure by a cross, becomes angular (square) for a living saint (El Greco's, *Christ Carrying the Cross,* mosaic of Pope John with the Church). If surrounding the entire body, it is termed *aureole or mandorla (tympanum at Arles, Autun, Moissac, and other Romanesque portals and foreshadowed in MSS–*Liber vitae*, British Museum). Renaissance realism shows halos in perspective as horizontal disks over the heads of saints (Piero della Francesco's works).

[M. J. DALY]

NIMROD, son of Cush, who was the son of Ham and grandson of Noah. He was "the first on earth to be a mighty man" and a "mighty hunter before the Lord." His kingdom was in Mesopotamia (Gen 10.8–12).

[T. EARLY]

NINA, LORENZO (1812–85), cardinal secretary of state for Leo XIII, 1878–80, who sought a settlement of the *Roman Question, dealt with the measures of the French Third Republic against religious orders, and concluded a settlement of the German *Kulturkampf.

[T. C. O'BRIEN]

NINE FRIDAYS, see FIRST FRIDAY.

NINETY-FIVE THESES, a series of statements proposed for theological debate by Martin Luther in 1517. The occasion was the dissemination among the faithful of exaggeration and error through the preaching of a papal indulgence by J. Tetzel. There is a tradition, seriously challenged by E. Iserloh, that Luther on Oct. 31, 1517, nailed his list of theses to the Wittenberg Castle church; the date is therefore marked as the birth date of the Reformation. The theses were made the basis for the canonical process against Luther that began his final break with Rome. Written in Latin and translated into German, they received a wide circulation that transformed the issues that had been personal or academic for Luther into a summons for reform of the Church. Luther challenged the extension of the papal ''power of the keys'' to the souls in purgatory; more importantly, the theses revealed, esp. in regard to sin, guilt, and forgiveness, that much of what Luther called ''my Gospel'' had already developed in his mind. Text: LW 31 (1957). BIBLIOGRAPHY: EncLuthCh 3:2388–91; R. Fife, *Revolt of Martin Luther* (1957); E. Iserloh, *Theses Were Not Posted* (tr. J. Wicks, 1968).

[P. DAMBORIENA]

NINEVEH, famous royal city of the Assyrian empire on the left bank of the Tigris River opposite modern Mosul, reduced to ruins since it was destroyed in 612 B.C.. Excavations of its ruins, dating from the 19th cent. have uncovered precious treasures of Assyrian art and a great hoard of cuneiform writings that have opened up the languages and history of ancient Akkadia, Sumeria, Babylon, and the whole Mesopotamian region. In biblical lore Nineveh was the symbol of oppressive arrogance that was bound to be punished by God (Nahum) and, in the parable of Jonah (Jon 1–2), it became the vast, pagan city that did penance and worshiped God in response to Jonah's preaching, in contrast to the unrepentant in Israel.

[J. F. FALLON]

NINIAN, ST. (fl.5th cent.), founder of a monastic settlement and church in Galloway, Scotland, mentioned in the Venerable Bede's *Ecclesiastical History*. N. was buried in the church he founded, called the *Candida casa*.

NINO, ST. (d. *c.*340). According to tradition N. was a Christian slave girl, to whom the name of N. was later given; she was brought to Georgia where her example of virtue and reputed miracles led to the introduction of Christianity into that country. To the early 5th cent. account of N. written by Rufinus many legendary elements have been added. BIBLIOGRAPHY: D. M. Lang, *Lives and Legends of the Georgian Saints* (1956); J.M. Sauget, BiblSanct 9:1018–21; P. Peeters, ''Les Débuts du Christianisme en Géorgie d'après les sources hagiographiques,'' AnalBoll 50(1932) 5–58.

[G. T. DENNIS]

NIŌ, pair of fierce guardians at a Japanese temple gate having powerfully muscular bodies partly bared, and carrying clubs. Greatest are those at the Middle Gate, Horyuji (711) and Southern Gate, Todaiji, executed by the master carvers Unkei, Kaikei, and followers (1203).

[M. J. DALY]

NIPPUR, ancient Mesopotamian city, founded *c.*4000 B.C.; undisputed religious and cultural center of Sumer from early in the 3d millennium B.C. until the time of Hamurabi. It was never the seat of a Sumerian dynasty, nor a center of political power. But its local deity, Enlil, became the chief of the Sumerian pantheon and was worshiped as the monarch of the entire universe. Enlil's temple was Sumer's leading shrine and its priests legitimized the various dynasties. It was the site of Sumer's leading academy, whose library provided archeologists with much of what is known of Sumerian literature, including: a Sumerian paradise myth; a Sumerian version of the Flood story; a text containing the acts of what may be the most ancient political assemblies ever recorded; a story of a descent to the underworld that reflects Sumerian attitudes toward the afterlife; a more prosaic description of daily activity in a scribal school. By the time of Hamurabi, Babylon had replaced Nippur as religious and cultural center. The city retained importance down to Parthian times. Its site is located S of ancient Kish and Babylon, NW of ancient Ur, and 100 miles S of modern Baghdad. The extremely important archeological work was conducted there by the University Museum of the University of Pennsylvania (1888–1900), and then jointly with the Oriental Institute of the University of Chicago (1948–67).

[E. J. DILLON]

NIRVĀṆA, state of ultimate bliss, as taught in Buddhism, Jainism, and some forms of Hinduism. The term is Sanskrit for blowing out, as a candle, and suggests the extinguishing of desires, ending worldly ties, and the cycle of rebirths. It is achieved by accepting correct views of reality, practicing correct moral discipline, and meditating. The state is differently understood in the various schools and religions. In Mahayana Buddhism a bodhisattva forgoes nirvana to aid others. In Jainism it is often interpreted as the void, nothingness. In Vedanta it expresses union with the Brahma. BIBLIOGRAPHY: E. J. Thomas, *History of Buddhist Thought* (2d ed., 1951).

[T. EARLY]

NISIBIS (Nusaybin), a city in SE Turkey, formerly an important military and commercial center and the site of a famous Nestorian theological school. By the 5th cent. it had become the third-ranked see in the Persian Church. About the middle of the 4th cent. it was already reputed as a theological center, counting among its teachers St. *Ephrem. After their condemnation at the Council of *Ephesus (431) many *Nestorians were forced to take refuge outside the Roman Empire and settled in Nisibis where they were protected by the Persian rulers. The real beginning of the theological school coincided with the arrival in 457 of its first great teacher *Narses. Graduates of the school filled the bishoprics in Persia and contributed to the spread of Nestorianism. During the 8th and 9th cent. the school rapidly declined. The teaching at Nisibis was based on the writings of *Nestorius, *Diodorus of Tarsus and esp. *Theodore of Mopsuestia. The very detailed curriculum and statutes of the school have been preserved and are probably the oldest of any Christian academy. BIBLIOGRAPHY: PSO 107–111.

[G. T. DENNIS]

NITHARD (d. 844–845), Carolingian historian. He and Hartnid were sons (natural but legitimated) of Charlemagne's daughter Bertha and of Angilbert, poet, abbot of St. Riquier, and archchaplain. N. participated in struggles following the death of Louis I as adherent of his cousin, Charles the Bald. Requested in 841 to write a history of the times, he composed *Historiarum libri IV*. The first book was a life of Louis I; the other three, a valuable record of the years 839–843. His work contains first literary evidence of the French language (Strasbourg oaths). He died in battle either against Pepin II (844) of Aquitaine or against Northmen (845). Works: *Histoire des fils de Louis le Pieux* (ed. and tr. P. Lauer 1926). BIBLIOGRAPHY: A. Cabaniss, NCE 10:475.

[A. CABANISS]

NITRIA, a monastery in early Christian Egypt.

NITRIAN VALLEY (WADI-NATRÛN), a site, 50 miles S of Alexandria, of the beginnings of Egyptian monasticism. The "Sayings of the Fathers" (see APOPHTHEGMATA PATRUM) gives evidence of the early monastic life of chiefly Coptic monks there, beginning *c.* 320. Many of the *Desert Fathers dwelt in the Nitrian Valley, and John *Cassian, as well as Rufinus of Aquileia and others recorded their visiting the monastic settlements. There still survive monasteries of the 9th century.

NIVARD, BL. (d. after 1153), Cistercian monk. Born at Fontaines-les-Dijon, the youngest brother of St. Bernard of Clairvaux, N. joined the Cistercians at Cîteaux and followed Bernard to Clairvaux. He assisted his brother in several new foundations. The earliest traces of his cult are from the 17th century. BIBLIOGRAPHY: J. Jobin, *St. Bernard et sa famille* (1891); G. Müller, "Der selige Nivard," *Cistercienser-Chronik,* 8 (1896), 43–51; L. J. Lekai, NCE 10:475; G. Picasso, BiblSanct 9:1022–24.

[L. J. LEKAI]

NIVARD OF GHENT, 12th cent. writer. Little is known about his life and it is not even certain that he was an ecclesiastic. Possibly he was born at Cologne, of German ancestry, and may have been a monk of St. Pierre-au-Mont-Blandin, Ghent. His famous work *Ysengrimus,* a beast epic, is a satire in fable style of current ecclesiastic controversies and manners, without moralizing. The author inveighs against papal imperialism, but also satirizes current figures such as Roger of Sicily, Bernard of Clairvaux, Pope Eugene III, and others. His work, with animals bearing names, may well be the source of the French "Reynard" stories. But in turn, it may owe debts to the "Ecbasis captivi" by a monk of Toul, in the 10th cent., and a fable-poem of the 8th cent., possibly by Paulus the Deacon. N.'s genius lay in the anthropomorphisms he projected into his animal characters—i.e., the fox in his fable was not merely an artful deceiver, but a danger to domestic happiness, satirizing some court morals of the day. With reason N. has been called the premier Latin poet of the 12th cent. BIBLIOGRAPHY: L. Willems, *Biographie Nationale de Belgique,* 15:753–759.

[N. F. GAUGHAN]

NIVERS, GUILLAUME GABRIEL (1632–1714), French composer, theorist, organist of St.-Sulpice in Paris (1640) and to the king, music master to the queen (1667). His influential organ works and treatises (3 v.) resulted in a marked change in French style in the late 17th cent., and in the end to solmization (use of syllables to designate notes) in musical theory. N.'s compositions include motets, organ pieces, and editions of the Gregorian chant.

[R. J. LITZ]

NIZA, MARCOS DE (d. 1558), Franciscan missionary, explorer. A native of Nice in Savoy, N. became a Franciscan of the Regular Observance and went to Santo Domingo as a missionary in 1531. He later went to Peru and is reputed to have founded the Franciscan province of Lima. N. is credited with having given information to B. de *Las Casas on the Spanish treatment of Indians in Peru. From Peru he went to New Spain and ultimately to Nueva Galicia, governed by Coronado. He was successively vicar commissary general of the Franciscans in New Spain, and provincial. In 1539 he was sent by the viceroy to investigate reports of a flourishing civilization in what is now New Mexico and Arizona. His glowing but inaccurate reports led to the Coronado expedition of 1540 which N. accompanied as guide. The disappointment of the Spanish at finding a mediocre Indian center led to a loss of credibility for N., who returned to New Spain.

[J. R. AHERNE]

NIZARIS, a sub-sect of the **Fâtimid* *Shiites that broke off following the death of Caliph al-Mustanṣir (A.D. 1094), insisting that the imamate (see IMAM) had passed to his son Nizâr (d. 1095) rather than to al-Musta'lî, who became caliph. Through the efforts of the propagandist Ḥasan al-Sabbâḥ (d. 1124) the sect spread widely in the East, subsequently giving rise to a number of subgroups, among them the *Assassins of Syria. Their greatest and most enduring success was in Persia and the Indian subcontinent, where they are represented by the Khojas and the Qâsim-Shâhis, who have been active in the spread of *Ismaili Islam in East Africa. BIBLIOGRAPHY: J. N. Hollister, *Shi'a in India* (1953); A. S. Mujtaba, *Origin of the Khojahs and Their Religious Life Today* (1936).

[R. M. FRANK]

NOAH (NOE), son of Lamech, chiefly known for the miraculous survival of himself, his family, and a representative number of animals for breeding purposes from the destruction of the Flood. This was ordained by God in order to repopulate and restock the earth after its destruction for sin, and was achieved by the building of an ark under his direction. The tradition of a vast destructive deluge has survived in several Mesopotamian accounts, and the similarities between these and the biblical account of the Flood are so strong that they must, in effect, rest upon a common tradition, though of course the inspired religious interpretation in the biblical account is proper to the Hebrews. In fact, however, Noah is also said to be the originator of viniculture (Gen 9.20), the recipient of the divine covenant and blessing which assure the future stability and permanence of the natural order (Gen 8.20–23; 9.9–16); the first to receive permission from God to eat flesh, though without blood (Gen 9.3–6); and the father of Sham, Ham, and Japheth, the three originators in popular Hebrew tradition of the major ethnic groups into which the world they knew was divided. This means that several previously disparate traditions have artificially been united in this single figure. The figure of Noah has, however, made little impact upon subsequent Hebrew tradition, though he is praised in Sir 44.17–18 for his perfect righteousness, and in Heb 11.7 and 2 Pet 2.5, for his righteousness and faith. BIBLIOGRAPHY: A. Parrot, *Déluge et arche de Noé, Cahiers d'archéologie biblique* (2d ed., 1953); P. A. Lewis, *Study of the Interpretation of Noah and the Flood in Jewish and Christian Literature* (1968); J. C. Whitcomb and H. M. Morris, *Genesis Flood* (1966).

[D. J. BOURKE]

NOAILLES, ANNA ELIZABETH DE (1876–1933), novelist and poet. Of French origin, N. was the author of several novels, *La Nouvelle espérance* (1903), *La Domination* (1905), and *Le Livre de ma vie* (1932). As a poet she published verse strongly lyrical and colored by the influence of the East. Her collections included *Le Coeur innombrable* (1901), *Les Vivants et les morts* (1913), and *Le Poème de l'Amour* (1925). In 1921 she was elected to the Académie Royale de Belgique and in 1924 she was given in France the title *Princesse des Lettres*.

[J. R. AHERNE]

NOAILLES, LOUIS ANTOINE DE (1651–1729), abp. of Paris from 1695, card. from 1700, ambivalent figure in the doctrinal controversies of the times. Before coming to Paris he was bp. of Cahors from 1679, then abp. of Châlons-sur-Mer from 1680, and a participant in the 1682 Assembly of the French Clergy that approved the four Gallican articles (see GALLICANISM). At Paris in 1696 N. condemned a work of the Jansenist, Martin de Baco, that repeated teaching he had approved at Châlons the year before in P. *Quesnel's *Nouveau testament avec des réflexions morales*. Personally favorable to *Jansenism, he first resisted the **Vineam Domini* (1705) of Clement XI, condemning *obsequious silence; yet he also enacted harsh measures against Port Royal and allowed suppression and destruction of the abbey in 1709. He also accused the Jesuits of a laxist moral theology and deprived them of the right to preach or hear confessions in Paris (1713). N.'s greatest struggle was against the anti-Quietist bull *Unigenitus* (1713), also of Clement XI. In 1718 he publicly appealed, in Gallican fashion, to a future general council to correct it; in 1719 he wrote a pastoral against it, supporting Quesnel, that was condemned by the Holy Office (Aug. 3, 1719). He accepted the bull finally in 1728; it is said that in the end he regretted his opposition.

[T. C. O'BRIEN]

NOAILLES, PIERRE BIENVENU (1793–1861), founder of the Holy Family Sisters of Bordeaux. He experienced a conversion from a dissolute life in 1813, was ordained in 1819, and founded his religious community to further the apostolate to the sick and poor. In his lifetime he saw 124 houses established. His cause for beatification was introduced in 1944.

[T. C. O'BRIEN]

NOBILI, JOHN (1812–1856), Italian Jesuit, founder of the Univ. of Santa Clara, Cal., missionary. Nobili became a Jesuit in 1828 and was ordained in 1843. His brief career as a priest was marked by extraordinary achievement. Volunteering in 1843 to accompany Father De Smet to the Indian missions of the Pacific Northwest, Nobili endured six years of incredible hardship while converting large numbers of Indians. Moved to California because of broken health, he labored in San Francisco among the rough "forty-niners." In the cholera epidemic of 1850 he rendered heroic service. In 1851 at the request of Bp. J. *Alemany, he founded and was first president of what became the Univ. of Santa Clara, unrivalled in the frontier country for its excellence. BIBLIOGRAPHY: DAB 7:536.

[J. R. AHERNE]

NOBILI, ROBERTO DE (1577–1656), Italian Jesuit missionary to India. Born in Montepulciano, Tuscany, the son of a papal general, he entered the Society in 1596 and in 1604 was sent to Portuguese Goa, where he began a novel, but highly successful career in south India that spanned 60 years. The establishment in 1606 of a mission at Madura was only the first and most prosperous of many such missions he was to found in the hitherto untapped hinterlands of the subcontinent. In this work he was greatly aided by his linguistic proficiency, which enabled him to teach and write in Tamil, Telugu, and Sanskrit. More important still were the innovative methods he adopted in order to make headway among the Hindus, and esp. among the Brahmin elite, who were inimical to Christianity, not only because it cut across the rigid caste system of the country, but also because until then conversion had required acceptance of Western customs that were considered repugnant. In contrast to his predecessors, N. decided to accommodate himself to the dress, diet, and mores of the Hindus, for which purpose he embraced the life style of an Indian penitent and—rather more questionably—so as to ingratiate himself with the Brahmins, eschewed public contact with the outcastes of Hindu society. His methods proved successful—in 1609 he even converted the Brahmin Sanskirt scholar Sivadarma through whom he had become acquainted with the ancient language and religious literature of the Hindus—but they were opposed by many of his fellow missionaries and aroused sufficient controversy that for 5 years after 1618 N. was not permitted to baptize. Supported provisionally by the general of his order, who was reluctant to erode the progress of the mission, he was finally vindicated by Pope Gregory XV in 1623 and thereafter was free to pursue his work, which ultimately brought several thousand converts into the Christian fold. It is generally conceded that N.'s missionary adaptation made it possible for Christianity at least to gain a foothold among the higher castes in Indian society; but such success, admittedly, was purchased at the price of a compromise that left the basic defects of the caste system intact. *RICCI, M; *CHINESE RITES CONTROVERSY.

[E. M. GATES]

NOBIS QUOQUE PECCATORIBUS (To us sinners also), the opening words of the next to last prayer in the first Eucharistic Prayer. The English text begins, "For ourselves, too, we ask . . ." The opening words were spoken aloud in the Latin Canon, and the celebrant struck his breast while pronouncing them. In the English translation, the reference to ourselves as sinners is transferred to the concluding section in an effort to simplify the prayer's complexity without departing from its thought. This leaves the initial gesture less obviously relevant. This prayer contains a list of saints whose place we ask to share; the first four of these are mentioned in the Scriptures, and the remaining eleven were martyrs venerated at Rome. The Peter of this list is not the Apostle, but a Roman martyr whose name is linked with that of Marcellinus. The Alexander is not certainly identifiable. The seven women here named were added to the list, according to Adalbert, by Gregory I, who thought it unfitting that no female saints apart from the Virgin Mary were commemorated in the Canon.

[P. K. MEAGHER]

NOBLE ECCLESIASTICS, ACADEMY OF, see PONTIFICAL ECCLESIASTICAL ACADEMY.

NOBLE GUARD, former Guard of Honor of the Holy Father, attending him at public functions. Members were to be Roman princes. The Noble Guard, established in 1801, was abolished by Paul VI's reorganization of the papal household in 1970.

NÓBREGA, MANUEL DA (1517–70), Portuguese Jesuit, one of the founders of Portuguese Brazil. He was received into the Society after his studies at Salamanca and Coimbra. He headed the first Jesuit expedition to Brazil, landing at Bahia in 1549. He served as Jesuit superior and provincial, accompanied numerous expeditions, and was a trusted adviser to governors. He is considered cofounder of Rio de Janeiro and São Paulo, and shares with Anchieta the credit of establishing Brazilian civilization.

[P. DAMBORIENA]

NOCK, ARTHUR DARBY (1902–63), authority on religion and magic in Graeco-Roman paganism. Editor of the *Hermetica,* he also wrote extensively on early Christianity and Hellenistic Judaism. While making full use of literary and philosophical sources, he contributed esp. to our knowledge of the beliefs of common men as seen in inscriptions, papyri, and lesser-known technical or inspirational writings. See bibliography in his *Essays on Religion and the Ancient World* (ed. Z. Stewart, 2 v., 1970).

[Z. STEWART]

NOE, see NOAH.

NOËTUS OF SMYRNA (fl. end of 2d cent.), the first to teach *Monarchianism. His followers are known as Noëtians. He propounded his doctrines at Smyrna between 180 and 200. In an effort to avoid ditheism, he refused to admit the existence of more than one divine person, whom he declared to be the Father, even going so far as to say that it was the Father who had been born, suffered, and died (*see* PATRIPASSIANISM). He denied the doctrine of the Logos and held that the prologue of the Fourth Gospel and other passages had to be interpreted allegorically. He admitted no real distinction between the Divine Persons, who were to be regarded simply as different modes of action within the Godhead. Hence the term modalistic Monarchianism was applied to his teaching. His disciple Epigonus carried his doctrines to Rome. BIBLIOGRAPHY: G. Bardy, DTC 10:2195–96 s.v. "Monarchianisme"; LTK 8:180–181 s.v. "Patripassianismus."

[L. G. MÜLLER]

NOGARET, GUILLAUME DE (*c.*1260–1313), French legist, minister of Philip IV of France. After the death of Pierre Flotte, N. became the principal antagonist of Boniface VIII whom he accused of immorality and heresy. He was associated with the Sciarra and Colonna families in the capture of Boniface at Anagni where a popular uprising forced the release of the pope. N. was excommunicated by Benedict XI (1304) but absolved by Clement V (1311). He led Philip's attack against the Templars (1307) and was the principal influence in attempts to have the memory of Boniface VIII condemned. His writings against the pope were scandalous and calumnious. His political philosophy indicative of the spirit of later Gallicanism emphasized the omnipotence of the king. BIBLIOGRAPHY: R. Holtzmann, *Wilhelm von Nogaret* (1898); J. Rivière, *Le Problème de l'église et de l'état au temps de Philippe le Bel* (1926); J. R. Strayer, NCE 10:481.

[J. J. SMITH]

NOH MASK, Japanese mask initially representing a divinity, demon, or human character, developed from dance and music at shrines and temples, reaching a peak in the Momoyama period. Certain families of importance, independent makers and artists of note (Kōetsu, 1558–1637, important painter and calligrapher) engaged in their production. The Noh drama finally developed as refined tragedy owes much to the great patron Ashikaga Shogun Yoshimitsu (1358–1408).

[M. J. DALY]

NOLDE, EMIL (Emil Hansen, 1867–1956), German painter and graphic artist born in Nolde. An expressionist, N. taught at St. Gall (1892–98), joined Die Brucke (1906), produced first significant woodcuts and further powerful religious works (1909–12). His *Life of Christ* triptych was rejected. Long interest in primitive art confirmed by meeting Belgian J. Ensor (1911), N. traveled to the Far East (1913), England, and Paris. In 1927 a *Festschrift* was published in his honor. The Nazis, condemning him as "degenerate," confiscated 1000 paintings and graphics by 1937. N. won the International Venice Biennale prize in 1952. *The Pentecost, Last Supper, Christ Among the Children, Life of Mary of Egypt, Christ and the Adulteress, Prophet* (woodcut), of medieval intensity in brilliantly opposed colors, violently brushed, disturbing and provocative, establish N.'s work as central to German expressionism. BIBLIOGRAPHY: P. Selz, *Emil Nolde* (1963).

[M. J. DALY]

NOLDE, OTTO FREDERICK (1899–1972), Lutheran clergyman-educator and first director of the Commission of the Churches on International Affairs. After graduation from Lutheran Theological Seminary, Philadelphia, in 1923, he taught there until 1962, serving as dean from 1943. He was also CCIA director from the organization's beginning in 1946 until his retirement at the end of 1968. On the founding of the World Council of Churches in 1948, the CCIA became a part of the Council and Nolde an associate general secretary of the WCC.

[T. EARLY]

NOLDIN, HIERONYMUS (1838–1922), Jesuit moralist. N. was rector of the Jesuit seminary at Innsbruck and taught moral theology at that university. In 1902, he published a three-volume compendium of moral theology which was widely used as a seminary manual. The text, entitled *Summa theologiae moralis,* has gone through numerous editions, some under the direction of A. Schmitt and the latest edited by G. Heinzel in 1961.

[T. M. MCFADDEN]

NOLE, COLYNS DE, FAMILY (16th cent.), Netherlandish sculptors, Guillaume, his sons John and Robert, and probably Jacques. In 1515 G. executed the tomb of Canon Jehan Leporis, Cambrai, the sons working in Utrecht, and in Antwerp, where a great-grandson was finally engaged on the tomb of Cardinal Guillaume de Croy (1613) and in the Chapel of the Jesuit church.

[M. J. DALY]

NOLL, JOHN FRANCIS (1875–1956) bp. of Fort Wayne, Ind., journalist. Ordained for the Diocese of Fort Wayne in 1898, he embarked on a career as priest and bp. which had considerable national influence. His output as a writer and editor was prodigious. In 1912 he founded *Our Sunday Visitor,* a weekly newspaper that achieved national circulation; and in 1925, *Acolyte,* which in 1945 became the *Priest* magazine. His particular apostolate was directed toward informing non-Catholics about Catholic belief and practice. *Father Smith Instructs Jackson* (1913) was widely used throughout the U.S. A prolific pamphleteer, he also wrote a number of books, among them *A Vest Pocket of Catholic Facts* (1927) and *Our National Enemy Number One: Education without Religion* (1942). N. was named bp. of Fort Wayne in 1925. He proved to be a vigorous administrator and strengthened religious and educational resources of his diocese. His influence nationally was great through his activity on committees of the National Catholic Welfare Conference. He was a force in establishing the Legion of Decency to fight immorality in motion pictures and the National Organization for Decent Literature. In 1953 Pius XII bestowed on him the personal rank of archbishop.

[J. R. AHERNE]

NOMINALISM, a term with two meanings, one ontological and the other historical. (1) Ontologically, nominalism is a philosophical doctrine concerning the problem of universals. It holds that only individual things exist. In opposition to Platonism, which explains the similarity of two individuals by saying that they share a common property or nature, i.e., by assuming the existence of a universal, nominalism holds that if individuals similar to one another may be said to share anything at all, this can only be a spoken or written name (Lat. *nomen*) or a mental image, i.e., another individual. In the strict sense nominalism is also opposed to conceptualism, for it rejects universals even as objects of thought. Ontological nominalism has often led to a skeptical attitude concerning the objective value of intellectual knowledge (Hume). The term is therefore frequently used in a loose way, as if it were synonymous with conventionalism, empiricism, positivism. (2) Historically, nominalism is a term applied to certain movements in early and late scholasticism, whose representatives were called *nominales*. Their doctrines included, among others, ontological nominalism in the broad sense, i.e., not excluding conceptualism. The lasting contribution of the early nominalists (Roscelin of Compiègne, Abelard) to scholasticism was that they introduced logic, not as a science of disembodied platonist "things" (*res*), but as a formal science of expressions (*voces*), esp. meaningful expressions (*sermones*). They also continued the tradition of earlier dialecticians of applying logical analysis to theological matters, but they were not professional theologians and their formulations were condemned as heretical.

The ontological nominalism of *William of Ockham, the father of the nominalist school, can be interpreted as a reaction against the many subtle distinctions of the Scotists. According to the principle that later became known as Ockham's razor, plurality is never to be posited without necessity; Ockham accepted only real distinctions where each component is real and individual. He defended his ontological viewpoint by revising the logic of the suppositions of terms accordingly. Characteristically his first followers in Paris were censured in 1339 because of their zeal for logical analysis; they had claimed that certain propositions of accepted authorities were "false in virtue of their formulation" (*falsae de virtute sermonis*). But Ockham was not only an eminent logician, he was also a recognized theologian. His ontological nominalism was intimately connected with his view of a free, all-powerful, and all-merciful God. For him, the affirmation of a real distinction implied that God could create one component without the other. In view of God's absolute power (*potentia absoluta*), the coexistence of individuals was entirely contingent; the actual order of nature and grace was necessary only insofar as God had in fact directed his power in this way (*potentia ordinata*). As a consequence, arguments based on man's experience of the *de facto* order of nature could lead only to probable conclusions. Furthermore, observation of regular sequence became the only ground for asserting a causal relation between two natural phenomena. Ockham has therefore been hailed as a forerunner of empirical science. But he himself had shown no particular interest in scientific experiments, and although many 14th-cent. physicists (e.g., Buridan, Oresme) belonged to the nominalist school, they did not follow the physical theories of Ockham but continued rather those of their realist predecessors.

Ockham extended the radical contingency even to the moral order, stressing that commandments were free, even arbitrary, dictates of God's will. Proponents of today's "situation ethics" find this denial of an objective natural law much to their liking, but Ockham did not deny that God had in fact established a particular moral code that all men must obey. Furthermore, it is doubtful that the advocates of situation ethics would follow Ockham's logic to the end and agree that even the first commandment was contingent; that God could also have commanded us to hate him and not to love him. The followers of Ockham formed a new school, the *via moderna,* in opposition to the old schools of *Scotism and *Thomism, the *via antiqua*. It is important to realize that the bitter quarrels that sprang up between these movements took place within theological orthodoxy. It is true that two contemporaries of Ockham, Nicholas of Autrecourt and John of Mirecourt, whose philosophy was similar to Ockham's, were condemned by the Church. But the theology of Ockham himself was never condemned as heretical, despite the fact that he had been personally excommunicated in his quarrel with Pope John XXII (see POVERTY CONTROVERSY).

In the 14th and 15th cent. the leaders of the conciliar movement (Peter of Ailly, Jean Gerson) belonged to the *via moderna,* and, since Ockham's criticism had made philosophical reasonings doubtful, the nominalist theologians (e.g., Gabriel Biel) were especially attracted by the practical Christianity of the *Devotio moderna. The nominalist school has therefore been characterized as "the late medieval ecumenical movement" (H. A. Oberman). The Reformation has to be understood with this background in mind. But it would be wrong to see Protestantism as the direct and necessary outcome of nominalism. Actually Wycliffe, Hus, and Calvin came from the Scotist, and Zwingli from the Thomist school. It is true that Luther was strongly influenced by Biel, but so was his Catholic antagonist J. *Eck, and even some formulations of the Council of Trent go back to Biel. In the important doctrine of justification Luther rejected the Semi-Pelagianism of the nominalists, which said that man could do his very best (*facere quod in se est*) and put himself in the proper disposition for the infusion of grace. BIBLIOGRAPHY: G. Küng, NCE 10:483–485; E. A. Moody, EncPhil 5:533–534; 8:306–317; H. A. Oberman, *Harvest of Medieval Theology* (1963).

[G. KÜNG]

NOMOCANON (Gr. *nomos,* law, and *kanon,* rule), a collection of civil laws (*nomoi*) and ecclesiastical laws (canons) used by the Eastern Churches. Since the Byzantine emperors promulgated laws affecting the Church which also had its own canon law, there was always the possibility of conflict between the two. It became the task of Byzantine jurists, both civil and ecclesiastical, to compile and reconcile them. This led to the formation of the nomocanons. Under a rubric designating the subject matter were given the text or a summary of the canon and the corresponding civil legislation. Commentaries and opinions with supporting texts were often added. They are generally referred to by the number of titles or chapters they contain (e.g., *Nomocanon of XIV Titles*) or by the name of their compiler. The role of the nomocanons in lands subjected to Islam acquired particular importance. The law of the Koran did not apply to non-Muslims so that, apart from certain criminal and civil cases, Christians were not tried in Muslim courts. Instead, they formed semi-independent juridico-religious communities headed by their patriarchs and bishops. The nomocanons, then, became the basis of civil law for Christians in Muslim countries, although they are not legal codes in the modern sense but serve more as a guide for legislators and judges. BIBLIOGRAPHY: J. M. Buckley, NCE 10:486.

[E. EL-HAYEK]

NOMOCANON OF ABDISO, the legislation of the Nestorian Church compiled by Abdiso (Ebedjesus) Bar-Brika, Nestorian metropolitan of Nisibis (d. 1318) and the last writer in Syriac. He also wrote *Paradise of Eden* and *The Book of the Pearl about the Truth of the Christian Religion*. His nomocanon follows that of *Bar Hebraeus. It is an epitome of the synodal canons, assembled according to their subject matter. It contains three series of pseudo-Apostolic canons accepted by the Nestorians, a treatise on the notion of synodical canons, laws concerning marriage, inheritance laws, procedural and civil laws (derived from the Syro-Roman Book), and finally the duties of Christians. The second section deals with the hierarchy and its organization, concluding with a treatise on the institution of patriarchs. The patriarch of Rome is recognized as having primacy over all other patriarchs, and the patriarch of Babylon ranks as fifth and last. BIBLIOGRAPHY: J. Sauviller, DDC 3:292–388.

[E. EL-HAYEK]

NOMOCANON OF BAR HEBRAEUS, the principal canonical collection of the Syrian Jacobite Church. Its author was the historian and theologian, Gregory Abul-Faradj (1226–86), known as Bar Hebraeus because of his Jewish parentage. Metropolitan of Aleppo, he was named *maphrian in 1264 and was greatly admired by Christians of all rites and by non-Christians. His nomocanon, entitled *The Book of Guidance*, is divided into 40 ch., 8 of which treat of ecclesiastical laws, while the rest are concerned with civil legislation of the time. Most of this derives from Roman-Byzantine and from Islamic law. It also includes the canons of the Council of Chalcedon. To the present it is, at least in principle, the only canon law of the Jacobite Church. BIBLIOGRAPHY: A. Coussa, *Epitome praelectionum de iure ecclesiastico orientali* (3 v., 1941–50; suppl., 1958) 2:180.

[E. EL-HAYEK]

NOMOCANON OF IBN-AL'ASSAL, one of the most important collections of canon and civil law of the Coptic Church, published in 1236. The first section (22 ch.) deals with church laws, the second with civil laws. In addition to conciliar canons, it contains a compilation of canons of the Fathers and those of the patriarchs of Alexandria of later date. In the second section there is a peculiar list of canons in 4 ch. called Canons of Kings, which are attributed to Emperor Constantine and the 318 Fathers of Nicaea. In fact it contains: (1) an Arabic version of the code of Basil I and of the *Procheiros Nomos*; (2) the 130 canons in Arabic of the so-called *Syro-Roman Book of Laws;* (3) 26 canons including those of Nicaea and the laws of four emperors before Constantine; (4) the laws taken from the OT that are still binding on Christians. BIBLIOGRAPHY: S. Jargy, DDC 5:1237–42.

[E. EL-HAYEK]

NON EXPEDIT (Lat. for it is not expedient), an expression used in reference to the Holy See's policy of forbidding Italian Catholics to participate in the political life of the Italian nation because unification had been achieved at the territorial expense of the papacy. The Sacred Penitentiary gave its formal approval to the policy in 1874, but inasmuch as doubt existed as to whether abstention from politics was mandatory or advisable, Pius IX issued a brief (1877) that declared abstention a duty, and this viewpoint was solemnly reiterated by Leo XIII in his encyclical *Immortale Dei* (1885). At the beginning of the 20th cent., the Church became alarmed over the electoral successes of leftist or anticlerical candidates, and the *non expedit* was consequently modified. In *Il fermo proposito* (1905), Pius X stated that a dispensation could be granted by bps. when the good of the Church and of society required it. Thereafter Italian Catholics made their weight felt in politics. In 1919 Benedict XV formally abrogated the *non expedit*. In the same year, Luigi *Sturzo organized the first Catholic political party, the Partito Popolare. BIBLIOGRAPHY: A. C. Jemolo, *Church and State in Italy, 1850–1950* (tr. D. Moore, 1960).

[E. A. CARRILLO]

NONANTOLA, ABBEY OF, ancient Benedictine monastery near Modena, Italy. Founded in 752, it played a major role in the ecclesiastical, cultural, and economic life of medieval Italy. In the investiture conflict, Placid of Nonantola wrote *Liber de honore ecclesiae* (1111) in support of the papacy. Under commendatory abbots (after 1449), gradual decline set in. The house was suppressed in 1797, restored as an abbey *nullius* in 1815, but in 1821 was united with the archbishopric of Modena. Secularized in 1866, it was restored in 1926, now having its own chapter and seminary and serving a number of parishes. BIBLIOGRAPHY: G. Penco, *Storia del monachesimo in Italia* (1961) 113–116.

[L. J. LEKAI]

NONBEING, the opposite of being and in any of these senses the term "being" has. The oppositeness may be divided generally into contradictory or contrary oppositeness.

Contradictorily opposed to factual being as this means the existent or the whole existing universe is absolute nothingness. This is purely imaginable, i.e. it is a purely conceptual opposite. Given that anything exists, absolute nothingness is an impossibility. But the hypothesis or conceptualization of absolute nothingness can be entertained, as in St. Thomas Aquinas's *tertia via* for proving the existence of God (ThAq ST 1a,2,3; see GOD, PROOFS FOR THE EXISTENCE OF). There are some notions allied to this conception of absolute nothingness. One is the hypothetical nonfactuality of any being other than God; that no created being exist is a possibility; that all created being cease to exist is also a possibility (ThAq ST 104.4; see ANNIHILATION). Since it is impossible that God not exist, the hypothetical nonfactuality of creation still is not equivalent to absolute nothingness. A second allied notion is the imaginary nothingness prior to creation as creation is taken to be the production of the whole being from nothingness (*ex nihilo*). The mind necessarily thinks of creation as a form of change or production and in so doing conceives of an antecedent nonbeing as the "subject" out of which being is created. The fact of creation in time is, according to St. Thomas, known only because of the Christian understanding of Genesis; philosophy cannot demonstrate the impossibility of an eternally existing but created universe (ibid 46.2). The Christian understanding of creation involves thinking of God as pre-existing the beginning of time and consequently of the nonbeing of creation as prior to being. This mode of thinking makes it "easier" to imagine nonbeing. It is of interest to note that the existentialism of M. *Heidegger involves these senses of contradictory opposition to being as a condition for the project of grasping "to be."

A further sense of nonbeing as contradictorily opposed to being is also conceptual: the apprehension of being as the first known involves the apprehension of nonbeing as its opposite (ThAq ST 1a2ae, 94.2). Thus the first principle of thought and of reality is the principle of noncontradiction: a thing cannot be and not be at the same time and in the same sense. This meaning of nonbeing does not involve simply the facticity of existing; rather it means the positive consistency and coherence of being that "resists" its contradictory; being rejects, as it were, the opposite of the coherence it requires as an existent. The meaning of nonbeing in this sense is implied by St. Thomas when he says: "The *esse* of a thing, though other than its essence, is, nevertheless, not to be understood as something superadded in the manner of an accident, but as though constituted by the principles of the essence" (*In Meta*.4,lect.2; see ESSENCE AND ESSE). Nonbeing in this meaning implies that the existent is a substance with a definite kind of being (essence) by reason of which it can stand in being. The opposition of being to its contradictory in this sense is the basis for the intelligibility of being and founds the transcendental property of being called "truth." Being is "apt" to be the object of intelligence and is in fact conformed (that is its inner consistence) to the divine intelligence. Nonbeing in this context is also conceptual: thus God's knowledge of nonbeing is inherent in his self-knowledge, as matching the coherence of the divine essence itself, the exemplar of all participated, definite beings; their definiteness stands as the repudiation of nonbeing, their contradictories.

Nonbeing also stands in an opposition of contrariety to being; the opposition here, however, is between "this being" and "not this being." Potential being is nonbeing by reference to actual being. In this sense nonbeing does not mean nothingness; rather an actual being is denominated as "nonbeing" when it is potential with reference to another actual being or quality of actual being. The meaning of potential being is at the basis of the Aristotelian explanation of change; it is Aristotle's answer to Parmenides' denial of change on the grounds that change means prior nonbeing and "from nothing, nothing comes to be." Change is not the emergence from nonbeing or nothingness, but involves an actual being that is not yet the being that it becomes.

Another form of contrariety to being is the privative. Privation is not mere negation, but the lack in a being of something that should be present; it is the lack of the completeness that should be there. The "nonbeing" of evil is explained through the privative sense of nonbeing. It has special application to the meaning of sin as an act, a way of being, which lacks the fullness of being it should have (ThAq ST 1a2ae,18.1).

Finally, nonbeing sometimes describes a type of being that has no real existence but which is given existence in thought. The thought itself, of course, as a psychological phenomenon is as real as a sensation; but the content of thought in some of its aspects may have purely mental existence; it is a quality attached to the content purely as existing in thought: thus the logical classifications "genus" or "species."

[T. C. O'BRIEN]

NONBELIEVERS, SECRETARIAT FOR, established April 7, 1965, by Pope Paul VI as part of the RC Church's dialogue with the world, esp. with those who do not believe in God. Unbelief here includes systematic atheism, agnosticism, and indifferentism. Pope John's encyclical *Pacem in terris,* Pope Paul's letter *Ecclesiam suam,* and the Vatican Council II's *Pastoral Constitution on the Church in the Modern World* (esp. nn. 19–21) provided the general guidelines for the secretariat's work. Cardinal Koenig was named its first president. The initial activity of the secretariat was to define the limits and sphere of the dialogue with nonbelievers, esp. through participation or sponsorship of conferences and congresses. Particular attention has been given to identifying the motives of unbelief. The secretariat is loosely structured. Its core unit is a selected number of bps., representing episcopal conferences or other units of the Church, which make up the deliberative assembly. A staff of bps. and experts is aided by consultors, Catholic and non-Catholic, from around the world. BIBLIOGRAPHY: AAS (1966) 58: 37–40; V. Miano, "Tasks Facing the Secretariat for Nonbelievers," *Pastoral Approach to Atheism* (Concilium 23 (1967) 122–29).

[L. B. GUILLOT]

NON-CATHOLIC, negatively inclusive term used to designate persons, Churches, ecclesial groups, and elements relating to the same, which are not RC or in union with the RC Church. The English term translates the Latin *acatholici* which has been used principally in older RC documents, e.g., CIC cc. 1258, 1325, 1350, 1399. Roman Catholics were forbidden with various qualifications to take an active part in non-Catholic worship services, to hold discussions with non-Catholics on matters of faith, or to use editions of Scripture or books treating professedly of religion which were published by non-Catholics. The disadvantages of the term are (1) esp. that it refers without distinction to the Orthodox, Anglicans, Protestants, and even to nonbelievers, and (2) that today it seems to mean all those who do not accept the primacy of the Roman Pontiff, though many non-Romans share in the Catholic tradition in various ways. The documents of Vatican II use in its place various descriptive phrases, such as separated brothers, Churches and ecclesial communities not in communion with Rome, or the Apostolic See, or the successor of Peter.

[L. B. GUILLOT]

NON-CATHOLIC SERVICES, an obsolescent generalization used in older RC theological and canonical literature (cf. CIC c. 1258); often used to include the various and particular forms of worship of Orthodox, Anglican, and Protestant Churches, and other worshiping communities.

More recently, the documents of Vatican II and the literature deriving from them, such as the *Directory* of the Secretariat for Promoting Christian Unity (25 ff.), distinguish more precisely between (a) various spiritual endowments, activities, and resources to be found among Christians not in full communion with the RC Church, and (b) those more official or sanctioned forms of worship celebrated according to the liturgical books or norms of a particular Church or ecclesial community. Roman Catholic appreciation and participation norms for both are intended to reflect this diversity and vary according to the Churches, communities, and cultures concerned.

Most Christian Churches have been profoundly influenced by the contemporary liturgical movement, so that a balance of Word and sacrament has generally been restored, removing a former major difference in Protestant and Catholic services. Under the same influence, the basic shape of eucharistic worship has become more and more identifiable. BIBLIOGRAPHY: R. P. Marshall and M. J. Taylor, *Liturgy and Christian Unity* (1965).

[L. B. GUILLOT]

NON-CHRISTIANS, SECRETARIAT FOR, established May 17, 1964, by Pope Paul VI, in order to implement the initiatives of Vatican II (Vat. II NonChrRel No. 1). The first chairman of the new secretariat was Cardinal Marella. Its scope and aims have been carefully distinguished from those of the Congregation for Evangelization. The secretariat seeks cordial fraternal relations, mutual understanding, and help between the RC Church and members of non-Christian religions, whereas the congregation is concerned for preaching the Gospel and conversions. The secretariat's initial work was more practical and contact-establishing than doctrinal and regulatory. Its staff structure includes a chairman, secretary, undersecretary, the head of an Islamic department, and several assistants. The basic staff is supplemented by specialist consultors and correspondents. The secretariat began by publishing a trimestral *Bulletin,* monographs, a series of *Guides* on various faiths, and some manuals of religion for use by seminaries and theological faculties. BIBLIOGRAPHY: *Toward the Meeting of Religions* (n.d.); and P. Humbertclaude, "Clarification of the Nature and Role of the Secretariat for Non-Christians," *Bulletin* 4 (1969) 76–96.

[L. B. GUILLOT]

NONCONFORMISTS, a term first used to refer to English Puritans who objected to subscription to the *Acts of Uniformity but also declined to leave the C of E; it became interchangeable with *Dissenters during the *Restoration. During the reign of Elizabeth I, Puritanism emerged within the C of E and fragmented into several parties. Some accepted episcopal government but wanted further reforms of ceremonies; others favored a Presbyterian polity for the English Church; another group adopted a *congregational view of the Church and separated from the C of E; but a large number of those who favored congregational principles abhorred schism and remained within the Church. When James I became king, the Presbyterians and nonseparating Congregationalists hoped for his support. The *Millenary Petition was presented to him in 1603, setting forth desired religious reforms, but at the *Hampton Court Conference (1604) he ordered all to conform or he would harry them out of the land. Supported by the King, Richard Bancroft (1544–1610), abp. of Canterbury, ordered that all clergy accept the Royal Supremacy, vestments, and the Book of Common Prayer. Nonconformity continued to grow, reinforced by those who objected to James's absolutist concept of monarchy. Charles I inherited the religious problem, and in 1628 appointed William *Laud abp. of Canterbury with a mandate to purge the Church's ranks of all who would not accept the Book of Common Prayer. Laud's rigorous policies caused thousands to migrate to Massachusetts Bay and elsewhere. Political and religious opponents of the King combined with parliamentary forces to engage in the civil war that culminated in the beheading of Charles I. Under the Commonwealth and Protectorate of Oliver *Cromwell, a large measure of toleration was granted to Protestants, and new sects (Friends, Diggers, Levelers, Familists, etc.) multiplied. The Restoration began in 1660 with the coronation of Charles II, who in the *Declaration of Breda gave assurances of wider toleration. The Presbyterians hoped for a more comprehensive establishment broad enough to include them; and the Independents, Baptists, and other groups expected freedom of worship. A new Act of Uniformity (1662) indicated the intention to enforce a rigid uniformity of religion, and about 2,000 clergy were ejected from their livings because they could not subscribe. Those who had been in the state Church without conforming to the required rites became Dissenters instead of simply Nonconformists. With ministers squeezed out of the Church by the Act of Uniformity, the people forbidden to worship in private by the *Conventicle Act (1664), and all dissenters eliminated from political and military offices by the *Corporation Act (1661) and *Test Act (1673), great pressure was exerted to compel conformity to the Church of England.

The accession of William and Mary was accompanied by the *Toleration Act (1689), which granted freedom of worship to all Protestants who met certain conditions (an oath of allegiance and acceptance of the *Thirty-Nine Articles, with slight exceptions), but the Test and Corporation Acts and other disabilities remained in force. The main Nonconformist bodies were the Baptists, Presbyterians, and Congregationalists, referred to often as "the three denominations." Greater freedom did not lead to more growth, since the Presbyterians and General Baptists were decimated by Unitarianism, and Particular Baptists and Congregationalists were afflicted with a hyper-Calvinism that opposed evangelistic effort. After 1738, the Methodists became an important religious force, but originally they were not classed as Nonconformists or Dissenters, since John *Wesley insisted throughout his life on their remaining within the Church of England. The 19th cent. witnessed a vigorous growth of Baptists, Congregationalists, and Methodists and a revival of the almost defunct Presbyterians. Noted preachers emerged from the Baptists (Charles H. Spurgeon, Robert Hall), the Congregationalists (R. W. Dale, Joseph Parker), and the Methodists (Hugh Price Hughes, John Scott Lidgett). Strong lay leaders were active both in church affairs and in political and social movements. In 1828 the Test and Corporation Acts were abolished; in 1836 marriages were allowed in Nonconformist meeting houses; in 1880 burial services by Dissenters were permitted in churchyards; in 1868 the payment of church rates was made voluntary; and in 1871 religious tests for Oxford and Cambridge degrees were removed, except for theology. The "Nonconformist conscience" played an important role in effecting social reforms during the century. By the 20th cent. the term Nonconformist was being replaced by *free Churches; these cooperated in various ways. In the 20th cent. all the free Churches have suffered losses of membership and influence along with the C of E, and various proposals for church union have been under way in recent years. BIBLIOGRAPHY: H. W. Clark, *History of English Nonconformity* (2 v., 1911–13); H. Davies, *English Free Churches* (1952); R. G. Cowherd, *Politics of English Dissent* (1956).

[N. H. MARING]

NONCONFORMITY, aloofness from this world, a major doctrine of the *Mennonites. It is based on Rom 12.2, "Be not conformed to this world," and on other NT passages. Christians in all ages have wrestled with the problem of their relation to the world, to society, and to culture; the term nonconformity particularly denotes the Mennonite response to the problem. Mennonite settlement groups as a rule have had no written regulations for their practices on nonconformity, but where the cultural environment is a threat, specific rules have been adopted by conferences and by ministerial leadership. Every area of life is affected. In business, nonconformity forbids partnership with non-Christians and enforces strict standards of justice and brotherly aid. Some lenders even refuse to accept interest from the needy. In civil life, it rules out standing for office and at times even voting. *Nonresistance and refusal of military service are applications of the rule of nonconformity. In dress, nonconformity means rejection of fashion, sumptuousness, and the use of jewelry and cosmetics. Mustaches are avoided because of their military association, but the men of some Mennonite groups are required to wear beards. Luxury and most forms of recreation—card playing, the theater, and television—are avoided. Prohibition of tobacco and liquor dates only from the late 19th cent., and as the result of outside influences like the temperance movement rather than from Mennonite tradition. Personal demeanor is restrained and quiet. Some conservative Mennonites also cling to the language of their forefathers and to remote rural life, opposing all modern inventions and industrial work.

Nonconformity is maintained chiefly in three ways: through tradition, indoctrination, and discipline. At times, worldliness, has been confusedly identified with variations in cultural conventions, and repressive and authoritarian measures have been used to ensure uniformity. The Mennonite ideal seeks to assert the positive aspect of nonconformity, i.e., that it is conformity to God's will and nature, as well as a way of imitating Christ's life. BIBLIOGRAPHY: H. S. Bender et al., MennEnc 3:890–897.

NONIUS MARCELLUS (fl. *c.*323 A.D.), compiler of *De compendiosa doctrina per litteras ad filium,* one of the primary encyclopedic sources on Latin letters available both to *Isidore of Seville and to the early medieval revivers of learning. BIBLIOGRAPHY: OCD 610.

[T. C. O'BRIEN]

NONJURORS, members of the C of E who, because they had previously taken oaths of loyalty to James II and his lawful heirs, refused to swear allegiance to William and Mary. Holding to a divine-right doctrine of kingship, they denied Parliament's authority to depose the lawful sovereign. Paradoxically, five of the nonjuring bps. had been among those who had helped precipitate the Revolution of 1688 by their disobedience to James's order that his *Declaration of Indulgence be read in all the churches. Their dilemma was that belief in passive obedience to a king conflicted with the conviction that the Church was autonomous in spiritual matters. Among those whose consciences kept them from taking the new oaths was William Sancroft, abp. of Canterbury, who until his death was the spiritual leader of the nonjurors' movement. Seven other bps. and about 400 of the lower clergy also scrupled to take the oaths. Prominent laymen were also nonjurors. Sancroft would not officiate in the coronation of the new sovereigns, but allowed his suffragan to do so. In 1690, he and five bps. were deprived of their offices, two other objectors having already died. When their successors were appointed, they claimed that the choice was unlawful because it was made solely by secular authority; they insisted that although they could not carry out the duties, they were still the rightful incumbents of their offices. Thus they became a schismatic party within the C of E, and after 1694 they began to ordain new bps., although they could assign them to no districts. After 1715, the movement ceased to have real significance, although the schism existed until the death of the last bishop, Boothe, in 1805. BIBLIOGRAPHY: J. H. Overton, *Nonjurors, Their Lives, Principles, and Writings* (1903).

[N. H. MARING]

NONNBERG, ABBEY OF, Benedictine convent in Salzburg, Austria. Founded by St. Rupert *c.*700, it is the oldest Benedictine monastery in either Germany or Austria. Rebuilt in 1043, the abbey was dedicated to its first abbess, St. Erentrude—believed to have been St. Rupert's niece. After a fire in 1423 the church was again rebuilt (1464–1509). In 1623, Abp. Paris Lodron introduced the Tridentine reform. Known for its wealth, Nonnberg was never suppressed and remained a noble abbey until the 18th century. Always regarded as a center of learning and education, Nonnberg continues to maintain a college for women.

[M. A. MCFADDEN]

NONNUS OF PANOPOLIS (fl. *c.*400), Greek poet from Upper Egypt, the probable author of two long poems. The first was the *Dionysiaca*, an epic in 48 books, describing the journey of the Greek god Dionysius to India and pagan both in theme and language; the later *Paraphrase of the Gospel of St. John,* in hexameters, is, by contrast, Christian in inspiration. Once thought to be the works of two separate authors, the poems, by their similarities in style and meter, led finally to the probable conclusion that they were penned by the same man, one who had evidently converted to Christianity.

[E. M. GATES]

NONRESISTANCE, a doctrine developed by the 16th-cent. Swiss Anabaptists and particularly associated with the Mennonites. Nonresistance is the renunciation of any coercive means, whether employed by individuals or society, to redress wrongs or to achieve objectives; *pacifism and *conscientious objection are allied but not synonymous terms. The *Schleitheim Confession (1529) expressed the doctrinal basis of nonresistance as a religious tenet: "The sword is ordained of God outside the perfection of Christ." The Swiss Anabaptists taught nonparticipation in civil affairs, regarding the civil power as alien to the Gospel, a relic of OT law. Unlike the *Zwickau Prophets or the Anabaptists at Münster, they did not seek to establish a theocratic kingdom by the sword but adopted an attitude of passive obedience; nonresistance was part of this. The *Dordrecht Confession of Faith (1632) includes nonresistance in the practice of Christian love, quoting Jesus' teaching to avoid revenge and to love enemies.

Historically, the practice of nonresistance has varied among the Mennonites with regard to military service. Because of persecution in their early history, those who were not martyred fled into isolated settlements in the Swiss Alps, the steppes of Russia, and later to the frontiers of N America. Nonresistance, nonparticipation, and nonconformity developed as characteristics that to this day continue among such conservative Mennonites as the Amish. In W Europe the Mennonites had almost completely given up traditional nonresistance by the time of World War I. Since World War II a revitalization of the peace witness has taken place, particularly in The Netherlands and Germany. In Russia, Mennonites served as noncombatants from 1880 to 1930, when it became impossible to claim complete exemption from military service. In N America the first real challenge came to Mennonite nonresistance during World War I. Since that time many traditional Mennonites have served in the armed forces. Nevertheless, the peace witness has been intensified in an effort to express a total Christian way of life in times of strife. Civilian public service, "pax service," and many channels of relief activities are signs of this intensification. Some Mennonites are involved in the struggle for social and racial equality by making use of the legal processes of democracy and even by political involvement. Their isolation belongs to the past. BIBLIOGRAPHY: MennEnc 3:897–907.

[T. C. O'BRIEN]

NONSECTARIAN, uncommitted to sectarian principles or spirit; unaffiliated with any denomination. The term may imply a desire to emphasize things on which Christians agree; or it may be used by *independent Churches that consider all major denominations as tainted with unorthodoxy and regard denominational distinctions with indifference.

[N. H. MARING]

NONVIOLENT RESISTANCE, a form of civil disobedience that seeks to change a law, a policy, or even the form of government by peaceful means or passive noncompliance. The *nonresistance of the *Anabaptists and *Mennonites represented, in its beginnings at least, the theological view that participation in civil life is alien to the Gospel, and it particularly involved refusal of military service. Nonviolent resistance has a more active meaning: it is not simple passivity, the renunciation of violence, but an active course of political participation. The first and foremost modern example of such a course was M. *Ghandi. It became a prominent part of the campaign of M.L. *King for racial justice, and of many adherents of the peace movement during the Viet Nam war. The moral rightness of resistance to law or to a form of government requires that the resistance be against a genuine injustice and not simply in favor of a factional cause; that whatever form the resistance takes, it does not create a greater upheaval in the community that is more harmful than the injustice it seeks to remedy; that its pursance not trample on the legitimate rights of others.

[T. C. O'BRIEN]

NOORT, ADAM VAN (1562–1641), Flemish painter of religious subjects, teacher of Rubens, and Jordaens, showing early elegant figure drawing with mannerist exaggerations, developing into plump forms and a richer ''palette'' from Italy, seen in *St. John Baptist Preaching* (1601), the rediscovered *Holy Family* (Georgetown Univ., Washington, D.C.) and *Suffer Little Children to Come unto Me* (Brussels). BIBLIOGRAPHY: E. Larsen, ''Ein 'Heilige Familie' von Adam van Noort,'' *Speculum artis,* 15 (1963).

[M. J. DALY]

NOOSPHERE, Teilhard de Chardin's term for the sphere of self-reflective consciousness circumscribing the earth through man and his media of communication. Within the process of evolution, the noosphere is the most recent layer added to the planet earth. Prior to the noosphere, non-self-reflective conscious life had spread around the earth, covering it with an infinite variety of living organisms. This biosphere had itself sprung forth from the hydrosphere, which at one time covered our earth. Beneath the hydrosphere lay the molecular spheres of rock and metal. The noosphere, then, is the latest layer to surround our planet earth. It is the sphere of thought which, like life itself, is multiplied in the population explosion of individual particles of thinking matter called man. BIBLIOGRAPHY: Teilhard de Chardin, *Phenomenon of Man,* (1959); *idem, Future of Man.* (1964).

[W. J. DUGGAN]

NORBERT OF XANTEN, ST. (*c.*1080–1134), founder of the Premonstratensians. A canon of Xanten, N. passed many years at the court of Frederick, abp. of Cologne, and of Emperor Henry V; he was in Rome at the humiliation of Paschal II in 1111. An accident shook him into a realization of his vocation, and he returned to Xanten after being ordained a priest in Cologne (1115) and for 3 years did penance. After being arrested for preaching without a license, N. sought and was granted authorization to preach by Gelasius. Callistus II and Bartholomew of Laon granted him permission to found a monastery at a ruined church near Laon in the valley of Prémontré in 1121. Here N. combined contemplation with his pastoral work, in some way foreshadowing the poverty of St. Francis, and concern with life in urban centers. With St. Bernard at Soissons, he condemned Abelard. In 1126, N. was elected abp. of Magdeburg, where the clergy were in urgent need of reform. Hugh of Fosse was elected head of the order and engaged in the mission to the Wends. In 1130, again with St. Bernard, N. went to Italy with the emperor to put an end to the schism. He returned to his see, fell ill, died, and was buried in Magdeburg. In 1627 his remains were moved to Strahov, near Prague. BIBLIOGRAPHY: J. R. Sommerfeldt, NCE 10:492; N. Backmund, LTK 7:1030–31; DTC 13:2–5; MGS 12:663–706; PL 170: 1253–1344; Butler 2:484–487; J.-B. Valvekens, BiblSanct 9:1050–68.

[S. WILLIAMS]

NORFOLK, DUKE OF, English title long held by Catholics. The early holders of the title were of the Mowbray family (1425–76) and from them the office of Earl Marshall, in charge of coronations, was attached to the title beginning with Thomas de Mowbray, the first duke of Norfolk (d. 1399). The more famous Howard family, related to the sovereign, received the dukedom of Norfolk in the person of John Howard (1430?–85) in 1485. He held many vital political and military positions and died in battle at Bosworth Field. Thomas Howard (1443–1524), created Earl of Surrey and Lord Treasurer to Henry VII (1501–22), was responsible for the English victory over the Scots at Flodden Field in 1513, for which he was given the dukedom. Thomas Howard (1473–1554) succeeded his father and was also Lord Treasurer; a rival of Card. Wolsey he was responsible for the latter's fall and became close adviser to Henry VIII. Presiding at the trial of Ann Boleyn, his niece, he agreed to her execution. He led the expedition that destroyed the Pilgrimage of Grace, an attempt by northern Catholics to stem the Reformation in England. His son, Henry Howard, Earl of Surrey, was a famous poet; he sought the regency and quartered the royal armies with his own; for the son's audacity the Duke of Norfolk, his father, was condemned, but the death of Henry VIII saved his life. With the coming of Mary to the throne, Norfolk was restored as Lord Treasurer and Earl Marshall. Thomas Howard (1538–72) was fourth Duke of Norfolk. His life was a web of conspiracy and intrigue, much of it concerned with his plan to marry Mary, Queen of Scots, and depose Elizabeth. He was also on the periphery of the Spanish plan to invade England and restore the old Faith. Reluctantly, Elizabeth signed his death warrant and he was executed in 1572 for treason. There was a gap in the succession, no Howard being granted the dukedom until Henry (1628–84) was restored to the title by Charles II in 1660. The eleventh Duke, Charles Howard turned Protestant. His successor Bernard Howard returned to Catholicism. Henry Fitzalan-Howard (1847–1917) was the titular head of the Catholic laity and played a prominent role in securing the cardinalate for John Henry Newman; he officiated at the coronation of Edward VII and George V. The 16th Duke, Bernard Fitzalan-Howard (1908–76) was a prominent Catholic layman; he officiated at the coronation of George VI and Elizabeth II, and supervised Winston Churchill's state funeral. The 17th Duke of Norfolk, a cousin of the preceding, is Miles Francis Stapleton Fitzalan Howard, who succeeded to the title in 1975; he also is Earl Marshal, Hereditary Marshal, and Chief Butler of England. Among his Catholic interests is the upkeep of Westminster Cathedral and he has lectured in the U.S. to attract American Catholic support for the project.

[J. R. AHERNE]

NORIS, HENRY (1631–1704), Augustinian theologian and historian. Created cardinal by Innocent XII in 1695, N. was later called to Rome as custodian of the Vatican Library and consultor to the Holy Office. He is the so-called founder and principal exponent of the later Augustinian school of the

17th and 18th cent. whose theologians are sometimes known as *Augustinenses*. In theology, including his doctrine on grace, he follows the main tradition of his predecessors, particularly Gregory of Rimini. His chief concern was to restore the authority of St. Augustine by a new and timely presentation of his theology of grace to counteract earlier Protestant and Jansenistic interpretations. Among the more crucial and controversial points of doctrine defended by N. and his school are those concerning man's ordination to beatific vision and the nature of efficacious grace. According to N., the impossibility of a purely natural state for man arises, not from God's "absolute" power, but from his "ordered" power, namely a power directed by his goodness and wisdom. Accordingly, the gifts originally conferred upon man, including sanctifying grace, though absolutely gratuitous on man's part, were owing to his nature by a title of benevolence on the part of the Creator (*ex decentia bonitatis Creatoris*). In consequence of original sin, man needs efficacious grace to enable his will to do good, namely, a grace that infallibly, but freely, produces its effect by a spiritual delectation (*delectatio victrix*) strong enough to overcome the contrary attraction of concupiscence. Although N.'s writings were strongly attacked for their alleged Jansenism, they were declared orthodox in a brief of Benedict XIV, issued on July 31, 1748, which also accorded the Augustinian system the same status allowed to Bañezianism and Molinism with respect to the problem of grace and free will. N.'s more important works include: *Vindiciae Augustinianae, Historia Pelagiana,* and *Dissertatio de synodo V oecumenica*. BIBLIOGRAPHY: F. Rojo, "Ensayo bibliográfico de Noris, Bellelli y Berti," *Analecta Augustiniana* 26 (1956) 146–222; H. de Lubac, *Augustinisme et théologie moderne* (1965).

[R. P. RUSSELL]

NORMA NORMATA (the rule ruled), a phrase describing confessions of faith esp. in Lutheranism. The *norma normans* (the rule ruling) is Holy Scripture, "the only rule and norm according to which all doctrine and teachers must be appraised and judged" (*Formula of Concord, Epitome). The confessions of faith are held to be genuine rules of faith because they, in fact, conform to the Scriptures; but they are a ruled rule, i.e., subordinate or derived. The Formula of Concord lists as such rules of faith the *Augsburg Confession, the *Apology for the Augsburg Confession, the *Schmalkaldic Articles, and Luther's *Catechisms. Adherence to the confessional principle has varied throughout Lutheran history, and is now strong, esp. with regard to the Augsburg Confession. Other Protestant confessional bodies agree in the principle that all doctrinal standards are rules of faith solely as subordinate to the Bible. BIBLIOGRAPHY: T. E. Schmauk and C. T. Benze, *Confessional Principle* (1911); Mayer RB 142–144.

[T. C. O'BRIEN]

NORMAN ARCHITECTURE, 11th-cent. church building by the Normans of NW France, most progressive of French local Romanesque styles and major influence in the evolution of Gothic architecture. The abbey of Jumièges (1037–1067), St. Étienne at Caen, in Normandy, begun (1067) by William the Conqueror in its W façade with two towers, tripartite divisions vertically and horizontally, and compound piers rising to sexpartite vaults showing earliest "ribs," are foreshadowings of Early Gothic. In England the cathedral of Durham (1093) with huge supporting columns, "ribs" of the choir vaults (1104) and slightly pointed arches (1130) determined the course of Gothic building. And in Sicily (after the Norman conquest in the mid-11th cent., at the crossroads of Byzantine, Arabic, and French-Norman cultures) in Palermo and at Monreale where the beautiful French "storied" capitals of the cloisters (one pair depicting William I offering the church to the Virgin), and glorious mosaics are magnificent in a Norman-Islamic-Byzantine plastic and decorative efflorescence.

[M. J. DALY]

NORMANS, also called Vikings, Norsemen, Northmen, were the Teutonic ancestors of the modern Swedes, Danes, and Norwegians who in the course of their incursions, settlement, and colonization in other European lands became an essential and vital constituent of medieval society and culture. During the latter half of the 9th cent., they held more than half of England and Ireland; attacked all the coast and river towns of France, pillaged Utrecht and Bremen, but made no permanent home in Germany; sailed into the Mediterranean, attacked Spain and Morocco, ravaged Provence and sacked Luna in Tuscany; pushed their settlement north and west into Iceland, Greenland, and temporarily to the North American coast; and, possibly as early as the 8th cent., advanced southeastward, laying the first trade routes through eastern Europe as far as the Caspian and Black Sea regions, and established themselves in Kiev around 852—an event usually accepted as the beginning of Russian history.

There is a discernible pattern in Norse activity in the 9th and 10th cent. pillaging forays, increasing in frequency and intensity, then permanent settlement followed by colonization. Norse settlement began in England when the Normans wintered at the mouth of the Thames in 851. Then followed a continuous conquest of land which left standing only one Anglo-Saxon kingdom, Wessex, whose king, Alfred the Great (871–899), checked the invaders and kept them north of the Thames. Alfred's son and grandson succeeded in regaining the conquered land and restoring Anglo-Saxon dominion. Succeeding Saxon kings were too weak to stem the tide of the massive Norse invasion of the 11th cent., and the Danish King Canute became the recognized King of all England. He gave to England an interval of good government and, being a convert to Christianity, an active support to the Church. Canute's sons were less capable rulers, and Alfred's line was restored in Edward the Confessor (1042) only to fall before the assault of William of Normandy (1066).

The ravages of the Norsemen in Frankish Gaul were even more serious than those in England. In 841 the first Norse fleet entered the Seine. The succeeding years saw Paris pillaged and burned and practically all the other important towns along the seacoasts and rivers plundered. In 866 and again in 877, Charles the Bald bought off the invaders. By the early 10th cent. leaders of Church and State realized that the enemy could no longer be bought or driven off; their goal was now land for permanent settlement. Charles the Simple, therefore, ceded in fief to the Norman leader Rollo and his followers (911–912) the whole Channel coast from the Somme to Brittany, which they promptly set out to enlarge and ultimately more than doubled. Thus was created the great fief of Normandy, which under relative prosperity and strong government became one of the best ruled lands of 11th-cent. Europe and where, once Christianity had been established, Christian life flourished. Its monasteries, such as Bec and Saint-Évroult, became famous centers of Benedictine learning under scholars lured from other parts of Europe, e.g., Lanfranc of Pavia and Anselm of Aosta. Normandy was prominent in the great religious and ecclesiastical renewal of the 11th century. After the conquest of 1066, Norman bps. and abbots undertook the reform of the English Church.

Bands of Norman adventurers brought Norman influence also to southern Italy and Sicily, where after a century of conquest they created the kingdom of Sicily (1139). So the Normans may be said to have created a Russian, a Sicilian, an English, and a French "Normandy," in each of which they were absorbed by their environment, adapting themselves to the language, culture, and institutions of the land in which they settled. The Normans were not, however, only receivers; they brought to their new homes the dynamism of their enterprise, daring, and leadership. BIBLIOGRAPHY: C. H. Haskins, *Normans in European History* (1916); for an extensive bibliography, R. Foreville, NCE 10:501–502.

[G. M. COOK]

NORRIS, JAMES (1917–1976), Catholic lay leader in antipoverty and refugee work. He was for many years associated with Catholic Relief Services and was associate executive director at the time of his death. He also labored for the U.S. bps.' overseas aid and development agency. After World War II he worked in Italy with G. Montini, afterwards Paul VI, in refugee resettlement. He was the only layman to address a session of Vatican Council II. He became a member after the council of the Pontifical Commission for Justice and Peace and was an assistant to the Synod of Bishops' special secretariat for world justice.

[T. C. O'BRIEN]

NORTH AMERICAN COLLEGE, a pontifical seminary in Rome for the education of diocesan clergy of the United States. Founded in 1859 by Pius IX, it was located in Via dell'Umiltà in the center of Rome; since 1953 it has been housed in a new building on the Janiculum Hill, overlooking St. Peter's. It has played a major role in the American Church, not only in the education of clergy for service in the U.S., but as a point of representation for the American hierarchy in Rome. The rector, appointed by the pope from names submitted by the American bps., has been an unofficial envoy of the hierarchy to the Holy See. From 1859 to 1932, undergraduate students attended the Urban College (Propaganda) but since then have attended the Gregorian University. Soon after Italy took over the Papal States in 1870, the American College was threatened with confiscation, but President Chester A. Arthur intervened to save it. During World War II the students at the American College were sent home, and the building was used to house Italian refugees. In 1953 a new location housed the college. In its long history the American College has provided the American Church with over a hundred bps. and a number of cardinals. It has also served as a hostel for American prelates visiting Rome and a service center for American visitors to Rome generally. BIBLIOGRAPHY: R. McNamara, *American College in Rome, 1855–1955* (1956).

[J. R. AHERNE]

NORTH AMERICAN MARTYRS. Six Jesuits and two laymen killed by Indians in Canada and the Northeastern U.S. from 1642 to 1649 were canonized by Pius XI in 1930. (See BRÉBEUF, JOHN DE, ST.; CHABANEL, NOËL, ST.; DANIEL, ANTONY, ST.; GARNIER, CHARLES, ST.; GOUPIL, RENÉ, ST.; JOGUES, ISAAC, ST.; LALANDE, JOHN, ST.; LALEMANT, GABRIEL, ST.) See also Butler 3:645–652; R. G. Thwaites, *Jesuit Relations* (73 v., 1897–1901); J. Wynne, *Jesuit Martyrs of North America* (1925); H. Fouqueray, *Martyrs du Canada* (1930), contains excellent bibliog.

[P. K. MEAGHER]

NORTH CAROLINA, S Atlantic state admitted to the Union (1789) as the 12th of the original Thirteen States. Giovanni da Verrazano's French expedition (1524) discovered the coast of North Carolina, and in 1540 Hernando de Soto entered the mountains of the region. Neither French nor Spanish settlement followed, however; Indians controlled the area until the arrival of the British. Walter Raleigh established the first English colony in America at Roanoke Island off the North Carolina coast (1585), and Virginians established permanent Carolina settlements in the 1650s and 1660s. Created as a proprietary colony by Charles II (1663), Carolina adopted (1669) John Locke's Fundamental Constitutions as the frame of government. After years of misgovernment by proprietors, North Carolina became a royal colony (1729). Thereafter legal discrimination against non-Anglican Protestants ended, but until 1835 only Protestants could hold public office.

Catholicism was almost nonexistent in North Carolina throughout the colonial and early national period. When the vicariate apostolic of North Carolina was established (1868), there were only 700 known Catholics in the state.

By 1924, when the Diocese of Raleigh was erected, there were still but 8,000 Catholics. A second diocese was established at Charlotte in 1972. Belmont Abbey was an abbey nullius from 1910–76, when its jurisdiction was integrated into that of Charlotte. The Dioceses of Raleigh and Charlotte are suffragan to the metropolitan see of Atlanta, Georgia. In 1976 North Carolina's Catholics numbered 86,530, about 1.6% of the total state population. The major Protestant denominations are the Southern Baptist Convention, with 24.8% of the total population in 1971, and the Methodist Church with 10.5%. Other Protestant denominations comprised 14% of the population. The Jewish population (1968) was 9,450, or 0.19%. There are two Catholic colleges in North Carolina, with a total enrollment of 975 students. Three Catholic high schools serve the educational needs of 1,081 students, and 9,253 pupils attend 39 Catholic elementary schools in the state. BIBLIOGRAPHY: H. T. Lefler and A. R. Newsome, *North Carolina: The History of a Southern State* (1963); J. J. O'Connell, *Catholicity in the Carolinas and Georgia 1820–78* (1879).

[J. L. MORRISON; R. M. PRESTON]

NORTH DAKOTA, a north central state admitted to the Union (1889) as the 39th state. Early settlements were made by the Hudson's Bay Company and other trading firms. The part of North Dakota drained by the Missouri River was acquired by the U.S. through the Louisiana Purchase (1803) and explored by the Lewis and Clark expedition. One of the first Catholics in the area was the fur trader Toussaint Charbonneau, whose Catholic wife, Sacajawea, served as a guide to Lewis and Clark. The first permanent pastor was S. N. Dumoulin, who came to Pembina on the Red River in 1818. Pioneering missionary work in the Dakota region was performed by Pierre J. *De Smet (1840–68). When North Dakota became a state, the Diocese of Jamestown (now Fargo) was established, its boundaries coextensive with those of the state. After Bismarck was created as the state's second diocese (1910), both dioceses became suffragans of the Archdiocese of St. Paul, Minnesota.

In 1976 North Dakota's Catholics numbered 171,471 or 27.7 of the total state population. The major Protestant denominations are the American Lutheran Church with 27.4% of the total population in 1971, and the United Methodist Church, with 4.9%. Other Protestant denominations comprised 16.4% of the population. The Jewish population (1968) was 1,285, or 0.21%. There are 2 Catholic colleges in North Dakota, with a total enrollment of 1,071 students. Over 2,800 students attend the state's 9 Catholic high schools, while 7,145 pupils attend 36 Catholic elementary schools. BIBLIOGRAPHY: H. C. Fish and R. M. Black, *Brief History of North Dakota* (1925); L. Pfaller, *Catholic Church in Western N. D., 1738–1960* (1960).

[J. L. MORRISON; R. M. PRESTON]

NORTHCOTE, JAMES SPENCER (1821–1907), English cleric and expert on the Roman catacombs. N. studied at Oxford where he was influenced by J. H. *Newman. He resigned his Anglican orders in 1845 and was ordained a Roman Catholic priest in 1855 after studies at the Collegio Pio in Rome. He became an authority on early Roman Christianity and published *Roma Sotterranea*, an authoritative study of the catacombs. He was president of Oscott College for 17 years.

[T. M. MCFADDEN]

NORTHERN IRELAND, a political division of the United Kingdom of Great Britain and Northern Ireland including the six counties of Antrim, Armagh, Down, Fermanagh, Londonderry and Tyrone and the boroughs of Belfast and Londonderry. Established in 1920 by an act of the British Parliament, its own parliament meets at Stormont with 12 members elected to Westminister. It is 5,452 sq mi in area or about one-sixth of the whole island, but its population is more than half of the total population. It is two-thirds Protestant and one-third Catholic, a reflection of the 17th-cent. colonization of plantations by Protestants from England and Scotland. The Anglican and the Presbyterian are the dominant Protestant bodies. Protestants have maintained a united stand against Catholics as enemies of the stability of the six counties or as anti-Protestant nationalists. Active discrimination has continued in education, politics, business, and social welfare, though policy statements would appear to encourage reform. Relations between the Catholic hierarchy and the government have been amicable and the diocesan boundaries are the same now as they were before the partition of 1920. The Archdiocese of Armagh includes portions of the Republic as well as the North. In 1968, discrimination in housing and employment, franchise for local government based on property ownership favoring Protestants, tardy social reform, and economic insecurity for the Catholic minority polarized long-standing differences and precipitated escalation of violence on both sides. This caused Great Britain to suspend Parliament and self-government in 1972 and effect direct rule from London with military occupation by British troops.

Lay and religious leaders from both sides responded with a significant peace movement against all violence. While it has succeeded in reducing some destruction of life and property, the movement has yet to effect a resolution of the political impasse between the Catholic minority and Protestant majority. BIBLIOGRAPHY: *Violence in Ireland: A Report to the Churches* (1976). [F. H. BRIGHAM]

NORTHUMBRIAN ART, evidences of rich Christian culture centered in 6th-cent. Anglo-Saxon kingdom of Northumbria in England. With Augustine's see established at Canterbury (597) and King Aethelbert accepting Christianity, conversions were completed by SS. Cuthbert and Chad from Lindisfarne. The Greek, Theodore of Tarsus, later appointed abp. of Canterbury, founded schools for secular and religious education. Benedict Biscop (628?–

690) founded monasteries at Wearmouth and Jarrow, and brought back from Italy many antique MSS for copying, which accounts for the classical aspects of Northumbrian art. Important are the stone crosses—impressive, enigmatic, decorated with interlace and flat stylized figures—and illuminated MSS, not Celtic, as at Durrow, but humanistic. The *Codex Amiatinus* (650–700), copied from the *Codex Grandior* of Cassiodorus, was the source for Lindisfarne figures (late 7th cent.). The Canterbury school produced the *Codex Aureus* (8th cent.), most classical of Northumbrian works, unique in pre-Carolingian illumination—modeling in color with repeated quotations from the antique—and the *Canterbury Psalter* (*c.*785), a blend of Byzantine, Celtic, and classical styles.

[M. J. DALY]

NORWAY, predominantly Lutheran country of Scandinavia; a constitutional monarchy with capital in Oslo. Norway was first unified by Kings Harold I (late 9th–early 10th cent.) and Haakon I (935–61). The latter sought to introduce Christianity, aided by English missionaries. But it finally prevailed only under Olaf I (995–1000) and Olaf II (1016–28). The latter lost his kingdom to Canute of Denmark and England, but became Norway's patron saint. In the 9th–11th cents. Norwegian influence spread through the Viking raids and settlements in the British Isles, Normandy, Iceland, Greenland, and elsewhere. Ecclesiastically, Norway was under the See of Bremen until 1104, when it came under Lund. In 1152 the English Nicholas Breakspear (*Hadrian IV) was sent to organize the Norwegian Church. He established the metropolitan see at Trondheim (Nidaros), site of St. Olaf's shrine and then capital of Norway. From 1380 Norway was ruled by Denmark, and Lutheranism became established in both countries under Christian III (1534–59). In 1814 Norway was taken from Denmark, which had sided with Napoleon, and given to Sweden. Though under the Swedish crown, Norway had its own constitution and parliament (*storting*). The Dissenter Act of 1845 gave religious tolerance to all Christians, though Lutheranism remained the state religion. In 1905 Norway became independent, but voted to remain a monarchy, choosing Haakon VII (1905–57), son of Denmark's Frederick VIII. Coronations are at Trondheim cathedral.

In a population of nearly 3 million, the Catholics of the Diocese of Oslo number just over ten thousand (*Annuario Pontificio* 1977). The diocese was established in 1953; Oslo had been made a prefecture apostolic in 1869 and a vicariate apostolic in 1931. There are 17 parishes, 20 diocesan and 30 religious priests, about 350 religious women. BIBLIOGRAPHY: R.G. Popperwell, *Norway* (1972).

[T. EARLY]

NOSTRADAMUS, MICHAEL (Michel de Nostredame; 1503–66), French physician and occultist. Although he attained some reputation in medicine, N.'s chief fame comes from the rhymed prophecies he began publishing in 1547. They were couched in language so ambiguous that it was possible both to claim and to deny the fulfillment of some of them. However, they attracted much attention and N. was received with honor in court circles. The prophecies were condemned by the Congregation of the Index in 1781. BIBLIOGRAPHY: A. M. Bozzone, DE 2:1162.

[M. J. SUELZER]

NOTARY (CANON LAW), ecclesiastical official who acts as secretary in formal procedures: trials, elections, depositions, the hearings of matrimonial tribunals, meetings of congregations of the *Curia Romana. In some instances he is elected; in others, appointed by competent authority. His obligation is to record the acta or minutes, testimony, etc., of the proceedings in which he serves (CIC, c. 374;1585, 1).

[T. C. O'BRIEN]

NOTBURGA, ST. (fl. 9th or 10th cent.), maidservant. She was a domestic who worked first for a farmer and later for the count of Rottenburg and was noted for her charity to the poor. Her cult was confirmed in 1862 and is popular among farmers and peasants of Slovakia and Bavaria. No contemporary documents concerning her are extant. What is known of her derives from a 13th-cent. legend, though this appears to have had some historical foundation. BIBLIOGRAPHY: R. Mieler, BiblSanct 9:1070–73; Butler 3:553–554.

[P. K. MEAGHER]

NOTES, THEOLOGICAL, technical formulas that express the binding character and certitude of doctrinal teachings of the Catholic Church. They are called notes because they distinguish one doctrine (or its aspect) from another in terms of human knowledge; and they are theological because they belong to the science of theology as a systematic analysis of divine revelation.

The notes are graded from the highest (dogma of faith) to the lowest (probable), depending on several factors that can be expressed in questions. Was the doctrine formally revealed by God? How authoritatively does the Catholic Church teach it? How closely (and logically) is it related to revealed truth? How widely is it held among theologians? The more affirmative the answer to these questions and the more certain, the higher is the theological note of the doctrine about which the questions are asked.

Comparable to the objective side of theological notes is a subjective counterpart that pertains to the individual believer. His response to religious teaching is either obligatory or optional, depending on whether or not a doctrine is revealed and authoritatively taught. If obligatory, it is either a grave or a minor duty, according to how certainly the matter is revealed and how definitively the Church proposes it for acceptance by the faithful. Where the teaching is optional, notes serve at least two valuable functions. They clarify what areas of theological insight are valid and so may become useful premises for sound dogmatic development; and they identify what areas are still theologically obscure or not firmly grounded and therefore need further investigation.

Each advancement in doctrinal progress is based on at least an implicit use of theological notes. They continually open up new prospects of exploration by sifting what is already certain from what remains speculative and by testing the value of tentative opinions through comparison with the established principles of faith. BIBLIOGRAPHY: E. J. Fortman, NCE 10:523–524; S. Cartechini, *De valore notarum theologicarum* (1951).

[J. A. HARDON]

NOTES ON THE NEW TESTAMENT (1755), one of John *Wesley's principal works. *Explanatory Notes upon the New Testament* was written to "help serious men, who have not the advantage of learning . . . to understand the New Testament" (from Wesley's introduction). He began it in Jan. 1754, when he was seriously ill, staying at Hot Well, Bristol. He based the *Notes* on *Gnomon Novi Testamenti* by Johann Albrecht Bengel but was indebted also to John Heylyn, John Guyse, and Philip Doddridge. Wesley's brother Charles assisted him, particularly in the third and best edition. The *Notes* are short and manifest Wesley's originality of thought, his evangelical doctrines, and his *Arminianism. The *Notes* have been regarded by some, esp. English Methodist bodies, as a *doctrinal standard. With the *Notes,* Wesley published a new translation of the NT and anticipated modern scholarship by dividing the text into paragraphs. In 1790 he published a pocket edition of the translation without notes but with the analysis of the books and the chapters. He replaced "charity" by "love" in 1 Cor ch. 13, and "blessed" by "happy" in the Sermon on the Mount. There are about 1,200 departures from the AV; about three-quarters of them have been incorporated into later English versions of the New Testament. BIBLIOGRAPHY: J. S. Simon, *John Wesley and the Advance of Methodism* (1925); F. E. Maser, *Story of John Wesley's New Testament* (1955).

[F. E. MASER]

NOTICIAS SECRETAS DE AMERICA, confidential report written in 1749 by two Spanish scientists dealing with the political, legal, and clerical abuses in the Spanish viceroyalty of Peru. The report was submitted to the Spanish king and was based on the personal observations of Jorge Juan and Antonio Ulloa during a scientific expedition from 1736 to 1744. It was widely accepted then, but, modern scholarship has come to regard the report as exaggerated, prejudiced, and based on limited evidence. The present title was attached to the report by David Barry, an English editor who published it in 1826. Barry also substituted a preface that distorted the purpose and value of the manuscript.

[T. M. MCFADDEN]

NOTIONAL ACTS, also called origins, are acts related to the Trinitarian *notions; they are the acts implied in the two immanent Trinitarian processions as revelatory of the Trinity and the Persons and are four in number: active generation, passive generation, active spiration, and passive spiration. Between active and passive generation, on the one hand, and active spiration on the other, there is no relation of opposition, and so no real distinction between them. The existence of notional acts in God, of course, is not to be understood to imply any imperfection in him. BIBLIOGRAPHY: STS BAC 1.1:373; 459–462, 526–539; Lampe 3:666–668.

[E. A. WEIS]

NOTIONS, the five properties predicated in Trinitarian theology of the divine Persons but understood to be not common to all the three Persons *(idiōmata gnōristika)*. Such predicates are called notions because by them either the Trinity becomes known (*nota*) to men or the Persons become known in their distinct and proper characteristics. These notions are: innascibility, paternity, filiation, active spiration, and passive spiration.

[E. A. WEIS]

NOTKE, BERNT (1440–1509), German sculptor and painter, chief master at Lübeck (15th cent.). In a dramatic decorative yet realistic style, N. executed *Triumphal Cross* (1477) in the cathedral, Lübeck, altarpiece (1479, Denmark), his major work *St. George and the Dragon* (1489, Sweden), and was Werkmeister of Petrikirche, Lübeck (1505).

[M. J. DALY]

NOTKER BALBULUS, BL. ("the Stammerer"; *c.*840–912), monk at the Benedictine monastery of Sankt Gallen in Switzerland, where he was teacher, librarian, and guest master. He composed the largely fictional *Gesta Caroli* (*c.*884), the *Breviarium regum Francorum* (*c.*881), the fragmentary *Vita Sancti Galli*, and four hymns in honor of St. Stephen. But he is most famous for his Sequences, i.e., unrhymed rhythmical texts to be sung to the *jubilus* at the end of the *Alleluia* after the Gradual of the Mass. He was beatified in 1512. BIBLIOGRAPHY: M. F. McCarthy, NCE 10:525–526.

[M. F. MCCARTHY]

NOTKER LABEO ("the thick-lipped"; *c.*950–1022), Benedictine monk and director of the monastery school at Sankt Gallen in Switzerland; early master of German literature in the vernacular (hence often referred to as "Teutonicus"). His original writings and translations from Latin into Old High German (those from Boethius, Martianus Capella, Aristotle, and the Psalter are still extant) were intended primarily as texts for his pupils. His orthographical rules, contained in a letter to Bp. Hugo of Sitten, are valuable contributions to our knowledge of the Alemannian dialect as N. spoke it. BIBLIOGRAPHY: J. K. Bostock, *Handbook on Old High German Literature* (1955) 245–

257; W. von den Steinen, *Notker, der Dichter und seine geistige Welt* (2 v., 1948).

[M. F. MCCARTHY]

NOTKER OF LIÈGE, BL. (*c.*940–1008), prince bishop. Born in Swabia, N. studied at the Abbey of Sankt Gallen and served at the court of Otto I. As bishop of Liège from 969, he made his cathedral school an outstanding center of education, built numerous churches, and strengthened the town fortifications. Intensely loyal to the Saxon imperial dynasty, N. staunchly maintained German influence and power in Lower Lorraine. He took part in the political activity of his age and was often in the emperors' entourage. His mental outlook was that of the Ottonian Renaissance, glorifying the ideals of ancient Rome; he reached the peak of his influence under Otto III. BIBLIOGRAPHY: G. Kurth, *Notker de Liège et la civilisation au Xe siècle* (2 v. 1905); E. N. Johnson, *Secular Activities of the German Episcopate 919–1024* (1932).

[R. H. SCHMANDT]

NOTKER PHYSICUS (also Notker II and *Piperis Granum,* or Pfefferkorn; d. 975), physician at Sankt Gallen and painter. Nephew of Ekkehard II at Sankt Gallen, he became cellarer of the monastery in 956 and physician in 965. He is reported to have painted miniatures, and his composition of hymns was praised by Abbot Ekkehard IV. N.'s medical skill was so great that he was once called to the imperial court for consultation and possibly is to be identified with the Notker Notarius well known there. BIBLIOGRAPHY: J. M. Clark, *Abbey of St. Gall* (1926) *passim*.

[N. F. GAUGHAN]

NOTRE DAME, SISTERS OF (SND; Coesfelder Schwestern), a pontifical congregation for education and teacher training, founded in 1850 in Coesfeld, Germany by Aldegonda Wolbring (1828–89), Lisette Kuehling (1822–69) and their spiritual director, Rev. Theodore Elting (1819–62). Trained by the Sisters of Notre Dame of Amersfoort, they adapted their rule from that of St. Julie *Billiart. Their generalate is now in Rome. The community opened a teacher-training school for women in 1853, and taught in parochial schools until 1871 when the Kulturkampf seriously restricted their apostolate in Europe. They arrived in the U.S. in 1874, where now are four provincialates: in Ohio, at Chardon and Toledo; in Covington, Ky.; and Thousand Oaks, California. There were (1975) 3,699 members in 335 houses; 1,582 in the U.S., in 5 archdioceses and 13 dioceses. Missions are maintained likewise in Patna, India, and at Mt. Hagen, New Guinea. Staffing many elementary and high schools, they conduct also in the U.S. Notre Dame College of Cleveland. Activities in behalf of the sick and the handicapped also engage them.

[M. R. BROWN]

NOTRE DAME, UNIVERSITY OF, a university for men conducted by the Congregation of the Holy Cross at Notre Dame, Ind. It was founded in 1842 by a group of French missionaries headed by E. F. Sorin, CSC, who became the first president, and was chartered as a university in 1844. A replica of the log cabin chapel, the outpost of S. T. *Badin, the first Catholic priest ordained in the U.S., stands on the campus to mark the humble beginnings of the university's 70 buildings. Notre Dame, which confers undergraduate, graduate, and professional degrees, comprises a graduate school, a school of law (the oldest in the U.S.); and undergraduate colleges of arts and letters; science; engineering; and business administration. Specialized units include research laboratories for botany, geology, metallurgy, and engineering; the Lobund Laboratories, noted for research in life sciences; the laboratory for radiation research built in 1963 by the U.S. Atomic Energy Commission; the research institutes in the humanities, notably, the Jacques Maritain Philosophical Center; the Medieval Institute, engaged in filming the 30,000 classical, medieval, and Renaissance MSS of the Ambrosian Library in Milan, to be housed in the Notre Dame Memorial Library; the Center for the Study of Man in Contemporary Society, which made a 3-year study of Catholic elementary and secondary schools, published as *Catholic Schools in Action* (1966); the Committee on International Relations, for research in contemporary international political problems, and the East European and Soviet Studies Center founded with the support of the Ford Foundation (1954), to deal with Soviet policy. The library houses more than 780,000 vols.; among its collections are the Dante Library, the Hiberniana, the Ambrosiana Collections, and rare books on medieval life and universities. On the library façade is Millard Sheet's "Christ the Teacher," and in the Gothic Sacred Heart Church, Ivan Meštrovič's *Pietà*. The O'Shaughnessy Hall of Liberal and Fine Arts contains the university's collection of 300 paintings. The university is administered by the president and his advisory councils. Student enrollment averages about 8,700 men and women in the academic year. BIBLIOGRAPHY: A.J. Hope, *Notre Dame: One Hundred Years* (1943); R. Sullivan, *Notre Dame: Reminiscences of an Era* (pa. 1951); F.Wallace, *Notre Dame: Its People and Its Legends* (1969).

[M. B. MURPHY]

NOTRE-DAME-DE-LA-BASSE-OEUVRE, BEAUVAIS, early French Carolingian structure of which only three W bays remain, following its destruction with that of the superstructure, the 10th-cent. church of St. Pierre, for construction of the third and present Gothic building. The Basse-Oeuvre had an unvaulted nave and clerestory. The exterior in Roman style, small-cut stones and bricks, is patterned over windows, the unadorned portal surmounted by a large window having archivolt and voussoirs ornamented with small diagonal crosses, and above, three interesting and primitive figures, deduced to be God with Adam and Eve, carved on two apparently displaced stones. BIBLIOGRAPHY: K. J. Conant,

Carolingian and Romanesque Architecture, 800–1200 (1959).

[M. J. DALY]

NOTRE DAME DE LIESSE, see LIPCHITZ. J.

NOTRE DAME DE NAMUR, SISTERS OF (SND de Namur), a pontifical congregation, founded in France in 1804, for the education apostolate, by St. Julie *Billiart with Françoise Blin de Bourdon, under direction of Joseph Desiré D'Ainville *Varin. Begun at Amiens, they were established shortly after in Namur, Belgium; since 1957 the motherhouse is in Rome. Sister Louise van der Schriek (1813–86) in 1840 led the first group to the U.S., where presently are six provincialates: Boston and Ipswich in Mass.; Fairfield, Conn.; Ilchester, Md.; Cincinnati, Ohio; Saratoga, California. Sisters number 2,444 in the U.S. (including Honolulu) in 3 archdioceses and 21 dioceses, and are also in Africa (Kenya, Rhodesia, Zaire), England, Brazil, Japan, and Italy (Botzona and Rome). Total membership (1975) was 3,685 in 342 houses. They maintain clinics for exceptional children, and teach in elementary and secondary schools, private and parochial. They conduct numerous colleges; their first college (1856) was Notre Dame Training College for teachers, Liverpool, England; their first in the U.S., Trinity College, Washington, D.C. (chartered 1897). From the U.S. after World War II they opened colleges in Japan.

[M. R. BROWN]

NOTRE-DAME DE PARIS (1163–1320), cathedral built on the site of two 9th-cent. Carolingian churches, St.-Étienne and Notre-Dame, begun (1163) by Bp. Maurice de Sully, the choir and transepts erected (1163–82), bays of the nave and finally the façade and towers added (1190–1245). It is a five-aisled basilica with deep choir and double ambulatory; the elevation was effected in four stages: open arcades (ground story), tribune galleries, windows, and clerestory. Though modified in the 13th cent., the bays near the crossing were restored by Viollet-le-Duc (19th century). Capitals of columns evolve from severe to naturalistic leaf forms. Impressive sculpture of the W facade in portals of the Virgin, Last Judgment, and St. Anne, moves from early Gothic, through monumental 13th-cent. style, to the more naturalistic mode insinuating the "precious" style of Reims (*c.* 1250). Chapels were added, windows enlarged, new flying buttresses erected. The N façade of Master Jean de Chelles and the S transept (1258), completed by Pierre de Montreuil upon the master's death, have rose windows elegant as jeweler's work, and rich sculptural decorations of the life of the Virgin, the stories of Theophilus and of St. Stephen (patron of the original church), all defaced in the French Revolution. Ambulatory chapels (1254–1320) and the *Porte Rouge* (*c.* 1265) with animal figures, voussoirs of the life of St. Marcel, and figures of St. Louis and Margaret of Provence before the Virgin, completed construction. On the interior the fine 14th-cent. Virgin at the transept comes from a chapel in the cloister. Tombs, choir stalls, and lecterns date from the 17th and 18th centuries. Restorations in façades, gargoyles, and flèche by Viollet-le-Duc (1845–64), though filling the need, are of questionable aesthetic value. BIBLIOGRAPHY: R. Branner, *St. Louis and the Court Style in Gothic Architecture* (1965); M. Aubert, *La Cathédrale Notre-Dame-de Paris,* 1950.

[M. J. DALY]

NOTRE-DAME DU HAUT, see RONCHAMP.

NOTRE-DAME-DU-PORT, CLERMONT-FERRAND, French structure of the 6th cent., rebuilt (1099–13th cent.) in the distinctive Auvergne Romanesque style. The exterior is boldly decorated in black and white stone in geometric designs with brackets suggesting Oriental influence. Four apsidal chapels radiate from the round choir richly decorated as is the façade. The tunnel-vaulted nave of four bays carries a strong geometric band under the triforium where cusped arches suggest Moorish influence. The S portal tympanum framing an enthroned Christ with figures is flanked by Isaiah, John the Baptist, and reliefs of the lives of Christ and of the Virgin which, in crude vigor are most significant of the region. Capitals of soft limestone cut in thick masses, signed by a master Robert, are vigorous and naively expressive showing God seizing Adam's beard, Adam kicking Eve, and Virtues armed, warring against Vices, in an Auvergnat exuberance of monumental figural sculpture, poignant, refreshing and disarmingly crude, with exotic (Moorish) and geometric motifs in unbridled ornamentation. BIBLIOGRAPHY: K.J. Conant, *Carolingian and Romanesque Architecture, 800–1200* (1959).

[M. J. DALY]

NOTRE-DAME-LA-GRANDE, see POITIERS.

NOTTINGHAM SCHOOL (14th–16th cent.), group of alabaster carvers in Nottingham, England, near quarries, and producing widely exported altarpieces. King Edward III, as royal patron, commissioned an altarpiece (1367) for Windsor Castle. Extant pieces have lost their original coloring. The Nottingham school ended with the Reformation.

[M. J. DALY]

NOUMENA, a Kantian concept, referring to things-in-themselves, as they are, beyond and independent of human cognition. In his *1770 Dissertation*, Kant distinguished between noumena and *phenomena, generally following the Platonic line that phenomena are objects of senses, noumena objects of intellect, though, even then, Kant considered the human intellect to be limited. In his *Critique of Pure Reason,* he maintained the distinction but claimed that senses and intellect complement each other in all experience and knowledge. As he explained: "With us understanding and sensuality cannot determine objects unless they are joined together. If we separate them we have intuitions without concepts, or concepts without intuition; in both cases, representation which we cannot refer to any definite object'' (B:312). In his moral inquiries, Kant maintained that human will operates in the noumenal realm as a free subject and is perceived by others as a phenomenon, an object of sensibility. *KANT, I.

[R. J. LITZ]

NOVALIS (Friedrich Von Hardenberg; 1772–1801), German romantic writer. His mystic tendencies inspired the *Hymnen an die Nacht* (1800); his romantic glorification of the Catholic Middle Ages found expression in the treatise *Die Christenheit oder Europa* (1798; published in 1826). But he is most famous for the unfinished novel *Heinrich von Ofterdingen* (published 1802), which, in its portrayal of the hero's search for *die blaue Blume,* gave Romanticism its central symbol. BIBLIOGRAPHY: W. Kosch, *Deutsches Literatur-Lexikon* (1965) 303, bibliog.; O. Walzel, *German Romanticism* (1932) 81–95, *passim*.

[M. F. MCCARTHY]

NOVATIAN, ANTIPOPE (d.258), advocate of a Church made up only of the elect. N. was a prominent Roman priest who wrote to the Churches of the world as the spokesman of the Roman clergy during the vacancy after Pope St. Fabian's death (250). Two of his letters to St. Cyprian at Carthage foreshadow N.'s later rigorism toward the *lapsi,* those who had apostatized during the Decian persecution. He was severely disappointed when in 251 Cornelius was chosen pope, and with the support of some of the clergy had himself consecrated bishop and opposed Cornelius, whom he accused of overindulgence toward the *lapsi*. N. gained many adherents to the view that the Church was made up of saints alone and that not only the *lapsi* but all who sinned gravely were excluded. In 251 he was condemned by a synod of 60 bps. in Rome, but Novatianist Churches with their own bps. spread, especially in Africa and the East. N. fled from Rome during the imperial persecutions of Gallus and Volusianus; he died, possibly as a martyr or confessor, under the Emperor Valerian. He was the first Roman theologian to write in Latin. His works show him an accomplished stylist and theologian. Of the many works that Jerome mentions, only a few survive. Two, the *De cibis judaicis* and the *De Trinitate*, were preserved among the works of Tertullian; two others, probably N.'s, survived among the works of Cyprian, *De bono pudicitiae* and *De spectaculis*. The *De Trinitate* is the principal work, and except for subordinationist expressions, one of high merit. BIBLIOGRAPHY: Altaner 191–193, with bibliog.; Daniélou-Marrou 194–200; P. H. Weyer, NCE 10:534–535.

NOVATIANISTS, members of a schismatic sect founded by the Roman priest *Novatian, who after the election of Pope Cornelius in March 251, had himself consecrated bishop and proclaimed as a rival pope. To give a theological basis to his schism, he adopted a rigorous attitude toward the *lapsi,* those who had lapsed during time of persecution. He excluded them forever from his Church, and this penalty was later applied to adulterers and murderers as well. Novatian and his followers were excommunicated by a synod of 60 bishops held at Rome in 251. His active proselytizing (Cyprian, *Ep*. 55.24) and the natural attraction his rigorism had for those who had suffered for the faith, favored the rapid spread of the schism, particularly in Syria, Asia Minor, and Palestine, where it numbered *Montanists as well as Catholics among its converts. They were opposed by Cyprian of Carthage, Dionysius of Alexandria, Pacian of Barcelona, and Ambrose of Milan. The Council of Nicaea declared the Novatianist priests to be validly ordained. Constantine permitted them to have their own Churches and cemeteries, but Honorius and Theodosius included the Novatianists in their legislation repressing heresies. In the East the schism persisted at least until the end of the 6th century. BIBLIOGRAPHY: E. Peterson, EncCatt. 8:1976–80; J. Quasten, LTK 7:1062–64.

[M. J. COSTELLOE]

NOVECENTO MOVEMENT, group of artists in Milan, returning (1922) to great Italian figurative art of the past, included painters C. Carrà, M. Campigli, and master sculptor Marino Marini.

[M. J. DALY]

NOVELLO, VINCENT (1781–1861), British composer, organist at the Royal Portuguese Chapel (1797–1822), London publisher and editor of Novello and Co. founded 1811. The first-published volume of his sacred organ music was successful because it could be played by less accomplished organists. He edited and revived a great body of work including *Sacred Music* by Purcell (5 v.), Masses of Beethoven, Haydn, and Mozart, and anthems by Croft, Boyce, and Greene. N. himself composed sacred music including Masses, motets, Kyries, and anthems.

[R. J. LITZ]

NOVELS OF JUSTINIAN or *Novellae Constitutiones,* laws decreed by Emperor *Justinian after the publication of the *Corpus Iuris Civilis*. It is the work of private jurists and is contained in three different collections: (1) *The Epitome of Julian,* containing an abbreviated text of the 122 novels published in Latin by Julian during the lifetime of Justinian (*c*.555); (2) the collection of 134 novels up to the year 556 contains the complete text of the novels in a somewhat inaccurate Latin translation from the Greek; (3) the more complete and accurate collection of 168 novels of which 153 belong to Justinian, most of them in Greek; and the rest to Justin II and Tiberius. BIBLIOGRAPHY: H. Scheltema, CMedH (1967) 4.2:55.

[E. EL-HAYEK]

NOVENA, 9 successive days of prayer for a special intention or in preparation for a feast. The devotional novena, as distinguished from the classical 9 days of mourning, is said to have begun in the early Middle Ages as preparation for Christmas, the 9 days representing the 9 months of Mary's pregnancy. Novenas grew out of popular piety; it was not until the 19th cent. that the Church promoted them by granting indulgences.

[J. DALLEN]

NOVENA OF GRACE, a novena in honor of St. Francis Xavier, esp. for a happy death. A prayer for this novena may be found in the *Enchiridion Indulgentiarum* (Raccolta) #500.

[J. DALLEN]

NOVGOROD, a Russian city important for its political, artistic, and religious history. Center of a huge territory uninfluenced by the Tatar conquest. Novgorod was the home of Joseph of Volokolamsk and Philotheus of Pskov, ideologists of the *''third Rome theory.'' Novgorod called itself ''the Holy, Catholic, and Apostolic Church of St. Sophia'' and from the 12th to the 15th cent. was a democratic, theocratic republic presided over by the archbishop. *Fools in Christ (*Yurodivy*) first appeared here. With Tver, Novgorod was a center of the anti-simonist *Strigolniki movement. The area is site of Russia's famous monasteries: Ferapontov, Kirillov, Solovki, and *Valamo. BIBLIOGRAPHY: G. P. Fedotov, *Russian Religious Mind* (1966), 2:186–194.

[T. BIRD]

NOVGOROD SCHOOL, artistic works of Novgorod, the only free city in Russia from the 12th cent. until the rise of Moscow (*c.* 1400). It resisted the Tatars and maintained the art tradition, so that all late medieval icons, murals, and objects of superior quality were termed ''Novgorod.'' Hieratic, frontal, and highly linear in style, the Novgorod school developed the narrative icon and introduced the iconostasis. Theophanese the Greek painted in Novgorod in the late 14th and early 15th cent., then in Moscow after 1395, when Novgorod shared leadership with that city.

[M. J. DALY]

NOVICE, a candidate for first, temporary religious profession who has been clothed with the religious habit and must spend at least one full canonical year of strictly religious formation and probation under the direction of a master or mistress of novices.

NOVITIATE, the period of at least 1 full year of religious formation required before admission of a candidate to religious profession. The religious house or a part of it, where the probationary period is passed is also called the novitiate. Awkwardly, if not incorrectly, English usage applies the term also to a novice.

NOYES, ALFRED (1880–1958), poet, critic, biographer. From Oxford days he determined upon the writing of poetry as his lifework. At 22 he published *The Loom of Years,* a collection of poetry which won him critical acceptance. His early enthusiasm for English heroes such as Drake created some superficial poems, but as a thinker he was not content with this narrowness, and pursuing a deeper philosophical purpose, he composed the poetic trilogy *The Torchbearers*. Ultimately he found his way to Catholicism in 1927. A major autobiographical account, *The Unknown God,* (1934) gives a record of his thinking. N. was a frequent and popular lecturer in the U.S. at Harvard, Princeton, and Columbia. His attempt to clear Voltaire of the charge of anti-Catholicism caused a painful dispute with Rome. N. was preeminently a lyric poet, but his *A Pageant of Letters* showed him to be a sensitive critic, and *The Opalescent Parrott* reveals an essayist of distinction. A work that should be noted is *No Other Man*, a futuristic excursion into a post-atomic world which was used as a framework for N.'s philosophical views. His autobiography, *Two Worlds for Memory* (1953), reveals his affection for America.

[J. R. AHERNE]

NUCLEAR WEAPONS. In a 1954 address to the World Medical Assn., Pius XII declared: ''Should the evil consequences of adopting this method of warfare ever become so extensive as to pass utterly beyond the control of man, then indeed its use must be rejected as immoral. In that event it would no longer be a question of defense against injustice and necessary protection of legitimate possessions, but of the annihilation, pure and simple, of all human life within the affected area. That is not lawful on any title.'' In the encyclical *Pacem in terris* (1963) John XXIII stated: ''In this age of ours, which prides itself on its atomic power, it is irrational to believe that war is still an apt means of vindicating violated rights.'' Vatican Council II made these declarations on nuclear weapons: ''Acts of war involving these weapons can inflict massive and indiscriminate destruction far exceeding the bounds of legitimate defense''; ''Any act of war aimed indiscriminately at the destruction of entire cities is a crime against God and man himself. It merits unequivocal and unhesitating condemnation'' (Vat II ChModWorld,n.80). Yet the Council held back, principally because of the intervention of American and some European bps., from condemning absolutely the defensive use of nuclear weapons, or from condemning stockpiling them. Many theologians, however, feel that nuclear annihilation is an evil effect necessarily greater than any evil against which nuclear weapons could be employed. *BOMB, ATOMIC.

[T. C. O'BRIEN]

NUDITY. Nakedness is a natural condition, and thus obviously not immoral; it is a physical fact. But even as clothing has meaning and purpose because of reason, so does complete nakedness, i.e., the human action of being naked. Thus anthropology and the history of religions have pointed out a ritual nakedness, connected with magic, myth, or cult. The shame of the first couple over their nakedness (Gen 3.10–11) describes, not a sexual awakening, but the loss of openness and spontaneity, and the subjection to the harshness of physical existence. In the OT complete nudity is taken to be a disgrace (Gen 3.10–11), and as a penalty inflicted on the adulteress (Jer 13.26), or on captives (Is 47.3). The moral rightness or wrongness of nudity in the presence of others is governed by the meaning and purposes of *purity, the virtue safeguarding manners and actions accessory or related to sexual intercourse (ThAq ST 2a2ae,142.4;151.4; 154.9). Nudity as intentionally sexual exposure is right where sexual intercourse is right. Nudity as the simple fact of disrobing is right in proper circumstances and for proper purposes: medical examination, sexually segregated showering or swimming. Nudity within a sexually mixed group normally directly provokes sexual arousal (whatever the gratuitous physical and psychological claims of nudism cults), and so is against purity. As to semi-exposure in dress, according to styles of fashion, the meaning and measure varies with standards and conventions of time and place, and also with the intent of the individual. Nudity in the plastic, pictorial, or dramatic arts may serve genuine artistic expression; nudity that is mere exhibitionism or an appeal to prurience is wrong.

[T. C. O'BRIEN]

NUDITY (IN THE BIBLE). Disapproval of nakedness in the OT is unmistakable and this seems to have been based on two reasons. First, it appears to have been associated with pagan and idolatrous forms of worship (cf., e.g., Ex 32.25); second, it implies a deprivation of due human dignity, a state of shame (*boshet*) specifically connected with lack of sexual modesty. It is this that prompts the filial reverence of Noah's sons in refusing to look at their father's nakedness (Gen 9.22–23). The humiliation of being stripped naked is often imposed on captives in war (cf. Is 20.4; Amos 2.16, etc.). The personified Israel is threatened with this deprivation of dignity for her adulteries and unfaithfulness to Yahweh, who will "pull your skirts up over your face" (Jer 13.26; Nah 3.5; cf. Is 47.3 on Babylon, etc.). Clearly, the exposure of nakedness is immediately connected with the arousal of sexual desire, and this underlies the story of Adam and Eve seeking to cover their nakedness (Gen 3.7,21). Again in certain contexts, to "uncover the nakedness" of someone is a euphemism for sexual intimacy (cf. Lev 18.6–19).

[D. J. BOURKE]

NUGENT, FRANCIS (1569–1635), Irish Capuchin, active during the Counter Reformation. Born in County Meath, he studied at Louvain and in 1591 joined the Capuchin Order in Brussels, where he became an exponent of the contemplative, or mystical, movement then flourishing in the Netherlands. For this he was twice required to defend himself before the Roman Inquisition, but he completely vindicated himself. After teaching theology in France for 5 years, he returned in 1605 to Belgium and ruled this province as guardian and definitor. N. had his greatest success as head of the Capuchin mission to Germany after 1610 (the Cologne convent was founded 1611) and as director of the order's foundation in Ireland, starting 1615. In 1624 he founded a house in Dublin while on a secret visit to the country and between 1628 and 1630 served as apostolic visitor in Ireland, and agent of the hierarchy in Rome. Internal disputes among the Belgian Capuchins led to his loss of guardianship in 1632, after which he retired to Charleville, one of several locales in N France and Belgium, where he had established Capuchin houses.

[E. M. GATES]

NÛHRĀ (Light), first word of the refrain accompanying two metrical hymns sung in the East Syrian festive morning office. The first letters of the strophes of the first hymn, attributed to St. Ephraem and sung in the Maronite daily morning office also, form acrostically the name Jesus Christ in Syriac.

[A. CODY]

NUMBER OF THE BEAST, a cryptic number, 666, taken from Rev 13.18, which reads, "He who has understanding, let him calculate the number of the beast, for it is the number of a man; and its number is six hundred and sixty-six." It stands probably for some personal world power. Since the number 6 was considered imperfect, it could be merely symbolic, signifying supreme imperfection. Various attempts of actual identification have been made, based on the numerical value of Hebrew or Greek letters. Most popular of these have been either the Hebrew *neron gesar*, the Emperor Nero, or the Greek abbreviation for the title of the Emperor Domitian, who was probably ruling at the time that the Apocalypse (Rev) was written.

BIBLIOGRAPHY: EDB 1652–53.

[J. A. GRASSI]

NUMBERS, BOOK OF, the third book of the OT which derives its name from the numbering of the tribes of Israel referred to in the opening chapters (1–4). The name is not descriptive of the general contents. As with the other books of the Pentateuch, Num is a mixture of law and history, the latter providing the framework for the former. This artificial arrangement is based on the concept of the covenant in which law follows on Yahweh's saving action in history.

The narrative section takes Israel from Sinai to the Eastern banks of the Jordan, opposite Canaan. Related here are: the march from Sinai to Paran, with accounts of Israel's murmuring and of Miriam's punishment (10.11–12.16); the sending of scouts into Canaan from the South, their report, and the defeat of Israel at Hormah (13–14); the revolts of Korah, Dothan, and Abiram against Moses (16); the vindication of the rights of the tribe of Levi (17); the march from Kadesh to Moab, with accounts of Aaron's death and the incident of the bronze serpent (20–21); the oracles of Balaam of Moab (22–24); apostasy of Israel at Peor (25); the defeat of the Midianites (31); the settlement of Reuben, Gad, and part of Manasseh in Transjordan (32).

The expressly legal sections contain regulations on: defilements demanding exclusion from the camp (5.1–4); ''breaking faith'' with Yahweh (5.5–10); the trial of the suspected adulteress (5.11–31); the Nazirite (6.1–21); the priestly blessing (6.22–27); the Levites (8.5–26); the Passover (9.1–14); the silver trumpets (10.1–10) various offerings (15.1–31); tassels (15.37–41); duties and privileges of priests and Levites (18.1–32); rites of purification (19.1–22); inheritance (27.1–11); the sacrificial calendar (28–29); women's vows (30); Levitical cities and cities of refuge (35); inheritance by daughters (36). Besides these, there is statistical information: the censuses (1–4; 26), the tribal leaders' offerings (7), the stages of Israel's journey (33), and the ideal boundaries of the land of Canaan (34). Almost all the legal and statistical material stems from various stages of the priestly tradition. In the narrative sections both the Yahwist and the Elohist are represented, as in the preceding books of the Pentateuch. The legal and midrashic development here indicates the significance attached to this period of her history by later Israel. BIBLIOGRAPHY: EDB 1653–55.

[E. H. MALY]

NUMBERS AND NUMBER SYMBOLISM, a usage of varying importance in all cultures. In some it is distinctly magical, philosophical and religious. In others, it is hard to determine the predominate emphasis. Mystic and/or symbolic meaning has enhanced the significance of certain numbers such as 1,2,3,4,7,10,12,40,70,100.

The number 1 is the Monad of Pythagoras, the One of Plato and in the Bible God as the ''Wholly Other''. (Dt 6.4; Sir 1.6, Jn 17.11.) The number 2 brings together pairs or opposites in terms of their relationship to one another e.g. sun–moon; day–night; yang–yin (Chinese). The number 3 is associated with perfection in God and the most common of all symbolic numbers e.g. the Divine Triads, Zeus, Athena, Apollo (Greece); Jupiter, Juno, Minerva (Rome); Osiris, Isis, Horus (Egypt); in the Bible, God's perfection in act (Gen 18.2). The number 4 is the symbol of completeness e.g. the 4 cardinal virtues of Plato, the seasons of the year, the 4 beatitudes (Lk 6.20–22). The number 7 was the ultimate number in the religion and astrology of Babylonia as the sum of the sacred numbers 3 and 4. In the Bible 7 is associated with a full series; it has special reference to cult and sacred objects (feasts, sacrifices, the Sabbath). Its multiples and its half are found passim to designate perfection (Dan 7.25).

The number 10 meant completeness to the Pythagoreans whereas in the Bible as a symbol of totality there is an uneven usage (10 plagues of Egypt, 10 commandments). The number 12 reflected cosmic order and government e.g. the twelve tribes of Israel and the Twelve Apostles, 12 as the symbol of the people of God passim in the Bible. The number 40 is significant in the Bible and Islamic Literature. In the former it frequently is associated with periods of man's struggle with all manner of evil and ultimate victory through God, e.g., the Flood (Gen 7.17), Israelites 40 years in the desert (Num 14.33), Christ in the desert (Mt 4.2).

The numbers 70 (7x10) and 72 (one-fifth of 360 degrees) indicated size and multiplicity. 100 is often used as a round number. BIBLIOGRAPHY: M. R. P. McGuire, NCE 10:567-568; H. J. Rose, OCD 614; T. Davidson et al, Hastings ERE 9:406-417; N. Turchi, EncCatt 8:995-997; H. J. Sorensen, NCE 10:569–570; E. T. Bell, *Magic of Numbers* (1952); M. N. Pope, InterDB 3:561–567.

[F. H. BRIGHAM]

NUMENIUS OF APAMEA (2d half of 2d cent. A.D.), Neo-Pythagorean philosopher and precursor of Neoplatonism. He was acquainted with the Jewish philosophy at Alexandria, for according to Clement of Alexandria he described Plato as a ''Moses speaking Attic Greek.'' However, it is an open question whether he was influenced by the **Chaldaean Oracles*, as is so often assumed. He regarded the philosophies of Plato and Pythagoras as basically identical. He is primarily important for his teaching that there are three Gods: the *prōtos Theos,* the Principle of Being, Pure Thought, and *Patēr*, Father; the second God, the Demiurge of the Timaeus, and the *poiētēs,* maker of the world; the third God is the *poiēma*, the world itself, formed by the Demiurge. He held that there are two souls in man, one rational and the other irrational, and that the entry of the soul into the body is an evil and is to be regarded as a ''fall.'' The ''fallen'' soul must strive stage by stage to return to its origin. The syncretism of Numenius and his special emphasis on the divine transcendence exercised a marked influence on the beginnings of Neoplatonism. BIBLIOGRAPHY: Copleston 1:448; CHGMP 96–104 (excellent).

[M. R. P. MCGUIRE]

NUN, strictly, the title applies only to a religious woman of solemn vows (*monialis*) in a monastery. The life of a nun is primarily one of contemplation and mortification. In popular speech the term refers to any woman religious. *SISTERS, RELIGIOUS.

[C. J. NOONE]

NUN OF KENT, see BARTON, ELIZABETH.

NUNC DIMITTIS, see CANTICLE OF SIMEON.

NUNCIATURE, the papal diplomatic counterpart of a civil embassy presided over by an apostolic nuncio who ranks as an ambassador among diplomatic envoys. BIBLIOGRAPHY: J.A. Abbo, NCE 8:607; R.A. Graham, *Vatican Diplomacy,* (1959).

[F. H. BRIGHAM]

NUNCIO, a prelate (usually titular archbishop) who represents the Pope before a civil government and its local Church. He is expected to effect continued positive diplomatic communication with the former and relay appropriate needs and information to and from Rome for the latter. BIBLIOGRAPHY: J.A. Abbo, NCE 8:607; G. Paro, *The Right of Papal Legation* (CUA CLS 211, 1947).

[F. H. BRIGHAM]

NUNES BARRETO, JOÃO (d. 1562), Portuguese Jesuit and patriarch of Abyssinia. N. first worked in Morocco caring for the Christian slaves there, and was consecrated patriarch of Abyssinia upon the recommendation of St. Ignatius Loyola and King John III of Portugal. N. attempted, through legates, to establish good relations with the Abyssinian Emperor Caludius (Calāwēdōs) and ultimately to persuade him to unite with Rome. These efforts were unsuccessful, and N. died in Goa awaiting some positive responses to his diplomatic efforts.

[T. M. MCFADDEN]

NÚÑEZ, JUAN (fl. 1480), Spanish painter in Seville, whose *Pietà* in the cathedral is Flemish in style, but Spanish in the crowding of space and in iconography from Bermejo.

[M. J. DALY]

NUNRAW, ABBEY OF, a Cistercian monastery near Edinburgh, founded in 1946 on the site of a medieval Cistercian convent which had survived into the 16th century. Established as a daughterhouse of Ireland's Roscrea, Nunraw was made an abbey in 1948 and presently has an active religious community.

[M. A. MCFADDEN]

NUN'S RULE, see ANCREN RIWLE.

NUPTIAL BLESSING, the blessing of spouses at their marriage. Prior to the rite of 1969 this was a blessing of the bride and could be given only to a Catholic. Various forms are provided, praying for loyalty and fidelity, continued growth in love and grace, and the blessing of children.

[J. DALLEN]

NUPTIAL MASS, the celebration of Mass within which marriage is solemnized. Special scripture readings are used. The ceremony of marriage itself consists of the declaration of intention, exchange of vows (and of rings) after the homily. Following the Lord's Prayer the nuptial blessing is given. In the early centuries the Church called for public marriage but did not require the presence of the priest. It gradually became customary to seek the priest's blessing, to marry in the church, and, finally, to do so at Mass. The revised Roman rite for marriage was published in 1969. It makes provision for the celebration of Mass even when one of the spouses is not Catholic.

[J. DALLEN]

NUREMBERG, DECLARATION, protest of German professors against the decrees of Vatican Council I. J. F. von *Schulte called a meeting at Nuremberg, Aug. 25–26, 1870; 14 professors, including I. von *Döllinger and F. *Reusch, attended. Their manifesto denied the validity of the Council on the grounds that it lacked freedom and moral unanimity; noted that certain chapters of the constitution *Pastor aeternus* lacked conditions necessary for a dogmatic definition; held that the dogma of the pope's immediate ordinary jurisdiction destroyed the divinely appointed nature of episcopacy; declared that papal infallibility would revive papal control of civil affairs and foment boundless discord; affirmed the signatories' solidarity with bps. opposing the conciliar decrees; and demanded a true general council on German soil. Thirty-three faculty members (priests and laymen) from seven universities signed the Declaration, which greatly sparked Old Catholicism. *OLD CATHOLICS; *VATICAN COUNCILS.

[E. E. BEAUREGARD]

NURTURE, CHRISTIAN, see CHRISTIAN NURTURE.

NUSAIRIS (Arab., *al-Nuṣayrîya*), also called the Alawis Arab., *al-'Alawîya*), a *Shiïte sect originating in the teaching of Ibn Nuṣair who taught that he was the divinely appointed spokesman (*Bâb*, literally, ''gate'') of 'Alî al-Hâdî al-'Askarî (the 10th Imām of the Shiïtes, d. A.D. 868), whom he considered as an incarnation of the Holy Spirit. According to Nusairi doctrine, God himself is completely unknowable but was incarnate in 'Alî ibn abî Ṭâlib whose divinity was expressed by *Mohammed, the incarnation of God's Name, while his *Bâb* was Salmân Pâk. Their esoteric teaching is granted to elected adepts through initiation, like that of the *Ismailis with which it has some kinship in its origin; though unlike the latter, the N.'s use a number of Christian symbols including a kind of eucharistic meal. They hold also that women have no souls and consequently speak of *Fâṭima, a divine figure in their hierarchy, using the masculine form of the name (i.e., *Fâṭim*) or the near homophone *Fâṭir* (creator). A sizeable community of Nusairis still survives in Syria. BIBLIOGRAPHY: R. Dussaud, *Histoire et religion des Nosairis* (1900); ''Nuṣayrîa,'' L. Massignon, EncIslam.

[R. M. FRANK]

NUZI, ALLEGRETTO (*c.*1315–73), Italian painter from Umbria, of Giottesque style, working in Florence (1346) and influenced by B. Daddi. Prior of his monastery (Fabriano) 1350–1363, N. painted *St. Anthony Abbot* (1353) and a *Madonna and Child* (1366 and 1372). Beautifully executed small triptychs in the Vatican (1365) and the National Gallery of Art, Washington, D.C., showing an Umbrian blending of Giottesque and Sienese elements with the Orcagna style, are richly ornamented and bright in color.

[M. J. DALY]

NUZU (NUZI), an ancient city of NW Mesopotamia, located at the site of modern Yorghan Tepe, near the foothills of South Kurdistan, 9 miles W of modern Kirkūk (ancient Arrapkha), and 150 miles N of Baghdad. The American School of Oriental Research in Baghdad and Harvard Univ. undertook a joint archeological expedition at the site (1925–31). The results throw much light on the social customs of the patriarchal age, constitute the primary source of knowledge concerning the Habirū, and in general confirm the biblical tradition about a NW Mesopotamian origin of the patriarchs. Old Akkadian, Old Assyrian, Middle Assyrian/Hurrian levels were unearthed, and the site was occupied down through Roman, Parthian, and Sāsānian times. In Akkadian times (2334–2154 B.C.) it was called Gasur. Early in the second millennium Hurrians from N Mesopotamia occupied the city and called it Nuzu. It reached its greatest prosperity and importance at mid-millennium, and then rapidly declined after the Assyrian conquest in the 13th century. The over 4,000 cuneiform tablets uncovered reveal a mix of Hurrian and Akkadian elements in language, family law, and social institutions, and throw light on some incidents narrated in Genesis. These Nuzu texts, for example, show that property could pass to a daughter's husband, if the father had handed over his household gods to his son-in-law (cf. the Rachel-Laban interplay in Gen 31). It was shrewd use of legitimate Hurrian custom for the patriarchs on three occasions to introduce their wives as sisters. It was custom for upper-class wives to present a slave-girl to their husbands as concubines and adopt the children of such a union. Slave girls could be presented to a new bride. Childless couples could adopt a slave as an heir. Birthright was not automatically determined by chronological age, but could be decided by paternal decree, which was especially binding in the form of a death-bed declaration introduced by the formula: "Now that I have grown old." The Habirū recur in texts which seem to refer to them as a particular class of people, not an ethnic group. They were underprivileged foreigners. This may shed light on the origins of the Hebrews in Canaan.

[E. J. DILLON]

NYGREN, ANDERS (1890–), Lutheran bishop of Lund in Sweden, theologian, and ecumenist. N., prominent in the World Council of Churches, was a delegate to its major conferences, as well as to those, beginning at Lausanne in 1907, that led to its formation. He served (1947–52) as president of the Lutheran World Federation. As a theologian he is chiefly associated with the *motif-research method in theology. Especially in his great work *Agape and Eros* (v.1, 1930; v.2, 1936; rev. Eng. ed., 1961), he presented the distinctive note of Christianity to be *agapē*—the unmotivated, completely gracious divine love that alone establishes man's relationship to God and enables him to live in love of neighbor. To N. the glory of the Reformation was the reassertion of this theme after it had been obscured by other motifs dominating Christian theology—*nomos* (law), the characteristic of Judaism, and *eros,* the egocentric human search for God as fulfillment of man, the essence of Greek religious thought. *AULÉN, G; *LUNDENSIAN THEOLOGY.

[T. C. O'BRIEN]

SISTERS OF SAINT JOSEPH
PHILADELPHIA